EDITION

ACCOUNTING

CONCEPTS & APPLICATIONS

W. STEVE ALBRECHT, PhD, CPA, CIA, CFE
Brigham Young University

JAMES D. STICE, PhD
Brigham Young University

EARL K. STICE, PhD
Brigham Young University

K. FRED SKOUSEN, PhD, CPA
Brigham Young University

MONTE R. SWAIN, PhD, CPA, CMA
(Consulting Editor)
Brigham Young University

Australia · Canada · Mexico · Singapore · Spain · United Kingdom · United States

Accounting: Concepts and Applications, 8e, by W. Steve Albrecht, James D. Stice, Earl K. Stice, K. Fred Skousen, and Monte R. Swain (Consulting Editor)

Publisher: Dave Shaut
Acquisitions Editor: Sharon Oblinger
Developmental Editor: Leslie Kauffman, Litten Editing and Production, Inc.
Production Editor: Kara ZumBahlen
Manufacturing Coordinator: Doug Wilke
Marketing Manager: Dan Silverburg
Promotions Manager: Jon Schneider
Photo Research: Fred Middendorf
Photo Manager: Cary Benbow
Cover Design: Lamson Design/Cincinnati
Cover Photography: Greg Grosse Photography/Cincinnati
Internal Design: Michael H. Stratton
Production House: Peggy Shelton, Litten Editing and Production, Inc.
Compositor: GGS Information Services
Printer: R.R. Donnelley, Willard

Printed in the United States of America
2 3 4 5 04 03 02

For more information contact South-Western, 5191 Natorp Boulevard, Mason, Ohio, 45040 or find us on the Internet at http://www.swcollege.com

ISBN: 0-324-06669-4 (text and CD)
ISBN: 0-324-11170-3 (text only)
ISBN: 0-324-06760-7 (CD only)

Library of Congress Cataloging-in-Publication Data

Accounting concepts and applications/W. Steve Albrecht ... [et al.] — 8th ed.
p. cm.
Rev. ed. of: Accounting concepts and applications/K. Fred Skousen, W. Steve Albrecht, James D. Stice, 5th ed. c1996
Includes bibliographical references and index.
ISBN 0-324-06669-4
1. Accounting I. Albrecht, W. Steve. II. Skousen, K. Fred. Accounting concepts and applications.

HF5635 .S618 2001
657—dc21 00-067080

photo credits

Page f2	© AFP/CORBIS
Page f18	© Kevin Fleming/CORBIS
Page f30	© Bonnie Kamin/PhotoEdit
Page f55	© Duomo/CORBIS
Page f78	© Sandy Felsenthal/CORBIS
Page f80	© Bonnie Kamin/PhotoEdit
Page f130	© Donald Johnston/Tony Stone Images
Page f141	© Zigy Kaluzny/Tony Stone Images
Page f204	© AP/Wide World Photos
Page f213	© Michael Newman/PhotoEdit
Page f236	© Mark Richards/PhotoEdit
Page f239	© 2000 Choice Hotels International, Inc. Photo reprinted with the express consent of Choice Hotels International, Inc. Choice Hotels is the registered owner of the marks COMFORT, CLARION, ECONO LODGE, MAINSTAY, QUALITY, RODEWAY and SLEEP.
Page f292	Sears, Roebuck and Co.
Page f300	© Robert Brenner/PhotoEdit
Page f350	© Bill Ross/CORBIS
Page f370	Photo by Austin Post—Courtesy of U.S. Geological Survey Photographic Library
Page f394	© 2001/PhotoDisc, Inc.
Page f400	© Barbara Stitzer/PhotoEdit
Page f454	© Kelly-Mooney Photography/CORBIS
Page f466	© 2001/PhotoDisc, Inc.
Page f510	© Mark Adams/CORBIS
Page f515	© Wolfgang Kaehler/CORBIS
Page f568	© Michael S. Yamashita/CORBIS
Page f572	© Kevin R. Morris/CORBIS
Page f620	© 2001/PhotoDisc, Inc.
Page m12	© Bettmann/CORBIS
Page m38	© Manfred Vollmer/CORBIS
Page m53	© 2001/PhotoDisc, Inc.
Page m104	© Bettmann/CORBIS
Page m111	© 2001/PhotoDisc, Inc.
Page m182	© George Hall/CORBIS
Page m193	© Michael S. Yamashita/CORBIS
Page m232	© 2001/PhotoDisc, Inc.
Page m248	© 2001/PhotoDisc, Inc.
Page m298	© Sergio Dorantes/CORBIS
Page m315	© 2001/PhotoDisc, Inc.
Page m344	© Bob Rowan; Progressive Image/CORBIS
Page m353	© Dave Bartruff/CORBIS
Page m406	© 2001/PhotoDisc, Inc.
Page m410	© Philip Gould/CORBIS
Page m456	© 2001/PhotoDisc, Inc.
Page m474	© 2001/PhotoDisc, Inc.
Page m522	© Premium Stock/CORBIS
Page m529	© 2001/PhotoDisc, Inc.

brief contents

Part f1
Financial Reporting and the Accounting Cycle

Part f2
Operating Activities

Part f3
Investing and Financing Activities

Part f4
Other Dimensions of Financial Reporting

Part m1
Foundations

Part m2
Planning

Part m3
Control

Part m4
Evaluation

contents

Appendices

Financial Accounting Indexes

Management Accounting Indexes

The Best Team

Authors **W. Steve Albrecht, James D. Stice, Earl K. Stice,** and **K. Fred Skousen,** and Consulting Editor **Monte R. Swain** are all key players in the curriculum change process at Brigham Young University. Individually and as a team, the authors feel passionately about making this the most relevant and useful book you will ever use.

W. Steve Albrecht is the Arthur Andersen & Co. Alumni Professor of Accountancy and the Director of the School of Accountancy & Information Systems at Brigham Young University. He received a bachelor's degree in accounting from Brigham Young University and MBA and Ph.D. degrees from the University of Wisconsin at Madison. Dr. Albrecht, a certified public accountant, certified internal auditor, and certified fraud examiner, came to BYU in 1977 after teaching at Stanford and at the University of Illinois. Earlier in his career, he worked as a staff accountant for Deloitte & Touche. Dr. Albrecht has received numerous awards and honors, including the BYU School of Management's Outstanding Faculty Award and the BYU Outstanding Researcher Award, and was recognized, as part of Utah's Centennial Celebration, as one of 131 Utahians who have made outstanding contributions or brought unusual recognition to the state. Dr. Albrecht has served as President of the American Accounting Association, the Administrators of Accounting Programs Group, and the Association of Certified Fraud Examiners and is currently president-elect of Beta Alpha Psi.

James D. Stice is the Distinguished Teaching Professor of Accounting at Brigham Young University. He is also the Associate Director of BYU's MBA program. He holds bachelor's and master's degrees from BYU and a Ph.D. from the University of Washington, all in accounting. He has been on the faculty at BYU since 1988. During that time, he has been selected by graduating accounting students as "Teacher of the Year" on numerous occasions, selected by his peers in the Marriott School of Management at BYU to receive the "Outstanding Teaching Award," and received the University's top award for teaching excellence, the Maeser Award, in 1999. Professor Stice has published articles in *The Accounting Review, Decision Sciences, Issues in Accounting Education, The CPA Journal,* and other academic and professional journals.

Earl K. Stice is the PricewaterhouseCoopers Professor of Accounting in the School of Accountancy & Information Systems at Brigham Young University. He holds bachelor's and master's degrees from Brigham Young University and a Ph.D. from Cornell University. Dr. Stice has taught at Rice University, the University of Arizona, Cornell University, and the Hong Kong University of Science and Technology (HKUST). He won the Phi Beta Kappa teaching award at Rice University and was twice selected at HKUST as one of the ten best lecturers on campus. Dr. Stice has also taught in a variety of executive education and corporate training programs in the United States, Hong Kong, and South Africa. He has published papers in the *Journal of Financial and Quantitative Analysis, The Accounting Review, Review of Accounting Studies,* and *Issues in Accounting Education*, and his research on stock splits has been cited in *Business Week, Money,* and *Forbes.*

K. Fred Skousen is Advancement Vice President at Brigham Young University. Previously, he was Dean of the Marriott School of Management and Director of the School of Accountancy at BYU. He earned a bachelor's degree from BYU and master's and Ph.D. degrees from the University of Illinois. Dr. Skousen taught at the University of Illinois and the University of Minnesota prior to joining the faculty at Brigham Young University. In 1983, Dr. Skousen was awarded the Peat Marwick Professorship at BYU. In 1984, Dr. Skousen was elected to the AICPA Council, and in 1985, he received the UACPA Outstanding Faculty Award.

Monte R. Swain is an Associate Professor of management accounting and information systems at Brigham Young University. He received his undergraduate degree in accounting and his master's degree in management accounting from BYU. In 1992, Dr. Swain received his Ph.D. in management accounting and information systems from Michigan State University, received a university-wide teaching award, and was honored with the department's Outstanding Doctoral Scholar Award. At BYU, he has received the college Teaching Excellence Award several times, was named the Marriott School of Management Outstanding Teacher in 1999, and is listed on the Outstanding Faculty List in *Business Week's* "Guide to the Best Business Schools." Dr. Swain has published papers in a number of journals, including *Decision Sciences, Behavioral Research in Accounting,* the *Journal of Accounting Case Research,* the *Case Research Journal, Advances in Accounting Education,* and the *Journal of Accounting Education.*

How the Best got Better.

Text—Raising the Bar Even Higher

Through each successful edition, **Accounting: Concepts and Applications** has come to be the text by which all others are judged. With the perfect blend of procedure and concepts, the text gives students an inside, realistic view of how accounting is done in leading companies across the nation and around the world. Now in its eighth successful edition, the book takes the bar up a notch by offering a combination of new and proven features that make the best even better:

- An enhanced integration of real company financial statements and real-world examples in every chapter gives students a clear picture of how to use accounting information

- A completely integrated learning system that includes elements for classroom learning, technology-assisted learning, and distance learning
- An organization that focuses on the principal activities of a business—financing, investing, and operating

- A cumulative spreadsheet assignment that reinforces each chapter's topics
- Specialized customer service through trained and personal consultants

How the Best got Better

The Best Language for Business

In order for today's student to be the best, they must have a complete understanding of the numbers. Understanding what the numbers reveal, and what they do not reveal, allows business managers and investors to make every type of business decision: expand, merge, close, launch, subcontract, downsize, invest, reposition, lease, replace. As the basis for all these decisions, accounting is the universal language of business. This edition makes it even easier to understand what the numbers mean.

Take, for instance, the case of Safeway, a major supermarket chain, as examined in the opening vignette of **Chapter f2: Financial Statements: An Overview**. In the last twenty years, Safeway has experienced, at various times: falling market share, challenging union demands, high overhead, significant job cuts, an aggressive construction and remodeling program, a leveraged buyout, and reintroduction of the firm as a public company.

Safeway has the third largest sales of major supermarket chains today. Its current net income is higher than that of Kroger and Albertson's stores, which have higher sales volumes. What does the Safeway experience tell us? It tells us that to truly comprehend what is going on in a business, whether in the grocery store or in the corporate boardroom, one must understand accounting data—both how it is prepared and why it is meaningful.

Changing for the Better

The past few years have seen many calls for improving accounting education. This call for change drove past editions of **Accounting: Concepts and Applications** to be the best book on the market. The central themes in all these calls for change have been (1) that the business world and accounting professions are changing rapidly, (2) that accountants of the past must become the premier information professionals of the future, and (3) that accounting and business graduates need new skills and knowledge if they are to effectively meet tomorrow's professional demands. We answered those calls by creating a textbook that teaches students both how to prepare financial statements and how to use that accounting information to make smart business decisions.

In creating this Eighth Edition, we crafted a textbook that does an even better job of addressing the needs of an ever-changing world of accounting education. **Accounting: Concepts and Applications,** Eighth Edition is written and organized in a manner that allows students and instructors at all institutions to capitalize on our positive curriculum development experience and strive to make the best education even better.

The Best Approach

Real Numbers, Real Understanding

Today's business students need to have an understanding of the basics of accounting, no matter what their future career plans include. Most will be business managers that use accounting information to make business decisions, but even then, in order to make sound decisions, one must understand how the accounting information was derived. And, of course, those students who plan an accounting career need a strong foundation upon which to build. **Accounting: Concepts and Applications** has built a reputation as the best balance of these attributes by using real company financials to give students an understanding of why and how accounting works. Our approach to this book is to introduce students to basic accounting concepts, excite them by using lots of real-world examples (both U.S. and international), provide them with some basic accounting knowledge, and then show them how accounting is used and analyzed in actual case situations.

The Eighth Edition continues this rich tradition and makes it better. The authors have taken great care to fully integrate the use of real company financials within the content of the chapters. For instance, in Chapter f2 *(Financial Statements: An Overview)*, the Setting the Stage opening vignette focuses on Safeway. Safeway's balance sheet and income statement are analyzed within the chapter. Also, several basic ratio calculations are taught in the chapter, and examples are shown using Safeway's numbers. In the CEO material at the end of the chapter, one of the *Analyzing Real Company Information* exercises centers on Safeway and further analysis of its financial statements.

The Best Business is Real Business

On the road from better to best, every company, regardless of its industry or type, must manage its business to acquire and sell products or services, make financing decisions, and invest in assets that will help the company generate growth and income. One of the reasons that **Accounting: Concepts and Applications** is the best is that we use an organizational format that is consistent with business activities and cycles (as opposed to the more traditional financial statement organization). This same approach was used in the last edition of the book, which was well received by reviewers and adopters. Specifically, after introducing and explaining financial reporting and the accounting cycle in Part f1 (Chapters 1-5), we discuss the operating activities of a business in Part f2 (Chapters 6-8) and the investing and financing activities in Part f3 (Chapters 9-12). We conclude the financial portion of the text by discussing the statement of cash flows in Part f4 (Chapter 13). This focus on business activities helps students understand functions of business and see accounting as a tool to assist in making business decisions, not as an end in itself.

Ahead of the Curve

With the Best Technology

Today's students learn in more visual and interactive ways than ever before. These are students that have grown up in a multimedia- and technology-enhanced world. In order to educate these students, technology must be employed as an efficient means for both teaching and learning accounting. Educators now have the opportunity to bring more information to students in more media than ever before. **Accounting: Concepts and Applications** takes full advantage of these possibilities with the best technology package that fills a variety of needs. The technology package consists of three distinct elements that can effectively be woven together. The three elements are *Product Web Site, Personal Trainer,* and the *Personal Web Tutor.* Some key facets to this package include:

- Lecture Replacement/Enhancement
- Concept Reinforcement
- Application
- Competency/Testing/Quizzing
- Remediation

Flexible Coverage

Brings out the Best in Instructors

Because the authors know that the best instructors continually try to make their classrooms better, we have preserved the text's innovation of dividing most chapters into two parts. This flexibility allows the instructor the chance to easily alter what they cover in class to fit the needs of their particular students. The first part includes material that needs to be covered to understand essential accounting concepts, while the second part features "expanded material" dealing with additional topics to be covered at the instructor's discretion.

This strategy of dividing chapters into basic and expanded material was universally applauded by users of our last edition. It allows significant flexibility in covering desired material, without the disruption of skipping to appendices for more advanced material. Also note that end-of-chapter materials are divided and labeled to coincide with the essential/expanded division in the chapters.

The Best of the Best

Outstanding Features

Special Margin Features

This edition makes the connection to real-life business even better with the use of many insightful pedagogical features and real-world examples. As real companies and current events are examined, the focus is not only on how business managers collect and record data, but also why the information is important as the basis for decisions. For example, Microsoft's annual report is provided at the end of the text and referenced throughout.

Other Pedagogy

LEARNING OBJECTIVES Each chapter begins with specific learning objectives to guide students in their study of the chapter. Where applicable, chapters include expanded learning objectives.

SETTING THE STAGE An interesting, real-life scenario sets the stage for each chapter. These scenarios tie directly to materials covered in the chapter and help students relate chapter topics to actual business happenings. For example, Chapter f6 begins with a discussion of Yahoo!, and many examples using Yahoo!'s financial data are featured throughout the chapter.

BUSINESS ENVIRONMENT ESSAYS The text contains numerous real-world vignettes, adapted from financial newspapers and business publications, which illustrate important concepts being discussed. These examples enable students to see how the accounting topics they are studying are applied and interpreted in real-world situations.

KEY TERMS Throughout each chapter, key terms are defined in the margins. A list of key terms (with Page references) is presented at the end of each chapter, and all key terms are defined in a comprehensive glossary at the end of the book.

SUMMARIES Several concise summaries are presented within each chapter to help students remember the important points just discussed, and each chapter concludes with a comprehensive summary, organized by learning objectives.

FYI
FYI features provide relevant information for students, drawing from real business events or situations.

STOP & THINK
Students are encouraged to take a step back occasionally to consider thought-provoking issues.

CAUTION
These reminders speak directly to students, helping them avoid common mistakes or misconceptions.

NET WORK
These exercises give students practice in seeking out information on the Internet.

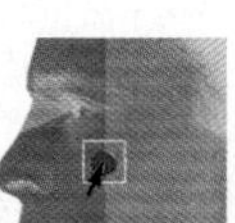

More Outstanding Features

REVIEW PROBLEMS A review problem is provided at the end of each chapter (where applicable). These review problems (with solutions) demonstrate the application of the major concepts and procedures covered in the chapter.

CUMULATIVE SPREADSHEET PROJECT The cumulative spreadsheet project builds in Chapters f2-f13. It is based on cash flow difficulties faced by The Home Depot at the end of 1985, but a fictitious name (Handyman) is used. The early assignments simply have the students construct a spreadsheet balance sheet and do a couple of simple manipulations, ratio calculations, and so forth. By the end of the text, the spreadsheet grows to a five-year forecast of operating cash flows that depends on assumptions about different operating parameters (speed of receivables collection, inventory efficiency, interest rates, sales growth, profitability).

COMPREHENSIVE PROBLEMS Five comprehensive problems, integrating multiple issues and methods, are found throughout the text.

FOCUS ON GLOBAL ECONOMY As mentioned, the focus in today's business world is on a global economy. To help students develop this global perspective, many international examples are provided throughout the Eighth Edition. In addition, there is at least one International Case provided at the end of each chapter.

FOCUS ON ETHICS Ethical considerations are increasingly important in all aspects of business. A section in Chapter f1 introduces the topic of ethics in financial accounting. Each chapter contains an Ethics Case relating to the topics covered in the chapter. These cases present ethical dilemmas that require students to think about behavioral and moral issues in business and accounting. We believe these ethics cases will provide a basis for rich classroom discussions and more responsible business conduct by students exposed to them.

Practice Makes the Best Better

The old adage *"practice makes perfect"* holds true in accounting. This book has all the traditional end-of-chapter assignments which has rendered it the best. Before describing the traditional material, however, we want you to understand our excitement for what makes this book even better: the **Competency Enhancement Opportunities** (CEO) that are included in the end-of-chapter material. Responding to well-justified calls for changes in accounting education, this material is included to help students develop critical thinking, ethical perspectives, oral and written communication skills, experience with electronic research, and team skills.

In each chapter's assignments, the CEO section begins with *Analyzing Real Company Information* exercises, based on actual company annual reports and data. CEO also includes:

- *International cases,* focusing on businesses that operate across international borders
- *Ethics cases,* examining issues of personal and business responsibilities
- *Writing assignments,* to be completed individually or in groups
- *Debates,* requiring two teams to argue the opposing sides of an accounting issue
- *Cumulative spreadsheet project,* building from one chapter to the next (included in the financial accounting chapters only)
- *Internet search exercises,* requiring students to find specific information on the Net

We believe students will find these assignments very relevant, interesting, and beneficial in their business careers. Users have responded favorably to the traditional end-of-chapter assignments in previous editions. The discussion questions are intended to refine students' understanding of specific accounting terms and concepts. Discussion cases encourage classroom discussion of real-world business situations. Exercises deal with single concepts, and each can be completed fairly quickly. Problems probe for a deeper level of understanding. Those problems identified as "Unifying Concepts" and those with "Interpretive Questions" require students to analyze or interpret the computed results.

The Best Support, the Best Service

Because we know how difficult Introductory Accounting can be to both teach and learn, we are not satisfied with merely offering the best textbook. We take it one step better by offering the most comprehensive and carefully prepared educational package available today.
The package accompanying **Accounting: Concepts and Applications** consists of more than simple "supplements." Taken in whole, it is a comprehensive teaching and learning system that incorporates the Internet, powerful multimedia, and exceptional printed materials—all coming together to create an educational experience unlike any other. Using the text in combination with these well-designed ancillaries makes it simple—and smart—to integrate technology into your course and makes it easy to be the best that you can be.

For more information on any of these supplements, don't hesitate to contact your South-Western/Thomson Learning™ sales representative. They are committed to providing you with unparalleled service and support.

Ancillary Materials

Available to Instructors

Thomson Learning is committed to providing you, our educational partners, with the best educational resources available. Because we prepare our instructor resources with a variety of teaching environments in mind, it is likely that you will need only a portion of these for your course. Before you request an item, we ask that you please read thoroughly the description of each resource. If you still need more information about resources, we urge you to contact your local Thomson Learning sales representative or visit our Web site at http://albrecht.swcollege.com. Many teaching and learning resources can be downloaded directly from this site.

Instructor's Resource CD This CD contains all the resources listed below (except the videos) in an easily accessible format. No longer will you have to lug heavy print items from school to home back to school again. This CD is your one-stop resource for assistance in teaching your course.

Web Site This site, http://albrecht.swcollege.com, contains downloadable supplements, current articles related to chapter content from academic periodicals, Internet exercises and related URLs, accounting career information, lecture enhancement slides, and numerous other teaching resources.

Solutions Manuals (Prepared by W. Steve Albrecht, James D. Stice, Earl K. Stice, and Monte R. Swain) These manuals contain independently verified answers to all end-of-chapter discussion questions, discussion cases, exercises, problems, and Competency Enhancement Opportunities (CEO). Suggested solutions to the Stop & Think questions are also included.

Instructor's Manuals (Prepared by Michael Shapeero, Bloomsburg University) These manuals contain learning objectives, chapter outlines, topical overviews of end-of-chapter materials, and assignment classifications with level of difficulty and estimated completion time. Transparency masters for each chapter are also provided.

Test Banks (*Financial Accounting* chapters prepared by Dick Wasson, Southwestern College; *Management Accounting* chapters prepared by Peggy Hussey)
The revised and expanded test banks contain a collection of more than 2,000 examination problems, multiple-choice questions, true-false questions, and matching exercises, all accompanied by solutions.

ExamView® Computerized Testing Software This supplement contains all of the questions in the printed test bank. This program is an easy-to-use test creation software compatible with Microsoft Windows®. Instructors can add or edit questions, instructions, and answers, and select questions (randomly or numerically) by previewing them on the screen. Instructors can also create and administer quizzes online, whether over the Internet, a local area network (LAN), or a wide area network (WAN).

Solutions Transparencies Acetate transparencies of solutions for all end-of-chapter exercises and problems are available to text adopters.

PowerPoint™ Slides (Prepared by Michael Blue, Bloomsburg University) Selected teaching transparency slides of key concepts and exhibits are available in PowerPoint presentation software, improving lecture organization and reducing preparation time.

Teaching Transparencies Acetate transparencies of key concepts and exhibits are available to text adopters.

BusinessLink™ Videos Two videos, one for financial accounting and one for management accounting, feature segments of actual companies illustrating key accounting concepts. Instructor's Manuals are available to assist in the use of the videos and the optional student workbooks.

Available to Students

Personal Trainer Online (Hints and Tips prepared by Suneel Maheshwari, Marshall University)
This Internet-based resource is designed to help students complete end-of-chapter assignments with helpful hints and interactive tips. By giving students this additional assistance in applying the concepts of the course you are ensuring their understanding of complex topics.

Study Guides (Prepared by W. Steve Albrecht, James D. Stice, Earl K. Stice, and Monte R. Swain)
The study guides provide a means for students to re-examine the concepts and procedures in each chapter from several different perspectives. These publications include learning objectives; detailed chapter summaries; discussions of topics that typically cause problems for students and suggestions for overcoming those problems; and tests for student self-assessment.

Working Papers Forms for solving end-of-chapter problems are perforated for easy removal and use.

Homework Assistant and Tutor (HAT) Software (Prepared by Rayman Meservy, Brigham Young University) This user-friendly software for Windows visually teaches the relationships among journals, ledgers, and financial statements. A built-in tutor function offers numerous hints and help screens. The software can be used to solve selected end-of-chapter exercises and problems, identified with the HAT icon. It is also an ideal teaching aid.

General Ledger Software (Prepared by Warren Allen and Dale Klooster)
This best-selling educational general ledger package may be used to solve selected end-of-chapter problems, which are identified with the general ledger icon.

Spreadsheet Templates (Prepared by Michael Blue, Bloomsburg University)
Excel templates are provided for solving selected end-of-chapter exercises and problems, which are identified with the spreadsheet icon.

BusinessLink™ Video Workbooks These workbooks enrich understanding of the BusinessLink videos through questions and related activities.

Personal Finance Resource CD-ROM This supplement helps students understand how the concepts they learn in the textbook can assist them in making better personal financial decisions. Topics have been chosen and ordered to correlate with the chapters in the textbook.

Related Products

Annual Report Project and Readings (0-324-02473-8)

This highly popular project by Bruce Baldwin of Arizona State University West is designed for use by either learning teams or individual students. It is tailored to reinforce the concepts presented in the financial accounting chapters of the text. Students work with annual reports of real companies to understand, interpret, and analyze the information. The project guides them through this process. Interesting readings from publications like *The Wall Street Journal* along with supporting Questions for Consideration provide additional material for discussion.

INTACCT (rama.swcollege.com)

This software and online tutorial by Dasaratha Rama reviews each major step in the accounting cycle in a short, user-friendly manner that is easily integrated into classroom use. It is designed for use in a financial accounting course or any course where a review of the accounting cycle is desired.

Using QuickBooks Pro '99 for Accounting (0-324-02831-8)

Written by Glenn Owen of Alan Hancock College, this book provides a self-paced environment where students use commercial software to analyze, interpret, and investigate accounting information to make business decisions.

preface 8e

Hazzard Travel (0-538-86552-0)

With this computerized simulation, students maintain an accounting system for the first two months of operation of Hazzard Travel, a small service business. Created by Donna Ulmer, St. Louis Community College at Meramec, and M. Robert Carver, Southern Illinois University–Edwardsville, this practice set familiarizes students with basic accounting documents, procedures, and concepts. Students make investing, financing, and operating decisions that may result in a different financial outcome from their classmates. The problems are unstructured, encouraging creativity and individual judgment.

Excel Applications for Accounting Principles (0-538-88887-3)

These text-workbooks, by Gaylord Smith, Albion College, include a software tutorial and accounting application with an accompanying template disk. Preprogrammed problems require students to develop formulas and enter data to complete partially constructed spreadsheet models. Model-building problems give students experience in developing their own spreadsheet models.

Accounting Fundamentals 2nd Edition (0-324-02361-8)

William Ruland, CUNY-Baruch College, has designed this self-paced workbook to help financial statement users who may have had little or no exposure to the accounting system understand accounting procedures.

Acknowledgements

Throughout the textbook, relevant publications of standard-setting and professional organizations are discussed, quoted, or paraphrased. We are indebted to the American Accounting Association, the American Institute of Certified Public Accountants, and the Financial Accounting Standards Board for material from their publications.

The eighth edition of **Accounting: Concepts and Applications** reflects many comments and suggestions from colleagues and students, all of which are deeply appreciated. In particular, we wish to thank the following accounting educators who have served as reviewers, diary keepers, and focus group participants:

Anwer Ahmed	Syracuse University
Matthew J. Anderson	Michigan State University
James W. Bannister	University of Hartford
Benjamin W. Bean	Utah Valley State College
Patricia A. Doherty	Boston University
Janice Glatt	North Dakota State University
Jeri Griego	Laramie County Community College
Gerald Lobo	Syracuse University
Robert L. Putman	University of Tennessee at Martin
Donald J. Raux	Sienna College
Lola Rhodes	Southern Methodist University
Frederic M. Stiner, Jr.	University of Delaware
Cynthia VanGelderen	Aquinas College

We would like to thank Cathy Xanthaky Larson, Middlesex Community College, for checking the accuracy of the text and solutions manuals. Her meticulous review contributed to a more concise, higher-quality product. We would also like to thank James Emig, Villanova University, who served as verifier for the test banks and study guides.

Steve Albrecht
Jim Stice
Kay Stice
Fred Skousen
Monte Swain

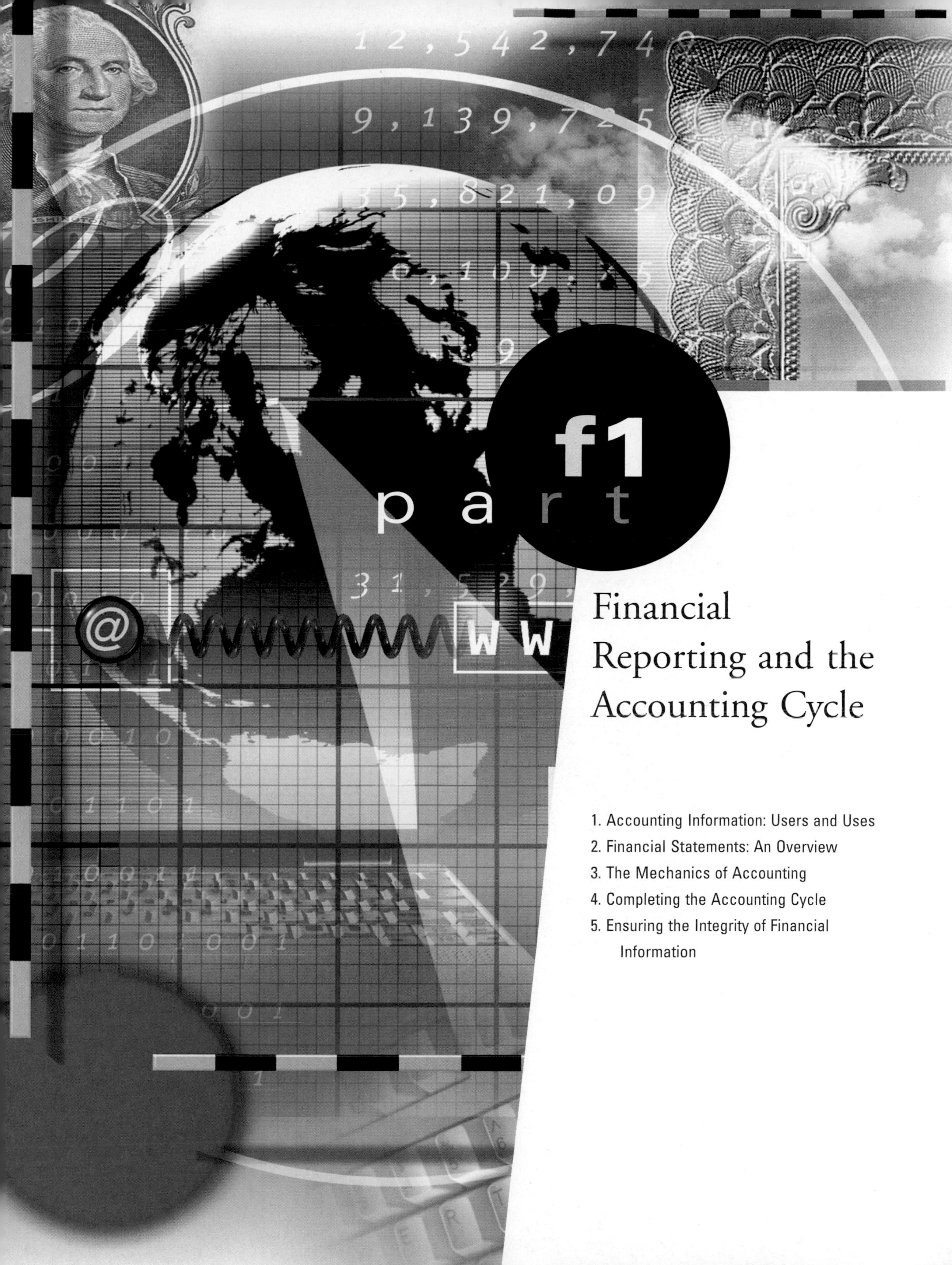

part f1

Financial Reporting and the Accounting Cycle

Accounting Information: Users and Uses

chapter f1

learning objectives

After studying this chapter, you should be able to:

1. Describe the purpose of accounting and explain its role in business and society.
2. Identify the primary users of accounting information.
3. Describe the environment of accounting, including the effects of generally accepted accounting principles, international business, ethical considerations, and technology.
4. Analyze the reasons for studying accounting.

setting the stage

In 1987, IBM was the most valuable company in the world, worth an estimated $105.8 billion. By the end of 1992, IBM had an estimated value of $28.8 billion. This decline in value can be traced to a strategic error made by IBM in the early 1980s. Prior to 1981, IBM was the major player in the computer market and was the primary provider of computers for government, universities, and businesses. At this time, believe it or not, virtually no computers were available at an affordable price for individuals. Then, in 1981, IBM introduced its personal computer (IBM PC), and it quickly established the standard by which other PCs would be measured. However, IBM elected to leave the software development for PCs to other companies. Instead of developing its own disk operating system (DOS), IBM elected to use a DOS developed by a small company located in Seattle—MICROSOFT.[1]

Microsoft was founded in 1975 by Bill Gates and Paul Allen.[2] When they founded Microsoft, Gates and Allen envisioned that computers would eventually find their way into everyday life (contrary to IBM's prediction in the 1950s when one IBM executive forecast the total worldwide demand for computers to be about five). While IBM's performance floundered in the mid- and late-1980s, Microsoft demonstrated an amazing ability to become a major player in practically every aspect of the computer software market—from operating systems to the Internet to networks to spreadsheets and word processors.

With Microsoft's many accomplishments comes the question: "Just how successful is the company?" The answer to that question depends on how you define "success." Measured in terms of number of employees, Microsoft has grown from just 32 employees in 1981 when IBM elected to use Microsoft's DOS to 31,575 as of the June 30, 1999, fiscal year. In terms of social impact, Microsoft and its employees donate millions of dollars each year to such charitable causes as Special Olympics, Boys and Girls Clubs, and the United Negro College Fund. Microsoft also supports elementary and high schools throughout the country in their efforts to incorporate technology into the curriculum, and the company has established scholarship programs to encourage minorities and women to pursue careers in computer science and related technical fields. In addition, Bill Gates and his wife Melinda have started a foundation dedicated primarily to health and education. Thus far they have contributed several billion dollars to their foundation.

In fact, many people are of the opinion that Microsoft has succeeded too well. Several of Microsoft's competitors allege that Microsoft is involved in monopolistic practices that stifle competition. As this book goes to press, the government is considering several options relating to Microsoft's business practices including breaking the company into several smaller entities.

In terms of stock price, Microsoft's per share stock price (adjusted for stock splits) has gone from $0.17 in 1986 to over $70 in April of 2000 (see Exhibit 1-1). On virtually every dimension you can think of, Microsoft has succeeded. But most of these dimensions are a by-product of Microsoft's ability to produce products that are valued by the market. If Microsoft were unable to produce and sell quality products, the company would not be in a position to employ so many people, to give so much money to charities, to dominate (some would say monopolize) its markets, or to experience such an incredible increase in stock price. And this is where accounting enters the picture.

1 The decision to have another company develop the software for its personal computer was not IBM's only strategic error. At the same time, IBM decided to use another company's microprocessors—the "brains" of the computer. As a result, another successful company was born—INTEL. IBM lost the opportunity to dominate the software market as well as the computer chip market. By May 2000, Microsoft, Intel, and IBM had market values exceeding $364 billion, $398 billion, and $195 billion, respectively.

2 Everybody knows Bill Gates, but few people know about Paul Allen. Allen was Microsoft's head of research and new product development until 1983 when a serious illness caused him to leave the company. He still remains on the company's board of directors and is Microsoft's second largest shareholder. He now spends much of his time investing in technology companies and watching the Seattle Seahawks, a professional football team, and the Portland Trailblazers, a professional basketball team—both of which he owns.

exhibit 1-1 History of Microsoft's Stock Price Per Share

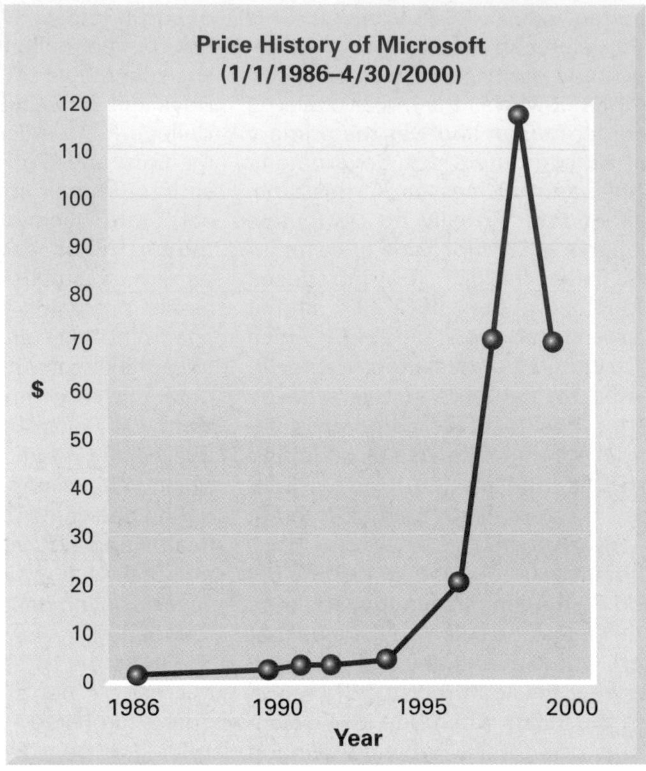

In this textbook, you will begin your study of accounting. You will learn to speak and understand accounting, "the language of business." Without an understanding of accounting, business investments, taxes, and money management will be like a foreign language to you. In brief, an understanding of accounting facilitates the interpretation of financial information, which allows for better economic decisions.

caution

Don't be too concerned with all the new and unfamiliar terms you see in the first chapter of the book. Learning a "new language" takes time. Be patient. Before too long, you will be speaking the "language of business" (accounting) quite fluently.

The major objectives of this text are to provide you with a basic understanding of the language of accounting and with the ability to interpret and use financial information prepared using accounting techniques and procedures. With the knowledge you obtain from this exposure to accounting, you will be able to "read" the financial statements of companies such as Microsoft, understand the information that is being conveyed, and use accounting information to make good business decisions. Also, through discussion of the business environment in which accounting is used, you will increase your understanding of general business concepts such as corporations, leases, annuities, leverage, derivatives (the financial kind, not the calculus kind), and so forth.

You will become convinced that accounting is not "bean counting." Time after time you will see that accountants must exercise judgment about how to best summarize and report the results of business transactions. As a result, you will gain a respect for the complexity of accounting and develop a healthy skepticism about the precision of any financial reports you see.

Finally, you will see the power of accounting. Financial statements are not just paper reports that get filed away and forgotten. You will see that financial statement numbers, and, indirectly, the accountants who prepare them, determine who receives loans and who doesn't, which companies attract investors and which don't, which managers receive salary bonuses and which don't, and which companies are praised in the financial press and which aren't.

So, let's get started.

1

Describe the purpose of accounting and explain its role in business and society.

WHAT'S THE PURPOSE OF ACCOUNTING?

Imagine a long distance telephone company with no system in place to document who calls whom and how long they talk. Or a manager of a 300-unit apartment complex who has forgotten to write down which tenants have and have not paid this month's rent. Or an accounting professor who, the day before final grades are due, loses the only copy of the disk containing the spreadsheet of all the homework, quiz, and exam scores. Each of these scenarios illustrates a problem with bookkeeping, the least glamorous aspect of accounting. **Bookkeeping** is the preservation of a systematic, quantitative record of an activity. Bookkeeping systems can be very primitive—cutting notches in a stick to tally how many sheep you have or moving beads on a string to track the score in a billiards game. But the importance of routine bookkeeping cannot be overstated; without bookkeeping, business is impossible.

bookkeeping The preservation of a systematic, quantitative record of an activity.

To evaluate the importance of bookkeeping records, we'll use a thought experiment. Suppose that sometime during the night, every copy of every novel ever written were to disappear. Could life proceed normally the next day? While the cultural loss would be incalculable, the normal activities of the next day would not be noticeably affected. What if television were suddenly gone when we woke up? While we might wander around wondering what to do with our time, life would go on. But what if we woke up tomorrow morning to find the bookkeeping records of all businesses worldwide destroyed during the night? Businesses that rely on up-to-the-minute customer account information, such as banks, simply could not open their doors. Retailers would have to insist on cash purchases, since no credit records could be verified. Manufacturers would have to do a quick count of existing inventories of raw materials and components to find out whether they could keep their production lines running. Suppliers would have to call all their customers, if they could remember who they were, to renegotiate purchase orders. Attorneys would find themselves in endless arguments about their fees because they would have no record of billable hours. Routine and dry as bookkeeping may seem, the world simply could not function for one day without it.

Rudimentary bookkeeping is ancient, probably predating both language and money. The modern system of double-entry bookkeeping still in use today (described in Chapter 3) was developed in the 1300s–1400s in Italy by the merchants in the trading and banking centers of Florence, Venice, and Genoa. The key development in accounting in the last 500 years has been the use of the bookkeeping data, not just to keep track of things, but to evaluate the performance and health of a business.

This use of bookkeeping data as an evaluation tool may seem obvious to you, but it is a step that is often not taken. Let's consider a bookkeeping system with which most of us are familiar—a checking account. Your checking account involves (or should involve) careful recording of the dates and amounts of all checks written and all deposits made, the maintenance of a running account total, and reconciliations with the monthly bank statement. Now, assume that you have a perfect checking account bookkeeping system. Will the system answer the following questions?

- Are you spending more for groceries this year than you did last year?
- What proportion of your monthly expenditures are fixed, meaning that you can't change them except through a drastic change in lifestyle?
- You plan to study abroad next year; will you be able to save enough between now and then to pay for it?

In order to answer these kinds of evaluation questions, each check must be analyzed to determine the type of expenditure, your checks must then be coded by type of expenditure, the data must be boiled down into summary reports, and past data must be used to forecast future patterns. How many of us use our checking account data like this? Not many. We do the bookkeeping (usually), but we don't structure the information to be used for evaluation.

accounting system The procedures and processes used by a business to analyze transactions, handle routine bookkeeping tasks, and structure information so it can be used to evaluate the performance and health of the business.

In summary, an **accounting system** is used by a business to (1) analyze transactions, (2) handle routine bookkeeping tasks, and (3) structure information so it can be used to evaluate the performance and health of the business. Exhibit 1-2 illustrates the three functions of the accounting system.

exhibit 1-2 Functions of an Accounting System

Analysis

Analyze business events to determine if information should be captured by the accounting system

Bookkeeping

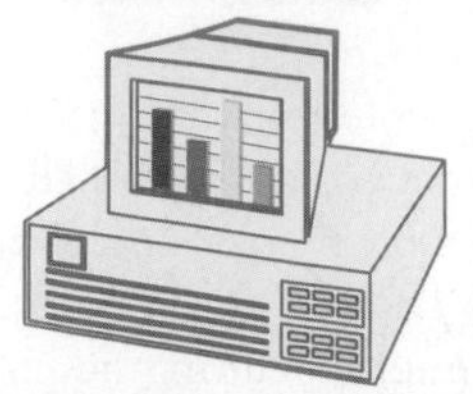

Day-to-day keeping track of things

Evaluation

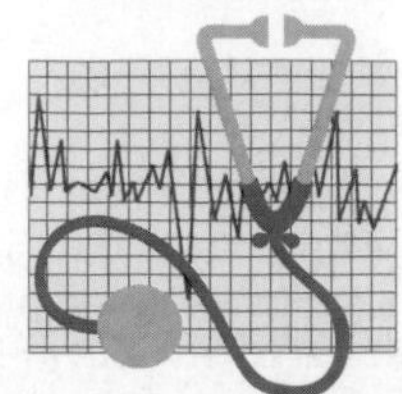

Use summary information to evaluate the financial health and performance of the business

accounting A system for providing quantitative, financial information about economic entities that is useful for making sound economic decisions. Accounting is often called the "language of business" because it provides the means of recording and communicating business activities and the results of those activities.

Accounting is formally defined as a system for providing "quantitative information, primarily financial in nature, about economic entities that is intended to be useful in making economic decisions."[3] The key components of this definition are:

- *Quantitative.* Accounting relates to numbers. This is a strength because numbers can be easily tabulated and summarized. It is a weakness because some important business events, such as a toxic waste spill and the associated lawsuits and countersuits, cannot be easily described by one or two numbers.
- *Financial.* The health and performance of a business are affected by and reflected in many dimensions—financial, personal relationships, community and environmental impact, and public image. Accounting focuses on just the financial dimension.
- *Useful.* The practice of accounting is supported by a long tradition of theory. U.S. accounting rules have a theoretical conceptual framework. Some people actually make a living as accounting theorists. However, in spite of its theoretical beauty, accounting exists only because it is useful.
- *Decisions.* Although accounting is the structured reporting of what has already occurred, this past information can only be useful if it impacts decisions about the future.

Making good decisions is critical for success in any business enterprise. When an important decision must be made, it is essential to use a rational decision-making process. The process is basically the same no matter how complex the issue. First, the issue or question must be clearly identified. Next, the facts surrounding the situation must be gathered and analyzed. Then, several alternative courses of action should be identified and considered before a decision is finally reached. This decision-making process is summarized in Exhibit 1-3.

One must be careful to make a distinction between a good decision and a good outcome. Often, many factors outside the control of the decision maker affect the outcome of a decision. The decision-making process does not guarantee a certain result; it only ensures that a good decision is made. To illustrate this process, let's consider an example. It's Friday afternoon, the sun is shining, your homework is done, and you have the rest of the afternoon and evening ahead of you. What to do? You check the movie listings in the newspaper to see if there are any new movies you haven't seen, you call several of your friends to see what they are doing, and you review your list of "things you always wanted to organize around your apartment but never had the time." With this information, you decide that you could either (1) go to the new Tom Hanks movie with a group of friends or (2) go over to your friend's house and watch TV. (Spending time at home organizing your sock drawer on a Friday night is out of the question.) You

3 Statement of the Accounting Principles Board No. 4, "Basic Concepts and Accounting Principles Underlying Financial Statements of Business Enterprises," New York: American Institute of Certified Public Accountants, 1970, par. 40.

exhibit 1-3 The Decision-Making Process

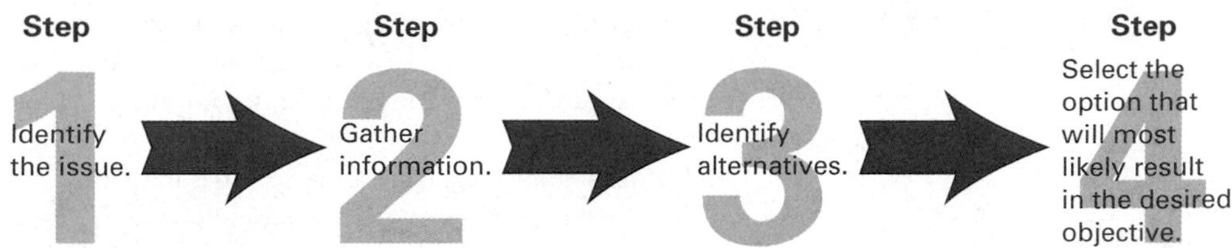

decide to go to the movies. You get to the movie theater, buy your ticket, your popcorn, and your drink, then select a seat. The lights dim, the movie starts, and the only empty seat left in the theater is right in front of you. It turns out you have the best seat in the house—until Shaquille O'Neal (7′2″, 300 pounds) comes in and sits in that seat. Good decision, bad outcome.

The four steps of the decision-making process lead to the best decision under the circumstances, but the outcome always has an element of chance. Part of business is learning how to protect yourself against bad outcomes. The first step in achieving a favorable outcome begins with making a good decision.

Accounting plays a vital role in the decision-making process. An accounting system provides information in a form that can be used to make knowledgeable financial decisions. The information supplied by accounting is in the form of quantitative data, primarily financial in nature, and relates to specific economic entities. An economic entity may be an individual, a business enterprise, or a nonprofit organization. A **business**, such as a grocery store or a car dealership, is operated with the objective of making a profit for its owners. The goal of a **nonprofit organization**, such as a city government or a university, is to provide services in an effective and efficient manner. Every entity, regardless of its size or purpose, must have a way to keep track of its economic activities and to measure how well it is accomplishing its goals. Accounting provides the means for tracking activities and measuring results.

business An organization operated with the objective of making a profit from the sale of goods or services.

nonprofit organization An entity without a profit objective, oriented toward providing services efficiently and effectively.

Without accounting information, many important financial decisions would be made blindly. Investors, for example, would have no way to distinguish between a profitable company and one that is on the verge of failure; bankers could not evaluate the riskiness of potential loans; corporate managers would have no basis for controlling costs, setting prices, or investing the company's resources; and governments would have no basis for taxing income. No list of examples could fully represent the pervasive use of accounting information throughout our economic, social, and political institutions. When accounting information is used effectively as a basis for making economic decisions, limited resources are more likely to be allocated efficiently. From a broad perspective, the result is a healthier economy and a higher standard of living.

The value of accounting information can also be illustrated on a personal level. Since very few of us will ever make more money than we can spend, we each will be making choices as to what to do with our limited incomes. For example, assume you have a job that results in take-home pay of $2,000 per month. What do you do with the money? If you are making monthly payments on a home and/or an automobile, you previously made choices to use part of your monthly income for these two items. How about a trip around the world, season tickets for your favorite basketball team, or a new home entertainment system? You could spend your money on these items, but that might not be the best use of your income. After all, you haven't eaten yet. Routine expenditures for food, clothing, and utilities must be made. How much money will you need for these and other everyday expenditures? By collecting financial information relating to prior months' inflows and outflows of cash, you will be able to approximate how much money you will need for this month. This process—called *budgeting* (discussed later)—is often used by individuals (and businesses) to ensure that monthly income is used in the best manner possible. While it is true that budgeting is not necessary, budgeting is part of good decision making.

The Relationship of Accounting to Business

Business is the general term applied to the activities involved in the production and distribution of goods and services. Accounting is used to record and report the financial effects of business activities. Thus, as mentioned earlier, accounting is often called the "language of business." It provides the means of recording and communicating the successes and failures of business organizations.

All business enterprises have some activities in common. As shown in Exhibit 1-4, one common activity is the acquisition of monetary resources. These resources, often referred to as "capital," come from three sources: (1) investors (owners), (2) creditors (lenders), and (3) the business itself in the form of earnings that have been retained. Once resources are obtained, they are used to buy land, buildings, and equipment; to purchase materials and supplies; to pay employees; and to meet any other operating expenses involved in the production and marketing of goods or services. When the product or service is sold, additional monetary resources (revenues) are generated. These resources can be used to pay loans, to pay taxes, and to buy new materials, equipment, and other items needed to continue the operations of the business. In addition,

exhibit 1-4 Activities Common to Business Organizations

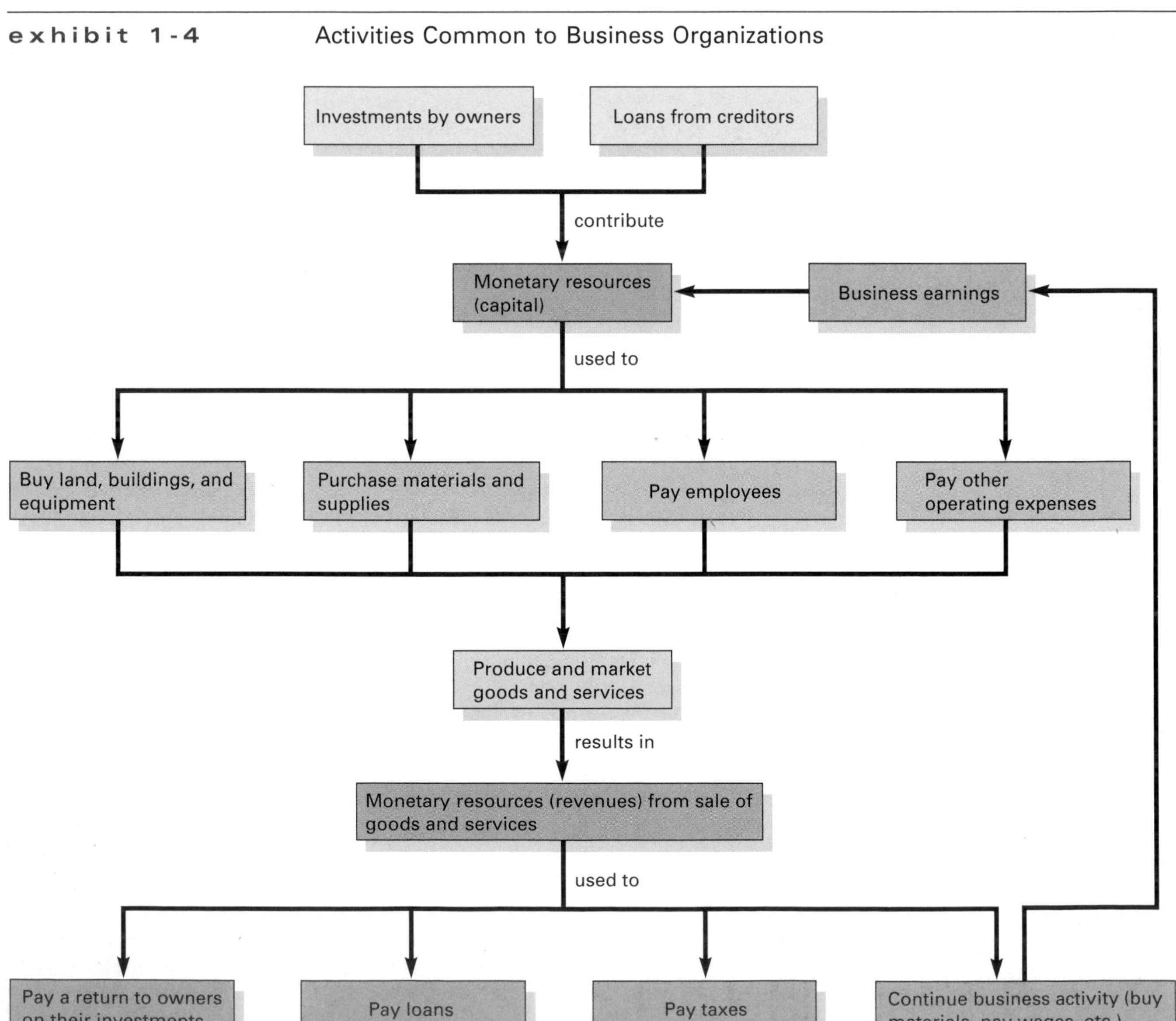

some of the resources may be distributed to owners as a return on their investment. MICROSOFT, for example, uses the earnings from its operations to fund research and development and to purchase other companies. The developed (or purchased) products can then be sold at a profit under the Microsoft name. This produces more funds that can then be used to purchase more companies or develop more products. Microsoft currently does not distribute its resources back to its owners. Owners receive a return on their investment through the growth in value of the stock.

accounting cycle The procedure for analyzing, recording, classifying, summarizing, and reporting the transactions of a business.

Accountants measure and communicate (report) the results of these activities. In order to measure these results as accurately as possible, accountants follow a fairly standard set of procedures, usually referred to as the **accounting cycle**. The cycle includes several steps, which involve analyzing, recording, classifying, summarizing, and reporting the transactions of a business. These steps are explained in detail in Chapters 3 and 4.

to summarize

Accounting is a service activity designed to accumulate, measure, and communicate financial information about economic entities—businesses and nonprofit organizations. Its purpose is to provide information used to make informed decisions about how to best use available resources. Accounting is often called the "language of business" because it provides the means of recording and communicating business activities and the results of those activities.

2

Identify the primary users of accounting information.

WHO USES ACCOUNTING INFORMATION?

management accounting The area of accounting concerned with providing internal financial reports to assist management in making decisions.

The accounting system generates output in the form of financial reports. As shown in Exhibit 1-5, there are two major categories of reports: internal and external. Internal reports are used by those who direct the day-to-day operations of a business enterprise. These individuals are collectively referred to as "management," and the related area of accounting is called **management accounting**. Management accounting focuses on the information needed for planning, implementing plans, and controlling costs. Managers and executives who work inside a company have access to specialized management accounting information that is not available to outsiders. For example, the management of McDONALD'S CORPORATION has detailed management accounting data on exactly how much it costs to produce each item on the menu. Further, if BURGER KING or WENDY'S starts a local burger price war in, say, Missouri, McDonald's managers can request daily sales summaries for each store in the area to measure the impact.

annual report A document that summarizes the results of operations and financial status of a company for the past year and outlines plans for the future.

financial statements Reports such as the balance sheet, income statement, and statement of cash flows, which summarize the financial status and results of operations of a business entity.

financial accounting The area of accounting concerned with reporting financial information to interested external parties.

Other examples of decisions made using management accounting information are whether to produce a product internally or purchase it from an outside supplier, what prices to charge, and which costs seem excessive. Consider those companies that produce computers. Most computers are shipped with an operating system already installed. Approximately 85% of computers have MICROSOFT's Windows pre-installed. The computer makers must decide whether to develop their own operating system or pay Microsoft a licensing fee to use Windows. Most computer manufacturers have determined it is cost effective to license from Microsoft. Companies such as SEARS and RADIO SHACK often use products produced by outside suppliers rather than manufacture the products themselves. The products are then labeled with the "Kenmore" or "Realistic" brand names and sold to customers. These are just two examples of decisions that must be made by management given available financial information.

External financial reports, included in the firm's **annual report**, are used by individuals and organizations that have an economic interest in the business but are not part of its management. Information is provided to these "external users" in the form of general-purpose **financial statements** and special reports required by government agencies. The general-purpose information provided by **financial accounting** is summarized in the three primary financial

exhibit 1-5 Output of the Accounting Cycle

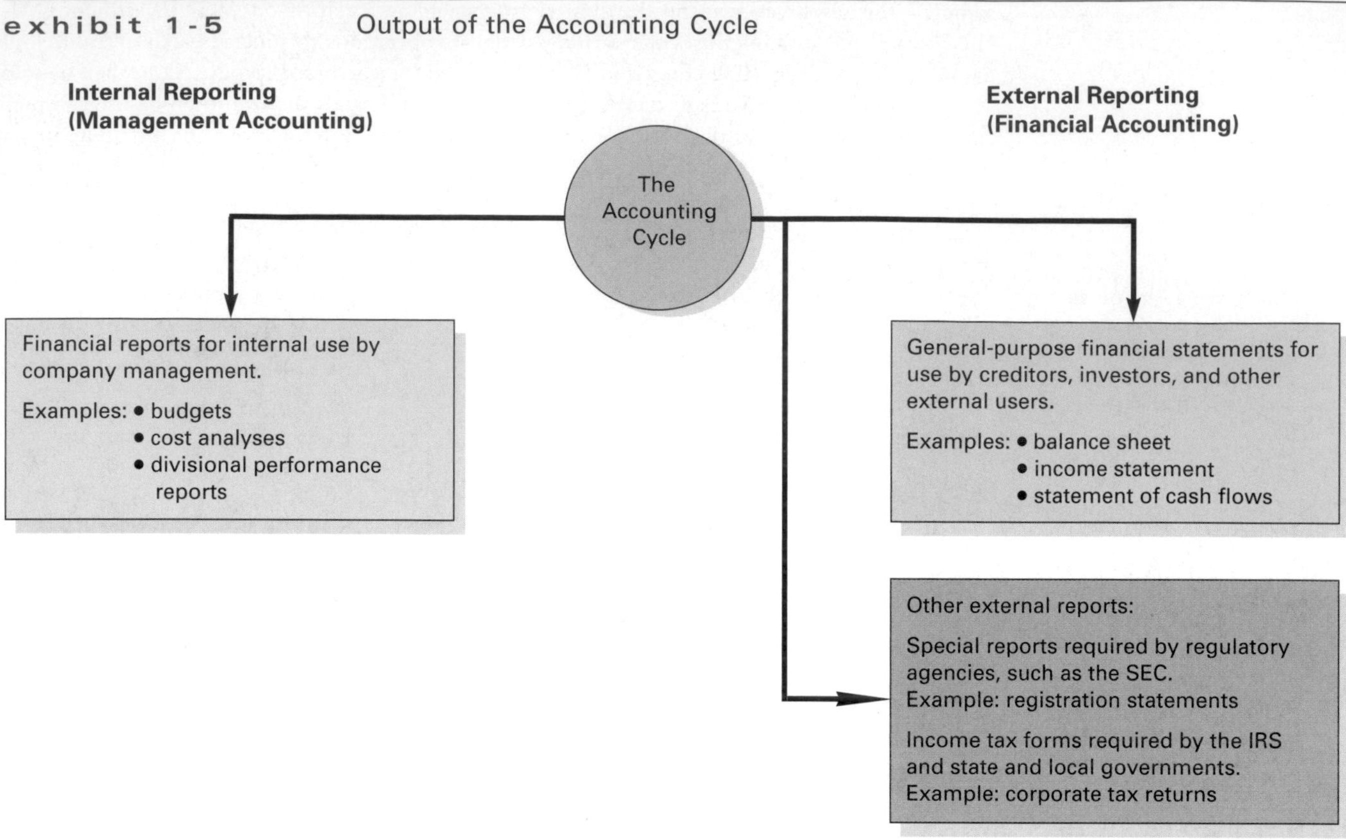

statements: balance sheet, income statement, and statement of cash flows (more formally introduced in Chapter 2).

- The *balance sheet* reports the resources of a company (the assets), the company's obligations (the liabilities), and the owners' equity, which represents the difference between what is owned (assets) and what is owed (liabilities).
- The *income statement* reports the amount of net income earned by a company during a period, with annual and quarterly income statements being the most common. Net income is the excess of a company's revenues over its expenses; if the expenses are more than the revenues, then the company has suffered a loss for the period. The income statement represents the accountant's best effort at measuring the economic performance of a company.
- The *statement of cash flows* reports the amount of cash collected and paid out by a company in the following three types of activities: operating, investing, and financing. The types of activities in each of these three categories will be explained in Chapter 2. The statement of cash flows is the most objective of the financial statements because, as you will see in subsequent chapters, it involves a minimum of accounting estimates and judgments.

Examples of external users of the information contained in these three financial statements, along with other available information, are described in the following paragraphs.

Lenders

Lenders (creditors) are interested in one thing—being repaid, with interest. If you were to approach a bank for a large loan, the bank would ask you for the following types of information in order to evaluate whether you would be able to repay the loan:

- A listing of your assets and liabilities
- Payroll stubs, tax returns, and other evidence of your income

- Details about any monthly payments (car, rent, credit cards, etc.) you are obligated to make
- Copies of recent bank statements to document the flow of cash into and out of your account

In essence, the bank would be asking you for a balance sheet, an income statement, and a statement of cash flows. Similarly, banks use companies' financial statements in making decisions about commercial loans. The financial statements are useful because they help the lender predict the future ability of the borrower to repay the loan.

In the case of Microsoft, a review of its balance sheet indicates that the company has no formal lenders. It does, however, report a balance in its "accounts payable" account. This amount represents amounts owed to vendors from whom Microsoft has purchased on credit. Considering Microsoft's reputation, this "lending" is very low risk.

Investors

Investors want information to help them estimate how much cash they can expect to receive in the future if they invest in a business now. Financial statements, coupled with a knowledge of business plans, market forecasts, and the character of management, can aid investors in assessing these future cash flows. Many companies have broad ownership with a few individuals owning a large portion of the company's stock. At Microsoft, Bill Gates owns 787,055,600 shares (15.3% of total shares outstanding); Paul Allen, Microsoft's cofounder, owns 260,723,896 shares (5.1%); and Steve Ballmer, Microsoft's chief executive officer, owns 239,626,854 shares (4.7%).

fyi

One of the concerns with online "day trading" is that investors make significant investment decisions without ever seeing, or even thinking about, a company's reported financial position.

Obviously, millions of Americans invest in McDonald's, Microsoft, **CISCO SYSTEMS**, and **GENERAL ELECTRIC** without ever seeing the financial statements of these companies. Investors can feel justifiably safe in doing this because large companies are followed by armies of financial analysts who would quickly blow the whistle if they found information suggesting that investors in these companies were at serious risk. But what about investing in a smaller company, one that the financial press doesn't follow, or in a local family business that is seeking outside investors for the first time? In cases such as these, investing without looking at the financial statements is like jumping off the high dive without looking first to see if there is any water in the pool.

Management

In addition to using management accounting information available only to those within the firm, managers of a company can use the general financial accounting information that is also made available to outsiders. Company goals are often stated in terms of financial accounting numbers, such as a target of sales growth in excess of 5%. Also, reported "net income" is frequently used in calculating management bonuses. Finally, managers of a company can analyze the general-purpose financial statements (using the techniques introduced in Chapter 2) in order to pinpoint areas of weakness about which more detailed management accounting information can be sought. Microsoft uses internally produced accounting reports to evaluate such things as the profitability of product lines, the success of international operations, and the performance of product and management teams.

Other Users of Financial Information

There are many other external users of financial information, including suppliers, customers, employees, competitors, government agencies, and the press. These are described below.

SUPPLIERS AND CUSTOMERS In some settings, suppliers and customers are interested in the long-run staying power of a company. On the supplier side, if **BOEING** receives an order from an airline for 30 new 747s over the next 10 years, Boeing wants to know whether the airline will be around in the future to take delivery of and pay for the planes. On the customer side, a homeowner who has foundation repair work done wants to know whether the company making the repairs will be around long enough to honor its 50-year guarantee. Financial statements provide information that suppliers and customers can use to assess the long-run prospects of a company. Each version of a software release has a limited life, and part of Microsoft's success has been its ability to provide product upgrades. Microsoft's customers can use financial information to help them ascertain the company's ability to survive and have the resources to fix glitches and provide upgrades as the technology improves.

EMPLOYEES Employees are interested in financial accounting information for a variety of reasons. As mentioned earlier, financial statement data are used in determining employee bonuses. In addition, financial accounting information can help an employee evaluate the likelihood that the employer will be able to fulfill its long-run promises, such as pensions and retiree health-care benefits. Financial statements are also important in contract negotiations between labor and management.

COMPETITORS If you were a manager at PEPSICO, would you be interested in knowing the relative profitability of COCA-COLA's operations in the United States, Brazil, Japan, and France? Of course you would, because that information could help you identify strategic opportunities for marketing pushes where potential profits are high or where your competitor is weak. Microsoft can use the information in financial statements to track its competitors and identify new opportunities to grow and use its market share in operating systems to increase its revenues in other software ventures. For example, Microsoft's recent antitrust troubles relate, in large part, to its competition with NETSCAPE, an Internet-browser alternative to Microsoft's Explorer. In 1997 (the last year that Netscape provided publicly available financial information), Netscape lost over $115 million on sales of almost $534 million. During that same period, Microsoft was earning a profit of almost $3.5 billion on sales of almost $12 billion.

GOVERNMENT AGENCIES Federal and state government agencies make frequent use of financial accounting information. For example, to make sure that investors have sufficient information to make informed investment decisions, the Securities and Exchange Commission monitors the financial accounting disclosures of companies (both U.S. and foreign) whose stocks trade on U.S. stock exchanges. The International Trade Commission uses financial accounting information to determine whether the importation of Ecuadorian roses or Chinese textiles is harming U.S. companies through unfair trade practices. The Justice Department uses financial statement data to evaluate whether companies (such as Microsoft) are earning excess monopolistic profits. In Microsoft's case, from 1994 through 1999, it reported profits of $0.34 on every dollar of sales. During that same period, General Electric, one of America's most admired companies, generated profits of $0.09 on every dollar of sales.

THE PRESS Financial statements are a great place for a reporter to find background information to flesh out a story about a company. For example, a story about Microsoft can be enhanced by using the sales data shown in its annual report. In addition, a surprising accounting announcement, such as a large drop in reported profits, is a trigger for an investigative reporter to write about what is going on in a company. When the Justice Department proposed the breakup of Microsoft, *The Wall Street Journal* reported analysts' estimates of the value of the company's various parts based on past revenue figures. For example, one analyst estimated that Microsoft's consumer business would be worth 50 times its revenue.[4]

In summary, who uses financial accounting information? Everyone does, or at least everyone should. External financial reports come within the area of accounting referred to as financial accounting. Most of the data needed to prepare both internal and external reports is provided by the same accounting system. A major difference between management and financial

4 Gregory Zuckerman, "Figuring Worth of a Split-Up, Microsoft Leaves Analysts Scattered All Over Map," *The Wall Street Journal*, May 2, 2000, p. C1.

accounting is the types of financial reports prepared. Internal reports are tailored to meet the needs of management and may vary considerably among businesses. General-purpose financial statements and other external reports, however, follow certain standards or guidelines and are thus more uniform among companies. The first thirteen chapters of *Accounting: Concepts and Applications* focus on financial accounting, specifically on the primary financial statements (discussed and illustrated in Chapter 2). The remaining chapters, 14 through 23, focus on management accounting.

---

to summarize

Two major categories of reports are generated by the accounting cycle: internal and external. Management accounting focuses on providing reports for internal use by management to assist in making operating decisions and in planning and controlling a company's activities. Financial accounting provides information to meet the needs of external users. General-purpose financial statements are used by investors, creditors, and other external parties who are interested in a company's activities and results.

3

Describe the environment of accounting, including the effects of generally accepted accounting principles, international business, ethical considerations, and technology.

WITHIN WHAT KIND OF ENVIRONMENT DOES ACCOUNTING OPERATE?

Accounting functions in a dynamic environment. Changes in technology as well as economic and political factors can significantly influence accounting practice. Four particularly important factors are the development of "generally accepted accounting principles" (GAAP), international business, ethical considerations, and technology.

The Significance and Development of Accounting Standards

Imagine a company that compensates a key employee in the following ways:

- Paying a cash salary of $80,000.
- Giving a new car with a value of $30,000.
- Offering the option to become, a year from now, a 10% owner of the company in exchange for an investment of $200,000.

If the company does well in the coming year, the company will increase in value, the $200,000 price tag for 10% ownership will look like a great deal, and the employee will exercise the option. If the company does poorly, it will decline in value, the $200,000 price will be too high, and the employee will throw the option away and forget the whole thing. Assume the company then sells the ownership option to interested outside investors for $25,000.

The accounting question is how to summarize in one number the company's compensation cost associated with this employee. We would probably all agree to include the $110,000 ($80,000 + $30,000) compensation cost from the cash salary and the new car. What about the option? Both of the following arguments could be put forward:

1. If the employee were to buy the option from the company, just like any other outside investor, the employee would have to pay $25,000. Therefore, giving the option to the employee is just like paying him or her $25,000 cash. The $25,000 value of the option should be added to compensation cost.
2. The option doesn't cost the company a thing. In fact, the option merely increases the probability that the employee will invest $200,000 in the company in the future. The option doesn't add a penny to compensation cost.

business environment essay

The Evolution of Accounting It can be argued that accounting as a profession is very young; as a service activity, however, it dates back several thousand years. Long before numerical figures were invented, people designated possessions and debts through natural means. Collections of pebbles, shells, or bones were used to represent exchanges between people. Some maintained records of debt by carving notches in rods or canes. The ancient Peruvians used knotted strings before numerical symbols were invented. Regardless of the rudiments put into practice through the generations, it is obvious that accounting for ownership between parties drove ancient peoples to invent new methods of record keeping and communication. In fact, in his book *The Temper of Our Times*, Eric Hoffer argues that accounting was the driving force behind written language:

> We are often told that the invention of writing in the Middle East about 3000 B.C. marked an epoch in man's career because it revolutionized the transmission of knowledge and ideas. Actually, for many centuries after its invention, writing was used solely to keep track of the intake and outgo of treasuries and warehouses. Writing was invented not to write books but to keep books. (Hoffer, p. 196)

Among the earliest known records are those of the Egyptians and Babylonians (from approximately 3000 B.C.), who recorded on clay tablets such transactions as the payment of wages and taxes. Multiple clay tablets listing valuable items in treasuries and temples have been found at excavation sites in Sumeria and Babylon. It makes sense that accountants of old would only take the time to carve in these clay tablets instead of writing on papyrus if they regarded the information to be of great importance. As a result, we have accurate knowledge of the wealth maintained in the treasuries, but little information relating to the persons who actually owned them.

With the development of a written language came the ability to represent measures of tallied items with a single symbol. Different numerical systems existed throughout the world. As empires gained and lost power, advances in culture and science spread among the different nations. In order to maintain their empires, rulers would dictate the use of more unified communication methods. Under Roman rule, people living in territories in Europe, Africa, the Middle East, and parts of Asia were forced to write and maintain business communications in Latin. During the Roman period (which lasted from approximately 500 B.C. to 500 A.D.), detailed tax records were maintained.

So, which argument is right? Should each company decide for itself whether to include the $25,000 option value as part of compensation cost, or should there be an overall accounting standard followed by all companies? And if there is a standard, who sets it?[5]

There are many situations in business, such as the option compensation case just described, in which reasonable people can disagree about how certain items should be handled for accounting purposes. And, since financial accounting information is designed to be used by people outside a company, it is important that outsiders understand the rules and assumptions used by the company in constructing its financial statements. This would be extremely difficult and costly for outsiders to find out if every company formulated its own set of accounting rules. Accordingly, in most countries in the world there exists a committee or board that establishes the accounting rules for that country.

The Financial Accounting Standards Board

Financial Accounting Standards Board (FASB) The private organization responsible for establishing the standards for financial accounting and reporting in the United States.

In the United States, accounting standards are set by the **Financial Accounting Standards Board (FASB)**. The FASB is based in Norwalk, Connecticut, and its seven full-time members

5 The answer to this surprisingly controversial question of the accounting for option compensation is given in Chapter 8. Just to show how influential accounting can be, this exact issue was debated on the floor of the U.S. Senate.

After the fall of Rome, trade continued to increase around the Mediterranean Sea. Italy found itself positioned between European consumers and Asian and Arabian producers. As trade increased in Italy's port cities, the need to borrow and purchase on credit also increased. In fact, the first bank of importance, Casa di San Georgio, was founded in Genoa, Italy, during the 12th century. During and after the era of the crusades from 1096 to about 1270, money from Italy's European neighbors streamed into and out of Italian cities. Credit transactions rose in volume as traders in Florence, Pisa, and Venice became merchant-bankers. Although accounting did not originate in Italy, its geographic location facilitated the formalization of a system of recording business transactions. In 1494, an Italian Franciscan monk, Luca Pacioli, published a treatise containing a small section titled "Particularis de Computis et Scripturis [Details of Accounting and Recording]," which contained the essential elements of the double-entry accounting system that is still in use today.

But accounting has not remained static. The Industrial Revolution brought about changes in business, and therefore in accounting. Beginning in England in the mid-1800s, manufacturing processes started to evolve from individualized, handicraft systems to mass-production, factory systems. Technological advances not only provided new machinery but required new types of expenditures as well. Cost accounting systems had to be developed to analyze and control the financial operations of these increasingly complex manufacturing processes.

Governmental laws and requirements also have caused changes in the business environment and have stimulated the growth of accounting services. For example, the Companies Act in England in the 1850s established compulsory independent audits by chartered accountants. In the United States, the 1913 Revenue Act instituted the personal federal income tax, which created a need for income tax accounting. The 1934 Securities Exchange Act established the Securities and Exchange Commission, which monitors the reporting procedures of companies that sell stock publicly.

These and other factors have produced changes in the types of accounting services needed, and in many instances they have affected the accounting procedures themselves. Thus, the profession of accounting has evolved to meet the needs of the people it serves in an ever-changing and increasingly complex business environment.

As this brief history makes clear, accounting is not a static science. It is constantly evolving, changing to meet the needs of users and adapting itself to the economic environment in which it operates.

Source: Eric Hoffer, *The Temper of Our Times* (New York: Harper & Row, 1966).

are selected from a variety of backgrounds—professional accounting, business, government, and academia. The FASB receives about one-third of its $20 million annual operating budget through donations from the accounting profession and from businesses. The remaining two-thirds is generated through sales of publications and other services (e.g., a CD-ROM version of all the existing accounting standards). An important thing to note about the FASB is that it is not a government agency; the FASB is a private body established and supported by the joint efforts of the U.S. business community, financial analysts, and practicing accountants. Because the FASB is not a government agency, it has no legal power to enforce the accounting standards it sets. The FASB gets its authority to establish rules from the Securities and Exchange Commission (discussed later).

The FASB maintains its influence as the accounting standard setter for the United States (and the most influential accounting body in the world) by carefully protecting its prestige and reputation for setting good standards. In doing so, the FASB must walk a fine line between constant improvement of accounting practices to provide more full and fair information for external users and practical constraints on financial disclosure to appease businesses that are reluctant to disclose too much information to outsiders. To balance these opposing forces, the FASB seeks consensus by requesting written comments and sponsoring public hearings on all its proposed standards. The end result of this public process is a set of accounting rules that are described as being **generally accepted accounting principles (GAAP)**. Without general acceptance by the

generally accepted accounting principles (GAAP) Authoritative guidelines that define accounting practice at a particular time.

business community, FASB standards would merely be theoretical essays by a powerless body, and the FASB would be disbanded. This may sound overly dramatic, but the FASB was created in 1973 to replace the previously existing accounting standards body (the Accounting Principles Board or APB), which had lost credibility with the business community because it was seen as being completely controlled by accountants.

As you study this text, you will be intrigued by the interesting conceptual issues the FASB must wrestle with in setting accounting standards. The FASB has deliberated over the correct way to compute motion picture profits, the appropriate treatment of the cost of dismantling a nuclear power plant, the best approach for reflecting the impact of changes in foreign currency exchange rates, and the proper accounting for complex financial instruments such as commodity futures and interest rate swaps. And since U.S. companies are always suspicious that any change in the accounting rules will make them look worse on paper, almost all FASB decisions are made in the midst of controversy.

STOP & THINK Why is it important for the FASB to remain completely independent?

Other Organizations

In addition to the FASB, several other organizations affect accounting standards and are important in other ways to the practice of accounting. Some of these organizations are discussed below.

SECURITIES AND EXCHANGE COMMISSION In response to the Stock Market Crash of 1929, Congress created the **Securities and Exchange Commission (SEC)** to regulate U.S. stock exchanges. Part of the job of the SEC is to make sure that investors are provided with full and fair information about publicly traded companies. The SEC is not charged with protecting investors from losing money; instead, the SEC seeks to create a fair information environment in which investors can buy and sell stocks without fear that companies are hiding or manipulating financial data.

Securities and Exchange Commission (SEC) The government body responsible for regulating the financial reporting practices of most publicly owned corporations in connection with the buying and selling of stocks and bonds.

As part of its regulatory role, the SEC has received from Congress specific legal authority to establish accounting standards for companies soliciting investment funds from the American public. For now, the SEC refrains from exercising this authority and allows the FASB to set U.S. accounting standards. The SEC has generally been content to be publicly supportive of the FASB and to work out any disagreements privately. Remember, however, that the SEC is always looming in the background, legally authorized to take over the setting of U.S. accounting standards should the FASB lose its credibility with the public.

certified public accountant (CPA) A special designation given to an accountant who has passed a national uniform examination and has met other certifying requirements.

American Institute of Certified Public Accountants (AICPA) The national organization of CPAs in the United States.

AMERICAN INSTITUTE OF CERTIFIED PUBLIC ACCOUNTANTS The label "CPA" has two different uses—there are individuals who are CPAs and there are CPA firms. A **certified public accountant (CPA)** is someone who has taken a minimum number of college-level accounting classes, has passed the CPA exam administered by the **American Institute of Certified Public Accountants (AICPA)**, and has met other requirements set by his or her state. In essence, the CPA label guarantees that the person has received substantial accounting training. Not all CPAs work as accountants, however. CPAs work in law firms, as business consultants, as corporate managers, for the government, and even some as accounting professors.

The second use of the label "CPA" is in association with a CPA firm. A CPA firm is a company that performs accounting services, just as a law firm performs legal services. Obviously, a CPA firm employs a large number of accountants, not all of whom have received the training necessary to be certified public accountants. CPA firms also employ attorneys, information technology specialists, experts in finance, and other business specialists. CPA firms help companies establish accounting systems, formulate business plans, redesign their operating procedures, and just about anything else you can think of. A good way to think of a CPA firm is as a freelance business-advising firm with a particular strength in accounting issues.

Other tasks accountants perform are planning for acquisitions and mergers, measuring efficiency improvements from new technology, managing quality, and developing accounting software.

fyi

Other accounting-related certifications also exist. Examples include the Certified Management Accountant (CMA), Certified Internal Auditor (CIA), and the Certified Fraud Examiner (CFE).

CPA firms are also hired to perform independent audits of the financial statements of a company. The important role of the independent audit in ensuring the reliability of the financial statements is discussed in Chapter 5.

INTERNAL REVENUE SERVICE Imagine that you have a contract to design a computerized accounting system for a local business. Your fee is $100,000, which will be paid in full when the job is finished. By the end of the year, you have collected nothing, but you estimate that you have completed 80% of the work on the contract.

If you are asked by a potential business partner how much money you have earned during the past year, what will you say? To say that you made $0, the amount you've collected on the contract, significantly understates the value of the work you have completed. If the 80% estimate is a fair reflection of the work you've done, it would seem reasonable for you to report to the potential partner that you've earned $80,000 ($100,000 × 0.80) during the year. And, as you'll see later in the text, this is exactly what you would report according to financial accounting rules.

Internal Revenue Service (IRS) A government agency that prescribes the rules and regulations that govern the collection of tax revenues in the United States.

Now, if you are asked by the **Internal Revenue Service (IRS)** to state your income for the year, how much should you report? You don't have much leeway in the matter, because the IRS has very specific rules about what is considered taxable income. Assume that IRS rules state that you must pay income tax on the $80,000 income from the estimated amount of the contract that you have completed. Two practical problems would arise:

1. You don't have the money to pay the tax. You won't be able to pay the tax until the job is completed and you have collected your entire fee.
2. You could have endless arguments with the IRS about the completion percentage. The IRS could send an agent to dispute your estimate. The whole thing might end up in Tax Court.

This example illustrates that what works for financial accounting purposes does not necessarily work for income tax purposes. Financial accounting reports are designed to provide information about the economic performance and health of a company. Tax rules are designed to tax income when the tax can be paid and to provide concrete rules to minimize inefficient arguing between taxpayers and the IRS. Accordingly, the IRS rules would probably allow you to report $0 income and delay paying income tax until you have actually collected the cash and could thus pay the tax.

International Accounting Standards Committee (IASC) The committee formed in 1973 to develop worldwide accounting standards.

The implication of this separation between financial accounting and tax accounting is that companies must maintain two sets of books—one set from which the financial statements can be prepared and the other set to comply with income tax regulations. There is nothing shady or underhanded about this. Financial accounting and tax accounting involve different sets of rules because they are designed for different purposes.

fyi

Since international accounting standards often differ from GAAP, foreign companies may be required to adjust their books to be listed on the New York Stock Exchange. For example, when Germany's DAIMLER-BENZ (makers of Mercedes Benz) became a NYSE-listed company in 1994, its GAAP-adjusted books showed a loss of $748 million, whereas its German standard books reported earnings of $636 million. Note: Daimler-Benz subsequently merged with CHRYSLER to become DAIMLER-CHRYSLER.

International Business

One of the significant environmental changes in recent years has been the expansion of business activity on a worldwide basis. As consumers, we are familiar with the wide array of products from other countries, such as electronics from Japan and clothing made in China. On the other hand, many U.S. companies have operating divisions in foreign countries. Other American companies are located totally within the United States but have extensive transactions with foreign companies. The economic environment of today's business is truly based on a global economy. As an example, in 1999 over 65% of MICROSOFT'S sales were to individuals and companies located outside the United States.

Accounting practices among countries vary widely. Attempts are being made to make those practices more consistent among countries. In an attempt to harmonize conflicting national standards, the **International Accounting Standards Committee (IASC)** was formed in 1973 to develop worldwide accounting standards. This body now represents more than 142 accountancy bodies from 103 countries (including the United States). Like the FASB, the IASC develops proposals, circulates them among interested organizations, receives feedback, and then issues a final pronouncement.

The accounting standards produced by the IASC are referred to as International Accounting Standards (IAS). IAS are envisioned to be a set of standards that can be used by

business environment essay

Do You Have What It Takes? There are many opportunities in the field of accounting. The Bureau of Labor Statistics forecasts that the demand for accounting graduates will increase 10 to 20 percent over the next decade. Accounting graduates use their education to obtain jobs in public accounting, for federal, state and local governments (including the Internal Revenue Service), and in commercial banking. In addition to becoming accountants, many accounting students use their undergraduate accounting education as a stepping-stone to law school or investment banking or to obtain other graduate degrees (like an MBA).

Many accounting students who go on to become accountants pursue the CPA designation. To be a CPA, specific requirements must be met. First, CPAs are re-

all companies regardless of where they are based. In the extreme, IAS could supplement or even replace standards set by national standard setters such as the FASB. IASC standards are gaining increasing acceptance throughout the world. For example, in April 2000, the IASC Web site (**http://www.iasc.org.uk**) listed more than 958 companies around the world that prepare financial statements according to IAS. Of these companies, 161 are located in Germany and 121 are located in China. Thus far, however, the SEC has not recognized IASC standards and has barred foreign companies from listing their shares on U.S. stock exchanges unless those companies agree to provide financial statements in accordance with U.S. accounting rules. Disclosure requirements in the United States are the strictest in the world, and foreign companies are reluctant to submit to the SEC requirement. This conflict will be interesting to watch in the coming years: Will the SEC maintain a hard line and ultimately force U.S. accounting rules on the rest of the world? Or will the IASC standards gain increasing acceptance and become the worldwide standard? We'll see.

STOP & THINK Why is it so difficult to make international accounting standards consistent?

At numerous points throughout this text, we will point out certain international applications of accounting as well as some differences that might exist in accounting rules between the United States and other countries. In addition, each chapter includes a case in the end-of-chapter material dealing with an international accounting issue.

Because of the expansion of international business, consumers are familiar with products from other countries, such as Hong Kong.

quired to have a formal education. For example, although individual state laws vary, as of April 17, 2000, 27 states require students to have completed 150 hours of college education to become CPAs. An additional 19 states have enacted legislation that will require 150 hours at some future date. Currently, only California, Delaware, New Hampshire, and Vermont have not enacted the 150-hour requirement. Next, aspiring CPAs must pass an examination based on the skills obtained from their education. This ensures that accountants are competent to perform independent services for the community. In addition to the examination, field experience requirements must be met to satisfy state licensing laws for CPAs.

If you are interested in someday working in a business environment, a degree in accounting can help you understand business issues, analyze accounting information, and make business decisions.

Ethics in Accounting

Another environmental factor affecting accounting, and business in general, is the growing concern over ethics. This concern was highlighted in a speech given by the chairman of the SEC, Arthur Levitt, in September 1998. In that speech, entitled "The Number's Game," Chairman Levitt identified several major accounting techniques that he believed were being used to undermine the integrity of financial reporting. As you will find, accounting involves significant judgment. Chairman Levitt expressed concern that this accounting judgment was giving way to pressure to "meet the numbers." In other words, Wall Street's expectations about a company, rather than the company's actual business performance, were driving the reported accounting numbers.

fyi

The AICPA's Code of Professional Conduct can be found on its Web site at www.aicpa.org. The Code of Conduct spells out what CPAs are famous for—they are required to be independent of their clients, to be good at what they do, and to keep client information confidential.

In his speech, Chairman Levitt mentioned the standards of objectivity, integrity, and judgment in reporting accounting numbers. These standards are an integral part of the public accounting profession's Code of Professional Conduct and form the foundation upon which audited financial statements are compiled and interpreted.

The ethical dilemmas facing businesses and their accountants often revolve around pressures placed on companies by investors, creditors, and potential investors and creditors. As Chairman Levitt mentioned, these pressures can sometimes cause company officials to become involved in "accounting hocus-pocus." Because accounting involves judgment, the reported accounting numbers can differ significantly depending on the assumptions made by those preparing the financial statements. As a simple example of how this can occur, consider again the case of Microsoft. When a customer buys a Microsoft product, part of the purchase price relates to promised customer service and future product upgrades. So the question is this: How much of the sales price should Microsoft report as a "sale" on the date of the sale, and how much relates to future services to be provided? As you can imagine, that is a difficult question to answer, and any answer will involve an estimate.

To quote again from Chairman Levitt's speech, accounting principles "allow for flexibility to adapt to changing circumstances." It is this flexibility that creates many of the ethical dilemmas faced by accountants. As businesses come under pressure to report favorable performance, accountants may also come under pressure to "flex" the rules just a little too far.

Fortunately, the public accounting profession is guided by a Code of Professional Conduct. Many other accounting organizations also have codes of conduct to provide guidance for their members.

Don't let yourself naively think that ethical dilemmas in business are rare. Such issues arise quite frequently. To help prepare you to enter the business world and to recognize and deal with ethical issues, we have included at least one ethics case at the end of each chapter. Ethics is an important topic that should be considered carefully, with the ultimate goal of improving individual and collective behavior in society.

Technology

Few developments have changed the way business is conducted as much as computers have. Computer technology allows businesses to do things that 20 years ago were unimaginable. Consider being able to use your desktop computer to track the status of a package shipped from Los Angeles to New York. Companies such as **UPS** and **FEDEX** incorporate this type of technology as an integral part of their business. Financial institutions use computer technology to wire billions of dollars each day to locations around the world.

So how have computers changed the way accounting is done? That question can be addressed on several levels. First, computer technology allows companies to easily gather vast amounts of information about individual transactions. For example, information relating to the customer, the salesperson, the product being sold, and the method of payment can be easily gathered for each transaction using computer technology. Prior to today's technology, the cost of gathering this information was prohibitive.

Access Microsoft's Web site at **http://www.microsoft.com**. Identify the different kinds of information found on Microsoft's home page, e.g., marketing, product information, etc. Can you find any financial information?

Second, computer technology allows large amounts of data to be compiled quickly and accurately, thereby significantly reducing the likelihood of errors. As you will soon discover, a large part of the mechanics of accounting involves moving numbers to and from various accounting records as well as adding and subtracting a lot of figures. Computers have made this process virtually invisible. What once occupied a large part of an accountant's time can now be done in an instant.

Third, in the precomputer world of limited analytical capacity, it was essential for lenders and investors to receive condensed summaries of a company's financial activities. Now, lenders and investors have the ability to receive and process gigabytes of information, so why should the report of Microsoft's financial performance be restricted to three short financial statements? Why can't Microsoft provide access to much more detailed information online? In fact, why can't Microsoft allow investors to directly tap into its own internal accounting database? Information technology has made this type of information acquisition and analysis possible; the question accountants face now is how much information companies should be required to make available to outsiders. Ten years ago, the only way you could get a copy of Microsoft's financial statements was to call or write to receive paper copies in the mail. Now you can download those summary financial statements from Microsoft's Web site. How will you get financial information 10 years from now? No one knows, but the rapid advances in information technology guarantee that it will be different from anything we are familiar with now.

Finally, and most importantly, although technology has changed the way certain aspects of accounting are carried out, on a fundamental level the mechanics of accounting are still the same as they were 500 years ago. People are still required to analyze complex business transactions and input the results of that analysis into the computer. Technology has not replaced judgment.

So if you are asking "Why do I need to understand accounting—can't computers just do it?"—the answer is a resounding "No!" You need to know what the computer is doing if you are to understand and interpret the information resulting from the accounting process. You need to understand that since judgment was required when the various pieces of information were put into the accounting systems, judgment will be required to appropriately use that information. We have included numerous end-of-chapter opportunities for you to experience how technology helps in the accounting process. These opportunities will illustrate the important role that technology can play in the accounting process as well as emphasize the critical role that the accountant plays as well.

---

to summarize

Accounting functions in a dynamic environment. Generally accepted accounting principles (GAAP) have developed over time. The primary standard-setting body for the private sector is the Financial Accounting Standards Board (FASB). The accounting environment includes business activity that is conducted on an international basis. Consequently, accounting practices often must be modified to reflect the accounting standards of different countries. Attempts are being made to establish comparable international accounting practices. There is increasing concern in society over ethics. High standards of ethical conduct are important, especially for accountants who assume a special responsibility to the public. CPAs have adopted standards of conduct that contain principles and rules as guidelines for the performance of accounting services. Technology has changed the way accounting information is collected, analyzed, and used. The use of computers in the accounting process has increased significantly, and although they allow more information to be gathered and used, computers have not replaced the accountant nor eliminated the need for qualified decision makers.

4

Analyze the reasons for studying accounting.

SO, WHY SHOULD I STUDY ACCOUNTING?

You may still be asking, "But why do I need to study accounting?" Even if you have no desire to be an accountant, at some point in your life you will need financial information to make certain decisions, such as whether to buy or lease an automobile, how to budget your monthly income, where to invest your savings, or how to finance your (or your child's) college education. You can make each of these decisions without using financial information and then hope everything turns out okay, but that would be bad decision making. As noted in the discussion of Exhibit 1–3, a good decision does not guarantee a good outcome, but a bad decision guarantees one of two things—a bad outcome or a lucky outcome. And you cannot count on lucky outcomes time after time. On a personal level, each of us needs to understand how to collect and use accounting information.

Odds are that each of you will have the responsibility of providing some form of income for yourself and your family. Would you prefer to work for a company that is doing well and has a promising future or one that is on the brink of bankruptcy? Of course we all want to work for companies that are doing well. But how would you know? Accounting information will allow you to evaluate your employer's short- and long-term potential.

When you graduate and secure employment, it is almost certain that accounting information will play some role in your job. Whether your responsibilities include sales (where you will need information about product availability and costs), production (where you will need information regarding the costs of materials, labor, and overhead), quality control (where you will need information relating to variances between expected and actual production), or human resources (where you will need information relating to the costs of employees), you will use accounting information. The more you know about where accounting information comes from, how it is accumulated, and how it is best used, the better you will be able to perform your job.

Everyone is affected by accounting information. Saying you don't need to know accounting doesn't change the fact that you are affected by accounting information. Ignoring the value of that information simply puts you at a disadvantage. Those who recognize the value of accounting information and learn how to use it to make better decisions will have a competitive advantage over those who don't. It's as simple as that.

review of learning objectives

1 Describe the purpose of accounting and explain its role in business and society. Accounting is a service activity designed to assist individuals and organizations in deciding how to allocate scarce resources and reach their financial objectives. It is used to accumulate, measure, and communicate economic data about organizations and to assist in the decision-making process.

2 Identify the primary users of accounting information. The primary users of accounting information are lenders, investors, management, and other interested individuals and organizations. Management accounting deals primarily with the internal accounting functions of planning, implementing, and control. Financial accounting is concerned with reporting business activities and results to external parties. The objectives of both areas of accounting are measurement and communication of information for decision-making purposes.

3 Describe the environment of accounting, including the effects of generally accepted accounting principles, international business, ethical considerations, and technology. Accounting functions in a dynamic environment. The principles of accounting have evolved over time to meet the changing demands of the business environment. They are therefore not absolute. Only if they prove useful do they become generally accepted. Accounting principles provide comparable data for external users and need to be applied with judgment.

Since the 1930s, several organizations have been involved in the development of accounting principles in the United States. The American Institute of Certified Public Accountants (AICPA), the Securities and Exchange Commission (SEC), and the Financial Accounting Standards Board (FASB) are among the most prominent. The FASB is currently the primary standard-setting body for accounting principles in the private sector.

Accounting is practiced in an international environment. Accounting procedures in the United States sometimes must be modified to accommodate foreign operations. Attempts are being made to establish consistent and comparable accounting practices throughout the world, primarily through the efforts of the International Accounting Standards Committee (IASC).

Ethical considerations affect society and are particularly important for accountants, who have a special responsibility to the public. CPAs have adopted standards of conduct to guide them in the performance of their duties.

Technology has changed the way accounting information is accumulated and analyzed. What once occupied a large part of an accountant's time is now done quickly by computers, thereby freeing the accountant to be involved in more productive tasks. But computer technology has not removed the accountant from the decision-making process. Accounting judgment is still essential.

4 Analyze the reasons for studying accounting. Knowing how to use accounting information will help individuals make better decisions in their personal life as well as in their employment. Whatever the job, it is likely that accounting information plays a part. Knowing where information comes from, how it is accumulated, and how it is best used will result in better decision making.

key terms and concepts

accounting 6
accounting cycle 9
accounting system 5
American Institute of Certified Public Accountants (AICPA) 16
annual report 9
bookkeeping 5
business 7
certified public accountant (CPA) 16
financial accounting 9
Financial Accounting Standards Board (FASB) 14
financial statements 9
generally accepted accounting principles (GAAP) 15
Internal Revenue Service (IRS) 17
International Accounting Standards Committee (IASC) 17
management accounting 9
nonprofit organization 7
Securities and Exchange Commission (SEC) 16

discussion questions

1. What are the three functions of an accounting system?
2. What are the essential elements in decision making, and how does accounting fit into the process?
3. What types of personal decisions have required you to use accounting information?
4. What does the term *business* mean to you?

5. Why is accounting often referred to as the "language of business"?
6. In what ways are the needs of internal and external users of accounting information the same? In what ways are they different?
7. What are generally accepted accounting principles (GAAP)? Who currently develops and issues GAAP? What is the purpose of GAAP?
8. Why is it important for financial statements and other external reports to be based on generally accepted accounting principles (GAAP)?
9. What are the respective roles of the Securities and Exchange Commission (SEC) and the Internal Revenue Service (IRS) in the setting of accounting standards?
10. For you as a potential investor, what is the problem with different countries having different accounting standards? For you as the president of a multinational company, what is the problem with different countries having different accounting standards?
11. Ethical considerations affect all society. Why are ethical considerations especially important for accountants?
12. Given significant technological advances, can we expect to see less demand for accountants and accounting-type services?
13. Other than that it is a requirement for your major or that your mom or dad is making you, why should you study accounting?

discussion cases

CASE 1-1

TO LEND OR NOT TO LEND—THAT IS THE QUESTION

Sam Love is vice president and chief lending officer of the Meeker First National Bank. Recently, Bill McCarthy, a new farmer, moved to town. Sam has not dealt with Bill previously and knows little about the Mountain Meadow Ranch that Bill operates. Bill would like to borrow $100,000 to purchase some equipment and yearling steers for his ranch. What information does Sam need to help make the lending decision? What type of information should Bill collect and analyze before even requesting the loan?

CASE 1-2

INFORMATION NEEDS TO REMAIN COMPETITIVE

In an article in *U.S. News & World Report,* Dan McGraw described how two computer giants, DELL and COMPAQ, were poised to do battle in the personal computer market. Compaq had 13.2% of the U.S. market share for personal computers to Dell's 8.8%. However, Dell's market share had more than doubled in the last four years while Compaq's share had increased less than 1%. What type of information, accounting or otherwise, do you think the management of Compaq may have wanted and needed as they competed with Dell and the other PC companies?

Source: Dan McGraw, "Shootout at PC Corral," *U.S. News & World Report,* June 23, 1997, pp. 37–38.

CASE 1-3

International

INTERNATIONAL HAPPENINGS

July 1, 1997, marked a historic date as Hong Kong reverted to political and economic control by mainland China. The Stock Exchange of Hong Kong offers the opportunity to invest in both local Hong Kong companies and in "red-chip offerings," which are stocks of companies that are listed in Hong Kong but controlled by mainland China interests. As an international investor, what accounting information might be helpful as you consider investing in the Hong Kong stock market? For which variables in this situation is accounting information unlikely to be very helpful?

EXERCISE 1-1

THE ROLE AND IMPORTANCE OF ACCOUNTING

Assume that you are applying for a part-time job as an accounting clerk in a retail clothing establishment. During the interview, the store manager asks how you expect to contribute to the business. How would you respond?

EXERCISE 1-2

BOOKKEEPING IS EVERYWHERE

Describe how bookkeeping is applied in each of the following settings:

a. Your college English class.
b. The National Basketball Association.
c. A hospital emergency room.
d. Jury selection for a major murder trial.
e. Four college roommates on a weekend skiing trip.

EXERCISE 1-3

ACCOUNTING INFORMATION AND DECISION MAKING

You are the owner of Automated Systems, Inc., which sells **APPLE** computers and related data processing equipment. You are currently trying to decide whether to continue selling the Apple computer line or to distribute the Windows-based computers instead. What information do you need to consider in order to determine how successful your business is or will be? What information would help you decide whether to sell the Apple or the Windows-based personal computer line? Use your imagination and general knowledge of business activity.

EXERCISE 1-4

USERS OF FINANCIAL INFORMATION

Why might each of the following individuals or groups be interested in a firm's financial statements? (a) The current stockholders of the firm; (b) the creditors of the firm; (c) the management of the firm; (d) the prospective stockholders of the firm; (e) the Internal Revenue Service (IRS); (f) the SEC; (g) the firm's major labor union.

EXERCISE 1-5

STRUCTURING INFORMATION FOR USE IN EVALUATION

You work in a small convenience store. The store is very low-tech; you ring up the sales on an old-style cash register that merely records the amount of the sale. The store owner uses this cash register tape at the end of each day to verify that the correct amount of cash is in the cash register drawer.

In addition to verifying the cash amount, how else could the information on the cash register tape be used to evaluate the store's operation? What additional bookkeeping procedures would be necessary to make these additional uses possible?

EXERCISE 1-6

INVESTING IN THE STOCK MARKET

Assume your grandparents have just given you $20,000 on the condition that you invest the money in the stock market. As you contemplate making your investment choices, what accounting information do you want to help identify companies that will have high future rates of return?

EXERCISE 1-7

ALLOCATION OF LIMITED RESOURCES

Assume you are a small business owner trying to increase your company's profits. How can accounting information help you efficiently allocate your limited resources to maximize your business profit?

EXERCISE 1-8

MANAGEMENT VERSUS FINANCIAL ACCOUNTING

This chapter discusses two areas of accounting: management and financial accounting. Contrast management and financial accounting with respect to the following:

- Overall purpose
- Type of financial reports used (i.e., external, internal, or both)
- Users of the information

Also, in what ways are these two fields of accounting similar?

EXERCISE 1-9

THE ROLE OF THE SEC

It is not often that the federal government has allowed the private sector to govern itself, but that is exactly what has happened with the field of accounting. The SEC has delegated the responsibility of rule making to the FASB, a group of seven individuals who are hired full-time to discuss issues, research areas of interest, and determine what GAAP is and will be. What are the advantages of allowing the private sector to determine accounting standards? Identify any advantages that the SEC might gain if it established the rules that govern the practice of accounting.

EXERCISE 1-10

WHY TWO SETS OF BOOKS?

This past year you were married. This coming April you will be faced with preparing your first tax return since mom and dad said "you are now on your own." As you review the IRS regulations, you notice several differences from what you learned in your accounting class. It appears that businesses must keep two sets of books: one for the IRS and one in accordance with GAAP. Why aren't GAAP and IRS rules the same?

EXERCISE 1-11

DIFFERENCES IN ACCOUNTING ACROSS BORDERS

In the United States, accounting for inventory is a difficult issue. Inventory is comprised of those items either purchased or manufactured to be resold at a profit. Numerous methods are available to account for inventory for financial reporting purposes. A very commonly used method—called LIFO (last-in, first-out)—minimizes a company's tax obligation. In the United Kingdom, however, LIFO is not permitted for tax purposes and thus is not used very often for financial reporting. In Turkey, the use of LIFO is severely restricted, and in Russia, LIFO is a foreign term. Only in Germany, where the tax laws have been modified to allow the use of LIFO, is LIFO being adopted. Different accounting methods are available for numerous other issues in accounting. Identify some major problems associated with comparing the financial statements of companies from different countries.

EXERCISE 1-12

ETHICS IN ACCOUNTING

The text has pointed out that ethics is an important topic, especially for CPAs. Derek Bok, former law professor and president of Harvard University, has suggested that colleges and universities have a special opportunity and obligation to train students to be more thoughtful and perceptive about moral and ethical issues. Other individuals have concluded that it is not possible to "teach" ethics. What do you think? Can ethics be taught? If you agree that colleges and universities can teach ethics, how might the ethical dimensions of accounting be presented to students?

EXERCISE 1-13

CAREER OPPORTUNITIES IN ACCOUNTING

You are scheduled to graduate from college with a degree in accounting, and your mother would like to know what you plan to do with the rest of your life. She assumes that your only option is to be a bookkeeper like Bob Cratchit in the story *A Christmas Carol.* What can you tell Mom regarding the options available to you with your degree in accounting?

EXERCISE 1-14

WHY DO I NEED TO KNOW ACCOUNTING?

One of your college friends recently graduated from school with a major in music (specifically piano). He has told you that he is going to start his own piano instructional business. He plans to operate the business from home. You ask him how he is going to account for his business, and his reply is, "I graduated in music, not accounting. I am going to teach music, not number crunching. I didn't need accounting in college and I don't need it now!" Is your friend right? What financial information might he find useful in operating his business?

EXERCISE 1-15

CHALLENGES TO THE ACCOUNTING PROFESSION

As the business world continues to change the way in which business is conducted, accountants are faced with the challenge of accounting for these changes. Who, for example, could have anticipated the risks associated with asbestos? Or the decline of communism? Or the increasingly litigious environment in the United States? Each of these events, and many more, has influenced business—which has, in turn, influenced accounting. From your general understanding of accounting and the current business environment, what are some of the challenges you see facing the accounting profession?

competency enhancement opportunities

- Analyzing Real Company Information
- International Case
- Ethics Case
- Writing Assignments
- The Debate
- Internet Search

The following additional assignments provide opportunities for students to develop critical thinking, ethical perspectives, oral and written communication skills, experience with electronic research, and teamwork through group and business activities.

ANALYZING REAL COMPANY INFORMATION

• ***Analyzing 1-1 (Microsoft)***

In the Appendix at the back of this text is MICROSOFT's complete annual report for the year ended June 30, 1999. Review the annual report and identify its major areas. How many pages of the report are devoted to a narrative of the prior three years' performance? How many pages focus on explaining technical accounting and business-related issues and procedures? In your opinion, given your limited knowledge of accounting, what is the most interesting part of the annual report? What is the least interesting?

• ***Analyzing 1-2 (General Motors)***

Below is a condensed listing of the assets and liabilities of GENERAL MOTORS as of December 31, 1999. All amounts are in millions of U.S. dollars.

Assets		*Liabilities*	
Cash	$ 21,250	Loans payable	$187,059
Loans receivable	80,627	Pensions	3,339
Inventories	10,638	Other retiree benefits	34,166
Property & equipment	69,186	Other liabilities	28,708
Other assets	92,572		
Total assets	$274,273	Total liabilities	$253,272

1. Among its assets, General Motors lists more than $80 billion in loans receivable. This represents loans that General Motors has made and expects to collect in the future. This is exactly the kind of asset reported among the assets of banks. Given what you know about General Motors' business, how do you think the company acquired these loans receivable?
2. The difference between the reported amount of General Motors' assets and liabilities is $21.001 billion ($274.273 − $253.272). What does this difference represent?

INTERNATIONAL CASE

International

• *Should the SEC choose the FASB or the IASC?*

The SEC has received from Congress the legal authority to set accounting standards in the United States. Historically, the SEC has allowed the FASB to set those standards. In addition, the SEC has refused to allow foreign companies to seek investment funds in the United States unless they agree to provide U.S. investors with financial statements prepared using FASB rules.

The number of foreign companies seeking to list their shares on U.S. stock exchanges is increasing. Even more would likely sell stock to the American public if the SEC were to agree to accept financial statements prepared according to usually less stringent IASC standards.

Why do you think the SEC has so far insisted on financial statements prepared using FASB rules? Do you agree with its policy? Explain.

ETHICS CASE

• *Disagreement With the Boss*

You recently graduated with your degree in accounting and have accepted an entry-level accounting position with BigTec, Inc. One of your first responsibilities is to review expense reports submitted by various executives. The expense reports include such items as receipts for taking clients to dinner and hotel receipts for business travel. In conducting this review, you note that your boss has submitted for reimbursement several items that are clearly outside the established guidelines of the corporation. In questioning your boss about the items, he told you to process the items and not worry about them. What would you do?

WRITING ASSIGNMENTS

• *The Language of Business*

Accounting is known as the "language of business." Prepare a one- to two-page paper explaining why all business students should have some accounting education. Also include a discussion of how accounting applies to at least five different types of businesses, such as a grocery store, a university, or a movie theater.

• *Visiting an Accounting Professional*

Select a field of accounting you are interested in. Visit a professional who works in that area and discuss the career opportunities available in that specific accounting field. After the visit, prepare a one- to two-page paper summarizing what you learned from your discussion with the accounting professional.

THE DEBATE

• *Insulate the FASB*

As mentioned in the text, the FASB conducts public hearings concerning any new accounting standards that it is considering. In addition, the FASB invites interested parties (businesses, trade groups, user groups, accounting professors) to send in written comments on proposed standards. This "due process" system occasionally exposes the FASB to intense lobbying pressure for and against proposed standards. For example, when the FASB was deliberating over the proper accounting for option compensation (see the example in the chapter), some companies, upset at the FASB's proposed approach, appealed to Congress to pass a bill outlawing the FASB's standard. Can the FASB establish good accounting standards in such a heated, public environment?

Divide your group into two teams.

- One team represents the "Open Door Policy." Prepare a two-minute oral argument supporting the continuation of the FASB's policy of adopting accounting standards only after public debate.
- The other team represents the "Insulate the FASB Movement." Prepare a two-minute oral argument outlining why it is impossible for the FASB to design conceptually correct accounting standards while being bombarded with the complaints and threats of self-interested companies and lobbyists.

INTERNET SEARCH

• The Financial Accounting Standards Board

The FASB's Web address is **http://www.fasb.org**. Sometimes Web addresses change; so if this address is out of commission, access the Web site for this textbook (**http://albrecht.swcollege.com**) for an updated link.

Once you have gained access to the site, answer the following questions.

1. What is the mission of the FASB?
2. How many FASB statements are there? When was the most recent statement issued?
3. When was the first statement issued and what is it about? What other statements are related to Statement No. 1?
4. In what ways are the following three types of FASB pronouncements different: (1) Statements of Financial Accounting Standards (SFAS), (2) Interpretations of SFAS, and (3) Statements of Financial Accounting Concepts?

Financial Statements: An Overview

chapter **f2**

learning objectives

After studying this chapter, you should be able to:

1. Understand the basic elements and formats of the three primary financial statements—balance sheet, income statement, and statement of cash flows.
2. Recognize the need for financial statement notes and identify the types of information included in the notes.
3. Describe the purpose of an audit report and the incentives the auditor has to perform a good audit.
4. Use financial ratios to identify a company's strengths and weaknesses and to forecast its future performance.
5. Explain the fundamental concepts and assumptions that underlie financial accounting.

setting the stage

In addition to founding the brokerage firm of MERRILL LYNCH, in 1926 Charles Merrill was instrumental in the consolidation of several grocery store chains in the western United States to form one big holding company called SAFEWAY. In 1955, control of Safeway passed to Robert Magowan, Merrill's son-in-law. Under Magowan's leadership, Safeway expanded to become the second largest supermarket chain in the United States. Shortly after Magowan retired in 1971, Safeway passed THE GREAT ATLANTIC AND PACIFIC TEA COMPANY (A&P) to become the largest supermarket chain.

During the 1970s, Safeway became too cautious and conservative (in the view of many). It was whispered that Safeway would become the A&P of the West—a fallen giant no longer willing to make the bold moves that had created its success in the first place. In 1980, Robert Magowan's 37-year-old son, Peter (who had started out in Safeway as a teenager bagging groceries), became chairman of the board of directors. As he assumed leadership of Safeway, Magowan faced a host of problems: an overall decrease in the size of the grocery market due to an increased tendency by Americans to eat at fast-food restaurants; union contracts that resulted in higher labor costs for Safeway than many of its competitors; high corporate overhead; and stores that were too small and too close together. As a result of these problems, between 1976 and 1980 Safeway lost market share in 9 of the 14 major markets in which it operated. As one executive put it, "[Losing market share] in the food business [is] a hell of an indicator you're not giving the customer what he wants." By 1981, Safeway's financial performance had hit disappointing lows.

Under Peter Magowan's leadership, Safeway eliminated 2,000 office and warehouse jobs and embarked upon an impressive program of new construction and remodeling. During much of the early 1980s, Safeway spent more on capital expenditures than any other U.S. company, averaging nearly $600 million per year. In November 1986, Safeway was acquired by KOHLBERG, KRAVIS, ROBERTS & CO. (KKR) for $5.3 billion in what was then the second-largest leveraged buyout (LBO) of all time. In an LBO, a group of private investors, sometimes joined by company managers, supply only a small amount of the money needed to buy an entire corporation. The bulk of the purchase price is provided by banks and other lenders, with the assets of the acquired company serving as collateral for the loans. As an indication of how leveraged the Safeway buyout was, the KKR investors put only $130 million of their own money into the $5.3 billion deal.

So, how is Safeway doing today? In the 1999 Fortune 500 survey, Safeway, with 1999 sales of $28.9 billion, ranks as the third-largest food and drug chain in the United States, behind KROGER ($45.3 billion in sales) and ALBERTSON'S ($37.5 billion in sales).[1] In fact, Safeway's 1999 sales increased 18% to reach this peak. Sales volume isn't the only financial measure that can be used to evaluate a company, however. For example, Safeway's net income in 1999 was $971 million, higher than the net income for both Kroger and Albertson's. Also, Safeway's cash income ("cash from operations") was $1,488.4 million. Further, Safeway earned 23.8 cents of profit for every dollar invested by its stockholders—a decent one-year return on investment (a dollar invested in a certificate of deposit during the same period would have earned only about 4 cents).

To adequately answer the question of how Safeway is doing today, one must have a working knowledge of financial statements. In this chapter, you will learn that the financial statements are summary reports that show how a business is doing and where its successes and failures lie. The financial statements covered in this chapter are the same as those used every day by millions of business owners, investors, and creditors to evaluate how well or poorly organizations are doing.

You will also be introduced to the use of financial ratios, which are the tools of financial statement analysis. You will learn how to compute and interpret ratios such as return on equity, asset

1 In 1999, Albertson's merged with AMERICAN STORES to form what was, at the time, the largest supermarket chain in the United States. Coincidentally, American Stores traces its roots back to the Skaggs family, whose stores also formed the backbone of the original Safeway chain organized by Charles Merrill in 1926.

turnover, and price-earnings (PE) ratio. Hopefully, you will come away from this chapter convinced that the purpose of accounting is not to fill out dull reports that are then filed away in dusty cabinets, but rather to prepare summary financial performance measures to be used as the basis for thousands of economic decisions every day.

1

Understand the basic elements and formats of the three primary financial statements—balance sheet, income statement, and statement of cash flows.

THE FINANCIAL STATEMENTS

The job of a mortgage loan officer is to evaluate each mortgage applicant to determine the likelihood that he or she will repay the mortgage loan. A key piece of evidence in each applicant's file is the financial information included as part of the loan application. A loan officer can use this information to evaluate whether an applicant will generate enough income to make the monthly mortgage payments and continue to make the required payments on other obligations. In fact, it is difficult to imagine how a mortgage loan officer could make an informed decision without this financial information.

Gaining access to an applicant's financial information clearly helps the mortgage lender make a better loan decision, but the applicant also benefits from making these financial disclosures. If no financial disclosures were provided, lenders would be forced to make loan decisions in the absence of reliable financial information about applicants. With greater uncertainty about applicants' ability to repay loans, a lender's risk would increase, causing the lender to raise the interest rate charged on loans. Thus, disclosure of financial information allows a lender to make better lending decisions and also allows an applicant to reduce the lender's uncertainty, leading to a lower interest rate on the loan.

The financial statements prepared by companies yield the same benefits as do the financial disclosures provided by mortgage applicants. Financial statement information provides potential lenders and investors with a reliable basis for evaluating the past performance and future prospects of a company. Because financial statements are used by so many different groups (investors, creditors, managers, etc.), they are sometimes called *general-purpose financial statements.* The three **primary financial statements** are the balance sheet, the income statement, and the statement of cash flows. These statements provide answers to the following questions:

primary financial statements The balance sheet, income statement, and statement of cash flows, used by external groups to assess a company's economic standing.

1. What is the company's current financial status?
2. What were the company's operating results for the period?
3. How did the company obtain and use cash during the period?

The **balance sheet** (or **statement of financial position**) reports the resources of a company (assets), the company's obligations (liabilities), and the difference between what is owned (assets) and what is owed (liabilities), called owners' equity. The **income statement** (or **statement of earnings**) reports the amount of net income earned by a company during a period, with annual and quarterly income statements being the most common. (Net income is discussed later in the chapter.) The income statement represents the accountant's best effort at measuring the economic performance of a company. The **statement of cash flows** reports the amount of cash collected and paid out by a company in the following three types of activities: operating, investing, and financing. As an illustration, the 1999 financial statements from MICROSOFT are reproduced in Appendix A at the end of the book. The Microsoft statements are referred to throughout this chapter and the rest of the book.

balance sheet (statement of financial position) The financial statement that reports a company's assets, liabilities, and owners' equity at a particular date.

income statement (statement of earnings) The financial statement that reports the amount of net income earned by a company during a period.

statement of cash flows The financial statement that reports the amount of cash collected and paid out by a company during a period of time.

The Balance Sheet

In the movie *The Princess Bride*, the hero, Wesley, was "mostly dead all day" until being revived by a miracle pill. Wesley was immediately challenged to come up with a plan to stop the imminent marriage of his true love, Buttercup, to the evil Prince Humperdinck. In formulating his plan, Wesley's first question to his conspirators was "What are our liabilities?" followed by "What are our assets?" In essence, the recently revived hero was saying, "Let me see a balance sheet." Similarly, the first questions asked about any business by potential investors and credi-

assets Economic resources that are owned or controlled by a company.

liabilities Obligations to pay cash, transfer other assets, or provide services to someone else.

tors are "What are the resources of the business?" and "What are its existing obligations?" The balance sheet answers these questions.

The three categories of the balance sheet—assets, liabilities, and owners' equity—are each explained below.

ASSETS **Assets** are economic resources that are owned or controlled[2] by a company. Assets for a typical company include cash, accounts receivable (amounts owed to the company by customers), inventory (goods held for sale), land, buildings, equipment, and even intangible items, such as copyrights and patents. To be summarized and aggregated on a balance sheet, each asset must be assigned a dollar amount. A balance sheet wouldn't be very useful with the following asset listing: one bank account, two warehouses full of goods, three trucks, and four customers who owe us money. As emphasized throughout this text, the monetary measurement and valuation of assets is an area in which accountants must exercise considerable professional judgment.

fyi

The insurmountable difficulties in valuing some assets can cause important economic assets to be excluded from a company's balance sheet. For example, how does one put a monetary value on the worldwide reputation of Coca-Cola or on the genius and leadership of Bill Gates? These assets, though incredibly valuable, are not listed in the balance sheets of THE COCA-COLA COMPANY or of Microsoft.

LIABILITIES **Liabilities** are obligations to pay cash, transfer other assets, or provide services to someone else. Your personal liabilities might include unpaid phone bills, the remaining balance on an automobile loan, or an obligation to complete work for which you have already been paid. Some common liabilities of a company are accounts payable (amounts owed by the company to suppliers), notes payable (amounts owed to banks or others), and mortgages payable (amounts owed for purchased property, such as land or buildings). Like assets, liabilities must be measured in monetary amounts. And, as with assets, quantifying the amount of a liability can require extensive judgment. As one example, consider the difficulties faced by a company to quantify its obligation to clean up a particular toxic waste site when the cleanup will take years to complete; the exact extent of the environmental damage at the site is still in dispute; and legal responsibility for the toxic mess is still debated in the courts. Properly valuing a company's liabilities is one of the biggest (if not *the* biggest) challenges that an accountant faces.

owners' equity The ownership interest in the net assets of an entity; equals total assets minus total liabilities.

net assets The owners' equity of a business; equal to total assets minus total liabilities.

OWNERS' EQUITY The remaining claim against the assets of a business, after the liabilities have been deducted, is **owners' equity**. Thus, owners' equity is a residual amount; it represents the **net assets** (total assets minus total liabilities) available after all obligations have been satisfied. Obviously, if there are no liabilities (an unlikely situation, except at the start of a business), then the total assets are exactly equal to the owners' claims against those assets—the owners' equity.

fyi

Although the emphasis in this book is on corporations, most of the same principles also apply to proprietorships and partnerships. Differences in accounting for proprietorships and partnerships are explained in detail in the expanded material in Chapter 11.

In order to get a business started, investors transfer resources, usually cash, to the business in return for part ownership. Ownership of a company can be restricted to one person (a sole proprietorship), to a small group (a partnership), or to a diffuse group of owners who often don't even know one another (a corporation). When owners initially invest money in a corporation, they receive evidence of their ownership in the form of shares of stock, represented by stock certificates. These shares of stock may then be privately traded among existing owners of the corporation, privately sold to new owners, or traded publicly on an organized stock exchange such as the New York Stock Exchange (NYSE) (where SAFEWAY's shares are traded) or the NASDAQ exchange (where Microsoft's shares are traded). The owners of a corporation are called **stockholders** or **shareholders**, and the owners' equity section of a corporate balance sheet is sometimes referred to as **stockholders' equity**.

stockholders (shareholders) The owners of a corporation.

stockholders' equity The owners' equity section of a corporate balance sheet.

Owners' equity is increased when owners make additional investments in a business or when the business generates profits that are retained in the business. Since business profits belong to the owners, retaining the profits in the business is equivalent to giving the profits to the owners and then having them immediately reinvest that amount back into the business.

2 An example of an asset that a company technically does not own, but does economically control, is a building that the company uses under a long-term, noncancelable lease agreement.

business environment essay

Should I Incorporate? Pick up just about any business newspaper or magazine, look in the classified section, and you are sure to see advertisements offering to help you set up a corporation. "Incorporate in USA by Fax or Phone!!!" "Incorporate: All 50 States and Offshore." "Typical Incorporating Fees: Delaware, $199; Wyoming, $285; the Bahamas, $500; Isle of Man, £250." With all this eagerness to incorporate, there must be some advantages. To understand these advantages, as well as the disadvantages, it is necessary to review the three major types of business entities: proprietorships, partnerships, and corporations.

1. *Proprietorship.* A proprietorship is a business owned by one person. Almost always, the owner of the business also manages the operation. For example, many owners of small businesses (especially those that provide personal services) manage the day-to-day activities of, and receive the profits directly from, those businesses. Legally, a proprietorship is merely an extension of the owner. The owner is personally responsible for all the activities and obligations of the business.
2. *Partnership.* A partnership is a business association of two or more individuals. As in a proprietorship, the partners generally own and manage the business and are personally responsible for all the obligations of the business. A partnership organization makes sense when the workload and financial requirements associated with starting and operating a business are too much for one person.
3. *Corporation.* A corporation is a business that is chartered (incorporated) as a separate legal entity under the laws of a particular state or country. With a proprietorship or a partnership, the owners are the business. With a corporation, the operations and obligations of the business are legally separated from the personal affairs of the owners. Typically, stockholders in a corporation can freely buy and sell their interests, thus allowing the corporate ownership to change without dissolving the business. The stock-

Owners' equity is decreased when the owners take back part of their investment. If the business is a corporation, distributions to the owners (stockholders) are called **dividends**. Owners' equity can also be decreased if operations generate a loss instead of a profit. In the extreme, very poor performance can result in the loss of all the assets originally invested by the owners. For a corporation, the amount of accumulated earnings of the business that have not been distributed to owners is called **retained earnings**. The portion of owners' equity contributed by owners in exchange for shares of stock is called **capital stock**. The amount of retained earnings plus the amount of capital stock equals the corporation's total owners' equity.

dividends Distributions to the owners (stockholders) of a corporation.

retained earnings The amount of accumulated earnings of the business that have not been distributed to owners.

capital stock The portion of a corporation's owners' equity contributed by owners in exchange for shares of stock.

ACCOUNTING EQUATION The balance sheet presents information based on the basic **accounting equation**:

$$\text{Assets} = \text{Liabilities} + \text{Owners' Equity}$$

accounting equation An algebraic equation that expresses the relationship between assets (resources), liabilities (obligations), and owners' equity (net assets, or the residual interest in a business after all liabilities have been met): Assets = Liabilities + Owners' Equity.

In fact, the name *balance sheet* comes from the fact that a proper balance sheet must always balance—total assets must equal the total of liabilities and owners' equity. The accounting equation is not some miraculous coincidence; it is true by definition. Liabilities and owners' equity are just the sources of funding used to buy the assets; that is, they are the claims (creditors' claims and owners' claims) against the assets. So, another way to view the accounting equation is that the total amount of the assets is equal to the total amount of funding needed to buy the assets. The total resources, therefore, equal the claims against those resources. This is illustrated in Exhibit 2-1.

The accounting equation is presented here merely to give you a glimpse of **double-entry accounting**. Chapter 3 gives an in-depth discussion of the equation elements and the mechanics of double-entry accounting.

holders elect a board of directors, which then hires executives to manage the corporation. The managers, as employees of the corporation, may or may not be stockholders. Thus, in a corporation there is a separation of ownership from management.

The primary advantages of incorporation are:

- Investment funds can be accumulated from many different individuals, allowing for the development of larger, more efficient companies.
- Individual owners can buy and sell their ownership shares without getting the permission of the other owners.
- The liability of the owners is limited. If the business does not flourish, the worst that can happen to the owners is that they lose their investment; their other personal assets are not at risk.

The primary disadvantages of incorporation are:

- Corporate income is taxed twice: once when it is earned by the corporation and again when it is paid out to shareholders in the form of dividends.
- Management of the business is separated from ownership. The owners must be cautious in monitoring the activities of their hired managers.

As shown below, the majority of business activity in the United States is conducted by corporations, although the actual number of proprietorships is greater.

Type of Business	Number of Businesses	Sales
Sole proprietorships	16.955 million	$ 843 billion
Partnerships	1.654 million	1,042 billion
Corporations	4.631 million	14,890 billion

Source: U.S. Bureau of the Census, *Statistical Abstract of the United States: 1999* (Washington, D.C., 1999). Data are based on IRS information for 1996.

exhibit 2-1 Elements of the Accounting Equation

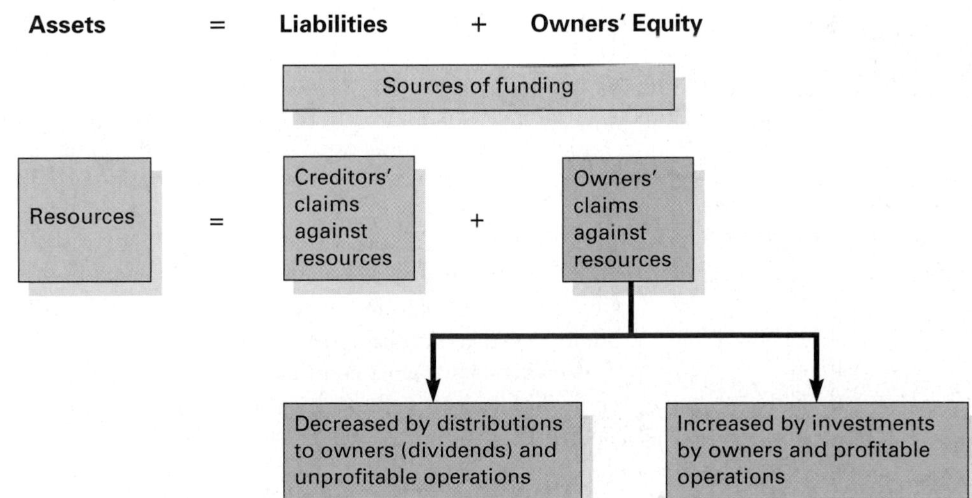

double-entry accounting A system of recording transactions in a way that maintains the equality of the accounting equation.

THE FORMAT OF A BALANCE SHEET A simple balance sheet, adapted from Microsoft's 1999 balance sheet reproduced in Appendix A at the end of the book, is shown in Exhibit 2-2.

Note that a balance sheet is presented for a particular date because it reports a company's financial position at a point in time. The balance sheet in Exhibit 2-2 presents Microsoft's financial position as of June 30, 1999.

exhibit 2-2 Simplified Balance Sheet for Microsoft

Microsoft Corporation
Balance Sheet
June 30, 1999
(amounts in millions)

Assets		Liabilities	
Cash and short-term investments	$17,236	Accounts payable	$ 874
Accounts receivable	2,245	Accrued compensation	396
Other current assets	752	Income taxes payable	1,607
Property, plant, and equipment	1,611	Unearned revenue	4,239
Equity and other investments	14,372	Other current liabilities	1,602
Other assets	940	Long-term loans	0
		Total liabilities	$ 8,718
		Owners' Equity	
		Capital stock	$14,824
		Retained earnings	13,614
Total assets	$37,156	Total liabilities and owners' equity	$37,156

As illustrated, the balance sheet is divided into the three major sections we have described: assets, liabilities, and owners' equity. The asset section identifies the types of assets owned by Microsoft (cash, for example) and the monetary amounts associated with those assets. The liability section defines the extent and nature of Microsoft's debts (income taxes not yet paid, for example).

Remember that the balance sheet is not merely a report to be prepared and forgotten; it is a summary of important information that is useful to investors and creditors. For example, if you were a banker, would you give a loan to Microsoft based on the information from the June 30, 1999, balance sheet? Of course you would, because you see that Microsoft already has enough cash on hand ($17 billion) to be able to pay off all existing liabilities ($8.7 billion) almost two times over. Based on the balance sheet information, you can see that any loan to Microsoft could be easily repaid.

Actually, the Microsoft balance sheet is quite unusual. Very few companies have the large amount of cash ($17 billion) and low amount of long-term debt ($0) that Microsoft has. Is it good for a company to have so much cash?

Owners' equity completes the balance sheet. This section identifies the portion of Microsoft's resources that were contributed by owners, either in exchange for shares of stock or as undistributed earnings since Microsoft's inception. Together with liabilities, owners' equity indicates how a company is financed (whether by borrowing or by owner contributions and operating profits). You can see that Microsoft has been financed primarily through owner investment. Almost half of this owner investment ($13.6 billion) has been in the form of retained earnings.

CLASSIFIED AND COMPARATIVE BALANCE SHEETS Imagine that two people each owe you $10,000. You ask to see the balance sheets of each. Borrower A has assets of $10,000 in the form of cash. Borrower B has assets of $10,000 in the form of undeveloped land. If you need to collect the loan in the next two weeks, which of the two borrowers is more likely to be able to pay you back? Borrower A is more likely to be able to repay you quickly because the assets of A are more *liquid*, meaning that they are in the form of cash or can be easily converted into cash. Assets such as undeveloped land are said to be *illiquid* in that it takes time and effort to convert them into cash. This illustration shows that not all assets are the same. For some purposes, it is very important to distinguish between current assets, which are generally more liq-

caution

Don't worry about fully understanding all the items in Safeway's classified balance sheet, such as the "Property under capital leases" and the "Cumulative translation adjustments." If there was nothing else to learn, this book would be much shorter and this accounting class would last only two weeks.

uid, and long-term assets. A balance sheet that distinguishes between current and long-term assets is called a **classified balance sheet**.

To illustrate a classified balance sheet, we consider the balance sheet for Safeway, the supermarket chain described in the opening scenario of this chapter. In Exhibit 2-3, Safeway's assets are classified as current, or short-term, and long-term.

Current assets include cash and other assets that are expected to be converted to cash within a year. Current assets generally are listed in decreasing order of **liquidity**; cash is listed first, followed by the other current assets, such as accounts receivable. **Long-term assets**, such as land, buildings, and equipment, are those that a company needs in order to operate its business over an extended period of time.

Like assets, liabilities usually are classified as either current (obligations expected to be paid within a year) or long-term. Accounts payable, for example, usually would be paid within 30 to 60 days, whereas a mortgage may remain on the books for 20 to 30 years before it is fully paid.

classified balance sheet A balance sheet in which assets and liabilities are subdivided into current and long-term categories.

current assets Cash and other assets that can be easily converted to cash within a year.

liquidity The ability of a company to pay its debts in the short run.

long-term assets Assets that a company needs in order to operate its business over an extended period of time.

comparative financial statements Financial statements in which data for two or more years are shown together.

market value The value of a company as measured by the number of shares of stock outstanding multiplied by the current market price of the stock; the current value of a business.

book value The value of a company as measured by the amount of owners' equity; that is, assets less liabilities.

Safeway's balance sheet in Exhibit 2-3 includes financial information for both the current year and the preceding year. Most companies prepare such **comparative financial statements** so that readers can identify any significant changes in particular items. For example, notice that Safeway's total assets increased by \$3,510.7 million (\$14,900.3 million − \$11,389.6 million) from 1998 to 1999. Where did the money come from to finance this increase in assets? Most of it came from an increased amount of loans (liabilities increased by \$2,507 million).

LIMITATIONS OF A BALANCE SHEET Although the balance sheet is useful in showing the financial status of a company, it does have some limitations. The primary limitation of the balance sheet is that it does not reflect the current value or worth of a company. Refer back to the balance sheet numbers for Microsoft in Exhibit 2-2. If the balance sheet were perfect, meaning that it included all economic assets reported at their current market values, then the amount of owners' equity would be equal to the market value of the company. In the case of Microsoft, the value of the company would be \$28.438 billion, which is the amount of assets that would remain after all the liabilities were repaid. The actual market value of Microsoft on May 18, 2000, however, was \$348 billion. How could the balance sheet be so wrong?

The discrepancy between recorded balance sheet value and actual market value is the result of the following two factors:

1. Accountants record many assets at their purchase cost, not at their current market value. **Market value** is the price that would have to be paid to buy the same asset today. For example, if land was obtained ten years ago, it would still be reported on the balance sheet at its original cost, even though its market value may have increased dramatically.
2. Not all economic assets are included in the balance sheet. For example, important economic assets of Microsoft are its proven track record of successful products, the genius of Bill Gates, and a strong, established position in the marketplace (ask NOVELL, WORDPERFECT, LOTUS, and NETSCAPE what it is like to compete against Microsoft). These intangible factors are all very valuable economic assets. In fact, they are by far the most valuable assets Microsoft has. Nevertheless, these important economic assets are outside the normal accounting process.

Because the balance sheet can underreport the value of some long-term assets, and not report other important economic assets, the accounting **book value** of a company (measured by the amount of owners' equity) is usually less than the company's market value, measured by the market price per share times the number of shares of stock. This is illustrated in Exhibit 2-4 using data for the ten largest companies (in terms of market value) in the United States.

Despite its deficiencies, the balance sheet is a useful source of information regarding the financial position of a business. A lender would never loan a company money without knowing what assets the company has and what other loans the company is already obligated to repay. An investor shouldn't pay money in exchange for ownership in a company without knowing something about the company's existing resources and obligations. When a balance sheet is classified, and when comparative data are provided, the balance sheet provides an informative picture of a company's financial position.

exhibit 2-3 Classified Balance Sheets for Safeway

Safeway, Inc.
Comparative Balance Sheet
December 28, 1999 and December 30, 1998
(amounts in millions)

	1999	1998
Assets		
Current assets:		
Cash	$ 106.2	$ 45.7
Accounts receivable	292.9	200.1
Merchandise inventories	2,444.9	1,856.0
Prepaid expenses and other current assets	208.1	218.1
Total current assets	$ 3,052.1	$ 2,319.9
Property:		
Land	$ 996.2	$ 794.1
Buildings	2,502.3	2,069.9
Leasehold improvements	1,784.3	1,498.3
Fixtures and equipment	3,852.4	3,282.6
Property under capital leases	591.4	379.2
Total property	$ 9,726.6	$ 8,024.1
Less accumulated depreciation and amortization	3,281.9	2,841.5
Total property, net	$ 6,444.7	$ 5,182.6
Other assets:		
Goodwill	$ 4,786.6	$ 3,348.0
Prepaid pension costs	405.6	369.6
Investments in unconsolidated affiliates	131.6	115.2
Other assets	79.7	54.3
Total assets	$14,900.3	$11,389.6
Liabilities and Stockholders' Equity		
Current liabilities:		
Accounts payable	$ 1,878.4	$ 1,595.9
Accrued salaries and wages	387.7	348.9
Other current liabilities	1,316.5	948.8
Total current liabilities	$ 3,582.6	$ 2,893.6
Long-term debt:		
Notes and debentures	$ 5,922.0	$ 4,242.6
Obligations under capital leases	435.4	408.0
Total long-term debt	$ 6,357.4	$ 4,650.6
Deferred income taxes	379.1	216.9
Accrued claims and other liabilities	495.4	546.4
Total liabilities	$10,814.5	$ 8,307.5
Stockholders' equity:		
Common stock: par value $0.01 per share	$ 5.6	$ 5.5
Additional paid-in capital	1322.4	1,297.3
Unexercised warrants purchased	(126.6)	(126.0)
Cumulative translation adjustments	(11.5)	(19.7)
Retained earnings	2,895.9	1,925.0
Total stockholders' equity	$ 4,085.8	$ 3,082.1
Total liabilities and stockholders' equity	$14,900.3	$11,389.6

exhibit 2-4 Book Value and Market Value for the Ten Largest U.S. Firms

Rank	Company	Book Value*	Market Value*†
1	Microsoft	$28,438.0	$492,462
2	Cisco Systems	11,678.0	453,879
3	General Electric	42,557.0	417,175
4	Intel	32,535.0	391,817
5	ExxonMobil	63,466.0	268,598
6	AT&T	78,927.0	236,704
7	Oracle	3,695.3	217,258
8	Lucent Technologies	13,584.0	214,185
9	Wal-Mart Stores	25,848.0	212,666
10	International Business Machines (IBM)	20,511.0	193,810

*Accounting book value and market value are in millions of dollars.
†On a previous page we noted that Microsoft's market value was $348 billion on May 18, 2000. In this exhibit, Microsoft's value is listed as $492 billion as of March 14, 2000. The reason for the dramatic decrease in market value in two months is the government's theatened breakup of the company.

Source: Fortune 500 listing, 1999. Market values are as of March 14, 2000. Accounting book values are for the end of the immediately preceding fiscal year. Accessible at http://www.fortune.com.

to summarize

The balance sheet provides a summary of the financial position of a company at a particular date. It helps external users assess the financial relationship between assets (resources) and liabilities and owners' equity (claims against those resources). Assets and liabilities are usually classified as either current or long-term and are presented in descending order of liquidity. For a corporation, owners' equity consists of directly invested funds as well as retained earnings. Classified and comparative balance sheets provide useful information for readers of financial statements. Because not all economic assets are included on the balance sheet, the book value as shown in the balance sheet is usually less than the market value of the company.

The Income Statement

Almost every day, *The Wall Street Journal* includes a section called "Digest of Earnings Reports" that contains the net income, or earnings, figures announced by companies the day before. The stock prices of companies go up or down depending on whether their announced earnings meet the expectations of investors. For example, on April 19, 1997, Microsoft stock shot up from $98.125 to $107.625 per share in response to news of an 85% increase in Microsoft's net income as compared to the previous year. This high level of interest centered on net income makes it apparent that investors find this accounting number useful in evaluating the health and performance of a business.

Net income is reported in the income statement. The income statement shows the results of a company's operations for a period of time (a month, a quarter, or a year). The income statement summarizes the revenues generated and the costs incurred (expenses) to generate those revenues. The "bottom line" of an income statement is net income (or net loss), the difference between revenues and expenses. To help you understand an income statement, we must first define its elements—revenues, expenses, and net income (or net loss).

revenue Increase in a company's resources from the sale of goods or services.

REVENUES **Revenue** is the amount of assets created through business operations. Think of revenue as another way for a company to acquire assets. In the same way that assets can be acquired by borrowing or by owners' investment, assets can also be acquired by providing a product or service for which customers are willing to pay. Manufacturing and merchandising companies receive revenues from the sale of merchandise. For example, Safeway's revenue is the cash that customers pay in exchange for groceries. A service enterprise generates revenues from the fees it charges for the services it performs. For example, a portion of the sales price of Microsoft software is not payment for the software itself, but instead is an advance payment for the customer support service that Microsoft promises. Companies might also earn revenues from other activities, such as charging interest or collecting rent. When goods are sold or services performed, the resulting revenue is in the form of cash or accounts receivable (a promise from the buyer to pay for the goods or services by a specified date in the future). Revenues thus generally represent an increase in total assets. These new assets are not tied to any liability obligation; therefore, the assets belong to the owners and thus represent an increase in owners' equity.

expenses Costs incurred in the normal course of business to generate revenues.

EXPENSES **Expenses** are the amount of assets consumed through business operations. Expenses are the costs incurred in normal business operations to generate revenues. Employee salaries and utilities used during a period are two common examples of expenses. For Safeway, the primary expense is the wholesale cost of the groceries that it sells to its customers at retail. Just as revenues represent an increase in assets and equity, expenses generally represent a decrease in assets and in equity.

In considering revenues and expenses, remember that not all inflows of assets are revenues; nor are all outflows of assets considered to be expenses. For example, cash may be received by borrowing from a bank, which is an increase in a liability, not a revenue. Similarly, cash may be paid for supplies, which is an exchange of one asset for another asset, not an expense. The details of properly identifying revenues and expenses will be discussed further in Chapter 3.

net income (net loss) An overall measure of the performance of a company; equal to revenues minus expenses for the period.

NET INCOME (OR NET LOSS) **Net income**, sometimes called earnings or profit, is an overall measure of the performance of a company. Net income reflects the company's accomplishments (revenues) in relation to its efforts (expenses) during a particular period of time. If revenues exceed expenses, the result is called net income (revenues − expenses = net income). If expenses exceed revenues, the difference is called **net loss**. Because net income results in an increase in resources from operations, owners' equity is also increased; a net loss decreases owners' equity. Exhibit 2-5 lists the ten U.S. companies with the highest net incomes in 1999.

It is important to note the difference between revenues and net income. Both concepts represent an increase in the net assets (assets − liabilities) of a firm. However, revenues represent total resource increases; expenses are subtracted from revenues to derive net income or net loss. Thus, whereas revenue is a "gross" concept, income (or loss) is a "net" concept.

At its Web site (http://www.fortune.com), *Fortune* magazine provides selected stories from current issues as well as summaries of its famous lists: the Fortune 500 (largest companies in the United States) and the Global 500 (largest companies in the world).

1. Search the Fortune 500 Top Performers to find out which U.S. company has the most assets.
2. Search the Global 500 Top Performers and identify which company employs more people than any other company in the world.

THE FORMAT OF AN INCOME STATEMENT Comparative income statements, which have been modified to a "multi-step format," for Safeway are presented in Exhibit 2-6. In contrast to the balance sheet, which is "as of" a particular date, the income statement refers to the "year ended." Remember, the income statement covers a period of time; the balance sheet is a report at a point in time. The multi-step format illustrated here highlights several profit measurements including gross profit, operating income, and net income.

The income statement usually shows two main categories, revenues and expenses, although several subcategories may also be presented (as illustrated). Revenues are listed first. Typical operating expenses for most businesses are employee salaries, utilities, and advertising. For Safeway, as with any retail firm, the largest expense is for cost of goods sold. The difference between sales and cost of goods sold represents the difference between the retail price Safeway receives from a grocery sale and the wholesale cost of the groceries that are sold. This difference (sales − cost of goods sold) is called **gross profit** or **gross margin**.

gross profit (gross margin) The excess of net sales revenue over the cost of goods sold.

Expenses are sometimes divided into operating and nonoperating categories. The primary nonoperating expenses are interest and income taxes. These expenses are called nonoperating because they have no connection with the specific nature of the operation of the business. For ex-

exhibit 2-5 Top Ten U.S. Companies, Ranked by Net Income

Company Name	Net Income*
General Electric	$10,717.0
Citigroup	9,867.0
SBC Communications	8,159.0
ExxonMobil	7,910.0
Bank of America Corporation	7,882.0
Microsoft	7,785.0
International Business Machines	7,712.0
E.I. du Pont de Nemours	7,690.0
Philip Morris	7,675.0
Intel	7,314.0

*Net income is in millions of dollars.

Source: Fortune 500 listing, 1999. Accessible at http://www.fortune.com.

ample, Safeway and Microsoft deal with interest and income taxes in a similar way, even though the two companies operate in completely different industries.

gains (losses) Money made or lost on activities outside the normal operation of a company.

Two other items that frequently appear in the income statement are **gains** and **losses**. Gains and losses refer to money made or lost on activities outside the normal business of a company. For example, when Safeway receives cash for selling groceries, it is called revenue. But when

exhibit 2-6 Adapted Comparative Income Statements for Safeway

Safeway, Inc.
Comparative Income Statement
For the Years Ended December 28, 1999
and December 30, 1998
(in millions)

	1999	1998
Revenues:		
Sales	$28,859.9	$24,484.2
Less: Cost of goods sold	20,349.2	17,359.7
Gross profit	$ 8,510.7	$ 7,124.5
Less: Operating and administrative expense	6,411.4	5,466.5
Goodwill amortization	101.4	56.3
Operating income	$ 1,997.9	$ 1,601.7
Add: Other income	38.3	30.2
Less: Interest expense	362.2	235.1
Less: Income tax expense	703.1	590.2
Net income	$ 970.9	$ 806.6
Basic earnings per share	$ 1.95	$1.67

Safeway makes money by selling an old delivery truck, the amount is called a gain, not revenue, because Safeway is not in the business of selling trucks.

Recently, companies have been providing an additional measure of income—comprehensive income. The wealth of a company is affected in a variety of ways that have nothing to do with the business operations of the company. For example, changes in exchange rates can cause the U.S. dollar value of a company's foreign subsidiaries to increase or decrease. **Comprehensive income** is the number used to reflect an overall measure of the change in a company's wealth during the period.

comprehensive income A measure of the overall change in a company's wealth during a period; consists of net income plus changes in wealth resulting from changes in investment values and exchange rates.

In addition to net income, comprehensive income includes items that, in general, arise from changes in market conditions unrelated to the business operations of a company. These items are excluded from net income because they are viewed as yielding little information about the economic performance of a company's business operations. Nevertheless, they do affect the value of assets and liabilities reported in the balance sheet, so they are reported as part of comprehensive income.

The most common examples of items included in comprehensive income include changes in foreign currency exchange rates, changes in the value of certain investment securities, and changes in the value of certain derivative financial instruments. Each of these items is affected by market conditions, affects a company's reported assets and liabilities, yet cannot be influenced in any large degree by the company. Therefore, they are reported as part of a firm's comprehensive income. To summarize, net income is a measure of a company's performance during the period; comprehensive income includes the net income performance measure plus other wealth changes resulting from changes in investment values and exchange rates.

earnings (loss) per share (EPS) The amount of net income (earnings) related to each share of stock; computed by dividing net income by the number of shares of stock outstanding during the period.

One final bit of information required on the income statements of corporations is **earnings (loss) per share (EPS)**. This EPS amount is computed by dividing the net income (earnings or loss) for the current period by the number of shares of stock outstanding during the period. Earnings per share information tells the owner of a single share of stock how much of the net income for the year belongs to him or her.

Like the balance sheet, the income statement usually shows the comparative results for two or more periods, allowing investors and creditors to evaluate how profitable an enterprise has been during the current period as compared with earlier periods. For example, examination of Safeway's comparative income statements in Exhibit 2-6 shows that net income in 1999 was 20% higher [($970.9 − $806.6) ÷ $806.6] than in 1998. Further analysis of the income statement is introduced later in this chapter and reinforced throughout the text. (For another illustration of a comparative income statement, see the income statement for Microsoft in Appendix A at the back of the book.)

statement of retained earnings A report that shows the changes in retained earnings during a period of time.

THE STATEMENT OF RETAINED EARNINGS In addition to an income statement, corporations sometimes prepare a **statement of retained earnings**. This statement identifies changes in retained earnings from one accounting period to the next. As illustrated in Exhibit 2-7, the

exhibit 2-7 Illustrated Statement of Retained Earnings for Safeway

Safeway, Inc.
Illustrated Statement of Retained Earnings
For the Year Ended December 28, 1999
(in millions)

Retained earnings, January 1, 1999	$1,925.0
Add net income for the year	970.9
	$2,895.9
Less dividends	0
Retained earnings, December 28, 1999	$2,895.9

statement shows a beginning retained earnings balance, the net income for the period, a deduction for any dividends paid, and an ending retained earnings balance. For Safeway, which paid no dividends during 1999, its retained earnings would simply increase by the amount of reported net income.

Note how the accounting equation is affected by the elements reported in the statement of retained earnings. Net income results in an increase in net assets and a corresponding increase in Retained Earnings, which increases Owners' Equity.

(↑) Assets = Liabilities + Owners' Equity (↑)

Capital Stock Retained Earnings (↑)

Dividends reduce net assets (e.g., cash) and similarly reduce Retained Earnings, which reduces Owners' Equity.

(↓) Assets = Liabilities + Owners' Equity (↓)

Capital Stock Retained Earnings (↓)

Corporations sometimes present a *statement of stockholders' equity* instead of a statement of retained earnings. The statement of stockholders' equity, illustrated for Microsoft in Appendix A at the back of the book, is more detailed and includes changes in capital stock as well as changes in retained earnings.

to summarize

The income statement provides a measure of the success of an enterprise over a specified period of time. The income statement shows the major sources of revenues generated and the expenses associated with those revenues. The difference between those revenues and expenses is net income or net loss. Gains and losses refer to money made or lost on activities outside the normal activities of a business. The income statements of corporations must also include earnings per share figures. Comprehensive income includes net income as well as other wealth changes resulting from changes in investment values and exchange rates. Like balance sheets, income statements are usually prepared on a comparative basis. A statement of retained earnings or statement of stockholders' equity is often provided by corporations in their annual reports to shareholders.

The Statement of Cash Flows

Net income is the single best measure of a company's economic performance. However, anyone who has paid rent or college tuition knows that bills must be paid with cash, not with "economic performance." Accordingly, in addition to net income, investors and creditors also desire to know how much actual cash a company's operations generate during a period and how that cash is used. The statement of cash flows shows the cash inflows (receipts) and cash outflows (payments) of an entity during a period of time. As shown in Exhibit 2-8, companies receive cash primarily by selling goods or providing services, by selling other assets, by borrowing, and by receiving cash from investments by owners. Companies use cash to pay current operating expenses such as wages, utilities, and taxes; to purchase additional buildings, land, and otherwise expand operations; to repay loans; and to pay their owners a return on the investments that have been made.

In the statement of cash flows, individual cash flow items are classified according to three main activities: operating, investing, and financing.

exhibit 2-8 Cash Flows

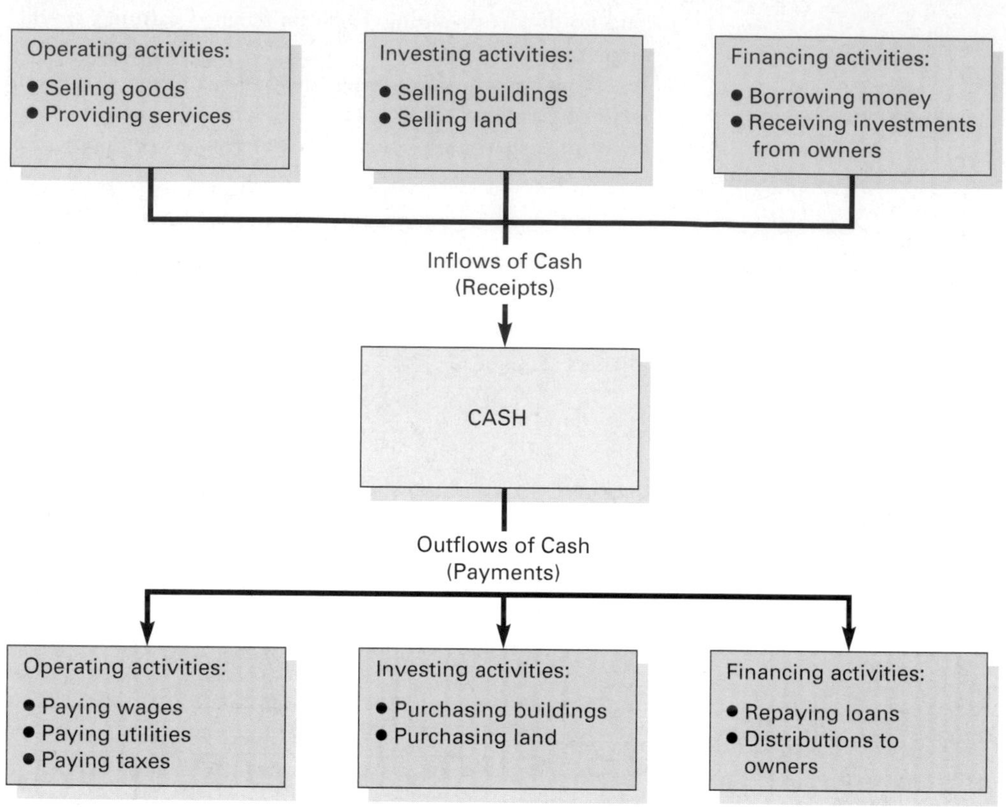

operating activities Activities that are part of the day-to-day business of a company.

OPERATING ACTIVITIES **Operating activities** are those activities that are part of the day-to-day business of a company. Cash receipts from selling goods or from providing services are the major operating cash inflow. Major operating cash outflows include payments to purchase inventory and to pay wages, taxes, interest, utilities, rent, and similar expenses.

investing activities Activities associated with buying and selling long-term assets.

INVESTING ACTIVITIES The primary **investing activities** are the purchase and sale of land, buildings, and equipment. You can think of investing activities as those activities associated with buying and selling long-term assets.

financing activities Activities whereby cash is obtained from or repaid to owners and creditors.

FINANCING ACTIVITIES **Financing activities** are those activities whereby cash is obtained from or repaid to owners and creditors. For example, cash received from owners' investments, cash proceeds from a loan, or cash payments to repay loans would all be classified under financing activities.

Conceptually, the statement of cash flows is the easiest to prepare of the three primary financial statements. Imagine examining every check and deposit slip you have written in the past year and sorting them into three piles—operating, investing, and financing. You would have to exercise some judgment in deciding which pile some items go into (for example, is the payment of interest an operating or a financing activity?). But overall, the three-way categorization of cash flows is not that difficult. In essence, this is all that is involved in the preparation of a statement of cash flows. As you will see in Chapter 13, however, actual preparation of a statement of cash flows can sometimes be challenging. The reason for this is that traditional accounting systems are designed to streamline the computation of net income. So, instead of preparing the statement of cash flows directly from the raw cash flow data, the process is as shown in Exhibit 2-9. The raw cash flow data are transformed into revenue and expense data using the accounting adjustments, assumptions, and estimates that you will learn about in this text. Then, to prepare the statement of cash flows, all of those adjustments must be undone to get back to the raw cash flow data. Challenging, but by the time we get to Chapter 13, you will be ready for it.

exhibit 2-9 Cash Flow to Net Income to Cash Flow

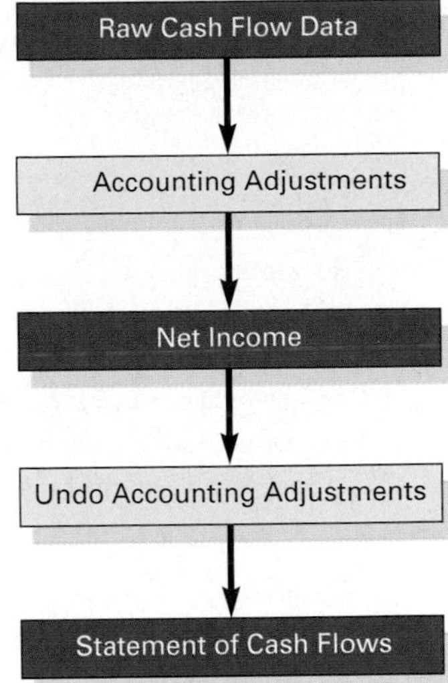

fyi

Notice that the Boston Celtics has chosen June 30 as the end of its fiscal year. About two-thirds of large U.S. companies choose December 31. The Boston Celtics uses June 30 because that coincides with a natural lull in its business (the playoffs are over and the next regular season is months away). Safeway chooses the last Saturday of the year to make sure that each fiscal year contains a whole number of weeks.

Exhibit 2-10 contains the statement of cash flows for the **BOSTON CELTICS** for the year ended June 30, 1996[3]. As sports fans know, the Boston Celtics is the NBA team with the most championships in history. What is not widely known is that ownership shares in the Boston Celtics could once be purchased by the general public and were traded on the New York Stock Exchange. Because the Celtics was a publicly traded company, it was required to make its financial statements publicly available, thus providing the information for Exhibit 2-10. As with balance sheets and income statements, companies usually provide comparative statements of cash flows. However, we have elected not to show comparative statements of cash flows in order to keep the Celtics illustration simple. (The Microsoft financial statements in Appendix A provide comparative statements of cash flows.)

One interesting item to note in the Celtics' cash flow statement is the $5.2 million payment for deferred compensation. This represents players' salaries that were earned (and reported as expenses) in prior years but not paid until 1996. Also notice the large amount of activity in buying and selling investment securities—$171 million in securities purchased and $157 million sold. And you thought that the Celtics only played basketball.

to summarize

The statement of cash flows is one of the three primary financial statements. It shows the significant cash inflows (receipts) and cash outflows (payments) of a company for a period of time. These cash flows are classified according to operating, investing, and financing activities. The statement of cash flows is discussed and illustrated in Chapter 13.

How the Financial Statements Tie Together

articulation The interrelationships among the financial statements.

Although we have introduced the primary financial statements as if they were independent of one another, they are interrelated and tie together. In accounting language, they "articulate." **Articulation** refers to the relationship between an operating statement (the income statement or the statement of cash flows) and comparative balance sheets, whereby an item on the operating statement helps explain the change in an item on the balance sheet from one period to the next.

3 Beginning in 1997, the Celtics were no longer publicly traded.

exhibit 2-10 Statement of Cash Flows for the Boston Celtics

BOSTON CELTICS LIMITED PARTNERSHIP
Statement of Cash Flows
For the Year Ended June 30, 1996

CASH FLOWS FROM OPERATING ACTIVITIES		
Receipts:		
Basketball regular season receipts:		
Ticket sales	$31,323,249	
Television and radio broadcast rights fees	19,908,800	
Other (principally promotional advertising)	8,424,038	
Basketball playoff receipts	360,895	
		60,016,982
Outflows:		
Basketball regular season expenditures:		
Team expenses	26,066,875	
Game expenses	2,481,007	
Basketball playoff expenses	0	
General and administrative expenses	13,996,805	
Selling and promotional expenses	1,333,238	
		43,877,925
		16,139,057
Interest income		9,553,938
Interest expense		(4,624,043)
Ticket refunds paid		(504)
Proceeds from league expansion		4,490,673
Payment of income taxes		(4,973,883)
Payment of deferred compensation		(5,226,095)
Other operating cash outflows		(2,931,742)
NET CASH FLOWS FROM OPERATING ACTIVITIES		12,427,401
CASH FLOWS FROM INVESTING ACTIVITIES		
Purchases of investment securities	(171,422,268)	
Proceeds from sales of investment securities	156,655,561	
Net cash proceeds from the sale of Boston Celtics Broadcasting Limited Partnership	77,597,929	
Capital expenditures	(796,424)	
Other investing receipts	293,503	
NET CASH FLOWS FROM INVESTING ACTIVITIES		62,328,301
CASH FLOWS (USED BY) FINANCING ACTIVITIES		
Repayment of bank borrowings	(80,000,000)	
Repurchase of Boston Celtics Limited Partnership shares from owners	(1,941,450)	
Cash distributions to owners	(26,395,139)	
NET CASH FLOWS (USED BY) FINANCING ACTIVITIES		(108,336,589)
NET (DECREASE) IN CASH		(33,580,887)
Cash at beginning of period		39,563,015
CASH AT END OF PERIOD		$ 5,982,128

Exhibit 2-11 shows how the financial statements tie together. Note that the beginning amount of cash from the 1998 balance sheet is added to the net increase or decrease in cash (from the statement of cash flows) to derive the cash balance as reported on the 1999 balance sheet. Similarly, the retained earnings balance as reported on the 1999 balance sheet comes from the beginning retained earnings balance (1998 balance sheet) plus net income for the period (from the income statement) less dividends paid. As you study financial statements, these relationships will become clearer and you will understand the concept of articulation better.

2

Recognize the need for financial statement notes and identify the types of information included in the notes.

notes to the financial statements Explanatory information considered an integral part of the financial statements.

NOTES TO THE FINANCIAL STATEMENTS

The three primary financial statements contain a lot of information. Still, three summary reports cannot possibly tell financial statement users everything they want to know about a company. Additional information is given in the **notes to the financial statements**. In fact, in a typical annual report, the notes go on for 15 pages or more, whereas the primary financial statements fill only 3 pages. The notes tell about the assumptions and methods used in preparing the financial statements and also give more detail about specific items.

The financial statement notes are of the following four general types:

1. Summary of significant accounting policies.
2. Additional information about the summary totals found in the financial statements.
3. Disclosure of important information that is not recognized in the financial statements.
4. Supplementary information required by the Financial Accounting Standards Board (FASB) or the Securities and Exchange Commission (SEC).

Summary of Significant Accounting Policies

As mentioned earlier, accounting involves making assumptions, estimates, and judgments. In addition, in some settings, there is more than one acceptable method of accounting for certain

exhibit 2-11 How the Financial Statements Tie Together

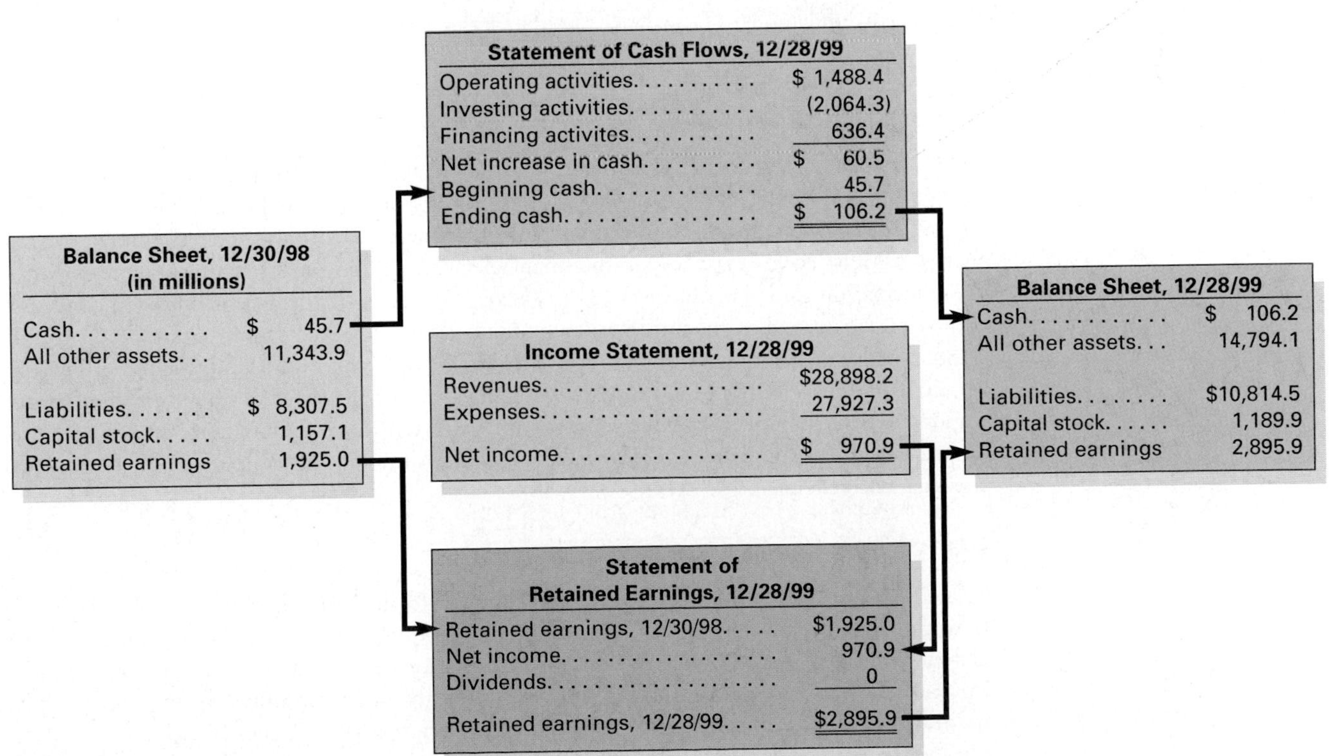

business environment essay

How to Get Your Own Copy of Microsoft's Financial Statements The complete Microsoft annual report containing the 1999 financial statements is reproduced at the end of this text. Is this secret information, available only to owners of this book? No. Anyone can get a copy of the most recent annual report of Microsoft or any other public corporation in the United States. Any of the following methods will work:

- Become an investor in Microsoft by buying shares of stock in the company. As a Microsoft investor, you are entitled to receive a copy of the annual report each year. In fact, according to U.S. government regulations, Microsoft is required to send a copy of the annual report to all of its investors within three months of the end of Microsoft's fiscal year on June 30.
- Call, write, fax, or e-mail Microsoft's Investor Relations department. The phone numbers and addresses are given in the Microsoft annual report re-

fyi

In its 1920 annual report, IBM included zero pages of notes (and the dollar amounts were carried out to the penny). In 1966, there were four pages of notes (and dollar amounts were rounded to the nearest dollar). In 1996, IBM's annual report included 26 pages of notes (and dollar amounts were rounded to the nearest million).

items. For example, there are a variety of acceptable ways of estimating how much a building depreciates (wears out) in a year. In order for financial statement users to be able to properly interpret the three primary financial statements, they must know what procedures were used in preparing those statements. This information about accounting policies and practices is given in the financial statement notes.

Additional Information about Summary Totals

For a large company, such as MICROSOFT or SAFEWAY, one summary number in the financial statements represents literally thousands of individual items. For example, the $5.922 billion in long-term notes and debentures included in Safeway's 1999 balance sheet (see Exhibit 2-3) represents loans of U.S. dollars, loans of Canadian dollars, mortgages, senior secured debentures, senior subordinated debentures, an unsecured bank credit agreement, and more. The balance sheet includes only one number, with the details in the notes.

Disclosure of Information Not Recognized

One way to report financial information is to boil down all the estimates and judgments into one number and then report that one number in the financial statements. This is called *recognition.* The key assumptions and estimates are then described in a note to the financial statements. Another approach is to skip the financial statements and just rely on the note to convey the information to users. This is called *disclosure.* Disclosure is the accepted way to convey information to users when the information is too uncertain to be recognized. For example, in July 1988, Safeway suffered a fire in one of its warehouses in Richmond, California. As of February 10, 2000, there were still 2,600 unsettled lawsuits against Safeway stemming from the fire. It is impossible to summarize the complexity of the potential outcome of these lawsuits in one financial statement number; so, Safeway describes the situation, in some detail, in the notes to the financial statements.

Supplementary Information

The FASB and SEC both require supplementary information that must be reported in the financial statement notes. For example, the FASB requires the disclosure of quarterly financial information and of business segment information. A sample of this type of disclosure can be seen in Microsoft's annual report in Appendix A. In the notes to its financial statements, Microsoft reports that 30% of its 1999 net income was generated outside of the United States.

produced at the back of this book. For promotional purposes, companies are happy to mail their annual report to anyone who asks.

- Download a copy of the annual report from Microsoft's Web site at microsoft.com. On the Web sites of most companies (Microsoft included), the annual report is not easy to find. You have to skirt past games, promotional material, and lots of nonfinancial information, but the annual report is usually there somewhere.
- Download a copy of the annual report (and lots of other information) from the U.S. government archives at sec.gov/edgarhp.htm. These government filings are pure text documents (no pictures) and are made available through the EDGAR (Electronic Data Gathering, Analysis, and Retrieval) system.

Now that you know how to get your own copy of the Microsoft annual report, make sure you study the rest of this book to learn how to use the report.

to summarize

The notes to the financial statements contain additional information not included in the financial statements themselves. The notes explain the company's accounting assumptions and practices, provide details of financial statement summary numbers and additional disclosure about complex events, and report supplementary information required by the SEC or the FASB.

3

Describe the purpose of an audit report and the incentives the auditor has to perform a good audit.

THE EXTERNAL AUDIT

Refer back to the opening scenario for this chapter. Following the November 1986 leveraged buyout by **KOHLBERG, KRAVIS, ROBERTS & CO. (KKR)**, **SAFEWAY** decided to again issue shares to the public. In April 1990, Safeway issued shares at a price of $11.25 per share. The $11.25 price implied that the market value of KKR's initial investment had risen from $130 million to $731 million. The $11.25 price was determined by investment bankers and potential investors after examining the financial statements of Safeway. Now, consider the following questions:

- Who controlled the preparation of the Safeway financial statements used by investors in arriving at the $11.25 price? The owners and managers of Safeway, led by KKR.
- Did KKR have any incentive to bias the reported financial statement numbers? Absolutely. The better the numbers, the higher the stock offering price and the more money raised by KKR.
- Since KKR had control of the preparation of the financial statements and stood to benefit substantially if those statements looked overly favorable, how could the financial statements be trusted? Good question.

audit report A report issued by an independent CPA that expresses an opinion about whether the financial statements fairly present a company's financial position, operating results, and cash flows in accordance with generally accepted accounting principles.

This situation illustrates a general truth: the owners and managers of a company have an incentive to report the most favorable results possible. Poor reported financial performance can make it harder to get loans, can lower the amount that managers receive as salary bonuses, and can lower the stock price when shares are issued to the public. With these incentives to stretch the truth, the financial statements would not be reliable unless they were reviewed by an external party.

To provide this external review, a company's financial statements are often audited by an independent certified public accountant (CPA). A CPA firm issues an **audit report** that ex-

fyi

Notice that **MICROSOFT**'s audit report is dated July 19, 1999. This means that it took less than three weeks (from the end of the fiscal year on June 30) for the completion of the audit. Obviously, much audit work was conducted during the year to make this happen.

presses an opinion about whether the statements fairly present a company's financial position, operating results, and cash flows in accordance with generally accepted accounting principles. Note that the financial statements are the responsibility of a company's management and not of the CPA. Although not all company records have to be audited, audits are needed for many purposes. For example, a banker may not make a loan without first receiving audited financial statements from a prospective borrower. As another example, most securities cannot be sold to the general public until they are registered with the SEC. Audited financial statements are required for this registration process.

Though an audit report does not guarantee accuracy, it does provide added assurance that the financial statements are not misleading since they have been examined by an independent professional. However, the CPA cannot examine every transaction upon which the summary figures in the financial statements are based. The accuracy of the statements must remain the responsibility of the company's management. An example of a typical audit report is found in Appendix A in Microsoft's 1999 annual report. Microsoft's financial statements were audited by **DELOITTE & TOUCHE LLP**, one of the large international audit firms.

One final question: Who hires and pays Deloitte & Touche to do the audit of Microsoft's financial statements? Microsoft does. At first glance, this situation appears to be similar to allowing students in an accounting class to choose and pay the graders of the examinations. However, two economic factors combine to allow us to trust the quality of the audit, even though the auditor was hired by the company being audited:

- *Reputation.* Deloitte & Touche, as one of the large accounting firms, has a reputation for doing high-quality audits (as do almost all independent auditors in the United States). It would be very reluctant to risk this reputation by signi ng off on a questionable set of financial statements.
- *Lawsuits.* Auditors are sued all the time, even when they conduct a perfect audit. Investors who lose money claim that they lost the money by relying on bogus financial statements that were certified by an external auditor. If even honest auditors get sued, then an auditor who intentionally approves a false set of financial statements is at great risk of losing a big lawsuit.

to summarize

An audit report is issued by an independent CPA firm attesting to the conformity of a set of financial statements with generally accepted accounting principles. CPA firms have an economic incentive to perform credible audits in order to preserve their reputations and to avoid lawsuits.

4

Use financial ratios to identify a company's strengths and weaknesses and to forecast its future performance.

FINANCIAL STATEMENT ANALYSIS

financial statement analysis Examining both the relationships among financial statement amounts and the trends in those numbers over time.

Financial statements are prepared so that they can be used. One important use is in analyzing a company's economic health. **Financial statement analysis** involves the examination of both the relationships among financial statement numbers and the trends in those numbers over time. One purpose of financial statement analysis is to use the past performance of a company to predict how it will do in the future. Another purpose of financial statement analysis is to evaluate the performance of a company with an eye toward identifying problem areas. Financial statement analysis is both diagnosis, identifying where a firm has problems, and prognosis, predicting how a firm will perform in the future.

Relationships between financial statement amounts are called **financial ratios**. For example, net income divided by sales is a financial ratio called "return on sales." Return on sales tells

financial ratios Ratios that show relationships between financial statement amounts.

you how many pennies of profit a company makes on each dollar of sales. The return on sales for MICROSOFT is 28.9%, meaning that Microsoft makes $0.289 worth of profit for every dollar of software sold. There are hundreds of different financial ratios, each shedding light on a different aspect of the health of a company. Some of the more common ratios are introduced in the following section. The numbers from the SAFEWAY balance sheet (Exhibit 2-3) and income statement (Exhibit 2-6) will be used to illustrate the ratio calculations.

Debt Ratio

debt ratio A measure of leverage, computed by dividing total liabilities by total assets.

Comparing the amount of liabilities to the amount of assets shows the extent to which a company has borrowed money to leverage the owners' investments and increase the size of the company. One frequently used measure of leverage is the **debt ratio**, computed as total liabilities divided by total assets. The debt ratio represents the proportion of borrowed funds used to acquire the company's assets. For Safeway, the 1999 debt ratio is computed as follows:

$$\text{Debt Ratio: } \frac{\text{Total Liabilities}}{\text{Total Assets}} = \frac{\$10{,}814.5}{\$14{,}900.3} = 72.6\%$$

In other words, Safeway borrowed 72.6% of the money it needed to buy its assets.

Is 72.6% a good debt ratio, a bad debt ratio, or is it impossible to tell? If you are a banker thinking of lending money to Safeway, you want Safeway to have a low debt ratio; a smaller amount of other liabilities increases your chances of being repaid. If you are a Safeway stockholder, you want a higher debt ratio; you want the company to add borrowed funds to your investment dollars to expand the business. There is some middle ground where the debt ratio is not too high for creditors, nor too low for investors. The general rule of thumb is that debt ratios should be around 50%. However, this general benchmark varies widely from one industry to the next. The 72.6% debt ratio for Safeway is not unusual for a supermarket chain.

Current Ratio

current (working capital) ratio A measure of the liquidity of a business; equal to current assets divided by current liabilities.

An important concern about any company is its *liquidity*. If a firm cannot meet its short-term obligations, it may not live to enjoy the long run. The most commonly used measure of liquidity is the **current** (or **working capital) ratio**, a comparison of the current assets (cash, receivables, and inventory) to the current liabilities. The current ratio is computed by dividing total current assets by total current liabilities. For Safeway, the 1999 current ratio is computed as follows:

$$\text{Current Ratio: } \frac{\text{Current Assets}}{\text{Current Liabilities}} = \frac{\$3{,}052.1}{\$3{,}582.6} = 0.852$$

Historically, a current ratio below 2.0 suggests the possibility of liquidity problems. However, advances in information technology have enabled companies to be much more effective in minimizing the need to hold cash, inventories, and other current assets. As a result, current ratios for successful companies are frequently less than 1.0. The 0.852 current ratio for Safeway is similar to that for other supermarket chains.

Minimum current ratio requirements are frequently included in loan agreements. A typical agreement might state that if the current ratio falls below a certain level, the lender can declare the loan in default and require immediate repayment. This type of minimum current ratio restriction forces the borrower to maintain its liquidity and gives the lender increased assurance that the loan will be repaid.

Asset Turnover

asset turnover A measure of company efficiency, computed by dividing sales by total assets.

The balance sheet of Safeway reveals total assets of $14,900.3 million at December 28, 1999. Are those assets being used efficiently? The **asset turnover** ratio gives an overall measure of company efficiency and is computed as follows:

$$\text{Asset Turnover: } \frac{\text{Sales}}{\text{Total Assets}} = \frac{\$28{,}859.9}{\$14{,}900.3} = 1.94$$

Safeway's 1999 asset turnover ratio of 1.94 means that for each dollar of assets, Safeway is able to generate $1.94 in sales. The higher the asset turnover ratio, the more efficient the company is at using its assets to generate sales.

Return on Sales

return on sales A measure of the amount of profit earned per dollar of sales, computed by dividing net income by sales.

As mentioned at the beginning of this section, Microsoft makes 28.9 cents of profit on each dollar of sales. This ratio is called **return on sales** and (using Safeway's 1999 numbers) is computed as follows:

$$\text{Return on Sales: } \frac{\text{Net Income}}{\text{Sales}} = \frac{\$970.9}{\$28{,}859.9} = 3.36\%$$

Clearly, the return on sales for Safeway of 3.36 cents per dollar is dramatically below that for Microsoft. As with all ratios, however, the return on sales value for Safeway must be evaluated within the appropriate industry. Return on sales in the supermarket industry is frequently between 1% and 2%; so, the Safeway value is very good indeed. In addition, Safeway's 1999 return on sales of 3.36% represents a small improvement over its 1998 return on sales of 3.29%.

Return on Equity

return on equity A measure of the amount of profit earned per dollar of investment, computed by dividing net income by equity.

What investors really want to know is how much profit they earn for each dollar they invest. This amount, called the **return on equity**, is the overall measure of the performance of a company. Return on equity for Safeway for 1999 is computed as follows:

$$\text{Return on Equity: } \frac{\text{Net Income}}{\text{Owners' Equity}} = \frac{\$970.9}{\$4{,}085.8} = 23.8\%$$

Safeway's return on equity of 23.8% means that 23.8 cents of profit was earned for each dollar of stockholder investment in 1999. If your intuition tells you that this seems high, you are right. Good companies typically have return on equity values between 15% and 25%. Safeway had a good year in 1999.

Price-Earnings Ratio

price-earnings (PE) ratio A measure of growth potential, earnings stability, and management capabilities; computed by dividing market price per share by earnings per share.

If a company earned $100 this year, how much should you pay to buy that company? If you expect the company to make more in the future, you would be willing to pay a higher price than if you expected the company to make less. Also, you would probably be willing to pay a bit more for a stable company than for one experiencing wild swings in earnings. The **price-earnings (PE) ratio** measures the relationship between the market value of a company and that company's current earnings. This ratio is computed by dividing the market price per share of stock by the earnings per share. Safeway's PE ratio at the end of 1999 was:

$$\text{PE Ratio: } \frac{\text{Market Price per Share}}{\text{Earnings per Share}} = \frac{\$35.75}{\$1.95} = 18.33$$

In the United States, PE ratios typically range between 5 and 30. High PE ratios are associated with firms for which strong growth is predicted in the future. Refer back to Exhibits 2-4 and 2-5 and notice that **CISCO SYSTEMS** and **ORACLE** are included in the list of companies with the highest market values but are not among those with high net incomes. The reason Cisco Systems and Oracle are valued so highly is that they are expected to continue to grow rapidly; their current incomes are small compared to what investors are expecting in the future. This expected future growth is reflected in the PE ratios for these companies, which, on August 9, 2000, were 123.6 for Cisco Systems and 39.5 for Oracle.

A summary of the financial ratios discussed in this section is presented in Exhibit 2-12. The values of financial ratios are most meaningful when they are compared with similar values for other companies. A comparison of ratio values for several large U.S. corporations is presented in Exhibit 2-13.

exhibit 2-12 Summary of Selected Financial Ratios

Ratio	Formula	Description
1. Debt ratio	$\frac{\text{Total liabilities}}{\text{Total assets}}$	Proportion of borrowed funds used to purchase assets.
2. Current ratio	$\frac{\text{Current assets}}{\text{Current liabilities}}$	Measure of liquidity; number of times current assets could cover current liabilities.
3. Asset turnover	$\frac{\text{Sales}}{\text{Total assets}}$	Number of dollars of sales generated by each dollar of assets.
4. Return on sales	$\frac{\text{Net income}}{\text{Sales}}$	Number of cents earned on each dollar of sales.
5. Return on equity	$\frac{\text{Net income}}{\text{Owners' equity}}$	Number of cents earned on each dollar invested.
6. Price-earnings ratio	$\frac{\text{Market price per share}}{\text{Earnings per share}}$	Amount investors are willing to pay for each dollar of earnings; indication of growth potential.

exhibit 2-13 Selected Ratios for Several Large U.S. Corporations for 1999

	Debt Ratio	Current Ratio	Asset Turnover	Return on Sales	Return on Equity	Price–Earnings Ratio
Microsoft	0.23	2.32	0.53	0.39	0.28	66.82
Cisco Systems	0.2	1.54	0.83	0.27	0.29	208.95
General Electric	0.92	1.09	0.15	0.12	0.27	48.33
Intel	0.26	2.51	0.67	0.25	0.22	62.53
ExxonMobil	0.56	0.8	1.26	0.043	0.125	34.67

to summarize

This overview of financial ratios is intended to emphasize that the preparation of the financial statements by the accountant is not the end of the process, but just the beginning. Those financial statements are then analyzed by investors, creditors, and management to detect signs of existing deficiencies in performance and to predict how the firm will perform in the future. Proper interpretation of a ratio depends on comparing a firm's ratio value to the value for the same firm in the previous year, as well as to values for other firms in the same industry.

5

Explain the fundamental concepts and assumptions that underlie financial accounting.

FUNDAMENTAL CONCEPTS AND ASSUMPTIONS

Certain fundamental concepts and assumptions underlie financial accounting practice and the resulting financial statements. These ideas are so fundamental to any economic activity that they usually are taken for granted in conducting business. Nevertheless, it is important to be aware of them because these assumptions, together with certain basic concepts and procedures, determine the rules and set the boundaries of accounting practice. They indicate which events will be accounted for and in what manner. In total, they provide the essential characteristics of the traditional **accounting model**.

accounting model The basic accounting assumptions, concepts, principles, and procedures that determine the manner of recording, measuring, and reporting a company's transactions.

This section will describe the separate entity concept, the assumption of arm's-length transactions, the cost principle, the monetary measurement concept, and the going concern assumption. The concept of double-entry accounting was already introduced on page 34 as the basis for the accounting equation. As noted, this concept will be explained in much more detail in Chapter 3. Additional concepts and assumptions will be covered in later chapters. Remember that accounting is the language of business, and it takes time to learn a new language. The terms and concepts we introduce here will become much more familiar as your study continues.

The Separate Entity Concept

entity An organizational unit (a person, partnership, or corporation) for which accounting records are kept and about which accounting reports are prepared.

separate entity concept The idea that the activities of an entity are to be separated from those of the individual owners.

Because business involves the exchange of goods or services between entities, it follows that accounting records should be kept for those entities. For accounting purposes, an **entity** is defined as the organizational unit for which accounting records are maintained—for example, IBM CORPORATION. It is a focal point for identifying, measuring, and communicating accounting data. Furthermore, the entity is considered to be *separate* from its individual owners.

We are all engaged in a variety of economic activities. For example, John Scott works for a large corporation, owns some real estate, is president of the local Little League baseball organization, and manages the family estate on behalf of his brothers and sister. The **separate entity concept** is the idea that, when John Scott is called upon to report the financial activities of the local Little League, he must make sure not to include any of his personal or family financial activities in the results. Similarly, the accounting records of a small business must be kept separate from the personal finances of the owner.

Applying the separate entity concept to large corporations can also be difficult. Large corporations, such as GENERAL ELECTRIC and IBM, own networks of subsidiaries (and those subsidiaries own subsidiaries) with complex business ties among the members of the group. A key part of the accounting process for such an organization is carefully defining what is part of General Electric and what is not. For example, one difficult accounting issue (covered in advanced accounting courses) is deciding how much of another company General Electric must own (20%? 45%? 51%? 100%?) before that other company is considered part of the General Electric reporting entity.

The Assumption of Arm's-Length Transactions

transactions Exchange of goods or services between entities (whether individuals, businesses, or other organizations), as well as other events having an economic impact on a business.

arm's-length transactions Business dealings between independent and rational parties who are looking out for their own interests.

Accounting is based on the recording of economic transactions. Viewed broadly, **transactions** include not only exchanges of economic resources between separate entities, but also events that have an economic impact on a business independently. The borrowing and lending of money and the sale and purchase of goods or services are examples of the former. The loss in value of equipment due to obsolescence or fire is an example of the latter. Collectively, transactions provide the data that are included in accounting records and reports.

Accounting for economic transactions enables us to measure the success of an entity. However, the data for a transaction will not accurately represent that transaction if any bias is involved. Therefore, unless there is evidence to the contrary, accountants assume **arm's-length transactions**. That is, they make the assumption that both parties—for example, a buyer and a seller—are rational and free to act independently; each trying to make the best deal possible in establishing the terms of the transaction.

To illustrate, assume you are preparing a personal balance sheet and want to list the value of your minivan. You bought the three-year-old minivan for $5,000. Of course, you should list the minivan on your balance sheet at the $5,000 price you paid for it. That should be a good reflection of the value of the vehicle. But, what if you bought the minivan from your brother (who gave you a good deal) and the real market value of the minivan is $11,000? The problem here is that the $5,000 price negotiated between you and your brother is not a market price. Market prices can be thought of as prices negotiated between two strangers who are both competing to get the best deal possible. Thus, a necessary assumption for financial statements to be informative is that the reported financial results come from arm's-length transactions. Without this assumption, the numbers in the financial statements (like the $5,000 for the minivan you bought from your brother) do not reflect true values.

historical cost The dollar amount originally exchanged in an arm's-length transaction; an amount assumed to reflect the fair market value of an item at the transaction date.

cost principle The idea that transactions are recorded at their historical costs or exchange prices at the transaction date.

An illustration of the accounting problems that can arise from the lack of arm's-length transactions is provided by the labor problems of major league baseball. The team owners and the players are always arguing about the profitability of the teams. The players do not believe the numbers in the owners' financial statements; many important transactions reported are between the baseball teams and other businesses controlled by the owners, such as television stations. Since the revenues received in these deals (between the baseball teams and related businesses) are not from arm's-length transactions, the players question whether the full value of the deals is reflected in the owners' financial reports.

caution

When reading accounting reports, remember that many reported values are historical costs, reflecting exchange prices at various transaction dates.

The Cost Principle

To further ensure objective measurements, accountants record transactions at **historical cost**, the amount originally paid or received for goods and services in arm's-length transactions. The historical cost is assumed to represent the fair market value of the item at the date of the transaction because it reflects the actual use of resources by independent parties. In accounting, this convention of recording transactions at cost is often referred to as the **cost principle**.

monetary measurement The idea that money, as the common medium of exchange, is the accounting unit of measurement, and that only economic activities measurable in monetary terms are included in the accounting model.

The Monetary Measurement Concept

Accountants do not record all the activities of economic entities. They record only those that can be measured in monetary terms. Thus, the concept of **monetary measurement** becomes another important characteristic of the accounting model. For example, employee morale cannot be measured directly in monetary terms and is not reported in the accounting records. Wages

Major league baseball salary disputes are frequently in the news. The lack of arm's-length transactions may contribute to some of the friction between players and owners.

paid or owed, however, are quantifiable in terms of money and are reported. In accounting, all transactions are recorded in monetary amounts, whether or not cash is involved. In the United States, the dollar is the unit of exchange and is thus the measuring unit for accounting purposes.

As noted earlier in discussing the limitations of a balance sheet, the listed values may not be the same as actual market values for two reasons. The first is due to the cost principle. Because of such factors as inflation (an increase in the general price level of goods and services), the recorded amount of an item may be quite different from the amount required at a later time to buy or replace the item. The second reason results from the monetary measurement concept. Not all economic assets are recorded, because they are too difficult or impossible to measure in monetary amounts.

The Going Concern Assumption

going concern assumption The idea that an accounting entity will have a continuing existence for the foreseeable future.

The **SAFEWAY** balance sheet in Exhibit 2-3 was prepared under the assumption that Safeway would continue in business for the foreseeable future. This is called the **going concern assumption**. Without this assumption, preparation of the balance sheet would be much more difficult. For example, the $2.4 billion inventory for Safeway in 1999 is reported at the cost originally paid to purchase the inventory. This is a reasonable figure because, in the normal course of business, Safeway can expect to sell the inventory for this amount, plus some profit. But if it were assumed that Safeway would go out of business tomorrow, the inventory would suddenly be worth a lot less. Imagine the low prices you could get on Safeway merchandise if it had to conduct a one-day, going-out-of-business sale! The going concern assumption allows the accountant to record assets at what they are worth to a company in normal use, rather than what they would sell for in a liquidation sale.

to summarize

In conducting economic activities, entities enter into transactions that form the basis of accounting records. An accounting model has been developed for recording, measuring, and reporting an entity's transactions. This model is founded on certain fundamental concepts and several important assumptions, principles, and procedures. First, the organizational unit being accounted for is a separate entity. The entity may be small or large, but it is the organizational unit for which accounting records are kept and financial reports prepared. Second, the transactions are assumed to be arm's-length. Third, transactions are recorded at historical cost. Fourth, transactions must be measurable in monetary amounts. Fifth, the accounting entity is assumed to be a going concern.

review of learning objectives

1 Understand the basic elements and formats of the three primary financial statements—balance sheet, income statement, and statement of cash flows. The balance sheet provides a summary of the financial position of a company at a particular date. It lists a company's assets, liabilities, and owners' equity. Assets and liabilities are usually classified as either current or long-term. For a corporation, owners' equity consists of directly invested funds as well as retained earnings.

The income statement shows the major sources of revenues generated and the expenses associated with those revenues. The difference between revenues and expenses is net income or net loss. The income statements of corporations must also include earnings per share.

The statement of cash flows shows the significant cash inflows (receipts) and cash outflows (payments) of a company for a period of time. These cash flows are classified according to operating, investing, and financing activities.

2 Recognize the need for financial statement notes and identify the types of information included in the notes. The notes to the financial statements contain additional information not included in the financial statements themselves. The notes explain the company's accounting assumptions and practices, provide details of financial statement summary numbers and additional disclosure about complex events, and report supplementary information required by the SEC and the FASB.

3 Describe the purpose of an audit report and the incentives the auditor has to perform a good audit. An audit report is issued by an independent CPA firm attesting to the conformity of a set of financial statements with generally accepted accounting principles. CPA firms have an economic incentive to perform credible audits in order to preserve their reputations and to avoid lawsuits.

4 Use financial ratios to identify a company's strengths and weaknesses and to forecast its future performance. Financial statements are analyzed by investors, creditors, and management to detect signs of existing deficiencies in performance and to predict how the firm will perform in the future. Proper interpretation of a financial ratio depends on comparing a firm's ratio value to the value for the same firm in the previous year, as well as to values for other firms in the same industry.

5 Explain the fundamental concepts and assumptions that underlie financial accounting. Certain fundamental concepts underlie the practice of accounting. First, a business must be accounted for as an economic entity separate from the personal affairs of the owners and separate from other businesses. Second, the transactions are assumed to be arm's-length, so that the negotiated prices reflect true market values at the dates of the transactions. Third, transactions are recorded at historical cost. Fourth, only those transactions and events that can be measured in monetary terms are reported. Fifth, the accounting entity is assumed to be a going concern.

key terms and concepts

review problem

The Income Statement and the Balance Sheet

Shirley Baum manages The Copy Shop. She has come to you for help in preparing an income statement and a balance sheet for the year ended December 31, 2003. Several amounts, determined as of December 31, 2003, are presented below. No dividends were paid this year.

Capital stock (10,000 shares outstanding)	$ 40,000	Mortgage payable	$72,000
Retained earnings (12/31/02)	12,400	Accounts payable	6,000
Advertising expense	2,000	Land	24,000
Cash	17,000	Supplies	2,000
Rent expense	2,400	Salary expense	20,000
Building (net)	100,000	Revenues	42,000
Interest expense	700	Other expenses	1,300
		Accounts receivable	3,000

Required

1. Prepare an income statement for the year ended December 31, 2003, including EPS.
2. Determine the amount of retained earnings at December 31, 2003.
3. Prepare a classified balance sheet as of December 31, 2003.
4. Calculate the current ratio for The Copy Shop. What does the current ratio tell you about the company?

Solution

1. Income Statement

The first step in solving this problem is to separate the balance sheet items from the income statement items. Asset, liability, and owners' equity items reflect the company's financial position and appear on the balance sheet; revenues and expenses are reported on the income statement.

Balance Sheet Items	Income Statement Items
Capital stock	Advertising expense
Retained earnings	Rent expense
Cash	Interest expense
Building (net)	Salary expense
Mortgage payable	Revenues
Accounts payable	Other expenses
Land	
Supplies	
Accounts receivable	

After the items have been separated, the income statement and the balance sheet may be prepared using a proper format.

The Copy Shop
Income Statement
For the Year Ended December 31, 2003

Revenues		$42,000
Expenses:		
Advertising expense	$2,000	
Rent expense	2,400	
Interest expense	700	
Salary expense	20,000	
Other expenses	1,300	26,400
Net income		$15,600
EPS = $15,600 ÷ 10,000 shares = $1.56		

2. Retained Earnings

The amount of Retained Earnings at December 31, 2003, may be calculated as follows:

Retained earnings (12/31/02)	$12,400
Add: Net income for year	15,600
Subtract: Dividends for year	(0)
Retained earnings (12/31/03)	$28,000

Since no dividends were paid during 2003, the ending balance in Retained Earnings is simply the beginning balance plus net income for the year.

3. Balance Sheet

The Copy Shop
Balance Sheet
December 31, 2003

Assets			**Liabilities and Owners' Equity**		
Current assets:			**Current liabilities:**		
Cash	$ 17,000		Accounts payable	$ 6,000	
Accounts receivable	3,000				
Supplies	2,000	$ 22,000	**Long-term liabilities:**		
			Mortgage payable	72,000	
Long-term assets:			Total liabilities		$ 78,000
Land	$ 24,000				
Building (net)	100,000	124,000	**Owners' equity:**		
			Capital stock	$40,000	
			Retained earnings	28,000*	68,000
			Total liabilities and		
Total assets		$146,000	owners' equity		$146,000

*See item 2 for calculation.

4. Current Ratio

CR = Current Assets/Current Liabilities
CR = $22,000/$6,000 = 3.67

The current ratio shows the relationship of total current assets to total current liabilities. It indicates whether a company can pay its current obligations with its current assets and therefore helps short-term creditors assess a company's liquidity. The amount of The Copy Shop's current assets is almost four times its current liabilities (3.67:1). In other words, The Copy Shop has $3.67 of current assets for every $1 of current liabilities, which shows a favorable liquidity position.

discussion questions

1. As an external user of financial statements, perhaps an investor or creditor, what type of accounting information do you need?
2. What is the major purpose of:
   a. A balance sheet?
   b. An income statement?
   c. A statement of cash flows?
3. Assume you want to invest in the stock market, and your friends tell you about a company's stock that is "guaranteed" to have an annual growth rate of 150 percent. Should you trust your friends and invest immediately, or should you research the company's financial statements before investing? Explain.

4. Why are classified and comparative financial statements generally presented in annual reports to shareholders?
5. Why are owners' equity and liabilities considered the "sources" of assets?
6. Owners' equity is not cash; it is not a liability; and it generally is not equal to the current worth of a business. What is the nature of owners' equity?
7. What are the limitations of the balance sheet? Why is it important to be aware of them when evaluating a company's growth potential?
8. Some people feel that the income statement is more important than the balance sheet. Do you agree? Why or why not?
9. How might an investor be misled by looking only at the "bottom line" (the net income or EPS number) on an income statement?
10. Why is it important to classify cash flows according to operating, investing, and financing activities?
11. You are thinking of investing in one of two companies. In one annual report, the auditor's opinion states that the financial statements were prepared in accordance with generally accepted accounting principles. The other makes no such claim. How important is that to you? Explain.
12. Some people think that auditors are responsible for ensuring the accuracy of financial statements. Are they correct? Why or why not?
13. What are the four general types of financial statement notes typically included in annual reports to stockholders?
14. What are the primary purposes of financial statement analysis?
15. Indicate how each of the following financial ratios is computed and describe what the ratio is attempting to explain:
    a. Debt ratio
    b. Current ratio
    c. Asset turnover
    d. Return on sales
    e. Return on equity
    f. Price-earnings ratio
16. Explain why each of the following is important in accounting:
    a. The separate entity concept
    b. The assumption of arm's-length transactions
    c. The cost principle
    d. The monetary measurement concept
    e. The going concern assumption

discussion cases

CASE 2-1

CREDITOR AND INVESTOR INFORMATION NEEDS

Ink Spot is a small company that has been in business for two years. Wilford Smith, the president of the company, has decided that it is time to expand. He needs $10,000 to purchase additional equipment and to pay for increased operating expenses. Wilford can either apply for a loan at First City Bank, or he can issue more stock (1,000 shares are outstanding) to new investors. Assuming that you are the loan officer at First City Bank, what information would you request from Ink Spot before deciding whether to make the loan? As a potential investor in Ink Spot, what information would you need to make a good investment decision? What financial ratios might you consider as a potential lender or investor before making a decision?

CASE 2-2

ANALYZING TRENDS AND KEY FINANCIAL RELATIONSHIPS

An investor may choose from several investment opportunities: the stocks of different companies; rental property or other real estate; or savings accounts, money market certificates, and similar financial instruments. When considering an investment in the stock of a particular company, comparative financial data presented in the annual report to stockholders helps an investor identify key relationships and trends. As an illustration, comparative operating results for Prime Properties, Inc., from its 2003 annual report are provided. (Dollars are presented in thousands except for earnings per share.)

	Year Ended December 31		
	2003	**2002**	**2001**
Revenues:			
Property management fees	$ 58,742	$ 63,902	$ 66,204
Appraisal fees	55,641	60,945	62,320
Total revenues	$114,383	$124,847	$128,524
Expenses:			
Selling and advertising	$ 64,371	$ 75,403	$ 80,478
Administrative expenses	30,671	31,115	31,618
Other expenses	9,265	9,540	9,446
Interest expense	2,047	1,468	26
Total expenses	$106,354	$117,526	$121,568
Income before taxes	$ 8,029	$ 7,321	$ 6,956
Income taxes	2,409	2,196	2,087
Net income	$ 5,620	$ 5,125	$ 4,869
*Earnings per share	$2.25	$2.05	$1.95

*2.5 million shares outstanding

What trends are indicated by the comparative income statement data for Prime Properties, Inc.? Which of these trends would be of concern to a potential investor? What additional information would an investor need in order to make a decision about whether to invest in this company?

CASE 2-3

ACCOUNTING FOR THE PROPER ENTITY

You have been hired to prepare the financial reports for White River Building Supply, a proprietorship owned by Bill Masters. Upon encountering several payments made from the company bank account to a nearby university, you contact Bill Masters to find out how to classify these payments. Masters explains that those checks were written to pay his daughter's tuition and to purchase her textbooks and miscellaneous supplies. He then tells you to include the payments with other expenses of the business. "This way," he explains, "I can deduct the payments on my tax return. Why not, since it all comes out of the same pocket?" How would you respond to Masters?

exercises

EXERCISE 2-1

CLASSIFICATION OF FINANCIAL STATEMENT ELEMENTS

Indicate for each of the following items whether it would appear on a balance sheet (BS) or an income statement (IS). If a balance sheet item, is it an asset (A), a liability (L), or an owners' equity item (OE)?

1. Accounts Payable
2. Sales Revenue
3. Accounts Receivable
4. Advertising Expense
5. Cash
6. Supplies
7. Consulting Revenue
8. Land
9. Capital Stock
10. Rent Expense
11. Equipment
12. Interest Receivable
13. Mortgage Payable
14. Notes Payable
15. Buildings
16. Salaries & Wages Expense
17. Retained Earnings
18. Utilities Expense

EXERCISE 2-2

ACCOUNTING EQUATION

Compute the missing amounts for companies A, B, and C.

	A	B	C
Cash	$25,000	$ 9,000	$12,000
Accounts receivable	20,000	15,000	7,000
Land and buildings	50,000	?	40,000
Accounts payable	?	6,000	14,000
Mortgage payable	30,000	10,000	15,000
Owners' equity	55,000	30,000	?

EXERCISE 2-3

COMPREHENSIVE ACCOUNTING EQUATION

Assuming no additional investments by or distributions to owners, compute the missing amounts for companies X, Y, and Z.

	X	Y	Z
Assets: January 1, 2003	$360	$?	$230
Liabilities: January 1, 2003	280	460	?
Owners' equity: January 1, 2003	?	620	150
Assets: December 31, 2003	380	?	310
Liabilities: December 31, 2003	?	520	90
Owners' equity: December 31, 2003	?	720	?
Revenues in 2003	80	?	400
Expenses in 2003	100	116	?

EXERCISE 2-4

COMPUTING ELEMENTS OF OWNERS' EQUITY

From the information provided, determine:

1. The amount of retained earnings at December 31.
2. The amount of revenues for the period.

Totals	January 1	December 31
Current assets	$ 5,000	$ 10,000
All other assets	150,000	160,000
Liabilities	25,000	30,000
Capital stock	50,000	?
Retained earnings	80,000	?

Additional data:
Expenses for the period were $35,000.
Dividends paid were $7,500.
Capital stock increased by $5,000 during the period.

EXERCISE 2-5

BALANCE SHEET RELATIONSHIPS

Correct the following balance sheet.

Canfield Corporation
Balance Sheet
December 31, 2003

Assets		Liabilities and Owners' Equity	
Cash	$ 55,000	Buildings	$325,000
Accounts payable	65,000	Accounts receivable	75,000
Interest receivable	20,000	Mortgage payable	150,000
Capital stock	200,000	Sales revenue	350,000
Rent expense	60,000	Equipment	85,000
Retained earnings	145,000	Utilities expense	5,000
		Total liabilities and	
Total assets	$545,000	owners' equity	$990,000

EXERCISE 2-6

Spread-Sheet Software

BALANCE SHEET PREPARATION

From the following data, prepare a classified balance sheet for Low Price Company at December 31, 2003.

Accounts payable	$ 46,500
Accounts receivable	99,000
Buildings	325,500
Owners' equity, 1/1/03	150,000
Cash	116,250
Distributions to owners during 2003	18,750
Supplies	2,250
Land	165,000
Mortgage payable	412,500
Net income for 2003	117,750
Owners' equity, 12/31/03	?

EXERCISE 2-7

INCOME STATEMENT COMPUTATIONS

Following are the operating data for an advertising firm for the year ended December 31, 2003.

Revenues	$175,000
Supplies expense	45,000
Salaries expense	70,000
Rent expense	1,500
Administrative expense	6,000
Income taxes (30% of income before taxes)	?

For 2003, determine:

1. Income before taxes.
2. Income taxes.
3. Net income.
4. Earnings per share (EPS), assuming there are 15,000 shares of stock outstanding.

EXERCISE 2-8

INCOME STATEMENT PREPARATION

The following selected information is taken from the records of Sel Tec Corporation.

Accounts payable	$ 25,000
Accounts receivable	49,000
Advertising expense	7,500
Cash	15,500
Supplies expense	23,000

(continued)

Rent expense	$ 5,000
Utilities expense	1,500
Income taxes (30% of income before taxes)	?
Miscellaneous expense	2,200
Owners' equity	125,000
Salaries expense	88,000
Fees (revenues)	242,000

1. Prepare an income statement for the year ended December 31, 2003. (Assume that 5,000 shares of stock are outstanding.)
2. Explain what the EPS ratio tells the reader about Sel Tec Corporation.

EXERCISE 2-9

CASH FLOW COMPUTATIONS

From the following selected data, compute:

1. Net cash flow provided (used) by operating activities.
2. Net cash flow provided (used) by investing activities.
3. Net cash flow provided (used) by financing activities.
4. Net increase (decrease) in cash during the year.
5. The cash balance at the end of the year.

Cash receipts from:	
Customers	$270,000
Investments by owners	54,000
Sale of building	90,000
Proceeds from bank loan	60,000
Cash payments for:	
Wages	$ 82,000
Utilities	3,000
Advertising	4,000
Rent	36,000
Taxes	67,000
Dividends	20,000
Repayment of principal on loan	40,000
Purchase of land	106,000
Cash balance at beginning of year	$386,000

EXERCISE 2-10

INCOME AND RETAINED EARNINGS RELATIONSHIPS

Assume that retained earnings increased by $240,000 from December 31, 2002, to December 31, 2003, for Miller Corporation. During the year, a cash dividend of $140,000 was paid.

1. Compute the net income for the year.
2. Assume that the revenues for the year were $920,000. Compute the expenses incurred for the year.

EXERCISE 2-11

RETAINED EARNINGS COMPUTATIONS

During 2003, Safe Lite Corporation had revenues of $180,000 and expenses, including income taxes, of $100,000. On December 31, 2002, Safe Lite had assets of $400,000, liabilities of $100,000, and capital stock of $250,000. Safe Lite paid a cash dividend of $40,000 in 2003. No additional stock was issued. Compute the retained earnings on December 31, 2002, and 2003.

EXERCISE 2-12

PREPARATION OF INCOME STATEMENT AND RETAINED EARNINGS STATEMENT

Prepare an income statement and a statement of retained earnings for Big Sky Corporation for the year ended June 30, 2003, based on the following information:

Capital stock (1,500 shares @ $100)		$150,000
Retained earnings, July 1, 2002		76,800
Dividends		6,500
Ski rental revenue		77,900
Expenses:		
Rent expense	$ 6,000	
Salaries expense	38,600	
Utilities expense	2,400	
Advertising expense	7,500	
Miscellaneous expense	7,700	
Income taxes	2,100	64,300

EXERCISE 2-13

ARTICULATION: RELATIONSHIPS BETWEEN A BALANCE SHEET AND AN INCOME STATEMENT

The total assets and liabilities of Roloflex Company at January 1 and December 31, 2003, are presented below.

	January 1	December 31
Assets	$76,000	$112,000
Liabilities	26,000	28,800

Determine the amount of net income or loss for 2003, applying each of the following assumptions concerning the additional issuance of stock and dividends paid by the firm. Each case is independent of the others.

1. Dividends of $10,800 were paid and no additional stock was issued during the year.
2. Additional stock of $4,800 was issued and no dividends were paid during the year.
3. Additional stock of $62,000 was issued and dividends of $15,600 were paid during the year.

EXERCISE 2-14

CASH FLOW CLASSIFICATIONS

For each of the following items, indicate whether it would be classified and reported under the Operating Activities (OA), Investing Activities (IA), or Financing Activities (FA) section of a statement of cash flows:

a. Cash receipts from selling merchandise
b. Cash payments for wages and salaries
c. Cash proceeds from sale of stock
d. Cash purchase of equipment
e. Cash dividends paid
f. Cash received from bank loan
g. Cash payments for inventory
h. Cash receipts from services rendered
i. Cash payments for taxes
j. Cash proceeds from sale of property no longer needed as expansion site

EXERCISE 2-15

CURRENT RATIO

Using the data in Exercise 2-6, compute the current ratio for Low Price Company. What does the current ratio show?

EXERCISE 2-16

DEBT RATIO

Using the data in Exercise 2-6, compute the debt ratio for Low Price Company. What does the debt ratio explain?

EXERCISE 2-17

RETURN ON EQUITY AND PRICE-EARNINGS RATIO

Using the data in Exercise 2-6, and assuming 20,000 shares of stock outstanding and a market price per share of $36.00, compute the return on equity and PE ratios for Low Price Company. Does the PE ratio seem reasonable relative to other U.S. stocks?

EXERCISE 2-18

NOTES TO FINANCIAL STATEMENTS

Refer to MICROSOFT's annual report in Appendix A at the end of the book. How important are the notes to financial statements? What are the major types of notes that Microsoft includes in its annual report?

EXERCISE 2-19

THE COST PRINCIPLE

On January 1, 2003, Save-More Construction Company paid $150,000 in cash for a parcel of land to be used as the site of a new office building. During March, the company petitioned the city council to rezone the area for professional office buildings. The city council refused, preferring to maintain the area as a residential zone. After nine months of negotiation, Save-More Construction convinced the council to rezone the property for commercial use, thus raising its value to $200,000.

For accounting purposes, what value should be used to record the transaction on January 1, 2003? At what value would the property be reported at year-end, after the city council rezoning? Explain why accountants use historical costs to record transactions.

EXERCISE 2-20

THE MONETARY MEASUREMENT CONCEPT

Many successful companies, such as FORD MOTOR COMPANY, EXXONMOBIL, and MARRIOTT CORPORATION, readily acknowledge the importance and value of their employees. In fact, the employees of a company are often viewed as the most valued asset of the company. Yet in the asset section of the balance sheets of these companies there is no mention of the asset Employees. What is the reason for this oversight and apparent inconsistency?

EXERCISE 2-21

THE GOING CONCERN ASSUMPTION

Assume that you open an auto repair business. You purchase a building and buy new equipment. What difference does the going concern assumption make with regard to how you would account for these assets?

problems

PROBLEM 2-1

BALANCE SHEET CLASSIFICATIONS AND RELATIONSHIPS

Tu'aa Corporation has the following balance sheet elements as of December 31, 2003.

Land	$ 69,000	Mortgage payable	$300,000
Cash	?	Capital stock	135,000
Building	178,000	Retained earnings	88,000
Accounts payable	100,000	Supplies	17,000
Notes payable (short-term)	105,000	Accounts receivable	88,000
Equipment	350,000		

Required:

Compute the total amount of:

1. Current assets.
2. Long-term assets.
3. Current liabilities.
4. Long-term liabilities.
5. Stockholders' equity

PROBLEM 2-2

PREPARATION OF A CLASSIFIED BALANCE SHEET

Following are the December 31, 2003, account balances for Siraco Company.

Cash	$ 1,950
Accounts receivable	2,500
Supplies	1,800
Equipment	11,275
Accounts payable	3,450
Wages payable	250
Dividends paid	1,500
Capital stock	775
Retained earnings, January 1, 2003	12,000
Revenues	10,000
Miscellaneous expense	1,550
Supplies expense	3,700
Wages expense	2,200

Required:

1. Prepare a classified balance sheet as of December 31, 2003.
2. **Interpretive Question:** On the basis of its 2003 earnings, was this company's decision to pay dividends of $1,500 a sound one?

PROBLEM 2-3

BALANCE SHEET PREPARATION WITH A MISSING ELEMENT

The following data are available for Sunshine Products Inc., as of December 31, 2003.

Cash	$10,000
Accounts payable	14,000
Capital stock	35,200
Accounts receivable	20,000
Building	28,000
Supplies	1,200
Retained earnings	?
Land	10,000

Required:

1. Prepare a balance sheet for Sunshine Products Inc.
2. Determine the amount of retained earnings at December 31, 2003.
3. **Interpretive Question:** In what way is a balance sheet a depiction of the basic accounting equation?

PROBLEM 2-4

INCOME STATEMENT PREPARATION

Listed below are the results of Rulon Candies' operations for 2002 and 2003. (Assume 4,000 shares of outstanding stock for both years.)

	2003	2002
Sales	$300,000	$350,000
Utilities expenses	15,000	8,500
Employee salaries	115,000	110,000
Advertising expenses	10,000	20,000
Income tax expense	9,000	36,500
Interest expense	25,000	15,000
Cost of goods sold	115,000	85,000
Interest revenue	10,000	10,000

Required:

1. Prepare a comparative income statement for Rulon Candies, Inc., for the years ended December 31, 2003 and 2002. Be sure to include figures for gross margin, operating income, income before taxes, net income, and earnings per share.
2. **Interpretive Question:** What advice would you give Rulon Candies, Inc., to improve its profitability for the year 2004?

PROBLEM 2-5

INCOME STATEMENT PREPARATION

The following information is taken from the records of Hill, Dunn, & Associates for the year ended December 31, 2003.

Income taxes	$ 10,800
Service revenues	150,000
Rent expense	5,500
Salaries expense	35,000
Miscellaneous expense	380
Utilities expense	1,230
Administrative expense	12,300

Required: Prepare an income statement for Hill, Dunn, & Associates for the year ended December 31, 2003. (Assume that 4,000 shares of stock are outstanding.)

PROBLEM 2-6

EXPANDED ACCOUNTING EQUATION

At the end of 2003, Morgan Systems, Inc., had a fire that destroyed the majority of its accounting records. Morgan Systems, Inc., was able to gather the following financial information for 2003.

a. Retained earnings was changed only as a result of net income and a $50,000 dividend payment to Morgan's investors.
b. All other account changes for the year are listed below. The amount of change for each account is shown as a net increase or decrease.

	Increase or (Decrease)
Cash	$ 25,000
Interest receivable	(15,000)
Inventory	100,000
Accounts receivable	(22,500)
Building	315,000
Accounts payable	45,000
Mortgage payable	275,000
Wages payable	(27,250)
Capital stock	52,500

Required: Using the accounting equation, compute Morgan's net income for 2003.

PROBLEM 2-7

INCOME STATEMENT PREPARATION

Precision Corporation has been a leading supplier of magnetic storage disks for three years. Following are the results of Precision's operations for 2003.

Sales revenue	$68,000
Advertising expense	1,530
Income taxes	4,360
Delivery expense	480
Packaging expense	355
Salaries expense	18,350
Supplies expense	8,410

EPS = $3.45

Required:

1. Prepare an income statement for the year ended December 31, 2003.
2. How many shares of stock were outstanding?

PROBLEM 2-8

STATEMENT OF CASH FLOWS

Southwestern Rentals, Inc., rents equipment to customers ranging from homeowners to large construction companies. The financial information shown below was gathered from its accounting records for 2003. Assume any increase or decrease in the balances from 1/1/03 to 12/31/03 resulted from either receiving or paying cash in the transaction. For example, during 2003 the balance on loans for land holdings increased $150,000 because the company received $150,000 in cash by taking out an additional loan on the land.

Items	Balance as of 1/1/03	Balance as of 12/31/03
Cash	$ 20,000	$ 50,000
Cash receipts from customers	—	600,000
Loans on land holdings	100,000	250,000
Cash distributions to owners	—	150,000
Loan on building	100,000	70,000
Investments in securities	850,000	1,050,000
Cash payments for other expenses	—	50,000
Cash payments for taxes	—	55,000
Cash payments for operating expenses	—	135,000
Cash payments for wages and salaries	—	100,000

Required:

1. Prepare a statement of cash flows for Southwestern Rentals, Inc., for the year ended December 31, 2003.
2. **Interpretive Question:** Does Southwestern Rentals, Inc., appear to be in good shape from a cash flow standpoint? What other information would help you analyze the situation?

PROBLEM 2-9

STATEMENT OF CASH FLOWS

The cash account for Kwon Enterprises shows the following for the year ended December 31, 2003.

Beginning cash balance	$?
Cash receipts during year from:	
Services	1,351,000
Investments by owners	82,000
Sale of land	135,000
Cash payments during year for:	
Operating expenses	963,000
Taxes	114,000
Purchase of building	326,000
Distributions to owners	55,000
Ending cash balance	850,000

Required: Prepare a statement of cash flows for Kwon Enterprises for the year ended December 31, 2003.

PROBLEM 2-10

UNIFYING CONCEPTS: NET INCOME AND FINANCIAL RATIO ANALYSIS

A summary of the operations of Streuling Company for the year ended May 31, 2003, is shown below.

Advertising expense	$ 2,760
Supplies expense	37,820
Rent expense	1,500
Salaries expense	18,150
Miscellaneous expense	4,170

(continued)

Dividends	$ 12,400
Retained earnings (6/1/02)	156,540
Income taxes	21,180
Consulting fees (revenues)	115,100
Administrative expense	7,250

Required:

1. Determine the net income for the year by preparing an income statement. (Assume that 3,000 shares of stock are outstanding.)
2. Compute the return on equity (ROE) for Streuling Company, assuming total owners' equity is $255,000.
3. **Interpretive Question:** What does the ROE ratio explain about Streuling's profitability?
4. **Interpretive Question:** Assuming an operating loss for the year, is it a good idea for Streuling to still pay its shareholders dividends?

PROBLEM 2-11

UNIFYING CONCEPTS: NET INCOME AND STATEMENT OF RETAINED EARNINGS

A summary of the operations of Stellenbach Company for the year ended May 31, 2003, is shown below.

Advertising expense	$ 2,760
Supplies expense	37,820
Rent expense	1,500
Salaries expense	18,150
Miscellaneous expense	4,170
Dividends	12,400
Retained earnings (6/1/02)	156,540
Income taxes	21,180
Consulting fees (revenues)	115,100
Administrative expense	7,250

Required:

1. Determine the net income for the year by preparing an income statement. (There are 2,000 shares of stock outstanding.)
2. Prepare a statement of retained earnings for the year ended May 31, 2003.
3. Prepare a statement of retained earnings assuming that Stellenbach had a net loss for the year of $25,000.
4. **Interpretive Question:** Assuming a loss as in (3), is it a good idea for Stellenbach to still pay its shareholders dividends?

PROBLEM 2-12

FINANCIAL RATIOS

The following information for High Flying Company is provided.

High Flying Company	
Current assets	$ 145,000
Long-term assets	750,000
Current liabilities	75,000
Long-term liabilities	300,000
Owners' equity	520,000
Sales for year	1,425,000
Net income for year	105,000
Average market price per share	145.00
Average number of shares outstanding	10,000

Required:

1. Compute the current ratio, debt ratio, return on sales, return on equity, asset turnover, and price-earnings ratio.
2. **Interpretive Question:** What do these ratios show for High Flying Company?

PROBLEM 2-13

COMPREHENSIVE FINANCIAL STATEMENT PREPARATION

The following information was obtained from the records of Uptown, Inc., as of December 31, 2003.

Land	$ 37,500
Buildings	145,050
Salaries expense	40,050
Utilities expense	9,750
Accounts payable	25,650
Revenues	397,800
Supplies	69,450
Retained earnings (1/1/03)	272,550
Capital stock (1,000 shares outstanding)	45,000
Accounts receivable	46,500
Supplies expense	207,900
Cash	?
Notes payable (long-term)	25,800
Rent expense	25,650
Dividends in 2003	60,750
Other expenses	13,050
Income taxes	52,800

Required:

1. Prepare an income statement for the year ended December 31, 2003.
2. Prepare a classified balance sheet as of December 31, 2003.
3. Compute the current ratio as of December 31, 2003.
4. Compute the debt ratio as of December 31, 2003.
5. **Interpretive Question:** What does the current ratio tell about Uptown's liquidity?
6. **Interpretive Question:** What does the debt ratio tell about Uptown's leverage?
7. **Interpretive Question:** Why is the balance in Retained Earnings so large as compared with the balance in Capital Stock?

PROBLEM 2-14

ELEMENTS OF COMPARATIVE FINANCIAL STATEMENTS

The following report is supplied by Smith Brothers Company.

Smith Brothers Company
Comparative Balance Sheets
As of December 31, 2003 and 2002

Assets	2003	2002	Liabilities and Owners' Equity	2003	2002
Cash	$13,000	$15,000	Accounts payable	$ 5,000	$ 4,000
Accounts receivable	18,000	11,000	Salaries and commissions payable	8,000	8,000
Notes receivable	11,000	10,000	Notes payable	25,000	27,000
Land	38,000	38,000	Capital stock	20,000	20,000
			Retained earnings	22,000	15,000
Total assets	$80,000	$74,000	Total liabilities and owners' equity	$80,000	$74,000

Operating expenses for the year included utilities of $4,500, salaries and commissions of $44,800, and miscellaneous expenses of $1,500. Income taxes for the year were $3,000, and the company paid dividends of $5,000.

Required:

1. Compute the total expenses, including taxes, incurred in 2003.
2. Compute the net income or net loss for 2003.
3. Compute the total revenue for 2003.
4. **Interpretive Question:** Why are comparative financial statements generally of more value to users than statements for a single period?

competency enhancement opportunities

- Analyzing Real Company Information
- International Case
- Ethics Case
- Writing Assignment
- The Debate
- Cumulative Spreadsheet Project
- Internet Search

The following additional assignments provide opportunities for students to develop critical thinking, ethical perspectives, oral and written communication skills, experience with electronic research, and teamwork through group and business activities.

ANALYZING REAL COMPANY INFORMATION

• *Analyzing 2-1 (Microsoft)*

The 1999 annual report for MICROSOFT is included in Appendix A. Locate that annual report and answer the following questions:

1. Locate Microsoft's 1999 balance sheet. What percentage of its total assets consists of cash and short-term investments? Compute Microsoft's current ratio. How does its current ratio compare to yours? How much long-term debt does Microsoft have?
2. Find Microsoft's 1999 income statement. Have revenues increased or decreased over the last three years? Is the rate of increase rising? Compute Microsoft's return on sales. Is it increasing?
3. Compute Microsoft's return on equity. How does that return compare to the rate of return you might earn if you were to invest your money in a savings account at a local bank?
4. Review Microsoft's statement of cash flows. What activity generates most of Microsoft's cash? What is Microsoft doing with all its money—buying back its own stock, investing in other companies, or something else?

• *Analyzing 2-2 (Safeway)*

At the start of this chapter you learned a little about SAFEWAY and its history. Now let's take a look at the company's financial performance in recent years. Refer back to Safeway's income statement (on page 41) and balance sheet (on page 38).

Based on information contained in these financial statements, answer the following questions:

1. Compute Safeway's debt ratio for the past two years. Has this ratio increased or decreased? Why?
2. Compute the company's current ratio. Do you notice anything unusual about Safeway's current ratio? How can a company stay in business with a current ratio this low?
3. Compute Safeway's return on sales for 1999. Does the size of this number surprise you? Now compute the company's asset turnover. Considering return on sales and asset turnover together, what does the result indicate?

INTERNATIONAL CASE

• ***Diageo***

DIAGEO is a United Kingdom (UK) consumer products firm, best known in the United States for the following brand names: Smirnoff, Johnnie Walker, J&B, Gordon's, Guinness, Pillsbury, Häagen-Dazs, and Burger King. Diageo's 1998 balance sheet is shown below.

Diageo
Consolidated Balance Sheet
30 June 1998
(in millions of pounds)

Fixed assets		
Intangible assets		4,727
Tangible assets		3,006
Investments		1,244
		8,977
Current assets		
Stocks	2,236	
Debtors—due within one year	2,037	
Debtors—due after more than one year	999	
Debtors subject to financing arrangements (franchisee loans of £145 million, less non-returnable proceeds of £127 million)	18	
Investments	484	
Cash at bank and in hand	2,503	
	8,277	
Creditors—due within one year		
Borrowings	(4,724)	
Other creditors	(3,524)	
	(8,248)	
Net current assets		29
Total assets less current liabilities		9,006
Creditors—due after more than one year		
Borrowings	(2,894)	
Other creditors	(243)	
		(3,137)
Provisions for liabilities and charges		(705)
		5,164
Shareholders' funds		
Equity share capital		1,034
Non-equity share capital		105
Called-up share capital		1,139
Share premium account	1,121	
Revaluation reserve	190	
Profit and loss account	2,179	
Reserves attributable to equity shareholders		3,490
		4,629
Minority interests		
Equity	169	
Non-equity	366	
		535
		5,164

1. Can you identify any major differences between Microsoft's and Diageo's balance sheets in terms of the order in which major categories are displayed?
2. What is Diageo's total assets? Is it as easy to determine as Microsoft's total assets?
3. Take a look at the following list of accounts and identify, given your knowledge of assets, liabilities, and owners' equity, what the American equivalent of those accounts might be (you might want to reference Microsoft's balance sheet for comparison):
   - Stocks
   - Debtors
   - Called-up share capital
   - Profit and loss account

ETHICS CASE

• Violating a Covenant

Often banks will require a company that borrows money to agree to certain restrictions on its activities in order to protect the lending institution. These restrictions are called "debt covenants." An example of a common debt covenant is requiring a company to maintain its current ratio at a certain level, say, 2.0.

Your boss has just come to you and asked, "How can you make our current ratio higher?" You know that the company has a line of credit with a local bank that requires the company to maintain its current ratio at 1.5. You also know that the company was dangerously close to violating this covenant during the previous quarter. The end of the fiscal period is next week, and some action must be taken to increase the current ratio. If the covenant is violated, the lending agreement allows the bank to significantly modify the terms of the debt (in the bank's favor) and also gives the bank a seat on the company's board of directors. Management would prefer not to have the bank involved in the day-to-day affairs of the business, nor do they want to alter the terms of the lending agreement.

Identify ways in which the current ratio can be increased. Would any of the alternatives you identify be good for the business, e.g., selling equipment might raise the current ratio but would that be good for the business? Should a company engage in these types of transactions?

WRITING ASSIGNMENT

• The Most Important Financial Statement

As you have discovered, there are three primary financial statements—balance sheet, income statement, and statement of cash flows. In no more than two pages, answer the following question: If you could have access to only one of the primary financial statements, which would it be and why? As you provide support for the financial statement of your choice, also provide reasons as to why you would not pick the other two statements.

THE DEBATE

• Save the Notes

As pointed out in the chapter, IBM's annual report in 1920 included zero pages of notes to the financial statements. In 1996, the notes had grown to 26 pages. While the number of financial statements has remained constant, the number of notes to the financial statements continues to grow.

Divide your group into two teams and prepare two-minute presentations representing the following points of view.

- The first team represents "Kill the Notes." You are to take the position that financial statements providing information relating to a firm's current asset and liability position, a summary of its operations, and its cash inflows and outflows are all that is needed to make good resource allocation decisions. The three primary financial statements are all that need to be provided to current and potential investors and creditors. In other words, the notes do not add value to the financial reports.
- The other team represents "Save the Notes." You are to argue that the notes represent essential information that must be used when interpreting the data contained in the financial statements themselves.

CUMULATIVE SPREADSHEET PROJECT

Starting with this chapter and continuing throughout the next twelve chapters, this text will include a spreadsheet assignment based on the financial information of a fictitious company named Handyman. The first assignments are simple—in this chapter you are asked to do little more than set up financial statement formats and input some numbers. In succeeding chapters, the spreadsheets will get more complex so that by the end of the course you will have constructed a spreadsheet that allows you to forecast operating cash flow for five years in the future and adjust your forecast depending on the operating parameters that you think are most reasonable.

So, let's get started with the first spreadsheet assignment.

1. The following numbers are for Handyman Company for 2003:

Short-term Loans Payable	$ 10	Long-term Debt	$207
Interest Expense	9	Income Tax Expense	4
Paid in Capital	50	Retained Earnings (as of 1/1/03)	31
Cash	10	Receivables	27
Dividends	0	Sales	700
Accumulated Depreciation	9	Accounts Payable	74
Inventory	153	Property, Plant, & Equipment	199
Cost of Goods Sold	519	Other Operating Expenses	160

   Your assignment is to create a spreadsheet containing a balance sheet and an income statement for Handyman Company.

2. Handyman is wondering what its balance sheet and income statement would have looked like if the following numbers were changed as indicated:

	CHANGE	
	From	**To**
Sales	700	730
Cost of Goods Sold	519	550
Other Operating Expenses	160	165

   Create a second spreadsheet with the numbers changed as indicated. Note: After making these changes, your balance sheet may no longer balance. Assume that any discrepancy is eliminated by increasing or decreasing Short-term Loans Payable as much as necessary.

INTERNET SEARCH

• *Microsoft*

While you have a copy of MICROSOFT's annual report in Appendix A, let's go see what its most current financial statements look like. Access Microsoft's Web site at http://www.microsoft.com. Sometimes addresses change, so if this Microsoft address doesn't work, access the Web site for this textbook (http://albrecht.swcollege.com) for an updated link to Microsoft.

Once you have accessed Microsoft's Web site, answer the following questions (you may have to search a bit to answer some of these questions):

1. When was Micro-Soft founded? (That's right, the company's name originally had a hyphen.)
2. Make your way to the shareholder information and locate the company's most recent income statement. Detail the steps you had to take to find this financial statement.
3. How has the company done since its 1999 financial statements were issued? Are sales still increasing? Are profits still on the rise?
4. Microsoft was one of the first companies to provide an income statement in multiple languages. Take a look at Microsoft's income statement based on accounting principles accepted in the United Kingdom. Do you recognize any of the terms? Now look at the German version of the income statement. Even though you probably don't speak German, can you guess what the German word is for "revenues"?

The Mechanics of Accounting

chapter

f3

learning objectives

After studying this chapter, you should be able to:

1 Understand the process of transforming transaction data into useful accounting information.

2 Analyze transactions and determine how those transactions affect the accounting equation (step one of the accounting cycle).

3 Record the effects of transactions using journal entries (step two of the accounting cycle).

4 Summarize the resulting journal entries through posting and prepare a trial balance (step three of the accounting cycle).

5 Describe how technology has affected the first three steps of the accounting cycle.

Ray Kroc, a 51-year-old milkshake machine distributor, first visited the McDonald brothers' drive-in (in San Bernardino, California) in July of 1954 because he wanted to know why a single "hamburger stand" needed ten milkshake machines. That first day, Kroc spent the lunch rush hour watching the incredible volume of business the small drive-in was able to handle. By the time he left town, Kroc had received a personal briefing on the "McDonald's Speedee System" from Dick and Mac McDonald and had secured the rights to duplicate the system throughout the United States.

In his first outlet in Chicago, Ray Kroc soon discovered that duplicating the McDonald's system involved more than just signing a licensing agreement. Kroc's french fries, for example, were mushy, even though he closely copied the McDonald brothers' process. Feverish detective work finally revealed that Dick and Mac McDonald had been storing their potatoes in an outside bin before turning them into french fries. This aging process allowed some of the natural sugars in the potatoes to turn into starch, resulting in fries that would cook all the way through without burning. Further research revealed the optimal temperature for the cooking oil, the best type of potato to use, and how to make frozen french fries that taste as good as fresh. The end product, the **McDONALD'S** french fry, was instrumental in establishing the McDonald's reputation for consistent quality.

As the number of McDonald's locations expanded (to 26,806 at the end of 1999), so did the menu. Originally, the McDonald's menu contained just 15-cent hamburgers, 12-cent french fries, 20-cent milkshakes, cheeseburgers, three flavors of soft drinks, milk, coffee, potato chips, and pie. The first addition to this menu was the Filet-O-Fish sandwich in the early 1960s. The Big Mac started in Pittsburgh in 1967, and the Egg McMuffin debuted in Santa Barbara in 1971. Not all of the McDonald's menu innovations caught on—the McLean Deluxe (a low-fat hamburger held together with a seaweed-based filler) and the Hulaburger, one of Ray Kroc's personal favorites (a cheeseburger with a big slice of pineapple), are among the items that are no longer offered.

The essence of McDonald's business seems fairly simple: revenues come from selling Big Macs, Happy Meals, Chicken McNuggets, etc.; operating costs include the costs of the raw materials to produce the food items, labor costs, building rentals, income taxes, and so forth. But the magnitude of McDonald's operations in terms of volume (sales average over $105 million per day) as well as geography (McDonald's has locations in 118 countries throughout the world) makes compiling this information a challenge. In order to prepare its year-end financial reports, McDonald's must accumulate financial information from its various locations throughout the world, summarize that information according to U.S. accounting standards, and make the report available to the public in less than four weeks. In fact, McDonald's annual report for the period ended December 31, 1999, was finished on January 26, 2000.

setting the stage

With the number of transactions that occur on a daily basis, the accounting for McDonald's would be impossible were it not for a systematic method for analyzing these transactions and collecting and recording transaction-related information. What is the process by which McDonald's and other entities transform raw transaction data into useful information? Certainly, shareholders and others would not understand how McDonald's has performed if the company merely published volumes of raw transaction data. How are millions of transactions summarized and eventually reported in the primary financial statements? This transformation process is referred to as the **accounting cycle**.

accounting cycle The procedure for analyzing, recording, summarizing, and reporting the transactions of a business.

In the first two chapters, we provided an overview of accounting. We discussed the environment of accounting and its objectives, some basic concepts and assumptions of accounting, and the primary financial statements. Now we begin our study of the "accounting cycle." This simply means that we will examine the procedures for analyzing, recording, summarizing, and reporting the transactions of a business. In this chapter, we describe the first three steps in the cycle. The remaining step (preparing reports for external users) is explained in Chapter 4.

1

Understand the process of transforming transaction data into useful accounting information.

HOW CAN WE COLLECT ALL THIS INFORMATION?

Suppose you were asked, "What was the total cost, to the nearest dollar, of your college education last year?" To answer this question would require that you (1) gather information (in the form of receipts, credit card statements, and canceled checks) for all your expenditures, (2) analyze that information to determine which outflows relate to your college education, and (3) summarize those outflows into one number—the cost of your college education. Once you have answered that question, answer this one, "How much did you spend on food last year?" Again you would have to go through the same process of collecting data, analyzing the information to identify those expenditures relating to food, and then summarizing those expenditures into one number. From these two examples you can see that, without a method for gathering and organizing day-to-day financial data, answers to seemingly routine questions can get quite complex.

Now you may be thinking, "Doesn't my checkbook allow me to easily answer these questions?" Your check register would certainly help, but it is limited in that it tracks only the transactions that go through your checking account. It does not track the cash in your pocket, in your savings accounts, or in other investment accounts. So, if any of your expenditures for food were made with cash, your check register would understate the amount you spent for food. In addition, you would still have to review each check and determine to what it related. Your check register provides good information for calculating exactly how much money you have in your checking account at any point in time, but it does not contain all the information necessary to determine exactly how your money was spent.

Now consider the dilemma for businesses. They typically have far more transactions than you, and the kinds of transactions are more varied. Businesses buy and sell goods or services; borrow and invest money; pay wages to employees; purchase land, buildings, and equipment; distribute earnings to owners; and pay taxes to the government. These activities are referred to as "exchange transactions" because the entity is actually trading (exchanging) one thing for another. A college bookstore, for example, exchanges textbooks for cash. **Business documents**, such as a sales invoice, a purchase order, or a check stub, are often used (1) to confirm that an arm's-length transaction has occurred, (2) to establish the amounts to be recorded, and (3) to facilitate the analysis of business events.

business documents Records of transactions used as the basis for recording accounting entries; include invoices, check stubs, receipts, and similar business papers.

Businesses, such as a college bookstore, have many exchange transactions in which they trade one thing for another—like textbooks for cash.

To determine how well an entity is managing its resources, the results of transactions must be analyzed. The accounting cycle makes the analysis possible by recording and summarizing an entity's transactions and preparing reports that present the summary results. Exhibit 3-1 shows the sequence of the accounting cycle. Later, we will discuss these general categories and the specific steps of the cycle.

Keeping track of a company's transactions requires a system of accounting that is tailor-made to the needs of that particular enterprise. Obviously, the accounting system of a large multinational corporation with millions of business transactions each day will be much more complex than the system needed by a small Internet start-up company. The more complex and detailed the accounting system, the more likely it is to be automated. Historically, of course, all accounting systems had to be maintained by hand. The image of the accountant with green eyeshade and quill pen, sitting on a high stool, meticulously maintaining the accounting records, reflects those early manual systems. Today, few accounting systems are completely manual. Even small companies generally use some type of inexpensive accounting software. Such software helps reduce the number of routine clerical functions and improves the accuracy and timeliness of the accounting records.

Although a computer-based system is faster and requires less labor than a manual system, the steps in the process are basically the same for both: transactions are recorded on source documents; they are then analyzed, journalized, and posted to the accounts; and the resulting information is summarized, reported, and used for evaluation purposes. The difference lies in who (or what) does the work. With a computer-based system, the software transforms the recorded data, summarizes the data into categories, and prepares the financial statements and other re-

exhibit 3-1 Sequence of the Accounting Cycle

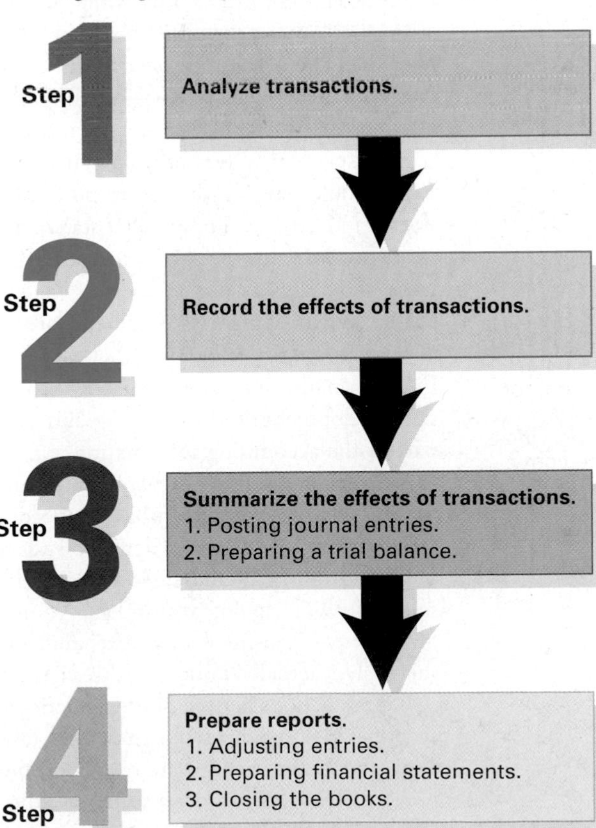

ports. Nevertheless, human judgment is still essential in analyzing and recording transactions, especially those of a nonroutine nature.

Because a manual accounting system is easier to understand, we will use a manual system for the examples in this text. As you begin studying the steps in the accounting cycle, it is important that you understand the accounting equation and double-entry accounting more fully. This concept was briefly introduced in Chapter 2. You will recall that the accounting model is built on this basic equation. You now need to learn how to use the equation in accounting for the transactions of a business.

---

to summarize

Businesses enter into exchange transactions. Evidence of these transactions is provided by business documents. Accounting is designed to accumulate and report in summary form the results of a company's transactions, therefore transforming the financial data into useful information for decision making.

2

Analyze transactions and determine how those transactions affect the accounting equation (step one of the accounting cycle).

HOW DO TRANSACTIONS AFFECT THE ACCOUNTING EQUATION?

Suppose you are the keeper of the archives at McDONALD'S assigned to protect the secret ingredient mix for the Big Mac special sauce. You came to work this morning only to hear that BURGER KING has cracked the secret ingredient recipe and plans to come out with a Big Mac clone at half the price. How would this event be reflected in the financial statements?

net work

Access McDONALD'S Web site (http://www.mcdonalds.com) and compare it to BURGER KING's (http://www.burgerking.com). In your opinion, which Web site is easier to navigate? How easy is it to find information on, for example, nutrition? Which site provides easier access to the company's financial information?

Often, the most difficult aspect of accounting is determining which events are to be reflected in the accounting records and which are not. In this example, the proliferation of Big Mac clones could have a serious impact on the future of the firm. However, as discussed in Chapter 2, events that cannot be measured in monetary terms will not be reflected in the financial statements. It would be virtually impossible to reliably quantify the impact that Big Mac clones could have on the future profitability of McDonald's, and thus, that information would not be reflected in the financial statements.

Now you may be saying to yourself, "We have an obligation to inform financial statement users about this attack on the Big Mac." We would all agree that this information should be shared, but the financial statements are not the place to do it. As you review MICROSOFT's annual report (in Appendix A), you'll notice that the financial statements are only one part of the information provided to users. Information relating to the competitive environment, product development, and marketing and sales efforts is included in the annual report, but not as part of the accounting information.

After quantifying an event's monetary impact, the event must be analyzed to determine if an arm's-length transaction has occurred. Accounting is concerned primarily with reflecting the effects of transactions between two independent entities. So a mining company's oil strike on the North Slope of Alaska would not be reflected in the financial statements until that oil is sold. Likewise, signing a promising young financial analyst directly out of college for a salary of $80,000 per year involves an exchange of promises. No accounting entry would be made until the analyst actually worked and received a paycheck.

Transactions between independent parties must be analyzed to determine their effect on the accounting equation. This analysis is often what separates an accountant from a bookkeeper. While many transactions are routine, some business events are quite complex and require a comprehensive analysis to determine how the event should be reflected in the financial statements. Consider the following examples:

- An employee works for one year, earning a base salary of $60,000. In addition, if the employee stays with the company for at least five years, the company promises to make a contribution to the employee's pension fund equal to 15% of salary. Approximately 60% of employees who start with the company stay for five years. Also, by working for one year, the employee earns 15 extra vacation days. Those vacation days can be saved and used any time in the future. How do we record compensation cost associated with this employee for the year?
- A company buys a building. In addition to paying $20,000 cash, the company agrees to pay $10,000 per year for the next ten years. The company will also pay a $2,000 property tax bill associated with the building from last year. As part of the purchase, the company gave the former owners of the building 500 shares of stock. Finally, the building will require $23,000 worth of repairs and renovations before it can be used. How much should be recorded as the cost of the building?

As these examples illustrate, transactions can become quite complex and the accounting for these types of transactions reflects that complexity. The good news is that the transaction analysis framework introduced in this chapter allows you to break complex transactions into manageable pieces and also provides a self-checking mechanism to ensure that you haven't forgotten anything. Once a transaction is properly analyzed and the affected accounts identified (along with the direction of those effects), the remainder of the accounting cycle can proceed without much difficulty.

The Accounting Equation

So let's begin our analysis of transactions by first reviewing some of the basics. Recall that the fundamental accounting equation is:

Assets	=	**Liabilities**	+	**Owners' Equity**
[Resources]		[Creditors' claims against resources]		[Owners' claims against resources]

Because the accounting equation is an equality, it must always remain in balance. To see how this balance is maintained when accounting for business transactions, consider the following activities:

Business Activity (Transaction)	**Effect in Terms of the Accounting Equation**
1. Investment of $50,000 by owners	Increase asset (Cash), increase owners' equity (Capital Stock): A ↑ $50,000 = OE ↑ $50,000
2. Borrowed $25,000 from bank	Increase asset (Cash), increase liability (Notes Payable): A ↑ $25,000 = L ↑ $25,000
3. Purchased $14,000 worth of inventory on credit. The inventory is to be resold at a later date.	Increase asset (Inventory), increase liability (Accounts Payable): A ↑ $14,000 = L ↑ $14,000
4. Purchased equipment costing $15,000 for cash	Decrease asset (Cash), increase asset (Equipment): A ↓ $15,000 = A ↑ $15,000

For each of the transactions, the terms in parentheses are the specific accounts affected by the transactions, as will be explained in the next section.

In each case, the equation remains in balance because an identical amount is added to both sides, subtracted from both sides, or added to and subtracted from the same side of the equation. Following each transaction, we can ensure that the accounting equation balances. Note how the following spreadsheet keeps track of the equality of the accounting equation:

TRANSACTION #	ASSETS		LIABILITIES		OWNERS' EQUITY
Beginning Balance	$ 0	=	$ 0	+	$ 0
1	+50,000				+50,000
Subtotal	$50,000	=	$ 0	+	$50,000
2	+25,000		+25,000		
Subtotal	$75,000	=	$25,000	+	$50,000
3	+14,000		+14,000		
Subtotal	$89,000	=	$39,000	+	$50,000
4	+15,000 −15,000				
Total	$89,000	=	$39,000	+	$50,000

Using Accounts to Categorize Transactions

In Chapter 2, the balance sheet and the income statement were introduced as two of the three primary financial statements, the third being the statement of cash flows. We learned that the elements of the balance sheet are assets, liabilities, and owners' equity; the elements of the income statement are revenues and expenses. Now we must learn how each of these elements is composed of many different accounts.

account An accounting record in which the results of transactions are accumulated; shows increases, decreases, and a balance.

An **account** is a specific accounting record that provides an efficient way to categorize transactions. Thus, we may designate asset accounts, liability accounts, and owners' equity accounts. Examples of asset accounts are Cash, Inventory, and Equipment. Liability accounts include Accounts Payable and Notes Payable. The equity accounts for a corporation are Capital Stock and Retained Earnings. You can think of an individual account as a summary of every transaction affecting a certain item (such as cash); the summary may be recorded on one page of a book, or in one computer file, or in one column of a spreadsheet (seen as follows).

business environment essay

Do Accountants Record the Most Important Events? Are all important economic events captured in a company's accounting records? No. In fact, the majority of events that affect the value of a company may fall outside the scope of traditional financial reporting. Consider the following selection of business events reported on the front page of *The Wall Street Journal* (Business and Finance column) on a typical day (Friday, August 11, 2000):

- DELL's earnings rose 19%, exceeding estimates, but revenue rose at its slowest rate in five years.
- AT&T's board of directors and management are considering breaking up the company by spinning off certain assets.
- FIRESTONE instigates the second biggest tire recall ever.
- The yield on 10-year Treasury notes fell to 5.754%, its lowest level this year.
- KMART and LAND'S END released operating results that fell short of already lowered market expectations.
- Brazil's PETROBAS began trading on the NYSE.

All of these events had impacts on the values of companies. For example, Dell's announcement caused the value of the company's shares to decrease by about

	ASSETS				LIABILITIES			OWNERS' EQUITY
Transaction #	Cash	Inventory	Equipment		Accounts Payable	Notes Payable		Capital Stock
Beginning Balance	$ 0	$ 0	$ 0	=	$ 0	$ 0	+	$ 0
1	+50,000							+50,000
Subtotal	$50,000	$ 0	$ 0	=	$ 0	$ 0	+	$50,000
2	+25,000					+25,000		
Subtotal	$75,000	$ 0	$ 0	=	$ 0	$25,000	+	$50,000
3		+14,000			+14,000			
Subtotal	$75,000	$14,000	$ 0	=	$14,000	$25,000	+	$50,000
4	−15,000		+15,000					
Total	$60,000	$14,000	$15,000	=	$14,000	$25,000	+	$50,000

Using the previous transactions, we can easily see how the accounting equation can be expanded to include specific accounts under the headings of assets, liabilities, and owners' equity. We can also see that after each transaction, the equality of the accounting equation can be determined simply by adding up the balances of all the asset accounts and comparing the total to the sum of all the liability and owners' equity accounts.

Now suppose that a company has 200 accounts and 10,000 transactions each month—this spreadsheet would quickly get very big. Today, computers help in compiling this massive amount of data. Five hundred years ago, when double-entry accounting was formalized, all the adding and subtracting was done by hand. You can imagine the difficulties of tracking multiple ac-

5%. And yet none of these value-relevant events would have been recorded in the accounting records of any company anywhere in the world.

Accounting academics have long been dismayed by the weak connection between a company's reported accounting numbers and the company's market value. In a famous paper, Professor Baruch Lev summarized this issue as follows:

> The correlation between earnings and stock returns is very low, sometimes negligible. . . . [T]he possibility that the fault lies with the low quality . . . of reported earnings looms large.

The challenge to accountants is to figure out how to bring more business events into the accounting model in order to increase the relevance of the financial statements. The risk of doing nothing to improve accounting is that potential investors and creditors will increasingly turn their backs on the financial statements when they can get more current, comprehensive, and relevant information merely by using an Internet search engine.

Source: Baruch Lev, "On the Usefulness of Earnings and Earnings Research: Lessons and Directions from Two Decades of Empirical Research," *Journal of Accounting Research,* Supplement 1989, p. 153.

counts, involving hundreds of transactions, using the spreadsheet method described above while doing all the computations by hand. Mixing "+" and "−" in one column would provide ample opportunity to make mistakes.

This problem was solved by separating the "+" and the "−" for each account into separate columns, totaling each column, and then computing the difference between the columns to arrive at an ending balance. The simplest, most fundamental format is the configuration of the letter T. This is called a **T-account**. Note that a T-account is an abbreviated representation of an actual account (illustrated later) and is used as a teaching and learning tool. The following are examples of T-accounts, representing the transactions described previously.

T-account A simplified depiction of an account in the form of a letter T.

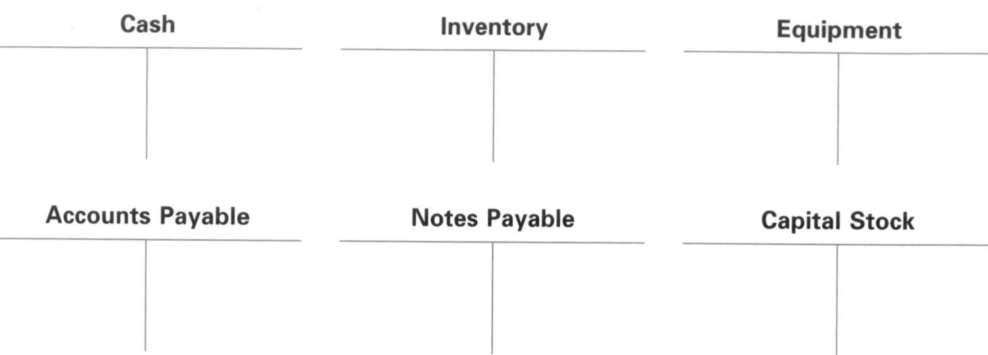

debit An entry on the left side of a T-account.

credit An entry on the right side of a T-account.

The account title (Cash, for example) appears at the top of the T-account. Transaction amounts may be recorded on both the left side and the right side of the T-account. Instead of using the terms left and right to indicate which side of a T-account is affected, terms unique to accounting were developed. **Debit** is used to indicate the left side of a T-account, and **credit** is used to indicate the right side of a T-account. Debit means left, credit means right—nothing more, nothing less.

Besides representing the left and right sides of an account, the terms *debit* (abbreviated DR) and *credit* (abbreviated CR) take on additional meaning when coupled with a specific account. By convention, for asset accounts, debits refer to increases and credits to decreases. For example, to increase the cash account, we debit it; to decrease the cash account, we credit it. Since we expect the total increases in the cash account to be greater than the decreases, the cash account will usually have a debit balance after accounting for all transactions. Thus, we can make this generalization—asset accounts will have debit balances. The opposite relationship is true of liability and owners' equity accounts; they are decreased by *debits* and increased by *credits*. As a result, liability and owners' equity accounts will typically have credit balances. The effect of this system is shown here, with an increase indicated by (+) and a decrease by (−).

fyi

Where does the "DR" come from when the term *debit* doesn't have an "r" in it? Recall that accounting, as we know it today, was formalized in the 1500s in Italy. The Italian and Latin (a common language back then) verb forms of debit are *addebitare* and *debere*, respectively. Thus, the "DR" represents an Italian or Latin abbreviation of debit.

Assets		=	**Liabilities**		+	**Owners' Equity**	
DR (+)	CR (−)		DR (−)	CR (+)		DR (−)	CR (+)

caution

Just a reminder that asset accounts will typically have debit balances, whereas liabilities and owners' equity accounts will typically have credit balances.

In addition to assets equaling liabilities and owners' equity, debits also equal credits. If you fully grasp the meaning of these two equalities, you are well on your way to mastering the mechanics of accounting. Debits and credits allow us to take a shortcut to ensure that the accounting equation balances. If, for every transaction, debits equal credits, then the accounting equation will balance.

To understand why this happens, keep in mind three basic facts regarding double-entry accounting:

> The word *credit* is associated with something good because your bank account increases when the bank "credits" your account. The bank uses this term because, from its standpoint, your account represents a liability—the bank owes you the amount of money in your account. Thus, when the bank credits your account (a liability), the bank is increasing the recorded amount it owes you.

1. Debits are always entered on the left side of an account and credits on the right side.
2. For every transaction, there must be at least one debit and one credit.
3. Debits must always equal credits for each transaction.

Now notice what this means for one of the business transactions shown earlier (page 83): investment by owners. An asset account (Cash) is debited; it is increased. An owners' equity account (Capital Stock) is credited; it is also increased. There is both a debit and a credit for the transaction, and we have increased accounts on both sides of the equation by an equal amount, thus keeping the accounting equation in balance.

Be careful not to let the general, nonaccounting meanings of the words *credit* and *debit* confuse you. In general conversation, credit has an association with plus and debit with minus. But on the asset side of the accounting equation, where debit means increase and credit means decrease, this association can lead you astray. In accounting, debit simply means left and credit simply means right. To make sure you understand the relationship between debits and credits, the various accounts, and the accounting equation, let us examine further the transactions listed on page 83.

Business Activity (Transaction)	**Effect in Terms of the Accounting Equation**							
	Assets		=	**Liabilities**		+	**Owners' Equity**	
1. Investment by owners	Cash DR (+)							Capital Stock CR (+)
2. Borrowed money from bank	Cash DR (+)				Notes Payable CR (+)			
3. Purchased inventory on credit	Inventory DR (+)				Accounts Payable CR (+)			
4. Purchased equipment for cash	Equipment DR (+)	Cash CR (−)						

Note that every time an account is debited, other accounts have to be credited for the same amount. This is the major characteristic of the double-entry accounting system: *the debits must always equal the credits.* This important characteristic creates a practical advantage: the opportunity for "self-checking." If debits do not equal credits, an error has been made in analyzing and recording the entity's activities.

Before proceeding any further, let's stop for a moment and review the relationship between the various types of accounts and debits and credits. It is in your best interest not to go on until you understand these relationships.

Account Type			**Debit or Credit?**	**Ending Balance**
Asset	Increase (+)	results in	Debit	Debit
	Decrease (−)	results in	Credit	
Liability	Increase (+)	results in	Credit	Credit
	Decrease (−)	results in	Debit	
Owners' Equity	Increase (+)	results in	Credit	Credit
	Decrease (−)	results in	Debit	

Expanding the Accounting Equation to Include Revenues, Expenses, and Dividends

At this point, we must bring revenues and expenses into the picture. Obviously, they are part of every ongoing business. Revenues provide resource inflows; they are increases in resources from the sale of goods or services. Expenses represent resource outflows; they are costs incurred in generating revenues. Note that revenues are not synonymous with cash or other assets, but are a way of describing where the assets came from. For example, cash received from the sale of a product would be considered revenue. Cash received by borrowing from the bank would not be revenue, but an increase in a liability. By the same token, expenses are a way of describing how an asset has been used. Thus, cash paid for interest on a loan is an expense, but cash paid to buy a building represents the exchange of one asset for another.

caution

We stated previously that owners' equity accounts will have credit balances. However, expenses, a component of Retained Earnings, will almost always have debit balances. Since revenues will usually exceed expenses, the net effect on Retained Earnings will result in a credit balance.

How do revenues and expenses fit into the accounting equation? Remember that revenues minus expenses equals net income; and net income is a major source of change in owners' equity from one accounting period to the next. Revenues and expenses, then, may be thought of as *temporary* subdivisions of owners' equity. Revenues increase owners' equity and so, like all owners' equity accounts, are increased by credits. Expenses reduce owners' equity and are therefore increased by debits. As will be explained in Chapter 4, all revenue and expense accounts are "closed" into the retained earnings account at the end of the accounting cycle.

dividends Distributions to the owners (stockholders) of a corporation.

One other temporary account affects owners' equity. It is the account that shows distributions of earnings to owners. For a corporation, this account is called **Dividends**. Since dividends reflect payments to the owners, therefore reducing owners' equity, the dividends account is increased by a debit and decreased by a credit. The dividends account, like revenues and expenses, is also "closed" into the retained earnings account.

Just a warning here: students who have trouble grasping debits and credits usually get hung up on the revenue and expense accounts. Remember that revenues and expenses are subcategories of Retained Earnings. When you credit a revenue account, you are essentially increasing Retained Earnings. When you debit an expense account, you are increasing the amount of expense, which in turn reduces Retained Earnings.

Using the corporate form of business as an example, the accounting equation may be expanded to include revenues, expenses, and dividends, as shown in Exhibit 3-2.

Keep in mind that in actual business practice, when a manual accounting system is used, the T-account is an integral feature of a more formal and complete account. Exhibit 3-3 is an example of such an account. Note that in addition to the debits and credits in the T-account portion (drawn in heavy lines in this example), the account has a title, Cash; an account number, 101; and columns for a transaction date, an explanation of the transaction, a posting reference (a cross-reference to other accounting records), and a balance.

Why Should I Understand the Mechanics of Accounting?

If computers now take care of all the routine accounting functions, why does a businessperson need to know anything about debits, credits, journals, posting, T-accounts, and trial balances? Good question. First of all, even though computers now do most of the dirty work, the essence of double-entry accounting is unchanged from the days of quill pens and handwritten ledgers. Thus, understanding the process explained in this chapter is still relevant to a computer-based accounting system. In addition, with or without computers, the use of debits, credits, and T-accounts still provides an efficient and widely used shorthand method of analyzing transactions. At a minimum, all businesspeople should be familiar enough with the language of accounting to understand, for example, why a credit balance in Cash or a debit balance in Retained Earnings is something unusual enough to merit investigation. Finally, an understanding of the accounting cycle—analyzing, recording, summarizing, and preparing—gives one insight into how information flows within an organization. And great advantages accrue to those who understand information flow.

exhibit 3-2 Expanded Accounting Equation

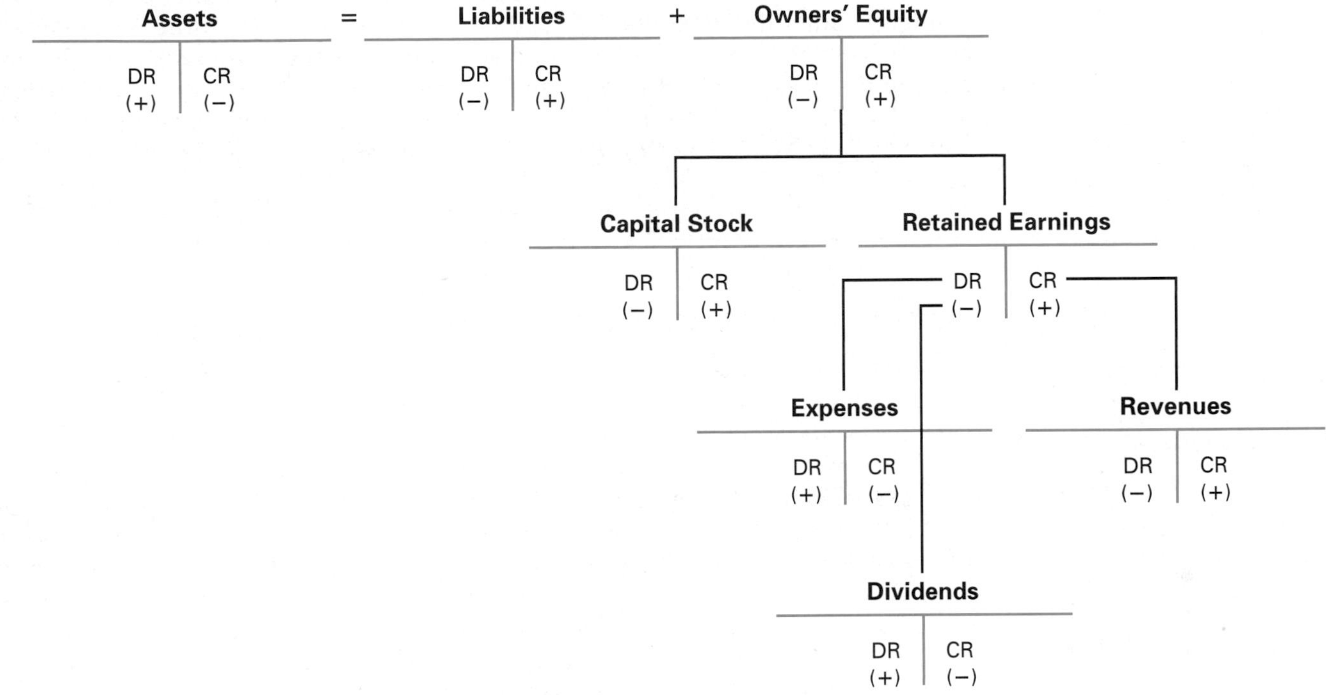

exhibit 3-3 Typical Account

ACCOUNT: Cash **ACCOUNT NO. 101**

Date	Explanation	Post. Ref.	Debits	Credits	Balance

to summarize

Regardless of the size or complexity of a business, or the manner in which the records are maintained (manual or automated system), the steps of the accounting cycle are the same. The entire process is based on double-entry accounting and the basic accounting equation. Accounts accumulate the results of transactions. Debits are always entered on the left side of an account, and credits are always entered on the right side. Debits increase asset, expense, and dividend accounts and decrease liability, owners' equity, and revenue accounts. Credits decrease asset, expense, and dividend accounts and increase liability, owners' equity, and revenue accounts. Revenues increase owners' equity, whereas expenses and dividends decrease owners' equity. Therefore, under a double-entry system of accounting, it is always possible to check the accounting records to see that Assets = Liabilities + Owners' Equity and debits equal credits.

3

Record the effects of transactions using journal entries (step two of the accounting cycle).

HOW DO WE RECORD THE EFFECTS OF TRANSACTIONS?

With our knowledge of the different types of accounts (assets, liabilities, and owners' equity) and the use of the terms *debit* and *credit* (debit means left and credit means right), we are now ready to actually record the effects of transactions.

journal An accounting record in which transactions are first entered; provides a chronological record of all business activities.

The second step in the accounting cycle is to record the results of transactions in a **journal**. Known as "books of original entry," journals provide a chronological record of all entity transactions. They show the dates of the transactions, the amounts involved, and the particular accounts affected by the transactions. Sometimes a detailed description of the transaction is also included.

This chronological recording of transactions provides a company with a complete record of its activities. If amounts were recorded directly in the accounts, it would be difficult, if not impossible, for a company to trace a transaction that occurred, say, six months previously.

Smaller companies, such as a locally owned pizza restaurant, may use only one book of original entry, called a "general journal," to record all transactions. Larger companies having thousands of transactions each year may use special journals (for example, a cash receipts journal) as well as a general journal.

journalizing Recording transactions in a journal.

journal entry A recording of a transaction where debits equal credits; usually includes a date and an explanation of the transaction.

A specific format is used in **journalizing** (recording) transactions in a general journal. The debit entry is listed first; the credit entry is listed second and is indented to the right. Normally, the date and a brief explanation of the transaction are considered essential parts of the **journal entry**. (In the text, we often ignore dates and explanations to simplify the examples.) Dollar signs usually are omitted. Unless otherwise noted, this format will be used whenever a journal entry is presented.

General Journal Entry Format

Date	Entry	Debit	Credit
Date	Debit Entry	xx	
	Credit Entry		xx
	Explanation.		

Exhibit 3-4 is a partial page from a general journal, showing typical journal entries. Study this exhibit carefully because the entire accounting cycle is based on journal entries. If journal entries are incorrect, the resulting financial information will be inaccurate.

To give you additional exposure to analyzing transactions and recording journal entries, we are going to start our own business. Rather than spend the summer flipping burgers at the local hamburger house, you decide that you want to have an outdoor job—one that allows you to enjoy the summer sun, engage in rigorous physical activity, and sharpen your skills as an entrepreneur. You are going to start your own landscaping business. This business will involve mowing lawns, pulling weeds, trimming and planting shrubs, and so forth. We will use your new business to illustrate the journal entries used to record some common transactions of a business enterprise.[1]

1 Normally, a small business like this one would be started as a sole proprietorship or as a partnership. We assume a corporation here to show a complete set of transactions.

exhibit 3-4 General Journal

JOURNAL **Page 1**

Date	Description	Post. Ref.	Debits	Credits
2003 July 1	Cash		2,000	
	Capital Stock			2,000
	Issued 200 shares of capital stock at $10 per share.			
5	Truck		800	
	Cash			800
	Purchased a used truck.			
5	Equipment		250	
	Accounts Payable			250
	Purchased a lawnmower on account.			
5	Supplies		180	
	Cash			180
	Purchased supplies for cash.			

These transactions fit into the following four general categories: acquiring cash, acquiring other assets, selling goods or providing services, and collecting cash and paying obligations. Obviously, we cannot present all possible transactions in this chapter. In studying the illustrations, strive to understand the conceptual basis of transaction analysis rather than memorizing specific journal entries. Pay particular attention to the dual effect of each transaction on the company in terms of the basic accounting equation (that is, its impact on assets and on liabilities and owners' equity). Remember that business activity involves revenues, expenses, and distributions to owners as well, and that these accounts eventually increase or decrease owners' equity (the retained earnings account for a corporation).

Acquiring Cash, Either from Owners or by Borrowing

Your first task in starting this business is to acquire cash, either through owners' investments or by borrowing. Your parents indicate that they will match any funds that you are going to put into your business. You have $1,000 in savings, and coupled with your parents' matching funds, you decide to issue 200 shares of stock.

EXAMPLE 1 The following transaction illustrates investments by owners:

		Debit	Credit
assets (+)	Cash.	2,000	
owners' equity (+)	Capital Stock.		2,000
	Issued 200 shares of capital stock at $10 per share.		

This transaction increases cash as a result of capital stock being issued to investors, or stockholders. The cash account is debited, and the capital stock account is credited. The economic impact of this situation may be summarized as follows:

	ASSETS					=	LIABILITIES		+	OWNERS' EQUITY
Transaction #	**Cash**	**Inventory**	**Equipment**	**Supplies**	**Truck**		**Accounts Payable**	**Notes Payable**		**Capital Stock**
Beginning Balance	$ 0	$0	$0	$0	$0	=	$0	$0	+	$ 0
Invested money in the business	2,000	–	–	–	–		–	–		2,000
Subtotal	$2,000	$0	$0	$0	$0	=	$0	$0	+	$2,000

EXAMPLE 2 Suppose that in addition to coming up with the money yourself or from your parents, you went to a bank and convinced the loan officer to lend you the money. The journal entry for such a transaction would be:

assets (+)
liabilities (+)

Cash.	2,000	
Notes Payable.		2,000
Borrowed $2,000 from First National Bank, signing a 12-month note at 12% interest.		

Here, the cash account is debited, and the notes payable account is credited. The accounting equation captures the economic impact of borrowing the money as follows:

	ASSETS					=	LIABILITIES		+	OWNERS' EQUITY
Transaction #	**Cash**	**Inventory**	**Equipment**	**Supplies**	**Truck**		**Accounts Payable**	**Notes Payable**		**Capital Stock**
Beginning Balance	$ 0	$0	$0	$0	$0	=	$0	$ 0	+	$ 0
Invested money in the business	2,000	–	–	–	–		–	–		2,000
Borrowed money from a bank	2,000	–	–	–	–		–	2,000		–
Subtotal	$4,000	$0	$0	$0	$0	=	$0	$2,000	+	$2,000

Acquiring Other Assets

Now that you have obtained the funds necessary to start your business, either from owner investment or by borrowing, you can use that money to acquire other assets needed to operate the business. Such assets include supplies (such as fertilizer), inventory (perhaps shrubs that you will plant), and equipment (for example, a lawnmower and a truck for hauling). These assets may be purchased with cash or on credit. Credit purchases require payment after a period of time, for example, 30 days. Normally, interest expense is incurred when assets are bought on a time-payment plan that extends beyond two or three months. (To keep our examples simple here, we will not include interest expense. We will show how to account for interest on page 98, where we discuss the payment of obligations.) Examples of transactions involving the acquisition of noncash assets follow.

EXAMPLE 1 The first thing you need is a lawnmower and some form of transportation. You find an old 1988 pickup truck for sale for $800, and you buy it paying cash.

assets (+)	Truck	800	
assets (−)	Cash		800
	Purchased a used truck.		

The accounting equation shows:

	ASSETS					=	LIABILITIES		+	OWNERS' EQUITY
Transaction #	**Cash**	**Inventory**	**Equipment**	**Supplies**	**Truck**		**Accounts Payable**	**Notes Payable**		**Capital Stock**
Beginning Balance	$ 0	$0	$0	$0	$ 0	=	$0	$ 0	+	$ 0
Invested money in the business	2,000	–	–	–	–		–	–		2,000
Borrowed money from a bank	2,000	–	–	–	–		–	2,000		–
Purchased a truck paying cash	−800	–	–	–	800		–	–		–
Subtotal	$3,200	$0	$0	$0	$800	=	$0	$2,000	+	$2,000

Next, you drive to the local Sears store and purchase a Craftsman lawnmower and gas can for $250. Instead of paying for the mower with cash, you open a charge account, which will allow you to pay for the mower in 30 days with no interest charge. (If you wait and pay beyond this 30-day grace period, an interest charge will apply.) The journal entry to record this purchase is:

assets (+)	Equipment	250	
liabilities (+)	Accounts Payable		250
	Purchased a lawnmower and gas can on account.		

The accounting equation shows:

	ASSETS					=	LIABILITIES		+	OWNERS' EQUITY
Transaction #	**Cash**	**Inventory**	**Equipment**	**Supplies**	**Truck**		**Accounts Payable**	**Notes Payable**		**Capital Stock**
Beginning Balance	$ 0	$0	$ 0	$0	$ 0	=	$ 0	$ 0	+	$ 0
Invested money in the business	2,000	–	–	–	–		–	–		2,000
Borrowed money from a bank	2,000	–	–	–	–		–	2,000		–
Purchased a truck paying cash	−800	–	–	–	800		–	–		–
Purchased a mower on account	–	–	250	–	–		250	–		–
Subtotal	$3,200	$0	$250	$0	$800	=	$250	$2,000	+	$2,000

When you pay for the mower, cash will be reduced, and the liability, Accounts Payable, will also be reduced, thus keeping the equation in balance.

EXAMPLE 2 Off you go to the neighborhood Eagle Hardware & Garden Shop to purchase fertilizer, gloves, a rake, a shovel, and other assorted supplies. The total cost is $180, which you pay in cash; an increase in one asset (supplies) results in a decrease in another asset (cash).

assets (+)	Supplies.	180	
assets (−)	Cash		180
	Purchased supplies for cash.		

The accounting equation shows:

	ASSETS					=	LIABILITIES		+	OWNERS' EQUITY
Transaction #	**Cash**	**Inventory**	**Equipment**	**Supplies**	**Truck**		**Accounts Payable**	**Notes Payable**		**Capital Stock**
Beginning Balance	$ 0	$0	$ 0	$ 0	$ 0	=	$ 0	$ 0	+	$ 0
Invested money in the business	2,000	–	–	–	–		–	–		2,000
Borrowed money from a bank	2,000	–	–	–	–		–	2,000		–
Purchased a truck paying cash	−800	–	–	–	800		–	–		–
Purchased a mower on account	–	–	250	–	–		250	–		–
Purchased supplies for cash	−180	–	–	180	–		–	–		–
Subtotal	$3,020	$0	$250	$180	$800	=	$250	$2,000	+	$2,000

EXAMPLE 3 On your way home from the hardware store, you drive past a greenhouse and notice a big sign advertising a "50% off" sale on shrubs. Since you anticipate that planting shrubs will be part of your business, you stop and purchase for cash $150 worth of shrubs as inventory. You plan to make money in two ways with the shrubs: (1) revenue from the labor associated with planting them and (2) a profit on selling the shrubs for more than you paid. (This is fair; after all, you are saving your client the time and trouble of having to go to the greenhouse.)

assets (+)	Inventory	150	
assets (−)	Cash		150
	Purchased inventory for cash.		

The accounting equation shows:

	ASSETS					=	LIABILITIES		+	OWNERS' EQUITY
Transaction #	**Cash**	**Inventory**	**Equipment**	**Supplies**	**Truck**		**Accounts Payable**	**Notes Payable**		**Capital Stock**
Beginning Balance	$ 0	$ 0	$ 0	$ 0	$ 0	=	$ 0	$ 0	+	$ 0
Invested money in the business	2,000	–	–	–	–		–	–		2,000
Borrowed money from a bank	2,000	–	–	–	–		–	2,000		–
Purchased a truck paying cash	−800	–	–	–	800		–	–		–
Purchased a mower on account	–	–	250	–	–		250	–		–
Purchased supplies for cash	−180	–	–	180	–		–	–		–
Purchased inventory for cash	−150	150	–	–	–		–	–		–
Subtotal	$2,870	$150	$250	$180	$800	=	$250	$2,000	+	$2,000

Selling Goods or Providing Services

Now that you have your lawnmower, your transportation, your supplies, and your inventory, it is time to go to work. The next category of common transactions involves the sale of services or merchandise. Revenues are generated and expenses incurred during this process. Sometimes services and merchandise are sold for cash; at other times, they are sold on credit (on account), and a receivable is established for collection at a later date. Therefore, revenues indicate the source not only of cash but of other assets as well, all of which are received in exchange for the merchandise or services provided. Similarly, expenses may be incurred and paid for immediately by cash, or they may be incurred on credit—that is, they may be "charged," with a cash payment to be made at a later date. Illustrative transactions follow. Note the effect of revenues and expenses on owners' equity is indicated in brackets for each transaction.

EXAMPLE 1 As soon as people find out that you are in the lawn care and landscaping business, your phone begins ringing off the hook. Although most of your clients pay you immediately when you perform the service, some prefer to pay you once a month. As a result, a portion of your revenues is received immediately in cash, while the balance becomes receivables. The journal entry to record your first week's revenue for lawn care services is:

assets (+)	Cash.	270	
assets (+)	Accounts Receivable	80	
revenues (+) [equity (+)]	Lawn Care Revenue		350
	To record revenue for lawn care services.		

compound journal entry A journal entry that involves more than one debit or more than one credit or both.

As the journal entry illustrates, more than two accounts can be involved in recording a transaction. This type of entry is called a **compound journal entry**.

Because revenues increase owners' equity, the accounting equation shows:

Assets	=	Liabilities	+	Owners' Equity (Revenues)
(increase $350)		(no change)		(increase $350)

The detailed effect of this transaction and of each of the following transactions is summarized in Exhibit 3-5 on page 100.

EXAMPLE 2 One of your customers asks if you will plant some shrubs in her backyard. You mention that you have some shrubs and describe them to her; she is thrilled that you have just the shrubs she wants, thereby saving her a trip to the greenhouse. You use one-half of your inventory of shrubs in this customer's yard, and it takes you three hours to complete the job. She pays you in cash. In this instance, we are dealing with two different types of revenue—profit from the sale of the shrubs and revenue from your labor. Let's deal with each type of revenue separately.

Sale of Shrubs Sales, whether made on account or for cash, require entries that reflect not only the sale, but also the cost of the inventory sold. The "cost of goods sold" is an expense and, as such, is offset with the sales revenue to determine the profitability of sales transactions. The special procedures for handling inventory are described in Chapter 7. It is sufficient here to show an example of the impact of the transaction on the accounting equation.

In this example, you charged your customer $90 for one-half of the shrubs you purchased earlier.

		Debit	Credit
assets (+)	Cash	90	
revenues (+) [equity (+)]	Sales Revenue		90
	Sold inventory for cash.		
expenses (+) [equity (−)]	Cost of Goods Sold	75	
assets (−)	Inventory		75
	To record the cost of inventory sold and to reduce inventory for its cost.		

In this example, inventory costing you $75 is being sold for $90. The effect on the accounting equation for each transaction is:

STOP & THINK Could the two journal entries relating to the sale of inventory be combined into one journal entry?

Sales on Account

Assets	=	Liabilities	+	Owners' Equity (Revenues)
(increase $90)		(no change)		(increase $90)

Cost of Goods Sold

Assets	=	Liabilities	+	Owners' Equity (Expenses)
(decrease $75)		(no change)		(decrease $75)

Labor for Planting In addition to making a profit on the sale of the shrubs, you also generated revenue planting them. The journal entry to record this revenue is:

		Debit	Credit
assets (+)	Cash	45	
revenues (+) [equity (+)]	Landscaping Revenue		45
	To record revenue for landscaping services.		

The effect of the transaction on the accounting equation is:

Assets	=	Liabilities	+	Owners' Equity (Revenues)
(increase $45)		(no change)		(increase $45)

EXAMPLE 3 In addition to expenses relating to the sale of inventory, other expenses are also incurred in operating a business. Examples include gas for your lawnmower and your truck and the wages you agreed to pay your little brother for working for you (Mom said you had to let him help). The following journal entries illustrate how these expenses would be accounted for:

expenses (+) [equity (−)]	Gasoline Expense	50	
assets (−)	Cash		50
	Paid cash for gas for the truck and the mower.		
expenses (+) [equity (−)]	Wages Expense	60	
assets (−)	Cash		60
	Paid wages expense.		

The effect on the accounting equation of the gasoline expense is:

Assets	=	Liabilities	+	Owners' Equity (Expense)
(decrease $50)		(no change)		(decrease $50)

The entry for Wages Expense affects the equation in the same manner, the only difference being the amount, $60.

Collecting Cash and Paying Obligations

Obviously, once merchandise or services are sold on account, the receivables must be collected. The cash received is generally used to meet daily operating expenses and to pay other obligations. Excess cash can be reinvested in the business or distributed to the owners as a return on their investment.

EXAMPLE 1 The collection of accounts receivable is an important aspect of most businesses. Receivables are created when you allow certain customers to pay for your services at a later date. When receivables are collected, that asset is reduced and cash is increased, as shown here.

assets (+)	Cash	80	
assets (−)	Accounts Receivable		80
	Collected $80 of receivables.		

The effect of collecting the receivables on the accounting equation is:

Assets	=	Liabilities	+	Owners' Equity
(increase $80; decrease $80)		(no change)		(no change)

Note that no revenue is involved here. Revenue is recorded when the original sales transaction creates the accounts receivable. The cash collection on account merely involves exchanging one asset for another.

EXAMPLE 2 Remember that lawnmower and gas can you purchased on account? Well, now you have to pay for them. The entry to record the payment of obligations with cash is:

liabilities (−)	Accounts Payable	250	
assets (−)	Cash		250
	Paid $250 for the lawnmower and gas can previously purchased.		

After payment of accounts payable, the accounting equation shows:

Assets	=	Liabilities	+	Owners' Equity
(decrease $250)		(decrease $250)		(no change)

Remember that two parties are always involved in exchange transactions. What one buys, the other sells. When sales are on credit, the seller will record a receivable and the buyer will record a payable. The two accounts are inversely related. The seller of merchandise records a receivable and a sale, and simultaneously records an expense for the cost of goods sold and a reduction of inventory (as in Example 2 on page 96). The buyer records the receipt of the merchandise and, at the same time, records an obligation to pay the seller at some future time. When payment is made, the buyer reduces Accounts Payable and Cash (as in this example), whereas the seller increases Cash and reduces Accounts Receivable (as in Example 1).

EXAMPLE 3 On page 92, we showed the entry required when cash was borrowed from the bank. In that entry, you borrowed $2,000 to be paid over 12 months. Suppose you are required to make monthly loan payments of $178 with a portion of each payment being attributed to interest and a portion to reducing the liability—just like a mortgage on a house. As the following compound journal entry shows, a note payable or similar obligation requires an entry for payment, as well as for the interest due. Note that "interest" is the amount charged for using money, as will be more fully explained in later chapters.

		Debit	Credit
liabilities (−)	Notes Payable	158	
expenses (+) [equity (−)]	Interest Expense	20	
assets (−)	Cash		178
	Paid first monthly payment on note with interest ($2,000 × 0.12 × 1/12).		

Analysis of this transaction reveals that assets have decreased for two reasons. First, a portion of a liability has been paid with cash. Second, interest expense at 12% for one month on the note payable has been paid. This relationship will generally be present in most long-term and some short-term liability transactions. Since the interest charge is an expense and decreases owners' equity, the impact of the entry on the accounting equation is:

Assets	=	Liabilities	+	Owners' Equity (Expense)
(decrease $178)		(decrease $158)		(decrease $20)

EXAMPLE 4 Recall that you obtained financing in two ways to start your business—investors (you, Mom, and Dad) and the bank. In the previous journal entry, we illustrated how the bank receives a return on its investment. Well, Mom and Dad would like a return as well. Corporations that are profitable generally pay dividends to their stockholders. "Dividends" represent a distribution to the stockholders of part of the earnings of a company. The following entry illustrates the payment of a cash dividend:

STOP & THINK Why are dividends NOT considered to be an expense?

		Debit	Credit
dividends (+) [equity (−)]	Dividends	50	
assets (−)	Cash		50
	Paid a $50 cash dividend.		

As noted earlier, dividends, like revenues and expenses, affect owners' equity. Unlike revenues and expenses, dividends are a distribution of profits and, therefore, are not considered in determining net income. Because dividends reduce the retained earnings accumulated by a corporation, they decrease owners' equity. The payment of a $50 dividend affects the accounting equation as follows:

Assets	=	Liabilities	+	Owners' Equity (Dividends)
(decrease $50)		(no change)		(decrease $50)

See Exhibit 3-5 for a summary of the transactions shown in this chapter and their effect on the accounting equation.

A Note on Journal Entries

When preparing a journal entry, a systematic method may be used in analyzing every transaction. A journal entry involves a three-step process:

1. Identify which accounts are involved.
2. For each account, determine if it is increased or decreased.
3. For each account, determine by how much it has changed.

fyi

Many students have a little trouble getting used to debits, credits, and journal entries. So you are not alone if you are feeling a little overwhelmed. But remember, riding a bike wasn't easy the first time either. Like riding a bike, you will soon find that debits, credits, and journal entries aren't that difficult.

The answer to step 1 tells you if the accounts involved are asset, liability, or owners' equity accounts. The answer to step 2, when considered in light of your answer to step 1, tells you if the accounts involved are to be debited or credited. Consider the instance where $25,000 is borrowed from a bank. The two accounts involved are Cash and Notes Payable. Cash increased, and since Cash is an asset and assets increase with debits, then Cash must be debited. Notes Payable increased (we owe more money), and since Notes Payable is a liability and liabilities increase with credits, then Notes Payable must be credited. The answer to step 3 completes the journal entry. Cash is debited for $25,000, and Notes Payable is credited for $25,000.

This three-step process will always work, even for complex transactions. Consider the case where inventory costing $60,000 is sold on account for $75,000. Using the three-step process results in the following:

1. *Step 1:* What accounts are involved?
    - Accounts Receivable (an asset), Inventory (an asset), Cost of Goods Sold (an expense—part of owners' equity), and Sales Revenue (a revenue account—part of owners' equity).
2. *Step 2:* Did the accounts increase or decrease?
    - Accounts Receivable increased (customers owe us more money). Since Accounts Receivable is an asset, it is increased with a debit.
    - Inventory decreased (we don't have it anymore). Since Inventory is an asset, it is decreased with a credit.
    - Cost of Goods Sold increased (an expense causing owners' equity to decrease). Since owners' equity decreases with a debit, Cost of Goods Sold must be debited.
    - Sales Revenue increased (a revenue causing owners' equity to increase). Since owners' equity increases with a credit, Sales Revenue must be credited.
3. *Step 3:* By how much did each account change?
    - The answer to step 3 results in the following journal entries:

Accounts Receivable	75,000	
Sales Revenue		75,000
Cost of Goods Sold	60,000	
Inventory		60,000

to summarize

Journal entries are used to summarize the effects of business transactions. Journal entries are prepared or analyzed by answering three questions: (1) What accounts are involved? (2) Did those accounts increase or decrease? (3) By how much did each account change? By correctly answering these three questions, transactions will be properly accounted for, and the accounting equation will always balance.

exhibit 3-5 Summary of Transactions

	ASSETS						=	LIABILITIES	
	Cash	Accounts Receivable	Inventory	Equipment	Supplies	Truck		Accounts Payable	Notes Payable
Balance	$2,870	–	$150	$250	$180	$800	=	$250	$2,000
Revenue from lawn care	270	80	–	–	–	–		–	–
Sold inventory for cash	90	–	−75	–	–	–		–	–
Revenue from landscaping	45	–	–	–	–	–		–	–
Paid for gasoline	−50	–	–	–	–	–		–	–
Paid wages	−60	–	–	–	–	–		–	–
Collected receivables	80	−80	–	–	–	–		–	–
Paid accounts payable	−250	–	–	–	–	–		−250	–
Paid loan payment	−178	–	–	–	–	–		–	−158
Paid dividend	−50	–	–	–	–	–		–	–
Total	$2,767	$ 0	$ 75	$250	$180	$800	=	$ 0	$1,842

business environment essay

A Bookkeeping Attack Starts a War Tom Clancy typed the first draft of his first novel, *The Hunt for Red October,* on an IBM Selectric typewriter while still holding down his full-time job as an insurance agent. The book was published in October 1984, and sales took off when it became known that the book was President Ronald Reagan's favorite. To date, Clancy has published a total of seven novels featuring the reluctant hero Jack Ryan, and the stories have been so popular that Clancy now commands a record $25 million advance per book.

In *The Hunt for Red October,* Jack Ryan, who was trained as a historian, is a part-time analyst for the CIA. By the sixth novel in the series, *Debt of Honor,* a well-earned reputation for being a "good man in a storm" has landed Ryan, against his wishes, in the position of serving as the president's National Security Adviser. Jack Ryan's abilities are tested as an international crisis is touched off when a group of Japanese businessmen gain control of their government and determine that the only way to save the Japanese economy is through neutralization of U.S. power in the Pacific.

The first act of war against the United States is an attack not on a military target but instead on the book-

+	OWNERS' EQUITY								
		Retained Earnings							
	Capital Stock	**Lawn Care Revenue**	**Sales Revenue**	**Landscaping Revenue**	**Cost of Goods Sold***	**Gasoline Expense***	**Wages Expense***	**Interest Expense***	**Dividends***
+	$2,000	–	–	–	–	–	–	–	–
	–	350	–	–	–	–	–	–	–
	–	–	90	–	−75	–	–	–	–
	–	–	–	45	–	–	–	–	–
	–	–	–	–	–	−50	–	–	–
	–	–	–	–	–	–	−60	–	–
	–	–	–	–	–	–	–	–	–
	–	–	–	–	–	–	–	–	–
	–	–	–	–	–	–	–	−20	–
	–	–	–	–	–	–	–	–	−50
+	$2,000	$350	$90	$45	−$75	−$50	−$60	−$20	−$50

*Recall that an increase in these accounts actually decreases owners' equity, hence the − (minus sign).

keeping system used by U.S. stock exchanges. A computer virus, injected into the program used to record trades on all the major U.S. stock exchanges, is activated at noon on Friday. The records of all trades made after that time are eliminated with this result:

> No trading house, institution, or private investor could know what it had bought or sold, to or from whom, or for how much, and none could therefore know how much money was available for other trades, or for that matter, to purchase groceries over the weekend. (Tom Clancy, *Debt of Honor,* p. 312)

The uncertainty created by the destruction of the stock exchange bookkeeping records threatens to throw the U.S. economy into a tailspin and distract U.S. policy makers from other moves being made by Japan in the Pacific. Jack Ryan saves the world as we know it and restores the U.S. economy to sound footing by . . . well, it wouldn't be fair to say—you'll have to read the book. Suffice it to say that a key part of the restoration plan is the repair of the stock exchange bookkeeping system.

4

Summarize the resulting journal entries through posting and prepare a trial balance (step three of the accounting cycle).

posting The process of transferring amounts from the journal to the ledger.

ledger A book of accounts in which data from transactions recorded in journals are posted and thereby summarized.

chart of accounts A systematic listing of all accounts used by a company.

POSTING JOURNAL ENTRIES AND PREPARING A TRIAL BALANCE

Once transactions have been analyzed and recorded in a journal, it is necessary to classify and group all similar items. This is accomplished by the bookkeeping procedure of **posting** all the journal entries to appropriate accounts. As indicated earlier, accounts are records of like items. They show transaction dates, increases and decreases, and balances. For example, all increases and decreases in cash arising from transactions recorded in the journal are accumulated in one account called Cash. Similarly, all sales transactions are grouped together in the sales revenue account.

Posting is no more than sorting all journal entry amounts by account and copying those amounts to the appropriate account. No analysis is needed; all the necessary analysis is performed when the transaction is first recorded in the journal.

All accounts are maintained in an accounting record called the "general ledger." A **ledger** is a "book of accounts." Exhibit 3-6 shows how the three cash transactions in the general journal would be posted to the cash account in the general ledger, with arrows depicting the posting procedures. Observe that a number has been inserted in the "posting reference" column in both books. This number serves as a cross-reference between the general journal and the accounts in the general ledger. In the journal, it identifies the account to which the journal entry has been posted. In the ledger, it identifies the page on which the entry appears in the general journal. For example, the GJ1 notation in the cash account for the July 1 entry means that the $2,000 has been posted from page 1 of the general journal. As you will discover, these posting references are useful in tracking down mistakes. With a computer system, the software automatically generates these posting references.

caution

Common mistakes when manually posting include posting a debit to the credit side of an account, transposing numbers (e.g., a 45 magically becomes a 54), and posting to the wrong account (e.g., Supplies instead of Inventory). The lesson—be very careful or mistakes will creep into your work. Thankfully, posting is a task done almost exclusively by computers these days.

A particular company will have as many (or as few) accounts as it needs to provide a reasonable classification of its transactions. The list of accounts used by a company is known as its **chart of accounts**. The normal order of a chart of accounts is assets (current and long-term), then liabilities (current and long-term), followed by owners' equity, sales, and expenses. Exhibit 3-7 shows some accounts that might appear in a typical company's chart of accounts.

Determining Account Balances

At the end of an accounting period, the accounts in the general ledger are reviewed to determine each account's balance. Asset, expense, and dividend accounts normally have debit balances; liability, owners' equity, and revenue accounts normally have credit balances. In other words, the balance is normally on the side that increases the account.

To illustrate how to determine an account balance, consider the following T-account depicting all the cash transactions from our landscaping business (with dates being added). The beginning cash account balance plus all Cash debit entries, less total credits to Cash, equals the ending balance in the cash account.

Cash

Beg. Bal.	0		
7/1	2,000		
7/1	2,000	7/5	800
7/9	270	7/5	180
7/14	90	7/7	150
7/14	45	7/18	50
7/30	80	7/23	60
		7/31	250
		7/31	178
		7/31	50
	4,485		(1,718)
	(1,718) ←		
End. Bal.	2,767		

exhibit 3-6 Posting to the General Ledger

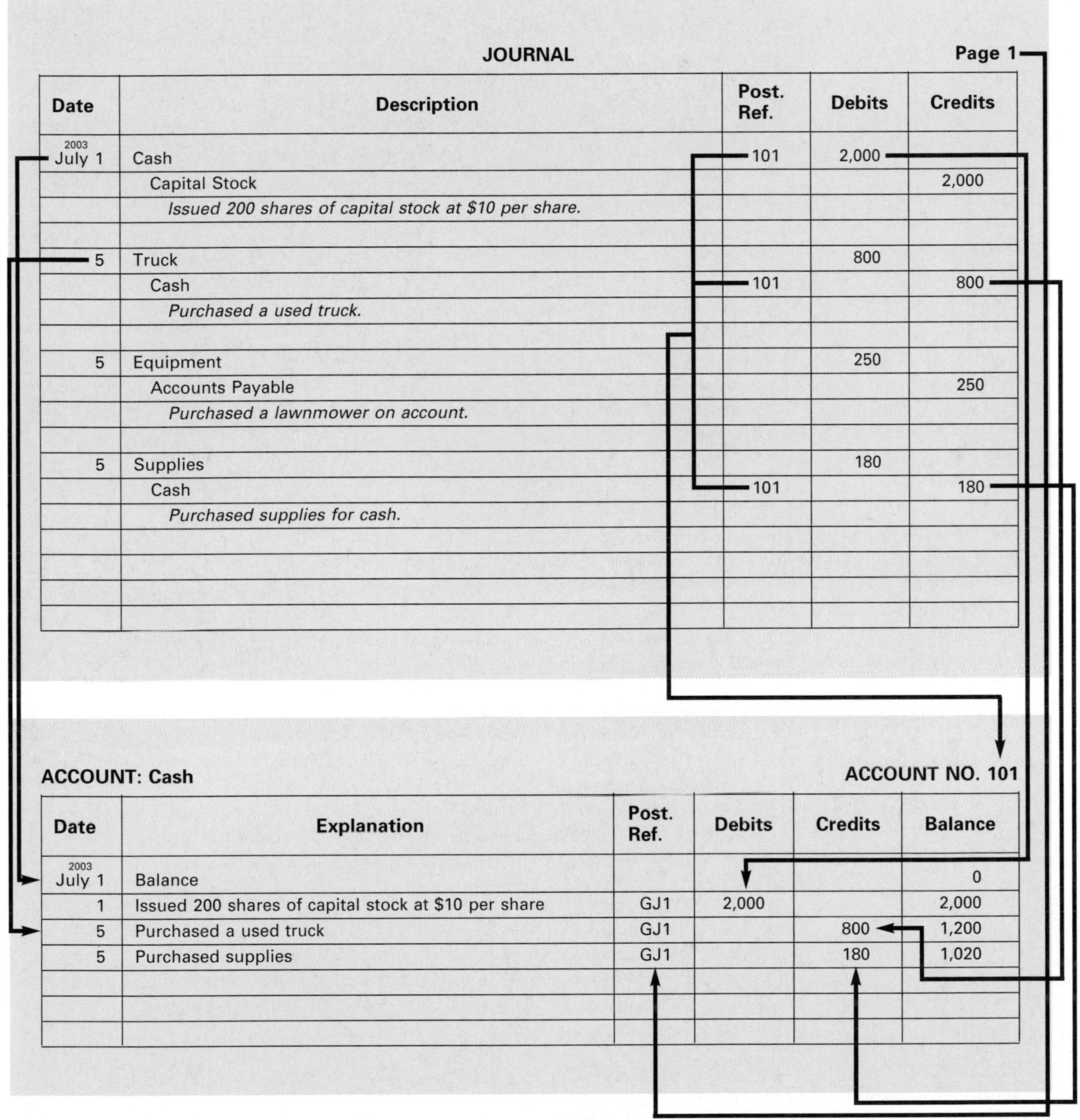

JOURNAL **Page 1**

Date	Description	Post. Ref.	Debits	Credits
2003 July 1	Cash	101	2,000	
	Capital Stock			2,000
	Issued 200 shares of capital stock at $10 per share.			
5	Truck		800	
	Cash	101		800
	Purchased a used truck.			
5	Equipment		250	
	Accounts Payable			250
	Purchased a lawnmower on account.			
5	Supplies		180	
	Cash	101		180
	Purchased supplies for cash.			

ACCOUNT: Cash **ACCOUNT NO. 101**

Date	Explanation	Post. Ref.	Debits	Credits	Balance
2003 July 1	Balance				0
1	Issued 200 shares of capital stock at $10 per share	GJ1	2,000		2,000
5	Purchased a used truck	GJ1		800	1,200
5	Purchased supplies	GJ1		180	1,020

Illustration of the First Three Steps in the Accounting Cycle

We have introduced the first three steps in the accounting cycle. A simple illustration will help reinforce what you have learned about the relationship of assets, liabilities, and owners' equity, as well as revenues, expenses, and dividends, and the mechanics of double-entry accounting. Katherine Kohler established the Double K Corporation in 2003. The following transactions occurred.

exhibit 3-7 Chart of Accounts for a Typical Company

Assets (100–199)	Owners' Equity (300–399)
Current Assets (100–150):	301 Capital Stock
101 Cash	330 Retained Earnings
103 Notes Receivable	
105 Accounts Receivable	**Sales (400–499)**
107 Inventory	400 Sales Revenue
108 Supplies	
Long-Term Assets (151–199):	**Expenses (500–599)**
151 Land	500 Cost of Goods Sold
152 Buildings	501 Sales Salaries and Commissions
154 Office Furniture or Equipment	523 Rent Expense
	525 Travel Expense
Liabilities (200–299)	528 Advertising Expense
Current Liabilities (200–219):	551 Officers' Salaries
201 Notes Payable	553 Administrative Salaries
202 Accounts Payable	570 Payroll Taxes
203 Salaries Payable	571 Office Supplies Expense
204 Interest Payable	573 Utilities Expense
206 Income Taxes Payable	578 Office Equipment Rent Expense
Long-Term Liabilities (220–239):	579 Accounting and Legal Fees
222 Mortgage Payable	

a. Initial capital contribution of $20,000, for which she received 1,000 shares of capital stock.
b. Double K Corporation paid $10,000 cash for inventory.
c. Borrowed $20,000 from a bank to buy some land, signing a long-term note with the bank.
d. Land was purchased for $25,000 cash.
e. During the year 2003, Double K Corporation sold 20%, or $2,000, of the inventory purchased. The company sold that inventory for $3,200, and the sale was originally made on credit.
f. The company paid $200 in selling expenses and $100 in miscellaneous expenses.
g. The company collected the full amount of the account receivable in cash.

The inventory purchases are verified by invoices showing the actual items purchased, dates, amounts, and so forth. There is a $20,000 note payable to the bank. Other business documents indicate the sale of inventory and the expenses incurred. Through analysis of these transactions and supporting documents (step 1), the pertinent facts are obtained and the transactions are recorded in a journal (step 2). The journal entries to record the transactions of Double K Corporation are as follows. (Note that letters are used in place of dates.)

Business Transaction	Account Category and Direction	Journal Entries	Debits	Credits
Issued stock	assets (+)	(a) Cash	20,000	
	owners' equity (+)	(a) Capital Stock		20,000
		Issued 1,000 shares of capital stock for $20,000.		
Purchased inventory	assets (+)	(b) Inventory	10,000	
	assets (−)	(b) Cash		10,000
		Purchased $10,000 of inventory for cash.		

(continued)

Business Transaction	Account Category and Direction	Journal Entries	Debits	Credits
Borrowed money	assets (+)	(c) Cash	20,000	
	liabilities (+)	(c) Notes Payable		20,000
		Borrowed $20,000 from a bank.		
Purchased land	assets (+)	(d) Land	25,000	
	assets (−)	(d) Cash		25,000
		Purchased land for cash.		
Sold inventory	assets (+)	(e) Accounts Receivable	3,200	
	revenues (+)	(e) Sales Revenue		3,200
		Sold inventory for $3,200 on account.		
	expenses (+)	(e) Cost of Goods Sold	2,000	
	assets (−)	(e) Inventory		2,000
		To record the cost of goods or inventory sold.		
Paid expenses	expenses (+)	(f) Selling Expenses	200	
	expenses (+)	(f) Miscellaneous Expenses	100	
	assets (−)	(f) Cash		300
		Paid selling and miscellaneous expenses.		
Collected cash	assets (+)	(g) Cash	3,200	
	assets (−)	(g) Accounts Receivable		3,200
		Collected accounts receivable.		

Next, the transactions are posted to the ledger accounts (step 3, part 1). T-accounts are used to illustrate this process, with the letters (a) through (g) showing the cross-references to the journal entries. A balance is shown for the end of the period. (Where only one transaction is involved, the amount of the transaction is also the account balance.)

Cash

	Debit		Credit
(a)	20,000	(b)	10,000
(c)	20,000	(d)	25,000
(g)	3,200	(f)	300
Bal.	7,900		

Accounts Receivable

	Debit		Credit
(e)	3,200	(g)	3,200
Bal.	0		

Inventory

	Debit		Credit
(b)	10,000	(e)	2,000
Bal.	8,000		

Land

	Debit		Credit
(d)	25,000		

Notes Payable

	Debit		Credit
		(c)	20,000

Capital Stock

	Debit		Credit
		(a)	20,000

Sales Revenue

	Debit		Credit
		(e)	3,200

Cost of Goods Sold

	Debit		Credit
(e)	2,000		

Selling Expenses

	Debit		Credit
(f)	200		

Miscellaneous Expenses

	Debit		Credit
(f)	100		

The effect of these transactions can also be visualized using a spreadsheet format as shown in Exhibit 3-8.

trial balance A listing of all account balances; provides a means of testing whether total debits equal total credits for all accounts.

After the account balances have been determined, a trial balance is usually prepared (step 3, part 2). A **trial balance** lists each account with its debit or credit balance, as shown in Exhibit 3-9. By adding all the debit balances and all the credit balances, the accountant can see whether total debits equal total credits. Even if the trial balance does show total debits equal to total credits, there may be errors. A transaction may have been omitted completely, or it may have been recorded incorrectly or posted to the wrong account. These types of errors will not be discovered by prepar-

exhibit 3-8 Effects of Business Transactions on the Accounting Equation

	ASSETS				=	LIABILITIES	+	OWNERS' EQUITY				
Transaction #	Cash	Inventory	Land	Accounts Receivable		Notes Payable		Capital Stock	Retained Earnings			
									Sales Revenue	Cost of Goods Sold*	Selling Expenses*	Misc. Expenses*
Beginning Balance	$ 0	$ 0	$ 0	$ 0	=	$ 0	+	$ 0				
a	20,000	–	–	–		–		20,000	–	–	–	–
b	−10,000	10,000	–	–		–		0	–	–	–	–
c	20,000	–	–	–		20,000		–	–	–	–	–
d	−25,000	–	25,000	–		–		–	–	–	–	–
e	–	−2,000	–	3,200		–		–	3,200	−2,000	–	–
f	−300	–	–	–		–		–	–	–	−200	−100
g	3,200	–	–	−3,200		–		–	–	–	–	–
Total	$ 7,900	$ 8,000	$25,000	$ 0	=	$20,000	+	$20,000	$3,200	−$2,000	−$200	−$100

*Recall that an increase in these accounts actually decreases owners' equity, hence the − (minus sign).

ing a trial balance; additional analysis would be required. In this case, total debits equal total credits. Thus, the accounting equation is in balance. The balances are taken from each ledger account.

Students frequently mistake a trial balance and the balance sheet for one another. In fact, they are very different reports. A trial balance is strictly an internal document used to summarize all of the account balances (assets, liabilities, owners' equity, revenues, expenses, and dividends) in a company's accounting system. Few people outside a company's accounting department ever see the trial balance; most businesspeople never see a real trial balance during their

exhibit 3-9 Trial Balance

Double K Corporation
Trial Balance
December 31, 2003

	Debits	Credits
Cash	$ 7,900	
Accounts Receivable	0	
Inventory	8,000	
Land	25,000	
Notes Payable		$20,000
Capital Stock		20,000
Sales Revenue		3,200
Cost of Goods Sold	2,000	
Selling Expenses	200	
Miscellaneous Expenses	100	
Totals	$43,200	$43,200

entire business career. The balance sheet, on the other hand, is a summary document that is frequently provided to interested parties both inside and outside a company.

From the data in the trial balance, an income statement and a balance sheet can be prepared. Exhibit 3-10 shows these two financial statements for Double K Corporation. Notice that there is no retained earnings account in the trial balance but there is one on the balance sheet. The reason for this is that all the income statement accounts such as Revenue, Cost of Goods Sold, and expenses are eventually accumulated into Retained Earnings. That is, earnings are re-

exhibit 3-10

Income Statement and Balance Sheet

Double K Corporation
Income Statement
For the Year Ended December 31, 2003

Sales revenue		$3,200
Expenses:		
Cost of goods sold	$2,000	
Selling expenses	200	
Miscellaneous expenses	100	2,300
Net income		$ 900
EPS ($900 ÷ 1,000 shares)		$ 0.90

Double K Corporation
Balance Sheet
December 31, 2003

Assets		Liabilities and Owners' Equity	
Cash	$ 7,900	Notes payable	$20,000
Inventory	8,000	Capital stock (1,000 shares)	20,000
Land	25,000	Retained earnings	900*
		Total liabilities and	
Total assets	$40,900	owners' equity	$40,900

*Beginning retained earnings + net income − dividends.

business environment essay

Nonfinancial Data Company annual reports provide more than just the financial statements and other financial information. They usually include nonfinancial information that provides insights into unusual circumstances, new trends, or significant changes, or that relate to important social issues, such as environmental concerns.

For example, **PHILIP MORRIS, INC.**, devoted more than seven pages in its 1999 annual report to litigation. In 1999, 510 new cases relating to the company's tobacco business were filed against Philip Morris. In its annual report, the company details the specific charges, the company's defense, the status of various cases, and the state of ongoing negotiations with the government.

Similarly, **EXXONMOBIL**'s 1999 annual report devotes a page to discussing the company's year 2000 plan and includes a brief note about the euro (the new currency of much of Europe).

Sources: The 1999 annual reports of Philip Morris and ExxonMobil.

exhibit 3-11 Statement of Cash Flows

Double K Corporation Statement of Cash Flows For the Year Ended December 31, 2003		
Operating activities:		
Collections from customers	$ 3,200	
Purchase of inventory	(10,000)	
Paid expenses	(300)	$ (7,100)
Investing activities:		
Purchased land		(25,000)
Financing activities:		
Issued stock	$20,000	
Borrowed from bank	20,000	40,000
Net increase in cash		$ 7,900
Beginning cash balance		0
Ending cash balance		$ 7,900

flected on the income statement. The business then decides the amount of those earnings to be retained. Those earnings that are to be retained are then disclosed on the balance sheet.

Also, the statement of cash flows can be prepared by categorizing the items in the cash account as operating, investing, or financing, as shown in Exhibit 3-11.

Two final notes: First, the preparation of financial statements is rarely so simple. In reality, the procedure also involves the adjustment of some ledger accounts, which need to be brought current before they can be included in the balance sheet or the income statement. In Chapter 4, we will explain how accounts are adjusted (step 4, part 1) so that the financial statements will accurately reflect the current financial position and operating results of an enterprise.

Second, net income does not usually equal the ending retained earnings balance. Only in the first year of a company's operations would this be the case. Double K Corporation began operations in 2003 and paid no dividends during the year; so, its $900 net income on the income statement equals the retained earnings figure on the balance sheet. In future years, the figures would be different, since retained earnings is an accumulation of earnings from past years adjusted for dividends and other special items.

to summarize

Once journal entries have been made and posted to the related accounts, account balances are computed by summing the debit and credit entries in each account. A trial balance is prepared by listing each account along with its balance. An income statement and a balance sheet can be prepared from this trial balance. A statement of cash flows is prepared by analyzing the inflows and outflows of cash as detailed in the cash account.

5

Describe how technology has affected the first three steps of the accounting cycle.

WHERE DO COMPUTERS FIT IN ALL THIS?

Students often ask, "Do I really need to know the difference between a debit and a credit? Haven't computers taken care of that?" Computers have greatly facilitated a business's ability to quickly process huge amounts of information without making mathematical errors. Most computers can make millions of calculations per second and produce more documents in ten minutes than a person could in an entire week. The time spent posting journal entries and summarizing accounts into a trial balance has been greatly reduced as a result of computers.

But computers still can't think. That's your job. Walk up to a computer terminal and show it a sales invoice and the computer will just sit there and wait. Wait for what? For the answers to three questions: (1) What accounts are involved? (2) Did those accounts increase or decrease? (3) By how much did each account change?

Let's consider how the best-selling money management software package, Quicken®, has changed the accounting process. Quicken works a lot like a check register. For each check, you indicate the date, the check number, the payee, and the amount. Quicken then prompts you to indicate the nature of the expenditure by selecting from a list of accounts. For example, if the expenditure relates to your purchase of groceries, you would select the account "Food." Thus, all your transactions relating to "Food" will be grouped together, allowing you to quickly determine all food expenditures.

Now let's review what Quicken has done. First of all, since you indicated the transaction involved a check, Quicken knows that cash decreased. Quicken is programmed to know that when cash decreases, it involves a credit to the cash account. Quicken also has been programmed to know that debits have to equal credits, and since Cash was credited, the program knows that something was debited. Since you indicated "Food" (an expense) was the other account, Quicken debits that account, causing your expense account to increase (we now know that expenses increase with debits). Instead of telling Quicken which accounts to debit and credit, you are required to identify the accounts (question 1) and indicate if they increased or decreased (question 2). Quicken is able to determine, based on the answer to these two questions, which accounts were debited and which accounts were credited.

So has Quicken fundamentally changed the accounting process? No. It has increased the accuracy and speed with which the posting process is done, as well as the speed with which a variety of reports can be prepared. Quicken has also eliminated the need for the user to specify debit or credit. Because computers are so fast, the two-step process of identifying accounts and the direction of their change can be done as quickly as you can say "credit Cash." So why don't accountants get rid of these 500-year-old terms, debit and credit? The reason is that all accountants are familiar with and comfortable using these terms. When someone says "credit Cash," accountants everywhere know exactly what that means. Thus, debit and credit provide a useful shorthand method of communication.

It should be noted that computers also bring with them several disadvantages. The acronym "GIGO" (garbage in, garbage out) refers to the problems that result when data are entered incorrectly. If you tell the computer the wrong account or wrong amount, all the related accounts and reports will be wrong. If bookkeepers or accountants had been doing the posting, they might have caught an unrealistic figure or account and corrected the mistake at its source; computers accept data without question.

A related problem has to do with fixing an error once it has been identified. Unlike someone familiar with the accounting process, a computer cannot grasp the double-entry nature of accounting and realize that, for example, an incorrect amount may be posted to two accounts, not just one. As an example, suppose a customer calls and notifies you of an error in her account—a sale to her was incorrectly recorded as $100 instead of $10. You can correct the customer's account by making a $90 adjustment to Accounts Receivable, but Sales would need to be adjusted by $90 as well. A computer couldn't extrapolate this and would end up overlooking this Sales adjustment.

The computer has enhanced step 3 of the accounting cycle—summarizing. In fact, only in the smallest of businesses will you find the posting of journal entries and the preparation of a trial balance being done by hand. But in every business, from the largest to the smallest, you will find accountants still actively involved in analyzing transactions and turning those transactions into journal entries and eventually into useful accounting reports.

to summarize

The computer has changed certain aspects of the accounting cycle. The posting process has been substantially improved through the use of computers. In addition, computers have made the preparation of reports and statements easier. But computers have not replaced the need to analyze transactions and determine their effect on the accounting equation.

review of learning objectives

1 Understand the process of transforming transaction data into useful accounting information. The objective of the accounting process is to gather and transform transaction data into useful information that measures and communicates the results of business activity. The accounting system used to keep track of the many financial activities of a business should be tailor-made for that business and may be a manual or an automated system, depending on the organization's needs.

2 Analyze transactions and determine how those transactions affect the accounting equation (step one of the accounting cycle). The procedures for processing accounting data are based on double-entry accounting and the fundamental accounting equation: Assets = Liabilities + Owners' Equity. Revenues increase retained earnings, whereas expenses and dividends decrease retained earnings. Thus, these accounts have a direct impact on the amount of owners' equity. In terms of the increase/decrease relationship of accounts, assets, expenses, and dividends are increased by debits; liabilities, owners' equity, and revenues are increased by credits. The double-entry system of accounting ensures that the accounting equation will always balance because debit entries require equal credit entries; that is, total debits must always equal total credits when transactions are properly recorded.

3 Record the effects of transactions using journal entries (step two of the accounting cycle). The effects of business events are recorded in the accounting system using journal entries. Journal entries detail the accounts involved in a transaction, whether the accounts increased or decreased, and the amount by which each account is affected. Each journal entry requires an equal amount of debits and credits. This equality ensures that the accounting equation will always be in balance.

4 Summarize the resulting journal entries through posting and prepare a trial balance (step three of the accounting cycle). Once journal entries are made, they are posted to individual accounts. The posting process involves simply copying each debit and credit from a journal entry into the associated account. A trial balance can be prepared to ensure that debits equal credits and that the accounting equation is in balance. From the trial balance, the primary financial statements can be prepared.

5 Describe how technology has affected the first three steps of the accounting cycle. Computers have changed the speed at which journal entries are processed through the accounting system. In most accounting systems, the posting process is done using computers. Computers ensure that no errors are made in transferring amounts from the journal entries to the accounts. Computers are also able to determine account balances and prepare reports quickly. Accountants are still required for the analysis and input of information into the accounting system.

key terms and concepts

account 84
accounting cycle 79
business documents 80
chart of accounts 102
compound journal entry 96
credit 86
debit 86
dividends 88
journal 90
journal entry 90
journalizing 90
ledger 102
posting 102
T-account 86
trial balance 105

review problem

The First Three Steps in the Accounting Cycle

Journal entries are given below for January 2003, the first month of operation for the Svendsen Service Company.

Date	Account	Debit	Credit
Jan. 2	Cash	40,000	
	Capital Stock		40,000
	Issued capital stock for cash.		
2	Insurance Expense	500	
	Cash		500
	Purchased a one-month insurance policy.		
2	Rent Expense	750	
	Cash		750
	Paid rent for the month of January.		
3	Shop Equipment	8,000	
	Cash		8,000
	Purchased shop equipment for cash.		
4	Supplies	3,000	
	Accounts Payable		3,000
	Purchased shop supplies on account.		
5	Automotive Equipment	11,500	
	Cash		3,500
	Notes Payable		8,000
	Purchased a truck. Paid $3,500 cash and issued a 30-day note for the balance.		
8	Cash	1,750	
	Service and Repair Revenue		1,750
	Received cash for repairs.		
9	Advertising Expense	300	
	Cash		300
	Paid cash for radio spot announcements.		
12	Automotive Expense	200	
	Cash		200
	Paid gas, oil, and service costs on the truck.		
14	Accounts Payable	3,000	
	Cash		3,000
	Paid $3,000 on account.		
16	Accounts Receivable	1,200	
	Service and Repair Revenue		1,200
	Repaired truck for Acme Drilling Company on account.		
18	Telephone Expense	75	
	Cash		75
	Paid for installation and telephone service for one month.		
19	Automotive Expense	180	
	Cash		180
	Paid for minor repairs on the truck.		
20	Cash	1,000	
	Notes Receivable	1,450	
	Service and Repair Revenue		2,450
	Collected $1,000 cash from Jones for truck repairs; accepted a 60-day note for the balance.		

(continued)

Jan. 24	Repairs and Maintenance Expense	150	
	Cash		150
	Paid cleaning and painting expenses on the building.		
25	Cash	1,500	
	Service and Repair Revenue		1,500
	Received cash for repairs and services from Hamilton, Inc.		
27	Supplies	2,500	
	Cash		2,500
	Purchased shop supplies.		
29	Office Equipment	1,250	
	Cash		1,250
	Purchased a computer.		
30	Cash	1,200	
	Accounts Receivable		1,200
	Collected receivables from Acme Drilling Company.		
31	Utilities Expense	900	
	Cash		900
	Paid the monthly utility bill.		
31	Automotive Expense	350	
	Cash		350
	Paid for gas, oil, and servicing of the truck.		

Required: Set up T-accounts, post all journal entries to the accounts, balance the accounts, and prepare a trial balance.

Solution The first step in solving this problem is to set up T-accounts for each item; then post all journal entries to the appropriate ledger accounts, as shown. Once the amounts are properly posted, account balances can be determined.

Cash

1/2	40,000	1/2	500
1/8	1,750	1/2	750
1/20	1,000	1/3	8,000
1/25	1,500	1/5	3,500
1/30	1,200	1/9	300
		1/12	200
		1/14	3,000
		1/18	75
		1/19	180
		1/24	150
		1/27	2,500
		1/29	1,250
		1/31	900
		1/31	350
Bal.	23,795		

Notes Receivable

1/20	1,450		

Accounts Receivable

1/16	1,200	1/30	1,200
Bal.	0		

Supplies

1/4	3,000		
1/27	2,500		
Bal.	5,500		

Shop Equipment

1/3	8,000		

Automotive Equipment

1/5	11,500		

Office Equipment

1/29	1,250		

Notes Payable

		1/5	8,000

Accounts Payable

1/14	3,000	1/4	3,000
		Bal.	0

Capital Stock

		1/2	40,000

Service and Repair Revenue

		1/8	1,750
		1/16	1,200
		1/20	2,450
		1/25	1,500
		Bal.	6,900

(continued)

Insurance Expense	
1/2 500	

Rent Expense	
1/2 750	

Advertising Expense	
1/9 300	

Automotive Expense	
1/12 200	
1/19 180	
1/31 350	
Bal. 730	

Telephone Expense	
1/18 75	

Repairs and Maintenance Expense	
1/24 150	

Utilities Expense	
1/31 900	

The final step is to prepare a trial balance to see whether total debits equal total credits for all accounts. List all the accounts with balances; then enter the balance in each account.

Svendsen Service Company
Trial Balance
January 31, 2003

	Debits	Credits
Cash	$23,795	
Accounts Receivable	0	
Notes Receivable	1,450	
Supplies	5,500	
Shop Equipment	8,000	
Automotive Equipment	11,500	
Office Equipment	1,250	
Accounts Payable		$ 0
Notes Payable		8,000
Capital Stock		40,000
Service and Repair Revenue		6,900
Insurance Expense	500	
Rent Expense	750	
Advertising Expense	300	
Automotive Expense	730	
Telephone Expense	75	
Repairs and Maintenance Expense	150	
Utilities Expense	900	
Totals	$54,900	$54,900

discussion questions

1. What is the basic objective of the accounting cycle?
2. Explain the first three steps in the accounting cycle.
3. What are the advantages of a computer-based accounting system? Does such a system eliminate the need for human judgment? Explain.
4. In a double-entry system of accounting, why must total debits always equal total credits?
5. Explain the increase/decrease, debit/credit relationship of asset, liability, and owners' equity accounts.

6. How are revenues, expenses, and dividends related to the basic accounting equation?
7. In what ways are dividend and expense accounts similar, and in what ways are they different?
8. How does understanding the mechanics of accounting help a businessperson who has no intention of practicing accounting?
9. Distinguish between a journal and a ledger.
10. Assume that Company A buys $1,500 of merchandise from Company B for cash. The merchandise originally cost Company B $1,000. What entries should the buyer and seller make, and what is the relationship of the accounts for this transaction?
11. Indicate how each of the following transactions affects the accounting equation.
    a. Purchase of supplies on account.
    b. Payment of wages.
    c. Cash sales of goods for more than their cost.
    d. Payment of monthly utility bills.
    e. Purchase of a building with a down payment of cash plus a mortgage.
    f. Cash investment by a stockholder.
    g. Payment of a cash dividend.
    h. Sale of goods on account for more than their cost.
    i. Sale of land at less than its cost.
12. What is a chart of accounts? What is its purpose?
13. If a trial balance appears to be correct (debits equal credits), does that guarantee complete accuracy in the accounting records? Explain.
14. What is the difference between a trial balance and a balance sheet?
15. Have computers eliminated the need to analyze transactions? Explain.

discussion cases

CASE 3-1

HOW DOES MICROSOFT (AND OTHER COMPANIES) DO IT?

MICROSOFT's revenues exceeded $19 billion in 1999. These revenues were generated by millions of transactions all over the world—in the United States, Canada, Europe, South America, and Asia. What is the process used by Microsoft to transform this tremendous amount of transaction data into summarized information reported to the general public in the form of financial statements?

CASE 3-2

ADVANTAGES AND DISADVANTAGES OF A COMPUTERIZED ACCOUNTING SYSTEM

Your soon-to-be father-in-law owns a small retail store. He has manually kept his business accounting records for over 20 years, but he is currently thinking about switching to a computerized accounting system. What advice would you give him about the advantages and the disadvantages of using a computerized accounting system?

CASE 3-3

WHEN IS A DEBIT A DEBIT?

Your new roommate, Susan, is confused. She has just received a notice from her bank indicating that her account has been debited for the cost of new checks. This has reduced her cash account. Susan just learned in her introductory accounting class that debiting Cash increases the account. She wonders why the bank has reduced her account by debiting it. How can you help Susan understand this situation?

CASE 3-4

UNDERSTANDING THE MECHANICS OF ACCOUNTING

As the CFO (Chief Financial Officer) of Rollins Engineering Company, you are looking for someone to fill the position of office manager. Part of the job description is to maintain the company's accounting records. This means that the office manager must be able to journalize transactions, post them to the ledger accounts, and prepare monthly trial balances. You have just interviewed the first applicant, Jay McMahon, who claims that he has studied accounting. As an initial check on his understanding of the basic mechanics of accounting, you give Jay a list of accounts randomly ordered and with assumed balances and ask him to prepare a trial balance. Jay prepares the following.

Trial Balance

	Debits	Credits
Accounts Payable		$ 4,500
Salaries Expense		175,000
Consulting Revenues	$269,000	
Cash	82,100	
Utilities Expense	12,000	
Accounts Receivable		44,000
Supplies	11,000	
Rent Expense	30,000	
Capital Stock		77,000
Supplies Expense	33,000	
Office Equipment	15,000	
Retained Earnings		24,000
Other Expenses	6,400	
Salaries Payable	34,000	
Totals	$492,500	$324,500

Based solely on your assessment of Jay McMahon's understanding of accounting, would you hire him as office manager? Explain. Prepare a corrected trial balance that you can use as a basis for your discussion with Jay and future applicants. Explain how the basic accounting equation and the system of double-entry accounting provide a check on the accounting records.

CASE 3-5

EXERCISING ACCOUNTING JUDGMENT

You have recently started business as an accounting consultant. Companies come to you when they face difficult decisions about how to make certain journal entries. You are currently working on the following two problems, which are independent of one another.

a. Baggins Company sells hamburgers for $1.00 each. The cost of the materials used to make each hamburger is 30 cents. Baggins has a compensation plan in which its employees are paid in the form of cash and hamburgers. During 2003, Baggins paid cash salaries of $500,000 and also issued certificates to employees entitling them to 200,000 free hamburgers. The certificates are not redeemable until 2004. What journal entry or entries should Baggins make in 2003 to record this employee compensation information?
b. Radagast Company purchased a building for $100,000 cash on January 1, 2003. Because of poor business decisions, as of December 31, 2003, the building is worthless. Make all journal entries necessary in 2003 in connection with this building.

EXERCISE 3-1

BASIC ACCOUNTING EQUATION

The fundamental accounting equation can be applied to your personal finances. For each of the following transactions, show how the accounting equation would be kept in balance. Example: Paid for semester's tuition (decrease assets: cash account; decrease owners' equity: expense account increases).

1. Took out a school loan for college.
2. Paid this month's rent.
3. Sold your old computer for cash at what it cost to buy it.
4. Received week's paycheck from part-time job.

5. Received interest on savings account.
6. Paid monthly payment on car loan (part of the payment is principal; the remainder is interest).

EXERCISE 3-2

ACCOUNTING ELEMENTS: INCREASE/DECREASE, DEBIT/CREDIT RELATIONSHIPS

The text describes the following accounting elements: assets, liabilities, owners' equity, capital stock, retained earnings, revenues, expenses, and dividends. Which of these elements are increased by a debit entry, and which are increased by a credit entry? Give a transaction for each item that would result in a net increase in its balance.

EXERCISE 3-3

EXPANDED ACCOUNTING EQUATION

Payless Department Store had the following transactions during the year:

1. Purchased inventory on account.
2. Sold merchandise for cash, assuming a profit on the sale.
3. Borrowed money from a bank.
4. Purchased land, making cash down payment and issuing a note for the balance.
5. Issued stock for cash.
6. Paid salaries for the year.
7. Paid a vendor for inventory purchased on account.
8. Sold a building for cash and notes receivable at no gain or loss.
9. Paid cash dividends to stockholders.
10. Paid utilities.

Using the following column headings, identify the accounts involved and indicate the net effect of each transaction on the accounting equation (+ increase; − decrease; 0 no effect). Transaction 1 has been completed as an example.

Transaction	Assets	=	Liabilities	+	Owners' Equity
1	+ (Inventory)		+ (Accounts Payable)		0

EXERCISE 3-4

CLASSIFICATION OF ACCOUNTS

For each of the accounts listed, indicate whether it is an asset (A), a liability (L), or an owners' equity (OE) account. If it is an account that affects owners' equity, indicate whether it is a revenue (R) or expense (E) account.

1. Cash
2. Sales
3. Accounts Receivable
4. Cost of Goods Sold
5. Insurance Expense
6. Capital Stock
7. Mortgage Payable
8. Salaries and Wages Expense
9. Retained Earnings
10. Salaries Payable
11. Accounts Payable
12. Interest Revenue
13. Inventory
14. Interest Receivable
15. Notes Payable
16. Equipment
17. Office Supplies
18. Utilities Expense
19. Interest Payable
20. Rent Expense

EXERCISE 3-5

NORMAL ACCOUNT BALANCES

For each account listed in Exercise 3-4, indicate whether it would normally have a debit (DR) balance or a credit (CR) balance.

EXERCISE 3-6

JOURNALIZING TRANSACTIONS

Record each of the following transactions in Chico's General Journal. (Omit explanations.)

1. Issued capital stock for $50,000 cash.
2. Borrowed $10,000 from a bank. Signed a note to secure the debt.
3. Purchased inventory from a supplier on credit for $8,000.

4. Paid the supplier for the inventory purchased in (3) above.
5. Sold inventory that cost $1,200 for $1,500 on credit.
6. Collected $1,500 from customers on transaction (5) above.
7. Paid salaries and rent of $25,000 and $1,200, respectively.

EXERCISE 3-7

JOURNALIZING TRANSACTIONS

Silva Company had the following transactions:

1. Purchased a new building, paying $20,000 cash and issuing a note for $50,000.
2. Purchased $15,000 of inventory on account.
3. Sold inventory costing $5,000 for $6,000 on account.
4. Paid for inventory purchased on account (item 2).
5. Issued capital stock for $25,000.
6. Collected $4,500 of accounts receivable.
7. Paid utility bills totaling $360.
8. Sold old building for $27,000, receiving $10,000 cash and a $17,000 note (no gain or loss on the sale).
9. Paid $2,000 cash dividends to stockholders.

Record the above transactions in general journal format. (Omit explanations.)

EXERCISE 3-8

JOURNAL ENTRIES

During June 2003, Husky, Inc., completed the following transactions. Prepare the journal entry for each transaction.

June	1	Received $200,000 for 2,000 shares of capital stock.
	2	Purchased $50,000 of equipment, with 25% down and 75% on a note payable.
	5	Paid utilities of $1,500 in cash.
	9	Sold equipment for $25,000 cash (no gain or loss).
	13	Purchased $100,000 of inventory, paying 50% down and 50% for credit.
	14	Paid $5,000 cash insurance premium for June.
	15	Sold inventory costing $30,000 for $45,000 to customers on account to be paid at a later date.
	20	Collected $3,000 from accounts receivable.
	24	Sold inventory costing $50,000 for $69,500 to customers for cash.
	25	Paid property taxes of $2,000.
	30	Paid $50,000 of accounts payable for inventory purchased on June 13.

EXERCISE 3-9

POSTING JOURNAL ENTRIES

Post the journal entries prepared in Exercise 3-8 to T-accounts, and determine the final balance for each account. (Assume all beginning account balances are zero.)

EXERCISE 3-10

CHALLENGING JOURNAL ENTRIES

The accountant for Han Company is considering how to journalize the following transactions:

a. The employees of Han Company earned $105,000. The employees received $90,000 in cash and were promised that they will receive the remaining $15,000 as a pension payment on the date that they retire.
b. On August 1, 2003, Han Company paid $1,800 cash for one year of rent on a building it is using. This one year of rent is scheduled to be in effect for the 12 months starting on August 1, 2003.

1. What journal entry should be made on the books of Han Company to record the employee compensation information in (a)?
2. Describe any assumptions necessary in making the employee compensation journal entry in (1).

3. Make the necessary journal entry on Han Company's books on August 1 to record the payment for the building rent described in (b).
4. Consider the journal entry made in (3). Is any adjustment to Han's books necessary as of December 31, 2003, as a consequence of the rent journal entry made on August 1?

EXERCISE 3-11

JOURNAL ENTRIES

The following transactions are for the Main Construction Corporation:

a. The firm purchased land for $300,000, $90,000 of which was paid in cash and a note payable signed for the balance.
b. The firm bought equipment for $75,000 on credit.
c. The firm paid $15,000 it owed to its suppliers.
d. The firm arranged for a $100,000 line of credit (the right to borrow funds as needed) from the bank. No funds have yet been borrowed.
e. One of the primary investors borrowed $50,000 from a bank. The loan is a personal loan.
f. The firm borrowed $65,000 on its line of credit.
g. The firm issued a $5,000 cash dividend to its stockholders.
h. An investor invested an additional $80,000 in the company in exchange for additional capital stock.
i. The firm repaid $7,500 of its line of credit.
j. The firm sold some of its products for $15,000—$5,000 for cash, the remainder on account.
k. Cost of sales in (j) are $8,000.
l. The firm received a $1,000 deposit from a customer for a product to be sold and delivered to that customer next month.

Analyze and record the transactions as journal entries. (Omit explanations.)

EXERCISE 3-12

ANALYSIS OF JOURNAL ENTRIES

The following journal entries are from the books of Kara Rachel Company:

	Account	Debit	Credit
a.	Cash	10,000	
	Capital Stock		10,000
b.	Cash	25,000	
	Loan Payable		25,000
c.	Buildings	50,000	
	Cash		5,000
	Mortgage Payable		45,000
d.	Inventory	25,000	
	Accounts Payable		25,000
e.	Accounts Receivable	42,000	
	Sales		42,000
	Cost of Goods Sold	21,000	
	Inventory		21,000
f.	Salary Expense	6,000	
	Cash		6,000
g.	Cash	37,000	
	Accounts Receivable		37,000
h.	Accounts Payable	20,000	
	Cash		20,000

For each of the journal entries, prepare an explanation of the business event that is being represented.

EXERCISE 3-13

JOURNALIZING AND POSTING TRANSACTIONS

Given the following T-accounts, describe the transaction that took place on each specified date during July:

Cash

7/5	9,500	7/1	3,420
7/28	8,000	7/23	2,000
		7/25	5,000
		7/30	5,500
Bal.	1,580		

Accounts Receivable

7/14	18,000	7/5	9,500
		7/28	8,000
Bal.	500		

Inventory

7/10	20,000	7/14	15,000
Bal.	5,000		

Equipment

7/30	1,500		

Land

7/30	4,000		

Accounts Payable

7/25	5,000	7/10	20,000
		Bal.	15,000

Sales Revenue

		7/14	18,000

Cost of Goods Sold

7/14	15,000		

Rent Expense

7/23	2,000		

Advertising Expense

7/1	3,420		

EXERCISE 3-14

TRIAL BALANCE

The account balances from the ledger of Yakamoto, Inc., as of July 31, 2003, are listed here in alphabetical order. The balance for Retained Earnings has been omitted. Prepare a trial balance, and insert the missing amount for Retained Earnings.

Accounts Payable	$ 8,600	Land	$19,000
Accounts Receivable	2,000	Miscellaneous Expenses	1,400
Buildings	20,000	Mortgage Payable (due 2006)	24,000
Capital Stock	10,000	Rent Expense	3,000
Cash	19,600	Retained Earnings	?
Equipment	16,000	Salary Expense	10,000
Fees Earned	26,000	Supplies	600
Insurance Expense	3,600	Utilities Expense	400

EXERCISE 3-15

TRIAL BALANCE

Assume you work in the accounting department at Marshall, Inc. Your boss has asked you to prepare a trial balance as of November 30, 2003, using the following account balances from the company's ledger. Prepare the trial balance and insert the missing amount for Cost of Goods Sold.

Accounts Payable	$ 55,000	Notes Payable	$250,000
Accounts Receivable	25,000	Notes Receivable	20,000
Advertising Expense	5,000	Other Expenses	1,000
Buildings	150,000	Property Tax Expense	1,500
Capital Stock	173,000	Rent Expense	7,500
Cash	35,000	Retained Earnings	40,000
Cost of Goods Sold	?	Salaries Expense	155,000
Equipment	55,000	Salaries Payable	2,000
Inventory	200,000	Sales Revenue	375,000
Land	125,000	Short-Term Investments	15,000
Mortgage Payable	95,000	Utilities Expense	7,000

EXERCISE 3-16

RELATIONSHIPS OF THE EXPANDED ACCOUNTING EQUATION

Domino, Inc., had the following information reported. From these data, determine the amount of:

1. Capital stock at December 31, 2002.
2. Retained earnings at December 31, 2003.
3. Revenues for the year 2003.

	December 31, 2002	December 31, 2003
Total assets	$250,000	$300,000
Total liabilities	60,000	70,000
Capital stock	?	50,000
Retained earnings	150,000	?
Revenues for 2003		?
Expenses for 2003		205,000
Dividends paid during 2003		5,000

EXERCISE 3-17

JOURNAL ENTRY TO CORRECT AN ERROR

Legolas Company paid $5,000 cash for executive salaries. When the journal entry to record this $5,000 payment was made, the payment was mistakenly added to the cost of land purchased by Legolas. The $5,000 should have been recorded as salary expense. Make the journal entry necessary to correct this error.

PROBLEM 3-1

JOURNAL ENTRIES AND TRIAL BALANCE

As of January 1, 2003, Kendrick Corporation had the following balances in its general ledger:

	Debits	Credits
Cash	$ 31,500	
Accounts Receivable	23,500	
Inventory	92,000	
Office Building	208,000	
Accounts Payable		$ 16,500
Mortgage Payable		180,000
Notes Payable		68,500
Capital Stock		57,500
Retained Earnings		32,500
Totals	$355,000	$355,000

Kendrick had the following transactions during 2003. All expenses were paid in cash, unless otherwise stated.

a. Accounts Payable as of January 1, 2003, were paid off.
b. Purchased inventory for $35,000 cash.
c. Collected $21,000 of receivables.
d. Sold $185,000 of merchandise, 85% for cash and 15% for credit. The Cost of Goods Sold was $98,500.
e. Paid $25,000 mortgage payment, of which $15,000 represents interest expense.

f. Paid salaries expense of $60,000.
g. Paid utilities of $6,300.
h. Paid installment of $5,000 on note.

Required:

1. Prepare journal entries to record each listed transaction. (Omit explanations.)
2. Set up T-accounts with the proper account balances at January 1, 2003, post the journal entries to the T-accounts, and prepare a trial balance for Kendrick Corporation at December 31, 2003.
3. **Interpretive Question:** If the debit and credit columns of the trial balance are in balance, does this mean that no errors have been made in journalizing the transactions? Explain.

PROBLEM 3-2

JOURNALIZING AND POSTING

Assume you are interviewing for a part-time accounting job at Spilker & Associates, Inc., and the interviewer gives you the following list of company transactions in September 2003.

Sept. 1 Received $150,000 for capital stock issued.
2 Paid $20,000 cash to employees for wages earned in September 2003.
4 Purchased $75,000 of running shoes and clothing on account for resale.
5 Paid utilities of $1,800 for September 2003.
9 Paid $1,500 cash for September's insurance premium.
11 Sold inventory of running shoes and clothing costing $35,000 for $70,000, with $20,000 received in cash and the remaining balance on credit.
15 Purchased $2,500 of supplies on account.
21 Received $25,000 from customers as payments on their accounts.
25 Paid $75,000 of accounts payable.

Using this list, you have been asked to do the following in the interview:

Required:

1. Journalize each of the transactions for September. (Omit explanations.)
2. Set up T-accounts, and post each of the journal entries made in (1).
3. **Interpretive Question:** If the business owners wanted to know at any given time how much cash the company had, where would you tell the owners to look? Why?

PROBLEM 3-3

JOURNAL ENTRIES FROM LEDGER ANALYSIS

T-accounts for RAM Technology, Inc., are shown below.

Cash

	Debit		Credit
(a)	100,000	(b)	45,000
(c)	50,000	(d)	5,000
(e)	25,000	(f)	20,000
(i)	15,000	(g)	53,500
		(h)	30,000

Accounts Receivable

	Debit		Credit
(e)	30,000	(i)	15,000

Inventory

	Debit		Credit
(d)	35,000	(e)	30,000

Building

	Debit		Credit
(b)	150,000		

Accounts Payable

	Debit		Credit
(h)	30,000	(d)	30,000

Mortgage Payable

	Debit		Credit
		(b)	105,000

Notes Payable

	Debit		Credit
(g)	50,000	(c)	50,000

Capital Stock

	Debit		Credit
		(a)	100,000

Sales Revenue

	Debit		Credit
		(e)	55,000

Cost of Goods Sold

	Debit		Credit
(e)	30,000		

Interest Expense

	Debit		Credit
(g)	3,500		

Wages Expense

	Debit		Credit
(f)	20,000		

Required:

1. Analyze these accounts and detail the appropriate journal entries that must have been made by RAM Technology, Inc. (Omit explanations.)
2. Determine the amount of net income/loss from the account information.

PROBLEM 3-4

JOURNALIZING AND POSTING TRANSACTIONS

Pat Bjornson, owner of Pat's Beauty Supply, completed the following business transactions during March 2003.

Mar.	1	Purchased $53,000 of inventory on credit.
	4	Collected $5,000 from customers as payments on their accounts.
	5	Purchased equipment for $3,000 cash.
	6	Sold inventory that cost $30,000 to customers on account for $40,000.
	10	Paid rent for March, $1,050.
	15	Paid utilities for March, $100.
	17	Paid a $300 monthly salary to the part-time helper.
	20	Collected $33,000 from customers as payments on their accounts.
	22	Paid $53,000 cash on account payable. (See March 1 entry.)
	25	Paid property taxes for March of $1,200.
	28	Sold inventory that cost $20,000 to customers for $30,000 cash.

Required:

1. For each transaction, give the entry to record it in the company's general journal. (Omit explanations.)
2. Set up T-accounts, and post the journal entries to their appropriate accounts.

PROBLEM 3-5

UNIFYING CONCEPTS: COMPOUND JOURNAL ENTRIES, POSTING, TRIAL BALANCE

J&W Merchandise Company had the following transactions during 2003.

a. Sam Jeakins began business by investing the following assets, receiving capital stock in exchange:

Cash	$ 20,000
Inventory	37,000
Land	25,500
Building	160,000
Equipment	12,500*
Totals	$255,000

*A note of $5,000 on the equipment was assumed by the company.

b. Sold merchandise that cost $30,000 for $45,000; $15,000 cash was received immediately, and the other $30,000 will be collected in 30 days.

c. Paid off the note of $5,000 plus $300 interest.

d. Purchased merchandise costing $12,000, paying $2,000 cash and issuing a note for $10,000.

e. Exchanged $2,000 cash and $8,000 in capital stock for office equipment costing $10,000.

f. Purchased a truck for $15,000 with $3,000 down and a one-year note for the balance.

Required:

1. Journalize the transactions. (Omit explanations.)
2. Post the journal entries using T-accounts for each account.
3. Prepare a trial balance at December 31, 2003.

PROBLEM 3-6

UNIFYING CONCEPTS: T-ACCOUNTS, TRIAL BALANCE, AND INCOME STATEMENT

The following list is a selection of transactions from Trafalga, Inc.'s business activities during 2003, the first year of operations.

a. Received $50,000 cash for capital stock.
b. Paid $5,000 cash for equipment.
c. Purchased inventory costing $18,000 on account.
d. Sold $25,000 of merchandise to customers on account. Cost of goods sold was $15,000.
e. Signed a note with a bank for a $10,000 loan.
f. Collected $9,500 cash from customers who had purchased merchandise on account.
g. Purchased land, $10,000, and a building, $60,000, for $15,000 cash and a 30-year mortgage of $55,000.
h. Made a first payment of $2,750 on the mortgage principal plus $2,750 in interest.
i. Paid $12,000 of accounts payable.
j. Purchased $1,500 of supplies on account.
k. Paid $2,500 of accounts payable.
l. Paid $7,500 in wages earned during the year.
m. Received $10,000 cash and $3,000 of notes in settlement of customers' accounts.
n. Received $3,250 in payment of a note receivable of $3,000 plus interest of $250.
o. Paid $600 cash for a utility bill.
p. Sold excess land for its cost of $3,000.
q. Received $1,500 in rent for an unused part of a building.
r. Paid off $10,000 note, plus interest of $1,200.

Required:

1. Set up T-accounts, and appropriately record the debits and credits for each transaction directly in the T-accounts. Leave room for a number of entries in the cash account.
2. Prepare a trial balance.
3. Prepare an income statement for the period. (Ignore income taxes and the EPS computation.)

PROBLEM 3-7

TRANSACTION ANALYSIS AND JOURNAL ENTRIES

Pacific Motors, Inc., entered into the following transactions during the month of August:

a. Purchased $1,500 of supplies on account from Major Supply Company. The cost of the supplies to Major Supply Company was $1,200.
b. Paid $600 to Valley Electric for the monthly utility bill.
c. Sold a truck to Fast Delivery, Inc. A $5,000 down payment was received with the balance of $12,000 due within 30 days. The cost of the delivery truck to Pacific Motors was $11,000.
d. Purchased a total of eight new cars and trucks from Japanese Motors, Inc., for a total of $96,000, one-half of which was paid in cash. The balance is due within 45 days. The total cost of the vehicles to Japanese Motors was $80,000.
e. Paid $1,875 to Silva's Automotive for repair work on cars for the current month.
f. Sold one of the new cars purchased from Japanese Motors to the town mayor, Ana Mecham. The sales price was $17,500, and was paid by Mecham upon delivery of the car. The cost of the particular car sold to Mecham was $12,100.
g. Borrowed $10,000 from a local bank to be repaid in one year with 12% interest.

Required:

1. For each of the transactions, make the proper journal entry on the books of Pacific Motors. (Omit explanations.)
2. For each of the transactions, make the proper journal entry on the books of the other party to the transaction, for example, (a) Major Supply Company, (b) Valley Electric. (Omit explanations.)
3. **Interpretive Question:** Why do some of the journal entries for Pacific Motors and other companies involved appear to be "mirror images" of each other?

PROBLEM 3-8

CORRECTING A TRIAL BALANCE

The following trial balance was prepared by a new employee.

Trial Balance
Alden Company, Inc.
For Year Ended November 30, 2003

	Credits	Debits
Cash	$ 18,250	
Mortgage Payable		$ 78,900
Advertising Expense	9,600	
Capital Stock		102,000
Equipment	36,900	
Notes Payable		187,350
Inventory	148,000	
Wages Expense	87,150	
Notes Receivable	5,000	
Accounts Payable		19,750
Accounts Receivable		5,300
Rent Expense		8,750
Wages Payable	9,000	
Furniture		15,000
Other Expenses	2,950	
Sales Revenue		235,600
Buildings	104,700	
Cost of Goods Sold	113,050	
Property Tax Expense		1,300
Land		87,850
Retained Earnings		14,400
Utilties Expense	3,200	
Totals	$537,800	$756,200

Required: Prepare the corrected company trial balance. (Assume all accounts have "normal" balances and the recorded amounts are correct.)

PROBLEM 3-9

UNIFYING CONCEPTS: JOURNAL ENTRIES, T-ACCOUNTS, TRIAL BALANCE

Downtown Company, a retailer, had the following account balances as of April 30, 2003:

Cash	$10,100	
Accounts Receivable	4,900	
Inventory	16,000	
Land	26,000	
Building	24,000	
Furniture	4,000	
Notes Payable		$25,000
Accounts Payable		12,000
Capital Stock		30,000
Retained Earnings		18,000
Totals	$85,000	$85,000

During May, the company completed the following transactions.

May 3 Paid one-half of 4/30/03 accounts payable.
6 Collected all of 4/30/03 accounts receivable.
7 Sold inventory costing $7,700 for $6,000 cash and $4,000 on account.

(continued)

May 8 Sold one-half of the land for $13,000, receiving $8,000 cash plus a note for $5,000.
10 Purchased inventory on account, $10,000.
15 Paid installment of $5,000 on notes payable (entire amount reduces the liability account).
21 Issued additional capital stock for $2,000 cash.
23 Sold inventory costing $4,000 for $7,500 cash.
25 Paid salaries of $2,000.
26 Paid rent of $500.
29 Purchased desk for $500 cash.

Required:

1. Prepare the journal entry for each transaction.
2. Set up T-accounts with the proper account balances at April 30, 2003, and post the entries to the T-accounts.
3. Prepare a trial balance as of May 31, 2003.

PROBLEM 3-10

UNIFYING CONCEPTS: FIRST STEPS IN THE ACCOUNTING CYCLE

The following balances were taken from the general ledger of Benson Company on January 1, 2003:

	Debits	Credits
Cash	$13,500	
Short-Term Investments	10,000	
Accounts Receivable	12,500	
Inventory	15,000	
Land	25,000	
Buildings	75,000	
Equipment	20,000	
Notes Payable		$17,500
Accounts Payable		12,500
Salaries and Wages Payable		2,500
Mortgage Payable		37,500
Capital Stock (7,000 shares outstanding)		70,000
Retained Earnings		31,000

During 2003, the company completed the following transactions:

a. Purchased inventory for $110,000 on credit.
b. Issued an additional $25,000 of capital stock (2,500 shares) for cash.
c. Paid property taxes of $4,500 for the year 2003.
d. Paid advertising and other selling expenses of $8,000.
e. Paid utilities expense of $6,500 for 2003.
f. Paid the salaries and wages owed for 2002. Paid additional salaries and wages of $18,000 during 2003.
g. Sold merchandise costing $105,000 for $175,000. Of total sales, $45,000 were cash sales and $130,000 were credit sales.
h. Paid off notes of $17,500 plus interest of $1,600.
i. On November 1, 2003, received a loan of $10,000 from the bank.
j. On December 30, 2003, made annual mortgage payment of $2,500 and paid interest of $3,700.
k. Collected receivables for the year of $140,000.
l. Paid off accounts payable of $112,500.
m. Received dividends and interest of $1,400 on short-term investments during 2003. (Record as Miscellaneous Revenue.)

n. Purchased additional short-term investments of $15,000 during 2003. (Note: Short-term investments are current assets.)
o. Paid 2003 corporate income taxes of $11,600.
p. Paid cash dividends of $7,600.

Required:

1. Journalize the 2003 transactions. (Omit explanations.)
2. Set up T-accounts with the proper account balances at January 1, 2003, and post the journal entries to the T-accounts.
3. Determine the account balances, and prepare a trial balance at December 31, 2003.
4. Prepare an income statement and a balance sheet. (Remember that the dividends account and all revenue and expense accounts are temporary retained earnings accounts.)
5. **Interpretive Question:** Why are revenue and expense accounts used at all?

competency enhancement opportunities

- Analyzing Real Company Information
- International Case
- Ethics Case
- Writing Assignment
- The Debate
- Cumulative Spreadsheet Project
- Internet Search

The following additional assignments provide opportunities for students to develop critical thinking, ethical perspectives, oral and written communication skills, experience with electronic research, and teamwork through group and business activities.

ANALYZING REAL COMPANY INFORMATION

• *Analyzing 3-1 (Microsoft)*

The 1999 annual report for **MICROSOFT** is included in Appendix A. Locate that annual report and consider the following questions:

1. Find Microsoft's 1999 income statement. Assume that research and development expenditures were paid in cash. What journal entry did Microsoft make in 1999 to record research and development?
2. Find Microsoft's 1999 cash flow statement. What journal entry did Microsoft make in 1999 to record the issuance of common stock?
3. Again, looking at the cash flow statement—what journal entry did Microsoft make in 1999 to record the purchase of property and equipment?
4. Using information from the cash flow statement, re-create the journal entry Microsoft made in 1999 to record the purchase of investments. Using the beginning and ending balances from the balance sheet, comment on the change in the balance of the equity and other investments account between the beginning of 1999 and the end of 1999.

• *Analyzing 3-2 (McDonald's)*

A brief history of the origin of the **McDONALD'S CORPORATION** is given at the start of this chapter. The following questions are adapted from information appearing in McDonald's 1999 annual report.

1. In 1999, total sales at all McDonald's stores worldwide were $38.5 billion. There were 26,806 McDonald's stores operating in 1999. *Estimate* how many customers per day visit an average McDonald's store.
2. For the stores owned by the McDonald's Corporation (as opposed to those owned by franchisees), total sales in 1999 were $9.512 billion, and total cost of food and packaging was $3.205 billion. What journal entries would McDonald's make to record a $10 sale and to record the cost of food and packaging associated with the $10 sale?
3. McDonald's reported payment of cash dividends of $264.7 million in 1999. What journal entry was required?
4. McDonald's reported that the total income tax it owed for 1999 was $936.2 million. However, only $642.2 million in cash was paid for taxes during the year. What compound journal entry did McDonald's make to record its income tax expense for the year?

INTERNATIONAL CASE

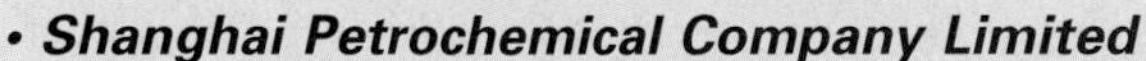

• *Shanghai Petrochemical Company Limited*

In July 1993, SHANGHAI PETROCHEMICAL COMPANY LIMITED became the first company organized under the laws of the People's Republic of China to publicly issue its shares on the worldwide market. Shanghai Petrochemical's shares now trade on the stock exchanges in Shanghai, Hong Kong, and New York. The following questions are adapted from information appearing in Shanghai Petrochemical's 1995 annual report.

1. In 1995, Shanghai Petrochemical reported sales of 11.835 billion renminbi (US$ 1 = 8.33 RMB) and cost of sales of RMB 9.016 billion. Make the necessary journal entries, using renminbi as the currency.
2. In 1995, Shanghai Petrochemical declared cash dividends of RMB 851.5 million. However, cash paid for dividends during the year was only RMB 818.8 million. Make the necessary compound journal entry to record the declaration and payment of cash dividends for the year.
3. In China, a 17% value added tax (VAT) is added to the invoiced value of all sales. This VAT is collected by the seller from the buyer and then held to be forwarded to the government. What journal entry would Shanghai Petrochemical make to record the sale, on account, of crude oil with an invoice sales value of $100 and a cost of $70?

ETHICS CASE

• *Should You Go the Extra Mile?*

You work in a small convenience store. The store is very low-tech; you ring up the sales on an old-style cash register that merely records the amount of the sale. The store owner uses this cash register tape at the end of each day to verify that the correct amount of cash is in the cash register drawer. On a day-to-day basis, no other financial information is collected about store operations.

Since you started studying accounting, you have become a bit uneasy about your job because you see many ways that store operations could be improved through the gathering and use of financial information. Even though you are not an expert, you are quite certain that you could help the store owner set up an improved information system. However, you also know that this will take extra effort on your part, with no real possibility of receiving an increase in pay.

Should you say anything to the store owner, or should you just keep quiet and save yourself the trouble?

WRITING ASSIGNMENT

• ***Accounting Is Everywhere!***

Financial accounting information is frequently used in newspaper and magazine articles to provide background data on companies. Prepare a one-page report on the use of financial accounting data by the press. Proceed as follows:

1. Scan the articles in a recent copy of one of the popular business periodicals (such as *The Wall Street Journal, Forbes, Fortune,* or *Business Week*) for examples of the use of financial accounting data.
2. Identify and describe three interesting examples:
   - Detail the nature of the accounting data used.
   - Outline the point that the writer is trying to make by using the particular accounting data.

THE DEBATE

• ***Are Computers the Hero or the Villain?***

As explained in the body of the chapter, computers have revolutionized the accounting process. In addition to taking over the mundane jobs of posting and report formatting, computers have also changed the way we think about information. When accounting was done by hand, it was not possible to match individual sales with specific products, specific customers, the exact time of day of the sale, the income level of the customer, the customer's favorite TV shows and magazines, and the like. In short, computers have made it possible to use the raw financial data to track much more than just revenues and expenses. How far should the use of computers go?

Divide your group into two teams.

- One team represents the computer technology group, "To Infinity, and Beyond!" Prepare a two-minute oral presentation supporting the notion that firms have a right to use their computer database systems to gather as much information about customers as possible, and even to sell that information to other firms. Now is the Information Age, and computers have made it possible to easily buy and sell information just like any other commodity.
- The other team represents "Right to Privacy." Prepare a two-minute oral presentation arguing that firms have no right to maintain databases containing individual customer information. A company's information system should relate to that company's products and processes, and customers have the right to interact with the firm anonymously.

CUMULATIVE SPREADSHEET PROJECT

This spreadsheet assignment is a continuation of the spreadsheet assignment given in Chapter 2. If you completed that spreadsheet, you have a head start on this one.

1. Refer back to the financial statement numbers for Handyman Company for 2003 [given in part (1) of the Cumulative Spreadsheet Project assignment in Chapter 2]. Using the balance sheet and income statement created with those numbers, create spreadsheet cell formulas to compute and display values for the following ratios:
   a. Current ratio
   b. Debt ratio

c. Asset turnover
d. Return on equity

2. Determine the impact of each of the following transactions on the ratio values computed in (1). Treat each transaction independently, meaning that before determining the impact of each new transaction, you should reset the financial statement values to their original amounts. Each of the hypothetical transactions is assumed to occur on the last day of the year.
   a. Collected $20 cash from customer receivables.
   b. Purchased $30 in inventory on account.
   c. Purchased $100 in property, plant, and equipment. The entire amount of the purchase was financed with a mortgage. Principal repayment for the mortgage is due in 10 years.
   d. Purchased $100 in property, plant, and equipment. The entire amount of the purchase was financed with new stockholder investment.
   e. Borrowed $20 with a short-term loan payable. The $20 was paid out as a dividend to stockholders.
   f. Received $20 as an investment from stockholders. The $20 was paid out as a dividend to stockholders.

INTERNET SEARCH

• McDonald's

Access McDONALD'S Web site at **http://www.mcdonalds.com**. Sometimes Web addresses change, so if this McDonald's address doesn't work, access the Web site for this textbook (**http://albrecht.swcollege.com**) for an updated link to McDonald's.

Once you've gained access to McDonald's Web site, answer the following questions:

1. Which has more calories—two hamburgers or one Big Mac?
2. How much money do you need to purchase a McDonald's franchise in the United States? What else is required to purchase a franchise?
3. Sometimes it isn't easy to find a company's financial statements in its Web site. Describe what you had to do to find a copy of McDonald's most recent annual report.
4. What information is contained in McDonald's most recent financial press release?

Completing the Accounting Cycle

chapter **f4**

learning objectives After studying this chapter, you should be able to:

1 Describe how accrual accounting allows for timely reporting and a better measure of a company's economic performance.

2 Explain the need for adjusting entries and make adjusting entries for unrecorded receivables, unrecorded liabilities, prepaid expenses, and unearned revenues.

3 Explain the preparation of the financial statements, the explanatory notes, and the audit report.

4 Perform a systematic analysis of financial statements.

5 Complete the closing process in the accounting cycle.

6 Understand how all the steps in the accounting cycle fit together.

expanded material

7 Make adjusting entries for prepaid expenses and unearned revenues when the original cash amounts are recorded as expenses and revenues.

GENERAL MOTORS, the brainchild of William Durant, was formed through the acquisition of a number of preexisting car makers. BUICK and OLDSMOBILE were acquired in 1908; CADILLAC and PONTIAC (originally called OAKLAND) were added in 1909. With so many acquisitions in those early years, General Motors' financing was quickly depleted, and Durant lost control of his company. With Durant fighting to regain the reins of General Motors, the company was in such turmoil that, at one point, CHEVROLET MOTOR COMPANY (another Durant creation) owned a majority of GM stock. After many deals, Durant found himself back in charge in 1916, and Chevrolet became a subsidiary of GM in 1918.

Following the end of World War I, an economic slowdown stretched Durant's financial resources past the breaking point, and in 1920 he lost control of General Motors for good. Pierre S. du Pont, a GM investor since 1914, became the company's new president. Du Pont brought to General Motors the financial resources and business connections associated with his own family's chemical empire. He was also instrumental in instituting the du Pont style of management and control. Implemented at General Motors by Alfred P. Sloan (who later went on to head GM until 1956), this system emphasized decentralized decision making; evaluations of managers of autonomous divisions were based on reaching specific financial goals. This "DuPont" system of evaluation is discussed later in the chapter.

Under Sloan's leadership, General Motors became the dominant car maker in the world, a position it still holds. In addition to implementing the DuPont system of evaluation and control, Sloan also formalized the caste system among GM's different automobile lines. For example, Chevrolets were targeted at the lower-income end of the market, while Cadillacs were aimed at the higher end. Sloan was also instrumental in creating the annual ritual of the "car model year" to encourage owners of older models to trade them in on new cars with the latest innovations.

Although General Motors' global market share has declined with stiff competition from Japanese, European (including DAIMLERCHRYSLER), and domestic (FORD) competitors, General Motors still sells more cars and trucks than any other company in the world. In 1999, GM sold 8.7 million vehicles, 15.8% of the worldwide total. GM also remains one of the largest private employers in the United States, ranking second behind WAL-MART in the 2000 Fortune 500 listing (see Exhibit 4-1).

In addition to being the most prolific car maker in the world, General Motors has the unenviable distinction of having posted the world record largest annual net loss. In 1992, GM reported a loss for the year of $23.5 billion. This record loss followed losses of $2.0 billion in 1990 and $4.5 billion in 1991.

How was General Motors able to stay in business while reporting these huge losses? During the same period it was reporting large losses on its income statement, GM was reporting healthy cash from operations on its cash flow statement. In fact, in 1992 (the year of the record loss), GM's positive cash from operations was $9.8 billion. This strong cash flow enabled GM to continue normal operations, pay its

exhibit 4-1 U.S. Companies with the Most Employees, 1999

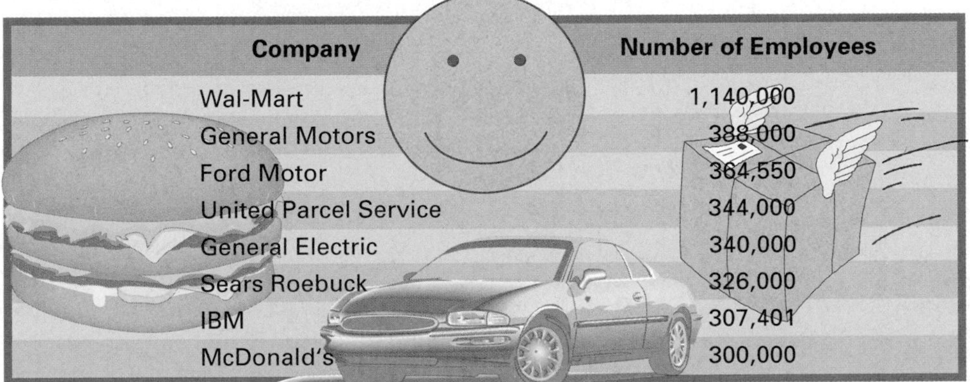

Company	Number of Employees
Wal-Mart	1,140,000
General Motors	388,000
Ford Motor	364,550
United Parcel Service	344,000
General Electric	340,000
Sears Roebuck	326,000
IBM	307,401
McDonald's	300,000

Source: 2000 Fortune 500 listing available at http://www.fortune.com

suppliers, repay its loans, and maintain investor confidence even while reporting significant losses.

Where did these losses come from if they weren't the result of a shortfall in cash from operations? The losses came from business expenses that General Motors had incurred as part of its operations but which had not yet been paid in cash. For example, the record $23.5 billion loss was primarily due to recording the large business expense from postretirement medical benefits that have been promised to GM employees. General Motors won't actually have to make the cash payments related to these benefits until the employees retire in the future. The benefits have already been earned, however, so they should be reported as a cost of business now. The art of accounting involves recording all business expenses—both those that are paid in cash and those that involve promises of payment in the future. As GM's $23.5 billion loss illustrates, those promises of future payment can really add up.

As the General Motors scenario illustrates, adjustments (to the raw transaction data recorded in the accounts) usually are needed so that the financial statements will accurately reflect a company's economic performance during the period and its economic condition as of the end of the period. This is a part of completing the accounting cycle. In addition, certain accounts must be "closed" at the end of an accounting period to prepare the records for a new accounting cycle. The nature of year-end adjustments, the remaining steps in the accounting cycle, and general techniques for analyzing the information contained in financial statements are discussed in this chapter.

1

Describe how accrual accounting allows for timely reporting and a better measure of a company's economic performance.

ACCRUAL ACCOUNTING

In 2002, two brothers sign a contract for a consulting project. The total contract price is $20,000. The brothers do most of the consulting work in 2002 and finish the job in 2003. They receive a $2,000 cash payment from the contract in 2002 and receive the remaining $18,000 cash in 2003. On December 31, 2002, the brothers prepare a 2002 income statement to use in applying for a bank loan. What amount of revenue should the brothers report for 2002?

This example illustrates why accounting is much more than merely tabulating cash receipts and cash payments. A proper measure of the brothers' economic performance in 2002 requires estimating the value of the work completed in 2002; to report 2002 revenue as only the $2,000 cash received grossly understates the actual economic output produced during the year. In addition, the need for the year-end income statement means that the brothers can't wait until after the final contract payment is received before preparing a summary of their activities; the bank wants the income statement now.

Accrual accounting is the process of adjusting raw transaction data into refined measures of a firm's past economic performance and current economic condition. As the following sections explain, this accrual process is necessary because a business requires periodic, timely financial reports and accrual information better measures a firm's performance than do cash flow data.

The difficulty in using accrual accounting to generate a performance measure is represented in Exhibit 4-2. Each horizontal bar in the exhibit represents a business deal such as the production and sale of a car, the delivery of legal services for a specific lawsuit, or the development, delivery, and support of a piece of software. Some deals last less than a day from start to finish, such as when a barber provides a haircut in exchange for cash. The obligations and responsibilities associated with other deals can stretch on for years. For example, when you buy a GENERAL MOTORS car, the deal is not done from your standpoint until four or five years later after you have received all of the GM warranty services promised to you. And, from GM's standpoint, the deal is not done until 40 or 50 years later after GM has paid the assembly-line workers all of the pension benefits they earned through the labor hours spent assembling your car. Even though the economic loose ends of some business deals extend for years, financial statement users still require periodic reports about a company's operating performance. As you can see in Exhibit 4-2, the beginning and the end of a year are arbitrary breaks in the life of an ongoing business. The job of accountants is to consider all business deals that were at least par-

exhibit 4-2 The Problem of Income Measurement

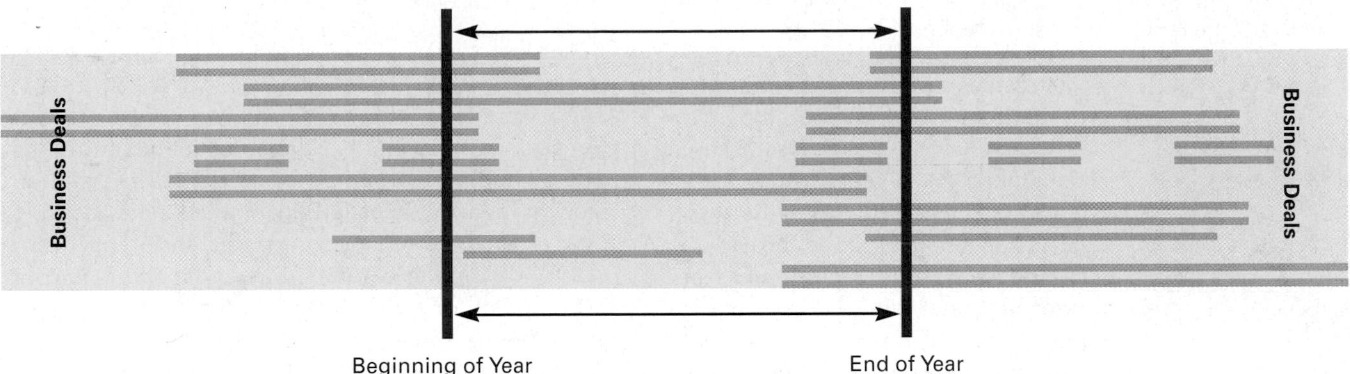

tially completed during a year and to measure the profit associated with those deals. This profit is then reported as net income for the year. As you can see, accrual accounting is much more than mere "bean counting."

Periodic Reporting

time-period concept The idea that the life of a business is divided into distinct and relatively short time periods so that accounting information can be timely.

fiscal year An entity's reporting year, covering a 12-month accounting period.

calendar year An entity's reporting year, covering 12 months and ending on December 31.

All businesses, large or small, periodically issue their financial statements so that users can make sound economic decisions. Current owners, prospective investors, bankers, and others need up-to-date reports in order to compare and judge a company's financial position and operating results on a continuing, timely basis. They need to know the financial position of a company (from the balance sheet), the relative success or failure of current operations (from the income statement), and the nature and extent of cash flows (from the statement of cash flows).

The financial picture of a company—its success or failure in meeting its economic objectives—cannot really be complete until the "life" of a business is over. However, managers, owners, and creditors cannot wait 10, 20, or 100 years to receive an exact accounting of a business. In order to provide timely accounting information, the **time-period concept** divides the life of an enterprise into distinct and relatively short (generally 12 months or less) accounting periods. The 12-month accounting period is referred to as the **fiscal year**. When an entity closes its books on December 31, its reports are based on a **calendar year**.

fyi

As mentioned in Chapter 2, about two-thirds of large U.S. companies choose December 31 as the end of their fiscal year.

Most large corporations, and even many small companies, issue a report to stockholders as of a fiscal year-end. As noted in Chapters 1 and 2, this annual report includes the primary financial statements (balance sheet, income statement, and statement of cash flows) and other financial data, such as a management discussion and analysis of operations. Other financial reports are prepared more frequently, perhaps quarterly or monthly. Indeed, some reports, such as sales reports for use by management, may be prepared on a daily basis.

Although periodic reporting is vital to a firm's success, the frequency of reporting forces accountants to use some data that are based on judgments and estimates. As you will see, the shorter the reporting period (for example, a month instead of a year), the less exact are the measurements of assets and liabilities and the recognition of revenues and expenses. Ideally, accounting judgments are made carefully and estimates are based on reliable evidence, but the limitations of accounting reports should be understood and kept in mind.

STOP & THINK Since almost all companies have their financial records on computer, what stops them from preparing financial statements every day?

accrual-basis accounting A system of accounting in which revenues and expenses are recorded as they are earned and incurred, not necessarily when cash is received or paid.

Accrual- versus Cash-Basis Accounting

Closely related to the time-period concept is the concept of **accrual-basis accounting**. This important characteristic of the traditional accounting model simply means that revenues are recognized (recorded) when earned without regard for when cash is received; expenses are recorded

business environment essay

Net Income versus Cash Flow and EVA® Accountants are proud of the set of accrual accounting rules that they have developed over the years. According to accountants, when these rules are applied to raw cash flow data, the resulting net income number provides a superior measure of a company's performance. Some financial analysts and many finance professors have long been skeptical about the value of accrual accounting. These skeptics contend that an investor is better off analyzing a company using cash flow data because the accounting rules distort a company's reported performance.

Recently, accrual accounting has been attacked from another direction. STERN STEWART & COMPANY has marketed an alternative measure of financial performance that it claims is superior to the net income number computed by accountants. The Stern Stewart measure is called Economic Value Added, or EVA®. Many prominent companies, including COCA-COLA, AT&T, and SPRINT, have paid Stern Stewart & Company for the right to use EVA® as an internal performance measure. Stern Stewart & Company claims that EVA® is "almost 50% better than its closest accounting-based competitor in explaining changes in shareholder wealth."

Three accounting professors decided to test the validity of these challenges to the usefulness of ac-

as incurred without regard for when they are paid. Accrual accounting requires that revenues and expenses be assigned to their proper accounting periods, which do not necessarily coincide with the periods in which cash is received or paid.

revenue recognition principle The idea that revenues should be recorded when (1) the earnings process has been substantially completed and (2) cash has either been collected or collectibility is reasonably assured.

REVENUE RECOGNITION How do we assign revenues to particular periods? First, we must determine when revenues have actually been earned. The **revenue recognition principle** states that revenues are recorded when two main criteria have been met.

1. The earnings process is substantially complete; generally, a sale has been made or services have been performed.
2. Cash has been collected or collectibility is reasonably assured.

These two criteria ensure that both parties to the transaction have fulfilled their commitment or are formally obligated to do so. In simple terms, satisfying the first criterion demonstrates that the seller has done something; satisfying the second criterion demonstrates that the buyer has done something. The seller generally records sales revenue when goods are shipped or when services are performed. When this occurs, the seller has completed his or her part of the transaction. The seller assumes, when shipment is made or services performed, that the buyer has given a valid promise to pay (if this promise is not implied, then the seller probably will not ship). The promise to pay, or the actual payment, would complete the buyer's part of the transaction. If, for example, General Motors sold and shipped $800 million of cars in 2003, but will not receive the cash proceeds until 2004, the $800 million would still be recognized as revenue in 2003, when it is earned and a promise of payment is received. Both of the revenue recognition principle criteria have been met. On the other hand, if General Motors is paid in 2003 for cars to be shipped in 2004, it would not record those payments as revenues until the cars are actually shipped.

matching principle The concept that all costs and expenses incurred in generating revenues must be recognized in the same reporting period as the related revenues.

THE MATCHING PRINCIPLE Once a company determines which revenues should be recognized during a period, how does it identify the expenses incurred? The **matching principle** requires that all costs and expenses incurred to generate revenues must be recognized in the same accounting period as the related revenues. The cost of the merchandise sold, for example, should be matched to the revenue derived from the sale of that merchandise during the period. Expenses that cannot be matched with revenues are assigned to the accounting period in which

crual accounting. Professors Biddle, Bowen, and Wallace constructed statistical tests to determine which performance measure—accrual accounting net income, EVA®, or cash flow from operations—is most closely associated with the ultimate performance measure, the annual change in the market value of a company. Using data for 773 U.S. companies for 11 years, Professors Biddle, Bowen, and Wallace computed a statistic called "adjusted R^2," which reflects the degree of association between a performance measure number for a given company in a given year and the company's market value change in the same year. The higher the adjusted R^2 value, the closer the association between the performance measure and the company's change in market value. The computed adjusted R^2 values were:

Net income (excluding extraordinary items)	12.8%
EVA®	6.5%
Cash flow from operations	2.8%

So, accrual accounting is still the undisputed champion of performance measures.

Source: Gary C. Biddle, Robert M. Bowen, and James S. Wallace. "Does EVA® Beat Earnings? Evidence on Associations with Stock Returns and Firm Values," *Journal of Accounting and Economics*, December 1997, p. 301.

they are incurred. For example, the exact amount of electricity used to make an automobile generally cannot be determined, but since the amount used for a month or a year is known, that amount can be matched to the revenues earned during the same period.

As shown in Exhibit 4-3, this process of matching expenses with recognized revenues determines the amount of net income reported on the income statement. Net income is the most widely used indicator of how well a company has performed during a period. The subject of income determination, including revenue recognition and expense matching, is discussed more completely in Chapters 6, 7, and 8.

To illustrate the difference between cash- and accrual-basis accounting, and to demonstrate why accrual-basis accounting provides a more meaningful measure of income, assume that Karas Brothers billed clients $50,500 for consulting services in 2003. By December 31, Karas had received $22,000, with the $28,500 balance expected in 2004. During 2003, Karas paid $21,900 for various expenses. At December 31, Karas still owed $11,200 for additional expenses incurred. These expenses will be paid during January 2004. How much income should Karas Brothers report for 2003? The answer depends on whether cash-basis or accrual-basis accounting is used. As shown on the next page, with cash-basis accounting, reported income would be $100. With accrual-basis accounting, reported income would be $17,400.

exhibit 4-3 Determining Accrual Income

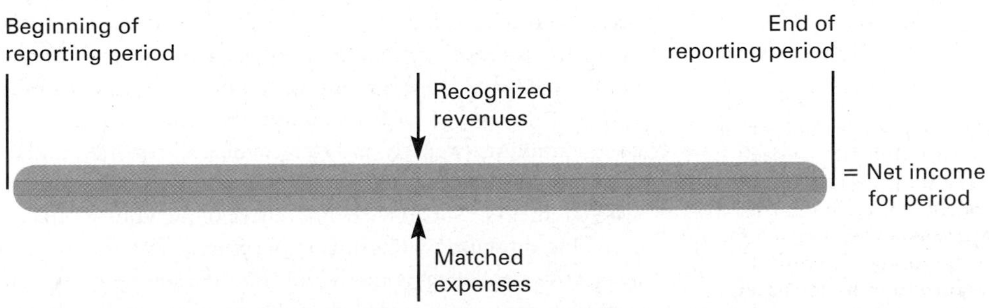

Recognized Revenues – Matched Expenses = Net Income for Period

Karas Brothers
Reported Income for 2003

Cash-Basis Accounting		Accrual-Basis Accounting	
Cash receipts	$22,000	Revenues earned	$50,500
Cash disbursements	21,900	Expenses incurred	33,100
Income	$ 100	Income	$17,400

cash-basis accounting A system of accounting in which transactions are recorded and revenues and expenses are recognized only when cash is received or paid.

caution

Although accrual-basis net income is the measure of Karas Brothers' economic performance for the year, the cash flow information is useful in evaluating the need to obtain short-term loans, the ability to repay existing loans, and the like. The statement of cash flows is an essential companion to the accrual-basis income statement.

How do we explain this $17,300 difference? Under **cash-basis accounting**, Karas Brothers would report only $22,000 in revenue, the total amount of cash received during 2003. Similarly, the company would report only $21,900 of expenses (the amount actually paid) during 2003. The additional $11,200 of expenses incurred but not yet paid would not be reported. Using accrual-basis accounting, however, Karas earned $50,500 in revenues, which is the total increase in resources for the period (an increase of $22,000 in cash plus $28,500 in receivables). Similarly, Karas incurred a total of $33,100 in expenses, which should be matched with revenues earned to produce a realistic income measurement. The combined result of increasing revenues by $28,500 while increasing expenses by only $11,200 creates the $17,300 difference in net income ($28,500 − $11,200 = $17,300).

As this example shows, accrual-basis accounting provides a more accurate picture of a company's profitability. It matches earned revenues with the expenses incurred to generate those revenues. This helps investors, creditors, and others to better assess the operating results of a company and make more informed judgments concerning its profitability and earnings potential. Accrual-basis accounting is required by generally accepted accounting principles (GAAP).

to summarize

Users of accounting information need timely, periodic financial reports to make decisions. The revenue recognition and matching principles provide guidelines for assigning the appropriate amounts of revenues and expenses to each period under accrual accounting. Accrual-basis accounting provides a better measure of net income than does cash-basis accounting; it is therefore required by GAAP in reporting the results of company operations.

2

Explain the need for adjusting entries and make adjusting entries for unrecorded receivables, unrecorded liabilities, prepaid expenses, and unearned revenues.

ADJUSTING ENTRIES

adjusting entries Entries required at the end of each accounting period to recognize, on an accrual basis, revenues and expenses for the period and to report proper amounts for asset, liability, and owners' equity accounts.

As discussed in Chapter 3, transactions generally are recorded in a journal in chronological order and then posted to the ledger accounts. The entries are based on the best information available at the time. Although the majority of accounts are up-to-date at the end of an accounting period and their balances can be included in the financial statements, some accounts require adjustment to reflect current circumstances. In general, these accounts are not updated throughout the period because it is impractical or inconvenient to make such entries on a daily or weekly basis. At the end of each accounting period, in order to report all asset, liability, and owners' equity amounts properly and to recognize all revenues and expenses for the period on an accrual basis, accountants are required to make any necessary adjustments prior to preparing the financial statements. The entries that reflect these adjustments are called **adjusting entries**.

One difficulty with adjusting entries is that the need for an adjustment is not signaled by a specific event such as the receipt of a bill or the receipt of cash from a customer. Rather, adjusting entries are recorded on the basis of an analysis of the circumstances at the close of each accounting period. This analysis involves just two steps:

1. Determine whether the amounts recorded for all assets and liabilities are correct. If not, debit or credit the appropriate asset or liability account. In short, fix the balance sheet.
2. Determine what revenue or expense adjustments are required as a result of the changes in recorded amounts of assets and liabilities indicated in step 1. Debit or credit the appropriate revenue or expense account. In short, fix the income statement.

It should be noted that these two steps are interrelated and may be reversed. That is, revenue and expense adjustments may be considered first to fix the income statement, indicating which asset and liability accounts need adjustment to fix the balance sheet. As you will see, each adjusting entry involves at least one income statement account and one balance sheet account. T-accounts are helpful in analyzing adjusting entries and will be used in the illustrations that follow.

The areas most commonly requiring analysis to see whether adjusting entries are needed are:

1. Unrecorded receivables
2. Unrecorded liabilities
3. Prepaid expenses
4. Unearned revenues

As we illustrate and discuss adjusting entries, remember that the basic purpose of adjustments is to make account balances current in order to report all asset, liability, and owners' equity amounts properly and to recognize all revenues and expenses for the period on an accrual basis. This is done so that the income statement and the balance sheet will reflect the proper operating results and financial position, respectively, at the end of the accounting period.

Unrecorded Receivables

In accordance with the revenue recognition principle of accrual accounting, revenues should be recorded when earned, regardless of when the cash is received. If revenue is earned but not yet collected in cash, a receivable exists. To ensure that all receivables are properly reported on the balance sheet in the correct amounts, an analysis should be made at the end of each accounting period to see whether there are any revenues that have been earned but have not yet been collected or recorded. These **unrecorded receivables** are earned and represent amounts that are receivable in the future; therefore, they should be recognized as assets.

unrecorded receivables Revenues earned during a period that have not been recorded by the end of that period.

To illustrate, we will pick up with the landscaping business we started in Chapter 3. Recall that we mow lawns, pull weeds, plant shrubs, and perform other related services. We are able to provide these services year round because we live in a region with a very mild climate. Our company reports on a calendar-year basis and has determined the following on December 31, 2003:

> On November 1, we entered into a year-long contract with an apartment complex to provide general landscaping services each week and bill the customer every three months. The terms of the contract state that we will earn $400 per month. As of December 31, Lawn Care Revenue of $800 ($400 for November and $400 for December) has not been recorded and will not be received until the end of January 2004. No entry has been made with regard to the contract.

As of year-end, no asset has been recorded, but an $800 receivable exists ($400 × 2), because two months' worth of revenue has been earned. To record this receivable, we must debit (increase) the asset Accounts Receivable for $800. With the debit, we have accomplished step 1 by fixing the balance sheet with regard to this transaction. Step 2 requires that we use the other half of the adjusting entry, the credit of $800, to fix the income statement. We know that the credit must be to a revenue or an expense account, and the nature of the transaction suggests that we should credit Lawn Care Revenue for $800. The adjusting entry is:

Dec. 31	Accounts Receivable	800	
	Lawn Care Revenue		800
	To record earned revenue not yet received.		

Adjusting entries are recorded in the general journal and are posted to the accounts in the general ledger in the same manner as other journal entries. Again note that each adjusting entry must involve at least one balance sheet account and at least one income statement account.

After this adjusting entry has been journalized and posted, the receivable will appear as an asset on the balance sheet, and the lawn care revenue is reported on the income statement. Through the adjusting entry, the asset (receivable) accounts are properly stated and revenues are appropriately reported.

Unrecorded Liabilities

unrecorded liabilities Expenses incurred during a period that have not been recorded by the end of that period.

Just as assets are created from revenues being earned before they are collected or recorded, liabilities can be created by expenses being incurred prior to being paid or recorded. These expenses, along with their corresponding liabilities, should be recorded when incurred, no matter when they are paid. Thus, adjusting entries are required at the end of an accounting period to recognize any **unrecorded liabilities** in the proper period and to record the corresponding expenses. As the expense is recorded (increased by a debit), the offsetting liability is also recorded (increased by a credit), showing the entity's obligation to pay for the expense. If such adjustments are not made, the net income measurement for the period will not reflect all appropriate expenses and the corresponding liabilities will be understated on the balance sheet.

To illustrate, we will assume that on December 31, 2003, our landscaping company has determined the following:

fyi

Most companies don't have to be reminded to search out unrecorded assets and revenues and recognize them. On the other hand, unrecorded liabilities and expenses are things companies would rather forget. Auditors must take care to ensure that all unrecorded liabilities and expenses are properly reported.

1. Your brother has worked for the company since its inception. He is paid every two weeks. The next payday is on Friday, January 5, 2004. On that day, your brother will be paid $700, the amount he earns every two weeks. Since December 31 falls halfway through the pay period, one-half of his wages should be allocated to 2003.
2. Recall from Chapter 3 that one of our options for financing our company was to borrow money from a bank. We borrowed $2,000 with the promise that on the first of every month we would make a $178 payment—a portion of that payment being attributed to interest[1] and a portion to principal. Our next payment is due on January 1, 2004, but the interest expense associated with that payment should be attributed to the period in which the money was actually used—December 2003. Assume that interest of $20 must be recognized on December 31, 2003.

To represent its current financial position and earnings, our landscaping company must record the impact of these events in the accounts, even though cash transactions have not yet occurred. The wages will not be paid until 2004. Under accrual-basis accounting, however, these costs are expenses of 2003 and should be recognized on this year's income statement, with the corresponding liability shown on the balance sheet as of the end of the year. To fix the balance sheet, Wages Payable must be credited (increased) for $350; recognition of this liability ensures that the balance sheet properly reports this liability, which was created during 2003 and exists as of the end of the year. The debit of this adjusting entry is to Wages Expense, resulting in the proper inclusion of this expense in the 2003 income statement. The adjusting journal entry is as follows:

Dec. 31	Wages Expense	350	
	Wages Payable		350
	To record obligation for wages.		

The liability for the interest for the month of December is recorded by a credit (increase) to Interest Payable; this fixes the balance sheet. The debit of the adjusting entry is to Interest

1 As noted in Chapter 3, *interest* is the cost of using money. The amount borrowed or lent is the *principal*. The *interest rate* is an annual rate stated as a percentage. The *period of time* involved may be stated in terms of a year. For example, if interest is to be paid for 3 months, time is 3/12, or 1/4 of a year. If interest is to be paid for 90 days, time is 90/365 of a year. Thus, the formula for computing interest is Interest = Principal × Interest Rate × Time (fraction of a year).

> **caution**
>
> A liability is not recorded for the total amount of interest that will have to be paid over the entire life of the loan. If we repay the loan on December 31, the future interest will not have to be paid, but the interest for the month of December that has passed will still be due.

Expense, which properly includes this expense on the 2003 income statement. The adjusting entry is:

Dec. 31	Interest Expense.	20	
	Interest Payable.		20
	To record interest incurred.		

The wages expense and interest expense would be shown on the income statement for the year ended December 31, and the liabilities (wages payable and interest payable) would be shown on the balance sheet as of December 31. Because of the adjusting entries, both the income statement and the balance sheet will more accurately reflect the financial situation of our landscaping company.

Prepaid Expenses

prepaid expenses Payments made in advance for items normally charged to expense.

Payments that a company makes in advance for items normally charged to expense are known as **prepaid expenses**. An example would be the payment of an insurance premium for three years. Theoretically, every resource acquisition is an asset, at least temporarily. Thus, the entry to record an advance payment should be a debit to an asset account (Prepaid Expenses) and a credit to Cash, showing the exchange of cash for another asset.

> **caution**
>
> Prepaid Expenses is a tricky name for an asset. Assets are reported in the balance sheet. Don't make the mistake of including Prepaid Expenses with the expenses on the income statement.

An expense is the using up of an asset. For example, when supplies are purchased, they are recorded as assets; when they are used, their cost is transferred to an expense account. The purpose of making adjusting entries for prepaid expenses is to show the complete or partial consumption of an asset. If the original entry is to an asset account, the adjusting entry reduces the asset to an amount that reflects its remaining future benefit and at the same time recognizes the actual expense incurred for the period.

For the unrecorded assets and liabilities discussed earlier, there was no original entry; the adjusting entry was the first time these items were recorded in the accounting records. For prepaid expenses, this is not the case. Because cash has already been paid (in the case of prepaid expenses), an original entry has been made to record the cash transaction. Therefore, the amount of the adjusting entry is the difference between what the updated balance should be and the amount of the original entry already recorded.

To illustrate adjustments for Prepaid Expenses, we will assume the following about our landscaping company:

1. On November 1, 2003, we purchased a six-month insurance policy on our old truck, paying a $600 premium.
2. On December 15, 2003, we purchased several months' worth of supplies (fertilizer, weed killer, etc.) at a total cost of $350. At year-end, $225 worth of supplies were still on hand.

For the prepaid insurance, we record the payment of $600 on November 1 as follows:

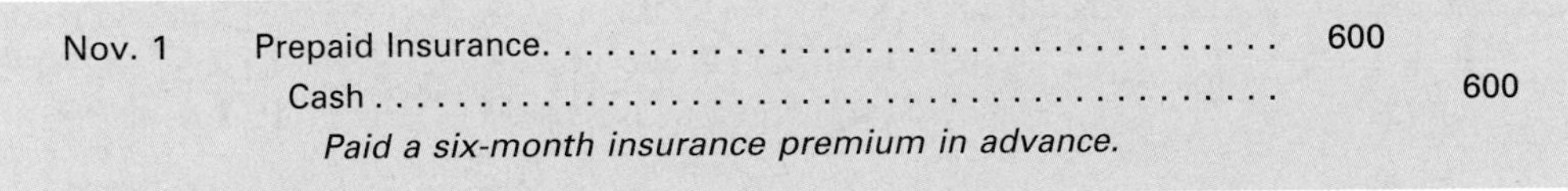

Nov. 1	Prepaid Insurance.	600	
	Cash		600
	Paid a six-month insurance premium in advance.		

This entry shows that one asset (Cash) has been exchanged for another asset (Prepaid Insurance). Over the next six months we will use the auto insurance and the asset, Prepaid Insurance, will slowly be used up. As the asset is used, its cost is recorded as an expense.

At year-end, only those assets that still offer future benefits to the company should be reported on the balance sheet. Thus, an adjustment is required to reduce the prepaid insurance account to reflect the fact that only four months of prepaid insurance remain. See the following time line.

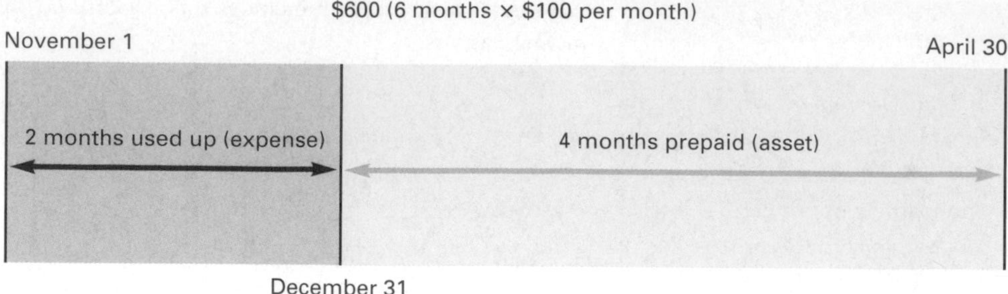

The adjusting journal entry to bring the original amounts to their updated balances at year-end is:

Dec. 31	Insurance Expense	200	
	Prepaid Insurance		200
	To record insurance expense for two months: 2 × $100 = $200.		

When the adjusting entry is journalized and posted, the proper amount of insurance expense ($200) will be shown as an expense on the income statement and the proper amount of prepaid insurance ($400) will be carried forward to the next period as an asset on the balance sheet. This is illustrated in the following T-accounts:

	Prepaid Insurance (Dr.)	Prepaid Insurance (Cr.)	Cash (Dr.)	Cash (Cr.)	Insurance Expense (Dr.)	Insurance Expense (Cr.)
Original entry (11/1/03)	600			600		
Adjusting entry (12/31/03)		200			200	
Updated balances (12/31/03)	400				200	
	To balance sheet				To income statement	

caution

The terms *supplies* and *inventory* are often confused. Supplies include such items as paper, pencils, and soap that might be used in an office or a warehouse. Inventory includes only those items held for resale to customers or for direct use in the manufacture of products.

When supplies are consumed in the normal course of business, the asset account (Supplies on Hand) must be adjusted and the used up portion charged as an operating expense (Supplies Expense) on the income statement. Thus, the adjustment for supplies is handled the same way as for any other prepaid asset.

We initially recorded $350 of supplies as an asset:

Dec. 15	Supplies on Hand	350	
	Cash		350
	Purchased supplies.		

At year-end, an adjustment must be made to recognize that only $225 worth of supplies remains. This also implies that $125 ($350 − $225) of the supplies have been used and should be charged to expense. The entries are summarized in the following T-accounts:

	Supplies on Hand (Dr.)	Supplies on Hand (Cr.)	Cash (Dr.)	Cash (Cr.)	Supplies Expense (Dr.)	Supplies Expense (Cr.)
Original entry (12/15/03)	350			350		
Adjusting entry (12/31/03)		125			125	
Updated balances (12/31/03)	225				125	
	To balance sheet				To income statement	

The adjusting entry is:

Dec. 31	Supplies Expense	125	
	Supplies on Hand		125
	To record the use of supplies.		

Unearned Revenues

unearned revenues Cash amounts received before they have been earned.

Amounts received before the actual earning of revenues are known as **unearned revenues**. They arise when customers pay in advance of the receipt of goods or services. Because the company has received cash but has not yet given the customer the purchased goods or services, the unearned revenues are in fact liabilities. That is, the company must provide something in return for the amounts received. For example, a building contractor may require a deposit before proceeding on construction of a house. Upon receipt of the deposit, the contractor has unearned revenue, a liability. The contractor must construct the house to earn the revenue. If the house is not built, the contractor will be obligated to repay the deposit.

caution

Unearned Revenue is a tricky name for a liability. Liabilities are reported in the balance sheet. Don't make the mistake of including Unearned Revenue with the revenues on the income statement.

To illustrate the adjustments for unearned revenues, we will assume the following about our landscaping company:

> On December 1, a client pays you $225 for three months of landscaping services to be provided for the period beginning December 1, 2003, and ending February 29, 2004. This client is going to Hawaii for an extended vacation and would like you to take care of the grounds in her absence.

Typically, the original entry to record unearned revenue involves a debit to Cash and a credit to a liability account. In our example of landscaping revenue received three months in advance, the liability account would be Unearned Revenue, as shown on the next page.

The deposit received by a building contractor prior to the construction of a house is classified as unearned revenue.

Dec. 1	Cash.	225	
	Unearned Revenue		225
	Received three months' revenue in advance:		
	$75 × 3 = $225.		

The credit to the liability account, Unearned Revenue, is logically correct; until we provide the landscaping service, the revenue received in advance is unearned and is thus an obligation (liability).

The next step is to compute the updated balances at year-end. As illustrated with the following time line, on December 31, two months' services (2 × $75 = $150) are still unearned and should be shown as a liability, Unearned Revenue, on the balance sheet. At the same time, $75, or one month's services, has been earned (1 × $75 = $75) and should be reported as Landscaping Revenue on the income statement.

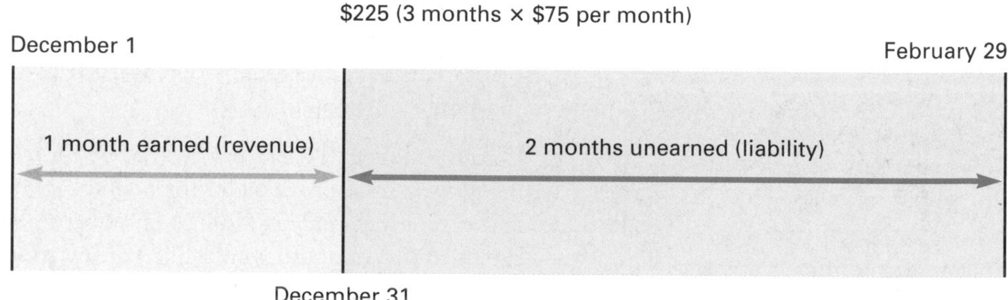

Step 1 of the adjusting entry is to fix the balance sheet. The reported liability of $225 is too much since some of the unearned revenue has been earned. The remaining obligation is $150 (2 × $75), so the liability must be reduced (debited) by $75 ($225 − $150). The second half of the adjusting entry is used to correct the income statement. The $75 credit is made to Landscaping Revenue, reflecting the fact that one month's revenue has now been earned. The appropriate adjusting entry is:

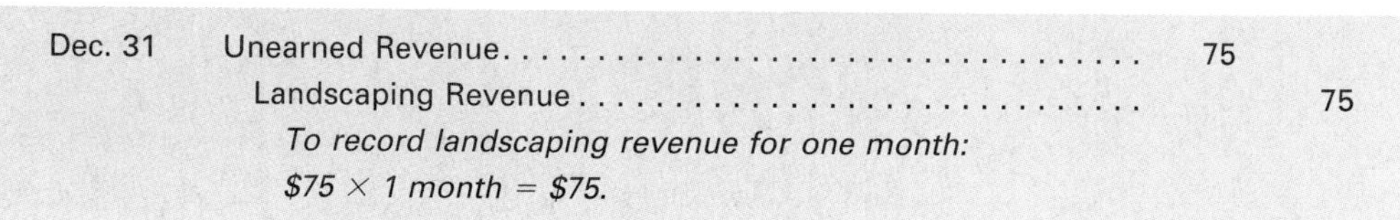

Dec. 31	Unearned Revenue.	75	
	Landscaping Revenue		75
	To record landscaping revenue for one month:		
	$75 × 1 month = $75.		

These results are illustrated in the following T-accounts:

	Unearned Revenue		Cash		Landscaping Revenue	
Original entry (12/1/03)		225	225			
Adjusting entry (12/31/03)	75					75
Updated balances (12/31/03)		150				75
		To balance sheet				To income statement

After the adjusting entry has been made on December 31, our accounts show $225 of cash received. Of this amount, $75 has been earned (1 month's service × $75) and would be reported as Landscaping Revenue on the income statement; $150 will not be earned until the next reporting period and would be shown as a liability on the balance sheet.

We should emphasize two characteristics of adjusting entries. First, adjusting entries made at the end of an accounting period *do not involve cash.* Cash has either changed hands prior to the end of the period (as is the case with prepaid expenses or unearned revenues), or cash will

Airlines have a large amount of unearned revenue because customers pay for their tickets before the airlines provide the travel service. Visit the Web site of UNITED AIRLINES: http://www.ual.com

What title is given to Unearned Revenue for an airline? What liability was reported for Unearned Revenue in the most recent annual report?

change hands in a future period (as is the case with many unrecorded receivables and unrecorded liabilities). It is precisely because cash is *not* changing hands on the last day of the accounting period that most adjusting entries must be made.

Second, each adjusting entry involves a balance sheet account and an income statement account. In each case requiring adjustment, we are either generating an asset, using up an asset, recording an incurred but unrecorded expense, or recording revenue that has yet to be earned. Knowing that each adjusting entry has at least one balance sheet and one income statement account makes the adjustment process a little easier. Once you have determined that an adjusting entry involves a certain balance sheet account, you can then focus on identifying the corresponding income statement account that requires adjustment.

The 1999 financial statements for GENERAL MOTORS offer several illustrations of the potential impact of failing to make adjusting entries. GM reports that, as of December 31, 1999, it had unearned revenue totaling $9.504 billion. If GM had failed to make the adjustment necessary to record this unearned revenue, total revenue for 1999 would have been overstated by $9.504 billion, or 5.4%. In addition, GM reported that its total warranty liability as of December 31, 1999, was $15.284 billion. This warranty liability falls in the category of unrecorded liabilities that are not reported in the financial statements unless an appropriate adjusting entry is made. Finally, GM also reported a $35.521 billion asset related to future tax deductions; this asset would remain unrecorded unless a special adjusting entry were made at the end of the year to reflect the future tax benefits of events that had occurred in 1999 and preceding years.

to summarize

To present financial statements that accurately report the financial position and the results of operations on an accrual basis for specific periods of time, adjusting entries must be made. The four main categories of adjustments are unrecorded receivables, unrecorded liabilities, prepaid expenses, and unearned revenues. In analyzing accounts at the end of an accounting cycle, adjusting entries are made in order to recognize all earned revenues and all incurred expenses and to report the proper balances in the asset, liability, and owners' equity accounts. This requires a two-step analysis: (1) determine what adjustments are necessary to ensure that all asset and liability amounts have been properly recorded, and (2) determine which revenues or expenses must be adjusted to correspond with the changes in assets and liabilities recorded in step 1. With unrecorded receivables and unrecorded liabilities, there is no original entry. With prepaid expenses, the original entry includes a credit to Cash and a debit to an asset account. With unearned revenues, the original entry includes a debit to Cash and a credit to a liability account.

3

Explain the preparation of the financial statements, the explanatory notes, and the audit report.

PREPARING FINANCIAL STATEMENTS

Once all transactions have been analyzed, journalized, and posted and all adjusting entries have been made, the accounts can be summarized and presented in the form of financial statements. Financial statements can be prepared directly from the data in the adjusted ledger accounts. The data must only be organized into appropriate sections and categories so as to present them as simply and clearly as possible. Once the financial statements are prepared, explanatory notes are written. These notes clarify the methods and assumptions used in preparing the statements. In addition, the auditor must review the financial statements to make sure they are accurate, reasonable, and in accordance with generally accepted accounting principles. Finally, the financial statements are distributed to external users who analyze them in order to learn more about the financial condition of the company.

Financial Statement Preparation

To illustrate the preparation of financial statements from adjusted ledger accounts, a simplified adjusted trial balance for **GENERAL MOTORS** as of December 31, 1999, is provided in Exhibit 4-4.

From these data, an income statement and a balance sheet may be prepared for General Motors, as shown in Exhibits 4-5 and 4-6 on pages 145 and 146.

The ending retained earnings balance for General Motors for 1999 ($6,961), as reported on the balance sheet, is computed as follows:

Beginning retained earnings balance (from the adjusted trial balance)	$2,326
Add: Net income for the period (from the income statement)	6,002
Subtract: Dividends for the period (from the adjusted trial balance)	(1,367)
Ending retained earnings balance	$6,961

exhibit 4-4 Simplified Adjusted Trial Balance

General Motors Corporation
Simplified Adjusted Trial Balance
December 31, 1999
(in millions)

	Debits	Credits
Cash	$ 10,442	
Investments	12,519	
Receivables	86,721	
Inventories	10,638	
Property and Equipment	38,523	
Intangible Assets	8,527	
Deferred Taxes	15,277	
Other Assets	55,676	
Investment in Leases	36,407	
Accounts Payable		$ 21,516
Accrued Expenses		32,854
Current Debt		70,934
Long-Term Debt		62,745
Pensions and Other Retirement Benefits		37,505
Other Liabilities		28,532
Capital Stock and Other		13,683
Retained Earnings		2,326
Dividends	1,367	
Revenue from Sales		152,635
Financing Revenues		14,734
Other Income		9,189
Cost of Sales	126,809	
Selling, General and Administrative Expenses	18,845	
Depreciation and Amortization	12,318	
Interest Expense	7,750	
Income Tax Expense	3,118	
Other Expenses	1,716	
Totals	$446,653	$446,653

exhibit 4-5 Income Statement

General Motors Corporation
Statement of Income
For the Year Ended December 31, 1999
(in millions)

Revenue from sales		$152,635
Financing revenues		14,734
Total revenues		$167,369
Cost of sales	$126,809	
Selling, general and administrative expenses	18,845	
Depreciation and amortization	12,318	
Total operating expenses		157,972
Operating income		$ 9,397
Other income	$ 9,189	
Interest expense	(7,750)	
Income tax expense	(3,118)	
Other expenses	(1,716)	
Total other revenues and expenses		(3,395)
Net income		$ 6,002

This follows the computation of retained earnings discussed in Chapter 2.

A statement of cash flows is not shown here. To prepare a statement of cash flows, we need more detailed information about the nature of the cash receipts and cash disbursements during the year. The preparation of a statement of cash flows will be illustrated in Chapter 13.

The Notes

As discussed in Chapter 2, the notes to the financial statements tell about the assumptions and methods used in preparing the financial statements and also give more detail about specific items. A sample of the kind of information that appears in the notes for General Motors' financial statements is illustrated in Exhibit 4-7 on page 147. The first two notes, on revenue recognition and credit losses, illustrate how financial statement notes can summarize the accounting policies and assumptions that underlie the financial statements. The third note, on the debt associated with GM's financing subsidiary (GMAC), provides detailed information about a summary number that was reported in the financial statements. The fourth note, on GM's labor force, provides information that is deemed to be important to financial statement users, such as future labor costs, but that does not directly affect any of the reported historical financial statement numbers.

The financial statement notes serve to augment the summarized, numerical information contained in the financial statements. To highlight the importance of the notes, many financial statements have the following message printed at the bottom: "The notes are an integral part of these financial statements."

The Audit

As mentioned in Chapter 2, an independent audit, by CPAs from outside the company, is often conducted to ensure that the financial statements have been prepared in conformity with generally accepted accounting principles. With respect to the financial statements of General Motors, the audit procedures conducted by the external auditor, DELOITTE & TOUCHE, would probably include the following checks.

REVIEW OF ADJUSTMENTS As you learned in the first part of this chapter, adjusting entries usually require more analysis, and more judgment, than do the regular journal entries recorded throughout the year. As part of the audit, the auditor will review these adjusting en-

exhibit 4-6 Balance Sheet

General Motors Corporation
Balance Sheet
December 31, 1999
(in millions)

Assets		
Current assets:		
Cash	$10,442	
Investments	12,519	
Receivables	86,721	
Inventories	10,638	
Total current assets		$120,320
Long-term assets:		
Property and equipment	$38,523	
Intangible assets	8,527	
Deferred taxes	15,277	
Other assets	55,676	
Investment in leases	36,407	
Total long-term assets		154,410
Total assets		$274,730
Liabilities and Owners' Equity		
Current liabilities:		
Accounts payable	$21,516	
Accrued expenses	32,854	
Current debt	70,934	
Total current liabilities		$125,304
Long-term debt		62,745
Pensions and other retirement benefits		37,505
Other liabilities		28,532
Total liabilities		$254,086
Owners' equity		
Capital stock and other	$13,683	
Retained earnings	6,961	
Total owners' equity		20,644
Total liabilities and owners' equity		$274,730

Note: This balance sheet is not an exact replica of General Motors' actual balance sheet due to simplifying modifications for this exhibit.

tries. Auditors pay particular attention to the adjustments involving unrecorded expenses. As mentioned in the text, companies don't like making these adjusting entries, because they increase reported liabilities and reduce reported net income. Accordingly, the auditor should review the business events of the year to make sure that no expenses have been left unrecorded.

SAMPLE OF SELECTED ACCOUNTS For a number of accounts, the auditor undertakes a sampling process to see whether the items reported in the balance sheet actually exist. For example, General Motors reports an ending cash and equivalents balance of $10,442,000,000. The auditor will ask to see bank statements and will probably call the bank(s) to verify the existence of the cash. For inventory, the auditor will ask to physically see the inventory and will conduct a spot check to see whether the company inventory records match what is actually in the warehouse.

REVIEW OF ACCOUNTING SYSTEMS The auditor will also evaluate General Motors' accounting systems. If a company has a good accounting system, with all transactions being recorded

exhibit 4-7 General Motors: Notes to the Financial Statements

General Motors Corporation
Notes to the Financial Statements (partial list)
For the Year Ended December 31, 1999

Revenue Recognition: Sales are generally recorded when products are shipped . . . to independent dealers.

Allowance for Credit Losses: Receivables are charged off [i.e., removed from the books] as soon as it is determined that the collateral cannot be repossessed, generally not more than 150 days after default.

Debt: Debt was as follows (in millions):

	Weighted-Average Interest Rate	December 31, 1999	December 31, 1998
Payable within one year:			
Current portion of debt	6.6%	$ 14,996	$ 12,701
Commercial paper	5.8%	33,229	34,487
All other	4.6%	18,727	15,208
Payable beyond one year:			
2000	—	—	13,154
2001	6.0%	16,854	10,322
2002	5.7%	15,100	8,561
2003	6.1%	8,786	7,919
2004	6.6%	5,550	1,208
2005 and after	7.4%	9,662	4,864
Unamortized discount		(622)	(671)
Total debt		$122,282	$107,753

Labor Force: The 1999 United Auto Workers (UAW) labor contract was ratified on October 13, 1999, covering a four-year term from 1999–2003. The contract included an annual salary increase of 3% per year, an up-front signing bonus of $1,350 per UAW employee. . . . The 1999 contract includes job security and sourcing provisions containing an employment floor set at 95% of 1996 employment levels in the event of net outsourcing.

in an efficient, orderly way, then the auditor has greater reason to be confident that the financial statements are reliable. On the other hand, if the company's accounting system is haphazard, with many missing documents and unexplained discrepancies, then the auditor must do more detailed work to verify the financial statements.

If the auditor finds that the financial statements have been prepared in conformance with generally accepted accounting principles, then the auditor provides a report to that effect. This report is attached and distributed as part of the financial statements. The audit report is discussed in more detail in Chapter 5.

to summarize

The adjusted trial balance provides the raw material for the preparation of the balance sheet and the income statement. The notes to the financial statements provide further information about the methods and assumptions used in preparing the financial statements as well as further detail about certain financial statement items. The audit is conducted by a CPA from outside the company who reviews the adjusting entries, performs tests to check the balances of selected accounts, and reviews the condition of the accounting systems.

4

Perform a systematic analysis of financial statements.

ANALYZING FINANCIAL STATEMENTS

Financial statements are prepared in order to be used. Once the balance sheet, income statement, statement of cash flows, notes, and audit report of a company are completed, the whole package is distributed to bankers, suppliers, and investors to be used in evaluating the company's financial health. Financial statement analysis was introduced in Chapter 2 with illustrations of the computation and interpretation of selected financial ratios. That discussion is extended here with the introduction of two general tools of financial statement analysis: the DuPont framework and common-size financial statements.

DuPont Framework

return on equity A measure of the amount of profit earned per dollar of investment, computed by dividing net income by equity.

As discussed in Chapter 2, **return on equity** (Net Income/Equity) is the single measure that summarizes the financial health of a company. Return on equity can be interpreted as the number of cents of net income an investor earns in one year by investing one dollar in the company. Return on equity (ROE) for **GENERAL MOTORS** for the year 1999 is computed below ($ in millions):

Net Income	$6,002
Equity	$20,644
Return on Equity	29.1%

DuPont framework A systematic approach for breaking down return on equity into three ratios: profit margin, asset turnover, and assets-to-equity ratio.

The **DuPont framework** (named after a system of ratio analysis developed internally at DuPont in the early part of the twentieth century) provides a systematic approach to identifying general factors contributing to return on equity. The insight behind the DuPont framework is that ROE can be decomposed into three components, as shown below.

$$\text{Return on Equity} = \text{Profitability} \times \text{Efficiency} \times \text{Leverage}$$

$$= \text{Profit Margin} \times \text{Asset Turnover} \times \text{Assets-to-Equity Ratio}$$

$$\frac{\text{Net Income}}{\text{Equity}} = \frac{\text{Net Income}}{\text{Revenue}} \times \frac{\text{Revenue}}{\text{Assets}} \times \frac{\text{Assets}}{\text{Equity}}$$

For each of the three ROE components—profitability, efficiency, and leverage—there is a correlating ratio that summarizes a company's performance in that area. These ratios are as follows:

profit margin A measure of the number of pennies in profit generated from each dollar of revenue; calculated by dividing net income by revenue.

asset turnover A measure of company efficiency, computed by dividing revenue by total assets.

assets-to-equity ratio A measure of the number of dollars of assets a company is able to acquire using each dollar of equity; calculated by dividing assets by equity.

- **Profit margin** is computed as (Net Income/Revenue) and is interpreted as the number of pennies in profit generated from each dollar of revenue.
- **Asset turnover** is computed as (Revenue/Assets) and is interpreted as the number of dollars in revenue generated by each dollar of assets.
- **Assets-to-equity ratio** is computed as (Assets/Equity) and is interpreted as the number of dollars of assets a company is able to acquire using each dollar invested by stockholders.

The DuPont analysis of General Motors' ROE for 1999 is as follows:

$$\text{Return on Equity} = \frac{\text{Net Income}}{\text{Revenue}} \times \frac{\text{Revenue}}{\text{Assets}} \times \frac{\text{Assets}}{\text{Equity}}$$

$$\frac{\$6{,}002}{\$20{,}644} = \frac{\$6{,}002}{\$176{,}558} \times \frac{\$176{,}558}{\$274{,}730} \times \frac{\$274{,}730}{\$20{,}644}$$

$$29.1\% = 3.4\% \times 0.64 \times 13.31$$

These three ratio values can be interpreted as follows:

- GM earned 3.4 cents in profit for each dollar in revenue.
- GM generated $0.64 in revenue for every dollar of assets.
- For every dollar invested by GM shareholders, GM was able to acquire $13.31 in assets; additional assets were acquired with borrowed funds.

Evaluation of whether these ratio values are too high or too low involves comparing the computed values to the ratio values of other companies in the same industry as General Motors. In addition, this year's ratio values can be compared to GM's own ratio values in past years. For example, if other companies in the auto industry have profit margins of 7.0%, it appears that GM's profitability (3.4%) is lower than that of its competitors. If the asset turnover value for GM's competitors is 1.00, the 0.64 value for GM suggests that GM is less efficient at using its assets to generate sales.

STOP & THINK Is it good for a company to have a high assets-to-equity ratio?

Common-Size Financial Statements

common-size financial statements Financial statements achieved by dividing all financial statement numbers by total revenues for the year.

A quick and easy way to get more information out of the financial statements is to divide all financial statement numbers for a given year by the total revenues for the year. The resulting financial statements, called **common-size financial statements**, show all amounts for a given year as a percentage of revenues for that year. A common-size income statement for General Motors, based on the income statement in Exhibit 4-5, is shown in Exhibit 4-8.

If General Motors' overall profitability is lower than its industry competitors, the common-size income statement can be used to pinpoint exactly where the problem lies. For example, if General Motors' competitors have cost of sales that is just 65.0% of total revenue, then the 71.8% for GM suggests that this expense may be too high.

A common-size balance sheet also expresses each amount as a percentage of total revenue for the year. A common-size balance sheet for General Motors, based on the balance sheet in Exhibit 4-6, is shown in Exhibit 4-9.

The most informative section of the common-size balance sheet is the asset section, which can be used to determine how efficiently a company is using its assets. For example, assume that GM's competitors have inventory levels equal to 5.0% of total revenues. This suggests that GM is maintaining higher inventory levels (6.0% of revenues) and is thus using its inventory less efficiently.

fyi

The amount of cash held by General Motors is quite low—5.9% of revenues. For comparison, look at **MICROSOFT**'s financial statements at the end of the text and you'll see that Microsoft has a very high 1999 cash balance equal to 87.3% of total revenues.

to summarize

Financial statements are used by various interested parties to examine a company's financial health. Two general techniques for financial statement

exhibit 4-8 Common-Size Income Statement

General Motors Corporation
Common-Size Income Statement
For the Year Ended December 31, 1999
(in millions)

	Amounts		% of Revenue
Revenue from sales		$152,635	
Financing revenues		14,734	
Other income		9,189	
Total revenues		$176,558	100.0%
Cost of sales	$126,809		71.8%
Selling, general and administrative expenses	18,845		10.7%
Depreciation and amortization	12,318		7.0%
Interest expense	7,750		4.4%
Income tax expense	3,118		1.8%
Other expenses	1,716	170,556	1.0%
Net income		$ 6,002	3.4%

exhibit 4-9 Common-Size Balance Sheet

General Motors Corporation
Common-Size Balance Sheet
December 31, 1999
(in millions)

	Amounts	% of Revenue
Assets		
Cash	$ 10,442	5.9%
Investments	12,519	7.1%
Receivables	86,721	49.1%
Inventories	10,638	6.0%
Property and equipment	38,523	21.8%
Intangible assets	8,527	4.8%
Deferred taxes	15,277	8.7%
Other assets	55,676	31.5%
Investment in leases	36,407	20.6%
Total assets	$274,730	155.6%*
Liabilities and Owners' Equity		
Accounts payable	$ 21,516	12.2%
Accrued expenses	32,854	18.6%
Current debt	70,934	40.2%
Long-term debt	62,745	35.5%
Pensions and other retirement benefits	37,505	21.2%
Other liabilities	28,532	16.2%
Capital stock and other	13,683	7.7%
Retained earnings	6,961	3.9%
Total liabilities and equities	$274,730	155.6%*

*Difference due to rounding.

business environment essay

Market Efficiency: Can Financial Statement Analysis Help You Win in the Stock Market? An efficient market is one in which information is reflected rapidly in prices. For example, if the real estate market in a city is efficient, then news of an impending layoff at a major employer in the city should quickly result in lower housing prices because of an anticipated decrease in demand. The major stock exchanges in the United States are often considered to be efficient markets in the sense that information about specific companies or about the economy in general is reflected almost immediately in stock prices. One implication of market efficiency is that, since current stock prices reflect all available information, future movements in stock prices should be unpredictable.

It seems clear that stock markets in the United States are efficient in a general sense, but accumulated evidence suggests the existence of a number of puzzling "anomalies" in the form of predictable patterns of stock returns. For example, prices tend to continue to drift upward for weeks or months after favorable earnings news is released. In addition, prices continue to climb for at least a year after a stock split is announced.

From an accounting standpoint, market efficiency relates to the usefulness of so-called fundamental analysis. Fundamental analysis is the practice of using financial data to calculate the underlying value of a firm and using this underlying value to identify over-

analysis are the DuPont framework and common-size financial statements. The DuPont framework is based on the insight that return on equity can be separated into three components, each with a correlating ratio: profitability (profit margin), efficiency (asset turnover), and leverage (assets-to-equity). Preparing common-size financial statements involves dividing all financial statement numbers by total revenue for the year.

5
Complete the closing process in the accounting cycle.

CLOSING THE BOOKS

We have almost reached the end of the accounting cycle. Thus far, the accounting cycle has included analyzing documents, journalizing transactions, posting to the ledger accounts, determining account balances, preparing a trial balance, making adjusting entries, and preparing the financial statements. Just two additional steps are needed: (1) journalizing and posting closing entries and (2) preparing a post-closing trial balance.

Real and Nominal Accounts

real accounts Accounts that are not closed to a zero balance at the end of each accounting period; permanent accounts appearing on the balance sheet.

nominal accounts Accounts that are closed to a zero balance at the end of each accounting period; temporary accounts generally appearing on the income statement.

To explain the closing process, we must first define two new terms. Certain accounts are referred to as **real accounts**. These accounts report the cumulative increases and decreases in certain account balances from the date the company was organized. Real accounts (assets, liabilities, and owners' equity) appear on the balance sheet and are permanent; they are not closed to a zero balance at the end of each accounting period. Balances existing in real accounts at the end of a period are carried forward to the next period.

Other accounts are known as **nominal accounts**. These accounts (revenues, expenses, and dividends) are temporary; they are really just subcategories of Retained Earnings and are reduced to a zero balance through the closing process at the end of each accounting period. Thus, nominal accounts begin with a zero balance at the start of each accounting cycle. Transactions throughout the period (generally a year) are journalized and posted to the nominal accounts. These are used to accumulate and classify all revenue and expense items, and also dividends, for that

and underpriced stocks. The notion of fundamental analysis is in conflict with market efficiency, because the analysis works only if current stock prices do not fully reflect all available accounting information. For this reason, fundamental analysis has frequently been regarded with skepticism by academics. A growing body of academic research, however, suggests that accounting data may be useful in predicting future stock returns. Ou and Penman (1989) and Holthausen and Larcker (1992) were the first to demonstrate that financial ratios derived from publicly available financial statements can be used to successfully forecast stock returns for the coming year. More recently, Abarbanell and Bushee (1998) showed that, using financial ratios to predict future earnings performance, one can selectively invest in companies and earn an abnormal return of 13.2% per year. An abnormal return is the return over and above what one would earn with a diversified portfolio of stocks. So, contrary to what is expected of an efficient stock market, it looks like you *can* use publicly available accounting data to make money in the U.S. stock market.

Sources: Jane A. Ou and Stephen H. Penman, "Financial Statement Analysis and the Prediction of Stock Returns," *Journal of Accounting and Economics*, November 1989, p. 295; Robert W. Holthausen and David F. Larcker, "The Prediction of Stock Returns Using Financial Statement Information," *Journal of Accounting and Economics*, June 1992, p. 373; Jeffery S. Abarbanell and Brian J. Bushee, "Abnormal Returns to a Fundamental Analysis Strategy," *The Accounting Review*, January 1998, p. 19.

fyi

In a proprietorship or a partnership, the nominal accounts are closed to the owners' permanent capital accounts instead of to Retained Earnings.

period. At the end of the accounting period, adjustments are made, the income statement is prepared, and the balances in the temporary accounts are then closed to Retained Earnings, a permanent account. These closing entries bring the income statement accounts back to a zero balance, which makes the accounts ready for a new accounting period. In addition, the closing entries transfer the net income or loss for the accounting period to Retained Earnings and reduce Retained Earnings for any dividends. Without closing entries, revenue and expense balances would extend from period to period, making it difficult to isolate the operating results of each accounting period.

Closing Entries

The actual mechanics of the closing process are not complicated. Revenue accounts normally have credit balances and are closed by being debited; expense accounts generally have debit balances and are closed by being credited. The difference between total revenues and total expenses represents the net income (or net loss) of the entity. For a corporation, net income is credited to Retained Earnings because income increases owners' equity. A net loss would be debited to Retained Earnings because a loss decreases owners' equity.

To illustrate the closing process, we will again refer to **GENERAL MOTORS'** financial information as discussed earlier on pages 144–146. The closing journal entry is:

closing entries Entries that reduce all nominal, or temporary, accounts to a zero balance at the end of each accounting period, transferring their preclosing balances to a permanent balance sheet account.

Dec. 31	Revenue from Sales	152,635	
	Financing Revenues	14,734	
	Other Income	9,189	
	Cost of Sales		126,809
	Selling, General and Administrative Expenses		18,845
	Depreciation and Amortization		12,318
	Interest Expense		7,750
	Income Tax Expense		3,118
	Other Expenses		1,716
	Retained Earnings		6,002
	To close revenues and expenses to Retained Earnings.		

caution

Don't close real accounts! Consider the negative implications of eliminating all your asset accounts at the end of the year. Nominal accounts are closed because they are just temporary subaccounts of Retained Earnings.

Closing entries must be posted to the appropriate ledger accounts. Once posted, all nominal accounts will have a zero balance; that is, they will be "closed."

The dividends account is also a nominal (temporary) account that must be closed at the end of the accounting period. However, dividends are not expenses and will not be reported on an income statement; they are distributions to stockholders of part of a corporation's earnings. Thus, dividends reduce retained earnings. When dividends are declared by the board of directors of a corporation, the amount that will be paid is debited to Dividends and credited to a liability account, Dividends Payable, or to Cash if paid immediately. Because Dividends is a temporary account, it must be closed to Retained Earnings at the end of the accounting period. The dividends account is closed by crediting it and by debiting Retained Earnings, thereby reducing owners' equity, as illustrated below for General Motors.

Dec. 31	Retained Earnings	1,367	
	Dividends		1,367
	To close Dividends to Retained Earnings.		

post-closing trial balance A listing of all real account balances after the closing process has been completed; provides a means of testing whether total debits equal total credits for all real accounts prior to beginning a new accounting cycle.

The books are now ready for a new accounting cycle. The closing process for the revenues, expenses, and dividends of a corporation is shown schematically in Exhibit 4-10.

Preparing a Post-Closing Trial Balance

An optional last step in the accounting cycle is to balance the accounts and to prepare a **post-closing trial balance**. The accounts are to be balanced—debits and credits added and a balance

exhibit 4-10 The Closing Process

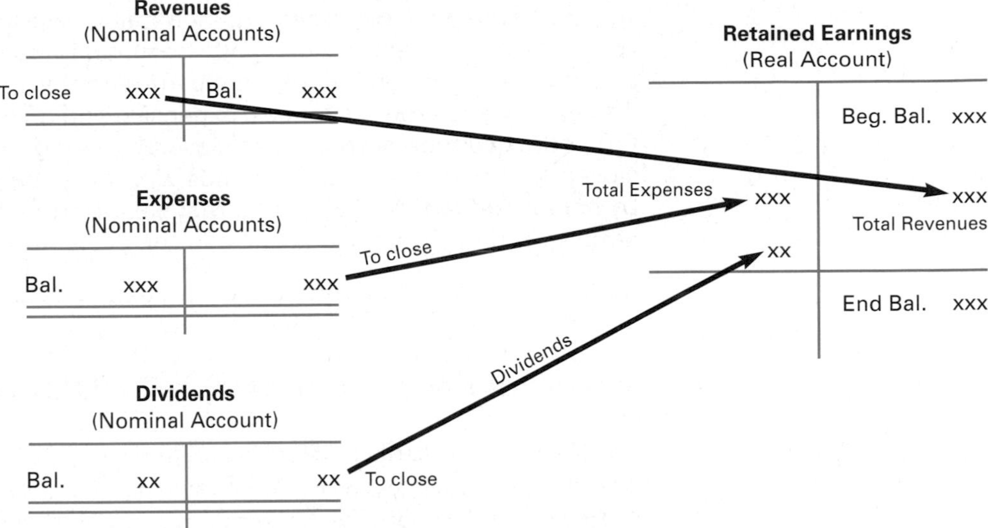

determined—only after the closing entries have been recorded and posted in the general ledger. The information for the post-closing trial balance is then taken from the ledger. The nominal accounts will not be shown since they have been closed and thus have zero balances. Only the real accounts will have current balances. This step is designed to provide some assurance that the previous steps in the cycle have been performed properly, prior to the start of a new accounting period. Exhibit 4-11 illustrates a post-closing trial balance for General Motors Corporation.

exhibit 4-11 Post-Closing Trial Balance

General Motors Corporation
Post-Closing Trial Balance
December 31, 1999
(in millions)

	Debits	Credits
Cash	$ 10,442	
Investments	12,519	
Receivables	86,721	
Inventories	10,638	
Property and Equipment	38,523	
Intangible Assets	8,527	
Deferred Taxes	15,277	
Other Assets	55,676	
Investment in Leases	36,407	
Accounts Payable		$ 21,516
Accrued Expenses		32,854
Current Debt		70,934
Long-Term Debt		62,745
Pensions and Other Retirement Benefits		37,505
Other Liabilities		28,532
Capital Stock and Other		13,683
Retained Earnings		6,961
Totals	$274,730	$274,730

to summarize

As part of the closing process, all nominal (temporary) accounts are closed to a zero balance. All real (permanent) accounts (balance sheet accounts for assets, liabilities, and owners' equity) are carried forward to the new reporting period. All nominal accounts (revenues, expenses, and dividends) are closed to Retained Earnings. Revenue accounts are closed by being debited; expense accounts are closed by being credited. Dividends also must be closed to Retained Earnings by being credited. A post-closing trial balance may be prepared to provide some assurance that the previous steps in the cycle have been performed properly.

6

Understand how all the steps in the accounting cycle fit together.

A SUMMARY OF THE ACCOUNTING CYCLE

We have now completed our discussion of the steps in the accounting cycle. By way of review, Exhibit 4-12 lists the sequence of the accounting cycle (presented earlier in Chapter 3). Many of the steps, such as analyzing transactions, occur continuously. Other steps, such as preparing the financial statements, generally occur only once during the cycle.

The financial statements that result from the accounting cycle provide useful information to investors, creditors, and other external users. These statements are included in the annual re-

exhibit 4-12 Sequence of the Accounting Cycle

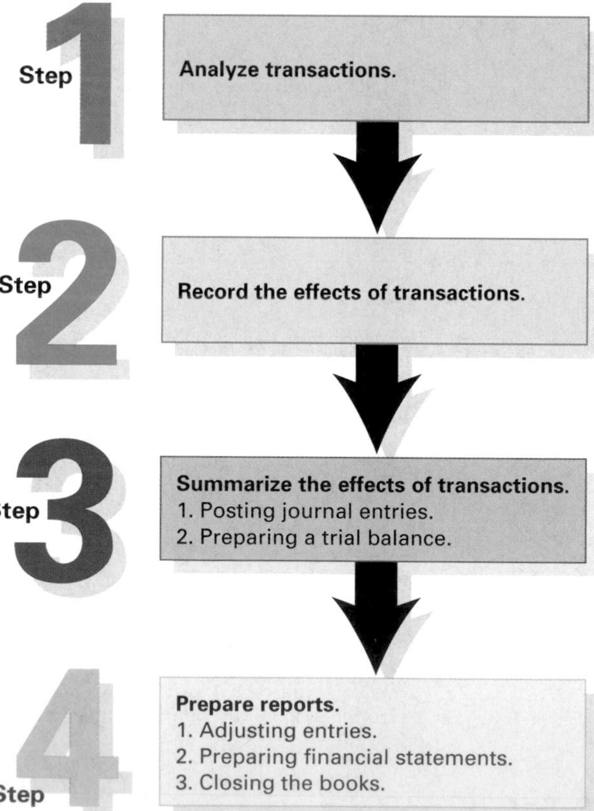

expanded material

ports provided to stockholders. As illustrated earlier in the chapter, once the financial statements are made available to users, they can then be analyzed and compared to the financial statements of similar firms to detect strengths and weaknesses.

expanded material

Earlier in the chapter, the adjusting entries for prepaid expenses were made assuming that the prepayments were initially recorded as assets. Alternatively, the prepayments can be initially recorded as expenses; the correct amounts of assets and expenses can still be achieved through an appropriate year-end adjusting entry. Similarly, cash receipts in advance are sometimes initially recorded as revenues instead of as liabilities. Again, although not conceptually correct, it is done in the normal course of bookkeeping; any necessary adjustments can be made at year-end.

7
Make adjusting entries for prepaid expenses and unearned revenues when the original cash amounts are recorded as expenses and revenues.

ADJUSTING ENTRIES: ORIGINAL ENTRIES TO EXPENSE OR REVENUE

To illustrate the necessary adjusting process when expense prepayments are debited to an expense account, we will use the prepaid insurance example for the landscaping company that was illustrated earlier:

> On November 1, 2003, the landscaping company purchased a six-month insurance policy on its old truck, paying a $600 premium.

Assume that the $600 insurance prepayment was initially recorded as follows:

Nov. 1	Insurance Expense	600	
	Cash		600
	Paid six months' insurance in advance:		
	6 × $100 = $600.		

Notice that the debit is to Insurance Expense instead of Prepaid Insurance (as illustrated earlier). In order to fix the balance sheet at December 31, the asset Prepaid Insurance must be debited (increased) for $400 (4 × $100) to reflect the fact that four months of prepaid insurance still remain. The entire $400 is debited to Prepaid Insurance because, with the original debit to Insurance Expense, the existing balance in Prepaid Insurance is $0. The credit half of the adjusting entry is used to fix the income statement. The $400 credit is to Insurance Expense, representing the fact that too much insurance expense was initially recorded and some is being removed. The appropriate adjusting entry is as follows:

Dec. 31	Prepaid Insurance	400	
	Insurance Expense		400
	To record prepaid insurance for four months:		
	4 × $100 = $400.		

Although this adjusting entry is different from the one shown previously, the net effect of the original and adjusting entries is exactly the same, as illustrated below.

Original debit to Insurance Expense:

	Prepaid Insurance		Cash		Insurance Expense	
	Dr.	Cr.	Dr.	Cr.	Dr.	Cr.
Original entry (11/1/03)				600	600	
Adjusting entry (12/31/03)	400					400
Updated balances (12/31/03)	400				200	
	To balance sheet				To income statement	

Original debit to Prepaid Insurance (illustrated earlier on page 140):

	Prepaid Insurance		Cash		Insurance Expense	
	Dr.	Cr.	Dr.	Cr.	Dr.	Cr.
Original entry (11/1/03)	600			600		
Adjusting entry (12/31/03)		200			200	
Updated balances (12/31/03)	400				200	
	To balance sheet				To income statement	

Whether the initial debit for a prepaid expense is to a prepaid asset or to an expense, the key thing to remember in constructing the necessary adjusting entry is to first fix the balance sheet; the other half of the adjusting entry is used to fix the income statement.

STOP & THINK Why would a company debit an insurance prepayment to Insurance Expense rather than adopting a more theoretically sound policy of debiting Prepaid Insurance?

To illustrate the necessary adjusting process when revenue received in advance is initially credited to a revenue account, we will use the unearned revenue example for our landscaping company that was illustrated earlier:

On December 1, a client pays $225 for landscaping services to be provided over the period December 1, 2003, to February 29, 2004.

Assume that the $225 cash received for services was initially recorded as follows:

Dec. 1	Cash.	225	
	Landscaping Revenue		225
	Received three months' revenue in advance: $75 × 3 = $225.		

On December 31, an adjusting entry must be made to reflect the fact that two months' worth of this revenue is still unearned and represents a liability. This adjustment is made through a credit (increase) to Unearned Revenue of $150 ($75 × 2), thereby fixing the balance sheet. The corresponding debit is used to fix the income statement. A debit to Landscaping Revenue represents a decrease in revenue because some of the revenue originally recorded on December 1 has not yet been earned. The necessary adjusting entry is as follows:

Dec. 31	Landscaping Revenue.	150	
	Unearned Revenue		150
	To record unearned revenue for two months: $75 × 2 = $150.		

The sequence of entries differs when the original credit is to Landscaping Revenue rather than Unearned Revenue, but the end result is the same. Compare the ending balances in the following T-accounts:

Original credit to Landscaping Revenue:

	Unearned Revenue (Dr.)	Unearned Revenue (Cr.)	Cash (Dr.)	Cash (Cr.)	Landscaping Revenue (Dr.)	Landscaping Revenue (Cr.)
Original entry (12/1/03)			225			225
Adjusting entry (12/31/03)		150			150	
Updated balances (12/31/03)		150				75
		To balance sheet				To income statement

Original credit to Unearned Revenue (illustrated earlier on page 142):

	Unearned Revenue (Dr.)	Unearned Revenue (Cr.)	Cash (Dr.)	Cash (Cr.)	Landscaping Revenue (Dr.)	Landscaping Revenue (Cr.)
Original entry (12/1/03)		225	225			
Adjusting entry (12/31/03)	75					75
Updated balances (12/31/03)		150				75
		To balance sheet				To income statement

to summarize

Prepayments are sometimes initially recorded as expenses instead of as prepaid expenses (assets); cash receipts for revenue in advance are sometimes initially recorded as revenues instead of as unearned revenues (liabilities). This requires an adjusting process that differs somewhat from that illustrated earlier in the chapter. No matter which approach is used, however, the resulting amounts reported in the balance sheet and the income statement are the same if the adjusting entries are made correctly.

APPENDIX A: USING A WORK SHEET

work sheet A columnar schedule used to summarize accounting data.

A **work sheet** is a tool used by accountants to facilitate the preparation of financial statements. Unlike the financial statements, work sheets are for internal use only; they are not distributed to "outsiders." Although the use of work sheets is optional, most accountants find them helpful for organizing large quantities of data. Many work sheets are now prepared on electronic spreadsheets, using a software package such as Lotus 1-2-3, Excel, or Quattro Pro.

Preparing a Work Sheet

In preparing a work sheet, accountants first list the trial balance, then add any adjusting entries, and finally extend the combined amounts into the appropriate financial statement columns. The figures in these columns are used in preparing the income statement and the balance sheet. Additional analysis is required to prepare the statement of cash flows (see Chapter 13).

A work sheet will usually have a minimum of eight columns, as shown in Exhibit 4-13. The accounts are listed on the left side, and columns 1 and 2 indicate the account balances prior to adjustments (the unadjusted trial balance). Columns 3 and 4 are for adjusting entries. It should be noted that even when a work sheet is used to prepare financial statements, the adjusting entries still must be journalized and posted to the ledger accounts, as explained earlier in the chapter.

exhibit 4-13 Eight-Column Work Sheet

ITEC, Inc.
Work Sheet
December 31, 2003

	Trial Balance		Adjustments		Income Statement		Balance Sheet	
Account Titles	**Debits**	**Credits**	**Debits**	**Credits**	**Debits**	**Credits**	**Debits**	**Credits**
Cash	24,270						24,270	
Accounts Receivable	3,000						3,000	
Inventory	3,000						3,000	
Supplies on Hand	250			(d) 140			110	
Prepaid Insurance	480			(b) 40			440	
Accounts Payable		3,000						3,000
Unearned Rent Revenue		600	(c) 100					500
Capital Stock		20,000						20,000
Sales		34,700				34,700		
Cost of Goods Sold	21,000				21,000			
Salaries Expense	1,500		(a) 700		2,200			
Truck Rental Expense	4,800			(e) 4,400	400			
	58,300	58,300						
Salaries Payable				(a) 700				700
Insurance Expense			(b) 40		40			
Rent Revenue				(c) 100		100		
Supplies Expense			(d) 140		140			
Prepaid Truck Rental			(e) 4,400				4,400	
			5,380	5,380	23,780	34,800	35,220	24,200
Net Income (to balance)					11,020			11,020
					34,800	34,800	35,220	35,220

Adjustments:
(a) Salaries Payable, $700
(b) Insurance Expense, $40
($480 ÷ 12 = $40 a month)
(c) Rent Revenue Earned, $100
(d) Supplies Expense, $140 ($250 − $110)
(e) Prepaid Truck Rental, $4,400
($4,800 ÷ 12 = $400; $400 × 11 months)

The last four columns of a work sheet are used for extending the unadjusted trial balance figures, plus or minus adjustments, into the appropriate financial statement columns. Revenue and expense accounts are extended into the income statement columns; asset, liability, and owners' equity accounts into the balance sheet columns. The exact form of a work sheet is flexible, and its content depends on the type of business and the way a company handles certain transactions.

To illustrate the use of a work sheet, we will examine the operating activities for one year for ITEC, Inc. The work sheet for ITEC, Inc., using the eight-column format, is shown in Exhibit 4-13. The amounts in the trial balance columns are based on the following transactions. (Note that the company was organized on January 1, 2003.)

1. Issued capital stock for $20,000 cash.
2. Paid $4,800 cash to lease a truck for one year; one month's expense applicable to 2003.
3. Received $600 on December 1 from a tenant for six months' rent ($100 per month).

4. Paid $480 for a one-year insurance policy; one month is expense applicable to 2003.
5. Purchased supplies for $250 cash.
6. Purchased inventory for $10,000 on account.
7. Sold inventory for $15,000 on account; cost of the merchandise sold was $8,000.
8. Collected $12,000 cash from customers' accounts receivable.
9. Paid $7,000 cash for inventories bought in item (6) above.
10. Paid $1,500 for sales representatives' salaries.
11. Purchased inventory for $14,000 cash.
12. Sold inventory for $19,700 cash; cost of the merchandise sold was $13,000.

After all transactions have been journalized and posted, the balances in the accounts can be listed in the first two columns of the work sheet as the unadjusted trial balance (see Exhibit 4-13). The columns are then added to make sure that total debits equal total credits. The following data are applicable to the necessary adjusting entries at December 31:

a. Salaries payable, $700. In item (10), $1,500 was paid to sales representatives. By the end of the year, an additional $700 in sales salaries had been earned but not yet paid.
b. Insurance expense, $40. In item (4), $480 was paid for insurance, debiting Prepaid Insurance. At the end of the year, only one-twelfth of this annual fee should be expensed ($480 ÷ 12 = $40); the balance ($440) should be shown as an asset, Prepaid Insurance.
c. Monthly rent revenue earned, $100. See item (3).
d. Supplies on hand, $110. Of the supplies purchased in item (5), some remain on hand and some have been used.
e. Prepaid truck rental, $4,400. In item (2), a truck was leased for one year for $4,800, payable in advance. (A lease is a formal rental agreement.) At the end of December, eleven-twelfths of the annual lease should be shown as an asset, Prepaid Truck Rental ($4,800 ÷ 12 = $400; $400 × 11 months = $4,400); one-twelfth ($400) should be shown as an expense.

As illustrated in Exhibit 4-13, these adjustments appear in the adjustments columns and are identified as entries (a) through (e). A key for the adjustments is usually included at the bottom of the work sheet. Some accounts that are involved in the adjusting entries have a zero balance before adjustments and are therefore not included in the trial balance. These accounts are added below those listed on the trial balance. The adjustments are then added to or subtracted from the account balances. If an eight-column work sheet is used, as in Exhibit 4-13, the results are extended to the appropriate income statement or balance sheet columns as debits or credits, respectively.

Note in Exhibit 4-13 that the income statement and the balance sheet column subtotals do not show the equality of debits and credits. A balancing figure must be added to both the income statement and the balance sheet to make total debits equal total credits. If credits (revenues) exceed debits (expenses) for the income statement column subtotals, a balancing debit amount ($11,020 in this case) must be added, reflecting pretax net income for the period. The same amount must also be added as a credit to the balance sheet columns, showing an increase in owners' equity. If debits exceed credits for the income statement subtotals, there is a net loss for the period. This would be presented as a balancing credit amount on the income statement and a balancing debit amount on the balance sheet, showing a reduction in owners' equity. In either case, a balancing figure is required to bring total debits equal to total credits for each set of columns.

Special Considerations in Using a Work Sheet

Two items relating to ITEC's work sheet (Exhibit 4-13) require additional explanation: (1) the work sheet adjustment for income taxes and (2) reporting the ending retained earnings balance.

WORK SHEET ADJUSTMENT FOR INCOME TAXES To keep the ITEC illustration simple, we ignored income taxes. When a corporation earns income, however, it must pay income taxes. A year-end adjustment is required, debiting Income Tax Expense and crediting Income

Taxes Payable for the appropriate amount. When the taxes are actually paid, Income Taxes Payable is debited, and Cash is credited.

The adjustment for income taxes presents a minor problem on the work sheet because the amount of income taxes to be paid cannot be determined until net income (net loss) has been computed. One way to solve this problem is to subtotal the work sheet columns, determine the balancing figure for pretax income, multiply that figure by the tax rate to determine the amount of the tax, and then make the adjusting entry for Income Tax Expense and Income Taxes Payable the same way as other adjustments are made.

With this approach, both income tax accounts—Income Tax Expense and Income Taxes Payable—are added on the work sheet following the column subtotals. To illustrate, we assume that ITEC, Inc., is subject to a tax rate of 25%. The work sheet shown in Exhibit 4-13 would be completed as follows:

	Adjustments		Income Statement		Balance Sheet	
	Debits	Credits	Debits	Credits	Debits	Credits
Subtotals	5,380	5,380	23,780	34,800	35,220	24,200
Income Tax Expense	2,755		2,755			
Income Taxes Payable		2,755				2,755
Totals	8,135	8,135	26,535	34,800	35,220	26,955
Net Income (to balance)			8,265*			8,265
Totals			34,800	34,800	35,220	35,220

*[$34,800 − $23,780 = $11,020 to balance the income statement columns: $11,020 × 0.25 = $2,755 Income Tax Expense and Income Taxes Payable; the balance ($11,020 − $2,755 = $8,265) is net income.]

REPORTING THE ENDING RETAINED EARNINGS BALANCE We have explained and illustrated how the financial statements can be prepared from the income statement and balance sheet columns on the work sheet. To simplify the illustration (Exhibit 4-13), we assumed that ITEC, Inc., was organized on January 1, 2003, and therefore had no previous retained earnings balance. Normally, a work sheet will show the beginning retained earnings on the trial balance, which will be extended as a credit to the balance sheet columns. In addition, if a corporation has paid its stockholders dividends during the period, the dividends account will be shown on the trial balance and extended as a debit to the balance sheet columns. When preparing the balance sheet, these amounts must be considered in determining the ending retained earnings balance. The net income balancing figure on the work sheet is added to the beginning retained earnings amount; any amount shown for dividends is subtracted. The resulting figure is the amount of ending retained earnings to be reported on the balance sheet; thus:

Beginning Retained Earnings
\+ Net Income
− Dividends

Ending Retained Earnings

For the ITEC illustration, the beginning Retained Earnings balance was zero since the company had just been established. There also were no dividends paid. Therefore, the ending balance for retained earnings ($8,265) was simply the amount of net income for the period. For the next accounting period, ITEC would start with a balance of $8,265 in its retained earnings account, add the net income balancing figure for that period, and subtract any dividends to determine the ending retained earnings balance to report on the balance sheet.

The income statement and balance sheet for ITEC, Inc., as prepared from the work sheet, are shown in Exhibits 4-14 and 4-15, respectively.

exhibit 4-14 Income Statement for ITEC, Inc.

ITEC, Inc.
Income Statement
For the Year Ended December 31, 2003

Sales revenue	$34,700	
Rent revenue	100	
Total revenues		$34,800
Less cost of goods sold		21,000
Gross profit		$13,800
Less operating expenses:		
Salaries expense	$ 2,200	
Truck rental expense	400	
Insurance expense	40	
Supplies expense	140	2,780
Income before income taxes		$11,020
Income tax expense		2,755
Net income		$ 8,265

exhibit 4-15 Balance Sheet for ITEC, Inc.

ITEC, Inc.
Balance Sheet
December 31, 2003

Assets		
Cash	$24,270	
Accounts receivable	3,000	
Inventory	3,000	
Supplies on hand	110	
Prepaid insurance	440	
Prepaid truck rental	4,400	
Total assets		$35,220
Liabilities and Owners' Equity		
Liabilities:		
Accounts payable	$ 3,000	
Unearned rent revenue	500	
Salaries payable	700	
Income taxes payable	2,755	$ 6,955
Owners' equity:		
Capital stock	$20,000	
Retained earnings	8,265*	28,265
Total liabilities and owners' equity		$35,220

*Beginning Retained Earnings + Net Income − Dividends = Ending Retained Earnings.

APPENDIX B: SPECIAL JOURNALS

special journal A book of original entry for recording similar transactions that occur frequently.

So far we have shown all journal entries in general journal format, as explained in Chapter 3. With many businesses having hundreds or even thousands of transactions every day, it is impractical and inefficient to use only one journal. Instead, they group transactions into similar classes and use a **special journal** for each. These special journals can be maintained on paper or in a computerized system; the basic principles are the same. In this appendix, we refer to a manual system.

The Sales Journal

sales journal A special journal in which credit sales are recorded.

One of the most frequently occurring business transactions involves the sale of goods or services, either for cash or on credit. Cash sales are generally recorded in a cash receipts journal. When merchandise is sold on credit, a prenumbered sales invoice is prepared. This invoice specifies the date of the sale, the amount and kinds of merchandise sold, and the price. One copy of the invoice is sent to the accounting department to be used as the basis for an entry in the **sales journal**. This journal is a chronological listing of all credit sales, as shown in Exhibit 4-16.

This sales journal page has no columns for sales discounts (reductions in price offered to customers who pay within a specified period), sales returns, or sales taxes. Antler Corporation records all credit sales at their gross amounts and notes sales discounts at the time of collection (in the Cash Receipts Journal). Sales returns, which involve a debit to Sales Returns and Allowances and a credit to Accounts Receivable, are recorded by Antler in the general journal. Many companies include sales discounts and returns in the sales journal, but we have omitted them here for the sake of simplicity. (The concepts of sales discounts and returns are covered more fully in Chapter 6.) If Antler were operating in a state with sales taxes, the taxes would be entered in a Sales Taxes Payable (credit) column, with the total posted to the sales taxes payable account at the same time Accounts Receivable and Sales Revenue are posted. (The concept of sales taxes is covered more fully in Chapter 8.)

exhibit 4-16 A Sample Page in a Sales Journal for Antler Corporation

SALES JOURNAL

Date	Customer	Invoice No.	Post. Ref.	Amount
2003 Jan. 2	Lee Smith	125	105.7	600
5	Roger Jameson	126	105.5	250
6	Ralph Smith	127	105.8	315
8	John Anderson	128	105.1	216
9	Carl Hartford	129	105.4	822
12	Mike Taylor	130	105.9	610
16	Marvin Brinkerhoff	131	105.3	507
23	Roy Avondet	132	105.2	125
27	Jay Rasmussen	133	105.6	350
28	Jerry Woolsey	134	105.11	816
				4,611
				(105) (400)

The sales journal differs from the general journal in several respects. First, because all transactions are similar, the entries do not require separate explanations. Second, there are no debit and credit columns because the total is always posted as a debit to Accounts Receivable (account 105) and a credit to Sales Revenue (account 400). Third, the sales journal includes a column for the sales invoice number for easy reference to a source of additional information.

Having a single total posted to Accounts Receivable saves time and keeps the general ledger in manageable form. However, it does make it difficult, if not impossible, for a company to monitor the activity of individual accounts. Maintaining a separate account for each customer within the general ledger creates a different sort of problem—a voluminous general ledger with many accounts receivable accounts, plus Cash, Inventory, and so forth. The same problem exists for Accounts Payable.

subsidiary ledger A grouping of individual accounts that in total equal the balance of a control account in the general ledger.

control account A summary account in the general ledger that is supported by detailed individual accounts in a subsidiary ledger.

To handle this problem, companies generally keep at least three ledgers: the general ledger, which contains all the balance sheet and income statement accounts; the accounts receivable subsidiary ledger; and the accounts payable subsidiary ledger. The **subsidiary ledgers** contain separate accounts (in alphabetical order) for each customer and creditor, showing all debits, credits, and a balance. They are called subsidiary ledgers because they back up, or support, the account balances in the general ledger. The total of all accounts in the accounts receivable subsidiary ledger, for example, equals the balance in Accounts Receivable in the general ledger. Accounts Receivable is called a **control account** because it summarizes the individual accounts in the accounts receivable subsidiary ledger. Exhibit 4-17 illustrates the relationship between the general and subsidiary ledgers.

As the sales journal entries are posted to the accounts receivable subsidiary ledger accounts, the individual account numbers are entered in the sales journal posting reference column. The number of the sales journal page and the date of the transaction are similarly entered as a posting reference in the subsidiary accounts. These cross-references quickly direct accountants to the source of additional information, while serving as a means of checking their work. Exhibit 4-18 shows the posting of the sales transactions to the general ledger. Note that the total posted to Accounts Receivable in the general ledger equals the total of all postings to the accounts receivable subsidiary ledger.

The Purchases Journal

purchases journal A special journal in which credit purchases are recorded.

A second frequently occurring transaction involves the purchase of merchandise for resale, either for cash or on credit. Cash purchases are recorded in a cash disbursements journal and will be discussed later. Credit purchases are chronologically recorded in a **purchases journal**. The individual entries are posted to accounts in the accounts payable subsidiary ledger throughout the accounting period. At the end of the period, the total is posted to both Accounts Payable and Purchases.

The purchases and sales journals are similar, except that the sales journal includes invoice numbers and the purchases journal includes invoice dates. The date is useful for identifying the beginning of a discount period. A sample page from a purchases journal is shown in Exhibit 4-19 on page 166. As with the sales journal, Antler Corporation handles discounts at the time of payment. (The concept of purchase discounts is covered more fully in Chapter 7.)

This purchases journal is used for recording credit purchases of inventory only. Credit purchases of equipment, supplies, other such items, and purchase returns would be recorded in the general journal. Exhibit 4-20 on page 167 illustrates the posting of the purchases journal to the accounts payable subsidiary ledger and to the general ledger.

Each purchase is posted to the individual creditor's account in the accounts payable subsidiary ledger; the total of $4,851 is posted to Accounts Payable (202) and Purchases (450) in the general ledger. Like the sales journal, the purchases journal is cross-referenced to the general and subsidiary ledgers. The cumulative total of all balances in the accounts payable subsidiary ledger equals the balance in the accounts payable account.

exhibit 4-17 The General and Subsidiary Ledgers

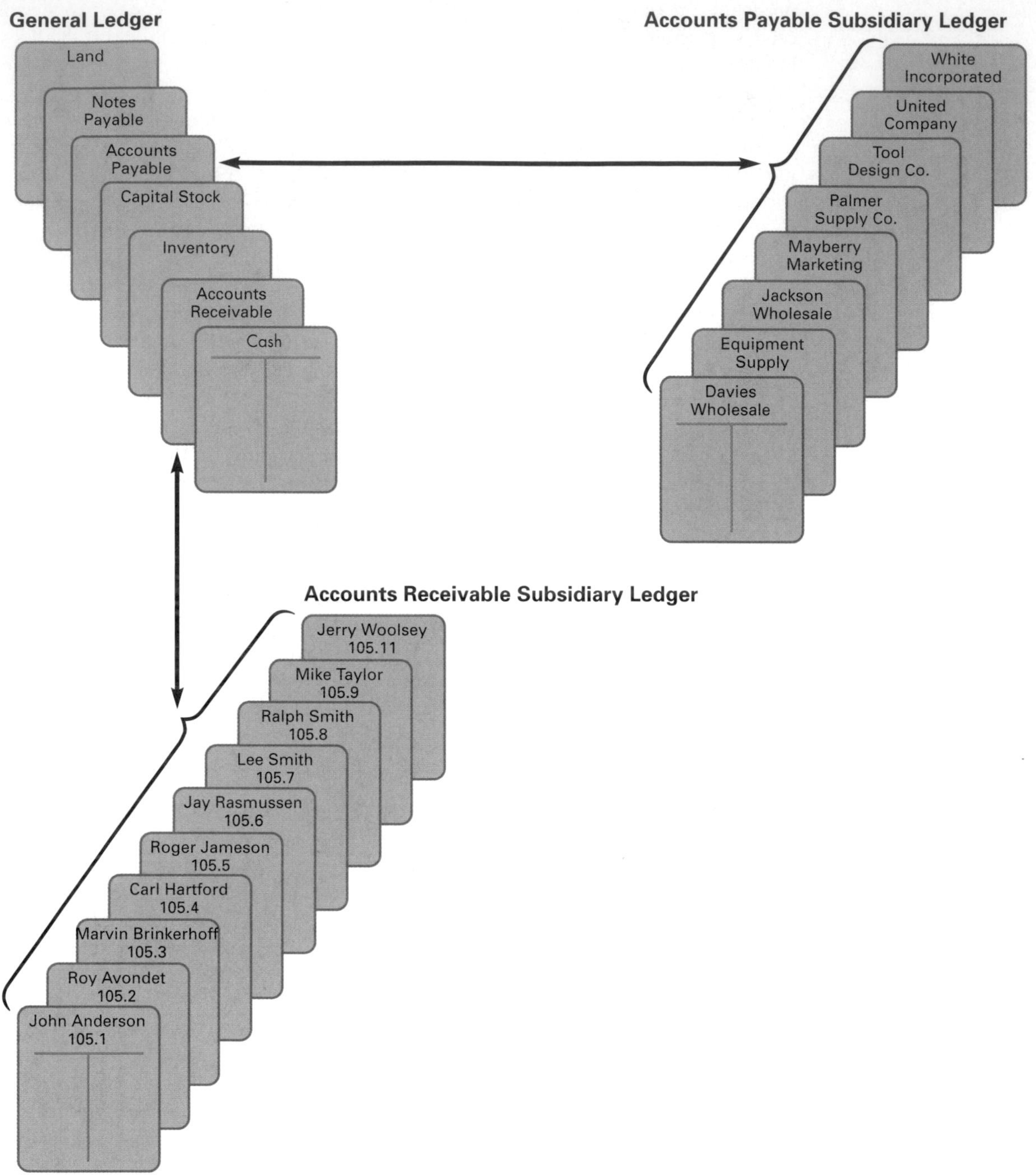

The Cash Receipts Journal

cash receipts journal A special journal in which all cash received, from sales, interest, rent, or other sources, is recorded.

Another special journal is the **cash receipts journal**, which includes all cash received from sales, interest, rent, or other sources. Exhibit 4-21 on page 168 shows a typical page from a cash receipts journal and the posting of its entries.

The cash receipts journal usually includes columns for Cash (DR), Sales Discounts (DR), Accounts Receivable (CR), and Sales Revenue (CR). In addition, an Other Accounts (CR) column is used to record all "irregular" cash transactions, that is, all items that do not fall naturally into a labeled column such as Cash or Accounts Receivable. Examples are collections of in-

exhibit 4-18 Posting from the Sales Journal

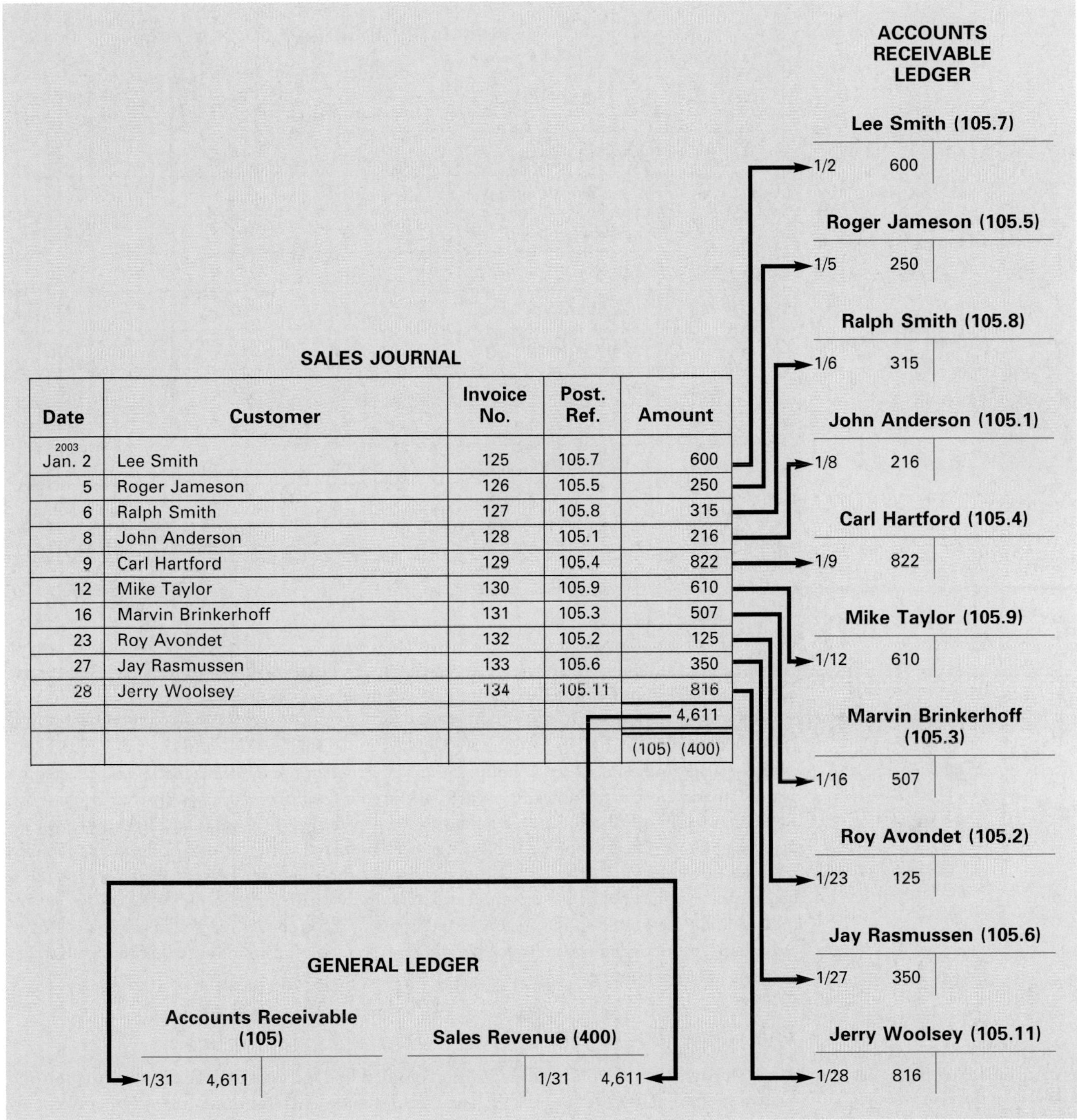

SALES JOURNAL

Date	Customer	Invoice No.	Post. Ref.	Amount
2003 Jan. 2	Lee Smith	125	105.7	600
5	Roger Jameson	126	105.5	250
6	Ralph Smith	127	105.8	315
8	John Anderson	128	105.1	216
9	Carl Hartford	129	105.4	822
12	Mike Taylor	130	105.9	610
16	Marvin Brinkerhoff	131	105.3	507
23	Roy Avondet	132	105.2	125
27	Jay Rasmussen	133	105.6	350
28	Jerry Woolsey	134	105.11	816
				4,611
				(105) (400)

terest, rents, or notes receivable. The Other Accounts column is added for cross-checking purposes. A check mark (√) is placed below the total to indicate that the individual items have been posted.

Exhibit 4-21 shows that on January 7, $588 was received from Lee Smith in payment of a $600 bill (debit Cash, credit Accounts Receivable). The $12 difference is a 2% discount ($600 × 0.02 = $12) offered by Antler to customers who pay within 10 days (debit Sales Discounts). The $125 cash sale on January 12 was debited to Cash and credited to Sales Revenue. The in-

exhibit 4-19 A Sample Page in a Purchases Journal for Antler Corporation

PURCHASES JOURNAL

Date	Supplier	Invoice Date	Post. Ref.	Amount
2003 Jan. 2	Mayberry Marketing	2003 Jan. 1	202.4	300
5	Jackson Wholesale	4	202.3	616
6	Equipment Supply	5	202.2	485
12	Davies Wholesale	11	202.1	690
14	Jackson Wholesale	12	202.3	150
15	Palmer Supply Co.	14	202.5	810
22	White Incorporated	22	202.8	800
29	United Company	28	202.7	600
30	Tool Design Co.	29	202.6	400
				4,851
				(202) (450)

terest revenue collected on January 18 was credited to Other Accounts. Mike Taylor did not receive a sales discount because he did not pay within the 10-day discount period.

In posting the entries from the cash receipts journal to the general ledger, only those amounts in the Other Accounts (CR) column are handled individually; the number of each ledger account appears in the Post. Ref. column. For example, when the $150 payment was collected on January 9 and posted to Notes Receivable, the account number 103 was entered in the Post. Ref. column. All other columns are posted to the general ledger as totals at the end of each accounting period. The total of the debit columns is compared with the total of the credit columns to make sure that total debits equal total credits. As the totals are posted, their account numbers are entered just below the column totals. The individual entries in the Accounts Receivable (CR) column are posted to the customers' accounts in the accounts receivable subsidiary ledger. Subsidiary account numbers are placed in the Post. Ref. column to indicate that these subsidiary postings have been made.

The Cash Disbursements Journal

cash disbursements journal A special journal in which all cash paid out for supplies, merchandise, salaries, and other items is recorded.

The cash payments of a business are usually recorded in a separate **cash disbursements journal** (shown in Exhibit 4-22 on page 169). The cash disbursements journal contains Other Accounts (CR), Cash (CR), Purchase Discounts (CR), Accounts Payable (DR), Sales Salaries Expense (DR), General and Administrative Salaries Expense (DR), and Other Accounts (DR) columns. The Purchase Discounts and Accounts Payable columns are used to account for payments for merchandise previously purchased. The Sales and the General and Administrative Salaries Expense columns are used to record the payment of salaries (if a separate payroll journal is not kept). The Other Accounts (DR) column is used to record cash purchases of merchandise and other payments for which there are no special columns. As with the other journals, the parenthetical numbers at the bottoms of the columns mean those column totals have been posted to their respective general ledger accounts.

exhibit 4-20 Posting from the Purchases Journal

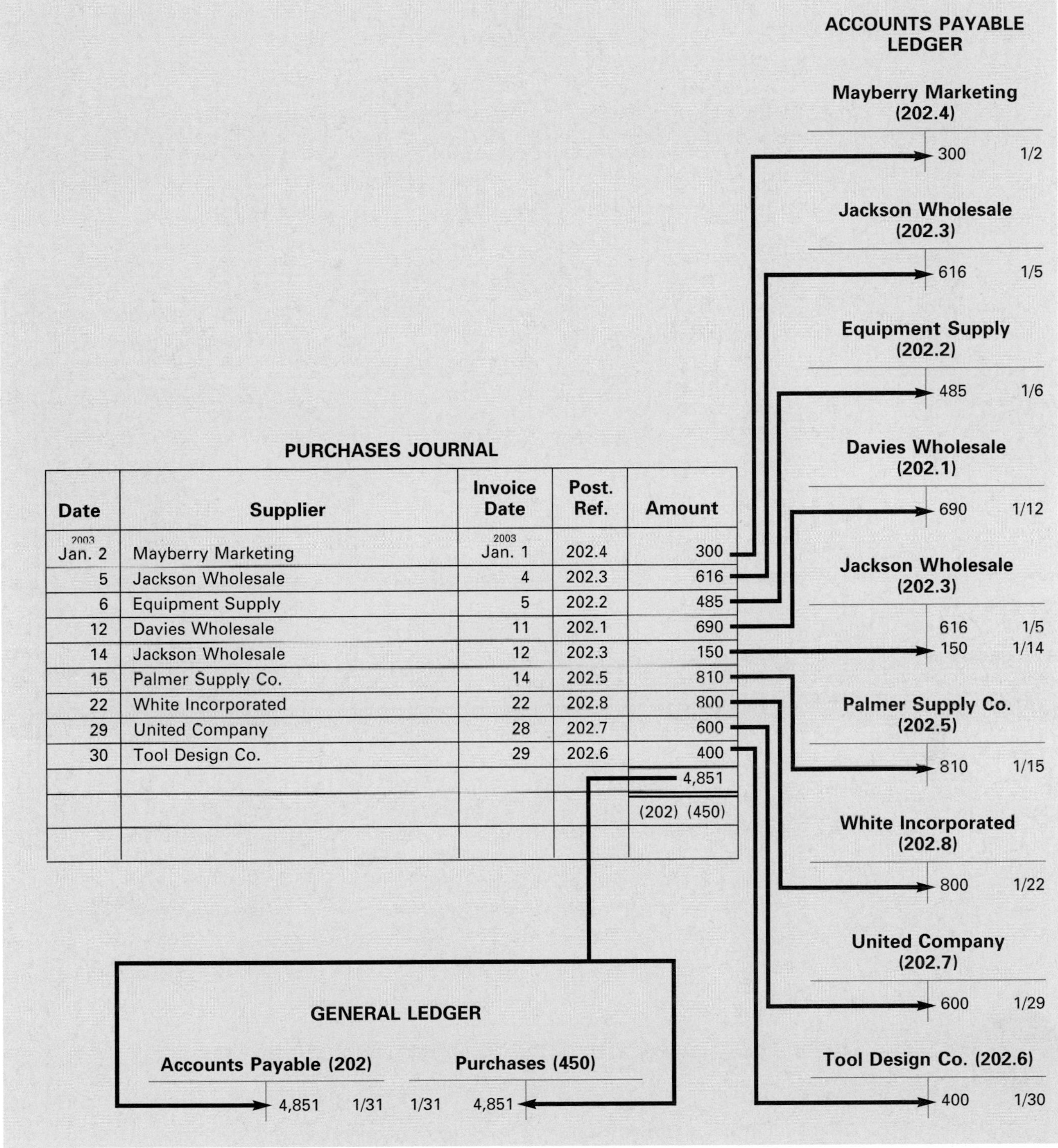

PURCHASES JOURNAL

Date	Supplier	Invoice Date	Post. Ref.	Amount
2003 Jan. 2	Mayberry Marketing	2003 Jan. 1	202.4	300
5	Jackson Wholesale	4	202.3	616
6	Equipment Supply	5	202.2	485
12	Davies Wholesale	11	202.1	690
14	Jackson Wholesale	12	202.3	150
15	Palmer Supply Co.	14	202.5	810
22	White Incorporated	22	202.8	800
29	United Company	28	202.7	600
30	Tool Design Co.	29	202.6	400
				4,851
				(202) (450)

In reading Exhibit 4-22, notice that on February 1 the company made a $588 payment to satisfy the $600 payable to United Company. The 2% discount of $12 was taken because payment was made within 10 days of purchase. The payments to Equipment Supply and Mayberry Marketing were for the full amounts because they were not made within the 10-day discount period (see the purchases journal in Exhibit 4-20).

exhibit 4-21 The Cash Receipts Journal

CASH RECEIPTS JOURNAL

Cash DR	Sales Discounts DR	Date	Receipt No.	Account Name	Post. Ref.	Accounts Receivable CR	Sales Revenue CR	Other Accounts	
								Post. Ref.	Amount CR
		2003							
588.00	12.00	Jan. 7	621	Lee Smith	105.7	600.00			
150.00		9	622	Notes Receivable				103	150.00
125.00		12	623	Cash Sales			125.00		
805.56	16.44	15	624	Carl Hartford	105.4	822.00			
50.00		18	625	Interest Revenue				513	50.00
30.00		22	626	Cash Sales			30.00		
122.50	2.50	29	627	Roy Avondet	105.2	125.00			
610.00		29	628	Mike Taylor	105.9	610.00			
2,481.06	30.94					2,157.00	155.00		200.00
(101)	(404)					(105)	(400)		(✔)

GENERAL LEDGER

Cash (101)		Notes Receivable (103)		Accounts Receivable (105)	
1/31 2,481.06			1/31 150.00		1/31 2,157.00

Sales Revenue (400)		Sales Discounts (404)		Interest Revenue (513)	
	1/31 155.00	1/31 30.94			1/31 50.00

ACCOUNTS RECEIVABLE SUBSIDIARY LEDGER

Roy Avondet (105.2)		Carl Hartford (105.4)		Lee Smith (105.7)		Mike Taylor (105.9)	
	1/29 125.00		1/15 822.00		1/7 600.00		1/29 610.00

review of learning objectives

1 Describe how accrual accounting allows for timely reporting and a better measure of a company's economic performance. Accounting information is needed on a timely basis for decision-making purposes. This requires that the total life of a business be divided into accounting periods, generally a year or less, for which reports are prepared. Some of the data presented in the periodic reports must be tentative because dividing a company's life into relatively short reporting periods requires that allocations and estimates be made.

The necessity for periodic reporting further requires that accrual accounting be used to provide accurate statements of financial position and results of operations for an accounting period. Accrual-basis accounting means that revenues are recognized as they are earned, not necessarily when cash is received; expenses are recognized as they are incurred, not necessarily when cash is paid. Accrual-basis accounting provides a more accurate picture of a company's financial position and operating results than does cash-basis accounting. The cash

exhibit 4-22 The Cash Disbursements Journal

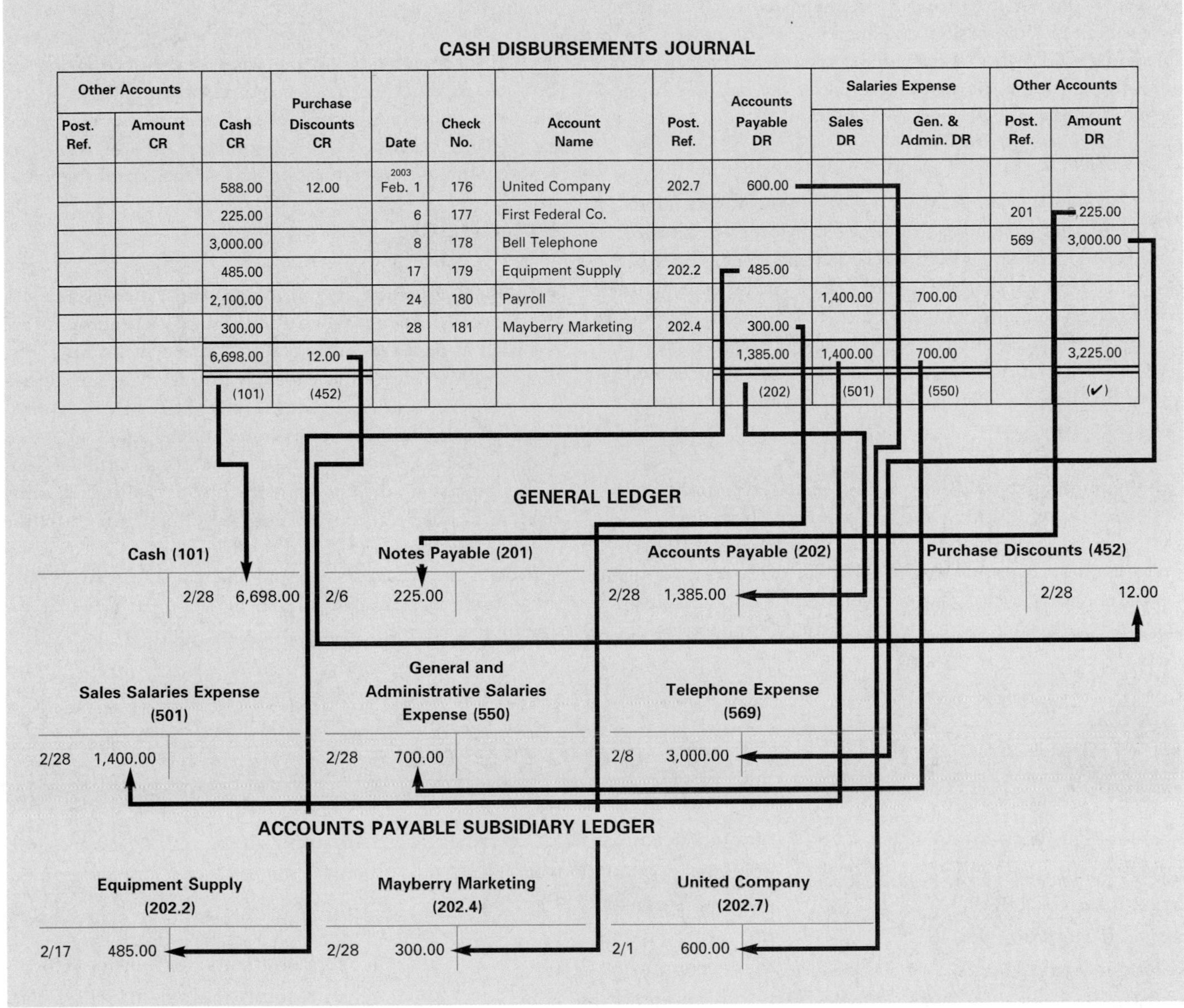

CASH DISBURSEMENTS JOURNAL

Other Accounts									Salaries Expense		Other Accounts	
Post. Ref.	Amount CR	Cash CR	Purchase Discounts CR	Date	Check No.	Account Name	Post. Ref.	Accounts Payable DR	Sales DR	Gen. & Admin. DR	Post. Ref.	Amount DR
		588.00	12.00	2003 Feb. 1	176	United Company	202.7	600.00				
		225.00		6	177	First Federal Co.					201	225.00
		3,000.00		8	178	Bell Telephone					569	3,000.00
		485.00		17	179	Equipment Supply	202.2	485.00				
		2,100.00		24	180	Payroll			1,400.00	700.00		
		300.00		28	181	Mayberry Marketing	202.4	300.00				
		6,698.00	12.00					1,385.00	1,400.00	700.00		3,225.00
		(101)	(452)					(202)	(501)	(550)		(✔)

flow statement is also very important in the financial position analysis.

2 **Explain the need for adjusting entries and make adjusting entries for unrecorded receivables, unrecorded liabilities, prepaid expenses, and unearned revenues.** At the end of an accounting period, there are potentially many important events that have as yet not been recorded. Some important events occur outside the normal accounting process, while other events occur slowly over time. An important part of the accounting process is to review the financial condition and operating activities of the company for the period to make sure that all assets, liabilities, revenues, and expenses have been recorded. These year-end adjustments are called adjusting entries and may be classified under four headings: unrecorded receivables, unrecorded liabilities, prepaid expenses, and unearned revenues. The analysis process involved in making an adjusting entry involves two steps. First, determine whether an asset or liability has been recorded for the proper amount and, if not, correct it (fix the balance sheet). Second, determine what revenue or expense adjustment is needed because of the asset or liability adjustment just made (fix the income statement).

3 **Explain the preparation of the financial statements, the explanatory notes, and the audit report.** After the adjusting entries have been posted to the accounts, an adjusted trial balance is prepared. This adjusted trial balance provides the raw data for the preparation of the balance sheet and the income statement; preparation of the statement of cash flows requires more detailed information about cash receipts and cash disbursements. The notes to the financial statements provide further information about the methods and assumptions used in preparing the financial statements as well as further detail about certain financial statement items. The audit is conducted by a CPA from outside the company who reviews the adjusting entries, performs tests to check the balances of selected accounts, and reviews the condition of the accounting systems.

4 **Perform a systematic analysis of financial statements.** Financial statements are prepared in order to be used. Two general techniques for financial statement analysis are the DuPont framework and common-size financial statements. The DuPont framework involves the decomposition of return on equity into three components: profitability, efficiency, and leverage. Preparation of common-size financial statements involves dividing all financial statement amounts by total revenue for the period.

5 **Complete the closing process in the accounting cycle.** Once adjusting entries have been journalized and posted to the accounts and the financia l statements have been prepared, the accounting records should be made ready for the next accounting cycle. This is accomplished by journalizing and posting closing entries for all nominal (temporary) accounts. Revenue accounts are closed by being debited; expense accounts and the dividends account are closed by being credited. Revenues, expenses, and dividends are closed to Retained Earnings.

6 **Understand how all the steps in the accounting cycle fit together.** The accounting cycle consists of specific steps to analyze, record, classify, summarize, and report the exchange transactions of economic entities. By way of review, Exhibit 4-12 identifies the steps in the accounting cycle.

expanded material

7 **Make adjusting entries for prepaid expenses and unearned revenues when the original cash amounts are recorded as expenses and revenues.** Prepayments are sometimes initially recorded as expenses instead of as prepaid expenses (assets); cash receipts for revenue in advance are sometimes initially recorded as revenues instead of as unearned revenues (liabilities). However, the concepts governing the adjusting process are the same: use the first part of the adjusting entry to fix the balance sheet and the second part to fix the income statement. The end result (the updated balances reported on the balance sheet and income statement, respectively) is the same regardless of which approach is used, assuming that adjusting entries are made correctly.

key terms and concepts

review problem

The Accounting Cycle

This review problem provides a useful summary of the entire accounting cycle. The following post-closing trial balance is for Sports Haven Company as of December 31, 2002.

Sports Haven Company
Post-Closing Trial Balance
December 31, 2002

	Debits	Credits
Cash	$17,500	
Accounts Receivable	17,000	
Inventory	28,800	
Supplies on Hand	1,200	
Prepaid Building Rental	24,000	
Accounts Payable		$18,000
Capital Stock (3,600 shares outstanding)		54,000
Retained Earnings		16,500
Totals	$88,500	$88,500

Following is a summary of the company's transactions for 2003.

a. At the beginning of 2003, the company issued 1,500 new shares of stock at $20 per share.
b. Total inventory purchases were $49,500; all purchases were made on credit and are recorded in the inventory account.
c. Total sales were $125,000; $102,900 were on credit, the rest were for cash. The cost of goods sold was $47,500; the inventory account is reduced at the time of each sale.
d. In December, a customer paid $3,500 cash in advance for merchandise that was temporarily out of stock. The advance payments received from customers are initially recorded as liabilities. The $3,500 is not included in the sales figures in (c) above.
e. The company paid $66,500 on accounts payable during the year.
f. The company collected $102,000 of accounts receivable during the year.
g. The company purchased $600 of supplies for cash during 2003, debiting Supplies on Hand.
h. The company paid $850 for advertising during the year, debiting Prepaid Advertising.
i. Total salaries paid during the year were $45,000.
j. The company paid $650 during the year for utilities.
k. Dividends of $7,500 were paid to stockholders in December.

On December 31, 2003, the company's accountant gathers the following information to adjust the accounts:

l. As of December 31, salaries of $750 had been earned by employees but will not be paid until January 3, 2004.
m. A count at December 31 shows $800 of supplies still on hand.
n. The prepaid advertising paid during 2003 includes $400 paid on December 1, 2003, for a series of radio advertisements to be broadcast throughout December 2003 and January 2004. The balance in the account, $450, represents advertisements that were broadcast during 2003.
o. On December 31, 2002, the company rented an office building for two years and paid $24,000 in cash (the full rental fee for 2003 and 2004). The payment was recorded with a debit to Prepaid Building Rental. No entries have been made for building rent in 2003.
p. On December 20, 2003, a bill for $150 was received for utilities. No entry was made to record the receipt of the bill, which is to be paid on January 4, 2004.
q. As of December 31, 2003, the merchandise paid for in advance [transaction (d)] was still out of stock. The company expects to receive the merchandise and fill the order by January 15, 2004.
r. The company's income is taxed at a rate of 15%.

Required:

1. Make entries in the general journal to record each of the transactions [items (a) through (k)].
2. Using T-accounts to represent the general ledger accounts, post the transactions recorded in the general journal. Enter the beginning balances in the accounts that appear in the De-

cember 31, 2002, post-closing trial balance before posting 2003 transactions. When all transactions have been posted to the T-accounts, determine the balance for each account.

3. Prepare a trial balance as of December 31, 2003.
4. Record adjusting entries [items (l) through (r)] in the general journal; post these entries to the general ledger (T-accounts).
5. Prepare an income statement and balance sheet for 2003.
6. Record closing entries [label (s) and (t)] in the general journal; post these entries to the general ledger (T-accounts).
7. Prepare a post-closing trial balance.

Solution

1. Following are the journal entries to record the transactions for the year. Several of these are summary entries representing numerous individual transactions.

(a)	Cash	30,000	
	Capital Stock		30,000

The company issued additional shares of stock, so Capital Stock must be credited to reflect the increase in owners' equity. Since the company received cash of $30,000 (1,500 shares at $20 per share), Cash is also increased.

(b)	Inventory	49,500	
	Accounts Payable		49,500

The company purchased $49,500 of goods on credit. Inventory is increased (debited) for this amount. Accounts Payable is credited to show the increase in liabilities.

(c)	Accounts Receivable	102,900	
	Cash	22,100	
	Sales Revenue		125,000

Total sales were $125,000, so Sales Revenue must be increased (credited) by that amount. Of this amount, $102,900 were on credit, and $22,100 were cash sales. We increase the asset accounts, Accounts Receivable and Cash, by debiting them.

(c)	Cost of Goods Sold	47,500	
	Inventory		47,500

The cost of the merchandise sold during the year was $47,500. Cost of Goods Sold (expense) must be increased (debited) by this amount. Since the goods were sold, Inventory (asset) must be reduced by a credit of $47,500.

(d)	Cash	3,500	
	Unearned Sales Revenue		3,500

Cash is debited (increased) by the amount received from the customer. The company recorded the advance payments for merchandise by crediting a liability account, Unearned Sales Revenue.

(e)	Accounts Payable	66,500	
	Cash		66,500

The company's payments on its accounts reduce the amount of its obligation to creditors, so Accounts Payable (liability) is debited to decrease it by the amount paid. Cash must also be decreased (credited).

(f)	Cash	102,000	
	Accounts Receivable		102,000

Since the company has collected some of its receivables from customers, Accounts Receivable is credited to show a decrease. Cash is increased (debited).

(g)	Supplies on Hand	600	
	Cash		600

The company purchased $600 of supplies. By debiting Supplies on Hand, an increase is shown in that asset account. Cash must be credited to show a decrease.

(h)	Prepaid Advertising	850	
	Cash		850

The company purchased $850 of advertising and chose to initially debit an asset account, Prepaid Advertising. Since cash was paid, it must be reduced by a credit.

(i)	Salaries Expense	45,000	
	Cash		45,000
(j)	Utilities Expense	650	
	Cash		650

For transactions (i) and (j), an expense account must be debited to show that expenses have been incurred. Cash must be credited (reduced).

(k)	Dividends	7,500	
	Cash		7,500

Dividends must be debited to show a decrease in owners' equity resulting from a distribution of earnings. Cash must be reduced by a credit.

2. T-accounts with the beginning balances and journal entries posted are shown here. (Note that accounts with more than one entry must be "balanced" by drawing a rule and entering the debit or credit balance below it.)

Cash

Debit		Credit	
Beg. bal.	17,500	(e)	66,500
(a)	30,000	(g)	600
(c)	22,100	(h)	850
(d)	3,500	(i)	45,000
(f)	102,000	(j)	650
		(k)	7,500
Updated bal.	54,000		

Accounts Receivable

Debit		Credit	
Beg. bal.	17,000	(f)	102,000
(c)	102,900		
Updated bal.	17,900		

Inventory

Debit		Credit	
Beg. bal.	28,800	(c)	47,500
(b)	49,500		
Updated bal.	30,800		

Supplies on Hand

Debit		Credit	
Beg. bal.	1,200		
(g)	600		
Updated bal.	1,800		

Prepaid Building Rental

Debit		Credit	
Beg. bal.	24,000		

Prepaid Advertising

Debit		Credit	
(h)	850		

Accounts Payable

Debit		Credit	
(e)	66,500	Beg. bal.	18,000
		(b)	49,500
		Updated bal.	1,000

Unearned Sales Revenue

Debit		Credit	
		(d)	3,500

Capital Stock

Debit		Credit	
		Beg. bal.	54,000
		(a)	30,000
		Updated bal.	84,000

Retained Earnings

Debit		Credit	
		Beg. bal.	16,500

Dividends

Debit		Credit	
(k)	7,500		

Sales Revenue

Debit		Credit	
		(c)	125,000

Cost of Goods Sold

Debit		Credit	
(c)	47,500		

Salaries Expense

Debit		Credit	
(i)	45,000		

Utilities Expense

Debit		Credit	
(j)	650		

3. The balance of each account is entered in a trial balance. Each column in the trial balance is totaled to determine that total debits equal total credits.

Sports Haven Company
Trial Balance
December 31, 2003

	Debits	Credits
Cash	$ 54,000	
Accounts Receivable	17,900	
Inventory	30,800	
Supplies on Hand	1,800	
Prepaid Building Rental	24,000	
Prepaid Advertising	850	
Accounts Payable		$ 1,000
Unearned Sales Revenue		3,500
Capital Stock		84,000
Retained Earnings		16,500
Dividends	7,500	
Sales Revenue		125,000
Cost of Goods Sold	47,500	
Salaries Expense	45,000	
Utilities Expense	650	
Totals	$230,000	$230,000

4. The adjusting entries for Sports Haven Company are presented in journal form and explained. Updated T-accounts are provided showing the posting of the adjusting entries.

(l)	Salaries Expense	750	
	Salaries Payable		750

As of December 31, there is an unrecorded liability and expense of $750 for salaries owed to employees. Because the salaries were earned in 2003, the liability and related expense must be recorded in 2003.

(m)	Supplies Expense	1,000	
	Supplies on Hand		1,000

Supplies on Hand (asset) has a debit balance before adjustment of $1,800 [beginning balance of $1,200 plus $600 of supplies purchased during the year, transaction (g)]. Since $800 of supplies are on hand at the end of the year, Supplies on Hand should be reduced (credited) by $1,000. Supplies Expense must be debited to show that $1,000 of supplies were used during the period.

(n)	Advertising Expense	650	
	Prepaid Advertising		650

Prepaid Advertising has a debit balance before adjustment of $850, the total amount paid for advertising during the year [transaction (h)]. This amount includes $400 that was paid for radio advertising throughout December 2003 and January 2004. Only that portion that applies to 2004 should be shown as Prepaid Advertising, $200 ($400 ÷ 2 months), since it is not an expense of the current year. The remainder, $650, is advertising expense for the period. Thus, the asset account, Prepaid Advertising, must be credited for $650, and Advertising Expense must be increased by a debit of $650.

(o)	Building Rent Expense	12,000	
	Prepaid Building Rental.		12,000

The original entry at the end of 2002 was a debit to the asset account, Prepaid Building Rental, and a credit to Cash. An adjusting entry is needed to record rent expense of $12,000 for 2003 ($24,000 ÷ 2 years). The expense account must be debited and the asset account must be reduced by a credit. The remaining $12,000 in Prepaid Building Rental reflects the portion of the total payment for building rent expense in 2004.

(p)	Utilities Expense.	150	
	Utilities Payable.		150

As of December 31, 2003, there is an unrecorded liability and expense of $150 for utilities. Because the expense was incurred in 2003, an adjusting entry is needed to record the liability and related expense.

(q) No entry required.

The original entry to record the advance payment from a customer was made by crediting a liability [transaction (d)]. As of December 31, no revenue has been earned. The company still has an obligation to deliver goods or refund the advanced payment. Therefore, no adjustment is required, since the liability is already properly recorded.

(r)	Income Tax Expense	2,595	
	Income Taxes Payable		2,595

The remaining adjustment is for income taxes. The difference between total revenues and total expenses is the amount of income before taxes, $17,300. This amount is multiplied by the applicable tax rate of 15% to determine income taxes for the period. The expense account is debited to show the income taxes incurred for the year and the liability account is credited to show the obligation to the government.

Cash

Beg. bal.	17,500	(e)	66,500
(a)	30,000	(g)	600
(c)	22,100	(h)	850
(d)	3,500	(i)	45,000
(f)	102,000	(j)	650
		(k)	7,500
Updated bal.	54,000		

Accounts Receivable

Beg. bal.	17,000	(f)	102,000
(c)	102,900		
Updated bal.	17,900		

Inventory

Beg. bal.	28,800	(c)	47,500
(b)	49,500		
Updated bal.	30,800		

Supplies on Hand

Beg. bal.	1,200	(m)	1,000
(g)	600		
Updated bal.	800		

Prepaid Building Rental

Beg. bal.	24,000	(o)	12,000
Updated bal.	12,000		

Prepaid Advertising

(h)	850	(n)	650
Updated bal.	200		

Accounts Payable

(e)	66,500	Beg. bal.	18,000
		(b)	49,500
		Updated bal.	1,000

Salaries Payable

		(l)	750

Utilities Payable

		(p)	150

Income Taxes Payable

Debit	Credit
	(r) 2,595

Unearned Sales Revenue

Debit	Credit
	(d) 3,500

Capital Stock

Debit	Credit
	Beg. bal. 54,000
	(a) 30,000
	Updated bal. 84,000

Retained Earnings

Debit	Credit
	Beg. bal. 16,500

Dividends

Debit	Credit
(k) 7,500	

Sales Revenue

Debit	Credit
	(c) 125,000

Cost of Goods Sold

Debit	Credit
(c) 47,500	

Salaries Expense

Debit	Credit
(i) 45,000	
(l) 750	
Updated bal. 45,750	

Utilities Expense

Debit	Credit
(j) 650	
(p) 150	
Updated bal. 800	

Advertising Expense

Debit	Credit
(n) 650	

Supplies Expense

Debit	Credit
(m) 1,000	

Building Rent Expense

Debit	Credit
(o) 12,000	

Income Tax Expense

Debit	Credit
(r) 2,595	

5. Data for the financial statements may be taken from the adjusted ledger accounts and reported as follows:

Sports Haven Company
Income Statement
For the Year Ended December 31, 2003

Sales revenue	$125,000	
Less cost of goods sold	47,500	
Gross profit		$77,500
Less operating expenses:		
Salaries expense	$ 45,750	
Utilities expense	800	
Advertising expense	650	
Supplies expense	1,000	
Building rent expense	12,000	60,200
Income before income taxes		$17,300
Income tax expense		2,595
Net income		$14,705

Earnings per share:
$14,705 ÷ 5,100 shares = $2.88 (rounded)

Sports Haven Company
Balance Sheet
December 31, 2003

Assets		
Cash	$54,000	
Accounts receivable	17,900	
Inventory	30,800	
Supplies on hand	800	
Prepaid building rental	12,000	
Prepaid advertising	200	
Total assets		$115,700
Liabilities and Owners' Equity		
Liabilities:		
Accounts payable	$ 1,000	
Salaries payable	750	
Utilities payable	150	
Income taxes payable	2,595	
Unearned sales revenue	3,500	
Total liabilities		$ 7,995
Owners' equity:		
Capital stock (5,100 shares outstanding)	$84,000	
Retained earnings	23,705*	
Total owners' equity		107,705
Total liabilities and owners' equity		$115,700

*Note that in preparing the balance sheet, net income must be added to the beginning balance in Retained Earnings and dividends must be subtracted ($16,500 + $14,705 − $7,500 = $23,705).

6. The next step is to record the closing entries in the general journal and then post those entries to the general ledger (T-accounts). T-accounts are shown with all previous entries and the closing entries [items (s) and (t)] posted.

   The first entry is to close the revenue account and each of the expense accounts. Sales Revenue has a credit balance; it is debited to reduce the balance to zero. The expense accounts are closed by crediting them. The difference in total revenues and total expenses is $14,705 (net income for the period). Net income represents an increase in retained earnings. All of this is captured in the single, compound closing entry (s), as follows:

(s)	Sales Revenue	125,000	
	Cost of Goods Sold		47,500
	Salaries Expense		45,750
	Utilities Expense		800
	Advertising Expense		650
	Supplies Expense		1,000
	Building Rent Expense		12,000
	Income Tax Expense		2,595
	Retained Earnings		14,705

Second, Dividends, a nominal account, must also be closed to Retained Earnings.

(t)	Retained Earnings	7,500	
	Dividends		7,500

Cash

Debit		Credit	
Beg. bal.	17,500	(e)	66,500
(a)	30,000	(g)	600
(c)	22,100	(h)	850
(d)	3,500	(i)	45,000
(f)	102,000	(j)	650
		(k)	7,500
Updated bal.	54,000		

Accounts Receivable

Debit		Credit	
Beg. bal.	17,000	(f)	102,000
(c)	102,900		
Updated bal.	17,900		

Inventory

Debit		Credit	
Beg. bal.	28,800	(c)	47,500
(b)	49,500		
Updated bal.	30,800		

Supplies on Hand

Debit		Credit	
Beg. bal.	1,200	(m)	1,000
(g)	600		
Updated bal.	800		

Prepaid Building Rental

Debit		Credit	
Beg. bal.	24,000	(o)	12,000
Updated bal.	12,000		

Prepaid Advertising

Debit		Credit	
(h)	850	(n)	650
Updated bal.	200		

Accounts Payable

Debit		Credit	
(e)	66,500	Beg. bal.	18,000
		(b)	49,500
		Updated bal.	1,000

Salaries Payable

Debit		Credit	
		(l)	750

Utilities Payable

Debit		Credit	
		(p)	150

Income Taxes Payable

Debit		Credit	
		(r)	2,595

Unearned Sales Revenue

Debit		Credit	
		(d)	3,500

Capital Stock

Debit		Credit	
		Beg. bal.	54,000
		(a)	30,000
		Updated bal.	84,000

Retained Earnings

Debit		Credit	
(t)	7,500	Beg. bal.	16,500
		(s)	14,705
		Updated bal.	23,705

Dividends

Debit		Credit	
(k)	7,500	(t)	7,500

Sales Revenue

Debit		Credit	
(s)	125,000	(c)	125,000

Cost of Goods Sold

Debit		Credit	
(c)	47,500	(s)	47,500

Salaries Expense

Debit		Credit	
(i)	45,000	(s)	45,750
(l)	750		

Utilities Expense

Debit		Credit	
(j)	650	(s)	800
(p)	150		

Advertising Expense

Debit		Credit	
(n)	650	(s)	650

Supplies Expense

Debit		Credit	
(m)	1,000	(s)	1,000

Building Rent Expense

Debit		Credit	
(o)	12,000	(s)	12,000

Income Tax Expense

Debit		Credit	
(r)	2,595	(s)	2,595

7. The final (optional) step in the accounting cycle is to prepare a post-closing trial balance. This procedure is a check on the accuracy of the closing process. It is a listing of all ledger account balances at year-end. Note that only real accounts appear because all nominal accounts have been closed to a zero balance in preparation for the next accounting cycle.

Sports Haven Company
Post-Closing Trial Balance
December 31, 2003

	Debits	Credits
Cash	$ 54,000	
Accounts Receivable	17,900	
Inventory	30,800	
Supplies on Hand	800	
Prepaid Building Rental	12,000	
Prepaid Advertising	200	
Accounts Payable		$ 1,000
Salaries Payable		750
Utilities Payable		150
Income Taxes Payable		2,595
Unearned Sales Revenue		3,500
Capital Stock		84,000
Retained Earnings		23,705
Totals	$115,700	$115,700

discussion questions

1. Why are financial reports prepared on a periodic basis?
2. Distinguish between reporting on a calendar-year and on a fiscal-year basis.
3. When are revenues generally recognized (recorded)?
4. What is the matching principle?
5. Explain why accrual-basis accounting is more appropriate than cash-basis accounting for most businesses.
6. Why are accrual-based financial statements considered somewhat tentative?
7. Why are adjusting entries necessary?
8. Since there are usually no source documents for adjusting entries, how does the accountant know when to make adjusting entries and for what amounts?
9. The analysis process for preparing adjusting entries involves two basic steps. Identify the two steps and explain why both are necessary.
10. Why are supplies not considered inventory? What type of account is Supplies on Hand?
11. Cash is not one of the accounts increased or decreased in an adjusting entry. Why?
12. Which are prepared first: the year-end financial statements or the general journal adjusting entries? Explain.
13. Of what value are the notes to the financial statements and the audit report, both of which are usually included in the annual report to shareholders?
14. Describe the DuPont framework for analysis of financial statements.
15. What is a common-size financial statement? What are its advantages?
16. What is the most informative section of the common-size balance sheet? Explain.
17. Distinguish between real and nominal accounts.
18. What is the purpose of closing entries?
19. What is the purpose of the post-closing trial balance? Explain where the information for the post-closing trial balance comes from.

expanded material

20. Explain why there are alternative ways of recording certain transactions, either as assets or expenses, or as liabilities or revenues.

discussion cases

CASE 4-1

USING FINANCIAL STATEMENTS FOR INVESTMENT DECISIONS

Several doctors are considering the purchase of a small real estate business as an investment. Because you have some training in the mechanics of the accounting cycle, they have hired you to review the real estate company's accounting records and to prepare a balance sheet and an income statement for their use. In analyzing various business documents, you verify the following data.

The account balances at the beginning of the current year were as follows:

Cash in Bank	$ 7,800
Notes Receivable (from Current Owner)	10,000
Supplies on Hand	750
Prepaid Office Rent	4,500
Accounts Payable	450
Owners' Equity	22,600

During the current year, the following summarized transactions took place:

a. The owner paid $1,200 to the business to cover the interest on the note receivable ($10,000 × 0.12 × 1 year). Nothing was paid on the principal.
b. Real estate commissions earned during the year totaled $45,500. Of this amount, $1,000 has not been received by year-end.
c. The company purchased $500 of supplies during the year. A count at year-end shows $300 worth still on hand.
d. The $4,500 paid for office rental was for 18 months, beginning in January of this year.
e. Utilities paid during the year amounted to $1,500.
f. During the year, $400 of accounts payable were paid; the balance in Accounts Payable at year-end is $300, with the adjustment being debited to Miscellaneous Office Expense.
g. The owner paid himself $1,500 a month as a salary and paid a part-time secretary $2,400 for the year. (Ignore payroll taxes.)

On the basis of the above data, prepare a balance sheet and an income statement for the real estate business. Does the business appear profitable? Does the balance sheet raise any questions or concerns? What other information might the doctors want to consider in making this investment decision?

CASE 4-2

ACCOUNTING AND ETHICAL ISSUES INVOLVING THE CLOSING PROCESS

Silva and Wanita Rodriques are the owners of Year-Round Landscape, Inc., a small landscape and yard service business in southern California. The business is three years old and has grown significantly, especially during the past year. To sustain this growth, Year-Round Landscape must expand operations.

In the past, the Rodriques have been able to secure funds for the business from personal resources. Now those resources are exhausted, and the Rodriques are seeking a loan from a local bank.

To satisfy bank requirements, Year-Round Landscape, Inc., must provide a set of financial statements, including comparative income statements showing the growth in earnings over the past three years. In analyzing the records, Silva notices that the nominal accounts have not yet been closed for this year. Furthermore, Silva is aware of a major contract that is to be signed on January 3, only three days after the December 31 year-end for the business. Silva suggests that the closing process be delayed one week so that this major contract can be included in this year's operating results. Silva estimates that this contract will increase current year earnings by 20%.

What accounting issues are involved in this case? What are the ethical issues?

CASE 4-3

WRESTLING WITH YOUR CONSCIENCE AND GAAP

You are the controller for South Valley Industries. Your assistant has just completed the financial statements for the current year and has given them to you for review. A copy of the statements also has been given to the president of the company. The income statement reports a net income for the year of $50,000 and earnings per share of $2.50.

In reviewing the statements, you realize the assistant neglected to record adjusting entries. After making the necessary adjustments, the company shows a net loss of $10,000. The difference is due to an unusually large amount of unrecorded expenses at year-end. You realize that these expenses are not likely to be found by the independent auditors.

You wonder if it would be better to delay the recording of the expenses until the first part of the subsequent year in order to avoid reporting a net loss on the income statement for the current year. A significant increase in revenues is expected in the coming year, and the expenses in question could be "absorbed" by the higher revenues.

What issues are involved in this case? What course of action would you take?

CASE 4-4

expanded material

MAKING SURE OPERATING RESULTS ARE ACCURATE

Dian Karen and Kathy Gillen are considering forming a company to purchase a small business that specializes in interior decoration services. The business records show a modest profit over each of the past five years (approximately $5,000 net income per year). However, the past year's operating results appear to be much better, as shown by the unaudited income statement.

Fashion Design, Inc.
Income Statement
For the Year Ended December 31, 2003

Revenues:		
Consulting revenues	$51,000	
Commissions on furnishings sold	18,000	
Total revenues		$69,000
Expenses:		
Advertising expense	$ 1,200	
Rent expense	4,800	
Salaries expense	36,000	
Supplies expense	500	
Utilities expense	1,800	
Other expenses	1,500	45,800
Income before taxes		$23,200
Income taxes (estimated at 25%)		5,800
Net income		$17,400
EPS: $17,400 ÷ 1,000 shares = $17.40 per share		

In an attempt to verify what appears to be unusually high net income for 2003, Karen and Gillen hire a CPA to audit the records. The CPA discovers the following:

a. The company pays salaries on the 1st and 15th of each month. Salaries amounting to $2,500 have been earned by employees by December 31 but will not be paid until January 1. No adjusting entry has been made.

b. Of the $18,000 in commissions received by December 31, 30% will not be earned until completion of a job in mid-February of 2004. All commissions received have been recorded as revenues.

c. A $10,000 payment was received on November 1 for a consulting assignment that is only one-half earned at December 31. The total amount was credited to Consulting Revenues when received.

d. The rent is $400 per month and must be paid in advance on a one-year lease. A check for $4,800 was given to the landlord on March 1, 2003, and recorded as rent expense on that date.

According to the CPA, except for these data, the income statement appears to accurately reflect the operating results of Fashion Design, Inc.

Answer the following questions:

1. Do the 2003 operating results offer encouragement to Karen and Gillen as potential investors? Explain.
2. What adjustments (if any) are required to make the income statement more accurately reflect the results of operations for the year?
3. What is the impact on the balance sheet (if any) of the data discovered by the CPA?

EXERCISE 4-1

REPORTING INCOME: CASH VERSUS ACCRUAL ACCOUNTING

On December 31, 2003, Matt Morgan completed the first year of operations for his new computer retail store. The following data were obtained from the company's accounting records:

Sales to customers	$197,000
Collections from customers	145,000
Interest earned and received on savings accounts	2,500
Cost of goods sold	98,500
Amounts paid to suppliers for inventory	103,000
Wages owed to employees at year-end	3,500
Wages paid to employees	40,000
Utility bill owed: to be paid next month	1,100
Interest due at 12/31 on loan to be paid in March of next year	1,200
Amount paid for one and one-half years' rent, beginning Jan. 1, 2003	17,500
Income taxes owed at year-end	4,000

1. How much net income (loss) should Matt report for the year ended December 31, 2003, according to (a) cash-basis accounting and (b) accrual-basis accounting?
2. Which basis of accounting provides the better measure of operating results for Matt?

EXERCISE 4-2

REPORTING INCOME: CASH VERSUS ACCRUAL ACCOUNTING

On December 31, Brian Silvaggi completed the first year of operations for his new business. The following data are available from the company's accounting records:

Sales to customers	$145,000
Collections from customers	125,000
Interest earned and received on savings accounts	1,500
Amount paid for one and one-half years' rent	3,600
Utility bill owed: to be paid next month	960
Cost of goods sold	80,000
Amount paid to suppliers for materials	83,000
Wages paid to employees	47,500
Wages owed to employees at year-end	1,200
Interest due at 12/31 on a loan to be paid the middle of next year	800

1. How much net income (loss) should Brian report for the year ended December 31 according to (a) cash-basis accounting and (b) accrual-basis accounting?
2. Which basis of accounting provides the better measure of operating results for Brian?

EXERCISE 4-3

CLASSIFYING ACCOUNT BALANCES

For each of the following accounts, indicate whether it would be found in the income statement or in the balance sheet.

1. Cash
2. Inventory
3. Salaries Expense
4. Prepaid Salaries
5. Retained Earnings
6. Office Supplies Expense
7. Accounts Receivable
8. Cost of Goods Sold
9. Maintenance Expense
10. Interest Receivable
11. Capital Stock
12. Accounts Payable
13. Buildings
14. Mortgage Payable
15. Interest Expense
16. Accounts Payable
17. Notes Receivable
18. Office Supplies
19. Sales Revenue
20. Insurance Expense
21. Machinery
22. Land
23. Salaries Payable
24. Prepaid Insurance
25. Notes Payable
26. Dividends

EXERCISE 4-4

CLASSIFICATIONS OF ACCOUNTS REQUIRING ADJUSTING ENTRIES

For each type of adjustment listed, indicate whether it is an unrecorded receivable, an unrecorded liability, an unearned revenue, or a prepaid expense at December 31, 2003.

1. Property taxes that are for the year 2003, but are not to be paid until 2004.
2. Rent revenue earned during 2003, but not collected until 2004.
3. Salaries earned by employees in December 2003, but not to be paid until January 5, 2004.
4. A payment received from a customer in December 2003 for services that will not be performed until February 2004.
5. An insurance premium paid on December 29, 2003, for the period January 1, 2004, to December 31, 2004.
6. Gasoline charged on a credit card during December 2003. The bill will not be received until January 15, 2004.
7. Interest on a certificate of deposit held during 2003. The interest will not be received until January 7, 2004.
8. A deposit received on December 15, 2003, for rental of storage space. The rental period is from January 1, 2004, to December 31, 2004.

EXERCISE 4-5

ADJUSTING ENTRIES: PREPAID EXPENSES AND UNEARNED REVENUES

Boswell Group is a professional corporation providing management consulting services. The company initially debits assets in recording prepaid expenses and credits liabilities in recording unearned revenues. Give the entry that Boswell would use to record each of the following transactions on the date it occurred. Prepare the adjusting entries needed on December 31, 2003.

1. On July 1, 2003, the company paid a three-year premium of $7,200 on an insurance policy that is effective July 1, 2003, and expires June 30, 2006.
2. On February 1, 2003, Boswell paid its property taxes for the year February 1, 2003, to January 31, 2004. The tax bill was $1,800.
3. On May 1, 2003, the company paid $180 for a three-year subscription to an advertising journal. The subscription starts May 1, 2003, and expires April 30, 2006.
4. Boswell received $1,800 on September 15, 2003, in return for which the company agreed to provide consulting services for 18 months beginning immediately.
5. Boswell rented part of its office space to Bristle Brush Company. Bristle paid $1,200 on November 1, 2003, for the next six months' rent.

6. Boswell loaned $100,000 to a client. On November 1 the client paid $24,000, which represents two years' interest in advance (November 1, 2003, through October 31, 2005).

EXERCISE 4-6

ADJUSTING ENTRIES: PREPAID EXPENSES AND UNEARNED REVENUES

Cannon Group provides computer network consulting services. The company initially debits assets in recording prepaid expenses and credits liabilities in recording unearned revenues. Give the appropriate entry that Cannon would use to record each of the following transactions on the date it occurred. Prepare the adjusting entries needed on December 31, 2003. (Round all numbers to the nearest dollar.)

1. On April 1, 2003, the company paid $250 for a two-year subscription to a computer networking journal. The subscription starts April 1, 2003, and expires March 31, 2005.
2. On May 1, 2003, Cannon paid $2,300 in property taxes for the year May 1, 2003, to April 30, 2004.
3. On June 15, 2003, Cannon received $25,000 for a contract to provide consulting services for 18 months beginning immediately.
4. On July 1, 2003, the company paid a two-year premium of $15,000 on an insurance policy that is effective July 1, 2003, and expires June 30, 2005.
5. Cannon rented part of its office building to Ross Graphics, LLC. Ross paid $1,500 on September 1, 2003, for the next six months' rent.
6. Cannon loaned $150,000 to a client. On October 1, 2003, the client paid $18,000 for interest in advance (October 1, 2003, to September 30, 2004).

EXERCISE 4-7

ADJUSTING ENTRIES

Shop Rite Services is ready to prepare its financial statements for the year ended December 31, 2003. The following information can be determined by analyzing the accounts:

1. On August 1, 2003, Shop Rite received a $4,800 payment in advance for rental of office space. The rental period is for one year beginning on the date payment was received. Shop Rite recorded the receipt as unearned rent.
2. On March 1, 2003, Shop Rite paid its insurance agent $3,000 for the premium due on a 24-month corporate policy. Shop Rite recorded the payment as prepaid insurance.
3. Shop Rite pays its employee wages the middle of each month. The monthly payroll (ignoring payroll taxes) is $22,000.
4. Shop Rite received a note from a customer on June 1, 2003, as payment for services. The amount of the note is $1,000 with interest at 12%. The note and interest will be paid on June 1, 2005.
5. On December 20, 2003, Shop Rite received a $2,500 check for services. The transaction was recorded as unearned revenue. By year-end, Shop Rite had completed three-fourths of the contracted services. The rest of the services won't be completed until at least the middle of January 2004.
6. On September 1, Shop Rite purchased $500 worth of supplies. At December 31, 2003, one-fourth of the supplies had been used. Shop Rite initially recorded the purchase of supplies as an asset.

Where appropriate, prepare adjusting journal entries at December 31, 2003, for each of these items.

EXERCISE 4-8

ADJUSTING ENTRIES

Consider the following two independent situations:

1. On June 1, Brown Company received $4,800 cash for a two-year subscription to its monthly magazine. The term of the subscription begins on June 1. Make the entry to record the receipt of the subscription on June 1. Also make the necessary adjusting entry at December 31. The company uses an account called Unearned Subscription Revenue.

2. Clark Company pays its employees every Friday for a five-day workweek. Salaries of $200,000 are earned equally throughout the week. December 31 of the current year is a Tuesday.
   a. Make the adjusting entry at December 31.
   b. Make the entry to pay the week's salaries on Friday, January 3, of the next year. Assume that all employees are paid for New Year's Day.

EXERCISE 4-9

ADJUSTING ENTRIES

Consider the following items for Burton Company:

1. On November 1 of the current year, Burton Company borrowed $150,000 at 8% interest. As of December 31, no interest expense has been recognized.
2. On September 1 of the current year, Burton Company rented to another company some excess space in one of its buildings. Burton Company received $18,000 cash on September 1. The rental period extends for six months, starting on September 1. Burton Company credited the account Unearned Rent Revenue upon receipt of the rent paid in advance.
3. At the beginning of the year, Burton Company had $900 of supplies on hand. During the year, another $5,400 of supplies were purchased for cash and recorded in the asset account Office Supplies. At the end of the year, Burton Company determined that $1,400 of supplies remained on hand.
4. On February 1 of the current year, Burton Company loaned Dridge Company $100,000 at 9% interest. The loan amount, plus accrued interest, will be repaid in one year.

For each of the items, make the appropriate adjusting journal entry, if any, necessary in Burton Company's books as of December 31.

EXERCISE 4-10

ADJUSTING ENTRIES

Davis Company opened a Web page design business on January 1 of the current year. The following information relates to Davis Company's operations during the current year:

1. On February 1, Davis Company rented a new office. Before moving in, it prepaid a year's rent of $24,000 cash.
2. On March 31, Davis Company borrowed $50,000 from a local bank at 15%. The loan is to be repaid, with interest, after one year. As of December 31, no interest payments had yet been made.
3. Davis Company bills some of its customers in advance for its design services. During the year Davis received $60,000 cash in advance from its customers. As of December 31, Davis's accountant determined that 40% of that amount had not yet been earned.
4. On June 15, Davis Company purchased $1,400 of supplies for cash. On September 14, Davis made another cash purchase of $1,100. As of December 31, Davis's accountant determined that $1,700 of supplies had been used during the year.
5. Before closing its books, Davis Company found a bill for $800 from a free-lance programmer who had done work for the company in November. Davis had not yet recorded anything in its books with respect to this bill. Davis plans to pay the bill in January of next year.

For each of the items, make the initial entry, where appropriate, to record the transaction and, if necessary, the adjusting entry at December 31.

EXERCISE 4-11

ANALYSIS OF ACCOUNTS

Answer the following questions:

1. If office supplies on hand amounted to $4,000 at the beginning of the period and total purchases of office supplies during the period amounted to $22,000, determine the ending balance of office supplies on hand if office supplies expense for the period amounted to $20,000.

2. If beginning and ending accounts receivable were $10,000 and $12,000, respectively, and total sales made on account for the period amounted to $52,000, determine the amount of cash collections from customers on account for the period.
3. Assume all rent revenues are received in advance and accounted for as unearned rent, and beginning and ending balances of unearned rent are $3,000 and $2,500, respectively. If total rent revenue for the period amounts to $15,000, determine the amount of rent collections in advance for the period.

EXERCISE 4-12

DUPONT FRAMEWORK

The following information is for Ina Company:

	2003	2002	2001
Total assets	$200,000	$160,000	$180,000
Total liabilities	90,000	80,000	100,000
Stockholders' equity	110,000	80,000	80,000
Sales	800,000	600,000	600,000
Net income	40,000	20,000	10,000

For the years 2001, 2002, and 2003, compute:

1. Return on equity
2. Profit margin
3. Asset turnover
4. Assets-to-equity ratio

EXERCISE 4-13

DUPONT FRAMEWORK

The numbers below are for Iffy Company and Model Company for the year 2003:

	Iffy	Model
Cash	$ 120	$ 900
Accounts receivable	600	4,500
Inventory	480	6,000
Property, plant, and equipment	3,440	15,000
Total liabilities	3,190	18,150
Stockholders' equity	1,450	8,250
Sales	10,000	75,000
Cost of goods sold	9,200	66,750
Wages expense	700	5,250
Net income	100	3,000

1. Compute return on equity, profit margin, asset turnover, and the assets-to-equity ratio for both Iffy and Model.
2. Briefly explain why Iffy's return on equity is lower than Model's.

EXERCISE 4-14

DUPONT FRAMEWORK

The numbers below are for Question Company and Standard Company for the year 2003:

	Question	Standard
Cash	$ 60	$ 300
Accounts receivable	600	4,000
Inventory	1,400	3,650
Plant and equipment	1,000	8,650

(continued)

	Question	Standard
Total liabilities	$ 2,448	$13,280
Stockholders' equity	612	3,320
Sales	10,000	50,000
Cost of goods sold	7,350	36,750
Wages expense	700	3,500
Other expenses	1,900	8,500
Net income	50	1,250

1. Compute return on equity, profit margin, asset turnover, and the assets-to-equity ratio for both Question and Standard.
2. Briefly explain why Question's return on equity is lower than Standard's.

EXERCISE 4-15

DUPONT FRAMEWORK FOR ANALYZING FINANCIAL STATEMENTS

The income statement and balance sheet for the Rollins Company are provided below. Using the DuPont framework, compute the profit margin, asset turnover, assets-to-equity ratio, and resulting return on equity for the year 2003.

Rollins Company
Income Statement
For the Year Ended December 31, 2003

Revenue from services		$151,920
Operating expenses:		
Insurance expense	$ 5,480	
Rent expense	500	
Office supplies expense	2,960	
Salaries expense	55,000	63,940
Net income		$ 87,980

Rollins Company
Balance Sheet
December 31, 2003

Assets		Liabilities and Owners' Equity	
Cash	$ 22,000	Accounts payable	$ 54,800
Accounts receivable	40,000	Capital stock	50,000
Notes receivable	12,800	Retained earnings	150,000
Machinery	180,000		
		Total liabilities	
Total assets	$254,800	and owners' equity	$254,800

EXERCISE 4-16

DUPONT FRAMEWORK FOR ANALYZING FINANCIAL STATEMENTS

Using the income statement and balance sheet for the Jacobson and Sons Company, compute the three components of return on equity—profitability, efficiency, and leverage—based on the DuPont framework, for the year 2003.

Jacobson and Sons Co.
Income Statement
For the Year Ended December 31, 2003

Revenues		$265,000
Expenses:		
Supplies expense	$138,600	
Salaries expense	26,700	
Utilities expense	6,500	
Rent expense	17,100	
Other expenses	8,700	197,600
Net income		$ 67,400

Jacobson and Sons Co.
Balance Sheet
December 31, 2003

Assets		Liabilities and Owners' Equity	
Cash	$ 38,900	Accounts payable	$ 17,100
Accounts receivable	31,000	Notes payable	17,200
Supplies	46,300	Capital stock	30,000
Land	25,000	Retained earnings	173,600
Buildings	96,700		
Total assets	$237,900	Total liabilities and owners' equity	$237,900

EXERCISE 4-17

COMMON-SIZE BALANCE SHEET

The following data are taken from the comparative balance sheet prepared for Elison Company:

	2003	2002
Cash	$ 68,000	$ 50,000
Accounts receivable	86,000	80,000
Inventory	136,000	60,000
Property, plant, and equipment	182,000	110,000
Total assets	$472,000	$300,000

Sales for 2003 were $2,000,000. Sales for 2002 were $1,600,000.

1. Prepare the asset section of a common-size balance sheet for Elison Company for 2003 and 2002.
2. Overall, Elison is less efficient at using its assets to generate sales in 2003 than in 2002. What asset or assets are responsible for this decreased efficiency?

EXERCISE 4-18

COMMON-SIZE INCOME STATEMENT

Comparative income statements for Callister Company for 2003 and 2002 are given on the following page.

1. Prepare common-size income statements for Callister Company for 2003 and 2002.
2. The profit margin for Callister is lower in 2003 than in 2002. What expense or expenses are causing this lower profitability?

	2003	2002
Sales	$1,600,000	$900,000
Cost of goods sold	1,020,000	480,000
Gross profit	$ 580,000	$420,000
Selling and administrative expenses	200,000	160,000
Operating income	$ 380,000	$260,000
Interest expense	80,000	60,000
Income before taxes	$ 300,000	$200,000
Income tax expense	90,000	60,000
Net income	$ 210,000	$140,000

EXERCISE 4-19

REAL AND NOMINAL ACCOUNTS

Classify each of the following accounts as either a real account (R) or a nominal account (N):

1. Cash
2. Sales Revenue
3. Accounts Receivable
4. Cost of Goods Sold
5. Prepaid Insurance
6. Capital Stock
7. Retained Earnings
8. Insurance Expense
9. Salaries Payable
10. Interest Expense
11. Insurance Premiums Payable
12. Salaries Expense
13. Accounts Payable
14. Prepaid Salaries
15. Utilities Expense
16. Notes Payable
17. Inventory
18. Property Tax Expense
19. Rent Expense
20. Interest Payable
21. Income Taxes Payable
22. Dividends
23. Buildings
24. Office Supplies
25. Income Tax Expense

EXERCISE 4-20

CLOSING ENTRY

The income statement for Eriksen Enterprises for the year ended June 30, 2003, is provided.

Eriksen Enterprises
Income Statement
For the Year Ended June 30, 2003

Sales revenue	$187,000
Cost of goods sold	(122,000)
Selling and general expenses	(20,500)
Income before income taxes	$ 44,500
Income tax expense	(17,800)
Net income	$ 26,700

1. Prepare a journal entry to close the accounts to Retained Earnings.
2. What problem may arise in closing the accounts if the information from the income statement is used?

EXERCISE 4-21

CLOSING ENTRY

Revenue and expense accounts of Rushford Publishing Company for November 30, 2003, are given as follows. Prepare a compound journal entry that will close the revenue and expense accounts to the retained earnings account.

	Debits	Credits
Sales Revenue		$250,500
Cost of Goods Sold	$124,500	
Salaries Expense	35,000	
Interest Expense	1,000	

(continued)

	Debits	Credits
Rent Expense	$ 9,300	
Insurance Expense	1,700	
Property Tax Expense	800	
Supplies Expense	1,000	
Advertising Expense	10,000	

EXERCISE 4-22

CLOSING DIVIDENDS AND PREPARING A POST-CLOSING TRIAL BALANCE

A listing of account balances taken from the adjusted ledger account balances of Farmers' Co-Op shows the following:

Cash	$ 22,580
Accounts Receivable	56,480
Inventory	78,360
Prepaid Insurance	6,520
Land	136,000
Accounts Payable	28,640
Notes Payable	40,000
Salaries Payable	9,000
Taxes Payable	24,400
Unearned Rent	15,200
Mortgage Payable	90,000
Capital Stock	44,000
Dividends	20,000
Retained Earnings	68,700

All revenue and expense accounts have been closed to Retained Earnings. Dividends has not yet been closed.

Prepare (1) the closing entry for Dividends and (2) a post-closing trial balance for December 31, 2003.

EXERCISE 4-23

CLOSING DIVIDENDS AND PREPARING A POST-CLOSING TRIAL BALANCE

Below is a listing of account balances taken from the adjusted ledger account balances of Goldsmith Corporation.

Cash	$25,500
Accounts Receivable	24,000
Inventory	60,000
Prepaid Advertising	5,500
Building	95,000
Land	35,000
Accounts Payable	20,000
Wages Payable	5,000
Income Taxes Payable	4,000
Mortgage Payable	55,000
Notes Payable	27,500
Unearned Rent	2,500
Capital Stock	95,500
Dividends	15,500
Retained Earnings	51,000

All revenues and expense accounts have been closed to Retained Earnings. Dividends has not yet been closed.

Prepare (1) the closing entry for Dividends and (2) a post-closing trial balance for December 31, 2003.

EXERCISE 4-24

ADJUSTING ENTRIES

The trial balance of Dallas Company shows the following balances, among others, on December 31, 2003, the end of its first fiscal year:

Rent Revenue	$ 36,800
Office Supplies Expense	2,700
Mortgage Payable	130,000

Inspection of the company's records reveals that:

1. Rent revenue of $2,800 is unearned at December 31, 2003.
2. Interest of $7,800 on the mortgage is payable semiannually on March 1 and September 1.
3. Office supplies of $500 are on hand on December 31. When purchases of office supplies were made during the year, they were charged to the office supplies expense account.

Given this information, prepare journal entries to adjust the books as of December 31, 2003.

problems

PROBLEM 4-1

CASH- AND ACCRUAL-BASIS ACCOUNTING

In the course of your examination of the books and records of Hickory Company, you find the following data:

Salaries earned by employees in 2003	$ 53,000
Salaries paid in 2003	55,000
Total sales revenue in 2003	838,000
Cash collected from sales in 2003	900,000
Utilities expense incurred in 2003	5,000
Utility bills paid in 2003	4,800
Cost of goods sold in 2003	532,000
Cash paid on purchases in 2003	411,000
Inventory at December 31, 2003	320,000
Tax assessment for 2003	5,000
Taxes paid in 2003	4,900
Rent expense for 2003	30,000
Rent paid in 2003	25,000

Required:

1. Compute Hickory's net income for 2003 using cash-basis accounting.
2. Compute Hickory's net income for 2003 using accrual-basis accounting.
3. **Interpretive Question:** Why is accrual-basis accounting normally used? Can you see any opportunities for improperly reporting income under cash-basis accounting? Explain.

PROBLEM 4-2

ADJUSTING ENTRIES

The information presented below is for Sun Marketing, Inc.

a. Salaries for the period December 26, 2003, through December 31, 2003, amounted to $14,240 and have not been recorded or paid. (Ignore payroll taxes.)
b. Interest of $6,000 is payable for three months on a 15%, $160,000 loan and has not been recorded.
c. Rent of $24,000 was paid for six months in advance on December 1 and debited to Prepaid Rent.
d. Rent of $82,000 was credited to an unearned revenue account when received. Of this amount, $33,400 is still unearned at year-end.
e. The expired portion of an insurance policy is $1,000. Prepaid Insurance was originally debited.

f. Interest revenue of $300 from a $2,000 note has been earned but not collected or recorded.

Required: Prepare the adjusting entries that should be made on December 31, 2003. (Omit explanations.)

PROBLEM 4-3

ADJUSTING ENTRIES

The information presented below is for Averrett Marketing, Inc.

a. Rent of $56,500 was credited to an unearned revenue account when received. Of this amount, $24,750 is still unearned at year-end.
b. Interest revenue of $4,500 from a $65,000 note has been earned but not collected or recorded.
c. Salaries for the period December 26, 2003, to December 31, 2003, amounted to $11,500 and have not been recorded or paid. (Ignore payroll taxes.)
d. Interest of $8,000 is payable for September 2003 through December 2003 on a 12%, $200,000 loan and has not been recorded.
e. The expired portion of an insurance policy is $2,150. Prepaid Insurance was originally debited.
f. Rent of $18,000 was paid for six months in advance on November 15, 2003, and debited to Prepaid Rent.

Required: Prepare the adjusting entries that should be made on December 31, 2003. (Omit explanations.)

PROBLEM 4-4

YEAR-END ANALYSIS OF ACCOUNTS

An analysis of cash records and account balances of Wells, Inc., for 2003 is as follows:

	Account Balances Jan. 1, 2003	Account Balances Dec. 31, 2003	Cash Received or Paid in 2003
Wages Payable	$2,600	$3,000	
Unearned Rent	4,500	5,000	
Prepaid Insurance	100	120	
Paid for wages			$29,600
Received for rent			12,000
Paid for insurance			720

Required: Determine the amounts that should be included on the 2003 income statement for (1) wages expense, (2) rent revenue, and (3) insurance expense.

PROBLEM 4-5

YEAR-END ANALYSIS OF ACCOUNTS

An analysis of cash records and account balances of Computer Networking, Inc., for 2003 is as follows:

	Account Balances Jan. 1, 2003	Account Balances Dec. 31, 2003	Cash Received or Paid in 2003
Salaries Payable	$10,750	$12,750	
Unearned Rent	23,250	26,500	
Prepaid Insurance	2,000	3,100	
Paid for salaries			$125,000
Received for rent			64,250
Paid for insurance			12,600

Required: Determine the amounts that should be included on the 2003 income statement for (1) salaries expense, (2) rent revenue, and (3) insurance expense.

PROBLEM 4-6

ACCOUNT CLASSIFICATIONS AND DEBIT-CREDIT RELATIONSHIPS

Using the format provided, for each account identify (1) whether the account is a balance sheet (B/S) or an income statement (I/S) account; (2) whether it is an asset (A), a liability (L), an owners' equity (OE), a revenue (R), or an expense (E) account; (3) whether the account is a real or a nominal account; (4) whether the account will be "closed" or left "open" at year-end; and (5) whether the account normally has a debit or a credit balance. The following example is provided:

Account Title	(1) B/S or I/S	(2) A, L, OE, R, E	(3) Real or Nominal	(4) Closed or Open	(5) Debit/ Credit
Cash	B/S	A	Real	Open	Debit

1. Accounts Receivable
2. Accounts Payable
3. Prepaid Insurance
4. Mortgage Payable
5. Rent Expense
6. Sales Revenue
7. Cost of Goods Sold
8. Dividends
9. Capital Stock
10. Inventory
11. Retained Earnings
12. Prepaid Rent
13. Supplies on Hand
14. Utilities Expense
15. Income Taxes Payable
16. Interest Revenue
17. Notes Payable
18. Income Tax Expense
19. Wages Payable
20. Unearned Rent Revenue
21. Land
22. Unearned Consulting Fees
23. Interest Receivable
24. Consulting Fees

PROBLEM 4-7

ANALYZING FINANCIAL STATEMENTS

Refer to the financial statements for Sports Haven Company for the year-ended December 31, 2003 (shown in the review problem for this chapter, pp. 176–177).

Required:

1. Using the DuPont framework, compute:
   a. The profit margin
   b. The asset turnover
   c. The assets-to-equity ratio
   d. The overall return on equity
2. Prepare a common-size income statement.
3. **Interpretive Question:** What is the value of common-size financial statements?

PROBLEM 4-8

ANALYZING FINANCIAL STATEMENTS

The income statement and the balance sheet for the Hamblin Company for the year ended December 31, 2003, are provided below.

Hamblin Company
Income Statement
For the Year Ended December 31, 2003

Sales revenue		$270,000
Expenses:		
Cost of goods sold	$150,000	
Salaries expense	45,000	
Interest expense	10,500	205,500
Net income		$ 64,500

Hamblin Company
Balance Sheet
December 31, 2003

Assets		
Cash	$ 49,500	
Accounts receivable	22,500	
Inventory	15,000	
Land	225,000	
Total assets		$312,000
Liabilities and Owners' Equity		
Liabilities:		
Accounts payable		$ 15,000
Owners' equity:		
Capital stock	$202,500	
Retained earnings	94,500	
Total owners' equity		297,000
Total liabilities and owners' equity		$312,000

Required:

1. Using the DuPont framework, compute Hamblin's return on equity (ROE).
2. Prepare a common-size balance sheet, using total revenue as the basis for comparison.
3. **Interpretive Question:** Based on your analysis in (1) and (2), does Hamblin Company appear to be in good shape?

PROBLEM 4-9

CLOSING ENTRIES

The income statement for Home Light, Inc., for the year ended December 31, 2003, is as follows:

Home Light, Inc.
Income Statement
For the Year Ended December 31, 2003

Sales revenue		$452,000
Less expenses:		
Cost of goods sold	$363,000	
Salaries expense	72,000	
Interest expense	5,250	
Office supplies expense	3,820	
Insurance expense	4,930	
Property tax expense	11,200	
Total expenses		460,200
Net loss		$ (8,200)

Required:

Dividends of $20,000 were paid on December 30, 2003.

1. Give the entry required on December 31, 2003, to properly close the income statement accounts.
2. Give the entry required to close the dividends account at December 31, 2003.

PROBLEM 4-10

CLOSING ENTRIES

The income statement for Quality Plumbing, Inc., for the year ended December 31, 2003, is as follows:

Quality Plumbing, Inc.
Income Statement
For the Year Ended December 31, 2003

Sales revenue		$623,400
Less expenses:		
Cost of goods sold	$447,000	
Wages expense	98,350	
Utilities expense	1,720	
Insurance expense	2,790	
Property tax expense	2,110	
Rent expense	26,000	
Advertising expense	9,830	
Interest expense	4,300	
Total expenses		592,100
Net income		$ 31,300

Dividends of $23,200 were paid on December 30, 2003.

Required:

1. Give the entry required on December 31, 2003, to properly close the income statement accounts.
2. Give the entry required to close the dividends account at December 31, 2003.

PROBLEM 4-11 UNIFYING CONCEPTS: ADJUSTING AND CLOSING ENTRIES

The unadjusted and adjusted trial balances of White Company as of December 31, 2003, are presented below.

White Company
Trial Balance
December 31, 2003

	Unadjusted		Adjusted	
	Debits	**Credits**	**Debits**	**Credits**
Cash	$ 21,250		$ 21,250	
Accounts Receivable	11,250		11,250	
Supplies on Hand	5,195		3,895	
Prepaid Rent	17,545		7,545	
Prepaid Insurance	1,985		1,100	
Buildings (net)	95,000		95,000	
Land	45,720		45,720	
Accounts Payable		$ 9,350		$ 9,350
Wages Payable				5,700
Income Taxes Payable				580
Interest Payable		450		1,050
Notes Payable		65,000		65,000
Capital Stock		84,320		84,320
Consulting Fees Earned		142,380		142,380
Wages Expense	92,335		98,035	
Rent Expense			10,000	
Interest Expense	3,500		4,100	
Insurance Expense	585		1,470	
Supplies Expenses	4,365		5,665	
Income Tax Expense	2,770		3,350	
Totals	$301,500	$301,500	$308,380	$308,380

Required:

1. Prepare the journal entries that are required to adjust the accounts at December 31, 2003.
2. Prepare the journal entry that is required to close the accounts at December 31, 2003.

PROBLEM 4-12

UNIFYING CONCEPTS: ANALYSIS OF ACCOUNTS

The bookkeeper for Careless Company accidentally pressed the wrong computer key and erased the amount of Retained Earnings. You have been asked to analyze the following data and provide some key numbers for the board of directors meeting, which is to take place in 30 minutes. With the exception of Retained Earnings, the following account balances are available at December 31, 2003.

Cash	$122,000	Accounts Receivable	$ 98,000
Furniture (net)	80,000	Inventory	320,000
Accounts Payable	240,000	Notes Payable	500,000
Land	520,000	Supplies on Hand	20,000
Buildings (net)	480,000	Capital Stock	600,000
Sales Revenue	830,000	Dividends	40,000
Salaries Expense	100,000	Retained Earnings	?
Cost of Goods Sold	440,000		

Required:

1. Compute the amount of total assets at December 31, 2003.
2. Compute the amount of net income for the year ended December 31, 2003.
3. After all closing entries are made, what is the amount of Retained Earnings at December 31, 2003?
4. What was the beginning Retained Earnings balance at January 1, 2003?

PROBLEM 4-13

UNIFYING CONCEPTS: ANALYSIS AND CORRECTION OF ERRORS

At the end of November 2003, the general ledger of Porridge Milling Company showed the following amounts:

Assets	$64,250
Liabilities	28,800
Owners' Equity	62,000

The company's bookkeeper is new on the job and does not have much accounting experience. Because the bookkeeper has made numerous errors, total assets do not equal liabilities plus owners' equity. The following is a list of errors made.

a. Inventory that cost $42,000 was sold, but the entry to record cost of goods sold was not made.
b. Credit sales of $12,100 were posted to the general ledger as $21,100. The accounts receivable were posted correctly.
c. Inventory of $12,500 was purchased on account and received before the end of November, but no entry to record the purchase was made until December.
d. November salaries payable of $5,000 were not recorded until paid in December.
e. Common stock was issued for $18,500 and credited to Accounts Payable.
f. Inventory purchased for $31,050 was incorrectly posted to the asset account as $13,500. No error was made in the liability account.

Required: Determine the correct balances of assets, liabilities, and owners' equity at the end of November.

PROBLEM 4-14

UNIFYING CONCEPTS: THE ACCOUNTING CYCLE

The post-closing trial balance of Anderson Company at December 31, 2002, is shown here.

Anderson Company
Post-Closing Trial Balance
December 31, 2002

	Debits	Credits
Cash	$ 15,000	
Accounts Receivable	20,000	
Inventory	30,000	
Land	150,000	
Accounts Payable		$ 25,000
Notes Payable		35,000
Capital Stock		125,000
Retained Earnings		30,000
Totals	$215,000	$215,000

During 2003, Anderson Company had the following transactions:

a. Inventory purchases were $80,000, all on credit (debit Inventory).
b. An additional $10,000 of capital stock was issued for cash.
c. Merchandise that cost $100,000 was sold for $180,000; $100,000 were credit sales and the balance were cash sales. (Debit Cost of Goods Sold and credit Inventory for sale of merchandise.)
d. The notes were paid, including $7,000 interest.
e. $105,000 was collected from customers.
f. $95,000 was paid to reduce accounts payable.
g. Salaries expense was $30,000, all paid in cash.
h. A $10,000 cash dividend was declared and paid.

Required:

1. Prepare journal entries to record each of the 2003 transactions.
2. Set up T-accounts with the proper balances at January 1, 2003, and post the journal entries to the T-accounts.
3. Prepare an income statement for the year ended December 31, 2003, and a balance sheet as of that date. Also prepare a statement of retained earnings.
4. Prepare the entries necessary to close the nominal accounts, including Dividends.
5. Post the closing entries to the ledger accounts [label (i) and (j)] and prepare a post-closing trial balance at December 31, 2003.

competency enhancement opportunities

- Analyzing Real Company Information
- International Case
- Ethics Case
- Writing Assignment
- The Debate
- Cumulative Spreadsheet Project
- Internet Search

The following additional assignments provide opportunities for students to develop critical thinking, ethical perspectives, oral and written communication skills, experience with electronic research, and teamwork through group and business activities.

ANALYZING REAL COMPANY INFORMATION

• ***Analyzing 4-1 (Microsoft)***

Using MICROSOFT's 1999 annual report contained in Appendix A, answer the following questions:

1. Microsoft discloses that as of June 30, 1999, the company had received cash of $4.239 billion that had not been earned as of that date. Accordingly, the company made an adjusting entry to recognize the unearned revenue. Provide the adjusting entry that was made by Microsoft.
2. Read the note related to Microsoft's unearned revenue and determine what this amount relates to—operating systems, applications, and so forth.
3. Using the DuPont framework, determine Microsoft's return on equity.

• ***Analyzing 4-2 (Hewlett-Packard and Compaq)***

Selected financial statement information for HEWLETT-PACKARD and COMPAQ is given in the table below. Using this information, answer the following questions.

(in millions)	Hewlett-Packard	Compaq
Assets	$35,297	$27,277
Equity	18,295	14,834
Net income	3,491	569
Sales	42,370	38,525

1. Compute each firm's return on equity using the DuPont framework.
2. Identify the primary reason for the significant difference between the two return on equity ratios.
3. Based on the ratios used in the DuPont framework, can you determine which firm has more debt? Which ratio provided this insight?

• ***Analyzing 4-3 (Campbell Soup)***

Information from the 1999 income statement for CAMPBELL SOUP COMPANY is shown below.

(in millions)	1999 52 weeks	1998 52 weeks	1997 52 weeks
Net Sales	**$6,424**	$6,696	$6,614
Costs and expenses			
Cost of products sold	**3,050**	3,233	3,412
Marketing and selling expenses	**1,634**	1,518	1,370
Administrative expenses	**304**	300	271
Research and development expenses	**66**	71	68
Other expenses (Note 7)	**64**	64	140
Restructuring charges (Note 6)	**36**	262	204
Total costs and expenses	**5,154**	5,448	5,465

(continued)

Earnings Before Interest and Taxes	**$1,270**	$1,248	$1,149
Interest expense (Note 8)	**184**	189	166
Interest income	**11**	14	8
Earnings before taxes	**1,097**	1,073	991
Taxes on earnings (Note 11)	**373**	384	357
Earnings from Continuing Operations	**724**	689	634
Earnings (Loss) from Discontinued Operations (Note 3)		(18)	79
Cumulative Effect of Change in Accounting Principle (Note 4)		(11)	
Net Earnings	**$ 724**	$ 660	$ 713

Using the information from the income statement, perform the following:

1. Prepare common-size income statements for 1999 and 1998. Can you identify any significant changes in expenses and revenues as a percentage of total revenue over the two-year period?
2. Using the information from the 1999 income statement, prepare the journal entry that would be required to close the nominal accounts to Retained Earnings.

INTERNATIONAL CASE

• *Exchange Rate Adjustments*

Given the international economy in which many firms operate, it is not unusual for companies to have transactions with companies in foreign countries. Relatedly, it is becoming common for some of those transactions to be denominated in a foreign currency. That is, if a company in the United States makes a purchase from a company in Japan, it is possible that the U.S. company will have to pay Japanese yen when the invoice comes due.

For example, suppose American, Inc., purchased inventory from Japan, Inc., on December 15, 2002. Japan, Inc., expects to receive 1,000,000 Japanese yen in 30 days. To record a journal entry for this purchase, you would need to know what 1,000,000 yen are worth today. Suppose that on December 15, 2002, one yen is worth $0.07 (this is called an exchange rate). What journal entry would be made on American, Inc.'s books?

Since exchange rates change every day, the amount of U.S. dollars to be paid on January 15, 2003, will likely be different than the originally recorded $70,000. In addition, to correctly state the liability on December 31, 2002, an adjustment will be required. Suppose that at year-end, one Japanese yen is worth $0.08. What adjusting entry would be made to reflect this change in exchange rates as of December 31, 2002? (HINT: The accounts being adjusted with this journal entry will be the accounts payable account and an exchange gain or loss.)

When the invoice is paid on January 15, 2003, it is likely that the number of U.S. dollars required to purchase 1,000,000 Japanese yen will again have changed. Suppose exchange rates have increased to $0.09. Provide the journal entry to pay the invoice.

ETHICS CASE

• *Do Two Wrongs Make a Right?*

Jex Varner, chief financial officer of Wyndam, Inc., is involved in a meeting with the firm's newly hired external auditors, Ernst & Price. The external auditors have noted several adjusting entries that they believe should be reflected in the current period's financial statements. Specifically, there are questions regarding $400,000 of cash that has been received (and recorded as revenue) but not yet earned. The auditors feel that this amount should be recognized as a liability.

Jex counters that the firm's policy has always been to recognize revenue when the cash is received. He states that $350,000 of cash was received in December of last year, earned in January, and no adjustment was made. To be consistent, he continues, he doesn't believe any adjustments should be made this year.

As a member of the external auditing team, do you agree with Jex's reasoning? If you think that an adjustment needs to be made, what journal entry would you propose? What should be done about the $350,000 that has been earned this year even though the cash was received last year?

WRITING ASSIGNMENT

• *Are Adjusting Entries More Trouble Than They Are Worth?*

You are taking an introductory accounting class. You think that making regular journal entries is not too difficult, but making adjusting entries is still a bit of a mystery. You have found that your answers to homework questions on adjusting entries are incorrect at least half the time. You mentioned your difficulties to the other members of your study group, and they all agreed—adjusting entries are brutal. As you and your study colleagues shared your frustration with adjusting entries, the following consensus formed: adjusting entries are more trouble than they are worth. You were selected by your study group to pass this sentiment along to your accounting instructor. She agreed that adjusting entries can be difficult, but she insisted that they are worth the effort. She has now given you the following writing assignment: write a one-page paper describing the value of adjusting entries.

THE DEBATE

• *Standardizing Ratios*

Up to this point in the text, you have been introduced to numerous ratios—current ratio, profit margin, return on equity, and so forth. The DuPont framework introduced in this chapter provides a meaningful way of using ratios to compare a company's performance both across time and across companies. Using ratios for comparison purposes could be facilitated by standardizing certain ratios and requiring all companies to compute a specified set of ratios in exactly the same way. For example, when computing a debt-to-equity ratio, should debt include all liabilities or only long-term liabilities? Having a specified definition of what should be included in the debt number and what should be included in the equity number might facilitate comparison.

Divide your group into two teams and defend the following positions:

- Team 1 represents "Standardize the Ratios." The FASB (or some other group) should establish standards for computing ratios. All firms would be required to compute certain ratios and include them with other financial statement information. In addition, definitions should be provided that specify what account balances are to be included in the numerator and denominator of each ratio.
- Team 2 represents "Freedom of Ratios." Ratios should be neither defined nor required by standard setters. Different financial statement users use the information for different purposes and in different ways. Requiring ratios for all companies may result in inappropriate comparisons being made.

CUMULATIVE SPREADSHEET PROJECT

This spreadsheet assignment is a continuation of the spreadsheet assignments given in earlier chapters. If you completed those spreadsheets, you have a head start on this one.

1. Refer back to the balance sheet and income statement created using the financial statement numbers for Handyman Company for 2003 [given in part (1) of the Cumulative Spreadsheet Project assignment in Chapter 2]. With these historical numbers for 2003 as a starting point, Handyman wishes to prepare a forecasted balance sheet and a forecasted income statement for 2004. In preparing the forecasted financial statements for 2004, consider the following additional information:
   a. Sales in 2004 are expected to increase by 40% over 2003 sales of $700.
   b. In the forecasted balance sheet for 2004, cash, receivables, inventory, and accounts payable will all increase at the same rate as sales (40%) relative to 2003. These increases occur because, with the planned 40% increase in the volume of business and no plans to significantly change its methods of operation, Handyman will probably also experience a 40% increase in the levels of its current operating assets and liabilities.
   c. In 2004, Handyman expects to acquire new property, plant, and equipment costing $80.
   d. Accumulated depreciation is the cumulative amount of depreciation expense that Handyman has reported over its years in business. Thus, the forecasted amount of accumulated depreciation for 2004 can be computed as accumulated depreciation as of the end of 2003 plus the forecasted depreciation expense for 2004.
   e. New short-term loans payable will be acquired in an amount sufficient to make Handyman's current ratio (current assets divided by current liabilities) in 2004 exactly equal to 2.0.
   f. No new long-term debt will be acquired in 2004.
   g. No cash dividends will be paid in 2004. Remember that the amount of retained earnings at the end of any year is the beginning retained earnings amount plus net income minus dividends.
   h. In this exercise, the forecasted amount of paid-in capital is the "plug" figure. In other words, the forecasted balance in paid-in capital at the end of 2004 is the amount necessary to make the forecasted balance sheet balance such that forecasted total assets equal forecasted total liabilities. A key reason for preparing forecasted financial statements is to identify in advance whether any additional financing will be required.
   i. The $160 in operating expenses reported in 2003 breaks down as follows: $5 depreciation expense, $155 other operating expenses.
   j. In the forecasted income statement for 2004, cost of goods sold and other operating expenses will both increase at the same rate as sales (40%) relative to 2003. This is another way of saying that the amount of these expenses, relative to the amount of sales, will probably stay about the same year to year unless Handyman plans to significantly change the way it does business.
   k. The amount of Handyman's depreciation expense is determined by how much property, plant, and equipment the company has. In 2003, Handyman had $5 of depreciation expense on $199 of property, plant, and equipment, meaning that depreciation was equal to 2.5% ($5/$199) of the amount of property, plant, and equipment. It is expected that the same relationship will hold in 2004.

l. Interest expense depends on how much interest-bearing debt a company has. In 2003, Handyman reported interest expense of $9 on long-term debt of $207. [Note: To simplify this exercise, we will ignore interest expense on the short-term loan payable.] Because Handyman is expected to have the same amount of long-term debt in 2004, our best guess is that interest expense will remain the same.

m. Income tax expense is determined by how much pretax income a company has. And, the most reasonable assumption to make is that a company's tax rate, equal to income tax expense divided by pretax income, will stay constant from year to year. Handyman's income tax rate in 2003 was 33% ($4/$12).

2. Repeat (1) assuming that forecasted sales growth in 2004 is 20% instead of 40%. Clearly state any assumptions that you make.

INTERNET SEARCH

• General Motors

We began this chapter with an introduction to GENERAL MOTORS; we will end this chapter with a look at its Web site. Access GM's Web site at **http://www.gm.com**. Sometimes Web addresses change, so if this address doesn't work, access the Web site for this textbook (**http://albrecht.swcollege.com**) for an updated link to GM.

Once you have located the company's Web site, answer the following questions:

1. Locate GM's financial statements. Write down the path you took to get to the statements. In your opinion, is GM's Web site easy to navigate relative to others you have accessed?
2. In the chapter, we computed GM's return on equity for 1999. Using the information contained in GM's most recent annual report, compute the company's return on equity using the DuPont framework. Provide these computations for the two most recent periods. Using the DuPont framework, identify the ratio(s) that highlight the reasons for any changes in return on equity over the two-year period and compare the results with those obtained from 1999.
3. Access the company's note information relating to accounting estimates. Since these estimates result in most adjusting entries, identify who makes these estimates and, as a result, who is responsible for making the adjusting entries.
4. As pointed out in the chapter, revenue is recognized when it is earned and a promise of payment has been received. Using the note relating to revenue recognition, identify when GM recognizes revenue for its various segments within the firm.

Ensuring the Integrity of Financial Information

chapter f5

learning objectives

After studying this chapter, you should be able to:

1. Identify the types of problems that can appear in financial statements.
2. Describe the safeguards employed within a firm to ensure that financial statements are free from problems.
3. Understand the need for monitoring by independent parties.
4. Describe the role of auditors and how their presence affects the integrity of financial statements.
5. Explain the role of the Securities and Exchange Commission in adding credibility to financial statements.

setting the stage

PHAR-MOR,[1] a dry goods retailer based in Youngstown, Ohio, was founded in 1982 by Mickey Monus. Within 10 years, Phar-Mor, with over 300 stores, was operating in nearly every state in the United States. Phar-Mor's strategy was to sell household products and prescription drugs at prices lower than those of other discount stores. Phar-Mor's prices were so low and its expansion was conducted so quickly that even WAL-MART, the king of discount prices, was nervous. Sam Walton once said that the only company he feared at all in the expansion of Wal-Mart was Phar-Mor.[2]

Today, with fewer than 140 stores, Phar-Mor is struggling to build a profitable business from the rubble of a financial statement fraud that exceeded $1 billion. Apparently, certain Phar-Mor executives used financial statements showing healthy profits to obtain more than $1 billion in credit and capital for the company. Investors in Phar-Mor included SEARS, ROEBUCK & CO., WESTINGHOUSE ELECTRIC CORPORATION, and mall developer Edward DeBartolo Sr. (the former owner of the San Francisco 49ers).

Phar-Mor's financial statements appeared to present an extremely profitable company. In reality, the company never made a legitimate profit. Phar-Mor actually had $238 million in pretax losses in 1992 alone. Schemers at the company kept two sets of accounting records: an official ledger that they sometimes manipulated with false entries, called "raisins," and another, nicknamed the "cookies," where they kept track of the false entries. They would refer to their fraud as "putting raisins in the cookies."

For six years, some company officials seemingly used the company as their personal plaything, falsifying financial ledgers and allegedly raiding company coffers. Officers diverted more than $10 million from Phar-Mor to prop up the WORLD BASKETBALL LEAGUE (the defunct minor-league basketball venture) and stole more than $500,000 for personal use. How could a company appear in its financial statements to be so profitable and yet in reality be losing money? How could a company with a reputation as good as Phar-Mor's deceive the public by misrepresenting its profitability, and what was the price of this deception?

Phar-Mor emerged from bankruptcy in September 1995 with 102 stores. In July 1999, the company had 139 stores in 24 states and reported a profit from its operations of $15 million. However, the debt incurred by the company to finance its recovery wiped out all that profit. For the fiscal year ended July 3, 1999, Phar-Mor reported a net loss of $1.6 million.

In Chapters 1 and 2, you were introduced to financial accounting and shown the outputs (financial statements) of the financial reporting process. You learned that the balance sheet, income statement, and statement of cash flows are reports used by organizations to summarize their financial results for various users. In Chapters 3 and 4, the accounting cycle, the method of entering and processing financial transaction information in the accounting records, was described. You learned that transaction data are captured by journal entries, journal entry data are summarized in accounts and ledgers, ledger information is summarized on trial balances, and trial balance information provides the basis for the balance sheet, income statement, and statement of cash flows.

In Chapters 1 through 4, the assumption was made that the financial reporting process always works the way it should and that the resulting financial statements are accurate. In reality, however, because of unintentional errors, as well as intentional deception or fraud (such as in the Phar-Mor case), the resulting financial statements sometimes contain errors or omissions that can mislead investors, creditors, and other users.

In this chapter, we show how financial statements might be manipulated, and we discuss the safeguards built into the financial reporting system to prevent these abuses. We also examine the role that auditors play in ensuring that the financial statements fairly represent the financial performance of the firm.

1 Most of these facts relating to Phar-Mor appeared in Gabriella Stern, "Chicanery at Phar-Mor Ran Deep, Close Look at Discounter Shows," *The Wall Street Journal*, January 20, 1994, p. 1.
2 Mark F. Murray, "When a Client Is a Liability," *Journal of Accountancy*, September 1992, pp. 54–58.

1

Identify the types of problems that can appear in financial statements.

THE TYPES OF PROBLEMS THAT CAN OCCUR

Obviously, most businesses do not engage in the massive frauds that occurred at PHAR-MOR. Financial deception does not come about mainly for two reasons: (1) the vast majority of business managers are honest, possess integrity, and would not be associated with fraudulent activity, and (2) safeguards have been built into the accounting system to prevent and detect activities that are inconsistent with the objectives of a business. These safeguards attempt to eliminate problems from being introduced into the financial statements.

Before proceeding further, we need to make an important distinction regarding these problems. Problems in the financial statements can result for several different reasons.

1. *Error*—results when care is not taken in recording transactions, posting transactions, summarizing accounts, and so forth. Errors are not intentional and when detected are immediately corrected.
2. *Disagreement*—results when different people arrive at different conclusions based on the same set of facts. Because accounting involves judgment and estimates, opportunities for honest disagreements in judgment abound. These disagreements often come about because of the different incentives that motivate those involved with producing the financial statements.
3. *Fraud*—results from intentional errors. As in the Phar-Mor case, fraudulent financial reporting occurs when management chooses to intentionally manipulate the financial statements to serve their own purposes.

An accounting system should be designed to significantly reduce the possibility that problems, in whatever form, will make their way into financial statements.

Types of Errors in the Reporting Process

Errors, and other problems, can occur in most stages of the accounting cycle. We will first describe the kinds of errors that can occur and then identify controls to minimize these errors.

ERRORS IN TRANSACTIONS AND JOURNAL ENTRIES Transactions, such as selling products or services, paying salaries, buying inventory, and paying taxes, are entered into the accounting records through journal entries. For example, if $5,000 is paid to an attorney for legal services, the following journal entry is made:

Legal Expense	5,000	
Cash		5,000
Paid an attorney $5,000 for legal services.		

An invoice from the law firm should support this entry. Errors could be introduced into the financial reporting process if (1) the invoice from the law firm was lost and the legal expense was not entered into the accounting records, (2) the amount entered into the accounting records was incorrect, or (3) the accounts involved were incorrectly identified.

ERRORS IN ACCOUNTS AND LEDGERS Even when journal entries properly summarize legitimate transactions, errors and misstatements can be introduced into the financial records because journal entry data are not summarized appropriately or accurately in the ledgers. Using the previous example of paying an attorney $5,000, errors could occur at the posting stage of the accounting cycle if the legal expense is entered in the wrong account in the ledger or if an incorrect amount is posted to the correct account. Posting the correct amount to the wrong expense account would result in the correct total for all expenses, but individual expense account balances would be incorrect.

A more severe error occurs at the ledger stage if amounts that should be included in asset or liability accounts are improperly included in expense or revenue accounts, or vice versa. Examples include (1) recording insurance expense as prepaid insurance (an asset), (2) recording purchases of goods for resale as inventory (an asset) when they should be reported as cost of goods sold (an expense), (3) recording a receipt of cash as revenue when it should be recorded as unearned revenue (a liability), or (4) not reporting supplies used as an expense.

Disagreements in Judgment

Many think that the accounting profession involves exactness and precision and that the accountant simply records the facts, totals the numbers, and presents unbiased results. Nothing could be further from the truth. Accountants are constantly making judgments and estimates regarding the past and the future. Let's return to the landscaping business that we introduced in Chapters 3 and 4 to illustrate some of the judgments involved in the accounting process.

As your lawn care and landscaping business has become more and more successful, you have been able to obtain bigger and better jobs. Recently, you signed a contract to provide all the landscaping for a new condominium complex currently under construction. The terms of the contract call for payment of one-half of the contract amount up front and the remaining one-half upon completion. You begin working on the condominium landscaping in early December, but it looks as though you will not finish until well into January. To prepare financial statements at the end of the calendar year, how much of the condominium contract should you report as revenue? Well, that depends on how close to completion the job is. If you are 25% complete, it makes sense to report 25% of the contract amount as revenue. If you are 75% complete, report 75% of the contract amount as revenue. The hard part is determining how much of the job has been completed.

Suppose you contact two landscapers (friendly competitors) and ask them to provide you with an estimate of how complete the landscaping job is at year-end. Would it be possible for these two people to arrive at different conclusions regarding the percentage of completion? Which one would be right? Different people can look at the same set of facts and arrive at different conclusions. They're not wrong, just different. In this case, the different estimates would result in different financial statement numbers. These different numbers could make the difference between your company showing a profit or reporting a loss.

Consider another example. Most of your customers pay promptly, but some take a little longer to pay. A few customers discontinue their lawn care service and never pay for some of the services they received. Your problem is that when you provide a service for a customer, you do not know if that customer will be a "prompt payer," a "slow payer," or a "no payer." Recognizing that a certain percentage of your customers will be "no payers," should you record a receivable (and a revenue) for the full amount of every sale? As you will learn in Chapter 6, most businesses recognize that a certain percentage of receivables will be uncollectible. How should you arrive at the amount of your receivables that won't be collected? Is it possible that your estimate will be slightly off? Could different people legitimately arrive at different estimates? Of course. These different estimates will then affect the results reported in the financial statements.

Fraudulent Financial Reporting

As mentioned previously, fraudulent financial reporting is intentional. To illustrate, consider the journal entry made previously related to legal expense. Assume that a company's accountant embezzles $5,000 and prepares the following journal entry to conceal the fraud:

Legal Expense	5,000	
Cash		5,000
Paid an attorney $5,000 for legal services.		

The accountant could prepare the journal entry without supporting documentation (e.g., an invoice) or create a fictitious invoice from a phantom law firm.

Unless someone is watching closely, the theft may go undetected. Because the accountant made a fictitious entry to Legal Expense, the accounting records appear to be correct, and the

business environment essay

Manipulation of Journal Entries Adam F.* graduated in accounting from a large university. Upon graduation, he accepted a job with one of the "Big 5" CPA firms. He worked there for three years, during which time he became a CPA and served as the in-charge auditor on a number of audit engagements.

After three years, he left the CPA firm to accept a job as controller in a small bank. Along with two other individuals, he invested in a farm implement dealership. Unfortunately, business wasn't as good as expected, and the dealership lost large sums of money. To keep the business afloat, Adam began embezzling money from the bank. At first he stole small amounts. As the business's cash needs became greater, he increased the amounts until he was stealing more than $15,000 per month. He concealed his frauds by creating journal entries debiting Advertising Expense and crediting Cash, as shown:

Advertising Expense	15,000	
Cash		15,000
Paid monthly advertising cost.		

accounting equation still balances. Cash, an asset, is stolen, and the recognition of an expense results in owners' equity being reduced by the same amount.

Assets	=	Liabilities	+	Owners' Equity
(decreased by $5,000)				(decreased by $5,000)

STOP & THINK Before reading about the safeguards designed to minimize the types of problems we have just discussed, can you think of things that could be done to ensure that errors, disagreements in judgment, and fraudulent financial reporting do not occur?

In addition, sometimes amounts for which there are no legitimate transactions are added or deducted directly from financial statement balances. Examples are listing sales that don't exist (as was the case with BAUSCH & LOMB, the eye care company, which was making false shipments to distributors at year-end resulting in an overstatement of profits by over $80 million); not recording sales returns or uncollectible receivables (as was the case with the vacuum maker, REGINA, which did not record the return of over 40,000 vacuums); and not recording various expenses, understating liabilities, and overstating assets such as inventory or receivables (as was the case with Phar-Mor). Sometimes these types of errors are unintentional, but in many cases they are intentional.

---

to summarize

The accounting cycle and resulting financial reports of most organizations are accurate and can be relied on. Nevertheless, unintentional errors, disagreements in judgment, and fraudulent financial reporting can occur in the accounting process, thereby producing erroneous financial reports.

2

Describe the safeguards employed within a firm to ensure that financial statements are free from problems.

SAFEGUARDS DESIGNED TO MINIMIZE PROBLEMS

Accounting is a language just as English is. In the same way that a falsehood can be written in English, a misleading story can be expressed by financial statements. By far, the vast majority of financial statements are as accurate as possible, and the preparers are honest. Most organizations

Adam's fraud went undetected until he became greedy and expanded his methods of embezzling. He was caught when a customer of the bank twice made interest payments of $10,000. Adam took the second $10,000 payment and deposited it in his own account at the bank. The customer, realizing the error, notified the bank. The search for the missing $10,000 revealed Adam's thefts.

As a result of his fraud, Adam was sentenced to four years in prison and entered into a restitution agreement to repay the bank. The IRS also informed Adam that his embezzled funds were taxable, and since he hadn't paid timely taxes, he owed fines, penalties, interest, and taxes totaling nearly $100,000. When released from jail, Adam will probably spend the rest of his life paying back the bank and the IRS the $250,000 he now owes.

*All Business Environment Essays in this chapter are real cases. In some instances, such as here, the names have been changed.

Source: This case is from the video *The Red Flags of Fraud*, The Association of Certified Fraud Examiners, Austin, Texas.

prepare accounting records and financial reports with integrity, and in most cases, preparers are even conservative when judgments and estimates are required. To help ensure that financial reports are accurate, and to prevent problems such as those that occurred at PHAR-MOR, several safeguards have been built into the financial reporting structure of most organizations in the United States. As a future user of accounting information, you should be aware of these safeguards and the reasons for their existence.

internal control structure Safeguards in the form of policies and procedures established to provide management with reasonable assurance that the objectives of an entity will be achieved.

Most organizations build controls into their organization and financial reporting processes so that abuses are difficult. These safeguards, called the **internal control structure**, are internal to the organization preparing the financial statements. The American Institute of Certified Public Accountants (AICPA) has defined *internal control* as "the policies and procedures established to provide reasonable assurance that specific entity objectives will be achieved."[3] These internal controls protect investors and creditors and even help management in their efforts to run their organizations as effectively and efficiently as possible. As a future investor and financial statement user, you should be aware of these controls. When you encounter an organization or financial statements that do not have these controls and safeguards, you should exercise extreme care. Most companies have the following five concerns in mind when they are designing internal controls:

1. To provide accurate accounting records and financial statements containing reliable data for business decisions.
2. To safeguard assets and records. Most companies think of their assets as including their financial assets (such as cash or property), their employees, their confidential information, and their reputation and image.
3. To effectively and efficiently run their operations, without duplication of effort or waste.
4. To follow management policies.
5. To comply with the Foreign Corrupt Practices Act, which requires companies to maintain proper record-keeping systems and controls.

Foreign Corrupt Practices Act (FCPA) Legislation requiring any company that has publicly traded stock to maintain records that accurately and fairly represent the company's transactions; additionally, requires any publicly traded company to have an adequate system of internal accounting controls.

The responsibility for establishing and maintaining the internal control structure belongs to a company's management. Until several years ago, this responsibility was only implied; there was no formal legal requirement. However, in the wake of illegal political campaign contributions, business frauds, and numerous illegal payments to foreign officials in exchange for business favors, Congress passed the **Foreign Corrupt Practices Act (FCPA)** of 1977. As a result of this legislation, all companies whose stock is publicly traded are required by law to keep records

3 AU Section 319, par. 06, Codification of Statements on Auditing Standards, CCH Inc., 1994, p. 98.

business environment essay

Manipulating the Ledgers Jane W. was the bookkeeper and proof operator for a small bank. Over a period of four years she embezzled over $3 million—an amount that exceeded 10% of the bank's assets. Jane's method of theft was simple. She would find something she wanted such as a new automobile. She would write the dealer a check for the car. Then, when her check came back from the Federal Reserve, she would allow it to be deducted from the bank's master demand deposit account (the general ledger), but not from her specific account (in the subsidiary ledger). As a result, the master account total was reduced and became out of balance with the sum of the individual account balances. To cover the shortage, at the end of each month she would pull some of her bank's previously used cashier's checks and send them to the Federal Reserve. For one day, until it sorted the checks, the Fed-

that represent the firm's transactions accurately and fairly. In addition, they must maintain adequate systems of internal accounting control.

A company's internal control structure can be divided into five basic categories: (1) the control environment, (2) risk assessment, (3) control activities, (4) information and communication, and (5) monitoring. In this chapter, we will cover the control environment and control activities (sometimes called control procedures), as well as the need for monitoring. We will also discuss elements of accounting systems that are important from a control perspective.

The Control Environment

control environment The actions, policies, and procedures that reflect the overall attitudes of top management, the directors, and the owners about control and its importance to the entity.

The **control environment** consists of the actions, policies, and procedures that reflect the overall attitudes of top management, the directors, and the owners about control and its importance to the company. In a strong control environment, management believes control is important and makes sure that everyone responds conscientiously to the control policies and procedures. Some of the key components of the control environment that relate to financial reporting are described below.

MANAGEMENT PHILOSOPHY AND OPERATING STYLE Does management set a good example by following controls? Do they stress the importance of controls to other employees? What is their management style? Are they, for example, risk averse or apt to take risks, dominated by one or two individuals or open to input from others, realistic or unrealistic about goals?

An example of a company with a poor management philosophy and operating style was EQUITY FUNDING. Equity Funding was a life insurance company that sold policies to individuals and then resold those policies to other insurance companies called reinsurers. Equity Funding's top managers were extremely dominant and dishonest; there were no clear lines of responsibility, budgets were unrealistic, and the company had no system of organizational checks and balances in place. In that environment, top management wrote $2 billion of fictitious life insurance policies and reported the sales and profits from those transactions on the company's financial statements. Management's dishonest actions were so blatant that a climate of moral decay filtered throughout the organization, resulting in widespread cheating by employees on travel reimbursements and other abuses.

organizational structure Lines of authority and responsibility.

ORGANIZATIONAL STRUCTURE Does the **organizational structure** identify clear lines of authority and responsibility? Is the organizational structure so complex that dishonest transactions can be concealed?

An example of a complex organizational structure that was used to conceal a large fraud (approximately $300 million) is the ESM COMPANY in Ohio. ESM was a brokerage business

eral Reserve would treat her bank's canceled checks as if they were legitimate checks received by the bank from its customers, and for which the Federal Reserve should credit her bank. Jane was caught when someone at the Federal Reserve noticed that a cashier's check she sent had been processed so many times that it was completely black.

As a result of her fraud, Jane was sentenced to eight years in prison. She also entered into a restitution agreement to repay her company and ended up owing considerable taxes to the IRS on her stolen funds. Jane and her husband (who assisted with the fraud) now owe a total of nearly $5 million to the bank and the IRS. For the rest of their lives, they will be in financial bondage.

Source: W. S. Albrecht, G. Wernz, and T. Williams, *Fraud: Bringing Light to the Dark Side of Business*, Irwin, 1995, p. 265.

that bought and sold government securities. Over a period of seven years, the officers of the company funneled cash to themselves until the company owed approximately $300 million more in payables than it had in receivables. This net payable was concealed by setting up related entities and reporting a fictitious receivable from one of those companies in ESM Company's financial statements. If anyone had investigated the receivable, he or she would have found that the related company from which it was supposedly collectible was bankrupt.

A good organizational structure requires that only one person in a department be responsible for each function, such as cash receipts, cash disbursements, purchasing, payroll preparation, or credit approval. It takes little imagination to envision the confusion that would result if a business gave every employee unlimited purchasing authority, for example. There would be overstocking, duplication of orders, loss of quantity discounts, and tremendous waste. By designating responsibility for the purchasing function, or any other function, the organization runs more smoothly and maintains control.

Normally, each company will have an organizational chart that not only specifies the formal lines of authority, but also indicates departmental responsibilities. In addition to formal lines of authority, each organization will have an informal hierarchy that develops based on the personalities of the individuals and the group dynamics of the situation.

audit committee Members of a company's board of directors who are responsible for dealing with the external and internal auditors.

AUDIT COMMITTEE Every major company has a board of directors. A good control environment would suggest that a subset of these directors should form an **audit committee**. Generally, the audit committee should be comprised of outside directors (members of the board who are not officers of the company). The internal and external auditors would then be accountable to this audit committee.

Companies listed on the New York Stock Exchange are required to have audit committees comprised entirely of outside directors who are not employees of the company. The audit committee is usually charged with the responsibility of supervising the company's financial reporting process, including internal control and compliance with applicable laws and regulations. Auditors who suspect wrongdoing in financial reporting should forward those concerns to the audit committee.

accounting system The set of manual and computerized procedures and controls that provide for identifying relevant transactions or events, preparing accurate source documents, entering data into the accounting records accurately, processing transactions precisely, updating master files properly, and generating correct documents and reports.

The Accounting System

The purpose of a company's accounting system is to identify, assemble, classify, analyze, record, and report the entity's transactions and to maintain accountability for assets. To be effective, the **accounting system** should contain adequate controls to ensure that seven control objectives are met.

1. *Validity.* Only valid transactions are recorded. If fictitious sales are recorded, for example, reported revenues will be too high, and the integrity of the financial statements will be lost.
2. *Authorization.* All transactions are properly authorized. If, for example, any employee could authorize purchases, a company might make duplicate purchases of the same items or purchase unneeded items.
3. *Completeness.* All legitimate transactions are recorded and the records are complete. If, for example, all liabilities are not recorded, a company will report a more favorable financial condition than actually exists.
4. *Classification.* All transactions are properly classified. For example, the current portion of long-term debt should be classified as a current liability. Incorrect classification would result in incorrect liability subtotals that would affect such ratios as the current ratio.
5. *Timeliness.* All transactions are recorded in the proper time period. A company might try to make its revenues and income look better than they are, for example, by recording early January sales in December.
6. *Valuation.* All transactions are properly valued. For example, if a receivable is uncollectible, it should not be classified as a current asset.
7. *Posting and summarization.* All transactions are properly included in subsidiary records and correctly summarized. Errors could occur, for example, if an accounts receivable entry was posted to the accounts payable account.

Control Activities (Procedures)

control activities (procedures) Policies and procedures used by management to meet their objectives; generally divided into adequate segregation of duties, proper procedures for authorization of transactions and activities, adequate documents and records, physical control over assets and records, and independent checks on performance.

segregation of duties A strategy to provide an internal check on performance through separation of authorization of transactions from custody of related assets, separation of operational responsibilities from record-keeping responsibilities, and separation of custody of assets from accounting personnel.

Control activities or **control procedures** are those policies and procedures, in addition to the control environment and accounting system, that management has adopted to provide reasonable assurance that the company's established objectives will be met and that financial reports are accurate. Generally, control activities fall into five categories: adequate segregation of duties, proper procedures for authorization, adequate documents and records, physical control over assets and records, and independent checks on performance.

ADEQUATE SEGREGATION OF DUTIES A good internal control system should provide for the appropriate **segregation of duties**. This means that no one department or individual should be responsible for handling all phases of a transaction. In some small businesses, this segregation is not possible because the limited number of employees prevents division of all the different functions. Nevertheless, there are three functions that should be performed by separate departments or by different people.

1. *Authorization.* Authorizing and approving the execution of transactions; for example, approving the sale of a building or land.
2. *Record keeping.* Recording the transactions in the accounting journals.
3. *Custody.* Having physical possession of or control over the assets involved in transactions, including operational responsibility; for example, having the key to the safe in which cash or investment securities are kept or, more generally, having control over the production function.

By separating the responsibilities for these duties, a company realizes the efficiency derived from specialization and also reduces the errors, both intentional and unintentional, that might otherwise occur.

An example of a problem resulting from the nonsegregation of the custody and record-keeping functions occurred when a young employee of a wholesale candy distributor both opened incoming mail and kept the accounts receivable file. Needing money for a family emergency, she stole $300 and did not show the receivable as collected. After realizing how easy it was, over time she took $76,000 by delaying the recording of receivables collected. She was eventually caught, but her theft affected the financial statements because receivables were misstated, as was the financial health of the company.

PROPER PROCEDURES FOR AUTHORIZATION A strong system of internal control requires proper authorization for every transaction. In the typical corporate organization, this authorization originates with the stockholders who elect a board of directors. It is then delegated from the board of directors to upper-level management and eventually throughout the organization. While the board of directors and upper-level management possess a fairly general power of authorization, a clerk usually has limited authority. Thus, the board would authorize dividends, a general change in policies, or a merger; a clerk would be restricted to authorizing credit or a specific cash transaction. Only certain people should be authorized to enter data into accounting records and prepare accounting reports.

ADEQUATE DOCUMENTS AND RECORDS A key to good controls is an adequate system of documentation and records. As explained in Chapter 3, documents are the physical, objective evidence of accounting transactions. Their existence allows management to review any transaction for appropriate authorization. Documents are also the means by which information is communicated throughout an organization. In short, adequate documentation provides evidence that the recording and summarizing functions that lead to financial reports are being performed properly. A well-designed document has several characteristics: (1) it is easily interpreted and understood, (2) it has been designed with all possible uses in mind, (3) it has been prenumbered for easy identification and tracking, and (4) it is formatted so that it can be handled quickly and efficiently. Documents can be actual pieces of paper or information in a computer database.

physical safeguards Physical precautions used to protect assets and records, such as locks on doors, fireproof vaults, password verification, and security guards.

PHYSICAL CONTROL OVER ASSETS AND RECORDS Some of the most crucial policies and procedures involve the use of adequate **physical safeguards** to protect resources. For example, a bank would not allow significant amounts of money to be transported in an ordinary car. Similarly, a company should not leave its valuable assets unprotected. Examples of physical safeguards are fireproof vaults for the storage of classified information, currency, and marketable securities; and guards, fences, and remote control cameras for the protection of equipment, materials, and merchandise. Records and documents are also important resources and must be protected. Re-creating lost or destroyed records can be costly and time-consuming, so companies make backup copies of records. The high cost of backup records (often on microfilm) is usually more than justified in protecting such valuable resources.

Providing proper safeguards reduces opportunities for employees to misappropriate assets. Each firm needs a comprehensive security program specifically engineered to protect its corporate assets. An example of a fraud committed in a setting of poor physical safeguards was the

Many companies use physical safeguards, such as surveillance cameras, to protect their resources.

business environment essay

An Example of Poor Controls Earlier in this chapter (pages 210–211), the $3.01 million theft by Jane W., proof operator in a bank, was discussed. Her fraud was possible because of poor internal controls in her bank. Here are some of the major control weaknesses that existed.

1. All documents were to be accessible to external auditors. Yet Jane kept a locked cabinet next to her desk and only she had a key. A customer whose statement had been altered by Jane complained, but was told that he would have to wait until Jane returned from vacation; the documentation relating to his account was in Jane's locked cabinet.
2. The bank required every employee and every officer to take a consecutive two-week vacation. At Jane's request, management allowed this control to be broken. Based on her memos that "proof would get behind if she took a two-week vacation," Jane was allowed to take her vacation one day at a time. In addition, no one was allowed to perform Jane's most sensitive duties while she was away.
3. General ledger entries were supposed to be approved by an individual other than the person who completed the entries. In order to override this control, Jane had her employees presign 10 or 12 general ledger approvals, so she wouldn't have to "bother" them when they were busy.
4. Opening and closing procedures were supposed to be in place to protect the bank, but many employees had all the keys necessary and could enter the bank at will.

crime against the PERINI CORPORATION. Approximately $1,150,000 of checks were written on the company's accounts by an employee. Access to the checks was easy because Perini kept its supply of unused checks in the same unlocked storeroom where the styrofoam coffee cups were stored. Every clerk and secretary had access to the storeroom. The checks had been written on a check-writing machine, which automatically signed the president's name. Despite inherent control procedures in the machine, and its CPA firm's warning to implement specific control procedures, the company found it inconvenient to use most of the control procedures. For example, the machine deposited signed checks into a box that was supposed to be locked; the key was supposed to be kept by an employee in a different department. No such employee was assigned, however, and the box was left unlocked. Furthermore, no one paid attention to the machine's counter, which kept track of the number of checks written for comparison with vouchers authorized for payment.

independent checks Procedures for continual internal verification of other controls.

INDEPENDENT CHECKS ON PERFORMANCE Having **independent checks** on performance is a valuable control technique. Independent checks incorporate reviews of functions, as well as the internal checks created from a proper segregation of duties.

There are many ways to independently check performance. Using independent reviewers, such as auditors, is one of the most common. In addition, mandatory vacations, where another employee performs the vacationing person's duties, periodic rotations or transfers, or merely having someone independent of the accounting records reconcile the bank statement are all types of independent checks.

Reporting on Internal Controls

Public companies are required to include in their annual report a statement signed by management that acknowledges their responsibility for maintaining a good system of internal controls. The statement shown in Exhibit 5-1 on page 216 was included in the 1999 annual report of SARA LEE CORPORATION.

5. An effective internal audit function was supposed to be in place. For a period of two years, however, no internal audit reports were issued. Even when the reports were issued, internal auditors did not check employees' bank accounts or perform a critical control test, such as surprise openings of the bank's incoming and outgoing mail to and from the Federal Reserve.
6. Employees' bank accounts were not regularly reviewed by internal audit or by management. On the rare occasions when they were reviewed, numerous deposits to and checks drawn on Jane's account that exceeded her annual salary were not questioned.
7. Loans were supposed to be made to employees only if the employees met all lending standards required of normal customers. At one point, the bank made a $170,000 mortgage loan to Jane, without requiring any explanation as to how the loan would be repaid or how she could afford such a house.
8. Managers were supposed to be reviewing key documents and reports daily. Either managers didn't review these reports, or they didn't pay close attention to the reports when they did perform the reviews. There were daily fluctuations in the reports of over $3 million. The reports revealed huge deposits to and checks drawn on Jane's account. In addition, Jane appeared on the overdraft report 97 times during the first four years she was employed.

Source: W. S. Albrecht, G. Wernz, and T. Williams, *Fraud: Bringing Light to the Dark Side of Business*, Irwin, 1995, p. 265.

to summarize

Most organizations have an internal control system that, among other things, helps ensure integrity in financial reports. The various elements of control that relate to financial reporting are summarized as follows:

Control Environment	Accounting System	Control Procedures
1. Management philosophy and operating style.	1. Valid transactions.	1. Segregation of duties.
2. Organizational structure.	2. Properly authorized transactions.	2. Proper procedures for authorization.
3. Audit committee.	3. Completeness.	3. Adequate documents and records.
	4. Proper classification.	4. Physical control over assets and records.
	5. Proper timing.	5. Independent checks on performance.
	6. Proper valuation.	
	7. Correct summarization.	

Public companies are required to include in their annual report a statement signed by management that describes and accepts responsibility for the internal controls of the company.

3

Understand the need for monitoring by independent parties.

THE NEED FOR MONITORING

A firm's internal control structure is designed to minimize the occurrence of intentional and unintentional problems in a firm's financial statements. But a system of internal controls provides

exhibit 5-1 Sara Lee's 1999 Management Letter

Management's Report on Financial Information

Management of Sara Lee Corporation is responsible for the preparation and integrity of the financial information included in this annual report. The financial statements have been prepared in accordance with generally accepted accounting principles and, where required, reflect our best estimates and judgments.

It is the corporation's policy to maintain a control-conscious environment through an effective system of internal accounting controls supported by formal policies and procedures communicated throughout the corporation. These controls are adequate to provide reasonable assurance that assets are safeguarded against loss or unauthorized use and to produce the records necessary for the preparation of financial information. There are limits inherent in all systems of internal control based on the recognition that the costs of such systems should be related to the benefits to be derived. We believe the corporation's systems provide this appropriate balance.

The control environment is complemented by the corporation's internal auditors, who perform extensive audits and evaluate the adequacy of and the adherence to these controls, policies and procedures. In addition, the corporation's independent public accountants have developed an understanding of our accounting and financial controls, and have conducted such tests as they consider necessary to support their report below.

The Board of Directors pursues its oversight role for the financial statements through the Audit Committee, which is composed solely of outside directors. The Audit Committee meets regularly with management, the corporate internal auditors and Arthur Andersen LLP, jointly and separately, to receive reports on management's process of implementation and administration of internal accounting controls, as well as auditing and financial reporting matters. Both Arthur Andersen LLP and the internal auditors have unrestricted access to the Audit Committee.

The corporation maintains high standards in selecting, training and developing personnel to help ensure that management's objectives of maintaining strong, effective internal controls and unbiased, uniform reporting standards are attained. We believe it is essential for the corporation to conduct its business affairs in accordance with the highest ethical practices as expressed in Sara Lee Corporation's Global Business Standards.

John H. Bryan *Judith A. Sprieser*

John H. Bryan
Chairman of the Board
and Chief Executive Officer

Judith A. Sprieser
Senior Vice President
and Chief Financial Officer

assurance as to the quality of the resulting financial information only if the system is functioning properly. What, or who, makes sure the system is functioning properly? What happens when disagreements in judgment arise? Who referees to ensure that the estimates and judgments that are reflected in the financial statements are reasonable? In this section, we discuss a mechanism, developed over time, that attempts to ensure that the financial statements provide an accurate and fair presentation of a company's financial status.

Let's return to our landscaping example. You have determined that your annual salary is a fixed monthly amount plus an annual bonus based on the net income of the business. The better the business performs, the higher your pay. Many companies actually reward their top executives using similar incentive plans (though many of these incentive plans can become quite complex). Now, what is your incentive? Well, it seems pretty clear that your incentive is to report as high a net income figure as possible. The higher your company's net income, the higher your annual bonus.

How can you increase net income given your current level of operations? Since you are a person of integrity and honor, falsifying transactions (e.g., fraudulent financial reporting) is out of the question. One possibility is to review your estimates regarding the percentage of revenues to be recognized and the percentage of accounts receivable that may be uncollectible.

Recall from a previous section that we had two of our landscaping friends provide us with independent estimates of the percentage of completion on our condominium landscaping project. Suppose that one estimate was that the project was 50% complete. The other was that the project was 60% complete. Which would you select as being more accurate? Well, the 60% estimate would result in a higher net income, which would mean a higher year-end bonus this year. Also, using the 60% estimate would be reasonable because it was provided by an independent source.

You also examine your accounts receivable to determine what percentage of those receivables might be uncollectible in the future.[4] Since you are dealing with estimates about future events, there is no right answer. You estimate that uncollectible receivables could be anywhere from 2 to 4% of the existing Accounts Receivable balance. Should you split the difference and say 3%? You could, but why not say 2%? After all, 2% is a possible outcome, and if you use the estimate of 2%, net income will be higher, again resulting in a higher year-end bonus for you.

fyi

In 1999, **GENERAL MOTORS** estimated that the amount of its total pension and postretirement health-care obligations to be paid in the future relating to past and current employees exceeded $127 billion.

Financial statements are full of estimates and judgments. Here we have illustrated just two areas involving estimates—revenues and uncollectible accounts. The financial statements of large companies involve many estimates relating to the future life of equipment and buildings, the amount to be paid in the future for warranties on products and services, and the amount of future benefits to be paid to retirees, to name a few. You might expect all these estimates to average out. That is, sometimes those that have a favorable effect on net income are used, and sometimes those that have an unfavorable effect are used. If estimates were randomly chosen, this would probably happen. But remember that these estimates aren't randomly chosen. In the case of your landscaping business, you are choosing the estimates.

Suppose that in every case involving an estimate, you elected to present the estimate that was most favorable to the firm's net income. Your annual bonus would certainly look nice, but would the resulting financial statements provide a fair assessment of your company's financial performance? Maybe, maybe not.

caution

We are not accusing management of misrepresenting the financial results of their companies. What we are saying is that management has an incentive to make things look as favorable (within the bounds of ethical disclosure) as possible.

As part owner[5] of the landscaping company, and with your compensation based on net income, you might have a tough time being objective when it comes to making estimates; you have an economic incentive to influence net income in a certain direction. But you also recognize the need to provide relevant and reliable financial information relating to the performance of the company.

As you wrestle with this issue of estimates in the financial statements, there is another issue to consider as well. We stated that an internal control system is designed to minimize the occurrence of errors and irregularities in the financial reporting process. While the system should not allow errors in posting or transactions to be fabricated, how do we know that the internal control system is running as designed? How can you obtain some assurance that errors, biased disagreements in judgment, and fraudulent financial reporting are not a part of your accounting system? In the next section, we discuss another major factor that ensures that financial information is presented with reliability and integrity.

to summarize

Because accounting involves estimates and judgment, management has an opportunity to influence the outputs of the accounting process. Managers of a business often have an incentive to provide financial statement information that appears as favorable as possible. While the vast majority of managers would not intentionally bias the financial statements, their incentives may cause them to influence the process.

4 As you will learn in Chapter 6, the estimate of uncollectible accounts receivable will affect the expense for the period, thereby affecting net income.

5 Recall that you own only part of the company. Your parents and the bank (we illustrated both of these possibilities) own the other part.

4

Describe the role of auditors and how their presence affects the integrity of financial statements.

THE ROLE OF AUDITORS IN THE ACCOUNTING PROCESS

Someone needs to check and make sure that the accounting system is running as designed and that the resulting financial statements fairly present the financial performance of the company. Auditors are that "someone." Auditors provide management (and stockholders) with some assurance that the internal control system is functioning properly and that the financial statements fairly represent the financial performance of the firm. Two types of auditors are typically employed by management—internal and external auditors.

Internal Auditors

internal auditors An independent group of experts (in controls, accounting, and operations) who monitor operating results and financial records, evaluate internal controls, assist with increasing the efficiency and effectiveness of operations, and detect fraud.

Most large organizations have a staff of **internal auditors**, an independent group of experts in controls, accounting, and operations. This group's major purpose is to monitor operating results and financial records, evaluate internal controls, assist with increasing the efficiency and effectiveness of operations, and even detect fraud. The internal audit staffs in some large organizations include over 100 individuals. The audit manager reports directly to the president (or other high-level executive officer) and to the audit committee of the board of directors. By performing independent evaluations of an organization's internal controls, the internal auditors are helping preserve integrity in the reporting process. Employees who know that internal auditors are reviewing operations and reports are less likely to manipulate records. Even if they do, their actions may be revealed by the work of the internal auditors.

Internal auditors' responsibilities vary considerably, depending upon the organization. Some internal audit staffs consist of only one or two employees who spend most of their time performing reviews of financial records or internal controls. Other organizations may have a large number of auditors who search for and investigate fraud, work to improve operational efficiency and effectiveness, and make sure their organization is complying with various laws and regulations.

Organizations that have a competent group of internal auditors generally have fewer financial reporting problems than do organizations that don't have internal auditors. An example of an industry that generally did not have effective internal audit staffs is the savings and loan industry, where many companies went bankrupt during the late 1980s. In many of those companies, managers who were committing fraud did not want internal auditors, who would have made it more difficult for management to manipulate financial statements.

external auditors Independent CPAs who are retained by organizations to perform audits of financial statements.

generally accepted auditing standards (GAAS) Auditing standards developed by the AICPA.

External Auditors

Probably the greatest safeguard in the financial reporting system in the United States is the requirement that firms have external audits. **External auditors** examine an organization's financial statements to determine if they are prepared and presented in accordance with generally accepted accounting principles and are free from material (significant) misstatement. External audits are performed by certified public accounting (CPA) firms. CPA audits are required by the Securities and Exchange Commission and the major stock exchanges for all companies whose stock is publicly traded. Even companies that are not public, however, often employ CPAs to perform audits of their financial statements. Banks and other lenders usually require audits, and audits can instill confidence in users of financial reports. In conducting audits, CPAs are required by **generally accepted auditing standards (GAAS)** to provide reasonable assurance that significant fraud or misstatement is not present in financial statements. Because CPAs cannot audit every transaction of an organization, and because detecting collusive management deception is sometimes impossible, it is not possible for auditors to guarantee that financial statements are "correct." Instead, they can only provide reasonable assurance that financial statements are "presented fairly." Even with audits, there are still a few occasions when major financial statement fraud is not detected.

fyi

As of September 1, 2000, five international public accounting firms—the "Big 5"—were responsible for auditing the majority of the Fortune 500 companies, as well as most other large, publicly traded companies in the United States.

CPA audits of financial statements have become very important in the United States because of the enormous size of many corporations. Because the stockholders, who own corporations, are usually different individuals from a company's management, audits provide comfort to these owners/investors that management is carrying out its stewardship function appropriately.

STOP & THINK What could auditors do to ensure that the financial reporting system is working properly? Be specific.

What Do Auditors Do?

caution

Auditors are responsible for evaluating the assumptions and estimates of management as well as testing the internal control system. The auditors do not make the assumptions and estimates, nor are they responsible for designing the internal control system.

While management has the primary responsibility of ensuring that the internal control system is functioning properly, internal auditors provide an independent assessment of how well the controls are working. External auditors usually study the internal control system to see if they can rely on it as they perform their audits. After all, if the internal control system is functioning correctly, it increases the likelihood that the resulting financial information is reliable. Often the external auditors will rely on the assessment of the internal controls made by the internal auditors.

Auditors gain confidence in the quality of the reporting process using several different processes: interviews, observation, sampling, confirmation, and analytical procedures. Several of these processes are used by both internal and external auditors, while some are used primarily by external auditors. Exhibit 5-2 provides a summary of these procedures and indicates who uses them most often. A brief discussion of each process then follows.

INTERVIEWS Auditors *interview* employees to ensure that procedures are understood, proper documentation is being made, and proper authorization is being obtained. Through interviews, auditors identify potential weaknesses in the control system that will be examined using testing procedures.

Access the AICPA's Web site at http://www.aicpa.org and locate the section on Assurance Services.

In addition to auditing, with what other assurance services are CPAs involved?

OBSERVATION *Observation* is done to verify compliance with procedures and to ensure that accounting records agree with physical records. For example, auditors in a bank will count the cash in a vault to ensure that recorded amounts agree with the actual cash on hand. Auditors will also verify the existence of inventory by doing a physical count of product. In addition to using observation to verify the existence of assets, auditors will also use observation to ensure that employees are complying with proper procedures.

SAMPLING As mentioned previously, auditors cannot examine every transaction. Typically, they will select a *sample of transactions* for analysis. Based on the results of their analysis of the sample, they may conclude that the internal control procedures are being complied with, resulting in reliable financial information. Auditors may also conclude from the results that the internal control system is not reliable, resulting in further testing being required.

CONFIRMATION Used primarily by external auditors, *confirmations* are used to verify the balances in accounts that result from transactions with outsiders. For example, customers are often contacted and asked to verify account balances. Banks are contacted to verify loan amounts, lines of credit, and other account balances. This procedure ensures that the balances listed on the financial statements do, in fact, exist.

ANALYTICAL PROCEDURES *Analytical procedures* are used to provide guidance to external auditors as they attempt to identify areas that may deserve attention. Analytical procedures involve the use of such techniques as comparative ratio analysis (the same ratio analysis we have been doing in Chapters 2, 3, and 4). By comparing the results of ratio analysis from one period to the next, auditors may be able to identify areas where additional investigation may be appropriate.

exhibit 5-2 Audit Processes Used by Auditors

	Internal Auditors	External Auditors
Interviews	X	X
Observation	X	X
Sampling	X	X
Confirmation	—	X
Analytical procedures	—	X

At the completion of an audit, the auditors issue a report that accompanies the financial statements and describes to readers, in very general terms, what was done by the audit firm and whether accounting rules were followed; the report also indicates an opinion as to whether the financial statements and the accompanying notes fairly represent the financial condition of the firm. As an example of an auditors' report, **PHAR-MOR**'s 1999 auditors' report, taken from the company's 1999 financial statements, is included in Exhibit 5-3.

Are Auditors Independent?

Auditors are hired by *management* to make sure that the financial statements prepared by *management* fairly represent the financial performance of the company. Since management is paying the auditors, is there a danger that the auditors may not be independent? Is there a possibility that auditors will go along with whatever management says because management is paying them? That possibility exists, but there are a number of factors that work as a counterbalance.

First, recall from our discussion of the internal control structure that the Foreign Corrupt Practices Act requires companies to maintain an adequate system of internal controls. If management knowingly violate this law, they can go to jail (a number of top managers have) and would be subject to personal fines. In addition, the company is subject to corporate fines. Thus, management would be taking a big risk if they interfere with the auditors.

exhibit 5-3 Phar-Mor's 1999 Independent Auditors' Report

INDEPENDENT AUDITORS' REPORT

To the Board of Directors and Stockholders of Phar-Mor, Inc.:

We have audited the accompanying consolidated balance sheets of Phar-Mor, Inc. and subsidiaries (the "Company") as of July 3, 1999 and June 27, 1998, and the related consolidated statements of operations, changes in stockholders' equity and cash flows for the fifty-three weeks ended July 3, 1999, the fifty-two weeks ended June 27, 1998 and the fifty-two weeks ended June 28, 1997. Our audits also included consolidated financial statement Schedule II, Valuation and Qualifying Accounts. These financial statements and financial statement schedules are the responsibility of the Company's management. Our responsibility is to express an opinion on these financial statements and financial statement schedules based on our audits.

We conducted our audits in accordance with generally accepted auditing standards. Those standards require that we plan and perform the audit to obtain reasonable assurance about whether the financial statements are free of material misstatement. An audit includes examining, on a test basis, evidence supporting the amounts and disclosures in the financial statements. An audit also includes assessing the accounting principles used and significant estimates made by management, as well as evaluating the overall financial statement presentation. We believe that our audits provide a reasonable basis for our opinion.

In our opinion, the consolidated financial statements referred to above present fairly, in all material respects, the financial position of Phar-Mor, Inc. and subsidiaries as of July 3, 1999 and June 27, 1998 and the results of its operations and its cash flows for the fifty-three weeks ended July 3, 1999, the fifty-two weeks ended June 27, 1998 and the fifty-two weeks ended June 28, 1997, in conformity with generally accepted accounting principles.

In our opinion, the financial statement schedules, when considered in relation to the basic consolidated financial statements taken as a whole, present fairly in all material respects the information set forth therein.

Deloitte & Touche LLP
Pittsburgh, Pennsylvania
September 17, 1999

Second, external auditors have a responsibility to financial statement users to ensure that financial statements are fairly presented. The legal system in the United States provides auditors with financial incentives to remain independent. As an example, the auditors in the Phar-Mor case were sued by plaintiffs for over $1 billion. A jury held the audit firm liable, and that firm settled with the plaintiffs for a lesser, though undisclosed (but not insignificant), amount. Thus, external auditors are taking a big risk if they allow their independence and integrity to be compromised.

Third, auditors have a reputation to protect. The reason auditors are hired at all is because the investing public believes they provide an independent check on the reliability and integrity of the financial information. If an audit firm were no longer perceived in this manner, companies would cease to employ it. CPA firms obtain audit clients based on the quality of their reputation. Would they sell that reputation to the highest bidder? That would be very shortsighted indeed.

Knowing the incentives that influence auditors to provide fair and reliable financial information, we can now begin to see how the issues relating to disagreements in judgment can work themselves out. On the one hand, we have a management team that has an incentive to provide financial statement information that portrays the company in the most favorable position possible. On the other hand, we have auditors who are responsible to ensure that the information being provided is unbiased and fair. If auditors don't live up to their charge, they can end up paying to litigants much more than they ever received in audit fees.

fyi

This give and take between the auditors and management typically results in financial statements that fairly reflect the financial performance of a business. For example, in 1998, of 7,016 audits conducted for firms listed on the New York, American, and NASDAQ stock exchanges, only eight involved significant issues on which auditors and management could not reach agreement on disclosure.

The Securities and Exchange Commission (SEC) is working with public accounting firms to ensure that independence remains a keystone of the auditing profession. To that end, in a speech given at the New York University Center for Business and Law on May 10, 2000, SEC chairman Arthur Levitt discussed the issue of independence and outlined the SEC's plan for safeguarding the independence of the auditing profession. That plan includes (1) enhancing the role of the Public Oversight Board, an entity charged with oversight of the profession; (2) working with the Independence Standards Board to modernize investment rules that affect public accounting; and (3) developing initiatives to deal with conflicts that might arise because of the ever-expanding menu of services offered by public accounting firms.

If management is allowed to paint an overly optimistic picture of the firm's performance by using estimates that bias the financial reports, the audit firm will pay (via litigation) if those estimates prove to be materially wrong in the future. To protect itself, the audit firm would actually prefer that management use conservative estimates, but management will not always go along with the auditors in this regard. It is this tension, resulting from differing incentives, that provides financial statement users with information that, taken as a whole, fairly represents the financial performance of a business.

to summarize

Auditors provide a check and balance to ensure that the financial statements fairly reflect the financial performance of a business. Most large organizations have internal auditors whose role it is to ensure integrity in the financial records and to evaluate and encourage adherence to the organization's internal controls. Internal auditors are a very effective deterrent to fraud by employees and to the overriding of controls by management. Integrity in the financial reporting process is ensured with independent audits of financial statements by external certified public accountants. Such independent financial statement audits are required for all public companies, and often by creditors and other users. While audits can't "guarantee" accuracy in the financial statements, they do add credibility.

5

Explain the role of the Securities and Exchange Commission in adding credibility to financial statements.

Securities and Exchange Commission (SEC) The government body responsible for regulating the financial reporting practices of most publicly owned corporations in connection with the buying and selling of stocks and bonds.

THE SECURITIES AND EXCHANGE COMMISSION

In addition to the role of independent internal and external auditors, the U.S. government plays a role in ensuring the integrity of financial information. The **Securities and Exchange Commission (SEC)** is responsible for ensuring that investors, creditors, and other financial statement users are provided with reliable information upon which to make investment decisions.

The SEC is an agency of the federal government.[6] The SEC was organized in the 1930s because of financial reporting and stock market abuses. One such abuse was price manipulation. It was not uncommon in the 1920s for stockbrokers or dealers to indulge in "wash sales" or "matched orders," in which successive buy and sell orders created a false impression of stock activity and forced prices up. This maneuver allowed those involved to reap huge profits before the price fell back to its true market level. Outright deceit by issuing false and misleading financial statements was another improper practice. The objective of these manipulative procedures was to make profits at the expense of unwary investors.

One classic example of a major fraud that may have contributed to the formation of the SEC is the Ivar Kreugar case. During the 1920s, the most widely held securities in the United States, and perhaps the world, were the stocks and bonds of KREUGAR & TOLL, INC., a Swedish match company. These securities were popular because they paid high dividends (over 20% annually) and were sold in small denominations, making them attractive to both large and small investors. Ivar Kreugar, known as the "Match King," became wealthy and famous as a financial genius, building his business into a multibillion-dollar international enterprise. In fact, Kreugar defrauded millions of investors by personally creating false and misleading financial statements. Instead of being paid out of profits, the dividends were paid out of capital that was raised by selling securities to unsuspecting investors. Eventually, the giant pyramid collapsed, Kreugar committed suicide, and Kreugar & Toll, Inc., went bankrupt. On the day Kreugar died, his company's stock was selling for $5 a share. Within weeks, it was selling for five cents a share. The American public was outraged, and some have speculated that this major fraud was instrumental in causing Congress to enact securities legislation to prevent such deception from happening again.

f.y.i.

The first chairman of the SEC was Joseph P. Kennedy, father of the late President John F. Kennedy.

The Securities Act of 1933 requires most companies planning to issue new debt or stock securities to the public to submit a registration statement to the SEC for approval. The SEC examines these statements for completeness and adequacy before permitting companies to sell securities through securities exchanges. The Securities Exchange Act of 1934 requires all public companies to file detailed periodic reports with the SEC.

The SEC requires a considerable amount of information to be included in these filings. Among other things, a company must submit financial statements that have been audited by CPAs and that contain an opinion issued by those CPAs.

Of the many reports required by the SEC, the following have the most direct impact on financial reporting:

- *Registration statements.* These include various forms that must be filed and approved before a company can sell securities through the securities exchanges.
- *Form 10-K.* This report must be filed annually within 90 days after the close of each fiscal year. The report contains extensive financial information, including audited financial statements by independent CPAs. The 10-K also requires additional disclosure beyond that typically provided in the audited financial statements. Examples of additional information include the executive compensation of top management and the details of property, plant, and equipment transactions.
- *Form 10-Q.* This report must be filed quarterly for all publicly held companies. It contains certain financial information and requires a CPA's involvement.

Because the SEC has statutory power to mandate any reporting requirement it feels is needed, it has considerable influence in setting generally accepted accounting principles and disclosure

6 Most of the information on the SEC was taken from K. Fred Skousen, *An Introduction to the SEC,* 5th ed., South-Western Publishing Co., 1991, pp. 3–6.

requirements for financial statements. Generally, the SEC accepts the accounting pronouncements of the Financial Accounting Standards Board and other bodies such as the AICPA. In addition, the SEC has the power to establish rules for any CPA associated with audited financial statements submitted to the commission.

The SEC is given broad enforcement powers under the 1934 Act. If the rules of operation for stock exchanges prove to be ineffectual in implementing the requirements of the SEC, the SEC can alter or supplement them. The SEC can suspend trading of a company's stock for not more than 10 days (a series of orders has enabled the SEC to suspend trading for extended periods, however) and can suspend all trading on any exchange for up to 90 days. If substantive hearings show that the issuer failed to comply with the requirements of the securities laws, the SEC can "de-list" any security. Brokers and dealers can be prevented, either temporarily or permanently, from working in the securities market, and investigations can be initiated, if deemed necessary, to determine violations of any of the Acts or rules administered by the SEC.

The Effect of the 1934 Act on Independent Accountants

Accountants are involved in the preparation and review of a major portion of the reports and statements required by the 1934 Act. Accountants also can be censured, and their work is subject to approval by the SEC. The financial statements in the annual report to stockholders and in the 10-K report must be audited. In addition, accountants consult and assist in the preparation of the quarterly 10-Q reports and the other periodic reports.

More recently, the SEC under Chairman Arthur Levitt has initiated a major push to reduce the manipulation of reported earnings by a company's management. In a speech given on September 28, 1998, Mr. Levitt identified several techniques of what he called "Accounting Hocus Pocus." The SEC's objective is to prevent the manipulation of earnings and reduce fraudulent financial reporting by limiting the flexibility with which management is currently interpreting certain auditing and accounting standards.

---

to summarize

The Securities and Exchange Commission is an agency of the federal government whose purpose is to assist investors in public companies by regulating stock and bond markets and by requiring certain disclosures. Although the SEC has statutory authority to establish accounting principles, it basically accepts pronouncements of the FASB and AICPA as authoritative. Common reports required by the SEC are registration statements and Forms 10-K and 10-Q. Because the SEC can suspend trading and even de-list securities, it is a powerful organization that significantly influences financial reporting in the United States.

---

review of learning objectives

1 Identify the types of problems that can appear in financial statements. Three types of problems can affect financial statements: (1) Errors involve unintentional mistakes that can enter the accounting system at the transaction and journal entry stage or when journal entries are posted to accounts. These errors, when detected, are immediately fixed. (2) Disagreements in judgment occur because of the differing incentives of those associated with the financial statements. While management may have an incentive to present an optimistic view of the company's performance, auditors have an incentive to ensure full disclosure of all relevant issues. These differing incentives typically result in financial statements that fairly reflect the financial performance of the company. (3) Fraudulent financial reporting involves intentional misrepresentations in the financial statements. Safeguards are built into the accounting and reporting system to minimize the possibility that these problems will be reflected in the financial statements.

2 **Describe the safeguards employed within a firm to ensure that financial statements are free from problems.** Internal controls are safeguards built into an organization that help to protect assets and increase reliability of the accounting records. The three basic internal control structure categories are (1) the control environment, (2) the accounting systems, and (3) the control procedures. The five types of control procedures are (1) segregation of duties, (2) procedures for authorizations, (3) documents and records, (4) physical safeguards, and (5) independent checks. The control environment is comprised of such things as management's philosophy and operating style, the organizational structure, and the audit committee.

3 **Understand the need for monitoring by independent parties.** Because management has an incentive to portray the performance of the firm as positively as possible, there may be a tendency to be overly optimistic when it comes to making estimates and assessments regarding future events. As a result, there is a need for someone to independently evaluate the projections made by management to ensure that those projections, taken as a whole, result in financial statements that fairly reflect the financial performance of the business.

4 **Describe the role of auditors and how their presence affects the integrity of financial statements.** Most large organizations have internal auditors who are "independent" internal control experts. They examine the various functions and divisions of the business to evaluate internal controls, operating efficiency and effectiveness, and compliance with laws and company policy. Internal auditors usually report to top management or the board of directors and increase the reliability of financial statements by ensuring that internal controls function as they should.

External audits are required of most public companies by the Securities and Exchange Commission. By conducting audits of financial statements according to generally accepted auditing standards put into effect by the AICPA, external audits provide "reasonable assurance" that financial statements are presented fairly and are not materially misstated. External audits must be performed by CPAs who are licensed by the individual states in which they practice.

5 **Explain the role of the Securities and Exchange Commission in adding credibility to financial statements.** The SEC is the agency of the federal government charged with the responsibility of assisting investors by making sure they are provided with reliable information upon which to make investment decisions. The SEC was organized in the 1930s and requires certain periodic reports such as the Forms 10-Q and 10-K of companies that sell stock publicly in the United States. It adds credibility to financial statements by requiring independent audits, reviewing financial statements itself, and sanctioning firms that violate its standards.

key terms and concepts

accounting system 211
audit committee 211
control activities (procedures) 212
control environment 210
external auditors 218
Foreign Corrupt Practices Act (FCPA) 209
generally accepted auditing standards (GAAS) 218
independent checks 214
internal auditors 218
internal control structure 209
organizational structure 210
physical safeguards 213
Securities and Exchange Commission (SEC) 222
segregation of duties 212

discussion questions

1. How can a person tell whether an entry to an expense account is payment for a legitimate expenditure or a means of concealing a theft of cash?
2. How would it be possible to overstate revenues? What effect would an overstatement of revenues have on total assets?

3. What is the Foreign Corrupt Practices Act, and how is it important to financial reporting?
4. What are the major elements of a system of internal controls?
5. Identify five different types of control procedures.
6. How do internal auditors add to the credibility of financial statements?
7. What is the purpose of a financial statement audit by CPAs?
8. Do you believe that outside auditors (CPAs) who examine the financial statements of a company, while being paid by that company, can be truly independent?
9. The SEC requires companies to register with it when they sell stocks or bonds and also requires periodic reporting thereafter. Which of these reports, the initial registration statements or the subsequent periodic reports, do you believe would be scrutinized more closely by the SEC?
10. What do you suspect is the relationship between the FASB and the SEC?

discussion cases

CASE 5-1

AUDITING A COMPANY

Jerry Stillwell, the owner of a small company, asked Jones, a CPA, to conduct an audit of the company's financial statements. Stillwell told Jones that the audit needed to be completed in time to submit audited financial statements to a bank as part of a loan application. Jones immediately accepted the assignment and agreed to provide an auditor's report within two weeks.

Because Jones was busy, he hired two accounting students to perform the audit. After two hours of instruction, he sent them off to conduct the audit. Jones told the students not to spend time reviewing the internal controls, but instead to concentrate on proving the mathematical accuracy of the ledgers and other financial records.

The students followed Jones's instructions, and after 10 days, they provided the financial statements, which did not include notes. Jones reviewed the statements and prepared an auditor's report. The report did not refer to generally accepted accounting principles and contained no mention of any qualifications or disclosures. Briefly describe the problems with this audit.

CASE 5-2

AUDITING PRACTICE

A few years ago, the owners of an electronics wholesale company committed massive fraud by overstating revenues on the financial statements. They recorded three large fictitious sales near the end of the year to the retailers **SILO**, **CIRCUIT CITY**, and **WAL-MART**. The three transactions overstated revenues, receivables, and income by nearly $20 million. As part of the audit procedures, the external auditors sent requests for confirmation to the three stores to ensure that they did, in fact, owe the electronics company $20 million. In the meantime, the owners of the electronics company rented mailboxes in the cities where the three "customers" were headquartered, using names very similar to those of the three "customers." The requests for confirmation were sent to the mailboxes. The owners completed the confirmations and sent them back to the auditors, confirming the $20 million in receivables. With respect to the fraud, answer the following two questions:

1. What journal entries would the fraud perpetrators have entered into the financial records to overstate revenues?
2. Should the external auditors be held liable for not catching the fraud?

exercises

EXERCISE 5-1

ACCOUNTING ERRORS—TRANSACTION ERRORS

How would the following errors affect the account balances and the basic accounting equation, *Assets* = *Liabilities* + *Owners' Equity*? How do the misstatements affect income?

a. The purchase of a truck is recorded as an expense instead of an asset.
b. A cash payment on accounts receivable is received but not recorded.
c. Fictitious sales on account are recorded.
d. A clerk misreads a handwritten invoice for repairs and records it as $1,500 instead of $1,800.
e. Payment is received on December 31 for the next three months' rent and is recorded as revenue.

EXERCISE 5-2

ERRORS IN FINANCIAL STATEMENTS

The following financial statements are available for **SHERWOOD REAL ESTATE COMPANY**:

Balance Sheet

Assets		Liabilities		
Cash	$ 1,300	Accounts payable	$ 100,000	
Receivable from sale of real estate	5,000,000	Mortgage payable	6,000,000	
Interest receivable*	180,000	Total liabilities		$ 6,100,000
Real estate properties	6,000,000	**Stockholders' Equity**		
		Capital stock	$ 10,000	
		Retained earnings	5,071,300	
		Total stockholders' equity		5,081,300
Total assets	$11,181,300	Total liabilities and stockholders' equity		$11,181,300

*Interest Receivable applies to Receivable from sale of real estate.

Income Statement

Gain on sale of real estate	$3,200,000
Interest income*	180,000
Total revenues	$3,380,000
Expenses	1,200,000
Net income	$2,180,000

*Interest Income applies to Receivable from sale of real estate.

Sherwood Company is using these financial statements to entice investors to buy stock in the company. However, a recent FBI investigation revealed that the sale of real estate was a fabricated transaction with a fictitious company that was recorded to make the financial statements look better. The sales price was $5,000,000 with a zero cash down payment and a $5,000,000 receivable. Prepare financial statements for Sherwood Company showing what its total assets, liabilities, stockholders' equity, and income really are with the sale of real estate removed.

EXERCISE 5-3

APPROPRIATENESS OF ACCOUNTING RULES

In the early 1990s, the top executive of a large oil refining company (based in New York) was convicted of financial statement fraud. One of the issues in the case involved the way the company accounted for its oil inventories. In particular, the company would purchase crude oil from exploration companies and then process the oil into finished oil products, such as jet fuel, diesel fuel, and so forth. Because there was a ready market for these finished products, as soon as the company purchased the crude oil, it would value its oil inventory at the selling prices of the finished products less the cost to refine the oil. Although the case involved fraud, the type of accounting used was also questioned because it allowed the company to recognize profit before the actual sale (and even refining) of the oil. Nevertheless, one of the large CPA firms attested to the use of this method. If you were the judge in this case, would you be critical of this accounting practice?

EXERCISE 5-4

INTERNAL CONTROL PROCEDURES

As an auditor, you have discovered the following problems with the accounting system control procedures of Jefferson Retailers. For each of the following occurrences, tell which of the five internal control procedures was lacking. Also, recommend how the company should change its procedures to avoid the problem in the future.

a. Jefferson Retailers' losses due to bad debts have increased dramatically over the past year. In an effort to increase sales, the managers of certain stores have allowed large credit sales to occur without review or approval.
b. An accountant hid his theft of $200 from the company's bank account by changing the monthly reconciliation. He knew the manipulation would not be discovered.
c. Steve Meyer works in the storeroom. He maintains the inventory records, counts the inventory, and has unlimited access to the storeroom. He occasionally steals items of inventory and hides the theft by including the value of the stolen goods in his inventory count.
d. Receiving reports are sometimes filled out days after shipments have arrived.

EXERCISE 5-5

INTERNAL AUDITING—STAFFING INTERNAL AUDITS

A manufacturing corporation recently reassigned one of its accounting managers to the internal audit department. He had successfully directed the western-area accounting office, and the corporation thought his skills would be valuable to the internal audit department. The director of the internal audit division knew of this individual's experience in the western-area accounting office and assigned him to audit that same office.

Should the internal auditor be assigned to audit the same office in which he recently worked? What problems could arise in this situation?

EXERCISE 5-6

INTERNAL AUDITING

Which of the following is not applicable to the internal audit function?

a. Deter or catch employee fraud.
b. Issue an opinion for investors regarding the reliability of the financial statements.
c. Be guided by its own set of professional standards.
d. Help to ensure that the accounting function is performed correctly and that the financial statements are prepared accurately.

EXERCISE 5-7

INTERNAL AUDITING—EXTERNAL AUDITOR'S RELIANCE ON INTERNAL AUDITORS

North, CPA, is planning an audit of the financial statements of General Company. In determining the nature, timing, and extent of the auditing procedures, North is considering General's internal audit function, which is staffed by Tyler.

1. In what ways may Tyler's work be relevant to North?
2. What factors should North consider and what inquiries should North make in deciding whether to rely on Tyler's work?

EXERCISE 5-8

ENSURING THE INTEGRITY OF FINANCIAL REPORTING

Three college seniors with majors in accounting are discussing alternative career plans. All three want to enter careers that will help to ensure the integrity of financial reporting. The first wants to become an internal auditor. She believes that by ensuring appropriate internal controls within a company, the financial statements will be reliable. The second wants to go to work in public accounting and perform external audits of companies. He believes that external auditors are independent and can make sure that financial statements are correct. The third student believes that neither choice will be adding much value to the integrity of financial statements because, in both cases, the auditors will be receiving their pay (either directly or indirectly) from the companies they audit. He believes the only way to make a real difference is to work for the Securities and Exchange Commission, using the "arm of government regulation" to force companies to issue appropriate financial statements and then punishing them (through jail sentences and large fines) when their financial statements are misleading. In your opinion, which of these three students will make the largest contribution toward ensuring integrity in the financial statements?

EXERCISE 5-9

EXTERNAL AUDITORS—PURPOSE OF AN AUDIT

What is the purpose of external auditors providing an opinion on a company's financial statements?

EXERCISE 5-10

AUDITING FINANCIAL STATEMENTS

The Utah Lakers professional basketball team has recently decided to sell stock and become a public company. In determining what it must do to file a registration statement with the SEC, the company realizes that it needs to have an audit opinion to accompany its financial statements. The company has recently approached two accounting students at a major university and asked them to "audit" its financial statements to be submitted to the SEC. Should the two accounting students accept the work and perform the audit?

EXERCISE 5-11

SECURITIES AND EXCHANGE COMMISSION—AUTHORITY TO SET ACCOUNTING STANDARDS

Which organization—the Securities and Exchange Commission, the American Institute of Certified Public Accountants, or the Financial Accounting Standards Board—has federal government authority to set accounting standards and reporting requirements? Some people have argued that all accounting rule making should be done by the federal government. Do you agree? Why or why not?

EXERCISE 5-12

SECURITIES AND EXCHANGE COMMISSION—ROLE OF THE SEC

Describe the role of the Securities and Exchange Commission and its influence on the practice of auditing.

EXERCISE 5-13

SECURITIES AND EXCHANGE COMMISSION—INFORMATION NEEDED FOR INVESTING

As an investor you are considering buying stock in a relatively new company. American Shipping, Ltd., has been in existence for 10 years and is now about to go public. The first stock offering will be listed on the New York Stock Exchange next week.

1. What kind of information would you like to know before investing in the company? Where can you find this information?
2. How does the SEC protect the securities market from companies that are fraudulent or in poor financial condition?
3. Besides stock market investors, what other parties might be interested in knowing financial data about companies?

EXERCISE 5-14

AUDITING NEGLIGENCE

A few years ago, the officers of **PHAR-MOR**, a discount retail chain, were convicted of issuing fraudulent financial statements. It was learned at the trial that the company overstated its inventory by moving inventory from store to store and counting the same inventory several times. For example, a case of Coca-Cola would be counted at one store and then moved to another store and counted again. In a separate civil trial, Phar-Mor's auditors were accused of performing negligent audits because they didn't catch these inventory movements. Do you believe that the external auditors were negligent in this case?

EXERCISE 5-15

SECURITIES AND EXCHANGE COMMISSION

Many people have argued that the purpose of the SEC is to protect investors. Some believe that the best way to do this is by preventing weak companies from issuing stock. Others say that the SEC should require full disclosure and then let the buyer beware. Which do you think is more appropriate: a preventive role or a disclosure role?

competency enhancement opportunities

- Analyzing Real Company Information
- International Case
- Ethics Case
- Writing Assignment
- The Debate
- Cumulative Spreadsheet Project
- Internet Search

The following additional assignments provide opportunities for students to develop critical thinking, ethical perspectives, oral and written communication skills, experience with electronic research, and teamwork through group and business activities.

ANALYZING REAL COMPANY INFORMATION

• ***Analyzing 5-1 (Microsoft)***

The 1999 annual report for MICROSOFT is included in Appendix A. Locate that annual report and consider the following questions:

1. With respect to the report of the external auditors to "the Board of Directors and Stockholders of Microsoft Corporation":
   a. Who is Microsoft's external auditor?
   b. How long after the end of Microsoft's fiscal year did the external auditor complete the audit?
2. With respect to the report of management concerning the financial statements:
   a. Who is responsible for the financial statements?
   b. After reading the paragraph on internal control, indicate whether you agree or disagree with the following statement: "The purpose of an internal control system is to ensure that all transactions are always recorded and that all assets are always completely safeguarded."
   c. After looking at the description of the members of the audit committee, do you think that Bill Gates is a member of that committee?

• ***Analyzing 5-2 (Circle K)***

At one time, CIRCLE K was the second-largest convenience store chain in the United States (behind 7-ELEVEN). At its peak, Circle K, based in Phoenix, Arizona, operated 4,685 stores in 32 states. Circle K's rapid expansion was financed through long-term borrowing. Interest on this large debt, combined with increased price competition from convenience stores operated by oil companies, squeezed the profits of Circle K. For the fiscal year ended April 30, 1990, Circle K reported a loss of $773 million. In May 1990, Circle K filed for Chapter 11 bankruptcy protection. Subsequently, Circle K was taken over by TOSCO, a large independent oil company.

1. In the fiscal year ended April 30, 1989, Circle K experienced significant financial difficulty. Reported profits were down 74.5% from the year before. In the president's letter to the shareholders, Circle K explained that 1989 was a "disappointing" year and that management was seeking some outside company to come in and buy out the Circle K shareholders. How do you think all this bad news was reflected in the auditor's report accompanying the financial statements dated April 30, 1989?

2. As mentioned, Circle K reported a loss of $773 million for the year ended April 30, 1990. Just a week after the end of the fiscal year, the CEO was fired. One week after that, Circle K declared bankruptcy. The audit report was completed approximately two months later. How do you think the news of the bankruptcy was reflected in the auditor's report accompanying the financial statements dated April 30, 1990?

INTERNATIONAL CASE

• *Do the Financial Statements Give a True and Fair View?*

SWIRE PACIFIC, LTD., based in Hong Kong, is one of the largest companies in the world. The primary operations of the company are in the region of Hong Kong, China, and Taiwan where it has operated for over 125 years. Swire operates CATHAY PACIFIC AIRWAYS and has extensive real estate holdings in Hong Kong. The 1996 auditor's report (prepared by PRICE WATERHOUSE) for Swire Pacific, dated March 14, 1997, read as follows (in part):

> An audit includes examination, on a test basis, of evidence relevant to the amounts and disclosures in the accounts. It also includes an assessment of the significant estimates and judgments made by the directors in the preparation of the accounts, and of whether the accounting policies are appropriate to the Company's and the Group's circumstances, consistently applied and adequately disclosed. . . .
>
> In our opinion the accounts give a true and fair view, in all material respects, of the state of affairs of the Company and the Group as at 31st December 1996. . . .

Although the concept of a "true and fair view" is not part of the auditor's terminology in the United States, it is used by auditors all over the world and is also discussed as part of International Accounting Standards (IAS). The "true and fair view" concept states that an auditor must make sure that the financial statements give an honest representation of the economic status of the company, even if the company violates generally accepted accounting principles in order to do so.

1. Review the opinion language in the auditor's report for MICROSOFT (see Appendix A). Does the audit report state unconditionally that Microsoft's financial statements are a fair representation of the economic status of the company?
2. Auditors in the United States concentrate on performing audits to ensure that financial statements are prepared in accordance with generally accepted accounting principles. What economic and legal realities in the United States would make it difficult for U.S. auditors to apply the "true and fair view" concept?

ETHICS CASE

• *Blowing the Whistle on Former Partners*

On St. Patrick's Day in 1992, CHAMBERS DEVELOPMENT COMPANY, one of the largest landfill and waste management firms in the United States, announced that it had been engaging in improper accounting for years. Wall Street fear (over what this announcement implied about the company's track record of steady earnings growth) sent Chambers' stock price plunging by 62% in one day.

The improper accounting by Chambers had been discovered in the course of the external audit. The auditors found that $362 million in expenses had not been reported since Chambers first became a public company in 1985. If this amount of additional expense had been reported, it would have completely wiped out all the profit reported by Chambers since it first went public. The difficult part of this situation was that a large number of the financial staff working for Chambers were former partners in the audit firm performing the audit. These accountants had first worked as independent external auditors at Chambers, then were hired by Chambers, and subsequently were audited by their old partners.

What ethical and economic issues did the auditors of Chambers Development Company face as they considered whether to blow the whistle on their former partners?

WRITING ASSIGNMENT

• ***External Auditors***

Visit or call a local CPA firm (or the local office of a multi-office CPA firm). Ask about career opportunities, the size of the firm's staff, who some of its major clients are, and other facts about the firm. Then, write a one-page summary of your visit.

THE DEBATE

• ***Who Needs Internal Control?***

An internal control system is intended to ensure that all transactions are properly approved and recorded, that assets and records are safeguarded, and that operations run efficiently. As with any other system in a business, an internal control system costs money to operate.

Divide your group into two teams.

- One team represents the "Hire Honest and Smart" group. Prepare a two-minute oral presentation supporting the notion that if a company would focus on hiring only honest and smart employees, it would not need to spend money designing and operating an internal control system. Most of the functions of internal control are to prevent employees from stealing and to make it difficult for inept employees to commit costly mistakes.
- The other team represents the "No Trust" group. Prepare a two-minute oral presentation arguing that a company must set up a careful internal control system because, given the right opportunity and motive, any employee can turn into a thief. In addition, a company cannot rely on the good intentions of employees to keep the business running smoothly. Instead, top management must design systems that will keep things running smoothly in spite of the mistakes of employees.

CUMULATIVE SPREADSHEET PROJECT

This spreadsheet assignment is a continuation of the spreadsheet assignment given in Chapter 2. If you completed that spreadsheet, you have a head start on this one.

1. Refer back to the financial statement numbers for Handyman Company for 2003 [given in part (1) of the Cumulative Spreadsheet Project assignment in Chapter 2]. Using the balance sheet and income statement created with those numbers, create spreadsheet cell formulas to compute and display values for the following ratios:

a. Current ratio
b. Debt ratio
c. Asset turnover
d. Return on equity

2. To observe the impact that errors and fraudulent transactions can have on the financial statements, determine what the ratios computed in (1) would have been if (1) each of the following transactions was recorded as described and (2) the transaction was recorded correctly. Treat each transaction independently, meaning that before determining the impact of each new transaction you should reset the financial statement values to their original amounts. Each of the hypothetical transactions is assumed to occur on the last day of the year.
   a. Created receivables by creating fictitious sales of $140 all on account.
   b. Purchased $80 of inventory on account but incorrectly increased the property, plant, and equipment account instead of increasing Inventory.
   c. Borrowed $60 with a short-term payable. The liability was incorrectly recorded as Long-Term Debt.
   d. An inventory purchase on account in the amount of $90 was not recorded until the next year.

INTERNET SEARCH

• ***Phar-Mor***

Access the Web site of **PHAR-MOR** at **http://www.pharmor.com**. Sometimes Web addresses change, so if this address doesn't work, access the Web site for this textbook (**http://albrecht.swcollege.com**) for an updated link.

Once you've gained access to the site, answer the following questions:

1. When was Phar-Mor founded? How many stores does the company have today? In how many states is the company doing business?
2. Locate Phar-Mor's most recent press release. What is the topic of the press release?
3. Review Phar-Mor's annual report to determine any lingering effects of the fraud that was revealed by the company in 1992.
4. Evaluate Phar-Mor's current financial position as compared to 1999.

comprehensive problem 1–5

As a recently hired accountant for a small business, SMC, Inc., you are provided with last year's balance sheet, income statement, and post-closing trial balance to familiarize yourself with the business.

SMC, Inc.
Balance Sheet
December 31, 2002

Assets		
Cash	$34,500	
Accounts receivable	25,000	
Inventory	10,000	
Supplies	200	
Total assets		$69,700
Liabilities and Stockholders' Equity		
Liabilities:		
Accounts payable	$12,000	
Salaries payable	1,000	
Income taxes payable	3,675	
Total liabilities		$16,675
Stockholders' equity:		
Capital stock (10,000 shares outstanding)	$25,000	
Retained earnings	28,025	
Total stockholders' equity		53,025
Total liabilities and stockholders' equity		$69,700

SMC, Inc.
Income Statement
For the Year Ended December 31, 2002

Sales revenue	$110,000	
Rent revenue	1,000	
Total revenues		$111,000
Less cost of goods sold		60,000
Gross margin		$ 51,000
Less operating expenses:		
Supplies expense	$ 400	
Salaries expense	22,000	
Miscellaneous expense	4,100	26,500
Income before taxes		$ 24,500
Less income taxes		3,675
Net income		$ 20,825
Earnings per share ($20,825 ÷ 10,000 shares)		$ 2.08

SMC, Inc.
Post-Closing Trial Balance
December 31, 2002

	Debits	Credits
Cash	$34,500	
Accounts Receivable	25,000	
Inventory	10,000	
Supplies	200	
Accounts Payable		$12,000
Salaries Payable		1,000
Income Taxes Payable		3,675
Capital Stock		25,000
Retained Earnings		28,025
Totals	$69,700	$69,700

You are also given the following information that summarizes the business activity for the current year, 2003.

a. Issued 5,000 additional shares of capital stock for $10,000 cash.
b. Borrowed $5,000 on January 2, 2003, from Downtown Bank as a long-term loan. Interest for the year is $500, payable on January 2, 2004.
c. Paid $3,600 cash on November 1 to lease a truck for one year.
d. Received $1,200 on November 1 from a tenant for six months' rent.
e. Paid $600 on October 1 for a one-year insurance policy.
f. Purchased $500 of supplies for cash.
g. Purchased inventory for $100,000 on account.
h. Sold inventory for $150,000 on account; cost of the merchandise sold was $80,000.
i. Collected $120,000 cash from customers' accounts receivable.
j. Paid $70,000 cash for inventories purchased during the year.
k. Paid $25,000 for sales reps' salaries, including $1,000 owed at the beginning of 2003.
l. No dividends were paid during the year.
m. The income taxes payable for the year were paid. Income taxes are based on a 15% corporate tax rate.
n. For adjusting entries, all prepaid expenses are initially recorded as assets, and all unearned revenues are initially recorded as liabilities.
o. At year-end, $150 worth of supplies are on hand.
p. At year-end, an additional $5,000 of sales salaries are owed, but have not yet been paid.

You are asked to do the following:

1. Journalize the transactions for the current year, 2003, using the accounts listed on the financial statements and other appropriate accounts (you may omit explanations).
2. Set up T-accounts and enter the beginning balances from the December 31, 2002, post-closing trial balance for SMC. Post all current year journal entries to the T-accounts.
3. Journalize and post any necessary adjusting entries at the end of 2003. (Hint: Items b, c, d, e, m, o, and p require adjustment.)
4. After the adjusting entries are posted, prepare a trial balance, a balance sheet, and an income statement for 2003. (Hint: Income before income taxes should equal $39,600.)
5. Journalize and post closing entries for 2003 and prepare a post-closing trial balance.
6. Using the DuPont framework, compute the return on equity for SMC for 2002 and 2003.
7. **Interpretive Question:** What is your overall assessment of the financial health of SMC, Inc.?

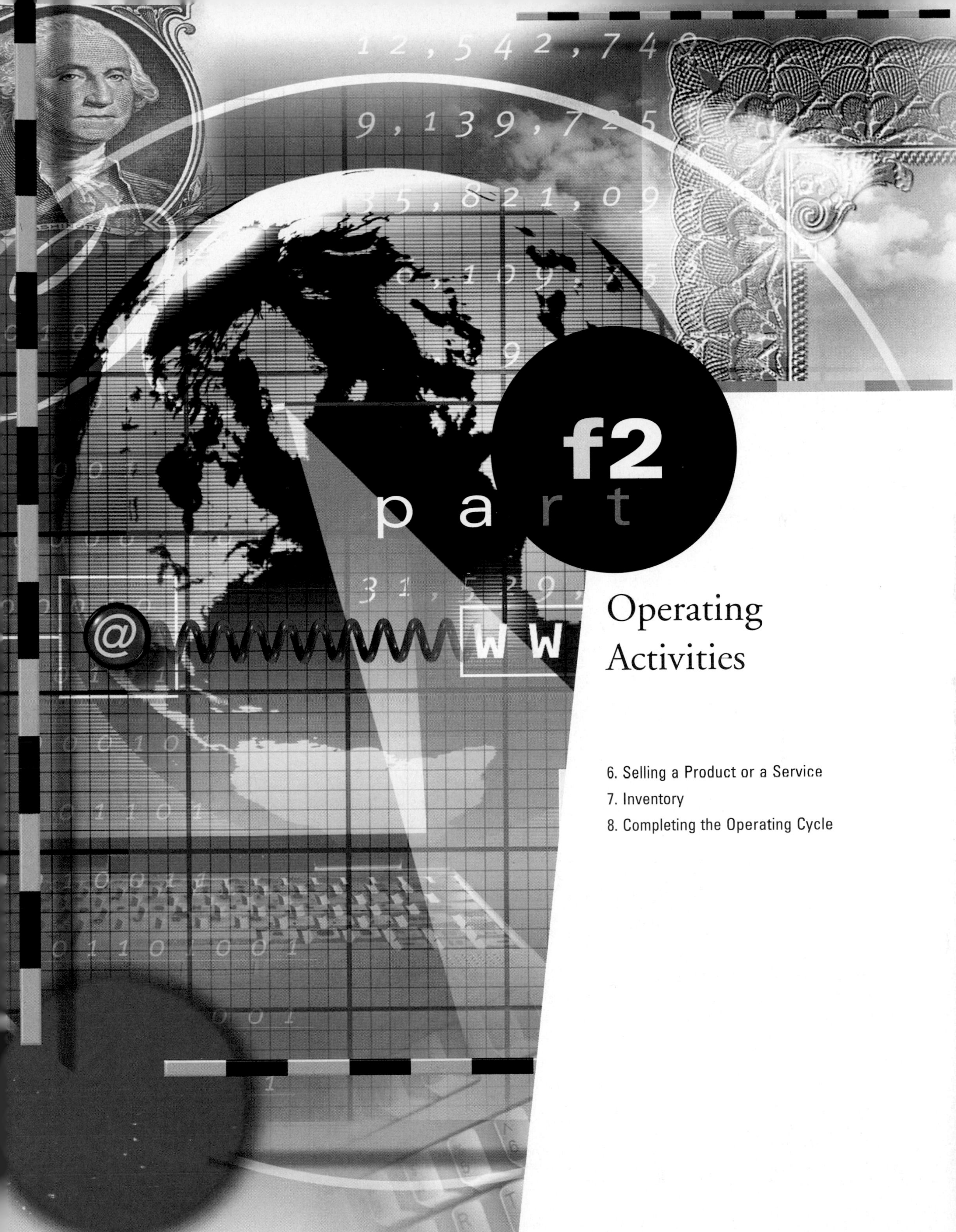

f2 part

Operating Activities

Selling a Product or a Service

chapter

f6

learning objectives After studying this chapter, you should be able to:

1 Understand the three basic types of business activities: operating, investing, and financing.

2 Use the two revenue recognition criteria to decide when the revenue from a sale or service should be recorded in the accounting records.

3 Properly account for the collection of cash and describe the business controls necessary to safeguard cash.

4 Record the losses resulting from credit customers who do not pay their bills.

5 Evaluate a company's management of its receivables by computing and analyzing appropriate financial ratios.

6 Match revenues and expenses by estimating and recording future warranty and service costs associated with a sale.

expanded material

7 Reconcile a checking account.

8 Understand how receivables can be used by a company to get cash immediately.

9 Account for the impact of changing exchange rates on the value of accounts receivable denominated in foreign currencies.

Jerry Yang was born in Taiwan in 1968. His father died when he was just two, so Jerry and his brother were raised by their mother, an English professor at a university in Taipei. Jerry's mother moved the family to San Jose, California, in 1978. In spite of what he calls a "very short attention span," Jerry was an excellent student—he was valedictorian of his high school class, and he completed his bachelor's and master's degrees in electrical engineering at Stanford University in a total of just four years.[1]

David Filo was born in Wisconsin in 1966. He describes his parents as "hippie wannabes," who moved their family to Moss Bluff, Louisiana, to join a commune. David eventually left the commune to attend Tulane University where he studied computer engineering. David then went to Stanford as a graduate student, working part-time as a teaching assistant. As luck would have it, one of his students was Jerry Yang. Jerry and David's friendship was strengthened when they both went on a six-month academic exchange program to Japan in 1992.

In 1993, Jerry and David were supposed to be working on their Ph.D. theses in computer-aided design at Stanford. Instead, they found themselves spending more and more research time surfing through the incredible amount of information available on the newly created "World Wide Web." Their first project was to write software that scanned the Web for NBA player statistics. The first Web site that Jerry designed was dedicated to another of his sports passions—sumo wrestling.

Jerry and David quickly learned that the key to surfing the vast quantities of information on the Web was to be able to organize the information. They compiled a list of their favorite Web sites, which they e-mailed to friends and posted on the Web under the title "Jerry's Guide to the World Wide Web." This title was a bit unwieldy, so they came up with the shorthand title "**YAHOO!**" Jerry and David liked the irreverent, lively tone of the name; they then went back and developed a "formal" title to fit the Yahoo! acronym: Yet Another Hierarchical Officious Oracle.

By 1994, thousands were using Yahoo! to access information on the Web. In fact, the demand was so great that Jerry and David were spending 20-plus hours a day on their "hobby." In addition, the resources of the Stanford computer network were being taxed by Yahoo! users, and university officials asked Jerry and David to find another computer to host their service. Interest in hosting the Yahoo! service was high, and representatives from **MCI WORLDCOM**, **AOL**, and **NETSCAPE** visited Jerry and David in their disheveled 10-by-10-foot work space in a trailer on the Stanford campus. Jerry and David accepted Netscape's offer of help, and the Yahoo! service moved over to the Netscape computer network in 1995.

fyi

Jonathan Swift coined the word *yahoo* in his book *Gulliver's Travels*. The "yahoos" were savage humans who lived in a land where horses were the dominant species. Swift, a noted satirist, used the term *yahoo* to illustrate how easy it is to justify committing atrocities against people once they are categorized with an unfavorable label.

In March 1995, Jerry and David were finally convinced that their Web search hobby could actually be turned into a business. They accepted a $4 million investment from **SEQUOIA**, a venture capital firm. Realizing that they lacked business expertise, they chose Tim Koogle, another Stanford graduate who was running a $400 million high-tech equipment company, to join them in running their company. In essence, Jerry and David hired Koogle to be their boss. In Yahoo!'s organizational hierarchy, Koogle bears the title of chief executive officer (CEO), and Jerry and David are officially titled the "Chief Yahoos." This team has turned Yahoo! into the most recognized name among Internet companies. As of June 2000, Yahoo! had a total market value of $76 billion.

So, how does Yahoo! make money? Throughout its history, Yahoo! has generated almost all of its revenue through the sale of advertising space on its Web pages. For example, in 1999, 90.4% of Yahoo!'s $588.6 million in revenue was generated through advertising. Yahoo!'s advertising fees are described as follows in the company's 1998 annual report:

> The Company's standard rates for banner advertising currently range from approximately $6.00 per thousand impressions for run of network [general advertising] to approxi-

setting the stage

1 The Yahoo! background material was obtained from the following sources: Beverly Schuch, "Yang and Filo: Chief Yahoos!" *CNN Pinnacle*, November 14, 1999, Transcript #99111400V39; and Brent Schlender, "How a Virtuoso Plays the Web," *Fortune*, March 6, 2000, p. F-79.

mately $90.00 per thousand impressions for highly targeted audiences and properties.

The key factor in generating this advertising revenue is maintaining high traffic through its Web sites. In March 2000, Yahoo!'s traffic averaged 625 million page views per day, originating from a pool of 145 million different Yahoo! users worldwide. Yahoo!'s growth in annual revenues from 1995 through 1999 averaged 353% per year, as illustrated in Exhibit 6-1. The challenge facing Yahoo! is to expand its revenue base from advertising into the exploding realm of e-commerce. For example, Yahoo! plans to significantly increase the amount of revenue it generates through commissions on e-commerce transactions facilitated through services such as Yahoo! Shopping and Yahoo! Auctions.

For Internet companies such as Yahoo!, investors are extremely interested in the amount of revenue reported in the income statement. In fact, in the gold rush of e-commerce, investors are more concerned about how much e-business a company is doing than about whether the company is able to generate immediate profits. The amount of revenue reported by an Internet company is a key indicator of how large the company is in the Internet economy. For example, as of 1999, **AMAZON.COM** *had never reported a profit (revenue minus expenses) in its history; the company lost $720 million in 1999 alone. Yet, because of the $1.6 billion in revenue it reported in 1999, Amazon.com is viewed as a major player in the burgeoning Internet economy. As a result, Amazon.com had a market value of $16.4 billion in May 2000.*

The amount of revenue reported by traditional companies, such as **GENERAL MOTORS, WAL-MART,** *and* **GENERAL ELECTRIC,** *is also of interest to investors because increased revenues almost always lead to increased profits. Consequently, there is sometimes great pressure on companies to report as much revenue as possible. To balance this pressure, accounting rules have been established to govern exactly when it is appropriate for a company to report the revenue from a transaction in the income statement. These accounting rules are not just conceptual toys for accountants; investor*

exhibit 6-1 Growth in Yahoo! Revenue: 1995–1999

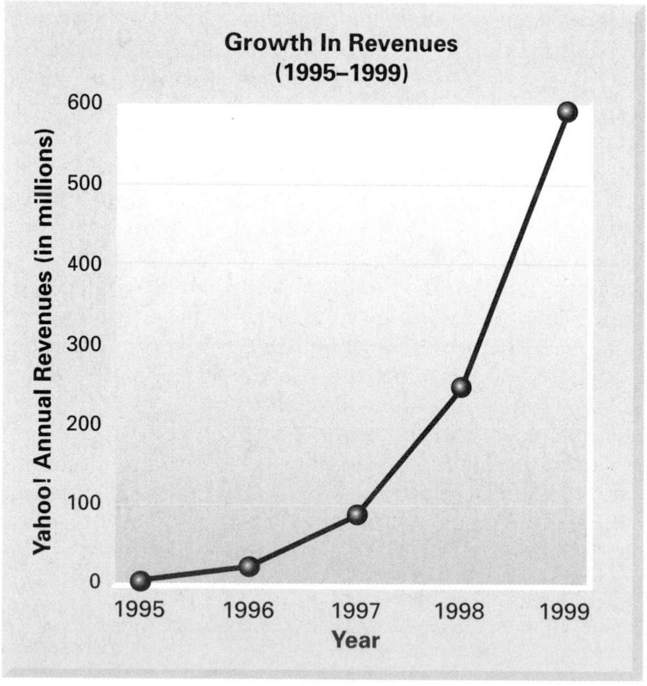

concern about whether MICROSTRATEGY, a software company, was correctly applying the accounting rules associated with revenue caused the company's stock price to drop from $333 per share on March 10, 2000, to $22.25 per share just 10 weeks later.[2]

In this chapter, you will study the accounting rules governing the proper recognition of revenue. You will also learn how to account for cash collections and how to handle customer accounts that are uncollectible. Selling goods and services, collecting the cash, and handling customer accounts are fundamental to the operation of any business. Accordingly, properly recording these activities is fundamental to the practice of accounting.

MAJOR ACTIVITIES OF A BUSINESS

1

Understand the three basic types of business activities: operating, investing, and financing.

In the first five chapters, you were introduced to the accounting environment, the basic financial statements, and the accounting cycle (the way business transactions are entered into the accounting records). That material was necessary for you to understand some basic terminology and procedures used in accounting. Accounting has often been called the language of business. By studying the first five chapters, you should now be somewhat familiar with this new business language.

With the basics behind us, it is now time to use accounting to understand how businesses work, how the various activities of business are accounted for, and how businesses report their operating results to investors. The activities of most businesses can be divided into three groups:

- Operating activities
- Investing activities
- Financing activities

operating activities Transactions and events that involve selling products or services and incurring the necessary expenses associated with the primary activities of the business.

Operating activities involve selling products or services, buying inventory for resale, and incurring and paying for necessary expenses associated with the primary activities of the business. The operating activities of a motel, for example, would include renting rooms (the selling activity); buying soap, shampoo, and other supplies to operate the motel; and incurring and paying for electricity, heat, water, cleaning, television and telephone service, and salaries and taxes of workers. The operating activities of a grocery store would include buying produce, meats, canned goods, and other items for resale; selling products to customers; and incurring and paying for expenses associated with the store's operations such as utilities, salaries, and taxes. The operating activities of YAHOO! include selling advertising space on the company's Web pages, paying employees to maintain the Yahoo! system and to develop new software, and paying to advertise the Yahoo! brand name on TV and in magazines. It is easy to identify operating activities because they are always associated with the primary purpose of a business.

A motel deals with operating activities on a daily basis when renting rooms, buying supplies, and paying utility expenses.

In this chapter we cover the operating activities for selling products and services, the recognition of revenues from those sales, accounting for cash, and problems associated with collecting receivables arising from sales. In Chapter 7 we examine the purchase of inventory for resale to customers and the necessary accounting procedures. In Chapter 8 we conclude our discussion of operating activities by considering other operating expenses and how revenues and expenses are combined to compute the net income of a business. Incurring and paying for operating expenses such

2 Michael Schroeder, "SEC Widens MicroStrategy Investigation," *The Wall Street Journal*, May 24, 2000, p. C1.

as employee compensation, insurance, advertising, research and development, and income taxes are also covered in Chapter 8.

investing activities Transactions and events that involve the purchase and sale of property, plant, equipment, and other assets not generally held for resale.

Investing activities involve the purchase of assets for use in the business. The assets purchased as part of investing activities include property, plant, and equipment, as well as financial assets such as investments in stocks and bonds of other companies. Investing activities are distinguishable from operating activities because they occur less frequently and the amounts involved in each transaction are usually quite large. For example, while most businesses buy and sell inventory or services to customers on a daily basis (operating activities), only rarely do they buy and sell buildings, equipment, and stocks and bonds of other companies. It is important to note that buying inventory for resale is an operating activity, not an investing activity. Investing activities are covered in Chapters 9 and 12.

financing activities Transactions and events whereby resources are obtained from, or repaid to, owners (equity financing) and creditors (debt financing).

Financing activities involve raising money to finance a business by means other than operations. In addition to earning money through profitable operations, there are two other ways to fund a business: (1) money can be borrowed from creditors (debt financing), or (2) money can be raised by selling stock or ownership interests in the business to investors (equity financing). Debt financing is the subject of Chapter 10, while equity financing will be discussed in Chapter 11.

Once you have studied Chapters 6 through 12, you will have a good understanding of how businesses operate, invest, and are financed. That knowledge should be helpful in the future if you own your own business, invest in companies as a stockholder, work for a financial institution (or other lender of funds), or work in any position where a knowledge of business is essential.

After studying the operating, investing, and financing activities of a business, you will be ready to combine your knowledge of how businesses operate with the basic accounting knowledge you gained from Chapters 1 through 5. To do this, we will study in detail the statement of cash flows, which is structured around the three activities of a business (Chapter 13). You will discover that preparation of a statement of cash flows requires a sound understanding of the balance sheet and the income statement, as well as a good grasp of how the activities of a business tie together. Exhibit 6-2 provides a graphical road map of the business and reporting activities that will be discussed in the subsequent eight chapters.

Although Chapters 6 through 12 are organized around business activities, it is important to understand how these activities relate to the basic financial statements. To help you understand these relationships, at the beginning of each of the next seven chapters, we present basic financial statements that highlight the accounts that will be covered in that chapter. As you can

exhibit 6-2 Major Activities of a Business

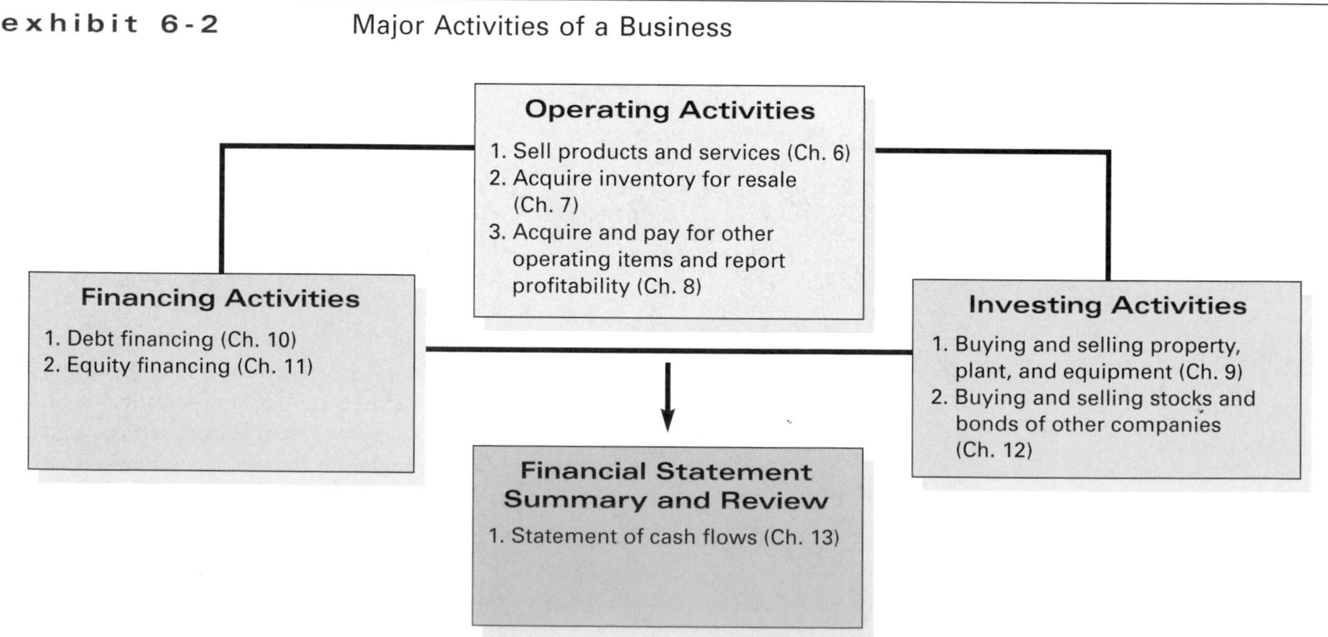

exhibit 6-3 Financial Statement Items Covered in This Chapter

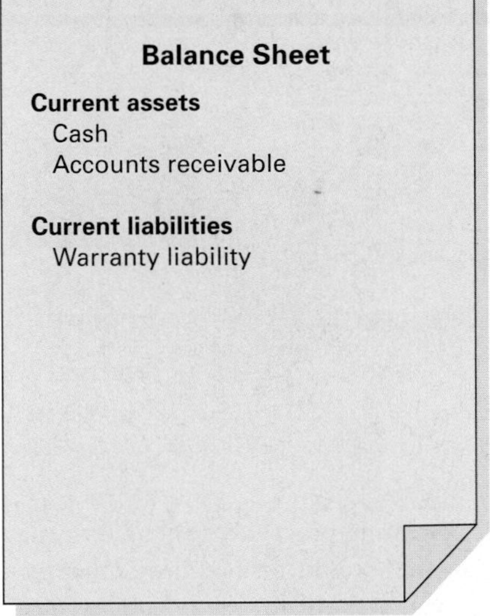

Statement of Cash Flows

Operating activities
Receipts from customers

Income Statement

Revenue
Sales of goods and services

Expenses
Bad debt expense
Warranty expense

see in Exhibit 6-3, Cash, Accounts Receivable, and Warranty Liability on the balance sheet; Sales, Bad Debt Expense, and Warranty Expense on the income statement; and Receipts from Customers on the statement of cash flows are covered in Chapter 6.

---

to summarize

Activities of a business can be divided into (1) operating activities, (2) investing activities, and (3) financing activities. Operating activities involve selling products or services, buying inventory for resale, and incurring and paying for necessary expenses associated with the primary activities of a business. Investing activities include purchasing assets for use in the business and making investments in such items as stocks and bonds. Financing activities include raising money to finance a business by means other than operations.

2

Use the two revenue recognition criteria to decide when the revenue from a sale or service should be recorded in the accounting records.

RECOGNIZING REVENUE

The operations of a business revolve around the sale of a product or a service. MCDONALD'S sells fast food; MICROSOFT sells software and continuing customer support; BANK OF AMERICA loans money and sells financial services; YAHOO! sells advertising space on its Web pages. Just as the sale of a product or service is at the heart of any business, proper recording of the revenue from sales and services is fundamental to the practice of accounting. A simple time line illustrating the business issues involved with a sale is given in Exhibit 6-4.

Consideration of this time line raises a number of very interesting accounting questions:

- When should revenue be recognized—when the initial order is placed, when the good or service is provided, when the cash is collected, or later, when there is no longer any chance that the customer will return the product or demand a refund because of faulty service?

exhibit 6-4 Time Line of Business Issues Involved with a Sale

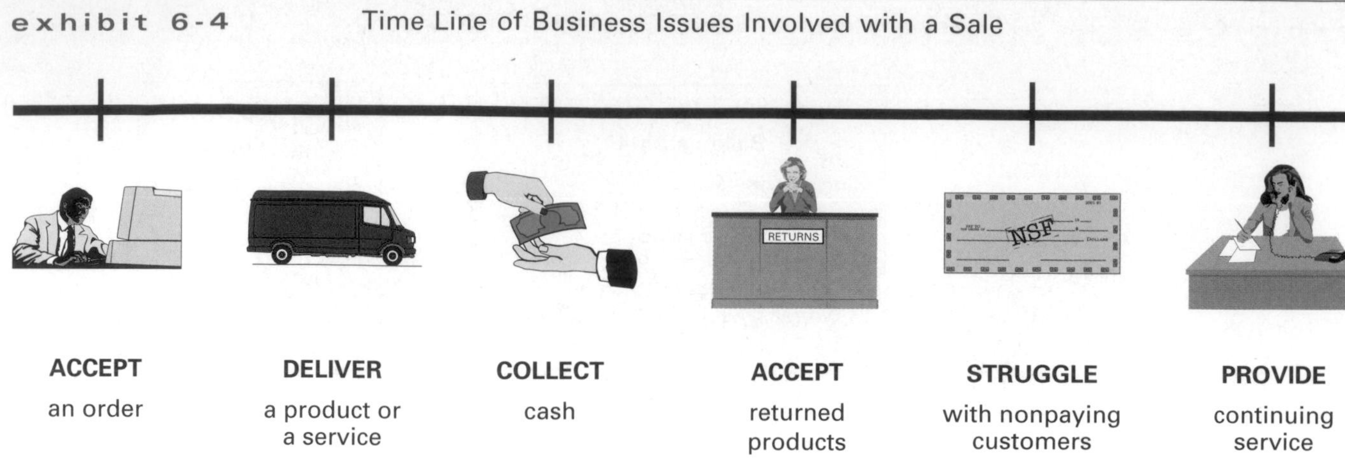

- What accounting procedures are used to manage and safeguard cash as it is collected?
- How do you account for bad debts, that is, customers who don't pay their bills?
- How do you account for the possibility that sales this year may obligate you to make warranty repairs and provide continuing customer service for many years to come?

The following sections will address these accounting issues, beginning with the important question of when to recognize revenue.

When Should Revenue Be Recognized?

revenue recognition The process of recording revenue in the accounting records; occurs after (1) the work has been substantially completed and (2) cash collection is reasonably assured.

Revenue recognition is the phrase that accountants use to refer to the recording of a sale through a journal entry in the formal accounting records. Revenue is usually recognized when two important criteria have been met:

1. The work has been substantially completed (the company has done something), and
2. Cash, or a valid promise of future payment, has been received (the company has received something in return).

As a practical matter, most companies record sales when goods are shipped to customers. Credit sales are recognized as revenues before cash is collected, and revenue from services is usually recognized when the service is performed, not necessarily when cash is received.

To illustrate, we will assume that on a typical business day Farm Land Products sells 30 sacks of fertilizer for cash and 20 sacks on credit, all at $10 per sack. Given these data, the $500 of revenue is recorded as follows:

Cash	300	
Accounts Receivable	200	
Sales Revenue		500
Sold 30 sacks of fertilizer for cash and 20 sacks on credit.		

fyi

In the majority of companies, the most frequent types of journal entries are those to record sales, cash collections, purchases, and payments to suppliers. Because such transactions are so frequent, most firms maintain four separate special journals: (1) the sales journal, (2) the purchases journal, (3) the cash receipts journal, and (4) the cash disbursements journal. These journals were noted in Appendix B (Special Journals) at the end of Chapter 4.

Although the debit entries are made to different accounts, the credit entry for the full amount is to a revenue account. Thus, accrual-basis accounting requires the recognition of $500 in revenue instead of the $300 that would be recognized if the focus were merely on cash collection.

This example is a simple illustration of how sales are recorded and revenue is recognized. In reality, sales transactions are usually more complex, involving such things as uncertainty about exactly when the transaction is actually completed and whether a valid promise of payment has actually been received from the customer. These difficulties are compounded by the fact that companies often have an understandable desire to report revenue as soon as possible in order to enhance their reported performance and make it easier to get loans or attract investors. The discussion below will further examine the two revenue recognition criteria (work done and cash collectible) to see how accountants apply these rules to ensure that reported revenue fairly reflects the economic performance of a business.

Application of the Revenue Recognition Criteria

The Farm Land example was used to illustrate a straightforward case of revenue recognition at the time a sale is made. The Farm Land customers bought $500 worth of fertilizer, paying $300 cash and promising to pay $200 later; the $500 of revenue was recognized immediately. But what if the terms of the sale had also required Farm Land to deliver the fertilizer to the customers at no extra charge? In this case, proper application of the "work done" revenue recognition criterion would require that the revenue not be recorded until actual delivery had taken place. Alternatively, assume that the fertilizer sale was accompanied by a guarantee that, within 30 days, customers could return the unused portion of fertilizer for a full refund. If very few customers ever seek a refund, revenue should still be recognized at the time of sale. But, for example, if over 70% of fertilizer customers later seek refunds, the "cash collectible" revenue recognition criterion suggests that no revenue should be recognized until the completion of the 30-day return period; Farm Land then becomes reasonably assured of the amount of cash it will collect from the $500 in sales. This situation illustrates the need for accountants to exercise professional judgment and account for the economic reality of a transaction instead of blindly relying on technical legal rules about whether a sale has taken place. Other examples of the application of the revenue recognition criteria are given below.

You have probably accessed Yahoo!'s Web site (**http://www.yahoo.com**) hundreds of times, but you were always on your way to somewhere else. This time, stop to find out something about Yahoo! itself. First, access Yahoo!'s company press release file to find out how much revenue Yahoo! reported in the most recent fiscal year. Then, use Yahoo!'s stock quote search engine to find out Yahoo!'s current market value (ticker symbol: YHOO). Comment on the relationship between reported revenue and current market value.

YAHOO! As mentioned in the opening scenario of this chapter, Yahoo! derives most of its revenue from the sale of banner advertising space on its Web pages. In 1998, Yahoo!'s standard rates ranged from 0.6 cents per "impression" (the appearance of an advertisement on a page viewed by a user) for general markets to 9 cents per impression for more focused markets. In general, Yahoo! recognizes advertising revenue as the impressions occur. This revenue recognition practice makes sense if Yahoo! is reasonably certain of collecting payment for these impressions because Yahoo! has completed its work of providing the impressions. Yahoo! often guarantees an advertiser a minimum number of impressions. To the extent that the minimum guaranteed impressions are not met as of the date the financial statements are prepared, Yahoo! delays recognizing the advertising revenue until the guaranteed number of impressions is reached.

STOP & THINK As you might expect, not all software companies support this revenue recognition practice; they would prefer to recognize all of the revenue from a software sale immediately at the time of the sale. Microsoft, on the other hand, has been very supportive of the rule. Why do you think Microsoft supports the accounting rule that many other software firms oppose?

MICROSOFT The nature of the computer software industry presents several sticky revenue recognition issues. The installation of software and the promise of software upgrades require software companies to consider when the earnings process is substantially complete. Are the revenue recognition criteria satisfied at the point of sale, when the software is installed, or after promised upgrades are delivered? Microsoft recognizes a portion (80% for the Office 97 software) of the software price as revenue immediately upon delivery of the software to you. The rest of the software price is recognized as revenue gradually over time as the technical support service is provided.

BOEING BOEING recognizes revenue from commercial aircraft sales at the time the aircraft is delivered to the airline. For example, in 1999 Boeing recognized revenue from the delivery of 620 commercial aircraft, including 320 737s. In contrast, many of Boeing's government contracts require years of work before any product is delivered. If Boeing did not recognize any revenue during this extended production period, its economic activity for that period would be understated. Thus, the accounting rules allow Boeing to recognize revenue piecemeal as it reaches "scheduled performance milestones." This type of "pro-

business environment essay

Worried about Revenues! Today the tobacco industry faces an unprecedented antismoking onslaught. An increasing number of lawsuits are alleging that smoking, and even secondhand smoke, causes cancer and other diseases and that the tobacco companies are at fault because their sales practices get people hooked on addictive drugs. (By the way, if you wish to read a careful assessment of the health risks associated with cigarettes, read the financial reports of the tobacco companies. By federal law, these reports must be provided to all interested investors, and, to ensure that investors are not misled, the Securities and Exchange Commission monitors these disclosures to make sure that they are not overly optimistic. Accordingly, these financial statement disclosures contain a much more evenhanded view than do most public statements on this controversial issue.) Although they are very large and extremely profitable, the tobacco companies are worried about future revenues. They are concerned that antismoking activity will result in fewer smokers and fewer sales. As a result, the big tobacco companies have been diversifying into other businesses, so that now a significant amount of their revenues comes from nontobacco sales. For example, two large tobacco companies now own the following:

portional performance" technique is commonly used to recognize revenue from transactions that extend over a long time period, such as for highway construction projects or season tickets for a professional sports team.

RENT-A-CENTER RENT-A-CENTER operates 2,440 rent-to-own stores in the United States under both its own name and the name "ColorTyme." Customers rent furniture, VCRs, and other consumer goods under an agreement giving them ownership of the item if they continue to make their payments for the entire rental period. Rent-to-own stores attract customers who cannot afford the outright purchase of consumer goods and who anticipate difficulty in receiving credit through normal channels. Thus, a big concern for Rent-A-Center is collecting the full amount of cash due under a rental contract. In fact, Rent-A-Center states that only about 25% of its customers complete the full term of their agreement. With such a high likelihood of customers stopping payments on their rental agreements, Rent-A-Center recognizes revenue from a specific contract only gradually as the cash is actually collected.

fyi

According to generally accepted auditing standards, auditors are often required to confirm Accounts Receivable balances directly with the company that supposedly owes the money. This can provide an independent check on the existence of the receivables.

CENDANT Discount-club retailers, such as SAM'S CLUB, are an increasing presence in the market. In 1999, for example, Sam's Club locations had total sales of $24.8 billion. The revenue recognition issue with these clubs is when to recognize the revenue from the up-front membership fees. In 1998, a dispute about the accounting for membership fees exploded in the face of CENDANT, which markets consumer goods and travel services to its members. Cendant had been recognizing its membership fees evenly over the 12-month membership period. However, the Securities and Exchange Commission ruled that, because members can cancel at any time and get their money back, Cendant should not recognize any revenue until the end of the membership period. The change caused Cendant to revise its reported 1997 results from a net income of $55.4 million to a net loss of $217.2 million. The uproar over this change caused the company's market value to plummet by $20 billion.

	Philip Morris	**Loews**
Major Cigarette Brands	Marlboro	Newport
	Benson & Hedges	Maverick
	Merit	Kent
	Virginia Slims	True
	Basic	Old Gold
Other Major Businesses	Post Cereals	14 hotels
and Products	Jell-O	Diamond Offshore Drilling
	Kool-Aid	CNA Financial
	Oscar Mayer	Bulova
	Miller Beer	
	Kraft	
1999 Revenues (billions)	$78.6	$21.5
% of Revenue from Tobacco Sales	60%	18.9%

Sources: 1999 Form 10-K filings by Philip Morris and Loews. In addition to these two tobacco companies, R.J. Reynolds Tobacco was, until 1999, part of the same company as Nabisco. Those two have now been split.

STOP & THINK Many colleges and universities prepare financial statements that are released to the public. When do you think a college or university should recognize revenue from student tuition?

As mentioned initially, the accounting for most sales transactions is straightforward—the revenue is recognized when the sale is made. However, as illustrated by the examples in this section, when the "work" associated with a sale extends over a significant period of time, or when cash collectibility is in doubt, the accountant must use professional judgment in applying the revenue recognition criteria to determine the proper time to record the sale.

Properly recognizing revenue is made more difficult by the fact that companies often have an understandable desire to report revenue as soon as possible. For example, for a company that is applying for a large loan or making an initial public offering of stock, it is critical that reported revenue, and thus reported net income, be as high as possible. In addition, company managers are often scrambling to make revenue or profit targets. In many cases, the managers' bonuses depend on whether these targets are met. Accordingly, managers often have great interest in making sure that revenue is recognized this year rather than waiting until next year. Receivables and revenue continue to be ripe areas for abuse or outright fraud because the associated accounting journal entry is so temptingly easy to make: debit Accounts Receivable and credit Revenue.

to summarize

Revenue is recognized when the work is done and when cash collectibility is reasonably assured. The entries to record revenue from the sale of merchandise or from the performance of a service involve debits to Cash or Accounts Receivable and credits to Sales Revenue or Service Revenue.

3
Properly account for the collection of cash and describe the business controls necessary to safeguard cash.

CASH COLLECTION

Recall the Farm Land Products example in which fertilizer was sold, partially for cash and partially on credit. Farm Land recorded the sales as follows:

Cash.	300	
Accounts Receivable	200	
Sales Revenue		500
Sold 30 sacks of fertilizer for cash and 20 sacks on credit.		

Subsequent collection of the $200 accounts receivable is recorded as follows:

Cash.	200	
Accounts Receivable		200
Collected cash for $200 credit sale.		

Note that Sales Revenue is not credited again when the cash is collected; the revenue was already recognized when the sale was made.

The following T-accounts show that the net result of these two transactions is an increase in Cash and Sales Revenue of $500.

	Cash (Dr.)	Cash (Cr.)	Accounts Receivable (Dr.)	Accounts Receivable (Cr.)	Sales Revenue (Dr.)	Sales Revenue (Cr.)
Original sale	300		200			500
Collection of account	200			200		
Final balances	500					500
	To balance sheet					To income statement

These two entries illustrate simple sales and collection transactions. Many companies, however, offer sales discounts and must deal with merchandise returns. The accounting for discounts and returns is explained below.

Sales Discounts

sales discount A reduction in the selling price that is allowed if payment is received within a specified period.

In many sales transactions, the buyer is given a discount if the bill is paid promptly. Such incentives to pay quickly are called **sales discounts**, or cash discounts, and the discount terms are typically expressed in abbreviated form. For example, 2/10, n/30 means that a buyer will receive a 2% discount from the selling price if payment is made within 10 days of the date of purchase, but that the full amount must be paid within 30 days or it will be considered past due. (Other common terms are 1/10, n/30 and 2/10, EOM. The latter means that a 2% discount is granted if payment is made within 10 days after the date of sale; otherwise the balance is due at the end of the month.) A 2% discount is a strong incentive for a customer to pay within 10 days because it is equivalent to paying an annual interest rate of about 36% to wait and pay after the discount period.[3] In fact, if the amount owed is substantial, most firms will borrow money, if necessary, to take advantage of a sales discount. The interest rate they will have to pay a lending institution to borrow the money is considerably less than the effective interest rate of missing the sales discount.

If an account receivable is paid within a specified discount period, the entry to record the receipt of cash is different from the cash receipt entry shown earlier. Thus, if the $200 in Farm

3 This is calculated by computing an annual interest rate for the period that the money is "sacrificed." With terms 2/10, n/30, a buyer who pays on the 10th day instead of the 30th "sacrifices" the money for 20 days. Since 2% is earned in 20 days, and there are just over 18 periods of 20 days in a year, earnings would be 18 × 2%, or approximately 36% annual interest.

Land credit sales were made with discount terms of 2/10, n/30, and if the customers paid within the discount period, the entry to record the receipt of cash is:

Cash	196	
Sales Discounts ($200 × 0.02)	4	
Accounts Receivable		200
Collected cash within the discount period for $200 credit sale.		

contra account An account that is offset or deducted from another account.

Sales Discounts is a **contra account** (specifically, a contra-revenue account), which means that it is deducted from sales revenue on the income statement. This account is included with other revenue accounts in the general ledger, but unlike other revenue accounts, it has a debit balance rather than a credit balance.

Sales Returns and Allowances

Customers often return merchandise, either because the item is defective or for a variety of other reasons. Most companies generally accept merchandise returns in order to maintain good customer relations. When merchandise is returned, the company must make an entry to reduce revenues and to reduce either Cash (a cash refund) or Accounts Receivable (an adjustment to the customer's account). A similar entry is required when the sales price is reduced because the merchandise was defective or damaged during shipment to the customer.

To illustrate the type of entry needed, we will assume that before any payments on account are made, Farm Land customers return goods costing $150; $100 in returns were made by cash customers, and $50 in returns were made by credit customers. The entry to record the return of merchandise is:

Sales Returns and Allowances	150	
Cash		100
Accounts Receivable		50
Received $150 of returned merchandise; $100 from cash customers and $50 from credit customers.		

sales returns and allowances A contra-revenue account in which the return of, or allowance for reduction in the price of, merchandise previously sold is recorded.

The credit customers will be sent a credit memorandum for the return, stating that credit has been granted and that the balance of their accounts (in total) is now $150 ($200 original credit purchase − $50 returns). Like Sales Discounts, **Sales Returns and Allowances** is a contra account that is deducted from sales revenue on the income statement. The income statement presentation for the revenue accounts, assuming payment within the discount period on the $150 balance in Accounts Receivable, is as follows:

Income Statement

Sales revenue	$500	
Less: Sales discounts*	(3)	
Less: Sales returns and allowances	(150)	
Net sales revenue		$347

*($200 − $50) × 0.02 = $3
Note that when merchandise is returned, sales discounts for the subsequent payment are granted only on the selling price of the merchandise not returned.

It might seem that the use of contra accounts (Sales Discounts and Sales Returns and Allowances) involves extra steps that would not be necessary if discounts and returns of merchandise were deducted directly from Sales Revenue. Although such direct deductions would have the same final effect on net income, the contra accounts separate initial sales from all returns,

gross sales Total recorded sales before deducting any sales discounts or sales returns and allowances.

net sales Gross sales less sales discounts and sales returns and allowances.

cash Coins, currency, money orders, checks, and funds on deposit with financial institutions; the most liquid of assets.

allowances, and discounts. This permits a company's management to analyze the extent to which customers are returning merchandise, receiving allowances, and taking advantage of discounts. If management find that excessive amounts of merchandise are being returned, they may decide that the company's sales returns policy is too liberal or that the quality of its merchandise needs improvement.

A company's total recorded sales, before any discounts or returns and allowances, are referred to as **gross sales**. When sales discounts or sales returns and allowances are deducted from gross sales, the resulting amount is referred to as **net sales**.

Control of Cash

Cash includes coins, currency, money orders and checks (made payable or endorsed to the company), and money on deposit with banks or savings institutions that are available for use to satisfy the company's obligations. All the various transactions involving these forms of cash are usually summarized and reported under a single balance sheet account, Cash.

fyi

In its balance sheet (see Appendix A), MICROSOFT follows the common practice of combining cash and short-term investments (bonds and U.S. Treasury securities) for the total Cash amount.

Because it is the easiest asset to spend if it is stolen, cash is a tempting target and must be carefully safeguarded. Several control procedures have been developed to help management monitor and protect cash. In Chapter 5, internal controls for cash and other assets were discussed. Because cash is particularly vulnerable to loss or misuse, however, we will discuss three important controls that are an integral part of accounting for cash.

One of the most important controls is that the handling of cash be separated from the recording of cash. The purpose of this separation of duties is that it becomes more difficult for theft or errors to occur when two or more people are involved. If the cash records are maintained by an employee who also has access to the cash itself, cash can be stolen or "borrowed," and the employee can cover up the shortage by falsifying the accounting records.

fyi

Consider the case of an employee who both receives payments and keeps the books. He or she could pocket a cash payment from one customer and not record the receipt until payment is received from a second customer. The second customer's payment could be recorded when a third customer pays, and so on. This type of delayed recording of payments is called *lapping*; it allows an employee to use company money for extended periods of time.

A second cash control practice is to require that all cash receipts be deposited daily in bank accounts. This disciplined, rigid process ensures that personal responsibility for the handling of cash is focused on the individual assigned to make the regular deposit. In addition, this process prevents the accumulation of a large amount of cash—even the most trusted employee can be tempted by a large cash hoard.

A third cash control practice is to require that all cash expenditures (except those paid out of a miscellaneous petty cash fund) be made with prenumbered checks. As we all know from managing our personal finances, payments made with pocket cash are quickly forgotten and easily concealed. In contrast, payments made by check are well documented, both in our personal check registers and by our bank.

In addition to safeguarding cash, a business must ensure that cash is wisely managed. In fact, many businesses establish elaborate control and budgeting procedures for monitoring cash balances and estimating future cash needs. Companies also try to keep only minimum balances in no-interest or low-interest checking accounts; other cash is kept in more high-yielding investments such as certificates of deposit.

to summarize

The amount of cash collected from customers can be reduced because of sales discounts and sales returns and allowances. On the income statement, sales discounts and sales returns and allowances are subtracted from gross sales to arrive at net sales. Cash is a tempting target for fraud or theft, so companies must carefully monitor and control the way cash is handled and accounted for. Common controls include (1) separation of duties in handling and accounting for cash, (2) daily deposits of all cash receipts, and (3) payment of all expenditures by prenumbered checks.

4

Record the losses resulting from credit customers who do not pay their bills.

ACCOUNTING FOR CREDIT CUSTOMERS WHO DON'T PAY

receivables Claims for money, goods, or services.

accounts receivable A current asset representing money due for services performed or merchandise sold on credit.

The term **receivables** refers to a company's claims for money, goods, or services. Receivables are created through various types of transactions, the two most common being the sale of merchandise or services on credit and the lending of money. On a personal level, we are all familiar with credit. Because credit is so readily available, we can buy such items as cars, refrigerators, and big-screen TVs, even when we cannot afford to pay cash for them. Major retail companies such as SEARS, oil companies such as SHELL, and credit card companies such as VISA, MASTERCARD, and AMERICAN EXPRESS have made credit available to almost every person in the United States. We live in a credit world—not only on the individual level, but also at the wholesale and manufacturing business levels.

fyi

Credit card sales can be viewed as a way for a business to reap the benefit of increased credit sales without having to set up a bookkeeping and collection service for accounts receivable. The credit card company screens customers based on their creditworthiness, sends out the bills, collects the cash, and bears the cost of any uncollectible accounts. A business that accepts credit card sales pays a fee ranging from 1 to 5 percent of credit card sales.

In business, credit sales give rise to the most common type of receivables: accounts receivable. **Accounts receivable** are the amounts owed to a business by its credit customers and are usually collected in cash within 10 to 60 days. Accounts receivable result from informal agreements between a company and its credit customers; a more formal contract, including interest on the unpaid balance, is called a note receivable. Other receivables may result from loans to officers or employees of a company, for example. To identify and maintain the distinction between these receivables, businesses establish a separate general ledger account for each classification. If the amount of a receivable is material, it is separately identified on the balance sheet. Receivables that are to be converted to cash within a year (or the normal operating cycle) are classified as current assets and listed on the balance sheet below Cash. In this section of the chapter, we discuss the accounting issues associated with credit customers who don't pay.

bad debt An uncollectible account receivable.

When companies sell goods and services on credit (as most do), there are usually some customers who do not pay for the merchandise they purchase; these are referred to as **bad debts**. In fact, most businesses expect a small percentage of their receivables to be uncollectible. If a firm tries too hard to eliminate the possibility of losses from nonpaying customers, it usually makes its credit policy so restrictive that valuable sales are lost. On the other hand, if a firm extends credit too easily, the total cost of maintaining the accounts receivable system may exceed the benefit gained from attracting customers by allowing them to buy on credit (due to the number of accounts to track and uncollectible receivables to try to collect). Because of this dilemma, most firms carefully monitor their credit sales and accounts receivable to ensure that their policies are neither too restrictive nor too liberal.

When an account receivable becomes uncollectible, a firm incurs a bad debt loss. This loss is recognized as a cost of doing business, so it is classified as a selling expense. There are two ways to account for losses from uncollectible accounts: the direct write-off method and the allowance method.

Direct Write-Off Method

direct write-off method The recording of actual losses from uncollectible accounts as expenses during the period in which accounts receivable are determined to be uncollectible.

With the **direct write-off method**, an uncollectible account is recognized as an expense at the time it is determined to be uncollectible. For example, assume that during the year 2003, Farm Land Products had total credit sales of \$300,000. Of this amount, \$250,000 was subsequently collected in cash during the year, leaving a year-end balance in Accounts Receivable of \$50,000 (\$300,000 − \$250,000). The summary journal entries to record this information are:

Accounts Receivable	300,000	
Sales Revenue		300,000
To record total credit sales for the year.		
Cash	250,000	
Accounts Receivable.		250,000
To record total cash collections for the year.		

business environment essay

Overstating Receivables One of the easiest ways to overstate income is to overstate receivables. For example, Michael Weinstein, former chairman and CEO of COATED SALES, INC., orchestrated a financial fraud scheme that ultimately cost investors close to $100 million. Coated Sales, Inc., was a New Jersey company that manufactured textiles coated with special chemicals, used for making such products as yacht sails, bullet-proof vests, conveyor belts, and parachutes. The company was best known for supplying the fabric used in the sails of the America's Cup–winning yacht *Stars and Stripes*.

Coated Sales was started as the second career of millionaire entrepreneur Michael Weinstein, who had "retired" in his 30s and sold the discount drug store chain he had built. Looking for a new business, he became interested in textiles through a friend. The proposition was simple: take unfinished textiles, known as gray goods, and finish them with specialized coatings or treatments. The company's earnings, though minuscule at first, began to double and even triple every year—sometimes every six months.

The fraud was instigated by inflating Coated's sales and earnings through the creation of phony invoices purporting to show sales of goods. Coated officials "prebilled" invoices to customers so they could obtain payment for goods before they were shipped.

Assume that one credit customer, Jake Palmer, has an account balance of $1,500 that remains unpaid for several months in 2004. If, after receiving several past-due notices, Palmer still does not pay, Farm Land will probably turn the account over to an attorney or a collection agency. Then, if collection attempts fail, the company may decide that the Palmer account will not be collected and write it off as a loss. The entry to record the expense under the direct write-off method is:

Bad Debt Expense	1,500	
Accounts Receivable.		1,500
To write off the uncollectible account of Jake Palmer.		

bad debt expense An account that represents the portion of the current period's credit sales that are estimated to be uncollectible.

Bad Debt Expense is usually considered a selling expense on the income statement. Although the direct write-off method is objective (the account is written off at the time it proves to be uncollectible), it most likely would violate the matching principle, which requires that all costs and expenses incurred in generating revenues be identified with those revenues period by period. With the direct write-off method, sales made near the end of one accounting period may not be recognized as uncollectible until the next period. In this example, the revenue from the sale to Jake Palmer is recognized in 2003, but the expense from the bad debt is not recognized until 2004. As a result, expenses are understated in 2003 and overstated in 2004. This makes the direct write-off method unacceptable from a theoretical point of view. The direct write-off method is allowable only if bad debts involve small, insignificant amounts.

The Allowance Method

allowance method The recording of estimated losses due to uncollectible accounts as expenses during the period in which the sales occurred.

The **allowance method** satisfies the matching principle because it accounts for uncollectibles during the same period in which the sales occurred. With this method, a firm uses its experience (or industry averages) to estimate the amount of receivables arising from this year's credit sales that will ultimately become uncollectible. That estimate is recorded as bad debt expense in the period of sale. Although the use of estimates may result in a somewhat imprecise expense figure, this is generally thought to be a less serious problem than the direct write-off method's failure to match bad debt expenses with the sales that caused them. In addition, with experience, these estimates tend to be quite accurate.

Coated then began sending out false invoices to customers, recording receivables, and obtaining funds for sales that never occurred. To prevent the customers from denying the sales, the company involved the customers in the racket. For example, Robert Solomon of **GLOBE SPORTS PRODUCTS** paid the fictitious bills and would then receive the money back from Weinstein. Due to the inflated sales and receivables, the value of Coated's stock rose from $1.50 per share in its initial public offering to over $12 per share in 1987. From 1984 to 1987, sales allegedly rose from $9.9 million to over $90 million.

In addition, Weinstein inflated accounts receivable by billing fictitious customers. He used the inflated accounts receivable account to secure large bank loans. For example, **BANCBOSTON FINANCIAL COMPANY** loaned Coated $45 million, based on the supposed existence of $51 million in accounts receivable that served as collateral for the loan.

Coated's auditor, **KPMG PEAT MARWICK**, withdrew because of its suspicions. Within days, Coated Sales' stock value tumbled from $8 to $2 a share. Shortly thereafter, the corporation's credit dried up, forcing it to declare bankruptcy.

Source: Graham Button, "Homeless Jailbird," *Forbes*, August 17, 1992, p. 13.

To illustrate the allowance method, assume that Farm Land Products estimates that the bad debts created by its $300,000 in credit sales in 2003 will ultimately total $4,500. Note that this is a statistical estimate—on average, bad debts will be $4,500, but Farm Land does not yet know exactly which customers will be the ones who will fail to pay. The entry to record this estimated bad debt expense for 2003 is:

Bad Debt Expense	4,500	
Allowance for Bad Debts		4,500
To record the estimated bad debt expense for the current year.		

allowance for bad debts A contra account, deducted from Accounts Receivable, that shows the estimated losses from uncollectible accounts.

Bad Debt Expense is a selling expense on the income statement, and **Allowance for Bad Debts** is a contra account to Accounts Receivable on the balance sheet. An allowance account is used because the company does not yet know which receivables will not be collected. Later on, for example, in 2004, as actual losses are recognized, the balance in Allowance for Bad Debts is reduced. For example, if in 2004 Jake Palmer's receivable for $1,500 is specifically identified as being uncollectible, the entry is:

Allowance for Bad Debts	1,500	
Accounts Receivable		1,500
To write off the uncollectible account of Jake Palmer.		

Note that the write-off entry in 2004 does not affect net income in 2004. Instead, the net income in 2003, when the credit sale to Jake Palmer was originally made, already reflects the estimated bad debt expense. Think of this entry as follows: The $1,500 Jake Palmer account has been shown to be bad, so it is "thrown away" via a credit to Accounts Receivable. In addition, Allowance for Bad Debts, which is a general estimate of the amount of bad accounts, is reduced by $1,500 because the bad Palmer account has been specifically identified and eliminated. In one entry, the amounts in Accounts Receivable and Allowance for Bad Debts have been reduced. Assume that the balance in Accounts Receivable was $50,000 and the balance in Allowance for Bad Debts was $4,500 before the Palmer account was written off. The net amount in Accounts

Receivable after the $1,500 write-off is exactly the same as it was before the entry, as shown here.

Before Write-Off Entry		After Write-Off Entry	
Accounts receivable	$50,000	Accounts receivable ($50,000 − $1,500)	$48,500
Less allowance for bad debts	4,500	Less allowance for bad debts ($4,500 − $1,500)	3,000
Net balance	$45,500	Net balance	$45,500

net realizable value of accounts receivable The net amount that would be received if all receivables considered collectible were collected; equal to total accounts receivable less the allowance for bad debts.

The net balance of $45,500 reflects the estimated **net realizable value of accounts receivable**, that is, the amount of receivables the company actually expects to collect.

The following T-account shows the kinds of entries that are made to Allowance for Bad Debts:

Allowance for Bad Debts	
Actual write-offs of uncollectible accounts	Estimates of uncollectible accounts

fyi

Sears discloses in its 1999 annual report that it writes an account off as uncollectible after a customer has failed to make a required payment for eight billing cycles in a row.

Occasionally, a customer whose account has been written off as uncollectible later pays the outstanding balance. When this happens, the company reverses the entry that was used to write off the account and then recognizes the payment. For example, if Jake Palmer pays the $1,500 after his account has already been written off, the entries to correct the accounting records are:

Accounts Receivable	1,500	
Allowance for Bad Debts		1,500
To reinstate the balance previously written off as uncollectible.		
Cash	1,500	
Accounts Receivable		1,500
Received payment in full of previously written-off accounts receivable.		

fyi

Banks often recover loan amounts that were previously written off as uncollectible. For example, for the three-year period ending in 1997, CITICORP managed to collect a total of $2.053 billion in loans that had been written off in prior years.

Because customers sometimes pay their balances after their accounts are written off, it is important for a company to have good control over both the cash collection procedures and the accounting for accounts receivable. Otherwise, such payments as the previously written-off $1,500 could be pocketed by the employee who receives the cash, and it would never be missed. This is one reason that most companies separate the handling of cash from the recording of cash transactions in the accounts.

Because the amount recorded in Bad Debt Expense affects both the reported net realizable value of the receivables and net income, companies must be careful to use good estimation procedures. These estimates can focus on an examination of either the total number of credit sales during the period or the outstanding receivables at year-end to determine their collectibility.

ESTIMATING UNCOLLECTIBLE ACCOUNTS RECEIVABLE AS A PERCENTAGE OF CREDIT SALES One method of estimating bad debt expense is to estimate uncollectible receivables as a percentage of credit sales for the period. If a company uses this method, the amount of uncollectibles will be a straight percentage of the current year's credit sales. That percentage will be a projection based on experience in prior years, modified for any changes expected for the current period. For example, in the Farm Land example, credit sales for the year of $300,000 are expected to generate bad debts of $4,500, indicating that 1.5% of all credit sales are expected to be uncollectible ($4,500 ÷ $300,000 = 1.5%). Farm Land would evaluate the percentage each year, in light of its continued experience, to see whether the same percentage still seems reasonable. In addition, if economic conditions have changed for Farm Land's customers (such as the onset of a recession making it more likely that debts will remain uncollected), the percentage would be adjusted.

When this percentage of sales method is used, the existing balance (if there is one) in Allowance for Bad Debts does not affect the amount computed and is not included in the adjusting entry to record bad debt expense. The 1.5% of the current year's sales that is estimated to be uncollectible is calculated and entered separately, and then added to the existing balance. For example, if the existing credit balance is $2,000, the $4,500 will be added, making the new credit balance $6,500. The rationale for not considering the existing $2,000 balance in Allowance for Bad Debts is that it relates to previous periods' sales and reflects the company's estimate (as of the beginning of the year) of prior years' accounts receivable that are expected to be uncollectible.

STOP & THINK Should a company work to reduce its bad debt expense to zero? Explain.

In determining the percentage of credit sales that will be uncollectible, a company must estimate the total amount of loss on the basis of experience or industry averages. Obviously, a company that has been in business for several years should be able to make more accurate estimates than a new company. Many established companies use a three- or five-year average as the basis for estimating losses from uncollectible accounts.

ESTIMATING UNCOLLECTIBLE ACCOUNTS RECEIVABLE AS A PERCENTAGE OF TOTAL RECEIVABLES Another way to estimate uncollectible receivables is to use a percentage of total receivables. Using this method, the amount of uncollectibles is a percentage of the total receivables balance at the end of the period. Assume that Farm Land decides to use this method and determines that 12% of the $50,000 in the year-end Accounts Receivable will ultimately be uncollectible. Accordingly, the credit balance in Allowance for Bad Debts should be $6,000 ($50,000 × 0.12). If there is no existing balance in Allowance for Bad Debts representing the estimate of bad accounts left over from prior years, then an entry for $6,000 is made. If the account has an existing balance, however, only the net amount needed to bring the credit balance to $6,000 is added. For example, an existing credit balance of $2,000 in Allowance for Bad Debts results in the following adjusting entry:

Bad Debt Expense	4,000	
Allowance for Bad Debts		4,000
To adjust the allowance account to the desired balance ($6,000 − $2,000 = $4,000).		

In all cases, the ending balance in Allowance for Bad Debts should be the amount of total receivables estimated to be uncollectible.

In estimating bad debt expense, the percentage of sales method focuses on an estimation based directly on the level of the current year's credit sales. With the percentage of total receivables method, the focus is on estimating total bad debts existing at the end of the period; this number is compared to the leftover bad debts from prior years, and the difference is bad debt expense, the new bad debts created in the current period. These two techniques are merely alternative estimation approaches. In practice, as a check, a company would probably use both procedures to ensure that they yield roughly consistent results.

aging accounts receivable The process of categorizing each account receivable by the number of days it has been outstanding.

Aging Accounts Receivable In the example just given, the correct amount of the ending Allowance for Bad Debts balance was computed by applying the estimated uncollectible percentage (12%) to the entire Accounts Receivable balance ($50,000). In a more refined method of estimating the appropriate ending balance in Allowance for Bad Debts, a company bases its calculations on how long its receivables have been outstanding. With this procedure, called **aging accounts receivable**, each receivable is categorized according to age, such as current, 1–30 days past due, 31–60 days past due, 61–90 days past due, 91–120 days past due, and over 120 days past due. Once the receivables in each age classification are totaled, each total is multiplied by

exhibit 6-5 Aging Accounts Receivable

Customer	Balance	Current	Days Past Due 1–30	31–60	61–90	91–120	Over 120
A. Adams	$10,000	$10,000					
R. Bartholomew	6,500			$ 5,000			$1,500
F. Christiansen	6,250	5,000	$1,250				
G. Dover	7,260			7,260			
M. Ellis	4,000	4,000					
G. Erkland	2,250				$2,250		
R. Fisher	1,500		500			$1,000	
J. Palmer	1,500		1,500				
E. Zeigler	10,740	4,000	6,740				
Totals	$50,000	$23,000	$9,990	$12,260	$2,250	$1,000	$1,500

Estimate of Losses from Uncollectible Accounts

Age	Balance	Percentage Estimated to Be Uncollectible	Amount
Current	$23,000	1.5	$ 345
1–30 days past due	9,990	4.0	400
31–60 days past due	12,260	20.0	2,452
61–90 days past due	2,250	40.0	900
91–120 days past due	1,000	60.0	600
Over 120 days past due	1,500	80.0	1,200
Totals	$50,000		$5,897*

*Receivables that are likely to be uncollectible.

an appropriate uncollectible percentage (as determined by experience), recognizing that the older the receivable, the less likely the company is to collect. Exhibit 6-5 shows how Farm Land could use an aging accounts receivable analysis to estimate the amount of its $50,000 ending balance in Accounts Receivable that will ultimately be uncollectible.

The allowance for bad debts estimate obtained using the aging method is $5,897. If the existing credit balance in Allowance for Bad Debts is $2,000, the required adjusting entry is:

Bad Debt Expense	3,897	
Allowance for Bad Debts.		3,897
To adjust the allowance account to the desired ending balance ($5,897 − $2,000 = $3,897).		

caution

The aging method is merely a more refined technique for estimating the desired balance in Allowance for Bad Debts.

The aging of accounts receivable is probably the most accurate method of estimating uncollectible accounts. It also enables a company to identify its problem customers. Companies that base their estimates of uncollectible accounts on credit sales or total outstanding receivables also often age their receivables as a way of monitoring the individual accounts receivable balances.

Real-World Illustration of Accounting for Bad Debts

The application of bad debt accounting is illustrated using the financial statements of YAHOO! for 1997–1999. As shown in Exhibit 6-6, Yahoo! reported accounts receivable at the end of 1999

exhibit 6-6

Bad Debt Expense for Yahoo!

Year	Ending Accounts Receivable	Ending Bad Debt Allowance	Bad Debt Allowance as a Percentage of Accounts Receivable
1999	$65,748*	$11,322	17.2%
1998	40,036	5,947	14.9%
1997	14,683	2,772	18.9%

*Dollar amounts are in millions.

of $65.7 million and a bad debt allowance for bad debts of $11.3 million. In other words, credit customers owed Yahoo! $65.7 million as of the end of 1999; however, Yahoo!'s best estimate was that $11.3 million of this amount would never be collected. This bad debt allowance amounted to 17.2% of the Accounts Receivable balance, down from 18.9% in 1997 but up from 14.9% in 1998. For a company operating in a stable economic environment with little change in the nature of its credit customers, this percentage would be expected to be about the same from year to year. In the case of Yahoo!, operating in the volatile Internet economy, it appears that there has been some variation in the collectibility of accounts receivable from one year to the next.

to summarize

Accounts receivable arise from credit sales to customers. Even though companies monitor their customers carefully, there are usually some who do not pay for the merchandise they purchase. There are two ways of accounting for losses from uncollectible receivables: the direct write-off method and the allowance method. The allowance method is generally accepted in practice because it is consistent with the matching principle. Two ways of estimating losses from uncollectible receivables are (1) as a percentage of credit sales and (2) as some fraction of total outstanding receivables. A common method for applying the latter technique uses an aging accounts receivable analysis.

5

Evaluate a company's management of its receivables by computing and analyzing appropriate financial ratios.

ASSESSING HOW WELL COMPANIES MANAGE THEIR RECEIVABLES

As you recall from the DuPont framework explained in Chapter 4, an important element of overall company performance is the efficient use of assets. With regard to accounts receivable, inefficient use means that too much cash is tied up in the form of receivables. A company that collects its receivables on a timely basis has cash to pay its bills. Companies that do not do a good job of collecting receivables are often cash poor, paying interest on short-term loans to cover their cash shortage or losing interest that could be earned by investing cash.

There are several methods of evaluating how well an organization is managing its accounts receivable. The most common method involves computing two ratios, accounts receivable turnover and average collection period. The **accounts receivable turnover** ratio is an attempt to determine how many times during the year a company is "turning over" or collecting its receivables. It is a measure of how many times old receivables are collected and replaced by new receivables. Accounts receivable turnover is calculated as follows:

accounts receivable turnover A measure used to indicate how fast a company collects its receivables; computed by dividing sales by average accounts receivable.

$$\text{Accounts Receivable Turnover} = \frac{\text{Sales Revenue}}{\text{Average Accounts Receivable}}$$

Notice that the numerator of this ratio is sales revenue, not credit sales. Conceptually, one might consider comparing the level of accounts receivable to the amount of credit sales instead of total sales. However, companies rarely, if ever, disclose how much of their sales are credit sales. For this ratio, you can think of cash sales as credit sales with a very short collection time (0 days). Also note that the denominator uses average accounts receivable instead of the ending balance. This recognizes that sales are generated throughout the year; the average Accounts Receivable balance is an approximation of the amount that prevailed during the year. If the Accounts Receivable balance is relatively unchanged during the year, then using the ending balance is acceptable and common. The following are the accounts receivable turnover ratios for two well-known companies for 1999:

$$\text{Wal-Mart} \quad \frac{\$165.013 \text{ billion}}{\$1.230 \text{ billion}} = 134.2 \text{ times}$$

$$\text{Boeing} \quad \frac{\$57.993 \text{ billion}}{\$3.371 \text{ billion}} = 17.2 \text{ times}$$

From this analysis, you can see that WAL-MART turns its receivables over much more often than does BOEING. This is not surprising given the different nature of the two businesses. Wal-Mart sells primarily to retail customers for cash. Remember, from Wal-Mart's standpoint, a credit card sale is the same as a cash sale since Wal-Mart receives its money instantly; it is the credit card company that must worry about collecting the receivable. Boeing, on the other hand, sells to airlines and governments that have established business credit relationships with Boeing. Thus, the nature of its business dictates that Boeing has a much larger fraction of its sales tied up in the form of accounts receivable than does Wal-Mart.

Accounts receivable turnover can then be converted into the number of days it takes to collect receivables by computing a ratio called **average collection period**. This ratio is computed by dividing 365 (or the number of days in a year) by the accounts receivable turnover as follows:

average collection period A measure of the average number of days it takes to collect a credit sale; computed by dividing 365 days by the accounts receivable turnover.

$$\text{Average Collection Period} = \frac{365}{\text{Accounts Receivable Turnover}}$$

Computing this ratio for both Wal-Mart and Boeing shows that it takes Wal-Mart only 2.7 days (365 ÷ 134.2) on average to collect its receivables, while Boeing takes an average of 21.2 days (365 ÷ 17.2).

Consider what might happen to Boeing's average collection period during an economic recession. During a recession, purchasers are often strapped for cash and try to delay paying on their accounts for as long as possible. Boeing might be faced with airlines that still want to buy airplanes but wish to stretch out the payment period. The result would be a rise in Boeing's average collection period; more of Boeing's resources would be tied up in the form of accounts receivable. In turn, Boeing would have to increase its borrowing in order to pay its own bills since it would be collecting less cash from its slow-paying customers. Proper receivables management involves balancing the desire to extend credit in order to increase sales with the need to collect the cash quickly in order to pay off your own bills.

to summarize

Careful management of accounts receivable is a balance between extending credit to increase your sales and collecting cash quickly to reduce your need to borrow. Two ratios commonly used in monitoring the level of receivables are accounts receivable turnover and average collection period. The level of these ratios is determined by how well a company manages its receivables, as well as by what kind of business the company is in.

6
Match revenues and expenses by estimating and recording future warranty and service costs associated with a sale.

RECORDING WARRANTY AND SERVICE COSTS ASSOCIATED WITH A SALE

Let's return to the Farm Land example in which 50 sacks of fertilizer were sold for $500. Assume that as part of each sale, Farm Land offers to send a customer service representative to the home or place of business of any purchaser who wants more detailed instructions on how to apply the fertilizer. Historical experience suggests that the buyer of one fertilizer sack in ten will request a visit from a Farm Land representative, and the material and labor cost of each visit averages $35. So, with 50 sacks of fertilizer sold, Farm Land has obligated itself to provide, on average, $175 in future customer service [(50 ÷ 10) × $35]. Proper matching requires that this $175 expense be estimated and recognized in the same period in which the associated sale is recognized. Otherwise, if the company waited to record customer service expense until the actual visits are requested, this period's sales revenue would be reported in the same income statement with customer service expense arising from last period's sales. The accountant is giving up some precision because the service expense must be estimated in advance. This sacrifice in precision is worth the benefit of being able to better match revenues and expenses.

The entry to recognize Farm Land's estimated service expense from the sale of 50 sacks of fertilizer is as follows:

Customer Service Expense	175	
Estimated Liability for Service		175
Estimated customer service costs on sales [(50 ÷ 10) × $35].		

The credit entry, Estimated Liability for Service, is a liability. When actual expenses are incurred in providing the customer service, the liability is eliminated with the following type of entry:

Estimated Liability for Service	145	
Wages Payable (to service employees)		100
Supplies		45
Actual customer service costs incurred.		

This entry shows that supplies and labor were required to honor the service agreements. This procedure results in the service expense being recognized at the time of sale, not necessarily when the actual service occurs.

After these two journal entries are made, the remaining balance in Estimated Liability for Service will be $30, shown as follows:

Estimated Liability for Service

	Debit	Credit
Estimate at time of sale		175
Actual service costs incurred	145	
Remaining balance		30

The $30 balance represents the estimated amount of service that still must be provided in the future resulting from the sale of the 50 sacks of fertilizer. If actual experience suggests that the estimated service cost is too high, a lower estimate would be made in connection with subsequent fertilizer sales. If estimated liability for service is too low, a higher estimate is made for subsequent sales. The important point is that the accountant would not try to go back and "fix" an estimate that later proves to be inexact; the accountant merely monitors the relationship between the estimated and actual service costs in order to adjust future estimates accordingly.

The accounting just shown for estimated service costs is the same procedure used for estimated warranty costs. For example, **GENERAL MOTORS** promises automobile buyers that it will fix, at no charge to the buyer, certain mechanical problems for a certain period of time. GM estimates and records this warranty expense at the time the automobile sales are made. At the end of 1999, GM reported an existing liability for warranty costs of $15.3 billion. This amount is what GM estimates it will have to spend on warranty repairs in 2000 (and later years) on cars sold in 1999 (and earlier).

to summarize

In addition to bad debt expense, there are other costs that must be estimated and recognized at the time a sale is made in order to ensure the proper matching of revenues and expenses. If a company makes promises about future warranty repairs or continued customer service as part of the sale, the value of these promises should be estimated and recorded as an expense at the time of the sale.

expanded material

Thus far the chapter has covered the main topics associated with selling goods or services, collecting the proceeds from those sales, and estimating and recording bad debt expense and service expense. The expanded material will cover three additional topics. First, an important tool of cash control, the bank reconciliation, will be explained. Second, the use of receivables to get cash immediately will be illustrated. Finally, the financial statement implications of making sales denominated in foreign currencies will be illustrated.

7

Reconcile a checking account.

RECONCILING THE BANK ACCOUNT

With the exception of small amounts of petty cash kept for miscellaneous purposes, most cash is kept in various bank accounts. Generally, only a few employees are authorized to sign checks, and they must have their signatures on file with the bank.

Each month the business receives a bank statement that shows the cash balance at the beginning of the period, the deposits, the amounts of the checks processed, and the cash balance at the end of the period. With the statement, the bank includes all of that month's canceled checks (or at least a listing of the checks), as well as debit and credit memos (for example, an explanation of charges for **NSF [not sufficient funds] checks** and service fees). From a bank's perspective, customers' deposits are liabilities; hence, debit memos reduce the company's cash balance, and credit memos increase the balance.

NSF (not sufficient funds) check A check that is not honored by a bank because of insufficient cash in the check writer's account.

The July bank statement for one of Hunt Company's accounts is presented in Exhibit 6-7. This statement shows all activity in the cash account as recorded by the bank and includes four bank adjustments to Hunt's balance—a bank service charge of $7 (the bank's monthly fee), $60 of interest paid by First Security Bank on Hunt's average balance, a $425 transfer into another account, and a $3,200 direct deposit made by a customer who regularly deposits payments directly to Hunt's bank account. Other adjustments that are commonly made by a bank to a company's account include:

exhibit 6-7 July Bank Statement for Hunt Company

First Security Bank
Helena, Montana 59601

Statement of Account

HUNT COMPANY
1900 S. PARK LANE
HELENA, MT 59601

Account Number 325-78126

Date of Statement JULY 31, 2003

Check Number	Checks and Withdrawals	Deposits and Additions	Date	Balance
			6/30	13,000
620	140		7/01	12,860
621	250	1,500	7/03	14,110
622	860		7/05	13,250
623	210		7/08	13,040
		2,140	7/09	15,180
624	205		7/10	14,975
626	310		7/14	14,665
	425 T		7/15	14,240
		3,200 D	7/18	17,440
628	765		7/19	16,675
629	4,825		7/22	11,850
630	420		7/24	11,430
632	326	1,600	7/25	12,704
		2,100	7/26	14,804
633	210		7/29	14,594
635	225		7/31	14,369
	7 SC	60 I	7/31	14,422
	9,178 TOTAL CHECKS AND WITHDRAWALS	10,600 TOTAL DEPOSITS AND ADDITIONS		14,422 BALANCE

NSF = Not Sufficient Funds D = Direct Deposit SC = Service Charge I = Interest MS = Miscellaneous T = Transfer Out of Account ATM = Automated Teller Machine Transaction

1. *NSF (not sufficient funds).* This is the cancellation of a prior deposit that could not be collected because of insufficient funds in the check writer's (payer's) account. When a check is received and deposited in the payee's account, the check is assumed to represent funds that will be collected from the payer's bank. When a bank refuses to honor a check because of insufficient funds in the account on which it was written, the check is returned to the payee's bank and is marked "NSF." The amount of the check, which was originally recorded as a deposit (addition) to the payee's account, is deducted from the account when the check is returned unpaid.
2. *MS (miscellaneous).* Other adjustments made by a bank.
3. *ATM (automated teller machine) transactions.* These are deposits and withdrawals made by the depositor at automated teller machines.
4. *Withdrawals for credit card transactions paid directly from accounts.* These types of cards, called debit cards, are like using plastic checks. Instead of the card holder getting a bill or statement, the amount charged is deducted from the card holder's bank balance.

It is unusual for the ending balance on the bank statement to equal the amount of cash recorded in a company's cash account. The most common reasons for differences are:

1. *Time period differences.* The time period of the bank statement does not coincide with the timing of the company's postings to the cash account.
2. *Deposits in transit.* These are deposits that have not been processed by the bank as of the bank statement date, usually because they were made at or near the end of the month.
3. *Outstanding checks.* These are checks that have been written and deducted from a company's cash account but have not cleared or been deducted by the bank as of the bank statement date.
4. *Bank debits.* These are deductions made by the bank that have not yet been recorded by the company. The most common are monthly service charges, NSF checks, and bank transfers out of the account.
5. *Bank credits.* These are additions made by the bank to a company's account before they are recorded by the company. The most common source is interest paid by the bank on the account balance.
6. *Accounting errors.* These are numerical errors made by either the company or the bank. The most common is transposition of numbers.

bank reconciliation The process of systematically comparing the cash balance as reported by the bank with the cash balance on the company's books and explaining any differences.

The process of determining the reasons for the differences between the bank balance and the company's cash account balance is called a **bank reconciliation**. This usually results in adjusting both the bank statement and the book (cash account) balances. If the balances were not reconciled (if the cash balance were left as is), the figure used on the financial statements would probably be incorrect, and external users would not have accurate information for decision making. More importantly, the bank reconciliation can serve as an independent check to ensure that the cash is being accounted for correctly within the company.

We will use Hunt Company's bank account to illustrate a bank reconciliation. The statement shown in Exhibit 6-7 indicates an ending balance of $14,422 for the month of July. After arranging the month's canceled checks in numerical order and examining the bank statement, Hunt's accountant notes the following:

1. A deposit of $3,100 on July 31 was not shown on the bank statement. (It was in transit at the end of the month.)
2. Checks No. 625 for $326, No. 631 for $426, and No. 634 for $185 are outstanding. Check No. 627 was voided at the time it was written.
3. The bank's service charge for the month is $7.
4. A direct deposit of $3,200 was made by Joy Company, a regular customer.
5. A transfer of $425 was made out of Hunt's account into the account of Martin Custodial Service for payment owed.
6. The bank paid interest of $60 on Hunt's average balance.
7. Check No. 630 for Thelma Jones's wages was recorded in the accounting records as $240 instead of the correct amount, $420.
8. The cash account in the general ledger shows a balance on July 31 of $13,937.

The bank reconciliation is shown in Exhibit 6-8. Since the bank and book balances now agree, the $16,585 adjusted cash balance is the amount that will be reported on the financial statements. If the adjusted book and bank balances had not agreed, the accountant would have had to search for errors in bookkeeping or in the bank's figures. When the balances finally agree, any necessary adjustments are made to the cash account to bring it to the correct balance. The entries to correct the balance include debits to Cash for all reconciling additions to the book balance and credits to Cash for all reconciling deductions from the book balance. Additions and deductions from the bank balance do not require adjustments to the company's books; the deposits in transit and the outstanding checks have already been recorded by the company, and, of course, bank errors are corrected by notifying the bank and having the bank make corrections. The adjustments required to correct Hunt's cash account are:

Cash.	3,260	
Accounts Receivable		3,200
Interest Revenue		60
To record the additions due to the July bank reconciliation (a $3,200 deposit made by Joy Company and $60 interest).		
Custodial Expense	425	
Miscellaneous Expense	7	
Wages Expense	180	
Cash		612
To record the deductions due to the July bank reconciliation (service charge, $7; a $180 recording error, check No. 630; bank transfer of $425 to Martin Custodial Service).		

to summarize

Because most payments are made by check, companies need to reconcile monthly bank statements with the cash balance reported on the company's books. This reconciliation process involves determining reasons for the differences and bringing the book and bank balances into agreement. Adjusting entries are then made for additions to and deductions from the book balance.

8

Understand how receivables can be used by a company to get cash immediately.

USING RECEIVABLES TO GET CASH IMMEDIATELY

Sometimes companies need cash prior to the due dates of their receivables. Often, in these circumstances, such companies will sell or "factor" their accounts receivables to financing or factoring companies. Factoring companies charge a percentage of the receivable, usually ranging

exhibit 6-8 July Bank Reconciliation for Hunt Company

Hunt Company
Bank Reconciliation
July 31, 2003

Balance per bank statement		$14,422	Balance per books		$13,937
Additions to bank balance:			*Additions to book balance:*		
Deposit in transit.		3,100	Direct deposit	$ 3,200	
Total		$17,522	Interest	60	3,260
			Total		$17,197
Deductions from bank balance:			*Deductions from book balance:*		
Outstanding checks: 625	$326		Service charge	$ 7	
631	426		Bank transfer	425	
634	185	(937)	Error in recording check No. 630		
			(for Jones's wages)	180	(612)
Adjusted bank balance		**$16,585**	**Adjusted book balance**		**$16,585**

from 2 to 15%, to buy receivables. If a company has notes receivable, these notes can be sold to a bank or finance company; selling a note is called "discounting" the note.

Selling or "Factoring" Accounts Receivable

To illustrate, assume that Reno Trucking Company has a $1,000 receivable from Bunker Metals that has terms n/30. Rather than wait the 30 days to collect the receivable, Reno Trucking could sell or "factor" the receivable at the Easy-Money Factoring Company for a 5% discount fee. If Reno Trucking needs the money to pay drivers' salaries and other expenses and factors the receivable, it would receive 95% of the $1,000, or $950, from Easy-Money Factoring. Sometimes accounts receivable are factored with "recourse," meaning that Reno Trucking must pay the receivable if Bunker Metals defaults. At times, usually for a larger discount fee, receivables are sold "without recourse," meaning that Reno Trucking has no obligation to pay, even if Bunker Metals defaults.

As an actual example, there is a small trucking company in Salt Lake City that owns five trucks and has another seven owner-operated trucks leased to it. The company primarily hauls steel from a large manufacturing plant in Utah to Chicago and hauls reclining chairs back to Utah from Chicago. Because the company is always pressed for cash, every receivable it has is factored at a rate of 6%. This means that the company receives only $94 on every $100 of receivables. Since the trucking company generally collects the receivables in 60 days, and there are approximately six 60-day periods in a year, the company is effectively paying 36% interest (6% × 6). Better cash management could make the company much more profitable.

Discounting Notes Receivable

An account receivable is an informal agreement between the seller and the credit buyer. No formal contract is drawn up, and no interest rate is specified on the account (unless the customer fails to pay within the specified time). Sometimes customers sign formal contracts, called notes, when they buy merchandise or services on credit. Even more often, customers from whom accounts receivable are past due sign interest-bearing notes to receive additional time to make payment. A **note receivable** is a claim against someone, evidenced by an unconditional written promise to pay a sum of money on or before a specified future date. Depending on the length of time until the due date, the note may be classified as a current asset or a long-term asset. In addition, it may be either a trade note receivable or a nontrade note receivable. A trade note receivable represents an amount due from a customer who purchased merchandise. Businesses often accept notes receivable from customers because they are contractual obligations that usually earn interest. A nontrade note receivable arises from the lending of money to an individual or company other than a customer (for example, an employee). Exhibit 6-9 shows a typical note receivable.

note receivable A claim against a debtor, evidenced by an unconditional written promise to pay a certain sum of money on or before a specified future date.

There are several key terms associated with a note receivable. The **maker** of a note is the person or entity who signs the note and who must make payment on or before the due date. The **payee** is the person or entity to whom payment will be made. The **principal** is the face amount of the note. The **maturity date** is the date the note becomes due. The **interest rate** is the percentage of the principal that the payee annually charges the maker for the loan; the interest is the dollar amount paid by the maker in accordance with this rate. Interest can also be thought of as the service charge, or rent, for the use of money. The formula for computing the interest on a note is:

maker A person (entity) who signs a note to borrow money and who assumes responsibility to pay the note at maturity.

payee The person (entity) to whom payment on a note is to be made.

principal The amount that will be paid on a note or other obligation at the maturity date.

maturity date The date on which a note or other obligation becomes due.

interest rate The cost of using money, expressed as an annual percentage.

Principal × Interest Rate × Time (in terms of a year) = Interest

For example, if Komatsu Company accepts from Solomon Company a 12%, three-month, $2,000 note receivable, the interest is calculated as:

$$\$2,000 \times 0.12 \times 3/12 = \$60$$

Note that the 12% stated interest rate is based on a one-year period, even though the note is only for three months. Interest rates are traditionally stated in annual terms no matter what

exhibit 6-9 Note Receivable

$2,000	Helena, Montana	July 15, 2003
PRINCIPAL	LOCATION	DATE

Ninety (90) days AFTER DATE Solomon Company PROMISES

TO PAY TO THE ORDER OF Komatsu Company
PAYEE

Two thousand and no/100 DOLLARS

PAYABLE AT First Security Bank

FOR VALUE RECEIVED, WITH INTEREST AT 12 percent per annum

John Doe
SIGNATURE OF MAKER

the term length of the credit agreement. If the $2,000 note is accepted in settlement of Solomon's unpaid account with Komatsu Company, the journal entry to record the note in Komatsu's books is:

Notes Receivable	2,000	
Accounts Receivable		2,000
Accepted 3-month, 12% note from Solomon Company in lieu of payment of its account receivable.		

When the note matures and payment is made (three months later), Komatsu's entry to record the receipt of cash would be:

Cash	2,060	
Notes Receivable		2,000
Interest Revenue		60
Received payment from Solomon Company for $2,000 note plus interest.		

maturity value The amount of an obligation to be collected or paid at maturity; equal to principal plus any interest.

Principal plus interest ($2,060 in this example) is known as the **maturity value** of the note. If the note is not paid by the maturity date, negotiations with the maker usually result in the company extending the period for payment, issuing a new note, or retaining an attorney or collection agency to collect the money. If the note eventually proves to be worthless, it is written off as a loss against Allowance for Bad Debts. Often, when an agency or attorney is attempting to collect notes receivable, they are classified on the balance sheet as special receivables.

discounting a note receivable The process of the payee's selling notes to a financial institution for less than the maturity value.

Because notes receivable are contractual promises to pay money in the future, they are negotiable. They can be sold to banks and other financial institutions. The selling of a note to a financial institution is referred to as **discounting a note receivable**. This means that the holder of a note who needs cash before a note matures can sell the note (simply by endorsing it) to a financial institution. The maker of the note, therefore, owes the money to the financial institution or other endorsee. To a financial institution, purchasing a note for cash is just like making a loan; cash is given out now in return for repayment of principal with interest in the future. To a company selling a note, discounting is a way of receiving cash earlier than would otherwise be possible.

to summarize

Companies that need cash prior to the time their accounts receivable are due often "factor" or sell those receivables to factoring companies that charge a factoring fee. Notes receivable are formal, interest-bearing credit agreements between a company and credit customers. Notes receivable are negotiable and can be discounted, or sold.

9

Account for the impact of changing exchange rates on the value of accounts receivable denominated in foreign currencies.

FOREIGN CURRENCY TRANSACTIONS

All of the sales illustrated to this point in the text have been denominated in U.S. dollars. However, many U.S. companies do a large portion of their business in foreign countries. For example, 29% of MICROSOFT's sales in 1999 were denominated in currencies other than the U.S. dollar. So, what would Microsoft have to do to record a software sale denominated in Japanese yen or British pounds? This section answers that question.

When a U.S. company sells a good or provides a service to a party in a foreign country, the transaction amount is frequently denominated in U.S. dollars. The U.S. dollar is a relatively stable currency, and buyers from Azerbaijan to Zimbabwe are often eager to avoid the uncertainty associated with payments denominated in their local currencies. For example, no matter where they are located, buyers and sellers of crude oil almost always write the contract price in terms of U.S. dollars. A U.S. company accounts for a sales contract with a foreign buyer with the sales price denominated in U.S. dollars in the way illustrated previously in this chapter; no new accounting issues are raised. However, if a U.S. company enters into a transaction in which the price is denominated in a foreign currency, the U.S. company must use special accounting procedures to recognize the change in the value of the transaction as foreign currency exchange rates fluctuate. For example, if Microsoft makes a sale with a price of 100,000 Indonesian rupiah, Microsoft knows that it will eventually collect 100,000 rupiah, but Microsoft does not know what those rupiah will be worth, in U.S. dollar terms, until the actual rupiah payment is received. Such a transaction is called a **foreign currency transaction**; the accounting for these transactions is demonstrated in the following section.

foreign currency transaction A sale in which the price is denominated in a currency other than the currency of the seller's home country.

Foreign Currency Transaction Example

To illustrate the accounting for a sale denominated in a foreign currency, assume that American Company sold goods with a price of 20,000,000 Korean won on March 23 to one of its Korean customers. Payment in Korean won is due July 12. American Company prepares quarterly financial statements on June 30. The following exchange rates apply:

	U.S. Dollar Value of One Korean Won	Event
March 23	$0.0010	Sale
June 30	0.0007	Financial statements prepared
July 12	0.0008	Payment received on account

On March 23, each Korean won is worth one-tenth of one U.S. cent. In other words, it takes 1,000 Korean won (1/0.0010) to buy one U.S. dollar. At this exchange rate, the 20,000,000-Korean-won contract is worth $20,000 (20,000,000 × $0.0010).

On March 23, American Company records the sale and the account receivable in its books as follows:

Accounts Receivable (fc)	20,000	
Sales Revenue		20,000

Note that this journal entry is exactly the same as those illustrated earlier in the chapter. The (fc) indicates that the Accounts Receivable asset is denominated in a foreign currency and, thus, subject to exchange rate fluctuations. Because the financial statements of American Company are reported in U.S. dollars, all transaction amounts must be converted into their U.S. dollar equivalents when they are entered into the formal accounting system.

fyi

The wide fluctuations in exchange rates in this illustration are unusual, but not unprecedented. For example, as part of the Asian financial crisis of 1997, the number of Korean won needed to purchase one U.S. dollar increased from 917.77 on October 23, 1997, to 1,952.68 on December 23, 1997.

On June 30, American Company prepares its quarterly financial statements. Because the 20,000,000-Korean-won contract price has not yet been collected in cash, American Company still has a receivable denominated in Korean won and must reflect the effect of the change in the exchange rate on the U.S. dollar value of that receivable. In this case the Korean won has decreased in value and is worth only $0.0007 on June 30. If American Company had to settle the contract on June 30, it would receive only $14,000 (20,000,000 × $0.0007). Thus, American Company must recognize an exchange loss of $6,000, or 20,000,000 × ($0.0010 − $0.0007). On July 12, American Company receives payment from its Korean customer. In the interim the value of the Korean won has increased slightly to $0.0008. When the receivable is collected, the 20,000,000 Korean won are worth $16,000 (20,000,000 × $0.0008), so now American Company has experienced a gain relative to its position on June 30. The effects of the fluctuation in the value of the Korean won can be summarized as follows:

	U.S. Dollar Value of the Receivable	Gain or Loss
March 23	$20,000	Not applicable
June 30	14,000	$6,000 loss
July 12	16,000	$2,000 gain

This information would be reported in American Company's three primary financial statements in the second quarter (ending June 30) and the third quarter (beginning July 1) as follows:

Second Quarter:

Income Statement		Balance Sheet		Statement of Cash Flows	
Sales revenue	$20,000	Accounts receivable	$14,000	Cash collected from customers	$ 0
Foreign exchange loss	(6,000)				

Third Quarter:

Income Statement		Balance Sheet		Statement of Cash Flows	
Sales revenue	$ 0	Cash	$16,000	Cash collected from customers	$16,000
Foreign exchange gain	2,000	Accounts receivable	0		

The net result of the sale in the second quarter, the collection of cash in the third quarter, and the changing exchange rates in between is to record a sale of $20,000, the collection of cash of $16,000, and a net exchange loss of $4,000 (a $6,000 loss in the second quarter and a $2,000 gain in the third quarter). The important point to note is that the sale is measured at the exchange rate on the date of sale and that any fluctuations between the sale date and the settlement date are recognized as exchange gains or losses.

What could American Company have done in the previous example to reduce its exposure to the risk associated with changing exchange rates? The easiest thing would have been to denominate the transaction in U.S. dollars. Then the risk of exchange rate changes would have fallen on the Korean company. Secondly, American Company could have locked in the price of Korean won by entering into a forward contract with a foreign currency broker. A forward contract is an example of a derivative contract. Derivatives are becoming more and more commonplace in today's business environment, and in Chapter 12 we examine derivatives and their uses and risks.

---

to summarize

When a U.S. company makes a sale that is denominated in a foreign currency, the sale is called a foreign currency transaction. The sale is measured at the exchange rate on the date of sale, and any fluctuations between the sale date and the settlement date are recognized as exchange gains or losses.

---

review of learning objectives

1 Understand the three basic types of business activities: operating, investing, and financing. The three major types of business activities are: (1) operating activities, (2) investing activities, and (3) financing activities. Operating activities include selling products or services, buying inventory for resale, and incurring and paying for necessary expenses associated with the primary activities of a business. Investing activities include purchasing property, plant, and equipment for use in the business or purchasing investments, such as stocks and bonds of other companies. Financing activities include raising money by means other than operations to finance a business. The two common financing activities are borrowing (debt financing) and selling ownership or equity interests (equity financing) in the company.

2 Use the two revenue recognition criteria to decide when the revenue from a sale or service should be recorded in the accounting records. Revenue is recognized when the work is done and when cash collectibility is reasonably assured. The entries to record revenue from the sale of merchandise or from the performance of a service involve debits to Cash or Accounts Receivable and credits to Sales Revenue or Service Revenue. In general, revenues are recognized at the time of a sale. If cash is collected before a service is provided or a product is delivered, however, then revenue should not be recognized until the promised action has been completed. Revenue for long-term contracts is recognized in proportion to the amount of the contract completed.

3 Properly account for the collection of cash and describe the business controls necessary to safeguard cash. The amount of cash collected from customers can be reduced because of sales discounts and sales returns and allowances. Sales discounts are reductions in the payments required of customers who pay their accounts quickly. Sales returns and allowances are payment reductions granted to dissatisfied customers. On an income statement, sales discounts and sales returns and allowances are subtracted from gross sales to arrive at net sales. Cash is a tempting target for fraud or theft, so companies must carefully monitor and control the way cash is handled and accounted for. Common controls include (1) separation of duties in the handling of and accounting for cash, (2) daily deposits of all cash receipts, and (3) payment of all expenditures by prenumbered checks.

4 Record the losses resulting from credit customers who do not pay their bills. Accounts receivable balances are generally collected from 10 to 60 days after the date of sale. There are two ways to account for losses from uncollectible receivables: the direct write-off method and the allowance method. Only the allowance method is generally acceptable because it matches expenses with revenues. Losses from uncollectible receivables can be estimated (1) as a percentage of total credit sales for the period or (2) as a percentage of total outstanding receivables. One technique for estimating uncollectible receivables as a percentage of total receivables is to perform an aging of accounts receivable.

5 Evaluate a company's management of its receivables by computing and analyzing appropriate financial ratios. Careful management of accounts receivable is a balance between extending credit to increase sales and collecting cash quickly to reduce the need to borrow. Two ratios commonly used in monitoring the level of receivables are accounts receivable turnover and average collection period. The level of these ratios is determined by how well a company manages its receivables, as well as by what kind of business the company is in.

6 Match revenues and expenses by estimating and recording future warranty and service costs associated with a sale. If a company makes promises about future warranty repairs or continued customer service as part of a sale, the value of these promises is estimated and recorded as an expense at the time of the sale. If experience suggests that the original estimate was in error, adjustments are made to the estimates made in relation to subsequent sales; however, no attempt is made to go back and "fix" the original estimates.

expanded material

7 Reconcile a checking account. Most cash is kept in bank accounts, which are reconciled each month. Bank reconciliations adjust the bank and book balances so that they are the same correct amount. Differences arise between the book and bank balances because the company knows about some cash transactions before the bank does (such as deposits in transit and outstanding checks) and because the bank knows about some cash transactions before the company does (such as bank service charges).

8 Understand how receivables can be used by a company to get cash immediately. Sometimes companies that need cash in a hurry sell or "factor" their receivables. Companies buying receivables, known as factoring or financing companies, usually charge a discount of 2 to 15% of the receivable. Receivables can be factored with or without recourse. A note receivable is a claim against a debtor, evidenced by an unconditional written promise to pay a sum of money on or before a specified future date. The amount of interest to be earned annually is equal to: principal × interest rate × time period (in terms of one year) of the note. Notes can be discounted at a bank or other financial institution. Discounting allows the original payee of a note to receive money prior to the maturity date.

9 Account for the impact of changing exchange rates on the value of accounts receivable denominated in foreign currencies. U.S. companies transact large amounts of business with foreign parties. When the transaction is denominated in U.S. dollars, no new accounting issues are introduced. However, when a U.S. company enters into a transaction in which the price is denominated in a foreign currency, the U.S. company must use special accounting procedures to recognize the change in the value of the transaction as foreign currency exchange rates fluctuate. The sale is measured at the exchange rate on the date of sale, and any fluctuations between the sale date and the settlement date are recognized as exchange gains or losses.

key terms and concepts

accounts receivable 249
accounts receivable turnover 255
aging accounts receivable 253
allowance for bad debts 251
allowance method 250
average collection period 256
bad debt expense 250
bad debts 249
cash 248
contra account 247
direct write-off method 249
financing activities 240
gross sales 248
investing activities 240
net realizable value of accounts receivable 252
net sales 248
operating activities 239
receivables 249
revenue recognition 242
sales discounts 246
sales returns and allowances 247

expanded material

bank reconciliation 260
discounting a note receivable 263
foreign currency transaction 264
interest rate 262
maker 262
maturity date 262
maturity value 263
note receivable 262
NSF (not sufficient funds) checks 258
payee 262
principal 262

review problem

Accounting for Receivables and Warranty Obligations

Douglas Company sells furniture. Approximately 10% of its sales are cash; the remainder are on credit. During the year ended December 31, 2003, the company had net credit sales of $2,200,000. As of December 31, 2003, total accounts receivable were $800,000, and Allowance for Bad Debts had a debit balance of $1,100 prior to adjustment. In the past, approximately 1% of credit sales have proved to be uncollectible. An aging analysis of the individual accounts receivable revealed that $32,000 of the Accounts Receivable balance appeared to be uncollectible.

The largest credit sale during the year occurred on December 4, 2003, for $72,000 to Aaron Company. Terms of the sale were 2/10, n/30. On December 13, Aaron Company paid $60,000 of the receivable balance and took advantage of the 2% discount. The remaining $12,000 was still outstanding on March 31, 2004, when Douglas Company learned that Aaron Company had declared bankruptcy. Douglas wrote the receivable off as uncollectible.

On December 31, 2003, Douglas Company estimated that it would cost $11,000 in labor and various expenditures to service the furniture it had sold (under 90-day warranty agreements) during the last three months of 2003. During January 2004, the company spent $430 in labor and $600 for supplies to perform service on defective furniture that was sold during the year 2003.

Required:

Prepare the following journal entries:

1. The sale of $72,000 of furniture on December 4, 2003, to Aaron Company on credit.
2. The collection of $58,800 from Aaron Company on December 13, 2003, assuming the company allows the discount on partial payment.
3. Record Bad Debt Expense on December 31, 2003, using the percentage of credit sales method.
4. Record Bad Debt Expense on December 31, 2003, using the aging of receivables method.
5. Record estimated warranty expense on December 31, 2003.
6. Record actual expenditures to service defective furniture under the warranty agreements on January 31, 2004.
7. Write off the balance of the Aaron Company receivable as uncollectible, March 31, 2004.

Solution

The journal entries would be recorded as follows:

Date	Account	Debit	Credit
1. Dec. 4, 2003	Accounts Receivable	72,000	
	Sales Revenue		72,000
	Sold $72,000 of furniture to Aaron Company on credit.		
2. Dec. 13, 2003	Cash	58,800	
	Sales Discounts	1,200	
	Accounts Receivable		60,000
	Collected $58,800 from Aaron Company on December 4 sale and recognized the 2% discount taken (0.02 × $60,000 = $1,200).		
3. Dec. 31, 2003	Bad Debt Expense	22,000	
	Allowance for Bad Debts		22,000
	Recorded bad debt expense as 1% of credit sales of $2,200,000 ($2,200,000 × 0.01 = $22,000).		

Note: When using the percentage of credit sales method to estimate bad debt expense, the existing balance in the allowance for bad debts account is ignored.

Date	Account	Debit	Credit
4. Dec. 31, 2003	Bad Debt Expense	33,100	
	Allowance for Bad Debts		33,100
	Recorded bad debt expense using the aging of accounts receivable method ($32,000 + $1,100 debit balance).		

Note: When using the percentage of total receivables method (e.g., by aging receivables) to estimate bad debt expense, the existing balance in Allowance for Bad Debts must be taken into consideration so that the new balance is the amount of receivables not expected to be collected.

5. Dec. 31, 2003	Customer Service Expense	11,000	
	Estimated Liability for Service		11,000
	Estimated customer service (warranty) costs on furniture sold during the last three months of 2003. (The warranty period is 90 days.)		
6. Jan. 31, 2004	Estimated Liability for Service	1,030	
	Wages Payable (to service employees)		430
	Supplies		600
	Actual customer service costs incurred.		
7. March 31, 2004	Allowance for Bad Debts	12,000	
	Accounts Receivable		12,000
	Wrote off the balance in the Aaron Company account as uncollectible.		

discussion questions

1. What are the three types of basic business activities?
2. Why is the purchase of inventory for resale to customers classified as an operating activity rather than an investing activity?
3. When should revenues be recognized and reported?
4. Why do you think misstatements of revenues (e.g., recognizing revenues before they are earned) is one of the most common ways to manipulate financial statements?
5. Why is it important to have separate sales returns and allowances and sales discounts accounts? Wouldn't it be much easier to directly reduce the sales revenue account for these adjustments?
6. Why do companies usually have more controls for cash than for other assets?
7. What are three generally practiced controls for cash, and what is the purpose of each control?
8. Why do most companies tolerate having a small percentage of uncollectible accounts receivable?
9. Why does the accounting profession require the use of the allowance method of accounting for losses due to bad debts rather than the direct write-off method?
10. With the allowance method, why is the net balance, or net realizable value, of Accounts Receivable the same after the write-off of a receivable as it was prior to the write-off of the uncollectible account?
11. Why is the "aging" of accounts receivable usually more accurate than basing the estimate on total receivables?
12. Why is it important to monitor operating ratios such as accounts receivable turnover?
13. Why must the customer service expense (warranty) sometimes be recorded in the period prior to when the actual customer services will be performed?

expanded material

14. What are the major reasons that the balance of a bank statement is usually different from the cash book balance (Cash per the general ledger)?
15. Why don't the additions and deductions from the bank balance on a bank reconciliation require adjustment by the company?
16. What is the advantage of having a note receivable over having an account receivable?
17. Why would someone discount a note receivable?
18. Why would someone factor an account receivable?
19. Do all transactions by U.S. companies with foreign parties require special accounting procedures by the U.S. companies? Explain.

discussion cases

CASE 6-1

ZZZZ BEST AND FICTITIOUS RECEIVABLES

ZZZZ BEST was a Los Angeles–based company specializing in carpet cleaning and insurance restoration. Prior to allegations of fraud and its declaration of bankruptcy in 1988, ZZZZ Best was touted as one of the hottest stocks on Wall Street. In 1987, after only six years in business, the company had a market valuation exceeding $211 million, giving its "genius" president a paper fortune of $109 million. Lawsuits, however, alleged that the company was nothing more than a massive fraud scheme that fooled major banks, two CPA firms, an investment banker, and a prestigious law firm.

ZZZZ Best was started as a carpet-cleaning business by Barry Minkow, a 15-year-old high school student, in 1981. Although ZZZZ Best had impressive growth as a carpet-cleaning business, the growth was not nearly fast enough for the impatient Minkow. In 1985, ZZZZ Best announced that it was expanding into the insurance restoration business, restoring buildings that had been damaged by fire, floods, and other disasters. During 1985 and 1986, ZZZZ Best reported undertaking several large insurance restoration projects. The company reported high profits from these restoration jobs. A public stock offering in 1986 stated that 86% of ZZZZ Best Corporation's business was in the insurance restoration area.

Based on the company's high growth and reported income in 1987, a spokesperson for a large brokerage house was quoted in *Business Week* as saying that "Barry Minkow is a great manager and ZZZZ Best is a great company." He recommended that his clients buy ZZZZ Best stock. That same year, the Association of Collegiate Entrepreneurs and the Young Entrepreneurs' Organization placed Minkow on their list of the top 100 young entrepreneurs in America; and the mayor of Los Angeles honored Minkow with a commendation that said that he had "set a fine entrepreneurial example of obtaining the status of a millionaire at the age of 18."

Unfortunately, ZZZZ Best's insurance business, its impressive growth, and its high reported income were totally fictitious. In fact, the company never once made a legitimate profit. Barry Minkow himself later said that he was a "fraudster" who convincingly deceived almost everyone involved with the company. Through the use of widespread collusion among company officials, Minkow was even able to hide the fraud from ZZZZ Best's external auditor. For example, when ZZZZ Best reported an $8.2 million contract to restore a building in San Diego, the external auditor demanded to see the building; this was difficult since neither the building nor the job existed. However, officials of ZZZZ Best gained access to a construction site and led the auditor through a tour of an unfinished building in San Diego to show that the "restoration" work was ongoing. The situation became very complicated for ZZZZ Best when the auditor later asked to see the finished job. ZZZZ Best had to spend $1 million to lease the building and hire contractors to finish six of the eight floors in ten days. The auditor was led on another tour and wrote a memo saying, "Job looks very good." The auditor was subsequently faulted for looking only at what ZZZZ Best officials chose to show, without making independent inquiries.

Minkow's house of cards finally came crashing down as it became apparent to banks, suppliers, investors, and the auditors that the increasing difficulty ZZZZ Best was having with paying its bills was entirely inconsistent with a company reporting so much revenue and profit. In January 1988, a federal grand jury in Los Angeles returned a 57-count indictment, charging 11 individuals—including ZZZZ Best founder and president, Barry Minkow—with engaging in a massive fraud scheme. Minkow was later convicted and sentenced to 25 years in a federal penitentiary in Colorado.

ZZZZ Best grossly inflated its operating results by reporting bogus revenue and receivables. What factors prevent a company from continuing to report fraudulent results indefinitely? What could the auditor have done to uncover the ZZZZ Best fraud?

Source: This description is based on articles in *The Wall Street Journal*, *Forbes*, and investigative proceedings of the U.S. House of Representatives, Subcommittee on Energy and Commerce hearings: *The Wall Street Journal*, July 7, 1987, p. 1; July 9, 1987, p. 1; August 23, 1988, p. 1; U.S. House of Representatives, Subcommittee on Oversight and Investigation of the Committee on Energy and Commerce, January 27, 1988; U.S. House of Representatives, Subcommittee on Oversight and Investigation of the Committee on Energy and Commerce, February 1, 1988; Daniel Akst, "How Barry Minkow Fooled the Auditors," *Forbes*, October 2, 1989, p. 126.

CASE 6-2 RECOGNIZING REVENUE

HealthCare, Inc.,* operates a number of medical testing facilities around the United States. Drug manufacturers, such as **MERCK** and **BRISTOL-MYERS SQUIBB**, contract with HealthCare

*The name of the actual company has been changed.

for testing of their newly developed drugs and other medical treatments. HealthCare advertises, gets patients, and then administers the drugs or other experimental treatments, under a doctor's care, to determine their effectiveness. The Food and Drug Administration requires such human testing before allowing drugs to be prescribed by doctors and sold by pharmacists. A typical contract might read as follows:

> HealthCare, Inc., will administer the new drug, "Lexitol," to 50 patients, once a week for 10 weeks, to determine its effectiveness in treating male baldness. Merck will pay HealthCare, Inc., $100 per patient visit, to be billed at the conclusion of the test period. The total amount of the contract is $50,000 (50 patients × 10 visits × $100 per visit).

Given these kinds of contracts, when should HealthCare recognize revenue—when contracts are signed, when patient visits take place, when drug manufacturers are billed, or when cash is collected?

CASE 6-3

CREDIT POLICY REVIEW

The president, vice president, and sales manager of Moorer Corporation were discussing the company's present credit policy. The sales manager suggested that potential sales were being lost to competitors because of Moorer Corporation's tight restrictions on granting credit to consumers. He stated that if credit policies were loosened, the current year's estimated credit sales of $3,000,000 could be increased by at least 20% next year with an increase in uncollectible accounts receivable of only $10,000 over this year's amount of $37,500. He argued that because the company's cost of sales is only 25% of revenues, the company would certainly come out ahead.

The vice president, however, suggested that a better alternative to easier credit terms would be to accept consumer credit cards such as **VISA** or **MASTERCARD**. She argued that this alternative could increase sales by 40%. The credit card finance charges to Moorer Corporation would be 4% of the additional sales.

At this point, the president interrupted by saying that he wasn't at all sure that increasing credit sales of any kind was a good thing. In fact, he suggested that the $37,500 of uncollectible accounts receivable was altogether too high. He wondered whether the company should discontinue offering sales on account.

With the information given, determine whether Moorer Corporation would be better off under the sales manager's proposal or the vice president's proposal. Also, address the president's suggestion that credit sales of all types be abolished.

exercises

EXERCISE 6-1

RECOGNIZING REVENUE

Supposedly, there is an over 200-year wait to buy **GREEN BAY PACKERS** season football tickets. The fiscal year-end (when they close their books) for the Green Bay Packers is March 30 of each year. If the Packers sell their season football tickets in February for the coming football season, when should the revenue from those ticket sales be recognized?

EXERCISE 6-2

RECOGNIZING REVENUE

James Dee Company cleans the outside walls of buildings. The average job generates revenue of $800,000 and takes about two weeks to complete. Customers are required to pay for a job within 30 days after its completion. James Dee Company guarantees its work for five years—

if the building walls get dirty within five years, James Dee will clean them again at no charge. James Dee is considering recognizing revenue using one of the following methods:

a. Recognize revenue when James Dee signs the contract to do the job.
b. Recognize revenue when James Dee begins the work.
c. Recognize revenue immediately after the completion of the job.
d. Recognize revenue 30 days after the completion of the job when the cash is collected.
e. Wait until the five-year guarantee period is over before recognizing any revenue.

Which revenue recognition option would you recommend to James Dee? Explain your answer.

EXERCISE 6-3

RECOGNIZING REVENUE—LONG-TERM CONSTRUCTION PROJECTS

In the year 2002, Salt Lake City, Utah, will host the Winter Olympics. To get ready for the Olympics, most of the major roads and highways in and around Salt Lake City are being renovated. It will take over three years to complete the highway projects, and **WASATCH CONSTRUCTORS**, the construction company performing the work, probably doesn't want to wait until the work is completed to recognize revenue. How would you suggest that the revenue on these highway construction projects be recognized?

EXERCISE 6-4

REVENUE RECOGNITION

Yummy, Inc., is a franchiser that offers for sale an exclusive franchise agreement for $30,000. Under the terms of the agreement, the purchaser of a franchise receives a variety of services associated with the construction of a Yummy Submarine and Yogurt Shop, access to various product supply services, and continuing management advice and assistance once the retail unit is up and running. The contract calls for the franchise purchaser to make cash payments of $10,000 per year for three years to Yummy, Inc.

How should Yummy, Inc., account for the sale of a franchise contract? Specifically, when should the revenue and receivable be recognized?

EXERCISE 6-5

CONTROL OF CASH

Molly Maloney is an employee of Marshall Company, a small manufacturing concern. Her responsibilities include opening the daily mail, depositing the cash and checks received into the bank, and making the accounting entries to record the receipt of cash and the reduction of receivables. Explain how Maloney might be able to misuse some of Marshall's cash receipts. As a consultant, what control procedures would you recommend?

EXERCISE 6-6

RECORDING SALES TRANSACTIONS

On June 24, 2003, Hansen Company sold merchandise to Jill Selby for $80,000 with terms 2/10, n/30. On June 30, Selby paid $39,200 on her account and was allowed a discount for the timely payment. On July 20, Selby paid $24,000 on her account and returned $16,000 of merchandise, claiming that it did not meet contract terms.

Record the necessary journal entries on June 24, June 30, and July 20.

EXERCISE 6-7

RECORDING SALES TRANSACTIONS

Lopez Company sold merchandise on account to Atlantic Company for $4,000 on June 3, 2003, with terms 2/10, n/30. On June 7, 2003, Lopez Company received $200 of returned merchandise from Atlantic Company and issued a credit memorandum for the appropriate amount. Lopez Company received payment for the balance of the bill on June 21, 2003.

Record the necessary journal entries on June 3, June 7, and June 21.

EXERCISE 6-8

ESTIMATING BAD DEBTS

The trial balance of Stardust Company at the end of its 2003 fiscal year included the following account balances:

Account	
Accounts receivable	$48,900
Allowance for bad debts	2,500 (debit balance)

The company has *not yet* recorded any bad debt expense for 2003.

Determine the amount of bad debt expense to be recognized by Stardust Company for 2003, assuming the following independent situations:

1. An aging accounts receivable analysis indicates that probable uncollectible accounts receivable at year-end amount to $4,500.
2. Company policy is to maintain a provision for uncollectible accounts receivable equal to 3% of outstanding accounts receivable.
3. Company policy is to estimate uncollectible accounts receivable as equal to 0.5% of the previous year's annual sales, which were $200,000.

EXERCISE 6-9

ACCOUNTING FOR BAD DEBTS

The following data were associated with the accounts receivable and uncollectible accounts of Hilton, Inc., during 2003:

a. The opening credit balance in Allowance for Bad Debts was $900,000 at January 1, 2003.
b. During 2003, the company realized that specific accounts receivable totaling $920,000 had gone bad and had been written off.
c. An account receivable of $50,000 was collected during 2003. This account had previously been written off as a bad debt in 2002.
d. The company decided that Allowance for Bad Debts would be $920,000 at the end of 2003.

1. Prepare journal entries to show how these events would be recognized in the accounting system using:
   a. The direct write-off method.
   b. The allowance method.
2. Discuss the advantages and disadvantages of each method with respect to the matching principle.

EXERCISE 6-10

ACCOUNTING FOR UNCOLLECTIBLE ACCOUNTS RECEIVABLE

Dodge Company had the following information relating to its accounts receivable at December 31, 2002, and for the year ended December 31, 2003:

Accounts receivable balance at 12/31/02	$ 900,000
Allowance for bad debts at 12/31/02 (credit balance)	50,000
Gross sales during 2003 (all credit)	5,000,000
Collections from customers during 2003	4,500,000
Accounts written off as uncollectible during 2003	60,000
Estimated uncollectible receivables at 12/31/03	110,000

Dodge Company uses the percentage of receivables method to estimate bad debt expense.

1. At December 31, 2003, what is the balance of Dodge Company's Allowance for Bad Debts? What is the bad debt expense for 2003?
2. At December 31, 2003, what is the balance of Dodge Company's gross accounts receivable?

EXERCISE 6-11

AGING OF ACCOUNTS RECEIVABLE

Cicero Company's accounts receivable reveal the following balances:

Age of Accounts	Receivable Balance
Current	$600,000
1–30 days past due	320,000
31–60 days past due	80,000
61–90 days past due	50,000
91–120 days past due	9,000

The credit balance in Allowance for Bad Debts is now $26,000. After a thorough analysis of its collection history, the company estimates that the following percentages of receivables will eventually prove uncollectible:

Current	0.4%
1–30 days past due	3.0
31–60 days past due	12.0
61–90 days past due	60.0
91–120 days past due	90.0

Prepare an aging schedule for the accounts receivable, and give the journal entry for recording the necessary change in the allowance for bad debts account.

EXERCISE 6-12

AGING OF ACCOUNTS RECEIVABLE

The following aging of accounts receivable is for Harry Company at the end of its first year of business:

Aging of Accounts Receivable
December 31, 2003

	Overall	Less Than 30 Days	31 to 60 Days	61 to 90 Days	Over 90 Days
Ken Nelson	$ 10,000	$ 8,000		$1,000	$1,000
Elaine Anderson	40,000	31,000	$ 4,000		5,000
Bryan Crist	12,000	3,000	4,000	2,000	3,000
Renee Warner	60,000	50,000	10,000		
Nelson Hsia	16,000	10,000	6,000		
Stella Valerio	25,000	20,000		5,000	
Totals	$163,000	$122,000	$24,000	$8,000	$9,000

Harry Company has collected the following bad debt information from a consultant familiar with Harry's industry:

Age of Account	Percentage Ultimately Uncollectible
Less than 30 days	2%
31–60 days	10
61–90 days	30
Over 90 days	75

1. Compute the appropriate Allowance for Bad Debts as of December 31, 2003.
2. Make the journal entry required to record this allowance. Remember that, since this is Harry's first year of operations, the allowance account at the beginning of the year was $0.
3. What is Harry's net accounts receivable balance as of December 31, 2003?

EXERCISE 6-13

DIRECT WRITE-OFF VERSUS ALLOWANCE METHOD

The vice president for Tres Corporation provides you with the following list of accounts receivable written off in the current year. (These accounts were recognized as bad debt expense at the time they were written off; i.e., the company was using the direct write-off method.)

Date	Customer	Amount
March 30	Rasmussen Company	$12,000
July 31	Dodge Company	7,500
September 30	Larsen Company	10,000
December 31	Peterson Company	12,000

Tres Corporation's sales are all on an n/30 credit basis. Sales for the current year total $3,600,000, and analysis has indicated that uncollectible receivable losses historically approximate 1.5% of sales.

1. Do you agree or disagree with Tres Corporation's policy concerning recognition of bad debt expense? Why or why not?
2. If Tres were to use the percentage of sales method for recording bad debt expense, by how much would income before income taxes change for the current year?

EXERCISE 6-14 ACCOUNTING FOR UNCOLLECTIBLE RECEIVABLES—PERCENTAGE OF SALES METHOD

The trial balance of Sporting House, Inc., shows a $100,000 outstanding balance in Accounts Receivable at the end of 2002. During 2003, 75% of the total credit sales of $4,000,000 was collected, and no receivables were written off as uncollectible. The company estimated that 1.5% of the credit sales would be uncollectible. During 2004, the account of Larry Johnson, who owed $1,200, was judged to be uncollectible and was written off. At the end of 2004, the amount previously written off was collected in full from Mr. Johnson.

Prepare the necessary journal entries for recording all the preceding transactions relating to uncollectibles on the books of Sporting House, Inc.

EXERCISE 6-15 COMPARING THE PERCENTAGE OF SALES AND THE PERCENTAGE OF RECEIVABLES METHODS

Keefer Company uses the percentage of sales method for computing bad debt expense. As of January 1, 2003, the balance of Allowance for Bad Debts was $200,000. Write-offs of uncollectible accounts during 2003 totaled $240,000. Reported bad debt expense for 2003 was $320,000, computed using the percentage of sales method.

Keith & Harding, the auditors of Keefer's financial statements, compiled an aging accounts receivable analysis of Keefer's accounts at the end of 2003. This analysis has led Keith & Harding to estimate that, of the accounts receivable Keefer has as of the end of 2003, $700,000 will ultimately prove to be uncollectible.

Given their analysis, Keith & Harding, the auditors, think that Keefer should make an adjustment to its 2003 financial statements. What adjusting journal entry should Keith & Harding suggest?

EXERCISE 6-16 RATIO ANALYSIS

The following are summary financial data for Parker Enterprises, Inc., and Boulder, Inc., for three recent years:

	Year 3	Year 2	Year 1
Net sales (in millions):			
Parker Enterprises, Inc.	$ 3,700	$ 3,875	$ 3,882
Boulder, Inc.	17,825	16,549	15,242
Net accounts receivable (in millions):			
Parker Enterprises, Inc.	1,400	1,800	1,725
Boulder, Inc.	5,525	5,800	6,205

1. Using the above data, compute the accounts receivable turnover and average collection period for each company for years 2 and 3.
2. Which company appears to have the better credit management policy?

EXERCISE 6-17

ASSESSING HOW WELL COMPANIES MANAGE THEIR RECEIVABLES

Assume that Hickory Company has the following data related to its accounts receivable:

	2002	2003
Net sales	$1,425,000	$1,650,000
Net receivables:		
Beginning of year	375,000	333,500
End of year	420,000	375,000

Use these data to compute accounts receivable turnover ratios and average collection periods for 2002 and 2003. Based on your analysis, is Hickory Company managing its receivables better or worse in 2003 than it did in 2002?

EXERCISE 6-18

MEASURING ACCOUNTS RECEIVABLE QUALITY

The following accounts receivable information is for Happy Tiny Company:

	2003	2002	2001
Accounts receivable	$300,000	$260,000	$220,000
Allowance for bad debts	18,000	17,000	16,000

Did the creditworthiness of Happy Tiny's customers increase or decrease between 2001 and 2003? Explain.

EXERCISE 6-19

ACCOUNTING FOR WARRANTIES

Rick Procter, president of Sharp Television Stores, has been concerned recently about declining sales due to increased competition in the area. Rick has noticed that many of the national stores selling television sets and appliances have been placing heavy emphasis on warranties in their marketing programs. In an effort to revitalize sales, Rick has decided to offer free service and repairs for one year as a warranty on his television sets. Based on experience, Rick believes that first-year service and repair costs on the television sets will be approximately 5% of sales. The first month of operations following the initiation of Rick's new marketing plan showed significant increases in sales of TV sets. Total sales of TV sets for the first three months under the warranty plan were $10,000, $8,000, and $12,000, respectively.

1. Assuming that Rick prepares adjusting entries and financial statements for his own use at the end of each month, prepare the appropriate entry to recognize customer service (warranty) expense for each of these first three months.
2. Prepare the appropriate entry to record services provided to repair sets under warranty in the second month, assuming that the following costs were incurred: labor (paid in cash), $550; supplies, $330.

EXERCISE 6-20

ACCOUNTING FOR WARRANTIES

Johnson Auto sells used cars and trucks. During 2003, it sold 51 cars and trucks for a total of $1,350,000. Johnson provides a 12-month, 12,000-mile warranty on the used cars and trucks sold. Johnson estimates that it will cost $25,000 in labor and $13,000 in parts to service (during the following year) the cars and trucks sold in 2003.

In January 2004, Steve Martin brought his truck in for warranty repairs. Johnson Auto fixed the truck under its warranty agreement. It cost Johnson $400 in labor and $275 in parts to fix Steve Martin's truck. Prepare the journal entries to record (1) Johnson Auto's estimated customer service liability as of December 31, 2003, and (2) the costs incurred in repairing the truck in January 2004.

expanded material

EXERCISE 6-21

PREPARING A BANK RECONCILIATION

Prepare a bank reconciliation for Oldroyd Company at January 31, 2003, using the information shown.

1. Cash per the accounting records at January 31 amounted to $72,802; the bank statement on this same date showed a balance of $64,502.
2. The canceled checks returned by the bank included a check written by the Oldham Company for $1,764 that had been deducted from Oldroyd's account in error.
3. Deposits in transit as of January 31, 2003, amounted to $10,928.
4. The following amounts were adjustments to Oldroyd Company's account on the bank statement:
   a. Service charges of $26.
   b. An NSF check of $1,400.
   c. Interest earned on the account, $40.
5. Checks written by Oldroyd Company that have not yet cleared the bank include four checks totaling $5,778.

EXERCISE 6-22

PREPARING A BANK RECONCILIATION

The records of Denna Corporation show the following bank statement information for December:

a. Bank balance, December 31, 2003, $87,450
b. Service charges for December, $50
c. Rent collected by bank, $1,000
d. Note receivable collected by bank (including $300 interest), $2,300
e. December check returned marked NSF (check was a payment of an account receivable), $200
f. Bank erroneously reduced Denna's account for a check written by Dunna Company, $1,000
g. Cash account balance, December 31, 2003, $81,200
h. Outstanding checks, $9,200
i. Deposits in transit, $5,000

1. Prepare a bank reconciliation for December.
2. Prepare the entry to correct the cash account as of December 31, 2003.

EXERCISE 6-23

RECONCILING BOOK AND BANK BALANCES

Jensen Company has just received the September 30, 2003, bank statement summarized in the following schedule:

	Charges	Deposits	Balance
Balance, September 1			$ 5,100
Deposits recorded during September		$27,000	32,100
Checks cleared during September	$27,300		4,800
NSF check, J. J. Jones	50		4,750
Bank service charges	10		4,740
Balance, September 30			4,740

Cash on hand (recorded on Jensen's books but not deposited) on September 1 and September 30 amounted to $200. There were no deposits in transit or checks outstanding at September 1, 2003. The cash account for September reflected the following:

Cash			
Sept. 1 Balance	5,300	Sept. Checks	28,000
Sept. Deposits	29,500		

Answer the following questions. (Hint: It may be helpful to prepare a complete bank reconciliation.)

1. What is the ending balance per the cash account before adjustments?
2. What adjustments should be added to the depositor's books?
3. What is the total amount of the deductions from the depositor's books?
4. What is the total amount to be added to the bank's balance?
5. What is the total amount to be deducted from the bank's balance?

EXERCISE 6-24

JOURNAL ENTRIES FOR NOTES RECEIVABLE

Prepare journal entries for the following transactions for Stansworth Plumbing for 2003:

July 1	Installed a sprinkling system for Chuck's Engineering and billed $12,600 for the job.
Sept. 1	Chuck's had not yet paid for the sprinkling system. Stansworth agreed to accept a three-month note for the full amount with interest at an annual rate of 14%.
Dec. 1	Chuck's Engineering paid the note in full.

EXERCISE 6-25

FACTORING RECEIVABLES AND BORROWING MONEY

Nixon Enterprises is experiencing a temporary shortage of cash. To cover the shortage, the financial vice president of the company proposed that some of the company's accounts receivable be sold (factored). A factoring company has offered to buy up to $2 million of the company's receivables on a without recourse basis at a fee of 16% of the amount factored.

As an alternative, another vice president of the company has proposed borrowing an equivalent amount from South Willow Bank, pledging the outstanding receivables as collateral for the loan. Under the terms of the borrowing agreement, Nixon Enterprises would receive 80% of the value of all receivables assigned to the bank and would be charged a 1% loan origination (service) fee based on the actual dollar amount of cash received and 12% annual interest on the outstanding loan. The company estimates that the loan will be repaid in two months.

Evaluate the two alternatives. Which one is better from the company's perspective?

EXERCISE 6-26

General Ledger Software

ACCOUNTING FOR NOTES RECEIVABLE

Escondido Company frequently sells merchandise on promissory notes. The following transactions relate to one such note:

Feb. 1	Sold merchandise for $9,000 to Marta Tabor; accepted a 6-month, 11% note.
Aug. 1	On this date (due date of the note), Marta Tabor did not make payment.
Oct. 1	Collected the maturity value (principal plus interest as of August 1) of the note from Marta Tabor, together with 15% interest on the maturity value from August 1.

Prepare the journal entries to record the above transactions.

EXERCISE 6-27

FOREIGN CURRENCY TRANSACTION

Rabona Slice, a U.S. company, sold 100,000 cases of tropical fruit to Ben Thanh Market, a Vietnamese firm, for 2.5 billion Vietnamese dong. The sale was made on November 17, 2003, when one U.S. dollar equaled 14,000 dong. Payment of 2.5 billion Vietnamese dong was due to Rabona Slice on January 16, 2004. At December 31, 2003, one U.S. dollar equaled 15,000 dong, and on January 16, 2004, one U.S. dollar equaled 15,600 dong.

1. What will be the value of the accounts receivable on December 31, 2003, in Vietnamese dong?

2. What will be the value of the accounts receivable on December 31, 2003, in U.S. dollars?
3. Will Rabona Slice recognize an exchange gain or loss at December 31, 2003? Explain.
4. Will Rabona Slice recognize an exchange gain or loss on January 16, 2004? Explain.
5. In connection with this sale, what amount will Rabona Slice report as Sales Revenue in its income statement for 2003?
6. In connection with this sale, what amount will Rabona Slice report as Cash Collected from Customers in its statement of cash flows for 2004?

EXERCISE 6-28

FOREIGN CURRENCY TRANSACTION

American, Inc., sells one widget to Japanese Company at an agreed-upon price of 1,000,000 yen. On the day of the sale, one yen is equal to $0.01. American, Inc., maintains its accounting records in U.S. dollars. Therefore, the amount in yen must be converted to U.S. dollars.

1. Provide the journal entry that would be made by American, Inc., on the day of the sale, assuming Japanese Company pays for the widget on the day of the sale.
2. Most sales are on account, meaning that payment will not be received for 30 days or even longer. What issues will arise for American, Inc., if the sale is made with payment due in 30 days? (Hint: What might happen to the value of the yen in relation to the dollar during the 30-day period?)
3. Suppose that 30 days from the date of the sale the value of one yen is equal to $0.008. What journal entry would be made when the 1,000,000 yen are received by American, Inc.?

problems

PROBLEM 6-1

RECOGNIZING REVENUE

Brad Company sells ships. Each ship sells for over $25 million. Brad never starts building a ship until it receives a specific order from a customer. Brad usually takes about four years to build a ship. After construction is completed and during the first three years the customer uses the ship, Brad agrees to repair anything on the ship free of charge. The customers pay for the ships over a period of ten years after the date of delivery.

Brad Company is considering the following alternatives for recognizing revenue from its sale of ships:

a. Recognize revenue when Brad receives the order to do the job.
b. Recognize revenue when Brad begins the work.
c. Recognize revenue proportionately during the four-year construction period.
d. Recognize revenue immediately after the customer takes possession of the ship.
e. Wait until the three-year guarantee period is over before recognizing any revenue.
f. Wait until the ten-year payment period is over before recognizing any revenue.

Required:

1. Which of the methods, (a) through (f), should Brad use to recognize revenue? Support your answer.
2. **Interpretive Question:** A member of Congress has introduced a bill that would require the SEC to crack down on lenient revenue recognition practices by shipbuilding companies. This bill would require Brad Company to use method (f) above. The "logic" behind the congressperson's bill is that no revenue should ever be recognized until the complete amount of cash is in hand. You have been hired as a lobbyist by Brad Company to speak against this bill. What arguments would you use on Capitol Hill to sway representatives to vote against this bill?

PROBLEM 6-2

RECOGNIZING REVENUE

The Ho Man Tin Tennis Club sells lifetime memberships for $20,000 each. A lifetime membership entitles a person to unlimited access to the club's tennis courts, weight room, exercise equipment, and swimming pool. Once a lifetime membership fee is paid, it is not refundable for any reason.

Judy Chan and her partners are the owners of Ho Man Tin Tennis Club. In order to overcome a cash shortage, they intend to seek investment funds from new partners. Judy and her partners are meeting with their accountant to provide information for preparation of financial statements. They are considering when they should recognize revenue from the sale of lifetime memberships.

Required: Answer the following questions:

1. When should the lifetime membership fees be recognized as revenue? Remember, they are nonrefundable.
2. **Interpretive Question:** What incentives would Judy and her partners have for recognizing the entire amount of the lifetime membership fee as revenue at the time it is collected? Since the entire amount will ultimately be recognized anyway, what difference does the timing make?

PROBLEM 6-3

General Ledger Software

SALES TRANSACTIONS

Company R and Company S entered into the following transactions:

a. Company R sold merchandise to Company S for $40,000, terms 2/10, n/30.
b. Prior to payment, Company S returned $3,000 of the merchandise for credit.
c. Company S paid Company R in full within the discount period.
d. Company S paid Company R in full after the discount period. [Assume that transaction (c) did not occur.]

Required: Prepare journal entries to record the transactions for Company R (the seller).

PROBLEM 6-4

CASH FRAUD

Mac Faber was the controller of the Lewiston National Bank. In his position of controller, he was in charge of all accounting functions. He wrote cashier's checks for the bank and reconciled the bank statement. He alone could approve exceptions to credit limits for bank customers, and even the internal auditors reported to him. Unknown to the bank, Mac had recently divorced and was supporting two households. In addition, many of his personal investments had soured, including a major farm implement dealership that had lost $40,000 in the last year. Several months after Mac had left the bank for another job, it was discovered that a vendor had paid twice and that the second payment had been deposited in Mac's personal account. Because Mac was not there to cover his tracks (as he had been on previous occasions), an investigation ensued. It was determined that Mac had used his position in the bank to steal $117,000 over a period of two years. Mac was prosecuted and sentenced to 30 months in a federal penitentiary.

Required:

1. What internal control weaknesses allowed Mac to perpetrate the fraud?
2. What motivated Mac to perpetrate the fraud?

PROBLEM 6-5

ANALYSIS OF ALLOWANCE FOR BAD DEBTS

Boulder View Corporation accounts for uncollectible accounts receivable using the allowance method.

As of December 31, 2002, the credit balance in Allowance for Bad Debts was $130,000. During 2003, credit sales totaled $10,000,000, $90,000 of accounts receivable were written off as uncollectible, and recoveries of accounts previously written off amounted to $15,000. An aging of accounts receivable at December 31, 2003, showed the following:

Classification of Receivable	Accounts Receivable Balance as of December 31, 2003	Percentage Estimated Uncollectible
Current	$1,140,000	2%
1–30 days past due	600,000	10
31–60 days past due	400,000	23
Over 60 days past due	120,000	75
	$2,260,000	

Required:

1. Prepare the journal entry to record bad debt expense for 2003, assuming bad debts are estimated using the aging of receivables method.
2. Record journal entries to account for the actual write-off of $90,000 uncollectible accounts receivable and the collection of $15,000 in receivables that had previously been written off.

PROBLEM 6-6

ACCOUNTING FOR ACCOUNTS RECEIVABLE

Assume that Dome Company had the following balances in its receivable accounts on December 31, 2002:

Accounts receivable	$400,000	
Allowance for bad debts	10,200	(credit balance)

Transactions during 2003 were as follows:

Gross credit sales	$1,600,000
Collections of accounts receivable ($1,560,000 less cash discounts of $20,000)	1,540,000
Sales returns and allowances (from credit sales)	10,000
Accounts receivable written off as uncollectible	6,000
Balance in Allowance for Bad Debts on December 31, 2003 (based on percent of total accounts receivable)	12,000

Required:

1. Prepare entries for the 2003 transactions.
2. What amount will Dome Company report for:
   a. Net sales in its 2003 income statement?
   b. Total accounts receivable on its balance sheet of December 31, 2003?

PROBLEM 6-7

ANALYSIS OF RECEIVABLES

Juniper Company was formed in 1993. Sales have increased on the average of 5% per year during its first ten years of existence, with total sales for 2002 amounting to $400,000. Since incorporation, Juniper Company has used the allowance method to account for uncollectible accounts receivable.

On January 1, 2003, the company's Allowance for Bad Debts had a credit balance of $5,000. During 2003, accounts totaling $3,500 were written off as uncollectible.

Required:

1. What does the January 1, 2003, credit balance of $5,000 in Allowance for Bad Debts represent?
2. Since Juniper Company wrote off $3,500 in uncollectible accounts receivable during 2003, was the prior year's estimate of uncollectible accounts receivable overstated?
3. Prepare journal entries to record:
   a. The $3,500 write-off of receivables during 2003.
   b. Juniper Company's 2003 bad debt expense, assuming an aging of the December 31, 2003, accounts receivable indicates that potential uncollectible accounts at year-end total $9,000.

PROBLEM 6-8

COMPUTING AND RECORDING BAD DEBT EXPENSE

During 2003, Wishbone Corporation had a total of $5,000,000 in sales, of which 80% were on credit. At year-end, the Accounts Receivable balance showed a total of $2,300,000, which had been aged as follows:

Age	Amount
Current	$1,900,000
1–30 days past due	200,000
31–60 days past due	100,000
61–90 days past due	70,000
Over 90 days past due	30,000
	$2,300,000

Prepare the journal entry required at year-end to record the bad debt expense under each of the following independent conditions. Assume, where applicable, that Allowance for Bad Debts had a credit balance of $5,500 immediately before these adjustments.

Required:

1. Use the direct write-off method. (Assume that $60,000 of accounts are determined to be uncollectible and are written off in a single year-end entry.)
2. Based on experience, uncollectible accounts existing at year-end are estimated to be 3% of total accounts receivable.
3. Based on experience, uncollectible accounts are estimated to be the sum of:

   1% of current accounts receivable
   6% of accounts 1–30 days past due
   10% of accounts 31–60 days past due
   20% of accounts 61–90 days past due
   30% of accounts over 90 days past due

PROBLEM 6-9

UNIFYING CONCEPTS: AGING OF ACCOUNTS RECEIVABLE AND UNCOLLECTIBLE ACCOUNTS

Delta Company has found that, historically, 0.5% of its current accounts receivable, 1% of accounts 1 to 30 days past due, 1.5% of accounts 31 to 60 days past due, 3% of accounts 61 to 90 days past due, and 10% of accounts over 90 days past due are uncollectible. The following schedule shows an aging of the accounts receivable as of December 31, 2003:

		Days Past Due			
	Current	1–30	31–60	61–90	Over 90
Balance	$45,600	$9,850	$4,100	$850	$195

The balances at December 31, 2003, in selected accounts are as follows. (Assume that the allowance method is used.)

Sales revenue	$120,096
Sales returns	1,209
Allowance for bad debts	113 (credit balance)

Required:

1. Given these data, make the necessary adjusting entry (or entries) for uncollectible accounts receivable on December 31, 2003.
2. On February 14, 2004, Lori Jacobs, a customer, informed Delta Company that she was going bankrupt and would not be able to pay her account of $46. Make the appropriate entry (or entries).
3. On June 29, 2004, Lori Jacobs was able to pay the amount she owed in full. Make the appropriate entry (or entries).

4. Assume that Allowance for Bad Debts at December 31, 2003, had a debit balance of $113 instead of a credit balance of $113. Make the necessary adjusting journal entry that would be needed on December 31, 2003.

PROBLEM 6-10

ESTIMATING UNCOLLECTIBLE ACCOUNTS

Ulysis Corporation makes and sells clothing to fashion stores throughout the country. On December 31, 2003, before adjusting entries were made, it had the following account balances on its books:

Accounts receivable	$ 2,320,000
Sales revenue, 2003 (60% were credit sales)	16,000,000
Allowance for bad debts (credit balance)	4,000

Required:

1. Make the appropriate adjusting entry on December 31, 2003, to record the allowance for bad debts if uncollectible accounts receivable are estimated to be 3% of accounts receivable.
2. Make the appropriate adjusting entry on December 31, 2003, to record the allowance for bad debts if uncollectible accounts receivable are estimated on the basis of an aging of accounts receivable; the aging schedule reveals the following:

	Balance of Accounts Receivable	Percent Estimated to Become Uncollectible
Current	$1,200,000	0.5%
1–30 days past due	800,000	1
31–60 days past due	200,000	4
61–90 days past due	80,000	20
Over 90 days past due	40,000	30

3. Now assume that on March 3, 2004, it was determined that a $64,000 account receivable from Petite Corners is uncollectible. Record the bad debt, assuming:
   a. The direct write-off method is used.
   b. The allowance method is used.
4. Further assume that on June 4, 2004, Petite Corners paid this previously written-off debt of $64,000. Record the payment, assuming:
   a. The direct write-off method had been used on March 3 to record the bad debt.
   b. The allowance method had been used on March 3 to record the bad debt.
5. **Interpretive Question:** Which method of accounting for bad debts, direct write-off or allowance, is generally used? Why?

PROBLEM 6-11

THE AGING METHOD

The following aging of accounts receivable is for Coby Company at the end of 2003:

Aging of Accounts Receivable
December 31, 2003

	Overall	Less Than 30 Days	31 to 60 Days	61 to 90 Days	Over 90 Days
Travis Campbell	$ 50,000	$ 40,000	$ 5,000	$ 2,000	$ 3,000
Linda Reed	35,000	31,000	4,000		
Jack Riding	110,000	100,000	10,000		
Joy Riddle	20,000	3,000	10,000	4,000	3,000
Afzal Shah	90,000	60,000	21,000	4,000	5,000
Edna Ramos	80,000	60,000	16,000		4,000
Totals	$385,000	$294,000	$66,000	$10,000	$15,000

Coby Company had a credit balance of $20,000 in its allowance for bad debts account at the beginning of 2003. Write-offs for the year totaled $16,500. Coby Company makes only one adjusting entry to record bad debt expense at the end of the year. Historically, Coby Company has experienced the following with respect to the collection of its accounts receivable:

Age of Account	Percentage Ultimately Uncollectible
Less than 30 days	1%
31–60 days	5
61–90 days	30
Over 90 days	90

Required:

1. Compute the appropriate balance of allowance for bad debts as of December 31, 2003.
2. Make the journal entry required to record this allowance for bad debts balance. Remember that the allowance account already has an existing balance.
3. What is Coby's net accounts receivable balance as of December 31, 2003?

PROBLEM 6-12

ANALYSIS OF ACCOUNTS RECEIVABLE QUANTITY AND QUALITY

The following accounts receivable information is for MaScare Company:

	2003	2002	2001
Accounts receivable	$100,000	$ 30,000	$ 50,000
Allowance for bad debts	4,000	2,000	3,000
Sales revenue	210,000	180,000	170,000

Required:

1. With the big increase in the Allowance for Bad Debts in 2003, MaScare Company is concerned that the creditworthiness of its customers declined from 2002 to 2003. Is there any support for this view in the accounts receivable data? Explain.
2. **Interpretive Question:** Is there any cause for alarm in the accounts receivable data for 2003? Explain.

expanded material

PROBLEM 6-13

PREPARING A BANK RECONCILIATION

Milton Company has just received the following monthly bank statement for June 2003.

Date	Checks	Deposits	Balance
June 01			$25,000
June 02	$ 150		24,850
June 03		$ 6,000	30,850
June 04	750		30,100
June 05	1,500		28,600
June 07	8,050		20,550

(continued)

Date	Checks	Deposits	Balance
June 09		$ 8,000	$28,550
June 10	$ 3,660		24,890
June 11	2,690		22,200
June 12		9,000	31,200
June 13	550		30,650
June 17	7,500		23,150
June 20		5,500	28,650
June 21	650		28,000
June 22	700		27,300
June 23		4,140†	31,440
June 25	1,000		30,440
June 30	50*		30,390
Totals	$27,250	$32,640	

*Bank service charge.
†Note collected, including $140 interest.

Data from the cash account of Milton Company for June are as follows:

June 1 balance $20,440

Checks written:		Deposits:	
June 1	$ 1,500	June 2	$ 6,000
4	8,500	5	8,000
6	2,690	10	9,000
8	550	18	5,500
9	7,500	30	6,000
12	650		$34,500
19	700		
22	1,000		
26	1,300		
27	1,360		
	$25,750		

At the end of May, Milton had three checks outstanding for a total of $4,560. All three checks were processed by the bank during June. There were no deposits outstanding at the end of May. It was discovered during the reconciliation process that a check for $8,050, written on June 4 for supplies, was improperly recorded on the books as $8,500.

Required:

1. Determine the amount of deposits in transit at the end of June.
2. Determine the amount of outstanding checks at the end of June.
3. Prepare a June bank reconciliation.
4. Prepare the journal entries to correct the cash account.
5. **Interpretive Question:** Why is it important that the cash account be reconciled on a timely basis?

PROBLEM 6-14

DETERMINING WHERE THE CASH WENT

Kim Lee, the bookkeeper for Briton Company, had never missed a day's work for the past ten years until last week. Since that time, he has not been located. You now suspect that Kim may have embezzled money from the company. The following bank reconciliation, prepared by Kim last month, is available to help you determine if a theft occurred:

Briton Company
Bank Reconciliation for August 2003
Prepared by Kim Lee

Balance per bank statement	$192,056	Balance per books.	$169,598
Additions to bank balance:		*Additions to book balance:*	
Deposits in transit.	8,000	Note collected by bank	250
		Interest earned	600
Deductions from bank balance:		*Deductions from book balance:*	
Outstanding checks:		NSF check.	(1,800)
#201.	(19,200)	Bank service charges.	(48)
#204.	(5,000)		
#205.	(4,058)		
#295.	(195)		
#565.	(1,920)		
#567.	(615)		
#568.	(468)		
Adjusted bank balance	**$168,600**	**Adjusted book balance**	**$168,600**

In examining the bank reconciliation, you decide to review canceled checks returned by the bank. You find that check stubs for check nos. 201, 204, 205, and 295 indicate that these checks were supposedly voided when written. All other bank reconciliation data have been verified as correct.

Required:

1. Compute the amount suspected stolen by Kim.
2. **Interpretive Question:** Describe how Kim accounted for the stolen money. What would have prevented the theft?

PROBLEM 6-15

ACCOUNTING FOR A NOTE RECEIVABLE

The following information is for Lyman Irrigation Company:

Mar. 1	Sold sprinkling pipe to Federated Farms for $16,000, terms 2/10, n/30 (omit entries for cost of goods sold or inventory).
Mar. 12	Accepted a $16,000, three-month, 10% note from Federated Farms in payment of its account.
June 12	Collected the note plus interest.

Required:

1. Prepare journal entries for the transactions.
2. **Interpretive Question:** What would be the purpose of Lyman "discounting" the note at a bank on April 30?

PROBLEM 6-16

ACCOUNTING FOR A NOTE RECEIVABLE

On May 1, your company accepted a $24,000, three-month, 12% note from a customer in exchange for services rendered.

Required:

1. As the accountant for the company, prepare an appropriate journal entry to record the acceptance of the note.
2. On August 1, the customer notified you that the note amount could not be repaid until October 1. You agreed on a new, two-month note with an interest rate of 18%. The face amount of this note includes the principal and accrued interest on the original note. Prepare the appropriate journal entry on August 1.
3. Prepare the appropriate entry to record the collection in full of the note plus interest on October 1.

PROBLEM 6-17

ACCOUNTING FOR A FOREIGN CURRENCY TRANSACTION

On December 19, 2003, Mr. Kitty Company performed services for Cartour Company. The contracted price for the services was 20,000 euros, to be paid on March 23, 2004. On Decem-

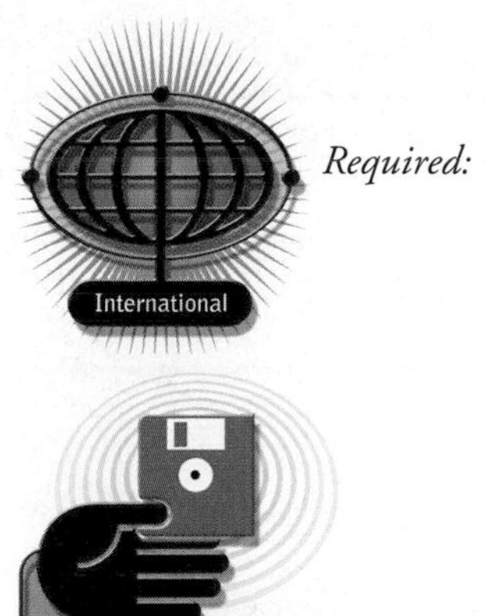

ber 19, 2003, one euro equaled $0.94. On December 31, 2003, one euro equaled $0.98, and on March 23, 2004, one euro equaled $0.91. Mr. Kitty is a U.S. company.

Required:

1. Make the journal entry on Mr. Kitty's books to record the provision of services on December 19, 2003.
2. Make the necessary adjusting entry on Mr. Kitty's books on December 31 to adjust the account receivable to its appropriate U.S. dollar value.
3. Make the journal entry on Mr. Kitty's books to record the collection of the 20,000 euros on March 23.
4. **Interpretive Question:** Why would Mr. Kitty, a U.S. company, agree to denominate the contract in euros instead of in U.S. dollars?

competency enhancement opportunities

- Analyzing Real Company Information
- International Case
- Ethics Case
- Writing Assignment
- The Debate
- Cumulative Spreadsheet Project
- Internet Search

The following additional assignments provide opportunities for students to develop critical thinking, ethical perspectives, oral and written communication skills, experience with electronic research, and teamwork through group and business activities.

ANALYZING REAL COMPANY INFORMATION

• *Analyzing 6-1 (Microsoft)*

The 1999 annual report for MICROSOFT is included in Appendix A. Locate that annual report and consider the following questions:

1. Provide the summary journal entry that Microsoft would have made to record its revenue for the fiscal year ended June 30, 1999 (assume all sales were on account).
2. Given Microsoft's beginning and ending balances in accounts receivable, along with your journal entry from Part 1, estimate the amount of cash collected from customers during the year.
3. Notice that Microsoft has an unearned revenue account. The balance in that account increased from 1998 to 1999. Provide the summary journal entry that was made to record that increase.
4. Locate Microsoft's note on revenue recognition. What is Microsoft's revenue recognition policy?

• *Analyzing 6-2 (Bank of America)*

BANK OF AMERICA is one of the oldest banks in America, as well as one of the largest. Founded in the late 1800s, Bank of America has grown from a strictly California-based bank to one with operations in over 20 states. Information from Bank of America's annual report follows. (Amounts are in millions.)

	1999	1998
Bad debt expense	$1,820	$2,920
Write-off of uncollectible accounts	2,582	3,050
Allowance for bad debts (year-end)	6,828	7,122

Using this information, answer the following questions:

1. Provide the journal entry made by Bank of America to record bad debt expense for 1999.
2. Provide the journal entry made by Bank of America to record the write-off of actual bad debts during 1999.
3. Estimate the amount of bad debts previously written off that Bank of America recovered in 1999.

• Analyzing 6-3 (Microsoft and IBM)

Information from comparative income statements and balance sheets for **MICROSOFT** and **IBM** is given below. (Amounts are in millions.)

	Microsoft		IBM	
	1999	1998	1999	1998
Sales	$19,747	$15,262	$87,548	$81,667
Accounts receivable	2,245	1,460	20,039	18,958

Use this information to answer the following questions:

1. Compute Microsoft's average collection period for 1999.
2. Compute IBM's average collection period for 1999.
3. Why do you think these two very profitable companies can have such large differences in their average collection period?

INTERNATIONAL CASE

• Samsung

The economic downturn in South Korea in late 1997 focused world attention on what had heretofore been viewed as one of the world's economic powerhouses. Symptomatic of the economic collapse was the freefall in Korea's currency, the won, which declined in value from 845 won per U.S. dollar on December 31, 1996, to 1,695 won per dollar on December 31, 1997.

When Korea's economy soured, many sought to blame the economy's unusual structure, which concentrates a large fraction of the economic activity in the hands of just a few companies, called *chaebol*. *Chaebol* are large Korean conglomerates (groups of loosely connected firms with central ownership) that are usually centered around a family-owned parent company. The growth of the *chaebol* in the years since the Korean War has been aided by government nurturing—it is said that the *chaebol* have received government assistance in getting loans and obtaining trading licenses, for example.

In Korea there are now four super-*chaebol*—**HYUNDAI**, **SAMSUNG**, **DAEWOO**, and **LUCKY GOLDSTAR**. Collectively, these four conglomerates account for between 40 and 45% of South Korea's gross national product.

Samsung, one of the four super-*chaebol*, was founded in 1938 in Taegu, Korea. The company had humble beginnings; its original products included fruit, dried seafood, flour, and noodles, and its original exports were squid and apples. Now, Samsung has a worldwide presence in electronics, machinery, automobiles, chemicals, and financial services. To illustrate the size of Samsung's operations, it is estimated that one out of every five televisions or monitors in the world was made by Samsung.

The following information is from Samsung's 1997 annual report. All numbers are in trillions of Korean won.

	1997	**1996**
Net sales	91.519	74.641
Accounts receivable	10.064	6.233

1. Did Samsung's sales increase in 1997, relative to 1996, in terms of U.S. dollars? Explain. What exchange rate information would allow you to make a more accurate calculation?
2. Compute Samsung's average collection period for both 1996 and 1997. Instead of using the average accounts receivable balance, use the end-of-year balance.
3. Comment on the change in the average collection period from 1996 to 1997, especially in light of the economic conditions in Korea in 1997.
4. What do you think happened to Samsung's accounts payable balance in 1997, relative to 1996? Explain.

ETHICS CASE

• Changing Our Estimates in Order to Meet Analysts' Expectations

John Verner is the controller for BioMedic, Inc., a biotechnology company. John is finishing his preparation of the preliminary financial statements for a meeting of the board of directors scheduled for later in the day. At the board's prior meeting, members discussed the need to report earnings of at least $1.32 per share. It was not mentioned specifically at the meeting, but everyone on the board knows that financial analysts have forecast that BioMedic will report earnings per share (EPS) of $1.32; failure to meet analysts' expectations could hurt BioMedic's chances of going forward with its planned initial public offering (IPO) later this year.

Unfortunately for John and the company, the preliminary EPS figure is coming up short. John knows that the board will take a serious look at the estimates and assumptions made in preparing the income statement. In anticipation of the board's review, John has identified the following two issues:

1. In the past, bad debt expense has been computed using the percentage of sales method. The percentage used has varied between 3 and 3.5%. This year, John assumed a rate of 3%. If he were to modify his estimate of bad debt expense to 2.5% of sales, income would increase by $700,000.
2. BioMedic, Inc., offers a warranty on many of the products it sells. Like bad debt expense, warranty expense is computed as a percentage of sales. John is considering modifying his estimate of warranty expense from 1.4% of sales down to 1.1%. This modification would result in a $420,000 increase in net income.

These two changes, considered together, would result in BioMedic being able to report EPS of $1.33 per share, thereby allowing the company to publicly announce that it had exceeded analysts' expectations. Without these changes, BioMedic will report EPS of $1.21 per share.

What issues should John consider before he makes the changes to the income statement? Would John be doing something wrong by making these changes? Would John be breaking the law?

WRITING ASSIGNMENT

• *Revenue Recognition for Health Clubs*

The health fitness business has become increasingly popular as the sedentary lifestyle of most Americans has caused a large percentage of the population to feel, and be, out of shape. Health clubs have popped up all over, and with these clubs come some interesting accounting issues. Members typically sign up for one year and pay an up-front fee, followed by a monthly payment. The up-front fee covers, among other things, a health assessment by a club expert as well as a customized training program. For the monthly fee, members get the use of the facilities. The big accounting question is: How should the up-front fee be accounted for? Can the entire amount of the up-front fee be recognized at the beginning of the contract, or should it be recognized over the course of the year? Prepare a one-page paper explaining your point of view.

THE DEBATE

• *Bad Debt Expense: Relevance Versus Reliability*

When it comes to recognizing bad debt expense, the allowance method is used because it complies with the matching principle (e.g., expenses are matched with revenues in the period in which those revenues are earned). However, the allowance method requires estimation, and the estimates may not be reliable. An alternative is to use the direct write-off method. Under the direct write-off method, when a receivable is deemed worthless it is written off, and the bad debt expense is recognized at that time. This method requires no estimates and is thus more reliable.

Divide your group into two teams.

- One team represents "The Direct Write-Off Method." Prepare a two-minute oral argument supporting the use of this method.
- The other team represents "The Allowance Method." Prepare a two-minute presentation supporting your position.

CUMULATIVE SPREADSHEET PROJECT

This spreadsheet assignment is a continuation of the spreadsheet assignments given in earlier chapters. If you completed those spreadsheets, you have a head start on this one. If needed, review the spreadsheet assignment for Chapter 4 to refresh your memory on how to construct forecasted financial statements.

1. Handyman wishes to prepare a forecasted balance sheet and income statement for 2004. Use the original financial statement numbers for 2003 [given in part (1) of the Cumulative Spreadsheet Project assignment in Chapter 2] as the basis for the forecast, along with the following additional information:
   a. Sales in 2004 are expected to increase by 40% over 2003 sales of $700.
   b. In 2004, Handyman expects to acquire new property, plant, and equipment costing $80.

c. The $160 in other operating expenses reported in 2003 includes $5 of depreciation expense.
d. No new long-term debt will be acquired in 2004.
e. No cash dividends will be paid in 2004.
f. New short-term loans payable will be acquired in an amount sufficient to make Handyman's current ratio in 2004 exactly equal to 2.0.

Note: These statements were constructed as part of the spreadsheet assignment in Chapter 4; you can use that spreadsheet as a starting point if you have completed that assignment.

For this exercise, the current assets are expected to behave as follows:

i. Cash and inventory will increase at the same rate as sales.
ii. The forecasted amount of accounts receivable in 2004 is determined using the forecasted value for the average collection period. For simplicity, do the computations using the end-of-period accounts receivable balance instead of the average balance. The average collection period for 2004 is expected to be 14.08 days.

Clearly state any additional assumptions that you make.

2. Repeat (1), with the following change in assumptions:
   a. Average collection period is expected to be 9.06 days.
   b. Average collection period is expected to be 20.00 days.
3. Comment on the differences in the forecasted values of accounts receivable in 2004 under each of the following assumptions about the average collection period: 14.08 days, 9.06 days, and 20.00 days. Under which assumption will Handyman's forecasted cash flow from operating activities be higher? Explain.

INTERNET SEARCH

• *Yahoo!*

YAHOO! is one of the best-known Internet brand names in the world. Access Yahoo!'s Web site at **http://www.yahoo.com** and answer the following questions. Sometimes Web addresses change, so if this address doesn't work, access the Web site for this textbook (**http://albrecht.swcollege.com**) for an updated link.

1. On its home page, Yahoo! has a link to information about job openings at the company. Use that link to find out what kind of benefits Yahoo! offers its employees.
2. Look at the current job openings at Yahoo! and identify one opening in the general field of finance.
3. Yahoo! is proud of the proliferation of "local Yahoos!" based in foreign countries. List the Asian countries in which a local Yahoo! is currently in operation.
4. Search the Yahoo! press release archive to find the most recent announcement about quarterly financial results. What was Yahoo!'s reported total revenue in the most recent quarter?

Inventory

chapter **f7**

learning objectives

After studying this chapter, you should be able to:

1. Identify what items and costs should be included in inventory and cost of goods sold.
2. Account for inventory purchases and sales using both a perpetual and a periodic inventory system.
3. Calculate cost of goods sold using the results of an inventory count and understand the impact of errors in ending inventory on reported cost of goods sold.
4. Apply the four inventory cost flow alternatives: specific identification, FIFO, LIFO, and average cost.
5. Use financial ratios to evaluate a company's inventory level.

expanded material

6. Analyze the impact of inventory errors on reported cost of goods sold.
7. Describe the complications that arise when LIFO or average cost is used with a perpetual inventory system.
8. Apply the lower-of-cost-or-market method of accounting for inventory.
9. Explain the gross margin method of estimating inventories.

SEARS, ROEBUCK & COMPANY began as the result of an inventory mistake. In 1886, a shipment of gold watches was mistakenly sent to a jeweler in Redwood Falls, Minnesota. When the jeweler refused to accept delivery of the unwanted watches, they were purchased by an enterprising railroad agent who saw an opportunity to make some money. Richard Sears sold all of those watches, ordered more, and started the **R. W. SEARS WATCH COMPANY**. The next year, Sears moved his operation to Chicago, where he found a partner in watchmaker Alvah Roebuck, and in 1893 they incorporated under the name "Sears, Roebuck & Co."

The company's initial growth was fueled by mail-order sales to farmers. Sears bought goods in volume from manufacturers. Then, taking advantage of cheap parcel post and rural free delivery (RFD) rates, Sears shipped the goods directly to the customers, thereby bypassing the profit markups of the chain of middlemen usually standing between manufacturers and farmers. Sales growth was partially driven by the persuasive advertising copy written by Richard Sears for the famous Sears catalog. In fact, his product descriptions have been politely called "fanciful." But the company compensated by backing its products with an unconditional money-back guarantee for dissatisfied customers.

The next wave of growth at Sears began in 1925 when the first Sears retail store was opened in Chicago. The shift from mail-order catalog sales to retail outlet sales paralleled the rise in popularity of the automobile in the United States. The automobile made it practical for rural customers to shop in the city. Reflecting the importance of the automobile, Sears pioneered the provision of free parking lots next to its stores. In the post–World War II boom, Sears' sales skyrocketed, leaving chief rival **MONTGOMERY WARD** far behind.

The 1980s was a decade of diversification at Sears. Actually, the diversification had begun in 1931 when Sears started selling **ALLSTATE** auto insurance, first by mail and then from its retail locations. In the 1980s, Sears acquired **DEAN WITTER**, a financial services firm, and **COLDWELL BANKER**, a real estate firm. In addition, Sears launched the Discover® credit card and backed Prodigy®, the first widespread online service (a joint project with **IBM** and **CBS**).

In the early 1990s, the diversified Sears empire began to show increasing weakness, culminating in a reported loss of almost $2.3 billion in 1992. The company's management responded by going back to the basics of retail marketing. The financial services operations (including the Discover card) and the real estate operations (along with the famous Sears Tower in Chicago) were sold. Sears focused on clothing sales in its mall-based stores and appliance and automotive product sales in its off-the-mall stores. In addition, Sears returned to emphasizing its in-house Sears credit card. In 1999, almost half of all Sears' sales were financed with the Sears credit card. During 1999, over 39 million people used the Sears card, and over 21 million owed Sears money as of the end of the year.

setting the stage

Sears is continuing to leverage one of its biggest assets—its in-house brand names such as Kenmore and Craftsman. In fact, sales of Sears appliances and tools make up two-thirds of the company's annual revenue. Currently, Sears is the leader in appliance sales and outsells the next 12 competitors combined. Sears has also streamlined its purchasing, cut 30% of its dealer network, and is keeping more popular fashions in stock in its clothing department. This streamlining has resulted in higher inventory turnover. As a result of these changes and others, Sears' stock price has risen from $15 per share in 1992 to as high as $50 per share in 1999.[1]

Like Sears, every business has products or services that it sells. Some companies, usually referred to as diversified companies or conglomerates, sell many unrelated products and services, just as Sears did in the 1980s. Other companies focus on a core set of products or services, as Sears did in the 1990s.

In Chapter 6, the focus was on revenues and receivables arising from the sale of products and services. In this chapter, the focus is on accounting for the products and services that are sold.

1 This description is based on the Sears Company History at http://www.sears.com; "Sears, Roebuck and Co.," *International Directory of Company Histories*, Vol. 18 (Detroit: St. James Press, 1997), pp. 475–479.

Exhibit 7-1 shows how the financial statements are affected by the material covered in this chapter. The inventory and accounts payable accounts on the balance sheet, cost of goods sold on the income statement, and payments for inventory on the statement of cash flows are discussed in this chapter.

Traditionally, companies have been divided into two groups: service companies and product companies. Companies such as hotels, cable TV networks, banks, carpet cleaners, and firms of lawyers, accountants, or engineers sell services. In contrast, supermarkets, steel mills, and book stores sell products. Because the practice of accounting evolved in a business environment dominated by manufacturing and merchandising firms, the accounting for service companies is significantly less developed than the accounting for companies that sell products. In this chapter we discuss traditional accounting for product companies, emphasizing cost of goods sold and inventory. In Chapter 8 we will discuss operating expenses that are common to both service and product firms. Further discussion of the developing area of accounting for service companies is included in Chapter 3 in the management accounting part of this text.

STOP & THINK The clear separation between product and service companies is disappearing. For example, does **MICROSOFT** sell a product or a service? What about **MCDONALD'S**—product or service?

Inventory accounting is considerably more complex for manufacturing firms than for merchandising firms. In a retail or wholesale business, the cost of goods sold is simply the costs incurred in purchasing the merchandise sold during the period; inventory is simply the cost of products purchased and not yet sold. Manufacturing firms, however, produce the goods they sell, so inventory and cost of goods sold must include all manufacturing costs of the products produced and sold. Because it is much easier to understand the concept of inventory and cost of goods sold in the context of retail and wholesale firms, manufacturing firms will not be considered in detail in this chapter. The details of inventory accounting for manufacturing firms will be covered in Chapter 2 in the management accounting part of this text.

Fifty years ago, inventory was arguably the most important asset on the balance sheet. However, changes in the economy have led to a decrease in the relative importance of inventory. For example, as illustrated in Exhibit 7-2, inventory for the 50 largest companies in the United States declined steadily from 15.4% of total assets in 1987 to 7.4% of total assets in 1998. This trend is a

exhibit 7-1 Financial Statement Items Covered in This Chapter

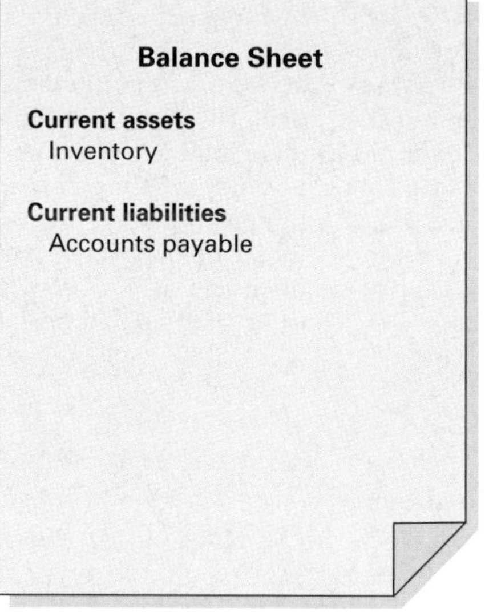

Statement of Cash Flows

Operating activities
Payments for inventory

Income Statement

Cost of goods sold

exhibit 7-2 How Much Inventory Do Companies Have?

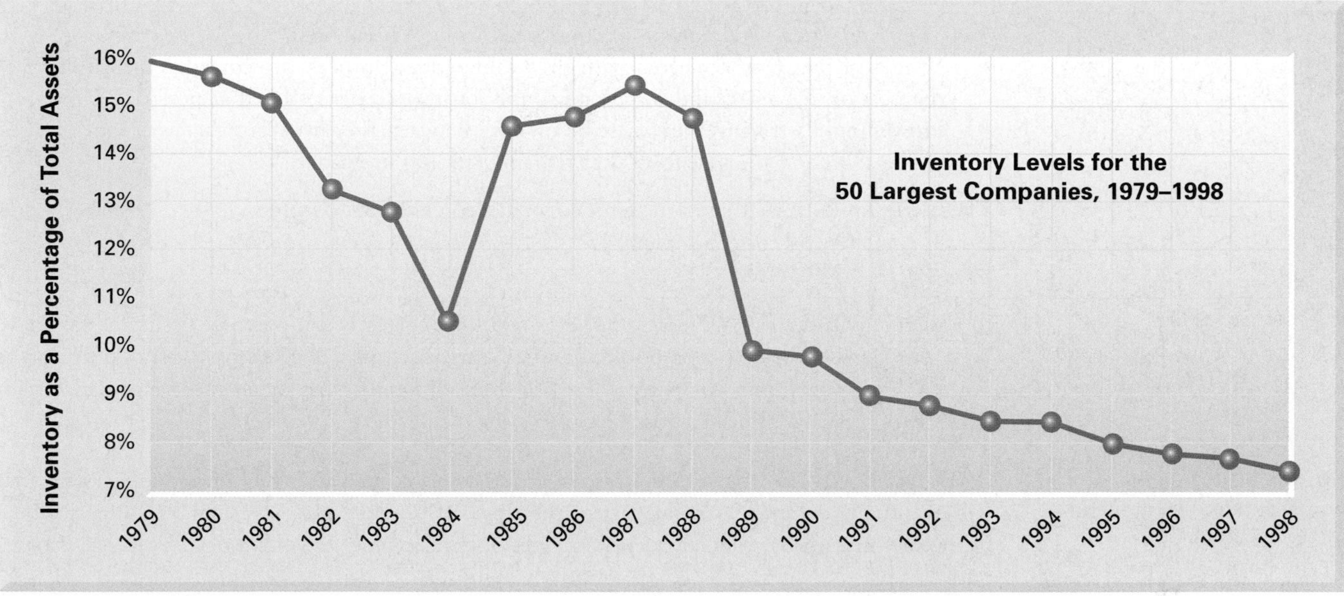

Source: Standard and Poor's *COMPUSTAT.*

result of two factors: more efficient management of inventory because of improved information technology and a decrease in the prominence of old-style, smokestack industries that carried large inventories. Companies in the growth industries of services, technology, and information often have little or no inventory.

1

Identify what items and costs should be included in inventory and cost of goods sold.

inventory Goods held for resale.

cost of goods sold The expenses incurred to purchase or manufacture the merchandise sold during a period.

INVENTORY AND COST OF GOODS SOLD

Inventory is the name given to goods that are either manufactured or purchased for resale in the normal course of business. A car dealer's inventory is comprised of automobiles; a grocery store's inventory consists of vegetables, meats, dairy products, canned goods, and bakery items; SEARS' inventory is composed of shirts, appliances, DieHard® batteries, and more. Like other items of value, such as cash or equipment, inventory is classified as an asset and reported on the balance sheet. When products are sold, they are no longer assets. The costs to purchase or manufacture the products must be removed from the asset classification (inventory) on the balance sheet and reported on the income statement as an expense—**cost of goods sold.**

The time line in Exhibit 7-3 illustrates the business issues involved with inventory.

exhibit 7-3 Time Line of Business Issues Involved with Inventory

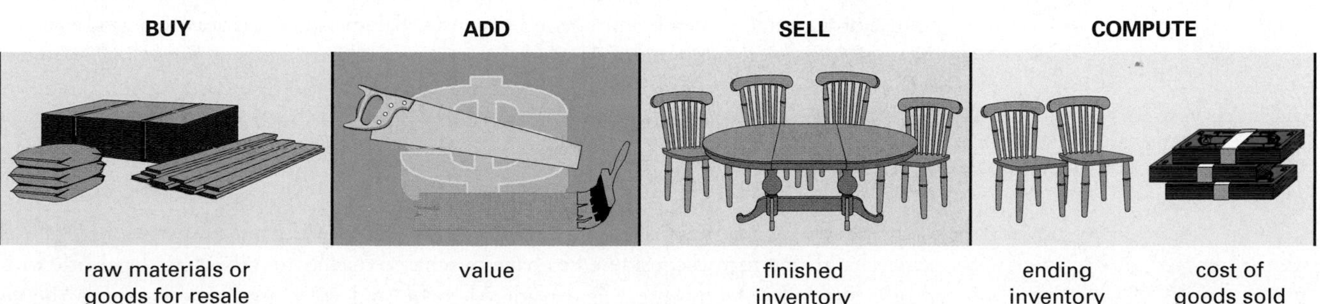

The accounting questions associated with the items in the time line are as follows:

- When is inventory considered to have been purchased—when it is ordered, shipped, received, or paid for?
- Similarly, when is the inventory considered to have been sold?
- Which of the costs associated with the "value added" process are considered to be part of the cost of inventory, and which are simply business expenses for that period?
- How should total inventory cost be divided between the inventory that was sold (cost of goods sold) and the inventory that remains (ending inventory)?

These questions are addressed in the following sections of the chapter.

What Is Inventory?

In a merchandising firm, either wholesale or retail, inventory is composed of the items that have been purchased in order to be resold. In a supermarket, milk is inventory, a shopping cart is not. In a manufacturing company, there are three different types of inventory: raw materials, work in process, and finished goods.

raw materials Materials purchased for use in manufacturing products.

RAW MATERIALS **Raw materials** are goods acquired in a relatively undeveloped state that will eventually compose a major part of the finished product. If you are making bicycles, one of the raw materials is tubular steel. For a computer assembler, raw materials inventory is composed of plastic, wires, and INTEL Pentium® chips.

work in process Partially completed units in production.

WORK IN PROCESS **Work in process** consists of partially finished products. When you take a tour of a manufacturing plant, you are seeing work-in-process inventory.

finished goods Manufactured products ready for sale.

FINISHED GOODS **Finished goods** are the completed products waiting for sale. A completed car rolling off the automobile assembly line is part of finished goods inventory.

What Costs Are Included in Inventory Cost?

Inventory cost consists of all costs involved in buying the inventory and preparing it for sale. In the case of raw materials or goods acquired for resale by a merchandising firm, cost includes the purchase price, freight, and receiving and storage costs.

The cost of work-in-process inventory is the sum of the costs of the raw materials, the production labor, and some share of the manufacturing overhead required to keep the factory running. The cost of an item in finished goods inventory is the total of the materials, labor, and overhead costs used in the production process for that item. As you can imagine, accumulating these costs and calculating a cost per unit is quite a demanding task. The cost of a finished automobile includes the cost of the steel and rubber; the salaries and wages of assembly workers, inspectors, and testers; the factory insurance; the workers' pension benefits; and much more. This costing process is a key part of management accounting and is covered in Chapter 2 in the management accounting part of the text.

The costs just described are all costs expended in order to get inventory produced and ready to sell. These costs are appropriately included in inventory costs. Those costs incurred in the sales effort itself are *not* inventory costs, but instead should be reported as operating expenses in the period in which they are incurred. For example, the costs of maintaining the finished goods warehouse or the retail showroom are period expenses. Salespersons' salaries are period expenses, as is the cost of advertising (a more detailed discussion of advertising is included in Chapter 8). In addition, general nonfactory administrative costs are also period expenses. Examples are the costs of the corporate headquarters and the company president's salary.

Who Owns the Inventory?

As a general rule, goods should be included in the inventory of the business holding legal title. So, a merchandising firm is considered to have purchased inventory once it has legal title to the inventory. Similarly, the inventory is considered to be sold when legal title passes to the customer. In most cases, this "legal title" rule is easy to apply—if you go into a business and look around, it is probably safe to assume that the inventory you see belongs to that business. In the case of goods in transit and goods on consignment, however, this "legal title" rule can be rather difficult to apply.

FOB (free-on-board) destination A business term meaning that the seller of merchandise bears the shipping costs and maintains ownership until the merchandise is delivered to the buyer.

FOB (free-on-board) shipping point A business term meaning that the buyer of merchandise bears the shipping costs and acquires ownership at the point of shipment.

consignment An arrangement whereby merchandise owned by one party, the consignor, is sold by another party, the consignee, usually on a commission basis.

GOODS IN TRANSIT When goods are being shipped from the seller to the buyer, who owns the inventory that is on a truck or railroad car—the seller or the buyer? If the seller pays for the shipping costs, the arrangement is known as **FOB (free-on-board) destination**, and the seller owns the merchandise from the time it is shipped until it is delivered to the buyer. If the buyer pays the shipping costs, the arrangement is known as **FOB (free-on-board) shipping point**, and the buyer owns the merchandise during transit. Thus, in determining which items should be counted and included in the inventory balance for a period, a company must note the amount of merchandise in transit and the terms under which it is being shipped. In all cases, merchandise should be included in the inventory of the party who owns it; for goods in transit, this is generally the party who is paying the shipping costs. The impact of shipping terms on the ownership of goods in transit is summarized in Exhibit 7-4.

GOODS ON CONSIGNMENT Sometimes the inventory a firm stocks in its warehouse has not actually been purchased from suppliers. With a **consignment** arrangement, suppliers (the consignors) provide inventory for resale while retaining ownership of the inventory until it is sold. The firm selling the merchandise (the consignee) merely stocks and sells the merchandise for the supplier/owner and receives a commission on any sales as payment for services rendered. Through a consignment arrangement, the manufacturer enables dealers to acquire a broad sample of inventory without incurring the purchase and finance charges required to actually buy the inventory. It is extremely important that goods being held on consignment not be included in the inventory of the firm holding the goods for sale even though they are physically on that firm's premises. It is equally important that the supplier/owner properly include all such goods in its records even though the inventory is not on its premises.

Auditing goods in transit and consigned inventory presents the auditor with a special set of problems. Inventory that is on the premises may not belong to the company because the goods are held on consignment. On the other hand, goods that are in transit in trucks and boats scattered around the world may belong to the company and should be included in the inventory count.

An example of a company that successfully uses consignment sales as part of its business strategy is INTERNATIONAL AIRLINE SUPPORT GROUP, INC. This company is a leading distributor of aircraft spare parts for large jet airplanes. The company uses consignments because, as stated in its annual report, this arrangement allows it "to obtain parts inventory on a favorable basis without committing its capital to purchasing inventory." In the fourth quarter of 1999, the company realized a 35% increase in earnings as a result of selling surplus BOEING 747 parts on behalf of GATX CORPORATION.

exhibit 7-4 Ownership Transfer for Goods in Transit

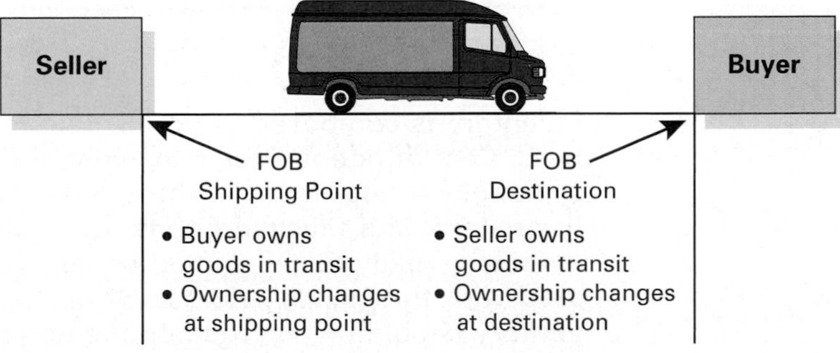

business environment essay

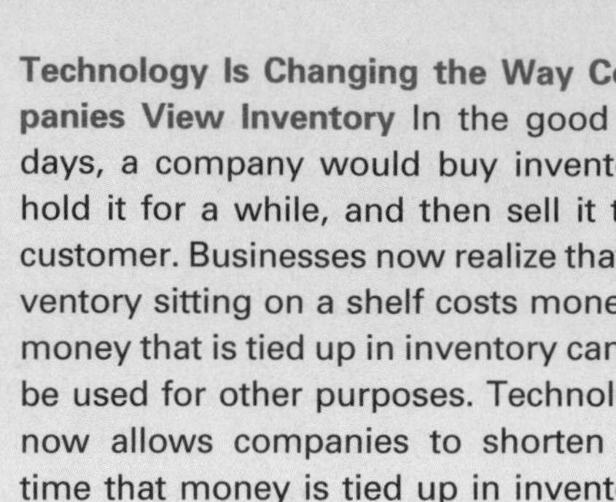

Technology Is Changing the Way Companies View Inventory In the good old days, a company would buy inventory, hold it for a while, and then sell it to a customer. Businesses now realize that inventory sitting on a shelf costs money—money that is tied up in inventory cannot be used for other purposes. Technology now allows companies to shorten the time that money is tied up in inventory. An entire discipline, supply-chain management, has developed to determine the most cost-efficient method for procuring and moving raw materials, work in process, finished goods, and items that have been sold from the supplier to the producer to the eventual end user.

The relationship between PROCTER & GAMBLE (P&G) and WAL-MART provides an example of how technology is being used to manage inventory. In 1999, Wal-Mart was easily P&G's largest customer, accounting for 12% of its sales. Using electronic data interchange (EDI), P&G has access to certain portions of Wal-Mart's inventory data. When Wal-Mart's inventory reaches a certain level, P&G automatically processes and ships an order to the appropriate Wal-Mart warehouse to ensure that Wal-Mart never is out of stock of P&G products. Companies are able to establish such mutually beneficial relationships because technology now allows the sharing of information at a very low cost.

Ending Inventory and Cost of Goods Sold

cost of goods available for sale The cost of all merchandise available for sale during the period; equal to the sum of beginning inventory and net purchases.

Inventory purchased or manufactured during the period is added to beginning inventory, and the total cost of this inventory is called the **cost of goods available for sale**. At the end of an accounting period, total cost of goods available for sale must be allocated between inventory still remaining (to be reported in the balance sheet as an asset) and inventory sold during the period (to be reported in the income statement as an expense, Cost of Goods Sold).

This cost allocation process is extremely important because the more cost that is said to remain in ending inventory, the less cost is reported as cost of goods sold in the income statement. This is why accurately determining who owns the inventory is such a big issue. Making a mistake with inventory ownership will result in misstating both the income statement and the balance sheet. For this reason, accountants must be careful of inventory errors because they directly affect reported net income. The impact of inventory errors is illustrated later in the chapter.

The cost allocation process also involves a significant amount of accounting judgment. Identical inventory items are usually purchased at varying prices throughout the year, so to calculate the amount of ending inventory and cost of goods sold, the accountant must determine which items (the low cost or high cost) remain and which were sold. Again, this decision can directly affect the amount of reported cost of goods sold and net income. The use of inventory cost flow assumptions is discussed later in the chapter.

to summarize

Inventory is composed of goods held for sale in the normal course of business. Cost of goods sold is the cost of inventory sold during the period. For a manufacturing firm, the three types of inventory are raw materials, work in process, and finished goods. All costs incurred in producing and getting inventory ready to sell should be added to inventory cost. The costs associated with the selling effort itself are operating expenses of the period. Inventory should be recorded on the books of the company holding legal title.

At the end of an accounting period, the total cost of goods available for sale during the period must be allocated between ending inventory and cost of goods sold.

2

Account for inventory purchases and sales using both a perpetual and a periodic inventory system.

ACCOUNTING FOR INVENTORY PURCHASES AND SALES

To begin a more detailed study of inventory accounting, we must first establish a solid understanding of the journal entries used to record inventory transactions. The accounting procedures for recording purchases and sales using both a periodic and a perpetual inventory system are detailed in this section.

Overview of Perpetual and Periodic Systems

Some businesses track changes in inventory levels on a continuous basis, recording each individual purchase and sale to maintain a running total of the inventory balance. This is called a perpetual inventory system. Other businesses rely on quarterly or yearly inventory counts to reveal which inventory items have been sold. This is called a periodic inventory system.

PERPETUAL You own a discount appliance superstore. Your biggest-selling items are washers, dryers, refrigerators, microwaves, and dishwashers. You advertise your weekly sale items on local TV stations, and your sales volume is quite heavy. You have 50 salespeople who work independently of one another. You have found that customers get very upset if they come to buy an advertised item and you have run out. In this business environment, would it make sense to keep a running total of the quantity remaining of each inventory item and update it each time a sale is made? Yes, the benefit of having current information on each inventory item would make it worthwhile to spend a little extra time to update the inventory records when a sale is made.

perpetual inventory system A system of accounting for inventory in which detailed records of the number of units and the cost of each purchase and sales transaction are prepared throughout the accounting period.

This appliance store would probably use a **perpetual inventory system**. With a perpetual system, inventory records are updated whenever a purchase or a sale is made. In this way, the inventory records at any given time reflect how many of each inventory item should be in the warehouse or out on the store shelves. A perpetual system is most often used when each individual inventory item has a relatively high value or when there are large costs to running out of or overstocking specific items.

PERIODIC You operate a newsstand in a busy metropolitan subway station. Almost all of your sales occur during the morning and the evening rush hours. You sell a diverse array of items—newspapers, magazines, pens, snacks, and other odds and ends. During rush hour, your business is a fast-paced pressure cooker; the longer you take with one customer, the more chance that the busy commuters waiting in line for service will tire of waiting and you will lose sales. In this business environment, would it make sense to make each customer wait while you meticulously check off on an inventory sheet exactly which items were sold? No, the delay caused by this detailed bookkeeping would cause you to lose customers. It makes more sense to wait until the end of the day, count up what inventory you still have left, compare that to what you started with, and use those numbers to deduce how many of each inventory item you sold during the day.

periodic inventory system A system of accounting for inventory in which cost of goods sold is determined and inventory is adjusted at the end of the accounting period, not when merchandise is purchased or sold.

This subway newsstand scenario is an example of a situation where a **periodic inventory system** is appropriate. With a periodic system, inventory records are not updated when a sale is made; only the dollar amount of the sale is recorded. Periodic systems are most often used when inventory is composed of a large number of diverse items, each with a relatively low value.

IMPACT OF INFORMATION TECHNOLOGY Over the past 25 years, advances in information technology have lowered the cost of maintaining a perpetual inventory system. As a result, more businesses have adopted perpetual systems so that they can more closely track inven-

A newsstand will wait until the end of the day to count inventory by comparing what items it started with to what is left. This is an example of a periodic inventory system.

tory levels. The most visible manifestation of this trend is in supermarkets. Twenty years ago, the checkout clerk rang up the price of each item on a cash register. After the customers walked out of the store with their groceries, the store knew the total amount of the purchase but did not know which individual items had been sold. This was a periodic inventory system. Now, with laser scanning equipment tied into the supermarket's computer system, most supermarkets operate under a perpetual system. The store manager knows exactly what you bought and exactly how many of each item should still be left on the store shelves.

STOP & THINK If you buy your groceries with a credit card or a bank debit card, what kind of information can the supermarket accumulate about you?

Perpetual and Periodic Journal Entries

The following transactions for Grantsville Clothing Store will be used to illustrate the differences in bookkeeping procedures between a business using a perpetual inventory system and one using a periodic inventory system:

a. Purchased on account: 1,000 shirts at a cost of $10 each for a total of $10,000.
b. Purchased on account: 300 pairs of pants at a cost of $18 each for a total of $5,400.
c. Paid cash for separate shipping costs on the shirts purchased in (a), $970. The supplier of the pants purchased in (b) included the shipping costs in the $18 purchase price.
d. Returned 30 of the shirts (costing $300) to the supplier because they were stained.
e. Paid for the shirt purchase. A 2% discount was given on the $9,700 bill [(1,000 purchased − 30 returned) × $10] because of payment within the ten-day discount period (payment terms were 2/10, n/30).
f. Paid $5,400 for the pants purchase. No discount was allowed because payment was made after the discount period.
g. Sold on account: 600 shirts at a price of $25 each for a total of $15,000.
h. Sold on account: 200 pairs of pants at a price of $40 each for a total of $8,000.
i. Accepted return of 50 shirts by dissatisfied customers.

The journal entries for the perpetual inventory system should seem familiar to you—a perpetual system has been assumed in all earlier chapters of the text. A perpetual system was assumed because it is logical and is the system all companies would choose if there were no cost to updating the inventory records each time a sale or purchase is made. As mentioned, a periodic inventory system is sometimes a practical necessity.

PURCHASES With a perpetual system, all purchases are added (debited) directly to Inventory. With a periodic system, the inventory balance is only updated using an inventory count at the end of the period; inventory purchases during the period are recorded in a temporary holding account called Purchases. As will be illustrated later, at the end of the period, the balance in Purchases is closed to Inventory in connection with the computation of cost of goods sold.

Entries (a) and (b) to record the shirt and pants purchases are given below:

	Perpetual			Periodic		
a.	Inventory	10,000		Purchases	10,000	
	Accounts Payable		10,000	Accounts Payable		10,000
b.	Inventory	5,400		Purchases	5,400	
	Accounts Payable		5,400	Accounts Payable		5,400

TRANSPORTATION COSTS The cost of transporting the inventory is an additional inventory cost. Sometimes, as with the pants in the Grantsville Clothing example, the shipping cost is already included in the purchase price, so a separate entry to record the transportation costs is not needed. When a separate payment is made for transportation costs, it is recorded as follows:

	Perpetual			Periodic		
c.	Inventory	970		Freight In	970	
	Cash		970	Cash		970

With a perpetual inventory system, transportation costs are added directly to the inventory balance. With a periodic inventory system, another temporary holding account, Freight In, is created, and transportation costs are accumulated in this account during the period. Like the purchases account, Freight In is closed to Inventory at the end of the period in connection with the computation of cost of goods sold.

PURCHASE RETURNS With a perpetual system, the return of unsatisfactory merchandise to the supplier results in a decrease in Inventory. In addition, since no payment will have to be made for the returned merchandise, Accounts Payable is reduced by the same amount. With a periodic system, the amount of the returned merchandise is recorded in yet another temporary holding account called Purchase Returns. Purchase Returns is a contra account to Purchases and is also closed to Inventory as part of the computation of cost of goods sold.

	Perpetual			Periodic		
d.	Accounts Payable	300		Accounts Payable	300	
	Inventory		300	Purchase Returns		300

If the returned merchandise had already been paid for, the supplier would most likely return the purchase price. In this case, the debit would be to Cash instead of to Accounts Payable.

PURCHASE DISCOUNTS As discussed in Chapter 6, sellers sometimes offer inducements for credit customers to pay quickly. In this example, Grantsville Clothing takes advantage of purchase discounts to save money on the payment for the shirts. The amount of the purchase discount is $194 ($9,700 × 0.02), so the total payment for the shirts is $9,506 ($9,700 − $194). The amount recorded for inventory should reflect the actual amount paid to purchase the inventory. With a perpetual inventory system, this is shown by subtracting the purchase discount amount from the inventory account. With a periodic inventory system, another holding account is created to accumulate purchase discounts taken during the period.

	Perpetual			Periodic		
e.	Accounts Payable	9,700		Accounts Payable	9,700	
	Inventory		194	Purchase Discounts		194
	Cash		9,506	Cash		9,506
f.	Accounts Payable	5,400		Accounts Payable	5,400	
	Cash		5,400	Cash		5,400

fyi

In practice, this same inventory adjustment information (e.g., Freight In, Purchase Returns, etc.) would be maintained in supplemental records under a perpetual inventory system. Such information is useful to management in evaluating company purchasing practices.

Note that the payment for the pants is made after the discount period, so the full amount must be paid. Since this transaction had no impact on Inventory, the entry is the same for both the perpetual and the periodic system.

In terms of journal entries, you should recognize that the difference between a perpetual and a periodic inventory system is that all adjustments to inventory under a perpetual system are entered directly in the inventory account; with a periodic system, all inventory adjustments are accumulated in an array of temporary holding accounts: Purchases, Freight In, Purchase Returns, and Purchase Discounts.

SALES The sales of shirts and pants would be recorded as follows:

	Perpetual			Periodic		
g.	Accounts Receivable	15,000		Accounts Receivable	15,000	
	Sales (600 × $25)		15,000	Sales		15,000
	Cost of Goods Sold	6,000				
	Inventory (600 × $10)		6,000			
h.	Accounts Receivable	8,000		Accounts Receivable	8,000	
	Sales (200 × $40)		8,000	Sales		8,000
	Cost of Goods Sold	3,600				
	Inventory (200 × $18)		3,600			

These entries reflect the primary difference between a perpetual and a periodic inventory system—with a periodic system, no attempt is made to recognize cost of goods sold on a transaction-by-transaction basis. In fact, with a periodic system, Grantsville Clothing would not even know how many shirts and how many pairs of pants had been sold. Instead, only total sales of $23,000 ($15,000 + $8,000) would be known.

For simplicity, we have recorded the cost of goods sold for the shirts as $10 each. The actual cost per shirt, after adjusting for freight in and purchase discounts, is $10.80, computed as follows:

Total purchase price (1,000 shirts)	$10,000
Plus: Freight in	970
Less: Purchase returns (30 shirts)	(300)
Less: Purchase discounts	(194)
Total cost of shirts (970 shirts)	$10,476

Total cost $10,476 ÷ 970 shirts = $10.80 per shirt

In practice, it is unlikely that a firm using a perpetual inventory system would bother to adjust unit costs for the effects of freight cost and purchase discounts on an ongoing basis. The cost of doing these calculations could easily outweigh any resulting improvement in the quality of cost information.

SALES RETURNS As discussed in Chapter 6, dissatisfied customers sometimes return their purchases. The journal entries to record the return of 50 shirts are as follows:

	Perpetual			Periodic		
i.	Sales Returns (50 × $25)	1,250		Sales Returns	1,250	
	Accounts Receivable		1,250	Accounts Receivable		1,250
	Inventory (50 × $10)	500				
	Cost of Goods Sold		500			

STOP & THINK Should the returned inventory be recorded at its original cost of $10 per shirt?

Under the perpetual system, not only are the sales for the returned items canceled, but the cost of the returned inventory is also removed from Cost of Goods Sold and restored to the inventory account.

CLOSING ENTRIES After all of the journal entries are posted to the ledger, the T-accounts for Inventory and Cost of Goods Sold, under a perpetual system, would appear as follows:

Inventory

	Debit		Credit
(a)	10,000	(d)	300
(b)	5,400	(e)	194
(c)	970	(g)	6,000
(i)	500	(h)	3,600
Bal.	6,776		

Cost of Goods Sold

	Debit		Credit
(g)	6,000	(i)	500
(h)	3,600		
Bal.	9,100		

These numbers, after being verified by a physical count of the inventory (as described in the next section), would be reported in the financial statements—the $6,776 of Inventory in the balance sheet and the $9,100 of Cost of Goods Sold in the income statement.

Review the journal entries (a) through (i) under the periodic inventory system and notice that none of the amounts have been entered in either Inventory or Cost of Goods Sold. As a result, both of these accounts will have zero balances at year-end. Actually, the inventory account would have the same balance it had at the beginning of the period, which, in this example, we will assume to be zero.

With a periodic inventory system, the correct balances are recorded in Inventory and Cost of Goods Sold through a series of closing entries. Two entries are made:

1. Transfer all the temporary holding accounts to the inventory account balance. At this point, the inventory account balance is equal to the cost of goods available for sale (beginning inventory plus the net cost of purchases for the period).
2. Reduce Inventory by the amount of Cost of Goods Sold. At this point, the inventory account balance is equal to the ending inventory amount, and the appropriate cost of goods sold amount is also recognized.

To illustrate, the information for Grantsville Clothing will be used. The entry to transfer all the temporary holding accounts to the inventory account is as follows:

Inventory	15,876	
Purchase Returns	300	
Purchase Discounts	194	
Freight In		970
Purchases		15,400
Closing of temporary inventory accounts for periodic system.		

net purchases The net cost of inventory purchased during a period, after adding the cost of freight in and subtracting returns and discounts.

The inventory debit of $15,876 is the amount of **net purchases** for the period. Notice that, after this entry has been posted, the balances in all the temporary holding accounts will have been reduced to zero. As mentioned, after the addition of net purchases, the inventory account balance represents cost of goods available for sale (the sum of beginning inventory and net purchases). Remember that, in this example, beginning inventory is assumed to be zero.

The second closing entry involves the adjustment of Inventory to its appropriate ending balance and the creation of the cost of goods sold account. This cost of goods sold account would be closed when other nominal accounts (e.g., Sales Salaries, Interest Expense, etc.) are closed. If the year-end physical count indicates that the ending inventory balance should be $6,776, the appropriate entry is as follows:

Cost of Goods Sold	9,100	
Inventory ($15,876 − $6,776)		9,100
Adjustment of inventory account to appropriate ending balance.		

In this example, the values for both ending inventory ($6,776) and cost of goods sold ($9,100) are the same with either a perpetual or a periodic inventory system. So, what is the practical difference between the two systems? One difference is that a perpetual system can tell you the inventory balance and the cumulative cost of goods sold at any time during the period. With a periodic system, on the other hand, you must wait until the inventory is counted at the end of the period to compute the amount of inventory or cost of goods sold. Another difference is that, with a perpetual system, you can compare the inventory records to the amount of inventory actually on hand and thus determine whether any inventory has been lost or stolen. As described in the next section, this comparison is not possible with a periodic system.

---

to summarize

With a perpetual inventory system, the amount of inventory and cost of goods sold for the period are tracked on an ongoing basis. With a periodic inventory system, inventory and cost of goods sold are computed using an end-of-period inventory count. With a periodic system, inventory-related items are recorded in temporary holding accounts that are transferred to the inventory account at the end of the period.

3

Calculate cost of goods sold using the results of an inventory count and understand the impact of errors in ending inventory on reported cost of goods sold.

COUNTING INVENTORY AND CALCULATING COST OF GOODS SOLD

Regular physical counts of the existing inventory are essential to maintaining reliable inventory accounting records. With a perpetual system, the physical count can be compared to the recorded inventory balance to see whether any inventory has been lost or stolen. With a periodic system, a physical count is the only way to get the information necessary to compute cost of goods sold.

Taking a Physical Count of Inventory

No matter which inventory system a company is using, periodic physical counts are a necessary and important part of accounting for inventory. With a perpetual inventory system, the physical count either confirms that the amount entered in the accounting records is accurate or highlights shortages and clerical errors. If, for example, employees have been stealing inventory, the theft will show up as a difference between the balance in the inventory account and the amount physically counted.

A physical count of inventory involves two steps:

1. *Quantity count.* In most companies, physically counting all inventory is a time-consuming activity. Because sales transactions and merchandise deliveries can complicate matters, in-

ventory is usually counted on holidays or after the close of business on the inventory day. Special care must be taken to ensure that all inventory owned, wherever its location, is counted and that inventory on hand but not owned (consignment inventory) is not counted.

2. *Inventory costing.* When the physical count has been completed, each type of merchandise is assigned a unit cost. The quantity of each type of merchandise is multiplied by its unit cost to determine the dollar value of the inventory. These amounts are then added to obtain the total ending inventory for the business. This is the amount reported as Inventory on the balance sheet. The ending balance in the inventory account may have to be adjusted for any shortages discovered.

To illustrate the impact of a physical inventory count on the accounting records for both a periodic and a perpetual system, we will refer back to the Grantsville Clothing Store example used earlier. Assume that a physical count, combined with inventory costing analysis, suggests that the correct amount for ending inventory is $5,950. This information can be combined with previous information from the accounting system as follows:

	Periodic System	Perpetual System	
Beginning inventory	$ 0	$ 0	
Plus: Net purchases	15,876	15,876	
Cost of goods available for sale	$15,876	$15,876	
Less: Ending inventory	5,950	6,776	(from inventory system)
Cost of goods sold	$ 9,926	$ 9,100	(from inventory system)
Goods lost or stolen	unknown	826	($6,776 − $5,950)
Total cost of goods sold, lost, or stolen	$ 9,926	$ 9,926	

Recall that, in this example, the beginning inventory is assumed to be zero. The amount of net purchases is a combination of the items affecting the amount paid for inventory purchases during the period: purchase price, freight in, purchase returns, and purchase discounts. The $15,876 amount for net purchases was computed earlier in connection with the closing entry for the periodic system.

This cost of goods sold computation highlights the key difference between a periodic and a perpetual inventory system. With a periodic system, the company does not know what ending inventory *should be* when the inventory count is performed. The best the company can do is count the inventory and assume that the difference between the cost of goods available for sale and the cost of goods still remaining (ending inventory) must represent the cost of goods that were sold. Actually, a business using a periodic system has no way of knowing whether these goods were sold, lost, stolen, or spoiled—all it knows for sure is that the goods are gone.

With a perpetual system, the accounting records themselves yield the cost of goods sold during the period, as well as the amount of inventory that should be found when the physical count is made. In the Grantsville Clothing example, the predicted ending inventory is $6,776 (from the T-account shown earlier); the actual ending inventory, according to the physical count, is only $5,950. The difference of $826 ($6,776 − $5,950) represents inventory lost, stolen, or spoiled during the period. This amount is called **inventory shrinkage**. The adjusting entry needed to record this inventory shrinkage is as follows:

inventory shrinkage The amount of inventory that is lost, stolen, or spoiled during a period; determined by comparing perpetual inventory records to the physical count of inventory.

Inventory Shrinkage	826	
Inventory ($6,776 − $5,950).		826
Adjustment of perpetual inventory balance to reflect inventory shrinkage.		

For internal management purposes, the amount of inventory shrinkage would be tracked from one period to the next to detect whether the amount of "shrinkage" for any given period is un-

business environment essay

Inventory Fraud: The Great Salad Oil Case One of the most common ways of committing major financial statement fraud and reporting income that is higher than it should be is to overstate a company's inventory. If ending inventory is overstated, cost of goods sold is understated and net income is overstated. The overstatement of inventory and income can attract investors and boost the stock price. In addition, since inventory can often be pledged as collateral to borrow money from banks, its overstatement increases a company's borrowing power. Consider the famous case of ALLIED CRUDE VEGETABLE OIL, one of the best-known inventory frauds of all time.

Founded in 1957 by Tino De Angelis, Allied Crude Vegetable Oil was set up on an old petroleum tank farm in Bayonne, New Jersey. De Angelis used the soybean oil that was supposedly in the tanks as collateral to borrow money from financial institutions. He then hired AMERICAN EXPRESS WAREHOUSING, LTD. (a subsidiary of AMERICAN EXPRESS) to take charge of storing, inspecting, and documenting the oil. The warehousing receipts issued by the warehouse workers were used as evidence of the oil.

De Angelis handpicked 22 men to work at the tank farm, and they fooled the American Express inspectors with considerable ease. For example, one of them would climb to the top of a tank, drop in a weighted tape measure, and then shout down to the inspector that the tank was full. In most cases the tanks were

fyi

CVS is a leader in the retail drugstore industry in the United States with net sales of $18.1 billion in fiscal 1999. Inventory shrinkage for CVS for 1999 was $163 million, or almost 1% of sales.

usually high. For external reporting purposes, the shrinkage amount would probably be combined with normal cost of goods sold, and the title "Cost of Goods Sold" would be given to the total. Notice that if this practice is followed, reported cost of goods sold would be the same under both a perpetual and a periodic inventory system. The difference is that, with a perpetual system, company management knows how much of the goods was actually sold and how much represents inventory shrinkage.

With a periodic inventory system, no journal entry for inventory shrinkage is made because the amount of shrinkage is unknown. Instead, the ending inventory amount derived from the physical count is used to make the second periodic inventory closing entry (refer back to the previous section). Using the $5,950 ending inventory amount, the appropriate periodic inventory closing entry is:

Cost of Goods Sold	9,926	
Inventory ($15,876 − $5,950).		9,926
Adjustment of inventory account to appropriate ending balance.		

The Income Effect of an Error in Ending Inventory

As shown in the previous section, the results of the physical inventory count directly affect the computation of cost of goods sold with a periodic system and inventory shrinkage with a perpetual system. Errors in the inventory count will cause the amount of cost of goods sold or inventory shrinkage to be misstated. To illustrate, assume that the correct inventory count for Grantsville Clothing is $5,950 but that the ending inventory value is mistakenly computed to be $6,450. The impact of this $500 ($6,450 − $5,950) inventory overstatement is as follows:

empty, although some were filled with seawater and topped with a thin slick of oil. Moreover, the tanks were connected by a jungle of pipes that allowed the workers to pump whatever oil there was from one tank to another.

The maneuvers gave De Angelis an "endless" supply of oil and borrowing power. If anyone had checked a statistical report issued by the U.S. Census Bureau, he or she would have found that the oil supposedly stored at the tank farm totaled twice as much as all the oil in the country. By the close of 1963, the warehouse receipts represented 937 million pounds of oil when actually only 100 million pounds existed.

The salad oil scandal was revealed when De Angelis was unable to make payments on an investment. The ensuing investigation revealed a fraud that was conservatively estimated at $200 million. Most of the losses were borne by 51 major banking and brokerage houses in the United States and Europe, 20 of which collapsed.

De Angelis pleaded guilty to four federal counts of fraud and conspiracy and was given a 20-year sentence. The millions of dollars loaned to De Angelis were never found, and it is generally believed that the missing oil never existed. In fact, when one oil tank that supposedly contained $3,575,000 worth of oil was opened, seawater ran out for 12 consecutive days.

Source: Marshall B. Romney and W. Steve Albrecht, "The Use of Investigative Agencies by Auditors," *The Journal of Accountancy*, October 1979, p. 61.

	Periodic System	Perpetual System
Beginning inventory	$ 0	$ 0
Plus: Net purchases	15,876	15,876
Cost of goods available for sale	$15,876	$15,876
Less: Ending inventory	6,450	6,776 (from inventory system)
Cost of goods sold	$ 9,426	$ 9,100 (from inventory system)
Goods lost or stolen	unknown	326 ($6,776 − $6,450)
Total cost of goods sold, lost, or stolen	$ 9,426	$ 9,426

The $500 inventory overstatement reduces the reported cost of goods sold, lost, or stolen by $500, from $9,926 (computed earlier) to $9,426. This is because if we mistakenly think that we have more inventory remaining, then we will also mistakenly think that we must have sold less. Conversely, if the physical count understates ending inventory, total cost of goods sold will be overstated.

Since an inventory overstatement decreases reported cost of goods sold, it will also increase reported gross margin and net income. For this reason, the managers of a firm that is having difficulty meeting profit targets are sometimes tempted to "mistakenly" overstate ending inventory. Because of this temptation, auditors must take care to review a company's inventory counting process and also to physically observe a sample of the actual inventory. Many new accounting graduates who are hired by public accounting firms spend a portion of their first year on the job checking the inventory counts done by clients. The benefits of this exposure are twofold: (1) these new auditors get an opportunity to see what a business actually does, and (2) the inventory count provides assurance that the inventory amount stated on the financial statements is accurate.

to summarize

A physical inventory count is necessary to ensure that inventory records match the actual existing inventory. If a perpetual system is used, an inventory count can be used to compute the amount of inventory shrinkage during the period. An error in the reported ending inventory amount can have a significant effect on reported cost of goods sold, gross margin, and net income. For example, overstatement of ending inventory results in understatement of cost of goods sold and overstatement of net income.

4

Apply the four inventory cost flow alternatives: specific identification, FIFO, LIFO, and average cost.

INVENTORY COST FLOW ASSUMPTIONS

Consider the following transactions for the Ramona Rice Company for the year 2003.

Mar. 23 Purchased 10 kilos of rice, $4 per kilo.
Nov. 17 Purchased 10 kilos of rice, $9 per kilo.
Dec. 31 Sold 10 kilos of rice, $10 per kilo.

The surprisingly difficult question to answer with this simple example is "How much money did Ramona make in 2003?" As you can see, it depends on which rice was sold on December 31. There are three possibilities:

	Case #1 Sold Old Rice	Case #2 Sold New Rice	Case #3 Sold Mixed Rice
Sales ($10 × 10 kilos)	$100	$100	$100
Cost of goods sold (10 kilos)	40	90	65
Gross margin	$ 60	$ 10	$ 35

FIFO (first in, first out) An inventory cost flow assumption whereby the first goods purchased are assumed to be the first goods sold so that the ending inventory consists of the most recently purchased goods.

LIFO (last in, first out) An inventory cost flow assumption whereby the last goods purchased are assumed to be the first goods sold so that the ending inventory consists of the first goods purchased.

average cost An inventory cost flow assumption whereby cost of goods sold and the cost of ending inventory are determined by using an average cost of all merchandise available for sale during the period.

In Case #1, it is assumed that the 10 kilos of rice sold on December 31 were the old ones, purchased on March 23 for $4 per kilo. Accountants call this a **FIFO (first in, first out)** assumption. In Case #2, it is assumed that the company sold the new rice, purchased on November 17 for $9 per kilo. Accountants call this a **LIFO (last in, first out)** assumption. In Case #3, it is assumed that all the rice is mixed together, so the cost per kilo is the average cost of all the rice available for sale, or $6.50 per kilo [($40 + $90) ÷ 20 kilos]. Accountants call this an **average cost** assumption.

The point of the Ramona Rice example is this: in most cases, there is no feasible way to track exactly which units were sold. Accordingly, in order to compute cost of goods sold, the accountant must make an assumption. Note that this is not a case of tricky accountants trying to manipulate the reported numbers; instead, this is a case in which income simply cannot be computed unless the accountant uses his or her judgment and makes an assumption.

All three of the assumptions described in the example—FIFO, LIFO, and average cost—are acceptable under U.S. accounting rules. An interesting question is whether a company would randomly choose one of the three acceptable methods, or whether the choice would be made more strategically. For example, if Ramona Rice were preparing financial statements to be used to support a bank loan application, which assumption would you suggest that the company make? On the other hand, if Ramona were completing its income tax return, which assumption would be the best? This topic of strategic accounting choice will be discussed later in this chapter.

In the following sections, we will examine in more detail the different cost flow assumptions used by companies to determine inventories and cost of goods sold.

Specific Identification Inventory Cost Flow

specific identification A method of valuing inventory and determining cost of goods sold whereby the actual costs of specific inventory items are assigned to them.

An alternative to the assumptions just described is to specifically identify the cost of each particular unit that is sold. This approach, called **specific identification**, is often used by automobile dealers and other businesses that sell a limited number of units at a high price. To illustrate the specific identification inventory costing method, we will consider the September 2003 records of Nephi Company, which sells one type of bicycle.

Sept. 1	Beginning inventory consisted of 10 bicycles costing $200 each.
3	Purchased 8 bicycles costing $250 each.
18	Purchased 16 bicycles costing $300 each.
20	Purchased 10 bicycles costing $320 each.
25	Sold 28 bicycles, $400 each.

These inventory records show that during September the company had 44 bicycles (10 from beginning inventory and 34 that were purchased during the month) that it could have sold. However, only 28 bicycles were sold, leaving 16 on hand at the end of September. Using the specific identification method of inventory costing requires that the individual costs of the actual units sold be charged against revenue as cost of goods sold. To compute cost of goods sold and ending inventory amounts with this alternative, a company must know which units were actually sold and what the unit cost of each was.

Suppose that of the 28 bicycles sold by Nephi on September 25, 8 came from the beginning inventory, 4 came from the September 3 purchase, and 16 came from the September 18 purchase. With this information, cost of goods sold and ending inventory are computed as follows:

	Bicycles	Costs
Beginning inventory	10	$ 2,000
Net purchases	34	10,000
Goods available for sale	44	$12,000
Ending inventory	16	4,600
Cost of goods sold	28	$ 7,400

The cost of ending inventory is the total of the individual costs of the bicycles still on hand at the end of the month, or:

2 bicycles from beginning inventory, $200 each	$ 400
4 bicycles purchased on September 3, $250 each	1,000
0 bicycles purchased on September 18, $300 each	0
10 bicycles purchased on September 20, $320 each	3,200
Total ending inventory (16 units)	$4,600

Similarly, the cost of goods sold is the total of the costs of the specific bicycles sold, or:

8 bicycles from beginning inventory, $200 each	$1,600
4 bicycles purchased on September 3, $250 each	1,000
16 bicycles purchased on September 18, $300 each	4,800
0 bicycles purchased on September 20, $320 each	0
Total cost of goods sold (28 units)	$7,400

For many companies, it is impractical, if not impossible, to keep track of specific units. In that case, an assumption must be made as to which units were sold during the period and which are still in inventory, as illustrated earlier in the Ramona Rice example.

It is very important to remember that the accounting rules do not require that the assumed flow of goods for costing purposes match the actual physical movement of goods purchased and sold. In some cases, the assumed cost flow may be similar to the physical flow, but firms are not required to match the assumed accounting cost flow to the physical flow. A grocery store, for example, usually tries to sell the oldest units first to minimize spoilage. Thus, the physical flow of goods would reflect a FIFO pattern, but the grocery store could use a FIFO, LIFO, or average cost assumption in determining the ending inventory and cost of goods sold numbers to be reported in the financial statements. On the other hand, a company that stockpiles coal must first sell the coal purchased last since it is on top of the pile. That company might use the LIFO cost assumption, which reflects physical flow, or it might use one of the other alternatives.

In the next few sections, we will illustrate the FIFO, LIFO, and average inventory costing methods. The bicycle inventory data for Nephi Company will again be used in illustrating the different inventory cost flows.

FIFO Cost Flow Assumption

With FIFO, it is assumed that the oldest units are sold and the newest units remain in inventory. Using the FIFO inventory cost flow assumption, the ending inventory and cost of goods sold for Nephi Company are:

	Bicycles	Costs
Beginning inventory	10	$ 2,000
Net purchases	34	10,000
Goods available for sale	44	$12,000
Ending inventory	16	5,000
Cost of goods sold	28	$ 7,000

The $7,000 cost of goods sold and $5,000 cost of ending inventory are determined as follows:

FIFO cost of goods sold (oldest 28 units):	
10 bicycles from beginning inventory, $200 each	$2,000
8 bicycles purchased on September 3, $250 each	2,000
10 bicycles purchased on September 18, $300 each	3,000
Total FIFO cost of goods sold	$7,000

FIFO ending inventory (newest 16 units):	
6 bicycles purchased on September 18, $300 each	$1,800
10 bicycles purchased on September 20, $320 each	3,200
Total FIFO ending inventory	$5,000

LIFO Cost Flow Assumption

LIFO is the opposite of FIFO. With LIFO, the cost of the most recent units purchased is transferred to cost of goods sold. When prices are rising, as they are in the Nephi Company example, LIFO provides higher cost of goods sold, and hence lower net income, than FIFO. This is because the newest (high-priced) goods are assumed to have been sold. Using the LIFO inventory cost flow assumption, the ending inventory and cost of goods sold for Nephi Company are:

	Bicycles	Costs
Beginning inventory	10	$ 2,000
Net purchases	34	10,000
Goods available for sale	44	$12,000
Ending inventory	16	3,500
Cost of goods sold	28	$ 8,500

The $8,500 cost of goods sold and $3,500 cost of ending inventory are determined as follows:

LIFO cost of goods sold (newest 28 units):	
10 bicycles purchased on September 20, $320 each	$3,200
16 bicycles purchased on September 18, $300 each	4,800
2 bicycles purchased on September 3, $250 each	500
Total LIFO cost of goods sold	$8,500

LIFO ending inventory (oldest 16 units):	
10 bicycles from beginning inventory, $200 each	$2,000
6 bicycles purchased on September 3, $250 each	1,500
Total LIFO ending inventory	$3,500

Average Cost Flow Assumption

With average costing, an average cost must be computed for all the inventory available for sale during the period. The average unit cost for Nephi Company during September is computed as follows:

	Bicycles	Costs
Beginning inventory	10	$ 2,000
Net purchases	34	10,000
Goods available for sale	44	$12,000
$12,000 ÷ 44 units = $272.73 per unit		

With the average cost assumption, cost of goods sold is computed by multiplying the number of units sold by the average cost per unit. Similarly, the cost of ending inventory is computed by multiplying the number of units in ending inventory by the average cost per unit. These calculations are as follows:

Average Cost of Goods Sold: 28 Units × $272.73 per Unit = $7,636 (rounded)

Average Ending Inventory: 16 Units × $272.73 per Unit = $4,364 (rounded)

This information can be shown as follows:

	Bicycles	Costs
Beginning inventory	10	$ 2,000
Net purchases	34	10,000
Goods available for sale	44	$12,000
Ending inventory	16	4,364
Cost of goods sold	28	$ 7,636

A Comparison of All Inventory Costing Methods

The cost of goods sold and ending inventory amounts we have calculated using the three cost flow assumptions are summarized along with the resultant gross margins as follows:

	FIFO	LIFO	Average
Sales revenue (28 × $400)	$11,200	$11,200	$11,200
Cost of goods sold	7,000	8,500	7,636
Gross margin	$ 4,200	$ 2,700	$ 3,564
Ending inventory	$ 5,000	$ 3,500	$ 4,364

Note that the net result of each of the inventory cost flow assumptions is to allocate the total cost of goods available for sale of $12,000 between cost of goods sold and ending inventory.

CONCEPTUAL COMPARISON From a conceptual standpoint, LIFO gives a better reflection of cost of goods sold in the income statement than does FIFO because the most recent goods ("last in"), with the most recent costs, are assumed to have been sold. Thus, LIFO cost of goods sold matches current revenues with current costs. Average cost is somewhere between LIFO and FIFO. On the balance sheet, however, FIFO gives a better measure of inventory value because, with the FIFO assumption, the "first in" units are sold and the remaining units are the newest ones with the most recent costs. In summary, LIFO gives a conceptually better measure of income, but FIFO gives a conceptually better measure of inventory value on the balance sheet.

FINANCIAL STATEMENT IMPACT COMPARISON As illustrated in the Nephi Company example, in times of rising inventory prices (the most common situation in the majority of industries today), cost of goods sold is highest with LIFO and lowest with FIFO. As a result, gross margin, net income, and ending inventory are lowest with LIFO and highest with FIFO. With the impact on the reported financial statement numbers being so uniformly bad, you may be wondering why any company would ever voluntarily choose to use LIFO (during times of inflation). It might further surprise you to learn that, since 1974, hundreds of U.S. companies have voluntarily switched from FIFO to LIFO and that over half of the large companies in the United States currently use LIFO in accounting for at least some of their inventories.

STOP & THINK Over the entire life of a company—from its beginning with zero inventory until its final closeout when the last inventory item is sold—is aggregate cost of goods sold more, less, or the same as aggregate purchases? How is this relationship affected by the inventory cost flow assumption used?

The attractiveness of LIFO can be explained with one word—TAXES. If a company uses LIFO in a time of rising prices, reported cost of goods sold is higher, reported taxable income is lower, and cash paid for income taxes is lower. In fact, LIFO was invented in the 1930s in the United States for the sole purpose of allowing companies to lower their income tax payments. In most instances where accounting alternatives exist, firms are allowed to use one accounting method for tax purposes and another for financial reporting. In 1939, however, when the Internal Revenue Service (IRS) approved the use of LIFO, it ruled that firms may use LIFO for tax purposes only if they also use LIFO for financial reporting purposes. Therefore, companies must choose between reporting higher profits and paying higher taxes with FIFO or reporting lower profits and paying lower taxes with LIFO.

---

to summarize

Some companies can use specific identification as a method of valuing inventory and determining cost of goods sold. In most cases, however, an accountant must make an inventory cost flow assumption in order to compute cost of goods sold and ending inventory. With FIFO (first in, first out), it is assumed that the oldest inventory units are sold first. With LIFO (last in, first out), it is assumed that the newest units are sold first. With the average cost assumption, the total goods available for sale are used to compute an average cost per unit for the period; this average cost is then used in calculating cost of goods sold and ending inventory. LIFO produces a better matching of current revenues and current expenses in the income statement; FIFO yields a balance sheet inventory value that is closer to the current value of the inventory. The primary practical attraction of LIFO is that it lowers income tax payments.

5

Use financial ratios to evaluate a company's inventory level.

ASSESSING HOW WELL COMPANIES MANAGE THEIR INVENTORIES

Money tied up in the form of inventories cannot be used for other purposes. Therefore, companies try hard to minimize the necessary investment in inventories while at the same time assuring that they have enough inventory on hand to meet customer demand. In recent years a method of inventory management called just-in-time (JIT) inventory has become popular. JIT, which will be described in Chapter 7 in the management accounting section of this text, is an inventory management method that attempts to have exactly enough inventory arrive just in time for sale. Its purpose is to minimize the amount of money needed to purchase and hold inventory.

Evaluating the Level of Inventory

inventory turnover A measure of the efficiency with which inventory is managed; computed by dividing cost of goods sold by average inventory for a period.

Two widely used measurements of how effectively a company is managing its inventory are the inventory turnover ratio and number of days' sales in inventory. **Inventory turnover** provides a measure of how many times a company turns over, or replenishes, its inventory during a year. The calculation is similar to the accounts receivable turnover discussed in Chapter 6. It is calculated by dividing cost of goods sold by average inventory as follows:

$$\text{Inventory Turnover} = \frac{\text{Cost of Goods Sold}}{\text{Average Inventory}}$$

The average inventory amount is the average of the beginning and ending inventory balances. The inventory turnover ratios for SEARS, SAFEWAY, and CATERPILLAR for 1999 are as follows (dollar amounts are in billions):

	Sears	Safeway	Caterpillar
Cost of goods sold	$27.212	$20.349	$14.481
Beginning inventory	5.322	1.856	2.842
Ending inventory	5.648	2.445	2.594
Average inventory	5.485	2.151	2.718
Inventory turnover	4.96	9.46	5.33

From this analysis, you can see that Safeway, the supermarket, turns its inventory over more frequently than Sears, the department store, and Caterpillar, the equipment dealer. This result is what we would have predicted given that the companies are in different businesses and have different types of inventory.

number of days' sales in inventory An alternative measure of how well inventory is being managed; computed by dividing 365 days by the inventory turnover ratio.

Inventory turnover can also be converted into the **number of days' sales in inventory**. This ratio is computed by dividing 365, or the number of days in a year, by the inventory turnover, as follows:

$$\text{Number of Days' Sales in Inventory} = \frac{365}{\text{Inventory Turnover}}$$

caution

Sometimes these two inventory ratios are computed using ending inventory rather than average inventory. This is appropriate if the inventory balance does not change much from the beginning to the end of the year.

Computing this ratio for Sears, Safeway, and Caterpillar yields the following:

	Number of Days' Sales in Inventory
Sears	73.6 days
Safeway	38.6 days
Caterpillar	68.5 days

business environment essay

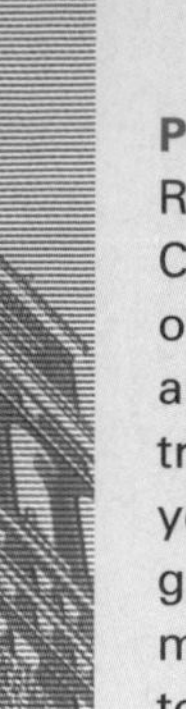

Phar-Mor Cooks Up Inventory Fraud Recall the introductory scenario from Chapter 5 that detailed the rise and fall of PHAR-MOR. That case resulted from an elaborate inventory fraud perpetrated by top management over several years. Phar-Mor's inventory ostensibly grew from $11 million in 1989 to $153 million in 1991, but much of this inventory had been "created" by fabricating financial data and misleading the external auditors.

Because Phar-Mor did not keep a perpetual inventory system, the company estimated the value of its inventory by using a ratio involving the cost of the items purchased and their retail value. Inventory was counted, valued at its retail price, and then multiplied by this ratio to obtain an approximation of its cost. Phar-Mor officials manipulated the ratio to ensure that inventory was inflated and that cost of goods sold was understated. In addition, when Phar-Mor's accountants made journal entries reducing Inventory (with a credit), the corresponding debit (which should have

net work

In addition to Safeway, another large supermarket chain is KROGER, based in Cincinnati. Access Kroger's Web site at http://kroger.com.

Is Kroger's inventory turnover higher or lower than Safeway's? Does Kroger use LIFO or FIFO?

Individuals analyzing how effective a company's inventory management is would compare these ratios with those of other firms in the same industry and with comparable ratios for the same firm in previous years.

Impact of the Inventory Cost Flow Assumption

As mentioned previously, in times of rising prices, the use of LIFO results in higher cost of goods sold and lower inventory values. All three of the companies in the ratio illustration on the previous page use LIFO. Each company includes supplemental disclosures in the financial statement notes that allow users to compute what reported inventory and cost of goods sold would have been if the company had used FIFO. To illustrate the impact that the choice of inventory cost flow assumption can have on the reported numbers, consider the following comparison for Caterpillar for 1999:

	Reported LIFO Numbers	Numbers if Using FIFO
Cost of goods sold	$14.481	$12.481
Average inventory	2.718	4.718
Inventory turnover	5.33	2.65
Number of days' sales in inventory	68.5 days	137.7 days

The difference in cost of goods sold for 1999 is not great because inflation was relatively low in that year. However, the difference in the reported average inventory balance reflects the cumulative effect of inflation for the many years since Caterpillar first started using LIFO. The impact on the ratio values is dramatic. Of course, the difference between LIFO and FIFO is not as great for most companies as shown here for Caterpillar, but the general point is that the choice of inventory cost flow assumption can affect the conclusions drawn about the financial statements—if the financial statement user is not careful.

Number of Days' Purchases in Accounts Payable

In Chapter 6, we introduced the average collection period ratio. In this chapter we have discussed the computation of the number of days' sales in inventory. Taken together, these two ratios indicate the length of a firm's operating cycle. The two ratios measure the amount of time it takes, on average, from the point when inventory is purchased to the point when cash is col-

been made to Cost of Goods Sold) was made to an asset account (with the clever name of "Cookies"). This "cookies" account would then be broken into smaller pieces and reallocated to individual stores. Because the "Cookies" were broken into pieces, the smaller numbers avoided attracting the external auditors' attention. Another tactic used by Phar-Mor was to artificially inflate the inventory numbers at the company's fiscal year-end (June 30) and attribute the inflated numbers to a buildup of inventory in preparation for the 4th of July.

These falsifications and more resulted in financial statement fraud amounting to over $1 billion in losses. The external auditors in the case were found guilty of fraud—not because the audit firm was an active participant in the scheme, but because the auditors were reckless with regard to the conduct of the audit.

Sources: Most of these facts relating to Phar-Mor appeared in Gabriella Stern, "Chicanery at Phar-Mor Ran Deep, Close Look at Discounter Shows," *The Wall Street Journal*, January 20, 1994, p. 1; Mark F. Murray, "When a Client is a Liability," *Journal of Accountancy*, September 1992, pp. 54–58.

lected from the customer who purchased the inventory. For example, Sears' 253-day operating cycle for 1999 is depicted below:

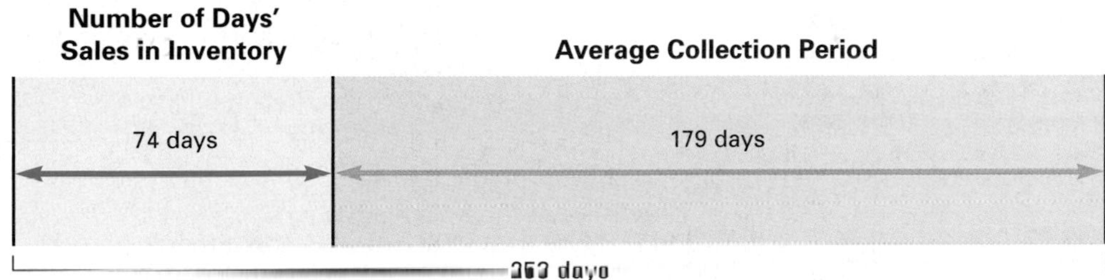

Is Sears' operating cycle too long, too short, or just right? That is difficult to tell without information from prior years and from competitors. But by including one additional ratio in the analysis, we can learn more about how Sears is managing its operating cash flow. The **number of days' purchases in accounts payable** reveals the average length of time that elapses between the purchase of inventory on account and the cash payment for that inventory. The number of days' purchases in accounts payable is computed by dividing total inventory purchases by average accounts payable and then dividing the result into 365 days:

number of days' purchases in accounts payable A measure of how well operating cash flow is being managed; computed by dividing total inventory purchases by average accounts payable and then dividing 365 days by the result.

$$\text{Number of Days' Purchases in Accounts Payable} = \frac{\text{365 Days}}{\text{Purchases/Average Accounts Payable}}$$

The amount of inventory purchased during a year is computed by combining cost of goods sold with the change in the inventory balance for the year. If inventory increased during the year, then inventory purchases are equal to cost of goods sold plus the increase in the inventory balance. Similarly, if inventory decreased during the year, inventory purchases are equal to cost of goods sold minus the decrease in the inventory balance.

The number of days' purchases in accounts payable indicates how long a company takes to pay its suppliers. For example, Sears' number of days' purchases in accounts payable for 1999 is computed as follows (dollar figures are in millions):

Cost of goods sold for 1999	$27,212
Add increase in inventory during 1999	326
Inventory purchases during 1999	$27,538
Average accounts payable during 1999	$ 6,862

$$\text{Number of Days' Purchases in Accounts Payable} = \frac{365 \text{ Days}}{\$27{,}538/\$6{,}862} = 91 \text{ Days}$$

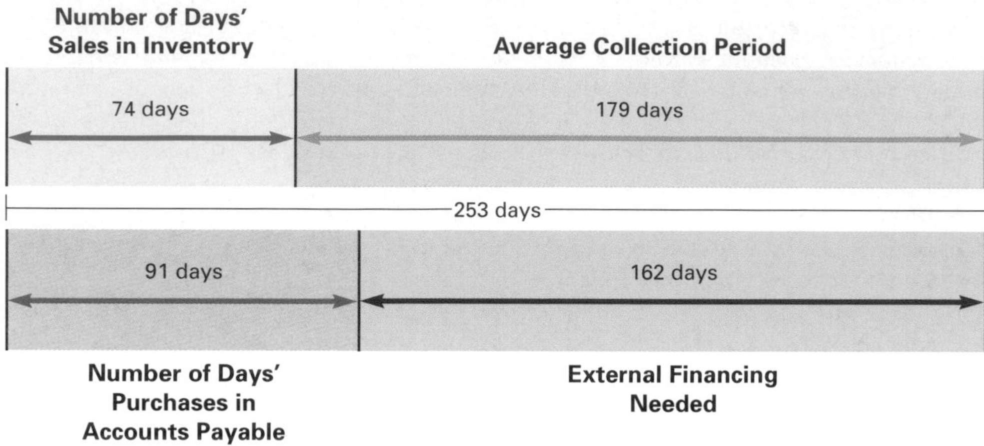

> **caution**
>
> This computation of the number of days' purchases in accounts payable assumes that only inventory purchases on account are included in accounts payable. It is likely that the accounts payable balance also includes such items as supplies purchased on account. Nevertheless, the purchase of inventory is typically the most significant element of accounts payable.

Sears must pay its suppliers in 91 days but must wait for 253 days before receiving the cash from its customers. Sears must finance the remaining 162 days (253 days − 91 days) of its operating cycle with bank loans or additional stockholder investment or by charging interest to those using its credit card debt. Sears is famous for using the last option—charging customers for the use of credit. In 1999 alone, Sears reported revenue from its credit card activities of over $4.3 billion.

These calculations illustrate that proper management of the sales/collection cycle, coupled with prudent financing of inventory purchases on account, can reduce a company's reliance on external financing.

to summarize

Proper inventory management seeks a balance between keeping a lower inventory level to avoid tying up excess resources and maintaining a sufficient inventory balance to ensure smooth business operation. Companies assess how well their inventory is being managed by using two ratios: (1) inventory turnover and (2) number of days' sales in inventory. A company's choice of inventory cost flow assumption can significantly affect the values of these inventory ratios; intelligent ratio analysis requires considering possible accounting differences among companies. Comparison of the average collection period, number of days' sales in inventory, and number of days' purchases in accounts payable reveals how much of a company's operating cycle it must finance through external financing.

expanded material

Thus far we have defined inventory and cost of goods sold; we have described the perpetual and periodic inventory systems, three inventory cost flow assumptions, and the use of financial ratios to evaluate a company's manage-

ment of its inventory. These topics are all sufficient for a basic understanding of the nature of inventory and cost of goods sold, as well as the most common ways of accounting for inventory. The four topics that will be discussed in the expanded material are (1) the impact of more complicated inventory errors, (2) complications that arise in using LIFO and average cost with a perpetual inventory system, (3) reporting inventory at amounts below cost, and (4) a method for estimating inventory without taking a physical count.

6

Analyze the impact of inventory errors on reported cost of goods sold.

FURTHER COVERAGE OF INVENTORY ERRORS

Incorrect amounts for inventory on the balance sheet and cost of goods sold on the income statement can result from errors in counting inventories, recording inventory transactions, or both. The effect of an error in the end-of-period inventory count was discussed earlier in the chapter. To examine the effects of other types of inventory errors, we will assume that Richfield Company had the following inventory records for 2003:

Inventory balance, January 1, 2003	$ 8,000
Purchases through December 30, 2003	20,000
Inventory balance, December 30, 2003	12,000

We will further assume that on December 31 the company purchased and received another $1,000 of inventory. The following comparison shows the kinds of inventory situations that might result:

The $1,000 of merchandise purchased on December 31 was	Incorrect*	Incorrect	Incorrect	Correct
	not recorded as a purchase and not counted as inventory	recorded as a purchase but not counted as inventory	not recorded as a purchase but counted as inventory	recorded as a purchase and counted as inventory
Beginning inventory	$ 8,000 (OK)**	$ 8,000 (OK)	$ 8,000 (OK)	$ 8,000 (OK)
Net purchases	20,000 (↓)	21,000 (OK)	20,000 (↓)	21,000 (OK)
Cost of goods available for sale	$28,000 (↓)	$29,000 (OK)	$28,000 (↓)	$29,000 (OK)
Ending inventory	12,000 (↓)	12,000 (↓)	13,000 (OK)	13,000 (OK)
Cost of goods sold	$16,000 (OK)	$17,000 (↑)	$15,000 (↓)	$16,000 (OK)

*This calculation produces the correct cost of goods sold but by an incorrect route—the errors in purchases and ending inventory offset each other.
**For the amount, ↓ indicates it is too low, ↑ means it is too high, and OK means it is correct.

In these calculations, the beginning inventory plus purchases equals the cost of goods that were "available for sale." In other words, everything that "could be sold" must have either been on hand at the beginning of the period (beginning inventory) or purchased during the period (net purchases). Then, ending inventory (what wasn't sold) was subtracted from the cost of goods available for sale. The result is the cost of goods that were sold. Everything on hand (available) had to be either sold or left in ending inventory. From this example, you can see how inventory and cost of goods sold can be misstated by the improper recording of inventory purchases or counting of inventory.

Similar errors can occur when inventory is sold. If a sale is recorded but the merchandise remains in the warehouse and is counted in the ending inventory, cost of goods sold will be understated, whereas gross margin and net income will be overstated. If a sale is not recorded but inventory is shipped and not counted in the ending inventory, gross margin and net income will be understated, and cost of goods sold will be overstated.

To illustrate these potential inventory errors, we will again consider the data of Richfield Company. Note that sales figures have been added and the ending inventory and the 2003 purchases now correctly include the $1,000 purchase of merchandise made on December 31, 2003.

Sales revenue through December 30, 2003 (200% of cost)	$32,000
Inventory balance, January 1, 2003	8,000
Net purchases during 2003	21,000
Inventory balance, December 31, 2003	13,000

In addition, assume that on December 31, inventory that cost $1,000 was sold for $2,000. The merchandise was delivered to the buyer on December 31. The following analysis shows the kinds of situations that might result:

	Incorrect	Incorrect	Incorrect	Correct
The $2,000 sale on December 31 was	not recorded and the merchandise was counted as inventory	recorded and the merchandise was counted as inventory	not recorded and the merchandise was excluded from inventory	recorded and the merchandise was excluded from inventory
Sales revenue	$32,000 (↓)*	$34,000 (OK)	$32,000 (↓)	$34,000 (OK)
Cost of goods sold:				
Beginning inventory	$ 8,000 (OK)	$ 8,000 (OK)	$ 8,000 (OK)	$ 8,000 (OK)
Net purchases	21,000 (OK)	21,000 (OK)	21,000 (OK)	21,000 (OK)
Cost of goods available for sale	$29,000 (OK)	$29,000 (OK)	$29,000 (OK)	$29,000 (OK)
Ending inventory	13,000 (↑)	13,000 (↑)	12,000 (OK)	12,000 (OK)
Cost of goods sold	$16,000 (↓)	$16,000 (↓)	$17,000 (OK)	$17,000 (OK)
Gross margin	$16,000 (↓)	$18,000 (↑)	$15,000 (↓)	$17,000 (OK)

*For the amount, ↓ indicates it is too low, ↑ means it is too high, and OK means it is correct.

To reduce the possibility of these types of inventory cutoff errors, most businesses close their warehouses at year-end while they count inventory. If they are retailers, they will probably count inventory after hours. During the inventory counting period, businesses do not accept or ship merchandise, nor do they enter purchase or sales transactions in their accounting records.

As explained, an error in inventory results in cost of goods sold being overstated or understated. This error has the opposite effect on gross margin and, hence, on net income. For example, if at the end of the accounting period $2,000 of inventory is not counted, cost of goods sold will be $2,000 higher than it should be, and gross margin and net income will be understated by $2,000. Such inventory errors affect gross margin and net income not only in the current year but in the following year as well. A recording delay resulting in an understatement of purchases in one year, for example, results in an overstatement in the next year.

To illustrate how inventory errors affect gross margin and net income, let us first assume the following correct data for Salina Corporation:

		2002		2003
Sales revenue		$50,000		$40,000
Cost of goods sold:				
Beginning inventory	$10,000		$ 5,000	
Net purchases	20,000		25,000	
Cost of goods available for sale	$30,000		$30,000	
Ending inventory	5,000		10,000	
Cost of goods sold		25,000		20,000
Gross margin		$25,000		$20,000
Operating expenses		10,000		10,000
Net income		$15,000		$10,000

Now suppose that ending inventory in 2002 was overstated; that is, instead of the correct amount of $5,000, the count erroneously showed $7,000 of inventory on hand. The following analysis shows the effect of the error on net income in both 2002 and 2003:

		2002		2003
Sales revenue		$50,000		$40,000
Cost of goods sold:				
Beginning inventory	$10,000		→ $ 7,000 (↑)	
Net purchases	20,000		25,000	
Cost of goods available for sale	$30,000		$32,000 (↑)	
Ending inventory	7,000 (↑)*		10,000	
Cost of goods sold		23,000 (↓)		22,000 (↑)
Gross margin		$27,000 (↑)		$18,000 (↓)
Operating expenses		10,000		10,000
Net income		$17,000 (↑)		$ 8,000 (↓)

*For the amount, ↑ means it is too high, ↓ means it is too low.

When the amount of ending inventory is overstated (as it was in 2002), both gross margin and net income are overstated by the same amount ($2,000 in 2002). If the ending inventory amount had been understated, net income and gross margin would also have been understated, again by the same amount.

Since the ending inventory in 2002 becomes the beginning inventory in 2003, the net income and gross margin for 2003 are also misstated. In 2003, however, beginning inventory is overstated, so gross margin and net income are understated, again by $2,000. Thus, the errors in the two years offset or counterbalance each other, and if the count taken at the end of 2003 is correct, income in subsequent years will not be affected by this error.

to summarize

Inventory errors can have a significant effect on cost of goods sold, gross margin, and net income. In addition, a misstatement of an ending inventory balance affects net income, both in the current year and in the next year. Errors in beginning and ending inventory have the opposite effect on cost of goods sold, gross margin, and net income. Errors in inventory correct themselves after two years if the physical count at the end of the second year shows the correct amount of ending inventory for that period.

7

Describe the complications that arise when LIFO or average cost is used with a perpetual inventory system.

COMPLICATIONS OF THE PERPETUAL METHOD WITH LIFO AND AVERAGE COST

In the Nephi Company bicycle example used earlier in the chapter, the simplifying assumption was made that all 28 bicycles were sold at the end of the month. In essence, this is the assumption made when a periodic inventory system is used—goods are assumed to be sold at the end of the period because the exact time when particular goods are sold is not recorded. Computation of average cost and LIFO under a perpetual system is complicated because the average cost of units available for sale changes every time a purchase is made, and the identification of the "last in" units also changes with every purchase.

These perpetual system complications are illustrated below using the same Nephi Company example used earlier, but now assuming that sales occurred at different times during the month.

Sept.	1	Beginning inventory consisted of 10 bicycles costing $200 each.
	3	Purchased 8 bicycles costing $250 each.
	5	Sold 12 bicycles, $400 each.
	18	Purchased 16 bicycles costing $300 each.
	20	Purchased 10 bicycles costing $320 each.
	25	Sold 16 bicycles, $400 each.

When a perpetual system is used and sales occur during the period, the identification of the "last in" units must be evaluated at the time of each individual sale, as follows:

September 5 sale of 12 bicycles, identification of "last in" units:		
8 bicycles purchased on September 3, $250 each	$2,000	
4 bicycles in beginning inventory, $200 each	800	
		$2,800
September 25 sale of 16 bicycles, identification of "last in" units:		
10 bicycles purchased on September 20, $320 each	$3,200	
6 bicycles purchased on September 18, $300 each	1,800	
		5,000
Total perpetual LIFO cost of goods sold		$7,800

This $7,800 amount for LIFO cost of goods sold under a perpetual inventory system compares to the $8,500 LIFO cost of goods sold computed earlier in the chapter assuming a periodic inventory system. Again, the difference arises because the "last in" units are identified at the end of the period with a periodic system; with a perpetual system, the "last in" units are identified at the time of each individual sale.

A similar difference arises with the average cost method because, with a perpetual system, a new average cost per unit must be determined at the time each individual sale is made. This process is illustrated as follows:

September 5 sale of 12 bicycles, determination of average cost:		
10 bicycles in beginning inventory, $200 each	$2,000	
8 bicycles purchased on September 3, $250 each	2,000	
Total cost of goods available for sale on September 5		$4,000

Average cost on September 5: $4,000 ÷ 18 bicycles = $222.22 per bicycle
September 5 cost of goods sold:
12 bicycles × $222.22 per bicycle = $2,667 (rounded)

September 25 sale of 16 bicycles, determination of average cost:		
6 (18 − 12) bicycles; remaining cost ($4,000 − $2,667)	$1,333	
16 bicycles purchased on September 18, $300 each	4,800	
10 bicycles purchased on September 20, $320 each	3,200	
Total cost of goods available for sale on September 25		$9,333

Average cost on September 25: $9,333 ÷ 32 bicycles = $291.66 per bicycle
September 25 cost of goods sold:
16 bicycles × $291.66 per bicycle = $4,667 (rounded)
Total cost of goods sold: $2,667 + $4,667 = $7,334

This $7,334 cost of goods sold under the perpetual average method compares with $7,636 cost of goods sold under the periodic average method. Again, the difference is that one overall average cost for all goods available for sale during the period is used with a periodic system; with a perpetual system, a new average cost is computed at the time of each sale.

By the way, no complications arise in using FIFO with a perpetual system. This is because, no matter when sales occur, the "first in" units are always the same ones. So, FIFO periodic and FIFO perpetual yield the same numbers for cost of goods sold and ending inventory.

Because of the complications associated with computing perpetual LIFO and perpetual average cost, many businesses that use average cost or LIFO for financial reporting purposes use a simple FIFO assumption in maintaining their day-to-day perpetual inventory records. The perpetual FIFO records are then converted to periodic average cost or LIFO for the financial reports.

to summarize

Using the average cost and LIFO inventory cost flow assumptions with a perpetual inventory system leads to some complications. These complications arise because the identity of the "last in" units changes with each new inventory purchase, as does the average cost of units purchased up to that point.

8

Apply the lower-of-cost-or-market method of accounting for inventory.

REPORTING INVENTORY AT AMOUNTS BELOW COST

All the inventory costing alternatives we have discussed in this chapter have one thing in common: they report inventory at cost. Occasionally, however, it becomes necessary to report inventory at an amount that is less than cost. This happens when the future value of the inventory is in doubt—when it is damaged, used, or obsolete, or when it can be replaced new at a price that is less than its original cost.

Inventory Valued at Net Realizable Value

net realizable value The selling price of an item less reasonable selling costs.

When inventory is damaged, used, or obsolete, it should be reported at no more than its **net realizable value**. This is the amount the inventory can be sold for, minus any selling costs. Suppose, for example, that an automobile dealer has a demonstrator car that originally cost $18,000 and now can be sold for only $16,000. The car should be reported at its net realizable value. If a commission of $500 must be paid to sell the car, the net realizable value is $15,500, or $2,500 less than cost. This loss is calculated as follows:

Cost		$18,000
Estimated selling price	$16,000	
Less selling commission	500	15,500
Loss		$ 2,500

To achieve a good matching of revenues and expenses, a company must recognize this estimated loss as soon as it is determined that an economic loss has occurred (even before the car is sold). The journal entry required to recognize the loss and reduce the inventory amount of the car is:

Loss on Write-Down of Inventory (Expense)	2,500	
Inventory		2,500
To write down inventory to its net realizable value.		

By writing down inventory to its net realizable value, a company recognizes a loss when it happens and shows no profit or loss when the inventory is finally sold. Using net realizable values means that assets are not being reported at amounts that exceed their future economic benefits.

Inventory Valued at Lower of Cost or Market

Inventory must also be written down to an amount below cost if it can be replaced new at a price that is less than its original cost. In the electronics industry, for instance, the costs of computers and compact disc players have fallen dramatically in recent years. When goods remaining in ending inventory can be replaced with identical goods at a lower cost, the lower unit cost must be used in valuing the inventory (provided that the replacement cost is not higher than net realizable value or lower than net realizable value minus a normal profit). This is known as the **lower-of-cost-or-market (LCM) rule**. (In a sense, a more precise name would be the lower-of-actual-or-replacement-cost rule.)

lower-of-cost-or-market (LCM) rule A basis for valuing inventory at the lower of original cost or current market value.

ceiling The maximum market amount at which inventory can be carried on the books; equal to net realizable value.

floor The minimum market amount at which inventory can be carried on the books; equal to net realizable value minus a normal profit.

The **ceiling**, or maximum market amount at which inventory can be carried on the books, is equivalent to net realizable value, which is the selling price less estimated selling costs. The ceiling is imposed because it makes no sense to value an inventory item above the amount that can be realized upon sale. For example, assume that a company purchased an inventory item for $10 and expected to sell it for $14. If the selling costs of the item amounted to $3, the ceiling or net realizable value would be $11 ($14 − $3).

The **floor** is defined as the net realizable value minus a normal profit. Thus, if the inventory item costing $10 had a normal profit margin of 20%, or $2, the floor would be $9 (net realizable value of $11 less normal profit of $2). This is the lowest amount at which inventory should be carried in order to prevent showing losses in one period and large profits in subsequent periods.

In applying this LCM rule, you can follow certain basic guidelines:

1. Define market value as:
   a. replacement cost, if it falls between the ceiling and the floor.
   b. the floor, if the replacement cost is less than the floor.
   c. the ceiling, if the replacement cost is higher than the ceiling.
   (As a practical matter, when replacement cost, ceiling, and floor are compared, market is always the middle value.)
2. Compare the defined market value with the original cost and choose the lower amount.

The following chart gives four separate examples of the application of the LCM rule; the resulting LCM amount is highlighted in each case.

			Market		
Item	Number of Items in Inventory	Original Cost (LIFO, FIFO, etc.)	Replacement Cost	Net Realizable Value (Ceiling)	Net Realizable Value Minus Normal Profit (Floor)
A	10	$17	$16	$15	$10
B	8	21	18	23	16
C	30	26	21	31	22
D	20	19	16	34	25

The LCM rule can be applied in one of three ways: (1) by computing cost and market figures for each item in inventory and using the lower of the two amounts in each case, (2) by computing cost and market figures for the total inventory and then applying the LCM rule to that total, or (3) by applying the LCM rule to categories of inventory. For a clothing store, categories of inventory might be all shirts, all pants, all suits, or all dresses.

To illustrate, we will use the above data to show how the LCM rule would be applied to each inventory item separately and to total inventory. (The third method is similar to the second, except that it may involve several totals, one for each category of inventory.)

Item	Number of Items in Inventory	Original Cost	Market Value	LCM for Individual Items
A	10	$17 × 10 units = $ 170	$15 × 10 units = $ 150	$ 150
B	8	$21 × 8 units = 168	$18 × 8 units = 144	144
C	30	$26 × 30 units = 780	$22 × 30 units = 660	660
D	20	$19 × 20 units = 380	$25 × 20 units = 500	380
		$1,498	$1,454	$1,334

$44 (difference between $1,498 and $1,454)

$164 (difference between $1,498 and $1,334)

Using the first method, applying the LCM rule to individual items, inventory is valued at $1,334, a write-down of $164 from the original cost. With the second method, using total inventory, the lower of total cost ($1,498) or total market value ($1,454) is used for a write-down of $44. The write-down is smaller when total inventory is used because the increase in market value of $120 in item D offsets decreases in items A, B, and C. In practice, each of the three methods is acceptable, but once a method has been selected, it should be followed consistently.

The journal entry to write down the inventory to the lower of cost or market applying the LCM rule to individual items is:

Loss on Write-Down of Inventory (Expense)	164	
Inventory		164
To write down inventory to lower of cost or market.		

The amount of this entry would have been $44 if the LCM rule had been applied to total inventory.

The LCM rule has gained wide acceptance because it reports inventory on the balance sheet at amounts that are consistent with future economic benefits. With this method, losses are recognized when they occur, not necessarily when a sale is made.

to summarize

The recorded amount of inventory should be written down (1) when it is damaged, used, or obsolete and (2) when it can be replaced (purchased new) at an amount that is less than its original cost. In the first case, inventory is reported at its net realizable value, an amount that allows a company to break even when the inventory is sold. In the second case, inventory is written down to the lower of cost or market. When using the lower-of-cost-or-market rule, market is defined as falling between the ceiling and floor. Ceiling is defined as the net realizable value; floor is net realizable value minus a normal profit margin. In no case should inventory be reported at an amount that exceeds the ceiling or is less than the floor. These reporting alternatives are attempts to show assets at amounts that reflect realistic future economic benefits.

Explain the gross margin method of estimating inventories.

METHOD OF ESTIMATING INVENTORIES

We have assumed that the number of inventory units on hand is known by a physical count that takes place at the end of each accounting period. For the periodic inventory method, this physical count is the only way to determine how much inventory is on hand at the end of a period. For the perpetual inventory method, the physical count verifies the quantity on hand or indicates the amount of inventory shrinkage or theft. There are times, however, when a company needs to know the dollar amount of ending inventory, but a physical count is either impossible or impractical. For example, many firms prepare quarterly, or even monthly, financial statements, but it is too expensive and time-consuming to count the inventory at the end of each period. In such cases, if the perpetual inventory method is being used, the balance in the inventory account is usually assumed to be correct. With the periodic inventory method, however, some estimate of the inventory balance must be made. A common method of estimating the dollar amount of ending inventory is the gross margin method.

The Gross Margin Method

gross margin method A procedure for estimating the amount of ending inventory; the historical relationship of cost of goods sold to sales revenue is used in computing ending inventory.

With the **gross margin method**, a firm uses available information about the dollar amounts of beginning inventory and purchases, and the historical gross margin percentage to estimate the dollar amounts of cost of goods sold and ending inventory.

To illustrate, we will assume the following data for Payson Brick Company:

Net sales revenue, January 1 to March 31	$100,000
Inventory balance, January 1	15,000
Net purchases, January 1 to March 31	65,000
Gross margin percentage	
(historically determined percentage of net sales)	40%

With this information, the dollar amount of inventory on hand on March 31 is estimated as follows:

		Dollars	Percentage of Sales
Net sales revenue		$100,000	100%
Cost of goods sold:			
Beginning inventory	$15,000		
Net purchases	65,000		
Total cost of goods available for sale	$80,000		
Ending inventory ($80,000 − $60,000)	20,000 (3)*		
Cost of goods sold ($100,000 − $40,000)		60,000 (2)*	60%
Gross margin ($100,000 × 0.40)		$ 40,000 (1)*	40%

*The numbers indicate the order of calculation.

In this example, gross margin is first determined by calculating 40% of sales (step 1). Next, cost of goods sold is found by subtracting gross margin from sales (step 2). Finally, the dollar amount of ending inventory is obtained by subtracting cost of goods sold from total cost of goods available for sale (step 3). Obviously, the gross margin method of estimating cost of goods sold and ending inventory assumes that the historical gross margin percentage is appropriate for the current period. This assumption is a realistic one in many fields of business. In cases where the gross margin percentage has changed, this method should be used with caution.

The gross margin method of estimating ending inventories is also useful when a fire or other calamity destroys a company's inventory. In these cases, the dollar amount of inventory lost must be determined before insurance claims can be made. The dollar amounts of sales, purchases, and beginning inventory can be obtained from prior years' financial statements and from customers, suppliers, and other sources. Then the gross margin method can be used to estimate the dollar amount of inventory lost.

to summarize

The gross margin method is a common technique for estimating the dollar amount of inventory. The historical gross margin percentage is used in conjunction with sales to estimate cost of goods sold. This estimated cost of goods sold amount is subtracted from cost of goods available for sale to yield an estimate of ending inventory.

review of learning objectives

1 Identify what items and costs should be included in inventory and cost of goods sold. Inventory is composed of goods held for sale in the normal course of business. Cost of goods sold is the cost of inventory sold during the period. For a manufacturing firm, the three types of inventory are raw materials, work in process, and finished goods. All costs incurred in producing and getting inventory ready to sell should be added to inventory cost. The costs associated with the selling effort itself are operating expenses of the period. Inventory should be recorded on the books of the company holding legal title. Goods in transit belong to the company paying for the shipping. Goods on consignment belong to the supplier/owner, not to the business holding the inventory for possible sale. At the end of an accounting period, the total cost of goods available for sale during the period must be allocated between ending inventory and cost of goods sold.

2 Account for inventory purchases and sales using both a perpetual and a periodic inventory system. With a perpetual inventory system, the inventory account is adjusted for every sale or purchase transaction. Discounts on purchases, returns of merchandise, and the cost of transporting goods intended for resale into the firm are also adjustments made directly to the inventory account. With a periodic inventory system, inventory-related items are recorded in temporary holding accounts that are closed to Inventory at the end of the period. The closing entries for a periodic system involve closing Purchases, Freight In, Purchase Returns, and Purchase Discounts to Inventory, and then adjusting the inventory account balance to reflect the appropriate amount given the results of the ending inventory physical count.

3 Calculate cost of goods sold using the results of an inventory count and understand the impact of errors in ending inventory on reported cost of goods sold. Obtaining an accurate inventory amount involves counting the physical units and then properly computing the cost of those units. Special care must be taken in dealing with goods in transit and consigned goods. When a perpetual inventory system is used, the ending inventory count provides an opportunity to compute inventory shrinkage. When ending inventory is not correctly counted, both cost of goods sold and net income will be reported incorrectly. For example, an overstatement in ending inventory leads to an overstatement in reported net income.

4 Apply the four inventory cost flow alternatives: specific identification, FIFO, LIFO, and average cost. The four major costing methods used in accounting for inventories are specific identification, FIFO, LIFO, and average cost. Each of these may result in different dollar amounts of ending inventory, cost of goods sold, gross margin, and net income. A firm may choose any costing alternative without regard to the way goods physically flow through that firm. With FIFO, the oldest units are assumed to be sold first; with LIFO, the newest units are assumed to be sold first. LIFO matches current revenues and current expenses in the income statement; FIFO results in current values being reported in the balance sheet. During an inflationary period, LIFO provides the lowest reported income and, therefore, lower taxes.

5 Use financial ratios to evaluate a company's inventory level. Companies assess how well their inventory is being managed by using two ratios: (1) inventory turnover and (2) number of days' sales in inventory. Inventory turnover is computed as cost of goods sold divided by average inventory; it tells how many times during the period the company turned over, or replenished, its inventory. The number of days' sales in inventory is computed by dividing 365 by the inventory turnover value. A company's choice of inventory cost flow assumption can significantly affect the values of these inventory ratios. The sum of the average collection period and the number of days' sales in inventory is the length of time between the purchase of inventory and the collection of cash from the sale of that inventory. Comparing this sum to the number of days' purchases in accounts payable reveals how much of a company's operating cycle it must finance through external financing.

expanded material

6 Analyze the impact of inventory errors on reported cost of goods sold. Inventory errors can have a significant effect on reported cost of goods sold, gross margin, and net income. In addition, a misstatement of an ending inventory balance affects net income, both in the current year and in the next year. Errors in beginning and ending inventory have the opposite effect on cost of goods sold, gross margin, and net income. Errors in inventory correct themselves after two years if the physical count at the end of the second year shows the correct amount of ending inventory for that period.

7 Describe the complications that arise when LIFO or average cost is used with a perpetual inventory system. Using the average cost and LIFO inventory cost flow assumptions with a perpetual inventory system leads to some complications. These complications arise because the identity of the "last in" units changes with each new inventory purchase, as does the average cost of units purchased up to that point.

8 Apply the lower-of-cost-or-market method of accounting for inventory. Sometimes inventory must be reported at amounts below cost. This occurs (1) when inventory is damaged, used, or obsolete, or (2) when the replacement cost drops below the original inventory cost. In the first case, inventory is valued at a net realizable value; in the second, it is valued at the lower of cost or market. When lower-of-cost-or-market valuation is used, market is defined as the replacement cost of the inventory; in no case can the value be greater than the item's net realizable value (the ceiling) or less than net realizable value minus a normal profit (the floor).

9 Explain the gross margin method of estimating inventories. Although most firms take a physical count of inventory at the end of each year, they sometimes need to estimate the value of inventory prior to year-end. The gross margin method is a common technique for estimating the dollar amount of inventory. The historical gross margin percentage is used in conjunction with sales to estimate cost of goods sold. This estimated cost of goods sold amount is subtracted from cost of goods available for sale to yield an estimate of ending inventory.

key terms and concepts

average cost 308
consignment 297
cost of goods available for sale 298
cost of goods sold 295
FIFO (first in, first out) 308
finished goods 296
FOB (free-on-board) destination 297
FOB (free-on-board) shipping point 297
inventory 295
inventory shrinkage 305
inventory turnover 313
LIFO (last in, first out) 308
net purchases 304
number of days' purchases in accounts payable 315
number of days' sales in inventory 313
periodic inventory system 299
perpetual inventory system 299
raw materials 296
specific identification 309
work in process 296

expanded material

ceiling 322
floor 322
gross margin method 324
lower-of-cost-or-market (LCM) rule 322
net realizable value 321

review problem

Inventory Cost Flow Alternatives

Lehi Wholesale Distributors buys printers from manufacturers and sells them to office supply stores. During January 2003, its periodic inventory records showed the following:

Jan. 1	Beginning inventory consisted of 26 printers at $200 each.
10	Purchased 10 printers at $220 each.
15	Purchased 20 printers at $250 each.
28	Purchased 9 printers at $270 each.
31	Sold 37 printers.

Required: Calculate ending inventory and cost of goods sold, using:

1. FIFO inventory.
2. LIFO inventory.
3. Average cost.

Solution

When computing ending inventory and cost of goods sold, it is usually easiest to get an overview first. The following calculations are helpful:

Beginning inventory, 26 units at $200 each	$ 5,200
Purchases: 10 units at $220	$ 2,200
20 units at $250	5,000
9 units at $270	2,430
Total purchases (39 units)	$ 9,630
Cost of goods available for sale (65 units)	$14,830
Less ending inventory (28 units)	?
Cost of goods sold (37 units)	?

Given a beginning inventory, only ending inventory and cost of goods sold will vary with the different inventory costing alternatives. Because ending inventory and cost of goods sold are complementary numbers whose sum must equal total goods available for sale, you can calculate only one of the two missing numbers in each case and then compute the other by subtracting the first number from goods available for sale. Thus, in the calculations that follow, we will always calculate ending inventory first.

1. FIFO Inventory

Since we know that 28 units are left in ending inventory, we look for the last 28 units purchased because the first units purchased would all be sold. The last 28 units purchased were:

9 units at $270 each on January 28 =	$2,430
19 units at $250 each on January 15 =	4,750
Ending inventory	$7,180

Ending inventory is $7,180, and cost of goods sold is $7,650 ($14,830 − $7,180).

2. LIFO Inventory

The first 28 units available would be considered the ending inventory (since the last ones purchased are the first ones sold). The first 28 units available were:

Beginning inventory: 26 units at $200 =	$5,200
January 10 purchase: 2 units at $220 =	440
Ending inventory	$5,640

Thus,

Cost of goods available for sale	$14,830
Ending inventory	5,640
Cost of goods sold	$ 9,190

3. Average Cost

The total cost of goods available for sale is divided by total units available for sale to get a weighted average cost:

$$\frac{\text{Cost of Goods Available for Sale}}{\text{Units Available for Sale}} = \frac{\$14{,}830}{65} = \$228.15 \text{ per Unit}$$

Cost of goods available for sale.	$14,830
Less ending inventory (28 units at $228.15)	6,388
Cost of goods sold (37 units at $228.15)	$ 8,442

Note: With the average cost alternative, the computed amounts may vary slightly due to rounding.

expanded material

Perpetual Inventory Cost Flow Alternatives

Using the above example, we assume Lehi Wholesale Distributors buys printers from manufacturers and sells them to office supply stores. During January 2003, its inventory records showed the following:

Jan. 1 Beginning inventory consisted of 26 printers at $200 each.
10 Purchased 10 printers at $220 each.
12 Sold 15 printers.
15 Purchased 20 printers at $250 each.
17 Sold 14 printers.
19 Sold 8 printers.
28 Purchased 9 printers at $270 each.

Required: Calculate ending inventory and cost of goods sold, using:

1. Perpetual FIFO inventory.
2. Perpetual LIFO inventory.
3. Perpetual average cost.

Solution When computing ending inventory and cost of goods sold, it is usually easiest to get an overview first. The following calculations are helpful:

Beginning inventory, 26 units at $200 each . . .	$ 5,200
Purchases: 10 units at $220 . . .	$ 2,200
20 units at $250 . . .	5,000
9 units at $270 . . .	2,430
Total purchases (39 units). . .	$ 9,630
Cost of goods available for sale (65 units) . . .	$14,830
Less ending inventory (28 units) . . .	?
Cost of goods sold (37 units) . . .	?

Given a beginning inventory, only ending inventory and cost of goods sold will vary with the different inventory costing alternatives. Because ending inventory and cost of goods sold are complementary numbers whose sum must equal total goods available for sale, you can calculate only one of the two missing numbers in each case, and then compute the other by subtracting the first number from goods available for sale. Thus, in the calculations that follow, we will always calculate ending inventory first.

1. Perpetual FIFO Inventory

With this alternative, records must be maintained throughout the period, as shown. The final calculation is:

Cost of goods available for sale. . . .	$14,830
Ending inventory [(19 × $250) + (9 × $270)]	7,180
Cost of goods sold	$ 7,650

PERPETUAL FIFO CALCULATIONS

Date	Purchased Number of Units	Purchased Unit Cost	Purchased Total Cost	Sold Number of Units	Sold Unit Cost	Sold Total Cost	Remaining Number of Units	Remaining Unit Cost	Remaining Total Cost
Beginning inventory							26	$200	$5,200
January 10	10	$220	$2,200				36	26 at $200 10 at $220	$7,400
12				15	15 at $200	$3,000	21	11 at $200 10 at $220	$4,400
15	20	$250	5,000				41	11 at $200 10 at $220 20 at $250	$9,400
17				14	11 at $200 3 at $220	2,860	27	7 at $220 20 at $250	$6,540
19				8	7 at $220 1 at $250	1,790	19	19 at $250	$4,750
28	9	$270	2,430	—			28	19 at $250 9 at $270	$7,180
Totals	39		$9,630	37		$7,650			

2. Perpetual LIFO Inventory

With this alternative, as shown below, the calculation is:

Cost of goods available for sale	$14,830
Ending inventory	6,230
Cost of goods sold	$ 8,600

PERPETUAL LIFO CALCULATIONS

Date	Purchased Number of Units	Purchased Unit Cost	Purchased Total Cost	Sold Number of Units	Sold Unit Cost	Sold Total Cost	Remaining Number of Units	Remaining Unit Cost	Remaining Total Cost
Beginning inventory							26	$200	$5,200
January 10	10	$220	$2,200				36	26 at $200 10 at $220	$7,400
12				15	10 at $220 5 at $200	$3,200	21	21 at $200	$4,200
15	20	$250	5,000				41	21 at $200 20 at $250	$9,200
17				14	14 at $250	3,500	27	21 at $200 6 at $250	$5,700
19				8	6 at $250 2 at $200	1,900	19	19 at $200	$3,800
28	9	$270	2,430	—			28	19 at $200 9 at $270	$6,230
Totals	39		$9,630	37		$8,600			

3. Perpetual Average Cost

With this alternative, a new average cost of inventory items must be calculated each time a purchase is made, as shown in the following table:

Cost of goods available for sale	$14,830
Ending inventory	6,748
Cost of goods sold	$ 8,082

PERPETUAL AVERAGE COST CALCULATIONS

	Purchased	Sold	Remaining	Computations
Beginning inventory			26 units at $200.00 = $5,200	
January 10	10 units at $220 = $2,200		36 units at $205.56 = $7,400	$5,200 + $2,200 = $7,400; $7,400 ÷ 36 = $205.56
12		15 units at $205.56 = $3,083	21 units at $205.56 = $4,317	
15	20 units at $250 = $5,000		41 units at $227.24 = $9,317	$4,317 + $5,000 = $9,317; $9,317 ÷ 41 = $227.24
17		14 units at $227.24 = $3,181	27 units at $227.24 = $6,135	
19		8 units at $227.24 = $1,818	19 units at $227.24 = $4,318	
28	9 units at $270 = $2,430		28 units at $241.00 = $6,748	$4,318 + $2,430 = $6,748; $6,748 ÷ 28 = $241.00

discussion questions

1. In wholesale and retail companies, inventory is composed of the items that have been purchased for resale. What types of inventory does a manufacturing firm have?
2. What comprises the cost of inventory?
3. Why is it more difficult to account for the inventory of a manufacturing firm than for that of a merchandising firm?
4. Who owns merchandise during shipment under the terms FOB shipping point?
5. When is the cost of inventory transferred from an asset to an expense?
6. Which inventory method (perpetual or periodic) provides better control over a firm's inventory?
7. Is the accounting for purchase discounts and purchase returns the same with the perpetual and the periodic inventory methods? If not, what are the differences?
8. Are the costs of transporting inventory into and out of a firm treated the same way? If not, what are the differences?
9. Why is it usually important to take advantage of purchase discounts?
10. Why are the closing entries for inventory under a periodic system more complicated than those for a perpetual system?
11. Why is it necessary to physically count inventory when the perpetual inventory method is being used?
12. What adjusting entries to Inventory are required when the perpetual inventory method is used?
13. What is the effect on net income when goods held on consignment are included in the ending inventory balance?
14. Explain the difference between cost flow and the movement of goods.
15. Which inventory cost flow alternative results in paying the least amount of taxes when prices are rising?
16. Would a firm ever be prohibited from using one inventory costing alternative for tax purposes and another for financial reporting purposes?
17. Why is it necessary to know which inventory cost flow alternative is being used before the financial performances of different firms can be compared?
18. What can the inventory turnover ratio tell us?

expanded material

19. Is net income under- or overstated when purchased merchandise is counted and included in the inventory balance but not recorded as a purchase?
20. Is net income under- or overstated if inventory is sold and shipped but not recorded as a sale?
21. Why do the LIFO and average cost inventory cost flow assumptions result in different inventory numbers for the perpetual and periodic inventory methods?
22. When should inventory be valued at its net realizable value?
23. When should inventory be valued at the lower of cost or market?
24. When firms cannot count their inventory, how do they determine how much inventory is on hand for the financial statements?

discussion cases

CASE 7-1

WHY USE A PERPETUAL SYSTEM?

You are a consultant for the ABC Consulting Company. You have been hired by Eddie's Electronics, a company that owns 25 electronics stores selling radios, televisions, compact disc players, stereos, and other electronic equipment. Since the company began business ten years ago, it has been using a periodic inventory system. However, Mark Eddie just returned from a seminar where some of his competitors told him he should be using the perpetual inventory method. Mr. Eddie is not sure he should believe his competitors. He wants you to advise him about his inventory choices and make a recommendation about the inventory method he should use.

CASE 7-2

SHOULD WE REDUCE INVENTORY?

It has now been two years since you advised Mr. Eddie to switch to the perpetual inventory method. He is very happy with the additional information he has about inventory levels and theft. He has hired you for advice once again. This time, Mr. Eddie has been to an inventory management seminar where he heard that most companies have too much money tied up in inventory. He wonders if his company could be much more profitable if it reduced its inventory levels. What would you tell him?

exercises

EXERCISE 7-1

GOODS ON CONSIGNMENT

Company A has consignment arrangements with Supplier B and with Customer C. In particular, Supplier B ships some of its goods to Company A on consignment, and Company A ships some of its goods to Customer C on consignment. At the end of 2003, Company A's accounting records showed:

Goods on consignment from Supplier B.	$ 8,000
Goods on consignment with Customer C	$10,000

1. If a physical count of inventory reveals that $30,000 of goods are on hand, what amount of ending inventory should be reported?
2. If the amount of the beginning inventory for the year was $27,000 and purchases during the year were $59,000, then what is the cost of goods sold for the year? (Assume the ending inventory from question 1.)

3. If, instead of these facts, Company A had only $4,000 of goods on consignment with Customer C, but had $10,000 of consigned goods from Supplier B, and physical goods on hand totaled $36,000, what would the correct amount of the ending inventory be?
4. With respect to question 3, if beginning inventory totaled $24,000 and the cost of goods sold was $47,500, what were the purchases?

EXERCISE 7-2

RECORDING SALES TRANSACTIONS—PERPETUAL INVENTORY METHOD

On June 24, 2003, Hansen Company sold merchandise to Jill Selby for $80,000 with terms 2/10, n/30. On June 30, Selby paid $39,200, receiving the cash discount on her payment, and returned $16,000 of merchandise, claiming that it did not meet contract terms.

Assuming that Hansen uses the perpetual inventory method, record the necessary journal entries on June 24 and June 30. The cost of merchandise to Hansen Company is 70% of its selling price.

EXERCISE 7-3

PERPETUAL INVENTORY METHOD

Oakwood Furniture purchases and sells dining room furniture. Its management uses the perpetual method of inventory accounting. Journalize the following transactions that occurred during April 2003:

Apr. 2	Purchased on account $15,000 of inventory with payment terms 2/10, n/30, and paid $250 in cash to have it shipped from the vendor's warehouse to the Oakwood showroom.
5	Sold inventory costing $3,000 for $5,400 on account.
10	Paid $6,860 on account (from April 2 purchase).
14	Returned two damaged tables purchased on April 2 (costing $800 each) to the vendor.
19	Received payment of $1,000 from customers.
20	Paid the balance of the account from April 2 purchase.
22	Sold inventory costing $6,000 for $7,000 on account.
26	A customer returned a dining room set that she decided didn't match her home. She paid $2,500 for it, and its cost to Oakwood was $1,500.

Assuming the balance in the inventory account is $8,000 on April 1, and no other transactions relating to inventory occurred during the month, what is the inventory balance at the end of April?

EXERCISE 7-4

ADJUSTING INVENTORY (PERPETUAL METHOD)

Deer Company's perpetual inventory records show an inventory balance of $120,000. Deer Company's records also show cost of goods sold totaling $240,000. A physical count of inventory on December 31, 2003, showed $92,000 of ending inventory.

Adjust the inventory records assuming that the perpetual inventory method is used.

EXERCISE 7-5

RECORDING SALES TRANSACTIONS—PERIODIC INVENTORY METHOD

On June 24, 2003, Mowen Company sold merchandise to Jack Simpson for $80,000 with terms 2/10, n/30. On June 30, Simpson paid $39,200, receiving the cash discount on his payment, and returned $16,000 of merchandise, claiming that it did not meet contract terms.

Assuming that Mowen Company uses the periodic inventory method, record the necessary journal entries on June 24 and June 30.

EXERCISE 7-6

ADJUSTING INVENTORY AND CLOSING ENTRIES (PERIODIC METHOD)

As of December 31, 2003, Deer Company had the following account balances:

Inventory (beginning)	$120,000
Purchases	220,000
Purchase returns	4,000

A physical count of inventory on December 31, 2003, showed $92,000 of ending inventory. Prepare the closing entries that are needed to adjust the inventory records and close the related purchases accounts, assuming that the periodic inventory method is used.

EXERCISE 7-7

COST OF GOODS SOLD CALCULATION

The accounts of Meeks Company have the following balances for 2003:

Purchases	$260,000
Inventory, January 1, 2003	40,000
Purchase returns	7,640
Purchase discounts	880
Freight in	12,400
Freight out (selling expense)	2,400
Cash	4,000

The inventory count on December 31, 2003, is $48,000. Using the information given, compute the cost of goods sold for Meeks Company for 2003.

EXERCISE 7-8

Spread-Sheet Software

COST OF GOODS SOLD CALCULATIONS

Complete the Cost of Goods Sold section for the income statements of the following five companies:

	Able Company	Baker Company	Carter Company	Delmont Company	Eureka Company
Beginning inventory	$16,000	$24,800	______	______	$19,200
Purchases	26,500	______	$43,000	$89,500	______
Purchase returns	______	1,000	1,800	200	2,200
Cost of goods available for sale	42,100	______	58,300	______	81,500
Ending inventory	______	22,200	15,200	28,800	______
Cost of goods sold	33,400	67,200	______	93,400	68,400

EXERCISE 7-9

JOURNALIZING INVENTORY TRANSACTIONS

Fleming Machinery uses the periodic method of inventory accounting.

1. Journalize the following transactions relating to the company's purchases in 2003:

Jan. 21	Purchased $8,000 of inventory on credit, terms 2/10, n/30.
30	Paid $7,840 to pay off the debt from the January 21 purchase.
Mar. 14	Purchased $125,000 of inventory on credit, terms 2/10, n/30. Paid $500 in cash for transportation.
Apr. 1	Returned defective machinery worth $20,000 to manufacturer.
13	Paid $105,000 to pay off the debt from the March 14 purchase.

2. Assuming these were the only purchases in 2003, compute the cost of goods sold. Beginning inventory was $13,000 and ending inventory was $22,000.

EXERCISE 7-10

ADJUSTING INVENTORY RECORDS FOR PHYSICAL COUNTS

Spartacas, Inc., which uses the perpetual inventory method, recently had an agency count its inventory of frozen chickens. The agency left the following inventory sheet:

Type of Merchandise	Date Purchased	Quantity on Hand	Unit Cost	Inventory Amount
Chicken grade A	2/12/03	30	$5.00	(a)
Chicken grade B	2/18/03	16	(b)	$54.40
Chicken grade C	2/08/03	(c)	$2.50	$60.00
Chicken grade D	2/15/03	46	(d)	$52.90

Complete the inventory calculations for Spartacas (items a–d) and provide the journal entry necessary to adjust ending inventory, if necessary. The balance in Inventory before the physical count was $305.05.

EXERCISE 7-11

SPECIFIC IDENTIFICATION METHOD

E's Diamond Shop is computing its inventory and cost of goods sold for November 2003. At the beginning of the month, these items were in stock:

	Quantity	Cost	Total
Ring A	8	$600	$ 4,800
Ring A	10	650	6,500
Ring B	5	300	1,500
Ring B	6	350	2,100
Ring B	3	450	1,350
Ring C	7	200	1,400
Ring C	8	250	2,000
			$19,650

During the month, the shop purchased four type A rings at $600, two type B rings at $450, and five type C rings at $300 and made the following sales:

Ring Type	Quantity Sold	Price	Cost
A	2	$1,000	$600
A	3	1,050	600
A	1	1,200	650
B	2	850	450
B	2	800	350
C	4	450	200
C	3	500	250
C	1	550	250

Because of the high cost per item, E's uses specific identification inventory costing.

1. Calculate the cost of goods sold and ending inventory balances for November.
2. Calculate the gross margin for the month.

EXERCISE 7-12

INVENTORY COSTING METHODS

For each of the descriptions listed below, identify the inventory costing method to which it applies. The costing methods are: average cost, LIFO, and FIFO.

1. The value of ending inventory does not include the cost of the most recently acquired goods.
2. In a period of rising prices, cost of goods sold is highest.
3. In a period of rising prices, ending inventory is highest.
4. Ending inventory is between the levels of the other two methods.
5. The balance of the inventory account may be unrealistic because inventory on hand is valued at old prices.

EXERCISE 7-13

FIFO AND LIFO INVENTORY COSTING

Jefferson's Jewelry Store is computing its inventory and cost of goods sold for November 2003. At the beginning of the month, the following jewelry items were in stock (rings were purchased in the order listed):

	Quantity	Cost	Total
Ring A	8	$600	$ 4,800
Ring A	10	650	6,500
Ring B	5	300	1,500
Ring B	6	350	2,100
Ring B	3	450	1,350
Ring C	7	200	1,400
Ring C	8	250	2,000
			$19,650

During the month, the following rings were purchased: four type A rings at $600, two type B rings at $450, and five type C rings at $300. Also during the month, these sales were made:

Ring Type	Quantity Sold	Price
A	2	$1,000
A	3	1,050
A	1	1,200
B	2	850
B	2	800
C	4	450
C	3	500
C	1	550

Jefferson's uses the periodic inventory method. Calculate the cost of goods sold and ending inventory balances for November using FIFO and LIFO.

EXERCISE 7-14

FIFO, LIFO, AND AVERAGE COST CALCULATIONS (PERIODIC INVENTORY METHOD)

The following transactions took place with respect to Model M computers in Alpha's Computer Store during April 2003:

April 1	Beginning inventory	40 computers at $1,200
5	Purchase of Model M computers	15 computers at $1,300
11	Purchase of Model M computers	16 computers at $1,350
24	Purchase of Model M computers	10 computers at $1,400
30	Sale of Model M computers	32 computers at $3,000

Assuming the periodic inventory method, compute cost of goods sold and ending inventory using the following inventory costing alternatives: (a) FIFO, (b) LIFO, and (c) average cost.

EXERCISE 7-15

INVENTORY RATIOS

The following data are available for 2003, regarding the inventory of two companies:

	Atkins Computers	Burbank Electronics
Beginning inventory	$ 40,000	$ 80,000
Ending inventory	48,000	95,000
Cost of goods sold	690,000	910,000

Compute inventory turnover and number of days' sales in inventory for both companies. Which company is handling its inventory more efficiently?

expanded material

EXERCISE 7-16

INVENTORY ERRORS

As the accountant for Mt. Pleasant Enterprises, you are in the process of preparing the income statement for the year ended December 31, 2003. In doing so, you have noticed that merchandise costing $2,000 was sold for $4,000 on December 31.

Before the effects of the $4,000 sale were taken into account, the relevant income statement figures were:

Sales revenue	$80,000
Beginning inventory	18,000
Purchases	44,000
Ending inventory	13,000

1. Prepare a partial income statement through gross margin under each of the following three assumptions:
   a. The sale is recorded in the 2003 accounting record; the inventory is included in the ending physical inventory count.
   b. The sale is recorded in 2003; the inventory is not included in ending inventory.
   c. The sale is not recorded in the 2003 accounting records; the merchandise is not included in the ending inventory count.
2. Under the given circumstances, which of the three assumptions is correct?
3. Which assumption overstates gross margin (and therefore net income)?

EXERCISE 7-17

FIFO, LIFO, AND AVERAGE COST CALCULATIONS (PERPETUAL INVENTORY METHOD)

The July 2003 inventory records of Mario's Bookstore showed the following:

July 1	Beginning inventory	28,000	at $2.00 =	$56,000
5	Sold	4,000		
13	Purchased	6,000	at $2.25 =	13,500
17	Sold	3,000		
25	Purchased	8,000	at $2.50 =	20,000
27	Sold	5,000		
				$89,500

1. Using the perpetual inventory method, compute the ending inventory and cost of goods sold balances with (a) FIFO, (b) LIFO, and (c) average cost. Compute unit costs to the nearest cent.
2. Which of the three alternatives is best? Why?

EXERCISE 7-18

LOWER OF COST OR MARKET

Prepare the necessary journal entries to account for the purchases and year-end adjustments of the inventory of Payson Manufacturing Company. All purchases are made on account. Payson uses the periodic inventory method.

1. Purchased 50 standard widgets for $8 each to sell at $14 per unit.
2. Purchased 15 deluxe widgets at $20 each to sell for $30 per unit.
3. At the end of the year, the standard widgets could be purchased for $9 and are selling for $15.
4. At the end of the year, the deluxe widgets could be purchased for $10 and are selling for $16 per unit. Selling costs are $4 per unit, and normal profit is $6 per unit. Inventory is 15 units.

5. At the end of the second year, standard widgets could be purchased for $6 and are selling for $8. Selling costs are $1 per widget, and normal profit is $2 per widget. Inventory is 50 units.
6. At the end of the second year, the deluxe widgets could be purchased for $9 and are selling for $20. Selling costs and normal profit remain as in (4). Inventory is 15 units.

EXERCISE 7-19

LOWER OF COST OR MARKET

Broderick Company sells lumber. Inventory cost data per 1,000 board feet of lumber for the Broderick Company are as follows:

Item	Plywood	Oak	Pine	Redwood
Quantity on hand	25	20	43	12
Original cost	$600	$2,000	$800	$1,400
Current replacement cost	600	1,800	700	1,800
Net realizable value	500	1,900	800	1,600
Net realizable value minus normal profit	400	1,850	600	1,300

1. By what amount, if any, should each item (considered separately) be written down?
2. Make the appropriate journal entry (or entries):
   a. Assuming that each inventory item is considered separately.
   b. Assuming that LCM is applied to total inventory.

EXERCISE 7-20

GROSS MARGIN METHOD OF ESTIMATING INVENTORY

Jason Company needs to estimate the inventory balance for its quarterly financial statements. The periodic inventory method is used. Records show that quarterly sales totaled $400,000, beginning inventory was $80,000, and net purchases totaled $280,000; the historical gross margin percentage has averaged approximately 40%.

1. What is the approximate amount of ending inventory?
2. If a physical count shows only $100,000 in inventory, what could be the explanation for the difference?

EXERCISE 7-21

ESTIMATING INVENTORY AMOUNTS

Sandra's Boutique was recently destroyed by fire. For insurance purposes, she must determine the value of the destroyed inventory. She knows the following information about her 2003 operations before the fire occurred:

Beginning inventory	$11,500
Net purchases	62,000
Sales	84,500
Profit margin	30%

Estimate the cost of Sandra's destroyed inventory.

EXERCISE 7-22

ESTIMATING INVENTORY

Ted Smyth manages an electronics store. He suspects that some employees are stealing items from inventory. Determine the cost of the missing inventory. The following information is available from the accounting records:

Beginning inventory	$ 300,000
Sales	2,000,000
Net purchases	1,600,000
Actual ending inventory	450,000
Historical profit margin	30%

EXERCISE 7-23

ANALYSIS OF THE OPERATING CYCLE

The following information was taken from the records of Dallen Company for the year 2004:

Sales	$600,000
Beginning inventory	114,000
Ending inventory	87,000
Beginning accounts receivable	68,000
Average collection period	44 days
Beginning accounts payable	36,000
Ending accounts payable	42,000
Gross profit percentage	37%

1. Compute the number of days' sales in inventory.
2. Compute the ending balance in Accounts Receivable.
3. Compute the number of days' purchases in accounts payable.
4. How many days elapse, on average, between the time Dallen must pay its suppliers for inventory purchases and the time Dallen collects cash from its customers for the sale of that same purchased inventory?
5. Repeat the computations in (1), (2), (3), and (4) using the end-of-year balance sheet balances rather than the average balances.

PROBLEM 7-1

WHAT SHOULD BE INCLUDED IN INVENTORY?

Demetrius is trying to compute the inventory balance for the December 31, 2002, financial statements of his automotive parts shop. He has computed a tentative balance of $52,600 but suspects that several adjustments still need to be made. In particular, he believes that the following could affect his inventory balance:

a. A shipment of goods that cost $3,000 was received on December 28, 2002. It was properly recorded as a purchase in 2002 but not counted with the ending inventory.
b. Another shipment of goods (FOB destination) was received on January 2, 2003, and cost $800. It was properly recorded as a purchase in 2003 but was counted with 2002's ending inventory.
c. A $2,800 shipment of goods to a customer on January 3 was recorded as a sale in 2003 but was not included in the December 31, 2002, ending inventory balance. The goods cost $2,000.
d. The company had goods costing $6,000 on consignment with a customer, and $5,000 of merchandise was on consignment from a vendor. Neither amount was included in the $52,600 figure.
e. The following amounts represent merchandise that was in transit on December 31, 2002, and recorded as purchases and sales in 2002 but not included in the December 31 inventory.
   1. Ordered by Demetrius, $1,800, FOB destination.
   2. Ordered by Demetrius, $600, FOB shipping point.
   3. Sold by Demetrius, cost $4,000, FOB shipping point.
   4. Sold by Demetrius, cost $4,600, FOB destination.

Required:

1. Determine the correct amount of ending inventory at December 31, 2002.
2. Assuming net purchases (before any adjustment, if any) totaled $86,400 and beginning inventory (January 1, 2002) totaled $31,600, determine the cost of goods sold in 2002.

PROBLEM 7-2

PERPETUAL AND PERIODIC JOURNAL ENTRIES

The following transactions for Goodmonth Tire Company occurred during the month of March 2003:

a. Purchased 500 automobile tires on account at a cost of $40 each for a total of $20,000.
b. Purchased 300 truck tires on account at a cost of $80 each for a total of $24,000.
c. Paid cash of $1,300 for separate shipping costs on the automobile tires purchased in (a). The supplier of the truck tires included the shipping costs in the $80 price.
d. Returned 12 automobile tires to the supplier because they were defective.
e. Paid for the automobile tires. A 1% discount was given on the amount owed. (HINT: Remember that some of the automobile tires were returned.) Payment terms were 1/20, n/30.
f. Paid for half the truck tires, receiving a discount of 2%. Terms were 2/10, n/30.
g. Paid the remaining balance owed on the truck tires. No discount was received because payment was made after the discount period.
h. Sold on account 400 automobile tires at a price of $90 each for a total of $36,000.
i. Sold on account 200 truck tires at a price of $150 each for a total of $30,000.
j. Accepted return of 7 automobile tires from dissatisfied customers.

Required:

1. Prepare journal entries to account for the above transactions assuming a periodic inventory system.
2. Prepare journal entries to account for the above transactions assuming a perpetual inventory system.
3. Assume that inventory levels at the beginning of March (before these transactions) were 100 automobile tires that cost $40 each and 70 truck tires that cost $80 each. Also, assume that a physical count of inventory at the end of March revealed that 184 automobile tires and 164 truck tires were on hand. Given these inventory amounts, prepare the closing entries to account for inventory and related accounts as of the end of March.

PROBLEM 7-3

INCOME STATEMENT CALCULATIONS

Waukesha Company has gross sales of 160% of cost of goods sold. It has also provided the following information for the calendar year 2003:

Inventory balance, January 1, 2003	$100,000
Total cost of goods available for sale	300,000
Sales returns	13,000
Purchase returns	5,000
Freight in	2,000
Sales (net of returns)	407,000
Operating expenses	27,000

Required:

Using the available information, compute the following. (Ignore income taxes.)

1. Gross sales for 2003.
2. Net purchases and gross purchases for 2003.
3. Cost of goods sold for 2003.
4. Inventory balance at December 31, 2003.
5. Gross margin for 2003.
6. Net income for 2003.

PROBLEM 7-4

INCOME STATEMENT CALCULATIONS

	Company A	Company B	Company C	Company D
Sales revenue	$2,000	(4) ____	$480	$1,310
Beginning inventory	200	76	0	600
Purchases	(1) ____	423	480	249
Purchase returns	(20)	(19)	(0)	(8) ____
Ending inventory	300	110	(6) ____	195
Cost of goods sold	1,200	370	(7) ____	(9) ____
Gross margin	(2) ____	(5) ____	155	(10) ____
Operating expenses	108	22	34	129
Net income	(3) ____	107	121	546

Required: Complete the income statement calculations by filling in all missing numbers.

PROBLEM 7-5

INVENTORY COST FLOW ALTERNATIVES

Stocks, Inc., sells weight-lifting equipment. The sales and inventory records of the company for January through March 2003 were as follows:

	Weight Sets	Unit Cost	Total Cost
Beginning inventory, Jan. 1	460	$30	$13,800
Purchase, Jan. 16	110	32	3,520
Sale, Jan. 25 ($45 per set)	216		
Purchase, Feb. 16	105	36	3,780
Sale, Feb. 27 ($40 per set)	307		
Purchase, March 10	150	28	4,200
Sale, March 30 ($50 per set)	190		

Required:

1. Determine the amounts for ending inventory, cost of goods sold, and gross margin under the following costing alternatives. Use the periodic inventory method, which means that all sales are assumed to occur at the end of the period no matter when they actually occurred. Round amounts to the nearest dollar.
   a. FIFO
   b. LIFO
   c. Average cost
2. **Interpretive Question:** Which alternative results in the highest gross margin? Why?

PROBLEM 7-6

PERIODIC INVENTORY COST FLOW METHOD

Dudley Wholesale buys peaches from farmers and sells them to canneries. During August 2003, Dudley's inventory records showed the following:

		Cases	Price
August 1	Beginning inventory	4,100	$10.50
4	Purchase	1,500	11.00
9	Sale	950	19.95
13	Purchase	1,000	11.00
19	Sale	1,450	19.95
26	Purchase	1,700	11.50
30	Sale	1,900	19.95

Dudley Wholesale uses the periodic inventory method to account for its inventory, which means that all sales are assumed to occur at the end of the period no matter when they actually occurred.

Required: Calculate the cost of goods sold and ending inventory using the following cost flow alternatives. (Calculate unit costs to the nearest cent.)

1. FIFO
2. LIFO
3. Average cost

PROBLEM 7-7

CALCULATING AND INTERPRETING INVENTORY RATIOS

Captain Geech Boating Company sells fishing boats to fishermen. Its beginning and ending inventories for 2003 are $462 million and $653 million, respectively. It had cost of goods sold of $1,578 million for the year ended December 31, 2003. Merchant Marine Company also sells fishing boats. Its beginning and ending inventories for the year 2003 are $120 million and $90 million, respectively. It had cost of goods sold of $1,100 million for the year ended December 31, 2003.

Required:

1. Calculate the inventory turnover and number of days' sales in inventory for the two companies.
2. **Interpretive Question:** Are the results of these ratios what you expected? Which company is managing its inventory more efficiently?

expanded material

PROBLEM 7-8

THE EFFECT OF INVENTORY ERRORS

The accountant for Steele Company reported the following accounting treatments for several purchase transactions (FOB shipping point) that took place near December 31, 2003, the company's year-end:

Date Inventory Was Shipped	Was the Purchase Recorded in the Books on or before December 31, 2003?	Amount	Was the Inventory Counted and Included in Inventory Balance on December 31, 2003?
2003:			
December 26	Yes	$1,100	Yes
December 29	Yes	800	No
December 31	No	1,800	Yes
2004:			
January 1	No	300	Yes
January 1	Yes	3,000	No
January 1	No	600	No

Required:

1. If Steele Company's records reported purchases and ending inventory balances of $80,800 and $29,800, respectively, for 2003, what would the proper amounts in these accounts have been?
2. What would be the correct amount of cost of goods sold for 2003, if the beginning inventory balance on January 1, 2003, was $20,200?
3. By how much would cost of goods sold be over- or understated if the corrections in question (1) were not made?

PROBLEM 7-9

CORRECTION OF INVENTORY ERRORS

The annual reported income for Salazar Company for the years 2000–2003 is shown here. However, a review of the inventory records reveals inventory misstatements.

	2000	2001	2002	2003
Reported net income	$30,000	$40,000	$35,000	$45,000
Inventory overstatement, end of year		3,000		2,000
Inventory understatement, end of year	4,000		1,000	

Required: Using the data provided, calculate the correct net income for each year.

PROBLEM 7-10

THE EFFECT OF INVENTORY ERRORS

You have been hired as the accountant for Tracy Company, which uses the periodic inventory method. In reviewing the firm's records, you have noted what you think are several accounting errors made during the current year, 2003. These potential mistakes are listed as follows:

a. A $43,000 purchase of merchandise was properly recorded in the purchases account, but the related accounts payable account was credited for only $2,000.
b. A $3,500 shipment of merchandise received just before the end of the year was properly recorded in the purchases account but was not physically counted in the inventory and, hence, was excluded from the ending inventory balance.
c. A $6,700 purchase of merchandise was erroneously recorded as a $7,600 purchase.
d. A $500 purchase of merchandise was not recorded either as a purchase or as an account payable.
e. During the year, $1,200 of defective merchandise was sent back to a supplier. The original purchase had been recorded, but the merchandise return entry was not recorded.
f. During the physical inventory count, inventory that cost $400 was counted twice.

Required:

1. If the previous accountant had tentatively computed the 2003 gross margin to be $10,000, what would be the correct gross margin for the year?
2. If these mistakes are not corrected, by how much will the 2004 net income be in error?

PROBLEM 7-11

UNIFYING CONCEPTS: INVENTORY COST FLOW ALTERNATIVES

Stan's Wholesale buys canned tomatoes from canneries and sells them to retail markets. During August 2003, Stan's inventory records showed the following:

		Cases	Price
August 1	Beginning inventory.	4,100	$10.50
4	Purchase	1,500	11.00
9	Sale	950	19.95
13	Purchase	1,000	11.00
19	Sale	1,450	19.95
26	Purchase	1,700	11.50
30	Sale	1,900	19.95

Even though it requires more computational effort, Stan's uses the perpetual inventory method because management feels that the advantage of always having current knowledge of inventory levels justifies the extra cost.

Required: Calculate the cost of goods sold and ending inventory using the following cost flow alternatives. (Calculate unit costs to the nearest cent.)

1. FIFO
2. LIFO
3. Average cost

PROBLEM 7-12

PERPETUAL INVENTORY COST FLOW ALTERNATIVES

Pump-It, Inc., sells weight-lifting equipment. The sales and inventory records of the company for January through March 2003 were as follows:

	Weight Sets	Unit Cost	Total Cost
Beginning inventory, Jan. 1	460	$30	$13,800
Purchase, Jan. 16	110	32	3,520
Sale, Jan. 25 ($45 per set).	216		
Purchase, Feb. 16	105	36	3,780
Sale, Feb. 27 ($40 per set).	307		
Purchase, March 10	150	28	4,200
Sale, March 30 ($50 per set)	190		

Required:

1. Determine the amounts for ending inventory, cost of goods sold, and gross margin under the following costing alternatives. Use the perpetual inventory method. Round amounts to the nearest dollar.
   a. FIFO
   b. LIFO
   c. Average cost (calculate unit costs to the nearest cent)
2. **Interpretive Question:** Which alternative results in the highest gross margin? Why?

PROBLEM 7-13

UNIFYING CONCEPTS: INVENTORY ESTIMATION METHOD

Jamestown Clothing Store has the following information available:

	Cost	Selling Price	Other
Purchases during January 2003	$120,000	$170,000	
Inventory balance January 1, 2003	48,000	62,000	
Sales during January		180,000	
Average gross margin rate for the last three years			25%

Required:

1. On the basis of this information, estimate the cost of inventory on hand at January 31, 2003, using the gross margin method. Round to the nearest whole percent.
2. How accurate do you think this method is?

competency enhancement opportunities

- Analyzing Real Company Information
- International Case
- Ethics Case
- Writing Assignment
- The Debate
- Cumulative Spreadsheet Project
- Internet Search

The following additional assignments provide opportunities for students to develop critical thinking, ethical perspectives, oral and written communication skills, experience with electronic research, and teamwork through group and business activities.

ANALYZING REAL COMPANY INFORMATION

• ***Analyzing 7-1 (Microsoft)***

Using MICROSOFT's 1999 annual report in Appendix A, answer the following questions:

1. What type of items compose Microsoft's inventory?
2. Review Microsoft's balance sheet to determine the amount of inventory on hand on June 30, 1999. Does this mean Microsoft has absolutely no inventory? Where would Microsoft's inventory probably be disclosed?
3. Review the management's discussion note disclosure on operating expenses, specifically the discussion relating to cost of revenue. Does this discussion help explain what might make up some of Microsoft's inventory?

• ***Analyzing 7-2 (Archer Daniels Midland)***

Selected financial statement information relating to inventories for ARCHER DANIELS MIDLAND (ADM) is given below:

	1999	1998
Cost of goods sold	$13,051,306	$14,727,670
Inventory—FIFO valuation	2,734,054	2,608,167
Inventory—LIFO valuation	2,732,694	2,562,650

ADM accounts for approximately 75% of its inventories using the FIFO method, but accounts for some of its inventories using the LIFO method. Thus, the differences reflected in the above table represent those inventories accounted for using the two methods.

1. Compute ADM's number of days' sales in inventory for 1999 using (a) the FIFO valuation for inventory and (b) the LIFO valuation for inventory. Are the differences significant enough to concern you?
2. Suppose that ADM purchases its inventory with the terms "net 30 days." That is, ADM's creditors expect payment in 30 days. Is ADM going to have a cash flow problem?

• *Analyzing 7-3 (La-Z-Boy and McDonald's)*

The following information is taken from the 1998 financial statements of LA-Z-BOY, INC., maker of recliners and other home furnishings, and the 1999 financial statements of MCDONALD'S, maker of the Big Mac® and other fast foods.

	La-Z-Boy	McDonald's
Cost of goods sold	$825.3*	$3,204.6
Beginning inventory	78.8	77.3
Ending inventory	91.9	82.7

*Amounts in millions.

1. Before you do any computations, forecast which of the two companies will have a lower number of days' sales in inventory.
2. Compute each company's number of days' sales in inventory. Was your forecast in (1) correct?
3. How can these two very successful companies have number of days' sales in inventory that are so different?

INTERNATIONAL CASE

• *Why No LIFO?*

The LIFO method of accounting for inventory is primarily a U.S. invention. Many countries around the world will not allow LIFO to be used, and other countries discourage its use. For example, the International Accounting Standards Committee calls LIFO an undesirable but "allowable" method. In the United Kingdom, LIFO is allowable under corporate law but is unacceptable under professional accounting standards.

Why do you think other countries have such an unfavorable opinion of LIFO? Think about these issues: In periods of rising prices, does the amount shown on the balance sheet relating to inventory reflect current cost? If a company's inventory on the balance sheet reflected costs from years past, what would happen to the income statement if those inventory costs were suddenly moved to Cost of Goods Sold? Would the result reflect a firm's actual performance?

ETHICS CASE

• *Shipping Bricks*

In 1989 the U.S. Department of Justice Criminal Division discovered a massive inventory fraud that was being conducted by managers at MINISCRIBE CORPORATION. MiniScribe manufactured and sold computer disk drives. The fraud included placing bricks in disk drive boxes, shipping those boxes to customers, and recording a sale when the box was shipped. MiniScribe managers also knowingly shipped defective drives and recorded sales even though they knew those drives would be returned.

What would be the effect on the income statement and the balance sheet of shipping bricks and recording those shipments as sales? (HINT: Think about the journal entry that would have been made by MiniScribe accountants when a box of bricks was shipped to customers who were expecting disk drives.)

Would company officials be able to fool financial statement users for a long time using this type of deception? What could financial statement users have looked for to detect this type of fraud?

WRITING ASSIGNMENT

• *Estimating Inventory*

Jon Johnson, an accountant with a local CPA firm, has just completed an inventory count for Mom & Pop's Groceries. Mom and Pop provide audited financial statements to their bank annually, and part of that audit requires an inventory count. Don Squire, a partner with the CPA firm, has also conducted an analysis to estimate this period's ending inventory. Don used the gross margin method, a method whereby the prior period's gross margin percentage is used to infer this period's percentage, to estimate ending inventory. In addition, the store is equipped with cash registers that scan each product as it is sold and, as a result, provide a perpetual inventory record.

These three inventory analysis methods have resulted in three very different answers, which are summarized in the following table:

Method	Inventory Value
Inventory count	$ 98,500
Gross margin analysis	119,750
Point-of-sale scanners	111,500

In evaluating the results, Jon and Don are curious as to why the three methods result in such large differences. Since the inventory count reports actual inventory on hand, they begin to wonder if Mom and Pop have an inventory theft problem. Write a short memo explaining why the other two methods, gross margin analysis and point-of-sale scanners, can result in significantly different answers without there being a theft problem.

THE DEBATE

• *One Method for All*

As you know, we have periodic and perpetual inventory methods, along with LIFO, FIFO, and average cost variations of each. How can we compare the financial statements of different companies if they are using different inventory methods? This debate focuses on the question of whether financial statement users would be better able to compare information if all companies used the same inventory method.

Divide your group into two teams and prepare a five-minute presentation defending the following positions:

- One team represents "What's Good for One Is Good for All." To make financial statements comparable, all companies should be required to use the same inventory method. Which one? Rather than fight over the pros and cons of LIFO and FIFO, a compromise position would be to require all firms to use perpetual average cost. With the availability of computers, the computational problems associated with this method no longer exist. The resulting information would then allow more comparability across firms.
- The other team represents "It's OK to Be Different." Firms are different. One size does not fit all, and one inventory method is not appropriate for

all firms. Firms should be allowed to use the inventory method(s) that are best suited for their unique operations.

CUMULATIVE SPREADSHEET PROJECT

This spreadsheet assignment is a continuation of the spreadsheet assignments given in earlier chapters. If you completed those spreadsheets, you have a head start on this one. If needed, review the spreadsheet assignment for Chapter 4 to refresh your memory on how to construct forecasted financial statements.

1. Handyman wishes to prepare a forecasted balance sheet and income statement for 2004. Use the original financial statement numbers for 2003 [given in part (1) of the Cumulative Spreadsheet Project assignment in Chapter 2] as the basis for the forecast, along with the following additional information:
   a. Sales in 2004 are expected to increase by 40% over 2003 sales of $700.
   b. Cash will increase at the same rate as sales.
   c. The forecasted amount of accounts receivable in 2004 is determined using the forecasted value for the average collection period. For simplicity, do the computations using the end-of-period accounts receivable balance instead of the average balance. The average collection period for 2004 is expected to be 14.08 days.
   d. In 2004, Handyman expects to acquire new property, plant, and equipment costing $80.
   e. The $160 in operating expenses reported in 2003 breaks down as follows: $5 depreciation expense, $155 other operating expenses.
   f. No new long-term debt will be acquired in 2004.
   g. No cash dividends will be paid in 2004.
   h. New short-term loans payable will be acquired in an amount sufficient to make Handyman's current ratio in 2004 exactly equal to 2.0.

   Note: These statements were constructed as part of the spreadsheet assignment in Chapter 6; you can use that spreadsheet as a starting point if you have completed that assignment. *Clearly state any additional assumptions that you make.*

   For this exercise, add the following additional assumptions:
   i. The forecasted amount of inventory in 2004 is determined using the forecasted value for the number of days' sales in inventory (computed using the end-of-period inventory balance). The number of days' sales in inventory for 2004 is expected to be 107.6 days.
   ii. The forecasted amount of accounts payable in 2004 is determined using the forecasted value for the number of days' purchases in accounts payable (computed using the end-of-period accounts payable balance). The number of days' purchases in accounts payable for 2004 is expected to be 48.34 days.
2. Repeat (1), with the following changes in assumptions:
   a. Number of days' sales in inventory is expected to be 66.2 days.
   b. Number of days' sales in inventory is expected to be 150.0 days.
3. Comment on the differences in the forecasted values of cash from operating activities in 2004 under each of the following assumptions about the number of days' sales in inventory: 107.6 days, 66.2 days, and 150.0 days.
4. Is there any impact on the forecasted level of accounts payable when the number of days' sales in inventory is changed? Why or why not?
5. What happens to the forecasted level of short-term loans payable when the number of days' sales in inventory is reduced to 66.2 days? Explain.

INTERNET SEARCH

• ***Sears***

We began this chapter with a discussion of **SEARS ROEBUCK & COMPANY**. Access its Web site at **http://www.sears.com**. Sometimes Web addresses change, so if this address doesn't work, access the Web site for this textbook (**http://albrecht.swcollege.com**) for an updated link.

Once you have located the company's Web site, answer the following questions:

1. Locate the portion of the Web site dedicated to Sears' history. Can you find information about Sears' beginnings (similar to the narrative at the beginning of this chapter)? In what year did Sears issue its first large general catalog?
2. Locate Sears' balance sheet. Have inventories, as a percentage of total assets, increased or decreased over the time period presented?
3. Compute Sears' number of days' sales in inventory. Is it increasing or decreasing over the time period presented?
4. Locate Sears' note information relating to inventory. Which inventory methods does Sears employ?

Completing the Operating Cycle

chapter f8

learning objectives

After studying this chapter, you should be able to:

1. Account for the various components of employee compensation expense.
2. Compute income tax expense, including appropriate consideration of deferred tax items.
3. Distinguish between contingent items that should be recognized in the financial statements and those that should be merely disclosed in the financial statement notes.
4. Understand when an expenditure should be recorded as an asset and when it should be recorded as an expense.
5. Prepare an income statement summarizing operating activities as well as other revenues and expenses, extraordinary items, and earnings per share.

Before 1850, the primary use for petroleum was as a medicine. Known variously as Seneca oil, American oil, and rock oil, a mixture of water and petroleum was reportedly good for rheumatism, chronic cough, ague, toothache, corns, neuralgia, urinary disorders, indigestion, and liver ailments. The oil was collected by wringing out woolen blankets that had been thrown onto the surfaces of ponds that had been fouled by seeping oil. Oil was also a nuisance by-product of drilling wells in search of underground salt brine deposits.

Gradually, additional properties of oil were discovered. It was found that oil could serve as a lubricant for the machinery that was becoming more common as the Industrial Revolution progressed. In addition, distilled oil was found to burn well in the household lamps that had traditionally burned vegetable oil or sperm whale oil. As the demand for petroleum increased, the search for oil began in earnest. A group of investors hired Edwin L. Drake to drill for oil in northwestern Pennsylvania, where oil had long been found in springs and wells. In late August 1859, Drake struck oil at a depth of 69½ feet, creating an oil well that yielded 25 barrels per day. This discovery touched off an oil rush in western Pennsylvania, and the opportunities to get rich were soon fanned by the increased demand for lubricating oil associated with the North's war production during the Civil War.

fyi

The oil boom did not hit Texas until 1901 when a well on Spindletop Hill, south of Beaumont, Texas, began to gush 100,000 barrels of oil a day.

In those early days, Cleveland, Ohio, was the center of oil refining, and one of the earliest players in the refining business was John D. Rockefeller. Rockefeller had started his business career in Cleveland as a bookkeeper(!) in 1855. By saving his earnings, he acquired some investment capital, and, with a partner, he put up $4,000 to begin a refinery in Cleveland in 1862. Rockefeller's aggressive business tactics aroused controversy almost from the beginning. In particular, Rockefeller was accused of negotiating favorable freight rates with the railroads hauling his oil whereas his competitors were required to pay the stated rates. In 1872, Rockefeller was able to persuade a large number of his Cleveland refining competitors to sell out to him by convincing them that he had arranged such a favorable deal with the railroads that competing head-to-head with him would be impossible.

Rockefeller was eager to expand the business interests of his **STANDARD OIL COMPANY OF OHIO** into other areas, but the incorporation laws in existence at the time made it difficult for corporations to merge. Therefore, Rockefeller created a "trust," which was basically a corporation of corporations. The stockholders of each corporation transferred their shares to the care of the nine trustees of the **STANDARD OIL TRUST**; in exchange, the stockholders received trust certificates. Thereafter, the nine trustees ran the businesses and the stockholders received the dividends. When the Ohio Supreme Court ruled this trust illegal in 1892, lawyers for Standard Oil sought another business structure that would preserve the essence of the trust. They found the answer in the incorporation laws of the state of New Jersey, which allowed the formation of a holding company that would own shares of various corporations, duplicating the function of the central trust. In 1899, legal ownership of the companies controlled by Rockefeller was transferred to a holding company called the **STANDARD OIL COMPANY OF NEW JERSEY**.

fyi

John D. Rockefeller used some of his Standard Oil profits to found the University of Chicago in 1891.

setting the stage

In the early 1890s, the spirit of reform spread over the United States. Many people felt that Big Business was too powerful and must be reined in by the federal government. President Theodore Roosevelt set the tone by proclaiming himself a "trust-buster," and his administration vigorously pursued an antitrust case against Standard Oil. In 1911, the U.S. Supreme Court mandated the breakup of the Standard Oil Company into 34 smaller companies. Many of those companies are still very well known, as evidenced by the partial list contained in Exhibit 8-1.

fyi

The federal antitrust case against **MICROSOFT** has been compared to the Standard Oil case of 1911, with Bill Gates playing the role of a modern-day Rockefeller.

The largest piece of the dismembered Standard Oil Trust was the Standard Oil Company of New Jersey, which changed its named to **EXXON** in 1972. Exxon now operates in over 100 countries, exploring for oil, producing petrochemical products, and transporting oil and natural gas. In

exhibit 8-1 Companies Descended from the Original Standard Oil

	Total Revenue for 1999 (in millions)
Amoco (subsidiary of BP Amoco)	$ 33,000*
Ashland	20,293
Atlantic Richfield (merger with BP Amoco pending)	13,055
Chevron	36,586
Conoco	27,309
ExxonMobil	185,527
Pennzoil–Quaker State	2,989
Total	$318,759

By contrast, the #1 company in the Fortune 500 revenue listing in 1999 was General Motors with revenues of $189,058 million.
*Estimated
Source: *The Wall Street Journal*, December 2, 1998, p. B1, updated.

many places, the company is known as ESSO, representing the initials "SO" for Standard Oil. To illustrate the size of Exxon's operations, the company had worldwide proved oil reserves of 11.3 billion barrels and proved natural gas reserves of 56.8 trillion cubic feet as of December 31, 1999. On December 1, 1998, Exxon (the former Standard Oil Company of New Jersey) announced an agreement to merge with MOBIL (the former STANDARD OIL COMPANY OF NEW YORK), thus reuniting these two pieces of the vast empire built by John D. Rockefeller. The formal joining of the two companies was completed on November 30, 1999, creating EXXONMOBIL.[1]

In Chapters 6 and 7, we discussed the accounting for sales and the cost of inventory sold. For firms that sell a product, the cost of the inventory sold typically represents the largest expense. For example, cost of goods sold was the largest expense category for EXXONMOBIL in 1999, totaling 42% of sales. For WAL-MART, cost of goods sold was 79% of sales in 1999. Although cost of goods sold represents a significant expense for those companies such as ExxonMobil and Wal-Mart that manufacture and/or sell a product, it is certainly not the only expense. And for those companies that sell a service, other expenses such as employee compensation or advertising can be far more significant than cost of goods sold.

In this chapter, we discuss a number of these other significant operating issues. We will begin with a discussion of two significant operating expenses that are incurred by almost every firm: employee compensation and income taxes. We also discuss the accounting for the costs associated with contingencies, which are items that are not fully resolved at the time the financial statements are prepared. Two common examples of contingencies are lawsuits and environmental cleanup obligations. Also in this chapter we discuss how one determines whether a cost should be recorded as an asset (capitalized) or recorded as an expense. The expense versus capitalize issue has arisen many

1 Information for this description was obtained from Daniel J. Boorstin, *The Americans: The Democratic Experience* (New York: Random House, 1973) and Ida M. Tarbell, *The History of the Standard Oil Company* (New York: MacMillan Company, 1904).

times over the years as accountants have wrestled with how to account for advertising costs, research costs, and others.

The financial statement items covered in this chapter are illustrated in Exhibit 8-2. Various operating items affecting the income statement are covered in the chapter. The two most significant are employee compensation and income taxes. The balance sheet items discussed are pension liabilities, deferred income tax liabilities, and contingent liabilities. The accounting aspects of these balance sheet items are intriguing in that both the pension and deferred tax items are sometimes reported as assets rather than liabilities. In addition, contingent liabilities are frequently not reported on the balance sheet at all. The details of all these topics, and more, are discussed in this chapter.

1

Account for the various components of employee compensation expense.

EMPLOYEE COMPENSATION

Often, one of the largest operating expenses of a business is the salaries and wages of its employees. But the cost of employees is not simply the expense associated with the current period's wages. As the following time line illustrates, issues associated with employee compensation can extend long after the employee has retired.

Employee Compensation Event Line

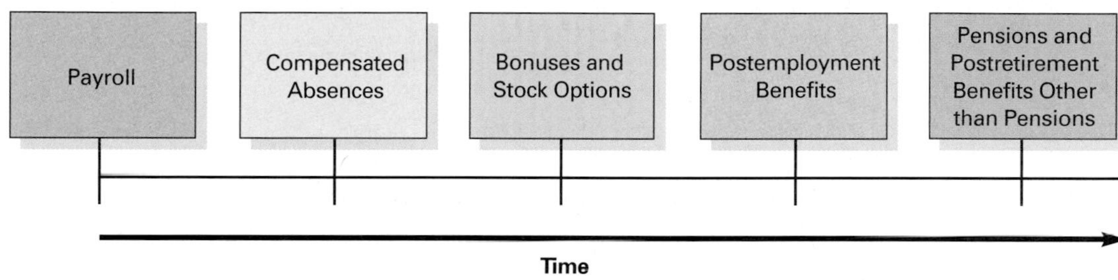

exhibit 8-2 Financial Statement Items Covered in This Chapter

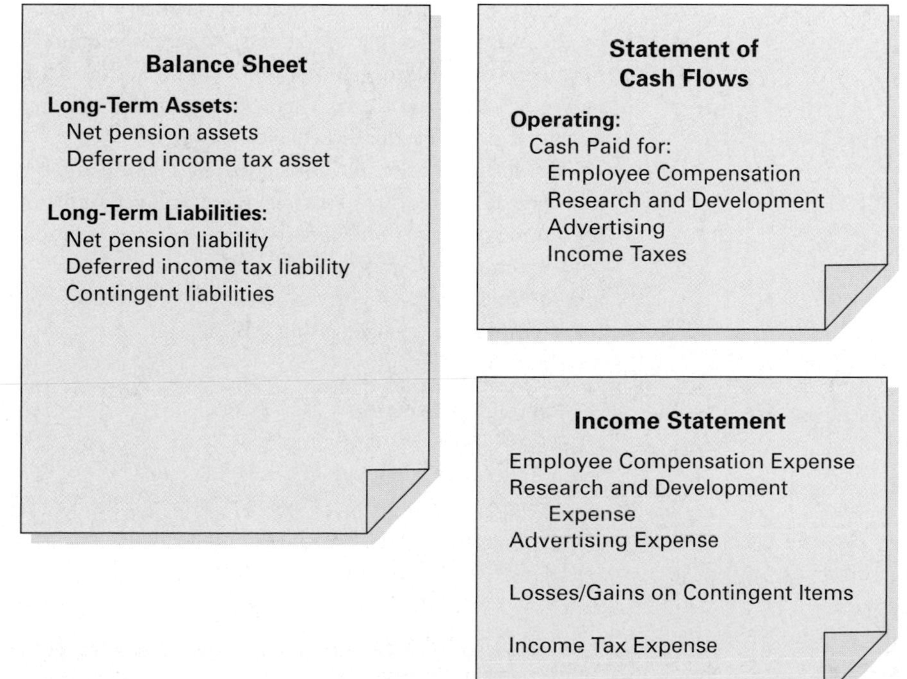

Payroll relates to the salaries and wages earned by employees for work done in the current period. Wages are paid anywhere from weekly to monthly, depending on the company. Compensated absences exist when an employer agrees to pay workers for sick days or vacation days. These obligations must be estimated and accrued in the period that the employee earns those days off. Many employees are paid bonuses based on some measure of performance (such as income or sales volume). Those bonuses are often paid quarterly or annually. One way to provide bonuses to employees is through the granting of stock options. In some cases, employees may earn what are termed "postemployment benefits," which kick in if an employee is laid off or terminated. Finally, firms offer benefits to their employees upon retirement. We will discuss each of these items in further detail in the sections that follow.

Payroll

In its simplest form, accounting for payroll involves debiting Salaries Expense and crediting Salaries Payable when employees work and then debiting Salaries Payable and crediting Cash when wages are paid. However, accounting for salaries and related payroll taxes is never quite that simple and can, in fact, be quite complex. This is primarily because every business is legally required to withhold certain taxes from employees' salaries and wages.

Very few people receive their full salary as take-home pay. For example, an employee who earns $30,000 a year probably takes home between $20,000 and $25,000. The remainder is withheld by the employer to pay the employee's federal and state income taxes, **Social Security (FICA) taxes**,[2] and any voluntary or contractual withholdings that the employee has authorized (such as union dues, medical insurance premiums, and charitable contributions). Thus, the accounting entry to record the expense for an employee's monthly salary (computed as 1/12 of $30,000) might be:

Social Security (FICA) taxes Federal Insurance Distributions Act taxes imposed on the employee and the employer; used mainly to provide retirement benefits.

Salaries Expense	2,500	
FICA Taxes Payable, Employees		191
Federal Withholding Taxes Payable		400
State Withholding Taxes Payable		200
Salaries Payable		1,709
To record Mary Perrico's salary for July.		

All the credit amounts (which are arbitrary in this example) are liabilities that must be paid by the employer to the federal and state governments and to the employee. It should be noted that these withholdings do not represent an additional expense to the employer because the employee actually pays them. The employer merely serves as an agent for the governments for collecting and paying these withheld amounts.

In addition to remitting employees' income and FICA taxes, companies must also pay certain payroll-related taxes, such as the employer's portion of the FICA tax (an amount equal to the employee's portion) and state and federal unemployment taxes. The payroll-related taxes paid by employers are expenses to the company and are included in operating expenses on the income statement. An entry to record the company's share of payroll taxes relating to Mary Perrico's employment (again using arbitrary amounts) would be:

Payroll Tax Expense	279	
FICA Taxes Payable, Employer		191
Federal Unemployment Taxes Payable		18
State Unemployment Taxes Payable		70
To record employer payroll tax liabilities associated with Mary Perrico's salary for July.		

2 Congress has split FICA taxes into two parts—Social Security and Medicare. For the purposes of this chapter, we will combine the two.

The different liabilities recorded in the preceding two entries for payroll would be eliminated as payments are made. The entries to account for the payments are:

FICA Taxes Payable	382	
Federal Withholding Taxes Payable	400	
Federal Unemployment Taxes Payable	18	
Cash		800
Paid July withholdings and payroll taxes to federal government.		
State Withholding Taxes Payable	200	
State Unemployment Taxes Payable	70	
Cash		270
Paid July withholdings and payroll taxes to state government.		
Salaries Payable	1,709	
Cash		1,709
Paid July salary to Mary Perrico.		

As these entries show, three checks are written for payroll-related expenses: one to the federal government, one to the state, and one to the employee.

One further point about salaries and wages needs to be made. The period of time covered by the payroll may not coincide with the last day of the year for financial reporting. Thus, if the reporting year ends on Wednesday, December 31, and the salaries and wages for that week will be paid Monday, January 5 of the following year, then the company must show the salaries and wages earned from Monday through Wednesday (December 29, 30, and 31) as a liability on the December 31 balance sheet. To accomplish this, the company would record an end-of-year adjusting entry to record the salaries and wages earned for those three days.

Compensated Absences

Suppose that you work for a business that provides each employee one day of sick leave for each full month of employment. When should that sick day (or compensated absence) be accounted for? When it is taken by the employee? When it is earned by the employee? And how much of an accrual should be associated with the compensated absences?

The matching principle requires that the expense associated with the compensated absence be accounted for in the period in which it is earned by the employee. Some of the conceptual issues associated with accounting for compensated absences are similar to those addressed in accounting for bad debts. In the case of bad debts, if we waited until we were sure a customer wasn't going to pay, then we could be certain about our bad debt expense. But we may not find out that we are not going to be paid until several periods later, and as a result, the bad debt expense would be reflected in the wrong accounting period. So instead of waiting until accounts are dishonored, we estimate the expense for each period. The same is true with compensated absences. Although we could wait until those sick days are taken and then know exactly what they will cost, it may be years before we know. Rather than wait, we estimate instead. For example, if you earn both $100 a day and one sick day per month, then it makes sense for your employer to recognize an expense (and accrue a liability) of $100 per month related to your sick pay. This would be done with the following journal entry:

Salaries Expense	100	
Sick Days Payable		100
To recognize accrued sick pay.		

When you take that sick day (and let's not forget that the government will take its share of your sick pay also), the journal entry would be:

Sick Days Payable	100	
Various Taxes Payable		20
Cash.		80
To record payment of sick day net of FICA, federal, and state taxes.		

Now suppose that you don't take your sick day until next year. Assume also that you received a $10 raise per day. This makes our estimate of $100 incorrect, so we will fix that estimate in the period in which you take the sick day. The journal entry in this instance would be:

Sick Days Payable	100	
Salaries Expense	10	
Various Taxes Payable		22
Cash.		88
To record payment of sick day net of FICA, federal, and state taxes.		

The same procedures would apply when accounting for accrued vacation pay or other types of compensated absences.

Bonuses

bonus Additional compensation, beyond the regular compensation, that is paid to employees if certain objectives are achieved.

Many companies offer employee **bonus** plans that allow employees to receive additional compensation should certain objectives be achieved. These bonus plans sometimes apply to all employees although more often they are restricted to members of top management. In many instances, the terms of the bonus plan are defined using financial statement numbers. For example, in its 1999 proxy statement filed with the Securities and Exchange Commission (SEC), EXXONMOBIL disclosed that it has a management bonus plan targeted at 1,000 of its managers. The plan grants a certain number of award units to the managers; a manager is entitled to receive cash equal to the company's reported earnings per share for each award unit held. For example, ExxonMobil's chief executive officer (CEO), Lee R. Raymond, received 301,140 of these award units in 1999. With ExxonMobil's earnings per share in 1999 being $2.25, these award units added $677,565 (301,140 award units × $2.25) to Raymond's base salary of $2,110,417.

The purpose of an earnings-based bonus plan is to encourage managers to work harder and smarter to improve the performance of the company. However, such a plan also increases the incentive of managers to manipulate reported earnings. In fact, one of the factors looked at by auditors in evaluating the risk of financial statement fraud in a company is whether the company has an earnings-based management bonus plan.

Stock Options

employee stock options Rights given to employees to purchase shares of stock of a company at a predetermined price.

Employee stock options have become an increasingly popular way to compensate top executives. Under a stock option plan, managers are given the option of purchasing shares of the company's stock in the future at a price that is specified today. For example, in 1999, Lee Raymond, CEO of ExxonMobil, was granted 425,000 options, each allowing him to buy one share of ExxonMobil stock in the future for $83.56, which was the market value of ExxonMobil shares on the date the options were granted. Raymond will make money from these options if he is able to improve the performance of ExxonMobil and increase its stock price. If, for example, the company's stock price were to increase to $100.00 per share, these 425,000 options, allowing Raymond to buy ExxonMobil shares at the fixed price of $83.56, would be worth $6,987,000 [425,000 × ($100.00 − $83.56)]. Stock options are an attractive way to compensate top management because the options pay off only if the managers are able to increase the value of the company, which is exactly what the owners of the company (the stockholders) desire.

There has been significant debate in the United States about how to compute the compensation expense associated with employee stock options. The debate centers around the issue of what the value of an option is. Two methods for valuing employee options for accounting purposes are described below.

INTRINSIC VALUE METHOD The "intrinsic value" of an option is the value it has if it must be exercised immediately. For example, if a company's stock price is $50 and it issues an option allowing an employee to buy a share of stock for $50, the option has no "intrinsic value" because the employee would be just as well off purchasing the company's stock in the market for $50, just as anyone not holding an option could do.

FAIR VALUE METHOD The "fair value" of an option stems from the possibility that the employee may want to exercise the option in the future if the company's stock price goes up. For example, even if an option exercise price of $50 is equal to the stock price on the date the option is granted to an employee, there is a chance that the stock price may increase during the life of the option. This means that an option with no "intrinsic value" can still have substantial economic value because the employee holding the option may be able to buy the stock at less than its market value some time in the future. Exact computation of the fair value of options involves complex formulas derived using stochastic calculus, but commercially available software packages make option valuation no more difficult than using a spreadsheet.

The fair value method, with its theoretically correct emphasis on estimating the actual value of the options granted to employees, is backed by the FASB. Nevertheless, the vast majority of U.S. corporations opposed the FASB's attempt in 1994 to require recognition of a stock option compensation expense. The reason for this opposition was simple: recognition of a stock option compensation expense would reduce reported earnings. The surprising vigor of the opposition to the fair value method caused the FASB to reluctantly approve the following accounting treatment:

- Companies are allowed to use the intrinsic value method. For most stock option plans, this means that no expense is recognized.
- Companies are encouraged, but not required, to adopt the fair value method for employee stock options. The fair value method results in compensation expense being recognized for almost all stock option plans.
- Those companies choosing to use the intrinsic value method must disclose what their net income would have been if they had used the fair value method.

Like most U.S. companies, ExxonMobil uses the intrinsic value method. In 1999, ExxonMobil granted over 22 million employee stock options, all with intrinsic values of $0 as of the grant date. Thus, ExxonMobil reported no compensation expense in relation to these 22 million options. In the notes to its financial statements, ExxonMobil discloses that these 22 million options had a total fair value of $149 million. This amount would have been recognized as compensation expense (spread over the number of years employees are required to stay with the company to earn the options) if ExxonMobil had used the fair value method.

fyi

MICROSOFT reports that if it had used the fair value method instead of the intrinsic value method in 1999, its reported compensation expense would have been increased by $1.1 billion.

Postemployment Benefits

postemployment benefits Benefits paid to employees who have been laid off or terminated.

Postemployment benefits are perhaps the least common of the topics covered in this section on employee compensation. **Postemployment benefits** are those benefits that are incurred after an employee has ceased to work for an employer but before that employee retires. A common example is a company-provided severance package for employees who have been laid off. This severance package might include salary for a certain time period, retraining costs, education costs, and the like. Although the company may not know the exact postemployment cost, accounting standards require that the amount be estimated and accrued in the period in which the decision is made to cut back the labor force. For example, suppose a company decides to close a segment of its operations, thereby laying off a certain percentage of its labor force. The company must estimate the costs associated with the benefits offered to those laid-off employees and would record the following journal entry:

business environment essay

What Goes into Pensions? A pension is an agreement between an employer and the employees that the employees will receive a certain sum of money upon retirement. That money may be paid in a single sum or over several years. In addition, employers often offer other postretirement benefits such as medical and life insurance. Consider how difficult it can be to account for these items.

Let's assume that you are 25 years old when you start working for your current employer. Your employer's pension plan states that upon retirement you will receive medical and life insurance benefits in addition to a monthly pension check. The pension will be a percentage, commonly 2%, of your average annual salary over the last five years of your employment multiplied by the number of years of employment. What factors need to be considered in determining the employer's future liability?

As you can imagine, estimating these various factors involves some enormous assumptions. Plus, once the estimates have been made, the fact that those expenditures will not be made for 40 years (assuming you retire when you turn 65) must be factored in.

As if that isn't enough, the employer must do this computation for every employee. In the case of large companies, such as EXXONMOBIL with 106,000 employees, the computations are staggering. Fortunately, businesses have help in the form of actuaries. Actuaries make their living predicting the future. They

pension An agreement between an employer and employees that provides for benefits upon retirement.

defined contribution plan A pension plan under which the employer contributes a defined amount to the pension fund; after retirement, the employees receive the amount contributed plus whatever it has earned.

defined benefit plan A pension plan under which the employer defines the amount that retiring employees will receive and contributes enough to the pension fund to pay that amount.

Salaries Expense	xxx	
Benefits Payable		xxx
To record postemployment benefits for laid-off employees.		

When the benefits are paid, a journal entry would be made to reduce the payable and to record the cash outflow.

Pensions

A **pension** is cash compensation received by an employee after that employee has retired. Two primary types of pension plans exist. A **defined contribution plan** requires the company to place a certain amount of money into a pension fund each year on behalf of the employees. Then, after the employees retire, they receive the money contributed to the pension fund plus the earnings on those contributions. With a **defined benefit plan**, on the other hand, the company promises the employees a certain monthly cash amount after they retire, based on factors such as number of years worked by the employee, employee's highest salary, and so forth.

The accounting for a defined contribution plan is quite simple—a company merely reports pension expense equal to the amount of cash it is required to contribute to its employees' pension fund during the year. Normally, no balance sheet liability is reported in connection with a defined contribution plan because, once the company has made the required contribution to the pension fund, it has no remaining obligation to the employees.

STOP & THINK Who bears the risks associated with a defined contribution plan—the employer or the employee? Which party bears the risks associated with a defined benefit plan?

The accounting issues associated with defined benefit plans are much more complex because the ultimate amount that a company will have to pay into its employees' pension fund depends on how long the employees work before retiring, what their highest salaries are, how long the employees live after they retire, and how well the investments in the pension fund perform. The accounting concept underlying this complexity, however, is still the same basic idea of matching: the income statement this year should contain all expenses related to generating revenue this year, whether those expenses are paid in cash this year (like cash wages) or are not expected to be paid for many years (like pension benefits).

estimate birth and death rates, trends in inflation, health-care costs, salaries, and other relevant information. There are about 14,000 actuaries in the United States, compared to over 1 million accountants.

So, if you start thinking that accounting is difficult and you become uncomfortable with all the assumptions and estimates, remember that it could be worse: you could be studying to be an actuary!

Postretirement Benefit	Factors to Consider
Medical insurance	What will health-care costs be in the future? How long will you live to enjoy those health insurance benefits? (The longer you live, the greater the cost.)
Life insurance	What will insurance premiums be for the remainder of your employment?
Pension check	How long will you work? What will your average annual salary be in your last five years of employment? How long will you or your spouse live after you retire?

PENSION-RELATED ITEMS IN THE FINANCIAL STATEMENTS Each of the major balance sheet and income statement items related to pension accounting is briefly introduced below.

- *Pension fund.* When a company has a defined benefit pension plan, it is required by U.S. federal law to establish a separate pension fund to ensure that employees receive the defined benefits promised under the plan. The pension fund is basically a large investment fund of stocks and bonds. The company still owns these pension fund assets, but it cannot use them for any purpose except to pay pension benefits to employees.
- *Pension obligation.* The promise to make defined benefit pension payments to employees represents a liability to the company making the promise. The amount of this liability is quite difficult to estimate because it depends on future salary increases, employee turnover, employee life span, and so forth. The estimation of the liability is done by professionals called actuaries. These are the same individuals who provide the computations that life insurance companies use in setting premiums.
- *Net pension asset or liability.* One possible way to present the pension information on a balance sheet is to list the pension plan assets among the long-term assets and the pension liability as a long-term liability. However, the accounting standards stipulate that these two items be offset against one another and a single net amount be shown as either a net pension asset or a net pension liability.
- *Pension-related interest cost.* The estimated pension obligation represents an amount owed by a company to its employees. Accordingly, a pension-related interest cost is recognized each year; the amount of this interest cost is the increase in the pension obligation resulting from interest on the unpaid pension obligation.
- *Service cost.* The amount of a company's pension obligation increases each year as employees work and earn more pension benefits. This increase in the pension obligation is an expense associated with work done during the year and is called the pension service cost.
- *Return on pension fund assets.* The cost of a company's pension plan is partially offset by the return that the company earns on the assets in its pension fund.
- *Pension expense.* Just as pension liabilities and assets are offset against one another to arrive at a single net liability or asset to be reported on the balance sheet, the three components of pension expense (interest cost, service cost, and return on pension fund assets) are netted against one another to yield a single number that is reported on the income statement.

ILLUSTRATION FROM EXXONMOBIL'S FINANCIAL STATEMENTS In the notes to its 1999 financial statements, ExxonMobil discloses the following about its pension benefit obligation and its pension fund. All numbers are in millions of dollars.

	U.S. Plans	Non-U.S. Plans	Total
Pension benefit obligation	$8,032	$11,628	$19,660
Pension fund assets	7,965	8,689	16,654
Net pension liability	$ 67	$ 2,939	$ 3,006

Note that ExxonMobil has separated its pension plans into those covering employees in the United States and those covering employees located outside the United States. This is a useful separation because the laws governing the maintenance of pension plans vary from country to country; U.S. laws are generally viewed as giving more protection to the rights of the employees covered by pension plans than foreign laws do. Also note that ExxonMobil's pension plans are "underfunded," meaning that the market value of the assets in the pension funds is less than the estimated pension liability. ExxonMobil also provides the following information about its pension expense in 1999. Again, all of the numbers are in millions.

	U.S. Plans	Non-U.S. Plans	Total
Service cost	$ 249	$ 312	$ 561
Interest cost	555	608	1,163
Less: Expected return on fund assets	(601)	(599)	(1,200)
Other miscellaneous items	(35)	217	182
Net pension expense	$ 168	$ 538	$ 706

caution

The *expected*, not the actual, return on the pension fund assets is subtracted in computing pension expense. The accounting for the difference between expected and actual return involves deferring gains and losses, corridor amounts, and other complexities best left for an intermediate accounting course.

Note the significant reduction in reported pension expense caused by the expected return on pension fund assets; without the return on the pension fund, ExxonMobil's pension expense would be more than twice as high.

Postretirement Benefits Other Than Pensions

In addition to pension benefits, employers often offer employees other benefits after their retirement. For example, ExxonMobil promises its employees that it will continue to cover them with health-care and life insurance plans after retirement. These types of plans are typically less formal than pension plans and often are not backed by assets accumulated in a separate fund. For example, ExxonMobil has only a $600 million separate fund set up to cover its estimated $2.6 billion obligation to cover the health-care needs of employees.

The accounting rules require companies to currently recognize the expense and long-term liability associated with the postretirement benefits that are earned in the current year, in keeping with the normal practice of matching expenses to the period in which they are initially incurred. The actual accounting is complex but similar to that required for pensions. The potential liabilities for these future payments can be quite significant for many firms. GENERAL MOTORS has the largest postretirement benefit plan in the United States, with a nonpension postretirement obligation totaling $44.683 billion as of December 31, 1999. Interestingly, General Motors clearly indicates that although it is reporting a liability for these postretirement benefits, it does not recognize these benefits as a legal obligation. In the notes to the 1999 financial statements, GM's management states:

> GM has disclosed in the consolidated financial statements certain amounts associated with estimated future postretirement benefits other than pensions and characterized such amounts as "accumulated postretirement benefit obligations," "liabilities," or "obligations." Notwithstanding the recording of such amounts and the use of these terms, GM

does not admit or otherwise acknowledge that such amounts or existing postretirement benefit plans of GM (other than pensions) represent legally enforceable liabilities of GM.

NORTHERN LIFE INSURANCE COMPANY's Web site, **http://www.northernlifetsa.com**, features a set of retirement and investment calculators to help in financial planning. How much money do you need to save per month in order to accumulate $1 million by the time you are 65?

As illustrated in this section, compensation expense includes much more than just wages and salaries. Companies presumably have calculated that the value of the services provided by employees justifies the additional compensation cost beyond salaries and wages. The fact that employees earn benefits in one year that they do not receive until later, sometimes many years later, necessitates careful accounting to ensure that compensation expense is reported in the year in which it is earned.

---

to summarize

Employee compensation is not limited to just the current period's payroll. The cost of employees also includes compensated absences, bonuses, stock options, postemployment benefits, pensions, and other postretirement benefits. Most companies account for employee stock options using the intrinsic value method, meaning that, typically, no compensation expense is recognized. A pension obligation is reported on the balance sheet as the difference between the obligation and the amount in an associated pension fund. Pension expense is the sum of interest cost and service cost, less the expected return on the pension fund assets.

2

Compute income tax expense, including appropriate consideration of deferred tax items.

TAXES

In addition to the payroll taxes described in the previous section, companies are responsible for paying several other taxes to federal, state, and/or local governments, including sales taxes, property taxes, and income taxes. The accounting for these taxes is described next.

Sales Taxes

Most states and some cities charge a sales tax on retail transactions. These taxes are paid by customers to the seller, who in turn forwards them to the state or city. Sales taxes collected from customers represent a current liability until remitted to the appropriate governmental agency. For example, assume that a sporting goods store in Denver prices a pair of skis at $200 and that the combination of state and city sales tax is 6.5%. When the store sells the skis, it collects $213 and records the transaction as follows:

Cash	213	
Sales Revenue		200
Sales Tax Payable		13
Sold a pair of skis for $200. Collected $213, including 6.5% sales tax.		

sales tax payable Money collected from customers for sales taxes that must be remitted to local governments and other taxing authorities.

The sales revenue is properly recorded at $200, and the $13 is recorded as **Sales Tax Payable**, a liability. Then, on a regular basis, a sales tax return is completed and filed with the state or city tax commission, and sales taxes collected are paid to those agencies. Note that the collection of the sales tax from customers creates a liability to the state but does not result in the recognition of revenue when collected or an expense when paid to the state. The company acts as an agent of the state in collecting the sales tax and recognizes a liability only until the collected amount is remitted to the state.

Property Taxes

Property taxes are usually assessed by county or city governments on land, buildings, and other company assets. The period covered by the assessment of property taxes is often from July 1 of one year to June 30 of the next year. If a property taxpayer is on a calendar-year financial reporting basis (or on a fiscal-year basis ending on a day other than June 30), the property tax assessment year and the company's financial reporting year will not coincide. Therefore, when the company prepares its financial statements at calendar-year end, it must report a prepaid tax asset (if taxes are paid at the beginning of the tax year) or a property tax liability (if taxes are paid at the end of the tax year) for the taxes associated with the first portion of the assessment year. To illustrate, assume that Yokum Company pays its property taxes of $3,600 on June 30, 2002, for the period July 1, 2002, to June 30, 2003. If the company is on a calender-year basis and records the prepayment as an asset, then the adjusting entry at December 31, 2002, would be:

Property Tax Expense	1,800	
Prepaid Property Taxes		1,800
To record property tax expense for 6 months.		

The prepaid property taxes account balance of $1,800 would be shown on Yokum's balance sheet at December 31, 2002, as a current asset. On June 30, 2003, property tax expense would be recognized for the period January 1, 2003, through June 30, 2003, with the following entry:

Property Tax Expense	1,800	
Prepaid Property Taxes		1,800
To record property tax expense for the property assessment period January 1–June 30, 2003.		

Income Taxes

Corporations pay income taxes just as individuals do. This corporate income tax is usually reported as the final expense on the income statement. For example, in 1999, the final three lines in EXXONMOBIL's income statement were as follows, with all numbers in millions:

	1999	1998	1997
Income before income taxes	$11,150	$12,083	$19,337
Income taxes	3,240	3,939	7,605
Net income	$ 7,910	$ 8,144	$11,732

The $3.240 billion in income tax expense reported by ExxonMobil in 1999 is not necessarily equal to the amount of cash paid for income taxes during the year. In fact, ExxonMobil paid $3.805 billion for income taxes in 1999. Reported income tax expense may differ from the actual amount of cash paid for taxes for two reasons. First, like many other expenses, income taxes are not necessarily paid in cash in the year in which they are incurred. The important point to remember is that reported income tax expense reflects the amount of income taxes attributable to income earned during the year, whether the tax was actually paid in cash during the year or not.

The second reason reported income tax expense may differ from the actual amount of cash paid for taxes is that income tax expense is based on reported financial accounting income, whereas the amount of cash paid for income taxes is dictated by the applicable government tax law. The $3.240 billion income tax expense reported by ExxonMobil in 1999 reflects the total estimated amount of income tax the company expects will eventually be paid based on the income reported in the current year's income statement. However, because the income computed using the tax rules is almost always different from the income computed using financial accounting standards, some of this tax may not have to be paid for several years. In addition, tax rules may require income tax to be paid on income before the financial accounting standards consider that income to be "earned." These differences in tax law income and financial accounting income give rise to deferred income tax items, which are discussed in this section.

Corporations in the United States compute two different income numbers—financial income for reporting to stockholders and taxable income for reporting to the Internal Revenue Service (IRS). The existence of these two "sets of books" seems unethical to some, illegal to others. However, the difference between the stockholders' need for information and the government's need for efficient revenue collection makes the computation of the two different income numbers essential. The different purposes of these reporting systems were summarized by the U.S. Supreme Court in the *Thor Power Tool* case (1979):

> The primary goal of financial accounting is to provide useful information to management, shareholders, creditors, and others properly interested; the major responsibility of the accountant is to protect these parties from being misled. The primary goal of the income tax system, in contrast, is the equitable collection of revenue.

In summary, U.S. corporations compute income in two different ways, and rightly so. Nevertheless, the existence of these two different numbers that can each be called "income before taxes" makes it surprisingly difficult to define what is meant by "income tax expense."

Deferred Tax Example

Assume that you invest $1,000 by buying shares in a mutual fund on January 1. Also assume that the income tax rate is 40%. According to the tax law, any economic gain you experience through an increase in the value of your mutual fund shares is not taxed until you actually sell your shares. The rationale behind this tax rule is that until you sell your shares, you don't have the cash to pay any tax. Now, assume further that the economy does well and that the value of your mutual fund shares increases to $1,600 by December 31. You decide to prepare partial financial statements to summarize your holdings and the performance of your shares during the year. These financial statements are as follows:

Balance Sheet		**Income Statement**	
Assets:		Revenues:	
Mutual Fund Shares	$1,600	Gain on Mutual Fund Investment	$600

A moment's consideration reveals that this balance sheet and income statement are misleading. Yes, it is true that your shares are now worth $1,600, but if and when you liquidate the shares, you will have to pay income tax of $240 [($1,600 − $1,000) × .40]. Thus, you are overstating your economic position by only reporting the $1,600 in mutual fund shares; you should also report that a liability of $240 exists in relation to these shares. Similarly, it is misleading to report the $600 gain on your income statement without also reporting that, at some future time, you will have to pay $240 in income tax on that gain. A more accurate set of financial statements would appear as follows:

Balance Sheet		**Income Statement**	
Assets:		Revenues:	
Mutual Fund Shares	$1,600	Gain on Mutual Fund Investment	$600
Liabilities:		Expenses:	
Deferred Income Tax Liability	$ 240	Income Tax Expense	$240

The appropriate journal entry to recognize income tax expense in this case is as follows:

Income Tax Expense	240	
Deferred Income Tax Liability		240

Note that the deferred income tax liability is not a legal liability because, as far as the IRS is concerned, you do not currently owe any tax on the increase in the value of your mutual fund. Nevertheless, the deferred tax liability is an economic liability that should be reported now because it reflects an obligation that will have to be paid in the future as a result of an event (the increase in the value of the mutual fund shares) that occurred this year.

Now, what if the mutual fund shares had decreased in value from $1,000 to $400? Consider whether the following set of financial statements would accurately reflect your economic position and performance:

Balance Sheet		**Income Statement**	
Assets:		Expenses:	
Mutual Fund Shares	$400	Loss on Mutual Fund Investment	$600

Again, these financial statements are somewhat misleading because they ignore the future tax implications of the change in the value of the mutual fund shares. In this case, when the shares are sold, you will realize a taxable loss of $600. If you have other investment income, that loss can be used to reduce your total taxable income by $600, which will save you $240 ($600 × .40 in income taxes. Thus, in a real sense, this loss on the mutual funds is not all bad because it will provide you with a $240 reduction in income taxes in the year in which you sell the shares. This reduction in taxes is an asset, a deferred income tax asset, because it represents a probable future economic benefit that has arisen from an event (the drop in the value of the mutual fund shares) that occurred this year. Similarly, the income statement effect of this future savings in taxes is to soften the blow of the reported $600 loss. The loss that occurred this year will result in an income tax benefit in the future, so the benefit is reported on this year's income statement, as follows:

Balance Sheet		**Income Statement**	
Assets:		Expenses:	
Mutual Fund Shares	$400	Loss on Mutual Fund Investment	$ 600
		Less: Income Tax Benefit	(240)
Deferred Income Tax Asset	$240		
		Net Loss	$ 360

The journal entry to recognize the income tax "expense" is as follows:

Deferred Income Tax Asset	240	
Income Tax Expense..		240

Notice that Income Tax Expense is credited, or reduced, in this entry. If there are other income taxes for the year, this credit will result in a reduction in reported income tax expense. If there are no other income taxes, then the credit amount will be reported on the income statement as an addition to income under the title "income tax benefit."

As this simple mutual fund example illustrates, the amount of income tax expense reported on a company's income statement is not necessarily the same as the amount of income tax the company must pay on taxable income generated during the year. There are literally hundreds

fyi

The value of the deferred tax asset depends on your having other investment income in the future against which the loss on the mutual fund shares can be offset. Thus, accounting for deferred tax assets is complicated by the fact that one must make an assumption about the likelihood that a company will have enough taxable income in the future to be able to take advantage of the deferred tax benefit.

of accounting areas in which income is taxed by the taxing authorities in a different year than the year in which the income is reported to the financial statement users in the income statement. The details of deferred income tax accounting are among the most complicated issues covered in intermediate accounting courses.

to summarize

The amount of sales tax collected is reported as a liability until the funds are forwarded to the appropriate government agency. When property taxes are paid in advance, the amount is reported as a prepaid asset until the time period covered by the property tax has expired. Reported income tax expense is not merely the amount of income tax that a company legally owes for a given year. Because of differences between financial accounting rules and income tax rules, revenues and expense can enter into the computation of income in different years for financial accounting purposes and for income tax purposes. Proper accounting for deferred income taxes ensures that reported income tax expense for a year represents all of the income tax consequences arising from transactions undertaken during the year.

3

Distinguish between contingent items that should be recognized in the financial statements and those that should be merely disclosed in the financial statement notes.

CONTINGENCIES

contingency Circumstances involving potential losses or gains that will not be resolved until some future event occurs.

By its very nature, business is full of uncertainty. As discussed in relation to employee compensation and taxes, proper recording of an expense in the current period frequently requires making estimates about what will occur in future periods. Sometimes the very existence of an asset or liability depends on the occurrence, or nonoccurrence, of a future event. For example, whether a company will have to make a payment as a result of a lawsuit arising from events occurring this year depends on a judge or jury ruling that may not be known for several years. In accounting terms, a **contingency** is an uncertain circumstance involving a potential gain or loss that will not be resolved until some future event occurs. In this section, we discuss the conceptual issues associated with contingencies and the accounting for events for which the outcome is uncertain.

If you were a financial statement user, would you want to be informed of events known to management that might have an adverse effect on the company's future? Consider as an example a lawsuit filed against a company. Because litigation can take years, how should that company account for the possibility of a loss? Would you want the company to wait until the lawsuit is resolved before informing financial statement users of the litigation? Of course not. You would want to know about the lawsuit if the outcome could potentially materially affect the operations of the company. But would you want to know about every lawsuit filed against the company? Probably not.

Accounting standard-setters have addressed this issue and determined that the proper disclosure for a contingency depends upon the assessed outcome. The first thing to note is that accounting standard-setters determined that accounting for contingent gains is, in most cases, inappropriate. Contingent gains are typically not accounted for until the future event relating to the contingent gain resolves itself. Contingent liabilities are to be accounted for differently depending on an assessment of the likely outcome of the contingency. Exhibit 8-3 contains the relevant terms, definitions, and proper accounting for contingent liabilities.

If you think about it, this probability spectrum makes a great deal of sense. For example, if it is likely that your company will lose a lawsuit in which it is the defendant, then it would be appropriate to account for that outcome now by recognizing a loss and establishing a payable. If the likelihood of your company losing the case is slight, then it makes sense to do nothing. And if you are unsure of the outcome, then disclosure in the notes seems appropriate.

exhibit 8-3 Accounting for Contingent Liabilities

Term	Definition	Accounting
Probable	The future event is likely to occur.	Estimate the amount of the contingency and make the appropriate journal entry; provide detailed disclosure in the notes.
Reasonably possible	The chance of the future event occurring is more than remote but less than likely.	Provide detailed disclosure of the possible liability in the notes.
Remote	The chance of the future event occurring is slight.	No disclosure required.

STOP & THINK Why might a company hesitate to assess the likelihood of losing an ongoing lawsuit as being probable? If you were the attorney for the plaintiff, how could you use the resulting information from the financial statements?

The problem in implementing these terms relates to assessing the likelihood of an outcome. Who is to say if your company will lose a lawsuit? The company must obtain objective assessments as to the possible outcome of future events. In the case of litigation, the company would ask its attorneys about the possible outcome. The firm auditing the company might use its own attorneys to assess the possible outcome. In any case, companies are required to make objective assessments as to the likely outcome of contingent events and then account for those events based on that assessment.

MICROSOFT's 1999 annual report (see Appendix A) contains the company's disclosure relating to contingencies. At the time, the company was being investigated by the Justice Department for potential monopolistic practices. Note that the disclosure relating to the antitrust contingency is minimal, consisting of just two paragraphs. Contrast Microsoft's disclosure with the 1999 disclosure provided by PHILIP MORRIS, the tobacco company, relating to its involvement in ongoing tobacco litigation. The company provides over seven pages of disclosure relating to its potential liability.

Environmental Liabilities

environmental liabilities Obligations incurred because of damage done to the environment.

Environmental liabilities have gained increasing attention of late because of their potential magnitude. **Environmental liabilities** are obligations incurred because of damage done by companies to the environment. Common environmental liabilities include cleanup costs associated with oil spills, toxic waste dumps, or air pollution. These liabilities are usually brought to the company's attention as a result of fines or penalties imposed by the federal government or when damage that is caused by the company is recognized. Although the accounting and disclosures associated with environmental liabilities fall under the guidelines for contingencies discussed in the previous section, environmental liabilities present a unique problem.

In the case of a lawsuit, one can typically make a reasonable estimate as to the upper bound of the potential settlement. For example, if your company is being sued for $4 million, it is unlikely that any potential settlement will be higher than that amount. In the case of environmental liabilities, it is often very difficult to estimate the cost of environmental cleanup. Thus, while the company may deem it probable that a liability exists, estimating that liability can be difficult. Recall that the contingency standard requires a liability to be recorded on the company's books if it is probable and estimable. If a potential liability is possible and estimable, the standards require note disclosure.

What about the situation where a potential liability is probable but cannot be estimated with much accuracy, as is often the case with environmental liabilities? Obviously, if a company cannot estimate a probable obligation, it makes sense to provide extensive note disclosure. Most companies will estimate a least a minimum amount and provide note disclosure as to the possibility of additional costs. As an illustration, EXXONMOBIL disclosed the information in Exhibit 8-4 in its 1991 and 1999 annual reports in connection with lawsuits filed as a result of the *Exxon Valdez* oil spill. Note that in 1991, the company sounds quite optimistic that it has set-

exhibit 8-4 ExxonMobil—1991 and 1999 Disclosures Concerning *Exxon Valdez* Oil Spill

Disclosure in 1991

On March 24, 1989, the Exxon Valdez, a tanker owned by Exxon Shipping Company, a subsidiary of Exxon Corporation, ran aground on Bligh Reef in Prince William Sound off the port of Valdez, Alaska, and released approximately 260,000 barrels of crude oil. More than 315 lawsuits, including class actions, have been brought in various courts against Exxon Corporation and certain of its subsidiaries.

On October 8, 1991, the United States District Court for the District of Alaska approved a civil agreement and consent decree. . . . These agreements provided for guilty pleas to certain misdemeanors, the dismissal of all felony charges and the remaining misdemeanor charges by the United States, and the release of all civil claims against Exxon . . . by the United States and the state of Alaska. The agreements also released all claims related to or arising from the oil spill by Exxon. . . .

Payments under the plea agreement totaled $125 million—$25 million in fines and $100 million in payments to the United States and Alaska for restoration projects in Alaska. Payments under the civil agreement and consent decree will total $900 million over a ten-year period. The civil agreement also provides for the possible payment, between September 1, 2002, and September 1, 2006, of up to $100 million for substantial loss or decline in populations, habitats, or species in areas affected by the oil spill which could not have been reasonably anticipated on September 25, 1991.

The remaining cost to the corporation from the Valdez accident is difficult to predict and cannot be determined at this time. It is believed the final outcome, net of reserves already provided, will not have a materially adverse effect upon the corporation's operations or financial condition.

Disclosure in 1999

On September 24, 1996, the United States District Court for the District of Alaska entered a judgment in the amount of $5.058 billion in the Exxon Valdez civil trial that began in May 1994. The District Court awarded approximately $19.6 million in compensatory damages to fisher plaintiffs, $38 million in prejudgment interest on the compensatory damages and $5 billion in punitive damages to a class composed of all persons and entities who asserted claims for punitive damages from the corporation as a result of the Exxon Valdez grounding. The District Court also ordered that these awards shall bear interest from and after entry of the judgment. The District Court stayed execution on the judgment pending appeal based on a $6.75 billion letter of credit posted by the corporation. The corporation has appealed the judgment. The corporation has also appealed the District Court's denial of its renewed motion for a new trial. The United States Court of Appeals for the Ninth Circuit heard oral arguments on the appeals on May 3, 1999. The corporation continues to believe that the punitive damages in this case are unwarranted and that the judgment should be set aside or substantially reduced by the appellate courts.

The ultimate cost to ExxonMobil from the lawsuits arising from the Exxon Valdez grounding is not possible to predict and may not be resolved for a number of years.

tled the bulk of the claims related to the oil spill and that any further claims "will not have a materially adverse effect" upon the company. This optimistic disclosure is particularly interesting in light of the $5 billion adverse judgment discussed in the 1999 disclosure.

to summarize

Contingent liabilities depend on some future event to determine if a liability actually exists. Companies are required to assess the likelihood of certain future events occurring and then, based on that assessment, provide appropriate disclosure. If the company deems the future event to be likely, the journal

entries are made and the liability is accrued. If the future event is deemed reasonably possible, note disclosure is required. For those events considered remote, no disclosure is required. Environmental liabilities represent a case where a liability exists but measurement is difficult. A minimum liability is typically established along with extensive note disclosure.

4

Understand when an expenditure should be recorded as an asset and when it should be recorded as an expense.

CAPITALIZE VERSUS EXPENSE

To this point in the text, we have assumed that the decision of expensing a cost to the income statement or capitalizing an expenditure and placing it on the balance sheet as an asset is an easy one. In reality, that decision is often difficult and one that makes accounting judgment critical. For example, should a building that cost $1 million and is expected to benefit 20 future periods be capitalized and placed on the balance sheet? The answer is pretty clear—of course. What about office supplies that are used this period? Will they benefit future periods? No, and as a result, the costs of those supplies should be expensed. What about research and development costs? Should they be capitalized as an asset or expensed to the income statement? Now you see the problem. Sometimes it is difficult to determine whether an expenditure will benefit the future. Exhibit 8-5 provides an expense/asset continuum that demonstrates the difficulty of the decision to capitalize or expense a cost.

The endpoints of the continuum are easy. The decision starts to get fuzzy, though, once you leave the endpoints. Do repairs and maintenance benefit future periods (and therefore need to be capitalized), or are they necessary expenditures just to keep a machine running (and should be expensed)? To illustrate the issues involved in deciding whether an expenditure should be capitalized or expensed, two specific areas will be discussed—research and development (R&D) and advertising.

Research and Development

Research is an activity undertaken to discover new knowledge that will be useful in developing new products, services, or processes. Development involves the application of research findings to develop a plan or design for new or improved products and processes. **EXXONMOBIL** reports that, from 1997 through 1999, it spent an average of $715 million per year on R&D activities.

STOP & THINK Would you expect that a rule requiring all firms to expense R&D outlays would cause R&D expenditures to decrease? Why or why not?

Because of the uncertainty surrounding the future economic benefit of R&D activities, the FASB decided in 1974 that research and development expenditures should be expensed in the period incurred. Among the arguments for expensing R&D costs is the frequent inability to find a definite causal re-

---

exhibit 8-5 Expense/Asset Continuum

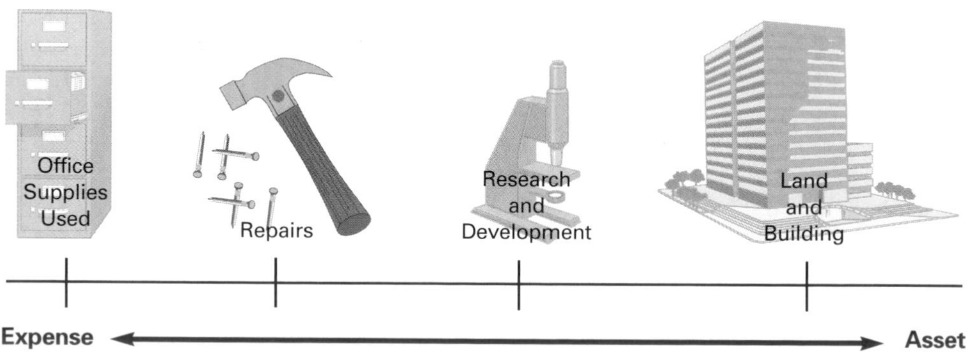

The International Accounting Standards Committee (IASC) has established an R&D accounting rule that many think is superior to the FASB rule. The IASC rule requires research costs to be expensed and development costs to be capitalized. Research costs are defined as those R&D costs incurred before technological feasibility has been established.

lationship between the expenditures and future revenues. Sometimes very large expenditures do not generate any future revenue, while relatively small expenditures lead to significant discoveries that generate large revenues. The FASB found it difficult to establish criteria that would distinguish between those R&D expenditures that would most likely benefit future periods and those that would not.

In summary, the FASB concluded that R&D expenditures are undertaken to benefit future periods, but that it is impractical to identify which R&D expenditures actually do provide future economic benefit. Accordingly, all R&D costs are to be recorded as expenses in the year they are incurred. This rule leads to a systematic overstatement of R&D expenses and a systematic understatement of R&D assets. The rule was roundly criticized in 1974 as the FASB prepared to release it. The FASB received many comments predicting that if firms were required to expense all R&D costs, they would be forced to significantly cut back on research expenditures to avoid hurting reported earnings. This, according to these comment letters, would cripple the U.S. economy. And the U.S. economy did indeed suffer in the mid-1970s, and R&D expenditures did decrease, but these occurrences may have had more to do with skyrocketing oil prices and double-digit inflation than with the R&D accounting rule passed by the FASB.

Advertising

Every year in the two weeks of hype preceding the Super Bowl, we hear about the incredible number of media people covering the event and about how much money advertisers are paying for a 30-second spot during the broadcast. We also hear a little bit about the football teams. With advertising costs running in excess of $2 million for 30 seconds, one has to believe that the advertisers expect some future economic benefit from the advertising. So, should advertising costs be capitalized or expensed?

For accounting purposes, the general presumption is that advertising costs should be expensed because of the uncertainty of the future benefits. However, in selected cases in which the future benefits are more certain, advertising costs should be capitalized. This type of advertising involves targeted advertising to customers who have purchased products in the past. Such advertising is also characterized by the ability to estimate how many customers will respond favorably. For example, **SEARS** discloses in the notes to its 1999 financial statements that it expenses newspaper, television, and radio advertising costs but capitalizes the cost of specialty catalogs and other direct response advertising. As of December 31, 1999, Sears reported an "advertising asset" of $180 million in its balance sheet. Of course, this is a rather small amount compared to the $1.63 billion in advertising that Sears expensed during 1999.

As these discussions of R&D and advertising illustrate, capitalize-or-expense decisions can be quite difficult from a conceptual standpoint. The general rule of thumb is that, when there is significant uncertainty about whether an expenditure should be capitalized or expensed, expense it. This approach is in line with the traditional conservatism of accounting, but be aware that it can result in a significant understatement of the economic assets of a company.

to summarize

Conceptually, a cost should be recorded as an asset whenever it has a probable future economic benefit. In practice, it is frequently quite difficult to tell when a cost should be recorded as an asset (capitalized) and when it should be recorded as an expense. In some areas, such as research and development (R&D) and advertising, specific accounting rules have been developed to create more uniformity about which costs should be expensed and which should be capitalized.

5

Prepare an income statement summarizing operating activities as well as other revenues and expenses, extraordinary items, and earnings per share.

SUMMARIZING OPERATIONS ON AN INCOME STATEMENT

Having now completed our discussion of operating revenues and expenses (in Chapters 6, 7, and thus far in 8), you are ready to examine an income statement, such as the one in Exhibit 8-6, and see how operating results are communicated to investors and creditors. The numbers in the income statement do not relate to any previous examples; they are shown here for illustrative purposes only.

This income statement shows that with net sales revenue of $2,475,000, P & L Company had net income of $385,000. The income statement classifies and accounts for the other $2,090,000 ($2,475,000 − $385,000). Sales revenue, cost of goods sold, and operating expenses (which are separated into selling expenses and general and administrative expenses on the income statement) have already been explained. It is important to note that operating income of $726,000 shows how much P & L Company earned from carrying on its major operations. These items constitute the major ongoing components of the income statement. Items shown at the bottom of the income statement are not part of the main operations of the business or are unusual and nonrecurring in nature.

fyi

Another item that is reported in a separate section of the income statement relates to discontinued operations. When a company decides to cease the operations of a segment or a division, it must provide careful disclosure as to the past profitability of the segment and the expected costs associated with closing the segment.

Other Revenues and Expenses

Other revenues and expenses are those items incurred or earned from activities outside of, or peripheral to, the normal operations of a firm. For example, a manufacturing company that receives dividends from its investments in the stock of another firm would show those dividend revenues as "Other Revenues and Expenses." This way, investors can see how much of a firm's income is from its major operating activity and how much is from peripheral activities, such as investing in other companies. The most common items reported in this section are interest and investment revenues and expenses. The other revenues and expenses category also includes gains and losses from the sale of assets other than inventory, such as land and buildings.

other revenues and expenses Items incurred or earned from activities that are outside of, or peripheral to, the normal operations of a firm.

Extraordinary Items

extraordinary items Nonoperating gains and losses that are unusual in nature, infrequent in occurrence, and material in amount.

The **extraordinary items** section of an income statement is reserved for reporting special nonoperating gains and losses. This category is restrictive and includes only those items that are (1) unusual in nature, (2) infrequent in occurrence, and (3) material in amount. They are separated from other revenues and expenses so that readers can identify them as onetime, or nonrecurring, events. Extraordinary items are rare but can include losses or gains from floods, fires, earthquakes, and so on. For example, in 1980 when Mount St. Helens erupted in Washington, mudslides and flooding adversely affected much of the WEYERHAEUSER COMPANY's timberlands. Weyerhaeuser reported an extraordinary loss of $66.7 million in 1980 to cover standing timber, buildings, equipment, and other damaged items. Certain other types of gains and losses are required by generally accepted accounting principles to be reported as extraordinary items. These involve technical accounting issues that are discussed in more advanced texts.

The 1980 eruption of Mount St. Helens caused WEYERHAEUSER COMPANY to report an extraordinary loss of $66.7 million. However, it's not likely Weyerhaeuser will have to worry about that extraordinary event happening again anytime soon!

If a firm has an extraordinary loss, its taxes are lower than they would be on the basis of ordinary operations. P & L Company, for example, actually paid only $165,000 ($195,000 based on operations less a $30,000 tax benefit from the extraordinary loss) in taxes. On the other hand, if a firm has an extraordinary gain, its taxes are increased. Therefore, to ensure that the full effect of the gain or loss is presented, extraordinary items are always shown together with their tax effects so

exhibit 8-6 Sample Income Statement

P & L Company
Income Statement
For the Year Ended December 31, 2003

Revenues:			
Gross sales revenue		$2,500,000	
Less: Sales returns		(12,000)	
Less: Sales discounts		(13,000)	
Net sales revenue			$2,475,000
Cost of goods sold			1,086,000
Gross margin			$1,389,000
Operating expenses:			
Selling expenses:			
Sales salaries expense	$200,000		
Sales commissions expense	60,000		
Advertising expense	45,000		
Delivery expense	14,000		
Total selling expenses		$ 319,000	
General and administrative expenses:			
Administrative salaries expense	$278,000		
Rent expense, office equipment	36,000		
Property tax expense	22,000		
Miscellaneous expenses	8,000		
Total general and administrative expenses		344,000	
Total operating expenses			663,000
Operating income			$ 726,000
Other revenues and expenses:			
Dividend revenue		$ 5,000	
Gain on sale of land		4,000	
Interest expense		(85,000)	
Net other revenues and expenses			(76,000)
Income from operations before income taxes			$ 650,000
Income taxes on operations (30%)			195,000
Income before extraordinary item			$ 455,000
Extraordinary item:			
Flood loss		$ (100,000)	
Income tax effect (30%)		30,000	(70,000)
Net income			$ 385,000
Earnings per share (100,000 shares outstanding):			
Income before extraordinary item			$4.55
Extraordinary loss			(0.70)
Net income			$3.85

that a net-of-tax amount can be seen. Thus, income tax expense may appear in two places on the income statement: below operating income before income taxes and in the extraordinary items section.

earnings per share (EPS) The amount of net income (earnings) related to each share of stock; computed by dividing net income by the number of shares of stock outstanding during the period.

Earnings per Share

As noted in Chapter 2, a company is required to show **earnings per share (EPS)** on the income statement. If extraordinary items are included on the income statement, a firm will report EPS figures on income before extraordinary items, on extraordinary items, and on net income.

> **caution**
>
> Actual EPS computations are much more complicated than shown here. Changes in the shares outstanding during the period must be considered when calculating EPS. In addition, there is another EPS figure, called diluted earnings per share, that considers the potential effect on EPS of things like the exercising of stock options by shareholders.

Earnings per share is calculated by dividing a firm's net income by the number of shares of stock outstanding during the period. Exhibit 8-6 assumes that 100,000 shares of stock are outstanding. Earnings per share amounts are important because they allow potential investors to compare the profitability of all firms, whether large or small. Thus, the performance of a company earning $200 million and having 200,000 shares of stock outstanding can be compared with a company earning $60,000 and with 30,000 shares outstanding.

Differing Income Statement Formats

The income statement featured in Exhibit 8-6 demonstrates detailed disclosure of a company's operations. Most companies do not provide that level of detail. The information contained in income statements varies from company to company. For example, MICROSOFT (see Appendix A) summarizes the results of its operations in 16 lines. IBM, on the other hand, provides detailed revenue and cost figures on the face of its income statements for each of its five operating segments (hardware sales, services, software, maintenance, and rentals). FORD MOTOR COMPANY provides detail in its income statements as to the operations of its two very different lines of business—automotive and financial services. Keep in mind that the format of the income statement will vary across companies but the information contained in the income statement is the same—revenues and expenses.

---

to summarize

The results of operating activities are summarized and reported on an income statement. On an income statement, cost of goods sold is subtracted from net sales to arrive at gross margin, or the amount a company marks up its inventory. Operating expenses are then subtracted from gross margin to arrive at operating income. Nonoperating items, such as other revenues and expenses, extraordinary items, and earnings per share, are reported on the income statement below operating income.

---

review of learning objectives

1 Account for the various components of employee compensation expense. Total employee compensation can involve some or all of the following:

- *Payroll.* Companies serve as the agents of federal, state, and local governments in withholding necessary taxes from employees' wages and salaries. These withholdings are then periodically forwarded to the appropriate government unit.
- *Compensated absences.* The value of vacation and sick days earned this year should be reported as an expense this year even though the actual vacation or sick days are not expected to be used until a future year.
- *Bonuses.* Employee bonuses, especially those for top management, are frequently based on reported accounting numbers such as net income. This creates some incentive for managers to manipulate reported earnings in order to boost their own bonuses.
- *Stock options.* The receipt of stock options gives managers an incentive to take value-enhancing actions that will increase their company's stock price. The intrinsic value method of accounting for stock options assumes that options have potential value only on the day that they are granted; this method almost always results in no reported compensation expense. A more theoretically satisfying accounting method is the fair value method, which results in reported compensation expense being equal to the estimated value of the options granted. The FASB encourages use of the fair value method, but almost all companies continue to use the intrinsic value method.

- *Postemployment benefits.* When a company makes a decision to terminate employees as part of a restructuring, an expense equal to the expected value of the employee severance benefits is reported in the year in which the termination decision is made.
- *Pensions.* The difference between the pension obligation liability and the market value of the pension fund assets is reported as a net asset or liability in the balance sheet. Net pension expense is composed of interest cost and service cost, which are offset by the expected return on the pension fund assets.
- *Postretirement benefits other than pensions.* Companies are required to report an annual expense equal to the value of retiree benefits such as health care and life insurance that were earned during the year. These benefit plans are not structured as formally as pension plans.

2 **Compute income tax expense, including appropriate consideration of deferred tax items.** Sales taxes collected are reported as a liability until the funds are forwarded to the appropriate government agency. When property taxes are paid in advance, the amount is reported as a prepaid asset until the time period covered by the property tax has expired. With respect to income tax, corporations in the United States compute two different income numbers—financial income for reporting to stockholders and taxable income for reporting to the IRS. For income tax purposes, some income is not taxed until after it has already been reported as financial accounting income in a previous year. In this case, a deferred income tax liability is recognized in the year when the income is first reported in the income statement to reflect that the income will be taxed in a subsequent year. Similarly, some income tax deductions are not allowed for income tax purposes until after they have been reported as a financial accounting expense in a prior year. These items represent potentially valuable future deductions and are recorded as deferred income tax assets.

3 **Distinguish between contingent items that should be recognized in the financial statements and those that should be merely disclosed in the financial statement notes.** A contingent item is one for which the existence of a liability or asset depends on the outcome of uncertain future events. An example is litigation. A company must make an assessment as to the likely outcome and then account for the event accordingly. An event that is "probable" will be recognized on the financial statements. An event for which the outcome is reasonably possible will be disclosed in the notes to the financial statements, and an event considered remote is not disclosed.

Environmental liabilities represent another difficulty for businesses. These liabilities result when firms damage the environment. The difficulty with these liabilities is determining an amount. Typically, estimates are made along with extensive note disclosure.

4 **Understand when an expenditure should be recorded as an asset and when it should be recorded as an expense.** Many expenditures fall into a gray area where it isn't certain whether they should be expensed immediately or capitalized as assets. Specific practices have arisen with respect to many of these difficult-to-classify expenditures. For research and development expenditures, all regular R&D costs are expensed as incurred. For advertising expenditures, most advertising costs are expensed immediately. However, the cost of targeted advertising for which customer response can be reasonably estimated is capitalized.

5 **Prepare an income statement summarizing operating activities as well as other revenues and expenses, extraordinary items, and earnings per share.** The income statement is the means of reporting net income. Its major sections are revenues, cost of goods sold, operating expenses, operating income, other revenues and expenses, extraordinary items, net income, and earnings per share.

In addition to cost of goods sold expense, businesses incur many other operating expenses. With accrual accounting these are reported on the income statement as they are incurred, not when they are paid. Interest and other nonoperating revenues and expenses are classified separately below operating income. The income statement is not complete until all extraordinary items and earnings-per-share amounts have been included.

key terms and concepts

bonus 356
contingency 365
defined benefit plan 358
defined contribution plan 358
earnings per share (EPS) 371
employee stock options 356
environmental liabilities 366
extraordinary items 370
other revenues and expenses 370
pension 358
postemployment benefits 357
sales tax payable 361
Social Security (FICA) taxes 354

review problem

The Income Statement

From the following information prepare an income statement for Southern Corporation for the year ended December 31, 2003. Assume that there are 200,000 shares of stock outstanding.

Sales Returns	$ 50,000
Sales Discounts	70,000
Gross Sales Revenue	9,000,000
Flood Loss	80,000
Income Taxes on Operations	500,000
Administrative Salaries Expense	360,000
Sales Salaries Expense	800,000
Rent Expense (General and Administrative)	32,000
Utilities Expense (General and Administrative)	4,000
Supplies Expense (General and Administrative)	16,000
Delivery Expense (Selling)	6,300
Payroll Tax Expense (Selling)	6,000
Automobile Expense (General and Administrative)	3,800
Insurance Expense (General and Administrative)	34,000
Advertising Expense (Selling)	398,000
Interest Revenue	6,000
Interest Expense	92,000
Insurance Expense (Selling)	7,000
Entertainment Expense (Selling)	7,200
Miscellaneous Selling Expenses	15,000
Miscellaneous General and Administrative Expenses	10,800
Tax rate applicable to flood loss	30%
Cost of Goods Sold	5,950,000

Solution

The first step in preparing an income statement is classifying items, as follows:

Revenue Accounts	
Sales Returns	$ 50,000
Sales Discounts	70,000
Gross Sales Revenue	9,000,000

Cost of Goods Sold Accounts	
Cost of Goods Sold	$5,950,000

Selling Expense Accounts	
Sales Salaries Expense	$800,000
Delivery Expense	6,300
Payroll Tax Expense	6,000
Advertising Expense	398,000
Insurance Expense	7,000
Entertainment Expense	7,200
Miscellaneous Selling Expenses	15,000

General and Administrative Expense Accounts	
Administrative Salaries Expense	$360,000
Rent Expense	32,000
Utilities Expense	4,000
Supplies Expense	16,000
Automobile Expense	3,800
Insurance Expense	34,000
Miscellaneous General and Administrative Expenses	10,800

Other Revenue and Expense Accounts	
Interest Revenue	$ 6,000
Interest Expense	92,000

Miscellaneous Accounts	
Income Taxes on Operations	$500,000

Extraordinary Item Accounts	
Flood Loss	$80,000
Tax rate	30%

Once the accounts are classified, the income statement is prepared by including the accounts in the following format:

	Net Sales Revenue (Gross Sales Revenue − Sales Returns − Sales Discounts)
−	Cost of Goods Sold
=	Gross Margin
−	Selling Expenses
−	General and Administrative Expenses
=	Operating Income
+/−	Other Revenues and Expenses (add Net Revenues, subtract Net Expenses)
=	Income before Income Taxes
−	Income Taxes on Operations
=	Income before Extraordinary Items
+/−	Extraordinary Items (add Extraordinary Gains, subtract Extraordinary Losses, net of applicable taxes)
=	Net Income

After net income has been computed, earnings per share is calculated and added to the bottom of the statement. It is important that the proper heading be included.

Southern Corporation
Income Statement
For the Year Ended December 31, 2003

Revenues:		
Gross sales revenue	$9,000,000	
Less: Sales returns	(50,000)	
Less: Sales discounts	(70,000)	
Net sales revenue		$8,880,000

(continued)

Cost of goods sold			5,950,000
Gross margin			$2,930,000
Operating expenses:			
Selling expenses:			
Sales salaries expense	$800,000		
Delivery expense	6,300		
Payroll tax expense	6,000		
Advertising expense	398,000		
Insurance expense	7,000		
Entertainment expense	7,200		
Miscellaneous expenses	15,000		
Total selling expenses		$1,239,500	
General and administrative expenses:			
Administrative salaries expense	$360,000		
Rent expense	32,000		
Utilities expense	4,000		
Supplies expense	16,000		
Automobile expense	3,800		
Insurance expense	34,000		
Miscellaneous expenses	10,800		
Total general and administrative expenses		460,600	
Total operating expenses			1,700,100
Operating income			$1,229,900
Other revenues and expenses:			
Interest revenue		$ 6,000	
Interest expense		(92,000)	
Net other revenues and expenses			(86,000)
Income from operations before income taxes			$1,143,900
Income taxes on operations			500,000
Income before extraordinary item			$ 643,900
Extraordinary item:			
Flood loss		$ (80,000)	
Income tax effect (30%)		24,000	(56,000)
Net income			$ 587,900
Earnings per share:			
Before extraordinary items	$3.22 ($643,900 ÷ 200,000 shares)		
Extraordinary loss	(0.28) ($ 56,000 ÷ 200,000 shares)		
Net income	$2.94 ($587,900 ÷ 200,000 shares)		

discussion questions

1. Why is the accounting for payroll-related liabilities more complicated than the accounting for other current liabilities?
2. If the period of time covered by a company's payroll does not coincide with the last day of the year for financial reporting, how is accounting for the payroll affected by this situation?
3. What is a compensated absence?
4. What danger is there in basing a manager's bonus on reported net income?
5. What is the primary difference between the intrinsic value method and the fair value method of accounting for stock-based compensation plans? Which method does the FASB recommend?
6. What additional disclosure is required of companies that use the intrinsic value method?
7. Severance benefits resulting from a company restructuring are reported as an expense in the period that the restructuring decision is made rather than when the benefits are actually paid. Why?

8. What is the difference between a defined contribution pension plan and a defined benefit pension plan?
9. How is a company's pension obligation reported in its balance sheet?
10. List and briefly discuss the three components of pension expense discussed in the chapter.
11. In what ways do postretirement health-care and life insurance benefit plans differ from postretirement pension plans?
12. Why is an end-of-year adjusting entry for property taxes often necessary?
13. In your opinion, what is the primary objective of determining pretax financial accounting income? How does this objective differ from the objectives of determining taxable income as defined by the IRS?
14. When and how does a company record the amount owed to the government for income taxes for a given year?
15. What causes deferred income taxes?
16. What is the difference between a "contingent liability" and a "liability"?
17. Escalating environmental liabilities are a major concern of companies today. How does a company know when to record such liabilities?
18. Currently **MICROSOFT** spends a tremendous amount of money on research and development costs to continuously develop new products. How are such R&D costs accounted for?
19. XYZ Corporation pays for advertising costs all the time. Sometimes the company records these payments as assets, and sometimes it records them as expenses. Why would XYZ use different accounting treatments?
20. What types of items would be included on an income statement as "other revenues and expenses"?
21. More than ever before, tremendous attention is being paid to a company's earnings-per-share number. Why do you think investors and creditors pay so much attention to earnings per share?

discussion cases

CASE 8-1

RECORDING LIABILITIES AND THE EFFECT ON BONUSES

John Flowers, president of Marquette Company, is paid a salary plus a bonus equal to 10% of pretax income. The company has just computed its pretax income to be $3.4 million. Based on this income, Flowers expects to receive a bonus of $340,000. However, the company has just been told by outside experts that it may have an environmental liability of $2.1 million and that, based on new actuarial estimates, the recorded amount of postretirement benefits is too low by $1.2 million. The experts recommend that both of these liabilities be recorded, which would reduce income to $100,000 and Flowers's bonus to $10,000. Flowers believes he does not need to record the adjustments for the following reasons: the environmental liability is not certain, the amount of the potential liability can't be accurately estimated, and "actuarial estimates" are always changing. Is Flowers violating GAAP if he refuses to allow the company to adjust pretax income, or is the decision to not record the adjustments acceptable because of the uncertainty of the liabilities and the amounts?

CASE 8-2

QUESTIONING THE ACCOUNTING FOR PENSIONS, RESEARCH, AND INCOME TAXES

Tatia Wilks, the president of Lewbacca Company, is concerned about the low earnings that Lewbacca is scheduled to report this year. She called the company's accounting staff into her office to question them about the accounting treatment of several items. She raised the following points:

a. Why do we have to report an expense this year associated with our pension plan? Our company is new, and none of our employees is within even 15 years of retirement. Accordingly, the pension plan won't cost us anything for at least 15 years.
b. Research to find new products and improve our old products is one of our key competitive advantages. However, you tell me that all of the money we spend on research is reported as an expense this year. This is silly because the results of our research comprise our biggest economic asset.

c. We have an excellent staff of tax planners who work hard to legally minimize the amount of income taxes we pay each year. However, I see in the notes to the financial statements that you are requiring our company to report a "deferred income tax expense" for taxes that we don't even owe yet! Why?

How would you respond to each of these points?

EXERCISE 8-1

PAYROLL ACCOUNTING

Stockbridge Stores, Inc., has three employees, Frank Wall, Mary Jones, and Susan Wright. Summaries of their 2003 salaries and withholdings are as follows:

Employee	Gross Salaries	Federal Income Taxes Withheld	State Income Taxes Withheld	FICA Taxes Withheld
Frank Wall	$54,000	$6,500	$2,500	$4,131
Mary Jones	39,000	4,800	1,900	2,984
Susan Wright	34,000	4,250	1,500	2,601

1. Prepare the summary entry for salaries paid to the employees for the year 2003.
2. Assume that, in addition to FICA taxes, the employer has incurred $192 for federal unemployment taxes and $720 for state unemployment taxes. Prepare the summary journal entry to record the payroll tax liability for 2003, assuming no taxes have yet been paid.
3. **Interpretive Question:** What other types of items are frequently withheld from employees' paychecks in addition to income taxes and FICA taxes?

EXERCISE 8-2

BONUS COMPUTATION AND JOURNAL ENTRY

Pete Mehling is the president of Mehling Company, and his cousin, John Mehling, is the vice president. Their compensation package includes bonuses of 3% for Pete Mehling and 2% for John Mehling of net income that exceeds $200,000. Net income for the year 2003 has just been computed to be $990,000.

1. Compute the amount of bonuses to be paid to Pete and John Mehling.
2. Prepare the journal entries to record the accrual and payment of the bonuses. Summarize all withholding taxes related to the bonuses in an account called Various Taxes Payable. Taxes payable on the bonuses total $9,200 for Pete and $6,300 for John.

EXERCISE 8-3

STOCK OPTIONS: INTRINSIC AND FAIR VALUE METHODS

On January 1, 2003, the Magily Company established a stock option plan for its senior employees. A total of 60,000 options were granted that permit employees to purchase 60,000 shares of stock at $48 per share. Each option had a fair value of $11 on the date the options were granted. The market price for Magily stock on January 1, 2003, was $50. The employees are required to remain with Magily Company for the entire year of 2003 in order to be able to exercise these options.

Compute the total amount of compensation expense to be associated with these options under the:

1. fair value method.
2. intrinsic value method.

EXERCISE 8-4

STOCK OPTIONS: REQUIRED DISCLOSURE

Refer to the information in Exercise 8-3. Magily's income for 2003, before subtracting any compensation expense associated with the stock option plan, is $500,000.

Prepare the required supplemental disclosure for 2003 assuming that Magily decides to use the intrinsic value method.

EXERCISE 8-5

PENSIONS ON THE BALANCE SHEET

Pension plan information for Rabona Company is as follows:

December 31, 2003	
Pension obligation liability	$3,000,000
December 31, 2003	
Pension fund assets	3,150,000
During 2003	
Total pension expense	200,000

How will this information be reported on Rabona's balance sheet as of December 31, 2003?

EXERCISE 8-6

COMPUTING PENSION EXPENSE

Lorien Company reports the following pension information for 2003:

Pension-related interest cost for the year	$ 80,000
Pension fund assets, end of year	925,000
Pension obligation liability, end of year	870,000
Pension service cost for the year	75,000
Return on pension fund assets for the year	100,000

1. What pension amount would Lorien report on its balance sheet as of the end of the year?
2. Compute the amount to be reported on the income statement as pension expense for the year.

EXERCISE 8-7

PENSION COMPUTATIONS

The following pension information is for three different companies. For each company, compute the missing amount or amounts.

	Company 1	Company 2	Company 3
Pension fund assets	$100,000	$75,000	$ (e)
Pension obligation liability	(a)	80,000	100,000
Net pension asset (liability)	20,000	(c)	(25,000)
Pension-related interest cost	$ 10,000	(d)	$ 20,000
Service cost	8,000	6,000	23,000
Return on pension plan assets	5,000	8,000	(f)
Pension expense	(b)	10,000	35,000

EXERCISE 8-8

ACCOUNTING FOR PROPERTY TAXES

In July 2003, Reynolds Company received a bill from the county government for property taxes on its land and buildings for the period July 1, 2002, through June 30, 2003. The amount of the tax bill is $7,600, and payment is due August 1, 2003. The tax rate will not change for the period July 1, 2003, to June 30, 2004, and the company does not plan to acquire any additional taxable assets during that period. Reynolds Company uses the calendar year for financial reporting purposes.

1. Prepare the journal entries to record payment of the property taxes on August 1, 2003.
2. Prepare the adjusting entry for property taxes on December 31, 2003.

EXERCISE 8-9

DEFERRED INCOME TAXES

Yosef Company began operating on January 1, 2003. At the end of the first year of operations, Yosef reported $750,000 income before income taxes on its income statement but only $660,000 taxable income on its tax return. This difference arose because $90,000 in income earned during 2003 was not yet taxable according to the income tax regulations. The tax rate is 35%.

1. Compute the amount of income tax that Yosef legally owes for taxable income generated during 2003.
2. Compute the amount of income tax expense to be reported on Yosef's income statement for 2003.
3. State whether Yosef has a deferred income tax asset or a deferred income tax liability as of the end of 2003. What is the amount of the asset or liability?

EXERCISE 8-10

DEFERRED INCOME TAXES

Boatogooso Company began operating on January 1, 2003. At the end of the first year of operations, Boatogooso reported $500,000 income before income taxes on its income statement but taxable income of $600,000 on its tax return. This difference arose because $100,000 in expenses incurred during 2003 were not yet deductible for income tax purposes according to the income tax regulations. The tax rate is 40%.

1. Compute the amount of income tax that Boatogooso legally owes for taxable income generated during 2003.
2. Compute the amount of income tax expense to be reported on Boatogooso's income statement for 2003.
3. State whether Boatogooso has a deferred income tax asset or a deferred income tax liability as of the end of 2003. What is the amount of the asset or liability?

EXERCISE 8-11

CONTINGENT LIABILITIES

Rayn Company is involved in the following legal matters:

a. A customer is suing Rayn for allegedly selling a faulty and dangerous product. Rayn's attorneys believe that there is a 40% chance of Rayn's losing the suit.
b. A federal agency has accused Rayn of violating numerous employee safety laws. The company faces significant fines if found guilty. Rayn's attorneys feel that the company has complied with all applicable laws, and they therefore place the probability of incurring the fines at less than 10%.
c. Rayn has been named in a gender discrimination lawsuit. In the past, Rayn has systematically promoted its male employees at a faster rate than it has promoted its female employees. Rayn's attorneys judge the probability that Rayn will lose this lawsuit at more than 90%.

For each item, determine the appropriate accounting treatment.

EXERCISE 8-12

CLASSIFYING EXPENDITURES AS ASSETS OR EXPENSES

Determining whether an expenditure should be expensed or capitalized is often difficult. Consider each of the following independent situations and indicate whether you would recommend that the cost be expensed or capitalized as an asset. Explain your answer.

1. Splash.com has spent $1.5 million for a 30-second advertisement to be aired during the Super Bowl. The ad introduces the company's new Web-based product, and the company expects the ad to increase sales for at least 18 months.
2. Chromosome.com has spent $8 million on research related to genetic diseases. The company expects this research to lead to substantial revenues, beginning in the next year.
3. Catalog.com is an online catalog sales company. Catalog.com has just spent $5 million designing a targeted advertising campaign that will encourage regular customers of the company's online catalog service to buy new products.
4. Food.com is an online seller of groceries. The company just spent $4 million building a new warehouse. The warehouse is expected to be useful for the next 15 years.

EXERCISE 8-13

PREPARING AN INCOME STATEMENT

Willow Company is preparing financial statements for the calendar year 2003. The following totals for each account have been verified as correct:

Office Supplies on Hand	$ 300
Insurance Expense	120
Gross Sales Revenue	6,000
Cost of Goods Sold	3,220
Sales Returns	200
Interest Expense	100
Accounts Payable	120
Accounts Receivable	260
Extraordinary Loss	1,080
Selling Expenses	360
Office Supplies Used	80
Cash	300
Revenue from Investments	280
Number of Shares of Capital Stock	90

Prepare an income statement. Assume a 20% income tax rate on both income from operations and extraordinary items. Include EPS numbers.

EXERCISE 8-14

UNIFYING CONCEPTS: THE INCOME STATEMENT

Use the following information to prepare an income statement for Fairchild Corporation for the year ended December 31, 2003. You should show separate classifications for revenues, cost of goods sold, gross margin, selling expenses, general and administrative expenses, operating income, other revenues and expenses, income before income taxes, income taxes, and net income. (HINT: Net income is $27,276.)

Sales Returns	$ 4,280
Income Taxes	26,000
Interest Revenue	2,400
Office Supplies Expense (General and Administrative)	400
Utilities Expense (General and Administrative)	3,980
Office Salaries Expense (General and Administrative)	12,064
Miscellaneous Selling Expenses	460
Insurance Expense (Selling)	1,160
Advertising Expense	6,922
Sales Salaries Expense	40,088
Sales Discounts	3,644
Interest Expense	1,170
Miscellaneous General and Administrative Expenses	620
Insurance Expense (General and Administrative)	600
Payroll Tax Expense (General and Administrative)	3,600
Store Supplies Expense (Selling)	800
Delivery Expense (Selling)	2,198
Inventory, January 1, 2003	79,400
Sales Revenue	395,472
Average number of shares of stock outstanding	10,000
Cost of Goods Sold	262,610
Purchases	230,560
Purchases Discounts	3,050
Inventory, December 31, 2003	44,300

problems

PROBLEM 8-1

PAYROLL ACCOUNTING

Orange County Bank has three employees, Albert Myers, Juan Moreno, and Michi Endo. During January 2003, these three employees earned $6,000, $4,200, and $4,000, respectively. The following table summarizes the required withholding rates on each individual's income for the month of January:

Employee	Federal Income Tax Withholdings	State Income Tax Withholdings	FICA Tax
Albert Myers	33%	3%	7.65%
Juan Moreno	28	4	7.65
Michi Endo	28	5	7.65

You are also informed that the bank is subject to the following unemployment tax rates on the salaries earned by the employees during January 2003:

Federal unemployment tax 0.8%
State unemployment tax 3.0%

Required:

1. Prepare the journal entry to record salaries payable for the month of January.
2. Prepare the journal entry to record payment of the January salaries to employees.
3. Prepare the journal entry to record the bank's payroll taxes for the month of January.

PROBLEM 8-2

DETERMINING PAYROLL COSTS

Orson Nutrition pays its salespeople a base salary of $1,000 per month plus a commission. Each salesperson starts with a commission of 1% of total gross sales for the month. The commission is increased thereafter according to seniority and productivity, up to a maximum of 5%. Orson has five salespeople with gross sales for the month of March and commission rates as follows:

	Commission Rate	Gross Sales
JD	4.5%	$100,000
Derrald	5.0	120,000
Cierra	2.5	80,000
Hannah	3.0	50,000
Skyler	1.0	200,000

The FICA tax rate is 7.65%. In addition, state and federal income taxes of 20% are withheld from each employee.

Required:

1. Compute Orson's total payroll expense (base salary plus commissions) for the month.
2. Compute the total amount of cash paid to employees for compensation for the month.
3. **Interpretive Question:** Briefly outline the advantages and disadvantages of having *no* income taxes withheld, but instead relying on individual taxpayers to pay the entire amount of their income tax at the end of the year when they file their tax return.

PROBLEM 8-3

STOCK OPTIONS

On January 1, 2003, Tiger Man Company established a stock option plan for its senior employees. A total of 400,000 options were granted that permit employees to purchase 400,000 shares of stock at $20 per share. Each option had a fair value of $5 on the grant date. The market price for Tiger Man stock on January 1, 2003, was $20. The employees are required to remain with Tiger Man for three years (2003, 2004, and 2005) in order to be able to exercise these options. Tiger Man's net income for 2003, before including any consideration of compensation expense, is $675,000.

Required:

1. Compute the compensation expense associated with these options for 2003 under the fair value method. Note that the period of time that the employees must work to be able to exercise the options is three years.
2. Repeat (1) using the intrinsic value method.
3. Prepare any supplemental disclosures needed if Tiger Man uses the intrinsic value method.
4. **Interpretive Question:** You are a Tiger Man stockholder. What objections might you have to Tiger Man's employee stock option plan?

PROBLEM 8-4

ACCOUNTING FOR PENSIONS

The following information is available from Haan Company relating to its defined benefit pension plan:

Balances as of January 1, 2003:	
Pension obligation liability	$3,500
Pension fund assets	3,000
Activity for 2003:	
Service cost	$ 400
Contributions to pension fund	230
Benefit payments to retirees	170
Return on plan assets	330
Pension-related interest cost	280

Required:

1. Compute the amount of pension expense to be reported on the income statement for 2003.
2. Determine the net pension amount to be reported on the balance sheet at the end of the year. Note: The benefit payments to retirees are made out of the pension fund assets. These payments reduce both the amount in the pension fund and the amount of the remaining pension obligation.
3. **Interpretive Question:** You are an employee of Haan Company and have just received the above information as part of the company's annual report to the employees on the status of the pension plan. Does anything in this information cause you concern? Explain.

PROBLEM 8-5

ACCOUNTING FOR PENSIONS

Kiev Company reported the following information relating to its pension plan for the years 2001 through 2004:

	Year-End Obligation	Year-End Plan Assets	Interest Cost	Service Cost	Return on Assets
2001	$522,500	$469,000	—	—	—
2002	581,250	505,050	$52,250	$61,500	$62,750
2003	643,000	549,700	58,125	65,625	71,650
2004	681,500	615,600	64,300	37,900	68,500

Required:

1. Compute the amount of pension expense to be reported on the income statement for each of the years 2002 through 2004.
2. Determine the net pension amount to be reported on the balance sheet at the end of each year 2001 through 2004. Clearly indicate whether the amount is an asset or a liability.

3. Each year, the amount of the pension obligation is increased by the interest cost and the service cost. The pension obligation is reduced by the amount of pension benefits paid. Compute the amount of pension benefits paid in each of the years 2002 through 2004.
4. Each year, the amount in the pension fund is increased by contributions to the fund and by the return earned on the fund assets. The pension fund amount is reduced by the amount of pension benefits paid. Compute the amount of contributions to the pension fund in each of the years 2002 through 2004.

PROBLEM 8-6

LIFE CYCLE OF A DEFERRED TAX ITEM

Black Kitty Company recorded certain revenues of $10,000 and $20,000 on its books in 2001 and 2002, respectively. However, these revenues were not subject to income taxation until 2003. Company records reveal pretax financial accounting income and taxable income for the three-year period as follows:

	Financial Income	Taxable Income
2001	$44,000	$34,000
2002	38,000	18,000
2003	21,000	51,000

Assume Black Kitty's tax rate is 40% for all periods.

Required:

1. Determine the amount of income tax that will be *paid* each year from 2001 through 2003.
2. Determine the amount of income tax expense that will be reported on the income statement each year from 2001 through 2003.
3. Compute the amount of deferred tax liability that would be reported on the balance sheet at the end of each year.
4. **Interpretive Question:** Why would the IRS allow Black Kitty to defer payment of taxes on some of the revenue earned in 2001 and 2002?

PROBLEM 8-7

UNIFYING CONCEPTS: THE INCOME STATEMENT

From the following information, prepare an income statement for Notem, Inc., for the year ended December 31, 2003. (HINT: Net income is $119,100.) Assume that there are 10,000 shares of capital stock outstanding.

Gross Sales Revenue	$3,625,000
Income Taxes	140,000
Cost of Goods Sold	2,415,000
Sales Salaries Expense	410,000
Rent Expense (Selling)	16,000
Payroll Tax Expense (Selling)	3,100
Entertainment Expense (Selling)	2,000
Miscellaneous Selling Expenses	7,800
Miscellaneous General and Administrative Expenses	5,400
Automobile Expense (Selling)	3,500
Insurance Expense (General and Administrative)	1,900
Interest Expense	46,000
Interest Revenue	3,000
Sales Returns	10,000
Advertising and Promotion Expense	199,000
Insurance Expense (Selling)	17,000
Delivery Expense (Selling)	3,100
Office Supplies Expense (General and Administrative)	8,000
Utilities Expense (General and Administrative)	1,100
Administrative Salaries Expense	180,000
Fire Loss (net of tax)	40,000

PROBLEM 8-8

INCOME STATEMENT ANALYSIS

The following table represents portions of the income statements of Brinkerhoff Company for the years 2001–2003:

	2003	2002	2001
Gross sales revenue	$42,000	$ (9)	$25,800
Sales discounts	0	100	100
Sales returns	0	200	700
Net sales revenue	42,000	(10)	(1)
Beginning inventory	(15)	8,000	(2)
Purchases	24,800	(11)	15,000
Purchases discounts	700	300	500
Freight-in	(16)	0	500
Cost of goods available for sale	29,000	25,000	(3)
Ending inventory	3,800	(12)	(4)
Cost of goods sold	(17)	(13)	(5)
Gross margin	(18)	14,000	(6)
Selling expenses	4,000	(14)	(7)
General and administrative expenses	(19)	3,200	3,000
Income before income taxes	9,000	8,000	4,000
Income taxes	4,500	4,000	(8)
Net income	(20)	4,000	2,000

Required: Fill in the missing numbers. Assume that gross margin is 40% of net sales revenue.

competency enhancement opportunities

- Analyzing Real Company Information
- International Case
- Ethics Case
- Writing Assignment
- The Debate
- Cumulative Spreadsheet Project
- Internet Search

The following additional assignments provide opportunities for students to develop critical thinking, ethical perspectives, oral and written communication skills, experience with electronic research, and teamwork through group and business activities.

ANALYZING REAL COMPANY INFORMATION

• ***Analyzing 8-1 (Microsoft)***

The 1999 annual report for **MICROSOFT** is included in Appendix A. Locate that annual report and consider the following questions:

1. Find Microsoft's financial statement note on "Income taxes."
   a. Using the current tax information and the information given on income before income taxes, compute Microsoft's 1999 effective tax rate for

both U.S. and international income. The effective tax rate is computed by dividing current taxes by income before income taxes.

b. As of June 30, 1999, Microsoft had $1,709 million in deferred income tax liabilities. What was the source of most of this deferred tax liability?

2. Find Microsoft's financial statement note concerning "employee stock and savings plans."
   a. Briefly describe Microsoft's employee stock purchase plan.
   b. Microsoft also has an employee stock option plan whereby certain key employees are granted incentive stock options that allow them to buy Microsoft stock at a fixed price in the future. If Microsoft's stock price continues to rise, these options could be very valuable. Microsoft is not required to report any expense associated with the granting of these options. However, Microsoft is required to estimate the value of these options and disclose what net income would have been if this value had been recognized as an expense. How much would Microsoft's 1999 net income have decreased if the value of the incentive stock options had been recognized as an expense?

• *Analyzing 8-2 (General Motors)*

GENERAL MOTORS has the largest set of private pension plans in the world. The company has many different pension plans covering different groups of employees. The following information was extracted from the notes to GM's 1999 financial statements. All numbers are in millions of U.S. dollars. As you can see, for reporting purposes these plans are separated into U.S. plans and non-U.S. plans.

	U.S. Plans Pension Benefits		Non-U.S. Plans Pension Benefits	
	1999	**1998**	**1999**	**1998**
Projected benefit obligation at end of year	$73,269	$76,963	$ 9,728	$10,283
Fair value of plan assets at end of year	80,462	75,007	7,062	5,976
Funded status	$ 7,193	$ (1,956)	$(2,666)	$ (4,307)

1. The projected benefit obligation is the measure of the value of the pension benefits earned by GM's employees that has not yet been paid. What is GM's total projected benefit obligation?
2. To ensure that employees will be able to collect their pension benefits, GM is required by law to set aside funds in a pension plan. What is the total value of assets in all of these pension funds?
3. Why do you think GM is required to separate its disclosure of pension plans into U.S. and non-U.S. plans?

• *Analyzing 8-3 (IBM)*

Note P to **IBM**'s 1999 financial statements describes how taxes affect IBM's operations. Among the information given is the following (all amounts are in millions of U.S. dollars):

	1999	1998	1997
Earnings before income taxes:			
U.S. operations	$ 5,892	$2,960	$3,193
Non-U.S. operations	5,865	6,080	5,834
Total earnings before income taxes	$11,757	$9,040	$9,027
Provision for income taxes:			
U.S. operations	$ 2,005	$ 991	$ 974
Non-U.S. operations	2,040	1,721	1,960
Total income taxes	$ 4,045	$2,712	$2,934
Total other taxes (Social Security, real estate, personal property, and other taxes)	$ 2,831	$2,859	$2,774

1. a. Compute the effective tax rate (income taxes/earnings before income taxes) for both U.S. and non-U.S. operations for 1997, 1998, and 1999.
   b. For each year 1997–1999, compute the percentage of the total tax burden that was made up of income taxes.
2. A deferred tax asset is a tax deduction that has already occurred and has been reported as a financial accounting expense but cannot be used to reduce income taxes until a future year. As of December 31, 1999, IBM reports that it has a deferred tax asset of $3.737 billion related to employee benefits. How would such a deferred tax asset arise?

INTERNATIONAL CASE

• *Hutchison Whampoa*

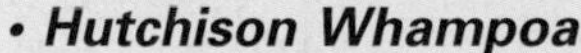

In Hong Kong, Li Ka-shing is known as "Superman." Li's personal wealth is estimated to be in excess of $1 billion, and there is a saying in Hong Kong that for every dollar spent, five cents goes into Li's pocket. Li and his family fled from China in 1940 in order to escape the advancing Japanese army. Li dropped out of school at age 13 to support his family by selling plastic trinkets on the streets of Hong Kong. Later, he scraped together enough money to buy a company that produced plastic flowers. His big success came when he bought the real estate surrounding his factory and watched the land skyrocket in value. Today, Li continues his simple lifestyle even though the companies he controls comprise over 10% of the value of the Hong Kong stock market. When asked why his sons have much nicer houses and cars than he does, Li responded, "My sons have a rich father; I did not."

Li is chairman of **HUTCHISON WHAMPOA LIMITED**. Hutchison has five major business segments: property development, container port operations, retailing, telecommunications, and energy. In 1999, Hutchison Whampoa reported net income of HK$118.735 billion (equivalent to approximately US$15.3 billion).

1. Assume that one of Hutchison Whampoa's overseas subsidiaries earns income of $1,000. The income tax rate in Hong Kong is 15%. When this income of $1,000 is transferred to the parent company in Hong Kong, it will be taxed, but no income tax is owed until then. What journal entry should Hutchison Whampoa make to record the income tax consequences of this $1,000 in income?

2. In 1999, Hutchison Whampoa reported earnings per share of HK$30.28. How many shares were outstanding during the year? (*Note:* See the net income information given above.)
3. Hutchison Whampoa reports that it records as assets the costs it incurs to sign up new subscribers to its cellular phone service network. These signup costs are then systematically transferred to expense over the following three years. What is the theoretical justification for this accounting practice?

ETHICS CASE

• *Twisting the Contingency Rules to Save the Environment*

You are a member of an environmental group that is working to clean up Valley River, which runs through your town. Right now, the group is focusing on forcing Allied Industrial, a manufacturer with a large plant located on the river, to conduct its operations in a more environmentally friendly way.

The leader of your group, Frank Bowers, is a political science major at the local university. Frank discovers that Allied Industrial is involved in ongoing litigation with respect to toxic waste cleanup at 13 factory sites in other states. Frank is shocked to learn that Allied itself estimates that the total cost to clean up the toxic waste at these 13 sites could be as much as $140 million yet has not reported any liability on its balance sheet. Frank found this information buried in the notes to Allied Industrial's financial statements.

Frank is convinced that he has found a public relations tool that can be used to force Allied Industrial to clean up Valley River. He has called a press conference and plans to accuse Allied of covering up its $140 million obligation to clean up the toxic waste at the 13 sites. His primary piece of evidence is the fact that the $140 million obligation is not mentioned anywhere in Allied's primary financial statements.

You have taken a class in accounting and are somewhat troubled by Frank's interpretation of Allied's financial statement disclosures. You look at Allied's annual report and see that it does give complete disclosure about the possible obligation although it does not report the $140 million as a liability. The report also states that, in the opinion of its legal counsel, it is possible but not probable that Allied will be found liable for the $140 million toxic waste cleanup cost.

The press conference is scheduled for 3 P.M. What should you do?

WRITING ASSIGNMENT

• *Computing the Total Compensation for a Professor*

Eunice Burns is a new assistant professor of phrenology at the University of Winnemucca. Her academic year salary is $30,000. In addition, she receives a summer salary equal to two-ninths (approximately 22%) of her academic year salary. The university agrees to contribute an amount equal to 7% of Eunice's academic year salary to a pension fund. Eunice acquires legal title to these pension contributions only if she stays at the university for five years or more. Historically, approximately 60% of new assistant professors have remained with the university at least five years. The university withholds $840 per year from Eunice's salary as her contribution to medical coverage. It costs the university $3,000 per year per employee for medical coverage. Eunice has a term-life insurance policy through the university because of the favorable group rate she can get. The $300 annual cost is withheld from her salary. If she were to get the same insurance on her own, it would cost $450. The FICA tax rate is 7.65%.

This amount is withheld from Eunice's pay, and in addition, the university must match this amount and pay it to the federal government. Federal income taxes totaling 15% of income are withheld from Eunice's pay. Both the FICA tax and the federal income tax withholding are applied only to Eunice's academic year salary; no amounts are withheld from her summer salary.

You have just been hired as an assistant to the chief financial officer of the university. You have been asked to compute the total cost to the university of having Eunice Burns on the faculty. Write a one-page memo to the chief financial officer of the university outlining your calculations. Be sure to explain any assumptions that you make.

THE DEBATE

• Is Research and Development an Asset or an Expense?

According to U.S. accounting rules (FASB Statement No. 2), all research and development expenditures should be recognized as expenses in the period in which they are incurred. This accounting treatment basically assumes that any expected benefit from the R&D is so uncertain or unpredictable that the R&D benefit should not be recorded as an asset. In contrast, international accounting rules (IAS No. 9) provide for R&D expenditures to be recorded as an asset if the technological feasibility of the research project has been established.

Divide your group into two teams.

- The first team represents the "Expense All R&D!" group. Prepare a two-minute oral presentation supporting the notion that the benefit of R&D activity is so uncertain that no assets should be recorded in conjunction with R&D.
- The second team represents the "R&D is an Asset!" group. Prepare a two-minute oral presentation arguing that the whole point of R&D is to generate future economic benefit. Accordingly, R&D should be recorded as an asset.

CUMULATIVE SPREADSHEET PROJECT

This spreadsheet assignment is a continuation of the spreadsheet assignments given in earlier chapters. If you completed those spreadsheets, you have a head start on this one.

This assignment is based on the spreadsheet prepared in part (1) of the spreadsheet assignment for Chapter 7. Review that assignment for a summary of the assumptions made in preparing a forecasted balance sheet and income statement for 2004 for Handyman Company. Using those financial statements, complete the following two independent sensitivity exercises.

1. Handyman is involved in a class-action lawsuit in which a number of customers allege that they injured their thumbs while using hammers purchased at Handyman. These customers are seeking $50 million in compensatory and punitive damages. [Note: All of the numbers in Handyman's financial statements are in millions.] In making the financial statement projections for Handyman for 2004, it has been assumed that losing this lawsuit is possible, but not probable. *Compute* how each of the following quantities would be affected if a loss in this lawsuit becomes probable during 2004:
   a. Debt ratio (total liabilities/total assets) as of the end of 2004.
   b. Return on equity (net income/ending stockholders' equity) for 2004.

2. Ignore the lawsuit described in (1). It is expected that Handyman's total "other operating expenses" will be $217 million in 2004. Of this amount, $20 million is for expected development costs that would be capitalized if Handyman were allowed to use International Accounting Standards. *Compute* how the capitalization of these development costs in 2004 would affect the following quantities. (Note: This is a hypothetical exercise because, as a U.S. company, Handyman is not currently allowed to use International Accounting Standards in preparing its financial statements.)
   a. Debt ratio (total liabilities/total assets) as of the end of 2004.
   b. Return on equity (net income/ending stockholders' equity) for 2004.

INTERNET SEARCH

• *ExxonMobil*

Access **EXXONMOBIL**'s Web site at **http://www.exxonmobil.com**. Sometimes Web addresses change, so if this ExxonMobil address doesn't work, access the Web site for this textbook (**http://albrecht.swcollege.com**) for an updated link to ExxonMobil. Once you've gained access to ExxonMobil's Web site, answer the following questions:

1. Using ExxonMobil's "history" site, determine the original names of the two companies that later became Exxon and Mobil.
2. Review ExxonMobil's note disclosure relating to litigation and other contingencies. What significant legal actions are being taken against the company, and what is their status?
3. Locate ExxonMobil's note relating to income taxes. What is the company's effective tax rate (income tax expense/income before taxes)? How does it compare to the U.S. statutory rate (as of 1999) of 35%?
4. Review ExxonMobil's disclosure relating to its pension plans. Does the amount of funding the company has set aside to satisfy its pension obligation exceed the company's pension obligation?

comprehensive problem 6-8

Zepplin Enterprises is a small business that purchases electronic personal information managers (PIM) from manufacturers and sells them to consumers. These PIMs keep track of appointments, phone numbers, to-do lists, and the like. Zepplin conducts business via the Internet and, at this point, carries only one model of PIM, the YO-660. Zepplin provides the following trial balance as of January 1, 2003.

Zepplin Enterprises
Trial Balance
January 1, 2003

	Debits	Credits
Cash	$ 8,500	
Accounts Receivable	28,400	
Allowance for Bad Debts		$ 568
Inventory	34,855	
Prepaid Rent	1,500	
Office Supplies	1,000	
Accounts Payable		19,700
Wages Payable		3,200
Taxes Payable		4,500
Common Stock (10,000 shares)		25,000
Retained Earnings		21,287
Total	$74,255	$74,255

Zepplin uses the periodic FIFO inventory method in accounting for its inventory. The inventory of YO-660 consists of the following inventory layers:

Layer	Units	Price per Unit	Total Price
1 (oldest purchase)	60	$150	$ 9,000
2	70	155	10,850
3	65	157	10,205
4 (most recent purchase)	30	160	4,800
Total	225		$34,855

Zepplin provides the following additional relevant information:

- The company uses the percentage of receivables method in estimating bad debts; 2% of the ending receivables balance is deemed to be uncollectible.
- Zepplin conducts an actual physical count of its inventory and office supplies at the end of each month.
- Zepplin rents its warehouse, office facilities, and computer equipment. Rent on the computer equipment is paid at the beginning of each month. Rent on the warehouse and office space is paid on the 15th of each month.
- Payroll is paid on the 5th and the 20th (pay periods end on the 15th and the last day of the month).
- Taxes Payable represents payroll taxes that are due by the 5th of the following month.
- All sales and all inventory purchases are on account.

The following transactions occurred for Zepplin during January of 2003:

Jan. 1 Paid rent on the computer equipment, $1,800.

5 Recorded sales for the week, 125 units at $220 per unit. (The company uses a periodic inventory system.)

5 Paid wages payable and taxes payable from the prior period.

5 Collected $15,000 from customers on account during the week.

8 Purchased office supplies for cash, $350.

10 Received 50 YO-660s from the manufacturer at a cost of $160 per unit.

11 Paid accounts payable, $17,500.

12 Collected $27,000 from customers on account during the week.

12 Recorded sales for the week, 140 units at $220 per unit.

15 Paid monthly rent for the office and warehouse, $3,000.

15 Received 140 YO-660s from the manufacturer at a cost of $162 per unit.

18 A customer returned a YO-660 and requested a refund. A check was immediately mailed to the customer in the amount of $220.

19 Collected $38,000 from customers on account during the week.

19 Recorded sales for the week, 115 units at $220 per unit.

20 Paid the semimonthly payroll for the pay period ending on January 15. Salaries and wages total $5,300 and payroll taxes were as follows: FICA taxes payable, employee, $405; FICA taxes payable, employer, $405; state withholding taxes payable, $280; federal withholding taxes payable, $810; federal unemployment taxes payable, $50; state unemployment taxes payable, $150.

22 Received notice that a customer owing Zepplin $440 had filed bankruptcy and would be unable to pay.

23 Paid the taxes payable from the payroll on January 20.

24 Received 190 YO-660s from the manufacturer at a cost of $160 per unit.

25 Purchased office supplies for cash, $730.

25 Paid accounts payable, $39,000.

26 Collected $44,500 from customers on account during the week.

26 Recorded sales for the week, 135 units at $225 per unit.

29 Customers returned 5 YO-660s and requested refunds. Checks were immediately mailed to each customer in the amount of $220 each.

30 Received 130 YO-660s from the manufacturer at a cost of $160 per unit.

31 Collected $21,800 from customers on account.

31 Recorded sales for the partial week, 65 units at $225 per unit.

31 Accrued the semimonthly payroll for the pay period ending on January 31. Salaries and wages total $5,400 and payroll taxes were as follows: FICA taxes payable, employee, $410; FICA taxes payable, employer, $410; state withholding taxes payable, $285; federal withholding taxes payable, $820; federal unemployment taxes payable, $55; state unemployment taxes payable, $160.

Required:

1. Provide the required journal entries to record each of the above events.
2. Make the adjusting entries necessary to (1) record bad debt expense for the period and (2) to adjust inventory and office supplies. A count of inventory and office supplies revealed 160 YO-660s on hand and supplies valued at $800.
3. Prepare a trial balance as of January 31, 2003.
4. Prepare an income statement and a balance sheet for Zepplin Enterprises.
5. Prepare a common-size income statement for Zepplin Enterprises.
6. Compute Zepplin's number of days' sales in inventory, number of days' sales in accounts receivable, and number of days' sales in accounts payable ratios. What can you conclude about the company's liquidity position based on this analysis?

Part 3

Investing and Financing Activities

Investments in Property, Plant, and Equipment and in Intangible Assets

chapter **f9**

learning objectives

After studying this chapter, you should be able to:

1 Identify the two major categories of long-term operating assets: property, plant, and equipment and intangible assets.

2 Understand the factors important in deciding whether to acquire a long-term operating asset.

3 Record the acquisition of property, plant, and equipment through a simple purchase as well as through a lease, by self-construction, and as part of the purchase of several assets at once.

4 Compute straight-line and units-of-production depreciation expense for plant and equipment.

5 Account for repairs and improvements of property, plant, and equipment.

6 Identify whether a long-term operating asset has suffered a decline in value and record the decline.

7 Record the discarding and selling of property, plant, and equipment.

8 Account for the acquisition and amortization of intangible assets and understand the special difficulties associated with accounting for intangibles.

9 Use the fixed asset turnover ratio as a measure of how efficiently a company is using its property, plant, and equipment.

expanded material

10 Compute declining-balance and sum-of-the-years'-digits depreciation expense for plant and equipment.

11 Account for changes in depreciation estimates.

setting the stage

Thomas Edison received $300,000 in investment funds in 1878 in order to start his **EDISON ELECTRIC LIGHT COMPANY**. Today, **GENERAL ELECTRIC** is the direct descendant of Edison's company and, with a market value of $583 billion (as of October 2000), is the most valuable company in the world. General Electric has been a fixture in corporate America since the late 1800s and is the only one of the 12 companies in the original Dow Jones Industrial Average that is still included among the 30 companies making up the Dow today.[1]

The stated purpose of the creation of the Edison Electric Light Company was the development of an economically practical electric light bulb. After a year of experimentation, Thomas Edison discovered that carbonized bamboo would provide a long-lasting light filament that was also easy to produce. Edison quickly found that delivering electric light to people's homes required more than a light bulb, however. So, he developed an entire electricity generation and distribution system, inventing new pieces of equipment when he couldn't find what he needed. The first public electric light system was built in London, followed soon after by the Pearl Street Station system in New York City in 1882. In 1892, Edison's company merged with the **THOMSON-HOUSTON ELECTRIC COMPANY** (developer of alternating-current [AC] equipment that could transmit over longer distances than Edison's direct-current [DC] system), and the General Electric Company (GE) was born.

From the beginning, General Electric's strength has been research. In addition to improving the design of the light bulb (including the development in the early 1900s of gas-filled, tungsten-filament bulbs that are the model for bulbs still used today), GE was also instrumental in developing almost every familiar household appliance—the iron, washing machine, refrigerator, range, air conditioner, dishwasher, and more. In addition, GE research scientists helped create FM radio, aircraft jet engines, and nuclear-power reactors.

Today, General Electric operates in a diverse array of businesses, ranging from train locomotives to medical CT scanners to consumer financing to the NBC television network. When Jack Welch became CEO of GE in 1981, his goal was to make GE number one or number two in each market segment in which it operates, or else get out of that particular line of business. This strategy has enabled GE's success to continue—its market value has grown by an average of 25% per year over the past 19 years.

To support its broad array of businesses, General Electric maintains a vast quantity of long-term assets that cost over $101 billion to acquire. In 1999 alone, GE spent an additional $15.5 billion in acquiring long-term operating assets and received $6.3 billion for disposing of old assets. Its long-term assets include $3.3 billion in rail cars, $6.7 billion in buildings, $20.8 billion in machinery, and $26.0 billion in "intangible" assets.

In Chapters 6 through 8, operating activities of a business and the assets and liabilities arising from those operations were discussed. In this and the next three chapters, investing and financing activities are covered. In this chapter, investments in long-term assets that are used in the business, such as buildings, property, land, and equipment, are discussed. In Chapter 10, long-term debt financing is covered. In Chapter 11, equity financing is discussed. Once you understand debt and equity securities, as discussed in Chapters 10 and 11, you will understand how these same securities can be purchased as investments. Therefore, in Chapter 12, investments in stocks and bonds (securities) of other companies are discussed. Exhibit 9-1 shows the balance sheet and income statement accounts as well as the cash flow items that will be covered in this chapter.

The two primary categories of long-term assets discussed in this chapter are (1) property, plant, and equipment and (2) intangible assets. Because property, plant, and equipment and intangible assets are essential to a business in carrying out its operating activities, they are sometimes called

1 This description is based on General Electric Company History at **http://ge.com/ibhis0.htm**; General Electric Company, *International Directory of Company Histories*, vol. 12 (Detroit: St. James Press, 1996), pp. 193–197; 1999 Annual Report of the General Electric Company.

long-term operating assets Assets expected to be held and used over the course of several years to facilitate operating activities.

long-term operating assets. *Unlike inventories, these long-term operating assets are not acquired for resale to customers but are held and used by a business to generate revenues. As illustrated by the numbers given for* ***GENERAL ELECTRIC*** *at the beginning of the chapter, long-term operating assets often comprise a significant portion of the total assets of a company.*

1

Identify the two major categories of long-term operating assets: property, plant, and equipment and intangible assets.

NATURE OF LONG-TERM OPERATING ASSETS

Businesses make money by selling products and services. A company needs an infrastructure of long-term operating assets in order to profitably produce and distribute these products and services. For example, **GENERAL ELECTRIC** needs factories in which to manufacture the locomotives and light bulbs that it sells. GE also needs patents on its unique technology to protect its competitive edge in the marketplace. A factory is an example of a long-term operating asset that is classified as property, plant, and equipment. A patent is an example of an intangible asset. **Property, plant, and equipment** refers to tangible, long-lived assets acquired for use in business operations. This category includes land, buildings, machinery, equipment, and furniture. **Intangible assets** are long-lived assets that are used in the operation of a business but do not have physical substance. In most cases, they provide their owners with competitive advantages over other firms. Typical intangible assets are patents, licenses, franchises, and goodwill. The time line in Exhibit 9-2 illustrates the important business issues associated with long-term operating assets.

property, plant, and equipment Tangible, long-lived assets acquired for use in business operations; include land, buildings, machinery, equipment, and furniture.

intangible assets Long-lived assets without physical substance that are used in business, such as licenses, patents, franchises, and goodwill.

The following section outlines the process used in deciding whether to acquire a long-term operating asset. The subsequent sections discuss the accounting issues that arise when a long-term operating asset is acquired: accounting for the acquisition of the asset, recording periodic depreciation, accounting for new costs and changes in asset value, and properly removing the asset from the books upon disposition.

exhibit 9-1 Financial Statement Items Covered in This Chapter

Balance Sheet

Property, plant, and equipment
Intangible assets

Statement of Cash Flows

Investing activities
Purchase of property, plant, and equipment
Proceeds from sale of property, plant, and equipment

Income Statement

Expenses
Depreciation expense
Amortization expense

exhibit 9-2 Time Line of Business Issues Involved with Long-Term Operating Assets

FOR SALE

EVALUATE possible acquisition of long-term operating assets

ACQUIRE long-term operating assets

ESTIMATE and RECOGNIZE periodic depreciation and amortization

MONITOR asset value for possible declines

DISPOSE of assets

to summarize

Long-term operating assets provide an infrastructure in which to conduct operating activities. The category of property, plant, and equipment refers to tangible, long-lived assets such as land and equipment. Examples of intangible assets are patents and licenses.

2

Understand the factors important in deciding whether to acquire a long-term operating asset.

DECIDING WHETHER TO ACQUIRE A LONG-TERM OPERATING ASSET

capital budgeting Systematic planning for long-term investments in operating assets.

As mentioned in the previous section, long-term operating assets are acquired to be used over the course of several years. The decision to acquire a long-term asset depends on whether the future cash flows generated by the asset are expected to be large enough to justify the asset cost. The process of evaluating a long-term project is called **capital budgeting**. This process is briefly introduced here and is covered in more detail in Chapter 9 in the management accounting section of this book.

Assume that Yosef Manufacturing makes joysticks and other computer game accessories. Yosef is considering expanding its operations by buying an additional production facility. The cost of the new factory is $100 million. Yosef expects to be able to sell the joysticks and other items made in the factory for $80 million per year. At that level of production, the annual cost of operating the factory (wages, insurance, materials, maintenance, etc.) is expected to total $65 million. The factory is expected to remain in operation for 20 years. Should Yosef buy the new factory for $100 million?

To summarize the information in the preceding paragraph, Yosef must decide whether to pay $100 million for a factory that will generate a net profit of $15 million ($80 million − $65 million) per year for 20 years. At first glance, you might think that the decision is obvious because the factory costs only $100 million but will generate $300 million in profit ($15 million × 20 years) during its 20-year life. But this analysis ignores the important fact that dollars received far in the future are not worth as much as dollars received right now. For example, if you can invest your money and earn 10%, receiving $1 today is the same as receiving $6.73 20 years from now because the $1 received today could be invested and would grow to $6.73 in 20 years. This important concept is called the **time value of money** and is essential to properly evaluating whether to acquire any long-term asset.

time value of money The concept that a dollar received now is worth more than a dollar received far in the future.

Using the time value of money calculations that will be explained in detail in Chapter 10, it can be shown that receiving the future cash flows from the factory of $15 million per year for 20 years is the same as receiving $128 million in one lump sum right now, if the prevailing interest rate is 10%. Thus, the decision to acquire the factory boils down to the following comparison: Should we pay $100 million to buy a factory now if the factory will generate future cash flows that are worth the equivalent of $128 million now? The decision is yes, because the $128 million value of the expected cash inflows is greater than the $100 million cost of the factory. On the other hand, if the factory were expected to generate only $10 million per year, then, using the computations that will be explained in Chapter 10, it can be calculated that the value of the cash flows would be only $85 million, and the factory should not be purchased for $100 million.

The important concept to remember here is that long-term operating assets have value because they are expected to help a company generate cash flows in the future. If events occur that change the expectation concerning those future cash flows, then the value of the asset changes. For example, if consumer demand for computer joysticks dries up, the value of a factory built to produce joysticks can plunge overnight even though the factory itself is still as productive as it ever was. Accounting for this type of decline in the value of a long-term operating asset is discussed later in the chapter.

---

to summarize

Long-term operating assets have value because they help companies generate future cash flows. The decision to acquire a long-term operating asset involves comparing the cost of the asset to the value of the expected cash inflows, after adjusting for the time value of money. An asset's value can decline or disappear if events cause a decrease in the expected future cash flows generated by the asset.

3

Record the acquisition of property, plant, and equipment through a simple purchase as well as through a lease, by self-construction, and as part of the purchase of several assets at once.

ACCOUNTING FOR ACQUISITION OF PROPERTY, PLANT, AND EQUIPMENT

Like all other assets, property, plant, and equipment are initially recorded at cost. The cost of an asset includes not only the purchase price but also any other costs incurred in acquiring the asset and getting it ready for its intended use. Examples of these other costs include shipping, installation, and sales taxes. The items that should be included in the acquisition cost of various types of property, plant, and equipment are outlined in Exhibit 9-3.

exhibit 9-3 Items Included in the Acquisition Cost of Property, Plant, and Equipment

Land	Purchase price, commissions, legal fees, escrow fees, surveying fees, clearing and grading costs.
Land improvements (e.g., landscaping, paving, fencing)	Cost of improvements, including expenditures for materials, labor, and overhead.
Buildings	Purchase price, commissions, reconditioning costs.
Equipment	Purchase price, taxes, freight, insurance, installation, and any expenditures incurred in preparing the asset for its intended use, e.g., reconditioning and testing costs.

Property, plant, and equipment are usually acquired by purchase. In some cases, assets are acquired by leasing but are accounted for as assets in much the same way as purchased assets. Plant and equipment can also be constructed by a business for its own use. Also, a company can in one transaction purchase several different assets or even another entire company. The accounting for each of these types of acquisition is explained below.

Assets Acquired by Purchase

A company can purchase an asset by paying cash, incurring a liability, exchanging another asset, or by a combination of these methods. If a single asset is purchased for cash, the accounting is relatively simple. To illustrate, we assume that Wheeler Resorts, Inc., purchases a new delivery truck for $15,096 (purchase price, $15,000, less 2% discount for paying cash, plus sales tax of $396). The entry to record this purchase is:

Delivery Truck	15,096	
Cash		15,096
Purchased a delivery truck for $15,096 ($15,000 – $300 cash discount + $396 sales tax).		

In this instance, cash was paid for a single asset, the truck. An alternative would be to borrow part of the purchase price. If the company had borrowed $12,000 of the $15,096 from a bank, the entry would have been:

Delivery Truck	15,096	
Cash		3,096
Notes Payable		12,000
Purchased a delivery truck for $15,096; paid $3,096 cash and issued a note for $12,000 to Chemical Bank.		

The $12,000 represents the principal of the note; it does not include any interest charged by the lending institution. (The interest is recognized later as interest expense.)

When one long-term operating asset is acquired in exchange for another, the cost of the new asset is usually set equal to the market value of the asset given up in exchange.

Assets Acquired by Leasing

lease A contract that specifies the terms under which the owner of an asset (the lessor) agrees to transfer the right to use the asset to another party (the lessee).

lessee The party that is granted the right to use property under the terms of a lease.

lessor The owner of property that is leased (rented) to another party.

operating lease A simple rental agreement.

Leases are often short-term rental agreements in which one party, the **lessee**, is granted the right to use property owned by another party, the **lessor**. For example, as a student, you may decide to lease (rent) an apartment to live in while you are attending college. The owner of the apartment (lessor) will probably require you to sign a lease specifying the terms of the arrangement. The lease states the period of time in which you will live in the apartment, the amount of rent you will pay, and when each rent payment is due. When the lease expires, you will either sign a new lease or move out of the apartment, which would then be rented to someone else.

Companies enter into similar types of lease arrangements. For example, Wheeler Resorts might decide to lease a building because it needs additional office space. Assume Wheeler signs a two-year lease requiring monthly rental payments of $1,000. When the lease expires, Wheeler will either move out of the building or negotiate a new lease with the owner. Accounting for this type of rental agreement, called an **operating lease**, is straightforward. When rent is paid each month, Wheeler records the following journal entry:

Rent (or Lease) Expense	1,000	
Cash		1,000
To record monthly rent of office building.		

A college student (lessee) often rents an apartment while attending college. The apartment owner (lessor) will require the student to sign a lease stating the terms of the arrangement.

Some lease agreements, however, are not so simple. Suppose Wheeler has decided to expand its operations and wants to acquire a hotel in the Phoenix, Arizona area. Wheeler's alternatives are to buy land and build a new hotel, purchase an existing hotel, or lease a hotel. Assume Wheeler locates a desirable piece of land, and the owner of the land agrees to build a hotel and lease the property to Wheeler. The lease agreement is noncancelable and requires Wheeler to make annual lease payments of $100,000 for 20 years. At the end of 20 years, Wheeler will become the owner of the property. Clearly, this is not a simple rental agreement, even though the transaction is called a lease by the parties involved. In reality, this transaction is a purchase of the property with the payments being spread over 20 years. The result is the same as if Wheeler had borrowed money on a 20-year mortgage and purchased the property.

Generally accepted accounting principles require that the recording of a transaction reflect its true economic nature, not its form. Instead of recognizing the individual lease payments as an expense as was done with the operating lease, Wheeler records the property as an asset and also records a liability reflecting the obligation to the lessor. The amount to be recorded is the cash amount that Wheeler would have to pay right now in order to completely pay off the obligation to make the future lease payments. This amount is called the present value of the lease payments (in the Wheeler example, the present value of 20 annual payments of $100,000) and takes into account the time value of money. As mentioned earlier, the time value concept will be explained in more detail in Chapter 10.

Continuing the example, assume that, at the beginning of the lease term, the present value of the future lease payments is $851,360. Wheeler makes the following journal entry to record the lease:

Leased Property	851,360	
Lease Liability		851,360
To record hotel acquired under a 20-year noncancelable lease.		

capital lease A leasing transaction that is recorded as a purchase by the lessee.

This type of lease is called a **capital lease** because the lessee records (capitalizes) the leased asset the same as if the asset had been acquired in an outright purchase. The asset is reported with Property, Plant, and Equipment on the lessee's balance sheet. The lessee (Wheeler Resorts) also shows the lease liability on the balance sheet as a long-term liability.

When annual lease payments are made, Wheeler will not record the payment as rent expense. Instead, the payment will be recorded as a reduction in the lease liability, with part of each payment being interest on the outstanding obligation. The difference between the total lease payments (20 years × $100,000, or $2 million) and the "cost" or present value of the property is the amount of interest that will be paid over the term of the lease. To illustrate, assume that the first payment is made one year after the lease term begins and includes interest of $85,136 and a $14,864 reduction in the liability. The payment is recorded as follows:

Lease Liability	14,864	
Interest Expense	85,136	
Cash		100,000
To record annual lease payment under capital lease.		

Accounting for payments on capital leases is discussed in more detail in Chapter 10.

CLASSIFYING LEASES As illustrated, an operating lease is accounted for as a simple rental, whereas a capital lease is accounted for as a purchase of the leased asset. Because the accounting treatment of a lease can have a major impact on the financial statements, the accounting profession has established criteria for determining whether a lease should be classified as an operating or a capital lease. If a lease is noncancelable and meets any one of the following four criteria, it is recorded as a capital lease:

1. The lease transfers ownership of the leased asset to the lessee by the end of the lease term (as in the Wheeler Resorts example).
2. The lease contains an option allowing the lessee to purchase the asset at the end of the lease term at a bargain price, essentially guaranteeing that ownership will eventually transfer to the lessee.
3. The lease term is equal to 75% or more of the estimated economic life of the asset, meaning that the lessee will use the asset for most of its economic life.
4. The present value of the lease payments at the beginning of the lease is 90% or more of the fair market value of the leased asset. Meeting this criterion means that, in agreeing to make the lease payments, the lessee is agreeing to pay almost as much as the cash price to purchase the asset outright.

If just one of the above criteria is met, then the lease agreement is classified as a capital lease and is accounted for by the lessee as a debt-financed purchase. A lease that does not meet any of the capital lease criteria is considered an operating lease. Keep in mind that these two types of leases are not alternatives for the same transaction. If the terms of the lease agreement meet any one of the capital lease criteria, the lease must be accounted for as a capital lease.

The accounting for leases has been a thorn in the side of accounting standard-setters for at least 50 years. From the beginning, the crucial issue has been how to require companies to report leased assets and lease liabilities in the balance sheet when a lease constitutes an effective transfer of ownership. The four lease criteria outlined above were issued by the FASB in 1976, with the thought that the rigidity and strictness of the criteria would result in most leases being reported on lessee companies' balance sheets as capital leases. In practice, U.S. companies have taken these four criteria as a challenge and have carefully crafted their lease agreements so that none of the criteria is satisfied, allowing the leases to continue to be accounted for as operating leases.

> **fyi**
>
> One of the most interesting accounting manipulations involving the four lease criteria relates to the 90% threshold for the present value of the minimum lease payments. By hiring an insurance company to guarantee a portion of the lease payments, a lessee is able to exclude these payments from the present value computations, lowering the present value below the 90% threshold.

One of the largest leasing companies in the United States is a subsidiary of **GENERAL ELECTRIC** called **GE CAPITAL SERVICES**. GE Capital Services leases industrial equipment, factory buildings, rail cars, shipping containers, computers, medical equip-

business environment essay

Lease or Buy? Leasing is an integral part of American business. From its beginning, a major aspect of IBM's business has been the leasing, rather than the outright sale, of its equipment. Over the years, Ray Kroc's MCDONALD'S empire has made more money leasing land and buildings to franchisees than it has made selling hamburgers. In short, leasing has long been a popular method of acquiring and financing operating assets. For example, airlines such as AMERICAN, DELTA, SOUTHWEST, and UNITED often lease many of their airplanes. Retail chains such as WAL-MART and SAFEWAY often lease their stores.

Virtually any type of operating asset can be acquired by leasing. Companies often lease such assets as rail cars, automobiles and trucks, airplanes, and various other types of equipment, as well as real estate. There are several reasons why a company might choose to lease rather than purchase an asset. A purchase transaction often requires a significant cash outlay in the form of a down payment at the date of purchase; leasing, therefore, can be used to minimize the amount of

ment, and more. In 1999, the total original cost of assets leased by GE Capital Services to other companies was $31.0 billion.

Assets Acquired by Self-Construction

Sometimes buildings or equipment are constructed by a company for its own use. This may be done to save on construction costs, to utilize idle facilities or idle workers, or to meet a special set of technical specifications. Self-constructed assets, like purchased assets, are recorded at cost, including all expenditures incurred to build the asset and make it ready for its intended use. These costs include the materials used to build the asset, the construction labor, and some reasonable share of the general company overhead (electricity, insurance, supervisors' salaries, etc.) during the time of construction.

capitalized interest Interest that is recorded as part of the cost of a self-constructed asset.

Another cost that is included in the cost of a self-constructed asset is the interest cost associated with money borrowed to finance the construction project. Just as the cost to rent a crane to be used to construct a building would be included in the cost of the building, the cost to "rent" money to finance the construction project should also be included in the building cost. Interest that is recorded as part of the cost of a self-constructed asset is called **capitalized interest**. The amount of interest that should be capitalized is that amount that could have been saved if the money used on the construction project had instead been used to repay loans.

The following illustration demonstrates the computation of the cost of a self-constructed asset. Wheeler Resorts decided to construct a new hotel using its own workers. The construction project lasted from January 1 to December 31, 2000. Building materials costs for the project were $4,500,000. Total labor costs attributable to the project were $2,500,000. Total company overhead (costs other than materials and labor) for the year was $10,000,000; of this amount, it is determined that 15% can be reasonably assigned as part of the cost of the construction project. A construction loan was negotiated with Wheeler's bank; during the year, Wheeler was able to borrow from the bank to pay for materials, labor, etc. The total amount of interest paid on this construction loan during the year was $500,000. The total cost of the self-constructed hotel is computed as follows:

Materials	$4,500,000
Labor	2,500,000
Overhead allocation ($10,000,000 × 0.15)	1,500,000
Capitalized interest	500,000
Total hotel cost	$9,000,000

cash paid initially to acquire the asset. For some types of assets, such as computers, leasing enables the lessee to avoid risks of obsolescence if the appropriate terms are written into the lease agreement.

Another potential advantage of leasing is that if the agreement can be recorded as an operating lease, the lessee does not have to report any related liability. This is an important consideration if a company is concerned about the effect of reporting additional debt on the balance sheet. Before criteria were established for classifying leases as operating or capital, almost all leases were treated as operating leases. Often the primary purpose of a leasing arrangement was to acquire an asset without reporting any related liability. Some companies are still using leasing for this purpose. They do so by writing the terms of a lease agreement in a manner that circumvents the generally accepted accounting capitalization criteria. The result is that some leasing transactions are reported as simple rental agreements (operating leases) when in fact they have many characteristics of a purchase transaction. Leasing and other forms of "off-balance-sheet financing" are of major concern to the accounting profession and financial statement users.

What is the difference between capitalized interest and regular interest?

The new hotel would be reported in Wheeler's balance sheet at a total cost of $9,000,000. As with other long-term operating assets, self-constructed assets are reported at the total cost necessary to get them ready for their intended use.

The amount of capitalized interest reported by several large U.S. companies, relative to their total interest expense, is displayed in Exhibit 9-4. As you can see, General Electric capitalized only an insignificant amount of its $10.013 billion in interest during 1999. On the other hand, **EXXONMOBIL** capitalized more than one-third of its interest during 1999.

Acquisition of Several Assets at Once

basket purchase The purchase of two or more assets acquired together at a single price.

A **basket purchase** occurs when two or more assets are acquired together at a single price. A typical basket purchase is the purchase of a building along with the land on which the building sits. Because there are differences in the accounting for land and buildings, the purchase price

exhibit 9-4 Magnitude of Capitalized Interest for Several Large U.S. Companies

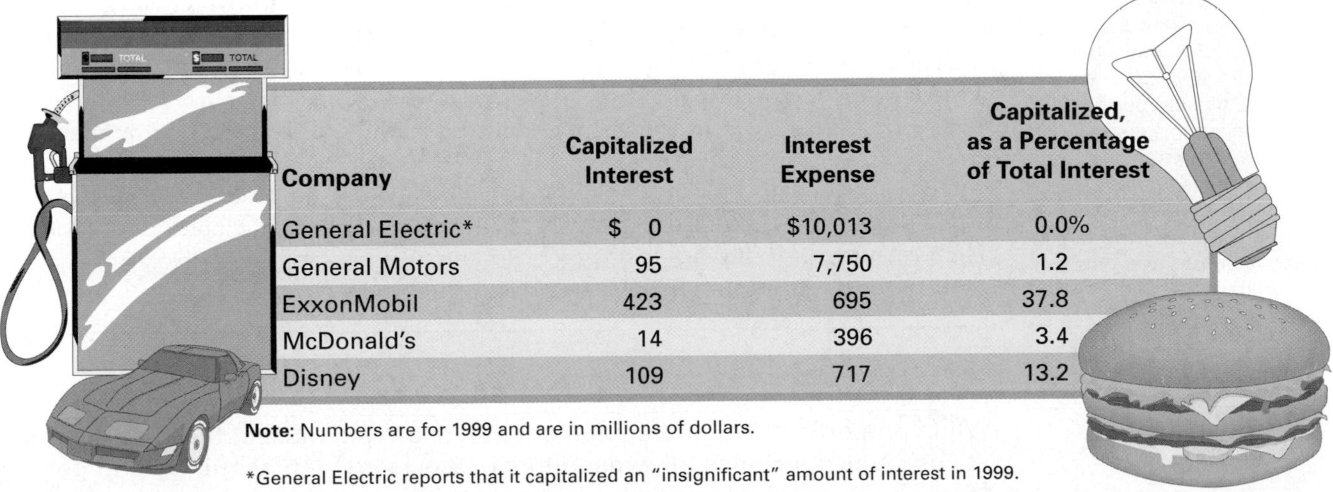

Company	Capitalized Interest	Interest Expense	Capitalized, as a Percentage of Total Interest
General Electric*	$ 0	$10,013	0.0%
General Motors	95	7,750	1.2
ExxonMobil	423	695	37.8
McDonald's	14	396	3.4
Disney	109	717	13.2

Note: Numbers are for 1999 and are in millions of dollars.

*General Electric reports that it capitalized an "insignificant" amount of interest in 1999.

must be allocated between the two assets on some reasonable basis. The relative fair market values of the assets are usually used to determine the respective costs to be assigned to the land and the building.

To illustrate, we will assume that Wheeler Resorts purchases a 40,000-square-foot building on 2.6 acres of land for $3,600,000. How much of the total cost should be assigned to the land and how much to the building? If an appraisal indicates that the fair market values of the land and the building are $1,000,000 and $3,000,000, respectively, the resulting allocated costs would be $900,000 and $2,700,000, calculated as follows:

Asset	Fair Market Value	Percentage of Total Value	Apportionment of Lump-Sum Cost
Land	$1,000,000	25%	0.25 × $3,600,000 = $ 900,000
Building	3,000,000	75	0.75 × $3,600,000 = 2,700,000
Total	$4,000,000	100%	$3,600,000

In this case, the fair market value of the land is $1,000,000, or 25% of the total market value of the land and building. Therefore, 25% of the actual cost, or $900,000, is allocated to the land, and 75% of the actual cost, or $2,700,000, is allocated to the building. The journal entry to record this basket purchase is:

Land	900,000	
Building.	2,700,000	
Cash.		3,600,000
Purchased 2.6 acres of land and a 40,000-square-foot building.		

If part of the purchase price is financed by a bank, an additional credit to Notes Payable or Mortgage Payable would be included in the entry.

Sometimes one company will buy all the assets of another company. For example, in its 1999 annual report, General Electric discloses that its financing subsidiary, GE Capital Services, acquired JAPAN LEASING, which leases fleets of automobiles to Japanese corporations. Similarly, in its 1999 annual report (included in Appendix A), MICROSOFT discloses that, in November 1998, it purchased LINKEXCHANGE for $265 million. The purchase of an entire company raises a number of accounting issues. The first, already discussed above, is how to allocate the purchase price to the various assets acquired. In general, all acquired assets are recorded on the books of the acquiring company at their fair values as of the acquisition date.

goodwill An intangible asset that exists when a business is valued at more than the fair market value of its net assets, usually due to strategic location, reputation, good customer relations, or similar factors; equal to the excess of the purchase price over the fair market value of the net assets purchased.

The second major accounting issue associated with the purchase of an entire company is the recording of goodwill. **Goodwill** represents all the special competitive advantages enjoyed by a company, such as a trained staff, good credit rating, reputation for superior products and services, and an established network of suppliers and customers. These factors allow an established business to earn more profits than would a new business, even though the new business might have the same type of building, the same equipment, and the same type of production processes.

When one company purchases another established business, the excess of the purchase price over the value of the identifiable net assets is assumed to represent the purchase of goodwill. The accounting for goodwill is illustrated later in the chapter.

to summarize

When property, plant, and equipment assets are purchased, they are recorded at cost, which includes all expenditures associated with acquiring and getting them ready for their intended use, such as sales tax, shipping, and installation.

Sometimes assets are acquired by lease rather than purchase. A lease may be a simple short-term rental agreement, called an operating lease, or it may be substantially the same as a purchase transaction. In the latter case, called a capital lease, the party acquiring the asset (the lessee) records the asset and related liability as if the property had been purchased and financed with long-term debt. When a company constructs an asset for its own use, the recorded cost includes materials, labor, a reasonable allocation of overhead, and the cost of interest used to finance the construction. When two or more assets are acquired for a single price in a basket purchase, the relative fair market values are used to determine the respective costs.

4

Compute straight-line and units-of-production depreciation expense for plant and equipment.

CALCULATING AND RECORDING DEPRECIATION EXPENSE

depreciation The process of cost allocation that assigns the original cost of plant and equipment to the periods benefited.

book value For a long-term operating asset, the asset's original cost less any accumulated depreciation.

salvage value The amount expected to be received when an asset is sold at the end of its useful life.

straight-line depreciation method The depreciation method in which the cost of an asset is allocated equally over the periods of an asset's estimated useful life.

units-of-production method The depreciation method in which the cost of an asset is allocated to each period on the basis of the productive output or use of the asset during the period.

The second element in accounting for plant and equipment is the allocation of an asset's cost over its useful life. The matching principle requires that this cost be assigned to expense in the periods benefited from the use of the asset. The allocation procedure is called **depreciation**, and the allocated amount, recorded in a period-ending adjusting entry, is an expense that is deducted from revenues in order to determine income. It should be noted that the asset "plant" normally refers to buildings only; land is recorded as a separate asset and is not depreciated because it is usually assumed to have an unlimited useful life.

Accounting for depreciation is often confusing because students tend to think that depreciation expense reflects the decline in an asset's value. The concept of depreciation is nothing more than a systematic write-off of the original cost of an asset. The undepreciated cost is referred to as **book value**, which represents that portion of the original cost not yet assigned to the income statement as an expense. A company never claims that an asset's recorded book value is equal to its market value. In fact, market values of assets could increase at the same time that depreciation expense is being recorded.

To calculate depreciation expense for an asset, you need to know (1) its original cost, (2) its estimated useful life, and (3) its estimated salvage, or residual, value. **Salvage value** is the amount expected to be received when the asset is sold at the end of its useful life. When an asset is purchased, its actual life and salvage value are obviously unknown. They must be estimated as realistically as is feasible, usually on the basis of experience with similar assets. In some cases, an asset will have little or no salvage value. If the salvage value is not significant, it is usually ignored in computing depreciation.

Several methods can be used for depreciating the costs of assets for financial reporting. In the main part of this chapter, we describe two: straight-line and units-of-production. In the expanded material section of this chapter, we describe two more depreciation methods: sum-of-the-years'-digits and declining-balance.

The **straight-line depreciation method** assumes that an asset will benefit all periods equally and that the cost of the asset should be assigned on a uniform basis for all accounting periods. If an asset's benefits are thought to be related to its productive output (miles driven in an automobile, for example), the **units-of-production method** is usually appropriate.

To illustrate straight-line and units-of-production depreciation methods, we assume that Wheeler Resorts purchased a van on January 1 for transporting hotel guests to and from the airport. The following facts apply:

Acquisition cost	$24,000
Estimated salvage value	$2,000
Estimated life:	
In years	4 years
In miles driven	60,000 miles

Straight-Line Method of Depreciation

The straight-line depreciation method is the simplest depreciation method. It assumes that an asset's cost should be assigned equally to all periods benefited. The formula for calculating annual straight-line depreciation is:

$$\frac{\text{Cost} - \text{Salvage value}}{\text{Estimated useful life (years)}} = \text{Annual depreciation expense}$$

With this formula, the annual depreciation expense for the van is calculated as:

$$\frac{\$24{,}000 - \$2{,}000}{4 \text{ years}} = \$5{,}500 \text{ depreciation expense per year}$$

When the depreciation expense for an asset has been calculated, a schedule showing the annual depreciation expense, the total accumulated depreciation, and the asset's book value (undepreciated cost) for each year can be prepared. The depreciation schedule for the van (using straight-line depreciation) is shown in Exhibit 9-5.

exhibit 9-5

Depreciation Schedule with Straight-Line Depreciation

	Annual Depreciation Expense	Accumulated Depreciation	Book Value
Acquisition date	—	—	$24,000
End of year 1	$ 5,500	$ 5,500	18,500
End of year 2	5,500	11,000	13,000
End of year 3	5,500	16,500	7,500
End of year 4	5,500	22,000	2,000
	$22,000		

The entry to record straight-line depreciation each year is:

Depreciation Expense.	5,500	
Accumulated Depreciation, Hotel Van		5,500
To record annual depreciation for the hotel van.		

fyi

A comparison of the amounts of cost and accumulated depreciation reveals how old the plant and equipment is relative to its total expected life.

Depreciation Expense is reported on the income statement. Accumulated Depreciation is a contra-asset account that is offset against the cost of the asset on the balance sheet. Book value is equal to the asset account balance, which retains the original cost of the asset as a debit balance, minus the credit balance in the accumulated depreciation account.

At the end of the first year, the acquisition cost, accumulated depreciation, and book value of the van are presented on the balance sheet as follows:

Property, Plant, and Equipment:	
Hotel van	$24,000
Less: Accumulated depreciation	5,500
Book value	$18,500

Similar information is provided in the annual reports of all companies with property, plant, and equipment. For example, **GENERAL ELECTRIC** reported the following in the notes to its 1999 financial statements:

	Original Cost (in millions)	
	1999	**1998**
GE		
Land and improvements	$ 526	$ 483
Buildings, structures, and related equipment	6,674	6,579
Machinery and equipment	20,849	19,491
Leasehold costs and manufacturing plant under construction	2,150	1,757
	$30,199	$28,310
GE Capital Services		
Buildings and equipment	$ 7,163	$ 4,828
Equipment leased to others		
Vehicles	10,942	9,825
Aircraft	10,591	9,321
Railroad rolling stock	3,323	2,804
Marine shipping containers	2,309	2,565
Other	3,832	3,447
	$38,160	$32,790
	$68,359	$61,100
	Accumulated Depreciation and Amortization	
GE	$17,818	$16,616
GE Capital Services		
Buildings and equipment	2,127	1,733
Equipment leased to others	7,392	7,021
	$27,337	$25,370

Using this information, one can calculate that the property, plant, and equipment used by General Electric had been used for 59% ($17,818/$30,199) of its useful life as of the end of 1999. Similarly, the buildings and equipment used by **GE CAPITAL SERVICES** had been used for 30% ($2,127/$7,163) of its life, and the equipment leased by GE Capital Services to others had been used for 24% ($7,392/$30,997) of its useful life.

Units-of-Production Method of Depreciation

The units-of-production depreciation method allocates an asset's cost on the basis of use rather than time. This method is used primarily when a company expects that asset usage will vary significantly from year to year. If the asset's usage pattern is uniform from year to year, the units-of-production method will produce the same depreciation pattern as the straight-line method. Assets with varying usage patterns for which this method of depreciation may be appropriate include automobiles and other vehicles whose life is estimated in terms of number of miles driven. It is also used for certain machines whose life is estimated in terms of number of units produced or number of hours of operating life. The formula for calculating the units-of-production depreciation for the year is:

$$\frac{\text{Cost} - \text{Salvage value}}{\text{Total estimated life in units, hours, or miles}} \times \text{Number of units produced, hours used, or miles driven during the year} = \text{Current year's depreciation expense}$$

To illustrate, we again consider Wheeler Resorts' van, which has an expected life of 60,000 miles. With the units-of-production method, if the van is driven 12,000 miles during the first year, the depreciation expense for that year is calculated as follows:

$$\frac{\$24{,}000 - \$2{,}000}{60{,}000 \text{ miles}} \times 12{,}000 \text{ miles} = \$4{,}400 \text{ depreciation expense}$$

The entry to record units-of-production depreciation at the end of the first year of the van's life is:

Depreciation Expense	4,400	
Accumulated Depreciation, Hotel Van		4,400
To record depreciation for the first year of the hotel van's life.		

The depreciation schedule for the four years is shown in Exhibit 9-6. This exhibit assumes that 18,000 miles were driven the second year, 21,000 the third year, and 9,000 the fourth year.

exhibit 9-6 Depreciation Schedule with Units-of-Production Depreciation

	Miles Driven	Depreciation Expense	Accumulated Depreciation	Book Value
Acquisition date	—	—	—	$24,000
End of year 1	12,000	$ 4,400	$ 4,400	19,600
End of year 2	18,000	6,600	11,000	13,000
End of year 3	21,000	7,700	18,700	5,300
End of year 4	9,000	3,300	22,000	2,000
		$22,000		

Note that part of the formulas for straight-line and units-of-production depreciation is the same. In both cases, cost − salvage value is divided by the asset's useful life. With straight-line, life is measured in years; with units-of-production, life is in miles or hours. With units-of-production, the depreciation per mile or hour must then be multiplied by the usage for the year to determine depreciation expense.

What if the van lasts longer than four years or is driven for more than 60,000 miles? Once the $22,000 difference between cost and salvage value has been recorded as depreciation expense, there is no further expense to record. Thus, any additional years or miles are "free" in the sense that no depreciation expense will be recognized in connection with them. However, as other vans are purchased in the future, the initial estimates of their useful lives will be adjusted to reflect the experience with previous vans.

What if the van lasts less than four years or is driven fewer than 60,000 miles? This topic is covered later in the chapter in connection with the accounting for the disposal of property, plant, and equipment.

A Comparison of Depreciation Methods

The amount of depreciation expense will vary according to the depreciation method used by a company. Exhibit 9-7 compares the annual depreciation expense for Wheeler Resorts' van under the straight-line and units-of-production depreciation methods. As this schedule makes clear, the total amount of depreciation is the same regardless of which method is used.

Straight-line is by far the most commonly used depreciation method because it is the simplest to apply and makes intuitive sense. For example, in the notes to its 1999 financial statements (see Appendix A), MICROSOFT discloses that it depreciates its property, plant, and equipment using the straight-line method over useful lives ranging from 1 to 15 years.

exhibit 9-7

Comparison of Depreciation Expense Using Different Depreciation Methods

	Straight-Line Depreciation	Units-of-Production Depreciation
End of year 1	$ 5,500	$ 4,400
End of year 2	5,500	6,600
End of year 3	5,500	7,700
End of year 4	5,500	3,300
Totals	$22,000	$22,000

Partial-Year Depreciation Calculations

Thus far, depreciation expense has been calculated on the basis of a full year. Businesses purchase assets at all times during the year, however, so partial-year depreciation calculations are often required. To compute depreciation expense for less than a full year, first calculate the depreciation expense for the year and then distribute it evenly over the number of months the asset is held during the year.

To illustrate, assume that Wheeler Resorts purchased its $24,000 van on July 1 instead of January 1. The depreciation calculations for the first one and one-half years, using straight-line depreciation, are shown in Exhibit 9-8. The units-of-production method has been omitted from the exhibit; midyear purchases do not complicate the calculations with this method because it involves number of miles driven, hours flown, and so on, rather than time periods.

exhibit 9-8

Partial-Year Depreciation

Method	Full-Year Depreciation	Depreciation 1st Year (6 months)	Depreciation 2nd Year (12 months)
Straight-line	$5,500	$2,750 ($5,500 × ½)	$5,500

In practice, many companies simplify their depreciation computations by taking a full year of depreciation in the year an asset is purchased and none in the year the asset is sold, or vice versa. This is allowed because depreciation is based on estimates, and in the long run, the difference in the amounts is usually immaterial.

Units-of-Production Method with Natural Resources

natural resources Assets that are physically consumed or waste away, such as oil, minerals, gravel, and timber.

depletion The process of cost allocation that assigns the original cost of a natural resource to the periods benefited.

Another common use for the units-of-production method is with natural resources. **Natural resources** include such assets as oil wells, timber tracts, coal mines, and gravel deposits. Like all other assets, newly purchased or developed natural resources are recorded at cost. This cost must be written off as the assets are extracted or otherwise depleted. This process of writing off the cost of natural resources is called **depletion** and involves the calculation of a depletion rate for each unit of the natural resource. Conceptually, depletion is exactly the same as depreciation; with plant and equipment, the accounting process is called depreciation, whereas with natural resources it is called depletion.

To illustrate, assume that Power-T Company purchases a coal mine for $1,200,000 cash. The entry to record the purchase is:

Coal Mine	1,200,000	
Cash		1,200,000
Purchased a coal mine for $1,200,000.		

If the mine contains an estimated 200,000 tons of coal deposits (based on a geologist's estimate), the depletion expense for each ton of coal extracted and sold will be $6 ($1,200,000/200,000 tons). Here, the unit of production is the extraction of one ton of coal. If 12,000 tons of coal are mined and sold in the current year, the depletion entry is:

Depletion Expense	72,000	
Accumulated Depletion, Coal Mine		72,000
To record depletion for the year: 12,000 tons at $6 per ton.		

After the first year's depletion expense has been recorded, the coal mine is shown on the balance sheet as follows:

Coal mine	$1,200,000
Less: Accumulated depletion	72,000
Book value	$1,128,000

But how do you determine the number of tons of coal in a mine? Because most natural resources cannot be counted, the amount of the resource owned is an estimate. The depletion calculation is therefore likely to be revised as new information becomes available. When an estimate is changed, a new depletion rate per unit is calculated and used to compute depletion during the remaining life of the natural resource or until another new estimate is made. Coverage of accounting for changes in estimates is included in the expanded material section of this chapter.

---

to summarize

Depreciation is the process whereby the cost of an asset is allocated over its useful life. Two common and simple methods of depreciation are straight-line and units-of-production. The straight-line and units-of-production methods allocate cost proportionately over an asset's life on the bases of time and use, respectively. Regardless of which method is used, depreciation is only an allocation of an asset's cost over the periods benefited and is not a method of valuation. Natural resources are assets, such as gravel deposits or coal mines, that are consumed or that waste away. The accounting process of depreciation for natural resources is called depletion.

5

Account for repairs and improvements of property, plant, and equipment.

REPAIRING AND IMPROVING PROPERTY, PLANT, AND EQUIPMENT

Sometime during its useful life, an asset will probably need to be repaired or improved. The accounting issue associated with these postacquisition expenditures is whether they should be immediately recognized as an expense or be added to the cost of the asset (capitalized). Remember from the discussion in Chapter 8 that an expenditure should be capitalized if it is expected to have an identifiable benefit in future periods.

Two types of expenditures can be made on existing assets. The first is ordinary expenditures for repairs, maintenance, and minor improvements. For example, a truck requires oil changes and periodic maintenance. Because these types of expenditures typically benefit only the period in which they are made, they are expenses of the current period.

The second type is an expenditure that lengthens an asset's useful life, increases its capacity, or changes its use. These expenditures are capitalized; that is, they are added to the asset's cost instead of being expensed in the current period. For example, overhauling the engine of a delivery truck involves a major expenditure to extend the useful life of the truck. To qualify for capitalization, an expenditure should meet three criteria: (1) it must be significant in amount; (2) it should benefit the company over several periods, not just during the current one; and (3) it should increase the productive life or capacity of the asset.

To illustrate the differences in accounting for capital and ordinary expenditures, assume that Wheeler Resorts also purchases a delivery truck for $42,000. This truck has an estimated useful life of eight years and a salvage value of $2,000. The straight-line depreciation is $5,000 per year [($42,000 − $2,000)/8 years]. If the company spends $1,500 each year for normal maintenance, its annual recording of these expenditures is:

Repairs and Maintenance Expense	1,500	
Cash		1,500
Spent $1,500 for maintenance of delivery truck.		

This entry has no effect on either the recorded cost or the depreciation expense of the truck. Now suppose that at the end of the sixth year of the truck's useful life, Wheeler spends $8,000 to overhaul the engine. This expenditure will increase the truck's remaining life from two to four years, but will not change its estimated salvage value. The depreciation for the last four years will be $4,500 per year, calculated as shown below.

	Depreciation before Overhaul		**Depreciation after Overhaul**
Original cost	$42,000	Original cost	$42,000
Less salvage value	2,000	Accumulated depreciation	
Cost to be allocated (depreciable amount)	$40,000	(prior to overhaul)	30,000
Original life of asset	8 years	Remaining book value	$12,000
Original depreciation per year ($40,000/8)	$5,000	Capital expenditure (overhaul)	8,000
Usage before overhaul	× 6 years	New book value	$20,000
Accumulated depreciation prior to overhaul	$30,000	Less salvage value	2,000
		New depreciable amount	$18,000
		Remaining life	4 years
		New annual depreciation ($18,000/4)	$4,500

The journal entry to record the $8,000 capitalized expenditure is:

Delivery Truck	8,000	
Cash		8,000
Spent $8,000 to overhaul the engine of the $42,000 truck.		

Another example of a capital expenditure is the cost of land improvements. Certain improvements are considered permanent, such as moving earth to change the land contour. Such an expenditure would be capitalized as part of the land account. Other expenditures may have a limited life, such as those incurred in building a road, a sidewalk, or a fence. These expenditures would be capitalized in a separate land improvements account and be depreciated over their useful lives.

It is often difficult to determine whether a given expenditure should be capitalized or expensed. The two procedures produce a different net income, however, so it is extremely important that such expenditures be properly classified. When in doubt, accepted practice is to record an expenditure as an expense to ensure that the asset is not reported at an amount that exceeds its future benefit.

to summarize

There are two types of expenditures for existing long-term operating assets: capital and ordinary. In general, for an expenditure to be capitalized, it must (1) be significant in amount, (2) provide benefits for more than one period, and (3) increase the productive life or capacity of an asset. Ordinary expenditures merely maintain an asset's productive capacity at the level originally projected. Capital expenditures are added to the cost of an asset and thus affect future depreciation, whereas ordinary expenditures are expenses of the current period.

6

Identify whether a long-term operating asset has suffered a decline in value and record the decline.

RECORDING IMPAIRMENTS OF ASSET VALUE

impairment A decline in the value of a long-term operating asset.

As mentioned earlier, the value of a long-term asset depends on the future cash flows expected to be generated by that asset. Occasionally, events occur after the purchase of an asset that significantly reduce its value. For example, a decline in the consumer demand for high-priced athletic shoes can cause the value of a shoe-manufacturing plant to plummet. Accountants call this **impairment**. When an asset is impaired, the event should be recognized in the financial statements, both as a reduction in the reported value of the asset in the balance sheet and as a loss in the income statement. Of course, the value of long-term assets can also increase after the purchase date. In the United States, these increases are not recorded, as explained more fully later in this section.

Recording Decreases in the Value of Property, Plant, and Equipment

According to U.S. accounting rules, the value of an asset is impaired when the sum of estimated future cash flows from that asset is less than the book value of the asset. This computation ignores the time value of money. As illustrated in the example below, this is a strange impairment threshold—a more reasonable test would be to compare the book value to the fair value of the asset.

Once it has been determined that an asset is impaired, the amount of the impairment is measured as the difference between the book value of the asset and the fair value. To summarize, the existence of an impairment loss is determined using the sum of the estimated future cash flows from the asset, ignoring the time value of money. The amount of the impairment loss is measured using the fair value of the asset, which does incorporate the time value of money. The practical result of this two-step process is that an impairment loss is not recorded unless it is quite certain that the asset has suffered a permanent decline in value.

To illustrate, assume that Wheeler Resorts purchased a fitness center building five years ago for $600,000. The building has been depreciated using the straight-line method with a 20-year useful life and no residual value. Wheeler estimates that the building has a remaining useful life of 15 years, that net cash inflow from the building will be $25,000 per year, and that the fair value of the building is $230,000.

Annual depreciation for the building has been $30,000 ($600,000 ÷ 20 years). The current book value of the building is computed as follows:

Original cost	$600,000
Accumulated depreciation ($30,000 × 5 years)	150,000
Book value	$450,000

The book value of $450,000 is compared with the $375,000 ($25,000 × 15 years) sum of future cash flows (ignoring the time value of money) to determine whether the building is impaired. The sum of future cash flows is only $375,000, which is less than the $450,000 book value, so an impairment loss should be recognized. The loss is equal to the $220,000 ($450,000 − $230,000) difference between the book value of the building and its fair value. The impairment loss would be recorded as follows:

Accumulated Depreciation, Building	150,000	
Loss on Impairment of Building	220,000	
Building ($600,000 − $230,000)		370,000
Recognized $220,000 impairment loss on building.		

This journal entry basically records the asset as if it were being acquired brand new at its fair value of $230,000. The existing accumulated depreciation balance is wiped clean, and the new recorded value of the asset is its fair value of $230,000 ($600,000 − $370,000). After an impairment loss is recognized, no restoration of the loss is allowed even if the fair value of the asset later recovers.

The odd nature of the impairment test can be seen if the facts in the Wheeler example are changed slightly. Assume that net cash inflow from the building will be $35,000 per year and that the fair value of the building is $330,000. With these numbers, no impairment loss is recognized, even though the fair value of $330,000 is less than the book value of $450,000, because the sum of future cash flows of $525,000 ($35,000 × 15 years) exceeds the book value. Thus, in this case the asset would still be recorded at its book value of $450,000, even though its fair value is actually less. As mentioned above, the practical impact of the two-step impairment test is that no impairment losses are recorded unless the future cash flow calculations offer very strong evidence of a permanent decline in asset value. The impairment test is summarized in Exhibit 9-9.

STOP & THINK Do you think businesses would prefer an impairment test involving only the comparison of the book value of an asset to its fair value? Explain.

RITE AID, one of the largest retail drugstore chains in the United States, provides an example of the reporting of an impairment loss. As of February 27, 1999, Rite Aid operated 3,821 drugstores. During 1998 and 1999, Rite Aid experienced significant financial difficulties and initiated a plan to vacate some markets and to close or consolidate some stores in other markets. In connection with this plan, Rite Aid recorded a $94 million loss "for impairment losses associated with land, buildings, fixtures, leasehold improvements, prescription files, lease acquisition costs and goodwill."

exhibit 9-9 Impairment Test

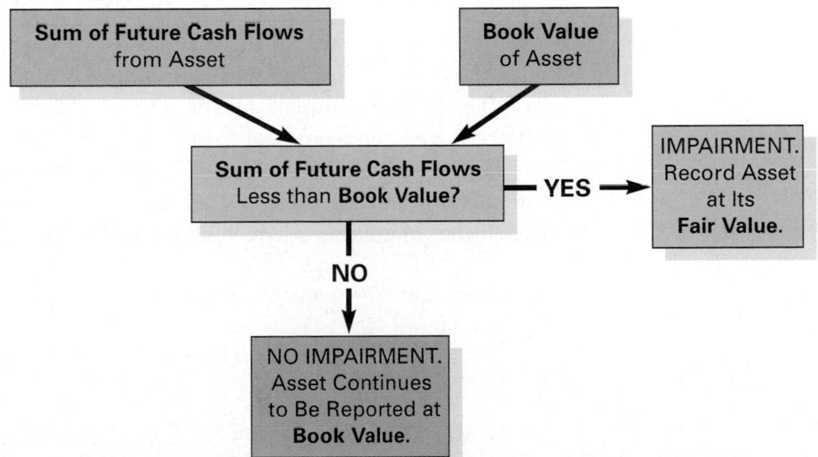

Recording Increases in the Value of Property, Plant, and Equipment

Under U.S. accounting standards, increases in the value of property, plant, and equipment are not recognized. Gains from increases in asset value are recorded only if and when the asset is sold. Thus, in the Wheeler example discussed above, if the fair value of the building rises to $800,000, the building would still be reported in the financial statements at its depreciated book value of $450,000. This is an example of the conservative bias that often exists in the accounting rules: losses are recognized when they occur, but the recognition of gains is deferred until the asset is sold.

Although increases in the value of property, plant, and equipment are not recognized in the United States, accounting rules in other countries do allow for their recognition. For example, companies in Great Britain often report their long-term operating assets at their fair values. Because this upward revaluation of property, plant, and equipment is allowable under international accounting standards, it will be interesting to watch over the next decade or so to see whether sentiment grows to allow this practice in the United States as well.

---

to summarize

When an asset's value declines after it is purchased, it is said to be impaired. Recording an impairment loss is a two-step process. First, the recorded book value of the asset is compared with the sum of future cash flows expected to be generated by the asset. Second, if the book value is lower, then a loss is recognized in an amount equal to the difference between the book value of the asset and its fair value. According to U.S. accounting rules, increases in the value of property, plant, and equipment are not recognized.

7

Record the discarding and selling of property, plant, and equipment.

DISPOSAL OF PROPERTY, PLANT, AND EQUIPMENT

Plant and equipment eventually become worthless or are sold. When a company removes one of these assets from service, it has to eliminate the asset's cost and accumulated depreciation from the accounting records. There are basically three ways to dispose of an asset: (1) discard or scrap it, (2) sell it, or (3) exchange it for another asset.

Discarding Property, Plant, and Equipment

When an asset becomes worthless and must be scrapped, its cost and its accumulated depreciation balance should be removed from the accounting records. If the asset's total cost has been depreciated, there is no loss on the disposal. If, on the other hand, the cost is not completely depreciated, the undepreciated cost represents a loss on disposal.

To illustrate, we assume that Wheeler Resorts, Inc., purchases a computer for $15,000. The computer has a five-year life and no estimated salvage value and is depreciated on a straight-line basis. If the computer is scrapped after five full years, the entry to record the disposal is as follows:

Accumulated Depreciation, Computer.	15,000	
Computer		15,000
Scrapped $15,000 computer.		

If Wheeler must pay $300 to have the computer dismantled and removed, the entry to record the disposal is:

Accumulated Depreciation, Computer	15,000	
Loss on Disposal of Computer.	300	
Computer.		15,000
Cash		300
Scrapped $15,000 computer and paid disposal costs of $300.		

If the computer had been scrapped after only four years of service (and after $12,000 of the original cost has been depreciated), there would have been a loss on disposal of $3,300 (including the disposal cost), and the entry would have been:

Accumulated Depreciation, Computer	12,000	
Loss on Disposal of Computer	3,300	
Computer.		15,000
Cash		300
Scrapped $15,000 computer and recognized loss of $3,300 (including $300 disposal costs).		

Don't think of the losses recognized above as "bad" or the gains as "good." A loss on disposal simply means that, given the information we now have, it appears that we didn't record enough depreciation expense in previous years. As a result, the book value of the asset is higher than the amount we can get on disposal. Similarly, a gain means that too much depreciation expense was recognized in prior years, making the book value of the asset lower than its actual disposal value.

Selling Property, Plant, and Equipment

A second way of disposing of property, plant, and equipment is to sell it. If the sales price of the asset exceeds its book value (the original cost less accumulated depreciation), there is a gain on the sale. Conversely, if the sales price is less than the book value, there is a loss.

To illustrate, we refer again to Wheeler's $15,000 computer. If the computer is sold for $600 after five full years of service, assuming no disposal costs, the entry to record the sale is:

Cash	600	
Accumulated Depreciation, Computer	15,000	
Computer.		15,000
Gain on Sale of Computer		600
Sold $15,000 computer at a gain of $600.		

Because the asset was fully depreciated, its book value was zero and the $600 cash received represents a gain. If the computer had been sold for $600 after only four years of service, there would have been a loss of $2,400 on the sale, and the entry to record the sale would have been:

Cash	600	
Accumulated Depreciation, Computer	12,000	
Loss on Sale of Computer.	2,400	
Computer.		15,000
Sold $15,000 computer at a loss of $2,400.		

The $2,400 loss is the difference between the sales price of $600 and the book value of $3,000 ($15,000 − $12,000). The amount of a gain or loss is thus a function of two factors: (1) the amount of cash received from the sale, and (2) the book value of the asset at the date of sale. The book value can vary from the market price of the asset for two reasons: (1) the accounting for the asset is not intended to show market value in the financial statements, and (2) it is difficult to estimate salvage value and useful life at the outset of an asset's life.

Exchanging Property, Plant, and Equipment

A third way of disposing of property, plant, and equipment is to exchange it for another asset. Such exchanges occur regularly with cars, trucks, machines, and other types of large equipment. When dissimilar assets are exchanged, such as a truck for a computer, the transaction is accounted for exactly as outlined previously: the acquired asset is recorded in the books at its fair market value, and a gain or loss may be recognized depending on the difference between this market value and the book value of the asset that was disposed of. Accounting for exchanges of similar assets can be more complicated and therefore is not discussed in this text. For a full treatment of the accounting for the exchange of similar assets, see an intermediate accounting text.

---

to summarize

There are three ways of disposing of assets: (1) discarding (scrapping), (2) selling, and (3) exchanging. If a scrapped asset has not been fully depreciated, a loss equal to the undepreciated cost or book value is recognized. When an asset is sold, there is a gain if the sales price exceeds the book value and a loss if the sales price is less than the book value.

---

8 Account for the acquisition and amortization of intangible assets and understand the special difficulties associated with accounting for intangibles.

ACCOUNTING FOR INTANGIBLE ASSETS

Intangible assets are rights and privileges that are long-lived, are not held for resale, have no physical substance, and usually provide their owner with competitive advantages over other firms. Familiar examples are patents, franchises, licenses, and goodwill. Although intangible assets have no physical substance, they are accounted for in the same way as other long-term operating assets. That is, they are originally recorded at cost, and the cost is allocated over the useful or legal life, whichever is shorter. The periodic allocation to expense of an intangible asset's cost is called **amortization**. Conceptually, depreciation (with plant and equipment), depletion (with natural resources), and amortization (with intangible assets) are exactly the same thing. Straight-line amortization is generally used for intangible assets.

amortization The process of cost allocation that assigns the original cost of an intangible asset to the periods benefited.

The traditional accounting model is designed for manufacturing and merchandising companies. Accordingly, accountants have developed intricate and sophisticated accounting methods for use with buildings, equipment, inventory, and receivables. The accounting procedures for gathering and reporting useful information about intangible assets are not as well developed. As the business environment is increasingly dominated by information, service, and reputation, the accounting profession is facing the challenge of improving the accounting for intangible assets.

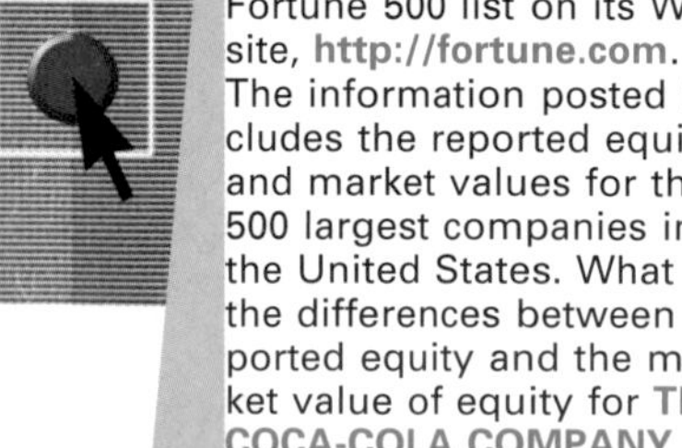

Fortune magazine posts its Fortune 500 list on its Web site, **http://fortune.com**. The information posted includes the reported equity and market values for the 500 largest companies in the United States. What are the differences between reported equity and the market value of equity for **THE COCA-COLA COMPANY** and for **GENERAL MOTORS CORPORATION**?

The importance of intangible assets can be illustrated by considering **GENERAL ELECTRIC**. As mentioned in Chapter 2, if the balance sheet were perfect, the amount of owners' equity would be equal to the market value of the company. On December 31, 1999, GE's reported equity was equal to $42.557 billion. The actual market value of GE on December 31, 1999, was $511 billion. The reason for the large difference between the recorded value and the actual value is that a traditional balance sheet excludes many important intangible economic assets. Examples of GE's important intangible economic assets are its track record of successful products and its entrenched market position in the many industries in which it operates. These intangible factors are by far the most valuable assets owned by GE, but they fall outside the traditional accounting process.

As with many accounting issues, accounting for intangibles involves a trade-off between relevance and reliability. Information concerning intangible assets is relevant, but to meet the standard for recognition in the financial statements, the recorded amount for the intangible must also be reliable. As a result, accounting for intangibles focuses on identifying the costs associated with securing or developing the intangible assets.

Because intangible assets are characterized by a lack of physical qualities, it is difficult to determine the value and life of any future benefits those assets might produce. As a result, it is difficult to separate expenditures that are essentially operating expenses from those that give rise to intangible assets. For example, advertising and promotion campaigns and training programs provide future benefits to the firm. If this were not the case, firms would not spend the millions of dollars on these programs that they do. From an accounting perspective, however, it is extremely difficult to measure the amount and life of the benefits generated by such programs. Therefore, as discussed in Chapter 8, expenditures for these and similar items are typically written off as an expenses in the period incurred.

The accounting for intangible assets is illustrated below with a discussion of the accounting for patents, franchises, and licenses.

patent An exclusive right granted for 17 years by the federal government to manufacture and sell an invention.

Patents

A **patent** is an exclusive right to produce and sell a commodity that has one or more unique features. In the United States, patents are issued to inventors by the federal government and have a legal life of 17 years. Patents may be obtained on new products developed in a company's own research laboratories, or they may be purchased from others. If a patent is purchased from others, its cost is simply the purchase price, and it is recorded as an asset (patent). The cost of the patent is amortized over the useful life of the patent, which may or may not coincide with the patent's legal life.

fyi

The U.S. rule for accounting for research and development differs from the international rule. According to international accounting rules, research and development costs that are incurred after the technological feasibility of a project has been demonstrated should be capitalized as an asset.

The cost of a patent for a product developed within a firm is difficult to determine. Should it include research and development costs as well as legal fees to obtain the patent? Should other company expenses such as administrative costs be included? Because of the high degree of uncertainty about their future benefits, U.S. accounting rules dictate that research and development costs must be expensed in the period in which they are incurred. Therefore, all research and development costs of internally developed patents are expensed as they are incurred.

To illustrate the accounting for patents, assume that Wheeler Resorts, Inc., acquires, for $200,000, a patent granted seven years earlier to another firm. The entry to record the purchase of the patent is:

Patent	200,000	
Cash		200,000
Purchased patent for $200,000.		

Because 7 years of its 17-year legal life have already elapsed, the patent now has a legal life of only 10 years, although it may have a shorter useful life. If its useful life is assumed to be eight years, one-eighth of the $200,000 cost should be amortized each year for the next eight years. The entry each year to record the patent amortization expense is:

Amortization Expense, Patent	25,000	
Patent		25,000
To amortize one-eighth of the cost of the patent.		

Notice that in the above entry, the patent account was credited. Alternatively, a contra-asset account, such as Accumulated Amortization, could have been credited. In practice, however, crediting the intangible asset account directly is more common. This is different from the normal practice of crediting Accumulated Depreciation for buildings or equipment.

Franchises and Licenses

franchise An entity that has been licensed to sell the product of a manufacturer or to offer a particular service in a given area.

license The right to perform certain activities, generally granted by a governmental agency.

Issued either by companies or by government agencies, **franchises** and **licenses** are exclusive rights to perform services in certain geographic areas. For example, MCDONALD'S CORPORATION sells franchises to individuals to operate its fast-food outlets in specific locations. Similarly, local airports issue licenses to airlines allowing them to use a specified number of boarding gates for a specified length of time. As with patents, the cost of a franchise or license is amortized over its useful or legal life, whichever is shorter.

Goodwill

caution

Goodwill is recorded only when it is purchased. A company's reported goodwill balance does not reflect the company's own homegrown goodwill. So, MICROSOFT's goodwill is not recognized in Microsoft's balance sheet, but it would be recognized in your balance sheet if you were to purchase Microsoft.

fyi

In 2001, the FASB was considering whether to lower the maximum allowable estimated life for goodwill to 20 years.

When a business is purchased, the negotiated price often exceeds the total fair market value of the individual assets purchased minus the outstanding liabilities assumed by the buyer. As mentioned earlier, this excess in purchase price that cannot be allocated to specific assets is called goodwill and is an intangible asset. The emergence of goodwill in such a transaction is considered an indication that the purchased business is worth more than its net assets, due to such favorable characteristics as a good reputation, a strategic location, product superiority, or management skill.

Goodwill is recorded only if its value can be objectively determined by a transaction. Therefore, even though two businesses may enjoy the same favorable characteristics, goodwill will be recognized only when it is purchased, that is, when one company buys another company. This disparity in accounting exists because the action of a buyer in paying a premium for a firm is objective evidence that goodwill exists and has a specific value.

As you can imagine, estimating the useful life of goodwill is extremely difficult. To give companies some direction in estimating the useful life of goodwill, accounting standard-setters have established some guidelines. In the United States, for example, historically the accounting rule has been that the estimated life of goodwill must be 40 years or less. According to international accounting standards, goodwill usually is assumed to have a life of 5 years or less, although a life of up to 20 years is sometimes justifiable. Most U.S. companies simply assume that any goodwill they purchase has a life of 40 years.

To illustrate the accounting for goodwill, assume that, in order to cater to the medicinal needs of its guests, Wheeler Resorts purchases Valley Drug Store for $400,000. At the time of purchase, the recorded assets and liabilities of Valley Drug have the following fair market values:

Inventory	$220,000
Long-term operating assets	110,000
Other assets (prepaid expenses, etc.)	10,000
Liabilities	(20,000)
Total net assets	$320,000

Note that Wheeler Resorts records these items at their fair market values on the date purchased, just as it does when purchasing individual assets.

Because Wheeler was willing to pay $400,000 for Valley Drug, there must have been other favorable, intangible factors worth approximately $80,000. These factors are called goodwill, and the entry to record the purchase of the drug store is:

Inventory	220,000	
Long-Term Operating Assets	110,000	
Other Assets	10,000	
Goodwill	80,000	
Liabilities		20,000
Cash		400,000
Purchased Valley Drug Store for $400,000.		

If Wheeler decides to use 40 years as the useful life of the goodwill, the yearly amortization entry is:

Amortization Expense, Goodwill	2,000	
Goodwill		2,000
To record annual straight-line amortization of goodwill ($80,000/40 years).		

An extreme example of the amount of goodwill that can be involved in a transaction occurred when **DISNEY** acquired **ABC** in 1996. At the time of the acquisition, ABC had identifiable assets worth $4.0 billion and identifiable liabilities of $4.3 billion, indicating a fair market value of net identifiable assets of −$0.3 billion. In spite of this apparent negative net worth, Disney paid $18.9 billion for ABC, a price that exceeded the fair market value of ABC's net identifiable assets by more than $19 billion. Presumably, Disney knew what it was doing in paying this much for ABC, and the $19 billion, which was recorded as goodwill on Disney's books, represents the fair market value of ABC's market position, reputation, network of radio and television affiliates, and creative staff under contract.

Difficulties of Accounting for Intangible Assets: The Case of Brand Names

Brand names offer a good illustration of the difficulty associated with accounting for intangible assets. As shown in Exhibit 9-10, a brand name can be an extremely valuable asset. According to **INTERBRAND**, a consulting firm specializing in valuing brand names, if you were to try to buy the worldwide rights to the exclusive use of the name "*Coca-Cola,*" you would have to pay in excess of $85 billion. A valuable brand name such as "*Coca-Cola*" or "*Disney*" arises as an integral part of improving products, advertising, strategic expansion, and so forth. Accordingly, it is very difficult to identify which costs associated with brand name sales are normal business expenses and which actually contribute to brand name value. Therefore, even though a brand name might have significant economic value, it is unlikely that the value, or the costs associated with developing the brand name, could be separately and reliably identified.

exhibit 9-10 Ten Most Valuable Brands in the World for 1999

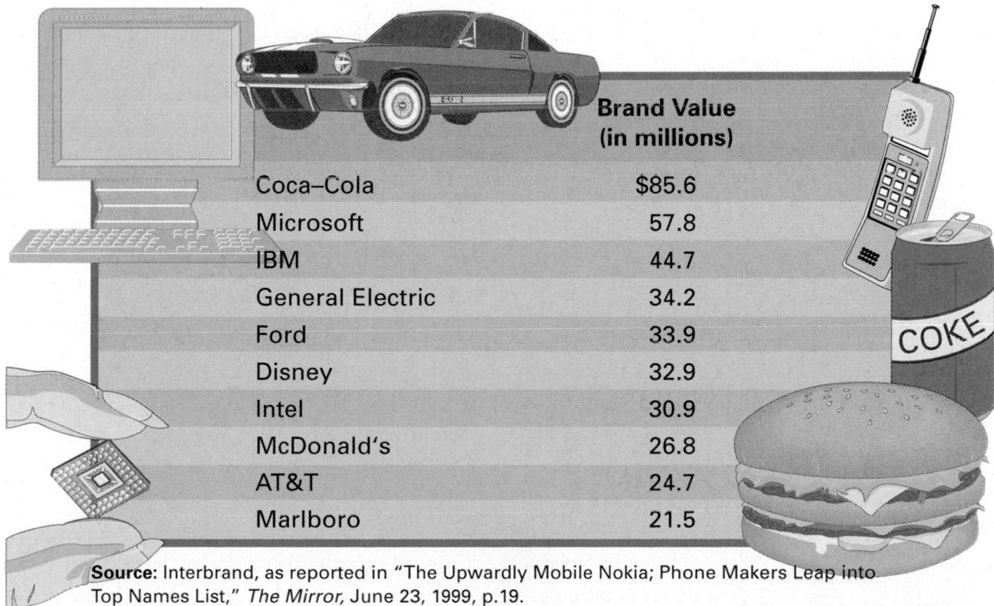

	Brand Value (in millions)
Coca–Cola	$85.6
Microsoft	57.8
IBM	44.7
General Electric	34.2
Ford	33.9
Disney	32.9
Intel	30.9
McDonald's	26.8
AT&T	24.7
Marlboro	21.5

Source: Interbrand, as reported in "The Upwardly Mobile Nokia; Phone Makers Leap into Top Names List," *The Mirror,* June 23, 1999, p.19.

As mentioned earlier in the chapter, a useful technique for valuing tangible long-term assets is to estimate the present value of the future cash flows expected to be associated with the asset. This technique is impractical for most intangible assets because the value of the intangible is inextricably connected with its use in conjunction with other assets. Thus, identifying the future cash flows associated with the intangible asset itself is nearly impossible.

In summary, the accounting for intangibles is still in its infancy. As accountants strive to meet the information demands of business decision makers, we will see a rapid development in the standards of accounting for intangibles.

---

to summarize

Intangible assets are long-term rights and privileges that have no physical substance but provide competitive advantages to owners. Common intangible assets are patents, franchises, licenses, and goodwill. The cost of an intangible asset is amortized over the economic life of the asset. Because it is often difficult to trace the development of specific intangible assets to specific costs, it is difficult to reliably recognize the assets in the financial statements.

9

Use the fixed asset turnover ratio as a measure of how efficiently a company is using its property, plant, and equipment.

MEASURING PROPERTY, PLANT, AND EQUIPMENT EFFICIENCY

In this section we discuss the fixed asset turnover ratio, which uses financial statement data to give a rough indication of how efficiently a company is utilizing its property, plant, and equipment to generate sales. We also illustrate that the fixed asset turnover ratio must be interpreted carefully because, as with most other financial ratios, acceptable values for this ratio differ significantly from one industry to the next.

Evaluating the Level of Property, Plant, and Equipment

fixed asset turnover The number of dollars in sales generated by each dollar of fixed assets; computed as sales divided by property, plant, and equipment.

Fixed asset turnover can be used to evaluate the appropriateness of the level of a company's property, plant, and equipment. Fixed asset turnover is computed as sales divided by average property, plant, and equipment (fixed assets) and is interpreted as the number of dollars in sales generated by each dollar of fixed assets. This ratio is also often called PP&E turnover. The computation of the fixed asset turnover for GENERAL ELECTRIC is given below. All financial statement numbers are in millions.

	1999	1998
Sales	$111,630	$100,469
Property, plant, and equipment:		
Beginning of year	$ 35,730	$ 32,316
End of year	41,022	35,730
Average fixed assets [(beginning balance + ending balance) ÷ 2]	$ 38,376	$ 34,023
Fixed asset turnover	2.91 times	2.95 times

The fixed asset turnover calculations suggest that GE used its fixed assets to generate sales about as efficiently in 1999 as in 1998. In 1999, each dollar of fixed assets generated $2.91 in sales, down just slightly from $2.95 in 1998.

Industry Differences in Fixed Asset Turnover

As with all ratios, the fixed asset turnover ratio must be used carefully to ensure that erroneous conclusions are not made. For example, fixed asset turnover ratio values for two companies in different industries cannot be meaningfully compared. This point can be illustrated using the fact that General Electric is composed of two primary parts—General Electric, the manufacturing company, and GE Capital Services, the financial services firm. The fixed asset turnover ratio computed earlier was for both these parts combined. Because GE Capital Services does not use property, plant, and equipment for manufacturing but instead leases the assets to other companies in order to earn financial revenue, one would expect its fixed asset turnover ratio to be quite unlike that for a manufacturing firm. In fact, as shown below, the fixed asset turnover ratio for the manufacturing segments of General Electric was 5.06 in 1999, nearly double the ratio value for the company as a whole.

Fixed Asset Turnover Ratio
General Electric—Manufacturing Segments Only

	1999	1998
Sales	$60,944	$56,026
Property, plant, and equipment:		
Beginning of year	$11,694	$11,118
End of year	12,381	11,694
Average fixed assets [(beginning balance + ending balance) ÷ 2]	$12,038	$11,406
Fixed asset turnover	5.06 times	4.91 times

to summarize

The fixed asset turnover ratio can be used as a general measure of how efficiently a company is using its property, plant, and equipment. Fixed asset turnover is computed as sales divided by average property, plant, and equipment and is interpreted as the number of dollars in sales generated by each dollar of fixed assets. Standard values for this ratio differ significantly from industry to industry.

expanded material

Two topics related to operational assets that are traditionally covered in introductory accounting classes were not covered in the main part of this chapter. These two topics relate to depreciation—accelerated depreciation methods and changes in depreciation estimates.

10

Compute declining-balance and sum-of-the-years'-digits depreciation expense for plant and equipment.

ACCELERATED DEPRECIATION METHODS

Earlier in the chapter, straight-line and units-of-production depreciation methods were discussed. Both of these methods allocate the cost of an asset evenly over its life. With straight-line depreciation, each time period during the asset's useful life is assigned an equal amount of depreciation. With units-of-production depreciation, each mile driven, hour used, or other measurement of useful life is assigned an equal amount of depreciation. Sometimes, a depreciation method that does not assign costs equally over the life of the asset is preferred. For example, if most of an asset's benefits will be realized in the earlier periods of the asset's life, the method used should assign more depreciation to the earlier years and less to the later years. Examples of these "accelerated" depreciation methods are the declining-balance and the sum-of-the-years'-digits methods. These methods are merely ways of assigning more of an asset's depreciation to earlier periods and less to later periods.

To illustrate these depreciation methods, we will again use the Wheeler Resorts example from earlier in the chapter. Assume again that Wheeler Resorts purchased a van for transporting hotel guests to and from the airport. The following facts apply:

Acquisition cost	$24,000
Estimated salvage value	$2,000
Estimated life:	
In years	4 years
In miles driven	60,000 miles

Declining-Balance Method of Depreciation

declining-balance depreciation method An accelerated depreciation method in which an asset's book value is multiplied by a constant depreciation rate (such as double the straight-line percentage, in the case of double-declining-balance).

The **declining-balance depreciation method** provides for higher depreciation charges in the earlier years of an asset's life than does the straight-line method. The declining-balance method involves multiplying a fixed rate, or percentage, by a decreasing book value. This rate is a multiple of the straight-line rate. Typically, it is twice the straight-line rate, but it also can be 175, 150, or 125% of the straight-line rate. Our depreciation of Wheeler's hotel van will illustrate the declining-balance method using a fixed rate equal to twice the straight-line rate. This method is often referred to as the double-declining-balance depreciation method.

Declining-balance depreciation differs from the other depreciation methods in two respects: (1) the initial computation ignores the asset's salvage value, and (2) a constant depreciation rate is multiplied by a decreasing book value. The salvage value is not ignored completely because the depreciation taken during the asset's life cannot reduce the asset's book value below the estimated salvage value.

The double-declining-balance (DDB) rate is twice the straight-line rate, computed as follows:

$$\frac{1}{\text{Estimated life (years)}} \times 2 = \text{DDB rate}$$

This rate is multiplied times the book value at the beginning of each year (cost − accumulated depreciation) to compute the annual depreciation expense for the year. If the 150% declining

business environment essay

"Pay Me Now or Pay Me Later?" Given the choice of paying income taxes now or later, an overwhelming majority of U.S. taxpayers would choose to pay later. Although it is illegal to evade income taxes, the postponement or "deferral" of tax payments is not only legal but is also a fundamental principle of good tax planning.

One way that businesses can defer income taxes is through the selection of accounting methods. The LIFO (last-in, first-out) method of inventory valuation, for example, is used primarily for the purpose of postponing tax payments. In some cases, companies use one accounting method for their financial statements and another for their tax returns.

Depreciation is the most common cause of differences between net income on the income statement

balance were being used instead, the 2 in the rate formula would be replaced by 1.5 and so on for any other percentages.

To illustrate, the depreciation calculation for the van using the 200% (or double) declining-balance method is:

Straight-line rate	4 years = ¼ = 25%
Double the straight-line rate	25% × 2 = 50%
Annual depreciation	50% × undepreciated cost (book value)

caution

With declining-balance depreciation, the asset is not depreciated below its salvage value, though this figure is ignored in the initial computations.

Based on this information, the formula for double-declining-balance depreciation can be expressed as (straight-line rate × 2) × (cost − accumulated depreciation) = current year's depreciation expense. The double-declining-balance depreciation for the four years is shown in Exhibit 9-11. As you review this exhibit, note that the book value of the van at the end of year 4 is $2,000, its salvage value.

If Wheeler had applied the declining-balance method to depreciate the hotel van on the basis of 150% of the straight-line rate, the fixed rate would have been 37.5%, computed as follows: 25% × 1.50 = 37.5%. Using the 37.5% fixed rate, the annual depreciation of the hotel van would have been as follows:

First year:	$24,000 × 37.5% = $9,000
Second year:	$24,000 − $9,000 = $15,000 × 37.5% = $5,625
Third year:	$15,000 − $5,625 = $9,375 × 37.5% = $3,516
Fourth year:	$9,375 − $3,516 = $5,859 − $2,000 salvage value = $3,859

exhibit 9-11 Depreciation Schedule with Double-Declining-Balance Depreciation

	Computation	Annual Depreciation Expense	Accumulated Depreciation	Book Value
Acquisition date	—	—	—	$24,000
End of year 1	$24,000 × 0.50	$12,000	$12,000	12,000
End of year 2	12,000 × 0.50	6,000	18,000	6,000
End of year 3	6,000 × 0.50	3,000	21,000	3,000
End of year 4	*	1,000	22,000	2,000
		$22,000		

*In year 4, depreciation expense cannot exceed $1,000 because the book value cannot be reduced below salvage value.

and taxable income on the tax return. Most companies use straight-line depreciation for financial statements to maximize income reported to stockholders while using the accelerated methods permitted by the tax rules to minimize taxable income in the early years of asset life. This allows companies to save cash by reducing the amount of taxes paid currently. Although the total amount of asset cost to be deducted will ultimately be the same for tax and financial reporting, the deferral of income taxes enables a business to earn additional income by investing cash that is retained as a result of delaying tax payments to future years.

The amount of income taxes that companies can defer is by no means insignificant. For example, GENERAL ELECTRIC was able to delay the payment of $1.499 billion in taxes in 1999 because of differences between financial accounting rules and income tax regulations.

Since a total book value of $5,859 remains at the end of year 3, the remaining book value less the estimated salvage value is expensed in year 4.

DEPRECIATION FOR INCOME TAX PURPOSES Net income reported on the financial statements prepared for stockholders, creditors, and other external users often differs from taxable income reported on income tax returns. The most common cause of differences between financial reporting and tax returns is the computation of depreciation. Depreciation for income tax purposes must be computed in accordance with federal income tax law, which specifies rules to be applied in computing tax depreciation for various categories of assets. Income tax rules are designed to achieve economic objectives, such as stimulating investment in productive assets.

The income tax depreciation system in the United States is called the Modified Accelerated Cost Recovery System (MACRS). MACRS is based on declining-balance depreciation and is designed to allow taxpayers to quickly deduct the cost of assets acquired. Allowing this accelerated depreciation deduction for income tax purposes gives companies tax benefits for investing in new productive assets. Presumably, this will spur investment, create jobs, and make voters more likely to reelect their representatives.

Sum-of-the-Years'-Digits Method of Depreciation

sum-of-the-years'-digits (SYD) depreciation method The accelerated depreciation method in which a constant balance (cost minus salvage value) is multiplied by a declining depreciation rate.

Like the declining-balance method, the **sum-of-the-years'-digits (SYD) depreciation method** provides for a proportionately higher depreciation expense in the early years of an asset's life. It is therefore appropriate for assets that provide greater benefits in their earlier years (such as trucks, machinery, and equipment) as opposed to assets that benefit all years equally (as buildings do). The formula for calculating SYD is:

$$\frac{\text{Number of years of life remaining at beginning of year}}{\text{Sum-of-the-years'-digits}} \times (\text{Cost} - \text{Salvage value}) = \text{Depreciation expense}$$

The numerator is the number of years of estimated life remaining at the beginning of the current year. The van, with a four-year life, would have four years remaining at the beginning of the first year, three at the beginning of the second, and so on. The denominator is the sum of the years of the asset's life. The sum of the years' digits for the van is 10 ($4 + 3 + 2 + 1$). In other words, the numerator decreases by one year each year, whereas the denominator remains the same for each year's calculation of depreciation. Also note that the asset's cost is reduced by the salvage value in computing the annual depreciation expense as is done for the straight-line method but not for the declining-balance method.

The depreciation on the van for the first two years is:

First year: $\frac{4}{10} \times (\$24,000 - \$2,000) = \$8,800$

Second year: $\frac{3}{10} \times (\$24,000 - \$2,000) = \$6,600$

The depreciation schedule for four years is shown in Exhibit 9-12.

exhibit 9-12 Depreciation Schedule with Sum-of-the-Years'-Digits Depreciation

	Annual Depreciation Expense	Accumulated Depreciation	Book Value
Acquisition date	—	—	$24,000
End of year 1	$ 8,800	$ 8,800	15,200
End of year 2	6,600	15,400	8,600
End of year 3	4,400	19,800	4,200
End of year 4	2,200	22,000	2,000
Total	$22,000		

The entry to record the sum-of-the-years'-digits depreciation for the first year is:

Depreciation Expense	8,800	
Accumulated Depreciation, Hotel Van		8,800
To record the first year's depreciation for the hotel van.		

Subsequent years' depreciation entries would show depreciation expense of $6,600, $4,400, and $2,200.

When an asset has a long life, the computation of the denominator (the sum-of-the-years'-digits) can become quite involved. There is, however, a simple formula for determining the denominator. It is:

$$\frac{n(n + 1)}{2} \quad \text{where n is the life (in years) of the asset}$$

Given that the van has a useful life of four years, the formula works as follows:

$$\frac{4(5)}{2} = 10$$

fyi

General Electric is one of the few large companies that continues to use the sum-of-the-years'-digits method of depreciation.

As you can see, the answer is the same as if you had added the years' digits (4 + 3 + 2 + 1). If an asset has a 10-year life, the sum of the years' digits is:

$$\frac{10(11)}{2} = 55$$

The depreciation fraction in year 1 would be 10/55, in year 2, 9/55, and so on.

A Comparison of Depreciation Methods

Now that you have been introduced to the four most common depreciation methods, we can compare them both graphically and by using the Wheeler Resorts van example. Exhibit 9-13 compares the straight-line, sum-of-the-years'-digits, and declining-balance depreciation methods with regard to the relative amount of depreciation expense incurred in each year for an asset that has a five-year life. The units-of-production method is not illustrated because there would not be a standard pattern of cost allocation. Exhibit 9-14 shows the results for the Wheeler Resorts' van for all four depreciation methods.

exhibit 9-13 Comparison of Depreciation Methods

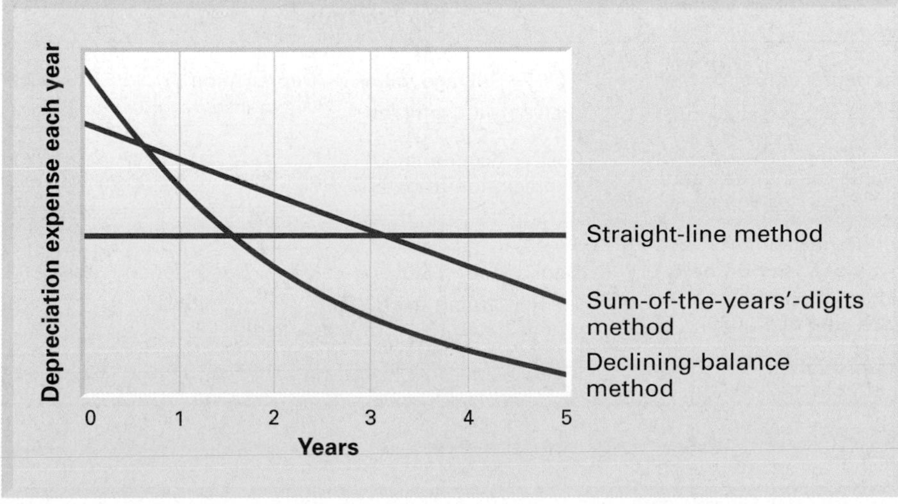

exhibit 9-14 Comparison of Depreciation Expense Using Different Depreciation Methods

	Straight-Line Depreciation	Units-of-Production Depreciation	DDB Depreciation	SYD Depreciation
Year 1	$ 5,500	$ 4,400	$12,000	$ 8,800
Year 2	5,500	6,600	6,000	6,600
Year 3	5,500	7,700	3,000	4,400
Year 4	5,500	3,300	1,000	2,200
Totals	$22,000	$22,000	$22,000	$22,000

to summarize

Two depreciation methods that allow for more depreciation expense in the early years of an asset's life are the declining-balance and the sum-of-the-years'-digits methods. The declining-balance method involves multiplying the asset's declining book value by a fixed rate that is a multiple of the straight-line rate. Sum-of-the-years'-digits depreciation is computed by multiplying (cost − salvage value) by a declining ratio based on the number of years in the asset's estimated life.

11 Account for changes in depreciation estimates.

CHANGES IN DEPRECIATION ESTIMATES

As mentioned earlier in the chapter, useful lives and salvage values are only estimates. Wheeler Resorts' van, for example, was assumed to have a useful life of four years and a salvage value of $2,000. In reality, the van's life and salvage value may be different from the original estimates. If, after three years, Wheeler realizes that the van will last another three years and that the salvage value will be $3,000 instead of $2,000, the accountant would need to calculate a new depreciation expense for the remaining three years. Using straight-line depreciation, the calculations would be as follows:

	Formula	Calculation	Total Depreciation
Annual depreciation for the first three years	$\frac{\text{Cost} - \text{Salvage value}}{\text{Estimated useful life}} = \text{Depreciation expense}$	$\frac{\$24,000 - \$2,000}{4 \text{ years}} = \$5,500$	$16,500
Book value after three years	Cost − Accumulated depreciation to date = Book value	$24,000 − $16,500 = $7,500	
Annual depreciation for last three years (based on new total life of six years and new salvage value of $3,000)	$\frac{\text{Book value} - \text{Salvage value}}{\text{Remaining useful life}} = \text{Depreciation expense}$	$\frac{\$7,500 - \$3,000}{3 \text{ years}} = \$1,500$	4,500
Total depreciation			$21,000

exhibit 9-15 Depreciation Schedule When There Is a Change in Estimate

	Annual Depreciation Expense	Accumulated Depreciation	Book Value
Acquisition date	—	—	$24,000
Year 1	$ 5,500	$ 5,500	18,500
Year 2	5,500	11,000	13,000
Year 3	5,500	16,500	7,500
Change			
Year 4	1,500	18,000	6,000
Year 5	1,500	19,500	4,500
Year 6	1,500	21,000	3,000
Total	$21,000		

fyi

To illustrate the uncertainty about depreciation life estimates, consider that BOEING 727 airplanes are lasting a lot longer than initially expected. The first Boeing 727 was delivered in 1963; the last was built in 1984. As of December 1998, almost 1,500 of the 1,831 727s delivered were still in service.

The example shows that a change in the estimate of useful life or salvage value does not require a modification of the depreciation expense already taken. New information affects depreciation only in future years. Exhibit 9-15 shows the revised depreciation expense. Similar calculations, although more complex, would apply if either the sum-of-the-years'-digits or the declining-balance depreciation method had been used.

to summarize

Because depreciation is only an estimate, changes in estimates of useful life or salvage value may be required as new information becomes available. When there is a change in estimate, past periods' depreciation amounts remain the same. The only change is in future years' depreciation where the remaining book value is allocated over the new life (in the case of a change in useful life), or the difference between the book value and the new salvage value is allocated over the remaining life (in the case of a change in salvage value).

review of learning objectives

1 Identify the two major categories of long-term operating assets: property, plant, and equipment and intangible assets. There are two major types of operating assets. Property, plant, and equipment are long-lived, tangible assets acquired for use in a business. This category includes land, buildings, machinery, equipment, and furniture. Intangible assets are long-lived assets used in a business, but they have no physical substance. Common intangible assets are patents, licenses, franchises, and goodwill.

2 Understand the factors important in deciding whether to acquire a long-term operating asset. The value of long-term operating assets stems from the fact that they help companies generate future cash flows. Capital budgeting is the name given to the process whereby decisions are made about acquiring long-term operating assets. Capital budgeting involves comparing the cost of the asset to the value of the expected cash inflows, after adjusting for the time value of money. The value of a long-term operating asset can disappear instantly if events lower the expectations about the future cash flows generated by the asset.

3 Record the acquisition of property, plant, and equipment through a simple purchase as well as through a lease, by self-construction, and as part of the purchase of several assets at once. Property, plant, and equipment may be acquired by purchase, lease, or self-construction. When purchased, the assets are recorded at cost, which includes all expenditures associated with acquiring them and getting them ready for their intended use. When these types of assets are leased, the lease agreement may be classified as an operating lease or as a capital lease. An operating lease results in a short-term use of the asset without recording the asset on the books of the user, the lessee. Instead, the lessee records only the rental expense paid each period. If the lease is for a longer term and meets the conditions of a capital lease, the lessee records the leased property as an asset and the related liability as if the property had been purchased and financed with long-term debt. The asset is recorded at the present value of the lease rental payments, which usually is equivalent to the current market value or the cash equivalent price. When a company constructs an asset for its own use, the recorded cost includes building materials, labor, a reasonable allocation of general administrative costs, and capitalized interest equal to the amount of interest that could have been avoided if the construction expenditures had been used to repay loans.

If two or more assets are acquired in a "basket" purchase, the relative fair market value method is used to assign costs to individual assets. If one company buys all the assets of another company, the excess of the purchase price over the aggregate fair value of the acquired net assets is recorded as goodwill, an intangible asset.

4 Compute straight-line and units-of-production depreciation expense for plant and equipment. Depreciation is the process of allocating the cost of plant and equipment to expense in the periods that are benefited from the use of the asset. The two most common and simple methods of depreciation are straight-line and units-of-production.

The straight-line method is the only method that results in the same amount of depreciation for each full year. The units-of-production method allocates cost over the useful life measured in units of output or usage. Both methods require salvage value to be subtracted from the original cost in computing depreciation expense.

The units-of-production method is also used with natural resources such as coal, gravel, and timber. Depletion expense for a year is computed by first computing a depletion rate by dividing the cost assigned to the natural resource by the estimated number of remaining units to be extracted. This depletion rate is multiplied by the number of units extracted for the year to arrive at the dollar amount of depletion for the year.

5 Account for repairs and improvements of property, plant, and equipment. Expenditures incurred for property, plant, and equipment after acquisition may be classified as either ordinary expenditures or capital expenditures. Since ordinary expenditures merely maintain an asset's productive capacity at the level originally projected, they are reported as repairs and maintenance expense and do not affect the asset's reported cost. For an expenditure to be classified as a capital expenditure, it must (1) increase the productive life or annual capacity of the asset, (2) be significant in amount, and (3) benefit the company over several periods. Because capital expenditures are added to the cost of an asset, they affect future depreciation, whereas ordinary expenditures are expenses of the current period.

6 Identify whether a long-term operating asset has suffered a decline in value and record the decline. Impairment is the decline in a long-term operating asset's value after it is purchased. In recording an impairment loss, the recorded book value of the asset is first compared with the sum of future cash flows to be generated by the asset. Next, if the book value is lower, a loss is recognized. The amount of the loss is the difference between the book value of the asset and its fair value. According to U.S. accounting rules, increases in the value of property, plant, and equipment are not recognized.

7 Record the discarding and selling of property, plant, and equipment. Property, plant, and equipment may be disposed of by discarding, selling, or exchanging. When an asset is sold, a gain is reported if the sales price exceeds the book value, or a loss is reported if the book value exceeds the sales price.

8 Account for the acquisition and amortization of intangible assets and understand the special difficulties associated with accounting for intangibles. Intangible assets are rights and privileges that are long-lived, are not held for resale, have no physical substance, and usually provide competitive advantages for the owner. Common examples are patents, franchises, licenses, and goodwill. Patents acquired by purchase are recorded at cost and amortized over the shorter of their economic life or their 17-year legal life. Research and development costs incurred internally in a firm are expensed as incurred even if they may result in the development of a legal patent. Franchises and licenses are exclusive rights to perform services or sell a product in certain geographic areas. The cost of acquiring a franchise or license is recorded as an asset, which is then amortized over its useful or legal life, whichever is shorter. Goodwill occurs when a business is purchased and the purchase price exceeds the total value of the identifiable assets less outstanding liabilities assumed. The excess purchase price that cannot be allocated to specific assets is called goodwill and is recorded as an intangible asset. Goodwill is amortized as an expense over its expected life, not to exceed 40 years. Because it is often difficult to trace the development of specific intangible assets to specific costs, it is difficult to reliably recognize the assets in the financial statements.

9 Use the fixed asset turnover ratio as a measure of how efficiently a company is using its property, plant, and equipment. Fixed asset turnover is computed as sales divided by average property, plant, and equipment (fixed assets) and is interpreted as the number of dollars in sales generated by each dollar of fixed assets. Fixed asset turnover ratios can be meaningfully compared only between firms in similar industries.

expanded material

10 Compute declining-balance and sum-of-the-years'-digits depreciation expense for plant and equipment. The two most common accelerated depreciation methods are declining-balance and sum-of-the-years'-digits. The declining- balance method is different from straight-line, units-of-production, and sum-of-the-years'-digits depreciation. The salvage value is ignored in the declining-balance method in the annual computation, but the book value of the asset cannot be less than the salvage value at the end of any reporting year. With declining-balance, the depreciation rate is calculated by multiplying a desired factor (such as 1.5 or 2.0) by the straight-line depreciation rate. This rate is then multiplied times the book value to determine annual depreciation expense. The declining-balance method is the basis for the MACRS income tax depreciation calculations in the United States. With sum-of-the-years'-digits depreciation, a ratio, computed by dividing the number of years of estimated life remaining at the beginning of the year by the sum of the years of the asset's life, is multiplied by the book value (cost − salvage value) of the asset to determine annual depreciation expense.

11 Account for changes in depreciation estimates. Useful lives and salvage values of plant and equipment are only estimates and may need adjustment during an asset's life. Changes in estimates of useful life or salvage value do not require modification of depreciation expense already taken. Rather, only future depreciation amounts are affected by changes in estimates.

key terms and concepts

amortization 416
basket purchase 403
book value 405
capital budgeting 397
capital lease 400
capitalized interest 402
depletion 409
depreciation 405
fixed asset turnover 420
franchise 418
goodwill 404
impairment 412
intangible assets 396
lease 399
lessee 399
lessor 399
license 418
long-term operating assets 396
natural resources 409
operating lease 399
patent 417
property, plant, and equipment 396
salvage value 405
straight-line depreciation method 405
time value of money 397
units-of-production method 405

expanded material

declining-balance depreciation method 422
sum-of-the-years'-digits (SYD) depreciation method 424

review problems

Property, Plant, and Equipment

Swift Motor Lines is a trucking company that hauls crude oil in the Rocky Mountain states. It currently has 20 trucks. The following information relates to a single truck:

a. Date truck was purchased, July 1, 2000.
b. Cost of truck:

Truck	$125,000
Paint job	3,000
Sales tax	7,000

c. Estimated useful life of truck, 120,000 miles.
d. Estimated salvage value of truck, $27,000.
e. 2002 expenditures on truck:
   (1) $6,000 on new tires and regular maintenance.
   (2) On January 1, spent $44,000 to completely rework the truck's engine; increased the total life to 200,000 miles but left expected salvage value unchanged.
f. Miles driven:

2000	11,000
2001	24,000
2002 (after reworking of engine)	20,000
2003	14,000

Required: Record journal entries to account for the following. (Use the units-of-production depreciation method.)

1. The purchase of the truck.
2. The expenditures on the truck during 2002.
3. Depreciation expense for:
   a. 2000
   b. 2001
   c. 2002
   d. 2003

Solution

1. Truck Purchase

The cost of the truck includes both the amount paid for it and all costs incurred to get it in working condition. In this case, the cost includes both the paint job and the sales tax. Thus, the entry to record the purchase is:

Truck	135,000	
Cash		135,000
Purchased truck for cash.		

2. Expenditures

The expenditure of $6,000 is an ordinary expenditure and is expensed in the current year. The engine overhaul is capitalized. The entries are:

Repairs and Maintenance Expense	6,000	
Cash		6,000
Recorded purchase of new tires and regular maintenance on truck.		
Truck	44,000	
Cash		44,000
Recorded major overhaul to truck's engine.		

3. Depreciation Expense

The formula for units-of-production depreciation on the truck is:

$$\frac{\text{Cost} - \text{Salvage value}}{\text{Total miles expected to be driven}} \times \begin{array}{c}\text{Number of miles}\\ \text{driven in any year}\end{array} = \text{Depreciation expense}$$

Journal entries and calculations are as follows:

a. 2000:

Depreciation Expense	9,900	
Accumulated Depreciation, Truck		9,900
Recorded depreciation expense for 2000.		

$$\frac{\$135{,}000 - \$27{,}000}{120{,}000 \text{ miles}} \times 11{,}000 \text{ miles} = \$9{,}900 \text{ or } \$0.90 \text{ per mile} \times 11{,}000 \text{ miles}$$

b. 2001:

Depreciation Expense	21,600	
Accumulated Depreciation, Truck		21,600
Recorded depreciation expense for 2001.		

$0.90 × 24,000 miles = $21,600

c. 2002:

Depreciation Expense	14,600	
Accumulated Depreciation, Truck		14,600
Recorded depreciation expense for 2002.		

$$\frac{\$135{,}000 - \$9{,}900 - \$21{,}600 + \$44{,}000 - \$27{,}000}{165{,}000 \text{ miles } (200{,}000 - 11{,}000 - 24{,}000)} \times 20{,}000 \text{ miles} = \$14{,}600 \text{ or } \$0.73^{*} \text{ per mile} \times 20{,}000 \text{ miles}$$

*Rounded to the nearest cent.

d. 2003:

Depreciation Expense	10,220	
Accumulated Depreciation, Truck		10,220
Recorded depreciation expense for 2003.		

$0.73 × 14,000 miles = $10,220

expanded material

Property, Plant, and Equipment

Swift Motor Lines is a trucking company that hauls crude oil in the Rocky Mountain states. It currently has 20 trucks. The following information relates to a single truck:

a. Date truck was purchased, July 1, 2000.
b. Cost of truck:

Truck	$125,000
Paint job	3,000
Sales tax	7,000

c. Estimated useful life of truck, eight years.
d. Estimated salvage value of truck, $27,000
e. 2002 expenditures on truck:
   (1) $6,000 on new tires and regular maintenance.
   (2) On January 1, spent $44,000 to completely rework the truck's engine. As a result of the engine work, the remaining life of the truck is increased to nine years, but the expected salvage value remains the same.

Required: Record journal entries to account for the following. (Use the sum-of-the-years'-digits depreciation method.)

1. The purchase of the truck.
2. Depreciation expense for:
   a. 2000
   b. 2001
   c. 2002
3. The expenditures on the truck during 2002.

Solution

1. Truck Purchase

The cost of the truck includes both the amount paid for it and all costs incurred to get it in working condition. In this case, the cost includes both the paint job and the sales tax. Thus, the entry to record the purchase is:

Truck	135,000	
Cash		135,000
Purchased truck for cash.		

2. Depreciation Expense

The formula for sum-of-the-years'-digits depreciation on the truck is:

$$\frac{\text{Number of years of life remaining at beginning of year}}{\text{Sum-of-the-years'-digits}} \times (\text{Cost} - \text{Salvage value}) = \text{Depreciation expense}$$

Depreciation for the three years is calculated as follows:

$$2000: \frac{8}{36} \times (\$135{,}000 - \$27{,}000) = \$24{,}000; \$24{,}000 \times ½ \text{ year} = \$12{,}000$$

$$2001: \frac{7.5}{36} \times (\$135{,}000 - \$27{,}000) = \$22{,}500$$

$$2002: \frac{9}{45} \times [(\$135{,}000 + \$44{,}000) - (\$12{,}000 + \$22{,}500) - \$27{,}000] = \$23{,}500$$

The depreciation entries are:

a. 2000:

Depreciation Expense	12,000	
Accumulated Depreciation, Truck		12,000
Recorded depreciation expense for 2000.		

b. 2001:

Depreciation Expense	22,500	
Accumulated Depreciation, Truck		22,500
Recorded depreciation expense for 2001.		

c. 2002:

Depreciation Expense	23,500	
Accumulated Depreciation, Truck		23,500
Recorded depreciation expense for 2002.		

3. Expenditures

The first expenditure of $6,000 is an ordinary expenditure and is expensed in the current year. The $44,000 expenditure is capitalized because it lengthens the truck's life. The entries are:

Repairs and Maintenance Expense	6,000	
Cash		6,000
Recorded purchase of new tires and regular maintenance on truck.		
Truck	44,000	
Cash		44,000
Recorded major overhaul of truck engine.		

discussion questions

1. What are the major characteristics of property, plant, and equipment?
2. When buying a long-term asset such as a building or piece of equipment, the time value of money must be considered. With respect to time value, it is often said that the last payment (say, 20 years in the future) doesn't cost as much as the next payment today. Explain.
3. Why are expenditures other than the net purchase price included in the cost of an asset?
4. Why would a company include leased assets in the property, plant, and equipment section of its balance sheet when the assets are owned by another entity?
5. A company that borrows money to construct its own building generally should include the interest paid on the loan during the construction period in the cost of the building. Why?
6. Why are fair market values used to determine the cost of operating assets acquired in a basket purchase?
7. Companies usually depreciate assets such as buildings even though those assets may be increasing in value. Why?
8. How does the company accountant decide whether an expenditure should be capitalized or expensed?
9. If a firm is uncertain whether an expenditure will benefit one or more than one accounting period, or whether it will increase the capacity or useful life of an operational asset, most firms will expense rather than capitalize the expenditure. Why?
10. Sometimes long-term assets experience sudden dramatic decreases in value. For example, a waste dump might suddenly be constructed next to an office building. When such impairment of value occurs, should the decrease in value be recognized immediately, or should the same amount of depreciation expense be recognized as in past years?
11. Accountants in other countries sometimes write up the recorded amounts of long-term assets when their values increase. Why are U.S. accountants reluctant to increase the recorded value of property, plant, and equipment when their value increases?
12. Why is it common to have a gain or loss on the disposal of a long-term operating asset? Is it true that if the useful life and salvage value of an asset could be known with certainty and were realized, there would never be such a gain or loss?
13. When recording the disposal of a long-term operating asset, why is it necessary to debit the accumulated depreciation of the old asset?
14. Why are intangible assets considered assets although they have no physical substance?
15. Goodwill can be recorded only when a business is purchased. Does this result in similar businesses having incomparable financial statements?
16. How is fixed asset turnover calculated, and what does the resulting ratio value mean?

expanded material

17. Which of the depreciation methods discussed in this chapter will usually result in the highest net income in the early years of an asset's life?
18. How does the declining-balance method of depreciation differ from other methods of depreciation?
19. Modified accelerated cost recovery system (MACRS) depreciation is allowed by the IRS but usually is not used in financial reporting. Why do you think this is the case?
20. When changing the estimate of the useful life of an asset, should depreciation expense for all the previous years be recalculated? If not, how do you account for a change in this estimate?
21. Why is it often necessary to recalculate the depletion rate for natural resources?

discussion cases

CASE 9-1

INTANGIBLE ASSETS

Renford Company owns two restaurants. One, located in Tacoma, was purchased from a previous owner and the other, located in Seattle, was built by Renford Company after purchasing the franchise. The restaurant in Seattle has a $20,000 unamortized franchise on the books. (The franchise originally cost $200,000 and is being amortized over 10 years.) The restaurant was built nine years ago. The Tacoma restaurant was purchased last year and has goodwill of $550,000 on the books. As it turns out, the Seattle restaurant does twice as much business as the Tacoma restaurant and is much more profitable. The Seattle restaurant is in a prime location, and business keeps increasing each year. The Tacoma restaurant does about the same amount of business each year, and it doesn't look as if it will ever do any better. Does it make sense to you to have goodwill on the books of the less profitable restaurant? Should Renford record goodwill on the books of the Seattle restaurant, or should it write off the goodwill on the Tacoma restaurant's books (which is being amortized over a 20-year period)?

expanded material

CASE 9-2

STRAIGHT-LINE VERSUS ACCELERATED DEPRECIATION

Dennis Company currently depreciates its assets using the straight-line method for both tax and financial accounting. Total depreciation expense for this year will be $250,000 using straight-line depreciation. A consultant has just advised the company that it should use accelerated depreciation methods for both tax and financial accounting because "paying lower taxes is better than recognizing higher income." Using accelerated depreciation methods, total depreciation expense this year would be $400,000. The company has an effective tax rate of 40%. Do you agree with the consultant? Why or why not?

exercises

EXERCISE 9-1

ACQUISITION DECISION

Johnson Company is considering acquiring a new airplane. It has looked at two financing options. The first is to lease the airplane for 10 years with lease payments of $70,000 each year. The second is to purchase the airplane, making a down payment of $250,000 and annual payments of $40,000 for 10 years. If the present value of the two financing options is the same, what other factors must be considered in deciding whether to purchase or to lease?

EXERCISE 9-2

ACCOUNTING FOR THE ACQUISITION OF A LONG-TERM ASSET

Chong Lai Company acquired a new machine in order to expand its productive capacity. The costs associated with the machine purchase were as follows:

Purchase price	$10,000
Installation costs	500
Cost of initial testing	600
Sales tax	750

1. Make the journal entry to record the acquisition of the machine. Assume that all costs were paid in cash.
2. Make the journal entry to record the acquisition of the machine. Assume that Chong Lai Company signed a note payable for the $10,000 purchase price and paid the remaining costs in cash.

EXERCISE 9-3

COMPUTING ASSET COST AND DEPRECIATION EXPENSE

Antique Furniture Company decided to purchase a new furniture-polishing machine for its store in New York City. After a long search, it found the appropriate polisher in Chicago. The machine costs $75,000 and has an estimated 10-year life and no salvage value. Antique Furniture Company made the following additional expenditures with respect to this purchase:

Sales tax	$4,000
Delivery costs (FOB shipping point)	1,500
Installation costs	2,200
Painting of machine to match the decor	300

1. What is the cost of the machine to Antique Furniture Company?
2. What is the amount of the first full year's depreciation if Antique uses the straight-line method?

EXERCISE 9-4

ACQUISITION AND DEPRECIATION OF ASSETS

Western Oil Company, which prepares financial statements on a calendar-year basis, purchased new drilling equipment on July 1, 2003, using check numbers 1015 and 1016. The check totals are shown here, along with a breakdown of the charges.

1015 (Payee—Oil Equipment, Inc.):	
Cost of drilling equipment	$ 75,000
Cost of cement platform	25,000
Installation charges	13,000
Total	$113,000
1016 (Payee—Red Ball Freight):	
Freight costs for drilling equipment	$ 2,000

Assume that the estimated life of the drilling equipment is 10 years and its salvage value is $5,000.

1. Record the disbursements on July 1, 2003, assuming that no entry had been recorded for the drilling equipment.
2. Disregarding the information given about the two checks, assume that the drilling equipment was recorded at a total cost of $95,000. Calculate the depreciation expense for 2003 using the straight-line method.

EXERCISE 9-5

ACCOUNTING FOR LEASED ASSETS

On January 1, 2003, Hartmeyer Company leased a fax machine with a laser printer from Teleproducts, Inc. The five-year lease is noncancelable and requires monthly payments of $150 at the end of each month, with the first payment due on January 31, 2003. At the end of five years, Hartmeyer will own the equipment. The present value of the lease payments at the beginning of the lease is determined to be $6,740.

1. Prepare journal entries to record:
   a. The lease agreement on January 1, 2003.
   b. The first lease payment on January 31, 2003, assuming that $68 of the $150 payment is interest.
2. Now assume that the lease expires after one year at which time a new lease can be negotiated or Hartmeyer can return the equipment to Teleproducts. Prepare any journal entries relating to the lease that would be required on January 1 and January 31, 2003.

EXERCISE 9-6

INTEREST CAPITALIZATION

Litton Company is constructing a new office building. Costs of the building are as follows:

Wages paid to construction workers	$185,000
Building materials purchased	456,000
Interest expense on construction loan	13,800
Interest expense on mortgage loan during the first year subsequent to the building's completion	22,000

Given the above costs, at what amount should the building be recorded in the accounting records?

EXERCISE 9-7

ACCOUNTING FOR THE ACQUISITION OF ASSETS—BASKET PURCHASE

Sealise Corporation purchased land, a building, and equipment for a total cost of $450,000. After the purchase, the property was appraised. Fair market values were determined to be $120,000 for the land, $280,000 for the building, and $80,000 for the equipment. Given these appraisals, record the purchase of the property by Sealise Corporation.

EXERCISE 9-8

DEPRECIATION CALCULATIONS

Luric Company purchased a new car on July 1, 2002, for $15,000. The estimated life of the car was four years or 104,000 miles, and its salvage value was estimated to be $2,000. The car was driven 9,000 miles in 2002 and 27,000 miles in 2003.

1. Compute the amount of depreciation expense for 2002 and 2003 using the following methods:
   a. Straight-line.
   b. Units-of-production.
2. Which depreciation method more closely reflects the used-up service potential of the car? Explain.

EXERCISE 9-9

DEPRECIATION CALCULATIONS

Denver Hardware Company has a giant paint mixer that cost $31,500 plus $400 to install. The estimated salvage value of the paint mixer at the end of its useful life in 15 years is estimated to be $1,900. Denver estimates that the machine can mix 850,000 cans of paint during its lifetime. Compute the second full year's depreciation expense, using the following methods:

1. Straight-line.
2. Units-of-production, assuming that the machine mixes 51,000 cans of paint during the second year.

EXERCISE 9-10

ACQUISITION AND IMPROVEMENT OF ASSETS

Prepare entries in the books of Sanmara, Inc., to reflect the following. (Assume cash transactions.)

1. Purchased a lathing machine to be used by the firm in its production process.

Invoice price	$45,000
Cash discount taken	900
Installation costs	1,200
Sales tax on machine	1,800

2. Performed normal periodic maintenance on the lathing machine at a cost of $200.
3. Added to the lathing machine a governor costing $400, which is expected to increase the machine's useful life.

EXERCISE 9-11

ASSET IMPAIRMENT

Consider the following three independent scenarios:

	1	2	3
Original cost of asset	$1,400	$1,400	$1,400
Accumulated depreciation	400	400	400
Sum of future cash flows	1,500	1,500	900
Fair value of the asset	1,100	800	800

1. For each of the three scenarios, answer the following questions:
   a. Is the asset impaired?
   b. At what amount (net of accumulated depreciation) should the asset be reported?
2. Make the journal entry required in Scenario 3.

EXERCISE 9-12

ASSET IMPAIRMENT

In 1998, Rhode Company purchased land and a building at a cost of $800,000, of which $200,000 was allocated to the land and $600,000 was allocated to the building. As of December 31, 2002, the accounting records related to these assets were as follows:

Land	$200,000
Building	600,000
Accumulated Depreciation, Building	100,000

On January 1, 2003, it is determined that there is toxic waste under the building and the future cash flows associated with the land and building are less than the recorded total book value for those two assets. The fair value of the land and building together is now only $100,000, of which $40,000 is land and $60,000 is the building. How should this impairment in value be recognized? Make the entry on January 1, 2003, to record the impairment of the land and building.

EXERCISE 9-13

Spread-Sheet Software

ACCOUNTING FOR THE DISPOSAL OF ASSETS

Zimer Concrete Company has a truck that it wants to sell. The truck had an original cost of $60,000, was purchased three years ago, and was expected to have a useful life of five years with no salvage value.

Using straight-line depreciation, and assuming that depreciation expense for three full years has been recorded, prepare journal entries to record the disposal of the truck under each of the following independent conditions:

1. Zimer Concrete Company sells the truck for $25,000 cash.
2. Zimer Concrete Company sells the truck for $20,000 cash.
3. The old truck is wrecked and Zimer Concrete Company hauls it to the junkyard.

EXERCISE 9-14

DISPOSAL OF AN ASSET

Honey Bee Company purchased a machine for $91,000. The machine has an estimated useful life of seven years and a salvage value of $7,000. Journalize the disposal of the machine under each of the following conditions. (Assume straight-line depreciation.)

1. Sold the machine for $72,000 cash after two years.
2. Sold the machine for $28,000 cash after five years.

EXERCISE 9-15

ACCOUNTING FOR INTANGIBLE ASSETS

Gaylord Research, Inc., has the following intangible assets:

Asset	Cost	Date Purchased	Expected Useful or Legal Life
Goodwill	$ 16,000	January 1, 1994	20 years
Patent	136,000	January 1, 1996	17 years
Franchise	180,000	January 1, 1997	10 years

1. Record the amortization expense for each of these intangible assets for 2003.
2. Prepare the intangible assets section of the balance sheet for Gaylord Research, Inc., as of December 31, 2003.

EXERCISE 9-16

INTANGIBLE ASSETS

On January 1, 2002, Landon Company purchased a franchise to operate a regionally owned fast-food restaurant for a cost of $250,000. On July 1, 2002, Landon Company purchased another existing business in a nearby city for a total cost of $750,000. The market value of the land, building, and equipment, and other tangible assets was $550,000. The excess $200,000 was recorded as goodwill, to be amortized over a 20-year period.

Assuming Landon Company amortizes franchises over a 10-year period, record the following:

1. The purchase of the franchise on January 1, 2002.
2. The amortization of the franchise and goodwill at December 31, 2002.
3. The amortization of the franchise and goodwill at December 31, 2003.

EXERCISE 9-17

COMPUTING GOODWILL

Stringtown Company purchased Stansbury Island Manufacturing for $1,800,000 cash. The book value and fair value of the assets of Stansbury Island as of the date of the acquisition are listed below:

	Book Value	Market Value
Cash	$ 30,000	$ 30,000
Accounts receivable	300,000	300,000
Inventory	350,000	600,000
Property, plant, and equipment	500,000	900,000
Totals	$1,180,000	$1,830,000

In addition, Stansbury Island had liabilities totaling $400,000 at the time of the acquisition.

1. At what amounts will the individual assets of Stansbury Island be recorded on the books of Stringtown, the acquiring company?
2. How will Stringtown account for the liabilities of Stansbury Island?
3. How much goodwill will be recorded as part of this acquisition?

EXERCISE 9-18

FIXED ASSET TURNOVER

Handy Corner Stores reported the following asset values in 2002 and 2003:

	2003	2002
Cash	$ 30,000	$ 20,000
Accounts receivable	400,000	300,000
Inventory	600,000	350,000
Land	200,000	150,000
Buildings	600,000	500,000
Equipment	300,000	200,000

In addition, Handy Corner had sales of $2,000,000 in 2003. Cost of goods sold for the year was $1,500,000.

Compute Handy Corner's fixed asset turnover ratio for 2003.

expanded material

EXERCISE 9-19

ACQUISITION AND DEPRECIATION OF ASSETS

Montana Oil Company, which prepares financial statements on a calendar-year basis, purchased new drilling equipment on July 1, 2003. A breakdown of the cost follows:

Cost of drilling equipment	$ 75,000
Cost of cement platform	25,000
Installation charges	13,000
Freight costs for drilling equipment	2,000
Total	$115,000

Assuming that the estimated life of the drilling equipment is 10 years and its salvage value is $5,000:

1. Record the purchase on July 1, 2003.
2. Assume that the drilling equipment was recorded at a total cost of $95,000. Calculate the depreciation expense for 2003 using the following methods:
   a. Sum-of-the-years'-digits.
   b. Double-declining-balance.
   c. 150% declining-balance.
3. Prepare the journal entry to record the depreciation for 2003 in accordance with 2(a).

EXERCISE 9-20

ACQUISITION AND DEPRECIATION

At the beginning of 2003, Lowham's Guest Ranch constructed a new walk-in freezer that had a useful life of 10 years. At the end of 10 years, the motor could be salvaged for $2,000. In addition to construction costs that totaled $10,000, the following costs were incurred:

Sales taxes on components.	$1,250
Delivery costs	800
Installation of motor	200
Painting of both interior and exterior of freezer.	100

1. What is the cost of the walk-in freezer to Lowham's Guest Ranch?
2. Compute the amount of depreciation to be taken in the first year assuming Lowham's Guest Ranch uses the
   a. Double-declining-balance method.
   b. Sum-of-the-years'-digits method.

EXERCISE 9-21

DEPRECIATION COMPUTATIONS

Techno Company purchases a $400,000 piece of equipment on January 2, 2001, for use in its manufacturing process. The equipment's estimated useful life is 10 years with no salvage value. Techno uses 150% declining-balance depreciation for all its equipment.

1. Compute the depreciation expense for 2001, 2002, and 2003.
2. Compute the book value of the equipment on December 31, 2003.

EXERCISE 9-22

DEPRECIATION CALCULATIONS

The University of Northern Utah purchased a new van on January 1, 2002, for $30,000. The estimated life of the van was five years or 95,000 miles, and its salvage value was estimated to be $2,000. Compute the amount of depreciation expense for 2002, 2003, and 2004 using the following methods:

1. Double-declining-balance.
2. 175% declining-balance.
3. Sum-of-the-years'-digits.

EXERCISE 9-23

DEPRECIATION CALCULATIONS

On January 1, 2002, MAC Corporation purchased a machine for $60,000. The machine cost $800 to deliver and $2,000 to install. At the end of 10 years, MAC expects to sell the machine for $2,000. Compute depreciation expense for 2002 and 2003 using the following methods:

1. Double-declining-balance.
2. 150% declining-balance.
3. Sum-of-the-years'-digits.

EXERCISE 9-24

ACCOUNTING FOR NATURAL RESOURCES

On January 1, 2002, Castle Investment Corporation purchased a coal mine for cash, having taken into consideration the favorable tax consequences and the inevitable energy crunch in the future. Castle paid $800,000 for the mine. Shortly before the purchase, an engineer estimated that there were 80,000 tons of coal in the mine.

1. Record the purchase of the mine on January 1, 2002.
2. Record the depletion expense for 2002, assuming that 20,000 tons of coal were mined during the year.
3. Assume that on January 1, 2003, the company received a new estimate that the mine now contained 120,000 tons of coal. Record the entry (if any) to show the change in estimate.
4. Record the depletion expense for 2003, assuming that another 20,000 tons of coal were mined.

EXERCISE 9-25

CHANGE IN ESTIMATED USEFUL LIFE

On January 1, 2001, Landon Excavation Company purchased a new bulldozer for $120,000. The equipment had an estimated useful life of 10 years and an estimated residual value of $10,000. On January 1, 2003, Landon determined that the bulldozer would have a total useful life of only 8 years instead of 10 years with no change in residual value. Landon uses straight-line depreciation.

Compute depreciation expense on this bulldozer for 2001, 2002, and 2003.

PROBLEM 9-1

ACQUISITION, DEPRECIATION, AND DISPOSAL OF ASSETS

On January 2, 2003, Scott Company purchased a building and land for $440,000. The most recent appraisal values for the building and the land are $360,000 and $120,000, respectively. The building has an estimated useful life of 20 years and a salvage value of $10,000.

Required:

1. Assuming cash transactions and straight-line depreciation, prepare journal entries to record:
   a. Purchase of the building and land on January 2, 2003.
   b. Depreciation expense on December 31, 2003.
2. Assume that after three years the property (land and building) was sold for $350,000. Prepare the journal entry to record the sale.

PROBLEM 9-2

PURCHASING PROPERTY, PLANT, AND EQUIPMENT

Jordon Company is considering replacing its automated stamping machine. The machine is specialized and very expensive. Jordon is considering three acquisition alternatives. The first is to lease a machine for 10 years at $1 million per year, after which time Jordon can buy the machine for $1 million. The second alternative is to pay cash for the machine at a cost of $7 million. The third alternative is to make a down payment of $3 million, followed by 10 annual payments of $550,000. The company is trying to decide which alternative to select.

Required:

1. Assuming the present value of the lease payments is $7.2 million and the present value of the 10 loan payments of $550,000 is $4.1 million, determine which alternative Jordon should choose.
2. **Interpretive Question:** Your decision in part (1) was based only on financial factors. What other qualitative issues might influence your decision?

PROBLEM 9-3

ACQUISITION OF AN ASSET

Pacific Printing Company purchased a new printing press. The invoice price was $158,500. The company paid for the press within 30 days, so it was allowed a 3% discount. The freight cost for delivering the press was $2,500. A premium of $900 was paid for a special insurance policy to cover the transportation of the press. The company spent $2,800 to install the press and an additional $400 in start-up costs to get the press ready for regular production.

Required:

1. At what amount should the press be recorded as an asset?
2. What additional information must be known before the depreciation expense for the first year of operation of the new press can be computed?
3. **Interpretive Question:** What criterion is used to determine whether the start-up costs of $400 are included in the cost of the asset? Explain.

PROBLEM 9-4

ACCOUNTING FOR LEASED ASSETS

On January 2, 2003, Cameron Company contracted to lease a computer on a noncancelable basis for five years at an annual rental of $63,000, payable at the end of each year. The computer has an estimated economic life of six years. There is no bargain purchase option, and the computer will be returned to the lessor at the end of the five-year term of the lease. At the beginning of the lease, the computer has a fair market value of $240,000, and the present value of the lease payments equals $238,820.

Required:

1. Is this a capital lease or an operating lease? Explain.
2. Assuming that the lease is an operating lease, prepare the journal entries for Cameron Company for 2003.
3. Assuming that the lease is a capital lease, prepare the journal entries for Cameron Company for 2003. Assume the lease payment at the end of 2003 includes interest of $23,882.

PROBLEM 9-5

ACCOUNTING FOR LEASED ASSETS

The board of directors of Swogen Company authorized the president to lease a corporate jet to facilitate her travels to domestic and international subsidiaries of the company. After extensive investigation of the alternatives, the company agreed to lease a jet for $300,548 each year for five years, payable at the end of each year. Title to the jet will pass to Swogen Company at the end of five years with no further payments required. The lease agreement starts on January 2, 2003. The jet has an economic life of eight years. The lease contract is noncancelable and contains an interest rate of 8%, resulting in a present value of the lease payments of $1,200,000 as of January 2, 2003.

Required:

1. Does this lease contract meet the requirements to be accounted for as a capital lease? Why or why not?
2. Assuming that the lease contract is to be accounted for as a capital lease, prepare the journal entries for Swogen Company for 2003. Interest included in the first payment is $96,000.

PROBLEM 9-6

INTEREST CAPITALIZATION

Jennifer Cosmetics wants to construct a new building. It has three building options, as follows:

a. Hire a contractor to do all the work. Jennifer has a bid of $850,000 from a reputable contractor to complete the project.
b. Construct the building itself by taking out a construction loan of $800,000. Using this alternative, Jennifer believes materials and labor will cost $800,000, and interest on the construction loan will be calculated as follows:

   $200,000 @ 12% for 9 months
   $300,000 @ 12% for 6 months
   $200,000 @ 12% for 3 months
   $100,000 @ 12% for 1 month

Required:

1. What will be the recorded cost of the building under each alternative?
2. Assuming the building is depreciated over a 20-year period using straight-line depreciation with no salvage value, how much is the annual depreciation expense under each alternative?

PROBLEM 9-7

DEPRECIATION CALCULATIONS

On January 1, VICOM Company purchased a $68,000 machine. The estimated life of the machine was five years, and the estimated salvage value was $5,000. The machine had an estimated useful life in productive output of 75,000 units. Actual output for the first two years was: year 1, 20,000 units; year 2, 15,000 units.

Required:

1. Compute the amount of depreciation expense for the first year, using each of the following methods:
   a. Straight-line.
   b. Units-of-production.
2. What was the book value of the machine at the end of the first year, assuming that straight-line depreciation was used?
3. If the machine is sold at the end of the fourth year for $15,000, how much should the company report as a gain or loss (assuming straight-line depreciation)?

PROBLEM 9-8

PURCHASE OF MULTIPLE ASSETS FOR A SINGLE SUM

On April 1, 2003, Mission Company paid $360,000 in cash to purchase land, a building, and equipment. The appraised fair market values of the assets were as follows: land, $90,000; building, $260,000; and equipment, $50,000. The company incurred legal fees of $3,000 to determine that it would have a clear title to the land. Before the facilities could be used, Mission had to spend $2,500 to grade and landscape the land, $4,000 to put the equipment in working order, and $15,000 to renovate the building. The equipment was then estimated to have a useful life of six years with no salvage value, and the building would have a useful life of 20 years with a net salvage value of $15,000. Both the equipment and the building are to be depreciated on a straight-line basis. The company is on a calendar-year reporting basis.

Required:

1. Allocate the single purchase price to the individual assets acquired.
2. Prepare the journal entry to acquire the land, building, and equipment.
3. Prepare the journal entry to record the title search, landscape, put the equipment in working order, and renovate the building.
4. Prepare the journal entries on December 31, 2003, to record the depreciation on the building and the equipment.

PROBLEM 9-9

BASKET PURCHASE AND PARTIAL-YEAR DEPRECIATION

On April 1, 2003, Rosenberg Company purchased for $200,000 a tract of land on which was located a fully equipped factory. The following information was compiled regarding this purchase:

	Market Value	Seller's Book Value
Land	$ 75,000	$ 30,000
Building	100,000	75,000
Equipment	50,000	60,000
Totals	$225,000	$165,000

Required:

1. Prepare the journal entry to record the purchase of these assets.
2. Assume that the building is depreciated on a straight-line basis over a remaining life of 20 years and the equipment is depreciated on a straight-line basis over five years. Neither the building nor the equipment is expected to have any salvage value. Compute the depreciation expense for 2003 assuming the assets were placed in service immediately upon acquisition.

PROBLEM 9-10

ACQUISITION, DEPRECIATION, AND SALE OF AN ASSET

On January 2, 2001, Union Oil Company purchased a new airplane. The following costs are related to the purchase:

Airplane, base price	$112,000
Cash discount	3,000
Sales tax	4,000
Delivery charges	1,000

Required:

1. Prepare the journal entry to record the payment of these items on January 2, 2001.
2. Ignore your answer to part 1 and assume that the airplane cost $90,000 and has an expected useful life of five years or 1,500 hours. The estimated salvage value is $3,000. Using units-of-production depreciation and assuming that 300 hours are flown in 2002, calculate the amount of depreciation expense to be recorded for the second year.
3. Ignore the information in parts 1 and 2 and assume that the airplane costs $90,000, that its expected useful life is five years, and that its estimated salvage value is $5,000. The company now uses the straight-line depreciation method. On January 1, 2004, the following balances are in the related accounts:

Airplane	$90,000
Accumulated Depreciation, Airplane	51,000

Prepare the necessary journal entries to record the sale of this airplane on July 1, 2004, for $40,000.

PROBLEM 9-11

ACQUISITION, DEPRECIATION, AND SALE OF AN ASSET

On July 1, 2003, Philip Ward bought a used pickup truck at a cost of $5,300 for use in his business. On the same day, Ward had the truck painted blue and white (his company's colors) at a cost of $800. Mr. Ward estimates the life of the truck to be three years or 40,000 miles. He further estimates that the truck will have a $450 scrap value at the end of its life, but that it will also cost him $50 to transfer the truck to the junkyard.

Required:

1. Record the following journal entries:
   a. July 1, 2003: Paid all bills pertaining to the truck. (No previous entries have been recorded concerning these bills.)
   b. December 31, 2003: The depreciation expense for the year, using the straight-line method.
   c. December 31, 2004: The depreciation expense for 2004, again using the straight-line method.
   d. January 2, 2005: Sold the truck for $2,600 cash.
2. What would the depreciation expense for 2003 have been if the truck had been driven 8,000 miles and the units-of-production method of depreciation had been used?
3. **Interpretive Question:** In part 1(d), there is a loss of $650. Why did this loss occur?

PROBLEM 9-12

ACCOUNTING FOR NATURAL RESOURCES

On April 30, 2001, Lindon Oil Company purchased an oil well, with estimated reserves of 100,000 barrels of oil, for $1 million cash.

Required:

Prepare journal entries for the following:

1. Record the purchase of the oil well.
2. During 2001, 10,000 barrels of oil were extracted from the well. Record the depletion expense for 2001.
3. During 2002, 18,000 barrels of oil were extracted from the well. Record the depletion expense for 2002.

PROBLEM 9-13

ASSET IMPAIRMENT

Delta Company owns plant and equipment on the island of Lagos. The cost and book value of the building are $2,800,000 and $2,400,000, respectively. Until this year, the market value of the factory was $7 million. However, a new dictator just came to power and declared martial law. As a result of the changed political status, the future cash inflows from the use of the factory are expected to be greatly reduced. Delta now believes that the output from the factory will generate cash inflows of $100,000 per year for the next 20 years. In addition, the market value of the factory building is now just $1,300,000. Delta is not sure how to account for the sudden impairment in value.

Required:

1. Explain how to decide whether an impairment loss is to be recognized.
2. Prepare the necessary journal entry, if any, to account for an impairment in the value of the factory.

PROBLEM 9-14

ACCOUNTING FOR INTANGIBLE ASSETS (GOODWILL)

On January 1, 2003, Universal Company purchased the following assets and liabilities from Grand Company for $250,000:

	Book Value	Fair Market Value
Inventory	$40,000	$ 50,000
Building	80,000	100,000
Land	50,000	60,000
Accounts receivable	20,000	20,000
Accounts payable	(10,000)	(10,000)

Required:

1. Prepare a journal entry to record the purchase of Grand by Universal.
2. Record amortization of goodwill as of December 31, 2003. (Assume a 40-year amortization period for the goodwill.)

PROBLEM 9-15

ACCOUNTING FOR GOODWILL

On January 1, 2003, Fishing Creek Company purchased Skull Valley Technologies for $8,800,000 cash. The book value and fair value of Skull Valley's assets as of the date of the acquisition are listed below:

	Book Value	Market Value
Cash	$ 100,000	$ 100,000
Accounts receivable	500,000	500,000
Inventory	950,000	1,200,000
Property, plant, and equipment	1,500,000	1,900,000
Trademark	0	2,000,000
Totals	$3,050,000	$5,700,000

In addition, Skull Valley had liabilities totaling $4,000,000 at the time of the acquisition.

Required:

1. At what amount will Skull Valley's trademark be recorded on the books of Fishing Creek, the acquiring company?
2. How much goodwill will be recorded as part of this acquisition?
3. How much goodwill amortization expense will Fishing Creek recognize in 2003? What assumptions are necessary to answer this question?
4. **Interpretive Question:** What was Skull Valley's recorded stockholders' equity immediately before the acquisition? Under what circumstances does stockholders' equity yield a poor measure of the fair value of a company?

PROBLEM 9-16

FIXED ASSET TURNOVER RATIO

Waystation Company reported the following asset values in 2002 and 2003:

	2003	2002
Cash	$ 40,000	$ 30,000
Accounts receivable	500,000	400,000
Inventory	700,000	500,000
Land	300,000	200,000
Buildings	800,000	600,000
Equipment	400,000	300,000

In addition, Waystation had sales of $4,000,000 in 2003. Cost of goods sold for the year was $2,500,000.

As of the end of 2002, the fair value of Waystation's total assets was $2,500,000. Of the excess of fair value over book value, $50,000 resulted because the fair value of Waystation's inventory was greater than its recorded book value. As of the end of 2003, the fair value of Waystation's total assets was $3,500,000. As of December 31, 2003, the fair value of Waystation's inventory was $100,000 greater than the inventory's recorded book value.

Required:

1. Compute Waystation's fixed asset turnover ratio for 2003.
2. Using the fair value of fixed assets instead of the book value of fixed assets, recompute Waystation's fixed asset turnover ratio for 2003. State any assumptions that you make.
3. **Interpretive Question:** Waystation's primary competitor is Handy Corner. Handy Corner's fixed asset turnover ratio for 2003, based on publicly available information, is 2.8 times. Is Waystation more or less efficient at using its fixed assets than is Handy Corner? Explain your answer.

expanded material

PROBLEM 9-17

DEPRECIATION CALCULATIONS

Springs Hardware Company has a giant paint mixer that cost $31,500 plus $400 to install. The estimated salvage value of the paint mixer at the end of its useful life in 15 years is estimated to be $1,900. Springs estimates that the machine can mix 850,000 cans of paint during its lifetime.

Required:

Compute the second full year's depreciation expense, using the following methods:

1. Double-declining-balance.
2. Sum-of-the-years'-digits.

PROBLEM 9-18

DEPRECIATION CALCULATIONS

On January 1, Top Flight Company purchased a $68,000 machine. The estimated life of the machine was five years, and the estimated salvage value was $5,000. The machine had an estimated useful life in productive output of 75,000 units. Actual output for the first two years was: year 1, 20,000 units; year 2, 15,000 units.

Required:

1. Compute the amount of depreciation expense for the first year, using each of the following methods:
   a. Straight-line.
   b. Units-of-production.
   c. Sum-of-the-years'-digits.
   d. Double-declining-balance.
2. What was the book value of the machine at the end of the first year, assuming that straight-line depreciation was used?
3. If the machine is sold at the end of the fourth year for $15,000, how much should the company report as a gain or loss (assuming straight-line depreciation)?

PROBLEM 9-19

FINANCIAL STATEMENT EFFECTS OF DEPRECIATION METHODS

On July 1, 2002, the consulting firm of Little, Smart, and Quick bought a new computer for $120,000 to help it service its clients more efficiently. The new computer was estimated to have a useful life of five years with an estimated salvage value of $20,000 at the end of five years. It was further estimated that the computer would be in operation about 1,500 hours in each of the five years with some variation of use from year to year. Janet Little, who manages the firm's internal operations, has asked you to help her decide which depreciation method should be selected for the new computer. The methods being considered are straight-line, double-declining-balance, and sum-of-the-years'-digits.

Required:

1. Prepare a schedule showing depreciation for 2002, 2003, and 2004 for each of the three methods being considered.
2. For each of the three methods, compute the asset book value that would be reported on the balance sheet at December 31, 2004.
3. **Interpretive Question:** Which method would maximize income for the three years (2002–2004), and which would minimize income for the same period?

PROBLEM 9-20

DEPRECIATION CALCULATIONS

Curtis, Inc., a firm that makes oversized boots, purchased a machine for its factory. The following data relate to the machine:

Price	$16,000
Delivery charges	$200
Installation charges	$600
Date purchased	May 1, 2002
Estimated useful life:	
In years	8 years
In hours of production	30,000 hours of operating time
Salvage value	$1,800

During 2002, the machine was used 4,400 hours. During 2003, the machine was used 3,200 hours.

Required:

Determine the depreciation expense and the year-end book values for the machine for the years 2002 and 2003, assuming that:

1. The straight-line method is used.
2. The double-declining-balance method is used.
3. The units-of-production method is used.
4. The sum-of-the-years'-digits method is used.
5. **Interpretive Question:** If you were Curtis, which method would you use in order to report the highest profits in 2002 and 2003 combined?

PROBLEM 9-21

CHANGES IN DEPRECIATION ESTIMATES AND CAPITALIZATION OF EXPENDITURES

Ironic Metal Products, Inc., acquired a machine on January 2, 2001, for $76,600. The useful life of the machine was estimated to be eight years with a salvage value of $4,600. Depreciation is recorded on December 31 of each year using the sum-of-the-years'-digits method.

At the beginning of 2003, the company estimated the remaining useful life of the machine to be four years and changed the estimated salvage value from $4,600 to $2,600. On January 2, 2004, major repairs on the machine cost the company $34,000. The repairs added two years to the machine's useful life and increased the salvage value to $3,000.

Required:

1. Prepare journal entries to record:
   a. The purchase of the machine.
   b. Annual depreciation expense for the years 2001 and 2002.
   c. Depreciation in 2003 under the revised estimates of useful life and salvage value.
   d. The expenditure for major repairs in 2004.
   e. Depreciation expense for 2004.
2. Compute the book value of the machine at the end of 2004.

PROBLEM 9-22

UNIFYING CONCEPTS: ACCOUNTING FOR NATURAL RESOURCES

Forest Products, Inc., buys and develops natural resources for profit. Since 2000, it has had the following activities:

1/1/00	Purchased for $800,000 a tract of timber estimated to contain 1,600,000 board feet of lumber.
1/1/01	Purchased for $600,000 a silver mine estimated to contain 30,000 tons of silver ore.
7/1/01	Purchased for $60,000 a uranium mine estimated to contain 5,000 tons of uranium ore.
1/1/02	Purchased for $500,000 an oil well estimated to contain 100,000 barrels of oil.

Required:

1. Provide the necessary journal entries to account for the following:
   a. The purchase of these assets.
   b. The depletion expense for 2002 on all four assets, assuming that the following were extracted:
      (1) 200,000 board feet of lumber.
      (2) 5,000 tons of silver.
      (3) 1,000 tons of uranium.
      (4) 10,000 barrels of oil.
2. Assume that on January 1, 2003, after 20,000 tons of silver had been mined, engineers' estimates revealed that only 4,000 tons of silver remained. Record the depletion expense for 2003, assuming that 2,000 tons were mined.
3. Compute the book values of all four assets as of December 31, 2003, assuming that the total extracted to date is:
   a. Timber tract, 800,000 board feet.
   b. Silver mine, 22,000 tons [only 2,000 tons are left per (2)].
   c. Uranium mine, 3,000 tons.
   d. Oil well, 80,000 barrels.

PROBLEM 9-23

UNIFYING CONCEPTS: PROPERTY, PLANT, AND EQUIPMENT

Smithfield Corportation owns and operates three sawmills that make lumber for building homes. The operations consist of cutting logs in the forest, hauling them to the various sawmills, sawing the lumber, and shipping it to building supply warehouses throughout the western part of the United States. To haul the logs, Smithfield has several trucks. Relevant data pertaining to one truck are:

a. Date of purchase, July 1, 2001.
b. Cost:

Truck	$60,000
Trailer	20,000
Paint job (to match company colors)	1,500
Sales tax	3,500

c. Estimated useful life of the truck, 150,000 miles.
d. Estimated salvage value, zero.
e. 2002 expenditures on truck:
   (1) Spent $5,000 on tires, oil changes, greasing, and other miscellaneous items.
   (2) Spent $22,000 to overhaul the engine and replace the transmission on January 1, 2002. This expenditure increased the life of the truck by 135,000 miles.

Required:

Record journal entries to account for:

1. The purchase of the truck.
2. The 2001 depreciation expense using units-of-production depreciation and assuming the truck was driven 45,000 miles.
3. The expenditures relating to the truck during 2002.
4. The 2002 depreciation expense using the units-of-production method and assuming the truck was driven 60,000 miles.

competency enhancement opportunities

- Analyzing Real Company Information
- International Case
- Ethics Case
- Writing Assignment
- The Debate
- Cumulative Spreadsheet Project
- Internet Search

The following additional assignments provide opportunities for students to develop critical thinking, ethical perspectives, oral and written communication skills, experience with electronic research, and teamwork through group and business activities.

ANALYZING REAL COMPANY INFORMATION

• *Analyzing 9-1 (Microsoft)*

Using MICROSOFT's 1999 annual report contained in Appendix A, answer the following questions:

1. As a percentage of total assets, is Microsoft's investment in property, plant, and equipment increasing or decreasing over time? Which of Microsoft's assets is increasing the fastest as a percentage of total assets? What does that indicate Microsoft is doing?
2. Reference the notes to the financial statements. Which depreciation method does Microsoft use? Estimate the average useful life of Microsoft's depreciable assets (i.e., not including land) by dividing the ending balance in the depreciable asset accounts by the depreciation expense for the year. Does the resulting estimated useful life seem reasonable?
3. Microsoft notes in its statement of cash flows that $583 million of property, plant, and equipment was purchased in 1999. Using that information along with the detailed information from the notes, compute (a) the original cost of the equipment disposed of during 1999 and (b) the accumulated depreciation associated with that equipment. (HINT: For property, plant, and equipment, beginning balance + purchases − disposals = ending balance; a similar calculation is used for accumulated depreciation.)

• *Analyzing 9-2 (FedEx)*

FEDEX delivers packages around the world. To accomplish this task, FedEx has made huge investments in long-term assets.

1. Identify what you consider to be the major long-term assets of FedEx. Review the information shown at the top of the next page from FedEx's balance sheet (numbers are in thousands) to see how well you did.

	2000	1999
Property and Equipment, at Cost (Notes 1, 3, 4 and 12):		
Flight equipment	**$ 4,960,204**	$ 4,556,747
Package handling and ground support equipment	**3,430,316**	3,193,620
Computer and electronic equipment	**2,088,510**	2,114,492
Other	**2,479,540**	2,332,227
	$12,958,570	$12,197,086
Less accumulated depreciation and amortization	**6,846,647**	6,454,579
Net property and equipment	**$ 6,111,923**	$ 5,742,507

2. FedEx uses the straight-line depreciation method in depreciating most of its assets. For each major category—flight equipment, package handling and ground support equipment (mainly trucks and buildings), and computer and electronic equipment—provide an estimate (or a range) as to what you would deem a reasonable useful life for each category.
3. Using the information above, compute the accumulated depreciation associated with the property and equipment sold during 2000 given that depreciation for the year was $997,735,000.
4. FedEx reports a balance of $328 million in its goodwill account at the end of 2000. In the notes to its annual report, the company reported amortization for the period of $11.7 million. Given that the company uses the straight-line method for amortizing its intangible assets, compute the approximate number of years left for amortizing goodwill.

• ***Analyzing 9-3 (U.S. Steel)***

1. U.S. STEEL provides the following information in the notes to its financial statements relating to its use of the straight-line method of depreciation. Can you interpret the information contained in the note?

> *Long-lived assets*—Depreciation is generally computed using a modified straight-line method based upon estimated lives of assets and production levels. The modification factors range from a minimum of 85% at a production level below 81% of capability, to a maximum of 105% for a 100% production level. No modification is made at the 95% production level, considered the normal long-range level.

2. U.S. Steel also provides information relating to the balances in its individual property, plant and equipment accounts, as shown at the top of the next page. In very general terms, how old is the company's property, plant, and equipment? Provide support for your answer.

18. Property, Plant and Equipment

(In millions)	December 31 1999	1998
Land and depletable property	$ 152	$ 151
Buildings	484	469
Machinery and equipment	8,007	7,711
Leased assets	105	108
Total	$8,748	$8,439
Less accumulated depreciation, depletion and amortization	6,232	5,939
Net	$2,516	$2,500

INTERNATIONAL CASE

International

• *Cadbury Schweppes*

CADBURY SCHWEPPES is a company based in the United Kingdom. You can probably guess some of the company's products from its name. The company produces Cadbury chocolates and Schweppes tonic water, among other things. But the company also owns the brands Dr. Pepper, A&W, 7 Up, and Crush. The company licenses these brands to distributors around the world.

Although most accounting rules in the United Kingdom are similar to those used in the United States, there are some differences. For example, companies in the United Kingdom are allowed to revalue their property, plant, and equipment upward based on the appraisals of experts. Cadbury Schweppes notes in its 1996 annual report that assets are revalued every five years and that, "The Group properties were professionally revalued at 30 September 1995." Information contained in the company's notes indicates that the company's land and buildings had an appraised value of 392 million British pounds and a book value of 314 million British pounds.

1. Can you compose the journal entry made by Cadbury Schweppes accountants to write the assets up in value? What would be the credit portion of the journal entry? (HINT: Although you may not know the exact answer, think about it and make an educated guess. Would the credit be to another asset account? Would it be to a liability account?)
2. Suppose that in the next year, the assets were again revalued and it was determined that a difference existed between market value and book value of only 70 million British pounds. How would this year's journal entry differ from the previous year's?

ETHICS CASE

• *Strategic Accounting Method Choices*

You saw in Chapter 6 that a company's management selects the percentage to be used when computing bad debt expense. You noted in Chapter 7 that management is allowed to choose the method for valuing inventory. In this chapter you found that management gets to choose the method used for depreciating assets, the estimated salvage value, and the estimated useful life.

Suppose that you are involved in negotiations with the local labor union regarding wages for your company's employees. Labor leaders are asking that their members be given an average annual raise of 12%. The company president has asked you to prepare a set of financial statements that portrays the company's performance as being mediocre at best. The president also makes it clear that she does not want you to prepare fraudulent financial statements. All estimates must be within the bounds of reason.

So you come up with the following:

- Change the percentage used for estimating bad debts from 1.5% to 2%.
- Elect to use the LIFO method for valuing inventory because the prices associated with inventory have been rising.
- Change the average estimated salvage value of long-term assets from 15% to 10% of historical cost.
- Change the depreciation method from straight-line to an accelerated method.
- Change the average estimated useful life of long-term assets from 10 years to 7 years.

As you know, each of these changes will result in net income being lower. Each of these changes is also still within the bounds of reason required by the company president.

1. Would it be appropriate to make the changes described above in order to obtain favorable terms from the labor union negotiators?
2. If the above changes are made, what sort of disclosure do you think should be required?

WRITING ASSIGNMENT

• *Gains Are Good, Losses Are Bad—Right?*

When a long-term asset is sold for more than its book value, we record a gain. When a long-term asset is sold for less than its book value, we record a loss.

Your assignment is to write a two-page memo addressing the following questions:

1. What factors affect a long-term asset's book value?
2. What factors affect a long-term asset's fair value?
3. Should financial statement users expect an asset's book value to equal its fair value?
4. In the case of an asset sold for a loss, if we knew when we purchased the asset what we know at the point of sale, how would depreciation expense have differed if our objective was to ensure that book value equaled fair value when the asset was sold?
5. Is recognizing a loss on the sale of a long-term asset a bad thing? Is a gain good?

THE DEBATE

• *Depreciating an Asset with an Increasing Value*

Paul Didericksen owns and operates a limousine service. He purchases luxury cars and hires drivers to transport people from place to place. Last year, Paul expanded his operations by renting out luxury vehicles on a daily basis for such events as weddings, proms, etc. One car Paul purchased for rental is a 1957 FORD Thunderbird. He paid $45,000 for the car and rents it for $250 per day.

Paul's accountant recently provided financial information indicating that the Thunderbird has a book value of $36,000. Paul questions this figure because he recently received an offer of $53,000 for the Thunderbird. Paul thinks that the car should not be depreciated because its value is increasing. In fact, Paul argues that the asset should be written up in value rather than down.

Divide your group into two teams and prepare to represent the following positions:

- The first team supports the position that the Thunderbird should be depreciated because it is used in generating revenues. You are also to provide support against writing the asset up to its fair market value.
- The second team argues that the Thunderbird should not be depreciated because its value is increasing rather than decreasing. Also, your group is to argue that the car should be written up to its fair value on the company's books.

CUMULATIVE SPREADSHEET PROJECT

This spreadsheet project is a continuation of the spreadsheet projects in earlier chapters. If you completed those spreadsheets, you have a head start on this one.

1. Handyman wishes to prepare a forecasted balance sheet and income statement for 2004. Use the original financial statement numbers for 2003 [given in part (1) of the Cumulative Spreadsheet Project assignment in Chapter 2] as the basis for the forecast, along with the following additional information:
   a. Sales in 2004 are expected to increase by 40% over 2003 sales of $700.
   b. Cash will increase at the same rate as sales.
   c. The forecasted amount of accounts receivable in 2004 is determined using the forecasted value for the average collection period. For simplicity, do the computations using the end-of-period accounts receivable balance instead of the average balance. The average collection period for 2004 is expected to be 14.08 days.
   d. The forecasted amount of inventory in 2004 is determined using the forecasted value for the number of days' sales in inventory (computed using the end-of-period inventory balance). The number of days' sales in inventory for 2004 is expected to be 107.6 days.
   e. The forecasted amount of accounts payable in 2004 is determined using the forecasted value for the number of days' purchases in accounts payable (computed using the end-of-period accounts payable balance). The number of days' purchases in accounts payable for 2004 is expected to be 48.34 days.
   f. The $160 in operating expenses reported in 2003 breaks down as follows: $5 depreciation expense, $155 other operating expenses.
   g. No new long-term debt will be acquired in 2004.
   h. No cash dividends will be paid in 2004.
   i. New short-term loans payable will be acquired in an amount sufficient to make Handyman's current ratio in 2004 exactly equal to 2.0.

   Note: These statements were constructed as part of the spreadsheet assignment in Chapter 7; you can use that spreadsheet as a starting point if you have completed that assignment. *Clearly state any additional assumptions that you make.*

   For this exercise, add the following additional assumptions:

   j. The forecasted amount of property, plant, and equipment (PP&E) in 2004 is determined using the forecasted value for the fixed asset turnover ratio. For simplicity, compute the fixed asset turnover ratio using the end-of-period *gross* PP&E balance. The fixed asset turnover ratio for 2004 is expected to be 3.518 times.

k. In computing depreciation expense for 2004, use straight-line depreciation and assume a 30-year useful life with no residual value. Gross PP&E acquired during the year is only depreciated for half the year. In other words, depreciation expense for 2004 is the sum of two parts: (1) a full year of depreciation on the beginning balance in PP&E, assuming a 30-year life and no residual value, and (2) a half-year of depreciation on any new PP&E acquired during the year, based on the change in the Gross PP&E balance.

Clearly state any additional assumptions that you make.

2. Repeat (1), with the following changes in assumptions:
   a. Fixed asset turnover ratio is expected to be 6.000 times.
   b. Fixed asset turnover ratio is expected to be 2.000 times.
3. Comment on the differences in the forecasted values of the following items in 2004 under each of the following assumptions about the fixed asset turnover ratio: 3.518 times, 6.000 times, and 2.000 times:
   a. Property, plant, and equipment.
   b. Depreciation expense.
   c. Income tax expense.
   d. Paid-in capital.
4. Return the fixed asset turnover ratio to 3.518 times. Now, repeat (1), with the following changes in assumptions:
   a. Estimated useful life is expected to be 15 years.
   b. Estimated useful life is expected to be 60 years.
5. Comment on the differences in the forecasted values of the following items in 2004 under each of the following assumptions about the estimated useful life of property, plant, and equipment: 30 years, 15 years, and 60 years.
   a. Depreciation expense.
   b. Income tax expense.

INTERNET SEARCH

• General Electric

We began this chapter with a review of the history of **GENERAL ELECTRIC**. Let's go to GE's Web site at **http://www.ge.com** and learn a little more about the company and its financial position. Sometimes Web addresses change, so if this address doesn't work, access the Web site for this textbook (**http://albrecht.swcollege.com**) for an updated link to GE.

Once you have gained access to General Electric's Web site, answer the following questions:

1. General Electric was formed in 1892 and constructed the nation's first industrial research laboratory In 1900. Can you identify where this laboratory was located?
2. Locate the company's most recent balance sheet. What percentage of total assets does property, plant, and equipment represent for General Electric? Is that percentage increasing, decreasing, or remaining constant?
3. Access the notes to the financial statements. What depreciation method does General Electric use for most of its manufacturing plant and equipment?
4. Find the note relating specifically to property, plant, and equipment. What types of property, plant, and equipment does General Electric own? Is GE involved strictly in producing light bulbs?

Long-Term Debt Financing

chapter

f10

learning objectives After studying this chapter, you should be able to:

1 Use present value concepts to measure long-term liabilities.

2 Account for long-term liabilities, including notes payable and mortgages payable.

3 Account for capital lease obligations and understand the significance of operating leases being excluded from the balance sheet.

4 Account for bonds, including the original issuance, the payment of interest, and the retirement of bonds.

5 Use debt-related financial ratios to determine the degree of a company's financial leverage and its ability to repay loans.

expanded material

6 Amortize bond discounts and bond premiums using either the straight-line method or the effective-interest method.

setting the stage

In 1923, two brothers, Walt and Roy Disney, founded the **DISNEY BROTHERS STUDIO** as a partnership to produce animated features for film. Five years later, the Disney Brothers Studio released its first animated film with sound effects and dialogue, *Steamboat Willie*, featuring a soon-to-become-famous mouse, Mickey. Pluto was introduced to American audiences in 1930, and Goofy was created just two years later. Walt Disney earned his first Academy Award in 1932 with the release of *Flowers and Trees*, the first full-color animated film. Donald Duck appeared on the scene in 1934, and in 1937 *Snow White and the Seven Dwarfs* was released, accompanied by the first comprehensive merchandising campaign.

But Walt Disney's vision encompassed more than animated films. In 1952, Disney began designing and creating Disneyland, which opened on July 17, 1955. Beginning in the late 1950s, the television shows *Disneyland* (which ran for 29 seasons under various names) and *The Mickey Mouse Club* were also successful Disney ventures. Though Walt Disney passed away in 1966, his influence is still felt around the world. We have Walt Disney World in Florida and Disneylands in Anaheim, California; Paris; and Tokyo. In November 2000, Disney was even scheduled to open an indoor theme park, DisneyQuest, in Chicago.

Disney's company has expanded far beyond what even he could have foreseen. **THE WALT DISNEY COMPANY** is now involved in television and radio stations; international film distribution; home video production; live theatrical entertainment; online computer programs; interactive computer games; telephone company partnerships; cruise lines; Disney Stores; newspaper, magazine, and book publishing; Internet marketing; and the convention business. In the past decade, The Walt Disney Company has grown over 600%. How has the company financed this growth? In part through very successful operations, but these have not been enough. The company has also borrowed to finance its expansion. As of September 30, 1999, The Walt Disney Company had long-term debt totaling over $9 billion. This long-term financing includes lines of credits with U.S. banks as well as loans denominated (or made) in Japanese yen and Italian lira. The effective interest rates on Disney's loans range from 2.7 to 6.4%.[1]

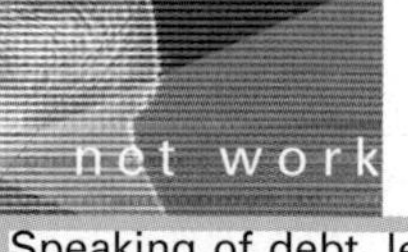

Speaking of debt, let's take a look at our government's debt situation. To see what the national debt is to the penny, go to **http://www.publicdebt.treas.gov/opd/opd.htm**. What was the national debt 100 years ago? 200 years ago?

How does the market determine the appropriate rate of interest that Disney, or any company, must pay when it borrows money? What factors affect interest rates, and how do interest rate changes influence the value of a liability? What other types of liabilities are affected by interest rates? In this chapter, we will introduce various types of long-term liabilities. We will explain a concept used in measuring the present value of an obligation due in the future. This concept—the time value of money—is useful for computing the value of bonds and notes, as in the Disney example, as well as for computing mortgage payments and pension obligations. In the main part of this chapter, we discuss the measurement of long-term liabilities and introduce numerous types of long-term liabilities—notes, mortgages, leases, and bonds. The basic accounting procedures associated with several of these liabilities are also discussed. In the expanded material, the complexities associated with the amortization of a bond issued at a premium or discount are discussed. Exhibit 10-1 highlights the financial statement accounts discussed in this chapter.

MEASURING LONG-TERM LIABILITIES

1

Use present value concepts to measure long-term liabilities.

Conceptually, the value of a liability is the cash that would be required to pay the liability in full today. Because money has a time value, most people are willing to accept less money today than they would if a liability were paid in the future. Therefore, with the exception of Accounts Payable, liabilities to be paid in the future usually involve interest.

1 The information for this scenario was obtained from Disney's Web site at **http://www.disney.com**.

exhibit 10-1 Financial Statement Items Discussed in This Chapter

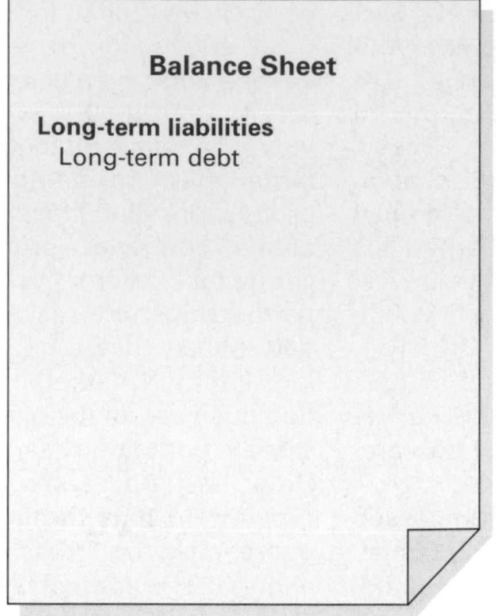

Statement of Cash Flows

Operating activities
Payments for interest
Financing activities
Proceeds from borrowing
Repayments of borrowing

Income Statement

Other revenues and expenses
Interest expense

long-term liabilities Debts or other obligations that will not be paid within one year.

Accounting for **long-term liabilities** is complex because usually payments of interest, or in some cases principal and interest, are made periodically over the period in which the liability is outstanding. Further, in some cases the amount of the liability in a noncash transaction may not be readily apparent. The time value of money concept is used in measuring and recording these liabilities.

Present Value and Future Value Concepts

present value of $1 The value today of $1 to be received or paid at some future date, given a specified interest rate.

The concepts of present value and future value are used to measure the effect of time on the value of money. To illustrate, if you are to receive $100 one year from today, is it worth $100 today? Obviously not, because if you had the $100 today you could either use it now or invest it and earn interest. If the $100 isn't to be received for one year, those options are not available. The **present value of $1** is the value today of $1 to be received or paid in the future, given a specified interest rate. To determine the value today of money to be received or paid in the future, we must "discount" the future amount (reduce the amount to its present value) by an appropriate interest rate. For example, if money can earn 10% per year, $100 to be received one year from now is approximately equal to $90.91 received today.

Putting it another way, if $90.91 is invested today in an account that earns 10% interest for one year, the interest earned will be $9.09 ($90.91 × 10% × 1 year = $9.09). The sum of the $90.91 principal and the $9.09 interest will equal $100 at the end of one year. Thus, the present value of $100 to be received (or paid) in one year with 10% interest is $90.91. This present value relationship can be diagrammed as follows:

Present Value (Computed)		Future Amount (Known)
$90.91	(One-Year Period @ 10%)	$100

$90.91 is the present value of the $100 future amount.

The relationships in this diagram can be described in two ways. We have just seen that the $90.91 is the present value of $100 to be received one year from now when interest is 10%. In this example, the $100 to be received one year from now is known, and the present value of $90.91 must be computed. We are computing a present value amount from a known future value amount.

Another way to look at the relationship is on a future value basis. Future values apply when the amount today ($90.91) is known, and the future amount must be calculated. Future values are exactly the opposite of present values. Thinking in terms of future values, $100 is the future amount we can expect to receive in one year, given a present known amount of $90.91 when the interest rate is 10%. We can diagram this relationship as follows:

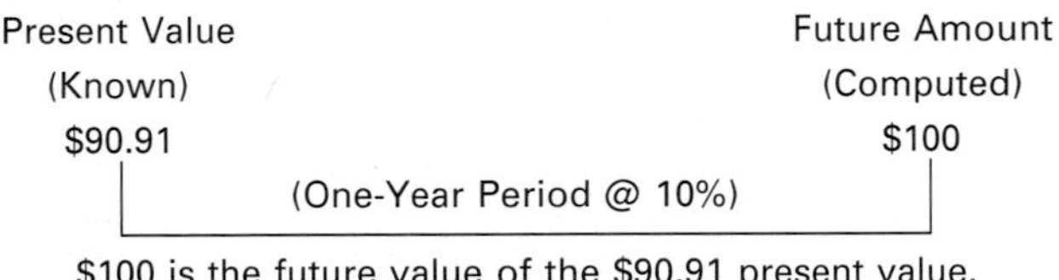

$100 is the future value of the $90.91 present value.

Present and future values can be calculated using formulas. If more than one period is involved, however, the formula is exponential, and the calculations become rather complicated. Therefore, it is more convenient to use either a present value table or a calculator that gives the present value of $1 for various numbers of periods and interest rates (see Table I, page 483) or a future value table that gives the future value of $1 for various numbers of periods and interest rates (see Table III, page 485). We will illustrate the use of both a present value table and a future value table as well as the keystrokes needed when using a standard business calculator.

COMPUTING THE PRESENT VALUE OF A SINGLE AMOUNT To use a present value table, you simply locate the appropriate number of periods in the leftmost column and the interest rate in the row at the top of the table. The intersection of the row and column is the factor representing the present value of $1 for the number of periods and the relevant interest rate. To find the present value of an amount other than $1, multiply the factor in the table by that amount.

To illustrate the use of a present value table (Table I) to find the present value of a known future amount, assume that $10,000 is to be paid four years from today when the interest rate is 10%. What is the present value of the $10,000 payment?

Amount of payment	$10,000
Present value factor of $1 to be paid in 4 periods at 10% interest (from Table I)	× 0.6830
Present value of payment	$ 6,830

This present value amount, $6,830, is the amount that could be paid today to satisfy the obligation that is due four years from now. As indicated, this procedure is sometimes referred to as "discounting." Thus, we say that $10,000 discounted for four years at 10% is $6,830. Stated another way, if $6,830 is invested today in an account that pays 10% interest, in four years the balance in that account will be $10,000.

Another way to compute this same amount is to use a business calculator. The keystrokes described below are for a Hewlett-Packard 10B business calculator; similar keystrokes are used with other business calculators. To compute the present value of $10,000 to be received four years from today, with a prevailing interest rate of 10%, make the following keystrokes:

Hewlett-Packard Keystrokes:

a. Always **CLEAR ALL** before doing anything else. With a Hewlett-Packard 10B, one does this by pressing the yellow key, then pressing "Input." This has the effect of clearing out any information left over from a prior computation.

b. Always set **P/YR** (payments per year) to the correct number—"1" in this case. With a Hewlett-Packard 10B, one does this by pressing "1," then pressing the yellow key, then pressing "PMT." This has the effect of telling the calculator that each year is being viewed as a separate period. As described later in this chapter, interest can be compounded over different periods, such as monthly, quarterly, daily, or even continuously. Setting **P/YR** equal to 1 means that the interest rate is compounded annually. Sometimes, the default for this amount is "12" because the calculator is set to compute monthly payments. Until you are comfortable using your calculator, your best strategy is to set this amount to "1" to avoid having the calculator doing too many mysterious things automatically.

1. 10,000 Press **FV**.
2. 4 Press **N**.
3. 10 Press **I/YR**.
4. Press **PV** for the answer of $6,830.13.

COMPUTING THE FUTURE VALUE OF A SINGLE AMOUNT To find the future value of an amount that is known today, use a future value table. When using a future value table, simply locate the appropriate number of periods in the leftmost column and the interest rate in the row at the top of the table. The intersection of the row and column is the factor representing the future value of $1 for the number of periods and the relevant interest rate. To find the future value of an amount other than $1, multiply the factor in the table by that amount.

To illustrate the use of a future value table (Table III), we will use the same information as before, except that we will now assume that the present value of $6,830 is known, not the future amount of $10,000. Assume that we have a savings account with a current balance of $6,830 that earns interest of 10%. What will be the balance in that account in four years?

Present value in savings account	$ 6,830*
Future value factor of $1 in 4 periods at 10% interest (from Table III)	× 1.4641*
Future value	$10,000*

*Rounded; other calculations in chapter will also be rounded.

Hewlett-Packard Keystrokes:

a. **CLEAR ALL.**
b. Set **P/YR** to 1.

1. 6,830 Press **PV**.
2. 4 Press **N**.
3. 10 Press **I/YR**.
4. Press **FV** for the answer of $9,999.80.

When computing future values, we often use the term *compounding* to mean the frequency with which interest is added to the principal. Thus, we say that interest of 10% has been compounded once a year (annually) to arrive at a future value at the end of four years of $10,000. If the interest is added more or less frequently than once a year, the future amount will be different.

compounding period The period of time for which interest is computed.

The preceding example assumed an annual **compounding period** for interest. If the 10% interest had been compounded semiannually (twice a year) for four years, the calculation would have used a 5% (one-half of the 10%) rate for eight periods (4 years × 2 periods per year) instead of 10% for four periods. To illustrate, what is the present value of $10,000 to be paid in four years if interest of 10% is compounded semiannually?

Amount of payment	$10,000
Present value factor of $1 to be paid in 8 periods	
at 5% interest (from Table I)	× 0.6768
Present value of payment	$ 6,768

Thus, the present value of $10,000 to be paid in four years is $6,768 if interest is compounded semiannually. Likewise, if semiannual compounding is used to determine the future value of $6,768 in four years at 10% compounded semiannually, the result is as follows:

Present value in savings account	$ 6,768
Future value factor of $1 in 8 periods	
at 5% interest (from Table III)	× 1.4775
Future value	$10,000

Note that the present value ($6,768) is lower with semiannual compounding than with annual compounding ($6,830). The more frequently interest is compounded, the greater the total amount of interest deducted (in computing present values) or added (in computing future values).

For practice using semiannual compounding with a business calculator, try the following set of keystrokes:

Hewlett-Packard Keystrokes:

a. CLEAR ALL.
b. Set **P/YR** to 1. There is a simple way to tell the calculator to automatically compute the impact of semiannual compounding. Look in your calculator instruction book if you are interested in knowing how to do this. Alternatively, you can do some of the calculations yourself (divide the interest rate by two and double the number of periods) and use the keystrokes below.

1. 6,768 Press **PV**.
2. 8 Press **N**.
3. 5 Press **I/YR**.
4. Press **FV** for the answer of $9,999.72.

STOP & THINK Without referencing the present value tables, answer these questions: As interest rates increase, would you expect the present value factors to increase or decrease? Why?

Because interest may also be compounded quarterly, monthly, or for some other period, you should learn the relationship of interest to the compounding period. Semiannual interest means that you double the interest periods and halve the annual interest rate; with quarterly interest, you quadruple the periods and take one-fourth of the annual interest rate. The formula for interest rate is:

$$\frac{\text{Yearly interest rate}}{\text{Compounding periods per year}} = \text{Interest rate per compounding period}$$

The number of interest periods is simply the number of periods per year times the number of years. That formula is:

$$\text{Compounding periods per year} \times \text{Number of years} = \text{Number of interest periods}$$

Computing the Present Value of an Annuity

In discussing present values and future values, we have assumed only a single present value or future value with one of the amounts known and the other to be computed. With liabilities, we generally know the future amount that must be paid and would like to compute the present value of that future payment. Because this chapter focuses on liabilities, we will concentrate on present value calculations.

annuity A series of equal amounts to be received or paid at the end of equal time intervals.

present value of an annuity The value today of a series of equally spaced, equal-amount payments to be made or received in the future given a specified interest rate.

Many long-term liabilities involve a series of payments rather than one lump-sum payment. For example, a company might purchase equipment under an installment agreement requiring payments of $5,000 each year for five years. Determining the value today (present value) of a series of equally spaced, equal-amount payments (called an **annuity**) is more complicated than determining the present value of a single future payment. If you were to try to calculate the **present value of an annuity** by hand, you would have to discount the first payment for one period, the second payment for two periods, and so on, and then add all the present values together. Because such calculations are time-consuming, a table is generally used (see Table II, page 484). The factors in the table are the sums of the individual present values of all future payments. Based on the present value of an annuity of $1, the table provides factors for various interest rates and number of payments.

caution

Use care when referencing the present value and future value tables. You can do all your computations correctly, but if you pull the factor from the wrong table, your answer will be wrong.

To illustrate the use of a present value of an annuity table (Table II), we will assume that $10,000 is to be paid at the end of each of the next 10 years. This series of payments is illustrated below:

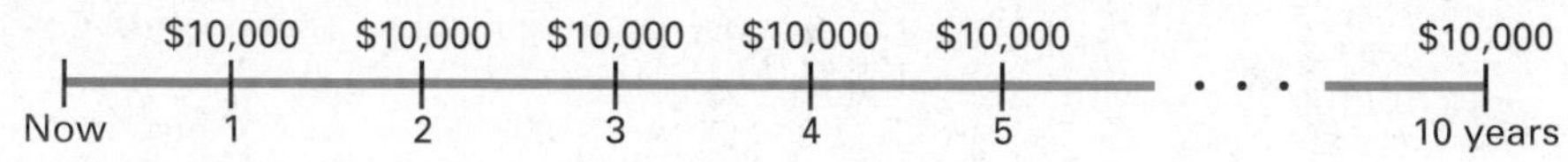

If the interest rate is 12% compounded annually, Table II shows a present value factor of 5.6502. This factor means that the present value of $1 paid each year for 10 years discounted at 12% is approximately $5.65. Applying this factor to payments of $10,000 results in the following:

Amount of the annual payment	$10,000
Present value factor of an annuity of $1 discounted for 10 payments at 12%	× 5.6502
Present value	$56,502

fyi

The underlying mathematical formula for computing the present value of an annuity is actually an elegant simplification of a long series of present value formulas, one for each payment. Unfortunately, it is beyond the scope of this text to illustrate how this annuity formula can be derived as the difference between two infinite sums.

This amount, $56,502, is the amount (present value) that could be paid today to satisfy the obligation if the interest rate is 12%.

The present value of an annuity can also be computed with a business calculator as follows:

Hewlett-Packard Keystrokes:

a. CLEAR ALL.
b. Set **P/YR** to 1.

1. 10,000 Press **PMT**.
2. 10 Press **N**.
3. 12 Press **I/YR**.
4. Press **PV** for the answer of $56,502.23.

COMPUTING PERIODIC PAYMENTS With some modifications, the same calculations used to compute the present value of an annuity can be used to compute the proper amount of a periodic loan payment. For example, consider the task of computing the appropriate monthly payment on an automobile loan of $20,000 if the interest rate is 12% compounded monthly (i.e., 1% per month) and the loan period is 60 months. This problem can be viewed as follows:

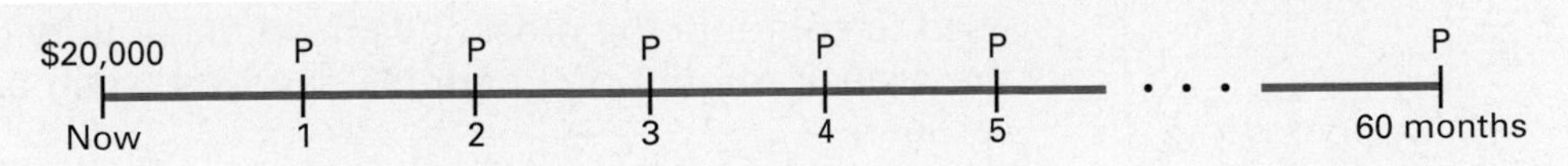

In this case, we know the present value of the annuity—it is $20,000, or the amount we would have to pay today to pay off the entire loan. What we want to know is what series of 60 payments (P in the diagram) has a present value exactly equal to the $20,000 that we owe. The calculation of the payment amount can be set up as follows:

Amount of the annual payment	Payment
Present value factor of an annuity of $1	
discounted for 60 payments at 1%	× 44.9550
Present value.	$20,000

In equation format, this can be written as follows:

$$\$20{,}000 = \text{Payment} \times 44.9550$$

$$\text{Payment} = \$20{,}000/44.9550$$

$$\text{Payment} = \$444.89$$

In other words, paying $444.89 per month for 60 months is the same as paying $20,000 right now, if the interest rate on borrowed money is 12% compounded monthly (1% per month).

This payment amount can also be computed with a business calculator as follows:

Hewlett-Packard Keystrokes:

a. **CLEAR ALL.**
b. Set **P/YR** to 1.

1. 20,000 Press **PV**.
2. 60 Press **N**.
3. 1 Press **I/YR**.
4. Press **PMT** for the answer of $444.88895.

---

to summarize

Long-term liabilities are debts or other obligations that will not be paid or satisfied within one year. Present value concepts, which equate the value of money received or paid in different periods, are used to measure long-term liabilities. Although present values can be computed using formulas, it is usually more convenient to use a table, such as Table I or II on pages 483–484, or a business calculator. If a future lump-sum payment is involved, Table I can be used to determine the present value. Table II is used to compute the present value of an annuity, which is a series of equally spaced, equal-amount payments. To determine the value of an amount at some point in the future, future value tables can be used. Tables III and IV allow one to compute the future value of a lump sum or an annuity, respectively. In calculating present and future values, you must consider the compounding period and the interest rate. For other than annual payments, the number of periods used is the number of periods per year times the number of years; the interest rate used is the annual rate divided by the number of periods per year. The same type of computations used to compute the present value of an annuity can also be used to compute the proper amount of a periodic payment, such as the monthly payment on a car loan.

2

Account for long-term liabilities, including notes payable and mortgages payable.

ACCOUNTING FOR LONG-TERM LIABILITIES

Now that we have explained how present value concepts are applied in measuring long-term liabilities, we are ready to discuss the accounting for those liabilities. The time line in Exhibit 10-2 illustrates the business events associated with long-term liabilities.

A company's first decision is to determine the type of long-term financing to use. In this chapter we will discuss four different types of financing: notes payable, mortgages payable, leasing, and bonds. There are advantages and disadvantages to each type of financing. For example, bonds (which are sold in $1,000 increments) allow a company to borrow a little bit of money from a lot of different people, whereas notes involve borrowing a lot of money from one lender (or perhaps a consortium of lenders). The benefit of a mortgage is typically a lower interest rate because the property being purchased is used as collateral on the loan, thereby providing the lender with less risk. Leases have the advantage of typically requiring a lower down payment as there are no risks associated with product obsolescence. (At the end of many leases, the asset being leased is returned to the owner.) Once the pros and cons of the various types of financing are analyzed, and the company selects an option, the accounting differs, depending upon the type of financing chosen. In this section, we will discuss the recording of long-term debt, including notes payable and mortgages payable.

Interest-Bearing Notes

To illustrate the accounting for a long-term interest-bearing note payable, assume that on January 1, 2003, Giraffe Company borrowed $10,000 from City Bank for three years at 10% interest. Assume also that interest is payable annually on December 31. The entries to account for the note are:

exhibit 10-2 Time Line of Business Issues Involved with Long-Term Liabilities

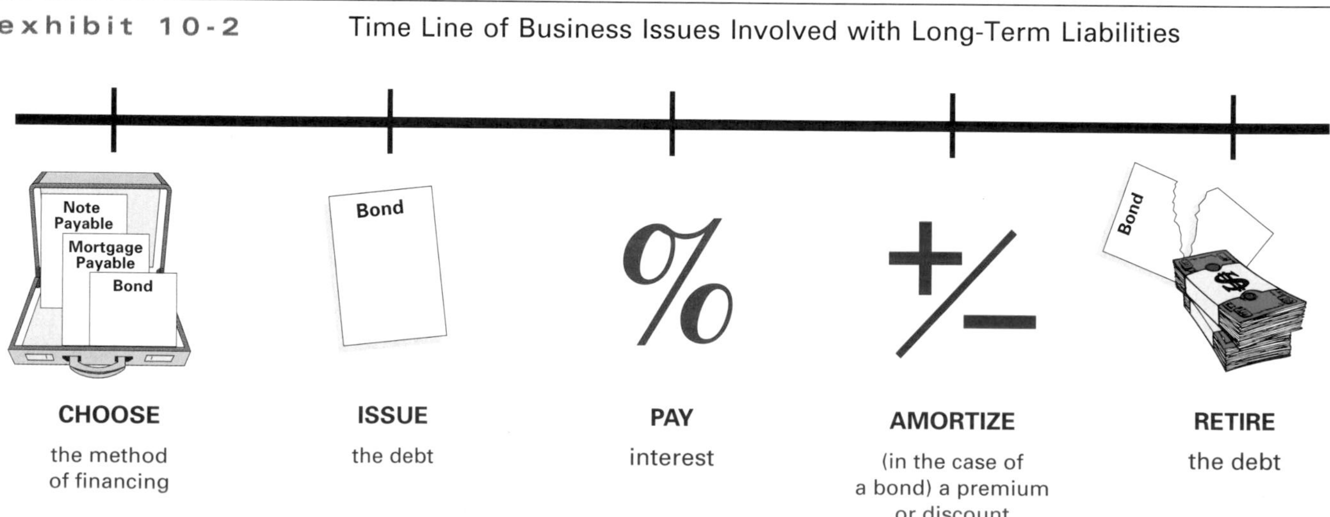

2003			
Jan. 1	Cash	10,000	
	Note Payable		10,000
	Borrowed $10,000 from City Bank for three years.		
Dec. 31	Interest Expense	1,000	
	Cash		1,000
	Made first annual interest payment on City Bank note ($10,000 × 0.10).		
2004			
Dec. 31	Interest Expense	1,000	
	Cash		1,000
	Made second annual interest payment on City Bank note ($10,000 × 0.10).		
2005			
Dec. 31	Interest Expense	1,000	
	Note Payable	10,000	
	Cash		11,000
	Made final interest payment ($10,000 × 0.10) and repaid principal on City Bank note.		

A long-term note such as this three-year note should be recorded in the books at the present value of the future cash payments to be made in connection with the note. If the market interest rate is 10%, then the present value of the cash payments on the note is computed as follows:

Present value of interest payments:		
Amount of each interest payment	$ 1,000	
Table II factor for 3 payments at 10%	× 2.4869	
Present value of annuity		$ 2,487
Present value of principal payment:		
Amount of principal payment	$ 10,000	
Table I factor for 3 periods at 10%	× 0.7513	
Present value of single payment		7,513
Present value of interest and principal		$10,000

fyi

As illustrated later in the chapter in the discussion of accounting for bonds, if the market rate of interest differs from the annual interest rate to be paid on a loan, then the present value of the cash payments will not be the same as the face amount of the loan. For example, if no interest payments were to be made on the note in the example given here, then the present value of the cash flows associated with the note would be just $7,513, which is the present value of the $10,000 payment to be made at the end of three years.

The total present value is the sum of the present values of the interest payments (an annuity) and the single principal payment due in three years. In this case, the present value of the cash payments on the note is exactly equal to the note's face amount of $10,000. This is because the annual interest payments of 10% are equal to the market rate of interest, or the rate of interest that lenders would insist on earning for lending money in exchange for the note.

In the notes to its 1999 financial statements, THE WALT DISNEY COMPANY reported the existence of a variety of notes payable, including notes for which the amounts to be repaid were stated in Japanese yen and Italian lira. In addition, Disney reported the existence of $1.247 billion in "participating" notes; the rate of interest to be paid on these notes depends on the financial performance of the films whose production was financed through the issuance of the notes.

mortgage payable A written promise to pay a stated amount of money at one or more specified future dates; a mortgage is secured by the pledging of certain assets, usually real estate, as collateral.

Mortgages Payable

A **mortgage payable** is similar to a note payable in that it is a written promise to pay a stated sum of money at one or more specified future dates. It differs from a note in the way it is applied. Whereas money borrowed with a note can often be used for any business purpose, mortgage money is usually related to a specific asset, typically real estate. Assets purchased with a

business environment essay

How Interest Rates Affect Mortgage Payments The interest rate on a mortgage is as important as the amount of the loan in determining whether a person can afford a mortgage. This is because the amount of interest paid over an extended period of time will be at least equal to, or even two or three times, the amount of the loan. The table on the next page shows the monthly payments on a $100,000, 25-year mortgage at interest rates from 7 to 14%, as well as the qualifying annual income.

The qualifying annual income is the minimum amount a person must earn to afford the payments at each interest rate. The FEDERAL HOME LOAN MORTGAGE CORPORATION and most lending institutions recommend that the monthly payment not exceed 28% of a person's monthly gross income. If, for example, you earn $30,000 a year, you should pay no more than $700 a month on a mortgage, which would be a $100,000 mortgage at 7% or a $58,000 mortgage at 14%. For this reason, most people "shop around" for the lowest mortgage rates—and even then, many will not qualify for a loan.

To calculate the monthly payments on a smaller or larger mortgage, divide the amount by $100,000, then multiply that percentage by the figure in the table. For example, the monthly payment on a $60,000 mortgage at 9% is $503.40 [($60,000/$100,000) × $839].

mortgage are usually pledged as security or collateral on the loan. Individuals commonly obtain home mortgages, and companies frequently use plant mortgages. In either case, a mortgage generally requires periodic (usually monthly) payments of principal plus interest.

To illustrate the accounting for a mortgage, we will assume that McGiven Automobile Company borrows $100,000 on January 1 to purchase a new showroom and signs a mortgage agreement pledging the showroom as collateral on the loan. If the mortgage is at 8% for 30 years, and the monthly payment is $733.76, payable on January 31 with subsequent payments due at the end of each month thereafter, the entries to record the acquisition of the mortgage and the first monthly payment are:

Jan. 1	Cash	100,000	
	Mortgage Payable		100,000
	Borrowed $100,000 to purchase the automobile showroom.		
Jan. 31	Mortgage Payable	67.09	
	Interest Expense	666.67	
	Cash		733.76
	Made first month's mortgage payment.		

As this entry shows, only $67.09 of the $733.76 payment is applied to reduce the mortgage; the remainder is interest ($100,000 × 0.08 × 1/12). In each successive month, the amount applied to reduce the mortgage will increase slightly until, toward the end of the 30-year mortgage, almost all of the payment will be for principal. A **mortgage amortization schedule** identifies how much of each mortgage payment is interest and how much is principal reduction, as shown in Exhibit 10-3. Note that during the first 20 years of McGiven's $100,000, 8%, 30-year mortgage, more of each mortgage payment is for interest than for principal.

mortgage amortization schedule A schedule that shows the breakdown between interest and principal for each payment over the life of a mortgage.

At the end of each year, a mortgage is reported on the balance sheet in two places: (1) the principal to be paid during the next year is shown as a current liability, and (2) the balance of the mortgage payable is shown as a long-term liability. Further, any accrued interest on the mort-

$100,000, 25-Year Mortgage			
Interest Rate	**Monthly Payment**	**Total Amount Paid**	**Qualifying Annual Income**
7%	$ 707	$212,100	$30,300
8%	772	231,600	33,086
9%	839	251,700	35,957
10%	909	272,700	38,957
11%	980	294,000	42,000
12%	1,053	315,900	45,129
13%	1,128	338,400	48,343
14%	1,204	361,200	51,600

exhibit 10-3 Mortgage Amortization Schedule ($100,000, 30-Year Mortgage at 8%)

		End-of-Year Totals		
Year	**Monthly Payment**	**Principal Paid during Year**	**Interest Paid during Year**	**Outstanding Mortgage Balance**
1	$733.76	$ 835	$7,970	$99,165
2	733.76	905	7,900	98,260
3	733.76	980	7,825	97,280
4	733.76	1,061	7,744	96,219
5	733.76	1,149	7,656	95,070
10	733.76	1,712	7,093	87,725
15	733.76	2,551	6,254	76,783
20	733.76	3,800	5,005	60,080
25	733.76	5,661	3,144	36,793
30	733.76	8,434	371	0

Total payments over life of mortgage: $264,154*
*$733.76 × 360 payments = $264,154.

gage is reported as a current liability, and the interest expense for the year is included with other expenses on the income statement.

to summarize

Long-term interest-bearing notes are obligations that will be repaid over several years. Interest on the note is computed by multiplying the outstanding balance of the note times the rate of interest. Mortgages payable are long-term liabilities that arise when companies borrow money to buy land, construct buildings, or purchase additional operating assets. Mortgages are tied to specific assets. They are amortized over a period of time and involve periodic, usually monthly, payments that include both principal and interest.

3

Account for capital lease obligations and understand the significance of operating leases being excluded from the balance sheet.

ACCOUNTING FOR LEASE OBLIGATIONS

As discussed in Chapter 9, a company may choose to lease rather than purchase an asset. If a lease is a simple, short-term rental agreement, called an operating lease, lease payments are recorded as Rent Expense by the lessee and as Rent Revenue by the lessor. However, if the terms of a lease agreement meet specific criteria (see Chapter 9, page 401), the transaction is classified as a capital lease and is accounted for as if the asset had been purchased with long-term debt. The lessee records the leased property as an asset and recognizes a liability to the lessor.

In Chapter 9, we focused on the recording of assets acquired under capital leases, using assumed amounts for the present value. Here we will explain how the present value of a capital lease is determined. To illustrate the measurement and recording of a capital lease, we will assume that Malone Corporation leases a mainframe computer from Macro Data, Inc., on December 31, 2002. The lease requires annual payments of $10,000 for 10 years, with the first payment due on December 31, 2003.[2] The rate of interest applicable to the lease is 14% compounded annually.

Assuming the lease meets the criteria for a capital lease, Malone Corporation will record the computer and the related liability at the present value of the future lease payments. From Table II, on page 484, the factor for the present value of an annuity for 10 payments at 14% is 5.2161.

A construction company may choose to lease large equipment rather than purchase such an asset.

2 Readers should be aware that the illustration of a capital lease presented here assumes that lease payments are made at the end of each year, with the present values based on an ordinary annuity. Usually, lease payments are made at the beginning of each lease period, which requires present value calculations using the concept of an annuity in advance or "annuity due." These calculations are explained in intermediate accounting texts.

fyi

Many companies structure their lease agreements so as not to meet the lease capitalization criteria. In these cases, the companies must still disclose their expected future lease payments in the notes to the financial statements.

This factor is multiplied by the annual lease payment to determine the present value. The entry to record the lease on Malone's books is:

2002			
Dec. 31	Leased Computer.	52,161	
	Lease Liability		52,161
	Leased a computer from Macro Data, Inc., for $10,000 a year for 10 years discounted at 14% ($10,000 × 5.2161 = $52,161).		

If Malone Corporation uses a calendar year for financial reporting, the December 31, 2003 balance sheet will report the leased asset in the property, plant, and equipment section and the lease liability in the liabilities section.

A schedule of the computer lease payments is presented in Exhibit 10-4. Each year the lease liability account balance is multiplied by 14% to determine the amount of interest included in each of the annual $10,000 lease payments.

exhibit 10-4

Schedule of Computer Lease Payments

Year	Annual Payment	Interest Expense (0.14 × Lease Liability)	Principal	Lease Liability
				$52,161
1	$10,000	(0.14 × $52,161) = $7,303	$2,697	49,464
2	10,000	(0.14 × 49,464) = 6,925	3,075	46,389
3	10,000	(0.14 × 46,389) = 6,494	3,506	42,883
4	10,000	(0.14 × 42,883) = 6,004	3,996	38,887
5	10,000	(0.14 × 38,887) = 5,444	4,556	34,331
6	10,000	(0.14 × 34,331) = 4,806	5,194	29,137
7	10,000	(0.14 × 29,137) = 4,079	5,921	23,216
8	10,000	(0.14 × 23,216) = 3,250	6,750	16,466
9	10,000	(0.14 × 16,466) = 2,305	7,695	8,771
10	10,000	(0.14 × 8,771) = 1,229*	8,771	0

*Rounded.

Note that this is the same procedure used with a mortgage when determining the amount of each payment that is applied to reduce the principal and the amount that is considered interest expense.

The remainder of the payment is a reduction in the liability. For example, the first lease payment is recorded as follows:

2003			
Dec. 31	Interest Expense	7,303	
	Lease Liability	2,697	
	Cash		10,000
	Paid annual lease payment for computer ($52,161 × 0.14 = $7,303; $10,000 − $7,303 = $2,697).		

Similar entries would be made in each of the remaining nine years of the lease, except that the principal payment (reduction in Lease Liability) would increase while the interest expense would decrease. Interest expense decreases over the lease term because a constant rate (14%) is applied to a decreasing principal balance.

Although the asset and liability accounts have the same balance at the beginning of the lease term, they seldom remain the same during the lease period. The asset and the liability are accounted for separately, with the asset being depreciated using one of the methods discussed in Chapter 9.

Operating Leases

When a lease is accounted for as a capital lease, the lease obligation (and an associated leased asset) will appear on the balance sheet of the company using the leased asset. If, on the other hand, a company is able to classify a lease as an operating lease according to the criteria outlined in Chapter 9, *nothing will appear on the balance sheet.* Neither the leased asset nor the lease liability will be recognized. For this reason, an operating lease is often referred to as a form of "off-balance-sheet financing"—the economic obligation associated with the financing arrangement entered into to secure the use of an asset is not reported on the balance sheet.

Because operating leases are not reported on the balance sheet, accounting rules require companies to disclose operating lease details in the financial statement notes so that financial statement users will be aware of these off-balance-sheet obligations. The information from the operating lease note from **DISNEY**'s 1999 financial statements is reproduced below:

The company has various real estate operating leases, including retail outlets for the distribution of consumer products and office space for general and administrative purposes. Future minimum lease payments under these non-cancelable operating leases totaled $2.2 billion at September 30, 1999, payable as follows [in millions]:

2000	$ 297
2001	262
2002	239
2003	216
2004	185
Thereafter	1,019

Recall that the obligation to make this $2.2 billion in operating lease payments is *not* reported as a liability on Disney's balance sheet.

to summarize

A lease is a contract whereby the lessee makes periodic payments to the lessor for the use of an asset. A simple short-term rental agreement, or operating lease, involves only the recording of rent expense by the lessee and rent revenue by the lessor. A capital lease is accounted for as a debt-financed purchase of the leased asset. Both the asset and the liability are initially recorded by the lessee at the present value of the future lease payments discounted at the applicable interest rate. Subsequently, the asset is depreciated and the lease liability is written off as periodic payments are made. Part of each lease payment is interest expense, computed at a constant interest rate, and the remainder is a reduction of the principal amount of the liability. Operating leases are a form of off-balance-sheet financing because the obligation to make future operating lease payments is not recognized as a liability on the balance sheet. Companies are required to disclose the amount of their future operating lease payments in the notes to the financial statements.

4

Account for bonds, including the original issuance, the payment of interest, and the retirement of bonds.

THE NATURE OF BONDS

A **bond** is a contract between the borrowing company (issuer) and the lender (investor) in which the borrower promises to pay a specified amount of interest at the end of each period the bond is outstanding and to repay the principal at the maturity date of the bond contract. Bonds generally have maturity dates exceeding 10 years and, as a result, are another example of a long-term liability.

bond A contract between a borrower and a lender in which the borrower promises to pay a specified rate of interest for each period the bond is outstanding and repay the principal at the maturity date.

debentures (unsecured bonds) Bonds for which no collateral has been pledged.

secured bonds Bonds for which assets have been pledged in order to guarantee repayment.

registered bonds Bonds for which the names and addresses of the bondholders are kept on file by the issuing company.

coupon bonds Unregistered bonds for which owners receive periodic interest payments by clipping a coupon from the bond and sending it to the issuer as evidence of ownership.

term bonds Bonds that mature in one single sum at a specified future date.

serial bonds Bonds that mature in a series of installments at specified future dates.

callable bonds Bonds for which the issuer reserves the right to pay the obligation before its maturity date.

convertible bonds Bonds that can be traded for, or converted to, other securities after a specified period of time.

zero-coupon bonds Bonds issued with no promise of interest payments; only a single payment will be made.

Types of Bonds

Bonds can be categorized on the basis of various characteristics. The following classification system considers three characteristics:

1. The extent to which bondholders are protected.
   a. **Debentures** (or **unsecured bonds**). Bonds that have no underlying assets pledged as security, or collateral, to guarantee their repayment.
   b. **Secured bonds**. Bonds that have a pledge of company assets, such as land or buildings, as a protection for lenders. If the company fails to meet its bond obligations, the pledged assets can be sold and used to pay the bondholders. Bonds that are secured with the issuer's assets are often referred to as "mortgage bonds."
2. How the bond interest is paid.
   a. **Registered bonds**. Bonds for which the issuing company keeps a record of the names and addresses of all bondholders and pays interest only to those whose names are on file.
   b. **Coupon bonds**. Unregistered bonds for which the issuer has no record of current bondholders but instead pays interest to anyone who can show evidence of ownership. Usually, these bonds have a printed coupon for each interest payment. When a payment is due, the bondholder clips the coupon from the certificate and sends it to the issuer as evidence of bond ownership. The issuer then sends an interest payment to the bondholder.
3. How the bonds mature.
   a. **Term bonds**. Bonds that mature in one single sum on a specified future date.
   b. **Serial bonds**. Bonds that mature in a series of installments.
   c. **Callable bonds**. Term or serial bonds that the issuer can redeem at any time at a specified price.
   d. **Convertible bonds**. Term or serial bonds that can be converted to other securities, such as stocks, after a specified period, at the option of the bondholder. (The accounting for this type of bond is discussed in advanced accounting texts.)

Two other types of bonds that are often encountered are zero-coupon bonds and junk bonds. **Zero-coupon bonds** are issued with no promise of interest payments. The company issuing the bonds promises only to repay a fixed amount at the maturity date. While the idea of having to make no interest payments might be initially appealing to the issuer, remember that the present value of the bond is affected by both the single payment at the end of the bond's life and the annuity payment. If this annuity (interest) payment will not be part of the bond, potential buyers will pay much less for the bond. For this reason, zero-coupon bonds are often referred to as *deep-discount bonds.*

Junk bonds are high-risk bonds issued by companies in weak financial condition or with large amounts of debt already outstanding. These bonds typically yield returns of at least 12%, but some may return in excess of 20%. Of course, with these high returns comes greater risk.

Characteristics of Bonds

When an organization issues bonds, it usually sells them to underwriters (brokers and investment bankers), who in turn sell them to various institutions and to the public. At the time of the original sale, the company issuing the bonds chooses a trustee to represent the bondholders. In most cases, the trustee is a large bank or trust company to which the company issuing the bonds delivers a contract called a bond indenture, deed of trust, or trust indenture. The

junk bonds Bonds issued by companies in weak financial condition with large amounts of debt already outstanding; these bonds yield high rates of return because of high risk.

bond indenture A contract between a bond issuer and a bond purchaser that specifies the terms of a bond.

principal (face value or maturity value) The amount that will be paid on a bond at the maturity date.

bond maturity date The date at which a bond principal or face amount becomes payable.

bond indenture specifies that in return for an investment of cash by investors, the company promises to pay a specific amount of interest (based on a specified, or stated, rate of interest) each period the bonds are outstanding and to repay the **principal** (also called **face value** or **maturity value**) of the bonds at a specified future date (the **bond maturity date**). It is the duty of the trustee to protect investors and to make sure that the bond issuer fulfills its responsibilities.

The total value of a single "bond issue" often exceeds several million dollars. A bond issue is generally divided into a number of individual bonds, which may be of varying denominations. The principal, or face value, of each bond is usually $1,000 or a multiple thereof. Note that the price of bonds is quoted as a percentage of $1,000 face value. Thus, a bond quoted at 98 is selling for $980 (98% × $1,000), and a bond quoted at 103 is selling for $1,030 (103% × $1,000). By issuing bonds in small denominations, a company increases the chances that a broad range of investors will be able to compete for the purchase of the bonds. This increased demand usually results in the bonds selling for a higher price.

In most cases, the market price of bonds is influenced by (1) the riskiness of the bonds and (2) the interest rate at which the bonds are issued. The first factor, riskiness of the bonds, is determined by general economic conditions and the financial status of the company selling the bonds, as measured by organizations (MOODY'S or STANDARD AND POOR'S, for instance) that regularly assign a rating, or a grade, to all corporate bonds.

Companies strive to earn as high a bond rating as possible because the higher the rating, the lower the interest rate they will have to pay to attract buyers. For example, using the widely cited Moody's bond rating, an Aaa bond is a bond of the highest quality with the least risk of nonpayment. As of October 2000, bonds with this rating were paying interest of approximately 6.6%. A high-risk bond, on the other hand, will have a low rating, which means the company will have to offer a higher rate of interest to attract buyers. For example, as of October 2000, the bonds of financially troubled CHIQUITA BRANDS (the banana company) were rated B1 by Moody's, a rating indicating that the bonds were "highly speculative." Lenders were requiring an interest rate of more than 30% to induce them to purchase these bonds.

fyi

Another type of bond that has arisen in recent years is the "Yankee bond." A Yankee bond is a bond issued by a non-U.S. company with all bond-related payments made in U.S. dollars. Non-U.S. companies sometimes choose to pay principal and interest on bonds in U.S. dollars because U.S. dollar amounts are associated with less risk of currency exchange fluctuations than are payments in less stable currencies such as Indonesian rupiah. Lower risk means that the company can pay a lower interest rate to lenders.

fyi

Bonds are bought and sold on trading markets just like stocks. The New York Bond Exchange is the largest exchange of this type.

to summarize

Bonds are certificates of debt issued by companies or government agencies, guaranteeing a stated interest rate and repayment of the principal at a specified maturity date. Corporations issue bonds as a form of long-term borrowing to finance the acquisition of operating assets, such as land, buildings, and equipment. Bonds can be classified by their level of security (debentures versus secured bonds), by the way interest is paid (registered versus coupon bonds), and by the way they mature (term bonds, serial bonds, callable bonds, and convertible bonds).

Determining a Bond's Issuance Price

When a company issues bonds, it is generally promising to make two types of payments: (1) a payment of interest of a fixed amount at equal intervals (usually semiannually but sometimes quarterly or annually) over the life of the bond and (2) a single payment—the principal, or face value, of the bond—at the maturity date. For example, assume that Denver Company issues 10%, five-year bonds with a total face value of $800,000. Interest is to be paid semiannually. This information tells us that Denver Company agrees to pay $40,000 ($800,000 × 0.10 × ½ year) in interest every six months and also agrees to pay to the investors the principal amount of $800,000 at the end of five years. The following diagram reflects this agreement between Denver Company and the bond investors:

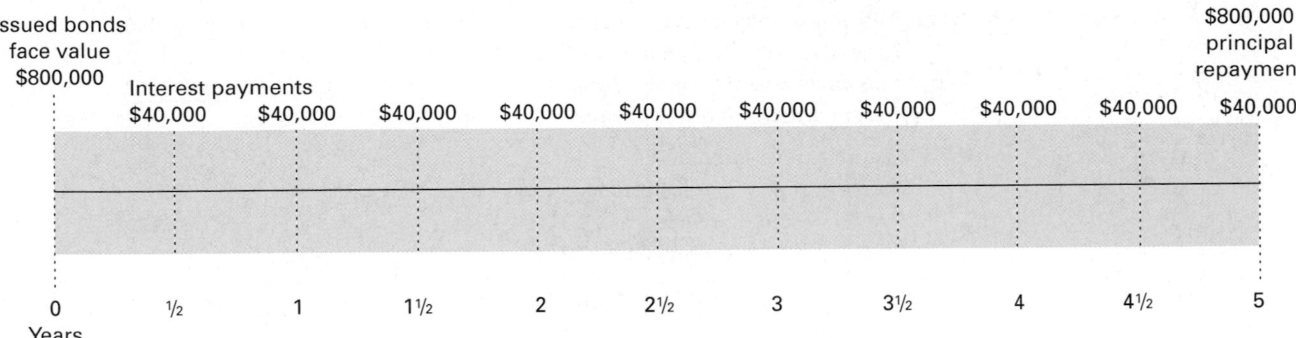

In this example, we assumed that the bonds were issued at their face value of $800,000. However, bonds are frequently issued at a price that is more or less than their face value. The actual price at which bonds are issued is affected by the interest rate investors are seeking at the time the bonds are sold in relation to the interest rate specified by the borrower in the bond indenture. How, then, is the issuance price of bonds determined?

STOP & THINK If the market rate of interest is higher than the rate of interest stated on the bonds, will the bonds sell at a price higher or lower than the face value? Think about the question this way: Is the higher rate more attractive to investors, and if it is, what would investors do as a result?

market rate (effective rate or yield rate) of interest The actual interest rate earned or paid on a bond investment.

stated rate of interest The rate of interest printed on the bond.

bond discount The difference between the face value and the sales price when bonds are sold below their face value.

bond premium The difference between the face value and the sales price when bonds are sold above their face value.

Essentially, present value concepts are used to measure the effect of time on the value of money. The price should equal the present value of the interest payments (an annuity) plus the present value of the bond's face value at maturity. These present values are computed using the **market rate of interest** (also called the **effective rate** or **yield rate**), which is the rate investors expect to earn on their investment. It is contrasted with the **stated rate of interest**, which is the rate printed on the bond (10% in the Denver Company example).

If the effective rate is equal to the stated rate, the bonds will sell at face value (that is, at $800,000). If the effective rate is higher than the stated rate, the bonds will sell at a **bond discount** (at less than the face value) because the investors desire a higher rate than the company is promising to pay. Likewise, if the effective rate is lower than the stated rate, the bonds will sell at a **bond premium** (at more than face value) because the company is promising to pay a higher rate than the market is paying at that time.

Consider the following scenario: If Company A is issuing bonds with a stated rate of 12% and the market rate for similar bonds is 10%, what will happen to the price of Company A's bonds? Investors, eager to receive a 12% return, will bid the price of the bonds up until the price at which the bonds sell yields a 10% return. The amount paid for the bonds over and above the maturity value is the bond premium. If Company A were issuing bonds with a stated rate of 8%, no one would buy the bonds until the price was lowered sufficiently to allow investors to earn a return of 10%. The difference between the selling price and the maturity value would be the amount of the bond discount.

We will use the Denver Company bonds example (from page 470) to explain how the price is computed in each situation.

BONDS ISSUED AT FACE VALUE Denver Company has agreed to issue $800,000 bonds and pay 10% interest, compounded semiannually. Assume that the effective interest rate demanded by investors for bonds of this level of risk is also 10%. Using the effective interest rate, which happens to be the same as the stated rate, the calculation to determine the price at which the bonds will be issued is shown at the top of the next page. (Note that because the interest is compounded semiannually, the interest rate is halved and the five-year bond life is treated as 10 six-month periods.)

The calculation shows why the bonds sell at face value. At the effective rate, the sum of the present value of the interest payments and the payment at maturity is $800,000, which is the issuance price at the stated rate. This equality of present values will occur only when the effective rate and the stated rate are the same.

1.	Semiannual interest payments	$ 40,000	
	Present value of an annuity of 10 payments of $1 at 5% (Table II)	× 7.7217	
	Present value of interest payments		$308,868
2.	Maturity value of bonds	$800,000	
	Present value of $1 received 10 periods in the future discounted at 5% (Table I)	× 0.6139	
	Present value of principal amount		491,132*
3.	Issuance price of bonds (total present value)		$800,000

*Difference is due to the rounding of the present value factor.

The value of the bonds can also be computed using a business calculator as follows:

Hewlett-Packard Keystrokes:

a. CLEAR ALL.
b. Set **P/YR** to 1.

1. 800,000 Press **FV**.
2. 40,000 Press **PMT**.
3. 10 Press **N**.
4. 5 Press **I/YR**.
5. Press **PV** for the answer of $800,000.

BONDS ISSUED AT A DISCOUNT Denver Company will sell its bonds at less than the face value of $800,000 (at a discount) if the stated rate of interest is less than the effective rate that investors are seeking. To illustrate the issuance of bonds at a discount, assume that the effective rate is 12% compounded semiannually; the stated rate remains 10% compounded semiannually. In this case, the bonds will be issued at a price of $741,124, as shown here:

1.	Semiannual interest payments	$40,000	
	Present value of an annuity of 10 payments of $1 at 6% (Table II)	× 7.3601	
	Present value of interest payments		$294,404
2.	Maturity value of bonds	$800,000	
	Present value of $1 received 10 periods in the future discounted at 6% (Table I)	× 0.5584	
	Present value of principal amount		446,720
3.	Issuance price of bonds (total present value)		$741,124

Denver Company will receive less than the $800,000 face value because the stated rate of interest is lower than the effective rate. In this case, there is a discount of $58,876 ($800,000 − $741,124).

The following keystrokes are used to compute the value of the bonds using a business calculator:

caution

The most common mistake made in computing bond values is to use the stated rate of interest in calculating the present value of the cash flows. The stated rate of interest is used *only* to compute the amount of the semiannual interest payments. The present value computations are done using the current market rate of interest.

Hewlett-Packard Keystrokes:

a. CLEAR ALL.
b. Set **P/YR** to 1.

1. 800,000 Press **FV**.
2. 40,000 Press **PMT**.
3. 10 Press **N**.
4. 6 Press **I/YR**.
5. Press **PV** for the answer of $741,119.30. This answer differs slightly from the value computed using the tables because of rounding.

BONDS ISSUED AT A PREMIUM The Denver Company bonds will be issued for more than $800,000 (at a premium) when the stated interest rate is higher than the effective rate. Let us now assume that the effective rate is 8% compounded semiannually and that the stated rate is still 10% compounded semiannually. In this case, the bonds will be issued at $864,916, as shown here:

1.	Interest payments	$ 40,000	
	Present value of an annuity of 10 payments of $1 at 4% (Table II)	× 8.1109	
	Present value of interest payments		$324,436
2.	Maturity value of bonds	$800,000	
	Present value of $1 received 10 periods in the future discounted at 4% (Table I)	× 0.6756	
	Present value of principal amount		540,480
3.	Issuance price of bonds (total present value)		$864,916

Denver Company will receive more than the $800,000 face value when the bonds are issued because the company has agreed to pay the investors a higher rate of interest than the market rate.

The same calculation can be done using a business calculator as follows:

Hewlett-Packard Keystrokes:

a. **CLEAR ALL.**
b. Set **P/YR** to 1.

1. 800,000 Press **FV**.
2. 40,000 Press **PMT**.
3. 10 Press **N**.
4. 4 Press **I/YR**.
5. Press **PV** for the answer of $864,887.17. This answer differs slightly from the value computed using the tables because of rounding.

In all three situations, the 10% stated rate determined the amount of each interest payment. The price of the bonds was determined by discounting the $40,000 of interest payments and the $800,000 face amount at maturity by the effective rate of interest, which may vary from day to day, depending on market conditions. In essence, the issuance price depends on four factors: (1) face value of the bonds, (2) periodic interest payments (face value × stated interest rate), (3) time period, and (4) effective interest rate. Although the bond price is the exact amount that allows investors to earn the interest rate they are seeking, it also reflects the real cost of money to the borrowing company.

Now that you know how to calculate bond values, you may feel ready to move to New York City and become a Wall Street bond trader. Not so fast. There are four steps to computing bond values, as outlined below:

1. Determine the market interest rate.
2. Compute the present value of the maturity amount (using the market interest rate as the discount rate).
3. Compute the present value of the annuity of annual interest payments (using the market interest rate as the discount rate).
4. Add the quantities computed in (2) and (3).

Three of these steps—2, 3, and 4—are very straightforward. These are the steps that you have learned in this chapter. The initial step of determining the market interest rate is where the art and analysis of bond trading are brought to bear. For example, how can you tell whether a company's riskiness requires that the market interest rate on its bonds should be 7.2% or 7.3%? This is an extremely difficult determination to make, and yet it is exactly the type of decision that bond traders must make many times each day.

to summarize

The price at which bonds are issued is a function of the interest rate investors are seeking when the bonds are issued in relation to the interest rate the borrowing company is promising to pay. The bond's face value, or principal, and future interest payments (face value × stated interest rate) are discounted by the interest rate desired by investors (the effective, yield, or market rate) to arrive at the issuance price of the bonds. Bonds will sell at their face value if the stated interest rate is equal to the effective rate. If the effective rate is higher than the stated rate, the bonds will sell at a discount. If the effective rate is lower than the stated rate, the bonds will sell at a premium. The effective rate used to discount the payments promised by the borrower reflects the real cost of the money borrowed.

Accounting for Bonds Payable Issued at Face Value

When a company issues bonds, it must account for the issuance (sale) of the bonds, for the interest payments, and for the amortization of any bond premium or discount. Then, at or before maturity, the company must account for the bond's retirement.

The accounting for these four elements depends on the issuance price of the bonds and on the date of issuance in relation to the date on which interest is paid. In the following sections, we explain the accounting for bonds when the issue price is equal to face value. The accounting for bonds issued at a premium or at a discount is discussed in the expanded material section of the chapter. For most of this discussion, we will use the following data:

Issuing company	Central Trucking Company
Accounting year	Calendar year ending December 31
Face value of bonds issued	$100,000
Stated interest rate	12%
Effective interest rate when issued	12%
Initial date of issuance	January 1, 2003
Date of maturity	January 1, 2013
Interest payment dates	January 1 and July 1

Central Trucking Company issued $100,000 bonds with a stated interest rate of 12% on January 1, 2003. The bonds were issued at face value because 12% is the effective, or market, rate of interest for similar bonds. The journal entry to record their issuance on January 1, 2003, is as follows:

Cash	100,000	
Bonds Payable		100,000
Issued $100,000, 12%, 10-year bonds at face value.		

The entry to record the first payment of interest on July 1, 2003, is:

Bond Interest Expense	6,000	
Cash		6,000
Paid semiannual interest on the $100,000, 12%, 10-year bonds ($100,000 × 0.12 × ½ year).		

Because Central Trucking operates on a calendar-year basis, it will need to make the following adjusting entry on December 31, 2003, to account for the interest expense between July 1 and December 31, 2003:

Bond Interest Expense	6,000	
Bond Interest Payable		6,000
To recognize expense for the six months July 1 to December 31, 2003 ($100,000 × 0.12 × ½ year).		

At the end of the accounting period (December 31, 2003), the financial statements will report the following:

Income Statement	
Bond interest expense ($6,000 × 2)	$ 12,000
Balance Sheet	
Current liabilities:	
Bond interest payable	$ 6,000
Long-term liabilities:	
Bonds payable (12%, due January 1, 2013)	$100,000

On January 1, 2004, when the semiannual interest is paid, the bond interest payable account is eliminated. The January 1 entry is:

Bond Interest Payable	6,000	
Cash		6,000
Paid semiannual bond interest.		

The entries to record the interest expense payments during the remaining nine years will be the same as those made during 2003 and on January 1, 2004. The only other entry required in accounting for these bonds is the recording of their retirement on January 1, 2013. That entry, assuming that all interest has been accounted for, will be:

Bonds Payable	100,000	
Cash		100,000
Retired the $100,000, 10-year, 12% bonds.		

As the preceding entries illustrate, accounting for the issuance of bonds, the payment of the interest, and the retirement of the bonds is relatively simple when the bonds are issued at face value.

Bond Retirements before Maturity

Bond issues are, by definition, an inflexible form of long-term debt. The issuing company has a set schedule of interest payments and a specified maturity date, usually at least 5 or 10 years from the issuance date. In many cases, however, a company may want to pay off (redeem) and retire its bonds before maturity. This situation might occur when interest rates fall—a company uses the money obtained by issuing new bonds at a lower interest rate to retire the older, higher-interest bonds. As a result, the company retains the money it needs for expansion or other long-range projects but pays less interest for using that money.

As noted earlier, callable bonds are issued with an early redemption provision. Although the company usually has to pay a premium (penalty) for the privilege of redeeming (calling) the bonds, the amount of the penalty will probably be less than the amount gained by paying a lower interest rate. With bonds that are not callable, the company simply purchases the bonds in the open market, as available, at the going price.

To illustrate the retirement of bonds before maturity, assume that the Central Trucking Company bonds are now selling in the bond market at 109 and are callable at 110. The company decides to take advantage of the lower interest rate (8%) by issuing new bonds and using the proceeds to pay off the outstanding bonds. Given that the bonds were issued at their face value, the penalty (the call premium) is $10,000. The entry to record the retirement of the bonds at 110 is:

Bonds Payable.	100,000	
Loss on Bond Retirement	10,000	
Cash ($100,000 × 1.10).		110,000
To retire $100,000 of bonds at a call price of 110.		

In this case, the bonds were retired at a loss of $10,000. The loss is probably tolerable because the company expects to pay significantly less interest over the life of the new bond issue than it would have had to continue to pay on the old bonds. Gains and losses on the early retirement of bonds are reported on the income statement as extraordinary gains and losses.

---

to summarize

Accounting for bonds involves three steps: (1) accounting for their issuance, (2) accounting for the periodic interest payments, and (3) accounting for their retirement. When bonds are retired at maturity, there is no gain or loss because the amount paid is equal to the face value of the bonds. When bonds are retired before maturity, a gain or loss often results because the price paid to retire the bonds can be different from the carrying value of the bonds. The gain or loss on retirement of bonds is reported on the income statement as an extraordinary item.

5

Use debt-related financial ratios to determine the degree of a company's financial leverage and its ability to repay loans.

USING DEBT-RELATED FINANCIAL RATIOS

As illustrated earlier in the chapter in Exhibit 10-2, an important business issue associated with long-term debt is the determination of how a company wishes to obtain the money it needs to buy necessary assets. A company's leverage is the degree to which the company has borrowed the funds needed for asset acquisitions. This section describes the financial ratios that are commonly used to evaluate the level of a company's financial leverage.

Debt Ratio and Debt-to-Equity Ratio

debt ratio A measure of leverage, computed by dividing total liabilities by total assets.

The **debt ratio** measures the amount of assets supplied by lenders. It is calculated as follows:

$$\text{Debt ratio} = \frac{\text{Total liabilities}}{\text{Total assets}}$$

The computed value of the debt ratio indicates the percentage of a company's funding that has come through borrowing.

The debt ratio for DISNEY for 1999 is calculated as follows (the numbers are in millions):

debt-to-equity ratio The number of dollars of borrowed funds for every dollar invested by owners; computed as total liabilities divided by total stockholders' equity.

$$\text{Debt ratio} = \frac{\$22{,}704}{\$43{,}679} = 52\%$$

Thus, 52% of Disney's assets are provided by lenders and 48% by stockholders.

The **debt-to-equity ratio** also measures the balance of funds being provided by creditors and stockholders. This ratio is calculated by dividing total liabilities by total stockholders' eq-

expanded material

uity. The higher the debt-to-equity ratio, the more debt the company has. The debt-to-equity ratio for Disney is calculated as follows:

$$\text{Debt-to-equity ratio} = \frac{\text{Total liabilities}}{\text{Total stockholders' equity}}$$

$$\text{Debt-to-equity ratio} = \frac{\$22{,}704}{\$20{,}975} = 1.08$$

In this case, the debt-to-equity ratio indicates that Disney's debt is about 8% higher than its equity. Note that the debt ratio and the debt-to-equity ratio both indicate the same thing—that Disney has acquired just a little bit more of its total financing from borrowing than from stockholders. It doesn't matter which of these two ratios you use to measure a company's leverage; the important thing is that you are consistent and that any ratios you use for comparison have been computed using the same formula.

Times Interest Earned Ratio

times interest earned A measure of a borrower's ability to make required interest payments; computed as income before interest and taxes divided by annual interest expense.

Lenders like to have an indication of the borrowing company's ability to meet the required interest payments. **Times interest earned** is the ratio of the income that is available for interest payments to the annual interest expense. Times interest earned is computed as follows:

$$\text{Times interest earned} = \frac{\text{Income before interest and taxes (operating profit)}}{\text{Annual interest expense}}$$

To illustrate the computation of this ratio, we will return to Disney. For year-end 1999, Disney's interest expense was $612 million, and its operating profit was $4,056 million. This results in times interest earned of 6.6 times, computed as follows:

$$\text{Times interest earned} = \frac{\$4{,}056}{\$612} = 6.6 \text{ times}$$

Disney's times interest earned value of 6.6 times means that its operations in 1999 generated enough profit to be able to pay Disney's interest expense for the year 6.6 times. This suggests that Disney's creditors have a substantial cushion before they need to be concerned about Disney's ability to meet its required periodic interest payments.

---

expanded material

The present value techniques discussed in this chapter are useful in determining the value of obligations due at some future time. The computations and accounting are similar for interest-bearing notes, mortgages, capital leases, and bonds. However, there are certain complexities associated with these liabilities that deserve additional attention. In this section of the chapter, we discuss the procedures associated with the amortization of a bond discount or premium.

6

Amortize bond discounts and bond premiums using either the straight-line method or the effective-interest method.

BONDS ISSUED AT A DISCOUNT OR AT A PREMIUM

As we have explained, bonds may be issued at a discount or a premium because their stated interest rate may be (and often is) lower or higher than the effective rate. The two rates often differ because economic conditions in the marketplace change between the date the stated interest is set and the date the bonds are actually sold. Various factors determine this second date—for example, the time it takes to print the bonds and the investment banker's decision regarding the best time to offer the bonds. Because the cost to the company for the use of the bond money is really the effective interest rate rather than the stated rate, the discount or premium must be written off (amortized) over the period the bonds are outstanding, and the amortization is treated as an adjustment to bond interest expense.

straight-line amortization A method of systematically writing off a bond discount or premium in equal amounts each period until maturity.

effective-interest amortization A method of systematically writing off a bond premium or discount that takes into consideration the time value of money and results in an equal interest rate being used for amortization for each period.

There are two methods of amortizing bond discounts and bond premiums: straight-line amortization and effective-interest amortization. With **straight-line amortization**, a company writes off the same amount of discount or premium each period the bonds are held. For example, with a $4,000 discount on a 10-year bond, $400 is amortized each year. **Effective-interest amortization** takes the time value of money into consideration. The amount of discount or premium amortized is the difference between the interest actually incurred (based on the effective rate) and the interest actually paid (based on the stated rate). The straight-line amortization method will be used to explain the accounting for the amortization of discounts and premiums; then the effective-interest method will be explained and illustrated.

Accounting for Bonds Issued at a Discount

When bonds are issued at a discount, a contra-liability account is used to keep a separate record of the discounted amount. To illustrate, we will assume that the $100,000, 10-year, 12% bonds issued by Central Trucking on January 1, 2003, sold for $98,000. The entry to record the issuance of the bonds is:

Cash	98,000	
Discount on Bonds	2,000	
Bonds Payable		100,000
Issued $100,000, 12%, 10-year bonds at 98.		

The discount on bonds account represents the difference between the face value of the bonds and the issuance price. This discount is accounted for as additional bond interest expense over the life of the bonds. In other words, if the company receives only $98,000 when the bonds are issued and is required to pay $100,000 at maturity, the $2,000 difference is additional interest. The following analysis shows that total interest on the bonds is $122,000, comprised of the periodic interest payments ($120,000) plus the $2,000 discount.

Amount to be paid to bondholders:	
Interest paid each year for 10 years ($100,000 × 0.12 × 10)	$120,000
Face value to be paid at maturity	100,000
Total amount to be paid to bondholders	$220,000
Proceeds received from sale of bonds ($100,000 × 0.98)	98,000
Total interest expense	$122,000
Average annual interest expense ($122,000/10 years)	$ 12,200

Although the $2,000 of additional interest arising from the discount will not be paid until the bonds mature, interest accrues, or accumulates, over time. Thus, each year that the bonds are outstanding, Central Trucking will record bond interest expense for the amount paid at the stated rate ($100,000 × 0.12 = $12,000) and will also recognize a portion of the discount as bond interest expense. In recording the additional bond interest expense, the contra account Discount on Bonds is amortized or written off over the life of the bonds. Using straight-line amortization, an even amount is amortized each period. In the Central Trucking Company example, the semiannual amortization would be $100 ($2,000 discount/10 years × ½). Bond amortization is recorded when interest payments are made, and the entry on July 1, 2003, is:

Bond Interest Expense	6,100	
Discount on Bonds		100
Cash		6,000
Paid semiannual interest on the $100,000, 12%, 10-year bonds ($100,000 × 0.12 × ½ year) and amortized the bond discount ($2,000/10 years × ½ year).		

As illustrated, amortization of a discount increases bond interest expense. In this case, the bond interest expense is $6,100, or the sum of the semiannual interest payment and the semiannual amortization of the bond discount. Over the 10-year life of the bonds, the bond interest expense will be increased by $2,000 (20 periods × $100), the amount of the discount. Thus, these bonds pay an effective interest rate of approximately 12.45%[3] per year ($12,200 interest/$98,000 received on the bonds).

The adjusting entry to record the bond interest expense on December 31, 2003, is:

Bond Interest Expense	6,100	
Discount on Bonds		100
Bond Interest Payable		6,000
To recognize bond interest expense for the six months July 1 to December 31, 2003.		

The financial statements prepared at December 31, 2003, would report the following:

Income Statement		
Bond interest expense ($6,100 × 2)		$12,200
Balance Sheet		
Current liabilities:		
Bond interest payable		$ 6,000
Long-term liabilities:		
Bonds payable (12%, due January 1, 2013)	$100,000	
Less unamortized discount ($2,000 − $200)	1,800	$98,200

The entries to account for the bond interest expense and bond discount amortization during the remaining nine years will be the same as those illustrated. And because the bond discount will be completely amortized at the end of the 10 years, the entry to record the retirement of the bonds will be the same as that for bonds issued at face value. That entry is:

Bonds Payable	100,000	
Cash		100,000
Retired the $100,000, 12%, 10-year bonds.		

Accounting for Bonds Issued at a Premium

Like discounts, premiums must be amortized over the life of the bonds. To illustrate the accounting for bonds sold at a premium, we will assume that Central Trucking was able to sell its

3 Because straight-line amortization was used, this effective rate of 12.45% is only an approximation that will change slightly each period. An accurate effective rate can be calculated only if the effective-interest method of amortization is used.

$100,000, 12%, 10-year bonds at 103 (that is, at 103% of face value). The entry to record the issuance of these bonds on January 1, 2003, is:

Cash	103,000	
Premium on Bonds		3,000
Bonds Payable		100,000
Sold $100,000, 12%, 10-year bonds at 103.		

Premium on Bonds is added to Bonds Payable on the balance sheet and, like Discount on Bonds, is amortized using either the straight-line method or the effective-interest method. Thus, if Central Trucking uses the straight-line method, the annual amortization of the premium will be $300 ($3,000/10 years), or $150 every six months. The entry to record the first semiannual interest payment and the premium amortization of July 1, 2003, is:

Bond Interest Expense	5,850	
Premium on Bonds	150	
Cash		6,000
Paid semiannual interest on the $100,000, 12%, 10-year bonds ($100,000 × 0.12 × ½ year) and amortized the bond premium ($3,000/10 years × ½).		

The amortization of a premium on bonds reduces the actual bond interest expense. The following analysis shows why bond interest expense is reduced when bonds are sold at a premium:

Amount to be paid to bondholders:	
[($12,000 interest × 10 years) + $100,000 face value]	$220,000
Proceeds received from sale of bonds	103,000
Total interest to be paid	$117,000
Average annual interest expense ($117,000/10 years)	$ 11,700

In this case, the annual payments of $12,000 include interest of $11,700 and $300, which represents a partial repayment (one-tenth) of the bond premium. Thus, the effective interest rate is approximately 11.36% ($11,700/$103,000), which is less than the stated rate of 12%.

The adjusting entry to record the accrual of the interest expense on December 31, 2003, is:

caution

If bonds issued at a premium or discount are retired before maturity, remember that the bond payable and any associated premium or discount would be taken off the books.

Bond Interest Expense	5,850	
Premium on Bonds	150	
Bond Interest Payable		6,000
To recognize bond interest expense for the six months July 1 to December 31, 2003.		

The financial statements prepared at December 31, 2003, would report the following:

Income Statement		
Bond interest expense ($5,850 × 2)		$ 11,700
Balance Sheet		
Current liabilities:		
Bond interest payable		$ 6,000
Long-term liabilities:		
Bonds payable (12%, due January 1, 2013)	$100,000	
Plus unamortized premium ($3,000 − $300)	2,700	$102,700

Effective-Interest Amortization

bond carrying value The face value of bonds minus the unamortized discount or plus the unamortized premium.

Companies can often justify use of the straight-line method of amortizing bond premiums and discounts on the grounds that its results are not significantly different from those of the theoretically more accurate effective-interest method. Nevertheless, because the effective-interest method considers the time value of money, it is required by generally accepted accounting principles if it leads to results that differ significantly from those obtained by the straight-line method.

Note that the table below looks a lot like the mortgage amortization schedule on page 465 and the schedule of computer lease payments on page 467. The reason is that these other schedules also use the effective-interest amortization method.

The effective-interest method amortizes a varying amount each period, which is the difference between the interest actually incurred and the cash actually paid. The amount actually incurred is the changing **bond carrying value** (the face value of the bond minus the unamortized discount or plus the unamortized premium) multiplied by a constant rate, the effective interest rate.

To illustrate the effective-interest method, let's continue with the Central Trucking Company example we have used previously. We will assume that the Central Trucking Company $100,000, 12%, 10-year bonds were issued on January 1, 2003, for $112,463. The bonds pay interest semiannually on January 1 and July 1, so their effective interest rate is approximately 10%[4] a year, or 5% every six months. Because the actual bond interest expense for each interest period is equal to the effective rate of 5% multiplied by the bond carrying value, the amortization (rounded to the nearest $1) for the 10 years is calculated as shown in the following table.

Period	1 Cash Paid for Interest	2 Semiannual Interest Expense (0.05 × Bond Carrying Value)	3 Premium Amortization (1) − (2)	4 Carrying Value
Issuance date				$112,463
Year 1, first six months	$6,000	$5,623	$377	112,086
Year 1, second six months	6,000	5,604	396	111,690
Year 2, first six months	6,000	5,585	415	111,275
Year 2, second six months	6,000	5,564	436	110,839
Year 3, first six months	6,000	5,542	458	110,381
Year 3, second six months	6,000	5,519	481	109,900
Year 4, first six months	6,000	5,495	505	109,395
Year 4, second six months	6,000	5,470	530	108,865
Year 5, first six months	6,000	5,443	557	108,308
Year 5, second six months	6,000	5,415	585	107,723
Year 6, first six months	6,000	5,386	614	107,109
Year 6, second six months	6,000	5,355	645	106,464
Year 7, first six months	6,000	5,323	677	105,787
Year 7, second six months	6,000	5,289	711	105,076
Year 8, first six months	6,000	5,254	746	104,330
Year 8, second six months	6,000	5,217	783	103,547
Year 9, first six months	6,000	5,177	823	102,724
Year 9, second six months	6,000	5,136	864	101,860
Year 10, first six months	6,000	5,093	907	100,953
Year 10, second six months	6,000	5,047	953	100,000

4 The 10% rate is the rate that will discount the face value of the bonds and the semiannual interest payments to a present value that equals the issuance price of the bonds, computed as follows:

Present value of $100,000 at 5% for 20 payments	$100,000 × 0.3769 =	$ 37,690
Present value of $6,000 at 5% for 20 payments	$ 6,000 × 12.4622 =	74,773
Total present value = issuance price of the bonds		$112,463

In this computation, the $6,000 in column (1) is the actual cash paid each six months. Column (2) shows the interest expense for each six months, which is the amount that will be reported on the income statement. Column (3), which is the difference between columns (1) and (2), represents the amortization of the premium. Column (4) shows the carrying, or book, value of the bonds (that is, the total of the bonds payable and the unamortized bond premium), which is the amount that will be reported on the balance sheet each period. Using the effective-interest method, the bond carrying value is always equal to the present value of the bond obligation. As the carrying value decreases, while the effective rate of interest remains constant, the interest expense also decreases from one period to the next, as illustrated in column (2) of the amortization schedule.

To help you translate this table into the entries for the interest payments and premium amortization at the end of each six-month period, we have provided the semiannual journal entries for year 3.

Year 3, End of First Six Months		
Bond Interest Expense	5,542	
Bond Premium.	458	
Cash		6,000
To record effective-interest expense on Central Trucking Company bonds for the first six months of year 3.		
Year 3, End of Second Six Months		
Bond Interest Expense	5,519	
Bond Premium.	481	
Bond Interest Payable.		6,000
To record effective-interest expense on Central Trucking Company bonds for the second six months of year 3.		

Because the straight-line method would show a constant amortization ($12,463/20 = $623.15 per six-month period) on a decreasing bond balance, the straight-line interest rate cannot be constant. When the straight-line results differ significantly from the effective-interest results, generally accepted accounting principles require use of the effective-interest method.

The effective-interest method of amortizing a bond discount is essentially the same as amortizing a bond premium. The main difference is that the bond carrying value is increasing instead of decreasing.

to summarize

When bonds are issued at a premium or a discount, the premium or discount must be amortized over the life of the bond. A discount or premium results when the market rate and the stated rate are different. Because of this difference, bond interest expense recognized on the income statement is not equal to the amount of cash paid for interest. The objective of amortization is to reflect the actual bond interest expense incurred over the life of the bond. Two methods of amortization are available—the straight-line method and the effective-interest method. The straight-line method amortizes an equal amount of premium or discount every period. When the effective-interest method is used, the amount of discount or premium amortized each period is equal to the market rate of interest multiplied by the bond's carrying value.

table I The Present Value of $1 Due in *n* Periods*

Period	1%	2%	3%	4%	5%	6%	7%	8%	9%	10%	12%	14%	15%	16%	18%	20%
1	.9901	.9804	.9709	.9615	.9524	.9434	.9346	.9259	.9174	.9091	.8929	.8772	.8696	.8621	.8475	.8333
2	.9803	.9612	.9426	.9246	.9070	.8900	.8734	.8573	.8417	.8264	.7972	.7695	.7561	.7432	.7182	.6944
3	.9706	.9423	.9151	.8890	.8638	.8396	.8163	.7938	.7722	.7513	.7118	.6750	.6575	.6407	.6086	.5787
4	.9610	.9238	.8885	.8548	.8227	.7921	.7629	.7350	.7084	.6830	.6355	.5921	.5718	.5523	.5158	.4823
5	.9515	.9057	.8626	.8219	.7835	.7473	.7130	.6806	.6499	.6209	.5674	.5194	.4972	.4761	.4371	.4019
6	.9420	.8880	.8375	.7903	.7462	.7050	.6663	.6302	.5963	.5645	.5066	.4556	.4323	.4104	.3704	.3349
7	.9327	.8706	.8131	.7599	.7107	.6651	.6227	.5835	.5470	.5132	.4523	.3996	.3759	.3538	.3139	.2791
8	.9235	.8535	.7894	.7307	.6768	.6274	.5820	.5403	.5019	.4665	.4039	.3506	.3269	.3050	.2660	.2326
9	.9143	.8368	.7664	.7026	.6446	.5919	.5439	.5002	.4604	.4241	.3606	.3075	.2843	.2630	.2255	.1938
10	.9053	.8203	.7441	.6756	.6139	.5584	.5083	.4632	.4224	.3855	.3220	.2697	.2472	.2267	.1911	.1615
11	.8963	.8043	.7224	.6496	.5847	.5268	.4751	.4289	.3875	.3503	.2875	.2366	.2149	.1954	.1619	.1346
12	.8874	.7885	.7014	.6246	.5568	.4970	.4440	.3971	.3555	.3186	.2567	.2076	.1869	.1685	.1372	.1122
13	.8787	.7730	.6810	.6006	.5303	.4688	.4150	.3677	.3262	.2897	.2292	.1821	.1625	.1452	.1163	.0935
14	.8700	.7579	.6611	.5775	.5051	.4423	.3878	.3405	.2992	.2633	.2046	.1597	.1413	.1252	.0985	.0779
15	.8613	.7430	.6419	.5553	.4810	.4173	.3624	.3152	.2745	.2394	.1827	.1401	.1229	.1079	.0835	.0649
16	.8528	.7284	.6232	.5339	.4581	.3936	.3387	.2919	.2519	.2176	.1631	.1229	.1069	.0930	.0708	.0541
17	.8444	.7142	.6050	.5134	.4363	.3714	.3166	.2703	.2311	.1978	.1456	.1078	.0929	.0802	.0600	.0451
18	.8360	.7002	.5874	.4936	.4155	.3503	.2959	.2502	.2120	.1799	.1300	.0946	.0808	.0691	.0508	.0376
19	.8277	.6864	.5703	.4746	.3957	.3305	.2765	.2317	.1945	.1635	.1161	.0829	.0703	.0596	.0431	.0313
20	.8195	.6730	.5537	.4564	.3769	.3118	.2584	.2145	.1784	.1486	.1037	.0728	.0611	.0514	.0365	.0261
25	.7798	.6095	.4476	.3751	.2953	.2330	.1842	.1460	.1160	.0923	.0588	.0378	.0304	.0245	.0160	.0105
30	.7419	.5521	.4120	.3083	.2314	.1741	.1314	.0994	.0754	.0573	.0334	.0196	.0151	.0116	.0070	.0042
40	.6717	.4529	.3066	.2083	.1420	.0972	.0668	.0460	.0318	.0221	.0107	.0053	.0037	.0026	.0013	.0007
50	.6080	.3715	.2281	.1407	.0872	.0543	.0339	.0213	.0134	.0085	.0035	.0014	.0009	.0006	.0003	.0001
60	.5504	.3048	.1697	.0951	.0535	.0303	.0173	.0099	.0057	.0033	.0011	.0004	.0002	.0001	†	†

*The formula used to derive the values in this table was $PV = F \frac{1}{(1 + i)^n}$ where PV = present value, F = future amount to be discounted, i = interest rate, and n = number of periods.
†The value of 0 to four decimal places.

table II The Present Value of an Annuity of $1 per Number of Payments*

Number of Payments	1%	2%	3%	4%	5%	6%	7%	8%	9%	10%	12%	14%	15%	16%	18%	20%
1	0.9901	0.9804	0.9709	0.9615	0.9524	0.9434	0.9346	0.9259	0.9174	0.9091	0.8929	0.8772	0.8596	0.8621	0.8475	0.8333
2	1.9704	1.9416	1.9135	1.8861	1.8594	1.8334	1.8080	1.7833	1.7591	1.7355	1.6901	1.6467	1.6257	1.6052	1.5656	1.5278
3	2.9410	2.8839	2.8286	2.7751	2.7232	2.6730	2.6243	2.5771	2.5313	2.4869	2.4018	2.3216	2.2832	2.2459	2.1743	2.1065
4	3.9820	3.8077	3.7171	3.6299	3.5460	3.4651	3.3872	3.3121	3.2397	3.1699	3.0373	2.9137	2.8550	2.7982	2.6901	2.5887
5	4.8884	4.7135	4.5797	4.4518	4.3295	4.2124	4.1002	3.9927	3.8897	3.7908	3.6048	3.4331	3.3522	3.2743	3.1272	2.9906
6	5.7985	5.6014	5.4172	5.2421	5.0757	4.9173	4.7665	4.6229	4.4859	4.3553	4.1114	3.8887	3.7845	3.6847	3.4976	3.3255
7	6.7282	6.4720	6.2303	6.0021	5.7864	5.5824	5.3893	5.2064	5.0330	4.8684	4.5638	4.2883	4.1604	4.0386	3.8115	3.6046
8	7.6517	7.3255	7.0197	6.7327	6.4632	6.2098	5.9713	5.7466	5.5348	5.3349	4.9676	4.6389	4.4873	4.3436	4.0776	3.8372
9	8.5660	8.1622	7.7861	7.4353	7.1078	6.8017	6.5152	6.2469	5.9952	5.7590	5.3282	4.9464	4.7716	4.6065	4.3030	4.0310
10	9.4713	8.9826	8.5302	8.1109	7.7217	7.3601	7.0236	6.7101	6.4177	6.1446	5.6502	5.2161	5.0188	4.8332	4.4941	4.1925
11	10.3676	9.7868	9.2526	8.7605	8.3064	7.8869	7.4987	7.1390	6.8052	6.4951	5.9377	5.4527	5.2337	5.0286	4.6560	4.3271
12	11.2551	10.5733	9.9540	9.3851	8.8633	8.3838	7.9427	7.5361	7.1607	6.8137	6.1944	5.6603	5.4206	5.1971	4.7932	4.4392
13	12.1337	11.3484	10.6350	9.9856	9.3936	8.8527	8.3577	7.9038	7.4869	7.1034	6.4235	5.8424	5.5831	5.3423	4.9095	4.5327
14	13.0037	12.1062	11.2961	10.5631	9.8986	9.2950	8.7455	8.2442	7.7862	7.3667	6.6282	6.0021	5.7245	5.4675	5.0081	4.6106
15	13.8651	12.8493	11.9379	11.1184	10.3797	9.7122	9.1079	8.5595	8.0607	7.6061	6.8109	6.1422	5.8474	5.5755	5.0916	4.6755
16	14.7179	13.5777	12.5611	11.6523	10.8378	10.1059	9.4466	8.8514	8.3126	7.8237	6.9740	6.2651	5.9542	5.6685	5.1624	4.7296
17	15.5623	14.2919	13.1661	12.1657	11.2741	10.4773	9.7632	9.1216	8.5436	8.0216	7.1196	6.3729	6.0472	5.7487	5.2223	4.7746
18	16.3983	14.9920	13.7535	12.6593	11.6896	10.8276	10.0591	9.3719	8.7556	8.2014	7.2497	6.4674	6.1280	5.8178	5.2732	4.8122
19	17.2260	15.6785	14.3238	13.1339	12.0853	11.1581	10.3356	9.6036	8.9501	8.3649	7.3658	6.5504	6.1982	5.8775	5.3162	4.8435
20	18.0456	16.3514	14.8775	13.5903	12.4622	11.4699	10.5940	9.8181	9.1285	8.5136	7.4694	6.6231	6.2593	5.9288	5.3527	4.8696
25	22.0232	19.5235	17.4131	15.6221	14.0939	12.7834	11.6536	10.6748	9.8226	9.0770	7.8431	6.8729	6.4641	6.0971	5.4669	4.9476
30	25.8077	22.3965	19.6004	17.2920	15.3725	13.7648	12.4090	11.2578	10.2737	9.4269	8.0552	7.0027	6.5660	6.1772	5.5168	4.9789
40	32.8347	27.3555	23.1148	19.7928	17.1591	15.0463	13.3317	11.9246	10.7574	9.7791	8.2438	7.1050	6.6418	6.2335	5.5482	4.9966
50	39.1961	31.4236	25.7298	21.4822	18.2559	15.7619	13.8007	12.2335	10.9617	9.9148	8.3045	7.1327	6.6605	6.2463	5.5641	4.9995
60	44.9550	34.7609	27.6756	22.6235	18.9293	16.1614	14.0392	12.3766	11.0480	9.9672	8.3240	7.1401	6.6651	6.2482	5.5553	4.9999

*The formula used to derive the values in this table was $PV = F\left(\frac{1 - \frac{1}{(1+i)^n}}{i}\right)$ where PV = present value, F = periodic payment to be discounted, i = interest rate, and n = number of payments.

table III Amount of $1 Due in *n* Periods

Period	1%	2%	3%	4%	5%	6%	7%	8%	9%	10%	12%	14%	15%	16%	18%	20%
1	1.0100	1.0200	1.0300	1.0400	1.0500	1.0600	1.0700	1.0800	1.0900	1.1000	1.1200	1.1400	1.1500	1.1600	1.1800	1.2000
2	1.0201	1.0404	1.0609	1.0816	1.1025	1.1236	1.1449	1.1664	1.1881	1.2100	1.2544	1.2996	1.3225	1.3456	1.3924	1.4400
3	1.0303	1.0612	1.0927	1.1249	1.1576	1.1910	1.2250	1.2597	1.2950	1.3310	1.4049	1.4815	1.5209	1.5609	1.6430	1.7280
4	1.0406	1.0824	1.1255	1.1699	1.2155	1.2625	1.3108	1.3605	1.4116	1.4641	1.5735	1.6890	1.7490	1.8106	1.9388	2.0736
5	1.0510	1.1041	1.1593	1.2167	1.2763	1.3382	1.4026	1.4693	1.5386	1.6105	1.7623	1.9254	2.0114	2.1003	2.2878	2.4883
6	1.0615	1.1262	1.1941	1.2653	1.3401	1.4185	1.5007	1.5869	1.6771	1.7716	1.9738	2.1950	2.3131	2.4364	2.6996	2.9860
7	1.0721	1.1487	1.2299	1.3159	1.4071	1.5036	1.6058	1.7138	1.8280	1.9487	2.2107	2.5023	2.6600	2.8262	3.1855	3.5832
8	1.0829	1.1717	1.2668	1.3686	1.4775	1.5938	1.7182	1.8509	1.9926	2.1436	2.4760	2.8526	3.0590	3.2784	3.7589	4.2998
9	1.0937	1.1951	1.3048	1.4233	1.5513	1.6895	1.8385	1.9990	2.1719	2.3579	2.7731	3.2519	3.5179	3.8030	4.4355	5.1598
10	1.1046	1.2190	1.3439	1.4802	1.6289	1.7908	1.9672	2.1589	2.3674	2.5937	3.1058	3.7072	4.0456	4.4114	5.2338	6.1917
11	1.1157	1.2434	1.3842	1.5395	1.7103	1.8983	2.1049	2.3316	2.5804	2.8531	3.4785	4.2262	4.6524	5.1173	6.1759	7.4031
12	1.1268	1.2682	1.4258	1.6010	1.7959	2.0122	2.2522	2.5182	2.8127	3.1384	3.8960	4.8179	5.3502	5.9360	7.2876	8.9161
13	1.1381	1.2936	1.4685	1.6651	1.8856	2.1329	2.4098	2.7196	3.0658	3.4523	4.3635	5.4924	6.1528	6.8858	8.5994	10.699
14	1.1495	1.3195	1.5126	1.7317	1.9799	2.2609	2.5785	2.9372	3.3417	3.7975	4.8871	6.2613	7.0757	7.9875	10.147	12.839
15	1.1610	1.3459	1.5580	1.8009	2.0789	2.3966	2.7590	3.1722	3.6425	4.1772	5.4736	7.1379	8.1371	9.2655	11.973	15.407
16	1.1726	1.3728	1.6047	1.8730	2.1829	2.5404	2.9522	3.4259	3.9703	4.5950	6.1304	8.1372	9.3576	10.748	14.129	18.488
17	1.1843	1.4002	1.6528	1.9479	2.2920	2.6928	3.1588	3.7000	4.3276	5.0545	6.8660	9.2765	10.761	12.467	16.672	22.186
18	1.1961	1.4282	1.7024	2.0258	2.4066	2.8543	3.3799	3.9960	4.7171	5.5599	7.6900	10.575	12.375	14.462	19.673	26.623
19	1.2081	1.4568	1.7535	2.1068	2.5270	3.0256	3.6165	4.3157	5.1417	6.1159	8.6128	12.055	14.231	16.776	23.214	31.948
20	1.2202	1.4859	1.8061	2.1911	2.6533	3.2071	3.8697	4.6610	5.6044	6.7275	9.6463	13.743	16.366	19.460	27.393	38.337
30	1.3478	1.8114	2.4273	3.2434	4.3219	5.7435	7.6123	10.062	13.267	17.449	29.959	50.950	66.211	85.849	143.37	237.37
40	1.4889	2.2080	3.2620	4.8010	7.0400	10.285	14.974	21.724	31.409	45.259	93.050	188.88	267.86	378.72	750.37	1469.7
50	1.6446	2.6916	4.3839	7.1067	11.467	18.420	29.457	46.901	74.357	117.39	289.00	700.23	1083.6	1670.7	3927.3	9100.4
60	1.8167	3.2810	5.8916	10.519	18.679	32.987	57.946	101.25	176.03	304.48	897.59	2595.9	4383.9	7370.1	20555.	56347.

table IV Amount of an Annuity of $1 per Number of Payments

Number of Payments	1%	2%	3%	4%	5%	6%	7%	8%	9%	10%	12%	14%	15%	16%	18%	20%
1	1.0000	1.0000	1.0000	1.0000	1.0000	1.0000	1.0000	1.0000	1.0000	1.0000	1.0000	1.0000	1.0000	1.0000	1.0000	1.0000
2	2.0100	2.0200	2.0300	2.0400	2.0500	2.0600	2.0700	2.0800	2.0900	2.1000	2.1200	2.1400	2.1500	2.1600	2.1800	2.2000
3	3.0301	3.0604	3.0909	3.1216	3.1525	3.1836	3.2149	3.2464	3.2781	3.3100	3.3744	3.4396	3.4725	3.5056	3.5724	3.6400
4	4.0604	4.1216	4.1836	4.2465	4.3101	4.3746	4.4399	4.5061	4.5731	4.6410	4.7793	4.9211	4.9934	5.0665	5.2154	5.3680
5	5.1010	5.2040	5.3091	5.4163	5.5256	5.6371	5.7507	5.8666	5.9847	6.1051	6.3528	6.6101	6.7424	6.8771	7.1542	7.4416
6	6.1520	6.3081	6.4684	6.6330	6.8019	6.9753	7.1533	7.3359	7.5233	7.7156	8.1152	8.5355	8.7537	8.9775	9.4420	9.9299
7	7.2135	7.4343	7.6625	7.8983	8.1420	8.3938	8.6540	8.9228	9.2004	9.4872	10.8090	10.7305	11.0668	11.4139	12.1415	12.9159
8	8.2857	8.5830	8.8923	9.2142	9.5491	9.8975	10.2598	10.6366	11.0285	11.4359	12.2997	13.2328	13.7268	14.2401	15.3270	16.4991
9	9.3685	9.7546	10.1591	10.5828	11.0266	11.4913	11.9780	12.4876	13.0210	13.5795	14.7757	16.0853	16.7858	17.5185	19.0859	20.7989
10	10.4622	10.9497	11.4639	12.0061	12.5779	13.1808	13.8164	14.4866	15.1929	15.9374	17.5487	19.3373	20.3037	21.3215	23.5213	25.9587
11	11.5668	12.1687	12.8078	13.4864	14.2068	14.9716	15.7836	16.6455	17.5603	18.5312	20.6546	23.0445	24.3493	25.7329	28.7551	32.1504
12	12.6825	13.4121	14.1920	15.0258	15.9171	16.8699	17.8885	18.9771	20.1407	21.2843	24.1331	27.2707	29.0017	30.8502	34.9311	39.5805
13	13.8093	14.6803	15.6178	16.6268	17.7130	18.8821	20.1406	21.4953	22.9534	24.5227	28.0291	32.0887	34.3519	36.7862	42.2187	48.4966
14	14.9474	15.9739	17.0863	18.2919	19.5986	21.0151	22.5505	24.2149	26.0192	27.9750	32.3926	37.5811	40.5047	43.6720	50.8180	59.1959
15	16.0969	17.2934	18.5989	20.0236	21.5786	23.2760	25.1290	27.1521	29.3609	31.7725	37.2797	43.8424	47.5804	51.6595	60.9653	72.0351
16	17.2579	18.6393	20.1569	21.8248	23.6575	25.6725	27.8881	30.3243	33.0034	35.9497	42.7535	50.9804	55.7178	60.9250	72.9390	87.4421
17	18.4304	20.0121	21.7616	23.6975	25.8404	28.2129	30.8402	33.7502	36.9737	40.5447	48.8837	59.1176	65.0751	71.6730	87.0680	105.9306
18	19.6147	21.4123	23.4144	25.6454	28.1324	30.9057	33.9990	37.4502	41.3013	45.5992	55.7497	68.3941	75.8364	84.1407	103.7403	128.1167
19	20.8190	22.8406	25.1169	27.6712	30.5390	33.7600	37.3790	41.4463	46.0185	51.1591	63.4397	78.9692	88.2118	98.6032	123.4135	154.7400
20	22.0190	24.2974	26.8704	29.7781	33.0660	36.7856	40.9955	45.7620	51.1601	57.2750	72.0524	91.0249	102.4436	115.3797	146.6280	186.6880
30	34.7849	40.5681	47.5754	56.0849	66.4388	79.0582	94.4608	113.2832	136.3075	164.4940	241.3327	356.7868	434.7451	530.3117	790.9480	1181.8816
40	48.8864	60.4020	75.4013	95.0255	120.7998	154.7620	199.6351	259.0565	337.8824	442.5926	767.0914	1342.0251	1779.0903	2360.7572	4163.2130	7343.8578
50	64.4632	84.5794	112.7969	152.6671	209.3480	290.3359	406.5289	573.7702	815.0836	1163.9085	2400.0182	4994.5213	7217.7163	10435.6488	21813.0937	45497.1908
60	81.6697	114.0515	163.0534	237.9907	353.5837	533.1282	813.5204	1253.2133	1944.7921	3034.8164	7471.6411	18535.1333	29219.9916	46057.5085	114189.6665	281732.5718

review of learning objectives

1 Use present value concepts to measure long-term liabilities. Obligations that will not be paid or otherwise satisfied within one year are classified on the balance sheet as long-term liabilities. Some common types of long-term liabilities are notes payable, mortgages payable, lease obligations, and pension obligations. The present value of a long-term liability is the current value, which is computed by discounting the known future amount using the current interest rate. If the present value amounts of assets or liabilities are known and a future amount is desired, then the present value must be compounded to arrive at a future amount that includes both principal and interest.

2 Account for long-term liabilities, including notes payable and mortgages payable. Interest-bearing notes are recorded on the books of the issuer at face value. Interest expense is incurred based on the rate of interest, the carrying value of the note, and the passage of time. Interest Expense is debited for the amount of interest incurred and Cash or Interest Payable is credited.

Mortgage liabilities are paid by a series of regular payments that include interest expense and a reduction of the principal of the mortgage note. The balance sheet liability at any given time is the present value of the remaining mortgage payments.

3 Account for capital lease obligations and understand the significance of operating leases being excluded from the balance sheet. A firm can acquire new assets by either purchasing or leasing them. Leasing involves periodic payments over the life of the lease. The lease is classified as an operating lease if it is short term and does not meet any of the criteria of a capital lease. If the lease meets one of the specified capital lease criteria, it is treated as a purchase and referred to as a capital lease. As such, it is recorded as both an asset and a long-term liability. The asset is depreciated and the liability is reduced as lease payments are made. Operating leases are a form of off-balance-sheet financing because the obligation to make the future operating lease payments is not recognized on the balance sheet. However, the amount of future operating lease payments is disclosed in the notes to the financial statements.

4 Account for bonds, including the original issuance, the payment of interest, and the retirement of bonds. Accounting for bonds by the borrowing company (the issuer) includes three elements: accounting for their issuance, for interest payments, and for their retirement. If bonds are sold at face value, Cash is debited and Bonds Payable is credited. More often, however, bonds are sold at a premium or a discount. The bond liability is recorded at face value in the bonds payable account, and the premium or discount is recorded in a separate account and added to (in the case of a premium) or subtracted from (in the case of a discount) Bonds Payable on the balance sheet. When interest is paid, Bond Interest Expense is debited and Cash is credited. An adjustment is made to bond interest expense if the bond is sold at a premium or discount. At the date a bond matures, the borrowing company pays the face value to the investors, and the bonds are canceled. If the bonds are retired before maturity, a gain or loss will be recognized when the carrying value of the bonds differs from the amount paid to retire the bonds.

5 Use debt-related financial ratios to determine the degree of a company's financial leverage and its ability to repay loans. Higher leverage allows a company to expand without requiring additional stockholder investment. However, higher leverage also makes repayment of debt less certain. Both the debt ratio (total liabilities divided by total assets) and the debt-to-equity ratio (total liabilities divided by total stockholders' equity) measure the level of a company's leverage. These ratios are also sometimes computed using only interest-bearing debt instead of total liabilities. The times interest earned ratio (operating income divided by interest expense) measures how much cushion a company has in terms of being able to make its periodic interest payments.

expanded material

6 Amortize bond discounts and bond premiums using either the straight-line method or the effective-interest method. If bonds are issued at a discount, the bond interest expense for the year is the amount of interest paid plus the bond discount amortized during that year. If the bonds are sold at a premium, the bond interest expense for the year is the interest paid minus the bond premium amortized that year. Bond premiums and discounts generally should be amortized using the effective-interest method. The straight-line method is allowed provided that the two methods produce similar results.

key terms

annuity 460
bond 469
bond discount 471
bond indenture 470
bond maturity date 470
bond premium 471
callable bonds 469
compounding period 458
convertible bonds 469
coupon bonds 469
debentures (unsecured bonds) 469
debt ratio 476
debt-to-equity ratio 476
junk bonds 469
long-term liabilities 456
market rate (effective rate or yield rate) of interest 471
mortgage amortization schedule 464
mortgage payable 463
present value of $1 456
present value of an annuity 460
principal (face value or maturity value) 470
registered bonds 469
secured bonds 469
serial bonds 469
stated rate of interest 471
term bonds 469
times interest earned 477
zero-coupon bonds 469

expanded material

bond carrying value 481
effective-interest amortization 478
straight-line amortization 478

review problems

Accounting for Long-Term Liabilities

Energy Corporation had the following transactions relating to its long-term liabilities for the year:

a. Issued a $30,000, three-year, 8% note payable to White Corporation for a truck purchased on January 2. Interest is payable annually on December 31 of each year.
b. Issued $300,000 of 12%, 10-year bonds on July 1. The market rate on the date of issuance was 12%. Interest payments are made on June 30 and December 31 of each year.
c. Purchased a warehouse on December 1 by borrowing $250,000. The terms of the mortgage call for monthly payments of $2,194 for 30 years to be made at the end of each month. The interest rate on the mortgage is 10%.

Required: Make all journal entries required during the year to account for the above liabilities. Energy Corporation reports on a calendar-year basis.

Solution

Date	Account	Debit	Credit
Jan. 2	Truck	30,000	
	Note Payable		30,000
	Purchased a truck by issuing a note.		
July 1	Cash	300,000	
	Bonds Payable		300,000
	Issued 12%, 10-year bonds with a face value of $300,000.		
Dec. 1	Warehouse	250,000	
	Mortgage Payable		250,000
	Purchased a warehouse by issuing a 10%, 30-year mortgage.		
31	Interest Expense	2,400	
	Cash		2,400
	Paid yearly interest on the 3-year, 8% note ($30,000 × 8% = $2,400).		
	Bond Interest Expense	18,000	
	Cash		18,000
	Paid semiannual interest payment on 12%, 10-year bonds ($300,000 × 0.12 × 6/12 = $18,000).		

(continued)

Interest Expense	2,083	
Mortgage Payable	111	
Cash		2,194
Paid first monthly payment on 30-year mortgage (interest: $250,000 × 0.10 × 1/12 = $2,083; reduction in principal: $2,194 − $2,083 = $111).		

expanded material

Bonds Payable

Scientific Engineering Company received authorization on July 1, 2003, to issue $300,000 of 12% bonds. The maturity date of the bonds is July 1, 2023. Interest is payable on January 1 and July 1 of each year. The bonds were sold for $289,200 on July 1, 2003 (the same day as authorized). Scientific Engineering uses straight-line amortization.

Required:

1. Compute the approximate effective interest rate for the bonds.
2. Record the journal entries on:
   a. July 1, 2003.
   b. December 31, 2003.
   c. January 1, 2004.
   d. July 1, 2004.
   e. December 31, 2004.
3. Record the journal entries on July 1, 2023, for the final interest payment and the retirement of the bonds.

Solution

1. Effective Interest Rate

Because the bonds sold at a discount, the actual or effective rate of interest is higher than the stated interest rate of 12%. The effective interest rate can be approximated as follows:

Bond discount amortized per year = $10,800/20 periods = $540
Annual interest expense = ($300,000 × 12%) + $540 = $36,540
Effective interest rate = $36,540/$289,200 = 12.63%

2. Journal Entries

	Date	Account	Debit	Credit
a.	2003 July 1	Cash	289,200	
		Discount on Bonds	10,800	
		Bonds Payable		300,000
		To record the sale of $300,000 of 12% bonds due on July 1, 2023.		
b.	2003 Dec. 31	Bond Interest Expense	18,270	
		Discount on Bonds		270
		Bond Interest Payable		18,000
		To record semiannual bond interest expense on $300,000, 12%, 20-year bonds ($300,000 × 0.12 × ½ year) and amortize bond discount ($10,800 ÷ 20 years × ½ year).		
c.	2004 Jan. 1	Bond Interest Payable	18,000	
		Cash		18,000
		Paid semiannual interest on $300,000 bonds.		
d.	2004 July 1	Bond Interest Expense	18,270	
		Discount on Bonds		270
		Cash		18,000
		Paid semiannual interest on $300,000 bonds and amortized bond discount.		

(continued)

e.	2004			
	Dec. 31	Bond Interest Expense	18,270	
		Discount on Bonds		270
		Bond Interest Payable		18,000
		To record semiannual bond interest expense on $300,000 bonds and amortize bond discount.		

3. Retirement of the Bonds

2023			
July 1	Bond Interest Expense	18,270	
	Discount on Bonds		270
	Bond Interest Payable		18,000
	To record the bond interest expense and discount amortization up to the date of maturity.		
	Bonds Payable	300,000	
	Bond Interest Payable	18,000	
	Cash		318,000
	To record the payment of interest for six months and retire the bonds at maturity.		

The first entry on July 1, 2023, updates the amortization of the bond discount to the retirement date and reflects the cash owed for interest for the period January 1–July 1, 2023. The second entry reflects payment for retiring the bonds plus payment of the interest owed. Alternatively, Cash could have been credited for $18,000 in the first entry. If Cash had been credited, the second entry would have included only a debit to Bonds Payable and a credit to Cash for $300,000.

discussion questions

1. The higher the interest rate, the lower the present value of a future amount. Why?
2. What is an annuity?
3. When does the stated amount of a liability equal its present value?
4. What is the difference between a note payable and a mortgage payable?
5. When a mortgage payment is made, a portion of it is applied to interest, and the balance is applied to reduce the principal. How is the amount applied to reduce the principal computed?
6. If a lease is recorded as a capital lease, what is the relationship of the lease payments and the lease liability?
7. Why do companies prefer to classify leases as operating leases rather than as capital leases?
8. To whom do companies usually sell bonds?
9. What are two important characteristics that determine the issuance price of a bond?
10. Identify four different ways in which bonds can mature or be eliminated as liabilities.
11. If a bond's stated interest rate is below the market interest rate, will the bond sell at a premium or at a discount? Why?
12. If you think the market interest rate is going to drop in the near future, should you invest in bonds?
13. When do you think bonds will sell at or near face value?
14. Explain why bonds retired before maturity may result in a gain or loss to the issuing company.
15. What does the debt ratio measure?
16. From the standpoint of a lender, which is more attractive: a high times interest earned ratio or a low times interest earned ratio? Explain.

expanded material

17. What type of account is Discount on Bonds?
18. Why does the amortization of a bond discount increase the book value of bonds?
19. Why is the effective-interest amortization method more theoretically appropriate than the straight-line amortization method?
20. What is the carrying value of a bond?
21. How does the carrying value of a bond affect the accounting for bonds payable under the effective-interest method?
22. If the effective rate of interest for a bond is greater than its stated rate of interest, explain why the annual bond interest expense will be different from the periodic cash interest payments to the bondholders.

discussion cases

CASE 10-1

PRESENT VALUE CONCEPTS

Hamburg Company recently began business and purchased a large facility to make beach clothing. Hamburg Company managed to make a small profit in its initial year of operations, although it used all its cash to purchase inventory and equipment. After preparing its tax return for the year, Hamburg's managers realized that they could pay less taxes than they thought. Because IRS accelerated depreciation methods allow for higher depreciation expense than the straight-line method the company is using for financial reporting purposes, Hamburg can claim more depreciation expense than it thought it could and can reduce taxable income by $30,000. However, Hamburg's managers know that the two depreciation methods will eventually even out because the difference is only temporary and will create a deferred income tax liability, which must be recorded on the books. The managers are very conservative, though, and would rather pay the additional taxes now than record a liability that must be paid in the future, even if they must borrow the money from a bank to pay the extra taxes. They have come to you for advice. What would you tell them?

CASE 10-2

DEBT AND EQUITY FINANCING

Berlin Company is in a world of hurt. For the past 15 years, the company has been the exclusive toy supplier to Infants-R-Us toy stores. Unfortunately for Berlin Company, Infants-R-Us just declared bankruptcy and went out of business. Berlin is the supplier for a few local toy stores, but Infants-R-Us was by far its largest customer. Berlin's managers believe that they can save the company if they can raise enough money to develop a new product line of a popular toy, "Nano Babies." Developing the new product line will require a considerable investment, however. Berlin is trying to decide the best way to finance the investment. It has found a bank that will loan it the money at 18%, a very high rate but the only one it can get because of its precarious financial position. Berlin can also issue bonds to raise the money, but because of investors' concerns about the future viability of the company, the only kind of bonds investors will buy are high-interest junk bonds at an interest rate of 17%. Even then, there is concern that the bonds will be discounted when they are marketed. Which financing alternative would you recommend to the company? If you were an investor, would you buy Berlin Company's bonds?

exercises

EXERCISE 10-1

COMPUTING THE PRESENT VALUE OF A SINGLE SUM

Find the present value (rounded to the nearest dollar) of:

1. $15,000 due in 5 years at 8% compounded annually.
2. $25,000 due in $8\frac{1}{2}$ years at 10% compounded semiannually.
3. $9,500 due in 4 years at 12% compounded quarterly.
4. $20,000 due in 20 years at 8% compounded semiannually.

EXERCISE 10-2

COMPUTING THE FUTURE VALUE OF A SINGLE SUM

Compute the future value (rounded to the nearest dollar) of the following investments:

1. $10,209 invested to earn interest at 8% compounded annually for 5 years.
2. $10,908 invested to earn interest at 10% compounded semiannually for $8\frac{1}{2}$ years.

3. $5,920 invested to earn interest at 12% compounded quarterly for 4 years.
4. $4,166 invested to earn interest at 8% compounded semiannually for 20 years.

EXERCISE 10-3

COMPUTING THE PRESENT VALUE OF AN ANNUITY

What is the present value (rounded to the nearest dollar) of an annuity of $8,000 per year for five years if the interest rate is:

1. 8% compounded annually.
2. 10% compounded annually.

EXERCISE 10-4

COMPUTING THE AMOUNT OF PERIODIC PAYMENTS

U-Crane Company has just borrowed $100,000. The loan is to be repaid in regular annual payments made at the end of each year. What is the amount of each annual payment under the following sets of terms:

1. Interest rate of 10% compounded annually; repayment in five annual payments.
2. Interest rate of 12% compounded annually; repayment in 10 annual payments.

EXERCISE 10-5

ACCOUNTING FOR LONG-TERM NOTE PAYABLE

Karl Company borrowed $25,000 on a two-year, 12% note dated October 1, 2002. Interest is payable annually on October 1, 2003, and October 1, 2004, the maturity date of the note. The company prepares its financial statements on a calendar-year basis. Prepare all journal entries relating to the note for 2002, 2003, and 2004.

EXERCISE 10-6

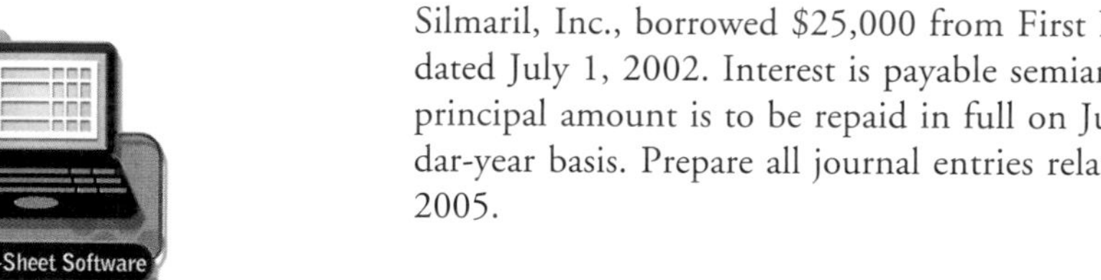

ACCOUNTING FOR LONG-TERM NOTE PAYABLE

Silmaril, Inc., borrowed $25,000 from First National Bank by issuing a three-year, 10% note dated July 1, 2002. Interest is payable semiannually on December 31 and June 30. The principal amount is to be repaid in full on June 30, 2005. Silmaril, Inc., reports on a calendar-year basis. Prepare all journal entries relating to the note during 2002, 2003, 2004, and 2005.

EXERCISE 10-7

ACCOUNTING FOR A MORTGAGE

Johnson Enterprises borrowed $100,000 on July 1, 2003, to finance the purchase of a building. The mortgage requires payments of $1,075 to be made at the end of every month for 15 years with the first payment being due on July 31, 2003. The interest rate on the mortgage is 10%.

1. Prepare a mortgage amortization schedule for 2003.
2. How much interest will be paid in 2003?
3. By how much will the principal amount of the mortgage be reduced by the end of 2003?

EXERCISE 10-8

ACCOUNTING FOR A MORTGAGE

On January 1, 2003, Gandalf, Inc., borrowed $50,000 to finance the purchase of machinery. The terms of the mortgage require payments to be made at the end of every month with the first payment being due on January 31, 2003. The length of the mortgage is five years, and the mortgage carries an interest rate of 12%.

1. Compute the amount of the monthly payment.
2. Prepare a mortgage amortization schedule for 2003.
3. Prepare the journal entry to be made on January 31, 2003, when the first payment is made.
4. For the remainder of the year, how will the journal entries relating to the mortgage differ from the one made on January 31?

EXERCISE 10-9

LEASE ACCOUNTING

Temple Corporation signed a lease to use a machine for four years. The annual lease payment is $10,500 payable at the end of each year.

1. Record the lease, assuming that the lease should be accounted for as a capital lease and the applicable interest rate is 10%. (Round to the nearest dollar.)
2. For the initial year, record the annual lease payment.

EXERCISE 10-10

LEASE ACCOUNTING

Digital, Inc., leased computer equipment from Young Leasing Company on January 2, 2003. The terms of the lease required annual payments of $4,141 for five years beginning on December 31, 2003. The interest rate on the lease is 14%.

1. Assuming the lease qualifies as an operating lease, what journal entry would be made on January 2 to record the leased asset?
2. If the lease qualifies as an operating lease, what journal entry would be made when the first payment is made on December 31, 2003?
3. Provide the journal entry made on January 2, 2003, assuming the lease qualifies as a capital lease.
4. Provide the journal entry made on December 31, 2003, to record the first lease payment, assuming a capital lease.

EXERCISE 10-11

ISSUANCE PRICE OF BONDS

Hanover Company issued five-year bonds on January 1. The face value of the bonds is $56,000. The stated interest rate on the bonds is 10%. The market rate of interest at the time of issuance was 8%. The bonds pay interest semiannually. Calculate the issuance price of the bonds.

EXERCISE 10-12

ISSUANCE PRICE OF BONDS

Bremen Company issued five-year bonds on January 1. The face value of the bonds is $56,000. The stated interest rate on the bonds is 8%. The market rate of interest at the time of issuance was 10%. The bonds pay interest semiannually. Calculate the issuance price of the bonds.

EXERCISE 10-13

ACCOUNTING FOR BONDS ISSUED AT FACE VALUE

Romulus, Inc., issued $500,000 of 10%, five-year bonds at face value on July 1, 2003. Interest on the bonds is payable semiannually on December 31 and June 30.

1. Provide the journal entry to record the issuance of the bonds on July 1, 2003.
2. Provide the journal entry made on December 31, 2003, to account for these bonds.
3. On September 29, 2004, Romulus elected to retire the bonds early. The market price of the bonds on this date was $486,000. Provide the journal entries to record the early retirement.
4. Why do you think Romulus elected to retire the bonds early?

EXERCISE 10-14

ACCOUNTING FOR BONDS ISSUED AT FACE VALUE

Rikker Company issued $600,000 of 12%, 10-year bonds at face value on October 1, 2003. The bonds pay interest on April 1 and October 1. Rikker uses the calendar year for financial reporting purposes.

1. Provide the journal entry to record the bond issuance on October 1, 2003.
2. Provide the journal entry to record interest expense on December 31, 2003.
3. Provide the journal entries made during 2004 relating to the bond.
4. On February 14, 2004, Rikker elected to retire the bond issue early. The market price on the day of retirement was $605,000. Provide the journal entries to record the bond retirement.
5. Why do you think Rikker elected to retire the bonds early?

EXERCISE 10-15

COMPUTATION OF DEBT-RELATED FINANCIAL RATIOS

The following information comes from the financial statements of Willard Hammond Company:

Long-term debt	$30,000
Total liabilities	48,000
Total stockholders' equity	25,000
Operating income	7,000
Interest expense	3,000

Compute the following ratio values:

1. Debt ratio.
2. Debt-to-equity ratio.
3. Times interest earned.

EXERCISE 10-16

IMPACT OF CAPITALIZING THE VALUE OF OPERATING LEASES

The following information comes from the financial statements of Karlla Peterson Company:

Total liabilities	$100,000
Total stockholders' equity	80,000

In addition, Karlla Peterson has a large number of operating leases. The payments on these operating leases total $20,000 per year for the next 15 years. The present value of the economic obligation associated with these operating leases is $150,000. Of course, because these are operating leases, this economic obligation is off the balance sheet.

Compute the following ratio values:

1. Debt ratio. HINT: Remember the accounting equation.
2. Debt-to-equity ratio.
3. Debt-to-equity ratio assuming that Karlla Peterson's operating leases are accounted for as capital leases.
4. Debt ratio assuming that Karlla Peterson's operating leases are accounted for as capital leases.

expanded material

EXERCISE 10-17

ACCOUNTING FOR BONDS ISSUED AT A DISCOUNT

Hawaii Equipment Company issued $300,000 of 8%, five-year bonds at 97 on June 30, 2003. Interest is payable on June 30 and December 31. The company uses the straight-line method to amortize bond premiums and discounts. The company's fiscal year is from February 1 through January 31.

Prepare all necessary journal entries to account for the bonds from the date of issuance through June 30, 2004. Also record the retirement of the bonds on June 30, 2008, assuming that all interest has been paid and that the discount has been fully amortized.

EXERCISE 10-18

ACCOUNTING FOR BONDS ISSUED AT A PREMIUM

Sealon Corporation issued $100,000 of 10%, 10-year bonds at 102 on April 1, 2003. Interest is payable semiannually on April 1 and October 1. Sealon Corporation uses the calendar year for financial reporting.

1. Record the necessary entries to account for these bonds on the following three dates. (Use the straight-line method to amortize the bond premium.)
   a. April 1, 2003.
   b. October 1, 2003.
   c. December 31, 2003.
2. Show how the bonds would be reported on the balance sheet of Sealon Corporation on December 31, 2003.

EXERCISE 10-19

EFFECTIVE-INTEREST CALCULATION

Determine the *approximate* effective rate of interest for $300,000, 8%, five-year bonds issued at 95. (Assume straight-line amortization.)

EXERCISE 10-20

BOND AMORTIZATION SCHEDULE

The following is a partially completed amortization schedule prepared for the Liggett Company to account for its three-year bond issue with a face value of $50,000. The schedule covers the first three semiannual interest payment dates. Amounts are rounded to the nearest dollar. Compute the missing numbers.

Year	Interest Paid	Bond Expense	Premium Amortized	Bonds Payable Carrying Value
0				$52,537
½	(1)	$2,627	(2)	52,164
1	$3,000	(3)	$392	(4)
1½	(5)	(6)	(7)	(8)

EXERCISE 10-21

ACCOUNTING FOR BONDS

Tanner Corporation, a calendar-year firm, is authorized to issue $400,000 of 12%, 10-year bonds dated May 1, 2003, with interest payable semiannually on May 1 and November 1.

Amortization of bond premiums or discounts is recorded using the straight-line amortization method. Prepare journal entries to record the following events, assuming that the bonds are sold at 96 on May 1, 2003.

1. The bond issuance on May 1, 2003.
2. Payment of interest on November 1, 2003.
3. Adjusting entry on December 31, 2003.
4. Payment of the interest on May 1, 2004.

problems

PROBLEM 10-1

PRESENT AND FUTURE VALUE COMPUTATIONS

Required:

1. Determine the present value in each of the following situations:
   a. A $5,000 loan to be repaid in full at the end of three years. Interest on the loan is payable quarterly. The interest rate is 12% compounded quarterly.
   b. A two-year note for $8,000 bearing interest at an annual rate of 10%, compounded semiannually. Interest is payable semiannually.
   c. A five-year mortgage to be paid in monthly installments of $1,000. The interest rate is 12% compounded monthly.
2. Determine the future value in each of the following situations:
   a. An investment of $10,000 today to earn interest at 6% compounded semiannually to provide for a down payment on a house five years from now.
   b. An investment of $25,000 today to earn interest at 8% compounded quarterly that is designated for a charitable contribution 10 years from now when the donor retires.

PROBLEM 10-2

PRESENT AND FUTURE VALUE COMPUTATIONS

Required:

1. Compute the present value for each of the following situations, assuming an interest rate of 10% compounded annually. (Round amounts to the nearest dollar.)
   a. A single payment of $30,000 due on a mortgage five years from now.
   b. A series of payments of $5,000 each, due at the end of each year for five years.
   c. A five-year, 10% loan of $25,000, with interest payable annually, and the principal due in five years.
2. Compute the future value amounts (rounded to the nearest dollar) in each of the following situations:
   a. A $20,000 lump-sum investment today that will earn interest at 10% compounded annually over five years.

b. A $5,000 lump-sum investment today that will earn interest at 8%, compounded quarterly to provide money for a child's college education 15 years from now.

PROBLEM 10-3

COMPUTING THE AMOUNT OF PERIODIC PAYMENTS

Kenneth J. Nelson has just purchased a new car for $35,000. He paid $5,000 down and signed a note for the remaining $30,000. The interest rate on the note is 12% compounded monthly, or 1% per month.

Required:

1. Compute the amount of Mr. Nelson's monthly payment if he plans to pay off the $30,000 note in 30 monthly payments. Remember: The interest rate is 1% per month.
2. Repeat (1) assuming that Mr. Nelson wishes to repay the note in 60 monthly payments.
3. Assume that Mr. Nelson decides to repay the note in 60 monthly payments. What is the balance remaining on the note immediately after he makes the 30th payment? HINT: Compute the present value of the remaining 30 payments.

PROBLEM 10-4

ACCOUNTING FOR NOTES PAYABLE

Sweet's Candy Company needed cash for its current business operations. On January 1, 2002, the company borrowed $8,000 on a two-year, interest-bearing note from Peterson Bank at an annual interest rate of 10%. Interest is payable annually on January 1, and the note matures January 1, 2004. Sweet's Candy Company also borrowed $4,500 from Laurence National Bank on January 1, 2002, signing a three-year, 11% note due on January 1, 2005, with interest payable annually on January 1.

Required:

Prepare all journal entries relating to the two notes for 2002, 2003, 2004, and 2005. Assume that Sweet's Candy Company uses the calendar year for financial reporting. (Round all amounts to the nearest dollar.)

PROBLEM 10-5

ACCOUNTING FOR NOTES PAYABLE

During 2002, Kenan Corporation had the following transactions relating to long-term liabilities:

Apr. 1 Purchased a machine costing $200,000 from Perry Corporation. Issued a two-year, interest-bearing note with interest payable on April 1 of each year. The note matures on April 1, 2004, and carries an interest rate of 9%.

July 1 Borrowed $30,000 from Northern National Bank. The terms of the note require semi-annual payments of interest on December 31 and June 30. The note matures in two years and carries an interest rate of 8%.

Required:

1. Prepare the journal entries made on April 1 and July 1 to record the issuance of these two notes.
2. Prepare all journal entries made on December 31, 2002.
3. Prepare all journal entries made during 2003.

PROBLEM 10-6

ACCOUNTING FOR A MORTGAGE

On November 1, 2003, Hill Company arranges with an insurance company to borrow $200,000 on a 20-year mortgage to purchase land and a building to be used in its operations. The land and the building are pledged as collateral for the loan, which has an annual interest rate of 12%, compounded monthly. The monthly payments of $2,200 are made at the end of each month, beginning on November 30, 2003.

Required:

1. Prepare the journal entry to record the purchase of the land and building, assuming that $40,000 of the purchase price is assignable to the land.
2. Prepare the journal entries on November 30 and December 31 for the monthly payments on the mortgage.
3. **Interpretive Question:** Explain generally how the remaining liability at December 31, 2003, will be reported on the company's balance sheet dated December 31, 2003.

PROBLEM 10-7

LEASE ACCOUNTING

On January 1, 2002, Linda Lou Foods, Inc., leased a tractor. The lease agreement qualifies as a capital lease and calls for payments of $7,000 per year (payable each year on January 1, starting in 2003) for eight years. The annual interest rate on the lease is 8%. Linda Lou Foods uses a calendar-year reporting period.

Required:

1. Prepare the journal entries for the following dates:
   a. January 1, 2002, to record the leasing of the tractor.
   b. December 31, 2002, to recognize the interest expense for the year 2002.
   c. January 1, 2003, to record the first lease payment.
2. Prepare the appropriate journal entries at December 31, 2003, and January 1, 2004.
3. **Interpretive Question:** Explain briefly how the leased asset is accounted for annually.

PROBLEM 10-8

LEASE ACCOUNTING

Exploration, Inc., leased a starship on January 2, 2003. Terms of the lease require annual payments of $41,208 per year for five years. The interest rate on the lease is 12%, and the first payment is due on December 31, 2003.

Required:

1. Compute the present value of the lease payments.
2. Assuming the lease qualifies as a capital lease, prepare the journal entry to record the lease.
3. Prepare the journal entry to record the first lease payment on December 31, 2003, and to depreciate the leased asset. Exploration, Inc., uses the straight-line method for depreciating all long-term assets.
4. **Interpretive Question:** How would the leased asset, and its associated liability, be disclosed on the balance sheet prepared on December 31, 2003?

PROBLEM 10-9

ISSUANCE PRICE OF BONDS

Patterson Company issued 30-year bonds on June 30. The face value of the bonds is $750,000. The stated interest rate on the bonds is 6%. The market rate of interest at the time of issuance was 4%. Patterson also issued another set of bonds on August 31. These bonds were 20-year bonds and had a face value of $556,000. The stated rate of interest on these bonds was 5%. The market rate of interest at the time these bonds were issued was 8%. Both sets of bonds pay interest semiannually.

Required:

Calculate the issuance price of these bonds.

PROBLEM 10-10

ACCOUNTING FOR BONDS

On July 1, 2003, Paramount, Inc. issued $500,000, 8%, 30-year bonds with interest paid semiannually on January 1 and July 1. The bonds were sold when the market rate of interest was 8%. On October 1, 2006, the bonds were retired when their fair market value was $495,000.

Required:

1. Demonstrate, using the present value tables, that the bonds were sold for $500,000.
2. Provide the journal entry made on July 1 to record the issuance of the bonds.
3. Provide the journal entry made on December 31, 2003, relating to interest.
4. Provide the journal entries to record the retirement of the bonds.

PROBLEM 10-11

ACCOUNTING FOR BONDS

Columbia Enterprises issued $1 million, 10%, 20-year bonds on October 1, 2002. Interest payment dates are April 1 and October 1. The bonds were sold at face value.

Required:

1. Provide the journal entry to record the initial issuance of the bonds.
2. Provide the required journal entry on December 31, 2002.
3. Provide all journal entries relating to the bonds made during 2003.

PROBLEM 10-12

REPORTING LIABILITIES ON THE BALANCE SHEET

The following list of accounts is taken from the adjusted trial balance of Goforth Company.

Accounts Payable	$45,000
Notes Payable (due in 6 months)	24,000
Income Taxes Payable	18,000
Unearned Sales Revenue	27,500
Notes Payable (due in 2 years)	40,000
Prepaid Insurance	6,200
Accounts Receivable	53,000
Current Portion of Mortgage Payable	12,300
Mortgage Payable (due beyond 1 year)	93,000
Retained Earnings	91,400
Property Taxes Payable	8,700
Salaries & Wages Payable	15,200
Sales Tax Payable	3,100

Required: Prepare the liabilities section of the company's balance sheet.

PROBLEM 10-13

REPORTING LIABILITIES ON THE BALANCE SHEET

The following amounts are shown on the Plymouth Company's adjusted trial balance for the year 2003:

Accounts Payable	$ 36,000
Property Taxes Payable	6,300
Short-Term Notes Payable	44,000
Mortgage Payable (due within 1 year)	28,000
Mortgage Payable (due after 1 year)	300,000
Accrued Interest on Mortgage Payable	3,000
Lease Liability (Current Portion)	58,000
Lease Liability (Long Term)	414,000
Rent Payable	70,000
Income Taxes Payable	50,000
Federal & State Unemployment Taxes Payable	16,000

Required: Prepare the liabilities section of Plymouth Company's balance sheet at December 31, 2003.

PROBLEM 10-14

COMPUTATION OF DEBT-RELATED FINANCIAL RATIOS

The following information comes from the financial statements of Ron Winmill Company:

Long-term debt	$180,000
Total liabilities	230,000
Total stockholders' equity	150,000
Current assets	80,000
Earnings before income taxes	11,000
Interest expense	23,000

Required: Compute the following ratio values. State any assumptions that you make.

1. Current ratio.
2. Debt ratio.
3. Debt-to-equity ratio.
4. Times interest earned.
5. **Interpretive Question:** You are a bank manager considering making a new $20,000 loan to Ron Winmill that would replace part of the existing long-term debt. You expect Ron Winmill to repay your loan in two years. Which of the ratios computed in (1) through (4) would be most useful to you in evaluating whether to make the loan to Ron Winmill?

PROBLEM 10-15

IMPACT OF CAPITALIZING THE VALUE OF OPERATING LEASES

The following information comes from the financial statements of Travis Campbell Company:

Total liabilities	$100,000
Total stockholders' equity	80,000
Property, plant, and equipment	110,000
Sales	500,000
Earnings before income taxes	11,000
Interest expense	23,000

In addition, Travis Campbell has a large number of operating leases. The payments on these operating leases total $30,000 per year for the next 10 years. The present value of the economic obligation associated with these operating leases is $180,000. Of course, because these are operating leases, this economic obligation is off the balance sheet.

Required: Compute the following ratio values:

1. Debt ratio. HINT: Remember the accounting equation.
2. Debt ratio assuming that Travis Campbell's operating leases are accounted for as capital leases.
3. Asset turnover (sales/total assets).
4. Asset turnover assuming that Travis Campbell's operating leases are accounted for as capital leases.
5. **Interpretive Question:** You are Travis Campbell's banker. You are concerned that the times interest earned ratio is not accurately reflecting the risk that Travis Campbell will not meet its fixed annual payments because most of those fixed payments are operating lease payments, not interest payments. Design an alternative ratio that will reflect the fact that, like interest payments, operating lease payments are fixed obligations that must be covered through operating profits each year. Compute the value for the ratio that you have designed.

expanded material

PROBLEM 10-16

ACCOUNTING FOR BONDS

Nemo Company authorized and sold $90,000 of 10%, 15-year bonds on April 1, 2003. The bonds pay interest each April 1, and Nemo's year-end is December 31.

Required:

1. Prepare journal entries to record the issuance of Nemo Company's bonds under each of the following three assumptions:
   a. Sold at 97.
   b. Sold at face value.
   c. Sold at 105.
2. Prepare adjusting entries for the bonds on December 31, 2003, under all three assumptions. (Use the straight-line amortization method.)
3. Show how the bond liabilities would appear on the December 31, 2003, balance sheet under each of the three assumptions.
4. **Interpretive Question:** What condition would cause the bonds to sell at 97? At 105?

PROBLEM 10-17

ACCOUNTING FOR BONDS ISSUED AT A PREMIUM

On March 1, 2003, Devone Corporation issued $50,000 of 10%, five-year bonds at 118. The bonds were dated March 1, 2003, and interest is payable on March 1 and September 1. Devone records amortization using the straight-line method. Devone's financial reporting year ends on December 31.

Required: Provide all necessary journal entries on each of the following dates:

1. March 1, 2003.
2. September 1, 2003.
3. December 31, 2003.
4. March 1, 2008.

PROBLEM 10-18

BONDS RETIRED AT MATURITY

Stottard Company issued $450,000 of 10%, 10-year bonds on June 1, 2002, at 103. The bonds were dated June 1, and interest is payable on June 1 and December 1 of each year.

Required:

1. Record the issuance of the bonds on June 1, 2002. (Round to the nearest dollar.)
2. Record the interest payment on December 1, 2002. Stottard uses the straight-line method of amortization.
3. Record the interest accrual on December 31, 2002, including amortization.
4. Record the journal entries required on June 1, 2012, when the bonds mature.

PROBLEM 10-19

STRAIGHT-LINE VERSUS EFFECTIVE-INTEREST AMORTIZATION

Cyprus Corporation issued $150,000 of bonds on January 1, 2003, to raise funds to buy some special machinery. The maturity date of the bonds is January 1, 2008, with interest payable each January 1 and July 1. The stated rate of interest is 10%. When the bonds were sold, the effective rate of interest was 12%. The company's financial reporting year ends December 31.

Required:

1. Determine the price at which the bonds would be sold.
2. Prepare the amortization schedule using the effective-interest method.
3. Prepare a comparative schedule of interest expense for each year (2003–2008) for the effective-interest and straight-line methods of amortization.
4. Record the journal entry for the last payment using the amortization schedule in (2).
5. Record the journal entry for the retirement of the bonds.
6. **Interpretive Question:** Is the difference between the interest expense each year between the straight-line and effective-interest methods sufficient to require the use of the effective-interest method? How do you think this question would be answered in practice?

PROBLEM 10-20

EFFECTIVE-INTEREST AMORTIZATION

Lancell Corporation issued $100,000 of three-year, 10% bonds on January 1, 2002. The bonds pay interest on January 1 and July 1 each year. The bonds were sold to yield an 8% return, compounded semiannually.

Required:

1. At what price were the bonds issued?
2. Prepare a schedule to amortize the premium or discount on the bonds using the effective-interest amortization method.
3. Use the information in the amortization schedule prepared for (2) to record the interest payment on July 1, 2004, including the appropriate amortization of the premium or discount.
4. **Interpretive Question:** Explain why these bonds sold for more or less than face value.

PROBLEM 10-21

ACCOUNTING FOR BONDS

Bell Company sold $200,000 of 10-year bonds on January 1, 2002, to Brown Corporation. The bond indenture included the following information:

Face value	$200,000
Date of bonds	January 1, 2002
Maturity date	January 1, 2012
Stated rate of interest	14%*
Effective (market) rate of interest	12%*

*Compounded semiannually

Required:

1. Prepare the journal entry to record the issuance of the bonds.
2. What is the interest expense on the Bell Company books for the years ending December 31, 2002, and December 31, 2003, using straight-line amortization?
3. Explain how the bonds would be presented on Bell's balance sheet at December 31, 2003.

PROBLEM 10-22

STRAIGHT-LINE VERSUS EFFECTIVE-INTEREST AMORTIZATION

Foster Corporation issued three-year bonds with a $180,000 face value on March 1, 2002, in order to pay for a new computer system. The bonds mature on March 1, 2005, with interest payable on March 1 and September 1. The contract rate of interest is 10%. (Interest is compounded semiannually.) When the bonds were sold, the effective rate of interest was 12%. The company's fiscal year ends on February 28.

Required:

1. At what price were the bonds issued based on the information presented?
2. Prepare an amortization schedule using the effective-interest method.
3. Prepare a schedule of interest expense for each year (2002–2005), comparing the annual interest expense for straight-line and effective-interest amortization.
4. Using the amortization schedule prepared in (2), prepare the journal entry to record the interest payment on September 1, 2002.
5. Prepare the adjusting journal entry to record accrued interest on February 28, 2003.
6. Prepare the journal entry to retire the bonds on March 1, 2005, assuming all interest has been paid prior to retirement.

PROBLEM 10-23

BONDS RETIRED BEFORE MATURITY

Amity Construction Company issued $100,000 of 10% bonds on January 1, 2003. The maturity date of the bonds is January 1, 2013. Interest is payable January 1 and July 1. The bonds were sold at 111.4 on July 1, 2003. The company uses the straight-line method of amortizing bond premiums and discounts.

Required:

1. Make the required journal entries for each of the following dates:
   a. July 1, 2003.
   b. December 31, 2003.
   c. January 1, 2004.
   d. July 1, 2004.
2. Because of a substantial decline in the market rate of interest, Amity Construction Company purchased all the bonds on the open market at face value (100) on July 1, 2006. The following entry had just been made on that day:

Bond Interest Expense	4,400	
Premium on Bonds	600	
Cash		5,000
Made semiannual interest payment on the bonds and amortized bond premium for six months.		

   Prepare the journal entry to record the retirement of the bonds on July 1, 2006.

PROBLEM 10-24

UNIFYING CONCEPTS: ACCOUNTING FOR BONDS PAYABLE

Durham Corporation was authorized to issue $500,000 of 8%, four-year bonds, dated May 1, 2003. All the bonds were sold on that date when the effective interest rate was 10%. Interest is payable on May 1 and November 1 each year. The company follows a policy of amortizing premium or discount using the effective-interest method. The company closes its books on December 31 of each year.

Required:

1. Calculate the issuance price of the bonds.
2. Prepare an amortization schedule that covers the life of the bond.
3. Prepare journal entries at the following dates based on the information shown in the amortization schedule prepared for requirement (2).
   a. December 31, 2003.
   b. May 1, 2004.

c. November 1, 2004.
d. December 31, 2004.

4. Based on the journal entries prepared for requirement (3), how much interest expense related to this bond issue did the company report on its income statement for the year 2004?
5. What was the carrying value of this bond issue on the balance sheet of the company at December 31, 2004?
6. **Interpretive Question:** Explain why another company in the same industry, which issued bonds with the same amount of face value, the same date of issuance, and the same stated rate of interest, might have had an issuance price of more or less than the price you computed for the issuance of the Durham Corporation bonds.

PROBLEM 10-25 ANALYSIS OF BONDS

Bonds with a face value of $200,000 and a stated interest rate of 12% were issued on March 1, 2003. The bonds pay interest each February 28 and August 31 and mature on March 1, 2013. The issuing company uses the calendar year for financial reporting.

Required: Using these data, complete the following tables for each of the conditions listed. (Show computations and assume straight-line amortization.)

1. The bonds sold at face value.
2. The bonds sold at 97.
3. The bonds sold at 103.

	Case 1	Case 2	Case 3
Cash received at issuance date	_____	_____	_____
Total cash paid to bondholders through maturity	_____	_____	_____
Income Statement for 2003:			
Bond interest expense	_____	_____	_____
Balance Sheet at December 31, 2003:			
Long-term liabilities:			
Bonds payable, 12%	_____	_____	_____
Unamortized discount	_____	_____	_____
Unamortized premium	_____	_____	_____
Bond carrying value	_____	_____	_____
Approximate effective interest rate*	_____	_____	_____

*Round to the nearest tenth of a percent.

competency enhancement opportunities

- Analyzing Real Company Information
- International Case
- Ethics Case
- Writing Assignment
- The Debate
- Cumulative Spreadsheet Project
- Internet Search

The following additional assignments provide opportunities for students to develop critical thinking, ethical perspectives, oral and written communication skills, experience with electronic research, and teamwork through group and business activities.

ANALYZING REAL COMPANY INFORMATION

• *Analyzing 10-1 (Microsoft)*

The 1999 annual report for MICROSOFT is included in Appendix A. Locate that annual report and consider the following questions:

1. Examine Microsoft's balance sheet as of June 30, 1999. Do you notice anything unusual in connection with Microsoft's reported long-term debt?
2. During fiscal 1997, Microsoft issued $980 million in convertible preferred stock. The terms of this preferred stock are that the investors agreed to give Microsoft $980 million, and Microsoft agreed to pay them a fixed amount of $27 million per year in dividends. Starting in 1999, these preferred stockholders can exchange their shares for Microsoft common stock, which will entitle them to all the rights of Microsoft owners. In what ways is this $980 million investment in Microsoft similar to a loan? In what ways is it different from a loan?

• *Analyzing 10-2 (IBM)*

INTERNATIONAL BUSINESS MACHINES (IBM) included the following information in Note J to its 1999 financial statements:

Long-Term Debt
At December 31, 1999
(dollars in millions)

	Maturity Dates	Amount
Items denominated in U.S. dollars:		
DEBENTURES:		
6.22% debentures	2027	$ 500
6½% debentures	2028	700
7% debentures	2025	600
7% debentures	2045	150
7⅛% debentures	2096	850
7½% debentures	2013	550
8⅜% debentures	2019	750

(continued)

NOTES:		
6.3% average	2000–2014	$ 4,191
Medium-term note		
Program: 5.8% average	2000–2014	6,230
Other: 6.5% average	2000–2012	1,227
		$15,748
Items denominated in other currencies:		
Japanese yen (3.0% average rate)	2000 through 2014	$ 3,141
Canadian dollars (5.7% average rate)	2000 through 2005	707
German marks (4.9% average rate)	2002	103
Swiss francs (2.5% average rate)	2001	78
U.K. pounds (7.0% average rate)	2000 through 2003	33
Other currencies (13.6% average rate)	2000 through 2014	159
		$19,969

1. IBM lists seven different issues of debentures. What is a debenture?
2. What is unusual about the 7⅛% debentures?
3. IBM has borrowed the equivalent of $4.221 billion in the form of foreign currency loans. Why would IBM get loans denominated in foreign currencies rather than get all of its loans in U.S. dollars?
4. The average interest rates on the foreign currency loans range from a low of 2.5% for loans of Swiss francs to 7.0% for loans of U.K. pounds. What factors would cause IBM to pay a higher interest rate when it borrows U.K. pounds than when it borrows Swiss francs?

• *Analyzing 10-3 (Citicorp)*

The CITY BANK OF NEW YORK was chartered on June 16, 1812, just two days before the start of the War of 1812 between the United States and Great Britain. To get around twentieth-century bank holding laws, a holding company was organized to own the bank. This holding company took the name of CITICORP in 1974, and the bank itself is now called CITIBANK. Citibank is one of the largest banks in the United States.

Below are a simplified balance sheet for Citicorp as of December 31, 1999, and a schedule outlining the interest rate on Citicorp's outstanding long-term debt:

Citicorp
Balance Sheet
December 31, 1999

	(millions of dollars)
Cash	$ 10,648
Investment securities	90,310
Loans receivable	203,288
Other assets	23,653
Total	$327,899
Deposit liabilities	$234,832
Other liabilities	59,753
Long-term debt	11,752
Stockholders' equity	21,562
Total	$327,899

Interest Rates Prevailing on Parent and Subsidiary Loans for Loans Outstanding on December 31, 1999

Type of Loan	Average Interest Rate
PARENT COMPANY	
Senior notes	05.94%
Subordinated notes	07.07%
SUBSIDIARIES	
Senior notes	08.22%
Subordinated notes	07.78%

1. Citicorp's simplified balance sheet is representative of most banks' balance sheets. Using the information about relative sizes of assets and liabilities given in that balance sheet, write a brief description of the primary operating activity of a bank.
2. Compute Citicorp's debt ratio (total liabilities divided by total assets). Comment on whether the value seems high or low to you.
3. In its long-term debt of $11.752 billion, Citicorp has both fixed-rate loans and floating-rate (or variable-rate) loans. What is the advantage of borrowing with a fixed-rate loan? What is the advantage of borrowing with a variable-rate loan?
4. Citicorp includes the following information in its 1999 financial statement note on long-term debt: "Approximately 59% . . . of subsidiary long-term debt was guaranteed by Citicorp, and of the debt not guaranteed by Citicorp, approximately 23% . . . was secured by the assets of the subsidiary." When Citicorp guarantees the long-term debt of one of its subsidiaries, does that raise or lower the interest rate that the subsidiary must pay on the debt? Explain. Is the interest rate on a loan higher when it is secured by assets or when it is unsecured? Explain.

INTERNATIONAL CASE

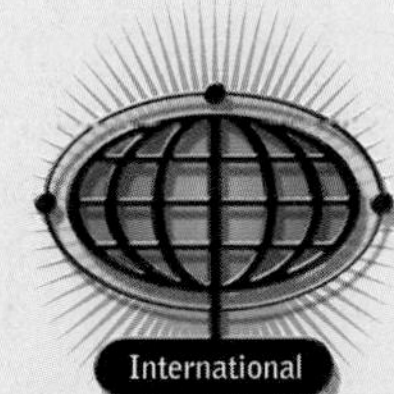

• *British Petroleum*

In May 1901, William Knox D'Arcy convinced the Shah of Persia (present-day Iran) to allow him to hunt for oil. The oil discovered in Persia in 1908 was the first commercially significant amount of oil found in the Middle East. The company making the discovery called itself the ANGLO-PERSIAN OIL COMPANY, later named BRITISH PETROLEUM, or BP. Today, BP Amoco is one of the largest oil and gas exploration and refining companies in the world.

The information on the next page comes from Note 23 (Finance debt) of British Petroleum's 1999 financial statements. All amounts are in millions of British pounds.

	Loans	Finance Leases
Payments due within:		
1 year	£ 4,812	£ 103
2 to 5 years	4,646	725
after 5 years	3,261	3,569
	£12,719	£4,397
Less finance charge	0	2,572
Net obligation	£12,719	£1,825

1. In Great Britain, a finance lease is what we in the United States would call a capital lease. According to Note 23, British Petroleum expects to make total lease payments of £4.397 billion under finance leases. However, a liability of only £1.825 billion is reported on the balance sheet. Why is there a difference between the two amounts?
2. The £4.397 billion payment amount for the finance leases reflects the total of all lease payments that will be made under the agreements. Does the £12.719 billion amount reported for loans reflect the amount of all payments that will be made under the loan agreements? Explain.
3. The future loan and finance lease payments are separated into amounts to be repaid within one year, within two to five years, and after five years. How would a financial statement user find this payment timing information to be useful?

ETHICS CASE

• *Hiding an Obligation By Calling It a Lease*

You and your partner own Miss Karma's Preschool, which provides preschool and day care services for about 100 children per day. Business is booming, and you are right in the middle of expanding your operation. Three months ago you took your financial statements to the local bank and applied for a five-year, $145,000 loan. The bank approved the loan, but it included as part of the loan agreement a condition that you would incur no other long-term liabilities during the five-year loan period. You cheerfully agreed to this condition because you didn't anticipate any further financing needs.

Two weeks ago a state government inspector came to your facility and said that your square footage was not enough for the number of children enrolled in your programs. The inspector gave you one month to find another facility, or else you would have to shut down. Luckily, you were able to find another building to use. However, the owner of the building insists on having you sign a 20-year lease. Alternatively, you can buy the building for $220,000. To buy the building, you would have to get a mortgage, which would, of course, violate the agreement on your five-year bank loan.

Your partner suggests that the lease is the way to solve all of your problems. Your partner has studied some accounting and reports that you can sign the lease but carefully construct the lease contract so that the lease will be accounted for as an operating lease. In this way, the lease obligation will not be reported as an accounting liability, the loan agreement will not be violated, and you can move to the new facility without any problem.

Is your partner right? Is it possible to avoid reporting the 20-year lease contract as an accounting liability? By signing the lease, are you violating the bank loan agreement? What do you think is the best course of action?

WRITING ASSIGNMENT

• ***My Contract's Bigger Than Your Contract!***
You are an agent for professional athletes. One of your clients is a superstar in the NBA. Last month you negotiated a new deal for your client that pays him $22 million per year for each of the next six years. Your client was very pleased with this $132 million contract, especially because it was a bigger contract than any of the other players on his team received.

This morning, while you were relaxing in your Jacuzzi, you got an angry cellular call from your client. It seems that one of his teammates just signed a $150 million deal, paying him $15 million per year for each of the next 10 years. Your client is outraged because you guaranteed that no one on his team would be receiving a bigger contract this season. Your client has threatened to terminate his agreement with you and also to spread the word among all his friends that you are not trustworthy.

Write a one-page memo to your client explaining that the actual value of his $132 million contract is greater than the $150 million contract signed by his teammate. Your client has a marketing degree from an ACC school, so he has had some exposure to the concept of the time value of money.

THE DEBATE

• ***Which is the Better Way to Borrow—Bank Loan or Bonds?***
When a major corporation is seeking to borrow a large sum of money, it can choose to arrange a loan through a single bank (or group of banks), or it can issue bonds and essentially borrow the money from the public.

Divide your group into two teams.

- One team represents "Bank Loans." Prepare a two-minute oral presentation arguing that the best way for a major corporation to borrow money is through bank loans negotiated directly with a single bank or group of banks.
- The other team represents "Bonds." Prepare a two-minute oral presentation arguing that bonds offer the best way for a major corporation to borrow a large sum of money.

CUMULATIVE SPREADSHEET PROJECT

This spreadsheet assignment is a continuation of the spreadsheet assignments given in earlier chapters. If you completed those spreadsheets, you have a head start on this one.

1. Handyman wishes to prepare a forecasted balance sheet and income statement for 2004. Use the original financial statement numbers for 2003 [given in part (1) of the Cumulative Spreadsheet Project assignment in Chapter 2] as the basis for the forecast, along with the following additional information:
   a. Sales in 2004 are expected to increase by 40% over 2003 sales of $700.
   b. Cash will increase at the same rate as sales.
   c. The forecasted amount of accounts receivable in 2004 is determined using the forecasted value for the average collection period. For simplicity, do the computations using the end-of-period accounts receiv-

able balance instead of the average balance. The average collection period for 2004 is expected to be 14.08 days.

d. The forecasted amount of inventory in 2004 is determined using the forecasted value for the number of days' sales in inventory (computed using the end-of-period inventory balance). The number of days' sales in inventory for 2004 is expected to be 107.6 days.
e. The forecasted amount of accounts payable in 2004 is determined using the forecasted value for the number of days' purchases in accounts payable (computed using the end-of-period accounts payable balance). The number of days' purchases in accounts payable for 2004 is expected to be 48.34 days.
f. The $160 in operating expenses reported in 2003 breaks down as follows: $5 depreciation expense, $155 other operating expenses.
g. See item (l) for the assumption concerning the amount of new long-term debt that will be acquired in 2004.
h. No cash dividends will be paid in 2004.
i. New short-term loans payable will be acquired in an amount sufficient to make Handyman's current ratio in 2004 exactly equal to 2.0.
j. The forecasted amount of property, plant, and equipment (PP&E) in 2004 is determined using the forecasted value for the fixed asset turnover ratio. For simplicity, compute the fixed asset turnover ratio using the end-of-period *gross PP&E* balance. The fixed asset turnover ratio for 2004 is expected to be 3.518 times.
k. In computing depreciation expense for 2004, use straight-line depreciation and assume a 30-year useful life with no residual value. Gross PP&E acquired during the year is depreciated for only half the year. In other words, depreciation expense for 2004 is the sum of two parts: (1) a full year of depreciation on the beginning balance in PP&E, assuming a 30-year life and no residual value and (2) a half-year of depreciation on any new PP&E acquired during the year, based on the change in the gross PP&E balance.

Note: These statements were constructed as part of the spreadsheet assignment in Chapter 9; you can use that spreadsheet as a starting point if you have completed that assignment. *Clearly state any additional assumptions that you make.*

For this exercise, add the following additional assumptions:

l. New long-term debt will be acquired (or repaid) in an amount sufficient to make Handyman's debt ratio (total liabilities divided by total assets) in 2004 exactly equal to 0.80.
m. Assume an interest rate on short-term loans payable of *6.0%* and on long-term debt of *8.0%*. Only a half year's interest is charged on loans taken out during the year. For example, if short-term loans payable at the end of 2004 are $15 and given that short-term loans payable at the end of 2003 were $10, total short-term interest expense for 2004 would be $0.75 [($10 × 0.06) + ($5 × 0.06 × $^1/_2$)].

Clearly state any additional assumptions that you make.

2. Repeat (1), with the following changes in assumptions:
   a. The debt ratio in 2004 is exactly equal to 0.70.
   b. The debt ratio in 2004 is exactly equal to 0.90.

3. Prepare a table displaying the forecasted values of long-term debt and paid-in capital in 2004 under each of the following assumptions about the debt ratio: 0.70, 0.80, and 0.90. The sum of these two items can be viewed as the total amount of long-term financing (both debt and equity) received from outsiders. Comment on why the total of these two items is not the same under each debt ratio assumption.

INTERNET SEARCH

International

• Disney

The history of DISNEY was outlined at the beginning of the chapter. Access Disney's Web site at http://www.disney.com. Sometimes Web addresses change, so if this Disney address doesn't work, access the Web site for this textbook (http://albrecht.swcollege.com) for an updated link to Disney.

Once you've gained access to Disney's Web site, answer the following questions:

1. Disney's home page offers a link to a site promoting Disney's current movies. What movie is currently featured at that site?
2. Use Disney's link to its international operations in France to see if you can find the Web site for Disneyland Paris. What is the Web address? Is the site in English or in French?
3. If you wish to enroll in Disney's direct stock purchase plan, meaning that you will buy ownership shares from Disney itself rather than going through a stockbroker, what is the minimum amount you must invest?
4. According to Disney's most recent statement of cash flows, how much new borrowing did Disney do in the most recent year? How much was spent to repay loans in the most recent year?

Equity Financing

chapter

f11

learning objectives After studying this chapter, you should be able to:

1 Distinguish between debt and equity financing, and describe the advantages and disadvantages of organizing a business as a proprietorship or a partnership.

2 Describe the basic characteristics of a corporation and the nature of common and preferred stock.

3 Account for the issuance and repurchase of common and preferred stock.

4 Understand the factors that affect retained earnings, describe the factors determining whether a company can and should pay cash dividends, and account for cash dividends.

5 Describe the purpose of reporting comprehensive income in the equity section of the balance sheet, and prepare a statement of stockholders' equity.

expanded material

6 Account for stock dividends and distinguish them from stock splits.

7 Explain prior-period adjustments and prepare a statement of retained earnings.

8 Understand basic proprietorship and partnership accounting.

In 1882, two young newspaper reporters, Charles Dow and Edward Jones, teamed up to provide the Wall Street financial community with handwritten news bulletins. In 1889, when the staff of **DOW JONES & COMPANY** had grown to 50, they decided to convert the bulletin service into a daily newspaper. The first issue of *The Wall Street Journal* appeared on July 8, 1889. Clarence Barron, who operated a financial news service in Boston, was the paper's first out-of-town reporter. Barron purchased Dow Jones & Company in 1902 for $130,000, and his heirs still hold majority control of the company today.

In the 1940s, *The Wall Street Journal* began publishing more than just business news, expanding its coverage to include economics, politics, and general news. Today, *The Wall Street Journal* has a paid circulation of 1.8 million and is read by an estimated 4.9 million people every day. Dow Jones also publishes *The Wall Street Journal Europe* and *The Asian Wall Street Journal*, and each day it contributes special business pages to 23 Spanish and Portuguese language newspapers in Latin American countries. *The Wall Street Journal* is also a leader in Web-based news, with more than 500,000 paid subscribers for **http://wsj.com** as of September 30, 2000. This is particularly impressive in that the public is accustomed to getting information for free on the Web.

The Wall Street Journal is the flagship of the company, but the name "Dow Jones" is best known because of the Dow Jones Industrial Average that is cited in the news every day. "The Dow" is widely used to reflect the general health of the U.S. economy. So, what is it? Simply put, the Dow Jones Industrial Average measures the average movement of the stock prices of selected U.S. companies. The very first value of the average was 40.94 on May 26, 1896. Charles Dow computed this value by adding the share prices of 12 important companies chosen by him (**GENERAL ELECTRIC** was one of them) and then dividing by 12. Thus, the average price per share for these 12 companies was $40.94. Since 1928, the average has included 30 companies selected by the editors of *The Wall Street Journal*. The average is no longer computed by simply averaging share prices, but the underlying concept remains the same. Changes in the companies included in the average are rare. Nevertheless, since 1990, 11 companies have been replaced to reflect the decreasing importance of manufacturing in the U.S. economy. For example, **BETHLEHEM STEEL**, which had been in "The Dow" since 1928, was replaced in March 1997 by **WAL-MART**. In 1999, the first two NASDAQ companies were added to "The Dow"—**MICROSOFT** and **INTEL**. The 30 companies included in the average as of October 16, 2000, are listed in Exhibit 11-1. The 30 companies in the average are listed every day in *The Wall Street Journal*, often on page C3.[1]

setting the stage

DOW JONES & COMPANY is an appropriate symbol of capitalism—a corporation that has done business in and around the spiritual heart of capitalistic finance, the New York Stock Exchange, for over one hundred years. With the disintegration of the former Soviet Union and the rapid conversion of China into a "socialist market" economy, it seems that the economic battle of capitalism and communism has been won by capitalism. As the history of many of the companies profiled in earlier chapters (MICROSOFT, SEARS, YAHOO!, GENERAL ELECTRIC) illustrates, the true story of capitalism is not the story of rich "capitalists" exploiting the masses, but rather the story of unknown individuals using a free market to find outside investor financing that will turn their ideas into reality. Accounting for investor financing is the topic of this chapter.

This is the second chapter on financing activities. In the previous chapter, financing through borrowing (debt) was discussed. Another way organizations raise money to finance operations is from investments by owners. In corporations, those investments take the form of stock purchases. In proprietorships and partnerships, they take the form of capital investments in the business. Exhibit 11-2 shows the financial statement items that will be covered in this chapter.

1 This description is based on information obtained from Dow Jones & Company History at **http://dowjones.com**; Dow Jones & Company, *International Directory of Company Histories*, vol. 19 (Detroit: St. James Press, 1998), pp. 128–131.

exhibit 11-1 The 30 Firms Included in the Dow Jones Industrial Average (as of October 16, 2000)

Aluminum Co. of America	General Electric Co.	McDonald's Corp.
American Express Co.	General Motors Corp.	Merck & Co.
AT&T Corp.	Hewlett-Packard Co.	Microsoft
Boeing Co.	Home Depot	Minnesota Mining & Manufacturing Co.
Caterpillar, Inc.	Honeywell	Philip Morris Cos.
Citigroup, Inc.	Intel	Procter & Gamble Co.
Coca-Cola Co.	International Business Machines Corp.	SBC Communications
DuPont Co.	International Paper Co.	United Technologies Corp.
Eastman Kodak Co.	J. P. Morgan & Co.	Wal-Mart Stores, Inc.
ExxonMobil Corp.	Johnson & Johnson	Walt Disney Co.

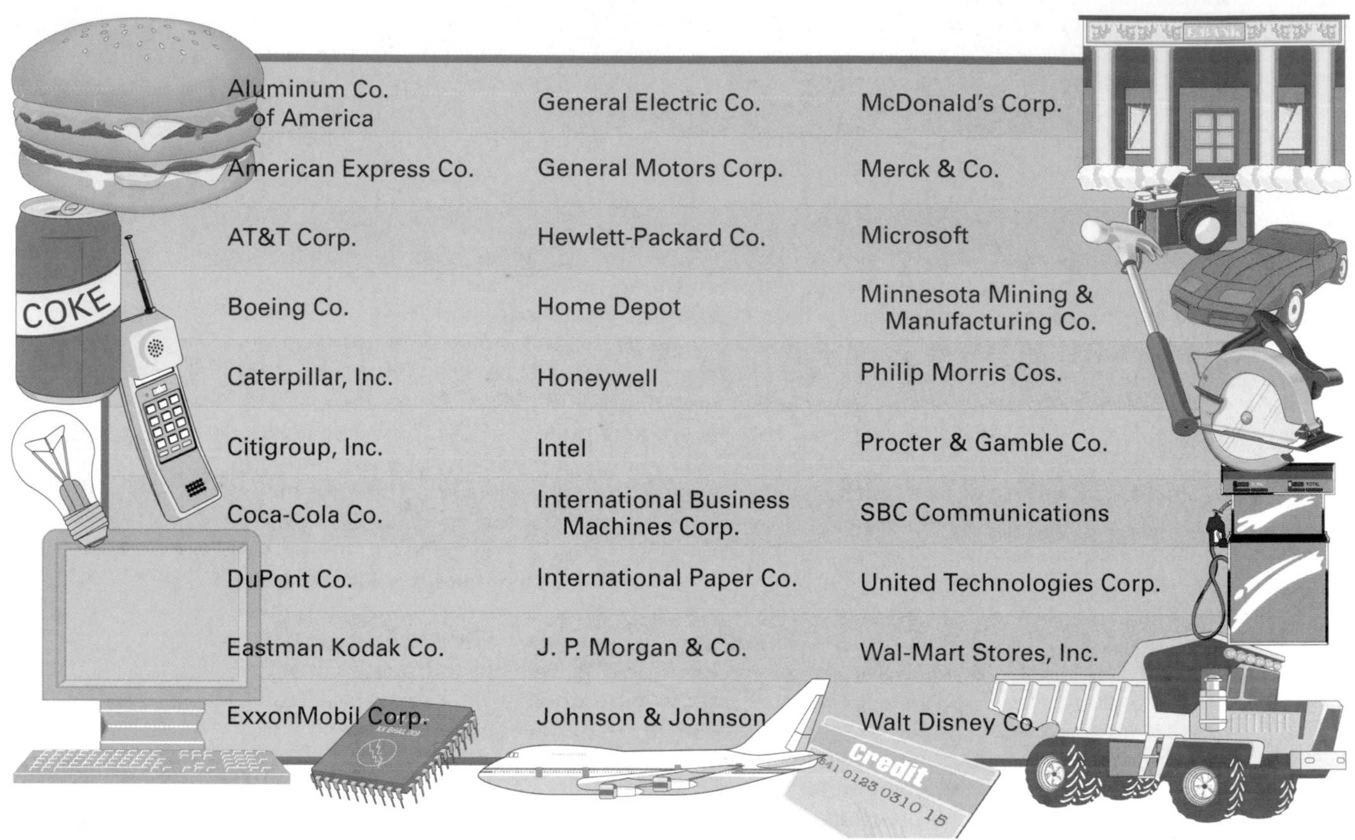

exhibit 11-2 Financial Statement Items Covered in This Chapter

Balance Sheet

Stockholders' equity
- Contributed capital
- Retained earnings
- Treasury stock

Statement of Cash Flows

Financing activities
- Sale of stock
- Purchase of treasury stock
- Payments of dividends

Certain basic characteristics are common to all investor financing, no matter what the form of business. The first is that owner investments affect the equity accounts of the business. Second, together with the liabilities, these owners' equity accounts show the sources of the cash that was used to buy the assets. There are three primary ways to bring money into a business: borrowing (debt financing), selling owners' interests (equity financing), and earning profits (also reflected in the equity accounts through the retained earnings account).

In the first part of this chapter, we illustrate the accounting for equity financing in the context of corporations. In the expanded material section of the chapter, we show how equity financing is accounted for in proprietorships and partnerships.

1

Distinguish between debt and equity financing, and describe the advantages and disadvantages of organizing a business as a proprietorship or a partnership.

RAISING EQUITY FINANCING

Most business owners do not have enough excess personal cash to establish and expand their companies. Therefore, they eventually need to look for money from outsiders, either in the form of loans or as funds contributed by investors. The business issues associated with investor financing are summarized in the time line in Exhibit 11-3.

The factors affecting the choice between borrowing and seeking additional investment funds are described in this section of the chapter. This section also outlines the advantages and disadvantages of organizing a business as a proprietorship or a partnership. The decision to incorporate and the process that a corporation follows in soliciting investor funds are described in the next section. The bulk of the chapter is devoted to the accounting procedures used to give a proper reporting of stockholders' equity to the investors. Of course, proper financial reporting to current and potential investors is one of the primary reasons for the existence of financial accounting.

Difference between a Loan and an Investment

Imagine that you own a small business and need $40,000 for expansion. What is the difference between borrowing the $40,000 and finding a partner who will invest the $40,000? If you borrow the money, you must guarantee to repay the $40,000 with interest. If you fail to make these payments, the lender can haul you into court and use the power of the law to force repayment. On the other hand, if your company does very well and you generate more than enough cash to repay the $40,000 plus interest, the lender does not get to share in your success. You owe the lender $40,000 plus interest and not a penny more. So, a loan is characterized by a fixed, legal obligation to repay a specified amount, whether the borrowing company performs poorly or performs well.

If you receive $40,000 in investment funds from a new partner, the partner now shares in your company's failures and successes. If business is bad and the investor is never able to recover

exhibit 11-3 Time Line of Business Issues Involved with Investor Financing

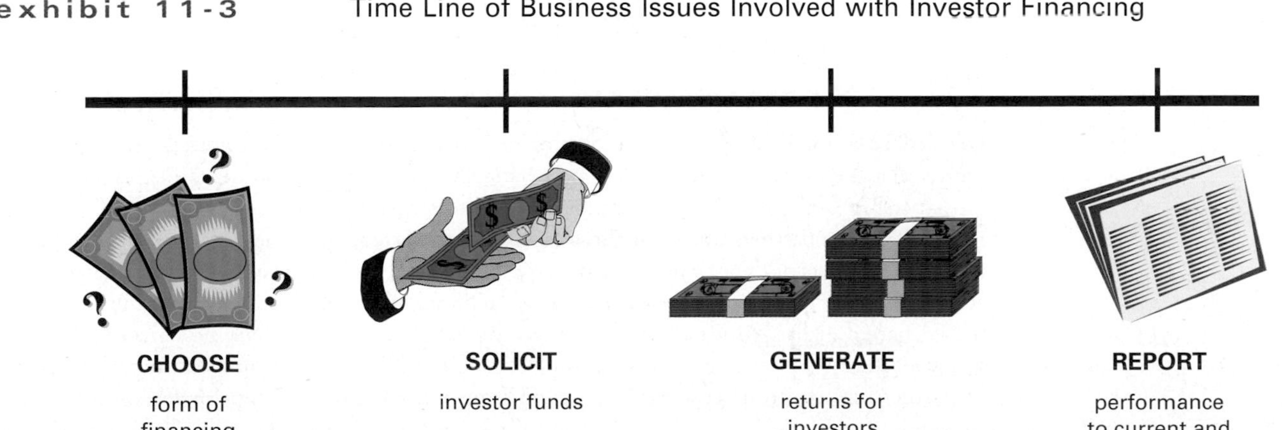

fyi

The law does not help investors recover lost investment funds unless the investors can show that they were tricked (by false financial reports, for example) into making the investment.

his or her $40,000 investment—well, that's the way it goes. The law will not help the investor recover the investment because the very nature of an investment is that the investor accepts the risk of losing everything. However, in exchange for accepting this risk, the investor also gets to share in the success if the company does well. For example, if you had loaned $40,000 to Bill Gates for MICROSOFT's expansion back in 1986, you would have been repaid the $40,000 plus a little interest. If you had invested that same $40,000 in Microsoft, however, your investment would have grown in value to $14.4 million by October 2000. Thus, an investment is characterized by a higher risk of losing your money, balanced by the chance of sharing in the wealth if the company does well.

Proprietorships and Partnerships

As explained in Chapter 2, a business can be organized as a proprietorship, a partnership, or a corporation. These three types of organization are merely different types of legal contracts that define the rights and responsibilities of the owner or owners of the business. The advantages and disadvantages of proprietorships and partnerships are discussed below. Corporations are discussed in the next section.

proprietorship A business owned by one person.

partnership An association of two or more individuals or organizations to carry on economic activity.

A **proprietorship** is a business owned by one person. A **partnership** is a business owned by two or more persons or entities. In most respects, proprietorships and partnerships are similar to each other but very different from corporations. Both a proprietorship and a partnership are characterized by ease of formation, limited life, and unlimited liability.

EASE OF FORMATION Proprietorships and partnerships can be formed with few legal formalities. When a person decides to establish a proprietorship, he or she merely acquires the necessary cash, inventory, equipment, and other assets; obtains a business license; and begins providing goods or services to customers. The same is true for a partnership, except that because two or more persons are involved, they must decide together which assets will be acquired and how business will be conducted.

LIMITED LIFE Because proprietorships and partnerships are not legal entities that are separate and distinct from their owners, they are easily terminated. In the case of a proprietorship, the owner can decide to dissolve the business at any time. For a partnership, anything that terminates or changes the contract between the partners legally dissolves the partnership. Among the events that dissolve a partnership are

1. the death or withdrawal of a partner,
2. the bankruptcy of a partner,
3. the admission of a new partner,
4. the retirement of a partner, or
5. the completion of the project for which the partnership was formed.

The occurrence of any of these events does not necessarily mean that a partnership must cease business; rather, the existing partnership is legally terminated, and another partnership must be formed.

UNLIMITED LIABILITY Proprietorships and partnerships have unlimited liability, which means that the proprietor or partners are personally responsible for all debts of the business. If a partnership is in poor financial condition, creditors first attempt to satisfy their claims from the assets of the partnership. After those assets are exhausted, creditors may seek payment from the personal assets of the partners. In addition, because partners are responsible for one another's actions (within the scope of the partnership), creditors may seek payment for liabilities created by a departed or bankrupt partner from the personal assets of the remaining partners. This unlimited liability feature is probably the single most significant disadvantage of a proprietorship or partnership. It can deter a wealthy person from joining a partnership for fear of losing personal assets.

to summarize

A loan is a fixed, legal obligation to repay a specified amount, whether the borrowing company performs poorly or performs well. With an investment, the investor risks losing the investment funds if the company performs poorly but shares in the wealth if the company does well. A proprietorship is a business owned by one person. A partnership is a business owned by two or more persons. Both types of businesses are easy to start and easy to terminate. A major disadvantage of proprietorships and partnerships is the unlimited liability of the owner or partners.

2

Describe the basic characteristics of a corporation and the nature of common and preferred stock.

corporation A legal entity chartered by a state; ownership is represented by transferable shares of stock.

CORPORATIONS AND CORPORATE STOCK

Corporations are the dominant form of business enterprise in the United States. Established as separate legal entities, **corporations** are legally distinct from the persons responsible for their creation. In many respects, they are accorded the same rights as individuals; they can conduct business, be sued, enter into contracts, and own property. Firms are incorporated by the state in which they are organized and are subject to that state's laws and requirements.

Characteristics of a Corporation

Corporations have several characteristics that distinguish them from proprietorships and partnerships. These characteristics are discussed below.

limited liability The legal protection given stockholders whereby they are responsible for the debts and obligations of a corporation only to the extent of their capital contributions.

LIMITED LIABILITY **Limited liability** means that in the event of corporate bankruptcy, the maximum financial loss any stockholder can sustain is his or her investment in the corporation (unless fraud can be proved). Because a corporation is a separate legal entity and is responsible for its own acts and obligations, creditors usually cannot look beyond the corporation's assets for satisfaction of their claims. This limited liability feature is probably the main reason for the

Corporations are the dominant form of business in the United States. As a corporation, MICROSOFT is a legal entity, and its ownership is represented by transferable shares of stock.

business environment essay

Going Public with a Dot.com Company It used to be that initial public offerings (IPOs) created millionaires overnight. Now, with the high values of many high-tech start-up companies, IPOs are creating billionaires overnight. For example, CORVIS, a provider of all-optical network switching equipment, went public on July 28, 2000. As of that date, Corvis had not yet reported any revenue in its history. Nevertheless, favorable expectations about the company's future potential caused the shares to trade for $84 per share at the end of the first day of trading, making the company worth over $20 billion on paper. As of the end of the IPO day, founder David Huber was personally worth $10 billion.

The eight steps involved in "going public" are outlined below by reference to the IPO of THEGLOBE.COM, a company that facilitates many online clubs and thus serves as an Internet portal for members of those clubs.

1. *Issuer conducts "bake-off" to select underwriter.* In September 1998, theglobe.com chose BEAR STEARNS to be the underwriter for its IPO. An underwriter guides the company through the IPO process.
2. *Underwriter benchmarks issuer's financial statements with competitors.* Bear Stearns analyzed theglobe.com's financial statements to determine how the company should be valued in light of the stock prices of other, similar companies that had already gone public.
3. *Underwriter sets the preliminary IPO price per share.* Based on its analysis of theglobe.com's financial statements, Bear Stearns determined that theglobe.com's shares should be issued at a price between $11 and $13 per share.
4. *Issuer and underwriter hold a "roadshow" to promote the IPO to large investors.* Bear Stearns and executives from theglobe.com gave a series of presentations to large investors to convince them to invest in the IPO shares of theglobe.com.

fyi

There are some hybrid organizations that have characteristics of both partnerships and corporations. For example, several of the large international accounting firms are organized as limited liability partnerships (LLPs). An LLP offers the advantages of a partnership structure but also provides each partner with limited liability for the costs of lawsuits caused by the actions of his or her partners.

fyi

An LLC (limited liability company) offers the limited liability legal protection of a corporation as well as the favorable partnership treatment for income tax purposes.

phenomenal growth of the corporate form of business because it protects investors from sustaining losses beyond their investments. In most cases of bankruptcy, however, stockholders will lose most of their investment because the claims of creditors must be satisfied before stockholders receive anything.

EASY TRANSFERABILITY OF OWNERSHIP Shares of stock in a corporation can be bought, sold, passed from one generation to another, or otherwise transferred without affecting the legal or economic status of the corporation. In other words, most corporations have perpetual existence—the life of the corporation continues by the transfer of shares of stock to new owners.

ABILITY TO RAISE LARGE AMOUNTS OF CAPITAL Raising large amounts of capital can be easier for a corporation than for a proprietorship or a partnership because a corporation can sell shares of its stock. The sale of shares of stock permits many investors, both large and small, to participate in ownership of the business. Some corporations actually have thousands of individual stockholders. In its 1999 annual report, DOW JONES & COMPANY reports that it has 15,508 stockholders of record. Because of this widespread ownership, large corporations are said to be publicly owned.

DOUBLE TAXATION Because corporations are separate legal entities, they are taxed independently of their owners. This often results in a disadvantage, however, because the portion of corporate profits that is paid out in dividends is taxed twice. First, the profits are taxed to the corporation; second, the owners, or stockholders, are taxed on their dividend income.

CLOSE GOVERNMENT REGULATION Because large corporations may have thousands of stockholders, each with only a small ownership interest, the government has assumed the task of monitoring certain corporate activities. For example, the government

5. *Underwriter "builds a book" of tentative orders to see how much interest there is in the IPO.* In October 1998, a downturn in the market caused some hesitancy among potential investors in theglobe.com's IPO. The price range was lowered to $8 to $10 per share, and Bear Stearns people called large investors to determine their interest.
6. *Final IPO price is set.* The day before the IPO, Bear Stearns set the final IPO price at $9 per share. This is the amount (less the Bear Stearns commission) that the founders of theglobe.com would receive for the shares that they intended to sell as part of the IPO.
7. *IPO shares are issued.* On November 13, 1998, theglobe.com's shares were issued.
8. *Trading begins.* As frequently happens with IPO shares, the price per share skyrocketed during the first day of trading. During the day on November 13, 1998, shares of theglobe.com stock traded for as high as $97 per share, a 928 percent increase over the IPO price of $9. This huge first-day price increase indicates that the founders of theglobe.com could have sold their shares for more. However, the publicity benefit of having all of Wall Street clamor to buy shares of theglobe.com stock may more than make up for this cost.

Frequently, the initial euphoria surrounding an IPO quickly dissipates and the share price sinks accordingly. For every MICROSOFT, where a share purchased in the IPO for $21 in 1986 was worth $7,560 in October 2000, there are dozens of less successful IPOs, such as theglobe.com. As of October 17, 2000, shares of theglobe.com stock that had traded as high as $97 per share on the IPO date were trading for just $1 per share.

Source: "The IPO Machine: From Start to Finish," *The Wall Street Journal,* April 14, 1999, p. C1.

requires that all major corporations be audited and that they issue periodic financial statements. As a result, in certain respects, major corporations often enjoy less freedom than do partnerships and proprietorships.

Starting a Corporation

Suppose that you want to start a corporation. First, you should study your state's corporate laws (usually with the aid of an attorney). Then you must apply to the appropriate state official for a charter. Your application will include the intended name of your corporation, its purpose (that is, the type of activity it will engage in), the type and amount of stock you plan to have authorized for your corporation, and, in some cases, the names and addresses of the potential stockholders. Finally, if the state approves your application, you will be issued a "charter" (also called "articles of incorporation"), giving legal status to your corporation.

prospectus A report provided to potential investors that represents a company's financial statements and explains its business plan, sources of financing, and significant risks.

stockholders Individuals or organizations that own a portion (shares of stock) of a corporation.

board of directors Individuals elected by the stockholders to govern a corporation.

Of course, the primary purpose of forming a corporation is to then sell stock in the corporation in order to obtain business financing. If the business you intend to establish will operate across state lines and if you intend to seek investment funds from the general public, then you must register your intended stock issue with the Securities and Exchange Commission in Washington, D.C. You are required to provide a **prospectus** to each potential investor; the prospectus outlines your business plan, sources of financing, significant risks, and the like. Finally, you can sell your shares to the public in what is called an "initial public offering" (IPO). You will receive the proceeds from the IPO, minus the commission charged by the investment banker sponsoring the issue.

When an investor buys stock in a corporation, he or she receives a stock certificate as evidence of ownership. For convenience, these stock certificates are frequently held by the stockbroker through whom the investor purchased the shares. The investors in a corporation are called **stockholders**, and they govern the corporation through an elected **board of directors**. In most corporations, the board of directors then chooses a management team to direct the daily affairs

business environment essay

Investing in the Stock Market "October," said Mark Twain, "is one of the peculiarly dangerous months to speculate in stocks. Others are July, January, September, April, November, May, March, June, December, August, and February." Despite Mark Twain's warning, stocks have always been one of the most prestigious and desired investments. These days, stock trading is easier than ever. There are scores of Internet stock trading firms that will allow you to buy and sell as many shares as you wish for less than $10 per trade. For some people, Internet stock trading has become the ultimate video game, with shooting lasers and fighting ninjas being replaced by stock price charts and the Federal Reserve Board.

This textbook won't make you an expert in picking promising stocks. In fact, you should be suspicious of any book or investment adviser claiming to have the secrets to deciphering the stock market. Here are some practical guidelines to help you avoid some of the pitfalls when deciding to buy stock:

of the corporation. In smaller companies, the board of directors is usually made up of members of that management team.

Several types of stock can be authorized by the charter and issued by the corporation. The most familiar types are common stock and preferred stock, and the major difference between them concerns the degree to which their holders are allowed to participate in the rights of ownership of the corporation.

Common Stock

common stock The most frequently issued class of stock; usually, it provides a voting right but is secondary to preferred stock in dividend and liquidation rights.

Certain basic rights are inherent in the ownership of **common stock**. These rights are as follows:

1. The right to vote in corporate matters such as the election of the board of directors or the undertaking of major actions such as the purchase of another company.
2. The preemptive right, which permits existing stockholders to purchase additional shares whenever stock is issued by the corporation. This allows common stockholders to maintain the same percentage of ownership in the company if they choose to do so.
3. The right to receive cash dividends if they are paid. As explained later, corporations do not have to pay cash dividends, and the amount received by common stockholders is sometimes limited.
4. The right to ownership of all corporate assets once obligations to everyone else have been satisfied. This means that once all loans have been repaid and the claims of the preferred stockholders have been met (as discussed below), all the excess assets belong to the common stockholders.

fyi

Occasionally, a corporation will have more than one class of common stock. For example, Dow Jones & Company has common stock and Class B common stock. Each Class B share gets 10 votes in corporate matters, and most of the Class B shares are owned by the descendants of Clarence Barron.

In essence, the common stockholders of a corporation are the true owners of the business. They delegate their decision-making authority to the board of directors, who in turn delegate authority for day-to-day operations to managers hired for that purpose. Thus, a distinguishing characteristic of business ownership as a common stockholder of a corporation is a clear separation between owning the business and operating the business.

Preferred Stock

preferred stock A class of stock that usually provides dividend and liquidation preferences over common stock.

The term "preferred stock" is somewhat misleading because it gives the impression that **preferred stock** is better than common stock. Preferred stock isn't better; it's different. A good way to think of preferred stock is that preferred stockholders give up some of the ownership rights of the common stockholders in exchange for some of the protection enjoyed by lenders.

In most cases, preferred stockholders are not allowed to vote for the corporate board of directors. In addition, preferred stockholders are usually allowed to receive only a fixed cash dividend, meaning that if the company does well, preferred stockholders do not get to share in the

1. Do not make hasty, emotional decisions about buying and selling stocks.
2. Do not "fall in love" with stocks so that you are no longer objective in appraising them.
3. Remember, you will seldom, if ever, buy stocks at their lowest price and sell them at their highest price.
4. There are stock market "fads," so when you buy at the height of a stock's popularity, you almost always pay too much.
5. Don't invest in stocks unless you can afford to lose the money you invest or at least have no access to it for a long time.
6. Plan to hold your stock investments for a long time. Most stock market millionaires were not speculators, and commissions on frequent sales and purchases will eat up your short-term gains.

Source: W. S. Albrecht, *Money Wise* (Salt Lake City, Utah: Deseret Book Company, 1983), pp. 134–139.

success. In exchange for these limitations, in the event that the corporation is liquidated, preferred stockholders are entitled to receive their cash dividends and have their claims fully paid before any cash is paid to common stockholders.

convertible preferred stock Preferred stock that can be converted to common stock at a specified conversion rate.

Preferred stock may also include other types of privileges, the most common of which is convertibility. **Convertible preferred stock** is preferred stock that can be converted to common stock at a specified conversion rate. For example, the notes to MICROSOFT's 1999 financial statements (see Appendix A) reveal that the investors who purchased 12.5 million shares of Microsoft convertible preferred stock in December 1996 were able to exchange those preferred shares (if they wish) for Microsoft common stock beginning in December 1999. Convertible preferred stock can be very appealing to investors. They can enjoy the dividend privileges of the preferred stock while having the option to convert to common stock if the market value of the common stock increases significantly. By issuing shares of stock with varying rights and privileges, companies can appeal to a wider range of investors.

to summarize

A corporation is a business entity that has a legal existence separate from that of its owners; it can conduct business, own property, and enter into contracts. The five major features of a corporation are (1) limited liability for stockholders, (2) easy transferability of ownership, (3) the ability to raise large amounts of capital, (4) separate taxation, and (5) for large corporations, closer regulation by government. Common stock confers four basic rights upon its owners: (1) the right to vote in corporate matters, (2) the right to maintain proportionate ownership, (3) the right to receive cash dividends, and (4) the ownership of all excess corporate assets upon liquidation of the corporation. Preferred stock typically carries preferential claims to dividend and liquidation privileges but has no voting rights.

3

Account for the issuance and repurchase of common and preferred stock.

ACCOUNTING FOR STOCK

In this section we focus on the accounting for the issuance of stock as well as the accounting for stock repurchases.

Issuance of Stock

par value A nominal value assigned to and printed on the face of each share of a corporation's stock.

Each share of common stock usually has a **par value** printed on the face of the stock certificate. For example, the common stock of DOW JONES & COMPANY has a $1 par value. This par value has little to do with the market value of the shares. In October 2000, each Dow Jones common share with a $1 par value was selling for about $55 per share. When par-value stock sells for a price above par, it is said to sell at a premium. In most states it is illegal to issue stock for a price below par value. If stock were issued at a discount (below par), stockholders could later be held liable to make up the difference between their investment and the par value of the shares they purchased. The par value multiplied by the total number of shares outstanding is usually equal to a company's "legal capital," and it represents the amount of the invested funds that cannot be returned to the investors as long as the corporation is in existence. This legal capital requirement was originally intended to protect a company's creditors; without it, excessive dividends could be paid, leaving nothing for creditors. The par value really was of more importance a hundred years ago and is something of a historical oddity today. These days, most states allow the sale of no-par stock.

fyi

Most companies establish a very low par value, such as $0.10 or $1.00 per share. In fact, in 1998, 40% of the publicly traded companies in the United States had par values of exactly $0.01.

When par-value stock is issued by a corporation, usually Cash is debited, and the appropriate stockholders' equity accounts are credited. For par-value common stock, the equity accounts credited are Common Stock, for an amount equal to the par value, and Paid-In Capital in Excess of Par, Common Stock, for the premium on the common stock.

To illustrate, we will assume that the Boston Lakers Basketball Team (a corporation) issued 1,000 shares of $1 par-value common stock for $50 per share. The entry to record the stock issuance is:

Cash (1,000 shares × $50)	50,000	
Common Stock (1,000 shares × $1 par value)		1,000
Paid-In Capital in Excess of Par,		
Common Stock (1,000 shares × $49)		49,000
Issued 1,000 shares of $1 par-value common stock at $50 per share.		

A similar entry would be made if the stock being issued were preferred stock. The total par value of the common and preferred stock, along with the associated amounts of paid-in capital in excess of par, constitutes a corporation's **contributed capital**.

contributed capital The portion of owners' equity contributed by investors (the owners) in exchange for shares of stock.

This illustration points out two important elements in accounting for the issuance of stock: (1) the equity accounts identify the type of stock being issued (common or preferred), and (2) the proceeds from the sale of the stock are divided into the portion attributable to its par value and the portion paid in excess of par value. These distinctions are important because the owners' equity section of the balance sheet should correctly identify the specific sources of capital so that the respective rights of the various stockholders can be known.

net work

Do you want to try your hand at buying some shares of stock? Go to http://ameritrade.com, the Web site for one of the leading Internet stock trading companies. How much is the commission for executing one stock trade?

If the stock being issued has no par value, only one credit is included in the entry. To illustrate, assume that the Lakers' stock does not have a par value and that the corporation issued 1,000 shares for $50 per share. The entry to record this stock issuance would be:

Cash	50,000	
Common Stock		50,000
Issued 1,000 shares of no-par stock at $50 per share.		

Although stock is usually issued for cash, other considerations may be involved. To illustrate the kinds of entries made when stock is issued for noncash considerations, we will assume that a prospective stockholder exchanged a piece of land for 5,000 shares of the Boston Lakers' $1 par-value common stock. Assuming the market value of the stock at the date of the exchange was $40 per share, the entry is:

Land (5,000 shares × $40)	200,000	
Common Stock (5,000 shares × $1)		5,000
Paid-In Capital in Excess of Par, Common Stock (5,000 shares × $39)		195,000
Issued 5,000 shares of $1 par-value common stock for land (5,000 shares × $40 per share = $200,000).		

When noncash considerations are received in payment for stock, the assets or services received should be recorded at the current market value of the stock issued. If the market value of the stock cannot be determined, the market value of the assets or services received should be used as the basis for recording the transaction.

Accounting for Stock Repurchases

treasury stock Issued stock that has subsequently been reacquired by the corporation.

Sometimes, when a company has excess cash or needs some of its shares of stock back from investors, it may purchase some of its own outstanding stock. This repurchased stock is called **treasury stock** by accountants. There are many reasons for a firm to buy its own stock. Five of the most common are that management:

1. wants the stock for a profit-sharing, bonus, or stock-option plan for employees,
2. feels that the stock is selling for an unusually low price and is a good buy,
3. wants to stimulate trading in the company's stock,
4. wants to remove some shares from the market in order to avoid a hostile takeover, or
5. wants to increase reported earnings per share by reducing the number of shares of stock outstanding.

Many successful U.S. companies have ongoing stock repurchase plans. For example, MICROSOFT disclosed in its 1999 annual report (Appendix A) that it spent $2.95 billion in 1999 to repurchase 44 million of its own shares. COCA-COLA spent $2.8 billion in the years 1997–1999 repurchasing its own shares. The most aggressive stock buyback program is GENERAL ELECTRIC's—a number of years ago GE announced its intention to spend a total of $13 billion buying back its own shares. As of the end of 1999, GE had already exceeded this amount, spending a cumulative total of $22.6 billion on stock repurchases.

When a firm purchases stock of another company, the investment is included as an asset on the balance sheet. However, a corporation cannot own part of itself, so treasury stock is not considered an asset. Instead, it is a contra-equity account and is included on the balance sheet as a deduction from stockholders' equity. Think of it this way: when a corporation issues shares, its equity is increased; when the corporation buys those shares back, its equity is reduced. The reporting of treasury stock is illustrated in the stockholders' equity section of the balance sheet for General Electric in Exhibit 11-4.

STOP & THINK For General Electric, the total amount invested by stockholders is $11,384 million, which is the sum of common stock at par ($594 million) and paid-in capital in excess of par (other capital of $10,790 million). And yet GE has spent $22,567 million buying back shares from stockholders. How is this possible?

Notice that the $22.567 billion spent by General Electric to buy back its own shares as of December 31, 1999, is shown as a subtraction from total share owners' equity. By the way, the "other capital" included in GE's equity section is primarily composed of paid-in capital in excess of par. Also, the "unrealized gains" and "currency translation adjustment" items are quite interesting and controversial, as will be explained in a later section.

Treasury stock is usually accounted for on a cost basis; that is, the stock is debited at its cost (market value) on the date of repurchase. To illustrate, we assume that 100 shares of the $1 par-value common stock were reacquired by the Boston Lakers for $60 per share. The entry to record the repurchase is:

Treasury Stock, Common	6,000	
Cash (100 shares × $60)		6,000
Purchased 100 shares of treasury stock at $60 per share.		

exhibit 11-4 Share Owners' Equity for General Electric

General Electric Company December 31, 1999 and 1998 Share Owners' Equity (in millions of U.S. dollars)	**1999**	**1998**
Common stock	$ 594	$ 594
Unrealized gains on investment securities—net	626	2,402
Accumulated currency translation adjustments	(1,370)	(738)
Other capital	10,790	6,808
Retained earnings	54,484	48,553
Less common stock held in treasury	(22,567)	(18,739)
Total share owners' equity	$42,557	$38,880

An alternative way to account for stock repurchases is called the par-value method. This method, though not used as frequently as the cost method illustrated in this section, is the method of choice for a number of large U.S. companies including Microsoft, INTEL, and WAL-MART. The par-value method of accounting for stock repurchases is covered in intermediate accounting courses.

The effect of this entry is to reduce both total assets (Cash) and total stockholders' equity by $6,000.

When treasury stock is reissued, the treasury stock account must be credited for the original amount paid to reacquire the stock. If the treasury stock's reissuance price is greater than its cost, an additional credit must be made to an account called Paid-In Capital, Treasury Stock. Together, these credits show the net increase in total stockholders' equity. At the same time, the cash account is increased by the total amount received upon reissuance of the treasury stock.

To illustrate, we assume that 40 of the 100 shares of the treasury stock that were originally purchased for $60 per share are reissued at $80 per share. The entry to record that reissuance is:

Cash (40 shares × $80)	3,200	
Treasury Stock, Common (40 shares × $60 cost)		2,400
Paid-In Capital, Treasury Stock [40 × ($80 − $60)]		800
Reissued 40 shares of treasury stock at $80 per share.		

caution

Do not credit a gain when treasury stock is reissued at a price greater than its cost. Gains are associated with a company's operations, not with a company buying and selling its own shares.

The company now has a balance of $3,600 in the treasury stock account (60 shares at $60 per share).

Sometimes the reissuance price of treasury stock is less than its cost. As before, the entry involves a debit to Cash for the amount received and a credit to Treasury Stock for the cost of the stock. However, because an amount less than the repurchase cost has been received, an additional debit is required. The debit is to Paid-In Capital, Treasury Stock if there is a balance in that account from previous transactions, or to Retained Earnings if there is no balance in the paid-in capital, treasury stock account.

To illustrate, we will consider two more treasury stock transactions. First, we assume that another 30 shares of treasury stock are reissued for $40 per share, $20 less than their cost. Because Paid-In Capital, Treasury Stock has a balance of $800, the entry to record this transaction is:

Cash (30 shares × $40)	1,200	
Paid-In Capital, Treasury Stock	600	
Treasury Stock, Common (30 shares × $60 cost)		1,800
Reissued 30 shares of treasury stock at $40 per share; original cost was $60 per share.		

Note that after this transaction is recorded, the balance in Paid-In Capital, Treasury Stock is $200 ($800 − $600).

Next, we assume that the company reissues 20 additional shares at $45 per share. The entry to record this transaction is:

Cash (20 shares × $45)	900	
Paid-In Capital, Treasury Stock	200	
Retained Earnings	100	
Treasury Stock (20 shares × $60 cost)		1,200
Reissued 20 shares of treasury stock at $45 per share; original cost was $60 per share.		

In this transaction, the selling price was $300 less than the cost of the treasury stock. Because the paid-in capital, treasury stock account had a balance of only $200, Retained Earnings was debited for the remaining $100.

Balance Sheet Presentation

We have discussed the ways in which stock transactions affect owners' equity accounts. We will now show how these accounts are summarized and presented on the balance sheet. The following data, with the addition of the preferred stock information in (1), summarize the stock transactions of the Boston Lakers shown earlier:

1. $40 par-value preferred stock: issued 1,000 shares at $45 per share.
2. $1 par-value common stock: issued 1,000 shares at $50 per share.
3. $1 par-value common stock: issued 5,000 shares for land with a fair market value of $200,000.
4. Treasury stock, common: purchased 100 shares at $60; reissued 40 shares at $80; reissued 30 shares at $40; reissued 20 shares at $45.

With these data, and assuming a Retained Earnings balance of $100,000, the stockholders' equity section would be as shown in Exhibit 11-5.

exhibit 11-5 Stockholders' Equity for Boston Lakers

Boston Lakers Basketball Team
Stockholders' Equity

Preferred stock ($40 par value, 1,000 shares issued and outstanding)	$ 40,000
Common stock ($1 par value, 6,000 shares issued, 5,990 shares outstanding)*	6,000
Paid-in capital in excess of par, preferred stock	5,000
Paid-in capital in excess of par, common stock	244,000
Total contributed capital	$295,000
Retained earnings (to be discussed)	100,000
Total contributed capital and retained earnings	$395,000
Less treasury stock (10 shares of $1 par common at cost of $60 per share)	(600)
Total stockholders' equity	$394,400

*Treasury shares are described as being issued but not outstanding. Thus, 6,000 common shares have been issued, but only 5,990 are outstanding because 10 are held by the Boston Lakers as treasury shares.

to summarize

When a company issues stock, it debits Cash or a noncash account (Property, for example) and credits various stockholders' equity accounts. Shares typically are assigned a par value, which is usually small in relation to the market value of the shares. Amounts received upon issuance of shares are divided into par value and paid-in capital in excess of par. A company's own stock that is repurchased is known as treasury stock and is included in the financial statements as a contra-stockholders' equity account. Treasury stock is usually accounted for on a cost basis. The stockholders' equity section of a balance sheet contains separate accounts for each type of stock issued, amounts paid in excess of par values, treasury stock, and retained earnings.

4

Understand the factors that affect retained earnings, describe the factors determining whether a company can and should pay cash dividends, and account for cash dividends.

RETAINED EARNINGS

Common stockholders can invest money in a corporation in two ways. First, as described in the previous section, common stockholders can buy shares of stock. Second, when the corporation makes money, the common stockholders can allow the corporation to keep those earnings to be reinvested in the business. **Retained earnings** is the name given to the aggregate amount of corporate earnings that have been reinvested in the business. The retained earnings balance is increased each year by net income and decreased by losses, dividends, and some treasury stock transactions (as illustrated earlier).

retained earnings The portion of a corporation's owners' equity that has been earned from profitable operations and not distributed to stockholders.

Remember, retained earnings is not the same as cash. In fact, a company can have a large Retained Earnings balance and be without cash, or it can have a lot of cash and a very small Retained Earnings balance. For example, on December 31, 1999, DOW JONES & COMPANY had a Cash balance of $86 million but a Retained Earnings balance of $810 million. Although both Cash and Retained Earnings are usually increased when a company has earnings, they typically are increased by different amounts. This occurs for two reasons: (1) the company's net income, which increases Retained Earnings, is accrual-based, not cash-based; and (2) cash from earnings may be invested in productive assets such as inventories, used to pay off loans, or spent in any number of ways, many of which do not affect net income or retained earnings. In summary, cash is an asset; retained earnings is one source of financing (along with borrowing and direct stockholder investment) that a corporation can use to get funds to acquire assets.

dividends Distributions to the owners (stockholders) of a corporation.

cash dividend A cash distribution of earnings to stockholders.

fyi

Fortune magazine maintains a list of the top 50 e-companies, called the Fortune e-50. A random sample of 10 of these companies indicated that only one of the 10 paid cash dividends to common stockholders in 1999. Thus, we see that high-tech, high-growth companies are not likely to pay cash dividends. By the way, the only one of the sampled e-50 companies to pay cash dividends to common stockholders was IBM, not exactly a young start-up.

Cash Dividends

If you had your own business and wanted to withdraw money for personal use, you would simply withdraw it from the company's checking account or cash register. In a corporation, a formal action by the board of directors is required before money can be distributed to the owners. In addition, such payments must be made on a pro rata basis. That is, each owner must receive a proportionate amount on the basis of ownership percentage. These pro rata distributions to owners are called **dividends**. When paid in the form of cash, they are called **cash dividends**. The amount of dividends an individual stockholder receives depends on the number of shares owned and on the per-share amount of the dividend.

SHOULD A COMPANY PAY CASH DIVIDENDS? Note that a company does not have to pay cash dividends. Theoretically, a company that does not pay dividends should be able to reinvest its earnings in assets that will enable it to grow more rapidly than its dividend-paying competitors. This added growth will presumably be reflected in increases in the per-share price of the stock. In practice, most public companies pay regular cash dividends, but some well-known companies do not. For example, MICROSOFT has never paid cash dividends to its common stockholders.

So, should a corporation pay cash dividends or not? Well, the surprising answer is that no one knows the answer to that question. Ask your finance professor what he or she thinks. Although no one knows the theoretically best dividend policy, three general observations can be made:

- Stable companies pay out a large portion of their income as cash dividends.
- Growing companies (such as Microsoft) pay out a small portion of their income as cash dividends. They keep the funds inside the company for expansion.
- Companies are very cautious about raising dividends to a new level because once investors come to expect a certain level of dividends, they see it as very bad news if the company reduces the dividends back to the old level.

STOP & THINK If you were a Microsoft shareholder, would you want to receive a high level of cash dividends, or would you prefer that Bill Gates use your share of the profits for business expansion?

Although cash dividends are the most common type of dividend, corporations can distribute other types of dividends as well. A stock dividend is a distribution of additional shares of stock to stockholders. Stock dividends will be discussed in the expanded material section of this chapter. A property dividend is a distribution of corporate assets (for example, the stock of another firm) to stockholders. Property dividends are quite rare. In this section, only the accounting for cash dividends will be discussed.

ACCOUNTING FOR CASH DIVIDENDS Three important dates are associated with dividends: (1) declaration date, (2) date of record, and (3) payment date. The first is when the board of directors formally declares its intent to pay a dividend. On this **declaration date**, the company becomes legally obligated to pay the dividend. Assuming that the board of directors votes on December 15, 2003, to declare an $8,000 dividend, this liability may be recorded as follows:

declaration date The date on which a corporation's board of directors formally decides to pay a dividend to stockholders.

Dividends	8,000	
Dividends Payable		8,000
Declared dividend on December 15, 2003.		

At the end of the year, the dividends account is closed to Retained Earnings by the following entry:

Retained Earnings	8,000	
Dividends		8,000
To close Dividends to Retained Earnings.		

From this entry, you can see that a declaration of dividends reduces Retained Earnings and, eventually, the amount of cash on hand. Thus, though not considered to be an expense, dividends do reduce the amount a company could otherwise invest in productive assets.

Alternatively, a declaration of dividends can be recorded by debiting Retained Earnings directly. However, using the dividends account instead of Retained Earnings allows a company to keep separate records of dividends paid to preferred and common stockholders. Whichever method is used, the end result is the same: a decrease in Retained Earnings.

date of record The date selected by a corporation's board of directors on which the stockholders of record are identified as those who will receive dividends.

The second important dividend date is the **date of record**. Falling somewhere between the declaration date and the payment date, this is the date selected by the board of directors on which the stockholders of record are identified as those who will receive dividends. Because many corporate stocks are in flux—being bought and sold daily—it is important that the stockholders who will receive the dividends be identified. No journal entry is required on the date of record; the date of record is simply noted in the minutes of the directors' meeting and in a letter to stockholders.

dividend payment date The date on which a corporation pays dividends to its stockholders.

As you might expect, the third important date is the **dividend payment date**. This is the date on which, by order of the board of directors, dividends will be paid. The entry to record a dividend payment would typically be:

Dividends Payable	8,000	
Cash		8,000
Paid dividends declared on December 15, 2003.		

The following press release, made by Dow Jones on January 19, 2000 (declaration date), identifies both the date of record and the dividend payment date:

> Dow Jones & Company announced that its Board of Directors voted today to increase the quarterly dividend on the common stock and Class B common stock to 25 cents a share from 24 cents a share. The 4.2% increase, the first for Dow Jones in four years, raises the indicated annual dividend rate to one dollar per share. The first new quarterly dividend is payable March 1 to shareholders of record as of February 1.

fyi

When Dow Jones announced its dividend increase on January 19, 2000, its stock price increased by just 1.9% over the following two days. This is a small price rise and may suggest that investors already were aware of the planned dividend increase.

As mentioned earlier, once a dividend-paying pattern has been established, the expectation of dividends is built into the per-share price of the stock. A reduction in the dividend usually produces a sharp drop in the price. Similarly, an increased dividend usually triggers an increase in the stock price. Dividend increases are usually considered to set a precedent, indicating that future dividends will be at this per-share amount or more. With this in mind, boards of directors are careful about increasing or decreasing dividends.

DIVIDEND PREFERENCES When cash dividends are declared by a corporation that has both common and preferred stock outstanding, how the dividends are allocated to the two classes of investors depends on the rights of the preferred stockholders. These rights are identified when the stock is approved by the state. Two "dividend preferences," as they are called, are (1) current-dividend preference and (2) cumulative-dividend preference.

Current-Dividend Preference Preferred stock has a dividend percentage associated with it and is typically described as follows: "5% preferred, $40 par-value stock, 1,000 shares outstanding." The first figure—"5%" in this example—is a percentage of the par value and can be any amount, depending on the particular stock. So, $2 per share (0.05 × $40 par) is the amount that will be paid in dividends to preferred stockholders each year that dividends are declared. The fact that preferred stock dividends are fixed at a specific percentage of their par value makes them somewhat similar to the interest paid to bondholders. The **current-dividend preference** requires that when dividends are paid, this percentage of the preferred stock's par value be paid to preferred stockholders before common stockholders receive any dividends.

current-dividend preference The right of preferred stockholders to receive current dividends before common stockholders receive dividends.

To illustrate the payment of different types of dividends, the following data from the Boston Lakers Basketball Team will be used throughout this section. (The various combinations of dividend preferences illustrated over the next few pages are summarized in Cases 1 to 4 in Exhibit 11-6.) As a reminder, the outstanding stock includes:

- Preferred stock: 5%, $40 par value, 1,000 shares issued and outstanding.
- Common stock: $1 par value, 6,000 shares issued, 5,990 shares outstanding.

exhibit 11-6 Dividend Preferences: Summary of Cases 1 to 4

Case	Preferred Dividend Feature	Years in Arrears	Total Dividend	Preferred Dividend	Common Dividend
1	5%, Noncumulative	Not applicable	$ 1,500	$1,500	$ 0
2	5%, Noncumulative	Not applicable	3,000	2,000	1,000
3	5%, Cumulative	2	5,000	5,000	0
4	5%, Cumulative	2	11,000	6,000	5,000

To begin, note that, as with all preferred stock, the Lakers' 5% preferred stock has a current-dividend preference: Before any dividends can be paid to common stockholders, preferred stockholders must be paid a total of $2,000 ($40 × 0.05 × 1,000 shares). Thus, if only $1,500 of dividends are declared (Case 1), preferred stockholders will receive the entire dividend payment. If $3,000 are declared (Case 2), preferred stockholders will receive $2,000 and common stockholders, $1,000.

cumulative-dividend preference The right of preferred stockholders to receive current dividends plus all dividends in arrears before common stockholders receive any dividends.

Cumulative-Dividend Preference The **cumulative-dividend preference** can be quite costly for common stockholders because it requires that preferred stockholders be paid current dividends plus all unpaid dividends from past years before common stockholders receive anything. If dividends have been paid in all previous years, then only the current 5% must be paid to preferred stockholders. But if dividends on preferred stock were not paid in full in prior years, the cumulative deficiency must be paid before common stockholders receive anything.

dividends in arrears Missed dividends for past years that preferred stockholders have a right to receive under the cumulative-dividend preference if and when dividends are declared.

With respect to the cumulative feature, it is important to repeat that companies are not required to pay dividends. Any past unpaid dividends are called **dividends in arrears**. Because they do not have to be paid unless dividends are declared in the future, dividends in arrears do not represent actual liabilities and thus are not recorded in the accounts. Instead, they are reported in the notes to the financial statements.

To illustrate the distribution of dividends for cumulative preferred stock, we will assume that the Boston Lakers Basketball Team has not paid any dividends for the last two years but has declared a dividend in the current year. The Lakers must pay $6,000 in dividends to preferred stockholders before they can give anything to the common stockholders. The calculation is as follows:

Dividends in arrears, 2 years	$4,000
Current dividend preference ($40 × 0.05 × 1,000 shares)	2,000
Total	$6,000

Therefore, if the Lakers pay only $5,000 in dividends (Case 3), preferred stockholders will receive all the dividends, common stockholders will receive nothing, and there will still be dividends in arrears of $1,000 the next year. If $11,000 in dividends are paid (Case 4), preferred stockholders will receive $6,000, and common stockholders will receive $5,000.

The entries to record the declaration and payment of dividends in Case 4 are:

Date of Declaration

	Debit	Credit
Dividends, Preferred Stock	6,000	
Dividends, Common Stock	5,000	
Dividends Payable		11,000
Declared dividends on preferred and common stock.		

Date of Payment

	Debit	Credit
Dividends Payable	11,000	
Cash		11,000
Paid dividends on preferred and common stock.		

CONSTRAINTS ON PAYMENT OF CASH DIVIDENDS Earlier in this section, the question was asked whether a company should pay cash dividends. A related question is: Can the company legally pay cash dividends? To illustrate, consider the following exaggerated scenario. Tricky Company obtains a corporate charter, borrows $1 million from Naïve Bank, pays out a $1 million cash dividend to the stockholders, and all the stockholders disappear to the Bahamas. Is this a legal possibility? No, it isn't, because the corporate right to declare cash dividends is regulated by state law in order to protect creditors. The right to declare cash dividends is often linked to a company's Retained Earnings balance.

fyi

Delaware has a reputation for having the least restrictive dividend laws. This is one reason many of the major U.S. companies are incorporated in the state of Delaware.

In many states, a company is not allowed to pay cash dividends in an amount that would cause the retained earnings balance to be negative. Thus, if the retained earnings balance of the Boston Lakers were $8,500, the $11,000 dividend in Case 4 discussed above could not be paid, even if the Lakers had the available cash to make the payment. The incorporation laws in many states are less restrictive and allow the payment of cash dividends in excess of the retained earnings balance if, for example, current earnings are strong or the market value of the assets is high.

Frequently, lenders do not rely on state incorporation laws to protect them from excess cash dividend payments by corporations to which they lend money. Instead, the loan contract itself includes restrictions on the payment of cash dividends during the period that the loan is outstanding. In this way, lenders are able to prevent cash that should be used to repay loans from being paid to stockholders as dividends.

Dividend Payout Ratio

dividend payout ratio A measure of the percentage of earnings paid out in dividends; computed by dividing cash dividends by net income.

A ratio of interest to stockholders is the **dividend payout ratio**. This ratio indicates the percentage of net income paid out during the year in the form of cash dividends and is computed as follows:

$$\text{Dividend payout ratio} = \frac{\text{Cash dividends}}{\text{Net income}}$$

Dividend payout ratio values for Dow Jones, Microsoft, and GENERAL ELECTRIC for 1999 are computed below. The numbers are in millions.

	Dow Jones	Microsoft	General Electric
Cash dividends	$87	$28	$4,786
Net income	$272	$7,785	$10,717
Dividend payout ratio	32.0%	0.4%	44.7%

Both Dow Jones and General Electric pay out between 30 and 50% of their annual income as dividends, a normal level for large U.S. corporations. Microsoft's low dividend payout ratio is indicative of a rapidly expanding company. In fact, all of the Microsoft cash dividends are preferred stock dividends; as mentioned earlier, Microsoft has never paid any cash dividends to its common stockholders.

to summarize

The retained earnings account reflects the total undistributed earnings of a business since incorporation. It is increased by net income and decreased by dividends, net losses, and some treasury stock transactions. The important dates associated with a cash dividend are the date of declaration, the date of record, and the payment date. Preferred stockholders can be granted a current and a cumulative preference for dividends over the rights of common stockholders. In some states, the payment of cash dividends is limited to an amount not to exceed the existing Retained Earnings balance. The dividend payout ratio (cash dividends divided by net income) reveals the percentage of net income that is paid out as cash dividends.

5

Describe the purpose of reporting comprehensive income in the equity section of the balance sheet, and prepare a statement of stockholders' equity.

OTHER EQUITY ITEMS

In addition to the two major categories of contributed capital and retained earnings, the equity section of a balance sheet often includes a number of miscellaneous items. These items are gains or losses that bypass the income statement when they are recognized. A further discussion of these items is given below.

Equity Items That Bypass the Income Statement

Since 1980, the equity sections of U.S. balance sheets have begun to fill up with a strange collection of items, each the subject of an accounting controversy. Two of these items are summarized below:

- *Foreign currency translation adjustment.* The foreign currency translation adjustment arises from the change in the equity of foreign subsidiaries (as measured in terms of U.S. dollars) that occurs as a result of changes in foreign currency exchange rates. For example, if the Japanese yen weakens relative to the U.S. dollar, the equity of Japanese subsidiaries of U.S. firms will decrease, in dollar terms. Before 1981, these changes were recognized as losses or gains on the income statement. Multinational firms disliked this treatment because it added volatility to reported earnings. The FASB changed the accounting rule, and now these changes are reported as direct adjustments to equity on the balance sheet, insulating the income statement from this aspect of foreign currency fluctuations.
- *Unrealized gains and losses on available-for-sale securities.* As will be explained in Chapter 12, available-for-sale securities are securities that a company purchased without intending to resell them immediately but also not necessarily planning to hold them forever. When the FASB was considering requiring securities to be reported at their market values on the balance sheet, companies complained about the income volatility that would be caused by recognizing these changes as gains or losses on the income statement. The FASB made the standard more acceptable to businesses by allowing unrealized gains and losses on available-for-sale securities to bypass the income statement and go straight to the equity section of the balance sheet.

The hodgepodge of direct equity adjustments described above is conceptually unsatisfying. These adjustments have arisen on a case-by-case basis as part of the FASB's effort to establish accounting standards that are accepted by the business community. As mentioned, many businesspeople are opposed to including these categories on the income statement because, they say, the income statement would become cluttered with gains and losses from market value changes, distracting from the purpose of the income statement, which is to focus on reporting profits from the activities of the business. The compromise that allows market values in the balance sheet while keeping the income statement uncluttered is the creation of a separate category of equity called **accumulated other comprehensive income**. Accumulated other comprehensive income is composed of certain market-related gains and losses that are not included in the computation of net income. It is important to remember that accumulated other comprehensive income is not income at all, but an equity category that summarizes the changes in equity that result during the period from market-related increases and decreases in the reported values of assets and liabilities. The reporting of accumulated other comprehensive income equity is illustrated in the 1999 equity section of DOW JONES & COMPANY, shown in Exhibit 11-7.

accumulated other comprehensive income Certain market-related gains and losses that are not included in the computation of net income; for example, foreign currency translation adjustments and unrealized gains or losses on investments.

statement of comprehensive income A statement outlining the changes in accumulated comprehensive income that arose during the period.

A **statement of comprehensive income** provides a place, outside the regular income statement, for reporting all the unrealized gains and losses that are reported as equity adjustments. The appeal of comprehensive income is that this approach preserves the traditional income statement (calming the fears of the business community) but allows unrealized gains and losses to be reported. In essence, comprehensive income makes it possible to recognize unrealized gains and losses so that current market values can be reported on the balance sheet without having those unrealized gains and losses affect the income statement.

STOP & THINK Which will have a greater impact on a company's stock price: net income of $100 million or a $100 million unrealized gain from a change in exchange rates or securities prices? Explain your answer.

The statement of comprehensive income is very new; U.S. companies have been required to present it starting December 31, 1998. Dow Jones &

exhibit 11-7

Equity Section for Dow Jones & Company

Dow Jones & Company's Equity Section (amounts in millions of dollars)

	1999	1998
Common stocks		
Common stock, par value $1 per share	$ 81,004	$ 80,899
Class B common stock, convertible, par value $1 per share	21,177	21,282
	$ 102,181	$102,181
Additional paid-in capital	137,487	137,479
Retained earnings	809,517	624,239
Accumulated other comprehensive income:		
Unrealized (loss) gain on investments	(941)	35,775
Cumulative translation adjustment	(1,257)	38
	$1,046,987	$899,712
Less treasury stock	493,497	390,372
Total stockholders' equity	$ 553,490	$509,340

Company's comprehensive income presentation for 1999 is shown in Exhibit 11-8. Note that net income is one component in the computation of comprehensive income. For Dow Jones, 1997 was a particularly bad year, with each of the three reported elements of comprehensive income being negative. By the way, the large loss reported by Dow Jones in 1997 resulted from a $1 billion restructuring charge.

Statement of Stockholders' Equity

statement of stockholders' equity A financial statement that reports all changes in stockholders' equity.

Companies that have numerous changes in their stockholders' equity accounts during the year usually include a **statement of stockholders' equity** (also called a statement of changes in stockholders' equity) with their financial statements. This statement reconciles the beginning and ending balances for all stockholders' equity accounts reported on the balance sheet.

An illustrative statement of stockholders' equity from the 1999 annual report of Dow Jones & Company is presented in Exhibit 11-9. Note the following items in the statement:

- As mentioned earlier in the chapter, Dow Jones has two classes of common stock. Class B common shares with a par value of $105,000 were converted into ordinary common shares during the year.
- Dow Jones both bought and sold treasury shares during the year. The $4,539,000 decrease in Additional Paid-In Capital from treasury stock sales indicates that these treasury shares were resold for less than the $43,604,000 Dow Jones spent to repurchase them.

exhibit 11-8

Statement of Comprehensive Income for Dow Jones & Company

(in thousands)	**1999**	**1998**	**1997**
Net income (loss)	$272,429	$ 8,362	$(802,132)
Unrealized gain (loss) on investments	2,124	32,379	(8,957)
Foreign currency translation adjustments	(1,295)	555	(3,644)
Other	(38,840)	9,023	—
Comprehensive income	$234,418	$50,319	$(814,733)

exhibit 11-9 Statement of Stockholders' Equity for Dow Jones & Company

CONSOLIDATED STATEMENT OF STOCKHOLDERS' EQUITY
Dow Jones & Company, Inc.
For the Year Ended December 31, 1999
(amounts in thousands of U.S. dollars)

	Common Stock	Class B Common Stock	Additional Paid-In Capital	Retained Earnings	Accumulated Other Comprehensive Income	Treasury Stock	Total
Balance, December 31, 1998	$80,899	$21,282	$137,479	$624,239	$35,813	$(390,372)	$509,340
Net income—1999				272,429			$272,429
Unrealized gain on investments					2,124		2,124
Translation adjustment					(1,295)		(1,295)
Other					(38,840)		(38,840)
Comprehensive income							$234,418
Dividends, $0.96 per share				(87,151)			(87,151)
Conversion of class B common stock into common stock	105	(105)					
Other equity changes			4,547				4,547
Sales under stock compensation plans			(4,539)			43,604	39,065
Purchase of treasury stock						(146,729)	(146,729)
Balance, December 31, 1999	$81,004	$21,177	$137,487	$809,517	$(2,198)	$(493,497)	$553,490

The last column in the statement reflects the total beginning and ending stockholders' equity account balances and all increases and decreases. Both the individual account balances and total Stockholders' Equity at December 31, 1999, are reported on the balance sheet of Dow Jones & Company.

to summarize

Accumulated other comprehensive income is not income at all, but an equity category that summarizes the effect on equity of certain market-related gains and losses. Two examples of items giving rise to accumulated other comprehensive income are market fluctuations in the value of some investment securities and changes in the value of assets and liabilities held by foreign subsidiaries that are caused by exchange rate changes. A statement of stockholders' equity summarizes the changes affecting all the different categories of equity during the year.

expanded material

Three topics related to equity financing need additional explanation. These topics are stock dividends and stock splits, prior-period adjustments, and accounting for equity financing in proprietorships and partnerships.

6

Account for stock dividends and distinguish them from stock splits.

stock dividend A pro rata distribution of additional shares of stock to stockholders.

ACCOUNTING FOR STOCK DIVIDENDS

Corporations sometimes distribute additional shares of their own stock to stockholders instead of paying a cash dividend. These **stock dividends** must be distributed to each stockholder in proportion to the number of shares held. For example, if a company issues a 10% stock dividend, each stockholder will receive one additional share for every 10 shares owned.

There is considerable disagreement as to whether stockholders receive anything of value from a stock dividend. Certainly, they do not receive corporate assets, as with a cash dividend. Nor does any stockholder own a larger percentage of the corporation after the stock dividend than before, because each stockholder receives a pro rata share of the stock issued. In fact, one way to view a stock dividend is that the company has just cut the total ownership up into smaller pieces, with each stockholder owning proportionately more pieces, and nothing has really changed.

Those who argue that stock dividends have value to stockholders point out that companies frequently maintain the same level of cash dividends per share after the stock dividend as before. Accordingly, a stock dividend is an indirect method of increasing the amount of total cash dividends to be received in the future by each stockholder.

Stock dividends are also sometimes used to mollify investors and lull them into thinking that a company is maintaining its record of paying dividends when, in fact, it is not. Corporations that issue dividends each year do not want to miss a year, so for them a stock dividend can be a useful substitute for cash when poor financial circumstances make payment of cash dividends difficult. It isn't clear whether investors are actually fooled by this tactic.

To illustrate the accounting for a stock dividend and to keep the example simple, we will assume that the stockholders' equity of the Boston Lakers Basketball Team is:

Common stock ($1 par value, 10,000 shares issued and outstanding)	$ 10,000
Paid-in capital in excess of par	40,000
Retained earnings	80,000
Total stockholders' equity	$130,000

If a 10% stock dividend is declared and issued when the stock's current market price is $70, the entry to record the stock dividend is:

Retained Earnings (1,000 shares × $70)	70,000	
Common Stock (1,000 shares × $1 par)		1,000
Paid-In Capital in Excess of Par, Common Stock		69,000
Declared and issued a 10% common stock dividend.		

business environment essay

Do You Want a Stock Tip? The conventional wisdom is that the announcement of a stock split is good news. Academic research has confirmed this—a company's share value goes up an average of 3% in the one or two days after a 2-for-1 split announcement appears in *The Wall Street Journal.* But for most of us, this market reaction to the split news is too fast to allow us to make any money. By the time we learn about the split announcement and buy the shares, the share price will have already increased.

All is not lost, however. Additional academic research suggests that the share values of splitting firms continue to go up for at least a year after the split announcement. In fact, if you buy the shares of a company one week after that company announces a stock split, you will earn, on average, an extra 7.9% on your investment during the following year. This extra 7.9%

STOP & THINK Look at the Boston Lakers example and explain how the accounting rules discourage companies from declaring small stock dividends on a regular basis.

Because the dividend was 10% and there were previously 10,000 common shares outstanding, 1,000 additional shares were issued for the dividend. The accounting rules dictate that when a "small" stock dividend is issued, the market value of the newly issued shares is transferred out of Retained Earnings, just as if that same amount had been paid out in cash. If a stock dividend is relatively large, the accounting rules state that only the par value of the newly issued shares is to be transferred out of Retained Earnings. A small stock dividend is one that is less than 25%.

To illustrate the accounting for a large stock dividend, we assume the same stockholders' equity for the Boston Lakers Basketball Team, except that the stock dividend is now 30%. The entry is:

Retained Earnings	3,000	
Common Stock (3,000 shares × $1 par)		3,000
Declared and issued a 30% common stock dividend (10,000 shares × 0.30 = 3,000 shares).		

The impact of the 10 and 30% stock dividends on the Boston Lakers' stockholders' equity is detailed below:

	Before Stock Dividend	With 10% Stock Dividend	With 30% Stock Dividend
Common stock, $1 par value	$ 10,000	$ 11,000	$ 13,000
Paid-in capital in excess of par	40,000	109,000	40,000
Retained earnings	80,000	10,000	77,000
Total stockholders' equity	$130,000	$130,000	$130,000

Note that a stock dividend does not change the total amount of stockholders' equity, regardless of the size of the dividend. The only effect is to reallocate some of the stockholders' equity into different categories.

Stock Splits

Many investors, particularly individuals with limited amounts to invest, will not purchase stocks with high market prices per share. For example, consider the case of **BERKSHIRE HATH-**

is over and above what you would have earned if you had invested in a similar company that had not announced a stock split.

Before you run off to buy *The Wall Street Journal* or subscribe to an online service that will alert you to stock split announcements, here are two more pieces of advice. First, always be suspicious of unsolicited stock tips (such as the one just given). You should ask yourself: "If this is such a good idea, why hasn't the person who told me about it become rich?" Second, always remember that academic research is a good thing to keep professors occupied during their spare time but is a notoriously unreliable (and unprofitable) basis for investment strategy.

Source: David L. Ikenberry, Graeme Rankine, and Earl K. Stice, "What Do Stock Splits Really Signal?" *Journal of Financial and Quantitative Analysis*, September 1996, pp. 357–375.

AWAY, which will be spotlighted in Chapter 12 and is the holding company controlled by Warren Buffett (one of the richest people in the United States). In October 2000, the shares of Berkshire Hathaway were selling for over $58,000 per share! At that price, not many of us can own even one share. To encourage more investors to buy their stocks, companies sometimes enact a **stock split**, replacing the outstanding shares with a larger number of new shares that sell at a lower price per share. MICROSOFT, for example, has split its stock eight times in order to bring down the price per share. Because of these splits, a single original share of Microsoft stock is now the equivalent (as of October 2000) of 144 shares.

stock split The replacement of outstanding shares of stock with a greater number of new shares.

In essence, the difference between a stock dividend and a stock split is that a stock split is usually bigger. Whereas a stock dividend might increase the number of shares outstanding by 10 or 25%, a stock split is likely to increase the number of shares outstanding by 50% (3-for-2 stock split), by 100% (2-for-1 stock split), or more. Actually, there is no clear distinction between a stock split and a stock dividend. For example, there are 50% stock dividends and there are also 5-for-4 stock splits.

From an accounting standpoint, stock splits are accounted for in one of two ways. The most common way is to simply account for the stock split as if it were a large stock dividend. Thus, a 2-for-1 stock split would be accounted for as a 100% stock dividend with the par value of the newly created shares transferred from Retained Earnings. Alternatively, a stock split can be accounted for by reducing the par value of all outstanding shares. For a 2-for-1 stock split accounted for in this way, the par value is halved and the number of shares is doubled. Thus, the total par value of stock outstanding is unchanged. For example, a firm with 20,000 shares of $10 par-value common stock outstanding may reduce the par value to $5 and increase the number of shares outstanding to 40,000. No journal entry is needed to account for a stock split in this way; the company merely makes note of the fact that the par value and number of shares outstanding have changed.

---

to summarize

Stock dividends are distributions of additional stock to stockholders. Although a stock dividend does not increase a stockholder's percentage of ownership in a corporation, the additional stock may provide the expectation of increased future cash dividends. With small stock dividends, Retained Earnings is debited at the stock's market value; with large stock dividends (25% or more), Retained Earnings is debited at the stock's par value. A stock split is also an increase in the number of shares outstanding. Generally, stock splits are authorized so that companies can attract more investors with a lower market price per share. A stock split can be accounted for as a large stock dividend or by lowering the par value of each share.

7

Explain prior-period adjustments and prepare a statement of retained earnings.

PRIOR-PERIOD ADJUSTMENTS

In the first part of this chapter, it was shown that profits and losses, dividends, and certain treasury stock transactions affect retained earnings. In addition to these three events, there is one other type of event that affects retained earnings directly. This category includes adjustments to restate the net income of prior periods; these are called, appropriately, **prior-period adjustments**. Prior-period adjustments are relatively infrequent. In addition to some technical adjustments involving taxes and bonds, which are beyond the scope of this book, the main event that qualifies as a prior-period adjustment is the correction of an error in previous financial statements, such as an error in accounting for revenues or expenses of a previous period. In accounting for prior-period adjustments, Retained Earnings is increased or decreased directly because the net income for the years affected by the adjustments has already been closed to the retained earnings account.

prior-period adjustments Adjustments made directly to Retained Earnings in order to correct errors in the financial statements of prior periods.

exhibit 11-10 Statement of Retained Earnings for Boston Lakers

Boston Lakers Basketball Team
Statement of Retained Earnings
For the Year Ended December 31, 2003

Retained earnings, January 1, 2003		$300,000
Prior-period adjustment:		
Deduct adjustment for 2002 inventory correction		(25,000)
Balance as restated		$275,000
Net income for 2003		50,000
Less dividends declared in 2003:		
Preferred stock	$10,000	
Common stock	12,000	(22,000)
Retained earnings, December 31, 2003		$303,000

statement of retained earnings A report that shows the changes in the retained earnings account during a period of time.

Prior-period adjustments (if there are any) and dividends are usually disclosed in a **statement of retained earnings**. Exhibit 11-10 shows how the Boston Lakers Basketball Team might present a statement of retained earnings, using arbitrary numbers.

to summarize

In addition to net income, dividends, and certain treasury stock transactions, retained earnings can also be either increased or decreased by prior-period adjustments, which do not occur often. Prior-period adjustments usually involve corrections of errors in previous financial statements. Prior-period adjustments are disclosed in a statement of retained earnings.

8 Understand basic proprietorship and partnership accounting.

PROPRIETORSHIP AND PARTNERSHIP ACCOUNTING

capital account An account in which a proprietor's or partner's interest in a firm is recorded; it is increased by owner investments and net income and decreased by withdrawals and net losses.

drawings account The account used to reflect periodic withdrawals of earnings by the owner (proprietor) or owners (partners) of a proprietorship or partnership.

Because the majority of businesses organized in the United States are proprietorships and partnerships, it is important to understand the accounting for equity financing in these types of businesses.

The difference between accounting for proprietorships and partnerships and accounting for a corporation is the owners' equity accounts. In a corporation, owners' equity is divided into contributed capital and retained earnings (and some other equity items, as explained earlier in the chapter), with each of these categories possibly having several different accounts. In proprietorships and partnerships, all owners' equity transactions are recorded in only two accounts, **Capital** and **Drawings**.

Accounting for Equity Financing in a Proprietorship

To illustrate the accounting for the owner's equity of a proprietorship, we will assume that Megan Wilkes decides to start a small, independent real estate brokerage business. On January 1, 2003, she deposits $40,000 into a bank account to finance the business. The entry to record the $40,000 deposit is:

Cash	40,000	
Megan Wilkes, Capital		40,000
Invested $40,000 to start a real estate business.		

Once the business is established, the entries to account for the purchase of assets, the payment of business expenses, and the receipt of revenues are similar to those for corporations. There is one exception, however. Whereas in a corporation salaries paid to management are accounted for as expenses, in a proprietorship the salary paid to the owner is a distribution of earnings. The managers of a corporation are considered to be employees, even if they are also stockholders in the company. The owners of a corporation receive dividends, which are deducted directly from Retained Earnings. In a proprietorship, the owner receives no dividends, so any "drawing out" of funds is considered to be a distribution to the owner. Hence, the name "drawings" account. If Megan Wilkes decides to withdraw $650 cash for personal use or as salary, the entry is:

Megan Wilkes, Drawings	650	
Cash		650
Withdrew $650 for personal use.		

The account Megan Wilkes, Drawings is similar to a dividends account in a corporation: at year-end, it is closed to the owner's equity account, Megan Wilkes, Capital.

Assuming that Megan Wilkes withdrew only $650 during the year, the closing entry to eliminate the balance in the drawings account is:

Megan Wilkes, Capital	650	
Megan Wilkes, Drawings		650
To close the drawings account for the year.		

If we also assume revenues of $100,000 and expenses of $86,000, Megan Wilkes's closing entry for net income is:

Revenues (individual revenue accounts)	100,000	
Expenses (individual expense accounts)		86,000
Megan Wilkes, Capital		14,000
To close net income for the year to the owner's capital account.		

From the preceding two entries, we see that Megan Wilkes's capital account has increased by $13,350 since January 1. Adding this amount to her original contribution results in a $53,350 balance at year-end, as the following statement of owner's capital shows:

Megan Wilkes
Statement of Owner's Capital
For the Year Ending December 31, 2003

Megan Wilkes, capital, January 1, 2003	$40,000
Add net income	14,000
Total	$54,000
Less withdrawals	(650)
Megan Wilkes, capital, December 31, 2003	$53,350

The owner's equity section of Megan Wilkes's balance sheet would have only one item:

Megan Wilkes, capital	$53,350

Accounting for Equity Financing in a Partnership

Like a proprietorship, a partnership differs from a corporation primarily in accounting for owners' equity. That is, a partnership has only two types of owners' equity accounts, Capital and Drawings. Whereas a proprietorship has only one of each type of account, a partnership maintains separate capital and drawings accounts for each partner.

FORMING A PARTNERSHIP To illustrate the accounting for the formation of a partnership, assume that Dr. Mary Adams and Dr. Jim Bell decide to form a partnership on January 1, 2003. Their partnership agreement specifies that Dr. Adams will contribute land valued at $30,000, a building valued at $50,000, and $10,000 cash to the business and that Dr. Bell will contribute medical equipment valued at $40,000 plus $50,000 cash. The entry to record the capital contributions of the two partners is:

Cash	60,000	
Equipment	40,000	
Land	30,000	
Building	50,000	
Adams, Capital		90,000
Bell, Capital		90,000
To record the investments of Adams and Bell in a partnership.		

The valuation of noncash assets invested in a business is one of the most difficult tasks in accounting for the formation of a partnership. Generally, the fair market values on the date of transfer should be used, but these values must be agreed upon by all partners. For example, if the assets contributed by either Bell or Adams had been used in another business prior to the partnership, the values assigned to them for the partnership might be quite different from the amounts that were being carried on the previous business's books. Although the equipment invested by Bell may have had a book value of only $30,000, or the land and building invested by Adams may have cost only $15,000 several years ago, it is only fair to give each partner credit for the current market values of the assets at the time they are transferred to the partnership.

PARTNERS' DRAWINGS ACCOUNTS As mentioned previously, in a corporation the managers are employees, so their salaries are accounted for as expenses; the stockholders are the owners, and distributions to them are in the form of dividends. In a partnership the managers are usually the owners, and any amounts they withdraw, either as salary or as a distribution of profits, are debited to their drawings accounts, which eventually reduces the capital accounts. Each partner has a drawings account in which his or her withdrawals are recorded for the year. For example, assume that sufficient income was earned during the year and that Adams withdrew $70,000 and Bell withdrew $55,000 as salary for the year. The entry is:

Adams, Drawings	70,000	
Bell, Drawings	55,000	
Cash		125,000
To record cash taken from the partnership as salary.		

Note that any salaries paid to employees who are not partners are expenses of the business.

If Adams or Bell had withdrawn funds, for example, for living expenses, that amount would also be debited to the drawings account. At year-end, the debits in the drawings accounts are totaled, and the accounts are closed to the partners' capital accounts. Assuming that the total in each drawings account was the salary, the entry to close the drawings accounts for the year is:

Adams, Capital	70,000	
Bell, Capital	55,000	
Adams, Drawings		70,000
Bell, Drawings		55,000
To close the drawings accounts for the year.		

statement of partners' capital A partnership report showing the changes in the capital balances; similar to a statement of retained earnings for a corporation.

THE STATEMENT OF PARTNERS' CAPITAL Because most partners want an explanation of how their capital accounts change from year to year, a **statement of partners' capital** is usually prepared. This statement, which is similar to a retained earnings statement for a corporation, lists the beginning Capital balances, additional investments, profits or losses from operations, withdrawals, and each partner's ending Capital balance. For example, given the preceding information and assuming that the Adams and Bell partnership had a 2003 profit of $140,000, the statement of partners' capital for the year ended December 31, 2003, would be as shown in Exhibit 11-11. Note that the partnership agreement specifies that Adams is to receive 60% of the profits and Bell is to receive 40%.

exhibit 11-11 Statement of Partners' Capital

Adams and Bell Partnership
Statement of Partners' Capital
For the Year Ended December 31, 2003

	Dr. Adams	Dr. Bell	Total
Investments, January 1, 2003.	$ 90,000	$ 90,000	$180,000
Add net income for 2003	84,000	56,000	140,000
Subtotal	$174,000	$146,000	$320,000
Less withdrawals during 2003	(70,000)	(55,000)	(125,000)
Capital balances, December 31, 2003.	$104,000	$ 91,000	$195,000

to summarize

The assets and liabilities of a proprietorship are accounted for in the same way as they are in a corporation, but equity is handled differently. Whereas the accounting for corporate equity may involve several accounts, the accounting for proprietorship equity requires only two accounts, Drawings and Capital. The drawings account is used for recording withdrawals of funds by the owner. It is closed to the capital account at year-end. The capital account is increased when capital is invested in the business and when profits are earned; it is decreased when cash or other assets are withdrawn from the business or when losses occur. The basic elements in accounting for the owners' equity of a partnership are (1) accounting for investments by the partners, (2) recording withdrawals of assets by the partners, (3) closing the drawings accounts, and (4) preparing a statement of partners' capital. Investments by owners are usually recorded at the fair market value and are credited to the owners' capital balances. Owners' withdrawals of cash, inventory, and other business assets are recorded in drawings accounts, which are closed to the capital accounts at year-end. There is one capital and one drawings account for each partner. A statement of partners' capital reconciles the beginning and ending capital balances by adding any profits and additional investments to the beginning capital balances and subtracting any losses and withdrawals.

review of learning objectives

1 **Distinguish between debt and equity financing, and describe the advantages and disadvantages of organizing a business as a proprietorship or a partnership.** Borrowing money imposes a legal obligation to repay the amount borrowed, plus interest. Receiving investment funds does not obligate the company to repay investors. Investors stand to lose their investments if the company does poorly, but they also stand to share in the wealth if the company does well. Proprietorships are owned by one person; partnerships are owned by two or more persons or entities. Partnerships and proprietorships share three characteristics: (1) ease of formation, (2) limited life, and (3) unlimited liability.

2 **Describe the basic characteristics of a corporation and the nature of common and preferred stock.** A corporation is a business entity that is legally separate from its owners and is chartered by a state. It is independently taxed, and it can incur debts, conduct business, own property, and enter into contracts. Among the benefits of the corporate form of business are that ownership interests are easily transferred and that the liability of the owners is limited to the amount of their investment. Common stockholders are the true owners of a corporation. They have the right to vote in corporate matters and own all corporate assets that are left after the claims of others have been satisfied. Preferred stockholders are entitled to receive their full cash dividend payments before any dividends can be paid to common stockholders. Preferred stockholders are entitled to a fixed amount of the corporate assets, and that amount does not increase when the company is successful.

3 **Account for the issuance and repurchase of common and preferred stock.** Stock that is issued often has a par value associated with each share. This par value is a legal technicality and represents the minimum amount that must be invested. When stock is issued in exchange for a noncash item, the transaction is recorded at the market value of the noncash item. Repurchased stock is called treasury stock. When treasury stock is purchased by a corporation, it is accounted for at cost and deducted from total stockholders' equity as a contra-equity account.

4 **Understand the factors that affect retained earnings, describe the factors determining whether a company can and should pay cash dividends, and account for cash dividends.** Retained earnings is increased by net income and is decreased by a net loss, by dividends, and by some treasury stock transactions. Corporations usually distribute cash dividends to their owners. The three important dates in accounting for cash dividends are the declaration date, the date of record, and the payment date. Dividends are not a liability until they are declared. If a company has common and preferred stock, the allocation of dividends between the two types of stock depends on the dividend preferences of the preferred stock. According to the incorporation laws in some states, the ability of a company to pay cash dividends can be restricted by the balance in Retained Earnings. In addition, private lending agreements sometimes constrain a company's ability to pay cash dividends. The dividend payout ratio, which is cash dividends divided by net income, reveals what percentage of a company's income it is paying out in dividends.

5 **Describe the purpose of reporting comprehensive income in the equity section of the balance sheet, and prepare a statement of stockholders' equity.** The accumulated amount of comprehensive income is reported in the equity section of the balance sheet. Comprehensive income items result from changes in market values of certain assets and liabilities. Comprehensive income is not income in the traditional sense but instead represents unrealized gains and losses that are excluded from the income statement. The statement of stockholders' equity summarizes the changes in each equity category during a year.

expanded material

6 **Account for stock dividends and distinguish them from stock splits.** Stock dividends and stock splits involve dividing the ownership of the corporation into smaller pieces but giving shareholders proportionately more of these smaller pieces. Generally speaking, stock dividends are smaller than stock splits. A small stock dividend is one that is less than 25% and is accounted for by transferring the market value of the newly created shares out of Retained Earnings. With a large stock dividend, only the par value of the new shares is transferred. A stock split can be accounted for as a large stock dividend or by decreasing the par value of the shares.

7 **Explain prior-period adjustments and prepare a statement of retained earnings.** Prior-period adjustments are

adjustments to restate net income of prior periods. The most common prior-period adjustments stem from past accounting errors that have been discovered in the current period. Because past periods' net income has already been closed to Retained Earnings, the corrections are made directly to the retained earnings account. Companies often include a statement of retained earnings with their financial statements. A statement of retained earnings reconciles the ending retained earnings balance with beginning retained earnings.

8 Understand basic proprietorship and partnership accounting. There are two owner's equity accounts in a proprietorship: a capital account and a drawings account. The capital account is increased by owner contributions and profits and decreased by owner withdrawals and losses. Events commonly accounted for in a partnership are investments by owners, withdrawals by partners, and allocation of partnership profits and losses. Investments and withdrawals by partners are treated in the same way as they are in a proprietorship. That is, investments increase the partners' Capital balances, and withdrawals decrease the partners' Capital balances. A statement of partners' capital is usually prepared at year end. This statement reconciles the ending Capital balances with the beginning Capital balances by adding profits and additional investments and deducting losses and partner withdrawals.

key terms and concepts

accumulated other comprehensive income 529
board of directors 517
cash dividend 524
common stock 518
contributed capital 520
convertible preferred stock 519
corporation 515
cumulative-dividend preference 527
current-dividend preference 526
date of record 525
declaration date 525
dividend payment date 525
dividend payout ratio 528
dividends 524
dividends in arrears 527
limited liability 515
par value 520
partnership 514
preferred stock 518
proprietorship 514
prospectus 517
retained earnings 524
statement of comprehensive income 529
statement of stockholders' equity 530
stockholders 517
treasury stock 521

expanded material

capital account 535
drawings account 535
prior-period adjustments 534
statement of partners' capital 538
statement of retained earnings 535
stock dividend 532
stock split 534

review problem

Stockholders' Equity

Clarke Corporation was organized during 1973. At the end of 2003, the equity section of the balance sheet was:

Contributed capital:	
Preferred stock (8%, $30 par, 6,000 shares authorized, 5,000 shares issued and outstanding)	$150,000
Common stock ($5 par, 50,000 shares authorized, 20,000 shares issued, 17,000 shares outstanding)	100,000
Paid-in capital in excess of par, common stock	80,000
Total contributed capital	$330,000
Retained earnings	140,000
Total contributed capital plus retained earnings	$470,000
Less treasury stock (3,000 shares of common stock at cost, $10 per share)	(30,000)
Total stockholders' equity	$440,000

During 2003, the following stockholders' equity transactions occurred in chronological sequence:

a. Issued 800 shares of common stock at $11 per share.
b. Reissued 1,200 shares of treasury stock at $12 per share.
c. Issued 300 shares of preferred stock at $33 per share.
d. Reissued 400 shares of treasury stock at $9 per share.
e. Declared and paid a dividend large enough to meet the current-dividend preference on the preferred stock and to pay the common stockholders $1.50 per share.
f. Net income for 2003 was $70,000, which included $400,000 of revenues and $330,000 of expenses.
g. Closed the dividends accounts for 2003.

Required:

1. Journalize the transactions.
2. Set up T-accounts with beginning balances and post the journal entries to the T-accounts, adding any necessary new accounts. (Assume a beginning balance of $20,000 for the cash account.)
3. Prepare the stockholders' equity section of the balance sheet as of December 31, 2003.

Solution

1. Journalize the Transactions

a.	Cash	8,800	
	Common Stock		4,000
	Paid-In Capital in Excess of Par, Common Stock		4,800
	Issued 800 shares of common stock at $11 per share.		

Cash received is $11 × 800 shares; common stock is par value times the number of shares ($5 × 800); paid-in capital is the excess.

b.	Cash	14,400	
	Treasury Stock		12,000
	Paid-In Capital, Treasury Stock		2,400
	Reissued 1,200 shares of treasury stock at $12 per share.		

Cash is $12 × 1,200 shares; treasury stock is the cost times the number of shares sold ($10 × 1,200 shares); paid-in capital is the excess.

c.	Cash	9,900	
	Preferred Stock		9,000
	Paid-In Capital in Excess of Par, Preferred Stock		900
	Issued 300 shares of preferred stock at $33 per share.		

Cash is $33 × 300 shares; preferred stock is par value times the number of shares issued ($30 × 300); paid-in capital is the excess.

d.	Cash	3,600	
	Paid-In Capital, Treasury Stock	400	
	Treasury Stock		4,000
	Reissued 400 shares of treasury stock at $9 per share.		

Cash is $9 × 400 shares; treasury stock is the cost times the number of shares sold ($10 × 400); paid-in capital is decreased for the difference. If no Paid-In Capital, Treasury Stock balance had existed, Retained Earnings would have been debited.

e.	Dividends, Preferred Stock	12,720	
	Dividends, Common Stock	29,100	
	Cash		41,820
	Declared and paid cash dividend.		

Calculations:

Preferred Stock	Number of Shares	Par-Value Amount
Original balance	5,000	$150,000
Entry (c)	300	9,000
Total	5,300	$159,000
		× 0.08
		$ 12,720

Common Stock	Number of Shares
Original balance (excludes treasury stock)	17,000
Entry (a)	800
Entry (b)	1,200
Entry (d)	400
Total	19,400 shares
	× $1.50
	$29,100
Total preferred stock dividend	$12,720
Total common stock dividend	29,100
Total dividend	$41,820

f.	Revenues (individual revenue accounts)	400,000	
	Expenses (individual expense accounts)		330,000
	Retained Earnings		70,000
	To close net income to Retained Earnings.		
g.	Retained Earnings	41,820	
	Dividends, Preferred Stock		12,720
	Dividends, Common Stock		29,100
	To close the dividends accounts for 2003.		

2. Set Up T-Accounts and Post to the Accounts

Cash

Debit		Credit	
Beg. Bal.	20,000	(e)	41,820
(a)	8,800		
(b)	14,400		
(c)	9,900		
(d)	3,600		
Bal.	14,880		

Preferred Stock

Debit		Credit	
		Beg. Bal.	150,000
		(c)	9,000
		Bal.	159,000

Paid-In Capital in Excess of Par, Preferred Stock

Debit		Credit	
		(c)	900
		Bal.	900

Common Stock

Debit		Credit	
		Beg. Bal.	100,000
		(a)	4,000
		Bal.	104,000

Paid-In Capital in Excess of Par, Common Stock

Debit		Credit	
		Beg. Bal.	80,000
		(a)	4,800
		Bal.	84,800

Treasury Stock

Debit		Credit	
Beg. Bal.	30,000	(b)	12,000
		(d)	4,000
Bal.	14,000		

Paid-In Capital, Treasury Stock

(d)	400	(b)	2,400
		Bal.	2,000

Retained Earnings

(g)	41,820	Beg. Bal.	140,000
		(f)	70,000
		Bal.	168,180

Dividends, Preferred Stock

(e)	12,720	(g)	12,720
Bal.	0		

Dividends, Common Stock

(e)	29,100	(g)	29,100
Bal.	0		

Revenues

(f)	400,000	Beg. Bal.	400,000
		Bal.	0

Expenses

Beg. Bal.	330,000	(f)	330,000
Bal.	0		

3. Prepare Stockholders' Equity Section of the Balance Sheet

Clarke Corporation
Partial Balance Sheet
December 31, 2003

Stockholders' Equity

Contributed Capital:	
Preferred stock (8%, $30 par, 6,000 shares authorized, 5,300 shares issued and outstanding)	$159,000
Common stock ($5 par, 50,000 shares authorized, 20,800 shares issued, 19,400 outstanding)	104,000
Paid-in capital in excess of par, preferred stock	900
Paid-in capital in excess of par, common stock	84,800
Paid-in capital, treasury stock	2,000
Total contributed capital	$350,700
Retained earnings	168,180
Total contributed capital plus retained earnings	$518,880
Less treasury stock (1,400 shares of common stock at cost, $10 per share)	(14,000)
Total stockholders' equity	$504,880

Transaction	Common Stock Issued	Common Stock Authorized	Treasury Stock
Number of shares originally issued	20,000	50,000	3,000
Entry (a)	800		
Entry (b)			(1,200)
Entry (d)			(400)
Total	20,800	50,000	1,400

discussion questions

1. What are the primary differences between debt financing and equity financing?
2. What are the major differences between a partnership and a corporation?
3. How is a proprietorship or partnership established?
4. Does the death of a partner legally terminate a partnership? If so, does it mean that the partnership must cease operating?

5. Are partners legally liable for the actions of other partners? Explain.
6. In which type of business entity do all owners have limited liability?
7. In what way are corporate profits subject to double taxation?
8. How do common and preferred stock differ?
9. What is the purpose of having a par value for stock?
10. Why would a company repurchase its own shares of stock that it had previously issued?
11. Is treasury stock an asset? If not, why not?
12. How is treasury stock usually accounted for?
13. In what way does the stockholders' equity section of a balance sheet identify the sources of the assets?
14. What factors affect the retained earnings balance of a corporation?
15. Is it possible for a firm to have a large Retained Earnings balance and no cash? Explain.
16. When is a company legally barred from paying cash dividends?
17. Why should a potential common stockholder carefully examine the dividend preferences of a company's preferred stock?
18. The dividend payout ratio for Deedle Company is 40%. What does this mean?
19. What is accumulated other comprehensive income? Why was this concept adopted by accounting standard-setters?
20. Give two examples of other equity items (items that bypass the income statement and go directly to the equity section of the balance sheet).

expanded material

21. Does a stock dividend have value to stockholders? Explain.
22. What is the difference between large and small stock dividends?
23. Why are prior-period adjustments entered directly into Retained Earnings instead of being reflected on the income statement?
24. Is the payment of salary to a proprietor an expense that would be deducted on a proprietorship's income statement? Explain.
25. In a corporation, contributions by owners and accumulated earnings of the business are separated into contributed capital and retained earnings accounts. Are earnings and contributions separated into different accounts in a partnership? Explain.

discussion cases

CASE 11-1

DOES STOCKHOLDERS' EQUITY TELL THE REAL STORY?

Last year, Shades International (a hypothetical company) invented the famous Shades Sunglasses that are widely popular around the world and especially in Japan and the Far East. Citizens of these countries love the new-age sunglasses and are buying them as fast as they can. Shades International owns the patent but contracts out to other companies to manufacture the glasses. Shades International also leases its research and development facility, the only building it occupies. Royalties from the glasses exceeded $10 million last year and are expected to increase dramatically this year. Selected data (in millions of dollars) from Shades International's financial statements are as follows:

Patent	$0.3
Other assets	0.9
Total liabilities	4.5
Total stockholders' equity	(3.3)

In the next two months, Shades International will be offering stock for sale to the public. Your friend is encouraging you to buy some of the stock. You are leery about the negative stockholders' equity balance. Is Shades International worth even considering as a possible investment?

CASE 11-2

TO PAY OR NOT TO PAY DIVIDENDS

Assume Lenny Company manufactures specialized computer peripheral parts such as speakers and modems. It is a new company that has been in operation for just two years. During those two years, Lenny Company's stock price has increased over 400%. Lenny Company does not pay dividends nor does the company plan to do so in the future. However, the company's stock seems to be heavily traded. Why do you think there is so much interest in buying Lenny Company's stock if stockholders do not receive dividends?

EXERCISE 11-1

ISSUANCE OF STOCK

Brockbank Corporation was organized on July 15, 2003. Record the journal entries for Brockbank to account for the following:

a. The state authorized 30,000 shares of 7% preferred stock ($20 par) and 100,000 shares of no-par common stock.
b. The company gave 6,000 shares of common stock to its attorney in return for her help in incorporating the business. Fees for this work are normally about $18,000. (Note: The debit is to Legal Expense.)
c. Brockbank Corporation gave 15,000 shares of common stock to an individual who contributed a building worth $50,000.
d. Brockbank Corporation issued 5,000 shares of preferred stock at $25 per share.
e. Peter Brockbank paid $70,000 cash for 30,000 shares of common stock.
f. Another individual donated a $15,000 machine and received 4,000 shares of common stock.
g. The attorney sold all her shares to her brother-in-law for $18,000.

EXERCISE 11-2

NO-PAR STOCK TRANSACTIONS

Parker Maintenance Corporation was organized in early 2003 with 40,000 shares of no-par common stock authorized. During 2003, the following transactions occurred:

a. Issued 17,000 shares of stock at $36 per share.
b. Issued another 2,400 shares of stock at $38 per share.
c. Issued 2,000 shares for a building appraised at $40,000.
d. Declared dividends of $1 per share.
e. Earned net income of $99,000 for the year, including $200,000 of revenues and $101,000 of expenses.
f. Closed the dividends accounts.

Given this information:

1. Journalize the transactions.
2. Present the stockholders' equity section of the balance sheet as it would appear on December 31, 2003.

EXERCISE 11-3

TREASURY STOCK TRANSACTIONS

Provide the necessary journal entries to record the following:

a. Fayette Corporation was granted a charter authorizing the issuance of 100,000 shares of $16 par-value common stock.
b. The company issued 40,000 shares of common stock at $20 per share.
c. The company reacquired 2,000 shares of its own stock at $22 per share, to be held in treasury.
d. Another 2,000 shares of stock were reacquired at $24 per share.
e. Of the shares reacquired in (c), 800 were reissued for $26 per share.
f. Of the shares reacquired in (d), 1,400 were reissued for $18 per share.
g. Given the preceding transactions, what is the balance in the treasury stock account?

EXERCISE 11-4

STOCK ISSUANCE AND CASH DIVIDENDS

Stillwater Corporation was organized in January 2003. The state authorized 100,000 shares of no-par common stock and 50,000 shares of 10%, $20 par, preferred stock. Record the following transactions that occurred in 2003:

a. Issued 10,000 shares of common stock at $30 per share.
b. Issued 2,000 shares of preferred stock for a building appraised at $60,000.
c. Declared a cash dividend sufficient to meet the current-dividend preference on preferred stock and pay common shareholders $2 per share.

EXERCISE 11-5

STOCK ISSUANCE, TREASURY STOCK, AND DIVIDENDS

On January 1, 2003, Abbott Corporation was granted a charter authorizing the following capital stock: common stock, $20 par, 100,000 shares; preferred stock, $10 par, 6%, 30,000 shares. Record the following 2003 transactions:

a. Issued 80,000 shares of common stock at $30 per share.
b. Issued 14,000 shares of preferred stock at $12 per share.
c. Bought back 5,000 shares of common stock at $40 per share.
d. Reissued 500 shares of treasury stock at $25 per share.
e. Declared cash dividends of $38,600 to be allocated between common and preferred stockholders. (The preferred stock, which has a current-dividend preference, is noncumulative.)
f. Paid dividends of $38,600.

EXERCISE 11-6

STOCK ISSUANCE, TREASURY STOCK, AND DIVIDENDS

On January 1, 2003, Snow Company was authorized to issue 100,000 shares of common stock, par value $10 per share and 10,000 shares of 8% preferred stock, par value $20 per share. Record the following transactions for 2003:

a. Issued 70,000 shares of common stock at $25 per share.
b. Issued 8,000 shares of preferred stock at $30 per share.
c. Reacquired 5,000 shares of common stock at $20 per share.
d. Reissued 2,000 shares of treasury stock for $46,000.
e. Declared a cash dividend sufficient to meet the current-dividend preference on preferred stock and pay common shareholders $1 per share.

EXERCISE 11-7

STOCK TRANSACTIONS AND DIVIDENDS

Marion Corporation was organized in January 2003. The state authorized 200,000 shares of no-par common stock and 100,000 shares of 10%, $10 par, preferred stock. Record the following transactions that occurred in 2003:

a. Issued 20,000 shares of common stock at $20 per share.
b. Issued 8,000 shares of preferred stock for a piece of land appraised at $90,000.
c. Declared a cash dividend sufficient to meet the current-dividend preference on preferred stock and paid common shareholders $1 per share.
d. How would your answer to (c) change if the dividend declared were not sufficient to meet the current-dividend preference on preferred stock?

EXERCISE 11-8

DIVIDEND CALCULATIONS

On January 1, 2003, Oldroyd Corporation had 130,000 shares of common stock issued and outstanding. During 2003, the following transactions occurred (in chronological order):

a. Oldroyd issued 10,000 new shares of common stock.
b. The company reacquired 2,000 shares of stock for use in its employee stock option plan.
c. At the end of the option period, 1,200 shares of treasury stock had been purchased by corporate officials.

Given this information, compute the following:

1. After the foregoing three transactions have occurred, what amount of dividends must Oldroyd Corporation declare in order to pay 50 cents per share? To pay $1 per share?

2. What is the dividend per share if $236,640 is paid?
3. If all 2,000 treasury shares had been purchased by corporate officials through the stock option plan, what would the dividends per share have been, again assuming $236,640 in dividends were paid? (Round to the nearest cent.)

EXERCISE 11-9

DIVIDEND CALCULATIONS

Stewart Corporation has the following stock outstanding:

Preferred stock (5%, $20 par value, 20,000 shares)	$400,000
Common stock ($5 par value, 80,000 shares)	400,000

For the two independent cases that follow, compute the amount of dividends that would be paid to preferred and common shareholders. Assume that total dividends paid are $86,000. No dividends have been paid for the past two years.

Case A, Preferred is noncumulative.
Case B, Preferred is cumulative.

EXERCISE 11-10

STOCK ISSUANCE, TREASURY STOCK, AND DIVIDENDS

During 2003, Doxey Corporation had the following transactions and related events:

Jan. 15	Issued 6,500 shares of common stock at par ($16 per share), bringing the total number of shares outstanding to 121,300.
Feb. 6	Declared a 50-cent-per-share dividend on common stock for stockholders of record on March 6.
Mar. 6	Date of record.
8	Pedro Garcia, a prominent banker, purchased 20,000 shares of Doxey Corporation common stock from the company for $346,000.
Apr. 6	Paid dividends declared on February 6.
June 19	Reacquired 800 shares of common stock as treasury stock at a total cost of $9,350.
Sept. 6	Declared dividends of 55 cents per share to be paid to common stockholders of record on October 15, 2003.
Oct. 6	The Dow Jones Industrial Average plummeted 300 points, and Doxey's stock price fell $3 per share.
15	Date of record.
Nov. 16	Paid dividends declared on September 6.
Dec. 15	Declared and paid a 6% cash dividend on 18,000 outstanding shares of preferred stock (par value $32).

Given this information:

1. Prepare the journal entries for these transactions.
2. What is the total amount of dividends paid to common and preferred stockholders during 2003?

EXERCISE 11-11

DIVIDEND PAYOUT RATIO

The following numbers are for three different companies:

	A	B	C
Total assets	$1,000	$2,500	$2,000
Cash dividends	50	200	400
Total liabilities	600	800	1,400
Net income	200	500	500

For each company, compute the dividend payout ratio.

EXERCISE 11-12

ANALYSIS OF STOCKHOLDERS' EQUITY

The stockholders' equity section of Kay Corporation at the end of the current year showed:

Preferred stock (6%, $40 par, 10,000 shares authorized, 6,000 shares issued and outstanding)	$?
Common stock ($6 par, 80,000 shares authorized, 53,000 issued, 52,650 shares outstanding)	318,000
Paid-in capital in excess of par, preferred stock	?
Paid-in capital in excess of par, common stock	129,000
Retained earnings	86,000
Less treasury stock (350 shares at cost)	(2,000)
Total stockholders' equity	$?

1. What is the dollar amount to be reported for preferred stock?
2. What is the average price for which common stock was issued? (Round to the nearest cent.)
3. If preferred stock was issued at an average price of $43 per share, what amount should appear in the paid-in capital in excess of par, preferred stock account?
4. What is the average cost per share of treasury stock? (Round to the nearest cent.)
5. Assuming that the preferred stock was issued for an average price of $43 per share, what is total stockholders' equity?
6. If net income for the year were $67,000 and if only dividends on preferred stock were paid, by how much would retained earnings increase?

EXERCISE 11-13

PREPARING THE STOCKHOLDERS' EQUITY SECTION

The following account balances, before any closing entries, appear on the books of Spring Company as of December 31, 2003:

Retained Earnings (balance at Jan. 1, 2003)	$240,000
Dividends, Preferred Stock	15,000
Dividends, Common Stock	35,000
Common Stock ($5 par, 100,000 shares authorized, 70,000 issued and outstanding)	350,000
Paid-In Capital in Excess of Par, Common Stock	350,000
Preferred Stock (6%, $50 par, 50,000 shares authorized, 5,000 issued and outstanding)	250,000
Paid-In Capital in Excess of Par, Preferred Stock	25,000

Based on these account balances, and assuming net income for 2003 of $80,000, prepare the stockholders' equity section of the December 31, 2003, balance sheet for Spring Company.

EXERCISE 11-14

COMPREHENSIVE INCOME

The following information relates to Lily Company:

a. Lily Company's net income for the year was $10,000.
b. Lily Company has an investment portfolio for long-term investment purposes. That portfolio increased in value by $2,000 during the year.
c. Lily Company has several foreign subsidiaries. The currencies in the countries where those subsidiaries are located declined in value (relative to the U.S. dollar) during the year. Accordingly, the computed value of the equity of those subsidiaries, in U.S. dollars, decreased by $3,000.

Compute Lily's comprehensive income for the year.

EXERCISE 11-15

OTHER EQUITY ITEMS

Red Rider Company has the following stockholders' equity section on its balance sheet as of December 31, 2003 and 2002.

Red Rider Company
(in millions)

	2003	2002
Stockholders' Equity		
Preferred stock	$ 2.0	$ 2.0
Common stock	32.0	32.0
Paid-in capital—various	12.4	11.2
Retained earnings	24.5	24.6
Subtotal	$ 70.9	$69.8
Accumulated foreign currency translation adjustments	5.2	4.5
Net unrealized gains on investments in certain debt and equity securities	25.6	20.0
Total stockholders' equity	$101.7	$94.3

Based on this stockholders' equity section, answer the following questions:

1. At the end of 2003, what was the total amount of equity financing provided by Red Rider's investors?
2. At the end of 2003, how much of Red Rider's earnings had not been distributed to investors?
3. What is the total amount of "other equity items" contained in the 2003 stockholders' equity section?
4. What contributed most to the increased equity from 2002 to 2003?

expanded material

EXERCISE 11-16

STOCK DIVIDENDS AND STOCK SPLITS

The stockholders' equity section of Ardvark Corporation's December 31, 2002, balance sheet included the following items:

Common stock ($20 par, 250,000 shares authorized, 50,000 shares issued and outstanding)	$1,000,000
Paid-in capital in excess of par, common stock	1,500,000
Retained earnings	2,000,000

Record the following transactions for 2003:

a. On March 1, Ardvark declared and issued a 25% stock dividend on common stock. The market price of the stock was $40 per share on that date.
b. On June 30, a 4-for-1 stock split was declared.
c. On September 15, a 10% stock dividend on common stock was declared and distributed. The market price of the stock was $30 per share on the dividend date.

EXERCISE 11-17

STOCK DIVIDENDS

Allred Company has issued 90,000 shares of common stock with a par value of $5. Of the shares issued, 80,000 shares are outstanding. Allred's board of directors has decided to issue a stock dividend. The current market price of the stock is $30 per share. Provide journal entries to record the issuance of the dividend under each of the following independent circumstances:

1. The dividend is a 20% stock dividend.
2. The dividend is a 30% stock dividend.

EXERCISE 11-18

STOCK DIVIDENDS

On July 1, 2003, Sanford Corporation's balance sheet reported the following account balances in the stockholders' equity section:

Common stock, $5 par	$150,000
Paid-in capital in excess of par, common stock	20,000
Retained earnings	180,000
Total stockholders' equity	$350,000

On August 31, 2003, Sanford's board of directors declared and issued a 10% stock dividend. The market value on August 31 is $12 per share.

1. Compare the book value per share before and after the issuance of the stock dividend.
2. Compute the new balance for all stockholders' equity accounts after the stock dividend.

EXERCISE 11-19

STOCKHOLDERS' EQUITY TRANSACTIONS

On December 31, 2002, White Lighting Corporation's stockholders' equity section of the balance sheet showed the following:

Common stock ($10 par, 50,000 shares authorized, 25,000 issued and 17,000 outstanding)	$250,000
Paid-in capital in excess of par, common stock	375,000
Retained earnings	450,000
Treasury stock (8,000 shares, at cost)	(90,000)
Total stockholders' equity	$985,000

During 2003, the following transactions occurred:

a. On March 1, 2003, White Lighting purchased 5,000 shares of its stock at $20 per share.
b. On April 15, 2003, White Lighting reissued the 5,000 shares of its stock purchased in (a); the market price on that day was $30 per share.
c. On June 10, 2003, White Lighting declared and paid a 10% stock dividend. Market price of the stock was $32 per share.
d. On June 30, 2003, White Lighting declared a cash dividend of 50 cents per share. The dividend was paid on July 30. The record date was July 15.
e. On October 1, 2003, White Lighting issued 5,000 shares of new stock for $40 per share.

Prepare journal entries to record each of the above transactions.

EXERCISE 11-20

STATEMENT OF RETAINED EARNINGS

The stockholders' equity section of Summer Corporation's balance sheet shows the following as of the end of 2003:

Preferred stock (5%, $30 par, 10,000 shares authorized, 5,000 shares issued and outstanding)	$?
Common stock ($12 par, 50,000 shares authorized, 28,000 issued, 27,500 outstanding)	336,000
Paid-in capital in excess of par, preferred stock	?
Paid-in capital in excess of par, common stock	424,000
Retained earnings	78,000
Treasury stock (purchased at $14)	?
Total stockholders' equity	$?

Prepare a statement of retained earnings for the year ended December 31, 2003. Assume the following additional facts:

a. Retained earnings as of December 31, 2002, was $25,500.
b. Net income as of 2003 was $72,000.
c. Dividends equal to the current-dividend preference on preferred stock were declared and issued.

d. A prior-period adjustment was made to retained earnings to correct an overstatement of 2002 net income in the amount of $12,000.
e. Common stock was sold for $12.

EXERCISE 11-21

ACCOUNTING FOR A PROPRIETORSHIP

At the beginning of 2003, Marena Sanchez decided to go into business making and selling decorative artificial plants. During the year ended December 31, 2003, Sanchez had the following transactions:

a. Withdrew $20,000 from a personal savings account and deposited that amount in a new checking account to be used solely for the business.
b. Paid cash to purchase $12,000 of materials needed to make plants.
c. Invested another $24,000 in the business.
d. Sold 450 plants during the year at $60 each for cash.
e. Incurred and paid operating expenses for the year of $10,500.
f. At the end of the year, $4,000 of materials remained on hand. The cost of materials used was transferred to a cost of goods sold account.
g. Withdrew $5,000 for personal use.

Prepare journal entries to record the transactions, and prepare a statement of owner's capital for the year.

EXERCISE 11-22

PARTNERSHIP ACCOUNTING

Jill Emerson owned a pet shop. On August 1, 2003, Emerson accepted Allan Jacobs as a partner. At that time, Emerson's capital account showed a balance of $135,000. Jacobs contributed $90,000 cash for a 40% share in both capital and earnings. During the rest of 2003, the following transactions took place:

a. Emerson withdrew $12,000 and Jacobs withdrew $4,000.
b. Emerson invested another $4,500 cash, and Jacobs contributed a truck valued at $6,000.
c. Net income from August 1, 2003, through December 31, 2003, was $26,700, which included $66,700 of revenues and $40,000 of expenses.

Given this information:

1. Prepare the journal entries (including closing entries) for the transactions.
2. Prepare a statement of partners' capital for the 5 months ending December 31, 2003, for the Emerson and Jacobs partnership.

EXERCISE 11-23

STARTING A PARTNERSHIP

On July 1, 2003, Dr. Wright and Dr. O'Flaherty decided to form a partnership by combining all the assets and liabilities of their respective dental practices. The partnership will have a new and separate set of books. Dr. Wright's balance sheet at June 30, 2003, was as follows:

Assets		
Cash		$ 27,000
Accounts receivable	$116,000	
Less allowance for uncollectible accounts	6,600	109,400
Dental equipment	$ 52,900	
Less accumulated depreciation	24,200	28,700
Building	$169,400	
Less accumulated depreciation	13,500	155,900
Total assets		$321,000
Liabilities and Owner's Equity		
Accounts payable		$ 22,700
Mortgage payable		150,000
Dr. Wright, capital		148,300
Total liabilities and owner's equity		$321,000

The partners agreed that $5,600 of the accounts receivable were uncollectible and that $2,400 was a reasonable allowance for the uncollectibility of the remaining receivables. They also agreed that the dental equipment and the building should be recorded at their respective fair market values of $46,000 and $182,000.

Prepare the journal entry to record Dr. Wright's investment in the partnership.

PROBLEM 11-1

STOCK TRANSACTIONS AND ANALYSIS

The following selected items and amounts were taken from the balance sheet of Quale Company as of December 31, 2003:

Cash	$ 93,000
Property, plant, and equipment	850,000
Accumulated depreciation	150,000
Liabilities	50,000
Preferred stock (7%, $100 par, noncumulative, 10,000 shares authorized, 5,000 shares issued and outstanding)	500,000
Common stock ($10 par, 100,000 shares authorized, 80,000 shares issued and outstanding)	800,000
Paid-in capital in excess of par, preferred stock	1,000
Paid-in capital in excess of par, common stock	125,000
Paid-in capital, treasury stock	1,000
Retained earnings	310,000

Required: For each of parts (1) to (5), (a) prepare the necessary journal entry (or entries) to record each transaction, and (b) calculate the amount that would appear on the December 31, 2003, balance sheet as a consequence of this transaction only for the account given. (Note: In your answer to each part of this problem, consider this to be the only transaction that took place during 2003.)

1. Quale Company issued 200 shares of common stock in exchange for cash of $4,000.
   a. Entry
   b. Paid-In Capital in Excess of Par, Common Stock
2. The company issued 200 shares of preferred stock at a price of $102 per share.
   a. Entry
   b. Paid-In Capital in Excess of Par, Preferred Stock
3. The company issued 500 shares of common stock in exchange for a building. The common stock is not actively traded, but the building was recently appraised at $11,000.
   a. Entry
   b. Property, Plant, and Equipment
4. The company reacquired 1,000 shares of common stock from a stockholder for $23,000 and subsequently reissued the shares to a different investor for $21,500. (Note: Make two entries.)
   a. Entries
   b. Paid-In Capital, Treasury Stock
5. The board of directors declared dividends of $75,000. This amount includes the current-year dividend preference on preferred stock, with the remainder to be paid to common shareholders.
   a. Entry
   b. Retained Earnings

PROBLEM 11-2

STOCK TRANSACTIONS AND THE STOCKHOLDERS' EQUITY SECTION

The following is West Valley Company's stockholders' equity section of the balance sheet on December 31, 2002:

Preferred stock (8%, $60 par, noncumulative, 16,000 shares authorized, 8,000 shares issued and outstanding)	$480,000
Common stock ($10 par, 120,000 shares authorized, 80,000 shares issued and outstanding)	800,000
Paid-in capital in excess of par, preferred stock	130,000
Paid-in capital in excess of par, common stock	252,000
Retained earnings	330,000

Required:

1. Journalize the following 2003 transactions:
   a. Issued 2,000 preferred shares at $70 per share.
   b. Reacquired 1,000 common shares for the treasury at $13 per share.
   c. Declared and paid a $2-per-share dividend on common stock in addition to paying the required preferred dividends. (Note: Debit Retained Earnings directly.)
   d. Reissued 600 treasury shares at $14 per share.
   e. Reissued the remaining treasury shares at $12 per share.
   f. Earnings for the year were $92,000, including $200,000 of revenues and $108,000 of expenses.
2. Prepare the stockholders' equity section of the balance sheet for the company at December 31, 2003.

PROBLEM 11-3

RECORDING STOCKHOLDERS' EQUITY TRANSACTIONS

Zina Corporation was organized during 2002. At the end of 2002, the stockholders' equity section of the balance sheet appeared as follows:

Contributed capital:	
Preferred stock (8%, $40 par, 10,000 shares authorized, 5,000 shares issued and outstanding)	$200,000
Common stock ($20 par, 30,000 shares authorized, 12,000 issued, 10,000 outstanding)	240,000
Paid-in capital in excess of par, preferred stock	50,000
Total contributed capital	$490,000
Retained earnings	110,000
Total contributed capital plus retained earnings	$600,000
Less treasury stock (2,000 shares at cost of $25 per share)	(50,000)
Total stockholders' equity	$550,000

During 2003, the following transactions occurred in the order given:

a. Issued 1,000 shares of common stock at $24 per share.
b. Reissued 1,000 shares of treasury stock at $27 per share.
c. Reissued 500 shares of treasury stock at $20 per share.

Required: Record the transactions.

PROBLEM 11-4

STOCK TRANSACTIONS AND STOCKHOLDERS' EQUITY SECTION

The balance sheet for Lakeland Corporation as of December 31, 2002, is as follows:

Assets		$750,000
Liabilities		$410,000
Stockholders' equity:		
Preferred stock, convertible (5%, $20 par)	$ 50,000	
Common stock ($10 par)	150,000	
Paid-in capital in excess of par, common stock	30,000	
Retained earnings	116,000	
	$346,000	
Less treasury stock, common (500 shares at cost)	(6,000)	340,000
Total liabilities and stockholders' equity		$750,000

During 2003, the following transactions were completed in the order given:

a. The company reacquired 750 shares of outstanding common stock at $7 per share.
b. The company reacquired 150 shares of common stock in settlement of an account receivable of $1,500.
c. Semiannual cash dividends of 75 cents per share on common stock and 50 cents per share on preferred stock were declared and paid.
d. Each share of preferred stock is convertible into three shares of common stock. Five hundred shares of preferred stock were converted into common stock. (HINT: Shares are converted at par values, and any excess reduces Retained Earnings.)
e. The 900 shares of common treasury stock acquired during 2003 were sold at $13. The remaining treasury shares were exchanged for a machine with a fair market value of $6,300.
f. The company issued 3,000 shares of common stock in exchange for land appraised at $39,000.
g. Semiannual cash dividends of 75 cents per share on common stock and 50 cents per share on preferred stock were declared and paid.
h. Closed net income of $35,000 to Retained Earnings, which included $135,000 of revenues and $100,000 of expenses.
i. Closed dividends accounts to Retained Earnings.

Required:

1. Give the necessary journal entries to record the transactions listed.
2. Prepare the stockholders' equity section of the balance sheet as of December 31, 2003.

PROBLEM 11-5

STOCKHOLDERS' EQUITY, DIVIDENDS, AND TREASURY STOCK

The stockholders' equity section of Nielsen Corporation's December 31, 2002, balance sheet is as follows:

Stockholders' equity:	
Preferred stock (10%, $50 par, 10,000 shares authorized, 1,000 shares issued and outstanding)	$ 50,000
Common stock ($15 par, 100,000 shares authorized, 5,000 shares issued and outstanding)	75,000
Paid-in capital in excess of par, preferred stock	2,000
Paid-in capital in excess of par, common stock	25,000
Total contributed capital	$152,000
Retained earnings	102,000
Total stockholders' equity	$254,000

During 2003, Nielsen Corporation had the following transactions affecting stockholders' equity:

Jan. 20 Paid a cash dividend of $2 per share on common stock. The dividend was declared on December 15, 2002.
Aug. 15 Reacquired 1,000 shares of common stock at $20 per share.
Sept. 30 Reissued 500 shares of treasury stock at $21 per share.
Oct. 15 Declared and paid cash dividends of $3 per share on the common stock.
Nov. 1 Reissued 200 shares of treasury stock at $18 per share.
Dec. 15 Declared and paid the 10% preferred cash dividend.
31 Closed net income of $40,000 to Retained Earnings. (Revenues were $260,000; expenses were $220,000.) Also closed the dividends accounts to Retained Earnings.

Required:

1. Journalize the transactions.
2. Prepare the stockholders' equity section of Nielsen Corporation's December 31, 2003, balance sheet.
3. **Interpretive Question:** What is the effect on earnings per share when a company purchases treasury stock?

PROBLEM 11-6

DIVIDEND CALCULATIONS

Salty Corporation was organized in January 2000 and issued shares of preferred and common stock as shown. As of December 31, 2003, there have been no changes in outstanding stock.

Preferred stock (8%, $10 par, 20,000 shares issued and outstanding)	$200,000
Common stock ($40 par, 10,000 shares issued and outstanding)	400,000

Required:

For each of the following independent situations, compute the amount of dividends that would be paid for each class of stock in 2002 and 2003. Assume that total dividends of $10,000 and $80,000 are paid in 2002 and 2003, respectively.

1. Preferred stock is noncumulative.
2. Preferred stock is cumulative, and no dividends are in arrears in 2002.
3. Preferred stock is cumulative, and no dividends have been paid during 2000 and 2001.

PROBLEM 11-7

DIVIDEND CALCULATIONS

Rasmussen Corporation had authorization for 40,000 shares of 6% preferred stock, par value $10 per share, and 8,000 shares of common stock, par value $100 per share, all of which are issued and outstanding. During the years beginning in 2002, Rasmussen Corporation maintained a policy of paying out 50% of net income in cash dividends. One-half the net income for the three years beginning in 2002 was $16,000, $160,000, and $128,000. There are no dividends in arrears for years prior to 2002.

Required:

Compute the amount of dividends paid to each class of stock for each year under the following separate cases:

1. Preferred stock is noncumulative.
2. Preferred stock is cumulative.
3. **Interpretive Question:** Why is it important that a common stockholder know about the dividend privileges of the preferred stock?

PROBLEM 11-8

DIVIDEND PAYOUT RATIO

The following numbers are for three different companies:

	A	B	C
Cash	$ 50	$ 200	$ 400
Retained earnings	900	800	3,500
Cash dividends	80	0	500
Paid-in capital	1,000	2,500	2,000
Total liabilities	600	300	1,400
Sales	5,000	10,000	4,000
Net income	200	500	800

Required:

1. For each company, compute the dividend payout ratio.
2. **Interpretive Question:** Which of the three companies is most likely to be a high-growth Internet company? Which is most likely to be an old, stable company? Explain.

PROBLEM 11-9

PREPARING THE STOCKHOLDERS' EQUITY SECTION AND RECORDING DIVIDENDS

In 2001, Lee Ann Adams and some college friends organized The Candy Jar, a gourmet candy company. In 2001, The Candy Jar issued 150,000 of the 300,000 authorized shares of common stock, par value $15, for $3,000,000 and all the 50,000 authorized shares of 10%, $20 par, cumulative preferred stock for $1,100,000. Combined earnings for 2001, 2002, 2003, and 2004 amounted to $1,250,000. Dividends paid in the four years were as follows: 2001—$100,000; 2002—$300,000; 2003—$0; 2004—$150,000.

Required:

1. Prepare the stockholders' equity section of the balance sheet as of December 31, 2004, for The Candy Jar.
2. Prepare the journal entry that would be necessary to record the dividends paid in 2004.

PROBLEM 11-10 STOCKHOLDERS' EQUITY CALCULATIONS

A computer virus destroyed important financial information pertaining to Denton Company's stockholders' equity section. Your expertise is needed to compute the missing account balances. The only information you can recover from the computer's backup system is as follows:

a. During 2003, 8,000 shares of common stock with a par value of $10 were issued when the market price per share was $22.
b. Cash dividends of $30,000 were paid to preferred shareholders.
c. Denton Company acquired 4,000 shares of common stock at $15 to hold as treasury stock.
d. Denton Company reissued 3,000 shares of treasury stock for $18.

	December 31, 2002	December 31, 2003
Preferred stock	$ 2,000	$ 2,000
Common stock	6,000	?
Paid-in capital in excess of par, preferred stock	750	750
Paid-in capital in excess of par, common stock	1,750	?
Paid-in capital, treasury stock	0	?
Retained earnings	4,500	5,250
Treasury stock	0	(15,000)
Total stockholders' equity	15,000	?

Required:

1. Calculate the account balances for the following accounts:
   a. Common Stock
   b. Paid-In Capital in Excess of Par, Common Stock
   c. Paid-In Capital, Treasury Stock
   d. Stockholders' Equity
2. How much net income did Denton Company report for 2003?

PROBLEM 11-11 STOCK CALCULATIONS AND THE STOCKHOLDERS' EQUITY SECTION

The following account balances appear on the books of World Corporation as of December 31, 2003:

Preferred stock (7%, $40 par, 70,000 shares authorized, 50,000 shares issued and outstanding)	$2,000,000
Common stock ($3 par, 500,000 shares authorized, 300,000 shares issued and outstanding)	900,000
Paid-in capital in excess of par, preferred stock	310,000
Paid-in capital in excess of par, common stock	490,000
Net income for 2003	130,000
Dividends paid during 2003	70,000
Retained earnings, January 1, 2003	1,360,000

Required:

1. If the preferred stock is selling at $45 per share, what is the maximum amount of cash that World Corporation can obtain by issuing additional preferred stock given the present number of authorized shares?
2. If common stock is selling for $12 per share, what is the maximum amount of cash that can be obtained by issuing additional common stock given the present number of authorized shares?
3. Given the account balances at December 31, 2003, and ignoring parts (1) and (2), prepare, in good form, the stockholders' equity section of the balance sheet.

PROBLEM 11-12

UNIFYING CONCEPTS: STOCK TRANSACTIONS AND THE STOCKHOLDERS' EQUITY SECTION

Richard Corporation was founded on January 1, 2003, and entered into the following stock transactions during 2003.

a. Received authorization for 100,000 shares of $20 par-value common stock, 50,000 shares of 6% preferred stock with a par value of $5, and 50,000 shares of no-par common stock.
b. Issued 25,000 shares of the $20 par-value common stock at $24 per share.
c. Issued 10,000 shares of the preferred stock at $8 per share.
d. Issued 5,000 shares of the no-par common stock at $22 per share.
e. Reacquired 1,000 shares of the $20 par-value common stock at $25 per share.
f. Reacquired 500 shares of the no-par common stock at $20 per share.
g. Reissued 250 of the 1,000 reacquired shares of $20 par-value common stock at $23 per share.
h. Reissued all the 500 reacquired shares of no-par common stock at $23 per share.
i. Closed the $14,000 net income to Retained Earnings. Revenues and expenses for the year were $90,000 and $76,000, respectively.

Required:

1. Prepare journal entries to record the 2003 transactions in Richard Corporation's books.
2. Prepare the stockholders' equity section of Richard Corporation's balance sheet at December 31, 2003. Assume that the transactions represent all the events involving equity accounts during 2003.

PROBLEM 11-13

UNIFYING CONCEPTS: STOCK TRANSACTIONS, THE STOCKHOLDERS' EQUITY SECTION, AND THE STATEMENT OF STOCKHOLDERS' EQUITY

The condensed balance sheet of IBC Corporation at December 31, 2002, is shown below.

IBC Corporation
Balance Sheet
December 31, 2002

Assets	
Cash	$ 400,000
All other assets	1,042,000
	$1,442,000
Liabilities and Stockholders' Equity	
Current liabilities	$ 164,000
Long-term liabilities	230,000
	$ 394,000
Contributed capital:	
Common stock ($10 par, 100,000 shares authorized, 80,000 shares outstanding)	$ 800,000
Paid-in capital in excess of par, common stock	80,000
Retained earnings	168,000
	$1,048,000
	$1,442,000

During 2003, the following transactions affected stockholders' equity:

Feb. 15 Purchased 2,000 shares of IBC outstanding common stock at $15 per share.
May 21 Sold 1,200 of the shares purchased on February 15 at $19 per share.
Sept. 15 Issued 8,000 shares of previously unissued common stock at $21 per share.
Dec. 21 Sold the remaining 800 shares of treasury stock at $22 per share.
31 Closed net income of $85,360 to Retained Earnings. Revenues were $185,360; expenses were $100,000.

Required:

1. Prepare the journal entries to record the 2003 transactions.
2. Prepare the stockholders' equity section of the balance sheet at December 31, 2003.
3. Prepare a statement of stockholders' equity for the year ended December 31, 2003.

PROBLEM 11-14

UNIFYING CONCEPTS: STOCKHOLDERS' EQUITY

Icon Corporation was organized during 2001. At the end of 2002, the equity section of its balance sheet appeared as follows:

Contributed capital:	
Preferred stock (6%, $20 par, 10,000 shares authorized, 5,000 shares issued and outstanding)	$100,000
Common stock ($10 par, 50,000 shares authorized, 11,000 shares issued, 10,000 outstanding)	110,000
Paid-in capital in excess of par, preferred stock	20,000
Total contributed capital	$230,000
Retained earnings	100,000
Total contributed capital plus retained earnings	$330,000
Less treasury stock (1,000 shares of common at cost)	(12,000)
Total stockholders' equity	$318,000

During 2003, the following stockholders' equity transactions occurred (in chronological sequence):

a. Issued 500 shares of common stock at $13 per share.
b. Reissued 500 shares of treasury stock at $13 per share.
c. Issued 1,000 shares of preferred stock at $25 per share.
d. Reissued 500 shares of treasury stock at $10 per share.
e. Declared a dividend large enough to meet the current-dividend preference of the preferred stock and to pay the common stockholders $2 per share. Dividends are recorded directly in the retained earnings account.
f. Closed net income of $65,000 to Retained Earnings. Revenues were $400,000; expenses were $335,000.

Required:

1. Journalize the transactions.
2. Prepare the stockholders' equity section of the balance sheet at December 31, 2003.

PROBLEM 11-15

COMPREHENSIVE INCOME

The following information relates to Pecos Yo Company:

Sales	$15,000
Cost of goods sold	6,000
Other operating expenses	2,500
Interest expense	400
Income tax expense	3,000

In addition, the following events occurred during the year:

a. Pecos Yo Company has an investment portfolio for long-term investment purposes. That portfolio decreased in value by $7,000 during the year.
b. Pecos Yo Company owns a substantial amount of land. During the year, the land increased in value by $11,000.
c. Pecos Yo Company has several foreign subsidiaries. The currencies in the countries where those subsidiaries are located declined in value (relative to the U.S. dollar) during the year. Accordingly, the computed value of the equity of those subsidiaries, in U.S. dollars, decreased by $5,000.

Required:

1. Compute Pecos Yo's comprehensive income for the year.
2. **Interpretive Question:** Is comprehensive income a good measure of the change in a company's value during the year?

PROBLEM 11-16

STOCKHOLDERS' EQUITY SECTION WITH SELECTED "OTHER INFORMATION"

The stockholders' equity section of Glory Company's balance sheet was as follows as of December 31, 2003, and December 31, 2002:

Glory Company
Stockholders' Equity Sections of Balance Sheet
December 31, 2003 and 2002
(in millions)

	2003	2002
Preferred stock	$ 21.4	$ 21.4
Common stock	48.4	43.2
Paid-in capital, various types	22.6	15.3
Retained earnings	51.8	41.2
Subtotal	$144.2	$121.1
Accumulated foreign currency translation adjustments	21.4	57.3
Net unrealized gains (losses) on investments in certain debt and equity securities	(46.4)	(8.8)
Total stockholders' equity	$119.2	$169.6

Required:

Based on the stockholders' equity section for Glory Company, answer the following questions:

1. Do you believe Glory Company made a profit during the year 2003? Assuming that only net income and dividends changed the retained earnings balance from 2002 to 2003, by how much did net income exceed dividends?
2. What was the total amount of money raised during 2003 from the selling of stock? (Assume that only the selling of stock affected the contributed capital accounts.)
3. Did the market value of Glory Company's securities that affect the equity section increase or decrease in 2003? By how much?
4. **Interpretive Question:** The board of directors believes it should fire the current management of the company because total stockholders' equity decreased substantially. Do you agree? Why or why not?

expanded material

PROBLEM 11-17

RECORDING STOCKHOLDERS' EQUITY TRANSACTIONS

The stockholders' equity section of Hathaway Corporation's December 31, 2002, balance sheet is as follows:

Stockholders' Equity

Contributed capital:	
Preferred stock (5%, $25 par, 2,000 shares issued and outstanding)	$ 50,000
Common stock ($30 par, 10,000 shares issued and outstanding)	300,000
Paid-in capital in excess of par, preferred stock	10,000
Paid-in capital in excess of par, common stock	100,000
Total contributed capital	$460,000
Retained earnings	340,000
Total stockholders' equity	$800,000

During 2003, Hathaway Corporation had the following transactions:

Feb. 1	Paid a cash dividend of $3 per share on common stock. The dividend was declared December 31, 2002.
Mar. 15	Declared and issued a 19% common stock dividend. The market price of the stock on this date was $40 per share.
June 1	Reacquired 3,000 shares of common stock at $35 per share.
Sept. 1	Reissued 500 shares of treasury stock at $40 per share.
Nov. 15	Reissued 500 shares of treasury stock at $32 per share.

Required: Record the transactions.

PROBLEM 11-18 DIVIDEND TRANSACTIONS AND CALCULATIONS

As of December 31, 2002, First Corporation has 200,000 shares of $10 par-value common stock authorized, with 100,000 of these shares issued and outstanding.

Required:

1. Prepare journal entries to record the following 2003 transactions:

Jan. 1	Received authorization for 200,000 shares of 7%, cumulative preferred stock with a par value of $10.
2	Issued 10,000 shares of the preferred stock at $15 per share.
June 1	Reacquired 40% of the common stock outstanding for $18 per share.
2	Declared a cash dividend of $10,000. The date of record is June 15.
June 30	Paid the previously declared cash dividend of $10,000.

2. Determine the proper allocation to preferred and common stockholders of a $100,000 cash dividend declared on December 31, 2003. (This dividend is in addition to the June 2 dividend.)
3. **Interpretive Question:** Why didn't the preferred stockholders receive their current-dividend preference of $7,000 in part (2)?

PROBLEM 11-19 RECORDING DIVIDEND TRANSACTIONS AND REPORTING STOCKHOLDERS' EQUITY

Murtry, Inc., reported the following stockholders' equity balances in its June 30, 2002, balance sheet:

Preferred stock (6%, $100 par, cumulative; 20,000 shares authorized, 6,000 shares issued and outstanding)	$ 600,000
Common stock ($20 par; 250,000 shares authorized, 60,000 shares issued and outstanding)	1,200,000
Retained earnings	950,000

Required:

1. The following stockholders' equity transactions occurred (in the order presented) during the fiscal year ending June 30, 2003. Prepare the necessary journal entries to record the transactions.
   a. Murtry declared and issued a 5% dividend on common stock; the market value of the stock was $30 per share on the date of the dividend.
   b. A 50% stock dividend on common stock was declared and issued when the stock was trading at a market price of $40 per share.
   c. A cash dividend was declared at the end of the fiscal year. The common stockholders will receive 50 cents per share after the current and cumulative preference on the preferred stock is satisfied. Preferred stock dividends are one year in arrears.
2. Assuming Murtry's net income for the year ended June 30, 2003, is $310,000, prepare the stockholders' equity section of the June 30, 2003, balance sheet and a statement of stockholders' equity for the 2002–2003 fiscal year.
3. **Interpretive Question:** What is the effect on earnings per share when a company has a stock dividend or stock split?

PROBLEM 11-20

STATEMENT OF RETAINED EARNINGS AND STOCKHOLDERS' EQUITY

The following balances appear in the accounts of Iron Corporation as of December 31, 2003:

Retained earnings, January 1, 2003	$128,000
Prior-period adjustment (tax adjustment for 2001)	(57,000)
Net income for 2003	60,000
Preferred stock (7%, $12 par, 20,000 shares authorized, 5,000 shares issued and outstanding)	60,000
Common stock ($5 par, 100,000 shares authorized, 16,000 shares issued, 200 held as treasury stock)	80,000
Paid-in capital in excess of par, preferred stock	13,400
Paid-in capital in excess of par, common stock	42,800
Treasury stock	3,600
Cash dividends (declared during 2003)	10,000

Required:

1. Prepare the statement of retained earnings for Iron Corporation as of December 31, 2003.
2. Prepare the stockholders' equity section of Iron Corporation's balance sheet as of December 31, 2003.

PROBLEM 11-21

STATEMENT OF RETAINED EARNINGS

Marsh Corporation records show the following at December 31, 2003:

Extraordinary loss (net of tax)	$(50,000)
Cash dividends declared during 2003	30,000
Stock dividends issued during 2003	14,000
January 1, 2003, retained earnings balance	690,000
Prior-period adjustment (net of tax)	(36,000)
Net income before extraordinary items and taxes (assume a 40% tax rate)	160,000

Required: Prepare a 2003 statement of retained earnings.

PROBLEM 11-22

ACCOUNTING FOR A PROPRIETORSHIP

On January 1, 2003, Pat Larsen decided to open the Donut Shop. Pat deposited $40,000 of her own money in a company bank account and obtained a $30,000 loan from a local bank. During its first year of operation, the shop had net income of $84,000, which included $150,000 of revenues and $66,000 of expenses. Pat withdrew a lump sum of $48,000 from the business that year to cover personal living expenses.

H.A.T.

Required:

1. Prepare journal entries to record:
   a. Pat's original contribution to the firm.
   b. The bank loan.
   c. Pat's withdrawal for her living expenses.
   d. Any closing entries required at year-end.
2. Prepare a statement of owner's capital for 2003.
3. **Interpretive Question:** How would the accounting for the transactions in part (1) be different if Pat's business were a corporation?

PROBLEM 11-23

PARTNERSHIP ACCOUNTING

On January 1, 2003, Reed and Bailey established a partnership to sell fruit.

a. Reed invested $42,000 cash in the partnership, and Bailey invested $20,000 cash and a building valued at $25,000.
b. Reed invested another $6,000 cash. Bailey donated a truck valued at $7,000.
c. Reed withdrew $11,000 cash, and Bailey withdrew $6,300 cash.
d. A fire destroyed half of the building donated by Bailey. There was no insurance on the building. The partners share profits and losses equally.

e. Reed and Bailey agree to admit a third partner on March 1 of the next year. This partner, Kiefer, promises to invest $50,000 cash.

Required:

1. Journalize the transactions.
2. Journalize the closing entries. Assume revenues totaled $50,000 and expenses totaled $31,000.
3. Compute each partner's capital balance at the end of 2003.
4. **Interpretive Question:** What is the relationship between the amount of capital contributed by each owner and the way profits are to be allocated?

competency enhancement opportunities

- Analyzing Real Company Information
- International Case
- Ethics Case
- Writing Assignment
- The Debate
- Cumulative Spreadsheet Project
- Internet Search

The following additional assignments provide opportunities for students to develop critical thinking, ethical perspectives, oral and written communication skills, experience with electronic research, and teamwork through group and business activities.

ANALYZING REAL COMPANY INFORMATION

• ***Analyzing 11-1 (Microsoft)***

The 1999 annual report for **MICROSOFT** is included in Appendix A. Microsoft's stockholders' equity statements provide details of equity transactions of the company during the 1999 fiscal year. Locate the statements and consider the following questions:

1. What was the major reason that stockholders' equity increased for the year?
2. How much did common stockholders receive in dividends during the year? How much did preferred stockholders receive?
3. Did Microsoft issue more shares than it repurchased during the year or vice versa? How can you tell? (HINT: You should look in the notes to the statements to answer this question.)

• ***Analyzing 11-2 (Wal-Mart Stores, Inc.)***

WAL-MART has a simple, straightforward statement of shareholders' equity. That statement for the years 1998 and 1999 is reproduced on the top of the next page.

Consolidated Statements of Shareholders' Equity

(Amounts in millions except per share data)	Number of Shares	Common Stock	Capital in Excess of Par Value	Retained Earnings	Other Accumulated Comprehensive Income	Total
Balance—January 31, 1998	2,241	$224	$585	$18,167	$(473)	$18,503
Net income				4,430		4,430
Cash dividends ($0.16 per share)				(693)		(693)
Foreign currency translation adjustment					(36)	(36)
Purchase of company stock	(21)	(2)	(37)	(1,163)		(1,202)
Two-for-one stock split	2,224	223	(223)			—
Other	4		110			110
Balance—January 31, 1999	4,448	445	435	20,741	(509)	21,112
Net income				5,377		5,377
Cash dividends ($0.20 per share)				(890)		(890)
Foreign currency translation adjustment					54	54
Purchase of company stock	(2)		(2)	(99)		(101)
Other	11	1	281			282
Balance—January 31, 2000	4,457	$446	$714	$25,129	$(455)	$25,834

1. Based on the dividends paid during each year, how many shares of stock were outstanding when the dividends were paid?
2. Why isn't the number of shares receiving dividends exactly the same as the number of shares outstanding on January 31 of each year as indicated in the statement?
3. Estimate Wal-Mart's dividend payout ratio for each year. (HINT: You will need to estimate an earnings-per-share figure given the available data.)

INTERNATIONAL CASE

• *The EMI Group*

The shareholders' equity section of the balance sheet of THE EMI GROUP, a company based in the United Kingdom, is reproduced below. Review this information and answer the questions below.

Balance Sheets at 31 March 1999

	Group	
	1999 £m	Pro Forma 1998 £m
Capital and reserves		
Called-up share capital	**110.2**	110.1
Share premium reserve	**441.2**	439.0
Capital redemption reserve	**495.8**	495.8
Other reserves	**636.9**	786.3
Profit and loss reserve (including goodwill previously written off)	**710.5**	529.3
Equity shareholders' funds	**2,394.6**	2,360.5

1. What do you think the term "called-up share capital" means?
2. What does the term "profit and loss reserve" mean?
3. In the United Kingdom, goodwill has historically not been recorded as an asset. Instead, it has frequently been recorded as a contra-equity account. As of March 31, 1997, The EMI Group reported a goodwill contra-equity amount of 524.7 million pounds. Assuming that The EMI Group paid cash of 524.7 million pounds for the goodwill it purchased, provide the journal entry that would have been made at the time. How does this journal entry differ from the one that would have been made had EMI been a U.S.-based company? [Note: Since 1997, The EMI Group has changed its accounting for goodwill; EMI now uses the same approach used in the United States.]

ETHICS CASE

• Buying Your Own Shares Back

You are the chief financial officer for Esoteric, Inc., a company whose stock is publicly traded. The stock market has recently experienced an overall downturn, and the price of your company's stock has decreased by about 15%. This significantly affects the compensation of the executives of your company as their bonuses are based on the company's stock price. The bonus plan rewards company executives who take actions to increase the value of the company to shareholders. The reasoning is that if management increases the value of the company to shareholders, management should be rewarded.

As you consider ways to increase the value of the company, when the market itself is slumping, the following idea pops into your head: We will buy back our own stock. That will cause the remaining outstanding stock to increase in value, which is good for those individuals holding that stock. And it will also result in you and the other corporate executives receiving sizable bonuses.

Do you think this plan of action to increase stock price was what the designers of the compensation plan had in mind when they linked executive bonuses to company stock price? Does buying back the company's own stock add value to the company as a whole? Should the compensation plan prohibit activities like buying stock back? Consider these issues and be prepared to discuss them.

expanded material

WRITING ASSIGNMENT

• Stock Splits Versus Stock Dividends

In this chapter, you learned that we account for stock dividends differently than we account for stock splits. For stock dividends, the accounting also varies, depending on the size of the dividend. Prepare a two-page memo summarizing the following points:

1. To an investor who holds stock in a company, what is the difference between a small stock dividend, a large stock dividend, and a stock split?
2. To the accountant who must account for business transactions, what is the difference between a small stock dividend, a large stock dividend, and a stock split?
3. If you held stock in a company that was contemplating the declaration of a stock dividend or a stock split, which would you prefer?

THE DEBATE

• ***Microsoft Should Share the Wealth!***

Turn to MICROSOFT's annual report in Appendix A and notice its cash balance. As of June 30, 1999, the company had over $17 billion in cash and short-term investments. It is likely that the company has a lot more cash on hand now. Should Microsoft use some of that cash to pay a dividend to its common shareholders?

Divide your group into two teams.

- The first team represents the position that "Bill Knows Best—Don't Pay a Dividend." Prepare a two-minute presentation outlining the reasons why Microsoft's no-dividend policy is appropriate.
- The second team represents the position that "A Dividend Should Be Paid." Prepare a two-minute presentation outlining reasons why Microsoft should use some of its stockpile of cash to reward common shareholders who have never received a dividend.

CUMULATIVE SPREADSHEET PROJECT

This spreadsheet assignment is a continuation of the spreadsheet assignments given in earlier chapters. If you completed those spreadsheets, you have a head start on this one.

1. Handyman wishes to prepare a forecasted balance sheet and income statement for 2004. Use the original financial statement numbers for 2003 [given in part (1) of the Cumulative Spreadsheet Project assignment in Chapter 2] as the basis for the forecast, along with the following additional information:
   a. Sales in 2004 are expected to increase by 40% over 2003 sales of $700.
   b. Cash will increase at the same rate as sales.
   c. The forecasted amount of accounts receivable in 2004 is determined using the forecasted value for the average collection period. For simplicity, do the computations using the end-of-period accounts receivable balance instead of the average balance. The average collection period for 2004 is expected to be 14.08 days.
   d. The forecasted amount of inventory in 2004 is determined using the forecasted value for the number of days' sales in inventory (computed using the end-of-period inventory balance). The number of days' sales in inventory for 2004 is expected to be 107.6 days.
   e. The forecasted amount of accounts payable in 2004 is determined using the forecasted value for the number of days' purchases in accounts payable (computed using the end-of-period accounts payable balance). The number of days' purchases in accounts payable for 2004 is expected to be 48.34 days.
   f. The $160 in operating expenses reported in 2003 breaks down as follows: $5 depreciation expense, $155 other operating expenses.
   g. New long-term debt will be acquired (or repaid) in an amount sufficient to make Handyman's debt ratio (total liabilities divided by total assets) in 2004 exactly equal to 0.80.
   h. No cash dividends will be paid in 2004.
   i. New short-term loans payable will be acquired in an amount sufficient to make Handyman's current ratio in 2004 exactly equal to 2.0.
   j. The forecasted amount of property, plant, and equipment (PP&E) in 2004 is determined using the forecasted value for the fixed asset turnover ratio. For simplicity, compute the fixed asset turnover ratio using the end-of-period *gross* PP&E balance. The fixed asset turnover ratio for 2004 is expected to be 3.518 times.

k. In computing depreciation expense for 2004, use straight-line depreciation and assume a 30-year useful life with no residual value. Gross PP&E acquired during the year is depreciated for only half the year. In other words, depreciation expense for 2004 is the sum of two parts: (1) a full year of depreciation on the beginning balance in PP&E, assuming a 30-year life and no residual value and (2) a half-year of depreciation on any new PP&E acquired during the year, based on the change in the gross PP&E balance.

l. Assume an interest rate on short-term loans payable of *6.0%* and on long-term debt of *8.0%*. Only a half-year's interest is charged on loans taken out during the year. For example, if short-term loans payable at the end of 2004 are $15 and given that short-term loans payable at the end of 2003 were $10, total short-term interest expense for 2004 would be $0.75 [($10 × .06) + ($5 × .06 × ½)].

Note: These statements were constructed as part of the spreadsheet assignment in Chapter 10; you can use that spreadsheet as a starting point if you have completed that assignment.

For this exercise, add the following additional assumptions:

- In addition to preparing forecasted financial statements for 2004, Handyman also wishes to prepare forecasted financial statements for 2005. All assumptions applicable to 2004 are also assumed to be applicable to 2005. Sales in 2005 are expected to be 40% higher than sales in 2004.

Clearly state any additional assumptions that you make.

2. For each forecasted year, 2004 and 2005, state whether Handyman is expected to issue new shares of stock or to repurchase shares of stock.
3. Repeat (2), with the following changes in assumptions:
   a. The debt ratio in 2004 and 2005 is exactly equal to 0.70.
   b. The debt ratio in 2004 and 2005 is exactly equal to 0.95.
4. Comment on how it is possible for a company to have negative paid-in capital.

INTERNET SEARCH

• *Dow Jones & Company*

We began this chapter with a look at the history of **DOW JONES & COMPANY**. Let's continue our examination of this company using its Internet site. Access Dow Jones' site at **http://dowjones.com**. Sometimes Web addresses change, so if this address doesn't work, access the Web site for this book (**http://albrecht.swcollege.com**) for an updated link to Dow Jones & Company.

Once you have gained access to the company's Web site, answer the following questions:

1. What business publications is the company responsible for? What other services does the company provide?
2. Locate the company's most recent annual report. Which of the company's business segments is the most profitable as measured by operating income as a percentage of revenues?
3. Did the company pay a dividend in the most recent year? If so, how much per share? Compute the company's dividend payout ratio.
4. Review the note disclosure relating to the company's executive incentive plan (employee stock compensation plans). What is the objective of this plan?

Investments in Debt and Equity Securities

chapter

f12

learning objectives

After studying this chapter, you should be able to:

1. Understand why companies invest in other companies.
2. Understand the different classifications for securities.
3. Account for the purchase, recognition of revenue, and sale of trading and available-for-sale securities.
4. Account for changes in the value of securities.

expanded material

5. Account for held-to-maturity securities.
6. Account for securities using the equity method.

setting the stage

Warren Buffett, who has been called "the world's greatest investor," has lived most of his life not far from the house in which he grew up in Omaha, Nebraska.[1] He attended the Wharton School at the University of Pennsylvania (but dropped out because he thought he wasn't learning anything); received a bachelor's degree from the University of Nebraska; applied for admission to do graduate work at Harvard but was rejected; and instead earned a master's degree in economics at Columbia.

Buffett began his professional career as a stock trader and eventually created an investment fund called the Buffett Partnership, which earned a 32% average annual return over its life from 1956 to 1969. Buffett also began purchasing shares in a small textile manufacturer called **BERKSHIRE HATHAWAY**. His first 2,000 shares of Berkshire Hathaway stock cost $7.50 per share (plus $0.10 per share in commissions). Buffett transformed Berkshire Hathaway from a textile manufacturer into a holding company that invests in the stock of other companies. A selection of the companies controlled by Berkshire Hathaway, along with some of Berkshire Hathaway's major investments, is shown in Exhibit 12-1.

How has Berkshire Hathaway's stock performed under Warren Buffett's leader-

exhibit 12-1 Berkshire Hathaway's Operations and Investments

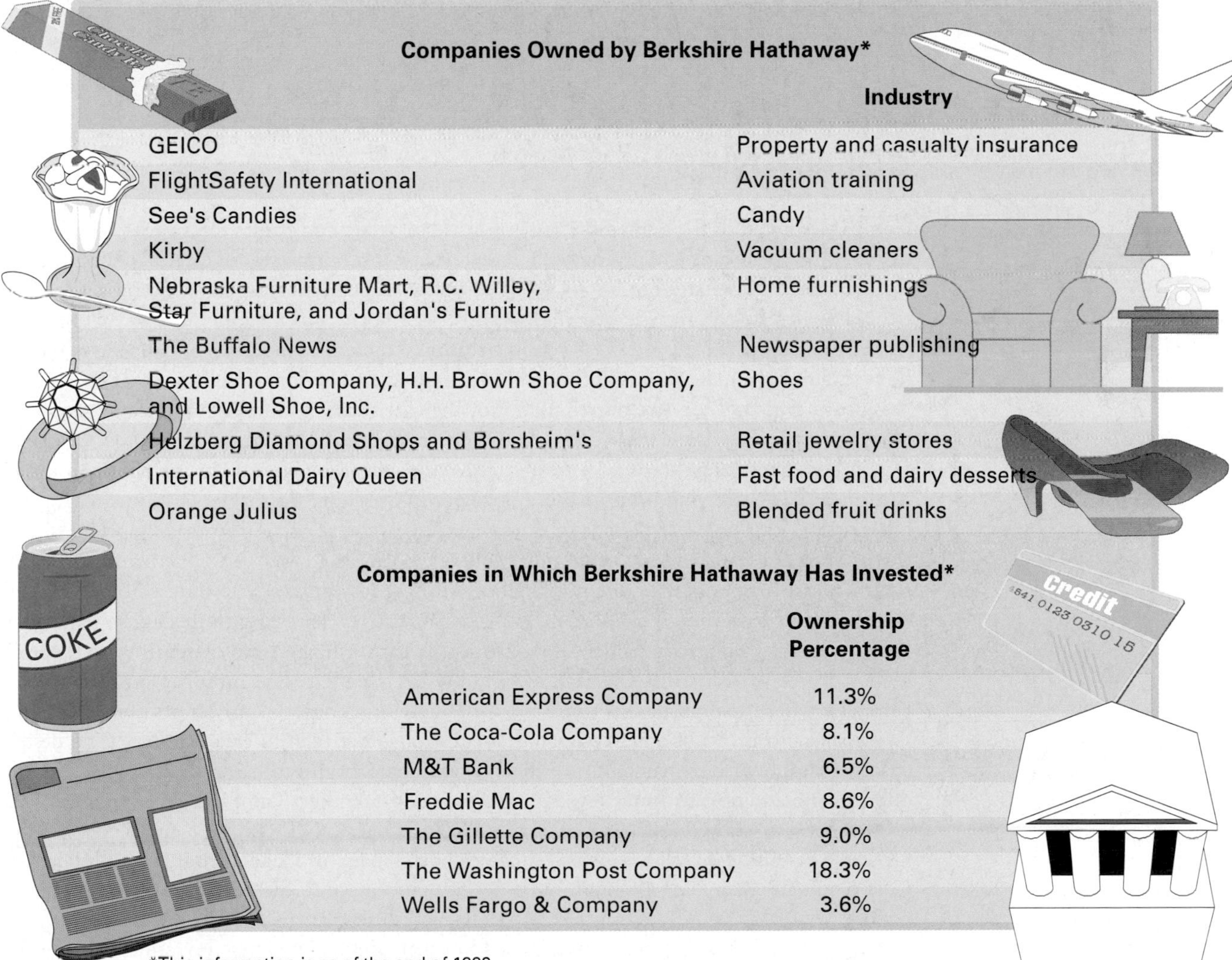

Companies Owned by Berkshire Hathaway*

	Industry
GEICO	Property and casualty insurance
FlightSafety International	Aviation training
See's Candies	Candy
Kirby	Vacuum cleaners
Nebraska Furniture Mart, R.C. Willey, Star Furniture, and Jordan's Furniture	Home furnishings
The Buffalo News	Newspaper publishing
Dexter Shoe Company, H.H. Brown Shoe Company, and Lowell Shoe, Inc.	Shoes
Helzberg Diamond Shops and Borsheim's	Retail jewelry stores
International Dairy Queen	Fast food and dairy desserts
Orange Julius	Blended fruit drinks

Companies in Which Berkshire Hathaway Has Invested*

	Ownership Percentage
American Express Company	11.3%
The Coca-Cola Company	8.1%
M&T Bank	6.5%
Freddie Mac	8.6%
The Gillette Company	9.0%
The Washington Post Company	18.3%
Wells Fargo & Company	3.6%

*This information is as of the end of 1999.

1 Janet Lowe, *Warren Buffett Speaks: Wit and Wisdom from the World's Greatest Investor* (New York: John Wiley & Sons, 1997).

ship? Well, on October 23, 2000, the company's stock closed at $58,600 per share! How has Warren Buffett done personally? He receives a salary of only $100,000 per year (making him the lowest paid CEO among the nation's top 200 companies). But don't feel sorry for Mr. Buffett. He was smart enough to purchase a large number of Berkshire Hathaway shares when the price was low. With a personal worth of approximately $25.6 billion, he ranks fourth on the list of the world's richest people.[2]

In this chapter we focus on why companies invest in other companies and how to account for those investments. When a company purchases the debt or equity securities of another company, several accounting issues are raised: how to account for the initial purchase, how to account for the receipt of dividends or interest, how to account for any subsequent changes in value of the security, and how to account for the security if it is sold or matures. The remainder of this chapter focuses on each of these issues. First, we examine how securities are classified and the different accounting implications of these classifications. We then introduce proper accounting for the purchase, receipt of revenue, sale, and valuation of securities. In the expanded material section of the chapter, we review the computations and accounting for a bond premium or discount from the point of view of the purchaser (we focused on the seller's perspective in Chapter 10). We also introduce the equity method of accounting and discuss when its application is appropriate. Exhibit 12-2 highlights the financial statement accounts that will be discussed in this chapter.

1

Understand why companies invest in other companies.

WHY COMPANIES INVEST IN OTHER COMPANIES

Companies invest in the debt and equity securities of other companies for a variety of reasons. A major reason is to earn a return on their excess cash. Most businesses are cyclical or seasonal; that is, their cash inflows and outflows vary significantly throughout the year. At certain times (particularly when inventories are being purchased), a company's cash supply is low. At other times (usually during or shortly after heavy selling seasons), there is excess cash on hand. A typical cash flow pattern for a retail firm is illustrated in Exhibit 12-3. The time line shows that the company has insufficient cash for inventory buildup for the Christmas rush, followed by large amounts of accounts receivable (from credit sales), and then an excess of cash immediately after Christmas.

When a company needs cash to meet current obligations, funds can be obtained through such means as borrowing from financial institutions or selling (factoring) accounts receivable or other assets. During those periods of time when excess cash exists, firms usually prefer to invest that money and earn a return. One possibility is to place the money in a bank and earn a fixed return. Most firms, however, are not satisfied with the low interest rates offered by financial institutions and have turned to other investment alternatives. Investing in the stocks (equity) and bonds (debt) of other companies allows a firm to earn a higher rate of return by accepting a higher degree of risk. BERKSHIRE HATHAWAY is perhaps the most famous example of a company whose sole purpose is to invest in the debt and equity securities of other companies.

Firms also invest in other companies for reasons other than to earn a return. The desire to ensure a supply of raw materials, to influence the board of directors, or to diversify its product offerings are additional reasons for a company to invest in other companies. For example, THE COCA-COLA COMPANY owns 40% of COCA-COLA ENTERPRISES and 37% of COCA-COLA AMATIL LTD. These two companies bottle many of Coke's products, and The Coca-Cola Company maintains a significant ownership percentage to ensure that the bottling facilities remain available. As indicated in Exhibit 12-1, Berkshire Hathaway owns a number of companies outright and has significant investments in other companies. These investments allow Berkshire Hathaway to significantly influence or even control the operating decisions of the investees.

2 If you have never had the pleasure of reading one of Warren Buffett's "Chairman's Letter to the Shareholders," you should take the opportunity now. No one writes a funnier, more insightful letter than Mr. Buffett. The company's Internet address is http://www.berkshirehathaway.com.

exhibit 12-2 Financial Statement Items Covered in This Chapter

Balance Sheet

Current assets
Investments

Long-term investments

Stockholders' equity
Unrealized increase/decrease in value of securities

Statement of Cash Flows

Operating activities
Purchase of trading securities
Sale of trading securities

Investing activities
Purchase of debt and equity securities other than trading securities
Sale of debt and equity securities other than trading securities

Income Statement

Other revenues and expenses
Gains and losses on sales of securities
Unrealized gains and losses on securities
Interest revenue

exhibit 12-3 A Cash Flow Pattern

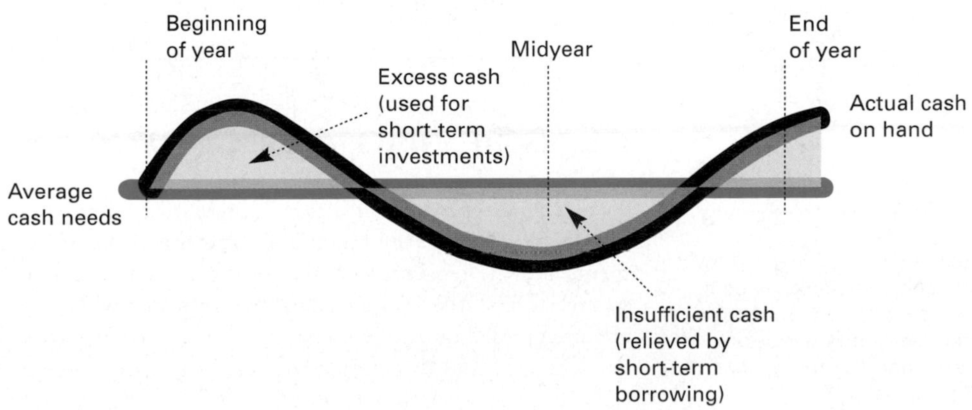

COCA-COLA COMPANY owns significant stakes in companies that bottle its products. Such investments allow Coca-Cola to ensure that its bottling facilities remain available and that its soft-drink products consistently meet the company's quality standards.

STOP & THINK Can you think of additional reasons why companies would purchase interests in other companies?

Rather than investing in the research and development required to develop a product or an area of expertise, many companies find it cheaper to purchase all or part of another company that has already expended the effort and the time to develop the desired product or know-how. As an example, to complement its existing software, NOVELL (a computer company specializing in networking) purchased WordPerfect and Quattro Pro, word-processing and spreadsheet software packages, respectively. This purchase then allowed Novell to assemble a menu of software packages to compete with MICROSOFT's Word, Excel, PowerPoint, and Access software packages. Novell's attempt to compete with Microsoft failed, however, and the company eventually sold WordPerfect to COREL.

to summarize

Companies invest in other companies for a variety of reasons. In most cases, the objective is to earn a return on the investment, either through the receipt of interest or dividends, or through an increase in the value of the investment. A firm may also invest in other companies so that it will be able to influence their operating decisions. In some cases, companies find it cheaper to buy another company to gain access to its assets than to expend the resources necessary to develop the assets on their own.

2

Understand the different classifications for securities.

CLASSIFYING A SECURITY

debt securities Financial instruments issued by a company that carry with them a promise of interest payments and the repayment of principal.

Two general types of securities are purchased by companies—debt securities and equity securities. **Debt securities** are financial instruments that carry with them the promise of interest payments and the repayment of the principal amount. Bonds are the most common type of debt security. Debt securities are issued by companies when the need for cash arises. These securities are often traded on public exchanges such as the New York Bond Exchange. Investors often prefer debt securities to equity securities because of the certainty of the income stream (interest) and the relative safety (low risk) of debt as an investment. Investors in corporate debt securities have priority over investors in equity securities, both for the yearly interest payments and for the return of principal if the issuing corporation gets into financial difficulty. Bonds issued by corporations are the most common type of debt securities (recall from Chapter 10 that bonds are typically issued in multiples of $1,000). Once the bonds are issued, ownership of the entire bond issuance, or just a portion, can change hands frequently.

equity securities (stock) Shares of ownership in a corporation that can change significantly in value and that provide for a return to investors in the form of dividends.

Unlike bonds, **equity securities** (or **stock**), which are also traded on public exchanges, represent actual ownership interest in a corporation. The owner of equity securities is allowed to vote on such corporate matters as executive compensation policies, who will serve on the board of directors of the corporation, and who will be the outside auditor. In addition to voting, the owner of stock often receives a return on that investment in the form of a dividend. A second type of return often accumulates to the stockholder as well—appreciation in stock price. Many investors invest in a company not for the dividend but for the potential increase in stock price. High-tech companies typically do not pay dividends, instead electing to funnel their profits back into the company. Investors know that their return in high-tech companies will come in the form of an increased stock price, not a dividend. With the potential for increased stock price also comes a risk—the stock price could fall. Holders of debt securities, barring extreme financial difficulties by the issuer, will always receive the face amount of the bond upon maturity. Equity holders do not have that same promise. Stock can greatly increase in value or become worthless.

Do you follow the stock price of individual companies? How can you get a company's stock price history? You can find the current stock price for any company that is publicly traded on the major stock exchanges at http://finance.yahoo.com. At what price is BERKSHIRE HATHAWAY (trading symbol BRKa) currently trading?

As mentioned earlier, investors can purchase both debt and equity securities with different goals in mind. Some may purchase to receive interest or dividend payments or to realize quick gains on price changes, while others may invest for more long-term reasons. Accounting standard-setters have developed different methods of accounting for investments depending on the intentions of the holder of the security. Exhibit 12-4 outlines the major classifications of debt and equity securities.

Held-to-Maturity Securities

held-to-maturity security A debt security purchased by an investor with the intent of holding the security until it matures.

If an investor purchases a debt security with the intent of holding the security until it matures, it is classified as a **held-to-maturity security** and is accounted for using techniques similar to those discussed in Chapter 10 for the bond issuer. The investor and the issuer record the same amounts but in a different way. With bond liabilities, the face value of the bonds is recorded in Bonds Payable, and a separate contra account is maintained for any discount or premium. Amortization of the discount or premium is then recorded in these contra accounts. With bond investments, the actual amount paid for the bonds (the cost of the asset), not the face value, is originally debited to the investment account. The amortization of any bond premium or discount

exhibit 12-4 Classifications of Debt and Equity Securities

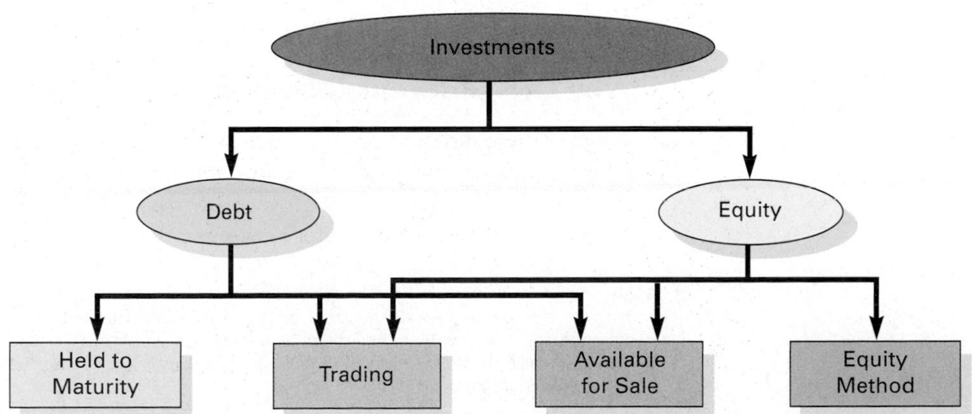

fyi

Equity securities cannot be classified as held-to-maturity securities.

is then recorded directly in the investment account. Thus, if you recall the accounting for Bonds Payable as presented in Chapter 10, you already know most of the accounting for a bond investment that is expected to be held to maturity. The procedures relating to amortizing premiums and discounts for the investors are discussed in the expanded material section of this chapter. Note that equity securities cannot be classified as held-to-maturity securities; equity securities typically do not mature.[3]

Equity Method Securities

equity method A method used to account for an investment in the stock of another company when significant influence can be imposed (presumed to exist when 20 to 50% of the outstanding voting stock is owned).

In the case of equity securities, accounting standard-setters have determined that if securities are held with the objective of significantly influencing the operations of the investee, then the securities should be accounted for using the **equity method**. The equity method records changes in the value of the investment as the net assets of the investee change. The assumption underlying the equity method is that if the investor can influence the operating decisions of the investee, then any change in the net assets of the investee should be reflected on the books of the investor. In determining what constitutes significant influence, the Accounting Principles Board suggests that, unless evidence exists to the contrary, ownership of at least 20% of the outstanding common stock of a company, but less than 50%, indicates the existence of significant influence. Because accounting for a security using the equity method can get complicated, details of the equity method are presented in the expanded material section of this chapter. If ownership exceeds 50%, then a controlling interest is assumed, and the accounting becomes far more complex. The FASB is examining the issue of control and has suggested that companies look beyond ownership percentage and examine other factors that may indicate control.[4] Two factors the FASB has highlighted are (1) ownership of a large minority voting interest (approximately 40%) with no other group owning a significant interest and (2) a company's domination of the process for electing the investee's board of directors. In cases where it is determined that control exists, the parent company (the acquiring company) and the subsidiary company (the acquired company) are required to combine their financial statements into one set of statements as if they were one economic entity. Such combined statements are called **consolidated financial statements**. The preparation of consolidated financial statements is covered in advanced accounting courses.

fyi

Debt securities cannot be classified as equity method securities.

consolidated financial statements Statements that report the combined operating results, financial position, and cash flows of two or more legally separate but affiliated companies as if they were one economic entity.

Trading and Available-for-Sale Securities

trading securities Debt and equity securities purchased with the intent of selling them should the need for cash arise or to realize short-term gains.

available-for-sale securities Debt and equity securities not classified as trading, held-to-maturity, or equity method securities.

In those instances where securities are not being held to maturity (in the case of debt) or to control or significantly influence an investee (in the case of equity), the Financial Accounting Standards Board has developed two other classes of securities—trading and available-for-sale. **Trading securities** are those debt and equity securities held with the intent of selling the securities should the need for cash arise or to realize gains arising from short-term changes in price. These types of securities are purchased simply to earn a return on excess cash. **Available-for-sale securities** are publicly traded securities that are classified as neither held-to-maturity nor trading (in the case of debt securities). In the case of equity securities, they represent securities that are not classified as trading securities or accounted for using the equity method.

Why the Different Classifications?

Why are there different classifications for debt and equity securities? Why not simply classify all securities as "investments"? The reason for the distinction lies in the different treatments of accounting for changes in market value. In the case of securities classified as held-to-maturity, changes in the securities' value between the date of purchase and the maturity date do not

3 There are exceptions to this rule, as in the case of "mandatorily redeemable preferred stock," but the accounting for these types of securities is beyond the scope of this text.

4 Exposure Draft: Consolidated Financial Statements: Purpose and Policy (Stamford: Financial Accounting Standards Board, 1999).

affect the amount to be received at maturity. That amount is fixed on the day the bonds are issued. Thus, temporary changes in the value of securities classified as held-to-maturity are not recognized on the investor's books. Similar reasoning applies to securities accounted for under the equity method. These securities are purchased, not with the intent of selling them in the future, but instead to be able to exercise influence over a corporation. Again, temporary changes in the value of these securities are not recognized on the investor's books.

Trading securities are purchased with the intent of earning a return—through interest or dividends and through short-term resale of the securities. Firms are required to recognize these two types of returns on the income statement. For example, assume that XYZ Company purchases 100 shares of ABC, Inc. stock for $5 per share. During the year, ABC pays a $1 dividend per share, and the value of the stock increases to $7 per share. XYZ will recognize, as income, $100 in dividend income as well as $200 in unrealized market gains. While the $100 in dividends was actually received, the $200 gain was not. The securities would have to have been sold in order to actually receive the $200 increase in value. Recognizing this gain, even though it was not realized through an arm's-length transaction, represents a major departure from the historical cost principle that has guided accounting for centuries. In 1994, the FASB determined that because the fair market value of many debt and equity securities can be objectively determined (via market quotes) and they can easily be sold (one phone call to a broker), it would be appropriate to include any unrealized gains or losses on changes in value of trading securities on the income statement.

fyi

Many companies avoid the issue of what to include on the income statement by classifying all their investment securities as being available-for-sale. Berkshire Hathaway and MICROSOFT are examples of companies that use this classification scheme.

Changes in the value of securities classified as available-for-sale are recorded on the balance sheet. However, no gain or loss is realized on the income statement. Instead, an adjustment is made directly to a stockholders' equity account—Unrealized Increase/Decrease in Value of Available-for-Sale Securities Equity. The obvious question is "Why aren't changes in the value of these securities reflected on the income statement?" The answer lies in the intent behind holding the securities. Trading securities will probably be sold sooner rather than later. We cannot make that same assumption with available-for-sale securities. We are less certain they will be sold. Because of this uncertainty as to when the change in value will actually be realized, the FASB elected to go around the income statement in reporting changes in value relating to available-for-sale securities. Whatever the classification used, companies disclose their classification in the notes to the financial statements. For example, BERKSHIRE HATHAWAY provides the following note disclosure relating to its investments:

> Berkshire's management determines the appropriate classifications of investments at the time of acquisition and re-evaluates the classifications at each balance sheet date. Investments may be classified as held for trading, held to maturity, or, when neither of those classifications is appropriate, as available-for-sale. Berkshire's investments in fixed maturity and equity securities are classified as available-for-sale. Available-for-sale securities are stated at fair value with unrealized gains or losses, net of taxes and minority interest, reported as a separate component in shareholders' equity. Realized gains and losses, which arise when available-for-sale investments are sold (as determined on a specific identification basis) or other than temporarily impaired, are included in the Consolidated Statements of Earnings.

As you can see, Berkshire Hathaway classifies every security as available-for-sale and is very specific as to what this classification means for the financial statements: current values go on the balance sheet, with unrealized gains and losses disclosed in stockholders' equity, while realized gains and losses are reported on the income statement.

Exhibit 12-5 summarizes the classification and disclosure issues relating to investments in debt and equity securities.

business environment essay

Following the Stock Market Stocks are sold in a variety of markets in the same way that bonds are sold. Original issues of stocks are usually sold by an investment banking group, referred to as the underwriters. After stocks are originally sold, they are traded in the marketplace, either on the New York Stock Exchange, the American Stock Exchange, regional market exchanges, or the over-the-counter market. A selected portion of stocks traded on the New York Stock Exchange on Monday, October 23, 2000, is listed here as they were reported in *The Wall Street Journal* on Tuesday, October 24, 2000. The quotations show the following information for each stock: (1) 52-week high and low; (2) the name of the company; (3) the trading symbol for that company; (4) the current dividend; (5) the yield percentage in relation to the purchase price; (6) the price-earnings (PE) ratio; (7) the volume of sales for that day; (8) the high, low, and closing prices for that day; and (9) the net change from the closing price of the previous day's trading. To illustrate how to read the quotation, the information for **BERKSHIRE HATHAWAY** class A common stock is as follows: The 52-week high was $66,900, and the low was $40,800. Berkshire does not pay a dividend. Thus, the dividend amount and dividend yield are blank. The current price is 47 times the annual earnings. A total of 90 (the z indicates that the 90 is actual number of shares sold) shares were traded on Monday, October 23, 2000, with the high price for the day being $59,200 and the low price being $58,600. The stock closed for the day at $58,600, which was $800 lower than the close on Friday, October 20, 2000.

exhibit 12-5 Classification and Disclosure of Securities

Classification of Securities	Types of Securities	Disclosed at	Reporting of Temporary Changes in Fair Value
Trading	Debt and equity	Fair value	Income statement
Available-for-sale	Debt and equity	Fair value	Stockholders' equity
Held-to-maturity	Debt	Amortized cost	Not recognized
Equity method	Equity	Cost adjusted for changes in net assets of investee	Not recognized

to summarize

Securities are classified depending upon the intent of management. If management's intent is to hold the investment until maturity (debt) or to influence the decisions of an investee (equity), then the held-to-maturity (debt) and eq-

NEW YORK STOCK EXCHANGE COMPOSITE TRANSACTIONS

Quotations as of 5 p.m. Eastern Time
Monday, October 23, 2000

	52 Weeks Hi	52 Weeks Lo		Stock	Sym	Div	Yld %	PE	Vol 100s	Hi	Lo	Close		Net Chg
▼	39^{31}	27^{06}	♣	Bemis	BMS	.96	3.9	10	10189	29^{19}	23^{75}	24^{69}	–	5^{44}
	64^{25}	12		BenchmkElec	BHE		...	92	774	47	44^{38}	45^{25}	–	1^{13}
	50^{94}	35^{38}		Benetton	BNG	3.78e	10.6	...	3	35^{81}	35^{81}	35^{81}	–	0^{13}
	4^{50}	1^{44}		BentonOG	BNO		...	dd	458	2^{25}	2^{06}	2^{13}		...
	12^{19}	4^{50}		BergnBruns	BBC	.04	.4	5	11056	9^{13}	8^{75}	9	+	0^{19}
	17^{94}	7^{75}		BergenCapTr	TOPrS	1.95	13.9	...	153	14^{25}	13^{94}	14	+	0^{13}
	66900	40800		BerkHathwy A	BRKA		...	47	z90	59200	58600	58600	–	800
	2219	1351		BerkHathwy B	BRKB		...	...	z6160	1953	1923	1928	–	28
	19^{94}	12^{13}	♣	BerryPete A	BRY	.40	2.3	12	55	17^{56}	17^{25}	17^{25}	–	0^{25}
	88^{88}	39		BestBuy	BBY		...	25	52393	44^{44}	40^{50}	43^{88}	+	3^{75}
	9^{31}	2^{25}		BethStl	BS		...	dd	7107	2^{44}	2^{25}	2^{38}	+	0^{13}
▼	51^{50}	30^{75}		BethStl pf		5.00	17.5	...	98	30^{50}	28^{13}	28^{63}	–	2^{25}
▼	26^{13}	14^{63}		BethStl pfB		2.50	18.7	...	208	14^{94}	13^{38}	13^{38}	–	1^{50}
	6^{38}	2^{50}		BeverlyEnt	BEV		...	dd	2166	4^{38}	4^{13}	4^{31}	–	0^{06}
	41^{50}	11^{75}	♣	BndlyWest	BDY	.08	.2	35	4888	41^{50}	39^{75}	41^{50}	+	1^{56}
	38^{50}	15^{81}		Biomatrx	BXM		...	27	682	18^{25}	17^{63}	17^{63}	–	0^{19}
s	43^{50}	12^{72}		Biovail g	BVF	g	...	...	4270	39^{69}	38	39^{06}	–	0^{06}
n	79	39^{25}		Biovail pf		1.76e	2.4	...	55	73^{38}	71^{06}	72^{26}	–	1^{31}
	134^{50}	23^{19}		Biovail wt			...	...	5	120	116^{44}	120	+	3^{25}

Source: *The Wall Street Journal,* October, 24, 2000.

uity method (equity) classifications are appropriate. If the securities are being held for other reasons, then management may classify them as either trading or available-for-sale. The importance of the classification becomes apparent when accounting for changes in value.

3

Account for the purchase, recognition of revenue, and sale of trading and available-for-sale securities.

ACCOUNTING FOR TRADING AND AVAILABLE-FOR-SALE SECURITIES

Four issues are associated with accounting for securities: (1) accounting for the purchase, (2) accounting for the revenue earned, (3) accounting for the sale, and (4) accounting for the changes in value. The first three issues are fairly straightforward and are presented in this section. Accounting for changes in the value of securities is discussed in the following section. The time line in Exhibit 12-6 illustrates the important business issues associated with buying and selling investment securities.

Accounting for the Purchase of Securities

Investments in securities, like all other assets, are recorded at cost when purchased. This is the case whether the security being purchased is debt or equity or whether it is being held with the intent to sell it quickly or hold it for the long term. Cost includes the market price of the security plus any extra expenditures required in making the purchase (such as a stockbroker's fee).

exhibit 12-6 Time Line of Business Issues Associated with Buying and Selling Investment Securities

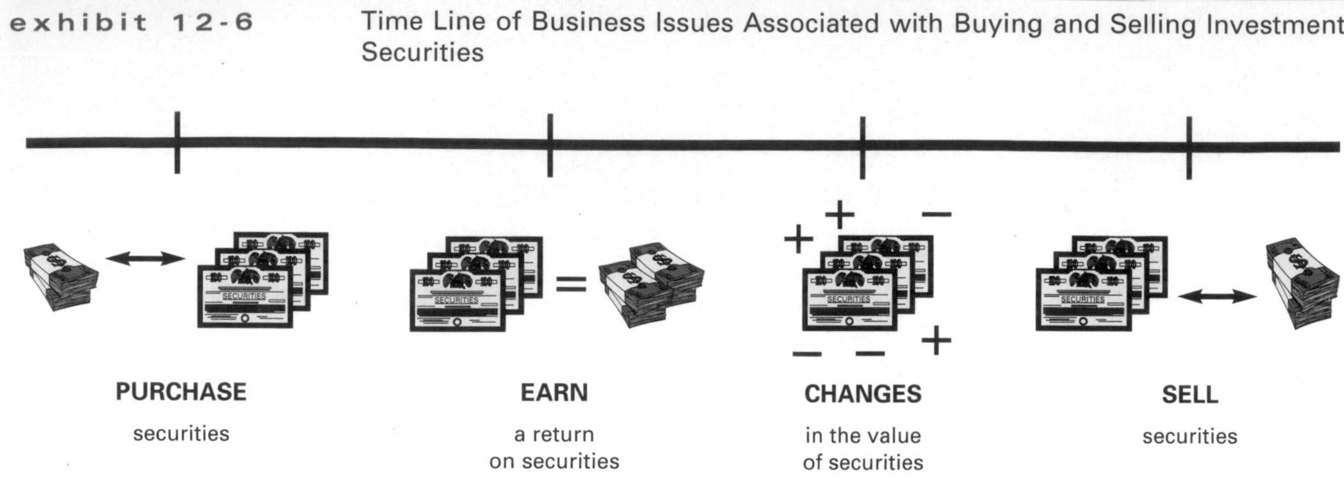

To illustrate the accounting for securities, we will use the following information throughout the chapter. On July 1, 2002, Far Side, Inc. purchased the following securities:

Security	Type	Classification	Cost (including Broker's Fees)
1	Debt	Trading	$ 5,000
2	Equity	Trading	27,500
3	Debt	Available-for-sale	17,000
4	Equity	Available-for-sale	9,200

The initial entry to record the investments is as follows:

Investment in Trading Securities	32,500	
Investment in Available-for-Sale Securities	26,200	
Cash		58,700

Though investments in securities are all recorded at cost, each of the four classifications of securities is accounted for differently subsequent to purchase. As a result, separate accounts are used to record the initial purchase. Management purchased Securities 1 and 2 with the intent of earning a return on the investment and selling the securities should the need for cash arise. Therefore, those securities are classified as "trading." Securities 3 and 4 were also purchased to earn a return on excess cash, but management has classified them as "available-for-sale." While the journal entry illustrated above combines all securities of the same classification into one account, subsidiary records will be kept for each individual security purchased.

fyi

BERKSHIRE HATHAWAY purchased with cash over $22 billion of securities in 1999.

Accounting for the Return Earned on an Investment

When a firm invests in the debt or equity of another firm with the intent of earning a return on its investment, how that return is accounted for varies depending on the classification of the investment. Recall from Chapter 10 that when debt securities are sold, a premium or discount can arise as a result of differences between the stated rate of interest and the market rate of interest. The resulting premium or discount must then be amortized over the life of the investment, thereby affecting the amount of interest expense recorded by the issuer. Theoretically, the purchaser of that debt security must also account for the difference between the purchase price and the eventual maturity value. In the discussion that follows, however, we are assuming that the time for which the investor anticipates holding debt securities classified as "trading" or as "available-for-sale" is not long enough for any amortization of premium or discount to materially affect interest expense. Amortization of premiums and discounts on debt securities is illustrated for "held-to-maturity" securities in the expanded material section of this chapter.

With this caveat in mind, the accounting for dividends and interest received on trading and available-for-sale securities becomes relatively straightforward. Cash received relating to interest and dividends is credited to Interest Revenue and Dividend Revenue, respectively. Interest earned but not yet received or dividends that have been declared but not paid are also recorded as revenue with a corresponding receivable. Continuing our example, interest and dividends received during 2002 relating to Far Side's securities investments were as follows:

fyi

BERKSHIRE HATHAWAY reported interest, dividends, and other investment income earned of $1.4 billion during 1999.

Security	Interest	Dividends
1	$225	
2		$825
3	850	
4		644

The appropriate journal entry to record the receipt of interest and dividends is:

Cash	2,544	
Interest Revenue		1,075
Dividend Revenue		1,469

Accounting for the Sale of Securities

Suppose that Far Side sells all of its investment in Security 2 for $28,450 on October 31, 2002. As Security 2 was purchased for $27,500, the security has increased in value and that increase must be recorded. The journal entry to record the sale is:

Cash	28,450	
Investment in Trading Securities		27,500
Realized Gain on Sale of Trading Securities		950

If Security 2 had been sold for less then $27,500, a loss would have been recorded. If a broker's fee had been charged on the transaction, the fee would reduce the amount of cash received and decrease the gain recognized. If the broker's fee exceeded $950, a loss would be recorded on the books of the seller.

At the end of the accounting period, any gain or loss on the sale of securities must be included on the income statement. In the above example, the "Realized Gain on Sale of Trading Securities" would be included with Other Revenues and Expenses on the income statement. Note the term *realized.* **Realized gains and losses** indicate that an arm's-length transaction has occurred and that the securities have actually been sold. This distinction is important because in the next section we focus on accounting for unrealized gains and losses—those gains and losses that occur while a security is still being held and no arm's-length transaction has taken place.

realized gains and losses Gains and losses resulting from the sale of securities in an arm's-length transaction.

On its statement of cash flows, BERKSHIRE HATHAWAY reported proceeds of $8,864 million from the sale of debt securities and equity securities. On its income statement, the company reported net realized gains of $1,365 million from the sale of securities. With this information, we can compute the historical cost of the securities sold during the period. Proceeds of $8,864 million less a gain of $1,365 million indicate that the cost of the securities was $7,499 million. A summary journal entry indicating the effects of these transactions for Berkshire Hathaway is as follows:

Cash	8,864	
Available-for-Sale Securities		7,499
Realized Gain on Sale of Securities		1,365

business environment essay

Following the Bond Market Bonds are sold in a variety of markets. Original issues of bonds, both industrial and governmental, are usually sold by an investment banking group, referred to as the underwriters. Bonds are then traded in the marketplace, either on the New York Bond Exchange or over-the-counter through brokers who make a market for a particular company's bonds. Following is an excerpt from *The Wall Street Journal* showing some composite information regarding bond transactions, as well as price quotations for specific bond issues. The composite information gives investors a sense of the overall activity level of the bond market in relation to previous years. In this case, it shows that sales through October 24, 2000, were lower than in either 1999 or 1998 for comparable time periods. Using a representative sample of bonds trading in the marketplace, it also gives the high and low prices for 2000 and 1999.

The listings for specific bonds give the stated interest rate, the year of maturity, the current yield (effective rate), the sales volume for that trading date (with 000s omitted), the closing price for the day, and the net change from the closing price on the previous day that the bond market was open. Looking at the IBM bond issue listed, we can deduce the following: the bonds have a stated interest rate of 7¼% and mature in 2002. The current yield (effective interest) on the bonds is 7.2%. Trading volume for the day was $35,000 face value, and the market price of the bonds at the end of the day was 100¾% (100.75%) of face value, a decrease of ¼ point from the previous day's closing price. Thus, each $1,000 bond was selling for $1,007.50.

Source: *The Wall Street Journal,* October 25, 2000.

U.S. EXCHANGE BONDS

Tuesday, October 24, 2000
Quotations as of 4 p.m. Eastern Time

SALES SINCE JAN. 1

New York	
2000	$1,912,572,000
1999	$2,659,930,000
1998	$3,139,412,000
AMEX	
2000	$86,633,000
1999	$144,567,000
1998	$220,938,000

Dow Jones Bond Averages

— 1999 —		— 2000 —			— — — 2000 — — —			— — 1999 — —	
High	Low	High	Low		Close	Chg.	%Yld	Close	Chg.
106.88	96.80	97.01	93.23	20 Bonds	95.71	−0.32	8.23	98.55	+0.08
104.72	94.96	95.09	90.69	10 Utilities	94.18	−0.03	7.93	95.86	+0.18
109.44	98.31	99.86	95.53	10 Industrials	97.25	−0.61	8.54	101.23	−0.03

Bonds	Cur Yld.	Vol.	Close		Net Chg.
ChaseM 6¾08	7.1	3	95	−	⅛
ChespkE 9⅝05	9.6	10	99¾	+	1¾
ChespkE 9⅛06	9.5	25	96⅛	−	½
ChespkE 8½12	9.8	40	87		...
ChiqBr 10s09	20.8	10	48	+	1⅛
CitigpCap 7¾36	8.7	10	89	+	1
vjClardg 11¾02f	...	10	69⅞	+	1⅜
ClrkOil 9½04	10.5	28	90⅛	−	1⅝
Coeur 6⅜04	cv	56	29⅛	−	3⅞
Consec 8⅛03	10.3	20	78⅞	−	1⅞
Conseco 10¼02	14.6	22	70⅛		...
ConNG 6s10	6.8	25	88⅞	+	1⅜
DelcoR 8⅝07	9.9	20	87	−	⅞
DevonE 4.9s08	cv	9	91¼	−	1¾
Dole 7s03	7.5	20	93¼	−	¾
Dole 7⅞13	9.0	43	88	+	⅛
DukeEn 5⅞01	5.9	30	99		...
DukeEn 6⅞23	7.7	1	89¼	+	¾
DukeEn 7½25	7.9	35	95½	−	⅛
DukeEn 7s33	7.8	50	90	−	¼
Finova 9⅛02	12.2	105	75	−	5
Florsh 12¾02	36.6	20	34⅞	+	1⅞

Bonds	Cur Yld.	Vol.	Close		Net Chg.
FordCr 6⅜08	7.0	10	90¾	−	1¾
GMA 6¾02	6.8	18	99½	+	⅝
GMA 5⅞03	6.0	9	97¾		...
GMA dc6s11	6.9	14	87½	+	¾
GMA zr12	...	1	390½	+	¼
GMA zr15	...	1	315⅛	−	⅞
vjGenesH 9¾05f	...	200	11¼	+	2⅛
HewlPkd zr17	...	6	71⅛	−	2⅞
Honywll zr01	...	5	93 17/32	−	1 7/32
Honywll zr07	...	65	62	+	¾
Honywll zr09	...	10	53	...	...
IBM 7¼02	7.2	35	100¾	−	¼
IBM 6.45s07	6.6	30	98¼	+	1⅜
IPap dc5⅛12	6.9	26	74¾	+	¾
KaufB 9⅜03	9.7	66	96¾	−	⅝
KaufB 7¾04	8.2	25	94	+	2
KaufB 9⅝06	9.8	117	98⅜	+	⅜
KentE 4½04	cv	40	85		...
KerrM 7½14	cv	14	97	−	⅛
Leucadia 8¼05	8.4	12	98	+	½
Leucadia 7⅞06	8.5	20	92¾		...
Leucadia 7¾13	8.8	11	88½	−	3

to summarize

Investments in debt and equity securities are recorded at cost, which includes the fair value of the securities plus any other expenditures required to purchase the securities. When purchased, the securities are classified into one of four categories: held-to-maturity, equity method, trading, or available-for-sale securities. Revenues from securities take the form of interest, dividends, or gains or losses from selling the securities and are included under Other Revenues and Expenses on the income statement.

4
Account for changes in the value of securities.

ACCOUNTING FOR CHANGES IN THE VALUE OF SECURITIES

Investments in debt and equity securities are initially recorded at cost. If the value of a security changes after it is purchased, should that change in value be recorded on the investor's books? As stated previously in the chapter, the answer is "it depends." It depends on management's intent regarding that security. In the case of trading and available-for-sale securities, changes in market value are recorded on the books of the investor. For held-to-maturity securities and equity method securities, changes in value are not recorded unless they are considered permanent. To illustrate the accounting for changes in value of securities, we will continue the Far Side example. On December 31, 2002, the following market values were available:[5]

Security	Classification	Historical Cost	Market Value (December 31, 2002)
1	Trading	$ 5,000	$ 5,200
3	Available-for-sale	17,000	16,700
4	Available-for-sale	9,200	9,250

Changes in the Value of Trading Securities

At the end of 2002, Far Side computes the market value of its trading securities portfolio and compares it to the historical cost of the portfolio. In this instance, market value is $200 greater than historical cost. The journal entry to record this increase in value is:

Market Adjustment—Trading Securities	200	
Unrealized Gain on Trading Securities—Income		200

unrealized gains and losses Gains and losses resulting from changes in the value of securities that are still being held.

Market Adjustment—Trading Securities An account used to track the difference between the historical cost and the market value of a company's portfolio of trading securities.

This journal entry recognizes the $200 increase in the value of the trading securities and records the unrealized gain on the income statement. **Unrealized gains and losses** indicate that the securities have changed in value and are still being held. This journal entry also introduces a new account—**Market Adjustment—Trading Securities.** This account is combined with the trading securities account and reported on the balance sheet. Thus, the balance sheet will reflect the trading securities at their fair market value. Why not adjust the trading securities account directly instead of creating this market adjustment account? The reason is that the use of a valuation account, Market Adjustment—Trading Securities, allows a record of historical cost to be

5 Remember that Security 2 was sold on October 31, 2002.

maintained. With this approach, a company can easily determine realized and unrealized gains. Perhaps the most important reason for keeping a record of historical cost is that, for tax purposes, only realized gains and losses are relevant. Other decisions made within a firm also rely on this historical cost information.

STOP & THINK In Chapter 7, we were not to write inventory up if its value increased, though we were to write it down if its value declined. In Chapter 9, we were not to write property, plant, and equipment up if its value increased, though we were to write it down if its value declined. Why can we write up the value of securities if their price increases above the original cost?

Changes in the Value of Available-for-Sale Securities

A market adjustment account is also employed when adjusting available-for-sale securities to their fair market value. However, the change in value is not recorded on the income statement but is instead recorded in the account "Unrealized Increase/Decrease in Value of Available-for-Sale Securities—Equity." The "equity" used in the account title refers to the fact that this account is disclosed in the stockholders' equity section of the balance sheet, and its balance is carried forward from year to year. To illustrate, the available-for-sale portfolio of Far Side has a fair market value of $25,950 at year-end and a historical cost of $26,200. The appropriate adjustment is:

Unrealized Increase/Decrease in Value of Available-for-Sale Securities—Equity	250	
Market Adjustment—Available-for-Sale Securities		250

This journal entry adjusts the portfolio of available-for-sale securities to its fair market value at year-end and records the difference in the equity account.

Subsequent Changes in Value

Assume that no securities were bought or sold by Far Side, Inc., during 2003. At the end of 2003, its portfolio of securities had the following fair market values:

Security	Classification	Historical Cost	Market Value (December 31, 2003)
1	Trading	$ 5,000	$ 4,850
3	Available-for-sale	17,000	16,900
4	Available-for-sale	9,200	9,150

The value of the trading securities has declined to $4,850. Since the market adjustment account relating to trading securities should reflect the difference between historical cost and market, an entry is made to adjust the balance in Market Adjustment—Trading Securities from its previous $200 debit balance to the required $150 credit balance ($5,000 − $4,850). Where did this $200 debit balance come from? It came from the adjusting entry made on December 31, 2002. Remember that the market adjustment account is a real (balance sheet) account and is not closed at the end of an accounting period. Its balance carries forward from year to year. The required adjusting entry is:

Unrealized Loss on Trading Securities—Income	350	
Market Adjustment—Trading Securities		350

When this entry is posted, the Market Adjustment—Trading Securities T-account will appear as follows:

**Market Adjustment—
Trading Securities**

12/31/02	200		
		Adjustment	350
		12/31/03	150

caution

The amount of the adjustment for the current period depends on the balance in the market adjustment account. Don't forget to factor that balance into your calculations.

The $150 credit balance will be netted against the $5,000 balance in the trading securities account and disclosed on the balance sheet as "Investment in Trading Securities (net)" for $4,850. The $350 unrealized loss will be included in the current period's net income and reported on the income statement. This adjustment procedure ensures that changes in the value of the trading securities portfolio are reflected in the period in which those changes in value occurred.

A similar procedure is employed in valuing the available-for-sale securities portfolio, except that the stockholders' equity account is used instead of the income statement account. For Far Side, the market value of the available-for-sale securities portfolio is $26,050. In comparing this to the historical cost of $26,200, a $150 credit balance in the market adjustment account is required. Take a moment and read the information again. An adjustment *to* get to a $150 credit balance is required—not an adjustment *of* $150. Given the previous credit balance in Market Adjustment—Available-for-Sale Securities of $250, the following adjusting entry is required:

Market Adjustment—Available-for-Sale Securities.	100	
Unrealized Increase/Decrease in Value of Available-for-Sale Securities—Equity		100

Once this entry is posted, Market Adjustment—Available-for-Sale Securities will have the required $150 credit balance as follows:

**Market Adjustment—
Available-for-Sale Securities**

		12/31/02	250
Adjustment	100		
		12/31/03	150

When individual securities from a portfolio are sold, a realized gain or loss is recognized for the difference between the original cost of the securities and the selling price, without regard to previous adjustments made to a market adjustment account. At the end of the period, the cost of the remaining securities is compared to the fair market value of the remaining securities, and the market adjustment account is updated to account for the difference.

As mentioned earlier, BERKSHIRE HATHAWAY classifies all of its securities as available-for-sale. To determine how well Warren Buffett has managed the portfolio during the year, the financial statement reader must review both the income statement and the statement of stockholders' equity. Comparing the performance of the company's portfolio of securities for the years 1997 through 1999 results in the following (in millions):

	1997	1998	1999
Realized investment gains (from the income statement)	$ 1,106	$2,415	$1,365
Unrealized appreciation of investments (from the statement of shareholders' equity)	10,574	3,011	(795)
Total portfolio performance	$11,680	$5,426	$ 570

This declining performance, particularly in 1999, prompted Mr. Buffett to state the following in his 1999 letter to shareholders:

> The numbers ... show just how poor our 1999 record was. We had the worst absolute performance of my tenure and, compared to the S&P, the worst relative performance as well. Relative results are what concern us: Over time, bad relative numbers will produce unsatisfactory absolute results. Even Inspector Clouseau could find last year's guilty party: your Chairman.

to summarize

When the value of a trading or available-for-sale security changes, that change is reflected on the balance sheet using a market adjustment account. For trading securities, the unrealized gain or loss is reflected on the income statement for the period. For available-for-sale securities, the unrealized increase or decrease is recorded in a stockholders' equity account.

expanded material

In this section of the chapter, we turn our attention to some of the complexities associated with purchasing debt and equity securities. First, we examine held-to-maturity securities and how any associated premium or discount associated with these securities is amortized. We also address the issue of purchasing a debt security between interest payment dates. The accounting issues associated with an equity security accounted for under the equity method are also presented.

5

Account for held-to-maturity securities.

ACCOUNTING FOR HELD-TO-MATURITY SECURITIES

Held-to-maturity securities are debt securities issued by companies to raise needed funding for expansion, acquisitions, or other business reasons. Bonds (discussed in Chapter 10 from the point of view of the issuer) are by far the most common type of debt instrument that can be readily bought and sold. Because bonds represent the most common type of publicly traded debt instrument, the following discussion will focus on bonds purchased as investments to be held to maturity.

Accounting for the Initial Purchase

Bonds can be purchased at amounts either above face value (at a premium), below face value (at a discount), or at face value. Regardless of the purchase price, like all other assets, bonds are initially recorded at cost. The cost is the total amount paid to acquire the bonds; this includes the actual price paid for the bonds and any other purchasing expenditures, such as commissions or broker's fees.

To illustrate, assume that Far Side, Inc., purchased a fifth security and classified it as held-to-maturity. Security 5 consists of twenty $1,000 bonds of Chicago Company. The bonds were issued on July 1, 2002, and will mature five years from the date of issuance. The bonds will pay interest at a stated annual rate of 12%, with payments to be made semiannually on June 30 and December 31. In determining the value of the bonds, the present value of these future cash flows must be determined at the market rate on the date of the purchase. Assuming the market rate on bonds of similar risk is 16%, the purchase price of the bonds is obtained by adding the present value of $20,000 (received 10 periods in the future and discounted at 8%) to the present value of the annuity of the 10 interest payments of $1,200 each (discounted at 8%). The reason 8% is used is that interest is received semiannually; recall that in calculating present value, you must halve the interest rate (16%/2) for semiannual compounding periods. Likewise, you must double the number of years to determine the number of periods (5 years × 2 periods per year = 10 periods). The calculations are:

1.	Semiannual interest payment	$ 1,200	
	Present value of an annuity of 10 payments of $1 at 8% (Table II, page 484)	× 6.7101	
	Present value of interest payments		$ 8,052
2.	Principal (face value) of bonds	$20,000	
	Present value of $1 received 10 periods in the future discounted at 8% (Table I, page 483)	× 0.4632	
	Present value of principal		9,264
3.	Total present value of investment		$17,316

In this example, 16% is the effective rate of interest because that is the amount of interest actually earned; 12% is the stated, or nominal, rate of interest on Chicago Company's bonds. Note that the 12% stated rate determines the size of the annuity payments ($20,000 × 0.12 × ½ year) but not the purchase price of the bonds; the purchase price varies according to market conditions. The 16% effective rate depends on three amounts: the purchase price, the interest payments, and the face value of the bonds. The $17,316 bond price is the amount that earns Far Side exactly 16%. The journal entry to record the acquisition is:

Investment in Held-to-Maturity Securities	17,316	
Cash		17,316

Note that the investment account is debited for the cost of the bonds with no separate amount shown for the discount of $2,684 ($20,000 − $17,316). Although the discount could be recorded in a separate contra-asset account, in practice it is more common for investors to record the asset cost in the investment account as shown.

Accounting for Bonds Purchased between Interest Dates

The preceding entry assumes that the investing company purchased the bonds on the issuance date, which was also the beginning date for the first interest period. In many cases, however, the date bonds are actually issued does not coincide with an interest date. Further, investors often acquire bonds in the "secondary market"; that is, they purchase bonds from other investors rather than from the issuing company. The secondary market for bonds includes the New York Bond Exchange and the over-the-counter bond market as described in the Business Environment Essay on page 580. Since bonds are traded actively in this market each weekday, investors often acquire bonds between interest dates.

An investor who buys bonds between interest dates, either from the issuing company or in the secondary market, has to pay for the interest that has accrued since the last interest payment date. As explained in Chapter 10, this is necessary because whoever owns the bonds at the time interest is paid receives interest for one full interest period, usually six months, regardless of how long the bonds have been held.

To illustrate, we will assume that Far Side purchased the Chicago Company bonds in the secondary market for $17,316 on November 1, 2002. Semiannual interest of $1,200 ($20,000 × 0.12 × ½) is paid on the bonds on June 30 and December 31 of each year. On December 31, 2002, Far Side will receive $1,200 even though the bonds were purchased only two months

exhibit 12-7 Investing between Interest Dates

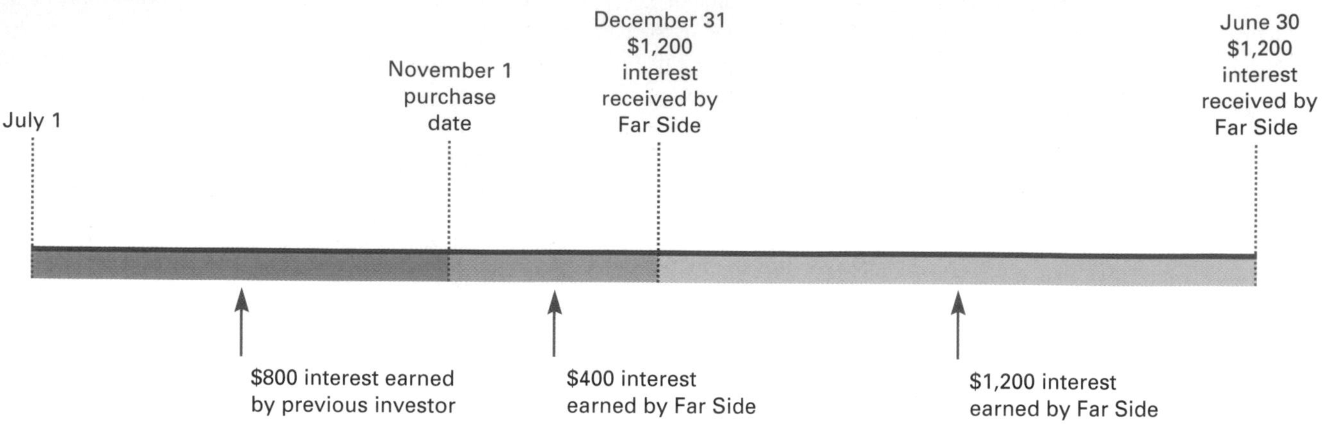

earlier. Since the previous owner is entitled to 4 months' interest on November 1, Far Side will have to pay that individual or company the interest for the period July 1 to October 31. This is illustrated in Exhibit 12-7.

The entry to record the investment in bonds on November 1 (between interest dates) is:

Investment in Held-to-Maturity Securities	17,316	
Bond Interest Receivable	800	
Cash		18,116
Purchased $20,000 of Chicago Company bonds for $17,316 and paid four months' accrued interest.		

When Far Side receives $1,200 in interest on December 31, it will make the following entry:

Cash	1,200	
Interest Receivable		800
Interest Revenue		400
Received interest on Chicago Company bonds.		

Accounting for the Amortization of Bond Discounts and Premiums

Only in those rare instances when the stated interest rate of a bond is exactly equivalent to the prevailing market (or yield) rate for similar investments is a bond purchased at face value. At all other times, bonds are purchased either at a discount (below face value) or at a premium (above face value). Because the face amount of a bond is received at maturity, discounts and premiums must be written off (amortized) over the period that a bond is held.

As you learned in Chapter 10, there are two common methods of amortizing bond discounts and premiums: the straight-line method and the effective-interest method. Because straight-line amortization is simpler, it will be used first to illustrate the amortization process; then the effective-interest method will be described.

straight-line amortization A method of systematically writing off a bond discount or premium in equal amounts each period until maturity.

STRAIGHT-LINE AMORTIZATION To illustrate the **straight-line amortization** of a bond discount, we will assume again that Far Side purchased the Chicago Company $20,000, 12%, five-year bonds for $17,316 on the issuance date, July 1, 2002. The entry to record this investment was given on page 585. Far Side will record amortization of $268.40 ($2,684/5 years × ½) on each interest date. Thus, every six months, beginning on December 31, 2002, Far Side will make the following entry:

Cash	1,200.00	
Investment in Held-to-Maturity Securities	268.40	
Bond Interest Revenue		1,468.40
Received semiannual bond interest and amortized bond discount.		

At the end of five years, the investment in the held-to-maturity securities account will have a balance of $20,000.

The discount amortization is revenue earned on the bonds; when the bonds mature, Far Side will receive $20,000 (the face value) in return for an original investment of $17,316. It is this additional revenue of $2,684 that increases the return the investor actually earns from the 12% stated interest rate to the effective interest rate of 16%. The following analysis shows how this works:

Maturity value to be received	$20,000
Interest to be received ($1,200 × 10 payments)	12,000
Total amount to be received	$32,000
Investment	17,316
Total interest revenue to be earned	$14,684

Interest earned per year:

Stated amount of interest ($20,000 × 0.12)	$2,400.00	12%
Additional interest from discount ($2,684/5 years)	536.80	4%*
Total	$2,936.80	16%

*This is an approximation; with the straight-line method, the actual interest earned each year changes.

When accounting for the amortization of a bond discount, a company must be careful to amortize the discount only over the period the bonds are actually held. For example, if Far Side had purchased the Chicago Company bonds four months after the issuance date, the discount would have been amortized over a period of 56 months (4 full years plus 8 months of the first year). The amortization for the first year would then have been approximately $383.43 ($2,684 × 8/56), and the amortization for each of the succeeding four years would be approximately $575.14 ($2,684 × 12/56).

Accounting for the amortization of a premium on investments is essentially the opposite of accounting for a discount. Amortization of a premium decreases revenue earned, and the effect of the amortization entry is to reduce Investment in Held-to-Maturity Securities to the face value of the bonds by the maturity date.

To illustrate the amortization of a bond premium by the investor, assume that Far Side acquired the $20,000, 12%, five-year Chicago Company bonds for $21,540 on July 1, 2002, the date of issuance. The entry to record the purchase is:

Investment in Held-to-Maturity Securities	21,540	
Cash		21,540
Purchased $20,000 of Chicago Company bonds for $21,540.		

At each interest payment date, beginning December 31, 2002, Far Side will make the following entry:

Cash	1,200	
Investment in Held-to-Maturity Securities		154
Bond Interest Revenue		1,046
Received semiannual bond interest and amortized bond premium ($1,540/5 years × ½).		

The effect of the amortization entries is to reduce the return earned on the bonds from the stated annual interest rate of 12% to the rate actually earned on the investment (approximately 10%).

effective-interest amortization A method of systematically writing off a bond premium or discount that takes into consideration the time value of money and results in an equal rate of amortization for each period.

EFFECTIVE-INTEREST AMORTIZATION To illustrate the computations involved in using the **effective-interest amortization** method, we will again consider Far Side's purchase of the 12%, five-year, $20,000 bonds of Chicago Company for $17,316 on the issuance date. The amount of discount amortized in each of the five years using the effective-interest method is computed as shown in Exhibit 12-8.

In the computation, column (2) represents the cash received at the end of each interest period; column (3) shows the amount of effective interest earned, which is the amount that will be reported on the income statement each period; column (4) is the difference between columns (3) and (2) and so represents the amortization; and column (5) shows the investment balance that will be reported on the balance sheet at the end of each period. Note that the interest rate used to compute the actual interest earned is the effective rate of 8% (16%/2) and not the stated rate of 12%. Also note that the total discount is the same as it was when the straight-line method was used, $2,684.

fyi

Note the similarities between this table and the amortization tables prepared in Chapter 10. The computations are identical—the only difference is that in Chapter 10, we were paying cash, whereas in Chapter 12, we are receiving cash.

When bonds are purchased at a discount, the amount of amortization increases each successive period. This is so because the investment balance of the bonds increases, and a constant interest rate times an increasing balance results in an increasing amount of interest income. If bonds are purchased at a premium, the effective-interest amortization method will involve a constant interest rate being multiplied by a declining investment balance each period. The result will be a decline in actual interest earned each period.

Since the effective-interest amortization method takes into account the time value of money, and thus shows the true revenue earned each period (whereas the straight-line method represents only approximations), companies normally should use the effective-interest amortization method. As an exception to this rule, companies are allowed to use the straight-line method when the two methods produce amortization amounts that are not significantly different. Because that is often the case, both methods continue to be used.

exhibit 12-8 Amortization Table for Chicago Company Bonds

(1) Time Period	(2) Cash Received	(3) Interest Actually Earned (0.16 x ½ × Investment Balance)	(4) Amount of Amortization (3) − (2)	(5) Investment Balance
Acquisition date				$17,316
Year 1, first six months	$1,200	(0.08 × $17,316) = $1,385	$ 185	17,501
Year 1, second six months	1,200	(0.08 × $17,501) = 1,400	200	17,701
Year 2, first six months	1,200	(0.08 × $17,701) = 1,416	216	17,917
Year 2, second six months	1,200	(0.08 × $17,917) = 1,433	233	18,150
Year 3, first six months	1,200	(0.08 × $18,150) = 1,452	252	18,402
Year 3, second six months	1,200	(0.08 × $18,402) = 1,472	272	18,674
Year 4, first six months	1,200	(0.08 × $18,674) = 1,494	294	18,968
Year 4, second six months	1,200	(0.08 × $18,968) = 1,517	317	19,285
Year 5, first six months	1,200	(0.08 × $19,285) = 1,543	343	19,628
Year 5, second six months	1,200	(0.08 × $19,628) = 1,572*	372	20,000
			$2,684	

*Difference due to rounding.

Accounting for the Sale or Maturity of Bond Investments

If bonds are held until their maturity date, the accounting for the proceeds at maturity includes a debit to Cash and a credit to the investment account for the principal amount. For example, if Far Side, Inc., holds the $20,000, 12% bonds from Chicago Company to maturity, the entry to record the receipt of the bond principal on the maturity date will be:

Cash	20,000	
Investment in Held-to-Maturity Securities.		20,000
Received the principal of Chicago Company bonds at maturity.		

This entry assumes, of course, that all previous receipts of interest and bond amortizations have been properly recorded.

Because held-to-maturity securities are usually traded on major exchanges, thus providing a continuous and ready market, they can be sold to other investors prior to their maturity. When these securities are sold prior to their maturity, the difference between the sales price and the investment balance is recognized as a gain or loss on the sale of the investment.

To illustrate, we will assume that Sawyer Company purchased ten $1,000, 8%, five-year bonds of REX Company. We will also assume that the bonds were originally purchased on January 1, 2002, at 101% of their face value; on January 1, 2003, Sawyer showed a balance of $10,040 for these bonds. If the bonds are sold on that day for $10,300, the entry to record the sale and recognize the gain is (assuming no sales commission):

Cash	10,300	
Gain on Sale of Bonds.		260
Investment in Held-to-Maturity Securities.		10,040
Sold the REX bonds for $10,300.		

If held-to-maturity securities are sold prior to their maturity date, it is important that the amortization of the bond premium or discount be recorded up to the date of sale. If the amortization of the discount or premium is not updated, the gain or loss recognized on the sale will be incorrect.

---

to summarize

Accounting for investments in held-to-maturity securities involves four steps: (1) accounting for the purchase of the securities, (2) accounting for interest received on the securities, (3) accounting for amortization of the premium or discount, and (4) accounting for the sale or maturity of the securities. Amortization of premiums and discounts is usually accounted for by the simple straight-line amortization method or the theoretically more correct effective-interest method. The amortization adjusts the interest earned on the bonds from the stated to the effective rate. Investments in held-to-maturity securities are generally reported at cost (adjusted for premium or discount amortization), regardless of whether the current market value is less than or greater than their historical cost. When held-to-maturity securities are sold before maturity, the premium or discount must be amortized to the date of sale; a gain or loss would be reflected in the income statement for the difference between the selling price and the carrying value on the date of sale. Debt securities held until maturity result in no gain or loss on retirement because the carrying value after amortization of a premium or discount should be equal to the face value of the securities.

ACCOUNTING FOR EQUITY INVESTMENTS USING THE EQUITY METHOD

6 Account for securities using the equity method.

When enough of the outstanding common stock of a company is purchased by another company, the acquiring company may have the ability to significantly influence the operating decisions of the investee. If the ability to influence is present, then accounting standards require the use of the equity method in accounting for the investment. As stated previously, significant influence is presumed if a company owns between 20 and 50% of a company. Keep in mind that the percentage ownership criterion serves only as a guideline. The ability to influence is the key criterion. For example, assume that a company owns 35% of a firm that is headquartered in a foreign country whose government is undergoing a period of volatility. Some of the radical leaders in that country are calling for more internal investment and less outside interference from U.S. corporations. These leaders, if able to gain positions of power, have threatened to expropriate (take over all operations owned by U.S. companies). Even though the U.S. company meets the percentage ownership criterion, it may not be able to significantly influence the operations of the foreign subsidiary. Consider another example of a firm whose ownership is widespread, with no single shareholder owning more than 2% of the corporation. If one stockholder were able to acquire 15% of the outstanding common stock, that investor might be able to influence the decisions of the investee simply because of the size of the ownership percentage relative to that of all other stockholders. The important point is that the ability to influence is the key criterion for using the equity method of accounting.

Under the equity method, dividend payments represent a return of investment; they do not represent revenue, as they do when accounting for trading or available-for-sale securities. Revenue is recognized when the investee company has earnings. When earnings are announced, the carrying (book) value of the investment is increased because the investor owns a fixed percentage of a company that is worth more now than it was when the investment was originally made.

fyi

Although temporary changes in the value of equity method securities are not accounted for, permanent changes are recognized. This treatment is consistent with the concept of asset impairment discussed in Chapter 9.

In accounting for investments with the equity method, the original investment is first recorded on the books at cost and is subsequently modified to reflect the investor's share of the investee's reported income, losses, and dividends. In this way, book value is increased to recognize the investor's share of earnings and decreased by the dividends received or to recognize the investor's share of losses. Temporary changes in value of investments accounted for using the equity method are not recorded.

There are two reasons why the procedures employed under the equity method are preferred over those used when accounting for trading or available-for-sale securities. First, the equity method assumes that significant influence can be exerted. Thus, the accounting procedures prevent the investing company from manipulating earnings by dictating the dividend policy of the investee. For a trading or available-for-sale security, where dividend payments are reported as revenue, an influential investor could increase its income by putting pressure on the investee to pay larger and more frequent dividends. With the equity method, dividends do not affect earnings. Second, the equity method provides more timely recognition of the investee's earnings and losses than do the procedures employed for trading or available-for-sale securities.

caution

A common mistake in accounting for equity method securities is to debit or credit the investment account for the entire amount of the investee's income or dividends. Remember, the investor accounts only for its share of the investee's income and dividends.

Illustrating the Equity Method

To illustrate the accounting for the equity method, we will use the following information: Kimball, Inc. purchases 20% (2,000 shares) of Holland Enterprises outstanding common stock (10,000 shares), paying $100 per share. Later in the year, Kimball receives a dividend of $2.50 per share; at year-end Kimball receives Holland's income statement showing that the company earned $50,000 for the year. To ensure that you understand how the equity method differs from the accounting demonstrated earlier in the chapter, we will proceed with two scenarios: (1) Kimball is not able to exercise significant influence on Holland and, as a result, classifies the security as available-for-sale, and (2) Kimball is able to exercise significant influence and uses the equity method. The accounting for this purchase of stock and subsequent events is shown in Exhibit 12-9. Column 1 shows the journal entries as-

exhibit 12-9 Accounting for Equity Securities

	(1) Available-for-Sale Security			(2) Equity Method Security		
Accounting for the initial purchase of the stock	Investment in Available-for-Sale Securities	200,000		Investment in Equity Method Securities	200,000	
	Cash		200,000	Cash		200,000
Payment of a $2.50 per share dividend by Holland Company	Cash	5,000		Cash	5,000	
	Dividend Revenue		5,000	Investment in Equity Method Securities		5,000
Announcement by Holland of net income for the year of $50,000	No entry			Investment in Equity Method Securities	10,000	
				Revenue from Investments. .		10,000
Holland stock is selling at $102 per share at year-end	Market Adjustment—Available-for-Sale Securities	4,000		No entry		
	Unrealized Increase in Available-for-Sale Securities—Equity		4,000			

suming that the Holland stock is considered an available-for-sale security. Column 2 illustrates the equity method. It is assumed that the Holland stock is selling for $102 per share at year-end.

> **fyi**
>
> COCA-COLA, a company in which BERKSHIRE HATHAWAY owns over 8%, has a number of subsidiaries that it accounts for using the equity method. In 1999, Coca-Cola reported equity income from those subsidiaries of a negative $184 million accounted for using the equity method.

Although accounting for the holding of equity method securities is different from the accounting for available-for-sale or trading securities, accounting for the sale of a stock investment is the same regardless of the classification. If the selling price exceeds the balance in the investment account, the difference is recognized as a gain. If the selling price is less than the recorded investment balance, the difference is recognized as a loss. To illustrate, assume that Kimball sells its 2,000 shares of Holland Enterprises stock (previously accounted for under the equity method) for $225,000 shortly after the year-end recognition of its $10,000 share of Holland's earnings. The entry to record the sale is:

Cash	225,000	
Investment in Equity Method Securities		205,000
Realized Gain on Sale of Investment		20,000

The $205,000 is obtained by adding Kimball's share of Holland's reported net income to the original investment cost and subtracting the dividends received from Holland ($200,000 + $10,000 − $5,000).

to summarize

All investments in stock are initially accounted for at cost. However, because different levels of investment provide different degrees of influence over investee companies, accounting for subsequent events relating to the investee will differ depending on the degree of influence. When the percentage of outstanding voting common stock owned is sufficient to exercise influence (as is usually true with ownership of 20 to 50%), the equity method is used. This method involves increasing the book value of the investment for earnings and decreasing it for dividends and losses.

review of learning objectives

1 **Understand why companies invest in other companies.** Companies invest in the debt and equity securities of other companies for a variety of reasons. The primary reason is to earn a return on invested funds. Bonds and stocks offer a higher potential return for investors than the interest rates offered by government-backed securities or savings rates offered by banks and other financial institutions. Along with the potential for higher returns comes the prospect of higher risks; the investor faces the possibility of earning little return or even losing money. Besides earning a return, companies invest in the securities of other companies for additional reasons, including establishing a long-term business relationship, ensuring an adequate supply of raw materials, ensuring a sales network for inventory, or gaining access to developed assets, such as software programs or oil reserves.

2 **Understand the different classifications for securities.** Debt and equity securities are classified according to management's intent in holding the securities. If the securities are being held for the short term with the intent to sell the securities if cash is needed, the securities are accounted for as "trading" securities. If debt securities are expected to be held until they mature, the securities are classified as "held-to-maturity." If equity securities are purchased with the intent of being able to significantly influence the operating decisions of the investee (ownership of between 20 and 50% of outstanding common stock typically reflects the ability to significantly influence), the securities are accounted for using the equity method. Debt and equity securities not classified as trading, held-to-maturity, or equity method securities are classified as "available-for-sale." The importance of these distinctions becomes clear when changes in the value of the securities are accounted for by the investor.

3 **Account for the purchase, recognition of revenue, and sale of trading and available-for-sale securities.** Investments in securities are initially recorded at cost. Cost includes the fair market value of the securities as well as broker's fees. For trading and available-for-sale securities, dividends or interest earned is recorded as revenue. For held-to-maturity securities and equity method securities, the recognition of revenue is more complex. When a security is sold, regardless of its classification, its carrying (book) value is compared to the selling price to determine any realized gain or loss on the sale. These realized gains and losses are disclosed on the income statement with Other Revenues and Expenses.

4 **Account for changes in the value of securities.** When the market value of a security changes, the classification of the security determines whether the change in value is recorded on the financial statements. With held-to-maturity securities and equity method securities, because the intent of management is to hold these types of securities for long periods of time, changes in market value are not recognized. For securities classified as trading, any unrealized gains and losses are recognized on the income statement. A market adjustment account is offset against Investment in Trading Securities to value the securities at their fair market value on the balance sheet. Available-for-sale securities are also adjusted to fair market value using a market adjustment account. However, the offset is recorded in a stockholders' equity account.

expanded material

5 **Account for held-to-maturity securities.** The purchase price of a held-to-maturity security may be less than face value, resulting in a discount, or it may be more than face value, resulting in a premium. The discount or premium is amortized over the life of the bond by adjusting the cost upward if purchased at a discount and downward if purchased at a premium. Adjusting the cost of the bond up or down ensures that the recorded cost will be equal to the face value of the bond at the maturity date. This adjustment is accomplished through the amortization of the premiums and discounts, which adjusts the interest earned on the bonds from the stated to the effective rate. Bond discounts and premiums can be amortized using either the straight-line or the effective-interest method. The latter is theoretically more correct, but if the differences between the two are insignificant, either can be used.

6 **Account for securities using the equity method.** If ownership of the outstanding stock of another company gives the investor the ability to significantly influence the company (as generally happens with 20 to 50% ownership), the equity method is used to account for the investment. With the equity method, the purchase is recorded at cost. The investment balance (its book value) is decreased by dividends and losses and increased by the investor's share of the investee company's earnings.

key terms and concepts

available-for-sale securities 574
consolidated financial statements 574
debt securities 572
equity method 574
equity securities (stock) 573
held-to-maturity security 573
Market Adjustment—Trading Securities 581
realized gains and losses 579
trading securities 574
unrealized gains and losses 581

expanded material

effective-interest amortization 588
straight-line amortization 586

review problem

Investments in Debt and Equity Securities

On January 1, 2003, Schultz, Inc., purchased the following securities:

Security	Type	Classification	Cost
1	Debt	Trading	$2,500
2	Debt	Trading	1,500
3	Equity	Trading	1,750
4	Debt	Available-for-sale	4,300
5	Equity	Available-for-sale	2,750

On March 31, one-half of Security 2 was sold for $900. During the year, interest and dividends were received as follows:

Security	Interest	Dividends
1	$200	
2	85	
3		none
4	435	
5		$200

The following fair market values are available on December 31, 2003. Schultz had no balance in its market adjustment accounts on January 1, 2003.

Security	Market Value
1	$2,400
2	950
3	1,600
4	4,250
5	2,900

Required: Record all necessary journal entries to account for these investments during 2003.

Solution To account for these investments, four events must be accounted for:

1. The initial purchase on January 1.
2. The sale of one-half of Security 2 on March 31.
3. The receipt of interest and dividends during the year.
4. The changes in value as of December 31.

The initial purchase

Jan. 1	Investment in Trading Securities	5,750	
	Investment in Available-for-Sale Securities	7,050	
	Cash		12,800
	To record the purchase of trading and available-for-sale securities.		

The sale of one-half of Security 2 on March 31

Mar. 31	Cash	900	
	Realized Gain on Sale of Securities		150
	Investment in Trading Securities		750
	Sold one-half of Security 2 ($750 book value) for $900. Recorded the $150 realized gain ($900 − $750).		

The receipt of interest and dividends during the year

	Cash	920	
	Interest Revenue		720
	Dividend Revenue		200
	Received $720 in interest during the year and $200 in dividends.		

Note: Even if cash were not received by year-end, the interest and dividends earned would need to be recorded, with the offsetting debit to a receivable account(s).

The changes in value as of December 31, 2003

Dec. 31	Unrealized Loss on Trading Securities	50	
	Market Adjustment—Trading Securities		50
	To account for the difference between book value ($5,000) and fair market value ($4,950) of trading securities.		

Note: Remember that one-half of Security 2 was sold during the year.

Dec. 31	Market Adjustment—Available-for-Sale Securities	100	
	Unrealized Increase/Decrease in Value of Available-for-Sale Securities—Equity		100
	To account for the difference between book value ($7,050) and fair market value ($7,150) of available-for-sale securities.		

discussion questions

1. Why do firms invest in assets that are not directly related to their primary business operations?
2. Describe the risk and return trade-off of investments.
3. What are the four different classifications of debt and equity securities?
4. When will a security be classified as "trading"?
5. What types of securities can be classified as "held-to-maturity"?
6. To be classified as an equity method security, the investor must typically own at least a certain percentage of the outstanding common stock of the investee. What is that minimum percentage? That percentage of ownership represents the investor's ability to do what?
7. Identify the different types of returns an investor can realize when investing in debt and equity securities.
8. When a security is sold, what information must be known to account for that transaction?
9. What is the difference between a realized gain or loss and an unrealized gain or loss?
10. What does the account "Market Adjustment" represent?
11. How are changes in the value of trading securities accounted for on the books of the investor?
12. How are changes in the value of available-for-sale securities accounted for on the books of the investor?
13. What is the process for adjusting the value of a trading or available-for-sale security after a valuation account has been established?

14. Why aren't premiums and discounts on available-for-sale securities amortized?
15. Why aren't changes in the value of held-to-maturity and equity method securities accounted for on the books of the investor?
16. How does the accounting for changes in the value of trading and available-for-sale securities differ?

expanded material

17. What future cash inflows is a company buying when it purchases a held-to-maturity security?
18. When would a company be willing to pay more than the face amount (a premium) for a held-to-maturity security?
19. Why does the amortization of a discount increase the amount of interest revenue earned on a held-to-maturity security?
20. Why must an investor purchasing held-to-maturity securities between interest payment dates pay the previous owner for accrued interest on those securities?
21. Why is the effective-interest amortization method theoretically superior to the straight-line method?
22. What is the key criterion for using the equity method of accounting for equity securities?
23. What guidelines have been provided to determine if the ability to significantly influence the decisions of an investee exists?
24. How does the equity method of accounting for securities differ from the procedures employed for a trading security?

discussion cases

CASE 12-1

WHICH INVESTMENT SHOULD WE MAKE?

Pentron Data Corporation has a significant amount of excess cash on hand and has decided to make a long-term investment in either debt or equity securities. After a careful analysis, the investment committee has recommended to the company treasurer that Pentron purchase either one of the following two investments. The first investment involves purchasing sixty $1,000, 8% bonds issued by the Andrea Company. The bonds mature in four years, pay interest semi-annually, and are currently selling at 92. The second investment alternative involves purchasing 3,000 shares of Franklin Corporation common stock at $30 per share (including brokerage fees). The investment committee believes that the Franklin stock will pay an annual dividend of $3.50 per share and is likely to be salable at the end of four years for $36 per share.

Discuss the following questions:

1. If Pentron wants to earn 12% per year, should it make either investment?
2. Which of the two investments would you advise the treasurer to invest in assuming the inherent risk is approximately equal? Your decision should be based on which investment provides the more attractive return, ignoring income tax effects.

CASE 12-2

CLASSIFICATION OF SECURITIES

Memphis Company has just purchased five securities; it intends to hold the stock until the price increases to a sufficiently high level, at which time it plans to sell the stock. In fact, it is unlikely that the company will hold the securities for more than a few months. Nevertheless, Memphis's management has decided to classify the securities as available-for-sale rather than as trading securities. Why is Memphis choosing this type of classification, and would you allow it if you were the auditor?

EXERCISE 12-1

INVESTMENT IN TRADING SECURITIES—JOURNAL ENTRIES

Prepare the journal entries to account for the following investment transactions of Clyde Company:

2002

July 1	Purchased 200 shares of Nickle Company stock at $36 per share plus a brokerage fee of $450. The Nickle stock is classified as trading.
Oct. 31	Received a cash dividend of $1.50 per share on the Nickle Company stock.
Dec. 31	At year-end, Nickle Company stock had a market price of $33 per share.

2003

Feb. 20	Sold 100 shares of the Nickle Company stock for $37 per share.
Oct. 31	Received a cash dividend of $1.70 per share on the Nickle Company stock.
Dec. 31	At year-end, Nickle Company stock had a market price of $39 per share.

EXERCISE 12-2

INVESTMENT IN TRADING SECURITIES—JOURNAL ENTRIES

In June 2003, Hatch Company had no investment securities but had excess cash that would not be needed for nine months. Management decided to use this money to purchase trading securities as a short-term investment. The following transactions relate to the investments:

July 16	Purchased 4,000 shares of Eli Corporation stock. The price paid, including brokerage fees, was $41,880.
Sep. 23	Received a cash dividend of $0.90 per share on the Eli stock.
28	Sold 2,000 shares of Eli Corporation stock at $11 per share. Paid a selling commission of $160.
Dec. 31	The market value of Eli's stock was $11.25 per share.

Given these data, prepare the journal entries to account for Hatch's investment in Eli Corporation stock.

EXERCISE 12-3

INVESTMENT IN AVAILABLE-FOR-SALE SECURITIES—JOURNAL ENTRIES

Wishbone Corporation made the following available-for-sale securities transactions:

Jan. 14	Purchased 2,000 shares of Clarke Corporation common stock at $31.60 per share.
Mar. 31	Received a cash dividend of $0.30 per share on the Clarke Corporation stock.
Aug. 28	Sold 800 shares of Clarke Corporation stock at $37.50 per share.
Dec. 31	The market value of the Clarke Corporation stock was $36 per share.

Prepare journal entries to record the transactions.

EXERCISE 12-4

INVESTMENT IN SECURITIES

In January 2001, Solitron, Inc., determined that it had excess cash on hand and decided to invest in Horner Company stock. The company intends to hold the stock for a period of three to five years, thereby making the investment an available-for-sale security. The following transactions took place in 2001, 2002, and 2003.

2001

Jan 17	Purchased 2,750 shares of Horner Company stock for $89,500.
May 10	Received a cash dividend of $1.30 per share on Horner Company stock.
Dec. 31	The market value of the Horner Company stock was $30 per share.

2002

May 22	Purchased 750 shares of Horner Company stock at $40 per share.
July 18	Received a cash dividend of $0.90 per share on the Horner Company stock.
Dec. 31	The market value of the Horner Company stock was $42 per share.

2003

June 7	Received a cash dividend of $1 per share on the Horner Company stock.
Oct. 5	Sold the Horner Company stock at $27 per share for cash.
Dec. 31	The market value of the Horner Company stock was $25 per share.

Prepare the journal entries required to record each of these events.

EXERCISE 12-5

INVESTMENT IN EQUITY SECURITIES

During 2001, Litten Company purchased trading securities as a short-term investment. The costs of the securities and their market values on December 31, 2003, are listed below:

Security	Cost	Market Value (December 31, 2003)
A	$ 65,000	$ 81,000
B	100,000	54,000
C	220,000	226,000

Litten had no trading securities in the years before 2003. Before any adjustments related to these trading securities, Litten had net income of $300,000 in 2003.

1. What is net income (ignoring income taxes) after making any necessary trading security adjustments?
2. What would net income be if the market value of Security B were $95,000?

EXERCISE 12-6

INVESTMENT IN DEBT AND EQUITY SECURITIES

In February 2003, Packard Corporation purchased the following securities. Prior to these purchases, Packard had no portfolio of investment securities.

Security	Type	Classification	Cost
1	Debt	Trading	$11,500
2	Equity	Trading	9,000
3	Equity	Available-for-sale	7,250
4	Debt	Available-for-sale	12,300

During 2003, Packard received $2,400 in interest and $1,800 in dividends. On December 31, 2003, Packard's portfolio of securities had the following market values:

Security	Fair Market Value
1	$12,000
2	8,750
3	7,500
4	12,500

Prepare the journal entries required to record each of these transactions.

EXERCISE 12-7

INVESTMENT IN DEBT AND EQUITY SECURITIES

CIB, Inc., purchased the following securities during 2003:

Security	Type	Classification	Cost
1	Debt	Trading	$1,200
2	Equity	Trading	1,750
3	Debt	Available-for-sale	2,100
4	Equity	Available-for-sale	900
5	Debt	Held-to-maturity	5,500

During 2003, CIB received interest of $700 and dividends of $300 on its investments. On September 29, 2003, CIB sold one-half of Security 1 for $800. On December 31, 2003, the portfolio of securities had the following fair market values:

Security	Fair Market Value
1	$ 850
2	1,800
3	2,000
4	950
5	6,000

CIB had no balance in its market adjustment accounts at the beginning of the year.

Prepare the journal entries required to record the purchase of the securities, the receipt of interest and dividends, the sale of securities, and the adjustments required at year-end.

EXERCISE 12-8

INVESTMENT IN SECURITIES—CHANGES IN VALUE

Sharp, Inc., had the following portfolio of investment securities on January 1, 2003:

Security	Type	Classification	Historical Cost	Fair Market Value (1/1/03)
1	Debt	Trading	$1,000	$ 800
2	Equity	Trading	1,250	1,100
3	Debt	Trading	1,700	1,650
4	Debt	Available-for-sale	2,200	2,150
5	Debt	Held-to-maturity	1,800	1,750

Appropriate adjustments have been made in prior years. No securities were bought or sold during 2003. On December 31, 2003, Sharp's portfolio of securities had the following fair market values:

Security	Fair Market Value (12/31/03)
1	$ 650
2	1,200
3	1,700
4	2,250
5	1,850

Prepare the necessary adjusting entry(ies) on December 31, 2003.

EXERCISE 12-9

INVESTMENT IN SECURITIES—CHANGES IN VALUE

Atlantic, Inc., held the following portfolio of securities on December 31, 2002 (the end of its first year of operations):

	Cost	Market Value (12/31/02)
Trading securities	$18,700	$17,500
Available-for-sale securities	21,350	22,000
Held-to-maturity securities	15,000	15,700

No additional securities were bought or sold during 2003. On December 31, 2003, Atlantic's securities had a fair market value of:

Trading securities	$18,250
Available-for-sale securities	22,500
Held-to-maturity securities	15,300

Prepare the entries required at the end of 2002 and 2003 to properly adjust Atlantic's portfolio of securities.

EXERCISE 12-10

ACCOUNTING FOR THE PURCHASE OF SECURITIES

The Fishing Store is a chain of sporting goods stores. The Fishing Store is interested in using some of its excess cash to invest in securities. It decides to buy the following securities:

Security	Type	Price
Fea Company	Available-for-sale	$ 4,000
Herdsman, Inc.	Trading	7,500
Lenny Company	Available-for-sale	3,200
White Company	Held-to-maturity	10,000

Prepare the journal entry to record the purchase of these securities.

EXERCISE 12-11

ACCOUNTING FOR THE SALE OF SECURITIES

Jerrod Company owns the following securities, which it is interested in selling:

Security	Type	Cost	Market Adjustments	Market Price
Monsen Company	Available-for-sale	$ 4,000	$ 300 increase	$ 5,000
Jensen Company	Trading	7,500	1,000 decrease	5,500
Stic Company	Available-for-sale	3,200	500 increase	4,000
Larouse Company	Held-to-maturity	10,000	None	11,000

Prepare the journal entry to record the sale of these securities.

expanded material

EXERCISE 12-12

HELD-TO-MATURITY SECURITY PRICE DETERMINATION

1. How much should an investor pay for $100,000 of debenture bonds that pay interest every six months at an annual rate of 8%, assuming that the bonds mature in 10 years and that the effective interest rate at the date of purchase is also 8%?
2. How much should an investor pay for $100,000 of debenture bonds that pay $5,000 of interest every six months, have a maturity date in 10 years, and are sold to yield 8% interest, compounded semiannually?

EXERCISE 12-13

HELD-TO-MATURITY SECURITY PRICE DETERMINATION

Flat Rock Corporation has decided to purchase bonds of Vicon Corporation as a long-term investment. The eight-year bonds have a stated rate of interest of 10%, with interest payments being made semiannually. How much should Flat Rock be willing to pay for $35,000 of the bonds if:

1. A rate of return of 12% is deemed necessary to justify the investment?
2. A rate of return of 8% is considered to be an adequate return?

EXERCISE 12-14

INVESTMENTS IN HELD-TO-MATURITY SECURITIES

Control Group purchased thirty $1,000, 10%, 20-year bonds of Natchez Corporation on January 1, 2003, as a long-term investment. The bonds mature on January 1, 2023, and interest is payable every January 1 and July 1. Control Group's reporting year ends December 31, and the company uses the straight-line method of amortizing premiums and discounts.

Make all necessary journal entries relating to the bonds for 2003, assuming:

1. The purchase price is 104% of face value.
2. The purchase price is 94% of face value.

EXERCISE 12-15

STRAIGHT-LINE AMORTIZATION OF PREMIUM

On their issuance date, Color Company purchased 20 $1,000, 8%, five-year bonds of Morton Company as a long-term investment for $21,706. Interest payments are made semiannually. Prepare a schedule showing the amortization of the bond premium over the five-year life of the bonds. Use the straight-line method of amortization.

EXERCISE 12-16

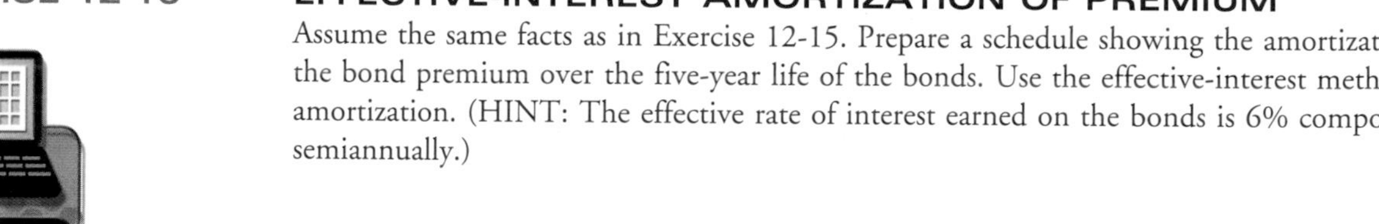

EFFECTIVE-INTEREST AMORTIZATION OF PREMIUM

Assume the same facts as in Exercise 12-15. Prepare a schedule showing the amortization of the bond premium over the five-year life of the bonds. Use the effective-interest method of amortization. (HINT: The effective rate of interest earned on the bonds is 6% compounded semiannually.)

EXERCISE 12-17

INVESTMENTS IN STOCK—EQUITY METHOD

On January 3, 2003, SW, Inc., purchased 8,000 shares of the outstanding common stock of IM Corporation. At the time of this transaction, IM has 20,000 shares of common stock outstanding. The cost of the purchase (including brokerage fees) was $47 per share. During the year, IM reported income of $18,000 and paid dividends of $10,000. On December 31, 2003, IM's stock was valued at $51 per share.

Provide the entries necessary to record the above transactions.

EXERCISE 12-18

EQUITY METHOD

Foster Enterprises purchased 20% of the outstanding common stock of Novelties, Inc., on January 2, 2003, paying $150,000. During 2003, Novelties, Inc., reported net income of $20,000 and paid dividends to shareholders of $15,000. On December 31, 2003, Foster's investment in Novelties stock had a fair market value of $158,000. Assuming this is the only security owned by Foster, prepare all journal entries required by Foster in 2003 assuming:

1. The security is classified as a trading security.
2. The security is classified as an available-for-sale security.
3. The equity method is applied to the investment.

EXERCISE 12-19

INVESTMENTS IN STOCK—EQUITY METHOD

During 2003, Genco Corporation purchased 10,000 shares of Wiener Company stock for $85 per share. Wiener had a total of 40,000 shares of stock outstanding.

1. Prepare journal entries for the following transactions:

Jan.	1	Purchased 10,000 shares of common stock at $85.
Dec.	31	Wiener Company declared and paid a $4.60-per-share dividend.
	31	Wiener Company reported net income for 2003 of $360,000.

2. On December 31, 2003, the market price of Wiener's stock was $79 per share. Show how this investment would be reported on Genco's balance sheet at December 31, 2003, assuming that this is the only stock investment owned by Genco.

PROBLEM 12-1

INVESTMENT IN SECURITIES—RECORDING AND ANALYSIS

The following data pertain to the securities of Linford Company during 2003, the company's first year of operations:

a. Purchased 400 shares of Corporation A stock at $40 per share plus a commission of $200. This security is classified as trading.
b. Purchased $6,000 of Corporation B bonds. These bonds are classified as trading.
c. Received a cash dividend of $0.50 per share on the Corporation A stock.
d. Sold 100 shares of Corporation A stock for $46 per share.
e. Received interest of $240 on the Corporation B bonds.
f. Purchased 50 shares of Corporation C stock for $3,500. Classified the stock as available-for-sale.
g. Received interest of $240 on the Corporation B bonds.
h. Sold 150 shares of Corporation A stock for $28 per share.
i. Received a cash dividend of $1.40 per share on the Corporation C stock.
j. Interest receivable at year-end on the Corporation B bonds amounts to $60.

Required: Prepare journal entries to record the preceding transactions. Post the entries to T-accounts, and determine the amount of each of the following for the year:

1. Dividend revenue.
2. Bond interest revenue.
3. Net gain or loss from selling securities.

PROBLEM 12-2

BUYING AND SELLING TRADING SECURITIES

Fox Company incurred the following transactions relating to the common stock of NOP Company:

July 10, 2001	Purchased 10,000 shares at $45 per share.
Sep. 29, 2002	Sold 2,000 shares at $51 per share.
Aug. 17, 2003	Sold 2,500 shares at $33 per share.

The end-of-year market prices for the shares were as follows:

Dec. 31, 2001	$47 per share
Dec. 31, 2002	$39 per share
Dec. 31, 2003	$31 per share

Fox Company classifies the NOP stock as trading securities.

Required:

1. Determine the amount of (a) realized gain or loss and (b) unrealized gain or loss to be reported on the income statement each year relating to the NOP stock.
2. How would your answer to (1) change if the securities were classified as available-for-sale? Explain.

PROBLEM 12-3

TRADING AND AVAILABLE-FOR-SALE SECURITIES

Lorien Technologies, Inc., purchased the following securities during 2002:

Security	Classification	Cost	Market Value (12/31/02)
A	Trading	$ 5,000	$ 4,000
B	Trading	7,000	10,000
C	Available-for-sale	10,000	8,000
D	Available-for-sale	6,000	3,500

The following transactions occurred during 2003:

a. On January 1, 2003, Lorien purchased Security E for $12,000. Security E is classified as available-for-sale.
b. On March 23, 2003, Security B was sold for $4,700.
c. On July 23, 2003, Security C was sold for $19,500.

The remaining securities had the following market values as of December 31, 2003:

Security	Market Value
A	$ 4,500
D	5,000
E	13,000

Required:

1. Determine the amount of (a) realized gain or loss and (b) unrealized gain or loss to be reported relating to Lorien's trading securities for 2003.
2. Determine the amount of (a) realized gain or loss and (b) unrealized gain or loss to be reported relating to Lorien's available-for-sale securities for 2003. Which amounts will appear on the income statement?

PROBLEM 12-4

INVESTMENTS IN TRADING SECURITIES

In December 2003, the treasurer of Marble Company concluded that the company had excess cash on hand and decided to invest in Sandy Corporation stock. The company intends to hold the stock for a period of 6 to 12 months and classifies the security as trading. The following transactions took place:

Jan. 1	Purchased 5,500 shares of Sandy Corporation stock for $82,500.
Apr. 15	Received a cash dividend of $0.65 per share on the Sandy Corporation stock.
May 22	Sold 1,500 shares of the Sandy Corporation stock at $20 per share for cash.
July 15	Received a cash dividend of $0.45 per share on the Sandy Corporation stock.
Aug. 31	Sold the balance of the Sandy Corporation stock at $8 per share for cash.

Required: Prepare the appropriate journal entries to record each of these transactions.

PROBLEM 12-5

INVESTMENTS IN DEBT AND EQUITY SECURITIES

Menlo Company often invests in the debt and equity securities of other companies as short-term investments. During 2003, the following events occurred:

July 1 Menlo purchased the securities listed here:

Security	Type	Classification	Cost
1	Debt	Trading	$28,800
2	Equity	Trading	27,600
3	Equity	Trading	46,800
4	Equity	Available-for-sale	16,800

Sep. 30 Menlo received a cash dividend of $1,500 on Security 2.
Dec. 1 Menlo sold Security 4 for $14,800.
31 Menlo received interest of $2,600 on Security 1.
31 The market prices were quoted as follows: Security 1, $25,600; Security 2, $28,800; Security 3, $45,000.

Required:

1. Prepare journal entries to record the events.
2. Illustrate how these investments would be reported on the balance sheet at December 31.
3. What items and amounts would be reported on the income statement for the year?

PROBLEM 12-6

UNIFYING CONCEPTS: SHORT-TERM INVESTMENTS IN STOCKS AND BONDS

FRC Manufacturing Company produces and sells one main product. There is significant seasonality in demand, and the unit price is quite high. As a result, during the heavy selling season, the company generates cash that is idle for a few months. The company uses this cash to acquire investments. The following transactions relate to FRC's investments during 2003:

Mar. 15 Purchased 800 shares of Lewis Corporation stock at $25 per share, plus brokerage fees of $624. This stock is classified as trading.
Apr. 1 Purchased $42,000 of 12% bonds of Martin Company. This investment is classified as available-for-sale.
June 3 Received a cash dividend of $1.80 per share on the Lewis Corporation stock.
Oct. 1 Received a semiannual interest payment of $2,520 on the Martin Company bonds.
10 Sold 600 shares of the Lewis Corporation stock at $29 per share less a $325 brokerage fee.
Dec. 31 Recorded $1,260 of interest earned on the Martin Company bonds for the period October 1, 2003, through December 31, 2003.
31 The market price of the Lewis Corporation stock was $22 per share; the market price of the Martin Company bonds was $40,320.

Required: Prepare journal entries to record these transactions.

PROBLEM 12-7

RECORDING INVESTMENT TRANSACTIONS

General Ledger Software

The following data pertain to the investments of Sumner Company during 2003, the company's first year of operations:

a. Purchased 200 shares of Corporation A stock at $40 per share, plus brokerage fees of $100. Classified as trading.
b. Purchased $10,000 of Corporation B bonds at face value. Classified as trading.
c. Received a cash dividend of $0.50 per share on the Corporation A stock.
d. Received interest of $600 on the Corporation B bonds.
e. Purchased 50 shares of Corporation C stock for $3,500. Classified as available-for-sale.
f. Received interest of $600 on the Corporation B bonds.
g. Sold 80 shares of Corporation A stock for $32 per share due to a significant decline in the market.
h. Received a cash dividend of $1.40 per share on the Corporation C stock.
i. Interest receivable at year-end on the Corporation B bonds amounts to $200.
j. Market value of securities at year-end: Corporation A stock, $42 per share; Corporation B bonds, $10,200; Corporation C stock, $3,450.

Required: Enter these transactions in T-accounts, and determine each of the following for the year:

1. Dividend revenue.
2. Bond interest revenue.
3. Net gain or loss from selling securities.
4. Unrealized gain or loss from holding securities.

PROBLEM 12-8

INVESTMENTS IN AVAILABLE-FOR-SALE SECURITIES

Durham Company often purchases common stocks of other companies as long-term investments. At the end of 2002, Durham held the common stocks listed. (Assume that Durham Company exercises no significant influence over these companies; that is, they are classified as available-for-sale securities.)

Corporation	Number of Shares	Cost per Share
A	2,000	$ 70
B	3,000	50
C	1,500	148
D	1,000	82

Additional information for 2002:

Sep. 30 Durham received a cash dividend of $2.50 per share on Corporation A stock.
Dec. 31 The market prices were quoted as follows:
Corporation A stock, $64; Corporation B stock, $48;
Corporation C stock, $150; Corporation D stock, $78.

Required:

1. Illustrate how these investments would be reported on the balance sheet at December 31, 2002, and prepare the adjusting entry at that date.
2. What items and amounts would be reported on the income statement for 2002?
3. Prepare the journal entry for the sale of Corporation D stock for $74 per share in 2003.
4. **Interpretive Question:** Why are losses from the write-down of available-for-sale securities not included in the current year's income, whereas similar losses for trading securities are included?

PROBLEM 12-9

UNIFYING CONCEPTS: INVESTMENTS IN DEBT AND EQUITY SECURITIES

On January 1, Draxton Company had surplus cash and decided to make some long-term investments. The following transactions occurred during the year:

Jan. 1 Purchased twenty $1,000, 12% bonds of Sifco Corporation at face value. Semiannual interest payment dates are January 1 and July 1 each year. The bonds are classified as available-for-sale.
Feb. 15 Purchased 4,000 shares of Porto Corporation stock at $35 per share, plus brokerage fees of $1,500. The stock is classified as available-for-sale.
July 1 Received a semiannual interest payment on the Sifco Corporation bonds.
Sep. 30 Received an annual cash dividend of $1.50 per share on Porto Corporation stock.
Oct. 15 Sold 1,000 shares of the Porto Corporation stock at $42 per share.
Dec. 31 Adjusted the accounts to accrue interest on the Sifco Corporation bonds.

Required:

1. Prepare journal entries for these transactions.
2. The market quote for Sifco Corporation's bonds at closing on December 31 was 104. The Porto Corporation stock closed at $40 per share. Prepare a partial balance sheet showing all the necessary data for these securities. Assume that Draxton exercises no significant influence over its investees.

PROBLEM 12-10

INVESTMENTS IN EQUITY SECURITIES

On March 15, 2003, Boston Company acquired 5,000 shares of Richfield Corporation common stock at $45 per share as a long-term investment. Richfield has 50,000 shares of outstanding voting common stock. Boston does not own any other stocks. The following additional events occurred during the fiscal year ended December 31, 2003:

Dec. 1 Boston received a cash dividend of $2.50 per share from Richfield Corporation.
31 Richfield Corporation announced earnings for the year of $150,000.
31 Richfield common stock had a closing market price of $42 per share.

Required:

1. What accounting method should be used to account for this investment? Why?
2. Prepare journal entries for the above transactions.
3. Prepare a partial income statement and balance sheet to show how the investments accounts would be shown on the financial statements.

PROBLEM 12-11

INVESTMENT PORTFOLIO

General Corporation has the following investments in equity securities at December 31, 2002 (there are no existing balances in the market adjustment account):

Company	Classification	Shares	Percentage of Shares Owned	Cost	Market Price at 12/31/02
Clarke Corporation	Trading	1,000	2%	$75	$78
Marlin Company	Available-for-sale	4,000	15	34	32
Air Products, Inc.	Available-for-sale	3,000	10	46	43

Required:

1. Prepare any adjusting entries required at December 31, 2002.
2. Illustrate how these investments would be presented on General Corporation's balance sheet at December 31, 2002. The available-for-sale securities are expected to be held for two to five years.
3. Prepare the journal entry on April 10, 2003, when General Corporation sold the Clarke Corporation investment for $72 per share.
4. Assume that General Corporation still owns its investment in Marlin Company and Air Products at December 31, 2003; the market prices on that date are $37 for Marlin and $44 for Air Products. Prepare all adjusting journal entries needed at December 31, 2003.

expanded material

PROBLEM 12-12

INVESTMENTS IN HELD-TO-MATURITY SECURITIES

Cyril Corporation purchased $25,000 of Baker Construction Company's 12% bonds at 102½ plus accrued interest on February 1, 2002. The bonds mature on April 1, 2009, and interest is payable on April 1 and October 1. Cyril Corporation uses the straight-line method of amortizing bond premiums and discounts.

Required:

1. Record all journal entries to account for this investment during the years 2002 and 2003, assuming that Cyril closes its books annually on December 31.
2. **Interpretive Question:** At the time these bonds were purchased (February 1, 2002), was the market rate of interest above or below 12%? Explain.

PROBLEM 12-13

INVESTMENTS IN HELD-TO-MATURITY SECURITIES

On January 1, 2003, Eurowest Company purchased a $25,000, 12% bond at 104 as a long-term investment. The bond pays interest annually on each December 31 and matures on December 31, 2005.

Required:

Assuming straight-line amortization, answer the following questions:

1. What will be the net amount of cash received (total inflows minus total outflows) from this investment over its life?
2. How much cash will be collected each year?
3. How much premium will be amortized each year?
4. By how much will Investment in Held-to-Maturity Securities decrease each year?
5. How much revenue will be reported on the income statement each year relating to this security?

PROBLEM 12-14

DETERMINING THE PURCHASE PRICE OF HELD-TO-MATURITY SECURITIES AND EFFECTIVE-INTEREST AMORTIZATION

Corbett Corporation decided to purchase twenty $1,000, 10%, six-year bonds of Texas Manufacturing Company as a long-term investment on February 1, 2002. The bonds mature on February 1, 2008, and interest payments are made semiannually on February 1 and August 1.

Required:

1. How much should Corbett Corporation be willing to pay for the bonds if the current interest rate on similar bonds is 8%?
2. Prepare a schedule showing the amortization of the bond premium or discount over the remaining life of the bonds, assuming that Corbett Corporation uses the effective-interest method of amortization.
3. How much bond interest revenue would be recorded each year if the straight-line method of amortization were used? Show how these amounts differ from the annual interest recognized using the effective-interest method. (Assume a fiscal year ending July 31.)
4. **Interpretive Question:** Which of the two amortization methods is preferable? Why?

PROBLEM 12-15

INVESTMENTS IN HELD-TO-MATURITY SECURITIES

Strong Equipment Company made the following purchases of debt securities during 2003. All are classified as held-to-maturity, and all pay interest semiannually.

Purchase Date	Corp.	Face Amount	Cost	Interest Rate, %	Maturity Date	Last Interest Payment Date
10/15/03	A	$ 5,000	102	9	1/1/08	7/1/03
11/30/03	B	10,000	96	12	4/1/06	10/1/03
12/15/03	C	15,000	98	14	6/1/07	12/1/03
12/31/03	D	12,000	105	10¼	5/1/04	11/1/03

Required:

1. Prepare journal entries for the purchases.
2. Show all adjusting entries relating to the bonds on December 31, 2003, assuming that Strong Equipment Company closes its book on that date and uses the straight-line amortization method.

PROBLEM 12-16

LONG-TERM INVESTMENTS IN EQUITY SECURITIES

Century Corporation acquired 8,400 common shares of Fidelity Company on January 10, 2003, for $12 per share and acquired 15,000 common shares of Essem Corporation on January 25, 2003, for $22 per share. Fidelity has 60,000 shares of common stock outstanding, and Essem has 50,000 shares outstanding. At December 31, 2003, the following information was obtained about the operations of Fidelity and Essem:

	Fidelity	Essem
Net income	$36,000.00	$100,000.00
Dividends paid per share	0.40	1.00
Market value per share at December 31, 2003	10.00	20.00

Assume that Century Corporation exerted significant influence over the policies of Essem Corporation, but influenced the policies of Fidelity Corporation only to a very limited extent. Century classified its investment in Fidelity as an available-for-sale security.

Required:

1. How should Century account for its investments in Essem Corporation?
2. Prepare the journal entries for each investment for the year 2003 using the method or methods you selected in (1).

PROBLEM 12-17

INVESTMENTS IN STOCKS—EQUITY METHOD

On April 20, 2003, Samson Company acquired 20,000 shares of Salem Industries common stock at $38 per share as a long-term investment. Salem has 50,000 shares of outstanding voting common stock. The following additional information is presented for the calendar year ended December 31, 2003:

Nov. 20	Samson received a cash dividend of $2 per share from Salem Industries.
Dec. 31	Salem announced earnings for the year of $135,000.
31	Salem Industries common stock had a closing market price of $35 per share.

Required:

1. **Interpretive Question:** What accounting method should be used by Samson Company to account for this investment? Why?
2. Prepare journal entries for the transactions and events described.

PROBLEM 12-18

LONG-TERM INVESTMENTS IN STOCK—AVAILABLE-FOR-SALE AND EQUITY METHOD

The following activities relate to the Hilton Company during the years 2002 and 2003:

2002

Feb. 15	Hilton purchased 5,000 shares of Brock Equipment stock for $35 per share.
Dec. 1	Hilton received a $1.25-per-share cash dividend from Brock Equipment.
31	Brock Equipment common stock had a closing market price of $32 per share. Brock's 2002 net income was $60,000.

2003

July 1	Hilton sold all 5,000 shares of Brock Equipment stock for $37 per share.

Additional information: Brock Equipment had 25,000 shares of common stock outstanding on January 1, 2002.

Required:

1. Prepare journal entries to record the transactions assuming:
   a. The securities are classified as available-for-sale.
   b. The equity method is used.
2. Show the amounts that would be reported on the financial statements of Hilton Company at December 31, 2002, under each assumption.
3. **Interpretive Question:** What is the minimum number of shares of stock that Brock could have outstanding in order for Hilton to use the equity method?

PROBLEM 12-19

LONG-TERM INVESTMENTS IN EQUITY SECURITIES

During January 2003, Danbury, Inc., acquired 40,000 shares of Corporation A common stock for $24 per share. In addition, it purchased 5,000 shares of Corporation B preferred (nonvoting) stock for $112 per share. Corporation A has 160,000 shares of common stock outstanding, and Corporation B has 12,000 shares of nonvoting stock outstanding. Danbury anticipates holding both securities for at least five years.

The following data were obtained from operations during 2003:

	2003
Net income:	
Corporation A	$190,000
Corporation B	80,000
Dividends paid (per share):	
Corporation A	$0.60
Corporation B	2.50
Market value per share at December 31:	
Corporation A	$ 25
Corporation B	109

Required:

1. **Interpretive Question:** What method should Danbury, Inc., use in accounting for the investment in Corporation A stock? Why? What accounting method should be used in accounting for Corporation B nonvoting stock? Why?
2. Prepare the journal entries necessary to record the transactions for 2003.

PROBLEM 12-20

UNIFYING CONCEPTS: LONG-TERM INVESTMENTS IN STOCKS AND BONDS

On January 2, 2003, Drexello, Inc., purchased $75,000 of 10%, five-year bonds of Greasy Trucking as a held-to-maturity security at a price of $77,610 plus accrued interest. The bonds mature on November 1, 2007, and interest is payable semiannually on May 1 and November 1. Drexello uses the straight-line method of amortizing bond premiums and discounts.

In addition to the bonds, Drexello purchased 30% of the 50,000 shares of outstanding common stock of Mellon Company at $42 per share, plus brokerage fees of $450, on January 10, 2003. On December 31, 2003, Mellon announced that its net income for the year was $150,000 and paid an annual dividend of $2 per share as advised by the board of directors of Drexello. The closing market price of Mellon common stock on December 31 was $38 per share.

Required:

1. Record all the 2003 transactions relating to these two investments in general journal form.
2. Show how the long-term investments and the related revenues would be reported on the financial statements of Drexello at December 31, 2003.

competency enhancement opportunities

- Analyzing Real Company Information
- International Case
- Ethics Case
- Writing Assignment
- The Debate
- Cumulative Spreadsheet Project
- Internet Search

The following additional assignments provide opportunities for students to develop critical thinking, ethical perspectives, oral and written communication skills, experience with electronic research, and teamwork through group and business activities.

ANALYZING REAL COMPANY INFORMATION

• *Analyzing 12-1 (Microsoft)*

The 1999 annual report for MICROSOFT is included in Appendix A. Locate that annual report and consider the following questions:

1. Find Microsoft's note on accounting policies. Using the information in that note (under the heading "Financial Instruments"), determine what fraction of Microsoft's investment securities are classified as "available-for-sale."
2. In its note on "Cash and short-term investments," Microsoft lists the general types of investments that make up its $17.236 billion portfolio. Certificates of deposit are listed both as "cash and cash equivalents" and as

"short-term investments." What is the difference between these two categories? HINT: Go back to the note you looked at to answer (1).

3. Look at Microsoft's stockholders' equity statement. Where in the equity section does Microsoft report the unrealized gains and losses from available-for-sale securities?

• ***Analyzing 12-2 (Berkshire Hathaway)***

The following note comes from the 1999 annual report of BERKSHIRE HATHAWAY:

(5) Investments in equity securities

Aggregate data with respect to the consolidated investment in equity securities are shown below (in millions):

December 31, 1999

	Cost	Unrealized Gains	Fair Value
Common stock of:			
American Express Company	$ 1,470	$ 6,932	$ 8,402
The Coca-Cola Company	1,299	10,351	11,650
The Gillette Company	600	3,354	3,954
Other equity securities	6,305	7,461	13,766
Other investments	1,651	85	1,736
	$11,325	$28,183	$39,508

December 31, 1998

	Cost	Unrealized Gains	Fair Value
Common stock of:			
American Express Company	$ 1,470	$ 3,710	$ 5,180
The Coca-Cola Company	1,299	12,101	13,400
The Gillette Company	600	3,990	4,590
Other equity securities	5,889	9,062	14,951
Other investments	1,639	1	1,640
	$10,897	$28,864	$39,761

Berkshire Hathaway also discloses that it classifies each of these investments as an available-for-sale security.

1. All securities included in the tables in Berkshire Hathaway's Note 5 are classified as available-for-sale. Make all journal entries that were required in 1999 to account for Berkshire Hathaway's investments in:
   a. AMERICAN EXPRESS COMPANY.
   b. Other equity securities.
2. Did the performance of Berkshire Hathaway's portfolio of equity securities have any bright spots in 1999?
3. How has Berkshire Hathaway's portfolio of equity securities performed over time?

INTERNATIONAL CASE

• ***Sony***

SONY CORPORATION was organized in 1946 under the name TOKYO TSUSHIN KOGYO. The name "Sony" is a combination of the Latin word *sonus* (sound)

and the English word *sonny*; it was given to a small transistor radio sold by the company in the United States, starting in 1954. The radio was so popular that the entire company changed its name to Sony in 1958.

In its 2000 annual report, Sony included the note to its financial statements shown below.

(10) Marketable securities and securities investments

	Yen in millions							
	March 31, 1999				March 31, 2000			
	Cost	Gross unrealized gains	Gross unrealized losses	Fair value	Cost	Gross unrealized gains	Gross unrealized losses	Fair value
Available-for-sale:								
Debt securities	¥746,005	¥36,632	¥12,187	¥770,450	¥739,563	¥ 40,646	¥7,268	¥772,941
Equity securities	57,712	13,774	3,156	68,330	55,321	66,905	2,594	119,632
Total	¥803,717	¥50,406	¥15,343	¥838,780	¥794,884	¥107,551	¥9,862	¥892,573

	Dollars in millions			
	March 31, 2000			
	Cost	Gross unrealized gains	Gross unrealized losses	Fair value
Available-for-sale:				
Debt securities	$6,977	$ 384	$69	$7,292
Equity securities	522	631	24	1,129
Total	$7,499	$1,015	$93	$8,421

1. In the notes to its English-language financial statements, Sony states that those statements "conform with accounting principles generally accepted in the United States." However, Sony's official accounting records are maintained using Japanese accounting principles. Why would Sony go to the trouble of preparing a separate set of English-language financial statements using U.S. accounting principles?
2. Assuming that approximately the same available-for-sale securities were on hand in both 1999 and 2000, how well did Sony's investments perform in 2000?
3. What journal entries did Sony make during the year to record the revaluation of available-for-sale securities? Use only the total amounts (that is, don't use the separate amounts for debt and equity securities), and ignore the fact that securities were bought and sold during the year.

ETHICS CASE

• *Is It OK to Strategically Classify Securities?*

You have recently been hired as a staff assistant in the office of the chairman of the board of directors of Clefton, Inc. Because you have some background in accounting, the chairman has asked you to review the preliminary financial statements that have been prepared by the company's accounting staff. After the financial statements are approved by the chairman of the board, they will be audited by external auditors. This is the first year that Clefton has had its financial statements audited by external auditors.

In examining the financial statement note on investment securities, you notice that all of the securities that had unrealized gains for the year have been classified as trading, whereas all of the securities that had unrealized losses have been classified as available-for-sale. You realize that this has the impact of placing all the gains on the income statement and hiding all the losses in the equity section of the balance sheet. You call the chief accountant who confirms that the securities are not classified until the end of the year and that the classification depends on whether a particular security has experienced a gain or a loss during the year. The chief accountant states that this policy was adopted, with the approval of the chairman of the board, in order to maximize the reported net income of the company. The chief accountant tells you that investment security classification is based on how management intends to use those securities; therefore, management is free to classify the securities in any way it wishes.

You are uncomfortable with this investment security classification strategy. You are also dismayed that the chief accountant and the chairman of the board seem to have agreed on this scheme to maximize reported income. You are also worried about what the external auditors will do when they find out about this classification scheme. You have been asked to report to the chairman of the board this afternoon to give your summary of the status of the preliminary financial statements. What should you do?

WRITING ASSIGNMENT

• ***Why Doesn't the Gain Go on the Income Statement?***

You are the controller for Chong Lai Company. You just received a very strongly worded e-mail message from the president of the company. The president has learned that a $627,000 gain on a stock investment made by the company last year will not be reported in the income statement because you have classified the security as available-for-sale. With the gain, the company would report a record profit for the year. Without the gain, profits are actually down slightly from the year before. The president wants an explanation—*now*.

It has been your policy for the past several years to routinely classify all investments as available-for-sale. Your company is not in the business of actively buying and selling stocks and bonds. Instead, all investments are made to strengthen relationships with either suppliers or major customers. As such, your practice is to buy securities and hold them for several years.

Write a one-page memo to the president explaining the rationale behind your policy of security classification.

THE DEBATE

• ***Market Values Do Not Belong in the Financial Statements!***

Accounting traditionalists opposed the move to report investment securities in the balance sheet at their current market value. These traditionalists complain that inclusion of market values reduces the reliability of the financial statements and introduces an unnecessary amount of variability in the reported numbers. On the other hand, supporters of reporting market values claim that market values are extremely relevant and, for investment securities traded on active markets, are reliable as well.

Divide your group into two teams.

- One team represents "Market Value." Prepare a two-minute oral presentation arguing that the market value of investment securities should be reported in the balance sheet. To do otherwise is to make the statements an out-of-date curiosity rather than a useful tool.
- The other team represents "Historical Cost." Prepare a two-minute oral presentation arguing for a return to strict historical cost in the balance sheet.

CUMULATIVE SPREADSHEET PROJECT

This spreadsheet assignment is a continuation of the spreadsheet assignments given in earlier chapters. If you completed those spreadsheets, you have a head start on this one.

This assignment is based on the spreadsheet prepared in part (1) of the spreadsheet assignment for Chapter 9. Review that assignment for a summary of the assumptions made in preparing a forecasted balance sheet, income statement, and statement of cash flows for 2003 for Handyman Company. Using those financial statements, complete the following exercise.

Handyman has decided that, in 2003, it will create an available-for-sale investment portfolio. Handyman plans to invest $20 million in a variety of stocks and bonds. (Recall that the numbers in the Handyman spreadsheet are in millions.) As of the end of 2002, Handyman has no investment portfolio. Adapt your spreadsheet to include this expected $20 million investment portfolio as a current asset in 2003. Ignore the possibility of any interest, dividends, gains, or losses on this portfolio. Answer the following questions:

1. With the assumptions built into your spreadsheet, where will Handyman get the $20 million in funding necessary to acquire these investment securities?
2. Where in the statement of cash flows did you put the cash outflow associated with the acquisition of these investment securities? Explain your placement.

INTERNET SEARCH

• ***Berkshire Hathaway***

The history of **BERKSHIRE HATHAWAY** was outlined at the beginning of this chapter. Access Berkshire Hathaway's Web site at **http://www.berkshirehathaway.com**. Sometimes Web addresses change, so if this address doesn't work, access the Web site for this textbook (**http://albrecht.swcollege.com**) for an updated link.

Once you've gained access to the site, answer the following questions:

1. Berkshire Hathaway can be described as primarily a holding company, which is a company that has no real operations of its own but instead holds ownership shares of other companies. Berkshire Hathaway's Web site offers links to a number of the subsidiaries that it holds. What are some of these subsidiaries?
2. Warren Buffett writes the best "Chairman's Letters to Shareholders" in corporate America. A historical collection of these letters is included in Berkshire Hathaway's Web site. Look at the 1994 letter and find out whom Warren Buffett quoted on the dangers of hard work.
3. Berkshire Hathaway has two classes of common stock. What does the Web site say about the difference between them?
4. Berkshire Hathaway is constantly making new investments. Search the Web site for recent news releases and identify the most recent investments.

comprehensive problem 9–12

Hannah Company started business on January 1, 2002. The following transactions and events occurred in 2002 and 2003. For simplicity, information for sales, inventory purchases, collections on account, and payments on account is given in summary form at the end of each year.

2002

Jan. 1	Issued 100,000 shares of $1-par common stock to investors at $20 per share.
1	Purchased a building for $550,000. The building has a 25-year expected useful life and a $50,000 expected salvage value. Hannah uses the straight-line method of depreciation.
1	Leased equipment under a five-year lease. The five lease payments of $30,000 each are to be made on December 31 of each year. The cash price of the equipment is $113,724. This lease is accounted for as a capital lease with an implicit interest rate of 10%. The equipment has a five-year useful life and zero expected salvage value; Hannah uses straight-line depreciation with all of its equipment.
Feb. 1	Borrowed $1.5 million from Burtone Bank. The loan bears an 11% annual interest rate. Interest is to be paid each year on February 1. The principal on the loan will be repaid in four years.
Mar. 1	Purchased 40,000 shares of Larry Company for $35 per share. Hannah classifies this as an investment in trading securities. These securities are reported as a current asset.
July 15	Purchased 50,000 shares of Frances Ann Company for $21 per share. Hannah classifies this as an investment in available-for-sale securities. These securities are reported as a long-term asset.
Nov. 17	Declared a cash dividend of $0.25 per share, payable on January 15, 2003.
Dec. 31	Made the lease payment.
31	The Larry Company shares had a market value of $30 per share. The Frances Ann Company shares had a market value of $27 per share.

Summary

a. Sales for the year (all on credit) totaled $800,000. The cost of inventory sold was $350,000.
b. Cash collections on credit sales for the year were $370,000.
c. Inventory costing $420,000 was purchased on account. (Hannah Company uses the perpetual inventory method.)
d. Payments on account totaled $400,000.

2003

Jan. 1	Issued $500,000 in bonds at par value. The bonds have a stated interest rate of 8%, payable semiannually on July 1 and January 1.
1	The estimated useful life and salvage value for the building were changed. It is now estimated that the building has a remaining life (as of January 1, 2003) of 20 years. Also, it is now estimated that the building will have no salvage value. These changes in estimate are to take effect for the year 2003 and subsequent years.
15	Paid the cash dividend declared in November 2002.
Feb. 1	Hannah Company repurchased 10,000 shares of its own common stock to be held as treasury stock. The price paid was $37 per share.
1	Paid the interest on the loan from Burtone Bank.
Apr. 10	Sold all 40,000 shares of the Larry Company stock. The shares were sold for $28 per share.
July 1	Paid the interest on the bonds.
Oct. 1	Retired the bonds that were issued on January 1. Hannah had to pay $470,000 to retire the bonds. This amount included interest that had accrued since July 1.
Nov 20	Declared a cash dividend of $0.40 per share. The dividend applies only to outstanding shares, not to treasury shares.

Dec. 31 Made the lease payment.

31 After recording depreciation expense for the year, the building was evaluated for possible impairment. The building is expected to generate cash flows of $20,000 per year for its 19-year remaining life. The building has a current market value of $325,000.

31 The Frances Ann Company shares had a market value of $18 per share.

Summary

a. Sales for the year (all on credit) totaled $1.7 million. The cost of inventory sold was $800,000.
b. Cash collections on credit sales for the year were $1.43 million.
c. Inventory costing $900,000 was purchased on account.
d. Payments on account totaled $880,000.

Required:

1. Prepare all journal entries to record the information for 2002. Also prepare any necessary adjusting entries.
2. Prepare a trial balance as of December 31, 2002. There is no need to show your ledger T-accounts; however, preparing and posting to T-accounts may aid in the preparation of the trial balance.
3. Prepare an income statement for the year ended December 31, 2002, and a balance sheet as of December 31, 2002.
4. Prepare all journal entries to record the information for 2003. Also prepare any necessary adjusting entries.
5. Prepare a trial balance as of December 31, 2003. (As you compute the amounts to include in the trial balance, don't forget the beginning balances left over from 2002.)
6. Prepare an income statement for the year ended December 31, 2003, and a balance sheet as of December 31, 2003.

part 4

Other Dimensions of Financial Reporting

The Statement of Cash Flows

chapter **f13**

learning objectives

After studying this chapter, you should be able to:

1. Understand the purpose of a statement of cash flows.
2. Recognize the different types of information reported in the statement of cash flows.
3. Prepare a simple statement of cash flows.
4. Analyze financial statements to prepare a statement of cash flows.
5. Use information from the statement of cash flows to make decisions.

setting the stage

HOME DEPOT is the leading retailer in the "do-it-yourself" home handyman market. In January 2000, Home Depot had 913 stores in the United States, five Canadian provinces, and Chile. With each store averaging 108,000 square feet (and an additional 24,000 square feet in the outside garden center), a lot of shelf space is filled with paint, lumber, hardware, and plumbing fixtures. If plumbing fixtures don't seem very exciting to you, consider this: Home Depot is the 22nd largest company in the United States (in terms of market value), with a 2000 market value of $122.9 billion.[1] And if lumber and hardware seem obsolete in this high-tech world, consider that, for the past 10 years, Home Depot's earnings per share (EPS) have grown an average of 30.4% per year, close to the 32.2% annual growth in EPS experienced by high-flying **INTEL** during the same period. In fiscal 1999, Home Depot's sales reached $38.4 billion.[2]

But Home Depot's prospects weren't always so rosy. Back in 1985, when sales were only $700 million, Home Depot experienced cash flow problems, in large part due to rapid increases in the level of inventory. Part of this inventory increase was the natural result of Home Depot's expansion. But Home Depot stores were also starting to fill up with excess inventory because of lax inventory management. In 1983, the average Home Depot store contained enough inventory to support average sales for 75 days. By 1985, the number of days' sales in inventory had increased to 83 days. Combined with Home Depot's rapid growth, this inventory inefficiency caused total inventory to increase by $69 million in 1985, and this increase in inventory was instrumental in Home Depot's negative cash from operations of $43 million. Concerns about this declining profitability and negative cash flow caused Home Depot's stock value to take a dive in 1985, and the beginning of 1986 found Home Depot wondering where it would find the investors and creditors to finance its aggressive expansion plans. Exhibit 13-1 summarizes the differences between Home Depot's reported net income and the company's cash flow from operations for the fiscal years 1984 through 1986 as well as the company's recent performance.

Home Depot's current success is the result of an incredible operating cash flow turnaround that the company pulled off in fiscal 1987. Operating income almost tripled compared to fiscal 1986, and net income increased from $8.2 million to $23.9 million. A computerized inventory management program was instituted, and the number of days' sales in inventory dropped to 80 days. Improved profitability and more efficient management of inventory combined to transform the negative $43 million operating cash flow in fiscal 1986 into positive cash from operations of $66 million in fiscal 1987.

exhibit 13-1 Home Depot's Net Income and Cash Flows from Operations

	Fiscal Year Ended		
(in thousands)	**February 2, 1986**	**February 3, 1985**	**January 29, 1984**
Net earnings	$ 8,219	$14,122	$ 10,261
Net cash provided by operations	**(43,120)**	**(3,056)**	**(10,574)**

	Fiscal Year Ended		
(in thousands)	**January 30, 2000**	**January 31, 1999**	**February 1, 1998**
Net earnings	$2,320,000	$1,614,000	$1,160,000
Net cash provided by operations	2,446,000	1,917,000	1,029,000

1 See the Fortune 500 listing at **http://www.fortune.com**.
2 January 30, 2000, 10-K filing of The Home Depot, Inc.

In this chapter, we will study the statement of cash flows. You will learn that this statement provides one of the earliest warning signs of cash concerns of the type experienced by Home Depot. The statement of cash flows alerts financial statement readers to increases and decreases in cash as well as to the reasons and trends for the changes.

In today's business environment, it is not enough simply to monitor earnings and earnings per share measurements. An entity's financial position and especially its inflows and outflows of cash are also critical to its financial success.

The three primary financial statements were introduced and illustrated in Chapter 2. In subsequent chapters, we examined in detail the components of the balance sheet and income statement. For our discussion of the statement of cash flows, we will first describe the purpose and general format of a statement of cash flows. We will then show how easy it is to prepare a statement of cash flows if detailed cash flow information is available. A statement of cash flows can also be prepared based on an analysis of balance sheet and income statement accounts. We will also distinguish between the direct and indirect methods of reporting operating cash flows and discuss the usefulness of the statement of cash flows. Finally, we will explain how the statement of cash flows can be used to make investment and lending decisions.

1

Understand the purpose of a statement of cash flows.

statement of cash flows The financial statement that shows an entity's cash inflows (receipts) and outflows (payments) during a period of time.

WHAT'S THE PURPOSE OF A STATEMENT OF CASH FLOWS?

The **statement of cash flows**, as its name implies, summarizes a company's cash flows for a period of time. It provides answers to such questions as, "Where did our money come from?" and "Where did our money go?" The statement of cash flows explains how a company's cash was generated during the period and how that cash was used.

You might think that the statement of cash flows is a replacement for the income statement, but the two statements have two different objectives. The income statement, as you know, measures the results of operations for a period of time. Net income is the accountant's best estimate at reflecting a company's economic performance for a period. The income statement provides details as to how the retained earnings account changes during a period and ties together, in part, the owners' equity sections of comparative balance sheets.

The statement of cash flows, on the other hand, provides details as to how the cash account changed during a period. The statement of cash flows reports the period's transactions and events in terms of their impact on cash. In Chapter 4, we compared the cash-basis and accrual-basis methods of measuring income and explained why accrual-basis income is considered a better measure of periodic income. The statement of cash flows provides important information from a cash-basis perspective that complements the income statement and balance sheet, thus providing a more complete picture of a company's operations and financial position. It is important to note that the statement of cash flows does not include any transactions or accounts that are not already reflected in the balance sheet or the income statement. Rather, the statement of cash flows simply provides information relating to the cash flow effects of those transactions.

Users of financial statements, particularly investors and creditors, need information about a company's cash flows in order to evaluate the company's ability to generate positive net cash flows in the future to meet its obligations and to pay dividends. In some cases, careful analysis of cash flows can provide early warning of impending financial problems, as was the case with HOME DEPOT.

Before moving on, it is important to reiterate that the statement of cash flows does not replace the income statement. The income statement summarizes the results of a company's operations, whereas the statement of cash flows summarizes a company's inflows and outflows of cash. Information contained in the income statement can be used to facilitate the preparation of a statement of cash flows; information in the statement of cash flows sheds some light on the company's ability to generate income in the future. The statement of cash flows and the income statement provide complementary information about different aspects of a business.

to summarize

The statement of cash flows, one of the three primary financial statements, provides information about the cash receipts and payments of an entity during a period. It provides important information that complements the income statement and balance sheet.

2

Recognize the different types of information reported in the statement of cash flows.

cash equivalents Short-term, highly liquid investments that can easily be converted into cash.

Speaking of cash, what is the largest denomination ever printed by the U.S. Treasury Department? Go to http://www.ustreas.gov/currency to find out.

operating activities Transactions and events that enter into the determination of net income.

WHAT INFORMATION IS REPORTED IN THE STATEMENT OF CASH FLOWS?

Accounting standards include specific requirements for the reporting of cash flows. The general format for a statement of cash flows, with details and dollar amounts omitted, is presented in Exhibit 13-2. As illustrated, the inflows and outflows of cash must be divided into three main categories: operating activities, investing activities, and financing activities. Further, the statement of cash flows is presented in a manner that reconciles the beginning and ending balances of cash and cash equivalents. **Cash equivalents** are short-term, highly liquid investments that can easily be converted into cash. Generally, only investments with maturities of three months or less qualify as cash equivalents. Examples are U.S. Treasury bills, money market funds, and commercial paper (short-term debt issued by corporations). In this chapter, as is common in practice, the term *cash* will be used to include cash and cash equivalents.

Major Classifications of Cash Flows

Exhibit 13-3 shows the three main categories of cash inflows and outflows—operating, investing, and financing. Exhibit 13-4 summarizes the specific activities included in each category. Beginning with operating activities, each of the cash flow categories will be explained. We will also discuss the reporting of significant noncash transactions and events.

OPERATING ACTIVITIES **Operating activities** include those transactions and events that enter into the determination of net income. Cash receipts from the sale of goods or services are the major cash inflows for most businesses. Other inflows are cash receipts for interest revenue, dividend revenue, and similar items. Major outflows of cash are for the purchase of inventory and for the payment of wages, taxes, interest, utilities, rent, and similar expenses. As we will explain later, the amount of cash provided by (or used in) operating activities is a key figure and should be highlighted on the statement of cash flows.

Note that our focus in analyzing operating activities is to determine cash flows from operations. An analysis is required to convert income from an accrual-basis to a cash-basis number.

exhibit 13-2 General Format for a Statement of Cash Flows

Cash provided by (used in):	
Operating activities	$XXX
Investing activities	XXX
Financing activities	XXX
Net increase (decrease) in cash and cash equivalents	$XXX
Cash and cash equivalents at beginning of year	XXX
Cash and cash equivalents at end of year	$XXX

exhibit 13-3 The Flow of Cash

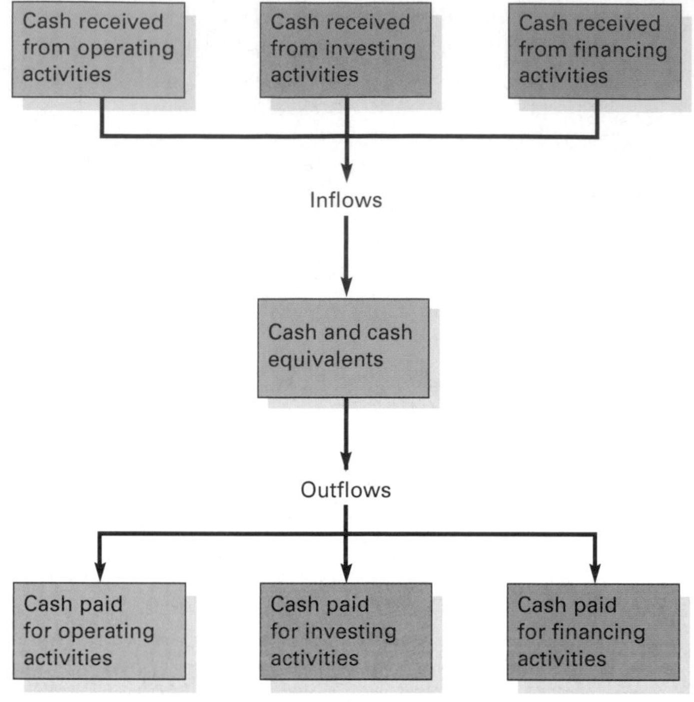

fyi

Although cash inflows from interest and dividends logically might be classified as financing activities, the FASB has decided to classify them as operating activities, which conforms to their presentation on the income statement.

To do this, we begin with the net income figure, remove all items relating to investing activities (such as depreciation and gains/losses on the sale of equipment) and financing activities (such as gains/losses on retirement of debt), and then adjust for changes in those current assets and current liabilities that involve cash and relate to operations (which are most of the current assets and current liabilities).

Operating activities, including the sale of goods, help determine net income and are reported on the statement of cash flows.

exhibit 13-4 Major Classifications of Cash Flows

Operating Activities
Cash receipts from:
- Sale of goods or services
- Interest revenue
- Dividend revenue
- Sale of investments in trading securities

Cash payments to:
- Suppliers for inventory purchases
- Employees for services
- Governments for taxes
- Lenders for interest expense
- Brokers for purchase of trading securities
- Others for other expenses (e.g., utilities, rent)

Investing Activities
Cash receipts from:
- Sale of property, plant, and equipment
- Sale of a business segment
- Sale of investments in securities other than trading securities
- Collection of principal on loans made to other entities

Cash payments to:
- Purchase property, plant, and equipment
- Purchase debt or equity securities of other entities (other than trading securities)
- Make loans to other entities

Financing Activities
Cash receipts from:
- Issuance of own stock
- Borrowing (e.g., bonds, notes, mortgages)

Cash payments to:
- Stockholders as dividends
- Repay principal amounts borrowed
- Repurchase an entity's own stock (treasury stock)

investing activities Transactions and events that involve the purchase and sale of securities (excluding cash equivalents), property, plant, equipment, and other assets not generally held for resale, and the making and collecting of loans.

fyi

The purchase and sale of trading securities is classified as an operating activity.

INVESTING ACTIVITIES Transactions and events that involve the purchase and sale of securities (other than trading securities), property, buildings, equipment, and other assets not generally held for resale, and the making and collecting of loans are classified as **investing activities**. These activities occur regularly and result in cash inflows and outflows. They are not classified under operating activities because they relate only indirectly to the entity's central, ongoing operations, which usually involve the sale of goods or services.

The analysis of investing activities involves identifying those accounts on the balance sheet relating to investments (typically long-term asset accounts) and then explaining how those accounts changed and how those changes affected the cash flows for the period.

financing activities Transactions and events whereby resources are obtained from, or repaid to, owners (equity financing) and creditors (debt financing).

FINANCING ACTIVITIES **Financing activities** include transactions and events whereby resources are obtained from or paid to owners (equity financing) and creditors (debt financing). Dividend payments, for example, fit this definition. As noted earlier, the receipt of dividends and interest and the payment of interest are classified under operating activities sim-

business environment essay

The W. T. Grant Company's Negative Cash Flows Perhaps the most famous case highlighting the deficiencies of accrual-basis net income was that of the W. T. GRANT COMPANY. In 1906, William T. Grant opened his first 25-cent store in Lynn, Massachusetts. Twenty-two years later, stock of the W. T. Grant Company was offered for sale to the public. By 1953, the company had expanded to include over 500 stores, and the expansion continued into the 1960s. In 1969 alone, 410 new stores were opened. In 1973, the company's stock was selling at nearly 20 times earnings and peaked at $70⅝ per share. As late as September 1974, a group of banks loaned the company $600 million.

A careful analysis of W. T. Grant's financial statements, however, would have indicated that although the company was reporting profits through 1974, cash flows from operations were almost always negative from 1966 to 1975. Once the market realized the magnitude of W. T. Grant's cash flow problems, it reacted quickly. In December 1974, the company's stock was trading at $2 per share. The company closed 107 stores and laid off 7,000 employees in September 1975. On October 2, 1975, the nation's largest retailer filed for protection under Chapter 11 of the National Bankruptcy Act. Only four months later, the creditors' committee voted for liquidation, and W. T. Grant ceased to exist.

Why didn't creditors and stockholders see W. T. Grant's impending problems sooner? As the chart shows, net income and working capital provided by operations were of little help in predicting W. T. Grant's problems, but a careful analysis of the company's cash flows would have revealed the problems as much as a decade before the collapse.

How could this happen? Oddly enough, firms were not required to provide investors and creditors with information about cash flows until 1987. Prior to that time, companies prepared a statement of changes in financial position, which measured changes in current assets and current liabilities. This statement of changes in financial position provided information that, if not carefully interpreted, could lead one to believe that a buildup of inventory and receivables was as good as money in the bank (as was the case with W. T. Grant).

The requirement of a statement of cash flows eliminated many of the alternatives used by companies to detail their liquidity position. Now, under generally accepted accounting principles, companies must disclose their liquidity position in terms of cash. Had this standard been applied to W. T. Grant, the negative cash flows from operations would have been highlighted and easily detected.

ply because they are reported as a part of income on the income statement. The receipt or payment of the principal amount borrowed or repaid (but not the interest) is considered a financing activity.

Analyzing the cash flow effects of financing activities involves identifying those accounts relating to financing (typically long-term debt and common stock) and explaining how changes in those accounts affected the company's cash flows. Exhibit 13-5 summarizes the activities reflected on the statement of cash flows and indicates how the balance sheet and income statement accounts relate to the various activities.

> The activities are typically listed in this order: operating, investing, and financing. However, there is no requirement that they be listed in this way. MICROSOFT, for example, uses this order: operating, financing, and investing.

Noncash Investing and Financing Activities

Some investing and financing activities do not affect cash. For example, equipment may be purchased with a note payable, or land may be acquired by issuing stock. These noncash transactions are not reported in the statement of cash flows. However, if a company has significant noncash financing and investing activities, they should be disclosed in a separate schedule or in a narrative explanation. The disclosures may be presented below the statement of cash flows or in the notes to the financial statements.

Financial History of the W. T. Grant Company 1966–1975

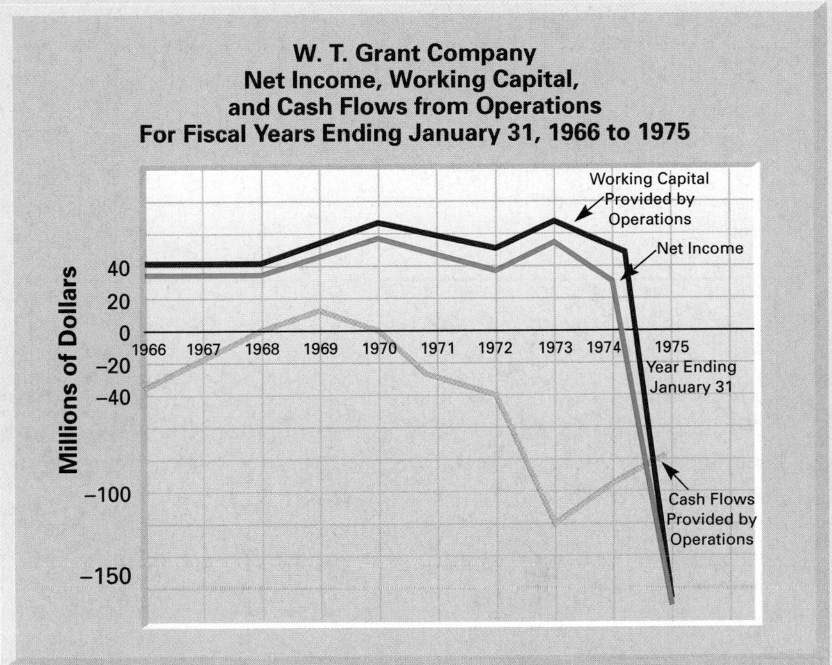

exhibit 13-5 How Balance Sheet and Income Statement Accounts Relate to the Statement of Cash Flows

Cash Flow Activity	Related Balance Sheet and Income Statement Accounts	Examples	Chapters in Which Accounts Were Covered
Operating	All income statement accounts **except** those income statement items relating to:	Sales, Cost of Goods Sold, Salaries Expense, etc.	Chs. 6–8
	• Investing	Depreciation, Gains/Losses on Sale of Equipment	Ch. 9
	• Financing	Gains/Losses on Retirement of Debt	Ch. 10
	Current assets	Accounts Receivable	Ch. 6
		Inventory	Ch. 7
	Current liabilities	Accounts Payable	Ch. 7
Investing	Long-term assets	Property, Plant, and Equipment	Ch. 9
	Long-term investments	Available-for-Sale and Held-to-Maturity Securities	Ch. 12
Financing	Long-term debt	Bonds and Mortgages	Ch. 10
	Stockholders' equity (except for net income in Retained Earnings)	Common Stock	Ch. 11
		Dividends	Ch. 11

Cash Flow Patterns

Most U.S. companies (about 70%) report positive cash flows from operations. That shouldn't come as a big surprise because companies need to generate cash from operating activities to survive in the long term. In addition, about 85% of U.S. companies report negative cash flows from investing activities. Again, this is expected as companies must expand, enhance, or replace long-term assets. Predicting whether the sign for cash from financing activities will be positive or negative is more difficult. That sign depends on whether the company is young, growing, and in need of cash, or mature, stable, and flush with cash. As a company proceeds through the normal life cycle of a business, cash from financing typically will vary between positive and negative. As an example, in fiscal 2000 Home Depot reported positive cash flows from operations ($2.4 billion), negative cash flows from investing ($2.6 billion), and a small positive cash flow from financing ($281 million).

to summarize

The statement of cash flows is presented in a manner that highlights three major categories of cash flows: operating activities, investing activities, and financing activities. In addition, the format of the statement should provide a reconciliation of the beginning and ending balances of cash and cash equivalents (short-term, highly liquid investments). Any significant noncash investing and financing activities should be disclosed separately, either below the statement of cash flows or in the notes to the financial statements.

3

Prepare a simple statement of cash flows.

PREPARING A STATEMENT OF CASH FLOWS—A SIMPLE EXAMPLE

Now that we have reviewed the three types of cash flow activities disclosed on the statement of cash flows, let's start with a simple example to see how easy (conceptually) a statement of cash flows is to prepare. For this example, we will begin with the following trial balance information for Silmaril, Inc.

Silmaril, Inc.
Trial Balance
January 1, 2002

	Debit	Credit
Cash	$ 300	
Accounts Receivable	2,500	
Inventory	1,900	
Property, Plant, and Equipment	4,000	
Accumulated Depreciation		$1,200
Accounts Payable		1,700
Taxes Payable		40
Long-Term Debt		2,200
Common Stock		1,000
Retained Earnings		2,560
Totals	$8,700	$8,700

The following transactions were conducted by Silmaril, Inc., during 2002:

1. Sales on account, $13,500.
2. Collections on account, $14,000.
3. Purchased inventory on account, $7,900.
4. Cost of goods sold, $8,000.
5. Paid accounts payable, $8,100.
6. Purchased property, plant, and equipment for cash, $1,700.
7. Sold property, plant, and equipment for cash, $500 (original cost, $1,200; accumulated depreciation, $800).
8. Paid long-term debt, $200.
9. Issued stock at par value, $450.
10. Recorded depreciation expense, $500.
11. Paid interest on debt, $180.
12. Recorded interest owed (accrued) but not paid, $20.
13. Paid miscellaneous expenses (e.g., wages, supplies, etc.) for the period, $3,200.
14. Recorded tax expense for the period, $450.
15. Paid taxes during the period, $440.

With this information, we can reconstruct the journal entries made by Silmaril, Inc., during the year:

	Account	Debit	Credit
1.	Accounts Receivable	13,500	
	Sales		13,500
2.	Cash	14,000	
	Accounts Receivable		14,000
3.	Inventory	7,900	
	Accounts Payable		7,900
4.	Cost of Goods Sold	8,000	
	Inventory		8,000
5.	Accounts Payable	8,100	
	Cash		8,100
6.	Property, Plant, and Equipment	1,700	
	Cash		1,700
7.	Cash	500	
	Accumulated Depreciation	800	
	Property, Plant, and Equipment		1,200
	Gain on Sale of Equipment		100
8.	Long-Term Debt	200	
	Cash		200
9.	Cash	450	
	Common Stock		450
10.	Depreciation Expense	500	
	Accumulated Depreciation		500
11.	Interest Expense	180	
	Cash		180
12.	Interest Expense	20	
	Interest Payable		20
13.	Miscellaneous Expenses	3,200	
	Cash		3,200
14.	Tax Expense	450	
	Taxes Payable		450
15.	Taxes Payable	440	
	Cash		440

business environment essay

The Statement of Cash Flows—A Historical Perspective The statement of cash flows is a relatively new financial statement. In 1987, the Financial Accounting Standards Board (FASB) issued an accounting standard, FASB Statement No. 95, requiring that the statement of cash flows be presented as one of the three primary financial statements. Previously, companies had been required to present a statement of changes in financial position, often called the funds statement. In 1971, APB Opinion No. 19 made the funds statement a required financial statement although many companies had begun reporting funds flow information several years earlier. The funds statement provided useful information, but it had several limitations. First, APB Opinion No. 19 allowed considerable flexibility in how funds could be defined and how they were reported on the statement. As a result, many companies reported on a working-capital basis (current assets minus current liabilities), whereas others reported on a cash basis or some other basis. Further, in each case, the individual company selected its own format. This inconsistency across companies made comparisons difficult.

Second, the funds statement, even when prepared on a cash basis, did not provide a complete and clear

When these journal entries are posted, the following trial balance results:

Silmaril, Inc.
Trial Balance
December 31, 2002

	Debit	Credit
Cash	$ 1,430	
Accounts Receivable	2,000	
Inventory	1,800	
Property, Plant, and Equipment	4,500	
Accumulated Depreciation		$ 900
Accounts Payable		1,500
Interest Payable		20
Taxes Payable		50
Long-Term Debt		2,000
Common Stock		1,450
Retained Earnings		2,560
Sales		13,500
Gain on Sale of Equipment		100
Cost of Goods Sold	8,000	
Depreciation Expense	500	
Interest Expense	200	
Tax Expense	450	
Miscellaneous Expenses	3,200	
Totals	$22,080	$22,080

To this point, this is all a review—journalizing transactions, posting journal entries, and preparing a trial balance. From this trial balance, we can easily prepare an income statement

picture of a company's ability to generate positive cash flows. One reason is that APB Opinion No. 19 required that all investing and financing activities be reported in the statement, even those that did not affect cash or working capital. Another problem was that the funds statement usually included two sections—sources (inflows) and uses (outflows) of funds. Thus, the amount of working capital or cash provided or used by each major type of activity (operating, investing, and financing) was not identified.

The limitations of the funds statement often made it difficult to assess a company's ability to generate sufficient cash. Some companies were able to report favorable earnings in the income statement, even while experiencing serious cash flow problems that were not readily apparent from the information reported in the funds statement. For example, **ENDO-LASE**, a distributor of medical lasers, reported a 200% increase in sales in one year. Unfortunately, due to poor collection performance, receivables increased at an even faster rate than sales, and much of the reported increase in revenues took the form of IOUs. When many of these receivables were determined to be uncollectible, Endo-Lase had to restate its previously reported earnings. So, although reported earnings appeared strong, Endo-Lase's cash flows were actually negative, and eventually the company had to file for bankruptcy protection.

and a balance sheet; but our objective here is to prepare a statement of cash flows. With information from the Cash T-account, we can prepare a statement of cash flows. The Cash T-account would contain the following information (journal entry reference numbers are in parentheses):

Cash

Beg. Bal.	300		
(2)	14,000	(5)	8,100
(7)	500	(6)	1,700
(9)	450	(8)	200
		(11)	180
		(13)	3,200
		(15)	440
End. Bal.	1,430		

Our task at this point is simply to categorize each cash inflow and outflow as an operating, investing, or financing activity. The inflows and outflows break down as follows:

Operating Activities:		
Collections on account (2)		$14,000
Payments for inventory (5)	$ 8,100	
Payments for miscellaneous expenses (13)	3,200	
Payment for interest (11)	180	
Payment for taxes (15)	440	(11,920)
Cash flows from operating activities		$ 2,080
Investing Activities:		
Sold equipment (7)	$ 500	
Purchased equipment (6)	(1,700)	
Cash flows from investing activities		(1,200)

Financing Activities:		
Issued stock (9)	$ 450	
Paid debt (8)	(200)	
Cash flows from financing activities		250
Net increase in cash		$ 1,130
Beginning cash balance		300
Ending cash balance		$ 1,430

As you can see, if we have access to the detailed transaction data from the Cash T-account, preparing a statement of cash flows involves determining the proper cash flow category (operating, investing, or financing) for each inflow or outflow and then properly formatting the statement. More advanced accounting software programs allow financial statement preparers to categorize each cash inflow and outflow as an operating, investing, or financing activity and to prepare a statement of cash flows with the press of a key. Once considered one of the most difficult parts of accounting, preparing a statement of cash flows has been greatly simplified as a result of computer technology.

If information is properly coded when input into a computerized accounting system, the preparation of a statement of cash flows is easy. As mentioned, the more advanced accounting software facilitates this process. But what happens if an accounting system does not classify cash transactions according to their activities? In the next section, we discuss how a statement of cash flows is prepared if one does not have ready access to detailed cash inflow and outflow information.

to summarize

If transactions are properly classified when input into the accounting system, the preparation of a statement of cash flows is straightforward. Cash inflows and outflows are segregated according to type of activity (operating, investing, or financing), and a statement of cash flows is prepared based on that information. As technology continues to advance, the preparation of a statement of cash flows is becoming easier.

4

Analyze financial statements to prepare a statement of cash flows.

ANALYZING THE OTHER PRIMARY FINANCIAL STATEMENTS TO PREPARE A STATEMENT OF CASH FLOWS

If detailed cash flow information is not accessible, the preparation of a statement of cash flows is more difficult. The income statement and comparative balance sheets must be analyzed to determine how cash was generated and how cash was used by a business. How can we determine a company's cash inflows and outflows by looking at balance sheets and an income statement? The secret lies in remembering the basics of double-entry accounting: each journal entry has two parts—a debit and a credit. In the case of the cash account, every time Cash is debited, some other account is credited; every time Cash is credited, some other account is debited. If we don't have access to the details of the cash account, we can infer those details based on our knowledge of accounting and by analyzing changes in accounts other than Cash.

For example, consider the accounts receivable account. A debit to that account means what? Ninety-nine percent of the time, a debit to Accounts Receivable is associated with a sale on account. A credit to Accounts Receivable means what? Most likely, cash was collected. If we have the beginning and ending balances for the accounts receivable account (from comparative balance sheets) and sales for the period (from the income statement), we can infer the cash collected for the period. Consider the information taken from Silmaril's beginning trial balance and the year-end trial balance relating to Accounts Receivable (remember, we are assuming that the detailed journal entries are not available to us, only the resulting financial statements):

Accounts Receivable

Beg. Bal.	2,500		
Sales	13,500	Collections	?
End. Bal.	2,000		

To reconcile the accounts receivable account, we can only assume that cash collections of $14,000 occurred. With any other amount the account will not reconcile.[3] In other words, we can infer that the following journal entry must have been made:

Cash	14,000	
Accounts Receivable.		14,000

As you can see from this analysis, we don't necessarily need the detailed cash account information to prepare a statement of cash flows. We can use our knowledge of double-entry accounting to infer those details.

caution

Every balance sheet account (except Cash) must be analyzed to determine any cash flow effects. Then those effects must be classified by activity.

A similar analysis is conducted for every balance sheet account (except Cash). The analyses draw on our knowledge of the relationship between the income statement and balance sheet accounts and of what accounts are associated with operating, investing, and financing activities. Consider another example—Common Stock. First of all, we know that changes in the common stock account are considered financing activities. Second, what do we know about credits to the common stock account? They typically are associated with the issuance (sale) of stock. Debits to the common stock account? They are associated with the retirement of common stock. Assume we are given comparative balance sheet information (transactions in a company's own stock are not reflected on the income statement) relating to the common stock account of Silmaril, Inc., as follows:

	Beginning Balance	Ending Balance
Common stock	$1,000	$1,450

What would you infer about Silmaril's cash flow activities relating to its common stock account? Without any additional information, it would be safe to assume that the company sold stock

3 Some of you may be thinking that Accounts Receivable can be credited when accounts are written off. This is true, and write-offs would affect our analysis. However, our purpose here is to understand the concepts. A more complicated analysis including write-offs will be covered in an intermediate accounting class.

for $450. If something out of the ordinary happened in the common stock account (like the retirement of stock), that information would generally be available in the notes to the financial statements and would be used to modify the analysis.

As an illustration of this type of complexity, consider Silmaril's property, plant, and equipment (PP&E) account. First of all, the PP&E account is associated with what type of cash flow activity? Investing. Increases in property, plant, and equipment correspond to purchases of PP&E, and decreases relate to the sale of PP&E. Because the sale of PP&E is typically an out-of-the-ordinary type of transaction, we could look at the notes to the financial statements for information relating to any sales. In the case of Silmaril, Inc., we find that equipment costing $1,200, with accumulated depreciation of $800, was sold for $500. Based on this information, and using information from the comparative balance sheets, we can infer the purchases made during the period as follows:

fyi

Buying and using PP&E would be considered common activities. Selling PP&E would be considered less common.

Property, Plant, and Equipment

Beg. Bal.	4,000		
Purchases	?	Sold	1,200
End. Bal.	4,500		

How much PP&E was purchased during the period? The only amount that will reconcile the PP&E account is $1,700. The journal entry would have been a debit to PP&E and a credit to Cash. Again, we find that we don't need the details of the cash account to be able to infer the cash inflows and outflows for the company. Our knowledge of double-entry accounting allows us to do a little detective work and infer what went on in the cash account.

A Six-Step Process for Preparing a Statement of Cash Flows

Is there a systematic method for analyzing the income statement and comparative balance sheets to prepare a statement of cash flows? Yes, the following six-step process can be used in preparing a statement of cash flows:

1. Compute the change in the cash and cash-equivalent accounts for the period of the statement. Seldom is one handed a check figure in real life, but such is the case when preparing a statement of cash flows. The statement of cash flows is not complete until you have explained the change from the beginning balance in the cash account to the balance at year-end.
2. Convert the income statement from an accrual-basis to a cash-basis summary of operations. This is done in three steps: (1) eliminate from the income statement those expenses that do not involve cash (such **noncash items** would include depreciation expense that does not involve an outflow of cash in the current period even though income was reduced); (2) eliminate from the income statement the effects of nonoperating activity items (such items include gains and losses on the sale of long-term assets and gains and losses associated with the retirement of debt); and (3) identify those current asset and current liability accounts associated with the income statement accounts, and adjust those income statement accounts for the changes in the associated current assets and current liabilities. For example, Sales will be adjusted for the change between the beginning and ending balance in Accounts Receivable to derive the cash collections for the period. The final result will be cash flows from operating activities.
3. Analyze the long-term assets to identify the cash flow effects of investing activities. Changes in property, plant, and equipment and in long-term investments may indicate that cash has either been spent or been received.

noncash items Items included in the determination of net income on an accrual basis that do not affect cash; for example, depreciation and amortization.

STOP & THINK Why must gains (losses) on the sale of equipment be subtracted (added) when computing cash flows from operations?

caution

Make sure that the total net cash flows from the statement (the sum of net cash flows from operating, investing, and financing activities) are equal to the net increase (decrease) in cash as computed in step 1.

4. Analyze the long-term debt and stockholders' equity accounts to determine the cash flow effects of any financing transactions. These transactions could be borrowing or repaying debt, issuing or buying back stock, or paying dividends.
5. Prepare a formal statement of cash flows by classifying all cash inflows and outflows according to operating, investing, and financing activities. The net cash flows provided by (used in) each of the three main activities of an entity should be highlighted. The net cash flows amount for the period is then added (subtracted) from the beginning Cash balance to report the ending Cash balance.
6. Report any significant investing or financing transactions that did not involve cash in a narrative explanation or in a separate schedule to the statement of cash flows. This would include such transactions as the purchase of land by issuing stock or the retirement of bonds by issuing stock.

An Illustration of the Six-Step Process

We will illustrate this six-step process for preparing the statement of cash flows using the information from the Silmaril, Inc., example presented earlier. Remember that in this case we are assuming that we do not have access to the detailed cash flow information. Thus, we are going to have to make inferences about cash flows by examining all other balance sheet and income statement accounts other than the cash account.

STEP 1. COMPUTE THE CHANGE IN THE CASH AND CASH-EQUIVALENT ACCOUNTS FOR THE PERIOD OF THE STATEMENT Recall that Silmaril began the year with a Cash balance of $300 and ended with a Cash balance of $1,430. Thus, our objective in preparing the statement of cash flows is to explain why the cash account changed by $1,130 during the year.

STEP 2. CONVERT THE INCOME STATEMENT FROM AN ACCRUAL BASIS TO A CASH BASIS From the trial balance prepared at the end of the year, we can prepare the following income statement for Silmaril, Inc.:

Sales	$13,500
Cost of goods sold	8,000
Gross margin	$ 5,500
Miscellaneous expenses	3,200
Depreciation expense	500
Income from operations	$ 1,800
Interest expense	(200)
Gain on sale of equipment	100
Income before taxes	$ 1,700
Tax expense	450
Net income	$ 1,250

Our objective at this point is to convert the income statement to cash flows from operations. Recall that this involves three steps: (1) eliminating expenses not involving cash, (2) eliminating the effects of nonoperating activities, and (3) adjusting the remaining figures from an accrual basis to a cash basis. We will use a work sheet to track the adjustments that will be made. The first two adjustments involve removing depreciation expense (because it does not involve an outflow of cash) and eliminating the gain on the sale of the equipment (because the sale of equipment is an investing activity, the effect of which will be disclosed in the investing activities section of the statement). The following work sheet reflects these adjustments:

	Income Statement	Adjustments	Cash Flows from Operations
Sales	$13,500		
Cost of goods sold	(8,000)		
Miscellaneous expenses	(3,200)		
Depreciation expense	(500)	**+500 (not a cash flow item)**	0
Interest expense	(200)		
Gain on sale of equipment	100	**−100 (not an operating activity)**	0
Tax expense	(450)		
	$ 1,250		

caution

When equipment is initially purchased, the cash outflow is reported as an investing activity. When the equipment is used, this use is recorded as depreciation and does not involve any cash flow even though it is reported as an expense on the income statement.

Note that because depreciation expense was initially subtracted to arrive at net income, our adjustment involves adding $500 back because no cash actually flowed out of the company relating to depreciation. The cash flow effect of the sale of the equipment should be reflected in the investing activities section of the statement of cash flows. Therefore, the effect of the gain must be removed from the operating activities section. Because the gain was initially added, we must subtract $100 as an adjustment to remove the effects of this investing activity from the operating activities section.

The adjustments now involve converting the remaining revenue and expense items from an accrual basis to a cash basis. Recall from our analysis earlier in this section that the amount of cash collected from customers differed from sales for the period. In fact, collections exceeded sales by $500 (explaining how the accounts receivable account declined by $500). An adjustment must be made to increase the accrual-basis sales figure to its cash-basis counterpart. We add $500 as illustrated below.

	Income Statement	Adjustments	Cash Flows from Operations
Sales	$13,500	**+500 (decrease in accounts receivable)**	$14,000
Cost of goods sold	(8,000)		
Miscellaneous expenses	(3,200)		
Depreciation expense	(500)	+500 (not a cash flow item)	0
Interest expense	(200)		
Gain on sale of equipment	100	−100 (not an operating activity)	0
Tax expense	(450)		
	$ 1,250		

caution

Remember that Cost of Goods Sold is subtracted from Sales. Adding $100 serves to reduce the negative number, and subtracting $200 makes the cost of goods sold figure a larger negative number.

Next, we turn our attention to Cost of Goods Sold. The statement of cash flows should reflect the amount of cash paid for inventory during the period. We can compute that amount by adjusting Cost of Goods Sold to reflect the inventory used this period but purchased last period, as well as inventory that was purchased last period and paid for this period.

Because Inventory declined for the period from a beginning balance of $1,900 to an ending balance of $1,800, we must adjust Cost of Goods Sold to reflect that it includes inventory that was purchased last period and used this period (explaining how the inventory balance declined). To reduce Cost of Goods Sold, our adjustment involves adding $100. The resulting number represents the amount of inventory purchased during the year. A similar adjustment is made for the change in the balance in Accounts Payable and reflects the amount of inventory paid for during the year. What event would cause Accounts Payable to decline?

Obviously, Accounts Payable would most likely decline because more was paid for this period than was purchased this period. If more was paid for this period, we are required to subtract an additional $200 to reflect the additional cash outflow. The net effect of these two adjustments is to convert the accrual-basis Cost of Goods Sold figure to the amount of inventory paid for during the year. The following T-account analysis shows the net effect of these two adjustments:

Cash	
	8,100[C]

Inventory	
1,900	8,000[A]
7,900[B]	
1,800	

Accounts Payable	
	1,700
	7,900[B]
8,100[C]	
	1,500

Cost of Goods Sold	
8,000[A]	

[A]Cost of inventory sold during the period (from the income statement).
[B]Inventory purchased during the period [solved for based on the beginning and ending Inventory balances and the cost of goods sold (A)].
[C]Inventory paid for during the period [solved for based on the beginning and ending Accounts Payable balances and the inventory purchased during the period (B)].

Updating our work sheet results in the following:

	Income Statement	Adjustments	Cash Flows from Operations
Sales	$13,500	+500 (decrease in accounts receivable)	$14,000
Cost of goods sold	(8,000)	+100 (decrease in inventory) −200 (decrease in accounts payable)	(8,100)
Miscellaneous expenses	(3,200)		
Depreciation expense	(500)	+500 (not a cash flow item)	0
Interest expense	(200)		
Gain on sale of equipment	100	−100 (not an operating activity)	0
Tax expense	(450)		
	$ 1,250		

Because neither a miscellaneous expenses payable account nor a prepaid expenses account exists, we can safely assume that all the miscellaneous expenses were paid for in cash. Therefore, there would be no adjustment.

Both Interest Expense and Tax Expense require adjustments similar to that done for Accounts Payable and/or Inventory. Let's first adjust Interest Expense from an accrual basis to a cash basis. Note that Interest Payable increased from $0 at the beginning of the period to $20 at the end of the period. How would that happen? Obviously, if a payable account increases, the company owes for products and services it has purchased or used. In this case what was used is money. Interest expense for the period was $200, of which Silmaril has yet to pay $20. Thus, the cash flow related to interest must be $180—requiring an adjustment of $20.

Tax Expense is adjusted in a similar fashion. Because the amount of taxes owed increased from the beginning to the end of the period, Silmaril must have paid a lesser amount relating to taxes than is reflected on the income statement. Reviewing the T-account for Taxes Payable helps us see how that can be:

Taxes Payable			
		Beg. Bal.	40
Taxes paid during the period	?	Amount related to tax expense	450
		End. Bal.	50

As you can determine, the only amount that will balance the above T-account is $440—the amount paid for taxes during the period. Because the income statement reflects expense of $450 related to taxes, yet the cash outflow was only $440, we must make an adjustment of $10. The work sheet, with these final adjustments, appears as follows:

	Income Statement	Adjustments	Cash Flows from Operations
Sales	$13,500	+500 (decrease in accounts receivable)	$14,000
Cost of goods sold	(8,000)	+100 (decrease in inventory)	(8,100)
		−200 (decrease in accounts payable)	
Miscellaneous expenses	(3,200)	+0	(3,200)
Depreciation expense	(500)	+500 (not a cash flow item)	0
Interest expense	(200)	**+20 (increase in interest payable)**	(180)
Gain on sale of equipment	100	−100 (not an operating activity)	0
Tax expense	(450)	**+10 (increase in taxes payable)**	(440)
	$ 1,250	+830 net adjustment	$ 2,080

Note that the cash flows from operations figure obtained through an analysis of the income statement accounts and current asset and current liability accounts is the same figure obtained previously when we assumed access to the detailed cash account information. We should always get the same answer when the question is the same—"What were cash flows from operations?"

The Direct and Indirect Methods Our final task relating to cash flows from operations relates to preparing the operating activities section of the statement of cash flows. At this point, we have two alternatives—the indirect method or the direct method.

indirect method A method of reporting net cash flows from operations that involves converting accrual-basis net income to a cash basis.

The **indirect method** begins with net income as reported on the income statement and then details the adjustments made to arrive at cash flows from operations. For Silmaril, Inc., it involves beginning with the net income figure and then listing the adjustments from the work sheet. In other words, the following highlighted portions of the work sheet are used.

	Income Statement	Adjustments	Cash Flows from Operations
Sales	$13,500	+500 (decrease in accounts receivable)	$14,000
Cost of goods sold	(8,000)	+100 (decrease in inventory)	(8,100)
		−200 (decrease in accounts payable)	
Miscellaneous expenses	(3,200)	+0	(3,200)
Depreciation expense	(500)	+500 (not a cash flow item)	0
Interest expense	(200)	+20 (increase in interest payable)	(180)
Gain on sale of equipment	100	−100 (not an operating activity)	0
Tax expense	(450)	+10 (increase in taxes payable)	(440)
	$ 1,250	+830 net adjustment	$ 2,080

The operating activities section is formatted as follows:

Operating Activities:		
Net income		$1,250
Add: Depreciation expense	$500	
Decrease in accounts receivable	500	
Decrease in inventory	100	
Increase in interest payable	20	
Increase in taxes payable	10	
Less: Gain on sale of equipment	(100)	
Decrease in accounts payable	(200)	830
Cash flows from operations		$2,080

direct method A method of reporting net cash flows from operations that shows the major classes of cash receipts and payments for a period of time.

Using the **direct method**, the operating activities section of a statement of cash flows is, in effect, a cash-basis income statement. Unlike the indirect method, the direct method does not start with net income. Instead, this method directly reports the major classes of operating cash receipts and payments of an entity during a period. This information is obtained from the last column of the work sheet as follows:

	Income Statement	Adjustments	Cash Flows from Operations
Sales	$13,500	+500 (decrease in accounts receivable)	$14,000
Cost of goods sold	(8,000)	+100 (decrease in inventory) −200 (decrease in accounts payable)	(8,100)
Miscellaneous expenses	(3,200)	+0	(3,200)
Depreciation expense	(500)	+500 (not a cash flow item)	0
Interest expense	(200)	+20 (increase in interest payable)	(180)
Gain on sale of equipment	100	−100 (not an operating activity)	0
Tax expense	(450)	+10 (increase in taxes payable)	(440)
	$ 1,250	+830 net adjustment	$ 2,080

The resulting operating activities section, given below, looks a lot like the operating activities section we prepared when we had access to the detailed cash flow information.

Operating Activities:		
Collections from customers		$14,000
Payments for inventory	$8,100	
Payments for miscellaneous expenses	3,200	
Payments for interest	180	
Payments for taxes	440	(11,920)
Cash flows from operating activities		$ 2,080

STOP & THINK Now that you have seen both methods for preparing the operating activities section of the statement of cash flows, which method do you prefer? Which method do you think is used most often by companies?

Note that the same amount of cash flows from operating activities is derived using either the indirect method or the direct method.

Why Two Methods? You may be wondering, "Why are there two methods for preparing a statement of cash flows when both methods always result in the same answer?" Good question. Each method has advantages and disadvantages. Most companies prefer and use the indirect method because it is relatively easy to apply and reconciles the difference between net income and the net cash flows provided by operations. Many users of financial statements favor the direct method because it reports the sources of cash inflows and outflows directly without the potentially confusing adjustments to net income. The accounting standard-setters considered the arguments for both methods, and although they preferred the clarity of the direct method, they permitted either method to be used. Because they can choose either method and already have to compute net income, approximately 95% of large U.S. corporations use the indirect method when preparing a statement of cash flows.

Some Rules of Thumb Although all this analysis may seem complex, the guidelines below will help you as you analyze accounts and prepare a statement of cash flows.

Accounts	Direction of Change during the Period	Adjustment to Be Made
Current assets	Increase	Subtracted
Current assets	Decrease	Added
Current liabilities	Increase	Added
Current liabilities	Decrease	Subtracted

caution

These guidelines will help you to understand *how* certain adjustments are made, but they will not help you understand *why* the adjustments are being made. To understand why, you must use your knowledge of accounting.

When current assets increase (decrease) during the period, the difference between the beginning and ending balances is subtracted (added) from the appropriate income statement account to arrive at cash flows for the period. As an example, if accounts receivable increase during the period, that means sales exceed collections and Sales on the income statement must be reduced to reflect the cash collected for the period. The reverse would be true when accounts receivable decrease.

In the case of current liabilities, an increase (decrease) requires that an adjustment be made to add (subtract) the difference between the beginning and ending balances. For example, when interest payable increases from the beginning to the end of the period, interest expense exceeds the cash paid during the period. Interest Expense must be reduced (by adding back) to reflect the cash paid during the period. Again, the reverse would be true if interest payable were to decrease during the period. Exhibit 13-6 summarizes the procedures for converting selected accounts from an accrual to a cash basis.

STEP 3. ANALYZE THE LONG-TERM ASSETS TO IDENTIFY THE CASH FLOWS EFFECT OF INVESTING ACTIVITIES The only long-term asset account for Silmaril, Inc., is the property, plant, and equipment (PP&E) account with its associated accumulated depreciation. The balance in the PP&E account increased by $500 during the period. What does an increase in the PP&E account indicate? Obviously, something was purchased. If we had no additional information, we would assume that PP&E was purchased by paying $500. But we do have additional information. We know that PP&E was purchased during the period by paying $1,700. With that information, we can prepare the following PP&E T-account:

Property, Plant, and Equipment

Beg. Bal.	4,000		
Purchased	1,700	Sold	?
End. Bal.	4,500		

To make the T-account balance, equipment must have been sold. What was the original cost of the equipment that was sold? It must have been $1,200 (that is the only number that will make the T-account balance). What was the accumulated depreciation associated with the sold equipment? Let's take a look at the accumulated depreciation T-account. Entries on the debit side of that account track the accumulated depreciation associated with

exhibit 13-6 Guidelines for Converting from Accrual to Cash Basis

Accrual Basis	±	Adjustments Required	=	Cash Basis
Net sales	+	Beginning accounts receivable*	=	Cash receipts
	−	Ending accounts receivable*		from customers
Other revenues (e.g., rent and interest):				
Rent revenue	+	Ending unearned rent	=	Cash received
	−	Beginning unearned rent		for rent
Interest revenue	+	Beginning interest receivable	=	Cash received
	−	Ending interest receivable		for interest
Cost of goods sold	+	Ending inventory	=	Cash paid
	−	Beginning inventory		for inventory
	+	Beginning accounts payable		
	−	Ending accounts payable		
Operating expenses** (e.g., insurance and wages)				
Insurance expense	+	Ending prepaid insurance	=	Cash paid
	−	Beginning prepaid insurance		for insurance
Wages expense	+	Beginning wages payable	=	Cash paid
	−	Ending wages payable		for wages
Income tax expense	+	Beginning income taxes payable	=	Cash paid for income taxes
	−	Ending income taxes payable		
				Net cash flows provided by (used in) operating activities

* Net of allowance for uncollectible accounts.
**Excluding depreciation and other noncash items.

equipment that has been sold. Entries to the credit side are associated with depreciation expense for the period. Because we know depreciation expense for the period (from the income statement), and we know the beginning and ending balances in the account (from the balance sheet), we can infer the accumulated depreciation associated with the equipment that was sold.

Accumulated Depreciation

		Beg. Bal.	1,200
Sold	?	Depreciation Expense	500
		End. Bal.	900

The accumulated depreciation associated with the equipment that was sold must have been $800. In addition, we know from the income statement that the sale resulted in a gain of $100. With this information, we can infer that the following journal entry was made relating to the sale of PP&E:

Cash	500	
Accumulated Depreciation	800	
Property, Plant, and Equipment		1,200
Gain on Sale of Equipment		100

As you can see, we can determine the amount of cash received from the sale of PP&E by monitoring the change in other related accounts on the income statement and balance sheet.

As Silmaril's only investing activity related to the PP&E account, we have analyzed all the changes in that account and are now ready to prepare the investing activities section of the statement of cash flows. Had Silmaril bought or sold available-for-sale or held-to-maturity securities during the year, we would need to analyze these accounts to determine any cash flow effects. The investing activities section of the statement of cash flows for Silmaril, Inc., would be as follows:

Investing Activities:		
Proceeds from the sale of property, plant, and equipment	$ 500	
Purchased property, plant, and equipment	(1,700)	
Cash flows from investing activities		(1,200)

STEP 4. ANALYZE THE LONG-TERM DEBT AND STOCKHOLDERS' EQUITY ACCOUNTS TO DETERMINE THE CASH FLOW EFFECTS OF ANY FINANCING TRANSACTIONS Consider long-term debt accounts. What would make them increase? What would make them decrease? Obviously, these debt accounts would increase when a company borrows more money (an inflow of cash) and decrease when the company pays back the debt (an outflow of cash). In the case of Silmaril, we observe that the company's long-term debt account declined from $2,200 to $2,000. Unless something unusual happened (such as additional debt was issued and then some debt was repaid), we assume that the reason for the decrease was that cash was used to reduce the liability.

In the case of stockholders' equity accounts, we examine both the common stock and retained earnings accounts for increases and decreases resulting from cash flows. The common stock account will increase as a result of the sale of stock and decrease if any stock is repurchased and retired. Because the common stock account increased by $450 during the period, we assume that the increase resulted from the sale of stock. Again, if an unusual transaction had occurred, information relating to the transaction would be available in the notes. Retained Earnings increases from the recognition of net income (an operating activity) and decreases as a result of net losses (also an operating activity) or through the payment of dividends (a financing activity). In the case of Silmaril, Inc., because no dividends are disclosed on the trial balance, the entire change in Retained Earnings results from net income; the cash flow effect has already been included in operating activities.

Silmaril, Inc., would prepare the following information relating to its financing activities:

Financing Activities:		
Proceeds from the sale of stock	$ 450	
Repayment of long-term debt	(200)	
Cash flows from financing activities		250

STEP 5. PREPARE A FORMAL STATEMENT OF CASH FLOWS Based on our analysis of all income statement and balance sheet accounts, we have identified all inflows and outflows of cash for Silmaril, Inc., and categorized those cash flows based on the type of activity. The resulting statement of cash flows (prepared using the direct method)[4] would be as follows:

4 A statement of cash flows prepared using the indirect method is shown in the Review Problem on pages 644–646. The statement of cash flows for MICROSOFT, shown in Appendix A, was also prepared using the indirect method.

Operating Activities:		
Collections from customers		$14,000
Payments for inventory	$ 8,100	
Payments for miscellaneous expenses	3,200	
Payments for interest	180	
Payments for taxes	440	(11,920)
Cash flows from operating activities		$ 2,080
Investing Activities:		
Proceeds from the sale of property, plant, and equipment	$ 500	
Purchased property, plant, and equipment	(1,700)	
Cash flows from investing activities		(1,200)
Financing Activities:		
Proceeds from the sale of stock	$ 450	
Repayment of long-term debt	(200)	
Cash flows from financing activities		250
Net increase in cash		$ 1,130
Beginning cash balance		300
Ending cash balance		$ 1,430

Additional disclosure is required in the notes to the financial statements depending on the method used. Other disclosures required by FASB Statement No. 95 include the amounts paid for interest and income taxes. When the indirect method is used to report cash flows from operating activities, cash paid for interest and income taxes is disclosed as supplemental. When the direct method is used to report cash flows from operating activities, these amounts are included in the statement of cash flows.

An additional disclosure required when the direct method is used is a schedule reconciling net income with net cash flows provided by (used in) operating activities. This schedule is, in effect, the same as the operating activities section of a statement of cash flows prepared using the indirect method.

noncash transactions Investing and financing activities that do not affect cash; if significant, they are disclosed below the statement of cash flows or in the notes to the financial statements.

STEP 6. REPORT ANY SIGNIFICANT INVESTING OR FINANCING TRANSACTIONS THAT DID NOT INVOLVE CASH If Silmaril had any significant **noncash transactions**, such as purchasing PP&E by issuing debt or trading Silmaril stock for that of another company, these transactions would be disclosed in the notes to the financial statements or in a separate schedule below the statement of cash flows. In this example, no such transactions occurred.

to summarize

The cash inflows and outflows of an organization must be analyzed and classified into one of three categories: operating, investing, and financing. Operating activities include those transactions that enter into the determination of net income. The direct or the indirect method may be used to show the net cash flows provided by (used in) operating activities. The indirect method starts with net income, as reported on the income statement, and adds or subtracts adjustments to convert accrual net income to net cash flows from operations. Adjustments to net income are made for increases and decreases in operating account balances, noncash items such as depreciation, and gains and losses from the sale of assets. The direct method shows the major classes of operating cash receipts and payments. The direct method requires analysis of cash transactions or an analysis of accrual revenues and expenses in

order to convert them to cash receipts and payments. Both methods produce the same results, and either method is allowed under generally accepted accounting principles. Investing activities involve the purchase or sale of long-term assets like property, plant, and equipment or investment securities. Financing activities include transactions in which cash is obtained from or paid to owners and creditors.

5
Use information from the statement of cash flows to make decisions.

USING INFORMATION FROM THE STATEMENT OF CASH FLOWS TO MAKE DECISIONS

To this point in the text, we have reviewed numerous financial statement analysis techniques involving the income statement and the balance sheet. We have introduced and discussed vertical and horizontal analysis, and we have used numerous ratios that were computed using numbers from the income statement and the balance sheet. We can also use information from the statement of cash flows for analysis purposes.

Analysis using cash flow information is often restricted to examining the relationships among the categories in the statement of cash flows. We do not perform vertical or horizontal analysis because, unlike the balance sheet and income statement, there is no guarantee that a specific number from the statement of cash flows will consistently serve as the denominator for scaling purposes. For example, all balance sheet accounts are compared to total assets when preparing a vertical analysis of the balance sheet. Why? The reason is that total assets is always going to be the biggest number on the balance sheet. The same is true for the income statement. Revenue is used because it is, in almost every case, the biggest number on the income statement. In the case of the statement of cash flows, some years the cash flow from operations may be the largest number on the statement. In subsequent years, that number may be negative. Thus, horizontal and vertical analyses are rarely performed using the statement of cash flows because of scaling problems.

Although the statement of cash flows, like the other financial statements, reports information about the past, careful analysis of this information can help investors, creditors, and others assess the amounts, timing, and uncertainty of future cash flows. Specifically, the statement helps users answer questions such as how a company is able to pay dividends when it had a net loss, or why a company is short of cash despite increased earnings. A statement of cash flows may show, for example, that external borrowing or the issuance of capital stock provided the cash from which dividends were paid even though a net loss was reported for that year. Similarly, a company may be short on cash, even with increased earnings, because of increased inventory purchases, plant expansion, or debt retirement.

Trends are often more important than absolute numbers for any one period. Accordingly, cash flow statements usually are presented on a comparative basis. This enables users to analyze a company's cash flows over time.

Because companies are required to highlight cash flows from operating, investing, and financing activities, a company's operating cash flows and investing and financing policies can be compared with those of other companies. We can learn much about a company by examining patterns that appear among the three cash flow categories in the statement of cash flows. Exhibit 13-7 shows eight possible cash flow patterns and provides some insight into what each cash flow pattern indicates about the company.

Positive cash flows from operations are necessary if a company is to succeed over the long term (patterns 1 through 4). The most common cash flow pattern is 2. Companies use cash flows from operations to purchase fixed assets or to pay down debt. Growing companies follow cash flow pattern 6. Cash is being borrowed to cover a shortage of cash from operations as well as to purchase fixed assets. Most (about 80%) of the publicly traded companies in the United States follow patterns 2, 4, and 6.

exhibit 13-7 Analysis of Cash Flows Statement: Patterns

	CF from Operating	CF from Investing	CF from Financing	General Explanation
#1	+	+	+	Company is using cash generated from operations, from sale of assets, and from financing to build up pile of cash—very liquid company—possibly looking for acquisition.
#2	+	–	–	Company is using cash flows generated from operations to buy fixed assets and to pay down debt or pay owners.
#3	+	+	–	Company is using cash from operations and from sale of fixed assets to pay down debt or pay owners.
#4	+	–	+	Company is using cash from operations and from borrowing (or from owner investment) to expand.
#5	–	+	+	Company's operating cash flow problems are covered by sale of fixed assets, by borrowing, or by stockholder contributions.
#6	–	–	+	Company is growing rapidly, but has shortfalls in cash flows from operations and from purchase of fixed assets financed by long-term debt or new investment.
#7	–	+	–	Company is financing operating cash flow shortages and payments to creditors and/or stockholders via sale of fixed assets.
#8	–	–	–	Company is using cash reserves to finance operation shortfall and pay long-term creditors and/or investors.

Source: Michael T. Dugan, Benton E. Gup, and William D. Samson, "Teaching the Statement of Cash Flows," *Journal of Accounting Education*, Vol. 9, 1991, p. 36.

to summarize

Conducting financial statement analysis using information from the statement of cash flows is more difficult than analyses using information from the income statement and the balance sheet. The primary reason is that it is common for cash flows for certain categories to be negative, thereby making interpretation difficult. Nevertheless, an analysis of the relationships among the categories on the statement of cash flows can provide insight into a company's performance.

review of learning objectives

1 Understand the purpose of a statement of cash flows. The statement of cash flows is one of the three primary financial statements presented by companies in their annual reports. Its primary purpose is to provide information about the cash receipts and payments of an entity during a period. The statement of cash flows also explains the changes in the balance sheet accounts and the cash effects of the accrual-basis amounts reported in the income statement.

2 Recognize the different types of information reported in the statement of cash flows. The statement of cash flows reports an entity's inflows and outflows of cash for a period of time and reconciles the beginning and ending balances of cash and cash equivalents.

The inflows and outflows of cash should be classified and reported for three main categories: operating activities, investing activities, and financing activities. Cash receipts and payments classified under operating activities generally include all items that enter into the determination of net income. Examples include receipts from the sale of goods or services and from interest, and the payments for inventory, wages, utilities, taxes, and interest.

Investing activities include the purchase and sale of certain securities (other than cash equivalents, which are included with cash), buildings and equipment, and other assets that generally are not purchased for resale by the entity. Also included are the making and collecting of loans.

Financing activities include obtaining and repaying cash from owners (equity financing) and from creditors (debt financing). Selling stock, paying cash dividends, and borrowing money, for example, are included under this category.

Significant noncash transactions involving investing and financing activities should be reported in a note or in a separate schedule to the financial statements. Because such transactions do not involve cash flows, they should not be reported in the statement of cash flows. An example would be the purchase of land by the issuance of stock.

3 Prepare a simple statement of cash flows. If cash inflows and outflows can be categorized according to the activity (operating, investing, or financing) when entered into the accounting system, the preparation of a statement of cash flows is straightforward. At the end of the period, inflows and outflows are divided by category and type of cash flow, e.g., collections from customers, payments for inventory, etc. A statement of cash flows then simply lists those inflows and outflows by activity.

4 Analyze financial statements to prepare a statement of cash flows. Often, detailed cash flow information is not available. When that happens, the statement of cash flows is prepared by analyzing comparative balance sheets and the income statement. A six-step process can be employed to assist in the analysis. First, the change in the cash balance for the period is computed. Second, the income statement is converted from an accrual basis to a cash basis. The result is cash flows from operating activities. Third, long-term assets are analyzed to determine the cash flow effects of investing activities. Fourth, long-term liabilities and stockholders' equity accounts are analyzed to determine the cash flow effects of financing activities. Fifth, a formal statement of cash flows is prepared. And sixth, significant noncash transactions are disclosed in the notes to the financial statements or in a separate schedule at the bottom of the statement of cash flows.

5 Use information from the statement of cash flows to make decisions. A careful analysis of the statement of cash flows will indicate shifts in a company's operating, investing, and financing policies. The statement explains the change in the cash balance during the period by identifying the inflows and outflows of cash. This helps investors and creditors observe trends related to a company's use of operating income and to its use of external sources of capital such as the issuance of stock or bonds. Used with the income statement and the balance sheet, the statement of cash flows is a valuable source of information.

key terms and concepts

cash equivalents 619
direct method 635
financing activities 621
indirect method 634
investing activities 621
noncash items 630
noncash transactions 639
operating activities 619
statement of cash flows 618

review problems

Classifying Cash Flows

Anna Dimetros is the bookkeeper for Russia Imports, Inc. (RII), a New York City–based company. Anna has collected the following cash flow information about RII for the most current year of operations. The cash balance at the beginning of the year was $105,000.

Cash receipts:	
Cash received from issuance of stock	$ 50,000
Cash received from customers	252,300
Cash received from interest at bank	4,600
Cash received from borrowing at bank	25,000
Total cash receipts	$331,900
Cash payments:	
Cash paid for wages of employees	$134,600
Cash paid to stockholders as dividends	5,500
Cash paid to bank for interest	7,200
Cash paid to bank to repay earlier loan	10,000
Cash paid for taxes	23,500
Cash paid for operating expenses	128,100
Cash paid for equipment	15,000
Total cash payments	$323,900

Required:

1. From the information provided, classify the cash flows for Russia Imports, Inc., according to operating, investing, and financing activities.
2. Determine the ending cash balance.

Solution

Russia Imports, Inc.
Cash Flows
20XX

1. *Cash flows from operating activities:*		
Cash receipts from:		
Customers	$252,300	
Bank (interest)	4,600	$256,900
Cash payments to:		
Employees (wages)	$134,600	
Bank (interest)	7,200	
Government (taxes)	23,500	
Various entities (operating expenses)	128,100	293,400
Net cash flows used in operating activities		$ (36,500)
Cash flows from investing activities:		
Cash payments to:		
Purchase equipment	$ (15,000)	
Net cash flows used in investing activities		$ (15,000)

(continued)

Cash flows from financing activities:		
Cash receipts from:		
Issuance of stock	$ 50,000	
Borrowing at bank	25,000	$ 75,000
Cash payments to:		
Stockholders (dividends)	$ (5,500)	
Repay earlier loan	(10,000)	(15,500)
Net cash flows provided by financing activities		$ 59,500
Total net cash flows for period		$ 8,000

2. Beginning cash balance	$105,000
Total net cash flows for period	8,000
Ending cash balance	$113,000*

*Alternatively, beginning balance ($105,000) + receipts ($331,900) − payments ($323,900) = ending balance ($113,000).

Preparing a Statement of Cash Flows

Snow Corporation produces clock radios. Comparative income statements and balance sheets for the years ended December 31, 2003 and 2002, are presented.

Snow Corporation
Comparative Income Statements
For the Years Ended December 31, 2003 and 2002

	2003	2002
Net sales revenue	$600,000	$575,000
Cost of goods sold	500,000	460,000
Gross margin	$100,000	$115,000
Operating expenses	66,000	60,000
Operating income	$ 34,000	$ 55,000
Interest expense	4,000	3,000
Income before taxes	$ 30,000	$ 52,000
Income taxes	12,000	21,000
Net income	$ 18,000	$ 31,000

Snow Corporation
Comparative Balance Sheets
December 31, 2003 and 2002

	2003	2002
Assets		
Current assets:		
Cash and cash equivalents	$ 11,000	$ 13,000
Accounts receivable (net)	92,000	77,000
Inventory	103,000	92,000
Prepaid expenses	6,000	5,000
Total current assets	$212,000	$187,000
Property, plant, and equipment:		
Land	$ 69,000	$ 66,000
Machinery and equipment	172,000	156,000
Accumulated depreciation, machinery and equipment	(113,000)	(102,000)
Total property, plant, and equipment	$128,000	$120,000
Total assets	$340,000	$307,000

(continued)

	2003	2002
Liabilities and Stockholders' Equity		
Current liabilities:		
Accounts payable	$ 66,000	$ 78,000
Dividends payable	2,000	0
Income taxes payable	3,000	5,000
Total current liabilities	$ 71,000	$ 83,000
Long-term debt	75,000	42,000
Total liabilities	$146,000	$125,000
Stockholders' equity:		
Common stock, no par	$ 26,000	$ 26,000
Retained earnings	168,000	156,000
Total stockholders' equity	$194,000	$182,000
Total liabilities and stockholders' equity	$340,000	$307,000

The following additional information is available.

a. Dividends declared during 2003 were $6,000.
b. The market price per share of stock on December 31, 2003, was $14.50.
c. Equipment worth $16,000 was acquired by the issuance of a long-term note ($10,000) and by paying cash ($6,000).
d. Land was acquired for $3,000 cash.
e. Depreciation of $11,000 was included in operating expenses for 2003.
f. There were no accruals or prepaid amounts for interest.

Required: Analyze the data provided to prepare a statement of cash flows. Use (1) the indirect method and (2) the direct method to report cash flows from operating activities.

Solution 1. Indirect Method

Snow Corporation
Statement of Cash Flows (Indirect Method)
For the Year Ended December 31, 2003

Cash flows from operating activities:		
Net income	$ 18,000	
Add (deduct) adjustments to cash basis:		
Depreciation expense	11,000	
Increase in accounts receivable	(15,000)	
Increase in inventory	(11,000)	
Increase in prepaid expenses	(1,000)	
Decrease in accounts payable	(12,000)	
Decrease in income taxes payable	(2,000)	
Net cash flows used in operating activities		$(12,000)
Cash flows from investing activities:		
Cash payments for:		
Land	$ (3,000)	
Machinery and equipment	(6,000)	
Net cash flows used in investing activities		(9,000)
Cash flows from financing activities:		
Cash receipts from long-term borrowing	$ 23,000	
Cash payments for dividends	(4,000)*	
Net cash flows provided by financing activities		19,000
Net decrease in cash		$ (2,000)
Cash and cash equivalents at beginning of year		13,000
Cash and cash equivalents at end of year		$ 11,000

*Cash dividends declared ($6,000) less increase in dividends payable ($2,000).

(continued)

Supplemental disclosure:	
Cash payments for:	
Interest	$ 4,000
Income taxes	14,000
Noncash transaction:	
Equipment was purchased by issuing a long-term note for $10,000.	

The statement of cash flows for Snow Corporation shows that although reported net income was positive for 2003, the net cash flows generated from operating activities were negative. Only by borrowing cash was Snow Corporation able to pay dividends and purchase land and equipment. Even then the cash account decreased by $2,000 during the period.

2. Direct Method

Snow Corporation
Statement of Cash Flows (Direct Method)
For the Year Ended December 31, 2003

Cash flows from operating activities:		
Cash receipts from customers		$585,000
Cash payments for:		
Inventory	$523,000	
Operating expenses	56,000	
Interest expense	4,000	
Income tax expense	14,000	(597,000)
Net cash flows used in operating activities		$ (12,000)
Cash flows from investing activities:		
Cash payments for:		
Land	$ (3,000)	
Machinery and equipment	(6,000)	
Net cash flows used in investing activities		(9,000)
Cash flows from financing activities:		
Cash receipts from long-term borrowing	$ 23,000	
Cash payments for dividends	(4,000)	
Net cash flows provided by financing activities		19,000
Net decrease in cash		$ (2,000)
Cash and cash equivalents at beginning of year		13,000
Cash and cash equivalents at end of year		$ 11,000

*Supplemental Disclosure**
Equipment was purchased by issuing a long-term note for $10,000.

*A schedule reconciling net income with net cash flow used by operating activities would also be presented, either with the statement of cash flows or in the notes to the financial statements. The information provided in the schedule is the same as the operating activities section of the statement of cash flows prepared using the indirect method (see part 1).

discussion questions

1. What is the main purpose of a statement of cash flows?
2. What are cash equivalents, and how are they treated on a statement of cash flows?
3. Distinguish among cash flows from operating, investing, and financing activities, providing examples for each type of activity.

4. How are significant noncash investing and financing transactions to be reported?
5. Describe the process of converting from accrual revenues to cash receipts.
6. Describe the six-step process that can be used to prepare a statement of cash flows by analyzing the income statement and comparative balance sheets.
7. Distinguish between the indirect and direct methods of reporting net cash flows provided by (used in) operating activities.
8. How are depreciation and similar noncash items treated on a statement of cash flows?
9. What supplemental disclosures are likely to be required in connection with a statement of cash flows?
10. How might investors and creditors use a statement of cash flows?

discussion cases

CASE 13-1

SHOULD WE MAKE THE LOAN?

Save More, Inc., a discount department store, has applied to its bankers for a loan. Although the company has been profitable, it is short of cash. The loan application includes the following information about current assets, current liabilities, net income, depreciation expense, and dividends for the past five years. (All numbers are rounded to the nearest thousand, with the 000s omitted.)

	Dec. 31, 1998	Dec. 31, 1999	Dec. 31, 2000	Dec. 31, 2001	Dec. 31, 2002
Cash and cash equivalents	$ 5	$ 73	$ 10	$158	$ (189)
Accounts receivable (net)	403	555	516	576	654
Inventory	253	142	383	385	1,022
Accounts payable	19	17	281	253	52
Net income	454	492	467	440	481
Depreciation expense	50	50	55	60	60
Dividends paid	177	197	208	211	211

As a bank loan officer, you have been asked to review these figures in order to determine whether the bank should loan money to Save More, Inc.

1. Compute the net cash flows from operations for the last four years.
2. What caused the sudden decrease in cash flows from operations?
3. What factors would you focus on and what additional information would you need before deciding whether to make the loan?

CASE 13-2

ANALYZING THE CASH POSITION OF GOOD TIME, INC.

The following data show the account balances of Good Time, Inc., at the beginning and end of the company's fiscal year:

Debits	Aug. 31, 2003	Sept. 1, 2002
Cash and cash equivalents	$ 88,200	$ 29,000
Accounts receivable (net)	15,000	13,300
Inventory	10,500	12,700
Prepaid insurance	2,800	2,000
Long-term investments (cost equals market)	3,000	8,400
Equipment	40,000	33,000
Treasury stock (at cost)	5,000	10,000
Cost of goods sold	184,000	
Operating expenses	93,500	
Income taxes	18,800	
Loss on sale of equipment	500	
Total debits	$461,300	$108,400
Credits		
Accumulated depreciation—equipment	$ 9,500	$ 9,000
Accounts payable	3,500	5,600
Interest payable	500	1,000
Income taxes payable	6,000	4,000
Notes payable—long-term	8,000	12,000
Common stock	55,000	50,000
Paid-in capital in excess of par	16,000	15,000
Retained earnings	9,800*	11,800
Sales	352,000	
Gain on sale of long-term investments	1,000	
Total credits	$461,300	$108,400

*Preclosing balance

The following information concerning this year was also available:

a. All purchases and sales were on account.
b. Equipment with an original cost of $5,000 was sold for $1,500; a loss of $500 was recognized on the sale.
c. Among other items, the operating expenses included depreciation expense of $3,500; interest expense of $1,400; and insurance expense of $1,200.
d. Equipment was purchased by issuing common stock and paying the balance ($6,000) in cash.
e. Treasury stock was sold for $2,000 less than it cost; the decrease in stockholders' equity was recorded by reducing Retained Earnings.
f. No dividends were paid this year.

You are to examine Good Time's cash position by:

1. Preparing schedules showing the amount of cash collected from accounts receivable, cash paid for accounts payable, cash paid for interest, and cash paid for insurance.
2. Preparing a statement of cash flows for Good Time for the fiscal year 2003 using the direct method.
3. Identifying the major reasons why Good Time's cash and cash equivalents increased so dramatically during the year.
4. Comment on whether the dividend policy seems appropriate under the current circumstances.

CASE 13-3

ANALYZING CASH FLOW PATTERNS

Paula Dalton is a security analyst for DJM, Inc. She claims that she can tell a great deal about companies by analyzing their cash flow patterns. Specifically, she looks at the negative or positive cash flow trends in the three categories on cash flow statements. Paula thinks this information is even more valuable than net income trend data from income statements. She illustrates her theory with the following patterns of cash flows for Abbott Company over the past three years.

	2003	2002	2001
Net income	−	+	+
Cash flows from:			
Operating activities	−	−	+
Investing activities	+	+	+
Financing activities	+	+	+

How do you think Paula would analyze these results? Do you agree that analyzing cash flow patterns provides superior analytical information?

EXERCISE 13-1

CLASSIFICATION OF CASH FLOWS

Indicate whether each of the following items would be associated with a cash inflow (I), cash outflow (O), or noncash item (N) and under which category each would be reported on a statement of cash flows: Operating Activities (OA); Investing Activities (IA); Financing Activities (FA); or not on the statement (NOS). An example is provided.

Item	Classified as	Reported under
Example: Sales Revenue	I	OA

1. Fees collected for services
2. Interest paid
3. Proceeds from sale of equipment
4. Cash (principal) received from bank on long-term note
5. Purchase of treasury stock for cash
6. Collection of loan made to company officer
7. Cash dividends paid
8. Taxes paid
9. Depreciation expense
10. Wages paid to employees
11. Cash paid for inventory purchases
12. Proceeds from sale of common stock
13. Interest received on loan to company officer
14. Purchase of land by issuing stock
15. Utility bill paid

EXERCISE 13-2

CLASSIFICATION OF CASH FLOWS

The following items summarize certain transactions that occurred during the past year for Alta Inc. Show in which section of the statement of cash flows the information would be reported by placing an X in the appropriate column. (Assume the direct method is used to report operating cash flows.)

Transaction	Reported In Statement of Cash Flows: Operating	Investing	Financing	Not Reported in Statement of Cash Flows
a. Collections from customers				
b. Depreciation expense				
c. Wages and salaries paid				
d. Cash dividends paid				
e. Taxes paid				
f. Utilities paid				
g. Building purchased in exchange for stock				
h. Stock of Western Co. purchased				
i. Inventory purchased for cash				
j. Interest on Alta's note to local bank paid				
k. Interest received from a note with a customer				
l. Delivery truck sold at no gain or loss				

EXERCISE 13-3

TRANSACTION ANALYSIS

Following are the transactions of Equine Company:

a. Sold equipment for $1,000. The original cost was $15,700; the book value is $1,700.
b. Purchased equipment costing $110,000 by paying cash of $20,000 and signing a $90,000 long-term note at 12% interest.
c. Received $5,000 of the principal and $450 in interest on a long-term note receivable.
d. Received $2,500 in cash dividends on stock held as a trading security. (Assume that the cost method is used.)
e. Purchased treasury stock for $3,000.

Complete the following:

1. Prepare journal entries for each of the transactions. (Omit explanations.)
2. For each transaction, indicate the amount of cash inflow or outflow. Then, note how each transaction would be classified on a statement of cash flows.

EXERCISE 13-4

TRANSACTION ANALYSIS

The Vikon Company had the following selected transactions during the past year:

a. Sold (issued) 1,000 shares of common stock, $10 par, for $25 per share.
b. Collected $100,000 of accounts receivable.
c. Paid dividends to current stockholders in the amount of $50,000 (assume dividends declared earlier establishing a dividends payable account).
d. Received $1,500 interest on a note receivable from a company officer.
e. Paid the annual insurance premium of $1,200.
f. Recorded depreciation expense of $5,000.

1. Prepare appropriate journal entries for each of the above transactions. (Omit explanations.)
2. For each transaction, indicate the amount of cash inflow or outflow and also how each cash flow would be classified on a statement of cash flows.

EXERCISE 13-5

PREPARING A SIMPLE CASH FLOW STATEMENT

Assume you have access to the ledger (specifically, the detail of the cash account) for New Company, represented by the following T-account:

Cash

Beg. Bal.	11,500	(2)	75,000
(1)	150,000	(3)	60,000
(4)	6,000	(5)	5,500
(6)	30,000	(7)	25,000
(8)	12,000	(9)	15,000
End. Bal.	29,000		

The transactions that are represented by posting entries (1) through (9) in the cash account are as follows:

1. Collections on account
2. Payments for wages and salaries
3. Payments for inventory
4. Proceeds from sale of equipment
5. Payments of dividends
6. Proceeds from new bank loan
7. Payments for other cash operating expenses
8. Proceeds from sale of nontrading securities
9. Payments for taxes

From these data, prepare a statement of cash flows for New Company for the year ended December 31, 2002.

EXERCISE 13-6

DETERMINING CASH RECEIPTS AND PAYMENTS

Assuming the following data, compute:

1. Cash collected from customers.
2. Cash paid for wages and salaries.
3. Cash paid for inventory purchases.
4. Cash paid for taxes.

	Income Statement Amount for Year	Balance Sheet Beg. of Year	Balance Sheet End of Year
Sales revenue	$225,000		
Accounts receivable (net)		$20,000	$22,000
Wages and salaries expense	55,000		
Wages and salaries payable		14,000	11,000
Cost of goods sold	105,000		
Accounts payable		24,500	26,000
Inventory		34,000	28,000
Income tax expense	35,000		
Income taxes payable		15,500	18,000

EXERCISE 13-7

ADJUSTMENTS TO CASH FLOWS FROM OPERATIONS (INDIRECT METHOD)

Assume that you are using the indirect method of preparing a statement of cash flows. For each of the changes listed, indicate whether it would be added to or subtracted from net income in computing net cash flows provided by (used in) operating activities. If the change does not affect net cash flows provided by (used in) operating activities, so indicate.

1. Increase in Accounts Receivable (net)
2. Decrease in Accounts Payable
3. Increase in securities classified as cash equivalents

4. Gain on sale of equipment
5. Decrease in Inventory
6. Increase in Prepaid Insurance
7. Depreciation
8. Increase in Wages Payable
9. Decrease in Dividends Payable
10. Decrease in Interest Receivable

EXERCISE 13-8

CASH FLOWS FROM OPERATIONS (DIRECT METHOD)

Jane Ortiz is the proprietor of a small company. The results of operations for last year are shown, along with selected balance sheet data. From the information provided, determine the amount of net cash flows provided from operations, using the direct method.

Sales revenue	$200,000	
Cost of goods sold	140,000	
Gross margin		$60,000
Operating expenses:		
Wages expense	$ 25,000	
Utilities expense	1,800	
Rent expense	12,000	
Insurance expense	3,000	41,800
Net income		$18,200

	Beginning of Year	End of Year
Accounts receivable (net)	$22,000	$25,000
Inventory	35,000	30,000
Prepaid insurance	3,000	2,500
Accounts payable	14,000	17,000
Wages payable	4,000	2,000

EXERCISE 13-9

CASH FLOWS FROM OPERATIONS (INDIRECT METHOD)

Given the data in Exercise 13-8, show how the amount of net cash flows from operating activities would be calculated using the indirect method.

EXERCISE 13-10

CASH FLOWS PROVIDED BY OPERATIONS (DIRECT METHOD)

The following information was taken from the comparative financial statements of Imperial Corporation for the years ended December 31, 2002 and 2003:

Net income for 2003	$ 90,000
Sales revenue	500,000
Cost of goods sold	300,000
Depreciation expense for 2003	60,000
Amortization of goodwill for 2003	10,000
Interest expense on short-term debt for 2003	3,500
Dividends declared and paid in 2003	65,000

	Dec. 31, 2003	Dec. 31, 2002
Accounts receivable (net)	$30,000	$43,000
Inventory	50,000	42,000
Accounts payable	56,000	59,400

Use the direct method to compute cash flows provided by operating activities in 2003. (HINT: You need to calculate cash paid for operating expenses.)

EXERCISE 13-11

CASH FLOWS PROVIDED BY OPERATIONS (INDIRECT METHOD)

Given the data in Exercise 13-10, show how the amount of cash provided by operations for 2003 is computed using the indirect method.

EXERCISE 13-12

CASH FLOWS PROVIDED BY OPERATIONS (DIRECT METHOD)

The following information was taken from the comparative financial statements of Altec Industries, Inc., for the years ended December 31, 2002 and 2003:

Net income for 2003	$175,000
Sales revenue	750,000
Cost of goods sold	425,000
Depreciation expense for 2003	45,000
Amortization of goodwill for 2003	5,000
Interest expense on short-term debt for 2003	8,000
Dividends declared and paid in 2003	30,000
Utilities expense	3,000

	Dec. 31, 2003	Dec. 31, 2002
Accounts receivable (net)	$45,000	$57,000
Inventory	62,500	50,000
Accounts payable	70,000	51,500

Use the direct method to compute cash flows provided by operating activities in 2003. (HINT: You need to calculate cash paid for operating expenses.)

EXERCISE 13-13

CASH FLOWS PROVIDED BY OPERATIONS (INDIRECT METHOD)

Given the data in Exercise 13-12, show how the amount of cash flows provided by operations for 2003 is computed using the indirect method.

EXERCISE 13-14

NET CASH FLOWS (INDIRECT METHOD)

Given the following selected data for Milton Corporation, using the indirect method to report cash flows from operating activities, determine the net increase (decrease) in cash for the year ended December 31, 2003.

Net income	$ 95,000
Depreciation	25,000
Other operating expenses	140,000
Cost of goods sold	240,000
Sales revenue	500,000
Increase in accounts receivable (net)	10,000
Decrease in accounts payable	5,000
Decrease in inventory	3,000
Increase in prepaid assets	7,000
Increase in wages payable	15,000
Equipment purchased for cash	40,000
Increase in bonds payable	100,000
Dividends declared and paid	40,000
Decrease in dividends payable	2,000

EXERCISE 13-15

NET CASH FLOWS (DIRECT METHOD)

Based on the following information, determine the net increase (decrease) in cash for Porter Corporation for the year ended December 31, 2003. Use the direct method to report cash flows from operating activities.

Cash received from interest revenue	$ 14,000
Cash paid for dividends	45,000
Cash collected from customers	349,000
Cash paid for wages	254,000
Depreciation expense for the period	25,000
Cash received from issuance of common stock	200,000
Cash paid for retirement of bonds at par	100,000
Cash received on sale of equipment at book value	5,000
Cash paid for land	85,000

EXERCISE 13-16

STATEMENT OF CASH FLOWS (INDIRECT METHOD)

North Western Company provides the following financial information. Prepare a statement of cash flows for 2003, using the indirect method to report cash flows from operating activities.

North Western Company
Comparative Balance Sheets
For the Years Ended December 31, 2003 and 2002

	2003	2002
Assets		
Cash and cash equivalents	$ 4,500	$ 9,000
Accounts receivable (net)	33,000	36,000
Inventory	75,000	60,000
Plant and equipment (net)	262,500	225,000
Total assets	$375,000	$330,000
Liabilities and Stockholders' Equity		
Accounts payable	$ 60,000	$ 54,000
Capital stock	225,000	217,500
Retained earnings	90,000	58,500
Total liabilities and stockholders' equity	$375,000	$330,000

North Western Company
Income Statement
For the Year Ended December 31, 2003

Sales	$412,500
Cost of goods sold	225,000
Gross margin	$187,500
Operating expenses	135,000
Net income	$ 52,500

Note: Dividends of $21,000 were declared and paid during 2003. Depreciation expense for the year was $22,500.

EXERCISE 13-17

STATEMENT OF CASH FLOWS (DIRECT METHOD)

By analyzing the information in Exercise 13-16, prepare a statement of cash flows. Use the direct method to report cash flows from operating activities.

EXERCISE 13-18

CASH FLOW PATTERNS

Below are recent financial statement data for the following companies:

- AMAZON.COM
- COCA-COLA
- EXXONMOBIL
- MICROSOFT

Use the financial statement data to match each company with its numbers. All numbers are in millions.

	Net Income	Cash Flow from Operating Activities	Cash Flow from Investing Activities	Cash Flow from Financing Activities
1	$ (720)	$ (91)	$ (922)	$ 1,104
2	7,910	15,013	(10,985)	(4,779)
3	7,785	10,030	(11,191)	2,245
4	2,431	3,883	(3,421)	(471)

Consider the following information as you match the companies:

1. Start-ups have high positive financing cash flows relative to investing cash flows.
2. Companies with lots of property, plant, and equipment have cash from operations that is greater than net income because of lots of depreciation expense.
3. Old cash cows are spending money on investing but still have plenty left over for a net cash outflow from financing activities.

EXERCISE 13-19

ANALYZING CASH FLOWS

Study the comparative cash flow statements for MICROSOFT in Appendix A. What observations do you have about Microsoft's cash flow position? From a liquidity standpoint, is the trend over the last few years positive or negative? Explain.

problems

PROBLEM 13-1

TRANSACTION ANALYSIS

Development Corporation reports the following summary data for the current year:

a. Sales revenue totaled $251,500.
b. Interest revenue for the period was $2,200.
c. Interest expense for the period was $800.
d. Cost of goods sold for the period was $156,000.
e. Operating expenses, all paid in cash (except for depreciation of $15,000), were $48,000.
f. Income tax expense for the period was $8,000.
g. Accounts receivable (net) increased by $10,000 during the period.
h. Accounts payable decreased by $5,000 during the period.
i. Inventory at the beginning and end of the period was $25,000 and $35,000, respectively.
j. Cash increased during the period by $5,000.

Assume all other current asset and current liability accounts remained constant during the period.

Required:

1. Compute the amount of cash collected from customers.
2. Compute the amount of cash paid for inventory.
3. Compute the amount of cash paid for operating expenses.
4. Compute the amount of cash flows provided by (used in) operations.
5. **Interpretive Question:** What must have been the combined amount of cash flows provided by (used in) investing and financing activities?

PROBLEM 13-2

ANALYSIS OF THE CASH ACCOUNT

The following information, in T-account format, is provided for the M & M Company for the year 2003:

Cash Account

Beg. Bal.	15,400	(b)	56,500
(a)	147,000	(c)	23,000
(d)	3,500	(f)	59,700
(e)	15,000	(g)	1,600
		(h)	2,400
End. Bal.	37,700		

Additional information:

a. Sales revenue for the period was $145,000. Accounts receivable (net) decreased $2,000 during the period.
b. Net purchases of $58,000 were made during 2003, all on account. Accounts payable increased $1,500 during the period.
c. The equipment account increased by $18,000 during the year.
d. One piece of equipment that cost $5,000, with a net book value of $3,000, was sold for a $500 gain.
e. The company borrowed $15,000 from its bank during the year.
f. Various operating expenses were all paid in cash, except for depreciation of $1,800. Total operating expenses were $61,500.
g. Interest expense for the year was $1,200. The interest payable account decreased by $400 during the year.
h. Income tax expense for the year was $3,600. The income taxes payable account increased by $1,200 during the year.

Required:

1. From the information given, reconstruct the journal entries that must have been made during the year (omit explanations).
2. Prepare a statement of cash flows for M & M Company for the year ended December 31, 2003.

PROBLEM 13-3

ANALYZING CASH FLOWS

The following information was provided by the treasurer of Surety, Inc., for the year 2003:

a. Cash sales for the year were $50,000; sales on account totaled $60,000.
b. Cost of goods sold was 50% of total sales.
c. All inventory is purchased on account.
d. Depreciation on equipment was $31,000 for the year.
e. Amortization of goodwill was $2,000.
f. Collections of accounts receivable were $38,000.
g. Payments on accounts payable for inventory equaled $39,000.
h. Rent expense paid in cash was $11,000.
i. The company issued 20,000 shares of $10-par stock for $240,000.
j. Land valued at $106,000 was acquired by issuance of a bond with a par value of $100,000.
k. Equipment was purchased for cash at a cost of $84,000.

l. Dividends of $46,000 were declared but not yet paid.
m. The company paid $15,000 of dividends that had been declared the previous year.
n. A machine used on the assembly line was sold for $12,000. The machine had a book value of $7,000.
o. Another machine with a book value of $500 was scrapped and was reported as an ordinary loss. No cash was received on this transaction.
p. The cash account increased $191,000 during the year to a total of $274,000.

Required:

1. Compute the beginning balance in the cash account.
2. How much cash was provided by (or used in) operating activities?
3. How much cash was provided by (or used in) investing activities?
4. How much cash was provided by (or used in) financing activities?
5. Would all the above items, (a) through (p), be reported on a cash flow statement? Explain.

PROBLEM 13-4

CASH FLOWS FROM OPERATIONS (INDIRECT METHOD)

Gardner Enterprises reported a net loss of $40,000 for the year just ended. Relevant data for the company follow.

	Beginning of Year	End of Year
Cash and cash equivalents	$ 50,000	$ 20,000
Accounts receivable (net)	80,000	65,000
Inventory	123,000	130,000
Prepaid expenses	7,500	4,500
Accounts payable	55,000	60,000
Accrued liabilities	10,000	4,000
Dividends payable	25,000	35,000
Depreciation for the year, $43,000		
Dividends declared, $35,000		

Required:

1. Using the indirect method, determine the net cash flows provided by (used in) operating activities for Gardner Enterprises.
2. **Interpretive Question:** Explain how Gardner Enterprises can pay cash dividends during a year when it reports a net loss.

PROBLEM 13-5

CASH FLOWS FROM OPERATIONS (DIRECT METHOD)

Super Sales, Inc., shows the following information in its accounting records at year-end:

Sales revenue	$890,000
Interest revenue	12,000
Cost of goods sold	425,000
Wages expense	225,000
Depreciation expense	50,000
Other (cash) operating expenses	84,000
Dividends declared	40,000

Selected balance sheet data are as follows:

	Beginning of Year	End of Year
Accounts receivable (net)	$ 55,000	$ 78,000
Interest receivable	10,000	12,000
Inventory	225,000	220,000
Accounts payable	42,000	35,000
Wages payable	20,000	25,000
Dividends payable	35,000	40,000

Required:

1. Using the direct method, compute the net cash flows provided by (used in) operating activities for Super Sales, Inc.
2. **Interpretive Question:** Explain the main differences between the net amount of cash flows from operations and net income (loss).

PROBLEM 13-6

CASH FLOWS FROM OPERATIONS (INDIRECT AND DIRECT METHODS)

The following combined income and retained earnings statement, along with selected balance sheet data, are provided for Roper Company:

Roper Company
Combined Income and Retained Earnings Statement
For the Year Ended December 31, 2003

Net sales revenue		$85,000
Other revenues		4,500*
Total revenues		$89,500
Expenses:		
Cost of goods sold	$51,000	
Selling and administrative expenses	14,700	
Depreciation expense	3,200	
Interest expense	1,400	
Total expenses		70,300
Income before taxes		$19,200
Income taxes		5,760
Net income		$13,440
Retained earnings, January 1, 2003		33,500
		$46,940
Dividends declared and paid		2,500
Retained earnings, December 31, 2003		$44,440

*Gain on sale of equipment (cost, $9,500; book value, $6,000; sales price $10,500).

	Beginning of Year	End of Year
Accounts receivable (net)	$10,500	$11,000
Inventory	19,300	18,000
Prepaid expenses	950	700
Accounts payable	7,200	8,000
Interest payable	1,500	1,000
Income taxes payable	500	2,500

Required:

1. Using the indirect method, compute the net cash flows from operations for Roper Company for 2003.
2. Using the direct method, compute the net cash flows from operations for Roper Company for 2003.
3. What is the impact of dividends paid on net cash flows from operations? Explain.

PROBLEM 13-7

COMPUTATION OF NET INCOME FROM CASH FLOWS FROM OPERATIONS (DIRECT METHOD)

The following partially completed work sheet is provided for ATM Corporation, which uses the direct method in computing net cash flows from operations:

ATM Corporation
Partial Work Sheet—Cash Flows from Operations
(Direct Method)
For the Year Ended December 31, 2003

	Accrual Basis	Adjustments		Cash Basis
		Debits	Credits	
Net sales revenue				$150,000
Expenses:				
Cost of goods sold				$ 75,000
Depreciation				0
Loss on sale of equipment				0
Other (cash) expenses				26,000
Total expenses				$101,000
Net income (net cash flows from operations)				$ 49,000

Key:

1. Decrease in Accounts Receivable (net), $4,500.
2. Loss on sale of equipment, $1,500.
3. Increase in Inventory, $10,000.
4. Incrcasc in Accounts Payable, $3,000.
5. Depreciation for the year, $8,000.
6. Decrease in Prepaid Expenses, $1,000.
7. Increase in Accrued Liabilities, $2,500.

Required: Complete the work sheet with the key items above and compute the net income (loss) to be reported by ATM Corporation on its income statement for 2003.

PROBLEM 13-8

INCOME STATEMENT FROM CASH FLOW DATA

Jackson Corporation computed the amount of cash flows from operations using both the direct and indirect methods, as follows:

Direct method:	
Collections from customers	$445,000
Payments to suppliers	(130,000)
Payments for operating expenses	(210,000)
Cash flows provided by operating activities	$105,000
Indirect method:	
Net income	$ 95,000
Depreciation	20,000
Gain on sale of equipment	(7,500)
Decrease in inventory	1,000
Decrease in accounts receivable (net)	1,500
Decrease in accounts payable	(7,500)
Increase in miscellaneous accrued payable	2,500
Cash flows provided by operating activities	$105,000

Required: Using the data provided, prepare an income statement for Jackson Corporation for the year 2003.

PROBLEM 13-9

STATEMENT OF CASH FLOWS (INDIRECT METHOD)

JEM Company's comparative balance sheets for 2002 and 2003 are provided.

JEM Company
Comparative Balance Sheets
December 31, 2003 and 2002

	2003	2002
Assets		
Cash and cash equivalents	$ 30,500	$ 10,000
Accounts receivable (net)	64,500	51,000
Inventory	100,000	115,000
Equipment	55,000	30,000
Accumulated depreciation—equipment	(21,500)	(14,000)
Total assets	$228,500	$192,000
Liabilities and Stockholders' Equity		
Accounts payable	$ 52,500	$ 46,000
Long-term notes payable	70,000	50,000
Capital stock	60,000	60,000
Retained earnings	46,000	36,000
Total liabilities and stockholders' equity	$228,500	$192,000

The following additional information is available:

a. Net income for the year 2003 (as reported on the income statement) was $50,000.
b. Dividends of $40,000 were declared and paid.
c. Equipment that cost $8,000 and had a book value of $1,000 was sold during the year for $2,500.

Required: Based on the information provided, prepare a statement of cash flows for JEM Company for the year ended December 31, 2003. Use the indirect method to report cash flows from operating activities.

PROBLEM 13-10

STATEMENT OF CASH FLOWS (DIRECT METHOD)

Financial statement data for Continental Stores, Inc., are provided. (All numbers are shown rounded to the nearest thousand, with 000's omitted.)

Continental Stores, Inc.
Income and Retained Earnings Statements
For the Year Ended December 31, 2003

Sales revenue	$1,290
Cost of goods sold	978
Gross margin	$ 312
Operating expenses:	
Sales and administrative expenses	$ 105
Depreciation expense	14
Other expenses	87
Total operating expenses	$ 206
Income before taxes	$ 106
Income taxes	51
Net income	$ 55
Dividends paid	10
Increase in retained earnings	$ 45

Continental Stores, Inc.
Comparative Balance Sheets
December 31, 2003 and 2002

	2003	2002
Assets		
Cash and cash equivalents	$ 752	$ 725
Accounts receivable (net)	461	448
Inventory	226	953
Land	1,340	1,240
Store fixtures	369	369
Accumulated depreciation, store fixtures	(51)	(37)
Total assets	$3,097	$3,698
Liabilities and Stockholders' Equity		
Liabilities:		
Accounts payable	$ 175	$ 378
Short-term notes payable	525	768
Long-term debt	804	1,004
Total liabilities	$1,504	$2,150
Stockholders' equity:		
Common stock	$ 448	$ 448
Paid-in capital in excess of par	500	500
Retained earnings	645	600
Total stockholders' equity	$1,593	$1,548
Total liabilities and stockholders' equity	$3,097	$3,698

Required:

1. Compute the net cash flows from operations using the direct method.
2. **Interpretive Question:** Comment on the difference between net income and net cash flows from operations.
3. Prepare a statement of cash flows for Continental Stores, Inc., for the year ended December 31, 2003.

PROBLEM 13-11

STATEMENT OF CASH FLOWS (INDIRECT METHOD)

1. Using the data from Problem 13-10, prepare a statement of cash flows. Use the indirect method to report cash flows from operating activities.
2. **Interpretive Question:** What are the main differences between a statement of cash flows prepared using the indirect method and one prepared using the direct method?

PROBLEM 13-12

UNIFYING CONCEPTS: ANALYSIS OF OPERATING, INVESTING, AND FINANCING ACTIVITIES

Grant Kesler is the manager and one of three brothers who own the Rocky Mountain Auto Parts Company in Denver, Colorado. Grant is pleased that sales were up last year and that his new, small company has been able to expand and open a second store in Denver. After reviewing the balance sheet, however, Grant is concerned that Cash shows a negative balance. He can't understand how his company can show net income, based on increased sales, yet have a negative Cash position. He is concerned about what his banker is going to say when they meet next month to discuss a loan for the company to expand to a third store. Grant provides the following financial information and asks for your help.

Rocky Mountain Auto Parts Company
Income Statement
For the Year Ended December 31, 2003

Sales		$150,000
Less cost of goods sold		63,000
Gross margin		$ 87,000
Operating expenses:		
Salary and wages	$32,000	
Depreciation	4,500	
Other operating expenses	12,400	48,900
Operating income		$ 38,100
Income taxes		8,200
Net income		$ 29,900

Rocky Mountain Auto Parts Company
Comparative Balance Sheets
As of December 31, 2003 and 2002

	2003	2002
Assets		
Current assets:		
Cash	$ (3,200)	$ 6,400
Accounts receivable (net)	3,100	2,700
Inventory	63,000	42,000
Total current assets	$ 62,900	$51,100
Other assets:		
Property, plant, and equipment	$ 82,300	$39,000
Less accumulated depreciation	(20,100)	(15,600)
Total other assets	$ 62,200	$23,400
Total assets	$125,100	$74,500
Liabilities and Stockholders' Equity		
Current liabilities:		
Accounts payable	$ 6,400	$ 5,700
Wages payable	1,500	1,300
Taxes payable	1,900	2,100
Total current liabilities	$ 9,800	$ 9,100
Other liabilities:		
Notes payable	30,000	10,000
Total liabilities	$ 39,800	$19,100
Stockholders' equity:		
Capital stock	$ 40,000	$40,000
Retained earnings	45,300	15,400
Total stockholders' equity	$ 85,300	$55,400
Total liabilities and stockholders' equity	$125,100	$74,500

Required:

1. Using the direct method, compute the net cash flows from operations. Also determine net cash flows for investing and financing activities.
2. **Interpretive Question:** Is Rocky Mountain Auto Parts Company in a good liquidity position? As Mr. Kesler's banker, would you loan him more money to fund the company's expansion?

competency enhancement opportunities

- Analyzing Real Company Information
- International Case
- Ethics Case
- Writing Assignment
- The Debate
- Cumulative Spreadsheet Project
- Internet Search

The following additional assignments provide opportunities for students to develop critical thinking, ethical perspectives, oral and written communication skills, experience with electronic research, and teamwork through group and business activities.

ANALYZING REAL COMPANY INFORMATION

• ***Analyzing 13-1 (Microsoft)***

The 1999 annual report for MICROSOFT appears in Appendix A. Locate that annual report and consider the following questions:

1. Does Microsoft present the three cash flow statement categories—operating, investing, and financing—in the same order as that illustrated in the chapter?
2. In 1999, Microsoft spent $11.191 billion on various investing activities. Were the cash flows from operations sufficient to pay for these investments?
3. In its 1999 operating activities section, Microsoft reports both $5.877 billion and $4.526 billion in relation to unearned revenue. Exactly what does each of these numbers represent? Compare these numbers to the corresponding numbers in 1997 and comment on the reason for such a big difference.
4. Did Microsoft pay any cash dividends to common stockholders during 1999? Did Microsoft make any payments to common stockholders during the year?

• ***Analyzing 13-2 (The Coca-Cola Company)***

The 1999 statement of cash flows for THE COCA-COLA COMPANY is given on page 665. Use the statement to answer the following questions:

1. Compute Coca-Cola's "Net cash provided by operations after reinvestment." This amount is computed by subtracting "Net cash used in investing activities" from "Net cash provided by operating activities." Interpret the results of the calculation for Coca-Cola for the period 1997–1999.
2. In its operating activities section, Coca-Cola subtracts gains on sales of assets in computing net cash provided by operating activities. Why are these gains subtracted?
3. Think of the dealings that The Coca-Cola Company has with its shareholders. The shareholders give money to the company by purchasing new shares of stock. In turn, the company returns cash to shareholders by paying cash dividends and by repurchasing shares of stock. For the three-year period 1997–1999, did The Coca-Cola Company receive more cash from its shareholders than it paid back to them, or did it pay more cash to its shareholders than it received? Show your calculations.
4. Look carefully at the statement of cash flows. Did the U.S. dollar get stronger or weaker during the three-year period 1997–1999?

The Coca-Cola Company and Subsidiaries
Consolidated Statements of Cash Flows
For the Years Ended December 31, 1997, 1998, 1999
(in millions)

Year Ended December 31,	1999	1998	1997
Operating activities:			
Net income	$ 2,431	$ 3,533	$ 4,129
Depreciation and amortization	792	645	626
Deferred income taxes	97	(38)	380
Equity income, net of dividends	292	31	(108)
Foreign currency adjustments	(41)	21	37
Gains on issuances of stock by equity investees	—	(27)	(363)
Gains on sales of assets, including bottling interests	(49)	(306)	(639)
Other operating charges	799	73	60
Other items	119	51	(42)
Net change in operating assets and liabilities	(557)	(550)	(47)
Net cash provided by operating activities	$ 3,883	$ 3,433	$ 4,033
Investing activities:			
Acquisitions and investments, principally trademarks and bottling companies	$(1,876)	$(1,428)	$(1,100)
Purchases of investments and other assets	(518)	(610)	(459)
Proceeds from disposals of investments and other assets	176	1,036	1,999
Purchases of property, plant and equipment	(1,069)	(863)	(1,093)
Proceeds from disposals of property, plant and equipment	45	54	71
Other investing activities	(179)	(350)	82
Net cash used in investing activities	$(3,421)	$(2,161)	$ (500)
Financing activities:			
Issuances of debt	$ 3,411	$ 1,818	$ 155
Payments of debt	(2,455)	(410)	(751)
Issuances of stock	168	302	150
Purchases of stock for treasury	(15)	(1,563)	(1,262)
Dividends	(1,580)	(1,480)	(1,387)
Net cash used in financing activities	$ (471)	$(1,333)	$(3,095)
Effect of exchange rate changes on cash and cash equivalents	$ (28)	$ (28)	$ (134)
Cash and cash equivalents:			
Net increase (decrease) during the year	(37)	(89)	304
Balance at beginning of the year	1,648	1,737	1,433
Balance at end of year	$ 1,611	$ 1,648	$ 1,737

INTERNATIONAL CASE

• *Glaxo Wellcome*

GLAXO WELLCOME, a British company, is one of the largest pharmaceutical firms in the world. The name "Glaxo" comes from the company's first major product line, baby food products that were sold with the slogan, "Builds Bonnie Babies." Growth of the company in recent years has been driven by sales of Zantac, an anti-ulcer drug.

Glaxo Wellcome's 1999 statement of cash flows is shown on the next page. Look at the statement and answer the following questions. (Note: Translations of British accounting terms into American English are shown in square brackets.)

1. In a U.S. statement of cash flows, cash flows are sorted into three categories. How many categories does Glaxo Wellcome use?
2. List some of the items that Glaxo Wellcome has excluded from the computation of cash from operating activities that would be included if the statement of cash flows were prepared according to U.S. standards.
3. Given your answer in (2), which is a better indication of cash from operating activities: the number reported by Glaxo Wellcome using a British classification of cash flows, or the number that would be reported using a U.S. classification? Explain your answer.
4. If you were to redo Glaxo Wellcome's statement of cash flows for 1999 using the U.S. classification scheme with just three categories, the total of these three categories would result in the same net change in cash (36) reported by Glaxo Wellcome using the British classification. Why is this?

Glaxo Wellcome plc
Consolidated Statement of Cash Flows
31st December 1999
(in millions of £)

	1999	1998
Trading profit	2,625	2,683
Depreciation	360	358
Impairment	68	—
Amortization of goodwill	9	6
Loss/(profit) on sale of tangible fixed assets	7	7
Profit on sale of equity investments	(139)	(38)
Increase in stocks [inventory]	(391)	(297)
Decrease/(increase) in debtors [accounts receivable]	(126)	(250)
(Decrease)/increase in creditors [accounts payable]	64	30
(Decrease)/increase in pension and other provisions	166	(41)
Other	(37)	(110)
Net cash inflow from operating activities	**2,606**	**2,348**
Earnings from joint ventures and associated undertakings	**2**	**40**
Returns on investment and servicing of finance		
Interest received	110	112
Interest paid	(198)	(200)
Cost of financing	(2)	—
Dividends paid to minority shareholders	(31)	(9)
	(121)	**(97)**
Taxation paid		
Corporate taxation	**(672)**	**(626)**
Capital expenditure less disposals		
Purchase of tangible fixed assets	(597)	(475)
Sale of tangible fixed assets	82	55
	(515)	**(420)**
Acquisitions and disposals		
Purchase of businesses	(67)	(156)
Investment in joint ventures and associated undertakings	(3)	(16)
Dissolution of joint ventures	—	20
Disposal of interest in associate	41	—
Purchase of own shares	(421)	(10)
Purchase of equity investments	(7)	(51)
Sale of equity investments	118	54
	(339)	**(159)**
Equity dividends paid	**(1,305)**	**(1,255)**
Net cash inflows before financing	**(344)**	**(169)**
Financing		
Management of liquid resources	(42)	(251)
Issue of ordinary share capital	104	284
Increase in long-term loans	110	5
Repayment of long-term loans	(9)	(63)
Net repayment of short-term loans	150	117
New obligations under finance [capital] leases	(5)	(4)
Net cash inflow from financing activities	**308**	**88**
(Decrease)/increase in cash in the year	**(36)**	**(81)**

ETHICS CASE

• *Manipulating the Federal Budget Deficit*

Assume that you are the paymaster in charge of all U.S. Department of Defense (DOD) payroll matters. The total amount that you disburse in payroll checks in any given week is in excess of $1 billion.

Assume also that tax receipts have been lower than expected and that a federal budget deficit, and not a surplus, is now projected. Currently, Congress is struggling to reduce the projected budget deficit. It is an election year, and the members of Congress are worried that they will be stuck with a "tax and spend" label if the government runs a deficit this year. Of course, the DOD budget has been scrutinized very carefully to reduce reported expenditures as much as possible.

Yesterday, a congressional leader came to your office with a disturbing proposal. Because the federal budget numbers are reported on a cash basis, rather than on an accrual basis, expenses are reported when they are paid instead of when they are incurred. This year, the final DOD payday of the year happens to fall on the last day of the federal government's fiscal year (September 30). The congressional leader suggested that you delay issuing the payroll checks by one day. This would push the actual payment of the cash into the next fiscal year. Thus, even though the payment would be for services performed in the current fiscal year, the expense wouldn't be reported until next year. With this simple trick, the reported deficit for this year (an election year) can be reduced by $1 billion.

What should you do?

WRITING ASSIGNMENT

• *Convincing the Old-Timers of the Need for Cash Flow Data*

You are the chief accountant for Harry Monst Company. The president of the company is a former accountant who worked her way up through the management ranks over the course of 30 years. She is a great manager, but her knowledge of accounting is outdated.

Harry Monst Company has a revolving line of credit with Texas Commercial Bank. A new loan officer has just been put in charge of the Harry Monst account. The new loan officer is surprised to see that Harry Monst has not been submitting a statement of cash flows along with the rest of the financial statements that comprise the annual loan review packet. The new loan officer called you and asked for a statement of cash flows.

You were surprised when you took the completed statement of cash flows to the president for her signature. She refused to sign, stating that she had never looked at or prepared a statement of cash flows in her career and she wouldn't start now.

Write a one-page memo to the president with the objective of convincing her of the usefulness of the statement of cash flows.

THE DEBATE

• *No One Can Understand the Indirect Method!*

Companies have the option of reporting cash flows from operating activities using either the direct or the indirect method. Many financial statement users think that the information provided with the direct method is easier to understand. In spite of this, more than 95% of large U.S. companies use the indirect method.

Divide your group into two teams.

- One team represents the "Direct Method." Prepare a two-minute oral presentation arguing that the direct method is just what its name implies—direct and easy to understand. The indirect method is merely an attempt by accountants to confuse financial statement users.
- The other team represents the "Indirect Method." Prepare a two-minute oral presentation arguing that the direct method may seem easy to understand, but only to unsophisticated financial statement readers. The indirect method reveals much more useful information.

CUMULATIVE SPREADSHEET PROJECT

This spreadsheet assignment is a continuation of the spreadsheet assignments given in earlier chapters. If you completed those spreadsheets, you have a head start on this one.

1. Handyman wishes to prepare a forecasted balance sheet, income statement, and statement of cash flows for 2004. Use the original financial statement numbers for 2003 [given in part (1) of the Cumulative Spreadsheet Project assignment in Chapter 2] as the basis for the forecast along with the following additional information:
   a. Sales in 2004 are expected to increase by 40% over 2003 sales of $700.
   b. In 2004, Handyman expects to acquire new property, plant, and equipment costing $80.
   c. The $160 in operating expenses reported in 2003 breaks down as follows: $5 depreciation expense, $155 other operating expenses.
   d. No new long-term debt will be acquired in 2004.
   e. No cash dividends will be paid in 2004.
   f. New short-term loans payable will be acquired in an amount sufficient to make Handyman's current ratio in 2004 exactly equal to 2.0.

Construction of the forecasted statement of cash flows for 2004 involves analyzing the forecasted income statement for 2004, along with the balance sheets for 2003 (actual) and 2004 (forecasted).

For this exercise, the current assets are expected to behave as follows:

a. Cash will increase at the same rate as sales.
b. The forecasted amount of accounts receivable in 2004 is determined using the forecasted value for the average collection period (computed using the end-of-period Accounts Receivable balance). The average collection period for 2004 is expected to be 14.08 days. This is from the *Chapter 6 spreadsheet.*

c. The forecasted amount of inventory in 2004 is determined using the forecasted value for the number of days' sales in inventory (computed using the end-of-period Inventory balance). The number of days' sales in inventory for 2004 is expected to be 107.6 days. This is from the *Chapter 7 spreadsheet.*
d. The forecasted amount of accounts payable in 2004 is determined using the forecasted value of the number of days' purchases in accounts payable (computed using the end-of-period Accounts Payable balance). The number of days' purchases in accounts payable for 2004 is expected to be 48.34 days. This is from the *Chapter 7 spreadsheet.*

Clearly state any additional assumptions that you make.

2. Repeat (1), with the following changes in assumptions:
   a. The average collection period is expected to be 9.06 days with days' sales in inventory remaining at 107.6 days and days' purchases in payables remaining at 48.34 days.
   b. The average collection period is expected to be 20 days with days' sales in inventory remaining at 107.6 days and days' purchases in payables remaining at 48.34 days.
   c. Days' sales in inventory are expected to be 66.2 days with the average collection period remaining at 14.08 days and days' purchases in payables remaining at 48.34 days.
   d. Days' sales in inventory are expected to be 150 days with the average collection period remaining at 14.08 days and days' purchases in payables remaining at 48.34 days.
3. Comment on the forecasted values of cash from operating activities in 2004 under each of the scenarios given in (2).

INTERNET SEARCH

• *Home Depot*

Access HOME DEPOT's Web site at http://www.homedepot.com. Sometimes Web addresses change, so if this address does not work, access the Web site for this textbook (http://albrecht.swcollege.com) for an updated link.

Once you've gained access to the site, answer the following questions:

1. Locate Home Depot's services site and determine how many different ways Home Depot can help you finance your home improvement plans.
2. Home Depot is highly supportive of various community efforts. Use its Web site to identify the community activities that Home Depot sponsors or is associated with.
3. Home Depot's Web site also includes a number of calculators designed to help buyers determine how much of a given item they need to purchase. Access the calculator for ceramic tile and determine how many tiles you would have to purchase if the room is 10 feet by 20 feet, the surface tiles are 12 inches by 12 inches, and the border tiles are 6 inches by 6 inches.
4. Find Home Depot's most recent set of financial statements. In its statement of cash flows, does Home Depot use the direct method or the indirect method in reporting cash from operating activities?

5. In the most recent year, which is greater—Home Depot's net income or its cash flows from operating activities?
6. Did Home Depot pay any cash dividends in the most recent year?

part m1

Foundations

Introduction to Management Accounting

chapter m1

learning objectives After studying this chapter, you should be able to:

1 Understand the essential differences between management accounting and financial accounting, as illustrated by managerial use of the ROI formula.

2 Understand that successfully managing a company requires good information that supports effective planning, controlling, and evaluating processes.

3 Know how the concepts of fixed and variable costs are used in C-V-P analysis in the management planning process.

4 Realize how the product cost classifications of direct materials, direct labor, and overhead are used in the management controlling process.

5 Be able to perform a simple segment analysis using the concepts of direct, indirect, and opportunity costs in the management evaluating process.

6 Understand that management accounting still continues to evolve.

setting the stage

You've probably never heard of **E. I. DU PONT DE NEMOURS AND COMPANY**, but you may be familiar with its more common name, **DUPONT**. Some of this company's best-known brands are Teflon® resins, SilverStone® nonstick finish, Lycra® spandex fiber, Stainmaster® stain-resistant carpet, Kevlar® fiber, Corian® solid surface material, Mylar® polyester films, Tyvek® spunbonded olefin fabric, and Coolmax® and Cordura® textile fibers. With revenues of nearly $28 billion and net income of nearly $8 billion in 1999, DuPont ranked number 42 in the Fortune 500 list. DuPont operates in approximately 70 countries worldwide with roughly 135 manufacturing and processing facilities. Working in these facilities are 94,000 employees; nearly one-third of them work outside the United States. In addition to its manufacturing and processing facilities, DuPont has more than 40 research and development and customer service labs in the United States and more than 35 labs in 11 other countries. This is a big company! So what does this company have to do with you (other than that you probably use many of its products)? In 1903, the owners of DuPont created for themselves a challenge that no one had ever before attempted. The way they handled this challenge profoundly affected the way American companies are managed today and permanently changed our approach to management accounting. So, if you want to understand the importance of management accounting in America (as well as in many other countries around the world), you need to put yourself in the shoes of three cousins, Alfred, Coleman, and Pierre du Pont.

One of the oldest continuously operating industrial enterprises in the world, the DuPont company was established in 1802 near Wilmington, Delaware, by a French immigrant, Eleuthére Irénée du Pont de Nemours, to produce black powder. Essentially, E. I. du Pont built a product that ignited when it was supposed to. Public enthusiasm for du Pont's product continued, and the company grew into a major family corporation. The start of the twentieth century brought increased competition from other companies, however, and DuPont fell on hard times. Seizing the opportunity created by the crisis, three of E. I. du Pont's great-grandsons, Alfred I. du Pont, Thomas Coleman du Pont, and Pierre Samuel du Pont, offered to purchase the firm's assets from the family in exchange for bonds and stock in a new corporation (a transaction known today as a leveraged buyout). The offer was accepted. In 1902, the company was restructured to look for new business and create new products through research and development.

Alfred, Coleman, and Pierre had some pretty innovative ideas about running a business. In 1903, the gunpowder industry looked much like any other industry in America. All of DuPont's competitors in the industry focused primarily on manufacturing. They purchased raw materials (such as charcoal, sodium nitrate, and crude glycerin) from suppliers and distributed their gunpowder products to customers using independent wholesalers and general merchants. For the du Pont cousins, the business they purchased looked a lot like the left side of Exhibit 1-1. After the purchase, they decided to expand the business beyond the manufacturing of high explosives, smokeless gunpowder, and black blasting powder. The DuPonts started "forward integrating" into the distribution business by creating their own network of branch sales offices scattered across the United States. They also "backward integrated" by buying out many (but not all) of their suppliers. When the dust finally settled, DuPont was America's first large-scale "vertically integrated" company (the right side of Exhibit 1-1). Most of the profits usually earned by outside companies (either selling DuPont products to customers or selling raw materials to DuPont) were now consolidated within DuPont. This type of organization is quite common today, but it was a strange-looking company at the turn of the twentieth century. Although Alfred, Coleman, and Pierre were confident that their new way of doing business was going to make them a lot of money (they were right!), they had created a serious challenge for themselves. They knew how to run a manufacturing business, but now they were in the purchasing and sales business as well. These were three very different businesses, each with its own way of communicating results and measuring success. The three cousins had a limited amount of time and resources to invest in developing their company. How were they going to be able to effectively plan schedules, control operations, and evaluate each division to determine additional investment needs?

exhibit 1-1 A Comparative Look at the DuPont Company before and after 1903

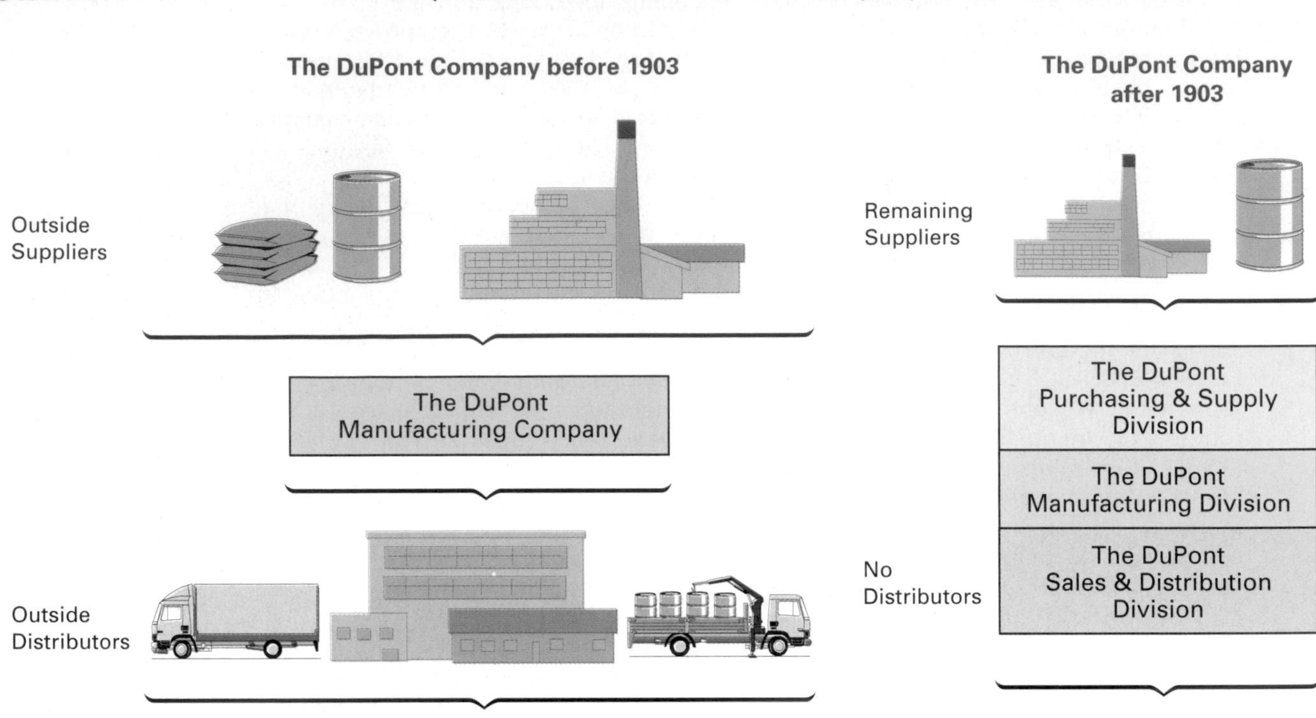

Essentially, Alfred, Coleman, and Pierre had an accounting problem. What would you have done if you were in their shoes in 1903? What the cousins did to handle the challenge was, to say the least, impressive.[1]

This chapter introduces management accounting and distinguishes it from financial accounting. We will use DuPont to introduce key management accounting concepts such as ROI. It is important to understand that the purpose of management accounting is to fulfill a competitive need. DuPont had a competitive need to manage a very large and diverse organization and so established ROI as an important management device. Accounting tools such as ROI are used to support the management process of planning, controlling, and evaluating. Every business organization uses a variety of accounting tools to support these important management processes. In this chapter we will use cost-volume-profit (C-V-P) analysis to introduce the planning process, product cost classifications to introduce the controlling process, and segment analysis to introduce the evaluating process. In working through a brief overview of these tools, you will be introduced to a variety of cost accounting terms. However, you also need to be aware that effective management in modern organizations requires management accountants to provide not only cost data, but also quality- and time-based information as well. Hence, this chapter has three purposes.

1. *To distinguish management accounting from financial accounting.*
2. *To outline the management process of planning, controlling, and evaluating, as well as the strategic issues of cost, quality, and time.*
3. *To introduce management accounting terminologies in the context of several key management tools.*

1 Historical sources: A. D. Chandler, *The Invisible Hand* (Boston: HBS Press, 1977); H. T. Johnson and R. S. Kaplan, *Relevance Lost* (Boston: HBS Press, 1987); the DuPont home page at http://www.dupont.com/corp/gbl-company/history.html; Microsoft Encarta 1994.

1

Understand the essential differences between management accounting and financial accounting, as illustrated by managerial use of the ROI formula.

MANAGEMENT ACCOUNTING VERSUS FINANCIAL ACCOUNTING

Knowing a little of the history of management accounting is very useful in understanding the differences between management accounting and financial accounting. Frankly, a lot of professionals have a difficult time separating the purposes of management accounting and financial accounting. Overall, the purpose of financial accounting, as determined by several regulatory groups, is to establish an objective and consistent format for all companies to use in reporting financial results to the public. In contrast, management accounting is established by individual companies that want to create proprietary information for internal use that has competitive value. The "rules" of management accounting are not governed by anything other than market forces.

The Return on Investment (ROI) Technique

By the time Alfred, Coleman, and Pierre du Pont had finished buying out suppliers and establishing sales offices throughout the country, they had created a giant organization. The fact that their company was big, however, is not what makes their situation interesting. Francis Cabot Lowell, Edward Henry Harriman, Andrew Carnegie, and Rowland H. Macy each had already created and successfully managed huge companies. Their companies, however, all focused on doing *one thing well*—making cloth, moving railway cars, producing steel, or selling goods. The du Ponts, on the other hand, were trying to combine within one company many different types of businesses: wholesale purchasing, raw materials and finished goods manufacturing, and retail distribution. They had a huge management hierarchy, complicated production processes, geographically dispersed business locations, and inventory that needed to turn over rapidly. Each of these divisions required constant attention and additional capital investments in order to grow and flourish. The du Ponts knew they could make or lose money in any part of this monstrous new company. Obviously, neither they nor their capital resources could be everywhere at once. They needed to make trade-off decisions. The problem was, with very diverse divisions, how could they decide which divisions should receive additional investments of time and money? They couldn't really compare the cost reports of retail stores in Denver with a black powder manufacturing factory in Delaware or with a sodium nitrate processing plant in Chile. Having all these unique business activities also made it quite difficult to relate various measures of efficiency directly to overall company profit. The first thing the new DUPONT management team did was develop extensive budgets to coordinate the flow of resources from raw materials to the final customer. But they still needed a measure for comparing performance in the firm's separate divisions with performance of the whole company. Enter the accountant. (Actually, he was an electrical engineer turned accountant. Nevertheless, if a management accountant hall of fame existed, the bust of F. Donaldson Brown would grace its entrance!)

return on investment (ROI) A measure of operating performance and efficiency in utilizing assets; computed in its simplest form by dividing net income by average total assets.

asset turnover An overall measure of how effectively assets are used during a period; computed by dividing revenue by total assets.

profit margin An overall measure of the profitability of operations during a period; computed by dividing profit by revenue.

Donaldson Brown, along with other executives at DuPont, realized that every division required an investment in capital (assets) in order to be in business. The overall goal of every business should be to effectively use its assets to make a profit. For example, an explosives plant earning \$50,000 in profit with required capital investments of \$1 million would not be performing as well as a major distributing division earning an equal \$50,000 in profit with only \$500,000 in required capital assets. If you had \$1 million to invest, which division would receive your money? The distributing division is earning a 10% return (\$50,000 ÷ \$500,000) on the DuPont investment in inventory, equipment, and buildings. The explosives plant is earning only a 5% return on investment. Although this simple formula was not really new to American business in the first part of the twentieth century, Brown took the idea of **return on investment (ROI)** and turned it into a management technique that could be used to manage any kind of business operation at DuPont. Exhibit 1-2 illustrates how the DuPont ROI formula could be expanded into a comprehensive measurement system for performance. Study this exhibit for a moment. If any company division (or the company as a whole) is generating low ROI, the DuPont management team can immediately begin analyzing the problem. Is **asset turnover** too low? Perhaps the division needs to reduce its investment in assets or work to improve sales. Is the **profit margin** less than adequate? Maybe the division needs to concentrate on reducing selling expenses or manufacturing costs. The ROI tool allowed the du Pont cousins to be hugely successful in managing the country's first integrated

exhibit 1-2 An Illustration of the DuPont ROI Formula (simple and complex)

The DuPont ROI Formula (simple)

$$\text{Return on Investment (ROI)} = \frac{\text{Profit}}{\text{Revenue}} \times \frac{\text{Revenue}}{\text{Assets}}$$

Note: Later development of the DuPont formula expanded the model to include a measure of leverage (Assets/Equity). The effect of this modification is to create a return on equity (ROE) instead of ROI.

The DuPont ROI Formula (complex)*

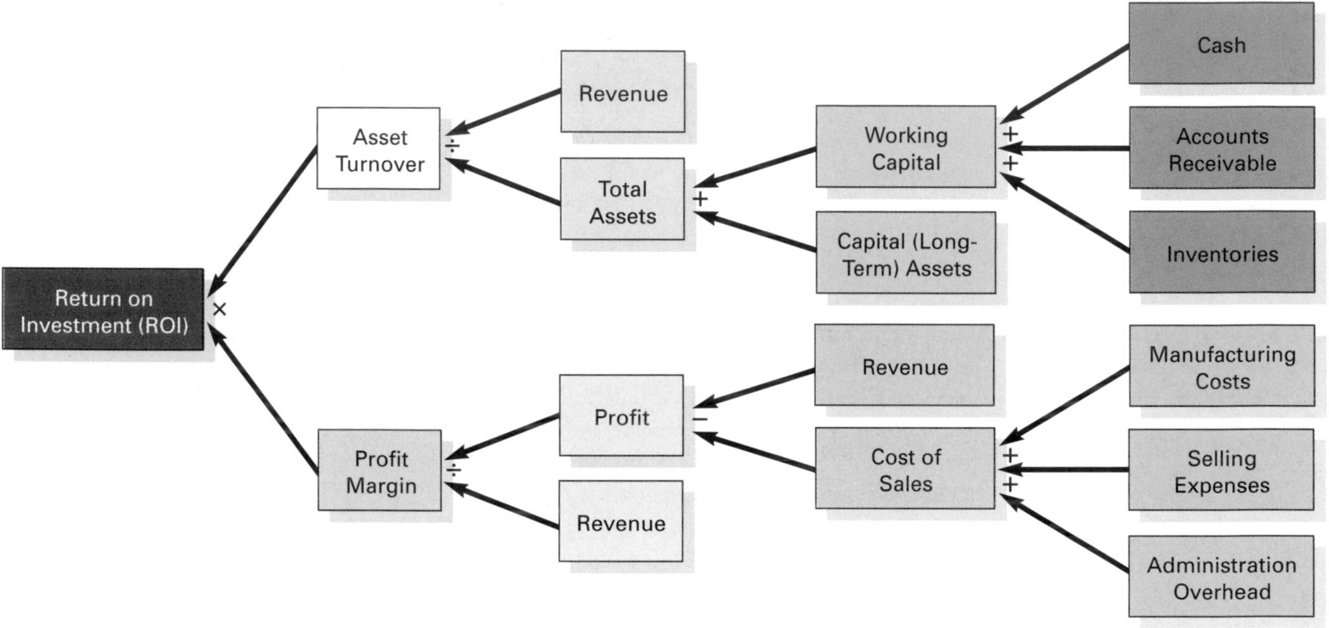

***Source:** T. C. Davis, "How the DuPont Organization Appraises Its Performance," in AMA *Financial Management Series No. 94* (New York: American Management Association, 1950), p. 7. Reprinted in Johnson and Kaplan, *Relevance Lost* (Boston: HBS Press, 1987), p. 85.

company by combining cost management with asset management and raising it to an art form! It's likely that no management accounting technique has had as great an impact on business management as the DuPont ROI formula. In fact, Donaldson Brown took the ROI approach with him when he followed Pierre du Pont to help rescue a little company in the midst of an inventory crisis in 1920. The name of the company was GENERAL MOTORS. The success of the DuPont technique at General Motors can be seen today in any parking lot in America.

Management Accounting and Financial Accounting

In addition to introducing the ROI formula, the DuPont story is an example of how management accounting evolves within organizations that have a particular need for good information. This development pattern has been playing out across companies for a long time. Since the first days of the Industrial Revolution, business owners and managers have generally adopted the best accounting ideas available from other companies and then created their own new accounting system that provided a competitive edge in terms of good management information. Over time, management accounting has, quite literally, evolved within and migrated between organizations and industries in the process of satisfying individual information needs in a competitive world. In fact, a company often regards a good management accounting system as *highly proprietary*—and rarely discloses its details to the public.

Conversely, primarily as a result of the Stock Market Crash of 1929, financial accounting has effectively developed in the United States to provide a *common reporting platform* to the public. In the rapidly rising stock market of the 1920s, many companies publicly issued shares for

caution

Don't think management accounting is not important just because it is not defined as precisely as financial accounting. As you study the story of ROI at DuPont, you will see that management accounting is critical to the success of businesses throughout the world.

the first time. These share issues were often accompanied by little or no financial disclosure. Thus, many stock traders were buying and selling shares based mainly on rumor, speculation, and deceit. In the aftermath of the crash, Congress established the Securities and Exchange Commission (SEC) to regulate the issuance and trading of securities in the United States. In addition to monitoring insider trading and stockbroker behavior, the SEC also ensures that companies issuing securities for purchase by U.S. investors provide full and fair disclosure of their financial status through the public release of financial statements prepared using a set of generally accepted accounting practices (GAAP). The SEC has the legal authority to prescribe accepted accounting standards, but has generally allowed the accounting profession in the United States to establish those rules. Currently, the Financial Accounting Standards Board (FASB), a nongovernmental body supported by the business community and the accounting profession, is the acknowledged source of authoritative accounting standards in the United States.

The important thing to remember is that the purpose of financial accounting, as defined by GAAP, is to comply with requests of outside investors, creditors, and regulators for fair and consistent reports of operations. Accordingly, all companies are required to apply the same general financial accounting rules so that outsiders can compare financial reports coming from many different companies. In contrast, no government regulator or auditor is going to insist that a company implement a good management accounting system; the choice of how to collect and use information within a company is part of a company's competitive strategy. For example, no one forced the du Pont cousins to use the ROI formula to better manage their business; however, because the ROI evaluation framework worked well for DuPont, it was subsequently mimicked by many (but not all) of DuPont's competitors. Remember, the only reason a company does management accounting is to satisfy a competitive need, and competitive need often dictates that one organization's management accounting system will not look like another's!

STOP & THINK We have described some differences in financial and management accounting. Why is it important for an accounting system to provide both types of accounting information?

to summarize

Among the successful innovators in management accounting were Donaldson Brown and the du Ponts who, at the beginning of the twentieth century, consolidated the previous work of others into the famous DuPont ROI management accounting model. The ROI story is typical of management accounting, which is the product of many years of business owners and managers experimenting with methods for capturing and using information about their organization that would give them a unique competitive edge. Organizations and managers are motivated to be innovative in developing and effective in deploying these new accounting tools by the need to compete in a growing economy. In contrast, financial accounting rules are established by an authoritative body in order to enhance company-to-company comparability of financial accounting reports.

2 Understand that successfully managing a company requires good information that supports effective planning, controlling, and evaluating processes.

THE MANAGEMENT PROCESS AND MANAGEMENT ACCOUNTING TERMINOLOGY

Critical to the success experienced by great companies like **DUPONT** is intelligent decision making by individuals supported by competitive management accounting information. Managers will always need to make choices. What should be produced? What should be sold? How should the service be delivered? What does this client need? Which supplier should be used? Who should be promoted? How should financing be obtained? Exhibit 1-3 illustrates the central role that decision making plays in the general management process.

Notice that the decision-making circle intersects three other circles, each representing a major management function. This intersection is meant to show that each of these functions re-

exhibit 1-3 The Management Process

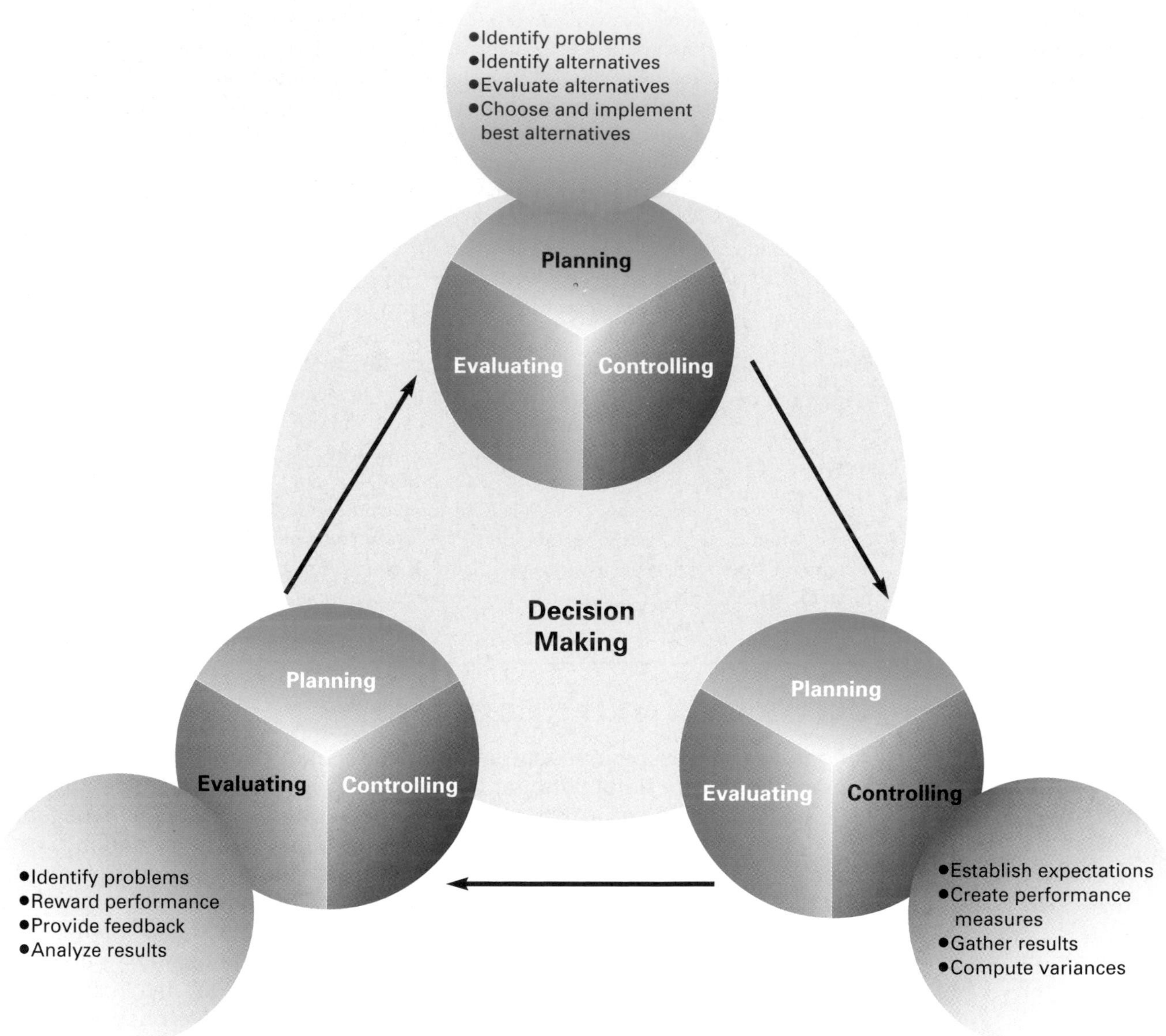

quires decision making. The three management functions of planning, controlling, and evaluating generally follow a natural order—at least in theory. In practice, managers and management accountants are often required to work with processes, customers, and employers requiring all three functions at once. Life can move pretty fast in business!

Planning

planning Outlining the activities that need to be performed for an organization to achieve its objectives.

Management **planning** involves a process of identifying problems or opportunities, identifying alternatives, evaluating alternatives, then choosing and implementing the best alternative(s). There are two basic types of planning:

1. Long-run planning, which includes:
   a. Strategic planning
   b. Capital budgeting

2. Short-run planning, which includes:
   a. Production and process prioritizing
   b. Operational budgeting (profit planning)

Long-run planning involves making decisions with effects that extend several years into the future—usually three to five years, but sometimes longer. This includes broad-based decisions about products, markets, productive facilities, and financial resources. Long-run planning is often called strategic planning. **Strategic planning**, likely the most critical decision-making process that takes place at the executive level in any organization today, usually involves identifying an organization's mission, the goals flowing from that mission, and strategies and action steps to accomplish those goals. Successful executives, such as Pierre du Pont or Andrew Carnegie, have always displayed great skill in studying the market, identifying customer needs, evaluating competitors' strengths and weaknesses, and defining the right investments and processes their organization needs for success. Good management accounting supports good strategic planning by providing the internal information needed by executives to evaluate and adjust their strategic plans. With strategic planning in place (or in process), the company can then plan for the purchase and use of major assets such as buildings or equipment to help the company meet its long-range goals. This type of long-run planning is called **capital budgeting**.

strategic planning Broad, long-range planning usually conducted by top management.

capital budgeting Systematic planning for long-term investments in operating assets.

Short-run planning is divided into two categories. Once the organization has made long-term resource commitments (e.g., land, buildings, equipment, management personnel, etc.), then managers need to determine how to best use those committed resources to maximize the return on their capital investments—a process often referred to as **production prioritizing**. Did you catch the phrase "return on capital investment" in the last sentence? Sound familiar? The DuPont ROI concept is one way to establish priorities on products, service processes, or divisions that make the largest contributions to the goals of the organization. In the next section, we'll introduce another popular method of prioritizing the production potential of an organization—cost-volume-profit (C-V-P) analysis. Once the organization has determined what to produce or otherwise provide to the marketplace in order to maximize its goals, then managers are ready to go on to the next phase of short-run planning—**operational budgeting**. Sometimes known as profit plans, operational budgets are used by managers to establish and communicate daily, weekly, and monthly goals (also known as "standards") for the organization. We will discuss operational budgets, along with production prioritizing, capital budgeting, and strategic planning, in subsequent chapters.

production prioritizing Management's continual evaluation of the profitability of the various product lines and divisions within an organization so that products or divisions that are performing below expectations can be analyzed to identify problems and potential solutions.

operational budgeting Managerial planning decisions regarding current operations and those of the immediate future (typically one year or less) that are characterized by regularity and frequency.

Controlling

Controlling involves a process of tracking actual performance in terms of costs, quality, and timeliness measures. These data are then used subsequently in the evaluating process to compare against the budgets previously prepared in the planning process to measure variances from the original goals or standards. The first management accounting systems focused on tracking costs within the organization. Today, sophisticated cost accounting systems carefully track prices paid for material, labor, overhead, and administrative costs. These systems often have built-in operational budgets so that they can simultaneously evaluate actual performance and compare it to expectations. These systems determine the desired amounts of labor, materials, and administrative support that should be used to efficiently achieve the right outputs of products and services. The foundation of management accounting is a carefully developed model of product and service costs. We'll explore this model later in this chapter.

controlling Implementing management plans and identifying how plans compare with actual performance.

Evaluating

Evaluating involves analyzing results, providing feedback to managers and other employees, rewarding performance, and identifying problems. Evaluating is typically a process of comparing actual performance against expected inputs of costs, expected outputs of quality, and expected timelines. This comparison typically results in information called *variances*, which tell management how well the organization is achieving its plans. If performance is in accordance with the plan, the variances signal that operations are in control and no unusual management action is

evaluating Analyzing results, rewarding performance, and identifying problems.

necessary. If performance is substantially different from the plan, management needs to decide how to alter operations in order to improve future performance.

One specific type of evaluation focuses on company personnel and their responsibilities within the organization. Upper-level management must evaluate how well lower-level managers have performed the activities assigned to them in the original planning stage. Feedback enables management to evaluate performance and provide direction for future improvements, an important aspect of growth in the organization. If performance is good, management needs to consider rewards; if performance is poor, corrective action must be taken. Too many companies fail to clearly link incentive compensation with management goals to ensure that everyone is focused on low cost, high quality, and timely delivery of goods and services expected by customers and clients.

Evaluating products and processes also takes place regularly. Managers need to assess the performance of their products or services, as well as the processes that have been put into place to create products and services. Such evaluation naturally leads to decisions that will affect future operations, including whether to enter or exit a market for a particular service or product, whether to make or buy a component, whether to sell a product before or after additional processing, and what prices to charge for services and products. This third function in the management process, evaluating, brings us back to the point where we started, planning. The information gained through the evaluating function is used in planning for the following period. Remember that as managers *evaluate* performance in the last period, they may also be making *planning* decisions to improve operations for the next period while gathering and receiving results to *control* the current period.

Introduction to Teflon® and Kevlar®

We all love to hear a good story about how hard work and good luck can collide to create history. To read about such a story, go to the DuPont Company Web site at http://www.dupont.com, click on its search engine, and enter the phrase "history of Teflon" (be sure to put the phrase in quotation marks). When was Teflon discovered? What was the name of the now-famous scientist who invented it? What other DuPont product was he working on when he came upon the "white, waxy solid" that eventually became Teflon?

To better understand the nature of planning, controlling, and evaluating, we will work through some typical decisions that managers at DuPont may, in fact, be working on at the moment. We will focus on two product lines at DuPont—Teflon® resins and Kevlar® fiber. These are flagship products at DuPont so you may already be familiar with them. Teflon is considered the most slippery material in existence. It begins as a mixture of chemicals that are then manipulated by DuPont's engineers to produce a product that has become a familiar household name through its use as a nonstick liner for pots and pans and as a soil and stain repellant for fabrics and clothing. One of Teflon's many less known uses is as a coating for fiberglass fabrics used in permanent structures such as the Pontiac Silverdome in Detroit, Michigan, and the Carrier Dome at Syracuse University in Syracuse, New York. Currently, Teflon has an average wholesale price of approximately $145 per gallon.

Kevlar is an even more interesting product. It is a specialty fabric that is extremely strong and tough—so tough that ordinary scissors will not cut through a piece of the fabric! Kevlar starts in a liquid form, is then spun to the point where the Kevlar fibers come together, and finally is heated to complete the process. It is used for boat hulls, bullet-resistant vests, coats, dress shirts, cut-resistant gloves, fiber-optic cables, tennis rackets, and skis. For example, a bullet-resistant vest that is made of seven layers of Kevlar weighs only 2.5 pounds, but can deflect a knife blade and stop a .38-caliber bullet shot from only 10 feet away. The average wholesale price for Kevlar is approximately $45 per pound. This is expensive fabric! Usually, DuPont ships Kevlar as a staple fiber (cotton balls), continuous filament (yarn), and chopped fiber.

The Interrelation of Planning, Controlling, and Evaluating

The use of the ROI model in the case of DuPont is a good example of how planning, control, and evaluation interrelate. DuPont makes 2,000 different products. And, although this is a very large company, its production capabilities are not limitless. So trade-off decisions need to be made. The bottom-line question is, "What product lines provide the most value to DuPont?" The original DuPont ROI formula provides some useful insights here. Consider DuPont's Teflon and Kevlar products. Teflon is part of Dupont's Performance Coatings Segment, and Kevlar belongs to the Specialty Fibers Segment, both critical business divisions within the DuPont organization. How are these segments doing? There are a lot of ways to answer this question, including using the ROI formula. You could use DuPont's annual report to calculate the ROI numbers on these divisions. You would find out if one division's ROI was outperforming the other. More importantly, you could determine how division performance was related to the ability to generate profit margins and the ability to turn over the investment in assets (i.e., asset turnover). Perhaps most importantly, if you were a manager at DuPont, you could then ask some really good questions, such as *why* the profit margin is low for one division. Are costs too high? Is competition forcing prices down? Or, why isn't the asset turnover higher in the other division? Should DuPont consider reducing the amount of assets being purchased and maintained in this segment? Interesting questions—all the result of management accounting providing useful information to help manage the company to be a stronger competitor in the marketplace.

Now review Exhibit 1-3 and think for a moment about the DuPont management process and ROI. As we make ROI calculations on DuPont divisions and ask direct questions as managers, are we clearly using ROI only to *evaluate* the two segments, or could this discussion be part of *planning* for changes in management of and investments in the two segments for the future? It's even possible that ROI measures could be used as a mechanism for gathering data and providing effective *control* of the two divisions in the current operating period. Do you see how the planning, controlling, and evaluating processes interrelate? Although planning, controlling, and evaluating are not always clear and distinct procedures in the management process, we'll use these three critical management functions throughout the remainder of this book to organize the structure of management accounting and discuss where and how the management accounting information is being used to support competitive business management.

to summarize

The essential purpose of management accounting is to support decision making that adds value to the organization. Effective decision making is the key to the management process, and it is central to the management functions of planning, controlling, and evaluating. Planning is the process of making decisions about future products and services, operations, and investments. Controlling involves tracking actual costs, quality, and timing performance within the organization. Evaluating is a process of analyzing results, computing variances, and providing feedback to assess personnel, divisions, products, and processes. The natural end result of evaluating is the identification of problems and opportunities, and from there, the next stage of planning begins. As can be demonstrated by ROI calculations for two divisions at DuPont, however, the management process may (and often does) involve evaluation of the past operating period while simultaneously planning for the future and working to effectively control current business operations. (Note: We'll return to ROI calculations again in Chapter 9 of management accounting.)

3

Know how the concepts of fixed and variable costs are used in C-V-P analysis in the management planning process.

cost-volume-profit (C-V-P) analysis Techniques for determining how changes in revenues, costs, and level of activity affect the profitability of an organization.

variable costs Costs that change in total in direct proportion to changes in activity level.

COST-VOLUME-PROFIT ANALYSIS AT DUPONT

At this point, you have had a good introduction to the ROI management tool. We'll explore this tool further in later chapters. It's time now to introduce a management tool primarily used in the planning process. It is called **cost-volume-profit (C-V-P) analysis**. C-V-P analysis is a very traditional technique in management accounting and is primarily used to plan for the products and services the organization will focus on in the future. The basic concept is to determine the volume of products or services that will be required to generate a desired profit. To use C-V-P analysis successfully, the management accountant must categorize costs as either fixed or variable costs. The concept of fixed and variable costs is fairly simple. Total **variable costs** change in *direct proportion* to changes in some particular activity level, such as production or sales volumes. One example of a variable cost is the costs of materials (such as bolts of cloth in a clothing factory), which vary proportionately with the number of units produced. Sales commissions, which vary proportionately with sales volume, are another example of a

The cost of bolts of cloth used in a clothing factory is classified as a variable cost because it varies proportionately by the number of units produced. The more cloth used in production, the more the total amount of this cost.

fixed costs Costs that remain constant in total, regardless of activity level, at least over a certain range of activity.

variable cost. **Fixed costs** remain constant in total, regardless of activity level, at least over a certain range of activity. Examples of fixed costs related to administration are institutional advertising, insurance, and executives' salaries. Fixed costs related to the manufacturing process might include plant depreciation and supervisors' salaries. Regardless of changes in sales or production output, these costs typically remain constant.

caution

In theory, distinguishing between variable and fixed costs sounds simple. If the activity, such as production volume or sales volume, increases and the cost in question increases, then it must be a variable cost. Otherwise, it is a fixed cost. In reality, however, identifying and managing variable and fixed costs can involve many complexities. Subsequent chapters, particularly Chapter 2 of management accounting, will focus more on identifying and using variable and fixed costs in the planning process.

To demonstrate C-V-P analysis in the planning process, let's return to the two DUPONT products, Teflon and Kevlar. Let's assume that DuPont currently needs to work through which product line to prioritize for the next year. It's not simply a matter of which product line is more profitable or which is expected to return the higher ROI. The decision also involves an assessment of the risk of these two products—in this case, the risk that either or both of these products will generate a loss instead of a profit. C-V-P analysis is used to assess this risk. The fundamental question addressed by C-V-P analysis is as follows: At what sales volume will the company "break even" (i.e., profit is exactly zero) in the Kevlar product line and in the Teflon product line? Answering this question requires the use of the concept of fixed and variable costs. Assume the following estimated price and cost data for the Kevlar and Teflon product lines for the upcoming year:

	Kevlar Product Line	Teflon Product Line
Wholesale price	$45.00 per lb.	$145.00 per gallon
Variable cost	$17.90 per lb.	$60.30 per gallon
Total monthly fixed costs	$3,210,000	$9,630,000

Typical variable costs are the costs of the raw chemicals used to produce Kevlar and Teflon and the labor costs of the workers involved in the manufacturing process. These costs are variable because the more Kevlar or Teflon produced, the more the total amount of these costs. Typical fixed costs are the cost of insurance on a chemical plant, the cost of plant supervisors, and the property taxes paid on a chemical facility. These costs are fixed because, within limits, they are the same no matter how much Kevlar or Teflon is produced.

Examination of the assumed cost numbers for Kevlar indicates that DuPont sells a pound of Kevlar for $27.10 ($45.00 sales price per pound − $17.90 variable cost per pound) more than the variable costs associated with making the product. A basic objective of C-V-P analysis is to determine how many pounds of Kevlar must be sold each month to generate enough profit to pay the $3,210,000 in fixed costs associated with manufacturing that product. The computation of this "break-even" amount is as follows:

$3,210,000 fixed cost ÷ ($45.00 sales price per lb. – $17.90 variable cost per lb.)
= 118,451 lb. (rounded up)

fyi

C-V-P analysis is often referred to as break-even analysis.

This computation means that DuPont must sell 118,451 pounds of Kevlar each month, generating a surplus of $27.10 on each pound, in order to be able to pay its fixed costs of $3,210,000 per month. If DuPont sells fewer than 118,451 pounds in a month, then the fixed costs will not be covered, and the Kevlar product line will report a loss. And remember, by definition the fixed costs of $3,210,000 will be there no matter how many pounds of Kevlar are sold.

STOP & THINK Refer back to the fixed and variable cost data for the Teflon product line. For some C-V-P analysis practice, compute the number of gallons of Teflon that DuPont must sell each month in order to break even.

The information from this simple C-V-P analysis can be used as DuPont makes its production plans with respect to Kevlar. For example, if current production plans, in conjunction with an assessment of the market demand, indicate that DuPont will consistently sell fewer than 118,451 pounds of Kevlar per month, the manager of the Kevlar product line will almost certainly wish to change his or her plans. Costs must be squeezed, new markets need to be sought, perhaps prices should be raised—in short, something has to change because the C-V-P analysis suggests that sales of less than 118,451 pounds per month will not result in profits.

to summarize

By defining costs as either fixed or variable, management accountants can add cost-volume-profit (C-V-P) analysis to the set of tools available in the management process of planning. Management accountants define fixed costs as those costs that will not change in relationship to a particular activity level such as sales volume. Conversely, variable costs are those costs that change in direct proportion to sales volume. Organizations can use C-V-P analysis to determine the sales volume necessary to break even (i.e., profit equals zero). Insights gained from C-V-P computations are extremely useful in the process of planning how and which product lines to emphasize for the future. We'll spend significant time on the C-V-P tool in Chapter 2 of management accounting.

PRODUCT AND PERIOD COSTS

4

Realize how the product cost classifications of direct materials, direct labor, and overhead are used in the management controlling process.

product costs Costs associated with products or services offered.

The concept of managing operations by controlling costs is certainly not a new technique. The early innovations in cost control made by Andrew Carnegie and other successful businesspersons established management accounting practices that continue today. Basically, costs associated with the products or services offered are called **product costs**. In a manufacturing company such as DUPONT or CARNEGIE STEEL, for example, product costs (often referred to as manufacturing costs) are all costs necessary to create finished goods ready for sale. They include all costs related to production: the factory manager's salary, depreciation and taxes on the factory building, wages of the factory workers, and the materials that go into the product. In a merchandising company such as MACY'S or SEARS, product costs are the costs incurred to purchase goods and get them ready for resale to customers. In a service company such as the UNION PACIFIC RAILROAD or KELLY SERVICES (which provides temporary employees), product costs (sometimes called cost of services) involve labor, supplies, and other costs directly related to providing services to customers. At Kelly Services, labor costs for all personnel who provide part-time or temporary services for clients are classified as contract service costs and are subtracted from revenues to arrive at gross margin. In manufacturing and merchandising organizations, the product costs of units still

business environment essay

The Steely-Eyed Business Tycoon In the nineteenth century and much of the twentieth century, management accounting, known then as cost accounting, focused strictly on cost measurement and cost management. Business owners were making a great deal of money using this information to build and expand large companies. And no one understood cost information quite like Andrew Carnegie, who controlled about 25% of the American iron and steel production in 1899. Carnegie was obsessed with costs. One of his favorite sayings was "Watch the costs and the profits will take care of themselves." Was Carnegie's management accounting focus successful? In 1901 he sold his company, **CARNEGIE STEEL**, to the **UNITED STATES STEEL CORPORATION** for $250 million and retired. During his lifetime he gave more than $350 million to various educational, cultural, and peace institutions, many of which bear his name. Not bad for an immigrant with no formal education.

on hand at the end of the accounting period (e.g., the month or year being reported) clearly form the basis for the dollar amount of inventory carried on the balance sheet. The product costs of units sold during the accounting period are used to determine cost of goods sold, which is shown on the income statement as part of the calculation of gross margin for the period.

period costs Costs not directly related to a product, service, or asset that are charged as expenses to the income statement in the period in which they are incurred.

Period costs are all costs incurred that cannot be associated with or assigned to a product or service. These costs are usually not associated with inventory or any other kind of asset. The most common period costs are selling and administrative costs. Examples of selling costs are sales salaries, advertising, and delivery costs. Examples of administrative costs are salaries of the president and controller, depreciation or rent on office buildings, taxes on assets used in administration, and other office expenditures such as postage, supplies, and utilities. The accountant typically treats period costs very differently from product costs. Instead of using these costs to establish a value for inventory, period costs are usually recognized as an expense on the income statement in the period in which they are incurred. For example, if Sears, Roebuck & Company sells two-thirds of the inventory it purchased during November, only the cost of the inventory sold becomes an expense (Cost of Goods Sold) on that month's income statement. The other third of the inventory cost remains an asset (Inventory) on the balance sheet. Regardless of how many products are sold during the month, however, the president's entire salary for November is recognized as an expense on the monthly income statement. You can see that these costs are called period costs because they are always expensed in the period (e.g., month) in which they are incurred.

STOP & THINK A major difference between Kelly Services and manufacturers or merchandisers is inventory. Kelly sells services. Can we put service labor into inventory? Think about this question; we'll discuss it later in Chapter 3 of management accounting.

Types of Product Costs

Now let's examine how we measure and control product and period costs in a variety of organizations. How would one measure product costs for a merchandiser? Actually, that is a fairly easy question. The resources Macy's spends to acquire store inventory for resale to customers clearly are product costs. As products are sold, these inventory costs become an expense on the income statement. What about the wages and salaries of Macy's store clerks and managers? Macy's will likely categorize these costs as part of its selling and administrative expenses and treat them as a period cost on the income statement. That's not too difficult. Now consider the same question for **ARTHUR ANDERSEN LLP**, one of the largest certified public accounting (CPA) firms in the world. What are the products sold by this service firm? Arthur Andersen sells the time of its tax accountants, auditors, and consultants. The salaries of these professionals represent the costs of its "product." Arthur Andersen also employs many other people (such as clerks, secretaries, and office managers) to support the professionals and administer office needs. The wages and salaries of these clerks and office managers, along with costs of office rent, desk supplies, and computers, are likely treated as period costs and recognized as selling and administrative expenses on the income statement.

When identifying product costs for control purposes, the most challenging organization to analyze is a manufacturing business. Does DuPont purchase inventory for resale? Actually, it does purchase some inventory, such as basic chemicals. But it doesn't simply turn around and sell these basic chemicals to customers. Significant processing has to take place before these raw materials become a finished product ready for sale. DuPont must employ laborers to work with these chemicals. In addition, DuPont builds factory buildings and purchases manufacturing equipment. DuPont must also employ managers and other support personnel (such as engineers and custodians) to support the line workers' efforts to convert basic chemicals into salable products. These are all product costs. Basically, any cost required to get the product manufactured and ready for sale is a product cost.

direct materials Materials that become part of the product and are traceable to it.

indirect materials Materials that are necessary to a manufacturing or service business but are not directly included in or are not a significant part of the actual product.

direct labor Wages that are paid to those who physically work on direct materials to transform them into a finished product and are traceable to specific products.

indirect labor Labor that is necessary to a manufacturing or service business but is not directly related to the actual production of the manufactured or service product.

manufacturing overhead All costs incurred in the manufacturing process other than direct materials and direct labor.

To help management analyze the manufacturing cost of its products, product costs are divided into three components: (1) direct materials, (2) direct labor, and (3) manufacturing overhead. **Direct materials** are materials that become part of the product and are traceable to it. Some materials, however, such as the glue and nails in a finished piece of furniture, are so minor and their use so difficult to trace to a specific product that they are not considered direct materials, but rather **indirect materials**. **Direct labor** consists of the wages that are paid to those who physically work on the direct materials to transform them into a finished product. Conversely, wages and salaries paid to factory supervisors and management, maintenance staff, and factory security guards are treated as **indirect labor**. **Manufacturing overhead** includes all other costs incurred in the manufacturing process not specifically identified as direct materials or direct labor. Both indirect materials and indirect labor are included in manufacturing overhead. Exhibit 1-4 summarizes the relationship between product costs and period costs in various types of organizations.

Product Costing and Overhead Cost Allocation

Kevlar and Teflon are rather complex products. The manufacturing process to create these products is also necessarily complex. Controlling the costs, quality, and timely delivery of these processes is key to DuPont's profitability. In this work, DuPont's manufacturing managers need a constant flow of information from management accountants and other information technologists. This is a *lot* of information, particularly in light of the fact that these are not the only products at DuPont (remember that this company manufactures and sells approximately 2,000 products). To control the costs of Kevlar production, DuPont needs accurate information about how much it currently costs to produce Kevlar. This is where the traditional cost accounting systems come into play.

exhibit 1-4 Product Costs and Period Costs in Business Organizations

Type of Company	Product Costs	Period Costs
Service company	Costs of providing services	Selling costs Administrative costs
Merchandising company (wholesale or retail)	Costs incurred in purchasing goods from suppliers	Selling costs Administrative costs
Manufacturing company	All manufacturing costs including direct materials, direct labor, and manufacturing overhead	Selling costs Administrative costs

business environment essay

Watch Your Language in Management Accounting! As good business professionals and management accountants work to compete in the marketplace, a set of common management accounting terms has evolved. Remember, this is not financial accounting—it is important to understand that no official regulatory body of professionals has defined these terms. As you work in various organizations later in your career, you will likely find that these definitions can become ambiguous. Depending on the decision context, a particular cost can have several names. You need to understand this fact and recognize that allowing these definitions to "shift about" can be completely appropriate!

To illustrate, if you like playing card games such as bridge or canasta, you understand that it is often very important in the game to distinguish between cards of different suits—hearts, spades, clubs, or diamonds. On the other hand, for some decisions in the card game it may be more useful to concentrate on the value of the card—ace, 10, deuce, and so on. Thus, sometimes you care about the ace of hearts because of its "heartness," and at other times you are really more interested in its "aceness." Similarly, a product cost may also be a variable cost. Depending on the management setting, you may choose to categorize costs as fixed or variable versus product or period or direct or indirect.

So, in business conversations (discussions concerning costs, for example), never assume you are talking about the same concept as another individual. You always need to be sure that everyone is using the same definition of a management accounting term or concept before you let the conversation get too far.

overhead cost allocation A system of assigning the indirect costs of the manufacturing or service process to the actual product being created for the customer.

As you now know, costs of manufacturing products can be broken down into three elements: (1) direct materials, (2) direct labor, and (3) manufacturing overhead. Although it is easy to assign direct materials and direct labor costs to specific products, it is extremely difficult to assign manufacturing overhead costs, such as rent or the custodian's salary, to specific manufactured products. Companies such as DuPont pay a great deal of attention to **overhead cost allocation** decisions. Unless all relevant costs are properly assigned, managers will not be able to effectively control costs and set prices. Lots of estimations must be made in allocating costs, however, and at some point, it simply isn't worth the effort to get the allocation exactly right (in other words, if management accountants aren't careful, they can start "spending dollars to manage dimes!"). Nevertheless, companies like DuPont are in a competitive market; they can't afford to not understand and manage their product and service costs. In that context, DuPont puts considerable effort into effective allocation of Kevlar and Teflon production costs.

STOP & THINK One of the major reasons it is difficult to assign overhead costs is that these overhead costs are "lumpy" in nature and cannot be precisely matched to the production of specific goods and services. For example, assume that you are the sole driver in a car pool; all the other individuals in the car pool have agreed to reimburse you for their respective shares of the cost of the daily commute. In computing this cost, how would you factor in the costs of insurance, maintenance, and repairs on your car?

How Low Can You Go?

Imagine that another company has recently introduced a new product on the market that competes directly with DuPont's Kevlar. Soon the intense competition between DuPont and the other company for customer orders starts to force down the market price of Kevlar. Now DuPont has a problem. How low can DuPont let the price of Kevlar drop before the company starts losing money? Answering this question requires that DuPont do a good job of measuring the costs of creating Kevlar. Measuring the costs of direct materials and direct labor is not really a problem. The challenge is accurately measuring (i.e., allocating) the cost of overhead to this product.

Overhead Cost Allocation at DuPont

At this point, you can probably imagine that the DuPont accountants could take several approaches to allocate overhead costs to a product such as Kevlar.

Let's explore one possibility by picking up where we left off in our C-V-P analysis for Kevlar. You'll recall from our earlier discussion that monthly fixed costs for Kevlar are estimated to be $3,210,000 and that variable costs are estimated at $17.90 per pound. Remember that fixed and variable costs are *one* way to define costs. These same fixed and variable costs can also be categorized as direct materials, direct labor, and manufacturing overhead costs. Consider the following list of variable costs required to produce a 300-pound batch of Kevlar:

Standard Variable Costs to Produce 300 Pounds of Kevlar

	Average Cost per Pound	Average Pounds per Batch	Total Costs
Direct materials:			
Material 1	$12	100	$1,200
Material 2	18	200	3,600
	Average Rate per Hour	**Average Hours per Batch**	
Direct labor	$18	10	180
Variable manufacturing overhead	39	10	390
Total variable costs*			**$5,370**

*You can verify the number for total variable costs. Remember from the previous C-V-P example that variable costs for Kevlar are $17.90 per pound. Divide the total variable costs of $5,370 by 300 pounds to see that this works out to $17.90 per pound.

Standard Monthly Fixed Costs Associated with the Kevlar Product Line

Manufacturing overhead	$1,560,000
Sales and administrative costs	1,650,000
Total fixed costs	**$3,210,000**

The variable manufacturing overhead costs might include some utility costs (e.g., power to run the equipment) and repairs and maintenance costs that change based on production volumes (similar to the way maintenance costs of your car increase the more you drive it).

Controlling these costs is a matter of continuously tracking what DuPont is spending on direct materials, direct labor, and variable manufacturing overhead and comparing those costs to what should be spent based on the actual volume of Kevlar being produced. Categorizing these costs provides both insight and the opportunity to make good management decisions on costs that are getting out of control; it also guides DuPont in making changes to Kevlar selling prices as costs change. This seems simple enough with one product like Kevlar. In a company as large and complex as DuPont, however, tracking these costs for Kevlar and 2,000 other products is a full-time job for a lot of people!

At this point, it should be clear that tracking the variable costs of producing Kevlar is insufficient to control total costs. A great deal of fixed costs must be managed as well. The Kevlar product generates approximately $1,560,000 in fixed manufacturing overhead costs monthly. Managers somehow need to relate these fixed costs to the production volume in order to manage and control (1) the costs of producing Kevlar and (2) the pricing of the Kevlar product. How would you go about relating the manufacturing overhead costs to Kevlar production? Assuming that DuPont expects to produce 1,000 batches (300 pounds per batch) in the next month, the fixed manufacturing overhead cost per pound can be computed as follows:

$$\$1{,}560{,}000 \div 1{,}000 \text{ batches} = \$1{,}560 \text{ per batch} \div 300 \text{ lb. per batch} = \$5.20 \text{ per lb.}$$

Adding together the fixed and variable manufacturing costs per batch, the expected total manufacturing cost is $23.10 ($17.90 variable costs + $5.20 fixed manufacturing overhead) per pound of Kevlar. Assuming that this method of allocating manufacturing overhead costs to Kevlar is appropriate, DuPont accountants can use this measure as a benchmark to track actual production costs as they come in throughout the year. Thus, use of the classic product cost classification scheme described in this section allows managers and accountants to closely monitor and control the impacts of changes in direct material prices, direct labor rates, and other costs in the effort to profitably provide Kevlar to the market.

The allocation of fixed overhead to products and services may appear to you to be a simple and straightforward process. If you've ever walked through a large manufacturing plant or a large bank, however, you were likely impressed with the complexity of the operation. You may wonder how such complex organizations can effectively control costs and aggressively compete in the marketplace using a cost allocation system that seems almost simplistic. Actually, most cost accounting systems are more involved than what is described here. Nevertheless, the Kevlar product costing example that you've just worked through exhibits the basic pattern found in most cost accounting systems—identifying a meaningful allocation basis (sometimes called an "activity basis") and using it to relate costs to products and services (as well as other critical objects of manager focus). Keep this pattern in mind as we turn to more advanced cost accounting issues in subsequent chapters (particularly Chapters 3, 6, and 7 of management accounting).

caution

Remember that this section began by distinguishing between product and period costs. In our Kevlar cost example, we've focused on assigning only the product costs to pounds of Kevlar. Don't forget that there are also $1,650,000 in period costs, that is, selling and administrative costs, to consider. Although many companies typically do not *directly* allocate these costs to individual products (e.g., pounds of Kevlar), these costs must be effectively tracked and considered in the management process of controlling (as well as planning and evaluating) specific products and services.

to summarize

Costs are initially categorized as either product or period costs. Most period costs are classified as sales and administrative overhead and are, generally, quite difficult to associate with any of the particular products or services that the company provides to the marketplace. Examples of period costs include salaries of selling and advertising personnel and rent or depreciation costs on administrative office buildings. On the other hand, product costs are closely related to the actual process of providing specific goods and services to customers. These costs are typically assigned to specific products or services in an effort to effectively control production costs. Product costs for manufacturing companies such as DuPont are traditionally divided into costs of direct materials, direct labor, and manufacturing overhead. Direct materials are those items that become part of the final product and are easily traceable to it. Direct labor costs are the wages of workers who are "hands on" involved in the production of the final product. Manufacturing overhead costs are essentially defined as all costs essential to the production of goods or services that cannot be categorized as direct materials and direct labor. The management process of controlling costs involves the effort to classify and track costs of providing specific goods and services. Perhaps the most challenging aspect of controlling costs for accountants is the process of assigning (i.e., allocating) overhead costs to specific products using an allocation basis such as production volume.

5

Be able to perform a simple segment analysis using the concepts of direct, indirect, and opportunity costs in the management evaluating process.

SEGMENT ANALYSIS

Managers and executives are typically paid well to make hard decisions. Managers must constantly evaluate the performance of divisions, personnel, processes, and products as markets for particular products change based on developments in technology, new fads and trends in consumer taste, and increased pressure from new and existing competitors. Occasionally, the situation requires a serious look at the potential need to exit from a particular market or drop a specific product line. Sometimes these decisions are motivated by the opportunity to enter a new market or add a new product line. The decision to drop a product line is critical because subsequently reversing the decision can be difficult or impossible. Good management accounting can do much to facilitate the process of evaluating divisions, personnel, processes, and products. Conversely, a poor understanding of some critical management accounting concepts can lead to painful, if not potentially lethal, company problems. To illustrate how accounting supports this evaluation process, we need to extend our vocabulary of key management accounting terms.

Direct and Indirect Costs

So far we have identified fixed and variable costs as a method of cost classification that provides good support to the planning process. We've also defined product and period costs and used those classifications to demonstrate the management controlling process. Now we introduce some new ways to classify costs that are useful for evaluating performance. One of these classifications is direct costs and indirect costs. **Direct costs** are costs that can be obviously and physically traced to a business unit or segment being analyzed. The unit may be a sales territory, product line, division, plant, or any other subdivision for which information is accumulated for analysis. Direct costs are often described as those costs that would be saved if the segment were to be discontinued. Typically, many types of direct costs are variable, but some are fixed. For example, if the segment being considered is a branch sales office, the cost of inventory and labor to run the store would be direct costs that are variable, while the cost to rent the building would be a direct cost that is fixed.

direct costs Costs that are specifically traceable to a unit of business or segment being analyzed.

indirect costs Costs normally incurred for the benefit of several segments within the organization; sometimes called common costs or joint costs.

Indirect costs—sometimes referred to as common costs or joint costs—are costs that are normally incurred for the benefit of several segments. Indirect costs can also be either fixed or variable, although these costs are often fixed. Sometimes these costs are allocated in order to be assigned to a segment. For example, consider a sales manager's salary. If a segment is defined as a branch sales office and a sales manager supervises only one segment, the manager's salary is likely a direct cost of that sales office. If the manager is responsible for several segments, however, the company may choose to allocate the manager's salary to each sales office. In this case, the salary would be an indirect cost to any one of the sales offices. Total indirect costs, such as the manager's salary, normally do not change if one or more of the segments (in this case, the sales offices) are discontinued. Another example of an indirect cost may be manufacturing overhead. Many (but not all) types of manufacturing overhead costs are usually not directly identifiable with any product line and are, therefore, indirect costs to those product lines. These types of costs are incurred as a consequence of general or overall operating activities.

fyi

Activity-based costing (ABC) is a relatively new method of cost assignment that we will fully discuss in Chapter 7 of management accounting. A major emphasis of ABC is to connect costs directly with certain activities. One result of ABC is an increase in the number of costs that can be classified as direct costs.

Costs are designated as either direct or indirect so that a business segment such as a division or product line can be evaluated on the basis of only those costs directly traceable or chargeable to it. Although companies sometimes allocate indirect costs among segments, such allocations often confuse the analysis of the segment's operations. By focusing only on direct costs, management can both identify segments where performance needs to be improved and recognize segments where performance is outstanding and should be rewarded.

Differential Costs and Sunk Costs

The difference between direct costs and indirect costs is similar to the difference between another set of cost terms—differential costs and sunk costs. The **differential costs**—sometimes called avoidable costs, incremental costs, or relevant costs—of a decision are the future costs that change as a result of that decision. In the context of making a decision as to whether to drop a product line, there is likely little difference between the terms *differential cost* and *direct cost.* (The term *differential* is also commonly applied to future *revenues* that will be affected by the decision.) **Sunk costs**, on the other hand, are past costs that cannot be changed as the result of a future decision. You need to note that the definition of sunk costs is not quite the same as that of indirect costs. Indirect costs are those costs that are not affected by a *particular* decision. For example, whether **DUPONT** decides to continue or discontinue its Kevlar product line will likely not affect its general and administrative costs. These costs are indirect to the Kevlar prod-

differential costs Future costs that change as a result of a decision; also called incremental or relevant costs.

sunk costs Costs, such as depreciation, that are past costs and do not change as a result of a future decision.

uct line. This does not mean that management cannot change any of DuPont's general and administrative costs. It just means that a different management decision process is required to change these costs than the process used in evaluating the feasibility of the Kevlar product line. If this sounds as though a cost could be indirect to one evaluation situation or focus and direct to another, you're right! Defining a cost as direct or indirect depends on the object of the decision. On the other hand, sunk costs are not dependent at all on any decision object. A sunk cost is exactly what it sounds like—sunk! There is nothing a company can reasonably do to change a sunk cost.

As an example of sunk costs, the costs that DuPont may have spent last year upgrading its Teflon manufacturing facilities are not relevant to the decision this year as to whether it should continue to compete in the market for performance coatings. Yet many individuals and companies make poor decisions because they fail to correctly distinguish between differential costs and sunk costs. As a personal example, assume you have season tickets to a school's basketball games. On the night of a game, a friend asks you to go to a movie with her. You have wanted to see the movie for a long time. If you decline because you have already purchased the basketball tickets and believe you must therefore go to the game, you may have made the wrong decision. The cost of the basketball tickets is a sunk cost. The only costs that are relevant to your decision are the costs associated with going to the movie, such as the ticket price and popcorn and other goodies you might buy.

Out-of-Pocket Costs and Opportunity Costs

out-of-pocket costs Costs that require an outlay of cash or other resources.

At the most general level, costs can be separated into out-of-pocket costs and opportunity costs. **Out-of-pocket costs** require an outlay of cash or other resources. Many of the costs discussed thus far in this chapter could be called out-of-pocket costs (though sunk costs are *never* considered an out-of-pocket cost). If a company is deciding whether to accept a special order, the costs of materials needed to produce that order are out-of-pocket costs. If a fast-food restaurant is considering installing a drive-up window, the cost of construction is an out-of-pocket cost. Naïve individuals and organizations usually consider only out-of-pocket costs when making decisions. For example, an individual deciding whether to attend a movie might consider only the $7 cost

business environment essay

Accounting and the "Shaq Impact" Opportunity costs are important in all organizations but are especially critical in situations where there are defined limits on available resources. Professional basketball teams, for example, have league-imposed salary caps that dictate the maximum total amount of salaries they can pay to team members. In the 2000/2001 season, the salary cap is $35.5 million per team. When an exceptional player, such as Shaquille O'Neal (Shaq) of the LOS ANGELES LAKERS, comes up for salary negotiations, the team's management must consider both out-of-pocket and opportunity costs when deciding whether to pay the salary requested. For example, Shaq signed a seven-year contract in 1996 with the Los Angeles Lakers for $123 million; that works out to more than $17 million per year! Before agreeing to the contract, the Lakers management had to decide whether yearly ticket sales and TV revenues would be sufficient to meet the out-of-pocket cost of $17 million. Management also had to consider what other player(s) it could sign for $17 million per year and whether, based on the existence of the salary cap, it would be able to pay other current and prospective players enough. For example, the Lakers recently signed Kobe Bryant at approximately $9 million per year. Paying $26 million per year to Shaq and Kobe makes it nearly impossible for the Lakers to pay other players that much money and thus is a high opportunity cost for a professional basketball team. (Note: The Lakers' total team salary payout for 1999/2000 was a little over $54 million. The NBA penalizes teams going over the salary cap with a hefty salary "luxury tax.")

of the ticket required to gain admittance. On the other hand, opportunity costs do not require an outlay of resources. Nevertheless, they are as important as out-of-pocket costs to good management decision making. **Opportunity costs** are the benefits lost or forfeited as a result of selecting one alternative course of action over another. For example, choosing to go to a movie instead of working two hours at $6 per hour has an opportunity cost of $12, as well as an out-of-pocket cost of $7 for the ticket. Installing a drive-up window at a fast-food outlet may have several opportunity costs, such as lost seating or lost parking available to customers.

opportunity costs The benefits lost or forfeited as a result of selecting one alternative course of action over another.

STOP & THINK Which of the following costs are typically recorded in a traditional accounting system: product costs, fixed costs, indirect costs, out-of-pocket costs, sunk costs, opportunity costs?

Segment Analysis at DuPont

Let's return once more to DuPont and apply these new cost concepts to the management process of evaluating the Kevlar and Teflon product lines to determine if the company can continue to profitably offer both products to the public. Assume that the following data represent the results of operations this last month for these two products:

Operating Statements	Kevlar	Teflon	Total
Batches produced and sold	900	920	
Sales revenue	$12,150,000	$13,340,000	$25,490,000
Direct materials	(4,320,000)	(3,864,000)	(8,184,000)
Direct labor	(162,000)	(607,200)	(769,200)
Variable manufacturing overhead	(351,000)	(1,076,400)	(1,427,400)
Fixed manufacturing overhead	(1,560,000)	(4,680,000)	(6,240,000)
Sales and administrative costs	(1,650,000)	(4,950,000)	(6,600,000)
Operating profit	**$ 4,107,000**	**$ (1,837,600)**	**$ 2,269,400**

It looks as though DuPont had a tough month with the Teflon product. In fact, let's assume that the past several months show similar losses on the Teflon product line. In evaluating these results, perhaps management should consider the possibility of dropping this product line. Doing so would certainly improve overall profits for the organization, wouldn't it? Actually, we need to be careful with this analysis. The operating statements above categorize the costs in terms of product costs and period costs. Is that the right way to view these costs for this particular decision? What are the *direct* costs in this decision? Stated another way, what are the *differential* (or *avoidable*) costs of producing Teflon? If DuPont exited from the market for Teflon products, could it avoid all the related costs of direct materials in the future? Yes, certainly. What about the costs of direct labor? With some effort, yes. Variable manufacturing overhead? Again, eliminating these costs would not be automatic, but these costs (such as indirect supplies and equipment maintenance work) could be substantially reduced or removed from the system over time with management effort. How about fixed manufacturing overhead? These costs are going to be more difficult to handle. Fixed manufacturing overhead includes items such as supervisors' salaries and depreciation on equipment and plant facilities. Can these costs be avoided? Actually, perhaps some of these costs can be avoided, but most of these costs are likely unavoidable. For example, let's assume that both Kevlar and Teflon are manufactured in the same building. The depreciation on this building, a fixed manufacturing cost, is allocated to both product lines (a classic example of an indirect cost). If DuPont drops the Teflon product line, the cost related to building depreciation does not go away. It is simply reallocated to the remaining products still being produced in the facility. Sales and administrative costs assigned to the Teflon product line are even less likely to be avoided by a decision to exit this market. These costs often remain within the company and then end up being the responsibility of the remaining product lines.

To better support a decision process involving the possibility of dropping Teflon from DuPont's mix of products, we really need to redo the cost classifications in the operating statements for these two products. We'll classify the product and period costs above as either direct or indirect to the product line. In making this new classification, we'll assume in this example that approximately 30% of the fixed manufacturing overhead can be avoided if Teflon is dropped. Hence, 30% of the fixed manufacturing overhead is a direct cost to the segment.

Operating Statements	Kevlar	Teflon	Total
Batches produced and sold	900	920	
Sales revenue	$12,150,000	$13,340,000	$25,490,000
Direct costs:			
Direct materials	(4,320,000)	(3,864,000)	(8,184,000)
Direct labor	(162,000)	(607,200)	(769,200)
Variable manufacturing overhead	(351,000)	(1,076,400)	(1,427,400)
Fixed manufacturing overhead (30%)	(468,000)	(1,404,000)	(1,872,000)
Segment profit	**$ 6,849,000**	**$ 6,388,400**	**$13,237,400**
Indirect costs:			
Fixed manufacturing overhead (70%)	(1,092,000)	(3,276,000)	(4,368,000)
Sales and administrative costs	(1,650,000)	(4,950,000)	(6,600,000)
Operating profit	**$ 4,107,000**	**$ (1,837,600)**	**$ 2,269,400**

These new cost classifications are very insightful. To grasp the message of these numbers, you need to be very clear about the distinction between direct and indirect costs. By definition, those costs that can be removed from the system by discontinuing the Teflon business segment are direct costs to the segment. All other costs assigned by the accounting system to the Teflon segment are actually indirect costs; that is, these are the common costs that have been allocated to the segments. As you can see, $8,226,000 ($3,276,000 + $4,950,000) of indirect costs is assigned to the Teflon product line. Should DuPont choose to exit the market for Teflon products, these costs will remain in the company and will likely be reallocated to the remaining business segments. So what will be the financial impact of dropping the Teflon product line? The "true" performance of Teflon last month was not a loss, but a $6,388,400 contribution to overall company profits.

Interestingly, some costs that are relevant to the decision of whether to drop the Teflon product line may not be reported in the analysis above. The evaluating process also needs to consider the opportunity costs to DuPont of producing Teflon. Suppose that DuPont has alternative uses for its Teflon production resources (e.g., personnel, equipment, expertise, etc.). If DuPont leaves the Teflon business, what else might it be able to produce and sell? If DuPont chooses to not drop Teflon from its product mix, then it will miss out on the profits possible from an alternative use of these resources. Suppose that DuPont could alternatively use the Teflon resources to enter the business of providing a different polymer product. After consulting with the engineering and marketing departments, DuPont's accountants determine that this alternative product could generate approximately $7 million monthly in incremental segment profit. This information could certainly change the evaluation decision. If there is a $7 million opportunity for the Teflon resources, one could argue that perhaps DuPont should drop the Teflon business segment. When the (very relevant) opportunity costs of Teflon are considered, Teflon's "true" profit is actually an economic loss of $611,600.

Segment profit	**$ 6,388,400**
Opportunity cost (alternative product profit)	(7,000,000)
Economic profit (loss)	**$ (611,600)**

It is important to understand that opportunity costs are very important costs that are not formally tracked in the company's accounting system. Nevertheless, the opportunity costs of Teflon are very real and, as you can see, need to factor into the decision of whether DuPont should continue to produce and sell Teflon. We will spend more time on opportunity costs and segment analysis in Chapters 8 and 9 of management accounting.

to summarize

Different terms are used to describe costs depending on the aspect of the management process involved—planning, controlling, or evaluating. In the evaluation of segments such as product lines or business divisions, managers need to be clear about the difference between direct and indirect costs. Direct costs are costs that are specifically traceable to a segment. Sometimes direct costs are referred to as differential costs, avoidable costs, incremental costs, or relevant costs. The direct costs of a particular segment will change based on future decisions affecting the segment. On the other hand, indirect costs, or common costs, are costs that are normally incurred for the benefit of several segments. Although indirect costs can be changed by some high-level decisions, decisions affecting any one of the segments will not affect indirect costs that are common across all the segments. On the other hand, sunk costs are costs that cannot be changed based on *any* decisions made by management. These are costs that have already been spent (such as depreciation on a purchased building) or costs that cannot be realistically avoided (such as the property tax on the administration building). Finally, opportunity costs are measured as the benefits lost by choosing one alternative over another. Opportunity costs, though not recorded formally in most companies' accounting systems, are relevant to most decisions. These cost terms are particularly useful in the management process of evaluating the contribution of product lines.

6

Understand that management accounting still continues to evolve.

EXPANDING MANAGEMENT ACCOUNTING: COST, QUALITY, AND TIME

just-in-time (JIT) A management philosophy that emphasizes removing all waste of effort, time, and inventory costs from the organization. One obvious result of JIT is the reduction or removal of needless inventory in a production process.

cycle time The total time a product spends moving through a particular process or cycle within the organization, such as the product design cycle, the production cycle, or the order and delivery cycle.

The DUPONT ROI formula is a terrific tool for managing most kinds of organizations. You realize, though, that ROI has been with us now for nearly a century. Most educated managers are fully aware of ROI and how to apply it within their particular organization. Remember that the development of management accounting is a function of the need for information and tools that provide a competitive edge. Would you expect then that the use of ROI provides managers a significant competitive edge in *today's* economy? The truth of the matter is that, in most industries, effective use of ROI and other traditional management accounting tools is still necessary, but using only these tools is probably not sufficient to successfully plan, control, and evaluate a business process. Today's managers need more and better information. In fact, beginning with the Japanese innovation of **just-in-time (JIT)** in the mid-twentieth century, accountants and other information providers have moved beyond just providing data on costs to include innovative methods of measuring the *quality* and the *timeliness* of products and production processes, as well as service and distribution systems. Businesses today create a competitive advantage by delivering more value to customers in less **cycle time** than competitors. As a firm creates and exploits a competitive advantage in cost, quality, and time, it creates increased shareholder value. In other words, if you make your customers happy, you create more profitable financial outcomes and, in the process, make the owners (shareholders) of the business happy! As a result, new performance measures related to cost, quality, and time are being accumulated, tracked, and monitored by firms in many modern industries and have become a hot topic for research among management accountants. Some examples of the new performance measures be-

business environment essay

One Company's Experience with Cost, Quality, and Time Developing measures of cost, quality, and time is a highly proprietary strategic activity. Many organizations are very reluctant to disclose the specifics of their efforts to develop competitive information in these three areas. One company (a medium-sized aerospace corporation in the Pacific Northwest that chooses to remain anonymous) provides a good illustration of the process of creating cost, quality, and time strategic measures. In 1989, the executive team started work to develop new competitive information for this company. It first conducted a survey of key customers, asking about product design, quality, and reliability; the company's ability to meet delivery schedules and other commitments; pricing and perceived value; service and the capability to recover from mistakes; and the overall ease of doing business with the company.

The results were surprising. Contrary to expectations, customers weren't concerned with the company's technological innovations that management had been proud of for years. Instead, customers were concerned with cost, quality, and delivery performance. To their dismay, the executives discovered that customers were dissatisfied with the company's performance in these three areas. Some said they continued to buy from the company only because it was easy to do business with and resolved problems quickly. Clearly, the company was at risk of losing its customers to a competitor unless some changes were made!

To refocus the company on the needs of its customers, an executive staff team was formed to meet weekly to develop a new performance measurement system. The meetings turned into prolonged debates over the number and kind of measures to use. Hours of brainstorming eventually led to the following list:

ing tracked by management accountants in the strategic areas of cost, quality, and time are displayed in Exhibit 1-5. We'll discuss many of these performance measures in later chapters.

The idea of extending beyond cost to also compete on quality and time is having a major impact in industries across the world. These competitive developments present a real opportunity for today's management accountants to jump in and be a part of the process! Frankly, some accountants are not paying attention to this recent shift in management information needs. These accountants continue to focus on providing cost data only. Apparently, they haven't learned their history lesson. Success and profits flow to the business that creates new views of information it can use to gain a competitive edge in the marketplace. On the other hand, some farsighted accountants see the trend and are currently bringing together "balanced scorecards" that combine cost, quality, and time data to support decision making that can literally redefine cus-

exhibit 1-5 New Measures of Cost, Quality, and Time

Cost Measures	Quality Measures	Time Measures
Engineering cost performance	Manufacturing first-pass yield	On-time delivery
Rework and scrap costs	Warranty returns	Master schedule stability
Cost versus features/benefits delivered	Vendor supply quality	New-product development cycle time
Costs of quality	Service and support events	Manufacturing cycle time
Life cycle costs	Successful availability events	Recovery-response time
Target costs	Alignment with customer expectations	Time to market
Learning costs	Six sigma error rate	Order fulfillment cycle time
Activity costs	Waste, scrap, and rework rates	Rework and other non-value-added time

Cost Measures

- Engineering cost performance
- Production efficiency
- Rework and scrap costs

Quality Measures

- Quality of supplier's products
- Manufacturing first-pass yield
- Warranty returns

Time Measures

- New-product development cycle time
- Master schedule stability
- Manufacturing cycle time
- On-time delivery

The executive team assigned the company's controller to collect performance data for each of these 10 measures and issue a monthly report. Graphs of the results were posted for employees and customers to see and became a critical part of any meeting in which management reviewed performance. Some adjustments to these measures were made based on feedback from employees and customers. Eventually, this new approach to performance measures played a crucial role in the company's overall efforts to increase its competitive position. By 1993, it achieved the following performance improvements:

- Customer-quoted delivery times were cut by 50%.
- On-time shipments rose 89%.
- Product-development cycle time fell 35%.
- Manufacturing costs as a percentage of manufacturing sales fell 10%.

Source: K. V. Ramanathan and D. S. Schaffer, "How Am I Doing?" *Journal of Accountancy,* May 1995, pp. 79–82.

tomer and client service. We'll talk more about balanced scorecards and other recent innovations in management accounting in Chapter 10 of management accounting.

fyi

In deciding how to make tradeoffs between costs, quality, and other factors, the lowest-cost alternative is not always best. Take major league baseball, for example. In 2000, the five teams with the highest player payrolls were the New York Yankees ($113.4 million), Atlanta Braves ($95.0 million), Los Angeles Dodgers ($94.2 million), Boston Red Sox ($93.9 million), and New York Mets ($89.7 million). Guess which teams were in the World Series in 2000? Hint: New Yorkers affectionately called it a "subway series." So, if winning the World Series is the most important measure of performance, then minimizing payroll costs is probably not a relevant goal.

to summarize

As we move into the twenty-first century, strategic performance measures of cost, quality, and time will continue to support and improve decisions that build organizations both in the profit and the not-for-profit sectors of our society. Management accountants, if they expect to have jobs as key decision-support professionals in the twenty-first century, must provide data that encompass all three of these strategic imperatives.

IN CONCLUSION—THE MANAGEMENT PROCESS

We have focused this chapter around DUPONT and the way this company uses management accounting to provide managers with information that has competitive value. To accomplish this, however, management accountants must understand the types of decisions being made and how these decisions affect management of a successful organization. In particular, we've introduced a number of important management accounting terms in the context of the management process of planning, controlling, and evaluating. Throughout the remainder of this text, we'll continue to organize management accounting topics around this management process.

review of learning objectives

1 Understand the essential differences between management accounting and financial accounting, as illustrated by managerial use of the ROI formula. Management accounting as we know it today is a product of managers and owners reacting to competitive forces. At the turn of the twentieth century, the DUPONT CORPORATION combined many management accounting innovations into a new performance evaluation model based on the return on investment (ROI) measure. Hence, the development trend of management accounting is in contrast to the legislative and regulatory forces that began defining financial accounting after the Stock Market Crash of 1929.

2 Understand that successfully managing a company requires good information that supports effective planning, controlling, and evaluating processes. Planning involves both long-term planning such as strategic planning and capital budgeting and short-term planning involving production and process prioritizing as well as operational budgeting. Effective control of costs in the organization requires good tracking of actual performance. Evaluating involves analyzing results, providing feedback to managers and other employees, rewarding performance, and identifying problems. Evaluating naturally leads management back to the planning process, illustrating the interrelationship of the management process.

3 Know how the concepts of fixed and variable costs are used in C-V-P analysis in the management planning process. It is important to understand how accounting terminology must change to support specific management settings. In the context of cost-volume-profit (C-V-P) analysis, costs are classified as variable costs or fixed costs. Using this classification, C-V-P analysis then follows a formula approach to determine the sales volumes necessary to achieve a specified profit level.

4 Realize how the product cost classifications of direct materials, direct labor, and overhead are used in the management controlling process. For manufacturing firms, product costs include direct materials, direct labor, and manufacturing overhead. In a merchandising company, product costs are costs incurred to purchase goods and get them ready for resale. For service firms, product costs are costs of providing a service to customers. These costs are used to determine both asset values on the balance sheet and costs of goods sold on the income statement. In contrast to product costs, period costs are used strictly to compute the selling and general administrative expenses on the income statement. The process of identifying, tracking, and controlling product costs requires an intelligent method of allocating overhead costs to goods and services.

5 Be able to perform a simple segment analysis using the concepts of direct, indirect, and opportunity costs in the management evaluating process. Costs can be distinguished as being direct or indirect depending on their relationship to a particular segment being evaluated. Essentially, all costs that would be eliminated if the business discontinued the segment are considered the direct costs of that particular segment. Other costs currently allocated to the segment being considered for removal that would essentially shift to other segments are indirect costs. Sunk costs are those costs in the organization that no reasonable decision of any kind can avoid. These costs are essentially irrelevant to any decisions in the organization. On the other hand, opportunity costs, which are rarely tracked in the formal accounting system, are nearly always relevant to decisions.

6 Understand that management accounting still continues to evolve. As competition has increased and markets have become more sophisticated, management accounting today is expanding beyond cost management to include performance measures of quality and timeliness.

key terms and concepts

discussion questions

1. DUPONT was America's first large-scale "vertically integrated" company. What does "vertically integrated" mean?
2. The chapter states that the focus of management accounting is to create information to fill a competitive need. Explain how management accounting can provide a competitive edge in business.
3. How can management accounting information help companies to be competitive and profitable?
4. What exactly did Donaldson Brown, the accountant for DuPont, develop, and why was it so revolutionary?
5. Management accounting and financial accounting provide different information for different purposes. Explain what this means and provide an example that illustrates the differences between management and financial accounting.
6. Managers need not be concerned about external financial statements. Do you agree or disagree with this statement? Explain.
7. Why is GAAP so important for external financial reporting but not for internal management reporting?
8. Identify the three management functions relating to the decision-making process. Briefly define each function.
9. How is strategic planning related to capital budgeting?
10. How do variable costs and fixed costs differ? Give an example of each.
11. Analyze your personal expenses on a variable and fixed basis. What are some of your personal fixed costs and variable costs? What would cause them to change?
12. What is C-V-P analysis used for?
13. Explain the difference between a product cost and a period cost.
14. What are the three components of manufacturing costs? Briefly describe them.
15. How do nonmanufacturing costs and indirect costs differ?
16. What classification determines whether materials used in the production of a product are direct materials or indirect materials? Is the classification always simple to determine? What are some examples of direct materials and indirect materials used in the production of a chair?
17. What are some of the major challenges in tracking and controlling manufacturing overhead costs?
18. Essentially, how are manufacturing overhead costs allocated to goods and services?
19. What is the difference between a direct cost and an indirect cost? Give an example of each in the context of teaching an accounting class at your school.
20. What is the difference between sunk costs and differential costs? Give an example of each.
21. How can out-of-pocket costs and opportunity costs be applied to your personal financial decisions?

discussion cases

CASE 1-1

DEVELOPING MANAGEMENT ACCOUNTING INFORMATION (DUPONT)

The story of E. I. DU PONT DE NEMOURS AND COMPANY detailed at the beginning of this chapter provides key insights into the development of management accounting. In particular, we see how the structure of a business affects the kinds of information required for planning, controlling, and evaluating purposes. Consider the decision to "vertically integrate" the company. What were the potential risks to DUPONT of this decision? What accounting information would have been required to determine if the decision to vertically integrate was successful? Does the traditional accounting system designed to produce external financial reports provide the required information in an easily obtainable fashion?

CASE 1-2

SUPPORTING THE MANAGEMENT PROCESS (IBM)

INTERNATIONAL BUSINESS MACHINES CORPORATION (IBM) has faced challenges this last decade due to increased competition in the home-consumer segment of the personal computer (PC) market. When IBM introduced the PC in the early 1980s, it was a huge success. Over time, however, the PC market grew immensely, and competition began to rise.

Although the PC was initially marketed toward businesses, a home-consumer market emerged as well. In 1995, IBM, under the direction of CEO Louis Gerstner, set up a home-consumer PC division to augment its business PC division. IBM hoped that with the two divisions, each employing its own design, manufacturing, and marketing personnel, it could better focus on the needs of its various customers and increase total sales.

IBM's consumer division quickly developed PCs that had high customer appeal. In early 1996, the division released its "Aptiva" PC in a sleek, dark gray color. The model was equipped with many high-tech features. Also, IBM's reputation for quality allowed the consumer division to charge a higher price for the PCs. (In December 1996, IBM PCs sold for an average of $1,880, whereas other companies charged as little as $1,300 to $1,400.)

Initially, the manufacturing department in IBM's consumer division could not keep up with consumer demand. Recently, however, IBM has been losing market share to companies such as **DELL, COMPAQ,** and **GATEWAY**. These companies are finding that consumers prefer low price to the extra "frills" that IBM offers in its computers. Furthermore, IBM is discovering that many consumers are no longer willing to pay higher prices for IBM's reputation. IBM, the company that once dominated the PC market, has plummeted in its market share and is currently at less than 5%.

1. Did IBM make a good decision in setting up its consumer division? How so?
2. Analyze IBM's decisions and actions involving the consumer division. Try to categorize these decisions and actions following the threefold management process of planning, controlling, and evaluating.
3. Based on the threefold management process of planning, controlling, and evaluating, where do you think IBM was weakest in its decision-making practice with respect to the consumer division? Where do you think it was strongest?
4. If you were Louis Gerstner, what information would you want from your management accountants in order to effectively plan, control, and evaluate the decision to either shut down or continue to operate the consumer division?

Source: Raju Narisetti, "IBM to Revamp Struggling Home-PC Business," *The Wall Street Journal,* October 14, 1997, p. B1.

EXERCISE 1-1

CHANGES IN BUSINESS AFFECTING MANAGEMENT ACCOUNTING

You are at the student union having lunch with a friend who is attending law school. In the course of your conversation, you tell your friend that, in contrast to financial accounting or tax accounting, management accounting has "competitive value" and is highly proprietary. Further, management accounting is more important in business today than ever before, and only those organizations that best control costs and improve quality are competitive. Your friend asks you two questions:

1. What do you mean by "competitive value"?
2. Why is it more important for management accountants to provide useful information to management today than it was before?

EXERCISE 1-2

CHARACTERISTICS OF ACCOUNTING REPORTS

Indicate whether each of the following is characteristic of financial accounting reports, management accounting reports, or both:

1. They are used primarily by creditors and investors.
2. They aid management in identifying problems.
3. They are based on generally accepted accounting principles.
4. They are standardized across companies.
5. They provide information for decision making by management.
6. They measure performance and isolate differences between planned and actual results.
7. They are created based on competitive needs that are unique to the organization.

EXERCISE 1-3

FINANCIAL AND MANAGEMENT ACCOUNTING

A friend who is thinking about majoring in accounting has asked you to distinguish between the work of a financial accountant and a management accountant. What is your response?

EXERCISE 1-4

PERIOD COSTS AND PRODUCT COSTS

Bright, Inc., a producer of educational toys for children, incurs the following types of costs:

a. Depreciation on the production plant
b. Depreciation on the corporate offices
c. Paper, toner, and miscellaneous supplies for the office copy machines
d. Wages of production-line employees
e. Raw materials used in the production of toys
f. Wages of the corporate headquarter's secretarial staff
g. Maintenance costs on the production equipment
h. Advertising costs
i. Shipping costs for products sold
j. Salaries of plant supervisors
k. Interest on bank loans
l. Property tax on the production plant
m. Property tax on the corporate offices
n. Commissions paid to sales personnel
o. Administrative salaries of corporate executives

Classify each cost as a period cost or a product cost. For each item classified as a product cost, indicate whether it would usually be included in direct materials, direct labor, or manufacturing overhead.

EXERCISE 1-5

Spread-Sheet Software

MANUFACTURING COSTS

Jordan Industries is a manufacturing company that produces solid oak office furniture. During the year, the following costs were incurred. The building depreciation and the utilities are allocated three-fourths to production and one-fourth to administration. The cost of furniture parts can be traced to specific production runs.

Oak wood	$ 50,000
Miscellaneous supplies (glue, saw blades, varnish, etc.)	10,000
Furniture parts (wheels, locks, etc.)	5,500
Payroll—plant manager's salary	25,000
Payroll—administrative salaries	100,000
Payroll—production-line employees' wages	45,500
Building depreciation	28,000
Maintenance—plant and equipment	5,000
Utilities	16,000
Income taxes	8,500

1. Classify the costs into the following four categories: direct materials, direct labor, manufacturing overhead, and period costs.
2. Calculate the total amount of cost for each category.

EXERCISE 1-6

MANUFACTURING AND NONMANUFACTURING COSTS

The Benson Manufacturing Company produces rides for amusement parks. Parts for the rides are purchased from other suppliers. Rides are then assembled in various company plants.

Recently, Benson Manufacturing hired two new employees. One will be working in an assembly plant, and the other will be working in the marketing division of the corporate offices as a sales representative.

The assembly plant employee will be paid an annual salary of $25,000, or $12.50 per hour. Her time will be charged to the individual rides that she assembles. The marketing division employee will receive an annual salary of $20,000 plus commission. He will be responsible for both advertising and selling. His salary is for advertising responsibilities, and he will be paid a commission on sales of amusement rides.

1. Should the salary of the assembly plant employee be classified as a manufacturing or a nonmanufacturing cost? Should the salary of the marketing division employee be classified as a manufacturing or a nonmanufacturing cost? How is this classification made?
2. After classifying the salaries as manufacturing or nonmanufacturing costs, determine how the salary costs will affect the cost of assembling the amusement rides. Classify the employee costs as direct, indirect, fixed, variable, product, or period. (Each cost can be classified in more than one way.)

EXERCISE 1-7

PERFORMANCE MEASUREMENT

The president of Radkline Corporation, Karen Pinkus, has asked you, the company's controller, to advise her on whether Radkline should develop a new inventory management system. Is the decision facing Karen Pinkus an example of a strategic planning decision, a capital budgeting decision, a production prioritization decision, or an operational budgeting decision? Be sure to defend your answer.

EXERCISE 1-8

COST CLASSIFICATIONS

The following are costs associated with manufacturing firms, merchandising firms, or service firms:

a. Miscellaneous materials used in production
b. Salesperson's commission in a real estate firm
c. Administrators' salaries for a furniture wholesaler
d. Administrators' salaries for a furniture manufacturer
e. Freight costs associated with inventories of a grocery store
f. Office manager's salary in a doctor's office
g. Utilities for the corporate offices of a toy manufacturer
h. Line supervisor's salary for a clothing manufacturing firm
i. Training seminar for sales staff of a service firm
j. Fuel used in a trucking firm
k. Paper used at a printing business
l. Oil for machinery at a plastics manufacturing firm
m. Food used at a restaurant
n. Windshields used for a car manufacturer

Classify the costs as (1) product or period; (2) variable or fixed; and (3) for those that are product costs, as direct materials, direct labor, or manufacturing overhead. Write "not applicable (N/A)" if a category doesn't apply.

EXERCISE 1-9

COST CLASSIFICATIONS

The following are costs associated with manufacturing firms, merchandising firms, or service firms:

a. Legal services for an accounting firm
b. Car leases for company management

c. Oil used to service manufacturing equipment
d. Office supplies for a grocery store
e. Entertainment expense
f. Travel expenses for doctors in a medical firm
g. Plastic used in making computers
h. Collection costs of accounts receivable
i. Electricity to run saws at a lumber yard
j. Food for a company banquet
k. Advertising expense
l. Continuing education for a doctor
m. Commissions paid to salespersons
n. Depreciation on sports equipment by a professional football team
o. Calculators used by office employees
p. Earplugs used at an airport
q. Toll charges incurred because of business travel
r. Fuel used in manufacturing equipment

Classify the costs as (1) product or period; (2) variable or fixed; and (3) for those that are product costs, as direct materials, direct labor, or manufacturing overhead. Write "not applicable (N/A)" if a category doesn't apply.

EXERCISE 1-10

C-V-P ANALYSIS

Phelps, Inc., located in Irvine, California, manufactures high-end baby chairs. The firm's cost accountant, Amy, has been assigned by the CEO to determine how many baby chairs Phelps, Inc., needs to make to break even. She is given the following data:

Baby chair sales price	$ 16
Variable cost per baby chair	6
Production worker salary	1,000

Determine how many baby chairs Phelps, Inc., needs to make to break even.

EXERCISE 1-11

C-V-P ANALYSIS

The Los Angeles Lakers basketball team has hired you as its new accountant. On your first day on the job, Lakers Vice President of Basketball Operations, Magic Johnson, comes to you and asks, "How many tickets must we sell to pay for Shaq's salary?" He then hands you a sheet of paper with the following information:

Shaq's salary	$17,000,000
Average ticket price	75
Printing cost of one ticket	1

1. Prepare your response to Magic's question.
2. How many tickets would the Lakers have to sell to pay for the entire Lakers team if the total team salary (including Shaq) is $54,000,000?

EXERCISE 1-12

PRODUCT COSTING

BatsRUs, Inc., has created a unique line of aluminum baseball bats that, while illegal for league use, are designed to nearly double the average length of a batted ball. They are a great "hit" in the personal and family use market. Recently, a new competitor, Awesome Bats, Inc., has introduced a competing bat to the market. Suddenly, BatsRUs is experiencing severe market pressure to significantly lower its normal market price of $175. The problem is that management is not very confident about the actual production cost per bat. With some effort, the following data have been developed for management to use in setting a new market price and, more importantly, beginning an effort to better control costs.

Standard Variable Costs to Produce One Batch of 10 Bats (600 batches are typically produced each month)			
	Average Cost per Pound	**Average Pounds per Batch**	**Total Costs**
Direct Materials	$ 3	16	$ 48
	Average Rate per Hour	**Average Hours per Batch**	
Direct labor	$15	2	30
Variable manufacturing overhead	20	2	40
Total variable costs			$118

Standard Monthly Fixed Costs	
Manufacturing overhead	$240,000
Sales and administrative costs	180,000
Total fixed costs	$420,000

1. What appears to be the average cost for BatsRUs to manufacture a single baseball bat?
2. Do you have any questions or concerns about how the data are being used to determine the cost of manufacturing a baseball bat at BatsRUs?

EXERCISE 1-13

PRODUCT COSTING AND C-V-P ANALYSIS

PrepNow, Inc., offers a CPA review course in cities throughout the eastern United States. PrepNow hires local CPAs to do the teaching. Each instructor is paid $110 an hour to teach the course; a course consists of 16 weeks of instruction with sessions taking place two evenings a week for three hours at each session. The other instruction costs to PrepNow are to pay for hotel conference rooms to host the course. Generally, PrepNow pays the hotel $500 per evening to rent a conference room. Also, tuition for the course includes all course materials, which cost the company $160 for each student.

1. What is the "product cost" of providing one evening of instruction for all students?
2. What is the "product cost" of training a student over the entire course (there are 50 students in this particular course)?
3. Assuming that PrepNow charges each student $1,100 for the course, how many students would be required to "break even" on this course?

EXERCISE 1-14

SEGMENT ANALYSIS

You are the accountant for the largest manufacturer of aluminum cans. The company's hottest product is the X-96, which provides most of the firm's revenue. Management is considering dropping the W-96 product line, which hasn't turned a profit for two consecutive years. The CFO comes to you and asks what you would do given the following data:

Operating Statements	**X-96**	**W-96**	**Total**
Batches produced and sold	100	120	
Sales revenue	$15,000	$21,600	$36,600
Direct materials	(1,000)	(4,200)	(5,200)
Direct labor	(2,000)	(3,840)	(5,840)
Variable manufacturing overhead	(500)	(2,400)	(2,900)
Fixed manufacturing overhead	(1,000)	(8,700)	(9,700)
Sales and administrative costs	(1,000)	(3,000)	(4,000)
Operating profit	$ 9,500	$ (540)	$ 8,960

Note: Approximately 20% of the fixed manufacturing overhead is directly related to (i.e., created within) each segment.

1. Distinguish between direct and indirect costs and find the segment profit for each product.
2. Determine the gain or loss that the firm would incur if it dropped the W-96 product line. What figure would you provide the CFO?
3. Explain your recommendation to continue or discontinue product line W-96.

EXERCISE 1-15

OPPORTUNITY COSTS

Mike is employed by a company that currently pays him $80,000 per year. He owns a new car that he bought for cash of $35,000. Mike is thinking about returning to school to obtain a law degree. Tuition for the school he wants to attend is $25,000 per year, books average $1,000 per year, and room and board average $10,000 per year.

Determine the total sunk cost and the total opportunity cost for Mike if he decides to go back to law school for three years.

competency enhancement opportunities

- Analyzing Real Company Information
- International Case
- Ethics Case
- Writing Assignment
- The Debate
- Internet Search

The following additional assignments provide opportunities for students to develop critical thinking, ethical perspectives, oral and written communication skills, experience with electronic research, and teamwork through group and business activities.

ANALYZING REAL COMPANY INFORMATION

• ***Analyzing 1-1 (Microsoft)***

1. Bill Gates wrote in his 1999 letter to MICROSOFT shareholders: "We are investing heavily in the future—from world-class customer support to the $3.8 billion we plan to spend in fiscal 2000 on research and development for the products of tomorrow." With the $2.970 billion that Microsoft spent on research and development (R&D) in 1999, it has increased its R&D spending by nearly 60% since 1997. R&D is more than 30% of its current operating expenses. Microsoft clearly spends a lot of its money on R&D. What are the potential advantages and disadvantages of this cost commitment to R&D?
2. A large part of Microsoft's R&D expenditures is for outside software developers who contract with Microsoft to work on specific projects. What factors does Microsoft need to consider in deciding to assign a research project to an outside contractor rather than to its internal software development staff?

• ***Analyzing 1-2 (DuPont)***

As described in the chapter, the challenge facing DUPONT in the early twentieth century was how to manage the diverse set of businesses operating under the control of the DuPont management team. This diversity still exists today. In its 1999 annual report, DuPont notes that its strategic business units (operating segments) are organized by product line. For purposes of financial reporting, these have been aggregated into nine reportable segments: Agriculture & Nutrition, Nylon Enterprise, Performance Coatings & Polymers, Pharmaceuticals, Pigments & Chemicals, Pioneer, Polyester Enterprise, Specialty Fibers, and Specialty Polymers.

Summary segment results for 1999 for six of these nine segments are as follows (dollars in millions):

	Agriculture & Nutrition	Nylon Enterprise	Polymers	Pharmaceuticals	Pioneer	Polyester Enterprise
Total revenue	$2,598	$4,487	$6,111	$1,630	$ 422	$2,649
After-tax operating income.	358	63	582	230	(2,309)	(119)
Identifiable assets at December 31, 1999.	3,184	3,004	4,061	1,939	7,762	2,679

1. Which segment has the highest profit margin? The lowest?
2. Which segment has the highest asset turnover? The lowest?
3. Which segment has the highest return on investment? The lowest?
4. How could the segment with the lowest return on investment improve its financial performance?

INTERNATIONAL CASE

• *Toyota*

TOYOTA MOTOR CORPORATION was the company that originally defined and implemented the just-in-time (JIT) management technique mentioned in this chapter. Toyota was started in 1918 by Sakichi Toyoda as the TOYOTA SPINNING AND WEAVING COMPANY; in fact, a subsidiary of Toyota still makes spinning and weaving equipment today. In 1995, Toyota was the third-largest motor vehicle producer in the world, manufacturing 4,512,076 vehicles (behind GENERAL MOTORS at 7,997,794 and FORD at 6,401,495). In January 1997, Toyota made its 100 millionth vehicle.

In its 1997 annual report, Toyota said the following about its performance:

> Consolidated net income rose 50.2%, to 385.9 billion yen ($3,112 million), in the fiscal year ended March 31, 1997. That rise in earnings is attributable principally to the weakening of the yen, continuing cost savings, and growth in sales volume. The yen/dollar exchange rate averaged 112 yen during the past fiscal year, compared with 96 yen in the previous year. . . . The capacity for achieving cost savings on a continuing basis is integral to management at Toyota. New cost savings therefore will continue to contribute to earnings in the years ahead. . . . Our cost savings resulted from value-engineering improvements in designs and also from improvements in manufacturing processes and in logistics. Unending, systematic improvements in product designs and production processes will yield continuing cost savings.

1. Toyota attributes its 50% increase in net income to three factors: the weakening of the yen, cost savings, and growth in sales volume. Consider conducting a performance evaluation on the following people, and decide which of the three factors should be considered in the evaluation of:
   a. an assembly-line worker
   b. a factory manager
   c. a sales manager
   d. the company president
2. In relation to its cost savings, Toyota reports that the savings stem from improvements in engineering design, improvements in manufacturing processes, and improved logistics. Consider conducting a performance evaluation on the following people, and decide which (and why!) of the three cost savings factors should be considered in the evaluation of:
   a. an assembly-line worker
   b. a factory manager
   c. a purchasing manager
   d. the company president

ETHICS CASE

• *Whom to Tell About Medicare Overbilling?*

Professor Mary Allen is sitting in her office one day when Mark Sullivan, an accounting graduate from five years ago, knocks on her door. Mark had been an exceptionally good student and had started with the CPA firm Peat & Price on graduation. After three years with that firm, he joined MiniCare Health Company as the chief accountant and is now serving as its controller. Mark asks if he can talk with Professor Allen in confidence and then tells her that he has a problem: "Two years ago, I started working for MiniCare. Not long after I was promoted to controller, I noticed that the officers of the company were doing things that I didn't think were right. They have overbilled Medicare on several occasions, and senior management executives are misusing their positions by taking company perks that are against the company code of ethics. I have talked to my superior, the financial vice president, and he has, in essence, told me to mind my own business—that accountants are to report results and assist management, not question them."

Mark informs Professor Allen that he is making $100,000 a year, far more than he could earn in another company at this stage in his career. He asks her for advice. What should Professor Allen recommend that he do? Should Mark quit his job? Should he talk to someone else? If so, who? Should he go public with his information?

WRITING ASSIGNMENT

• *Sunk Costs: They May Be Sunk, But They Aren't Forgotten.*

You are the manager of the tire manufacturing subdivision of Uniyear Diversified Products. Last year, you were successful in convincing corporate executives that your division needed to purchase a new warehouse facility costing $40 million to house raw materials. You argued at the time that you could be much more productive if delays in getting materials from suppliers could be eliminated.

During the past 18 months, your company has worked hard to adopt JIT inventory and total quality control. You have successfully placed online terminals at key supplier locations, and the lag time in getting the raw materials you need has dropped from an average of four weeks to six hours.

Your problem now is that you no longer need the $40 million warehouse. It is a sunk cost. However, you are afraid that if you reveal that fact to the corporate executives, they will penalize or even fire you for being so shortsighted.

Draft a one-page memo to the president of Uniyear Diversified Products that explains why the $40 million warehouse is no longer needed. Remember that the memo has two purposes: to inform the president that the warehouse is no longer needed and to do so in a way that doesn't cost you your job.

THE DEBATE

• *When Should You Surrender?*

You are a partner in a CPA firm. For over 15 years, you conducted the audit of XYZ Corporation. Three years ago, however, the company went bankrupt. To your surprise, a class-action lawsuit was filed against your firm for $5 million, alleging that you failed to warn stockholders that the company was in financial difficulty. Your audit fee for XYZ Corporation was only $15,000 per year. Thus far you have spent $957,000 on legal fees and expert witness costs. Your attorney has worked out a settlement that would involve you paying the plaintiffs $750,000. You believe your defense is excellent, that the quality of your audits of XYZ Corporation was high, and that you will win the lawsuit. However, you also believe that it will cost another $800,000 in legal fees to successfully defend the case. Should you settle?

Divide your group into two teams.

- One team represents the "Fight to the Death" group. Prepare a two-minute oral presentation supporting the notion that you should not pay a penny to settle the lawsuit when you know that you did nothing wrong. You believe that the best long-run business strategy is to vigorously fight every lawsuit in order to discourage future suits.
- The other team represents the "Cut Our Losses" group. Prepare a two-minute oral presentation arguing that the past litigation costs are sunk and that the only reasonable comparison is between the cost of settling now and the cost of continuing the lawsuit.

INTERNET SEARCH

• *DuPont*

Access DUPONT's Web site at http://www.dupont.com. Sometimes Web addresses change, so if this DuPont address doesn't work, access the Web site for this textbook (http://albrecht.swcollege.com) for an updated link to DuPont.

Once you've gained access to DuPont's Web site, answer the following questions:

1. Who is the current chief executive officer (CEO) of DuPont? How long has he or she been with the company? What is his or her background (e.g., legal, accounting, engineering, etc.)?
2. As mentioned in the chapter, the DuPont organization includes many diverse types of businesses. How many employees does DuPont have? In how many countries does DuPont operate? How many manufacturing facilities does DuPont operate? What fraction of DuPont's business is conducted outside the United States?

3. The history of DuPont, and some of its well-known products, is summarized in the chapter. DuPont's Web site offers further information. When did DuPont's polymer chemists invent nylon? What is Kevlar® used for?
4. DuPont reports a corporate commitment to moving toward zero emissions, zero employee injuries, and zero material waste. What progress does DuPont report in its effort to reduce air carcinogenic emissions?

Analyzing Cost-Volume-Profit Relationships

chapter **m2**

learning objectives

After studying this chapter, you should be able to:

1. Understand the key factors involved in cost-volume-profit (C-V-P) analysis and why it is such an important tool in management decision making.
2. Explain and analyze the basic cost behavior patterns—variable, fixed, mixed, and stepped.
3. Analyze mixed costs using the scattergraph and high-low methods.
4. Perform C-V-P analyses, and describe the effects potential changes in C-V-P variables have on company profitability.
5. Visualize C-V-P relationships using graphs.
6. Identify the limiting assumptions of C-V-P analysis, and explain the issues of quality and time relative to C-V-P analysis decisions.

expanded material

7. Analyze mixed costs using the least squares method.
8. Explain the effects of sales mix on profitability.
9. Describe how fixed and variable costs differ in manufacturing, service, merchandising, and e-commerce organizations, and illustrate these differences with the operating leverage concept.

setting the stage

Recently, a profitable two-plant manufacturing company (that wishes to remain anonymous) built a new manufacturing facility less than one mile from its largest operating facility. This new facility provided no new features; it was built solely to provide additional manufacturing capacity. The company was expert in the design and manufacture of its products and, with the new facility coming on line, would have the capacity to make and sell more of its products.

As the firm's management considered the new facility, all involved parties got caught up in the excitement of the new plant. Executive management wanted to be "a bigger player in the industry" and believed that the new plant was its key to being one. Marketing said that the company could easily sell the "new capacity." Operations suggested that the new capacity would help the firm run more efficiently and facilitate manufacturing flow, thereby causing costs per unit to drop dramatically. And Finance approved capital appropriations based on the most favorable scenarios provided by everyone else.

What actually happened to this company was that fixed costs tripled while sales increased marginally, by about 30%. Profits turned quickly into losses, inventory increased, and over time the stock price fell to less than one-fourth of the pre-new facility level. In reality, the company had more than enough capacity in its preexisting facility to manufacture 25 to 30% more product and, indeed, could have done so without incurring any additional fixed costs. As in so many cases, the data were available to all concerned, but the ability to analyze, interpret, and then act upon those data was missing or, worse, squandered.[1]

In Chapter 1 of management accounting, we discussed different ways to categorize costs. To review, some costs, such as direct materials and direct labor costs in a manufacturing firm, vary directly with the number of products or services produced. Other costs, such as some manufacturing overhead costs in a manufacturing firm, cannot be as easily traced to products. Costs that vary proportionately with the level of products produced or services offered are variable costs, while costs that do not vary in total with changes in the level of production are fixed costs. We used these definitions of variable costs and fixed costs to introduce you to ***cost-volume-profit (C-V-P) analysis****, a management accounting tool used to make planning decisions concerning appropriate levels of production and spending.*

In this chapter, you will further explore this important management tool to analyze relationships between variable costs, fixed costs, and revenues. You will learn that a key factor in making operating decisions is understanding ***cost behavior****—how costs change in relation to changes in activity levels, such as number of patients in a hospital or pounds of ore processed in a copper smelter. An understanding of how costs behave in relation to levels of activity helps managers predict the effects of their plans on future performance.*

cost-volume-profit (C-V-P) analysis Techniques for determining how changes in revenues, costs, and level of activity affect the profitability of an organization.

cost behavior The way a cost is affected by changes in activity levels.

You will also use the knowledge of cost behavior patterns to analyze the kinds of decisions facing companies like the one in the opening scenario. You will learn, for example, to make calculations that will determine how profits will change in relation to changes in sales volume, fixed costs, and variable costs. C-V-P analysis is critical in helping management plan future operations. Because the C-V-P analysis technique is applicable to all types of firms, we will also discuss the nature of costs in manufacturing, merchandising, service, and e-commerce firms. And while the focus will be primarily on examining the financial implications of cost-volume-profit analysis decisions, we will also pay attention to the effects these decisions have on quality and time issues as well.

1 John M. Brausch and Thomas C. Taylor, "Who Is Accounting for the Cost of Capacity?" *Management Accounting,* February 1997, p. 44.

1

Understand the key factors involved in cost-volume-profit (C-V-P) analysis and why it is such an important tool in management decision making.

UNDERSTANDING WHY C-V-P ANALYSIS IS IMPORTANT

Management must make many critical operating decisions that affect a firm's profitability. With respect to planning, management is often interested in the impact a particular action will have on profitability. C-V-P analysis can help managers assess that impact. The following are examples of questions that can be answered with C-V-P analysis:

- How will the profits of a bookstore be affected if the store raises its prices by 10%, resulting in a reduction of 2% in the number of books sold?
- How many customers must a scuba shop in the mall serve each month in order to break even and be able to pay the monthly rental fee?
- How many carpets must a fledgling entrepreneur clean in a month in order to generate a net profit of $3,000 each month?
- By how much will the profits of a discount computer store change if a $100,000 advertising campaign increases the number of units sold by 13%?
- How will the profits of a fast-food restaurant change if the restaurant stops selling milk shakes and instead focuses on raising the volume of soft drink sales by 25%?

It should be clear to you from these examples that C-V-P analysis involves studying the interrelationships among revenues, costs, levels of activity, and profits. However, quality of products and services and speed of production and delivery must also be considered as managers use C-V-P analysis to determine product prices, the mix of products, market strategy, appropriate sales commissions, advertising budgets, production schedules, and a host of other important planning decisions. Although C-V-P analysis is most useful for planning, it can also be used to assist with controlling decisions (e.g., are the costs too high for the level of sales?) and evaluating decisions (e.g., should we reward employees for holding costs down or be concerned that sales growth has slowed?). Indeed, the concept of C-V-P analysis is pervasive in management accounting. It offers tremendous potential for helping management increase the profitability and effectiveness of an organization. This chapter will help you learn the mechanics of C-V-P analysis as well as how to use this important concept. Before studying C-V-P analysis, however, you need to have a better understanding of basic cost behavior patterns. Once you understand these cost behavior patterns and how to determine them, you can use them to make the planning, controlling, and evaluating decisions discussed above.

---

to summarize

C-V-P analysis is a very important concept in management accounting. Key factors involved in C-V-P analysis include (1) the revenues derived from the sales prices charged for goods and services, (2) the fixed and variable costs, (3) the sales volume, (4) the mix of products, (5) the speed and quality of production, and (6) the resulting profits. Understanding the interrelationships of the key variables in C-V-P analysis can assist management in planning and in making critical controlling and evaluating decisions.

2

Explain and analyze the basic cost behavior patterns—variable, fixed, mixed, and stepped.

BASIC COST BEHAVIOR PATTERNS

The two basic cost behavior patterns—variable and fixed—were introduced in Chapter 1 of management accounting. Other cost behavior patterns, such as mixed costs, are variations of these two. Mixed costs exhibit characteristics of both variable and fixed costs. In this section, we will review both variable and fixed costs and examine the reality of how these costs often look in many organizations. We will also introduce mixed costs and stepped costs.

A cost is classified in one of the two basic categories by the way it reacts to changes in level of activity. The first task, then, is to define the activity involved and identify appropriate activity bases (often referred to as cost drivers). C-V-P analysis requires that we first determine what activity "drives" the costs. Once the activity is defined, measurements of changes in activity level can be used to determine cost behavior patterns.

Measuring Level of Activity

Level of activity is often measured in terms of output, input, or a combination of the two. Some of the most common activity bases used are number of units sold and number of units produced in manufacturing firms, number of units sold in merchandising firms, and number of contract hours paid for or billed in service firms. We will generally use production volume or sales volume as the activity basis in this chapter to demonstrate the use of C-V-P analysis. Note that just because a cost doesn't vary with a particular activity base (e.g., total units sold or units produced) does not mean it isn't a variable cost. For example, the total cost of wages for a convenience store may not vary with the amount of sales volume (the clerks get paid the same whether they serve a lot of customers or just a few), but total wages would vary based on the number of hours per week that the convenience store is open. So, if another type of activity other than sales volume is more relevant in determining changes in the variable costs being planned, the C-V-P analysis should be based on that activity. Managers must be careful to understand the various activity bases within their company so that they can properly plan for and control costs. We will discuss a number of alternative activity bases in Chapter 7 of management accounting.

Manufacturing and merchandising companies with a single product generally measure volume of activity in terms of output, for example, number of cars, television sets, or desks produced. However, many companies produce or sell several different products (refrigerators, toasters, and irons, for example), and a simple total of all the products manufactured or sold during a given period may not provide a good measure of activity. This is particularly true for manufacturing firms. For example, GENERAL ELECTRIC manufactures a wide variety of products, ranging from light bulbs to locomotives. It obviously takes more effort (and consequently costs more) to produce a locomotive than a light bulb; accordingly, it wouldn't make any sense to state that total production for a given day was 1,000,001—1,000,000 light bulbs and 1 locomotive. In multiproduct situations, these manufacturing firms usually use input measures, such as direct labor hours worked, machine time used, or the time needed to set up a job, as the activity base. Such measures are often better cost drivers than the more general output measures.

Variable Costs

variable costs Costs that change in total in direct proportion to changes in activity level.

Total **variable costs** change in direct proportion to changes in activity level. Examples are costs of direct materials, which vary proportionately with the number of units produced, and sales commissions, which vary proportionately with the sales volume. As an example, an automobile manufacturer might define the activity as the production of cars and the cost driver as the number of cars produced. If engines, tires, axles, and steering wheels are purchased from suppliers, the related costs would be variable because the total cost of steering wheels, for example, would vary proportionately with the number of cars produced. If no cars are produced, there are no steering wheel costs; if 1,000 cars are manufactured during a period, the total cost for steering wheels and other purchased parts is 1,000 times the unit cost of each item. As more cars are produced, the total cost of each item increases. The unit cost, however, remains constant. For example, if an auto company pays $150 per steering wheel, the total cost of steering wheels for 200 cars is $30,000; for 500 cars, it is $75,000. At both levels of activity, however, the unit cost is still $150. This relationship between variable costs and level of activity is shown graphically in Exhibit 2-1, which relates the number of cars produced to the total cost of the steering wheels used in production.

In addition to sales commissions and materials, many other costs (such as labor) have a variable cost behavior pattern. For example, if it takes four hours of labor to assemble a frame and

exhibit 2-1 An Example of Variable Costs

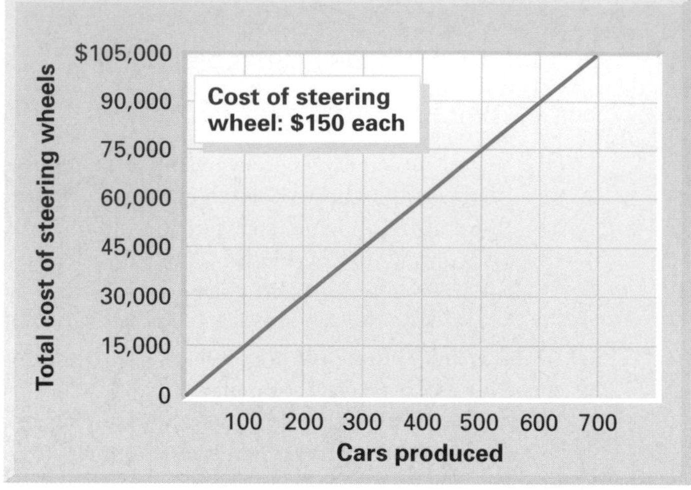

caution

Do not think that because a cost doesn't vary with production or sales, it cannot be a variable cost. For example, in a design engineering department, the activity base may be the number of changes to the architect's blueprints. Those costs that vary in total with the number of blueprint changes made would be classified as variable costs for that activity.

each hour costs $25, a unit labor cost of $100 per frame is a variable cost; the total labor cost would be $100 times the number of frames produced. As another example, if it generally requires $115 in materials and inspection time to do a quality check on a batch of chemicals being produced, then inspection costs of $115 per batch (regardless of the number of pounds of chemicals in the batch) is also a variable cost for batch-related activities. With respect to labor, however, a word of caution is in order. While the labor it takes to assemble a frame or perform quality checks varies proportionately with the number of frames assembled or quality checks performed, it isn't always easy to have exactly the right amount of labor on hand for various levels of production. When changes in production occur, it may take weeks or months to adjust labor costs to the amount that should be incurred. For example, automobile manufacturers understand (after years of negotiating with labor unions) that they cannot make sudden changes to their labor costs. If the market demand for cars goes down, rarely will manufacturers immediately lay off workers. Reductions in labor costs for these companies take time and must be handled appropriately. This does not necessarily mean that labor costs are fixed for a manufacturer. Given time, these costs can and will be adjusted.

curvilinear costs Variable costs that do not vary in direct proportion to changes in activity level but vary at decreasing or increasing rates due to economies of scale, productivity changes, and so on.

CURVILINEAR VARIABLE COSTS Our definition of the variable cost behavior pattern specifies that variable costs have a linear relationship to the level of activity; that is, when the level of activity increases, total variable costs rise at a directly proportional rate. For example, if the level of activity doubles, the total variable costs will also double; this is a called a linear relationship. The reality is that, in practice, a truly linear relationship usually does not exist. Overall, many variable costs are actually **curvilinear costs** when considered over many activity levels. That is, these curvilinear costs actually vary at increasing or decreasing rates with changes in activity level. To illustrate, assume that an ice cream manufacturer uses milk, sugar, and other ingredients purchased from suppliers to make ice cream. Assume that one gallon of milk is used to make one gallon of ice cream; so, if no ice cream is produced, there is no milk cost. If 1,000 gallons of ice cream are scheduled to be manufactured during the week, 1,000 gallons of milk will be purchased at a cost of $2.00 per gallon for a total of $2,000. As more ice cream is produced, the total cost of milk increases, but the price per gallon decreases because of quantity discounts. If 2,000 gallons of milk are purchased, the price is $1.85 per gallon; and if 3,000 gallons are purchased, the price is $1.70 per gallon. The price decreases $0.15 per gallon for each additional 1,000 gallons purchased until a price of $1.25 per gallon is reached. Thereafter, the price discounts start becoming smaller. Thus, this curvilinear cost increases at a decreasing rate, as depicted in the top graph in Exhibit 2-2.

exhibit 2-2 Curvilinear Variable Costs

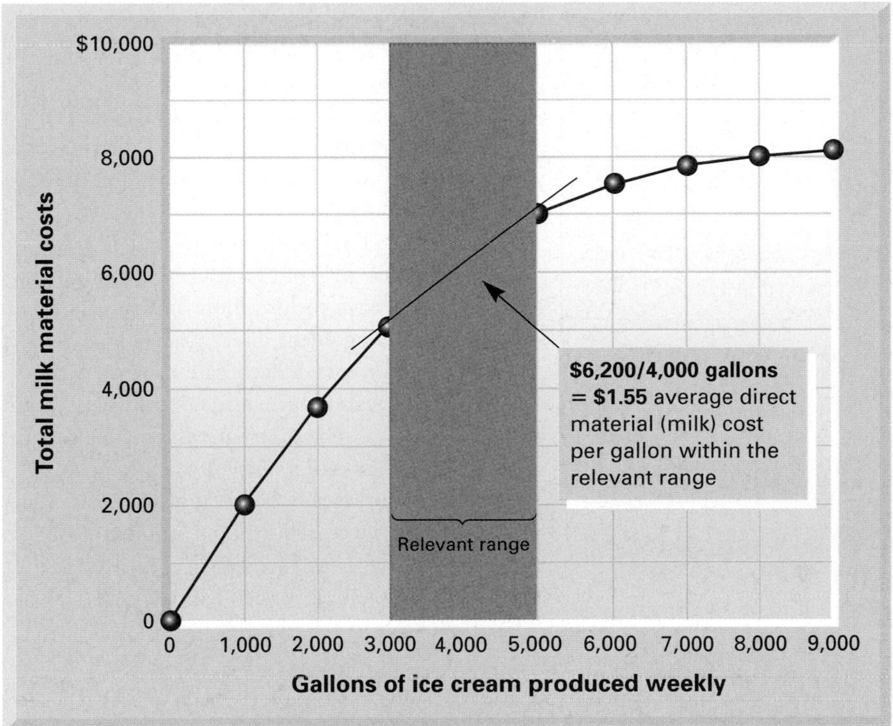

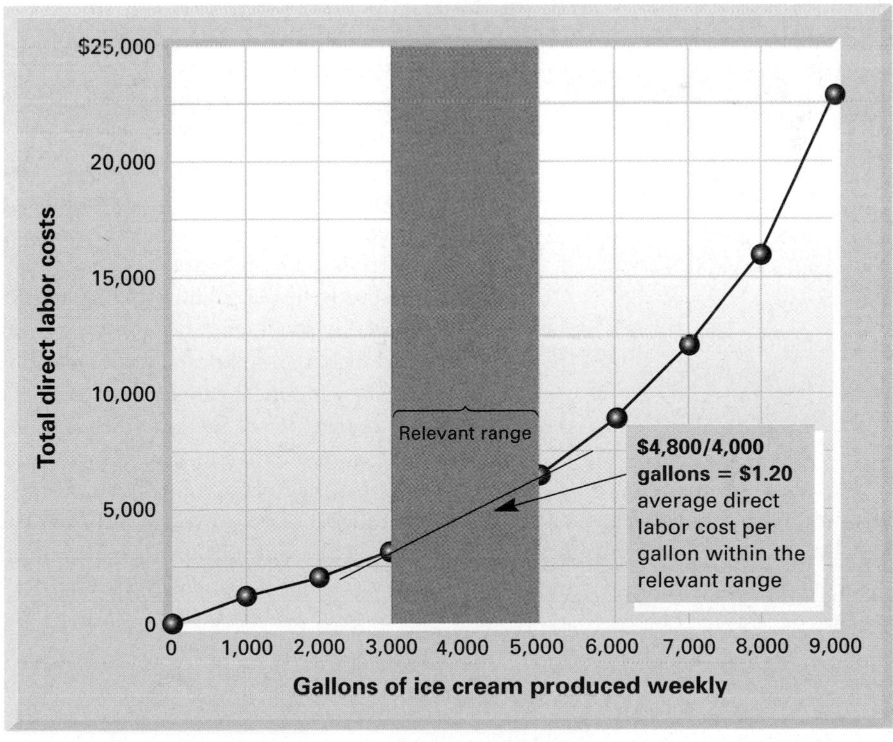

fyi

If you've had an introductory class in economics, you have likely been introduced to the term *economies of scale.* The cost of milk that becomes cheaper as production volume increases (top graph in Exhibit 2-2) is a cost that displays economies of scale. On the other hand, the direct labor costs to produce ice cream that become more costly as production increases (bottom graph in Exhibit 2-2) represent costs with *diseconomies* of scale.

To illustrate how curvilinear costs can increase at an increasing rate, let's assume that this particular ice cream manufacturer actually makes a very specialized "premium natural" ice cream that is handmade using a traditional preindustrial process. The problem for the manager of the ice cream production process is that it is difficult to find people who can make ice cream efficiently. Essentially, the production speed of an individual who makes ice cream can range from 4 to 12 gallons per hour. The manager of the production process has two top employees who can make 12 gallons of ice cream per hour. Because everyone on the ice cream production crew is paid $10 per hour, these two employees can produce 960 gallons of ice cream each week (12 gallons per hour × 40 hours per week × 2 employees) at a total cost of $800 ($10 per hour × 40 hours per week × 2 employees). That works out to a little more than 83 cents per gallon for direct labor costs. However, plans to increase the production volume of the operation mean that the manager will have to hire more individuals for the ice cream production crew, and the ice-cream-making talent of each new employee gets worse the more she hires! As a result, the direct labor cost of each gallon of ice cream will increase as planned production volumes go up because the average output per worker goes down. For example, based on the available pool of job applicants, the manager figures that weekly production of 3,000 gallons of ice cream will require 8 workers, resulting in an average direct labor cost of $1.07 per gallon of ice cream (total labor cost of $3,200 = $10 per hour × 40 hours per week × 8 employees), while a 5,000-gallon production week will require 16 workers, resulting in an average direct labor cost of $1.28 per gallon (total labor cost of $6,400 = $10 per hour × 40 hours per week × 16 employees). This curvilinear cost increases at an *increasing* rate, as depicted in the bottom graph in Exhibit 2-2.

relevant range The range of operating level, or volume of activity, over which the relationship between total costs (variable plus fixed) and activity level is approximately linear.

RELEVANT RANGE AND THE LINEARITY OF VARIABLE COSTS Curvilinear costs are very difficult to deal with when using C-V-P analysis to make planning decisions. In fact, as we'll discuss later, one of the limiting assumptions of C-V-P analysis is that all costs are assumed to be strictly linear! While this is never exactly true, it is usually safe to assume that variable costs are *approximately* linear within a certain range of production, called the **relevant range**. To illustrate the relevant range concept, let's return to our ice cream manufacturing business. Realistically, the production manager does not expect to vary weekly production volume outside the range of 3,000 to 5,000 gallons of ice cream. As displayed in Exhibit 2-2 for both milk material cost and direct labor cost, a linear segment within the relevant range of weekly production can effectively approximate the curvilinear cost relationship of producing between 3,000 and 5,000 gallons of ice cream. By assuming a linear (rather than a curvilinear) relationship, the variable costs of milk and direct labor are estimated at $1.55 and $1.20, respectively, per gallon of ice cream using the costs in the midpoint of the relevant range (weekly production of 4,000 gallons of ice cream).

caution

Remembering the concept of the relevant range is especially important when applying C-V-P analysis to companies in very high growth situations, such as high-tech start-ups. If a company's sales are increasing by 60% each quarter, for example, it is unlikely to remain in the same "relevant range" from quarter to quarter; so careful analysis of variable and fixed costs must be repeated on a regular basis.

Relevant range is an important concept and should be kept in mind when considering cost behavior patterns. If activity increases or decreases significantly, cost relationships will probably change. If production volume soars, for example, such factors as overtime work and bulk-purchase discounts may subject direct labor and materials costs to fluctuations that destroy their proportional relationship to volume. That is why we say that the definition of variable costs—costs that in total have a linear relationship with volume of activity—is applicable only within relevant ranges. The important point to remember is that whenever we define a particular variable cost, we are assuming that the cost is within the relevant range of activity.

Fixed Costs

fixed costs Costs that remain constant in total, regardless of activity level, at least over a certain range of activity.

Fixed costs remain constant in total, regardless of activity level, at least within the relevant range of activity. Examples include property taxes, insurance, executives' salaries, plant depreciation, and rent. Because total fixed costs remain constant as activity increases, the fixed cost per unit (total fixed cost ÷ level of activity) decreases. Similarly, as the level of activity decreases, the fixed cost per unit increases. This is in contrast to variable costs, where the costs

caution

While total variable costs increase as production increases, the per-unit variable cost is constant across activity levels within the relevant range. In contrast, while total fixed costs are constant over the relevant range, the per-unit fixed cost changes with increases or decreases in production.

per unit are assumed to remain constant through changes in the level of activity within the relevant range.

Before we go any further, it would be a good idea to put all this concern about identifying fixed and variable costs in context. Remember that this chapter is about managing the relationships among costs, volume, and profit. In Chapter 1 of management accounting, we briefly introduced the concept of C-V-P and break-even analysis. In the C-V-P formula below that we used previously in Chapter 1, you can see that predicting (i.e., calculating) what a company needs to do to "break even" and start making a profit requires a clear measure of total fixed costs and variable costs per unit:

$$\frac{\text{Total fixed costs}}{(\text{Sales price per unit} - \text{Variable cost per unit})} = \text{Break-even sales (in units)}$$

In an actual company, these costs are very challenging to identify. That is why it is important that you understand the nature of cost behavior and how to (hopefully) classify costs as either fixed or variable. Once we've completed our discussion of cost behavior, we'll be ready to spend some time on this very useful C-V-P formula later in this chapter.

fyi

Have you ever wondered why you always wait so long and why there are so many patients at one time in a dentist's office? Think about the nature of the dentist's costs. Most costs are fixed—dentists' salaries, rent or depreciation, and so forth. When costs are mostly fixed, seeing a high volume of patients is important to cover the fixed costs. Then, once fixed costs are covered, almost all additional patient revenue becomes profit. Thus, by seeing only a few additional patients, dentists can increase their profits substantially.

STEPPED FIXED COSTS The top graph in Exhibit 2-3 shows the relationship between the ice cream manufacturer's production line supervisor cost and the total number of gallons of ice cream produced. In this case, until weekly ice cream production reaches 1,000 gallons a week, the manufacturing manager is able to oversee all line workers. At 1,000 gallons a week production, however, the manager expects to hire a production line supervisor at $500 per week to provide more supervision of the workers. Further, the manager expects that she'll need to hire an additional supervisor each time weekly production is increased another 2,000 gallons. Yet, though the production line supervisor cost is changing as the scale of ice cream production changes, we still consider this cost to be fixed *within the relevant range.* Hence, as shown in the top graph in Exhibit 2-3, within a relevant range of activity of between 3,000 and 5,000 gallons of ice cream, the total fixed manufacturing supervisor cost of $1,000 does not change. On the other hand, the per-unit supervisor cost will drop considerably as production increases. For example, when the fixed supervisor cost is $1,000 and 3,000 gallons of ice cream are being produced, the supervisor cost per gallon of ice cream is $0.33 ($1,000 ÷ 3,000 gallons). With production of 4,000 gallons, however, the manufacturing supervisor cost is only $0.25 ($1,000 ÷ 4,000 gallons) per gallon.

As you can see in the top graph of Exhibit 2-3, the fixed cost of production line supervision "steps up" as the volume of ice cream production increases. **Stepped costs** are costs that change in total in a stair-step fashion (that is, in large amounts) with changes in volume of activity. Another example of a stepped cost might be the labor charges for the maintenance of the tools and machinery in a small manufacturing plant. One maintenance worker can handle the upkeep of all the equipment during normal levels of activity. When there is a significant increase in activity, a second worker must be hired, and the maintenance cost approximately doubles.

stepped costs Costs that change in total in a stair-step fashion (in large amounts) with changes in volume of activity.

RELEVANT RANGE AND THE LINEARITY OF FIXED COSTS How are stepped costs analyzed so that managers can make appropriate decisions? If the steps are wide compared to the relevant range (in other words, the costs essentially are unchanged within the relevant range), the costs are usually treated as fixed. This would be the case with the production line supervisor costs in Exhibit 2-3. If the steps are small and change throughout the relevant range, the costs are usually approximated with a variable cost line. Though this approximation is not perfect, it is better than making the more substantial error of ignoring the change in a stepped cost.

The bottom graph in Exhibit 2-3 illustrates a stepped cost that approximates a variable cost. This graph represents the depreciation and electricity costs required to operate a set of machines used to pack the ice cream in special cartons. Each machine can pack 10 half-gallon cartons per hour. The depreciation and electricity costs of each machine are approximately $50 per week.

exhibit 2-3 Stepped Fixed Costs

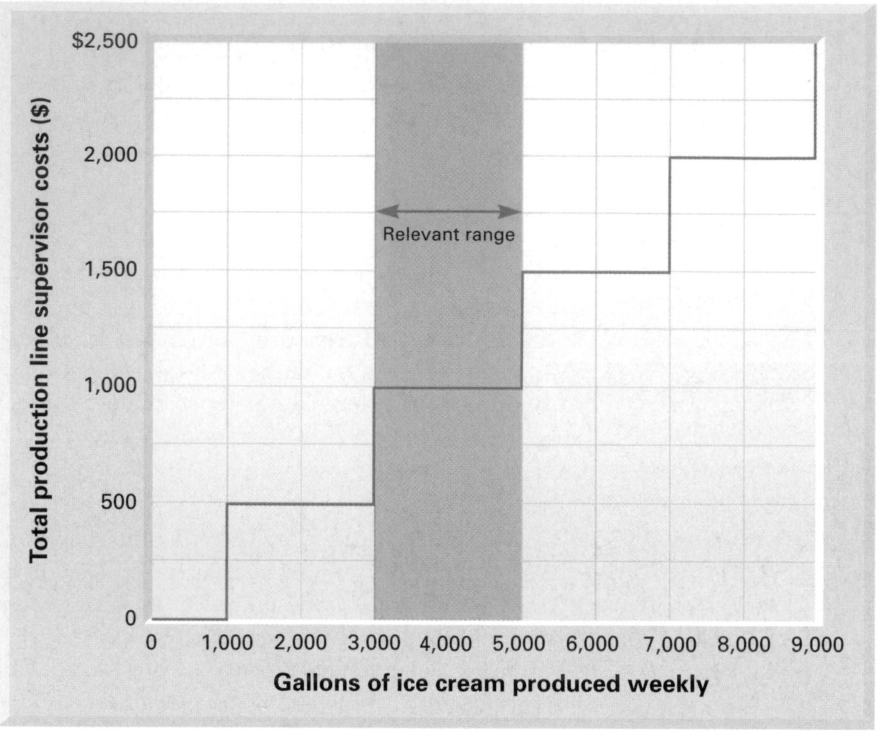

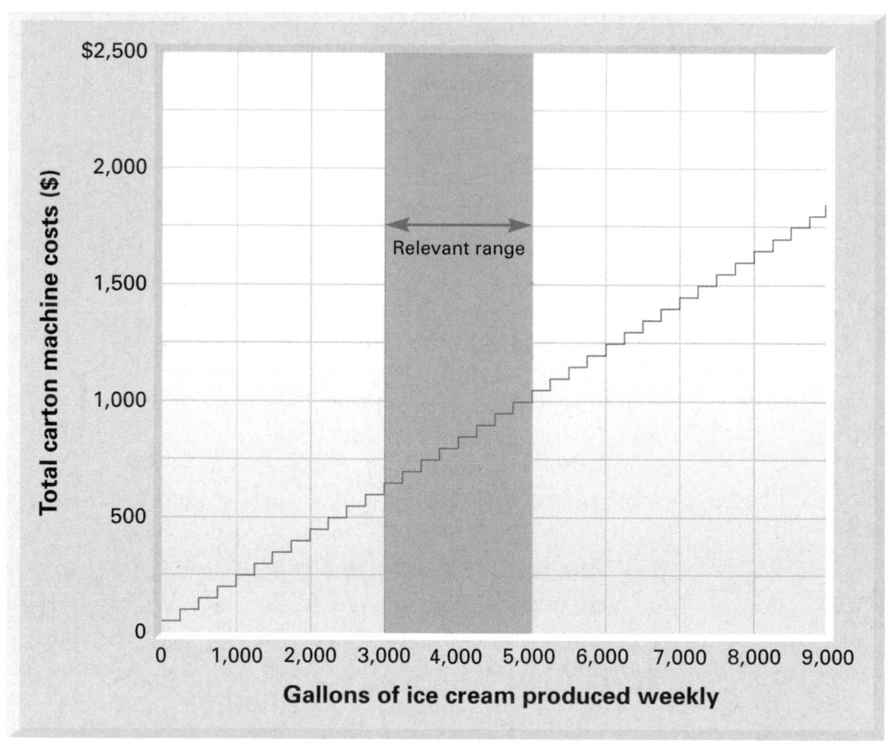

Each increase in planned weekly production of 200 gallons of ice cream will cause total carton machine costs to "step up" by $50. Therefore, at 1,000 gallons of production a week, total carton machine costs are $250; and at 3,000 gallons of production a week, total carton machine costs are $650. The management accounting question here is how to treat the behavior of carton machine costs in a C-V-P analysis. Clearly, the production line supervisor costs are fixed within the relevant range of between 3,000 and 5,000 gallons of production. But the carton machine costs are "stepping up" throughout the relevant range. Typically, though the carton machine costs are not actually linear variable costs with respect to incremental changes in each gallon of ice cream produced (as are the milk costs), accountants within the organization will treat these costs as if they were variable. In our example, the average carton machine cost per gallon of ice cream within the relevant range is $0.20.[2]

THE TREND TOWARD FIXED COSTS Over the past few decades, fixed costs have increased as a percentage of total costs for many manufacturing companies, primarily due to the increase in factory automation. As a machine replaces each manual job, costs change from variable labor costs to fixed depreciation or rental charges. It is important to note that many service companies have much higher ratios of fixed-to-variable costs than do manufacturing companies. The costs of providing services in companies such as banks, consulting agencies, and airlines typically do not vary much depending on the volume of banking transactions, consulting hours, or passengers carried. Perhaps more significantly, e-commerce organizations often have even fewer variable costs than service organizations do! Once the technology has been put in place to run an e-commerce business, there is typically very little additional cost of technology based on usage (within the relevant range). Personnel costs in e-commerce organizations, such as engineering personnel, marketing teams, and executive personnel, also do not change much based on customer use of the organization's technology.

As fixed costs in manufacturing organizations increase, and the economy continues to shift more and more to service and e-commerce organizations, this fixed cost emphasis has a significant effect on the decision-making process. When costs are fixed, management's ability to influence costs with activity-level decisions is limited. With variable costs, management has more flexibility to change activity levels and thereby increase or decrease total operating cost structures. This trend of replacing variable costs with fixed costs has an important impact on the cost structure of an organization that is captured in the concept of operating leverage, which is discussed in the expanded material section of this chapter.

Mixed Costs

mixed costs Costs that contain both variable and fixed cost components.

Mixed costs, like curvilinear costs and stepped costs, are variations of the basic fixed and variable cost behavior patterns. Specifically, mixed costs are costs that contain both variable and fixed components. An example is rent that is based on a fixed rental fee plus a percentage of total sales. Thus, the rental terms for an automobile dealer's showroom might include a flat payment of $4,000 per month plus 1% of each month's sales. The 1% of sales is the variable portion, and the $4,000 is the fixed cost. The total rent, therefore, would be considered a mixed cost and could be diagrammed as shown in Exhibit 2-4. As this exhibit shows, the cost of renting the showroom increases as sales increase. The total rent is $4,000 when there are no sales; $6,000 when sales are $200,000 [$4,000 + (0.01 × $200,000)]; and $8,000 when sales are $400,000 [$4,000 + (0.01 × $400,000)]. This increase is directly due to the variable cost element, which increases in total as activity level (car sales) increases.

One of the important challenges in using C-V-P analysis in the planning process is the need to effectively separate mixed costs into their fixed and variable cost components. Over the years several management accounting techniques have been developed by organizations for this purpose. We will explore these mixed cost analysis methods in the next section of this chapter.

2 This is calculated using the high-low method described later in this chapter. ($1,050 − $650)/(5,000 gallons − 3,000 gallons) = $0.20 per gallon

exhibit 2-4 An Example of a Mixed Cost

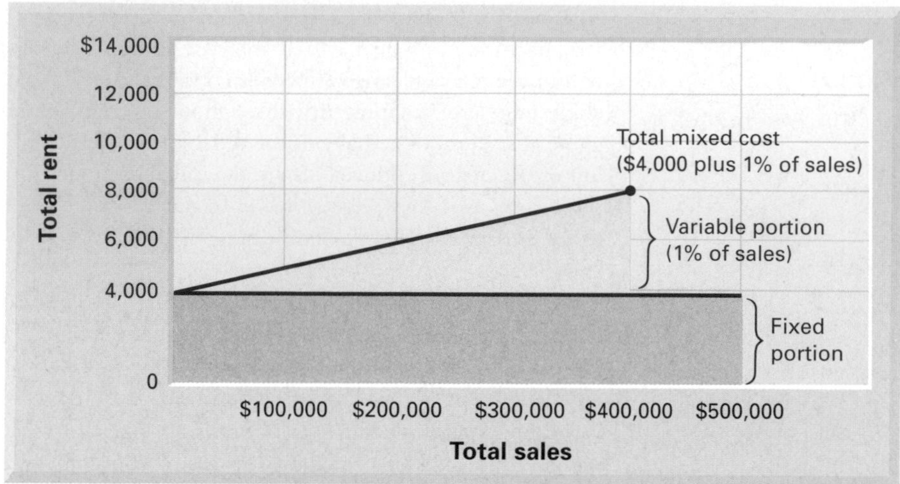

to summarize

Understanding cost behavior patterns is essential for the management process of effective planning. Cost behavior is the way a cost changes in response to changes in activity level. There are two basic cost behavior patterns, variable and fixed. Total variable costs change in direct proportion to changes in the level of activity over the relevant range; therefore, variable costs are constant per unit over this range. In analyzing variable costs, we generally assume a linear relationship between total costs and the level of activity within the relevant range; outside of this range, variable costs are usually curvilinear. Total fixed costs do not change over the relevant range; therefore, fixed costs decrease per unit as the level of activity increases within the relevant range. Stepped costs increase with the level of activity but not proportionately. If the steps are wide in relation to the relevant range, these costs can be treated as fixed; if the steps are narrow, they can be treated as variable. Because of such factors as technology and automation, many costs that were once variable now exhibit fixed cost behaviors. Mixed costs have both a variable and a fixed cost component. An increase in a mixed cost with a rising level of activity is due directly to the variable cost element.

3 Analyze mixed costs using the scattergraph and high-low methods.

ANALYSIS OF MIXED COSTS

So far in this chapter, we have introduced several types of behavior exhibited by costs. We will spend this section discussing and analyzing mixed costs for the purpose of making planning decisions using C-V-P analysis. Mixed costs are often difficult to separate into variable and fixed components. Usually, the fixed portion represents the cost necessary to maintain a service (such as a telephone) or a facility (such as a building), and the variable portion covers actual use. Recall the example of the automobile showroom's rental cost, part of which was a flat monthly fee and part a percentage of sales. Other common mixed costs are certain types of leases and such overhead costs as electricity, repairs, telephone, and maintenance.

The most accurate way to separate the actual fixed and variable components of mixed costs is to analyze each invoice. An electricity bill, for example, may include a flat monthly service charge that would be classified as a fixed cost. Additional variable costs are those based on the amount of electricity actually used during the month. This approach could be very time-consuming, however, and may not be cost-effective (that is, it would cost more than the detailed information is worth). A more useful approach would be to use, for each level of activity, the historical trend in past costs as the basis for classifying costs as fixed or variable. There are several methods of doing this. In this section we will concentrate on two: the scattergraph method and the high-low method. In the expanded material, we introduce least squares analysis, a more sophisticated method for analyzing mixed costs.

The Scattergraph, or Visual-Fit, Method

scattergraph (visual-fit) method A method of segregating the fixed and variable components of a mixed cost by plotting on a graph total costs at several activity levels and drawing a regression line through the points.

regression line On a scattergraph, the straight line that most closely expresses the relationship between the variables.

variable cost rate The change in cost divided by the change in activity; the slope of the regression line.

Probably the simplest method of segregating mixed costs into their variable and fixed components is the **scattergraph** (or **visual-fit**) **method**. The total mixed cost for each level of activity is plotted on a graph, and a straight line (called the **regression line**) is visually fitted through the points. The idea is to position the line through the set of plotted data points in a way that minimizes the average distance between all the data points and the fitted regression line. With the regression line inserted into the graph, the fixed portion of the mixed cost is estimated to be the amount on the cost (vertical) axis at the point where it is intercepted by the regression line. The variable cost per unit (referred to as the **variable cost rate**) is equal to the slope of the regression line, which is simply the change in cost divided by the change in activity.

To illustrate the scattergraph method, we will use the electricity costs for an automobile manufacturer. In the analysis and calculations that follow, all costs are assumed to fall within the relevant range of activity. In this example, we use direct labor hours as a measure of the activity level.

Exhibit 2-5 shows a scattergraph on which electricity costs and direct labor hours have been plotted. The regression line has been visually fitted to minimize the distance between data points. It appears that the total fixed portion of electricity cost is about $40,000 per month, which is where the regression line intersects the cost axis. The variable cost rate is approximately $4.29 per direct labor hour, which is the slope of the regression line. To calculate the slope, we use the following formula and the data points of zero and 7,000 direct labor hours, respectively.

$$\text{Variable cost rate} = \frac{\text{Change in (electricity) cost}}{\text{Change in activity (direct labor hours)}}$$

$$X = \frac{\$70{,}000 - \$40{,}000}{7{,}000 - 0}$$

$$X = \frac{\$30{,}000}{7{,}000}$$

$$X = \$4.29 \text{ (rounded)}$$

caution

Once the regression line has been fitted through the data points, the scattergraph method does not depend any longer on the *data points* to estimate fixed and variable costs. Cost estimations are entirely based on *points along the regression line.* For instance, notice that in this case we used the points 0 and 7,000 along the visually fitted regression line. However, we could have used any two points on the regression line to calculate the variable costs per direct labor hour.

Obviously, the scattergraph method has some limitations as a cost estimation tool. Perhaps the most critical limitation is that how the user fits the regression line through the data points is entirely subjective. Consider Exhibit 2-5 once more. If you were the one fitting the regression line to these data points, would you have set the line exactly where it is in this graph? Hopefully, your line would have been quite close to the current line. Still, it probably wouldn't have been exactly the same, resulting in some small differences in your own estimations of fixed and variable costs. Hence, the scattergraph method is a classic "quick and dirty" management accounting technique. Yet, although the scattergraph provides only subjective estimates of the fixed and variable portions of mixed costs, it can be an extremely useful tool to describe and discuss cost behavior in the planning process. It is also useful for controlling operating costs. For instance, it shows at a glance any trends and abrupt changes in cost behavior patterns. It is also a means of checking whether costs are rising at a directly

exhibit 2-5 Total Electricity Costs

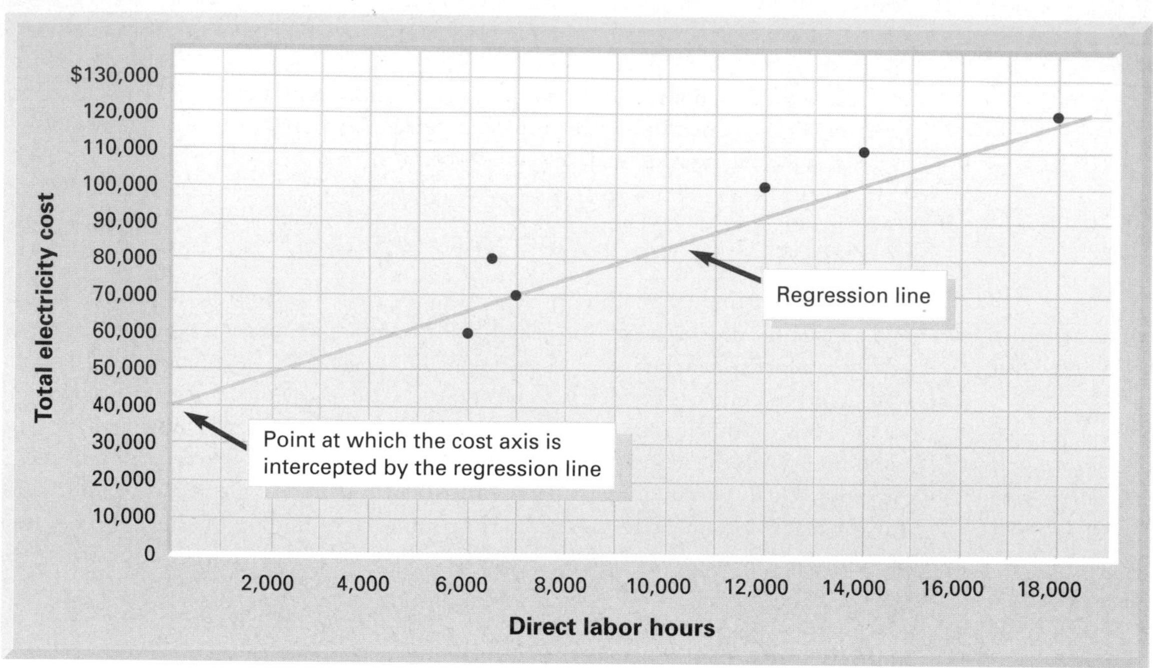

proportionate rate within the relevant range. As such, it can be used as a preliminary step before using more sophisticated methods of cost evaluation.

The High-Low Method

high-low method A method of segregating the fixed and variable components of a mixed cost by analyzing the costs at the highest and the lowest activity levels within a relevant range.

A second approach is the **high-low method**, which analyzes mixed costs on the basis of total costs incurred at both the highest and the lowest levels of activity. To illustrate this method, we refer again to the electricity costs of the automobile manufacturer. This time, however, we will focus on the following table of reported electricity costs and direct labor hours worked.

Month	Direct Labor Hours Worked	Total Electricity Cost
January	7,000	$ 70,000
February	6,000	60,000
March	12,000	100,000
April	6,600	80,000
May	18,000	120,000
June	14,000	110,000

Although these two columns of figures do not visually show trends as clearly as the scattergraph does, they do suggest that as the activity level (direct labor hours) increases, total electricity costs increase. Given this relationship, the high-low method can be used to determine the fixed and variable portions of the electricity cost as follows:

1. Identify the highest and lowest activity levels (18,000 hours in May and 6,000 hours in February). These two months also represent the highest and lowest levels of electricity costs, or $120,000 and $60,000, respectively (though this may not always be the case).
2. Determine the differences between the high and low points.

	Total Electricity Cost	Direct Labor Hours
High point (May)	$120,000	18,000
Low point (February)	60,000	6,000
Difference	$ 60,000	12,000

3. Calculate the variable cost rate (variable cost per unit). The formula is the same as the one used to compute the slope of the regression line in the scattergraph method. The results are different, of course, because the scattergraph method is based on a regression line that is plotted using all the data points, whereas the high-low method uses only the high and low data points.

$$\text{Variable cost rate} = \frac{\text{Change in costs}}{\text{Change in activity}}$$

$$= \frac{\$60,000}{12,000}$$

$$= \$5 \text{ per direct labor hour}$$

4. Determine fixed costs based on the variable cost rate ($5 in this case). The formula for this computation is:

$$\text{Fixed costs} = \text{Total costs} - \text{Variable costs}$$

At the high level of activity, the calculation would be:

$$X = \$120,000 - (18,000 \times \$5)$$
$$X = \$120,000 - \$90,000$$
$$X = \$30,000$$

You get the same results if you calculate fixed costs at the low level of activity:

$$X = \$60,000 - (6,000 \times \$5)$$
$$X = \$60,000 - \$30,000$$
$$X = \$30,000$$

In summary, using the high-low method of analyzing mixed costs, the variable portion of the total electricity cost is estimated to be $5 per direct labor hour, and the fixed portion is $30,000 per month. This means that $30,000 appears to be the amount the company pays each month just to have electricity available, and $5 is the average additional electricity cost for each hour of direct labor worked.

A Comparison of the Scattergraph and High-Low Methods

As we have illustrated, the scattergraph and high-low methods may produce different results.

Method	Variable Cost Rate	Fixed Cost
Scattergraph	$4.29	$40,000
High-low	5.00	30,000

Both methods are useful for a quick approximation. The scattergraph method takes all the data into account. Therefore, it tends to be more accurate, although it is somewhat subjective (depending on how the line is drawn) and inconsistent because different people might draw the

business environment essay

From Bankruptcy to 23 Consecutive Profitable Quarters CONTINENTAL AIRLINES has increased profits each of the last six years, an amazing turnaround for a company that once was protected from many of its creditors under Chapter 11 bankruptcy. In 1995, when Continental's last failure, Continental Lite (an attempt to copy SOUTHWEST AIRLINES' cheap commuter flights), ended up costing the company $110 million, new management was brought in. Today, Continental Airlines is the fifth largest airline in the United States, offering more than 2,200 departures daily to 136 domestic and 92 international destinations. And for the third year in a row, Continental was ranked among the 100 Best Companies to work for by *Fortune* magazine.

What has changed? How has Continental's management team taken what airline creditors wanted to liquidate and turned it into a viable competitor in its industry? For one thing, Continental Airlines management carefully analyzed its costs, divided those

line through the points differently. On the other hand, anyone using the high-low method will consistently get the same results. However, because only two data points are used, the high-low method may not be representative of the costs incurred at all levels of activity. Essentially, the math used in the high-low method plots the regression line through the two most extreme points in a scattergraph. Check whether the high and low points in our example are representative by plotting the data on the scattergraph of Exhibit 2-5. You will notice that the low point lies below the scattergraph regression line and the high point lies above the scattergraph regression line, indicating that, in this case, a straight line drawn through the high and the low points would not necessarily represent all six data points plotted. Nevertheless, both methods can be used to predict future costs. If, for example, management wants to know how much electricity will cost next month with 10,000 direct labor hours budgeted, the following calculations would be made:

Method	Formula	Estimated Cost
Scattergraph	$40,000 + 10,000($4.29) =	$82,900
High-low	$30,000 + 10,000($5.00) =	$80,000

As you can see, the total estimated costs resulting from these two methods, in this case, are reasonably close to each other.

caution

Once you have selected the high and low activity levels to use in the high-low method, you must base all cost calculations on those two activity levels and related costs. Otherwise, if you use any other activity level or cost to perform the calculations, you will have erroneous results that could produce significantly different cost estimations.

to summarize

Two common techniques for analyzing mixed costs are the scattergraph and high-low methods. The scattergraph method involves visually fitting a straight line (the regression line) through data points plotted on a graph, then noting where the line intercepts the cost axis (the fixed cost) and calculating the slope of the line (the variable cost rate). With the high-low method, the high and the low levels of activity are used to calculate first the variable cost rate and then the fixed cost component.

costs into fixed and variable components, and made several decisions to reduce fixed costs. For example, Continental grounded 41 planes and slashed capacity roughly 9% to rebound from its disaster in 1995. The airline cut more than 4,900 jobs, or approximately 12% of its workforce to reach profitability.

With fixed costs under control, Continental Airlines became profitable. In fact, it is now one of the most profitable airlines. Because it cut costs, Continental Airlines passengers pay lower fares than on other airlines and receive better service. These lower fares and better service enable Continental to fill more seats than most of its competitors. Because its costs are low, it is highly profitable. Fixed costs are now a smaller percentage of total costs at Continental Airlines than at almost all other airlines.

Sources: Adapted from PR Newswire, "Continental Airlines Earnings Per Share Jump 45 Percent; Six Straight Years of Profit," http://www.datek.com, January 17, 2001, Copyright 2001, Datek Online; Wendy Zellner, "Back to 'Coffee, Tea, or Milk?'" *Business Week*, July 3, 1995.

4

Perform C-V-P analyses, and describe the effects potential changes in C-V-P variables have on company profitability.

METHODS OF C-V-P ANALYSIS

Now that you have a better understanding of cost behaviors and can separate both mixed and stepped costs into their fixed and variable cost elements, you are ready to use your knowledge of cost behaviors to make planning decisions. Chapter 1 of management accounting provided a quick introduction to C-V-P analysis in the process of planning and analyzing decisions to prioritize Kevlar versus Teflon product at DUPONT. We will further explore C-V-P analysis now and extend your ability to use this valuable management accounting tool. First, we need to spend some time working with the concept of contribution margin.

contribution margin The difference between total sales and variable costs; the portion of sales revenue available to cover fixed costs and provide a profit.

Contribution Margin

Contribution margin is equal to sales revenue less variable costs; it is the amount of revenue that remains to cover fixed costs and provide a profit for an organization. For example, the con-

The contribution margin generated by the sale of an order of french fries can be used to pay fixed costs such as rent, insurance, and salaries. Now you know why you often hear that ever popular question "Would you like fries with that?" at fast-food restaurants.

tribution margin from the sale of one order of french fries by a fast-food restaurant is the selling price less the variables costs (potatoes, salt, container, cooking oil, wages of the cook) of producing the fries. Any contribution margin generated by the sale of an order of french fries can be used to pay the fixed costs of the fast-foot outlet, such as the monthly rent, the insurance, the supervisor's salary, and so forth. Contribution margin is one of the most important management accounting concepts you will study because many operating decisions are made on the basis of how it will be affected. A company may decide, for example, to advertise one product more than others because it has a higher contribution margin.

THE CONTRIBUTION MARGIN INCOME STATEMENT To illustrate the concept of contribution margin, we will use the following format of a contribution margin income statement. The statement data for Jewels Corporation, a producer of high-quality baseball gloves, follow.[3]

Jewels Corporation
Contribution Margin Income Statement
For the Month Ended November 30, 2003

	Total	Per Unit
Sales revenue (1,000 gloves)	$200,000	$200
Less variable costs	110,000	110
Contribution margin	$ 90,000	$ 90
Less fixed costs	63,000	
Profit*	$ 27,000	

*In this chapter, "profit" means pretax income; the terms *income* and *profit* are interchangeable.

per-unit contribution margin The excess of the sales price of one unit over its variable costs.

As this income statement shows, for internal decision-making purposes, Jewels Corporation computes its contribution margin on a per-unit (glove) and total-dollar basis. During November, Jewels' **per-unit contribution margin** is $90; the total contribution margin at a sales volume of 1,000 baseball gloves is $90,000.

The per-unit contribution margin tells us that $90 is available from each glove sold to cover fixed costs and provide a profit. By showing the $63,000 of fixed costs separately, this income statement also indicates that Jewels must generate sufficient contribution margin to cover these costs before a profit can be earned. With $200,000 of sales revenue, the contribution margin ($90,000) is sufficient to cover the fixed costs and provide a profit of $27,000.

This type of contribution margin income statement is particularly useful as a planning tool. It enables a company to project profits at any level of activity within the relevant range. For example, if Jewels Corporation forecasts sales at 1,200 baseball gloves next month, it could prepare a forecasted (or pro-forma) income statement (in contribution margin format) as follows:

Jewels Corporation
Pro-Forma Contribution Margin Income Statement
For the Month Ended December 31, 2003

Sales revenue (1,200 gloves × $200)	$240,000
Less variable costs (1,200 gloves × $110)	132,000
Contribution margin	$108,000
Less fixed costs	63,000
Profit	$ 45,000

Notice that with an increase in sales of 200 baseball gloves, the contribution margin increases $18,000 ($108,000 − $90,000). This can be confirmed by multiplying the per-unit con-

3 In this example, we assume that there is only one model of baseball glove, which sells for $200.

tribution margin by the increase in volume ($90 per unit × 200 gloves = $18,000). Because we assume that the increase in volume is still within the relevant range of activity (which is *very* important!), the fixed costs remain at $63,000, and profit increases by the $18,000 change in contribution margin. The critical thing to see here is that once the fixed costs are covered, each subsequent dollar in contribution margin goes straight to profit! In other words, when Jewels Corporation hits its break-even point (i.e., all fixed costs are covered), each additional glove sold will generate $90 in profit.

Notice the importance of accurately determining cost behavior when forecasting profit levels. If one ignores cost behavior, then the $27,000 profit generated by November sales of 1,000 gloves leads to the conclusion that each glove creates $27 ($27,000 profit/1,000 gloves) in profit. With this *incorrect* information, the forecasted level of profit for December sales of 1,200 gloves is $32,400 ($27 per glove × 1,200 gloves). This forecast differs significantly from the $45,000 profit forecast above that stems from a *correct* consideration of the behavior of Jewels Corporation's costs.

contribution margin ratio The percentage of net sales revenue left after variable costs are deducted; the contribution margin divided by net sales revenue.

THE CONTRIBUTION MARGIN RATIO The contribution margin may be expressed as a percentage of sales revenue as well as on a per-unit or total-dollar basis. Knowing the **contribution margin ratio**, which is the percentage of sales revenue left after variable costs are deducted, management can compare the profitability of various products. For example, if product A has a 45% contribution margin ratio and the contribution margin ratio of product B is only 30%, the company should emphasize product A, assuming that other factors are equal.

To illustrate the calculation of contribution margin ratios, we refer again to the initial Jewels Corporation example. The ratio is computed as follows:

	Total	Per Unit	Ratio (Percentage)
Sales revenue (1,000 gloves)	$200,000	$200	100%
Less variable costs	110,000	110	55%
Contribution margin	$ 90,000	$ 90	45%
Less fixed costs	63,000		
Profit	$ 27,000		

The contribution margin ratio is 45% of sales revenue ($90 ÷ $200), which means that for every $1.00 increase in sales revenue, the contribution margin increases by $0.45 (45% of $1.00). If fixed costs are already covered, profit will also increase by $0.45 for every $1.00 increase in sales. Notice also that the variable cost ratio ($110 ÷ $200 = 55%) plus the contribution margin ratio (45%) must equal 100%.

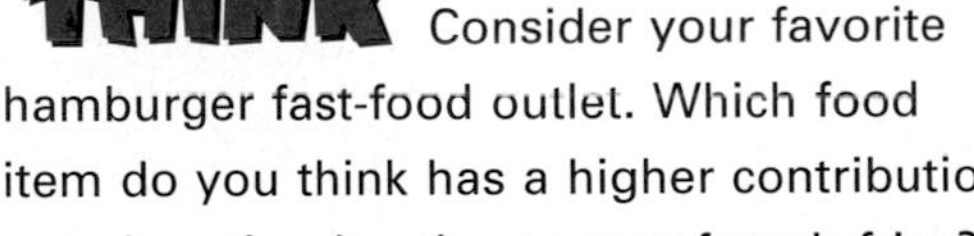

Consider your favorite hamburger fast-food outlet. Which food item do you think has a higher contribution margin ratio—hamburgers or french fries?

With contribution margin ratios, it is easy to analyze the impact of future changes in sales on the contribution margin. For example, if Jewels' management estimates that sales will increase by $20,000, it can apply the contribution margin ratio of 45% and estimate that the contribution margin will increase by $9,000 ($20,000 × 0.45). The higher the contribution margin ratio, the larger the share of each additional dollar of sales that goes toward covering fixed costs and increasing profit.

The C-V-P Equation

As you can see, contribution margin calculations are very useful for analyzing cost-volume-profit relationships in the management planning process. Doing C-V-P analysis using contribution margin calculations is a straightforward process of simple algebra. We began this chapter with the assumption that all costs can be described as either fixed or variable. To highlight the important idea that C-V-P analysis depends on dividing costs into fixed and variable behavior patterns, we will develop the C-V-P equation as follows:[4]

4 Granted, fixed and variable costs often get "mixed together" and can be difficult (and sometimes impossible) to separate. The fact that C-V-P analysis is based on an assumption that all costs can be divided clearly into fixed and variable is one of the limitations of this technique.

1. Because all costs can be classified as either variable or fixed, we can express the calculation of profit with the following basic formula:

$$\text{Revenues} - \text{Variable costs} - \text{Fixed costs} = \text{Profit}$$

2. We can specify the formula more precisely by expressing the equation in units:

$$(\text{Sales price} \times \text{Units}) - (\text{Variable cost} \times \text{Units}) - \text{Fixed costs} = \text{Profit}$$

3. Or, we can express the equation using ratios:

$$\text{Revenues} - (\text{Variable cost ratio} \times \text{Revenues}) - \text{Fixed costs} = \text{Profit}$$

These equations are quick and useful methods for examining the financial aspects of C-V-P analysis problems. To illustrate, we will use the data from the Jewels Corporation example and assume that sales of 1,200 baseball gloves are projected. What will Jewels' profit be using the equation based on units?

$$\begin{aligned}
\textbf{(Sales price} \times \textbf{Units)} - \textbf{(Variable cost} \times \textbf{Units)} - \textbf{Fixed costs} &= \textbf{Profit} \\
(\$200 \times 1{,}200) - (\$110 \times 1{,}200) - \$63{,}000 &= \text{Profit} \\
\$240{,}000 - \$132{,}000 - \$63{,}000 &= \text{Profit} \\
\$45{,}000 &= \text{Profit}
\end{aligned}$$

Alternatively, we could calculate Jewels' profits using the equation based on ratios.

$$\begin{aligned}
\textbf{Revenues} - \textbf{(Variable cost ratio} \times \textbf{Revenues)} - \textbf{Fixed costs} &= \textbf{Profit} \\
\$240{,}000 - [(\$110 \div \$200) \times \$240{,}000] - \$63{,}000 &= \text{Profit} \\
\$240{,}000 - (0.55 \times \$240{,}000) - \$63{,}000 &= \text{Profit} \\
\$240{,}000 - \$132{,}000 - \$63{,}000 &= \text{Profit} \\
\$45{,}000 &= \text{Profit}
\end{aligned}$$

Note that we obtained a profit of $45,000 using both formula approaches. This is no surprise because these are simply alternative routes to the same destination. Both methods are commonly used, depending on the data available for the analysis. So, although there may appear to be many alternative ways to write the C-V-P formula, there is really only one formula, and it is not hard to remember: Revenues − Variable costs − Fixed costs = Profit. Once you understand this fact, C-V-P analysis using the equation approach is basic math; you merely insert the known elements into the formula and solve for the one unknown element.

break-even point The amount of sales at which total costs of the number of units sold equal total revenues; the point at which there is no profit or loss.

BREAK-EVEN POINT Generally, management wants to know how many units need to be sold to break even, that is, to recover all costs. Thus, the **break-even point** is defined as the volume of activity at which total revenues equal total costs, or where profit is zero. The break-even point may also be thought of as the volume of activity at which the contribution margin equals the fixed costs.

Although the goal of business planning is to make a profit, not just to break even, knowing the break-even point can be useful in assessing the risk of selling a new product, setting sales goals and commission rates, deciding on marketing and advertising strategies, and other similar operating decisions. Because the break-even point is, by definition, that activity level at which no profit or loss is earned, the basic C-V-P equation can be modified to reflect a break-even point as follows:

$$\text{Revenues} - \text{Variable costs} - \text{Fixed costs} = \$0$$

As you can see, to compute the break-even point, we first set income equal to zero and then solve for the unknown—such as the number of units to be sold or the total revenues to be achieved.

Again using the Jewels Corporation example, how many units must Jewels sell to break even? (Note that we use *X* to represent the unknown element, in this case, the number of baseball gloves.)

$$\textbf{(Sales price} \times \textbf{Units)} - \textbf{(Variable cost} \times \textbf{Units)} - \textbf{Fixed costs} = \textbf{\$0}$$
$$[\text{Sales price} \times (X)] - [\text{Variable cost} \times (X)] - \text{Fixed costs} = \$0$$
$$\$200X - \$110X - \$63{,}000 = \$0$$
$$\$90X = \$63{,}000$$
$$X = \$63{,}000 \div \$90 = 700 \text{ units (baseball gloves)}$$

In this case, if Jewels sells 700 baseball gloves, it will generate enough revenues to cover its variable and fixed costs, earning zero profits [($200 × 700) − ($110 × 700) − $63,000 = $0]. Once you understand the basic C-V-P formula, you just set it up and solve for whatever unknown you're interested in planning. Think you've got it? Then try this one as a check on yourself: Assuming that Jewels can sell only 600 baseball gloves, what price per glove would the company have to use in order to break even?[5]

DETERMINING SALES VOLUME TO ACHIEVE TARGET INCOME Another way C-V-P analysis can be used in planning is to determine what level of activity is necessary to reach a target level of income. In this case, instead of setting profit at $0 to do a break-even analysis, we obviously set income in the formula at the targeted level and then use the formula to plan or predict what fixed costs, variable costs, sales prices, and sales volumes are needed to achieve the target level of income. **Target income** is usually defined as the amount of income that will enable management to reach its objectives—paying dividends, meeting analysts' predictions, purchasing a new plant and equipment, or paying off existing loans. Target income can be expressed as either a percentage of revenues or a fixed amount.

target income A profit level desired by management.

To illustrate target income, suppose the management of Jewels Corporation would like to know how many baseball gloves must be sold to achieve a target income of $36,000, assuming no changes in per-unit variable costs or total fixed costs. The calculation is as follows:

$$\textbf{(Sales price} \times \textbf{Units)} - \textbf{(Variable cost} \times \textbf{Units)} - \textbf{Fixed costs} = \textbf{Target income}$$
$$(\$200X - \$110X) - \$63{,}000 = \$36{,}000$$
$$\$90X = \$99{,}000$$
$$X = 1{,}100 \text{ units (baseball gloves)}$$

Thus, if Jewels could sell 1,100 baseball gloves at a contribution margin of $90 (assuming $63,000 of fixed costs), the company would earn a pretax profit of $36,000 [($90 × 1,100 units) − $63,000 = $36,000].

A fixed dollar amount of income, such as the $36,000 that would be earned by selling 1,100 baseball gloves, is probably the most typical way of expressing a target income goal for many companies. However, because investors often evaluate companies partially on the basis of the **return on sales revenue** (or simply "return on sales"), management may want to state its goal as a percentage return as opposed to a fixed amount of income. For example, if Jewels Corporation set a target income of a 20% return on sales, the computation would be:

return on sales revenue A measure of operating performance; computed by dividing net income by total sales revenue. Similar to profit margin.

$$\text{Sales revenue} - \text{Variable costs} - \text{Fixed costs} = 0.20 \text{ Sales revenue}$$
$$\$200X - \$110X - \$63{,}000 - 0.2(\$200X)$$
$$\$200X - \$110X - \$63{,}000 = \$40X$$
$$\$200X - \$110X - \$40X = \$63{,}000$$
$$\$50X = \$63{,}000$$
$$X = \$63{,}000 \div \$50 = 1{,}260 \text{ gloves}$$

5 $$\textbf{(Sales price} \times \textbf{Units)} - \textbf{(Variable cost} \times \textbf{Units)} - \textbf{Fixed costs} = \textbf{\$0}$$
$$[(X) \times \text{Units}] - (\text{Variable cost} \times \text{Units}) - \text{Fixed costs} = \$0$$
$$[(X) \times 600] - (\$110 \times 600) - \$63{,}000 = \$0$$
$$600X - \$66{,}000 - \$63{,}000 = \$0$$
$$600X = \$129{,}000$$
$$X = \$215 \text{ (new baseball glove price)}$$

business environment essay

Does Professional Soccer Have Any Real Future in the United States? Major League Soccer (MLS) had its fifth season in the United States in 2000. There have been many attempts to launch professional soccer as an American sport, but each attempt has failed. The last failure, that of the North American Soccer League (NASL)—which brought Pelé, Cruyff, Best, and Beckenbauer to the United States in the early 1970s—was especially painful because, with the big names, professional soccer looked so promising. One of the major reasons previous efforts failed is that player salaries and other fixed costs were too high for the small number of fans and meager TV revenues. Each attempt ended up with negative contribution margins and the team owners losing money.

Aware of past losses, this time the MLS has established itself in a different way. It has bet on an unusual single-entity structure, under which the league owns all the teams as well as all player contracts, and investors buy operating rights rather than setting up franchises. The MLS says the structure allows it to "eliminate the financial disparities between large and small markets, control player salaries and other fixed costs, and offer commercial affiliates an integrated sponsorship and licensing program." It also gives the

For Jewels Corporation, the 20% return on revenues would be earned by selling 1,260 baseball gloves.

SHORT-CUT FORMULAS FOR C-V-P ANALYSIS Notice that in the C-V-P analysis examples so far, the basic C-V-P equation has not changed. That's what makes this formula so powerful. Once you're comfortable with it, you can use it to manage any number of factors in planning for profits. However, you may remember from your brief introduction to C-V-P analysis in Chapter 1 of management accounting and from our C-V-P formula example on page 57 that we calculated break-even sales in units directly using the following formula.

$$\frac{\text{Total fixed costs}}{(\text{Sales price per unit} - \text{Variable cost per unit})} = \text{Break-even sales (in units)}$$

This formula is a "short-cut" version of the C-V-P formulas above. You can see that it is simply the last step in the C-V-P calculation above for Jewels' break-even point of 700 baseball gloves. So, if you understand the basic C-V-P equation, you can simply skip to the last step of the calculation. There are short cuts for computing the level of sales for both break-even volume and target income volume. The short-cut formula for both the break-even volume and the target income volume in units is:

$$\frac{\text{Fixed costs} + \text{Target income}}{\text{Contribution margin per unit}^{6}}$$

Note that if you use this formula to determine the break-even volume, then you will assume that target income is $0, giving you:

$$\frac{\text{Fixed costs}}{\text{Contribution margin per unit}}$$

Plugging in the numbers for Jewels Corporation, the results are the same as shown earlier. As you can see, the short-cut calculation for both the break-even volume and the target income volume is really the same formula. For target sales:

6 Remember that per-unit contribution margin is the sales price per unit less the variable cost per unit.

MLS significant economies of scale and allows it to allocate fixed costs across several teams.

Even though the fan base shrunk and TV ratings dropped during the first two years, financially the league is ahead of forecasts. The MLS lost $19 million in 1996, compared with anticipated losses of $22 million, and expected to lose $13 million more in 1997. The MLS is confident that the break-even point will come "by the end of the fourth year." That confidence may not be justified, however, as some report that the MLS has lost upwards of $100 million since its inception. The question is, does the MLS have the financial resources, the management expertise, and the fan and TV support to survive long term?

In the end, whether the MLS succeeds will depend on whether sufficient revenues can be generated to cover fixed and variable costs. While fixed costs, including player salaries, are low now, they may not always be. Already, 10 players, backed by the MLS Players Association, have filed a class action lawsuit arguing that the league's precious single-entity structure is designed expressly to hold down player salaries (fixed costs) and that, in doing so, it violates U.S. antitrust laws.

Sources: John McLaughlin, *Sky,* October 1997, pp. 27–32; and Willie Calderon, "Special to Soccer Times," March 28, 2000, http://www.soccertimes.com/mls/2000/mar28.htm.

Bank of America has a tool for analyzing the decision to rent an apartment versus buy a home. Go to http://www.bofa.com/mortgage/ and select the "Toolbox" connection. Then choose the "Rent vs. Buy Analysis" option. Use the following data: price of home, $150,000; down payment percentage, 10%; interest rate, 8%, property taxes, $950; insurance, $700; term of loan, 30 years; property appreciation, 3%; monthly rent, $850; savings growth rate, 6%; tax bracket, 28%.

If the above data represented your current rent situation, should you consider buying a house? What appear to be the two most important issues about renting versus buying?

$$\frac{\$63{,}000 + \$36{,}000}{\$90} = 1{,}100 \text{ units}$$

For the break-even volume:

$$\frac{\$63{,}000 + \$0}{\$90} = 700 \text{ units}$$

Always remember, though, that short cuts are useful, but they should not be applied until you fully understand the basic C-V-P relationships. In addition, managing some aspects of the C-V-P relationships can be tricky when you use shorts cuts. So if you ever get confused in solving a C-V-P analysis problem, just put the problem back in the original C-V-P equation:

$$\text{Revenues} - \text{Variable costs} - \text{Fixed costs} = \text{Target income}$$

COMPUTATION IN DOLLAR AMOUNTS VERSUS UNITS Before leaving the equation approach, we should note that a variable cost ratio is sometimes used instead of a per-unit variable cost. In such cases, the basic C-V-P equation is modified as follows:

$$\text{Sales} - (\text{Variable cost ratio} \times \text{Sales}) - \text{Fixed costs} = \text{Profit}$$

Because the variable costs are stated as a percentage of sales dollars rather than on a per-unit basis, this approach expresses activity in terms of sales dollars, not units. This is still the same basic C-V-P equation, but setting up the equation using the variable cost ratio will result in a break-even point in dollars instead of units. For example, the break-even point for Jewels Corporation would then be expressed as $140,000 in sales revenue ($200 per unit × 700 units) instead of 700 units as previously illustrated. This may be verified using the preceding equation and a 55% variable cost ratio as follows:

$$\begin{aligned} \text{Sales} - (0.55)\text{Sales} - \$63{,}000 &= \$0 \\ (0.45)\text{Sales} &= \$63{,}000 \\ \text{Sales} &= \$140{,}000 \end{aligned}$$

> **caution**
>
> Remember, if you want to use C-V-P analysis to calculate the necessary sales volume in terms of *dollars,* the per-unit variable cost is *not* used. Rather, use the variable cost *ratio* times sales to determine total variable costs. Many students make the mistake of multiplying the per-unit variable cost times sales instead of the variable cost ratio times sales to get total variable costs.

The short-cut formula for break-even volume and target income volume in sales dollars is:

$$\frac{\text{Fixed costs} + \text{Target income}}{\text{Contribution margin ratio}}$$

Measuring the Effect of Potential Changes in C-V-P Variables

The basic techniques of C-V-P analysis that we have covered in this chapter are used almost daily by organizations in the management processes of planning, controlling, and evaluating. Managers must be adept at evaluating the effects on profitability of the following common changes in C-V-P variables: (1) the amount of fixed costs, (2) the variable cost rate, (3) the sales price, (4) the sales volume or the number of units sold, and (5) combinations of these variables.

CHANGES IN FIXED COSTS Many factors, such as an increase in property taxes or an increase in management's salaries, for example, will cause an increase in fixed costs. (Recall also from the opening scenario for this chapter that building a new manufacturing facility can also increase fixed costs.) If all other factors remain constant, an increase in fixed costs always increases the number of units needed to break even. Obviously, the number of units needed to reach a target income will also increase. To illustrate, we will assume that Jewels Corporation's fixed costs increase from $63,000 to $81,000. Because of the added fixed costs, Jewels must now sell 1,300 baseball gloves, instead of 1,100, to earn a target income of $36,000.

Target income of $36,000:

$$\begin{aligned} \text{Revenues} - \text{Variable costs} - \text{Fixed costs} &= \text{Target income} \\ \$200X - \$110X - \$81,000 &= \$36,000 \\ \$90X &= \$117,000 \\ X &= 1,300 \text{ gloves} \end{aligned}$$

The computations are quite simple. In fact, you may have found them unnecessary, realizing that if fixed costs increase by $18,000 ($81,000 − $63,000), and if the unit contribution margin remains $90 per glove, 200 additional gloves ($18,000 ÷ $90) will have to be sold in order to reach the $36,000 target income (1,100 + 200 = 1,300).

CHANGES IN THE VARIABLE COST RATE Like an increase in fixed costs, an increase in the variable cost rate also increases the number of units needed to break even or to reach target income levels, when all other factors remain constant. Suppose that the variable cost rate increased from $110 per baseball glove to $130 per glove because of higher wages for factory personnel, increased costs of direct materials, or other factors. With this increase, the number of units needed to reach the target income would be calculated as follows (assuming that fixed costs are again $63,000 and rounding up to the next unit):

Target income of $36,000:

$$\begin{aligned} \text{Revenues} - \text{Variable costs} - \text{Fixed costs} &= \text{Target income} \\ \$200X - \$130X - \$63,000 &= \$36,000 \\ \$70X &= \$99,000 \\ X &= 1,415 \text{ gloves}^* \end{aligned}$$

*Technically, if the C-V-P analysis results in a fractional, you should always round the answer *up* to the next digit. In this case, if you round the calculated answer of 1,414.29 to 1,414 gloves, you won't quite achieve the target income of $36,000.

The increase in the variable cost rate reduces the unit contribution margin (from $90 to $70), which means that more gloves must be sold to maintain the same target income. With a unit contribution margin of $90, the company would make a $36,000 target income by selling 1,100 baseball gloves; with a unit contribution margin of only $70, an additional 315 (1,415 − 1,100) gloves must be sold to earn a $36,000 target income.

CHANGES IN SALES PRICE If all other variables remain constant, an increase in the sales price decreases the sales volume needed to reach a target income. This is because an increase in sales price increases the unit contribution margin per baseball glove, thereby decreasing the number of gloves that must be sold to earn the same amount of target income.

To illustrate, we will assume that the demand for baseball gloves is overwhelming and that Jewels cannot produce gloves fast enough. A decision is made to increase the price from $200 to $230 per glove. As a result of the price increase, the number of gloves that must be sold to reach the target income of $36,000 decreases:

Target income of $36,000:

$$\begin{aligned} \text{Revenues} - \text{Variable costs} - \text{Fixed costs} &= \text{Target income} \\ \$230X - \$110X - \$63{,}000 &= \$36{,}000 \\ \$120X &= \$99{,}000 \\ X &= 825 \text{ gloves} \end{aligned}$$

With the sales price increase of $30 per glove, the contribution margin also increased $30 per glove to $120; and with a $120 contribution margin per glove, only 825 gloves need to be sold to reach the $36,000 target income. Obviously, a decrease in the sales price would have the opposite effect; it would increase the number of units needed to reach the target income.

CHANGES IN SALES VOLUME As you have seen, the sales volume (the number of gloves to be sold) for the target income has varied with each change in one of the other variables. When other variables remain constant, an increase in the sales volume will result in an increase in income. Very simply, the more gloves sold, the higher the income (as long as the contribution margin is positive). The degree of change in profits resulting from volume change depends on the size of the unit contribution margin. To be specific, the change in income will be equal to the change in sales volume units multiplied by the contribution margin per unit. So, when the unit contribution margin is high, a slight change in volume results in a dramatic change in profit. With a lower unit contribution margin, the change in profit is less.

SIMULTANEOUS CHANGES IN SEVERAL VARIABLES Thus far, we have examined changes in only one variable at a time. Individual changes are quite rare, however; more often, a decision will affect several variables, all at the same time. For example, should Jewels Corporation increase fixed advertising costs by $20,000 and reduce the sales price by 10% if the result would be to increase sales volume by 500 units? The impact on the target income from these proposed changes is as follows:

Initial Data		Proposed Changes
Sales price per glove	$200	$180 ($200 × 90%)
Variable costs per glove	$110	$110
Fixed costs	$63,000	$83,000 ($63,000 + $20,000)
Target income	$36,000	*X*
Sales volume	1,100 gloves	1,600 gloves (1,100 + 500)

Computations and Result:

$$\begin{aligned} \text{Revenues} - \text{Variable costs} - \text{Fixed costs} &= \text{Target income} \\ (\$180 \times 1{,}600) - (\$110 \times 1{,}600) - \$83{,}000 &= X \\ \$288{,}000 - \$176{,}000 - \$83{,}000 &= X \\ \$29{,}000 &= X \text{ (target income)} \end{aligned}$$

The analysis shows that target income would drop by $7,000 ($36,000 − $29,000) as a result of these changes. So, the decision would be to not implement the proposed changes.

Consider another possible decision: Should Jewels automate part of its production, thereby reducing (by $10) variable costs to $100 per unit and increasing (by $5,000) fixed costs to $68,000? The computation would be:

business environment essay

Gathering Information for C-V-P Analysis Accurately determining fixed and variable costs and performing C-V-P analysis are not easy tasks, but the rewards of thorough work are well worth the effort. Through a detailed analysis of its costs, a manufacturing firm in the United Kingdom found that two of its three production processes were generating losses. Prices to its major customers had to be increased between 20 and 60%, yet only one customer stopped buying from the company as a result of the increase. To the company's surprise, that same customer returned not long after and confessed to being unable to find a better deal elsewhere. With inaccurate cost information, the company had simply been pricing its products too low.

Source: "Which Products Make a Profit?" *Management Accounting,* June 1993, pp. 34–36.

$$\begin{aligned} \text{Revenues} - \text{Variable costs} - \text{Fixed costs} &= \text{Target income} \\ (\$200 \times 1{,}100) - (\$100 \times 1{,}100) - \$68{,}000 &= X \\ \$220{,}000 - \$110{,}000 - \$68{,}000 &= X \\ \$42{,}000 &= X \text{ (target income)} \end{aligned}$$

caution

Remember, any change that affects the level of sales (such as a price decrease) also affects the total amount of variable costs. Some students change only the number of units of sales, and not the number of units multiplied by the variable cost per unit.

This analysis shows that management should implement these proposed changes because they would increase target income by $6,000 ($42,000 − $36,000). Obviously, this is true only if the assumptions can be relied on—that is, if fixed costs will rise by no more than $5,000 and unit variable costs will decrease by a full $10.

Consider another example. Suppose Jewels Corporation could use part of the excess capacity of its operating facilities to make baseball bats. These bats would sell for $90 per unit, increase fixed costs by $40,000, and have a variable cost per unit of $45. Jewels wants to add this new product line only if it can increase income by $25,000. How many baseball bats must Jewels sell to reach this target income? The computation follows:

$$\begin{aligned} \text{Revenues} - \text{Variable costs} - \text{Fixed costs} &= \text{Target income} \\ \$90X - \$45X - \$40{,}000 &= \$25{,}000 \\ \$45X &= \$65{,}000 \\ X &= 1{,}445 \text{ baseball bats (rounded up)} \end{aligned}$$

Management now must determine whether the company can produce and sell 1,445 baseball bats. If that sales goal seems attainable, the facilities should be used to make the bats.

to summarize

The contribution margin is sales revenue less variable costs. It is the amount of revenue left to cover fixed costs and provide a profit. The contribution margin can be expressed in total dollars, on a per-unit basis, or on a percentage basis. Because fixed costs remain constant within a relevant range, once fixed costs have been covered, income increases by the amount of the per-unit contribution margin for every additional unit sold. This relationship is used in C-V-P analysis. The basic C-V-P equation is:

$$\text{Revenues} - \text{Variable costs} - \text{Fixed costs} = \text{Target income}$$

Using this equation, management can plan, control, and evaluate the costs, prices, and sales output of the organization. The effects of changes in costs,

prices, and volume on profitability may be determined by C-V-P analysis. Changes in individual variables or simultaneous changes in several variables can be analyzed with this technique.

5
Visualize C-V-P relationships using graphs.

USING GRAPHS TO "SEE" C-V-P RELATIONSHIPS

Cost-volume-profit relationships can also be expressed in graphic form. In fact, the graphic format may be the most effective way to communicate information to management. It allows managers to visualize and examine cost and revenue data over a range of activity rather than at a single volume. Reading precise information from a graph can be difficult, however, so management will typically use the C-V-P equation to analyze specific proposals.

On a C-V-P graph, volume or activity level usually is shown on the horizontal axis, and total dollars of sales and costs are shown on the vertical axis. Lines are then drawn to represent total fixed costs, total costs, and total revenues. Exhibit 2-6 shows a C-V-P graph for Jewels Corporation.

Fixed and variable cost relationships are valid only for the relevant range of activity (the screened area on the graph in Exhibit 2-6). In this case, fixed costs are \$63,000, and variable costs are \$110 per glove over the range of activity between 400 and 1,200 gloves sold. Total costs are \$118,000 at 500 gloves [\$63,000 + (\$110 × 500 gloves)], \$129,000 at 600 gloves [\$63,000 + (\$110 × 600 gloves)], and so on. Similarly, total revenues are \$100,000 at 500 gloves

exhibit 2-6 A Cost-Volume-Profit Graph

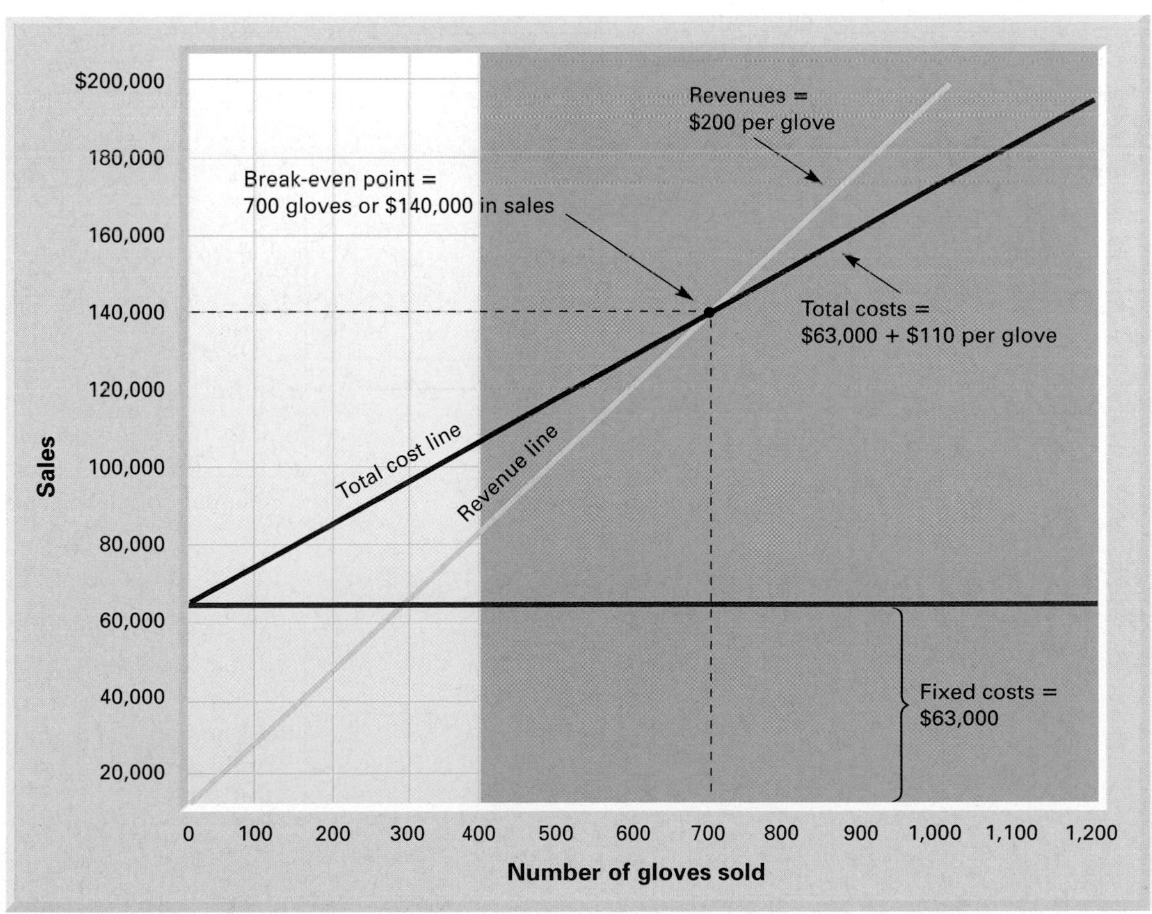

($200 × 500 gloves), $120,000 at 600 gloves, and so forth. The break-even point, the point at which total revenues equal total costs, is 700 gloves, or $140,000 in sales.

As shown in Exhibit 2-7, the graphic format can be used to isolate such items of interest as total variable costs, total fixed costs, the area in which losses occur, the area in which profits will be realized, and the break-even point. Because C-V-P graphs illustrate a wide range of activity, management can use them to quickly determine approximately how much profit or loss will be realized at various levels of sales.

The Profit Graph

profit graph A graph that shows how profits vary with changes in volume.

Some managers use another graphic approach, referred to as the **profit graph**, which plots only profits and losses and omits costs and revenues. Exhibit 2-8 shows a profit graph for Jewels Corporation.

Notice that, though the horizontal axis of the profit graph is the same as those of the previous graphs, the vertical axis represents only profits and losses. As long as the contribution margin is positive, the maximum amount of losses that can occur is at a zero level of sales. With no sales, total losses will be the amount of the fixed costs. With the axes properly labeled, the profit line is drawn as follows:

1. Locate the loss for zero sales volume on the vertical axis. This is the total fixed cost, or negative $63,000 in this case.
2. Locate the profit or loss at another sales volume. For example, at sales of 700 gloves, profits are zero [$140,000 − ($63,000 + $77,000)], or at sales of 1,000 gloves, profits are $27,000 [$200,000 − ($63,000 + $110,000)].
3. After the two profit or loss points have been identified, draw a line through them back to the vertical axis.

Because of its simplicity, the profit graph is widely used for comparing competing projects. It has the disadvantage, however, of not showing how costs vary with changes in sales volume.

exhibit 2-7 Cost-Volume-Profit Graphs

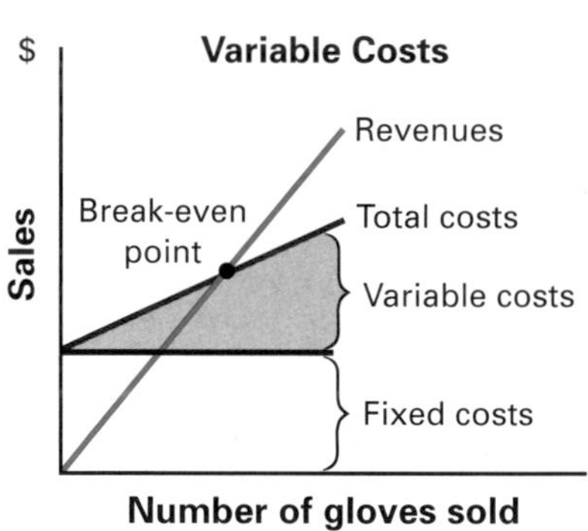

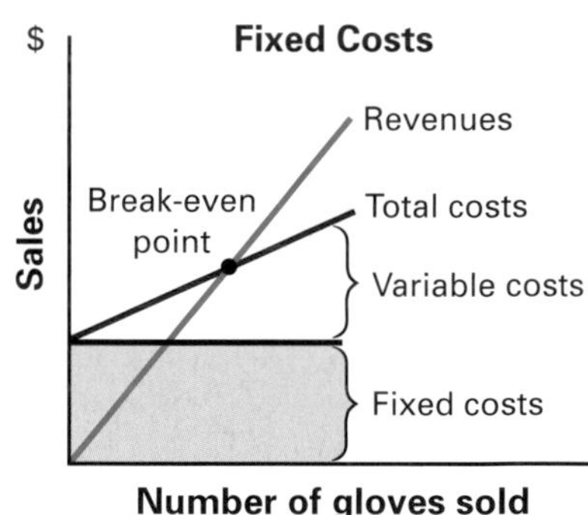

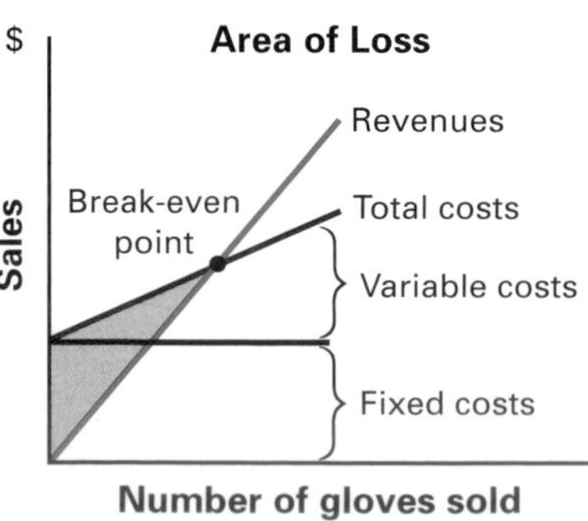

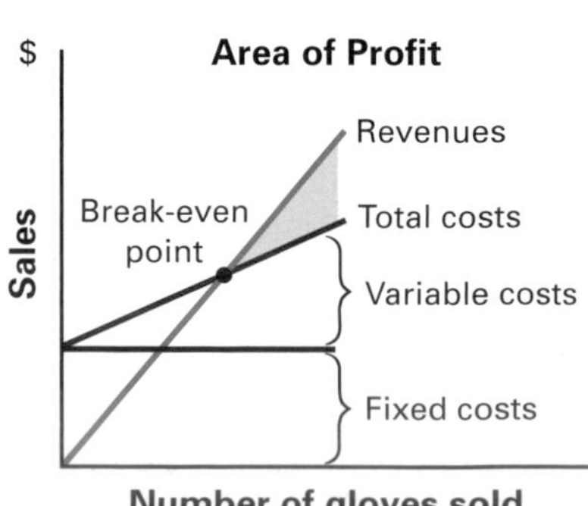

exhibit 2-8 Profit Graph for Jewels Corporation

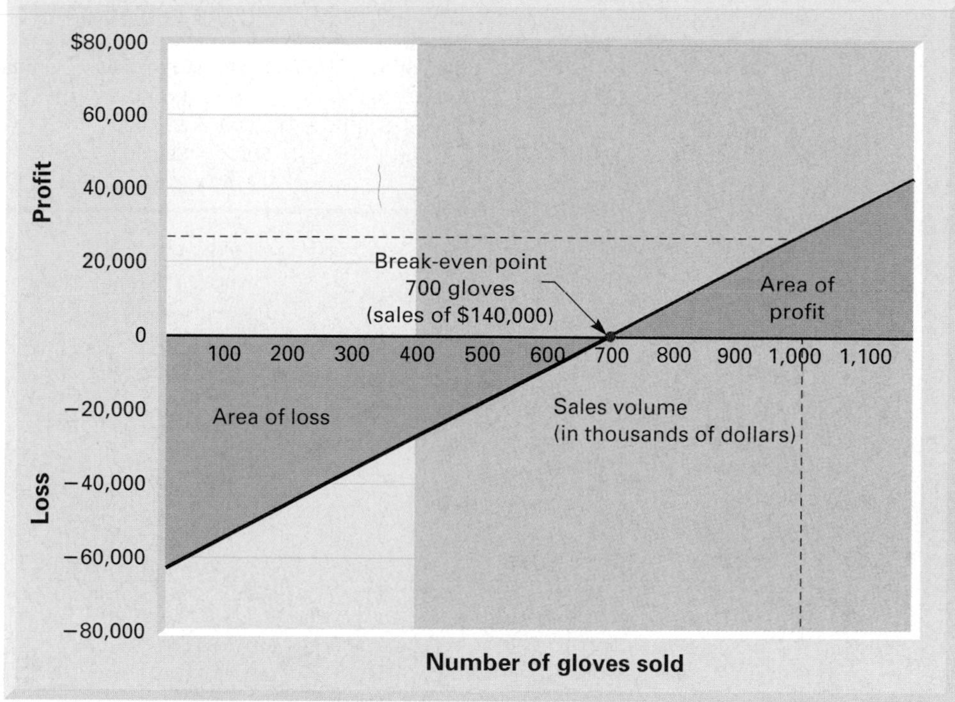

A Comparison of C-V-P Graphs with C-V-P Equations

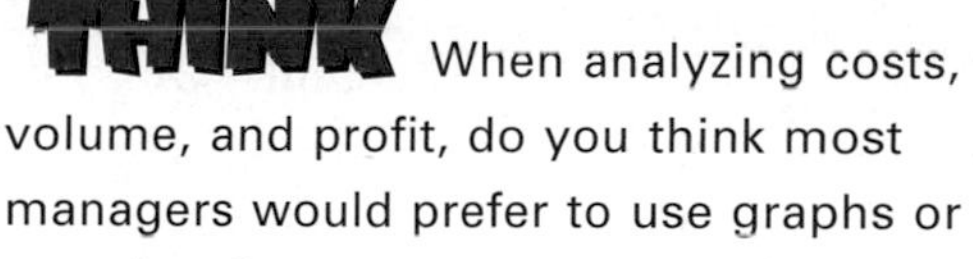
When analyzing costs, volume, and profit, do you think most managers would prefer to use graphs or equations?

C-V-P graphs are very useful for understanding the results of analyzing contribution margin statements with C-V-P equations. To illustrate this point, we will combine a C-V-P graph with a C-V-P equation to show you that both approaches are assessing the same contribution margin statement results. Again we'll explore the question of what volume of activity Jewels Corporation needs to reach a target income of $36,000. This was illustrated earlier with the equation approach, but it is repeated here to show that the graph approach will produce the same quantitative results. As shown in Exhibit 2-9, Jewels Corporation must sell 1,100 baseball gloves to reach a target income of $36,000.

to summarize

The financial effects on cost-volume-profit decisions can be examined by using either equations or graphs. These methods of analysis can be used to calculate the break-even point, which occurs at the point where total revenues equal total fixed costs plus total variable costs. These methods can also be used to project a target income level, with profit being equal to the excess of revenues over total costs. The graphic approaches can be useful because they highlight cost-volume-profit relationships over wide ranges of activity. The most common graphic approach involves plotting fixed costs as a horizontal line with variable costs above fixed costs. A profit graph, which shows only profit or loss and volume, is much simpler, but it does not show how costs vary with changes in sales volume. Regardless of the approach, C-V-P analysis is based on the same calculations and on the underlying concept of fixed and variable cost behavior patterns.

exhibit 2-9 Comparison of C-V-P Equation with C-V-P Graph

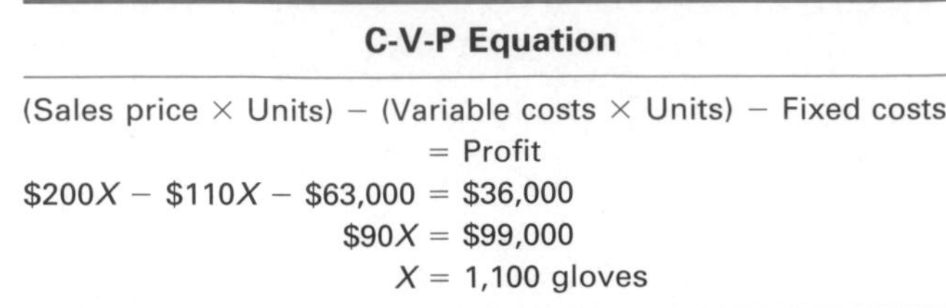

C-V-P Equation

(Sales price × Units) − (Variable costs × Units) − Fixed costs = Profit

$\$200X - \$110X - \$63{,}000 = \$36{,}000$

$\$90X = \$99{,}000$

$X = 1{,}100$ gloves

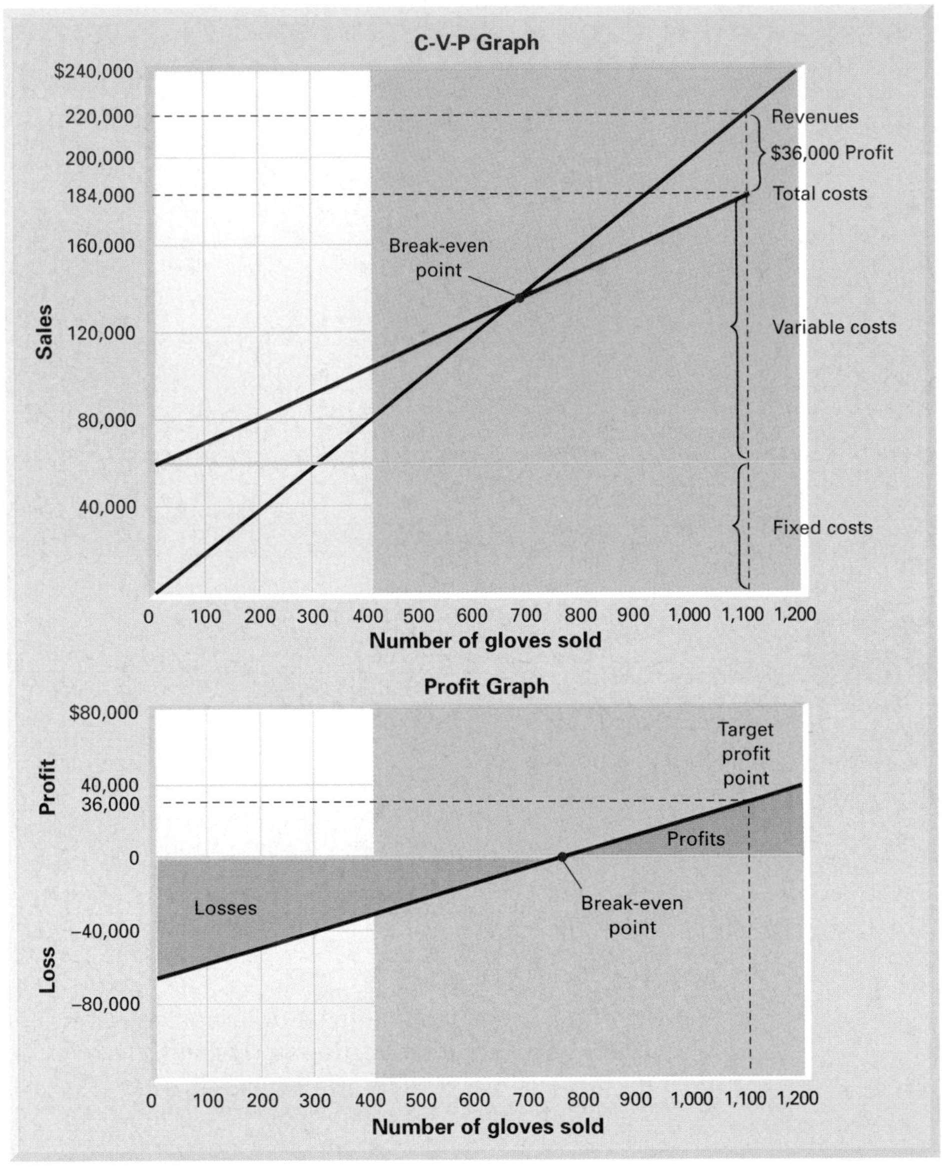

6 Identify the limiting assumptions of C-V-P analysis, and explain the issues of quality and time relative to C-V-P analysis decisions.

LIMITING ASSUMPTIONS OF C-V-P ANALYSIS

C-V-P analysis is an extremely useful tool for assisting management in making short-term operating decisions. However, C-V-P analysis has some limiting assumptions that must not be overlooked.

The key assumption is that the behavior of revenues and costs is linear throughout the relevant range. C-V-P analysis is valid only for a relevant range.

A second assumption is that all costs, including mixed costs, can be accurately divided into fixed and variable categories. As noted earlier in the chapter, some costs have characteristics of both fixed and variable costs. These costs sometimes are not easily classified into their fixed and variable components, which limits the accuracy of C-V-P analysis.

For companies with more than one product, a third major assumption in C-V-P analysis is required—that the mix of a company's products does not change over the relevant range. The sales mix is the proportion of the total units sold (or the total dollar sales) represented by each of a company's products. (Sales mix will be discussed in the expanded material section of this chapter.)

In addition to the three assumptions already identified, there are other limiting assumptions implicit in C-V-P analysis. For example, C-V-P analysis assumes that efficiency and productivity are held constant, that the prices of materials and other product components are constant, and that revenues and costs can be analyzed using a single activity base, such as volume. A related and very significant assumption, and one that clearly is not always valid, is that volume is the only, or even the primary, driver of costs.

Because of the limiting assumptions just described, the conclusions reached from C-V-P analysis must be considered with reasonable caution. Nevertheless, C-V-P analysis does provide a good model for predicting future operating results when specific relationships are defined and recognized.

Issues of Quality and Time

The emphasis in this chapter has been primarily on costs and profits and how they change when changes in variable costs, fixed costs, sales prices, and sales volume are made. Remember, however, that financial results are just one element of performance that management is interested in. Good managers are equally interested in how these changes will affect the quality of goods and services produced and sold and the speed at which products and services can be delivered to customers. If, for example, reducing fixed costs means that goods will be produced more slowly or that the quality of manufactured products will be reduced, the decision to reduce fixed costs may be a poor one. On the other hand, if management can automate a function using robotics instead of high-cost workers, for example, it may be possible to simultaneously reduce costs, increase quality and consistency, and improve speed of production. To determine whether quality and speed of production are good or bad, management may need to compare its results with those of other firms, a process called *benchmarking*, which will be introduced in Chapter 8 of management accounting.

---

to summarize

C-V-P analysis is based on three critical and limiting assumptions: (1) that the behavior of revenues and costs is linear throughout the relevant range, (2) that all costs can be categorized as either fixed or variable, and (3) that the sales mix does not change. When considering how changes in variable costs, fixed costs, sales prices, sales volume, and sales mix will affect profits, it is important to also consider how these changes will affect the quality of goods and services and the speed at which products and services can be delivered to customers. Changes that increase quality, reduce costs, and speed up production are good changes and should be made; changes that have a negative effect on one or more of these variables must be carefully analyzed and trade-offs considered.

Thus far, we have covered various types of costs, simple methods of analyzing mixed costs, and the basics of C-V-P analysis. In this expanded section we cover an additional, more advanced method of analyzing mixed costs—least squares analysis. We also cover the effect of the sales mix on profitability and use the concept of operating leverage to explore differences in cost structures among manufacturing, merchandising, service, and e-commerce organizations.

7

Analyze mixed costs using the least squares method.

ANALYSIS OF MIXED COSTS—THE LEAST SQUARES METHOD

least squares method A method of segregating the fixed and variable portions of a mixed cost; the regression line, a line of averages, is statistically fitted through all cost points.

Earlier, we described two common methods for analyzing mixed costs: the scattergraph and high-low methods. These methods are relatively easy to use and provide useful estimates of the fixed and variable components of mixed costs. A more sophisticated method for analyzing mixed costs is the **least squares method**, which is the most accurate method of determining the fixed and variable portions of a mixed cost. Like the scattergraph, the least squares method fits a straight line through all points on a graph. However, instead of visually fitting the regression line through the cost points, it uses statistical analysis to guarantee that the line is the best possible fit for the applicable costs. (Note here that regression overcomes the subjectivity weakness of scattergraphs and the limited data use of the high-low method.)

The formula for the least squares method is based on the equation for a straight line:

$$Y = a + bX$$

In this equation, Y represents the total predicted cost; a represents the intercept and the fixed cost (if in the relevant range); b represents the variable cost rate or the slope of the line; and X represents the activity level. Using cost and activity level data, this method involves the use of simultaneous equations to find the values of a and b. Once computed, these values can be combined with the projected activity level X to predict total future cost Y. For example, if the values of a and b are computed to be \$200 and \$5, respectively, then for an estimated activity level of 100 direct labor hours, we find that:

$$\begin{aligned} Y \text{ (total predicted cost)} &= \$200 + \$5(100 \text{ hours}) \\ Y &= \$200 + \$500 \\ Y &= \$700 \end{aligned}$$

Obviously, because the regression line is a line of averages, the actual total cost for 100 direct labor hours might be somewhat different from the predicted cost of \$700. The method of least squares, however, attempts to minimize the differences between predicted and actual costs. Once a regression line has been fitted to historical data, the fixed and variable costs represented by the line can be used to predict the level of future costs.

Calculating the estimates of a (the intercept, or the total fixed cost) and b (the slope, or variable cost rate) requires solving the following two simultaneous equations:

1. $\Sigma XY = a\Sigma X + b\Sigma X^2$
2. $\Sigma Y = na + b\Sigma X$

where

a = fixed cost
b = variable cost rate
n = number of observations
Σ = summation sign (which means the sum of all available historical data)
X = activity level, or independent variable
Y = total (predicted) mixed cost, or dependent variable

fyi

Use of the least squares equations results in the unique line that minimizes the sum of the squared distances between the actual observation points and the regression line. The equations are based on squared distances because the necessary derivation (based on differential calculus) is mathematically simple when squared quantities are included.

Solving these equations is easy with a calculator or computer, but difficult and tedious by hand. Because calculators and computers are so widely available and can analyze large amounts of data very quickly, we will focus on describing and interpreting the typical output from a computerized application of least squares analysis. We will leave it to math classes to illustrate the manual calculations of the least squares method.

To illustrate the concept of least squares, we return again to the electricity cost data used to describe the scattergraph and high-low methods. (Note that the data, e.g., 12 or 18 months of data, are given for only six months; thus, the resulting regression equation will be less accurate than it would be with more data.)

Month	Direct Labor Hours Worked	Total Electricity Cost
January	7,000	$ 70,000
February	6,000	60,000
March	12,000	100,000
April	6,600	80,000
May	18,000	120,000
June	14,000	110,000

Using these data, the following output, shown in Exhibit 2-10, was generated in just a matter of minutes using the "data analysis" tool in Excel®, a Microsoft database software program.[7] Comparing the least squares output with the results from our earlier examples of the scattergraph and high-low methods, we get the following:

	Fixed Costs	Variable Cost per Direct Labor Hour
Scattergraph method	$40,000 per month	$4.29 per direct labor hour
High-low method	30,000 per month	5.00 per direct labor hour
Least squares analysis	40,402 per month	4.68 per direct labor hour

exhibit 2-10 Output of Least Squares Analysis Application

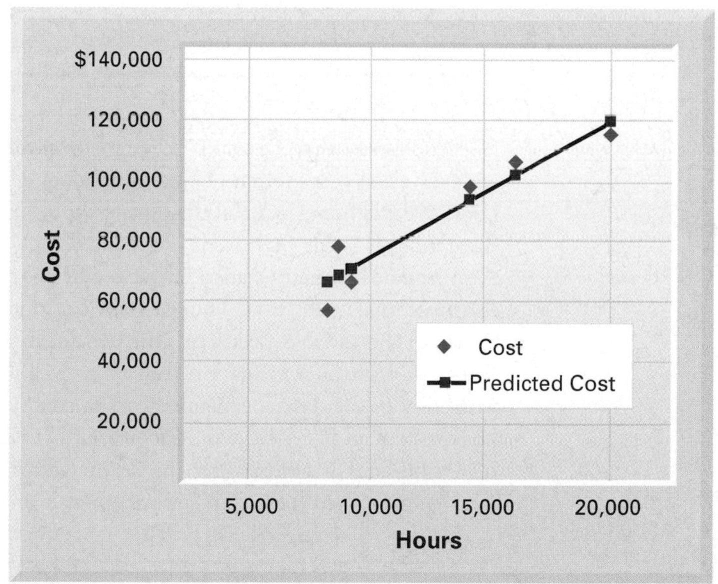

Month	Hours	Cost
January	7,000	$ 70,000
February	6,000	60,000
March	12,000	100,000
April	6,600	80,000
May	18,000	120,000
June	14,000	110,000

Summary Output	
Regression Statistics	
Multiple R	0.962
R square	0.926
Adjusted R square	0.907
Standard error	7207.705
Observations	6

(continued)

7 There are literally hundreds of software programs that can be used to run regressions or least squares analysis.

exhibit 2-10 (Concluded)

ANOVA					
	df	*SS*	*MS*	*F*	*Significance F*
Regression	1	2592195946	2.59E+09	49.89693	0.002118833
Residual	4	207804054.1	51951014		
Total	5	2800000000			

	Coefficients	*Standard Error*	*t Stat*	*P-value*	*Lower 95%*	*Upper 95%*
Intercept	$40,402.03	$7,613.10	$5.31	0.0061	$19,264.63	$61,539.43
Hours	$ 4.68	$ 0.66	$7.05	0.0021	$ 2.84	$ 6.52

Residual Output		
Observation	*Predicted Cost*	*Residuals*
1	$ 73,155.41	$(3,155.41)
2	68,476.35	(8,476.35)
3	96,550.68	3,449.32
4	71,283.78	8,716.22
5	124,625.00	(4,625.00)
6	105,908.78	4,091.22

You can see that the results are very similar for the least squares analysis and scattergraph method, with the fixed cost estimate being $40,402 and the variable cost rate being $4.68 per direct labor hour. We will not explain all the output shown in Exhibit 2-10; what is important is that you know three things: (1) the coefficient of the intercept, (2) the coefficient of the direct labor hours, and (3) the R square summary statistic. The coefficient of the intercept, or $40,402 in this case, is the estimate of total fixed costs. The coefficient of the direct labor hours, or $4.68 in this case, is the estimate of the variable electricity cost per direct labor hour. The R square (R^2) is a descriptive statistic that provides information about how well the regression line fits the data or how much of the variability in the data is explained by the computed regression statistics. For now, all you need to know is that an R^2 of 1.0 would represent a perfect fit (meaning all data points were exactly on the regression line) and the higher the R^2 the better. In this case, an R^2 of 0.926 is high and suggests that the computed regression statistics explain most of the variability in the data.[8]

to summarize

A more sophisticated technique for analyzing mixed costs is the least squares method. The least squares method is essentially equivalent to simple regression analysis, using the equation for a straight line ($Y = a + bX$) and simultaneous equations to calculate the fixed and variable portions of a mixed cost. Even though the least squares method is more mathematically correct than the scattergraph or high-low methods, it still should be used with caution in analyzing mixed costs. Least squares results can be quickly calculated using computer programs such as Microsoft's Excel®.

8 The adjusted R^2 of 0.907 is a more conservative estimate of the variance explained in the data and is preferred to the R^2 statistic in some circumstances.

8

Explain the effects of sales mix on profitability.

sales mix The relative proportion of total units sold (or total sales dollars) that is represented by each of a company's products.

SALES MIX

As we explained earlier in the chapter, **sales mix** is the proportion of the total units represented by each of a company's products. To keep our discussions simple, in previous sections of the chapter, we used examples of companies with only one product. Many companies have more than one product, however, so we need to illustrate how sales mix issues are resolved. To illustrate how a change in sales mix can affect a company's C-V-P relationships, we assume that Multi-Product, Inc., sells three different products. Following are the monthly revenues and costs for each type of product:

	Product A		Product B		Product C		Total	
	Amount	Percent	Amount	Percent	Amount	Percent	Amount	Percent
Sales revenue	$25,000	100%	$45,000	100.00%	$30,000	100%	$100,000	100%
Less variable costs	20,000	80	30,000	66.67	21,000	70	71,000	71
Contribution margin	$ 5,000	20%	$15,000	33.33%	$ 9,000	30%	$ 29,000	29%
Sales mix	25%		45%		30%		100%	

fyi

Obviously, a computer can make sales mix and other C-V-P analysis computations very easy. Using simulation or other programs, you can quickly calculate the financial effects of changes in the sales of one product or simultaneous changes in sales of several products.

Total sales are $100,000, which in this example includes $25,000 in sales of Product A, $45,000 of Product B, and $30,000 of Product C. Therefore, the sales mix is 25% Product A ($25,000 ÷ $100,000), 45% Product B ($45,000 ÷ $100,000), and 30% Product C ($30,000 ÷ $100,000). With this sales mix, the average contribution margin ratio is 29%, which is determined by subtracting total variable costs of $71,000 from total sales of $100,000, and dividing the result ($29,000) by $100,000. If Multi-Product, Inc., had fixed costs of $17,400 and desired a target income of $40,000, the necessary sales volume (in dollars) would be:

$$\begin{aligned} \text{Sales} - (0.71)\text{Sales} - \$17{,}400 &= \$40{,}000 \\ (0.29)\text{Sales} &= \$57{,}400 \\ \text{Sales} &= \$57{,}400 \div 0.29 \\ \text{Sales} &= \$197{,}932 \text{ (rounded up)} \end{aligned}$$

Alternatively, the company could divide the average contribution margin ratio (29%) into fixed costs plus target income ($17,400 + $40,000). As you can see, this revised, more compact formula is simply a restatement of the preceding equation.

$$\frac{\text{Fixed costs} + \text{Target income}}{\text{Average contribution margin ratio}} = \frac{\$57{,}400}{0.29} = \$197{,}932 \text{ (rounded up)}$$

Obviously, $197,932 in sales will make the target income only if the average contribution margin ratio, and therefore the sales mix, does not change. To illustrate the effect of a change in sales mix, assume that the total sales revenue and the sales price of each product remain the same but that the sales mix changes as follows:

	Product A		Product B		Product C		Total	
	Amount	Percent	Amount	Percent	Amount	Percent	Amount	Percent
Sales revenue	$50,000	100%	$30,000	100.00%	$20,000	100%	$100,000	100%
Less variable costs	40,000	80	20,000	66.67	14,000	70	74,000	74
Contribution margin	$10,000	20%	$10,000	33.33%	$ 6,000	30%	$ 26,000	26%
Sales mix	50%		30%		20%		100%	

In this example, the contribution margin ratio for each product remains the same, but the sales mix changes. Product A now comprises 50% of total sales instead of 25%. Because Product

A has a lower contribution margin ratio than Products B and C, the average contribution margin ratio decreases from 29 to 26%. Accordingly, the sales volume needed to generate $40,000 of target income increases to $220,770, computed as follows:

$$\frac{\text{Fixed costs + Target income}}{\text{Average contribution margin ratio}} = \frac{\$57,400}{0.26} = \$220,770 \text{ (rounded up)}$$

As you can see, a sensible profit-maximizing strategy for management would be to maintain as large a contribution margin as possible on all products and then to emphasize those products with the largest individual contribution margins. In the remaining chapters of this text we discuss procedures management can use to control costs and, hence, maintain high contribution margins. The second part of this strategy—emphasizing the products with the highest contribution margins—is a marketing function. Multi-Product, Inc., for example, should promote Product B more aggressively than Product A. With other factors being equal, a company should spend more advertising dollars and pay higher sales commissions on its higher contribution margin products. In fact, instead of paying commissions based on total sales, a good strategy would be to base sales commissions on the total contribution margin generated. This way, the mix of products that maximizes the sales staff's commissions will be the mix that provides the company with the greatest overall profit.

STOP & THINK Would maximizing the sales of the highest contribution margin products still be the best profit-maximizing strategy if the company experienced production constraints such that producing more of the highest contribution margin products severely limited the quality or production speed of other products?

to summarize

Sales mix is the proportion of the total units sold represented by each of a company's products. Changes in sales mix can affect profits because not all products have the same contribution margin. Other things being equal, to maximize profits, management should put greater emphasis on the sale of products with higher contribution margin ratios.

9

Describe how fixed and variable costs differ in manufacturing, service, merchandising, and e-commerce organizations, and illustrate these differences with the operating leverage concept.

COST STRUCTURE IN DIFFERENT TYPES OF ORGANIZATIONS

As noted earlier in the chapter, cost-volume-profit relationships and contribution margins, in particular, highlight the different effects that variable and fixed costs have on profitability. An important issue has to do with the amount of fixed costs a company has in its cost structure. The amount of fixed costs an organization commits itself to often has a lot to do with its type of business, e.g., merchandising, manufacturing, or service. In addition, a new type of organization has arrived in the economy—companies organized around the process of e-commerce. We'll talk more about differences between merchandising, manufacturing, service, and e-commerce companies throughout the remaining chapters in this textbook. For now, we'll simply illustrate the differences among these organizations using an example and then apply the concept of **operating leverage** to illustrate how a company can manage risk (in terms of profits) by the way it organizes its cost structure—in other words, how much the company is committed to using fixed costs versus variable costs to do business.

operating leverage The extent to which fixed costs are part of a company's cost structure; the higher the proportion of fixed costs to variable costs, the faster income increases or decreases with sales volume.

Imagine that three college students design a new computer software game that they would like to market to college campuses across the nation. They identify three ways that they can approach the market. First, they could take on the role of the merchant by contracting with a software manufacturing company to handle all the production of the packaged software. They would then concentrate on the sales and marketing of their new game. This approach won't require an expensive production facility, but the students know that they will have to pay a high price per unit to the company that handles the production of the packaged software. Second, they could take on the role of manufacturer by setting up their own production facilities. In this case, because all their effort would be dedicated to producing the game, they would need to wholesale their software product to another merchant company that would then resell the product to the actual customers. Finally, they could "virtually" sell their game to other college students by contracting with an e-commerce company that will host their software download site for a significant fixed fee per month. In any case, regardless of whether they will wholesale the game to another merchant or retail their game directly to the college student market, they determine that they will sell their game for $100. The costs of each of these methods of structuring their business are as follows:

Business Structure	Variable Cost per Unit to Manufacture or to Purchase from a Manufacturer	Fixed Cost per Year for the Merchandising, Manufacturing, or E-Commerce Facility
Traditional merchant	$80	$100,000
Manufacturer	25	375,000
E-commerce merchant	0	500,000

caution

Don't confuse the concept of operating leverage with the concept of financial leverage. While both concepts focus on risk and the sensitivity of profit to changes in sales volume, financial leverage has to do with the use of debt versus equity to provide financing for a company. In general, the financial leverage (and risk) of a company increases as management chooses to use debt, rather than equity, to raise funds for the company. Similarly, the operating leverage (and risk) of a company increases as management chooses to emphasize fixed cost, rather than variable cost, to create or obtain the product for sale to the marketplace.

As you can see, one of the issues that these students must decide when selecting their business structure is whether they want to commit to high fixed costs in order to have low variable costs, or vice versa. This trade-off of fixed versus variable costs is what we mean when we talk about operating leverage. As total fixed costs increase and variable costs per unit decrease, the operating leverage of the organization increases. In the example above, the operating leverage of the company will be very high if the students choose to structure their company as an e-commerce merchant. So, the question is, is it good or bad to have high operating leverage? The answer is, it depends on whether the company is operating above or below the break-even point.

Look at the C-V-P graphs in Exhibit 2-11 and you can see the impact of operating leverage for these three types of companies. The break-even point (which is the same for all three companies) is at a sales volume of 5,000 games sold each year. At this point, all three companies would generate the same level of profit—nothing. As sales move above or below the break-even point, however, there are significant differences in profit between the company structures. If sales are below the break-even point, then the e-commerce merchant structure will generate a lot of losses. If the three students can sell more than 5,000 games per year, however, then the e-commerce merchant structure will generate the most profit per year. Essentially, operating leverage is a measure of risk. With high levels of operating leverage, the company is at risk of losing a lot of money if sales go down. But business risk often has an upside. In the case of operating leverage, the risk of loss is balanced by the potential for large gains in income as sales go up. So the decision on how to structure a company partly depends on the impact on operating leverage and on how much risk the business owners are willing to accept.

to summarize

STOP & THINK Think about the level of operating leverage you would expect to find in a service organization such as a consulting company or a law firm. Would these kinds of organizations typically have high or low levels of operating leverage?

The relationship between fixed and variable costs differs across different types of organizations. Generally, traditional merchandising companies have relatively low levels of fixed costs and high levels of variable costs. On the other hand, manufacturing companies often have higher levels of fixed costs and lower levels of variable costs. The emergence of e-commerce in this economy has resulted in some companies that are even more extremely committed to fixed costs with little or no variable product

exhibit 2-11 "Seeing" Operating Leverages

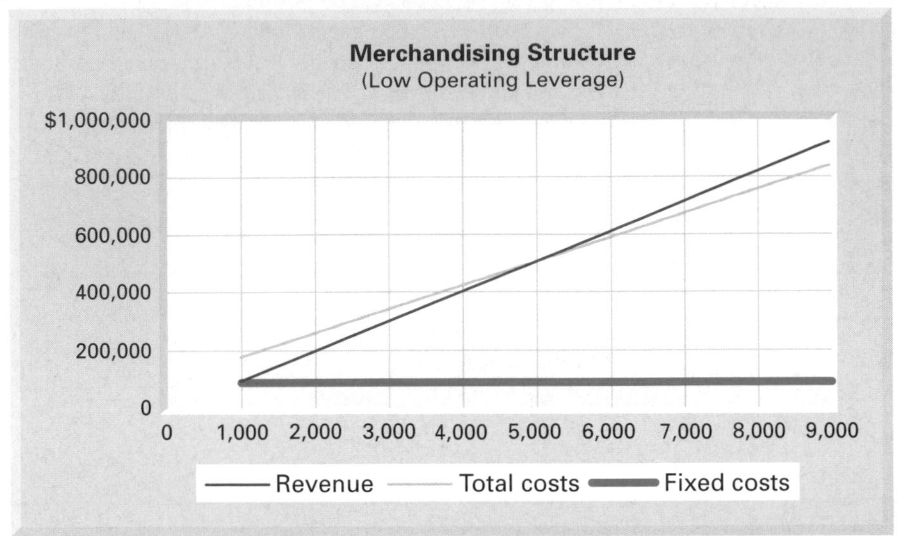

		Sales in Units	Revenue	Total Variable Costs	Contribution Margin	Total Fixed Costs	Operating Income
Price per unit	$ 100	3,000	$300,000	$(240,000)	$ 60,000	$(100,000)	$(40,000)
Variable cost per unit	80	5,000	500,000	(400,000)	100,000	(100,000)	—
Total fixed costs	100,000	7,000	700,000	(560,000)	140,000	(100,000)	40,000

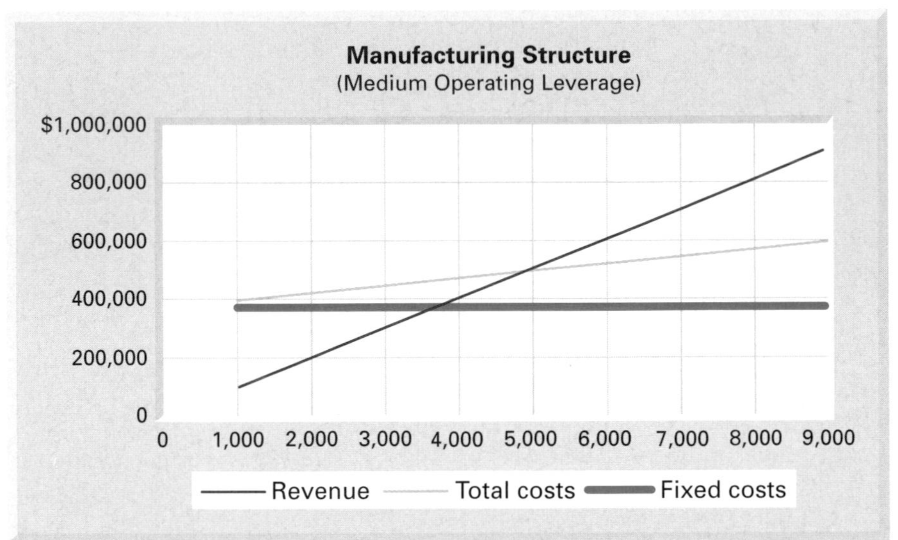

		Sales in Units	Revenue	Total Variable Costs	Contribution Margin	Total Fixed Costs	Operating Income
Price per unit	$ 100	3,000	$300,000	$ (75,000)	$225,000	$(375,000)	$(150,000)
Variable cost per unit	25	5,000	500,000	(125,000)	375,000	(375,000)	—
Total fixed costs	375,000	7,000	700,000	(175,000)	525,000	(375,000)	150,000

exhibit 2-11 (Concluded)

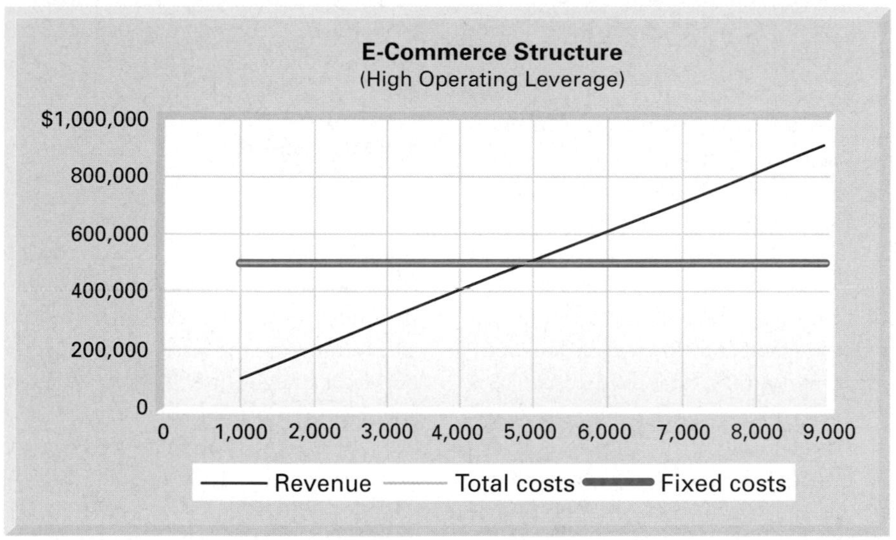

		Sales in Units	Revenue	Total Variable Costs	Contribution Margin	Total Fixed Costs	Operating Income
Price per unit	$ 100	3,000	$300,000	$ —	$300,000	$(500,000)	$(200,000)
Variable cost per unit	0	5,000	500,000	—	500,000	(500,000)	—
Total fixed costs	500,000	7,000	700,000	—	700,000	(500,000)	200,000

costs. These cost structure differences are important and are illustrated in the concept of operating leverage. Operating leverage relates to the amount of fixed costs a company has in its cost structure. When sales are expected to increase, high operating leverage results in higher income, and vice versa.

review of learning objectives

1 Understand the key factors involved in cost-volume-profit (C-V-P) analysis and why it is such an important tool in management decision making. C-V-P analysis is a very important management concept. It is a technique used by management to understand how profits may be expected to vary in relation to changes in key variables: sales price and volume, variable costs, fixed costs, and mix of products. C-V-P analysis is a particularly useful tool for planning and making operating decisions. It can provide data to stimulate increased sales efforts or cost reduction programs; assist in production scheduling or marketing strategy; and help establish company policies, for example, the appropriate product mix or the fixed cost structure of a company. Effective management requires a comprehensive understanding and use of C-V-P analysis.

2 Explain and analyze the basic cost behavior patterns—variable, fixed, mixed, and stepped. Understanding cost behavior patterns can assist management in making key operating decisions. The two basic cost behavior patterns are variable and fixed. Costs that vary in total in direct proportion to changes in the level of activity are variable costs. Therefore, per-unit variable costs remain constant. Generally, we assume a linear relationship between variable costs and level of activity within the relevant range; for other ranges, variable costs are curvilinear. Costs that do not change in total with changes in activity level, within the relevant range, are fixed costs; thus, per-unit fixed costs decrease as level of activity increases. Because of factors such as automation, fixed costs are becoming a greater percentage of total costs in most manufacturing companies. Costs that contain both fixed and variable components are mixed costs. Stepped costs increase in total in a stair-step fashion with the level of activity. If the steps are wide, the cost is treated as a fixed cost for analysis purposes; if the steps are narrow, the cost is approximated as a variable cost.

3 **Analyze mixed costs using the scattergraph and high-low methods.** Before mixed costs can be analyzed and used in decision making, they must be divided into their fixed and variable components. The scattergraph and high-low methods are commonly used to analyze mixed costs. The scattergraph method involves visually plotting a straight line (the regression line) through points on a graph of cost data at various activity levels. With the high-low method, the highest and lowest levels of activity and their associated highest and lowest costs are used to calculate the variable cost rate and the total fixed costs.

4 **Perform C-V-P analyses, and describe the effects potential changes in C-V-P variables have on company profitability.** C-V-P analysis is based on the computation of contribution margin, which is sales less variable costs. Contribution margin is the amount available to cover fixed costs and then provide a profit. C-V-P analysis is commonly used to assess break-even points (where contribution margin equals fixed costs) and to compute target income levels. The C-V-P equation is especially useful in assessing how profits can be expected to change when costs or revenues change. Increases in fixed or variable costs result in a larger number of sales being required to break even and reach target income levels. Increases in sales price result in a decreased number of sales being required to break even and reach target income levels.

5 **Visualize C-V-P relationships using graphs.** C-V-P graphs are an effective method for visualizing the effect of impacts on key variables in the C-V-P equation. In addition, the graphic approach effectively allows the simultaneous analysis of several different activity levels.

6 **Identify the limiting assumptions of C-V-P analysis, and explain the issues of quality and time relative to C-V-P analysis decisions.** C-V-P analysis has several limiting assumptions, including the following: (1) cost and revenue behavior patterns are linear and remain constant over the relevant range, (2) all costs can be categorized as either fixed or variable, and (3) the sales mix of products is constant over the relevant range. When making changes in costs, revenues, and volume, resulting changes in the quality of products or services and the speed at which those products and services can be delivered to customers must be considered. Changes that result in increased profits while decreasing product or service quality or slowing delivery of products or services may not be good decisions.

expanded material

7 **Analyze mixed costs using the least squares method.** The least squares method uses a simple regression analysis to identify the variable and fixed portions of mixed costs. The formula for the least squares method is based on the equation for a straight line, $Y = a + bX$, where a is total fixed cost and b is per-unit variable cost. Least square calculations can be easily performed using basic computer software programs or programmed calculators.

8 **Explain the effects of sales mix on profitability.** Sales mix is the proportion of total units sold represented by each of a company's products. Because all products do not have the same contribution margin ratios, changes in the sales mix of products sold can significantly affect total profits. The best profit-maximizing strategy is to maintain as large a contribution margin as possible on all products and then emphasize those products with the largest individual contribution margins.

9 **Describe how fixed and variable costs differ in manufacturing, service, merchandising, and e-commerce organizations, and illustrate these differences with the operating leverage concept.** The trade-off between fixed costs and variable costs is related to whether a company is structured as a manufacturing, merchandising, or service firm. The advent of e-commerce has created the potential for companies to have very high levels of fixed costs and very low levels of variable costs. The impact of the fixed cost/variable cost relationship on profits is captured in the concept of operating leverage. Operating leverage is a measure of the extent to which a company's costs are fixed rather than variable. Companies with higher fixed costs and lower per-unit variable costs will experience higher operating leverage and, therefore, a tendency for profits to increase at a faster rate when sales increase. A company with such a cost structure will be more profitable in good times but have higher losses in bad times.

key terms and concepts

break-even point 56
contribution margin 53
contribution margin ratio 55
cost behavior 39
cost-volume-profit (C-V-P) analysis 39
curvilinear costs 42
fixed costs 44
high-low method 50

mixed costs 47
per-unit contribution margin 54
profit graph 64
regression line 49
relevant range 44
return on sales revenue 57
scattergraph (visual-fit) method 49
stepped costs 45
target income 57
variable cost rate 49
variable costs 41

expanded material

least squares method 68
operating leverage 72
sales mix 71

review problems

1. Variable and Fixed Costs Analyses

Blade Corporation manufactures two types of inline skates—a basic model and a racing model. During the year 2003, Blade accumulated the following summary information about its two products:

	Racing Model	Basic Model
Selling price	$130	$65
Number of units manufactured and sold	14,000	9,000

	Racing Model		Basic Model	
	Units	Costs	Units	Costs
January	1,200	$ 112,000	800	$ 39,600
February	900	91,000	600	30,000
March	800	76,400	450	25,800
April	1,400	124,800	900	36,900
May	950	92,650	1,000	47,000
June	1,600	146,800	1,200	57,300
July	1,400	134,600	1,300	60,600
August	1,700	154,500	650	32,195
September	1,550	140,200	850	44,250
October	1,500	134,500	500	27,000
November	600	62,500	350	20,700
December	400	44,000	400	22,000
Totals	14,000	$1,313,950	9,000	$443,345

Required:

1. Use the high-low method to estimate the variable and fixed production costs of both the racing model and the basic model skates.
2. All selling costs are fixed, and they total $200,000 for the racing model and $80,000 for the basic model. Prepare a contribution margin income statement for each model at sales of 10,000 racing and 10,000 basic skates.

Solution

1. Variable and Fixed Costs

The high-low method involves finding the variable and fixed costs at the high and low levels of production. In this case:

	Racing Model	Basic Model
High-production month	1,700 (Aug.)	1,300 (July)
Low-production month	400 (Dec.)	350 (Nov.)
Difference	1,300	950
Total production costs of high month	$154,500	$60,600
Total production costs of low month	44,000	20,700
Difference	$110,500	$39,900

Once the differences are known, the change in units (production) is divided into the change in costs to determine the variable cost rate.

$$\frac{\text{Change in costs}}{\text{Change in units}} = \text{Variable cost rate}$$

$$\text{Racing model: } \frac{\$110,500}{1,300} = \$85$$

$$\text{Basic model: } \frac{\$39,900}{950} = \$42$$

Because total variable costs equal unit variable cost times number of units produced, and total costs equal total variable costs plus total fixed costs, fixed costs can now be calculated.

$$\text{Total costs} - (\text{Variable cost per unit} \times \text{Number of units}) = \text{Total fixed costs}$$

	Racing Model	Basic Model
High production level (X) =	\$154,500 − \$85(1,700)	\$60,600 − \$42(1,300)
	X = \$154,500 − \$144,500	X = \$60,600 − \$54,600
	X = \$10,000	X = \$6,000
Low production level (X) =	\$44,000 − \$85(400)	\$20,700 − \$42(350)
	X = \$44,000 − \$34,000	X = \$20,700 − \$14,700
	X = \$10,000	X = \$6,000

Thus, we have the following:

	Racing Model	Basic Model
Variable cost rate	\$ 85	\$ 42
Total fixed costs	10,000	6,000

2. Contribution Margin Income Statements

Blade Corporation
Contribution Margin Income Statements
For the Year Ended December 31, 2003

	Racing Model	Basic Model
Sales revenue (at 10,000 units)	\$1,300,000	\$650,000
Less variable cost of goods sold*	(850,000)	(420,000)
Contribution margin	\$ 450,000	\$230,000
Less fixed cost of goods sold	(10,000)	(6,000)
Less fixed selling costs	(200,000)	(80,000)
Income	\$ 240,000	\$144,000

*\$85 per unit for racing model; \$42 per unit for basic model.

2. Assessing the Effects of Changes in Costs, Prices, and Volume on Profitability

K&D Company plans the following for the coming year:

Sales volume	100,000 units
Sales price	$2.50 per unit
Variable costs	$1.30 per unit
Fixed costs	$60,000

Required:

1. Determine K&D's target income.
2. Compute what the target income would be under each of the following independent assumptions:
   a. The sales volume increases 20%.
   b. The sales price decreases 20%.
   c. Variable costs increase 20%.
   d. Fixed costs decrease 20%.

Solution

1. Target Income

Basic C-V-P equation: Revenues − Variable costs − Fixed costs = Target income

(Units sold × Sales price) − (Units sold × Variable unit cost) − Fixed costs = Target income
(100,000 × $2.50) − (100,000 × $1.30) − $60,000 = *X*
$250,000 − $130,000 − $60,000 = *X*
$60,000 = *X*

This answer can be validated by dividing fixed costs by the per-unit contribution margin to find the break-even point and then multiplying the excess units to be sold above the break-even point by the per-unit contribution margin of $1.20 ($2.50 − $1.30).

$$\frac{\text{Fixed costs}}{\text{Per-unit contribution margin}} = \text{Break-even point}$$

$$\frac{\$60{,}000}{\$1.20} = 50{,}000 \text{ units}$$

Units sold	100,000
Less break-even point (units)	50,000
Excess	50,000
Per-unit contribution margin	× $1.20
Target income	$60,000

2a. The sales volume increases 20%

(100,000 × 1.2 × $2.50) − (100,000 × 1.2 × $1.30) − $60,000 = *X*
$300,000 − $156,000 − $60,000 = *X*
$84,000 = *X*

In this case, the contribution margin does not change. Therefore, the answer can be validated by multiplying the units to be sold in excess of the break-even point by the per-unit contribution margin of $1.20 to find the target income.

Units sold	120,000
Less break-even point (units)	50,000
Excess	70,000
Per-unit contribution margin	× $1.20
Target income	$84,000

2b. The sales price decreases 20%

(100,000 × $2.50 × 0.8) − (100,000 × $1.30) − $60,000 = *X*
$200,000 − $130,000 − $60,000 = *X*
$10,000 = *X*

In this case, the contribution margin changes. Therefore, the answer can be validated by dividing fixed costs by the new per-unit contribution margin of \$0.70 (\$2.00 − \$1.30) to find the new break-even point and then multiplying the units to be sold in excess of the break-even point by the new per-unit contribution margin.

$$\frac{\$60{,}000 \text{ (fixed costs)}}{\$0.70 \text{ (new per-unit contribution margin)}} = 85{,}715 \text{ units (new break-even point, rounded up)}$$

Units sold	100,000
Less break-even point (units)	85,715
Excess	14,285
Per-unit contribution margin	× \$0.70
Target income	\$10,000 (rounded)

2c. Variable costs increase 20%

$$\begin{aligned}(100{,}000 \times \$2.50) - (100{,}000 \times \$1.30 \times 1.2) - \$60{,}000 &= X\\ \$250{,}000 - \$156{,}000 - \$60{,}000 &= X\\ \$34{,}000 &= X\end{aligned}$$

In this case, the contribution margin changes. Therefore, the answer can be validated by dividing fixed costs by the new per-unit contribution margin of \$0.94 (\$2.50 − \$1.56) to find the new break-even point and then multiplying the units to be sold in excess of the break-even point by the new per-unit contribution margin.

$$\frac{\$60{,}000 \text{ (fixed costs)}}{\$0.94 \text{ (new per-unit contribution margin)}} = 63{,}830 \text{ units (new break-even point, rounded up)}$$

Units sold	100,000
Less break-even point (units)	63,830
Excess	36,170
Per-unit contribution margin	× \$0.94
Target income	\$34,000 (rounded)

2d. Fixed costs decrease 20%

$$\begin{aligned}(100{,}000 \times \$2.50) - (100{,}000 \times \$1.30) - (\$60{,}000 \times 0.8) &= X\\ \$250{,}000 - \$130{,}000 - \$48{,}000 &= X\\ \$72{,}000 &= X\end{aligned}$$

In this case, the contribution margin does not change, but fixed costs, and hence the break-even point, do. Therefore, the answer can be validated by dividing the per-unit contribution margin of \$1.20 into the new fixed costs to find the break-even point and then multiplying the units to be sold in excess of the break-even point by the per-unit contribution margin.

$$\frac{\$48{,}000 \text{ (new fixed costs)}}{\$1.20 \text{ (per-unit contribution margin)}} = 40{,}000 \text{ units (new break-even point)}$$

Units sold	100,000
Less break-even point (units)	40,000
Excess	60,000
Per-unit contribution margin	× \$1.20
Target income	\$72,000

discussion questions

1. Explain how understanding cost behavior patterns can assist management.
2. Discuss how level of activity is measured in manufacturing, merchandising, and service firms.
3. What is meant by the linearity assumption, and why is it made? Relate this assumption to the relevant-range concept.
4. What factors seem to have caused the shift from variable to fixed cost patterns?
5. How should stepped costs be treated in the planning process?
6. Why must all mixed costs be segregated into their fixed and variable components?
7. What is the major weakness of the scattergraph, or visual-fit, method of analyzing mixed costs?
8. What is the major limitation of the high-low method of analyzing mixed costs?
9. What is the basic C-V-P equation?
10. What is the contribution margin, and why is it important for managers to know the contribution margins of their products?
11. How much will profits increase for every unit sold over the break-even point?
12. What is the major advantage of using C-V-P graphs?
13. When other factors are constant, what is the effect on profits of an increase in fixed costs? Of a decrease in variable costs?
14. What are the limiting assumptions of C-V-P analysis?
15. How do the issues of quality and time relate to C-V-P analysis decisions?

expanded material

16. How does the method of least squares differ from the scattergraph method?
17. What effect is a change in the sales mix likely to have on a firm's overall contribution margin ratio?

discussion cases

CASE 2-1

COLORADO OUTDOORS FEDERATION

The Colorado Outdoors Federation sponsors an annual banquet. This year the guest speaker is a noted wildlife photographer and lecturer. In planning for the event, the group's treasurer has determined the following costs:

Rental of meeting facility	$250
Honorarium for speaker	800
Tickets and advertising	300
Cost of dinner (per person)	20
Door prizes	500

Last year, tickets were sold at $20 per person, and 350 people attended the banquet. This year the planning committee is hoping for an attendance of 450 at a price of $25 each.

1. a. At $25 per person, how many people must attend the banquet for the Federation to break even?
   b. How much profit (loss) will occur if 450 people attend?
2. Should the Federation increase its advertising costs by $200 and its door prizes by $300 if it can expect another 100 people to attend the banquet?

3. If the Federation maintains its original expected costs but reduces the price per ticket from $25 to $22, it can expect 500 people to attend the banquet. Should the Federation reduce the price of its tickets to $22 per person?

CASE 2-2

ENTERTAINMENT ENTERPRISES

Entertainment Enterprises, a firm that sells magazine subscriptions, is experiencing increased competition from a number of companies. The president, Betty Kincher, has asked you, the controller, to prepare an income statement that will highlight the fixed and variable costs; this will provide more useful information for planning and control purposes. Sales revenues are $25 per subscription. An analysis of company costs for the past six months reveals the following:

Administrative salaries	$10,000 per month
Advertising expense	$2,000 per month
Cost of goods sold	$12.50 per subscription
Rent expense	$5,000 per month
Sales commissions	15% of sales

In addition, the company makes most sales contacts through an extensive telephone network. Consequently, the telephone expense is significant and has both fixed and variable components. Relevant data concerning the telephone expense for the past six months follow:

Month	Unit Sales	Telephone Expense
July	4,000	$10,200
August	5,000	12,300
September	3,500	9,150
October	4,500	11,250
November	5,200	12,720
December	5,500	13,350

Prepare a management report for the president that:

1. Computes the fixed and variable portions of the telephone expense using the high-low method. (*Note:* A scattergraph may be used to visually check your answer.)
2. Presents a budgeted (pro-forma) contribution margin income statement for Entertainment Enterprises for the next six months (January through June), assuming that it expects to sell 30,000 subscriptions at a price of $25 each.
3. Explains how the information provided in (3) might help the president make better management decisions.

exercises

EXERCISE 2-1

VARIABLE AND FIXED COSTS OVER THE RELEVANT RANGE

Cook Corporation manufactures plastic garbage cans. In a typical year, the firm produces between 40,000 and 50,000 cans. At this level of production, fixed costs are $10,000 and variable costs are $2 per can.

1. Graph the cost of producing cans, with cost as the vertical axis and production output as the horizontal axis.

2. Indicate on the graph the relevant range of the $10,000 in fixed costs, and explain the significance of the relevant range.
3. What would total production costs be if 46,000 cans were produced?

EXERCISE 2-2

FIXED COSTS—THE RELEVANT RANGE

Flying A Company manufactures airplanes. The following schedule shows total fixed costs at various levels of airplane production:

Units Produced	Total Fixed Costs
0–200	$200,000
201–500	300,000
501–800	400,000

1. What is the fixed cost per unit when 50 airplanes are produced?
2. What is the fixed cost per unit when 250 airplanes are produced?
3. What is the fixed cost per unit when 800 airplanes are produced?
4. Plot total fixed costs on a graph similar to that shown in Exhibit 2-3.

EXERCISE 2-3

SCATTERGRAPH METHOD OF ANALYZING MIXED COSTS

Wyoming Company makes windmills. The company has the following total costs at the given levels of windmill production:

Units Produced	Total Costs
20	$16,000
30	20,000
40	24,000
50	28,000

1. Use the scattergraph method to estimate the fixed and variable elements of Wyoming's total costs.
2. Compute the total cost of making 44 windmills, assuming that total fixed costs are $8,000 and that the variable cost rate computed in (1) does not change.

EXERCISE 2-4

SCATTERGRAPH METHOD OF ANALYZING MIXED COSTS

Given the following mixed costs at various levels of production, complete the requirements.

Month	Units Produced	Mixed Costs
January	2	$13.75
February	3	16.50
March	1	11.00
April	5	22.00
May	2	13.75

1. Plot the data on a scattergraph, and visually fit a straight line through the points.
2. Based on your graph, estimate the monthly fixed cost and the variable cost per unit produced.
3. Compute the total cost of producing eight units in a month, assuming that the same relevant range applies.
4. **Interpretive Question:** Why is it so important to be able to determine the components of a mixed cost?

EXERCISE 2-5

HIGH-LOW METHOD OF ANALYZING MIXED COSTS

Sailmaster makes boats and has the following costs at the given levels of production:

Units Produced	Total Costs
200	$200,000
250	225,000
300	250,000
350	275,000
400	300,000
450	325,000

1. Use the high-low method to compute the variable and fixed elements of Sailmaster's total costs.
2. Compute the total cost of making 500 boats, assuming that total fixed costs and the variable cost rate do not change.

EXERCISE 2-6

HIGH-LOW METHOD OF ANALYZING MIXED COSTS

The *San Fernando Herald* has determined that the annual printing of 600,000 newspapers costs 9 cents per copy. If production were to be increased to 900,000 copies per year, the per-unit cost would drop to 7 cents per copy.

1. Determine the total fixed and variable costs of printing 600,000 newspapers.
2. What would be the total cost of producing 800,000 copies?

EXERCISE 2-7

CONTRIBUTION MARGIN CALCULATIONS

Jerry Stone owns and operates a small beach shop in a mall on Sanibel Island, Florida. For the last six months, Jerry has had a display of sunglasses in the front window. Largely because of the display, Jerry has sold 100 pairs of sunglasses per month at an average cost of $26 and selling price of $50. The sales volume has doubled since the display was put in the window. One-fourth of Jerry's storage space is occupied by 190 ice coolers. The coolers have not been selling as well as Jerry hoped, but he is convinced that a front window display of coolers would increase sales by 50%. The coolers cost Jerry a total of $2,280 and have been selling at a rate of 100 per month at $28 each.

1. Assuming that cost of goods sold is the only variable cost, compute the contribution margin per unit for sunglasses and ice coolers.
2. Compute the total contribution margins for both sunglasses and ice coolers assuming window displays and no window displays for both items.
3. What are the economic costs associated with keeping the sunglass display in the store window?
4. What are the economic costs associated with replacing the sunglass display with an ice cooler display?

EXERCISE 2-8

CONTRIBUTION MARGIN INCOME STATEMENT

The following data apply to Gordon Company for 2003:

Sales revenue (10 units at $25 each)	$250
Variable selling expenses	45
Variable administrative expenses	25
Fixed selling expenses	30
Fixed administrative expenses	15
Direct labor	50
Direct materials	60
Fixed manufacturing overhead	5
Variable manufacturing overhead	3

1. Prepare a contribution margin income statement. Assume there were no beginning or ending inventories in 2003.
2. How much would Gordon Company have lost if only five units had been sold during 2003?

EXERCISE 2-9

ANALYSIS OF A CONTRIBUTION MARGIN INCOME STATEMENT

Fill in the missing amounts for the following three cases:

	Case I	Case II	Case III
Sales revenue	$100,000	$120,000	$ (7) ?
Variable cost of goods sold:			
Direct materials	$ 25,000	$ (4) ?	$10,000
Direct labor	(1) ?	30,000	10,000
Variable selling and administrative costs	7,000	(5) ?	5,000
Contribution margin	$ (2) ?	$ 40,000	$ (8) ?
Gross margin	40,000	60,000	20,000
Fixed selling and administrative costs*	11,000	20,000	(9) ?
Rent expense on office building	(3) ?	10,000	1,000
Depreciation expense on delivery trucks	10,000	5,000	4,000
Profit	$ 8,000	$ (6) ?	$ -0-

*Except rent and depreciation.

EXERCISE 2-10

ANALYSIS OF THE CONTRIBUTION MARGIN

Dr. Hughes and Dr. Hawkins, owners of the Spanish Fork Care Clinic, have $150,000 of fixed costs per year. They receive 20,000 patient visits in a year, charging each patient an average of $20 per visit; variable costs average $2 per visit (needles, medicines, and so on).

1. What is the contribution margin per patient visit?
2. What is the total contribution margin per year?
3. What is the total pretax profit for a year?
4. Drs. Hughes and Hawkins can bring in another doctor at a salary of $100,000 per year. If this new doctor can handle 5,000 patient visits per year, should the new doctor be hired? (Assume no additional fixed costs will be incurred.)

EXERCISE 2-11

CONTRIBUTION MARGIN ANALYSIS

Compute the missing amounts for the following independent cases. (Assume zero beginning and ending inventories.)

	Case I	Case II	Case III
Sales volume (units)	12,000	(5) ?	8,000
Sales price per unit	$5	$4	(9) ?
Variable costs (total)	(1) ?	$50,000	$25,000
Contribution margin (total)	(2) ?	(6) ?	$15,000
Contribution margin per unit (rounded)	$2	$1.50	(10) ?
Fixed costs (total)	(3) ?	(7) ?	(11) ?
Fixed costs per unit (rounded)	(4) ?	$1.00	(12) ?
Profit	$10,000	(8) ?	$10,000

EXERCISE 2-12

BREAK-EVEN POINT AND TARGET INCOME

Detienne Company manufactures and sells one product for $20 per unit. The unit contribution margin is 40% of the sales price, and fixed costs total $80,000.

1. Using the equation approach, compute:
   a. The break-even point in sales dollars and units.
   b. The sales volume (in units) needed to generate a profit of $40,000.
   c. The break-even point (in units) if variable costs increase to 80% of the sales price and fixed costs increase to $100,000.
2. Using the contribution margin approach in units, recalculate 1(a), 1(b), and 1(c).

EXERCISE 2-13

BREAK-EVEN POINT AND TARGET INCOME

Household Products, Inc., estimates 2003 costs to be as follows:

Direct materials	$4 per unit
Direct labor	$6 per unit
Variable manufacturing overhead	$2 per unit
Variable selling and administrative expenses	$1 per unit
Fixed expenses	$50,000

1. Assuming that Household will sell 40,000 units, what sales price per unit will be needed to achieve a $60,000 profit?
2. Assuming that Household decides to sell its product for $16 per unit, determine the break-even sales volume in dollars and units.
3. Assuming that Household decides to sell its product for $16 per unit, determine the number of units it must sell to generate a $50,000 profit.

EXERCISE 2-14

BREAK-EVEN POINT—GRAPHIC ANALYSIS

Using the graph below, answer the following questions:

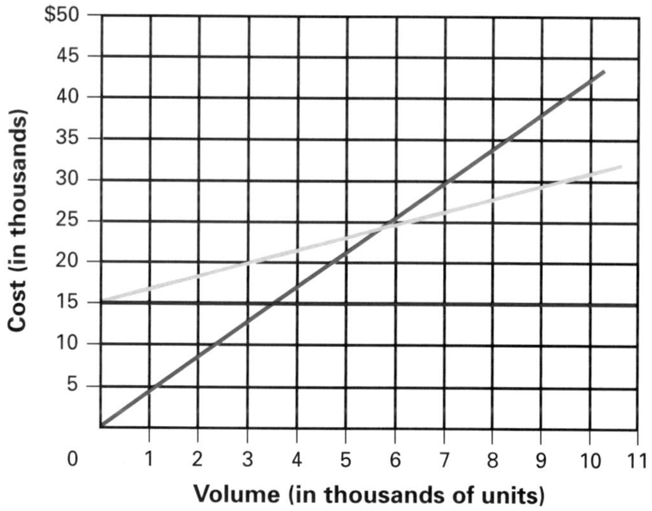

1. Copy the graph and identify (label) fixed costs, variable costs, total revenues, the total cost line, and the break-even point.
2. Determine the break-even point in both sales dollars and volume.
3. Suppose that as a manager you forecast sales volume at 7,000 units. At this level of sales, what would be your total fixed costs, approximate variable costs, and profit (or loss)?
4. At a sales volume of 3,000 units, what would be the level of fixed costs, variable costs, and approximate profit (or loss)?

EXERCISE 2-15

THE PROFIT GRAPH

Using the graph at the top of the next page, answer the following questions:

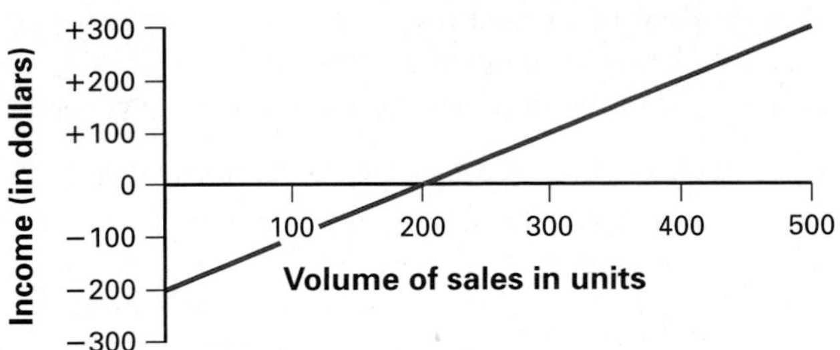

1. What is the break-even point in sales volume (in units)?
2. Approximately what volume of sales (in units) must this company have to generate an income of $300?
3. How much are the fixed costs?

EXERCISE 2-16

GRAPHING REVENUES AND COSTS

Montana Company manufactures chocolate candy. Its manufacturing costs are as follows:

Annual fixed costs	$15,000
Variable costs	$2 per box of candy

1. Plot variable costs, fixed costs, and total costs on a graph for activity levels of 0 to 30,000 boxes of candy.
2. Plot a revenue line on the graph, assuming that Montana sells the chocolates for $5 a box.

EXERCISE 2-17

C-V-P ANALYSIS

The Last Outpost is a tourist stop in a western resort community. Kerry Yost, the owner of the shop, sells hand-woven blankets for an average price of $30 per blanket. Kerry buys the blankets from Native Americans at an average cost of $21. In addition, he has selling expenses of $3 per blanket. Kerry rents the building for $300 per month and pays one employee a fixed salary of $500 per month.

1. Determine the number of blankets Kerry must sell to break even.
2. Determine the number of blankets Kerry must sell to generate a profit of $1,000 per month.
3. Assume that Kerry can produce and sell his own blankets at a total variable cost of $16 per blanket, but that he would need to hire one additional employee at a monthly salary of $600.
   a. Determine the number of blankets Kerry must sell to break even.
   b. Determine the number of blankets Kerry must sell to generate a profit of $1,000 per month.

EXERCISE 2-18

C-V-P ANALYSIS—CHANGES IN VARIABLES

Stop & Shop, Inc., estimates that next year's results will be:

Sales revenue (150,000 units)	$1,125,000
Less variable costs	(600,000)
Less fixed costs	(400,000)
Profit	$ 125,000

Recompute profit, assuming each of the following independent conditions:

1. A 10% increase in the contribution margin.
2. A 6% increase in the sales volume.
3. A 6% decrease in the sales volume.
4. A 6% increase in variable costs per unit.

5. A 7% decrease in fixed costs.
6. A 7% increase in fixed costs.
7. A 7% increase in the sales volume and a 5% increase in fixed costs.

EXERCISE 2-19

C-V-P ANALYSIS—CHANGES IN VARIABLES

Modern Fun Corporation sells electronic games. Its three salespersons are currently being paid fixed salaries of $30,000 each; however, the sales manager has suggested that it might be more profitable to pay the salespersons on a straight commission basis. He has suggested a commission of 15% of sales. Current data for Modern Fun Corporation are as follows:

Sales volume	15,000 units
Sales price	$40 per unit
Variable costs	$29 per unit
Fixed costs	$140,000

1. Assuming that Modern Fun Corporation has a target income of $50,000 for next year, which alternative is more attractive?
2. The sales manager believes that by switching to a commission basis, sales will increase 20%. If that is the case, which alternative is more attractive? (Assume that sales are expected to remain at 15,000 units under the fixed salary alternative.)

expanded material

EXERCISE 2-20

MIXED COSTS—LEAST SQUARES ANALYSIS

Given the following mixed costs at various levels of production, complete the requirements.

Month	Units Produced	Mixed Costs
January	2	$15
February	3	18
March	1	11
April	5	22
May	2	13

1. Using the least squares method (either the equation approach or a software package), calculate the monthly fixed and variable components of the mixed costs.
2. Using the estimates from (1), compute the total cost of producing four units in a month.
3. Describe a major advantage and a major disadvantage of the least squares method.

EXERCISE 2-21

SALES MIX

Klein Brothers sells products X and Y. Because of the nature of the products, Klein sells two units of product X for each unit of product Y. Relevant information about the products is as follows:

	X	Y
Sales price per unit	$20	$30
Variable cost per unit	16	24

1. Assuming that Klein's fixed costs total $140,000, compute Klein's break-even point in sales dollars and units of products X and Y.
2. Assuming that Klein sells two units of product Y for each unit of product X, and fixed costs remain at $140,000, compute Klein's break-even point in sales dollars and units of products X and Y.
3. Explain any differences in your answers to (1) and (2).

EXERCISE 2-22

C-V-P ANALYSIS

Mower Manufacturing's income statement for January 2003 is given below.

Sales (25,000 units × $25)	$625,000
Less variable costs	450,000
Contribution margin	$175,000
Less fixed costs	125,000
Profit	$ 50,000

1. Calculate the company's break-even point in sales dollars and units.
2. The company is contemplating the purchase of new production equipment that would reduce variable costs per unit to $16. However, fixed costs would increase to $175,000 per month. Assuming sales of 26,000 units next month, prepare an income statement for both the current and the proposed production methods. Calculate the break-even point (in dollars and units) for the new production method.

EXERCISE 2-23

OPERATING LEVERAGE

Relax Company and Recline Company both make rocking chairs. They have the same production capacity, but Relax is more automated than Recline. At an output of 1,000 chairs per year, the two companies have the following costs:

	Relax	Recline
Fixed costs	$40,000	$20,000
Variable costs at $10 per chair	10,000	
Variable costs at $30 per chair		30,000
Total cost	$50,000	$50,000
Unit cost (1,000 units)	$ 50	$ 50

Assuming that both companies sell chairs for $70 each and that there are no other costs or expenses for the two firms, complete the following:

1. Which company will lose the least money if production and sales fall to 500 chairs per year?
2. How much would each company lose at production and sales level of 500 chairs per year?
3. How much would each company make at production and sales levels of 2,000 chairs per year?

problems

PROBLEM 2-1

GRAPHING REVENUES AND COSTS

Cloward and Hawkins, CPAs, took in $350,000 of gross revenues this year. Besides themselves, they have two professional staff (one manager and one senior) and a full-time secretary. Fixed operating expenses for the office were $50,000 last year. This year the volume of activity is up 5%, and fixed operating expenses are still $50,000. Total variable operating costs, except for bonuses, average $5 per billable hour. The billable time for all professionals is as follows:

Partners:	3,000 hours at $75/hour
Manager:	1,800 hours at $40/hour
Senior:	2,120 hours at $25/hour

Salaries for the professional staff are $40,000 and $28,000, respectively; the secretary is paid $18,000. The partners each draw salaries of $60,000; plus they share a 5% bonus based on gross revenues. The manager is given a 2% bonus, also based on gross revenues.

Required:

1. Plot the data on a graph clearly showing (a) fixed costs, (b) variable costs, (c) total costs, and (d) total revenues.
2. How much profit did the CPA firm make this year (after partners' salaries)?

PROBLEM 2-2

HIGH-LOW AND SCATTERGRAPH METHODS OF ANALYSIS

Woodfield Company makes bed linens. During the first six months of 2003, Woodfield had the following production costs:

Month	Units Produced	Total Costs
January	10,000	$ 68,000
February	20,000	100,000
March	15,000	90,000
April	8,000	52,000
May	17,000	94,000
June	12,000	74,000

Required:

1. Use the high-low method to compute the monthly fixed cost and the variable cost rate.
2. Plot the costs on a scattergraph.
3. **Interpretive Question:** Based on your scattergraph, do you think the fixed costs and the variable cost rate determined in (1) are accurate? Why?

PROBLEM 2-3

CONTRIBUTION MARGIN INCOME STATEMENT

Early in 2004, Delta Company (a retailing firm) sent the following income statement to its stockholders:

Delta Company
Income Statement
For the Year Ended December 31, 2003

Sales revenue (1,000 units)	$60,000	
Less cost of goods sold (variable)	40,000	
Gross margin		$20,000
Operating expenses:		
Selling	$ 6,000	
Administrative	4,000	
Depreciation (fixed)	1,000	
Insurance (fixed)	50	
Utilities ($20 fixed and $30 variable)	50	11,100
Profit		$ 8,900

Required:

1. Prepare a contribution margin income statement. (Assume that the fixed components of the selling and administrative expenses are $3,000 and $2,000, respectively.)
2. **Interpretive Question:** Why is a contribution margin income statement helpful to management?
3. **Interpretive Question:** How would the analysis in (1) be different if the depreciation expense was considered a stepped cost with wide steps compared to the relevant range?

PROBLEM 2-4

CONTRIBUTION MARGIN INCOME STATEMENT

Susan Young is an attorney for a small law firm in Arizona. She is also a part-time inventor and an avid golfer. One day Susan's golf foursome included a man named Henry Jones, a manufacturer of Christmas ornaments. Henry explained to Susan that he manufactures an ornament everyone loves, but stores will not carry the ornaments because they are very fragile and often break during shipping. Susan told Henry about a plastic box she had developed recently that would protect such fragile items during shipping. After crash testing the plastic box, Henry offered Susan a contract to purchase 100,000 of the boxes for $2.20 each. Susan is convinced that the box has many applications and that she can obtain future orders. Production of the plastic boxes will take one year. Estimated costs for the first year are as follows:

Lease payments on building	$800 per month
Lease payments on machine	$2,200 per month
Cost to retool machine	$10,000
Depreciation on machine	$9,600
Direct materials	$0.70 per box
Direct labor	$0.30 per box
Indirect materials and other manufacturing overhead	$10,000
Interest on loan	$2,500
Administrative salaries	$15,000

Required:

1. Using the information provided, determine Susan's contribution margin and projected profit at a sales level of 100,000 boxes.
2. If Susan's salary as an attorney is $44,500, determine how many boxes Susan must sell to earn profits equal to her salary.

PROBLEM 2-5

FUNCTIONAL AND CONTRIBUTION MARGIN INCOME STATEMENTS

Smooth Surface, Inc. (SSI) is a retail outlet for customized speedboats. The average cost of a boat to the company is $12,500. SSI includes a markup of 30% of cost in the sales price. In 2003, SSI sold 33 boats and finished the year with the same amount of inventory it had at the beginning of the year. Additional operating costs for the year were as follows:

Selling expenses:	
Advertising (fixed)	$ 500 per month
Commissions (mixed)	4,500 per month plus 2% of sales
Depreciation (fixed)	300 per month
Utilities (fixed)	150 per month
Freight on delivery (variable)	100 per boat
Administrative expenses:	
Salaries (fixed)	$4,000 per month
Depreciation (fixed)	300 per month
Utilities (fixed)	150 per month
Clerical (variable)	25 per sale

Required:

1. Prepare a traditional income statement using the functional approach.
2. Prepare an income statement using the contribution margin format.
3. **Interpretive Question:** Which statement is more useful for decision making? Why?

PROBLEM 2-6

CONTRIBUTION MARGIN AND FUNCTIONAL INCOME STATEMENTS

The following information is available for Dabney Company for 2003:

Sales revenue (at $20 per unit)	$151,200
Fixed manufacturing costs	24,000
Variable manufacturing costs (at $8 per unit)	60,480
Fixed selling expenses	70,000
Variable selling expenses (at $2 per unit)	15,120

Required:

1. Prepare a contribution margin income statement.
2. Prepare a functional income statement.
3. Calculate the number of units sold.
4. Calculate the contribution margin per unit.
5. Calculate markup as a percentage of manufacturing costs.
6. **Interpretive Question:** Why is a knowledge of the contribution margin more useful than a knowledge of the markup per unit when management has to make a decision about profitability?

PROBLEM 2-7

UNIFYING CONCEPTS: HIGH-LOW METHOD, CONTRIBUTION MARGINS, AND ANALYSIS

Press Publishing Corporation has two major magazines: *Star Life* and *Weekly News.* During 2003, *Star Life* sold 3 million copies at $1.00 each, and *Weekly News* sold 2.1 million copies at $1.10 each. Press Publishing accumulated the following cost information:

	Star Life		*Weekly News*	
Month	Copies Produced	Manufacturing Cost	Copies Produced	Manufacturing Cost
January	400,000	$170,000	300,000	$170,000
February	300,000	150,000	150,000	105,000
March	400,000	180,000	130,000	100,000
April	200,000	120,000	120,000	90,000
May	250,000	140,000	200,000	130,000
June	200,000	125,000	250,000	150,000
July	240,000	130,000	150,000	110,000
August	200,000	130,000	200,000	135,000
September	180,000	110,000	150,000	105,000
October	230,000	130,000	150,000	108,000
November	200,000	125,000	150,000	115,000
December	200,000	126,000	150,000	112,500

Required:

1. Use the high-low method to estimate the variable and fixed manufacturing costs of each magazine. (Round the variable cost rate to three decimal places.)
2. If all selling expenses are fixed and they total $500,000 for *Star Life* and $400,000 for *Weekly News,* prepare contribution margin income statements for the two magazines at sales of 3 million copies each.
3. Which magazine is more profitable at sales of 2 million copies?
4. **Interpretive Question:** If the same total dollar amount spent on either magazine will result in the same number of new subscriptions, which magazine should be advertised?

PROBLEM 2-8

CONTRIBUTION MARGIN ANALYSIS

Sunrise Company is a manufacturer of alarm clocks. The following information pertains to Sunrise's 2003 sales:

Sales price per unit	$ 15
Variable costs per unit	11
Total fixed costs	300,000

Required:

1. Determine Sunrise Company's unit contribution margin.
2. Using the contribution margin approach, compute:
   a. The break-even point in sales dollars and units.
   b. The sales volume (in dollars and units) needed to generate a target income of $50,000.
3. Using the equation approach of C-V-P analysis, compute:
   a. The break-even point in sales dollars and units.
   b. The sales volume (in dollars and units) needed to generate a 20 percent return on sales.

PROBLEM 2-9

CONTRIBUTION MARGIN ANALYSIS

Porter Company manufactures products X, Y, and Z. The following information relates to the three products:

	Product X	Product Y	Product Z
Sales volume (in units)	50,000	25,000	10,000
Sales revenue	$150,000	$125,000	$100,000
Variable costs	$100,000	$ 85,000	$ 70,000
Fixed costs	$ 30,000	$ 30,000	$ 30,000

Required:

1. At the current level of sales, which product provides the most profit?
2. With each additional unit of sales, which product provides the least contribution to profit?
3. If you could sell only 5,000 units, but all 5,000 must be either product X, Y, or Z, which would you sell?
4. If you could sell only 50,000 units, but all 50,000 must be either product X, Y, or Z, which would you sell?
5. **Interpretive Question:** If you had $5,000 for advertising and each dollar of advertising resulted in a one-unit increase in sales volume, which product would you advertise?

PROBLEM 2-10

BREAK-EVEN ANALYSIS

Trudy Sorensen paid $150 to rent a carnival booth for four days. She has to decide whether to sell donuts or popcorn. Donuts cost $1.20 per dozen and can be sold for $2.40 per dozen. Popcorn will require a $75 rental fee for the popcorn maker and $0.05 per bag of popcorn for the popcorn, butter, salt, and bags; a bag of popcorn could sell for $0.30.

Required:

1. Compute the break-even point in dozens of donuts if Trudy decides to sell donuts exclusively and the break-even point in bags of popcorn if she decides to sell popcorn exclusively.
2. Trudy estimates that she can sell either 50 donuts or 30 bags of popcorn every hour the carnival is open (10 hours a day for four days). Which product should she sell?
3. Trudy can sell back to the baker at half cost any donuts she fails to sell at the carnival. Unused popcorn must be thrown away. If Trudy sells only 80% of her original estimate, which product should she sell? (Assume that she bought or produced just enough to satisfy the demands she originally estimated.)

PROBLEM 2-11

C-V-P GRAPHIC ANALYSIS

Using the graph below, complete the requirements.

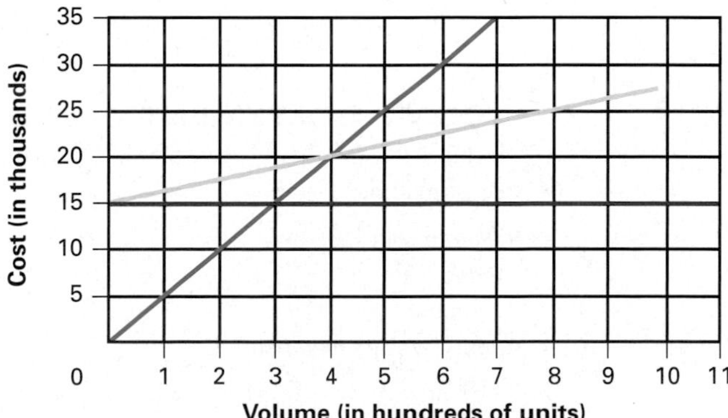

Required:

1. Determine the following:
   a. The break-even point in sales dollars and volume.
   b. The sales price per unit.

   c. Total fixed costs.
   d. Total variable costs at the break-even point.
   e. The variable cost per unit.
   f. The unit contribution margin.
2. What volume of sales must the company generate to reach a target income of $7,500?

PROBLEM 2-12

CONTRIBUTION MARGIN ANALYSIS—CHANGES IN VARIABLES

SMC, Inc., is a producer of hand-held electronic games. Its 2003 income statement was as follows:

SMC, Inc.
Contribution Margin Income Statement
For the Year Ended December 31, 2003

	Total	Per Unit
Sales revenue (150,000 games)	$5,250,000	$35
Less variable costs	3,750,000	25
Contribution margin	$1,500,000	$10
Less fixed costs	900,000	
Profit	$ 600,000	

In preparing its budget for 2004, SMC is evaluating the effects of changes in costs, prices, and volume on profit.

Required: Evaluate the following independent cases, and determine SMC's 2004 budgeted profit or loss in each case. (Assume that 2003 figures apply unless stated otherwise.)

1. Fixed costs increase $150,000.
2. Fixed costs decrease $100,000.
3. Variable costs increase $3 per unit.
4. Variable costs decrease $4 per unit.
5. Sales price increases $5 per unit.
6. Sales price decreases $5 per unit.
7. Sales volume increases 25,000 units.
8. Sales volume decreases 15,000 units.
9. Sales price decreases $4 per unit, sales volume increases 40,000 units, and variable costs decrease by $2.50 per unit.
10. Fixed costs decrease by $100,000, and variable costs increase $4 per unit.
11. Sales volume increases 30,000 units, with a decrease in sales price of $2 per unit. Variable costs drop $1.50 per unit, and fixed costs increase $50,000.

PROBLEM 2-13

INCOME STATEMENT AND BREAK-EVEN ANALYSIS

Zimmerman Company records the following costs associated with the production and sale of a steel slingshot:

Selling expenses:	
Fixed	$6,500
Variable	$0.50 per unit sold
Administrative expenses:	
Fixed	$4,500
Variable	$0.25 per unit sold
Manufacturing costs:	
Fixed	$15,500
Variable	$7.50 per unit produced

Required: Assume that in 2003 the beginning and ending inventories were the same. Also assume that 2003 sales were 11,000 units at $11.50 per slingshot.

1. Prepare a contribution margin income statement.
2. Determine the break-even point in sales dollars.
3. **Interpretive Question:** Zimmerman believes that sales volume could be improved 20% if an additional commission of $0.50 per unit were paid to the salespeople. Zimmerman also believes, however, that the same percentage increase could be achieved through an additional $3,000 investment in advertising. Which action, if either, should Zimmerman take? Why?

PROBLEM 2-14 C-V-P ANALYSIS—CHANGES IN VARIABLES

Rougely Manufacturing Company produces electric carving knives. The firm has not been as profitable as expected in the past three years. As a result, it has excess capacity that could be used to produce an additional 10,000 knives per year. However, any production above that amount would require a capital investment of $50,000. Operating results for the previous year are shown here. Assume that there is never any ending inventory.

Sales revenue (125,000 knives × $8)		$1,000,000
Variable costs (125,000 knives × $5)	$625,000	
Fixed costs	350,000	975,000
Profit		$ 25,000

Required: Respond to the following independent proposals, and support your recommendations:

1. The production manager believes that profits could be increased through the purchase of more automated production machinery, which would increase fixed costs by $100,000 and reduce the variable costs by $0.75 per knife. Is she correct if sales are to remain at 125,000 knives annually?
2. The sales manager believes that a 5% discount on the sales price would increase the sales volume to 135,000 units annually. If he is correct, would this action increase or decrease profits?
3. Would the implementation of both proposals be worthwhile?
4. The sales manager believes that an increase in sales commissions could improve the sales volume. In particular, he suggests that an increase of $0.50 per knife would increase the sales volume 30%. If he is correct, would this action increase profits?
5. The accountant suggests another alternative: Reduce administrative salaries by $10,000 so that prices can be reduced by $0.10 per unit. She believes that this action would increase the volume to 130,000 units annually. If she is correct, would this action increase profits?
6. The corporate executives finally decide to spend an additional $30,000 on advertising to bring the sales volume up to 135,000 units. If the increased advertising can bring in these extra sales, is this a good decision?

PROBLEM 2-15 C-V-P ANALYSIS—RETURN ON SALES

The federal government recently placed a ceiling on the selling price of sheet metal produced by MOB Company. In 2003, MOB was limited to charging a price that would earn a 20% return on gross sales. On the basis of this restriction, MOB had the following results for 2003:

Sales revenue (1,150,000 feet at $2.00 per foot)		$2,300,000
Variable costs (1,150,000 feet × $1.40)	$1,610,000	
Fixed costs	230,000	1,840,000
Profit		$ 460,000

In 2004, MOB predicted that the sales volume would decrease to 900,000 feet of sheet metal. With this level of sales, however, the company anticipated no changes in the levels of fixed and variable costs.

Required:

1. Determine MOB's profit for 2004 if all forecasts are realized. Compute both the dollar amount of profit and the percentage return on sales.

2. MOB plans to petition the government for a price increase so that the 2003 rate of return on sales (20%) can be maintained. What sales price should the company request, based on 2004 projections? (Round to the nearest cent.)
3. How much profit (in dollars) will MOB earn in 2004 if this sales price, as determined in (2), is approved?
4. **Interpretive Question:** What other factors must be considered by MOB and the government?

PROBLEM 2-16

UNIFYING CONCEPTS: C-V-P ANALYSIS AND CHANGES IN VARIABLES

The 2003 pro-forma income statement for Cedar Company is as follows (ignore taxes):

Cedar Company
Pro-Forma Income Statement
For the Year Ended December 31, 2003

Sales (60,000 units)		$660,000
Cost of goods sold:		
Direct materials	$40,000	
Direct labor	75,000	
Variable manufacturing overhead	18,000	
Fixed manufacturing overhead	11,000	
Total cost of goods sold		144,000
Gross margin		$516,000
Selling expenses:		
Variable	$45,000	
Fixed	98,000	
Administrative expenses:		
Variable	17,000	
Fixed	77,000	
Total selling and administrative expenses		237,000
Profit		$279,000

Required:

1. Compute how many units must be sold to break even.
2. Compute the increase (decrease) in profit under the following independent situations:
   a. Sales increase 30%.
   b. Fixed selling and administrative expenses decrease 10%.
   c. Contribution margin decreases 20%.
3. Compute sales in units and dollars at the break-even point if fixed costs increase from $186,000 to $260,400.
4. Compute the number of units that must be sold if expected profit is $1 million.

expanded material

PROBLEM 2-17

UNIFYING CONCEPTS: HIGH-LOW, SCATTERGRAPH, AND LEAST SQUARES METHODS

You have been hired as a consultant for MediaPro Inc. The company manufactures high-density floppy disks and sells them to a wide variety of business clients. Management is eager to learn more about the company's cost behavior. You have been provided the following data. Assume all production falls within the relevant range.

Month	Machine Hours	Utility Costs
January	145	$5,350
February	140	5,200
March	160	5,800
April	170	6,050
May	175	6,200
June	145	5,375
July	150	5,400
August	150	5,450
September	155	5,600
October	170	6,100
November	145	5,300
December	155	5,500

Required:

1. Using the high-low method, compute the variable and fixed elements of MediaPro's utility costs.
2. Plot the information on a scattergraph. Based on your graph, determine the unit variable cost and monthly fixed costs.
3. Using the least squares method (either the equation approach or a software package), calculate the variable and fixed cost components. Determine the cost formula.
4. **Interpretive Question:** Why are the variable cost per unit and fixed costs different for each of these methods of analysis? Which method is the most accurate for determining variable and fixed cost components?

PROBLEM 2-18

SALES MIX

Mike's Ice Cream Company produces and sells ice cream in three sizes: quart, half-gallon, and gallon. Relevant information for each of the sizes is as follows:

	Quart	Half-Gallon	Gallon
Average sales price	$1.00	$1.85	$3.60
Less variable cost	0.80	1.40	2.40
Unit contribution margin	$0.20	$0.45	$1.20
Sales mix (% of sales)	15%	60%	25%

Mike anticipates sales of $500,000 and fixed costs of $120,000 in 2003.

Required:

1. Determine the break-even sales volume in units and dollars for 2003.
2. Determine Mike's 2003 projected profit.
3. Assume that Mike's sales mix changes to 10% quarts, 40% half-gallons, and 50% gallons. Determine Mike's break-even sales volume in units and dollars.

PROBLEM 2-19

UNIFYING CONCEPTS: BREAK-EVEN POINT AND OPERATING LEVERAGE

The following summary data are provided for Basalt Mercantile Corporation and Sunshine Service, Inc. (000's omitted):

	Basalt Mercantile Corp.		Sunshine Service, Inc.
Sales revenue (100,000 units)	$520	(200,000 units)	$1,050
Less variable costs	260		315
Contribution margin	$260		$ 735
Less fixed costs	100		300
Income	$160		$ 435

Required:

1. Determine the break-even point for Basalt and Sunshine in both sales dollars and units.
2. **Interpretive Question:** Which company has a higher operating leverage? Why?
3. **Interpretive Question:** Based on your analysis of the cost structures of Basalt and Sunshine, which company's cost structure is better? What factors are important to consider in answering such a question?

competency enhancement opportunities

- Analyzing Real Company Information
- International Case
- Ethics Case
- Writing Assignment
- The Debate
- Internet Search

The following additional assignments provide opportunities for students to develop critical thinking, ethical perspectives, oral and written communication skills, experience with electronic research, and teamwork through group and business activities.

ANALYZING REAL COMPANY INFORMATION

• ***Analyzing 2-1 (Microsoft)***

Annual revenues, as well as sales and marketing expenses, for the 1988-1999 years are provided below for MICROSOFT CORPORATION:

Microsoft Corporation (millions)		
Year	**Sales and Marketing Expenses**	**Annual Revenue**
1988	$ 152	$ 591
1989	205	805
1990	300	1,186
1991	490	1,847
1992	758	2,777
1993	1,086	3,786
1994	1,135	4,714
1995	1,564	6,075
1996	2,185	9,050
1997	2,411	11,936
1998	2,887	15,262
1999	3,238	19,747

1. Operating output data, such as the number of computer products sold each year, are not provided in Microsoft's annual report. However, while it is a little odd to use revenues to predict marketing expense (instead of the other

way around), it seems sensible that changes in revenues should serve as an approximate measure of changes in the number of products sold by Microsoft. Use the high-low method to analyze the data above to determine if there is a relationship between revenues and sales and marketing expenses. (*Hint:* Don't round off the value you calculate for variable costs per revenue dollar.) What appears to be the amount of fixed costs in these expenses? Does this fixed cost amount make sense? (*Note:* Remember that the data are in millions of dollars!)

expanded material

2. Using your calculator (or some computer software program such as Microsoft Excel®), compute a regression analysis on the data above. What do you learn from the analysis? The Management's Discussion in Microsoft's 1999 Annual Report states: "The increase in the absolute dollar amount of sales and marketing expenses in the three-year period was due primarily to expanded product-specific marketing programs, such as Office 97 in 1997, Windows 98 in 1998, and Office 2000 in 1999. Sales and marketing costs as a percentage of revenue decreased primarily due to moderate headcount growth. Microsoft brand advertising expenses rose slightly in 1998, but declined in 1999." Does this statement provide any help in understanding the analysis?

• ***Analyzing 2-2 (Star Video)***

It is likely that a number of grocery stores in your town have video rental departments. Generally, however, grocery stores do not focus much management attention on their small video rental businesses. The main purpose of having a video department is to encourage more customers to come into the store and purchase groceries! Nevertheless, a grocery store cannot simply buy a large selection of videotapes, corner off a section of floor space, and start renting tapes. Successfully managing a rental business requires being aware of an unimaginably large number of video titles. Obviously, new movies are constantly being released, while old movies gradually lose their appeal and are eventually scrapped. Further, large-scale video rental chains such as BLOCKBUSTER constantly track shifting consumer tastes for certain titles and movie categories. These consumer preferences differ based on demographic data like geographic location, average age, ethnicity, average income, etc. A grocery store really can't manage all these data without losing focus on its main business. Hence, most grocery stores contract out their video rental business to a large-scale video management company. These management companies can purchase huge quantities of tapes, maintain large distribution warehouses, and track demographic data that allow them to manage and move specific inventories to the appropriate grocery store locations. In 1992, one such video management company, Star Video (not its real name), was managing 86 stores representing three supermarket chains in five states—Arizona, California, Montana, Washington, and Wyoming. Total revenue in 1992 for Star Video was $3.6 million. Star Video made all the inventory investments and handled all management activities involved in providing video rentals at each of the 86 stores. Video rental revenue was then split between Star Video and each grocery store, with Star Video keeping the lion's share. Stores liked this arrangement because they made most of their money on grocery sales to customers who came to rent videotapes. Star Video needed to carefully manage revenue and costs at each store in order to stay profitable. Following are the data for six stores located in Washington:

Store Name	Monthly Revenue	Monthly Operating Expenses
Moses Lake	$ 6,408	$ 3,295
W. Kennewick	4,064	2,289
Pasco	4,038	2,270
S. Kennewick	3,692	2,142
E. Wenatchee	1,395	1,316
Richland	2,104	1,516
Total	$21,701	$12,828

Use the high-low method to analyze the operating expenses at these six stores. Determine if operating expenses are related to store revenue. What appear to be the fixed costs of operating each store? Create a graph and plot these costs using revenue on the horizontal axis and operating expenses on the vertical axis. Does the scattergraph agree or disagree with the results of your high-low analysis?

INTERNATIONAL CASE

• ***The Paper Company***

The GHANATA GROUP OF COMPANIES (GGC) is a locally owned and controlled company in Ghana, West Africa. One of its principal operating divisions, THE PAPER COMPANY, is one of Africa's most modern and largest manufacturers/distributors of paper products. For both operating and reporting purposes, The Paper Company is organized into product lines: scholastic, envelope, and stationery. During the 1980s, the economy in Ghana was stagnant. The country faced severe economic problems as a result of unfavorable trade terms with other countries. The official exchange rate of U.S. $1.00 to the local currency, the *cedi*, was about 39.00 as of the end of 1984. (The unofficial rate, e.g., the black market rate, was at least five times worse!) As a result of the economy, it became very difficult for GGC to secure direct materials for its divisions. If a division could secure direct materials, it could sell almost everything it produced. Hence, in terms of being able to predict sales volumes, there was a great deal of risk for GGC divisions. The 1985 budgeted operating data for the three departments in The Paper Company were as follows:

The Paper Company
1985 Budgeted Operations Data
(*Cedi* 000's)

	Scholastic	Envelope	Stationery
Budgeted sales	$1,785,000	$984,000	$3,334,050
Budgeted variable costs	(410,550)	(442,800)	(2,200,473)
Contribution margin	$1,374,450	$541,200	$1,133,577
Budgeted fixed costs	(1,267,350)	(482,160)	(933,534)
Income	$ 107,100	$ 59,040	$ 200,043

Using these operating data, create C-V-P graphs for each department. (Note: Since you don't have per-unit prices and costs, you may assume that the product sales price for each department is $1 per unit, and then plot your graphs at 0, 2 million, and 4 million units.) Given the high-risk business environment in Ghana at this time, which department presents the highest risk to GGC? The lowest risk? Be sure to explain your answer in terms of operating leverage. You may also want to consider each department's break-even point compared to budgeted (expected) operations.

Source: A. Oppong, "The Paper Company," *The Journal of Accounting Case Research,* Vol. 3, No. 2 (1996), pp. 80–88. Permission to use has been granted by Captus Press, Inc. and the Accounting Education Resource Centre of The University of Lethbridge. [Journal Subscription: Captus Press, Inc., York University Campus, 4700 Keele Street, North York, Ontario, M3J 1P3, by calling (416) 736-5537, or by fax at (416) 736-5793, E-mail: info@captus.com, Internet: http://www.captus.com]

ETHICS CASE

• *Pickmore International*

Joan Hildabrand is analyzing some cost data for her boss, Ross Cumings. The data relate to a special sales order that Pickmore International is considering from a large customer in Singapore. The following data are applicable to the product being ordered:

Normal unit sales price	$49.95
Variable unit manufacturing costs	10.50
Variable unit selling and administrative expenses	18.25

The customer is requesting that the sales order be accepted on the following terms:

a. The unit sales price would equal the unit contribution margin plus 10%.
b. Freight would be paid by the customer.
c. Pickmore International would pay a $5,000 "facilitating payment" to a "friend of the customer" to get the product through customs more quickly.

In considering the order, Ross has indicated to Joan that this is a very important customer. Furthermore, this work would help some employees earn a little extra Christmas money with overtime.

1. What are the accounting and ethical issues involved in this case?
2. Should Joan recommend acceptance of the sales terms proposed for this special order?

WRITING ASSIGNMENT

• *Issues of Quality and Time on C-V-P Analysis Decisions*

This chapter described how to analyze whether the difference between sales price and variable costs, as well as the volume of sales, is sufficient to pay for all fixed costs in an organization and provide a sufficient profit. A number of methods have been presented for analyzing these costs, volume, and price relationships. These methods all focus on *quantitative* issues that affect how a company manages its resources to maximize overall profits. However, there are a number of *qualitative* issues involving quality and time that should also affect decisions about what sales prices to set, how to manage fixed and variable costs, and which products should be emphasized within the organization. One way to trade off fixed costs for variable costs is to consider making large fixed cost investments in technology that result in automated production, merchandising, and service processes. These kinds of investments allow some variable costs, such as direct labor, to be reduced. Managing this cost trade-off often has strong implications on the quality of the product or service, as well as the timeliness with which it can be delivered. Both of these qualitative issues eventually affect the quantitative issues of costs, volume, and price. Go to your library and find an article describing one organization's effort to invest in automation or other technologies in order to reduce costs. Determine what quality and time issues are affected by the investment. Write a one- to two-page memo describing what you found.

THE DEBATE

• *Which Cost Analysis Method is Better?*

Many costs within an organization are mixed costs, combining elements of both fixed and variable costs. Separating these types of costs into their fixed and variable cost components is necessary before C-V-P analysis work can be done. Two potential cost analysis methods are the scattergraph (visual-fit) approach and the high-low approach. Each of these methods has both disadvantages and advantages compared to the other.

Divide your group into two teams and prepare a two-minute oral argument supporting your assigned position.

- One team represents "The scattergraph (visual-fit) method is superior!" Explain why this method should be used for determining the variable and fixed cost components in a mixed cost.
- The other team represents "High-low; the way to go!" Explain why this method should be used for determining the variable and fixed cost components in a mixed cost.

INTERNET SEARCH

• *Centre for Applied Ethics*

We have discussed ethical issues for accountants in this text and have included an ethics case at the end of each chapter. Obviously, ethical issues are of concern to accountants and all other business professionals. There are a number of good resources on the Internet for those interested in better exploring ethical issues in business (hopefully, we're all interested in this topic!). One of the better sites is the Centre for Applied Ethics at the University of British Columbia (**http://www.ethics.ubc.ca/resources/**). Sometimes Web addresses change, so if this address doesn't work, access the Web site for this textbook (**http://albrecht.swcollege.com**) for an updated link to the Centre for Applied Ethics.

Go to this site and explore the materials regarding applied ethics resources on the World Wide Web. Find an article that discusses either business or professional ethics. Write a short paragraph that describes exactly where you found the article and give a brief summary.

Product Cost Flows and Business Organizations

chapter m3

learning objectives

After studying this chapter, you should be able to:

1. Understand the difficulty, yet importance, of having accurate product cost information.
2. Explain the flow of goods and services in a manufacturing organization and follow the accumulation of product costs in its accounting system.
3. Understand the process of accounting for overhead.
4. Explain the flow of goods and services in a merchandising organization and follow the accumulation of product costs in its accounting system.
5. Explain the flow of goods and services in a service organization and follow the accumulation of product costs in its accounting system.
6. Understand the impact of e-business on product costing.

expanded material

7. Use the FIFO method to do process costing.

setting the stage

Before 1810, American business was basically made up of a loose bunch of independent contractors, each focused on doing one thing well.[1] As you can imagine, the wheels of commerce turned rather slowly. These small businesses were fairly easy to manage. They had few employees and simple processes. Cost accounting, if it existed at all, was not a difficult procedure. If the wainwright wanted to know how much it cost to build a wagon for a customer, he simply added up the costs of buying lumber products from the sawmill, leather products from the tanner, and iron products from the blacksmith. He then set the price of the wagon high enough to compensate him for his assembly labor.

When the Industrial Revolution came to America sometime after 1812, big business started appearing on the East Coast, beginning with the mechanized, integrated cotton textile factories of New England. In 1814, at a cotton mill established by the American industrialist Francis Cabot Lowell in Waltham, Massachusetts, all the steps of an industrial process were combined under one roof for the first time. Instead of contracting with a dozen different little family-owned businesses to card, spin, and sew raw material into cloth, Lowell brought raw cotton fiber into a heavily equipped factory staffed with workers who were organized by specialty and created a finished product ready for sale! This was "big business," and it really complicated the accounting process. (Actually, it is more likely that the development of management accounting did a great deal to facilitate the growth of these large-scale firms.) In order to run this textile mill, Lowell and his managers required a reporting system that would provide the information needed to plan, control, and evaluate work they were not actually doing themselves. History shows that these early textile mills developed a remarkably good accounting system that tracked inventory, payroll, and production work.

Shortly after the textile manufacturing industry was launched, the advent of railroads as a service industry probably presented some of the most complex administrative problems of the nineteenth century. By 1869, the UNION PACIFIC RAILROAD from the East and the CENTRAL PACIFIC RAILROAD from the West were joined at Promontory Point, Utah. Railroad companies soon grew to sizes that dwarfed the scale of the largest textile factories, and names like J. P. Morgan and Edward Henry Harriman became famous (or infamous, depending on your perspective). Managing these huge administrative entities required special record-keeping systems that recorded enormous numbers of daily transactions and summarized essential information for frequent internal reports to management. The challenge for railroads was that employees and processes were literally spread all over the map! Senior managers needed some means of assessing the performance of submanagers at terminals and yards across the country. Management accounting expanded as "costs per ton-mile" (the average cost to move a ton of material one mile) and "operating ratio" (a ratio of operating expenses to revenues that railroads studied constantly) began providing competitive information to indicate how the performance of various submanagers would affect the company's total financial performance. These performance measures were used to delegate responsibilities and to control and evaluate the business from a distance. As management accounting matured and added competitive value, companies were able to spread out geographically.

The last quarter of the nineteenth century brought an incredible outpouring of inexpensive, mass-produced goods and services for consumers, leading to the emergence of the mass merchandising industry composed of wholesalers and retailers. Besides making many diverse items available for purchase from one source, these wholesalers and retailers provided other critical services, including distribution, delivery, and credit service on account. Companies such as R. H. MACY & COMPANY, INC., in New York City and SEARS, ROEBUCK & COMPANY in Chicago were achieving tremendous financial success by focusing on a very important idea: move the inventory! The success of the mass merchant hinged on **inventory turnover**, called "**stockturns**." By selling goods faster than smaller local merchants, large-scale wholesalers and retailers could charge lower prices and still realize tremendous profit. Up to this point, big business in

inventory turnover (stockturns) The number of times the inventory in an organization "turns over" during a period of time. It is often easier to think of inventory turnover as the number of times a dollar invested in inventory is sold during a period of time. Inventory turnover is computed as cost of goods sold divided by average inventory value.

1 Historical sources: A. D. Chandler, *The Invisible Hand* (Boston: HBS Press, 1977); H. T. Johnson and R. S. Kaplan, *Relevance Lost* (Boston: HBS Press, 1987).

America had focused almost exclusively on costs. But wholesalers and retailers introduced a new concept to management accounting. By controlling and evaluating the use of assets (in this case, inventory), merchandisers helped management accounting grow to include the process management technique of asset (or capital) management.

manufacturing organizations Organizations that focus on using labor and/or machinery to convert raw materials into marketable products.

merchandising organizations Organizations that focus on procuring tangible products, then distributing them to customers. These customers may include individuals or other business organizations such as manufacturing organizations.

service organizations Organizations that focus on delivery of marketable services, such as legal advice or education, to individuals or other organizations.

As described in the opening scenario, management accounting has developed as a mature discipline to support the needs of business organizations. You understand at this point that management accounting is essentially the result of the efforts of many individuals and organizations to create information that has a competitive value in the marketplace. To really understand management accounting, you need to grasp how ***manufacturing, merchandising*** *and* ***service organizations*** *do business. Management accounting historically began with a focus on planning, controlling, and evaluating costs. Cost accounting continues to be a central facet of management accounting. In fact, understanding cost flows is a useful way to understand how a business is structured or organized. And while accurately determining the costs of products and services is difficult, it is one of the most important aspects of management accounting and provides one of the most useful pieces of information for business decision makers. Without accurate cost information, it is difficult to set appropriate prices, evaluate performance, reward employees, or make production decisions. It is even difficult to know whether a company should be competing in a specific market.*

In this chapter, you will learn how goods and services flow in manufacturing, merchandising, and service companies and how product costs incurred in these organizations are tracked and accumulated. In subsequent chapters you will learn how to use product costs to manage and control manufacturing, merchandising, and service companies.

1

Understand the difficulty, yet importance, of having accurate product cost information.

WHY HAVING ACCURATE PRODUCT COSTS IS SO DIFFICULT, YET IMPORTANT

As discussed in Chapter 1 of management accounting, management is constantly making planning, controlling, and evaluating decisions. Managers need accurate product cost information to plan for the future, to control current operations, and to evaluate past performance. They also need accurate product cost information so that they can deliver high-quality products to customers at the lowest price and at the fastest speed.

Bad Product Cost Information Can "Hurt!"

net work

Access HONDA's Web site at http://www.honda.com. The base price for this year's Accord LX V-6 is $22,400. How much does the price increase if keyless entry, a security system, and a CD player are added? How do these features affect Honda's manufacturing costs?

For most companies, accurately determining their product costs is a difficult challenge. Regardless of the difficulty, however, having accurate product cost information is critical for a business. Without knowledge of accurate product costs, managers could easily over- or underprice products and make other poor decisions. What if, for example, HONDA sells its 2002 Accord LX for $23,945 (its intended sales price), but the actual cost of producing the car is $26,000? How long could Honda stay in business losing $2,055 ($26,000 − $23,945) per car? In this case, buyers will probably rush to buy Accords because they will likely be priced much lower than other comparable cars (assuming Honda's competitors have more accurate cost information and have priced their cars to cover their total manufacturing costs). Not only will Honda lose money on every car it sells, but the more cars Honda sells, the greater its losses will be. What if Honda attempts to sell its Accord LX for $23,945, not realizing that its cost of making the car is actually only $18,000? If the accurate cost is only $18,000, other manufacturers, such as FORD, may sell their cars for much less than Honda (assuming Ford has a better cost accounting system); sales of Accords will dwindle. If Honda really believes its costs are higher than $18,000, say, $22,500, it will not lower prices to the point where the company can compete with Ford and other manufacturers. The competitors that better understand their own costs will probably reduce prices, leaving Honda behind in the market. With lower (maybe even zero) sales, Honda may again lose money because it can't sell enough cars to cover its operating expenses. As you can see, having accurate product cost information helps managers in many ways, including making planning, controlling, and evaluating decisions such as the following:

1. As part of the *planning* process, a company can determine whether it can or should compete in certain markets. It is possible that prices of competitors in some markets are already lower than the manufacturing costs would be for a new company trying to compete.
2. When *controlling* operations, a company can analyze the relationship between production levels and costs and determine whether to increase or decrease production levels of certain products. These control data will help the company in planning future operations because it can determine if the increased cost of additional production would be less than the revenue that would be derived from sales of those products.
3. In the *evaluation* process, a company can compare actual costs against budgeted costs (a management accounting process know as variance analysis that we'll discuss in Chapter 9 of management accounting) and identify both progress and problems for subsequent management action.

Having accurate product cost information also allows a company to identify and eliminate costly, complicated processes so that higher-quality, lower-priced products and services can be delivered to customers in increasingly shorter **cycle times**. Accurate cost information allows management to determine the appropriate level at which to operate, to assess the long-term profitability of various products, and to manage the costs of production activities.

cycle time The total time a product spends moving through a particular process or cycle within the organization, such as the product design cycle, the production cycle, or the order and delivery cycle.

Overhead: The Problem in Determining Accurate Product Costs

In Chapter 1 of management accounting, you learned that costs of manufacturing products can be broken down into three elements: (1) direct materials, (2) direct labor, and (3) manufacturing overhead. Direct materials include the cost of raw materials that are used directly in the manufacture of products. Direct materials are kept in the raw materials warehouse until used and include such things as rubber used in making tires, steel used to make cars, wood used to make tables, and plastic used to make eyeglasses. Direct labor includes the wages and other payroll-related expenses of factory employees who work directly on products. Direct labor includes the cost of wages and benefits for assembly-line workers, but it does not include the wages and benefits of the factory custodians or the factory controller because, even though they work in the factory, they don't work directly on making products. Manufacturing overhead includes all manufacturing costs that are not classified as direct materials or direct labor. This includes miscellaneous materials used in production, such as glue or nails; wages for the factory supervisor, controller, and custodians who work in the factory, but not directly on products; and other manufacturing costs such as utilities, depreciation of manufacturing facilities, insurance, and property taxes.

caution

Product costs are only one element management must consider when establishing prices for its products. Pricing is a complex issue, and management usually looks to its own strategy and to the market to set prices (also considering competitors' prices, market's ability to pay, and so forth). Assuming that management uses only its product cost information to set prices is a wrong assumption.

While it is easy to assign direct materials and direct labor costs to specific products, it is extremely difficult to assign manufacturing costs, such as rent or the custodian's salary, to specific manufactured products. One of the major reasons for this difficulty is that many of these overhead costs are "lumpy" in nature and do not match the production of goods. To be more specific, production output in a manufacturing plant tends to occur in an even flow throughout the year. Similarly, the costs of raw materials and direct labor used also follow a generally even pattern throughout the year. On the other hand, most manufacturing overhead costs are not related to the flow of production. For example, think about the nature of maintenance and repair costs on your car (if you have one). If you're a careful car owner, then you get an oil change for your car every 3,000 to 4,000 miles. Occasionally, you need to rotate or replace the tires. Sometimes an alternator or battery (or worse!) goes out and needs replacement. The car gets used every day, and each day's use eventually leads to costs for oil changes, tires, and alternators. Paying for these costs on an occasional basis makes it difficult to budget for and to apply these costs to daily use. As a result, most of us don't have a good idea of what it costs per mile to drive our car. Companies face the same problem. They have insurance and tax bills that

business environment essay

The Commercialization of the Internet Who invented the Internet? The Internet began at the U.S. Department of Defense in the late 1950s at the direction of President Dwight D. Eisenhower. At the time of the Cold War and the Soviet Union's successful launch of *Sputnik*, the Eisenhower administration felt the need for a network of computers between major U.S. cities so that the Department of Defense could easily connect with them. Soon major universities began to tap into the network. The timeline below shows the network's origins and growth.

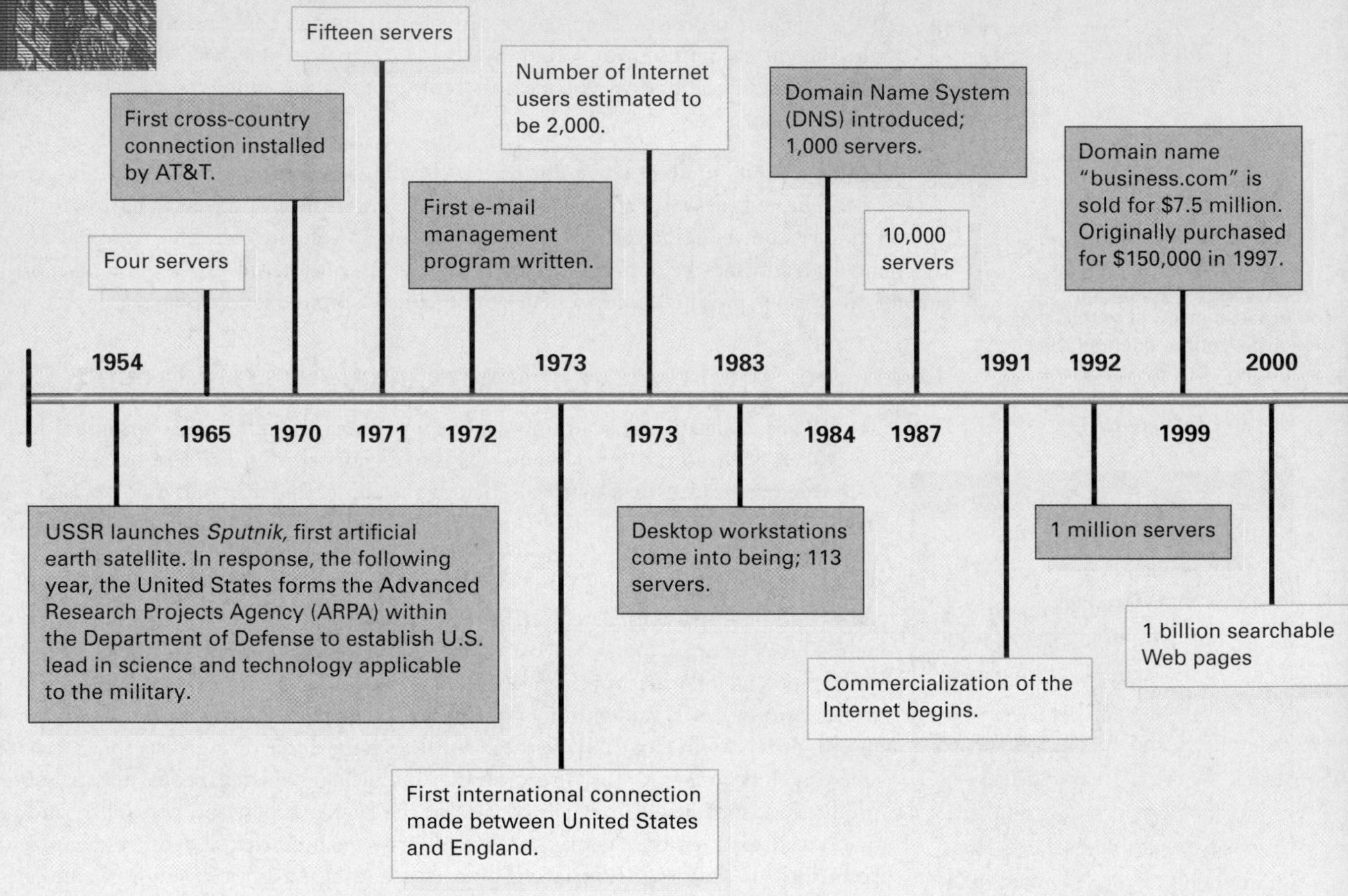

Source: Robert Hobbes, *Hobbes' Internet Timeline.* **http:// www.zakon.org/robert/internet/timeline/.**

are part of manufacturing overhead costs that must be paid only once or twice a year. Utility costs, like heating and air conditioning in the plant, vary from month to month, sometimes significantly! The occasional repairs and maintenance on equipment are difficult to predict and to budget for accurately. Nevertheless, most management accountants are required by their organizations to relate these "lumpy" costs back to the volume of production output. In addition, accurate product pricing is even more difficult because the actual amount of all manufacturing overhead costs isn't known until the end of the period, long after some products have been completed and even sold.

Exhibit 3-1 shows this product costing problem. While direct materials and direct labor are directly related or associated to the manufacture of certain products, the various expense items that

As early as 1988, pressure to commercialize the Internet began when businesses saw its potential as a means of communication and a way to create new marketplaces. Before the Internet could become commercial property, however, Congress had to enact new laws. A few years passed before the Internet was successfully commercialized. Then businesses jumped onto the "backbone" that the government had established and have since created a World Wide Web that enables businesses and consumers to enjoy the technology of the Internet that has been termed the "Technological Revolution" in business.

Like the Industrial Revolution, the Technological Revolution started with individuals who had a unique vision that eventually profited millions of people. For example, Barry Shein, a college dropout, created the first ISP (Internet service provider) in 1989. Barry's idea stemmed from the "withdrawal" he felt when he no longer had Internet access after leaving his university. Soon after, giants such as AMERICA ONLINE (AOL), PRODIGY, and COMPUSERVE began reaping the benefits of Barry's "withdrawal" symptoms. E-commerce on the Internet as we know it today is the result of the vision and efforts of many individuals such as Barry Shein. Without them, the explosive growth in e-commerce shown in the following graph would not have occurred.

Source: John Thomson, Jr., *Privatization of the New Communication Channel: Computer Networks and the Internet*, © 2000. http://www.sit.wisc.edu/%7Ejcthomsonjr/j561/.

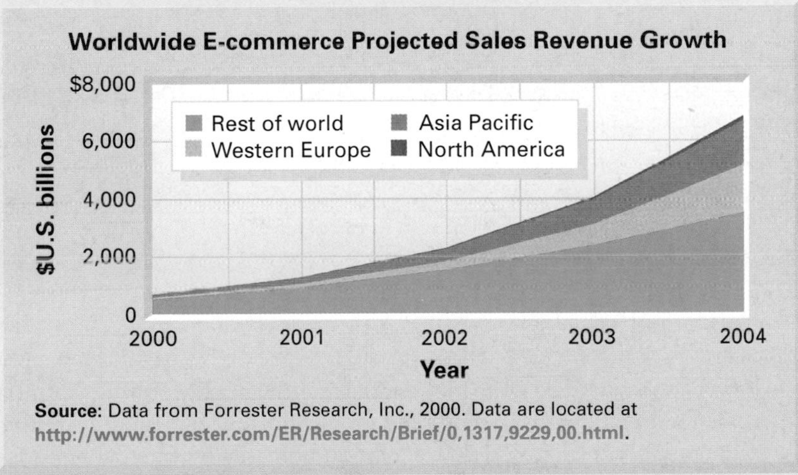

Source: Data from Forrester Research, Inc., 2000. Data are located at http://www.forrester.com/ER/Research/Brief/0,1317,9229,00.html.

comprise manufacturing overhead are not. Therefore, management accountants must find some artificial (but hopefully logical) and fair way to "allocate" or "assign" manufacturing overhead costs to products produced. This "artificial allocation" can result in inaccurate product costs and can lead to serious problems when making planning, controlling, and evaluating decisions.

Most product costing systems were initially designed for the purpose of assigning direct materials, direct labor, and manufacturing overhead costs to individual products. This would then determine which costs should flow to Cost of Goods Sold (as each product is sold) to be matched with revenues and which costs should be used to value the remaining inventory on the balance sheet. Because of the emphasis on financial and tax accounting, there sometimes wasn't much emphasis on accurately allocating manufacturing overhead to specific products. Product cost

exhibit 3-1 Production Flow and "Lumpy" Overhead Costs

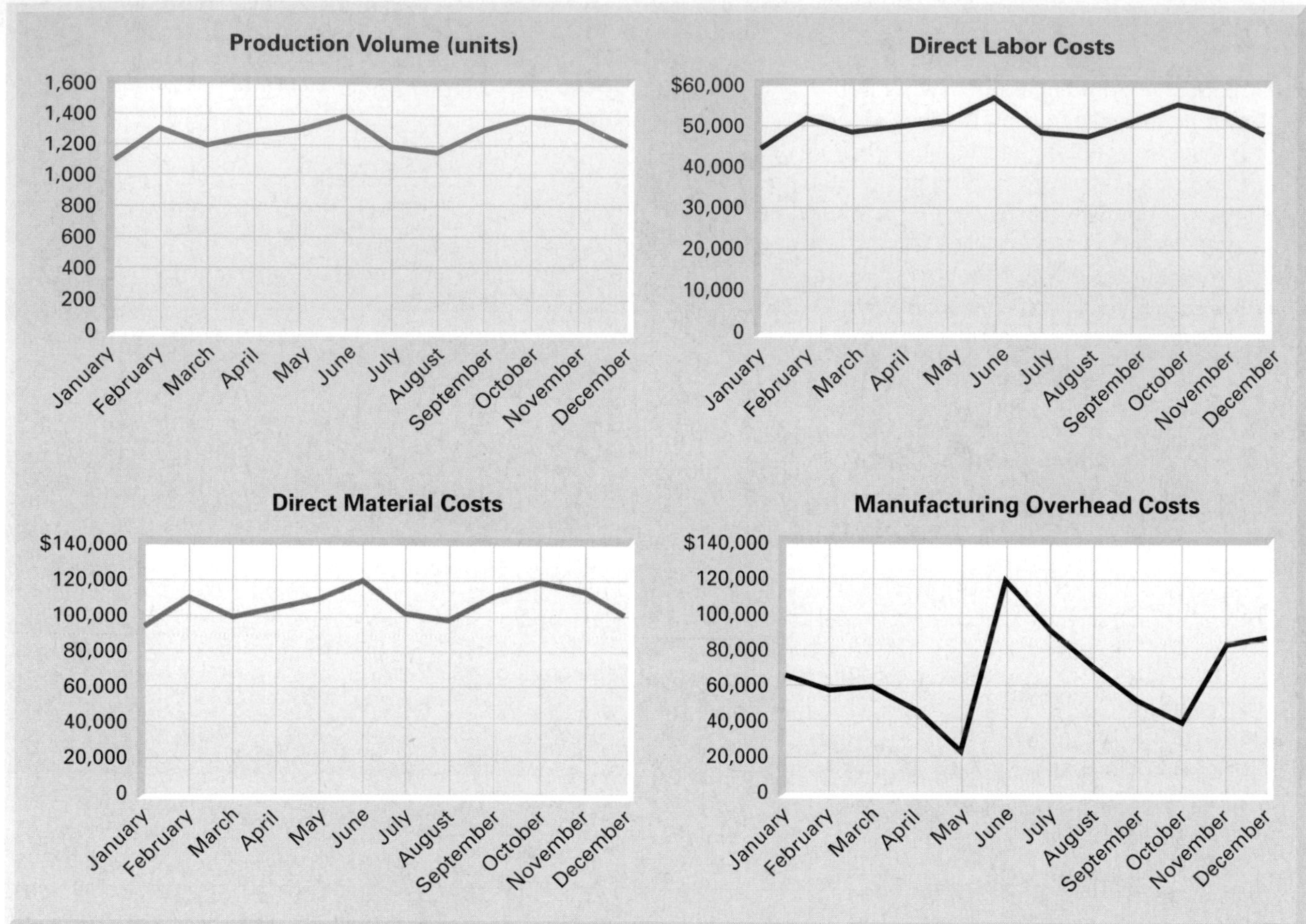

information was used primarily for external financial reporting (to measure the assets and income for an accounting period) and for income tax reporting (to measure taxable income). Because product costing systems were driven primarily by external reporting rules and needs, they did not necessarily provide the best information for management decision making. Only in recent years has emphasis been placed on developing good management accounting systems that provide cost information useful for decision making: planning (e.g., how much labor should we hire?); controlling (e.g., which products are costing more to produce than expected?); and evaluating (e.g., which processes are operating efficiently?).

New Methods of Cost Accumulation

As waves of modernization continue to sweep across the world, manufacturing, merchandising, and service companies are discovering that by integrating better technology into the process of creating and delivering goods and services, they can reduce overall costs, improve quality, and increase productivity. As investments in technology in the workplace continue, however, it can become virtually impossible for some companies to accurately measure costs of goods and services using traditional cost accounting systems. For example, as automation, robotics, and other innovations replace workers, significant changes are occurring in the types of costs that innovative companies must now manage. To provide accurate product costs, new and better ways of assigning costs to products have to be developed.

Management accountants are now working to develop radically different product costing systems. These new types of cost systems are providing information so different from that of

By integrating technology such as robotics into the production process, companies can reduce costs, improve quality, and increase productivity. However, technology also leads to significant changes in the types of costs companies must now manage.

conventional cost systems that many businesses have been able to refocus their manufacturing, merchandising, and service efforts and dramatically increase their profits while reducing prices. With better product cost information, some companies have been able to eliminate high-cost, low-productivity processes and replace them with lower-cost, less-complex processes. Researchers and manufacturers have spent more time trying to determine ways to provide accurate product cost information than they have spent on any other management accounting topic. The result has been the introduction of several new product costing methods including **activity-based costing (ABC)**. Because of these changes in management accounting and cost accumulation systems, many business organizations are currently in a state of transition. Companies such as DELUXE CORPORATION (the world's largest printer of bank checks as well as a provider of electronic products and services to financial institutions) have completely restructured strategies and operations based on new cost accounting systems.[2] Other companies have been slower to change and still use conventional cost accumulation systems. As a result, some companies struggle to compete effectively in their markets.

activity-based costing (ABC) A method of attributing costs to products based on first assigning costs of resources to activities and then costs of activities to products.

fyi

The very nature of the grocery business—selling perishable and dated products—makes inventory cost management crucial. One grocery food chain, HANNAFORD BROS., has implemented a new inventory management system that allows for quick and efficient communication between store managers and has saved several hundreds of thousands of dollars in paper reports, giving the company an important competitive advantage.

Source: Cisco Systems Customer Profiles at http://www.cisco.com/warp/public/cc/general/profile/hanna_cp.htm.

Most innovative companies have adopted costing approaches (such as ABC) that better track overhead costs and more accurately assign them to products. Advocates maintain that ABC can provide management with a more accurate assignment of overhead to products and, therefore, a better understanding of profitability. ABC systems use direct material and direct labor cost information in the same way as conventional systems. Where ABC systems differ is in their accounting for overhead costs. ABC advocates claim that traditional cost accounting distorts product costs by allocating overhead costs in irrelevant ways, which may lead to inaccurate and potentially damaging decisions. And despite the advances being made in new product costing systems, costs are only one of the strategic imperatives facing companies. Managers and accountants in companies that expect to remain competitive must always remember that the market demands high quality and timeliness, as well as low costs.

In view of the transitional state of accounting for product costs, we will cover both conventional product costing systems (in this chapter) and new cost accumulation systems (in later chapters). You need to understand both types of systems in order to facilitate organizational transitions to more competitive costing systems during your career. In the remainder of this chapter, we describe the conventional accumulation of product costs. The ABC concept will be defined and discussed in Chapter 7 of management accounting.

2 P. B. B. Turney, *Deluxe Corporation: A Strategic Need for Activity-Based Costing* (Charlottesville, Va.: University of Virginia Darden School Foundation, 1999).

business environment essay

Firestone Disaster Sometimes, a company's management will sacrifice the quality of its goods or services to obtain a cheaper product. Yet, in a world where consumers place absolute trust in the products they purchase, it is imperative that cost does not replace quality as the company's primary focus. This was not the case with FIRESTONE tires in 2000.

Lawsuits were brought against Firestone (whose parent company is BRIDGESTONE), claiming that its tires on sports utility vehicles, especially the FORD Explorer, were faulty and had caused accidents and even the deaths of numerous individuals (according to recent reports, 88 fatalities and 250 injuries have been blamed on Firestone tires). On further investigation, ex-employees of Firestone's plant in Decatur, Illinois, testified in court "that the facility was suffering from various quality-control problems. . . . [one] policy . . . shortened the time spent curing, or cooking, the tires—when the different layers are bonded together under intense heat—from 26 to 16 minutes." In an effort to cut down production time and costs, Firestone sacrificed the quality of its tires, which unfortunately led to unimaginable consequences for 88 individuals.

Needless to say, Firestone has lost most, if not all, consumer confidence. To date, Firestone has recalled approximately 6.5 million tires at an enormous cost, and some analysts doubt that the company will recover. As the graph on the next page shows, *Fortune* magazine ranked Bridgestone/Firestone as one of the worst companies in America. Management's decision to sacrifice quality for cost savings has left Firestone desperately hoping to survive.

to summarize

While it is difficult to determine true product costs, having accurate product cost information is extremely important. Without accurate costs, management can easily over- or underprice products and make bad business decisions. Although it is easy to allocate direct material and direct labor costs to specific products, manufacturing overhead costs make accurate product costing difficult. Traditionally, product cost information has been used primarily for financial reporting and tax purposes, and little emphasis has been placed on accurately assigning manufacturing overhead costs to manufacturing products. Recently, however, a number of innovative approaches to product costing have been developed. The new methods of cost accumulation, though challenging to implement, offer significant potential benefits to manufacturing, merchandising, and service companies. Management needs accurate product cost information to plan for the future, control current operations, and evaluate past performance.

2
Explain the flow of goods and services in a manufacturing organization and follow the accumulation of product costs in its accounting system.

THE FLOW OF GOODS AND COSTS IN A MANUFACTURING FIRM

It should be clear to you at this point that management accounting provides information with competitive value that supports management efforts to plan, control, and evaluate the organization's performance in providing goods and services to the world. In addition, you know that organizations compete on the basis of costs, quality, and timeliness, and that management ac-

The Bottom Ten of *Fortune*'s America's Most Admired Companies, 2001

Rank	Company	Rank	Company
526	TRANS WORLD AIRLINES	531	LTV
527	TRUMP RESORTS	532	US AIRWAYS GROUP
528	KMART	533	FEDERAL-MOGUL
529	BRIDGESTONE/FIRESTONE	534	WARNACO GROUP
530	AMERICA WEST HOLDINGS	535	CKE RESTAURANTS

Sources: D. Einsenberg, "Anatomy of a Recall," *Time*, September 11, 2000; and A. Diba and L. Munoz, "America's Most Admired Companies," *Fortune*, February 19, 2001.

counting needs to provide information regarding all three of these performance characteristics. As you read in the opening of this chapter, however, management accounting had its beginnings in tracking and reporting costs. Today, one of the best ways to understand how an organization works to provide goods and services is to "follow the money"; in other words, observe how costs flow through the organization. We'll use cost flows to introduce you to manufacturing, merchandising, and service organizations. For a long time, manufacturing was the basis of the U.S. economy. Today, relative to other industries, manufacturing is much smaller. Nevertheless, management accounting systems were originally built to support the manufacturing process, so we'll start there.

Consider the layout for a simple, hypothetical manufacturing company shown in Exhibit 3-2. This floor plan is for a manufacturer of furniture, Broyman Furniture Company. The floor plan shows a building that is partitioned into two sections. The administrative offices include office space for various vice presidents, the sales staff, the president, and the word-processing staff. The manufacturing facility encompasses the offices of the vice president of manufacturing, the plant manager, and the controller; the raw materials and finished goods warehouses; and the factory floor, where production takes place.

raw materials inventory The inventory of raw materials that have not yet begun the production process.

work-in-process inventory Inventory that is partly completed in the production process, but not yet ready for sale to customers.

finished goods inventory Inventory that has completed the production process and is ready for sale to customers.

The manufacturing process for Broyman is quite straightforward. When purchased, raw materials are delivered to the **raw materials inventory** warehouse where they are stored until requisitioned for production. When requisitioned, raw materials are moved out onto the factory floor for the actual manufacturing process; there all material is referred to as **work-in-process inventory** until the process is completed. The factory floor includes three different manufacturing departments: cutting, machining, and finishing. Whereas some furniture products require work in all three areas, others may require work in only one or two areas. On the factory floor, factory employees combine materials with their labor to produce finished products. The finished products are then moved into the **finished goods inventory** warehouse and stored until sold.

Although the movement of goods through this simple factory is straightforward, tracking the costs of goods manufactured (the product costs) is not always so simple. You remember from Chapter 1 of management accounting that product costs include all costs necessary to create the product: essentially, the costs of all people and processes within Broyman's manufacturing

exhibit 3-2 Broyman Furniture Company (A Manufacturing Firm's Layout)

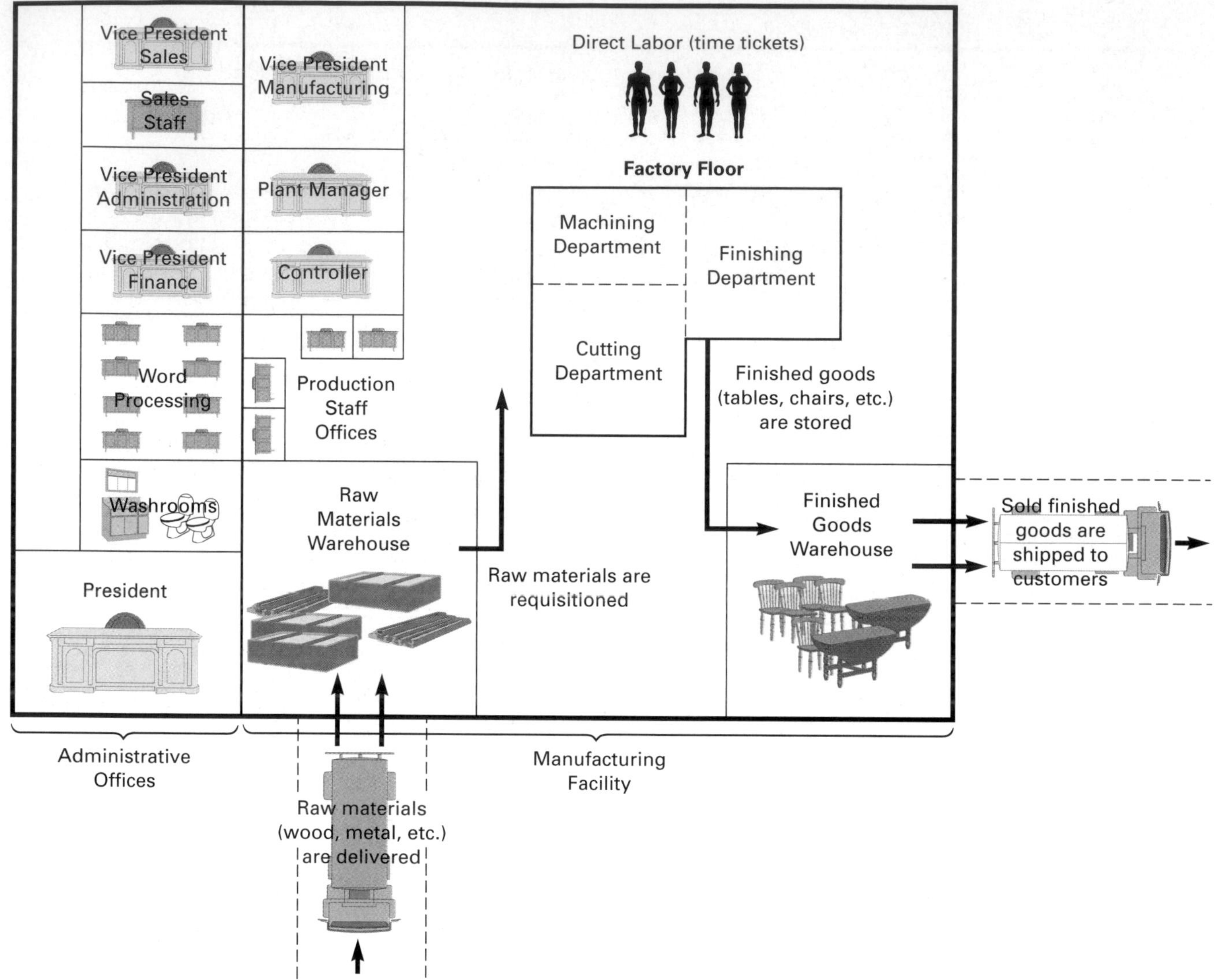

facility. On the other hand, the costs of people and processes in Broyman's administrative offices, which are not associated with the production of furniture, are period costs. The basic idea that defines product costs is that product costs can be associated with specific products. Certainly, the costs of the raw materials and the wages of factory employees who work on the factory floor are manufacturing costs that can be traced to specific products. But what about the salaries of the vice president of manufacturing, the plant manager, and the individuals working in the administrative offices? Should any part of their salaries be included in product costs? What about the utility bills to heat and light the building, the depreciation or rent on the building, the cost of the parking lot, the cost of paper towels for the washrooms, and other miscellaneous expenditures? Should any part of these expenses be included in manufacturing costs?

Because the individuals working in the administrative offices perform administrative and selling duties, rather than manufacturing functions, their salaries should probably not be classified as product costs. Likewise, the costs to pay for electricity, heat, and other expenses for the administrative offices are probably not manufacturing costs. However, the vice president of manufacturing and the plant manager perform functions related to manufacturing, so their salaries

In 1999, U.S corporations reported earnings of nearly $7.6 trillion. When we break this number down by industries, manufacturers earned $1.5 trillion, merchandisers earned another $1.5 trillion, and service companies (including transportation and finance companies) earned $4.6 trillion. Note, however, that nonprofit organizations do not report earnings. Therefore, service industries are even bigger than these numbers would indicate!

Source: U.S. Department of Commerce, Bureau of Economic Analysis, 1999.

should probably be included as product costs. Although these employees perform administrative functions within the manufacturing facility, the work they perform cannot easily be identified with or assigned to specific products, unlike the factory employees who work directly on the products. Similarly, the heat, power, and depreciation related to the manufacturing facility should be included as manufacturing costs but cannot be easily traced to specific products. What about the costs of delivering purchased raw materials to the plant or the delivery of finished goods to customers? Should these delivery costs be classified as manufacturing, administrative, or selling expenses?

As you can see, accurately determining the costs of manufactured products can be challenging, even in a simple firm with one product and one location. When the "real world" introduces the complexities of multiple products being produced in the same facility, changing prices and labor rates, multiple manufacturing locations (perhaps some international locations), and individuals performing multiple functions, it becomes very challenging to accurately determine product costs. Essentially, in order to accurately measure product costs, management accountants must be able to:

1. Determine which costs relate to manufacturing and which relate to administrative and selling functions.
2. Accurately identify and measure all costs associated with manufacturing.
3. Determine appropriate ways to assign costs incurred to products manufactured.

These issues are discussed in the following section.

The Product Costing System

Most accounting systems that track costs of producing and providing goods and services are based on a few key procedures.

- First, identify the product or project that needs cost measurement and track this project through the production process.[3]
- Second, specifically trace the direct costs (costs of direct materials and direct labor) to each product or project.
- Finally, allocate an appropriate amount of overhead costs to each product or project.

job order costing A method of product costing whereby each job, product, or batch of products is costed separately.

This accounting approach is traditionally called **job order costing**. As we discuss the mechanics of this product costing system, keep in the mind the overall procedure—identify the product or service (the "job"), trace the direct costs, and allocate the overhead. Also be sure to remember the big picture. In other words, why are we doing this? Product and service cost information is used to plan future operations (e.g., at what level of production should we operate?), to control current operations (e.g., are our costs too high?), and to evaluate performance (e.g., were our costs and performance last period good or bad?). This information is used by management to support continuous decisions about costs, quality, and time.

In our example, we will track product costs as we follow an order for a mahogany table that is manufactured by Broyman Furniture Company. The production of the table is a custom job requiring two operations: machining (preparing the mahogany) and finishing (assembling, staining, and packaging the table). (You will recall that there were three manufacturing areas in Exhibit 3-2. This table does not require work in the cutting department.)

Exhibit 3-3 shows that the mahogany table costs $393.50 to make. This amount includes $135 of direct materials, $134 of direct labor, and $124.50 of manufacturing overhead (which includes supervisor and production staff salaries, insurance, utilities, depreciation on plant and machinery, and so on). Looking at the cost summary in Exhibit 3-3, we can see that the hourly

3 In some organizations, it is not reasonable or possible to specifically track the product being produced. For example, a lumber mill that continuously processes timber into planks may not specifically track individual products. Instead, the mill would track the total production costs expended for a particular period of time (e.g., a day), then assign those costs to the total amount of timber processed during that same period of time. This management accounting approach is called process costing and will be discussed in the expanded material section of this chapter.

exhibit 3-3 Total Product Costs for One Mahogany Table

Machining Department Costs

Direct Materials	Direct Labor			Manufacturing Overhead (based on machine hours)		
Requisitioned	Hours	Wage Rate	Amount	Hours	Overhead Rate	Amount
$100	8	$10	$80	6	$11	$66

Finishing Department Costs

Direct Materials	Direct Labor			Manufacturing Overhead (based on direct labor hours)		
Requisitioned	Hours	Wage Rate	Amount	Hours	Overhead Rate	Amount
$30.00	3	$12.00	$36.00	3	$13.00	$39.00
5.00	1.5	$12.00	18.00	1.5	$13.00	19.50
$35.00			$54.00			$58.50

Final Product Cost for Mahogany Table

	Machining	Finishing	Total
Direct materials	$100.00	$ 35.00	$135.00
Direct labor	80.00	54.00	134.00
Manufacturing overhead	66.00	58.50	124.50
Total cost	$246.00	$147.50	$393.50

manufacturing overhead rate The rate at which manufacturing overhead is assigned to products; equals estimated manufacturing overhead for the period divided by the number of units of the activity base being used.

wage rate for direct labor is $10 per hour in machining and $12 per hour in finishing; the manufacturing overhead rate is $11 per machine hour in machining and $13 per direct labor hour in finishing. The **manufacturing overhead rate** is an estimate of the overhead that will be incurred for each unit (in this case, allocated on the basis of machine and direct labor hours). In this example, the company incurs an average of $11 of overhead for every hour the machine is run in the machining department. Thus, each table that requires the use of the machine is allocated a portion of the overhead costs. The use of different manufacturing overhead rates is common. Each department will allocate manufacturing overhead to products on the basis of the most meaningful activity in that department. (Remember the challenge discussed earlier of accurately estimating and allocating manufacturing overhead to products.) The machining department is more automated, so activity is tied more closely to machine hours; the finishing department requires more handwork, so activity is tied more closely to direct labor hours. With these "finished costs" in mind, let's talk about how Broyman Furniture Company actually created these data on the mahogany table. But first, take a brief look at Exhibit 3-4 on page 120. In this rather complicated-looking exhibit you can literally "see" how the costs follow the production process and flow through the accounting system. We'll work through the details of Exhibit 3-4 below. (Note: Don't worry if you are still a little confused about how Broyman creates and uses manufacturing overhead rates. We're going to discuss these concepts in detail later in this chapter.)

DIRECT MATERIALS COSTS To illustrate the accounting for direct materials costs, we will assume that Broyman purchased a supply of mahogany and placed it in a materials storeroom. The entry to record this purchase is:[4]

[4]In this chapter, we will use an *actual* cost accounting system. We will discuss standard cost accounting systems in Chapter 9.

business environment essay

Costs and the Medical Profession Have you ever gone to the doctor's office, spent 20 minutes in the waiting room, then another 20 minutes in the examination room before the doctor comes in? When she finally comes in, she examines you for 10 minutes and then sends you on your way, charging you $50 for the visit. No wonder medical doctors make so much money—or do they? Does the doctor put your $50 right in her pocket?

What costs must your $50 cover? Unfortunately, you must help the doctor pay for office medical supplies, rent on the office, utilities, salaries of nurses and office personnel, fees charged by hospitals to use their facilities, and costs of training seminars to remain current in her field. While these costs are expensive, perhaps the most rapidly rising cost is for malpractice insurance. As an example, in many communities in the United States, the cost of obstetrical malpractice insurance is so high that some doctors will no longer deliver babies.

Where does the doctor get the money to cover these costs? By charging you $50 for your visit. Medicine is a business. The doctor is pricing patient visits to cover all costs incurred in providing that service. Costs must be covered and we, the consumers, must pay for them. The next time you visit the doctor, take a look around the waiting room, enjoy those pictures, and read those magazines. After all, you paid for them!

Raw Materials Inventory	50,000	
Accounts Payable (or Cash)		50,000
Purchased 25,000 board feet of mahogany at $2 per foot.		

When raw materials are needed (such as for the manufacture of the table), the machining department sends a request (i.e., a requisition) to the storeroom (usually via computer) identifying the quantity and type of materials needed. When the raw materials warehouse fills the requisition, it records the transfer of goods to the factory floor by making an entry (usually by computer) that serves as the basis for the accounting records. The storeroom manager sends the requisition information to the accounting department, where the unit cost is entered and the total cost calculated. The accounting entry made to record the transfer of mahogany from storage to machining is:

Work-in-Process Inventory	100	
Raw Materials Inventory		100
Issued 50 board feet of mahogany to production at $2 per foot.		

Work-in-Process Inventory	35	
Raw Materials Inventory		35
Issued packaging material to production.		

The mahogany and packaging material were used directly in the production of the table ready to ship; the cost is assigned as direct materials for this particular job. Because the amount of direct materials used varies proportionately with the level of production, direct materials are almost always variable costs. Indirect materials and supplies used in production (classified as manufacturing overhead costs), such as glue, nails, and varnish, are ordered from the storeroom in the same manner. Although some inexpensive materials, such as glue, are used directly in the manufactured products and others are used to support production, it is generally not cost-beneficial to trace such miscellaneous items to a particular job. These miscellaneous items are treated as indirect materials costs and recorded in the manufacturing overhead account (explained later in the chapter). Manufacturing overhead consists of numerous expenditures such as indirect labor, indirect materials, utilities, rent, and the like. The sum of these various expenditures provides the balance in the manufacturing overhead account. The following entry records the sum of all the requisitions for indirect materials for the period:

Manufacturing Overhead (indirect materials)	15,000	
Raw Materials Inventory.		15,000
Issued miscellaneous materials and supplies to the production floor.		

At the end of a period, the amount of materials and supplies that remain on hand in the raw materials warehouse is shown on the balance sheet as Raw Materials Inventory.

DIRECT LABOR COSTS The method of charging direct labor costs to production jobs is similar to that for direct materials costs. Most factories have a time clock where employees punch in and record their hourly activities. These time clocks often allow workers to identify specific jobs worked on. When the time clocks do not capture specific job information, the information is noted by making entries in the computer or on manual time tickets. The product costs, shown in Exhibit 3-3, reveal that machining employees worked on the mahogany table for 8 hours. Because the wage rate was $10 per hour in machining, the total direct labor cost in machining was $80 ($10 per hour × 8 hours). Similar calculations provide the entry to record the direct labor costs in the finishing department. The entries to record all the direct labor costs (ignoring payroll taxes and benefits) for the mahogany table are:

Work-in-Process Inventory	80	
Wages Payable		80
To record the machining department's direct labor costs.		

Work-in-Process Inventory	54	
Wages Payable		54
To record the finishing department's direct labor costs.		

Remember that within certain limits, direct labor costs vary proportionately with the number of products made and, thus, are typically considered variable costs.

Like materials, labor costs can be either direct or indirect. Indirect labor costs include the wages of employees who perform functions not related to a specific job, such as maintenance and custodial. Usually, these employees still punch time clocks, but their wages become part of the indirect labor costs that are included in manufacturing overhead, as discussed in the next section. The following entry records the sum of all indirect labor for the period:

Manufacturing Overhead (indirect labor).	20,000	
Wages Payable		20,000
To record indirect labor costs.		

STOP & THINK In our example, the company makes a mahogany table using two operations: machining and finishing. When making a real table, how many separate operations do you think would be necessary?

MANUFACTURING OVERHEAD COSTS In contrast to direct materials and direct labor, manufacturing overhead (the third type of product cost) involves more complex accounting procedures and estimation problems. As we've discussed earlier, while direct materials and direct labor can be readily assigned to specific jobs or products, manufacturing overhead costs are difficult to trace directly to the production of a single item and must often be estimated in advance of their incurrence. By definition, most manufacturing overhead costs benefit all products made in a department or a company during a period. The depreciation on equipment and the wages paid for maintenance in the machining department, for example, ensure the smooth operation of the entire department for the period; these cannot be traced directly to individual items produced during the period. Some manufacturing overhead costs, such as property taxes and repairs, are not known until the end of an accounting period. However, managers need current product cost information (for pricing similar jobs, estimating costs for next year, and so forth), so each job is assigned a share of *estimated* (i.e., budgeted) manufacturing overhead costs. In accounting terminology, manufacturing overhead costs are applied to (or absorbed by) jobs or products. Overall, knowing how to set up and handle the accounting for overhead costs at Broyman Company is a tricky business, which we'll talk further about later in this chapter.

For now, as *actual* manufacturing overhead costs for Broyman are incurred, the management accounting system needs to recognize and record the costs. During the current production period, these costs include $1,200 for repairs to equipment, $6,450 for monthly rent allocated to the production facility, $850 for liability insurance, and $2,900 in depreciation of manufacturing equipment. The total of these costs is debited of Manufacturing Overhead, and the individual amounts are credited to their respective accounts, as shown here.

caution

Many students will make the mistake of debiting manufacturing overhead costs to an expense account. Although these costs eventually do become an expense, first they are debited to Manufacturing Overhead, then allocated to Work-in-Process Inventory, then transferred to Finished Goods Inventory, and finally expensed in Cost of Goods Sold.

Manufacturing Overhead	11,400	
Accounts Payable		1,200
Rent Payable		6,450
Prepaid Insurance		850
Accumulated Depreciation		2,900
To record actual manufacturing overhead costs.		

In addition to recording the actual costs of manufacturing overhead, Broyman's accountants need to allocate overhead costs to the mahogany table in production. As you can see in Exhibit 3-3, the Broyman management accountants follow a traditional approach of assigning manufacturing overhead costs by taking the expected annual costs of overhead for each department and dividing this estimated amount by the selected activity base (in this case, machine hours for the machining department and direct labor hours for the finishing department). Estimated overhead costs typically come from the company's annual budgets. Selection of the activity base is the result of experience and analysis. The result is an allocation rate for each department that is used to uniformly assign a "fair share" of manufacturing overhead costs to production volume throughout the year. This allocation rate is called the **predetermined overhead rate**. In this case, Broyman's accountants allocate to the mahogany table $66 based on activity in the machining department ($11 predetermined overhead rate × 6 machine hours) and $58.50 based on activity in the finishing department ($13 rate × 4.5 direct labor hours). The entries to record these allocations are:

predetermined overhead rate A rate at which estimated manufacturing overhead costs are assigned to products throughout the year; equals total estimated manufacturing overhead costs divided by a suitable allocation base, such as number of units produced, direct labor hours, direct materials used, or direct labor costs.

Work-in-Process Inventory	66.00	
Manufacturing Overhead		66.00
To apply manufacturing overhead from the machining department.		

Work-in-Process Inventory	58.50	
Manufacturing Overhead		58.50
To apply manufacturing overhead from the finishing department.		

Notice in Exhibit 3-4 that as *actual* overhead costs are incurred (as with indirect materials and indirect labor), the manufacturing overhead account is debited. As overhead costs are *applied* to products, the manufacturing overhead account is credited. This relationship is better illustrated and discussed later in this chapter.

exhibit 3-4 Flow of Product Costs in Broyman Company Job Order Cost Accounting System

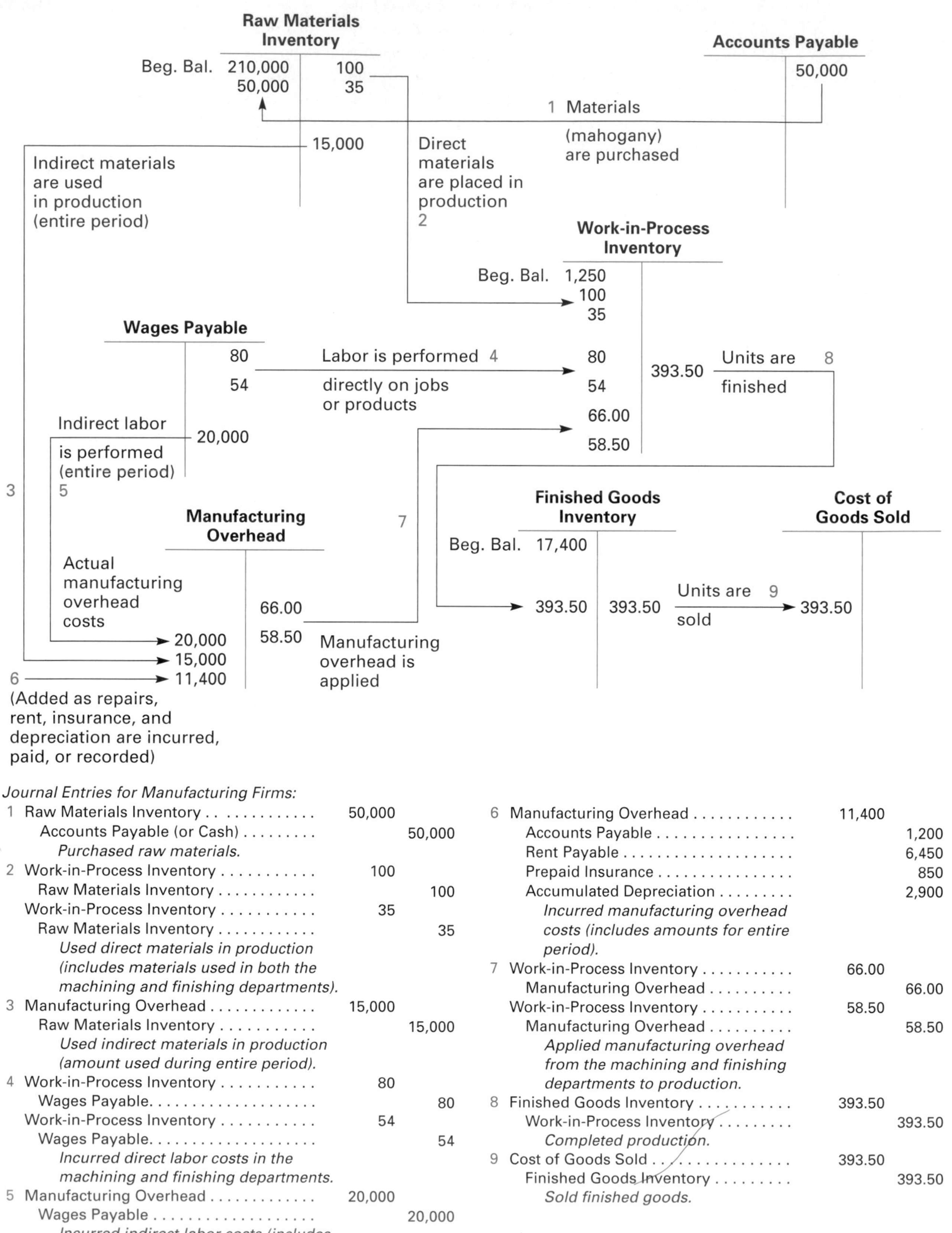

Journal Entries for Manufacturing Firms:

1	Raw Materials Inventory	50,000	
	Accounts Payable (or Cash)		50,000
	Purchased raw materials.		
2	Work-in-Process Inventory	100	
	Raw Materials Inventory		100
	Work-in-Process Inventory	35	
	Raw Materials Inventory		35
	Used direct materials in production (includes materials used in both the machining and finishing departments).		
3	Manufacturing Overhead	15,000	
	Raw Materials Inventory		15,000
	Used indirect materials in production (amount used during entire period).		
4	Work-in-Process Inventory	80	
	Wages Payable		80
	Work-in-Process Inventory	54	
	Wages Payable		54
	Incurred direct labor costs in the machining and finishing departments.		
5	Manufacturing Overhead	20,000	
	Wages Payable		20,000
	Incurred indirect labor costs (includes indirect labor costs for entire period).		
6	Manufacturing Overhead	11,400	
	Accounts Payable		1,200
	Rent Payable		6,450
	Prepaid Insurance		850
	Accumulated Depreciation		2,900
	Incurred manufacturing overhead costs (includes amounts for entire period).		
7	Work-in-Process Inventory	66.00	
	Manufacturing Overhead		66.00
	Work-in-Process Inventory	58.50	
	Manufacturing Overhead		58.50
	Applied manufacturing overhead from the machining and finishing departments to production.		
8	Finished Goods Inventory	393.50	
	Work-in-Process Inventory		393.50
	Completed production.		
9	Cost of Goods Sold	393.50	
	Finished Goods Inventory		393.50
	Sold finished goods.		

TRANSFERRING THE COSTS OF COMPLETED JOBS AND COMPUTING UNIT COSTS While a job is in process, the costs of direct materials, direct labor, and manufacturing overhead are accounted for separately. When the job is completed, however, these costs (in total) are transferred from Work-in-Process Inventory to Finished Goods Inventory. In the Broyman Furniture Company example, the total cost assigned to the mahogany table is $393.50, as illustrated in Exhibit 3-3. The entry to transfer the completed cost of the table to Finished Goods Inventory is:

Finished Goods Inventory	393.50	
Work-in-Process Inventory		393.50
To record the completion of the mahogany table.		

As you can see by comparing Exhibits 3-2 and 3-4, the product costs assigned to the table literally follow that table as it moves through the factory floor (and through the work-in-process inventory account) until the table is completed and moves into the finished goods warehouse (and into the finished goods inventory account). Once completed, cost data for the mahogany table are used in pricing similar jobs, estimating costs for the next year, and measuring income. Note that this process would be no different if, instead of a single table, Broyman were to identify and cost an entire batch of mahogany tables. In this case, at the completion of the job, the unit cost of each table is computed by adding the direct materials, direct labor, and manufacturing overhead costs for the batch and dividing the total by the number of tables produced in the batch (i.e., the job).

TRANSFERRING THE COSTS OF PRODUCTS THAT ARE SOLD When a product is sold, the costs assigned to it are transferred to Cost of Goods Sold. For example, when the mahogany table, which cost $393.50 to make, is shipped to a customer, the table is loaded from the warehouse onto the truck, and the cost of the table is transferred from Finished Goods Inventory to Cost of Goods Sold, using the following entry:

Cost of Goods Sold	393.50	
Finished Goods Inventory		393.50
To record the cost of goods sold for the mahogany table.		

With this entry, costs have been traced all the way through the production cycle and expensed onto the income statement. Once again, inspect Exhibit 3-4 and be sure that you can clearly see how all the costs flow through the manufacturing process for Broyman. Note that direct labor, when incurred, and raw materials, when used, are debited directly to Work-in-Process Inventory. Actual manufacturing overhead costs, on the other hand, are entered first as debits to Manufacturing Overhead and then are allocated to Work-in-Process Inventory by crediting Manufacturing Overhead. Be careful to note that in Exhibit 3-4, entry 1 is for mahogany that will be used on several jobs; entries 3, 5, and 6 are actual manufacturing costs incurred for the entire accounting period in which the table was manufactured. Entries 2, 4, 7, 8, and 9 are entries specifically associated with the mahogany table in our example. At the end of the period, the company will usually have three inventory balances: Raw Materials Inventory, Work-in-Process Inventory, and Finished Goods Inventory.

STOP & THINK Compare Exhibit 3-2 with Exhibit 3-4. Try to identify the physical location (from Exhibit 3-2) with each type of accounting cost in Exhibit 3-4.

to summarize

In traditional job order cost accounting systems for manufacturing organizations where a specific product can be identified, all direct labor, direct materials, and manufacturing overhead costs are accumulated for each unit or batch (generally referred to as a job). Because the exact amount of manufacturing overhead cannot be determined until the accounting period is completed, an estimated amount of manufacturing overhead is applied to jobs. To estimate the amount of manufacturing overhead to be applied to a job, a predetermined overhead rate is calculated for each department involved in production, using an appropriate measure of activity. This rate is multiplied by the actual quantity of the activity used to complete the job. Total costs for completed jobs are then transferred from Work-in-Process Inventory to Finished Goods Inventory. When manufactured goods are sold, costs are transferred from Finished Goods Inventory to Cost of Goods Sold.

3
Understand the process of accounting for overhead.

ACCOUNTING FOR OVERHEAD

In the Broyman Company example of producing a mahogany table and tracking its production costs, you can see that accounting for manufacturing overhead costs is not the same process as accounting for direct materials and direct labor costs. Because manufacturing overhead costs generally do not coincide with the flow of production (as was illustrated earlier in Exhibit 3-1), a few extra steps are required to handle the accounting. These steps are:

1. Before the year begins, budget the *estimated* manufacturing overhead, estimate the allocation activity, and establish the predetermined overhead rate.
2. During the year, as costs are incurred, record *actual* manufacturing overhead as debits to the manufacturing overhead account.
3. During the year, as activity takes place, record *applied* manufacturing overhead as credits to the manufacturing overhead account.
4. At the end of the year, compare *actual* and *applied* overhead balances and close out the difference in the manufacturing overhead account.

Estimated Manufacturing Overhead

estimated manufacturing overhead Budgeted manufacturing overhead costs that are used to establish the predetermined overhead rate.

As you can see, the list above includes three difference classifications of manufacturing overhead costs—estimated, actual, and applied. It is *critical* that you understand the differences among these numbers. **Estimated manufacturing overhead** is the amount of overhead costs that management has budgeted for the upcoming production period. The predetermined overhead rate is created by dividing estimated manufacturing overhead by the estimate of the expected level of activity (e.g., direct labor hours) to be used to allocate overhead during the year.

To illustrate the use of estimated manufacturing overhead to create the predetermined overhead rate for the machining department at Broyman Company, assume that at the beginning of the year the accountants and production personnel estimated that 24,500 machine hours would be used on the factory floor. Budgeted (estimated) overhead costs for the machining department are shown below. Note that these costs have been separated into fixed and variable components.

Variable manufacturing overhead:		
Indirect labor	$ 45,000	
Indirect materials	15,000	
Repairs	7,500	$ 67,500
Fixed manufacturing overhead:		
Rent	$105,000	
Depreciation	85,000	
Insurance	12,000	202,000
Total expected manufacturing overhead cost for the year (machining department)		$269,500

Using these data, the accountants then computed the predetermined overhead rate in the machining department to be $11 per machine hour, as follows:

$$\frac{\text{Total estimated manufacturing overhead cost for the year}}{\text{Total estimated machine hours}} = \frac{\$269{,}500}{24{,}500} = \$11 \text{ per machine hour in machining department}$$

Similar calculations were used to calculate the predetermined overhead rate of $13 per direct labor hour in the finishing department.

fyi

One useful way to think about the manufacturing overhead account is to consider it to be simply a temporary holding tank for overhead costs that we don't immediately know how to assign to production. By the end of the period, however, we will have sorted out how much was actually spent on overhead and how much actual production took place. At that point, we can clear out the "holding tank" and start over the process of tracking and applying overhead costs.

Actual Manufacturing Overhead

After studying financial accounting, some students have a difficult time with the accounting for actual manufacturing overhead. For example, in financial accounting, we accounted for salaries by debiting Salaries Expense and crediting Salaries Payable; the correct entry when the salaries are for sales or other nonmanufacturing personnel. However, as you saw in tracking production costs for Broyman's mahogany table, when the wages are related to manufacturing, the debit is to Work-in-Process Inventory for direct labor and to Manufacturing Overhead for indirect labor. Thus, in management accounting, it is important to determine first whether salaries are for manufacturing or for nonmanufacturing personnel. Then, for manufacturing personnel, it must be determined whether the individuals worked directly on the product (Work-in-Process Inventory) or indirectly on the product (Manufacturing Overhead). The same is true for other costs such as depreciation and rent. If these costs relate to manufacturing, they are debited to Manufacturing Overhead; costs not related to manufacturing are debited to Depreciation Expense, Rent Expense, and so forth. The manufacturing costs will eventually become expenses when the products are sold (Cost of Goods Sold).

Applied Manufacturing Overhead

It is important to understand that the debit side of the manufacturing overhead account is used to record actual overhead expenses. Conversely, the credit side of this account is used to record applied manufacturing overhead that is simultaneously debited to the work-in-process inventory account, as illustrated in Exhibit 3-5. In essence, this entry transfers the overhead cost from the temporary holding account called Manufacturing Overhead to the asset account called Work-in-Process Inventory.

Actual costs, including actual manufacturing overhead costs, are needed for accurate reporting of annual income and for computing a company's income tax liability at the end of the year. However, the management process of controlling and evaluating costs and setting prices cannot wait until the end of the year. Hence, while both actual and applied manufacturing overhead costs are accounted for constantly throughout the year, actual overhead costs are too sporadic (again, see Exhibit 3-1) to be effectively used for pricing and costing decisions that take place continuously. For this reason, predetermined overhead rates are used to apply overhead throughout the year.

exhibit 3-5 Recording Costs in the Manufacturing Overhead Account

Manufacturing Overhead	
Actual manufacturing overhead costs are entered as debits on a regular basis as they are incurred.	Applied overhead costs are entered as credits as production takes place; costs are applied to Work-in-Process on the basis of a predetermined overhead rate.

Disposition of Over- and Underapplied Manufacturing Overhead

If the beginning-of-the-year estimates of both manufacturing overhead costs *and* the activity basis (e.g., machine hours) are perfect, then at the end of the year the accountants at the Broyman Company will have applied as much overhead to Work-in-Process as was actually incurred, and the ending balance in the manufacturing overhead account will be $0 (this rarely happens). Typically, though, the ending balance in the manufacturing overhead account is not very large. Nevertheless, the manufacturing overhead account is a temporary account that must be closed out at the end of the year. Handling any balance left in Manufacturing Overhead is the process of disposing of over- and underapplied manufacturing overhead.

Note in Exhibit 3-4 that a total of $46,400 in actual costs have been debited to the manufacturing overhead account. To illustrate the accounting for the difference between actual and applied manufacturing overhead costs, we will assume that these costs represent the total actual manufacturing overhead for March 2003. Further, including the work done on the mahogany table in our example, the machining department at Broyman used a total of 1,600 machine hours and applied $17,600 to Work-in-Process Inventory, and the finishing department employed 1,250 direct labor hours and applied $16,250. Finally, the cutting department (using a similar overhead allocation procedure) applied $11,800. At the end of March, the manufacturing overhead account would appear as follows.

Manufacturing Overhead

(Actual costs)	(Applied costs)
20,000	17,600 applied in machining department
15,000	16,250 applied in finishing department
11,400	11,800 applied in cutting department
46,400	45,650
750 balance (underapplied)	

STOP & THINK What would it mean if the debit (actual overhead) and credit (applied overhead) amounts in the manufacturing overhead account were vastly different?

A comparison of the debit and credit sides of the manufacturing overhead account shows that actual manufacturing overhead costs incurred were $750 higher than applied costs. This difference is usually ignored until year-end because management is concerned with immediate decisions, for which current estimates are adequate. At year-end, however, this difference must be accounted for, not only to balance the books, but also to show actual costs in measuring income.

business environment essay

Simplifying Product Costing by Outsourcing One way to simplify operations and product costing is for a company to perform only the core, or strategic, functions inside the company and to outsource all support activities to a network of external companies that specialize in each function. These types of companies, sometimes referred to as virtual corporations, form functional alliances to manufacture products or provide services for customers. The goal of a virtual corporation is to position itself at the center of these relationships and serve as the catalyst that draws these cooperating companies together and organizes how the work will flow. Supposedly, this allows a company to maximize the return from these partnerships while making the minimum investment in permanent staff, fixed assets, and working capital. One such company is **SUPER BAKERY, INC.**, which was formed by former Pittsburgh Steelers' running back Franco Harris in 1983. Super Bakery, Inc., is a supplier of donuts and other

overapplied manufacturing overhead The excess of applied manufacturing overhead (based on a predetermined application rate) over the actual manufacturing overhead costs for a period.

underapplied manufacturing overhead The excess of actual manufacturing overhead costs over the applied overhead costs for a period (based on a predetermined application rate).

If, at the end of the year, total actual manufacturing overhead is less than the amount applied, the account will have a credit balance. This result is referred to as **overapplied manufacturing overhead**. Conversely, if applied manufacturing overhead is less than actual costs, the account will have a debit balance representing **underapplied manufacturing overhead**.

Which is better to have at the end of the year—under- or overapplied overhead? If overhead is underapplied, then the total cost of jobs will be understated. If a company were to price its products in the future based on this understated cost, the company could lose money because it might not cover its actual manufacturing overhead costs. On the other hand, overapplied manufacturing overhead indicates that jobs were overcharged for overhead and costs were overstated. If future pricing decisions were made based on these overstated costs, the company would soon find customers looking elsewhere for more reasonably priced products. Neither under- nor overapplied overhead is desirable. A company's objective is to attempt to anticipate overhead costs and accurately charge those costs to the various jobs.

There are two methods of treating over- and underapplied manufacturing overhead:

1. Close over- or underapplied manufacturing overhead directly to Cost of Goods Sold.
2. Allocate over- or underapplied manufacturing overhead to Work-in-Process Inventory, Finished Goods Inventory, and Costs of Goods Sold on the basis of the ending balances in these three accounts.

The first method is easier and more commonly used, especially if the over- or underapplied amount is small, because it requires only a single entry to correct the amount of manufacturing overhead applied. Let's assume that at year-end, when total actual and applied manufacturing overhead have been recorded, manufacturing overhead for Broyman was overapplied by $1,900. The entry to assign this overapplied manufacturing overhead to Cost of Goods Sold would be:

Manufacturing Overhead	1,900	
Cost of Goods Sold		1,900
To recognize the excess of applied manufacturing overhead costs over actual manufacturing overhead.		

This entry will decrease the cost of goods sold account for the year by $1,900 and will close out the manufacturing overhead account. Companies that have very small or zero inventory balances would normally charge any over- or underapplied overhead to Cost of Goods Sold.

baked goods to the institutional food market. Since its inception, it has been gaining market share and establishing a firm foothold in the highly competitive institutional baked goods market. Instead of creating a large multifunctional organization to administer the business, the management of Super Bakery outsources selling activities to a network of independent brokers and contracts out manufacturing, warehousing, and shipping processes. Super Bakery handles inhouse the strategic planning, marketing, research and development, and finance/accounting processes. The company also purchases ingredients and formulates and produces its own dough. Super Bakery's product costing problem is significantly reduced by outsourcing so many functions. In essence, Franco Harris is letting other companies worry about many different aspects of product costing.

Source: Tim R.V. Davis and B. L. Darling, "ABC in a Virtual Corporation," *Management Accounting*, October 1996, pp. 18–26.

The second method is more accurate because, theoretically, any difference between applied and actual manufacturing overhead should be allocated proportionately to all items in production during the period. The items in production include those produced and sold (Cost of Goods Sold), those produced and not sold (Finished Goods Inventory), and those still being produced (Work-in-Process Inventory). If the estimate had been accurate, manufacturing overhead costs would have been allocated proportionately to all products. Therefore, those products actually sold should not be burdened with, or relieved of, the entire amount of the estimation error. This alternative is more complicated, however, and requires detailed calculations and several journal entries, so it will not be illustrated here. When differences between actual and applied overhead are small, this more accurate method is usually not worth the extra effort.

to summarize

Actual manufacturing overhead costs are accumulated and debited to Manufacturing Overhead throughout the year. Applied (or estimated) manufacturing overhead costs are assigned to jobs on the basis of a predetermined overhead rate. These costs are credited to Manufacturing Overhead and debited to Work-in-Process Inventory. Any difference between actual and applied manufacturing overhead at the end of the period must be accounted for in order to properly measure income. When total actual manufacturing overhead exceeds total applied overhead, the excess is referred to as underapplied manufacturing overhead. When total applied overhead exceeds total actual overhead, the excess is referred to as overapplied manufacturing overhead. The easiest and most commonly used method of eliminating over- or underapplied manufacturing overhead is to transfer it directly to Cost of Goods Sold. In some cases, the over- or underapplied manufacturing overhead is allocated among Work-in-Process Inventory, Finished Goods Inventory, and Cost of Goods Sold to arrive at a more accurate assignment of costs.

business environment essay

Wholesalers You Never Knew The distribution process that makes it possible for you to purchase a product, such as a car stereo, from a store is complex. The average customer does not give much thought beyond the local retail store. Consumers focus on the reputation of the retail store and the manufacturer instead of the wholesaler that distributes the product.

The Fortune 500 list of top ten wholesalers is shown on the next page. These large, powerful companies tap into numerous facets of the nation's economy.

Most people are familiar with grocery stores such as ALBERTSON'S and SAVE-A-LOT. But how many people have heard of the wholesaler for these retailers, SUPERVALU? SuperValu, one of the nation's top food service distributors, is a major player in the U.S. economy. Even though SuperValu ranks fifth on the list, this wholesaler achieves startling annual revenues of more than $17 billion. It employs over 67,000 people to assist numerous grocery stores with inventory. The company operates approximately 1,100 stores in 38 states. Perhaps a wholesaler like SuperValu should be better known considering its role of supplying grocery stores with the products consumers demand, enabling consumer purchases to take place.

4

Explain the flow of goods and services in a merchandising organization and follow the accumulation of product costs in its accounting system.

channel The distribution line that a product travels from the original manufacturer to the eventual end-user customer. The channel is typically composed of a manufacturer, a wholesaler, a retailer, and the end-user customer.

THE FLOW OF GOODS AND COSTS IN A MERCHANDISING FIRM

For most of us, retailing is the most visible component of a wonderful economic system that has provided great benefits to us for most of our lives. Nevertheless, we probably fail to appreciate that what happens over the last three feet of counter in the store is the culmination of the efforts of a great industrial machine and the related mass distribution system. Similar to the concept of an ecosystem in nature, manufacturers, wholesalers, and retailers are linked together in an economic system called a **channel**. If retailers cannot move goods and services the last three feet into the hands of those who will use them, the whole distribution system of manufacturing, wholesaling, and retailing falls apart.

The Distribution Channel

Exhibit 3-6 illustrates the channel system that typically interrelates manufacturers, wholesalers, and retailers. We've discussed manufacturing operations (the starting point of the channel) and the related management accounting systems. In order to understand the full cycle of business, we now discuss the process of distributing goods to customers. As you can see in Exhibit 3-6, the distribution channel does not prevent retailers from occasionally dealing directly with manufacturers. For example, WAL-MART is noted for its ability to use technology to make direct contact with manufacturers to obtain a significant number of its inventory items. Similarly, some manufacturers may handle some (or even all) of their distribution to retailers. For example, HONDA and FORD work directly with their car dealerships and bypass the wholesalers to distribute their products directly to retailers. Finally, a limited number of manufacturers, particularly small manufacturers, have direct relationships with the ultimate end-user customers of their products. They do this by setting up the well-known factory outlet store or by allowing customers to order directly from them. A good example of this particular distribution approach is DELL COMPUTER CORPORATION. Dell is one of several large personal computer manufacturers in the United States that take orders directly from end-user customers, build computers to customer specifications, then ship the finished computers directly to the customers. The management accounting issues do not change if one member of the distribution channel

Company	Revenues (millions)	Products
MCKESSON CORPORATION	$30,382	Health care products
INGRAMMICRO, INC.	28,069	Microcomputer products
CARDINAL HEALTH, INC.	25,034	Health and beauty care products
SYSCO CORPORATION	17,423	Food service provider
SUPERVALU	17,421	Food service provider
BERGEN BRUNSWIG	17,245	Pharmaceutical products
TECH DATA	16,992	IT products
FLEMING	14,646	Food
AMERISOURCE HEALTH	9,760	Health care products
CHS ELECTRONICS	9,737	Electronics

Source: Fortune 500 Industry List, 2000.

exhibit 3-6 A Typical Channel of Distribution

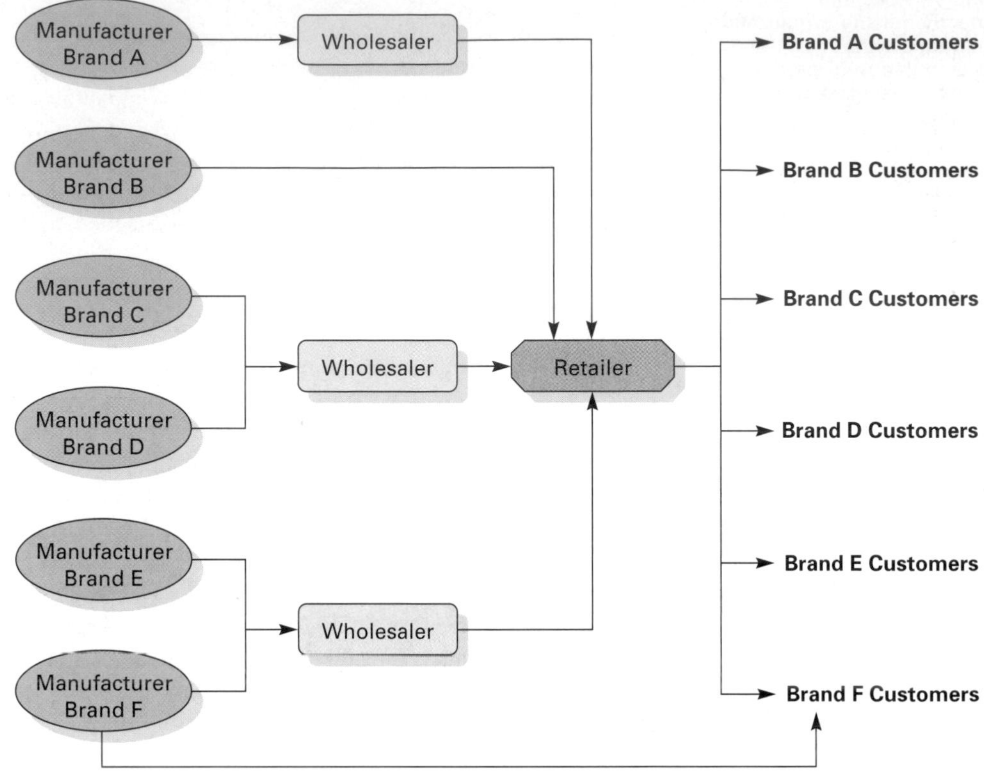

skips over another. Such "skipping" (or vertical integrating) in the chain simply means that the organization must handle a wider variety of management accounting issues. Exhibit 1-1 (page 4 of Chapter 1 of management accounting) shows the successful "skipping" accomplished by **DUPONT** owning nearly its entire distribution chain at the beginning of the twentieth century. Nevertheless, the process of manufacturers selling to wholesalers, wholesalers supplying retailers, and retailers selling to the final customers is the way most distribution works in the United States. We'll assume this to be the case for the rest of this textbook.

For many manufacturers, the only efficient way to get their products into the hands of the customer is through wholesalers and retailers. In a sense, these merchants are "middlemen." Some people argue that the presence of middlemen is economically inefficient and simply adds to the cost of getting products from manufacturers to consumers. In some cases, this is true. The furniture store probably adds to the consumer's cost of buying a rocking chair from our example manufacturer, the Broyman Furniture Company. But the reality is that most customers cannot buy directly from furniture manufacturers. Further, Broyman may not be interested in (nor equipped for) dealing directly with its many customers! Similarly, many retailers (such as your local grocery store) are not in a position to deal directly with the manufacturers of the items they sell to the public. On the other hand, some retailers can deal directly with manufacturers, but feel that dealing directly is more costly. A retailer may reap great benefits by using a wholesaler as a middleman between itself and the manufacturers. Wholesalers may be able to provide the retailer such things as next-day delivery, unlimited returns, expert advice on merchandise selection, and customized product mix. If the cost of using a wholesaler is less than the cost to the retailers of providing these services for themselves, then the use of a middleman makes good economic sense. Hence, in providing important options, services, and convenience, wholesalers and retailers can actually add to the efficiency of the distribution system and decrease costs for the ultimate consumer. In terms of costs, this is how merchants compete in the marketplace. Management accountants help merchandising companies carefully manage the costs of obtaining and distributing inventory. If costs become too high, then the merchant's customers may either go to a competitor to obtain the goods or skip over the middleman to negotiate directly with the supplier.

wholesalers Top-tier merchants who typically deal directly with the original manufacturers to distribute products to retailers.

logistics The management process involved in obtaining, managing, and transporting inventory and other assets in organizations.

Inventory Flow in the Distribution Channel

Spend a few minutes studying Exhibit 3-7. This exhibit shows the basic layout of a typical wholesaler's operation and a retailer's operation. Although the layouts of operations vary for both retailers and wholesalers, this exhibit will help us visualize the process of moving inventory from manufacturers into the hands of the ultimate end-user.

WHOLESALERS Let's begin with wholesalers. **Wholesalers** generally work within a particular industry (e.g., vegetable produce, running shoes, or calculators) to secure distribution contracts with a few key manufacturers. They receive goods in huge bulk shipments that they then break down for smaller shipments to retailers. This is a lot of inventory to manage, and a lot of money is at risk. Obviously, wholesalers will not make a profit unless there is a difference between the price at which they buy goods from manufacturers and the price at which they sell goods to retailers. However, the wholesaling process is much more involved than simply managing the cost of buying and selling goods. Quality and timelines are also important performance measures that are critical to successful wholesale management. Not only must wholesalers negotiate profitable contracts with manufacturers, but they must then handle the **logistics** of transporting those goods long distances to multiple retail locations. This requires wholesalers to work closely with large transportation companies to both receive and ship out goods as quickly and inexpensively as possible. To help control transportation costs and make the process as timely as possible, wholesalers often locate their distribution centers near large transit hubs such as train yards, shipping docks, airports, and major freeways. Usually, these distribution centers are very large buildings with little advertisement of their business to passersby. If you happen to live or travel near a large transit hub, see if you can spot these giant distribution warehouses, typically surrounded by lots of trucks, trains, or ships.

Managing the transportation of goods is not the only thing that wholesalers do. Manufacturers typically ship their goods in large bulk containers such as railway cars. Retailers, on the other hand, often require much smaller shipments. As a result, the logistics of the wholesale business will require many wholesalers to expand their distribution centers to include large areas where the manufacturers' shipping units can be opened and the goods repackaged for transportation to retail customers. Look at the wholesaler depicted in Exhibit 3-7. The large shipping crates received from manufacturers must be opened (or "broken down") and the goods designated for individual retailers (a process called "picking and packaging"). The process of repackaging goods for shipment to retailers often includes checks on both the quality of the goods and the accuracy of the packaged order. The key to success for wholesalers is to be sure that the right goods are received and shipped in the right manner to the right retailer for the right price at the right time.

fyi

Electronic Data Interchange (EDI) is a specialized computer link between companies that tremendously increases the efficiency with which companies can exchange the information necessary to handle supply transactions. WAL-MART, for example, requires all of its suppliers to use EDI links to tailor production and delivery of inventory to Wal-Mart stores based on customer demand. Recently, Wal-Mart has enabled its suppliers to monitor how each product is performing through real-time reports via the Internet. Using EDI, Wal-Mart has been able to reduce the time it takes to initiate a purchase, receive inventory, and pay the supplier from several weeks to just a few days. As a result of the collaborated effort, Wal-Mart is able to maintain an average level of inventory much lower than many of its competitors, resulting in increased return on investment (ROI).

Source: M. Cleary, "Wal-Mart Updates Supply System," *Interactive Week*, October 23, 2000. http://www.interactiveweek.com.

RETAILERS The business process for retailers is probably quite familiar to you. Most **retailers** place orders with and receive shipments from wholesalers. Because retailers need to provide a large variety of goods to their customers, they must often work with a large number of wholesalers (and, in some cases, manufacturers) to obtain their desired mix of inventory. As shown in the floor plan in Exhibit 3-7, many retailers have a receiving dock and a breakdown area used to prepare goods for display on their sales floor. Some retailers also keep a stock room for holding excess inventory. However, the cost of holding inventory in today's competitive environment is causing retailers to demand that wholesalers provide smaller and more frequent shipments. As a result, many retailers are able to avoid having a stock room. Inventory in these companies can then be moved directly from the breakdown area onto the sales floor.

retailers Second-tier merchants who typically purchase products from wholesalers to distribute to end-user customers. Many large retailers, however, often bypass wholesalers to purchase products directly from the original manufacturers.

Like wholesalers, retailers invest a lot of money in their inventory. Also similar to wholesalers, the big risk in the retailing business is having money tied up in inventory that is not selling. Obviously, having inventory is important to a retailer's business, but holding on to inventory for too long usually results in a significant opportunity cost. For example, as long as a shoe retailer has its money currently invested in a large inventory of running shoes, it is unable to use that money to purchase basketball shoes. These opportunity costs become particularly painful

exhibit 3-7 A Comparison of the Floor Plans for a Wholesaler and a Retailer

Wholesaler's Floor Plan

Inventory is delivered

Inventory is delivered

Inventory is delivered

Receiving Dock	Receiving Dock	Receiving Dock
	Breakdown Area	
	Pick and Package Area	
Shipping Dock	Shipping Dock	Shipping Dock

Inventory is shipped

Retailer's Floor Plan

Inventory is delivered

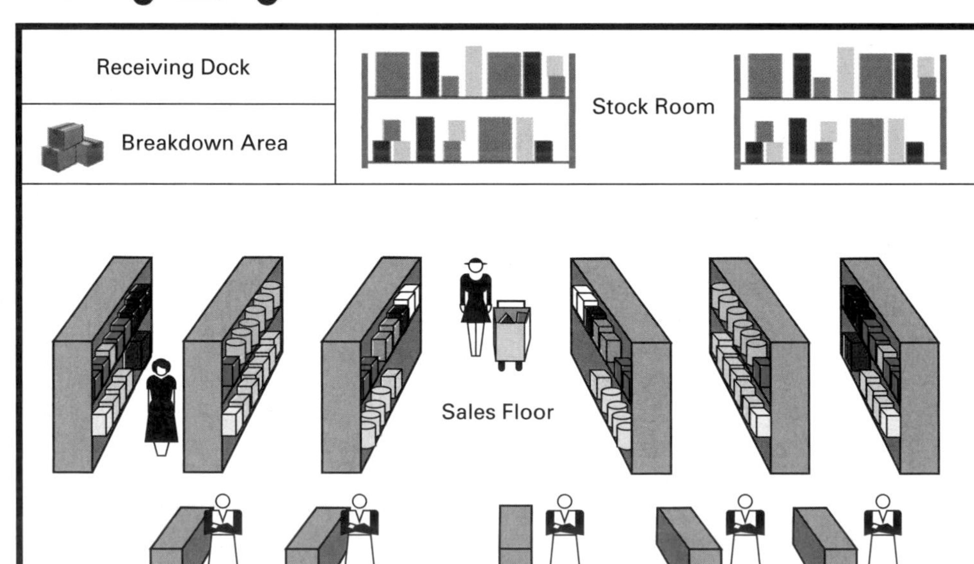

Some retailers do not have a physical store location where customers come to shop. Instead, they have created a virtual store on the Internet. One of the most successful examples of a retailer that exists solely in the virtual economy is **AMAZON BOOKS**. A brief tour of its virtual bookstore is quite impressive. Access the Web site for Amazon Books at **http://www.amazon.com/books**. What is the "Amazon Top 100" list? What book currently sits atop this list?

when the retailer is unable to sell its inventory of running shoes during the running season and, as a result, lacks the money to purchase basketball shoe inventory in time for the basketball season. This is why management accountants in the merchandising business are so focused on measuring stockturns. The faster you can turn your stock (i.e., inventory), the sooner you have the money available to purchase more inventory to sell. Obviously, retailers are just as concerned as wholesalers with the cost and timeliness involved in managing inventory. Further, given the demanding nature of today's informed consumer, management accountants must also provide retail managers with information on inventory quality. We'll talk more about the opportunity costs of holding inventory too long in Chapter 6 of management accounting.

Product Cost Accumulation in Merchandising Organizations

The bulk of this chapter so far has focused on manufacturing companies and how management accountants accumulate costs for these organizations. Traditionally, accounting textbooks have not gone much beyond manufacturing to discuss how management accounting works in merchandising and service organizations. This may have been appropriate given that manufacturing used to dominate the U.S. economy. However, as we have discussed in previous chapters, manufacturing is no longer the dominant type of business today. Merchandising and service organizations continue to increase their prevalence in the world economy. Although both merchandising and service organizations borrow much of their management accounting from the manufacturing industry, there are some important differences. Many of these differences result from the need to support management decision processes in merchandising and service organizations that are very different from the decision processes required in the manufacturing business.

INVENTORY FLOW AND THE INCOME STATEMENT In contrast to accounting for manufacturing businesses, the flow of costs through the merchandising accounting system is relatively simple. Examine Exhibit 3-8 and compare it to Exhibit 3-4 on page 120. Notice how simple the flow of inventory costs is in Exhibit 3-8. Essentially, accounting for inventory in merchandising organizations is a fairly straightforward process. There are no raw materials inventory, manufacturing overhead, or work-in-process inventory accounts. Merchandise inventory, by definition, is essentially complete and ready for sale when purchased. Hence, the cost of purchased inventory is debited to Merchandise Inventory throughout the year as it is acquired.[5] Conceptually, the inventory costs for a merchant should also include all costs required to purchase the inventory, transport it to the merchant's place of business, and ready it for sale (unpacking, displaying, etc.). Hence, the inventory cost should include the purchase price, shipping costs (freight in), insurance while in transit, administrative costs incurred by the merchant related to purchasing and handling activities, and storage costs prior to sale. In practice, though, most of these overhead-related costs, other than freight in costs, are difficult to allocate to specific inventory items. As a result, overhead costs related to merchandise inventory are often expensed as a period cost and included in Selling and General Administrative Expenses.

As inventory is sold, the cost of inventory is credited from Merchandise Inventory and debited to Cost of Goods Sold. When customers return merchandise that can be resold, Cost of Goods Sold is credited and the inventory account is debited (if the returned merchandise cannot be resold, then nothing happens in either of these particular accounts).

Tracking inventory costs in a merchant's accounting system may appear to be a fairly easy conceptual process. However, developing useful information on merchandise inventory for managers who need to plan, control, and evaluate inventory and inventory costs is a bit more involved. As the successful merchants learned historically, the key to profits is stockturns. Managing merchandise inventory is a significant topic for Chapter 6 of management accounting.

5 Recall that this method of continuously debiting and crediting Merchandise Inventory as inventory is purchased and sold (and debiting Cost of Goods Sold as inventory is sold) is called the *perpetual* inventory method of accounting. The alternative to the perpetual method is the *periodic* inventory method. There are several more accounts involved with the periodic inventory method, including Purchases, Purchase Discounts, and Purchase Returns. A significant difference between the perpetual and periodic inventory methods is that the periodic inventory method adjusts Merchandise Inventory *only at the end* of each period when cost of goods sold is calculated for the income statement.

exhibit 3-8 Flow of Product Costs in a Merchant's Cost Accounting System

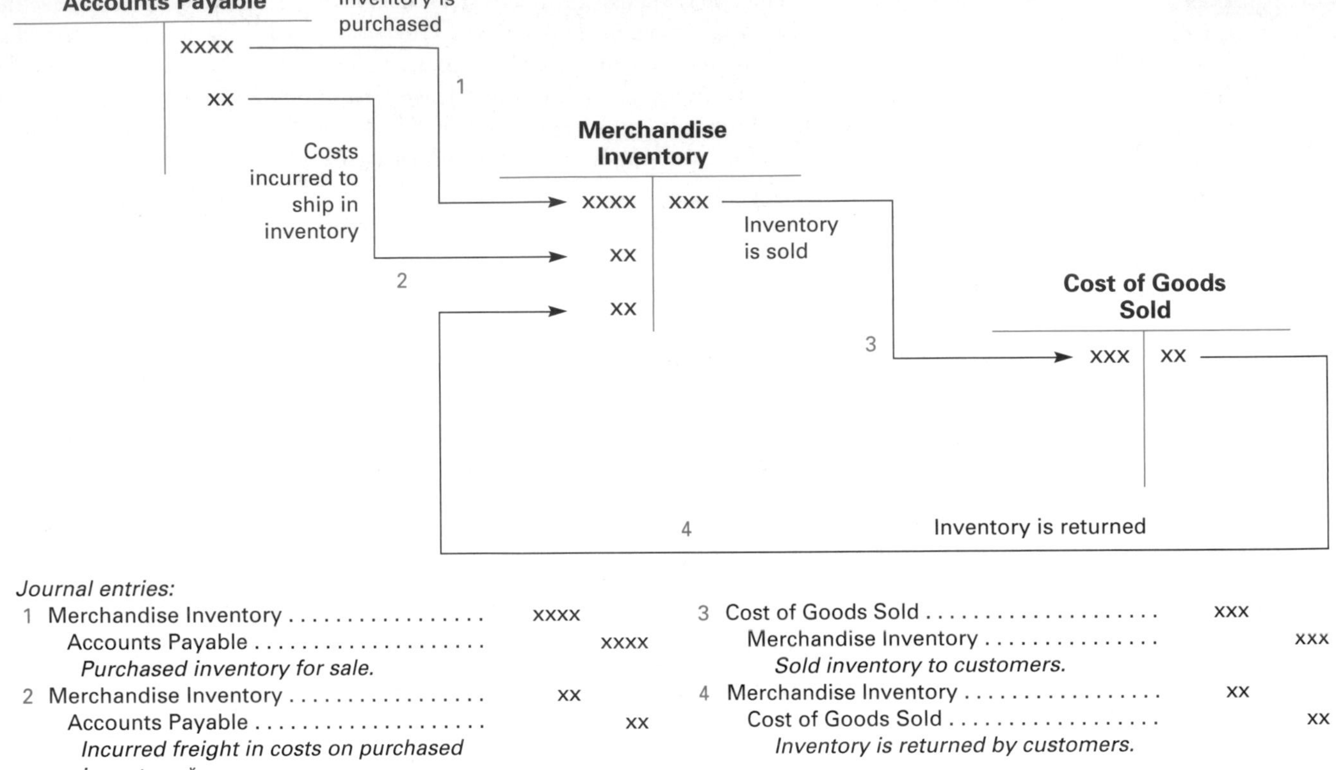

Journal entries:

1 Merchandise Inventory	xxxx	
Accounts Payable		xxxx
Purchased inventory for sale.		
2 Merchandise Inventory	xx	
Accounts Payable		xx
*Incurred freight in costs on purchased inventory.**		
3 Cost of Goods Sold	xxx	
Merchandise Inventory		xxx
Sold inventory to customers.		
4 Merchandise Inventory	xx	
Cost of Goods Sold		xx
Inventory is returned by customers.		

**Note:* Freight in is considered part of the purchase cost and should be added to inventory, eventually to be split between Cost of Goods Sold and the ending balance in Merchandise Inventory as goods are sold. In practice, the entire cost of freight in for a period is often simply debited directly to Cost of Goods Sold.

to summarize

Merchants are interconnected with manufacturers in a distribution channel that basically involves manufacturers selling to large-scale wholesalers, who then sell to retailers, who then sell to the end-user customer. Managing the movement (i.e., logistics) of inventory across the distribution channel is a critical business activity. Because wholesalers and retailers generally do not have to deal with raw materials or work in process, the process of accounting for inventory in a merchandising business is not nearly as complicated as it is in a manufacturing business. However, *managing* inventory costs (discussed in Chapter 6) is both complicated and critical for a merchant.

5

Explain the flow of goods and services in a service organization and follow the accumulation of product costs in its accounting system.

THE FLOW OF SERVICES AND COSTS IN SERVICE COMPANIES

So far in this chapter we have defined and discussed the nature of manufacturing and merchandising businesses and identified examples of companies in each type of business. The third type of business is service. What is a service business? Frankly, this is a rather difficult question. Simply stated, the service industry in the United States generally comprises all businesses that cannot be classified as merchandising or manufacturing (this assumes that we classify organizations that convert natural resources into useful products, such as farming or mining, as manufacturers). This is obviously a simple definition, but it is not very useful for us. It is important to more precisely define the service industry because nonmerchandising/nonmanufacturing businesses are the largest and fastest-growing sector in our economy. Hence, it is more likely that your career will involve working with service businesses than any other business type. For our purposes, we'll define a service business as follows:

> A service business is any organization whose main economic activity involves producing a nonphysical product that provides value to a customer.

The definition sounds pretty academic, but it needs to cover a lot of conceptual ground. As you'll see in the list in Exhibit 3-9, there is a lot of variety in the specific types of organizations that are neither merchandising nor manufacturing. As you study Exhibit 3-9, try to apply our definition of a service business to each of these categories and see if the definition fits.

Effects of Deregulation

Not very long ago, many service organizations were not nearly as concerned about cost management as they are today. Increasing global competition has put tremendous pressure on manufacturers and merchants to continuously improve their ability to compete on costs, quality, and time. In contrast, the nature of most service businesses means that they face little in the way of foreign-based competition. Nevertheless, it is becoming increasingly more important for service businesses to develop useful management accounting systems that support strategic imperatives of managing costs, quality, and timelines in creating and delivering a service product. The reason for this increased competition for service industries is really quite interesting. Prior to the 1980s, the communications, banking, health-care, utilities, and transportation industries were subject to tremendous government regulation. Even some professional services, such as accounting and legal services that have been essentially unregulated by government agencies, were more self-regulated than they are today. This self-regulation had the effect of discouraging competition by limiting the way these professionals could advertise their services. As a result of this regulation, most service-oriented companies were essentially sheltered. Government regulators restricted entry by low-cost suppliers and set prices in relationship to overall costs so that a minimum return on investment (ROI) could be earned. Essentially, prices were set to cover the least efficient producer. Self-regulation restricted information in the marketplace so that consumers were not well equipped to compare quality and price of services. **Deregulation** in the service sector has now changed the pricing and profitability picture for many industries. Now the most efficient producers establish

deregulation The term used to describe the process of removing restrictions on competition in the marketplace for a particular industry.

exhibit 3-9 Categories of Service Businesses

- Accounting/legal
- Architectural/engineering
- Communications (e.g., television, radio, etc.)
- Banking/financial (including insurance, investment brokers, consulting, etc.)
- Health care
- Software/systems integration (e.g., programming, installation, service, consulting, etc.)
- Marketing/advertising
- Public utilities
- Research and development
- Transportation
- Entertainment
- Education and training (not including state-owned schools and universities)

Source: Adapted from O. B. Martinson, *Cost Accounting in the Service Industry: A Critical Assessment* (Montvale, N.J.: Institute of Management Accountants, 1989).

business environment essay

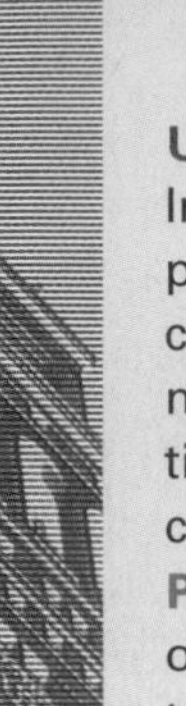

Union Pacific Had a Tough Year in 1996 Ineffective management of a single prominent service company can have catastrophic effects on the rest of the nation. In 1996, **UNION PACIFIC**, the nation's largest railway company, purchased **SOUTHERN PACIFIC RAIL CORPORATION**. Combining the service operations of these two companies turned out to be a lot more difficult than Union Pacific had anticipated. The operational problems resulting from the merger caused financial and production distress for numerous companies that depended on the railway industry as a primary means of transportation.

Stalled cars that caused trains to sit in limbo, congested lines that limited train movement, and shortages of crew members and locomotives were just a few of the problems Union Pacific faced as it worked to merge the two railway services. Every day, thousands of railroad cars failed to arrive at their destinations. Shipments that used to be delivered by Union Pacific in one week were taking two or three weeks. The economic effects of the clogged 36,000-mile system included factory production slowdowns and depleted inventory stock in stores. As a result, manufacturers' and merchants' costs rose as they switched to more expensive forms of delivery or halted production to wait for deliveries. As a result of delayed deliveries to its Michigan assembly plant, **FORD MO-**

prices. Today, service providers who don't know their costs will not be able to aggressively set prices, be responsive to consumer demands, and make enough money to stay in business.

Comparing Service and Manufacturing Business Activities

Service companies actually share more similarities with manufacturing companies than with merchandising companies. In this section, we will discuss the similarities of and the differences between service and manufacturing firms.

SIMILARITIES BETWEEN SERVICE AND MANUFACTURING FIRMS As you now understand, merchants purchase goods from manufacturers in finished condition. As a result, inventory in merchandising companies requires little, if any, conversion cost before being sold to customers. Inventory costs used to determine cost of goods sold on the merchant's income statement are relatively easy to determine. On the other hand, like manufacturers, most service companies perform a significant number of activities to prepare their service products for sale and delivery to their customers. Typically, a lot of direct labor and overhead is involved in a service business. Hence, the management process in service organizations shares a number of similarities with the process of managing a manufacturing business. Consider the following fundamental description of a service company; think about the similarities between this management process and what you now understand about the management process in manufacturing.

> A service organization identifies a need in the economy for which customers are willing to pay. Satisfying this need profitably involves creating a high-quality product that must be delivered in a timely manner while keeping costs low. The creative process often requires that the organization make investments in highly paid skilled labor or expensive capital equipment and buildings (or both!). In addition, a sophisticated management structure is important in order to effectively plan, control, and evaluate labor or equipment activities. Determining the total cost of the service product will require that a large amount of overhead be allocated to the direct service provided to the customer.

TOR COMPANY shut down factory lines for two days, causing a loss in the production of 600 cars. Even farmers in Nebraska became concerned about running out of molasses to feed their cattle.

Faced with the enormous task of fixing the mess created by the merger with Southern Pacific, executives at Union Pacific set forth a plan that would incrementally improve customer service, systems and facilities, safety, and efficiency. For example, throughout 1998, Union Pacific vigorously worked on expanding its capacity. Building new rail lines alleviated the "traffic jams" its locomotives were facing; this directly improved customer service and helped Union Pacific regain the confidence of its customers. These improvements did not come without significant capital expenditures that hurt operating margins, however.

Has Union Pacific's incremental plan worked? The company improved its net income from a *negative* $633 million in 1998 to a *positive* $842 million in 2000. During the implementation of the plan, Union Pacific's executives saw the company's stock price rise from $34.25 a share to $53.20 in February 2001. After the messy merger, it appears that Union Pacific is back on track and chugging along!

Sources: "Union Pacific Tie-Ups Reach across Economy," *Wall Street Journal*, October 8, 1997, pp. B1, B16; "Union Pacific Claims over Delays," *Wall Street Journal*, October 10, 1997, pp. A3, A6; Union Pacific home page at **http://www.up.com**.

The description sounds quite familiar, doesn't it? Most service companies engage in a very real production activity. However, what they provide is not nearly as tangible as the product provided by manufacturers. Yes, an architect or engineer does provide a tangible set of drawings or blueprints. But what is really being sold is the knowledge and customized advice that is represented by drawings. Public utilities provide heating or lighting that can be considered tangible in terms of watts or BTUs. What they are really selling, though, is the service of lighting or heating your home or business.

Service companies essentially build a product (the service) and deliver it to the customer (versus a merchant that resells a product built by another company). Consider the organizational effort required for a CPA firm to provide an audit service to a client. This organization is depicted in Exhibit 3-10. As you can see, there is direct labor (the auditing staff) involved in this audit that is supported by a complex system of supervisors, supplies, equipment, capital assets, and so forth. This support system essentially forms the overhead costs of the audit product, and these overhead costs will need to be appropriately allocated as part of the product cost of the audit. You can see, then, that there are many similarities between the process of manufacturing and service companies.

caution

When trying to decide whether a company is in the service business, consider the following old joke:

A plumber is called out to fix a clogged pipe. The plumber examines the situation for a few seconds, then pulls out a hammer and taps on the offending pipe. The problem is solved. However, the customer is a bit upset upon receiving the bill for $100.17. "All you did was tap on the pipe. I demand an itemized bill!" the customer complains. So, the plumber sends the following itemized bill:

Tapping on pipe	$ 0.17
Knowing where to tap	100.00
Total	$100.17

Remember that expertise is a significant component of most service companies.

DIFFERENCES BETWEEN SERVICE AND MANUFACTURING FIRMS Some service organizations do sound as though they are really in the manufacturing business. Notwithstanding, there are some important differences between most service and manufacturing businesses that affect the information provided by management accountants. For example, the use of distribution channels is not nearly as prevalent in the service sector. Whereas manufacturers are dependent on merchants to distribute their products to the final customers, most service businesses deal directly with the end-user customer. Also, there is probably a lot more customization in the service process than in the manufacturing process. Hence, most service businesses use a job order approach rather than a process approach to cost accounting (with some exceptions, such as public utilities). Additionally, very little raw material is involved in the process of converting labor or capital equipment into a service product (again, some public utilities will be the exception here, e.g., coal-burning power plants). Note, though, that items such as paper and syringes are sometimes included as part of the delivered service, but these items are not the main focus of what the customer is paying to

exhibit 3-10 The Service Process at a CPA Firm

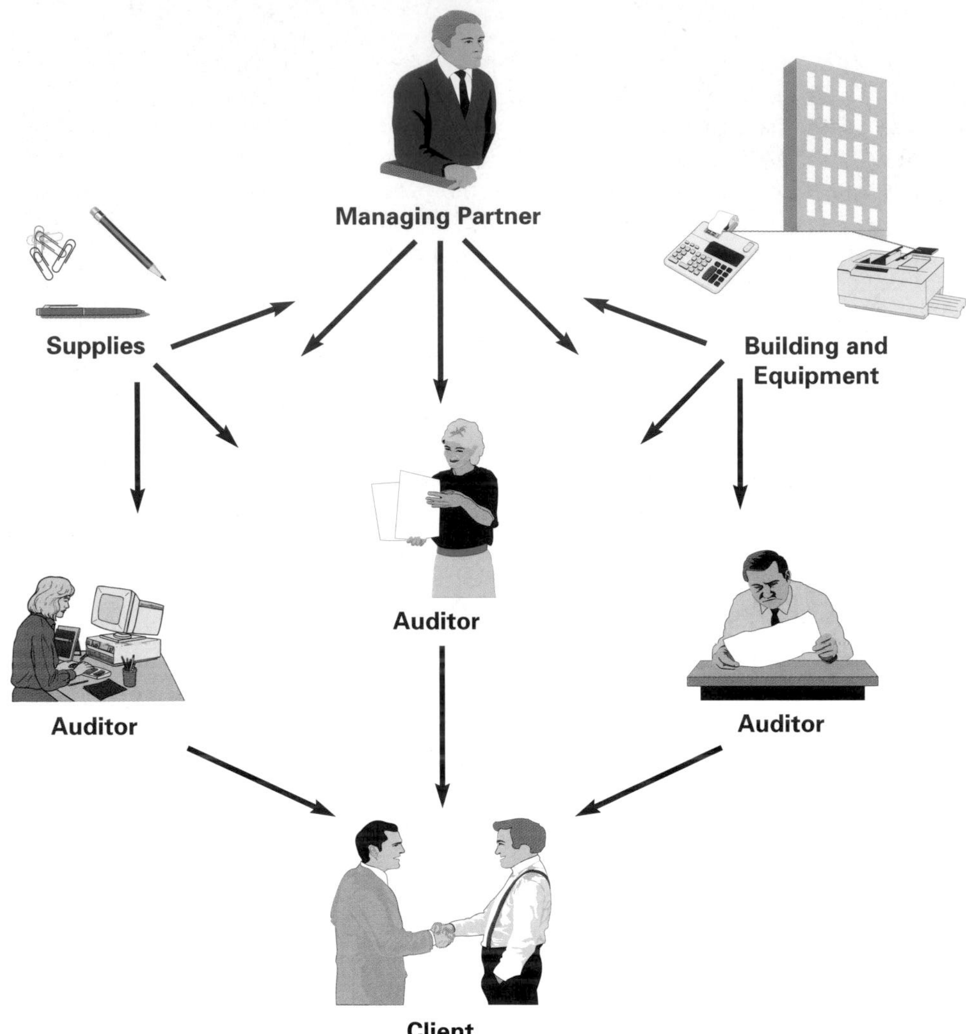

receive. As a result, raw material inventories are insignificant or nonexistent in a service business. Similarly, it is often difficult to store a finished service in anticipation of a later sale to customers, making finished goods inventories insignificant or nonexistent. At the close of a reporting period, however, most service companies will be in the process of completing a service for delivery to a customer. This suggests that work-in-process inventories exist and may be significant for many service organizations. (We will discuss work-in-process inventories further below.)

As you can see, defining a service business can be challenging. Don't worry too much about being able to perfectly identify every organization as either a manufacturer or a service business. An overall familiarity with the basic differences and similarities between service, manufacturing, and merchandising businesses will help in determining the relevant management accounting that adds competitive value as managers work to plan, control, and evaluate operations.

Product Cost Accumulation in Service Organizations

As you now understand, there are a number of accounting similarities between manufacturing and service organizations. The most important similarity is that both manufacturing and service organizations use a significant amount of direct labor in producing their products. In addition, large amounts of overhead costs typically are allocated to individual products. Similar to many manufacturers, service businesses often allocate overhead on the basis of direct labor hours. One

> **fyi**
>
> Over the past 100 years, costs for raw materials in manufacturing firms have averaged nearly 50% of total product costs.

important difference is that manufacturers must also manage large amounts of raw materials costs, while the materials included in the services sold by service companies are typically limited to insignificant amounts of supplies used in the service process.

"INVENTORY" FLOW AND THE INCOME STATEMENT IN SERVICE COMPANIES Exhibit 3-11 summarizes the flow of costs for a service company. Comparing Exhibit 3-11 to Exhibits 3-4 and 3-8 illustrates that accounting for service cost flows can be more complicated than accounting for merchandise inventory cost flows, but is quite similar to accounting for manufacturing cost flows. Materials (e.g., supplies), labor, and overhead costs are all involved in, and should be assigned to, the process of creating and delivering a service product to the customer.

The overhead for service firms can involve nearly any kind of management costs—service firms generally do not distinguish between manufacturing and administrative overhead costs. Allocating overhead to service activities generally involves factoring an overhead rate into the billing rate used to charge customers. Think about all the services you buy and use. Often some type

exhibit 3-11 Summary of Service Cost Flows

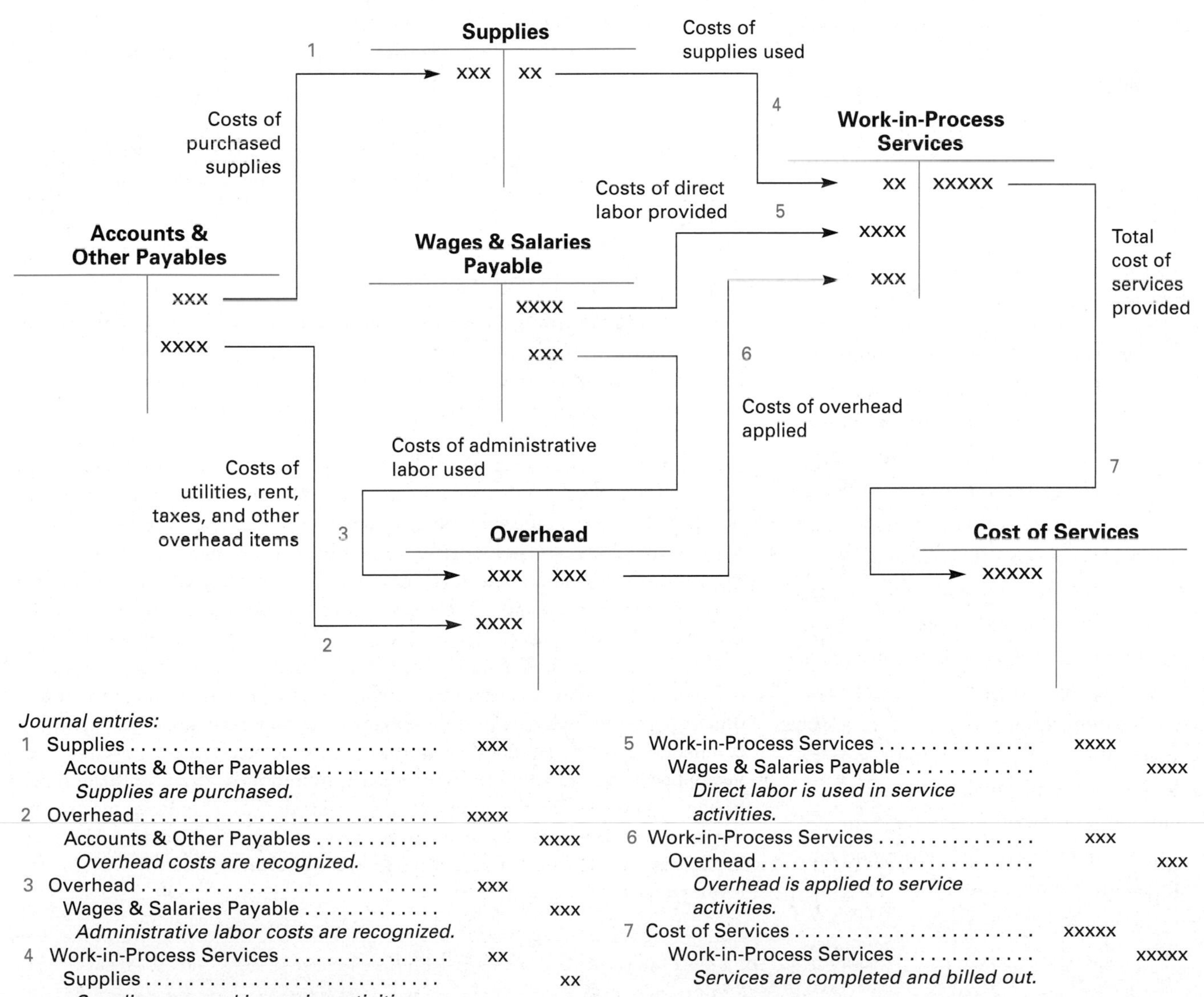

Journal entries:

1 Supplies	xxx	
Accounts & Other Payables		xxx
Supplies are purchased.		
2 Overhead	xxxx	
Accounts & Other Payables		xxxx
Overhead costs are recognized.		
3 Overhead	xxx	
Wages & Salaries Payable		xxx
Administrative labor costs are recognized.		
4 Work-in-Process Services	xx	
Supplies		xx
Supplies are used in service activities.		
5 Work-in-Process Services	xxxx	
Wages & Salaries Payable		xxxx
Direct labor is used in service activities.		
6 Work-in-Process Services	xxx	
Overhead		xxx
Overhead is applied to service activities.		
7 Cost of Services	xxxxx	
Work-in-Process Services		xxxxx
Services are completed and billed out.		

of a billing rate per hour or per event is used to determine the price you pay for the service. For example, accountants, lawyers, consultants, programmers, and repair shops often charge by the hour. When you get the bill, you understand that the huge rate per hour does not represent solely the wage or salary of the professional who provided a service to you. This rate has been enhanced (sometimes significantly!) in order to cover all the overhead and supplies costs necessary to support the work done by the service professional. Similarly, doctors, trainers, entertainers, and transportation companies usually charge by event. You understand that the doctor isn't paid the full $175 charge when he or she gives you a physical exam. Much of that amount goes to pay for the costs of staff, equipment, and building occupancy necessary to support the actual service provided by your doctor.

Assigning overhead costs to a service event follows a pattern very similar to that for manufacturing firms. Total overhead for the service organization is estimated for a period of time, generally a year. This estimated overhead is then divided by an appropriate activity measure. For an accountant, this activity measure may be billable hours. The measure for a bank could be the number of teller transactions or number of accounts. For a cable TV company, it could be the average number of accounts expected for the year. The activity measure for an electric company might be the expected number of kilowatts produced during the next year. Other examples of possible overhead rate calculations for several types of service companies are shown below.

STOP & THINK The selection of the activity base that is used to allocate overhead is a very important management decision because any particular activity base could have a significant impact on how much cost is assigned to one product versus another. For example, suppose that the academic advisement center at your college is trying to determine what it costs to provide advisement services to a specific student each semester. What are some possible activity bases this department might use to allocate the costs of the office equipment, supervisor salary, and other overhead items? Would your choice of a base have an effect on which students are then identified as "high-cost-to-serve" students?

With a predetermined overhead rate, service companies are able to allocate overhead costs to service events as they occur. This method of allocating overhead helps managers control overhead costs, establish prices for services provided, and measure profit on each service event or contract. The overhead account for a service company is used in much the same manner as in a manufacturing firm. As actual overhead costs are incurred, they are debited to the overhead account rather than being debited to an expense account. Then, as the appropriate overhead activities actually take place (e.g., consulting hours, teller transactions, and kilowatts), overhead costs are allocated to Work-in-Process Services (more about this account in the next section). As services are actually billed, these overhead costs are combined with the direct labor costs of the service professionals (if any) and any incidental costs of supplies and debited to Cost of Services (an account very similar to the cost of goods sold account used by manufacturers and merchants). At the end of the year (or any other time period relevant to the company), the total actual overhead costs are compared to the total allocated overhead costs to determine an over- or underapplied overhead amount. If overhead is overapplied, there will be a credit balance in the service company's overhead account. This balance means that too much overhead cost was allocated to the cost of service activities. The overapplied costs are removed (and the overhead account is closed) with the following entry:

Overhead	xxx	
Cost of Services		xxx

If overhead is underapplied, then there will be a debit balance in the overhead account, and Cost of Services is adjusted (increased) by closing the overhead account with the following entry:

Cost of Services	xxx	
Overhead		xxx

Similar to manufacturing firms, the service company may choose to apportion the over- or underapplied overhead amount between Cost of Services and Work-in-Process Services. The question you might be asking at this point is, "Why would a service organization have a work-in-process inventory account?" Good question! We'll talk about this account next.

WHO HAS WORK-IN-PROCESS INVENTORY? In manufacturing companies, accounting for work-in-process inventory is a significant part of the product cost accounting effort. Costs of resources used in the process of creating a product are attached to that product. Typically, at the end of an income period (e.g., a month, a quarter, or a year), a number of products are still in process. A significant amount of costs can be tied up in these in-process products. GAAP requires that these costs be capitalized (identified as assets) and assigned to the balance sheet until the products are actually sold. Only at the time that goods are sold and revenue is recognized can the related costs be charged to the income statement. The basic underlying accounting concept behind this approach is the all-important matching principle.

The logic for identifying work-in-process inventory as a balance sheet asset applies to both manufacturing and service businesses. Service companies typically earn revenue as the service is provided to the customer. At the end of an accounting period, however, significant effort and resources may have been invested in a service product that is not yet completed for the customer. As a result, revenue is not yet earned, and the costs invested at this point should not be recognized as expenses. In other words, until they actually complete the project and bill it to the client, service companies have work in process.

The following are some examples of work in process that are likely to exist at the end of an accounting period for various types of service companies:[6]

- Accounting/legal—An audit that will take three months to complete is in its initial stage.
- Architectural/engineering—The blueprints for a large construction project are only partially completed.
- Banking/financial—The fieldwork has been completed and the lending documents are being finalized for a large loan that will be closed next month.
- Marketing/advertising—Three weeks of effort have been expended on the development of a new advertising campaign that will not be ready for presentation to the client for another three weeks.
- Transportation—A large shipment of coal is being held in a midwestern freight yard en route to its shipping point on the East Coast.

In each of these examples, resources have been invested in creating a service that the customer has not yet received. As a result, work in process exists and should be recognized on the balance sheet. As you can see in Exhibit 3-11, as supplies and labor costs are directly invested in the process of creating a service for customers, these amounts are debited to Work-in-Process Services. As overhead costs such as utilities, rent, taxes, and support staff salaries are incurred, these costs are debited to the overhead account and are subsequently allocated to Work-in-Process Services using an overhead rate. When the service is completed and delivered to the customer, then the revenue earning process is complete and the service costs are transferred out of Work-in-Process Services and into Cost of Services.[7]

6 O. B. Martinson, *Cost Accounting in the Service Industry: A Critical Assessment* (Montvale, N.J.: Institute of Management Accountants, 1989), pp. 47–48.

7 Some fairly large long-term service contracts are sometimes designed to allow the provider to bill and receive partial payments as the contract is completed. In these cases, as the revenue process is partially completed, some service costs can be transferred out of Work-in-Process Services and into Cost of Services. Learning about this type of accounting is reserved for more advanced accounting courses.

business environment essay

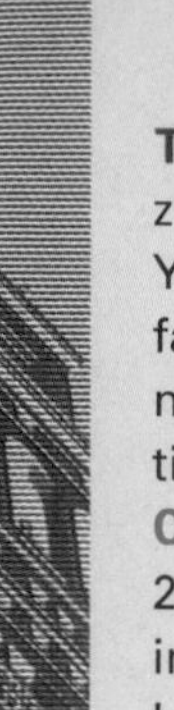

The Birth of an e-Business Jeffrey P. Bezos quit his lucrative job with a New York investment firm and moved his family to Seattle, Washington, to start a new company in a new industry. A short time later, on July 16, 1995, **AMAZON.COM**, the largest e-tailer in the world in 2001, opened its Web doors. After having 300 of his friends and family members test the site, Jeff asked them to tell everyone they knew about Amazon.com. Within 30 days, with no press or traditional advertising, Amazon.com had sold books in all 50 states and 45 countries—an instant Web success! How did this all begin?

Amazon.com began as a bookseller over the Internet that offered competitive prices, accessibility, and extreme convenience. It was readily apparent to Bezos, as his book-selling Web site grew exceptionally fast, that Amazon.com could become the "Earth's Biggest Store." In 1998, Amazon.com offered its first product other than books—music CDs. From there, Amazon.com has expanded into videos, DVD movies, toys, hardware, greeting cards, electronics, software, home improvement products, auctions, and more. How does Amazon.com manage this huge distribution channel?

With more than 2 million unique visitors a month currently, Amazon.com has established a highly au-

to summarize

Essentially, a service business is any organization whose main economic activity involves producing a nonphysical product that provides value to a customer. As service industries have been deregulated in the last few decades, the increased competition has forced these companies to develop better cost management. Because service companies generally create the service they provide, they have some similarities with manufacturing companies in both the management and the accounting processes, including the need to manage and account for work in process. A major difference between service and manufacturing operations is that raw materials typically are not a significant component of a service company's product. Costs flow through a service firm in a manner very similar to a manufacturing firm. Costs of supplies (usually insignificant in size) and direct labor (usually significant in size) accumulate in an account called Work-in-Process Services. This account performs much the same function as a work-in-process inventory account in a manufacturing firm. In addition, overhead must often be applied to Work-in-Process Services as service activities take place. The process of applying overhead is typically done using a predetermined overhead application rate.

6

Understand the impact of e-business on product costing.

THE EFFECT OF E-BUSINESS

Before we conclude the main part of this chapter, we should say a little about the impact of e-business on business organizations and the product costing process.[8] First of all, it is important to understand that e-business is not a separate new industry like manufacturing, merchandising, or service. Rather, e-business provides new platforms for conducting business *within* the current industries in the economy.

8 Some of the material in this section is based on information presented in S. M. Glover, S. W. Liddle, and D. F. Prawitt, *eBusiness: Principles & Strategies for Accountants* (Upper Saddle River, N.J.: Prentice Hall, 2001).

tomated system that prides itself on discovering and satisfying customer needs. In addition, the Amazon system must maintain a critical relationship with manufacturers and suppliers. One glitch in the system could spell disaster for the company and its end-users (us!). The life of an order begins well before a customer hits the "Buy it" button on the site. Management must forecast consumer needs, arrange to be able to ship merchandise from suppliers on demand, maintain a precise calculation of inventory available from its suppliers, and meet customer demands quickly and effectively. One of the original strengths of Amazon's business model was that it rarely held inventory (recently, Amazon expanded its business operations significantly by building some large distribution warehouses that do hold inventory). Instead, in many cases Amazon has direct connections to its suppliers that allow customer orders to be shipped directly from supplier to customer. Computers track most of this complicated distribution channel, but it is the knowledge of management that ultimately provides the success that Amazon.com enjoys.

Source: J. C. Ramo, "1999 Person of the Year," *Time*, December 27, 1999.

fyi

Many people originally predicted that the Internet would open up new, previously untapped markets. The reality is that, in 1999, only 6% of consumer e-business revenue was new spending. In other words, sales on the Internet are not, by and large, *new* sales, but represent commerce that is *replacing* business previously done within traditional manufacturing, merchandising, or service settings.

Source: Jupiter Communications, 1999.

You have probably had some experience in shopping on the Internet. Most organizations today have an Internet site. Generally, all you have to do is open your Internet browser and add a ".com" to the end of the name of your favorite company, and you can be doing business with that company in no time. Obviously, a lot of business is being transacted on the Internet. However, the lion's share of Internet business is *not* taking place with individual consumers like most of us. To help you understand this point, we need to distinguish between two kinds of e-business. One kind is conducted between companies and consumers (or end-users). This sort of business is often referred to as business-to-consumer (or "B2C"). When you shop at **WALMART.COM** or **NORDSTROMS.COM**, you're engaged in B2C e-business. B2C e-business in the United States amounted to $33 billion in 2000 and is expected to grow to between $200 billion and $400 billion by 2003. In addition, business also takes place between businesses, such as the purchase of raw materials, consulting, outsourcing of services, and important partnerships or joint ventures where companies work together to provide goods and services to the public. When this work is managed with Internet-type technology, it is referred to as a business-to-business process (or "B2B"). This aspect of e-business is, frankly, huge. B2B e-business amounted to $251 billion in 2000 and is expected to grow to between $1.5 trillion and $2 trillion by 2003!

As manufacturers, merchants, and service providers move more and more of their business onto the Internet, they expect to enjoy a number of significant benefits, including expanded sales opportunities; improved communications, customer service, and loyalty; and better management of human resources and supply channels. Perhaps most relevant to this chapter is the fact that companies expect to lower their costs of business using Internet technology. For example, bank transactions involving a teller cost an average of $1.07 per transaction. When you log on to your bank at its ".com" Internet site, however, an online banking transaction costs only $0.01. As another example, **IBM** bought $13 billion worth of goods and services over the Internet in 1999, saving more than $270 million in procurement costs. E-billing, the delivery of routine bills online, can save as much as 60% per bill in handling costs. Hence, cost savings in running a billing process at a large utility could be as much as $50 million per year when an e-billing process is implemented. **WAL-MART** has achieved tremendous improvements in the costs, quality, and timing of goods purchased from wholesalers through the use of inventory management systems that have direct Internet-based connections to its suppliers. Even hiring costs can be reduced, as evidenced by the fact that IBM has installed Internet software that has cut the cost of hiring temporary workers by $3 million annually.

fyi

In a *Business Week* article, GENERAL ELECTRIC's CEO Jack Welch was asked how high the Internet was on his company's agenda. Welch responded, "Where does the Internet rank in priority? It's No. 1, 2, 3, and 4."

Source: N. Byrnes and P. C. Judge, "Internet Anxiety," *Business Week*, June 28, 1999.

E-business can have tremendous impacts on product costs. Specifically, costs of raw materials are reduced as organizations use the Internet to find and demand better pricing and save significant costs in the process of ordering and managing raw material inventories. Costs of direct labor can also be better managed by using the Internet to identify, hire, and train the organization's workforce. In some cases, direct service labor, such as bank tellers, are redeployed to new assignments in the organization as Internet technology becomes the means of interacting with clients and customers. Perhaps most significantly, companies are making significant changes in the structure of their organizations, which can greatly affect the costs of overhead. At many companies, overhead costs are much higher than the costs of raw materials/supplies and direct labor combined, so finding new ways to handle the management and logistics of a company can have immediate and important impacts on costs. The example of IBM using the Internet to change the way it obtains goods and services (and temporary employees) demonstrates the savings that can result.

to summarize

E-business and Internet technology are dramatically changing all types of business organizations, including manufacturing, merchandising, and service organizations. As these companies make adjustments in both their organizational structure and in the way they connect to and do business with suppliers and customers within their distribution channel, there have been (and will continue to be) significant changes and improvements in the costs, quality, and timeliness of goods and services. These changes are affecting the process of both business-to-consumer (B2C) and business-to-business (B2B) operations.

expanded material

In the first part of the chapter we illustrated product costing using the job order costing method. This method is commonly used in both manufacturing and service organizations. In this expanded material section, we discuss how companies, predominantly manufacturers, use process costing when it is difficult to specifically identify unique products or jobs during the manufacturing process.

7

Use the FIFO method to do process costing.

THE PROCESS COSTING SYSTEM

All the product costing methods described so far in this chapter assume that the accountant is able to specifically identify the job (i.e., the product or service) being produced for customers. By identifying each specific job, the accountant is then able to specifically track a job as it moves through the work-in-process inventory and into the finished goods inventory. While it is in the production process, the accountant assigns the actual direct materials and direct labor costs, as well as allocates a specific amount of overhead costs, that are required to produce to a particular job. This cost accounting method is often referred to as job order costing. Some manufacturing companies cannot use job order costing because they cannot specifically identify each job (product) being produced. Examples of such companies include manufacturers of bricks, lumber, paint, soft drinks, and newspapers and most food processing plants. These companies manufacture large volumes of product using a series of uniform processes. For these companies, **process costing** is the appropriate product cost accounting method. Because these companies can't focus on costing a particular job, they focus on costing the amount of work done for a particular *period of time.* We'll talk more about this concept of work done in a particular time period below. For now, remember that for process costing to be appropriate, two general conditions typically exist:

process costing A method of product costing whereby costs are accumulated by process or work centers and averaged over all products manufactured in a center or department during a particular production period. There are two methods of process costing: The FIFO method separately tracks the costs of beginning work-in-process units and the costs of units started in the current production period. The weighted-average method (not discussed in this text) averages together the costs of beginning work-in-process units and the costs of units started in the current production period.

1. The activities performed in each process center are identical for all units.
2. The units produced as a result of passing through the process centers are basically the same.

Steps in Process Costing

A firm whose products and processes meet the preceding conditions would employ process costing using five steps:

1. Identify units that went into the process and identify where those units are at the end of the processing time. Determine the amount of "work done" (equivalents units of production) during the processing time period.
2. Determine the amount of production costs that went into the process and compute the product costs per unit for the processing time period.
3. Compute the total cost of units completed and transferred out (costs of goods manufactured) during the processing time period.
4. Compute the total cost of units remaining in process (ending work-in-process inventory) at the end of the processing time period.
5. Prepare the production cost report.

STEP 1. COMPUTE EQUIVALENT UNITS OF PRODUCTION The first step in process costing is to track the flow of units and compute the **equivalent units of production**. The concept of equivalent units of production essentially means to calculate the amount of work actually done during any particular period of time in terms of units of output. It's really a very simple concept. For example, let's assume that you are being paid by the hour to hand paint porcelain figurines for a small local art shop. It's an arduous process, taking several hours to paint a single figurine. On average, you can do only three or four figurines per day. At the end of your first day on the job, you have painted three figurines and have another one nearly complete. If your boss were to ask you how much work you did for the day, are you going to reply that you painted only three figurines? Of course not! Instead, you'll likely tell her that you completely painted three figurines and that you have another one nearly done (let's say it is 90% done). So, did you paint four figurines? Not really. The amount of work done on your first day is 3.9 figurines (three whole units plus 90% of a fourth unit), right? In other words, you did 3.9 equivalent units of production. Also note that you have one unit in ending work-in-process inventory (the figurine that is 90% done).

equivalent units of production A method used in a process costing system to measure the production output during a period. Equivalent units of production essentially measures the "work done" by the center or department in terms of units of output.

The real measure of equivalent units of production is what happens on your second day on the job. When you come back to the shop the next day, the first thing you will do is work on that day's beginning work-in-process inventory, which is the figurine that is 90% done from the day before.[9] Let's assume that you then start and complete three more figurines. Before it's time to go home, you are able to start one more figurine and get it about 30% done. Now how do you answer the boss's question about how much work was done on your second day? You completed a total of four figurines (the figurine that was work-in-process when you came to work plus three more that were both started and completed this same day), but to say that you did the work of four figurines isn't quite accurate, is it? To be accurate, you completed 10% of one figurine, 100% of three figurines, and 30% of a final figurine that is still work-in-process. In other words, the work done for the day was 3.4 figurines, computed as follows:

9 This is the reason we call this particular method of process costing the FIFO (first in, first out) method. It is based on the assumption that all beginning work-in-process inventory is completed before any new units are started.

	Physical Units		Percent Completed (i.e., "work done")		Equivalent Units of Production
Beginning work-in-process	1	×	10%	=	0.1
Started and completed	3	×	100%	=	3.0
Ending work-in-process	1	×	30%	=	0.3
Total equivalent units of production					**3.4**

With this example of equivalent units of production in mind, let's now use an example that's more representative of manufacturers that follow the process costing approach to accounting for product costs. Exhibit 3-12 shows how products and costs move through the two process centers (mixing and bagging) of the Allied Cement Company. For now, we will focus on the process costing for the mixing center at Allied Cement. Production units at Allied are measured in pounds of finished cement. When the mixing machines are shut down at the end of a production period (let's assume a production period at Allied is one month), not all pounds of cement started the last day of the month in the mixing center will have been completed. In fact, as at most manufacturers, units are usually in process at both the beginning and the end of a period. Were it not for these beginning and ending work-in-process inventories, the number of units actually produced in the mixing center for the period could be determined merely by counting all pounds of cement that were transferred out of the mixing center and into the bagging center. However, as you saw in our earlier example of hand painting figurines, the amount of work actually done in the mixing center for the period is partly based on how much work was done in the beginning and ending work-in-process inventories.

With this in mind, look at the report below on equivalent units of production for the mixing center.

Step 1: Compute equivalent units of production.

		Direct Materials Costs		Conversion Costs	
	Physical Units (pounds)	Percent Done	Equivalent Units	Percent Done	Equivalent Units
Beginning work-in-process	4,000	0%	0	80%	3,200
Started and completed	44,000	100%	44,000	100%	44,000
Ending work-in-process	2,000	100%	2,000	60%	1,200
Equivalent units of production			**46,000**		**48,400**
Transferred out (to Bagging)	48,000				

The "Physical Units" column reports that the mixing center had 4,000 pounds of cement in beginning work-in-process when the month started. The department finished mixing these 4,000 pounds and mixed an additional 44,000 pounds before the end of the month, allowing the mixing center to transfer a total of 48,000 pounds to the bagging center. At the end of the month, 2,000 pounds of cement remained in ending work-in-process.

Now look at the "Equivalent Units" column for the Direct Materials Costs. In this case, all of the materials necessary to mix a pound of cement are put in place at the beginning of the mixing process. In other words, when the month began, the 4,000 pounds of cement in beginning work-in-process were already 100% complete in terms of materials. Similarly, at the end of the month, the 2,000 pounds of cement in ending work-in-process were 100% complete in terms of materials. As a result, the equivalent units of production (i.e., "work

exhibit 3-12 The Flow of Products and Costs through Process Centers

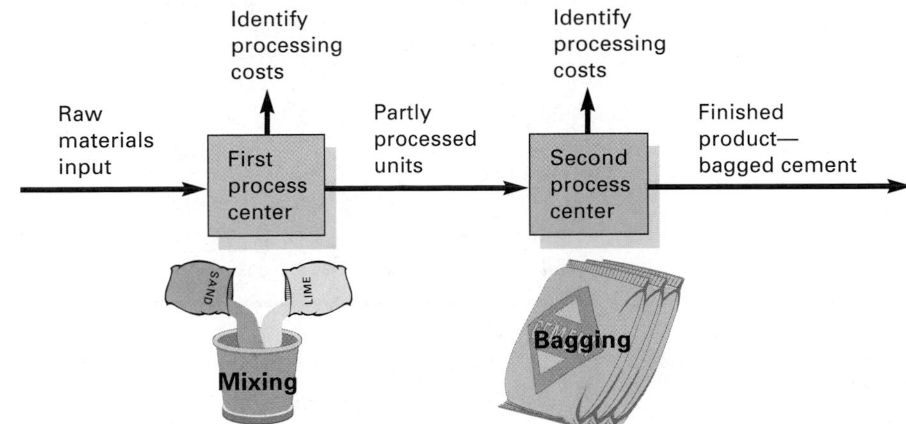

done") to be used when accounting for costs of direct materials for Allied is simply the number of pounds of cement *started* into production during the production period, or 100% of units started and completed plus 100% of units in ending work-in-process (and 0% of units in beginning work-in-process).[10]

conversion costs The costs of converting raw materials to finished products; include direct labor and manufacturing overhead costs.

Finally, look at the "Equivalent Units" column under "Conversion Costs." **Conversion costs** is the term we use to describe all product costs necessary to "convert" raw materials into finished goods. Hence, conversion costs include all costs of direct labor and manufacturing overhead.[11] In this example, at the beginning of the month, the beginning work-in-process inventory was 20% complete in terms of costs of direct labor and manufacturing overhead. As a result, the first work done in the mixing center for the current production period was to finish the remaining 80% of the effort required to complete these 4,000 pounds of cement. In other words, the mixing center did 3,200 equivalent units of production (4,000 × 80%) on beginning work-in-process. At the end of the month, there were 2,000 pounds in ending working-in-process that were 60% complete in terms of direct labor and manufacturing overhead costs, which means that the mixing center did 1,200 equivalent units of production (2,000 × 60%) on ending work-in-process. When combined with the work done on units started and completed, the mixing center's "work done" in terms of direct labor and manufacturing overhead was 48,400 equivalent units (3,200 + 44,000 + 1,200).

> In the FIFO approach to process costing, the total physical units "started" always equal total units "started and completed" plus total units in "ending work-in-process." Similarly, the total physical units "transferred out" always equal total units "started and completed" plus total units in "beginning work-in-process."

STEP 2. COMPUTE THE PRODUCT COSTS PER UNIT With Step 1 completed, we know how much work was done in terms of production output for the mixing center. Now, to compute the product cost per unit, we need to determine how much was spent on production. For the mixing center, we will assume that the beginning work-in-process of 4,000 pounds includes $800 in direct materials and $1,200 in direct labor and manufacturing overhead (i.e., conversion costs). Further, Allied spent $9,660 for direct materials and $70,180 for conversion costs in the current production period. Computing the product costs per unit (pound) for the mixing department is then a simple matter of dividing the product costs by the appropriate equivalent units of production, reported as follows:

10 When computing equivalent units in this chapter, we will always assume that direct materials are all added at the beginning of the process. However, this assumption is not always the case in actual companies.

11 Because we assume in this example that costs of manufacturing overhead are being allocated on the basis of direct labor, we can combine the equivalent units calculation for direct labor and for manufacturing overhead costs into one calculation for conversion costs. This is the assumption that we will follow for all subsequent equivalent unit calculations in this chapter.

Step 2: Compute the product costs per unit.

	Total Costs	Equivalent Units	Cost per Unit
Beginning work-in-process			
Direct materials costs	$ 800	4,000	$0.20
Conversion costs	1,200	800	1.50
Total	$ 2,000		**$1.70**
Current period			
Direct materials costs	$ 9,660	46,000	$0.21
Conversion costs	70,180	48,400	1.45
Total	$79,840		**$1.66**

caution

When using beginning work-in-process in the calculation of equivalent units of production for the current production period, remember to use the percentage *yet to be done.* In other words, the "work done" in the current period on *beginning* work-in-process is:

Number of physical units in inventory × (1 − Percent done)

The "work done" on *ending* work-in-process for the current period is:

Number of physical units in inventory × Percent done

As you can see in the report above on product costs per unit, Allied spent $0.21 per pound for direct materials in the mixing center in the current production period. This cost is based on dividing the total equivalent units of 46,000 for work done on direct materials into the total direct materials costs of $9,660. Bearing in mind that beginning work-in-process came from the previous production period, Allied can compare the current direct materials cost to the direct materials cost in the previous production period, which was $0.20 per pound. This cost is obtained by dividing the costs of direct materials in beginning work-in-process by the equivalent units in beginning work-in-process (remember that when the day begins, all 4,000 pounds in inventory are 100% done with respect to direct materials). The current-period conversion cost per unit is $1.45, based on dividing the total equivalent units of 48,400 for work done in terms of direct labor and manufacturing overhead into the total conversion costs of $70,180. Again, Allied's management can check their efforts to control conversion costs by comparing the current-period costs with the previous period's cost of $1.50 per pound, which is calculated by dividing conversion costs in beginning work-in-process by the work already done in beginning work-in-process when the month begins (800 equivalent pounds = 4,000 physical pounds × 20% "work done").

STEP 3. COMPUTE THE COSTS TRANSFERRED OUT Allied has spent a total of $79,840 in the current production period in the mixing center. In addition, when the production period began, there was work-in-process inventory in the mixing center that had a total value of $2,000. Hence, as you can see in the report above on product costs per unit, the mixing center needs to account for $81,840. Assuming that there has been no waste or pilferage in the mixing process, at the end of the production period all costs have either been transferred out to the bagging center or remain in ending work-in-process. To compute the costs transferred out to the bagging center, the mixing center needs to account for the costs of completing the cement in beginning work-in-process, as well as the cement that was started and completed in the current period. The following report shows the costs transferred out:

Step 3: Compute the costs transferred out.

	Cost per Unit	Equivalent Units	
Beginning work-in-process			
Initial direct materials costs			$ 800
Initial conversion costs			1,200
Costs to complete materials	$0.21	0	0
Costs to complete conversion	$1.45	3,200	4,640
Total			$ 6,640
Started and completed	$1.66	44,000	73,040
Total costs transferred out			**$79,680**

As you can see in the above report, the mixing center did not need to add any more direct materials costs to complete the beginning work-in-process. However, there were 3,200 equivalent units of work in terms of direct labor and manufacturing overhead that needed to be completed in the current period before the 4,000 pounds of cement in beginning work-in-process could be transferred out to the bagging center. Hence, the mixing department spent $4,640 in conversion costs ($1.45 per unit × 3,200 equivalent units) to complete the mixing on beginning work-in-process. When added to the initial beginning work-in-process costs of $2,000 ($800 + $1,200), the first 4,000 pounds of cement transferred to the bagging center carried total production costs of $6,640.

Of the total 48,000 pounds transferred to the bagging center, 44,000 pounds were started and completed in the current production period. At a total cost per unit of $1.66 ($0.21 per unit for direct materials + $1.45 per unit for direct labor and manufacturing overhead), the mixing department spent $73,040 to mix the remaining units transferred out of its operations in the current production period.

STEP 4. COMPUTE COSTS OF ENDING WORK-IN-PROCESS INVENTORY The fourth step in the mixing center's process costing effort is to determine the costs of the 2,000 pounds of cement remaining in work-in-process inventory at the end of the current production period. These calculations are reported below.

Step 4: Compute costs of ending work-in-process inventory.

	Cost per Unit	Equivalent Units	
Costs for direct materials.	$0.21	2,000	$ 420
Conversion costs.	$1.45	1,200	1,740
Cost of ending work-in-process.			**$2,160**

Because all 2,000 pounds are 100% complete in terms of direct materials, this inventory represents $420 ($0.21 per unit × 2,000 pounds × 100%) in direct materials costs. On the other hand, because these 2,000 pounds are only 60% complete in terms of direct labor and manufacturing overhead, there are $1,740 ($1.45 per unit × 2,000 pounds × 60%) in conversion costs residing in ending work-in-process inventory. In total, ending work-in-process contains $2,160 ($420 + $1,740) in product costs.

production cost report A document that compiles all the costs of a manufacturing center for a particular production period. The information on this report is used to control and evaluate production costs, as well as transfer costs and units of output from one manufacturing center to another.

STEP 5. PREPARE THE PRODUCTION COST REPORT All the data calculated so far are combined into the **production cost report** for the mixing center. This report is shown in Exhibit 3-13. As you can see, this report includes a large number of calculations. However, we've carefully worked through all the calculations in this report together, so you should feel fairly comfortable understanding how it all fits together. (You'll feel more comfortable once you've worked through the review problem at the end of this chapter and a few homework problems!) Remember that the report is composed of four overall steps, each of which should make sense to you.

When a lot of calculations are involved, as in the production cost report in Exhibit 3-13, a good check figure can be a wonderful tool! Notice in Exhibit 3-13 that the arrows point to a very good check figure—$81,840. This amount represents the total dollars that have gone into the mixing center in the current period ($2,000 in beginning work-in-process + $79,840 in current production costs), as well as the total dollars that have come out of the mixing process ($79,680 transferred out + $2,160 in ending work-in-process). If the production cost report can balance out to this check figure, you have good (though not perfect) assurance that the calculations have been done correctly.

to summarize

Process costing involves five steps: (1) determine the amount of "work done" (equivalents units of production) during the processing time period, (2) compute the product costs per unit by dividing total costs by "work done," (3)

exhibit 3-13 A Production Cost Report

Allied Cement Company
Mixing Center
Production Cost Report
For the Month of October 2003

Equivalent Units of Production

	Physical Units (pounds)	Direct Materials Costs: Percent Done	Direct Materials Costs: Equivalent Units	Conversion Costs: Percent Done	Conversion Costs: Equivalent Units
Beginning work-in-process	4,000	0%	0	80%	3,200
Started and completed	44,000	100%	44,000	100%	44,000
Ending work-in-process	2,000	100%	2,000	60%	1,200
Equivalent units of production			**46,000**		**48,400**
Transferred out	48,000				

Product Costs Per Unit

	Total Costs	Equivalent Units	Cost per Unit
Beginning work-in-process			
Direct materials costs	$ 800	4,000	$0.20
Conversion costs	1,200	800	1.50
Total	$ 2,000		**$1.70**
Current period			
Direct materials costs	$ 9,660	46,000	$0.21
Conversion costs	70,180	48,400	1.45
Total	$79,840		**$1.66**
TOTAL DOLLARS IN	**$81,840**		

Costs Transferred Out

	Cost per Unit	Equivalent Units	
Beginning work-in-process			
Initial direct materials costs			$ 800
Initial conversion costs			1,200
Costs to complete materials	$0.21	0	0
Costs to complete conversion	$1.45	3,200	4,640
Total			$ 6,640
Started and completed	$1.66	44,000	73,040
Total costs transferred out			**$79,680**

Costs of Ending Work-in-Process

	Cost per Unit	Equivalent Units	
Costs for direct materials	$0.21	2,000	$ 420
Conversion costs	$1.45	1,200	1,740
Cost of ending work-in-process			**$ 2,160**
TOTAL DOLLARS OUT			**$81,840**

compute the total cost of units completed and transferred out, (4) compute the total cost of units in ending work-in-process inventory, and (5) prepare the production cost report. With process costing, both units and costs must be transferred from one process center to the next until the final unit cost is accumulated at the end of the total production process. The production cost report provides a method of accounting for the flow of units and costs between process centers.

review of learning objectives

1 Understand the difficulty, yet importance, of having accurate product cost information. It is relatively easy to associate direct materials and direct labor costs with specific products. However, it is very difficult, and often even arbitrary, to assign overhead costs to specific products. Hence, it is difficult to accurately determine the cost of products because overhead costs have to be estimated before being incurred; they often cannot be easily assigned to units produced; and they are often "lumpy"—that is, overhead costs typically do not follow the same even flow pattern of production and service output as followed by direct materials and direct labor. Regardless of the difficulty, however, having accurate product cost information is critical for management to make good planning, controlling, and evaluation decisions.

2 Explain the flow of goods and services in a manufacturing organization and follow the accumulation of product costs in its accounting system. In a manufacturing firm, employees work with raw materials to make finished goods to be sold to customers. When purchased, raw materials are stored in a raw materials warehouse as raw materials inventory; as they are manufactured, goods move through the factory floor as work-in-process inventory; when completed, goods are stored in a finished goods warehouse as finished goods inventory. The costs of direct materials and direct labor (factory employees who work directly in production) are combined with manufacturing overhead costs as goods are being produced to make up the cost of finished goods. The process of tracing manufacturing costs to specific goods typically follows an accounting method traditionally known as job order costing. When a manufacturing firm purchases materials, the costs are recorded in a raw materials inventory account. As direct materials are used, costs are removed from this account and debited to Work-in-Process Inventory. Direct labor and manufacturing overhead costs are also debited to Work-in-Process Inventory. As units are completed, the costs in Work-in-Process Inventory are transferred to Finished Goods Inventory. When the units are sold, the costs are transferred to Cost of Goods Sold. Whereas direct materials and direct labor costs assigned to products are actual costs, manufacturing overhead is transferred to Work-in-Process Inventory and assigned to products on the basis of some predetermined overhead rate.

3 Understand the process of accounting for overhead. *Estimated* manufacturing overhead costs for a period are determined at the beginning of the period and combined with an estimated level of activity (such as direct labor hours) to create the predetermined overhead rate that is used to allocate overhead costs to products as they are produced. As *actual* manufacturing overhead costs are incurred, they are debited to Manufacturing Overhead. This account is credited (and Work-in-Process Inventory is debited) as overhead costs are applied to specific jobs on the basis of the predetermined rate. At the end of the period, if total *applied* manufacturing overhead costs are larger (smaller) than total *actual* manufacturing overhead costs, the manufacturing overhead account will have a credit (debit) balance, indicating that manufacturing overhead costs were overapplied (underapplied). The debit or credit balance in the manufacturing overhead account is either closed directly to Cost of Goods Sold or allocated among Cost of Goods Sold, Finished Goods Inventory, and Work-in-Process Inventory.

4 Explain the flow of goods and services in a merchandising organization and follow the accumulation of product costs in its accounting system. Manufacturers sell to large-scale wholesalers, who then sell to retailers, who then sell to the end-user customer. These interconnected business relationships are called a distribution channel. Within this system, wholesalers and retailers are the merchants who are most concerned with effectively managing the costs involved in the inventory movement along the distribution channel. Because merchants basically purchase inventory in a finished state, the process of accounting for inventory in a merchandising business is not nearly as complicated as it is in a manufacturing business.

5 Explain the flow of goods and services in a service organization and follow the accumulation of product costs in its accounting system. Essentially, a service business is any organization whose main economic activity involves producing a nonphysical product that provides value to a customer. As service industries have deregulated in the last few decades, increased competition has forced these companies to develop better cost management systems. There are a number of similarities between accounting for service organizations and accounting for manufacturing organizations. Although most service firms do not need to manage large investments in raw materials, some firms do have large investments in partially completed service projects and contracts. Partially completed service jobs require management accounting that is very similar to the process of accounting for work-in-process in manufacturing firms. Supplies, direct labor, and overhead costs accumulate in an account called Work-in-Process Services. This account performs much the same function as Work-in-Process Inventory in a manufacturing firm. In addition, as service activities take place, overhead is applied to Work-in-Process Services using a predetermined overhead application rate. When the firm has completed and delivered the contracted service, the relevant costs are transferred from Work-in-Process Services to Cost of Services (an account similar to the cost of goods sold account used by manufacturing and merchandising firms).

6 **Understand the impact of e-business on product costing.** As a result of the growth of e-business being conducted on the Internet, accountants and managers are experiencing tremendous change in the way business is conducted across all types of organizations (manufacturing, merchandising, and service). These changes in business processes are also dramatically changing the size of (and the process of managing) all three types of product costs, i.e., direct materials, direct labor, and overhead.

expanded material

7 **Use the FIFO method to do process costing.** Process costing involves five steps: (1) Identify units that went into the process and identify where those units are at the end of the processing time. Determine the amount of "work done" (equivalents units of production) during the processing time period. (2) Determine the amount of production costs that went into the process and compute the product costs per unit for the processing time period. (3) Compute the total cost of units completed and transferred out (costs of goods manufactured) during the processing time period. (4) Compute the total cost of units that remain in process (ending work-in-process inventory) at the end of the processing time period. (5) Prepare the production cost report. The production cost report provides unit cost data that are used to cost inventory as it transfers from one process center to the next and to cost the ending work-in-process inventory of each process center.

key terms and concepts

activity-based costing (ABC) 111
channel 127
cycle times 107
deregulation 133
estimated manufacturing overhead 122
finished goods inventory 113
inventory turnover (stockturns) 105
job cost sheet 116
job order costing 115
logistics 129
manufacturing organizations 106
manufacturing overhead rate 116
merchandising organizations 106
overapplied manufacturing overhead 125
predetermined overhead rate 119
raw materials inventory 113
retailers 129
service organizations 106
underapplied manufacturing overhead 125
wholesalers 129
work-in-process inventory 113

expanded material

conversion costs 145
equivalent units of production 143
process costing 143
production cost report 147

review problems

Job Order Costing

Salem Manufacturing Company applies manufacturing overhead costs on the basis of direct materials costs. The year 2003 estimates are:

Direct materials costs.	$300,000
Manufacturing overhead	180,000

For every dollar of direct materials costs, 60 cents of overhead is applied ($180,000 ÷ $300,000 = $0.60).

Following are the Salem Manufacturing Company transactions for 2003 (entries rounded to the nearest dollar):

a. Purchased materials for cash, $500,000.
b. Issued $400,000 of materials to production (80% direct, 20% indirect).
c. Incurred direct labor costs of $250,000.
d. Incurred indirect labor costs of $70,000.
e. Incurred costs for administrative and sales salaries of $70,000 and $60,000, respectively.
f. Incurred manufacturing overhead costs: property taxes on manufacturing plant, $6,000; plant utilities, $14,000; insurance on plant and equipment, $3,000. (Assume these expenses have not yet been paid.)
g. Recorded depreciation on manufacturing plant and equipment of $18,000 and $6,000, respectively.
h. Applied manufacturing overhead.
i. Transferred 65% of Work-in-Process Inventory to Finished Goods Inventory. Beginning Work-in-Process Inventory was $13,000.
j. Sold 90% of finished goods on account at a markup of 60% of cost. There was no beginning inventory of finished goods.
k. Closed the balance in Manufacturing Overhead to Cost of Goods Sold.

Required: Prepare a journal entry for each transaction.

Solution

a. Raw Materials Inventory	500,000	
Cash		500,000
Purchased raw materials.		
b. Manufacturing Overhead	80,000	
Work-in-Process Inventory	320,000	
Raw Materials Inventory		400,000
Issued materials to production.		
c. Work-in-Process Inventory	250,000	
Wages Payable (or Cash)		250,000
Incurred direct labor costs.		
d. Manufacturing Overhead	70,000	
Wages Payable (or Cash)		70,000
Incurred indirect labor costs.		
e. Salaries Expense, Administrative	70,000	
Salaries Expense, Sales	60,000	
Salaries Payable (or Cash)		130,000
Incurred sales and administrative salaries expense.		
f. Manufacturing Overhead	23,000	
Property Taxes Payable		6,000
Utilities Payable		14,000
Insurance Payable		3,000
Incurred manufacturing overhead costs.		
g. Manufacturing Overhead	24,000	
Accumulated Depreciation—Plant		18,000
Accumulated Depreciation—Equipment		6,000
Recorded depreciation on plant and equipment.		
h. Work-in-Process Inventory	192,000	
Manufacturing Overhead		192,000*
Applied manufacturing overhead to Work-in-Process Inventory.		

*The predetermined overhead rate is equal to estimated total manufacturing overhead divided by estimated direct materials costs ($180,000 ÷ $300,000), or 60% of direct materials costs. In this case, $192,000 ($320,000 × 0.60) is applied because direct materials costs were $320,000 ($400,000 × 0.80).

i. Finished Goods Inventory	503,750	
Work-in-Process Inventory		503,750*
Transferred Work-in-Process Inventory to Finished Goods Inventory (0.65 × $775,000).		

*The amount transferred is determined as follows:

Work-in-Process Inventory

Beginning Balance	13,000		
(b)	320,000		
(c)	250,000		
(h)	192,000		
	775,000	(i)	503,750
Ending Balance	271,250		

j. Accounts Receivable	725,400	
Sales		725,400*
Cost of Goods Sold	453,375*	
Finished Goods Inventory		453,375
Sold 90% of Finished Goods Inventory.		

*Because Finished Goods Inventory is $503,750 (i), Cost of Goods Sold is $453,375 ($503,750 × 0.90). Because Finished Goods Inventory is marked up 60%, Sales is $725,400 ($453,375 × 1.6).

k. Cost of Goods Sold	5,000	
Manufacturing Overhead		5,000*
Closed underapplied manufacturing overhead.		

*The amount of underapplied manufacturing overhead is determined as follows:

Manufacturing Overhead

Actual Overhead	(b)	80,000	(h)	192,000	Applied Overhead
	(d)	70,000			
	(f)	23,000			
	(g)	24,000			
	Balance	5,000			

Accounting for Overhead in a Service Business

Columbus & Hercules, a public accounting firm, is computing the overhead rates to use when billing customers and bidding on jobs. Columbus & Hercules provides the following estimates relating to overhead costs for the year 2003:

Utilities	$ 12,000
Rent	30,000
Equipment depreciation	22,000
Office supplies	20,000
Support staff salaries	120,000
Total estimated overhead costs	$204,000

In addition, Columbus & Hercules offers the following annual estimates (based on a 50-week work year) regarding the salaries and estimated hours associated with the professionals employed by the firm:

Position	Total Estimated Salaries	Total Estimated Billable Hours
Partners (2 × $100,000)	$200,000	4,400
Managers (3 × $70,000)	210,000	6,600
Seniors (6 × $50,000)	300,000	13,200
Staff auditors (10 × $25,000)	250,000	22,000

Columbus & Hercules computes a chargeable hourly rate for each position that is the sum of the following: (1) each position's hourly rate (based on salary), (2) an overhead rate, and (3) a markup of 20% of (1) and (2). The overhead rate allocates estimated overhead costs to each position, then relates the allocated costs to the hours expected to be worked by each position. Travel and materials costs are directly traceable and billed to each job.

Columbus & Hercules has no client projects in process on January 1, 2003. During January of 2003, Columbus & Hercules worked on several auditing and accounting jobs and incurred the following costs:

Jan. 1 Paid rent for January, $2,500.
4 Purchased office supplies on account, $1,200.
9 Paid $4,500 for payables from last year.
15 Paid office support salaries, $5,000.
15 Paid biweekly salaries of professionals: partners, $8,000; managers, $8,400; seniors, $12,000; staff, $10,000.
15 Applied overhead costs based on billable hours: partners, 170 hours; managers, 270 hours; seniors, 500 hours; staff, 900 hours.
18 Used office supplies totaling $800 to prepare client materials.
21 Purchased office supplies on account, $1,100.
25 Received and paid invoice from office supply store for purchase on January 4.
27 Billed clients for the following jobs using the computed hourly rate for each position:

	Job #1	Job #2
Partner	90 hours	80 hours
Manager	150 hours	140 hours
Senior	320 hours	200 hours
Staff	560 hours	400 hours

27 Transferred costs from Work-in-Process Services to Cost of Services based on information from January 27.
31 Estimated utility costs for the month of January to be $1,000.
31 Paid office support salaries, $5,400.
31 Recognized depreciation of office equipment, $1,900.
31 Paid biweekly salaries of professionals: partners, $8,000; managers, $8,400; seniors, $12,000; staff, $10,000.
31 Applied overhead costs based on billable hours: partners, 180 hours; managers, 280 hours; seniors, 525 hours; staff, 950 hours.

Required:

1. Compute the billing rate to be used for each position.
2. Provide the journal entries made by Columbus & Hercules for January.
3. Compute the ending balance in Work-in-Process Services.
4. Compute the ending balance in Overhead.

Solution

1. Billing rate

Overhead allocation rate: $204,000 ÷ $960,000 = $0.2125 per dollar of salary.

Position	Estimated Salaries	Preliminary Rate	Allocated Overhead	Billable Hours	Overhead Rate per Hour
Partner	$200,000	$0.2125	$ 42,500	4,400	$9.66
Manager	210,000	0.2125	44,625	6,600	6.76
Senior	300,000	0.2125	63,750	13,200	4.83
Staff	250,000	0.2125	53,125	22,000	2.41
Total	$960,000		$204,000		

		Billable Rate for Each Position		
Position	**Hourly Rate (1)**	**Overhead Rate (2)**	**Markup [(1) + (2)] × 0.20 = (3)**	**Billable Rate (1) + (2) + (3)**
Partner	$45.45[1]	$9.66	$11.02	$66.13
Manager	31.82[2]	6.76	7.72	46.30
Senior	22.73[3]	4.83	5.51	33.07
Staff	11.36[4]	2.41	2.75	16.52

[1]$200,000 ÷ 4,400 hours = $45.45 per hour
[2]$210,000 ÷ 6,600 hours = $31.82 per hour
[3]$300,000 ÷ 13,200 hours = $22.73 per hour
[4]$250,000 ÷ 22,000 hours = $11.36 per hour

2. Journal entries

Date	Account	Debit	Credit
Jan. 1	Overhead	2,500	
	Cash		2,500
	Paid rent for the month of January.		
4	Office Supplies	1,200	
	Accounts Payable		1,200
	Purchased office supplies on account.		
9	Accounts Payable	4,500	
	Cash		4,500
	Paid accounts payable from prior period.		
15	Overhead	5,000	
	Cash		5,000
	Paid office support salaries.		
15	Work-in-Process Services	38,400	
	Cash		38,400
	Paid salaries of professionals.		

Partners	$ 8,000
Managers	8,400
Seniors	12,000
Staff	10,000
Total	$38,400

Date	Account	Debit	Credit
15	Work-in-Process Services	8,051	
	Overhead		8,051
	Allocated overhead based on billable hours.		

Partners—170 hours × $9.66	$1,642
Managers—270 hours × $6.76	1,825
Seniors—500 hours × $4.83	2,415
Staff—900 hours × $2.41	2,169
Total	$8,051

Date	Account	Debit	Credit
18	Work-in-Process Services	800	
	Office Supplies		800
	Used office supplies on behalf of clients.		
21	Office Supplies	1,100	
	Accounts Payable		1,100
	Purchased office supplies on account.		
25	Accounts Payable	1,200	
	Cash		1,200
	Paid for supplies purchased on January 4.		

		Debit	Credit
27	Accounts Receivable	57,724	
	Service Revenue		57,724
	Billed clients for Jobs #1 and #2.		

Partners—170 hours × $66.13	$11,242
Managers—290 hours × $46.30	13,427
Seniors—520 hours × $33.07	17,196
Staff—960 hours × $16.52	15,859
Total	$57,724

		Debit	Credit
27	Cost of Services	48,107	
	Work-in-Process Services		48,107
	Transferred completed work in process to cost of services; comprised of each position's hourly rate and overhead rate.		

Partners—170 hours × ($45.45 + $9.66)	$ 9,369
Managers—290 hours × ($31.82 + $6.76)	11,188
Seniors—520 hours × ($22.73 + $4.83)	14,331
Staff—960 hours × ($11.36 + $2.41)	13,219
Total	$48,107

		Debit	Credit
31	Overhead	1,000	
	Utilities Payable		1,000
	To record estimated utilities expense for the month.		
31	Overhead	5,400	
	Cash		5,400
	Paid office support salaries.		
31	Overhead	1,900	
	Accumulated Depreciation—Office Equipment		1,900
	To record depreciation expense for the month.		
31	Work-in-Process Services	38,400	
	Cash		38,400
	Paid salaries of professionals.		

Partners	$ 8,000
Managers	8,400
Seniors	12,000
Staff	10,000
Total	$38,400

		Debit	Credit
31	Work-in-Process Services	8,458	
	Overhead		8,458
	Allocated overhead based on billable hours.		

Partners—180 hours × $9.66	$1,739
Managers—280 hours × $6.76	1,893
Seniors—525 hours × $4.83	2,536
Staff—950 hours × $2.41	2,290
Total	$8,458

3. Ending balance in Work-in-Process Services

Work-in-Process Services

1/15	38,400	1/27	48,107
1/15	8,051		
1/18	800		
1/31	38,400		
1/31	8,458		
End. bal.	46,002		

4. Ending balance in Overhead

Overhead			
1/1	2,500	1/15	8,051
1/15	5,000	1/31	8,458
1/31	1,000		
1/31	5,400		
1/31	1,900		
		End. bal. (overapplied)	709

expanded material

Process Costing

Cleveland Enterprises produces flour in a continuous manufacturing process. The flour is mixed in one step and transferred to the finished goods department. At the beginning of September, Cleveland had 1,600 bags of flour in process (100% complete as to materials and 20% complete as to processing) that held $2,800 in costs of direct materials and $800 in conversion costs. During September, 20,000 bags of flour were placed into production, and by the end of the month, only 2,000 bags of flour remained in process (100% complete as to materials and 30% complete as to processing). Production costs for September are as follows:

Direct materials	$36,000
Conversion costs	47,712

Required:

1. Prepare the production cost report for September.
2. Prepare the journal entries required to record the production of flour and the transfer of the finished bags to finished goods inventory. Assume that the processing costs are 75% direct labor and 25% manufacturing overhead.

Solution 1. Production cost report

Cleveland Enterprises
Production Cost Report
For the Month of September

EQUIVALENT UNITS OF PRODUCTION

		Direct Materials Costs		Conversion Costs	
	Physical Units	**Percent Done**	**Equivalent Units**	**Percent Done**	**Equivalent Units**
Beginning work-in-process	1,600	0%	0	80%	1,280
Started and completed	18,000	100%	18,000	100%	18,000
Ending work-in-process	2,000	100%	2,000	30%	600
Equivalent units of production			**20,000**		**19,880**
Transferred out	19,600				

PRODUCT COSTS PER UNIT

	Total Costs	Equivalent Units	Cost per Unit
Beginning work-in-process			
Direct materials costs	$ 2,800	1,600	$1.75
Conversion costs	800	320	2.50
Total	$ 3,600		**$4.25**
Current period			
Direct materials costs	$36,000	20,000	$1.80
Conversion costs	47,712	19,880	2.40
Total	$83,712		**$4.20**
TOTAL DOLLARS IN	**$87,312**		

COSTS TRANSFERRED OUT

	Cost per Unit	Equivalent Units	
Beginning work-in-process			
Initial direct materials costs			$ 2,800
Initial conversion costs			800
Costs to complete materials	$1.80	0	0
Costs to complete conversion	$2.40	1,280	3,072
Total			$ 6,672
Started and completed	$4.20	18,000	75,600
Total costs transferred out			**$82,272**

COSTS OF ENDING WORK-IN-PROCESS

	Cost per Unit	Equivalent Units	
Costs for direct materials	$1.80	2,000	$ 3,600
Conversion costs	$2.40	600	1,440
Cost of ending work-in-process			**$ 5,040**
TOTAL DOLLARS OUT			**$87,312**

2. Journal entries

Work-in-Process Inventory	36,000	
Direct Materials Inventory		36,000
Transferred direct materials to work-in-process inventory.		
Work-in-Process Inventory	47,712	
Wages Payable		35,784
Manufacturing Overhead		11,928
To record the department's payroll costs and applied manufacturing overhead ($47,712 × 75% = $35,784; $47,712 × 25% = $11,928).		
Finished Goods Inventory	82,272	
Work-in-Process Inventory		82,272
Transferred finished goods to the finished goods inventory.		

discussion questions

1. Why do managers need accurate product cost information?
2. For financial reporting, which costs are usually included as product costs in a manufacturing company?
3. Why should a firm know how much it costs to produce its goods and services?
4. How can companies improve quality while also reducing product costs?
5. Why is it difficult to track the costs of manufactured products?
6. What is the difference in the accounting treatment for direct materials and indirect materials?
7. Why are actual manufacturing overhead costs not assigned directly to products as they are incurred?
8. What is the normal flow of costs in a job order costing system?
9. What are some common bases for applying manufacturing overhead costs to products?
10. Why might Manufacturing Overhead be referred to as a "clearing account"?
11. How does a firm dispose of over- or underapplied overhead costs?
12. What is the difference between a manufacturing company and a merchandising company? Between a merchandising company and a service company?
13. What does a distribution channel consist of?
14. What is a service organization?
15. What effect does deregulation have on the service industry?

16. Name three ways in which the service industry differs from the manufacturing industry.
17. What is the principal "product cost" for a service company?
18. Which three costs go into the work-in-process services account for a service company? How does this account differ between service and manufacturing firms?
19. What similarities and differences exist among the costs of merchandising, manufacturing, and service firms?
20. Should managers concentrate only on the costs of production (e.g., the cost of goods sold), or should they also consider other costs and factors?

expanded material

21. What is the major difference between job order costing and process costing?
22. What two conditions generally exist for process costing to be appropriate?
23. What are the five steps involved in employing process costing?
24. What is meant by the term "equivalent units of production"?

discussion cases

CASE 3-1

PACKARD, INC.

Packard, Inc., produces and sells mousetraps. The cost of a mousetrap can be broken down as follows:

Direct materials	$0.23
Direct labor	0.09
Manufacturing overhead	0.12
Cost per trap	$0.44

The traps are then sold for 120% of cost, or $0.53 each. The manufacturing overhead is applied based on direct labor costs and was computed at the beginning of the year using the following estimates:

Estimated manufacturing overhead for the period	$540,000
Estimated direct labor costs	405,000
Predetermined overhead rate (per direct labor dollar)	1.33

During the year, several changes in the production process were made. As a result, expected manufacturing overhead costs have been significantly reduced below the original estimate of $540,000. For the first six months of the year, overhead costs of $272,000 were actually incurred. For that same time period, actual direct labor costs were $204,000. For the last six months of the year, overhead costs are expected to be $225,000, and direct labor costs are expected to be $202,500.

1. What changes (if any) should be made in the predetermined manufacturing overhead rate for Packard, Inc.?
2. Assuming that direct materials and direct labor costs will remain the same for the last six months of the year, determine the new cost of a single mousetrap.
3. Because the cost of producing mousetraps dropped during the second half of the year, Packard can reduce the price of its traps and still earn its 20% markup on cost. Should the company reduce the price of its mousetraps? What factors would affect your decision?

CASE 3-2

US MACDONALD CORPORATION

You work for US MacDonald Corporation (USMC), an airplane manufacturer. USMC makes airplanes for commercial airlines, such as **UNITED**, **AMERICAN**, and **DELTA**, and for the **U.S. AIR FORCE**. Many parts are common to all planes made by USMC. The market for commercial planes is extremely competitive with **GENERAL DYNAMICS**, **LOCKHEED**, and European manufacturer **AIRBUS** often bidding lower than USMC. However, USMC's contract with the Air Force allows it to bill them at cost plus a 9% profit.

Times have been tough lately for USMC. In fact, if you can't find a way to increase profits, the company may have to lay off 5,000 employees.

A colleague has just presented you with an idea that he believes will increase profits. He suggests that instead of using direct labor hours to allocate overhead costs among airplanes, you should allocate costs on the basis of the number of each type of airplane made. Because you make far more, smaller, less expensive planes for the Air Force, more of the overhead costs will be allocated to those planes. This action will not only decrease your cost per unit on commercial planes (allowing you to be competitive in that market), but will also increase your profits on Air Force planes because the cost per plane will be higher.

You are not sure about your colleague's suggested action. You do know that your allocation base of direct labor hours is quite arbitrary and probably does not correspond well to the way overhead costs are consumed.

1. What is an appropriate allocation basis? Would adopting the suggestion be ethical?
2. Would you change your mind if you learned that competitors were allocating overhead on the basis of number of each type of plane made?
3. Is your action appropriate, from both a business and an ethical point of view, if direct labor hours is not an accurate allocation base?

CASE 3-3

THE DISTRIBUTION CHANNEL

You have just been hired as a branch manager for Perkins Retailers, a chain of office-supply stores in the Midwest. Perkins often purchases inventory items from Walker Wholesalers, a local distributor. However, Perkins also has the option of purchasing directly from various manufacturers, all of whom ensure prompt delivery. A comparative price list is as follows:

Lined paper:	
Gates Paper Manufacturers	$ 0.25
Walker Wholesalers	0.35
Steno chairs:	
Sturdychairs Manufacturers	$27.80
Walker Wholesalers	30.00
Desk lamps:	
Illumination Manufacturers	$ 7.60
Walker Wholesalers	11.25
Day planners:	
Olsen Manufacturers	$12.50
Walker Wholesalers	15.40

While examining past purchase invoices, you are perplexed to discover that despite the significantly higher prices, the previous branch manager had made most of his purchases from Walker Wholesalers.

1. Why might the previous branch manager have purchased from Walker Wholesalers when purchasing directly from the manufacturers is less expensive?
2. Why do wholesalers need to charge higher prices than manufacturers? Are they justified from the customers' point of view?
3. Will you, the new branch manager, always purchase from the manufacturers? Why or why not?

CASE 3-4

SERVICE COST FLOWS

The CPA firm you work for has just been hired by Phillips Attorneys at Law to perform an audit. In the process of the audit, you notice that Phillips' accountant has been inconsistent in accounting for the company president's salary. You notice that sometimes he has accounted for the company president's salary as follows:

Overhead	20,000	
Salaries and Wages Payable		20,000
To record the company president's salary.		

Other times, the accountant has debited Salaries and Wages Expense instead of Overhead. When you confront the accountant about the inconsistency, he gets somewhat defensive and says that it doesn't matter which method is used because both methods result in an expense; net income will be the same either way.

1. Assuming that the company president's tasks are exclusively administrative, do you agree with the accountant? Why or why not?
2. Which journal entry is correct? Why?

EXERCISE 3-1

MANUFACTURING COSTS

Springville Manufacturing Company uses a job order costing system. For Job #151, the production manager requisitioned $1,200 of direct materials and used 40 hours of direct labor at $18 per hour. Manufacturing overhead is applied on the basis of direct labor hours, using a predetermined overhead rate. At the beginning of the year, $800,000 of manufacturing overhead costs were estimated based on a forecast of 200,000 direct labor hours. Prepare a summary of the costs for Job #151. (*Note:* You have to calculate the predetermined overhead rate.)

EXERCISE 3-2

MANUFACTURING COSTS

The Make-It-Right Company manufactures special wheelchairs for handicapped athletes. The company uses a job order costing system. Partial data for a particular job include:

Direct materials	$450
Direct labor	375
Manufacturing overhead	?
Total cost	$?

The company allocates manufacturing overhead on the basis of direct labor hours. The estimated total manufacturing costs for the year are $750,000, and the total estimated direct labor hours are 150,000. Factory workers are paid $15 per hour.

1. Compute the predetermined manufacturing overhead rate.
2. What is the allocated manufacturing overhead cost and the total cost of the above referenced job?

EXERCISE 3-3

PREDETERMINED MANUFACTURING OVERHEAD RATES

Memphis Corporation uses a job order costing system. Thus, management must establish a predetermined overhead rate for applying manufacturing overhead. During the past three years, the following data have been accumulated:

	2001	2002	2003
Direct labor hours	40,000	52,000	65,000
Machine hours	80,000	65,000	45,000
Direct materials costs	$400,000	$250,000	$390,000
Total budgeted manufacturing overhead	$80,000	$65,000	$45,000

1. What would the predetermined overhead rate be for each of the three years, if based on (a) direct labor hours, (b) machine hours, (c) direct materials costs?
2. **Interpretive Question:** Which allocation basis would you recommend be used in the future for applying manufacturing overhead? Why?

EXERCISE 3-4

PREDETERMINED MANUFACTURING OVERHEAD RATES

East Lake Corporation uses a job order costing system and applies manufacturing overhead using a predetermined overhead rate. The following data are available for the past two years.

	2002	2003
Direct labor hours	104,000	130,000
Direct materials costs	$500,000	$780,000
Machine hours	100,000	70,000
Total budgeted manufacturing overhead	$130,000	$90,000

1. Compute the predetermined overhead rate for each of the two years, based on (a) direct labor hours, (b) direct materials costs, and (c) machine hours.
2. **Interpretive Question:** Which allocation basis would you recommend for applying manufacturing overhead? Why?

EXERCISE 3-5

WORK-IN-PROCESS ANALYSIS IN A MANUFACTURING ORGANIZATION

Matt Jones, a recently hired internal auditor, is currently auditing the work-in-process inventory account. Matt has forgotten some basic cost accounting concepts and asks for your assistance. Identify the four types of transactions or events that affect the work-in-process inventory account in a manufacturing organization. Prepare and explain a sample journal entry for each type of transaction.

EXERCISE 3-6

FLOW OF MANUFACTURING COSTS

Post the following cost data to the appropriate T-accounts to trace the flow of costs from the time they are incurred until the product is completed and sold. (Assume that purchases and expenses are credited to Cash or Accounts Payable.)

a.	Direct materials purchased	$ 60,000
b.	Direct materials used	50,000
c.	Indirect materials purchased	9,000
d.	Indirect materials used	7,000
e.	Wages payable, direct	60,000
f.	Wages payable, indirect	12,000
g.	Selling and administrative expenses	32,000
h.	Actual manufacturing overhead costs other than indirect materials and indirect labor	25,000
i.	Manufacturing overhead applied	40,000
j.	Work-in-process completed	120,000
k.	Finished goods sold	135,000

Raw Materials Inventory

Beg. Bal. 9,000 |

Manufacturing Overhead

Work-in-Process Inventory

Beg. Bal. 30,000 |

Finished Goods Inventory

Beg. Bal. 20,000 |

Cash (Accounts Payable)

Wages Payable

Cost of Goods Sold

Selling and Administrative Expenses

EXERCISE 3-7

APPLYING MANUFACTURING OVERHEAD

Newstar Company has four manufacturing subsidiaries: A, B, C, and D. Each subsidiary keeps a separate set of accounting records. Manufacturing cost forecasts for 2003 for each subsidiary are:

	Subsidiaries			
	A	B	C	D
Materials to be used (lb.)	80,000	80,000	60,000	52,500
Direct labor hours	30,000	40,000	25,000	40,000
Direct labor costs	$12,000	$10,000	$3,750	$7,000
Machine hours	25,000	15,000	9,500	40,000
Manufacturing overhead	$30,000	$45,000	$20,000	$50,000

The predetermined overhead rates for each subsidiary are based on the following:

Subsidiary A: Machine hours
Subsidiary B: Direct labor costs
Subsidiary C: Materials to be used
Subsidiary D: Direct labor hours

1. Compute the predetermined overhead rate to be used in 2003 by each subsidiary.
2. If Subsidiary B actually had $8,000 of direct labor costs and $37,500 of manufacturing overhead, will overhead be over- or underapplied and by how much?
3. If Subsidiary C used 66,000 pounds of materials in 2003, what will be the applied manufacturing overhead?
4. **Interpretive Question:** Identify the two most commonly used methods to dispose of under- or overapplied manufacturing overhead. What is the major advantage of each method?

EXERCISE 3-8

APPLYING MANUFACTURING OVERHEAD

Valtec Company has three manufacturing divisions: A, B, and C. Each division has its own job order costing system and forecasts the following manufacturing costs for the year 2003:

	Division		
	A	B	C
Materials to be used (lb.)	120,000	100,000	80,000
Direct labor hours	45,000	60,000	25,000
Machine hours	40,000	25,000	15,000
Total budgeted manufacturing overhead	$50,000	$70,000	$45,000

The predetermined overhead rates for each division are based on the following:

Division A: Machine hours
Division B: Materials to be used
Division C: Direct labor hours

1. Compute the predetermined overhead rate to be used in 2003 by each division.
2. If Division A actually had 37,000 machine hours and $49,000 of manufacturing overhead, will overhead be over- or underapplied and by how much?
3. If Division B used 95,000 pounds of materials in 2003, what will be the applied manufacturing overhead?
4. **Interpretive Question:** Of the two commonly used methods to dispose of over- or underapplied manufacturing overhead, which method would you recommend and why?

EXERCISE 3-9

ASSIGNING MANUFACTURING COSTS TO JOBS

Noah Manufacturing Company uses a job order costing system. All relevant information for Jobs #609 and #610, which were completed during June, is provided here. No other jobs were in process during the month of June.

	Job #609	Job #610
Direct materials cost	$5,000	$6,500
Direct labor cost	$3,900	$5,400
Direct labor hours on job	400	700
Units produced	500	875

A predetermined overhead rate of $6 per direct labor hour is used to apply manufacturing overhead costs to jobs. Actual manufacturing overhead for the month of June totaled $9,000. All completed products are delivered to customers immediately after completion, so costs are transferred directly to Cost of Goods Sold without going through Finished Goods Inventory.

1. How much manufacturing overhead will be assigned to each job completed during June?
2. Compute the total cost of each job.
3. Compute the unit cost for each job.
4. Compute the over- or underapplied manufacturing overhead for June.
5. Prepare the journal entries to transfer the cost of direct materials, direct labor, and manufacturing overhead to Work-in-Process Inventory and to transfer the cost of completed jobs to Cost of Goods Sold. (Omit explanations.)
6. **Interpretive Question:** How would the company have computed its predetermined overhead rate of $6 per direct labor hour? Explain.

EXERCISE 3-10

ASSIGNING MANUFACTURING COSTS TO JOBS

Remington Company uses predetermined overhead rates in assigning manufacturing overhead costs to jobs. The rates are based on machine hours in the Machining Department and on direct labor hours in the Assembly Department. Estimated costs, machine hours, and direct labor hours for the year in each department are:

	Machining	Assembly
Direct labor cost	$64,000	$100,000
Manufacturing overhead	$90,000	$50,000
Direct labor hours	12,000	32,000
Machine hours	18,000	2,500

During the month of April, Job #402X had the following data for 50 completed units of product:

	Machining	Assembly
Direct materials cost	$400	$700
Direct labor cost	$650	$2,300
Direct labor hours	120	740
Machine hours	900	80

1. What predetermined overhead rates would be used by the company in assigning manufacturing overhead costs to Job #402X in machining and in assembly? (*Note:* You should round all rates you calculate to two decimal places.)
2. Using the overhead rates you calculated in (1), how much manufacturing overhead is applied to Job #402X?
3. What is the unit cost for Job #402X? (Round the unit cost to two decimal places.)

EXERCISE 3-11

ANALYZING MANUFACTURING COSTS

The following T-accounts represent inventory costs as of December 31, 2003:

Raw Materials Inventory

Debit		Credit
Bal. 12/31/02	140,000	400,000
	350,000	
Bal. 12/31/03	90,000	

Finished Goods Inventory

Debit		Credit
Bal. 12/31/02	79,000	673,000
	700,000	
Bal. 12/31/03	106,000	

Work-in-Process Inventory

Debit		Credit
Bal. 12/31/02	25,000	700,000
	400,000	
	249,000	
	172,000	
Bal. 12/31/03	146,000	

Manufacturing Overhead

Debit	Credit
49,000	249,000
52,000	
60,000	
72,000	

1. Determine the direct labor costs for 2003.
2. Determine the cost of goods manufactured for 2003.
3. Determine the cost of goods sold for 2003.
4. Compute over- or underapplied manufacturing overhead for 2003.
5. Determine actual indirect manufacturing costs for 2003.

EXERCISE 3-12

SERVICE COST FLOWS

Xavier & Associates Law Firm estimated its total overhead costs for 2003 to be $1.8 million. It allocates overhead based on direct labor hours. Xavier employs a total of 11 attorneys, each working an average of 2,000 hours per year. The average annual salary for Xavier attorneys is $140,000, or approximately $70 per hour. Xavier attorneys worked a total of 23 hours and used $150 of supplies in doing work for Mr. Bailey, one of Xavier's clients.

1. What is Xavier's overhead rate?
2. Prepare the journal entry to record the overhead for the Bailey job.
3. Prepare the journal entry to record the cost of supplies for the Bailey job.
4. Prepare the journal entry to record the cost of labor for the Bailey job.

EXERCISE 3-13

SERVICE COST FLOWS

Pierce Engineers incurred the following costs in 2003:

Use of supplies for clients	$ 3,500
Utilities	8,000
Property taxes	12,000
Engineers' salaries	100,000
Support staff salaries	35,000
Applied overhead	50,000

Prepare the journal entries to account for the costs given. Close the overhead account to Cost of Services.

EXERCISE 3-14

PREDETERMINED SERVICE OVERHEAD RATES

The following data are available for Haul-It-Away Truckers:

	2002	2003
Budgeted direct labor hours	135,000	140,000
Planned number of moving jobs	300	310
Total miles to be driven	450,000	597,000
Total budgeted overhead	$900,000	$1,200,000

1. Compute the predetermined overhead rate for each of the two years, if based on (a) direct labor hours, (b) number of moving jobs, and (c) total miles driven.
2. **Interpretive Question:** Which allocation basis would you recommend for applying overhead? Why?

EXERCISE 3-15

APPLYING OVERHEAD

Lemon Schools teaches private drivers' education courses. It applies overhead based on instructor hours, i.e., direct labor hours. The following information was forecasted for 2003:

Direct labor	$360,000
Property tax on cars	$3,600
Supplies	$12,000
Rent	$24,000
Support staff salaries	$160,000
Instructor hours	24,000

1. Calculate the predetermined overhead rate for 2003.
2. If Lemon actually had 23,000 instructor hours and spent $170,000 on overhead, will overhead be under- or overapplied for 2003? By how much?

EXERCISE 3-16

SERVICE COSTS

The following information is available for a particular job performed by Newland Business Consultants in 2003:

Direct labor	$4,000
Supplies	500
Overhead	?
Total cost	$?

Newland applies overhead on the basis of consulting hours, i.e., direct labor hours. The estimated total overhead costs for 2003 are $6.2 million, and the estimated total consulting hours are 150,000. Newland pays its consultants $40 per hour.

1. Compute the predetermined overhead rate.
2. What are the allocated overhead cost and the total cost of this particular job?

expanded material

EXERCISE 3-17

EQUIVALENT UNITS—PROCESS COSTING

Assume that you are the owner and sole employee of a bicycle service business that you run out of your home. Currently, you are running a spring special on a "super maintenance service" on bikes. The maintenance service you offer is quite comprehensive and includes (among other things) adjusting gears and brakes, cleaning and greasing all moving parts, "trueing" both wheels, and touching up the paint. It takes about 45 minutes to an hour to complete a bike. With the great price you're offering on this service, you immediately find yourself with about five days of customer order backlog. To catch up, you decide to spend the next week working solely on the "super maintenance service." Further, you want to track your output to see if you can improve the amount of maintenance work you do each of the next five days.

When you come to work the following Monday, you have one bike that is about 70% complete. At the end of the week, the results are as follows:

	Total Bikes Completed Each Day	End-of-Day Bike in Process
Monday	8	60% complete
Tuesday	8	90% complete
Wednesday	10	20% complete
Thursday	9	90% complete
Friday	10	10% complete

How much work did you get done each day? In other words, how many equivalent units of production did you have each day?

EXERCISE 3-18

EQUIVALENT UNITS AND UNIT COSTS—PROCESS COSTING

A large factory that manufactures wooden furniture has several assembly lines. One of the assembly lines is dedicated to assembly of wooden kitchen chairs. All raw materials necessary to complete each chair are requisitioned from the raw materials warehouse at the time each chair starts production on the assembly line. The following data relate to one week of production:

Beginning Work-in-Process
40 chairs; 80% complete; $350 in direct materials costs; $320 in conversion costs

Ending Work-in-Process
60 chairs; 40% complete

Current Week
550 chairs started and completed; $4,880 requisitioned from raw materials warehouse, $5,820 incurred in conversion costs

1. Compute the equivalent units of production for both direct materials and conversion costs for the week.
2. Compute the total production cost per chair for the week on the assembly line.
3. How does this week's production cost on the assembly line compare to last week's production cost?

EXERCISE 3-19

EQUIVALENT UNITS AND UNIT COSTS—PROCESS COSTING

Savana Corporation began producing "quick-stick glue" in April 2003 (i.e., there was no beginning work-in-process inventory on April 1). The manufacturing process involves only one step. In April, the costs were $8,000 for direct materials and $6,216 for conversion costs. During the month, 6,400 pounds of direct materials were placed in production. At the end of April, 1,200 pounds of direct materials were still being processed and were 60% complete. Assume that all direct materials are added at the beginning of production.

1. Compute the number of equivalent units of output in terms of materials costs and labor and overhead (conversion) costs for April, assuming FIFO cost flow.
2. Determine the total cost of goods transferred to Finished Goods Inventory and the total cost of Work-in-Process Inventory at the end of April.

problems

PROBLEM 3-1

JOB ORDER COSTING IN A MANUFACTURING ORGANIZATION—JOURNAL ENTRIES

Following are transactions for Montigo Manufacturing Company. Assume that the company has no beginning work-in-process inventory.

1. Montigo purchased $600,000 of raw materials, paying 10% down, with the remainder to be paid in 10 days.
2. The production manager requisitioned $260,000 of materials (90% for direct use and the remainder for indirect purposes).
3. The liability incurred in (1) was paid in full.
4. 24,000 hours of direct labor and 2,000 hours of indirect labor were incurred. (Assume an average hourly wage rate of $9 for both direct and indirect labor.)
5. The following salaries were paid:

Factory supervisor (a product cost)	$80,000
Administrative executives	70,000
Sales personnel	90,000

6. Rent and utilities for the building of $30,000 and $7,000, respectively, were paid. Three-fourths of these expenses are applicable to manufacturing and the remainder to administration.
7. Depreciation on factory equipment was $15,000.
8. Advertising costs for the year totaled $15,000.
9. Manufacturing overhead is applied at a rate of $6.90 per direct labor hour.
10. All but $35,000 of Work-in-Process Inventory was completed and transferred to Finished Goods Inventory.
11. The sales price of finished goods that were sold was 130% of manufacturing costs. Assume a perpetual inventory system and that all finished goods were sold.
12. Close over- or underapplied overhead directly to cost of goods sold.

Required: Prepare journal entries for the transactions.

PROBLEM 3-2

ACCOUNTING FOR MANUFACTURING TRANSACTIONS—JOURNAL ENTRIES

Payson Company uses a job order costing system. The following is a partial list of the company's accounts. (*Note:* Additional accounts may be needed.)

Cash
Manufacturing Overhead
Sales
Cost of Goods Sold
Sales Commissions Expense
Administrative Expenses
Accounts Receivable
Commissions Payable

Required:

1. Prepare journal entries for each of the following transactions (omit explanations).
2. Prepare T-accounts and post the journal entries to the T-accounts. Transaction (a) has been completed as an example.
   a. Raw materials previously purchased on account were paid for in cash, $700.

Cash				Accounts Payable	
	(a)	700	(a)	700	

   b. Raw materials were purchased for $1,500 on account.
   c. Direct labor costs of $3,000 were recorded.
   d. Direct materials costing $1,100 were issued directly to production.
   e. Depreciation of $1,500 on manufacturing equipment was recorded. (Assume this is a product cost.)
   f. Property taxes payable of $2,600 were recorded, half to manufacturing and half to administration.
   g. Manufacturing overhead costs of $400 were applied to a job in process.
   h. Materials previously purchased on account were paid for in cash, $1,500.
   i. Sales commissions of $240 were recorded.
   j. Goods costing $2,700 were transferred from Work-in-Process Inventory to Finished Goods Inventory.
   k. Finished goods costing $2,300 were sold for $3,200 on credit, and the cost of goods sold was recorded.

PROBLEM 3-3

MANUFACTURING COST FLOWS

Tremonton Corporation uses a job order costing system in its manufacturing operation. For the year 2003, Tremonton's predetermined overhead rate was 90% of direct labor costs. For September 2003, the company incurred the following costs:

Purchased raw materials on account	$140,000
Issued raw materials to manufacturing process	130,000
Incurred direct labor costs ($10 per hour × 15,000 hr)	150,000
Actual manufacturing overhead costs	128,500
Cost of goods completed and sold	483,000

The company's inventories at the beginning of September 2003 were as follows:

Raw materials	$ 24,000
Work-in-process	115,000

The costs of all completed orders are transferred directly from Work-in-Process Inventory to Cost of Goods Sold.

Required:

1. Compute the following amounts.
   a. Work-in-Process Inventory balance at the end of September 2003.
   b. Over- or underapplied manufacturing overhead for the month of September.
2. Prepare journal entries to reflect the flow of costs into and out of Work-in-Process Inventory during September (omit explanations).

PROBLEM 3-4

USING T-ACCOUNTS: COST FLOWS IN A JOB ORDER MANUFACTURING ORGANIZATION

High Country Furniture Company manufactures custom furniture only and uses a job order costing system to accumulate costs. Actual direct materials and direct labor costs are accumulated for each job, but a predetermined overhead rate is used to apply manufacturing overhead costs to individual jobs. Manufacturing overhead is applied on the basis of direct labor hours. In computing a predetermined overhead rate, the controller estimated that manufacturing overhead costs for 2003 would be $80,000 and direct labor hours would be 20,000. The following information is available for the year 2003:

a. Direct materials purchased, $22,000.
b. Direct materials used in production, $19,500.
c. Wages and salaries paid for the year: direct labor (18,000 hours), $117,000; indirect labor, $12,000; sales and administrative salaries, $21,000.
d. Depreciation on machinery and equipment, $9,000.
e. Rent and utilities for building (75% factory), $16,000.
f. Miscellaneous manufacturing overhead, $51,500.
g. Advertising costs, $12,000.
h. Manufacturing overhead is applied to Work-in-Process Inventory.
i. Eighty percent of Work-in-Process Inventory was completed and transferred to Finished Goods Inventory.

Required:

1. Compute the predetermined overhead rate at which manufacturing overhead costs will be applied to jobs.
2. Set up T-accounts and post the transactions.
3. Compute the under- or overapplied manufacturing overhead. Prepare a journal entry to close Manufacturing Overhead and transfer the balance to Cost of Goods Sold.

PROBLEM 3-5

APPLYING MANUFACTURING OVERHEAD

Pinegor Corporation has four independent manufacturing divisions. The following data apply to the divisions for the year ended December 31, 2003:

	A	B	C	D
Direct materials costs	$120,000	$140,000	$80,000	$65,000
Direct labor hours	40,000	30,000	24,000	14,000
Direct labor costs	$110,000	$65,000	$70,000	$42,000

(continued)

	A	B	C	D
Actual manufacturing overhead	$120,000	$60,000	$70,000	$16,500
Machine hours worked	20,000	6,000	14,000	8,000
Number of units produced	100,000	2,000	15,000	5,000
Predetermined overhead rate	90% of direct labor costs	57% of direct materials costs	$1.25 per direct labor hour	$2 per machine hour

Required:

1. For each of the four divisions, calculate:
   a. Applied manufacturing overhead.
   b. Over- or underapplied manufacturing overhead.
   c. Cost of goods manufactured, assuming no work-in-process inventories.
   d. Average cost per unit produced.
2. **Interpretive Question:** How would you recommend that the over- or underapplied manufacturing overhead be disposed of in each division? Why?

PROBLEM 3-6 APPLYING MANUFACTURING OVERHEAD

Openshaw Manufacturing Company made the following estimates at the beginning of the year:

	Department G	Department H
Direct labor costs	$219,000	$166,980
Manufacturing overhead	$86,700	$153,340
Machine hours	17,000	12,500
Direct labor hours	30,000	22,000

Manufacturing overhead is applied on the basis of machine hours in Department G, and on the basis of direct labor hours in Department H. During the year, the following two jobs were completed:

Job #29

	Department G	Department H
Direct materials used	$16,000	$9,200
Direct labor costs	$18,250	$14,420
Direct labor hours	2,500	1,900
Machine hours	1,410	1,080

Job #30

	Department G	Department H
Direct materials used	$17,500	$8,100
Direct labor costs	$19,710	$13,920
Direct labor hours	2,700	1,800
Machine hours	1,530	1,020

Required:

1. Compute the predetermined overhead rate for each department.
2. Determine the amount of manufacturing overhead to be applied to each job.
3. Determine the total cost of each job.
4. Given that the actual manufacturing overhead costs for the year in Departments G and H were $88,200 and $152,500, respectively; that the actual machine hours in Depart-

ment G were 18,100; and that the direct labor hours in Department H were 21,600; compute the amount of over- or underapplied manufacturing overhead.

5. **Interpretive Question:** Why is the predetermined overhead rate based on estimated rather than actual information?

PROBLEM 3-7

UNIFYING CONCEPTS: JOB ORDER COSTING, COST FLOWS, JOURNAL ENTRIES, AND PREDETERMINED OVERHEAD RATES

Itsu Manufacturing Company applies manufacturing overhead on the basis of direct materials costs. The estimates for 2003 were:

Direct materials costs	$500,000
Manufacturing overhead.	150,000

Following are the transactions of Itsu Manufacturing Company for 2003:

a. Raw materials purchased on account, $550,000.
b. Raw materials issued to production, 90% for direct use and 10% for indirect use, for a total of $350,000.
c. Direct labor costs, $500,000.
d. Indirect labor costs, $50,000.
e. Administrative and sales salaries, $140,000 and $90,000, respectively.
f. Utilities, $21,000; plant depreciation, $40,000; maintenance, $15,000; miscellaneous administrative expenses, $4,000. (These costs are allocated on the basis of plant floor space—administrative facilities, 500 square feet; manufacturing, 2,500 square feet; sales facilities, 1,000 square feet.)
g. Manufacturing equipment depreciation, $12,000.
h. Additional raw materials issued to production for direct use, $250,000.
i. Manufacturing overhead is applied.
j. Recorded factory foreman's salary, $54,000.
k. Ninety percent of existing Work-in-Process Inventory is transferred to Finished Goods Inventory. (Work-in-Process beginning inventory was $30,000.)
l. All finished goods are sold. (Assume no beginning or ending inventories. Sales are marked up 50% of cost.)
m. Over- or underapplied manufacturing overhead is closed to Cost of Goods Sold.

Required:

1. Prepare a journal entry for each of the transactions and show the T-accounts for Manufacturing Overhead and Work-in-Process Inventory. (Assume that all manufacturing overhead is a product cost.)
2. What is the ending balance in the cost of goods sold account?
3. **Interpretive Question:** Comparing actual manufacturing overhead with estimates for 2003, what would you recommend that Itsu Manufacturing Company estimate for manufacturing overhead costs in 2004?

PROBLEM 3-8

UNIFYING CONCEPTS: JOB ORDER COSTING

Jones Custom Furniture Manufacturing, Inc., made the following estimates at the beginning of the year, 2003:

Budgeted direct labor costs	$300,000
Budgeted direct labor hours	20,000
Budgeted manufacturing overhead	$520,000

Jones applies manufacturing overhead to specific job orders on the basis of direct labor hours.

During the month of January, the following transactions occurred for Job #345, an order for 10 custom oak chairs, manufactured in the first week of January 2003:

Jan. 3 Requisitioned direct materials (lumber, fabric, paint), $876; put into production on Job #345.

3 Requisitioned indirect materials (glue, staples, sandpaper, and equipment grease), $154, for use in manufacturing the 10 chairs for Job #345, as well as other subsequent jobs.

7 Processed time card for Employee #214; 25 direct labor hours attributed to Job #345 at wage rate of $15 per hour.

7 Applied manufacturing overhead at the predetermined rate to Job #345, based on the actual direct labor hours.

7 Processed the manufacturing supervisor's weekly salary of $1,000. (This salary is considered indirect labor because the supervisor oversees all jobs in process and does not account for her time on a job-by-job basis.)

7 Job #345 was completed and transferred to the finished goods warehouse to await shipment to the customer.

9 The 10 oak chairs (Job #345) were shipped to the customer. The sales invoice reflects a sales price of $3,000 on account.

In addition to Job #345, Jones completed 47 other job orders in January and had 7 others in process at month-end. The following information summarizes additional manufacturing transactions for Jones for the month of January (not relating to Job #345):

a. Raw materials purchased on account, $102,675.
b. Requisitioned raw materials to specific job orders, $90,430; 80% direct materials, and the remainder indirect materials not directly attributable to any one specific job.
c. Incurred and paid direct labor wages totaled, $24,600; an average of $15 per hour for 1,640 total direct labor hours for January.
d. Applied manufacturing overhead at the predetermined rate to all jobs in progress on the basis of the actual direct labor hours incurred by job.
e. Incurred and paid supervisor salaries and other indirect manufacturing labor (e.g., maintenance labor) totaled, $7,000.
f. Incurred and paid the following costs associated with the manufacturing process and facility:

Factory rent	$ 7,600
Factory utilities	2,700
Insurance	1,200
Miscellaneous	1,900
	$13,400

g. Recorded depreciation of manufacturing equipment for the month, $5,500.
h. The cost of the 47 jobs completed during the month totaled $125,446.
i. Shipped all completed jobs to customers by month-end at a total sales price of $200,714 on account.
j. Incurred and paid selling and administrative costs (e.g., administrative salaries, sales commissions, office supplies, office rent, etc.), $46,514.

Required:

1. a. Calculate Jones' predetermined overhead rate for the year 2003.
   b. Prepare journal entries for the first seven transactions (relating to Job #345). Omit explanations.
   c. Determine the total cost of manufacturing each of the 10 oak chairs.
   d. Determine the total gross margin earned on all 10 oak chairs.
2. Prepare the journal entries for transactions (a)–(j). Omit explanations.
3. Close Manufacturing Overhead to Cost of Goods Sold (include all transactions noted for Job #345).
4. Calculate Jones' total gross margin for January, including Job #345.
5. Calculate Jones' total operating income for January.

6. Determine the ending January balances in Raw Materials Inventory, Work-in-Process Inventory, and Finished Goods Inventory (assume no beginning balances).

PROBLEM 3-9

COMPUTING OVERHEAD RATES AND CLIENT BILLING IN A SERVICE FIRM

Morgan Engineering Company employs three professional engineers, each having a different specialty. Don Corbin specializes in structural engineering; Bob Rouse, electrical engineering; and Bill Phillips, mechanical engineering. The firm expects to incur the following operating costs for 2003; travel and materials costs are billed separately to clients.

Office salaries and wages	$ 36,000
Office supplies	20,000
Utilities and telephone	15,400
Depreciation	16,200
Taxes and insurance	10,300
Miscellaneous expenses	2,100
Total estimated costs for 2003	$100,000

The salaries and billable hours of the three engineers are expected to be as follows:

	Expected Salary	Expected Hours
Corbin.	$ 60,000	2,000
Rouse	48,000	1,760
Phillips	42,000	1,925
Total.	$150,000	5,685

Required:

1. Compute the overhead cost rate that should be used for each of the engineers (based on the expected hours to be billed, with overhead cost rates varying in proportion to each engineer's compensation) to ensure that the total expected operating costs for 2003 will be recovered from clients. (*Hint:* Allocate total estimated overhead costs to each engineer based on relative salaries, then relate the allocated costs to the hours expected to be worked by each.)
2. Using the overhead cost rates determined in (1), determine the costs associated with the firm's work for Seaside Company with the following engineering services and related costs: Corbin, 100 hours; Rouse, 40 hours; Phillips, 10 hours; transportation and supplies costs, $1,600.

PROBLEM 3-10

SERVICE COSTING—JOURNAL ENTRIES

Following are transactions for Andersen Custodial, Inc. Assume the company's beginning work-in-process services account balance is zero.

1. Purchased supplies costing $5,000 for cash.
2. Received and immediately paid a utility bill, $800.
3. Used supplies costing $3,000 in doing work for a customer.
4. 3,000 hours of direct labor and 1,500 hours of indirect labor were incurred and paid. The average hourly wage rate for both direct and indirect labor is $7.
5. Monthly rent payment was made, $2,000.
6. Applied overhead at $4.50 per direct labor hour.
7. Andersen bills its customers at a rate of $20 per direct labor hour. All work in process was moved to Cost of Services.
8. All under- or overapplied overhead is closed to Cost of Services.

Required: Prepare the journal entries for the above transactions.

PROBLEM 3-11

SERVICE COSTING—JOURNAL ENTRIES

Blake Accounting Services has the following transactions. Its beginning work-in-process services account balance is zero.

a. Purchased supplies costing $11,000 on account.
b. Paid property tax, $20,000.
c. Paid rent, $2,000; and utilities, $700.
d. Paid support staff salaries, $35,000.
e. Used supplies costing $9,000.
f. Paid direct labor salaries, $50,000. Average rate was $10 per hour.
g. Applied overhead at $11.50 per direct labor hour.
h. Transferred $100,000 from Work-in-Process to Cost of Services and billed customers for 4,500 hours of work. Blake bills its customers $40 per direct labor hour.
i. Closed under- or overapplied overhead to Cost of Services.

Required:

1. Prepare the journal entries for the above transactions.
2. Determine the ending balance in the work-in-process services account.

PROBLEM 3-12

SERVICE COST FLOWS

Tolman Company had the following balances at the beginning of 2003:

	Debit	Credit
Accounts receivable	$22,000	
Supplies	5,000	
Work-in-process services	15,000	
Accounts payable (related to supplies)		$ 3,500
Salaries and wages payable		35,000
Utilities payable		1,200
Rent payable		1,500

Tolman estimates that its total 2003 overhead will amount to $200,000. It allocates overhead based on direct labor hours. Tolman estimates that its total 2003 direct labor hours will be 50,000 hours. Because it produces monthly financial statements, Tolman makes adjusting entries at the end of each month. However, over- or underapplied overhead is not closed to Cost of Services until the end of the year.

During January 2003, Tolman had the following transactions:

Jan. 1 Paid rent. Tolman has a two-year, $72,000 lease. Rent is payable on the 1st of each month.
4 Paid all utilities payable from 2002.
5 Paid all salaries and wages payable from 2002. $23,000 was for direct labor; $12,000 was for indirect labor.
8 Paid for all supplies purchased in 2002.
10 Used supplies, $450.
19 Collected $15,000 from a customer for services performed and billed in December 2002.
23 Purchased supplies, $600.
25 Used supplies, $1,300.
31 Paid all employees for January labor. Total direct labor costs for the month of January were $25,000, direct labor hours, 4,000. Indirect labor costs were $15,000.
31 Tolman estimates its January utility expenses to be $1,000.
31 Tolman completed and billed jobs costing $40,000. The company billed customers $55,000.

Required:

1. Prepare all journal entries necessary for the month of January.
2. What is the balance in the work-in-process services account at the end of January?
3. Compute the balance in the overhead account on January 31.

expanded material

PROBLEM 3-13

FIFO COST FLOW—PROCESS COSTING

The cleaning division of Sunshine Grain Company had the following data for January 2003:

	Tons	Percentage Completed	Direct Materials Costs	Conversion Costs
Beginning work-in-process inventory . .	400	65%	$ 8,500	$ 1,200
Units started in production	26,600	—		
Costs added this month.			598,500	126,192
Ending work-in-process inventory	600	25%		
Units completed during month and transferred to packing	26,400	—		

Required:

1. Compute the per-ton cost of grain processed by the cleaning division in this period.
2. Using the FIFO cost flow method, compute the cost of the 26,000 tons of grain that were started and completed during January.
3. Compute the cost of the ending work-in-process inventory.

PROBLEM 3-14

FIFO COST FLOW—PROCESS COSTING

Western Oil Company has three process centers: drilling, processing, and distributing. During September 2003, the processing department had the following operating data:

	Barrels	Percentage Completed	Direct Materials Costs	Conversion Costs
Beginning work-in-process inventory . .	4,000	60%	$ 2,200	$ 4,200
Units started and completed this month	36,000	—		
Costs added this month.			33,150	88,410
Ending work-in-process inventory	15,000	30%		
Units completed during month and transferred to distributing	40,000	—		

Required:

Assuming a FIFO flow of costs, compute:

1. The "work done" for September (in equivalent units of production) for direct materials and for conversion costs.
2. The September cost per barrel of oil in the processing department.
3. The cost of all oil transferred to distributing.
4. The cost of ending work-in-process inventory in the processing department.

PROBLEM 3-15

FIFO COST FLOW—PROCESS COSTING

The Assembly Department of Southeastern Electronics Company reported the following data for the month of June 2003:

	Units	Costs
Beginning inventory (60% complete)	4,000	
Units transferred from prior department	30,000	
Ending inventory (50% complete)	6,000	
Cost of beginning inventory (materials $15,000, conversion $15,000)		$ 30,000
Cost of materials used in assembly department		90,000
Conversion costs for June in assembly department		157,300
Total cost		$277,300

(*Note:* Materials used in the assembly department are added at the beginning of the assembly process.)

Required: Prepare the production cost report for the assembly department. (Note: For purposes of this problem, prior department's manufacturing costs are not included in this department's production cost report.)

PROBLEM 3-16

EQUIVALENT UNITS AND FIFO COST FLOW—PROCESS COSTING

Midtown Manufacturing Company has two process centers—manufacturing and assembly. The data that follow show the production and cost results for the manufacturing center for the month of July 2003:

Production data:	
Units in process, July 1 (materials 50% complete, conversion 40% complete)	500
Units started in production	2,500
Units in process, July 31 (materials 100% complete, conversion 60% complete)	700
Cost data:	
Units in process, July 1:	
Direct materials	$ 3,000
Conversion costs	6,400
Direct materials used in July	27,500
Conversion costs for July	73,080
Total	$109,980

(*Note:* In this problem, materials are *not* added at the beginning of the manufacturing process.)

Required: Prepare the production cost report for the manufacturing center.

competency enhancement opportunities

- Analyzing Real Company Information
- International Case
- Ethics Case
- Writing Assignment
- The Debate
- Internet Search

The following additional assignments provide opportunities for students to develop critical thinking, ethical perspectives, oral and written communication skills, experience with electronic research, and teamwork through group and business activities.

ANALYZING REAL COMPANY INFORMATION

• *Analyzing 3-1 (Microsoft)*

1. Is MICROSOFT a service business, a manufacturing business, or a merchandising business? Explain.
2. Microsoft's 1999 income statement (Appendix A) lists research and development expense of $2,970 billion for the year. The notes to the financial statements say that "research and development costs are expensed as incurred" in accordance with generally accepted accounting principles. Do you think that Microsoft treats R&D costs any differently in its internal accounting reports? Explain.
3. In its management's discussion and analysis (Appendix A), Microsoft describes its three primary sales channels. What are they?

• *Analyzing 3-2 (Pump, Inc.)*

Acquiring management accounting data on real companies can be a challenge because this information is generally highly proprietary and of significant competitive value. The cost data below are for a medium-size family-owned pump manufacturing business located in the Midwest. (This business chooses to remain anonymous in order to keep its competitors from using these data to compete against it.) We'll refer to this company simply as Pump, Inc.

Pump, Inc., had reorganized much of its production into manufacturing "cells": self-supervising work centers that produce complete products. The cell program was initiated because of a strategic decision (with no management accounting data to support it) to improve customer service. The financial impact of the program was unclear; the operational causes and the financial effects were murky. As a result, the management team at Pump, Inc., was having a difficult time evaluating the effects of its strategic decision to change *most* of the company to manufacturing cells. (Some of the production process continued to be organized as a typical production line, similar to what is demonstrated in the chapter.) The current year's cost data are presented below in the standard format typically used by the management accountant for Pump, Inc.

Typical Cost Data Format

Cost Category	Cost	Percent of Cost
Direct materials	$433,966	54.55%
Direct labor	96,990	12.19
Manufacturing overhead	264,583	33.26
Total costs	$795,539	100.00%

The management team, however, had a difficult time using the cost data in the typical format to effectively control and evaluate its reorganization decision. The management accountant was asked to reformat the data to make them more useful for the management team. After some analysis, the accountant decided to provide more detail by breaking down Manufacturing Overhead into subcategories organized by function: Indirect Materials, Indirect Labor, Factory Support, Occupancy Costs, and Non-Factory Support. The accountant also realized that she could divide all costs into two additional categories: People Costs (represent costs for wages and salaries) and Purchased Costs (represent costs for materials, supplies, and services acquired from outside agencies). The new report format is presented below.

New Cost Data Format

Cost Category	**People Costs**	**Purchased Costs**	**Total Cost**
Direct materials		$433,966	$433,966
Indirect materials		9,460	9,460
Direct labor	$ 96,990		96,990
Indirect labor (production line supervision)	29,100		29,100
Factory support (material handling, equipment depreciation, utilities, expediting, engineering, etc.)	80,953	71,310	152,263
Occupancy costs (rents, taxes, maintenance, etc.)	15,180	32,550	47,730
Non-factory support (cost accounting, personnel, etc.)	23,390	2,640	26,030
Total costs	$245,613	$549,926	$795,539

Source: Adapted from J. S. McGroarty and C. T. Horngren, "Functional Costing for Better Teamwork and Decision Support," *Journal of Cost Management*, Winter 1993, pp. 24–36. Reprinted with permission.

Consider the two reports on cost data for Pump, Inc.

1. Do you think the new report format provides any additional information value for controlling and evaluating the decision to change most of the production process into manufacturing cells?
2. What costs do you think the management team at Pump, Inc., should pay careful attention to in its effort to better control costs in the production plant?
3. Most importantly, if you were on the management team at Pump, Inc., what *additional* data would you like to see the management accountant provide?

INTERNATIONAL CASE

• *Management Accounting in France*

France has a well-developed set of financial accounting rules, as embodied in the *Plan Comptable Général (PCG)*. The French PCG is comparable to U.S. GAAP. You may not have realized it, but the cost accounting for manufacturers we have studied in this chapter has a very clear connection to the way financial accounting is reported. Exhibit 3-2 in the text visibly demonstrates the difference between the production process and the administration process in a manufacturing organization. U.S. cost accounting makes a clear functional distinction between costs related to the production process (e.g., direct materials, direct labor, and manufacturing overhead) versus the administration process (e.g., selling costs and general administration costs). Further, Exhibit 3-4 demonstrates that the flow of direct materials costs and direct labor costs through the accounting system, as well as the allocation of manufacturing overhead costs, allows U.S. companies to determine product costs and easily compute cost of goods sold for financial reporting purposes. However, cost accounting (*comptabilité analytique*) in France is explicitly decoupled from financial accounting, as defined by the PCG. What this means is that the chart of accounts French companies use for cost accounting is completely different from the chart of accounts used for financial accounting. The reason is not necessarily because French companies perform cost accounting differently from U.S. companies, but that the nature of French financial accounting is quite different from financial accounting in the United States. The PCG requires financial accounting reports in France to organize and report costs by their inherent nature (materials, labor, depreciation, etc.). Costs are not assigned to products or to departments. Hence, one wouldn't expect to see a French company report Costs of Goods Sold or Selling and General Administrative Expense.

Think about this for a moment. If costs are not being assigned to products, departments, or operations within the organization, how does the organization perform the management processes of planning, controlling, and evaluating? Actually, French companies do not have a tradition of using costs to manage their companies. In fact, the traditional phrase used in France to describe the techniques and practices of planning, control, and evaluation has been *contróle de gestion*, literally, "management control." The absence of the word *comptabilité* (accounting) in this phrase is significant: it indicates that accounting numbers play a limited role in managerial reporting systems in France. Only very recently has the phrase *comptabilité de gestion* become more common. French business has had a long tradition of being led by engineers, not by accountants and financiers. Even today some 50% of managing directors in France are engineers by profession or training.

Costs are not being used as the main tool for managing companies in France. Given that a large number of the management executives of French companies have engineering backgrounds, how do French companies handle the management processes of planning, controlling, and evaluating (e.g., what kinds of numbers and reports might you expect to find in a French company)? Would you expect that French companies reconcile their *comptabilité analytique* systems with their financial accounting systems, as U.S. companies typically do?

Source: Reprinted from A. Roberts, "Management Accounting in France," *Management Accounting (UK)*, March 1995, pp. 44–46, by permission of the publisher Academic Press Limited, London.

ETHICS CASE

• *State Home Builders Inc.*

You have recently been hired as an accountant for the largest residential construction company in the state. Your primary responsibility is to track costs for each home being constructed. Tracking the costs for direct materials and direct labor is relatively straightforward. Materials requisitioned for each home site are carefully tracked, and the construction workers are very careful about assigning their time to the homes they work on.

Accounting for manufacturing overhead costs, on the other hand, presents quite a problem. In the past, overhead has been allocated on the basis of direct labor hours. As a result, because larger houses require more workers, those houses have been allocated a larger share of the overhead.

Your company was recently selected by the state to build a number of low-income housing complexes. The state has agreed to an arrangement whereby it will pay your costs plus a 10% profit. Construction of these low-income housing units will be relatively simple and will not require a great deal of materials or labor, compared to the average house the company builds.

At a meeting following the granting of the construction contract by the state, the production foreman proposes the following idea:

> Since the state has agreed to pay our costs plus 10%, the higher the costs on the project, the more money we make. What we need to do is to funnel as much of our costs as possible to this low-income housing project. Now I don't want anyone to think I am proposing something unethical. I am not saying that we should charge the state for fictitious costs. What I am saying is that we should allocate as much overhead as possible to the low-income project. Therefore, I propose that we allocate overhead on a per-house basis with each house, regardless of size, being allocated the same amount of overhead.

You have analyzed the activities that drive overhead costs and have found that bigger houses, in addition to requiring more direct materials and direct labor, require more inspections, more supervision, etc. You can see that most in attendance at the meeting are being persuaded by the production foreman's idea. You slowly raise your hand. It takes about 10 seconds before all the voices quiet. You look around the table and see 10 of your colleagues staring at you. You open your mouth and . . .

1. What would you do in this situation? Is the overhead allocation method being proposed by the production foreman illegal? Is it unethical?
2. Suppose you argue that overhead should continue to be allocated on the basis of direct labor hours. After hearing your points, the group votes to go with the production foreman and allocate the overhead on a per-house basis. What would you do next?

WRITING ASSIGNMENT

• ***Trends in Product Cost Relationships***

The ratios among the three types of product costs have changed quite a bit over the last 150 years of business. Generally, costs of direct materials have consistently formed approximately 50% of total product costs for manufacturing firms. However, the ratio of direct labor costs has been decreasing with an offsetting increase in the ratio of manufacturing overhead costs. What kinds of costing challenges does this shift from direct costs to manufacturing overhead costs pose for a manufacturing company? What factors do you think have contributed to this trend? Do you think that the advent of e-business will significantly affect the amount or ratio of direct labor costs in manufacturing products? If so, how? Write a one- to two-page paper on this topic.

THE DEBATE

• ***When Does a Direct Materials Cost Turn Into an Indirect Cost (e.g., Manufacturing Overhead)?***

Consider your automobile. What costs would be considered direct materials? What costs would be considered indirect materials? Are the fender panels direct or indirect materials? Are the rivets that connect the fender to the frame direct or indirect materials? Are the headlights direct or indirect materials? Are the screws that hold the headlights in place direct or indirect materials? In light of the intense price competition that takes place in the automobile industry, these are important cost questions: direct materials are assigned to a specific automobile (or automobile model), while indirect materials are gathered together in the pool of manufacturing overhead costs and generally allocated across all types of automobiles in the manufacturing plant.

Divide your group into two teams.

- One team represents: "Rivets and screws should be treated as direct costs." Prepare a two-minute oral argument supporting this view. Be careful that you don't make too many quick assumptions. Tracking direct materials costs to specific product units or product lines can be a very expensive process in a complex manufacturing organization.
- The other team represents: "Rivets and screws should be treated as indirect costs." Prepare a two-minute oral argument supporting this view. You must be careful that you don't make too many quick assumptions. Before you say that rivets and screws are indirect because their costs are small, consider that the bigger automakers spend tens of millions of dollars each year on rivets and screws.

INTERNET SEARCH

• *Wal-Mart*

Access **WAL-MART**'s customer web site at **http://www.walmart.com**. Sometimes Web addresses change, so if this address doesn't work, access the Web site for this textbook (**http://albrecht.swcollege.com**) for an updated link.

Once you've gained access to the site, answer the following questions.

1. Use Wal-Mart's Store Finder to find the store nearest you.
2. What is the current price on a paperback version of J. K. Rowling's *Harry Potter and the Sorcerer's Stone* (a popular children's book)?

Now access Wal-Mart's corporate Web site at **http://www.walmartstores.com** (you could also click on the "Wal-Mart Stores, Inc." link at the bottom of the customer Web site). Again, if this Web address should change, access the Web site for this textbook (**http://albrecht.swcollege.com**) for an updated link.

Once you've gained access to this site, answer the following questions:

3. In order to be a Wal-Mart supplier you would need to adhere to certain "Supplier Standards." Although these standards are very detailed, what are the nine basic categories of supplier standards?
4. Wal-Mart's first non-U.S. store opened in December 1991. Where? How many Wal-Mart stores are located in China?

part m2

Planning

Capital Investment Decisions

chapter m4

learning objectives

After studying this chapter, you should be able to:

1 Understand the importance of capital budgeting and the concepts underlying strategic and capital investment decisions.

2 Describe and use two nondiscounted capital budgeting techniques: the payback method and the unadjusted rate of return method.

3 Describe and use two discounted capital budgeting techniques: the net present value method and the internal rate of return method.

4 Understand the need for evaluating qualitative factors in strategic and capital investment decisions.

expanded material

5 Use sensitivity analysis to assess the potential effects of uncertainty in capital budgeting.

6 Explain how to use capital budgeting techniques in ranking capital investment projects.

7 Explain how income taxes affect capital budgeting decisions.

setting the stage

FEDERAL EXPRESS CORPORATION (FEDEX) is the largest air-freight company in the world. Fred Smith, founder of Federal Express, came up with his initial overnight-delivery idea as he was writing a term paper in 1965 as a Yale undergraduate. Smith's Yale professor was unimpressed with the idea and gave the paper a "C" grade. After serving two tours of duty in Vietnam as a Marine, Smith returned to the United States and began assembling the pieces to implement his idea. In 1971, Smith was optimistic about obtaining the contract to ship canceled checks around the country; he named his company "Federal Express" because the contract would have been with the Federal Reserve System. That contract never came to be, and Smith focused his attention on shipping small, time-sensitive packages through his hub-and-spoke air system centered in Memphis, Tennessee. The inaugural night of service was March 12, 1973, but only six packages arrived at the 10,000-per-hour package handling system in Memphis. After further marketing in an expanded set of cities, a second start was attempted on April 17, 1973. That night, Federal Express handled 186 packages, and daily volume has climbed steadily ever since. In 2000, FedEx Corporation delivered nearly 5 million shipments per day.

For FedEx and other firms in the air-freight industry, their most important investment is the airplanes that haul the freight. Indeed, making good airplane acquisition decisions is critical to the success of FedEx and its competitors. Though FedEx is profitable and expanding, questions have been raised about whether the company has made the right kind of airplane investment decisions. In early 1998, the Federal Aviation Administration (FAA) began public hearings to question the structural safety of scores of FedEx's aircraft. The FAA contended that the maximum allowed weight limit of these 727s should be cut from 8,000 pounds per modular cargo container to 3,000 pounds, which would significantly increase the per-pound cost of shipping cargo and reduce FedEx's profitability.

For years, the air-freight industry has relied heavily on the practice of converting retired passenger planes into cargo freighters. The safety questions raised by the FAA involve how cargo doors were installed and other structural changes made when the aircraft were modified. Safety concerns range from the stability of cargo doors to the ability of aircraft to survive a strong downward gust. FAA research has shown that under combinations of certain extreme conditions, the floor beams of 727s might fail, causing the aircraft to suddenly break apart in a massive midair convulsion. [Those who have seen the Tom Hanks movie *Cast Away* are familiar with this scenario.]

FedEx countered that the probability of the combination of conditions that would cause such an accident is highly remote. The FAA said it didn't want to wait until after an accident had occurred to raise safety issues about the 727s. In the end, the FAA compromised and only required FedEx to reduce its modular cargo container weights to 4,800 pounds in the 120 FedEx **BOEING** 727s in question. While FedEx was fighting the FAA claims and allegations, the company must have wondered if it made the right kind of investment decision by acquiring and converting the 727s. At a minimum, the questions raised about the safety of FedEx's operations represented a public relations nightmare for FedEx.

Sources: Douglas A. Blackmon, "FedEx Faults Claims by FAA Over Aircraft," *The Wall Street Journal*, Wednesday, February 18, 1998, p. A3; Paul Richfield, "FAA Issues Final Ruling on 727 Freighters," *The Wall Street Journal*, January 11, 1999, p. B2; Robert A. Sigafoos, *Absolutely Positively Overnight!: The Unofficial History of Federal Express* (Memphis: St. Lukes Press, 1988).

How do FedEx and other companies decide which types of equipment to buy and what other capital investments to make? In this chapter, we examine that part of planning called ***capital budgeting****, the systematic planning for long-term investments in operating assets (primarily property, plant, equipment, intangible assets, and natural resources). Capital budgeting techniques are also important in planning for a company's investments in people and information. For example, the most important*

capital budgeting Systematic planning for long-term investments in operating assets.

decisions a university makes are not about where or when to build buildings but instead are about whom to hire for the university's faculty.

Capital budgeting differs from the types of planning already discussed in that it is more permanent and less retractable. A decision to increase inventory levels, for example, can be reversed within a relatively short time by cutting back on future purchases or by lowering prices to increase sales. Even a nonroutine decision to purchase, rather than make or deliver internally, a component or service can generally be changed without too much disruption to operations. On the other hand, a capital investment decision to purchase 120 Model 727 freight aircraft at several million dollars each requires a long-term commitment of resources, a commitment that will probably be difficult and very expensive to change at a later date. Because of its long-term consequences, capital budgeting is an important part of a company's strategic plan. Strategic planning involves establishing the overall direction of a company's activities. Strategic planning is discussed in Chapter 5 of management accounting.

Because capital budgeting involves long-range planning, the time value of money must be considered. But before we begin to explain how capital budgeting provides management with information for evaluating long-term investments in operating assets, we must introduce some basic concepts.

1

Understand the importance of capital budgeting and the concepts underlying strategic and capital investment decisions.

CONCEPTUAL BASIS OF CAPITAL BUDGETING

The primary objective of a business is to generate a profit for its owners. Profitable businesses can be based on a low-cost strategy (such as WAL-MART), a customer service strategy (such as FEDEX), a product-branding strategy (such as COCA-COLA), and a variety of other business strategies. No matter what a company's underlying strategy, it must make long-term investment decisions in buildings, equipment, information technology, personnel, and so forth. Capital budgeting is the process of determining whether the future sales, cost savings, quality improvements, and other future benefits stemming from these strategic investment decisions are sufficient to justify the significant up-front costs associated with those decisions. In short, capital budgeting involves a comparison of the magnitude of up-front costs to the magnitude of estimated future multiyear benefits.

capital The total amount of money or other resources owned or used to acquire future income or benefits.

The term **capital** may be defined broadly as any form of material wealth. As used in business, it is more specifically defined as the total amount of money or other resources owned or used by an individual or a company to acquire future income or benefits.

Thus, capital is something to be invested with the expectation that it will be recovered along with a profit, and capital budgeting is the planning for that investment. From a quantitative viewpoint, the success of an investment depends on the amount of net future cash inflows (or future cash savings) in relation to the cost (current cash outlays) of the investment. Ignoring the time value of money for the moment, if a company invests $10,000 and receives only $10,000 in the future, there has been only a return of the investment but no profit. However, if $15,000 is received in the future, there is not only a return of the original investment but also an additional return, or profit, of $5,000. Other things being equal, investors obviously wish to receive the greatest future benefits for the least investment cost.

Importance of Capital Investment Decisions in Planning

Three aspects of capital investment decisions are critical to long-run profitability:

1. *Large initial outlay.* Decisions to invest in assets such as land, buildings, and equipment usually require large outlays of capital. Unless a reasonable return is received on such significant investments, the overall profitability of a firm will suffer.
2. *Potential long-term impact on earnings.* Long-term investments, by definition, extend over several years. Thus, poor capital budgeting, resulting in bad investment decisions, is likely to have an adverse effect on earnings over a long period.
3. *Difficult to reverse course.* Long-term investments in land, buildings, and specialized equipment are much less liquid than other investments. Investments in stocks and bonds, for example, can usually be terminated by sale through regularly established markets at almost any time; operating assets may not be so readily disposed of.

Each of these three factors can be seen in the FedEx scenario described at the beginning of the chapter. FedEx had expended millions of dollars on the 120 BOEING 727s that the FAA was concerned about. The efficient, or inefficient, use of this portion of FedEx's fleet would have implications for FedEx's reported earnings for many years; many 727s have now been in use for over 30 years. Finally, once FedEx had committed itself to using these converted 727 freighters, it was extremely costly to overhaul or retire the planes in response to the FAA concerns.

Uses of Capital Budgeting: Screening and Ranking

net work

The Web site for the U.S. President's Office of Management and Budget is http://www.whitehouse.gov/omb. This Web site can be used to find a copy of the most recent Federal budget. Associated with the budget itself is an analysis of different budget categories; this document is called Analytical Perspectives. In this Analytical Perspectives is an analysis of the "Federal Investment Spending and Capital Budgeting." For the most recent Federal budget year, determine how most of the direct Federal capital investment funds were spent.

Clearly, all long-term investment decisions are important. The larger the investment, however, the more critical is the need to budget for that expenditure. And the longer the time period, the more difficult it is to assess future outcomes and to plan accordingly. Following are some typical business situations that lend themselves to analysis with capital budgeting techniques:

1. A machine breaks down. Should the manager have the machine repaired or replaced?
2. Should a pharmaceutical company hire a renowned research scientist and commit to supporting this scientist and her staff for the next 10 years?
3. Should a company add to its manufacturing facility or build a new, larger factory?
4. Should a professional sports team sign a long-term guaranteed contract for $252 million with a key player?
5. Should Company A purchase Company B and, if so, on what terms?

Situations such as these require careful consideration of all factors, qualitative as well as quantitative, and it is just as important for nonprofit organizations to make sound strategic and capital investment decisions as for-profit organizations. Thus, the concepts and techniques discussed in this chapter are applicable to all types of organizations—companies, governmental agencies, school districts, hospitals, city governments, and so forth.

Capital budgeting analysis can help by answering two basic questions. First, does the investment make sense? That is, does it meet a minimum standard of financial acceptability? This is the **screening** function of capital budgeting. Second, is an investment the best among available acceptable alternatives? We determine this by **ranking** the alternatives. Before we discuss the screening and ranking of investment alternatives, we will briefly review the time value of money concept.

screening Determining whether a capital investment meets a minimum standard of financial acceptability.

ranking The ordering of acceptable investment alternatives from most to least desirable.

The Time Value of Money

Like other commodities, money has value because it is a scarce resource. Therefore, a payment is generally required for its use. This payment is called **interest**. Because the time value of money is widely recognized, few people would consider hiding money under a mattress or otherwise keeping large amounts of idle cash; they realize that there is a significant opportunity cost in doing so. Money left idle will not earn interest, nor will it earn the potentially higher returns that can be obtained from investments in corporate stocks and bonds or real estate, for example.

interest The payment (cost) for the use of money.

Because money has value over time, the timing of expected cash flows is important in investment decisions. This is the essence of capital budgeting—comparing the cost of an investment with the expected future net cash inflows to decide whether, given the risks and available alternatives, the project should be undertaken. An investment made today will not generate cash inflows until the future, either periodically over a number of years or in a lump sum several years hence. Thus, for the comparison of cash flows to be accurate, all amounts should be stated at their value at one point in time, generally the present; this means that all future cash flows should be stated in terms of their present values. This mathematical process of adjusting future cash flows to their present values is called discounting.

The choice of the correct interest rate, or discount rate, to use in doing time value of money computations is extremely important. In fact, this is one of the topics emphasized in the field of finance. Generally speaking, managers use relatively high discount rates when evaluating projects or investments that involve a high degree of risk; an expectation of a high rate of return is necessary to entice a rational manager into undertaking a very risky project. In addition, a manager must consider what it will cost to obtain the funds to finance the project. We will return later to the problem of selecting a discount rate for making capital investment decisions.

In the remainder of this chapter and in the end-of-chapter exercises and problems, we will assume that you understand the concepts of present value and the underlying notion of the time value of money. If you do not, or if you want to refresh your memory, you might want to review the appendix to this chapter.

Discounting Cash Flows

Because of the time value of money, a difference in the timing of cash flows can make one investment more attractive than another, even if both involve the same total amount of money. To illustrate, we assume that project A will produce $100,000 at the end of one year and that project B will return $50,000 at the end of each year for two years. Both projects will generate a total of $100,000. However, by using present value computations (reviewed in the chapter appendix) and assuming a discount (interest) rate of 10 percent per year, you will see that the discounted cash flows from project A are $90,910 and from project B are $86,775. In other words, if the appropriate discount rate is 10 percent, receiving $90,910 right now is the same as receiving $100,000 one year from now. Similarly, receiving $86,775 right now is the same as receiving $50,000 at the end of each year for the next two years. The difference in the present values of these two projects with the same total cash flows arises because with project A, the cash is received sooner. Cash received sooner is worth more because it can be put to productive use—invested, used to pay off loans, and so forth. If all other factors—that is, any qualitative considerations—are the same, an investor would be $4,135 (in today's dollars) better off by investing in project A.

Project A

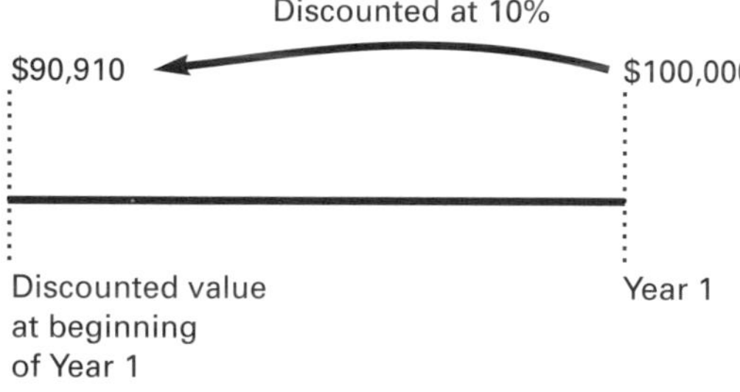

Project B

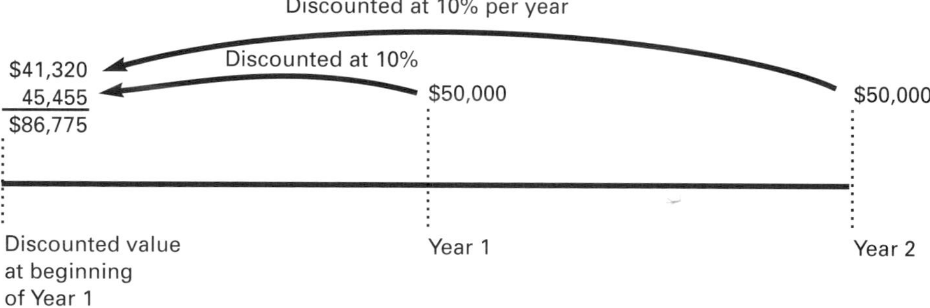

As this analysis shows, discounted cash flows reflect the time value of money and should be considered in capital budgeting. The determination of net income in accordance with GAAP is based, as you know, on accrual concepts that recognize income when it is earned, not when cash is actually received. Thus, accounting net income doesn't necessarily coincide with cash flows. For short-term investments, this approach does not significantly affect the results. Ignoring the time value of money can be misleading, however, for evaluating long-term projects.

To be able to compare cash outflows and inflows, you need a solid understanding of the discounting of cash flows. In the following paragraphs, we provide some definitions and examples.

cash outflows The initial cost and other expected outlays associated with an investment.

CASH OUTFLOWS **Cash outflows** include the initial cost of an investment plus any other expected future cash outlays associated with the investment. For example, suppose that a company purchases a drill press for $8,000 cash less a trade-in allowance of $500 for its old press. With maintenance expenses of $400 at the end of each year for the 5-year life of the press, and assuming a 12 percent discount rate, the present value of the cash outflows for the investment is:

	Time Period	Cash Outflows	Present Value Factor	Present Value of Cash Outflows
Initial cash outlay	Today	$7,500	1.0000	$7,500
Future cash outlays	Years 1–5	400	3.6048*	1,442
Total present value of cash outflows				$8,942

*From Table II, 5 years at 12 percent.

caution

In the examples used in this chapter, we provide the amounts of the future cash flows that are discounted. With real capital budgeting decisions, however, it is often very difficult to determine what the amounts of future cash inflows and outflows will be. With capital budgeting, we are dealing with future outcomes that are often difficult to project. It is this uncertainty about the future that makes capital budgeting so complex in the real world.

The $7,500 is invested immediately, so it is already stated at its present value. The $400 series of equal payments (an annuity) is to be extended over five years, so it must be discounted to its present value equivalent.

Maintenance expense is only one category of future cash outflows. Another is manufacturing overhead costs, such as heat, electricity, and rent, that may be incurred as a consequence of an investment. In addition, income taxes are expenses that must be considered in almost all capital budgeting decisions made by businesses. For simplicity, income taxes are ignored in the first part of this chapter; the impact of income taxes on capital budgeting decisions is explained in the expanded material section of the chapter. In brief, all current or expected cash outlays (expressed in terms of present values) should be considered as cash outflows in evaluating investments.

Note that some expenses, although deducted from revenues in arriving at accounting net income, do not involve actual cash disbursements and so should not be considered outflows in capital budgeting. It would obviously be wrong, for example, to include depreciation expense as an outflow, since no cash flow is directly involved.

cash inflows Any current or expected revenues or savings directly associated with an investment.

CASH INFLOWS **Cash inflows** include all current and expected future revenues or savings directly associated with an investment. For example, rent receipts, installment payments, and other revenues represent cash inflows. Returning to our earlier example, we now assume that the drill press is expected to generate annual revenues of $2,500 for five years, after which it can be sold as scrap for $750. The present value of the cash inflows for the investment is:

	Time Period	Cash Inflows	Present Value Factor	Present Value of Cash Inflows
Revenues	Years 1–5	$2,500	3.6048*	$9,012
Salvage value	Year 5	750	0.5674**	426
Total present value of cash inflows				$9,438

*From Table II, 5 years at 12 percent.
**From Table I, 5 years at 12 percent.

These revenues may be shown "net"—that is, reduced by any direct expenses, such as those for maintenance or materials and supplies. Thus, the net annual cash inflows from the drill press would be $2,100 per year ($2,500 − $400 maintenance expense).

Less obvious cash inflows are represented by the present value of the savings to be derived from an investment that reduces costs. In brief, the present value of all cash that is likely to be received or saved as a result of an investment should be included as cash inflows.

to summarize

Certain long-term investment decisions require significant capital outlays. Proper planning for these decisions is critical to long-run profitability. Capital budgeting techniques are designed to help in analyzing the quantitative factors relating to these decisions. Essentially, capital budgeting involves a comparison of the current and expected cash outflows and inflows in order to decide whether, given the risks and available alternatives, an investment should be made. To make comparisons more meaningful, all future cash flows should be discounted to the present.

2

Describe and use two nondiscounted capital budgeting techniques: the payback method and the unadjusted rate of return method.

NONDISCOUNTED CAPITAL BUDGETING TECHNIQUES

The four most commonly used capital budgeting techniques are (1) the payback method, (2) the unadjusted rate of return method, (3) the net present value method, and (4) the internal rate of return method. We will discuss the first two methods in this section and the latter two in the next section.

We have chosen the sequence of our discussion to parallel the pattern of most companies as they grow larger and become more sophisticated in the way that they make investment decisions. That is, companies generally first use the payback method or the unadjusted rate of return method because these techniques are relatively simple. Both of these techniques have a serious weakness, however, in that they ignore the time value of money. As a result, most companies eventually turn to either the net present value method or the internal rate of return method, both of which are more theoretically correct approaches to capital budgeting. The last two techniques are referred to as **discounted cash flow methods** because they use a discount rate in comparing the cash flows of investments.

discounted cash flow methods Capital budgeting techniques that take into account the time value of money by comparing discounted cash flows.

payback method A capital budgeting technique that determines the amount of time it takes the net cash inflows of an investment to repay the investment cost.

Payback Method

The **payback method** is widely used in business because it is simple to apply and it provides a preliminary screening of investment opportunities. It can also be used as a crude measure of a project's risk. Basically, this method is used to determine the length of time it will take the net cash inflows of an investment to equal the cash outlay. The payback period may be a particularly important consideration for companies in a tight credit position. Assuming that the payback period is to be computed in years (any time frame can be applied) and that equal cash flows are generated for each period, the formula for a project's payback period is:

$$\frac{\text{Investment cost}}{\text{Annual net cash inflows}} = \text{Payback period}$$

To illustrate the payback method, we will consider Kristi Felt's decision to purchase a personal computer, printer, and software for typing and printing essays and term papers for other students. A reasonably good PC, printer, and appropriate software will cost Kristi a total of \$1,500. She can borrow the \$1,500 from her parents, who require no interest but need to be repaid at the end of 18 months. Kristi expects to make $100 per month after paying for supplies and other related expenses. The payback period (in months) may be computed as follows:

$$\frac{\$1,500}{\$100} = 15 \text{ months}$$

Since Kristi would generate sufficient cash to recover the investment in 15 months, she could repay her parents within the agreed period of time (assuming she spends none of the money).

This is one of the strengths of the payback method: It can be used to determine whether an investment fits within an acceptable period for the use of funds. For example, a company's cash position may lead it to establish a rule of thumb that no investment with a payback period exceeding three years will be accepted. In such a situation, a manager may be obliged to select an investment alternative with a slightly lower rate of return but a shorter payback period.

The payback method has several weaknesses, however. One is that it measures the time needed to recover the initial outlay but does not consider the investment's profitability. Investments obviously are made in order to earn an acceptable return, not just to recover their costs. In our example, Kristi is not solely interested in recovering the $1,500 in the shortest time possible. Her purpose in buying the equipment is to earn some extra money. Assuming that the equipment will last for more than 15 months, Kristi not only will recover her initial investment, but will also generate subsequent earnings (at least $100 per month). Although the payback method may provide some clues about the advisability of investments, it does not directly measure profitability.

To clarify this last point and show why the payback method must be used with care, consider a manager's decision to purchase one of two machines. Machine A costs $5,500 and is expected to generate $1,000 of net cash inflows annually. Machine B costs $3,500 and will produce $800 of net cash inflows annually. The payback period for machine A is 5.5 years ($5,500 ÷ $1,000); for machine B, the payback period is 4.4 years ($3,500 ÷ $800). Other things being equal, the payback method would indicate that the manager should purchase machine B because it would result in a shorter payback period. That is, its original cost would be recovered in a shorter time. However, if machine B were expected to last less than 4.4 years, such an investment would be unwise. The machine would not last long enough to recover its original cost, let alone generate any earnings.

Now suppose that both machines were estimated to have a 7-year life. Which machine would be the better investment? What if the estimated lifetimes of both machines were more than 10 years? To answer these questions, we would have to use one of the discounted cash flow methods (to be discussed later) in conjunction with the payback period.

This example highlights the other major weakness of the payback method: It does not take into account the time value of money. As a result, incorrect investment decisions may result unless the payback period is relatively short.

Unadjusted Rate of Return Method

unadjusted rate of return method A capital budgeting technique in which a rate of return is calculated by dividing the increase in the average annual net income a project will generate by the initial investment cost.

Another commonly used capital budgeting technique is the **unadjusted rate of return method.** Also referred to as the simple rate of return method or the accounting rate of return method, it is computed as follows:

$$\frac{\text{Increase in future average annual net income}}{\text{Initial investment cost}} = \text{Unadjusted rate of return}$$

To illustrate the unadjusted rate of return method, consider the following situation. Seal Right Company manufactures cans for fruits, vegetables, and other farm produce. Management wants to add a new, larger can size to the product line in order to take advantage of a potential demand for food storage items in the western states. This new can is expected to increase the company's annual net income by an average of $30,000 a year for 10 years. The additional

While the payback and unadjusted rate of return methods do not consider the time value of money, they are widely used in practice because they involve simple computations and are so easy to use. In fact, smaller, unsophisticated companies rarely use the more complex discounted methods.

machinery needed to manufacture the can will cost $215,000. The expected return on the investment is $30,000 ÷ $215,000 = 14% (rounded).

Unlike the payback method, the unadjusted rate of return method attempts to measure the profitability of an investment. A company compares the unadjusted rate of return with a preselected rate that it considers acceptable. Management invests only in projects with rates of return that are equal to or greater than the established standard. Thus, if Seal Right's standard acceptance rate is less than or equal to 14 percent, the project would be acceptable.

The main weakness of the unadjusted rate of return method is that, like the payback method, it does not consider the time value of money. The computation uses average future net income rather than expected future earnings discounted to the present. A second problem is that this method counts the initial investment cost twice. This occurs because depreciation is a component in the computation of the average net income added by a project.

The problem of double counting can be eliminated by using refined models of the unadjusted rate of return method. The more serious problem—the omission of the time value of money—cannot be corrected. And since this omission can produce misleading results and incorrect long-term investment decisions, the unadjusted rate of return method must be used with extreme care.

to summarize

The payback method measures the time required to recover the initial cost of an investment from future net cash inflows (investment cost divided by annual net cash inflows). It may be useful as a preliminary screen of investment projects. The unadjusted rate of return method provides a measure of the profitability of an investment (increases in future average annual net income divided by the cost of the investment). If the resulting return is greater than the company's minimum standard of acceptability, the project is acceptable quantitatively. Because the payback and the unadjusted rate of return methods do not consider the time value of money, they should be used only in conjunction with one of the discounted cash flow methods.

3

Describe and use two discounted capital budgeting techniques: the net present value method and the internal rate of return method.

DISCOUNTED CAPITAL BUDGETING TECHNIQUES

Two widely used capital budgeting techniques recognize the time value of money—the net present value method and the internal rate of return method. Both methods apply discounted cash flow principles in determining the acceptability of an investment. The net present value method uses a standard discount rate to restate all cash flows in terms of present values and then makes comparisons. The internal rate of return method calculates the investment's "true" discounted rate of return and compares it with the firm's "hurdle" rate. Thus, an appropriate discount rate is extremely important in capital budgeting. Before explaining each of the two methods, we first discuss how to select an appropriate discount rate.

Selecting a Discount Rate

cost of capital The average cost of a firm's debt and equity capital; equals the rate of return that a company must earn in order to satisfy the demands of its owners and creditors.

An excellent starting point for computing the correct discount rate is a company's cost of capital. The **cost of capital** is basically an average cost of a firm's debt (primarily bank loans and bonds) and its equity (primarily common and preferred stock and retained earnings). These costs are measured in terms of effective interest rates on bank loans and bonds and the rate of return expected to be earned by the company's stockholders. In essence, then, the cost of capital is the rate a company must earn in order to satisfy its owners and creditors.

The computation of the cost of capital is complex and beyond the scope of this book. However, the following example should help you understand the concept. Assume that 30 percent of a company's total capital is debt, 20 percent is equity from the issuance of stock, and 50 percent is equity from retained earnings. Upon analysis, the company has determined that the cost of its debt capital is 10 percent, and the cost of its equity capital is 22 percent from stock and 16 percent from retained earnings. (Note: The cost of equity capital from the issuance of new shares is considered to be higher because of the commissions, registration fees, and so forth associated with the issuance of new shares.) The firm's cost of capital would be determined as follows:

Type	Cost of Capital	×	Weight	=	Average Cost of Capital
Debt (bonds)	10%	×	30%	=	3.0%
Equity (stocks)	22	×	20	=	4.4
Equity (retained earnings)	16	×	50	=	8.0
Total cost of capital			100%		15.4%

The weighting procedure may seem fairly simple. As you will learn in more advanced courses, however, it is not always easy to calculate the costs of the different types of capital. This is because the necessary information is often not readily available or absolutely verifiable. For example, debt costs must be adjusted to an after-tax basis, and equity costs include some subjective elements, such as the opportunity cost of retained earnings. Although you now have a general understanding of the cost of capital, you will need further study to use this concept.

STOP & THINK Assume you were trying to decide whether to purchase or lease an automobile and you wanted to use the net present value method to determine which alternative to choose. What factors would you consider in determining the rate at which to discount the future cash outflows (i.e., what factors would determine your personal cost of capital)?

As mentioned above, the cost of capital is a starting point in identifying an appropriate discount rate. The riskiness of a project should also be considered in choosing the appropriate discount rate. For example, the cost of capital computed earlier is 15.4 percent. If the company were considering a very risky project, a higher discount rate would be used because high-risk projects must yield higher-than-average returns in order to compensate for the increased probability of no returns at all. The techniques of correctly computing risk-adjusted discount rates are beyond the scope of this text; however, remember that the selection of the right discount rate is critical in the execution of a useful capital budgeting analysis.

Net Present Value Method

net present value method A capital budgeting technique that uses discounted cash flows to compare the present values of an investment's expected cash inflows and outflows.

The **net present value method** compares all expected cash inflows associated with an investment with the current and future cash outflows. All cash flows are discounted to their present values, giving recognition to the time value of money. For this reason, the net present value method is superior to both the payback method and the unadjusted rate of return method.

In general, the net present value method involves the following three steps:

1. *Compute.* Using a predetermined interest rate or discount factor, compute the present values of all the expected cash inflows and outflows of an investment. (Note that most present value tables assume end-of-year inflows and outflows.)
2. *Subtract.* Subtract the total present value of the cash outflows from the total present value of the cash inflows. The difference is the investment's net present value.
3. *Evaluate.* If the net present value of the investment is positive, or at least zero, the project is acceptable from a financial standpoint.

The following case illustrates the net present value method. The fleet manager of MBK Company is thinking of replacing an old truck before it begins to need major repairs. Because the company has limited funds and cannot spend more than $18,000, the manager is considering a small, fuel-efficient pickup truck that is presently selling for that amount. The truck would save the company $5,625 a year in gas and other expenses. The truck's estimated useful life is four years, and the expected salvage value is $1,800. The company uses a 10 percent discount rate. What is this investment's net present value? Should the truck be purchased?

Step 1 of the net present value method is to use the predetermined discount rate to state all cash flows at their present values (rounded to the nearest dollar in this example).

Cash inflows:

Annual cash savings	×	Discount factor	=	Present value
$5,625	×	3.1699*	=	$17,831
Salvage value	×	Discount factor	=	Present value
$1,800	×	0.6830**	=	$1,229

Cash outflows:

Initial cost	×	Discount factor	=	Present value
$18,000	×	1.0000	=	$18,000

*From Table II, 4 years at 10 percent.
**From Table I, 4 years at 10 percent.

net present value The difference between the present values of an investment's expected cash inflows and outflows.

Step 2 is to compute the **net present value**, that is, the difference between the present values of cash inflows and outflows.

Present value of inflows:	
Cash savings	$17,831
Salvage value	1,229
Total	$19,060
Less present value of outflows:	
Cost of truck	18,000
Net present value	$ 1,060

The analysis in Step 2 shows that investing in the truck would produce a positive net present value. In other words, after adjusting for the time value of money, purchasing the truck is like paying $18,000 in exchange for a stream of cash flows that is worth $19,060. Clearly, this is something that you would want to do. Thus, from a quantitative standpoint, it seems that the truck should be purchased. Exhibit 4-1 illustrates the process just described.

exhibit 4-1 Computing Net Present Value

	Present Time	Year 1	Year 2	Year 3	Year 4
Cost	$18,000				
Savings		$5,625	$5,625	$5,625	$5,625
Salvage value					1,800

	Time Period	Cash Flows	Present Value Factor	Present Value of Cash Flows
Present value of cash inflows:				
Savings	Years 1–4	$ 5,625	3.1699*	$17,831
Salvage value	Year 4	1,800	0.6830**	1,229
				$19,060
Present value of cash outflows:				
Cost	Today	(18,000)	1.0000	18,000
Net present value				$ 1,060

*From Table II, 4 years at 10 percent.
**From Table I, 4 years at 10 percent.

A common misinterpretation of the $1,060 net present value is that the acquisition of the truck will generate a net profit of just $1,060. Actually, because a 10 percent discount rate was used in evaluating the truck, the $1,060 net present value means that the investment in the truck will yield a net value gain of $1,060 OVER AND ABOVE the 10 percent minimum required rate of return. Similarly, a computed net present value of $0 does not mean that an investment just barely breaks even; instead, a $0 net present value means that the investment yields a return exactly equal to the discount rate used in evaluating the investment.

Before the company decides whether to purchase the truck, however, management must consider other factors. For example, a policy of support for U.S. car manufacturers or a lack of certain safety features on the pickup might dictate a particular course of action. Qualitative factors are discussed in greater detail later in the chapter.

LEAST-COST DECISIONS The net present value method generally assumes that an investment must be justified by cash savings or increased revenues. Sometimes, however, funds must be used to purchase assets regardless of whether they can be justified financially. Such situations arise, for example, when (1) government regulations require a firm to purchase safety or pollution-control equipment, (2) personnel contracts stipulate the establishment of retirement funds, or (3) a company is required to invest in cafeteria or recreational facilities, either to comply with a labor union contract or because management is persuaded that morale considerations warrant it.

Such situations may seem to be beyond help from capital budgeting. However, the net present value method may assist managers in making a **least-cost decision**—a decision that satisfies certain requirements at the lowest possible cost to the firm. The two major differences between least-cost decisions and all other capital budgeting decisions are:

least-cost decision A decision to undertake the project with the smallest negative net present value.

1. Least-cost decisions are limited to alternatives that fulfill certain imposed requirements.
2. None of the alternatives may produce a positive net present value.

To illustrate, we will assume that New England Steel Company has been told by the Environmental Protection Agency to install a pollution-control device. One alternative would cost $1,000,000 immediately but would not add to operating costs. It would last for 10 years. A second alternative is a device that costs $200,000 immediately but would add $125,000 to annual operating costs. Like the first device, it would last 10 years. Which device should be purchased? The firm uses a 12 percent discount rate.

The first alternative involves no future cash inflows or outflows. Its outlay cost in net present value terms is its initial cash outlay of $1,000,000. The second alternative has an initial cost

Managers must sometimes make least-cost decisions to fulfill certain imposed requirements at the lowest possible cost. For example, a company may be required to invest in a cafeteria to comply with a labor union contract.

business environment essay

Investing for a Cleaner World Businesses have traditionally used capital budgeting to guide them on making wise investments in property, plant, and equipment that will earn a return. However, in recent years, investments in environmental cleanup activities have become extremely common. Companies today face a climate with increasingly significant environmental concerns. Environmental costs have soared, in some cases to billion of dollars each year. Fines and penalties for violation of environmental regulations are substantial. And, due to new sentencing guidelines, strict liability for environmental losses has been imposed on directors and officers of companies. There is currently a myriad of environmental laws forcing companies to spend huge amounts of money to comply with these laws and to clean up environmental damage. Some of the most costly laws are the Clean Air Act, the Clean Water Act, the Resource Conservation and Recovery Act of 1976, the Comprehensive Environmental Response, the Compensation and Liability Act of 1980 (known as Superfund), and the Superfund Amendments Reauthorization Act of 1986 (SARA). The impact of these laws on capital in-

STOP & THINK Over your lifetime, you will make many personal, long-term investments such as buying automobiles and buying a home. Are the capital budgeting techniques we have discussed in this chapter relevant to these personal decisions? Since you probably won't be earning a return on your automobile and home investments, what type of capital budgeting decisions are these?

of $200,000 plus future cash outflows of $125,000 per year for the next 10 years. Therefore, its outlay cost in net present value terms would be:

Annual cash outflows	×	Discount factor	=	Present value
$125,000	×	5.6502*	=	$706,275
Initial cost				200,000
Outlay cost at net present value				$906,275

*From Table II, 10 years at 12 percent.

If the company had a choice between installing and not installing, neither alternative would be acceptable because both net present values are negative. However, one of the alternatives must be accepted. Because a cost of $906,275 is less than a cost of $1,000,000, the second alternative should be chosen to minimize costs.

Internal Rate of Return Method

internal rate of return method A capital budgeting technique that uses discounted cash flows to find the "true" discount rate of an investment; this true rate produces a net present value of zero.

internal rate of return The "true" discount rate that will produce a net present value of zero when applied to the cash flows of investment inventory goods held for resale.

The **internal rate of return method**, also known as the time-adjusted rate of return method or the discounted rate of return method, is similar to the net present value approach in that it emphasizes the profitability of investments and takes into account the time value of money. As a discounted cash flow method, it is superior to either the payback method or the unadjusted rate of return method. Some managers consider the internal rate of return method more tedious than the net present value method because, in the absence of a business calculator, the computations can be difficult. Some managers, however, prefer to analyze investment alternatives in terms of comparative rates of return rather than net present values.

The **internal rate of return** is defined as the "true" discount rate that an investment yields. For example, assume that your parents have $100,000 that they are considering investing in one of two ways—in a mutual fund containing the stocks of large U.S. companies or in your collegiate education. They learn that the mutual fund investment will yield an average return of 12 percent. They estimate the increased value of your lifetime annual output stemming from your college education and calculate that, after adjusting for the time value of money, the investment in your college education will yield an average return of, say, 20 percent per year. The 20 percent number is the internal rate of return generated by an investment in your education; be-

vestment decisions can be substantial. For example, under SARA, purchasers of real property are usually financially liable for environmental cleanup costs even if the property was contaminated before it was purchased.

Environmental concerns impact several stages of the capital budgeting decision. First, capital budgeting decision makers must expand traditional company boundaries to consider all entities affected by environmental degradation. Even though a project may be profitable from the firm's perspective, if it pollutes the environment, cleanup liability may make the investment a real loser. Second, environmental laws, current conditions, and trends can significantly affect the feasibility of an investment. Third, in deciding whether an investment is profitable, environmental costs and benefits, as well as environmental risk, must be considered. Finally, once an investment in a capital asset is made, attention must be given to environmental events such as accidents or increased regulation, which might affect the continued viability of the investment.

Source: Devaun Kite, "Capital Budgeting: Integrating Environmental Impact," *Journal of Cost Management*, Summer 1995, Vol. 9, No. 2, pp. 11–14.

caution

Of course, as mentioned earlier, there may be QUALITATIVE considerations that would cause your parents to invest in your education even if the MONETARY return were expected to be lower than what they could earn in the stock market.

cause this return is higher than the return your parents can earn on a mutual fund, they would naturally invest the $100,000 in your future.

Mathematically, the internal rate of return is the discount rate that yields a net present value of zero when applied to the cash flows of an investment—both inflows and outflows.

When using present value tables, the internal rate of return method involves three steps.

1. Calculate the present value factor by dividing the investment cost by the annual net cash inflows.
2. Using applicable present value tables and the life of the investment, find the present value factor closest to the number derived in step 1.
3. Using interpolation, if necessary, find the exact internal rate of return represented by the present value factor in step 1.

To help you understand this concept, we will again refer to MBK Company's plan to purchase a new truck. For the purpose of this explanation, however, we will ignore the truck's salvage value; later, we will show how to incorporate salvage value into the calculation. The calculations for the MBK example are as follows:

1. Calculate the present value factor with the following formula:

$$\frac{\text{Investment cost}}{\text{Annual net cash inflows}} = \text{Present value factor}$$

$$\frac{\$18{,}000}{\$5{,}625} = 3.2000$$

(Note that this is also the formula for calculating the payback period.)

2. In Present Value Table II, find the applicable row for the life of the investment. By moving across the table, you can find the present value factor closest to the number derived in step 1. In our example, the investment's life is known to be 4 years, so find row 4 and move across the row until you come to the factor 3.2397. This is the factor for 9 percent. The next factor, 3.1699, represents 10 percent. Since the factor is between these two numbers, the truck purchase yields between a 9 and 10 percent return.
3. If necessary, use **interpolation** to find the exact internal rate of return. Interpolation is most easily visualized by setting up a table as follows:

interpolation A method of determining the internal rate of return when the factor for that rate lies between the factors given in the present value table.

	Rate of Return (Discount Rate)	Present Value Factors: High and True Factors	Present Value Factors: High and Low Factors
High factor*	9%	3.2397	3.2397
True factor		3.2000	
Low factor	10		3.1699
Differences	1%	0.0397	0.0698

*Note that the high factor is associated with the low rate and that the low factor is associated with the high rate.

The number 0.0397 is the difference between the high factor and the true factor determined in step 1. The number 0.0698 is the difference between the high factor and the low factor. One percent is the difference between the discount rates for the high and the low factors. To find the exact rate of return in this example, you would make the following calculation:

$$\text{Internal rate of return} = 0.09 + \left(0.01 \times \frac{0.0397}{0.0698}\right) = 0.0957 \text{ or } 9.6 \text{ percent (rounded)}$$

caution

Although the internal rate of return and net present value capital budgeting methods provide answers that appear to be very precise, they should be used with caution. There are many assumptions made when using these methods. Some of these assumptions are (1) that the discount rate (cost of capital) is accurate and (2) that the future cash flows, useful lives of the assets, and salvage values are known. It is often easy in accounting to assume that precise calculations are accurate without giving due consideration to the assumptions underlying the calculations.

What we are doing is adding the proportion 0.0397 ÷ 0.0698 of the 1 percent difference to the low rate to get the true rate. The result, 9.6 percent, means that if the annual savings of $5,625 were discounted at 9.6 percent, the net present value of the investment would be zero. (Note that there may be slight differences due to rounding.)

The purpose of interpolation is to determine the "true" rate of interest indicated by the present value factor. Although the factor's true rate of interest is fairly easy to roughly estimate, interpolation produces a more precise estimate.

Computation of internal rates of return is one area in which knowledge of how to use a standard business calculator really pays off. For example, the internal rate of return in the MBK example could be computed using the following keystrokes with a Hewlett-Packard business calculator:

Hewlett-Packard Keystrokes:

1. −18,000: Press **PV** (you must enter the cash outflow as a NEGATIVE number)
2. 5,625: Press **PMT** (this is the annual cash inflow)
3. 4: Press **N** (number of years)
4. Press **I/YR** for the answer = 9.5642274%

USING THE INTERNAL RATE OF RETURN To determine the value of an investment, management must compare the project's internal rate of return with the company's usual discount rate, often called the **hurdle rate**, or the rate that must be cleared for a project to be acceptable. If the internal rate is higher than or equal to the company's hurdle rate, the project is acceptable. If the internal rate is lower than the hurdle rate, the project is usually rejected. As with any of the capital budgeting techniques, even if the investment is acceptable from an internal rate of return standpoint, qualitative factors must still be considered before a final decision can be made.

hurdle rate The minimum rate of return that an investment must provide in order to be acceptable.

fyi

A calculator actually computes the internal rate of return using a repeated interpolation process; most business calculators take a couple of seconds to come up with the final answer.

THE PROBLEM OF UNEVEN CASH FLOWS In the truck example, annual cash flows were the same because salvage value was ignored. However, when salvage value is considered, the investment will have uneven cash flows. When this occurs, an annuity table cannot be used. Each cash flow has to be discounted back at an assumed discount rate until the net present value of all the cash flows discounted at this rate approximates zero. The rate that results after a trial-and-error process or a computer simulation is the internal rate of return. A simplified example of this method is shown on page 199. Although this can be a tedious procedure, it is facilitated by using computers or calculators. For example, computing the internal rate of return of the MBK truck purchase, including consideration of the $1,800 salvage value cash inflow at the end of four years, would be done as follows using a Hewlett-Packard business calculator:

Hewlett-Packard Keystrokes:

1. −18,000: Press **PV**
2. 5,625: Press **PMT**
3. 4: Press **N** (number of years)
4. 1,800: Press **FV** (this is a single amount occurring at the end of the period of time indicated in step 3)
5. Press **I/YR** for the answer = 12.5774719%

Note that the internal rate of return is higher (12.6% vs. 9.6%) when the additional cash inflow from the salvage value is considered.

---

to summarize

The net present value method is a capital budgeting technique that takes into consideration the time value of money by discounting future cash flows to their present values. By comparing the discounted net cash inflows and outflows, this method derives a net present value figure. If the net present value is zero or positive, the project is acceptable from a quantitative standpoint. The discount rate used is the minimum rate of interest that a company will accept. The net present value method also may be used in making least-cost decisions. The internal rate of return is a capital budgeting technique that utilizes discounted cash flows. It derives the "true" rate of return for an investment by comparing the cost of the project with the amounts to be returned. This produces a present value factor that is associated with the internal rate of return for the project. Often, the rate must be derived by interpolation and, if uneven cash flows are involved, by trial and error, computer simulation, or business calculator.

COMPARATIVE EXAMPLE OF CAPITAL BUDGETING TECHNIQUES

To solidify your understanding of the capital budgeting techniques introduced thus far in this chapter, we present the example of Will's Pit Stop, a small service station that sells gasoline on a self-service basis as its only source of revenue. Because one wall of the enclosed station area is vacant, the manager has decided to install one or two food vending machines. A sales representative has suggested that a freezer for ice cream and other dairy items would do well. The freezer would cost $42,045. It has an estimated useful life of 10 years, with an expected salvage value of $4,000. The sales representative is confident that the freezer will generate revenues of $15,000 a year on goods that cost $7,600. The freezer will need $8,000 of servicing during its fifth year of operation. The increase in Will's average yearly net income if the freezer is purchased is estimated to be $3,500. Note that the difference between annual net cash inflows of $7,400 ($15,000 − $7,600) and the estimated average net income of $3,500 is due to noncash expenses, such as depreciation, which are deducted on the income statement.

The manager of the station has come to you for advice, indicating that the firm's hurdle rate is 12 percent—Will's estimated cost of capital. Compute the payback period, the unadjusted

business environment essay

McDonald's Probably the most successful fast-food restaurant of all time is MCDONALD'S. However, as of early 1997, things weren't going so well for McDonald's. Jokes about McDonald's food were rampant. Ronald McDonald had become a symbol for botched marketing schemes. McDonald's sales were off target. McDonald's image was off kilter. And, McDonald's solutions to problems were off the mark.

By 1997 McDonald's had realized that it needed to take drastic action to correct these problems and lift the company back above its competitors. So what was McDonald's solution? In 1997 and 1998, it started investing $500 million in a new cooking and food delivery system that would allow the company to serve hot food to every customer, made to order, faster than ever before. For the first time in decades, McDonald's planned to serve hotter, fresher food, in less than three-and-a-half minutes per customer.

rate of return, the net present value, and the internal rate of return of the project. Then give your recommendations. Note that companies generally do not analyze an investment with all these techniques. They are all used here for illustrative purposes.

1. *Payback period:*

$$\frac{\text{\$50,045 (investment cost)*}}{\text{\$7,400 (annual net cash inflows)}} = 6.76 \text{ years}$$

*$42,045 initial investment + $8,000 servicing cost after 5 years.

Note that the salvage value is not considered here because it is received in the tenth year.

2. *Unadjusted rate of return:*

$$\frac{\text{\$3,500 (increase in future average annual net income)}}{\text{\$42,045 (initial investment cost)}} = 8.3 \text{ percent}$$

3. *Net present value:*

	Time Period	Cash Flows	Present Value Factor	Present Value of Cash Flows
Present value of cash inflows:				
Net revenues				
($15,000 − $7,600)	Years 1–10	$ 7,400	5.6502*	$41,811
Salvage value	Year 10	4,000	0.3220**	1,288
Total cash inflows				$43,099
Present value of cash outflows:				
Initial cost	Today	$42,045	1.0000	$42,045
Servicing cost	Year 5	8,000	0.5674***	4,539
Total cash outflows				$46,584
Net present value				$ (3,485)

*From Table II, 10 years at 12 percent.
**From Table I, 10 years at 12 percent.
***From Table I, 5 years at 12 percent.

The new ad campaign was called "made for you." In two test stores, sales were up 20 percent, even without advertising. One thing was certain, however. Investing $500 million in new equipment and technology was a lot more risky than McDonald's earlier attempted solutions to resurrect its image. These involved offering new products such as the Arch Deluxe and McRib Sandwich. By early 1998, McDonald's was convinced that the investment would result in increased sales, higher profits, and an improved reputation. Franchise owners, who were being asked to pay $300 million of the $500 million total cost, weren't so sure. To some of them, the charge seemed like an awfully big and risky capital investment gamble. However, the market seemed to like the bold move—from January 1997 through January 1999, McDonald's stock price almost doubled, from $44 per share to $80 per share.

Source: Bruce Horovitz, "Fast-Food Giant's New Plan: Hot, Juicy, Made to Order," *USA Today*, February 20, 1998, p. B1.

4. *Internal rate of return:*

Since the cash flows are uneven due to the servicing cost and the salvage value, a trial-and-error process is required in computing the internal rate of return. From the net present value method, we can see that the 12 percent rate is too high. A 10 percent rate is selected for trial, and the net present value at that rate is calculated.

	Time Period	Cash Flows	Present Value Factor	Present Value of Cash Flows
Present value of cash inflows:				
Net revenues				
($15,000 − $7,600)	Years 1–10	$ 7,400	6.1446*	$45,470
Salvage value	Year 10	4,000	0.3855**	1,542
Total cash inflows				$47,012
Present value of cash outflows:				
Initial cost	Today	$42,045	1.0000	$42,045
Servicing cost	Year 5	8,000	0.6209***	4,967
Total cash outflows				$47,012
Net present value				$ 0

*From Table II, 10 years at 10 percent.
**From Table I, 10 years at 10 percent.
***From Table I, 5 years at 10 percent.

At 10 percent, the net present value is zero. Therefore, 10 percent is the internal rate of return.

On the basis of the foregoing information, you should recommend rejection. The payback period is well within the life of the investment; however, it is not short enough to warrant any special consideration. The unadjusted rate of return is only 8.3 percent, and the internal, or adjusted, rate of return of 10 percent is well under Will's hurdle rate, which means that the project's net present value is negative. Therefore, on the basis of the quantitative results, the manager should look for an opportunity that is more attractive financially. However, if the 10 percent rate is close enough to the 12 percent hurdle rate, perhaps qualitative factors, such as the probability that the additional customers attracted by the freezer items will also buy gas, might make the project acceptable.

4

Understand the need for evaluating qualitative factors in strategic and capital investment decisions.

QUALITATIVE FACTORS IN STRATEGIC AND CAPITAL INVESTMENT DECISIONS

In explaining the fundamental concepts of capital budgeting, we have focused on the financial (quantitative) aspects of analyzing investment alternatives. However, a discussion of capital budgeting is incomplete without mentioning factors that cannot be reduced to numbers. These qualitative factors are often of overriding importance in strategic and capital investment decisions. Here, we consider three types of qualitative factors: (1) an investment's effect on the *quality* of products and services offered, (2) an investment's effect on the *time* with which products and services can be produced and delivered to customers, and (3) other qualitative factors. Thus far in the chapter, we have made the determination of whether a capital investment decision is a good one solely on the basis of its financial return, computed using one of four methods. If the financial return was positive, our conclusion was to invest; if the financial return was negative, we recommended that the project not be undertaken. However, throughout the management accounting chapters of this book, we have focused on three aspects of decision making: cost, quality, and time.

fyi

In today's world economy, most companies have to be competitive on a cost basis. What makes good companies even better is their attention to quality and time (speed of delivery of products and services) considerations—the same factors that are important in capital investment decisions.

Quality and time considerations can sometimes dictate that a capital investment should be made even if the financial returns don't justify the expenditure. For example, if buying a new machine will help the company produce higher quality products or deliver those products to its customers faster, the machine may be a good investment. Companies know that their competitors are doing everything possible to speed up delivery and increase quality. Thus, even if a company has a cost of capital of 12 percent, and an investment will return only 8 percent, if buying a machine will allow the company to deliver products or services faster than competitors, the purchase may be a good one. Likewise, if buying a machine will mean fewer defects, higher quality, and more satisfied customers, the purchase may be a good one. Companies must always be continuously improving in order to keep up with or surpass their competition. Unfortunately, capital investments often are long-term decisions that make continuous improvement difficult. Thus, even if a company has not completely recovered its investment in a capital project, recognizing that competitors have better or more efficient equipment may motivate a company to abandon an investment (a machine that works fine, for example) and make a costlier new investment that will allow the company to remain competi-

business environment essay

Ethics in Capital Investment Decisions In 1990, after making substantial investments in two plants in Thailand and one in China, **HUNTSMAN CHEMICAL CORPORATION (HCC)** abruptly sold out its business interests when unethical practices were encountered. After winning a major bid in competition with worldwide firms, HCC was virtually guaranteed a significant profit on a $40 million investment. It became clear, however, that business practices involving bribes, payoffs, inflated invoices, and the like were going to be a part of the deal. As soon as Jon Huntsman, founder, chairman, and CEO of HCC, became aware of these unethical practices, he called his managers home and refused to participate further in the projects. HCC sold all its interests and walked away from the deal. When asked about this situation, Mr. Huntsman was quoted as saying, "We simply refuse to carry out negotiations based on factors other than competitiveness, quality, and productivity."

Although the quantitative factors led HCC to become involved in a major capital investment project, other factors caused the company to withdraw. As noted in the text, qualitative factors often override purely quantitative results.

Source: Adapted from "The Heart of the Deal," *Wharton Alumni Magazine* (Summer 1991), pp. 8–14.

tive. The impact of quality and time on capital budgeting decisions cannot be underestimated. In fact, because of the need to continuously improve, companies are always looking for shorter and shorter capital investment opportunities so that they are more flexible, such as leasing or renting equipment and other operating assets where possible.

In addition to quality and time, there are a number of other qualitative factors that must be considered when making capital budgeting decisions. Consider, for example, consumer safety. In one lawsuit, a major U.S. automobile manufacturer was cited for producing cars that were not as safe as they should have been. The company was essentially accused of comparing the present value of the legal and other costs that might result from the unsafe condition of the cars with the cash savings from manufacturing the cars more cheaply, and of choosing the less expensive route. The question was then posed: What is the value of a life? This situation provides a dramatic illustration of the need to include qualitative factors in capital investment decisions.

Other qualitative factors include such matters as (1) government regulations, (2) pollution control and environmental protection, (3) worker safety, (4) company image and prestige, (5) preferences of owners and management, and (6) the general welfare of the community in which the company operates. The business environment essay (on page 200) provides a specific example of one company that combined strategic objectives with humanitarian motives in making a major capital investment decision. Many more examples could be mentioned, but the point is that numbers alone do not control the investment decisions of a good manager. Quality, time, and other qualitative, as well as quantitative, factors should all be considered in reaching long-term investment decisions.

to summarize

In making capital budgeting decisions, the effects of a decision on the quality of and the time with which products can be delivered to customers must be considered. In addition, other qualitative factors such as litigation effects, government regulations, environmental impact, worker safety, company image, preferences of owners, and welfare of community must also be considered.

expanded material

In the previous sections of the chapter, we have explained the importance of capital budgeting and the concepts underlying strategic and capital investment decisions, including the time value of money. We have also described and illustrated the four most commonly used capital budgeting techniques. Finally, we have discussed briefly the need for evaluating qualitative factors in any investment decision. In the expanded material, we explain how to use sensitivity analysis in dealing with uncertainty in capital budgeting decisions and the concept of "capital rationing," i.e., the process of ranking capital investment projects. We also discuss the impact of taxes on capital budgeting decisions.

5

Use sensitivity analysis to assess the potential effects of uncertainty in capital budgeting.

sensitivity analysis A method of assessing the reasonableness of a decision that was based upon estimates; involves calculating how far reality can differ from an estimate without invalidating the decision.

DEALING WITH UNCERTAINTY IN STRATEGIC AND CAPITAL INVESTMENT DECISIONS

Throughout this chapter, we have applied capital budgeting techniques as though the future were certain. That is, we have assumed perfect knowledge of expected cash flows, the useful lives of assets, salvage values, and so forth. Actually, the future is almost always uncertain, and the applicable numbers are estimates. By using "sensitivity analysis," we can evaluate, at least to some extent, the degree to which an error in a particular estimate is likely to invalidate the decision reached. Essentially, **sensitivity analysis** is a method of examining the effect of changes in an estimate on the results of the calculations. We use sensitivity analysis to determine whether the conclusions still seem reasonable under modified circumstances.

To illustrate this approach, we will consider the following situation. An asset can be purchased for $100,000; it is expected to provide $20,000 of annual net cash inflows. It has a 10-year life and an expected salvage value of $10,000. The hurdle rate is 8 percent. We can use either of the discounted cash flow techniques to assess this investment opportunity. For illustrative purposes, we use both.

Net present value method:

Discounted expected cash inflows ($20,000 × 6.7101*)	$134,202
Discounted disposal value ($10,000 × 0.4632**)	4,632
Net cash inflows	$138,834
Net cash outflows	100,000
Net present value	$ 38,834

*From Table II, 10 years at 8 percent.
**From Table I, 10 years at 8 percent.

Internal rate of return method:

$$\frac{\text{Investment cost (\$100,000} - \text{\$4,632)}}{\text{Annual net cash inflows}} = \frac{\$95{,}368}{\$20{,}000} = 4.7684 \text{ present value factor}$$

For 10 years, the internal rate of return is between 16 and 18 percent.

The net present value is greater than zero, and the internal rate of return is considerably more than the minimum acceptable rate of 8 percent. Therefore, from a quantitative standpoint, we should accept this investment opportunity. But what about the uncertainties? What if $20,000 is not received each year? What if the asset does not last 10 years? What if the disposal value is less than $10,000? Sensitivity analysis enables us to evaluate the potential effect of each of these uncertainties.

If Expected Cash Flows Are Uncertain

To assess the amount of error we can tolerate in expected cash flows, we need to determine the break-even amount of net cash flow—that is, the annual cash flow that would earn the minimum rate of 8 percent. We accomplish this by determining the discounted net cost of the investment and dividing that amount by the present value factor for the minimum acceptable interest rate (8 percent) for 10 years.

Computations:

Initial cost	$100,000
Discounted disposal value	4,632
Net cost of investment	$ 95,368

$95,368 ÷ 6.7101 (present value factor of 8 percent) = $14,213 cash flow return in order to break even.

We could then assess how likely it is that this project will generate annual cash flows of at least $14,213. Any amount above that, of course, would be acceptable with an 8 percent hurdle rate.

If Useful Life Is Uncertain

To assess the amount of error we can tolerate in the estimate that the asset will have a useful life of 10 years, we take the discounted net cost of the investment and divide it by the expected cash flows. This produces a present value factor of 4.7684. Looking under 8 percent interest in Table II, we find that this factor falls between 6 and 7 years. Thus, assuming that the $20,000 estimate of cash inflows is reliable, the asset does not have to last a full 10 years for the investment to be acceptable. In fact, only 7 years are necessary.

Computations:

$$\frac{\text{Net cost of investment}}{\text{Annual net cash inflows}} = \frac{\$95{,}368}{\$20{,}000} = 4.7684 \text{ at 8 percent}$$

= Between 6 and 7 years of useful life in order to break even

If Disposal Value Is Uncertain

Usually, the disposal value is an insignificant factor in the investment decision. However, to see if it would make a difference in the acceptability of a project, we can assume it is zero. In our example, if the asset has a zero disposal value, the investment cost of $100,000 divided by $20,000 annual net cash inflows equals a 5.0 present value factor. For an assumed 10-year life, the return is between 15 and 16 percent, which is clearly acceptable according to our 8 percent hurdle rate.[1]

Computations:

$$\frac{\text{Initial investment cost}}{\text{Annual net cash inflows}} = \frac{\$100{,}000}{\$20{,}000} = 5.0 \text{ for 10 years}$$

= 15 to 16 percent return

to summarize

Capital budgeting decisions always involve estimates of future amounts, and estimates involve uncertainty. To evaluate the potential effect of this uncertainty, we can use sensitivity analysis, which shows how far reality can deviate from the estimate without invalidating an investment decision.

6

Explain how to use capital budgeting techniques in ranking capital investment projects.

CAPITAL RATIONING

Thus far, we have dealt exclusively with the screening function of capital budgeting—that is, determining whether an investment meets a minimum standard of acceptability. In many cases, however, a company has not one but several investment opportunities, all of which offer returns in excess of the company's hurdle rate. Since a company's resources are limited, some projects should be given priority. The ranking function of capital budgeting enables management to select the most profitable investments first. Projects should not be ranked, however, until the screening process is completed.

1 In this example, we looked at the uncertainty of each variable separately. Using computer simulation, uncertainty in all variables could have been examined simultaneously.

Another factor to consider in ranking projects is whether particular projects are compatible, complementary, or mutually exclusive. We assume mutually exclusive projects in this section on ranking, that is, that each project is independent and adds neither an advantage nor a disadvantage to other projects. Certainly, there are situations where the acceptance of one project adds value, directly or indirectly, to another project and might therefore alter a ranking consideration. These factors, like the qualitative factors that we discussed earlier, may significantly influence the strategy involved in a capital investment decision.

capital rationing Allocating limited resources among ranked acceptable investments.

The objective of ranking is to help a company use limited resources to the best advantage by investing only in the projects that offer the highest return. The process of allocating limited resources based on the ranking of projects is called **capital rationing**. Either the internal rate of return method or the net present value method may be used in ranking investments.

Ranking by the Internal Rate of Return Method

If the internal rate of return method is used, investments that pass the screening test are ranked in the order of their internal rate of return, from highest to lowest. This method is simple, requires no additional computations, and is widely used.

To illustrate the process, we will assume the following situation. Sundance Enterprises is considering six capital investment projects. Management requires a minimum return of 15 percent on its investments. The six projects are first screened, then ranked by their internal rates of return, as shown below.

Project	Expected Rate of Return	Screening Decision	Ranking Decision
A	10%	Reject	—
B	18	Accept	3
C	12	Reject	—
D	22	Accept	1
E	20	Accept	2
F	16	Accept	4

From a quantitative standpoint, Sundance should invest in all four of the projects that passed the screening test. If resources are limited, however, capital must be rationed. In this situation, the ranking process indicates that limited resources would be allocated to project D first, then to projects E, B, and F, respectively. This conclusion ignores the additional complications of the investments having different lives. It also does not consider differences in the size of the initial investment.

Ranking by the Net Present Value Method

If the net present value method is used for ranking investments, additional computations are necessary because the net present value of one investment usually cannot be directly compared with that of another. Only projects that require the same amount of investment are comparable. For example, you cannot readily compare an investment of $10,000 that produces a $2,000 net present value (project A) with a $20,000 investment that also results in a $2,000 net present value (project B), although project A certainly seems more desirable. To rank such projects, we need to compute a **profitability index**.

profitability index The present value of net cash inflows divided by the cost of an investment.

$$\frac{\text{Present value of net cash inflows}}{\text{Investment cost}} = \text{Profitability index}$$

Projects can then be ranked from highest to lowest in terms of their respective profitability indexes. The project with the highest profitability index should obviously be undertaken first; other projects will be undertaken according to the amount of resources available for investment.

To illustrate the ranking of projects using the net present value method, we will use the example in the preceding paragraph. The amount of the investment and its net present value are added to arrive at the present value of net cash inflows. Then, present value is divided by the investment cost to calculate a profitability index and respective ranking.

	Project A	Project B
Present value of net cash inflows	$12,000 (a)	$22,000 (a)
Investment cost	10,000 (b)	20,000 (b)
Net present value	$ 2,000	$ 2,000
Profitability index (a ÷ b)	1.20	1.10
Rank	1	2

Note that the profitability index must be 1.0 or greater for a project to be acceptable; this means that the net present value is at least zero.

Exhibit 4-2 summarizes the rules for making screening and ranking decisions using the net present value (with a profitability index) and the internal rate of return methods. Note that each technique leads management to the same screening decision. However, the methods may produce different rankings. In selecting between the two for the purposes of ranking, the profitability index is preferred because it considers directly the amount invested in each project, which results in the selection of the most profitable alternative.

to summarize

The screening function determines if projects are acceptable; the ranking function enables management to select the most profitable investment first and thus use limited resources to the best advantage. Ranking may be accomplished by the internal rate of return or by the net present value method.

7

Explain how income taxes affect capital budgeting decisions.

INCOME TAX CONSIDERATIONS IN CAPITAL BUDGETING DECISIONS

To keep the concepts simple, when considering capital budgeting decisions thus far in the chapter, we ignored the effects of income taxes on capital budgeting decisions. Unfortunately, ignoring

exhibit 4-2 Capital Budgeting Decision Rules

Selected Capital Budgeting Techniques	Decision Rules: Screening	Decision Rules: Ranking
Net present value method (NPV) using the profitability index (PI)	If PI > 1, invest If PI = 1, indifferent If PI < 1, don't invest	For two projects, a and b; If $PI_a > PI_b$, pick a, etc.
Internal rate of return (IRR)	If IRR > CC*, invest If IRR = CC, indifferent If IRR < CC, don't invest	For two projects, a and b; If $IRR_a > IRR_b$, pick a, etc.

*CC = cost of capital, or hurdle rate.

tax effects is not very realistic because capital budgeting decisions can be significantly affected by tax considerations. You will remember that an investment is acceptable financially if the net present value of the cash flows is zero or positive, given a desired rate of return. The discount rate used to compute the net present value is generally based on the company's cost of capital, which is usually the minimum rate of return a company must earn to satisfy its owners and creditors.

As an example of the income tax effects, a capital investment may allow a company to take an expense deduction for the cost of the asset and expense deductions for repairs and depreciation. Similarly, the resulting income from operations and any gain on the eventual sale of an asset are affected by taxes. Such tax effects can be so significant that the net present value of the cash flows changes from positive to negative, or vice versa.

To illustrate these income tax effects, we will use the Will's Pit Stop example discussed earlier. Recall that the gas station owner was considering installing a freezer for ice cream and other dairy products. The cost of the freezer was $42,045. It was expected to have a salvage value of $4,000 at the end of its 10-year useful life and to generate revenues of $15,000 per year on goods that cost $7,600. Thus, the cash flow was expected to be $7,400 ($15,000 − $7,600). At the end of the fifth year, the freezer would need $8,000 of repairs and servicing. Based on this information, the management of Will's Pit Stop decided not to buy the freezer because, at a hurdle rate of 12 percent, the net present value was negative. Furthermore, the internal rate of return was only 10 percent.

In making this decision, management neglected to consider the income tax effects. Here, we will incorporate the tax effects of the investment, based on the following initial assumptions: (1) Will's Pit Stop is a corporation with an effective tax rate of 25 percent, and (2) the hurdle rate of 12 percent is an after-tax rate. Assumption (2) means that the calculation of the cost of capital reflects the after-tax cost of interest expense, which is a deduction in computing a corporation's tax liability.

To compute the present values of the cash inflows and outflows, we must first convert them to after-tax amounts. This conversion is accomplished as follows:

1. Income on the freezer before taxes was $7,400 ($15,000 revenues − $7,600 cost of goods sold). At a 25 percent tax rate, net income is $5,550 ($7,400 × 0.25 = $1,850; $7,400 − $1,850 = $5,550). In other words, the company keeps 75 percent of the net revenues from the freezer ($7,400 × 0.75 = $5,550).
2. The U.S. income tax regulations allow a company to reduce its income tax liability by expensing some of the cost of tangible personal property immediately in the year of acquisition. If Will's Pit Stop elects to expense $10,000 of the cost of the freezer, this amount is deducted from the original cost in computing the depreciation base. The tax savings from taking this deduction in the year of acquisition is $2,500 ($10,000 × 0.25 tax rate).
3. Although the freezer has an estimated useful life of 10 years, the accelerated cost recovery system would allow Will's Pit Stop to write the freezer off over a 7-year period on an accelerated basis (using the double-declining-balance method) or over 10 or more years on a straight-line basis. We will assume that Will's Pit Stop elects to use the 7-year period to write off the remaining $32,045 ($42,045 − $10,000). The cost recovery for each year will be as follows:

Year	Pretax Cost Recovery
1	$ 4,578 ($32,045 on a double-declining-balance basis for ½ year)
2	7,848 [($32,045 − $4,578) ÷ 7 × 2]
3	5,605 [($27,467 − $7,848) ÷ 7 × 2]
4	4,004 [($19,619 − $5,605) ÷ 7 × 2]
5	2,860 [($14,014 − $4,004) ÷ 7 × 2]
6	2,860 [straight-line: ($10,010 − $2,860) ÷ 2½ years]
7	2,860 (straight-line)
8	1,430 (straight-line for ½ year)
	$32,045

Note that the company shifts to the straight-line method in year 6 in order to deduct as much depreciation as possible in that year and thereafter. As shown in Exhibit 4-3, at a 25 percent tax rate, the accelerated cost recovery deduction will save the company $1,145 in the first year in addition to the $2,500 saved by expensing the first $10,000 of the freezer's cost.

4. Under the IRS depreciation method known as the modified accelerated cost recovery system (MACRS), the entire cost of the freezer will have been written off in the first 8 years of its life. If the freezer is sold at the end of 10 years at its $4,000 estimated salvage value, there will be a $4,000 gain on the sale. This gain will be taxable as ordinary income at 25 percent (assuming no change in tax rates), so the after-tax cash inflow will be only $3,000 ($4,000 × 0.75).
5. The estimated repairs and servicing cost of $8,000 at the end of Year 5 is an expense deduction from the company's income for that year. Therefore, the net cost of this expense to the company is only $6,000 ($8,000 × 0.75).

These adjusted cash flows can now be used to compute the net present value of the cash inflows and outflows that would result if the freezer were purchased. The present values of these cash flows are presented in Exhibit 4-3 at three different hurdle rates: 8, 10, and 12 percent.

Three different rates are used to illustrate that the net present value decreases as the hurdle rate increases from 8 to 12 percent. In other words, as the rate of return increases, the present value of the cash inflows decreases in relation to the present value of the cash outflows, eventually changing the net present value from positive to negative. The point at which the present values of the inflows and outflows are equal reflects the expected internal rate of return. If the expected return is less than the company's hurdle rate, it is unlikely that the company will acquire the asset unless there are compensating qualitative factors.

Exhibit 4-3 shows that the tax effects on cash inflows and outflows, given a tax rate of 25 percent, reduce the rate of return on Will's Pit Stop's proposed freezer from a pretax 10 percent calculated earlier in the chapter to just over 8 percent. This occurs because taxes reduce the present value of the cash inflows more than they reduce the present value of the cash outflows. (Remember the initial cost is already at its present value.) If the tax rate were at the maximum corporate rate of 34 percent (when taxable income is in the $75,000 to $100,000 range), a likely event for many corporations, the internal rate of return would decrease even further. This is because the negative effect of the increased tax expense on gross margin is greater than the positive effect of the increased tax savings from expensing the first $10,000 of the freezer's cost and from the tax effects of the annual depreciation deduction and the deduction for repairs. In general, income taxes reduce the internal rate of return—and the higher the tax rate, the greater the reduction.

For the company to justify purchasing the freezer in the face of a 12 percent hurdle rate, the company would have to increase its gross margin significantly (increase sales volume with the same freezer capacity). You should also keep in mind that when the net present value at a selected hurdle rate is at or near zero, important qualitative factors not incorporated into the calculations of net present value will be the primary determinants of whether the asset is acquired.

to summarize

The cash inflows and outflows of capital budgeting decisions must be converted to after-tax amounts before the present values are computed in order to obtain a realistic measure of net present value. Cash inflows and outflows are converted to after-tax amounts by including such factors as the expense deduction, the modified accelerated cost recovery system (MACRS), any gain or loss on disposal, and the cash operating revenues and expenses.

exhibit 4-3 Income Tax Effects of Capital Budgeting

Will's Pit Stop
Net Present Value of Cash Inflows and Outflows (25% Tax Rate)

			8%		10%		12%	
Type of Cash Flow	**Period**	**After-Tax Cash Flow**	**Present Value**	**Amount***	**Present Value**	**Amount***	**Present Value**	**Amount***
Inflows:								
Revenue less cost of goods sold								
(net of tax): ($15,000 − $7,600) × 0.75 . .	Years 1–10	$ 5,550	6.7101	$37,241	6.1446	$34,103	5.6502	$31,359
MACRS expensing ($10,000 × 0.25)	Year 1	2,500	0.9259**	2,315	0.9091	2,273	0.8929	2,232
MACRS [($42,045 − $10,000): $32,045								
at 7-year, 200%]:								
$4,578 × 0.25	Year 1	$ 1,145	0.9259	$ 1,060	0.9091	$ 1,041	0.8929	$ 1,022
7,848 × 0.25	2	1,962	0.8573	1,682	0.8264	1,621	0.7972	1,564
5,605 × 0.25	3	1,401	0.7938	1,112	0.7513	1,053	0.7118	997
4,004 × 0.25	4	1,001	0.7350	736	0.6830	684	0.6355	636
2,860 × 0.25	5	715	0.6806	487	0.6209	444	0.5674	406
2,860 × 0.25	6	715	0.6302	451	0.5645	404	0.5066	362
2,860 × 0.25	7	715	0.5835	417	0.5132	367	0.4523	323
1,430 × 0.25	8	357	0.5403	193	0.4665	167	0.4039	144
				$ 6,138		$ 5,781		$ 5,454
Salvage value ($4,000 × 0.75).	End of Year 10	3,000	0.4632	$ 1,390	0.3855	$ 1,157	0.3220	$ 966
Total cash inflows				$47,084		$43,314		$40,011
Outflows:								
Initial freezer cost	Today	42,045	1.0000	$42,045	1.0000	$42,045	1.0000	$42,045
Repairs and servicing cost ($8,000 × 0.75) .	End of Year 5	6,000	0.6806	4,084	0.6209	3,725	0.5674	3,404
Total cash outflows				$46,129		$45,770		$45,449
Excess cash inflow (outflow).				$ 955		$ (2,456)		$ (5,438)

*After-tax cash flow × present value.
**Note that this is the present value of the cash flow discounted for 1 year.

APPENDIX: THE TIME VALUE OF MONEY

Present Value and Future Value Concepts

The concepts of present value and future value are used to measure the effect of time on the value of money. To illustrate, if you are to receive $100 one year from today, is it worth $100 today? Obviously not, because if you had the $100 today you could either use it now or invest it and earn interest. If the $100 isn't to be received for one year, those options are not available. The present value of $1 is the value today of $1 to be received or paid in the future, given a specified interest rate. To determine the value today of money to be received or paid in the future, we must "discount" the future amount (reduce the amount to its present value) by an appropriate interest rate. For example, if money can earn 10 percent per year, $100 to be received one year from now is approximately equal to $90.91 received today.

Putting it another way, if $90.91 is invested today in an account that earns 10 percent interest for one year, the interest earned will be $9.09 ($90.91 × 10% × 1 year = $9.09). The sum of the $90.91 principal plus $9.09 interest would equal $100 at the end of one year. Thus, the present value of $100 to be received (or paid) in one year with 10 percent interest is $90.91. This present value relationship can be diagramed as follows:

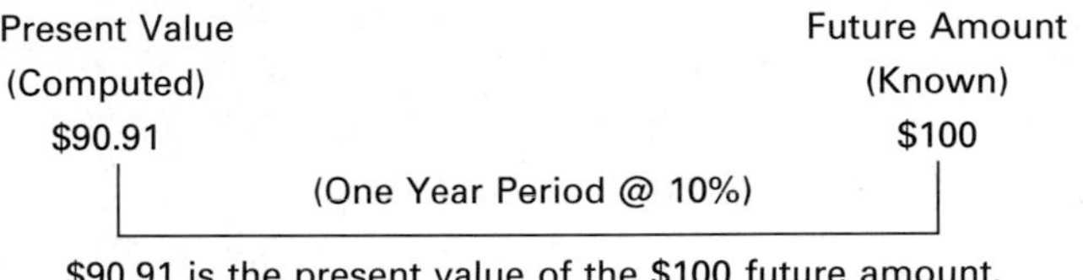

$90.91 is the present value of the $100 future amount.

The relationships in this diagram can be described in two ways. We have just looked at the relationship by recognizing that the $90.91 is the present value of $100 to be received one year from now when interest is 10 percent. In this example, the $100 to be received one year from now is known, and the present value of $90.91 must be computed. We are computing a present value amount from a known future value amount.

Another way to look at the relationship is on a future value basis. Future values apply when the amount today ($90.91) is known, and the future amount must be calculated. Future values are exactly the opposite of present values. Thinking in terms of future values, $100 is the future amount we can expect to receive in one year, given a present known amount of $90.91 when the interest rate is 10 percent. We can diagram this relationship as follows:

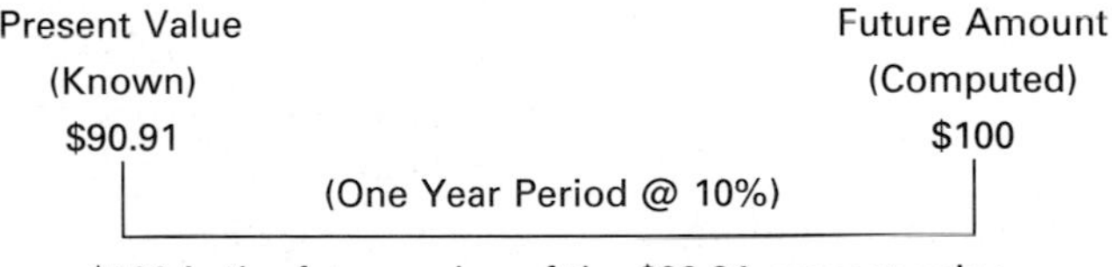

$100 is the future value of the $90.91 present value.

Present and future values can be calculated using formulas. However, if more than one period is involved, the calculations become rather complicated. Therefore, it is more convenient to use either a present value table or a calculator that gives the present value of $1 for various numbers of periods and interest rates (see Table I, page 212) or a future value table that gives the future value of $1 for various numbers of periods and interest rates (see Table III, page 214). We will illustrate the use of both a present value table and a future value table.

PRESENT VALUE TABLE To use a present value table, you simply locate the appropriate number of periods in the leftmost column and the interest rate in the row at the top of the table. The intersection of the row and column is the factor representing the present value of $1 for the number of periods and the relevant interest rate. To find the present value of an amount other than $1, multiply the factor in the table by that amount.

To illustrate the use of a present value table (Table I) to find the present value of a known future amount, assume that $10,000 is to be paid four years from today when the interest rate is 10 percent. What is the present value of the $10,000 payment?

Amount of payment.	$10,000
Present value factor of $1 to be paid in 4 periods	
at 10% interest (from Table I)	×0.6830
Present value of payment	$ 6,830

This present value amount, $6,830, is the amount that could be paid today to satisfy the obligation that is due four years from now. As indicated, this procedure is sometimes referred to as "discounting." Thus, we say that $10,000 discounted for four years at 10 percent is $6,830. Stated another way, if $6,830 is invested today in an account that pays 10 percent interest, in four years the balance in that account would be $10,000.

FUTURE VALUE TABLE To find the future value of an amount that is known today, you use a future value table. When using a future value table, you simply locate the appropriate number of periods in the leftmost column and the interest rate in the row at the top of the table. The intersection of the row and column is the factor representing the future value of $1 for the number of periods and the relevant interest rate. To find the future value of an amount other than $1, multiply the factor in the table by that amount.

To illustrate the use of a future value table (Table III), we will use the same information that was presented before, except that we will now assume that the present value of $6,830 is known, not the future amount of $10,000. Assume that we have a savings account with a current balance of $6,830 that earns interest of 10 percent. What will be the balance in that account in four years?

Present value in savings account	$ 6,830
Future value factor of $1 in 4 periods	
at 10% interest (from Table III)	×1.4641
Future value.	$10,000*

*Rounded

When computing future values, we often use the term *compounding* to mean the frequency with which interest is added to the principal. Thus, we say that interest of 10 percent has been compounded once a year (annually) to arrive at a future value at the end of four years of $10,000. If the interest is added more or less frequently than once a year, the future amount will be different.

The preceding example assumed an annual compounding period for interest. If the 10 percent interest had been compounded semiannually (twice a year) for four years, the calculation would have involved using a 5 percent (one-half of the 10 percent) rate for 8 periods (4 years × 2 periods per year) instead of 10 percent for 4 periods. To illustrate, what is the present value of $10,000 to be paid in four years if interest of 10 percent is compounded semiannually?

Amount of payment.	$10,000
Present value factor of $1 to be paid in 8 periods	
at 5% interest (from Table I)	×0.6768
Present value of payment	$ 6,768

Thus, the present value of $10,000 to be paid in four years is $6,768 if interest is compounded semiannually. Likewise, if semiannual compounding is used to determine the future value of $6,768 in four years at 10 percent compounded semiannually, the result is as follows:

Present value in savings account	$ 6,768
Future value factor of $1 in 8 periods	
at 5% interest (from Table III)	×1.4775
Future value.	$10,000*

*Rounded

Note that the present value ($6,768) is lower with semiannual compounding than with annual compounding ($6,830). The more frequently interest is compounded, the greater the total amount of interest deducted (in computing present values) or added (in computing future values).

Since interest may also be compounded quarterly, monthly, daily, or for some other period, you should learn the relationship of interest to the compounding period. Semiannual interest means that you double the interest periods and halve the annual interest rate; with quarterly interest you quadruple the periods and take one-fourth of the annual interest rate. The formula for interest rate is:

$$\frac{\text{Yearly interest rate}}{\text{Compounding periods per year}} = \text{Interest rate per compounding period}$$

The number of interest periods is simply the number of periods per year times the number of years. That formula is:

$$\text{Compounding periods per year} \times \text{Number of years} = \text{Number of interest periods}$$

The Present Value of an Annuity

In discussing present values and future values, we have assumed only a single present value or future value with one of the amounts known and the other to be computed. With liabilities, we generally know the future amount that must be paid and would like to compute the present value of that future payment.

Many long-term liabilities involve a series of payments rather than one lump-sum payment. For example, a company might purchase equipment under an installment agreement requiring payments of $5,000 each year for five years. Determining the value today (present value) of a series of equally spaced, equal amount payments (called annuities) is more complicated than determining the present value of a single future payment. If you were to try to calculate the present value of an annuity by hand, you would have to discount the first payment for one period, the second payment for two periods, and so on, and then add all the present values together. Because such calculations are time-consuming, a table is generally used (see Table II, page 213). The factors in the table are the sums of the individual present values of all future payments. Based on the present value of an annuity of $1, the table provides factors for various interest rates and payments.

To illustrate the use of a present value of an annuity table (Table II), we will assume that $10,000 is to be paid at the end of each of the next 10 years. If the interest rate is 12 percent compounded annually, Table II shows a present value factor of 5.6502. This factor means that the present value of $1 paid each year for 10 years discounted at 12 percent is approximately $5.65. Applying this factor to payments of $10,000 results in the following:

Amount of the annual payment.	$10,000
Present value factor of an annuity of $1 discounted for 10 payments at 12%	×5.6502
Present value	$56,502

This amount, $56,502, is the amount (present value) that could be paid today to satisfy the obligation if interest is 12 percent.

table I The Present Value of $1 Due in *n* Periods*

Period	1%	2%	3%	4%	5%	6%	7%	8%	9%	10%	12%	14%	15%	16%	18%	20%
1	.9901	.9804	.9709	.9615	.9524	.9434	.9346	.9259	.9174	.9091	.8929	.8772	.8696	.8621	.8475	.8333
2	.9803	.9612	.9426	.9246	.9070	.8900	.8734	.8573	.8417	.8264	.7972	.7695	.7561	.7432	.7182	.6944
3	.9706	.9423	.9151	.8890	.8638	.8396	.8163	.7938	.7722	.7513	.7118	.6750	.6575	.6407	.6086	.5787
4	.9610	.9238	.8885	.8548	.8227	.7921	.7629	.7350	.7084	.6830	.6355	.5921	.5718	.5523	.5158	.4823
5	.9515	.9057	.8626	.8219	.7835	.7473	.7130	.6806	.6499	.6209	.5674	.5194	.4972	.4761	.4371	.4019
6	.9420	.8880	.8375	.7903	.7462	.7050	.6663	.6302	.5963	.5645	.5066	.4556	.4323	.4104	.3704	.3349
7	.9327	.8706	.8131	.7599	.7107	.6651	.6227	.5835	.5470	.5132	.4523	.3996	.3759	.3538	.3139	.2791
8	.9235	.8535	.7894	.7307	.6768	.6274	.5820	.5403	.5019	.4665	.4039	.3506	.3269	.3050	.2660	.2326
9	.9143	.8368	.7664	.7026	.6446	.5919	.5439	.5002	.4604	.4241	.3606	.3075	.2843	.2630	.2255	.1938
10	.9053	.8203	.7441	.6756	.6139	.5584	.5083	.4632	.4224	.3855	.3220	.2697	.2472	.2267	.1911	.1615
11	.8963	.8043	.7224	.6496	.5847	.5268	.4751	.4289	.3875	.3503	.2875	.2366	.2149	.1954	.1619	.1346
12	.8874	.7885	.7014	.6246	.5568	.4970	.4440	.3971	.3555	.3186	.2567	.2076	.1869	.1685	.1372	.1122
13	.8787	.7730	.6810	.6006	.5303	.4688	.4150	.3677	.3262	.2897	.2292	.1821	.1625	.1452	.1163	.0935
14	.8700	.7579	.6611	.5775	.5051	.4423	.3878	.3405	.2992	.2633	.2046	.1597	.1413	.1252	.0985	.0779
15	.8613	.7430	.6419	.5553	.4810	.4173	.3624	.3152	.2745	.2394	.1827	.1401	.1229	.1079	.0835	.0649
16	.8528	.7284	.6232	.5339	.4581	.3936	.3387	.2919	.2519	.2176	.1631	.1229	.1069	.0930	.0708	.0541
17	.8444	.7142	.6050	.5134	.4363	.3714	.3166	.2703	.2311	.1978	.1456	.1078	.0929	.0802	.0600	.0451
18	.8360	.7002	.5874	.4936	.4155	.3503	.2959	.2502	.2120	.1799	.1300	.0946	.0808	.0691	.0508	.0376
19	.8277	.6864	.5703	.4746	.3957	.3305	.2765	.2317	.1945	.1635	.1161	.0829	.0703	.0596	.0431	.0313
20	.8195	.6730	.5537	.4564	.3769	.3118	.2584	.2145	.1784	.1486	.1037	.0728	.0611	.0514	.0365	.0261
25	.7798	.6095	.4476	.3751	.2953	.2330	.1842	.1460	.1160	.0923	.0588	.0378	.0304	.0245	.0160	.0105
30	.7419	.5521	.4120	.3083	.2314	.1741	.1314	.0994	.0754	.0573	.0334	.0196	.0151	.0116	.0070	.0042
40	.6717	.4529	.3066	.2083	.1420	.0972	.0668	.0460	.0318	.0221	.0107	.0053	.0037	.0026	.0013	.0007
50	.6080	.3715	.2281	.1407	.0872	.0543	.0339	.0213	.0134	.0085	.0035	.0014	.0009	.0006	.0003	.0001
60	.5504	.3048	.1697	.0951	.0535	.0303	.0173	.0099	.0057	.0033	.0011	.0004	.0002	.0001	†	†

*The formula used to derive the values in this table was $PV = F \frac{1}{(1+i)^n}$ where PV = present value, F = future amount to be discounted, i = interest rate, and n = number of periods.

†The value of 0 to four decimal places.

table II The Present Value of an Annuity of $1 per Number of Payments*

Number of Payments	1%	2%	3%	4%	5%	6%	7%	8%	9%	10%	12%	14%	15%	16%	18%	20%
1	0.9901	0.9804	0.9709	0.9615	0.9524	0.9434	0.9346	0.9259	0.9174	0.9091	0.8929	0.8772	0.8596	0.8621	0.8475	0.8333
2	1.9704	1.9416	1.9135	1.8861	1.8594	1.8334	1.8080	1.7833	1.7591	1.7355	1.6901	1.6467	1.6257	1.6052	1.5656	1.5278
3	2.9410	2.8839	2.8286	2.7751	2.7232	2.6730	2.6243	2.5771	2.5313	2.4869	2.4018	2.3216	2.2832	2.2459	2.1743	2.1065
4	3.9820	3.8077	3.7171	3.6299	3.5460	3.4651	3.3872	3.3121	3.2397	3.1699	3.0373	2.9137	2.8550	2.7982	2.6901	2.5887
5	4.8884	4.7135	4.5797	4.4518	4.3295	4.2124	4.1002	3.9927	3.8897	3.7908	3.6048	3.4331	3.3522	3.2743	3.1272	2.9906
6	5.7985	5.6014	5.4172	5.2421	5.0757	4.9173	4.7665	4.6229	4.4859	4.3553	4.1114	3.8887	3.7845	3.6847	3.4976	3.3255
7	6.7282	6.4720	6.2303	6.0021	5.7864	5.5824	5.3893	5.2064	5.0330	4.8684	4.5638	4.2883	4.1604	4.0386	3.8115	3.6046
8	7.6517	7.3255	7.0197	6.7327	6.4632	6.2098	5.9713	5.7466	5.5348	5.3349	4.9676	4.6389	4.4873	4.3436	4.0776	3.8372
9	8.5660	8.1622	7.7861	7.4353	7.1078	6.8017	6.5152	6.2469	5.9952	5.7590	5.3282	4.9464	4.7716	4.6065	4.3030	4.0310
10	9.4713	8.9826	8.5302	8.1109	7.7217	7.3601	7.0236	6.7101	6.4177	6.1446	5.6502	5.2161	5.0188	4.8332	4.4941	4.1925
11	10.3676	9.7868	9.2526	8.7605	8.3064	7.8869	7.4987	7.1390	6.8052	6.4951	5.9377	5.4527	5.2337	5.0286	4.6560	4.3271
12	11.2551	10.5733	9.9540	9.3851	8.8633	8.3838	7.9427	7.5361	7.1607	6.8137	6.1944	5.6603	5.4206	5.1971	4.7932	4.4392
13	12.1337	11.3484	10.6350	9.9856	9.3936	8.8527	8.3577	7.9038	7.4869	7.1034	6.4235	5.8424	5.5831	5.3423	4.9095	4.5327
14	13.0037	12.1062	11.2961	10.5631	9.8986	9.2950	8.7455	8.2442	7.7862	7.3667	6.6282	6.0021	5.7245	5.4675	5.0081	4.6106
15	13.8651	12.8493	11.9379	11.1184	10.3797	9.7122	9.1079	8.5595	8.0607	7.6061	6.8109	6.1422	5.8474	5.5755	5.0916	4.6755
16	14.7179	13.5777	12.5611	11.6523	10.8378	10.1059	9.4466	8.8514	8.3126	7.8237	6.9740	6.2651	5.9542	5.6685	5.1624	4.7296
17	15.5623	14.2919	13.1661	12.1657	11.2741	10.4773	9.7632	9.1216	8.5436	8.0216	7.1196	6.3729	6.0472	5.7487	5.2223	4.7746
18	16.3983	14.9920	13.7535	12.6593	11.6896	10.8276	10.0591	9.3719	8.7556	8.2014	7.2497	6.4674	6.1280	5.8178	5.2732	4.8122
19	17.2260	15.6785	14.3238	13.1339	12.0853	11.1581	10.3356	9.6036	8.9501	8.3649	7.3658	6.5504	6.1982	5.8775	5.3162	4.8435
20	18.0456	16.3514	14.8775	13.5903	12.4622	11.4699	10.5940	9.8181	9.1285	8.5136	7.4694	6.6231	6.2593	5.9288	5.3527	4.8696
25	22.0232	19.5235	17.4131	15.6221	14.0939	12.7834	11.6536	10.6748	9.8226	9.0770	7.8431	6.8729	6.4641	6.0971	5.4669	4.9476
30	25.8077	22.3965	19.6004	17.2920	15.3725	13.7648	12.4090	11.2578	10.2737	9.4269	8.0552	7.0027	6.5660	6.1772	5.5168	4.9789
40	32.8347	27.3555	23.1148	19.7928	17.1591	15.0463	13.3317	11.9246	10.7574	9.7791	8.2438	7.1050	6.6418	6.2335	5.5482	4.9966
50	39.1961	31.4236	25.7298	21.4822	18.2559	15.7619	13.8007	12.2335	10.9617	9.9148	8.3045	7.1327	6.6605	6.2463	5.5641	4.9995
60	44.9550	34.7609	27.6756	22.6235	18.9293	16.1614	14.0392	12.3766	11.0480	9.9672	8.3240	7.1401	6.6651	6.2482	5.5553	4.9999

*The formula used to derive the values in this table was $PV = F\left(\frac{1 - \frac{1}{(1+i)^n}}{i}\right)$ where PV = present value, F = periodic payment to be discounted, i = interest rate, and n = number of payments.

table III Amount of $1 Due in *n* Periods

Period	1%	2%	3%	4%	5%	6%	7%	8%	9%	10%	12%	14%	15%	16%	18%	20%
1	1.0100	1.0200	1.0300	1.0400	1.0500	1.0600	1.0700	1.0800	1.0900	1.1000	1.1200	1.1400	1.1500	1.1600	1.1800	1.2000
2	1.0201	1.0404	1.0609	1.0816	1.1025	1.1236	1.1449	1.1664	1.1881	1.2100	1.2544	1.2996	1.3225	1.3456	1.3924	1.4400
3	1.0303	1.0612	1.0927	1.1249	1.1576	1.1910	1.2250	1.2597	1.2950	1.3310	1.4049	1.4815	1.5209	1.5609	1.6430	1.7280
4	1.0406	1.0824	1.1255	1.1699	1.2155	1.2625	1.3108	1.3605	1.4116	1.4641	1.5735	1.6890	1.7490	1.8106	1.9388	2.0736
5	1.0510	1.1041	1.1593	1.2167	1.2763	1.3382	1.4026	1.4693	1.5386	1.6105	1.7623	1.9254	2.0114	2.1003	2.2878	2.4883
6	1.0615	1.1262	1.1941	1.2653	1.3401	1.4185	1.5007	1.5869	1.6771	1.7716	1.9738	2.1950	2.3131	2.4364	2.6996	2.9860
7	1.0721	1.1487	1.2299	1.3159	1.4071	1.5036	1.6058	1.7138	1.8280	1.9487	2.2107	2.5023	2.6600	2.8262	3.1855	3.5832
8	1.0829	1.1717	1.2668	1.3686	1.4775	1.5938	1.7182	1.8509	1.9926	2.1436	2.4760	2.8526	3.0590	3.2784	3.7589	4.2998
9	1.0937	1.1951	1.3048	1.4233	1.5513	1.6895	1.8385	1.9990	2.1719	2.3579	2.7731	3.2519	3.5179	3.8030	4.4355	5.1598
10	1.1046	1.2190	1.3439	1.4802	1.6289	1.7908	1.9672	2.1589	2.3674	2.5937	3.1058	3.7072	4.0456	4.4114	5.2338	6.1917
11	1.1157	1.2434	1.3842	1.5395	1.7103	1.8983	2.1049	2.3316	2.5804	2.8531	3.4785	4.2262	4.6524	5.1173	6.1759	7.4031
12	1.1268	1.2682	1.4258	1.6010	1.7959	2.0122	2.2522	2.5182	2.8127	3.1384	3.8960	4.8179	5.3502	5.9360	7.2876	8.9161
13	1.1381	1.2936	1.4685	1.6651	1.8856	2.1329	2.4098	2.7196	3.0658	3.4523	4.3635	5.4924	6.1528	6.8858	8.5994	10.699
14	1.1495	1.3195	1.5126	1.7317	1.9799	2.2609	2.5785	2.9372	3.3417	3.7975	4.8871	6.2613	7.0757	7.9875	10.147	12.839
15	1.1610	1.3459	1.5580	1.8009	2.0789	2.3966	2.7590	3.1722	3.6425	4.1772	5.4736	7.1379	8.1371	9.2655	11.973	15.407
16	1.1726	1.3728	1.6047	1.8730	2.1829	2.5404	2.9522	3.4259	3.9703	4.5950	6.1304	8.1372	9.3576	10.748	14.129	18.488
17	1.1843	1.4002	1.6528	1.9479	2.2920	2.6928	3.1588	3.7000	4.3276	5.0545	6.8660	9.2765	10.761	12.467	16.672	22.186
18	1.1961	1.4282	1.7024	2.0258	2.4066	2.8543	3.3799	3.9960	4.7171	5.5599	7.6900	10.575	12.375	14.462	19.673	26.623
19	1.2081	1.4568	1.7535	2.1068	2.5270	3.0256	3.6165	4.3157	5.1417	6.1159	8.6128	12.055	14.231	16.776	23.214	31.948
20	1.2202	1.4859	1.8061	2.1911	2.6533	3.2071	3.8697	4.6610	5.6044	6.7275	9.6463	13.743	16.366	19.460	27.393	38.337
30	1.3478	1.8114	2.4273	3.2434	4.3219	5.7435	7.6123	10.062	13.267	17.449	29.959	50.950	66.211	85.849	143.37	237.37
40	1.4889	2.2080	3.2620	4.8010	7.0400	10.285	14.974	21.724	31.409	45.259	93.050	188.88	267.86	378.72	750.37	1469.7
50	1.6446	2.6916	4.3839	7.1067	11.467	18.420	29.457	46.901	74.357	117.39	289.00	700.23	1083.6	1670.7	3927.3	9100.4
60	1.8167	3.2810	5.8916	10.519	18.679	32.987	57.946	101.25	176.03	304.48	897.59	2595.9	4383.9	7370.1	20555.	56347.

table IV Amount of an Annuity of $1 per Number of Payments

Number of Payments	1%	2%	3%	4%	5%	6%	7%	8%	9%	10%	12%	14%	15%	16%	18%	20%
1	1.0000	1.0000	1.0000	1.0000	1.0000	1.0000	1.0000	1.0000	1.0000	1.0000	1.0000	1.0000	1.0000	1.0000	1.0000	1.0000
2	2.0100	2.0200	2.0300	2.0400	2.0500	2.0600	2.0700	2.0800	2.0900	2.1000	2.1200	2.1400	2.1500	2.1600	2.1800	2.2000
3	3.0301	3.0604	3.0909	3.1216	3.1525	3.1836	3.2149	3.2464	3.2781	3.3100	3.3744	3.4396	3.4725	3.5056	3.5724	3.6400
4	4.0604	4.1216	4.1836	4.2465	4.3101	4.3746	4.4399	4.5061	4.5731	4.6410	4.7793	4.9211	4.9934	5.0665	5.2154	5.3680
5	5.1010	5.2040	5.3091	5.4163	5.5256	5.6371	5.7507	5.8666	5.9847	6.1051	6.3528	6.6101	6.7424	6.8771	7.1542	7.4416
6	6.1520	6.3081	6.4684	6.6330	6.8019	6.9753	7.1533	7.3359	7.5233	7.7156	8.1152	8.5355	8.7537	8.9775	9.4420	9.9299
7	7.2135	7.4343	7.6625	7.8983	8.1420	8.3938	8.6540	8.9228	9.2004	9.4872	10.8090	10.7305	11.0668	11.4139	12.1415	12.9159
8	8.2857	8.5830	8.8923	9.2142	9.5491	9.8975	10.2598	10.6366	11.0285	11.4359	12.2997	13.2328	13.7268	14.2401	15.3270	16.4991
9	9.3685	9.7546	10.1591	10.5828	11.0266	11.4913	11.9780	12.4876	13.0210	13.5795	14.7757	16.0853	16.7858	17.5185	19.0859	20.7989
10	10.4622	10.9497	11.4639	12.0061	12.5779	13.1808	13.8164	14.4866	15.1929	15.9374	17.5487	19.3373	20.3037	21.3215	23.5213	25.9587
11	11.5668	12.1687	12.8078	13.4864	14.2068	14.9716	15.7836	16.6455	17.5603	18.5312	20.6546	23.0445	24.3493	25.7329	28.7551	32.1504
12	12.6825	13.4121	14.1920	15.0258	15.9171	16.8699	17.8885	18.9771	20.1407	21.3843	24.1331	27.2707	29.0017	30.8502	34.9311	39.5805
13	13.8093	14.6803	15.6178	16.6268	17.7130	18.8821	20.1406	21.4953	22.9534	24.5227	28.0291	32.0887	34.3519	36.7862	42.2187	48.4966
14	14.9474	15.9739	17.0863	18.2919	19.5986	21.0151	22.5505	24.2149	26.0192	27.9750	32.3926	37.5811	40.5047	43.6720	50.8180	59.1959
15	16.0969	17.2934	18.5989	20.0236	21.5786	23.2760	25.1290	27.1521	29.3609	31.7725	37.2797	43.8424	47.5804	51.6595	60.9653	72.0351
16	17.2579	18.6393	20.1569	21.8245	23.6575	25.6725	27.8881	30.3243	33.0034	35.9497	42.7535	50.9804	55.7178	60.9250	72.9390	87.4421
17	18.4304	20.0121	21.7616	23.6975	25.8404	28.2129	30.8402	33.7502	36.9737	40.5447	48.8837	59.1176	65.0751	71.6730	87.0680	105.9306
18	19.6147	21.4123	23.4144	25.6454	28.1324	30.9057	33.9990	37.4502	41.3013	45.5992	55.7497	68.3941	75.8364	84.1407	103.7403	128.1167
19	20.8190	22.8406	25.1169	27.6712	30.5390	33.7600	37.3790	41.4463	46.0185	51.1591	63.4397	78.9692	88.2118	98.6032	123.4135	154.7400
20	22.0190	24.2974	26.8704	29.7781	33.0660	36.7856	40.9955	45.7620	51.1601	57.2750	72.0524	91.0249	102.4436	115.3797	146.6280	186.6880
30	34.7849	40.5681	47.5754	56.0849	66.4388	79.0582	94.4608	113.2832	136.3075	164.4940	241.3327	356.7868	434.7451	530.3117	790.9480	1181.8816
40	48.8864	60.4020	75.4013	95.0255	120.7998	154.7620	199.6351	259.0565	337.8824	442.5926	767.0914	1342.0251	1779.0903	2360.7572	4163.2130	7343.8578
50	64.4632	84.5794	112.7969	152.6671	209.3480	290.3359	406.5289	573.7702	815.0836	1163.9085	2400.0182	4994.5213	7217.7163	10435.6488	21813.0937	45497.1908
60	81.6697	114.0515	163.0534	237.9907	353.5837	533.1282	813.5204	1253.2133	1944.7921	3034.8164	7471.6411	18535.1333	29219.9916	46057.5085	114189.6665	281732.5718

review of learning objectives

1 Understand the importance of capital budgeting and the concepts underlying strategic and capital investment decisions. Strategic planning, especially as related to capital investment decisions, is critical to the success of organizations. The systematic planning for long-term investments in operating assets is known as capital budgeting. Long-term investments are usually large and represent commitments that are difficult to change, so capital budgeting is crucial to the long-run profitability of a company.

2 Describe and use two nondiscounted capital budgeting techniques: the payback method and the unadjusted rate of return method. Several capital budgeting techniques have been developed to assist in the decision-making process. The payback and unadjusted rate of return methods are commonly used in business because they are simple to apply. However, they generally should be used together with the discounted cash flow methods—net present value and internal rate of return—which are theoretically more correct because they consider the time value of money.

3 Describe and use two discounted capital budgeting techniques: the net present value method and the internal rate of return method. The net present value method uses a predetermined discount rate to state all the cash flows of an investment in present value terms. This rate is a company's cost of capital. The discounted cash inflows and outflows are then compared, and if the result is positive, or at least zero, the project is acceptable from a quantitative standpoint.

The internal rate of return method determines the "true" rate of return on an investment. This is the discount rate at which a project would have a net present value of zero. The internal rate is compared with the company's hurdle rate. If the internal rate is higher than or equal to the hurdle rate, the project is acceptable from a quantitative standpoint.

4 Understand the need for evaluating qualitative factors in strategic and capital investment decisions. Qualitative factors—such as the effect of an investment on quality and time, consumer and worker safety, and environmental and civic responsibility—are important considerations in capital investment decisions and may override the conclusions suggested by quantitative data.

expanded material

5 Use sensitivity analysis to assess the potential effects of uncertainty in capital budgeting. Sensitivity analysis is used to assess the potential effect of uncertainty with regard to capital budgeting. It enables management to examine how the results of the calculations would vary if certain estimates were to change and thereby to gauge how reasonable the decision is.

6 Explain how to use capital budgeting techniques in ranking capital investment projects. Capital budgeting deals with both the screening and the ranking of projects. Investments must first be screened to determine which are acceptable. They must then be ranked to ensure that a company's limited funds are invested in the projects that will earn the greatest rate of return and otherwise accomplish the company's overall objectives.

7 Explain how income taxes affect capital budgeting decisions. The cash inflows and outflows of capital budgeting decisions must be converted to after-tax amounts before the present values are computed in order to obtain realistic measures of net present values. Cash inflows and outflows are converted to after-tax amounts by taking into account such tax provisions as expense deductions for repairs and depreciation, the estimated gain on disposal of the asset at the end of its useful life, and annual operating revenues and expenses.

key terms and concepts

capital 184
capital budgeting 183
cash inflows 187
cash outflows 187
cost of capital 190
discounted cash flow methods 188
hurdle rate 196
interest 185
internal rate of return 194

review problem

Capital Budgeting

High Flying Company has an opportunity to make an investment that will yield $1,000 net cash inflow per year for the next 10 years. The investment will cost $6,000 and will have no salvage value. After cost reductions and depreciation related to the new investment, the future average annual net income will increase $800.

Required: Compute the following:

1. The payback period.
2. The unadjusted rate of return.
3. The net present value. (Use a 10 percent discount rate.)
4. The internal rate of return. (The hurdle rate is 10 percent.)

Solution

1. The Payback Period

To compute the payback period, divide the investment cost by the annual net cash inflows.

$$\frac{\text{Investment cost}}{\text{Annual net cash inflows}} = \frac{\$6{,}000}{\$1{,}000} = 6 \text{ years}$$

2. The Unadjusted Rate of Return

To compute the unadjusted rate of return, divide the increase in future average annual net income by the initial investment cost.

$$\frac{\text{Increase in future average annual net income}}{\text{Initial investment cost}} = \frac{\$800}{\$6{,}000} = 13.3 \text{ percent}$$

3. The Net Present Value

To compute the net present value, first state in present value terms all expected cash outflows and inflows.

Present value of 10 annual payments of $1,000 discounted at 10 percent	$6,145
Present value of payment of $6,000 now	6,000
Net present value of project (present value of cash inflows minus present value of cash outflow)	$ 145

Since this investment's net present value is greater than zero, it is acceptable from a quantitative standpoint.

4. The Internal Rate of Return

To compute the internal rate of return, first compute the present value factor, as follows:

$$\frac{\text{Investment cost}}{\text{Annual net cash inflows}} = \frac{\$6{,}000}{\$1{,}000} = 6.0000$$

Next, use this present value factor to find the investment's internal rate of return in a present value table. Using Table II, find the row for 10 years, the life of the investment. Move across the row until you find the present value factor closest to 6.0000, which is 6.1446. This is the factor for 10 percent. Since 6.0000 is between 6.1446 and 5.6502, the investment's internal rate of return is between 10 and 12 percent. Next, use interpolation to find a more exact internal rate of return.

	Rate of Return	Present Value Factors	
High factor	10%	6.1446	6.1446
True factor		6.0000	0.0000
Low factor	12		5.6502
Differences	2%	0.1446	0.4944

The number 0.1446 is the difference between the high factor and the true factor. The number 0.4944 is the difference between the high factor and the low factor. The difference between the high rate and the low rate is 2 percent. The proportion 0.1446 ÷ 0.4944 of this 2 percent difference must be added to the low rate to give the true internal rate of return.

$$\text{True internal rate of return} = 0.10 + \left(0.02 \times \frac{0.1446}{0.4944}\right) = 10.58 \text{ percent}$$

The internal rate of return could also be computed using the following keystrokes with a Hewlett-Packard business calculator:

Hewlett-Packard Keystrokes:

1. −6,000: Press **PV** (you must enter the cash outflow as a NEGATIVE number)
2. 1,000: Press **PMT** (this is the annual cash inflow)
3. 10: Press **N** (number of years)
4. Press **I/YR** for the answer = 10.56%

Note that the answer obtained using table interpolation (10.58 percent) is very close to the actual internal rate of return of 10.56 percent.

Next, this internal rate of return is compared with the hurdle rate. Since it is greater, the investment is acceptable quantitatively. Note that this is the same decision reached by calculating the net present value.

discussion questions

1. Define capital budgeting. Give two examples of long-term investment decisions that require capital budgeting.
2. Why do long-term capital investment decisions often have a significant effect on a company's profitability?
3. Why is the time value of money so important in capital budgeting decisions?
4. If the time value of money is so important, why isn't the timing of cash flows emphasized in the accounting cycle?
5. How is depreciation expense treated when the discounted cash flow methods are used? Why?
6. How are cost savings and increased revenues related in capital budgeting?
7. Identify four capital budgeting methods, and explain why some are considered better than others.
8. Why is the payback method inferior to the discounted cash flow methods? When is the payback method helpful?

9. What is the major weakness of the unadjusted rate of return method?
10. Does a net present value of zero indicate that a project should be rejected? Explain.
11. As the desired rate of return increases, does the net present value of a project increase? Explain.
12. Under what circumstances might a project with a negative net present value be accepted?
13. What discount rate yields a net present value of zero? How is it determined?
14. What is a company's hurdle rate? How is it used?
15. How do quality and time considerations affect capital budgeting decisions?
16. Identify several qualitative factors, other than quality and time considerations, that may affect strategic and capital investment decisions. Why are qualitative factors important?

expanded material

17. How can we deal with uncertainties involved in capital budgeting?
18. Distinguish between the screening and ranking functions of capital budgeting.
19. Of what value is a profitability index in capital budgeting?
20. How do income taxes influence capital budgeting decisions?

discussion cases

CASE 4-1

SHOULD WE PURCHASE THAT NEW COPIER?

Campus Print Shop is thinking of purchasing a new, modern copier that automatically collates pages. The machine would cost $22,000 cash. A service contract on the machine, considered a must because of its complexity, would be an additional $200 per month. The machine is expected to last eight years and have a resale value of $4,000. By purchasing the new machine, Campus would save $450 per month in labor costs and $100 per month in materials costs due to increased efficiency. Other operating costs are expected to remain the same. The old copier would be sold for its scrap value of $1,000. Campus requires a return of 14 percent on its capital investments.

1. As a consultant to Campus, compute:
   a. The payback period.
   b. The unadjusted rate of return.
   c. The net present value.
   d. The internal rate of return.
2. On the basis of these computations and any qualitative considerations, would you recommend that Campus purchase the new copier?

CASE 4-2

COST AND QUALITATIVE FACTORS IN CAPITAL INVESTMENT DECISIONS

Yoshika Landscaping is contemplating purchasing a new ditch-digging machine that promises savings of $5,600 per year for 10 years. The machine costs $21,970, and no salvage value is expected. The company's cost of capital is 12 percent. You have been asked to advise Yoshika relative to this capital investment decision. As part of your analysis, compute:

1. The payback period.
2. The unadjusted rate of return.
3. The net present value.
4. The internal rate of return.

What factors besides your quantitative analysis should be considered in making this decision?

Note: Unless otherwise indicated, the exercises and problems assume that all payments are made or received at the end of the year.

EXERCISE 4-1

PRESENT VALUES

Consider each part independently.

1. Super-Fix Company would like to move its auto repair shop to a downtown location in order to attract more customers. What is the maximum Super-Fix should pay to purchase a building at the new location, assuming that the company needs to earn 12 percent? The new building will last 40 years. Super-Fix estimates that moving to the new location will result in a $10,000 increase in annual income.
2. If Audrey Ostler buys a new small automobile that costs $14,000 and provides annual gasoline savings of $1,200, how long must she own the car before the savings justify its cost? Assume an 8 percent cost of capital.

EXERCISE 4-2

TIME VALUE OF MONEY

Your late, rich uncle left you $250,000. The executor of the estate has asked if you would rather receive the full amount now or $30,000 a year for the next 40 years.

Which of these options would you take, assuming that your desired rate of return is:

1. 10 percent?
2. 12 percent?

EXERCISE 4-3

PAYBACK METHOD

The manager of Simple Company must choose between two investments. Project A costs $50,000 and promises cash savings of $10,000 a year over a useful life of 10 years. Project B costs $60,000, and the estimated cash savings are $11,000 per year over a useful life of 11 years. Using the payback method, determine which project the manager should choose.

EXERCISE 4-4

UNADJUSTED RATE OF RETURN METHOD

Um Good, Inc., a candy maker, is thinking of purchasing a new machine. A marketing firm has estimated that the new machine could increase revenues by $30,000 a year for the next 5 years. The expenses directly relating to the machine total $60,000 ($12,000 × 5 years). The initial purchase cost would be $80,000. What is the unadjusted rate of return?

EXERCISE 4-5

NET PRESENT VALUE METHOD

The Carroll Broom Company is thinking of purchasing a new automatic straw-binding machine. The company president, Joan Carroll, has determined that such a machine would save the company $10,000 per year in labor costs. The machine would cost $46,500 and would have a useful life of 10 years and a scrap value of $500. The machine would require servicing after 5 years at a cost of $1,000. Carroll uses a discount rate of 16 percent. Compute the net present value. From a quantitative standpoint, should the machine be purchased?

EXERCISE 4-6

LEAST-COST DECISION

The local fire department has determined the Sleep-Eazy Mattress Company is not in full compliance with local fire regulations. To comply, Sleep-Eazy has two alternatives: It may install an automatic sprinkler system, or it may hire a fire safety expert to make weekly fire safety checks. The automatic sprinkler system will cost $125,000, including installation charges, and will last for 10 years. It will have no salvage value. The entire system is virtually maintenance-free. The fire safety expert's fee is $14,000 per year. The cost of capital is 10 percent. Which alternative should Sleep-Eazy Mattress Company choose? Why?

EXERCISE 4-7

INTERNAL RATE OF RETURN

Juan Gonzales, the president of Nogalis Corporation, is trying to decide whether he should buy a new machine that will improve production efficiency. The machine will increase cash inflows $5,000 a year for 5 years. It will cost $18,000, and there will be no salvage value. What is the internal rate of return?

EXERCISE 4-8

COST OF CAPITAL

Daphney Corporation has raised $200,000 in equity financing through the issuance of shares. Stockholders expect to earn an average of 20 percent per year on their equity investment in Daphney. In addition, the corporation has issued $100,000 of 10 percent bonds. The corporation has also accumulated $25,000 in earnings that have been retained in the company. Investors expect to earn about 16 percent on the earnings that are retained in the company. Using the weighting procedure discussed in the chapter, calculate Daphney Corporation's cost of capital. (Ignore taxes in calculating the cost of debt.)

EXERCISE 4-9

NET PRESENT VALUE AND INTERNAL RATE OF RETURN

A real estate investment requires an initial outlay of $150,000 in cash. The investment will return a single sum cash payment of $606,796 after 10 years. The rate of return required on projects as risky as this one is 18 percent.

1. What is the net present value of this real estate investment?
2. What is the internal rate of return of this real estate investment?
3. Is this an attractive investment?

EXERCISE 4-10

NET PRESENT VALUE AND INTERNAL RATE OF RETURN

A retired person has $700,000 in a retirement account. An insurance company is offering to give the retired person an annuity of $61,029 at the end of each year for the next 20 years in exchange for the $700,000. The retired person requires a rate of return of 8 percent on investments; this is the rate currently being earned in the retirement account.

1. What is the net present value of this exchange?
2. What is the internal rate of return implied in this exchange?
3. Should the retired person accept the exchange offered by the insurance company?

EXERCISE 4-11

QUALITY AND TIME FACTORS

Tucker Yard Service Company is contemplating purchasing a new riding lawnmower for its business. One particular model has special features that enhance the cutting and the collecting of the mowed grass, but that mower is quite expensive. Another model is more basic and costs $1,000 less. The payback period on the more expensive model is estimated to be 3.5 years and on the less expensive model 2.5 years. The "bumper-to-bumper" warranties are two years and one year, respectively. From these limited data, what factors should Tucker consider in making this decision?

EXERCISE 4-12

QUALITATIVE CONSIDERATIONS

The Upscale Department Store has been plagued with shoplifting. The president, Hector Conrad, has suggested that the store hire a security force to "frisk" all customers as they leave the store. It is estimated that annual shoplifting losses are $100,000. Expenses associated with the security force are estimated to be $50,000 annually. Before Mr. Conrad makes his final decision, what other factors might he consider?

expanded material

EXERCISE 4-13

SENSITIVITY ANALYSIS

You have accumulated $10,500 in a savings account that pays 10 percent interest. You are offered the opportunity to buy 30 ounces of gold at $350 per ounce. The price of gold is expected to rise to $700 per ounce by the end of 10 years. You realize, however, that this is only an estimate.

To what price would gold have to rise in order to earn a 10 percent return? (Note that the future value factor for $10,500 at 10 percent at the end of 10 years is 2.5937.)

EXERCISE 4-14

SCREENING FUNCTION

Your company's cost of capital was determined to be 12 percent. Several investment alternatives are being considered, and the discounted cash flows have given the following results:

Net present value:

1. A new machine was analyzed, and a net present value of zero resulted.
2. A new product line was analyzed, and a negative net present value of $60 resulted.
3. An investment was being considered. The analysis yielded a net present value of $250.

Internal rate of return:

1. A plant expansion project promised a yield of 12 percent.
2. An investment in additional transport trucks would yield an internal rate of return of 10 percent.
3. The addition of another assembly line would add cash flows that would give an internal rate of return of 16 percent.

Determine which projects should be accepted as investment opportunities and which should be rejected.

EXERCISE 4-15

RANKING PROJECTS

Using net present value (NPV) analysis, a manager can select those projects that will maximize the present value of future cash flows. NPV analysis is a powerful tool; however, surveys of current practice indicate that the internal rate of return (IRR) method enjoys considerable popularity among decision makers. What would account for IRR's appeal? What are the drawbacks to using only the IRR method to rank projects?

EXERCISE 4-16

PROFITABILITY INDEX

California Company is trying to determine the relative profitability of two alternative investments. Investment A requires an initial cash outlay of $10,000 and has a net present value of $500. Investment B requires an initial cash outlay of $2,000 and has a net present value of $150. Compute the profitability index of each investment. Which alternative is more profitable?

EXERCISE 4-17

INCOME TAX EFFECTS

Kade Corporation is considering purchasing a new piece of equipment. The equipment will cost $135,000 and is expected to have a useful life of five years. The gross cash flow savings is estimated to be $50,000 per year. The company elects not to take the expense deduction and will depreciate the full cost of the asset for tax purposes under MACRS using a 5-year recovery period and the straight-line method. The company is in the 40 percent tax bracket (including federal, state, and local taxes).

1. Compute the after-tax cash flow savings on the asset.
2. Compute the after-tax internal rate of return that will equate the present value of the savings with the net outlay cost.

PROBLEM 4-1

NET PRESENT VALUE METHOD

A fast-food establishment is thinking of buying a new cooking grill and refrigeration unit. The cost of these new machines is $12,500 and $9,000, respectively. The installation costs of the new equipment will run about $800. It is estimated that 10 percent more customers can be served

with the new equipment, which would mean an additional annual net cash flow of approximately $4,500. The salvage value of the old grill and refrigeration unit is estimated to be $1,000.

The firm's cost of capital is 12 percent. The equipment should last 10 years, at a minimum.

Required: Using the net present value method, should the company purchase the new equipment? (Ignore income tax effects.)

PROBLEM 4-2

NET PRESENT VALUE METHOD—UNEVEN CASH FLOWS

Southside Junk Yard needs to buy a car smasher. The machine would add the following revenues to the business over the next three years:

Year 1 Cash savings = $30,000
Year 2 Cash savings plus additional scrap sales = $40,000
Year 3 Cash savings plus additional scrap sales = $55,000

The initial cost of the machine is $100,000. At the end of three years, its salvage value is estimated at $20,000. The firm has a cost of capital of 12 percent.

Required: Using the net present value method, determine whether the company should purchase the machine. (Ignore income tax effects.)

PROBLEM 4-3

INTERNAL RATE OF RETURN

You have been offered the opportunity to purchase a franchise of Sunshine Juice Stores. You will have to pay $155,625 for the initial investment in the store and its equipment, plus $30,000 per year for the lease payments and the franchise fee. The franchise contract obligates you for 10 years. Operating costs for each year will be $125,000, and the expected revenue is $180,000 a year. Your hurdle rate is 10 percent. Ignore income taxes.

Required:

1. Does this investment yield a satisfactory rate of return?
2. What qualitative factors might be considered?

PROBLEM 4-4

INTERNAL RATE OF RETURN AND HURDLE RATE

Nina Roberts has the opportunity to invest in a timber forest. She would have to invest $100,000. Revenues of $20,000 per year are projected for 20 years. However, these revenues will not begin coming in for five years because the timber must be seasoned before cutting and selling can begin. Ms. Roberts's hurdle rate is 10 percent. Ignore income taxes.

Required:

1. Calculate the internal rate of return, and determine whether or not Ms. Roberts should make the investment.
2. If Ms. Roberts has to borrow the $100,000 necessary for the investment from her bank at 12 percent interest, should she make the investment?
3. **Interpretive Question:** Why is it important for Ms. Roberts to determine her cost of capital before making this investment decision?

PROBLEM 4-5

PAYBACK, NET PRESENT VALUE, AND INTERNAL RATE OF RETURN METHODS

Nucore Company is thinking of purchasing a new candy-wrapping machine at a cost of $370,000. The machine should save the company approximately $70,000 in operating costs per year over its estimated useful life of 10 years. The salvage value at the end of 10 years is expected to be $15,000. (Ignore income tax effects.)

Spread-Sheet Software

Required:

1. What is the machine's payback period?
2. Compute the net present value of the machine if the cost of capital is 12 percent.
3. What is the expected internal rate of return for this machine?

PROBLEM 4-6

INTERNAL RATE OF RETURN

The manager of Soft & Creamy Ice Cream is thinking of buying a new soft ice cream machine. The machine will cost $13,500 and will last 10 years. Soft ice cream sales are expected to generate $3,000 in income per year.

Required: What is the internal rate of return on this project?

PROBLEM 4-7

CHOOSING AMONG ALTERNATIVES

Tom Thurlow wants to buy a boat but is short of cash. Two alternatives are available: Tom can accept $2,000 per year from his brother for partial ownership in the boat, or he can earn money by renting the boat to others. Rental income would be $2,500 per year. Under either alternative, the boat will last eight years. If Tom rents the boat out, he will have to pay $3,000 to overhaul the engine at the end of the fourth year.

Required: Which alternative should Tom select, assuming that the cost of capital is 12 percent and that only quantitative considerations are involved?

PROBLEM 4-8

LEASE-OR-BUY DECISION

A small sales company is committed to supplying three sales representatives with new cars. The company has two alternatives. It can either buy the three cars and sell them after two years, or it can lease the cars for two years. The company uses a 16 percent discount rate. The information for each alternative is as follows:

Alternative 1: Buy

Cost	$36,000
Annual service costs	3,000
Anticipated repairs during the 1st year	700
Anticipated repairs during the 2nd year	1,500
Salvage value at the end of 2 years	10,000

Alternative 2: Lease

To lease the cars, the company would simply pay $20,000 a year for the two years.

Required: Assuming the lease is paid at the end of each year, determine the better alternative.

PROBLEM 4-9

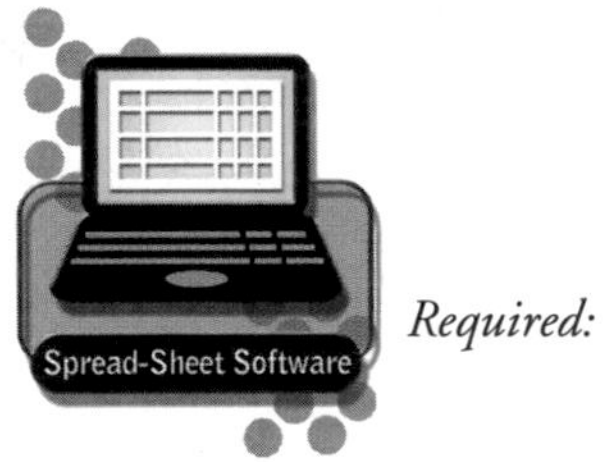

RENT-OR-PURCHASE DECISION

As one aspect of its business, New Lawn Company currently rents a ditch-digging machine for an average of $48 per job. A used machine is available for $995 but would cost $498 to repair. The machine, if purchased, would cost $800 a year to maintain and in two years would need a new chain costing $394. The used digger has a useful life of four years with no salvage value.

Required: If the company averages 30 jobs a year and has a cost of capital of 10 percent, which alternative is more profitable?

PROBLEM 4-10

SELL-OR-RENT DECISION

Clarence Gleason has inherited an apartment complex. He is now faced with the decision of whether to sell or to rent the property. A real estate adviser believes that Clarence should rent the property, because he could receive $65,000 per year for 10 years and then could sell the property for $400,000. A development company has offered Clarence $300,000 down and promises to pay $50,000 per year for the next 15 years. The land has a remaining mortgage of $130,000. If Clarence sells the complex, he will have to pay that sum now. If he rents the property, he will have to pay $20,000 per year for 10 years. The cost of capital is 16 percent.

Required:

1. Calculate the net present value of each alternative.
2. **Interpretive Question:** Discuss the qualitative factors that might affect the decision to sell or rent.

PROBLEM 4-11

UNIFYING CONCEPTS: NET PRESENT VALUE AND INTERNAL RATE OF RETURN METHODS

Julie Kowalis, an investment analyst, wants to know if her investments during the past four years have earned at least a 12 percent return. Four years ago, she had the following investments:

a. She purchased a small building for $50,000 and rented space in it. She received rental income of $8,000 for each of the four years and then sold the building this year for $55,000.
b. She purchased a small refreshment stand near the city park for $25,000. Annual income from the stand was $5,000 for each of the four years. She sold the stand for $20,000 this year.

c. She purchased an antique car for $5,000 four years ago. She sold it this year to a collector for $7,000.

Required:

1. Using the net present value method, determine whether or not each investment earned at least 12 percent.
2. Did the investments as a whole earn at least 12 percent? Explain.

expanded material

PROBLEM 4-12

SENSITIVITY ANALYSIS

Falcon Manufacturing is a leading manufacturer of airframe components for small aircraft. Heidi Saxton, Falcon's operations manager, has submitted a request for a new piece of production equipment. Using the new machine, the company will be able to reduce expenses for both maintenance and labor. Data on the project are as follows:

Initial investment	$80,000
Useful life	10 years
Salvage value of old machine	$1,500
Annual cash savings	$15,000
Salvage value of new machine	$10,000
Maintenance overhaul (Year 5)	$7,600
Cost of capital	12%

Assume all cash flows occur at the end of each year. (Ignore income tax effects.)

Required:

1. Using the above data, calculate the net present value of the investment. From a strictly quantitative standpoint, should the machine be purchased?
2. Suppose that Heidi receives another analysis that increases the cost of capital estimate to 14 percent and the new machine's salvage value to $17,000. Would the purchase still make sense?
3. Falcon's CEO, Kevin Davis, is responsible for approving all capital investment projects. Having spent his entire career dealing with one estimate after another, Davis has asked you to consider two specific changes:
   a. Reduce annual cash inflows by 10 percent.
   b. Cut in half the estimated salvage value of new equipment.

   Using the original problem data, calculate the net present value using the CEO's two changes.

PROBLEM 4-13

NET PRESENT VALUE USED TO RANK ALTERNATIVES

Taglioni's Pizza Company has to choose a new delivery car from among three alternatives. Assume that gasoline costs $1.30 per gallon and that the firm's cost of capital is 12 percent. The car will be driven 12,000 miles per year.

	Car 1	Car 2	Car 3
Cost	$12,000	$4,000	$8,000
Mileage per gallon	40	8	12
Useful life	5 years	5 years	5 years
Salvage value	$2,000	$500	$1,000

Required:

1. Which car should the company purchase?
2. How would your answer change if the price of gasoline increased to $2 per gallon?

PROBLEM 4-14

SCREENING AND RANKING ALTERNATIVES

Sunshine Corporation is considering several long-term investments. Management wants to accept the two best projects, given the following data:

	Project				
	A	B	C	D	E
Present value of net cash inflows	$24,000	$44,000	$15,000	$30,000	$50,000
Investment cost	20,000	40,000	16,000	24,000	41,000

Required:

1. Determine the net present value and the profitability index for each project.
2. Which projects are acceptable using the profitability index as a screening tool?
3. What would be the ranking of the acceptable projects according to the profitability indexes?
4. **Interpretive Question:** What additional information would be needed to screen and rank the projects using the internal rate of return method? What are the decision rules using the IRR method for screening and ranking capital budgeting projects?

PROBLEM 4-15 UNIFYING CONCEPTS: COMPARING THE INTERNAL RATE OF RETURN AND THE NET PRESENT VALUE METHODS

Get Rich Corporation has to choose between two investment opportunities. Investment A requires an immediate cash outlay of $100,000 and provides after-tax income of $20,000 per year for 10 years. Investment B requires an immediate cash outlay of $1,000 and generates after-tax income of $350 per year for 5 years.

Required:

1. Using a cost of capital of 12 percent, calculate the net present value of each investment, and determine which one Get Rich should select.
2. Calculate the internal rate of return of each investment. On the basis of this method, which investment should Get Rich select?
3. **Interpretive Question:** How do you account for the difference in rankings? Under the circumstances, which method would you rely on for your decision?

PROBLEM 4-16 UNIFYING CONCEPTS: PAYBACK AND INTERNAL RATE OF RETURN

The management of Kitchen Shop is thinking of buying a new drill press to aid in adapting parts for different machines. The press is expected to save Kitchen Shop $8,000 per year in costs. However, Kitchen Shop has an old punch machine that isn't worth anything on the market and that will probably last indefinitely. The new press will last 12 years and will cost $41,595. (Ignore income tax effects.)

Required:

1. Compute the payback period of the new machine.
2. Compute the internal rate of return.
3. **Interpretive Question:** What uncertainties are involved in this decision? Discuss how they might be dealt with.

PROBLEM 4-17 UNIFYING CONCEPTS: CAPITAL RATIONING USING THE PAYBACK AND NET PRESENT VALUE METHODS

Dino Corporation is trying to decide which of five investment opportunities it should undertake. The company's cost of capital is 16 percent. Owing to a cash shortage, the company has a policy that it will not undertake any investment unless it has a payback period of less than three years. The company is unwilling to undertake more than two investment projects. The following data apply to the alternatives:

Investment	Initial Cost	Expected Returns
A	$100,000	$30,000 per year for 5 years
B	50,000	25,000 per year for 6 years
C	30,000	8,000 per year for 10 years
D	20,000	7,000 per year for 6 years
E	10,000	3,500 per year for 3 years

Required:

1. Using the payback method, screen out any investment project that fails to meet the company's payback period requirement.
2. Using the net present value method, determine which of the remaining projects the company should undertake, keeping in mind the capital rationing constraint.
3. **Interpretive Question:** What advantages do you see in using the payback method together with other capital budgeting methods?

PROBLEM 4-18

INCOME TAX EFFECTS

Sylvania Manufacturing Company is considering the purchase of new equipment to perform operations currently being performed on less efficient equipment. The purchase price is $142,000 delivered and installed. The company elects to expense $10,000 of the purchase price in the first year. A company engineer estimates that the new equipment will save $28,000 in labor and other direct costs annually. The new equipment will have an estimated life of 10 years and zero salvage value at the end of the 10 years. The equipment will be depreciated over 10 years on the optional straight-line basis for income tax purposes, after taking the $10,000 expense election in the first year. The existing equipment has a book value of $4,000, a remaining economic life of five years, and can be disposed of now for $4,000. The company's average tax rate is 40 percent (including federal, state, and local taxes), and its after-tax cost of capital is 12 percent.

Required:

1. Should the new equipment be purchased?
2. What would the decision be if the cost of capital were 10 percent?
3. **Interpretive Question:** Assuming that the net present value of an investment in new equipment is so small that you are indifferent about whether to make the purchase or keep the old equipment, what other factors would you consider in making the decision?

competency enhancement opportunities

- Analyzing Real Company Information
- International Case
- Ethics Case
- Writing Assignment
- The Debate
- Internet Search

The following additional assignments provide opportunities for students to develop critical thinking, ethical perspectives, oral and written communication skills, experience with electronic research, and teamwork through group and business activities.

ANALYZING REAL COMPANY INFORMATION

• ***Analyzing 4-1 (Microsoft)***

The 1999 annual report for MICROSOFT is included in Appendix A. The section of the annual report relating to management's discussion and analysis provides detail as to factors that might affect Microsoft's future and, as a result, the company's long-term decisions. Review the financial statements and the "Management Discussion and Analysis" section, and answer the following questions:

1. Microsoft has no long-term debt. Does that mean its cost of capital is zero? Explain.

2. Microsoft specifically states that the company "does not provide forecasts of future financial performance." If that is the case, how can it make any capital budgeting decisions?
3. In Bill Gates's letter to shareholders, he makes the following comment:

   > We are investing heavily in the future—from world-class customer support to the $3.8 billion we plan to spend in fiscal 2000 on research and development for the products of tomorrow. There is, however, no guarantee of success. Competition continues to intensify, and regulatory pressures are unlikely to ease. Although global PC sales have proved remarkably robust, some slowdown is likely in the coming year. And as Microsoft's business becomes more complex, the strategic challenges and risks we face grow exponentially.

   Microsoft is committed to making heavy investments in the future. However, Bill notes that "there is no guarantee of success." How would such factors as competition, regulation, and a changing computer world affect the company's capital budgeting process? What specific inputs into the capital budgeting models would be affected by these factors?

• *Analyzing 4-2 (The Boeing Company)*

As you probably know, **BOEING** builds airplanes. While most famous for the big 747, Boeing is continually developing newer models. Over the past several years, Boeing has been developing the 737 and 777 families of airplanes. In 1996, Boeing formed a joint venture with **GENERAL ELECTRIC** to develop planes that can fly over 6,000 miles without refueling.

1. What factors must Boeing consider when making the decision to produce a new family of airplanes like the 777? What would be the expected cash inflows, and what would be the expected cash outflows? Categorize the outflows into two types: one-time outflows and annual outflows.
2. The costs of developing a new family of airplanes are enormous. Why would Boeing agree to incur these costs when it is able to continue producing older model planes like the 747 and the 767? Frame this discussion in terms of a capital budgeting decision. That is, evaluate the opportunities in terms of cash inflows and cash outflows.

INTERNATIONAL CASE

International

• *DaimlerChrysler*

DAIMLERCHRYSLER discloses the following information relating to its long-term debt in its 1999 annual report:

- 6.9 percent notes/bonds
- 5.6 percent commercial paper
- 4.7 percent liabilities to financial institutions

FORD MOTOR COMPANY also provides information relating to its debt in the notes to its annual report. That information is given below.

- Secured indebtedness, 8.3 percent
- Unsecured senior indebtedness—notes and bank debt, 6.4 percent
- Unsecured senior indebtedness—debentures, 3.2 percent
- Unsecured subordinated indebtedness—notes, 6.6 percent

1. Assume that each company's debt is distributed equally across the various categories. Compute an average cost interest rate for each company.
2. If your answer from (1) represented each firm's cost of capital, what would it tell you about the kinds of projects that DaimlerChrysler can undertake as compared to Ford?

ETHICS CASE

• *Wheeler, Nevada*

The city council of Wheeler, Nevada, is faced with an important decision: whether or not to rezone a parcel of property and allow ChemStor, Inc., to purchase the land and build a chemical waste storage facility on the property. Several factors enter into the decision.

a. The property is currently zoned for agricultural use and is surrounded by ranching operations in a rural community.
b. Several ranchers have joined together and offered to buy the property from the city over a 40-year period. In return for an agreed-upon interest rate of one point below prime, they will donate 20 acres of the land for a city park.
c. ChemStor has offered to pay cash for the land. Company management also points out that the facility will create about 25 new jobs for local residents and generate close to $100,000 a year in increased property taxes for the city.
d. ChemStor, a New Jersey-based company, learned of this property from its controller, who is a brother-in-law to one of the Wheeler City council members. ChemStor has offered a "finder's fee" for locating a waste storage site. The finder's fee would be split between the controller and the brother-in-law.

Identify the ethical and other issues involved in this capital investment decision.

WRITING ASSIGNMENT

• *Lease versus Buy*

You are fresh out of college, have your first real job, and just received your first big paycheck. You decide you need some wheels. Off you go to the car dealer. You carefully review the various makes and models of cars, determine the price range you can afford, and select "YOUR FIRST CAR." You thought that was the hard part. Now you need to decide on financing. The salesperson says you can either borrow money to purchase the vehicle or you can lease the car.

What factors should you consider in making this capital budgeting decision? Identify those factors that should enter into the lease versus buy decision. Prepare a short memo discussing the pros and cons of leasing versus buying and identifying the cash inflows and outflows associated with each option.

THE DEBATE

• *The Time Value of Money*

The text discusses two general types of capital budgeting techniques: nondiscounted and discounted. The nondiscounted methods involve comparing the outflows of cash to the inflows. These methods do not take into account the time value of money. The discounted capital budgeting techniques factor into the evaluation the time value of money.

Divide your group into two teams.

- Team 1 is to take the position that the nondiscounted methods provide the best means of evaluating capital budgeting alternatives. Prepare a short presentation that identifies the advantages of using the nondiscounted methods and discusses the disadvantages of the discounted capital budgeting techniques.
- Team 2 is to take the position that the discounted methods are preferred. Prepare a short presentation in support of the various methods that incorporate into their analysis the time value of money.

INTERNET SEARCH

• *Federal Express*

We began this chapter with a look at FEDERAL EXPRESS. Let's continue our examination of this company using its Internet site. Access Federal Express's site at http://www.fedex.com. Sometimes Web addresses change, so if this address doesn't work, access the Web site for this book at http://albrecht.swcollege.com for an updated link to Federal Express.

Once you have gained access to the company's Web site, answer the following questions:

1. Find the portion of the Web site containing information about the early history of FedEx Express. Why was Memphis, Tennessee, chosen as the company headquarters?
2. Find the portion of the Web site containing "FedEx Express Facts." How many aircraft does FedEx have in its worldwide fleet?
3. Find FedEx's most recent annual report. Does the company lease any of its aircraft or equipment? [Hint: Look in the notes to the financial statements.] What factors would the company have considered when determining whether to lease or buy its aircraft and equipment?

comprehensive problem 1-4

Imagine that one of your parents has traveled across the country to visit you at college. As the two of you have dinner together at one of your favorite restaurants, the discussion turns to your accounting class. You begin describing some of the new ideas and techniques you have been learning lately. Suddenly, your parent wants to talk about the family business. As the discussion goes on, it becomes clear that your parent is expecting you to provide some specific ideas about how to improve the management process in the family business using current accounting methods. You certainly want to impress your parent with all the detailed knowledge that you have gained since beginning your course work in accounting. However, you are also concerned that you may describe something incorrectly or say something misleading. One day you expect to inherit the family business, and you would hate to say anything during dinner that might later cause problems in the company!

Required: You need to respond to your parent using insights gained from the last four chapters (1–4 of management accounting) of this textbook. Further, answering your parent's questions will require you to carefully construct your remarks in light of the exact nature of the family business. Hence, we will assume three separate types of businesses for your family:

1. Computer manufacturing plant
2. Neighborhood grocery store
3. Large architectural firm

For each of these businesses, divide your comments into two parts:

- Return on investment

Discuss the nature of the family business in terms of the DuPont formulation of return on investment (Profit margin × Asset turnover = Return on investment). What aspects of this formula are most important for the type of strategy that the family business may choose to follow?

- Relevant topics

Listed below are a number of topics from Chapters 1–4 of management accounting. Briefly describe (three sentences or less) how each topic may relate to the family business.

1. Direct materials costs
2. Direct labor costs
3. Overhead costs
4. Direct materials inventory
5. Work-in-process inventory
6. Finished goods inventory
7. Job order costing
8. Process costing*
9. Cost behavior
10. Break-even analysis
11. Capital budgeting
12. Net present value
13. Internal rate of return

*Relates to expanded material.

Operating Budgets

chapter m5

learning objectives

After studying this chapter, you should be able to:

1 Describe different types of budgeting and identify the purposes of budgeting.

2 Describe the budgeting process and its behavioral implications.

3 Explain the master budget and its components for manufacturing firms, merchandising firms, and service firms.

expanded material

4 Prepare pro-forma financial statements.

5 Distinguish between static and flexible budgets.

setting the stage

Every organization needs to budget. Budgets help allocate resources effectively so that the organization can accomplish its mission. Consider how the federal government budgets, for example. The arrival of the president's budget on Capitol Hill signals the beginning of the annual budget process in Congress—a process that can last more than eight months and require the passage of scores of bills and resolutions.[1] Congress drafts a budget resolution—a spending plan that defines in broad terms how much the government will take in through taxes and other receipts and spend on all government accounts during the coming fiscal year. The House and Senate Budget Committees each draft their own version, bring the drafts to their respective chambers for approval, iron out differences in conference, and return the resulting version to their chambers for adoption. Because the president's signature is not required, the resolution does not carry the force of law—although Congress is forced to abide by the limits it sets for itself. Discretionary spending is allocated to the Appropriations Committees in both chambers. Throughout the budget process, Congress passes authorization bills that set the maximum amounts that may be spent in specific fiscal years for individual discretionary programs, as well as goals for those programs. The budget resolution serves as a blueprint for congressional spending decisions. It sets the total levels for budget authority, outlays, incoming revenues, direct-loan obligations, and loan guarantee commitments, as well as the public debt ceiling for the upcoming fiscal year.

In 1999, for example, the federal budget was broken down as follows:

As you can see, a significant portion of the budget goes to pay interest on the national debt. However, given that revenues are anticipated to be $1.75 trillion in fiscal year 2000 and grow to $2 trillion by 2004, large budget surpluses are expected. If Congress and the president can resist the urge to spend the excesses, the national debt can be reduced or even eliminated.

Budgeting probably consumes more congressional time than any other single activity. Even though you may argue that Congress and the president have not been as fiscally responsible as they could have been, the budgeting process has instilled some discipline in their spending habits and provided a sense of order for governmental expenditures and management of programs.

On a more local level, consider how budgeting can resolve problems at your university. The administration probably wants to hold down spending and keep tuition competitive and affordable. At the same time, however, the department chairs and deans probably want to spend more money to enhance the education of the students.

Shouldn't the arts and humanities departments get more money this year to help emphasize the importance of a liberal arts education? Already, salaries of faculty in those areas are near poverty levels. What about the business school? Shouldn't business and accounting receive more operating funds because their classes have the highest demand and are the largest on campus? Wait a minute, shouldn't more money be put into program diversity to help students become more aware of the differences between cultures, races, and sexes and enhance understanding? How about the buildings and grounds—the roofs need

Spending Category	Amount	Percentage of Total
Social Security	$387 billion	22.5%
Other discretionary spending	300 billion	17.5%
Defense	275 billion	16.0%
Interest on debt	231 billion	13.5%
Medicare	220 billion	12.8%
Other entitlements	196 billion	11.4%
Medicaid	108 billion	6.3%

1 Information on the federal budget process was obtained from **http://hillsource.house.gov/LegislativeDigest/Digest/DigestArchives/D99/Wk8pt2.htm**.

replacing and the sidewalks are cracking. Don't we need to make repairs? What's more, how can we have a winning basketball team without a new basketball arena?

The poor administration. How would you like to be responsible for resolving these questions and allocating the limited funds? Each department within the university has its own sense of mission, priorities, goals, objectives, and agendas. Furthermore, some departmental priorities may not be consistent with university goals. Prioritizing the funding requests may be difficult if the university has no clear, agreed-upon criteria to use in evaluating them. The difficulty of measuring the benefits of each program makes the process even more challenging. The budgeting process that we will discuss in this chapter can help the university resolve these conflicting objectives and facilitate order in its spending. Without budgeting, no matter how difficult, the university will never be able to accomplish its objectives.[2]

budget A quantitative expression of a plan of action that shows how a firm or an organization will acquire and use resources over some specified period of time.

*A **budget** is a quantitative expression of a plan of action that shows how a firm, an organization (such as the government or a university in the opening scenario), or an individual will acquire and use resources over a specified period of time. For a firm, implicit in most budgets is management's expectation of earning sufficient profit to provide a reasonable return on investment. The budget identifies and allocates resources necessary to effectively and efficiently carry out the mission of the organization. Although budgeting may sound to you like an unappealing activity (maybe you have tried budgeting your personal expenditures), successful budgeting is absolutely critical to the success of a business. In this chapter, we will briefly touch on personal budgeting and then cover budgeting for manufacturing, merchandising, and service firms.*

1

Describe different types of budgeting and identify the purposes of budgeting.

TYPES AND PURPOSES OF BUDGETING

As you learned in Chapter 1 of management accounting, budgeting is part of the management planning process, a process that involves identifying problems or opportunities, identifying alternative solutions, evaluating those alternatives, then choosing and implementing the best alternatives. As you learned in Chapter 1 of management accounting, there are two basic types of planning: (1) long-run planning, which includes strategic planning and capital budgeting, and (2) short-run planning, which includes production and process prioritizing and operational budgeting or profit planning. Long-run planning involves making decisions where the effects will extend several years into the future. Long-run planning includes broad-based decisions about products, markets, productive facilities, and financial resources. This type of planning is often referred to as strategic planning. Strategic planning takes place at the executive level in an organization and involves identifying the organization's mission, the goals flowing from that mission, and the strategies and actions that will be taken to accomplish those goals. With strategic planning in place, the company can then plan for the purchase and use of major assets such as buildings or equipment to help the company meet its long-range goals. This type of planning is called capital budgeting.

As you also learned in Chapter 1 of management accounting, short-run planning is divided into two categories. Once the organization has made long-term commitments to capital structure (land, buildings, equipment, management personnel, etc.), then managers need to determine how to best use those committed resources to maximize the return on their capital investments—a process often referred to as production prioritizing. Once the organization has determined what to produce or otherwise provide to the marketplace in order to maximize its goals, managers are ready to go to the next phase of short-run planning—operational budgeting. Sometimes known as profit plans, operational budgets are used by managers to establish and communicate daily, weekly, and monthly goals for the organization. Failure to carefully perform strategic planning, capital budgeting, or budgeting for operations can have adverse conse-

2 James C. Horsch, "Redesigning the Resource Allocation Process," *Management Accounting,* July 1995, pp. 55–59.

quences for organizations, even to the point of causing bankruptcy. The list of companies that have failed in recent years as a result of poor planning and execution is getting longer each day. Casualties of poor planning include such common names as EASTERN AIRLINES, MANVILLE CORPORATION, ATARI COMPUTERS, and CIRCLE K. In Chapter 4 of management accounting, we discussed strategic planning and capital budgeting elements of planning. In this chapter, our focus is on budgeting for operations.

operating (master) budget A network of many separate schedules and budgets that together constitute the overall operating and financing plan for the coming period.

The **operating (master) budget** is the most detailed and most heavily used budget in an organization. As the name implies, this budget details the immediate goals for revenues, production, expenses, and cash for the next period. Before we can examine the operating budget in detail, we need to identify its purposes, describe its evolution, and discuss the major issues involved in budget preparation. This will give us a framework for preparing an operating budget.

Purposes of Budgeting

The overall purpose of an operating budget is to quantify a general plan so that performance in relation to a goal can be carefully monitored. Thus, budgeting has a twofold purpose. The first purpose is to allow individuals or companies to develop a plan to meet a specified goal. The second purpose is to allow ongoing comparison between actual results and the plan in order to control operations or activities. To illustrate, let us assume that Dick Cotton earns $3,000 a month (and takes home only $2,000 after taxes) and has prepared a budget of his income and expenses.

disposable income Income left after withholdings and fixed expenses have been subtracted from gross salary; the amount left to cover variable expenditures.

The budget in Exhibit 5-1 contains an important warning that spending is exceeding earnings. The commitment of $1,300 to fixed expenses leaves only $680 to cover all of Dick's necessary expenditures for utilities, food, clothing, and the like. Because Dick cannot cover these expenditures using his **disposable income** of $680 a month, he must revise his plans; perhaps he could ask for a raise, get a second job or a new job that pays more, obtain a loan, or decrease his spending. This simple illustration shows that budgeting is extremely important. Unless Dick takes corrective action, he will soon join the growing number of individuals declaring bankruptcy. To learn more about personal budgeting, study the budgeting chapter of the personal financial planning supplement that accompanies this book.

exhibit 5-1 Monthly Budget for Dick Cotton

Gross salary		$ 3,000
Withholdings:		
Federal income taxes	$500	
State income taxes	150	
FICA taxes	230	
Other withholdings	140	(1,020)
Net take-home pay		$ 1,980
Fixed expenses:		
House mortgage expense	$750	
Car payment expense	350	
Insurance expense	200	(1,300)
Disposable income		$ 680
Utilities expense	$200	
Food expense	400	
Clothing expense	100	
Entertainment expense	100	
Miscellaneous expenses	200	(1,000)
Net surplus (deficit)		$ (320)

business environment essay

Budgeting Woes The budgeting process can be frustrating if the prepared budgets are not realistic. For example, if a married couple determine that they will spend only $100 per month on food when in reality food will cost at least $400 per month, communication and other problems will usually occur. The following list highlights some warning signs that the budgeting process needs revamping:

1. Decision makers who must comply with the budget become frustrated.
2. There is a lack of agreement on amounts budgeted.
3. Prioritizing expenditures or agreeing on the allocation of funds is difficult.
4. There is confusion about who is accountable for funding decisions.
5. Budgeting is not integrated across various segments of the firm.
6. The "squeaky wheel gets the grease" rule is used to allocate resources.
7. The budgeting process requires more effort than it is worth.
8. Managers are held responsible for budgets that include elements over which they have no control.
9. Long-term budgeting and strategic planning are absent.
10. The budgeting process is "political."

Source: Adapted from James C. Horsch, "Redesigning the Resource Allocation Process," *Management Accounting*, July 1995, pp. 55–59.

fyi

A study conducted several years ago revealed that only 4 of every 100 employees who join the workforce at age 25 have sufficient funds to retire at age 65. The other 96 must either keep working or depend on someone else for help.

In addition, someday Dick will want to retire. Currently, Dick's budget does not provide for any savings or investments. With all the planning tools available today, such as tax-sheltered retirement plans, investments, annuities, and so forth, an individual who plans and budgets well can prepare adequately for the future. Unfortunately, at his present rate, Dick will not be one of these individuals.

Indeed, the penalty for not budgeting is severe. Individuals who budget successfully have found that they can spend just as much if they budget as they can if they don't. The only difference is that those who budget spend money how, where, and when they want to.

The previous example was of a personal budget. The same advantages that budgeting provides on a personal level exist for organizations. Specifically, there are seven major reasons why budgeting is important to an organization's success:

1. *Planning and setting objectives.* The preparation of a budget forces managers to consider explicitly where the firm is going and how it is going to get there. Budgeting forces managers to quantify objectives for the organization and the means of achieving those objectives. The federal government, as described in the opening scenario, uses the budgeting process to plan its expenditures for the upcoming year. Similarly, by budgeting, an organization, such as the university described in the opening scenario, will be better prepared to decide where its scarce resources will be spent.
2. *Communication.* Budgets improve communication between the various management levels of a business, helping managers plan activities that enhance the smooth functioning of the enterprise. In general, budgets relay top management's expectations and show each segment how it fits into the overall plan. Budgets establish a benchmark to which actual performance will be compared. In both families and business organizations, it is usually not the lack of money that causes problems but the lack of communication about money. Couples and organizations that budget adequately find that their budgets are a great communication tool. For example, once the budget is established for the university in the opening scenario, the budget communicates to various departments and groups how university money will be spent.

3. *Coordination.* Budgets help management coordinate activities of business segments. By coordinating and integrating the goals of each segment, management ensures that its efforts to meet the overall objectives of the firm will be realized. In addition, budgeting helps to identify potential bottlenecks and allows management to develop plans to alleviate them. For example, the budgeting process may reveal that a resource, critical to the production process, is in short supply. Management can then take action to address this shortage. Budgets help guarantee that the combined expenditures of the various segments do not exceed the total budgeted expenditures for the organization.
4. *Authorization.* Once budgets are approved by top management, they provide authorization for investing, spending, ordering, producing, and borrowing by lower-level managers and employees. At most major companies, **IBM** for example, the budget becomes the law. If something is budgeted, it can be purchased. If not budgeted, the purchase cannot be made. This is one area where many personal budgets fail. Many individuals use their budget as a guide instead of as authorization to spend; as a result, they often "exceed" their budget.
5. *Motivation.* Budgets help motivate people. By providing a clear set of quantified objectives, budgets guide people to perform the activities that need to be accomplished. The motivational aspect of budgets can be quite strong. Care must be exercised in budgeting to ensure that budgets do not create a "success at any cost" attitude.
6. *Conflict resolution.* In most organizations, everyone usually wants additional resources. Budgeting forces up-front planning, which helps resolve conflicts over how limited resources will be allocated among an organization's various parts. (Remember the conflicting objectives of the university in the opening scenario?) Consider, for example, a family that will have $1,000 of disposable income next year. How shall they spend the money? Suppose the wife wants to spend $500 on clothes for the children because they are quickly outgrowing their wardrobes. In addition, she would like to spend the other $500 on piano lessons for the children. On the other hand, the husband would like to spend $500 to replace the garage door, which is falling down, and another $500 to fix the transmission on the car (it's starting to slip). A budget, prepared by the husband and wife together, could help them resolve these conflicting priorities.
7. *Performance measurement (evaluation).* Budgets provide quantitative measures of expectations and objectives. These objectives later serve as benchmarks against which the performance of managers and others in a firm can be evaluated. Employees and managers who meet or exceed budgets are often rewarded. When productivity is inadequate, as measured against budgeted performance, employees may be penalized or even terminated.

In recent years, a number of concerns have been expressed about operational budgeting and the way firms budget. As you will see with even a simple example in this chapter, the budgeting process can be a very time-consuming, "number-crunching" exercise. Even worse, some companies have found that their business environment is changing so rapidly that once the process is finally finished, the budget has little to do with the realities they face. In some companies, budgets analyze minute spending without recognizing the bigger picture, such as the fact that the company is losing customers or that a new product is selling far below expectations. In some cases, traditional budgets have undermined the growth potential of companies by forcing managers to focus exclusively on short-term financial numbers. The following are some of the problems with traditional budgeting that have led to revisions in the way companies budget:

- Departments and business units have tended to create budgets based on how much they spent in previous years.
- Once budgets are set, resource allocations have been inflexible and unable to adapt to change.
- In many companies, managers who have been evaluated and compensated according to how well they met their numbers have been powerless to step outside the budget and act on opportunities.
- Often budgeting time lines (e.g., calendar years) have not matched new product schedules.
- Frequently, because of fast-paced business changes, a budget is outdated before it is completed.

business environment essay

The Principles of Warfare: "The Art of War" Twenty-five hundred years ago, Sun Wu, general to the Chinese state of Wu, wrote a treatise entitled "The Art of War." It is one of those rare works that transcends time. It is the first text on budgeting and strategy, and some would argue that it is still the most important text on strategy ever written. Little did Sun Wu realize that his work would be absorbed by others of influence throughout history—from the fearless samurai of the sixteenth century to the shrewd business leaders of the twenty-first century. The following are a few quotations from the treatise. Although Sun Wu is talking about war and battle, see if you can determine which comments relate to short-term planning (budgeting) and which relate more to strategy.

- Calculate advantages by means of what was heard, then create force in order to assist outside missions (in other words, gather information before you proceed).
- The best warfare strategy is to attack the enemy's plans, next is to attack alliances, next is to attack the army, and the worst is to attack a walled city.
- Generally in warfare: If ten times the enemy's strength, surround them; if five times, attack them; if double, divide them; if equal, be able to fight them; if fewer, be able to evade them; if weaker, be able to avoid them.
- There are three ways the ruler can bring difficulty to the army: (1) To order an advance when not realizing the army is in no position to advance, or to order a withdrawal when not realizing the army is in no position to withdraw. This is called entangling the army. (2) By not knowing the army's matters,

fyi

While budgeting is very helpful for decision making, organizations are often required to prepare detailed budgets before bankers will loan money or before a company can issue stock or debt for sale to the public. When companies declare bankruptcy and are taken over by court-ordered trustees, one of the trustee's first steps is to prepare detailed budgets. These budgets help to determine whether the company should cease operations, or whether the trustee should ask the court to give the company time to work through its financial problems so that it can fully or partially repay its debts.

A high-level manager of a large company summed up the shortcomings of traditional budgets with this comment: "Trying to figure out how much fax paper you will need next November and what that will cost is like forecasting the weather."

Recognizing such concerns but also realizing that a well-conceived strategy and supporting budgets are essential to effective growth, in recent years some organizations have spent large sums of money to make their budgeting more relevant and timely to what they do. With developments in technology, companies can now measure results almost instantly. CISCO and DELL COMPUTER, for example, now receive immediate information about how they are doing (compared to processes that used to take several months) and can use these data to make real-time decisions on resource allocations and forecasts about profit margins and growth rates of different products. With such timely information, organizations can now both predict revenues and costs and measure them on a timely basis. Because companies can make real-time changes in their budgets, projections are much more accurate, and the budgeting process is much more meaningful. FUJITSU, for example, now uses a monthly, rolling forecast, which is part of its enterprise planning software, that allows financial managers to make corrective budget changes on a timely basis. Instead of the usual multi-iterative planning and budgeting process, where unsupported assumptions are repeated up and down the management ladder, Fujitsu's process now takes only about 10 to 15 days compared with six to eight weeks under the previous system.

Effective and timely budgets, aided by developments in technology, can help companies overcome the weaknesses in traditional budgeting. The right budgeting system provides financial managers with a map that can guide their company to competitive advantages. Effective budgets tie all the pieces together, providing goals and benchmarks against which performance can be measured as defined by a company's strategic plan. As noted earlier, however, the faster an industry moves, and the faster a company shifts its priorities, the more often plans must be adjusted and budgets changed. E-businesses, for example, need to plan and re-plan quickly. Fast, efficient budgeting, rolling forecasts, and effective management reporting and analysis are keys to success in these types of companies.

and administering the army the same as administering civil matters, the officers and troops will be confused. (3) By not knowing the army's calculations, and taking command of the army, the officers and troops will be hesitant. When the army is confused and hesitant, the neighboring rulers will take advantage.

- One who knows how to unite upper and lower ranks in purpose will be victorious.
- One who knows the enemy and knows himself will not be in danger in a hundred battles. One who does not know the enemy but knows himself will sometimes win, sometimes lose. One who does not know the enemy and does not know himself will be in danger in every battle.
- A victorious army first obtains conditions for victory, then seeks to do battle. A defeated army first seeks to do battle, then obtains conditions for victory.
- Generally, commanding of many is like commanding of a few. It is a matter of dividing them into groups.
- Generally, the principles of warfare are: The general receives his commands from the ruler, assembles the troops, mobilizes the army, and sets up camp.
- If the general is weak and not disciplined, his instructions not clear, the officers and troops lack discipline and their formation is in disarray. This is called chaos.
- The wise general thinks about it, and the good general executes it. If it is not advantageous, do not move; if there is no gain, do not use troops; if there is no danger, do not do battle.

Source: http://www.sonshi.com/suntintro.html.

The best-known budget in the United States is the budget of the federal government. The Congressional Budget Office offers a monthly update on the level of government receipts and outlays relative to budgeted levels. Go to the CBO's Web site at http://www.cbo.gov to get a budget review for the most recent month.

to summarize

Budgeting in most organizations is based on that organization's strategic plan. Using the strategic plan to guide decisions, organizations perform two types of budgeting: capital budgeting and operations budgeting. The operating budget has several purposes: (1) assist in planning and setting objectives, (2) facilitate communication, (3) coordinate activities, (4) authorize expenditures and actions, (5) motivate employees, (6) assist in resolving conflicts, and (7) provide a vehicle for performance measurement.

2

Describe the budgeting process and its behavioral implications.

budget committee A management group responsible for establishing budgeting policy and for coordinating the preparation of budgets.

THE BUDGETING PROCESS

Budgeting is such an important activity that the top executives of most companies coordinate and participate in the process. Large firms usually establish a **budget committee**, which includes among its members the vice presidents for sales, production, purchasing, and finance and the controller or chief financial officer. These executives coordinate the preparation of a detailed budget in their areas of responsibility and then together oversee the preparation of a comprehensive budget for the firm. As noted previously, recent developments in software have made the budgeting process much more useful and relevant. Using enterprise-wide software, such as that developed by ORACLE, SAP, BONN, and PEOPLESOFT, companies can now integrate

business environment essay

Losing Focus on Budgeting Goals XYZ was a sleepy little firm, barely making a profit, when it got a new CEO. He said, "I'm going to make this a go-go company. And pretty soon, instead of a price-earnings ratio (stock price divided by earnings per share) of 10:1, it's going to be 40:1. We're all going to get rich." In trying to make the company more profitable, he hired a group of high-powered executives, and the company as a whole, not just the CEO, adopted a new budgeting policy. Essentially, the CEO and division managers decided together on next year's earnings budgets for their respective divisions, and the managers were responsible for meeting these goals. Implied in the budgets was the idea that the budget represented a fair goal. However, as it turned out, the CEO leaned on managers at the start of the year. To one manager, for example, he said, "Look, this company is going to have an earnings per share of $1.90 next year. Your division's share of that is $0.42." As the year progressed, periodic meetings were held with the manager. If the division was not on target to earn $0.42 a

their budgeting process into their accounting systems, get immediate feedback about how they are doing, and use the feedback to make timely changes in their budgeting process. Two important issues faced by executives in the budgeting process are:

1. Behavioral considerations, and
2. Delegation of responsibility for preparing the budget—the top-down versus bottom-up issue.

Behavioral Considerations

Research has shown that several behavioral factors determine how successful the budgeting process will be. First, the process must have the support of top management. Without a clear indication from top management that the budgeting process is important to the organization, managers will not be motivated to devote the time necessary to formulate an effective and efficient budget.

Second, all managers, and as many employees as possible, should participate in the budgeting process. Managers will be more motivated to achieve budget goals that they understand and help design. For this process to work, managers must feel that their opinions are respected and given full consideration. In addition, this communication and participation process must remain open throughout the year. If internal or external circumstances change, all parties must meet to discuss the necessary budget adjustments. The most efficient and effective companies are those that involve employees in the decision-making process.

Third, deviations from the budget must be addressed by managers in a positive and constructive manner. Identifying deviations from the plan is simply a way to focus management's attention on areas needing improvement. Unfortunately, some managers treat these deviations as an opportunity to find fault and assign blame to lower-level managers. The result is usually a loss of motivation, accompanied by such dysfunctional behavior as interdepartmental bickering, defensive attitudes, and attempts to "build slack" into the budget. ("Building slack" is the process of inflating a department's budget request so that the department manager can more easily achieve the budget.) Obviously, all these behaviors waste an organization's resources and do not contribute to solving its problems. A more useful reaction to deviations is to focus on the action to be taken. As one CEO stated, "I never made a dime for the company by assessing blame or firing a manager. If I can provide help to a manager to solve a problem, though, we can see the benefit." In administering the budget process, it is extremely important that top management not use the budget as a "club" or "whipping stick." To illustrate the negative effects of using budgets inappropriately, consider what happened at XYZ Company, as described in the Business Environment Essay above.

share, the manager would be told by the CEO, "If you can't find a way to make your budget, we'll hire someone else who can."

One of the ways division managers met their budgets was to recognize sales before they occurred. "Who cares when you close the books at the end of the period? A sale is a sale, right? Does it really matter whether we reach a little into next week and take some of the sales we ship next week and include them with this week's sales? After all, the sales were all made in the same month." Soon, one week stretched into two weeks, then three, until eventually it wasn't too hard for managers to rationalize, "We know that a customer is going to buy our product eventually; let's record it as a sale now." Consequently, the company's managers were driven by their budgets rather than using budgets as goals, until finally they were so far beyond reality that the company was committing massive fraud, eventually causing it to collapse.

Source: Adapted from Robert J. Sack, "Ethical Issues in the Practice of Accounting." In W. Steve Albrecht, ed., *Ethical Issues in the Practice of Accounting* (Cincinnati: South-Western Publishing Co., 1992), pp. 24–25.

Who Prepares the Budget: Top-Down versus Bottom-Up

A firm-wide operating budget could be prepared by top management, apportioned to the major segments of the firm, and then distributed to each lower-level segment manager. This is the top-down approach. Its proponents argue that only top management knows the strategic direction of the firm and is aware of all the external factors influencing its operations. Further, since top management involves only a few people who have risen to positions where they should no longer have special interests to protect, they are in the best position to efficiently coordinate the competing needs of the segments.

The alternative approach is bottom-up, whereby each division manager prepares a budget request for his or her segment. These requests are combined and reviewed as they move up the organization hierarchy, with adjustments being made to coordinate the needs and goals of individual units. Proponents of this approach contend that segment managers have the best information on the products or services they provide, the customers they serve, and the technology that is emerging; they are therefore in the best position to identify segment needs and to weigh alternative courses of action. More importantly, as mentioned earlier, managers who have a role in setting segment goals are more motivated to achieve these goals. It is also good training for managers to develop their planning skills in preparation for promotions to positions of greater authority. Naturally, the organization also benefits when its managers are proficient in planning.

Because these are both legitimate approaches, most organizations use some combination of the two. Top managers know the strategic direction of the firm and the important external factors that affect it, so they prepare a set of planning guidelines that are communicated to lower-level managers. These guidelines include such things as a forecast of key economic variables and their potential impact on the firm, plans for introducing and advertising new products, and some broad sales targets and resource allocations. With these guidelines in mind, lower-level managers prepare their individual budgets. Although these budgets are always reviewed to be sure they are consistent with the objectives of other segments and of the company as a whole, from a behavioral point of view, any changes to a manager's budget should be made with great care. This is not to suggest that changes should not be made, only that reasons for those changes should be substantial and should be discussed with the managers involved.

The blending of these two approaches will vary among organizations. A smaller organization with few management levels will rely more on the top-down approach than a larger organization. Top management in smaller organizations tends to be more knowledgeable about and more involved in the operating details.

to summarize

The behavioral factors that contribute to the success of the budgeting process include the support of top management, the participation of all managers in the budgeting process, and the need to address deviations from the budget in a positive and constructive manner. With the top-down approach, top management prepares the entire budget. With bottom-up budgeting, each segment manager makes budget requests. Most firms use a combination of the two approaches.

3

Explain the master budget and its components for manufacturing firms, merchandising firms, and service firms.

THE MASTER BUDGET

The operating budget is called the *master budget*; it is an integrated group of detailed budgets that together constitute the overall operating and financing plans for a specific time period. In a manufacturing firm, the master budget begins with a forecast of sales; is followed by detailed budgets for the production, selling, administrative, and financial activities; and culminates in a set of pro-forma (or budgeted) financial statements. The flow of the preparation of the individual budgets within this master network is shown in Exhibit 5-2. (Notice that the final items are the budgeted or "pro-forma" financial statements. Preparing these pro-forma statements is discussed in the expanded material.) Review this exhibit carefully because we will follow these schedules in sequence in the next sections of this chapter.

exhibit 5-2 The Master Budget for a Manufacturing Firm

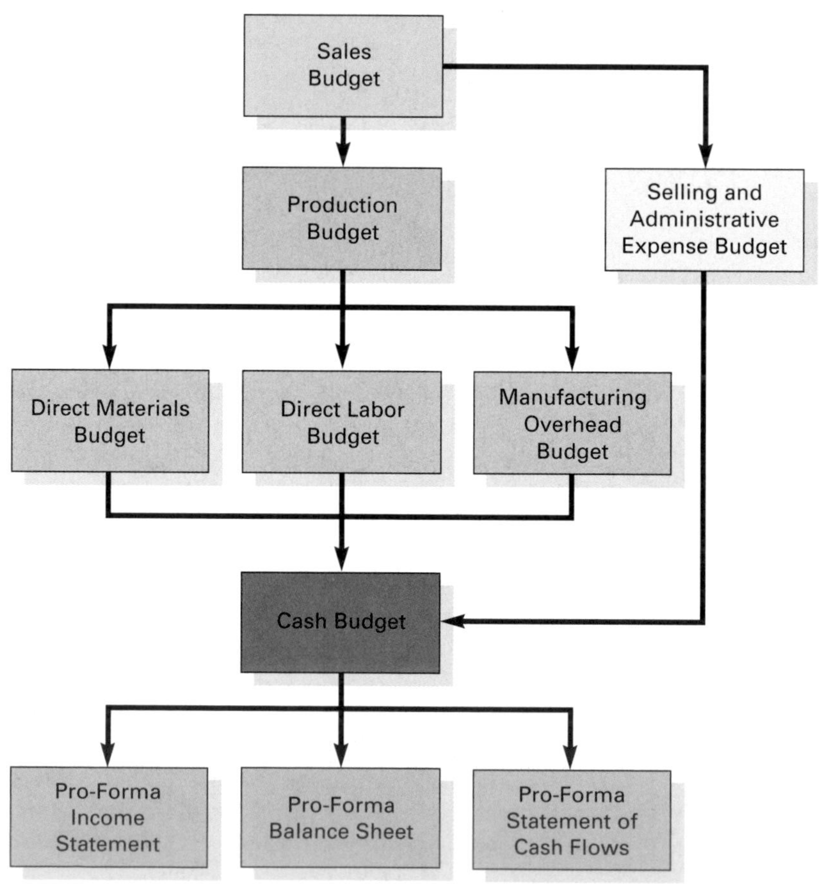

To help explain these steps, we will illustrate budgeting for three different kinds of companies. First, we will illustrate the budgeting process in a manufacturing firm using an integrated example of budgets for the Sunbird Boat Company, a manufacturer of small fishing boats. Second, we will illustrate budgeting in merchandising firms (retail and wholesale) for Wind River Boat Company, a company that buys its boats for resale from other manufacturers rather than making the boats itself. Third, we will illustrate budgeting in service firms by illustrating the budgeting process for a small motel, the Boulder View Inn. We thought seriously about including the budgeting process for an Internet or e-business company as well. In reality, however, these businesses represent either manufacturing, wholesale, retail, or service businesses. DELL COMPUTER, for example, makes and sells computers over the Internet and so is a manufacturing and retail company. AMAZON.COM sells books and other products and is also a retail company. PRICELINE.COM is a service company in that it matches buyers of airline tickets and other products with vendors selling those products and receives a commission for its matchmaking activities. Although the types of revenues these firms generate and even their cost structures often differ from those of traditional firms, their business models usually represent traditional types of firms.

As we examine our three companies, you will see similarities in the budgeting process for all three types of businesses. Basically, the budgeting process involves budgeting (or forecasting) revenues and cash that will be generated by those revenues, and budgeting costs that will be incurred and cash that will be expended. Budgeters—whether individuals, companies, or other entities—are always interested in how much revenues (inflows) and expenditures (outflows) they will have during each budgeted period, and how much cash and assets they will have at the end of each budgeted period. The budgeting discussions that follow may seem mechanical, but you should keep in mind that this formalized budgeting activity forces management to make many important decisions that guide a company toward its goals. For example, decisions regarding production scheduling, pricing, borrowing, investing, and research and development need to be made before the budget can be completed.

In most companies today, the actual preparation of the master budget is usually done on computerized spreadsheets and other software packages. Although automation takes care of much of the drudgery or tedious work, it is important that you understand the budgeting process and what is being done by the computer.

Another factor you should recognize is that many of the recent developments in management accounting, such as ABC and just-in-time (JIT) inventory systems, have a significant impact on the budgeting process. As we discuss the various elements of the master budget, we will explain how budgeting is affected by these developments.

Budgeting for Operations in a Manufacturing Firm

Our first illustration of the budgeting process is for Sunbird Boat Company, a manufacturing company that makes fishing boats. The boats are made of fiberglass and wood and come in 15-foot and 18-foot sizes. Because preparing actual budgets can be tedious and is usually done by computers, we will focus on the budgeting for only one product—the 15-foot boat—in this chapter. Our goal is to help you understand the budgeting process, not to force you to spend significant time following numbers through a complicated budgeting process. The budgeting process for the 18-foot boat would be similar to that illustated for the 15-foot boat. In explaining the budgeting for Sunbird Boat Company, we will begin with the sales budget and then discuss each budget identified in Exhibit 5-2.

sales budget A schedule of projected sales over the budget period.

SALES BUDGET The first step in developing a master budget is to prepare a **sales budget**. As shown in Exhibit 5-2, all the other budgets are developed from this budget. Projecting accurate sales is very difficult, however, because sales are a function of both external variables (customer tastes and economic conditions, for example) and internal variables (such as price, sales effort, and advertising expenditures). In fact, in preparing a sales budget, internal variables (such as how much production capacity do we have?) and external variables must first be analyzed separately.

Analysis of external variables is accomplished through sales-forecasting techniques. These techniques may be as simple as having the sales staff ask major customers about their buying plans for the next year or as sophisticated as statistical market research techniques. Some firms use quantitative forecasting models: these range from simple growth rate trends derived from the past year's sales (e.g., regression analysis) to complex forecasting models that attempt to measure the influence of many economic and industry variables.

Data on which to base sales forecasts are abundant. For example, economic data about the United States and many other countries are available from private vendors and from trade associations and sector specialists. Data about regions, cities, or markets are provided by vendors and trade groups, as well as by university business departments and forecasting centers.

Demographic data such as population projections, household spending patterns, and lifestyles (nationally and locally—down to city blocks) are available from vendors. These vendors use various statistical methods to project data from the national 10-year census to the current year. In their updating processes, they use other data sources such as the Current Population Survey (CPS) conducted annually by the Census Bureau, payroll taxes, home sales, apartment occupancy rates, state driver's licenses applications, school enrollments, and births and deaths. Government data often report economic conditions with some delay. The Consumer Price Index (CPI), a measure of inflation, is reported monthly at the national and regional levels with specific cities reported either monthly or semiannually. The CPI is a good indicator of a business's ability to pass along cost increases to its customers. The Producer Price Index (PPI), another measure of inflation, reports changes in business costs and is subject to larger fluctuations than the CPI. The Gross Domestic Product (GDP) Implicit Price Deflator measures inflation in the consumer and business sectors simultaneously.

Consumer spending patterns by region and income level are reported from the annual Consumer Expenditure Survey, conducted by the Census Bureau since 1980. Because consumer spending represents more than 65% of GDP, an understanding of how households allocate their expenditures can be very helpful in business planning. For example, if your business expects to sell home entertainment systems to middle-income consumers, it is helpful to know whether they are changing the share of income they spend on in-home entertainment. Production, capacity utilization, and shipment data by sector are estimated in the course of developing GDP estimates. This information also is valuable in forecasting the availability and cost of materials.

Business environment data include the regulatory climate and changes in regulations, product liability issues, competitive structure, technological changes, foreign markets, trends in consumer attitudes and behavior, and demographic trends. Government regulatory information is available on the Internet (for a price), and is available through many agency publications and reference sources such as the Commerce Clearing House. Business trends are tracked and reported by trade associations and magazines, as well as by consultants who specialize in various types of businesses.[3]

In analyzing the influence of internal variables, sales budgeting is viewed as an active process (what factors can we change to meet our sales targets?), not as a passive process (let us predict what customers will buy from us). Cost-volume-profit analysis (the subject of Chapter 2 of management accounting) is frequently used for analyzing the influence of internal variables.

Firms generally do not rely on a single approach to sales budgeting. Instead, they develop several tentative sales budgets, using different combinations of various forecasting and budgeting techniques. These budgets are then reconciled through discussions between the planning and marketing staffs and top management, and a final sales budget is agreed upon. Recent developments in management accounting that have focused on quality and continuous improvement have enabled many organizations to significantly reduce delivery times by using JIT inventory, electronic data interchange (EDI), and other techniques. MOTOROLA CORPORATION, for example, reduced the time needed from taking orders to delivery from four weeks to six hours. The effect of shorter lead times for production has significantly reduced the time horizons of sales and other budgets. Also, instead of the sales budget being fixed for an entire year (or period), there is flexibility to continuously revise the sales and other budgets. With full-time computer hookups to

3 Dianne Wilner Green, "Using Economic Data in Your Strategic Plan," *Management Accounting*, January 1997, p. 32.

suppliers and customers, and with automated budget preparation tools, the sales budget, as well as the entire budget process, is much more dynamic than ever before. With shorter lead times, management can more quickly adapt to increases, decreases, and other trends in revising budgets.

For purposes of this illustration, we will not go into the details about the development of data for the sales budget. Rather, assume that Sunbird Boat Company has projected the year 2003 sales to be 100 15-foot boats. The anticipated sales price for a 15-foot boat is $14,000.

Most organizations divide their yearly sales budget into monthly, weekly, or even daily budgets in order to plan production schedules and cash flows more precisely. Because this involves too much detail for our illustration, we will assume that Sunbird Boat Company projects its boat sales on a quarterly basis, as shown in Schedule 1. Note that we are using Microsoft Excel® as a tool for our budgeting examples.

Schedule 1

Microsoft Excel - sch-m0501.xls

Schedule 1

Sales Budget—2003

	Quarter 1	Quarter 2	Quarter 3	Quarter 4	Total
15-foot boats:					
Selling price per unit	$ 14,000	$ 14,000	$ 14,000	$ 14,000	$ 14,000
Expected sales (units)	x 24	x 28	x 30	x 18	x 100
Expected revenues	$ 336,000	$ 392,000	$ 420,000	$ 252,000	$ 1,400,000

PRODUCTION BUDGET The second detailed budget covers production, the number of units to be produced during the period. Factors to be considered in preparing this **production budget** are projected sales for the period, the desired amount of ending inventory, and the amount of time needed to obtain materials and then to make a unit of product.

production budget A schedule of production requirements for the budget period.

Ending inventory is an important figure because management wants enough units on hand to meet customer demands, but not so many that unnecessary costs will be incurred because of excessive inventory. Usually, the desired ending inventory for any period is expressed as a percentage of the following period's expected sales volume. Sunbird Boat Company has determined that its desired ending inventory for each quarter should be approximately 80% of projected sales for the next quarter. The fourth quarter's ending inventory is 20 15-foot boats, which is 80% of the next quarter's (first quarter of 2004) expected sales.

The production budget (Schedule 2) supplies information needed for all manufacturing cost budgets. Only after production quantities are known can management determine the amount of direct materials, direct labor, and manufacturing overhead needed during the period.

Schedule 2

Microsoft Excel - sch-m0502.xls

Schedule 2

Production Budget—2003

	Quarter 1	Quarter 2	Quarter 3	Quarter 4	Total
15-foot boats:					
Expected sales (Schedule 1)	24	28	30	18	100
Add desired ending inventory of finished boats	22	24	15	20	20
Total number of boats needed	46	52	45	38	120
Less beginning inventory of finished boats	18*	22	24	15	18
Total number of boats to be produced	28	30	21	23	102

*These numbers represent ending inventory in 2002; the 2002 ending inventory cost $150,000.

Although we are using quarterly production budgets in our example, the production budget has probably been most affected by recent developments in product costing and inventories. As was discussed in Chapter 7 of management accounting, JIT inventory is a "pull-through" rather than a "push" system. This means that raw materials arrive just in time for production and that finished goods arrive just in time for sale. With short production times, the sales order pulls production and procurement. In organizations where JIT inventory systems work well, there is less need for a production budget with desirable levels of ending inventory. Indeed, the optimum level of inventory in these organizations is zero. Most companies, however, do not have perfect JIT inventory systems; even those few companies that do often keep a minimal level of inventory on hand for unexpected or "walk-in" sales.

direct materials budget A schedule of direct materials to be used during the budget period and direct materials to be purchased during that period.

DIRECT MATERIALS BUDGET The next detailed budget to be prepared is the **direct materials budget** (Schedule 3). Based on the engineering department's estimates of the materials required to make a boat, this budget helps management schedule purchases from suppliers. Sunbird's engineers estimate that the amounts of wood and fiberglass needed per boat are as follows:

	15-Foot Boat
Direct materials requirements:	
Wood	70 board feet
Fiberglass	50 square feet

Based on these requirements for materials, the direct materials budget for Sunbird Boat Company for 2003 is shown in Schedule 3. The usage requirements are based not only on expected quarterly sales, but also on desired quarterly boat ending inventories. The materials purchase requirements are, in turn, based on the quarterly production requirements and the amount of raw materials inventory desired at the end of each quarter. Because raw materials can be obtained fairly soon after an order is placed, Sunbird has decided to maintain a supply of about 30% of the next quarter's production requirements for wood and fiberglass.

Like the production budget, the direct materials budget depends on the desired level of ending inventory. If management does not maintain sufficient materials inventory levels, costly work stoppages can occur; if inventories are excessive, inventory investment and storage costs may be unduly high.

As with the production budget, JIT inventory systems have decreased the time horizon, the amount of inventory needed, and, in some cases, even the need for the direct materials budget. When materials can be secured immediately on demand, the need for direct materials budgets is decreased. As stated before, however, relatively few companies have perfect JIT inventory systems.

direct labor budget A schedule of direct labor requirements for the budget period.

DIRECT LABOR BUDGET The fourth detailed budget is the **direct labor budget** (Schedule 4). The direct labor budget for Sunbird Boat Company is based on an hourly rate of $15 per hour for production workers and 80 labor hours to make a 15-foot boat.

Because labor is costly, the direct labor budget is often revised on a monthly or even weekly basis. Management must plan so that sufficient (but not excessive) labor is always available.[4] Otherwise, the company is likely to suffer the high cost of frequent hirings, firings, layoffs, and overtime work. Probably even more important than the high cost of employee turnover, however, is the feeling of demoralization among employees that such events

4 Just how variable labor costs are has aroused significant controversy in the management accounting literature. Some researchers argue that employees cannot easily be hired or terminated and, therefore, labor should be a fixed cost. Other researchers argue that labor can be easily hired and terminated—just read business newspapers where announcements of employee layoffs are printed every day. One thing is certain, though—management strives to be able to control labor costs.

Schedule 3

Schedule 3
Direct Materials Budget—2003

	Quarter 1	Quarter 2	Quarter 3	Quarter 4	Total	Unit Cost of Materials[1]	Cost of Materials Used
Direct materials usage per quarter:							
Wood (board feet):[2]							
15-foot boats (70 board feet per boat)	1,960	2,100	1,470	1,610	7,140	$10/bd. ft.	$71,400
Fiberglass (square feet):[3]							
15-foot boats (50 square feet per boat)	1,400	1,500	1,050	1,150	5,100	$5/sq. ft.	$25,500
Total materials cost							$96,900
Direct materials purchase requirements:							
Wood (board feet):							
Desired direct materials ending inventory	630	441	483	525[4]	525		
Direct materials needed for production	1,960	2,100	1,470	1,610	7,140		
Total direct materials needed	2,590	2,541	1,953	2,135	7,665		
Less beginning direct materials inventory	(588)[5]	(630)	(441)	(483)	(588)		
Direct materials to be purchased	2,002	1,911	1,512	1,652	7,077		
Unit cost	x $10	x $10	x $10	x $10	x $10		
Cost of wood purchases	$20,020	$19,110	$15,120	$16,520	$70,770		
Fiberglass (square feet):							
Desired direct materials ending inventory	450	315	345	375[4]	375		
Direct materials needed for production	1,400	1,500	1,050	1,150	5,100		
Total direct materials needed	1,850	1,815	1,395	1,525	5,475		
Less beginning direct materials inventory	(420)[5]	(450)	(315)	(345)	(420)		
Direct materials to be purchased	1,430	1,365	1,080	1,180	5,055		
Unit cost	x $5	x $5	x $5	x $5	x $5		
Cost of fiberglass purchases	$ 7,150	$ 6,825	$ 5,400	$ 5,900	$25,275		
Total direct materials to be purchased	$27,170	$25,935	$20,520	$22,420	$96,045		

[1]Supplier price quotations.
[2]Budgeted production in Schedule 2 multiplied by 70 board feet.
[3]Budgeted production in Schedule 2 multiplied by 50 square feet.
[4]Expected direct materials usage for the first quarter of 2004 is 1,750 board feet of wood (25 boats × 70 bd. ft.) and 1,250 square feet of fiberglass (25 boats × 50 sq. ft.).
[5]Ending direct materials figure from 2002.

Schedule 4

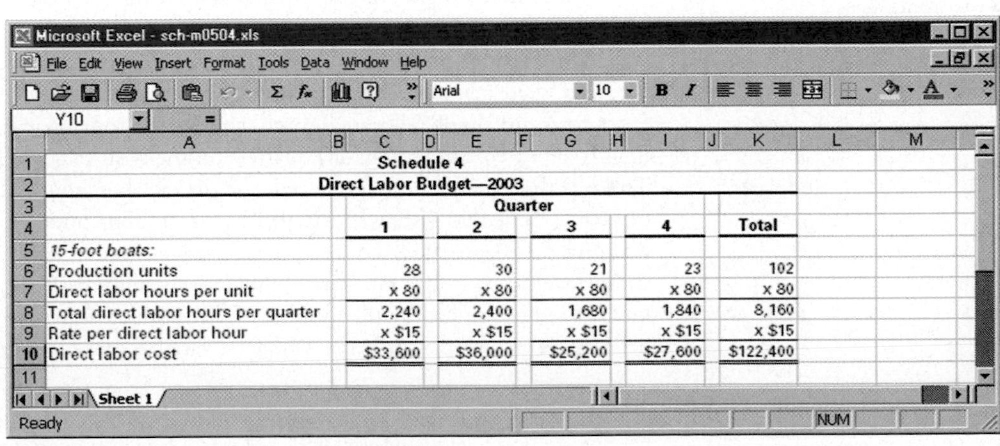

Schedule 4
Direct Labor Budget—2003

	Quarter 1	Quarter 2	Quarter 3	Quarter 4	Total
15-foot boats:					
Production units	28	30	21	23	102
Direct labor hours per unit	x 80	x 80	x 80	x 80	x 80
Total direct labor hours per quarter	2,240	2,400	1,680	1,840	8,160
Rate per direct labor hour	x $15	x $15	x $15	x $15	x $15
Direct labor cost	$33,600	$36,000	$25,200	$27,600	$122,400

Banks have replaced many of their full-time customer representatives with part-time employees. From management's perspective, the use of part-time workers makes direct labor budgeting easier.

can cause. If employees lack security, they usually behave in ways that maximize their own personal short-run benefits (e.g., they may slow down production, thus creating the need for overtime work).

The recent trend in many companies has been to keep a relatively small full-time staff and hire an increasing number of part-time employees. Not only are part-time employees much easier to hire and terminate, but the company does not have to pay retirement and other benefits for them. Banks, for example, have replaced many of their full-time customer representatives with part-time employees. As a result of the smaller full-time workforce, companies that provide temporary workers are increasing in both size and number. From management's perspective, both part-time and temporary workers increase workforce flexibility and make direct labor budgeting easier. Unfortunately, these same trends probably mean less stable and secure careers for more and more workers.

manufacturing overhead budget A schedule of production costs other than those for direct labor and direct materials.

MANUFACTURING OVERHEAD BUDGET The **manufacturing overhead budget** (Schedule 5) includes all production costs other than those for direct materials and direct labor. As noted in earlier chapters, manufacturing overhead is now a major element of total manufacturing costs in many organizations. As manufacturing overhead increases in size and complexity, it becomes much more important to use ABC and appropriate cost drivers.

In preparing this budget, Sunbird's accounting department first estimates the annual variable and fixed manufacturing overhead costs, as shown in the first column of Schedule 5. Total fixed costs are simply allocated evenly among the four quarters. The total variable cost of each item is allocated among the four quarters on the basis of some appropriate activity or cost driver. To keep the example simple, we will use direct labor hours to allocate manufacturing overhead to boats.[5] Schedule 4 showed that 8,160 direct labor hours are projected for the year 2003. By dividing 8,160 projected hours into the total estimated cost of each item of variable manufacturing overhead, we get the variable manufacturing overhead rate per hour for that item. This rate is then multiplied by the number of direct labor hours estimated for each quarter (also from Schedule 4) to figure that item's budgeted variable manufacturing overhead cost for that quarter.

5 Remember (from our discussions of ABC in Chapter 7 in management accounting), however, that direct labor hours is often not the relevant basis to allocate overhead in practice. We use direct labor hours here because using various cost drivers would unnecessarily complicate our examples.

Schedule 5

Schedule 5

Manufacturing Overhead Budget—2003

	Total Estimated Annual Manufacturing Overhead Costs	Manufacturing Overhead Costs Assigned to Each Quarter			
		1	2	3	4
Variable costs:					
Indirect materials costs ($1.50 rate)	$ 12,240	$ 3,360	$ 3,600	$ 2,520	$ 2,760
Indirect labor costs ($3.50 rate)	28,560	7,840	8,400	5,880	6,440
Other payroll costs ($2.00 rate)	16,320	4,480	4,800	3,360	3,680
Utilities expense ($1.00 rate)	8,160	2,240	2,400	1,680	1,840
Total variable costs	$ 65,280	$17,920	$19,200	$13,440	$14,720
Fixed costs:					
Property taxes expense	$ 3,000	$ 750	$ 750	$ 750	$ 750
Insurance expense	2,400	600	600	600	600
Depreciation expense—plant	10,000	2,500	2,500	2,500	2,500
Supervisors' salaries	33,560	8,390	8,390	8,390	8,390
Total fixed costs	$ 48,960	$12,240	$12,240	$12,240	$12,240
Total manufacturing overhead	$114,240	$30,160	$31,440	$25,680	$26,960

caution

Remember that the budgets being discussed in this chapter are for only one level of expected sales. If the level of sales changes, the variable cost and expense amounts budgeted will change also. This means that all the direct materials and direct labor budgets will change, as will some of the manufacturing overhead and selling and administrative expense budgets. This issue of changing levels of sales or operations is covered in the expanded material section of the chapter under the topic of flexible budgeting.

To illustrate, estimated total indirect materials costs are $12,240. Dividing that number by 8,160 direct labor hours yields a rate of $1.50 per hour. Multiplying the $1.50 rate by 2,240 direct labor hours produces $3,360 to be assigned to the first quarter as the budgeted cost of indirect materials. With 2,400 direct labor hours in the second quarter, the cost for that quarter is $3,600. The calculation is the same for the remaining quarters, as well as for other variable overhead items.

The manufacturing overhead budget serves two important purposes. First, when compared with actual manufacturing overhead costs, the data on this budget provide management with a basis for controlling costs and evaluating the performance of the managers responsible for those costs. Second, it is used in product costing. As you will recall from Chapter 2 in management accounting, the manufacturing overhead costs that flow through Work-in-Process Inventory to Finished Goods Inventory (and eventually to Cost of Goods Sold) are applied costs, based on one or more predetermined overhead rates. In our example, this rate is calculated by dividing estimated annual direct labor hours into estimated annual manufacturing overhead ($114,240/8,160 = $14).

When ABC is used, accurate measures of costs, identification of activities, and appropriate selection of cost drivers are important. As discussed in Chapter 7 of management accounting, properly budgeting and assigning overhead costs to products is often difficult and is an area where exciting advances are being made.

Now that we have discussed direct materials, direct labor, and manufacturing overhead (the three elements of a product's cost), we can compute the cost of making the 15-foot boats. Using information from the previous sections, the manufacturing costs are calculated as shown in Schedule 6 at the top of page 250.

selling and administrative expense budget A schedule of all nonproduction spending expected to occur during the budget period.

SELLING AND ADMINISTRATIVE EXPENSE BUDGET The **selling and administrative expense budget** (Schedule 7) includes planned expenditures for all areas other than production. The costs of supplies used by the office staff, the salaries of the sales manager and company president, and the depreciation of office buildings all belong in this category. Because this budget covers several areas, it is usually quite large and may be supported by individual budgets for specific departments within the selling and administrative functions.

The selling and administrative expense budget for Sunbird is prepared in a manner similar to the manufacturing overhead budget. Total selling and administrative expenses are estimated for the year, with each expense then being distributed among the four quarters. As shown in Schedule 7, fixed expenses are assigned equally to each quarter, whereas variable expenses

Schedule 6

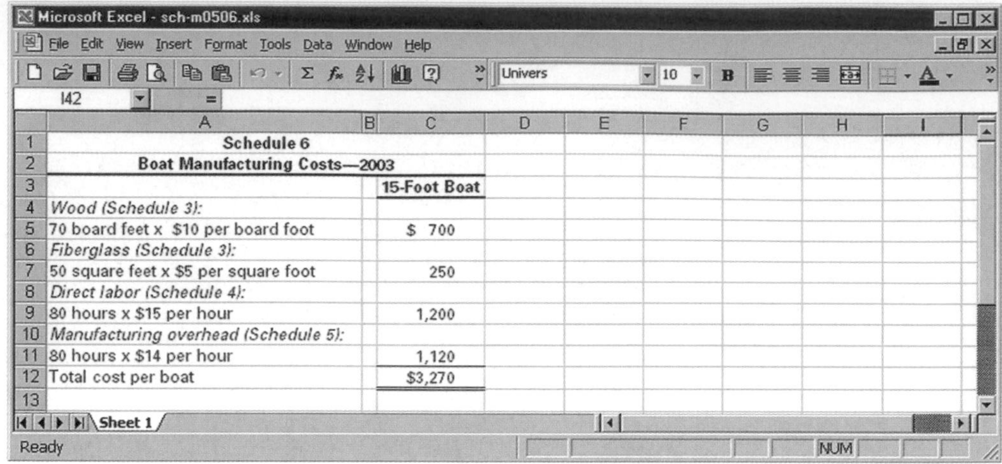

Schedule 6	
Boat Manufacturing Costs—2003	
	15-Foot Boat
Wood (Schedule 3):	
70 board feet x $10 per board foot	$ 700
Fiberglass (Schedule 3):	
50 square feet x $5 per square foot	250
Direct labor (Schedule 4):	
80 hours x $15 per hour	1,200
Manufacturing overhead (Schedule 5):	
80 hours x $14 per hour	1,120
Total cost per boat	$3,270

are allocated according to the number of boats to be sold. Variable delivery expenses, for example, are allocated to quarters by first determining the delivery expense rate ($50,000 estimated delivery expenses ÷ 100 boats expected to be sold during the year [from Schedule 1] = $500 per boat). This rate is multiplied by the number of boats sold in a quarter to determine the delivery expenses allocated to that quarter. Because Sunbird expects to sell 24 boats in the first quarter at a rate of $500 per boat, the amount of delivery expense budgeted for that quarter would be $12,000 ($500 × 24 boats). Sales commissions are allocated to each quarter in the same way.

Schedule 7

Schedule 7					
Selling and Administrative Expense Budget—2003					
	Estimated	Quarter			
	Annual Costs	1	2	3	4
Variable expenses:					
Delivery expenses ($500 rate)	$ 50,000	$ 12,000	$ 14,000	$ 15,000	$ 9,000
Sales commissions ($1,600 rate)	160,000	38,400	44,800	48,000	28,800
Total variable expenses	$210,000	$ 50,400	$ 58,800	$ 63,000	$ 37,800
Fixed expenses:					
Executives' salaries	$220,000	$ 55,000	$ 55,000	$ 55,000	$ 55,000
Depreciation expense	40,000	10,000	10,000	10,000	10,000
Advertising expense	80,000	20,000	20,000	20,000	20,000
Miscellaneous expenses	10,000	2,500	2,500	2,500	2,500
Total fixed expenses	$350,000	$ 87,500	$ 87,500	$ 87,500	$ 87,500
Total selling and administrative expenses	$560,000	$137,900	$146,300	$150,500	$125,300

cash budget A schedule of expected cash receipts and disbursements during the budget period.

CASH BUDGET The **cash budget**, which shows expected cash receipts and disbursements during a period, summarizes much of the information discussed thus far. A detailed cash budget will point out when a company has excess cash to invest and when it has to borrow funds. This allows a firm to earn maximum interest on excess funds and to avoid the costs of unnecessary borrowing. Most firms prepare a month-by-month, or even week-by-week, cash budget. Because of space limitations, however, we will continue to show Sunbird's budget on a quarterly basis.

Typically, a cash budget is divided into four sections:

1. Cash receipts
2. Cash disbursements

3. Cash excess or deficiency
4. Financing

The cash receipts section summarizes all cash expected to flow into the business during the budget period. Because companies generally extend credit to their customers, most of their sales are originally recorded as accounts receivable. The collection of accounts receivable is thus a major source of cash, and its timing is an important consideration in preparing a cash budget.

To illustrate how the collection of accounts receivable is budgeted, we will assume that all sales are on credit; that Sunbird's sales during the last quarter of 2002 were $280,000, and that expected sales for each quarter of 2003 (Schedule 1) are $336,000, $392,000, $420,000, and $252,000, respectively. On the basis of experience, Sunbird's accountants estimate that 80% of credit sales are collected during the quarter of sale and the remaining 20% are collected in the next quarter. Expected quarterly collections for the year 2003 would therefore be:

Collection of Accounts Receivable—2003

Sales Quarter	Sales Revenue	Collection Quarter 1	2	3	4	2003 Total
2002:						
Fourth	$ 280,000	$ 56,000 (20%)				$ 56,000
2003:						
First	336,000	268,800 (80%)	$ 67,200 (20%)			336,000
Second	392,000		313,600 (80%)	$ 78,400 (20%)		392,000
Third	420,000			336,000 (80%)	$ 84,000 (20%)	420,000
Fourth	252,000				201,600 (80%)	201,600
Total	$1,680,000	$324,800	$380,800	$414,400	$285,600	$1,405,600

This analysis shows that total collections during 2003 are budgeted to be $1,405,600. In this example, we have assumed that all proceeds from credit sales are eventually collected. Usually, however, some customers never pay, and these uncollectible accounts must be considered when analyzing estimated cash collections from accounts receivable. You should recognize that economic factors play a significant role in the timing of collections of accounts receivable. During recessionary periods, customers often drag out their payments much longer than in prosperous times.

caution

When preparing a cash budget, be careful not to include expenditures that do not require cash (e.g., depreciation expense from the manufacturing overhead and selling and administrative expense budgets).

The cash disbursements section of Schedule 8 summarizes all expected cash outlays by a firm during the budget period. These include payments of accounts payable, payroll, other costs and expenses, capital improvements, and dividends. Note that to compute cash disbursements for "other costs and expenses," depreciation and other noncash items must not be included.

The section related to cash excess or deficiency merely reports the difference between budgeted cash receipts and disbursements. With a prospective excess of cash, management should look for the most attractive short-term investments. A deficiency obviously means that additional short-term funds will be needed.

The financing section analyzes the timing and amounts of all projected borrowings and repayments during the period. It also estimates the amount of interest to be paid on borrowed funds. By accurately projecting these amounts and events, firms can give banks and other lending institutions advance notice of their needs. Banks appreciate, and sometimes insist, that companies plan their cash needs in advance. Because money has a time value, management always walks a tightrope between having too much or too little cash on hand.

Exhibit 5-3 shows how a typical company's cash balance and requirements fluctuate constantly. Most of this fluctuation is due to the varying amounts of raw materials and finished

business environment essay

Budgeting at Budget Not only do companies forecast their revenues and earnings, but analysts and various investment institutions forecast companies' earnings as well. And, when a company's actual earnings fall short of analysts' expectations, the company's stock price usually falls. Take the case of **BUDGET RENTAL CAR**, for example. Both analysts and the company had forecast that the company's third quarter, 2000 earnings would be approximately $1 per share. However, because of losses in the international portion of its car rental business, Budget reported actual earnings of only $.30 per share, down from $.86 per share a year earlier. Having revenues and income that were 70% lower than expected significantly hurt Budget's stock price. After the announcement, the company's stock hit a 52-week low of $2.31 per share, down from a high of $10.44 per share the previous January. Trying to forecast earnings and predict earnings in the highly volatile car and truck rental business is no easy task. But, when a company is as far off as Budget was in the third quarter of 2000, stock prices, which are based on investors' expectations, usually take a substantial hit.

Source: Anne Marie Chaker, *The Wall Street Journal,* October 30, 2000, p. A8.

goods that are needed in the different seasons of the year. A prosperous firm could, if it desired, maintain enough cash on hand so that short-term borrowing would never be necessary, but such a policy might not be cost-beneficial. Long-term investments in productive assets usually earn considerably more than short-term cash investments; firms are generally better off maintaining lower cash balances, keeping as much capital as possible "at work" in the company's productive assets, and borrowing from time to time for short periods. For this reason, most companies obtain a line of credit from banks. A **line of credit** is a prearranged agreement whereby an organization or individual can borrow money on demand, up to a specific amount at specific rates.

line of credit An arrangement whereby a bank agrees to loan an amount of money (up to a certain limit) on demand for short periods of time, usually less than a year.

Schedule 8 gives the quarterly cash budget for Sunbird Boat Company for 2003. This cash budget assumes that when the company's cash balance at the end of a quarter is less than the desired minimum balance, cash is borrowed (in multiples of $10,000) and repaid at the end of a subsequent period when funds are available. It also assumes that loans are repaid on a first-in,

exhibit 5-3 A Typical Relationship between Cash Balance and Cash Needs

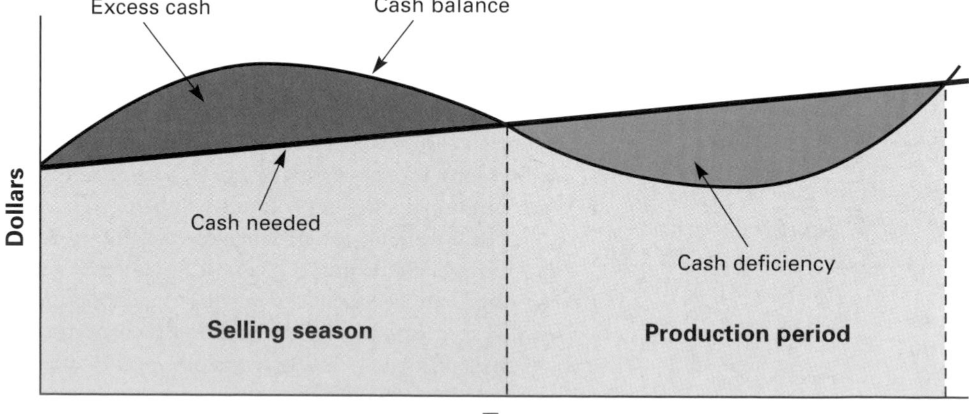

first-out basis and that interest is paid only when the principal is repaid. The $20,000 scheduled to be repaid in the third quarter has been outstanding for one quarter. Furthermore, note that the entries in the Total column do not always equal the sum of the four quarters; the beginning cash balance and the minimum cash balance desired are the same for the year as they are for the first quarter.

With the cash budget, the company is now able to make planning decisions regarding financing. For example, Sunbird is now aware that although the cash balance will be sufficient at the end of the year, there will probably be a cash shortage in the second quarter of 2003. With this knowledge, the company can take steps to deal with the situation. One solution would be to negotiate with a bank to obtain a loan. The company might also obtain money by attempting to get customers to pay sooner, trying to negotiate with creditors for a longer repayment period, or simply reducing the desired ending cash balance (currently at $140,000). The point is, with a knowledge of the coming cash shortfall, Sunbird is able to formulate a method of dealing with the problem now, rather than waiting until the company actually finds itself short of cash.

Schedule 8

Microsoft Excel - sch-m0508.xls

	Schedule 8				
	Cash Budget—2003				
	Quarter				
	1	2	3	4	Total
Cash balance, beginning	$135,000[1]	$147,470	$141,095	$325,595	$ 135,000
Add collections from customers	324,800	380,800	414,400	285,600	1,405,600
(1) Total cash available before disbursement and financing	$459,800	$528,270	$555,495	$611,195	$1,540,600
Less disbursement for:					
Direct materials (Schedule 3)	$ 27,170	$ 25,935	$ 20,520	$ 22,420	$ 96,045
Direct labor (Schedule 4)	33,600	36,000	25,200	27,600	122,400
Manufacturing overhead (Schedule 5)[2]	27,660	28,940	23,180	24,460	104,240
Income tax expense	96,000[3]				96,000
Equipment purchase		150,000[4]			150,000
Selling and administrative expenses (Schedule 7)	127,900[5]	136,300	140,500	115,300	520,000
Dividends		30,000[6]			30,000
(2) Total disbursements	$312,330	$407,175	$209,400	$189,780	$1,118,685
Minimum cash balance desired	140,000	140,000	140,000	140,000	140,000[7]
Total cash needed	$452,330	$547,175	$349,400	$329,780	$1,258,685
Excess (or deficiency) of cash available before financing	$ 7,470	$(18,905)	$206,095	$281,415	$ 281,915
Financing:					
Borrowings	$ 0	$ 20,000			$ 20,000
Repayments			$ (20,000)		(20,000)
Interest (at 10%)			(500)		(500)[8]
(3) Total effect of financing	$ 0	$ 20,000	$ (20,500)		$ (500)
(4) Ending cash balance [(1)−(2)+(3)]	$147,470	$141,095	$325,595	$421,415	$ 421,415

[1]Estimated 12/31/02 balance.
[2]Does not include depreciation expense.
[3]Income taxes owed at 12/31/02 are assumed to be $96,000.
[4]Equipment costing $150,000 is assumed to be purchased for cash during the second quarter.
[5]Does not include depreciation expense.
[6]The company pays dividends of $30,000 during the second quarter of each year.
[7]Not a total of the four quarters—management's policy or plan.
[8]Computed as follows: $20,000 × 0.10 × ¼ = $500.

to summarize

The master budget consists of detailed budgets for sales, production, selling and administrative expenses, and financing activities. Both the sales forecasting process and the development of the master budget may need to be repeated until the results are consistent with the company's strategic plan. The detailed budgets that make up the master budget are prepared in a logical sequence, as shown in Exhibit 5-2. The budgets related to sales, production, and other expenses allow the company to prepare a detailed cash budget. The cash budget shows expected cash receipts and disbursements; it also signals when the company can expect a cash shortage requiring outside financing, or a cash overage, which should be temporarily invested in income-producing assets.

Budgeting for Operations in a Merchandising Firm

The approach illustrated thus far in the chapter is the budgeting process used by most manufacturing companies. Many organizations, however, do not manufacture products; they either purchase products to resell or are organizations that sell services instead of "products."

As discussed previously in this text, organizations that purchase the products they resell are often referred to as merchandising companies; these include retailers that sell directly to consumers and wholesale distributors that buy products from manufacturers or other suppliers and sell to retailers. Well-known retail companies include WAL-MART, SEARS, and KMART. Although retail companies such as Wal-Mart buy many of the products they sell directly from manufacturers (e.g., COCA-COLA, NABISCO, WRIGLEY, etc.), they also buy from wholesalers who either buy from domestic manufacturers or import their products from other countries.

STOP & THINK In this chapter, the emphasis is on budgeting costs and revenues, only one of the three elements management is interested in managing. Do you think management performs any budgeting related to quality or delivery time of products or services to customers?

Because merchandising companies buy products (rather than make them), their budgeting process is less complicated than the budgeting done by manufacturing companies. For example, if Sunbird Boat Company were a merchandising firm rather than a manufacturing firm, the company would prepare a purchases budget rather than a production budget. The result of the purchases budget would be the number of units to be purchased rather than the number of units to be produced. The format of the purchases budget would be similar to the production budget, combining expected sales and desired ending inventory to arrive at needs for the period. Inventory on hand at the start of the period would then be subtracted to arrive at the amount to be purchased during the period.

Exhibit 5-4 compares the master budgeting process for a merchandising firm with that for manufacturing firms (from Exhibit 5-2).

Looking at Exhibit 5-4, you can see that in merchandising companies, one purchases budget replaces four budgets (production budget, direct materials budget, direct labor budget, and manufacturing overhead budget) used by manufacturing firms.

Because the sales budget, the selling and administrative expense budget, and the cash budget are similar to those prepared for manufacturing firms, we will not discuss them again. To illustrate budgeting in a merchandising company, we will assume that Wind River Boat Company is a retail company that buys boats from manufacturers and sells them to consumers.

purchases budget A schedule of projected purchases over the budget period.

PURCHASES BUDGET Assuming the same level of sales as we did for Sunbird, the **purchases budget** for Wind River Boat Company is shown in Schedule 9.

You can see from Schedule 9 that Wind River Boat Company pays its suppliers $8,000 for each 15-foot boat. (If you compare this cost with the total manufacturing cost for Sunbird Boat Company, you will see that it is higher. This is because manufacturing companies also need to make a profit.) In Schedule 9, we have assumed the same beginning and ending inventory numbers we used in Schedule 2 for Sunbird, the manufacturing company. Total purchases in this schedule replaces the direct materials, direct labor, and manufacturing overhead lines in the cash budget for a manufacturing firm.

exhibit 5-4 A Comparison of the Master Budgets for a Manufacturing and a Merchandising Firm

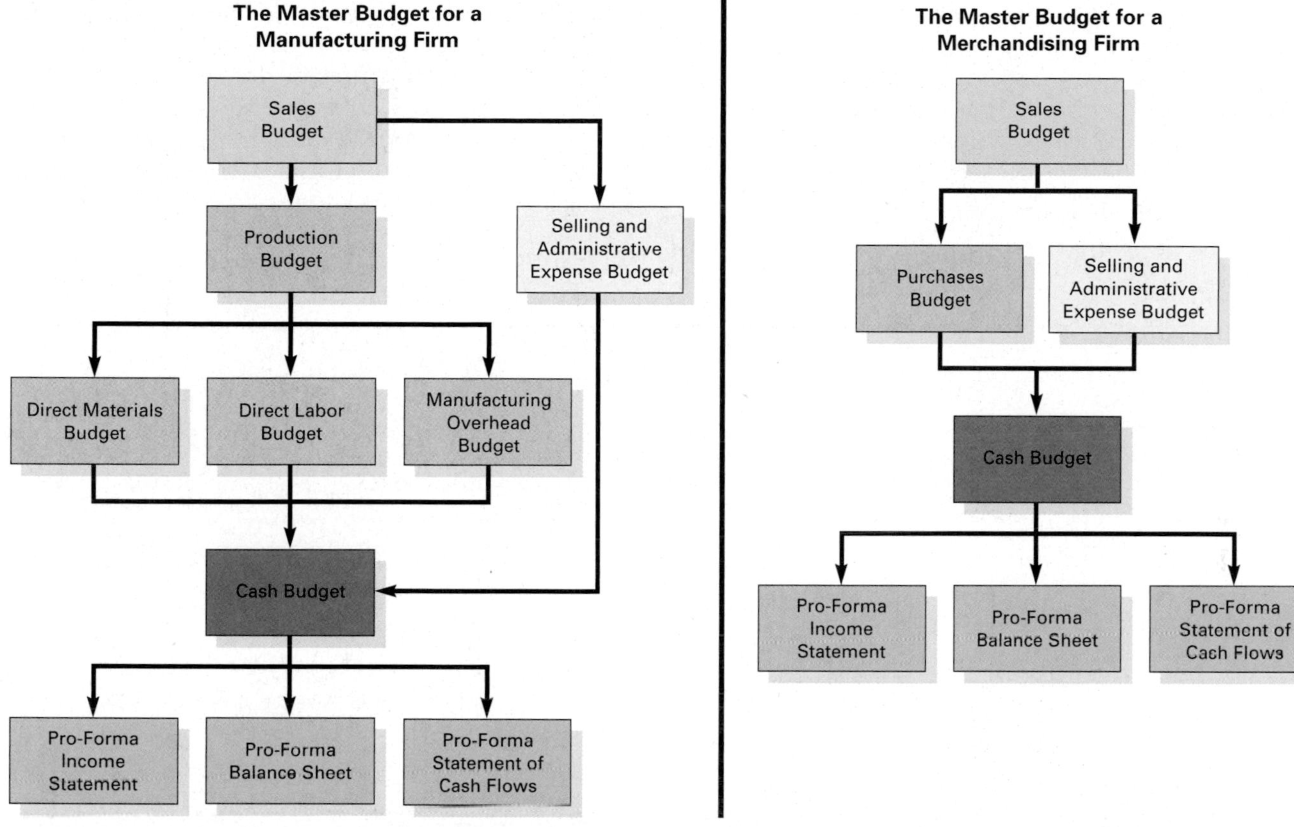

Schedule 9

Microsoft Excel - sch-m0509.xls

Schedule 9 Purchases Budget—2003	Quarter 1 15 ft.	Quarter 2 15 ft.	Quarter 3 15 ft.	Quarter 4 15 ft.	Total 15 ft.
Expected sales	24	28	30	18	100
Desired ending inventory	22	24	15	20	20
Boats needed	46	52	45	38	120
Less beginning inventory	(18)	(22)	(24)	(15)	(18)
Boats to be purchased	28	30	21	23	102
Cost per boat	x $8,000	x $8,000	x $8,000	x $8,000	x $8,000
Total purchases	$224,000	$240,000	$168,000	$184,000	$816,000

to summarize

The budgeting process for merchandising organizations (retail and wholesale companies) is similar, but easier, than that for manufacturing firms. The major difference is that a merchandising firm's purchases budget replaces four of a manufacturing firm's budgets—the production, direct materials, direct labor, and manufacturing overhead budgets. On the cash budget for a merchandis-

business environment essay

World's Largest Retailers In many industrialized countries, the growth rate for retail sales is barely keeping pace with the population growth rate. As a result, retailers are expanding into foreign markets to increase sales. Have you ever wondered which company is the largest retailer in the world? As of January 1, 2000, the largest retailer was **WAL-MART**, with 1999 sales of almost $167 billion. In addition to the United States, Wal-Mart operates stores in numerous other countries, including Argentina, Brazil, Canada, China, Indonesia, and Mexico. Here are the top nine global retailers as of December 1999.

Top Nine Global Retailers

Rank	Company	Country	Type of Store	1999 Sales (Millions of U.S. Dollars)*
1	WAL-MART	United States	Discount, warehouse	$166,809
2	SEARS, ROEBUCK	United States	Department, specialty	41,071
3	KMART	United States	Discount, warehouse	35,925
4	TARGET	United States	Discount	33,702
5	J.C. PENNEY	United States	Department	32,510
6	DAIEI	Japan	Department	25,320
7	GROUP PINAULT-PRINTEMPS	Europe	Department	20,144
8	FEDERATED DEPT. STORE	United States	Department	17,716
9	FONCIERE EURIS	Europe	Department	17,475

*Currency converted using average 1999 exchange rates.

Sources: http://Fortune500.com. Sales figures are from various sources.

ing company, total purchases replace cash expended for direct materials, direct labor, and manufacturing overhead. Otherwise, the entire master budgeting process is the same.

Budgeting for Operations in a Service Firm

Each year a larger and larger percentage of businesses in the United States are service entities. Service entities differ from manufacturing and merchandising companies in that they provide services to customers instead of products. Examples of service organizations are law, accounting, and engineering firms; doctors and dentists; hotels and motels; hunting and fishing guide services; automotive, home, and appliance repair services; and Internet providers. Budgeting for service firms is similar to budgeting for manufacturing firms. As was the case with both manufacturing and merchandising companies, the budgeting process for service firms begins with a sales budget. (For a service firm, this is usually called a revenue budget.) Expected revenues then drive the production budget, which is the number of billable hours in a CPA or law firm, the number of rooms to rent in a hotel, or the number of hours of service for an Internet provider. The production budget drives the separate budgets for supplies, wages and salaries, and overhead. These three budgets are similar to the direct materials, direct labor, and manufacturing overhead budgets for a manufacturing firm. These budgets, together with the revenue and selling and administrative expense budgets, provide the data needed for the cash budget. Once the cash budget is completed, pro-forma financial statements can be prepared. Exhibit 5-5 contrasts the budgeting process for a manufacturing and a service firm.

REVENUE BUDGET It is difficult to use either the Sunbird or Wind River examples discussed thus far to illustrate budgeting in service firms; both companies sold products—fishing boats. Therefore, to illustrate the budgeting process in service firms, we will use the example of the Boulder View Inn, a small motel that has 12 rooms to rent each night. The Boulder View Inn is located adjacent to a national park in southern Utah, and its business is highly seasonal, with April through December being busy (peak period) and January through March being very slow. The Boulder View Inn rents its rooms for an average rate of $55 per night during the peak period and $35 per night during the slow period. Guests who stay at the hotel either pay cash or use credit cards, such as VISA, MasterCard, American Express, or Discover. The motel has a direct link with its bank that immediately deposits credit card receipts in Boulder View Inn's bank account after charging a 4 to 5% discount fee, which covers the bank's costs as well as fees charged by the credit card companies. Historically, the Boulder View Inn has found that because most customers use credit cards to pay for their rooms, it pays an average of $2 per room per night to the credit card companies to cover the discount fee. After the discount fee, the net amount of revenues per room per night is $53 during peak periods and $33 during slow periods. Based on past experience, occupancy rates for the coming year are expected to be as follows:

January–March	25%
April–June	90%
July–September	80%
October–December	60%

exhibit 5-5 A Comparison of the Master Budgets for a Manufacturing and a Service Firm

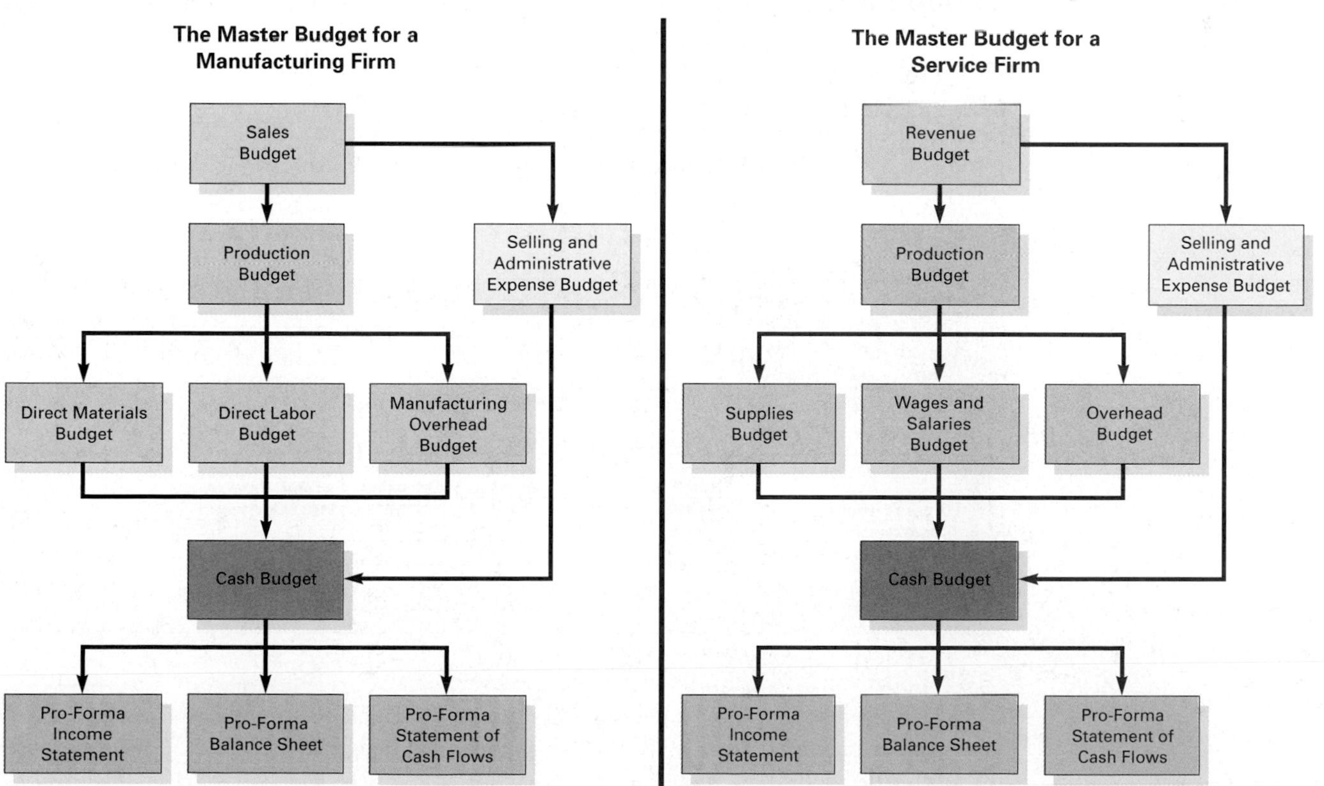

revenue budget A service entity's budget that identifies how much revenue (and often cash) will be generated during a period.

Using these data, the **revenue budget** for the Boulder View Inn would be as shown in Schedule 10.

This budget shows that the Boulder View Inn will generate gross revenues of $148,512 during the next year. Since the Boulder View Inn collects cash or its equivalent (credit cards) from each guest, there is no need to prepare a collection of accounts receivable budget as was done for the Sunbird Boat Company.

The revenue budget would be similar for other types of service firms, except that instead of a per-room revenue, the revenue would be based on per patient visit (for doctors and dentists), per service performed (for engineers, accountants, and lawyers), or per subscription (for Internet providers). Service companies that do not collect cash, but rather bill clients on a periodic basis (such as lawyers and accountants), would also prepare cash collection schedules to determine when the cash generated from revenues would be collected.

Schedule 10

Microsoft Excel - sch-m0510.xls

Schedule 10
Revenue Budget—2003

	January–March	April–June	July–September	October–December	Total
Gross revenue per room	$ 35	$ 55	$ 55	$ 55	
Number of days in quarter	x 90	x 91	x 92	x 92	
Total quarterly revenue per room	$ 3,150	$ 5,005	$ 5,060	$ 5,060	
Number of rooms to rent	x 12	x 12	x 12	x 12	
Possible revenues (at 100% occupancy)	$37,800	$60,060	$60,720	$60,720	
Occupancy rate	x 25%	x 90%	x 80%	x 60%	
Budgeted gross revenues	$ 9,450	$54,054	$48,576	$36,432	$148,512

PRODUCTION BUDGET The production budget for a service firm determines the total amount of services (the number of units of service) that will be used to earn the revenues budgeted. For a law firm, for example, the production budget would be the total number of billable hours at each billing rate used to generate the revenues. For a hunting and fishing guide service, the production budget would be the number of guide days. For Boulder View Inn, the production budget is the number of rooms that will be rented each quarter, as shown in Schedule 11.

Schedule 11

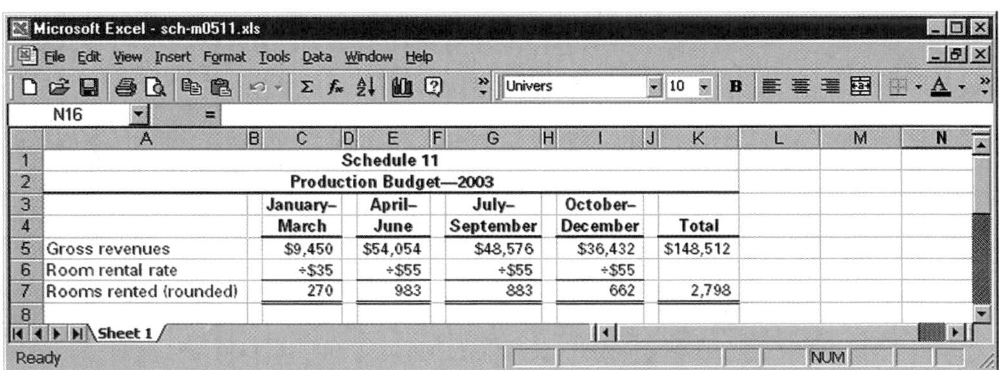
Microsoft Excel - sch-m0511.xls

Schedule 11
Production Budget—2003

	January–March	April–June	July–September	October–December	Total
Gross revenues	$9,450	$54,054	$48,576	$36,432	$148,512
Room rental rate	÷$35	÷$55	÷$55	÷$55	
Rooms rented (rounded)	270	983	883	662	2,798

This production budget is necessary in order to determine the supplies, wages and salaries, and overhead budgets. You can see from this production budget that Boulder View Inn expects to rent 2,798 rooms next year.

supplies budget The budget, prepared by service entities, that identifies projected supplies expenses over the budget period.

SUPPLIES BUDGET Most service businesses need supplies to operate their business. For a restaurant, supplies include the food used in preparing meals, napkins, afterdinner mints, and toothpicks. For a medical doctor, supplies might include needles, tape, bandages, and thread for stitching cuts. For Boulder View Inn, supplies include soap and shampoo for the guest rooms, as well as donuts, cereal, juice, and coffee for the continental breakfast. The **supplies budget** for the Boulder View Inn is shown in Schedule 12.

Schedule 12

Schedule 12

Supplies Budget—2003

Supplies Needed Per Room	January–March	April–June	July–September	October–December	Total
Soap	$ 0.40	$ 0.40	$ 0.40	$ 0.40	$ 0.40
Shampoo	0.60	0.60	0.60	0.60	0.60
Coffee	0.30	0.30	0.30	0.30	0.30
Juice	0.60	0.60	0.60	0.60	0.60
Cereal	0.40	0.40	0.40	0.40	0.40
Donuts	0.70	0.70	0.70	0.70	0.70
Total supplies per room	$ 3.00	$ 3.00	$ 3.00	$ 3.00	$ 3.00
Rooms rented	x 270	x 983	x 883	x 662	x 2,798
Total supplies cost	$ 810	$ 2,949	$ 2,649	$ 1,986	$ 8,394

wages and salaries budget The budget, prepared by service entities, that identifies projected labor costs involved directly in providing the service over the budget period.

WAGES AND SALARIES BUDGET The **wages and salaries budget** is reserved for labor costs involved directly in providing the service (similar to direct labor in a manufacturing firm). Administrative labor costs are not included in this budget; they are part of the selling and administrative expense budget. For a law firm, the wages and salaries budget would include salaries of lawyers (but not of paralegals), photocopy personnel, or computer specialists. For the Boulder View Inn, the only labor cost included in this budget is the $3 per room that is paid for cleaning the rooms. Schedule 13 is the wages and salaries budget for Boulder View Inn.

Schedule 13

Schedule 13

Wages and Salaries Budget—2003

	January–March	April–June	July–September	October–December	Total
Rooms rented	270	983	883	662	2,798
Cleaning fee	x $3	x $3	x $3	x $3	x $3
Total wages and salaries	$810	$2,949	$2,649	$1,986	$8,394

service overhead budget The budget, prepared by service entities, that identifies projected costs associated with providing the service.

OVERHEAD BUDGET As was the case with manufacturing firms, the **service overhead budget** includes all the costs associated with providing the product, or service in this case. The overhead budget does not include selling and administrative costs not directly associated with providing the service. For the Boulder View Inn, overhead includes utilities, depreciation, TV and telephone service, and miscellaneous expenses. Schedule 14 is the overhead budget for the Boulder View Inn.

The depreciation is calculated by dividing the motel cost of $300,000 by its 30-year life to arrive at $10,000 per year. The utilities include heat, lights, sewer, and garbage removal. Because the Boulder View Inn expects to rent 2,798 rooms during the year, the overhead assigned to each room rented is $9.29 ($26,000 ÷ 2,798 rooms).

Schedule 14

Schedule 14					
Overhead Budget—2003					
	January–March	April–June	July–September	October–December	Total
Utilities	$2,000	$2,000	$2,000	$2,000	$ 8,000
Depreciation expense	2,500	2,500	2,500	2,500	10,000
TV and telephone	800	800	800	800	3,200
Miscellaneous expenses	1,200	1,200	1,200	1,200	4,800
Total overhead	$6,500	$6,500	$6,500	$6,500	$26,000

Based on the three production-related budgets (supplies, wages and salaries, and overhead), we know it costs the Boulder View Inn approximately $15.29 to provide the services needed to rent one room for one night. The calculation of this cost is shown in Schedule 15.

Schedule 15

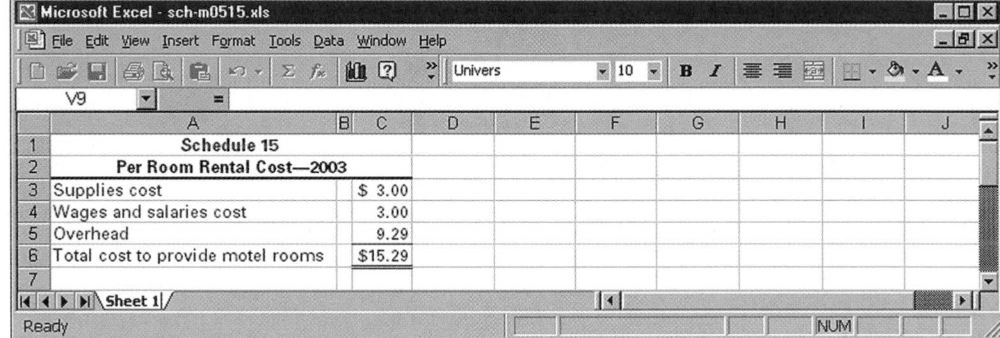

Schedule 15	
Per Room Rental Cost—2003	
Supplies cost	$ 3.00
Wages and salaries cost	3.00
Overhead	9.29
Total cost to provide motel rooms	$15.29

SELLING AND ADMINISTRATIVE EXPENSE BUDGET As was the case for Sunbird Boat Company, the selling and administrative expense budget includes planned expenditures for all selling and administrative expenses. As in manufacturing companies, the selling and administrative expense budget for a service firm can be quite large and is sometimes supported by individual budgets for specific elements included in this budget. The selling and administrative expense budget for the Boulder View Inn would be as shown in Schedule 16.

This selling and administration expense budget shows that the Boulder View Inn's total selling and administrative expense for the year is $29,596. The selling and administrative expenses include credit card charges, the manager's salary, and advertising expense, which includes yellow page directory advertisement and Internet listings.

Schedule 16

Schedule 16					
Selling and Administrative Expense Budget—2003					
	Quarter				Estimated
	1	2	3	4	Annual Cost
Credit card fees*	$ 540	$1,966	$1,766	$1,324	$ 5,596
Manager's salary	5,000	5,000	5,000	5,000	20,000
Advertising expense	1,000	1,000	1,000	1,000	4,000
Total selling and administrative expenses	$6,540	$7,966	$7,766	$7,324	$29,596

*At $2 per room.

CASH BUDGET The cash budget, which shows expected cash receipts and disbursements during a period, summarizes information contained in both the revenue and the selling and administrative expense budgets. For the Boulder View Inn, and for most service organizations, once the individual budgets are prepared, preparing the cash budget is quite simple. As is the case with all cash budgets, the Boulder View Inn's cash budget allows the motel to determine when it will have excess cash and when it will have to borrow cash. The cash budget for the Boulder View Inn is shown in Schedule 17.

This cash budget makes several assumptions. First, the Boulder View Inn is a partnership, so there is no income tax. Instead, as in all partnerships, the income is allocated among the partners and claimed as income on their personal tax returns. Many service organizations are partnerships, so this assumption is not unusual (many are also corporations). Second, it is assumed that all expenditures are paid in the quarter incurred. If the Boulder View Inn paid some of its expenses in the quarters following their incurrence, a cash payments schedule would need to be prepared.

This cash budget shows that the Boulder View Inn generates excess cash in quarters two, three, and four, but has a net cash outflow of $2,710 in the first quarter. The Boulder View Inn can solve its cash flow shortage in the first quarter either by keeping enough cash in its bank account to cover the shortage or by borrowing money in the first quarter and repaying it in the second quarter.

Schedule 17

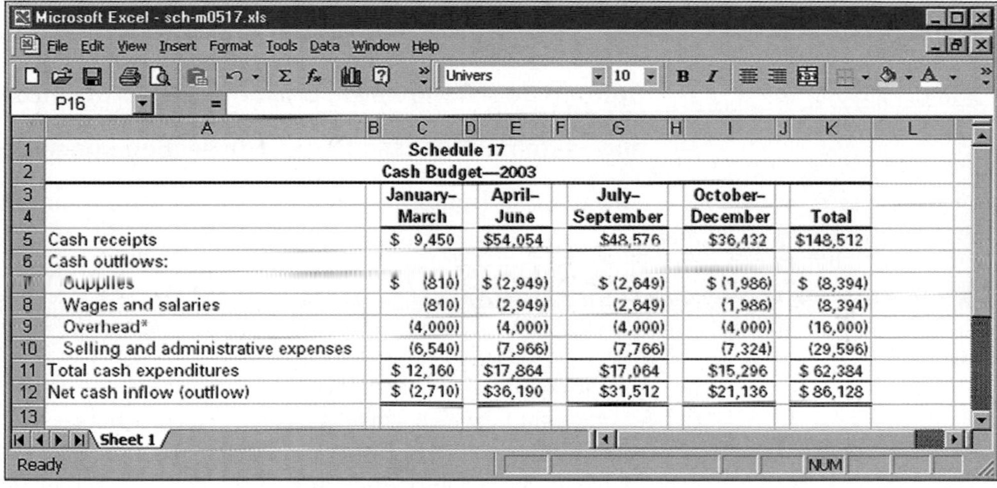

Schedule 17

Cash Budget—2003

	January–March	April–June	July–September	October–December	Total
Cash receipts	$ 9,450	$54,054	$48,576	$36,432	$148,512
Cash outflows:					
Supplies	$ (810)	$ (2,949)	$ (2,649)	$ (1,986)	$ (8,394)
Wages and salaries	(810)	(2,949)	(2,649)	(1,986)	(8,394)
Overhead*	(4,000)	(4,000)	(4,000)	(4,000)	(16,000)
Selling and administrative expenses	(6,540)	(7,966)	(7,766)	(7,324)	(29,596)
Total cash expenditures	$ 12,160	$17,864	$17,064	$15,296	$ 62,384
Net cash inflow (outflow)	$ (2,710)	$36,190	$31,512	$21,136	$ 86,128

*Depreciation expense is not included because it is not a cash expenditure.

to summarize

The master budget for a service company is similar to budgeting in a manufacturing company. As a result, in addition to the pro-forma financial statements (covered in the expanded material section of the chapter), seven budgets are prepared: the revenue budget, the production budget, the supplies budget, the wages and salaries budget, the overhead budget, the selling and administrative expense budget, and the cash budget. The revenue budget is usually based on whatever the service performed is (e.g., per room, per service performed, per patient, or per subscription basis). The production budget identifies the number of units of the service that will be performed so that supplies, wages and salaries, and overhead budgets can be prepared. The selling and administrative expense budget includes all costs not directly related to providing the service. The cash budget is net revenues received less cash spent for supplies, wages, overhead (not including depreciation expense), and selling and administrative expenses. As was the case with manufacturing and merchandising companies, the budgeting process allows a service company to determine when it will have excess cash and when it will experience cash shortages.

expanded material

The budgeting process discussed to this point allows management to plan various activities within the firm, such as purchasing and borrowing. Armed with these budgets, management is now prepared to monitor the firm's performance and compare actual results to budgeted results. If corrective action is needed, management can identify deviations from the budget early and take the appropriate steps to remedy problems. In addition to preparing the detailed budgets, management can combine the various budgets to arrive at pro-forma, or budgeted, financial statements. In this section, we use the budgets from the Sunbird Boat Company to prepare a pro-forma income statement, balance sheet, and statement of cash flows. The section concludes with a discussion of static and flexible budgeting and illustrates the advantages of flexible budgeting.

PRO-FORMA FINANCIAL STATEMENTS

4

Prepare pro-forma financial statements.

The pro-forma income statement (often called a budgeted income statement) projects income for the coming period and, therefore, is valuable to management in making key decisions. Such questions as how high a dividend to pay, whether to invest in a new plant, and how strenuously to bargain with unions are usually decided on the basis of projected and actual profits. Because budgeting for manufacturing firms is the most complicated, we will illustrate pro-forma financial statements using the Sunbird Boat Company example illustrated earlier in the chapter. Sunbird's pro-forma income statement is shown in Schedule 18. In the income statement, we assume an income tax rate of 27% for Sunbird.

How would the three financial statements be different if we assumed Sunbird was a merchandising company instead of a manufacturing company?

The final two items to be projected are the balance sheet and the statement of cash flows. These statements are presented in Schedules 19 and 20.

The master budget is now complete. It is ready for use to communicate information, coordinate and authorize activities, motivate employees, and measure performance. The decisions to be made on the basis of this budget depend on the answers to such questions as:

1. Is the net income of approximately $307,593 adequate? If not, how can it be increased?
2. How does the expected financial position at the end of the year fit with long-range objectives and goals?
3. Is the projected increase in cash sufficient to meet the firm's goals?
4. Are there sufficient liquid assets to purchase needed assets?
5. How should management be rewarded if these budgets are met?
6. Who should be responsible for meeting the goals set for sales, production, and costs?

These are only a few of the questions that management needs to answer. However, they should give you a sense of the master budget's usefulness. In fact, it is hard to imagine how a company could be profitable in the long run without such planning.

Schedule 18

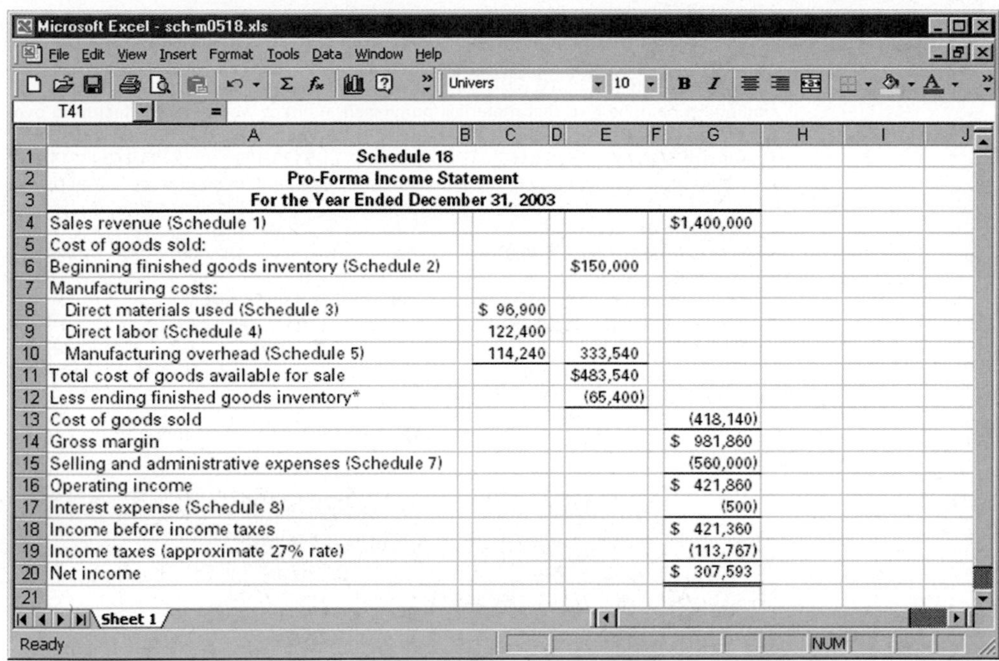

	A	C	E	G
1	Schedule 18			
2	Pro-Forma Income Statement			
3	For the Year Ended December 31, 2003			
4	Sales revenue (Schedule 1)			$1,400,000
5	Cost of goods sold:			
6	Beginning finished goods inventory (Schedule 2)		$150,000	
7	Manufacturing costs:			
8	Direct materials used (Schedule 3)	$ 96,900		
9	Direct labor (Schedule 4)	122,400		
10	Manufacturing overhead (Schedule 5)	114,240	333,540	
11	Total cost of goods available for sale		$483,540	
12	Less ending finished goods inventory*		(65,400)	
13	Cost of goods sold			(418,140)
14	Gross margin			$ 981,860
15	Selling and administrative expenses (Schedule 7)			(560,000)
16	Operating income			$ 421,860
17	Interest expense (Schedule 8)			(500)
18	Income before income taxes			$ 421,360
19	Income taxes (approximate 27% rate)			(113,767)
20	Net income			$ 307,593

*Calculation of ending Finished Goods Inventory. (Schedule 2 states that the desired ending inventory is 20 15-foot boats.) Per Schedule 6: Cost of 15-foot boat: $3,270 × 20 boats = $65,400.

Schedule 19

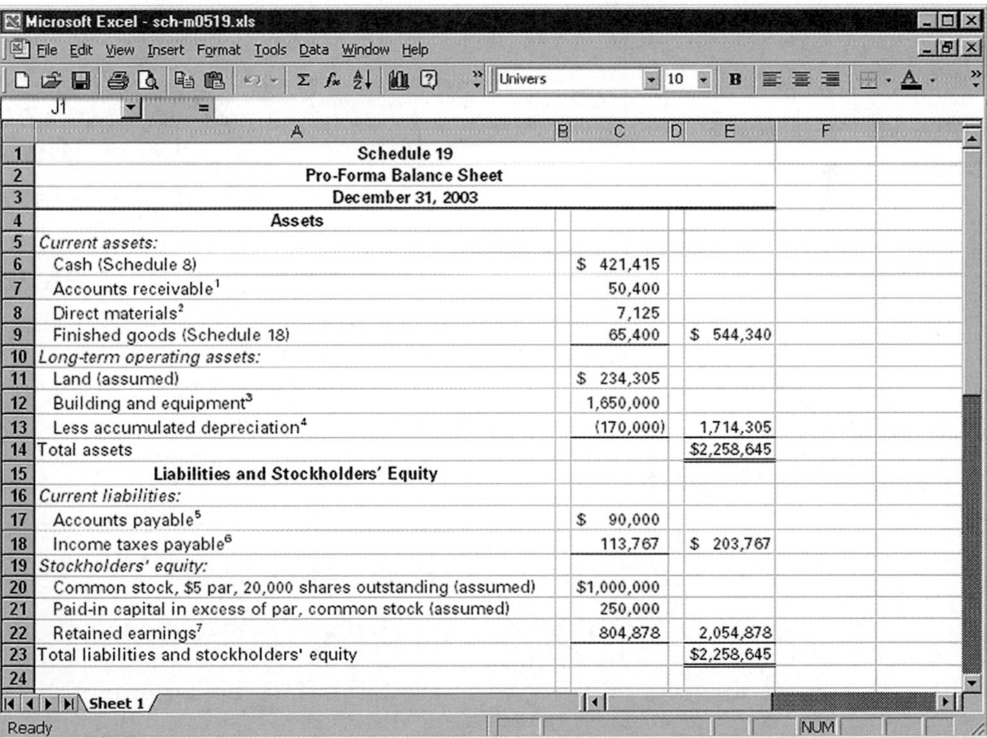

	A	C	E
1	Schedule 19		
2	Pro-Forma Balance Sheet		
3	December 31, 2003		
4	Assets		
5	*Current assets:*		
6	Cash (Schedule 8)	$ 421,415	
7	Accounts receivable[1]	50,400	
8	Direct materials[2]	7,125	
9	Finished goods (Schedule 18)	65,400	$ 544,340
10	*Long-term operating assets:*		
11	Land (assumed)	$ 234,305	
12	Building and equipment[3]	1,650,000	
13	Less accumulated depreciation[4]	(170,000)	1,714,305
14	Total assets		$2,258,645
15	Liabilities and Stockholders' Equity		
16	*Current liabilities:*		
17	Accounts payable[5]	$ 90,000	
18	Income taxes payable[6]	113,767	$ 203,767
19	*Stockholders' equity:*		
20	Common stock, $5 par, 20,000 shares outstanding (assumed)	$1,000,000	
21	Paid-in capital in excess of par, common stock (assumed)	250,000	
22	Retained earnings[7]	804,878	2,054,878
23	Total liabilities and stockholders' equity		$2,258,645

[1]Accounts receivable:
beginning balance + sales (Schedule 1) − collections (Schedule 8) = ending balance
(assumed) $56,000 + $1,400,000 − $1,405,600 = $50,400

[2]Direct materials:
Wood $5,250 (525 × $10 per board foot) + fiberglass $1,875 (375 × $5) = $7,125

[3]Building and equipment:
beginning balance + equipment purchase (Schedule 8) = ending balance
(assumed) $1,500,000 + $150,000 = $1,650,000

(continued)

[4]Accumulated depreciation:
beginning balance + plant overhead (Schedule 5) + selling and administrative expenses (Schedule 7) = ending balance
(assumed) $120,000 + $10,000 + $40,000 = $170,000

[5]Accounts payable:
beginning balance + direct materials purchased (Schedule 3) + direct labor (Schedule 4) + manufacturing overhead (less depreciation) (Schedule 5)
(assumed) $90,000 + $96,045 + $122,400 + $104,240 ($114,240 − $10,000)
+ selling and administrative expenses (less depreciation) (Schedule 7) + income tax expense (Schedule 8) + dividends (Schedule 8) + equipment (Schedule 8) − amount paid for cash payments (Schedule 8) = ending balance
+ $520,000 ($560,000 − $40,000) + $96,000 + $30,000 + $150,000 − $1,118,685 = $90,000

[6]Income taxes payable:
beginning balance + estimated taxes − payment = ending balance
(assumed) $96,000 + $113,767 − $96,000 = $113,767

[7]Retained earnings:
beginning balance + net income − dividends = ending balance
(assumed) $527,285 + $307,593 − $30,000 = $804,878

Schedule 20

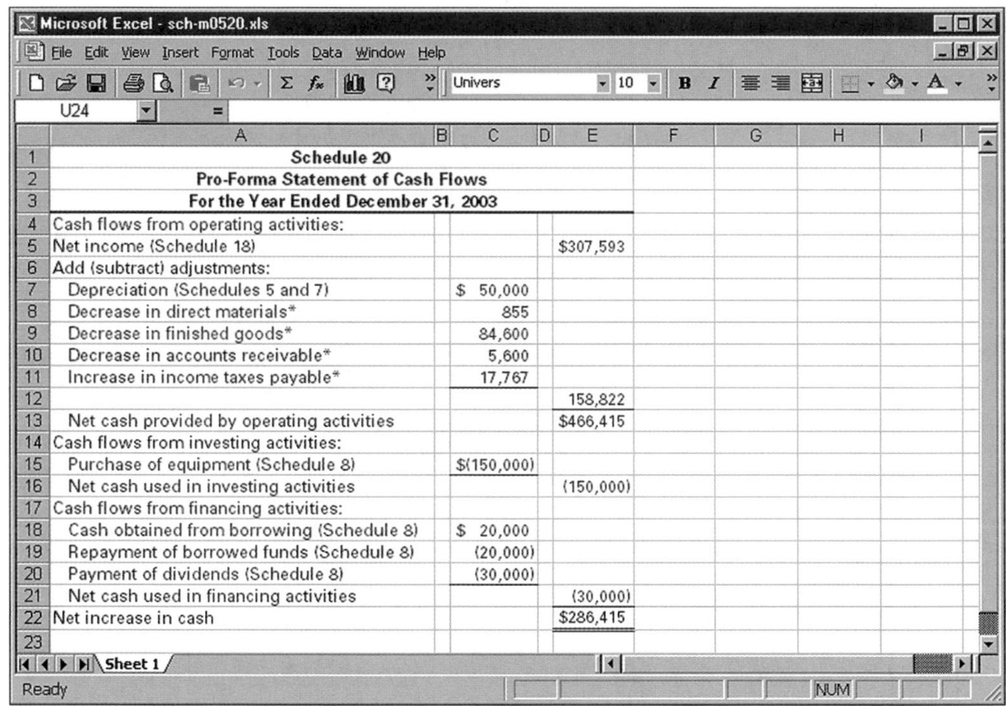

Microsoft Excel - sch-m0520.xls

	A	B	C	D	E
1	**Schedule 20**				
2	**Pro-Forma Statement of Cash Flows**				
3	**For the Year Ended December 31, 2003**				
4	Cash flows from operating activities:				
5	Net income (Schedule 18)				$307,593
6	Add (subtract) adjustments:				
7	Depreciation (Schedules 5 and 7)		$ 50,000		
8	Decrease in direct materials*		855		
9	Decrease in finished goods*		84,600		
10	Decrease in accounts receivable*		5,600		
11	Increase in income taxes payable*		17,767		
12					158,822
13	Net cash provided by operating activities				$466,415
14	Cash flows from investing activities:				
15	Purchase of equipment (Schedule 8)		$(150,000)		
16	Net cash used in investing activities				(150,000)
17	Cash flows from financing activities:				
18	Cash obtained from borrowing (Schedule 8)		$ 20,000		
19	Repayment of borrowed funds (Schedule 8)		(20,000)		
20	Payment of dividends (Schedule 8)		(30,000)		
21	Net cash used in financing activities				(30,000)
22	Net increase in cash				$286,415
23					

*2002 year-end balances are assumed to be $7,980 for direct materials, $150,000 for finished goods, $56,000 for accounts receivable, and $96,000 for income taxes payable.

to summarize

Following the preparation of the cash budget, which provides an indication of the financing activities of the business, pro-forma financial statements can be prepared. The pro-forma income statement, balance sheet, and statement of cash flows follow directly from the components of the master budget. The pro-forma balance sheet also relies heavily on beginning account balances. Once these pro-forma financial statements have been prepared, management can then determine if budgeted sales and production levels will allow the company to achieve its strategic goals. These pro-forma financial statements serve as a basis for key management decisions.

5 Distinguish between static and flexible budgets.

static budget A quantified plan that projects revenues and costs for only one level of activity.

flexible budget A quantified plan that projects revenues and costs for varying levels of activity.

STATIC VERSUS FLEXIBLE BUDGETING

The budgets discussed thus far were **static budgets**; that is, they were geared to only one level of activity. Actual results were compared to budgeted costs at the budgeted activity level. Although such budgets help in planning, they are not very useful for controlling costs and measuring performance because the actual level of activity may have differed significantly from the planned level.

A **flexible budget** is much more useful for control and performance evaluation because it is not confined to one level of activity. Flexible budgets are dynamic; that is, they can be tailored to any level of activity within the relevant range. Using flexible budgeting, a manager can look at the actual level of activity attained and then determine what costs should have been at that level.

Weaknesses in Static Budgeting

To illustrate why a static budget is inadequate for controlling operations, we will use an example for Kemper Manufacturing Company and assume only variable costs. We use this different example so as not to complicate the Sunbird Boat Company example used throughout the chapter. Here we are interested only in illustrating the concept of flexible budgets.

Using information from various sources, Kemper developed the following budgeted per-unit manufacturing costs for its product:

Direct materials	$0.90
Direct labor	0.74
Manufacturing overhead	1.36
Total	$3.00

Extending these per-unit costs to establish a total budgeted amount for the month of August, the company might prepare a static budget as follows:

Kemper Manufacturing Company
Budgeted Manufacturing Costs
For the Month of August 2003

Budgeted production (units)	4,000
Budgeted manufacturing costs:	
Direct materials ($0.90 × 4,000)	$ 3,600
Direct labor ($0.74 × 4,000)	2,960
Manufacturing overhead ($1.36 × 4,000)	5,440
Total manufacturing costs	$12,000

Now, let's assume that Kemper produced only 3,800 units in August and that actual costs incurred were $3,370 for direct materials, $2,900 for direct labor, and $5,400 for manufacturing overhead. Comparing actual results with the static budget information, the performance report for the month would be as follows:

Kemper Manufacturing Company
Static Budget Performance Report
For the Month of August 2003

	Actual	Budgeted	Difference
Production (units)	3,800	4,000	(200)
Manufacturing costs:			
Direct materials	$ 3,370	$ 3,600	$(230)
Direct labor	2,900	2,960	(60)
Manufacturing overhead	5,400	5,440	(40)
Total actual and budgeted manufacturing costs	$11,670	$12,000	$(330)

Obviously, something is wrong with this performance report. Producing fewer units than budgeted (3,800 actual units versus 4,000 budgeted units) has led to actual costs that are $330 less than budgeted costs. Should management be rewarded for keeping costs down or penalized for producing fewer units than budgeted? The deficiencies of this static budget performance report can be explained as follows: A production manager is responsible for controlling two things—production (output) and costs; that is, he or she must try to meet budgeted production volume and control costs in the process. To measure a manager's performance, the production and cost control functions must be separated. It makes no sense to note that the actual cost of producing 3,800 units is less than the budgeted cost of producing 4,000 units. It obviously should be. The manager in our example clearly has not met budgeted production volume, but to determine whether he or she has controlled costs adequately, we must be able to compare actual costs to budgeted costs at the same number of units of production.

Using the Flexible Budget

Instead of providing budgeted costs for only one level of activity, the flexible budget covers a range of activity levels so that managers can easily determine what costs should have been at the actual activity level. Because it is possible to prepare budgeted costs at every possible activity level, per-unit costs that can be applied to any activity level within the relevant range are developed. The actual steps in preparing a flexible budget are:

1. Determine a relevant range over which production is expected to vary during the coming period.
2. Analyze the projected manufacturing costs for the coming period.
3. Using the per-unit costs for each element, prepare a budget showing what costs are expected to be incurred at several points within the relevant range.

To illustrate the preparation of a flexible budget, let us assume that Kemper's relevant range of activity per month is between 3,600 and 4,200 units. As noted earlier, the per-unit costs are:

business environment essay

Budgeting at Theme Parks Although the rides are idle at many theme parks during the winter, theme park accountants are not without work. When the gates close for the last time each fall, accountants at SIX FLAGS GREAT AMERICA in Illinois use the off-period to prepare the annual operating budget for the coming season.

The process begins with the development of the park's anticipated attendance levels and the daily operating schedule. Attendance levels from the preceding season are used to make projections for the next year. Attendance is computed by summing the number of tickets sold at the entrance, the number of pre-sold tickets redeemed, and the number of season pass admissions. In addition, turnstiles are used at entrances and exits to count admissions and the number of guests riding each ride. Turnstile meters are "read" on an hourly basis to enable management to monitor varying attendance throughout the day. This information is used to anticipate and budget staffing needs.

Based on past performance and other information (such as planned improvements), revenues and expenses are projected for each area of the park. For example, gift shops, food outlets, movable carts, and support areas are budgeted individually. The master budget, then, is a consolidation of the several hundred budgets of individual activity centers.

Theme parks are an established cultural phenomenon in America. Those parks that budget and then execute their budgets most effectively are the most financially successful.

Source: Adapted from Kevin A. Roth, "Theme Park Accounting: What Do We Really Do All Winter?" *Management Accounting,* February 1994, pp. 48–51.

Direct materials	$0.90
Direct labor	0.74
Manufacturing overhead	1.36
Total	$3.00

These per-unit costs can now be used to prepare a flexible budget showing expected costs for several levels of production.

Kemper Manufacturing Company
Manufacturing Cost Flexible Budget
For the Month of August 2003

	Manufacturing Costs per Unit	Range of Production (units) 3,600	3,800	4,000	4,200
Direct materials	$0.90	$ 3,240	$ 3,420	$ 3,600	$ 3,780
Direct labor	0.74	2,664	2,812	2,960	3,108
Manufacturing overhead	1.36	4,896	5,168	5,440	5,712
Total	$3.00	$10,800	$11,400	$12,000	$12,600

With the flexible budget prepared, Kemper can compare actual amounts against budgeted amounts for the production level attained. In this case, 3,800 units were actually produced, so the actual costs for the period can be compared with the budget for 3,800 units. If actual production had been 3,700 units, a number not included in the budget, Kemper could simply multiply the per-unit cost of each item (direct materials, direct labor, and manufacturing overhead) by the actual activity level in order to judge performance. The performance report based on flexible budgeting for the 3,800 units actually produced now makes much more sense.

Kemper Manufacturing Company
Flexible Budget Performance Report
For the Month of August 2003

Actual production (units)	3,800
Budgeted production (units)	4,000
Difference	(200)

	Cost per Unit	Actual Costs Incurred at 3,800 Units	Budgeted Costs for 3,800 Units	Difference
Direct materials	$0.90	$ 3,370	$ 3,420	$ (50)
Direct labor	0.74	2,900	2,812	88
Manufacturing overhead	1.36	5,400	5,168	232
Total costs	$3.00	$11,670	$11,400	$270

Notice that the actual costs for both direct labor and manufacturing overhead exceeded budgeted costs for the actual level of activity. We are now comparing apples with apples, or actual costs of producing 3,800 units with budgeted costs of producing 3,800 units. Using the same activity level has revealed that total manufacturing costs exceeded budget by $270 during the month and that the most significant difference was in the cost of manufacturing overhead.

Flexible budgets provide management with useful information for investigating problem areas. This flexible budget performance report shows that not only was planned production not achieved, but also that the costs incurred exceeded those budgeted at the attained level of activity. Apparently, the manager is having problems with both production and cost control. Having meaningful cost comparisons is very useful for evaluating performance and overcoming breakdowns in cost control.

to summarize

The master budget described in this chapter was a static budget. A static budget is a budget that is prepared for only one level of activity. Static budgets are useful for planning purposes, but flexible budgets are much more useful for control and performance evaluation. A flexible budget is a budget prepared over a range of activity. Flexible budgets allow budgeted and actual costs to be compared at the same level of activity, thereby revealing cost and production effectiveness.

review of learning objectives

1 Describe different types of budgeting and identify the purposes of budgeting. A budget is a quantitative expression of a plan of action. The budget identifies and allocates resources necessary to carry out the mission of the organization. Based on the strategic plan, the organization prepares a capital budget and a budget for operations. The operating budget provides quantitative estimates of sales and expected costs for each activity to be performed during a specified period of time (usually, one year). The budgeting process has several purposes. Budgeting encourages planning, enhances communications, helps management at all levels coordinate activities, provides authorization for actions (investing, spending, borrowing, producing), helps motivate employees to perform, assists in reducing conflicts, and provides quantitative measures of expectations and objectives.

2 Describe the budgeting process and its behavioral implications. Most organizations establish a budget committee composed of several vice presidents who coordinate the preparation of detailed budgets in their areas of responsibility and oversee the preparation of the overall budget. There are significant behavioral ramifications to consider in preparing an operating budget. For the process to be successful, top management must give its full support, all members of management must actively participate in the process, and deviations from the budget must be addressed in a constructive manner. If only the top management is involved in budget preparation, it is referred to as top-down budgeting. When each segment manager prepares a budget for that segment's operations, it is called bottom-up budgeting. Most budgeting processes incorporate both approaches to some degree.

3 Explain the master budget and its components for manufacturing firms, merchandising firms, and service firms. The operating budget, also called a master budget, is an integrated group of detailed budgets that together provide overall operating and financing plans for a specific time period. The master budget for a manufacturing firm starts with a sales forecast, which serves as the basis for the sales budget. The sales budget is followed in sequence with detailed budgets for production, direct materials usage and purchases, direct labor, manufacturing overhead, selling and administrative expenses, and cash. These detailed budgets are usually prepared on a monthly or quarterly basis. For operations budgeting in merchandising companies, a purchases budget replaces the production, direct materials, direct labor, and manufacturing overhead budgets used in manufacturing companies. Operations budgeting in service firms includes preparing revenue, production, selling and administrative expense, and cash budgets. Together these budgets provide management with a master plan of action for the coming year.

expanded material

4 Prepare pro-forma financial statements. Once a cash budget is prepared to project the firm's ending cash balances and borrowing and investing activities, pro-forma financial statements can be prepared. The pro-forma balance sheet relies heavily on the balances at the beginning of the period, along with components of the master budget. The pro-forma income statement and statement of cash flows are prepared primarily from the detailed budgets included in the master budget. With these pro-forma financial statements, management is able to determine if budgeted results are consistent with the firm's master plan.

5 Distinguish between static and flexible budgets. Static budgets project expected results at only one activity level. When the actual production level differs significantly from the budgeted level, it is difficult to know what costs should have been for the actual production level. Flexible budgets estimate costs for various activity levels and allow actual costs to be compared to budgeted costs for the actual production level. Flexible budgets allow management to focus on both the production and cost control elements of budgeting.

budget 234
budget committee 239
cash budget 250
direct labor budget 246
direct materials budget 246
disposable income 235
line of credit 252
manufacturing overhead budget 248
operating (master) budget 235
production budget 245
purchases budget 254
revenue budget 258
sales budget 243
selling and administrative expense budget 249
service overhead budget 259
supplies budget 259
wages and salaries budget 259

expanded material

flexible budget 265
static budget 265

review problem

Budgeting in a Manufacturing Firm

The following information is available for the Call Company:

Expected sales (units):		
June	840	
July	980	
August	1,400	
Selling price per unit	$15	
Accounts receivable balance, June 1	$6,300	
Desired finished goods inventory, August 31 (units)	250	
Beginning finished goods inventory, June 1 (units)	270	
Direct materials needed per unit	11	feet
Desired direct materials inventory, August 31	2,800	feet
Beginning direct materials inventory, June 1	2,700	feet
Total direct labor time per finished unit	3	hours
Direct materials cost per foot	$0.60	
Direct labor cost per hour	$8	

Additional information:

a. Seventy-five percent of a month's sales is collected by the month's end; the remaining 25% is collected in the following month.
b. The desired ending finished goods inventory every month is 25% of the next month's sales.
c. The desired ending direct materials inventory every month is 20% of the next month's production needs.

Required:

1. Prepare sales budgets for June, July, and August (in dollars).
2. Prepare cash collection budgets for June, July, and August (in dollars).
3. Prepare production budgets for June, July, and August (in units).
4. Prepare direct materials budgets for June, July, and August (in dollars).
5. Prepare direct labor budgets for June, July, and August (in dollars).

Solution

1. **Sales Budgets**

	June	July	August
Expected sales (units)	840	980	1,400
Selling price per unit	× $15	× $15	× $15
Expected revenues	$12,600	$14,700	$21,000

2. Cash Collection Budgets

	June	July	August
From accounts receivable	$ 6,300		
From June's sales (75%/25%)	9,450	$ 3,150	
From July's sales (75%/25%)		11,025	$ 3,675
From August's sales (75%/25%)			15,750
Total	$15,750	$14,175	$19,425

3. Production Budgets

	June	July	August
Expected sales (units)	840	980	1,400
Add desired ending inventory			
(25% of next month's sales)	245	350	250*
Total needed	1,085	1,330	1,650
Less beginning inventory	(270)*	(245)	(350)
Budgeted production (units)	815	1,085	1,300

*Given.

4. Direct Materials Budgets

	June	July	August
Units to be produced	815	1,085	1,300
Direct materials needed per unit	× 11 feet	× 11 feet	× 11 feet
Total production needs	8,965 feet	11,935 feet	14,300 feet
Desired ending direct materials inventory (20% of next month's production needs)	2,387	2,860	2,800*
Total feet needed	11,352	14,795	17,100
Less beginning inventory	(2,700)*	(2,387)	(2,860)
Direct materials to be purchased	8,652	12,408	14,240
Cost per foot	× $0.60	× $0.60	× $0.60
Total direct materials cost (rounded)	$ 5,191	$ 7,445	$ 8,544

*Given.

5. Direct Labor Budgets

	June	July	August
Units to be produced	815	1,085	1,300
Direct labor hours per unit (given)	× 3	× 3	× 3
Total hours needed	2,445	3,255	3,900
Cost per hour	× $8	× $8	× $8
Direct labor cost	$19,560	$26,040	$31,200

discussion questions

1. How are strategic planning, capital budgeting, and operations budgeting different?
2. What are the advantages of budgeting?
3. How does management use the operating budget?
4. Describe the advantages of the top-down approach and the bottom-up approach to budgeting.
5. Why are budgets usually prepared for one year?
6. Why does the accuracy of the entire master budget depend on a reliable sales forecast?
7. Identify the sequence of schedules used in preparing a master budget for a manufacturing firm.
8. Describe the four sections of a cash budget.
9. How is the budgeting process for a merchandising firm different from the budgeting process for a manufacturing firm?
10. How is the budgeting process for a service firm similar to the budgeting process for a manufacturing firm? What are any differences?

expanded material

11. How does a cash budget differ from a pro-forma income statement?
12. How are flexible budgets useful in controlling costs?

discussion cases

CASE 5-1

WEST MOUNTAIN CANNING COMPANY

West Mountain Canning Company produces several food items, including certain tomato-based products. For about nine months during the year, the company is able to purchase tomatoes from various parts of the country. The tomatoes are then processed and canned for sale in grocery stores.

The processing department employs three highly skilled workers, who are paid an average of $15 per hour. Between January and March, tomatoes are not available, and the processing and canning departments are shut down. Rather than lay off these three specialists, who have excellent alternative job opportunities, the company transfers them to the shipping department, at the same $15 pay rate. The shipping department manager is not happy, however, because his five regular employees are paid only $9 per hour. His unhappiness has become particularly acute since he was told he was $9,000 over budget for wages during the January-to-March quarter (budget was $36,000; actual was $45,000). Note that the actual amount includes 1,500 hours (3 employees × 500 hours) at $15 per hour, and that each employee works 2,000 hours in a year.

The shipping department manager feels that he is being unduly penalized for two reasons: (1) $15 is too much to pay even a good shipping clerk, and (2) the three skilled workers do not work as hard as his regular employees because they know they are needed for tomato processing and will not be fired. Therefore, he has suggested to his boss that the wages in excess of the $9 he normally pays be assigned elsewhere or that he be allowed to hire his own temporary employees during this busy period.

Answer the following questions:

1. Does the shipping department manager have a legitimate complaint? Explain.
2. Explain how management arrived at the budgeted figure for shipping wages.
3. How might the quarterly figures be reported to satisfy the shipping department manager?
4. How would you recommend that the problem be solved?

CASE 5-2

TIP TOP COMPANY

Tip Top Company recently hired a new hot-shot CEO. Traditionally, the budgeting process at Tip Top has been pretty relaxed, with the executive vice president for sales providing "best-guess" sales projections and the controller providing "ballpark" cost estimates. Although the budget has been due each year 30 days prior to the new fiscal year, it generally is not finalized until two or three months into the new fiscal year. One of the first actions of the new CEO is to institute a formalized top-down budgeting process, complete with fairly sophisticated sales projections and cost data based on benchmark statistics from industry competitors.

Discuss the issues involved in the new budgeting process for Tip Top Company.

CASE 5-3

NEW AGE BUDGETING

Manes.com is an Internet company that searches out job listings on corporate home pages, organizes them by type of job, and lists them so that individuals seeking jobs can see the kinds of jobs that are available. The Internet site is free to all users. Manes.com hopes that by providing a job-matching service, its site will attract substantial traffic, and advertisers will be willing to pay large sums of money to advertise. The company has a $20 million investment from a venture capitalist to get started but must provide budget projections to secure additional funding. Assume you are the controller for the company. How would you go about forecasting revenues and preparing budgets and profit projections to show potential investors?

CASE 5-4

DISAGREEMENTS OVER THE VALUE OF BUDGETS

Tueller Enterprises is a large manufacturer of airplane parts for commercial and military aircraft. In addition to making parts, it also serves as a distributor for other, smaller manufacturers. Traditionally, the company has spent large amounts of time preparing operational budgets, only to find that they are rarely useful and often outdated. Some managers have even argued that because they are evaluated on the basis of how well they meet the budget, they have been unable to react to changing markets and take advantage of new opportunities that have become available. The managers argue that the entire budgeting process is too constraining and should be scrapped. The new controller agrees that the traditional budgeting process has been flawed but argues that with the new enterprise-wide information systems and the availability of up-to-date performance information, budgets can now be revised more frequently and will be much more useful than in the past. The company is trying to decide what to do. Should it scrap the entire budgeting process? Or, should it work to make the budgeting process more relevant and useful?

exercises

EXERCISE 5-1

PERSONAL BUDGETING

Jennifer Swartz works as an interior decorator for Modern Fashion Corporation. Her annual salary is $36,500. Of that amount, 20% is withheld for federal income taxes, 7.15% for state taxes, 7.65% for FICA taxes, and 2% as a contribution to the United Way. Another 5% is deposited directly into a company credit union for savings. Jennifer has four monthly payments: $225 for her car, $80 for furniture, $410 for rent, and $100 to repay college loans. Jennifer's other monthly expenses are approximately:

Food expense	$250
Clothing expense	100
Entertainment expense	125
Utilities expense	80
Insurance expense	30
Gas and maintenance expenses on car	180
Miscellaneous expenses	200
Total	$965

Prepare both a monthly budget and an annual budget for Jennifer that identifies gross salary, net take-home pay, net disposable income, and net surplus or deficit.

EXERCISE 5-2

PERSONAL BUDGETING

Trent Jones, a recent college graduate, has been hired by Midwest Corporation at a salary of $36,000 per year. In anticipation of his salary, Trent purchased a $14,000 automobile and will pay for it at a rate of $350 per month, including interest, for four years. He also rented a townhouse for $475 a month and bought some furniture on account for $230 a month. In addition, Trent figures that his other monthly expenses will be:

Food expense	$200
Clothing expense	100
Entertainment expense	175
Insurance expense	100
Gas and other car expenses	170
Utilities expense	100

1. On the assumption that Trent also pays income and FICA taxes of 20 and 7.65%, respectively, prepare his monthly budget.
2. Trent plans to get married soon and have a family, so he intends to save enough money for a down payment on a house. If a $15,000 down payment is needed, how long will it take him to save the needed amount? (Ignore interest on savings, and assume that Trent does not have any savings at the present time.)

EXERCISE 5-3

PRODUCTION BUDGETING

Daytona Electric makes and sells two kinds of portable radios—an AM-FM radio with CD player and an AM-FM radio. The sales forecasts for these radios for the next four quarters are as follows:

	AM-FM with CD Player	AM-FM Radio
1st quarter	170	130
2nd quarter	178	139
3rd quarter	166	127
4th quarter	190	145
Totals	704	541

At the beginning of the first quarter, Daytona has 140 AM-FM radios with CD players and 120 AM-FM radios in stock. Experience has shown that Daytona must maintain an inventory equal to two-thirds of the next quarter's sales.

How many radios of each type must be produced during each of the first three quarters to meet sales and inventory demands?

EXERCISE 5-4

PRODUCTION BUDGETING

James Seigel is the CEO of Seigel Monitor Company, a manufacturer of computer monitors. Seigel manufactures three types of computer monitors: SVGA, VGA, and EGA. The sales projections (in units) for 2003 and the first quarter of 2004 are:

	SVGA	VGA	EGA
1st quarter, 2003	3,000	5,000	2,000
2nd quarter, 2003	2,500	4,750	2,150
3rd quarter, 2003	2,850	4,900	1,800
4th quarter, 2003	3,200	4,876	2,150
1st quarter, 2004	2,900	5,100	2,200

Beginning inventory for SVGA, VGA, and EGA are 1,350, 1,500, and 1,275, respectively. Seigel requires that half of the next quarter's sales be maintained in inventory.

How many monitors must be manufactured for each quarter of 2003 to meet sales and inventory demand?

EXERCISE 5-5

DIRECT MATERIALS BUDGETING

Shaver Bicycle Shop assembles and sells tricycles and bicycles. The frames are purchased from one supplier and the wheels from another. The following materials are required:

Bicycles	Tricycles
One 22-inch frame, $35	One 12-inch frame, $15
Two 22-inch wheels, $10 each	Two 4-inch wheels, $10 each
	One 12-inch wheel, $7.50

Management anticipates that 150 bicycles and 160 tricycles will be assembled during the first quarter of 2003. On December 31, 2002, the following assembly parts are on hand:

22-inch frames	12
22-inch wheels	20
12-inch frames	8
4-inch wheels	24
12-inch wheels	10

Management also decides that, beginning in January, the inventory of parts on hand at the end of each month should be sufficient to make 10 bicycles and 10 tricycles.

Prepare a direct materials budget for the first quarter of 2003.

EXERCISE 5-6

DIRECT MATERIALS BUDGETING

Shanahan Corporation produces three types of videocassettes: VHS, S-VHS, and 8 millimeter. Shanahan purchases tape for the videocassettes from a firm in Mexico and purchases the cases from another supplier in Brazil. The following materials are required for production.

	VHS	S-VHS	8MM
Tape	$1.75	$2.30	$3.05
Cases	2.50	2.50	2.00

Beginning inventory for Shanahan Corporation is 5,000, 7,000, and 3,500 tapes for VHS, S-VHS, and 8 MM, respectively. Management wants to have 5,000 VHS and 8MM tapes and 2,500 S-VHS tapes in ending inventory. Projected sales for the first half of 2003 are 40,000 VHS tapes, 14,000 S-VHS tapes, and 21,000 8 MM tapes.

Prepare a direct materials budget for the first half of 2003.

EXERCISE 5-7

DIRECT LABOR BUDGETING

Super Good Chocolate Company makes and sells two kinds of candy: chocolate peanut bars and caramel bars. The production budget for the next three months for each of the bars is as follows:

	Boxes of Chocolate Peanut Bars	Boxes of Caramel Bars
January	640	700
February	870	450
March	920	630

From experience, Super Good's management knows that it takes approximately 20 minutes to make a box of chocolate peanut bars and 30 minutes to make a box of caramel bars. Super Good pays its direct labor employees $8 per hour.

Prepare a direct labor budget for each of the two products in both hours and costs for January, February, and March.

EXERCISE 5-8

DIRECT LABOR BUDGETING

Sanford Shoe Company makes three shoe styles: loafers, work boots, and tennis shoes. The production budget for the next three months for each type of shoe is:

	Loafers	Work Boots	Tennis Shoes
January	2,900	5,400	3,160
February	3,100	6,000	5,400
March	2,750	6,600	4,300

From experience, Sanford's management knows that it takes 15 minutes of direct labor to make a pair of loafers, 20 minutes to make a pair of work boots, and 12 minutes to make a pair of tennis shoes. At Sanford, direct labor employees are paid $5 per hour.

Prepare a direct labor budget in both hours and costs for each of the three months.

EXERCISE 5-9

COMPUTATION OF UNIT COSTS

High Lift Garage Door Company makes two types of garage doors: aluminum and wood. During the past several years, management has kept accurate records of costs and resource requirements and has determined that the following is needed to make the garage doors:

Wood Door	Production Requirements	Unit Cost
Wood	200 board feet	$1.70
Paint	2 gallons	7.50
Direct labor	6 hours	9.00
Manufacturing overhead	6 hours	5.50
Aluminum Door		
Aluminum	40 pounds	$3.50
Paint	1½ gallons	7.50
Direct labor	12 hours	9.00
Manufacturing overhead	12 hours	5.50

Compute the total unit costs of both the wood and aluminum garage doors.

EXERCISE 5-10

CASH BUDGETING—HOSPITAL

The management of West Valley Memorial Hospital needs to prepare a cash budget for July 2003. The following information is available:

a. The cash balance on July 1, 2003, is $236,000.
b. Actual services performed during May and June and projected services for July are:

	May	June	July
Cash services (bills paid by individuals as they leave the hospital)	$110,000	$ 90,000	$120,000
Credit services (bills paid by insurance companies and Medicare)	900,000	1,000,000	875,000

Credit sales are collected over a two-month period, with 60% collected during the month the service is performed and 40% in the following month.

c. Hospital personnel plan to purchase $80,000 of supplies during July on account. Accounts payable are usually paid one-half in the month of purchase and one-half in the following month. The accounts payable balance on July 1, 2003, is $35,000.
d. Salaries and wages paid during July will be approximately $600,000. (Ignore income and other tax withholdings.)
e. Depreciation on the hospital and equipment for July will be $100,000.
f. A short-term bank loan of $80,000 (including interest) will be repaid in July.
g. All other cash expenses for July will total $56,000.

Prepare the hospital's July cash budget.

EXERCISE 5-11

CASH BUDGETING

Medical Supplies, Inc., purchases first-aid items from large wholesalers. Medical Supplies then assembles and sells first-aid kits to businesses and contracts to maintain the first-aid kits. You have been asked to prepare a cash budget for January. The following information is provided:

a. Cash in the bank on January 1 is $33,000.
b. Actual sales for October, November, December, and projected sales for January are as follows:

	October	November	December	January
Cash	$12,000	$11,500	$ 8,200	$12,500
Credit	31,000	29,400	32,000	28,000

Payments on credit sales are received 50% in the month of sale, 31% in the month following the sale, and 15% and 4% in the second and third months, respectively, following the sale.

c. Total administrative and selling expenses (all cash) are $25,000.
d. Purchases are always paid 30 days after delivery. Purchases for October, November, and December were $28,000, $39,000, and $29,500, respectively.
e. Cash dividends of $22,000 are paid.
f. Any cash excess is used to purchase 30-day government securities, and any cash deficiency is compensated by short-term borrowing.
g. Management desires a minimum balance of $9,000 in the bank.

Prepare a cash budget for the month of January.

EXERCISE 5-12

CASH BUDGETING (MERCHANDISING COMPANY)

Whitlock, Inc., buys hardware parts from various manufacturers and sells them to retail stores. Management is currently trying to prepare a cash budget for August and has the following information available:

a. The cash balance on August 1 is $25,000.
b. Actual sales for June and July and projected sales for August are as follows:

	June	July	August
Cash sales	$ 30,000	$ 45,000	$ 50,000
Credit sales	100,000	120,000	130,000

Credit sales are collected 63% during the month of sale, 26% during the month following the sale, and 11% during the second month following the sale.

c. Whitlock's actual purchases for June and July and its projected purchases for August are as follows:

	June	July	August
Cash purchases	$10,000	$20,000	$25,000
Credit purchases	40,000	50,000	60,000

All accounts payable are paid in the month following the purchase.

d. Total administrative and selling expenses (including $14,000 depreciation) for August are expected to be $105,000.

e. Whitlock expects to pay a $26,000 dividend to stockholders and to purchase, for cash, a $25,000 piece of land during August.

f. Cash on hand should never drop below $25,000.

1. Prepare Whitlock's August cash budget, assuming that the company borrows any amounts needed to meet its minimum desired balance.
2. **Interpretive Question:** What types of expenses other than depreciation would be excluded from a cash budget?

EXERCISE 5-13

BUDGETING FOR A SERVICE COMPANY

Dr. Dawn Gifford is a new dentist specializing in treating children under the age of 18. Dr. Gifford has two primary sources of revenues: (1) fees from regular dental work (checkups, cleanings, fillings, etc.) and (2) fees from specialized dental reconstructive surgery. Last year, Gifford earned an average of $75 per patient visit from regular customers and $800 per surgery. The following operating expenses were incurred last year in running the office:

Variable operating expenses:	
Dental supplies (per patient)	$ 10
Hospital surgery room rental (per surgery)	200
Annual fixed operating expenses:	
Office manager's salary	$18,000
Dental hygienist's salary	26,000
Utilities	3,600
Rental of office space	12,000
Depreciation expense on office equipment*	20,000
Liability insurance	48,000
Other expenses	9,600

*Total equipment cost, $200,000; depreciated over 10 years on a straight-line basis.

Last year Dr. Gifford treated an average of 200 patients per month and performed an average of eight surgeries per month. She expects to increase the number of patients serviced by 10% this coming year and increase the number of surgeries by two per month. She also expects the average patient fee to be $80 and the average surgical fee to be $850. Gifford expects the variable expenses to remain constant this year, but is expecting to raise the manager's salary by 5% and the hygienist's by 15%. She thinks the other expenses will stay about the same.

Based on these data (and ignoring payroll and income taxes):

1. What was the operating profit (loss) for last year?
2. Prepare a revenue budget, operating expense budget, and cash budget for this coming year.

expanded material

EXERCISE 5-14

PRO-FORMA INCOME STATEMENT

Gold Manufacturing, Inc., is a manufacturer of electric pencil sharpeners. The following is information regarding Gold Manufacturing for the fiscal year-end, May 31, 2003:

Beginning finished goods inventory	$ 55,000
Ending finished goods inventory	42,000
Interest expense	28,000
Selling and administrative expenses	72,000
Sales revenue	425,000
Direct materials used	52,000
Direct labor	63,000
Manufacturing overhead	32,000

Assume a tax rate of 33%. Prepare a pro-forma income statement for the year ended May 31, 2003, for Gold Manufacturing, Inc.

EXERCISE 5-15

PRO-FORMA INCOME STATEMENT

Silver Company has asked you to prepare a pro-forma income statement for the coming year. The following information is available:

Expected sales revenue	$1,240,000
Manufacturing costs:	
Variable cost of goods sold	625,000
Fixed overhead	125,000
Selling expenses:	
Variable expenses	140,000
Fixed expenses	45,000
Administrative expenses:	
Variable expenses	45,000
Fixed expenses	160,000
Other:	
Interest expense	28,000
Income tax rate	35%

Prepare a pro-forma contribution margin income statement for Silver Company.

EXERCISE 5-16

PRO-FORMA STATEMENT OF CASH FLOWS

The accountants at Bryant Hardware Company are currently preparing the pro-forma statement of cash flows for August. In getting ready to prepare the statement, they have the following information available:

Dividends to be paid in August	$ 7,500
Bonds to be issued in August	44,000
Equipment to be sold in August	27,000
Repayment of short-term loans in August	24,000
Depreciation expense during August	6,000
Expected August net income	15,000
Expected changes in current assets and liabilities during August:	
Accounts receivable increase	3,500
Accounts payable decrease	2,750
Increase in inventory	4,200
Decrease in income taxes payable	8,400

Prepare Bryant's pro-forma statement of cash flows.

EXERCISE 5-17

PRO-FORMA INCOME STATEMENT AND BALANCE SHEET (SERVICE INDUSTRY)

Horrock's, Inc., is a small engineering corporation that surveys land for development. The company has grown rapidly over the past few years, and management has to decide whether to hire new engineers and open new offices. To assess future growth, the company's accountant has gathered budgeted information for the coming year, 2003:

Ending common stock balance	$ 48,000
Beginning retained earnings balance	34,000
Ending accounts payable balance	6,000
Ending equipment balance	159,000
Ending accumulated depreciation balance	24,000
Ending accounts receivable balance	19,500
Ending cash balance	18,000
Interest expense	3,000
Salary expense	105,000
Other expenses (including depreciation)	37,500
Service revenue	300,000
Income tax rate	33%

Income taxes due on the coming year's net income will be paid during 2004. Dividends of $70,000 are to be declared and paid during 2003.

1. Prepare a pro-forma income statement and balance sheet for 2003 from which the company president can make expansion decisions.
2. **Interpretive Question:** On the basis of this information, is the company very profitable? How should this level of profits affect its expansion plans?

EXERCISE 5-18 STATIC VERSUS FLEXIBLE BUDGETING—PERFORMANCE REPORTS (SERVICE FIRM)

Flannery Muffler Shop has budgeted to repair 10,000 mufflers during 2003. Each repair job takes 1½ hours, and employees are paid $12 per hour. During 2003, Flannery actually repaired 9,425 mufflers, and the salary expense amounted to $179,000.

1. Assuming a static budget, use the information to prepare a performance report for Flannery Muffler Shop for 2003.
2. Assuming a flexible budget, use the information to prepare a performance report for Flannery Muffler Shop for 2003.
3. **Interpretive Question:** The manager of the muffler shop believes he deserves a bonus because the actual salary expense ($179,000) was less than budgeted. Do you agree? Explain.

EXERCISE 5-19 FLEXIBLE BUDGETS (SERVICE FIRM)

Outdoors Unlimited operates a fishing lodge in northern Canada. The following cost information has been developed by the company's accountant:

Fixed costs:	
Salaries	$68,000
Mortgage payments	24,000
Taxes	4,000
Other	3,000
Variable costs (per guest):	
Fishing tackle	$20
Food	80
Other	16

1. In planning for its 2003 summer season, Outdoors Unlimited does not know exactly how many guests to expect and, hence, how much to charge per guest. Prepare a flexible budget showing expected total costs at 200, 300, 400, and 500 guests.
2. Assume that Outdoors Unlimited conservatively estimates 300 guests for the year. If it wants to earn profits of $100,000 for the 300 guests, how much should it charge per guest?

PROBLEM 5-1

PERSONAL BUDGETING

Ben Fleming has just received a job offer of $35,000 salary per year plus overtime pay, which will amount to 10% of his salary. Ben estimates his living costs as follows:

Federal, state, and FICA taxes amount to	35% of income
Rent	$550/month
Car payment	$210/month
IRA	$1,500/year
Other savings	4% of net take-home pay
Utilities	$90/month
Gas and maintenance—automobile	$130/month
Insurance	$75/month
Food	$240/month
Entertainment	$170/month
Clothing	$80/month

Required:

1. Prepare a budget for the year. Assume Ben starts his job on January 1.
2. Is Ben's offer sufficient to meet his projected expenses?
3. Ben has always dreamed of going to Africa to photograph wildlife. The trip will cost $5,000. How long will it take Ben to save for the trip? (Ignore interest earnings, and assume that he has no savings at the present time.)

PROBLEM 5-2

PERSONAL BUDGETING

Carol Baum is an advertising specialist for Success Advertising, Inc. Her annual salary is $37,500, of which 20% is withheld for federal income taxes, 7% for state income taxes, 7.65% for FICA taxes, and 5% for a tax-sheltered annuity. She estimates that her monthly expenses are approximately as follows:

Rent	$ 475
Automobile payment	250
Food	240
Automobile gasoline and maintenance	120
Utilities	70
Clothing	100
Entertainment	150
Miscellaneous	130
Total monthly expenses	$1,535

Required:

1. Prepare Carol's monthly budget, assuming that the car payments will continue for about three years.
2. Assume that Carol would like to accumulate savings of $12,000 in order to take an extended leave from her job. This will allow her to travel and take courses as a way of generating some fresh ideas she can use in creating new approaches to advertising. How long will it take her to save the needed amount? (Ignore interest earnings, and assume that she has no savings at the present time.)
3. **Interpretive Question:** If Carol asked you for advice on how she might reduce her expenses, what would you suggest?

PROBLEM 5-3

PRODUCTION BUDGETING

Rockville Cabinet Company makes and sells two products: two-drawer and four-drawer cabinets. The sales forecasts for these cabinets for the next four quarters are as follows:

	Two-Drawer Cabinets	Four-Drawer Cabinets
1st quarter	30	30
2nd quarter	50	60
3rd quarter	90	76
4th quarter	96	48
Total	266	214

On January 1, Rockville has a stock of 40 completed two-drawer cabinets and 30 four-drawer cabinets. Experience indicates that Rockville must maintain an inventory equal to one-half of the next quarter's sales.

Required:

1. How many two-drawer and four-drawer cabinets must be produced during each of the first three quarters to meet sales and inventory demands?
2. **Interpretive Question:** Assume Rockville is a wholesale merchandising company instead of a manufacturing company. How would the budget information provided in (1) change?

PROBLEM 5-4

PRODUCTION AND DIRECT MATERIALS BUDGET

Chandler Manufacturing Company makes two products: widgets and gidgets. The following information is available on May 1:

a. Direct materials needed to make a widget: six units of X, three units of Y. Direct materials needed to make a gidget: two units of X, six units of Y.

b. Number of units available at beginning of May:

Direct material X	72 units
Direct material Y	43 units
Finished widgets	12
Finished gidgets	15

c. Expected sales during May:

Widgets	100
Gidgets	95

d. Desired levels of ending inventory:

Direct material X	70 units
Direct material Y	35 units
Widgets	11
Gidgets	13

e. Cost of direct materials:

Direct material X	$3 per unit
Direct material Y	$2 per unit

Required:

Prepare a production budget and a direct materials budget for Chandler Company for the month of May.

PROBLEM 5-5

COMPUTATION OF UNIT COSTS

Jersey Candy Company makes and sells two kinds of candy bars: chocolate almond and coconut. During the past several years, the company has kept accurate records of costs and resource requirements and has determined that the following are needed to make the candy bars:

One Box of 24 Chocolate Almond Bars	Cost
Chocolate (1½ pounds)	$3.00/pound
Almonds (1 pound)	$5.00/pound
Sugar (2 pounds)	$0.50/pound
Direct labor (20 minutes)	$9.00/hour
Manufacturing overhead (20 minutes)	$7.00/direct labor hour

One Box of 24 Coconut Bars	Cost
Chocolate (1 pound)	$3.00/pound
Coconut (1¼ pounds)	$2.00/pound
Sugar (1¾ pounds)	$0.50/pound
Direct labor (30 minutes)	$9.00/hour
Manufacturing overhead (30 minutes)	$7.00/direct labor hour

Required:

1. Compute the unit cost of making a box of each type of candy bar.
2. If management wants to mark up each box of candy 30% to cover other costs and earn a profit, how much should be charged for a box of each type of candy bar?

PROBLEM 5-6

UNIFYING CONCEPTS: PRODUCTION AND DIRECT MATERIALS BUDGETS AND COST OF GOODS SOLD COMPUTATIONS

San Antonio Furniture Company makes two products: bookshelves and rocking chairs. The following information is available for September:

a. Production requirements:

	Bookshelves	Rocking Chairs
Materials needed:		
Wood	100 board feet at $0.90/ft.	90 board feet at $0.90/ft.
Stain	2 gallons at $9/gallon	3 gallons at $9/gallon
Bolts, nuts, etc.	1 dozen at $1.50/dozen	1½ dozen at $1.50/dozen
Direct labor	12 hours at $8.50/hour	10 hours at $8.50/hour
Variable manufacturing overhead	12 hours at $4/ direct labor hour	10 hours at $4/ direct labor hour
Fixed manufacturing overhead	$16 per unit	$15 per unit

b. Levels of inventories:

	Actual Beginning Inventory	Desired Ending Inventory
Wood	1,100 board feet	1,000 board feet
Stain	11 gallons	12 gallons
Bolts, nuts, etc.	15 dozen	9 dozen
Finished bookshelves	3	5
Finished rocking chairs	6	7

c. Total actual resources used in production during September:

Direct materials	$4,259
Direct labor	3,850
Variable manufacturing overhead	1,500
Fixed manufacturing overhead	700

Required:

1. Prepare the production budget, assuming that the company expects to sell 40 bookshelves and 50 rocking chairs in September.
2. Based on the production budget and the desired ending inventory level, prepare the direct materials usage and purchases budget for September.
3. If the company actually sold the number of bookshelves and rocking chairs projected, how much would the cost of goods sold be for September?

PROBLEM 5-7

UNIFYING CONCEPTS: SALES, CASH COLLECTIONS, PRODUCTION, DIRECT MATERIALS, AND DIRECT LABOR BUDGETS

The following information is available for Raleigh Company:

Expected sales volume:	
April	1,600 units
May	1,500 units
June	1,750 units
Selling price per unit	$12
Accounts receivable balance, April 1	$6,000
Desired finished goods inventory, June 30	200 units
Beginning finished goods inventory, April 1	210 units
Direct materials needed per unit	5 pounds
Desired direct materials inventory, June 30	550 pounds
Beginning direct materials inventory, April 1	420 pounds
Total direct labor time per finished product	2 hours
Direct materials cost per pound	$0.50
Direct labor cost per hour	$8

Additional information:

a. Each month 70% of sales is collected by month-end; the remaining 30% is collected in the following month.
b. The desired finished goods inventory every month is 20% of the next month's sales.
c. The desired direct materials inventory every month is 10% of the next month's production needs.

Required:

1. Prepare sales budgets for April, May, and June (in dollars).
2. Prepare cash collection budgets for April, May, and June (in dollars). Assume that all sales are on credit.
3. Prepare production budgets for April, May, and June (in units).
4. Prepare direct materials budgets for April, May, and June (in dollars).
5. Prepare direct labor budgets for April, May, and June (in dollars).

PROBLEM 5-8

UNIFYING CONCEPTS: SALES, CASH COLLECTIONS, AND PURCHASES BUDGETS

The following information is available for Durham Company, a merchandising retail company:

Expected sales volume:	
April	3,200 units
May	3,000 units
June	3,500 units
Selling price per unit	$25
Accounts receivable balance, April 1	$12,000
Desired ending inventory, June 30	650 units
Beginning inventory, April 1	420 units

Additional information:

a. Each month 70% of sales is collected by month-end; the remaining 30% is collected in the following month.
b. The desired inventory every month is 20% of the next month's sales.

Required:

1. Prepare sales budgets for April, May, and June (in dollars).
2. Prepare cash collection budgets for April, May, and June (in dollars). Assume that all sales are on credit.
3. Prepare purchases budgets for April, May, and June (in units).

PROBLEM 5-9

CASH BUDGETING (MANUFACTURING COMPANY)

Hare Manufacturing Company makes wax for automobiles. As part of overall planning, a cash budget is prepared quarterly each year. You have been asked to assist in preparing the cash budget for the fourth quarter of the company's fiscal year. The following information is available:

a. Sales:

Third quarter (actual)	$180,000
Fourth quarter (expected)	175,000

All sales are made on account, with 70% collected in the quarter in which the sales are made and 30% collected during the following quarter.

b. Materials purchases are scheduled as follows:

Third quarter (actual)	$90,000
Fourth quarter (expected)	80,000

Materials are purchased on account and paid for at the rate of 80% in the quarter of purchase and 20% in the following quarter.

c. Direct labor and manufacturing overhead costs (including $6,000 of depreciation) are expected to be $45,000 and $21,000, respectively, during the fourth quarter.
d. Selling and administrative expenses are expected to total $27,000 during the fourth quarter, including $2,000 of depreciation.
e. Plans have been made to purchase, for cash, $15,000 of equipment during the fourth quarter.
f. The cash balance at the beginning of the quarter is $16,000. The company can borrow money in $1,000 multiples at 12% interest from a local bank. The bank assesses interest for a full quarter, both for the quarter in which the money is borrowed and for the quarter in which it is repaid. All interest is paid at the time of note repayment. Hare ran short of cash during the third quarter and had to borrow $8,000 from the bank. Hare wishes to maintain a minimum cash balance of $16,000.

Required:

Prepare a schedule showing the cash budget and financing needs of Hare Manufacturing Company for the fourth quarter.

PROBLEM 5-10

CASH BUDGETING (MERCHANDISING COMPANY)

Keven Johnson, owner of Meyers Department Store, is negotiating a $50,000, 15%, four-month loan from the Lee County National Bank, effective October 1, 2003. The bank loan officer has requested that Meyers prepare a cash budget for each of the next four months as evidence of its ability to repay the loan. The following information is available as of September 30, 2003:

Cash on hand	$ 4,500
Accounts receivable	48,750
Inventory	32,000
Accounts payable	72,250

a. The accounts payable are for September merchandise purchases and operating expenses and will all be paid in October. Sales forecasts for the next few months are October, $110,000; November, $150,000; December, $200,000; January, $100,000; February, $70,000.

b. Collections on sales are usually made at the rate of 20% during the month of the sale, 60% during the month following the sale, and 16% during the second month after the sale. Four percent of accounts receivable are written off as uncollectible. Of the $48,750 of accounts receivable at September 30, $32,500 will be collected in October, and $16,250 will be collected in November. Cost of goods sold is 60% of sales, with all purchases paid for in the month following purchase. Ending inventory should always equal the cost of the goods that will be sold during the next month. Operating expenses are $12,000 a month plus 5% of sales, all paid in the month following their incurrence.

Required: Prepare a cash budget showing receipts and disbursements for October, November, December, and January. Also prepare supporting schedules for cash collections, purchases, and operating expenses. Assume that the loan plus interest will be paid on January 31.

PROBLEM 5-11 CASH BUDGETING

Athlete World is a sporting goods store. The following data are for use in preparing its forecast of cash needs for June:

a. Current assets (May 31):

Cash	$22,000
Inventory	17,500
Accounts receivable	29,400
Property, plant, and equipment	90,000
Accounts payable (merchandise purchases only)	13,100
Recent and estimated future sales:	
May	49,000
June	57,000
July	52,000

b. Sales are made 60% on credit and 40% for cash. All credit sales are collected in the month following the sale.

c. Athlete World's June expenses are estimated to be:

Salaries and wages expense	20% of sales
Rent expense	4% of sales
All other cash expenses	6% of sales
Depreciation expense	$600
Gross margin	40% of sales

d. Athlete World buys all its inventory from companies on the West Coast and wants to maintain an inventory level equal to one-half of the next month's sales. Payments for merchandise are made 50% during the month of purchase and 50% in the next month.

e. Other cash expenditures planned for June are:
   1. The purchase of $8,000 of furniture.
   2. The payment of $5,000 of dividends.

f. Athlete World desires to maintain a minimum cash balance of $10,000. The store has an arrangement with a local bank whereby it can borrow money in multiples of $1,000. Interest is charged on all loans at an annual rate of 10% and is assessed for a full quarter both in the quarter in which the money is borrowed and in the quarter in which the money is repaid. Interest is paid when the loan is repaid.

Required: Prepare Athlete World's cash budget for June.

PROBLEM 5-12 BUDGETING FOR A SERVICE COMPANY

Riverside Country Club has approximately 435 members. Each member has paid a $10,000 initiation fee and pays $100 a month in dues to remain an active member of the club. The club offers golf, tennis, and food and beverage services. The club is essentially run on a cash basis. Operating data for 2002 are as follows:

Riverside Country Club
Operating Data
For the Year 2002

Revenues:		
Dues[1]	$742,000	
Guest fees[2]	6,500	
Golf revenues	455,000	
Tennis revenues	145,000	
Food and beverage	325,000	
Miscellaneous	2,500	$1,676,000
Expenses:		
Golf course	$395,000	
Tennis courts	170,000	
Food and bar	272,000	
Administration and maintenance[3]	515,000	
Interest on debt[4]	50,000	
Miscellaneous	27,000	(1,429,000)
Net operating profit		$ 247,000

[1]Dues (410 × $1,200 = $492,000; 25 new members × $10,000 = $250,000).
[2]Guest fees (130 × $50 = $6,500).
[3]Maintenance includes $125,000 depreciation on facilities.
[4]Interest ($500,000 × 0.10 × 1 year).

Assume the following additional facts for the year 2003:

a. There are 425 members paying dues, as well as 10 additional new members.
b. Guest fees are 110% of 2002 fees.
c. Golf revenues are 125% of 2002 revenues.
d. Tennis revenues are 90% of 2002 revenues (due to courts being closed for one month).
e. Food and beverage revenues are the same as 2002.
f. Operating expenses (golf, tennis, and food and beverage) are up 5%.
g. Administration and maintenance will increase $40,000 due to expected repairs.
h. Principal payment of $50,000 during 2003 will reduce interest expense by 10% for 2003.
i. Miscellaneous revenues will stay the same; miscellaneous expenses are expected to be $25,000.

Required:

1. Prepare an annual budget for Riverside for the year 2003.
2. What is the expected cash flow for Riverside for the year 2003?
3. **Interpretive Question:** Is Riverside in better shape financially in 2003 as compared to 2002? What areas of concern do you see?

expanded material

PROBLEM 5-13

UNIFYING CONCEPTS: THE PRO-FORMA INCOME STATEMENT, BALANCE SHEET, AND STATEMENT OF CASH FLOWS

Alex Corporation makes trailers for trucks. During the past few days, the company's accountants have been preparing the master budget for 2003. To date, they have gathered the following projected data:

For the Year Ended December 31, 2003:	
Sales revenue	$10,127,200
Variable selling expenses	448,000
Variable administrative expenses	672,000
Interest expense	67,200
Cost of goods sold (variable costs only)	5,600,000
Fixed manufacturing expenses	784,000
Fixed administrative expenses	492,000
Fixed selling expenses	336,000

Account Balances at December 31, 2003:	
Cash	$448,000
Accounts receivable	168,000
Land	417,200
Buildings	504,000
Equipment	358,400
Accumulated depreciation—equipment	89,600
Accumulated depreciation—buildings	80,000
Direct materials inventory	106,400
Finished goods inventory	117,600
Accounts payable	45,240
Common stock	700,000
Retained earnings	?
Paid-in capital in excess of par	40,000
Income taxes payable	200,000

Other Information:	
Dividends to be declared and paid during 2003	$600,000
Income tax rate	33%

In addition, last year's balance sheet was as follows:

Alex Corporation
Balance Sheet
December 31, 2002

Assets		
Cash		$ 189,600
Accounts receivable		45,400
Direct materials inventory		90,000
Finished goods inventory		123,200
Land		336,000
Buildings	$448,000	
Less accumulated depreciation	(50,000)	398,000
Equipment	$324,800	
Less accumulated depreciation	(60,000)	264,800
Total assets		$1,447,000
Liabilities and Stockholders' Equity		
Liabilities:		
Accounts payable	$ 75,000	
Income taxes payable	225,000	
Total liabilities		$ 300,000
Stockholders' Equity:		
Common stock	$700,000	
Paid-in capital in excess of par, common stock	40,000	
Retained earnings	407,000	
Total stockholders' equity		1,147,000
Total liabilities and stockholders' equity		$1,447,000

Required:

1. Prepare a pro-forma income statement for 2003 (contribution margin approach).
2. Prepare a pro-forma balance sheet as of December 31, 2003.
3. Prepare a pro-forma statement of cash flows for 2003.

PROBLEM 5-14

PRO-FORMA INCOME STATEMENT AND BALANCE SHEET

Style Right Company makes hair dryers. During the past few days, its accountants have been preparing the master budget for the coming year, 2003. To date, they have gathered the following projected data:

Sales revenue (at $20 per unit)	$281,750
Variable selling expenses	17,250
Variable administrative expenses	40,250
Interest expense (not included in selling and administrative expenses)	1,725
Cost of goods sold (includes only variable costs)	103,500
Ending cash balance	30,475
Ending accounts receivable balance	47,150
Ending land balance	24,150
Ending buildings balance	71,300
Ending equipment balance	24,150
Ending accumulated depreciation—buildings balance	47,150
Ending accumulated depreciation—equipment balance	9,200
Ending direct materials inventory balance	16,100
Ending finished goods inventory balance	25,300
Ending accounts payable balance	6,900
Ending common stock balance	32,200
Retained earnings balance, January 1	64,050
Balance in paid-in capital in excess of par account	23,000
Fixed selling expenses	23,000
Fixed administrative expenses	28,750
Fixed manufacturing overhead	11,150
Income tax rate	35%

Required:

1. Prepare a pro-forma income statement (contribution margin approach) and balance sheet for the coming year. Any income taxes owed on the coming year's net income will be paid the following year.
2. By approximately how much would Style Right's profits increase if another 3,000 units were produced and sold for $20 each?

PROBLEM 5-15

PRO-FORMA STATEMENT OF CASH FLOWS

The accountants at Toledo Department Store are preparing the pro-forma statement of cash flows for 2003. The following information is available:

Expected net income	$70,000
Dividends to be paid	22,000
Equipment to be purchased	34,000
Expected short-term borrowing	8,000
Expected long-term borrowing	24,000
Expected depreciation expense for 2003	15,000
Expected issuance of common stock	80,000
Expected purchase of a new plant	71,000
Expected changes in current assets and liabilities during 2003:	
Increase in accounts receivable	$ 900
Increase in accounts payable	1,000
Increase in inventory	1,000
Decrease in income taxes payable	1,800

Required: Prepare the pro-forma statement of cash flows for Toledo Department Store.

PROBLEM 5-16

STATIC VERSUS FLEXIBLE BUDGETING (SERVICE FIRM)

Wasatch Medical Clinic has three doctors on staff. The clinic's budget for 2003 is as follows:

Wasatch Medical Clinic
Budget for the Year Ended December 31, 2003

Expected number of patient visits		26,000
Average charge per patient		× $25
Total revenues		$650,000
Budgeted costs:		
Variable costs:		
Supplies for each patient ($2 × 26,000)		$ 52,000
Fixed costs:		
Utilities	$ 2,400	
Rent	9,600	
Nurses' salaries	90,000	
Malpractice insurance	150,000	
Equipment leases	25,000	
Other	30,000	
Total fixed costs		307,000
Total budgeted costs		$359,000
Expected income		$291,000
Number of doctors on staff		÷ 3
Expected income per doctor		$ 97,000

Required:

1. Is this a static or flexible budget?
2. Prepare a flexible budget showing expected income per doctor at 22,000, 26,000, 30,000, and 34,000 total patient visits.
3. **Interpretive Question:** Why does the expected income per doctor increase so dramatically as the number of patient visits increases?

PROBLEM 5-17

STATIC VERSUS FLEXIBLE BUDGETING (SERVICE FIRM)

Peterson Management, Inc., is a small firm that sponsors time-management seminars in hotels throughout the country. It sponsors 20 two-day seminars during the year for a tuition fee of $200 per student. The following is a budget for a single seminar:

Peterson Management, Inc.
Budget Per Seminar

Expected enrollment	40
Tuition per person	×$200
Revenue per seminar	$8,000
Variable costs:	
Catering ($25 per person)	$1,000
Books and handouts ($10 per person)	400
Fixed costs:	
Airfare	425
Hotel rental fee	600
Advertising	1,000
Other	300
Total costs	$3,725
Expected income	$4,275

Required:

1. Bruce Peterson, owner of the company and the speaker at the seminars, would be pleased with an income of $4,275 per seminar. With 20 seminars per year, the company's annual

income would be $85,500. He is concerned, however, that every seminar may not have 40 participants. Prepare a flexible budget, showing what annual income would be if 10, 20, 40, or 50 people enroll in each seminar.

2. What is the break-even point per seminar in number of participants?

competency enhancement opportunities

- Analyzing Real Company Information
- International Case
- Ethics Case
- Writing Assignment
- The Debate
- Internet Search

The following additional assignments provide opportunities for students to develop critical thinking, ethical perspectives, oral and written communication skills, experience with electronic research, and teamwork through group and business activities.

ANALYZING REAL COMPANY INFORMATION

- ***Analyzing 5-1 (Microsoft)***

Auditors are extremely reluctant to publish any projections of future financial performance for the companies they are auditing. DELOITTE & TOUCHE LLP obviously has made no such predictions in its audit of MICROSOFT's 1999 financial performance (the annual report in Appendix A). However, the Management's Discussion of the Income Statement results, in the section titled "Outlook: Issues and Uncertainties," provide some hints about what executives may expect to affect future revenues. Elsewhere in the management discussion are insights useful in predicting future operating expenses, interest income, and income taxes. These discussions can be extremely useful to investors who are trying to understand what Microsoft plans to do in 2000. Essentially, these investors need to put together their own pro-forma financial statements on Microsoft for use in planning, controlling, and evaluating their investment decisions in this company.

Consider the 1999 income statement on the following page and use the information provided in Microsoft's Management Discussion of "Outlook: Issues and Uncertainties" to prepare your own pro-forma 2000 income statement for Microsoft. Be sure to read and consider each item in the management discussion relating to Microsoft's income statement in the annual report in Appendix A. You may also want to consider the 1997 and 1998 revenue and cost trends from the income statement published in this same annual report. For each line item (i.e., for each revenue and cost category), briefly defend the budget number you chose to use.

	1999
Revenue	$19,747
Operating expenses:	
Cost of revenue	$ 2,814
Research and development	2,970
Sales and marketing	3,231
General and administrative	689
Other expenses	115
Total operating expenses	$ 9,819
Operating income	$ 9,928
Investment income	1,803
Gains on sale of Softimage Inc.	160
Income before income taxes	$11,891
Provision for income taxes	4,106
Net income	$ 7,785

• ***Analyzing 5-2 (Participative Living, Inc.)***

Participative Living, Inc. (a fictitious name) is an actual charitable organization in a medium-size community in Canada. It was organized by parents of disabled adults to provide accommodation and training for severely disabled adults in the community. With the help of the Ministry of Community and Social Services, the parents eventually organized six different homes, each with two to four residents. In addition to the six homes, Participative Living also had an employment and education program that provided training and assistance for residents seeking employment or educational opportunities. Overall, the organization had eight divisions composed of six homes, the employment and education program, and an administrative program. A supervisor who reports to the Participative Living executive team staffs each division. The executive team, in turn, reports to a volunteer board of directors composed of 12 people from the community.

Participative Living is a not-for-profit organization. Hence, while surpluses and deficits are occasionally expected, each division is expected to break even each operating period. Seven of the eight divisions are established as break-even operations, with responsibility for both revenues and expenses. The main revenue source is the Ontario government, through the Ministry of Community and Social Services, which provides all funding necessary to support each home as well as the employment and education program. All costs of Participative Living's administrative division in excess of any donations from the community are allocated to its other seven divisions. The Ministry follows a procedure of disbursing operating funds for all social service agencies under its direction based on annual operating budgets submitted to the Ministry. Generally, the Ministry is not concerned about whether an individual budget item was overspent as long as the overall spending is within the approved budget. As a result, it became a common practice among agencies to transfer expenses from one budget line to another and, in the case of Participative Living, to transfer expenses from one division to another depending on which division had excess budgeted funds. As with most government organizations, the Ministry's administrative process of reviewing and approving a new home for Participative Living is often quite slow. As long as the Ministry is holding up the establishment of a proposed new home, it provides significant interest payments to Participative Living. The Ministry was making large interest payments during the first few months of Participative Living's 2000 fiscal year (which ended on March 31, 2000) while the organization waited for government approval and funding of the sixth group home.

In November 1999, Mr. Brad Dunford, the executive director of Participative Living, Inc., was reviewing the financial statements for the first seven months of the 2000 fiscal year. He was puzzled about how the agency could suddenly be $50,000 over budget in salaries and benefits when just last month the statements indicated that spending was slightly under budget.

1. As you review operating results for the last seven months at Participative Living, Inc., what problems do you foresee?
2. Consider the style of management and management accounting for this not-for-profit organization, as well as its relationship with the Ministry of Community and Social Services. What aspects of the way business is conducted here do you think have led to the current situation?

Participative Living, Inc.
Operating Results
For the Seven Months Ended October 31, 1999

YTD	Admin. Costs	Admin. Budget	Employ. and Edu. Costs	Employ. and Edu. Budget	Group Homes Costs	Group Homes Budget	Total Actual	Total Budget*	% of Budget
Revenues:									
Ministry**	$ —	$ —	$206,315	$297,675	$521,841	$476,714	$728,156	$774,389	94.0%
Interest	20,943	—	—	—	—	—	20,943	—	0%
Donations	1,567	—	—	—	—	—	1,567	—	0%
Total revenues	$ 22,510	$ —	$206,315	$297,675	$521,841	$476,714	$750,666	$774,389	96.9%
Expenses:									
Salaries	$ 59,029	$ 61,754	$141,034	$197,386	$434,014	$327,789	$634,077	$586,929	108.0%
Occupancy costs	10,392	12,264	39	2,205	61,598	68,761	72,029	83,230	86.5%
Services, supplies, and food	4,375	7,000	3,643	14,147	16,812	35,301	24,830	56,448	44.0%
Personal needs	—	—	3,077	—	35	26,327	3,112	26,327	11.8%
New furnishing and equip.	5	350	60	2,765	6,548	19,236	6,613	22,351	29.6%
Other expenses	1,176	4,669	197	7,707	15,681	7,868	17,054	20,244	84.2%
Travel and training	436	875	1,972	8,792	1,992	4,900	4,400	14,567	30.2%
Specific reimbursements	—	—	—	—	(32,119)	(35,707)	(32,119)	(35,707)	90.0%
Allocated admin. costs	(75,417)	(86,912)	56,293	64,673	19,123	22,239	(1)	—	0.0%
Total expenses	$ (4)	$ —	$206,315	$297,675	$523,684	$476,714	$729,995	$774,389	94.3%
Net surplus (deficit)	$ 22,514	$ —	$ —	$ —	$ (1,843)	$ —	$ 20,671	$ —	N/A

*Budget columns represent 7/12ths of the total annual budget (e.g., Participative Living is now seven months into its fiscal year).
**Ministry revenues are based on actual payments made by the Ministry. Total payments limited to maximum of total annual budget approved.

Source: Adapted from M. Heisz, "Participative Living, Inc.," *Journal of Accounting Case Research* 2(3), 1995, pp. 87–91. Permission to use has been granted by Captus Press, Inc. and the Accounting Education Resource Centre of The University of Lethbridge. [Journal Subscription: Captus Press Inc., York University Campus, 4700 Keele Street, North York, Ontario, M3J1P3, by calling (416) 736-5537, or by fax at (416) 736-5793, E-mail: info@captus.com, Internet: http://www.captus.com]

INTERNATIONAL CASE

• *It's Not Easy Being an Accountant in Poland*

The late 1980s and early 1990s were a very significant time for Eastern Europe. Several national boundaries and political ideologies, as well as the names of a few countries, changed during this period. Poland, like its neighbors, experienced tremendous upheaval in its political and economic climate during this time. In 1989, Poland changed to a non-Communist government and a free market economy. Since the end of World War II in 1945, Poland had been a centrally planned economy with government-enforced economic rules based on Marxism-Leninism. A Polish accountant's professional life during the 1945–1989 period was not very exciting. Most university-trained accountants worked in a state-owned enterprise, earning a reasonable salary. The work was not complicated, generally entailing only basic bookkeeping. Performing the accounting work essentially required simple mathematical operations. In addition, the nature of Poland's history since the fifteenth century had generally created disdain for business and profiteering in general. These traditions, coupled with the social environment engendered by a Marxist government, resulted in a serious lack of respect (sometimes bordering on distrust) for accountants, economists, and business managers from 1945 to 1989.

The failure of the Communist system in 1989 was the beginning of a new career stage for most accountants in Poland. The accounting profession suddenly became prestigious. It also became very challenging. Past accounting knowledge and skills were simply inadequate for the new economic situation, particularly for accountants moving out of state-owned enterprises and into the private sector. Business terminology, performance measures, and goals changed. Before 1989, the Communist regime promoted a view that everything a "capitalist" did was wrong and everything a Communist did was right. After the change in the political system, a lot of people began to see things in an opposite way; they expected that life in a capitalist country would be completely just and everyone would be employed with plenty of money. Obviously, life in a capitalist country is not perfect. There are problems, including injustice and unemployment. Complicating this reality, many people also carried over into the 1990s some of the prevailing pre-1989 attitudes that accountants and for-profit businesses were not trustworthy. Today Poland is making steady progress, but the accounting profession continues to face a number of challenges as attitudes and business processes are still in transition.

Assume that you have just been transferred by your U.S.-based company to an accounting or management position in the company's Poland division. Your assignment is to implement a traditional budgeting system (similar to the budget systems described in this chapter) in a large-scale manufacturing plant. Based on your understanding of Polish history and attitudes, what specific challenges would you expect to encounter in this new assignment? Do you have any ideas on how to handle these challenges?

Source: Adapted from P. Stec, "Mr. Kowalski: A Man Against All Odds," *Journal of Accounting Case Research* 2(3), 1995, pp. 52–54. Permission to use has been granted by Captus Press, Inc. and the Accounting Education Resource Centre of The University of Lethbridge. [Journal Subscription: Captus Press Inc., York University Campus, 4700 Keele Street, North York, Ontario, M3J1P3, by calling (416) 736-5537, or by fax at (416) 736-5793, E-mail: info@captus.com, Internet: http://www.captus.com]

ETHICS CASE

• Skipper Enterprises

You are the management accountant for Skipper Enterprises, a manufacturer of screen doors. Recently, one of the commissioned salespersons (your close personal friend) confided in you that a problem with the budgets is hurting the company's profitability.

Your friend explained that salespersons are paid a straight commission of $15 for every screen door they sell. If a salesperson meets the budgeted sales of 3,000 screen doors per year, he or she is paid an annual bonus of $5,000. Your friend stated that it is actually quite easy to reach budgeted sales of 3,000 doors by October or early November. Because there is no financial incentive to sell additional doors once the 3,000 sales level is met and the $5,000 bonus is earned, salespersons only "line up" sales for next year during the last couple of months of each year. In other words, instead of selling additional doors during November and December, they commit customers to buy during January of next year. This way, the doors count as next year's sales, ensuring that the commissioned salespersons are well on their way to meeting the sales budget for next year.

You realize the current bonus plan is causing two problems. First, valuable sales are being deferred each year because there is less incentive to sell near the end of the year. Second, customers are receiving less than optimum service because it can take as long as two months for customers to get their desired doors.

You don't know what to do with your new information.

1. Should you inform management that the sales plan is hurting company profits, or should you keep the information confidential as your friend requested?
2. If it becomes known that you had this information and didn't come forward, you could lose your job. On the other hand, you hate to lose a good friend. What should you do?

WRITING ASSIGNMENT

• Preparing a Personal Budget

Most people have the ability to spend more than they make. As a student, you probably fit in that category. This writing assignment requires you to prepare a personal budget for a one-month period. Forecast your income and expenses to determine what your cash position will be at the end of the month. If you forecast a cash shortage, what actions can you take to address the problem (e.g., increase income, reduce expenses, borrow money, etc.)? If you forecast a cash surplus, what are your options for the surplus?

THE DEBATE

• The Hatchet Has Arrived!

Assume that your local hospital has just hired a new COO (chief operating officer). Everyone in the hospital understands that the new COO was essentially hired to save the hospital. During the last five years, cost overruns have created tremendous spending deficits in the organization. The hospital is clearly headed for insolvency within three to five years if something isn't done. The new COO has a reputation as a focused manager, who is able to make difficult decisions. She doesn't waste any time proving her reputation in the new job. At the first meeting with the chief medical staff and administrators, the COO rolls out the new budget goals with the following statement:

> Everyone here knows that this hospital is in serious financial trouble, and it's not hard to understand why. After carefully reviewing cost reports for the last several years, it's obvious that there has been very little discipline in controlling costs. There are no improvement goals for cost savings, and no one is required to take responsibility when cost overruns occur. Looking at next quarter's operating budget doesn't give me much hope for improvement in this mess. Well, folks, that party is over! It's time to get to work saving this hospital. We will reconvene in one week; I expect each department head to provide a new departmental operating budget that demonstrates a reduction in costs that is equal to 5% of department revenues. Thereafter, until we turn this situation around, each new quarterly budget will reflect an *additional* decrease in operating costs equal to 2% of department revenues. Any questions?

There were no questions. Everyone filed out of the meeting in shocked silence. Five percent of revenues is a big number!

Divide your group into two teams and prepare a two-minute defense of your team's assigned position.

- One team represents "Support the COO!" A difficult situation requires a tough response. Defend the COO's new budget proposal. What should be the positive results in the hospital if the COO's budget instructions are fully implemented?
- The other team represents "Out with the new budget proposal!" Overreacting to a difficult situation only worsens the problem. Criticize the COO's new budget proposal. What could be the negative results in the hospital if the COO's budget instructions are fully implemented?

INTERNET SEARCH

• *Using the Internet to Budget Personal Finances*

There are a number of terrific tools on the Internet that can be very useful to you in managing your finances. For one example, go to **http://www.financenter.com**. Sometimes Web addresses change, so if this address does not work, access the Web site for this textbook (**http://albrecht.swcollege.com**) for an updated link. Once there, select the "Budgeting" link, then select "How much am I spending?" from the SmartCalcs™ menu. You will see here that FinanCenter provides a form on which you can enter your current income and budgeted expenditures, as well as your desired expenditures.

1. Complete the information on the input form, then hit the "Calculate" button. You should now learn whether your income is sufficient to handle your expenditures (actually, you probably already knew the answer to this question). Print out your budget.
2. Now go back to the input form and change the numbers in order to assess what might need to change in your future personal "operations." Put to-

gether a realistic budget. Try to create a little "extra" that can be used for investment. Note how the difference affects your long-term savings. When you're satisfied, print out your new budget.

3. Now that you have a better understanding of your cash budget, work through FinanCenter's tools to identify and answer another important personal finance and budgeting question for yourself. Go back to the SmartCalcs™ page and select an additional budgeting function to perform. When completed, list two important insights you learned about your personal budgeting process.

part 3

Control

Traditional Cost Management

chapter

m6

learning objectives After studying this chapter, you should be able to:

1 Outline the different cost flow patterns in manufacturing, merchandising, and service organizations and understand how these costs are reflected in the income statement and balance sheet.

2 Interpret a cost of goods manufactured schedule and analyze the levels of raw materials, work-in-process, and finished goods inventories in a manufacturing organization.

3 Understand how merchants manage cost information in their organizations.

4 Measure profitability and personnel utilization in a service organization.

expanded material

5 Calculate and interpret holding costs in merchandising and service businesses.

6 Use classic quantitative tools in inventory management (economic order quantity, reorder point, and safety stock).

Sam Walton didn't invent discount retailing, but the company he founded, WAL-MART, is now the undisputed giant in the field.[1] Sam Walton started his career in retailing at a J.C. PENNEY store in Des Moines, Iowa. Sam was a good salesperson, though he disliked the bookkeeping that went along with the job: "[I] couldn't stand to leave a new customer waiting while I fiddled with paperwork on a sale I'd already made."

After World War II, Sam borrowed $20,000 from his father-in-law and bought a variety store in Newport, Arkansas. By 1962, Sam Walton had built a chain of 16 variety stores located in Missouri, Arkansas, and Kansas. By this time, however, Walton had become convinced that there were big opportunities in opening discount retail locations in the smaller U.S. towns and cities that were being overlooked by the traditional retailers such as SEARS. Walton pitched his idea to a couple of retail chains, but he couldn't generate any interest. He finally had to fund the start-up of his first discount store with his own money, putting up 95% of the financing, with another 3% coming from his skeptical brother Bud and 2% from the person he hired to manage the store. On July 2, 1962, this first Wal-Mart opened its doors—the first of what has now grown into an international network of 2,985 stores (as of January 31, 2000).

fyi

Two other well-known discount retailers also began operations in 1962: KMART and TARGET.

The crucial idea behind discount retailing is that lower prices will lead to a large enough increase in sales volume to make up for the fact that a smaller profit is made on each sale. As the discount retailing industry has expanded and become more competitive, Wal-Mart has had to be ever more aggressive in cutting its profit margins in order to keep its prices low. For example, in 1980 Wal-Mart's gross profit percentage was 27%; by 1989, it had dropped to 23%, and by 2000, to 21%. For a company wrestling with tightening margins, inventory control is a crucial part of operations. Wal-Mart leased its first computer, an IBM 360, in 1969 in order to track the inventory flow at its new distribution center in Bentonville, Arkansas. Ever since, Wal-Mart has been a leader in using information technology to monitor and manage its inventory. In the late 1980s, Wal-Mart was a leader in implementing Electronic Data Interchange (EDI), which involves the electronic transfer of invoices, purchase orders, and shipping notices, thus speeding up the communication between Wal-Mart and its suppliers. Beyond this, Wal-Mart's "Retail Link" system now gives vendors access to Wal-Mart's own store-by-store sales information in real time, so that the vendors themselves can know when to make additional product shipments to specific Wal-Mart locations. The information partnership between Wal-Mart and PROCTER & GAMBLE, dating back to 1987, is legendary as an example of a buyer and a seller exchanging detailed transaction data in order to improve the operating efficiency of both companies.

fyi

In its 2000 financial statements, Procter & Gamble (P&G) disclosed that Wal-Mart is its single largest customer, accounting for 14% of P&G's sales in 2000.

Other elements contributing to Wal-Mart's success include a steadfast dedication to customer service, company policies designed to engender loyalty from employees, and sophisticated mechanisms for keeping overhead costs low. It is precisely because Wal-Mart carefully controls expenses that the company is able to consistently maintain its low price structure. Backing up Wal-Mart's cost control is the industry's most efficient and sophisticated distribution system, as well as significant cost-control relationships with the manufacturers and wholesalers it does business with.

Today, Wal-Mart employs over 1,140,000 people worldwide and has annual sales in excess of $165 billion. In addition, like many other merchandisers, Wal-Mart is experimenting with the retail distribution potential of the Internet (http://www.walmart.com). Providing the management accounting information necessary to effectively control this massive merchandising organization is no easy task. Providing merchandise at the right time, to the right place, and at the right price is how a retailer "wins" customers. However, winning the merchandising game also requires

setting the stage

1 Information from Sandra S. Vance and Roy V. Scott, *Wal-Mart: A History of Sam Walton's Retail Phenomenon* (New York: Twayne Publishers, 1994); Sam Walton and John Huey, *Sam Walton: Made in America* (New York: Doubleday, 1992).

that the merchandiser be able to provide these items at a cost that provides a reasonable profit to the organization. Sound simple? Consider that at any given moment, a typical Wal-Mart discount store has more than 70,000 different items of inventory in stock. Every one of these items must be identified, ordered, inventoried, and replenished—all the while keeping an eye on costs. (Inventory costs at a typical Supercenter are even tougher to manage because these stores also carry more than 20,000 grocery items, many of them perishable.) So how does Wal-Mart do it? With the wave of a magic wand! These "magic wands" are actually small handheld computers that link by radio frequency to in-store terminals. The next time you're in a Wal-Mart store, watch to see if you can spot an employee using these magic wands to manage inventory on the shelves. These small computers provide the critical link between Wal-Mart's suppliers and customers. With this technology, Wal-Mart management is able to get faster and more accurate information to plan, control, and evaluate every aspect of inventory management. This leads to better cost control and better merchandise and service. As a result of its leadership in technology, Wal-Mart is able to generate management accounting information that provides truly competitive cost, quality, and time information.

Some companies, such as COCA-COLA and NIKE, have become successful through convincing potential customers that their soft drinks or sports shoes are superior to all others. We talk of the marketing genius of Coca-Cola and Nike, not their cost management techniques. In contrast, WAL-MART does not offer unique products; to a large extent, Wal-Mart sells the same products sold by every other discount retailer in the world. Wal-Mart attracts us with its low prices, and consistent low prices are possible only in an organization that meticulously and relentlessly controls its costs. In this chapter, we will introduce techniques used to manage costs in manufacturing organizations, service organizations, and merchandising organizations (like Wal-Mart).

1

Outline the different cost flow patterns in manufacturing, merchandising, and service organizations and understand how these costs are reflected in the income statement and balance sheet.

COST FLOWS IN ORGANIZATIONS

In Chapter 3 of management accounting, we discussed the ways in which costs flow from one activity to the next in manufacturing, merchandising, and service organizations. These cost flow patterns are summarized in Exhibit 6-1. Recall that the extended production process characteristic of both manufacturing and service firms means that those organizations have significant levels of work-in-process inventory—goods or services that have not yet been completed but have already resulted in work being done and costs being incurred. In addition, note that both manufacturing and merchandising firms maintain significant inventories of goods that are ready for sale (finished goods or merchandise inventory); the nature of the service business means that once a service has been completed, typically it is delivered to the final customer and does not remain in inventory.

Exhibit 6-2 compares the income statements for three fictitious firms. The exhibit also presents selected balance sheet accounts. Carefully examine this exhibit to be sure you understand how the activities of manufacturing, service, and merchandising organizations are reflected in the financial statements.

As you can see, each income statement in Exhibit 6-2 follows a typical income statement format:

Sales revenue	$XXX,XXX
Costs of goods sold	(XX,XXX)
Gross margin	$XXX,XXX
Selling and administrative expenses	(X,XXX)
Operating income	$XXX,XXX

exhibit 6-1 Cost Flows in Manufacturing, Merchandising, and Service Organizations

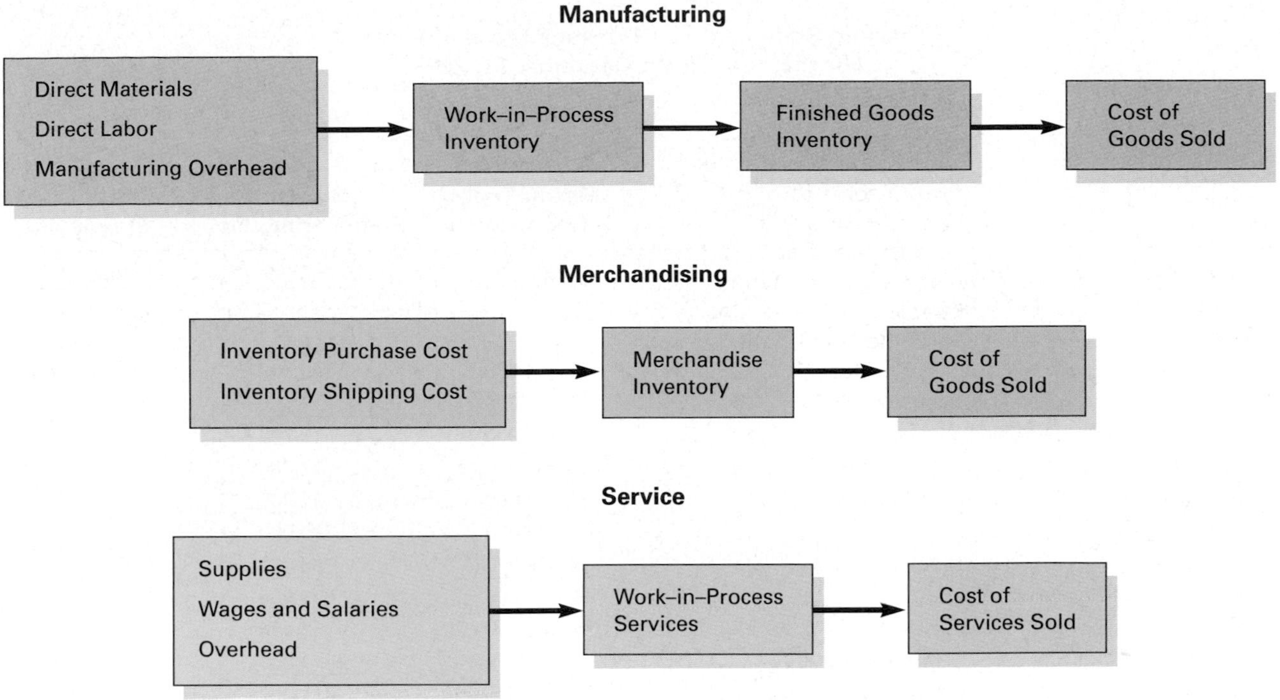

You should note two important items in Mason Tool's cost of goods sold calculation versus Brown Engineering's cost of services calculation. First of all, notice that Brown is using a rather insignificant amount of supplies ($11,900) to create its service product, especially when compared with Mason Tool, which is using a very significant amount of raw materials ($1,182,000) to create its tools. This difference underscores the fact that some supplies are often used in the process of creating and delivering a service product, but these costs are typically not a significant component of cost of services. Secondly, note that Brown Engineering does not hold finished service products for later sale to its customers. The very nature of a service business determines that a completed service is "delivered" to the customer almost instantly. In contrast, Brown Engineering does have a significant work-in-process inventory, representing service jobs that are not yet completed.

Smith Office Supply does not create the products it sells. As a result, Smith has no work-in-process inventory, and the cost of goods sold calculation only requires that Smith adjust the total amount of merchandise it purchased in 2003 by the change in its merchandise inventory account.

Balance sheet information for the three companies is presented at the bottom of Exhibit 6-2. As you can see, all three firms have accounts receivable, supplies inventory, and accounts payable accounts. Because Brown uses supplies directly in providing engineering services to its clients, this account is used in the cost of services calculation. On the other hand, cost of supplies for Mason Tool and Smith Office Supply is included in the overhead and administrative expenses accounts. In addition, you can see that Mason Tool has three inventory accounts; Smith Office Supply has one inventory account to record the costs of goods until the goods are sold to customers. Brown does not have a raw materials inventory, finished goods inventory, or merchandise inventory account. However, its work-in-process services account acts much like Mason Tool's work-in-process inventory account and is similarly used to adjust the Cost of Services account in Brown's income statement.

Exhibit 6-1 reviews the flow of costs through manufacturing, merchandising, and service organizations, and Exhibit 6-2 illustrates how these differing cost flows are reflected in the income

exhibit 6-2 Financial Statement Comparison: Manufacturing, Service, and Merchandising Firms

Income Statements for Different Types of Firms
For the Year Ended December 31, 2003

	Manufacturing Firm	Service Firm	Merchandising Firm
	Mason Tool Company	**Brown Engineering, Inc.**	**Smith Office Supply, Inc.**
Sales revenues	$4,000,000	$5,000,000	$2,500,000
Cost of goods sold/Cost of services:			
Cost of goods manufactured/Cost of services:			
Beginning raw materials/supplies inventory	$ 234,000	$ 2,300	
+ Purchases of raw materials/supplies	1,153,000	11,400	
Total raw materials/supplies available	$1,387,000	$ 13,700	
− Ending raw materials/supplies inventory	(205,000)	(1,800)	
Raw materials/supplies used	$1,182,000	$ 11,900	
+ Direct labor	445,000	1,890,000	
+ Manufacturing/service overhead	1,003,000	798,000	
Total manufacturing/service costs	$2,630,000	$2,699,900	
+ Beginning work in process	245,000	755,000	
− Ending work in process	(192,000)	(843,000)	
Cost of goods manufactured/Cost of services	$2,683,000	$2,611,900	
Underapplied overhead	307,000	22,100	
Adjusted cost of goods manufactured/Cost of services	$2,990,000	$2,634,000	
Merchandise purchases			$1,713,000
+ Beginning finished goods/merchandise inventory	354,000		378,000
− Ending finished goods/merchandise inventory	(407,000)		(356,000)
Total cost of goods sold/Cost of services	$2,937,000		$1,735,000
Gross margin	$1,063,000	$2,366,000	$ 765,000
Selling and administrative expenses:			
Selling expenses	$ 256,000	$ 367,000	$ 406,000
Administrative expenses	474,000	1,003,000	188,000
Total selling and administrative expenses	$ 730,000	$1,370,000	$ 594,000
Operating income	$ 333,000	$ 996,000	$ 171,000

Selected Balance Sheet Information
December 31, 2003

Accounts receivable	$744,000	$639,000	$ 39,000
Raw materials inventory	205,000		
Work-in-process inventory	192,000		
Work-in-process services		843,000	
Finished goods inventory	407,000		
Merchandise inventory			356,000
Supplies inventory	7,500	1,800	450
Accounts payable	298,000	106,000	489,000

statement and the balance sheet. In the remainder of this chapter, we will discuss how this cost information can be used to plan, control, and evaluate a company's operations. The extended production process of a manufacturing or service firm requires careful scrutiny of costs at each important stage of the process. For a merchandising company, cost management focuses on acquiring the right amount of inventory for the right price.

to summarize

Both manufacturing and service organizations maintain substantial production processes; an important managerial accounting function in these organizations is tracing the flow of costs through the various stages of production. Both manufacturing and merchandising organizations maintain significant inventory levels. These differences among manufacturing, merchandising, and service organizations are reflected in differences in their income statements and balance sheets.

2

Interpret a cost of goods manufactured schedule and analyze the levels of raw materials, work-in-process, and finished goods inventories in a manufacturing organization.

cost of goods manufactured schedule A schedule supporting the income statement; summarizes the total cost of goods manufactured during a period, including direct materials, direct labor, and manufacturing overhead.

COST OF GOODS MANUFACTURED SCHEDULE

The accounting for the flow of costs through a manufacturing organization was discussed in Chapter 3 of management accounting. In this section we will examine a single report, the cost of goods manufactured schedule, that summarizes the cost flows in a manufacturing organization during a given period. We will also see how this cost information can be used to evaluate both the management of costs incurred during the period and the levels of inventories that are maintained.

Exhibit 6-1 showed how manufacturing costs are accumulated in Work-in-Process Inventory, then flow to Finished Goods Inventory, and finally to Cost of Goods Sold. These costs are also usually summarized on a **cost of goods manufactured schedule**, which supports the cost of goods sold calculation on the income statement.

The cost of goods manufactured schedule shows the specific costs that have been incurred to manufacture goods during a period. Exhibit 6-3 shows the cost of goods manufactured schedule for Broyman Furniture Company, the hypothetical company that was used

exhibit 6-3 Cost of Goods Manufactured Schedule

Broyman Furniture Company
Cost of Goods Manufactured Schedule
For the Year Ended December 31, 2003

Raw materials:		
Beginning raw materials inventory	$ 50,000	
Add: Raw materials purchased	270,000	
Total raw materials available	$320,000	
Less: Ending raw materials inventory	30,000	
Raw materials used in production		$290,000
Direct labor		300,000
Manufacturing overhead:		
Indirect labor	$ 20,000	
Utilities	7,000	
Rent	72,000	
Depreciation	30,000	
Indirect materials	15,000	
Insurance	24,000	
Total actual manufacturing overhead	$168,000	
Add: Overapplied manufacturing overhead	6,000	
Applied manufacturing overhead		174,000
Total manufacturing costs		$764,000
Add: Beginning work-in-process inventory		90,000
Less: Ending work-in-process inventory		(80,000)
Cost of goods manufactured		$774,000

to illustrate manufacturing cost flows in Chapter 3 of management accounting. Most of the numbers in the schedule cannot be specifically traced back to the Chapter 3 illustration because it focused on the cost flows associated with the manufacture of one table. The important thing to focus on in Exhibit 6-3 is the format for summarizing and reporting manufacturing cost flows.

The cost of goods manufactured schedule provides the calculations that support the flow of costs for a manufacturing firm. In our example, the schedule shows that materials costing $290,000 were combined with direct labor costs of $300,000 and manufacturing overhead costs of $174,000 to transfer $764,000 of manufacturing costs to work-in-process inventory. This $764,000 amount of total manufacturing costs represents the new manufacturing costs incurred during the period and is a good representation of the level of production activity carried out during the period. The $764,000 was then adjusted for the beginning and ending work-in-process inventories to determine the $774,000 cost of goods manufactured for the period. The amount of cost of goods manufactured represents the total cost of items for which production was completed during the period; this cost includes some costs incurred in prior periods (from beginning work-in-process inventory) and some costs incurred during this period. Knowing the total cost of goods manufactured makes it easy to determine the total cost of goods sold. The cost of goods manufactured amount is added to beginning finished goods inventory (assume $60,000) and adjusted for any over- or underapplied manufacturing overhead (assume $6,000 overapplied) to arrive at cost of goods available for sale of $828,000. The ending finished goods inventory (assume $40,000) is then subtracted to determine the cost of goods sold ($788,000). This calculation of cost of goods sold is shown below.

caution

Remember that over- or underapplied overhead is usually charged to Cost of Goods Sold. Thus, in the cost of goods sold calculation, underapplied overhead is added to cost of goods manufactured, and overapplied overhead is subtracted from cost of goods manufactured.

Cost of Goods Sold

Beginning finished goods inventory	$ 60,000
Add: Cost of goods manufactured	774,000
Less: Overapplied manufacturing overhead	(6,000)
Total cost of goods available for sale	$828,000
Less: Ending finished goods inventory	(40,000)
Cost of goods sold	$788,000

Total cost of goods manufactured should include only those costs that have gone through the work-in-process inventory account during the period. Thus, as shown in Exhibit 6-3, applied (rather than actual) overhead costs are included in the cost of goods manufactured schedule. As illustrated, Cost of Goods Sold is then adjusted for the amount of over- or underapplied overhead.

Analyzing Production Costs and Inventory Levels

In the above example, cost of goods sold was determined to be $788,000. You should note that this is a summary number that is used in the financial statements and is the number to which auditors will attest. However, because it is a summary number, it is not useful for detailed internal decision making. To be useful, management would want to determine the cost of goods manufactured on a product-by-product basis, a period-by-period basis, and a department-by-department basis. By breaking costs down by product, period, and department, management can determine which units and products are performing well and which are performing poorly. For example, examine the table and bookcase production cost data for Broyman Furniture in Exhibit 6-4. The data are listed by month, and comparisons to the production cost in the same month in the preceding year are included. First, note that the production cost per unit for both the tables and the bookcases declines during the summer months; this seasonal decline probably occurs because the factory facility is used more heavily during these months, resulting in fixed production costs being spread over a larger number of manufactured units. Notice that, for the tables, the increase in production cost in 2003, relative to the same month in 2002, is

exhibit 6-4 Monthly Cost Information, by Product

Tables—Average Production Cost per Unit, by Month

	Jan.	Feb.	Mar.	Apr.	May	June	July	Aug.	Sep.	Oct.	Nov.	Dec.
2003	$310.12	$312.75	$308.49	$311.71	$306.23	$301.87	$298.44	$297.03	$305.60	$313.45	$315.79	$314.32
2002	300.37	302.24	298.24	302.04	297.81	293.49	292.12	288.43	294.05	306.32	310.89	309.75
Change in 2003	$9.75	$10.51	$10.25	$9.67	$8.42	$8.38	$6.32	$8.60	$11.55	$7.13	$4.90	$4.57
Percentage change	3.2%	3.5%	3.4%	3.2%	2.8%	2.9%	2.2%	3.0%	3.9%	2.3%	1.6%	1.5%

Bookcases—Average Production Cost per Unit, by Month

	Jan.	Feb.	Mar.	Apr.	May	June	July	Aug.	Sep.	Oct.	Nov.	Dec.
2003	$77.53	$78.18	$77.12	$77.92	$76.55	$75.46	$74.61	$74.25	$76.40	$78.36	$78.94	$78.58
2002	75.65	76.27	75.26	75.82	74.42	72.69	71.88	71.04	72.58	73.94	73.99	73.15
Change in 2003	$1.88	$1.91	$1.86	$2.10	$2.13	$2.77	$2.73	$3.21	$3.82	$4.42	$4.95	$5.43
Percentage change	2.5%	2.5%	2.5%	2.8%	2.9%	3.8%	3.8%	4.5%	5.3%	6.0%	6.7%	7.4%

much lower near the end of the year than at the beginning of the year. This evidence suggests that the production manager for the tables has improved the control of costs as the year has progressed. The bookcase numbers present exactly the opposite picture: cost per unit was up 7.4% in the month of December compared to the year before, whereas the cost increases in the early months of the year were just 2.5%.

Our brief analysis of the production cost data in Exhibit 6-4 is just the beginning of a thorough investigation into the performance of the table and the bookcase production units. As will be discussed in Chapter 9 of management accounting, cost variance analysis can be used to determine exactly which costs (material, labor, or manufacturing overhead) are causing the production cost per unit for bookcases to increase so dramatically.

Management would also use the manufacturing cost and inventory numbers to evaluate the levels of raw materials, work-in-process, and finished goods inventories. Two measures used to evaluate a company's inventory management practices are **inventory turnover** and **days in inventory.** Selected information from Exhibit 6-3 is repeated in Exhibit 6-5 and used to illustrate the computations of inventory turnover and days in inventory.

inventory turnover (stock-turns) The number of times the inventory in the organization "turns over" during a period of time. It is often easier to think of inventory turnover as the number of times a dollar invested in inventory is sold during a period of time. Inventory turnover is computed as cost of goods sold divided by average inventory value.

days in inventory Average number of days of sales that can be made using only the supply of inventory on hand.

The inventory turnover measures indicate how many times during the year Broyman has completely replenished or replaced the inventory, given the rate at which costs are flowing through the production process. For example, Exhibit 6-5 shows that the raw materials inventory "turned over" or was replaced 9.7 times during the year. Inventory turnover measures the intensity with which Broyman is managing its inventory—low inventory turnover indicates lots of idle inventory lying around whereas high inventory turnover indicates extremely active management with little excess inventory. The days in inventory measure provides an alternative measure of this same concept. For example, Exhibit 6-5 shows that Broyman's average manufacturing cost per day is $2,093.15. Given that the ending work-in-process inventory amount is $80,000, the amount of inventory still in process at the end of the year represents 38.2 days ($80,000 ÷ $2,093.15) days of manufacturing. A very streamlined production process would result in a low number of days of manufacturing in work-in-process inventory; a long, complex manufacturing process (such as the construction of a ship) could have more than a year's worth of manufacturing costs tied up in unfinished products.

fyi

Both inventory turnover and days in inventory measure the same thing. This can be seen by the fact that another way to compute days in inventory is as follows: Days in inventory = 365 ÷ Inventory turnover.

In evaluating products and departments, cost is only one criterion examined by management. In most cases, management is just as interested in indicators of product quality and production speed as in costs of production. Exhibit 6-6 shows cost, quality, and time data that would be examined by management for a hypothetical company with three divisions and six products. Obviously, management could have many different measures for

exhibit 6-5

Analysis of the Levels of Raw Materials, Work-in-Process, and Finished Goods Inventories

Raw Materials Inventory	
Ending raw materials inventory	$30,000
Total amount used during the year	$290,000
Average amount used per day (365 days)	$794.52
Inventory turnover (yearly cost ÷ inventory)	9.7
Days' supply of raw materials in ending inventory (inventory ÷ average daily cost)	37.8 days
Work-in-Process Inventory	
Ending work-in-process inventory	$80,000
Total manufacturing costs during the year	$764,000
Average manufacturing cost per day (365 days)	$2,093.15
Inventory turnover (yearly cost ÷ inventory)	9.6
Days of manufacturing represented by ending work-in-process inventory (inventory ÷ average daily cost)	38.2 days
Finished Goods Inventory	
Ending finished goods inventory	$40,000
Total cost of goods sold during the year	$788,000
Average cost of goods sold per day (365 days)	$2,158.90
Inventory turnover (yearly cost ÷ inventory)	19.7
Days of sales in ending inventory (inventory ÷ average daily cost)	18.5 days

the cost, quality, and time attributes it monitors. In this hypothetical example, the summary information suggests that both products in Division B have improved performance on each dimension (cost, quality, and time) over the last period, while both products in Division C show decreased performance over the prior period. Obviously, comparing performance with the last period is only one measure that could be used. Management may want to compare the performance of products versus each other or "benchmark" the performance of its products with those of other companies.

exhibit 6-6

Divisional Performance Report

	Division A		Division B		Division C	
	Product 1	Product 2	Product 3	Product 4	Product 5	Product 6
Cost to produce	Higher than last period	Same as last period	Lower than last period	Lower than last period	Higher than last period	Higher than last period
Quality of product	Happier customers, fewer defects	No change in customer attitudes	Happier customers, fewer defects	Happier customers, fewer defects	Increase in complaints	Increase in complaints
Average time to produce	Same as last period	One day less	Two days less	One day less	Two days more	Six days more

to summarize

Manufacturing costs are summarized on a cost of goods manufactured schedule. The cost of goods manufactured is added to the beginning finished goods inventory to determine cost of goods available for sale. Ending finished goods inventory is then subtracted from this number to compute cost of goods sold. Cost of goods sold is a summary number that is audited and used in the financial statements, but is not very useful for internal management decision making. For decision making, management would examine costs, as well as quality and time measures, on a product-by-product, period-by-period, and department-by-department basis. Inventory turnover measures can be used to evaluate the levels of raw materials, work-in process, and finished goods inventories.

3 Understand how merchants manage cost information in their organizations.

MANAGING COST INFORMATION

As discussed in the preceding section, cost data can be used in a manufacturing firm to evaluate the appropriateness of the levels of raw materials, work-in-process, and finished goods inventories. Merchants, or managers of merchandising organizations, are also very conscious of the total amount of inventory that is currently in the retail store or in the distribution center. Managing this inventory takes careful and detailed planning. The detail in these plans results from merchants having *many* different types of inventory items, each with its own particular supplier source and targeted customer. Merchants must also be very careful in planning their inventory levels because having either too little or too much inventory can involve critical issues. These issues are listed in Exhibit 6-7. If accountants are aware of these issues, they can help their organizations avoid a variety of unnecessary out-of-pocket costs or opportunity costs.

Carrying Too Much Inventory

holding costs The financial opportunity costs that result from investing money in an asset such as inventory. Whatever income the money could generate in an alternative investment is the holding cost of the current investment.

Having inventory is certainly necessary for most merchants if they expect to do business with their customers. However, accumulating as much inventory as possible is *not* the purpose of merchandising (or manufacturing) companies. Good business management entails having the right assets at the right place in the right time and in the right quantity (always a challenging endeavor!). The advent of the just-in-time (JIT) inventory management concept has clearly taught us that too much inventory creates a lot of management problems. First of all, clearly many out-of-pocket costs are involved in having inventory on site, including costs of storage, security, and record keeping. What may not be as clear is the financial opportunity cost (sometimes called the **holding cost**) of the inventory investment. Every dollar that is invested in inventory cannot be used in alternative business investments, such as expanding another part of the business

exhibit 6-7 Inventory Management Issues

Carrying Too Much Inventory	Carrying Too Little Inventory
• Increased overhead costs	• Increased risk of lost sales
• Increased financial holding costs	• Increased ordering costs
• Increased risk of loss of market value	• Increased risk of supplier price increases
• Decreased inventory flexibility	• Increased exposure to nondelivery
• Increased inventory shrinkage	• Decreased bulk order discounts

or simply investing in the stock market or in a bank savings account. Whatever money we *could* make by investing the money elsewhere is the holding cost of the current inventory investment. Accountants measure and report holding costs all the time. We will demonstrate the calculation of holding costs in the expanded material section of this chapter.

Increased overhead costs and holding costs are not the only issues involved in carrying too much inventory. The more inventory a merchant elects to carry, the more risk the merchant faces that the inventory will decrease in market value before it can be sold (of course, inventory may unexpectedly increase in market value as well). In addition, when a merchant invests in a lot of one type of inventory, it becomes difficult to shift to another inventory type that customers may suddenly want to buy. Finally, every merchant understands the tough reality that inventories "shrink" over time. **Inventory shrinkage** happens in a lot of ways. The type of shrinkage we hear about most often is theft (either by customers or employees). However, when inventory is being moved, stacked, stored, retrieved, and rotated, things get broken, parts get lost, and items become mislabeled. Liquid and gas stocks spill or evaporate. Cloth material becomes soiled. Grocery items spoil or become stale. As inventory is piled up around the store or distribution center, this disorder, spoilage, and theft are revealed every time the company takes an annual inventory count, resulting in additional out-of-pockets costs to replace the inventory.

inventory shrinkage The disorder, spoilage, and theft that result when a company chooses to maintain inventory on site, resulting in additional out-of-pocket costs to replace inventory.

Carrying Too Little Inventory

Clearly, having too much inventory is a poor use of resources. However, poor planning that results in not having enough inventory on hand can also be a source of trouble. It is obvious to most managers and owners that they lose potential sales when they have to turn away customers because of a lack of inventory. Accountants can support good inventory management when they are able to quantify these opportunity costs for decision makers. As can be seen in Exhibit 6-7, however, an organization that has inadequate inventory levels also incurs other costs. For example, initiating an order with a wholesaler or manufacturer for the delivery of goods often requires a number of business processes, including counting inventory, preparing purchase orders, receiving and inspecting shipments of goods, and initiating payments for purchases. Most merchants have to initiate and pay for each of these steps every time they purchase inventory. Merchants that maintain low inventory levels by buying in smaller quantities will generally have to make more purchases, and pay for additional employee time, to replenish their stock.

Prices for most types of inventory increase with time. Some items are particularly susceptible to sudden price increases. Have you ever awakened to hear the morning newscast report that automobile gasoline prices have suddenly surged? When you go out to your car and discover the gas tank nearly empty, don't you wish you had filled the tank yesterday? One reason some merchants purchase large amounts of inventory is to temporarily protect themselves from sudden increases in prices. Companies without similar foresight will experience greater out-of-pocket expenses if prices do increase. Companies that keep very low levels of inventory are most likely to have to pay for every price increase. In addition, these same companies are much more dependent on their suppliers to *always* meet their delivery commitments. If a supplier is late in making promised shipments or delivers inventory that is damaged or of the wrong type, the merchant may miss making sales to some customers. Finally, merchants that regularly purchase large levels of inventory often enjoy price discounts from their suppliers. Merchants making smaller purchases should be aware of the opportunity cost related to missing these potential bulk purchase discounts.

fyi

In 1999, FRUIT OF THE LOOM reported that it experienced inventory shrinkage totaling $70.4 million. This represented a 25% increase in shrinkage compared to the prior year. Fruit of the Loom attributed the shrinkage increase to its expansion of its network of contractors (factories where its clothing items are produced).

fyi

How important is the Christmas buying season for a toy merchant? The 1999 annual report for TOYS "R" US, INC., reports that approximately 42% of its sales occur in the months of November, December, and January.

Example of Inventory Management Costs

We'll use the fictitious example of two large retailers of children's toys, Kids N Toys, Inc., and Child's Delight, Inc., to illustrate the issues and costs involved in inventory management for merchandising organizations. As you might expect, the Christmas buying season is a big deal for a toy retailer. Management and buyers for these companies study trend reports and catalogs all year in order to properly plan their investments for December. Both companies have limited resources that can be invested in inventory for the holiday season. Given the necessary **lead time**, as well as the size of the investment, these decisions are absolutely critical to both companies.

lead time Generally, the time interval between initiating a request and finally fulfilling the request.

TOYS "R" US is the largest toy retailer in the United States. With its toysrus.com Web site, a partnership with AMAZON.COM, it has also sought to expand its success to the Internet. As discussed in the chapter, effective management of a merchandising company requires information about both profitability and inventory management. Go to the corporate Web site for Toys "R" Us at http://www.toysrus.com and find the company's most recent earnings press release. In addition to discussing the company's profitability, does this press release also discuss inventory management?

Once December has arrived, it becomes very difficult to make many adjustments to preplanned inventory types and levels.

A wholesaler of children's dolls has announced the availability of a new doll for Christmas this year, the Burzee Doll. Based on the manufacturer's reputation, as well as the fact that the manufacturer of the doll intends to do a lot of promotional advertising, the wholesaler is confident that the Burzee Doll will sell very well this year. To help make planning decisions, each retailer has its management accountants prepare some forecasts on potential revenues and costs related to the issues listed in Exhibit 6-7. Based on the projections of its management accountants, Kids N Toys, Inc., decides to invest very heavily in the Burzee Doll and orders 50,000 dolls for delivery on November 1. Because of the size of its order, the wholesaler offers Kids N Toys a discount of $2 per doll. On the other hand, the management accountants' projections of revenues and costs at Child's Delight, Inc., are not as optimistic. As a result, Child's Delight orders only 5,000 dolls and pays the full wholesale price of $12 per doll. Both retailers follow the manufacturer's recommendation to set the customer price at $30 per doll.

Exhibit 6-8 outlines all the Burzee Doll events that take place during the holiday season, as well as the resulting revenues and costs for the two companies. As it turns out, the Burzee Dolls are a real hit during the holiday buying season. Child's Delight keeps running out of inventory and must reorder dolls three times during the season. As you can see in Exhibit 6-8, each time Child's Delight reorders dolls, it is not hard for the accountants to note the amount of inventory shrinkage. Occasionally, dolls are stolen, misplaced, or destroyed in the process of moving, sorting, and stacking. On the other hand, Kids N Toys has dolls all over the store, making it difficult to know much about shrinkage without taking a very expensive inventory count. The accountants at Kids N Toys elect to wait until all the inventory is sold before measuring inventory shrinkage.

By the end of December, Child's Delight has sold all of its dolls and elects not to place a fifth order. On the other hand, Kids N Toys still has a large number of dolls remaining. Since the buying craze for Burzee Dolls appears to be finished, Kids N Toys puts the dolls on sale at cost ($10 per doll) in mid-January. At the end of January, the store liquidates the remaining 4,400 dolls to another retailer at $3 per doll.

STOP & THINK These two companies now have very different levels of inventory in Burzee Dolls. With its very large inventory investment, what additional inventory costs are now a factor for Kids N Toys? What additional inventory costs is Child's Delight susceptible to with its relatively small inventory investment?

THE GROSS MARGIN REPORT When all Burzee Doll sales are totaled, Kids N Toys sold 48,400 dolls (indicating inventory shrinkage over the last three months of 1,600 dolls); Child's Delight sold 19,850 dolls (indicating inventory shrinkage of 150 dolls). Which of the two retailers did better with the Burzee Dolls? Exhibit 6-9 provides a gross margin report based on what each company spent on inventory purchases and received in inventory sales. When you look at the gross margin of $793,200 for Kids N Toys, it appears that this company did a much better job selling Burzee Dolls than its competitor, Child's Delight, based on its gross margin of only $325,500.

STOP & THINK Is there anything wrong with using the gross margin analysis presented in Exhibit 6-9 to evaluate management performance in these two companies? What costs may be missing?

RETURN ON INVESTMENT (ROI) The gross margin numbers presented in Exhibit 6-9 suggest that Kids N Toys outperformed Child's Delight. However, if you had money to invest in these companies, you might actually like Child's Delight's retail work on Burzee Dolls better than the work done by Kids N Toys. Think about the average size of the inventory investment each company maintained. Kids N Toys initially spent $500,000 to acquire 50,000 dolls. By the end of January, this inventory had been fully liquidated back into cash. Hence, Kids N Toys had quite a bit of cash tied up in Burzee Doll inventory! On average, how much cash did it have invested in this inventory during its selling period? On November 1, Kids N Toys had $500,000 in Burzee Doll inventory. On January 30, it had no Burzee Doll inventory. On average, Kids N Toys had about a $250,000 investment in inventory during its three-month selling period ($500,000 ÷ 2).[2]

2 Be careful with this calculation! The fact that Kids N Toys held its doll inventory for three months (or two months, or four months) does not change the fact that average inventory for the company is $250,000. The formal calculation here is (Beginning balance + Ending balance) ÷ 2. Instead of having no inventory, what if Kids N Toys still had $50,000 worth of Burzee Dolls on January 31? The average inventory investment would then be $275,000 [($500,000 + $50,000) ÷ 2].

exhibit 6-8 Management Events in the Burzee Doll Inventory

Date	Event	Kids N Toys, Inc.	Child's Delight, Inc.
Nov. 1	Retailers prepare the Burzee Doll inventory.	Company buys 50,000 dolls at $10 per doll. Customer price is set at $30.	Company buys 5,000 dolls at $12 per doll. Customer price is set at $30.
30	Sales on the doll start increasing.	Company has sold 7,500 dolls.	Company has sold 4,950 dolls and is out of stock. Reorders another 5,000 dolls at $12 per doll.
Dec. 10	Sales on the doll are really strong.	Company has sold another 12,000 dolls.	Company has sold another 4,970 dolls and is out of stock again. Reorders another 5,000 dolls at $15 per doll (supplier has increased price).
20	Sales on the doll continue to be very strong.	Company has sold another 15,000 dolls.	Company has sold another 4,990 dolls and is out of stock again. Reorders another 5,000 dolls at $15 per doll.
31	Sales have nearly halted in the last few days.	Company has sold another 7,000 dolls.	Company has sold another 4,940 dolls and is out of stock again. Chooses not to reorder.
Jan. 15	Sales are nearly nonexistent.	Company has sold another 500 dolls and now puts dolls on sale at cost ($10).	Out of Burzee Doll business.
30	Sales pick up a little.	Company has sold another 2,000 dolls and now sells the remaining 4,400 usable dolls to a small merchant for $3 per doll.	Out of Burzee Doll business.
31	Evaluate inventory shrinkage.	Sold a total of 48,400 units indicating that 1,600 units were lost due to shrinkage.	Sold a total of 19,850 units indicating that 150 units were lost due to shrinkage.

How does Kids N Toys' average inventory investment compare to its competitor's investment? Rather than one large inventory purchase at the beginning of November, Child's Delight made four smaller investments as needed during November and December. The average inventory purchase amount was $67,500 [($60,000 + $60,000 + $75,000 + $75,000) ÷ 4]. On December 31, it had no Burzee Doll inventory. On average, then, Child's Delight had only about a $33,750 investment in inventory during its two-month selling period ($67,500 ÷ 2).

exhibit 6-9 Gross Margin Report on the Burzee Doll Inventory

	Kids N Toys, Inc.		Child's Delight, Inc.	
	42,000 units × $30	$1,260,000		
	2,000 units × $10	20,000		
	4,400 units × $3	13,200		
Sales revenue		$1,293,200	19,850 units × $30	$595,500
			10,000 units × $12	
Cost of purchases	50,000 units × $10	(500,000)	10,000 units × $15	(270,000)
Gross margin		$ 793,200		$325,500

Obviously, the difference between the two companies' gross margins reported in Exhibit 6-9 is dramatic. However, the difference in Kids N Toys' average inventory investment of $250,000 versus the $33,750 average inventory investment at Child's Delight is also impressive. Remember from Chapter 1 of management accounting, that the DuPont approach to business recognizes that it is just as important to manage the money outflow for asset investment as it is to manage the money inflow from profits. This is the logic underlying Pierre du Pont and Donaldson Brown's ROI (return on investment) formula. Remember that the ROI formula has two parts (see Exhibit 1-2 if you need a review):

$$\underset{(\text{Profit} \div \text{Revenue})}{\text{Profit margin}} \times \underset{(\text{Revenue} \div \text{Total assets})}{\text{Asset turnover}} = \text{ROI}$$

Based on ROI, which of these two companies has created the most revenue for each dollar invested in its Burzee Doll inventory asset? Answering this question is really a function of the "asset turnover" section of the ROI formula. Notice, however, that rather than *total* revenue and *total* assets, we are focusing only on Burzee Doll revenue and the value of the Burzee Doll inventory asset. This fact really doesn't present a problem. Rather than measuring how much total revenue is generated per dollar of total assets, we will simply measure *how much specific revenue is generated per dollar of a specific inventory item.* Hence, how many times does Kids N Toys turn over its Burzee Doll inventory compared to Child's Delight?

Kids N Toys: Revenue ÷ Average inventory
$1,293,200 ÷ $250,000 = 5.17

Child's Delight: Revenue ÷ Average inventory
$595,500 ÷ $33,750 = 17.64

Note that organizations have a limited amount of resources to invest. Using the ROI formula, the **DUPONT COMPANY** was able to wisely manage the task of maximizing the value of its investments by knowing where in the massive organization to invest its resources. Looking at the asset turnover numbers above, you can see that Child's Delight made the better use of limited purchasing dollars to manage the Burzee Doll inventory to create sales revenue.[3]

Combining the gross margin and inventory turnover data yields the following ROI calculations for Kids N Toys and Child's Delight:

(Gross margin ÷ Revenue) × (Revenue ÷ Inventory) = Return on investment in inventory

Kids N Toys: ($793,200 ÷ $1,293,200) × ($1,293,200 ÷ $250,000) = 317%

Child's Delight: ($325,500 ÷ $595,500) × ($595,500 ÷ $33,750) = 964%

These ROI numbers suggest that although Child's Delight generated a lower gross margin, it actually performed better than Kids N Toys because of superior inventory management. By the way, if these ROI numbers (317% and 964%) seem high to you, then you should congratulate yourself for paying attention. These numbers *are* high because we have focused on the utilization of just one asset—inventory. In order to sell Burzee Dolls, each merchandiser must also invest in buildings, store shelving and displays, cash registers, and so forth. However, these ROI numbers give a strong indication that, regardless of what the overall ROI of each company is, it appears that Child's Delight has been more effective at managing its acquisition and sales of Burzee Dolls.

The day-to-day effort to manage the Burzee Doll inventory involves many other important issues (as listed in Exhibit 6-7). Even the ROI measures above do not provide Kids N Toys and

3 In this case, inventory turnover was measured by dividing a retail number (revenue) by a wholesale, or purchase cost, number (inventory). As illustrated in the preceding section, inventory turnover is frequently measured using cost of goods sold rather than sales or revenue. Conceptually, comparing a wholesale number (inventory) to a wholesale number (cost of goods sold) makes more sense than comparing a wholesale number to a retail (sales) number. However, as long as a consistent approach is used, the insights gained are the same.

Child's Delight management with the data necessary to address all issues as they *plan* for future inventory investments and *control* and *evaluate* the current inventory acquisition and selling process. This is where good management accounting can provide real value in management's effort to improve a merchandising operation. Exhibit 6-10 provides a management accounting view of the two companies' retail work with the Burzee Doll line of operations. Study both Exhibit 6-10 and Exhibit 6-7 for a moment. What information in Exhibit 6-10 could help a manager trying to work with some of the issues described in Exhibit 6-7?

THE MANAGEMENT ACCOUNTING REPORT ON KIDS N TOYS' NET OPERATING PROFIT As you can see in Exhibit 6-10, we are identifying some additional out-of-pocket costs on the Burzee Doll operation for each company. Note that the gross margin for each company is the same as that calculated in the gross margin report in Exhibit 6-9. However, we're approaching the calculation of gross margin differently, as well as identifying some other relevant costs to calculate **net operating profit** for each company. Net operating profit is useful in measuring the performance of these operations. Much more important, though, are the insights gained in the management accounting numbers used to calculate gross margin and net operating profit. These numbers, presented in Exhibit 6-10, are extremely useful for planning, controlling, and evaluating the Burzee Doll retail operations.

net operating profit The difference between normal business sales and normal business expenses.

Let's work with Kids N Toys first. This company originally purchased 50,000 units with the intent of selling all of them for $30. Why didn't it then have $1.5 million in revenue? This question cannot be answered using the gross margin report in Exhibit 6-9, but the answer is obvious in the management accounting report in Exhibit 6-10. Somehow, 1,600 dolls that Kids N Toys planned to sell were broken, misplaced, or stolen. Based on an intended $30 selling price, this cost the company $48,000 in lost revenue. In addition, the market demand changed while Kids N Toys still had dolls to sell. As a result, the store had to sell some dolls for prices lower than the planned $30. Specifically, Kids N Toys reduced expected revenue by $40,000 when it sold 2,000 dolls for $10, and reduced expected revenue by another $118,800 when it sold 4,400 dolls for $3. This loss of market value is a risk that Kids N Toys management should consider when planning for next year's purchases. Further, management

exhibit 6-10 Management Accounting Report on the Burzee Doll Inventory

In addition to cost of purchases, note the following additional inventory costs:

- Average inventory overhead costs are $1.10 per unit per month.
- Average costs to initiate and receive a purchase order are $1,250 per event.

	Kids N Toys, Inc.		Child's Delight, Inc.	
Expected revenue	50,000 units × $30 standard price	$1,500,000	20,000 units × $30 standard price	$600,000
Shrinkage loss	1,600 units × $30	(48,000)	150 units × $30	(4,500)
Market loss	2,000 units × ($30 − $10) + 4,400 units × ($30 − $3)	(158,800)		(0)
Actual revenue		$1,293,200		$595,500
Purchase costs	50,000 units × $10 standard cost	(500,000)	20,000 units × $10 standard cost	(200,000)
Lost discount		(0)	20,000 units × $2 lost discount	(40,000)
Price increase		(0)	10,000 units × $3 price increase	(30,000)
Gross margin		$ 793,200		$325,500
Overhead costs	50,000 units ÷ 2 = 25,000 average inventory level × $1.10 × 3 months	(82,500)	5,000 units ÷ 2 = 2,500 average inventory level × $1.10 × 2 months	(5,500)
Order costs	1 order × $1,250	(1,250)	4 orders × $1,250	(5,000)
Net operating profit		$ 709,450		$315,000

should also evaluate the information on inventory shrinkage to better control the inventory operation.

We briefly discussed the concept of activity-based costing (ABC) in Chapter 3 of management accounting. We'll spend a lot of time on this concept in Chapter 7 of management accounting. Briefly, ABC is an approach to tracking the relationship between activities and costs that is generally used to better allocate manufacturing overhead costs to products. This concept can also be used to analyze overhead costs in merchandising organizations. Managing the Burzee Doll inventory requires some overhead costs. In this example, let's assume an ABC analysis reveals that the cost for storage, security, and other supervisory activities works out to be about $1.10 per doll per month. In addition, the effort to count inventory and prepare the purchase order, as well as to receive and pay for the inventory, requires about $1,250 in administrative costs each time inventory is purchased. In a standard income statement, only the direct cost of inventory purchases would be used to measure gross margin. Those overhead and purchasing costs related to managing the Burzee Doll inventory are typically combined with all other administrative costs to form Selling and Administrative Expenses on the income statement. However, the management accounting report in Exhibit 6-10 has specifically identified and related these costs to the Burzee Doll inventory. This information allows management to see exactly how the Burzee Doll product line is contributing to Kids N Toys' overall net operating profit. Further, management can evaluate how having a lot of inventory leads to higher overhead costs. On the other hand, though, purchasing all these dolls at once saved Kids N Toys additional purchasing costs.

THE MANAGEMENT ACCOUNTING REPORT ON CHILD'S DELIGHT'S NET OPERATING PROFIT Now let's evaluate operations at Child's Delight using the management accounting report in Exhibit 6-10. During November and December, Child's Delight purchased a total of 20,000 units with the intent of selling all of them for $30. Similar to Kids N Toys, the difference between expected revenue and actual revenue is explained by the inventory shrinkage of 150 units. Compared to Kids N Toys, why does Child's Delight have a much lower percentage of dolls being broken, misplaced, or stolen? It seems reasonable to expect that Child's Delight found it much easier to maintain and keep track of its much smaller level of inventory. Can this shrinkage be further reduced? Child's Delight should carefully consider this question as it plans for the next buying season.

As noted in Exhibit 6-7, keeping the inventory levels low helps protect the organization against certain types of costs and risks. However, this can be a challenging balance because other costs occur as a result of low inventory levels; Child's Delight incurred three of these costs. First, because Child's Delight made small inventory purchases, bulk discounts were unavailable to the company. The effect of losing these discounts, $40,000, was to pay $2 more per doll (20,000 dolls × $2). Second, each time Child's Delight ran out of inventory and had to reorder, it had to pay the current market rate. Given the high popularity of Burzee Dolls during the holiday buying spree, it is not surprising that the manufacturer raised the price. This cost was passed through the distributor to Child's Delight, which had to pay an additional $3 per doll for its last two shipments. Overall, this resulted in an additional $30,000 in cost (10,000 dolls × $3). Finally, each purchase event at Child's Delight adds to the management activities that must take place. If we assume that both companies have similar inventory acquisition activities, then Child's Delight must have $5,000 in purchase order costs (4 purchases × $1,250 activity costs). Again, though, low inventory levels have their advantage. Because Child's Delight orders only 5,000 dolls at a time, its inventory will range from 0 to 5,000 dolls. On average, it will generally have 2,500 dolls on hand. Based on an average monthly overhead cost of $1.10 per doll, selling Burzee Dolls led to relatively low overhead costs of $5,500 (again, assuming similar ABC costs for storage, security, and other supervisory activities for Child's Delight and Kids N Toys). Clearly, Child's Delight management should pay attention to all these numbers as it evaluates this year's operations and make plans for next year.

Remember that the format and content of financial accounting reports are standardized in order to allow external users to compare reports from many different companies. In contrast, the format and content of internal management accounting reports differ across organizations because each organization customizes the reports to fit specific needs. Hence, the format of the management accounting report in Exhibit 6-10 is not regulated by anyone! The accountants for one particular retailer will customize the report to best support their own management processes of planning, controlling, and evaluating. The cost calculations displayed in Exhibit 6-10 are used by many, but not all, organizations in the merchandising industry. In this case, we saw that a simple comparison of gross margins does not necessarily indicate which company, Kids N Toys (gross margin of $793,200) or Child's Delight (gross margin of $325,500), made the better decisions. By including information on inventory management, we concluded that Child's Delight had more successfully combined the activities of profitable sales with efficient asset utilization. The more detailed profit analysis contained in Exhibit 6-10 enabled us to look more closely at the specific factors affecting the net operating profit of Kids N Toys and Child's Delight.

to summarize

Because wholesalers and retailers generally do not have to deal with raw materials or work in process, the process of accounting for inventory in a merchandising business is not nearly as complicated as it is in a manufacturing business. However, *managing* inventory costs is both complicated and critical for a merchant. Having too much inventory creates unnecessary overhead costs, financial holding costs, costs due to loss of market value, and costs due to inventory shrinkage. Not having enough inventory may result in unnecessary ordering costs and loss of bulk order discounts, as well as opportunity costs due to lost sales and increased supplier prices. While measuring some of these costs presents a challenge to accountants, the information is very important to the processes of planning, controlling, and evaluating gross margins and net operating profits for individual product lines.

4

Measure profitability and personnel utilization in a service organization.

COST MANAGEMENT IN SERVICE ORGANIZATIONS

As discussed in Chapter 3 of management accounting, service organizations have many characteristics in common with manufacturing organizations. Both types of organizations engage in a substantial production process before delivering the final product to the customer. In a manufacturing organization, this production process involves people assembling materials using equipment located in factories. In a service organization, materials are of much smaller importance, and the production process focuses on people delivering a service within an infrastructure of tangible assets (hotels, delivery trucks, barbershops, doctors' offices, etc.). In some service organizations, such as airline service, the focus is on the tangible asset infrastructure—while the pilots, flight attendants, and ticket agents are important, most of our interest centers around the reliability of the planes and the baggage handling equipment. In other service organizations, such as legal services, the focus is on person-to-person delivery of customized service—we don't really care how nice the attorney's office is, as long as the attorney gives us good legal counsel. In this section, the evaluation of cost management will be discussed in the context of a service organization.

Characteristics of a Service Organization

Service organizations can be broadly categorized into three basic types: professional services, service shops, and mass services.[4] A professional services organization is associated with people pro-

4 See Lin Fitzgerald, Robert Johnson, Stan Brignall, Rhian Silvestro, and Christopher Voss, *Performance Measurement in Service Businesses* (London: CIMA, 1991).

A family doctor clinic is categorized as a professional services organization because the doctor provides a highly customized service—treatment is tailored to individual patients.

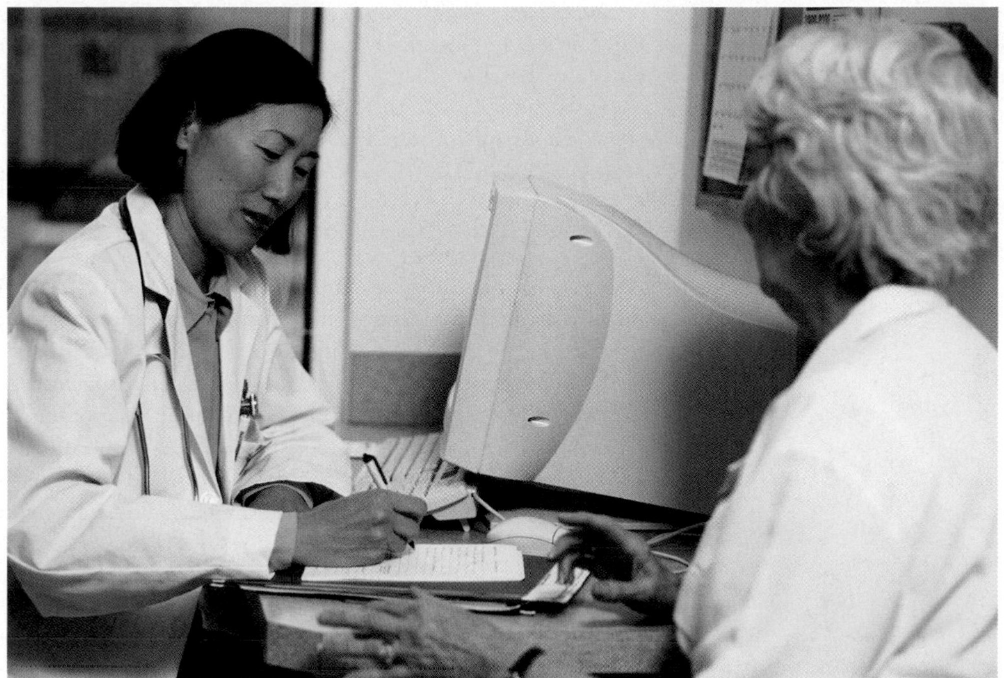

viding a highly customized service process. For example, a good family doctor tailors the treatment to the specific patient, after developing a personal rapport with the patient and carefully extracting a thorough case history. At the other end of the continuum, a mass service organization provides a standardized product with little emphasis on the person delivering the product. For example, MCDONALD'S has developed its fast-food business around the delivery of standard-quality food in a predictable atmosphere; we are pleased when the person serving us is competent and cheerful, but we are primarily interested in the taste of the food and the cleanliness of the restrooms. A service shop is somewhere between a professional service and a mass service. For example, in a large-scale laser eye surgery clinic, there is more emphasis on standardization and on the equipment itself than one finds in a family doctor clinic. Also, in a high-end sit-down restaurant, the taste of the food is still important, but the quality of the personal service is at least as important.

The different characteristics of professional services, service shops, and mass services are summarized in Exhibit 6-11. Professional services are those services that emphasize person-to-

exhibit 6-11 Characteristics of Service Organizations

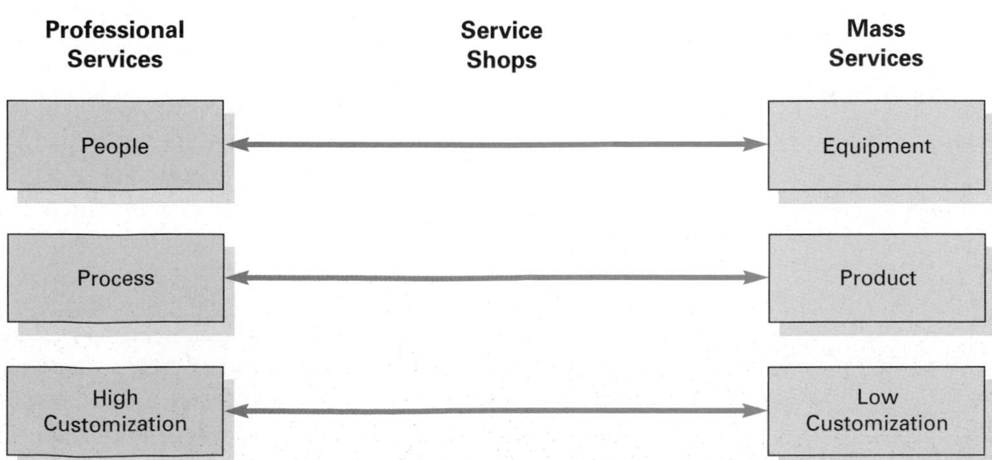

person delivery, that focus on the process of service delivery rather than the creation of some final, tangible product, and that are highly customized. Mass services are those services that rely on equipment more than people in delivering the service, that result in the customer taking away a tangible product, and that do little, if any, tailoring to individual customer needs. Service shops provide a mixture of the three dimensions of people/equipment, process/product, and high/low customization.

Cost Management in a Service Organization

As we saw earlier in the chapter in our discussion of cost management in manufacturing and merchandising organizations, it is important for an organization to evaluate the magnitude of its costs and the degree to which it is efficiently utilizing its resources. We looked at cost and profitability measures, as well as at indicators of inventory management (such as inventory turnover). The same two concepts—evaluation of profitability and efficiency—will be used in developing cost management tools for services organizations.

The magnitude of an organization's costs can be evaluated in at least three ways. First, the trend in the costs over time can be examined. For example, back in Exhibit 6-4, we evaluated the performance of Broyman Furniture by looking at the patterns in its monthly production cost numbers. Second, actual costs can be compared to budgeted costs. Preparation and use of cost budgets were discussed at length in Chapter 5 of management accounting. Finally, the magnitude of a cost can be evaluated by comparing it to the associated revenue. For example, as part of our evaluation of the sale of Burzee Dolls by Kids N Toys and Child's Delight, we looked at the gross margin (retail sales less wholesale cost of goods sold). In our illustration of cost management in a service organization in this section, we will use this latter approach of comparing costs to revenues in order to evaluate costs. Remember, however, that time-series cost trends and comparison of budgeted costs to actual costs can also be used.

For a manufacturing organization, key resources used in the production process are raw materials, machine hours, factory space, and labor. For a merchandising organization, the management of the level of inventory is crucial to the efficient use of the organization's resources. For a service organization, the management of materials inventories, building space, and equipment usage is also important. However, to emphasize the importance of people in service organizations, our illustration in this chapter will identify one way in which a service organization can measure the degree to which it is efficiently using its people.

Illustration: Cost Management in an Audit Firm

A large audit firm is a good example of a professional services organization. Actually, an "audit" firm is better characterized as being a professional services firm in the businesses of advising companies on how to improve their operating systems and processes; providing specialized accounting, tax, and information systems consulting; and conducting audits of financial statements. In fact, the broad-based nature of the services provided by audit firms has gotten them into a bit of trouble with the Securities and Exchange Commission (SEC)—in November 2000, the SEC adopted new regulations restricting the type of consulting services that an audit firm can provide to a company that it also audits.

The illustration in this section is for the hypothetical audit firm of LeviForrester. This illustration will center on the audit services offered in one large regional office of the firm. The office employs approximately 200 professionals and another 100 support staff. We will examine the costs associated with the professionals in the office. The costs of the support staff, as well as the training, recruiting, marketing, and technical analysis costs charged to the regional office by the national headquarters of LeviForrester, are also very important to the overall profitability of the regional office. However, assigning these support costs and national charges to specific jobs is quite difficult. The task of identifying cost drivers, common costs, and other concepts important to the proper treatment of these indirect support costs will be undertaken in Chapter 7 of management accounting, where we discuss activity-based costing. For the example in this chapter, we will restrict our attention to personnel costs that can be directly traced to specific client engagements.

The regional office of LeviForrester employs five types of professionals, as listed below.

	Average Years of Service with the Firm	Number of Professionals in the Office
Partner	More than 12 years	10
Senior manager	9 to 12 years	15
Manager	6 to 8 years	20
Senior	3 to 5 years	50
Staff	1 to 2 years	100

The partners exercise overall oversight of the audit practice. They review and approve the supporting documents (in electronic form) for each audit. They also seek to build the business by finding new clients. One of the 10 partners is designated the "managing partner" and is responsible for running the office and setting the strategic direction for the practice in that area. The senior managers and the managers are the professionals who are the primary interface between the audit firm and the clients. These managers keep the client informed about the progress of the audit and also supervise the other members of the audit team (the seniors and staff). The seniors spend much of their time at the clients' offices supervising and performing the actual work of the audit. The staff accountants do the bulk of the routine work of the audit.

Partners are expected to spend about half of their time working on specific client jobs during the year. This works out to be 1,000 hours out of the potential 2,000 working hours (50 weeks × 40 hours per week) during the year. At other times, partners are cultivating new client relationships and making proposals in order to get new client engagements. Senior managers and managers are expected to spend 75% of their time working on specific client engagements; seniors and staff are expected to spend all of their time working on specific client engagements. In fact, an important responsibility within the audit firm is the planning of the demands of various audit engagements to make sure that all of the seniors and the staff are always scheduled for specific engagements and are not sitting around the main office because of "unassigned" time.

These expectations about how much of a professional's time is to be spent in serving specific clients are used to develop billing rates and job cost charges. The computation of these billing rates and job cost charges is shown in Exhibit 6-12. The job cost charges are computed as a professional's total annual compensation divided by the number of client hours to be worked during a year. For example, a partner's annual compensation is $400,000, and each partner is expected to work on specific client engagements for 1,000 hours during a year. Thus, the partner compensation cost assigned to a job is $400 per hour ($400,000 ÷ 1,000 hours). These job cost charges are used by LeviForrester to compute the professional labor cost associated with each audit engagement.

exhibit 6-12 Billing Rates and Job Cost Charges for LeviForrester

	Annual Compensation	Expected Billable Hours	Compensation Cost per Billable Hour	Client Billing Rate per Billable Hour
Partner	$400,000	1,000	$400	$500
Senior manager	130,000	1,500	87	300
Manager	100,000	1,500	67	225
Senior	50,000	2,000	25	150
Staff	40,000	2,000	20	100

The billing rates are used in computing how much is to be charged to a client for an audit engagement. As explained in Chapter 3 of management accounting, the billing rate for professional services is large enough to cover both the payment to the professional and general administrative costs such as secretarial support, computers, supplies, travel, and so forth. LeviForrester's billing rates for each type of professional are shown in Exhibit 6-12. As you can imagine, the determination of these billing rates is an extremely important element in LeviForrester's success. Billing rates that are too high will drive away potential customers whereas billing rates that are too low will lead to low profitability and, perhaps, the inability to appropriately compensate the professionals.

On October 5, the managing partner for the regional office of LeviForrester received the profitability report contained in Exhibit 6-13. The report is generated in early October because LeviForrester's fiscal year ends on September 30—it is impossible for LeviForrester to analyze its own business operations at the end of the normal calendar year because January is the busiest month of the year for audit firms as they perform audit work for their clients with December 31 year-ends. The managing partner used the data in the profitability report to compute profit percentage from professionals (PPP), which is the fundamental measure of profitability used by LeviForrester. PPP is computed as follows:

$$\begin{aligned} \text{PPP} &= (\text{Revenue} - \text{Professional compensation cost}) \div \text{Revenue} \\ &= (\$60{,}975{,}000 - \$14{,}450{,}000) \div \$60{,}975{,}000 \\ &= 76.3\% \end{aligned}$$

The managing partner is quite pleased with this report because the firm-wide goal for PPP is just 73.0%. As the various regional offices within LeviForrester are evaluated, each region's PPP is used to allocate a firm-wide bonus pool—the professionals in regions with PPP in excess of 73.0% can expect to receive higher-than-average year-end bonuses.

The managing partner also received the personnel utilization report contained in Exhibit 6-14. The report contains personnel utilization rates (PUR) for each category of professional within the firm. The contents of this report are somewhat disturbing. The managing partner sees that the partners in the office spent only 82.0% of the time that they should have on specific client engagements. In addition, the hours billed by managers, seniors, and staff accountants were well in excess of 100% of the expected amount. This personnel utilization pattern suggests at least two potential future problems. First, existing clients may become concerned that the LeviForrester partners are not spending as much time with them as they had anticipated. The clients may feel that the LeviForrester partners are now spending too much time finding new clients and not enough time attending to the needs of the existing clients. Second, the high utilization rates for the managers, seniors, and staff are a warning sign that these key professionals may be being worked too hard. Hiring and training new professionals is an expensive process, and LeviForrester does not want to overwork its young professionals, resulting in abnormally high employee turnover.

exhibit 6-13 Profitability Report for LeviForrester

	Number of Professionals	Actual Billable Hours	Billing Rate	Total Revenue	Total Compensation Cost
Partners	10	8,200	$500	$ 4,100,000	$ 4,000,000
Senior managers . .	15	20,000	300	6,000,000	1,950,000
Managers.	20	35,000	225	7,875,000	2,000,000
Seniors.	50	120,000	150	18,000,000	2,500,000
Staff.	100	250,000	100	25,000,000	4,000,000
Total.				$60,975,000	$14,450,000

exhibit 6-14 Personnel Utilization Report for LeviForrester

	Actual Billable	Budgeted Billable	Utilization Rate
Partners	8,200	10,000	82.0%
Senior managers	20,000	22,500	88.9%
Managers	35,000	30,000	116.7%
Seniors	120,000	100,000	120.0%
Staff	250,000	200,000	125.0%

The two specific measures used in this example—PPP and PUR—are intended only as illustrations; measures with these specific names are not in use in any real professional services firm. However, measures similar to these are very commonly used in service organizations. These two measures are representative of a broad class of measures that indicate the performance of service organizations on two important dimensions—profitability and personnel utilization.

to summarize

Three broad types of service organizations are professional services, service shops, and mass services. The dimensions on which these types of organizations differ are people/equipment, process/product, and high/low customization. As with manufacturing and merchandising organizations, it is important to measure both profitability and resource utilization in a service organization. In a professional services firm, profitability is measured by comparing the service revenues with the compensation costs associated with the professionals. It is also important to monitor the degree to which the professionals are appropriately utilized within the firm.

expanded material

As mentioned earlier in the chapter, an important element of cost management is the evaluation of whether an organization is utilizing its resources efficiently. In the expanded material section of this chapter, you will learn further details about resource management. In particular, the expanded material discusses ways to determine the appropriate level of inventory that should be maintained by an organization.

5

Calculate and interpret holding costs in merchandising and service businesses.

OPPORTUNITY COSTS IN MANAGING INVENTORY AND WORK-IN-PROCESS SERVICES

Let's return to our Burzee Doll example to discuss opportunity costs involved in managing inventory. As discussed in Chapter 1 in management accounting, there are many types of costs involved in managing an organization. All the costs that we discussed in the management accounting report for Kids N Toys and Child's Delight involved out-of-pocket costs (see Exhibit 6-10). However, there are several cost issues listed in Exhibit 6-7 that we did not include in the earlier analysis for these two companies. For example, inventory flexibility involves potential opportunity costs related to investing in a lot of inventory. Kids N Toys tied up a lot of money in securing 50,000 Burzee Dolls for the Christmas season—a shopping season that is particularly critical for retailers in the United States. Kids N Toys may have been fortunate that the Burzee Doll line sold as well as it did. If fickle shopper tastes had turned instead to another toy, it would have been difficult for Kids N Toys to shift this part of its inventory investment out of Burzee Dolls and into an alternative item in time to take advantage of the Christmas shopping rush. Kids N Toys may not have had any real problems in this area, but it needs to pay attention to this issue in planning for next year.

Child's Delight was also exposed to some opportunity costs. For example, because it kept its inventory of Burzee Dolls much lower than its competitor, Child's Delight was much more at risk of losing sales due to problems with supplier delivery and other logistics beyond its control. We'll assume in this case that all its deliveries were on time and without problems. However, another opportunity cost that Child's Delight was clearly not so fortunate in avoiding was lost sales due to lack of inventory. During the same period of time that Child's Delight sold its 19,850 dolls, Kids N Toys sold 41,500 dolls. If these retailers were at all similar in terms of competitive factors such as location and advertising, then it appears certain that Child's Delight could have sold more dolls *if* it had had more dolls! How many more dolls could have been sold? Frankly, this is a very difficult number to measure—even for a good management accountant. You won't see it measured on any of the management accounting reports in this chapter. That does not at all imply that this number is less important than the others. There is a lot of discussion (and disagreement) on how to measure this number. The important thing is to somehow make decision makers aware of this cost. However, there is so much disagreement in practice as to how to specifically calculate this number that it is best in a textbook such as this to simply make you aware of this particular opportunity cost issue.

Holding Costs and Economic Profit in Merchandising Organizations

economic profit The difference between net operating profit and holding costs of inventory and other asset investments. Note that generally accepted accounting principles (GAAP) do not formally recognize opportunity costs such as holding costs.

cost of capital The weighted-average cost of a firm's debt and equity capital equals the rate of return that a company must earn in order to satisfy the demands of its owners and creditors.

Another opportunity cost that both companies in our example experienced is financial holding costs. Financial holding costs are very well defined in practice. We'll use this cost to calculate for these two merchants a third income number called **economic profit**. As we calculated before, during the three-month period of November, December, and January, Kids N Toys had an average of $250,000 invested in Burzee Doll inventory. (See pages 309–311 if you need help remembering how to calculate average inventory levels.) This money could alternatively have been earning money in a financial investment, or it could have been used to pay off loans or retire stock that Kids N Toys currently has outstanding. Every business has a **cost of capital** that relates to its cost of using money. In fact, you likely have your own individual cost of capital. Do you have any loans? What is the average interest rate on those loans? Let's assume it is 15%. Hopefully, you understand that as long as you have loans, every dollar you use for anything besides paying down your loan(s) costs you 15%. This 15% rate is your cost of capital. To be specific, for every dollar you spend buying a new stereo system, your loan(s) will increase by $0.15 at the end of the year. Hence, buying the stereo had better be worth this implicit financial holding cost. Even if you don't have any loans, you probably (hopefully!) have a savings account. Your cost of capital would then be the interest rate on your investment in the savings account. Let's assume you get a 4% return on your account. In this case, for every dollar you delay putting into the account (such as money spent on your new stereo), at the end of the year, your account will be $0.04 less than it could have been. Obviously, this cost information is important to all decisions involving the investment of limited resources. The formula to calculate a financial holding cost is the same approach traditionally used to calculate interest costs. We'll assume that the cost of capital for both Kids N Toys and Child's Delight is 20%. The financial holding cost of the average Burzee Doll inventory investment for Kids N Toys can be calculated in the following manner:

Financial holding cost = Average investment × Annual rate × Number of periods
$250,000 × 20% × 3/12 year = $12,500

The financial holding cost for Child's Delight can also be calculated. Remember, we calculated earlier that Child's Delight had a much lower average investment in inventory. In addition, this company's investment in Burzee Dolls lasted only for two months—November and December. As a result, its financial holding cost was much lower than Kids N Toys and is calculated as follows:

$33,750 × 20% × 2/12 year = $1,125

The financial holding cost is as much a cost of being in the business of selling Burzee Dolls as any other cost we calculated and listed earlier in Exhibit 6-10. Most accountants recognize that measuring financial holding costs is important to managing the economic well-being of the organization. Hence, in Exhibit 6-15 we have expanded the original management accounting report on the Burzee Doll inventory to include financial holding costs in order to calculate the organization's economic profit.

Before we leave this example and move on to discuss holding costs in service organizations, take one more opportunity to compare the gross margin report in Exhibit 6-9 and the management accounting report in Exhibit 6-15. These two merchandising reports would look basically the same regardless of whether Child's Delight and Kids N Toys were retailers or wholesalers of toys. You should now have a pretty clear understanding of how dramatically

exhibit 6-15 Expanded Management Accounting Report on the Burzee Doll Inventory

In addition to cost of purchases, note the following additional inventory costs:

- Average inventory overhead costs are $1.10 per unit per month.
- Average costs to initiate and receive a purchase order are $1,250 per event.
- Average costs of capital are 20%.

	Kids N Toys, Inc.		Child's Delight, Inc.	
Expected revenue	50,000 units × $30 standard price	$1,500,000	20,000 units × $30 standard price	$ 600,000
Shrinkage loss	1,600 units × $30	(48,000)	150 units × $30	(4,500)
Market loss	2,000 units × ($30 − $10) + 4,400 units × ($30 − $3)	(158,800)		(0)
Actual revenue		$1,293,200		$ 595,500
Purchase costs	50,000 units × $10 standard cost	(500,000)	20,000 units × $10 standard cost	(200,000)
Lost discount		(0)	20,000 units × $2 lost discount	(40,000)
Price increase		(0)	10,000 units × $3 price increase	(30,000)
Gross margin		$ 793,200		$ 325,500
Overhead costs	50,000 units ÷ 2 = 25,000 average inventory level × $1.10 × 3 months	(82,500)	5,000 units ÷ 2 = 2,500 average inventory level × $1.10 × 2 months	(5,500)
Order costs	1 order × $1,250	(1,250)	4 orders × $1,250	(5,000)
Net operating profit		$ 709,450		$ 315,000
Holding costs	$500,000 in purchases ÷ 2 = $250,000 average inventory investment × 20% × 3/12 year	(12,500)	($60,000 + $60,000 + $75,000 + $75,000) ÷ 4 = $67,500 average purchase ÷ 2 = $33,750 average inventory investment × 20% × 2/12 year	(1,125)
Economic profit		$ 696,950		$ 313,875

segment Any part of an organization requiring separate reports for evaluation by management.

Economic Value Added (EVA®) A commercialized performance measurement system that emphasizes the incremental profits an organization creates over and above the profit required to cover the costs of capital.

management accounting can differ from financial accounting in analyzing results of merchandising organizations. It is also important to point out that the reports in Exhibits 6-9 and 6-15 are both **segment** reports that are specific to inventory lines in these companies. A complete net operating profit analysis of all operations at either company should obviously include revenues and costs that are specific to all other inventory lines and overhead costs that are common across the organization (for example, the salaries for company executives). A complete economic profit analysis (sometimes called an **Economic Value Added** or **EVA™**) would include a "holding cost" on all assets belonging to the company (cash, investments, equipment, buildings, land, etc.).

Service Organizations and Holding Costs

Something you should realize about GAAP and the service industry is that there typically has *not* been nearly as much emphasis on measuring and reporting work-in-process costs as compared to the manufacturing industry. However, it is important that the management accountant support the management process by reporting on the costs invested in work-in-process services. Think about the economic facts of work-in-process services for a moment. What do these costs represent? They represent significant investments in services provided to a client that typically have yet to provide any kind of a ROI in terms of cash receipts. Work in process is obviously necessary in many service companies. However, service companies cannot allow work-in-process services to build up in their organizations without restraint. Otherwise, resources are tied up that could otherwise be used to provide additional salable services. These opportunity costs eventually reduce profits in the company. Doesn't this sound a lot like the same risk of holding costs we described for merchandising companies earlier in this section? Accountants can and should measure holding costs on large service projects. Such measures provide decision makers with the insight to assess the effects of not properly planning and controlling large service projects. For example, consider a large accounting firm that is planning an audit which is expected to take three months to complete. Suppose that by the end of the three months, this large accounting firm has invested $400,000 in supplies, labor, and overhead for the audit project. Because most service companies have outstanding debts that are accruing interest costs or investment opportunities that have a measurable rate of return, these companies will incur a cost of capital just like merchants and manufacturers. If the accounting firm's cost of capital is 20%, the holding costs on this project are:

fyi

A study on cost accounting in the service industry reported that 65% of service companies have significant levels of work in process at the end of their reporting periods.

Average investment during the three-month period—($0 + $400,000) ÷ 2 = $200,000
Holding cost—$200,000 × 20% × 3/12 months = $10,000

What if the accounting firm has not completed the audit at the end of three months? At this point, it appears that the audit will require another month and another $40,000 in costs to complete. What are the additional holding costs of this extra month?

Average investment during the fourth month—($400,000 + $440,000) ÷ 2 = $420,000
Additional holding cost—$420,000 × 20% × 1/12 months = $7,000[5]

Computing and understanding these cost data provide a lot of incentive for the audit manager to complete the job and collect fees as quickly as possible. In providing these data, the accountant is supporting good planning and control of work in process in the audit service process.

5 Note that ($440,000 ÷ 2) × 20% × (4/12) < $10,000 + $7,000. This is because the costs on this audit contract are building much faster in the first three months ($400,000 in three months) than in the last month ($40,000 in one month). Similarly, using $400,000 ÷ 2 assumes that the $400,000 in costs is growing evenly over the three-month period ($133,333 per month). A more accurate method of computing the total holding costs for the four-month period would involve calculating and summing the holding costs for each individual month.

to summarize

Both merchandising and service firms often experience several types of opportunity costs, such as lost sales due to not having enough inventory or delays in completing work in process for customers. These costs are extremely difficult to measure. One important category of opportunity costs that management accountants can measure is financial holding costs, which is a measure of the costs of having money tied up in inventory (for merchants) or in work-in-process services (for service companies). Measuring holding costs requires that the company's cost of capital first be identified. The holding cost formula is Average investment in inventory or Work-in-process services × Annual rate × Number of periods. Financial holding costs can be deducted from net operating profit to measure economic profit for a particular product line.

6

Use classic quantitative tools in inventory management (economic order quantity, reorder point, and safety stock).

QUANTITATIVE INVENTORY MANAGEMENT METHODS

We have spent a lot of time in this chapter discussing the many types of costs involved in managing inventory for merchants. These issues are listed in Exhibit 6-7. Generally, service companies do not carry significant levels of inventory and do not need to pay as much attention to inventory management costs. However, many manufacturing companies carry significant inventory levels of raw materials, work in process, and finished goods. These companies need to pay attention to issues involved in managing costs of carrying too much versus too little inventory. The primary question here is, "How much inventory should a company have?" This section will describe some quantitative methods that can be useful to accountants working to answer this question. We will use the example of a merchandising company to illustrate these methods; however, these inventory management calculations are equally applicable to manufacturing companies.

economic order quantity (EOQ) A specific calculation used to determine the most cost-effective size of a purchase order. The EOQ balances the costs of placing an order against the costs of carrying inventory in the organization.

Economic Order Quantity

It is a significant challenge to balance the costs (in Exhibit 6-7) of carrying too much inventory against the costs of carrying too little inventory. Determining how much inventory a company should have involves two important issues: (1) knowing *how much* inventory to order and (2) knowing *when* to place the inventory order. One well-known method used to handle the first issue is the **economic order quantity (EOQ)**. In calculating the optimal size of an inventory order, the EOQ attempts to balance the costs of carrying inventory (e.g., overhead costs, holding costs, risk of lost market values, shrinkage, etc.) against the costs involved in purchasing inventory.

caution

It is important that you understand that the purchase costs used to calculate the EOQ are *not* the inventory purchase prices, but the overhead costs involved in handling a purchase order (e.g., preparing purchase orders, receiving and inspecting shipments, initiating payment for purchases, etc.).

We'll use the Burzee Doll example to demonstrate how to balance carrying costs and purchasing costs to calculate EOQ. First, we need to determine a cost per doll that includes all the costs of carrying Burzee Dolls during the two-month holiday buying season (November and December). Look back at Exhibit 6-15. Carrying costs should include the cost due to shrinkage loss, cost due to market loss, overhead costs, and holding costs. You should realize that combining all these carrying costs into a single cost per unit requires a great deal of analysis and intuition on the part of the accountant. However, let's assume that carrying costs are approximately $5 per doll. In addition, purchase order costs are $1,250 per order. Finally, we'll assume that a merchant can sell as many as 40,000 dolls during the holiday buying season. Exhibit 6-16 demonstrates one method of calculating EOQ using a cost schedule approach. As you can see, as the order quantity gets higher, the average inventory level in the store increases, and total carrying costs increase; in addition, the total purchase orders for the buying season are reduced, resulting in lower total ordering costs. By calculating the total of both carrying and ordering costs, the accountant can get a general idea of the optimal (i.e., economic) order quantity. According to the numbers in Exhibit 6-16, it appears that the store should request approximately 4,500 dolls for each of its nine orders during the buying season.

STOP & THINK Think about EOQ and the relationship between the costs of carrying inventory versus the costs involved in purchasing inventory. As costs of carrying inventory increase, should the organization increase or decrease the size of its purchase orders? As costs of purchasing inventory increase, should the organization increase or decrease the size of its purchase orders?

There is an alternative, and more precise, approach to calculating the EOQ using a formula (derived by calculus). Without working through the calculus derivation, the EOQ formula is:

$$EOQ = \sqrt{\frac{2QP}{C}}$$

Q = The market demand in units for the period
P = The overhead cost of placing one order
C = The total carrying cost for one unit for the period

By inserting our Burzee Doll data into the EOQ formula, we can calculate the precise EOQ as follows:

$$EOQ = \sqrt{\frac{2(40{,}000)(\$1{,}250)}{\$5}} = \sqrt{\frac{\$100{,}000{,}000}{\$5}} = \sqrt{20{,}000{,}000} = 4{,}472 \text{ dolls}$$

Now that we have the EOQ, we can calculate the following exact costs:

Total carrying costs = 4,472 ÷ 2 = 2,236 average inventory × \$5 = \$11,180
Total ordering costs = 40,000 ÷ 4,472 = 9 orders × \$1,250 = \$11,250
Total inventory management costs = \$11,180 + \$11,250 = \$22,430

Using the EOQ formula is much faster and more precise than working through an EOQ cost schedule. With the EOQ, we can resolve the first of two important issues involved in determining how much inventory a company should have—knowing *how much* inventory to order. Now we will turn our attention to the second issue—knowing *when* to place the inventory order.

exhibit 6-16 Calculating EOQ Using a Cost Schedule

Base data:

- Total market demand for dolls for the period: 40,000 dolls
- Average carrying cost per doll for the period: \$5
- Average overhead costs per purchase order: \$1,250

Order Quantity	**1,500**	**2,250**	**3,000**	**3,750**	**4,500**	**5,250**	**6,000**	**6,750**
	÷ 2	÷ 2	÷ 2	÷ 2	÷ 2	÷ 2	÷ 2	÷ 2
Average inventory level	750	1,125	1,500	1,875	2,250	2,625	3,000	3,375
× Carrying cost	\$ 5	\$ 5	\$ 5	\$ 5	\$ 5	\$ 5	\$ 5	\$ 5
Total Carrying Costs	**\$ 3,750**	**\$ 5,625**	**\$ 7,500**	**\$ 9,375**	**\$11,250**	**\$13,125**	**\$15,000**	**\$16,875**
Total demand	40,000	40,000	40,000	40,000	40,000	40,000	40,000	40,000
÷ by Order quantity	1,500	2,250	3,000	3,750	4,500	5,250	6,000	6,750
Number of orders (rounded up)	27	18	14	11	9	8	7	6
× Costs per order	\$ 1,250	\$ 1,250	\$ 1,250	\$ 1,250	\$ 1,250	\$ 1,250	\$ 1,250	\$ 1,250
Total Ordering Costs	**\$33,750**	**\$22,500**	**\$17,500**	**\$13,750**	**\$11,250**	**\$10,000**	**\$ 8,750**	**\$ 7,500**
Total Costs	**\$37,500**	**\$28,125**	**\$25,000**	**\$23,125**	**\$22,500**	**\$23,125**	**\$23,750**	**\$24,375**

Reorder Point and Safety Stock

Knowing *when* to place the inventory order involves the reorder point and the desired safety stock. Assume for a moment that you are the manager of the Kids N Toys store. Now that you have calculated the EOQ, you need to know exactly when to place your order. You don't want to reorder Burzee Dolls too soon, or you'll end up with more inventory on hand than you need. This will result in unnecessary overhead costs, holding costs, and possibly increased inventory shrinkage. On the other hand, if you wait until you're nearly out of dolls before you place the order, you'll probably run out of inventory before the next shipment arrives. This will result in lost sales—a serious opportunity cost. Walking through your store, you watch the levels of dolls on your shelves and in your storeroom decline as customers make purchases. In terms of level of Burzee Doll inventory, at what point do you place your next order? Essentially, you need to calculate a **reorder point**. The calculation is quite simple:

reorder point The point at which the inventory level in the organization drops low enough to trigger a new purchase order.

Reorder point = Average lead time in days × Average daily sales

Lead time, in this case, is the time between when store management initiates a purchase order and when the inventory is finally delivered and ready for sale. Lead time for Burzee Dolls would include the time it takes for Kids N Toys to process any necessary paperwork to initiate the purchase order, for the distributor to process the purchase order and deliver the goods, and for Kids N Toys to receive and prepare the dolls for aisle display. Let's assume that lead time for the Burzee Doll is three days. Further, Kids N Toys sells, on average, 800 dolls per day. The reorder point calculation is:

Reorder point = 3 days × 800 dolls = 2,400 dolls

When the inventory falls to 2,400 dolls, you need to initiate a new purchase order. By the time the order arrives, the store should be selling its last doll.

At this point, a couple of things about this reorder point number may be bothering you. One possible problem is that the reorder point calculation is assuming a perfect world. In other words, the reorder point calculation shown assumes that sales are *always* 800 dolls per day and that the lead time is *always* three days. A sudden surge in customer demand or any problems in order processing or shipping could result in empty shelves. As manager for Kids N Toys, you may think you should build a little cushion into your reorder point calculation to allow for any unexpected problems. This is the purpose of **safety stock**. The calculation of the amount of safety stock has two parts: (1) to handle possible problems in the reorder process and (2) to handle an unexpected spike in sales demand. Let's assume that problems in the reorder process could result in a maximum lead time of four days. Further, as many as 875 dolls could sell in one day. The safety stock calculation would be as follows:

safety stock The minimal level of inventory required to ensure against the organization running out of inventory in the case of unforeseen problems in receiving its next purchase order.

Maximum lead time	4 days	
Average lead time in days	3 days	
Surplus	1 day	
Average expected sales per day	× 800 dolls	
Safety stock for reorder problem		800 dolls
Maximum expected sales per day	875 dolls	
Average expected sales per day	800 dolls	
Surplus	75 dolls	
Maximum lead time	× 4 days	
Safety stock for demand changes		300 dolls
Total safety stock		1,100 dolls

Based on these numbers, Kids N Toys will always want to keep at least 1,100 dolls on hand to handle unexpected situations involving either its suppliers or its customers. Hence, this safety stock number should be added to the original reorder point calculation, resulting in a new reorder point calculation that includes a cushion for safety stock:

caution

Perhaps you've heard of the saying "Garbage in, garbage out!" The quality of these three quantitative inventory management models (like all decision models and systems in business) is only as good as the quality of the information that is used in the calculations. Before using the EOQ, reorder point, or safety stock calculations, the accountant needs to be sure that all costs and risks of carrying and ordering inventory are understood. Current JIT thinking suggests that accountants in the past may have severely understated the costs of carrying inventory, resulting in unnecessarily large inventory orders and high levels of inventory in the organization.

Reorder point with safety stock = (Average lead time in days × Average daily sales) + Safety stock
= (3 days × 800 dolls) + 1,100 dolls = 3,500 dolls

You've likely noticed that the reorder point calculation that includes safety stock can be directly calculated as:

Reorder point with safety stock = Maximum lead time in days × Maximum daily sales
= 4 days × 875 dolls = 3,500 dolls

Combining these two calculations into one simple calculation is acceptable, assuming that management is not interested in knowing the specific level for safety stock. Usually, though, store management wants to know when sales are eating into the safety stock. Such a situation signals that special attention is needed to ensure that the store does not run out of stock and miss some customer sales. Exhibit 6-17 graphically depicts these relationships.

to summarize

Balancing costs of carrying too much inventory against the costs of carrying too little inventory is a significant challenge for accountants in both merchandising and manufacturing organizations. The economic order quantity, reorder point, and safety stock calculations can help. Exhibit 6-17 graphically summarizes the relationship between EOQ, reorder points, and safety stock inventory levels. Consider Exhibit 6-17 in light of the inventory management issues in Exhibit 6-7. The EOQ model is a useful tool for managing carrying costs (e.g., overhead costs, holding costs, losses

exhibit 6-17 Graphical Display of EOQ, Reorder Points, and Safety Stock Inventory Levels

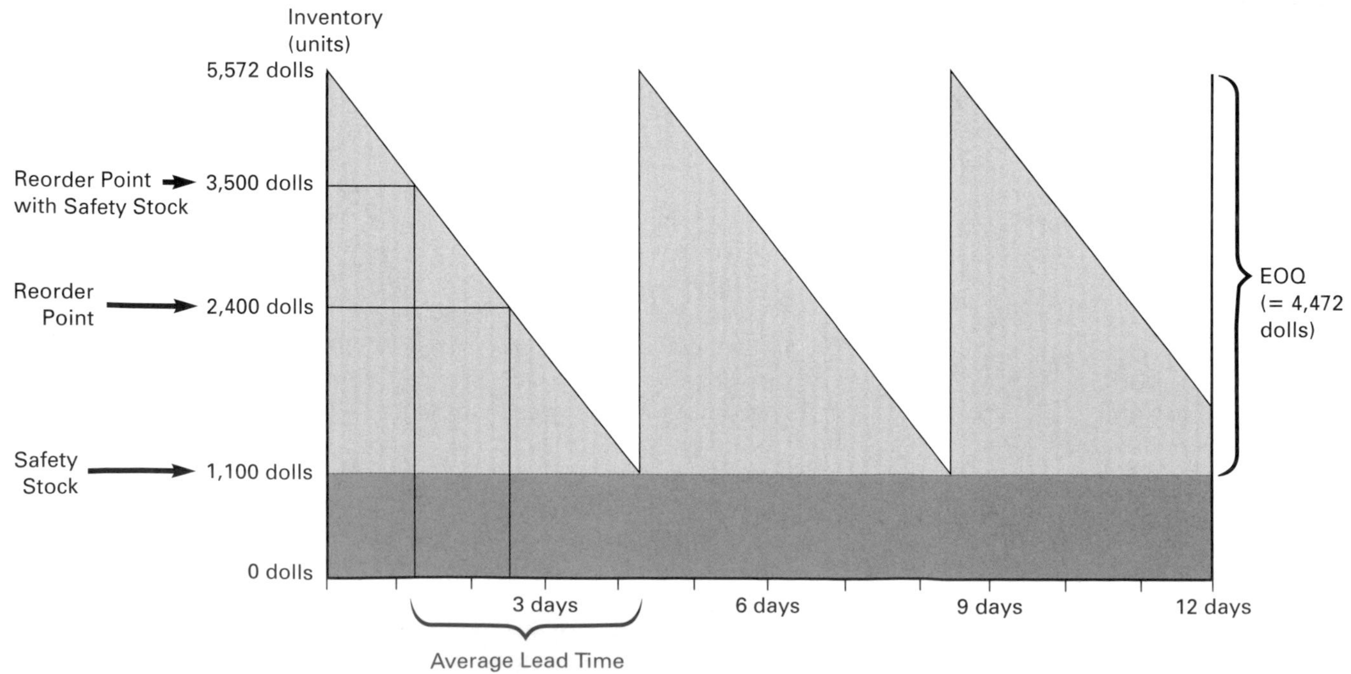

due to decreased market value, and the cost of inventory shrinkage). The EOQ model balances these carrying costs against ordering costs. In addition, the EOQ should be combined with intelligent calculations of reorder points and safety stock in order to guard against excessive risk of lost sales due to delivery problems and fluctuating market demand.

---

review of learning objectives

1 Outline the different cost flow patterns in manufacturing, merchandising, and service organizations and understand how these costs are reflected in the income statement and balance sheet. Both manufacturing and service organizations maintain substantial production processes. As a result, both types of organizations report work-in-process inventory in the balance sheet. In addition, the computation of cost of goods sold can be quite complex for these types of organizations because the computation involves combining information about materials, labor, and overhead costs. The computation of cost of goods sold in a merchandising organization is relatively simple because inventory is purchased in its final form and no substantial additional costs are incurred in getting it ready to sell. Both manufacturing and merchandising organizations maintain significant levels of ending inventory that are reported in the balance sheet.

2 Interpret a cost of goods manufactured schedule and analyze the levels of raw materials, work-in-process, and finished goods inventories in a manufacturing organization. Manufacturing costs are summarized on a cost of goods manufactured schedule. The total manufacturing cost for a period is the sum of the direct materials and direct labor costs incurred, as well as an addition for the amount of overhead applied to the goods in production during the period. The cost of goods manufactured is the cost of goods completed and transferred out of work-in-process inventory during the period. The cost of goods manufactured is added to the beginning finished goods inventory to determine cost of goods available for sale. Ending finished goods inventory is then subtracted from this number to compute cost of goods sold. Inventory turnover measures can be used to evaluate the levels of raw materials, work-in-process, and finished goods inventories. The level of raw materials inventory is compared to the amount of materials used during the period. Work-in-process inventory is compared to the total manufacturing costs incurred during the period. The level of finished goods inventory is compared to the cost of goods sold during the period.

3 Understand how merchants manage cost information in their organizations. Because merchants basically purchase inventory in a finished state, the process of accounting for inventory in a merchandising business is not nearly as complicated as it is in a manufacturing business. There are a number of important issues associated with managing the inventory in order to maximize sales and minimize a variety of inventory costs. For example, having too much inventory creates unnecessary overhead costs, financial holding costs, costs due to loss of market value, and costs due to inventory shrinkage. Not having enough inventory may result in unnecessary ordering costs and loss of bulk order discounts, as well as opportunity costs due to lost sales and increased supplier prices. Measuring these costs allows management accountants to prepare detailed cost reports that support effective management of gross margins and net operating profits for individual product lines.

4 Measure profitability and personnel utilization in a service organization. Like a manufacturing organization, a service organization involves a substantial process before delivering a final product to the customer. Three types of service organizations are professional services, service shops, and mass services. Professional service firms emphasize people-to-people service over automation, the delivery of a process rather than a final tangible product, and high customization. A mass service organization emphasizes the standardized, automated delivery of a tangible product. Service organizations, similar to manufacturing and merchandising organizations, must measure profitability and resource utilization. A professional services firm uses profitability measures based on a comparison of revenues to the compensation cost of the professionals. Personnel utilization can be measured by comparing the number of billable hours actually worked to the number that was expected.

expanded material

5 Calculate and interpret holding costs in merchandising and service businesses. Although opportunity costs can be extremely difficult to measure, one important type of opportunity cost that accountants can measure is financial holding costs. Financial holding costs measure the costs of having money tied up in inventory (for merchants) or in work-in-process services (for service companies). Measuring holding costs requires that the company's cost of capital first be identified. The holding cost formula is Average investment in inventory or work-in-process services × Annual rate × Number of periods. Financial holding costs can be deducted from net operating profit to measure economic profit for a particular product line. Measuring economic profit for an entire company is sometimes called Economic Value Added (EVA™).

6 Use classic quantitative tools in inventory management (economic order quantity, reorder point, and safety stock). Both merchandising and manufacturing organizations have significant investments in inventory costs. Accountants can balance the costs of carrying too much inventory against the costs of carrying too little inventory by calculating the economic order quantity (EOQ), reorder point, and safety stock. The EOQ model is a useful tool for managing carrying costs (e.g., overhead costs, holding costs, losses due to decreased market value, and the costs of inventory shrinkage). The EOQ model balances these carrying costs against ordering costs. The EOQ is combined with reorder point and safety stock calculations in order to guard against excessive risk of lost sales due to delivery problems and fluctuating market demand.

key terms and concepts

cost of goods manufactured schedule 303
days in inventory 305
holding costs 307
inventory shrinkage 308
inventory turnover (stockturns) 305
lead time 308
net operating profit 312

expanded material

cost of capital 320
economic order quantity (EOQ) 323
economic profit 320
Economic Value Added (EVA) 322
reorder point 325
safety stock 325
segment 322

review problem

Cost Management in a Service Business

[Note: This Review Problem combines the cost flow accounting tools learned in Chapter 3 of management accounting with the service organization cost management skills learned in this chapter.]

Columbus & Hercules, a public accounting firm, is computing the overhead rates to use when billing customers and bidding on jobs. Columbus & Hercules provides the following estimates relating to overhead costs for the year 2003:

Utilities	$ 12,000
Rent	30,000
Equipment depreciation	22,000
Office supplies	20,000
Support staff salaries	120,000
Total estimated overhead costs	$204,000

In addition, Columbus & Hercules offers the following annual estimates (based on a 50-week work year) regarding the salaries and estimated hours associated with the professionals employed by the firm:

Position	Total Estimated Salaries	Total Estimated Billable Hours
Partners (2 × $100,000)	$200,000	4,400
Managers (3 × $70,000)	210,000	6,600
Seniors (6 × $50,000)	300,000	13,200
Staff auditors (10 × $25,000)	250,000	22,000

Columbus & Hercules computes a chargeable hourly rate for each position that is the sum of the following: (1) each position's hourly rate (based on salary), (2) an overhead rate, and (3) a markup of 20% of (1) and (2). The overhead rate allocates estimated overhead costs to each position, then relates the allocated costs to the hours expected to be worked by each position. Travel and materials costs are directly traceable and billed to each job.

Columbus & Hercules have no client projects in process on January 1, 2003. During January of 2003, Columbus & Hercules worked on several auditing and accounting jobs and incurred the following costs:

Jan. 1 Paid rent for January, $2,500.
4 Purchased office supplies on account, $1,200.
9 Paid $4,500 for payables from last year.
15 Paid office support salaries, $5,000.
15 Paid biweekly salaries of professionals: partners, $8,000; managers, $8,400; seniors, $12,000; staff, $10,000.
15 Applied overhead costs based on billable hours: partners, 170 hours; managers, 270 hours; seniors, 500 hours; staff, 900 hours.
18 Used office supplies totaling $800 to prepare client materials.
21 Purchased office supplies on account, $1,100.
25 Received and paid invoice from office supply store for purchase on January 4.
27 Billed clients for the following jobs using the computed hourly rate for each position:

	Job #1	Job #2
Partner	90 hours	80 hours
Manager	150 hours	140 hours
Senior	320 hours	200 hours
Staff	560 hours	400 hours

28 Transferred costs from Work-in-Process Services to Cost of Services based on information from January 27.
31 Estimated utility costs for the month of January to be $1,000.
31 Paid office support salaries, $5,400.
31 Made an adjusting entry for the depreciation of office equipment, $1,900.
31 Paid biweekly salaries of professionals: partners, $8,000; managers, $8,400; seniors, $12,000; staff, $10,000.
31 Applied overhead costs based on billable hours: partners, 180 hours; managers, 280 hours; seniors, 525 hours; staff, 950 hours.

During the month, the 10 staff accountants were assigned to one of the three managers for the entire month. Managers 1 and 2 were assigned three staff accountants each; Manager 3 was assigned four staff accountants. At the end of the month, the following staff utilization report was generated:

Staff Working for:	Budgeted Billable Hours	Actual Billable Hours
Manager 1	528	690
Manager 2	528	530
Manager 3	704	630
Total	1,760	1,850

Required:

1. Compute the billing rate to be used for each position.
2. Provide the journal entries made by Columbus & Hercules for January.
3. Compute the ending balance in Work-in-Process Services.

4. Compute the ending balance in Overhead.
5. Using the January 27 billing and cost data for Jobs 1 and 2 (combined), compute a profitability percentage for the jobs. The profitability percentage is computed as [(Revenue − Cost) ÷ Revenue]. Comment, given that the target profitability percentage is 23%.
6. Use the staff utilization numbers to evaluate the staff usage practices by the three managers.

Solution

1. Billing rate

Overhead allocation rate: $204,000 ÷ $960,000 = $0.2125 per dollar of salary.

Position	Estimated Salaries	Preliminary Rate	Allocated Overhead	Hours	Overhead Rate per Hour
Partner	$200,000	$0.2125	$ 42,500	4,400	$9.66
Manager	210,000	0.2125	44,625	6,600	6.76
Senior	300,000	0.2125	63,750	13,200	4.83
Staff	250,000	0.2125	53,125	22,000	2.41
Total	$960,000		$204,000		

Billable Rate for Each Position

Position	Hourly Rate (1)	Overhead Rate (2)	Markup [(1) + (2)] × 0.20 = (3)	Billable Rate (1) + (2) + (3)
Partner	$45.45[1]	$9.66	$11.02	$66.13
Manager	31.82[2]	6.76	7.72	46.30
Senior	22.73[3]	4.83	5.51	33.07
Staff	11.36[4]	2.41	2.75	16.52

[1] $200,000 ÷ 4,400 hours = $45.45 per hour.
[2] $210,000 ÷ 6,600 hours = $31.82 per hour.
[3] $300,000 ÷ 13,200 hours = $22.73 per hour.
[4] $250,000 ÷ 22,000 hours = $11.36 per hour.

2. Journal entries

Date	Account	Debit	Credit
Jan. 1	Overhead	2,500	
	Cash		2,500
	Paid rent for the month of January.		
4	Office Supplies	1,200	
	Accounts Payable		1,200
	Purchased office supplies on account.		
9	Accounts Payable	4,500	
	Cash		4,500
	Paid accounts payable from prior period.		
15	Overhead	5,000	
	Cash		5,000
	Paid office support salaries.		
15	Work-in-Process Services	38,400	
	Cash		38,400
	Paid salaries of professionals.		

Partners	$ 8,000
Managers	8,400
Seniors	12,000
Staff	10,000
Total	$38,400

Date	Account / Explanation	Detail	Debit	Credit
15	Work-in-Process Services		8,051	
	Overhead			8,051
	Allocated overhead based on billable hours.			
	Partners—170 hours × $9.66	$1,642		
	Managers—270 hours × $6.76	1,825		
	Seniors—500 hours × $4.83	2,415		
	Staff—900 hours × $2.41	2,169		
	Total	$8,051		
18	Work-in-Process Services		800	
	Office Supplies			800
	Used office supplies on behalf of clients.			
21	Office Supplies		1,100	
	Accounts Payable			1,100
	Purchased office supplies on account.			
25	Accounts Payable		1,200	
	Cash			1,200
	Paid for supplies purchased on Jan. 4.			
27	Accounts Receivable		57,724	
	Service Revenue			57,724
	Billed clients for Jobs #1 and #2.			
	Partners—170 hours × $66.13	$11,242		
	Managers—290 hours × $46.30	13,427		
	Seniors—520 hours × $33.07	17,196		
	Staff—960 hours × $16.52	15,859		
	Total	$57,724		
28	Cost of Services		48,107	
	Work-in-Process Services			48,107
	Transferred completed work in process to cost of services; comprised of each position's hourly rate and overhead rate.			
	Partners—170 hours × ($45.45 + $9.66)	$ 9,369		
	Managers—290 hours × ($31.82 + $6.76)	11,188		
	Seniors—520 hours × ($22.73 + $4.83)	14,331		
	Staff—960 hours × ($11.36 + $2.41)	13,219		
	Total	$48,107		
31	Overhead		1,000	
	Utilities Payable			1,000
	To record estimated utilities expense for the month.			
31	Overhead		5,400	
	Cash			5,400
	Paid office support salaries.			
31	Overhead		1,900	
	Accumulated Depreciation—Office Equipment			1,900
	To record depreciation expense for the month.			
31	Work-in-Process Services		38,400	
	Cash			38,400
	Paid salaries of professionals.			
	Partners	$ 8,000		
	Managers	8,400		
	Seniors	12,000		
	Staff	10,000		
	Total	$38,400		

31	Work-in-Process Services	8,458	
	Overhead		8,458

Allocated overhead based on billable hours.

Partners—180 hours × $9.66	$1,739
Managers—280 hours × $6.76	1,893
Seniors—525 hours × $4.83	2,536
Staff—950 hours × $2.41	2,290
Total	$8,458

3. Ending balance in Work-in-Process Services

Work-in-Process Services

1/15	38,400	1/28	48,107
1/15	8,051		
1/18	800		
1/31	38,400		
1/31	8,458		
End. bal.	46,002		

4. Ending balance in Overhead

Overhead

1/1	2,500	1/15	8,051
1/15	5,000	1/31	8,458
1/31	1,000		
1/31	5,400		
1/31	1,900		
		End. bal.	709

5. Profitability percentage

[($57,724 − $48,107) ÷ $57,724] = 16.7%

The profitability percentage for Jobs 1 and 2 is just 16.7%, compared to the target of 23.0%. Columbus & Hercules should look at two things. First, was there anything about the way the firm did business this month that would have caused its costs to be unusually high? Second, if the firm's business practices during the month were the same as usual, the client engagements for Jobs 1 and 2 should be reevaluated to determine whether Columbus & Hercules has underbid for the jobs.

6. Staff utilization ratios

Staff Working for:	Budgeted Billable Hours	Actual Billable Hours	Staff Utilization Ratio
Manager 1	528	690	130.7%
Manager 2	528	530	100.4%
Manager 3	704	630	89.5%

Manager 3 was given four staff accountants for the month; it is apparent that Manager 3 did not have enough work to keep all four of those individuals occupied for the entire month. In addition, Manager 1 may be putting an excessive workload on the staff assigned to him or her. Manager 1 should be reminded that good staff accountants are expensive to replace, and excessively long hours can cause them to look elsewhere for work.

discussion questions

1. What similarities are there in the inventories of a manufacturing and a merchandising organization? What are the differences?
2. What similarities are there in the inventories of a manufacturing and a service organization? What are the differences?
3. How does the work-in-process inventory in a manufacturing organization differ from that in a service organization?
4. What is represented by total manufacturing cost?
5. What is represented by total cost of goods manufactured?
6. Why is the total cost of goods sold number of limited usefulness for detailed internal decision making?
7. What amount is compared to the level of raw materials inventory in computing a useful measure of raw materials inventory turnover? Of work-in-process inventory turnover? Of finished goods inventory turnover?
8. Name three problems associated with carrying too much inventory.
9. Name three problems associated with carrying too little inventory.
10. What is inventory shrinkage? Name three things that can cause inventory shrinkage.
11. How can the ROI formula be used to evaluate the management of inventory?
12. What are the three basic types of service organizations?
13. The different types of service organizations vary in the emphasis they place on three dimensions. What are these three dimensions?
14. The same two concepts that underlie cost management in manufacturing and merchandising organizations are also used in developing cost management tools for service organizations. What are these two concepts?
15. What are three ways in which the magnitude of an organization's costs can be evaluated?

expanded material

16. What causes holding costs to exist? How is it that holding costs exist in the service industry, which typically does not have inventories?
17. What are the advantages of purchasing inventory in large quantities? What are the advantages of purchasing it in small quantities?
18. What are carrying costs in the denominator of the economic order quantity (EOQ) formula? How do large carrying costs affect the economic order quantity?
19. Explain the reasoning behind the reorder point formula, Reorder point = Lead time × Average daily sales.

discussion cases

CASE 6-1

BUYING INVENTORY FOR THE HOLIDAY SELLING SEASON

Ryan Baird owns a small retail shop. Historically, her annual sales have been about $250,000, with 60% of that coming in the holiday selling season of November and December. This year on a buying trip to southern China, Ryan discovered an item that she is certain will be in huge demand. The item is a mechanical cricket powered by a photovoltaic cell—the cricket automatically silences at night when it gets dark and then starts chirping in the morning when the sun's rays hit it. Ryan can buy the crickets from her Guangdong supplier for $1.00 each; she plans to sell them for $9.95 each.

Ryan is trying to decide how many of the crickets she should order. If she orders 30,000 or more, she can get a volume discount and pay just $0.80 each. However, she does not have room to store that many crickets, and she will have to rent storage space for $3,000 per month (three-month minimum). Also, the Guangdong supplier will only accept cash, and, because Ryan does not have very good credit, she will have to pay 17% annual interest on any money she borrows. She expects any loan to be outstanding for about two months.

Ryan has come to you for advice about whether she should buy a large quantity of crickets or play it safe and order just 10,000. What advice would you give her?

CASE 6-2

FINANCIAL HOLDING COSTS

You work in the accounting department of Cox Company. You are having a debate with one of your co-workers about holding costs. Your co-worker insists that holding costs should not be considered in making decisions because they do not involve any cash flows. He believes that cash flows are all that the business really cares about. How do you respond to him?

exercises

EXERCISE 6-1

TOTAL MANUFACTURING COSTS AND COST OF GOODS MANUFACTURED

The following information is for Kiev Derrald Company:

Manufacturing overhead (actual)	$100,000
Ending raw materials inventory	12,000
Manufacturing overhead (applied)	95,000
Beginning work-in-process inventory	55,000
Manufacturing overhead (applied)	40,000
Ending work-in-process inventory	47,000
Beginning raw materials inventory	10,000
Direct labor costs	60,000

1. Compute total manufacturing costs.
2. Compute cost of goods manufactured.

EXERCISE 6-2

TOTAL MANUFACTURING COSTS, COST OF GOODS MANUFACTURED, AND COST OF GOODS SOLD

The following information is for MTC Harry Company:

Beginning raw materials inventory	$ 25,000
Raw materials *used* in production as direct materials	110,000
Ending raw materials inventory	40,000
Manufacturing overhead (actual)	300,000
Beginning work-in-process inventory	150,000
Ending work-in-process inventory	180,000
Direct labor costs	95,000
Beginning finished goods inventory	71,000
Ending finished goods inventory	86,000
Underapplied manufacturing overhead	19,000

1. Compute total manufacturing costs.
2. Compute cost of goods manufactured.
3. Compute cost of goods sold.

EXERCISE 6-3

INVENTORY TURNOVER IN A MANUFACTURING COMPANY

The following information is for Pecos Yo Company:

Raw materials used during the year	$200,000
Ending raw materials inventory	25,000
Applied manufacturing overhead	350,000
Direct labor costs	100,000
Ending work-in-process inventory	60,000
Cost of goods sold	600,000
Ending finished goods inventory	40,000

Compute the following:

1. Inventory turnover for ending raw materials inventory.
2. Days' supply of raw materials in ending inventory.
3. Inventory turnover for ending work-in-process inventory.
4. Days of manufacturing represented by ending work-in-process inventory.
5. Inventory turnover for ending finished goods inventory.
6. Number of days' sales in ending finished goods inventory.

EXERCISE 6-4

INVENTORY TURNOVER IN A MERCHANDISING COMPANY

Beanie Company is a merchandising company. Beanie had the following financial data for the years 2002 and 2003:

	2003	2002
Revenues	$200,000	$180,000
Cost of goods sold	110,000	109,000
Gross margin	$ 90,000	$ 71,000
Inventory	$ 40,000	$ 50,000

Calculate Beanie Company's turnover for inventory for 2003 and explain what it means.

EXERCISE 6-5

INVENTORY TURNOVER IN A MERCHANDISING COMPANY

Both Dave and Kelly own auto parts stores. The following information is available for 2002 and 2003:

	Dave	Kelly
Revenue		
2002	$150,000	$300,000
2003	130,000	350,000
Ending inventory		
2002	75,000	225,000
2003	55,000	255,000

1. Calculate each company's turnover for inventory for 2003.
2. Which owner manages inventory better? Explain your answer.

EXERCISE 6-6

PROFITABILITY IN A SERVICE ORGANIZATION

Lorien Company is an engineering firm composed of five engineers. The annual compensation for each engineer is $200,000. It is expected that each engineer will work 2,000 hours during a year on client jobs. To cover overhead costs, the billing rate per engineering hour has been set at $175 per hour. At the end of the most recent year, the managing partner of the engineering firm found that total billable hours during the year for the five engineers had been 9,200. Use this information to compute the firm's profitability percentage, computed as follows:

[(Revenue − Compensation cost) ÷ Revenue]

EXERCISE 6-7

PERSONNEL UTILIZATION IN A SERVICE ORGANIZATION

Magily Company is a mathematical model consulting firm. Magily's services are sought by oil exploration companies for interpreting seismic data, by NASA for deciphering signals from deep space probes, and by Wall Street derivatives speculators who want to predict the weather in order to know whether to buy or sell soybean futures. Magily has the following numbers of mathematicians on its professional staff:

	Number of Individuals	Client Billable Hours Expected to Be Worked per Year
Full mathematicians	5	700
Associate mathematicians	10	2,100
Assistant mathematicians	40	2,600

During the most recent year, full mathematicians worked a total of 3,000 hours; associate mathematicians worked a total of 25,000 hours; and assistant mathematicians worked a total of 140,000 hours. Compute personnel utilization ratios for each class of mathematician.

expanded material

EXERCISE 6-8

FINANCIAL HOLDING COSTS

On January 1, 2003, Owen Corporation has $350,000 in inventory. On May 1, 2003, Owen's inventory is at $400,000. Owen's cost of capital is 13%. What were Owen's financial holding costs for January through April?

EXERCISE 6-9

FINANCIAL HOLDING COSTS

Brady Company sells imported goods made in India. One product it sells is a wooden music box. The music boxes cost Brady $65, and Brady charges its customers a price of $250. Brady's cost of capital is 12%. On average, an entire year elapses between the time Brady pays for a music box and the time Brady collects the cash from the sale of the music box. What are Brady's annual financial holding costs per unit for the wooden music boxes?

EXERCISE 6-10

ECONOMIC ORDER QUANTITY

Pace Retailers' best-selling item is its reinforced bicycle tires. Pace sells 4,745 of these tires each year. Pace pays $200 to place an order, and it costs Pace $2.50 per year to hold one tire. The retail price of the tires is $12.50. What is the economic order quantity of tires Pace should order at one time?

EXERCISE 6-11

REORDER POINT

Refer to Exercise 6-10. Suppose the lead time for reinforced bicycle tires is 13 days. To ensure adequate inventories at all times, Pace maintains a safety stock of 80 tires. Assuming Pace sells the 4,745 bicycle tires uniformly over the 365 days of the year, what is Pace's reorder point?

EXERCISE 6-12

ECONOMIC ORDER QUANTITY

For the past three years, Hawkeye Army Surplus Store has had excessive inventory holding costs. Management believes the excessive costs are due to the large orders the company places. The company hires a consultant, Brad Miles, to analyze the problem and suggest a solution. Information about two products, combat boots and backpacks, is as follows:

	Combat Boots	Backpacks
Annual market demand	20,000 pairs	5,000
Cost per unit	$20	$55
Annual carrying cost per unit	$7	$16
Ordering cost	$500	$500

How many pairs of combat boots should Brad suggest Hawkeye purchase at a time? How many backpacks?

EXERCISE 6-13

REORDER POINT

Avery Grocery Store is the only grocery store in Rayville, a small town populated mostly by college students. Students have been complaining lately because Avery always runs out of macaroni and cheese, the students' favorite food. Avery management decides it needs to calculate a more suitable reorder point. Information about the macaroni and cheese is as follows:

Average daily sales	500 boxes
Average lead time	5 days
Avery's cost per unit	$0.30
Price charged to customers	$0.75

1. What should be the reorder point if Avery does not want to maintain any safety stock?
2. What should be the reorder point if Avery wants to maintain a safety stock of 1,000 boxes of macaroni and cheese?

PROBLEM 6-1

COST OF GOODS MANUFACTURED

The following data apply to the Newton and Alexander Companies:

	Newton	Alexander
Raw materials inventory, January 1, 2003	(1) $____	$ 4,000
Raw materials purchased	21,000	(4) ____
Raw materials inventory, December 31, 2003	6,000	3,000
Manufacturing overhead (actual)	8,000	(5) ____
Manufacturing overhead (applied)	(2) ____	16,000
Selling and administrative expenses	14,000	25,000
Work-in-process inventory, January 1, 2003	(3) ____	20,000
Work-in-process inventory, December 31, 2003	16,000	22,000
Direct (raw) materials used in production	15,000	(6) ____
Direct labor costs	25,000	30,000
Cost of goods manufactured	49,000	55,000
Overapplied (or underapplied) manufacturing overhead	(2,000)	4,000

Fill in the unknowns for the two cases. (*Hint:* Indirect materials are not used in either company.)

PROBLEM 6-2

COST OF GOODS MANUFACTURED SCHEDULE

[Note: The journal entries required as Part (1) of this problem are also a requirement in Problem 3-7 in management accounting.]

Itsu Manufacturing Company applies manufacturing overhead on the basis of direct materials costs. The estimates for 2003 were:

Direct materials costs	$500,000
Manufacturing overhead	150,000

Following are the transactions of Itsu Manufacturing Company for 2003:

a. Raw materials purchased on account, $550,000.
b. Raw materials issued to production, 90% for direct use and 10% for indirect use, for a total of $350,000.

c. Direct labor costs, $500,000.
d. Indirect labor costs, $50,000.
e. Administrative and sales salaries, $140,000 and $90,000, respectively.
f. Utilities, $21,000; plant depreciation, $40,000; maintenance, $15,000; miscellaneous manufacturing overhead, $4,000. (These costs are allocated on the basis of plant floor space—administrative facilities, 500 square feet; manufacturing, 2,500 square feet; sales facilities, 1,000 square feet.)
g. Manufacturing equipment depreciation, $12,000.
h. Additional raw materials issued to production for direct use, $250,000.
i. Manufacturing overhead is applied.
j. Recorded factory foreman's salary, $54,000.
k. Ninety percent of existing Work-in-Process Inventory is transferred to Finished Goods Inventory. (Work-in-Process beginning inventory was $30,000.)
l. All finished goods are sold. (Assume no beginning or ending inventories. Sales are marked up 50% of cost.)
m. Over- or underapplied manufacturing overhead is closed to Cost of Goods Sold.

Required:

1. Prepare a journal entry for each of the transactions. (Assume that all manufacturing overhead is a product cost.)
2. Given the following beginning inventory amounts, prepare a cost of goods manufactured schedule for 2003 for Itsu Manufacturing Company. Assume all beginning and ending raw materials amounts include only direct materials.

Raw materials inventory	$80,000
Work-in-process inventory	30,000
Finished goods inventory	-0-

PROBLEM 6-3

COST OF GOODS MANUFACTURED SCHEDULE

Delta Manufacturing Company applies manufacturing overhead to jobs on the basis of machine hours. The 2003 estimates of manufacturing overhead and machine hours were:

Manufacturing overhead	$1,825,000
Machine hours	365,000

Delta had the following transactions for October 2003:

a. Raw materials of $420,000 were purchased on account.
b. Raw materials of $400,000 were issued to production; 90% were direct materials, and the balance was indirect materials.
c. Direct labor costs incurred, $300,000.
d. Indirect labor costs incurred, $55,000.
e. Selling, general, and administrative expenses incurred, $150,000.
f. Manufacturing overhead costs incurred:

Plant depreciation (factory)	$25,000
Equipment depreciation (factory)	14,000
Utilities (factory)	7,000
Factory maintenance	9,000
Factory taxes and insurance	5,000
Miscellaneous manufacturing overhead	6,000

g. Machine hours for the month, 30,400.
h. Eighty-five percent of Work-in-Process Inventory was transferred to Finished Goods Inventory. Assume that beginning Work-in-Process Inventory amounted to $95,000.
i. *All* finished goods are sold. (There is no beginning or ending finished goods inventory.)
j. Over- or underapplied manufacturing overhead is charged to Cost of Goods Sold, and the overhead account is closed.

Required:

1. Prepare journal entries to reflect the flow of costs incurred during October.
2. Assuming that beginning raw materials inventory was $16,000 and beginning work-in-process inventory was $95,000, prepare a cost of goods manufactured schedule for October 2003.

PROBLEM 6-4

ANALYSIS OF MANUFACTURING COST FLOWS

The following T-accounts represent manufacturing cost flows for Kanton Manufacturing Company for the year 2003.

Direct Materials Inventory

	Debit	Credit
1/1	70,000	250,000
	210,000	
12/31	30,000	

Work-in-Process Inventory

	Debit	Credit
1/1	80,000	700,000
	250,000	
	310,000	
	140,000	
12/31	80,000	

Finished Goods Inventory

	Debit	Credit
1/1	90,000	740,000
	700,000	
12/31	50,000	

Manufacturing Overhead

Debit	Credit
30,000	140,000
22,000	
16,000	
38,000	
40,000	

Required:

1. Compute the following amounts for 2003:
   a. Direct labor cost.
   b. Cost of goods manufactured.
   c. Cost of goods sold.
   d. Actual manufacturing overhead costs.
2. Prepare a cost of goods manufactured schedule for 2003.
3. Prepare a cost of goods sold schedule for 2003.
4. **Interpretive Question:** Explain how the over- or underapplied manufacturing overhead is usually accounted for.

PROBLEM 6-5

INVENTORY TURNOVER IN A MANUFACTURING COMPANY

The following information is for Bun MaScare Company:

Beginning raw materials inventory	$ 25,000
Raw materials purchased	110,000
Ending raw materials inventory	15,000
Manufacturing overhead (actual)	300,000
Beginning work-in-process inventory	50,000
Ending work-in-process inventory	40,000
Direct labor costs	90,000
Beginning finished goods inventory	200,000
Ending finished goods inventory	270,000
Overapplied manufacturing overhead	15,000

Required: Compute the following:

1. Inventory turnover for ending raw materials inventory.
2. Days' supply of raw materials in ending inventory.
3. Inventory turnover for ending work-in-process inventory.
4. Days of manufacturing represented by ending work-in-process inventory.
5. Inventory turnover for ending finished goods inventory.
6. Number of days' sales in ending finished goods inventory.
7. **Interpretive Question:** What conclusions can you draw from your inventory turnover calculations?

PROBLEM 6-6

PROFITABILITY AND PERSONNEL UTILIZATION IN A SERVICE COMPANY

Diggy Company specializes in caring for the pets of the rich and famous. Diggy gives personal care to each and every pet, and its professional animal "consultants" are on call 24 hours per day. Some details about Diggy's business are given below.

	Number of Individuals	Client Billable Hours Expected to Be Worked per Year	Annual Compensation	Billing Rate
Partners	5	500	$500,000	$400
Consultants	40	2,500	35,000	250

During the most recent year, the five partners billed a total of 3,000 hours, and the 40 consultants billed a total of 56,000 hours.

Required:

1. Compute personnel utilization ratios for each of the two classes of professionals within the firm.
2. Compute the firm's profitability percentage as follows: [(Revenue − Compensation cost) ÷ Revenue].
3. **Interpretive Question:** Speculate on why the 40 consultants worked the number of billable hours that they did.

expanded material

PROBLEM 6-7

INVENTORY MANAGEMENT

Watersports, Inc., sells high-performance water skis. Because its sales are seasonal, Watersports calculates and uses different reorder points for summer and winter months. The following information is available:

	April–October	November–March
Lead time (days)	3	7
Total customer demand for the period	1,600	400

The water skis cost $150 each, and Watersports sells them to its customers for $300. Watersports' supplier charges $500 for each order placed. Watersports incurs an *annual* holding cost of $17 per set of skis.

Required: Calculate the appropriate economic order quantities and reorder points for the two seasons.

competency enhancement opportunities

- Analyzing Real Company Information
- International Case
- Ethics Case
- Writing Assignment
- The Debate
- Internet Search

The following additional assignments provide opportunities for students to develop critical thinking, ethical perspectives, oral and written communication skills, experience with electronic research, and teamwork through group and business activities.

ANALYZING REAL COMPANY INFORMATION

• *Analyzing 6-1 (Microsoft)*

1. For the year ended June 30, 1999, MICROSOFT's total cost of revenue was $2.814 billion. Can you compute Microsoft's total manufacturing costs for the year? Cost of goods manufactured for the year? Explain.
2. As of June 30, 1999, Microsoft reported the following about the number of its employees:

Employees engaged in research and development	12,090
Employees in sales and marketing	15,186
Employees in administration	2,850
Other employees	1,270
Total	31,396

   Refer to Microsoft's income statement in Appendix A and compute the following:

   a. Total revenue per employee.
   b. Total R&D cost per R&D employee.
   c. Total sales and marketing cost per sales and marketing employee.
   d. Total administrative cost per administrative employee.

• *Analyzing 6-2 (Wal-Mart)*

1. Through its Retail Link™ system, WAL-MART gives its suppliers access to detailed sales information "store by store, item by item, day by day." What advantages are there to Wal-Mart in sharing this kind of detailed data with suppliers? What disadvantages?
2. Wal-Mart reports (in its 2000 10-K report filed with the Securities and Exchange Commission) that 83% of the goods sold in Wal-Mart stores and Supercenters is first shipped to one of Wal-Mart's 45 regional distribution centers and then shipped to the individual stores. On the other hand, SAM'S CLUBS receive the majority of their goods directly from the supplier. Why is there a difference in the distribution procedure for these two groups of stores?
3. In recent years, SAM'S Clubs sales, as a percentage of total Wal-Mart sales, have decreased, from 19% of sales in fiscal 1997 to 15% of sales in fiscal 2000. What impact do you think this change in sales mix has had on Wal-Mart's overall gross margin percentage? Explain.

INTERNATIONAL CASE

• *Arthur Andersen*

ARTHUR ANDERSEN is one of the largest professional services firms in the world. In 2000, the company reported revenues of $8.4 billion generated from

its various business units—assurance and business advisory, tax and legal advisory, business consulting, and global corporate finance. Arthur Andersen has 385 offices in 83 countries, and over half of its revenues are generated outside North and South America.

1. What does Arthur Andersen sell?
2. Arthur Andersen has an office in Quito, Ecuador. What type of company operating in Ecuador would hire Arthur Andersen instead of a local Ecuadorian professional services firm?
3. Review the chapter discussion of cost information for service companies. What costs would be important to Arthur Andersen in deciding how much to bid on a consulting contract for a potential new client?

ETHICS CASE

• ***Performance Evaluation: The Illusion of Objectivity?***

You are a store manager for a large, regional department store chain. You have been asked by company headquarters to submit an evaluation of the performance of two of your assistant managers. The company is considering promoting one of them to be the manager of another store in the chain.

One of the assistant managers heads the Electronics department in your store. She is a long-time friend of yours and you would like her to get the promotion. The other candidate heads the Home and Garden department; she is a good assistant manager but you just don't know her well. You decide to recommend your friend, the head of the Electronics department, for the promotion.

In order to support your recommendation with objective evidence, you include the following departmental profit numbers for the most recent year:

	Electronics	Home and Garden
Sales	$500,000	$300,000
Net profit	$100,000	$ 40,000
Profit percentage	20%	13%

On this basis, arguing that the Electronics department has generated higher sales, higher net profit, and a higher profit margin percentage, you recommend that the promotion be given to your friend. However, you are a little troubled by the following two additional pieces of information:

1. The average value of inventory held in the Electronics department at any given time is $1.2 million. The comparable number for the Home and Garden department is $250,000.
2. The profit percentage in the Electronics department has been fairly stable over the last five years. On the other hand, the profit percentage in the Home and Garden department is at a 10-year high; the increase coincides with the hiring of the current head of the Home and Garden department.

Is it ethical for you to recommend the promotion for your friend, the head of the Electronics department? How should you use the numerical evidence in support of your recommendation?

WRITING ASSIGNMENT

• ***Consultant's Report for a Small-Town Supermarket***

You have been hired as a financial consultant by a small-town supermarket. The supermarket is considering building a new, larger store and requests your expertise in evaluating the feasibility of the project. You know that the construction of the store will cost $3 million. You also know that the average gross margin percentage in supermarkets is 27%.

Draft a one-page memo to the owner of the supermarket requesting additional cost information to be used in your analysis. The store owner is a clever businessperson but has no experience in using quantitative data in making decisions. Therefore, your memo must be very specific in identifying the information that you will need to perform a useful analysis.

THE DEBATE

• *Overutilization of Young Professionals*

As seen in this chapter, an important dimension of performance for a manufacturing, merchandising, or service organization is the efficient utilization of resources. The more intensively resources are used, the greater a company's return on investment. However, when talking about a service organization, this "resource" is often the time of young professionals who are just starting their careers. Competitive pressures on companies can translate into 70- and 80-hour work weeks for college graduates in the first few years of their careers. These work pressures make it difficult for young professionals to develop their lives outside work.

Divide your group into two teams and prepare a two-minute oral presentation supporting the following views.

- One team supports "Work/Life Balance." This group believes that young professionals should not be viewed as "resources" to be utilized but as human beings to be respected.
- The other team supports "Survival of the Fittest." This group believes that it is a dog-eat-dog world out there, and that those young professionals who can't stand the long hours should get out of the way of those who can.

INTERNET SEARCH

• *The Peninsula Hotel in Hong Kong*

The **PENINSULA HOTEL** is Hong Kong's oldest and finest hotel. The hotel epitomizes service. For example, the Peninsula maintains a fleet of chauffeur-driven Rolls-Royce limousines to transport guests to and from the Hong Kong airport. Access the Web site for the Peninsula Hotel at **http://www.peninsula.com/hotels/hk/hk.html**. Sometimes Web addresses change, so if this address doesn't work, access the Web site for this textbook (**http://albrecht.swcollege.com**) for an updated link. Once you've gained access to the site, answer the following questions:

1. Hong Kong is divided into three main parts: Hong Kong Island, Kowloon, and the New Territories. In which of these is the Peninsula Hotel located?
2. In its description of its "Accommodations," the Peninsula Hotel describes some of the special features offered to guests in the Peninsula, Garden, and Marco Polo suites. What are these special features?
3. What is the daily rate for the cheapest room at the Peninsula Hotel? For the most expensive room?
4. The Peninsula Hotel in Hong Kong is owned by the Peninsula Group. What other hotels does this group own?

Management Accounting Information in the New Business Environment

chapter **m7**

learning objectives After studying this chapter, you should be able to:

1 Explain the fundamentals of activity-based costing (ABC) and activity-based management (ABM).

2 Describe total quality management (TQM) and costs of quality (COQ).

3 Describe how just-in-time (JIT) management systems integrate with and extend ABC and TQM using time-based performance measures.

expanded material

4 Compute the opportunity cost of lost sales.

setting the stage

You most likely wouldn't want to be in Phil Condit's shoes anytime in the next few years; then again, maybe you would.[1] Condit is CEO of BOEING COMPANY, the largest manufacturer of commercial airplanes in the world. If you have ever flown on a commercial jet, odds are you were in one of Condit's (or one of his predecessor's) products. In fact, a Boeing airplane is taking off somewhere in the world every 3.5 seconds. By the end of each day, Boeing jets fly over 17 million miles; that's the equivalent of 35 round trips to the moon! With its $16.3 billion merger with MCDONNELL DOUGLAS, Boeing commands approximately two-thirds of the $65 billion global market for commercial planes with 100 seats or more. Further, just prior to the McDonnell Douglas merger, Boeing completed a $3.1 billion acquisition of the defense and space operations of ROCKWELL INTERNATIONAL, making Boeing the largest builder of military aircraft in the world, as well as the number one supplier of goods and services to both the Pentagon and NASA. Boeing is basically sitting in the catbird seat. So, why might you hesitate to take Condit's job right now if it were offered to you?

If you had taken a walking tour of Boeing's 747, 767, and 777 plant in Everett, Washington, within the last couple of years, two things would likely have impressed you. First, this cavernous plant is monstrous, able to house 74 football fields! Second, for the largest company in the world dealing in commercial and military aircraft technology, as well as a significant player in space rockets and satellites, there isn't much in the Everett plant that suggests a "future world" of production technology. You won't find robotics, flashing lights, or laser-guided tools. In fact, the place looks a lot like a very large version of a repair bay at your local automobile service station. Planes are everywhere in various stages of completion, and *a lot* of mechanics are running around with nothing more complicated than a set of hand tools. Is this the way a production operation works that builds something as sophisticated as a 747-400 jet, capable of flying 420 people in a three-class configuration across the Atlantic Ocean? In 1998, Boeing likely had one of the most inefficient large-scale production operations in the world. Phil Condit, and everyone else at Boeing, was painfully aware of this fact. In fact, one vice president said at that time, "You know the Baldrige prize for the manufacturing processes? Well, if there was a prize for the opposite, this system would win it hands down."

Boeing's Everett plant turns out four massive jets per month, each priced at about $170 million. Each jet is tailor-made to the desires of each customer. The company has always prided itself on giving customers *exactly* what they want. This customization doesn't end with engine specifications and landing systems. It includes choice of paint colors (e.g., if you want white, Boeing offers nearly 110 shades to choose from) and location in the cockpit where the pilot's clipboard will be placed. However, don't get the impression that these are simple adjustments. Every alteration, even a seemingly minor one such as moving the location of an emergency flashlight holder, consumes thousands of hours of engineering time, requires hundreds of pages of detailed drawings, and costs hundreds of thousands, if not millions, of dollars to execute. Much of this cost of product complexity is compounded by the fact that Boeing *manually* tracks many of the parts that go into each plane.

Today's air transportation market is changing. The profits of commercial airlines are no longer protected by government regulations. The once free-spending Department of Defense has had its wings clipped by Congress. Boeing's customers have become extremely cost-conscious, leading to major pricing battles with Boeing's last remaining major competitor, AIRBUS INDUSTRIE (a European consortium). The three-fold *strategic imperatives* of cost, quality, and time are more important to Boeing than ever before. Boeing has responded to new market demands by implementing a complete reengineering of all processes, information systems, and management procedures involved in the manufacturing of its products. It is working to better manage costs by reducing and streamlining activities in the production process. No longer can Boeing customers select every option in their plane without paying extra. The company is reducing parts and work-in-process inventories in order to significantly increase stockturns. It is working to correct problems

1 Information from "Boeing's BIG Problem," *Fortune*, January 12, 1998, pp. 96–103; Boeing Company's home page at http://www.boeing.com; "The Incentives Airbus Is Using to Sell Its A380 Now May Backfire Later," *Business Week*, March 5, 2001, pp. 52–53.

with receiving shipments of parts on time from suppliers and getting completed planes out the door on time to customers. And all these changes must be accomplished without diminishing the absolute quality that is expected of aircraft technology that carries satellites into space, carries military weapons into battle, and (most importantly) carries two million people daily—a number that exceeds the world's population over an eight-year period! If Phil Condit and his reformation team succeed, Boeing, a manufacturer of world-class airplanes, may become a world-class company—perhaps even a Baldrige Award winner.

The biggest challenge for Boeing, however, is increased competition from Airbus. Airbus is aggressively promoting its new superjumbo jet, the A380, touted to seat nearly 550 passengers (Boeing's 747 seats 416 passengers) and fly more efficiently than any Boeing aircraft. When questioned on the surprisingly low cost of the A380 (currently offered at a discount of $140 million), Airbus executives claim their factories and turnaround times are more efficient than Boeing's. The A380 poses a significant threat to Boeing, which has no plans for an airplane that would directly compete with the size of the A380. Some analysts view this battle between Boeing and Airbus as the "dogfight of the century." So the future certainly does look very exciting for Phil Condit. What do you think? Still want to trade places with him?

caution

Just because the science of product costing was first developed over 100 years ago, don't assume that there are no new issues today. Business is now more complicated and more competitive than ever before. Management accounting systems are expected today to provide cost and performance measures that are more accurate, more relevant, and more strategically focused than ever before!

If there is one thing that is constant in the history of business (and, for that matter, history at large), it is change. A hundred years ago, the executives and management accountants of successful companies such as CARNEGIE STEEL and DUPONT created cost accounting and performance measurement systems that were so new and unique at the time that the decision makers in these companies were able to plan, control, and evaluate critical business processes better than most of their competition. However, these management accounting practices are now well understood and serve as a minimum expectation of most organizations desiring to remain competitive and viable in today's business environment. New management accounting theories and techniques are being developed constantly and tested in the laboratory of the current international market economy. Some of these new ideas are gaining a lot of attention, and you need to be aware of them. This chapter will introduce three important topics that have had a significant impact in the last 10 to 20 years on the types of information that many management accounting systems are now providing to the management process in an effort to keep organizations competitive. These topics are activity-based costing (ABC), costs of quality (COQ), and just-in-time (JIT). In Chapter 10 of management accounting, we will introduce a new model of strategic performance measurement that has come into the spotlight in just the last five or six years. This new innovation, called the Balanced Scorecard, is getting a lot of attention and may be the next significant step in the innovation of management accounting.

1

Explain the fundamentals of activity-based costing (ABC) and activity-based management (ABM).

ACTIVITY-BASED COSTING

In the late 1800s, Andrew Carnegie competed very strongly in the steel market with an almost fanatical emphasis on product cost information. Since then, product costing has been a primary purpose of management accounting. Manufacturing processes of today don't look at all like the manufacturing processes of the late 1800s, however. Advances in technology, combined with increasingly intense global competition, have resulted in manufacturing systems that are very complex compared to their predecessors. Because the companies that best understand their costs generally compete well in the economy, product costing has also undergone some important changes that we will consider in this chapter. It is important, though, to remember that the economy has shifted dramatically since the days of Andrew Carnegie. Service companies, such as transportation, consulting, and financial institutions, are the dominant force in today's economy. As you know from your study of Chapter 3 of management accounting, the service provided by these companies to their clients is a "product" that requires a product costing system very similar to that of manufacturing companies. In fact, service companies are some of the heaviest users of the management accounting techniques discussed in this chapter.

activity-based costing (ABC) A method of attributing costs to products based on first assigning costs of resources to activities and then costs of activities to products.

One major development in product costing is **activity-based costing (ABC)**. Basically, ABC identifies and uses a number of critical activities within the organization to measure product costs. For many types of manufacturing and service companies, ABC is a more accurate product costing system than the traditional product costing systems introduced in Chapter 3 of management accounting. However, ABC requires more time and expense to administer than traditional costing systems.

Product Costing Review

Consider, for example, a small ice cream shop that is owned and managed by one person. Lucas, the owner, hires college students to run the daily operations of preparing and selling his various ice cream desserts. Lucas must decide how to properly price his ice cream desserts. One of his employees, Sally, who just completed her first economics class, tells him to simply "charge whatever the market will bear." Yet this advice provides Lucas only with a price ceiling. Obviously, he cannot charge more than his customers will pay. However, in response to important matters of profitability such as competition and market share, Lucas wonders about his price floor—how low can he go? The obvious answer is that he cannot price below cost (except on occasion). But this begs the elemental question: What does it *cost* Lucas to make each of his ice cream desserts? Frankly, despite being in the ice cream business for several years, Lucas is not sure.

In relatively "simple" operations like Lucas's ice cream shop, as well as in complex operations such as a car manufacturer or a large law firm, product costing is a critical management issue. Today, cost accountants are paid rather well to answer the question, "What does it cost to make a product ready to sell?" In working with Lucas and his ice cream shop, the classic approach to this question is to apply the traditional product cost models that we studied in Chapter 3 of management accounting. Essentially, for a manufacturing organization, this model states that:

$$\text{Cost of product} = \text{Direct materials} + \text{Direct labor} + \text{Manufacturing overhead}$$

conversion costs The costs of converting raw materials to finished products; include direct labor and manufacturing overhead costs.

prime costs The direct costs that are "primarily seen" in the product (i.e., direct materials and direct labor).

To calculate the direct materials cost of a banana split, for example, Lucas needs simply to determine the cost of materials directly involved in making a banana split; in other words, the cost of ingredients. The process of converting these "raw" materials into a banana split (the conversion process) requires direct labor and overhead costs, known together as **conversion costs**. Direct labor is simply the hourly wage Lucas pays his employees to physically assemble the ingredients of each dessert sold. Clearly, because each type of dessert requires different ingredients and different amounts of time to create, each will have a different set of direct materials and direct labor costs. Direct materials and direct labor, the **prime costs**, are obvious components in the ice cream dessert production process. Prime costs are easily understood and, typically, can be directly traced to each type of product produced.

The second cost of the conversion process, overhead, is a little more difficult to understand and directly trace to the dessert production operation. Typically, in a "manufacturing" company like Lucas's shop, manufacturing overhead costs are thought of as "manufacturing support costs." In order to produce banana splits and other desserts, Lucas must have several other components in place besides ice cream and an ice cream scooper. Lights, heat, and other utilities must be present in the kitchen area. Equipment, such as blenders and freezers, must be purchased and maintained. Indirect materials, such as cleaning supplies and light bulbs, must be provided. Likely, Lucas will have other personnel on the payroll besides the counter help. A shop manager and a nightly cleanup crew add additional production costs in the form of indirect labor. All these costs are necessary for Lucas to produce his wares; hence, all are included in manufacturing overhead. As you understand after studying previous chapters, manufacturing overhead is, in essence, a catchall category. In other words, the total cost of a product or service is the cost of everything necessary to produce the product or service. In the case of a manufacturing company, after identifying direct materials and direct labor costs, any remaining product costs are manufacturing overhead costs.

Direct materials, direct labor, and manufacturing overhead do not comprise the total set of costs in Lucas's ice cream shop. Traditionally, product costs are defined as only those costs necessary to actually produce the product. There are other nonproduction costs in Lucas's ice cream shop. These include selling costs, such as costs of advertising the shop and maintaining an area for customers to enjoy their ice cream. General administrative expenses, such as office expenses and Lucas's own salary, are also costs that must be planned and controlled. Because these selling and general administrative costs are not directly connected to any aspect of the production process, they are typically not included in the product cost category. Nonetheless, these are still essential costs. If Lucas does not invest in selling and general administrative activities, soon there will be no production. Costs related to selling and general administration come under the heading of "period costs." In contrast to product costs, which are incurred as products are produced, period costs seem to be strictly related to the passage of "periods" of time.

Hence, we can summarize all these costs (originally defined in Chapter 1 of management accounting) as follows:

- *Direct materials:* The cost of the materials that actually become part of the product.
- *Direct labor:* Wages paid to those who physically work to assemble direct materials into the finished product.
- *Manufacturing overhead:* All costs required to produce a product *other than* direct materials and direct labor.
- *Product costs:* Direct materials + Direct labor + Manufacturing overhead.
- *Period costs:* All costs in the company *other than* the product costs.

Hopefully, this quick discussion of Lucas's ice cream shop is simply a review of what you already understand about product costing. At this point, you may feel that it should be a simple task to track the total costs Lucas spends on direct materials, direct labor, and manufacturing overhead in order to answer his question, "What does it cost to make a dessert?" Frankly, tracking Lucas's *total* product costs in his shop is a fairly simple task. However, the key issue for Lucas (and all other product and service managers) is to break those total product costs down for *each type* of product being created. For an ice cream shop that makes and sells many types of desserts, the product cost question becomes much more difficult to answer. It is precisely this question that accountants and managers have been struggling to answer for the last several decades.

SeatJoy, Inc., Is in Trouble!

Consumers are better informed and more demanding than ever before. In addition, competition is increasing as industries are deregulated, technology improves, and national barriers to worldwide competition are removed. The bottom line in this business environment is that margins on goods and services are becoming increasingly tighter. In terms of the ROI model, because most companies cannot sell their goods and services for more money, they need to sell more of their products faster (i.e., increase turnover) in order to remain profitable. What does this mean to an organization that sells a large variety of goods or services? Basically, it means that the organization could be losing money on some of its products and not even realize what is happening. In addition, it may choose to stop providing a particular product based on the false assumption that the product is a money loser. We can better demonstrate this point with an example that we will use for the remainder of this section.

Exhibit 7-1 displays the 2002 operating results for SeatJoy, Inc. (a fictitious company in the business of making high-quality leather desk chairs). As you can see, SeatJoy has three lines of reclining desk chairs. The Cushman model is its "bread and butter" product. This is the original chair that SeatJoy introduced in 1989 when the company started business. Shortly thereafter, SeatJoy introduced a similar chair that included a swing-out leg rest when the chair reclined. SeatJoy called this chair the Cushman II. More recently (2000), SeatJoy came out with a premium chair made from exotic leathers called the Luxor. Compared to the Cushman lines, the Luxor production process requires closer supervision, as well as more specialized production equipment.

SeatJoy follows a traditional approach of applying manufacturing overhead to products using an overhead application rate based on direct labor hours. The computation of the 2002 over-

exhibit 7-1 SeatJoy, Inc.: 2002 Operating Results

Manufacturing Overhead Cost Analysis

Annual manufacturing overhead	$18,240,000
Total annual direct labor hours	÷ 456,000
Manufacturing overhead rate per direct labor hour	$40

Labor Cost Analysis

	Cushman	Cushman II	Luxor	Total
Direct labor hours per product	10.0 hours	15.0 hours	12.5 hours	
Annual sales volume	× 18,000 chairs	× 14,400 chairs	× 4,800 chairs	
Total annual direct labor hours	180,000 hours	216,000 hours	60,000 hours	456,000 hours
Wage rate per hour	× $20	× $20	× $20	× $20
Total annual direct labor costs	$3,600,000	$4,320,000	$1,200,000	$9,120,000

Individual Unit Analysis

	Cushman	Cushman II	Luxor
Sales price	$1,000	$ 1,500	$ 3,000
Direct materials per product	$ (335)	$ (650)	$(1,395)
Direct labor per product	(200)	(300)	(250)
Manufacturing overhead per product	(400)	(600)	(500)
Total cost per product	$ (935)	$(1,550)	$(2,145)
Margin per product	$ 65	$ (50)	$ 855
Margin percent	6.5%	(3.3)%	28.5%

Total Annual Results

	Cushman	Cushman II	Luxor	Total
Sales revenue	$ 18,000,000	$ 21,600,000	$ 14,400,000	$ 54,000,000
Total direct materials	$ (6,030,000)	$ (9,360,000)	$ (6,696,000)	$(22,086,000)
Total direct labor	(3,600,000)	(4,320,000)	(1,200,000)	(9,120,000)
Total manufacturing overhead	(7,200,000)	(8,640,000)	(2,400,000)	(18,240,000)
Total product costs	$(16,830,000)	$(22,320,000)	$(10,296,000)	$(49,446,000)
Total margin	$ 1,170,000	$ (720,000)	$ 4,104,000	$ 4,554,000
Selling and administrative expenses				(4,000,000)
Operating profit				$ 554,000

head rate is shown first in Exhibit 7-1. Now take a moment to look through all the numbers in SeatJoy's 2002 operating results. Based on an analysis of 2002 results, it appears that the Cushman II line is dragging down company profits. After evaluating these numbers, the management team decides to drop the Cushman II product line. As a result, some suppliers are notified that SeatJoy will be reducing or canceling orders for certain raw materials. Further, one supervisor and the entire Cushman II labor crew are laid off. These are difficult decisions, but management feels strongly that SeatJoy should not absorb in 2003 another $720,000 reduction in operating profit (the total loss on the Cushman II line in 2002). SeatJoy is now in a position to realize a significant jump in operating profit in 2003. Or is it?

As the accountant prepares and provides the first few monthly profit reports in 2003, it is obvious that there are problems in the operations of the remaining two product lines, particularly

STOP & THINK What do you think is the source of the problem with operations at SeatJoy, Inc.? Should SeatJoy now drop the Cushman product line? Why or why not?

in the Cushman line. By the end of the year, when the annual operating results are put together (Exhibit 7-2), the debacle is confirmed. SeatJoy is in serious trouble! What happened? Sales of both the Cushman and the Luxor product did not change from 2002 results. Further, labor and materials costs per product stayed consistent with 2002 costs, and total manufacturing overhead decreased in 2003. Why didn't company profits improve as management expected after making the decision to drop the Cushman II product line? It looks as if SeatJoy should now consider dropping the Cushman product line in order to save the company.

Comparing the operations reports for 2002 and 2003 should reveal the problem. Take a second look at the manufacturing overhead numbers at the top of each exhibit, particularly the overhead rate per direct labor hour. Yes, manufacturing overhead costs did decrease in 2003, as

exhibit 7-2 SeatJoy, Inc.: 2003 Operating Results

Manufacturing Overhead Cost Analysis

Annual manufacturing overhead	$11,920,000	
Total annual direct labor hours	÷ 240,000	
Manufacturing overhead rate per direct labor hour	$49.67	(rounded) (Note: All computations below are based on rounding the overhead rate to the nearest penny.)

Labor Cost Analysis

	Cushman	Luxor	Total
Direct labor hours per product	10.0 hours	12.5 hours	
Annual sales volume	× 18,000 chairs	× 4,800 chairs	
Total annual direct labor hours	180,000 hours	60,000 hours	240,000 hours
Wage rate per hour	× $20	× $20	× $20
Total annual direct labor costs	$3,600,000	$1,200,000	$4,800,000

Individual Unit Analysis

	Cushman	Luxor
Sales price	$ 1,000.00	$ 3,000.00
Direct materials per product	$ (335.00)	$(1,395.00)
Direct labor per product	(200.00)	(250.00)
Manufacturing overhead per product	(496.70)	(620.88)
Total cost per product	$(1,031.70)	$(2,265.88)
Margin per product	$ (31.70)	$ 734.12
Margin percent	(3.2)%	24.5%

Total Annual Results

	Cushman	Luxor	Total
Sales revenue	$ 18,000,000	$ 14,400,000	$ 32,400,000
Total direct materials	$ (6,030,000)	$ (6,696,000)	$(12,726,000)
Total direct labor	(3,600,000)	(1,200,000)	(4,800,000)
Total manufacturing overhead	(8,940,600)	(2,980,224)	(11,920,824)
Total product costs	$(18,570,600)	$(10,876,224)	$(29,446,824)
Total margin	$ (570,600)	$ 3,523,776	$ 2,953,176
Selling and administrative expenses			(4,000,000)
Operating loss			$ (1,046,824)

expected since some costs were saved by dropping the Cushman II product. However, these costs did not drop nearly as much as the direct labor hours, resulting in a sharp increase in the overhead application rate per direct labor hour ($40 in 2002 versus nearly $50 in 2003). When the management team decided to drop the Cushman II line, why didn't manufacturing overhead costs decrease as much as expected? Obviously, the current manufacturing overhead application system based on direct labor hours does not provide very accurate insight on cost behavior, particularly in decision-making situations that have strategic implications like adding or dropping a major product line. When management made the decision to drop the Cushman II line, it failed to consider two very important issues:

- First, if the allocation system based on direct labor hours is improper, then it is possible that the Cushman II product line was actually subsidizing some manufacturing overhead costs that should have been assigned to one or both of the other products (a problem called product cost **cross-subsidization**). When a poor cost accounting system allows cross-subsidization of product costs, then the management process of planning, controlling, and evaluating is severely compromised.
- Second, some manufacturing overhead costs (known as **common costs**) simply do not relate directly to any particular product line. Examples of these common costs include executive salaries, rent or property taxes on administrative buildings, and general liability insurance. Common costs cannot be allocated meaningfully to products without potentially creating confusion as the organization works to manage its costs effectively.

cross-subsidization A distortion of costs that occurs when costs of one product are erroneously assigned to another product.

common costs Manufacturing overhead costs, such as executive salaries or property taxes, that cannot be attributed to products. Costs of facility support activities are common costs.

Hierarchical Product Cost Model A method of categorizing costs based on types of activities. Activity types include unit-level activities, batch-level activities, product line activities, and facility support activities.

ABC-based accounting systems are designed to avoid problems related to cross-subsidization effects and common costs allocations by categorizing and assigning manufacturing overhead costs based on the **Hierarchical Product Cost Model**. Essentially, the Hierarchical Product Cost Model provides management accountants with a method for categorizing costs according to the types of activities those costs support. One important benefit of ABC and the Hierarchical Product Cost Model is the way these tools affect our view of variable and fixed costs (more on this below).

The ABC Hierarchical Product Cost Model

We provided some very simple definitions of fixed and variable costs in Chapter 1 of management accounting. Chapter 2 of management accounting spent considerable time describing how much variety there actually is in fixed and variable costs. The important thing to understand in this chapter is that, in practice, very few costs can be definitely categorized as fixed or variable with respect to a single type of activity in the organization, such as direct labor hours, machine hours, or units produced. In fact, every organization has many different kinds of activities, each of which directly affects certain costs. Stated differently, *given enough time and with respect to a particular activity, nearly every cost in the organization can be considered variable.* This is really quite an important concept in the theory of ABC. Before you can predict a cost behavior (which is necessary before you can begin managing the cost), you need to identify the activity that actually drives the cost in question.

Let's return to the situation at SeatJoy, Inc. As you now know, the traditional approach SeatJoy is using to assign manufacturing overhead costs to its products appears to be causing problems. This approach is demonstrated in Exhibit 7-3. As you can see, SeatJoy simply sums together all manufacturing overhead costs within the organization and assigns those costs to products based on a single activity, direct labor hours. However, consider the variety of costs that are being combined into a single pool of costs. The purpose of a manufacturing overhead allocation rate (in this case, based on direct labor hours) is to *meaningfully* allocate costs to products in a manner that relates to the behavior of the costs. Think about property taxes on the production facility for a moment. Do these costs adjust at all based on changes in total direct labor hours within the organization? Of course not! Neither do the costs of insuring these facilities against damage and liability claims. Perhaps engineering costs and supervision costs, as well as costs to set up a production run and perform quality checks on the output, are related to direct labor hours, but the relationship is not very strong. There likely are other activities in

exhibit 7-3 Traditional Overhead Costing at SeatJoy, Inc.

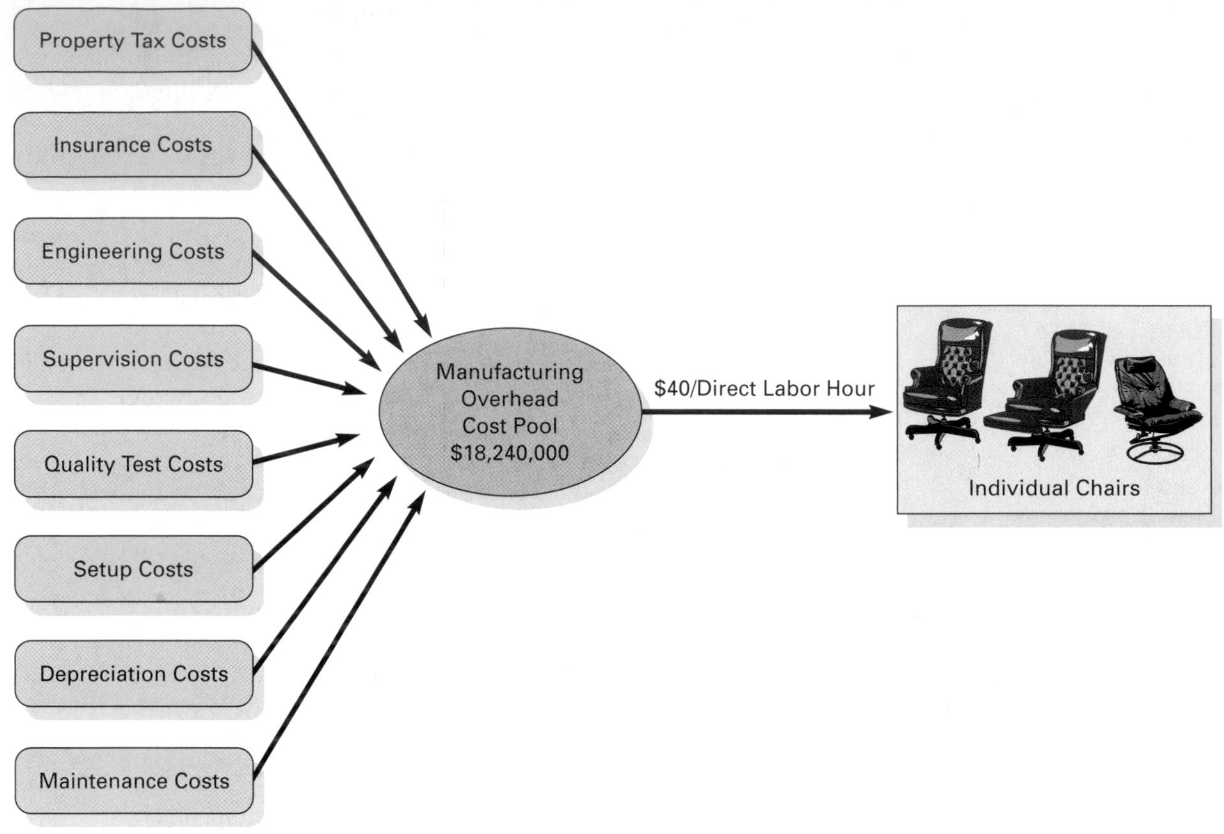

the SeatJoy organization that relate more closely to increases and decreases in these costs than direct labor hours. Identifying these activities is the intent of the Hierarchical Product Cost Model.

Look back at Exhibit 7-1 for a moment. How does SeatJoy determine how many direct labor hours are used in the plant? As you can see in the second table, annual labor hours for each product line are really just a function of how many chairs SeatJoy intends to produce and sell. Allocating manufacturing overhead on the basis of the number of direct labor hours per chair is essentially the same thing as allocating manufacturing overhead on the basis of the number of chairs produced. How much of manufacturing overhead costs will be assigned to the Luxor product line? Well, that really depends on how many units SeatJoy will produce in this product line (which then determines how many direct labor hours will be used). Because the allocated manufacturing overhead is really a function of the number of units produced, we call this method of allocating manufacturing overhead costs **unit-based costing (UBC)**. Think back to Chapter 3 of management accounting. Isn't this the basic approach we used in that chapter to allocate overhead in both manufacturing and service companies? UBC is a very traditional cost accounting method used in many types of organizations, and it is the cost allocation approach currently used by the SeatJoy organization in this example. UBC is a good method of cost allocation *in the right context.* However, a UBC approach usually creates problems in an organization with multiple products and services. Cost distortions can develop that make both strategic and short-term planning decisions difficult. The distortions are the result of using an oversimplified information system to represent the complex realities of modern business processes.

unit-based costing (UBC) The traditional method of allocating manufacturing overhead using an approach that is essentially based on the number of units produced.

STOP & THINK We have stated that the overhead allocation rate per direct labor hour for SeatJoy is really just a rate per chair (i.e., unit). Hence, we call this a UBC allocation system. Look at Exhibit 7-1. What is the manufacturing overhead allocation rate per chair (i.e., per unit)?

You have probably noticed by now that allocating manufacturing overhead costs to products is a two-stage process. First, we gather all the manufacturing overhead costs into a common pool of costs. Second, we allocate these costs to products based on a (hopefully) appropriate allocation rate. This rather simple UBC two-stage allocation process is characterized by the following relationship:

caution

Don't get the idea from the SeatJoy example that UBC is always a "bad" cost allocation method. On the contrary, UBC is a very good cost allocation method for manufacturing and service organizations with overhead that essentially does change based on the number of units of goods and services produced. Further, compared to ABC, UBC is typically easier and less costly. However, if UBC is causing reported product costs to be distorted, the management process in the organization can be seriously affected.

You can see this relationship demonstrated in Exhibit 7-3. All the support costs related to the production department at SeatJoy are gathered into a single cost pool. The costs are then allocated to individual chairs using a UBC rate based on direct labor hours.

The two-stage UBC relationship seems to say that products consume costs in production departments. However, that is not true. Costs are consumed by activities. And activities are necessary to create and deliver products and services. Based on this fact, the activity-based costing (ABC) method of allocating manufacturing overhead costs (which is also accomplished in two stages) makes a rather subtle change to the UBC relationship. The ABC two-stage allocation process is characterized by the following relationship:

In the ABC relationship, costs are first attributed to activities. Then, each activity is studied to determine its relationship to the product, and product costs are determined based on these activities. Using this relationship allows the management accountant to refine the categorization of costs as either variable or fixed. The UBC approach, with its focus on production units, strictly defines variable costs as those that proportionally shift when an additional unit is produced. This approach probably works well with direct labor, direct materials, and *some* overhead costs. All other remaining costs are then considered fixed and allocated to units using a unit-based driver such as direct labor hours.

However, in today's complex manufacturing and service environments, production costs are determined by many types of activities, not by the production of single units. An activity that affects a particular cost is called a **cost driver** for that cost. Given the right cost drivers and enough time, most costs are variable. For instance, many costs in a manufacturing organization are variable based on the number of and type of *batches* produced or the number of and the characteristics of *product lines* within the company's product mix. Conversely, these costs are fixed based on the number of units produced. Nearly every cost has at least one cost driver (an activity). Effectively managing costs of providing a product means that *activities, not products,*

cost driver A factor that determines an activity cost. An activity can have more than one cost driver.

An activity that affects a particular production cost is called a cost driver. Given the right cost drivers, most costs are variable. Many costs in a manufacturing organization, such as a candy factory, are variable based on the number of and type of batches produced.

must be managed. The bottom line is that the traditional management accounting approach to product costs, which states that

Individual cost of product = Direct materials + Direct labor + Manufacturing overhead,

may not be the best perspective of production costs when making planning decisions such as the one facing SeatJoy. Notice, though, that this is the approach used by SeatJoy's management accountants to analyze individual unit costs and total annual operating results in Exhibit 7-1. ABC recommends a different view of production costs based on production activities. Using the Hierarchical Product Cost Model, we can see that production costs are a function of many types of activities. As shown in Exhibit 7-4, there are four categories of activities that result in production costs. Rather than focusing on the cost for an individual product, the Hierarchical Product Cost Model recognizes that an organization's total production costs are a function of these four categories of activities. As a result, these categories need to be well understood in order to manage the costs related to production. We need to spend some time discussing these four types of activities in order to better assess the situation at SeatJoy, Inc. We'll start at the top with unit-level activities and work our way down.

unit-level activities Activities that take place each time a unit of product is produced.

UNIT-LEVEL ACTIVITIES In the Hierarchical Product Cost Model, activities that are performed each time a unit of a product or service is produced are classified together and called **unit-level activities**. Think about the SeatJoy production setting. Obviously, direct materials are released and direct labor is used each time a chair is produced. Perhaps many of the production processes are automated, minimizing the amount of direct labor involved in the production of a single chair. Nevertheless, each chair produced increases the amount of operating time on the machinery. Operating SeatJoy's assembly, sewing, and packing equipment generates machine maintenance activities. If SeatJoy uses the unit-based depreciation method on its machinery, then depreciation charges occur as chairs are produced. Energy costs required to run the production machinery are also directly tied to the number of hours the machines are operated. Costs related to all these activities are categorized as unit-based costs. Note that in the traditional UBC approach, all costs are treated as if they took place at the unit level. Direct materials and direct labor are attributed to each unit produced. Additionally, all manufacturing overhead is allocated to each unit produced. In the ABC approach, direct materials, direct labor, and *some types* of manufacturing overhead are handled at the unit level. Traditionally, these

exhibit 7-4 Hierarchical Product Cost Model

Total Production Costs

Costs of Products

Unit-Level Activities

Batch-Level Activities

Product Line Activities

Common Costs

Facility Support Activities

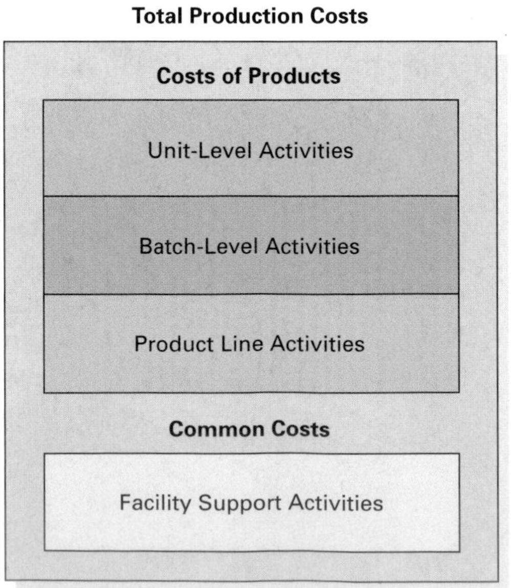

costs are considered to be the variable costs of production. The remaining manufacturing overhead costs are traditionally considered fixed. In ABC, however, these fixed manufacturing costs are related to batch-level, product line, or facility support activities. It is really this categorization, illustrated in Exhibit 7-5, that makes ABC quite different from UBC.

Let's assume that the accountants at SeatJoy determine that $3,420,000 of the $18,240,000 in annual manufacturing overhead costs is related to unit-level activities. SeatJoy can continue to use direct labor hours to allocate these costs to chairs. Based on 456,000 annual direct labor hours, this works out to $7.50 per direct labor hour ($3,420,000 ÷ 456,000 hours). As a result, a Cushman II chair is allocated $112.50 in manufacturing overhead for unit-level activities (based on 15 direct labor hours per Cushman II chair).

As you can see in Exhibit 7-5, ABC takes a hard look at manufacturing overhead costs historically considered fixed. Remember that ABC is based on the premise that, once the proper cost driver is identified, most costs can be managed as variable costs. In terms of both the traditional UBC approach and the more modern ABC approach, unit-level costs are variable. As a product unit is produced or a service is performed, unit-level costs increase. Traditional management accounting using UBC then maintains that all other costs are fixed. Frankly, if we're talking about using individual units of the product as a cost driver, then these costs are fixed. However, the ABC Hierarchical Product Cost Model looks for other activities, required by the production process, that make many (though not all) fixed costs act variable. The result is the categorization of batch-level and product line activities and their related costs.

BATCH-LEVEL ACTIVITIES Let's consider batch costs. Many production runs flow in batches. An automotive production line builds a particular line of cars until market orders are met. Then the current production line is changed over to produce a different car. A steel mill or a flour mill mixes different components into customized batches, then packages the output to meet customer specifications. These attempts to individually satisfy customer demands result in the need for batch setups on the production line. During setup, production must pause while employees recalibrate or install different machines. The new batch often requires a different mix of raw materials. Ordering, paying for, and moving raw materials into production position entail time and expense. Often some inspection takes place, such as testing the first item of the batch run, to ensure that the configuration and quality of the product are acceptable. These

exhibit 7-5 Relationship between Unit-Based Costs and Activity-Based Costs in a Manufacturing Organization

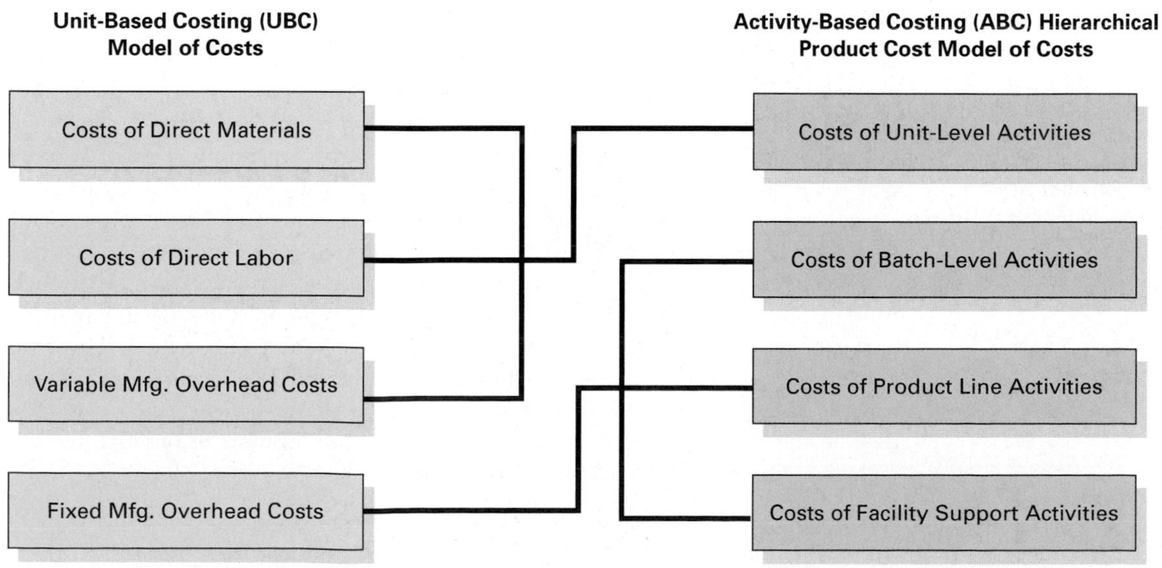

batch-level activities Activities that take place in order to support a batch or production run, regardless of the size.

activities that are necessary each time products or services are processed as a batch are known as **batch-level activities.**

Batch-level activities are more common in service firms where there is a lot of customization of the product for customers. A public accounting firm undertakes a lot of setup activities before work can begin on an audit, tax, or consulting job. A trucking company must perform many activities related to setting up a contract and organizing pickup and delivery details before transportation work can begin for a customer. A radio station that sells advertising often does a lot of design work before it can begin running a customer's advertising spot.

Regardless of the size of the batch (1 or 10,000 units, miles, or broadcasts), batch activities must take place, and batch-related costs must be spent. Each organization must evaluate its production operation to determine if and what activities take place to support a batch run. Then, the individual costs of each of these activities are determined. In line with the two-stage cost attribution process of ABC, once costs are assigned to activity cost pools, then batches that require a particular activity are assigned the attending costs. Examples of batch activities at a manufacturing company like SeatJoy include:

- number of setups,
- setup hours,
- movements of materials,
- orders for nonstocked items,
- purchase orders,
- number of inspections, and
- inspection hours.

By tracking batch costs in this manner, much product cost cross-subsidization is avoided. Batch costs can then be averaged out across the number of units in the batch (if desired). Units in small batches will then be required to carry a larger burden of these costs. Units in larger batches will experience favorable economies of scale. The cost information system begins reflecting what most managers and supervisors already know: poor scheduling leading to unnecessary production setups results in wasted resources. With this information available, managers can make better-informed decisions concerning the trade-off of large, cost-efficient batches versus production flexibility and low inventory levels. Later we will work through some calculations that demonstrate the negative impact that product cost cross-subsidization can have on decisions.

PRODUCT LINE ACTIVITIES Henry Ford infamously said that his customers were welcome to have their Model T car in any color, so long as it was black! That position has obviously changed at FORD MOTOR COMPANY, as well as at many other companies. Products, including the huge airplanes produced at BOEING, are often customized to satisfy rather small pockets of customers. This leads to the third level of activities in the Hierarchical Product Cost Model—product line activities. **Product line activities** are required to supply a particular product type to the market. These activities are constant regardless of the number of units or batches produced. The number of product line activities is tied to the diversity of the company's product mix and the individual complexity of each product. Organizations with many types of goods or services will require many more of these activities than organizations that produce only a few types of goods or services. As part of the effort to diversify the risk of market fluctuations and satisfy a myriad of demanding and informed customers, companies must develop and provide a diverse set of products. This results in increased overhead costs related to product line activities.

product line activities Activities that take place in order to support a product line, regardless of the number of batches or individual units actually produced. Costs of product line activities are also known as capability costs.

Management must be constantly aware of the costs of activities necessary to support an expanding product mix. As with batch activities, management must intelligently trade off the value of a large product mix against the cost of providing a variety of products. There are great opportunities for product cost savings through evaluating the inefficient use of resources by both batch-level and product line activities. Product lines that experience such cost savings should then be able to compete in the market at reduced prices. Sources of product line activities in a manufacturing firm like SeatJoy might include:

- engineering departments where product design changes in a product or production process take place,
- warehouses where materials necessary to each product line are stored and managed,

- supervisors who are dedicated to managing a particular product line,
- purchasing departments that initiate purchase orders, and
- receiving and shipping docks that receive raw materials and ship finished products.

In service organizations like a public accounting firm, a transportation company, or a bank, product line activities might include:

- in-house training resources dedicated to specific audit, tax, or consulting services,
- safety specialists dedicated to managing transportation of hazardous material, and
- loan officers dedicated to home mortgages versus commercial lending.

Only when the organization decides to permanently eliminate the product from its product mix can product line activities and their related costs be removed. Costs of product line activities are also referred to as **capability costs**—costs necessary to the capability of providing a particular product or service to the market.

capability costs Costs necessary to have the capability to produce a particular product or to provide a particular service. Capability costs are also known as the costs of product line activities.

FACILITY SUPPORT ACTIVITIES Up to this point we have discussed the top three layers of activities in the Hierarchical Product Cost Model: unit-level, batch-level, and product line (see Exhibit 7-4). The final level of activities in the Hierarchical Product Cost Model is facility support activities. Essentially, **facility support activities** are those activities that must be in place before development and production of any product or service can begin. Most of these activities are administrative in nature. Facility support activities are the source of the true common costs in the production facility. No single product or product line is responsible for the creation of these costs. Facility support activities are necessary for a business to create any products or services. Examples of facility support costs for a company like SeatJoy include:

facility support activities Activities necessary to have a facility in place in order to participate in the development and production of products or services. However, these activities are not related to any particular line of products or services. Costs of facility support activities are often called common costs.

- property taxes,
- plant security,
- landscaping,
- accounting, and
- salaries of the general administration (e.g., the vice president of manufacturing) and support staff.

The extent of facility support activities is unrelated to production volume or diversity. Therefore, it is impossible to sensibly relate these costs to the production of any particular product or product line. In the ABC model, there is no intervening activity that can connect costs of facility-sustaining activities to the products. Any assignment of these costs to products is doomed to be arbitrary. Therefore, the ABC approach is to *not* allocate these costs to products.[2] Allocating these costs simply distorts management's view of the relevant costs to be considered when strategically managing a product or product line.

Costs of facility support activities should be pooled together and kept separate from the other product costs. Only the costs of activities at the unit, batch, and product line levels are relevant to the production and management of a particular product line. For this reason, costs of facility support activities are part of the total production costs, but they should not be included in the costs of any specific line of products. Separating the costs of facility support activities from specific product costs is illustrated in the Hierarchical Product Cost Model in Exhibit 7-4.

Exhibit 7-6 illustrates how the two-stage ABC model is blended with the Hierarchical Product Cost Model. As you can see, the total manufacturing overhead costs shown in Exhibit 7-3 have been split into four separate cost pools based on how the costs relate to types of activities. The manufacturing overhead allocation rates per direct labor hour, per batch run, and per product line are discussed in the next section.

Resolving Cost Distortions

Poor management accounting can create tremendous problems within an organization, particularly when the competition starts driving down market prices. As profit margins are reduced

2 Actually, the idea that allocating common costs cannot be done sensibly does not belong solely to ABC theory. The traditional theory of responsibility accounting also supports not allocating the costs of facility support activities to products.

exhibit 7-6 Activity-Based Costing at SeatJoy, Inc.*

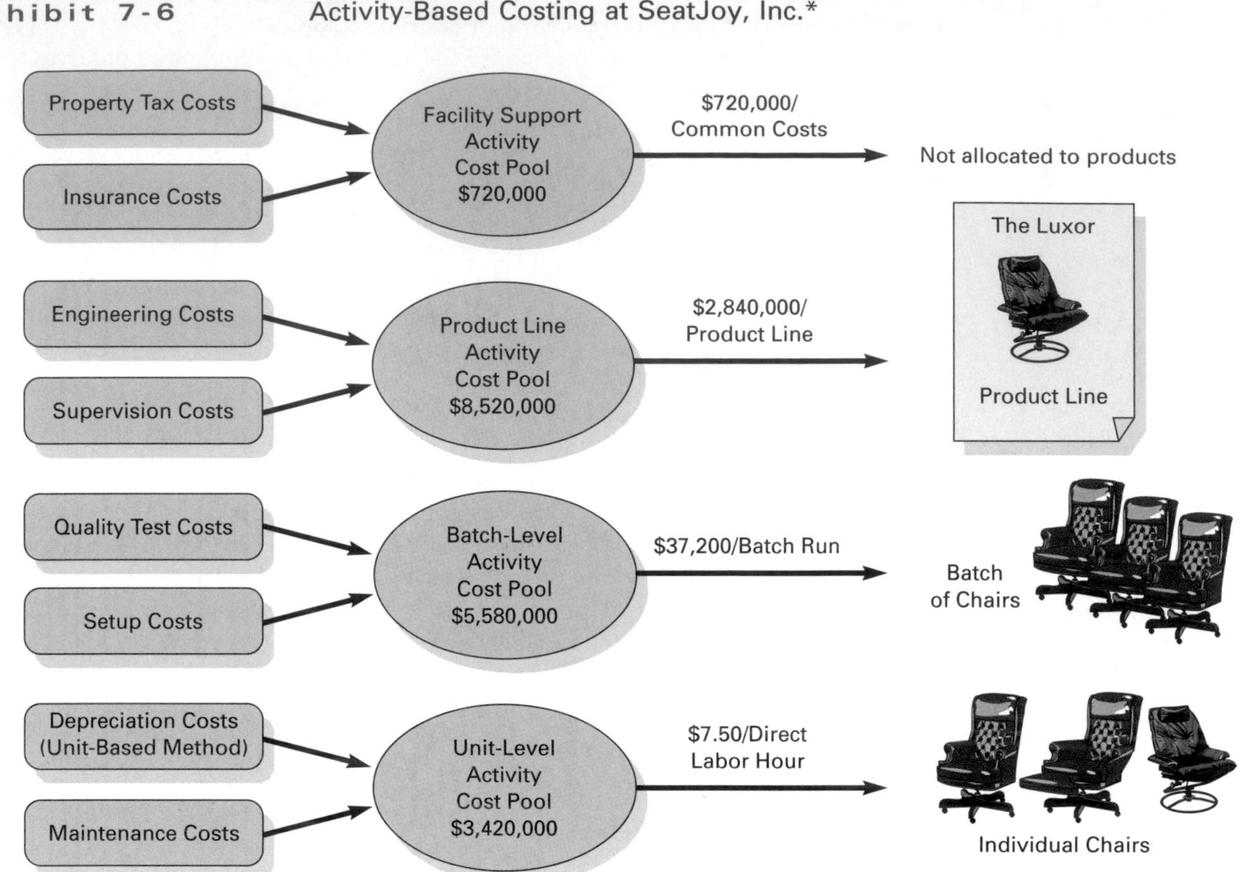

*Calculation of ABC allocation rates is demonstrated in Exhibit 7-7.

in a competitive market, it becomes increasingly more important for a manufacturing, merchandising, or service firm to accurately identify its product costs. The Boeing Company situation described at the beginning of this chapter is a classic example of an organization that produces multiple types of products in an environment with many batch-level and product line activities. Competition is pressuring Boeing to reduce its prices, requiring that Phil Condit and the other executives and managers at Boeing fully understand all production costs *and* how these costs relate to the aircraft they are manufacturing. There is little room for error. To the extent that management accountants provide poor data because of inappropriate cost allocation methods, Boeing will be susceptible to cost distortions such as cross-subsidization and inappropriate allocation of common costs. Each of these cost distortions can lead to decisions that reduce, rather than enhance, the organization's competitive strength.

PRODUCT COST CROSS-SUBSIDIZATION Let's return to SeatJoy, Inc. The production supervisors at SeatJoy have organized the production process by producing one batch run of each product each week. Typically, production workers spend Monday mornings setting up equipment to produce Cushman chairs. Once everything is set, some chairs are produced and evaluated for quality assurance. With the inspectors' OK, the production process begins, and company employees work until enough chairs are produced to fill all orders placed that week. Sometime Tuesday afternoon or Wednesday morning, they switch to producing Cushman II chairs, and all the setup and quality assurance activities again take place. Hopefully, by Friday morning SeatJoy can begin setting up the production equipment to make Luxor chairs. As you can see in Exhibit 7-3, SeatJoy has specific costs related to performing setup and quality test activities. Currently, SeatJoy combines these costs with all other manufacturing costs in order to create its manufacturing overhead allocation rate. However, because the weekly batch run of

Luxor chairs is much smaller than the weekly batch run of either Cushman or Cushman II chairs, some of the batch costs related to producing Luxor chairs are being subsidized by the other two products.

With a little additional data, we can compute the size of the product cost cross-subsidization taking place at SeatJoy. Of the $18,240,000 in 2002 manufacturing overhead costs, SeatJoy's management accountant determines that $5,580,000 is related to batch-level activities. SeatJoy works 50 weeks a year and produces one batch of each product weekly, which works out to 150 total batches each year (50 weeks × 1 batch per week × 3 product lines). As a result, SeatJoy should establish a manufacturing overhead allocation rate of $37,200 *per batch* ($5,580,000 ÷ 150 batches). The average cost *per chair* for batch-level activities at SeatJoy is computed as follows.[3]

MANUFACTURING OVERHEAD ALLOCATION USING BATCH-LEVEL ACTIVITIES

$5,580,000 ÷ 150 batches = $37,200 Manufacturing Overhead Costs per Batch

	Cushman	Cushman II	Luxor
Annual sales volume in chairs	18,000	14,400	4,800
Annual number of batches	÷ 50	÷ 50	÷ 50
Average batch size in chairs	360	288	96
Overhead costs per batch	$37,200	$37,200	$37,200
Average batch size in chairs	÷ 360	÷ 288	÷ 96
Average batch costs per chair	$103.33	$129.17	$387.50

How do these costs per chair compare when we allocate the $5,580,000 based on direct labor hours? Total direct labor hours for 2002, as well as the average number of direct labor hours per chair, are provided in Exhibit 7-1. The UBC allocation is computed below.

MANUFACTURING OVERHEAD ALLOCATION USING UNIT-LEVEL ACTIVITIES

$5,580,000 ÷ 456,000 hours = $12.24 Manufacturing Overhead Costs per Direct Labor Hour (rounded)

	Cushman	Cushman II	Luxor
Manufacturing overhead costs per direct labor hour	$ 12.24	$ 12.24	$ 12.24
Direct labor hours per product	× 10.0	× 15.0	× 12.5
Average batch costs per chair	$122.40	$183.60	$153.00

Look carefully at the difference in the calculations when using batches versus direct labor hours as the cost driver. If these manufacturing overhead costs are truly determined by batch-level activities, then the first set of calculations is more accurate than the second set. However, in Exhibits 7-1 and 7-2, SeatJoy is allocating manufacturing overhead costs using direct labor hours. As a result, Luxor chairs are receiving only *some* of the $387.50 average batch-level overhead costs per chair that this product is actually creating. The rest of these costs are being inappropriately allocated to the Cushman and Cushman II products. In other words, Luxor product costs are being *cross-subsidized* by the Cushman and Cushman II product lines. The result of this product cost cross-subsidization is that Cushman and Cushman II products will look less profitable than they really are, and conversely, Luxor chairs will look more profitable than they should.

Just like the product cost cross-subsidization that resulted from using direct labor hours to allocate costs of batch-level activities, SeatJoy is also likely cross-subsidizing costs of product line activities. Of the $18,240,000 in 2002 manufacturing overhead costs at SeatJoy, it is determined

3 It is critical to remember that we are computing *average* costs per chair here. Hence, because these are batch-level activities, SeatJoy *cannot* change these costs by changing the number of chairs produced. The cost driver for these costs is batches, not units (i.e., individual chairs).

that $8,520,000 is related to product line activities. That means that each product line should receive $2,840,000 of these costs ($8,520,000 ÷ 3 product lines). The average cost per chair for these manufacturing overhead costs is computed as follows:

PRODUCT LINE MANUFACTURING OVERHEAD ALLOCATION USING PRODUCT LINE ACTIVITIES

$8,520,000 ÷ 3 lines = $2,840,000 Manufacturing Overhead Costs per Product Line

	Cushman	Cushman II	Luxor
Manufacturing overhead costs per product line	$2,840,000	$2,840,000	$2,840,000
Annual sales volume in chairs	÷ 18,000	÷ 14,400	÷ 4,800
Average product line costs per chair	$ 157.78	$ 197.22	$ 591.67

How do these costs per chair compare when we allocate the $8,520,000 based on direct labor hours? Again, total direct labor hours for 2002, as well as the average number of direct labor hours per chair, are provided in Exhibit 7-1. The UBC allocation is computed below.

PRODUCT LINE MANUFACTURING OVERHEAD ALLOCATION USING UNIT-LEVEL ACTIVITIES

$8,520,000 ÷ 456,000 hours = $18.68 Manufacturing Overhead Costs per Direct Labor Hour (rounded)

	Cushman	Cushman II	Luxor
Manufacturing overhead costs per direct labor hour	$ 18.68	$ 18.68	$ 18.68
Direct labor hours per product	× 10.0	× 15.0	× 12.5
Average product line costs per chair	$186.80	$280.20	$233.50

business environment essay

City of Indianapolis Uses ABC Mayor Steve Goldsmith of Indianapolis understands the power of correctly allocating costs to their drivers. In his tenure as mayor of the twelfth largest city in the United States, Goldsmith has saved the local taxpayers roughly $400 million, has decreased the city's debt 3%, and has created nearly 30,000 jobs. How? Through ABC.

Before Goldsmith, ABC in the public sector was unexplored. Previously, the city of Indianapolis had broken down its costs only by function. In other words, the old accounting system identified money spent on salaries, equipment, capital investments, and professional service contracts, but never identified what specific activities were actually using these costs. But with his pioneering spirit and determination to save the taxpayers' money, Goldsmith undertook the challenge of painstakingly relating each cost to its appropriate activity by identifying the relevant cost driver. The result was significant insight into how money was being spent in his city.

With the help of KPMG (one of the "Big 5" CPA firms), Goldsmith and his finance team completed the analysis and then trained city employees on the importance of accounting correctly for money spent. The taxpayers of Indianapolis may not fully understand the power of ABC, but they are glad that Mayor Steve Goldsmith does!

Source: Adapted from H. Mayer, "Indianapolis Speeds Away," *Journal of Business Strategy*, May–June 1998, p. 41.

As you can see, there is a significant difference in the average costs per chair based on allocating these manufacturing overhead costs using product lines rather than direct labor hours. If these manufacturing overhead costs are truly determined by product line activities, then the first set of calculations is more accurate than the second set. However, since SeatJoy is allocating manufacturing overhead costs using direct labor hours, Luxor chairs are receiving only *some* of the $591.67 product line manufacturing overhead costs. Just like the previous situation involving batch-level activities, some of the product line manufacturing overhead costs belonging to Luxor products are being inappropriately allocated to the Cushman and Cushman II products. Luxor product costs are being *cross-subsidized* by the Cushman and Cushman II product lines in the case of manufacturing overhead costs related to both batch-level and product line activities.

By understanding that batch and product line activities act as cost drivers, costs previously considered to be fixed are actually variable with respect to these types of activities. Products that require these activities should be assigned the burden of these costs. As you can see, product cost cross-subsidization occurs when unit-level cost drivers such as direct labor costs are used to allocate costs of batch-level and product line activities.

ALLOCATING COMMON COSTS AND THE DEATH SPIRAL Suppose, for example, that it is a company's practice to allocate a share of the cost of property taxes to each product. Neither the product manager nor the production line supervisor has any control over this cost (other than to argue vehemently in management meetings for smaller allotments of this cost). When the company is trying to manage product lines to new levels of cost effectiveness and customer satisfaction, this cost allocation serves only to cloud the issues. The product line is not responsible for creating activities that lead to property taxes, so these costs should not be combined with costs of unit-level, batch-level, and product line activities in determining product costs.

Some individuals argue that allocating facility support costs is useful because these activities result in very real costs and must be "covered" by product revenues if the company is to be profitable. It is true that these costs are real. Management must be constantly aware of these costs and should be constantly working to ensure that all facility support activities are cost effective. However, consider a simple example. Suppose that a company's annual property taxes are $100,000 and are allocated evenly across four products (Products A, B, C, and D). The product cost information system indicates that the Product D line is generating a $10,000 loss. After several unsuccessful attempts to make the product more profitable, it is discontinued. However, property taxes remain unchanged and are now allocated evenly over the remaining three product lines. Thus, where the three remaining product lines were each previously receiving $25,000 in allocated common costs ($100,000 ÷ 4 product lines), now each receives $33,333 ($100,000 ÷ 3 product lines). Suppose that, with the new allocation, Product C turns unprofitable. Should management now consider discontinuing Product C?

It is doubtful that anyone would be fooled into making the mistake of discontinuing Product C in the simple example above. Hopefully, few would have originally discontinued Product D either. Such imprudent decisions result in a classic case of "death spiral." Essentially, a **death spiral** begins when a company does not fully understand its costs and then attempts to reduce costs by cutting products or other business segments that in fact do not create the costs in question. This results in the remaining costs being reallocated over fewer product lines. So, although the Product D line may be displaying a $10,000 loss, once the unavoidable $25,000 allocation is removed, it is clear that the Product D line is actually contributing $15,000 to help "cover" the $100,000 tax cost and provide overall profit for the company. Removing this product from the company only results in other products having to carry an even larger burden of facility support costs. Continuing to drop products in such a manner will leave the company with $100,000 in property taxes and no revenue-generating products.

death spiral A series of management decisions based on bad information that results in reducing or removing activities or segments from the organization that are actually profitable.

Given this simple example, you might expect few to fall into a death spiral trap. However, the product mix of most large-scale organizations is much more complex than this example. For example, the situation at Boeing Company involves many activities and much cost complexity. It would be quite easy to become confused about cost relationships in such a setting. There are several cases of companies falling into this trap and seriously damaging their competitive position before realizing what was happening.

The situation at SeatJoy certainly looks like the beginning of a death spiral. As demonstrated earlier, the accountants are allocating costs of batch-level and product line activities to the Cushman and Cushman II product lines that should belong to the Luxor product line. When SeatJoy management elects to drop the Cushman II product line, the Luxor manufacturing overhead costs being subsidized by the Cushman II line are reallocated to the remaining products. The result is that the Cushman product now looks as if it is unprofitable. Remember, though, that the Cushman line is subsidizing some Luxor costs. In addition, some common costs (i.e., costs of facility support activities) are being allocated to all three products. As demonstrated in Exhibit 7-6, property tax and insurance costs are facility support costs that really shouldn't be allocated to any of the products. Similar to the product cost cross-subsidization situation, dropping the Cushman II product line results only in a reallocation of these common costs. This reallocation also contributes to the Cushman product becoming unprofitable in 2003 as shown in Exhibit 7-2. Of the $18,240,000 in manufacturing overhead at SeatJoy, $720,000 is facility support costs. The average facility support cost per chair as allocated by the traditional manufacturing overhead allocation system is computed below.

FACILITY SUPPORT MANUFACTURING OVERHEAD ALLOCATION USING UNIT-LEVEL ACTIVITIES

$720,000 ÷ 456,000 hours = $1.58 Manufacturing Overhead Costs per Direct Labor Hour (rounded)

	Cushman	**Cushman II**	**Luxor**
Manufacturing overhead costs per direct labor hour	$ 1.58	$ 1.58	$ 1.58
Direct labor hours per product	× 10.0	× 15.0	× 12.5
Average facility support costs per chair	$15.80	$23.70	$19.75

As you can see, the UBC allocation approach assigns $23.70 per chair in common costs to the Cushman II product line. These costs, if removed from the 2002 operating results in Exhibit 7-1, would go a long way toward reversing what appears to be a loss in this product line. In fact, as you might suspect, once we have corrected accounting problems related to product cost cross-subsidization, removing these common costs should demonstrate that Cushman II is not an unprofitable product line. Exhibit 7-7 combines all the ABC allocations we've discussed into a new view of the 2002 operating results. With this information, SeatJoy management should clearly see that dropping the Cushman II product line is not a good decision and will drive overall SeatJoy operations into a loss situation in the year 2003. With the information shown in Exhibit 7-7, managers at SeatJoy should understand that to improve profits, they must focus on better controlling existing costs rather than making plans to drop any specific line of products.

Activity-Based Management (ABM)

Once SeatJoy has identified and classified activities according to the Hierarchical Product Cost Model, it is in a position to use the ABC data it has gathered to begin the process of improving activities. Remember that ABC is basically a two-stage process. The first stage of ABC involves tracing the flow of resources (and their costs) to activities. The result of the first stage of ABC is activity cost pools. Exhibit 7-6 illustrates activity cost pools for SeatJoy, Inc. It looks like a simple process to establish activity cost pools for an organization, right? Actually, this work can be both difficult and time-consuming. Allocating costs using UBC can often be done simply by using available records (such as payroll sheets or production reports) to identify the number of direct labor hours or number of chairs produced. All manufacturing overhead costs are then averaged across the total number of hours or units. On the other hand, to find out how costs *really* flow (i.e., to trace costs to activities), the accountant must leave the office and go out on the production floor or into the service area. Interacting with those

exhibit 7-7 SeatJoy, Inc.: ABC Analysis of 2002 Operating Results

	Unit-Level	Batch-Level	Product Line	Facility-Support
Activity cost pools	$3,420,000	$5,580,000	$8,520,000	$720,000
Cushman activity units	180,000 hours	50 batches	1 product line	
Cushman II activity units	216,000 hours	50 batches	1 product line	
Luxor activity units	60,000 hours	50 batches	1 product line	
Total activity units	456,000 hours	150 batches	3 product lines	1 facility
Cost per activity	$7.50	$37,200	$2,840,000	$720,000
	per direct labor hour	per batch	per product line	in common costs

Labor Cost Analysis

	Cushman	Cushman II	Luxor	Total
Labor hours per product	10.0 hours	15.0 hours	12.5 hours	
Annual sales volume	× 18,000 chairs	× 14,400 chairs	× 4,800 chairs	
Total annual direct labor hours	180,000 hours	216,000 hours	60,000 hours	456,000 hours
Wage rate per hour	× $20	× $20	× $20	× $20
Total annual direct labor costs	$3,600,000	$4,320,000	$1,200,000	$9,120,000

Total Annual Results

	Cushman	Cushman II	Luxor	Total
Sales revenue	$ 18,000,000	$ 21,600,000	$ 14,400,000	$ 54,000,000
Total direct materials	$ (6,030,000)	$ (9,360,000)	$ (6,696,000)	$(22,086,000)
Total direct labor	(3,600,000)	(4,320,000)	(1,200,000)	(9,120,000)
Unit-level overhead	(1,350,000)	(1,620,000)	(450,000)	(3,420,000)
Batch-level overhead	(1,860,000)	(1,860,000)	(1,860,000)	(5,580,000)
Product line overhead	(2,840,000)	(2,840,000)	(2,840,000)	(8,520,000)
Total product-related costs	$(15,680,000)	$(20,000,000)	$(13,046,000)	$(48,726,000)
Total product margin	$ 2,320,000	$ 1,600,000	$ 1,354,000	$ 5,274,000
Facility support overhead				(720,000)
Selling and administrative expenses				(4,000,000)
Operating profit				$ 554,000

Individual Unit Analysis

	Cushman	Cushman II	Luxor
Sales price	$1,000.00	$ 1,500.00	$ 3,000.00
Direct materials per product	$ (335.00)	$ (650.00)	$(1,395.00)
Direct labor per product	(200.00)	(300.00)	(250.00)
Average unit-level OH per product	(75.00)	(112.50)	(93.75)
Average batch-level OH per product	(103.33)	(129.17)	(387.50)
Average product line OH per product	(157.78)	(197.22)	(591.67)
Total cost per product	$ (871.11)	$(1,388.89)	$(2,717.92)
Margin per product	$ 128.89	$ 111.11	$ 282.08
Margin percent	12.9%	7.4%	9.4%

involved (department managers, line supervisors, etc.) is the only way to gather accurate insight about activities.

The second stage of ABC is assigning costs now pooled by activities to products. In the work of tracing resources to activity cost pools, much of the insight necessary to establish the second ABC stage is also developed. Typically, a budgeted cost is established for each activity. The expected use of the activity is also determined (e.g., number of direct labor hours for unit-level activities, number of batches for batch-level activities, number of product lines for product line activities). Similar to the traditional manufacturing overhead allocation rate, an activity cost allocation rate is established and used to transfer costs as an activity is actually employed.

For example, think of the activity "purchasing" for a merchandising company. The accountants and managers using ABC must assimilate what costs are required to purchase inventory for the company. The total cost of purchasing activities, as well as the number of expected purchase orders, is budgeted for the year. Using this information, costs per purchase order are set. Then, each time a purchase order is initiated, the costs are assigned to the object requiring a purchase order. Most merchants purchase inventory in large lots, or batches. If this is the case, then costs of purchase orders are related to batch-level activities. Hence, using ABC, the accountants and managers may be able to demonstrate and understand clearly that it is batches of products that must carry (and cover) the costs of purchasing. If the company wants to know the average purchasing costs of a particular inventory item, this is simply a function of the number of product units in each batch of products purchased.

ABC does not provide all the information a company needs to *manage* the costs of purchasing, however. Other things besides number of purchase orders requested may be driving the costs of purchasing activities. Further, the merchant also needs to manage the performance (i.e., the quality and timeliness) of its purchasing activities. With ABC, our focus is on activities. However, effectively tracing costs to products is a separate issue from managing the activity process. In order for the accountant to provide useful information for managing activities within the organization, we need to expand our ABC model as shown below.

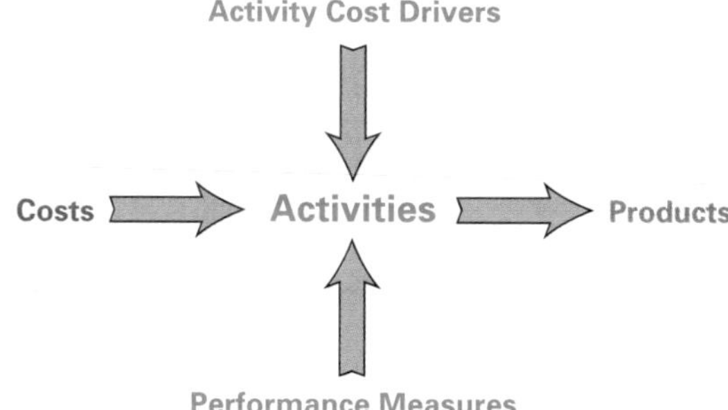

Assume that for our purchasing activity example, the ABC team finds that the number of line items in the purchase order and the amount of lead time provided for the purchase order drive the level of costs supporting this activity. In managing costs, it is important that this set of cost drivers be related to the purchasing activity. To better control costs, management needs to concentrate on controlling needlessly high levels of the cost drivers.[4]

In addition, activity performance measures should be established. The drive to improve the overall company so that it can better compete within its market means that every critical activity in the organization, not just those directly affecting customers, must be continuously improved. Every activity has a customer—either inside or outside the company. Performance measures used to evaluate the quality of purchasing might include the amount of time required to complete an order (i.e., lead time) and the level of errors in filling an order. Endeavoring to become a world-class merchandiser (or manufacturer or service provider) requires a company to

4 Often the allocation rate used to assign activity costs to cost objects is also included in the total set of activity cost drivers used to evaluate and control activity costs. However, an activity pool's set of cost drivers and the allocation rate used to assign its cost to products do not have to be the same.

clearly identify its strategy and then intelligently build performance measures that support the attainment of strategic goals.

activity-based management (ABM) The identification and use of cost drivers and performance measures to manage the costs, quality, and timeliness of activities.

Identifying and using multiple cost drivers and performance measures to manage an activity is called **activity-based management (ABM)**. As you can see in the previous diagram, ABM expands the basic ABC model by separating the task of product costing using activity-based relationships (Costs → Activities → Products) from the task of directly managing activities in order to achieve cost efficiencies and to enhance quality in business processes (Activity Cost Drivers → Activities ← Performance Measures). Using ABM, opportunities for cost efficiencies are created by separately tracking multiple cost drivers for each critical activity. Continuous improvement of the organization is then achieved using performance measures for strategically important activities in the organization. As you can see, managing activity cost drivers and performance measures for a particular activity is a management task that is actually exclusive of the processes of tracking a single cost driver that allocates the activity's costs to products. Exhibit 7-8 illustrates the application of ABM for two activities at SeatJoy.

exhibit 7-8 Activity-Based Management at SeatJoy, Inc.

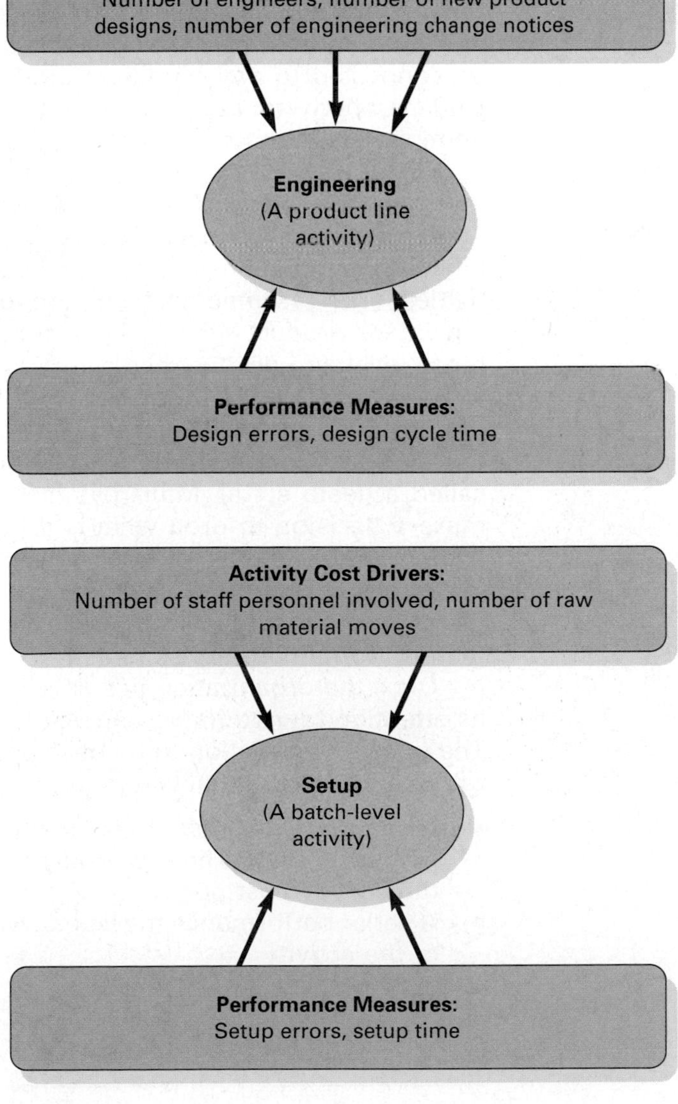

to summarize

Traditional product cost models generally focus on allocating overhead costs based on some measure that is a function of the number of products being produced or the amount of service being provided in the organization. This approach, called unit-based costing (UBC), works well in fairly simple settings with little diversity in the types of products or services offered to customers. In contrast, activity-based costing (ABC) recognizes that activities are the causes of costs. By understanding how activities relate to products, a manufacturing company with a diverse set of products and processes, such as Boeing Company, can more intelligently allocate manufacturing overhead costs to products.

Activities can be categorized across four levels: unit-level activities, batch-level activities, product line activities, and facility support activities. Generally, variable manufacturing overhead, such as machine maintenance or energy costs to run production equipment, is a function of the number of units produced. Setup costs, materials purchase orders, and route planning are examples of costs traditionally considered fixed that actually are variable in relation to the number of batch runs within the organization. Manufacturing overhead costs that are a function of product line activities are generally related to engineering, supervision, and warehousing. In contrast to unit-level, batch-level, and product line activities, costs of facility support activities cannot sensibly be connected to any particular product line. Examples of these activities include property taxes, plant security, landscaping, accounting, and executive administration.

Once costs have been pooled together according to the proper activity level (the first stage of ABC), new overhead allocation rates can then be created to separately allocate costs of unit-level, batch-level, and product line activities to product lines (the second stage of ABC). Costs of facility support activities are classified as common costs and should *not* be allocated to individual product lines; otherwise, product costs are distorted. If costs of batch-level and product line activities are allocated using UBC, then cost distortions called product cost cross-subsidization can also take place as one product is erroneously allocated another product's cost in the accounting system. Product cost distortions can lead to a series of management decisions called a death spiral. Managers inadvertently involved in a death spiral will make a decision to drop what is actually a profitable product or service line based on UBC data that erroneously suggest this product or service is unprofitable. Once one product line is dropped, the reallocation of overhead to the remaining products may result in another product looking unprofitable, thereby continuing the spiral.

Once the organization has developed an accurate ABC system, it can turn its attention toward improving activities that support its competitive strategy. The crucial information to be developed for important activities in the organization includes the following:

- A set of activity cost drivers that provides the greatest influence on the activity cost pool. The cost drivers become the focus of effort in controlling the activity cost pool.
- A set of performance measures used to evaluate the quality and timeliness of the activity.

This information is used to expand the ABC model in order to perform activity-based management (ABM).

2

Describe total quality management (TQM) and costs of quality (COQ).

TOTAL QUALITY MANAGEMENT

total quality management (TQM) A management philosophy focused on increasing profitability by improving the quality of products and processes and increasing customer satisfaction, while promoting the well-being and growth of employees.

We ended the last section on ABC by introducing the important concept that tracking and effectively allocating activity costs is not sufficient for managing activities. In today's highly competitive global markets, managing both the cost *and the performance* of activities is critical to the success of most organizations. This fact supports the importance of ABM to the management process of planning, controlling, and evaluating activities within the organization. In the last 20 years, an important management model known as **total quality management (TQM)** has had significant impacts on modern management accounting. TQM is a management philosophy that seeks to increase profitability by improving the quality of products and processes and increasing customer satisfaction while promoting the well-being and growth of the employees of the organization. Most managers, if asked, would say that their company seeks to improve quality, increase customer satisfaction, and take care of its employees. Implementing TQM, however, requires more than just endorsing the importance of quality in the company. An organization that has truly implemented TQM exhibits two defining characteristics. First, quality and continuous improvement are emphasized above all else within the organization. The premise here is one of priority. A company focused on TQM manages itself with the assumption that if product quality is high, customers will be satisfied and employees will be happy, and *then* profits can be expected. This contrasts with the assumption that the company cannot focus on quality until it is performing well financially. Second, TQM in the organization is the result of continuously planning, controlling, and evaluating improvement using specific measures. It is in this second assumption that accounting systems built to perform ABM can interface well with TQM. By tracking costs and performance related to TQM activities, the management accountant provides important support of this critical trend in business management.

TQM Comes to the United States

W. Edward Deming is widely credited with leading the quality revolution in Japan that started in the 1950s. Ironically, Deming received little attention as a consultant to U.S. companies prior to 1950. In contrast, the Japanese began to heed his advice on controlling processes, improving systems, and empowering workers in 1950. Soon, Deming moved to Japan where he remained for approximately 30 years. In honor of his work, Japan established the national Deming Prize to annually honor companies making significant improvements in the TQM process.

During the 1980s, concerns about American competitiveness spurred many U.S. companies to take a new interest in quality. Several companies invited Deming, then in his eighties, back to the United States to challenge the "old way" of thinking about costs and quality. A hundred years ago Andrew Carnegie essentially built an empire in the steel industry with the following motto: "Watch the costs and the profits will take care of themselves." Deming essentially revised this phrase to "Watch the *quality* and the profits will take care of themselves." The effect he and his colleagues have had on the way organizations work and compete is profound. Deming passed away in December 1993 at the age of 93.

TQM and Management Accounting

statistical process control (SPC) A statistical technique for identifying and measuring the quality status of a process by evaluating its output to determine if serious problems exist in the process.

Perhaps you've heard the term *statistical process control*. **Statistical process control (SPC)** is a technical tool that provides users with the ability to study, control, and improve processes of all types. Using statistical probability analysis, SPC provides management with the ability to know whether the errors in a production or service process are a signal that a serious problem exists in the process. Deming refined this early engineering tool and placed it squarely in the center of his TQM theory of management. Basically, Deming recognized that variation is a regular fact of life. No matter how carefully the fry cook at your local **MCDONALD'S** prepares a set of hamburgers, each one will be slightly different from the others. This is a natural fact of variation. Frankly, it's probably not very important to you as a consumer that every McDonald's hamburger you purchase is *exactly* like every other hamburger made that day in that store. However, if you're in the business of manufacturing or purchasing baseballs to be used in major league games throughout the summer, you're probably quite interested in consistent product

business environment essay

AT&T Is a Double Prize Winner! In 1951, the Union of Japanese Scientists and Engineers (JUSE) created the Deming Prize to commemorate the philosophy of W. Edward Deming. This distinguished award is given to companies that best exemplify Deming's methods by achieving outstanding quality management.

For years, Americans did not really grasp Deming's quality methods. It was not until the success of Japanese industries started to seriously affect America's world market share in the late 1970s that the American attitude regarding quality management changed. Now, American companies such as AT&T are impressing the Japanese. In 1994, AT&T received the two most prestigious quality awards—the U.S. Baldrige Award and the Japanese Deming Prize. AT&T is the first American manufacturer to receive the Deming Prize. Commenting on this accomplishment, AT&T's chairman, Robert E. Allen, said, "Receiving these awards is like winning both the World

net work

The NATIONAL INSTITUTE OF STANDARDS AND TECHNOLOGY (NIST) sponsors a site for the Malcolm Baldrige National Quality Award program at http://www.quality.nist.gov. This site will keep you up-to-date on the latest quality award winners, quality programs for students, presidential speeches on "Baldrige" quality, and descriptive portfolios of the award winners. Check out this site to answer the following fundamental question: Who was Malcolm Baldrige, and why is the award named after him?

quality. If you're in the business of manufacturing or purchasing surgical scalpels, computer chips, or rocket boosters for the U.S. Space Shuttle Program, then consistent product quality may be even more important.

SPC is having a large effect on management accounting in many organizations today. An accountant usually doesn't need to perform statistical analysis and probability procedures in order to participate in the TQM effort. SPC work is typically the responsibility of engineers and statisticians. Nevertheless, using SPC to support TQM in a company involves a lot of cost management issues. It costs money to create low-variation, high-quality products and services. It costs money to inspect and measure processes in order to know when problems exist. Finally, Deming and others have taught us that it costs a great deal of money to allow high-variation, low-quality products and services to exist in our organizations. Tracking and managing these costs is an important part of the TQM effort and is often the responsibility of accountants.

Costs of Quality (COQ)

Let's use baseball manufacturing to help understand exactly how management accounting works with SPC to measure and report quality costs. You may be interested to learn that, although China produces 80% of the world's baseballs, every single baseball pitched in the major leagues is made in a Costa Rican factory owned by RAWLINGS SPORTING GOODS COMPANY. A Rawlings baseball begins life as a "pill," a small sphere of cork and rubber enclosed in a rubber shell. The pill is tightly wound with three different layers of wool yarn, then finished with a winding of cotton/polyester yarn. This "core" is then coated with a latex adhesive. Over this gooey, hard lump, an extremely tight-fitting jacket of leather must be sewn. Sewing on the cover is a major effort. No one has been able to successfully create a machine that can automatically stitch the cover on a professional baseball. Hence, Rawlings employs about 1,000 baseball sewing experts. In its factory, top sewing pros can sew four to six baseballs an hour, achieving perfect string tension by feel. A wooden press rolls the seams flat, and finished balls are stored in a dehumidifying room that shrinks the covers tight and protects the balls from tropical humidity that might make them bloat illegally. Baseballs are carefully inspected at the Rawlings plant before being packed for shipping. A baseball that turns out too skinny, too hefty, or otherwise off-spec is "blemmed." It's stamped "blem" for blemish and sold as a practice ball.[5]

To be used in the major leagues, a Rawlings baseball should weigh 5.10 ounces and be 9.15 inches in diameter. As we pointed out, however, regardless of how hard the Rawlings Sporting

5 Hannah Holmes, "The Skinny on Sewing Up Baseballs," at http://www.discovery.com.

Series and the World Cup on the same day." AT&T's commitment to total quality management (TQM) that began in 1990 definitely paid off!

The Malcolm Baldrige National Quality Award was established in 1988 to recognize U.S. manufacturing, service, and small business companies that excel in quality management. The award's threefold purpose is to promote awareness of quality as an important competitive element, recognize quality achievements of U.S. companies, and publicize successful quality strategies. The award can be presented to a maximum of six companies each year that exemplify these characteristics. Due to the award's strict criteria, however, the Baldrige Award has *never* been given to six companies in one year.

Sources: "AT&T Wins Baldrige Award and Deming Prize in Quality Coup" and "Power Systems Is First U.S. Manufacturer to Win Deming Prize," AT&T Press Releases, October 18, 1994, http://www.att.com/press/; The Baldrige National Quality Program, http://www.quality.nist.gov.

fyi

A Rawlings baseball doesn't last long in a major league game (average life is about six minutes), but it has to be as perfect as possible. When a professional pitcher hurls a ball toward homeplate at nearly 100 miles per hour, the slightest blemish in stitching, size, or weight can be the difference between a strike and a home run, the difference between winning a Pennant and having a disappointing season.

Goods Company works to make sure its sewers are consistently producing baseballs of the perfect weight and size, variation occurs.[6] For the Rawlings plant, the important thing is to distinguish simple random variations in baseball weight and size that occasionally occur in a well-controlled production environment from systematic variations that occur more often when a poorly trained sewer is working or when low-quality leather is being used. Consider the following hypothetical example. Using probability rules, Rawlings has determined upper and lower control limits for a baseball. Specifically, baseballs must weigh between 5 and 5.25 ounces and have a circumference between 9 and 9.25 inches. Exhibit 7-9 shows an SPC chart of measurements of daily baseball weights at Rawlings. As you can see, some of these measurements are outside the control limits, indicating that there are potentially serious quality problems in the factory. Although getting the production process back in control will require some management effort, the problem cannot go on unchecked. Blemmed baseballs cost Rawlings money because the balls cannot be sold at game prices. Worse, though, is the cost to Rawlings' reputation. If Major League Baseball switches to another supplier because of inconsistent quality at Rawlings, the long-term opportunity costs to Rawlings could be devastating.

Before Rawlings' production managers can begin working on a potential quality problem on the production floor, the management accountants need to answer a couple of important questions: "What is it costing Rawlings when it produces blemmed baseballs? What will it cost to get the production process back within control limits?" These questions are the initial step in identifying an important set of costs called "costs of quality." **Costs of quality (COQ)** are costs spent to achieve TQM, as well as costs spent when products and processes fail to have high quality. Once activities that relate to quality in the organization have been identified, the accountant must be able to track the costs of those activities in order to measure COQ. Joseph M. Juran, another American quality guru who, like Deming, was enormously influential in the Japanese quality movement, originally identified COQ as an important accounting concept. Eventually, Juran also returned from Japan to the United States with his COQ theories to guide notable companies such as TEXAS INSTRUMENTS, DUPONT, and XEROX. He understood that organizations need to balance costs of achieving quality against the costs of poor quality. Most importantly, he specifically defined four types of quality costs that form the COQ model: prevention costs, appraisal costs, internal failure costs, and external failure costs.

costs of quality (COQ) Costs spent to achieve high quality of products and services, as well as costs spent when products fail to have high quality. The four types of costs of quality are prevention costs, appraisal costs, internal failure costs, and external failure costs.

6 *Note:* This example uses fictitious production standards and results in the setting of an actual company. Data used to illustrate quality concepts in this text should not be construed as actual production standards and results for the Rawlings Sporting Goods Company.

exhibit 7-9 Rawlings Baseball Production: Deming's SPC Analysis of Daily Operating Results

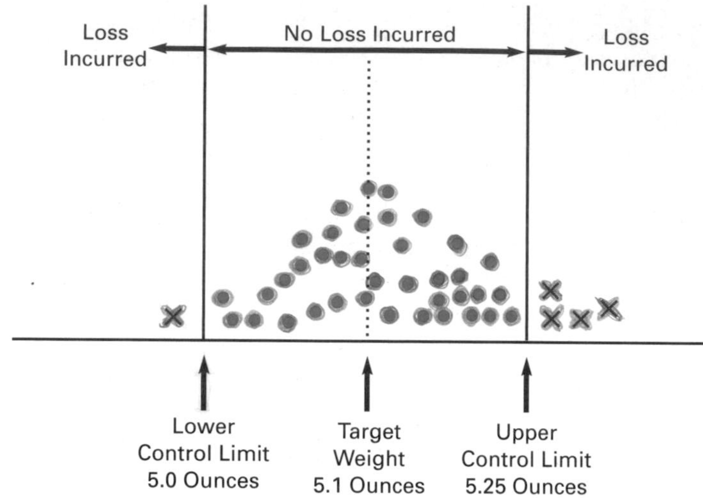

prevention costs Costs of quality that specifically relate to the effort to ensure that processes are performed correctly the first time and that products and services meet customers' expectations.

PREVENTION COSTS **Prevention costs** are costs incurred to ensure that tasks are performed correctly the first time and that the product or service meets customer requirements. Examples of prevention costs include costs of process or product design, employee training, education of suppliers, preventive maintenance, and other quality improvement meetings and projects. In the case of Rawlings Sporting Goods, the quality of its baseballs is highly dependent on the quality of its raw materials and on the expertise of those who stitch on the leather covers. This company will likely spend a lot of money working with its suppliers and training its employees to build a quality product.

appraisal costs Costs of quality that specifically relate to the effort of inspecting, testing, and sampling activities performed in order to identify and remove low-quality products and services from the system.

APPRAISAL COSTS **Appraisal costs** are the amounts spent on inspection, testing, and sampling of raw materials, work in process, and finished goods and services. They include overhead expenses for quality inspectors, costs to adjust measuring and test equipment, and costs of associated supplies and materials. Rawlings performs extensive inspections to gather data similar to that shown in Exhibit 7-9. These inspections require individuals to invest time using special equipment to evaluate each ball for size, weight, color, stitching, etc. Both appraisal and prevention costs can be viewed as investments in the process of providing quality baseballs to Major League Baseball.

internal failure costs Costs of quality that specifically relate to the expenses that occur when low-quality products and services fail before production and delivery to customers.

INTERNAL FAILURE COSTS Juran categorizes all the scrap and rework costs that are incurred to dispose of or fix defective products *before* they are shipped to the customer as **internal failure costs**. Costs of downtime or reduced yield due to production of defective parts or services are also included in this cost category. For example, if a Rawlings employee spends 10 minutes sewing a baseball, only to have the cover suddenly rip because of poor-quality leather, the company has lost money due to both the scrapped leather and the wages paid for 10 minutes of sewing a useless ball. In addition, all the materials and labor time spent previously winding, coating, and fitting the ball before the stitching work started are lost and become part of the internal failure costs. Clearly, Rawlings wants to be able to reduce scrap and sell more baseballs. Investments in prevention and appraisal work should reduce internal failure in the organization.

Most expensive

external failure costs Costs of quality that specifically relate to the costs that occur when low-quality products and services fail after production and delivery to customers.

EXTERNAL FAILURE COSTS Internal failure costs are very expensive. Nevertheless, Rawlings would *much* rather experience an internal failure than an external failure (defined as failure after the product has been delivered to the customers). **External failure costs** are generally the highest costs of a poor-quality process. Some examples are the costs of processing complaints, customer returns, warranty claims, product recalls, field service, and product liability. The most serious type of external failure cost likely results from unhappy customers; because bad news travels fast, defects found by a customer can cause the firm to lose both market share and future profits. In fact, a FORD MOTOR COMPANY survey indicates that a dissatisfied customer tells, on average, six other people. Sometimes the bad news can travel even faster. If a cover of a Rawlings baseball is pulled loose by a pitcher in the act of throwing a knuckleball during a game, the ball is immediately removed from the game. Obviously, more than six people instantly know about the product failure. Worse, though, is when product failure leads to news announcements and discussion in the media. In the last few years, you may recall some famous examples of publicized product failure involving software with bugs, unsafe tires on vehicles, and medicine or medical procedures with unexpected side effects.

Juran originally related all four of these COQ categories back to Deming's SPC model. He taught that if companies really understood the extent of failure costs, they would be willing to invest more in appraisal and prevention costs to keep more of their products performing within established control limits. Accountants should track these costs so that they can better manage the important relationship between costs of low-quality products and costs required to create high-quality products. This is an important relationship to manage. Obviously, high quality saves the company a lot of money as both internal and external product failures are reduced. On the other hand, high quality may require high investments in appraisal and prevention costs. Even though TQM requires that managers focus first on quality and then on profits, managers still need to understand how their commitment to TQM affects the company's bottom line (i.e., its profits). The dollar amounts involved in COQ are often quite large. Accountants add important competitive value to the organization when they are able to provide this important cost information. Hence, the ABC/ABM accounting system should identify appraisal and prevention activities, track the cost drivers of these activities, and establish performance measures that relate to reductions in failure costs and activities as a result of appraisal and prevention activities.

fyi

Most experts agree that losses on gross sales due to poor quality range from 20% to 30%. Most executives underestimate these losses because they consider only the most obvious costs such as scrap and rework to be the costs of low quality.

Source: K. G. Rust, "Measuring the Costs of Quality," *Management Accounting*, August 1995, pp. 33–37.

COQ Example

Let's return to our hypothetical example involving the production of baseballs at Rawlings Sporting Goods Company. Rawlings has invested expensive time and equipment to inspect all baseballs represented on the graph in Exhibit 7-9. As you can see, there are a few baseballs whose individual weights are outside the control limits. Balls failing the test are marked "blems" and sold very cheaply as practice balls. Other balls are not even usable as practice balls and must be scrapped. (Remember that weight is not the only quality criterion at Rawlings. The company is inspecting and scrapping balls for size, stitching, and color problems as well.) In addition to the balls failing the SPC tests, as displayed in Exhibit 7-9, Rawlings may also occasionally deal with complaints from merchants, athletes, and other organizations involving balls that fail in "the field" (pardon the pun). Because of the company's high commitment to customer satisfaction, it incurs significant costs in handling these calls, providing replacement balls, and investigating the cause of the product failure back at the factory. To counter these problems, Rawlings is considering making a large investment in its inspection equipment and in better training for its factory workers. Additionally, it is considering a new supplier for some of its raw materials, but significant costs are involved in establishing a new supplier relationship. Rawlings has a difficult planning decision to make that will likely require an intelligent evaluation of the trade-offs across all its quality costs. Rawlings will invest in an increasing level of appraisal and prevention costs in order to increase the percentage of baseballs that conform to all control limits. However, as the quality of baseballs increases, failure costs decrease dramatically. Balancing the decreasing costs of product failure with the increasing costs of high quality requires combining *all* costs in order to compute total COQ. The idea is to find the quality level where COQ is minimized. As an example, look at the fictitious cost numbers in the following table. As the percentage of baseballs that comply with all control limits (color, weight, diameter) increases, total appraisal and prevention costs increase. On the other hand, as the percentage of baseballs that comply with all control limits decreases, total failure costs increase. Rawlings needs to balance these costs by focusing on the appropriate level of quality in its production process. As you can see by inspecting the numbers presented, all quality costs are minimized in this example at 94% conformance where total COQ equals $2,237,155.

% of balls within all control limits	84%	86%	88%	90%	92%	**94%**	96%	98%	100%
Total appraisal & prevention costs	$ 100,037	$ 122,554	$ 156,347	$ 211,347	$ 311,850	**$ 530,663**	$1,164,270	$4,214,198	$44,172,984
Total failure costs	52,100,456	7,927,472	3,713,274	2,549,005	2,018,342	**1,706,492**	1,495,145	1,338,798	1,216,244
Total costs of quality (COQ)	$52,200,493	$8,050,026	$3,869,621	$2,760,352	$2,330,192	**$2,237,155**	$2,659,415	$5,552,996	$45,389,228

Locating COQ in the Accounting Records

It is important to see that tracking COQ within traditional accounting records can be challenging. Essentially, if the accountant desires to provide COQ data, most of these data are generally buried in the accounting records. As we discussed in previous chapters, many organizations traditionally categorize product costs as direct materials, direct labor, and overhead; and they categorize period costs as selling or general administrative. Quality costs used in the COQ model are typically spread throughout these traditional categories as shown below.

Prevention Costs		Appraisal Costs		Internal Failure Costs		External Failure Costs	
Cost Type	**Where Found**	**Cost Type**	**Where Found**	**Cost Type**	**Where Found**	**Cost Type**	**Where Found**
Process or product design	General administrative	Quality inspectors	Overhead	Scrap	Direct materials	Processing complaints & returns	Selling
Employee training	Overhead	Purchasing test equipment	Overhead (depreciation)	Rework	Direct labor	Product recalls	Selling or general administrative
Educating suppliers	General administrative	Adjusting test equipment	Overhead	Downtime	Direct labor and overhead or general administrative	Product liability	General administrative
Preventive maintenance	Overhead	Special supplies and materials	Overhead	Reduced yield	Direct materials and direct labor	Lost sales	Not found in the accounting system

Companies using a traditional cost accounting system may have some difficulty separating quality costs from other costs. However, companies using an ABC system should have already identified activities related to each of these quality processes. Often, it is much easier to implement a COQ accounting system in an organization that uses ABC. Note that lost sales (one type of failure costs) are *not* found in the accounting system. Remember that lost sales are an opportunity cost, and opportunity costs are typically not tracked within most accounting systems. Nevertheless, these are extremely important costs for the accountant to measure and provide to decision makers trying to plan, control, and evaluate the quality process in the organization. Lately, there has been some progress in the effort to track these important opportunity costs. Measuring the costs of lost sales is discussed in the expanded material section of this chapter.

to summarize

W. Edward Deming was extremely influential in helping companies understand that quality is an important competitive necessity in business. One of the main TQM (total quality management) tools he prescribed was SPC (statistical process control). Companies use SPC to identify an acceptable range of variation in their products and services. When the variation in the product or service exceeds the control limits established by the firm, then managers begin working to increase the quality of the production process.

A contemporary of Deming, Joseph M. Juran, developed a new categorization of costs called COQ (costs of quality) that can be used to manage decision making based on SPC. Keeping products or services in conformance with control limits requires investing in two types of quality costs: prevention costs (such as good product design and employee training) and appraisal costs (such as inspection and testing). When the production process starts creating variation outside the control limits, two types of quality costs result: internal failure costs (such as scrap and employee downtime) and external failure costs (such as handling complaints and product recalls). Perhaps the most important external failure costs are the opportunity costs of lost sales.

The COQ information that accountants provide managers should illustrate how decreasing failure costs may be offset by increasing prevention and appraisal costs. The level of quality conformance in a production process should be at the point where total quality costs are minimized. Identifying quality costs can be a challenge because these costs are generally intermingled across all the product and period costs within many organizations' accounting systems. Of all the quality costs identified in the COQ model (i.e., appraisal, prevention, internal failure, and external failure costs), the external failure costs are most difficult to measure because these costs include the opportunity costs of lost sales due to customer dissatisfaction.

3

Describe how just-in-time (JIT) management systems integrate with and extend ABC and TQM using time-based performance measures.

JUST-IN-TIME

Now that you are familiar with some of the newest concepts for managing costs and quality, it is "time" to talk about some modern methods of managing time. When discussing TQM in the previous section, we mentioned that managing quality was fundamentally a Japanese concept that was adopted by the United States in the 1980s. Remember that management accounting has evolved as a result of competition. When one company or industry (or, in the new global economy, country) develops a better management accounting technique or measure, it then competes more strongly in the marketplace. Eventually, the success of the innovator puts pressure on other organizations to adopt the same or a similar approach to their own management accounting systems. This was exactly the situation when U.S. companies began adjusting their management teams and management accounting systems to focus on quality and timeliness. In the 1980s, American manufacturers faced an assault from Japanese companies such as TOYOTA and NEC. These Japanese companies had mastered quality and inventory control, as well as speedier ways to get products to market. Western CEOs studied the competition, deconstructed what made it so good, adopted the better features of their rivals, and changed their management systems. Since then, this new management focus on quality and timeliness has had an impact on management accounting and has spread into U.S. merchandising and service industries, as well as into industries in other countries around the world.

business environment essay

The Japanese Focus on Inventory Henry Ford, the famous automotive production industrialist, lifted the FORD MOTOR COMPANY to great success during the early and mid-1900s by achieving tremendous cost efficiencies in producing cars. He believed in long production runs where low-skilled workers could build the same car part over and over again. As a result, high manufacturing costs per automobile plummeted, and he was able to offer cars to the public at extremely competitive prices. However, this production approach required high levels of raw materials, work-in-process, and finished goods inventories.

Meanwhile, across the ocean in Japan, Taiichi Ohno, an industrial scientist, and Eliji Toyoda, an executive vice president at TOYOTA MOTOR CORPORATION (and the son of the founder of Toyota), were experimenting with a different approach to large-scale production. While other Toyota executives thought that Toyoda's ideas were impractical, in 1949, in a machine shop in Koromo, Eliji Toyoda began experimenting with a new production control approach

JIT Inventory Systems

just-in-time (JIT) A management philosophy that emphasizes removing all waste of effort, time, and inventory costs from the organization. One obvious result of JIT is the reduction or removal of needless inventory in a production system.

The effort of management to compete on measures of time and to make improvements involving time is captured in the concept of **just-in-time (JIT)** management processes. To understand JIT, you need to first understand how JIT is used to manage inventory, including raw materials inventory, work-in-process inventory, and finished goods inventory. Let's talk for a moment about inventory. What is the purpose of inventory in a manufacturing plant? This may seem obvious. In the past, manufacturers stockpiled inventories in order to avoid shutdowns or slowdowns and to meet customer needs if suppliers were late or if production or delivery was slow. Occasionally (sometimes more than occasionally!), suppliers deliver raw materials that contain some defects, or the production process ruins some work-in-process, or a customer returns an unacceptable product. How do we deal with these unexpected surprises? Again the answer has been to "have a little extra on hand" so that bad parts or products can be replaced without having to interrupt the manufacturing process. Not surprisingly, production managers can get a little nervous when inventory levels get too low.

Because of concerns about risks due to scheduling and quality problems, companies establish policies to keep inventory levels at or above some minimal level. This minimum level of inventory is usually called a "safety stock" (as was discussed in the expanded material section of Chapter 6 of management accounting). However, several years ago some cagey accountants and business owners in Japan created a new competitive view of inventory management. They (like everyone else) realized that maintaining these inventories can be very expensive because of warehousing costs, interest costs incurred to finance inventory, and the opportunity cost of money tied up in stockpiled inventory. The real insight these Japanese business professionals had was that inventories are really only "buffers" that mask inefficient operations or product quality problems. Eliminate these timing and quality problems, and you no longer need the inventory buffers. By concentrating on improving product quality and timely deliveries, many Japanese companies became much more efficient and profitable at the same time that inventories were kept to a minimum or even eliminated. The emerging inventory systems that allow for the elimination of inventory stockpiles, inefficiency, and waste are referred to as just-in-time inventory systems. The competitive value of these new management systems eventually caught on and came to America.

JIT began as a management tool for manufacturing. So, when first learning about JIT, it's probably best to think of it in this context. In a manufacturing setting, JIT is a process by which only enough materials to satisfy immediate production are shipped to the job site. When JIT is functioning perfectly, companies take delivery from suppliers only as raw materials are needed for production and complete all inventory started during the day. In addition, inventory is completed only as it is ordered by customers and can be shipped immediately. As the name implies,

using the concepts of a just-in-time (JIT) inventory system. By 1953, the Koromo machine shop had a fully implemented *Kanban* system, which was based on the concept that supplies should be "pulled" through the production process as they are needed. (*Kanban* is essentially a signaling system that pulls parts forward through the production system.) Interestingly, Toyoda copied this idea from the sales methods of U.S. supermarkets. He was able to demonstrate that *Kanban* eliminated waste due to the overproduction of parts, reduced or eliminated the need for buffer inventories in the plant, and dramatically reduced production defects. In 1963, top management decided on the full application of *Kanban* as a means of transforming the production control system. Cost accountants were charged with developing and maintaining performance measures that tracked defects, excess inventory, and throughput time. Eliji Toyoda became chairman of Toyota in 1983. The rest, as they say, is history.

Source: M. Udagawa, "The Development of Production Management at the Toyota Motor Corporation," *Business History,* 1995, pp. 107–120.

materials are delivered "just in time" for production, and goods are manufactured "just in time" to meet customers' needs. As described earlier, JIT inventory systems started in Japan and have now been adopted successfully by a number of U.S. organizations. The results of JIT implementation are often dramatic. For example, one AT&T shop realized 54% improvement in quality yield, a 12-fold decrease in manufacturing time, an 88% reduction in scrap and rework, and a 95% increase in on-time deliveries.[7]

JIT and Value-Added Activities

Benefits such as those experienced by AT&T occur because companies that have adopted JIT have been able to avoid buildups of parts and materials and still ensure a smooth and orderly flow of goods to customers. JIT-based environments manage the flow of goods using a "pull" process. Essentially, this means that the final assembly stage for a product sends a signal (a *Kanban*; see the Business Environment Essay above) to the preceding workstation indicating what parts and materials will be needed during the next few hours. The preceding workstation then sends similar signals all the way back through the manufacturing cycle, ensuring an orderly flow of products. Thus, the demand at the final assembly stage "pulls" the inventory through the production process only as it is needed. Using this system, nothing is produced unless customers demand it. At all stages, inventories are eliminated or reduced to the lowest possible level. Obviously, then, progress toward successful implementation of JIT is inventory-related. Inventory reduction is not the primary purpose of JIT, but it generally is a consequence of JIT efforts to eliminate waste. The goal is to add value to the product or service and reduce or eliminate activities that do not. To be specific, **value-added activities** are essentially defined as those activities for which the customer is willing to pay. On the other hand, **non-value-added activities** are those for which the customer is not willing to pay. For example, clients in a law office are *not* interested in paying for the time spent running the payroll, organizing the file room, or computing billable hours. These are non-value-added activities. However, these clients should be willing to pay for court time and consultation time. These are clearly value-added activities that the law firm should emphasize. Under JIT, waste is considered to be anything other than the minimum amount of equipment, materials, parts, space, and workers' time that is essential to add desired value to a product. This results in careful management of time spent on value-added activities such as machining and assembly operations (for a manufacturer) and customer service and contact activities (for a service firm). More importantly, the JIT focus on eliminating waste emphasizes removing as much as possible the time spent on non-value-added activities such as setup work, materials handling, and inspection.

value-added activities Necessary activities in a production or service process that customers identify as valuable and for which they are willing to pay.

non-value-added activities Unnecessary activities in a production or service process that customers typically do not see or care about and for which they are unwilling to pay.

7 F. B. Green, F. Amenkhienan, and G. Johnson, "Performance Measures and JIT," *Management Accounting,* February 1991, pp. 50–54.

business environment essay

JIT and Speed, Speed, Speed The JIT philosophy originally focused on inventory. The objective of JIT was to reduce the amount of inventory on hand. Businesses learned that time is money, and if they could reduce the amount of time that inventory sat in storage, they could make more money. The JIT strategy was eventually incorporated into other areas of business as well. For BANK OF BOSTON CORPORATION (now part of FLEETBOSTON FINANCIAL), the objective was to reduce the time for processing mortgage applications. For GILLETTE COMPANY, it was accelerating the speed at which it introduces products.

Businesses are now differentiating themselves on speed. The faster they can provide a product or service, the more likely they are to obtain and retain business. As Kim Sheridan, chairman of AVALON SOFTWARE INC., said, "It's not the big companies that eat the small; it's the fast that eat the slow." BELL HELICOPTER obtained a $113 million Army con-

JIT and Time

Like ABC and COQ, the JIT management model focuses a lot of attention on cost and quality. It is important to understand that JIT also encourages accountants to emphasize providing time-based performance measures to management. Critical success factors for many JIT manufacturing, service, and merchandising firms include improving timeliness of customer delivery and increasing the product or service provider's flexibility in handling customers' needs. Exhibit 7-10 provides a sample of appropriate performance measures that support these factors of success, which are particularly important in today's dynamic, customer-oriented environment.

How JIT Works with ABC and COQ in the New Business Environment

Initially, JIT inventory systems dramatically changed the cost structures of many manufacturing companies. JIT has also had significant impacts on management processes at many merchandising and service companies. Inventory balances have been reduced significantly (including work-in-process in service organizations), and product costs have decreased, primarily because of increased efficiency and reduced costs of handling inventory. JIT systems support both ABC and COQ. All three systems work to improve quality and productivity and to reduce costs. All are focused on increasing the accuracy and relevance of product costing and thus provide better information for management decision making. COQ helps identify activities that either add value or do not add value to providing a product or service. JIT also improves quality, as well as reducing the number of costs that must be allocated, by eliminating non-value-added activities. ABC more accurately assigns the remaining value-added costs that must be allocated. Together, these new management methods and their resulting changes in the way we do management accounting today have dramatically improved overall planning, controlling, and evaluating processes. JIT, ABC, and COQ are being combined in an increasing number of companies today to create a win-win situation for everyone. With these methods, product costs are more accurate, quality is increased, and timeliness of product and service delivery improves as companies experience better control over their business processes.

to summarize

Fundamentally, just-in-time (JIT) is a method of removing all waste from a production or service process. Originally a Japanese management system, JIT has

tract to build helicopters by emphasizing the speed at which it could build its products. It reduced its production time from 24 months to 12 months between 1991 and 1994.

By pushing speed, CHRYSLER (now part of DAIMLERCHRYSLER) was able to introduce its small car, the Neon, in just 33 months. Typical development time for a new car is four to six years. It was also able to reduce by almost half the number of people required to develop a new car model—from 1,400 people to 741. Did this push for speed reduce quality at Chrysler? Quality ratings provided by J. D. POWER & ASSOCIATES indicated that quality improved by as much as 15% for cars such as the Dodge Intrepid, the Chrysler Concorde, and the Eagle Vision.

No longer is the focus of JIT on inventory alone. Companies are just-in-timing just about everything—including time itself.

Source: *The Wall Street Journal*, December 23, 1994, p. A1.

exhibit 7-10 Time-Based Performance Measures in a JIT Firm

Customer Delivery Success Factor (On-time delivery to customers can be affected by suppliers, product design time, and the production process and distribution time.)

Measure	Computation Method
Customer on-time delivery	Number of on-time deliveries divided by total deliveries. Goal: higher
Supplier on-time delivery	Number of on-time deliveries divided by total deliveries. Goal: higher
Design cycle time	Amount of time from initial idea to readied plans. Goal: lower
Number of contract changes	Number of times a contract is changed. Goal: lower
Schedule attainment	Number of unchanged schedules divided by total schedules. Goal: lower
Lead time	Amount of time from customer's initial request to final product or service delivery. Goal: lower
Setup time*	Amount of time required to set up a production run. Goal: lower
Throughput time*	Amount of time from beginning of production or service process until process conclusion. Goal: lower

Provider Flexibility Success Factor (Manufacturing, service, and merchandising flexibility includes the ability to respond quickly to changes in customer demand and product design changes.)

Measure	Computation Method
Lead time for new product introduction	Amount of time from idea to readiness for sale. Goal: lower
Parts and product availability	Number of times a part or product is unavailable when requested. Goal: lower
Number of common parts	Number of parts in a product design common to other products. Goal: higher
Inventory level	Average level of inventory. Goal: lower
Capacity utilization	Percentage of process capacity used in current operations. Goal: higher
Downtime	Amount of time a manufacturing or service process was unavailable. Goal: lower
Setup time*	Amount of time required to set up a production run. Goal: lower
Throughput time*	Amount of time from beginning of production or service process until process conclusion. Goal: lower

*Note that some performance measures are important to both customer delivery and flexibility success factors.

Source: Adapted from J. A. Hendricks, "Performance Measures for a JIT Manufacturer," *Management Accounting*, January 1994, pp. 26–30.

made a significant impact on the way manufacturing, service, and merchandising companies in the United States and other nations are managed. Like ABC and COQ, JIT has a strong emphasis on costs and quality. However, JIT adds an important third dimension to the management process—management of timeliness and flexibility. In a manufacturing setting, demand at the final assembly stage "pulls" the inventory through the production process only as it is needed. Using this system, nothing is produced until customers demand it.

The main goal of JIT is to add value to the product or service and to reduce or eliminate activities that do not. By focusing on removing non-value-added activities and managing time spent on value-added activities, inventories and costs are reduced, while quality and timeliness are improved. Timeliness issues include emphasis on reducing customer delivery times and increasing flexibility within the production, service, or merchandising process.

JIT, ABC, and COQ all interact well in manufacturing, merchandising, and service operations to support managers in the new business environment. COQ helps identify value- and non-value-added activities. JIT improves quality and timeliness by eliminating non-value-added activities. ABC more accurately assigns costs to the remaining value-added activities.

---

expanded material

The focus of this chapter is to introduce you to some of the "cutting-edge" issues in management accounting today. The topics in this chapter are organized around the threefold strategic imperatives of costs (e.g., activity-based costing or ABC), quality (e.g., total quality management or TQM), and time (e.g., just-in-time or JIT). Remember that management accounting is not dictated by some regulatory agency. Management accounting practice is determined by competition and the strategic needs of each organization. Accounting tools such as ABC and COQ essentially focus on new ways of measuring and reporting costs. These costs are often recorded somehow in the traditional accounting system. In this expanded section, we will explore a *very* new way of thinking about and reporting the opportunity costs of lost sales. The interesting thing about measuring the costs of lost sales is that this is a measure of costs that is rarely recorded anywhere within the traditional accounting system.

4
Compute the opportunity cost of lost sales.

MEASURING COSTS OF LOST SALES

Want to set a manager's teeth on edge? If you're in manufacturing, show the manager a pile of scrapped work-in-process inventory due to low-quality materials or mistakes made in the production process. If you're in merchandising, show the manager a pile of merchandise that can't be sold due to low-quality materials, poor design, or damage during shipping. These piles represent wasted costs and opportunities and translate into lost profits. The accountant using COQ in a manufacturing or merchandising organization will report these costs as internal failure costs. However, identifying internal failure costs within service companies is more challenging. Where are the piles of scrapped inventory in a service company? Actually, there is often no distinction between internal failures and external failures for a service company such as an airline, a law firm, or a bank. Baggage is misplaced, a client's phone calls are not returned, or deposits are recorded in the wrong account. Internal processes have failed at these service companies, and external customers are *immediately* affected. Instead of scrapped inventory that can't be sold, service companies identify their own kind of scrap heap: customers who will not come back. Frankly, all three types of companies (service firms, merchants, and manufacturers) experience lost opportunities due to disgruntled customers. Perhaps the most significant impact of the TQM revolution across businesses is an increasing determination to make sure the customers' experience with the company is exemplary. (Hopefully, you've had some personal experience as a customer with this corporate resolution.)

As we discussed earlier, disappointed customers can lead to a number of external failure costs, including costs of processing complaints, customer returns, warranty claims, product recalls, field service, and product liability. Many of these costs don't apply to service companies. As a result, these companies naturally focus on the effect of losing the goodwill of their customers, which in turn leads to loss of future sales. However, the risk to manufacturers and merchants is that they will focus too much on external failure costs that are easy to measure and will fail to fully appreciate the opportunity cost of lost sales.

Robust Quality

If the accountant is somehow able to identify and measure the cost of lost sales, then managers can use this information in better planning, controlling, and evaluating the process of delivering the products that customers want. What kinds of products do customers want? Let's return to our earlier discussion about baseball manufacturing. Think about a baseball player pitching for the Chicago Cubs. Does he care if a RAWLINGS baseball appropriately weighs between 5 and 5.25 ounces and has a circumference between 9 and 9.25 inches? Actually, no. What he cares about is that the baseball, when pitched, will perform as he intends—that it will have the desired curve, fade, slide, drop, or heat. Referring back to the SPC chart in Exhibit 7-9, a ball that weighs between 5 and 5.25 ounces and has a circumference between 9 and 9.25 inches has no defects. However, one-tenth of an ounce is pretty important to a professional baseball pitcher trying to throw a split-fingered fastball. Pitching performance will improve and be more consistent as Rawlings works to reduce variation in the weight and size of baseballs—even if the variation is within the limits imposed by Major League Baseball.

robust quality The capability of a product to perform according to customer expectations regardless of surroundings and circumstances.

The effort to reduce all variation is related to the concept of robust quality. **Robust quality** essentially means that the product will perform for the customer under all kinds of circumstances. In other words, you and I really don't care if the stereo, shirt, or sports car we buy was manufactured within some set of control limits or specifications. For us, the proof of a product's quality is in its performance when it is rapped, overloaded, stretched, or soaked. We all prefer stereos that continue to power up (even after a lightning storm has sent electrical surges throughout our neighborhood); we all prefer clothes that don't tear (even when a small child yanks on the sleeve to get our attention); we all prefer cars designed to steer safely and predictably (even on roads that are wet or full of potholes). We say these products are robust. They gain steadfast customer loyalty.

In the mid-1980s, FORD MOTOR COMPANY had a valuable experience with the importance of robust quality.[8] At that time, Ford owned 25% of MAZDA and asked the Japanese company to help build some of the transmissions for a car Ford was selling in the United States. Both Ford and Mazda built their transmissions using the same specifications. Yet, after the cars with Ford-built transmissions had been on the road for a while, they began developing much

8 G. Taguchi and D. Clausing, "Robust Quality," *Harvard Business Review*, January–February 1990, pp. 65–75.

higher warranty costs and more customer complaints about noise than the cars with Mazda-built transmissions. As a result, Ford engineers disassembled and inspected transmissions made by both companies. They were astounded at the comparison. The Ford transmissions were all built within the range of engineering specifications, but the Mazda transmissions displayed absolutely no variability from the target measures. The Ford transmissions that were breaking down were those shipped with components built quite close to the manufacturing control limits. Because the Mazda plant was working hard to reduce all variance—even variance within the acceptable control limits—its transmissions had lower production, scrap, rework, and warranty costs.

Taguchi's Quality Loss Function

Taguchi quality loss function A method developed by Genichi Taguchi for estimating the actual size of all external failure costs, particularly the opportunity costs of lost customer sales that result from dissatisfied customers.

Genichi Taguchi is a very famous Japanese quality expert who made an important adaptation to SPC charts that allows management accountants to actually measure the external failure costs of lost customers. U.S. companies have used Taguchi's famous quality loss function since the early 1980s. Essentially, the **Taguchi quality loss function** is a method of relating the amount of variation in a product to external failure costs due to dissatisfied customers. Managers and accountants who use the Taguchi quality loss function recognize that shipping a product that barely satisfies the corporate standard gains you virtually nothing over shipping a product that fails. Translation: There is a lot more difference between baseballs that weigh 5.10 ounces versus 5.24 ounces (both balls are within Major League Baseball tolerance specifications) than there is between baseballs weighing 5.24 ounces versus 5.26 ounces (only one ball is within tolerance specifications). Nevertheless, using the upper and lower limit controls displayed in Exhibit 7-9 would have Rawlings feeling just as confident shipping a baseball to the National League weighing 5.24 ounces as shipping a baseball weighing 5.10 ounces. Can you see why this might create a performance problem for Rawlings' customers? The Taguchi motto is: "Don't just try to stay within specifications, get on target!" Every time Rawlings ships a baseball that is more or less than the perfect size and weight, robust quality is reduced, and the likelihood increases that the ball will not perform in the field as expected. The result of being off target is dissatisfied customers, and dissatisfied customers talk to other customers, which can significantly reduce future sales.

The quality loss, as defined by Taguchi, is all the costs of external failure (including costs of lost customer sales). A simple formulation of Taguchi's loss function looks a bit like Einstein's

business environment essay

Real Customer Satisfaction Arrives at Ford Motor Company In 1981, FORD MOTOR COMPANY decided it was time to investigate what was behind the success of Japanese manufacturers. Japanese companies were quickly becoming the leaders in the car industry as well as other manufacturing industries. Edward Deming and Genichi Taguchi were responsible for making the Japanese companies strong competitors in the world economy. Using total quality management (TQM) and the Taguchi quality loss function enabled a company to achieve high levels of quality without the high costs. For example, Taguchi methods enabled some Japanese manufacturers to realize a large increase in quality gains—up to 80%!

Ford Motor Company was struggling to compete against the Japanese, so the company decided it was better "to join the cause than to fight the cause." In 1981, Taguchi first presented his ideas to Ford on how quality should be based on customer needs. After listening to Taguchi's presentation, Ford was motivated to become much more aggressive in implementing quality strategies and information.

Some time later, Ford began its Ford 2000 initiative to drastically reduce the number of defects per manufactured car made between 1995 and 2000. To make this goal possible, managers were provided with up-to-date, accurate information via the company's Intranet. The company's efforts did not go unnoticed. Customer satisfaction, the best measurement of reduction in external failure costs, increased. In

A recent study of the performance of Rawlings baseballs notes that even balls within Major League Baseball specifications (i.e., weigh between 5.00 and 5.25 ounces) can have approximately a 10% performance difference. In other words, the study showed that balls at the lightest and liveliest end of the tolerance specifications would typically travel 49.1 feet farther on a 400-foot hit than the heavier balls. That's within Major League Baseball's own specifications and could mean the difference between a lazy fly ball and a home run.

Source: J. Kaat, "Baseball's New Baseball," *Popular Mechanics*, October 13, 2000.

theory of relativity formula (remember $E = MC^2$?). Using Taguchi's formula, the cost of external failures is computed as follows:

$$L = CD^2$$

L = total quality loss due to external failures.
C = costs required to fix the problem and get the product back on target.
D = distance from the target measured in standard units.

If your geometry skills are reasonably fresh, you might note that this formula is a quadratic function (because of the D^2 term). If it has been a while since your last geometry class, you just need to note that quality loss increases very quickly as the distance between the product and the target increases. The implication here is that if management decides not to incur the voluntary expenses of reducing variation, it involuntarily incurs several times that amount in the form of warranty costs, lost sales due to customer ill will, and so forth. One important idea behind Taguchi's quality loss function is that it disagrees with the traditional notion of quality control limits. Look back at the SPC chart in Exhibit 7-9. This chart says that there is no loss as long as baseballs weigh between 5.0 and 5.25 ounces. Since the SPC chart is reporting that very few balls being shipped to the major leagues are outside the weight specifications, the data suggest that probably little loss is being incurred. But how much is Rawlings really losing in external failure costs, and how much would be saved if Rawlings reduced weight variation in baseballs? This is difficult to know precisely. Remember that Rawlings is trying to manufacture baseballs that weigh exactly 5.10 ounces. Let's assume that it would cost Rawlings $10,000 in prevention and appraisal costs to reduce average variation by each 0.01 ounce. Therefore, if baseballs varied on average only 0.01 ounce from the target of 5.10 ounces (i.e., from 5.09 to 5.11), then it would require only $10,000 to correct the problem. According to the Taguchi quality loss function, Rawlings would then save approximately $10,000 in external failure costs by making this reduction. It looks like an even trade-off between costs and cost savings, doesn't it? Remember, though, that Rawlings would also save some internal failure costs as well (waste, scrap, downtime, etc.). Now look at the chart of numbers on the following page. As you can

1997, the J. D. Power Initial Quality Study recognized the drastic leap in consumer quality ratings of Ford cars. In addition to the improved rankings, Ford's Atlanta plant received the Power's Platinum Award, which is given to the car manufacturing plant with the fewest facility problems.

The rankings and award seemed to confirm the company's efforts toward quality improvements and have acted as a catalyst to further inspire Ford to become a worldwide quality leader. However, the emphasis on quality improvements has not come without serious trade-offs. As part of the Ford 2000 initiative, a majority of management efforts concentrated on the North American market. The initial success of the program has aroused enthusiasm for the effort, pushing it forward. However, the emphasis on the North American market has come at an enormous cost in the foreign markets where Ford is engaged. Ford's net income in its foreign divisions dropped from a profit of $300 million in 1997 to a loss of $300 million in 1999. It seems that Ford's efforts to address the critical factor of quality have enabled it to compete with other car makers in North America, but have been less successful elsewhere. However, no one ever said that managing large companies such as Ford is easy. Ford will continue to work to implement quality performance measures while balancing its efforts across a global market.

Sources: M. Larson, "Ford Puts Quality Data in Human Hands," *Quality Magazine*, December 1997, http://www.qualitymag.com; D. Winter, "Ford's Nasser Still Upbeat Despite Firestone Fallout," *Ward's Auto World*, December 2000.

see, it will cost Rawlings more to get the baseball weight on target as the distance between the target weight and the actual weights increases. However, the opportunity loss (i.e., external failure costs) is much larger as the variation (i.e., the distance from target) increases. Hence, the Taguchi quality loss function really emphasizes the importance of reducing variation in order to increase robust quality within products and services.

Cost per 0.01 ounce unit to correct	$10,000	$10,000	$10,000	$10,000	$10,000	$10,000
Average distance from target	× 1 unit	× 2 units	× 3 units	× 4 units	× 5 units	× 6 units
Total cost to correct	$10,000	$20,000	$30,000	$40,000	$50,000	$60,000
Cost per 0.01 ounce unit to correct (C)	$10,000	$10,000	$10,000	$10,000	$10,000	$10,000
Distance squared (D^2)	× 1 unit	× 4 units	× 9 units	× 16 units	× 25 units	× 36 units
Total quality loss (L)	$10,000	$40,000	$90,000	$160,000	$250,000	$360,000

fyi

In 1989, Genichi Taguchi received the Ministry of International Trade and Industry (MITI) Purple Ribbon Award from the emperor of Japan for his contribution to Japanese industrial standards.

Obviously, Taguchi's quality loss measures are not very precise and objective. He is making general *approximations* about how quality problems affect all companies. Some companies may experience more or less loss due to quality problems than Taguchi suggests. Nevertheless, using the quality loss function, the management accounting system can provide a valuable signal to companies about the importance of continuously improving the quality of their goods and services. Measuring deviations from specifications has always been the job of engineers. However, by taking those deviations and translating them into costs, the accountant is able to draw a lot of attention to the problem.

Is Quality Free?

Before we leave this section on quality, you need to know that there is some disagreement in the profession on how to measure quality costs. In fact, you may have even noticed a discrepancy in the section you just read. Remember that earlier we discussed the importance of identifying the proper level of quality in the organization by offsetting prevention and appraisal costs against internal and external failure costs in order to minimize total costs of quality (COQ). It appears, therefore, that COQ trade-offs will typically justify a level of quality that is less than 100% conformance to all control limits. On the other hand, our discussion of measuring the costs of lost sales using the Taguchi quality loss function seems to indicate that "quality is free!" In other words, when one understands the *full extent* of external failure costs, the minimal quality cost trade-off point is very close to or exceeds 100% conformance. Hence, using the Taguchi quality loss function, companies should spend whatever it takes to have absolute quality and customer satisfaction. Remember that this is the essence of TQM—that quality is emphasized above all else, including costs. Not everyone feels this strongly about TQM. Some managers and accountants disagree with a "field of dreams" approach to managing quality costs (i.e., "if you build *perfect* quality, profits will come"). You should pay attention to this current debate, as there is good logic on both sides. The real test of this concept is in the competitive marketplace. In any event, management accounting systems need to measure COQ, including the cost of lost sales, in order to add competitive value to the organization's TQM efforts.

to summarize

The Taguchi quality loss function attempts to measure external failure costs using a formula where L (quality loss) = C (cost to correct) × D^2 (distance from target). The quality loss function is not a precise measure of external failure costs, but it provides an approximate signal of the significant opportunity costs organizations experience when less-than-perfect goods and services are provided to customers. Using the quality loss function, accountants can provide important insight to help their companies better compete in the marketplace. Some TQM advocates suggest that organizations should strive for 100% quality conformance. These individuals defend this position by suggesting that most organizations underestimate failure costs as a product or service process moves away from 100% quality conformance. Nevertheless, there is currently an active debate on the issue of whether perfect quality is too costly to achieve.

review of learning objectives

1 Explain the fundamentals of activity-based costing (ABC) and activity-based management (ABM). Unit-based costing (UBC) systems generally allocate all manufacturing overhead costs based on some measure related to the number of products being produced or the amount of service being provided in the organization (e.g., direct labor hours). In settings with little diversity in the types of products or services offered to customers, UBC may be an appropriate tool. On the other hand, activity-based costing (ABC) recognizes that activities are the causes of costs. Activities can be categorized across four levels: unit-level activities, batch-level activities, product line activities, and facility support activities. Generally, variable overhead such as machine maintenance or energy costs to run production equipment is a function of the number of units produced. Setup costs, materials purchase orders, and route planning are examples of costs traditionally considered fixed that actually are variable in relation to the number of batch runs within the organization. Overhead costs that are a function of product line activities are generally related to engineering, supervision, and warehousing. Once activity cost pools have been created, costs of unit-level, batch-level, and product line activities can be assigned to products. If costs of batch-level and product line activities are allocated using UBC, then some products may be inappropriately assigned costs that actually belong to another product. This particular cost distortion is referred to as product cost cross-subsidization.

Costs of facility support activities (e.g., property taxes, plant security, landscaping, accounting, and executive administration) cannot be sensibly connected to any particular product line. These costs (otherwise known as common costs) should *not* be allocated to individual product lines. Otherwise, product costs are distorted, which can lead to a series of management decisions called a death spiral. Managers inadvertently involved in a death spiral will make a decision to drop a product or service line based on UBC data that erroneously suggest that these products or services are unprofitable.

The point of ABC is to appropriately *assign* costs to products. However, ABC does not really provide useful information for managing activities. To *manage* costs of activities, a set of activity cost drivers that provides the greatest influence on the activity cost pool is identified. To manage activity performance, a set of quality- and time-based measures is also created and related to each critical activity in the organization. The process of managing activities using cost drivers and performance measures is called activity-based management (ABM). ABC and ABM combine to form the following model of activities:

Activity Cost Drivers
↓
Costs → Activities → Products
↑
Performance Measures

2 Describe total quality management (TQM) and costs of quality (COQ). Total quality management (TQM) is a philosophy in which (1) product and process quality is emphasized over profits and (2) quality must be measured in order to be realized. Using SPC (statistical process control), W. Edward Deming became one of the pioneers of TQM in both Japan and America. SPC establishes control limits. When the variation in the product or service exceeds the control limits established by the firm, then managers begin work to increase the quality of the production process. Joseph M. Juran expanded the process of SPC in order to manage four specific types of costs of quality (COQ). Prevention and appraisal costs are viewed as investments in the process of keeping products and services within established control limits. When the production process starts creating variation outside the control limits, internal failure costs (such as scrap and employee downtime) and external failure costs (such as handling complaints and product recalls) occur. If increasing prevention and appraisal costs offset decreasing failure costs, then management accountants should help companies understand how to minimize total quality costs. Identifying quality costs can be a challenge, however, because these costs are generally intermingled across both product and period costs within most organizations' accounting systems. Costs of lost sales due to customer dissatisfaction are important opportunity costs, yet they are particularly difficult to measure.

3 Describe how just-in-time (JIT) management systems integrate with and extend ABC and TQM using time-based performance measures. Just-in-time (JIT) has become an important tool for managing manufacturing, service, and merchandising companies across the world. In a manufacturing setting, demand at the final assembly stage "pulls" the inventory through the production process only as it is needed. Using this system, nothing is produced until customers demand it. Like ABC and COQ, JIT puts a strong emphasis on costs and quality. However, JIT also focuses on management of timeliness and flexibility. The main goal of JIT is to add value to the product or service and reduce or eliminate activities that do not. By focusing on removing non-value-added activities and reducing time spent on value-added activities, inventories and other costs are reduced, while quality and timeliness are improved. It is important to point out that JIT, ABC, and COQ all interact well to support managers in the new business environment. COQ helps identify value and non-value-added activities. JIT improves quality and timeliness by eliminating non-value-added activities. ABC more accurately assigns costs to the remaining value-added activities.

expanded material

4 **Compute the opportunity cost of lost sales.** The Taguchi quality loss function provides a means of approximately measuring the impact of *all* external failure costs on the company's costs—including the opportunity costs of lost sales due to customer dissatisfaction. The Taguchi quality loss function measures these costs using a formula where L (quality loss) $= C$ (cost to correct) $\times D^2$ (distance from target). Using this formula, accountants can provide an important signal of the significant opportunity costs organizations experience when less-than-perfect goods and services are provided to customers. Currently, in light of the likely size of cost of external failure, there is some debate on whether prevention and appraisal costs can ever increase enough to justify having less-than-perfect conformance to control limits (i.e., perfect quality).

key terms and concepts

activity-based costing (ABC) 347
activity-based management (ABM) 365
appraisal costs 370
batch-level activities 356
capability costs 357
common costs 351
conversion costs 347
cost driver 353
costs of quality (COQ) 369
cross-subsidization 351
death spiral 361
external failure costs 371
facility support activities 357
Hierarchical Product Cost Model 351
internal failure costs 370
just-in-time (JIT) 374
non-value-added activities 375
prevention costs 370
prime costs 347
product line activities 356
statistical process control (SPC) 367
total quality management (TQM) 367
unit-based costing (UBC) 352
unit-level activities 354
value-added activities 375

expanded material

robust quality 379
Taguchi quality loss function 380

review problem

ABC versus Conventional Product Costing

Willett Company makes two types of products: Product A and Product B. The company's management accountants accumulated the following production cost information for 2003:

	Product A	Product B	Total
Production volume (units)	1,000	500	
Number of engineering changes per product line	4	8	
Total cost of engineering changes			$12,000
Direct labor hours per unit	3	2	
Direct materials cost per unit	$5	$7	
Direct labor cost per hour	$6	$12	

Required: Assume Product A sells for $42 each and Product B sells for $50 each. Assume also that engineering changes are the only manufacturing overhead cost Willett Company incurs. If all products are sold, what is the gross margin of each product assuming the following:

1. Engineering change costs are allocated on the basis of direct labor hours.
2. Engineering change costs are allocated on the basis of the number of engineering changes made.

Solution **1. Allocation on the Basis of Direct Labor Hours**

	Product A (1,000 units)	Product B (500 units)
Sales	$42,000 (1,000 × $42)	$25,000 (500 × $50)
Cost of goods sold:		
Direct materials	$ 5,000 (1,000 × $5)	$ 3,500 (500 × $7)
Direct labor	18,000 (1,000 × 3 hr × $6)	12,000 (500 × 2 hr × $12)
Manufacturing overhead	9,000 (1,000 × 3 hr × $3*)	3,000 (500 × 2 hr × $3*)
Total cost of goods sold	$32,000	$18,500
Gross margin	$10,000	$ 6,500

*Overhead allocation per direct labor hour:

$$\frac{\$12{,}000 \text{ total costs}}{4{,}000 \text{ total direct labor hours}} = \$3 \text{ per direct labor hour}$$

Product A	(1,000 × 3 hr) =	3,000
Product B	(500 × 2 hr) =	1,000
Total		4,000 direct labor hours

2. Allocation on the Basis of Engineering Changes

Sales	$42,000	$25,000
Cost of goods sold:		
Direct materials	$ 5,000	$ 3,500
Direct labor	18,000	12,000
Manufacturing overhead	4,000*	8,000*
Total cost of goods sold	$27,000	$23,500
Gross margin	$15,000	$ 1,500

*Overhead allocation per engineering change:

$$\text{Cost per change: } \frac{\$12{,}000}{12} = \$1{,}000 \text{ per change}$$

Overhead allocations per product:

Product A: 4 changes × $1,000 per change =	$ 4,000
Product B: 8 changes × $1,000 per change =	8,000
Total	$12,000

discussion questions

1. What is the lowest price that a company should charge its customers?
2. What is the difference between a product cost and a period cost?
3. Traditionally, what basis has been used to allocate manufacturing overhead costs to products?
4. What type of incorrect decision can be made if a cost accounting system allows cross-subsidization of product costs?
5. "Given enough time, every cost is fixed." Do you agree or disagree? Explain.

6. In what context does a unit-based costing (UBC) system cause problems?
7. Under a Hierarchical Product Cost Model, what are the four classifications of production costs?
8. Give three examples of batch-level activities.
9. In general, which type of fast-food outlet would have higher overhead costs: an outlet selling hamburgers, pizza, and chicken or an outlet selling only hamburgers? Explain.
10. Give three examples of facility support costs.
11. How can the allocation of common costs potentially cause a death spiral?
12. ABC (activity-based costing) uses activity allocation rates in product costing. How are activity cost drivers used in ABM (activity-based management)?
13. In what way do Edward Deming's ideas of total quality management (TQM) change Andrew Carnegie's slogan, "Watch the costs and the profits will take care of themselves"?
14. Briefly describe the four types of costs in costs of quality (COQ).
15. Why are external failure costs generally the highest of the costs of quality (COQ)?
16. How did the concept of just-in-time (JIT) change the view of most companies that maintaining a minimum level of inventory was desirable? Use the measures of cost, quality, and time as you prepare your answer.
17. "The purpose of just-in-time (JIT) is to reduce inventory." Do you agree or disagree? Explain.

expanded material

18. Describe the concept of robust quality.
19. According to the Taguchi quality loss function, what happens to the total loss due to external failure as a product's quality gets further from target specifications?

discussion cases

CASE 7-1

PARAMOUNT SKIS

Paramount Skis produces three models of skis: Novice, Straightaway, and Mogulist. Sales and costing information for the three models are as follows:

	Novice	Straightaway	Mogulist
Selling price per unit	$130	$250	$300
Units produced	13,000	8,000	6,000
Direct materials cost	$780,000	$400,000	$240,000
Direct labor cost	$130,000	$52,000	$42,000

In the past, manufacturing overhead has been allocated based on number of units produced. Manufacturing overhead for the period is $1,620,000, and the predetermined overhead rate is $60 per unit produced.

Based on this information, management has determined that the Novice is barely breaking even. Because the market for skis is quite competitive, the price for each model is set by the market—not by management. Thus, increasing the price charged for products is not an option. As a result, management is considering discontinuing the Novice. Before making a final decision, management has come to you for advice. You collect the following information regarding manufacturing overhead:

Manufacturing Overhead	Manufacturing Overhead Costs	Allocation Bases
Engineering	$ 250,000	Engineering changes
Quality control	750,000	Number of units produced
Manufacturing support	620,000	Number of setups
Total overhead	$1,620,000	

Allocation Bases	Novice	Straightaway	Mogulist
Engineering changes	3	7	5
Number of units produced	13,000	8,000	6,000
Number of setups	29	78	63

Determine the gross profit for each model under the current manufacturing overhead allocation scheme. Determine the manufacturing overhead cost for each model using the information relating to activities. Determine the gross profit for each model using the ABC allocated manufacturing overhead. What recommendation would you make to management regarding its decision to discontinue the Novice?

CASE 7-2

COSTS OF QUALITY (SLEEPY INN MOTELS)

You are the leader of a group of investors that is planning to open a nationwide chain of low-cost motels that you will call "Sleepy Inn Motels." You are preparing for a strategy meeting that will be held tomorrow. The investor group is considering two strategies for how the motel chain will be operated. One strategy, which you have titled "Quality," proposes to market the motel chain as the quality leader among low-cost motels. The motels will be located in good neighborhoods, will offer swimming pools and other amenities, and will have well-appointed rooms. The motels will also have good maid service, a trained manager on site 24 hours per day to handle guest complaints, and a national troubleshooting team that will promptly fly to any location to investigate consistent patterns in customer complaints received via a toll-free complaint hotline.

You have titled the other strategy "Quick and Dirty." The motels will be located wherever cheap real estate can be found, will be staffed with the lowest-cost labor possible, and will offer no amenities, no reservations, and low-budget room furnishings. There will be no mechanism for receiving customer complaints, and the night manager will not be authorized to do anything more than distribute room keys and collect cash.

A significant portion of the investor group advocates the "Quick and Dirty" strategy, arguing that it offers the lowest operating costs and, therefore, the highest profit. You are worried that these investors may not have thought carefully about all the costs associated with this strategy. Using the costs of quality (COQ) categories, outline some of the major costs that will differ between these two motel strategies.

exercises

EXERCISE 7-1

PRODUCT COSTING REVIEW

Mad Dog Enterprises manufactures computer game control devices such as joysticks and steering wheels. Following is a list of the costs incurred by Mad Dog in 2003:

Wages paid to assembly workers	$100,000
Cost of plastic used in making devices	25,000
Insurance on factory building	12,000
Salary of factory supervisor	57,000
Interest on money borrowed to finance operations	34,000
Wages paid to factory maintenance workers	61,000
Cost of computer/controller boards installed in devices	38,000
Advertising costs	127,000
Cost of electricity used in factory	46,000

Compute the total cost for each of the following categories:

1. Direct materials
2. Direct labor
3. Manufacturing overhead
4. Period costs

EXERCISE 7-2

IMPORTANCE OF MANUFACTURING OVERHEAD ALLOCATION

The percentages of product costs comprised by direct materials, direct labor, and manufacturing overhead for three companies are as follows:

	Company A	Company B	Company C
Direct materials	45%	31%	13%
Direct labor	22	62	8
Manufacturing overhead	33	7	79
	100%	100%	100%

Based on this information, which of these three companies would probably improve its product-costing accuracy most by converting to activity-based costing (ABC)? Explain your answer.

EXERCISE 7-3

PRODUCT COST HIERARCHY

For the following list of costs, indicate by the appropriate letter which category of activities each cost applies to: unit level (U), batch level (B), product line (P), or facility support (F):

a. Machine fine-tuning adjustment cost (required after the production of each unit)
b. Salary of vice president of finance
c. Machine inspection cost (required after the completion of each day's production)
d. Cost of the external audit firm
e. Direct labor
f. Product testing cost (performed at the start of each day's production)
g. Direct materials
h. Factory security cost
i. Machine straight-line depreciation cost (Generally, machines are dedicated to producing a particular type of product.)
j. Warehousing cost (Each type of product has its own warehouse.)
k. Employee training cost (Training is generally specific to different types of products.)

EXERCISE 7-4

IDENTIFYING CROSS-SUBSIDIZATION

Cottrell Company manufactures three products. Gross margin computations for these three products for 2003 are given below.

	Product A	Product B	Product C
Sales	$ 300,000	$500,000	$600,000
Direct materials	(50,000)	(250,000)	(200,000)
Direct labor	(150,000)	(50,000)	(100,000)
Manufacturing overhead*	(225,000)	(75,000)	(150,000)
Gross margin	$(125,000)	$125,000	$150,000

*Manufacturing overhead is allocated to production based on the amount of direct labor cost.

Cottrell has reexamined the factors that cause its manufacturing overhead costs and has discovered that the annual amount of manufacturing overhead is more closely related to the number of product batches produced during the year than it is to direct labor costs. The number of batches of the three products for 2003 was as follows: Product A, 10 batches; Product B, 60 batches; Product C, 30 batches.

1. Prepare gross margin calculations for Cottrell's three products assuming that manufacturing overhead is allocated based on the number of batches.
2. Under the direct labor cost method of manufacturing overhead allocation, one of Cottrell's products received a cross-subsidization from the others. Which product received the subsidization, and what was the amount of the subsidization?

EXERCISE 7-5

ALLOCATING BATCH-LEVEL AND PRODUCT LINE MANUFACTURING OVERHEAD COSTS

Grantsville Company has two divisions. Gross margin computations for these two divisions for 2003 are given below.

	Industrial Products	Consumer Products
Sales	$600,000	$900,000
Direct materials	(100,000)	(150,000)
Direct labor	(300,000)	(300,000)
Manufacturing overhead*	(250,000)	(250,000)
Gross margin	$ (50,000)	$200,000

*Manufacturing overhead is allocated to production based on the amount of direct labor cost.

Grantsville has determined that its total manufacturing overhead cost of $500,000 is a mixture of batch-level costs and product line costs. Grantsville has assembled the following information concerning the manufacturing overhead costs, the annual number of production batches in each division, and the number of product lines in each division:

	Total Mfg. Overhead Costs	Industrial Products	Consumer Products
Batch-level manufacturing overhead	$300,000	10 batches	40 batches
Product line manufacturing overhead	200,000	5 lines	15 lines
	$500,000		

1. Prepare gross margin calculations for Grantsville's two divisions assuming that manufacturing overhead is allocated based on the number of batches and number of product lines.
2. Under the direct labor cost method of manufacturing overhead allocation, which division received a cross-subsidization, and what was the amount of the cross-subsidization?

EXERCISE 7-6

COMMON COSTS AND THE DEATH SPIRAL

Blaine Avenue Company manufactures three products. Gross margin computations for these three products for 2003 are given below.

	Product X	Product Y	Product Z
Sales	$800,000	$700,000	$ 600,000
Direct materials	(50,000)	(150,000)	(200,000)
Direct labor	(50,000)	(200,000)	(250,000)
Manufacturing overhead*	(80,000)	(320,000)	(400,000)
Gross margin	$620,000	$ 30,000	$(250,000)

*Manufacturing overhead is allocated to production based on the amount of direct labor cost.

Blaine Avenue has reexamined the activities that relate to its manufacturing overhead costs and has discovered that $500,000 of the annual amount of manufacturing overhead is directly related to the number of product batches produced during the year. The number of batches of the three products for 2003 was as follows: Product X, 100 batches; Product Y, 100 batches; Product Z, 50 batches. The remaining $300,000 in overhead is for facility support (property taxes, security costs, general administration, etc.) and does not vary at all with the level of activity.

1. Prepare gross margin calculations for Blaine Avenue's three products assuming that manufacturing overhead is allocated based on the number of batches. Also, show a "total" column. Facility support costs are not to be allocated to any of the products, but are to be subtracted in the "total" column in the computation of total company operating profit.
2. Using the gross margin numbers prepared under the direct labor cost method of manufacturing overhead allocation, Blaine Avenue's board of directors has tentatively decided to discontinue the Z product line. Assume that this was done at the beginning of 2003. What would have happened to total company operating profit for the year? Explain.

EXERCISE 7-7

COSTS OF QUALITY

Some of the costs in the list below are costs of quality. For each cost, indicate by the appropriate letter what type of cost it is: prevention cost (P), appraisal cost (A), internal failure cost (I), external failure cost (E), or not a cost of quality (N/A).

a. Cost of raw materials used in discarded, defective products
b. Salary of the president of the company
c. Cost to purchase product testing equipment
d. Lawsuit costs stemming from the sale of defective products
e. Cost to repair defective products before shipment
f. Employee quality training costs
g. Employee downtime caused by production halts to repair defective products
h. Cost of sampling raw materials to ensure quality
i. Customer warranty costs
j. Property taxes
k. Cost of lost reputation (i.e., lost sales)
l. Cost to help suppliers improve their product shipping procedures
m. Interest cost on short-term loans
n. Production process design costs

EXERCISE 7-8

OPTIMAL LEVEL OF COSTS OF QUALITY

Leslie Angel is planning to open her own textbook publishing company. Leslie is trying to decide whether to provide low-quality textbooks, average-quality textbooks, or high-quality textbooks. Leslie has analyzed the costs of quality related to publishing textbooks and has developed the following analysis of the costs of quality:

- *Prevention costs:* The best way to ensure the quality of a textbook is to hire good authors and to increase the amount of time the authors spend on researching and writing the text material. Of course, high-quality authors cost more.
- *Appraisal costs:* To improve the quality of the text material, Leslie can hire independent verifiers to determine whether the text is readable and correct and whether the homework problems are solvable.
- *Internal failure costs:* Sometimes an error in the text is found just before the book is to be printed. In such a case, Leslie must require the authors to spend extra time fixing the text.
- *External failure costs:* If a textbook containing lots of errors is sold, the bad reputation created will hurt potential future sales. To counteract this effect, Leslie must spend more on advertising.

Leslie has gathered the following numerical information about the costs of quality in relation to publishing textbooks:

	Low Quality	Average Quality	High Quality
Prevention costs:			
Author hours spent on text	100 hours	500 hours	1,000 hours
Author salary rate	$50/hour	$60/hour	$70/hour
Appraisal costs:			
Verifier hours spent on text	50 hours	200 hours	800 hours
Verifier salary rate	$20/hour	$20/hour	$20/hour
Internal failure costs:			
Author hours spent fixing text	400 hours	200 hours	20 hours
Author salary rate	$50/hour	$60/hour	$70/hour
External failure costs:			
Cost of advertising	$60,000	$20,000	$5,000

Which type of textbooks—low-, average-, or high-quality—should Leslie publish in order to minimize her total costs of quality? Show your calculations.

EXERCISE 7-9

JIT INVENTORY

The president of Penman Corporation, John Burton, has asked you, the company's controller, to advise him on whether Penman should develop a just-in-time (JIT) inventory system. Your research concludes that there is a high cost associated with inventory storage facilities; that inventories use a large portion of the company's cash flow; and that because of the nature of the inventory, there is a significant amount of shrinkage. Research also shows that neither of Penman's two competitors uses a JIT inventory system. Most of Penman's employees are trained to do only one job and belong to a local union. The union is strong and, in the past, has opposed major production changes. The union believes major changes will result in the loss of union employees' jobs. Your research indicates that Penman's major production item (a fairly new product in the market) should continue to have strong sales growth.

1. Using the information provided, advise John Burton to either continue the present system or work to develop a JIT inventory system.
2. Assume John decides to develop an inventory management system. He plans to evaluate the system after one year. List at least four possible performance measures John could use to evaluate the effectiveness of the system. Describe what information these measures would provide John.

EXERCISE 7-10

VALUE-ADDED AND NON-VALUE-ADDED ACTIVITIES

Below is a list of activities performed by the Ibapah Bijou, a movie theater. Indicate whether each activity is a value-added activity (VA) or a non-value-added activity (NVA).

a. Redesigning the staff uniforms.
b. Cooking popcorn.
c. Counting the ticket stubs at night to make sure no one got in free.
d. Servicing the quadraphonic speaker system.
e. Paying for the rights to show the next movie starring Julia Roberts.
f. Paying a management fee for the employee pension fund.
g. Renting a storage facility to store the excess inventory of candy, uncooked popcorn, and soft drinks.
h. Paying the accounts payable.
i. Cleaning the white movie screens.
j. Scrubbing the theater floor to remove the sticky residue of spilled soft drinks.

expanded material

EXERCISE 7-11

TAGUCHI QUALITY LOSS FUNCTION

Cooley Lane Company manufactures computer disk drives. Occasionally, a defective disk drive (one that spins at the wrong revolutions per minute) is shipped to a customer. Cooley Lane's policy is to fix the drive for free when it is returned by a complaining customer. Cooley Lane has a standardized statistical defect measure whereby each defective drive is given a score of 0 through 5 to indicate how bad it is, with 5 being the worst. A perfect drive receives a score of 0. The direct material and direct labor cost to fix a defective drive is only $25.

The manager in charge of product quality has recently been reading about the Taguchi quality loss function, and she thinks that Cooley Lane is underestimating the external failure costs associated with a defective disk drive. She thinks that Cooley Lane should consider increasing the amount it spends on prevention and appraisal in order to reduce the number of defective drives returned by customers. In the past month, 15 drives have been returned by customers. The drives had the following standardized defect scores:

Standardized Defect Score	Number of Defective Drives
1	2
2	1
3	1
4	4
5	7

Using the Taguchi quality loss function, estimate the dollar value of the quality loss associated with the external failure of these defective drives.

problems

PROBLEM 7-1

IDENTIFYING CROSS-SUBSIDIZATION

Dugway Company has three operating divisions. Gross margin computations for these three divisions for 2003 are given below.

	Division R	Division S	Division T
Sales	$300,000	$200,000	$150,000
Direct materials	(50,000)	(100,000)	(40,000)
Direct labor	(150,000)	(30,000)	(70,000)
Manufacturing overhead*	(105,000)	(21,000)	(49,000)
Gross margin	$ (5,000)	$ 49,000	$ (9,000)

*Manufacturing overhead is allocated to production based on the amount of direct labor cost.

Dugway has determined that its total manufacturing overhead cost of $175,000 is a mixture of batch-level costs and product line costs. Dugway has assembled the following information concerning the overhead costs, the annual number of production batches in each division, and the number of product lines in each division:

	Total Mfg. Overhead Costs	Division R	Division S	Division T
Batch-level overhead	$100,000	10 batches	40 batches	50 batches
Product line overhead	75,000	5 lines	15 lines	20 lines
	$175,000			

Required:

1. Prepare gross margin calculations for Dugway's three divisions assuming that manufacturing overhead is allocated based on the number of batches and the number of product lines.
2. Under the direct labor cost method of manufacturing overhead allocation, one or more of Dugway's divisions received a cross-subsidization from one or more of the others. Which division(s) received subsidizations, and what was the amount of the subsidizations?
3. After preparing the gross margin calculations in part (1), what advice do you have for Dugway concerning whether it should shut down any of its three divisions? Is this the same advice that would come from looking at the original gross margin calculations using manufacturing overhead allocated according to direct labor cost? Why is there a difference?

PROBLEM 7-2

ALLOCATING UNIT-LEVEL, BATCH-LEVEL, AND PRODUCT LINE MANUFACTURING OVERHEAD COSTS

Solar Salt Company has two divisions. Gross margin computations for these two divisions for 2003 are given below.

	Agricultural Products	Retail Products
Sales	$1,600,000	$900,000
Direct materials	(100,000)	(50,000)
Direct labor	(900,000)	(500,000)
Manufacturing overhead*	(450,000)	(250,000)
Gross margin	$ 150,000	$100,000

*Manufacturing overhead is allocated to production based on the amount of direct labor cost.

Solar Salt has determined that its total manufacturing overhead cost of $700,000 is a mixture of unit-level costs, batch-level costs, and product line costs. Solar Salt has assembled the following information concerning the manufacturing overhead costs, the annual number of units produced, production batches, and number of product lines in each division:

	Total Mfg. Overhead Costs	Agricultural Products	Retail Products
Unit-level overhead	$210,000	13,500 units	7,500 units
Batch-level overhead	280,000	90 batches	50 batches
Product line overhead	210,000	18 lines	10 lines
	$700,000		

Required:

1. Prepare gross margin calculations for Solar Salt's two divisions assuming that manufacturing overhead is allocated based on the number of units, number of batches, and number of product lines.

2. Comment on the comparison between the original overhead allocation done using direct labor cost and the manufacturing overhead allocation done in part (1).
3. Repeat part (1), assuming the following information concerning the number of units, batches, and product lines in each division.

	Total Mfg. Overhead Costs	Agricultural Products	Retail Products
Unit-level overhead	$210,000	13,500 units	7,500 units
Batch-level overhead	280,000	50 batches	90 batches
Product line overhead	210,000	10 lines	18 lines
	$700,000		

PROBLEM 7-3

IDENTIFYING AND USING VOLUME-BASED AND ACTIVITY-BASED COST ALLOCATION RATES

Rane Company produces electronic fish finders. It makes two different fish finders: the standard model, which is produced in bulk and sells for $150, and the deluxe model, which comes in various configurations and sells for $300. Rane's engineering and design overhead cost for 2003 is $60,000. The following information relates to production in 2003:

Number of different machine setups needed for a standard model production run	4
Number of different machine setups needed for a deluxe model production run	11
Number of standard fish finders produced	22,000
Number of deluxe fish finders produced	8,000
Average batch size per production run for standard model	400
Average batch size per production run for deluxe model	200

Required:

1. Determine the engineering and design costs to be assigned to standard and deluxe fish finders using the following allocation methods:
   a. Number of units produced
   b. Number of setups required
2. Which allocation method do you believe is more equitable?

PROBLEM 7-4

COMMON COSTS AND THE DEATH SPIRAL

Clark Street Company manufactures three products. Gross margin computations for these three products for 2003 are as follows:

	Product J	Product K	Product L
Sales	$800,000	$700,000	$ 600,000
Direct materials	(150,000)	(50,000)	(200,000)
Direct labor	(50,000)	(200,000)	(250,000)
Manufacturing overhead*	(80,000)	(320,000)	(400,000)
Gross margin	$520,000	$130,000	$(250,000)

*Manufacturing overhead is allocated to production based on the amount of direct labor cost.

Clark Street has reexamined the factors that cause its manufacturing overhead costs and has discovered that $300,000 of the annual amount of manufacturing overhead is directly related to the number of product batches produced during the year. The number of batches of the three products for 2003 was as follows: Product J, 150 batches; Product K, 100 batches; Product L, 50 batches. The remaining $500,000 in manufacturing overhead is for facility support (property taxes, security costs, general administration, etc.) and does not vary at all with levels of manufacturing activity in the company.

Required:

1. Assume that Product L was eliminated at the start of the year. Estimate what the gross margin for the remaining two products would have been. Use the direct labor cost method of overhead allocation.
2. Now, assume that both Product K and Product L were eliminated at the start of the year. Estimate what the gross margin for the remaining product, Product J, would have been. No manufacturing overhead allocation is needed because there is only one product.
3. In light of your answers in parts (1) and (2), what problems can arise when facility support manufacturing overhead costs are allocated?
4. Prepare gross margin calculations for Clark Street's three products assuming that manufacturing overhead is allocated based on the number of batches. Also, show a "total" column. Facility support costs are not to be allocated to any of the products, but are to be subtracted in the "total" column in the computation of total company operating profit.

PROBLEM 7-5

MANUFACTURING OVERHEAD ALLOCATION USING ACTIVITY-BASED COSTING

The following information is given for the Greenbaum Manufacturing Company:

	Product A	Product B	Product C	Product D
Units produced	3,000	3,450	2,875	2,400
Direct materials cost	$135,000	$169,050	$149,500	$103,200
Direct labor cost	$75,000	$124,200	$117,875	$93,600

Manufacturing Overhead	Mfg. Overhead Costs	Relevant Activities
Engineering	$209,950	Engineering changes
Quality control	129,500	Number of setups
Maintenance	41,065	Maintenance hours worked in each area of production
Manufacturing support	93,800	Production volume (units produced)

Activities	Product A	Product B	Product C	Product D
Engineering changes	300	150	275	125
Number of setups	12	5	9	11
Maintenance hours worked in each area of production	45	49	56	41
Production volume	3,000	3,450	2,875	2,400

Required:

1. Determine the ABC allocation rate for each activity (i.e., each manufacturing overhead cost pool).
2. Determine the manufacturing overhead cost for each product.
3. If products A, B, C, and D sell for $130, $125, $156, and $166, respectively, determine the gross margin for Greenbaum's four products. Assume all units are sold.

PROBLEM 7-6

MANUFACTURING OVERHEAD ALLOCATION USING ACTIVITY-BASED COSTING

Twigco Transmission Company manufactures three different automobile transmissions. The first model is an automatic transmission, the second model is a 4-gear manual transmission, and the third model is a 5-gear manual transmission. Relevant information for each transmission is provided as follows:

	Automatic		4-Gear		5-Gear	
	Total	Per Unit	Total	Per Unit	Total	Per Unit
Units produced	10,000		8,000		6,000	
Direct materials cost	$2,000,000	$200	$1,200,000	$150	$1,050,000	$175
Direct labor cost	$2,700,000	$270	$1,600,000	$200	$1,350,000	$225
Sales price		$505		$425		$455
Purchases per year	22		26		27	
Number of machine setups per unit	30		34		40	
Engineering change orders	36		42		50	

Total manufacturing overhead cost pools:

Engineering	$304,000
Quality control	260,000
Purchasing costs	150,000
Machine maintenance costs	240,000
Total costs	$954,000

Required:

1. Determine the gross margin for each product allocating manufacturing overhead costs on the basis of production volume (units produced).
2. Identify appropriate allocation bases for each of the four pools of manufacturing overhead costs.
3. Determine the ABC allocation rates for each of the four cost pools suggested in part (2).
4. Using the allocation bases suggested in part (2), determine manufacturing overhead costs per product.
5. a. Determine the gross margin per product using the manufacturing overhead costs determined in part (4).
   b. **Interpretive Question:** Which of the methods (unit-based costing or activity-based costing) is the better method to allocate the manufacturing overhead costs?

PROBLEM 7-7

MANUFACTURING OVERHEAD ALLOCATION WITH MULTIPLE PRODUCTS

Schmidt Electronics produces two products: CD105 and HD210. Relevant costing information for each product is as follows:

Per Unit	CD105	HD210
Direct materials	$10.50	$17.25
Direct labor	$10.00	$15.00
Direct labor hours per unit	1	2
Total number of machine setups	400	200
Units produced	6,000	7,000

Manufacturing overhead costs and associated ABC allocation bases are as follows:

	Mfg. Overhead Costs	Allocation Bases
Product inspection	$30,000	Units produced
Materials management	48,000	Number of machine setups
Manufacturing support	16,000	Product lines

Required:

1. If manufacturing overhead is allocated on the basis of direct labor hours, compute the cost per unit for CD105 and HD210.
2. Determine the allocation rate per activity for each ABC allocation basis.
3. Determine the manufacturing overhead cost for each product using your answer to part (2).
4. Using your answer to part (3), compute the cost per unit for CD105 and HD210.
5. Compare your answers to part (1) and part (4). Why the difference in costs?

PROBLEM 7-8

ACTIVITY-BASED COSTING AND GROSS MARGIN CALCULATIONS

Stafford Manufacturing, Inc., produces two different products. Product 1 sells for $950 each, and Product 2 sells for $700 each. Estimated annual production and sales for Product 1 and Product 2 are 2,100 units and 2,900 units, respectively. Direct materials are $350 for Product 1 and $200 for Product 2. Direct labor costs are $300 for Product 1 and $310 for Product 2. Stafford purchases materials for Product 1 every month and for Product 2 every two months. On average, Stafford performs 10 setups each month for Product 1 production and 8 setups each month for Product 2 production. The following are manufacturing overhead costs incurred by Stafford Manufacturing:

Quality control	$150,000
Purchasing costs	74,880
Miscellaneous manufacturing overhead	62,640

Required:

1. Assuming that the allocation bases for the three manufacturing overhead costs are production volume for quality control, number of purchases for purchasing costs, and number of setups for miscellaneous manufacturing overhead, calculate the cost per unit of each allocation basis.
2. Determine total manufacturing overhead costs for each product.
3. Determine the gross margin percent for Stafford Manufacturing for each product it produces.

PROBLEM 7-9

ALLOCATION OF MANUFACTURING OVERHEAD WITH MULTIPLE PRODUCTS

Central, Inc., is a manufacturing firm that manufactures two types of airplane motors. The Type 1 motor is a jet engine that is designed for medium-size military aircraft. Because of a long-term contract with the military, Type 1 motors need no modifications. Type 2 motors are designed for larger commercial aircraft. Because the Type 2 motor is designed for several different models of airplanes and the mounting hardware is different for each, retooling is regularly required. Costs for the two types of engines are presented here:

	Type 1 Engine (400 Units Produced)		Type 2 Engine (180 Units Produced)	
	Total	**Per Unit**	**Total**	**Per Unit**
Direct materials cost	$108,000,000	$270,000	$70,200,000	$390,000
Direct labor cost	72,000,000	180,000	46,800,000	260,000
Manufacturing overhead costs:				
Engineering costs				$576,000,000
Quality control				155,520,000
Utilities and maintenance				5,220,000

Required:

1. Determine the amount of manufacturing overhead to be assigned to each unit of activity assuming the following ABC information:

Manufacturing Overhead Cost	*Allocation Bases*
• Engineering costs	• Engineering change orders per unit
• Quality control	• Machine setups per unit
• Utilities and maintenance	• Production volume

Type 1 Engines
- 0 engineering change orders per unit
- 18 machine setups per unit
- 400 units produced

Type 2 Engines
- 16 engineering change orders per unit
- 32 machine setups per unit
- 180 units produced

2. Determine the amount of manufacturing overhead to be assigned to each type of engine.
3. Compute the gross margin on Type 1 and Type 2 engines assuming selling prices of $1 million and $4 million, respectively.

PROBLEM 7-10

ALLOCATION OF MANUFACTURING OVERHEAD WITH MULTIPLE PRODUCTS

Macey Sprinkling Company produces two types of pipe: (1) lawn sprinkler pipe and (2) building sprinkler pipe. Relevant information for the production of the two types of pipe for 2003 is as follows:

	Lawn Sprinkler Pipe	Building Sprinkler Pipe
Feet produced	325,000	150,000
Prime costs	$243,750	$123,000
Manufacturing overhead costs:		
Utilities	$ 75,000	$ 40,000
Support staff	63,000	35,750
Quality control	8,000	4,060
Purchasing	19,200	10,250

Macey allocates utilities and support staff costs on the basis of production volume, quality control costs on the basis of number of machine setups required, and purchasing department costs on the basis of number of purchase orders. During 2003, volume of these various activities per *product line* was:

	Lawn Sprinkler Pipe	Building Sprinkler Pipe
Production volume	325,000 ft.	150,000 ft.
Machine setups	12	24
Purchase orders	1	30

Required:

1. Determine the cost per unit for each cost driver.
2. Determine the amount of manufacturing overhead to be assigned to the two types of sprinkler pipe.
3. Determine the total cost for each type of pipe produced for the year.

PROBLEM 7-11

COSTS OF QUALITY

DeeAnn Martinez is preparing to open her own CPA firm. DeeAnn is a smart businessperson and wants to maximize her profits. She has not yet decided whether to run a low-quality CPA firm (basically offering to sign the financial statements of anyone who will pay her fee), an average CPA firm, or a premium-quality CPA firm (competing head-to-head with the large international accounting firms such as PRICEWATERHOUSE COOPERS).

DeeAnn has analyzed the costs of quality related to operating a CPA firm and has developed the following analysis:

- *Prevention costs:* The best way to ensure the quality of the audit is to increase the quality of the staff hired and to increase the time that the staff spends on each audit. DeeAnn realizes that hiring higher-quality staff will cost more.
- *Appraisal costs:* DeeAnn plans to inspect the work of the staff auditors by having audit managers review the work. The average salary rate for an audit manager (including all fringe benefits) is $50 per hour.

- *Internal failure costs:* Sometimes the audit team will do such a poor job that one of DeeAnn's audit partners will have to personally supervise the completion of the audit work. The average salary rate for an audit partner is $100 per hour.
- *External failure costs:* If investors or creditors rely on financial statements that later prove to be false, the audit firm that approved those financial statements will probably be sued. Of course, the frequency of being sued, and the cost of each lawsuit, will be higher if DeeAnn decides to provide low-quality audits.

DeeAnn has gathered the following numerical information about the costs of quality in relation to operating a CPA firm:

	Low Quality	Average Quality	Premium Quality
Prevention costs:			
Staff hours spent on audit	10 hours	30 hours	100 hours
Staff salary rate	$20/hour	$25/hour	$35/hour
Appraisal costs:			
Manager review of audit work	1 hour	5 hours	20 hours
Internal failure costs:			
Frequency of bad audits	1 in 3	1 in 10	1 in 50
Partner time to fix bad audit	10 hours	5 hours	3 hours
External failure costs:			
Frequency of lawsuits	1 in 5	1 in 40	1 in 100
Expected loss on each lawsuit	$200,000	$100,000	$100,000

Required:

1. Assume that the revenue from each audit is the same no matter what the quality of the audit. Therefore, in order to maximize her profits, DeeAnn must minimize the expected cost of each audit. Which type of audit firm—low quality, average quality, or premium quality—should DeeAnn operate in order to maximize her expected profit per audit? Show your calculations.
2. Comment on whether the assumption about revenue made in part (1) seems appropriate.

expanded material

PROBLEM 7-12

TAGUCHI QUALITY LOSS FUNCTION

TAC Computers is a nationwide distributor of personal computers for home and business use. Its main sales channels are the Internet and telephone sales. Customers either call in to TAC's customer sales center or log on to TAC's Web site to place orders for custom-made computers. One of TAC's distinguishing marketing strategies is its three-year 24 × 7 customer support call center. All TAC customers have the ability to call the customer support center 24 hours a day, seven days a week to receive technical assistance with their machine. TAC prides itself on the high quality of service in this call center. Every customer call is immediately followed with either an e-mail or a postcard survey that asks the customer to provide feedback on the experience and answer the following questions:

1. Was your concern or question thoroughly resolved by the TAC technician?
2. Did the TAC technician handle your call with courtesy and professionalism?

Technicians' performance on the first question is referred to as the "error rate." Performance on the second question is referred to as the "care rate." The customer support call center management team uses performance on the error rate and care rate to manage operations and determine additional training needed by individual call center technicians. Performance on these two measures has been quite good for TAC. The TAC standard for each technician is to have no more than 1% complaints per month on the first question and no more than 0.5% complaints per month on the second question (a full-time technician handles 600 calls per month on average). Management feels that 99% quality on error and 99.5% quality on care is an excellent performance level for this industry.

Currently, few technicians need additional training each month. However, if a technician's error rate exceeds 1% of any month's call volume, that technician goes through a skills verification test to identify areas of weakness in handling specific technical issues, then undergoes some customized training. The cost of running a technician through this analysis and training process is estimated to be about $600. In the event that a technician's care rate exceeds 0.5% of a month's call volume, a manager is assigned to observe the technician in order to identify specific problems in working with customers. Then the technician works through a specialized training program based on the manager's assessment. The average cost of running a technician through this process is about $900.

As the controller for TAC Computers, you've been reading lately about the opportunity costs of low quality, and you're concerned that management of the customer support call center may not recognize the significant cost of lost sales that result when the company's reputation is hurt by technician error or lack of care for the customer.

Required:

1. Assuming that the Taguchi quality loss function is approximately accurate in measuring TAC's quality loss due to the external failure of handling customer calls, calculate the opportunity cost of lost sales when a technician's error rate hits 1%. Calculate the opportunity cost of lost sales when a technician's care rate hits 0.5%.
2. Explain to the management team of the customer support call center how they should interpret and use these Taguchi calculations to improve the operations in their center.

competency enhancement opportunities

- Analyzing Real Company Information
- International Case
- Ethics Case
- Writing Assignment
- The Debate
- Internet Search

The following additional assignments provide opportunities for students to develop critical thinking, ethical perspectives, oral and written communication skills, experience with electronic research, and teamwork through group and business activities.

ANALYZING REAL COMPANY INFORMATION

• ***Analyzing 7-1 (Microsoft)***

MICROSOFT, like most other companies, is continually striving to appropriately allocate costs and to increase the quality of its products. We have studied Microsoft's financial statements in past chapters. Now it is time to think beyond the numbers and examine other factors that might affect a firm's performance. Use your knowledge of Microsoft and the computer software industry to answer the following questions:

1. What types of overhead costs might Microsoft incur associated with its software products? Identify several cost drivers that Microsoft might consider in allocating overhead using the ABC method of overhead allocation.
2. What sort of product quality issues might Microsoft face associated with its software? Identify the various costs of quality associated with a faulty software product.

• ***Analyzing 7-2 (Techtronics Technologies)***

Techtronics Technologies (a hypothetical company) produces mass storage devices for computers. The company produces three models: Model HD110, Model HD220, and Model HD330. Sales and costing information for these three products is as follows:

	HD110	HD220	HD330
Selling price per unit	$169	$185	$199
Units produced	2,500	3,800	4,100
Direct materials cost	$235,000	$444,600	$574,000
Direct labor cost	$37,500	$64,600	$77,900

In the past, manufacturing overhead has been allocated based on direct labor costs. Manufacturing overhead for this period is $416,000, and the predetermined overhead rate is $40 per unit produced.

Based on this information, management has determined that Model HD330 is barely breaking even. Because the market for mass storage devices is quite competitive, the price for each model is set by the market—not by management. Thus, increasing the price charged for products is not an option. As a result, management is considering discontinuing Model HD330. Before making a final decision, management has come to you for advice. You collect the following information regarding manufacturing overhead:

Mfg. Overhead	Mfg. Overhead Costs	Allocation Bases
Engineering	$198,000	Engineering changes
Quality control	34,000	Number of units produced
Manufacturing support	184,000	Number of setups
Total manufacturing overhead	$416,000	

Activity	HD110	HD220	HD330
Total number of engineering changes	210	114	126
Total number of units produced	2,500	3,800	4,100
Total number of setups	30	27	23

1. Determine the gross margin for each model under the current manufacturing overhead allocation scheme.
2. Determine the manufacturing overhead cost for each model using the information related to cost drivers.
3. Determine the gross margin for each model using cost drivers to allocate manufacturing overhead.
4. What recommendation would you make to management regarding their decision to discontinue Model HD330?

INTERNATIONAL CASE

• *Deming in Japan*

As noted in this chapter, the ideas of W. Edward Deming received little attention in the United States in the late 1940s and early 1950s. Deming then moved to Japan where his ideas were accepted and implemented almost immediately. The result was that industries in Japan, such as automobile production, quickly developed a reputation for producing quality products. In the 1980s, the United States found itself trying to catch up to the Japanese in the race for quality products. Can you speculate as to why Deming's ideas were not readily accepted in the United States, yet were quickly adopted in Japan? To answer this question, you may need to recall your world history during the 1940s.

ETHICS CASE

• *Minuteman Enterprises*

You are the controller for Minuteman Enterprises, a manufacturer of rocket booster engines and various aerospace products. Though there are many commercial customers for most of the company's products, the federal government is the only buyer of your rocket booster engines. Because you are the only provider for the engines, the government has agreed to buy these engines at a price equal to your cost plus a 10% markup.

As the controller, you have recently been studying the accuracy of your product costs. Traditionally, manufacturing overhead has been allocated on the basis of direct labor hours. Using this method, rocket boosters have borne a high percentage of manufacturing overhead because they take many more direct labor hours than do the other products.

You have just been presented an analysis by one of your staff members that shows that direct labor hours is not a very relevant base for allocating manufacturing overhead costs. Rather, she has made a very convincing case that manufacturing overhead should be allocated using activity-based costing with multiple cost drivers. Using her suggested approach, however, you discover that the rocket boosters bear a much smaller portion of manufacturing overhead costs, and therefore, the total cost of the boosters is considerably less than the amount you had been using to determine the price charged to the government.

You know that her calculations using ABC are likely more accurate than the current cost allocation method and that the commercial products should bear a larger amount of manufacturing overhead costs. Yet, you also know that by using ABC and the more accurate cost drivers, your profits from both the boosters and the commercial products will be reduced.

1. What should you do?
2. Is it ethical to continue to allocate manufacturing overhead costs on the basis of direct labor hours?
3. Would it be ethical to use direct labor hours if that were the basis used by other government contractors?
4. If you decide to switch to ABC, should you inform the government that you have overcharged it and return the excess profits?

WRITING ASSIGNMENT

• *Advantages and Disadvantages of ABC*

Your boss recently attended a conference where activity-based costing was discussed. She is intrigued by the ABC concept and wonders if the company is appropriately costing its products. Your company produces and sells four different styles of briefcases. The production process differs for each briefcase, as different features require different equipment. She returns from the conference and asks you to summarize the advantages and disadvantages of ABC. Your assignment is to write a two-page memo addressing these issues.

THE DEBATE

• *ABC or Bust!*

As the text indicates, activity-based costing has received much attention from businesses around the world. Yet some firms still resist adopting an ABC system, and others have adopted ABC and then reverted to their more traditional costing systems. Divide your group into two teams and prepare five-minute presentations defending the following positions:

- Team One is "In Support of ABC." Your team's task is to identify the benefits of using an activity-based product costing system. Briefly explain the advantages that a company will realize if it adopts ABC.
- Team Two is "In Support of Tradition." Your team's task is to identify the benefits of using a more traditional product costing system based on, for example, direct labor hours. Explain the advantages of a traditional system that cause many firms to still choose it over ABC.

INTERNET SEARCH

• *Toyota Motor Corporation*

W. Edward Deming helped TOYOTA become the company it is today. Go to Toyota's Web site at http://www.toyota.com. Sometimes Web addresses change, so if this Toyota address doesn't work, access the Web site for this textbook (http://albrecht.swcollege.com) for an updated link to Toyota. Once you have gained access to Toyota's Web site, answer the following questions:

1. Access Toyota's operations section and locate the company's history timeline. When did Toyota begin selling in North America? When did this company sell its millionth car in North America?
2. Next, look for the criteria and mission of Toyota's community-funding program. What is the mission of this program? Identify a couple of points in the funding guidelines that would limit a community's or a program's chance for funding.

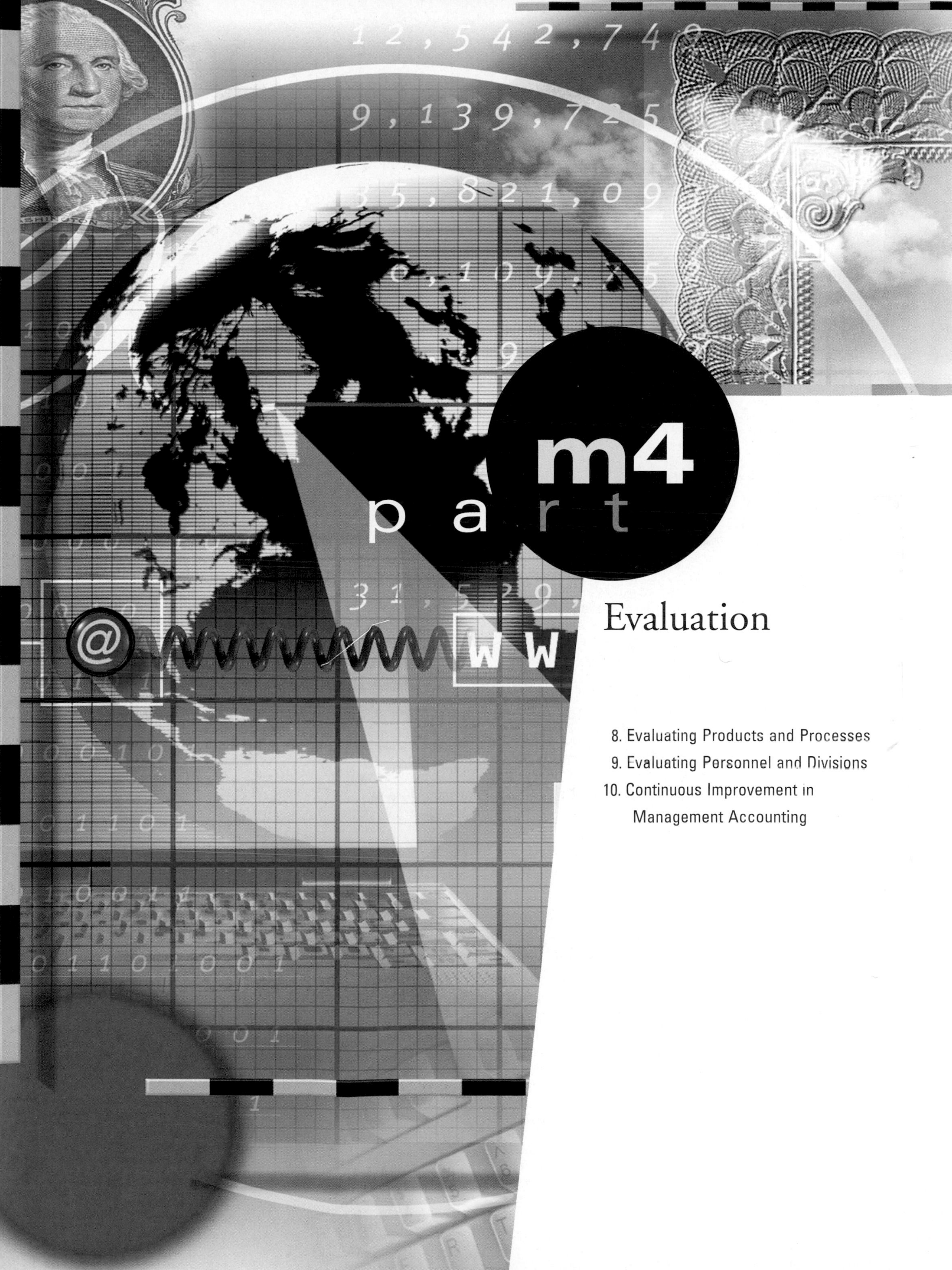

part 4

Evaluation

Evaluating Products and Processes

chapter

m8

learning objectives After studying this chapter, you should be able to:

1 Explain how evaluation leads to planning and why products and processes must be continuously evaluated.

2 Understand why benchmarking is so important and how it is conducted.

3 Understand the concept of differential costs and revenues, and be able to identify those costs and revenues that are relevant to making product and process decisions.

4 Identify several examples of product and process evaluation decisions, and be able to analyze and select the best alternative for each example.

expanded material

5 Understand the theory of constraints and how focusing on scarce resources can direct activities in manufacturing companies.

setting the stage

Every day in *The Wall Street Journal* and other publications, we read about companies that are either expanding into new business lines, dropping existing products, entering new markets, exiting existing markets, or making other major business decisions. These kinds of decisions have historically been referred to as nonroutine decisions. Take the October 6, 2000 issue of *The Wall Street Journal,* for example. On just the front page, there were stories about:

- TIME WARNER and EMI scrapping plans for a $20 billion music joint venture because of tough antitrust scrutiny from the European Commission.
- PRICELINE.COM's decision to close its WEBHOUSE service that allowed customers to bid for groceries and gasoline online.
- OWENS CORNING filing for Chapter 11 bankruptcy court protection, blaming escalating asbestos liability claims.
- SMITHKLINE's bid to acquire BLOCK DRUG for about $1.2 billion. (Block is the maker of Sensodyne and other dental products.)
- GENERAL MOTORS' SATURN division's plans to unveil and produce a new sports utility vehicle as part of its $1.5 billion investment to expand Saturn into a full-line automobile brand.
- POLO RALPH LAUREN's closing of its Polo Jeans stores and some Club Monaco outlets to focus on wealthier customers.
- TWA's plans to revamp its route network, including dropping flights from New York's Kennedy Airport to Milan, Italy, and Lisbon, Portugal.

Each of these actions represents a major product or process decision by the company. Consider the Priceline.com decision, for example. One year earlier, Priceline.com founder Jay Walker said that his "name-your-own-price system" would encompass every category of goods. His prediction that "there is no category we won't be in" turned out to be less than accurate. By shutting down its name-your-own-price grocery and gasoline sales operations, Priceline and its subsidiary, WebHouse Club, Inc., wrote off an investment of over $363 million.

In Chapter 1 of management accounting, you learned that management decision making involves the three functions of planning, controlling, and evaluating. Thus far, we have discussed the planning and controlling functions. You have learned that planning involves long-run planning, including strategic planning and capital budgeting, and short-run planning, including production prioritizing and operational budgeting. You have learned that controlling involves tracking actual performance in terms of costs, quality, and timeliness measures. These tracked measures (costs, quality, and timeliness) are then used in the evaluating process to compare against budgets previously prepared. Evaluating involves analyzing results, providing feedback to managers and other employees, rewarding performance, and identifying problems. One specific type of evaluation focuses on products and processes. As you learned in Chapter 1, managers need to assess the performance of their products or services, as well as the processes that are in place to create those products or services. A second type of evaluation focuses on the personnel and their divisions within the organization. Upper-level management must evaluate how well lower-level managers perform the activities assigned to them in the planning stages. In this chapter, we focus on the evaluation of products, services, and processes. In Chapter 9 of management accounting, we focus on evaluating personnel and their divisions.

1

Explain how evaluation leads to planning and why products and processes must be continuously evaluated.

EVALUATING PRODUCTS AND PROCESSES

Evaluation brings us back to the point where we started—planning. Information gained through the evaluation process is used for planning during the following period. When managers are evaluating last period's performance, they are also probably making planning decisions that will affect, and hopefully improve, performance in the next period. This planning, controlling, and evaluating cycle is diagrammed on the following page.

The evaluation of products, services, and processes leads to decisions that will affect future operations, including whether to enter or exit a market for a particular service or product, whether to make or buy a component, whether to sell a product before or after additional processing, and what prices to charge for services and products. In the opening scenario, most of the examples cited involved entering or exiting markets.

The evaluation decisions we will discuss in this chapter can have a significant impact on the profitability, quality, and timeliness of the products of an organization for several periods and so must be considered very carefully. In a manufacturing company, for example, evaluation can help a company decide whether to accept a special order, whether to make or buy manufacturing components, whether to build or sell plants, and how to best use limited raw materials in the manufacturing process. In a merchandising company, evaluation can lead to decisions about how to use limited store shelves and whether to open a new store. In a service company, evaluation can help the company decide whether to hire a particular specialist or contract that service to another firm, how to use scarce labor resources, and whether to merge with another company. In a governmental unit, evaluation can affect decisions about whether to collect garbage

business environment essay

A Better Bumper Factory Shahid Khan is the founder and owner of **BUMPER WORKS** in Danville, Illinois. Bumper Works designs and manufactures bumpers for lightweight pickup trucks for Japanese automakers, including **TOYOTA MOTOR CORPORATION**, whose standards are very exacting. "There was nothing Toyota could teach us," says Khan, "about engineering low-cost bumpers." But on how to run a bumper factory, Khan is more humble. "We had benchmarked ourselves against American industry," he says. "I don't think we knew how bad we were."

Toyota, a world leader in factory efficiency, did know. But rather than take its business elsewhere, Toyota dispatched a team of manufacturing experts to the bumper plant to conduct a crash course in the Toyota system. Productivity at Bumper Works rose 60% from the previous year, and the number of defects was reduced by 80%.

Khan made sales calls to Toyota for five years before landing his first contract with the company in 1985. Then, in 1987, Khan and two other bumper makers were told by Toyota to design new bumpers considerably more durable than the Big Three (**GM**, **CHRYSLER**, and **FORD**) specifications required. Such demands from Japanese companies are common. "We were the only company that could demonstrate we could do that," Khan says. As a result, in 1988, his firm became the sole supplier of bumpers to U.S. facilities where Toyota attaches rear bumpers and other accessories to trucks made in Japan.

In 1989, Toyota made additional demands. Toyota wanted annual price reductions despite rising costs for materials and labor. It also wanted better bumpers

at the curb or at the house site, whether to hire an in-house lawyer or contract out all legal services, and whether to develop a water system or buy water from a nearby community. In a dot.com company, evaluation could lead to decisions about how to price banner ads, whether to charge an access or user fee, or whether to add or drop existing lines (such as Priceline.com's decision to drop groceries and gasoline).

To illustrate how evaluation (and help from customers and vendors) can help companies improve their competitive position, see the Business Environment Essay below. Especially note the types of actions taken by **BUMPER WORKS** to improve product quality, cut production time, acquire new equipment, reduce inventory, and increase worker participation. All these actions involved changes in the fundamental operating process that Bumper Works had been using. The decisions made by Bumper Works enabled the company to continue to be successful in a very competitive market.

Why Evaluation Is So Important

Today, we live in an age when information is transmitted worldwide almost instantaneously and change is occurring faster than ever before. With accurate and timely information so readily available, it is absolutely critical that companies produce the highest-quality products at the lowest possible price and faster than anyone else. If a U.S. automobile manufacturer produces a car that is more expensive or of lower quality than cars made in Japan or Germany, for example, consumers will buy foreign automobiles because information about the Japanese and German cars is readily available to U.S. car buyers. Likewise, if a U.S. automobile company can buy higher-quality tires at a lower price from a Korean tire manufacturer than it can from a U.S. tire manufacturer, it will buy Korean tires because information about the foreign tires is easily accessible. Similarly, if investors have a limited amount of money to invest, they can just as easily buy stocks of European or Asian companies as stocks of U.S. companies because the information is available and the markets are easily accessible.

This increased availability of up-to-date information and the ease with which products, services, and investments can be acquired internationally have made it critically important that

and more punctual deliveries. Toyota wanted to help Khan meet these demands, but little could be done until Bumper Works cut the time it took to change dies in the metal-stamping presses from 90 minutes or more to less than 22 minutes. Only then would Bumper Works be flexible enough to make 20 different bumper models each day. Bumper Works could not afford new presses with quick-change features, so, with Toyota's help, Khan's workers improvised. They welded homemade metal tabs to their nine-ton dies to facilitate lining up the dies on pins attached to the presses. Workers also videotaped die-change procedures and produced an instruction manual—a Bumper Works first. "We had no organization," recalls the die coordinator. "There were a lot of simple things we didn't think about until the Toyota team came in."

By July 1990, Bumper Works achieved the die-change objective. Toyota then dispatched two more consultants from Japan to lead what Khan calls "boot camp." In about two weeks of 16-hour days, the plant was turned upside down. Virtually every piece of equipment, except the massive metal presses, was moved. Employees had to relearn their jobs. Toyota's goal was for a piece of raw steel to come in one end of the building and go out the other end on the same day as a finished bumper. The employees now schedule their own work rather than wait for a supervisor's direction. When a batch of Toyota bumpers is shipped, a card is returned to the press operators, and they press out more. Bumper quality improved significantly, and costs came down.

Source: Adapted from "Japanese Auto Makers Help U.S. Suppliers to Become More Efficient," *The Wall Street Journal*, September 9, 1991.

fyi

Much of the continuous improvement literature had its origin in Japan with Japanese companies. As a result, even in U.S. management accounting literature, you will frequently encounter the Japanese term *kaizen,* which means "continuous improvement." Continuous improvement can take the form of continuous reductions in product defects, delivery time, material waste, inventory size, setup time, and so on. Under continuous improvement programs, one of the major responsibilities of managers and workers is to reduce total costs by continuous improvement in both monetary and nonmonetary standards.

companies operate as efficiently and effectively as possible. Because it is so important to be a high-performing or "world-class" company, organizations are placing more and more emphasis on evaluating their performance and continuously improving. Managers recognize that, in this information age, it is "survival of the fittest" and that only the best-performing companies will be able to compete in the long run.

Companies can be poor performers for several reasons. Some companies do not perform well because they fail to develop appropriate corporate strategies or goals or because they lack vision (planning). Some companies do not perform well because their evaluation methods are poor or do not fit their organizational structures and, therefore, fail to accurately assess how well they are doing. Perhaps most commonly, some companies do not perform well because they fail to execute their strategies and planned actions.

In this chapter, we will discuss several ways companies organize and set goals and then evaluate their performance against those goals. As was the case with product cost determination discussed in Chapter 2 of management accounting, performance evaluation has been the subject of considerable research in the past few years and has undergone significant changes. Much emphasis has been placed on developing evaluation systems that align performance evaluation with an organization's strategic plan and objectives and that focus on customer and employee needs. Historically, many performance measures have been backward looking and have tended to report results too late to allow corrective action to be taken. New evaluation systems link daily activities with measures that help organizations guide decisions and actions.

Obviously, to effectively evaluate performance, organizations must have goals, objectives, or benchmarks against which to assess their performance. Most organizations establish these goals and benchmarks through a process called strategic planning, which we have already discussed.

Quality and Time Standards

In evaluating performance, it is important to focus on both monetary and nonmonetary measures. For example, one well-known fast-food chain's managers are evaluated not only on the profitability of their unit, but also on such quality standards as cleanliness and the kind of service provided to customers. In another company, some managers receive more points for developing new technologies and making innovations than for keeping costs in line. At another company, production employees are rewarded on how much they can reduce the delivery time of products to customers. Other nonmonetary measures of performance include creating good employee morale and maintaining equipment in good running order.

Fast-food managers can be evaluated on the kind of service provided to customers. Thus, it is important that employees offer fast service with a smile.

For an evaluation system to be successful, the criteria by which products and processes are evaluated should be well defined, objective, and measurable. Usually, qualitative criteria are much harder to evaluate than objective cost measures and resulting variances, but that does not diminish their importance. In fact, quality and time standards are often as important to a firm's success as financial results. Those companies that can deliver the highest-quality products quickest and at the most competitive price will usually be the most successful. Some companies have even developed "best supplier" awards to recognize those suppliers that deliver products at the lowest price, with the highest quality and with the fewest late orders. Criteria used in making these awards usually include such elements as cost reductions, delivery improvement (frequency as well as timeliness), and percentage of defects.

In evaluating quality and time considerations, quality is usually defined as the total features and characteristics of a product or service that bear on its ability to satisfy stated or implied needs. Generally, as a final measure, quality must be viewed from a customer perspective as determined by acceptance in the marketplace. One writer has suggested that quality includes the following eight dimensions:[1]

1. *Performance*—a product's primary operating characteristic. Examples are automobile acceleration and a television set's picture clarity.
2. *Features*—supplements to a product's basic functioning characteristics, such as power windows on a car.
3. *Reliability*—a probability of not malfunctioning during a specified period.
4. *Conformance*—the degree to which a product's design and operating characteristics meet established standards.
5. *Durability*—a measure of product life.
6. *Serviceability*—the speed and ease of repair.
7. *Aesthetics*—how a product looks, feels, tastes, and smells.
8. *Perceived quality*—as seen by a customer.

As an example of how management might apply these quality components to a specific product, consider an automobile tire. Its quality may be measured by tread-wear rate, handling, traction, impact on gas mileage, noise levels, resistance to punctures, and appearance. As another example, the tax service of a CPA may be measured by timely completion of tax returns, tax savings, number of audits or letters from the IRS, suggestions made for future investment opportunities, fees charged, and personal attention given.

This discussion of quality suggests that performance evaluation must be viewed more broadly and from a different perspective than it has been in the past. Controlling costs is still essential, but the emphasis should also be on quality and improvement in processes, products, and services. Some people argue that the competitive advantage of some Japanese companies is the direct result of acceptance of this quality philosophy, attributed to W. Edwards Deming. The Deming chain reaction is depicted in Exhibit 8-1.

With a broader perspective, managers can seek ways to measure all aspects of company performance. The emphasis should be on the critical activities of the company. The goal is to identify and concentrate on those activities that add the most value to products or services.

In addition to quality, performance evaluation now often considers the time it takes to get a product to the marketplace. By using technology and re-engineering processes, most companies today can deliver goods to customers faster than ever before.

The challenge is to integrate cost, quality, and speed considerations into evaluation systems effectively. The objectives of zero defects, continuous improvement, decreasing manufacturing and delivery time, and meeting customer expectations of quality are admirable. Developing and effectively implementing performance measures that help achieve these objectives is not an easy task, but it is certainly worthy of management's effort. In the end, those organizations that develop the most appropriate performance measures and provide the necessary encouragement and motivation for employees to achieve the organization's objectives will be the most successful.

STOP & THINK What do you think researchers mean when they say that current evaluation methods do not give enough consideration to intangible capabilities and focus too much on financial returns?

1 David A. Garvin, "Competing on the Eight Dimensions of Quality," *Harvard Business Review* 65 (November–December 1987): pp. 101–109.

exhibit 8-1 Deming Chain Reaction

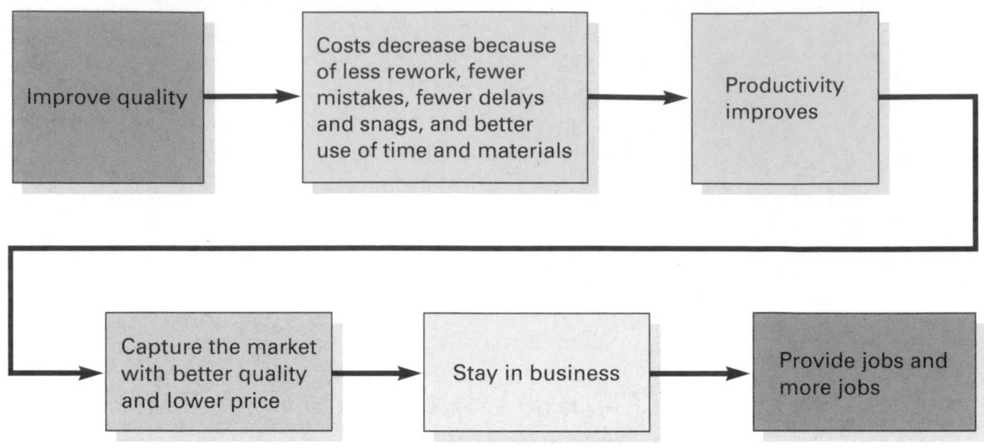

to summarize

In an age when information is inexpensive and readily available, it is important that companies offer the highest-quality products at the lowest possible price and faster than their competitors. Because quality, speed, and price are so important, it is critical that organizations establish good evaluation methods and continuously improve. A company cannot improve its performance until it knows how it is doing. Evaluation helps an organization plan better and control its operations more effectively. In addition to cost considerations, nonmonetary measures should be used in evaluating performance. To be effective, these criteria must be well defined, objective, and measurable. New approaches to performance evaluation include quality and time considerations. The new approaches are required because all aspects of a company's performance need to be monitored. In the final analysis, those organizations that can deliver the highest-quality products to their customers at the lowest

business environment essay

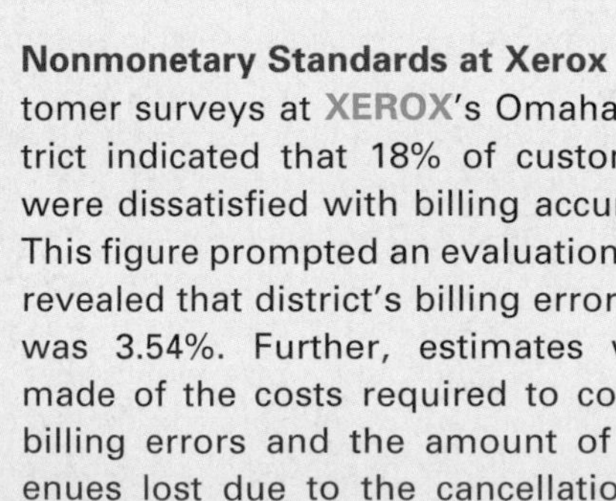

Nonmonetary Standards at Xerox Customer surveys at XEROX's Omaha district indicated that 18% of customers were dissatisfied with billing accuracy. This figure prompted an evaluation that revealed that district's billing error rate was 3.54%. Further, estimates were made of the costs required to correct billing errors and the amount of revenues lost due to the cancellation of contracts by those dissatisfied because of billing problems. The total cost to the company was estimated to be almost $200,000 during a six-month test period.

A team with representatives from the different departments that participated in the billing process was formed to improve billing performance. The team followed a multistep problem-solving process. First, the problem was identified and analyzed. During this stage, team members identified all those who might have an impact on billing errors and the likely causes of those errors. Next, possible solutions were con-

prices and in the shortest amount of time will be the most successful. Significant challenges exist in implementing new performance evaluation approaches.

2

Understand why benchmarking is so important and how it is conducted.

benchmarking A performance evaluation process used by companies to target areas for improvement by comparing the company's financial and operating performance against the performance of other companies or by comparing the performance of internal departments against each other.

BENCHMARKING

In recent years, there has been an evaluation revolution. Several new evaluation methods have been developed. In this chapter, we will describe only one—benchmarking. Two others (the balanced scorecard and the concept of continuous improvement) will be discussed in future chapters.

Benchmarking involves comparing a company's financial and operating performance against a competitor's performance or comparing the performance of various internal departments against each other. The benchmarking process usually consists of four steps. Step 1 is to analyze the company's practices, procedures, and performance in a given process and to set forth goals and objectives for improving them. Analysis of the company's practices and procedures is crucial because the practices of other firms will not prove very revealing unless a company has determined its own strengths and weaknesses.

Step 2 involves the selection of a benchmark (or benchmarks). These benchmarks can be departments within a company or competing companies that perform the process under analysis optimally. This step is critical as selection of the wrong benchmarks can result in identifying inappropriate procedures and unrealistic goals for a firm.

In step 3, detailed information on the benchmarks' practices and procedures for that process is collected and shared. Although collecting such data on competing companies may prove difficult, various sources offer benchmark data, and companies are often willing to share information with each other.

In step 4, a company must carefully analyze the data collected in step 3 to determine which of the policies and procedures used by benchmarked companies can best be employed.

Internal versus External Comparisons

The standards of comparison used for benchmarking can be based on the performance of departments or divisions within the same company or appropriate departments from other companies. When using internal units as benchmarks, a company can begin by identifying its

sidered. Here the focus was on ways to educate personnel about correct billing input and procedures. In the solution-planning stage, the team chose to create a cartoon character, Captain Xero, to attract attention to the improvement program and to convey the program's message. Cartoons would be published weekly to educate personnel about billing. Finally, the team implemented the program and evaluated its results.

The focus on improving billing accuracy paid off handsomely. During a one-year period, billing errors were reduced 52% as the billing error rate fell from 3.54% to 1.71%. Surveys revealed that customer satisfaction with billing accuracy also improved significantly. The estimated reduction in costs associated with billing errors exceeded $100,000 during the second six-month period after the program was implemented.

Source: Adapted from David M. Beuhlmann and Donald Stover, "How Xerox Solves Quality Problems," *Management Accounting*, September 1993, pp. 33–36.

best-performing units and then analyze their strategies and practices for performance. Once the approaches have been determined and quantified, less effective departments are encouraged to adopt the practices of the more successful units.

A drawback to internal comparisons alone, however, is that they may foster complacency and may not afford a realistic picture of a unit's potential within the industry. Internal comparisons are often of limited value because a company may be unable to recognize its own shortcomings and faults. Also, although one department within a company may outperform other departments substantially, that fact is not indicative of its performance relative to the industry as a whole. In essence, the department may be outperforming other units within the company, but still be falling short of the performance yields found in other similar companies. For example, it is easy to assume that a growth rate of 4 percent a year is satisfactory; yet, if outside competitors are realizing growth rates of 8 percent, there is clearly great room for improvement.

A second approach to benchmarking is to compare a company against top competitors. Most experts believe that this approach is the most relevant point of comparison for both services and products. As mentioned above, a major stumbling block is that obtaining the necessary data for an effective comparison may be difficult. Nevertheless, this type of analysis, peer group benchmarking, is beneficial because it not only allows a company to compare itself to another company with a similar set of attributes, but it may also afford a more invigorating view of what is possible within the industry. Thus, to the extent that key result measurement ratios of individual companies can be compared with averages of a select group of companies with generally similar attributes, peer group examinations can be quite revealing.

A third form of benchmarking is to compare a company with the "best-in-class." This approach entails comparing a company with top-performing firms sharing comparable functions or philosophies, although they may not be in the same industry. The advantage of this type of cross-industry comparison is that practices and procedures followed in other industries may prove very beneficial, even though they have not been used previously in the same industry. Best-in-class comparisons can bring new ideas, new thoughts, and even new concepts. On the downside, however, the introduction of new concepts is somewhat speculative. There is risk whenever a company adapts a new concept or procedure. Because a process performs well in one industry does not necessarily mean it can be carried over effectively to a different industry. This limitation has to be considered before implementing any new ideas.

Benchmarking can yield great benefits in the education of executives and the realized performance improvements of operations. In addition, benchmarking can be used to determine strategic areas of opportunity. In general, it is the application of what is learned in benchmarking that delivers the impressive results so often noted.

The benefits of benchmarking are realized when companies employ recommendations and embark on a change process leading to marked improvements in productivity, costs, and revenues. The following are examples of how companies improved their results through benchmarking:

- GLAXO WELLCOME had over 80 toll-free telephone numbers, over half of which failed to ring anywhere. By eliminating all but one telephone number, Glaxo greatly reduced customer frustration and confusion.
- NORWEST (now WELLS FARGO), the nation's largest mortgage company, embarked on a benchmarking campaign and was able to quantify the following benefits:
    - Sales brochure consolidation: $430,000 in savings.
    - Customer and direct mail consolidation: $1 million in savings.
    - Opportunity lending: $20 million in added growth.
    - Teller referrals: up 15%, 33% of which result in additional sales.
    - Use of sales road maps: sales increase up to 102%.
    - Use of partner letters: 150% increase in commercial sales.
    - Performance coaching: 5.08 products per new customer.
- MARRIOTT improved its guest check-in service process 500% by benchmarking the patient admittance process used by hospital emergency rooms.
- SOUTHWEST AIRLINES saved millions of dollars a year and was able to put more aircraft in the air while reducing the number on the ground by benchmarking Indy 500 pit crews.

- XEROX dramatically improved its warehouse order-picking process by benchmarking L.L. BEAN, a catalog order company.
- KPMG PEAT MARWICK borrowed the concept of a supermarket's express checkout to start an express line in its word-processing pools. The change enabled teams with minor document changes to go through an expedited process, which was of great value to the word-processing department and solved a long-standing problem of work assignments.[2]

to summarize

Several new performance measures have been developed in recent years. In this chapter we discuss one—benchmarking. Benchmarking is the process of comparing a unit's performance with other units either within or outside the company. Benchmarking can result in marked improvements in productivity, costs, and revenue.

3

Understand the concept of differential costs and revenues, and be able to identify those costs and revenues that are relevant to making product and process decisions.

DIFFERENTIAL COSTS AND REVENUES

Evaluation of products and processes usually leads to consideration of alternative courses of actions. For example, the evaluation of a particular product may lead a company to believe that it must expand capacity, outsource production, or even drop a product in favor of an alternative product. It may also result in the company deciding to buy a competitor. In the rest of this chapter, we provide examples of how products and processes are evaluated to make better decisions. These concepts are probably best understood by examining examples of decisions to change, add, or drop products or processes. Before you can understand how evaluation can lead to better product and process decisions, however, a framework is necessary. In building a framework, we will focus mostly on costs and revenues. Do not forget, however, that the evaluation of timeliness and quality must be considered as well. In making decisions about products and processes, the costs and revenues that are different for, and hence relevant to, various alternative courses of action must be identified. When evaluating costs and revenues, analysis of **differential costs** and revenues is the key to properly evaluating both products and processes. As discussed in Chapter 1 of management accounting, the differential costs of a decision are the future costs that change as a result of that decision. For example, recently GM estimated that it would cost nearly $4 billion to close some plants and lay off some employees. By doing so, however, it expected to save hundreds of millions of dollars in future years by being more efficient. The term *differential* is also commonly applied to future revenues that will be affected by these decisions.

differential costs Future costs that change as a result of a decision.

To illustrate, assume that you own the Speedy Print Shop. A customer wants you to print 500 copies of a one-page flyer immediately. To price the job, you need to know what it will cost. Exhibit 8-2 includes both an incorrect and a correct analysis of the available cost data. The left column (the incorrect analysis) includes all costs; the right column (the correct analysis) includes only the differential costs. We will explain each cost and how we determined whether it was relevant to the pricing decision.

1. *Paper.* The cost of the paper for the printing job is differential because it is a future expenditure that must be made as a result of the decision to accept the order. In a sense, therefore, it is a cost that changes as a result of the decision. If we do not accept the order, we do not need to purchase the paper. Note also that paper is a variable cost—its total cost increases proportionately to the size of the order.

2 These examples were taken from "Benefits and Values of Benchmarking," Best Practices, LLC, 6320 Quadrangle Drive, Suite 200, Chapel Hill, NC 27514.

exhibit 8-2 Speedy Print Shop Rush Order Analysis

	Incorrect Analysis (all costs)	Correct Analysis (differential costs)
Variable costs:		
Paper (500 at 10¢)	$ 50	$ 50
Printing labor (5 hours at $16; 5 hours at $24)	80	120
Fixed costs:		
Printing plates	100	100
Printing press depreciation (5 hours at $10)	50	
Manager's salary (5 hours at $20)	100	
Totals	$380	$270

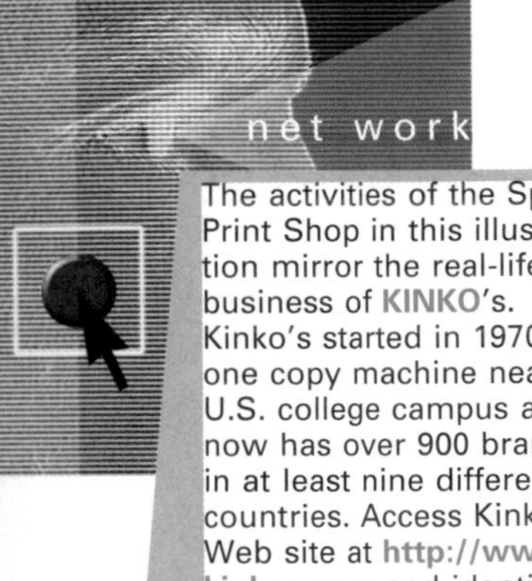

The activities of the Speedy Print Shop in this illustration mirror the real-life business of KINKO's. Kinko's started in 1970 with one copy machine near a U.S. college campus and now has over 900 branches in at least nine different countries. Access Kinko's Web site at http://www.kinkos.com and identify which college campus Kinko's opened next to and in which countries it now operates.

2. *Printing labor.* Accepting the order will require a future expenditure for additional labor to operate the press. This again obviously represents a change from the existing situation—without the order, we would not incur the cost of labor. Also, this example illustrates another important point about measuring future costs. Since this rush order will have to be printed during overtime hours, the appropriate labor rate is time and a half. (Given a normal hourly rate of $16, the labor rate for this job would be $24.) It is easy to overlook this and assume that the normal labor cost per hour ($16) applies. The differential cost of $24 per hour that will be incurred as a result of the decision, however, is the appropriate cost to use. Like paper, printing labor is a variable cost that increases in total proportionately to the size of the order.
3. *Printing plates.* New printing plates must be prepared for this order, so it is a future expenditure that changes as a result of the decision to accept the order. The important point here is that printing plates are a fixed cost (you can print as many copies as you want from the same set of plates), but the cost is still differential because it is an additional expenditure for this order. A common but incorrect assumption is that only variable costs are relevant (that fixed costs do not have to be taken into account). This is not the case. All future costs that change as a result of accepting the order, whether fixed or variable, are differential.
4. *Printing press depreciation.* This cannot be a differential cost because it is not a future cost (depreciation is an allocation of a past cost), and it does not change as a result of the decision to accept the order. (Assuming a time-based depreciation method, the press depreciates over time, whether or not it is used.) Costs such as depreciation, which are past costs and do not change, are referred to as **sunk costs**. No decision can change past, or sunk, costs; they are never relevant to a decision.
5. *Manager's salary.* Although the manager's salary is a future cost (we will be paying for future services), it will be paid whether or not the order is accepted. Consequently, the manager's salary is not a differential cost; it does not change as a result of the decision to accept this order.

sunk costs Costs, such as depreciation, that are past costs and do not change as the result of a future decision.

The differential costs for this rush order total $270. This means that in pricing the job, Speedy Print Shop will be losing money unless it charges at least this much. Similarly, if Speedy Print Shop declines the job at an offered price of $300 because that price is less than the incorrectly calculated differential cost of $380, the company will experience an opportunity cost (loss) of $30.

To further illustrate the role of differential and sunk costs in making a product or process decision, we assume that Dixon Wholesale Company is thinking of purchasing a delivery truck with an estimated useful life of five years. Following are the costs of acquiring and operating a truck:

Original cost		$10,000
Variable costs per mile:		
Gasoline and oil	$ 0.25	
Repairs and maintenance	0.03	
Tires	0.02	
Total variable costs per mile		$ 0.30
Fixed costs per year:		
Insurance	$ 500	
Licenses	110	
Depreciation expense ($10,000 ÷ 5 years)	2,000	
Total fixed costs per year		$ 2,610

These variable and fixed operating costs are incurred each year the truck is used. However, they are not all differential costs; they are not all relevant to every decision made about the truck. For the following decisions, we identify the differential costs, the sunk costs, and the reason for the classifications.

DECISION 1 Should the truck be purchased? Whether to purchase the truck is really a capital budgeting decision, a topic we discussed in Chapter 4 of management accounting. But the decision is based on differential (future) costs to be incurred if the truck is purchased.

- **Differential costs:** All variable costs (30 cents per mile driven); all fixed costs except depreciation (which is already included in the purchase cost); and the purchase cost ($10,000).
- **Sunk costs:** None.
- **Comment:** All costs except depreciation are differential costs because the truck has not yet been purchased; all costs can be avoided by an alternative decision.

DECISION 2 Let's now jump forward in time two years. The truck has now been owned and used for two years, but it has not been licensed or insured for the current (third) year. Should it be licensed and insured, or should some other means of transportation be used? (Assume for now that the truck will not be sold, even if not used.)

- **Differential costs:** All variable costs (30 cents per mile driven) and some fixed costs (insurance, $500; licenses, $110).
- **Sunk costs:** Remaining book value of the truck ($6,000 at the beginning of the year).
- **Comment:** As soon as the truck is purchased, its cost becomes a sunk cost. During its estimated life, its remaining book value is a sunk cost if we assume, for simplicity, that the truck has no resale value. The company must absorb the cost of the truck either by using the truck (and depreciating its cost each year) or by writing off the entire cost. All costs except depreciation and the remaining book value are, therefore, differential costs.

DECISION 3 The truck has been owned and used for two years and has been licensed and insured for the current (third) year. Should the truck be used for transporting inventory this year? Should other means be arranged?

- **Differential costs:** All variable costs (30 cents per mile driven) and no fixed costs.
- **Sunk costs:** Insurance ($500); licenses ($110); remaining book value ($6,000 at the beginning of the year).
- **Comment:** If insurance and license fees are not refundable, these are sunk costs, as is the remaining book value.

Analysis of the costs that are relevant in making these three decisions should help you understand how differential costs are determined. As you can see, variable costs are *usually* differential; fixed costs are *sometimes* differential; and past costs are *never* differential.

Total Costs versus Differential Costs

In trying to improve performance, managers usually prefer to use the differential-cost approach; that is, they disregard sunk costs and other costs that are the same for each alternative being considered. This approach highlights costs that make a difference, takes less time, and reduces the chance of error in the calculation (fewer numbers reduce the chances for mistakes). In some cases, however, a manager may want to review the **total cost** to ensure that some relevant costs are not overlooked.

total cost The total variable and fixed costs incurred in making a product or providing a service.

To illustrate this total-cost approach, we will assume that Dixon Wholesale Company has another decision to make about its truck.

DECISION 4 The truck has been owned for four years, but it has not yet been licensed or insured for the current (fifth) year. Should the truck be used for the last year of its economic life, or should it be traded for a new truck that will be driven five years?

Pertinent information is presented in the following table:

	Old Truck	New Truck
Original cost	$10,000	$12,500
Current book value	2,000	
Current resale value	1,700	
Resale value at end of year	0	10,000
Variable operating costs	$0.30 per mile	$0.27 per mile
Annual fixed costs:		
Insurance	$ 500	$ 550
Licenses	110	110
Depreciation expense	2,000	2,500
Estimated mileage per year	50,000 miles	50,000 miles

On the basis of this information, the total cost of operating the old truck and the total cost of operating a new truck are shown in Exhibit 8-3.

Note that the total cost of operating the old truck includes the yearly $2,000 depreciation expense. If the new truck is bought, the $2,000 book value of the old truck must still be writ-

exhibit 8-3 Total-Cost Analysis for the Current Year: Keeping the Old Truck versus Selling It and Buying a New Truck*

Total Costs	Old Truck	Difference	New Truck
Variable costs:			
$0.30 × 50,000 miles	$15,000		
$0.27 × 50,000 miles			$13,500
Fixed costs:			
Insurance	500		550
Licenses	110		110
Depreciation expense	2,000		2,500
Book value of old truck to be written off			2,000
Resale value of old truck	0		(1,700)
Total cost	$17,610		$16,960
Difference		$650	

*Be aware that in order to emphasize the total-cost and differential-cost approaches, this analysis ignores the time value of money and related income tax effects, which we discussed in Chapter 4 of management accounting.

ten off. Thus, the $2,000 is a sunk cost and is the same under both alternatives, so it is not relevant to the decision at hand. The current resale value of the old truck, however, is a reduction in cost that will occur only if the new truck is purchased.

Two observations should be made about the total-cost approach to analyzing alternatives. First, it highlights the more attractive alternative in terms of cost only. In our example, the data appear to favor buying a new truck. However, this requires an investment of additional funds, which forces consideration of other factors. Because these factors were covered in Chapter 4 of management accounting, we have tried to keep our example simple by assuming a fair market value of $10,000 for the new truck at the end of one year. This means that the new truck's annual depreciation expense of $2,500 is equal to the difference between its original cost and its resale value after one year. Had the drop in value been greater than the depreciation expense, the excess would have been an additional cost of using the new truck during its first year.

Second, the total-cost approach is time-consuming because it involves differential costs as well as costs that are the same for all alternatives under consideration. With the differential-cost approach, only costs that are different need to be accumulated and analyzed. Thus, the costs of licensing both trucks and the $2,000 book value of the old truck to be depreciated or written off would not be considered. Exhibit 8-4 provides a list of the differential costs taken from Exhibit 8-3.

Although the differential-cost approach accumulates comparative costs and revenues that are different from those of the total-cost approach, it does not alter the relative attractiveness of the alternatives. Both the total and the differential analyses show a savings of $650 if the new truck is purchased. Thus, the acquisition of the new truck should bring future benefits to the company.

It should be noted that in both the total analysis and the differential analysis, the resale value of the old truck was treated as a negative cost. Instead, it could have been treated as a differential revenue from which the differential costs had been subtracted. It should also be noted that since both methods of analysis provide the same answer, it is likely that a firm will use the differential analysis method to save time in the collection and analysis of data. The total-cost revenue method will likely be used only when there is considerable uncertainty about whether all differential costs and revenues have been accounted for in the differential-cost approach.

Qualitative Considerations

As has been the case with all management accounting decisions discussed in this book, the effect of product or process decisions on the time and quality with which products or services can be delivered must be considered. In deciding whether to accept the rush print job, for example, Speedy Print Shop must consider the possibility that while accepting the job might lead to additional business, it could affect the quality of printing services to other customers. Likewise, if accepting the rush print job will slow down service to other customers, accepting the job may not be a good decision, no matter how financially attractive it seems to be.

In making a final decision, the cost and qualitative factors may lead you to the same conclusion. If they do not, you must decide what to do to enhance your company's overall profitability

exhibit 8-4

Differential-Cost and Revenue Analysis for the Current Year: Operating the Old Truck versus Selling It and Buying a New Truck

Differential Costs and Revenues	Old Truck	New Truck	Difference
Variable costs	$15,000	$13,500	$ 1,500
Insurance	500	550	(50)
Depreciation expense		2,500	(2,500)
Resale value of old truck	0	(1,700)	1,700
Total differential costs and revenues	$15,500	$14,850	$ 650

in the future. You might decide, for example, to accept the rush print job for an amount near or even below your differential cost to ensure that you get the order.

---

to summarize

Differential costs are the future costs that change as a result of a decision. Differential costs and revenues are those costs and revenues that are relevant to decisions. Sunk costs are never relevant because they are past costs that cannot be changed. Care must be exercised when estimating future costs because past cost relationships may not continue into the future. Some future costs may not be differential because they do not change as a result of a decision. Both variable and fixed costs may be differential.

There are two approaches to analyzing alternatives: total cost and differential cost. With the total-cost approach, all costs (including sunk costs) are accumulated. The differential-cost approach excludes sunk costs and all common costs, dealing only with costs that are different for the alternatives being considered. Once the quantitative analysis has been completed, qualitative factors must be considered.

4

Identify several examples of product and process evaluation decisions, and be able to analyze and select the best alternative for each example.

special order An order that may be priced below the normal selling price in order to utilize excess capacity and thereby contribute to company profits.

STOP & THINK In addition to the specific examples covered in this chapter, identify two other types of decisions that organizations make that would involve evaluating products and/or processes.

EXAMPLES OF PRODUCT AND PROCESS EVALUATION DECISIONS

The concept of differential costs applies to all evaluation decisions covered in this and the next chapter. In the remainder of this chapter, we will apply differential costing to several examples of short-term product and process evaluation decisions. First, we will consider the issue of evaluating special orders. A **special order** is an order that may be priced below the normal price in order to utilize excess capacity, thus contributing to company profits. We will look at special orders from the perspective of both the buyer and the seller. Second, we will look at the decisions, based on evaluation of products, competition, and the like, of exiting or entering a market (dropping or adding plants, segments, product lines, geographic territories, etc.). Third, we will look at how an organization might evaluate the use of scarce resources, such as limited raw materials in a manufacturing firm, limited shelf space in a merchandising company, and limited expertise or labor in a service firm. Fourth, we will consider how firms evaluate the pricing of regular products and services. In the expanded material section of the chapter, we will discuss the theory of constraints and how focusing on critical, constrained resources can result in more efficient manufacturing processes. On the text Web site at **http://albrecht.swcollege.com**, you will find a discussion of another major decision for some companies: deciding how manufacturers of joint products decide at what stage to sell the products.

Special Orders

In the opening scenario, we mentioned that **SATURN** is introducing a new sports utility vehicle (SUV) as part of its effort to become a full-line automobile brand. In making SUVs, Saturn will have to decide which parts and services to outsource to suppliers and which to make itself. **TOYOTA**, for example, makes only 30% of its automobile parts while **GM** makes 65% of its parts. The decision to outsource the making of parts or services is the first decision we cover in this chapter. It would be made after calculating all the costs and other factors involved in outsourcing versus making the parts internally. These types of special order decisions can involve long-term purchase and sales arrangements (as would be the case with Saturn) or only one-time orders (as in the Speedy Print Shop example). In either case, both the buyer (Saturn in the opening scenario) and the seller (the parts manufacturer) have decisions to make. These decisions can be outlined as in the following diagram:

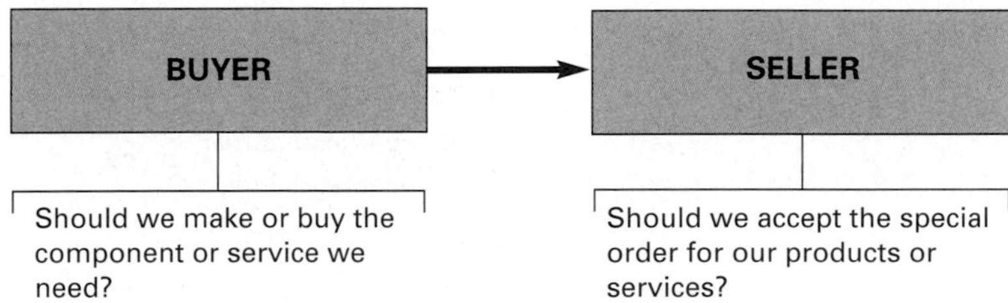

As the diagram shows, special orders can involve products or services. For example, in manufacturing companies, the special order might involve buying parts on a one-time basis from other companies because of a sudden surge in demand; or it could involve a company outsourcing or purchasing its internal audit services from a CPA firm. When parts are involved, both companies are manufacturing firms. When a service (such as internal auditing) is involved, the buyer may be a manufacturing, merchandising, or service company, but the provider is always a service company.

We will first look at special order decisions from the perspective of the buyer. Then, we will look at special order decisions from the perspective of the seller. In both cases, we will examine buying and selling products and services.

SPECIAL ORDERS—THE BUYER'S DECISION Many companies outsource virtually everything. Many Internet businesses, for example, are "virtual outsourcers." They take orders from customers and relay those orders to manufacturers, which, in turn, ship the products directly to the customers. Other organizations make or provide most of their products and services internally. In the following section, we describe the factors companies must consider when deciding whether to make or to buy products and services.

Making or Buying Manufactured Parts Companies, such as Toyota and Saturn, must decide which products and services they will produce and offer internally and which ones they will outsource or buy from outsiders. With respect to manufactured products, if a product consists of a number of parts, management must decide for each component whether to produce it or purchase it from an outside supplier. Over time, and based on a consideration of the relevant quantitative and qualitative factors, management develops a long-term policy regarding the use of its facilities to produce components for its products.

The fact that a long-term policy has been established does not mean that the issue is permanently closed. In fact, management is always reconsidering its decisions and looking for new ways to save money, improve quality, or speed up manufacturing and delivery processes. If a firm has idle facilities, for example, management may wish to find a use for those facilities. One possibility is to manufacture components that are normally purchased. Whether this decision is wise depends not only on cost considerations but also on a number of qualitative factors, such as the likely effect on the regular source of supply, the company's ability to produce a high-quality component, speed of delivery, and management's interest in keeping workers on the payroll. Thus, even though a firm has a long-term policy of purchasing some components and producing others, certain situations may require decisions that alter that policy.

Assuming that the qualitative factors favor the use of idle facilities to produce the part, what costs are relevant to a make-or-buy decision? In general, the purchase cost and all other costs that can be avoided if the part is manufactured are differential costs. Any cost that will be incurred regardless of whether the part is purchased or manufactured is not a differential cost and is irrelevant.

To illustrate how the differential costs in such a decision are identified, we assume that Ritter Manufacturing Company has excess capacity that could be used in producing wheel bearings. The accounting department has compiled the following projected total-cost figures for producing the bearings:

	Cost per Unit	Costs for 1,000 Units
Direct materials	$ 3.00	$ 3,000
Direct labor	8.00	8,000
Variable manufacturing overhead	4.00	4,000
Fixed manufacturing overhead, direct	2.50	2,500
Fixed manufacturing overhead, indirect	5.00	5,000*
Total costs	$22.50	$22,500

*Total indirect fixed costs are the same under both alternatives.

The company has been buying this bearing from a regular supplier in 1,000-unit quantities at a price of $19 per unit. Should Ritter continue to buy or start making the bearings? To answer this question, management must identify the differential costs of each alternative, taking into account any additional resources that may be needed, as well as alternative uses for the currently idle facilities. Two possible situations are presented here.

SITUATION 1 The currently idle facilities have no alternative uses. If the idle facilities do not have any practical alternative use, the opportunity cost is zero. With no opportunity cost, the differential costs would be the costs strictly associated with manufacturing (direct labor, direct materials, and so on).

The costs of the two alternatives can be presented on a total-cost or a differential-cost basis, as shown in Exhibit 8-5. Although each analysis produces different total costs, both demonstrate that the firm would save $1,500 per 1,000 units ($1.50 per unit) by making the component rather than buying it. The company's final decision would depend, of course, on whether there were negative qualitative factors that would, in the opinion of management, more than offset the $1.50 unit-cost advantage of making the part.

SITUATION 2 The idle facilities can be rented for $4,000 if they are not used to manufacture bearings. Management estimates that, if the facilities are used for manufacturing, 1,000 wheel bearings could be manufactured during this time.

In this case, the opportunity cost of producing the bearings is $4,000, or an average cost of $4 per unit ($4,000 ÷ 1,000 units). This opportunity cost is an important consideration in the firm's decision whether to buy or make the part, as shown in Exhibit 8-6. When the opportunity cost is considered, the cost of producing the part is $2,500 more than the cost of buying it.

exhibit 8-5 Analyses of the Costs of Using Idle Facilities (Situation 1)

	Total-Cost Analysis (per 1,000 Units)		Differential-Cost Analysis (per 1,000 Units)	
	Buy	Make	Buy	Make
Purchase cost	$19,000		$19,000	
Direct materials		$ 3,000		$ 3,000
Direct labor		8,000		8,000
Variable manufacturing overhead		4,000		4,000
Fixed manufacturing overhead:				
Direct		2,500		2,500
Indirect	5,000	5,000		
Total cost	$24,000	$22,500	$19,000	$17,500
Difference	$1,500		$1,500	

exhibit 8-6 The Effect of an Opportunity Cost on Analyses (Situation 2)

	Total-Cost Analysis (per 1,000 Units)			Differential-Cost Analysis (per 1,000 Units)		
	Buy		**Make**	**Buy**		**Make**
Purchase cost	$19,000			$19,000		
Direct materials			$ 3,000			$ 3,000
Direct labor			8,000			8,000
Variable manufacturing overhead			4,000			4,000
Fixed manufacturing overhead:						
Direct			2,500			2,500
Indirect	5,000		5,000			
Opportunity cost, rental			4,000			4,000
Total cost	$24,000		$26,500	$19,000		$21,500
Difference		$2,500			$2,500	

Unless there are quality, time, or other qualitative factors that override this cost, Ritter should buy the bearing and rent the idle facilities. Remember, the essence of the make-or-buy problem is management's desire to achieve the best utilization of existing facilities in the short term.

Because opportunity costs do not represent actual transactions, they are not recorded in the accounts. Yet they are always significant in the decision-making process because each situation has at least two alternatives. Thus, opportunity costs provide a good illustration of why a manager cannot rely solely on the data collected for external financial reports.

Purchasing Services or Providing Them Internally In recent years, companies have not only outsourced product parts, but more and more they are also outsourcing services such as cafeteria service, internal auditing, garbage removal, payroll accounting, legal services, and even basic accounting. In deciding whether to acquire services or provide them internally, companies go through the same kind of analysis as if they were buying products. That is, they consider the differential costs of each alternative, as well as qualitative factors, such as the quality of the service, whether space exists to house the service, whether services can be delivered on a timely basis, and management's interest in keeping workers on the payroll. Assuming management believes it can acquire high-quality services both within and outside the company, what costs are relevant to the purchase-or-provide decisions? Costs that will be incurred regardless of whether the service is purchased or provided internally are not differential costs and are irrelevant to the decision.

To illustrate how the differential costs are identified, we assume that Ritter Manufacturing Company is considering outsourcing its internal audit function. The following annual cost information relating to internal auditing is available.

Costs of Internal Auditing Department	
Salaries of internal audit employees	$1,200,000
Travel costs	1,400,000
Training costs	100,000
Depreciation on internal audit offices	50,000
Utilities for internal audit offices	40,000
Computers, software, and supplies	150,000
Other variable costs	75,000
Total costs of internal audit	$3,015,000

business environment essay

The Outsourcing Rage in America In recent years, organizations have outsourced more and more of their manufacturing and administrative functions. **GENERAL MOTORS**, for example, has outsourced its accounting functions. The **U.S. POST OFFICE** has outsourced much of its sales function and has asked supplier firms to teach customers how they can use the Post Office to ship their products. Everyone seems to be outsourcing everything, keeping only core activities in-house.

One exception to this trend is **WALT DISNEY**. Recognizing that it has a strong brand name, Disney decided that it could effectively sell clothes and other merchandise to customers. It had to decide whether to own its own retail outlets or enter into licensing agreements with other retailers. If it chose licensing, it would face some risk that contractual protections would be insufficient to prevent the licensee from degrading the value of the brand or from attempting to extract money from Disney by threatening to do so. On the other hand, entering into a new line of business, retail stores, where the company had no expertise was problematic as well. Disney chose to develop its own stores, but to enter into a long-term promotional relationship with **MCDONALD'S**.

Source: Information obtained from **http://as3.lib.byu.edu:8686/universe/document?_ansset=GeHauKO-EVYRMsSEVYRUUBRI** (accessed on September 29, 2000).

fyi

In recent years, major CPA firms have become professional service firms and are offering all kinds of new services. In fact, in other countries where accountants can practice law, three of the world's largest law firms are "Big 5" CPA firms. One of the fasting-growing services being offered by CPA firms is internal audit services for major corporations, such as the example in this chapter.

A CPA firm has offered to perform the internal audit services for $3,100,000 per year. You have determined that if internal audit services were contracted out to the CPA firm, the space currently used by the internal auditors could be used by the purchasing department, which is currently occupying rented space in a nearby city. The rent paid for offices used by the purchasing department is $10,000 per month.

Should Ritter continue to have its own internal audit department, or should it outsource its internal audit function to the CPA firm? From a strictly financial point of view, Ritter should not outsource, as shown below.

Cost of outsourcing:		
CPA firm cost		$3,100,000
Rent saved by relocating purchasing department ($10,000 per month × 12 months)		(120,000)
Net cost of outsourcing		$2,980,000
Cost of maintaining internal audit department:		
Total cost of internal audit department		$3,015,000
Less: nondifferential costs (incurred under either alternative)		
Depreciation expense	$50,000	
Utilities	40,000	
Total nondifferential costs		(90,000)
Differential cost of maintaining internal audit department		$2,925,000
Excess cost incurred by outsourcing internal auditing		$ 55,000

Of course, the one-year cost analysis is really an incomplete analysis. In making the decision, management must determine what the future costs of each alternative will be. If, for example, management can lock into a five-year commitment of $3,100,000 annually and it believes costs of keeping the internal audit department will rise $100,000 per year, from a cost perspective, the company may want to outsource even though the cost is higher in the current year.

In addition to costs, management must consider many other factors. For example, will the outside CPA firm provide audit services of the same or higher quality as those provided by the internal auditors? Having good internal audit services is important because the auditors can help ensure the efficiency and effectiveness of operations, assure that controls are implemented and

caution

Be careful to consider all differential costs and revenues in making evaluation decisions and to exclude the nondifferential costs. For example, in this internal audit example, if depreciation and utilities (which will be incurred whether or not internal audit services are outsourced) are not considered, an incorrect decision will be made.

followed, and even prevent and detect fraud and other problems. Quality of services is very important in an area like internal auditing, where it is difficult for management to judge whether the company is getting value for its money. Management would also want to consider other factors: (1) Will the CPA firm be able to provide the services in the long run? (2) Can the company use the displaced internal audit employees in other positions, or is the company willing to lay off employees? (3) Will outsourcing the internal audit services affect the cost of other services received by the company (for example, will outsourcing internal audit services reduce the cost of the external audit or the cost of cafeteria or other services)? (4) If internal auditing was used as a management trainee development area (as it is in many companies), are there other efficient and effective ways to train future managers?

SPECIAL ORDERS—THE SELLER'S DECISION If a seller can sell its services profitably at market prices, the decision is an easy one—provide the service. After all, that is the purpose of being in business. Where the difficulty comes is in deciding whether to reduce the normal price of a product or service in order to obtain a special order. Typical situations involving a possible price reduction when idle capacity exists are:

1. A manufacturer sells products under its own brand name, as well as to retail chain stores for sale under the chain's brand name.
2. A firm, such as a building contractor or an equipment manufacturer, sells its products or services in a competitive bidding situation.
3. A firm sells a product under distress conditions, for instance, when there has been a sharp decline in demand for its products because of a new product offered by a competitor.
4. A product has significant sales potential with a foreign distributor, whose market demands lower prices than those in the United States.
5. A provider of a service has extra capacity and has the opportunity to sign a large contract, at a lower-than-normal price, that would consume the excess capacity.

In each of these situations, we assume that a firm has available capacity that can be utilized to fill the special order. The relevant costs for this decision are the additional, or incremental, costs necessary to produce and deliver the special order. Management must therefore know the incremental costs. This information will indicate the lowest price at which the special order will begin to contribute to the firm's profits.

To illustrate, we will assume that Kent Electronics, which usually sells hand calculators for \$19, receives an order from a large department store chain for 10,000 calculators at a price of \$13 each. The requested calculators are to be sold under the store's brand name. Kent currently has excess capacity that could be used in producing enough calculators to fill the order. Should the company accept the order?

The answer to this question does not, of course, depend on cost and price factors alone. An obvious consideration, for example, would be whether the order would result in a significant loss of sales of the company's own brand of calculators. Let's assume that this is not a problem.

If the accounting department presents the data on a total-cost basis, the manager might erroneously reject the order. It appears from the following that the firm would have a loss if it accepted the special order:

Special Order for Calculators—Total-Cost Approach

Sales price		$ 13
Manufacturing costs:		
Direct materials	$3	
Direct labor	4	
Manufacturing overhead	9	
Total manufacturing costs		16
Loss per unit		$ (3)
Number of units in order		× 10,000
Expected loss exclusive of selling and administrative expenses		$(30,000)

It is not unusual for managers to base decisions on total-cost information because the data are readily available, having been collected in order to prepare financial statements and income tax returns. Unfortunately, such information may lead management to the wrong conclusion—in this case, to reject the order.

The only differential costs, however, are those future costs that change if the order is accepted. These include the variable product costs as well as the direct fixed costs. Fixed costs that are incurred regardless of whether the order is accepted should not be considered. The following analysis, prepared on a differential-cost basis, shows that Kent Electronics should accept the order.

Special Order for Calculators—Differential-Cost Approach

Sales price		$ 13
Variable and differential fixed costs:		
Direct materials	$3	
Direct labor	4	
Variable manufacturing overhead costs	2	
Differential fixed overhead costs	1	
Variable selling and administrative expenses	1	
Total variable and differential fixed costs		11
Remaining margin to cover fixed costs and provide a profit		$ 2
Number of units in order		×10,000
Expected contribution to fixed costs and profit		$ 20,000

These data assume that additional fixed costs of $1 per unit will be incurred if the order is accepted. If no additional fixed costs would be incurred, the margin would increase to $3. The analysis clearly suggests that, from a financial point of view, management should accept the order. This approach identifies not only the differential costs but also a price floor (the total variable and differential fixed costs of $11) below which management should probably not accept an order. As long as the price exceeds total variable and differential fixed costs, the firm will increase its profits by accepting the order. This analysis assumes that the company has no better alternative uses for its excess capacity and that special sales by the chain will have no adverse effect on Kent's normal sales. But what if regular customers hear about this special order and insist on lower prices, thus disrupting the normal pricing structure? Or, what if filling the special order will have an adverse effect on the quality of current products or the speed with which products can be offered to regular customers? These and other qualitative factors must also be considered.

A manager must also consider whether acceptance of such an order would be a violation of the Robinson-Patman Act. This legislation, enacted in 1936, prohibits firms from quoting different prices to competing customers for the same goods unless differences in price can be attributed to differences in cost. In the case of Kent Electronics, the sale is probably legal because the calculators are to be sold under the store's brand name, and the department store will assume all advertising costs.

The differential-cost approach to pricing can also be used in explaining why theater tickets are less expensive for matinees than for evening performances, why airline economy fares are less expensive than business-class fares, and why it is cheaper to make telephone calls at night and on weekends than on weekdays. If there is excess capacity that can be used to provide a service or make a product that will generate more revenue than the variable cost of providing the service or making the product, the firm will increase its profits by the amount of the margin remaining after deducting differential costs.

A few words of caution are in order when making these types of decisions. First, in some situations, there may also be some additional fixed costs that are relevant to the pricing decision. Second, a company must not accept too many orders that barely cover variable costs, or it will not be able to cover all its fixed costs. Third, using all extra capacity to fill a special order at a lower-than-normal price may prevent a company from being able to accept additional work at higher prices in the future. Fourth, accepting a special order may force a company to cut corners with normal customers, resulting in lower-quality products or services to those customers or decreasing the speed at which other customers are served.

to summarize

In choosing whether to make or buy a component or service, management must compare the differential costs of making the part or providing the service (including the opportunity costs of alternative uses of the facilities) with the cost of purchasing (outsourcing) the part or service. Qualitative factors must also be considered because they may be significant enough to reverse a decision based only on quantitative considerations. In deciding whether to accept special orders, the differential-cost approach is appropriate. Using this approach, only variable costs and differential fixed costs are considered.

Exiting or Entering a Market

The decision of whether to exit or enter a market is usually based on careful evaluation, although companies seem to be buying and selling businesses quite often these days. We will first consider the decision of whether to exit a market and then the decision of whether to enter a market.

EXITING A MARKET When a segment (product or line of products) is losing money, management must decide whether to drop it, as PRICELINE.COM did with its grocery and gasoline business. Such decisions are particularly difficult because the differential costs are not easy to identify, and this can lead to analyses based on invalid assumptions, as the following example demonstrates.

To illustrate, we will assume that Augusta Retail Company is thinking of closing one of its stores. The question of the store's value arose because of the July financial results for the company's three stores (amounts are in thousands):

	Store 1	Store 2	Store 3	Total
Sales revenue	$250,000	$90,000	$60,000	$400,000
Cost of goods sold	170,000	40,000	30,000	240,000
Gross margin	$ 80,000	$50,000	$30,000	$160,000
Operating expenses	55,000	30,000	35,000	120,000
Net income (or loss)	$ 25,000	$20,000	$ (5,000)	$ 40,000

If Store 3 is closed, it would seem reasonable to assume that Augusta Retail Company's profits will increase by $5 million, as shown here.

	Store 1	Store 2	Total
Sales revenue	$250,000	$90,000	$340,000
Cost of goods sold	170,000	40,000	210,000
Gross margin	$ 80,000	$50,000	$130,000
Operating expenses	55,000	30,000	85,000
Net income	$ 25,000	$20,000	$ 45,000

business environment essay

Dropping a Product Line In October 2000, **CIRCUIT CITY** suddenly decided that it would no longer sell major home appliances, such as washers, dryers, and dishwashers. Why would it make such a dramatic decision when sales of major appliances totaled $1.7 billion in 1999? According to Circuit City strategists, appliances were dropped for two reasons: (1) other companies such as **SEARS**, with 35% of the market; **HOME DEPOT**, quickly becoming a billion-dollar player; and **LOWE'S**, the number two seller, were too aggressive in their pricing and competitive strategies; and (2) softening volume, lower margins, and dim prospects for appliances were discouraging, especially compared to the higher margins on consumer electronic products. In dropping appliances, Circuit City embarked on a three-year plan to remodel virtually all of its 616 stores to concentrate exclusively on consumer electronics and home office equipment. The plan would cost about $1.2 billion and entail laying off about 1,000 employees. The price of Circuit City's stock dropped by 7% soon after the plan was announced.

Source: Information obtained from **http://library.northernlight.com/NC20000816060003696.html?inid=d1xbRwcTFkB5D34VBm** (accessed on October 2, 2000).

This analysis is based on three assumptions:

1. That all costs shown are differential and therefore relevant to the decision. In other words, there are no joint costs (costs that are common to two or more stores).
2. That the sales of the other stores will not be affected by dropping Store 3.
3. That no qualitative factors have a bearing on the decision.

Before closing Store 3, the company's general manager should check the validity of these assumptions. For simplicity, suppose that the second and third assumptions are valid, and that only the first assumption needs verification. First, the accounting department must separate the total costs of each store into variable costs, direct fixed costs, and indirect (or unavoidable) fixed costs. With this new information, the accounting department might prepare the following modified report for July (amounts are in thousands).

business environment essay

Avon Cosmetic Products in Department Stores? One of the most important decisions a company faces is what distribution channels to use to sell its products. Take Avon cosmetics, for example. **AVON PRODUCTS** is the world's largest direct seller of cosmetics. The company has sold its products through door-to-door sales representatives for the past 115 years. "Ding-dong, Avon calling," which debuted in 1954, is one of the best-known commercials and sales pitches. Now, for the first time, Avon will begin selling products in department stores. The Avon line will be called "Becoming," as in "Avon lets me become the woman that I am." Some 400 new products are being developed for the new line that will be sold in about 150 to 200 **J.C. PENNEY** and **SEARS, ROEBUCK** stores beginning in summer 2001.

Avon's retail strategy is part of its plan to reach new customers. Although Avon is the world's leading

	Store 1	Store 2	Store 3	Total
Sales revenue	$250,000	$90,000	$60,000	$400,000
Variable costs	190,000	50,000	40,000	280,000
Contribution margin	$ 60,000	$40,000	$20,000	$120,000
Direct fixed costs	20,000	15,000	18,000	53,000
Segment margin	$ 40,000	$25,000	$ 2,000	$ 67,000
Indirect fixed costs (not allocated)				27,000
Net income				$ 40,000

The manager can use this modified report to determine whether Store 3 made a positive contribution toward covering the indirect (unavoidable) fixed costs. In looking at this modified report, the manager would immediately see that the segment margin for Store 3 is a positive $2 million. This means that Store 3 is contributing $2 million to the company's overall profit. Thus, if Store 3 is dropped, profits will decrease by $2 million unless another store with greater profit potential is added or Store 3 can be sold to another company. To illustrate the potential decline in profits if Store 3 is dropped, the manager might ask the accounting department to prepare a report to indicate what the company's July financial results would show without Store 3. This pro-forma report would show the following information (amounts are in thousands):

	Store 1	Store 2	Total
Sales revenue	$250,000	$90,000	$340,000
Variable costs	190,000	50,000	240,000
Contribution margin	$ 60,000	$40,000	$100,000
Direct fixed costs	20,000	15,000	35,000
Segment margin	$ 40,000	$25,000	$ 65,000
Indirect fixed costs (not allocated)			27,000
Net income			$ 38,000

Although the original report suggested that profits would increase by $5 million if Store 3 were dropped, total profits would actually decrease by $2 million ($40 million − $38 million). The reason is that Store 3 is generating revenues that are $2 million greater than differential costs (variable costs and avoidable fixed costs). This analysis suggests that Store 3 should not be

direct seller of beauty and related products with sales of $5.3 billion in 1999, the company believes that it is missing sales to women who prefer to buy cosmetics in stores. The new line will be priced significantly higher than Avon's core direct selling brand, but well below prestige brands. For example, the new line may charge $7.50 for a tube of lipstick—higher than the $3 charged by Avon's core brand but lower than the $14 charged for most department store brands. Although the new distribution strategy may reach new customers, some people believe it will alienate committed, long-time, door-to-door sales representatives who have been the bread-and-butter sales force of the company. Only time will tell if the new distribution process is a good one.

Source: Information obtained from **http://www.businessweek.com/reprints/00-38/b3699003.htm**.

dropped, unless it can be replaced by another store or business that will contribute more than $2 million to cover unavoidable indirect fixed costs. (Obviously, we have not considered any sales price Augusta could receive from selling Store 3. Any money received from selling Store 3 would need to be deducted from the $2 million annual contribution Store 3 is making toward covering indirect costs.)

ENTERING A MARKET The considerations involved in deciding whether to enter a market are quite similar to those when deciding whether or not to exit a market. From a financial perspective, if adding a product line (segment) will contribute to the income of a firm, it is generally a good decision. The contribution can come in several forms. First, entering a new market can reduce the current cost of doing business. For example, assume that Augusta is considering purchasing a wholesale distribution company that will allow the company to buy directly from manufacturers, rather than from other wholesalers, when acquiring merchandise for its stores. Even if the new wholesale company is not profitable on its own, if it could reduce Augusta's costs enough so that overall profits are higher, the decision to buy might be a good one. Buying a new company or entering a new market could increase overall company profits by having the new segment cover some of the indirect fixed costs now being borne entirely by existing businesses. From a financial perspective, the important point to consider is whether total profits will be higher or lower after the purchase.

In addition to the financial considerations, organizations consider the effects on quality and time to deliver products to customers when deciding whether to enter a market. For example, suppose a small company has superior-quality products, manufacturing knowledge, or other attributes that could enhance the quality of the organization's products. Would it be wise to buy this smaller company even if the purchase doesn't increase overall short-term profits? Probably so. Or, what if a company occupies a strategic location for serving an organization's customers and buying the company would allow the organization to deliver its products more quickly to customers? Would buying the strategically located company be a good decision even if short-term overall profits aren't increased? Again, probably so. Both purchases would allow the organization to serve its customers better by increasing quality and decreasing delivery time. Hopefully, the result of both purchases would be a larger market share and higher profits in the long run. Unfortunately, it is hard to quantify by how much quality and/or delivery time must improve before a purchase is a good one. Because quality and time decisions are subjective, we will focus on the short-term financial considerations in deciding whether to enter a market. You should realize, however, that quality and time considerations are very important, and in considering some purchases, they may be the overriding factors that outweigh short-term financial considerations.

To illustrate entering a new market, assume that Augusta Retail Company now has only two stores. Further, assume that it is considering purchasing the wholesale company just discussed. The following data are available for Augusta Retail Company prior to making the purchase (amounts are in thousands):

	Store 1	Store 2	Total
Sales revenue	$250,000	$90,000	$340,000
Cost of goods sold	170,000	40,000	210,000
Other variable costs	20,000	10,000	30,000
Contribution margin	$ 60,000	$40,000	$100,000
Direct fixed costs	20,000	15,000	35,000
Segment margin	$ 40,000	$25,000	$ 65,000
Indirect fixed costs (not allocated)			27,000
Net income			$ 38,000

As these data show, Augusta currently makes a net income of $38 million. Now, assume that Augusta can purchase a wholesale company that will allow Augusta to buy directly from manufacturers, thus decreasing its cost of goods sold by 30%. However, the wholesale company is currently losing $10 million per year. Should Augusta buy the wholesale company? The following analysis shows that, from a financial perspective, buying the wholesale company would be a good decision (again, amounts are in thousands).

Effect on Current Stores

	Store 1		Store 2		Total (before and after purchase)		Wholesale Company	Total (including wholesale company)
	Before	After	Before	After	Before	After		
Sales revenue	$250,000	$250,000	$90,000	$90,000	$340,000	$340,000	$110,000	$450,000
Cost of goods sold	170,000	119,000[1]	40,000	28,000[2]	210,000	147,000	70,000	217,000
Other variable costs	20,000	20,000	10,000	10,000	30,000	30,000	15,000	45,000
Contribution margin	$ 60,000	$111,000	$40,000	$52,000	$100,000	$163,000	$ 25,000	$188,000
Direct fixed costs	20,000	20,000	15,000	15,000	35,000	35,000	35,000	70,000
Segment margin	$ 40,000	$ 91,000	$25,000	$37,000	$ 65,000	$128,000	$ (10,000)	$118,000
Indirect fixed costs (not allocated)					27,000	27,000	—	27,000
Net income					$ 38,000	$101,000	$ (10,000)	$ 91,000

[1]$170,000 − (0.3 × $170,000) = $119,000.
[2]$40,000 − (0.3 × $40,000) = $28,000.

fyi

Pick up practically any business newspaper or periodical and you'll read about companies exiting or entering markets. For example, the front page of the November 6, 2000 *Wall Street Journal* carried stories about VIACOM agreeing to buy BET, the nation's biggest African American–controlled media company; PEPSICO's offer to purchase QUAKER OATS; and the plans of BANK OF AMERICA, IBM, and PRUDENTIAL to purchase stakes in a Web firm that helps link tenants directly with landlords.

This analysis shows that even though the wholesale company is losing $10 million per year, purchasing the wholesale company will increase overall company profits by $53 million ($91 million − $38 million). Of course, this elaborate analysis really wasn't necessary since many costs (other variable costs, direct fixed costs, and indirect fixed costs) stayed the same. In fact, the only differential costs were the decrease in cost of goods sold (facilitated by being able to buy directly from manufacturers instead of wholesalers) and the $10 million loss the wholesale company incurs. Focusing only on the differential costs, you can see that the net income of the company would be increased by $53 million upon buying the wholesale company (numbers are in thousands).

Differential Costs of Deciding to Enter a Market

Decrease in cost of goods sold of Store 1	$51,000
Decrease in cost of goods sold of Store 2	12,000
Loss incurred by wholesaler	(10,000)
Increase in income from buying wholesaler	$53,000

This analysis suggests that, from a financial perspective, the wholesale company should be purchased. The decreases in cost of goods sold that will result in Store 1 and Store 2 more than compensate for the losses currently being incurred by the wholesaler.

to summarize

In deciding whether to exit or enter a market, the effect on profits, quality, and speed of delivery should be considered. When focusing on the financial aspects of exiting or entering a market, only the differential costs and revenues need be considered. A product or line of products should not be dropped unless it does not make a contribution toward covering indirect fixed costs. An alternative product or line of products can be added that will contribute more toward covering unavoidable indirect fixed costs. A segment should be added if it increases overall company profits. The increase in overall company profits can come from reduced costs in existing segments or from the profitable margin of the acquired segment.

Selecting the Best Use of a Scarce Resource

Organizations are often faced with the decision of how to best use scarce resources. In a manufacturing company, the scarce resource might be limited raw materials or limited production capacity. For a retail merchandising firm, such as **WAL-MART**, the scarce resource might be limited shelf space. For a service firm, the scarce resource might be limited expertise. We will illustrate the concept of scarce resources using limited shelf space for a retail merchandising firm.

When a retail merchandising firm sells more than one product and store shelves are inadequate to display all products equally, management has to decide to which products the store should allocate shelf space and how much space should be allocated to each product. With limited shelf space, stocking one product means that another product cannot be stocked or will have to be stocked on a more limited basis. In deciding which products to stock, management needs to know which products and how much of each product to stock in order to maximize net income. A retail store will normally maximize net income by stocking those products that contribute the most toward covering fixed costs and providing profit in relation to the "critical resource factor," in this case, shelf space. The **critical resource factor** is the resource that limits operating capacity by its availability. For example, in a manufacturing company, if machine hours are the most critical resource, a company should concentrate on the product for which revenues exceed variable costs by the highest margin per machine hour. Other critical resources in manufacturing companies might include labor hours, floor space, or special raw materials. Because shelf space is the critical resource factor for our retail store example, from a financial point of view, management should stock those products for which revenues exceed variable costs by the highest margin per square foot of shelf space.

critical resource factor The resource that limits operating capacity by its availability.

To illustrate, we assume that Bolten Retail Company stocks potato chips and cookies. Let's further assume that its capacity, at least in the short term, is limited by the availability of only 20 square feet of shelf space for these two products. The revenue and cost data for one package each of potato chips and cookies are:

	Potato Chips	Cookies
Selling price	$3.10	$3.50
Variable costs	2.48	3.15
Contribution margin per unit	$0.62	$0.35
Percentage contribution margin (contribution margin ÷ selling price)	20%	10%

On the basis of this limited information, it would appear that potato chips are more profitable than cookies. The sale of one bag of potato chips will contribute $0.62 toward fixed costs, whereas the sale of one package of cookies will contribute only $0.35.

Before Bolten can decide whether or not to emphasize potato chips, however, management must consider the extent to which each product uses the critical resource, limited shelf space. If a bag of potato chips takes up twice as much space as a package of cookies (two bags of potato chips occupy one square foot of shelf space, while four packages of cookies can occupy the same one square foot of shelf space), the sale of cookies will make a greater total contribution to profits than the sale of potato chips, as shown by the following calculations:[3]

3 We are assuming that the company can sell all the potato chips and cookies it stocks. If it can't, or if one product sells faster than the other, rate of turnover must be considered.

	Potato Chips	Cookies
Contribution margin per unit	$0.62	$0.35
Packages per square foot	× 2	× 4
Contribution margin per square foot of shelf space	$1.24	$1.40

STOP & THINK Why do you think that most grocery stores allocate more space to breakfast cereals than to most other products?

Even though potato chips have a higher contribution margin per unit of product ($0.62 versus $0.35), cookies have a higher contribution margin per square foot of shelf space ($1.40 versus $1.24), which is the critical resource. The management of Bolten Retail Company should stock cookies rather than potato chips, assuming that the company's only critical resource is shelf space.

However, if the demand for cookies is limited and Bolten never has potato chips for sale, will customers start shopping at other stores? In that case, Bolten should stock as many cookies as it can sell and use the balance of the critical resource for stocking potato chips. To illustrate, we assume that the market demand for cookies is 1,800 packages per month or an average of 60 per day. Because it takes only 15 square feet of shelf space (60 packages ÷ 4 packages per square foot) to store one day's worth of cookies, 5 square feet of shelf space are available to stock potato chips. This means that 10 bags of potato chips can be stocked. Assuming all 10 bags are sold during each day, the combined sales of cookies and potato chips will contribute $27.20 to cover fixed costs and provide a profit, as shown below.

caution

It is essential to carefully and accurately identify the scarce resource and the quantity of the scarce resource consumed by each product. For example, in the store shelf space decision, if you don't carefully calculate the amount of space needed for cookies and potato chips and instead look only at the contribution margin per unit, an incorrect decision will be made. It is only when you consider the contribution margin per square foot of shelf space that the correct decision is made.

	Daily Contribution Margin
Packages sold:	
Potato chips (10 bags × $0.62 per bag)	$ 6.20
Cookies (60 packages × $0.35 per package)	21.00
Total	$27.20

This analysis shows that from a financial perspective, the best use of the 20 square feet of shelf space is to use 15 square feet for cookies and 5 square feet for potato chips. Because demand for cookies is limited, only a $21 daily contribution margin can be earned by selling cookies. The other 5 feet of shelf space should be used to stock potato chips. Obviously, nonfinancial factors, such as customer satisfaction, would also have to be considered in making the final decision of how much of each product to stock.

The foregoing analysis dealt with only two constraints: store shelf space and product demand. If a firm is further limited by other factors (such as the ability to buy certain amounts of particular products), management generally has to use the quantitative techniques of linear programming or simulation to help decide how many of each product to produce and/or sell. You can learn about this technique in advanced accounting or business management courses. Regardless of the number of constraints, though, the essence of the decision is to achieve the best short-term utilization of available resources.

In the expanded material section of this chapter, you will find a discussion of the theory of constraints, a philosophical approach to focusing on "constraints" as a way to allocate limited resources and improve management processes.

to summarize

In deciding how to make the best use of critical resource factors, management should choose the item that provides the greatest contribution margin per unit of the most critical resource.

Setting Selling Prices

Some people argue that a discussion of setting prices in a book such as this is a waste of time because the market sets the price and there is nothing management can do to affect prices. Others argue that, especially in some markets, management does set prices or at least influence prices. In this section, we assume that management can influence prices and discuss those factors management should consider.

Pricing a product is partly a matter of guesswork because managers rarely know with any precision how price affects demand (e.g., how many more units could be sold if the price were to be lowered by a certain amount). In addition, other factors, such as advertising and packaging, affect the sale of a product.

The pricing process is further complicated by the fact that there are several broad categories of pricing decisions and the same cost information is not appropriate for all of them. Earlier, we considered the pricing of special orders. In this section, we cover the pricing of normal products. Other pricing categories, including the pricing of new products, are covered in advanced accounting and marketing texts.

NORMAL PRICING OF PRODUCTS In deciding whether to accept special orders, we stated that the price must be high enough to cover variable and incremental fixed costs. The price normally charged for a product or service, however, must be high enough to cover all costs (including production, selling, and administrative costs) and still provide a reasonable return on the owners' investments. Therefore, all costs (variable, as well as a fair share of fixed costs) are relevant to the pricing decision. In some cases, however, the final price may be set somewhat above or below the price suggested by total cost plus a reasonable return. This occurs when pricing decisions are based primarily on supply and demand, competition, and other market factors. For example, textbook prices are strictly competitive. Whether it costs $250,000 or $500,000 to produce a textbook, its price has to be close to that of the nearest competitors.

In supplying cost data to aid management in normal pricing decisions, accountants may use a functional approach, summarizing costs by function (manufacturing, selling, or administrative), or a contribution approach, classifying costs by behavior (fixed or variable). To illustrate the two approaches, we assume that Kent Electronics (from the calculator example earlier in the chapter) is pricing a desk calculator. The relevant costs for each approach are as follows:

Functional Cost Approach	
Direct materials	$ 6
Direct labor	8
Manufacturing overhead (200% × direct labor cost)	16
Total manufacturing cost	$30
Markup to cover selling and administrative expenses and provide a reasonable return on investment (0.40 × selling price)	20
Estimated normal selling price	$50

Contribution Approach	
Direct materials	$ 6
Direct labor	8
Variable manufacturing overhead	7
Variable selling and administrative overhead expenses	4
Total variable costs	$25
Markup to cover fixed costs and provide a reasonable return on investment (0.50 × selling price)	25
Estimated normal selling price	$50

The markups calculated here are based on the selling price because marketing people generally use this approach. How do we calculate the markup as a percentage of the selling price before that price is known? If the markup is to be 40% of the selling price, as in our first example, the total manufacturing cost must be 60% of the selling price. So we simply divide the manufacturing cost by 60% to get the selling price ($30 ÷ 0.60 = $50). Then, the selling price minus the manufacturing cost is the markup ($50 − $30 = $20).

If a functional cost approach is used, the markup must be large enough to cover all selling and administrative costs and provide a reasonable return on investment. If a contribution approach is used, the markup must be large enough to cover all fixed costs and generate a reasonable return on investment.

to summarize

For normal pricing of products, management should consider all costs, not just differential costs (as was the case with pricing special orders). The markups applied must be high enough to cover all costs and expenses and provide a reasonable return on investment.

expanded material

Thus far in this chapter, we have discussed how and why organizations evaluate products and processes, including the concepts of benchmarking and differential costs and revenues. We have also provided several examples of evaluation decisions, such as whether to accept special orders, whether to outsource or provide services and products internally, whether to continue or discontinue existing product lines or expand into new product lines or geographic regions, how best to use critical resources, and how to set selling prices. Another evaluation decision, whether to sell or continue processing products developed from joint manufacturing processes, is discussed on the Internet if you are interested. In the chapter, we have explained how to make product and process evaluation decisions by focusing on differential costs and revenues. In this expanded section, we discuss another approach to making product and process evaluation decisions—the theory of constraints. This approach or philosophy, which has gained in popularity in recent years, was developed during the 1980s and involves making production decisions by focusing on bottleneck resources. The theory of constraints advocates that only constraint resources should operate at full capacity.

5

Understand the theory of constraints and how focusing on scarce resources can direct activities in manufacturing companies.

theory of constraints (TOC) A management philosophy that focuses on constraint resources and holds that they should operate at full capacity.

THEORY OF CONSTRAINTS

To compete against global rivals in the early 1980s, managers from a variety of industries worked hard to revitalize their manufacturing practices. During this period, a manufacturing philosophy called the **theory of constraints (TOC)** or optimized production technology (OPT) received considerable attention. TOC was popularized by Eliyahu Goldratt, an Israeli physicist, in his book *The Goal.* Goldratt claimed that by scheduling production by focusing on bottleneck resources, a firm could develop and maintain a manufacturing-based competitive advantage over other firms. The premise of TOC is that only constraint resources should operate at full capacity. That is, a facility can produce a finished product no faster than the constraint resource can process the materials that go into the product. The constraint resource acts as the "drum," setting the production pace for the entire operation. Once material has been processed on the constraint resource, it should not sit idle but should be kept moving until shipped to the customer. By following a few basic rules, each of which focuses management's attention on the firm's constraint resource, managers can use TOC to maximize the throughout (amount of product produced in available facilities) of their production facility. The result is that the firm is better able to meet its customers' needs.

Constraint management can improve a company's competitive position by helping it better schedule and utilize its productive resources. When the constraint resource becomes the focal point, nonconstraint operations will operate below capacity, facilitating several positive outcomes. For example, nonconstraint resources no longer produce excess work-in-process (WIP) inventory; shop floor clutter and confusion are thereby reduced, production quality is improved, preventive maintenance activities are enhanced, and more time is available for employee training. By identifying the constraint resource and using it as the reference point for decision making, management can alter the very nature of key assumptions regarding product costing, performance measurement, product and process design, and make-versus-buy decisions. In general, the theory holds that more accurate assumptions lead to better decisions and enhanced competitiveness.

Employing TOC requires five basic steps:

1. *Understand the system's constraints.* The constraint may be a manufacturing process, a delivery process, or any other aspect of the process from taking delivery of raw materials to making sure finished products are sold and delivered.
2. *Decide how to exploit the system's constraints.* Production and pricing decisions should be based on the throughput yield per unit of constraint resource.
3. *Subordinate everything else to keeping the constraint resource operating at optimal capacity.* All nonconstraint activities should be coordinated with the constraint resource. This often requires a dramatic shift in managerial mindset, including allowing workers and machinery to sit idle or perform other, unrelated activities when not needed.
4. *Elevate the constraint.* By focusing on the constraint, it may be possible to offload some work to nonbottlenecks by acquiring more equipment or outsourcing some bottleneck work.
5. *If a constraint has been broken, go back to step 1.* Do not allow nonaction or inertia to cause a system constraint. Bottlenecks can, and will, shift around within an organization. Not properly identifying the relevant and current constraint can lead to a return of process inefficiencies and confused management policies.

Examples of companies that have adopted TOC are plentiful in the literature. For example, before employing TOC, a privately held metal tool manufacturing company used the ratio of indirect to direct labor hours as its key performance measure. Focusing on this measure caused the company to develop a "keep the workers busy at all costs" attitude, resulting in piles of excess WIP inventory, production inefficiencies, and a poorly focused pricing strategy. Under TOC, nonconstrained resources are allowed to sit idle, and the company uses this idle time to cross-train employees. As another example, a packing company struggled for a period of time with employees at nonbottlenecks who tried to stay busy by releasing WIP too early to the bottleneck operation. By implementing new, TOC-consistent performance measures, the company was able to eliminate buildups of WIP inventory and become more efficient.

As a simple example of the TOC, assume that Wilton Company requires five processes to make treadmills. The first process involves purchasing materials such as metal, rubber, and electronic components. There is no constraint on the amount of any of these materials that can be purchased. The second process involves manufacturing the various components of the treadmills. The equipment and personnel available to manufacture the components can produce parts for 20 treadmills per hour. The third process involves painting the various components. Painting equipment and personnel can process 18 treadmills per hour. The fourth process involves assembling the finished parts into completed treadmills. Assembly requires specially manufactured equipment that can process only 15 treadmills per hour. Finally, the fifth process, testing, has unlimited capacity because it involves labor only and additional workers can be hired. The following diagram shows the manufacturing processes and their capacities.

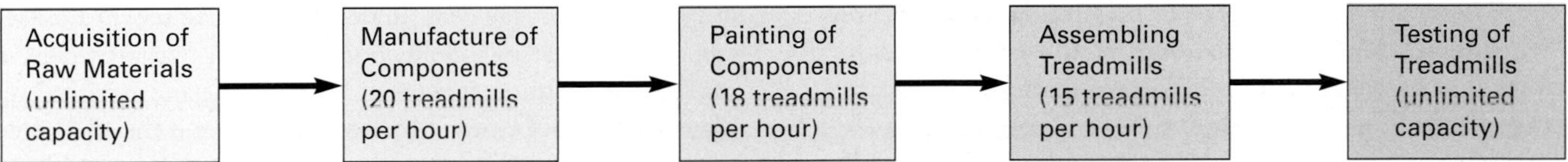

As you can see, if each process operated at full capacity, every hour the components for two treadmills would be produced that painting couldn't process, and three treadmills would be painted that couldn't be assembled. WIP inventory would accumulate in both the third and fourth processes, making production less efficient.

By focusing on the constraint resource—assembling in this case—the company might choose to purchase another specialized assembly machine, outsource some assembly, use the extra time in manufacturing components and painting to complete other jobs or cross-train, or even have some of the idle employees help out in testing treadmills. By focusing on constraint resources, management will know exactly where its bottlenecks are and can take action to fix the problem. Of course, if the constraint resource—assembly—is allowing the company to meet customer demands for treadmills, management may choose to undertake promotional campaigns or add additional products that can be made using excess capacity in component manufacturing and painting.

to summarize

TOC is a management philosophy that focuses management's attention on the bottlenecks or constraint resources. Other measures can result in excess WIP inventory or other inefficiencies. TOC helps management understand the kinds of decisions that will make the firm more productive.

review of learning objectives

1 Explain how evaluation leads to planning and why products and processes must be continuously evaluated. Evaluation is designed to improve the efficiency and cost-effectiveness of existing operations related to products and operating processes. Such decisions usually are in the form of corrective actions regarding machinery efficiency, reduction of waste, efficient task performance, and overcoming bottlenecks. Evaluation takes place regularly, often daily, weekly, or monthly. Sometimes evaluation leads to strategic decisions that deal with changes in the product or the processes. These decisions might be related to the type or quality of the company's products, fundamental changes in the production process, changing suppliers or types of raw materials, or changing the product distribution system.

2 **Understand why benchmarking is so important and how it is conducted.** Benchmarking involves comparing a company's financial and operating performance against a competitor's performance or comparing the performance of various internal departments against each other. It consists of four steps: (1) analyzing the company's practices, procedures, and performance in a given process; (2) selecting a benchmark or benchmarks; (3) gathering information on the benchmark's practices and procedures; and (4) analyzing the data collected in step 3 to determine which policies and procedures used by the benchmarked companies can best be employed.

3 **Understand the concept of differential costs and revenues, and be able to identify those costs and revenues that are relevant to making product and process decisions.** Making product and process decisions involves a consideration of differential costs and revenues. These are future costs and revenues that will change as a result of the decision and therefore are the relevant costs in determining whether the decision to change should be made. Differential costs may be variable, fixed, or both. Past costs that do not change as a result of a decision are not relevant to the decision and are called sunk costs.

4 **Identify several examples of product and process evaluation decisions, and be able to analyze and select the best alternative for each example.** Examples of product and process decisions are (1) special orders (including whether to make or buy a component or service and whether to accept special orders), (2) whether to exit or enter a market, (3) how to best utilize a critical resource, and (4) setting normal selling prices. In choosing whether to make or buy a component or service, management must compare the differential costs of making the part or providing the service (including the opportunity cost of alternative uses of the facilities or labor) with the cost of purchasing the part or service. In deciding whether or not to accept a special order in situations where there is excess capacity, the price should be high enough to provide a positive contribution toward covering normal fixed costs and increasing profit. A product or product line should not be dropped or a market exited unless that unit does not make a positive contribution toward covering indirect fixed costs. An alternative product or line of products can be added that will contribute more toward covering unavoidable indirect costs. A market should be entered only if it contributes to the overall profitability of the firm. In deciding how to use a scarce resource, management should choose the item that provides the greatest contribution margin per unit of the most critical resource. A product should be processed further if the additional revenues from further processing will exceed the additional costs of further processing. For normal pricing, management should consider all costs, not just differential costs.

expanded material

5 **Understand the theory of constraints and how focusing on scarce resources can direct activities in manufacturing companies.** The theory of constraints (TOC) suggests that management should focus on the few "constraints" that are found in any management setting. The premise of TOC is that only constraint resources should operate at full capacity and that a facility can produce a finished product no faster than the constraint resource can process the materials that go into the product.

key terms and concepts

benchmarking 413
critical resource factor 432
differential costs 415
special order 420
sunk costs 416
total cost 418

expanded material

theory of constraints (TOC) 436

review problem

Whether to Make or Buy a Part

Schill Manufacturing Company makes lawn mowers. It has been buying a component from a regular supplier for $11.50 per unit. Because Schill recently has been operating at less than full capacity, the president is considering whether to make the part rather than purchase it. The estimated total cost of making the part under the company's costing system is $14.40, computed as follows:

Direct materials	$ 3.20
Direct labor	5.60
Manufacturing overhead (100% of direct labor cost)	5.60
Estimated total cost to make	$14.40

Variable manufacturing overhead costs are estimated to be 40% of direct labor cost. Fixed manufacturing costs that are not differential are 60% of direct labor cost.

Required: Decide whether Schill should make or buy the component.

Solution

Differential-Cost Analysis

	Cost to Make	Cost to Buy
Purchase price		$11.50
Direct materials	$ 3.20	
Direct labor	5.60	
Variable manufacturing overhead (40% of direct labor cost)	2.24	
Differential cost to make the part	$11.04	
Differential cost to buy the part		$11.50
Cost savings by making the part	$ 0.46	

Total-Cost Analysis

	Cost to Make	Cost to Buy
Purchase price		$11.50
Direct materials	$ 3.20	
Direct labor	5.60	
Variable manufacturing overhead (40% of direct labor cost)	2.24	
Fixed manufacturing overhead	3.36	3.36
Total cost to make	$14.40	
Total cost to buy		$14.86
Cost savings by making the part	$ 0.46	

Calculations:

$5.60 × 0.40 = $2.24 variable manufacturing overhead

$5.60 × 0.60 = $3.36 fixed manufacturing overhead

Unless qualitative factors override the cost estimate, Schill should make the part rather than purchase it. The decision will be the same whether the calculation is based on differential costs only or on total costs. Note that the fixed manufacturing overhead cost applies to both making and buying the part under the total-cost analysis because these costs will be incurred whichever alternative is selected.

discussion questions

1. Why is it so important to continuously evaluate products and processes?
2. Many accounting systems are designed to collect financial information for the purpose of preparing financial statements. What problem does this create for an accountant who is asked to compile relevant data for use by managers to make product and process decisions? Explain.
3. What is a differential cost? Give an example of how differential costs are used by managers making product and process decisions.
4. Distinguish between variable costs and differential costs. Why is the distinction important?
5. Can a fixed cost be relevant to a decision? Explain.
6. What is a sunk cost? Why are sunk costs irrelevant in product and process decision making?
7. In deciding whether to replace an old asset with a new one, which of the following are differential revenues and costs?
   a. Cost of the new equipment
   b. Resale value of the old equipment
   c. Resale value of the new equipment
   d. Book value of the old equipment
   e. Operating costs of the new equipment
8. Distinguish between the total-cost approach and the differential-cost approach to analyzing data for product and process decisions.
9. What is the major limitation in using the total-cost approach to analyze data for product and process decisions?
10. Why must business decisions be based on qualitative as well as quantitative information? Explain.
11. Explain what costs are generally relevant to make-or-buy decisions.
12. Explain why opportunity costs are not included in the accounting records.
13. What is the significance of idle capacity in determining the price of a special order?
14. If total manufacturing costs, including fixed manufacturing overhead, are larger than the price offered by a purchaser for a special order, the order should not be accepted because the profits of the company will be adversely affected. Do you agree? Explain. (Ignore qualitative factors.)
15. In deciding whether to exit or enter a market, what factors should be considered?
16. When should a segment (product, product line, division, etc.) be dropped? When should a segment be added?
17. Why is the contribution margin per unit of a critical resource more important than the contribution margin per unit of product in deciding which products to produce and sell?

expanded material

18. Why does employing the TOC in manufacturing processes lead to less WIP inventory?
19. Proponents argue that the TOC helps management make better use of production resources and better decisions about whether or not to outsource and how to use employees effectively. Explain why this is so.

discussion cases

CASE 8-1

BUYING FROM INSIDE OR OUTSIDE THE COMPANY

E & B Company has two divisions, processing and finishing. The Finishing Division has been purchasing certain products from the Processing Division at a price of $80 per unit. (A unit consists of 100 yards of material.) The Processing Division has announced that, starting next month, it will raise its price to $100 per unit. As the manager of the Finishing Division, you object to this price and have indicated that you are planning to purchase these units of material from outside suppliers at a price of $85 per unit. You have asked the accounting department to furnish cost data to help you understand why the Processing Division's price has to be raised to $100 per unit. Following is the information supplied about the Processing Division's operations:

Units produced for Finishing Division	2,000
Variable production costs per unit	$60
Indirect fixed costs allocated to the Processing Division	$50,000
Normal profit per unit in Processing Division	$15

If the Finishing Division buys from outside suppliers, the facilities used by the Processing Division to manufacture these units for the Finishing Division will remain idle.

Answer the following questions:

1. If the Processing Division is successful in imposing the $100 price and the Finishing Division elects to buy from outside suppliers, what impact does this action have on the overall profit of E & B Company?
2. Explain why the variable production costs, the fixed costs, and the normal profit are, or are not, each relevant to this decision. (You are not being asked to discuss whether the $100 price is an appropriate price or whether the division managers should be allowed to maintain an autonomous posture in this decision.)
3. What additional factors should E & B Company's top management consider in resolving this matter?

CASE 8-2

SUNK COSTS

Sam Love owns and manages a small but growing service business. In fact, this year has been so good that Sam is moving his office to a larger, more centrally located site. In an effort to save on moving costs, Sam employs his brother Dan (who owns a large truck) to haul his office furniture and equipment. Unfortunately, Dan doesn't properly secure the rear door of the truck, and one of Sam's two copy machines winds up in a million pieces in the middle of the highway. As the two brothers survey the damage, Sam's office manager approaches and says, "Well, look on the bright side, the machine was half depreciated."

Should Sam take comfort from this statement? Explain your answer.

CASE 8-3

WHY MOST COMPANIES WANT TO BENCHMARK

Everyone wants to benchmark these days. Assume you are the dean of a business school with a highly successful MBA program. You have enjoyed increasing numbers of highly qualified applicants, recruiters love your students, and both *Business Week* and *U.S. News and World Report* have ranked you in the top 10 business schools in the United States. You have just been contacted by the deans of two other business schools, whose MBA programs rank well below yours. They would like to spend a couple of days at your school benchmarking against your admissions, advising, placement, and other services, as well as studying your curriculum, faculty development processes, and other ingredients of your success. You would like to help them but are not sure you want to reveal why you have been so successful. If you don't expose your secrets of success, however, their visits would largely be a waste of time. What should you do? Should you welcome your competitors with open arms, or should you refuse to allow them to benchmark against you? Or, should you allow them to come but hide your best secrets from them?

EXERCISE 8-1

CLASSIFYING DECISIONS

Indicate whether each of the following activities appears to be mostly related to planning, controlling, or evaluating:

1. Operational budgeting
2. Production prioritizing
3. Providing feedback to managers
4. Tracking performance
5. Strategic planning
6. Rewarding performance
7. Capital budgeting

8. Comparing costs, quality, and timeliness against previously prepared budgets
9. Analyzing results
10. Identification of problems

EXERCISE 8-2

RELEVANT COSTS

Quick Serve Company provides janitorial services for office buildings. Last year the firm acquired a cleaning machine for $100,000. The firm expected to use the machine for five years. However, this year a new, more efficient machine has been introduced on the market. The accountant for Quick Serve has determined that the annual total operating costs for the old machine are $240,000. The annual operating costs for the new machine would be $200,000, and the purchase price is $130,000. The president of Quick Serve feels the company should not buy the new machine. He points out that the operating costs of $200,000 and the purchase price of $130,000 for the new machine, plus the original cost of the old machine of $100,000, are greater than the operating costs of the old machine.

1. Do you agree with the president?
2. What type of cost is the $100,000 purchase price of the old machine?

EXERCISE 8-3

QUALITATIVE FACTORS

Sturdy Chair Company manufactures wooden chairs. In producing the chairs, a great deal of scrap wood is created. The company currently uses the wood as fuel in a factory furnace. However, it has the opportunity to send the scrap wood to a subcontractor, who would turn it into pressed board to be used to produce small end tables as a new product of Sturdy Chair.

Identify any qualitative factors that Sturdy Chair Company might want to consider in deciding how to use the scrap wood.

EXERCISE 8-4

SPECIAL-ORDER PRICING

You are the controller for Comfort Shoe Company. The company has excess shoes, which it has not been able to market through its own distribution outlets. To utilize the excess capacity, the president is negotiating with a large department store chain to sell Comfort shoes. He has asked you to estimate the minimum selling price below which Comfort should not accept an order from the retail chain. Cost information per pair of shoes is:

Direct materials	$8
Direct labor	5
Manufacturing overhead:	
Variable	3
Fixed	2
Selling and administrative expenses:	
Variable	1
Fixed	3

The fixed costs are the same whether or not the order is accepted.

1. What is the minimum selling price the company should accept based solely on cost information (not considering qualitative factors)?
2. Assume that the president agrees to sell 20,000 pairs at a price of $19 per pair. What would be the expected increase in profit?

EXERCISE 8-5

MAKE-OR-BUY DECISIONS

Tiny Toy Company needs 40,000 miniature engines to complete its toy fire trucks. If Tiny Toy Company buys rather than makes the part, some of the facilities still cannot be used in another manufacturing activity. Twenty-five percent of the fixed manufacturing overhead costs are indirect and will still be incurred regardless of which decision is made. The costs of making and buying the part are:

Cost to make the part:	
Direct materials	$ 5.00
Direct labor	10.00
Variable manufacturing overhead	7.00
Fixed manufacturing overhead	8.00
	$30.00
Cost to buy the part from another company	$28.80

Identify the differential costs of making the part as a basis for deciding whether to make or buy it.

EXERCISE 8-6

MAKE-OR-BUY DECISIONS

Miller Manufacturing builds and markets personal computers for home and small business use. The company has been approached by an outside supplier offering to provide monitors to the company for $65 each. The company's marketing director negotiated the deal personally and is thrilled about how much cheaper it will be to purchase the monitors from outside. Producing the cost data outlined below, the manager proudly proclaims, "Look, a $9 per-unit savings!"

	Per Unit	15,000 Units per Year
Direct materials	$28	$ 420,000
Direct labor	10	150,000
Variable manufacturing overhead	3	45,000
Fixed manufacturing overhead, direct	6	90,000
Fixed manufacturing overhead, indirect	27	405,000
Total cost	$74	$1,110,000

1. Assuming zero opportunity costs, should the company accept the outside offer?
2. If the monitors are purchased from outside, Miller can produce an alternative product that will contribute $250,000 per year toward covering indirect fixed overhead. Will this affect your decision in item (1) above?

EXERCISE 8-7

MAKE-OR-BUY DECISIONS

Alta Company has been manufacturing 8,000 units of part X for its products. The unit cost for the part is as follows:

Direct materials	$ 3
Direct labor	8
Variable manufacturing overhead	4
Fixed manufacturing overhead	6
Total	$21

A supplier has offered to sell 8,000 units of part X to Alta for $18 each. If the part is purchased, Alta can use its facilities to manufacture another product, which would generate a contribution margin of $4,000. Seventy-five percent of the fixed manufacturing overhead costs are indirect and will still be incurred even if the part is purchased.

Compute the net differential cost in deciding whether to make or buy the part.

EXERCISE 8-8

PURCHASING SERVICES FROM OUTSIDE

Dr. Anderson, a local dentist, is considering reducing his office staff and outsourcing the management of his accounts receivable. Currently, he has an office manager and two part-time workers on his staff. One part-time employee spends almost 100% of her time sending out billing notices and following up on collections. Even then, Dr. Anderson is able to collect on only about 80% of the receivables. A collection agency wants Dr. Anderson's business. It will handle all billing and collection details for a monthly fee of $1,500. The agency believes it can deliver a 90% collection of receivables. Another firm, We Collect, Inc., has approached Anderson with a proposal that would shift all accounts receivable risk to We Collect, Inc. Anderson would receive 85% of all receivables automatically. Additional information follows:

Anderson's average yearly accounts receivable	$400,000
Anderson's average annual bad debt expense	80,000
Part-time accounts receivable employee salary	12,000

Which of the following alternatives should Anderson pursue concerning his accounts receivable?

1. Maintain status quo (part-time employee handling accounts receivable).
2. Outsource to collection agency.
3. Outsource to We Collect, Inc.

EXERCISE 8-9

DISCONTINUING A PRODUCT LINE

Swanton Company currently sells three products: desk calendars, pen sets, and paper-clip holders. The company is thinking of discontinuing the production and sales of paper-clip holders. However, because many customers buy the products as a set, Swanton estimates that the sales of the other two products will decrease by 20% if the paper-clip holders are discontinued.

Current data on each of the three products are provided below.

	Desk Calendars	Pen Sets	Paper-Clip Holders	Total
Units	40,000	20,000	12,000	
Sales revenue	$280,000	$240,000	$24,000	$544,000
Variable costs	160,000	160,000	26,000	346,000
Direct fixed costs	40,000	20,000	5,000	65,000
Indirect fixed costs	30,000	40,000	6,000	76,000

1. What is the segment margin of the paper-clip holders?
2. **Interpretive Question:** Would you recommend dropping the paper-clip holder product line? Why or why not?

EXERCISE 8-10

ADDING A NEW PRODUCT

Lipston Corporation is thinking about adding a new product line. Marketing surveys indicate that sales of the new product would be 200,000 units. Each unit sells for $4. Direct variable costs would be $2.80 per unit, direct fixed costs would be $120,000, and $90,000 represents the company's indirect fixed costs. The company does not expect the new product to affect the sales of its other products.

Should Lipston add the new product? Why or why not?

EXERCISE 8-11

CONTRIBUTION MARGIN PER UNIT OF A CRITICAL RESOURCE

Santana Sports Company produces two products, soccer balls and volleyballs. Both products are extremely popular, and the company can sell as many of either ball as it can produce. Santana Sports can produce only a limited number of balls, however, because only 12,000 direct labor hours are available due to the isolated location of the community. It takes two hours of direct labor to produce a soccer ball and one-and-one-half hours to produce a volleyball. The selling price of a soccer ball is $34, and the variable costs are $20. The selling price of a volleyball is $26, with variable costs of $14.

Which product should Santana Sports Company produce if its direct labor hours are limited?

EXERCISE 8-12

CRITICAL RESOURCE CONSTRAINTS

Whiz Kids manufactures two computer games. Far Out is a quiz game about astronomy, and Dynamite is a mystery game. The company has a limited supply of skilled labor and has been able to obtain only a limited number of "chips," a necessary part in the production process.

Information on each product is as follows:

	Far Out	Dynamite
Contribution margin per unit	$4	$3
Units produced per hour	2	3
Units produced per 100 chips	80	60

Anticipated sales exceed capacity for both products.
Total labor hours available: 9,000 hours
Total chips available: 30,000 chips

1. Identify the critical resource constraint under which Whiz Kids must operate.
2. Which product should be produced?

EXERCISE 8-13

PRICING REGULAR PRODUCTS

Medical Care, Inc., is considering what price to charge for Sparkle, a toothpaste that is sold in its leased store at a hospital. The accountant has been asked to prepare an estimated normal selling price based on the costs that Medical Care incurs in making the product in a factory it operates. Costs of producing one tube of Sparkle are 20 cents for direct materials, 10 cents for direct labor, 20 cents for variable manufacturing overhead, and 10 cents for variable selling and administrative costs. Total direct fixed costs are $10,000. The company estimates that a markup of 40% of the selling price is necessary to cover the fixed costs and provide a reasonable return on investment.

1. Calculate the estimated normal selling price.
2. Would you recommend that the company obtain any other information before establishing a sales price?

expanded material

EXERCISE 8-14

THEORY OF CONSTRAINTS

Rudyard Company makes replacement engines for jet aircraft. Making the engines involves four processes: (1) purchasing materials, (2) assembling the engines, (3) testing the engines, and (4) delivering the completed engines to customers. Although each of these processes is critical, delivery to customers is very difficult because of the weight of the engine, the sensitivity of the calibration, and the stabilization required for shipment. Rudyard has no problem purchasing component parts for the engines. Upon order, suppliers can deliver needed parts in any quantity within one day. Assembling engines, however, requires highly skilled employees. Currently, the company has three employees who can each assemble one engine every three days. Testing also requires highly skilled engineers who use simulators made to the company's specifications. Right now, Rudyard has two simulators, each of which can test one engine every four days. Currently, there is only one trucking company that can deliver the engines to customers and ensure that they will be treated with the necessary care. The trucking company can haul three engines per truck, but given the location of customers, it can deliver only 15 engines per month.

1. What is the constraint resource in this company?
2. How many engines should Rudyard be making per month?
3. How much excess time is available in the other processes?
4. How would you suggest the company use its excess resources?

PROBLEM 8-1

SPECIAL-ORDER PRICING

Midwest Company manufactures portable radios. Shop Smart, a large retail merchandiser, wants to buy 200,000 radios from Midwest Company for $12 each. The radio would carry Shop Smart's name and would be sold in its stores.

Midwest Company normally sells 420,000 radios a year at $16 each; its production capacity is 540,000 units a year. Cost information for the radios is as follows:

Production costs:	
Variable production costs	$7
Fixed manufacturing overhead ($2,100,000 ÷ 420,000 units)	5
Selling and administrative expenses:	
Variable	1
Fixed ($420,000 ÷ 420,000 units)	1

The $1 variable selling and administrative expenses would not be applicable to the radios ordered by Shop Smart because that is a single large order. Shop Smart has indicated that the company is not interested in signing a contract for less than 200,000 radios. Total fixed costs will not change regardless of whether the Shop Smart order is accepted.

Required:

1. Identify any opportunity costs that Midwest Company should consider when making the decision.
2. Determine whether Midwest Company should accept Shop Smart's offer.
3. **Interpretive Question:** What qualitative factors might be relevant to this decision?

PROBLEM 8-2

MAKE-OR-BUY DECISIONS

Logan Company manufactures several toy products. One is a large plastic truck, which requires a plastic truck body, two metal axles, and four rubber wheels. Logan currently manufactures and assembles all the parts.

Another toy company has offered to sell the parts to Logan at $1.70 per truck if 20,000 or more parts are purchased each year, and at $2 per truck if less than 20,000 parts are purchased. Logan is considering this offer. The space used in producing the parts could be used for a new toy, which is scheduled to begin production next year. If Logan continues to produce the parts for the plastic truck, the company will have to lease space from another company in an adjacent building to produce the new toy. The rent would be $8,000 per year.

Other information related to the truck is:

	Produce Parts	Assemble Truck	Total
Direct materials	$1.10	$0.20	$1.30
Direct labor	0.30	0.20	0.50
Variable manufacturing overhead	0.20	0.15	0.35
Fixed manufacturing overhead	0.20	0.40	0.60
Total manufacturing costs	$1.80	$0.95	$2.75

The marketing department has estimated that sales for the plastic truck will be approximately 16,000 units per year for the next three years. The fixed manufacturing overhead is indirect and will still be incurred regardless of which decision is made.

Required:

1. Describe Logan Company's two alternatives for this decision.
2. What costs are relevant to the decision?
3. Which alternative should Logan Company select?
4. What would be the best decision had Logan not planned to produce the new toy?
5. **Interpretive Question:** What are some of the qualitative factors that Logan Company might consider in making the decision?

PROBLEM 8-3

CHOOSING BETWEEN TWO MACHINES

Tasty Burger is thinking of making the hamburger rolls for its chain of fast-food restaurants. Two machines, A and B, are being considered for purchase. The company now purchases the rolls from an outside supplier for 12 cents each. The cost information for producing the rolls would be:

	Machine A	Machine B
Variable costs per roll	$0.08	$0.07
Annual fixed costs	$1,750	$2,500
Initial cost of machine	$5,000	$12,000
Salvage value at end of five years	$0	$4,000
Estimated life of machine	5 years	5 years

Required:

1. At a sales volume of 300,000 rolls per year, which of these alternatives is best—buying the rolls, using machine A, or using machine B? (Ignore the time value of money, and assume straight-line depreciation.)
2. At what level of production would you be indifferent between machine A and machine B? Which machine is preferable if production exceeds this volume?

PROBLEM 8-4

PURCHASING SERVICES FROM OUTSIDE

Northeast Reinsurance Company is growing rapidly. As it has grown, it has added legal staff to provide for its legal services. One of the principals of the company is an attorney who has provided oversight over the growing legal department. However, she is now too busy to continue this "legal counsel" role. She suggests that the senior company attorney become an officer of the company and be given the title "legal counsel and secretary." Another of the principals is good friends with an attorney at a prestigious regional law firm. That law firm has offered to provide Northeast with legal services for an annual retainer of $500,000 plus an average billing rate of $100 per hour for all work done over 5,000 hours per year. It is expected that legal work, whether done inside or outside the company, will require about 6,000 hours this coming year and will probably increase by 10% a year thereafter. The current company legal staff may be able to handle the work load for two years before it will have to hire another attorney (at an expected salary and benefit package of $100,000). Other variable costs are expected to increase by 5% a year.

Additional information follows:

	Current Costs of Internal Legal Department
Salaries and benefits of legal staff	$350,000
Travel costs	80,000
Required continuing education costs	10,000
Legal support costs (library, computers, software, supplies, etc.)	100,000
Other variable costs	25,000
Allocated office overhead (depreciation, utilities, etc.)	40,000
Total costs of legal department	$605,000

Required:

1. What are the relevant costs for Northeast to consider in making this decision?
2. From a financial standpoint, should Northeast continue to use its own legal department for legal services or outsource this function to the regional law firm?
3. What other factors might Northeast consider in making this decision?

PROBLEM 8-5

UNIFYING CONCEPTS: MAKE-OR-BUY DECISIONS (DIFFERENTIAL COSTS AND OPPORTUNITY COSTS)

Snow Corporation manufactures freezers for residential use. The company is planning to produce a new freezer suitable for apartments. These smaller freezers require a component that Snow Corporation can either make or buy from a subcontractor. The subcontractor will sell the part for $46. The costs for making 12,000 units of the part are as follows:

Direct materials	$20 per unit
Direct labor	$15 per unit
Variable manufacturing overhead	$10 per unit
Fixed manufacturing overhead	$40,000*

*The $40,000 fixed manufacturing overhead includes $24,000 of indirect fixed costs allocated to the part and $16,000 for a production manager.

If the part is produced, Snow Corporation will use an idle machine it already owns. If the part is bought, the company plans to rent the machine and the factory space to another company for $8,000 and $14,000 a year, respectively.

Snow expects that, if the part is produced, the company will be able to schedule production so that no warehouse space will be needed. However, if the part is bought, Snow will need to use warehouse space, for which it will have to pay $2,000 a year in rent.

Required:

1. Identify any opportunity costs relevant to the decision to make or buy the component.
2. Determine the differential costs of making the product.
3. Determine the differential costs of buying the product.
4. **Interpretive Question:** Would you recommend that Snow make or buy the component? Why?

PROBLEM 8-6

DROPPING A PRODUCT LINE

Mountain Land, Inc., manufactures skis, ski boots, and ski poles for downhill skiing. The company is thinking of dropping ski poles as a product line. The following report was prepared by the accounting department:

	Skis	Ski Boots	Ski Poles	Total
Sales revenues	$480,000	$210,000	$50,000	$740,000
Variable costs	(370,000)	(140,000)	(24,000)	(534,000)
Contribution margin	$110,000	$ 70,000	$26,000	$206,000
Direct fixed costs	(40,000)	(20,000)	(27,000)	(87,000)
Segment margin	$ 70,000	$ 50,000	$ (1,000)	$119,000
Indirect fixed costs	(35,000)	(20,000)	(5,000)	(60,000)
Net income	$ 35,000	$ 30,000	$ (6,000)	$ 59,000

Required:

1. Should the ski pole line be dropped? Why or why not?
2. **Interpretive Question:** What qualitative factors should be considered in deciding whether to drop the ski pole line?

PROBLEM 8-7

ADDING AND DROPPING PRODUCT LINES

Hansig Manufacturing Company has been producing three products: A, B, and C. Now that the plant has been shifted to an assembly-line operation, a fourth product, D, has been added.

Each product has its own assembly-line operation, producing 10,000 units. Total indirect fixed costs of $23,000 are divided proportionately, based on the space allocated to each assembly line. Other pertinent information is given below.

	A	B	C	D
Selling price per unit	$3.00	$2.50	$2.70	$1.50
Variable cost per unit	$2.00	$1.80	$1.80	$1.30
Number of square feet	800	600	500	400

Required:

1. Prepare a schedule that shows net income for each product line.
2. Would total company income increase if product D were dropped? Why or why not?
3. **Interpretive Question:** If you could double the production of A, B, or C in place of having D, which would you choose? Why?

PROBLEM 8-8

SHUTTING DOWN OR CONTINUING OPERATIONS

End Trail Campground is open year-round. However, 80% of its revenues are generated from May through October. Because only 20% of the revenues are generated from November to April, the campground is considering closing during those months. The yearly revenues and cost information expected by End Trail for next year if the campground does not close are:

Camping fees	$1,800,000
Variable costs	990,000
Fixed costs ($40,000 per month)	480,000

The cost to close the campground at the end of October would be $20,000, and the cost to reopen in May would be $50,000. If the campground is closed, the total fixed costs are only $25,000 per month, rather than the $40,000 per month when the campground is open.

Required: Determine whether End Trail Campground should close from November to April or remain open for the entire year.

PROBLEM 8-9

DETERMINING PRODUCTION WITH A CRITICAL RESOURCE LIMITATION

Clarity Corporation produces three sizes of television sets: 10-inch screen, 19-inch screen, and 24-inch screen. The revenues and costs per unit for each size are as follows:

	Screen Size		
	10-inch	19-inch	24-inch
Selling price	$195	$325	$450
Variable costs:			
Direct materials	$ 55	$100	$126
Direct labor	80	120	180
Variable manufacturing overhead	40	60	90
Total variable costs	$175	$280	$396
Contribution margin	$ 20	$ 45	$ 54
Units ordered for next week	200	150	75

The company has a constraint on the amount of skilled labor available to produce television sets. Direct labor employees are paid $8 per hour. The total amount of labor time available for next week's production is 2,700 hours.

Required: Given the units ordered for next week, which size or sizes of television sets should be produced and sold to maximize the company's profit?

PROBLEM 8-10

DETERMINING PRODUCTION WITH A CRITICAL RESOURCE LIMITATION

A company is examining two of its products, X-121 and Y-707. The following information is being reviewed:

	X-121	Y-707
Unit selling price	$28.50	$21.00
Materials required per unit	$3.00	$1.50
Direct labor required per unit	$2.50	$1.25
Variable manufacturing overhead per unit	$0.50	$1.00
Production time per unit (in hours)	1.5	1

Required:

1. Which item should the company manufacture if there is no constraint on hours of production?
2. If full production capacity is 1,500 hours, and if the company can sell all the units it makes, which item should it manufacture? Why?

PROBLEM 8-11

CONTRIBUTION MARGIN PER UNIT OF A CRITICAL RESOURCE

Dresser, Inc., manufactures three super-sports-hero dolls: Super Dunk, Pete Tulip, and Zonk. Production, however, is limited by the skilled labor necessary to produce these unique dolls. Data on each of the dolls are as follows:

	Super Dunk	Pete Tulip	Zonk
Contribution margin per doll	$6	$4	$5
Dolls produced per hour	20	28	25
Expected total market volume (units)	20,000	9,000	100,000
Total skilled labor hours available: 4,500 hours.			

Required:

Assuming that there are no relevant qualitative factors, how many dolls of each type should Dresser produce?

PROBLEM 8-12

UNIFYING CONCEPTS: PRODUCTION AND ADVERTISING

Cole Company manufactures only two products—a battery charger and a testing machine for automobile engines. An average of 30,000 chargers and 50,000 testers are sold each year. This year, the company can afford only $60,000 for advertising the products, which is just enough to advertise one product effectively. The marketing manager expects that the sales of chargers will increase by 20% if they are advertised and that the sales of testers will increase by 10% if they are advertised.

The following information about the two products has been provided by the accountant:

	Charger	Tester
Selling price per unit	$70	$90
Variable cost per unit	$30	$40
Fixed cost per unit	$30	$40
Production time per unit (in hours)	2	4

Required:

1. If Cole had an unlimited number of labor hours, would you recommend that it advertise either of its products? If yes, which one and why?

2. Assume that Cole has a capacity of 260,000 labor hours. Should Cole still advertise? If so, which product should it advertise?

PROBLEM 8-13

NORMAL SELLING PRICE

TeleCom Products manufactures desktop and wall-mounted telephone units. The company is seeking to come up with a reasonable price for its desktop slimline model. Production costs for each unit follow:

Direct materials	$3.50 per unit
Direct labor	0.5 hour per unit
Direct labor rate	$6 per hour
Variable manufacturing overhead	$4 per labor hour
Variable selling and administrative costs	$1 per unit
Fixed overhead (direct)	$1.50 per unit
Markup of selling price to cover indirect overhead and expected profit	40%

Required: Calculate the estimated normal selling price.

expanded material

PROBLEM 8-14

THEORY OF CONSTRAINTS

Dalton Enterprises makes several products, including microwave ovens, dishwashers, and vacuum cleaners. Each manufacturing process requires several production processes. Right now, the company has large amounts of money tied up in work-in-process inventory at various locations throughout the company. Although Dalton has tried to eliminate this inventory, each month the inventory seems to increase. In addition, the company has a salary incentive system that pays production employees bonuses if they meet budgeted production quotas. The bonuses pay increasingly higher amounts for each unit that is produced in excess of the quota. In recent years, employees have been receiving large production bonuses under the incentive plan, so management knows that the employees are working hard and being productive. These higher bonuses, combined with the money tied up in work-in-process inventory, are creating a cash flow problem for the company.

You have been hired to help the company fix its cash flow problems. You have just attended a conference on the theory of constraints.

Required: Explain how you could apply what you have learned to help the company with its problems.

competency enhancement opportunities

- Analyzing Real Company Information
- International Case
- Ethics Case
- Writing Assignment
- The Debate
- Internet Search

The following additional assignments provide opportunities for students to develop critical thinking, ethical perspectives, oral and written communication skills, experience with electronic research, and teamwork through group and business activities.

ANALYZING REAL COMPANY INFORMATION

• ***Analyzing 8-1 (Microsoft)***

Go to the annual report for MICROSOFT provided in Appendix A at the back of this textbook. Read through the report to determine how many segments of business exist within Microsoft. What approach does Microsoft appear to use in identifying operating segments within the company at large?

• ***Analyzing 8-2 (Main Line Pictures, Inc. versus Kim Basinger)***

Hollywood produces a lot of entertainment, including accounting entertainment! In early 1993, the Superior Court of the State of California (Los Angeles County) heard a litigation suit filed by MAIN LINE PICTURES, INC., against the actress Kim Basinger for breach of contract. At issue was Basinger's decision to withdraw from a film project after making a verbal commitment to appear in it. The film, released in September 1993, was *Boxing Helena.* Didn't see it? That was the point of Main Line's lawsuit: the studio claimed a lot of people didn't see *Boxing Helena* because the actress who replaced Basinger (Sherilyn Fenn) did not have nearly the same box office appeal.

Main Line claimed damages due to an incremental difference in revenues and costs, which led to actual profits being less than expected, all due to not having Basinger in the film. An expert economist and an expert in film finance were called to testify regarding the appropriate size of the incremental revenue and cost differences. Hence, the case essentially became an accounting argument.

Main Line's lawyers argued that their client lost between \$5.1 million and \$9.7 million as a result of Basinger's withdrawal. The \$5.1 million loss calculation is shown below (all amounts are in millions).

Minimum Damages, Plaintiff

	With Basinger	Without Basinger	Difference
Foreign presales	\$ 7.60	\$ 2.70	\$4.90
Domestic presales	3.00		3.00
Total revenue	\$10.60	\$ 2.70	\$7.90
Production costs	(7.60)	(4.80)	(2.80)
Profit (loss)	\$ 3.00	\$(2.10)	\$5.10

To understand the numbers above, you need to know a couple of things about revenues and costs in the movie business and this film in particular.

- It is extremely difficult to predict what a film will actually earn when released. There are *plenty* of examples of big budget films that did poorly at the box office, as well as inexpensive, independent films that have done very well. Hence, presale revenue (guaranteed minimum payments by a film distributor to the film producer) is the only sure revenue the producer can bank on when budgeting costs of making the film. If the film does well, then the distributor and producer share in the profits.
- After Basinger dropped out of the film, one of Main Line's partners loaned \$1.7 million to the project, to be repaid out of domestic revenues.
- Often the producer will contract to share profits from presales, as well as incremental profits, with key actors. Basinger was to be paid a guaranteed \$1 million to star in the film. In addition, she, her proposed co-star Ed Har-

ris, and writer/director Jennifer Lynch were to be paid a total of 20.5% of the producer's net profits. On the other hand, Sherilyn Fenn and her co-star, Julian Sands, each received only a $100,000 guaranteed salary.

- After Basinger dropped from the film project, the producer made some changes to scale back production costs by $1.9 million.
- Often a movie project has many investing partners. Main Line had a partnership with Philippe Caland, who was, essentially, to receive 50% of net profits (after participation payments to the actors and writer), up to a maximum of $2 million.
- After withdrawing from *Boxing Helena,* Basinger received $3 million from a separate producer to star in *Final Analysis.*

Do you agree with the numbers presented above by the plaintiff? Consider all the information provided above and adjust the incremental profit analysis if needed. Be sure to defend your decision to use or not use each piece of information provided.

Source: Adapted from T. L. Barton, W. G. Shenkir, and B. C. Marinas, "Main Line vs. Basinger: A Case in Relevant Costs and Incremental Analysis," *Issues in Accounting Education*, Spring 1996, pp. 163–174.

INTERNATIONAL CASE

International

• *Ameripill Company*

Located in Bartow, Alabama, the Pharmaceutical Division of **AMERIPILL COMPANY** ranks among the top 15 drug companies in the world. The European Unit of the Pharmaceutical Division is divided into three markets: United Kingdom (U.K.), Germany, and France. Actual and budgeted operating reports for two recent years are presented below for these three markets.

	United Kingdom		Germany		France	
	Year 2 Budget	Year 1 Actual	Year 2 Budget	Year 1 Actual	Year 2 Budget	Year 1 Actual
Sales	$49,960	$48,080	$156,840	$137,440	$108,720	$102,560
Cost of sales	(21,982)	(21,155)	(65,872)	(57,995)	(53,414)	(50,254)
Direct expenses	(14,658)	(14,512)	(50,286)	(46,603)	(31,529)	(29,742)
Other income/expenses	(1,499)	(1,155)	(300)	(210)	(946)	(1,026)
Responsibility earnings	$11,821	$11,258	$ 40,382	$ 32,632	$ 22,831	$ 21,538
Interest income/expense*	(358)	(241)	(1,312)	(939)	(1,033)	(1,047)
Exchange gain/loss**	(142)	(338)	(150)	(210)	(272)	(286)
Division charges***	(1,629)	(1,640)	(4,700)	(4,123)	(3,262)	(3,077)
Earnings before taxes	$ 9,692	$ 9,039	$ 34,220	$ 27,360	$ 18,264	$ 17,128
Segment assets	$84,500	$88,860	$ 73,760	$ 72,900	$ 74,220	$ 73,460
Earnings before taxes	19.4%	18.8%	21.8%	19.9%	16.8%	16.7%
Return on assets	11.5%	10.2%	46.4%	37.5%	24.6%	23.3%

* Based on locally incurred debt.

** Based on the average Year 1 exchange rate with the United States.

*** Fixed charge negotiated annually between the Bartow Division and the market subsidiary.

1. Analyze these reports carefully. Assuming that Ameripill requires a minimum ROA of 12%, should the company consider dropping the U.K. market?
2. Ameripill currently has a problem with one of the drugs sold in France. In the French market, Saincoeur is a highly successful treatment for heart-attack victims. (It is also sold under other names in all of Ameripill's markets.) Because of regulatory pressure in France, Saincoeur is being sold at a much lower price in France than in Germany or the U.K. Despite the price ceiling, Saincoeur is a profitable product (barely) in France. However, word of the lower price is creating a lot of pressure in the neighboring markets to reduce the prices to a level similar to that of the French market. Saincoeur is a very profitable product in both Germany and the U.K. How do these facts affect your previous decision regarding the U.K. market in (1)?

Source: Adapted from S. F. Haka, B. A. Lamberton, and H. M. Sollenberger, "International Subsidiary Performance Evaluation: The Case of the Ameripill Company," *Issues in Accounting Education*, Spring 1994, pp. 168–190.

ETHICS CASE

• *Play World, Inc.*

Roger Smith, the controller of Play World, Inc., a toy company, has just completed an analysis of a make-or-buy decision with respect to a particular part for one of the new toys the company is planning to manufacture. The result of the analysis clearly shows that the company should buy the part from one of the three available suppliers (based on written price quotations received from those suppliers within the past few weeks). Based on this analysis, Smith and the division manager, Kate Pfirman, agreed to proceed with placing an order. They issued instructions to the purchasing department indicating that the order should be placed for a price not higher than $3.40 per part. A few days later, Smith received a phone call from the purchasing department indicating that all three suppliers had raised their price to $4.00 per unit. It was a normal business practice to raise prices after written quotations had been issued.

It was immediately clear to Smith that it would be disadvantageous to his company to buy the part at the higher price. He discussed the new information with Pfirman, and they agreed to proceed with manufacturing plans to make the part internally. Smith thought it was rather strange that all three suppliers had raised their price to the same amount, but felt there was nothing he could do about it.

A few days later, Smith's secretary, Lynn Berry, asked if she could have a private conversation with him. Berry was obviously upset, so Smith asked her to come into his office and shut the door. Berry told him she was good friends with the secretary for the president of one of the suppliers from which Play World had planned to buy the part for the new toy. Berry's friend had casually mentioned that her boss had been on the phone with the other suppliers and they had agreed to raise the price for certain parts they were manufacturing to specified dollar amounts. Berry said she was reluctant to tell Smith because she didn't want her friend to get in trouble for revealing confidential information outside her company. For Smith, this information was the missing piece that explained why the price for the part had been raised to $4.00 by all three companies. Smith thanked Berry for the information and told her not to worry; he would keep the information to himself but would give some thought to what he would eventually do with what she had told him.

1. Who are the parties that are affected by this bid-rigging scheme?
2. What should Smith do with the information he received from Berry (keep in mind his responsibilities to the accounting profession, to his company, and to Berry)?

WRITING ASSIGNMENT

• *Airline Ticket Prices*

If you have ever shopped for airline tickets, you are aware of the tremendous diversity in ticket prices for the same flight, even for those who sit in the same section (first-class, coach, etc.) Much of the difference is based on two factors: (1) when you bought your ticket and (2) whether you plan to stay over a Saturday night.

Write a one- to two-page paper describing why airline companies have so many different ticket prices. Also, why do you think it is important to the airline that clients fly back from their business trips on Sunday instead of Saturday?

THE DEBATE

• *Total Costs versus Differential Costs*

As discussed in this chapter, a management accountant can choose whether to present information using total costs or differential (e.g., incremental) costs. Divide your group into two teams. Each group will defend cost analysis for relevant decision making using either total costs or differential costs.

- One team represents "Total Costs." Present the advantages of using total costs for decision making. What are the disadvantages of using differential costs?
- The other team represents "Differential Costs." Present the advantages of using differential costs for decision making. What are the disadvantages of using total costs?

INTERNET SEARCH

• *Benchmarking in Europe*

Early in the chapter we discussed the concept of benchmarking, a new evaluation method that has been used extensively in recent years. We discussed benchmarking in the context of one company comparing its financial and operating performance against a competitor's performance or comparing the performance of various internal departments against each other. However, benchmarking is a concept that can be used in any type of organization or even for yourself. Take the **EUROPEAN COMMISSION**, for example. Since the mid-1990s, the commission has undertaken a number of benchmarking initiatives so that member countries can compare best practices at three levels: country and business environment, company or enterprise, and industry or sector. The European Commission discusses its benchmark initiatives at the following Web site: **http://www.benchmarking-in-europe.com**. (Sometimes Web addresses change, so if this address does not work, access the Web site for this textbook, **http://albrecht.swcollege.com**, for an updated link.) Go to this site and answer the following questions:

1. List the four basic steps in benchmarking it identifies.
2. Identify the objective of enterprise policy benchmarking.
3. What method has been used to benchmark in the area of enterprise policy?

Evaluating Personnel and Divisions

chapter m9

learning objectives After studying this chapter, you should be able to:

1 Explain why evaluating personnel and divisions is such an important activity in organizations.

2 Identify different kinds of organizational units in which evaluation occurs.

3 Explain how performance is evaluated in cost centers.

4 Explain how performance is evaluated in profit centers.

5 Explain how performance is evaluated in investment centers.

expanded material

6 Compute and interpret variable overhead variances in cost centers.

setting the stage

In deciding where to invest their money, potential investors, whether they are individuals or professionally managed investment funds, try to evaluate the company and its management. This evaluation has never been harder than with Internet or high-tech companies. Take the case of **ICG COMMUNICATIONS INC.**, for example.[1] ICG Communications is a provider of Internet services based in Englewood, Colorado. After being a high flier on Wall Street, its stock was selling for $.44 a share in January 2001, down from a high of $39.25 in March 2000. What went wrong, and why didn't investors do a better job of evaluating potential returns?

ICG is a story of big ambition and big money gone awry. The company borrowed heavily to grow as fast as possible, while paying too little attention to the details needed to manage its growth, such as customers, investment bankers, industry analysts, and current and former employees. While ICG's expansion made it one of the biggest players providing access to the Internet—by early 2000, 10% of Internet traffic crossed the ICG network—it overpromised and then underdelivered on its service. As a result, key customers, such as **MICROSOFT**, **NETZERO, INC.**, and **EARTHLINK, INC.**, responded to customer complaints about blocked connections, busy signals, and cutoff connections by shifting their business to ICG competitors.

ICG's strategy was to provide the systems—networks of switches, modem banks, and fiber-optic cable—that linked people at home via their local telephone company with the high-speed fiber-optic lines that carry Internet traffic. If the Internet is a superhighway, ICG would build the ramps that carried traffic from the local roads—i.e., the Baby Bells—onto the superhighway. Because more and more people wanted to get onto the Internet, the demand for the ramps was practically unlimited, ICG said, and it intended to dominate the ramp business.

ICG planned to get the bulk of its revenue in two ways: by getting paid for its systems and service by Internet providers such as NetZero, and by collecting a small toll from the local phone company for each minute a customer spent connected to the Internet through ICG's system. But building ramps was not going to be cheap. So, ICG went where the money is—Wall Street. With the help of **MORGAN STANLEY DEAN WITTER & COMPANY**, the company raised $2 billion starting in 1995. While some of the money was used to build ramps, some of it was used to build ICG's striking new headquarters, a tower that the architect described as "the curve of a ship's prow looking toward the mountains."

Meanwhile, in addition to leading the company, the CEO, J. Shelby Bryan, was hobnobbing on the social and political circuits in New York and Washington. Although the company was headquartered in Colorado, Bryan lived in Manhattan where he held fund-raising parties for President Clinton and Al Gore. In July 1999, Clinton named Bryan to the President's Foreign Intelligence Advisory Board where he was awarded top-secret security clearance. He also served as national finance chair of the Democratic Senatorial Campaign Committee in 1997 and 1998. Unfortunately, Bryan's growing public profile began to rankle investors, making it harder to raise new capital. One major investor nixed an earlier investment in 1999, in part due to its concerns that Bryan had too many distractions to keep a close eye on the company.

Today, although the company still hopes to solve its network problems and arrange a large credit line to make sure it is able to keep operating and pay new supplier debts and employees, ICG's frustrated investors have taken to ridiculing the company on Internet message boards. One ditty making the rounds, meant to be sung to the tune of the "Addams Family," goes:

Their tower's a museum
With art that's ad nauseam
The stockholders could scream
The Gang at ICG.

On November 14, 2000, ICG filed for Chapter 11 bankruptcy protection from creditors. Chapter 11 is a plan that allows the company some time to try to work out its financial matters.

With ICG, some investors have not only not earned a positive return, they have experienced a 98% loss on their investment. This case illustrates well the importance of the two topics that will be discussed in this chapter—the need to evaluate both divisions (or companies in

1 Paul M. Sherer and Gary McWilliams, "How a Brash Provider of Internet Services Became Unplugged," *The Wall Street Journal*, November 13, 2000, p. A1. Also, see Paul M. Sherer, "ICG Files for Protection from Creditors," *The Wall Street Journal*, November 15, 2000, p. A1.

this case) and people. In this case, the company seems to have overpromised and underperformed. Similarly, Bryan, the CEO, appears to have been distracted by political and social ambitions and interests. If the allegations of investors and potential investors are correct, this fixation on interests outside the company made it impossible for Bryan to perform to his best ability.

In this chapter, we will be examining ways that investors, managers, and others evaluate how well organizational units and their managers are performing. In Chapter 8 of management accounting, we focused on the performance of products and processes and introduced various evaluation methods, including benchmarking. Benchmarking and other overall evaluation methods are appropriate for divisions and units as well, but will not be repeated in this chapter. Rather, we will concentrate on evaluation measures that focus exclusively on the performance of divisions and people.

In evaluating divisions and people, it is often difficult to separate the performance of a unit from the performance of its managers. As a result, managers are most often evaluated on how well their units perform. If managers are responsible for costs only, they are usually evaluated on how well they control costs. If they are responsible for revenues and costs, they are usually evaluated on how profitable their units are. And, if they are responsible for costs, revenues, and investments, they are most frequently evaluated on the return those investments generate. In the case of ICG and CEO Bryan, he was responsible for costs, revenues, and investments. Since the company lost large sums of money, neither Bryan nor ICG would be evaluated very positively.

1

Explain why evaluating personnel and divisions is such an important activity in organizations.

EVALUATING PERSONNEL AND DIVISIONS

Today, we live in a new and different economy. At least three major developments have dramatically changed the environment in which businesses operate. First, new technology has made information inexpensive. While low-cost, high-speed digital and cable video and data transmission hardware produces information quickly and easily, new software has made preparation, data, and communication tools available to individuals who previously did not have access to needed information. With these technology developments, time, space, and other temporal constraints on information have been reduced and, in many cases, eliminated.

A second major development that has significantly affected business has been globalization. Faster methods of transportation, together with instantaneous information, have allowed the world to become one giant marketplace. Consumers can now buy products from foreign firms as easily as from a local store. Organizations such as GENERAL MOTORS have to worry not only about what CHRYSLER and FORD are doing, but also about what TOYOTA, VOLKSWAGEN, and BMW are doing as well. In fact, Chrysler is not just "Chrysler" anymore. It is now a conglomeration of European, North American, and Asian manufacturers known as DAIMLERCHRYSLER. Instead of having only two major American competitors, General Motors and all other business organizations now have to compete with similar companies throughout the world. In addition, with the increased availability of inexpensive information, more is known about these competitors and about General Motors than ever before. If a GM product has deficiencies, for example, the world knows about and can act on those problems instantly. If GM or one of its units is not performing well, investors will be reluctant to invest money and even GM's management will direct its resources to other operating units.

A third major change is the concentration of power in certain market investors, primarily large mutual and pension funds. Mutual funds such as FIDELITY and VANGUARD and pension funds such as CALPERS, for example, now hold major stock positions in many companies. The influence of these major market players is so significant that, if they are displeased, corporate executives will find that their positions within the company are in jeopardy. Armed with easily available and inexpensive information about investees and their competitors, large institutional investors raise the competitive bar very high and shorten the periods over which success is measured.

While these change drivers have significantly affected everything we do, including the way we live, they have had two dramatic effects on business and on how we evaluate business units and their managements. First, they have eliminated the old model that assumed information is expensive. Today, anyone, armed with the right access to data sources, can know almost as much about companies as corporate insiders. In addition, with better and more timely information, investors can make evaluations that tell them where they should put their money and which organizations are performing best. Second, these developments have dramatically increased the level of competition among organizations. Institutional investors and business executives want the best performance, and they want it now. They demand that organizations be market leaders and be highly profitable. Because global competitors often have different cost structures that can be exploited to render historically successful business models obsolete, and because information about all organizations is widely available, only organizations that are truly the best survive and remain successful.

A number of business developments have occurred because of these changes. Some of the most obvious are:

- An increased pace of change in the business world
- Shorter product life cycles and shorter competitive advantages
- A requirement for better, quicker, and more decisive actions by management
- The emergence of new companies and new industries
- The emergence of new professional services
- Outsourcing of non-value-added, but necessary, services
- Increased uncertainty and the explicit recognition of risk
- Increasingly complex business transactions
- Increased focus on customer satisfaction

To be able to react to fast-paced business changes, managers and investors must make timely evaluations of units and their managements. They must know as early as possible whether a unit's profit or market share is decreasing. They must be able to assess trends and changes in performance quickly. They must know when new competitors are getting stronger and encroaching on the business's success. They must know when management is performing in ways that are resulting in the organization losing ground to competitors. Only if they have accurate information about how well management and various organizational units are performing, can they make effective personnel, resource, and other decisions. In addition, as we have stated previously, good evaluation leads to good planning, which leads to good control. If managements do not accurately evaluate how they are doing, what needs to be improved, and where resources must be placed and withdrawn, their organizations will most likely be unsuccessful in the future. The result of faster-paced changes is that evaluations must be performed quicker and more frequently than ever before.

---

to summarize

The business world is changing faster than ever before. These fast-paced changes require that decision makers (managers and investors) have better information and perform more timely evaluations of organizational units and the individuals responsible for the organizations. Good evaluation leads to better planning and control decisions and the better allocation of resources.

---

business environment essay

Reducing Trauma Unit Costs As an example of how good evaluation can lead to better decisions and better performance, consider the case of the **UNIVERSITY OF MICHIGAN MEDICAL CENTER**'s trauma unit. Evaluation of the trauma (emergency) unit resulted in subdividing costs into six categories: (1) nursing, (2) surgery, (3) pharmacy, (4) laboratory, (5) radiology, and (6) emergency. Because medical practice continues to be pressured by increasing patient demands and decreasing reimbursement, and because trauma services are especially vulnerable to cost pressures as the ability of their patients to pay is often marginal and the care provided is extremely resource intensive, the medical center decided to work hard to reduce trauma unit costs.

Take nursing services, for example. To reduce costs, the hospital developed a coherent discharge plan for each patient early during hospitalization. The physician leader was responsible for coordination and oversight of the nursing staff, residents, case man-

2

Identify different kinds of organizational units in which evaluation occurs.

EVALUATION OF DIVISIONS AND PERSONNEL IN DIFFERENT TYPES OF OPERATING UNITS

segments Parts of an organization requiring separate reports for evaluation by management.

Most companies are made up of a number of relatively independent **segments** or subunits, sometimes called groups, divisions, or subsidiaries.

As an example, Exhibit 9-1 shows an organizational chart for a hypothetical company that we will call International Manufacturing Corporation (IMC). IMC has three operating (subsidiary) companies: Acme Computer, Edison Automobile, and Jennifer Cosmetics. Although each of these companies has several divisions and other subsegments, only a few of those for Edison Automobile are shown. Edison has three geographic bases: the United States, the Far East, and Europe. The making and selling of automobiles in the Far East division is further broken down into the Japanese and Korean units. The Japanese unit is separated into sales, manufacturing, and service. Edison Automobile's other geographic divisions have similar subsegments.

You will notice that IMC uses different criteria to define its segments at each level. At the highest level, product group (computers, autos, cosmetics) is used, probably because there is a significant difference in the business knowledge needed to produce and sell these products. At the middle level, segments are defined geographically because of the unique needs of each market and the distances involved. At the lowest level, each country unit is subdivided by function—sales, manufacturing, and service.

Given the organizational chart in Exhibit 9-1, how much autonomy should the executives of each division be granted by corporate management? If each company (Acme, Edison, and Jennifer) has its own president, vice presidents, and other officers, should these executives be allowed to operate independently of one another? If Acme, for example, is the most profitable company, should it be given more operating capital than Edison and Jennifer, or less? Should a decision for Acme to expand into hand-held computers be made by Acme's executives or by IMC's corporate officers? Within Edison Automobile, how much autonomy should each of the geographic offices have? Should a decision to double the advertising budget or offer consumer rebates in the Far East operations be made by the manager of that division, by the top management of Edison Automobile, or by the president of IMC?

decentralized company An organization in which managers at all levels have the authority to make decisions concerning the operations for which they are responsible.

Questions such as these are difficult to answer. In fact, it would probably be difficult to find two companies that would answer them the same way. Assuming that IMC is basically a **decentralized company**, managers at all levels will have the authority to make decisions concerning the operations for which they are directly responsible. Regarding the question of rebates

agers, and discharge planners in the discharge process. The net effect of the shorter stays was reduced nursing costs. As another example, radiology costs were reduced by utilizing outside hospital examinations and substituting less costly examinations for more expensive tests (abdominal ultrasound instead of abdominal CT, for example). The medical center also developed protocols for X-ray utilization so as to minimize "routine films." As a result, the center stopped performing lateral C spines in the trauma bays and discontinued routine daily chest X-rays in the ICU. Through close evaluation and follow-up in other areas, the overall variable cost of care per patient was reduced by 25%. The mean length of patient stay decreased from 8.72 days to 7.06 days, and significant cost reduction was achieved in all six cost areas. Nursing costs decreased 24%; surgical costs, 5%; laboratory costs, 27%; radiology costs, 7%; pharmacy costs, 57%; and emergency services, 36%.

Source: Information was obtained from **http://www.chcecon.org/traumacostpaper.asp**.

exhibit 9-1 An Organizational Chart

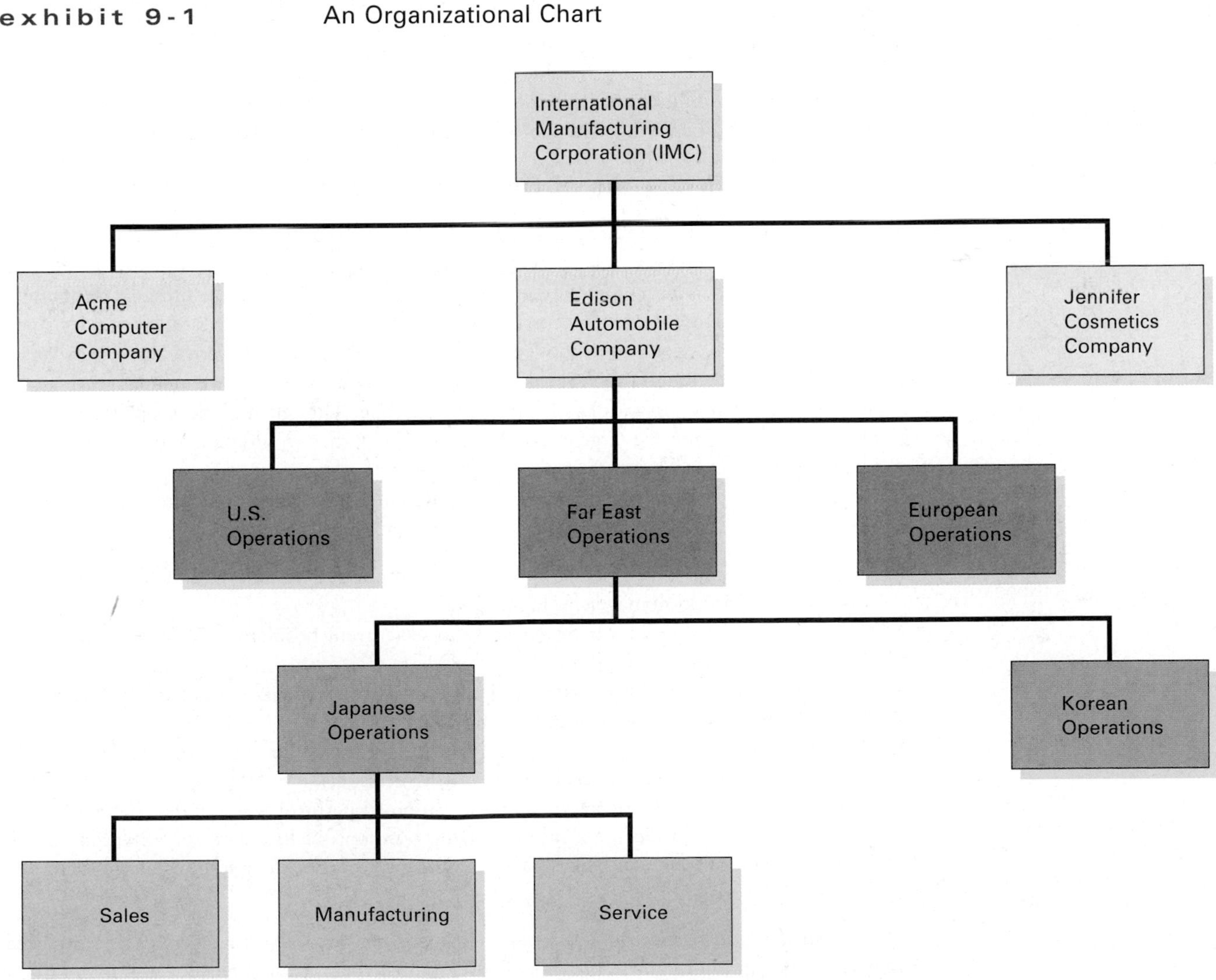

business environment essay

Berkshire Hathaway As an example of how businesses are divided into segments, consider BERKSHIRE HATHAWAY, INC., which is primarily owned by Warren E. Buffett, one of the richest individuals in the United States. In a 2000 SEC filing, Berkshire stated that its most important business is the property and casualty insurance business, which includes GEICO CORPORATION, the sixth largest auto insurer in the United States, and GENERAL RE CORPORATION, one of the four largest reinsurers in the world. In addition, it identified several other types of businesses, including the publication of a daily and Sunday newspaper in western New York (BUFFALO NEWS); the manufacture and sale of boxed chocolates and other confectionery products (SEE'S CANDIES); diversified manufacturing and distribution; the retail sale of home furnishings (NEBRASKA FURNITURE MART, R.C. WILLEY HOME FURNISHINGS, STAR FURNITURE COMPANY, and JORDAN'S, INC.); the manufacture, import, and distribution of footwear (H.H. BROWN SHOE COMPANY, LOWELL SHOE, INC., DEXTER SHOE COMPANY, and JUSTIN BRANDS); the retail sale of fine jewelry; the providing of training to operators of aircraft and ships throughout the world; the providing

in the Far East, for example, the operating manager of that geographic division should probably decide whether to offer them. Likewise, the manager of the Japanese Manufacturing division should decide where to buy engine parts, and the manager of the Service division should have primary responsibility for setting the price to charge for repairing a muffler in Japan. These managers would also be held accountable for the consequences of their decisions.

Benefits and Problems of Decentralization

To what degree should a company decentralize? BERKSHIRE HATHAWAY, for example, is very decentralized, allowing managers of its various business units to operate nearly autonomously. Clearly, a large company employing thousands of people in different geographic areas could not remain completely centralized, with top management making all the decisions. The president of IMC would not know enough about the costs and varieties of paint in Japan, for example, or have enough time to make all the operating decisions for the manufacturing subsegment of the Japanese operations of Edison Automobile. Though such decisions would never be made by the president of a large international company, they would be made at a higher level in a **centralized company** than in a decentralized one.

centralized company An organization in which top management makes most of the major decisions for the entire company rather than delegating decisions to managers at lower levels.

Currently, the trend in most companies is to decentralize. The reasons often cited for making decisions at the lowest possible level in an organization are:

1. Segment managers usually have more information about matters within their area of responsibility than do managers at higher levels.
2. Segment managers are in a better position to see current problems and to react quickly to local situations.
3. Higher-level management can spend more time on broader policy and strategic issues because the burden of daily decision making is distributed.
4. Segment managers have a greater incentive to perform well because they receive the credit (or blame) for performance resulting from their decisions.
5. Employees have greater incentives and motivation to perform well because there are more opportunities for advancement into leadership positions when a company is decentralized.
6. Managers and officers can be evaluated more easily because their responsibilities are more clearly defined.

Decentralization has its drawbacks as well. Decisions made by managers of decentralized units are sometimes not consistent with the overall objectives of the firm. For example, Edison

of fractional ownership programs for general aviation aircraft; the licensing and servicing of almost 6,000 DAIRY QUEEN stores; the rental of furniture and accessories; and the manufacturing and production of face brick and concrete masonry products.

In addition to its own business segments, Berkshire Hathaway also owns large segments of AMERICAN EXPRESS COMPANY, THE COCA-COLA COMPANY, FEDERAL HOME LOAN MORTGAGE CORPORATION, THE GILLETTE COMPANY, THE WASHINGTON POST COMPANY, and WELLS FARGO COMPANY. Warren Buffett is generally believed to be one of the most astute investors in the United States. As he states in his annual report, "We are interested in making investments that meet the following conditions:

1. It is a large purchase (at least $25 million of before-tax earnings).
2. The company has demonstrated consistent earning power.
3. The business earns a good return on equity with little or no debt.
4. The management of the company is good and in place.
5. The company is involved in a 'simple business.'
6. There is an offering price which is realistic."

Automobile might find it less expensive to buy computer parts for its automobiles from an outside source than from Acme Computer, or the Service division of Japanese operations may find it cheaper to buy repair parts from outsiders rather than from the Manufacturing division. Such decisions would allow the buying divisions to report lower costs, but the decisions might decrease the company's overall profitability.

There are two ways to prevent such problems. First, certain decisions should be centralized. For example, all decisions related to insurance coverage, which benefits the entire company, should probably be made at the corporate level. Second, a system of responsibility accounting should be established so that a manager's decisions will benefit not only the segment but also the firm as a whole. This **goal congruence**, whereby the goals of the company and all its segments are in harmony, can be achieved only if the responsibility accounting system is well designed.

goal congruence The selection of goals for responsibility centers that are consistent, or congruent, with those of the company as a whole.

Responsibility Accounting

responsibility accounting A system of evaluating performance; managers are held accountable for the costs, revenues, assets, or other elements over which they have control.

Responsibility accounting is a system in which managers are assigned and held accountable for certain costs, assets, and/or revenues. There are two important behavioral considerations in assigning responsibilities to managers. First, the responsible manager should be involved in developing the plan for the unit over which the manager has control. Current research indicates that people are more motivated to achieve a goal (budget or standard) if they participate in setting it. Such participation assures that the goals will be reasonable and, more importantly, that they will be perceived to be reasonable by the managers.

Second, a manager should be held accountable only for those costs, assets, or revenues over which the manager has substantial control. Some costs may be generated within a segment, but control over them lies outside that unit. The manager of the Japanese Manufacturing division, for example, may be responsible for labor costs, but employee wages may be determined by a union scale controlled elsewhere. Admittedly, determining "substantial control" requires a judgment based on the circumstances, but if all relevant factors are considered, careful and fair judgments can be made.

RESPONSIBILITY ACCOUNTING REPORTS Regardless of the degree of autonomy given to managers at various operating levels, responsibility accounting (performance) reports are needed at all levels of the organization. At the lowest levels, these reports tell managers where corrective action must be taken to control their segments' operations. At top levels, these reports keep management informed of the activities of all segments. The reports are then used to reward past performance and set incentives for future performance.

exception reports Reports that highlight variances from, or exceptions to, the budget.

Exhibit 9-2 illustrates the kind of responsibility accounting reports a company might use. Note that reporting begins at the bottom and works upward, with each manager receiving information on the operations for which that manager is responsible, as well as summary information on the performance of lower-level managers. Note also that these reports are **exception reports**, meaning that variances from, or exceptions to, the budget are highlighted. In the report, unfavorable or negative variances are labeled "U" while favorable variances are labeled "F." Such reports direct management immediately to the areas requiring corrective action. To keep

exhibit 9-2 Responsibility Accounting Reports for Edison Automobile Company of IMC

President, Edison Automobile	**Responsibility Centers**	**Budgeted Costs**	**Actual Costs**	**Variance***
The president receives from each geographic area of operations a report summarizing its performance. The president can see where corrective action needs to be made by tracing the differences between budget and actual downward to their sources.	General Administration	x	x	x
	United States	x	x	x
	Far East	$58,000	$65,000	$7,000 U
	Europe	x	x	x

Far East Operations	**Responsibility Centers**	**Budgeted Costs**	**Actual Costs**	**Variance**
The manager of Far East operations receives a report from each country segment's head. These reports are then summarized and passed on to the president of Edison Automobile.	Japanese Operations	$21,000	$23,000	$2,000 U
	Korean Operations	x	x	x
	Total costs	$58,000	$65,000	$7,000 U

Japanese Operations	**Responsibility Centers**	**Budgeted Costs**	**Actual Costs**	**Variance**
The manager of Japanese operations receives from each unit a report summarizing its performance. These reports are combined and sent up to the next level, the manager of Far East operations.	Sales	x	x	x
	Manufacturing	$ 9,000	$10,200	$1,200 U
	Service	x	x	x
	Total costs	$21,000	$23,000	$2,000 U

Japanese Manufacturing Division	**Variable Costs of Manufacturing**	**Budgeted Costs**	**Actual Costs**	**Variance**
The Manufacturing division supervisor receives a performance report on the supervisor's center of responsibility. The totals from these reports are then communicated to the manager of Japanese operations, the next level of responsibility.	Direct materials	$ 2,000	$ 2,500	$ 500 U
	Direct labor	6,000	6,400	400 U
	Manufacturing overhead	1,000	1,300	300 U
	Total costs	$ 9,000	$10,200	$1,200 U

*U means unfavorable.

the example simple, Exhibit 9-2 focuses only on costs. In a real company, some units would report their profitability and even a return on investment.

Responsibility accounting reports prepared for lower-level managers contain greater detail than those for upper-level managers. This is because lower-level managers are responsible for the detailed operations of the firm and need to take immediate action when some aspect of operations gets out of control; upper-level managers perform more of an overall review function. Furthermore, the responsibility accounting reports of lower-level managers in a decentralized operation would contain more items than they would in a centralized operation; with decentralization, managers are given broader areas of responsibility.

RESPONSIBILITY CENTERS In our example, the president of IMC is responsible for the entire organization and should be held accountable for the company's overall successes and failures. At lower levels, the president of Edison Automobile Company, the manager of Edison's operations in the Far East, the manager in charge of Japanese operations in Edison's Far East operations, and the manager of the Japanese Manufacturing division, for example, would be held responsible for operations within their respective units.

responsibility center An organizational unit in which a manager has control over and is held accountable for performance.

cost center An organizational unit in which a manager has control over and is held accountable for costs.

profit center An organizational unit in which a manager has control over and is held accountable for both costs and revenues.

investment center An organizational unit in which a manager has control over and is held accountable for costs, revenues, and assets.

Each unit is referred to as a **responsibility center**, and, depending on the operation, it may be a cost, profit, or investment center. As the name implies, a **cost center** is any organizational unit in which the manager of that unit has control over the costs incurred. The manager of a cost center has no responsibility for revenues or assets, either because revenues are not generated or because they are under the control of someone else. The manufacturing unit of Japanese operations of IMC, for example, could be designated a cost center. A **profit center** manager, however, has responsibility for both costs and revenues. Profit centers are usually found at higher levels in an organization than are cost centers. The geographic regions (United States, Far East, and Europe, as well as various country operations within the Far East region) of Edison Automobile would probably be profit centers.

In an **investment center**, the manager is responsible for costs, revenues, and assets. This means that the manager is responsible not only for operating costs, but also for determining the amount of funds to be invested in the center's plant and equipment and for the rate of return earned on those investments. Investment centers are usually found at relatively high levels in organizations. The different companies in IMC (Acme Computer, Edison Automobile, and Jennifer Cosmetics) would probably be investment centers.

to summarize

Most companies are divided into segments with specific responsibilities assigned to each segment manager. In a centralized organization, top management makes most of the operating decisions; in a decentralized organization, decision-making authority is delegated down the corporate ladder to the managers most immediately responsible. It is very important in a decentralized company that the goals of the company and all its segments are in harmony. This concept is referred to as goal congruence.

Regardless of the degree of decentralization, almost all companies use performance reports that show variances from budgeted amounts for each division, department, and unit. These reports pass upward through an organization so that supervisors and managers at all levels can assess the performance of the units serving under them. Decentralized companies are divided into fairly independent responsibility centers. There are three types of responsibility centers: cost, profit, and investment. Managers of responsibility centers usually have control over, and are held accountable for, the performance of the center.

3 Explain how performance is evaluated in cost centers.

EVALUATING PERFORMANCE IN COST CENTERS

As stated in the last section, managers of cost centers are responsible for costs incurred. Most cost centers usually have one type of cost that is more significant than any other. In service organizations, salaries are generally the major cost. In wholesale and retail businesses, the cost of merchandise purchased for resale is often the most significant cost. In manufacturing firms, costs incurred to make products (direct materials, direct labor, and manufacturing overhead) are usually most significant.

If managers are to be held responsible for the costs incurred in their centers, they must have control over those costs, have relevant information about those costs, and have a system that focuses on or engineers in effective cost controls. Historically, companies have used a *standard costing* system that isolates differences between actual and standard costs to determine whether costs are too high or too low, whether they are improving (decreasing) or getting worse (increasing), and whether they will allow the company to be competitive. With this method, standard costs are compared to actual costs, and variances are computed. Standard cost systems have been used effectively in service, merchandising, and manufacturing firms.

In recent years, however, some leading management accountants have argued that companies using standard costing have been missing out on a valuable competitive tool in controlling costs. They argue that instead of assessing, after the fact, whether costs were appropriate, it is more effective to design or engineer appropriate cost levels into products and services. They advocate a **target costing** approach that evaluates costs before production begins. Basically, target costing involves designing products based on prespecified costs by gathering marketing input on customer needs and getting everyone in the company to work toward hitting the target costs.

target costing A costing approach that designs a product to meet specific cost objectives based on target market prices less the target margin.

In this section, we will first cover standard costing systems and will then introduce the revolutionary target costing approach being advocated and tried by some accountants and companies.

Standard Cost System

standard cost system A cost-accumulation system in which standard costs are used as product costs instead of actual costs.

Companies that use standard costing design their accounting systems to incorporate standard costs and variances. This type of system, called a **standard cost system**, is a cost-accumulation process based on costs that should have been incurred rather than costs that were actually incurred. The steps in establishing and operating a standard cost system are:

Step 1 Develop standard costs. → **Step 2** Collect actual costs. → **Step 3** Compare actual costs to standard costs and identify variances. → **Step 4** Report results including variances to managers responsible for variances. → **Step 5** Analyze causes of significant controllable variances. → **Step 6** Take action to eliminate variances. → **Step 7** Journalize actual costs and standard costs and record the variances.

These steps describe a typical standard cost system. You can find some or all of these elements in most organizations, but you will not likely find all seven elements in all firms. You are most likely to find an extensive standard cost system in manufacturing firms, which usually have standard costs for direct materials and direct labor and, to a lesser extent, for manufacturing overhead. These standard costs usually are reported on **standard cost cards**, often stored in a computer. A standard cost card for Smell-Good Perfume made by Jennifer Cosmetics, a subsidiary of IMC, is shown in Exhibit 9-3. The data in Exhibit 9-3 will be used to illustrate how variances are calculated and analyzed.

standard cost cards An itemization of the components of the standard cost of a product.

DETERMINING STANDARD COSTS AND IDENTIFYING VARIANCES In a manufacturing firm, standard costs are determined on the basis of careful analysis and the experience of many people, including accountants, industrial engineers, purchasing agents, and the managers of the departments to be judged. Accountants play an important role in developing standard costs because they have the data needed to determine how costs have changed in the past in re-

exhibit 9-3 Standard Cost Card

Jennifer Cosmetics
Standard Cost Card—Smell-Good Perfume

	(1) Standard Quantity	(2) Standard Price or Rate	(3) Standard Cost (1) × (2)
Inputs:			
Direct materials	2 ounces	$ 2.000	$ 4.00
Direct labor	2 hours	16.000	32.00
Manufacturing overhead:			
Variable	2 hours	1.500	3.00
Fixed	2 hours	2.375	4.75
Total standard cost per unit.			$43.75

lation to levels of activity. This is not an easy task. Changes in methods of production, technology, worker efficiency, and plant layout, for example, can affect the behavior of costs. Before they can serve as standard costs, past costs often have to be adjusted to take changes in operating conditions into account. These changes sometimes occur gradually and may not be easily noticeable, making it difficult for management accountants to identify cost characteristics that will be useful in setting standards for the future.

Engineers are often involved in setting standard costs because of their knowledge of the most efficient way of performing each task in relation to the existing technology of the operation. Managers who will be judged by the standard costs should be involved in the standard-setting process; they are more likely to be motivated to meet standards if they have participated in setting the standards and have accepted them. Of course, the participation of such managers also makes effective use of their experience and judgment.

Once management has established a standard quantity and a standard price for each resource (direct materials, direct labor, and manufacturing overhead), the standard quantity is multiplied by the standard price to arrive at a standard dollar cost for the manufactured product. Actual costs are then compared with these standards to calculate the **variance**, the amount by which the actual cost differs from the standard. This variance, if significant, is a signal to management that costs may be "out of control" and that corrective action should be taken to eliminate the variance. This process of using variances from a standard to isolate problem areas is called **management by exception**. It is the basis of the control function.

variance Any deviation from standard.

management by exception The strategy of focusing attention on significant deviations from a standard.

Because standard costs have a price (or rate) component and a quantity (or usage) component, a comparison of actual and standard costs can result in two variances: a price (rate) variance and a quantity (usage) variance. These variances are usually computed for direct materials, direct labor, and variable manufacturing overhead.

Is it possible for a company to have positive variances (actual costs are less than standard costs) and still have problems?

Exhibit 9-4 is a general model for calculating variances. This model has two important characteristics. First, it is applicable to each of the manufacturing cost elements—direct materials, direct labor, and variable manufacturing overhead. Second, the analysis is essentially an input-output analysis. The price (rate) variance compares actual inputs used at the actual and standard prices. The actual quantities are used to isolate the effect of the price change on the cost of the resources actually acquired or used. The price variance, then, is the difference between the actual price and the standard price, times the actual quantity. The quantity (usage) variance compares the inputs actually used at the standard price with the inputs that should have been used at the standard price to produce the actual output. The standard price is used so that the quantity variances will not be influenced by price changes. The quantity variance is the difference between the actual quantity and the standard quantity, times the standard price.

exhibit 9-4 General Model for Variance Analysis

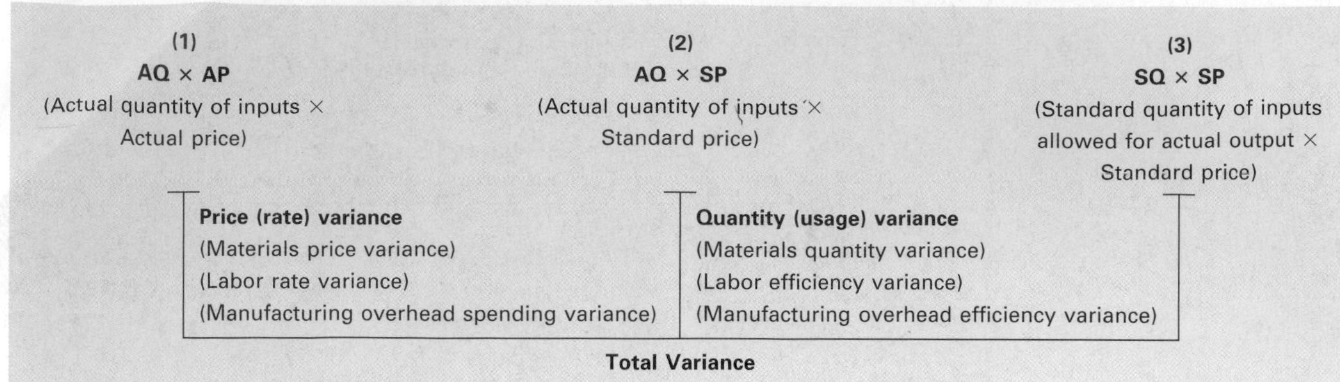

to summarize

Standard cost systems are used to accumulate costs based on standards rather than actual costs. Standard costs are predetermined costs that serve as benchmarks for judging what actual costs should be. Standard costs are usually expressed as the per-unit cost of materials, labor, and manufacturing overhead and are used by managers for planning, implementing, and controlling decisions. The total variance between actual and standard costs is made up of price or rate and quantity or efficiency variances. Standard costs are based on careful analysis by many people, including accountants, engineers, and managers. Standard costs are compared with actual costs incurred to determine variances, the amounts by which actual costs differ from standards. Significant variances alert management to specific problem areas that may require corrective action. The strategy of focusing on significant variances, called management by exception, is essential to the controlling function.

DIRECT MATERIALS VARIANCES Variance analysis is an essential part of an effective standard cost system. We will first explain how direct materials variances are computed and analyzed. Then, we will explain the computation and analysis of direct labor variances. The more complex variances for manufacturing overhead will be discussed and illustrated in the expanded material section of this chapter.

To illustrate the computation of the price and quantity variances for direct materials, we will assume the following actual results of Smell-Good Perfume made by Jennifer Cosmetics:

Direct materials purchased.	10,000 ounces at $1.85 per ounce
Direct materials used	8,300 ounces
Bottles of perfume produced	4,000

Keep in mind throughout the following discussion that the standard cost card (Exhibit 9-3) specifies that materials should cost $2 for each ounce and that each bottle produced should require 2 ounces of material. (Obviously, many ingredients would be mixed together to make perfume. To keep the example simple, we are assuming only one ingredient is used.)

materials price variance The extent to which the actual price varies from the standard price for the quantity of materials purchased or used; computed by multiplying the difference between the actual and standard prices by the quantity purchased or used.

Materials Price Variance The **materials price variance** reflects the extent to which the actual price varies from the standard price for the actual quantity of materials purchased or used. Although the price variance can be calculated either when materials are purchased or when they are used, it is generally best to isolate the variance at purchase and report the variance to the purchasing manager who has responsibility for controlling the purchase price. If management waits until the materials are used before calculating variances, the information needed by the purchasing managers to take corrective action is delayed.

In calculating the materials price variance, the standard price per unit of materials should reflect the final, delivered cost of materials, net of any discounts taken. For example, Jennifer Cosmetics may have determined its standard materials price per ounce as follows:

Purchase price	$ 1.84
Freight	0.17
Handling costs	0.04
Less purchase discounts	(0.05)
Standard materials cost per unit	$ 2.00

The standard cost above assumes that the materials were purchased in certain lot sizes (for example, 50-gallon quantities) and delivered a certain way (by rail, for example). Handling costs and purchase discounts have also been included.

Assuming that variances are determined when materials are purchased and that 10,000 ounces of materials are purchased, the price variance is computed as follows:

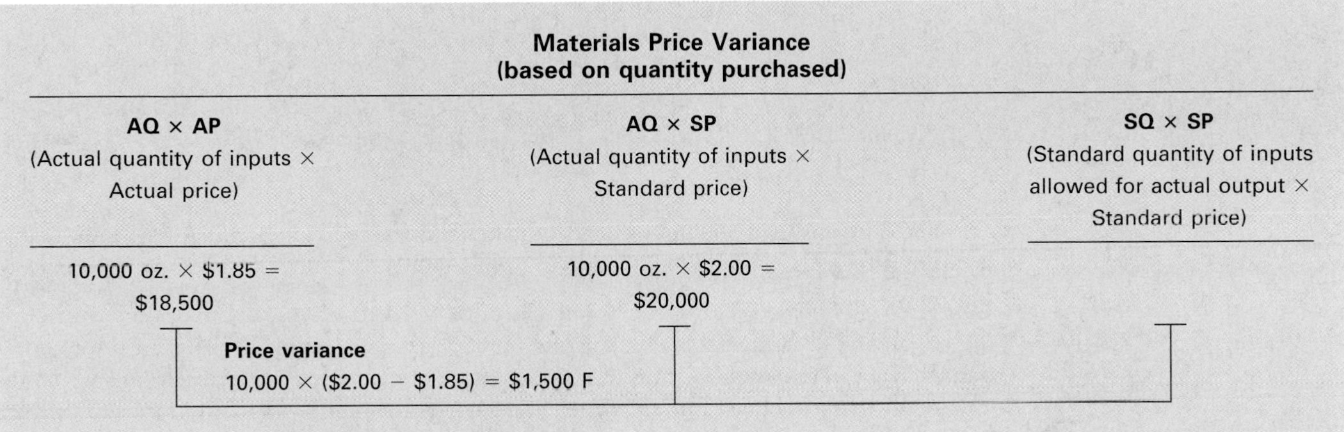

This variance indicates that the company spent $1,500 less than the standard cost for the direct materials purchased. Because less money was spent than the standard cost, the variance is labeled "F" meaning "favorable." If the amount expended had exceeded the standard cost, the variance would have been "unfavorable," designated with a "U."

Isolating materials price variances at the time of purchase has the advantage of providing immediate information on purchasing decisions. This also allows companies to carry inventory in the accounting records at the standard cost. Some companies, however, prefer to compute materials price variances at the time the materials are transferred to Work-in-Process Inventory. If 8,300 ounces were used in production, the variance would be based on that amount rather than on the 10,000 ounces purchased. In this case, a favorable price variance of $1,245 would result, as shown below.

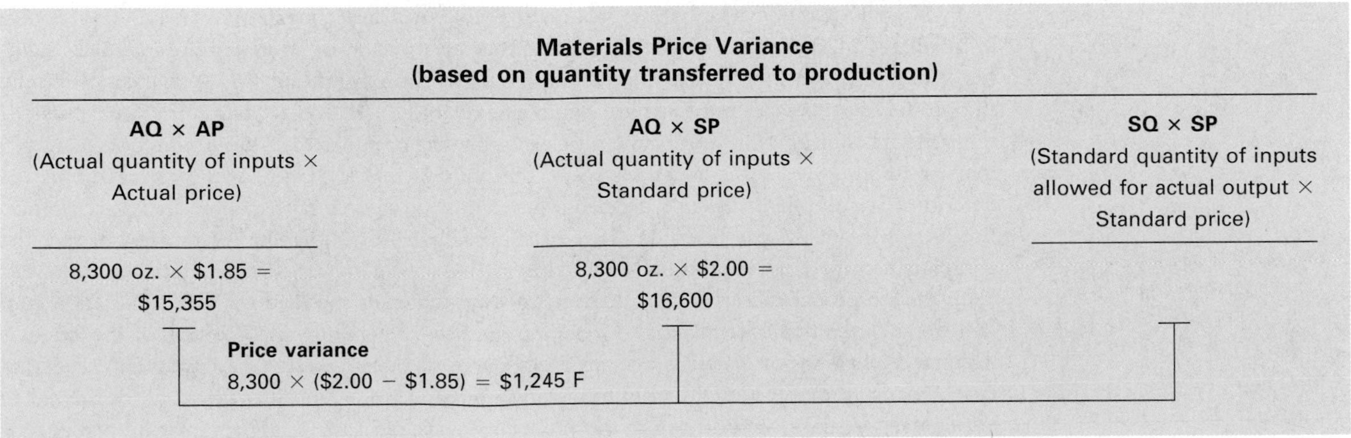

materials quantity variance The extent to which the actual quantity of materials varies from the standard quantity; computed by multiplying the difference between the actual quantity and the standard quantity of materials used by the standard price.

Materials Quantity Variance The standard quantity of materials should reflect the amount needed for each completed unit of product but should allow for normal waste, spoilage, and other unavoidable inefficiencies. The standard cost card indicates that 2 ounces of direct materials are allowed for each bottle of perfume produced. Because Jennifer Cosmetics produced 4,000 bottles of Smell-Good perfume last period, the standard quantity allowed is 8,000 ounces (2 ounces × 4,000 bottles). Actual use of materials amounted to 8,300 ounces. The computation of the **materials quantity variance** is:

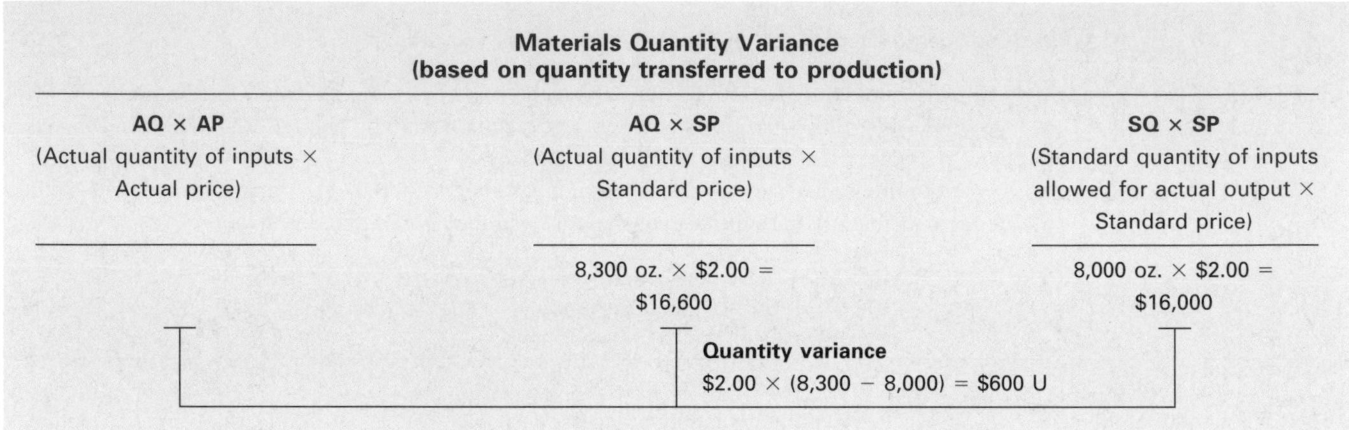

The company used 300 more ounces of material than expected, resulting in an unfavorable quantity variance of $600 (300 ounces × $2 per ounce).

Controlling Materials Variances Materials price variances are usually under the control of the purchasing department. The purchasing function involves getting a variety of price quotations, buying in economic lot sizes to take advantage of quantity discounts, buying and paying on a timely basis to obtain cash discounts, and paying attention to alternative forms of delivery to minimize shipping costs. Some of these factors will be less important when there are few suppliers or when purchase contracts with suppliers are for long periods. In any case, the existence of unfavorable price variances may suggest a problem that needs correcting.

The buyer responsible for these purchases should be able to explain the variance even though the buyer may not be able to control its occurrence. This may be the case, for example, when market prices change after the standard is set, which could be the explanation for the favorable price variance. Or materials may be damaged, requiring the reorder of a small quantity on a rush basis; this usually raises the price of the materials as well as the cost of shipping, causing an unfavorable price variance. The point is that the cause of any significant variance must be explained and steps taken to avoid such variances in the future. The purpose of variance analysis is not to browbeat employees for failing to meet impossible expectations, but rather to provide information that will help management identify ways of improving the production process.

Materials quantity variances may be caused by quality defects, poor workmanship, poor choice of materials, inexperienced workers, machines that need repair, or an inaccurate materials quantity standard. Just as the purchasing manager must explain significant price variances, generally the production manager must analyze significant quantity variances to determine their cause. If the material is of inferior quality, the purchasing manager, rather than the production manager, may be responsible for the variance. Again, the point is that the cause of the variance must be determined; only then can it be decided what action, if any, to take to prevent its recurrence. Production managers can be made aware of materials quantity variances on a timely basis if the company uses materials requisition forms. These forms should indicate when materials withdrawals from the storeroom exceed the standard quantity of materials specified for that production run. If the standard amount of materials for the production run is known at the start of the run, additional requisitions of materials can be "red-flagged" as being excessive. By using an excess materials requisition procedure as a nonmonetary standard, production managers will be alerted to a materials quantity variance before the monetary measure of the materials quantity variance is available. Thus, production managers can take quicker action to correct a problem than would be the case if they had to wait until the end of the reporting period to learn of materials quantity variances. Corrective action may involve returning excess materials to the storeroom rather than being careless about control in the production area, which could lead to waste or theft.

Accounting for Materials Variances The journal entries for recording the purchase and use of materials, as well as the materials price variance (isolated at purchase) and the quantity variance (isolated when materials are used), are:

Materials Price Variance:		
Direct Materials Inventory ($2.00 × 10,000 ounces)	20,000	
Materials Price Variance [($2.00 – $1.85) × 10,000 ounces]		1,500
Cash (or Accounts Payable) ($1.85 × 10,000 ounces)		18,500
Purchased 10,000 ounces of direct materials at $1.85 per ounce and entered the materials in inventory at the standard price of $2.00 per ounce.		
Materials Quantity Variance:		
Work-in-Process Inventory (8,000 ounces × $2.00)	16,000	
Materials Quantity Variance [(8,300 ounces – 8,000 ounces) × $2.00]	600	
Direct Materials Inventory (8,300 ounces × $2.00)		16,600
Transferred 8,300 ounces of materials out of inventory and recorded standard usage of 8,000 ounces of materials to produce 4,000 bottles of perfume.		

As shown, Materials Price Variance and Materials Quantity Variance are debited when the variances are unfavorable; they are credited when the variances are favorable. An unfavorable variance can be thought of as an expense; a favorable variance can be considered an expense reduction or savings. Note that the $16,000 debit to Work-in-Process Inventory is the standard cost for the 4,000 bottles (standard 8,000 ounces of materials × $2 standard price per ounce). The actual cost deviations from the standard costs are now in variance accounts. The variance accounts are usually transferred to Cost of Goods Sold at the end of the period. Thus, the income statement reports actual costs, where Work-in-Process Inventory and Finished Goods Inventory include only the standard costs of materials. Alternatively, as explained in Chapter 2 of management accounting, when variances are significant in amount, variance account balances at the end of a period should be allocated among Cost of Goods Sold, Work-in-Process Inventory, and Finished Goods Inventory instead of just transferred to Cost of Goods Sold.

to summarize

The difference between actual and standard costs of materials for a given production level can be separated into a materials price variance and a materials quantity variance. The materials price variance can be computed when the materials are purchased or when they are used in production. The managers responsible for the variances must determine their causes and, if the variances are outside an acceptable range, take action to eliminate them. The materials variances (price and quantity) are recorded in individual accounts when materials are acquired and used. The accounts for materials variances are generally closed into Cost of Goods Sold; work-in-process inventory and finished goods inventory accounts include only standard materials costs.

DIRECT LABOR VARIANCES A direct labor rate variance and a direct labor efficiency variance are usually determined for manufacturing labor when a standard cost system is being used. These variances are computed in a manner similar to the materials price and quantity variances.

labor rate variance The extent to which the actual labor rate varies from the standard rate for the quantity of labor used; computed by multiplying the difference between the actual rate and the standard rate by the quantity of labor used.

Labor Rate Variance A **labor rate variance** is a price variance; it shows the difference between actual and standard wage rates. Unfavorable labor rate variances may occur when skilled workers with high hourly pay rates are placed in jobs intended for less skilled or lower-wage-rate employees. Unfavorable labor rate variances may also occur when employees work overtime at premium pay (time and a half or double time). Conversely, favorable labor rate variances occur when less skilled or lower-wage-rate employees perform duties intended for higher-paid workers.

For Jennifer Cosmetics, the standard cost card (Exhibit 9-3) indicates that the standard direct labor rate per bottle of perfume was 2 hours at $16 per hour. Actual labor used during the month to make 4,000 bottles was 8,352 hours at $16.20 per hour. The labor rate variance was thus $1,670 unfavorable, computed as follows:

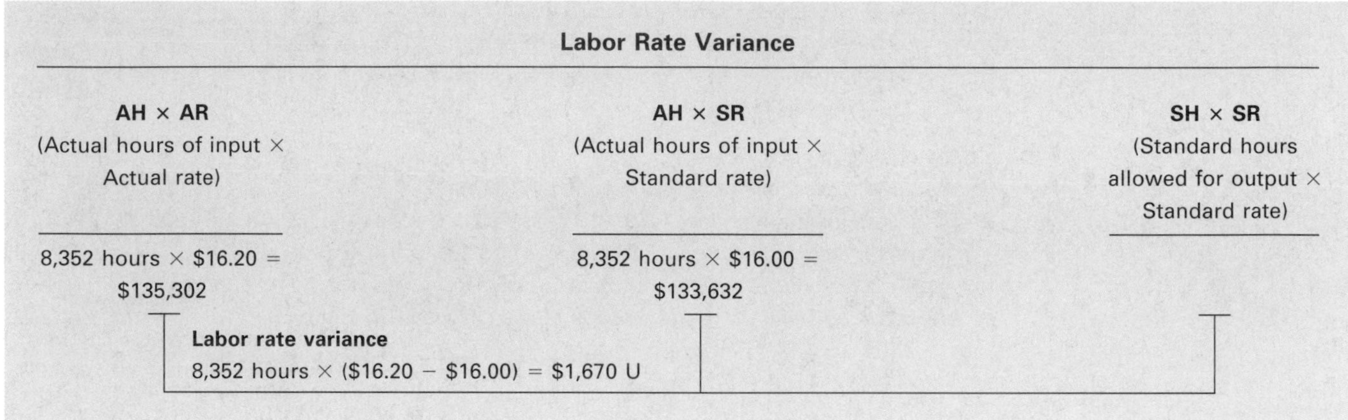

As this variance indicates, $1,670 more than the standard amount for the actual number of hours used was spent for direct labor because actual labor rates were higher than standard rates by $0.20 per hour. The company's guidelines would determine whether the variance should be investigated. Depending on the firm's hiring policies, and the degree of authority given to operating managers in setting wage rates and assigning workers to particular jobs, the operating managers may or may not be responsible for this labor rate variance. In general, labor rates are the responsibility of the manager who makes staffing decisions.

labor efficiency variance The extent to which the actual labor used varies from the standard quantity; computed by multiplying the difference between the actual quantity and the standard quantity of labor by the standard rate.

Labor Efficiency Variance The **labor efficiency variance** is a quantity variance. It measures the cost (or benefit) of using labor for more (or fewer) hours than prescribed by the standard. Computed in the same manner as the materials quantity variance, the labor efficiency variance computation is illustrated in the following schedule for Jennifer Cosmetics. Note that total standard hours are computed by multiplying the standard hours per unit by the actual number of bottles produced (2 hours × 4,000 bottles = 8,000 standard hours allowed).

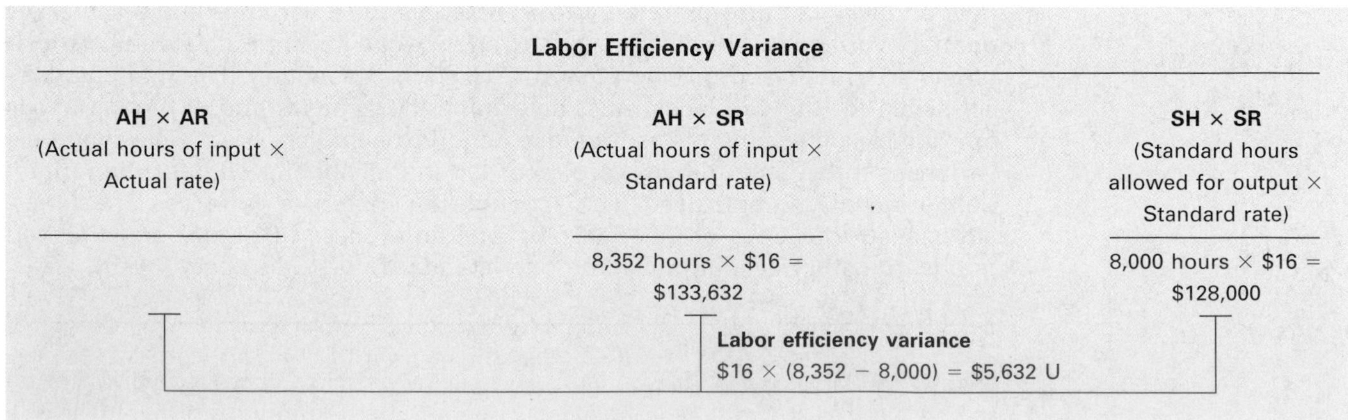

Organizations often try to encourage employees to work harder and faster by offering them rewards for productivity increases. However, employees are skeptical about whether rewards will actually be received. In 1997, for example, a survey reported the following results:

- 81% of workers surveyed said they would not receive any reward for productivity increases.
- 60% of managers surveyed felt their compensation would not increase if their performance improved.
- Only 3% of base salary separated average from outstanding employees at the companies surveyed.

Source: Craig Eric Schneider, "Capitalizing on Performance Management, Recognition, and Rewards Systems," *Compensation and Benefits Review*, March–April 1997, p. 23.

caution

When computing variances, be careful not to confuse actual and standard hours and actual and standard rates. The rate variance is always the difference between the standard and actual rate times the actual hours. (To multiply it times standard hours would not tell you how much the rate increase actually cost or saved the company in total.) On the other hand, the efficiency variance is a time-based variance; therefore, it is the difference between the standard and actual hours times the standard rate.

The manufacturing division used 352 more direct labor hours than the standard, which caused an unfavorable efficiency variance of $5,632 (352 hours × $16).

The labor efficiency variance shows how efficiently the workers performed and, hence, how productive a department was. The variances might be unfavorable for a variety of reasons, including poorly trained employees, poor-quality materials that require extra processing time, old or faulty equipment, and improper supervision of employees. Note that the labor efficiency variance is probably the most important and closely watched manufacturing variance. It has become even more important in recent years as U.S. industries have tried to increase their productivity to match that of Japan, Korea, and other countries.

Controlling Labor Variances Whereas a materials price variance is usually the responsibility of the purchasing department, labor "price" or rate variances are normally the responsibility of either the production manager who is responsible for employees' work assignments or the personnel responsible for hiring employees. As indicated, rate variances are likely to be due to (1) certain tasks being performed by workers with different pay rates or (2) working overtime at rates higher than the normal wage rate. These variances may be manageable if care is taken in assigning workers to jobs that are consistent with their skills and pay scales. Deviations may be necessary in certain situations because of vacations, sickness, or absences of other employees. If the variances are caused by factors beyond the manager's control, he or she should not be held responsible for the unfavorable variance.

In a labor-intensive company, the labor efficiency variance is much more important than in a company that has low labor costs. The labor efficiency variance can be expressed in standard hours for a given activity or in monetary terms (standard hours × standard labor rate). If time standards are set for each activity and workers are required to report their actual hours of work on time tickets, managers have a basis for checking labor efficiency by comparing standard hours with the actual hours shown on time tickets. The variances can be separated into categories by causes so that judgments can be made about what corrective action should be taken. Some typical causes of labor inefficiency variances are absenteeism, machinery breakdowns, poor-quality materials, poor work environment, inadequate machinery, lack of employee skills on a given job, poor employee attitudes, lazy employees, and inaccurate standards. If these causes can be identified by analyzing time tickets, corrective action can be taken promptly. If the labor efficiency variance is expressed in monetary terms, the variances may not be available until end-of-period accounting reports are issued.

Accounting for Labor Variances Because the labor rate and labor efficiency variances are both computed for a given period of time or for a given amount of production, the labor costs and variances for Jennifer Cosmetics can be accounted for in a single journal entry.

Work-in-Process Inventory (8,000 hours × $16.00)	128,000	
Labor Rate Variance [($16.20 − $16.00) × 8,352 hours]	1,670	
Labor Efficiency Variance [(8,352 hours − 8,000 hours) × $16.00]	5,632	
Wages Payable (8,352 hours × $16.20)		135,302
To charge Work-in-Process Inventory for standard labor hours at the standard wage rate to produce 4,000 bottles of perfume; to set up unfavorable labor rate and efficiency variances to reflect the use of 352 hours above standard at an average wage rate of $0.20 above standard.		

As with all production variances, labor variances are closed to Cost of Goods Sold at the end of the period or allocated among Cost of Goods Sold, Work-in-Process Inventory, and Finished Goods Inventory. By closing variances from standard into Cost of Goods Sold, actual cost of goods sold will be reported on the income statement. Work-in-Process Inventory and Finished Goods Inventory include only the standard costs of labor.

business environment essay

Satisfied Employees Are More Productive For many companies, labor costs are the highest cost. This is certainly true for service firms and may even be true for manufacturing firms. Labor rate and labor efficiency variances provide information about whether labor rates are higher than expected or standard and whether workers are performing as efficiently as expected or standard. Many labor costs that are not usually explicitly considered can significantly affect both of these ratios, however, and result in higher costs than expected. Take employee turnover, for example. Common estimates are that employee turnover costs range from $10,000 to $40,000 per person, depending on the position, while employee retention actually increases revenues. In addition, it has been estimated that a 5% increase in employee retention can result in a 10% decrease in labor costs and lead to productivity increases ranging from 25 to 65%.

Because of the high costs of employee turnover, most companies work hard to increase employee retention. The most common approach is to "buy" employee satisfaction with increased pay and benefits.

to summarize

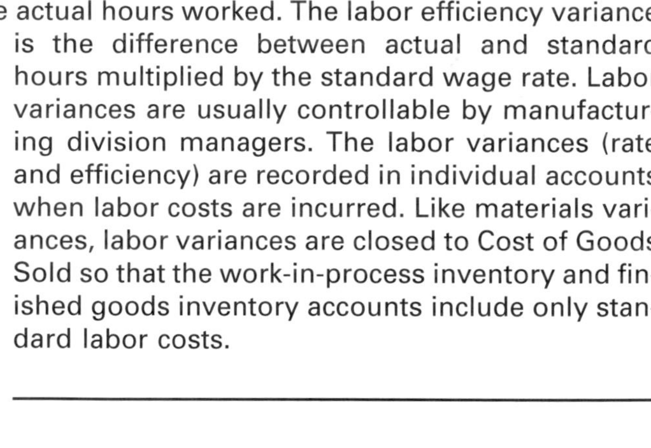

The labor rate variance is the difference between the actual and the standard labor rates multiplied by the actual hours worked. The labor efficiency variance is the difference between actual and standard hours multiplied by the standard wage rate. Labor variances are usually controllable by manufacturing division managers. The labor variances (rate and efficiency) are recorded in individual accounts when labor costs are incurred. Like materials variances, labor variances are closed to Cost of Goods Sold so that the work-in-process inventory and finished goods inventory accounts include only standard labor costs.

A nonmanufacturing organization sometimes expresses standards in quantitative terms. For example, a hospital might have standard times for activities such as taking blood samples.

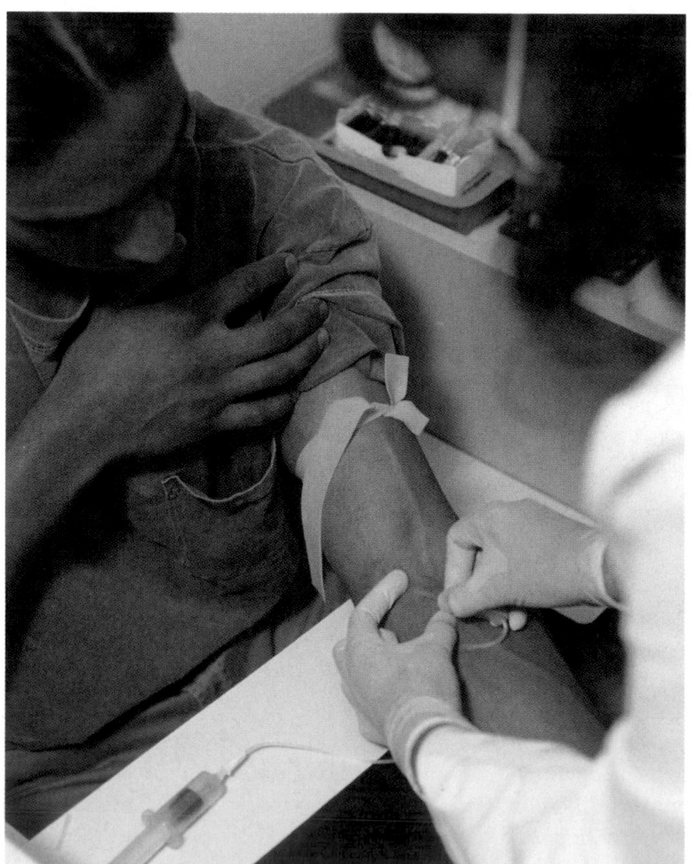

STANDARD COSTS IN NONMANUFACTURING FIRMS In nonmanufacturing environments, standards are sometimes expressed only in quantitative terms; in other situations, the quantitative standards are converted to monetary standards as a basis for identifying monetary variances. For example, automobile service centers have standard times and standard labor costs for automobile repairs, tune-ups, oil changes, muffler replacements, and so forth. Organizations might have standard times for such activities as cleaning hotel rooms, taking blood samples, completing income tax returns, and meeting delivery schedules. These types of standards can be applied in not-for-profit and service organizations as well as in restaurants and merchandising firms. In the fast-food area, for example, franchises, such as MCDONALD'S and BASKIN-ROBBINS, have standard quantities for meat in hamburgers and ice cream in cones.

However, a 1998 survey of 206 medium-to-large companies conducted by **WILLIAM M. MERCER, INC.**, found that in organizations with high turnover, compensation was the most common reason for dissatisfaction. In companies with very low turnover, 40% of the respondents said that emotional factors (work satisfaction, good relationships with managers and other employees) were the sole reasons for their retention; only 21% attributed their retention to financial factors (satisfaction with compensation and benefits).

This evidence suggests that creating a workplace where employees feel better about themselves is extremely important. If a work environment constantly raises employees' self-esteem to a higher level than they experience elsewhere, they will want to spend more time at work and will enjoy very high job satisfaction. It certainly makes sense: people do more of what they enjoy and less of what they don't enjoy. The consequence is that people who enjoy working are more productive.

Source: "Increasing Employee Satisfaction," http://www.performance-unlimited.com/satisfy.htm.

EVALUATION OF STANDARD COSTING Standard cost systems, such as those discussed here, have many advantages and disadvantages. The advantages include the following:

1. The setting of standard costs requires a careful analysis of operations. Such an analysis can lead to efficiencies and economies even before the standard cost system is fully operative.
2. Standard costs are useful for planning overall materials and labor.
3. A standard cost system is simpler to operate than a system using actual costs because the cost flows are recorded at standard.
4. A standard cost system helps identify and control problem areas; this leads to increased production efficiency.
5. Standard costs provide a basis for measuring performance by assigning variances to the responsible manager.
6. A standard cost system is compatible with the principle of management by exception, which contributes to the effective utilization of management's time and effort.

The disadvantages of standard costing include the following.

1. A standard cost system is expensive and time-consuming to develop.
2. It is easy to misinterpret the causes of a variance because so many factors are involved.
3. Standard costs must be changed as conditions change (e.g., as the product, the materials, or the production methods change). Sometimes these changes occur so quickly that standards become out-of-date before management realizes it.
4. Workers tend to view measures of efficiency with mistrust. Responsibility for significant variances may be erroneously assigned, leading to morale problems.
5. The setting of standards is not an exact science. Standards are reported as specific figures but are treated by managers as ranges of acceptable performance. Random fluctuations are to be expected but often are hard to distinguish from situations requiring action.
6. Standards do not support continuous improvement.
7. Standard costs are based on the simplistic cost model in which every cost has to be treated as either fixed or variable. In the real world, however, many costs do not behave according to these idealized models, which means that managers can always legitimately point to shortcomings in the variance analysis and standard costing.

Although the disadvantages noted here are real and should not be minimized, standard cost systems have generally been cost-beneficial and are widely used, even for nonmanufacturing activities. You should recognize that standards are also used for planning and controlling in nonmanufacturing activities and organizations. Manufacturing firms use standards and budgets for their nonmanufacturing activities, as do merchandising and service businesses. In essence, the concepts of standards and cost systems apply to all types of organizations in varying degrees.

---

to summarize

Standard costs can be used in nonmanufacturing firms, as well as manufacturing firms. Standard cost systems have both advantages and disadvantages. Most advantages center on achieving greater accuracy and efficiency. Most disadvantages center on the costs involved in setting standards and the inability to establish exact standards in a changing environment.

Target Costing

target market price The price that consumers will pay for a product or service.

Target costing is an alternative to standard costing. With this approach, the company designs a product based on prespecified costs by gathering input on customer needs and then gets everyone in the company to work toward hitting those target costs. Target costing begins by determining the **target market price**, the price required to win the customer's business, then subtracts the target profit to arrive at the target cost. Target costing has all the ingredients of strategic cost management: quality, cost, and time. It manages costs before they are incurred by setting a target cost for the product or service based on the market, the customer, and the amount of profit desired. It is externally focused on the competition. It organizes workers from different departments into cross-functional teams that strive for the same cost goal and form an integrated planning and execution system.

Target costing involves the following six steps:

1. *Establish the target market price.* The price consumers will pay for a product or service is based largely on the value they perceive in the item and the qualities that contribute to their perception. Target costing uses a product's or service's features to pin down a market price and involves assessing how similar products already on the market are priced. The goal is to determine customers' preferences, collect information about similar products marketed by competitors, and apply that information during the design phase.
2. *Determine the target profit margin.* Target profit margins should reflect the company's strategic business objectives and should be sufficient to offset the life-cycle costs of the product.
3. *Examine the reliability of current cost-management techniques.* A key step in the product-planning phase is analyzing the quality and accuracy of cost information and subsequently generating reliable estimates. For companies with existing products that are similar to the proposed product, cost information from the old product can be used to estimate the new costs.
4. *Establish the target cost.* The difference between the target price and the target profit margin is the allowable cost that the company can commit to the product or service. This cost goal should be attainable, but should still require considerable effort to achieve.
5. *Achieve the target cost.* Making the target cost a reality requires designing excess costs out of the product. Cost reduction efforts do not end with design considerations. Rather, they include eliminating waste, such as scrap and rework, and striving to make operational processes more cost-efficient.
6. *Identify further cost reductions once production begins.* Target costing is a continuous process. As product design unfolds, it is important to compare the target costing objects to actual costs. Companies need to ask: Are competitors still behaving as expected? Are customers' needs still being met? Maintaining an accurate assessment of current costs is also a key to staying on track.

Target costing assumes that companies have little power over customer behavior. Certainly, customers have more options than ever before. Continuing improvements in technology and reduced costs of logistics have not only expanded customer choices but have also created unrelenting downward pricing pressure. If companies are to remain profitable, they must operate with the assumption that the market sets the prices of products and services and that the customer is the ultimate judge in the marketplace.

The roots of target costing trace back to World War II when, due to a shortage of materials, U.S. manufacturers made an organized effort to build the most function into a product for the lowest cost. This approach was called value engineering. The Japanese adopted and expanded the concept in the 1960s, and target costing was born as a long-term profit-planning system that is customer driven and price led.

Today, target costing is used by 80 to 85% of Japanese manufacturing companies, including such well-known names as **SONY**, **TOYOTA**, **NISSAN**, **CANON**, **NEC**, and **OLYMPUS**. Historically, American companies have been slow to adopt target costing. Today, however, major companies such as **DAIMLERCHRYSLER** and **BOEING** are making concerted efforts to adopt target costing. Boeing has implemented target costing in producing the new 757-300, an innovative airplane design that stretches 24 feet longer than the standard passenger plane and is 10% more economical for airlines on a per-seat basis. Using target costing, DaimlerChrysler has established a program to reduce the total cost of the extended enterprise by eliminating stifling bureaucratic procedures, redundant checking and testing, and other practices that have historically hampered customer-supplier relationships. Companies that are adopting target costing believe that technology and globalization have given customers more power than ever before and that to be competitive, a company must adopt target costing.

As a specific example of the value of target costing, consider the case of a major manufacturing company that found itself on the losing end of a bidding competition. To respond, the company broke down the costs and compared them to the target cost allowed by the market. Although the company performed well in most areas, it determined that its cost for the product's power supply was grossly higher than the competition's. Further investigation revealed that the company produced unique power supplies for many of its different products. In contrast, the competitor had standardized its power supplies, which resulted in far less complexity and far higher production volumes. These two benefits allowed the competitor to drive down the overall cost of power supplies as well as the overall market price for the finished product. The manufacturing company's choices were clear—standardize power supplies to reduce costs or consider outsourcing the manufacturing of power supplies to a company that could produce them at the allowable component cost.

With target costing, companies can avoid the problem of producing a product, only to discover that the price they must charge to make a profit is too expensive for their customers. Standard costs that are too high, whether they are achieved or not, result in lost customers if other suppliers can meet customers' targeted costs. Because target costing is customer driven, it can improve customer satisfaction. Target costing also allows more people in the company to understand the company's objectives and how they are going to be achieved because it encourages people with different functions to work on the same team to meet the collective target costing goals. Ideally, target costing arrives at a price that works for the company as well as the customer. That makes it a more effective way to do business, and companies that have used target costing have found that they reach their profit goals more effectively.

IMPLEMENTING TARGET COSTING Although nearly everyone can see the advantages of a system that promises greater customer satisfaction and profitability, putting target costing into practice and getting all employees to accept a new way of doing their jobs can be difficult. Among the problems experienced by companies that have adopted or tried to adopt target costing are the following:

- The company may fail to clearly explain the reasons for implementing target costing. Specifically, the connection to business strategy may not be made clear.
- Top management may not support target costing.
- The company may underestimate the effort required to implement target costing and dedicate insufficient resources to its implementation.

- People may not be ready for change—old ideas change slowly.
- Managers may not respond quickly to the changes target costing brings.
- The company may not be able to accurately determine acceptable market prices.

Unlike standard costing, where the methods of setting standards and computing variances can be covered in this text, there is no easy template for teaching how target costing is performed. Whereas standard costing looks at actual costs and compares them to predetermined standards, implementing target costing involves determining what prices customers will support, specifying appropriate profit levels, and then engineering production processes and costs so that acceptable customer prices can be met. The way organizations complete that process varies from company to company, depending on the specific manufacturing processes the company uses and the individuals involved in the process. Further, some companies implement target costing only on an incremental basis whereas others use a more revolutionary approach, making it one of their highest priorities.

ADVANTAGES OF TARGET COSTING Companies that have successfully implemented and maintained an effective target costing system have experienced the following advantages:

- More effective determination of the expected cost of manufacturing a product or providing a service.
- Greater cost efficiencies.
- Spending money where it had the greatest impact.
- Appropriate identification of customers' real needs.
- Matching of the firm's activities to customers' requirements.
- Increased customer satisfaction.
- Better understanding of cost objectives among co-workers.
- Participation of co-workers in setting quality, cost, and time targets.
- Transformation of the image of management accountants into that of valued partners working on everyone's behalf.
- Greater ability to compete globally.

---

to summarize

Target costing is an approach that attempts to determine the price customers will pay for products and services, subtracts an appropriate level of profits, and then engineers and designs production and other processes so that predetermined costs can be met. Target costing involves cross-functional teams working together to meet target costs. While most people agree that target costing has great appeal, implementing it can often be very difficult. As a result, although target costing has been widely used by Japanese companies, American companies have been slow to adopt it.

4

Explain how performance is evaluated in profit centers.

EVALUATING PERFORMANCE IN PROFIT CENTERS

As defined earlier, a profit center is an organizational unit (segment) in which a manager has responsibility for both costs and revenues. Profit centers both produce and market goods or services. For example, the U.S., Far East, and European operations of the Edison Automobile Company of IMC, illustrated in Exhibit 9-1, might be profit centers.

The Segment-Margin Income Statement

To evaluate the performance of profit centers and to decide how limited resources will be divided among profit centers, management needs a report that compares the revenues and costs

segment-margin income statement An income statement that identifies costs directly chargeable to a segment and further divides them into variable and fixed cost behavior patterns.

direct costs Costs that are specifically traceable to a unit of business or segment being analyzed.

indirect costs Costs normally incurred for the benefit of several segments or activities.

caution

Many students confuse the terms *variable* and *fixed costs, controllable* and *noncontrollable costs*, and *direct* and *indirect costs*. Costs are variable if they fluctuate with activity. If they don't fluctuate with activity, costs are fixed. Costs are controllable if they can be adjusted by the activity manager. If they can't be adjusted by the activity manager, costs are noncontrollable. Costs are direct if removing the activity results in the costs being eliminated. Costs that remain after an activity is eliminated are indirect.

of the profit centers being evaluated. One such report that is often used is the **segment-margin income statement**, such as the one presented in Exhibit 9-5 for IMC on pages 480-481.

To keep Exhibit 9-5 simple, we are assuming that IMC has only two divisions: Acme Computer and Edison Automobile. Further, we have included only the regions of Edison Automobile. You will note that it includes three geographic regions; the Far East Region has operations in two countries—Japan and Korea. As you read across, note that the segment focus becomes narrower: from divisions to geographic regions to countries within geographic regions.

Before reviewing specific aspects of this segment-margin income statement, we want to remind you of a very important management accounting principle—segment managers should receive information about, and be evaluated on, only the items they can control or influence.

As was the case with cost centers, in evaluating profit centers it is important that managers be held responsible only for the controllable costs; the costs and revenues over which they have control are usually called **direct costs**. In Exhibit 9-5, we apply responsibility accounting to IMC by including in each segment report only the revenues and costs controlled by that segment manager. This implies that some costs, **indirect costs**, will not be assigned to a particular segment because the manager cannot control them. Company-wide, indirect costs total $1.5 million, which might include the president's salary and interest on company debt, for example.

Similarly, when Edison Automobile is broken down into smaller segments for analysis, we see an additional $200,000 of indirect costs that are not assigned to Edison Automobile's three regions. Costs such as the division manager's salary and advertising for all regions are not controlled by the division manager and so are not allocated to the regions. You will note that as we move down the organizational hierarchy, from divisions to geographic regions to countries, indirect costs increase in total; managers at the lower levels have the narrowest range of responsibility and the fewest costs to control. The manager of manufacturing in Japan, for example, will be responsible for the items ordered for that unit but not for setting the salary of the manager of Far East operations; this is the responsibility of the manager of Edison Automobile. The salary of the manager of Far East operations is thus a direct and controllable cost of Edison Automobile and is an indirect and noncontrollable cost to Japanese operations.

Managing Costs and Revenues in Profit Centers

Profit center managers manage their costs the same way cost center managers evaluate and manage costs. That is, they use either the standard or target costing concepts that we have already discussed. Unlike cost center managers, however, profit center managers are also responsible for managing revenues because the segment profit they are evaluated on is a function of both costs and revenues. In the next section, we examine one way management analyzes its revenues.

MANAGING REVENUES AND REVENUE VARIANCES A segment's actual and expected revenues may differ for several reasons including the following:

- Sales prices were higher or lower than expected.
- Sales volume was higher or lower than expected.
- The company's market share was higher or lower than expected.
- The industry, as a whole, sold fewer products than expected.
- The mix of products sold was different than expected.

Because management is interested in knowing which of these factors contributed to differences between actual and expected or standard[2] revenues, variances that help isolate these fac-

2 In this discussion, the terms *standard* and *expected* are used interchangeably. Some people refer to these prices and volumes as standard; others refer to them as expected because they aren't under the complete control of the company.

sales price variance The difference between the actual price and the expected or standard price multiplied by the actual quantity; measures the part of the difference between expected and actual sales revenue that is due to differences between expected and actual prices of goods.

sales volume variance The difference between the actual quantity and the expected quantity multiplied by the expected or standard price; measures the part of the difference between expected and actual sales revenue that is due to the difference between expected and actual volume of goods sold.

market share variance The part of the sales volume variance that accounts for the difference between the actual market share of each product sold and the expected market share of each product sold.

tors are calculated. To illustrate how revenue variances are calculated, assume the following data for one of Acme Computer's divisions. Assume that the division sells two types of computing devices: hand-held and laptop. Market share, industry volume, and sales data for the two computing devices are as follows:

	Actual Data (in thousands)			
	Units	**Sales Prices**	**Total Market**	**Percent of Market**
Hand-held	800	$240	9,500 units	8.42%
Laptops	2,300	290	10,100 units	22.77%
Total	3,100	277*	19,600 units	15.82%

*Weighted average price rounded to the nearest dollar. Calculated as [(800 × $240) + (2,300 × $290)]/3,100.

	Expected Data (in thousands)			
	Units	**Sales Prices**	**Total Market**	**Percent of Market**
Hand-held	900	$200	10,000 units	9.00%
Laptop	2,100	300	10,000 units	21.00%
Total	3,000	270*	20,000 units	15.00%

*Weighted average price rounded to the nearest dollar. Calculated as [(900 × $200) + (2,100 × $300)]/3,000.

exhibit 9-5 A Segment-Margin Income Statement

International Manufacturing Corporation (IMC)
Segment-Margin Income Statement
September 2003
(in thousands of dollars)

		Corporation Breakdown into Two Companies	
	Corporation as a Whole	**Acme Computer**	**Edison Automobile**
Net sales revenue	$25,000	$15,000	$10,000
Variable costs:			
Cost of goods sold	$15,000	$ 9,000	$ 6,000
Selling and administrative costs	3,000	1,700	1,300
Total variable costs	$18,000	$10,700	$ 7,300
Contribution margin	$ 7,000	$ 4,300	$ 2,700
Less fixed costs controllable by segment managers	2,000	1,300	700
Segment margin	$ 5,000	$ 3,000	$ 2,000
Less company indirect costs	1,500		
Net income	$ 3,500		
Segment-margin ratio		20%	20%

industry volume variance The part of the sales volume variance that accounts for the difference between the expected market share of the total market and the expected or standard quantity of goods sold.

Using these data, we can compute the **sales price variance** and the **sales volume variance.** Note that when actual sales exceed expected or standard sales, the variance is favorable. This is the opposite of the cost variances, where an actual cost that exceeds a standard cost was deemed to be an unfavorable variance. Once we have calculated the sales price variance and sales volume variance, we can then split the sales volume variance into a **market share variance** and an **industry volume variance.** These calculations are shown below and on the next page.

Sales Price Variance and Sales Volume Variance
For Hand-Helds

Actual quantity × Actual price	Actual quantity × Standard price	Standard quantity × Standard price
800 × \$240 = \$192,000	800 × \$200 = \$160,000	900 × \$200 = \$180,000

Sales price variance \$32,000 F | Sales volume variance \$20,000 U

Market Share Variance and Industry Volume Variance

Actual quantity × Standard price	Total actual market × Expected market share × Standard price	Standard quantity × Standard price
800 × \$200 = \$160,000	9,500 × .09 × \$200 = \$171,000	900 × \$200 = \$180,000

Market share variance \$11,000 U | Industry volume variance \$9,000 U

International Manufacturing Corporation (IMC)
Segment-Margin Income Statement (continued)
September 2003
(in thousands of dollars)

	Possible Breakdown of Edison Automobile (Only)			Possible Breakdown of Edison Automobile (Far East Operations)		
Not Allocated	**U.S. Operations**	**Far East Operations**	**European Operations**	**Not Allocated**	**Japanese Operations**	**Korean Operations**
—	\$5,000	\$2,000	\$3,000	—	\$1,200	\$800
—	\$2,900	\$1,100	\$2,000	—	\$ 700	\$400
—	700	300	300	—	170	130
—	\$3,600	\$1,400	\$2,300	—	\$ 870	\$530
—	\$1,400	\$ 600	\$ 700	—	\$ 330	\$270
\$ 200	250	100	150	\$ 30	60	10
\$(200)	\$1,150	\$ 500	\$ 550	\$(30)	\$ 270	\$260
	23%	25%	18%		23%	33%

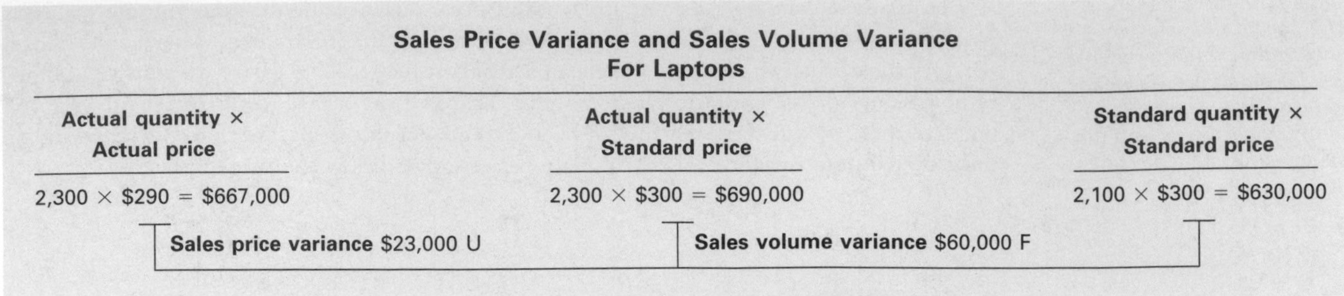

Market Share Variance and Industry Volume Variance

Actual quantity × Standard price	Total actual market × Expected market share × Standard price	Standard quantity × Standard price
2,300 × $300 = $690,000	10,100 × .21 × $300 = $636,300	2,100 × $300 = $630,000

Market share variance $53,700 F

Industry volume variance $6,300 F

Summarizing these variances, we see that the revenue variances for Acme's two products are as follows:

Variances	Hand-Held	Laptops	Total
Sales price	$32,000 F	$23,000 U	$ 9,000 F
Sales volume	20,000 U	60,000 F	40,000 F

Breakdown of Sales Volume Variance

	Hand-Held	Laptops	Total
Market share	$11,000 U	$53,700 F	$42,700 F
Industry volume	9,000 U	6,300 F	2,700 U

The sales price variance informs users whether actual sales prices were higher or lower than expected. The sales volume variance informs users whether the number of units sold was more or less than expected. The market share variance informs users whether the company's share of the total market was higher or lower than expected. Finally, the industry volume variance informs users whether the actual total market was higher or lower than expected.

Thus far, the revenue variance analysis has been on a product-by-product basis. By looking at products individually, we have answered four of the five questions raised earlier. We know from the sales price variances that the sales price for hand-held computers was higher than expected and the sales price for laptops was lower than expected. We know that sales volume for hand-held computers was less than expected and that the sales volume for laptops was greater than expected. In further analyzing the reason for the $20,000 negative sales volume variance for hand-held computers, we see that $11,000 was due to Acme's share of the market being less than expected and that $9,000 was due to the total market being less than expected. With respect to the $60,000 favorable sales volume variance, we know that $53,700 was due to Acme's share of the market being greater than expected and that $6,300 was due to the total market being higher than expected.

The one question we haven't answered relates to the sales mix of the two products. To answer the mix question, it is necessary to combine the analysis of the two products. We do this as follows:

Sales Price Variance and Sales Volume Variance
Hand-Helds and Laptops Combined

	Actual quantity × Actual price	Actual quantity × Standard price	Standard quantity × Standard price
Hand-held	800 × $240 = $192,000	800 × $200 = $160,000	900 × $200 = $180,000
Laptops	2,300 × $290 = $667,000	2,300 × $300 = $690,000	2,100 × $300 = $630,000
Total	3,100 × $277.09677* = $859,000	3,100 × $274.19354* = $850,000	$3,000 × $270* = $810,000

Sales price variance $9,000 F | **Sales volume variance** $40,000 F

*Weighted average price

sales mix variance The part of the sales volume variance that accounts for the difference between the actual quantity of each product sold and the percentage of the actual total products sold that was expected to be represented by each product based on expected market share of the products.

Note that the sales price variance and the sales volume variance for the two products combined is equal to the sum of the two products individually.

Now, we can split the sales volume variance into a **sales mix variance** and a **sales yield variance** (sometimes called the final sales volume). The sales mix variance is caused by selling a different mix (proportion) of hand-helds and laptops than expected. Note that the standard weighted average price for the two products at the expected sales volume is $270 per unit.

Actual quantity × Standard price	Actual total quantity × Standard weighted average price	Standard quantity × Standard price
800 × $200 = $160,000		900 × $200 = $180,000
2,300 × $300 = $690,000		2,100 × $300 = $630,000
3,100 × $274.19354* = $850,000	3,100 × $270 = $837,000	3,000 × $270* = $810,000

Sales mix variance $13,000 F | **Sales yield variance** $27,000 F

*Weighted average price

By examining the sales volume variance on a combined product basis, we see that the mix of products sold was positive—more of the higher-price laptops were sold than expected while fewer of the lower-price hand-held computers were sold.

A final analysis is to split the sales yield variance into the market share variance and industry volume variance, as follows:

Actual total quantity × Standard weighted average price	Total actual market × Expected market share × Standard price	Standard quantity × Standard price
		900 × $200 = $180,000
		2,100 × $300 = $630,000
3,100 × $270 = $837,000	19,600 × .15 × $270 = $793,800	3,000 × $270* = $810,000

Market share variance $43,200 F | **Industry volume variance** $16,200 U

*Weighted average price

On a weighted product basis, you can see that the sales yield variance is positive because of the positive market share variance, meaning that Acme sold a higher share of the weighted market than was expected. The sales yield variance is made lower because the total market in the industry was less than expected.

sales yield variance On a combined product basis, that part of the sales volume variance that is not explained by the mix of products sold. The sales yield variance is the amount of sales volume variance explained by differences between actual and expected market share and total industry sales. The sales yield variance is further broken down into the industry volume variance and market share variance and is also referred to as the "final volume variance."

Using this analysis, if we were evaluating the manager of this segment, we would probably:

- Congratulate him or her for:
  - Selling more laptops than expected.
  - Selling hand-helds at a higher price than expected.
  - Having a positive sales mix.
  - Getting a larger share of the combined market than was expected.
  - Gaining market share for laptops.
- Criticize him or her for:
  - Selling fewer hand-helds than expected.
  - Selling laptops at a lower price than expected.
  - Losing market share in the hand-held market.

When combined with cost variances, revenue variances can inform managers why the income or profit margin of a division or company wasn't as high as it should have been. It will tell them whether the lower net income is caused by expenses that are too high or revenues that are too low. Revenue variance information can help managers take corrective actions to improve their performance. If revenues, for example, are the problem, maybe an aggressive advertising campaign is warranted. If costs are the problem, maybe some cost-cutting or efficiency measures need to be implemented. With these variances, profit center managers now have the information they need to make intelligent planning, controlling, and evaluating decisions.

Interpreting Profit Center Performance Results

segment margins The difference between segment revenue and direct segment costs; a measure of the segment's contribution to cover indirect fixed costs and provide profits.

segment-margin ratios The segment margin divided by the segment's net sales revenue; a measure of the efficiency of the segment's operating performance and, therefore, of its profitability.

contribution-margin ratio The percentage of net sales revenue left after variable costs are deducted; the contribution margin divided by net sales revenue.

Given that the segment-margin income statement in Exhibit 9-5 was prepared in light of the principles of controllable and direct costs, how does management use the information it contains? First, the net income figure provides management with concrete information for evaluating the performance of the company as a whole. Second, the **segment margins** enable management to analyze company results by evaluating the performance of each segment.

We are now ready to examine the operations of IMC segments in detail. In absolute terms, Edison Automobile has a smaller segment margin than Acme Computer ($3 million versus $2 million). U.S. operations has earned more than the Far East and European operations; the Japanese operations has a larger segment margin than the Korean operations. Absolute profits, however, often favor those segments with a larger asset base—with larger manufacturing facilities, for example. A larger facility with more manufacturing capacity should naturally have higher production and higher sales and, hence, a higher segment margin and higher income. A more equitable way to assess performance is to compare **segment-margin ratios** (segment margin divided by net sales), because ratios focus on relationships rather than absolute dollar amounts. For example, though the segment margin of European operations is larger than that of Far East operations, the latter has a higher segment-margin ratio (25% versus 18%). Far East operations also has a higher **contribution-margin ratio** [30% versus 23% ($600 ÷ $2,000 = 30% for Far East; $700 ÷ $3,000 = 23% for Europe)].

In using segment-margin income statements to evaluate profit centers, it is important to review performance over several periods or months. A single period or month may not be typical of overall performance. In our example, September might have been an unusually bad profitability month for the Korean unit of Far East operations because of a slump in the Korean economy or a labor strike. In fact, the performance can be evaluated only by looking at cost and profit trends over several periods, and by comparing the results of these units with those of other similar units. (This comparison is consistent with the process of benchmarking introduced in Chapter 8 of management accounting.)

to summarize

Profit center managers are usually evaluated on both costs and revenues. The most common profit center measurement tool is the segment-margin income statement. This statement identifies both direct and indirect costs and charges only the direct costs to segments. Segment-margin income statements subdivide direct costs into their variable and fixed cost components. Nonmonetary as well as monetary measures should be used to evaluate profit centers. Costs in profit centers are analyzed and managed the same way they are in cost centers—using standard or target costing. Because profit center managers are also held responsible for revenues, a revenue variance analysis procedure that breaks down differences between actual and expected revenues into sales price variances, sales volume variances, sales mix variances, market share variances, and industry volume variances is used.

STOP & THINK Is it possible that a manager could be doing a poor job of managing revenues and revenue growth even though revenues were increasing from period to period?

5

Explain how performance is evaluated in investment centers.

EVALUATING PERFORMANCE IN INVESTMENT CENTERS

An investment center was defined earlier as an organizational unit in which a manager has responsibility for costs, revenues, and assets. Overall, companies would be considered investment centers, as would the independent segments of decentralized companies. For example, the Acme Computer, Edison Automobile, and Jennifer Cosmetics subsidiaries of IMC (see Exhibit 9-1) would probably all be investment centers. Officers of such segments are responsible for acquiring and managing the assets required to manufacture and market their products, as well as for managing the revenues and costs related to those products. The assets include inventory, accounts receivable, and long-term operating assets such as equipment and delivery trucks.

In business, the distinction between profit and investment centers often becomes blurred or even nonexistent. Many companies refer to segments as profit centers when they are really investment centers. Nevertheless, because the distinction between profit and investment centers is useful for defining responsibilities and determining how performance will be evaluated, we discuss them separately.

There are several methods of evaluating the performance of an investment center. When a segment operates almost as a separate company, the rate of return on invested assets and the residual income are usually measured.

Return on Investment (ROI)

return on investment (ROI) A measure of operating performance and efficiency in utilizing assets; computed in its simplest form by dividing net income by total assets.

As you will recall, we discussed **return on investment (ROI)** (sometimes called return on total assets[3]) to evaluate a company's overall performance. ROI is a measure of how much has been earned on the assets of a company; it is equal to net income divided by total assets. For example, if a company earned $1,000 on $10,000 of assets for one year, its ROI would be $1,000 ÷ $10,000, or 10%.

Because an investment center operates as if it were an independent company, its performance can also be evaluated using ROI. In calculating the ROI for an investment center, however, management must be sure to consider only the assets, revenues, and costs controlled by that center. In other words, assets used and costs incurred for the benefit of several investment centers should not be included in the calculation. To stress this concept, we will restate the basic ROI formula as:

$$\text{Investment center ROI} = \frac{\text{Investment center income}}{\text{Investment center assets}}$$

3 In this chapter, we will use the term *ROI* instead of *return on total assets* because it is more commonly used in management decision making. We also use total assets instead of average total assets to keep the calculations simple.

Generally, when an investment center's ROI is analyzed, this formula is divided into its components—the operations performance (sometimes called profit margin) and asset turnover ratios—as follows:

$$\text{Profit margin} \times \text{Asset turnover} = \text{ROI}$$

$$\frac{\text{Net income}}{\text{Revenue}} \times \frac{\text{Revenue}}{\text{Total assets}} = \frac{\text{Net income}}{\text{Total assets}}$$

Note from this formula that the new element is total assets or investments. Net income, which is a function of costs or expenses and revenues, and revenues were considered in profit centers. In evaluating investment centers, where management has responsibility for assets as well as profits, the ROI formula can be used where it couldn't be used before. It is this ROI calculation that investors commonly use to evaluate companies in which they are considering investing.

Clearly, in the above calculations, we could have eliminated the two revenue figures because they cancel each other out, making ROI equal to net income divided by total assets. However, including revenue draws attention to the important concept that ROI is a function of both operating performance and asset turnover.

profit margin (operating performance) ratio An overall measure of the profitability of operations during a period; computed by dividing net income by revenue.

asset turnover ratio An overall measure of how effectively assets are used during a period; computed by dividing revenue by total assets.

The expanded formula shown above helps us identify the three ways an investment center can improve its ROI: (1) it can decrease costs to increase its **profit margin (operating performance) ratio** (net income divided by revenue), (2) it can decrease assets to increase its **asset turnover ratio** (revenue divided by total assets), or (3) it can increase revenue with a corresponding increase in net income. An investment center requiring a major investment in assets (such as a steel mill) will necessarily have a low asset turnover and will therefore have to rely primarily on a higher operating performance to increase its return. An investment center with few operating assets (such as a grocery store) has a more rapid asset turnover and can sustain a lower profit margin ratio while still earning an attractive ROI. For example, a grocery store might make only 2 cents profit per dollar of product sold, but its asset turnover of 12 times a year makes its ROI 24%. A steel mill with an asset turnover of 2 times a year would have to earn 12 cents per dollar of sales to produce an ROI of 24%.

To illustrate the three ways of increasing ROI, we will assume that Acme Computer has revenue of $10,000,000, net income of $1,000,000, and total assets of $5,000,000. The ROI is:

$$\text{Profit margin} \times \text{Asset turnover} = \text{ROI}$$

$$\frac{\$1{,}000{,}000}{\$10{,}000{,}000} \times \frac{\$10{,}000{,}000}{\$5{,}000{,}000} = \text{ROI}$$

$$10\% \times 2 = 20\%$$

The following examples show how each of the three alternatives increases ROI:

1. Increase ROI by reducing expenses by $400,000, providing a net income of $1,400,000:

$$\frac{\$1{,}400{,}000}{\$10{,}000{,}000} \times \frac{\$10{,}000{,}000}{\$5{,}000{,}000} = \text{ROI}$$

$$14\% \times 2 = 28\%$$

2. Increase ROI by reducing total assets to $4,000,000:

$$\frac{\$1{,}000{,}000}{\$10{,}000{,}000} \times \frac{\$10{,}000{,}000}{\$4{,}000{,}000} = \text{ROI}$$

$$10\% \times 2.5 = 25\%$$

3. Increase ROI by increasing revenue to $12,000,000 (assume that profits increase proportionately):[4]

$$\frac{\$1{,}200{,}000}{\$12{,}000{,}000} \times \frac{\$12{,}000{,}000}{\$5{,}000{,}000} = \text{ROI}$$

$$10\% \times 2.4 = 24\%$$

Although ROI is an effective way of evaluating managers of investment centers, it has certain drawbacks. For example, assume that an investment center currently has an ROI of 22%, but the company has an overall ROI of only 16%. If a new project or investment that promises a return of 19% becomes available to the investment center manager, it might be rejected because the center's ROI would be reduced, even though the company's overall ROI would be increased.

Residual Income

residual income The amount of net income earned above a specified minimum rate of return on assets; used to evaluate investment centers.

Although ROI is widely used to evaluate investment centers, because of its drawbacks, some companies use a closely related measure called **residual income**, which is the amount of net income an investment center is able to earn above a certain minimum rate of return on assets. Exhibit 9-6 compares the residual income and ROI approaches. Assuming that the specified minimum rate of return on assets is 15% and that an investment center earns a $25,000 net income on total assets of $100,000, we see that residual income is $10,000 ($25,000 net income − $15,000 minimum return on assets).

To further illustrate why many companies prefer to use residual income over ROI for evaluating investment center performance, assume that the division for which data were given in Exhibit 9-6 has an opportunity to invest $40,000 in a new project that will generate a return of 20% ($8,000 per year). A manager being evaluated on ROI would probably reject this investment opportunity because, as the following analysis shows, it would reduce the division's overall ROI from 25 to 23.6%.

	Without the New Investment	The New Investment	With the New Investment
Total assets	$100,000	$40,000	$140,000
Net income	$ 25,000	$ 8,000	$ 33,000
ROI	25%	20%	23.6%

exhibit 9-6 A Comparison of ROI and Residual Income

	ROI	Residual Income
Total assets	$100,000	$100,000
Net income	$ 25,000	$ 25,000
ROI ($25,000 ÷ $100,000)	25%	
Minimum rate of return on assets (15% × $100,000)		15,000
Residual income		$ 10,000

4 As discussed in Chapter 2 of management accounting, because of the concept of operating leverage, profits are likely to increase more than proportionately when revenue rises. When revenue increases 10%, fixed costs may remain the same. The result is that both the operating performance and asset turnover ratios are likely to increase when revenue goes up. We are ignoring these CVP considerations in order to keep the example simple.

On the other hand, a manager being evaluated on residual income (with a minimum rate of return of 15%) would probably be quite enthusiastic about the project because it increases residual income from $10,000 to $12,000.

	Without the New Investment	The New Investment	With the New Investment
Total assets	$100,000	$40,000	$140,000
Net income	$ 25,000	$ 8,000	$ 33,000
Minimum rate of return	15,000*	6,000**	21,000
Residual income	$ 10,000	$ 2,000	$ 12,000

*$100,000 × 15% = $15,000
**$40,000 × 15% = $6,000

Whether or not the investment should actually be made also depends on several other factors, including what other alternatives are or will be available. The advantage of residual income is that it encourages managers to make as much profit as possible rather than merely achieving a certain ROI; this means making investments that benefit not only their centers but also the company as a whole.

to summarize

Managers of investment centers are usually held responsible for costs, revenues, and assets. The most common performance measures used in investment centers are ROI and residual income. ROI is a function of both operating performance and asset turnover. Residual income is the amount of net income left over after a certain minimum rate of return has been earned on assets. Both ROI and residual income must be used with care because they can encourage managers to maximize short-run profits at the expense of long-term profitability.

expanded material

Earlier in the chapter, you were introduced to standard costing as a way to evaluate performance in cost centers and were shown how standard costing can be used to compute variances for materials and labor. Information relating to these material and labor variances can be used by decision makers to evaluate the acquisition and use of these important resources. In this expanded material section, we introduce you to the variances associated with variable manufacturing overhead costs. (Fixed overhead variances, which are more complicated and less useful, will be left for future courses.) While the computations associated with variable overhead variances are similar to those used for materials and labor, they are generally more complicated. As a result, interpreting the results and assigning responsibility must be done with caution.

expanded material

Compute and interpret variable overhead variances in cost centers.

VARIABLE MANUFACTURING OVERHEAD VARIANCES IN COST CENTERS

Manufacturing overhead is the third type of product cost that must be controlled and accounted for. Manufacturing overhead includes such costs as indirect materials, indirect labor, utilities, and repairs and maintenance. Like direct materials and direct labor, variable manufacturing overhead is measured and controlled by establishing standard costs, measuring actual costs, analyzing variances from standard, and reporting the variances to managers so they can take necessary corrective action.

Measuring and Controlling Variable Manufacturing Overhead Costs

As you study this expanded material, keep in mind that we are covering only variable overhead in this book. Fixed overhead and its associated variances will be covered in later courses. In studying variable overhead, remember that the formal costing system generates only monetary variances, called spending and efficiency variances. In addition to these variances, control is often achieved by physical observation of activities and by using quality and time measures of results, such as scrap rates for materials, downtime for machines, overtime hours, defective parts, kilowatt-hour usage, and the number of hours needed for repairs. These nonmonetary measures are cost drivers that should be monitored on a regular basis to ensure efficient operations.

IDENTIFYING VARIABLE OVERHEAD ELEMENTS, COST DRIVERS, AND PER-UNIT COSTS The first step in controlling variable manufacturing overhead is to study the behavior of each overhead cost to determine whether it is fixed, variable, or mixed. (You will recall that the analysis of costs was discussed in Chapter 7 of management accounting.) The second step is to develop a cost driver (for each variable manufacturing overhead element) that relates the variable manufacturing overhead cost to specific activities or volume changes. As we explained in Chapter 7 of management accounting, traditional cost drivers have usually been output measures (number of items produced) or input measures (number of direct labor hours worked, machine hours used, or direct labor dollars spent). In Chapter 7 of management accounting, we introduced you to new product costing methods, including activity-based costing, where multiple cost drivers are used. For simplicity in illustrating variable overhead variances, we will assume that variable manufacturing overhead costs vary with direct labor hours. However, you should be aware that, where possible, costs are assigned to activities based on cost drivers that reflect the actual usage of costs for each activity. Thus, instead of using one cost driver, such as direct labor hours, a company might identify different cost drivers for each type of variable overhead cost.

To illustrate the calculation of variable manufacturing cost variances using direct labor hours as the cost driver, we will again use the Jennifer Cosmetics example discussed earlier in the chapter. Assume that, for Jennifer Cosmetics, direct labor hours worked fluctuate between 7,000 and 9,000 hours each month. A study of cost behavior patterns over this relevant range has revealed the following variable rates for each of the variable manufacturing overhead items:

Variable Manufacturing Overhead Items	Standard Variable Rates (per direct labor hour)
Indirect materials	$0.44
Indirect labor	0.38
Utilities	0.19
Repairs and maintenance	0.49
Total	$1.50

Summing these amounts, a total standard variable manufacturing overhead rate of $1.50 per direct labor hour is developed. The amount of standard variable overhead applied to each unit is $1.50 times the number of standard direct labor hours allowed for each bottle of perfume manufactured. Because Jennifer Cosmetics allows 2 standard direct labor hours for each bottle of perfume, the applied variable manufacturing overhead cost is $3.00 per unit ($1.50 × 2 hours).

VARIABLE MANUFACTURING OVERHEAD VARIANCES To illustrate how variances are calculated for variable manufacturing overhead costs, assume again that Jennifer Cosmetics actually used 8,352 direct labor hours to produce 4,000 bottles of perfume during the month. Also assume that the actual results, including the total variable manufacturing overhead costs incurred, are summarized as follows:

Bottles of perfume produced	4,000
Direct labor hours used	8,352
Standard direct labor hours for bottles produced (2 hours × 4,000 bottles)	8,000
Actual variable manufacturing overhead costs incurred:	
Indirect materials	$ 3,370
Indirect labor	2,900
Utilities	1,500
Repairs and maintenance	4,200
Total variable manufacturing overhead costs	$11,970

total variable manufacturing overhead variance The extent to which actual variable manufacturing overhead varies from the amount included in Work-in-Process Inventory; the difference between actual and applied variable manufacturing overhead.

On the basis of 8,000 standard direct labor hours to produce an actual output of 4,000 bottles, the standard cost for variable manufacturing overhead is $12,000 (8,000 hours × $1.50 per hour). The difference between the $11,970 actually incurred and the $12,000 standard cost is the **total variable manufacturing overhead variance.** This variance is the amount of under- or overapplied variable overhead. In this example, variable manufacturing overhead has been overapplied by $30 ($12,000 − $11,970). As with direct materials and direct labor, the total variable manufacturing overhead variance is separated into two major variances: spending and efficiency. The spending and efficiency variances are computed as follows:

Variable Manufacturing Overhead Variances

AH × AR (Actual hours of input × Actual rate)	AH × SR (Actual hours of input × Standard rate)	SH × SR (Standard hours allowed for output × Standard rate)
$11,970	8,352 hours × $1.50 = $12,528	8,000 hours × $1.50 = $12,000

Spending variance
$12,528 − $11,970 = $558 F

Efficiency variance
$12,528 − $12,000 = $528 U
[or $1.50 × (8,352 − 8,000)]

Total variable manufacturing overhead variance $30 F

variable manufacturing overhead spending variance The difference between actual manufacturing overhead incurred and the standard manufacturing overhead for the actual activity level.

Variable Manufacturing Overhead Spending Variance The **variable manufacturing overhead spending variance** ($558 F) is the difference between the actual variable manufacturing overhead costs incurred ($11,970) and the amount that should have been incurred at the actual activity level [$12,528 (8,352 direct labor hours × $1.50 standard rate)].

Because manufacturing overhead contains several different cost items, it is possible to compute a spending variance for each overhead item. This analysis helps managers determine which costs are creating the variances. For Jennifer Cosmetics, the analysis would be as follows:

	Actual Costs	Actual Hours of Input × Standard Rate	Variance
Indirect materials	$ 3,370	$0.44 × 8,352 hours = $ 3,675	$305 F
Indirect labor	2,900	0.38 × 8,352 hours = 3,174	274 F
Utilities	1,500	0.19 × 8,352 hours = 1,587	87 F
Repairs and maintenance	4,200	0.49 × 8,352 hours = 4,092	(108)U
	$11,970	$12,528	$558 F

Looking at the variance column, we see a $305 favorable variance for indirect materials, a $274 favorable variance for indirect labor, an $87 favorable variance for utilities, and a $108 unfavorable variance for repairs and maintenance. The favorable variances mean that less was spent than was expected for the actual hours worked, indicating either that spending is in control or that the standards are too high. The unfavorable variance for repairs and maintenance indicates that spending exceeded the standard and that there may be a problem. In both cases, managers and others responsible for any significant variances (favorable or unfavorable) should be asked to explain the reasons for their existence. Of course, this example assumes that variable overhead is a function of direct labor hours. If direct labor hours is not a good cost driver of (does not influence) variable overhead costs, the variances are highly suspect.

variable manufacturing overhead efficiency variance The difference between manufacturing overhead costs at actual hours and manufacturing overhead costs expected at standard hours.

Variable Manufacturing Overhead Efficiency Variance The $528 unfavorable **variable manufacturing overhead efficiency variance** is the standard variable overhead rate times the difference between the standard and actual activity levels [$1.50 × (8,352 actual direct labor hours − 8,000 standard)]. When direct labor hours are used as the basis for assigning manufacturing overhead, the efficiency variance indicates the number of dollars saved (or spent) as a result of using fewer (or more) actual direct labor hours than the standard number of hours for the actual output. As you will recall, the same relationship was used in computing the direct labor efficiency variance. The reason for computing the two efficiency variances is to show that inefficient use of labor causes variances not only in labor costs but also in variable manufacturing overhead. If you use more direct labor hours than planned, more variable manufacturing overhead cost is assigned to products. Since Jennifer Cosmetics' direct labor efficiency variance is unfavorable ($5,632), the variable manufacturing overhead efficiency variance also is unfavorable. Conversely, of course, a favorable direct labor efficiency variance would have produced a favorable variable manufacturing overhead efficiency variance. Again, it is important to note that we are assuming that direct labor hours is an appropriate cost driver for variable overhead costs.

The manager responsible for the control of direct labor hours should be held responsible for an unfavorable manufacturing overhead efficiency variance because the variance is a measure of the efficiency with which direct labor is used. Thus, the manufacturing overhead efficiency variance is really an additional aspect of the direct labor efficiency variance when using direct labor hours as the cost driver to assign variable overhead.

to summarize

Historically, standard costs for variable manufacturing overhead items have been developed using an input measure, such as direct labor hours or machine hours, as a cost driver. Recently, however, cost drivers that relate to individual overhead items have been used to reflect how overhead costs relate to activities. Regardless of the cost drivers used, standard overhead costs are computed for each variable overhead item to determine a standard variable rate that is used in applying variable manufacturing overhead to each unit of product.

The total variable manufacturing overhead variance can be segregated into two variances: spending and efficiency. The variable manufacturing overhead spending variance measures the difference between the costs actually incurred and the amount that should have been incurred at the actual activity level. The variable manufacturing overhead efficiency variance is the difference between variable manufacturing overhead costs at the actual and standard activity levels. Because the spending variance highlights the differences between actual costs incurred and standard amounts for individual manufacturing overhead items, it is generally the more useful overhead variance to analyze for control purposes.

---

review of learning objectives

1 Explain why evaluating personnel and divisions is such an important activity in organizations. Today, information about how efficiently and effectively an organization is operating is easily accessible worldwide. For a company to survive in this information age, it must deliver the highest-quality products to its customers at the least possible price in the shortest amount of time. The only way an organization can continue to improve on these dimensions is to assess its performance and identify areas for improvement. This need for continuous improvement makes performance evaluation more important than ever before.

2 Identify different types of organizational units in which evaluation occurs. Most companies are divided into segments with responsibilities assigned to segment managers. These segments may be defined in terms of product line, geographic area, or function, for example. In a centralized organization, top management makes most of the important operating decisions; in a decentralized organization, decision-making authority is delegated to lower-level managers as well. The current trend is toward decentralization because it usually results in better, more informed decisions.

With responsibility accounting, managers are held accountable for the costs, assets, or revenues over which they have control. The three types of responsibility centers are cost, profit, and investment. Cost centers are usually found at relatively low levels in the organization, and the managers are held accountable for the costs they incur. Profit and investment centers are found at higher levels, and the managers are held accountable for the profits or the return on investments in assets they generate.

3 Explain how performance is evaluated in cost centers. Traditionally, performance has been evaluated in cost centers using standard costs. In recent years, some organizations, including most Japanese companies, have adopted an alternative called target costing. A standard cost system involves setting standard (predetermined) costs that serve as a benchmark for judging what actual costs should be. Standard costs are usually expressed as the per-unit cost of materials, labor, and manufacturing overhead and are used by managers for planning, implementing, and controlling decisions. Standard costs are developed on the basis of careful analysis using the experience of many types of staff, including engineers, supervisors, accountants, purchasing agents, and others. Standard costs have a quantity component and a price component. A comparison of actual and standard costs usually results in two variances: a price (rate) variance and a quantity (usage) variance. Significant variances alert management to specific problem areas that require corrective action. The strategy of focusing on significant variances, called management by exception, is essential to the control function. A standard cost system is designed to accumulate actual costs, to compare actual and standard costs to identify variances, and to report operating results (including variances) to management for review and for corrective action when significant variances occur. Manufacturing firms make extensive use of standard costing systems. A complete standard cost system includes standards for materials, labor, and manufacturing overhead. Materials variances are usually called price variances and quantity variances. The materials price variance reflects the extent to which the actual price varies from the standard price for the actual quantity of materials purchased or used. The materials quantity variance measures the extent to which the quantity of materials used varies from the standard quantity allowed for the achieved level of production. Labor variances are called rate variances and efficiency variances. The labor rate variance is the difference between the actual and the standard labor rates multiplied by the actual hours worked. The labor efficiency variance is the difference between actual and standard hours multiplied by the standard wage rate. Target costing is a customer-focused approach that attempts to determine the price customers will pay for products and services. It involves six steps: (1) establishing target market prices, (2) determining target profit margins, (3) examining the reliability of current cost-management techniques, (4) establishing target costs, (5) achieving targeted costs, and (6) identifying further cost reductions once production begins. With target costing, cross-functional teams work together to meet the target costs. Although most people agree that target costing has great appeal, implementing it can often be very difficult. As a result, while target costing has been widely used by Japanese companies, American companies have been slow to adopt it.

4 **Explain how performance is evaluated in profit centers.** Profit center managers are responsible for revenues as well as costs. The best measure of performance in a profit center is a segment-margin income statement, which distinguishes between indirect and direct costs and reports a segment margin that is controllable by segment managers. Segment-margin income statements also divide direct segment costs into their variable and fixed components in order to compute the segment's contribution margin. Nonmonetary factors often must also be considered in assessing the performance of a profit center. In profit centers, costs are analyzed in the same way they are in cost centers. Revenues are analyzed by calculating sales price and sales volume variances. The sales volume variance is further broken down into market share and industry volume variances. And, in cases where profit centers sell more than one product, a sales mix variance can also be calculated.

5 **Explain how performance is evaluated in investment centers.** Investment centers are usually found at higher levels in an organization than profit centers. The managers of investment centers are responsible for costs, revenues, and assets. Commonly used measures of investment center performance are return on investment (ROI) and residual income. ROI is calculated by dividing net income by total assets. An investment center can improve its ROI by (1) decreasing its costs to increase its operating performance ratio, (2) decreasing its assets to increase its asset turnover ratio, or (3) increasing revenue with a corresponding increase in net income. Residual income is the amount of net income an investment center is able to earn above a certain minimum rate of return on assets. The problem with both ROI and residual income is that they tend to encourage managers to make decisions that increase short-run profits but may diminish profits in the long run.

expanded material

6 **Compute and interpret variable overhead variances in cost centers.** Using an appropriate cost driver, standard costs are computed for each variable overhead item to determine a standard variable overhead rate that is used in applying variable manufacturing overhead to each unit of product. The variable overhead variances may be divided into spending and efficiency variances. The spending variance measures the difference between the costs actually incurred and the amount that should have been incurred at the attained level of activity. The efficiency variance is the difference between variable manufacturing overhead costs at the actual and standard activity levels.

key terms and concepts

review problems

Material and Labor Variances

The standard cost sheet for Kendra Box Company shows the following unit costs for direct materials and direct labor for each box made:

Direct materials (4 board feet of lumber @ \$2)	\$ 8
Direct labor (2 standard hours @ \$6)	12
Total standard cost per unit (excluding overhead)	\$20

During the month of October, 83,000 board feet of lumber were used to produce 20,000 boxes, and the following actual costs were incurred:

Lumber purchased (100,000 board feet @ \$2.20)	\$220,000
Direct labor (39,600 hours @ \$6.05)	\$239,580

Required: Compute the materials and labor variances.

Solution

Materials Variances

The price variance is computed when the lumber is purchased, and the quantity variance is computed when the lumber is used.

Materials price variance:

Purchase price per board foot for 100,000 feet	\$ 2.20	
Standard price per board foot	(2.00)	
Difference	\$ 0.20	U
Feet of lumber purchased	× 100,000	
Total price variance	\$ 20,000	U

Materials quantity variance:

Actual lumber used	83,000	feet
Standard lumber required (20,000 boxes × 4 feet)	(80,000)	feet
Difference	3,000	feet U
Standard cost per board foot	× \$2.00	
Total quantity variance	\$ 6,000	U

Labor Variances

The labor rate and labor efficiency variances are both based on direct labor hours used; thus, they are computed at the same point in time.

Total direct labor variance:

Actual direct labor cost (39,600 hours at \$6.05)	\$239,580	
Standard direct labor cost (20,000 boxes × 2 hours = 40,000 hours × \$6.00)	240,000	
Total direct labor variance	\$ 420	F

Labor rate variance:	
Actual rate	$ 6.05
Standard rate	(6.00)
Difference	$ 0.05 U
Actual hours	× 39,600
Total labor rate variance	$ 1,980 U
Labor efficiency variance:	
Actual direct labor hours	39,600
Standard direct labor hours	40,000
Difference	400 F
Standard direct labor rate	× $6.00
Total labor efficiency variance	$ 2,400 F

expanded material

Variable Manufacturing Overhead Variances

Use the information given above, plus the following information, to address issues associated with Kendra Box Company's manufacturing overhead variances.

The company's budget shows the following monthly variable manufacturing overhead costs at several production levels:

	Percent of Standard Capacity		
	80%	**90%**	**100%**
Expected number of boxes	20,000	22,500	25,000
Expected direct labor hours	40,000	45,000	50,000
Variable manufacturing overhead costs	$80,000	$90,000	$100,000

The company normally produces at 100% of capacity. In addition to the information given above relating to production and the use of materials and overhead, the following actual information is also available:

Variable manufacturing overhead	$83,000

Required:

1. Compute variable manufacturing overhead cost rate (a) per box and (b) per direct labor hour.
2. Compute the variable manufacturing overhead spending and efficiency variances for October.

Solution

1. **Variable Manufacturing Overhead Cost Rates**

		Cost per Unit	Cost per Hour
Flexible budget at normal capacity:			
Boxes produced per month	25,000		
Labor hours per month	50,000		
Variable manufacturing overhead costs	$100,000	$4	$2

2. **Variable Manufacturing Overhead Variances**

The following diagram shows the computation of the variable overhead spending and efficiency variances:

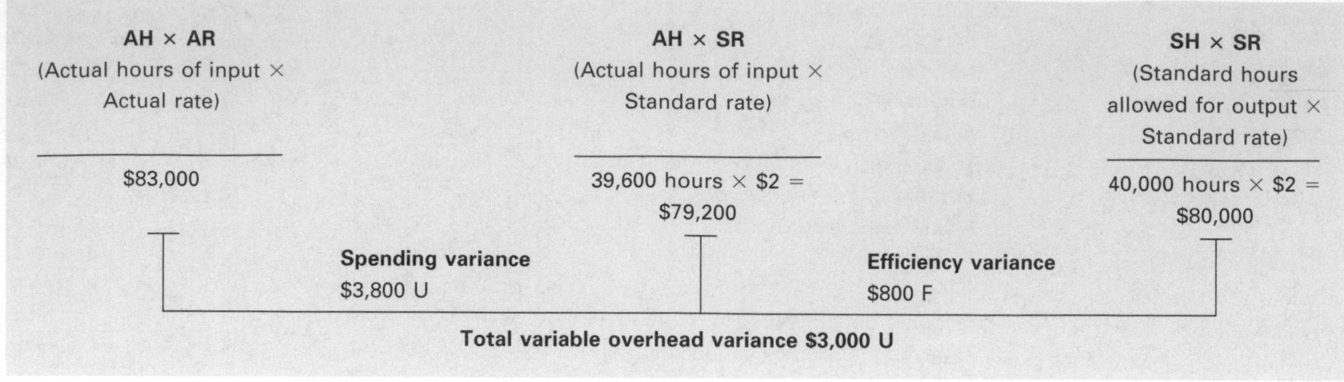

The variable overhead efficiency variance can also be computed by multiplying the difference between standard labor hours and actual labor hours by the standard variable overhead rate per hour (39,600 − 40,000 = 400 favorable hours × $2 variable overhead rate = $800 F).

discussion questions

1. Why is evaluating personnel and divisions so important to a business, especially in today's economy?
2. Why is it practically impossible for a firm to be completely centralized, that is, to have top management making all operating decisions?
3. Why is a system of responsibility accounting necessary in most businesses?
4. What are some important behavioral factors that must be considered when responsibilities are assigned to managers?
5. Why are most performance reports called exception reports?
6. What is the difference between a cost center and a profit center? Between a profit center and an investment center?
7. What is a standard cost?
8. What is the purpose of a standard cost system?
9. Who is responsible for the development of the standards to be used in a standard cost system?
10. What is a variance from standard?
11. What is the relationship of a standard cost system to the principle of management by exception?
12. What are the steps in establishing and operating a standard cost system?
13. What purpose is served by dividing the total direct materials variance into a price and a quantity variance, and dividing the total direct labor variance into a rate and an efficiency variance?
14. Who is usually responsible for each of the following variances?
    a. Direct materials price variance
    b. Direct materials quantity variance
    c. Direct labor rate variance
    d. Direct labor efficiency variance
15. What are the major advantages and disadvantages of a standard cost system?
16. What are the major advantages and disadvantages of using target costing?
17. If a profit center has a net loss, does that mean it is not making a contribution to the company as a whole?
18. What are the variances used to analyze revenues in profit and investment centers?
19. What is the major disadvantage of using ROI to evaluate the performance of investment centers?
20. What is the major advantage of using residual income to evaluate the performance of investment centers?

expanded material

21. What are the two steps in developing standards and measures for use in controlling variable manufacturing overhead?
22. What is a variable manufacturing overhead spending variance, and what does it indicate about variable manufacturing overhead costs?
23. What is a variable manufacturing overhead efficiency variance, and how does it relate to the labor efficiency variance?

discussion cases

CASE 9-1

CONTINUOUS IMPROVEMENT NEEDED

One evening after a strenuous day at the office, Janis Walker, president of Western Mills, Inc., a leading textile manufacturing firm, was out jogging to help relieve the tensions of that day's work. While jogging, she focused her thinking on the firm's commercial carpeting division. The major customers of the division are companies that are building new office buildings, hotels, and motels and need quality carpet in their buildings. The carpet division is doing quite well, but Walker has a nagging feeling that the division could be doing better. She decided to discuss the performance of the division with the division manager. When she arrived home after jogging, Walker called the division manager and arranged a meeting for the next day.

At the meeting, Walker asked the division manager how long it took to deliver an order to the building site after production started. The manager's answer was 17 days. Walker then asked what the industry average was for delivery. The answer was 15 days. Walker wanted to know why Western Mills took longer than competitors to meet order requirements. The manager answered that its product was of a higher quality, so customers were willing to wait longer for the order to be filled. With this information in hand and without hesitation, Walker said, "I will give you six months to reduce the delivery time to 10 days! You study the problem and tell me what resources you need to meet this 10-day delivery goal. I want a report from you as soon as possible."

1. Assuming that the division already has a standard cost system, what limitations of that system resulted in two more days of delivery time than its competitors?
2. Assuming this company has a standard cost system, what changes is the division manager likely to make in order to meet the president's 10-day delivery mandate?
3. How could the use of target costing have helped this company?

CASE 9-2

USING SEGMENT DATA TO MAKE KEY DECISIONS

Sure-Check Company, a calculator manufacturer, is considering dropping one of its calculator product lines because of consistent losses from this model over the past three years. The recent poor performance of this product (known as model A) is shown here (in thousands).

	2001	2002	2003
Revenue (average price $100 per unit)	$14,600	$14,400	$14,200
Variable costs:			
Direct materials cost ($40 per unit)	$ 5,840	$ 5,760	$ 5,680
Direct labor cost ($20 per unit)	2,920	2,880	2,840
Variable manufacturing overhead costs ($15 per unit)	2,190	2,160	2,130
Selling expenses (10% of sales)	1,460	1,440	1,420
Total variable costs	$12,410	$12,240	$12,070
Contribution margin	$ 2,190	$ 2,160	$ 2,130
Less fixed costs controllable by segment managers	2,022	1,997	1,972
Segment margin	$ 168	$ 163	$ 158
Less company indirect fixed costs	438	432	426
Operating loss	$ (270)	$ (269)	$ (268)

Revenue and fixed costs (controllable by segment managers) are expected to decrease again in 2004 by $200,000 and $25,000, respectively, whereas direct materials and direct labor are expected to increase by 5% unless the production department purchases a new attachment with a two-year life for $150,000. This new attachment would replace an attachment purchased only two years ago for $200,000 with, at that time, an expected four-year life. If the new attachment is purchased, direct materials and direct labor will not increase in 2004.

1. Assuming that the new attachment is not purchased, should Sure-Check Company continue to manufacture and sell the model A calculator? Explain.
2. Should the new attachment be purchased? Explain.
3. How, if at all, would the production capacity made available by discontinuing model A affect your decision regarding the purchase of the attachment?
4. What qualitative factors could affect your responses to (1) and (2)?

CASE 9-3

WHY IS MY GROSS MARGIN DECREASING?

Jenson Company sells three products: (1) a health food called *Gro-Gain,* (2) diet supplements called *Muscular,* and (3) a liquid medication called *Yupi Juice* that supposedly cures arthritis. Gro-Gain sells for $5 per bottle, Muscular sells for $10 for a package of 50 pills, and Yupi Juice sells for $15 per bottle. Gro-Gain has 2% of the health food market, Muscular has 10% of its niche market, and Yupi Juice has 50% of the liquid arthritis medication market. The gross margins are 20% for Gro-Gain, 25% for Muscular, and 30% for Yupi Juice. Even though total sales increased this period over last period while total industry sales and the expected and actual sales prices of the three products remained constant, Jenson's gross margin decreased slightly. You suspected that the cause of the decreased gross margin was an increase in costs of the three products. However, an investigation revealed that costs for the three products remained the same as they were last period. Considering the data given, what do you believe is causing the decreased gross margin?

CASE 9-4

WHAT ARE MY COSTS ANYWAY?

You have recently been promoted to be the manager of the camera division of a large corporation. Your most profitable product is an instant camera that takes pictures and then develops them immediately. Historically, the pictures taken by the camera were of a poor quality, but due to large investments in research and new breakthroughs in technology, the instantly developed pictures are of increasingly higher quality. You have just received your segment financial statements for the period, which report the following:

Revenue	$81,000,000
Cost of products sold	40,000,000
Gross margin	$41,000,000

On the basis of this performance you are due to receive a $3 million bonus. The top executives of the company are ecstatic about your performance because you have increased quality, reduced defects, and dramatically increased the productivity of your segment. Having studied management accounting, however, you know that the manufacturing costs are not the only ones that add value to your products. In fact, in your heart, you believe that were it not for research and development costs, aggressive marketing, and good customer service subsequent to sales, your segment would not be nearly so profitable. Yet, these costs are tracked in other departments and are not your responsibility.

As a manager who is benefiting from traditional performance evaluation methods, you wonder whether you should inform management that they are actually giving you a bonus that is too high. Apparently, you are the only one in your company that is aware that these other value-adding costs should be included in your performance evaluation. What should you do? Do you let well enough alone or should you go to management and let them know that you are probably being overpaid?

EXERCISE 9-1

RESPONSIBILITY ACCOUNTING REPORTS

Lorlily Company is an agricultural supply firm. The management of the company is decentralized, with division managers heading the two operating divisions: Machinery and Seed/Fertilizer. Within each division, the sales are split between the two states of Indiana and Illinois.

The following data are applicable to revenue in 2003:

	Budget	Actual
Machinery—Indiana	$800,000	$750,000
Seed/Fertilizer—Illinois	500,000	580,000
Seed/Fertilizer—Indiana	400,000	530,000
Machinery—Illinois	350,000	250,000

1. Prepare a responsibility accounting report for the head of the Machinery division. For each of the two geographic areas (Indiana and Illinois), show whether the variance between budgeted and actual machinery revenue is favorable or unfavorable.
2. Prepare a responsibility accounting report for the head of the entire company. The company head wants to see only the overall results for each of the two operating divisions (Machinery and Seed/Fertilizer); a detailed breakdown by geographic area is not requested.

EXERCISE 9-2

MATERIALS PRICE VARIANCE

Hogan Manufacturing Company has just adopted a standard cost system. You have been asked to analyze the materials purchases and usage for the month of August to determine the materials price variance to be recorded at the end of the month. During August, 5,000 gallons of a chemical were purchased at $3.20 per gallon. Only 4,200 gallons were put into production. The standard price per gallon is $3.15. Compute the following variances:

1. The materials price variance if the chemical is carried in inventory at standard price.
2. The materials price variance if the chemical is carried in inventory at actual price and is charged to Work-in-Process Inventory at the standard price.

EXERCISE 9-3

MATERIALS PRICE AND QUANTITY VARIANCES—JOURNAL ENTRIES

Genesis Enterprises produces one product—MX4. The following information relating to raw materials is available for the month of March:

Beginning direct materials inventory	1,500 pounds @ $3.10 per unit
Purchases made during the month	11,000 pounds @ $3.10 per unit
Direct materials placed in production	11,750 pounds

The standard materials usage for one unit of MX4 is 2 pounds with a standard price per pound of $3. Genesis produced 6,000 units of Product MX4 during the month.

1. Compute the materials price and quantity variances for Genesis assuming the materials price variance is computed at the time of purchase.
2. Provide the journal entries required to record:
   a. The purchase of direct materials and the materials price variance.
   b. Placing the direct materials in production and the materials quantity variance.

EXERCISE 9-4

DIRECT MATERIALS PURCHASED AND USED

Mary Clarke is concerned about her performance as a recently employed purchasing agent. The accounting department has provided her with the following data for the month of August:

Units produced	2,000
Materials used	1,078 tons
Materials purchased	1,400 tons at $43 per ton

The standard materials usage set by management for one unit of product is half a ton of materials per unit, at $45 per ton. Her performance report shows the following variances:

Used (1,078 tons − 1,000 tons standard) × $45 per ton	$3,510 U
Purchased ($45 per ton standard − $43 per ton actual) × 1,400 tons	2,800 F
	$ 710 U

If you were Mary Clarke, how would you explain this report, which indicates a $710 unfavorable variance?

EXERCISE 9-5

ANALYZING MATERIALS COST

Mr. Rogers, the production manager, has received a report showing a $16,500 unfavorable total materials variance. He knows that production used 10,000 pounds less than the budgeted amount for direct materials. Mr. Rogers also knows that the standard price for direct materials was determined to be 80 cents per pound.

What was the actual cost of direct materials used during the period if the budgeted amount was estimated to be 500,000 pounds?

EXERCISE 9-6

MATERIALS PRICE AND QUANTITY VARIANCES

John Clarke, production manager, has just received a report stating that the total materials variance for last month was $3,000 unfavorable. However, he is not certain whether the production foremen are overdrawing from inventory or the purchasing department has been unable to acquire materials at reasonable prices. The information he needs is contained in the following report:

Standard production	150,000 units
Actual production	146,000 units
Standard materials per unit	2 pounds
Materials used in March	300,000 pounds
Standard price for materials	$1.50 per pound
Actual price for materials	$1.47 per pound

1. Compute the materials price and quantity variances for the month.
2. **Interpretive Question:** What was the cause of the unfavorable variance, and what recommendation would you make to Mr. Clarke?

EXERCISE 9-7

MATERIALS PRICE AND QUANTITY VARIANCES—JOURNAL ENTRIES

Starship Enterprises produces and sells calibrators. The company began the period with the following inventory of raw material:

200 units at $5.50 per unit (the materials price variance is taken at the time of purchase)

A standard of four units of material for each calibrator produced has been established. During the period, Starship purchased an additional 1,500 units of material at a total cost of $8,220. The dollar amount of materials transferred to Work-in-Process Inventory during the period was $8,800. At the end of the period, Starship had an ending materials inventory of 50 units.

1. Provide the journal entry required to record the materials price variance.
2. Provide the journal entry required to record the materials quantity variance.

EXERCISE 9-8

LABOR RATE AND EFFICIENCY VARIANCES

To produce one unit of Product OU812 requires four hours of labor at a standard cost per hour of $8.50. During the month of September, 15,000 units were produced. Actual hours and costs for the month are as follows:

Actual direct labor hours	58,800
Actual direct labor costs	$498,000

1. Compute the actual cost per hour of direct labor for the month of September.
2. Compute the labor rate variance.
3. Compute the labor efficiency variance.

EXERCISE 9-9

RESPONSIBILITY FOR LABOR COSTS

Raymond Stone, a recent business school graduate, has taken a job with Farben Corporation as production manager. His job is to see that production is efficient. After his first month, he is given this memo.

Performance Report	
Ray Stone:	$8,000 Unfavorable

Given the following data, what justification would you give if you were in his position, keeping in mind that Stone is not responsible for hiring, firing, and wage rates?

Units produced	750 units
Direct labor used	7,600 hours at $20
Standard direct labor hours per unit	10 hours at $16

EXERCISE 9-10

RESPONSIBILITY FOR LABOR RATES

In Exercise 9-9, what is theoretically wrong with the conclusion that Raymond Stone is not responsible for labor rates?

EXERCISE 9-11

LABOR VARIANCES

During the year, Thompson Plastics was in negotiation with the local union over wages. A settlement was finally reached, and the average wage per hour was increased to $32.80. Production fell to 145,000 units, and 220,000 hours were incurred. Standard production has been set at 150,000 units; 1.5 hours of labor were expected to produce one unit at a standard labor cost of $48.75 per unit. Actual labor cost for the period was $7,216,000.

1. Calculate the labor variances at Thompson Plastics.
2. Prepare the journal entry to enter labor costs in Work-in-Process Inventory and set up the rate and efficiency variances for labor.
3. **Interpretive Question:** Are these variances significant in light of the new wage agreement?

EXERCISE 9-12

EMPLOYEE MORALE AND PRODUCTION EFFICIENCY

Crest Fabrics is a nonunion textile firm. Employee morale and production efficiency have dropped in the last few weeks, causing management some concern. Further, quality control problems have resulted in a 10% increase in rejects in the last two weeks. The following information may help management identify the causes of current problems:

Employee Production Efficiency Report (in percentages)

Employee	Wk 14	Wk 15	Wk 16	Wk 17	Wk 18	Wk 19	Wk 20
Baker	96	100	86	93	91	89	85
Johnson	101	97	89	90	93	91	87
Becker	105	109	93	96	95	92	90
Howard	99	98	88	93	97	94	88
Kettle	92	93	81	85	90	91	90

Additional information:

a. Standards for measuring worker efficiency were raised at the start of week 16.
b. Crest Fabrics changed its source of supply of materials in week 15.

1. From the production efficiency report can you identify trends in the efficiency of individual workers? Which ones might have low morale?
2. **Interpretive Question:** What clues to the causes of the diminishing efficiency and quality can you draw from the information given?

EXERCISE 9-13

LABOR VARIANCES

Compute the missing amounts.

Total labor variance	$ 47,500 U
Labor efficiency variance	42,000 U
Actual labor hours incurred	110,000
Standard labor hours allowed	(a)
Units produced	50,000
Standard hours allowed per unit	2
Total actual labor costs	$467,500
Actual labor cost per hour	(b)
Actual labor cost per unit	(c)
Labor rate variance	(d)
Standard labor cost per hour	(e)
Standard labor cost per unit	(f)

EXERCISE 9-14

TARGET COSTING AT NASA

By the time the National Aeronautics and Space Administration (NASA) launched the Viking missions to Mars, its costs had skyrocketed into the billions. So, as preparations were being made for the next Mars exploration mission, Pathfinder, NASA was told to tighten its belt considerably. NASA had a target cost goal (for Pathfinder) that was one-fifteenth of the cost of the Viking mission, which forced the agency along a different design path. One of the changes NASA's engineers made that saved huge amounts of money was to use inflated balloons to land the spacecraft rather than retro rockets, which the Viking mission had employed.

1. Why was NASA able to reduce costs so significantly when preparing for the Pathfinder mission?
2. Do you think applying target costing is easier for NASA than for for-profit organizations such as General Motors or General Mills? If so, why?

EXERCISE 9-15

SEGMENT-MARGIN INCOME STATEMENTS

Professional Management, Inc., is a company that sponsors seminars for executives. It has two profit centers, or divisions: a time-management group and a money-management group. Financial information for the two divisions for the year just ended follows:

	Time Management	Money Management
Revenue	$842,000	$965,000
Mailing costs	48,000	102,000
Printing costs	146,000	98,000
Hotel rental costs	425,000	501,000
Travel expenses	72,000	60,000
Advertising costs	108,000	106,000

Of these costs, printing and advertising are direct fixed costs, whereas mailing, hotel rental, and travel are variable costs. Using this information, prepare segment-margin income statements for the two divisions.

EXERCISE 9-16

EVALUATING PERFORMANCE WITH SEGMENT AND CONTRIBUTION MARGINS

Damond Corporation's three profit centers had the following operating data during 2003:

	North	East	West
Revenue (at $10 per unit)	$100,000	$150,000	$200,000
Fixed costs:			
Costs unique to the division	30,000	61,000	70,000
Costs allocated by corporate headquarters	20,000	30,000	40,000
Variable costs per unit	6	6	4

Damond's management is concerned because the company is losing money. They ask you to:

1. Calculate each profit center's contribution and segment margins, and overall company profits.
2. Determine, on the basis of these calculations, which center(s), if any, should be discontinued. (Assume that the 2003 performance is indicative of all future years. Ignore all nonfinancial factors.)

EXERCISE 9-17

MEASURING PERFORMANCE USING SEGMENT AND CONTRIBUTION MARGINS

El Pico Company has two divisions: Maya and Aztec. During 2003, they had the following operating data:

	Maya Division	Aztec Division
Revenue	$100,000	$120,000
Fixed costs:		
Costs unique to the division	50,000	45,000
Costs allocated by corporate headquarters	11,000	10,000
Variable costs per unit	4	4
Unit sales price of division's product	10	8

1. Compute each division's contribution and segment margins, and the contribution each makes to overall company profits.
2. **Interpretive Question:** Based on only the financial information given, should either division be discontinued? Why?

EXERCISE 9-18

REVENUE VARIANCES

Sweets, Inc., makes two products: caramel wafers and chocolate wafers. Actual and standard or expected revenue data for the two products are as follows:

	Actual Data (in 000s)		
	Units	Sales Price	Total Actual Market
Caramel wafers	5,000 boxes	$20.00	50,000 boxes
Chocolate wafers	4,000 boxes	25.00	60,000 boxes
Total	9,000 boxes	22.22	110,000 boxes

	Standard Data (in 000s)		
	Units	Sales Price	Expected Market Share
Caramel wafers	4,500 boxes	$22.00	12%
Chocolate wafers	4,400 boxes	26.00	7%
Total	8,900 boxes	23.98	10% (given)

Using the above data, calculate the sales price and sales volume variances for caramel and chocolate wafers for Sweets, Inc.

EXERCISE 9-19

REVENUE VARIANCES

Using the data in Exercise 9-18 and assuming that the sales volume variance for caramel wafers is $11,000 favorable and for chocolate wafers is $10,400 unfavorable, compute the market share and industry volume variances for both caramel and chocolate wafers.

EXERCISE 9-20

REVENUE VARIANCES

Using the data in Exercise 9-18, calculate the sales mix variance for Sweets, Inc.

EXERCISE 9-21

RETURN ON INVESTMENT

Compute the missing data, items (a) through (i), in the following table:

	Division X	Division Y	Division Z
Revenue	$600,000	$500,000	$ (g)
Net income.	30,000	25,000	(h)
Total assets	(a)	100,000	200,000
Operating performance ratio.	(b)	(d)	10%
Asset turnover ratio	(c)	(e)	4 times
ROI.	12%	(f)	(i)

EXERCISE 9-22

RETURN ON INVESTMENT

During 2003, the North and South divisions of Mayberry Company reported the following:

	North Division	South Division
ROI	18%	20%
Operating performance ratio	6%	5%
Revenue	$60,000	$80,000
Total assets	$20,000	$20,000

1. What was each division's asset turnover ratio in 2003?
2. What operating performance ratio would each division need in order to generate an ROI of 25%?

EXERCISE 9-23

MEASURING PERFORMANCE: RESIDUAL INCOME AND ROI

McCormick Corporation measures the performance of its divisions by using the residual income approach, with a minimum accepted rate of return of 16%. In 2003, the printing division, which has total assets of $250,000, generated a net income of $55,000, or 8% of sales. The operating results are expected to be the same in 2004. In early 2004, the printing division receives a proposal for a $50,000 investment that would generate an additional $10,000 of income per year.

1. Should the manager of the printing division make the investment?
2. Would your answer to (1) be different if McCormick Corporation used the ROI approach to evaluate the performance of its various divisions? Why or why not?

EXERCISE 9-24

MEASURING PERFORMANCE: RESIDUAL INCOME AND ROI

An investment center of Southwick Corporation made three investment proposals. Details of the proposals follow.

	Proposals		
	1	**2**	**3**
Required investment	$80,000	$50,000	$65,000
Annual return	13,000	9,000	9,500

Southwick Corporation uses the residual income method to evaluate all investment proposals. Its minimum rate of return is 15%.

1. As president of Southwick Corporation, which of the investments, if any, would you make? Why?
2. Assuming that Southwick Corporation uses the ROI approach to evaluate investment proposals, which investments, if any, would you make? (Southwick Corporation's current return on assets is 20%.)

expanded material

EXERCISE 9-25

VARIABLE MANUFACTURING OVERHEAD SPENDING AND EFFICIENCY VARIANCES

Lauder Company manufactures one product. The standard capacity is 20,000 units per month. Manufacturing overhead costs are budgeted on the basis of direct labor hours. At standard capacity, the monthly variable overhead budget would be $50,000 at two direct labor hours per unit. During February, 18,000 units of product were manufactured, and $46,000 of variable manufacturing overhead was incurred. Actual direct labor hours were 35,000.

Compute the variable manufacturing overhead spending and efficiency variances.

EXERCISE 9-26

VARIABLE MANUFACTURING OVERHEAD VARIANCES

Rollins Manufacturing Company estimates variable manufacturing overhead for the month of November to be $80,000 with an estimated activity level (in direct labor hours) of 10,000 hours. At standard capacity, each unit of finished product requires two direct labor hours to complete. During November, 4,900 units of finished product were produced at an actual overhead cost of $77,500. Actual direct labor hours during the month were 9,850.

1. Compute the amount of variable overhead applied during November.
2. Compute the amount of under- or overapplied overhead for the month.
3. Compute the variable manufacturing overhead spending and efficiency variances.

PROBLEM 9-1

RESPONSIBILITY ACCOUNTING REPORTS

Ryhan Company is a multinational computer services firm. The management of the company is decentralized, with division managers heading the following three divisions: Europe, Asia, and the Americas. Within each division, the three sources of revenue are software sales, service contracts, and consulting fees.

The following data are applicable to revenue in 2003:

	Budget	Actual
Europe—software sales	$200,000	$230,000
Asia—software sales	200,000	130,000
Americas—software sales	350,000	420,000
Europe—service contracts	120,000	90,000
Asia—service contracts	70,000	80,000
Americas—service contracts	250,000	190,000
Europe—consulting fees	40,000	90,000
Asia—consulting fees	50,000	35,000
Americas—consulting fees	100,000	60,000

Required:

1. Prepare a responsibility accounting report for the head of the Europe division. For each of the three revenue sources (software sales, service contracts, and consulting fees), show whether the variance between budget and actual is favorable or unfavorable.
2. Prepare a responsibility accounting report for the head of the entire company. The company head wants to see only the overall results for each of the three geographic divisions (budget versus actual); a detailed breakdown by revenue source is not requested.

PROBLEM 9-2

MATERIALS AND LABOR VARIANCES

The standard cost data for Madison Machinery Company show the following costs for producing one of its machines:

Direct materials	400 pounds at $8 = $3,200
Direct labor	150 hours at $15 = $2,250

During April, four machines were built, with actual total costs as follows:

Materials purchased	2,000 pounds at $8.20 = $16,400
Materials used	1,700 pounds
Direct labor incurred	625 hours at $14.80 = $9,250

Required:

1. Compute the following variances:
   a. Materials price variance (inventory is carried at standard cost)
   b. Materials quantity variance
   c. Labor rate variance
   d. Labor efficiency variance
2. Record the standard materials and labor costs in Work-in-Process Inventory, and enter the variances in appropriate journal entries.

PROBLEM 9-3

MATERIALS AND LABOR VARIANCES

Gemini, Inc., provides the following standard cost data for one of its products:

Direct materials	5 pounds at $4.25 per pound
Direct labor	2 hours at $6.00 per hour

During the month of August, the following actual cost data were accumulated:

Materials purchased	16,000 pounds at $4.15 per pound
Materials used	14,500 pounds
Direct labor incurred	6,450 hours at a total cost of $38,571
Units produced	3,150 units

Required: Compute the following variances:

1. Materials price variance (this variance is computed at the time of purchase)
2. Materials quantity variance
3. Labor rate variance
4. Labor efficiency variance

PROBLEM 9-4 MATERIALS AND LABOR VARIANCES

Actual materials	2,000 tons
Actual hours used	1,500 hours
Standard materials for output (tons)	(a)
Standard hours for output	(b)
Actual cost per ton of material	(c)
Standard cost per ton of material	$ 4
Actual cost per direct labor hour	$ 4
Standard cost per direct labor hour	(d)
Total direct labor variance	$1,625 U
Total direct materials variance	$ 400 F
Direct materials price variance	(e)
Direct materials quantity variance	$ 0
Direct labor rate variance	$ 750 U
Direct labor efficiency variance	(f)

Required: Compute the missing amounts.

PROBLEM 9-5 MATERIALS AND LABOR VARIANCES

Sports Manufacturing, Inc., produces and sells footballs. The standard cost for materials and labor for one regulation-size football is as follows:

Direct materials	2 feet of leather at $5.50 per foot
Direct labor	½ hour at $9.00 per hour

During the period, Sports Manufacturing recorded a materials price variance of $100 U and a materials quantity variance of $380 F. In addition, the company recorded a labor rate variance and a labor efficiency variance of $1,200 U and $450 U, respectively. Seven thousand footballs were produced during the period, and the materials inventory did not change during the period.

Required:

1. Compute the actual costs for materials and labor during the period.
2. Provide the journal entries to record the materials price and quantity variances. (Hint: the amount of materials purchased and used is the same.)
3. Provide the journal entries to record the labor rate and efficiency variances.

PROBLEM 9-6 MATERIALS AND LABOR VARIANCES

The following information was taken from the records of Liberty Manufacturing Company for the month of July:

Materials (actual):	
Purchases of material A:	1,300 pounds × $5.25
Purchases of material B:	750 pounds × $2.50
Used 900 pounds of material A	
Used 525 pounds of material B	
Direct labor (actual):	
Manufacturing:	1,050 hours × $8.90
Assembly:	450 hours × $4.50

Standard cost per unit:

Material A: 2 pounds × $5.20 per pound	$10.40
Material B: 1 pound × $2.60 per pound	2.60
Direct labor—manufacturing: 2 hours × $8.50	17.00
Direct labor—assembly: 1 hour × $4.60	4.60
Standard cost per unit	$34.60

Units produced: 500

Required:

1. Calculate the materials price and quantity variances, assuming that the materials price variance is recognized at the time of purchase.
2. Calculate the labor rate and labor efficiency variances.
3. **Interpretive Question:** What is the advantage, if any, of calculating the materials price variance at the time of purchase rather than at the time of use?

PROBLEM 9-7

MATERIALS AND LABOR VARIANCE ANALYSIS

Cooke Manufacturing Company produces high-quality men's pajamas for several large retail stores. The standard cost card for each dozen pairs of pajamas is as follows:

Direct materials, 30 yards at $0.80	$24
Direct labor, 4 hours at $5.00	20
Manufacturing overhead:	
Variable cost: 4 direct labor hours at $2.00	8
Fixed cost: 30% of direct labor cost	6
Total product cost per dozen pairs	$58

During the month of September, the company filled three orders of pajamas at the following costs:

Order	Number of Dozens	Yards Used	Labor Hours
8	400	12,200	1,500
9	900	26,750	3,750
10	500	15,450	2,140
	1,800	54,400	7,390

The following additional information involving materials and labor was supplied by the accounting department:

a. Purchases of materials during the month amounted to 60,000 yards at $0.82 per yard.
b. Total direct labor cost for the month was $37,689.

Required:

1. Compute the materials price variance for September. (Materials are carried in Direct Materials Inventory at standard.)
2. Compute the materials quantity variance for September.
3. Compute the labor rate and labor efficiency variances for September.

PROBLEM 9-8

DETERMINING HOW VARIANCES ARE COMPUTED

HIC Company uses a standard cost system in its accounting for the manufacturing costs of its only product. The standard cost information for materials and labor is as follows:

Direct materials: 3 pounds at $4	$12
Direct labor: 1 hour at $6	6

During April of its first year of operation, the company completed 4,400 units and had the following materials and labor variances:

Materials price variance	$ 700 F
Materials quantity variance	3,200 U
Labor rate variance	900 U
Labor efficiency variance	600 U

There was no Work-in-Process Inventory at the beginning or end of April.

Required: Compute the following amounts:

1. The amount of materials and labor debited to Work-in-Process Inventory during April.
2. The pounds of materials used in production.
3. The actual hours of labor used in production.
4. The actual labor rate per hour.

PROBLEM 9-9 TARGET COSTING

Hotstone, Inc., makes tires for automobiles and other vehicles. The company is currently under tremendous pressure by customers to hold down costs, increase quality, and provide tires on a more timely basis. Automakers have informed Hotstone that if improvements are not made soon, they will start using other providers. While one large customer is very concerned about the prices Hotstone charges for the tires, it is particularly concerned about the quality and safety of the tires. There have been several incidents where one particular type of tire has experienced rubber separation, resulting in costly and deadly rollovers of a particular type of sports utility vehicle.

In a meeting of Hotstone's top executives to determine how to meet these almost unrealistic customer demands, two proposals have emerged. The first, made by a marketing vice president, is that costs can be reduced and quality improved only by tightening the standards imposed on factory employees for costs, productivity, and quality. The marketing vice president believes that there is a lot of slack in the manufacturing process, that employees are enterprising, and that the employees will find ways to meet the standards if sufficient rewards are attached to meeting them. Others point out that the standards now in effect were established after significant time and motion studies and suggest that they cannot be arbitrarily tightened without significant employee unrest and compromises in quality.

As an alternative, a manufacturing vice president, who recently returned from studying several Japanese companies, argues that the only way to lower costs and simultaneously increase quality and timeliness is to engineer cost savings and quality into products using a process called target costing. She argues that it is essential to involve employees in a target costing effort so that they will understand the customers' demands for prices and quality and will work creatively on ways to reengineer the entire manufacturing process. She believes that significant cost reductions, quality improvements, and shortened manufacturing and delivery times can be developed if enough smart people work together to solve the problem. She argues that a target costing approach is the only way to make meaningful, long-term changes and to meet customer demands.

Required: As the CFO of Hotstone, Inc., you have been assigned to lead the effort to reduce costs, increase quality, and decrease manufacturing and delivery times. Considering the costs and benefits of the two proposed approaches, what should you do? Write a memo to the CEO informing him of your plan to adopt the target costing approach.

PROBLEM 9-10 EVALUATION OF PROFIT CENTERS—SEGMENT MARGIN

Della Brown is the manager of one of the stores in the nationwide EatRite supermarket chain. The following information has been gathered about the performance of Della's store in the most recent quarter:

Operating Departments	Revenue	Contribution-Margin Ratio
Groceries	$600,000	20%
Fresh produce	200,000	40%
Dry goods	500,000	35%
Fixed costs controllable by:		
Manager of grocery department	$ 50,000	
Manager of fresh produce department	70,000	
Manager of dry goods department	80,000	
Store manager	100,000	
Corporate headquarters	100,000	
Total	$400,000	

Required: Prepare a segment-margin income statement for corporate headquarters' use in evaluating the store manager, Della Brown, and which Della can use to evaluate the managers of the three departments within the store.

PROBLEM 9-11

EVALUATION OF PROFIT CENTERS—SEGMENT MARGIN

Derrald Pearl Company has two divisions, Computer Consulting and Construction. During the most recent year, the two divisions had the following operating data:

	Computer Consulting	Construction
Revenue	$600,000	$250,000
Contribution-margin percentage	45%	15%
Fixed costs controllable by division managers	$200,000	$30,000
Fixed costs allocated by corporate headquarters	$100,000	$100,000

Required:

1. Prepare a segment-margin income statement for Derrald Pearl Company. Include three columns—one for the company total and one for each of the two divisions.
2. Based on the segment-margin income statement prepared in (1), what would happen to overall company profits if the Construction Division were to be discontinued?
3. Should either of the divisions be discontinued? Explain.

PROBLEM 9-12

REVENUE VARIANCES

Menendez Company is a merchandiser that sells three products: Product X, Product Y, and Product Z. The following are the actual and expected (standard) data for the three products:

	Actual Data		
	Units	Sales Price	Total Actual Market
Product X	530	$5.00	2,250 units
Product Y	760	4.00	10,000 units
Product Z	660	7.00	2,500 units
Total	1,950	5.29	14,750 units

Standard Data

	Units	Sales Price	Total Market Share
Product X	500	$6.00	25%
Product Y	900	3.00	10%
Product Z	600	5.00	20%
Total	2,000	4.35	Total market = 20% (assumed)

Required:

1. Compute the sales price variance, the sales volume variance, the market share variance, and the industry volume variance for Product X.
2. Compute the sales price variance, the sales volume variance, the market share variance, and the industry volume variance for Product Y.
3. Compute the sales price variance, the sales volume variance, the market share variance, and the industry volume variance for Product Z.
4. Compute the sales price, sales volume, sales mix, market share, and industry volume variance for the three products combined.

PROBLEM 9-13

ROI AND CONTRIBUTION-MARGIN ANALYSIS

Macro Data Corporation's three divisions had the following operating data during 2003:

	Fax Machine	Calculator	Computer
Revenue	$100,000	$150,000	$200,000
Variable costs	50,000	90,000	135,000
Fixed costs	45,000	56,000	53,000
Total assets	50,000	38,000	120,000

Required:

1. Compute the contribution margin for each division.
2. Compute the segment margin for each division.
3. Compute the ROI for each division.
4. Which division had the highest operating performance ratio?
5. **Interpretive Question:** Which division had the best performance in 2003? Why?

PROBLEM 9-14

ROI

Marcos Trade Corporation has two divisions: the Pacific division and the Atlantic division. Following are their operating data for 2003:

	Pacific Division	Atlantic Division
Revenue	$100,000	$100,000
Net income	8,000	7,000
Total assets	50,000	40,000
Stockholders' equity	24,000	16,000
Long-term debt	23,000	20,000

1. Calculate the ROI for each division.
2. **Interpretive Question:** On the basis of this return, which division appears to have the better performance? Why?

PROBLEM 9-15

ROI

The following information for 2003 applies to the two sales divisions of Ward Enterprises:

	Division A	Division B
Total inventory	$33,333	$37,500
Operating performance ratio	12%	16%
Net income	$12,000	$10,000

Required:

1. Calculate each division's revenue.
2. Calculate each division's asset turnover ratio assuming that controllable assets include inventory only.
3. **Interpretive Question:** Which division had the better performance for the period? Why?

PROBLEM 9-16

ROI AND RESIDUAL INCOME

Pacific Corporation has a number of autonomous divisions. Its real estate division has recently reviewed a number of investment proposals.

a. A new office building would cost $450,000 and would generate yearly net income of $80,000.
b. A computer system would cost $350,000 and would reduce bookkeeping and clerical costs by $50,000 annually.
c. A new apartment house would cost $900,000 and would generate yearly net income of $150,000.

The real estate division currently has total assets of $1.8 million and net income of $350,000.

Required:

1. Assuming that the performance of the manager of the real estate division is evaluated on the basis of the division's ROI, evaluate each of the independent proposals, and determine whether it should be accepted or rejected.
2. Assuming that the manager's performance is evaluated on a residual income basis, determine whether each of the proposals should be accepted or rejected. (The division's minimum accepted rate of return is 15%.)

PROBLEM 9-17

ROI AND RESIDUAL INCOME

Albertson Furniture Company is a retailer of home furnishings. It currently has stores in three cities—San Francisco, Los Angeles, and Phoenix. Operating data for the three stores in 2003 were as follows:

	San Francisco	Los Angeles	Phoenix
Revenue	$1,500,000	$1,900,000	$1,800,000
Variable costs	900,000	1,200,000	1,200,000
Fixed costs	300,000	350,000	250,000
Total assets	1,800,000	2,500,000	1,300,000

Required:

1. Compute the segment margin for each store.
2. Compute the operating performance ratio for each store.
3. Compute the asset turnover for each store.
4. Compute the ROI for each store.
5. Compute the residual income for each store. (The minimum rates of return for the stores are San Francisco, 15%; Los Angeles, 13%; and Phoenix, 18%.)

PROBLEM 9-18

ROI AND RESIDUAL INCOME

	Division W	Division X	Division Y	Division Z
Revenue	$100,000	$300,000	$ (i)	$850,000
Net income	$ (a)	$ 90,000	$ (j)	$ (m)
Total assets	$ 85,000	$ (e)	$550,000	$ (n)
Operating performance ratio	15%	(f)	6%	(o)
Asset turnover ratio	(b)	0.75 times	(k)	4.0 times
ROI	(c)	(g)	(l)	21%
Minimum accepted rate of return	13%	(h)	15%	12%
Residual income	$ (d)	$ 12,000	$ 17,500	$ (p)

Required: Compute the missing data, labeled (a) through (p).

PROBLEM 9-19

MEASURING PERFORMANCE: RESIDUAL INCOME AND ROI

The gaming division of Nevada Corporation had income of $550,000 and total assets of $3 million in 2003. The figures are expected to be similar in 2004. The manager of the gaming division has an opportunity to purchase some new gambling machines for $250,000. He concludes that the new machines would increase annual net income by $44,000.

Required:

1. Calculate the current ROI and the expected return on the proposed investment.
2. Calculate the gaming division's current residual income and the expected residual income on the proposed investment. (Assume that the division's minimum accepted rate of return is 17%.)
3. Should the new machines be purchased:
   a. If the division uses the ROI method?
   b. If the division uses the residual income method?

PROBLEM 9-20

ROI AND RESIDUAL INCOME

The manager of the manufacturing division of Minolta Company is evaluated on a residual income basis. He is in the process of evaluating three investment proposals.

a. Pay $500,000 for a new machine that will increase production substantially. This will result in an increased income of $80,000 annually.
b. Pay $350,000 for a new machine that will reduce labor costs by $70,000 annually.
c. Pay $800,000 for a new machine that will increase annual net income by $115,000.

The manufacturing division currently has total assets of $1.2 million and net income of $200,000. Its minimum accepted rate of return is 15%.

Required:

1. Evaluate the three investment proposals independently, and determine which should be accepted.
2. Assuming that the division manager is evaluated on the basis of the division's ROI, determine whether each of the proposals should be accepted or rejected.

expanded material

PROBLEM 9-21

VARIABLE MANUFACTURING OVERHEAD VARIANCES

Engraph Manufacturing Company uses standard direct labor hours as a basis for charging variable manufacturing overhead to Work-in-Process Inventory. The following data were taken from the records:

Data for August:	
Budgeted units	9,000
Budgeted hours	36,000
Actual variable manufacturing overhead	$217,000
Actual units produced	8,000
Actual direct labor hours	33,000
Variable manufacturing overhead data (annual):	
Estimated variable manufacturing overhead cost	$2,560,000
Estimated direct labor hours	400,000
Estimated units of production	100,000

Required:

1. Compute the annual variable manufacturing overhead rate to be used to apply variable overhead to Work-in-Process Inventory per direct labor hour.
2. Determine the variable overhead spending variance for August.
3. Determine the variable overhead efficiency variance for August.
4. Prepare the journal entry to transfer standard variable overhead costs to Work-in-Process Inventory.

PROBLEM 9-22

VARIABLE MANUFACTURING OVERHEAD VARIANCES

Piedmont Tile Company attempts to control manufacturing overhead costs through the use of a flexible budget. Standards are set by studying historical overhead cost data, which are shown here. Actual total overhead costs for each month of the third quarter are also shown.

Standards:
Variable overhead: $1.70 per direct labor hour

Months	Direct Labor Hours	Total Variable Overhead Costs (actual)	Standard Hours Allowed
July	50,000	$150,000	47,500
August	60,000	185,000	60,500
September	40,000	90,000	39,000

Required:

1. Compute the variable overhead spending variance for each month.
2. **Interpretive Question:** Give several reasons why the variable overhead spending variances for all three months might be unfavorable.

PROBLEM 9-23

VARIABLE MANUFACTURING OVERHEAD SPENDING AND EFFICIENCY VARIANCES

The following production information is available for the Porter Corporation:

Standard production	150,000 units
Actual production	145,000 units
Actual variable manufacturing overhead	$175,000
Variable manufacturing overhead applied	$0.80 per machine hour
Actual machine hours	220,000 hours
Standard machine hours per unit produced	1.5 machine hours

Required:

1. Calculate the variable manufacturing overhead spending and efficiency variances for the Porter Corporation.
2. **Interpretive Question:** Explain how the spending variance and the efficiency variance are used to control overhead costs.
3. Identify cost drivers other than machine hours that might be better measures of spending and efficient use of variable overhead costs.

competency enhancement opportunities

- Analyzing Real Company Information
- International Case
- Ethics Case
- Writing Assignment
- The Debate
- Internet Search

The following additional assignments provide opportunities for students to develop critical thinking, ethical perspectives, oral and written communication skills, experience with electronic research, and teamwork through group and business activities.

ANALYZING REAL COMPANY INFORMATION

- ***Analyzing 9-1 (Microsoft)***

In the 2000 annual report for MICROSOFT (accessible at http://www.Microsoft.com), you will find Segment Information in footnote #16 in the Notes to the Financial Statements. That footnote is shown below:

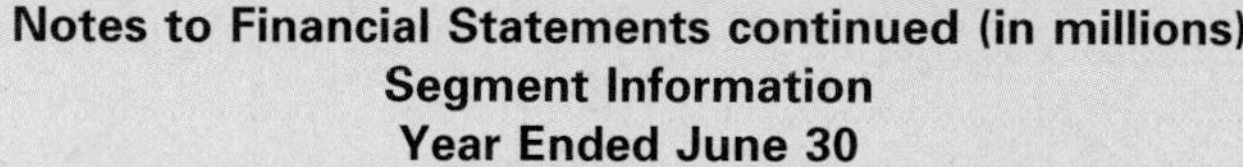
Notes to Financial Statements continued (in millions)
Segment Information
Year Ended June 30

	Windows Platforms	Productivity Applications and Developer	Consumer and Other	Reconciling Amounts	Consolidated
1998					
Revenue	$6,236	$ 7,458	$ 1,765	$ (197)	$15,262
Operating income . .	3,661	4,824	(1,050)	(1,021)	6,414
1999					
Revenue	$8,570	$ 8,636	$ 1,854	$ 687	$19,747
Operating income . .	5,476	4,950	(1,241)	743	9,928
2000					
Revenue	$9,265	$10,089	$ 2,718	$ 884	$22,956
Operating income . .	5,813	4,935	(1,455)	1,644	10,937

The Company's organizational structure and fundamental approach to business reflect the needs of its customers. As such, Microsoft has three major segments: Windows Platforms; Productivity Applications and Developer; and Consumer and Other. Windows Platforms includes the Windows Division, which is primarily responsible for developing and marketing Windows NT Workstation, Windows 2000 Professional, Windows 98, Windows 95, Windows NT Server, and Windows 2000 Server. Productivity Applications and Developer includes the Business Productivity Division, which is responsible for developing and marketing desktop applications, server applications, and developer tools. Consumer and Other products and services include primarily learning, entertainment, and PC input device products; WebTV and PC online access; and portal and vertical properties. Assets of the segment groups are not relevant for management of the businesses nor for disclosure. Segment information is presented in accordance with SFAS 131, Disclosures about Segments of an Enterprise and Related Information. This standard is based on a management approach, which requires segmentation based upon the Company's internal organization and disclosure of revenue and operating income based upon internal accounting methods. The Company's financial reporting systems present various data for management to run the business, including internal profit and loss statements (P&Ls) prepared on a basis not consistent with generally accepted accounting principles. Reconciling items include certain elements of unearned revenue, the treatment of certain channel inventory amounts and estimates, and the classification of revenue from product support and consulting. Additionally, the internal P&Ls use accelerated methods of depreciation and amortization. In fiscal 2000, the Company's internal P&Ls included the Black-Scholes value of employee stock option grants, amortized over the remaining months of the fiscal year of the grant, as well as minor changes to the segments' composition due to various internal reorganizations during the year. Fiscal 1999 disclosures have been restated for consistent presentation. It is not practicable to restate fiscal 1998 for these changes.

Revenue attributable to U.S. operations includes shipments to customers in the United States, licensing to OEMs and certain multinational organizations, and exports of finished goods, primarily to Asia, Latin America, and Canada. Revenue from U.S operations totaled \$10.1 billion, \$13.7 billion, and \$15.7 billion in 1998, 1999, and 2000, respectively. Revenue from outside the United States, excluding licensing to OEMs and certain multinational organizations and U.S. exports, totaled \$5.2 billion, \$6.0 billion, and \$7.3 billion in 1998, 1999, and 2000, respectively.

Long-lived assets totaled \$1.5 billion and \$1.8 billion in the United States in 1999 and 2000 and \$154 million and \$126 million in other countries in 1999 and 2000.

1. As you can see, Microsoft has three different segments: Windows Platforms, Productivity Applications and Developer, and Consumer, Commerce, and Other. How do you think Microsoft primarily evaluates these segments—as cost centers, as profit centers, or as investment centers?
2. Compute the margin (operating income/revenue) for the three divisions for 1998, 1999, and 2000. Which segment is the most profitable? Which is growing the fastest?

• *Analyzing 9-2 (Petersen Pottery)*

Just outside Elkins, West Virginia, Clive Petersen has been making ceramic bathroom fixtures (sinks, toilets, and bathtubs) since 1960. Petersen fixtures had become known over the years for their distinctive customer features, their high quality, and their long life. **PETERSEN POTTERY** started out as a two-man operation. By 1980 it had grown to 20 master potters. By this time, Clive Petersen felt that he had expanded to a point that he needed to institute a formal accounting control system. The insistence of his banker that he get a "real" management accounting system in place was also compelling. As a result, Petersen hired a formally trained management accountant who began working with his most experienced master potters to design cost standards. After some research, Petersen's accountant arrived at the following cost standards for a toilet (note that variable manufacturing overhead is allocated based on direct labor hours):

Direct materials:		
Raw clay	25 lb. × \$0.95 per lb. =	\$23.75
Glazing mix	5 lb. × \$0.75 per lb. =	3.75
Direct labor:		
Molding	1.0 hr. × \$15.00 per hour =	15.00
Glazing	0.5 hr. × \$15.00 per hour =	7.50
Variable manufacturing overhead	1.5 hr. × \$3.00 per hour =	4.50
Total per fixture		\$54.50

After six months of operations, Petersen was disturbed over the lack of attention paid to the standards by his potters. He felt that the potters were just too set in their ways to adhere to the new system. Many of the potters told Petersen that the new system was "confusing" and didn't help them in their work. In reviewing the June production results, the following actual costs were noted in connection with manufacturing 1,145 toilets:

Materials used:	
Raw clay	28,900 lb. @ $0.92 per lb.
Glazing mix	5,900 lb. @ $0.78 per lb.
Direct labor:	
Molding	1,200 hr. @ $15.25 per hour (average)
Glazing	600 hr. @ $15.00 per hour (average)
Actual variable manufacturing overhead	$5,120

1. Compute all cost variances for the month of June.
2. What suggestions do you have for Mr. Petersen regarding his new standard cost system?

Source: Adapted from J. K. Shank, "Petersen Pottery" case, *Cases in Cost Management: A Strategic Emphasis* (Cincinnati: South-Western, 1996).

INTERNATIONAL CASE

• *Target Costing in Japan*

Japan is always a good place for useful insight on innovative management accounting practice and technique. From early on, the Japanese recognized that the most efficient way to keep costs down was to *design* them out of their products, not to reduce them after the products entered production. This realization reflects a fundamental reality of cost management in Japan; the majority of a product's costs (as much as 90 to 95% according to some experts) are "designed in." Consequently, effective cost control programs in a Japanese business typically focus heavily on the design process for a particular product. This is done primarily through target costing and value engineering (VE). Target costing is used to determine what the market is willing to pay for a product, then VE is used to design the product in order to achieve a prespecified targeted level of costs.

What do you think is the effect of target costing and VE on the use of variances? Specifically, will materials usage variances and labor efficiency variances be more or less important to a firm that strictly uses target costing and VE versus a traditional firm that is more focused on controlling daily production processes?

ETHICS CASE

• *Cool Air, Inc.*

Jack Lear, an internal auditor for Cool Air, Inc., met with Paul Marsh, the manager of the cost accounting department, to discuss a concern about a possible "glitch" in the standard cost system. Jack explained that he had been reviewing the employee time cards in the company division where air-conditioning units and refrigerators were assembled. The time cards reflected how much employee time was devoted to the assembly of air-conditioning units and how much time applied to refrigerators. Jack's concern was that the hours actually charged for each of these operations always seemed to be right on target with the standard labor times for each air-conditioning unit and each refrigerator unit assembled; yet Jack had been told a number of times by employees in the assembly department that the standard hours for assembling air-conditioning units were too low. The employees felt that they could not meet these standards without "fudging" their time cards or sacrificing some quality work in the assembly process. Since company policy emphasized product quality, Jack suspected that time sheets were being modified by shifting hours worked on air-conditioning units to the time sheets for assembling refrigerators.

Paul Marsh, the cost manager, thought for a minute about what Jack was telling him and then made an interesting observation. He said that he had been concerned about the fact that the company's prices for its air-conditioning units were generally lower than its competitors' prices for the same size and quality of units, whereas its prices for refrigerators were generally higher than those of its competitors. He wondered if the company's pricing structure, which was tied to its standard costs, was out of line with competition. This position was reinforced when Paul and Jack looked at the company's sales of each of these products. Over the past year or so, the company had gained market share in air-conditioner sales and had lost market share in refrigerators! Based on this information, Paul asked Jack to do some "detective" work on the time cards in the assembly division and report back his findings.

A few days later, Jack reported that he had found convincing evidence that the foremen in the assembly division had been in collusion to "doctor" employee time sheets in order to more closely meet the time standards for both air-conditioner and refrigerator assembly.

1. Who are the stakeholders affected by the "doctoring" of time sheets?
2. What are the ethical issues in this situation?
3. What should Paul do?

WRITING ASSIGNMENT

• *Qualitative Variance Analysis*

With the push for continuous improvement, stable standards may become a thing of the past. As companies strive for and achieve zero defects and no waste, variances quantifiable in terms of dollars become more and more difficult to obtain. To determine variances from a standard, firms are now turning their attention to qualitative measures such as the number of customer complaints or the number of machine setups. In a one- to two-page paper, identify three standards that might be used in a manufacturing environment and three standards that might be used in a service environment that cannot be readily quantifiable in dollars. Discuss how each of those standards would be measured, as well as how variances from those standards would be measured.

THE DEBATE

• *When Might a Favorable Variance Turn "Bad"?*

Consider the labor efficiency variance. As you now understand after working through this chapter, a labor efficiency variance occurs when the hours actually used are more or less than the standard hours allowed based on actual production output. Assume that a team of internal auditors was able to complete a particular auditing project in one of the company's divisions in fewer hours than originally expected. Does this team have a favorable labor efficiency variance? More importantly, assuming there is a favorable labor efficiency variance, is this a good or a bad thing?

Divide your group into two teams and prepare a two-minute defense of your team's assigned position.

- One team represents "Favorable labor efficiency variance—GOOD!" Answer the following questions in your discussion. (1) Is measuring the difference between auditing hours *originally* budgeted and the actual hours used the proper way to measure a labor efficiency variance? (2) Your team should take the position that favorable labor efficiencies are a *good* result in this operation. What positive aspects concerning the audit team's work are indicated by a favorable labor efficiency variance?
- The other team represents "Favorable labor efficiency variance—BAD!" Answer the following in your discussion. (1) Respond to Team 1's report on whether measuring the difference between auditing hours *originally* budgeted and the actual hours used is the proper way to measure a labor efficiency variance. If you disagree, provide a correct response. (2) Your team should take the position that favorable labor efficiencies may *not* be a good result in this operation. What negative aspects concerning the audit team's work could be indicated by a favorable labor efficiency variance?

INTERNET SEARCH

• Motivating Employees to Be More Productive

In addition to evaluating employees, as was discussed in this chapter, it is also important to motivate employees and managers by providing appropriate incentives. Many companies provide consulting services to organizations to help them create winning incentives for their employees. For an example of the kinds of services that are offered and some examples of incentives that seemed to work, go to **http://www.goalmanager.com**. Sometimes Web addresses change, so if this address does not work, access the Web site for this textbook (**http://albrecht.swcollege.com**) for an updated link. Once you've gained access to the site, look over some of the success stories and answer the following questions:

1. Describe one employee motivation success story described at this Web site.
2. What was the key to motivating employees in that organization?

comprehensive problem 8–9

C-V-P Analysis, Variance Analysis, and Budgeting

Gonzales Company makes compact discs, which it sells to music companies. The following data are available for the company:

Expected sales in units:	
January	1,200 discs
February	1,400 discs
March	1,800 discs
Selling price	$10.00 per disc
Beginning accounts receivable balance, January 1	$4,000.00
Desired finished goods inventory, March 31	380 discs
Beginning finished goods inventory, January 1	300 discs*
Beginning direct materials inventory, January 1	400 ounces*
Desired direct materials inventory, March 31	600 ounces
Standard direct materials needed per disc	4 ounces
Standard direct labor time per finished product	10 minutes
Standard direct materials cost per ounce	$0.50
Standard direct labor cost per hour	$18.00

*The beginning inventory numbers for January were based on the best estimate of January sales in December. The expectations changed in January, and the new expected sales numbers should be used to estimate beginning inventory on hand for February and March.

Additional information:

- Of a month's sales, 60% is collected by month-end; the remaining 40% is collected the following month.
- The desired finished goods inventory each month is 20% of the next month's sales.
- The desired direct materials inventory every month is 10% of next month's production needs.

Required:

1. Using the standard costs for making the discs, prepare the following:
   a. Sales forecasts for January, February, and March (in dollars).
   b. Cash collections budgets for January, February, and March (in dollars). Assume that all sales are on credit.
   c. Production budgets for January, February, and March (in units).
   d. Direct materials usage budgets for January, February, and March (in ounces).
   e. Direct materials purchases budgets for January, February, and March (in ounces).
   f. Direct labor budgets for January, February, and March (in dollars).
2. Assume that actual usage of direct materials to make the discs was 4½ ounces at a cost of $0.60 per ounce. Compute the materials price and quantity variances for each month.
3. Assume that actual labor costs to make the discs were 12 minutes of labor at a cost of $19 per hour. Compute labor rate and efficiency variances for each month.
4. Assuming again that Gonzales is able to make the discs at the standard costs, how much will profits increase if it raises its price to $12 per disc in January, February, and March? Assume total fixed costs of $5,000 per month.
5. Assuming again that Gonzales is able to make the discs at its standard costs, if sales decrease by 300 discs during the three months at the increased price of $12 per disc, should Gonzales raise its price?

Continuous Improvement in Management Accounting

chapter **m10**

learning objectives After studying this chapter, you should be able to:

1. Explain the fundamentals of building a Balanced Scorecard.
2. Anticipate that both management accounting and financial accounting are poised for important changes.

setting the stage

It has been said, "knowledge is power!" The ability to compete effectively in the economy has always been a function of the knowledge and abilities that a company can pull together and emphasize in the process of creating new products, making good decisions, and implementing effective processes. Throughout this text, we have generally classified organizations as manufacturers, merchandisers, or service providers. However, in this new age, more and more successful companies really can't be classified in one of these three categories. We've often used **MICROSOFT** as an example company in this textbook. What kind of company is Microsoft? Does this company manufacture products? Does it distribute merchandise? Does it sell services? Actually, Microsoft does all three things, but that still doesn't adequately describe this company. Microsoft is one of the key citizens in what might be called a "New Economy" that runs more on intangible assets, such as intellectual property, than tangibles such as plants, equipment, and distribution channels. A lot of these New Economy companies have comparatively little in tangible assets, and yet they are obviously considered to be very valuable by the stock market. What this tells you is that traditional accounting models aren't capturing the value. Accounting, in other words, no longer delivers accountability.

Knowledge assets are very expensive both to acquire and to develop. And they're extremely difficult to manage. When a drug passes its clinical tests, huge value is created—but there's no transaction. Nothing changes hands. Nobody buys anything, and nobody sells anything. As a result, accounting, by tradition, does not measure or report this kind of information to managers (or investors). When software passes a beta-test, it suddenly becomes valuable—but there's no transaction, so there's no reporting. Or think about how value is destroyed: when a big, old company is late in figuring out how to enter the world of e-commerce, huge value is destroyed—but there's no transaction, and the company continues to be reported by accountants to its managers as doing well. Traditional measures of performance may ignore intangible corporate capabilities that can often lead to higher long-term returns than plant and equipment assets. In short, technology has created far more data than ever before. But what we all need—and what accounting now needs to work on—is the transformation of data into valuable information and knowledge.

For example, Bill Gates and Microsoft are continually hiring many of the world's smartest scientists and creating a giant research laboratory. Their goal is to control the future of computing. In the process, the value of Microsoft as a company rises and falls based on progress and problems in its (research and development) process. For example, a conflict is currently raging at Microsoft regarding its flagship Windows™ product and a rising new software called ".Net"—a technology that can link thousands of Web sites together in an Internet-style bucket brigade. This new software promises that one mouse click will have the wallop of dozens of steps on the Web today. Putting an accurate value on the Windows technology at Microsoft is difficult, but no one can question that much of the market value of Microsoft, one of the most important companies in the world today, is based on Windows—a proprietary technology that Microsoft guards with the ferocity of a rottweiler. However, .Net technology may be the biggest threat to the future of Windows that Microsoft has ever seen. And ironically, .Net is Microsoft's own technology. So far, about 4,000 of Microsoft's 40,000 employees are working exclusively on .Net. By the end of 2001, Bill Gates expects that virtually all of the company will be focused on creating new .Net products or updating old products with the new technology. In fact, Gates is committing half of Microsoft's current $4 billion budget to .Net breakthroughs. Not everyone at Microsoft, though, is committed to the vision of .Net. In fact, many key executives and scientists, including Bill Gates himself, have worried that .Net could totally undercut the value of Windows in the marketplace long before Microsoft is actually able to sell .Net products and technology to the world. The result of such a scenario could be significant reductions in Microsoft's revenues. On this argument, some key employees have even left Microsoft to join or start other companies that would directly compete with their former employer.

In the midst of all this effort and diverging opinions, the economic value of Microsoft is changing, though traditional accounting has no effective way of measuring or helping to manage these very real changes in the company's critical intangible assets. Only the future will reveal how Microsoft's bottom line will be affected by the efforts of its research teams and the strategic decisions of its executives. One thing is certain, however, traditional performance evaluation systems don't consider these kinds of changes.

Sources: A. Webber, "New Math for a New Economy," *Fast Company* (January–February 2000); J. Greene, "Microsoft's Big Bet," *Business Week* (October 30, 2000).

Competitive pressures in the marketplace require that companies continually look for ways to improve their information systems in order to obtain better insights into how to operate their businesses more effectively and more efficiently. Management accounting, being at the core of business information systems, is always evolving. Managers want management accounting information that supports the strategy of the company. They do not want the information limited to financial measures of performance only. Quality and time measures of performance in customer service (e.g., timely deliveries), internal business processes (e.g., production defects), and growth in the organization (e.g., employee education levels) are becoming more important all the time. As a result, we are at the intersection of new directions in accounting. It's time we take a brief look at the future of management accounting.

You are now in the last chapter of this textbook. You've spent a lot of time studying many details concerning the process of creating and using accounting to add value to an organization. We've established that the management process involves planning, controlling, and evaluating business activities in order to compete well on issues involving cost, quality, and time. We've also discussed managing these concerns across three different types of firms: manufacturing, merchandising, and service. It should be clear to you now that the accountant must customize a great variety of information sources to fit the specific strategic and operating needs of decision makers. Perhaps you're feeling a bit overwhelmed. Of all the information that is possible (and we've presented in this text only a subset of a growing list of possibilities), what information is best for a particular company? Does a model exist that helps accountants and managers identify specific performance measures critical to surviving and thriving in the fast-paced, highly competitive, worldwide economy of the twenty-first century? More importantly, how does management accounting continue to improve performance measures in pace with innovations in products and processes and changes in markets and competition? Actually, there's been a lot of discussion recently among managers and management accountants on this very question. One approach to answering this question is gaining attention in many companies. The approach is called the "Balanced Scorecard," and no education on management accounting is really complete without some awareness of this approach. We'll spend most of this chapter illustrating this new performance measurement model and how it could affect the nature of both management accounting and financial accounting.[1]

LET'S TAKE A FLIGHT!

Imagine that a friend of yours is getting her airplane pilot's license and has invited you to sit in the passenger seat of the airplane during her next pilot's lesson. Your friend has not been taking flying lessons very long. However, as you listen to her enthusiastic description of past lessons as the two of you drive out to the airfield the next afternoon, you begin to really look forward to the experience. After parking the car and walking to the Cessna plane that waits on the tar-

1 The Balanced Scorecard Model was first presented in a series of articles in the *Harvard Business Review* by Robert S. Kaplan and David P. Norton: "The Balanced Scorecard—Measures That Drive Performance" (January–February 1992); "Putting the Balanced Scorecard to Work" (September–October 1993); "Using the Balanced Scorecard as a Strategic Management System" (January–February 1996). The most complete discussion on this theory is found in Kaplan and Norton's *The Balanced Scorecard: Translating Strategy into Action* (Boston, MA: Harvard Business School Press, 1996) and *The Strategy-Focused Organization: How Balanced Scorecard Companies Thrive in the New Business Environment* (Boston, MA: Harvard Business School Press, 2001).

mac, your friend introduces you to the flight instructor, and the three of you climb into the plane. Soon after you take your seat and buckle the seatbelt, your friend revs the engine and the small plane surges forward. The instructor is sitting next to your friend, providing advice and guidance as the plane taxis down the runway gathering speed for takeoff. Suddenly, as you peer over the shoulders of the instructor and your friend in front of you, you notice with some concern that the small plane's instrument panel is noticeably bare of the assortment of instruments, dials, gauges, and controls that are typically part of an airplane's cockpit. In fact, there appears to be only one gauge on the whole panel. Trying to make your question sound casual, you ask about the barren panel and the sole gauge. The instructor looks back over his shoulder to tell you that the gauge measures airspeed. The plane is nearing the end of the runway and is just about to lift off. After swallowing once or twice, you brave more questions about direction, altitude, fuel, temperature, and thrust. Aren't these items also important in flying a plane? Don't most planes have gauges to provide feedback to the pilot on details other than simply airspeed? The instructor agrees but indicates that your friend is currently concentrating on airspeed in her flying lessons. Once she excels at managing airspeed, perhaps the airspeed gauge will be switched for an altimeter, and she can then concentrate on managing altitude. The instructor tells you that he feels it's important to not make the pilot concentrate on too many things at the same time. You notice that your friend is concentrating very hard on the airspeed gauge as the plane noses up and lifts off from the ground. You swallow hard and tighten your seatbelt until it is very snug around your waist. For some reason, you're suddenly imagining about a hundred others places you'd rather be than sitting in this plane.

Flying an airplane is a complicated process. To do it successfully requires that the pilot process a lot of information about various performance aspects of both the equipment and the environment. Managing a company is certainly no less complicated. A lot has to happen at once in order for a company to perform well in its competitive environment as the demands of products, customers, and regulatory agencies change constantly. One of a management accountant's most important functions is to identify and implement **performance measures** that are focused on key strategic and operating plans established by management. These performance measures then become the primary means of controlling and evaluating business processes in the organization. What is the best performance measure for an accountant to provide for an organization? Frankly, there is no one best performance measure.

performance measures A general term used to describe all measures designed to capture information about performance related to a particular activity or process.

THE BALANCED SCORECARD

1

Explain the fundamentals of building a Balanced Scorecard.

Previous chapters and sections in this textbook have typically focused on subsets of management accounting issues such as merchandising, cost measurement, or the evaluating process. However, in this chapter we are not going to focus the discussion on any particular type of firm, strategic imperative, or management process. Instead, we present a *framework* that a management accountant can use to work with any of these issues. That framework is the Balanced Scorecard.

The **Balanced Scorecard** is an approach to integrating performance measures in order to support directly the strategy an organization is trying to establish and follow. At first glance, this may not seem like a very new idea. Shouldn't all performance measures support the organization's strategy? Hasn't management accounting always been focused on supporting managers' and executives' efforts to create a profitable company? Actually, although the purpose of management accounting is to establish performance measures that add value to the organization, too often these measures have been limited to periodic reports composed solely of financial measures. Advances in computer systems technology today allow more information, more variety in information, and more timely information to be created and reported than ever before. The existence of better information capabilities provides an opportunity for accountants, working in conjunction with system technologists and organization executives, to significantly expand the definition of management accounting. As you study this chapter, you need to understand that the Balanced Scorecard is really a guiding theory of management, rather than an exact formula or blueprint that can be automatically implemented in any organization to improve its management processes. Once created, each organization's own Balanced Scorecard is a direct view

Balanced Scorecard A new management model designed to link together performance measures for financial, customer, internal process, and learning/growth perspectives that are unique to an organization's particular strategy.

of its strategy, its plans, and its management processes. The idea that a Balanced Scorecard is extremely personal for each organization is captured in the following comment made by an executive as his division completed work on its first Balanced Scorecard:

> In the past, if you had lost my strategic planning document on an airplane and a competitor found it, I would have been angry, but I would have gotten over it. In reality, it wouldn't have been that big a loss. Or if I had left my monthly operating review somewhere and a competitor obtained a copy, I would have been upset, but, again, it wouldn't have been that big a deal. This Balanced Scorecard, however, communicates my strategy so well that a competitor seeing this would be able to block the strategy and cause it to become ineffective.[2]

Hence, there is no such thing as a *standard* Balanced Scorecard that any organization can use to operate successfully in its environment. Therefore, as we use example performance measures throughout the chapter to describe the Balanced Scorecard theory, you should remember that each organization must design its own performance measures that support its own particular strategy.

Adding Value with Performance Measures

Think back on the last nine chapters involving management accounting and all the various performance measures we've studied involving cost, quality, and time. You should recognize that there are a number of problems associated with the performance evaluation methods currently used in many organizations. Some individuals argue that current performance measurement systems even encourage waste, inefficiency, and poor quality. For example, a measure that emphasizes purchase price may encourage the purchasing department to increase the purchase quantity to get a lower price but might ignore quality and speed of delivery. The results may be excess inventory, increased storage and other carrying costs, and failure to use suppliers with the best quality and service.

Another example may be allocating overhead costs based on direct labor hours. Direct labor may be a fixed cost that is small in relation to manufacturing overhead items, which are becoming more significant for many companies. The result of any overemphasis on direct labor as a mechanism for managing overhead costs may be missed opportunities for cost control since major overhead activities are not directly exposed to the management process of planning, controlling, and evaluating.

If machine utilization is the performance measure being emphasized, a supervisor may run a machine in excess of daily production requirements to maximize the performance measure. This may result in excess inventory or production that is not needed. Similarly, if only the number of units produced is the performance measure, poor-quality goods or inventory that is not desired by customers may be produced. A specific example from the former Soviet Union illustrates this point. Oil drillers, in competition with one another, received recognition and compensation based on the number of meters drilled. The award-winning team recognized by Pravda drilled meter upon meter but never struck oil. It seems that the first 100 meters of drilling do not require as much effort and expense as the second, third, fourth, and so on. The winning team drilled dry hole after dry hole. The depth of these wells never exceeded 100 meters.

Some prominent researchers believe that performance evaluation systems used in the United States are quite ineffective and have contributed to a decline in America's competitiveness. One major problem that these researchers identify with traditional performance evaluation methods is the limited focus of these methods. To be specific, they argue that current evaluation methods, which mostly focus on financial returns, are not designed to cope with such intangible corporate capabilities as an excellent work force, research and development, and information assets. They argue that we have moved from a manufacturing society to an information society and that performance evaluation systems have not kept pace. This argument certainly seems to have merit when considering the competitive position of MICROSOFT described at the beginning of this chapter. Are Mi-

2 R. S. Kaplan and D. P. Norton, *The Balanced Scorecard: Translating Strategy into Action* (Boston, MA: Harvard Business School Press, 1996), p. 148.

crosoft's real assets appropriately displayed on a balance sheet that focuses on inventory, equipment, and buildings? Does it make sense to evaluate performance at Microsoft based on controlling costs of materials, labor, and manufacturing overhead? Microsoft, like many other companies, needs a performance measurement system that is customized to fit its particular strategy.

Every company ultimately must perform well financially in order to survive. Even not-for-profit organizations must be able to consistently pay their bills, including payrolls and loans, in order to survive over time. Other companies must consistently show profits, build equity, and provide a return to stockholders. The **DUPONT COMPANY** made a lot of money by carefully tracking financial measures that contributed to consistent ROI and ROE performance. Remember, however, that successful management accounting methods are eventually copied by other organizations. Hence, strictly using ROI to manage an organization does not provide a competitive edge in today's economy. Organizations must continuously improve their management information processes in order to continue to compete. Traditional financial measures are now being vigorously supplemented in three new areas: customer service, internal process improvement, and learning and growth throughout the organization.

leading measures Measures that, if successfully implemented, will support desired performance in other business activities. Note that some leading measures can also serve as outcome measures.

outcome measures Measures of desired outcome performance in activities critical to an organization's strategic goals. Note that some outcome measures are also leading measures to support desired performance in other business activities.

Customers

The first key to strong financial performance is customer satisfaction. When companies understand what their customers value and what services and products they are willing to pay for, then these companies can design customer-focused performance measures that lead to growth in market share, increased revenues, and long-term profits. There are two types of customer performance measures: leading measures and outcome measures. **Leading measures** focus on fulfilling customer expectations regarding cost, quality, and time factors. **Outcome measures** determine if the improvements in leading measures result in more satisfied, loyal customers. Therefore, it is important that there be a clear link between the company's efforts to provide low-cost, high-quality, timely products and services and customer response to these efforts as demonstrated by increased market share and customer profitability (i.e., the company is able to earn sufficient profits by serving its customers). Exhibit 10-1 provides measures of customer-focused performance.

exhibit 10-1 Performance Measures of Customer Satisfaction

Leading Performance Measures

Cost	Quality	Time: Reliable Delivery	Time: Fastest Delivery
• Purchase cost to customer • Delivery cost to customer • Setup cost to customer • Maintenance and repair cost to customer	• Returns by customers • Quality rankings by other agencies • Customer survey response	• Percentage of on-time deliveries • Number of production interruptions	• Average response time for service call • Time to complete contract • Production cycle time

Outcome Performance Measures

Customer Retention Rates	Customer Acquisition Rates	Market Share
• Retention rates • Number of defecting customers • Costs to retain customers	• Acquisition rates • Number of new customers • Costs to recruit customers	• Percent of total number of customers • Percent of total dollars spent by customers • Percent of total units sold to customers

business environment essay

Volant, Inc. Hank Kashiwa (a 1975 Olympic skier) and his brother Bucky (who holds a Ph.D. in fluid mechanics) decided to combine their expertise and create VOLANT, INC., a ski manufacturing company. The Kashiwas wanted to manufacture a revolutionary product—skis made from steel. Steel would resist lateral twisting in the pressure of a ski turn and give the skis a tighter grip on the snow, as well as decrease production costs. This design quickly became popular among skiers; however, the company's production problems were clouding its success.

That is when Volant, Inc., turned to Mark Soderberg, a former BOEING employee who was very familiar with the manufacturing process. As Soderberg walked into Volant's factory for the first time, the immense inventory piles and the excessive product scrapping shocked him. Soderberg decided the best way to begin the company makeover was to stop the daily production problems by shutting down the factory for a few weeks.

Soderberg involved the entire company as he created problem-solving and process-analysis teams to generate ideas and strategies. During some of the brainstorming sessions, he encouraged everyone to throw out any and every idea; as an incentive, he

LEADING MEASURES OF CUSTOMER SATISFACTION We have discussed cost, quality, and time measures throughout the last nine chapters of this textbook. Naturally, most customers desire low-cost products and services. However, customer satisfaction is the result of the right combination of cost, quality, and time. As customers, we are willing to balance our demands for these three objectives. For example, when you mail a package across the nation, you are probably very comfortable making a trade-off decision. The U.S. POSTAL SERVICE, like other package delivery companies, provides various delivery schedules (overnight, two days, three to five days), as well as some options regarding quality of service (contents insurance and registered delivery); each mailing option carries an appropriate price.

Most companies have spent a great deal of effort understanding how their customers perceive value in terms of timeliness, quality, and price. For many companies, customers are more concerned with reliability than with the fastest delivery. This is particularly true in a JIT environment. TOYOTA demands deliveries from its suppliers to assembly plants within a one-hour time window. Early arrivals of parts are as unacceptable as late deliveries. Hence, observers have sometimes witnessed delivery trucks driving around and around a Toyota assembly plant until it is time to deliver their goods. If you think about it, this is not really strange behavior. Have you ever scheduled a telephone repairperson to come to your home during the day? Your definition of "on time" is probably not sometime between 9:00 A.M. and 3:00 P.M., is it? Further, given a 1:00 P.M. appointment, you probably would not be particularly pleased at the repairperson's effort to "delight the customer" by arriving two hours early. Performance measures regarding reliability versus fastest delivery of goods or services depend on both the strategy of the company and the demands of its customers. A few examples of these types of measures are provided in Exhibit 10-1. You can look back at Exhibit 7-10 on page 376 in Chapter 7 of management accounting for more examples of time-based performance measures.

As you remember from Chapter 7, total quality management (TQM) has been firmly rooted in the United States since the 1980s. Commitment to quality is now generally assumed for most products and services—it is a competitive necessity. Companies not committed to the total quality effort will typically struggle to survive. Hence, organizations must pay careful attention to what quality factors are important to their customers and then build measures that accurately track performance of these quality factors.

As mentioned earlier, customers compare timeliness and quality factors with price to evaluate the real value of a product or service. Many companies realize, however, that the purchase

would hand out $100 bills to the participating employees.

Through Soderberg's strategic framework and involvement of company employees, Volant, Inc., began witnessing major quality improvements along with decreasing costs. In addition, the manufacturing process was eased through a simple design change in the skis. Volant's output quickened and the company started making on-time deliveries. The inventory piles, the poor-quality cycles, and delivery problems that plagued the business were eliminated. For the first time in Volant's history, the company finished its preseason shipments ahead of schedule.

The Kashiwa brothers had a great business idea, but the company lacked a good planning, controlling, and evaluating system. Soderberg says that, "it was just the basics of manufacturing" that helped turn this ski company around. It is the combination of these company basics, strategies, and visions that creates a customized performance measurement system that enhances operations management and creates a competitive advantage.

Source: Thomas Petzinger Jr., "The Front Lines," *The Wall Street Journal* (October 3, 1997), p. B1.

life cycle costing The process of measuring all costs involved in creating, producing, and using a product or service. Life cycle costing is not limited to costs incurred by the organization measuring these costs but also includes all costs incurred by the suppliers and the customers of the product or service.

price of their product often does not represent the total cost to their customer. If you own a car, you may be painfully aware of this fact. The purchase price of your car is only part of its total cost. Maintenance, repairs, gas mileage, and insurance also combine with the original purchase price to determine the total cost of owning your car. Perhaps you wish you had spent a little more (or less) when purchasing your car in order to better balance the subsequent costs of owning your car. In an effort to account for costs that are an essential part of the total value of a product, some firms are turning to a concept known as life cycle costing. Essentially, **life cycle costing** is a method of costing that focuses on all costs that will be incurred throughout the entire life of a product. The life cycle approach to costing helps to ensure that no costs are omitted when evaluating performance and value. Hence, when evaluating customer satisfaction, an

When you buy a car the purchase price represents only part of the total cost of car ownership. You must also consider such costs as maintenance, repairs, and gas. In an effort to account for all costs incurred throughout the entire life of a product, some companies use life cycle costing.

organization also needs to measure performance of its product or service in terms of *all* its costs for its customers. These cost measures are listed in Exhibit 10-1.

market share The percentage share one company receives of the total sales revenue in the economy for a particular product or service.

OUTCOME MEASURES OF CUSTOMER SATISFACTION An organization's focus on customers must be twofold. First, the company works to measure up to customer expectations regarding cost, quality, and time. Then the company must determine if its efforts are being rewarded with increased market share and customer profitability. **Market share** is the proportion of industry sales of a particular product or service that is controlled by a specific firm. Companies increase their market share in two ways: retaining current customers and acquiring new customers. Clearly, companies that cannot service their current customers better than competitors will be hard-pressed to maintain market share. Absolute customer satisfaction is key in this regard. Interestingly, when management accountants ignore expected future cash flows over a customer's life, they miss reporting the real cost (the opportunity cost) of losing customers. Exhibit 10-2 shows how much profit a customer generates over time in four different industries. As you can see, customer profitability over time really takes off *if* the company can retain its customers' loyalty. This increased profitability over time is the result of increased purchases or higher account balances, reduced operating costs, and profits from referrals. Hence, customer retention rates are very important outcome measures that result from good performance of leading measures related to customers' overall costs, quality of product, and timeliness of delivery.

caution

Research indicates that adequate scores on customer satisfaction surveys are not sufficient to create the kind of loyalty that results in high customer retention rates. Companies that cannot consistently *delight* their customers on the most valued performance factors will lose business.

Source: T. O. Jones and W. E. Sasser, "Why Satisfied Customers Defect," *Harvard Business Review* (November–December 1995), pp. 88–99.

Once the company has established leading measures that result in high customer retention, it can turn its attention to acquiring new customers in order to grow its market share. Obviously, there is a strong relationship between loyal customers who speak enthusiastically about the company's product and the company's ability to win new customers. As a result, many companies identify customer loyalty as the best way to acquire new customers. In addition, companies also spend a great deal of effort and resources recruiting new customers. Hence, tracking performance in customer acquisition is a strategy of growth in market share. It is important to understand that there are many ways to successfully maintain and increase market share through customer retention and acquisition. However, retaining and recruiting customers *profitably* is important to strong financial performance. Hence, companies must track the costs spent recruiting new customers, as well as the costs spent retaining current customers. Using activity-based costing (ABC) to track the costs of activities necessary to recruit and retain customers can provide a company with the necessary information to identify desirable customers and to make important decisions to drop certain unprofitable customers. Management accountants who provide outcome measures of their companies' efforts to profitably grow market share can add competitive value to the management process. These customer outcome measures are listed in Exhibit 10-1.

fyi

On average, credit card companies spend $51 recruiting each new customer. Given the data in Exhibit 10-2, a company must then retain a new customer for about a year and a half in order just to pay back its initial investment in acquiring the customer.

Internal Processes

Management accountants can help their organizations better understand how satisfying customers (using leading performance measures) relates to growth in customer profitabil-

exhibit 10-2 How Much Profit an Average Customer Generates over Time

Industry	Year 1	Year 2	Year 3	Year 4	Year 5
Credit cards	$ 30	$ 42	$ 44	$ 49	$ 55
Industrial laundry	144	166	192	222	256
Industrial distribution	45	99	121	144	168
Auto servicing	25	35	70	88	88

Source: Adapted from F. F. Reichheld and W. E. Sasser, "Zero Defections: Quality Comes to Services," *Harvard Business Review* (September–October 1990), pp. 105–112.

net work

J.D. POWER AND ASSOCIATES, headquartered in Los Angeles, has achieved international recognition for its marketing information and consulting in the areas of consumer opinion and customer satisfaction. You may be familiar with the annual customer satisfaction awards this company provides in the automobile industry. In the last few years, J.D. Power and Associates has branched out into the financial, telecommunications, and travel service industries. Go to its home page at **http://www.jdpower.com** and research the awards for the most recent year. What automotive brand had the highest owner loyalty? What credit card had the highest customer satisfaction? What long-distance telephone company had the highest customer satisfaction? What rental car agency had the highest customer satisfaction?

ity (using outcome measures). The next issue to be resolved is what processes within the organization must take place in order to satisfy the customer completely? Most of your work in the last nine chapters has focused on building performance measures to support the manager's efforts to plan, control, and evaluate processes within the company. However, building performance measures that effectively support the goal of customer satisfaction requires that the management accountant first understand that there are three types of processes that must be in place in order to take care of the customer: innovation processes, operations processes, and service-after-sale processes. Examples of performance measures for management of internal processes are provided in Exhibit 10-3.

INNOVATION PROCESS MEASURES We've talked very little in this textbook about planning, controlling, and evaluating the *innovation process*, which involves identifying new products and services, and then creating and bringing those products to market. The reason for this is that most of the management accounting effort has historically been focused on the operations process, which involves building goods or providing services that already exist. For example, accountants spend a great deal of effort developing budgets of operations, then measuring variances from standard costs of direct materials, direct labor, and manufacturing overhead. However, the innovation process of identifying and creating new products is where much of a company's competitive edge is created. This is why Microsoft spends so much money hiring some of the best minds in the software industry—to ensure that it will continue to create new products that retain and recruit customers. As we move further into the new century, many businesses are spending more in their research, design, and development processes than they do to support their production and operating processes. Microsoft is a great example of this trend. If you look at its income statements for 1998 through 2000, you will see that this company is now spending more money on research and development of new products than it is spending to provide goods and services to its current customers. These data are provided below.

	1998	1999	2000
Cost of sales	$2,460 million	$2,814 million	$3,002 million
Research & development	$2,601 million	$2,970 million	$3,772 million

Admittedly, many companies do not spend the kind of money on the innovation process that Microsoft does. Nevertheless, the resources invested in the innovation process for most companies are significant. It's important to the ultimate financial success of the organization that the critical effort to identify and develop new products and services is effectively managed. At some point, the money invested in the research and development (R&D) effort must provide

exhibit 10-3 Performance Measures of Internal Processes

	Innovation Processes	Operations Processes	Service-after-Sale Processes
Cost measures	• R&D costs per new product • Payback on R&D costs	• Unit-level costs • Batch-level costs • Product line costs	• Costs per service incidence • Costs of replacement parts
Quality measures	• Number of modifications required per design • Percentage of sales from new products	• Defects-per-million opportunities (six sigma) • Errors in customer service	• Customer requests handled on first call • Satisfaction survey responses
Time measures	• Lead time (idea to working model) • Design cycle time	• Lead time (order to delivery) • Production cycle time	• Lead time (request to fulfillment) • Repair cycle time

business environment essay

The Balanced Scorecard—Code Red! The job of managing a hospital is extremely difficult! On the one end, you must deal with doctors who oppose any monetary label on patient care, and on the other end you must make financial decisions that will keep the hospital operational. Some of these decisions can be agonizing, leaving you to wonder where you draw the line. For example, do you make the questionably unethical decision of turning away needy patients because of money? These were the very problems facing Dr. Jon Meliones, chief medical director of **DUKE CHILDREN'S HOSPITAL** in Durham, North Carolina, in the mid-1990s.

The hospital was $11 million in the red. Critical programs were being canceled, the number of patient beds was being reduced, and the quality of patient care was in a miserable state. Dr. Meliones, faced with the disastrous state of the hospital, came across the Balanced Scorecard strategy and instantly decided that applying the principles from the Balanced Scorecard was the solution. Upon learning that the Balanced Scorecard dealt with finance, customer service, learning and growth, and internal processes, Dr. Meliones saw this model as a perfect fit for his hospital. Not only did it deal with the financial administration of running a hospital, but it also took into consideration the very real needs of the patients and doctors who receive and provide the care.

"We wanted everyone—from accountants to physicians to therapists—focusing on a common goal, not individual goals," explained Meliones. "We needed to become a strategy-focused organization if our Balanced Scorecard was to succeed and, in turn, if the hospital was to succeed." The Balanced Scorecard effort at Duke Children's Hospital involved distributing daily "report

financial returns. However, an R&D project can require a very long payback period. Many organizations begin significant R&D projects expecting that financial returns will not be realized for many years. Sometimes basic research is done in organizations with no clear idea of what profitable product or service may eventually result. Occasionally, some of our society's most useful innovations have resulted from these kinds of R&D investments. On the other hand, with this strategy it is possible that a lot of resources and energy will be needlessly spent in the innovation process, which means that the strategic imperatives of cost, quality, and time still apply here. Given the size of the investments made, it is important that organizations develop measures to evaluate the costs of their innovation processes. In addition, organizations should assess the effectiveness (e.g., the quality) of innovation work.

Finally, without proper controls, R&D work is at risk of simply taking too long. You're likely familiar with the old adage that "time is money." Clearly, any project that requires time extensions will cost more to complete. You'll remember from Chapter 6 of management accounting that additional costs due to time overruns will also include increased holding costs. However, in the case of R&D, "time is opportunity!" The market is always moving. Organizations that take longer than their competitors to complete the research and development of new products or services may quickly find themselves seriously disadvantaged in the marketplace. Hence, organizations that manage well their innovation processes will compete well in the marketplace. Performance measures that support the management of the innovation process will typically be custom-built for each organization based on its strategic intent and on the particular nature of its R&D work. Exhibit 10-3 provides examples of cost, quality, and time-based measures for the innovation process.

OPERATIONS PROCESS MEASURES *Operations processes* involve all the activities a customer generally experiences, including receipt of customer order, creation of product, and delivery of product or service. Ever since Francis Cabot Lowell established his cotton mill in Waltham, Massachusetts, in 1814 and created the "Waltham system" of accounting to track manufacturing costs, accountants have focused on adding value to the operations processes by measuring cost, quality, and time performance. In the effort to support operations processes, many valuable accounting methods have been developed. As a result, several of the previous

cards" to all hospital employees to ensure they understood where they stood within the strategic goals of the hospital. These report cards empowered the hospital staff to find creative ways to reduce costs, increase the quality of patient care, and help hospital administrators see more than just the bottom line. For example, physicians received information pertaining to their own patient loads, such as average length of stay and average cost per patient. They could then evaluate the results themselves and determine where to cut costs rather than having to follow a mandate issued by someone in management who doesn't understand the medical issues involved in these kinds of decisions.

Not only did these report cards allow doctors and other medical staff to evaluate where they could cut costs, but it also empowered them to look for other ways to improve quality of care. For example, a chief complaint of patients' parents was not being able to identify their child's primary caregiver. So a secretary decided that as patients were admitted, labels with the names of each one's primary doctor and nurse would be placed on their doors. "Prior to this simple solution, only 42 percent of parents could identify their child's doctor," said Meliones. "But as soon as we began labeling, that number rose to 99 percent. The Balanced Scorecard began turning everyone into a chief strategy officer of some sort."

As a result of the cooperative effort between management and medical staff to implement a Balanced Scorecard, Duke Children's Hospital has gone from $11 million in the red to $4 million in the black, an incredible turnaround!

Source: SAS Institute, Inc., News and Events, "Life in the Balance: Duke Children's Hospital," http://www.sas.com/news/success/dukehosp.html (accessed March 5, 2001).

chapters have focused on helping you understand these methods. Though management accounting for operations processes has been in place for a long time, new methods continue to evolve in an effort to create information that has competitive value.

The concepts of activity-based costing (ABC) and the Hierarchical Production Model (discussed in Chapter 7 of management accounting) represent some of the important cost measures created recently to fulfill competitive needs for organizations. An example of a fairly new quality measure for manufacturing processes that is having an impact in the marketplace is "six sigma quality." One of the famous measures of quality, six sigma quality is now gaining attention as an operations management tool for merchandising and service firms. Sigma[3] is a statistical measure of variation in a product or process and is used in statistical process control (SPC) charts to evaluate upper and lower control limits (see Chapter 7 for a review of SPC charts). Sigma measures also provide insight about probabilities. Specifically, when the incidence of a single error in the product or service process occurs at a distance of six sigma from the target value, then the probability that the process itself has quality problems is very low. To be precise (without getting into all the statistics involved), an operation process is said to have **six sigma quality** when defects in the process are occurring at the low rate of 3.4 defects per million opportunities—now that's a high-quality process! Other measures of cost, quality, and time that have competitive value continue to be developed and refined. Exhibit 10-3 provides some measures that exemplify the continuous improvements we now see in cost, quality, and time measures to support operations processes.

six sigma quality A measure of quality based on statistical analysis. Products or services with six sigma quality have no more than 3.4 defects per million opportunities (e.g., parts or events).

SERVICE-AFTER-SALE PROCESS MEASURES *Service-after-sale processes* are of two types. One type of service-after-sale process involves the billing and collection of payments from customers. The other type involves the organization's commitment to warranty its product, including efforts to repair or replace products and provide post-sale support and guidance in the use of the product. If you've purchased a personal computer lately, you have likely had some experience with technical support to help you resolve a computer problem or simply to figure out how to better use your new computer. Depending on your experience with your computer merchant's technical support (or, for that matter, the post-sale support of any other product or service you've purchased), you

3 Sigma is the Latin symbol for a statistical measure more commonly known as "standard deviation."

fyi

LANDS' END is a garment mail-order merchant that exemplifies the growing trend of excellent service-after-sale to customers. Despite being a very large company (on an average day, close to 300 phone lines handle between 40,000 and 50,000 calls, and during peak seasons, close to 1,100 phone lines handle over 100,000 calls per day), it has established a strong reputation for customer service. Lands' End offers one of the simplest guarantees in the industry—"GUARANTEED. PERIOD.®" This means letting the customer return the product at any time, for any reason. As an example of the extent of its guarantee, customers who need additional buttons, have lost a belt, or need a piece of luggage repaired can receive all these services at any time after purchase, free of charge. Even if a child loses a mitten from Lands' End the same season it was purchased, the "Lost Mitten Club" will replace it at half the price of a pair, and Lands' End will pick up the costs of shipping.

probably have strong positive or negative feelings about the quality and timeliness of the support you received, and about the company itself! Do organizations create a competitive edge when they provide quality, timely post-sale support while controlling the costs of that support? You bet! Is it important to effectively control the process of billing and collecting payments from customers? If you remember our extensive discussion of holding costs in Chapter 6 of management accounting, you know that companies can spend a lot of time and resources creating customer invoices and then following up to ensure prompt collection. Poor management of service-after-sale processes can result in many opportunity costs. Hence, management accountants also pay attention to management of these processes using effective performance measures, some examples of which are provided in Exhibit 10-3.

Learning and Growth

Perhaps the most interesting example of continuous improvement in management accounting is found in the very recent trend for accountants to help management teams better understand the process of building learning and growth within the organization. In order to survive and thrive in this competitive economy, an organization must continue to learn and grow. Or, to be more specific, the organization's employees, system, and structure must learn, grow, and change in order to continuously build and improve internal processes and satisfy customers. Certainly, the demand of customers today is well described by the question, "What have you done for me lately?" Without learning and growth, internal processes stop improving, customers grow restless and defect, and financial performance stagnates. However, many might react rather strongly to the trend to create performance measures on learning and growth by challenging whether this kind of work is really management accounting at all! How does one measure learning and growth? Frankly, it's not a well-developed accounting discipline. However, because development in this area is rather slight, there is much opportunity for management accountants to create significant competitive value for their organizations by working to build good measures. Don't forget the lesson of Donaldson Brown and the DuPont ROI formula. Accountants who are able to provide information useful to plan, control, and evaluate critical business processes, regardless of the initial difficulty of the effort, will add the most value to their organization. By dividing this effort into leading measures and outcome measures (somewhat similar to the effort of managing an organization's work with its customers), the Balanced Scorecard Model suggests some interesting possibilities for measuring performance in the learning and growth effort. Exhibit 10-4 illustrates some example measures that can be used for managing learning and growth performance.

LEADING MEASURES OF LEARNING AND GROWTH The ultimate result of building learning and growth in the organization is based on developing employee productivity. Employee productivity then leads to internal process improvements. Related to employee productivity is employee retention and employee satisfaction. These three issues form the desired outcome measures of learning and growth. Therefore, the organization should track performance in the productivity, retention rates, and satisfaction of its employees. However, managing improvements in these important outcome measures requires that management accountants identify the factors that result in high employee productivity, retention, and satisfaction. These factors form *leading* measures in learning and growth: employee capabilities, information system capabilities, and organizational structure capabilities.

Improvements in employee capabilities should lead to improvements in employee productivity. However, improving employee productivity does not necessarily mean that employees are satisfied with their work situation and are committed to staying with the company. To the extent investments in employee capabilities also lead to higher satisfaction and retention rates among employees, then companies may expect to see positive improvements in internal processes, customer care, and financial performance. Measures here can focus on the level of qualifications and certifications among employees, as well as investments made by the company in employee training and education.

In this information age, the strength of a company's information system structure is critical to employee productivity. To build an excellent organization, employees need relevant, accurate, and timely information on the effects of their efforts to improve processes, satisfy customers, and

Balanced Scorecards are often implemented with the help of an outside consultant. **METRUS GROUP** is an organization whose employees are experts in Balanced Scorecards and performance measurement strategies. Access the Web site at http://www.metrus.com and find "the balanced scorecard process" link, which will allow you to choose another link titled "Assessment." In what ways does the Balanced Scorecard approach open up opportunities for a firm's leaders?

strengthen financial performance within the organization. In addition to information systems, modern technology continues to provide significant opportunities for directly improving various business processes in all kinds of organizations. Performance measures on information systems and other types of technologies can focus on the quality of systems, accessibility to systems, and investments in systems.

Poorly run organizations can quickly damage employee satisfaction, as well as create confusion that limits employee productivity. Factors that define a well-run organization include effective communication; alignment of goals (i.e., everyone understands and is working toward the same goals); integration of team efforts across departments; and clearly defined planning, controlling, and evaluating processes. Measuring performance and capability in organizational structures is likely the most undefined and challenging "next step" for management accountants today. Nevertheless, this is important work. Organizations usually work very hard to create effective communication channels, to obtain buy-in from employees on company goals, to form an environment where people will work together, and to establish good management processes. Surveys of employees' perspectives are one good way to measure performance on the drive to create good organizational structure.

STOP & THINK *Market value* for a company is computed as the number of shares of stock outstanding multiplied by the average price per share. Essentially, market value measures how much money stockholders believe the company is worth. **MICROSOFT**'s stock price at the end of 1999 was $95.63 per share. Based on 5,028,000,000 common shares outstanding at the end of 1999, this works out to a market value of over $480 billion! However, if you look at Microsoft's 1999 balance sheet, you'll see that its net assets (total assets minus total liabilities) are valued at only $28.44 billion. Why the huge difference?

OUTCOME MEASURES OF LEARNING AND GROWTH Examples of leading and outcome measures of learning and growth are provided in Exhibit 10-4. As accountants track these measures, it is critical that good performance

exhibit 10-4 Performance Measures of Learning and Growth

Leading Performance Measures

	Employee Capabilities	Information Systems Capabilities	Organizational Structure Capabilities
Cost measures	• On-site training expense per employee • Off-site education expense per employee	• Total costs invested in computer systems within the organization • Systems R&D expense per total systems expense	• Costs invested in assessing and building new communication structures • Costs invested in activities to align goals within the company
Quality measures	• Number of new certifications or degrees • Percentage of employees participating in education activities	• System capability compared to competitor systems • Percentage of employees with access to personal computer	• Assessment of effective communication • Assessment of effective teamwork • Assessment of goal alignment
Time measures	• Average yearly training or education hours per employee • Time required to complete a training module	• Average life cycle time of personal computers (e.g., how often are machines upgraded?) • Time required to complete a system upgrade	• Amount of time spent in teamwork versus individual work • Average time to disseminate information or to receive employee feedback

Outcome Performance Measures

Employee Retention	Employee Satisfaction	Employee Productivity
• Employee turnover rate • Average employee years with company • Number of female managers • Average age of employees	• Survey of employee satisfaction • Percentage of employees having leadership opportunities • Management positions filled by inside versus outside recruits	• Output per employee • Billable hours per consultant • New ideas or patents per employee • Recognition of employees by customers

business environment essay

A Nose by Any Other Name . . . In 1996, GIVAUDAN ROURE (at that time a division of ROCHE HOLDINGS LTD., a $14 billion Swiss conglomerate) created a product that would go on to win two prestigious 1997 FiFi Awards. Haven't heard of the FiFi Awards? Are you also unfamiliar with Givaudan Roure or Roche Holdings? Don't worry. These are not exactly household names, but they are part of an industry with a very familiar "smell." FiFi Awards are given by the Fragrance Foundation, an international coalition of companies involved in the business of creating and selling perfume. Givaudan Roure is an inconspicuous research firm in Teaneck, New Jersey, whose business is perfumery—the art of blending natural and synthetic scents to make perfume. Givaudan Roure created Michael Jordan Cologne for BIJAN FRAGRANCES, INC. It was this cologne that won the two FiFi Awards—the industry's version of the Oscars: Men's Fragrance Star of the Year and Men's National Advertising Campaign of the Year. Givaudan Roure has had a major impact on the fragrance industry, having created CALVIN KLEIN's Obsession, CHRISTIAN DIOR's Poison, YVES SAINT LAURENT's Opium, CARTIER's So Pretty, ARMANI's Aqua di Gio, and HUGO BOSS's Hugo.

Remember the last time you smelled a perfume or cologne that you thought was really wonderful? Trying to describe the scent to another person is usually quite difficult—it must be experienced to be understood. Constantly inventing new scents to delight the noses of people across the world is a large, but financially rewarding, challenge. In 1999, the fragrance industry reported sales of approximately $8.3 billion in America alone. Givaudan Roure's CEO, Geoffrey Webster, understands that the success of his company is based on a strategy of learning and growth, and he is making significant investments in employee, systems, and organizational capabilities.

Givaudan Roure's main employees are perfumers who work in a perfumery laboratory. However, per-

in employee capabilities, information system capabilities, and organizational structure capabilities results in improvements in employee satisfaction, retention, and productivity. Obviously, then, management accountants can (and should) test the relationship between leading measures and outcome measures by evaluating satisfaction of employees using surveys; reporting on resignation trends within the company; and measuring employees' productivity in terms of volume, quality, and timeliness of output. When investments in employee education programs or improvements in information systems fail to improve employee outcome measures, then management accountants should provide useful information to better manage these critical processes. Otherwise, there is likely to be little improvement in internal processes, customer satisfaction, and (finally) financial performance. Are you getting the sense that linking together all performance measures within the organization may be a critical aspect of developing a Balanced Scorecard? If so, then you are on track with the final concept that we discuss in the next section.

Linking It All Together

So far in this chapter, and, for that matter, throughout this entire textbook, we have been discussing *a lot* of different performance measures! Do management accountants really need to track *all* these data in order to effectively support the management processes within their companies? Clearly, the answer is no. Too much information is often as harmful as too little. Managers and organizations can become overloaded with information. The key is to clearly identify the vision and strategy a company chooses to pursue, and then establish a set of performance measures that supports progress toward specific company goals. Thus far in this chapter, we have learned that a Balanced Scorecard approach recognizes that management of a company requires information on financial, customer, internal process, and learning and growth activities. Further, performance measures of these activities are not limited to financial measures, but should include nonfinancial measures as well (e.g., quality and time-based measures). Perhaps the most important aspect of a Balanced Scorecard approach is that all measures must *link together* to eventually support

fumers are not really scientists; they are artists who look everywhere for the necessary inspiration to design scent compounds called notes. Perfumers must complete a rigorous education that culminates in the ability to identify by smell nearly 3,000 synthetic natural scents. To make the most of these talents, Webster has designed an entire building to foster creativity among all perfumers. An immaculately kept Zen garden occupies the central courtyard in the New Jersey building. The building has a circular layout that is intended to inspire the circular process of fragrance invention. Givaudan Roure employees regularly participate in tasting sessions designed to inspire new combinations of fragrance notes. Edible floral sorbets, such as rose, lavender, and geranium, are some of the featured dishes prepared by the corporate chef. Some perfumers surround themselves with music to stimulate their creative abilities by listening for musical notes that can be replayed as fragrance notes.

In addition, Givaudan Roure is making significant investments in the capabilities of laboratory technologies. One important technological system is called ScentTrek. ScentTrek is used to identify previously undetected scents in nature. Using a clear plastic globe to surround a flower and take constant measures over a 24-hour period, ScentTrek is able to then reproduce natural scents too subtle to be consciously detected by the human nose. ScentTrek has been sent to golf courses, mountain glens, and seaside beaches to capture scents that can evoke for each of us pleasant memories and emotions. ScentTrek has even been used to analyze the wonderful smell of an old leather baseball glove. Using well-trained and inspired perfumers in combination with investments in advanced technologies like ScentTrek, Givaudan Roure is able to savor the sweet smell of success in a very competitive industry.

Source: Lisa Chadderdon, "The Sweet Smell of Success," *Fast Company* (April–May 1998), pp. 144–153.

the ultimate financial goals of a company.[4] Good performances on activities that do not directly or indirectly contribute to the ultimate goals the organization has established are obviously a waste of resources. Nevertheless, pointless investments in non-value-added activities probably occur in many organizations. Distinguishing non-value-added activities from value-added activities and identifying which performance measures successfully contribute to helping the company accomplish its strategic goals are the ideas behind linkages within a Balanced Scorecard.

To illustrate the importance of clearly linking performance measures in a Balanced Scorecard, look at Exhibit 10-5. It should be clear that the ability to achieve a positive ROI (return on investment) or ROE (return on equity) is closely linked to customer outcome measures (customer retention, customer acquisition, and market share). However, a company can increase its market share and still experience declining ROI because the type of customers it is serving, or the way it is serving its customers, does not lead to positive profits for the company. This is the concept of leading versus lagging indicators. **Leading indicators** are measures of performance that, if accomplished, should lead to a desired result. Measures of performance on the desired results are the **lagging indicators**. A company may desire positive ROI. However, the company does not really "manage" ROI directly; instead, it manages performance that *leads* to positive ROI. Hence, it is important that the company has clearly determined that there is a strong relationship between its leading and lagging indicators. In other words, a company may determine that high rates of customer acquisition should lead to improvements in its overall ROI. Nevertheless, if the company actually does acquire a lot of new customers but does not experience improved ROI performance, it likely needs to spend some time better identifying exactly what the real leading indicators are for improved profits in its industry.

leading indicators Measures that indicate the potential success of future business activities. Leading indicators are related to the concept "leading measures."

lagging indicators Measures that indicate the success of past business activities. Lagging indicators are related to the concept "outcome measures."

As you can see in Exhibit 10-5, cause-and-effect relationships between leading and lagging indicators should exist throughout a company's Balanced Scorecard. Customer outcome measures

4 The ultimate goals of an organization do not need to be financial profits in order to apply the Balanced Scorecard Model. For example, not-for-profit organizations (such as governments or charities) will likely emphasize service to constituents or clients as their ultimate strategic goals.

exhibit 10-5 Performance Measurement Linkages in a Balanced Scorecard

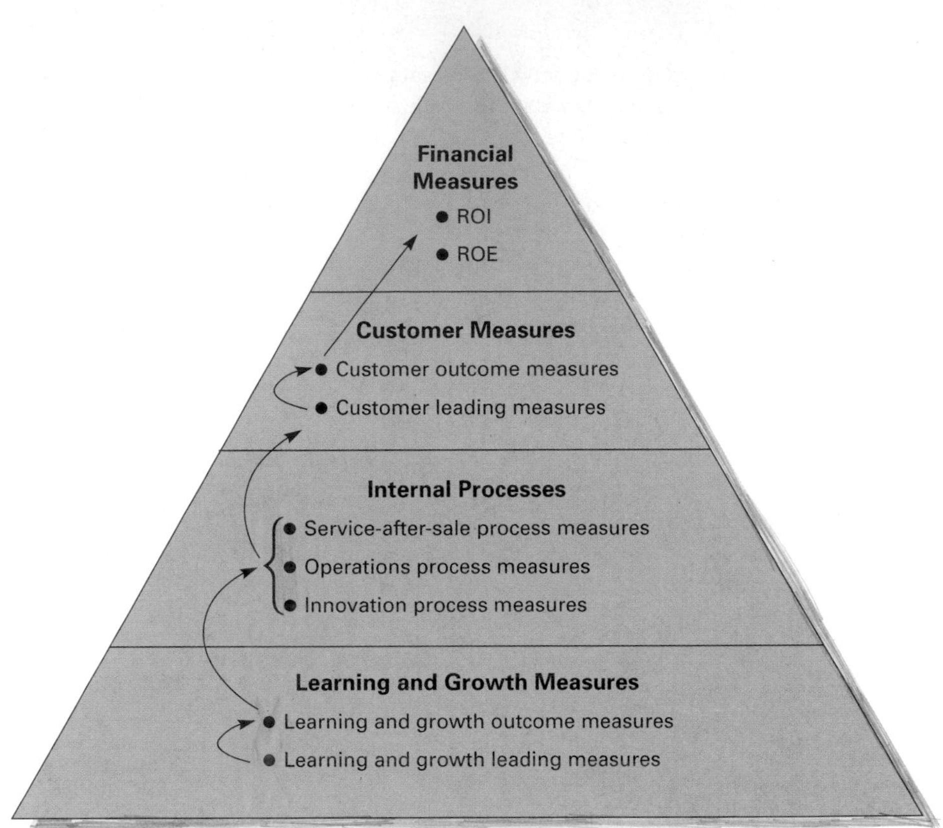

fyi

In Chapter 7 of management accounting, we described the Malcolm Baldrige National Quality Award for companies that have demonstrated excellence in quality management. Since 1988, 43 companies have received the Baldrige Award. However, high quality has not always translated into strong financial performance. Many Baldrige Award winners have struggled financially after winning the award. For example, FEDEX lost $1.5 billion on its European operation, the WALLACE COMPANY declared bankruptcy, and many RITZ-CARLTON hotels have lost money or become insolvent since winning the award. Furthermore, GM, IBM, KODAK, and WESTINGHOUSE each had Baldrige Award-winning divisions, yet each sustained substantial overall corporate losses that led to the replacement of their chairmen. Failure to invest in quality initiatives that translate (i.e., *link*) to desired financial performance may be one reason some Baldrige Award companies have struggled financially.

Source: D. Benson and M. Swain. "A Study of the Impact of TQM on the Financial Performance of Firms," *Academy of Accounting and Financial Studies Journal* (Vol. 3, no. 1, 1999, pp. 145–159).

are leading indicators for financial measures. If the company identifies the cost, quality, and time factors that customers care about, then improved performance in these activities will lead to good outcomes in customer retention, acquisition, and market share. Similarly, effective innovation, operations, and service-after-sale processes should lead to improved performance in customer leading measures. Continuous improvements in these internal processes are then linked to learning and growth outcome measures (i.e., employee retention, satisfaction, and productivity), which are linked to investments in leading measures of employee, information systems, and organizational structure capabilities. Exhibit 10-5 illustrates that most performance measures serve as both leading and lagging indicators. When an accountant builds a performance measurement system based on this perspective, it should be clear that financial performance is no more important than performance related to internal processes or learning and growth effort. This is the concept of "balance" in a Balanced Scorecard.

To illustrate this idea of linkages, suppose that a company has identified that repeat and expanded sales to current customers (e.g., the result of customer retention) is the most important factor leading to improved ROI. Next, customer loyalty is assured by continuous improvement in product design, coupled with short lead times on customer orders. Finally, improving the process of product design and delivery requires committed and well-educated employees working with state-of-the-art computer systems in an organization with clear communication channels. These cause-and-effect relationships form the company's strategy. By building a Balanced Scorecard that focuses on this particular set of performance measures, a management accountant is able to clearly support the company strategy. Accountants do not *traditionally* perform this kind of work. However, according to a survey, 80 percent of large American companies want to change their performance measurement systems to better support competitive company strategies.[5]

5 B. Birchard, "Making It Count," *CFO* (October 1995), pp. 42–48.

Traditional financial measures such as net income or ROI are really "after the fact." The fact that a company is reporting either positive or negative profits is the result of *past* performance with customers, internal processes, and learning and growth efforts. Can an ROI measure be used to predict future performance? As illustrated in Exhibit 10-5, financial measures are the ultimate lagging indicators of a successful strategy. Managing an organization's strategy requires insight on leading performance measures. What we see from this reality is that the Balanced Scorecard is really a management system. Management accountants who want to add value to the organization must build and support effective management systems.

An Example Scorecard

Exhibit 10-6 shows the Balanced Scorecard for a small company (between 100 and 1,000 employees) in the biotechnology industry. This scorecard is in an ever-constant state of evaluation

exhibit 10-6 Sample Balanced Scorecard

Scorecard for a Biotechnology Firm

Strategic Goals	**Performance Measures**
Financial Perspective	
• Growth	• Percent increase in revenue of top line products
• Profitability	• Return on equity; earnings per share
• Industry leadership	• Market share
Customer Perspective	
Outcome:	
• New products	• Percent of sales from new products
• Early purchase of seasonal products	• Percent of sales recorded by early purchase date
Leading:	
• Early payment	• Percent of customers who pay early
• Product quality	• Product performance vs. industry quality standards
• Customer satisfaction	• Customer satisfaction surveys
Internal Processes Perspective	
Service-after-sale:	
• Accurate invoices	• Percent of error-free invoices
Operations:	
• Low-cost producer	• Unit cost vs. competitors
• Reduce inventory	• Inventory as percent of sales
Innovation:	
• New products	• Number of actual introductions vs. target
• New active ingredients	• Number of new ingredients identified by research program
• Proprietary positions	• Number of patents that create exclusive marketing rights
Learning and Growth Perspective	
Outcome:	
• Employee retention	• Average employee years with company
• Employee satisfaction	• Employee satisfaction surveys
Leading:	
• Employee capabilities	• Training costs invested per employee; percent of employees participating annually in training
• Organizational structure capabilities	• Average weekly hours in teamwork settings; survey of effective teamwork

Source: Adapted from C. W. Chow, K. M. Haddad, and J. E. Williamson, "Applying the Balanced Scorecard to Small Companies," *Management Accounting* (August 1997), Institute of Management Accountants, Montvale, NJ, pp. 21–27.

business environment essay

Citibank's Balanced Scorecard CITIBANK PRIVATE BANK, one of the largest private banks in the world, realizes that a Balanced Scorecard of performance measurements is a necessity for success. Recently, Citibank has achieved revenue growth of 20 percent each year partly due to its focus on its Balanced Scorecard.

The company's Balanced Scorecard includes five components, one of which is Strategic Cost Management (SCM). The overall goal of SCM is to improve efficiency and cut costs while maintaining a high-quality service. This strategy was implemented after noticing that downsizing and one-time cost cuts do not help companies maintain permanent low costs. Therefore, Citibank's SCM is designed to be a continuous cost-management process that encourages reinvesting the saved money into the company to sustain growth.

and redesign as the company works to better understand the right strategy and the right performance measures to use in implementing its strategy to succeed in its particular market. Take a moment to examine this scorecard. Can you recognize the factors this company has identified as important to its strategy? Can you identify linkages between its measures?

The financial goals and measures are rather generic for this firm. The majority of companies in most industries are working to build return on equity, earnings per share, and market share. However, this biotechnology company has determined that it needs to be particularly aggressive in revenue growth in its top line (i.e., best selling) products.

The customer goals are divided into leading and outcome measures. The company has linked early customer payment, product performance, and customer satisfaction as important to its percent of sales from new products and percent of sales taking place early in the buying season. Further, growth in new products should provide future top line products. Getting customers to buy early in the season also seems to be important to building market share and profitability.

Innovation is likely the most important factor in internal processes for a research-intensive firm (such as in the biotechnology industry). Accordingly, you can see that there are a number of measures encouraging successful efforts in innovation processes, which should support customer and financial goals for this company. Additionally, this firm also emphasizes keeping product costs and inventory levels low in order to further support the effort to improve return on equity and earnings per share. Finally, providing accurate invoices should encourage customers to pay early.

At the foundation of this company's business are its investments in learning and growth. It is making substantial investments in training and desires to continually train as many employees as possible. In addition, it is also focusing on teamwork efforts. The expectation is that these leading measures of learning and growth will link to improved employee retention and satisfaction, as well as support internal processes and customer service.

As you consider this scorecard, you may feel that some measures and linkages among measures may be missing. You may be right! Nevertheless, in contrast to being solely focused on short-term financial performance, the management accountants in this company are on their way to creating a performance measurement system that truly incorporates the entire strategy of their company. Studying this scorecard should make it clear to you that good performance measures can capture a unique strategy for a specific firm.

There Is No "Quick Approach"

The Balanced Scorecard approach to performance measurement recognizes that every organization is unique. Hopefully, this textbook has made it clear for you that a manufacturing com-

Citibank collects its cost structure improvement ideas from all branches of the company, both formally and informally. These improvement ideas have been as simple as reducing copying costs by using both sides of paper to complex strategies such as creating a predictive model for filtering loan-application data.

Citibank's management and internal consultants actively support and manage SCM. In 1999, for example, this strategy reduced Citibank's annualized expenses by $2 billion and has enabled the bank to grow globally. Citibank now has offices in more than 90 countries. Its future growth looks great—as long as Citibank maintains its Balanced Scorecard objectives.

Sources: William A. Brindley and Michael J. Bear, "The Citibank Private Bank's Portfolio Balancing Act," *The Journal of Business Strategy* (July–August 1997), pp. 12–17; Citigroup press release, January 18, 2000, http://www.citigroup.com.

pany will not manage itself the same as a merchandising or service company. Further, even companies competing within the same industry will each have different sets of goals, objectives, and strategies to attain a specific mission. The process of building a Balanced Scorecard takes time and effort. The management accountant must have a clear knowledge of both financial and management accounting concepts. Then the organization's specific strategy must be clearly and specifically defined in terms of cause-and-effect relationships (i.e., linkages) for its particular industry. What cost, quality, and time issues are important to compete successfully within a particular market? An organization cannot expect to be financially rewarded for world-class performance in response time to customer repair requests unless that type of response time is truly valued by its customers. Finally, measures must be developed, tested, and implemented into clear reporting systems that support effective planning, controlling, and evaluating procedures.

Management accountants can easily build elegant looking but irrelevant performance measurement systems. There are examples of this in far too many organizations. The best example of this bad situation is when accounting is determined to be a non-value-added activity in an organization, and managers simply ignore accounting data as they work on their own to build the company. One of the authors of this textbook is reminded of an experience of having dinner with a plant manager who had established his plant as the most successful division within the company. When asked how the plant controller's work figured into the division's successful implementation of cutting-edge management principles such as JIT and TQM, the plant manager smiled grimly and indicated that the controller really had only two jobs in the organization. First, the controller was responsible for handling all requests from the external auditors. Second, the controller was simply to "stay out of his way!" He felt that the controller (the chief accountant in the organization) provided no information useful to him in his efforts to implement and execute strategy. Clearly, both the controller and the plant manager were missing important opportunities. The division was making significant investments in its accounting system without receiving any competitive benefits. The controller's reports were irrelevant to the core activities of the organization. How long before one of the competitors in this division's market can effectively use management accounting to better implement its own strategy and seize the market?

Good management accounting requires that both managers and accountants work together to create information systems and performance measures that add value—that support the organization's unique strategy. This kind of work is not easy, nor is it done quickly. Management accountants must clearly understand the nature of critical business processes in the organization, as well as how managers and executives intend to strategically plan, control, and evaluate those processes. Linkages between activities must be tested. If performance in one activity does not lead to desired outcomes in customer service or financial performance, then relationships need to be reexamined. This is exciting work! The history of business in America has clearly demonstrated that successful organizations are willing to spend the necessary creative energy to really understand how the work they do adds value to the marketplace. The spirit of continuous improvement that is now prevalent throughout our economy requires that management accounting continue to identify and support opportunities to improve the cost, quality, and timeliness of the information it provides.

to summarize

The Balanced Scorecard is a new theory that explicitly supports strategy by integrating performance measures of financial, customer, internal process, and learning and growth activities within an organization. Both financial and nonfinancial measures are used throughout this new management model. A Balanced Scorecard, once created, is unique to each organization. The process of building a Balanced Scorecard requires that management accountants work closely with managers, executives, and information technologists in order to clearly understand how measures link together to eventually support successful financial results for the company. This idea of linkages across performance measures is critical to a successful Balanced Scorecard. Financial performance is linked to customer outcome measures of customer retention, customer acquisition, and market share. These customer outcome measures in turn are linked to leading measures on customer service involving cost, quality, and time. Supporting customer service are the internal processes that take place within an organization. These internal processes include innovation processes (identifying and creating new products), operations processes (obtaining customer orders and producing and delivering products), and service-after-sale

business environment essay

What's in a Name? The accounting profession is facing profound changes. The marketplace, clients, and professional expectations are suddenly different. Accountants must develop new competencies, including improved communication skills, business knowledge, and the capacity to make inferences from the relationship between business circumstances and economic and industrial trends. Further, accountants must redefine themselves as being concerned with the definition, acquisition, analysis, reporting, and use of all kinds of information (both financial and nonfinancial, internal and external). Expanding the relationship between accountants and the information that they use in their work will allow these professionals to more effectively operate, manage, and assess organizations and their various activities in a global economy that is being constantly reshaped by technology advances.

In the midst of the increasing pressure to change and adapt within this new economy, some people are proposing that the terms "accounting" and "accountancy" may no longer adequately describe a profession moving to higher levels of information management. For instance, it may be appropriate for the accounting profession to rename itself the "information consultancy" profession. The body of knowledge that would qualify a person as an "information consultant" should include management techniques, computers, computerized information systems, and the various functions needed by an organization to carry out its mission (including accounting). Most importantly, to understand and manage essentially *all* of the critical information needed to effectively run an organization, one must clearly understand *all* of the key underlying business activities and processes.

The American Institute of Certified Public Accountants (AICPA) is currently working with several other

processes (handling warranties and providing support to customers). In order to continually improve its internal processes, an organization must emphasize its employees by measuring outcome performance on employee retention, satisfaction, and productivity. Finally, these employee outcome measures are linked to important investments in the capabilities of employees, information systems, and organizational structure.

2

Anticipate that both management accounting and financial accounting are poised for important changes.

ACCOUNTING FOR TOMORROW

"There is a bulldozer of change moving across America and if you are not part of the bulldozer, you will be part of the road." The Balanced Scorecard is one important example of continuous improvement that is characteristic of a competitive world economy that is always growing and changing. Managers and accountants in many organizations are creating new performance measurement systems that support dramatic improvements in products, processes, and people. These professionals understand that measures should focus on monitoring *all* critical activities in an organization in order to anticipate and prepare for future decisions, rather than simply report the financial effects of past decisions. Hence, in harmony with the idea of an instrument panel on an airplane, some companies prefer to refer to their measurement systems as dashboards rather than scoreboards.

In this atmosphere of healthy competition and change, you can expect that new models and methods of management accounting will continue to be developed. Even financial accounting is beginning to move in this direction. Investors, creditors, and regulators are beginning to put a lot of pressure on companies to make public more relevant and more timely information than is now contained in annual reports prepared using the financial accounting model first developed by Italian merchants in the 1300–1400s. The American Institute of Certified Public Accountants

leading accountancy institutions around the world to create a new professional designation that is global in scope and focused on knowledge integration that creates economic value. This new designation is not intended to replace the CPA designation, or any other designation, but rather is intended to complement existing credentials. At the time of the printing of this textbook, those working on this project have not yet decided what to call this new designation. For now, it is simply referred to as the "XYZ" designation; and it will be defined by four critical characteristics. It will be:

1. global in reach (it will be recognized throughout the world, not just in the United States);
2. based on a wide range of disciplines (including accountancy, management consulting, information technology, business law, finance, financial planning, marketing, economics, risk management, human resources, actuarial services, and engineering);
3. bound by global ethical standards; and
4. based on global standards of competency, with a commitment to continuing learning and periodic evaluation to ensure currency of knowledge and skills.

Overall, the intent is that this "XYZ" designation will be a recognized emblem of experience and ability to integrate knowledge and business experience to provide strategic business insight that creates economic value. So watch for future developments here, including its actual name. This may be a professional designation that you will hold one day.

Sources: P. Lowell and R. Fremgen, "What's in a Name Change?" *Journal of Accountancy* (August 1999); "Key Features of XYZ: The Proposed Designation," *The CPA Letter* (February–March 2001).

exhibit 10-7 The Future of Financial Accounting in Public Reports

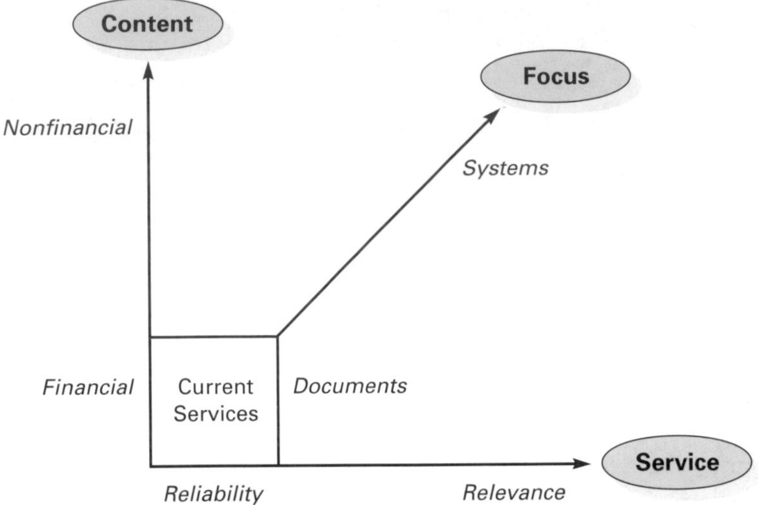

Source: From a 1996 presentation by Robert K. Elliott, Chairperson of the AICPA Special Committee on Assurance Services.

(AICPA) has commissioned special committees to study these demands for additional public data about companies and to propose new models of financial accounting. Robert Elliott, chairman of the AICPA in 2000/2001, represents many others in calling for accounting to continue to grow and mature as the global economy and technology grow. He describes the professional practice of a "new finance" that "encompasses hard-core management accounting topics such as cost management, discount rates, and capacity management; manufacturing issues including just-in-time production, distribution channel management, and competitive intelligence; and softer topics like benchmarking, performance measurement, and managing change." He says the new finance is "less about accounting and more about becoming strategic advisors and decision makers in our companies."[6]

Exhibit 10-7 illustrates one way to view the current direction of change that is necessary for accounting in today's marketplace. As you can see, the pressure on accounting to change is threefold. First, financial accounting is being pressured to provide *nonfinancial* data in public reports. Second, preparation of financial accounting reports has always focused on making reports objective, consistent, and reliable. However, users of financial accounting reports want these reports to emphasize more the *relevance* of information to important investing, lending, and regulatory decisions for individual companies. Finally, in an age when the Internet allows users to access and analyze huge amounts of data almost instantaneously, there is increased demand by decision makers trying to evaluate a company based on financial accounting to be able to access information *systems* throughout the year, rather than having to wait one to three months after the year-end for the company to release an annual report document; or, in the case of internal management accounting reports, having to wait days or weeks for cost, quality, and time analysis reports to be completed and delivered to management. It's difficult to predict how these demands will eventually affect the financial accounting reports provided by thousands of companies like MICROSOFT. However, it's not difficult to predict that changes are coming. This is a very exciting time to be preparing to enter the world of business. Regardless of whether you intend to actually work as an accountant, it is clear that accounting will dramatically impact the way you work. By understanding the concepts of financial and management accounting, as well as the great potential for continuous improvement in these areas, you will be better prepared to use accounting to personally add value to your organization.

6 P. Fleming, "Steering a Course for the Future," *Journal of Accountancy* (November 1999), pp. 35–38.

review of learning objectives

1 Explain the fundamentals of building a Balanced Scorecard. Competition requires that companies continually improve their performance measures in order to add value to the products and services they provide within their industries. Nonfinancial measures are growing in importance in today's marketplace as companies work to build better management systems. The Balanced Scorecard is being heralded as an important new management model that explicitly supports a successful strategy by integrating performance measures of financial, customer, internal process, and learning and growth activities within an organization. Management accountants must work closely with managers, executives, and information technologists in order to build a Balanced Scorecard that is unique to their own organization. One of the most important aspects of a successful scorecard is *linking* all performance measures either directly or indirectly to desired financial performance. The Balanced Scorecard approach to these linkages is to connect financial performance directly to customer outcome measures of customer retention, customer acquisition, and market share. These customer outcome measures in turn are linked to leading measures on customer service involving cost, quality, and time. Internal processes taking place within an organization that support value-added services expected by customers are then identified. These internal processes include innovation processes (identifying and creating new products), operations processes (obtaining customer orders and producing and delivering products), and service-after-sale processes (handling warranties and providing support to customers). Positive employee outcome performance in terms of employee retention, satisfaction, and productivity is necessary in order to support continual improvement of internal processes. Employee outcome measures on retention, satisfaction, and productivity are linked to important investments in the capabilities of employees, information systems, and organizational structure.

2 Anticipate that both management accounting and financial accounting are poised for important changes. This textbook has covered a lot of territory in an effort to introduce you to the world of accounting. You should understand that management accounting has always been a function of competitive need. In other words, the desire to compete well in the marketplace drives companies to develop better methods of management accounting. Hence, as you would expect, today's competitive markets continue to put pressure on both management and financial accounting to make some fundamental changes. The AICPA (American Institute of Certified Public Accountants) has commissioned special committees to investigate these trends. The pressure on accounting to grow and change involves three essential areas: (1) the need to include nonfinancial measures in public accounting reports; (2) the need to better emphasize relevant, rather than just reliable, data; and (3) the need to allow continual access to data systems rather than periodic report documents. Accountants, as well as other business professionals, who can anticipate these needs will be best positioned to add value to their organizations throughout the future.

key terms and concepts

discussion questions

1. Why is it unwise for a company to focus on only one performance measure while ignoring other performance measures?
2. Why do you think performance measures vary from company to company?
3. Why do you think there has been such a revolution in the way companies think about and measure their performance in recent years?
4. What is one way that traditional performance measurement systems, which have historically been tied to financial reporting, may be dysfunctional?

5. Why do you think some researchers argue that traditional performance measures are partly responsible for a decline in America's competitiveness?
6. Describe the two types of customer performance measures.
7. What are the key ingredients of customer satisfaction?
8. Why doesn't the purchase price of a product equal the product's total cost to customers?
9. What are two ways companies can increase the market share of their products?
10. What are the three types of processes that should be in place to effectively support customer satisfaction?
11. How can companies plan, control, and evaluate their innovation processes?
12. Is it possible for a company to spend more money on the innovation process than on providing goods and services to current customers?
13. What are the three leading measures of "learning and growth" in an organization?
14. What are some of the factors of effective organizational structures discussed in this chapter?
15. Why do you think the market value of many companies (as measured by per-share stock price times the number of shares outstanding) is greater than the book value of the net assets (as measured by total assets minus total liabilities) listed on the balance sheets of those companies?
16. How do companies go about managing their return on investment (ROI)?
17. Pressure to provide better information to support the competitive needs of today's marketplace is resulting in fundamental changes in the accounting information that is being provided to managers, investors, and creditors. Identify the three primary areas of change.

discussion cases

CASE 10-1 STRATEGY FOR DEVELOPING A BALANCED SCORECARD

A company is interested in developing a Balanced Scorecard approach to evaluating and enhancing its performance. It is looking at two ways of accomplishing the task. The first is for top management to develop the scorecard approach and impose it on managers throughout the organization. The second is to involve managers, customers, and other stakeholders in a grass-roots approach to determine what cost, quality, and time factors should be measured. Which of the two approaches would you recommend to the company?

CASE 10-2 HOW SOON CAN YOU MAKE US A BALANCED SCORECARD?

You are currently the controller for a large manufacturing company. The president of the company calls you to his office and states the following: "I just went to a round-table discussion with presidents of other companies, and they told me that the most important development they had made in their companies was to implement Balanced Scorecards. I want you to drop whatever you are doing this week and develop a Balanced Scorecard for our company." You are vaguely aware of the concept of Balanced Scorecards from your reading, but you aren't too sure what they are all about. As you begin to think about your upcoming task, you discover that your company does not have a strategic plan or mission statement. Is the task given you by the president one that can be accomplished in a week or accomplished at all? What is the effect of not having a strategic plan or mission statement on the development of a Balanced Scorecard for the company?

CASE 10-3 GET THOSE BUSINESS SCHOOL RATINGS UP!

You are the dean of the business school at North Central University. You have recently gone through a strategic planning process involving representatives from all your stakeholder groups (students, staff, faculty, recruiters, alumni, administration, etc.). The result is a newly refined strategic plan, including a mission statement, underlying values, specific objectives and strategies, and assessment outcomes (performance measurements). One of your objectives is to increase the ranking of your business school by *Business News*, a magazine that annually ranks business programs in your region. Given your understanding of the Balanced Scorecard approach and the material covered in this textbook, answer the following questions.

1. Even though it takes longer, is it wise to involve various stakeholders in developing your strategic plan? Why or why not?
2. What are some likely strategies that might be implemented to increase your business school ranking? Explain.

EXERCISE 10-1

CUSTOMER SATISFACTION PERFORMANCE MEASURES

The following are possible performance measures of customer satisfaction:

1. Purchase cost to customer
2. Customer defection rate
3. Returns by customers
4. Number of new customers
5. Time to complete contract
6. Percent of total units sold
7. Customer survey response
8. Costs to recruit customers

Identify which of these measures are most likely to be considered leading measures and which are outcome performance measures. Also, if they are leading performance measures, identify whether they relate to cost, quality, or time. If they are outcome performance measures, identify whether they relate to customer retention, customer acquisition, or market share.

EXERCISE 10-2

INTERNAL PROCESSES PERFORMANCE MEASURES

The following are possible performance measures of internal processes:

1. Cost of replacement parts
2. Lead time (order to delivery)
3. Lead time (idea to working model)
4. Payback on R&D costs
5. Percentage of sales from new products
6. Unit-level costs
7. Defects per million
8. Repair cycle time

Identify the type of performance measure (cost, quality, or time) and the related process (innovation, operations, or service-after-sale) for each of these measures.

EXERCISE 10-3

PERFORMANCE MEASURES OF LEARNING AND GROWTH

The following are performance measures of learning and growth:

1. Number of new certifications or degrees
2. Average life cycle time of personal computers
3. Assessment of effective communication
4. Employee turnover rate
5. Output per employee
6. Average yearly training or education hours per employee
7. Survey of employee satisfaction
8. Amount of time spent in teamwork versus individual work

Identify which of these learning and growth measures are leading performance measures and which are outcome performance measures. Also, if they are leading performance measures, identify whether they would be classified as cost, quality, or time measures and whether they relate to employee, information system, or organizational structure capabilities. If they are outcome performance measures, identify whether they relate to employee retention, employee satisfaction, or employee productivity.

EXERCISE 10-4

BALANCED SCORECARD LINKAGES

The following are examples of performance measures in a Balanced Scorecard:

1. ROI
2. Percentage of employees having leadership opportunities

3. Repair cycle time
4. Quality rankings by other agencies
5. ROE
6. Design cycle time
7. Six sigma
8. Systems R&D expense per total systems expense

Classify each of the above performance measures using the categories in Exhibit 10-5. For each measure, identify the type of lagging measure to which it links.

EXERCISE 10-5

CLASSIFYING BALANCED SCORECARD ELEMENTS

Listed below are a number of scorecard measures for a manufacturing company:

a. Number of new customers
b. Percentage of customers who place multiple orders
c. Percentage of on-time deliveries
d. Number of worker accidents
e. Number of customer complaints about products
f. Number of employees who attend training seminars
g. Percentage of product defects
h. Percentage of back-ordered products
i. Customer satisfaction, as measured through periodic surveys
j. Unit product cost
k. Percentage of revenues from new products
l. Earnings per share
m. Gross margin on products
n. Employee turnover
o. Costs to retain customers
p. Amount of time spent in teamwork

Classify each performance measure according to the following:

1. *Perspective:* financial, customer, internal processes, or learning and growth
2. *Focus:* cost, quality, time, or overall financial (*Note:* Some measures may have more than one focus.)
3. *Relationship:* leading or outcome (*Note:* As the measure relates to other measures within its own perspective)

EXERCISE 10-6

BALANCED SCORECARD AND INCENTIVES

Recall from the chapter the discussion of the oil drillers from the former Soviet Union who won a production competition based on the number of meters drilled. Those drillers determined that the first 100 meters of drilling were the easiest, so they simply drilled dry wells that never exceeded 100 meters in depth. Naturally, management would be upset when the drillers' tactics were exposed. After all, management's objective was to drill wells and find oil.

1. Can you suggest to management an incentive system that would have prevented such behavior and would instead encourage the desired behavior?
2. Do you consider what the drillers did to be wrong or smart?

EXERCISE 10-7

THINKING ABOUT THE BALANCED SCORECARD

Albert Einstein once commented that "sometimes what can be counted doesn't count, and what can't be counted is what really counts." A business executive stated, "The first indication we don't know what we are doing is a preoccupation with numbers." How do you think these two statements relate to the Balanced Scorecard approach to performance measurement?

PROBLEM 10-1

APPLYING THE BALANCED SCORECARD TO MANUFACTURING

Martin, Inc., manufactures pleasure and fishing boats. Management's goals and objectives for the company are:

1. *Goal:* To maintain strong financial health
   Objectives:
   - Maintain sufficient cash balances to assure liquidity and solvency
   - Achieve continued growth in sales and profits
   - Provide a good return to investors
   - Increase market share
2. *Goal:* Provide excellent customer service
   Objectives:
   - Provide boats that meet customer needs
   - Meet customer needs on a timely basis
   - Exceed customer quality standards
3. *Goal:* Be the industry leader in product innovations
   Objectives:
   - Bring new boats and features to the market before competitors
   - Increase efficiency and productivity faster than competitors

Required: For each of these objectives, provide one measure of performance the company could use.

PROBLEM 10-2

APPLYING THE BALANCED SCORECARD TO A SMALL BUSINESS

You are an optometrist with your own practice. For the past 20 years, you have focused almost exclusively on profitability of your practice as your sole performance measure. In fact, you have been quite profitable. However, during the past two years, a number of new, low-cost, commercial optometric offices including LENSCRAFTERS, WAL-MART, SHOPKO, and even KMART have opened in your practice area. As a result, your profitability has decreased to the point where you are barely breaking even. Because of your concern for your practice, you have asked a business consultant what you should do.

She has told you that your single-minded focus on profitability is no different than that of your new commercial competitors and has convinced you that these competitors will be more successful than you in making profits because they have lower cost structures than you do. She has suggested that you read her recently published book on the Balanced Scorecard measurement system and respond to the following questions:

Required:

1. Are your current success measures mostly financial, internal processes, learning and growth, or customer focused?
2. Has your focus been on financial, quality, or time measures, or on an appropriate balance of the three?
3. Thinking about your performance perspective (financial, customer, internal processes, and learning and growth), how could you distinguish yourself from the commercial optometrists and create value for your customers?
4. Are there ways you should change your focus regarding cost, quality, and time measures?

PROBLEM 10-3

APPLYING THE BALANCED SCORECARD TO AN INTERNET COMPANY

OnRamp, Inc., is a technology company that provides connections for Internet service providers (ISPs) to the information highway. If U.S. WEST and other long-distance companies that own fiber optic cable are the information highway, OnRamp, Inc., views itself as the on- and off-ramps that provide access to the highway for ISPs, such as EARTHLINK, INC., and their customers. Two years ago, OnRamp, Inc., had an initial public offering (IPO) where it raised $500 million in operating capital. With that money, it built a new office building and developed much of the infrastructure needed to serve as the on- and off-ramp market leader. The company gets its revenue from charging ISPs a small user fee for each customer connected to the information highway. In its prospectus for the IPO, OnRamp, Inc., stated that its only critical performance measure of success was the number of users that it served. It stated that if, in two years, it serviced 2 million individual users, then it would consider itself to be successful. Now, two years later, there are 5 million individual customer accounts within OnRamp's system. Unfortunately, however, OnRamp, Inc., is still losing considerable amounts of money and is experiencing serious complaints about delayed Internet access and server problems.

Required:

1. What do you think about OnRamp, Inc.'s "number of ISP customers" performance measure?
2. If, in fact, OnRamp Inc., measures its success solely on the basis of number of individual ISP customers, what important performance measures is it ignoring?

PROBLEM 10-4 APPLYING THE BALANCED SCORECARD TO A UNIVERSITY

The dean of your business school has determined that there are four major drivers of success for her business school. Those success drivers are having outstanding (1) faculty, (2) students, (3) curricula, and (4) alumni and recruiter support.

Required:

Based on these drivers of success, develop a Balanced Scorecard performance system that the dean could use to evaluate the operations of her school. Be specific and indicate the purpose of each measure. Make sure that you clearly include both leading and outcome measures in your Balanced Scorecard.

PROBLEM 10-5 APPLYING THE BALANCED SCORECARD TO A CHURCH

As an accountant and active member of a local church, you have been asked by your pastor to help him develop a Balanced Scorecard measurement system for the church. He is seriously interested in continuous improvement and believes that by identifying and monitoring the right performance measurements, the church will be more successful. In discussions with the pastor, you have determined that the scorecard should focus on the following four areas:

- Increase in learning and commitment of members
- Size of congregation and membership
- Respect in the community
- Amount of financial contributions

Required:

Develop a performance measurement system for these four areas that includes both leading and outcome measures that could be used by the pastor and his church to grow and measure the success of his ecumenical efforts.

competency enhancement opportunities

- International Case
- Ethics Case
- Writing Assignment
- The Debate
- Internet Search

The following additional assignments provide opportunities for students to develop critical thinking, ethical perspectives, oral and written communication skills, experience with electronic research, and teamwork through group and business activities.

Note: Due to the nature of this chapter, there are no Analyzing Real Company Information problems.

INTERNATIONAL CASE

• ***A Balanced Scorecard in Russia***

This chapter has discussed the need for companies to focus on more than just the numbers. Additional factors must be considered in addition to financial results. Thus, the concept of the Balanced Scorecard. Consider the case of a country where the economy is not as sophisticated as in the United States—Russia. Inflation runs rampant, shortages prevail, organized crime rules. How could a Balanced Scorecard approach help a company that finds itself in this situation? Or could it? Can you suggest areas from a Balanced Scorecard perspective that a company in Russia might emphasize?

ETHICS CASE

• ***"Family" Business***

Martin Beemer is the purchasing manager for the police department in a large metropolitan city. The city has 13,000 police officers. The city currently purchases police uniforms from three different manufacturers, one of which is SunKing, International (a Korean company). Martin recently agreed (in private) with SunKing's vice president to give SunKing increased business if SunKing would hire his daughter as a "ghost" salesperson in the United States at a salary of $350,000 per year.

1. Do you believe the actions of Martin and SunKing are unethical? Fraudulent?
2. What internal process performance measures could the city have had in place in the purchasing department that could have revealed the kickback arrangement?

WRITING ASSIGNMENT

• ***More Than Just the Numbers***

You have found in your study of accounting that accountants generally focus on the numbers. Their job is to summarize financial results and provide information for decision makers. In this chapter, you have read about additional measures that are critical to a company's success: items like customer loyalty and satisfaction and employee productivity. Your assignment is to prepare a one- to two-page memo summarizing the following points:

1. Select an internal process measure, like research and development, and map out how the careful monitoring of that process will eventually show up in a financial measure like ROI.
2. Are accountants the best people to collect information on items such as customer satisfaction and customer loyalty? If not, who in a business would be best suited to collect this type of information?

THE DEBATE

• *Quantitative vs. Qualitative*

The concept of the Balanced Scorecard suggests that instead of focusing on the financial aspects of business decisions, a company should manage such items as customer satisfaction, employee growth, and total quality, and the profits will follow. Divide your group into two teams. Each team should prepare a five-minute presentation addressing the following issues:

- One team supports "quantitative" measures. Defend the position that a company should manage by the numbers. The DuPonts and the Carnegies achieved the success they did because they focused on costs and profits. Provide reasons in support of your assigned position.
- The other team supports "qualitative" measures. Defend the position that a company's management should examine more than just the financial statement numbers. Other important information must be managed if a company is to be successful. In your presentation, identify some of that "other important information."

INTERNET SEARCH

• *Building a Balanced Scorecard*

How does one go about building a Balanced Scorecard? Let's go to the Internet to find some help. Go to **http://www.rens.com/viewpoint/papers.html** and access the site entitled "An Overview of The Balanced Scorecard." Sometimes Web addresses change, so if this address does not work, access the Web site for this textbook (**http://albrecht.swcollege.com**) for an updated link. Once you have gained access to this site, answer the following questions:

1. How do you recognize a "good" Balanced Scorecard?
2. How many steps are involved in developing a Balanced Scorecard? What are the steps?

appendix a

MICROSOFT CORPORATION 1999 ANNUAL REPORT

FINANCIAL HIGHLIGHTS

msft In millions, except earnings per share

Year Ended June 30	1995	1996	1997	1998	1999
Revenue	$6,075	$9,050	$11,936	$15,262	**$19,747**
Net income	1,453	2,195	3,454	4,490	**7,785**
Diluted earnings per share[1]	0.29	0.43	0.66	0.84	**1.42**
Cash and short-term investments	4,750	6,940	8,966	13,927	**17,236**
Total assets	7,210	10,093	14,387	22,357	**37,156**
Stockholders' equity	5,333	6,908	10,777	16,627	**28,438**

1 Diluted earnings per share have been restated to reflect a two-for-one stock split in March 1999.

FELLOW SHAREHOLDERS

> Microsoft continued to perform strongly in 1999. Our customers count on us to provide great software that helps them communicate more effectively, work more productively, learn more creatively, and make the most of their leisure time. We worked hard to meet those needs and to set the standard for features, functionality, simplicity, and seamless integration with the Internet in all of our products. The result was remarkable growth and record revenue.

In the years ahead, we will see accelerating change in the software industry, as the computing needs of our customers start to move beyond the PC into a "PC-Plus" world. The PC will undoubtedly remain at the heart of computing at home, work, and school, but it will be joined by numerous new intelligent devices and appliances, from handheld computers and auto PCs to Internet-enabled cellular phones. More software will be delivered over the Internet, and the boundary between online services and software products will blur. The Internet will continue to change everything by offering a level of connectivity that was unimaginable only a few years ago — and every home, business, and school will want to be hooked up to that incredible global database.

Microsoft's vision is to empower people through great software — any time, any place, and on any device. That means helping companies build friction-free knowledge-management systems, so information flows effortlessly through their businesses, and to implement flawless e-commerce operations. It means helping developers create great Web-enabled products for a wide range of devices. It means making PCs simpler and more reliable. It means helping consumers transform the Internet into their own "personal Internet" — a resource that learns from them over time and empowers them with all of the information they need, while protecting their privacy. Everything we do focuses on allowing people and organizations to create and manage their information.

BUILT AROUND YOU

> In a world of increasing technological complexity, one of our primary goals must be to make our products easier and more effective for customers to use. In part, this entails developing simpler interfaces, natural-language processing, and voice control to help hide the underlying complexity from users. We're working hard to achieve those breakthroughs. But it also means getting closer to our customers and working harder to understand their needs. We must help customers integrate technology by learning about how they work, how information flows through their organization, what they'll need in the future — and about where we're succeeding or failing. Customer-centric thinking must permeate everything we do.

Our growth is always forcing us to look at the best way to stay close to our customers and respond to their needs. This year we organized the company so that its structure is customer-based rather than product-based. The leaders of each of Microsoft's newly defined divisions now have end-to-end management accountability in their respective customer segments. Guided by the company's overall vision, they have total responsibility for setting a clear mission and priorities for their division, including all product planning and marketing strategies. The divisional leaders also have freedom to form business relationships both inside and outside Microsoft — freedom to work with the parties they need to do the best job for their customers.

Microsoft's mission has always been to connect customers with the information they need. But today there is more information to connect with than ever before, stored in more places than ever before, and accessible in more ways than ever before. By refocusing totally on offering customers what they want rather than what technology can provide, we will help them succeed in the PC-Plus world. We will also build a solid foundation for Microsoft well into the 21st century.

MANAGING KNOWLEDGE

> An organization's most valuable asset is its knowledge base. It is also the hardest to manage. For the majority of knowledge workers, getting the information they need is still more difficult than it should be. Mostly, it involves creating and distributing paper documents or telephoning and meeting with fellow employees. New digital approaches enabled by our software will make knowledge workers far more efficient.

With its Web-based collaboration tools, Microsoft® Office 2000 is already a powerful component of a knowledge management solution. In the coming year, we will augment it with several other key initiatives. Windows® 2000 Active Directory™ service will simplify administration and make it easier for knowledge workers to find resources throughout their organization. Future versions of Microsoft Exchange will offer both a platform for unified messaging and our Web Store technology, creating a powerful, centralized communications and knowledge management solution. In the future, we plan to introduce document library and search server technology that will help companies leverage their knowledge bases. Because 50% of work is now done in teams — compared with only 20% a decade ago — we have added team productivity features to the BackOffice® family and other products. And to help organizations realize the dream of a paperless office, our ClearType technology offers on-screen resolution and readability that equals or exceeds that of paper.

To help knowledge workers access information more efficiently, we're also developing what we call a digital dashboard. The digital dashboard is a customized Office 2000 solution that pulls together all of the information that is important to you — regardless of whether it's on your PC, corporate network, or the Internet — and makes it available in one place. A digital dashboard helps you manage and prioritize messages, tasks, information, meetings — in fact, whatever you want. It also gives you access to all of the analytical tools you need to process your data. And it makes all of this available wherever you are, whether on your handheld computer, PC, or smart telephone. The digital dashboard will bring the concept of empowerment any time, any place, and on any device even closer to reality.

CONNECTING EVERYWHERE

> Microsoft's fundamental vision for Windows is one of total scalability — from embedded operating systems in smart devices such as thermostats and light switches, through Windows CE on handheld PCs, and Web-enabled telephones, to the largest mission-critical server farms. Windows 2000, SQL Server™ 7.0, and the next version of Exchange will take our high-end scalability and around-the-clock availability

far beyond what was thought possible just five years ago, and we expect to make even greater progress in the years ahead. A key to this is using Windows 2000 breakthrough load-balancing to provide scaling and reliability beyond that of the most expensive systems of the past. Web sites can use Windows to easily add capacity and avoid having a single point of failure. The Windows 2000 load-balancing technology automatically redirects tasks to the server that is operating under the least load.

A core requirement of knowledge workers is access to their information wherever they are. Our IntelliMirror™ technology in Windows 2000 will help make that possible, by transparently and automatically backing up and synchronizing your data so that it is available on PCs or intelligent devices.

Your handheld computer, Web-enabled telephone, and PC will synchronize with each other wirelessly and automatically, whether you are in your office or on the road. At Microsoft, some of our employees already use Windows 2000 with a wireless network. When they walk into a meeting room, their laptop is automatically recognized and a "virtual workgroup" of everyone in the room is created. Wireless networks will transform the workplace.

Ubiquitous connectivity will also revolutionize the home, enabling consumers to leverage the power and richness of the PC on any intelligent device, thanks to fast, low-cost wireless networks that will make high-quality audio and video available in every room. For example, our Windows Media™ audio player downloads music twice as fast as previous formats, has double the storage capacity, and offers powerful anti-piracy protection. We're also evolving the WebTV Network™ service, which today has more than 800,000 subscribers, with on-demand programming, personalized viewing, more Web-enhanced content, great games, and powerful communications for the whole family. We aim to help millions of Americans enjoy the digital lifestyle at home as well as at work with exciting offerings such as the CarPoint™ online automotive service, HomeAdvisor™ online real estate service, MoneyCentral™ personal finance service, plus the MSN™ Hotmail Web-based e-mail service, which now has more than 40 million members.

EXPANDING BANDWIDTH

> Microsoft's vision of empowering people through great software — any time, any place, and on any device — depends on helping consumers and businesses advance from today's narrow-band world into a broadband future. Even now, the majority of consumers — along with many small and medium-sized businesses — still access the Internet via their regular telephone lines. The result is that the rich world of real-time interactivity remains a dream for most consumers, while many businesses are reluctant to put videoconferencing or multimedia on their networks, because they fear it will crowd out transaction traffic and other high-priority communications.

Our core strategy here is to make investments that will accelerate the deployment of high-speed broadband networks and to collaborate on the technology that will make interactive services for consumers and businesses run seamlessly across these networks. To that end, we are working with companies that will play a leading role in making broadband Internet and multimedia access widely available. We are enthusiastic about the many technologies that will deliver this, which is why we continue to invest in various infrastructures such as wired and wireless telecommunications, cable, and interactive television. Some of our exciting relationships include AT&T, Nextel Communications, NTL, Rogers Communications, WirelessKnowledge, Concentric Networks, Wink Communications, and more.

THE PC-PLUS ERA

> The enduring popularity of the PC — more than 100 million should be sold worldwide this year — is amazing, but not surprising. In a single, economical package, the PC offers individual students, knowledge workers, and consumers the kind of computing power that was found only in corporate computing departments just a decade ago. Whether you want to communicate, learn, work, or play, the PC can enrich and improve the experience.

In the new millennium, the remarkable power and flexibility of the PC will be available wherever it is needed. The PC-Plus era will be about connectivity, scalability, and simplicity. It will be an era when people are at the center, where technology is a natural extension of the way consumers and businesses think about themselves and their interactions with others. The combination of experience, resources, and research that is unique to Microsoft puts us in a strong position to transform this vision into reality.

We are investing heavily in the future — from world-class customer support to the $3.8 billion we plan to spend in fiscal 2000 on research and development for the products of tomorrow. There is, however, no guarantee of success. Competition continues to intensify, and regulatory pressures are unlikely to ease. Although global PC sales have proved remarkably robust, some slowdown is likely in the coming year. And as Microsoft's business becomes more complex, the strategic challenges and risks we face grow exponentially.

I remain optimistic, because the new opportunities for great software products are still incredible. I appreciate the unwavering support and trust of our shareholders and customers as Microsoft enters the 21st century.

Bill Gates

Bill Gates

INCOME STATEMENTS

msft In millions, except earnings per share			
Year Ended June 30	1997	1998	1999
Revenue	$11,936	$15,262	**$19,747**
Operating expenses:			
Cost of revenue	2,170	2,460	**2,814**
Research and development	1,863	2,601	**2,970**
Acquired in-process technology	–	296	**–**
Sales and marketing	2,411	2,828	**3,231**
General and administrative	362	433	**689**
Other expenses	259	230	**115**
Total operating expenses	7,065	8,848	**9,819**
Operating income	4,871	6,414	**9,928**
Investment income	443	703	**1,803**
Gain on sale of Softimage, Inc.	–	–	**160**
Income before income taxes	5,314	7,117	**11,891**
Provision for income taxes	1,860	2,627	**4,106**
Net income	$ 3,454	$ 4,490	**$ 7,785**
Earnings per share[1]:			
Basic	$ 0.72	$ 0.92	**$ 1.54**
Diluted	$ 0.66	$ 0.84	**$ 1.42**

1 Earnings per share have been restated to reflect a two-for-one stock split in March 1999.

See accompanying notes.

MANAGEMENT'S DISCUSSION AND ANALYSIS

msft

RESULTS OF OPERATIONS FOR 1997, 1998, AND 1999

> Microsoft develops, manufactures, licenses, and supports a wide range of software products for a multitude of computing devices. Microsoft software includes scalable operating systems for intelligent devices, personal computers (PCs), and servers; server applications for client/server environments; knowledge worker productivity applications; and software development tools. The Company's online efforts include the MSN network of Internet products and services; e-commerce platforms; and alliances with companies involved with broadband access and various forms of digital interactivity. Microsoft also licenses consumer software programs; sells PC input devices; trains and certifies system integrators; and researches and develops advanced technologies for future software products.

REVENUE

> The Company's revenue growth rate was 32% in fiscal 1997, 28% in fiscal 1998, and 29% in fiscal 1999. Revenue growth rates reflected the continued adoption of Windows operating systems and Microsoft Office, particularly as Microsoft software is deployed across entire corporate, academic, and governmental organizations. Software license volume increases have been the principal factor in the Company's revenue growth. The average selling price per license has decreased, primarily because of general shifts in the sales mix from retail packaged products to licensing programs, from new products to product upgrades, and from stand-alone desktop applications to integrated product suites. Average revenue per license from original equipment manufacturer (OEM) licenses and organizational license programs is lower than average revenue per license from retail versions. Likewise, product upgrades have lower prices than new products. Also, prices of integrated suites, such as Microsoft Office and BackOffice, are less than the sum of the prices for the individual programs included in these suites when such programs are licensed separately. During each of the three years, an increased percentage of products and programs included elements that were billed but unearned and recognized ratably, such as Microsoft Windows, Microsoft Office, maintenance, and other subscription models. See accompanying notes to financial statements.

As noted above, the Company's business model continues to evolve from selling packaged products to licensing organizational licenses and subscriptions. The Company's products are generally delivered to customers through a multi-tiered channel of distributors and resellers, but the distribution model is also changing for selected retail products that are now being shipped straight to resellers and other selected products that are now being shipped straight to customers. Due to these changes in channel mechanics and the business model, the risk of returns of product from distributors and resellers has declined. Accordingly, the estimate for future product returns was reduced by $250 million in the fourth quarter of fiscal 1999.

The Company changed the way it reports revenue and costs associated with product support, consulting, MSN Internet access, and training and certification of system integrators. Amounts received from customers for these activities have been classified as revenue in a manner more consistent with Microsoft's primary businesses. These amounts had been previously netted in sales and marketing expenses, except for MSN access fees, which had been netted in research and development expenses. Direct costs of these activities are classified as cost of revenue. Prior financial statements and disclosures have been reclassified for consistent presentation. Revenue from these activities was $578 million, $778 million, and $1.06 billion in 1997, 1998, and 1999.

Microsoft also made two changes related to the ratable recognition of revenue for a portion of its revenue for certain products. A new accounting rule that interprets American Institute of Certified Public Accountants (AICPA) Statement of Position (SOP) 97-2, *Software Revenue Recognition,* requires companies to use the average sales price of each undelivered element of software arrangements. Prior authoritative guidance allowed a comparison of the total price differential between a licensed product sold through different channels of distribution to derive the value of undelivered elements offered to customers acquiring product from one channel but not the other. Upon adoption of this new rule in the fourth quarter of fiscal 1999, the percentages of the total arrangement treated as unearned decreased. This change in the timing of revenue recognition reduced the amount of Microsoft Windows and Microsoft Office sales treated as unearned and increased the amount of revenue recognized upon shipment. Additionally, as part of the Company's long range planning process and a review of product shipment cycles, it was determined that the life cycle of Windows should be extended from two years to three years. The net impact of these changes was to increase reported revenue $80 million in the fourth quarter of 1999.

BUSINESS DIVISIONS > Microsoft has three major segments: Windows Platforms; Productivity Applications and Developer; and Consumer, Commerce, and Other.

> WINDOWS PLATFORMS revenue was $4.92 billion, $6.28 billion, and $8.50 billion in 1997, 1998, and 1999. Platform revenue is primarily licenses of PC operating systems and business and enterprise server systems with client/server, Internet, and intranet architectures.

The Company's principal PC operating systems are Windows 95, Windows 98, and Windows NT® Workstation. Windows 95 was released in August 1995, while its successor, Windows 98, became available at the end of fiscal 1998. Windows NT Workstation version 4.0 was released in fiscal 1997. Although the growth rate of new PC shipments slowed, PC operating systems contributed to revenue growth as shipments of new PCs preinstalled with such systems increased during the three-year period. Additionally, increased penetration of the higher value Windows NT Workstation led to growth in all three years.

WINDOWS PLATFORMS REVENUE

In billions

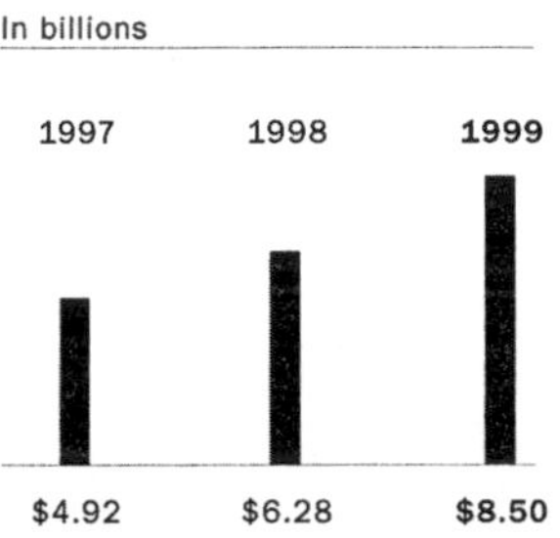

Windows NT Server is a comprehensive business and enterprise server operating system, combining application, file and print, communication, and Web services. Windows NT Server version 4.0 was released in fiscal 1997. Revenue from Windows NT Server increased strongly during each of the three years due to greater corporate demand, particularly for intranet computing solutions.

> PRODUCTIVITY APPLICATIONS AND DEVELOPER revenue was $5.62 billion, $7.04 billion, and $8.82 billion in 1997, 1998, and 1999. Products include primarily desktop applications, server applications, and software developer tools.

Microsoft Office integrated suites, including the Standard, Small Business, Professional, and Premium Editions, are the Company's principal desktop applications and a key driver of revenue growth. Microsoft Office 97 was released in fiscal 1997 and Microsoft Office 2000 was released at the end of fiscal 1999. The primary programs in Microsoft Office are the word processor Microsoft Word, Microsoft Excel spreadsheet, and Microsoft Outlook® messaging and collaboration client. Various versions of Office, which are available for the Windows and Macintosh operating systems, also include Microsoft Access database management program, Microsoft PowerPoint® presentation graphics program, Microsoft FrontPage® Web site creation and management program, or other programs. Revenue from stand-alone versions of Microsoft Excel, Word, and PowerPoint continued to decrease as the sales mix shifted to integrated product suites.

PRODUCTIVITY APPLICATIONS AND DEVELOPER REVENUE

In billions

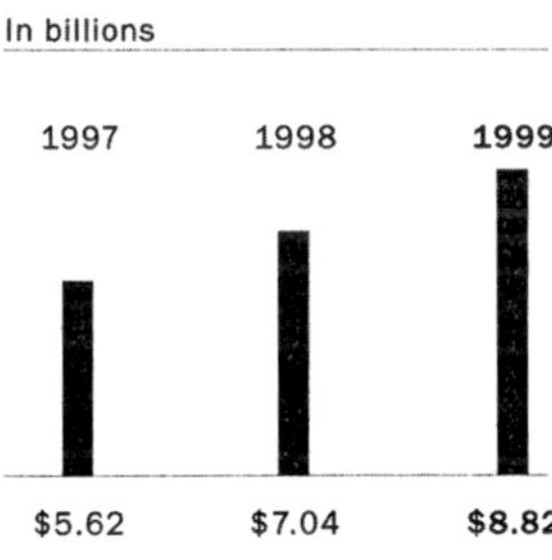

Server applications, based on Microsoft Windows NT Server, offer an enterprise-wide distributed client/server, Internet, and intranet environment. Products include Microsoft Exchange Server, Microsoft SQL Server, and other server applications in the Microsoft BackOffice family of products. Microsoft Exchange is an enterprise messaging and collaboration server while Microsoft SQL Server is a scalable database and data warehouse platform. Revenue from these products increased strongly over the three-year period, albeit with slowing growth rates in 1998 and 1999.

Independent software vendors, corporate developers, and solutions developers license tools such as the Microsoft Visual Studio® development system, which includes the Microsoft Visual Basic® development system, to develop software for the Windows operating systems and the Internet. Revenue from developer products increased moderately in 1997, was flat in 1998, and increased strongly in 1999.

Although revenue was not significant, preinstallations of Windows CE by OEMs on intelligent devices were strong in 1998 and 1999.

> CONSUMER, COMMERCE, AND OTHER revenue was $1.40 billion, $1.94 billion, and $2.43 billion in 1997, 1998, and 1999. This category of product revenue includes learning and entertainment software; PC input devices; training and certification fees; consulting; and the online services. The Company's Internet services include the MSN portal, MSN access, WebTV®, and vertical properties such as MSN Hotmail Web-based e-mail service, Expedia.com™ travel site, CarPoint car buying site, and MoneyCentral personal finance site.

Learning and entertainment revenue was relatively flat in all three years. Mouse, gaming device, and keyboard sales increased in 1997 and 1998, but were steady in 1999. Training and certification fees from system integrators, along with consulting services to large enterprise customers and technology solution providers, increased strongly in all three years. Revenue from MSN Internet access fees and WebTV services increased due to higher subscriber levels. Advertising revenue, although relatively small in amount, increased exceptionally well in 1999 for the online portal and vertical properties.

CONSUMER, COMMERCE, AND OTHER REVENUE

In billions

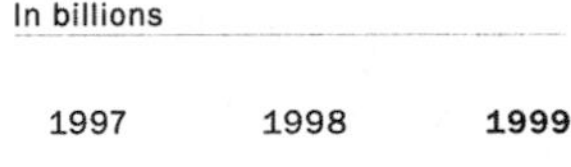

SALES CHANNELS > Microsoft distributes its products primarily through OEM licenses, organizational licenses, and retail packaged products. OEM channel revenue represents license fees from original equipment manufacturers who preinstall Microsoft products, primarily on PCs. Microsoft has three major geographic sales and marketing organizations: the South Pacific and Americas Region; the Europe, Middle East, and Africa Region; and the Asia Region. Sales of organizational licenses and packaged products via these channels are primarily to and through distributors and resellers.

OEM channel revenue was $3.49 billion in 1997, $4.72 billion in 1998, and $6.40 billion in 1999. The primary source of OEM revenue is the licensing of desktop operating systems, and OEM revenue is highly dependent on PC shipment volume. Growth was also enhanced by increased penetration of higher-value Windows NT Workstation licenses.

Revenue in the South Pacific and Americas Region was $4.39 billion, $5.57 billion, and $7.25 billion in 1997, 1998, and 1999. Revenue in the Europe, Middle East, and Africa Region was $2.77 billion, $3.50 billion, and $4.33 billion for the three years. Growth rates have been lower in Europe than in other geographic areas due to higher existing market shares and a faster shift to licensing programs. Asia Region revenue was $1.29 billion in 1997, $1.48 billion in 1998, and $1.78 billion in 1999. After strong growth in prior years, revenue was relatively flat in Japan and Southeast Asia in 1998 and the first half of fiscal 1999 due to economic issues and weak currencies.

The Company's operating results are affected by foreign exchange rates. Approximately 32%, 32%, and 29% of the Company's revenue was collected in foreign currencies during 1997, 1998, and 1999. Since a portion of local currency revenue is hedged and much of the Company's international manufacturing costs and operating expenses are also incurred in local currencies, the impact of exchange rates is partially mitigated.

OPERATING EXPENSES

> Microsoft encourages broad-based employee ownership of Microsoft stock through an employee stock option (ESO) program in which most employees are eligible to participate. Historically, exercise prices of grants of ESOs were struck at the lowest price in the 30 days following July 1 for annual grants and the 30 days after the start date for new employees. In connection with this practice, which is no longer employed, a charge of $217 million was recorded in the fourth quarter for fiscal 1999 compensation expense, calculated under the provisions of Accounting Principles Board Opinion 25 (APB 25). Charges related to ESO compensation were reflected in 1999 operating expenses as follows (in millions):

Cost of revenue	$ 44
Research and development	105
Sales and marketing	46
General and administrative	22
Total	$217

> COST OF REVENUE Cost of revenue as a percent of revenue was 18.2% in 1997, 16.1% in 1998, and 14.3% in 1999. The percentage decreases resulted primarily from the trend in mix shift to OEM and organizational licenses. The decrease was also due to the shifts in mix to CD-ROMs (which carry lower cost of goods than disks) and higher-margin Windows NT Server, other servers, and client access licenses in the BackOffice product family. Additionally, cost of revenue in 1999 was positively impacted by a reduction in estimates of obsolete inventory and other manufacturing costs of $67 million. As discussed above, the Company's business model continues to evolve toward licensing from sales of packaged products through distribution channels. Consequently, risks associated with manufacturing and holding physical product have declined.

> RESEARCH AND DEVELOPMENT Microsoft continued to invest heavily in the future by funding research and development (R&D). Expense increases in 1997, 1998, and 1999 resulted primarily from development staff headcount growth in many areas, particularly Windows platforms, including PC operating systems, servers, and Internet and intranet technologies. R&D costs also increased for productivity applications, development tools, and online services.

In 1998, the Company acquired WebTV Networks, Inc., an online service that enables consumers to experience the Internet through their televisions via set-top terminals. Microsoft paid $425 million in stock and cash. The accompanying income statement reflects a one-time write-off of in-process technologies under development by WebTV Networks of $296 million.

> SALES AND MARKETING The increase in the absolute dollar amount of sales and marketing expenses in the three-year period was due primarily to expanded product-specific marketing programs, such as Office 97 in 1997, Windows 98 in 1998, and Office 2000 in 1999. Sales and marketing costs as a percentage of revenue decreased primarily due to moderate headcount growth. Microsoft brand advertising expenses rose slightly in 1998, but declined in 1999.

> GENERAL AND ADMINISTRATIVE Increases in general and administrative expenses were attributable to higher legal fees, litigation costs, and growth in the number of people and computer systems necessary to support overall increases in the scope of the Company's operations.

> OTHER EXPENSES Other expenses include the recognition of Microsoft's share of joint venture activities, including DreamWorks Interactive and the MSNBC entities.

INVESTMENT INCOME, GAIN ON SALE, AND INCOME TAXES

> Investment income increased primarily as a result of a larger investment portfolio generated by cash from operations in 1997, 1998, and 1999, coupled with realized gains from the sale of certain bond and equity securities in 1999.

In fiscal 1999, Microsoft sold its Softimage, Inc. subsidiary to Avid Technology, Inc. for a pretax gain of $160 million.

The effective income tax rate was 35.0% in 1997. The effective income tax rate increased to 36.9% in 1998 due to the nondeductible write-off of WebTV in-process technologies. Excluding the impact of the gain on the sale of Softimage, Inc., the effective tax rate for fiscal 1999 was 35.0%.

NET INCOME

> Net income as a percent of revenue increased in 1997, 1998, and 1999 due primarily to the lower relative cost of revenue and sales and marketing expenses, combined with greater investment income.

FINANCIAL CONDITION

> The Company's cash and short-term investment portfolio totaled $17.24 billion at June 30, 1999. The portfolio is diversified among security types, industries, and individual issuers. Microsoft's investments are generally liquid and investment grade. The portfolio is invested predominantly in U.S. dollar denominated securities, but also includes foreign currency positions in anticipation of continued international expansion. The portfolio is primarily invested in short-term securities to minimize interest rate risk and facilitate rapid deployment in the event of immediate cash needs.

Microsoft also invests in equities, primarily strategic technology companies. The Company has made large-scale investments in access providers, including cable, telephony, and wireless communications companies. During 1999, the Company purchased $5.0 billion of AT&T convertible preferred securities and warrants, $600 million of Nextel Communications, Inc. common stock, $500 million of NTL, Inc. convertible preferred stock, $330 million of United Pan-Europe Communications common stock, and $200 million of Qwest Communications International Inc. common stock. In connection with AT&T's proposed merger with MediaOne Group, Inc., the Company agreed to acquire MediaOne's interest in Telewest Communications plc, a leading provider of cable television and residential and business cable telephony services in the United Kingdom, subject to certain regulatory approvals and other conditions. During 1997, Microsoft purchased $1.0 billion of Special Class A common stock and convertible preferred stock of Comcast Corporation. Microsoft also owns an interest in MCI WorldCom, Inc.

Microsoft and National Broadcasting Company (NBC) operate two MSNBC joint ventures: a 24-hour cable news and information channel, and an interactive online news service. Microsoft is paying $220 million over a five-year period that ends in 2001 for its interest in the cable venture and one-half of the operational funding of both joint ventures. Microsoft guarantees a portion of MSNBC debt.

Microsoft has no material long-term debt and has $100 million of standby multicurrency lines of credit to support foreign currency hedging and cash management. Stockholders' equity at June 30, 1999 was $28.44 billion.

Microsoft will continue to invest in sales, marketing, and product support infrastructure. Additionally, research and development activities will include investments in existing and advanced areas of technology, including using cash to acquire technology. Additions to property and equipment will continue, including new facilities and computer systems for R&D, sales and marketing, support, and administrative staff. Commitments for constructing new buildings were $275 million on June 30, 1999. Cash will also be used to fund ventures and other strategic opportunities.

In addition, cash will be used to repurchase common stock to provide shares for employee stock option and purchase plans. The buyback program has not kept pace with employee stock option grants or exercises. Beginning in fiscal 1990, Microsoft has repurchased 710 million common shares while 1.79 billion shares were issued under the Company's employee stock option and purchase plans. The market value of all outstanding stock options was $69 billion as of June 30, 1999. Microsoft enhances its repurchase program by selling put warrants. During December 1996, Microsoft issued 12.5 million shares of 2.75% convertible exchangeable preferred stock. Net proceeds of $980 million were used to repurchase common shares. In December 1999, each preferred share is convertible into common shares or an equivalent amount of cash determined by a formula that provides a floor price of $79.875 and a cap of $102.24 per preferred share, equivalent to $19.97 and $25.56 per common share.

Management believes existing cash and short-term investments together with funds generated from operations will be sufficient to meet operating requirements for the next 12 months. The Company's cash and short-term investments are available for strategic investments, mergers and acquisitions, other potential large-scale cash needs that may arise, and to fund an increased stock buyback program over historical levels to reduce the dilutive impact of the Company's employee stock option and purchase programs.

Microsoft has not paid cash dividends on its common stock. The preferred stock pays $2.196 per annum per share.

ISSUES AND UNCERTAINTIES

> While Microsoft management is optimistic about the Company's long-term prospects, the following issues and uncertainties, among others, should be considered in evaluating its growth outlook.

> RAPID TECHNOLOGICAL CHANGE AND COMPETITION Rapid change, uncertainty due to new and emerging technologies, and fierce competition characterize the PC software industry. The pace of change continues to accelerate, including "open source" software, new computing devices, new microprocessor architectures, the Internet, and Web-based computing models.

> FUTURE INITIATIVES The Company continues to expand its efforts to provide and support mission-critical systems to large enterprises. Microsoft is also developing a Windows Web-centric platform and simpler and new natural interfaces for PC users. Additionally, Microsoft is committed to providing technologies, operating systems, and online services for all types of computing devices, including PCs, televisions, and intelligent appliances. Future revenue from these initiatives may not duplicate historical revenue growth rates.

> PC GROWTH RATES The underlying PC unit growth rate and percentage of new PCs acquired as replacement units directly impact the Company's software revenue growth. Additionally, inexpensive PCs and specialty devices create less demand for Microsoft software than traditional PCs. The PC shipment growth rate may continue to decrease, the replacement rate may continue to increase, and limited-use PC growth may increase, reducing future software revenue opportunity.

> PRODUCT SHIP SCHEDULES Potential delays in new product releases, including seminal products such as Windows 2000, could dampen revenue growth rates and cause operational inefficiencies that impact manufacturing and distribution logistics and relationships with customers, OEMs, and independent software vendors.

> CUSTOMER ACCEPTANCE While the Company performs extensive usability and beta testing of new products, user acceptance and corporate penetration rates ultimately dictate the success of development and marketing efforts.

> PRICES Future product prices may decrease from historical levels, depending on competitive market and cost factors. European and Asian software prices vary by country and are generally higher than in the United States to cover localization costs and higher costs of distribution. Increased global license agreements, European monetary unification, or other factors could erode such price uplifts in the future.

> SATURATION Product upgrades, which enable users to upgrade from earlier versions of the Company's products or from competitors' products, have lower prices and margins than new products. Also, penetration of the Company's desktop applications into large organizations is becoming saturated. These factors are likely to depress future desktop applications revenue growth.

> ORGANIZATIONAL LICENSES Average revenue per unit from organizational license programs is lower than average revenue per unit from retail versions shipped through the finished goods channels. Unit sales under licensing programs may continue to increase.

> EARNINGS PROCESS An increasingly higher percentage of the Company's revenue is subject to ratable recognition, which impacts the timing of revenue and earnings recognition. This policy may be required for additional products, depending on specific license terms and conditions. Also, maintenance and other subscription programs may continue to increase in popularity, particularly with organizations.

> CHANNEL MIX Average revenue per license is lower from OEM licenses than from retail versions, reflecting the relatively lower direct costs of operations in the OEM channel. An increasingly higher percentage of revenue was achieved through the OEM channel during 1998 and 1999.

> COST OF REVENUE Decreases in cost of revenue as a percentage of revenue in 1998 and 1999 were due to general shifts from packaged products to OEM and organizational licenses, from lower-margin products to higher-margin products, and from disks to CD-ROMs. These shifts may not continue. Direct costs of product support; services such as consulting and training and certification of system integrators; and online operations comprise the majority of cost of revenue and are not likely to decrease. The trend of declining cost of revenue as a percentage of revenue is unlikely to continue in 2000.

> EMPLOYEE COMPENSATION Microsoft employees currently receive salaries, incentive bonuses, other benefits, and stock options. Fiscal 2000 salaries will be enhanced, with the mid-point salary range raised from the 50th to the 65th percentile of competitive positions. Additionally, new government regulations, poor stock price performance, or other factors could diminish the value of the option program to current and prospective employees and force the Company into more of a cash compensation model. Had the Company paid employees in cash the equivalent of the Black-Scholes value of options vested in 1997, 1998, and 1999, the incremental pretax expense would have been approximately $620 million, $850 million, and $1.10 billion.

> LONG-TERM R&D INVESTMENT CYCLE Developing and localizing software is expensive, and the investment in product development often involves a long payback cycle. The Company plans to continue significant investments in software research and development, including online initiatives. Significant revenue from these product opportunities is not anticipated for a number of years. Total spending for R&D in 2000 will increase over spending in 1999.

> SALES AND MARKETING INVESTMENTS The Company's plans for 2000 include accelerated investments in its sales groups, customer satisfaction, and marketing activities.

> INTERNATIONAL OPERATIONS Much of the Company's operations are conducted outside of the United States, and a large percentage of sales, costs of manufacturing, and marketing is transacted in local currencies. As a result, the Company's international results of operations are subject to local economic environments and foreign exchange rate fluctuations.

> MARKET RISK The Company is exposed to foreign currency, interest rate, and equity price risks. A portion of these risks is hedged, but fluctuations could impact the Company's results of operations and financial position. The Company hedges the exposure of accounts receivable and a portion of anticipated revenue to foreign currency fluctuations, primarily with option contracts. The Company monitors its foreign currency exposures daily to ensure the overall effectiveness of its foreign currency hedge positions. Principal currencies hedged include the Japanese yen, British pound, German mark, French franc, and Canadian dollar. Fixed income securities are subject to interest rate risk. The portfolio is diversified and consists primarily of investment grade securities to minimize credit risk. The Company routinely hedges its exposure to interest rate risk with options in the event of a catastrophic increase in interest rates. Many securities held in the Company's equity and other investments portfolio are subject to equity price risk. The Company hedges its equity price risk on certain highly volatile equity securities with options.

The Company used a value-at-risk (VAR) model to estimate and quantify its market risks. The VAR model is not intended to represent actual losses in fair value, but is used as a risk estimation and management tool. Assumptions applied to the VAR model at June 30, 1999 include the following: normal market conditions; Monte Carlo modeling with 10,000 simulated market price paths; a 97.5% confidence interval; and a 20-day estimated loss in fair value for each market risk category. Accordingly, 97.5% of the time the estimated 20-day loss in fair value would be nominal for foreign currency denominated investments and accounts receivable, and would not exceed $95 million for interest-sensitive investments or $1.38 billion for equity securities.

Previously, the Company used a sensitivity analysis to estimate interest rate and equity price risk. A 10% increase in interest rates would have reduced the carrying value of interest-sensitive securities by $128 million and $101 million at June 30, 1998 and 1999. A 10% decrease in market values would have reduced the carrying value of the Company's equity securities by $300 million and $1.37 billion at June 30, 1998 and 1999.

> INTELLECTUAL PROPERTY RIGHTS Microsoft diligently defends its intellectual property rights, but unlicensed copying of software represents a loss of revenue to the Company. While this adversely affects U.S. revenue, revenue loss is even more significant outside of the United States, particularly in countries where laws are less protective of intellectual property rights. Throughout the world, Microsoft actively educates consumers on the benefits of licensing genuine products and educates lawmakers on the advantages of a business climate where intellectual property rights are protected. However, continued efforts may not affect revenue positively.

> LITIGATION Litigation regarding intellectual property rights, patents, and copyrights occurs in the PC software industry. In addition, there are government regulation and investigation risks along with other general corporate legal risks.

> YEAR 2000 The Year 2000 presents potential concerns for business and consumer computing. In addition to the well-known calculation problems with the use of 2-digit date formats as the year changes from 1999 to 2000, the Year 2000 is a special case leap year and in many organizations using older technology, dates were used for special programmatic functions. The problem exists for many kinds of software and hardware, including mainframes, mini computers, PCs, and embedded systems. The consequences of this issue may include systems failures and business process interruption.

Microsoft has tested more than 3,000 versions/languages of its products. The vast majority of these tested products are Year 2000 compliant, as defined by Microsoft. There are a small number of older products that are identified as being non-compliant, and Microsoft will provide recommendations regarding these products. Not all versions of products or all products will be tested. All Year 2000 software updates, resources, and tools are available to customers at no charge from the Microsoft Year 2000 Portal Page or Microsoft Year 2000 Resource CD.

Current information needed to evaluate the impact of the Year 2000 on organizational and home computing environments is available at the Microsoft Year 2000 Portal Page (www.microsoft.com/year2000) and the Microsoft Year 2000 Resource CD, which is released on a quarterly basis. The Web site and Microsoft Year 2000 Resource CD detail specific Year 2000 information concerning Microsoft products and technologies for large organizations. The detailed information available on the Web site and Microsoft Year 2000 Resource CD is presented to assist information technology (IT) professionals in planning their transition to the Year 2000. The Microsoft Year 2000 Portal Page also contains information for small business and home PC users, including in-depth product information, answers to frequently asked questions, and links to the other Year 2000 sites.

Variability of definitions of "compliance" with the Year 2000 and of different combinations of software, firmware, and hardware will likely lead to lawsuits against the Company. The outcome of such lawsuits and the impact on the Company are not estimable at this time.

The Year 2000 issue also affects the Company's internal systems, including IT and non-IT systems. Microsoft has assessed the readiness of its mission-critical systems for handling the Year 2000. Although testing and remediation of all systems have not been completed, management currently believes that all mission-critical systems will be compliant by the Year 2000 and that the cost to address the issues is not material. Nevertheless, Microsoft is creating contingency plans for certain internal systems.

Microsoft is addressing the effect this issue will have on its third-party supply chain and has undertaken steps to formulate a system of working with key third parties to understand their ability to continue providing services and products through the change to 2000. Microsoft is working directly with its key vendors, distributors, and resellers to avoid material business interruptions in 2000. Contingency plans are being developed where practicable for these key third parties.

Resolving Year 2000 issues is a worldwide phenomenon that is absorbing a substantial portion of IT budgets and attention. Certain industry analysts believe the Year 2000 issue will accelerate the trend toward distributed PC-based systems from mainframe systems, while others believe a majority of IT resources will be devoted to fixing older mainframe software in lieu of large-scale transitions to systems based on software such as that developed by Microsoft. The impact of the Year 2000 on future Microsoft revenue is difficult to discern, but it is a risk to be considered in evaluating the future growth of the Company.

> FUTURE GROWTH RATE The revenue growth rate in 2000 may not approach the level attained in prior years. As discussed previously, operating expenses are expected to increase in 2000. Because of the fixed nature of a significant portion of such expenses, coupled with the possibility of slower revenue growth, operating margins in 2000 may decrease from those in 1999.

CASH FLOWS STATEMENTS

msft In millions

Year Ended June 30	1997	1998	1999
Operations			
Net income	$ 3,454	$ 4,490	$ 7,785
Depreciation and amortization	557	1,024	1,010
Write-off of acquired in-process technology	-	296	-
Gain on sale of Softimage, Inc.	-	-	(160)
Unearned revenue	1,601	3,268	5,877
Recognition of unearned revenue from prior periods	(743)	(1,798)	(4,526)
Other current liabilities	321	208	966
Accounts receivable	(336)	(520)	(687)
Other current assets	(165)	(88)	(235)
Net cash from operations	4,689	6,880	10,030
Financing			
Common stock issued	744	959	1,350
Common stock repurchased	(3,101)	(2,468)	(2,950)
Put warrant proceeds	95	538	766
Preferred stock issued	980	-	-
Preferred stock dividends	(15)	(28)	(28)
Stock option income tax benefits	796	1,553	3,107
Net cash from (used for) financing	(501)	554	2,245
Investing			
Additions to property and equipment	(499)	(656)	(583)
Cash portion of WebTV purchase price	-	(190)	-
Cash proceeds from sale of Softimage, Inc.	-	-	79
Purchases of investments	(18,216)	(19,114)	(36,441)
Maturities of investments	1,874	1,890	4,674
Sales of investments	13,752	10,798	21,080
Net cash used for investing	(3,089)	(7,272)	(11,191)
Net change in cash and equivalents	1,099	162	1,084
Effect of exchange rates on cash and equivalents	6	(29)	52
Cash and equivalents, beginning of year	2,601	3,706	3,839
Cash and equivalents, end of year	3,706	3,839	4,975
Short-term investments	5,260	10,088	12,261
Cash and short-term investments	$ 8,966	$ 13,927	$ 17,236

See accompanying notes.

BALANCE SHEETS

msft In millions

June 30	1998	1999
Assets		
Current assets:		
Cash and short-term investments	$13,927	**$17,236**
Accounts receivable	1,460	**2,245**
Other	502	**752**
Total current assets	15,889	**20,233**
Property and equipment	1,505	**1,611**
Equity and other investments	4,703	**14,372**
Other assets	260	**940**
Total assets	$22,357	**$37,156**
Liabilities and stockholders' equity		
Current liabilities:		
Accounts payable	$ 759	**$ 874**
Accrued compensation	359	**396**
Income taxes payable	915	**1,607**
Unearned revenue	2,888	**4,239**
Other	809	**1,602**
Total current liabilities	5,730	**8,718**
Commitments and contingencies		
Stockholders' equity:		
Convertible preferred stock - shares authorized 100; shares issued and outstanding 13	980	**980**
Common stock and paid-in capital - shares authorized 12,000; shares issued and outstanding 4,940 and 5,109	8,025	**13,844**
Retained earnings, including other comprehensive income of $666 and $1,787	7,622	**13,614**
Total stockholders' equity	16,627	**28,438**
Total liabilities and stockholders' equity	$22,357	**$37,156**

See accompanying notes.

STOCKHOLDERS' EQUITY STATEMENTS

msft In millions

Year Ended June 30	1997	1998	1999
Convertible preferred stock			
Balance, beginning of year	–	$ 980	$ 980
Convertible preferred stock issued	$ 980	–	–
Balance, end of year	980	980	980
Common stock and paid-in capital			
Balance, beginning of year	2,924	4,509	8,025
Common stock issued	744	1,262	2,338
Common stock repurchased	(91)	(165)	(64)
Structured repurchases price differential	–	328	(328)
Proceeds from sale of put warrants	95	538	766
Reclassification of put warrant obligation	45	–	–
Stock option income tax benefits	792	1,553	3,107
Balance, end of year	4,509	8,025	13,844
Retained earnings			
Balance, beginning of year	3,984	5,288	7,622
Net income	3,454	4,490	7,785
Other comprehensive income:			
Net unrealized investment gains	280	627	1,052
Translation adjustments and other	5	(124)	69
Comprehensive income	3,739	4,993	8,906
Preferred stock dividends	(15)	(28)	(28)
Common stock repurchased	(3,010)	(2,631)	(2,886)
Reclassification of put warrant obligation	590	–	–
Balance, end of year	5,288	7,622	13,614
Total stockholders' equity	$10,777	$16,627	$28,438

See accompanying notes.

NOTES TO FINANCIAL STATEMENTS

msft ACCOUNTING POLICIES

> ACCOUNTING PRINCIPLES The financial statements and accompanying notes are prepared in accordance with generally accepted accounting principles.

> PRINCIPLES OF CONSOLIDATION The financial statements include the accounts of Microsoft and its subsidiaries. Significant intercompany transactions and balances have been eliminated. Investments in 50% owned joint ventures are accounted for using the equity method; the Company's share of joint ventures' activities is reflected in other expenses.

> ESTIMATES AND ASSUMPTIONS Preparing financial statements requires management to make estimates and assumptions that affect the reported amounts of assets, liabilities, revenue, and expenses. Examples include provisions for returns and bad debts and the length of product life cycles and buildings' lives. Actual results may differ from these estimates.

> FOREIGN CURRENCIES Assets and liabilities recorded in foreign currencies are translated at the exchange rate on the balance sheet date. Translation adjustments resulting from this process are charged or credited to other comprehensive income. Revenue and expenses are translated at average rates of exchange prevailing during the year. Gains and losses on foreign currency transactions are included in other expenses.

> REVENUE RECOGNITION Revenue is recognized when earned. The Company's revenue recognition policies are in compliance with all applicable accounting regulations, including American Institute of Certified Public Accountants (AICPA) Statement of Position (SOP) 97-2, *Software Revenue Recognition,* and SOP 98-9, *Modification of SOP 97-2, With Respect to Certain Transactions.* Revenue from products licensed to original equipment manufacturers is recorded when OEMs ship licensed products while revenue from certain license programs is recorded when the software has been delivered and the customer is invoiced. Revenue from packaged product sales to and through distributors and resellers is recorded when related products are shipped. Maintenance and subscription revenue is recognized ratably over the contract period. Revenue attributable to undelivered elements, including technical support and Internet browser technologies, is based on the average sales price of those elements and is recognized ratably on a straight-line basis over the product's life cycle. When the revenue recognition criteria required for distributor and reseller arrangements are not met, revenue is recognized as payments are received. Costs related to insignificant obligations, which include telephone support for certain products, are accrued. Provisions are recorded for returns and bad debts.

> COST OF REVENUE Cost of revenue includes direct costs to produce and distribute product and direct costs to provide online services, consulting, product support, and training and certification of system integrators.

> RESEARCH AND DEVELOPMENT Research and development costs are expensed as incurred. Statement of Financial Accounting Standards (SFAS) 86, *Accounting for the Costs of Computer Software to Be Sold, Leased, or Otherwise Marketed,* does not materially affect the Company.

> INCOME TAXES Income tax expense includes U.S. and international income taxes, plus the provision for U.S. taxes on undistributed earnings of international subsidiaries. Certain items of income and expense are not reported in tax returns and financial statements in the same year. The tax effect of this difference is reported as deferred income taxes. Tax credits are accounted for as a reduction of tax expense in the year in which the credits reduce taxes payable.

NOTES continued

> STOCK SPLIT During March 1999, outstanding shares of common stock were split two-for-one. All share and per share amounts have been restated.

> FINANCIAL INSTRUMENTS The Company considers all liquid interest-earning investments with a maturity of three months or less at the date of purchase to be cash equivalents. Short-term investments generally mature between three months and six years from the purchase date. All cash and short-term investments are classified as available for sale and are recorded at market using the specific identification method; unrealized gains and losses are reflected in other comprehensive income. Cost approximates market for all classifications of cash and short-term investments; realized and unrealized gains and losses were not material.

Equity and other investments include debt and equity instruments. Debt securities and publicly traded equity securities are classified as available for sale and are recorded at market using the specific identification method. Unrealized gains and losses are reflected in other comprehensive income. All other investments, excluding joint venture arrangements, are recorded at cost.

Derivative financial instruments are used to hedge certain investments, international revenue, accounts receivable, and interest rate risks, and are, therefore, held primarily for purposes other than trading. These instruments may involve elements of credit and market risk in excess of the amounts recognized in the financial statements. The Company monitors its positions and the credit quality of counter parties, consisting primarily of major financial institutions, and does not anticipate nonperformance by any counter party.

During June 1999, the Financial Accounting Standards Board (FASB) issued SFAS 137, *Accounting for Derivative Instruments and Hedging Activities – Deferral of the Effective Date of FASB Statement 133*. The Statement defers the effective date of SFAS 133 to fiscal 2001. Management is evaluating SFAS 133 and does not believe that adoption of the Statement will have a material impact on its financial statements.

> PROPERTY AND EQUIPMENT Property and equipment is stated at cost and depreciated using the straight-line method over the shorter of the estimated life of the asset or the lease term, ranging from one to 15 years.

> RECLASSIFICATIONS The Company changed the way it reports revenue and costs associated with product support, consulting, MSN Internet access, and certification and training of system integrators. Amounts received from customers for these activities have been classified as revenue in a manner more consistent with Microsoft's primary businesses. Direct costs of these activities are classified as cost of revenue. Prior financial statements have been reclassified for consistent presentation. Certain other reclassifications have also been made for consistent presentation.

UNEARNED REVENUE

> A portion of Microsoft's revenue is earned ratably over the product life cycle or, in the case of subscriptions, over the period of the license agreement.

End users receive certain elements of the Company's products over a period of time. These elements include browser technologies and technical support. Consequently, Microsoft's earned revenue reflects the recognition of the fair value of these elements over the product's life cycle. Upon adoption of SOP 98-9 during the fourth quarter of fiscal 1999, the Company was required to change the methodology

NOTES continued

of attributing the fair value to undelivered elements. The percentages of undelivered elements in relation to the total arrangement decreased, reducing the amount of Windows and Office revenue treated as unearned, and increasing the amount of revenue recognized upon shipment. The percentage of revenue recognized ratably decreased from a range of 20% to 35% to a range of approximately 15% to 25% of Windows desktop operating systems. For desktop applications, the percentage decreased from approximately 20% to a range of approximately 10% to 20%. The ranges depend on the terms and conditions of the license and prices of the elements. The impact on fiscal 1999 was to increase reported revenue $170 million. In addition, the Company extended the life cycle of Windows from two to three years based upon management's review of product shipment cycles. The impact on fiscal 1999 was to decrease reported revenue $90 million. Product life cycles are currently estimated at 18 months for desktop applications. The Company also sells subscriptions to certain products via maintenance and certain organizational license agreements. At June 30, 1999, Windows platforms products unearned revenue was $2.17 billion and unearned revenue associated with productivity applications and developer products totaled $1.96 billion. Unearned revenue for other miscellaneous programs totaled $116 million at June 30, 1999.

FINANCIAL RISKS

> The Company's cash and short-term investment portfolio is diversified and consists primarily of investment grade securities. Investments are held with high-quality financial institutions, government and government agencies, and corporations, thereby reducing credit risk concentrations. Interest rate fluctuations impact the carrying value of the portfolio. The Company routinely hedges the portfolio's return with options in the event of a catastrophic increase in interest rates. At June 30, 1999, the notional amount of the options outstanding was $4.0 billion. The fair value and premiums paid for the options were not material. Much of the Company's equity security portfolio is highly volatile, so certain positions are hedged.

Finished goods sales to international customers in Europe, Japan, Canada, and Australia are primarily billed in local currencies. Payment cycles are relatively short, generally less than 90 days. Certain international manufacturing and operational costs are disbursed in local currencies. Local currency cash balances in excess of short-term operating needs are generally converted into U.S. dollar cash and short-term investments on receipt. Although foreign exchange rate fluctuations generally do not create a risk of material balance sheet gains or losses, the Company hedges a portion of accounts receivable balances denominated in local currencies, primarily with purchased options. At June 30, 1999, the notional amount of options outstanding was $662 million. The fair value and premiums paid for the options were not material.

Foreign exchange rates affect the translated results of operations of the Company's foreign subsidiaries. The Company hedges a portion of planned international revenue with purchased options. The notional amount of the options outstanding at June 30, 1999 was $2.25 billion. The fair value and premiums paid for the options were not material.

At June 30, 1998 and 1999, approximately 40% and 50% of accounts receivable represented amounts due from 10 customers. One customer accounted for approximately 12%, 8%, and 11% of revenue in 1997, 1998, and 1999.

Microsoft lends certain fixed income and equity securities to enhance investment income. Adequate collateral and/or security interest is determined based upon the underlying security and the credit worthiness of the borrower.

NOTES continued (in millions)

CASH AND SHORT-TERM INVESTMENTS

June 30	1998	1999
Cash and equivalents:		
Cash	$ 195	$ 635
Commercial paper	2,771	3,805
Certificates of deposit	419	522
Money market preferreds	454	13
Cash and equivalents	3,839	4,975
Short-term investments:		
Commercial paper	868	1,026
U.S. government and agency securities	3,511	3,592
Corporate notes and bonds	3,998	6,996
Municipal securities	1,361	247
Certificates of deposit	350	400
Short-term investments	10,088	12,261
Cash and short-term investments	$13,927	$17,236

PROPERTY AND EQUIPMENT

June 30	1998	1999
Land	$ 183	$ 158
Buildings	1,259	1,347
Computer equipment	1,182	1,433
Other	428	578
Property and equipment – at cost	3,052	3,516
Accumulated depreciation	(1,547)	(1,905)
Property and equipment – net	$ 1,505	$ 1,611

During 1997, 1998, and 1999, depreciation expense, of which the majority related to computer equipment, was $353 million, $528 million, and $483 million; disposals were not material.

NOTES continued (in millions)

EQUITY AND OTHER INVESTMENTS

June 30, 1999	Cost Basis	Net Unrealized Gains	Recorded Basis
Debt securities recorded at market, maturing:			
Within one year	$ 682	$ 8	$ 690
Between 10 and 15 years	533	(3)	530
Beyond 15 years (AT&T)	4,731	347	5,078
Debt securities recorded at market	5,946	352	6,298
Equity securities recorded at market:			
Comcast Corporation common stock	500	1,394	1,894
MCI Worldcom, Inc. common stock	14	1,088	1,102
Other	849	1,102	1,951
Unrealized hedge loss	-	(785)	(785)
Equity securities recorded at market	1,363	2,799	4,162
Equity securities and instruments recorded at cost:			
Nextel Communications, Inc. common stock	600	-	600
Comcast Corporation convertible preferred stock	555	-	555
NTL, Inc. convertible preferred stock	511	-	511
Other	2,179	-	2,179
Equity securities and instruments recorded at cost	3,845	-	3,845
Other investments	67	-	67
Equity and other investments	$11,221	$3,151	$14,372

Debt securities include corporate and government notes and bonds and derivative securities. Debt securities maturing beyond 15 years are composed entirely of AT&T 5% convertible preferred debt with a contractual maturity of 30 years. The debt is convertible into AT&T common stock on or after December 1, 2000, or may be redeemed by AT&T upon satisfaction of certain conditions on or after June 1, 2002. Unrealized gains on equity securities recorded at market were $1.4 billion on June 30, 1998. Equity securities and instruments recorded at cost include primarily preferred stock, common stock, and warrants that are restricted or not publicly traded. At June 30, 1998 and 1999, the estimated fair value of these investments was $2.4 billion and $6.1 billion, based on publicly available market information or other estimates determined by management. The Company hedges the risk of significant market declines on certain highly volatile equity securities with options. The options are recorded at market, consistent with the underlying equity securities. At June 30, 1999, the notional amount of the options outstanding was $2.1 billion; the fair value was $1.0 billion; and premiums paid for the options were not material. Realized gains and losses of equity and other investments in 1997 and 1998 were not material; realized gains were $623 million and losses were not material in 1999.

NOTES continued (in millions)

INCOME TAXES

> The provision for income taxes consisted of:

Year Ended June 30	1997	1998	1999
Current taxes:			
U.S. and state	$1,710	$2,518	**$4,027**
International	412	526	**281**
Current taxes	2,122	3,044	**4,308**
Deferred taxes	(262)	(417)	**(202)**
Provision for income taxes	$1,860	$2,627	**$4,106**

U.S. and international components of income before income taxes were:

Year Ended June 30	1997	1998	1999
U.S.	$3,775	$5,072	**$10,649**
International	1,539	2,045	**1,242**
Income before income taxes	$5,314	$7,117	**$11,891**

The effective income tax rate was 35.0% in 1997 and increased to 36.9% in 1998 due to the non-deductible write-off of WebTV in-process technologies. In 1999, the effective tax rate was 35.0%, excluding the impact of the gain on the sale of Softimage, Inc. The components of the differences between the U.S. statutory tax rate and the Company's effective tax rate were not significant.

Income taxes payable were:

June 30	1998	1999
Deferred income tax assets:		
Revenue items	$ 713	**$ 1,145**
Expense items	613	**648**
Deferred income tax assets	1,326	**1,793**
Deferred income tax liabilities:		
Unrealized gain on investments	(479)	**(1,046)**
International earnings	(373)	**(647)**
Other	(26)	**(16)**
Deferred income tax liabilities	(878)	**(1,709)**
Current income tax liabilities	(1,363)	**(1,691)**
Income taxes payable	$ (915)	**$(1,607)**

Income taxes have been settled with the Internal Revenue Service (IRS) for all years through 1989. The IRS has assessed taxes for 1990 and 1991, which the Company is contesting in U.S. Tax Court. The IRS is examining the Company's U.S. income tax returns for 1992 through 1994. Management believes any related adjustments that might be required will not be material to the financial statements. Income taxes paid were $1.1 billion in 1997, $1.1 billion in 1998, and $874 million in 1999.

NOTES continued (in millions)

CONVERTIBLE PREFERRED STOCK

> During 1996, Microsoft issued 12.5 million shares of 2.75% convertible exchangeable principal-protected preferred stock. Dividends are payable quarterly in arrears. Preferred stockholders have preference over common stockholders in dividends and liquidation rights. In December 1999, each preferred share is convertible into common shares or an equivalent amount of cash determined by a formula that provides a floor price of $79.875 and a cap of $102.24 per preferred share, equivalent to $19.97 and $25.56 per common share. Net proceeds of $980 million were used to repurchase common shares.

COMMON STOCK

> ISSUED AND OUTSTANDING Shares of common stock outstanding were as follows:

Year Ended June 30	1997	1998	1999
Balance, beginning of year	4,776	4,816	**4,940**
Issued	188	202	**213**
Repurchased	(148)	(78)	**(44)**
Balance, end of year	4,816	4,940	**5,109**

> REPURCHASE PROGRAM The Company repurchases its common stock in the open market to provide shares for issuing to employees under stock option and stock purchase plans. The Company's Board of Directors authorized continuation of this program in 2000.

During 1998, the Company executed two forward settlement structured repurchase agreements with an independent third party totaling 42 million shares of stock and paid cash for a portion of the purchase price. In 1999, the Company settled the agreements by returning 28 million shares of stock, based upon the stock price on the date of settlement. The timing and method of settlement were at the discretion of the Company. The differential between the cash paid and the price of Microsoft common stock on the date of the agreement was originally reflected in common stock and paid-in capital.

PUT WARRANTS

> To enhance its stock repurchase program, Microsoft sells put warrants to independent third parties. These put warrants entitle the holders to sell shares of Microsoft common stock to the Company on certain dates at specified prices. On June 30, 1999, 163 million warrants were outstanding with strike prices ranging from $59 to $65 per share. The put warrants expire between September 1999 and March 2002. The outstanding put warrants permit a net-share settlement at the Company's option and do not result in a put warrant liability on the balance sheet.

EMPLOYEE STOCK AND SAVINGS PLANS

> EMPLOYEE STOCK PURCHASE PLAN The Company has an employee stock purchase plan for all eligible employees. Under the plan, shares of the Company's common stock may be purchased at six-month intervals at 85% of the lower of the fair market value on the first or the last day of each six-month period. Employees may purchase shares having a value not exceeding 10% of their gross compensation during an offering period. During 1997, 1998, and 1999, employees purchased

NOTES continued (in millions, except per share amounts)

5.6 million, 4.4 million, and 2.7 million shares at average prices of $14.91, $27.21, and $52.59 per share. At June 30, 1999, 70.9 million shares were reserved for future issuance.

> SAVINGS PLAN The Company has a savings plan, which qualifies under Section 401(k) of the Internal Revenue Code. Participating employees may contribute up to 15% of their pretax salary, but not more than statutory limits. The Company contributes fifty cents for each dollar a participant contributes, with a maximum contribution of 3% of a participant's earnings. Matching contributions were $28 million, $39 million, and $49 million in 1997, 1998, and 1999.

> STOCK OPTION PLANS The Company has stock option plans for directors, officers, and employees, which provide for nonqualified and incentive stock options. Options granted prior to 1995 generally vest over four and one-half years and expire 10 years from the date of grant. Options granted during and after 1995 generally vest over four and one-half years and expire seven years from the date of grant, while certain options vest over seven and one-half years and expire after 10 years. At June 30, 1999, options for 406 million shares were vested and 998 million shares were available for future grants under the plans.

Stock options outstanding were as follows:

		Price per Share	
	Shares	Range	Weighted Average
Balance, June 30, 1996	952	$ 0.28 - $14.74	$ 5.52
Granted	220	13.83 - 29.80	14.58
Exercised	(180)	0.28 - 14.74	3.32
Canceled	(36)	4.25 - 24.29	9.71
Balance, June 30, 1997	956	0.56 - 29.80	7.86
Granted	138	16.56 - 43.63	31.28
Exercised	(176)	0.56 - 31.24	4.64
Canceled	(25)	4.25 - 41.94	14.69
Balance, June 30, 1998	893	0.56 - 43.63	11.94
Granted	78	45.59 - 83.28	54.62
Exercised	(175)	0.56 - 53.63	6.29
Canceled	(30)	4.25 - 74.28	21.06
Balance, June 30, 1999	766	0.56 - 83.28	17.28

For various price ranges, weighted average characteristics of outstanding stock options at June 30, 1999 were as follows:

	Outstanding Options			Exercisable Options	
Range of Exercise Prices	Shares	Remaining Life (Years)	Weighted Average Price	Shares	Weighted Average Price
$ 0.56 - $ 5.97	242	2.9	$ 4.31	230	$ 4.24
5.98 - 13.62	158	3.9	10.85	89	10.62
13.63 - 29.80	173	4.7	14.92	66	14.67
29.81 - 43.62	117	5.5	32.06	21	31.83
43.63 - 83.28	76	6.2	55.04	-	-

NOTES continued (in millions, except per share amounts)

The Company follows Accounting Principles Board Opinion 25, *Accounting for Stock Issued to Employees,* to account for stock option and employee stock purchase plans. Historically, exercise prices of grants of ESOs were struck at the lowest price in the 30 days following July 1 for annual grants and the 30 days after the start date for new employees. In connection with this practice, which is no longer employed, a charge of $217 million was recorded in the fourth quarter for fiscal 1999 compensation expense.

An alternative method of accounting for stock options is SFAS 123, *Accounting for Stock-Based Compensation.* Under SFAS 123, employee stock options are valued at grant date using the Black-Scholes valuation model, and compensation cost is recognized ratably over the vesting period. Had compensation cost for the Company's stock option and employee stock purchase plans been determined based on the Black-Scholes value at the grant dates for awards, pro forma income statements for 1997, 1998, and 1999 would have been as follows:

Year Ended June 30	1997		1998		**1999**	
	Reported	Pro forma	Reported	Pro forma	**Reported**	**Pro forma**
Revenue	$11,936	$11,936	$15,262	$15,262	**$19,747**	**$19,747**
Operating expenses:						
Cost of revenue	2,170	2,290	2,460	2,628	**2,814**	**3,024**
Research and development	1,863	2,168	2,601	3,023	**2,970**	**3,504**
Acquired in-process technology	–	–	296	296	**–**	**–**
Sales and marketing	2,411	2,539	2,828	3,003	**3,231**	**3,448**
General and administrative	362	424	433	520	**689**	**822**
Other expenses	259	259	230	230	**115**	**115**
Total operating expenses	7,065	7,680	8,848	9,700	**9,819**	**10,913**
Operating income	4,871	4,256	6,414	5,562	**9,928**	**8,834**
Investment income	443	443	703	703	**1,803**	**1,803**
Gain on sale of Softimage, Inc.	–	–	–	–	**160**	**160**
Income before income taxes	5,314	4,699	7,117	6,265	**11,891**	**10,797**
Provision for income taxes	1,860	1,646	2,627	2,325	**4,106**	**3,723**
Net income	3,454	3,053	4,490	3,940	**7,785**	**7,074**
Preferred stock dividends	15	15	28	28	**28**	**28**
Net income available for common shareholders	$ 3,439	$ 3,038	$ 4,462	$ 3,912	**$ 7,757**	**$ 7,046**
Diluted earnings per share	$ 0.66	$ 0.58	$ 0.84	$ 0.73	**$ 1.42**	**$ 1.29**

The pro forma disclosures in the previous table include the amortization of the fair value of all options vested during 1997, 1998, and 1999, regardless of the grant date. If only options granted after 1996 were valued, as prescribed by SFAS 123, pro forma net income would have been $3,179 million, $4,019 million, and $7,109 million, and earnings per share would have been $0.61, $0.75, and $1.30 for 1997, 1998, and 1999.

The weighted average Black-Scholes value of options granted under the stock option plans during 1997, 1998, and 1999 was $5.86, $11.81, and $20.90. Value was estimated using an expected life of five years, no dividends, volatility of .32 in 1999 and 1998 and .30 in 1997, and risk-free interest rates of 6.5%, 5.7%, and 4.9% in 1997, 1998, and 1999.

NOTES continued (in millions, except per share amounts)

EARNINGS PER SHARE

> Basic earnings per share is computed on the basis of the weighted average number of common shares outstanding. Diluted earnings per share is computed on the basis of the weighted average number of common shares outstanding plus the effect of outstanding preferred shares using the "if-converted" method, assumed net-share settlement of common stock structured repurchases, and outstanding stock options using the "treasury stock" method.

The components of basic and diluted earnings per share were as follows:

Year Ended June 30	1997	1998	1999
Net income	$3,454	$4,490	**$7,785**
Preferred stock dividends	15	28	**28**
Net income available for common shareholders	$3,439	$4,462	**$7,757**
Weighted average outstanding shares of common stock	4,782	4,864	**5,028**
Dilutive effect of:			
Common stock under structured repurchases	–	6	**13**
Preferred stock	26	34	**16**
Employee stock options	436	458	**425**
Common stock and common stock equivalents	5,244	5,362	**5,482**
Earnings per share:			
Basic	$ 0.72	$ 0.92	**$ 1.54**
Diluted	$ 0.66	$ 0.84	**$ 1.42**

OPERATIONAL TRANSACTIONS

> In August 1997, Microsoft acquired WebTV Networks, Inc., an online service that enables consumers to experience the Internet through their televisions via set-top terminals based on proprietary technologies. A director of the Company owned 10% of WebTV. Microsoft paid $425 million in stock and cash for WebTV. The Company recorded an in-process technologies write-off of $296 million in the first quarter of fiscal 1998.

In August 1998, the Company sold a wholly-owned subsidiary, Softimage, Inc. to Avid Technology, Inc. and recorded a pretax gain of $160 million. As part of a transitional service agreement, Microsoft agreed to make certain development tools and management systems available to Avid for use in the Softimage, Inc. business.

In November 1998, Microsoft acquired LinkExchange, Inc., a leading provider of online marketing services to Web site owners and small and medium-sized businesses. Microsoft paid $265 million in stock. During fiscal 1999, Microsoft also acquired several other entities primarily providing online technologies and services. The Company did not record significant in-process technology write-offs in connection with these transactions.

In July 1999, Ticketmaster Online CitySearch, Inc. agreed to purchase certain online properties of Sidewalk in exchange for stock and warrants at a price to be determined upon closing.

NOTES continued

COMMITMENTS

> The Company has operating leases for most U.S. and international sales and support offices and certain equipment. Rental expense for operating leases was $92 million, $95 million, and $135 million in 1997, 1998, and 1999. Future minimum rental commitments under noncancelable leases, in millions of dollars, are: 2000, $133; 2001, $121; 2002, $97; 2003, $83; 2004, $75; and thereafter, $194.

In connection with the Company's communications infrastructure and the operation of online services, Microsoft has certain communication usage commitments. Future related minimum commitments, in millions of dollars, are: 2000, $125 and 2001, $22. Also, Microsoft has committed to certain volumes of outsourced telephone support and manufacturing of packaged product and has committed $275 million for constructing new buildings.

During 1996, Microsoft and National Broadcasting Company (NBC) established two MSNBC joint ventures: a 24-hour cable news and information channel and an interactive online news service. Microsoft agreed to pay $220 million over a five-year period for its interest in the cable venture, to pay one-half of operational funding of both joint ventures for a multiyear period, and to guarantee a portion of MSNBC debt.

CONTINGENCIES

> On October 7, 1997, Sun Microsystems, Inc. brought suit against Microsoft in the U.S. District Court for the Northern District of California. Sun's complaint alleges several claims against Microsoft, all related to the parties' relationship under a March 11, 1996 Technology License and Distribution Agreement (Agreement) concerning certain Java programming language technology. The Complaint seeks: a preliminary and permanent injunction against Microsoft distributing certain products with the Java Compatibility logo, and against distributing Internet Explorer 4.0 browser technology unless certain alleged obligations are met; an order compelling Microsoft to perform certain alleged obligations; an accounting; termination of the Agreement; and an award of damages, including compensatory, exemplary, and punitive damages, and liquidated damages of $35 million for the alleged source code disclosure.

On March 24, 1998, the court entered an order enjoining Microsoft from using the Java Compatibility logo on Internet Explorer 4.0 and the Microsoft Software Developers Kit (SDK) for Java 2.0. Microsoft has taken steps to fully comply with the order.

On November 17, 1998, the court entered an order granting Sun's request for a preliminary injunction, holding that Sun had established a likelihood of success on its copyright infringement claims, because Microsoft's use of Sun's technology in its products was beyond the scope of the parties' license agreement. The court ordered Microsoft to make certain changes in its products that include Sun's Java technology and to make certain changes in its Java software development tools. The court also enjoined Microsoft from entering into any licensing agreements that were conditioned on exclusive use of Microsoft's Java Virtual Machine. Microsoft appealed that ruling to the 9th Circuit on December 16, 1998. Oral argument on that appeal was held on June 16, 1999. In the interim, Microsoft is complying with the ruling and has not sought a stay of the injunction pending appeal. On December 18, 1998, Microsoft filed a motion requesting an extension of the 90-day compliance period for certain Microsoft products, which was granted in part in January 1999. Microsoft filed a motion on February 5, 1999, seeking clarification of the court's order that Microsoft would not be prevented from engaging in independent development of Java technology under the order. The court granted that motion. On July 23, 1999 the court also granted Microsoft's motion to increase the bond on the preliminary injunction from $15 million to $35 million.

NOTES continued

On January 22, 1999, Microsoft and Sun filed a series of summary judgment motions regarding the interpretation of the contract and other issues. On May 20, 1999, the court issued tentative rulings on three of the motions. In the preliminary rulings, the court (1) granted Sun's motion for summary judgment that prior versions of Internet Explorer 4.0, Windows 98, Windows NT, Visual J++® 6.0 development system, and the SDK for Java infringe Sun's copyrights, because they contain Sun's program code but do not pass Sun's compatibility tests and, therefore, Microsoft's use of Sun's technology is outside the scope of the Agreement and unlicensed; (2) granted Microsoft's motion that the Agreement authorizes Microsoft to distribute independently developed Java technology that is not subject to the compatibility obligations in the Agreement; and (3) denied Sun's motion for summary judgment on the meaning of certain provisions of the Agreement, tentatively adopting Microsoft's interpretation that Sun is required to deliver certain new Java technology, called "Supplemental Java Classes," in working order on Microsoft's then existing and commercially distributed virtual machine. On June 24, 1999, the court heard oral argument on the three tentative rulings. No final orders have been issued. At the hearing, the court also directed the parties to identify other pending summary judgment motions that the court should next consider. There are no other hearing or trial dates set.

On May 18, 1998, the Antitrust Division of the U.S. Department of Justice (DOJ) and a group of 20 state Attorneys General filed two antitrust cases against Microsoft in the U.S. District Court for the District of Columbia. The DOJ complaint alleges violations of Sections 1 and 2 of the Sherman Act. The DOJ complaint seeks declaratory relief as to the violations it asserts and preliminary and permanent injunctive relief regarding: the inclusion of Internet browsing software (or other software products) as part of Windows; the terms of agreements regarding non-Microsoft Internet browsing software (or other software products); taking or threatening "action adverse" in consequence of a person's failure to license or distribute Microsoft Internet browsing software (or other software product) or distributing competing products or cooperating with the government; and restrictions on the screens, boot-up sequence, or functions of Microsoft's operating system products. The state Attorneys General allege largely the same claims and various pendent state claims. The states seek declaratory relief and preliminary and permanent injunctive relief similar to that sought by the DOJ, together with statutory penalties under the state law claims. The foregoing description is qualified in its entirety by reference to the full text of the complaints and other papers on file in those actions, case numbers 98-1232 and 98-1233.

On May 22, 1998, Judge Jackson consolidated the two actions. The judge granted Microsoft's motion for summary judgment as to the states' monopoly leverage claim and permitted the remaining claims to proceed to trial. Trial began on October 19, 1998. Microsoft believes the claims are without merit and is defending against them vigorously. In other ongoing investigations, the DOJ and several state Attorneys General have requested information from Microsoft concerning various issues.

Caldera, Inc. filed a lawsuit against Microsoft in July 1996. It alleges Sherman Act violations relating to Microsoft licensing practices of the MS-DOS® operating system and Windows in the late 80s and early 90s — essentially the same complaints that resulted in the 1994 DOJ consent decree. Caldera claims to own the rights of Novell, Inc. and Digital Research, Inc. relating to DR-DOS and Novell DOS products. It also asserts a claim that Windows 95 is a technological tie of Windows and MS-DOS. Trial is scheduled for January 2000. Some partial summary judgment motions are pending. Microsoft believes the claims are without merit and is vigorously defending the case.

The Securities and Exchange Commission is conducting a non-public investigation into the Company's accounting reserve practices. Microsoft is also subject to various legal proceedings and claims that arise in the ordinary course of business.

Management currently believes that resolving these matters will not have a material adverse impact on the Company's financial position or its results of operations.

NOTES continued (in millions)

SEGMENT INFORMATION

Year Ended June 30	Windows Platforms	Productivity Applications and Developer	Consumer, Commerce, and Other	Reconciling Amounts	Consolidated
1997					
Revenue	$5,213	$5,992	$ 1,129	$ (398)	$11,936
1998					
Revenue	$6,236	$7,458	$ 1,765	$ (197)	$15,262
Operating income	3,661	4,824	(1,050)	(1,021)	6,414
1999					
Revenue	**$8,590**	**$8,686**	**$ 1,784**	**$ 687**	**$ 19,747**
Operating income	**6,007**	**5,568**	**(1,072)**	**(575)**	**9,928**

The Company's organizational structure and fundamental approach to business reflect the needs of its customers. As such, Microsoft has three major segments: Windows Platforms; Productivity Applications and Developer; and Consumer, Commerce, and Other. Windows Platforms includes the Business and Enterprise Division, which is primarily responsible for Windows NT and developing Windows 2000. Windows Platforms also includes the Consumer Windows Division, which oversees Windows 98 and Windows 95. Productivity Applications and Developer includes the Business Productivity Division, which is responsible for developing and marketing desktop applications, server applications, and developer tools. Consumer, Commerce, and Other products and services include primarily learning, entertainment, and PC input device products; WebTV and PC online access; and portal and other Internet services. Assets of the segment groups are not relevant for management of the businesses nor for disclosure. In addition, it is not practicable to discern operating income for 1997 for the above segments due to previous internal reorganizations.

Segment information is presented in accordance with SFAS 131, *Disclosures about Segments of an Enterprise and Related Information*. This standard is based on a management approach, which requires segmentation based upon the Company's internal organization and disclosure of revenue and operating income based upon internal accounting methods. The Company's financial reporting systems present various data for management to run the business, including profit and loss statements (P&Ls) prepared on a basis not consistent with generally accepted accounting principles. Reconciling items include certain elements of unearned revenue, the treatment of certain channel inventory amounts and estimates, and revenue from product support, consulting, and training and certification of system integrators. Additionally, the internal P&Ls use accelerated methods of depreciation and amortization, but do not reflect the charge for the ESO exercise price methodology previously employed by the Company.

Revenue attributable to U.S. operations includes shipments to customers in the United States, licensing to OEMs and certain multinational organizations, and exports of finished goods primarily to Asia, Latin America, and Canada. Revenue from U.S. operations totaled $7.8 billion, $10.1 billion, and $13.7 billion in 1997, 1998, and 1999. Revenue from outside the United States, excluding licensing to OEMs and certain multinational organizations and U.S. exports, totaled $4.1 billion, $5.2 billion, and $6.0 billion in 1997, 1998, and 1999.

Long-lived assets totaled $1.2 billion and $1.5 billion in the United States in 1998 and 1999 and $287 million and $154 million in other countries in 1998 and 1999.

QUARTERLY INFORMATION (in millions, except per share amounts, unaudited)

	Quarter Ended				
	Sept. 30	Dec. 31	Mar. 31	June 30	Year
1997					
Revenue	$2,405	$2,808	$3,365	$3,358	$11,936
Gross profit	1,923	2,250	2,782	2,811	9,766
Net income	614	741	1,042	1,057	3,454
Basic earnings per share	0.13	0.15	0.22	0.22	0.72
Diluted earnings per share	0.12	0.14	0.20	0.20	0.66
Common stock price per share:					
High	17.33	21.54	25.88	33.74	33.74
Low	13.44	16.36	20.19	22.44	13.44
1998					
Revenue	$3,334	$3,792	$3,984	$4,152	$15,262
Gross profit	2,800	3,179	3,344	3,479	12,802
Net income	663	1,133	1,337	1,357	4,490
Basic earnings per share	0.14	0.24	0.27	0.27	0.92
Diluted earnings per share	0.13	0.21	0.25	0.25	0.84
Common stock price per share:					
High	37.69	36.66	45.47	54.28	54.28
Low	30.82	29.50	31.10	40.94	29.50
1999					
Revenue	**$4,193**	**$5,195**	**$4,595**	**$5,764**	**$19,747**
Gross profit	**3,544**	**4,407**	**3,887**	**5,095**	**16,933**
Net income	**1,683**	**1,983**	**1,917**	**2,202**	**7,785**
Basic earnings per share	**0.34**	**0.40**	**0.38**	**0.43**	**1.54**
Diluted earnings per share	**0.31**	**0.36**	**0.35**	**0.40**	**1.42**
Common stock price per share:					
High	**59.81**	**72.00**	**94.63**	**95.63**	**95.63**
Low	**47.25**	**48.13**	**68.00**	**75.50**	**47.25**

The Company's common stock is traded on The Nasdaq Stock Market under the symbol MSFT. On July 31, 1999, there were 92,169 registered holders of record of the Company's common stock. The Company has not paid cash dividends on its common stock.

REPORTS OF MANAGEMENT AND INDEPENDENT AUDITORS

Management is responsible for preparing the Company's financial statements and the other information that appears in this annual report. Management believes that the financial statements fairly reflect the form and substance of transactions and reasonably present the Company's financial condition and results of operations in conformity with generally accepted accounting principles. Management has included in the Company's financial statements amounts that are based on estimates and judgments, which it believes are reasonable under the circumstances.

The Company maintains a system of internal accounting policies, procedures, and controls intended to provide reasonable assurance, at appropriate cost, that transactions are executed in accordance with Company authorization and are properly recorded and reported in the financial statements, and that assets are adequately safeguarded.

Deloitte & Touche LLP audits the Company's financial statements in accordance with generally accepted auditing standards and provides an objective, independent review of the Company's internal controls and the fairness of its reported financial condition and results of operations.

The Microsoft Board of Directors has an Audit Committee composed of nonmanagement Directors. The Committee meets with financial management, internal auditors, and the independent auditors to review internal accounting controls and accounting, auditing, and financial reporting matters.

Gregory B. Maffei
Senior Vice President, Finance and Administration; Chief Financial Officer

To the Board of Directors and Stockholders of Microsoft Corporation:

We have audited the accompanying balance sheets of Microsoft Corporation and subsidiaries as of June 30, 1998 and 1999, and the related statements of income, cash flows, and stockholders' equity for each of the three years ended June 30, 1999, appearing on pages 17 and 27 through 42. These financial statements are the responsibility of the Company's management. Our responsibility is to express an opinion on these financial statements based on our audits.

We conducted our audits in accordance with generally accepted auditing standards. Those standards require that we plan and perform the audit to obtain reasonable assurance about whether the financial statements are free of material misstatement. An audit includes examining, on a test basis, evidence supporting the amounts and disclosures in the financial statements. An audit also includes assessing the accounting principles used and significant estimates made by management, as well as evaluating the overall financial statement presentation. We believe that our audits provide a reasonable basis for our opinion.

In our opinion, such financial statements present fairly, in all material respects, the financial position of Microsoft Corporation and subsidiaries as of June 30, 1998 and 1999, and the results of their operations and their cash flows for each of the three years ended June 30, 1999 in conformity with generally accepted accounting principles.

Deloitte & Touche LLP
Seattle, Washington
July 19, 1999

DIRECTORS AND OFFICERS

DIRECTORS

William H. Gates, III
Chairman of the Board;
Chief Executive Officer,
Microsoft Corporation

Paul G. Allen
Chairman of the Board,
Vulcan Northwest Inc.

Jill Barad
President and
Chief Executive Officer,
Mattel, Inc.

Richard A. Hackborn
Chairman-Elect of the Board,
Hewlett-Packard Company

David F. Marquardt
General Partner,
August Capital and
Technology Venture Investors

Wm. G. Reed, Jr.
Chairman of the Board,
Simpson Investment
Company (retired)

Jon A. Shirley
President and
Chief Operating Officer,
Microsoft Corporation
(retired)

EXECUTIVE OFFICERS

William H. Gates, III
Chairman of the Board;
Chief Executive Officer

Steven A. Ballmer
President

Robert J. Herbold
Executive Vice President;
Chief Operating Officer

Frank M. (Pete) Higgins
Group Vice President
(on leave)

Paul A. Maritz
Group Vice President,
Developer

Jeffrey S. Raikes
Group Vice President,
Sales and Support

James E. Allchin
Senior Vice President,
Platforms

Orlando Ayala Lozano
Senior Vice President,
South Pacific and Americas

Joachim Kempin
Senior Vice President,
OEM Sales

Michel Lacombe
Senior Vice President;
President, Microsoft
Europe, Middle East,
and Africa

Gregory B. Maffei
Senior Vice President,
Finance and Administration;
Chief Financial Officer

Robert L. Muglia
Senior Vice President,
Business Productivity

Craig Mundie
Senior Vice President,
Consumer Strategy

William H. Neukom
Senior Vice President,
Law and Corporate
Affairs; Secretary

Bernard P. Vergnes
Senior Vice President;
Chairman, Microsoft
Europe, Middle East,
and Africa

VICE PRESIDENTS

Robert J. Bach
Home and Retail

Dick Brass
eMerging Technologies

Brad Chase
Consumer and Commerce

Frank M. Clegg
Central United States
and Canada

David Cole
Consumer Windows

John G. Connors
Enterprise

Jean-Philippe Courtois
Customer Marketing

Jon DeVaan
Consumer and Commerce

Richard R. Devenuti
Information Technology;
Chief Information Officer

Richard W. Fade
OEM Multinational Accounts

Dianne Gregg
Eastern United States

Paul H. Gross
Server Applications

William V. Henningsgaard
Western United States
and South Pacific

Laura Jennings
Planning

Kevin Johnson
Product Support Services

Pieter Knook
Asia

Harel Kodesh
Productivity Appliances

Thomas Koll
Network Solutions

Bruce A. Leak
WebTV

John Leftwich
Europe, Middle East,
and Africa Marketing

Lewis Levin
TransPoint

Moshe Lichtman
Consumer and Commerce,
International

Nick N. MacPhee
Operations

Mich Mathews
Corporate Communications

Robert L. McDowell
Enterprise Business
Relationships

Tod Nielsen
Developer Marketing

Umberto Paolucci
Europe, Middle East,
and Africa

Richard F. Rashid
Research

Darryl E. Rubin
Software Strategy

Stephen A. Schiro
Home and Retail Sales

Steven J. Sinofsky
Office

Charles Stevens
Business Solutions

Rick Thompson
Hardware

Rich Tong
Business Audience
Management

Brian Valentine
Business and Enterprise

David Vaskevitch
Distributed Applications
Platform

Henry P. Vigil
Consumer Strategy
and Partnerships

Christopher L. Williams
Human Resources

Deborah N. Willingham
Business and
Enterprise Marketing

A

Account. An accounting record in which the results of transactions are accumulated; shows increases, decreases, and a balance.

Accounting. A system for providing quantitative, financial information about economic entities that is useful for making sound economic decisions. Accounting is often called the "language of business" because it provides the means of recording and communicating business activities and the results of those activities.

Accounting cycle. The procedure for analyzing, recording, classifying, summarizing, and reporting the transactions of a business.

Accounting equation. An algebraic equation that expresses the relationship between assets (resources), liabilities (obligations), and owners' equity (net assets, or the residual interest in a business after all liabilities have been met): Assets = Liabilities + Owners' equity.

Accounting model. The basic accounting assumptions, concepts, principles, and procedures that determine the manner of recording, measuring, and reporting a company's transactions.

Accounting system. The procedures and processes used by a business to analyze transactions, handle routine bookkeeping tasks, and structure information so it can be used to evaluate the performance and health of the business.

Accounts receivable. A current asset representing money due for services performed or merchandise sold on credit.

Accounts receivable turnover. A measure used to indicate how fast a company collects its receivables; computed by dividing sales by average accounts receivable.

Accrual-basis accounting. A system of accounting in which revenues and expenses are recorded as they are earned and incurred, not necessarily when cash is received or paid.

Accumulated other comprehensive income. Certain market-related gains and losses that are not included in the computation of net income; for example, foreign currency translation adjustments and unrealized gains or losses on investments.

Activity-based costing (ABC). A method of attributing costs to products based on first assigning costs of resources to activities and then costs of activities to products.

Activity-based management (ABM). The identification and use of cost drivers and performance measures to manage the costs, quality, and timeliness of activities.

Adjusting entries. Entries required at the end of each accounting period to recognize, on an accrual basis, revenues and expenses for the period and to report proper amounts for asset, liability, and owners' equity accounts.

Aging accounts receivable. The process of categorizing each account receivable by the number of days it has been outstanding.

Allowance for bad debts. A contra account, deducted from accounts receivable, that shows the estimated losses from uncollectible accounts.

Allowance method. The recording of estimated losses due to uncollectible accounts as expenses during the period in which the sales occurred.

American Institute of Certified Public Accountants (AICPA). The national organization of CPAs in the United States.

Amortization. The process of cost allocation that assigns the original cost of an intangible asset to the periods benefited.

Annual report. A document that summarizes the results of operations and financial status of a company for the past year and outlines plans for the future.

Annuity. A series of equal amounts to be received or paid at the end of equal time intervals.

Appraisal costs. Costs of quality that specifically relate to the effort of inspecting, testing, and sampling activities performed in order to identify and remove low-quality products and services from the system.

Arm's-length transactions. Business dealings between independent and rational parties who are looking out for their own interests.

Articulation. The interrelationships among the financial statements.

Asset turnover. A measure of company efficiency, computed by dividing revenue by total assets.

Asset turnover ratio. An overall measure of how effectively assets are used during a period; computed by dividing revenue by total assets.

Assets. Economic resources that are owned or controlled by a company.

Assets-to-equity ratio. A measure of the number of dollars of assets a company is able to acquire using each dollar of equity; calculated by dividing assets by equity.

Audit committee. Members of a company's board of directors who are responsible for dealing with the external and internal auditors.

Audit report. A report issued by an independent CPA that expresses an opinion about whether the financial statements fairly present a company's financial position, operating results, and cash flows in accordance with generally accepted accounting principles.

Available-for-sale securities. Debt and equity securities not classified as trading, held-to-maturity, or equity method securities.

Average collection period. A measure of the average number of days it takes to collect a credit sale; computed by dividing 365 days by the accounts receivable turnover.

Average cost. An inventory cost flow assumption whereby cost of goods sold and the cost of ending inventory are determined by using an average cost of all merchandise available for sale during the period.

B

Bad debt. An uncollectible account receivable.

Bad debt expense. An account that represents the portion of the current period's credit sales that are estimated to be uncollectible.

Balance sheet (statement of financial position). The financial statement that reports a company's assets, liabilities, and owners' equity at a particular date.

Balanced Scorecard. A new management model designed to link together performance measures for financial, customer, internal process, and learning/growth perspectives that are unique to an organization's particular strategy.

Bank reconciliation. The process of systematically comparing the cash balance as reported by the bank with the cash balance on the company's books and explaining any differences.

Basket purchase. The purchase of two or more assets acquired together at a single price.

Batch-level activities. Activities that take place in order to support a batch or production run, regardless of the size.

Benchmarking. A performance evaluation process used by companies to target areas for improvement by comparing the company's financial and operating performance against the performance of other companies or the performance of internal departments against each other.

Board of directors. Individuals elected by the stockholders to govern a corporation.

Bond. A contract between a borrower and a lender in which the borrower promises to pay a specified rate of interest for each period the bond is outstanding and repay the principal at the maturity date.

Bond carrying value. The face value of bonds minus the unamortized discount or plus the unamortized premium.

Bond discount. The difference between the face value and the sales price when bonds are sold below their face value.

Bond indenture. A contract between a bond issuer and a bond purchaser that specifies the terms of a bond.

Bond maturity date. The date at which a bond principal or face amount becomes payable.

Bond premium. The difference between the face value and the sales price when bonds are sold above their face value.

Bonus. Additional compensation, beyond the regular compensation, that is paid to employees if certain objectives are achieved.

Book value. The value of a company as measured by the amount of owners' equity; that is, assets less liabilities.

Bookkeeping. The preservation of a systematic, quantitative record of an activity.

Break-even point. The amount of sales at which total costs of the number of units sold equal total revenues; the point at which there is no profit or loss.

Budget. A quantitative expression of a plan of action that shows how a firm or an organization will acquire and use resources over some specified period of time.

Budget committee. A management group responsible for establishing budgeting policy and for coordinating the preparation of budgets.

Business. An organization operated with the objective of making a profit from the sale of goods or services.

Business documents. Records of transactions used as the basis for recording accounting entries; include invoices, check stubs, receipts, and similar business papers.

C

Calendar year. An entity's reporting year, covering 12 months and ending on December 31.

Callable bonds. Bonds for which the issuer reserves the right to pay the obligation before its maturity date.

Capability costs. Costs necessary to have the capability to produce a particular product or to provide a particular service. Capability costs are also known as the costs of product line activities.

Capital. The total amount of money or other resources owned or used to acquire future income or benefits.

Capital account. An account in which a proprietor's or partner's interest in a firm is recorded; it is increased by owner investments and net income and decreased by withdrawals and net losses.

Capital budgeting. Systematic planning for long-term investments in operating assets.

Capital lease. A leasing transaction that is recorded as a purchase by the lessee.

Capital rationing. Allocating limited resources among ranked acceptable investments.

Capital stock. The portion of a corporation's owners' equity contributed by owners in exchange for shares of stock.

Capitalized interest. Interest that is recorded as part of the cost of a self-constructed asset.

Cash. Coins, currency, money orders, checks, and funds on deposit with financial institutions; the most liquid of assets.

Cash budget. A schedule of expected cash receipts and disbursements during the budget period.

Cash disbursements journal. A special journal in which all cash paid out for supplies, merchandise, salaries, and other items is recorded.

Cash dividend. A cash distribution of earnings to stockholders.

Cash equivalents. Short-term, highly liquid investments that can be converted easily into cash.

Cash inflows. Any current or expected revenues or savings directly associated with an investment.

Cash outflows. The initial cost and other expected outlays associated with an investment.

Cash receipts journal. A special journal in which all cash received, from sales, interest, rent, or other sources, is recorded.

Cash-basis accounting. A system of accounting in which transactions are recorded and revenues and expenses are recognized only when cash is received or paid.

Ceiling. The maximum market amount at which inventory can be carried on the books; equal to net realizable value.

Centralized company. An organization in which top management makes most of the major decisions for the entire company rather than delegating them to managers at lower levels.

Certified Public Accountant (CPA). A special designation given to an accountant who has passed a national uniform examination and has met other certifying requirements.

Channel. The distribution line that a product travels from the original manufacturer to the eventual end-user customer. The channel is typically composed of a manufacturer, a wholesaler, a retailer, and the end-user customer.

Chart of accounts. A systematic listing of all accounts used by a company.

Classified balance sheet. A balance sheet in which assets and liabilities are subdivided into current and long-term categories.

Closing entries. Entries that reduce all nominal, or temporary, accounts to a zero balance at the end of each accounting period, transferring their preclosing balances to a permanent balance sheet account.

Common costs. Manufacturing overhead costs, such as executive salaries or property taxes, that cannot be attributed to products. Costs of facility support activities are common costs.

Common stock. The most frequently issued class of stock; usually it provides a voting right but is secondary to preferred stock in dividend and liquidation rights.

Common-size financial statements. Financial statements achieved by dividing all financial statement numbers by total revenues for the year.

Comparative financial statements. Financial statements in which data for two or more years are shown together.

Compound journal entry. A journal entry that involves more than one debit or more than one credit or both.

Compounding period. The period of time for which interest is computed.

Comprehensive income. A measure of the overall change in a company's wealth during a period; consists of net income plus changes in wealth resulting from changes in investment values and exchange rates.

Consignment. An arrangement whereby merchandise owned by one party, the consignor, is sold by another party, the consignee, usually on a commission basis.

Consolidated financial statements. Statements that report the combined operating results, financial position, and cash flows of two or more legally separate but affiliated companies as if they were one economic entity.

Contingency. Circumstances involving potential losses that will not be resolved until some future event occurs.

Contra account. An account that is offset or deducted from another account.

Contributed capital. The portion of owners' equity contributed by investors (the owners) in exchange for shares of stock.

Contribution margin. The difference between total sales and variable costs; the portion of sales revenue available to cover fixed costs and provide a profit.

Contribution-margin ratio. The percentage of net sales revenue left after variable costs are deducted; the contribution margin divided by net sales revenue.

Control account. A summary account in the general ledger that is supported by detailed individual accounts in a subsidiary ledger.

Control activities (procedures). Policies and procedures used by management to meet its objectives; generally divided into adequate segregation of duties, proper procedures for authorization of transactions and activities, adequate documents and records, physical control over assets and records, and independent checks on performance.

Control environment. The actions, policies, and procedures that reflect the overall attitudes of top management, the directors, and the owners about control and its importance to the entity.

Controlling. Implementing management plans and identifying how plans compare with actual performance.

Conversion costs. The costs of converting raw materials to finished products; include direct labor and manufacturing overhead costs.

Convertible bonds. Bonds that can be traded for, or converted to, other securities after a specified period of time.

Convertible preferred stock. Preferred stock that can be converted to common stock at a specified conversion rate.

Corporation. A legal entity chartered by a state; ownership is represented by transferable shares of stock.

Cost behavior. The way in which a cost is affected by changes in activity levels.

Cost center. An organizational unit in which a manager has control over and is held accountable for costs.

Cost driver. A factor that determines an activity cost. An activity can have more than one cost driver.

Cost of capital. The average cost of a firm's debt and equity capital; equals the rate of return that a company must earn in order to satisfy the demands of its owners and creditors.

Cost of goods available for sale. The cost of all merchandise available for sale during the period; equal to the sum of beginning inventory and net purchases.

Cost of goods manufactured schedule. A schedule supporting the income statement; summarizes the total cost of goods manufactured during a period, including direct materials, direct labor, and manufacturing overhead

Cost of goods sold. The expenses incurred to purchase or manufacture the merchandise sold during a period.

Costs of quality (COQ). Costs spent to achieve high quality of products and services, as well as costs spent when products fail to have high quality. The four types of costs of quality are prevention costs, appraisal costs, internal failure costs, and external failure costs.

Cost principle. The idea that transactions are recorded at their historical costs or exchange prices at the transaction date.

Cost-volume-profit (CVP) analysis. Techniques for determining how changes in revenues, costs, and level of activity affect the profitability of an organization.

Coupon bonds. Unregistered bonds for which owners receive periodic interest payments by clipping a coupon from the bond and sending it to the issuer as evidence of ownership.

Credit. An entry on the right side of a T-account.

Critical resource factor. The resource that limits operating capacity by its availability.

Cross-subsidization. A distortion of costs that occurs when costs of one product are erroneously assigned to another product.

Cumulative-dividend preference. The right of preferred stockholders to receive current dividends plus all dividends in arrears before common stockholders receive any dividends.

Current assets. Cash and other assets that can be easily converted to cash within a year.

Current (working capital) ratio. A measure of the liquidity of a business; equal to current assets divided by current liabilities.

Current-dividend preference. The right of preferred stockholders to receive current dividends before common stockholders receive dividends.

Curvilinear costs. Variable costs that do not vary in direct proportion to changes in activity level but at decreasing or increasing rates due to economies of scale, productivity changes, and so on.

Cycle time. The total time a product spends moving through a particular process or cycle within the organization, such as the product design cycle, the production cycle, or the order and delivery cycle.

D

Date of record. The date selected by a corporation's board of directors on which the stockholders of record are identified as those who will receive dividends.

Days in inventory. Average number of days of sales that can be made using only the supply of inventory on hand.

Death spiral. A series of management decisions based on bad information that results in reducing or removing the activities or segments from the organization that are actually profitable.

Debentures (unsecured bonds). Bonds for which no collateral has been pledged.

Debit. An entry on the left side of a T-account.

Debt ratio. A measure of leverage, computed by dividing total liabilities by total assets.

Debt securities. Financial instruments issued by a company that carry with them a promise of interest payments and the repayment of principal.

Debt-to-equity ratio. The number of dollars of borrowed funds for every dollar invested by owners; computed as total liabilities divided by total equity.

Decentralized company. An organization in which managers at all levels have the authority to make decisions concerning the operations for which they are responsible.

Declaration date. The date on which a corporation's board of directors formally decides to pay a dividend to stockholders.

Declining-balance depreciation method. An accelerated depreciation method in which an asset's book value is multiplied by a constant depreciation rate (such as double the straight-line percentage, in the case of double-declining-balance).

Defined benefit plan. A pension plan under which the employer defines the amount that retiring employees will receive and contributes enough to the pension fund to pay that amount.

Defined contribution plan. A pension plan under which the employer contributes a defined amount to the pension fund; after retirement, the employees receive the amount contributed plus whatever it has earned.

Depletion. The process of cost allocation that assigns the original cost of a natural resource to the periods benefited.

Depreciation. The process of cost allocation that assigns the original cost of plant and equipment to the periods benefited.

Deregulation. The term used to describe the process of removing restrictions on competition in the marketplace for a particular industry.

Differential costs. Future costs that change as a result of a decision; also called incremental or relevant costs.

Direct costs. Costs that are specifically traceable to a unit of business or segment being analyzed.

Direct labor. Wages that are paid to those who physically work on the direct materials to transform them into a finished product and are traceable to specific products.

Direct labor budget. A schedule of direct labor requirements for the budget period.

Direct materials. Materials that become part of the product and are traceable to it.

Direct materials budget. A schedule of direct materials to be used during the budget period and direct materials to be purchased during that period.

Direct method. A method of reporting net cash flows from operations that shows the major classes of cash receipts and payments for a period of time.

Direct write-off method. The recording of actual losses from uncollectible accounts as expenses during the period in which accounts receivable are determined to be uncollectible.

Discounted cash flow methods. Capital budgeting techniques that take into account the time value of money by comparing discounted cash flows.

Discounting a note receivable. The process of the payee's selling notes to a financial institution for less than the maturity value.

Disposable income. Income left after withholdings and fixed expenses have been subtracted from gross salary; the amount left to cover variable expenditures.

Dividend payment date. The date on which a corporation pays dividends to its stockholders.

Dividend payout ratio. A measure of the percentage of earnings paid out in dividends; computed by dividing cash dividends by net income.

Dividends. Distributions to the owners (stockholders) of a corporation.

Dividends in arrears. Missed dividends for past years that preferred stockholders have a right to receive under the cumulative-dividend preference if and when dividends are declared.

Double-entry accounting. A system of recording transactions in a way that maintains the equality of the accounting equation.

Drawings account. The account used to reflect periodic withdrawals of earnings by the owner (proprietor) or owners (partners) of a proprietorship or partnership.

Dupont framework. A systematic approach for breaking down return on equity into three ratios:

profit margin, asset turnover, and assets-to-equity ratio.

E

Earnings (loss) per share (EPS). The amount of net income (earnings) related to each share of stock; computed by dividing net income by the number of shares of stock outstanding during the period.

Economic order quantity (EOQ). A specific calculation used to determine the most cost-effective size of a purchase order. The EOQ balances the costs of placing an order against the costs of carrying inventory in the organization.

Economic profit. The difference between net operating profit and holding costs of inventory and other asset investments. Note that generally accepted accounting principles (GAAP) do not formally recognize opportunity costs such as holding costs.

Economic Value Added (EVA™). A commercialized performance measurement system that emphasizes the incremental profits an organization creates over and above the profit required to cover its costs of capital.

Effective-interest amortization. A method of systematically writing off a bond premium or discount that takes into consideration the time value of money and results in an equal rate of amortization for each period.

Employee stock options. Rights given to employees to purchase shares of stock of a company at a predetermined price.

Entity. An organizational unit (a person, partnership, or corporation) for which accounting records are kept and about which accounting reports are prepared.

Environmental liabilities. Obligations incurred because of damage done to the environment.

Equity method. Method used to account for an investment in the stock of another company when significant influence can be imposed (presumed to exist when 20 to 50 percent of the outstanding voting stock is owned).

Equity securities (stock). Shares of ownership in a corporation that can change significantly in value and that provide for a return to investors in the form of dividends.

Equivalent units of production. A method used in a process costing system to measure the production output during a period. Equivalent units of production essentially measures the "work done" by the center or department in terms of units of output.

Estimated manufacturing overhead. Budgeted manufacturing overhead costs that are used to establish the predetermined overhead rate.

Evaluating. Analyzing results, rewarding performance, and identifying problems.

Exception report. A report that highlights variances from, or exceptions to, the budget.

Expenses. Costs incurred in the normal course of business to generate revenues.

External auditors. Independent CPAs who are retained by organizations to perform audits of financial statements.

External failure costs. Costs of quality that specifically relate to the costs that occur when low-quality products and services fail after production and delivery to customers.

Extraordinary items. Nonoperating gains and losses that are unusual in nature, infrequent in occurrence, and material in amount.

F

Facility support activities. Activities necessary to have a facility in place in order to participate in the development and production of products or services. However, these activities are not related to any particular line of products or services. Costs of facility support activities are often called common costs.

FIFO (first in, first out). An inventory cost flow whereby the first goods purchased are assumed to be the first goods sold so that the ending inventory consists of the most recently purchased goods.

Financial accounting. The area of accounting concerned with reporting financial information to interested external parties.

Financial Accounting Standards Board (FASB). The private organization responsible for establishing the standards for financial accounting and reporting in the United States.

Financial ratios. Ratios that show relationships between financial statement amounts.

Financial statement analysis. Examining both the relationships among financial statement amounts and the trends in those numbers over time.

Financial statements. Reports such as the balance sheet, income statement, and statement of cash flows, which summarize the financial status and results of operations of a business entity.

Financing activities. Activities whereby cash is obtained from or repaid to owners and creditors.

Finished goods. Manufactured products ready for sale.

Finished goods inventory. Inventory that has completed the production process and is ready for sale to customers.

Fiscal year. An entity's reporting year, covering a 12-month accounting period.

Fixed asset turnover. The number of dollars in sales generated by each dollar of fixed assets; computed as sales divided by property, plant, and equipment.

Fixed costs. Costs that remain constant in total, regardless of activity level, at least over a certain range of activity.

Flexible budget. A quantified plan that projects revenues and costs for varying levels of activity.

Floor. The minimum market amount at which inventory can be carried on the books; equal to net realizable value minus a normal profit.

FOB (free on board) destination. A business term meaning that the seller of merchandise bears the shipping costs and maintains ownership until the merchandise is delivered to the buyer.

FOB (free on board) shipping point. A business term meaning that the buyer of merchandise bears the shipping costs and acquires ownership at the point of shipment.

Foreign Corrupt Practices Act (FCPA). Legislation requiring any company that has publicly traded stock to maintain records that accurately and fairly represent the company's transactions; additionally, requires any publicly traded company to have an adequate system of internal accounting controls.

Foreign currency transaction. A sale in which the price is denominated in a currency other than the currency of the seller's home country.

Franchise. An entity that has been licensed to sell the product of a manufacturer or to offer a particular service in a given area.

G

Gains (losses). Money made or lost on activities outside the normal operation of a company.

Generally accepted accounting principles (GAAP). Authoritative guidelines that define accounting practice at a particular time.

Generally accepted auditing standards (GAAS). Auditing standards developed by the AICPA.

Goal congruence. The selection of goals for responsibility centers that are consistent, or congruent, with those of the company as a whole.

Going concern assumption. The idea that an accounting entity will have a continuing existence for the foreseeable future.

Goodwill. An intangible asset that exists when a business is valued at more than the fair market value of its net assets, usually due to strategic location, reputation, good customer relations, or similar factors; equal to the excess of the purchase price over the fair market value of the net assets purchased.

Gross margin method. A procedure for estimating the amount of ending inventory; the historical relationship of cost of goods sold to sales revenue is used in computing ending inventory.

Gross profit (gross margin). The excess of net sales revenue over the cost of goods sold.

Gross sales. Total recorded sales before deducting any sales discounts or sales returns and allowances.

H

Held-to-maturity security. A debt security purchased by an investor with the intent of holding the security until it matures.

Hierarchical Product Cost Model. A method of categorizing costs based on types of activities. Activity types include unit-level activities, batch-level activities, product line activities, and facility support activities.

High-low method. A method of segregating the fixed and variable components of a mixed cost by analyzing the costs at the highest and the lowest activity levels within a relevant range.

Historical cost. The dollar amount originally exchanged in an arm's-length transaction; an amount assumed to reflect the fair market value of an item at the transaction date.

Holding costs. The financial opportunity costs that result from investing money in an asset such as inventory. Whatever income the money could generate in an alternative investment is the holding cost of the current investment.

Hurdle rate. The minimum rate of return that an investment must provide in order to be acceptable.

I

Impairment. A decline in the value of a long-term operating asset.

Income statement (statement of earnings). The financial statement that reports the amount of net income earned by a company during a period.

Independent checks. Procedures for continual internal verification of other controls.

Indirect costs. Costs normally incurred for the benefit of several segments within the organization; sometimes called common costs or joint costs.

Indirect labor. Labor that is necessary to a manufacturing or service business but is not directly related to the actual production of the manufactured or service product.

Indirect materials. Materials that are necessary to a manufacturing or service business but are not directly included in or are not a significant part of the actual product.

Indirect method. A method of reporting net cash flows from operations that involves converting accrual-basis net income to a cash basis.

Industry volume variance. The part of the sales volume variance that accounts for the difference between the expected market share of the total market and the expected or standard quantity of goods sold.

Intangible assets. Long-lived assets without physical substance that are used in business, such as licenses, patents, franchises, and goodwill.

Interest. The payment (cost) for the use of money.

Interest rate. The cost of using money, expressed as an annual percentage.

Internal auditors. An independent group of experts (in controls, accounting, and operations) who monitor operating results and financial records, evaluate internal controls, assist with increasing the efficiency and effectiveness of operations, and detect fraud.

Internal control structure. Safeguards in the form of policies and procedures established to provide management with reasonable assurance that the objectives of an entity will be achieved.

Internal failure costs. Costs of quality that specifically relate to the expenses that occur when low-quality products and services fail before production and delivery to customers.

Internal rate of return. The "true" discount rate that will produce a net present value of zero when applied to the cash flows of investment inventory goods held for resale.

Internal rate of return method. A capital budgeting technique that uses discounted cash flows to find the "true" discount rate of an investment; this true rate produces a net present value of zero.

Internal Revenue Service (IRS). A government agency that prescribes the rules and regulations that govern the collection of tax revenues in the United States.

International Accounting Standards Committee (IASC). The committee formed in 1973 to develop worldwide accounting standards.

Interpolation. A method of determining the internal rate of return when the factor for that rate lies between the factors given in the present value table.

Inventory. Goods held for resale.

Inventory shrinkage. The amount of inventory that is lost, stolen, or spoiled during a period; determined by comparing perpetual inventory records to the physical count of inventory.

Inventory turnover. A measure of the efficiency with which inventory is managed; computed by dividing cost of goods sold by average inventory for a period.

Inventory turnover (stockturns). The number of times the inventory in the organization "turns over" during a period of time. It is often easier to think of inventory turnover as the number of times a dollar invested is sold during a period of time. Inventory turnover is computed as Cost of goods sold ÷ Average inventory value.

Investing activities. Activities associated with buying and selling long-term assets.

Investment center. An organizational unit in which a manager has control over and is held accountable for costs, revenues, and assets.

J

Job order costing. A method of product costing whereby each job, product, or batch of products is costed separately.

Journal. An accounting record in which transactions are first entered; provides a chronological record of all business activities.

Journal entry. A recording of a transaction where debits equal credits; usually includes a date and an explanation of the transaction.

Journalizing. Recording transactions in a journal.

Junk bonds. Bonds issued by companies in weak financial condition with large amounts of debt already outstanding; these bonds yield high rates of return because of high risk.

Just-in-time (JIT). A management philosophy that emphasizes removing all waste of effort, time, and inventory costs from the organization. One obvious result of JIT is the reduction or removal of needless inventory in a production system.

L

Labor efficiency variance. The extent to which the actual labor used varies from the standard quantity; computed by multiplying the difference between the actual quantity and the standard quantity of labor by the standard rate.

Labor rate variance. The extent to which the actual labor rate varies from the standard rate for the quantity of labor used; computed by multiplying the difference between the actual rate and the standard rate by the quantity of labor used.

Lagging indicators. Measures that indicate the success of past business activities. Lagging indicators are related to the concept "outcome measures."

Lead time. Generally, the time interval between initiating a request and finally fulfilling the request.

Leading indicators. Measures that indicate the potential success of future business activities. Leading indicators are related to the concept "leading measures."

Leading measures. Measures that, if successfully implemented, will support desired performance in other business activities. Note that some leading measures can also serve as outcome measures.

Lease. A contract that specifies the terms under which the owner of an asset (the lessor) agrees to transfer the right to use the asset to another party (the lessee).

Least-cost decision. A decision to undertake the project with the smallest negative net present value.

Least squares method. A method of segregating the fixed and variable portions of a mixed cost; the regression line, a line of averages, is statistically fitted through all cost points.

Ledger. A book of accounts in which data from transactions recorded in journals are posted and thereby summarized.

Lessee. The party that is granted the right to use property under the terms of a lease.

Lessor. The owner of property that is leased (rented) to another party.

Liabilities. Obligations to pay cash, transfer other assets, or provide services to someone else.

License. The right to perform certain activities, generally granted by a governmental agency.

Life cycle costing. The process of measuring all costs involved in creating, producing, and using a product or service. Life cycle costing is not limited to costs incurred by the organization measuring these costs but also includes all costs incurred by the suppliers and the customers of the product or service.

LIFO (last in, first out). An inventory cost flow whereby the last goods purchased are assumed to be the first goods sold so that the ending inventory consists of the first goods purchased.

Limited liability. The legal protection given stockholders whereby they are responsible for the debts and obligations of a corporation only to the extent of their capital contributions.

Line of credit. An arrangement whereby a bank agrees to loan an amount of money (up to a certain limit) on demand for short periods of time, usually less than a year.

Liquidity. The ability of a company to pay its debts in the short run.

Logistics. The management process involved in obtaining, managing, and transporting inventory and other assets in organizations.

Long-term assets. Assets that a company needs in order to operate its business over an extended period of time.

Long-term liabilities. Debts or other obligations that will not be paid within one year.

Long-term operating assets. Assets expected to be held and used over the course of several years to facilitate operating activities.

Lower-of-cost-or-market (LCM) rule. A basis for valuing inventory at the lower of original cost or current market value.

M

Maker. A person (entity) who signs a note to borrow money and who assumes responsibility to pay the note at maturity.

Management accounting. The area of accounting concerned with providing internal financial reports to assist management in making decisions.

Management by exception. The strategy of focusing attention on significant deviations from a standard.

Manufacturing organizations. Organizations that focus on using labor and/or machinery to convert raw materials into marketable products.

Manufacturing overhead. All costs incurred in the manufacturing process other than direct materials and direct labor.

Manufacturing overhead budget. A schedule of production costs other than those for direct labor and direct materials.

Manufacturing overhead rate. The rate at which manufacturing overhead is assigned to products; equals estimated manufacturing overhead for the period divided by the number of units of the activity base being used.

Market Adjustment—Trading Securities. An account used to track the difference between the historical cost and the market value of a company's portfolio of trading securities.

Market rate (effective rate or yield rate) of interest. The actual interest rate earned or paid on a bond investment.

Market share. The percentage share one company receives of the total sales revenue in the economy for a particular product or service.

Market share variance. The part of the sales volume variance that accounts for the difference between the actual market share of each product sold and the expected market share of each product sold.

Market value. The value of a company as measured by the number of shares of stock outstanding multiplied by the current market price of the stock; the current value of a business.

Matching principle. The concept that all costs and expenses incurred in generating revenues must be recognized in the same reporting period as the related revenues.

Materials price variance. The extent to which the actual price varies from the standard price for the quantity of materials purchased or used; computed by multiplying the difference between the actual and standard prices by the quantity purchased or used.

Materials quantity variance. The extent to which the actual quantity of materials varies from the standard quantity; computed by multiplying the difference between the actual quantity and the standard quantity of materials used by the standard price.

Maturity date. The date on which a note or other obligation becomes due.

Maturity value. The amount of an obligation to be collected or paid at maturity; equal to principal plus any interest.

Merchandising organizations. Organizations that focus on procuring tangible products, then distributing them to customers. These customers may include individuals or other business organizations such as manufacturing organizations.

Mixed costs. Costs that contain both variable and fixed cost components.

Monetary measurement. The idea that money, as the common medium of exchange, is the accounting unit of measurement, and that only economic activities measurable in monetary terms are included in the accounting model.

Mortgage amortization schedule. A schedule that shows the breakdown between interest and principal for each payment over the life of a mortgage.

Mortgage payable. A written promise to pay a stated amount of money at one or more specified future dates; a mortgage is secured by the pledging of certain assets, usually real estate, as collateral.

N

Natural resources. Assets that are physically consumed or waste away, such as oil, minerals, gravel, and timber.

Net assets. The owner's equity of a business; equal to total assets minus total liabilities.

Net income (net loss). An overall measure of the performance of a company; equal to revenues minus expenses for the period.

Net operating profit. The difference between normal business sales and normal business expenses.

Net present value. The difference between the present values of an investment's expected cash inflows and outflows.

Net present value method. A capital budgeting technique that uses discounted cash flows to compare the present values of an investment's expected cash inflows and outflows.

Net purchases. The net cost of inventory purchased during a period, after adding the cost of freight in and subtracting returns and discounts.

Net realizable value. The selling price of an item less reasonable selling costs.

Net realizable value of accounts receivable. The net amount that would be received if all receivables considered collectible were collected; equal to total accounts receivable less the allowance for bad debts.

Net sales. Gross sales less sales discounts and sales returns and allowances.

Nominal accounts. Accounts that are closed to a zero balance at the end of each accounting period; temporary accounts generally appearing on the income statement.

Noncash items. Items included in the determination of net income on an accrual basis that do not affect cash; examples are depreciation and amortization.

Noncash transactions. Investing and financing activities that do not affect cash; if significant, they are disclosed below the statement of cash flows or in the notes to the financial statements.

Nonprofit organization. An entity without a profit objective, oriented toward providing services efficiently and effectively.

Non-value-added activities. Unnecessary activities in a production or service process that customers typically do not see or care about and for which they are unwilling to pay.

Note receivable. A claim against a debtor, evidenced by an unconditional written promise to pay a certain sum of money on or before a specified future date.

Notes to the financial statements. Explanatory information considered an integral part of the financial statements.

NSF (not sufficient funds) check. A check that is not honored by a bank because of insufficient cash in the check writer's account.

Number of days' purchases in accounts payable. A measure of how well operating cash flow is being managed; computed by dividing total inventory purchases by average accounts payable and then dividing 365 days by the result.

Number of days' sales in inventory. An alternative measure of how well inventory is being managed; computed by dividing 365 days by the inventory turnover ratio.

O

Operating activities. Activities that are part of the day-to-day business of a company.

Operating (master) budget. A network of many separate schedules and budgets that together constitute the overall operating and financing plan for the coming period.

Operating lease. A simple rental agreement.

Operating leverage. The extent to which fixed costs are part of a company's cost structure; the higher the proportion of fixed costs to variable costs, the faster income increases or decreases with sales volume.

Operational budgeting. Managerial planning decisions regarding current operations and those of the immediate future (typically one year or less) that are characterized by regularity and frequency.

Opportunity costs. The benefits lost or forfeited as a result of selecting one alternative course of action over another.

Organizational structure. Lines of authority and responsibility.

Other revenues and expenses. Items incurred or earned from activities that are outside, or peripheral to, the normal operations of a firm.

Outcome measures. Measures of desired outcome performance in activities critical to an organization's strategic goals. Note that some outcome measures are also leading measures to support desired performance in other business activities.

Out-of-pocket costs. Costs that require an outlay of cash or other resources.

Overapplied manufacturing overhead. The excess of applied manufacturing overhead (based on a predetermined application rate) over the actual manufacturing overhead costs for a period.

Overhead cost allocation. A system of assigning the indirect costs of the manufacturing or service process to the actual product being created for the customer.

Owners' equity. The ownership interest in the net assets of an entity; equals total assets minus total liabilities.

P

Par value. A nominal value assigned to and printed on the face of each share of a corporation's stock.

Partnership. An association of two or more individuals or organizations to carry on economic activity.

Patent. An exclusive right granted for 17 years by the federal government to manufacture and sell an invention.

Payback method. A capital budgeting technique that determines the amount of time it takes the net cash inflows of an investment to repay the investment cost.

Payee. The person (entity) to whom payment on a note is to be made.

Pension. An agreement between an employer and employees that provides for benefits upon retirement.

Performance measures. A general term used to describe all measures designed to capture information about performance related to a particular activity or process.

Period costs. Costs not directly related to a product, service, or asset that are charged as expenses to the income statement in the period in which they are incurred.

Periodic inventory system. A system of accounting for inventory in which cost of goods sold is determined and inventory is adjusted at the end of the accounting period, not when merchandise is purchased or sold.

Perpetual inventory system. A system of accounting for inventory in which detailed records of the number of units and the cost of each purchase and sales transaction are prepared throughout the accounting period.

Per-unit contribution margin. The excess of the sales price of one unit over its variable costs.

Physical safeguards. Physical precautions used to protect assets and records, such as locks on doors, fireproof vaults, password verification, and security guards.

Planning. Outlining the activities that need to be performed for an organization to achieve its objectives.

Post-closing trial balance. A listing of all real account balances after the closing process has been completed; provides a means of testing whether total debits equal total credits for all real accounts prior to beginning a new accounting cycle.

Postemployment benefits. Benefits paid to employees who have been laid off or terminated.

Posting. The process of transferring amounts from the journal to the ledger.

Predetermined overhead rate. A rate at which estimated manufacturing overhead costs are assigned to products throughout the year; equals total estimated manufacturing overhead costs divided by a suitable allocation base, such as number of units produced, direct labor hours, direct materials used, or direct labor costs.

Preferred stock. A class of stock that usually provides dividend and liquidation preferences over common stock.

Prepaid expenses. Payments made in advance for items normally charged to expense.

Present value of $1. The value today of $1 to be received or paid at some future date given a specified interest rate.

Present value of an annuity. The value today of a series of equally spaced, equal-amount payments to be made or received in the future given a specified interest rate.

Prevention costs. Costs of quality that specifically relate to the effort to ensure that processes are performed correctly the first time and that products and services meet customers' expectations.

Price-earnings (P/E) ratio. A measure of growth potential, earnings stability, and management capabilities; computed by dividing market price per share by earnings per share.

Primary financial statements. The balance sheet, income statement, and statement of cash flows, used by external groups to assess a company's economic standing.

Prime costs. The direct costs that are "primarily seen" in the product (i.e., direct materials and direct labor).

Principal (face value or maturity value). The amount that will be paid on a note or other obligation at the maturity date.

Prior-period adjustments. Adjustments made directly to Retained Earnings in order to correct errors in the financial statements of prior periods.

Process costing. A method of product costing whereby costs are accumulated by process or work centers and averaged over all products manufactured in a center or department during a particular production period.

Product costs. Costs associated with products or services offered.

Product line activities. Activities that take place in order to support a product line, regardless of the number of batches or individual units actually produced. Costs of product line activities are also known as capability costs.

Production budget. A schedule of production requirements for the budget period.

Production cost report. A document that compiles all the costs of a manufacturing center for a particular production period. The information on this report is used to control and evaluate production costs, as well as transfer costs and units of output from one manufacturing center to another.

Production prioritizing. Management's continual evaluation of the profitability of the various product lines and divisions within an organization so that products or divisions that are performing below expectations can be analyzed to identify problems and potential solutions.

Profit center. An organizational unit in which a manager has control over and is held accountable for both costs and revenues.

Profit graph. A graph that shows how profits vary with changes in volume.

Profit margin. A measure of the number of pennies in profit generated from each dollar of revenue; calculated by dividing net income by revenue.

Profit margin (operating performance) ratio. An overall measure of the profitability of operations during a period; computed by dividing net income by revenue.

Profitability index. The present value of net cash inflows divided by the cost of an investment.

Property, plant, and equipment. Tangible, long-lived assets acquired for use in business operations; includes land, buildings, machinery, equipment, and furniture.

Proprietorship. A business owned by one person.

Prospectus. Report provided to potential investors that presents a company's financial statements and explains its business plan, sources of financing, and significant risks.

Purchases budget. A schedule of projected purchases over the budget period.

Purchases journal. A special journal in which credit purchases are recorded.

R

Ranking. The ordering of acceptable investment alternatives from most to least desirable.

Raw materials. Materials purchased for use in manufacturing products.

Raw materials inventory. The inventory of raw materials that have not yet begun the production process.

Real accounts. Accounts that are not closed to a zero balance at the end of each accounting period; permanent accounts appearing on the balance sheet.

Realized gains and losses. Gains and losses resulting from the sale of securities in an arm's-length transaction.

Receivables. Claims for money, goods, or services.

Registered bonds. Bonds for which the names and addresses of the bondholders are kept on file by the issuing company.

Regression line. On a scattergraph, the straight line that most closely expresses the relationship between the variables.

Relevant range. The range of operating level, or volume of activity, over which the relationship between total costs (variable plus fixed) and activity level is approximately linear.

Reorder point. The point at which the inventory level in the organization drops low enough to trigger a new purchase order.

Residual income. The amount of net income earned above a specified minimum rate of return on assets; used to evaluate investment centers.

Responsibility accounting. A system of evaluating performance; managers are held accountable for the costs, revenues, assets, or other elements over which they have control.

Responsibility center. An organizational unit in which a manager has control over and is held accountable for performance.

Retailers. Second-tier merchants who typically purchase products from wholesalers to distribute to end-user customers. Many large retailers, however, will often bypass wholesalers to purchase products directly from original manufacturers.

Retained earnings. The amount of accumulated earnings of the business that have not been distributed to owners.

Return on equity. A measure of the amount of profit earned per dollar of investment, computed by dividing net income by equity.

Return on investment (ROI). A measure of operating performance and efficiency in utilizing assets; computed in its simplest form by dividing net income by average total assets.

Return on sales. A measure of the amount of profit earned per dollar of sales, computed by dividing net income by sales.

Return on sales revenue. A measure of operating performance; computed by dividing net income by total sales revenue. Similar to profit margin.

Revenue. Increase in a company's resources from the sale of goods or services.

Revenue budget. A service entity's budget that identifies how much revenue (and often cash) will be generated during a period.

Revenue recognition. The process of recording revenue in the accounting records; occurs after (1) the work has been substantially completed and (2) cash collection is reasonably assured.

Revenue recognition principle. The idea that revenues should be recorded when (1) the earnings process has been substantially completed and (2) cash has either been collected or collectibility is reasonably assured.

Robust quality. The capability of a product to perform according to customer expectations regardless of surroundings and circumstances.

S

Safety stock. The minimal level of inventory required to ensure against the organization running out of inventory in the case of unforeseen problems in receiving its next purchase order.

Sales budget. A schedule of projected sales over the budget period.

Sales discount. A reduction in the selling price that is allowed if payment is received within a specified period.

Sales journal. A special journal in which credit sales are recorded.

Sales mix. The relative proportion of total units sold (or total sales dollars) that is represented by each of a company's products.

Sales mix variance. The part of the sales volume variance that accounts for the difference between the actual quantity of each product sold and the percentage of the actual total products sold that was expected to be represented by each product based on expected market share of the products.

Sales price variance. The difference between the actual price and the expected or standard price multiplied by the actual quantity; measures the part of the difference between expected and actual sales revenue that is due to differences between expected and actual prices of goods.

Sales returns and allowances. A contra-revenue account in which the return of, or allowance for reduction in the price of, merchandise previously sold is recorded.

Sales tax payable. Money collected from customers for sales taxes that must be remitted to local governments and other taxing authorities.

Sales volume variance. The difference between the actual quantity and the expected quantity multiplied by the expected or standard price; measures the part of the difference between expected and actual sales revenue that is due to the difference between expected and actual volume of goods sold.

Sales yield variance. On a combined product basis, that part of the sales volume variance that is not explained by the mix of products sold. The sales yield variance is the amount of sales volume variance explained by differences between actual and expected market share and total industry sales. The sales yield variance is further broken down into the industry volume variance and market share variance and is also referred to as the "final volume variance."

Salvage value. The amount expected to be received when an asset is sold at the end of its useful life.

Scattergraph (visual-fit) method. A method of segregating the fixed and variable components of a mixed cost by plotting on a graph total costs at several activity levels and drawing a regression line through the points.

Screening. Determining whether a capital investment meets a minimum standard of financial acceptability.

Secured bonds. Bonds for which assets have been pledged in order to guarantee repayment.

Securities and Exchange Commission (SEC). The government body responsible for regulating the financial reporting practices of most publicly owned corporations in connection with the buying and selling of stocks and bonds.

Segment. Any part of an organization requiring separate reports for evaluation by management.

Segment margin. The difference between segment revenue and direct segment costs; a measure of the segment's contribution to cover indirect fixed costs and provide profits.

Segment-margin income statement. An income statement that identifies costs directly chargeable to a segment and further divides them into variable and fixed cost behavior patterns.

Segment-margin ratio. The segment margin divided by the segment's net sales revenue; a measure of the efficiency of the segment's operating performance, and therefore of its profitability.

Segregation of duties. A strategy to provide an internal check on performance through separation of authorization of transactions from custody of related assets; separation of operational responsibilities from record-keeping responsibilities; and separation of custody of assets from accounting personnel.

Selling and administrative expense budget. A schedule of all nonproduction spending expected to occur during the budget period.

Sensitivity analysis. A method of assessing the reasonableness of a decision that was based upon estimates; involves calculating how far reality can differ from an estimate without invalidating the decision.

Separate entity concept. The idea that the activities of an entity are to be separated from those of the individual owners.

Serial bonds. Bonds that mature in a series of installments at specified future dates.

Service organizations. Organizations that focus on delivery of marketable services, such as legal advice or education, to individuals or other organizations.

Service overhead budget. The budget, prepared by service entities, that identifies projected costs associated with providing the service.

Six sigma quality. A measure of quality based on statistical analysis. Products or services with six sigma quality have no more than 3.4 defects per million opportunities (e.g., parts or events).

Social security (FICA) taxes. Federal insurance contributions act taxes imposed on employee and employer; used mainly to provide retirement benefits.

Special journal. A book of original entry for recording similar transactions that occur frequently.

Special order. An order that may be priced below the normal selling price in order to utilize excess capacity and thereby contribute to company profits.

Specific identification. A method of valuing inventory and determining cost of goods sold whereby the actual costs of specific inventory items are assigned to them.

Standard cost card. An itemization of the components of the standard cost of a product.

Standard cost system. A cost-accumulation system in which standard costs are used as product costs instead of actual costs.

Stated rate of interest. The rate of interest printed on the bond.

Statement of cash flows. The financial statement that shows an entity's cash inflows (receipts) and outflows (payments) during a period of time.

Statement of comprehensive income. A statement outlining the changes in accumulated comprehensive income that arose during the period.

Statement of partners' capital. A partnership report showing the changes in the capital balances; similar to a statement of retained earnings for a corporation.

Statement of retained earnings. A report that shows the changes in the retained earnings account during a period of time.

Statement of stockholders' equity. A financial statement that reports all changes in stockholders' equity.

Static budget. A quantified plan that projects revenues and costs for only one level of activity.

Statistical process control (SPC). A statistical technique for identifying and measuring the quality status of a process by evaluating its output to determine if serious problems exist in the process.

Stepped costs. Costs that change in total in a stair-step fashion (in large amounts) with changes in volume of activity.

Stock dividend. A pro rata distribution of additional shares of stock to stockholders.

Stock split. The replacement of outstanding shares of stock with a greater number of new shares.

Stockholders (shareholders). The owners of a corporation.

Stockholders' equity. The owners' equity section of a corporate balance sheet.

Straight-line amortization. A method of systematically writing off a bond discount or premium in equal amounts each period until maturity.

Straight-line depreciation method. The depreciation method in which the cost of an asset is allocated equally over the periods of an asset's estimated useful life.

Strategic planning. Broad, long-range planning, usually conducted by top management.

Subsidiary ledger. A grouping of individual accounts that in total equal the balance of a control account in the general ledger.

Sum-of-the-years'-digits depreciation method. The accelerated depreciation method in which a constant balance (cost minus salvage value) is multiplied by a declining depreciation rate.

Sunk costs. Costs, such as depreciation, that are past costs and do not change as the result of a future decision.

Supplies budget. The budget, prepared by service entities, that identifies projected supplies expenses over the budget period.

T

T-account. A simplified depiction of an account in the form of a letter T.

Taguchi quality loss function. A method developed by Genichi Taguchi for measuring the actual size of all external failure costs, particularly the opportunity costs of lost customer sales that result from dissatisfied customers.

Target costing. A costing approach that designs a product to meet specific cost objectives based on target market prices less the target margin.

Target income. A profit level desired by management.

Target market price. The price that consumers will pay for a product or service.

Term bonds. Bonds that mature in one single sum at a specified future date.

Theory of constraints (TOC). A management philosophy that focuses on constraint resources and holds that they should operate at full capacity.

Time period concept. The idea that the life of a business is divided into distinct and relatively short time periods so that accounting information can be timely.

Time value of money. The concept that a dollar received now is worth more than a dollar received far in the future.

Times interest earned. A measure of a borrower's ability to make required interest payments; computed as income before interest and taxes divided by annual interest expense.

Total cost. The total variable and fixed costs incurred in making a product or providing a service.

Total quality management (TQM). A management philosophy focused on increasing profitability by improving the quality of products and processes and increasing customer satisfaction, while promoting the well-being and growth of employees.

Total variable manufacturing overhead variance. The extent to which actual manufacturing overhead varies from the amount included in work-in-process inventory; the difference between actual and applied variable manufacturing overhead.

Trading securities. Debt and equity securities purchased with the intent of selling them should the need for cash arise or to realize short-term gains.

Transactions. Exchange of goods or services between entities (whether individuals, businesses, or other organizations), as well as other events having an economic impact on a business.

Treasury stock. Issued stock that has subsequently been reacquired by the corporation.

Trial balance. A listing of all account balances; provides a means of testing whether total debits equal total credits for all accounts.

U

Unadjusted rate of return method. A capital budgeting technique in which a rate of return is calculated by dividing the increase in the average annual net income a project will generate by the initial investment cost.

Underapplied manufacturing overhead. The excess of actual manufacturing overhead costs over the applied overhead costs for a period (based on a predetermined application rate).

Unearned revenues. Cash amounts received before they have been earned.

Unit-based costing (UBC). The traditional method of allocating manufacturing overhead using an approach that is essentially based on the number of units produced.

Unit-level activities. Activities that take place each time a unit of product is produced.

Units-of-production method. The depreciation method in which the cost of an asset is allocated to each period on the basis of the productive output or use of the asset during the period.

Unrealized gains and losses. Gains and losses resulting from changes in the value of securities that are still being held.

Unrecorded liabilities. Expenses incurred during a period that have not been recorded by the end of that period.

Unrecorded receivables. Revenues earned during a period that have not been recorded by the end of that period.

V

Value-added activities. Necessary activities in a production or service process that customers identify as valuable and for which they are willing to pay.

Variable cost rate. The change in cost divided by the change in activity; the slope of the regression line.

Variable costs. Costs that change in total in direct proportion to changes in activity level.

Variable manufacturing overhead efficiency variance. The difference between manufacturing overhead costs expected at actual hours and manufacturing overhead costs expected at standard hours.

Variable manufacturing overhead spending variance. The difference between actual manufacturing overhead incurred and the standard manufacturing overhead for the actual activity level.

Variance. Any deviation from standard.

W

Wages and salaries budget. The budget, prepared by service entities, that identifies projected labor costs involved directly in providing the service over the budget period.

Wholesalers. Top-tier merchants who typically deal directly with the original manufacturers to distribute products to retailers.

Work in process. Partially completed units in production.

Work sheet. A columnar schedule used to summarize accounting data.

Work-in-process inventory. Inventory that is partly completed in the production process, yet not ready for sale to customers.

Z

Zero-coupon bonds. Bonds issued with no promise of interest payments; only a single payment will be made.

appendix c

CHECK FIGURES*

CHAPTER f1

Not Applicable

CHAPTER f2

Exercises

2-2 (c) Owners' equity = $30,000
2-4 Revenues = $47,500
2-6 12/31/03 Owners' equity = $249,000
2-8 Income Taxes = $34,440
2-10 (1) Net income = $380,000
2-12 EPS = $9.07
2-14 N/A
2-16 Debt ratio = 0.648
2-18 N/A
2-20 N/A

Problems

2-2 (1) Total assets = $17,525
2-4 (1) Net income for 2003 = $21,000
2-6 (5) Net Income = $107,250
2-8 Net increase in cash = $30,000
2-10 (2) ROE = 8.73%
2-12 PE ratio = 13.81
2-14 (3) Total revenue = $65,800

CHAPTER f3

Exercises

3-2 N/A
3-4 (2) OE—R
3-6 (3) Debit to Inventory = $8,000
3-8 6/14 Debit to Insurance Expense = $5,000
3-10 (1) Debit to Compensation Expense = $105,000
3-12 N/A
3-14 Retained Earnings = $27,000
3-16 (3) Revenues for 2003 = $240,000

Problems

3-2 (2) Cash balance = $96,700
3-4 (2) Cost of goods sold balance = $50,000
3-6 (3) Net loss = ($300)
3-8 Total debits = $647,000
3-10 (4) EPS = $1.84

CHAPTER f4

Exercises

4-2 (1) (b) Net income = $13,640
4-4 N/A
4-6 (5) Debit to Cash = $1,500
4-8 (1) Debit to Unearned Subscription Revenue = $1,400
4-10 (5) Debit to Programming Expense = $800
4-12 (2) Profit margin for 2003 = 5.0%
4-14 (1) Question Co. ROE = 8.2%
4-16 N/A
4-18 (1) Net income percentage of revenue = 13.1
4-20 Credit to Income Tax Expense = $17,800
4-22 Post-closing trial balance totals = $299,940
4-24 (3) Debit to Office Supplies on Hand = $500

Problems

4-2 (d) Credit to Rent Revenue = $48,600
4-4 (1) Wages expense = $30,000
4-6 N/A
4-8 (2) Total assets = $312,000
4-10 (1) Credit to Insurance Expense = $2,790
4-12 (4) Beginning RE = $50,000
4-14 (3) Net Income = $43,000

CHAPTER f5

Exercises

5-2 Total assets = $7,801,300
5-4 N/A
5-6 N/A
5-8 N/A
5-10 N/A
5-12 N/A
5-14 N/A

CHAPTER f6

Exercises

6-2 N/A
6-4 N/A
6-6 6/30 Debit to Sales Discount = $800

*Note: Check figures are provided for even-numbered exercises and problems, where applicable.

6-8 (1) Bad debt expense = $7,000
6-10 (2) Ending Accounts Receivable = $1,340,000
6-12 (3) Net Accounts Receivable = $149,010
6-14 2003 Debit to Bad Debt Expense = $60,000
6-16 (1) Boulder, Inc. average collection period for Year 3 = 118 days
6-18 N/A
6-20 (2) Debit to Estimated Liability for Service = $675
6-22 (2) Debit to Miscellaneous Expenses = $50
6-24 12/1 Debit to Cash = $13,041
6-26 10/1 Credit to Interest Revenue = $732
6-28 (1) Debit to Cash (Japanese yen) = $10,000

Problems

6-2 N/A
6-4 N/A
6-6 (2) (a) Net sales = $1,570,000
6-8 (2) Debit to Bad Debt Expense = $63,500
6-10 (1) Debit to Bad Debt Expense = $65,600
6-12 N/A
6-14 (1) Suspected stolen = $28,453
6-16 (3) Debit to Cash = 25,462

CHAPTER f7

Exercises

7-2 6/30 Debit to Sales Returns = $16,000
7-4 Debit to Inventory Shrinkage = $28,000
7-6 Debit to Cost of Goods Sold = $244,000
7-8 Carter Co. Cost of goods sold = $43,100
7-10 Credit to Inventory = $12.25
7-12 N/A
7-14 (b) Ending inventory LIFO = $59,700
7-16 (1) (a) Gross margin = $35,000
7-18 (5) Credit to Inventory = $100
7-20 (1) Gross margin = $160,000
7-22 Gross margin = $600,000

Problems

7-2 (2) (j) Debit to Sales Returns = $630
7-4 (10) Gross margin = $675
7-6 (2) Ending inventory LIFO = $42,000
7-8 (1) Net Purchases = $79,600
7-10 (1) 2003 Correct gross margin = $14,700
7-12 (1) (a) Gross margin = $9,336

CHAPTER f8

Exercises

8-2 (2) Credit to Bonus Payable = $24,000
8-4 N/A
8-6 (1) Pension = $55,000
8-8 (2) Debit to Property Tax Expense = $3,800
8-10 (2) Income Tax Expense = $200,000
8-12 N/A
8-14 Gross margin = $124,938

Problems

8-2 (2) Cash paid to employees = $15,193
8-4 (1) Pension expense = $350
8-6 (3) 2003 Deferred tax liability = $0
8-8 (10) Net sales revenue = $35,000

CHAPTER f9

Exercises

9-2 (1) Debit to Machine = $11,850
9-4 (1) Credit to Cash = $115,000
9-6 Building = $654,800
9-8 (1) (b) 2003 Depreciation expense = $3,375
9-10 (1) Credit to Cash = $47,100
9-12 Credit to Land = $160,000
9-14 (1) Credit to Gain on Sale of Machine = $5,000
9-16 (3) Credit to Franchise = $25,000
9-18 Fixed asset turnover = 2.05
9-20 (1) Total cost = $12,350
9-22 (2) 2003 = $6,825
9-24 (4) Credit to Accumulated Depletion, Coal Mine = $100,000

Problems

9-2 N/A
9-4 (3) 1/2 Debit to Leased Computer = $238,820
9-6 (2) Alternative B = $42,150 per year
9-8 (2) Debit to Equipment = $45,000
9-10 (1) Credit to Cash = $114,000
9-12 (3) Debit to Depletion Expense = $180,000
9-14 (2) Credit to Goodwill = $750
9-16 (1) Fixed asset turnover = 3.08
9-18 (3) Depreciation = $50,400
9-20 (2) 2003 Depreciation expense = $3,500
9-22 (3) Uranium book value = $24,000

CHAPTER f10

Exercises

10-2 (4) $20,000
10-4 (1) Payment = $26,380
10-6 12/31/03 Credit to Cash = $1,250
10-8 (2) Total interest paid = $5,582
10-10 (2) Debit to Rent Expense = $4,141

10-12 Total issuance price = $51,675
10-14 (3) 4/1 Debit to Bond Interest Expense = $18,000
10-16 (1) Debt ratio = 55.6%
10-18 (1) (b) Debit to Premium on Bonds = $100
10-20 (4) Bonds Payable Carrying Value = $51,772

Problems

10-2 (2) (a) $32,210
10-4 1/1/03 Debit to Interest Payable = $1,295
10-6 (2) 12/31/03 Debit to Interest Expense = $1,998
10-8 (2) Debit to Leased Starship = $148,547
10-10 (4) 10/1/06 Credit to Gain on Bond Retirement = $5,000
10-12 Total current liabilities = $153,800
10-14 (1) Current ratio = 1.6
10-16 (2) (a) Credit to Discount on Bonds = $135
10-18 (1) Debit to Cash = $463,500
10-20 (2) Total interest expense = $24,759
10-22 (2) Total discount amortization = $8,844
10-24 (1) Issuance price of bonds = $467,664

CHAPTER f11

Exercises

11-2 (2) Retained earnings = $77,600
11-4 (c) Credit to Dividends Payable = $24,000
11-6 (e) Credit to Dividends Payable = $79,800
11-8 (3) $1.69 per share
11-10 (2) Total dividends paid = $172,485
11-12 (2) $8.43 per share
11-14 Comprehensive income = $9,000
11-16 (c) Debit to Retained Earnings = $750,000
11-18 (2) Retained earnings = $144,000
11-20 Retained earnings, 12/31/03 = $78,000
11-22 (2) Total investments = $100,500

Problems

11-2 (2) Total contributed capital = $1,802,200
11-4 (2) Total stockholders' equity = $398,175
11-6 (3) Total preferred stock dividends = $64,000
11-8 (1) (a) Dividend payout ratio = 0.40
11-10 (1) (c) $9,000
11-12 (2) Total contributed capital = $791,500
11-14 (2) Total stockholders' equity = $395,800
11-16 (3) Decrease = $37.6 million
11-18 (2) Total dividends = $110,000
11-20 (2) Total contributed capital = $196,200
11-22 (2) Pat Larsen, capital, 12/31/03 = $76,000

CHAPTER f12

Exercises

12-2 12/31 Credit to Unrealized Gain on Trading Securities—Income = $1,560
12-4 12/31/03 Debit to Unrealized Increase/Decrease in Value of Available-for-Sale Securities—Equity = $27,500
12-6 Debit to Investment in Trading Securities = $20,500
12-8 Debit to Market Adjustment—Available-for-Sale Securities = $100
12-10 Credit to Cash = $24,700
12-12 (2) Total present value = $113,592
12-14 (1) 12/31 Debit to Bond Interest Receivable = $1,500
12-16 Total amount of amortization = $1,706
12-18 (2) Credit to Dividend Revenue = $3,000

Problems

12-2 (1) Unrealized gain/loss for 2002 = $68,000 loss
12-4 8/31 Debit to Realized Loss on Sale of Trading Securities = $28,000
12-6 12/31/03 Credit to Market Adjustment—Available-for-Sale Securities = $1,680
12-8 (3) Debit to Realized Loss on Sale of Available-for-Sale Securities = $8,000
12-10 (2) 12/31 Credit to Market Adjustment—Available-for-Sale Securities = $15,000
12-12 (1) 10/1/03 Credit to Investment in Held-to-Maturity Securities = $43.60
12-14 (2) Total interest revenue = $10,123
12-16 (2) 12/31/03 Credit to Investment in Equity Method Securities to record dividends from Essem = $15,000
12-18 (1) (a) 12/1/02 Credit to Dividend Revenue = $6,250
12-20 (2) Balance sheet—Investment in equity method securities = $645,450

CHAPTER f13

Exercises

13-2 N/A
13-4 (1) (d) Credit to Interest Revenue = $1,500
13-6 (1) Cash collected from customers = $223,000
13-8 Net cash flows provided by operations = $21,700
13-10 Net cash flows provided by operating activities = $161,600
13-12 Net cash flows provided by operating activities = $243,000

13-14 Net cash flows by operating activities = $116,000
13-16 Net cash flows used in investing activities = ($60,000)
13-18 N/A

Problems

13-2 (2) Net increase in cash = $22,300
13-4 (1) Net cash flows provided by operating activities = $13,000
13-6 (1) Net cash flows from operations = $15,490
13-8 Net income = $95,000
13-10 (1) Net cash flows from operating activities = $580
13-12 (1) Cash paid for taxes = $8,400

CHAPTER m1

Exercises

1-2 N/A
1-4 N/A
1-6 N/A
1-8 N/A
1-10 100 baby chairs
1-12 (1) Total manufacturing cost per bat = $51.80
1-14 (1) X-96 segment profit = $11,300

CHAPTER m2

Exercises

2-2 (3) $500 per unit
2-4 (3) $30.25
2-6 (2) Total cost = $60,000
2-8 (1) Profit = $17
2-10 (4) Additional fixed costs = $100,000
2-12 (1) (c) 25,000 units
2-14 (4) Loss of approximately $7,500
2-16 N/A
2-18 (7) Profit = $141,750
2-20 (2) $19.69
2-22 (1) Break-even units = 17,857 units

Problems

2-2 (1) Variable cost = $4 per unit
2-4 (1) Contribution margin = $110,000
2-6 (1) Loss = ($18,400)
2-8 (3) (b) $4,500,000
2-10 (1) Y = 900 bags
2-12 (7) Profit = $850,000
2-14 (1) Profit = $18,750
2-16 (4) 153,033 units
2-18 (2) Total sales = $500,000

CHAPTER m3

Exercises

3-2 (1) Predetermined manufacturing overhead rate = $5
3-4 (1) (b) 2002 Predetermined overhead rate = 26%
3-6 N/A
3-8 (3) Applied manufacturing overhead = $66,500
3-10 (3) Cost per unit = $194
3-12 (1) Overhead rate = $81.82 per direct labor hour
3-14 (1) (c) 2003 = $2.01 per mile
3-16 (1) Overhead rate = $41.33 per consulting hour
3-18 (1) Equivalent units of production for conversion costs = 582 units

Problems

3-2 (1) (g) Credit to Manufacturing Overhead = $400
3-4 (3) Underapplied manufacturing overhead = $12,500
3-6 (3) Total cost of Job #29 = $78,304
3-8 (5) Operating income = $28,003
3-10 (4) Debit to Work-in-Process Services = $21,000
3-12 (3) Overhead = $3,000 debit balance
3-14 (3) Total costs transferred out = $108,760
3-16 Equivalent units of production for direct materials costs = 2,750 units

CHAPTER m4

Exercises

4-2 (2) Present value = $247,314
4-4 Unadjusted rate of return = 22.5%
4-6 Alternative 2 net present value = ($86,024)
4-8 Average cost of capital = 16.7%
4-10 (1) Net persent value = ($100,811)
4-12 N/A
4-14 N/A
4-16 Investment B profitability index = 1.075

Problems

4-2 Net present value = $12,060
4-4 (1) IRR = 10.55%
4-6 Internal rate on return = 4.5 factor
4-8 Alternative 2 = $32,104

4-10 (1) Net present value to rent = $308,174
4-12 (2) Net present value = $380
4-14 (1) Project E net present value = $9,000
4-16 (1) Payback period = 5.2 years
4-18 (2) Net present value at 10 percent = $3,345

CHAPTER m5

Exercises

5-2 (1) Net income = $270
5-4 Quarter 4 EGA units to be produced = 2,175
5-6 VHS total direct materials cost = $170,000
5-8 March total direct labor cost = $18,740
5-10 Projected cash balance July 31, 2003 = $470,000
5-12 (1) Deficiency of cash = ($42,900)
5-14 Income before income taxes = $165,000
5-16 (2) Net increase in cash = $41,650
5-18 (1) Budgeted salary expense = $180,000

Problems

5-2 (2) 34 months
5-4 Total cost of material used = $4,050
5-6 (2) Direct materials costs, bolts = $168.75
5-8 (3) June budgeted purchases (units) = 3,450
5-10 January excess cash = $45,100
5-12 (1) Net operating profit = $140,050
5-14 (2) Additional net income = $16,714
5-16 Expected income per doctor at 34,000 visits = $158,333

CHAPTER m6

Exercises

6-2 (3) Cost of goods sold = $460,000
6-4 Asset turnover = 4.44
6-6 Profitability percentage = 37.9%
6-8 Financial holding costs = $16,250
6-10 EOQ = 872 tires
6-12 559 backpacks

Problems

6-2 (2) Cost of goods manufactured = $1,138,050
6-4 (1) (a) Direct labor cost = $310,000
6-6 (2) Profitability percentage = 74.3%

CHAPTER m7

Exercises

7-2 N/A
7-4 (1) Product A manufacturing overhead = $45,000
7-6 (1) Product Z gross margin = $50,000
7-8 Low quality total expected cost of quality = $86,000
7-10 N/A

Problems

7-2 (1) Agricultural products gross margin = $150,000
7-4 (2) Product J gross margin = ($50,000)
7-6 (3) Machine setups cost per activity = $2,500
7-8 (2) Product 1 manufacturing overhead costs = $147,720
7-10 (2) Lawn Pipe total overhead costs = $151,220
7-12 (1) Opportunity costs at an error rate of 1 percent = $21,600

CHAPTER m8

Exercises

8-2 New machine total relevant costs = $930,000
8-4 (2) Expected increase in profit if order is accepted = $40,000
8-6 (1) Total cost using total-cost analysis to buy the monitor = $1,380,000
8-8 Alternative 3 net expected benefit = $340,000
8-10 Product line contribution = $120,000
8-12 (2) Far Out maximum production = 18,000 units
8-14 (2) 10 engines per month

Problems

8-2 (2) Total cost per unit to make = $2.10
8-4 (2) Alternative 1 differential costs = $565,000
8-6 (1) Skis and ski boots net income = $60,000
8-8 Net cost of closing = ($142,000)
8-10 (1) Y-707 contribution margin = $17.25
8-12 (2) Charger lost contribution = ($150,000)
8-14 N/A

CHAPTER m9

Exercises

9-2 (1) Price variance = $250U
9-4 N/A
9-6 (1) Price variance = $9,000F

9-8 (3) Efficiency variance = $10,200F
9-10 N/A
9-12 N/A
9-14 N/A
9-16 (1) North's segment margin = $10,000
9-18 Caramel Wafers' sales price variance = $10,000U
9-20 Sales mix variance = $1,820U
9-22 (1) South Division asset turnover ratio = 4.0
9-24 (1) Proposal 1 residual income = $1,000
9-26 (2) Overapplied by $900

Problems

9-2 (1) (b) Quantity variance = $800U
9-4 (d) Standard cost per direct labor hour = $3.50 per hour
9-6 (2) Manufacturing rate variance = $420U
9-8 (4) Actual labor rate per hour = $6.20
9-10 Grocery department total margin = $70,000
9-12 (2) Product Y sales price variance = $760F
9-14 (1) Atlantic Division ROI = 17.5%
9-16 (1) (a) ROI without investment = 19.4%
9-18 (d) Residual income = $3,950
9-20 (1) (a) Total residual income = $25,000
9-22 (1) August spending variance = $83,000U

CHAPTER m10

Not Applicable

indexes

FINANCIAL ACCOUNTING SUBJECT INDEX

D

R

S

T

U

V

W

Y

Z

indexes

FINANCIAL ACCOUNTING REAL WORLD COMPANY INDEX

FINANCIAL ACCOUNTING INTERNET INDEX*

*Note: These Web site addresses may also be accessed at **http://albrecht.swcollege.com**

indexes

MANAGEMENT ACCOUNTING SUBJECT INDEX

A

B

C

D

indexes

MANAGEMENT ACCOUNTING REAL WORLD COMPANY INDEX

N

O

P

Q

R

S

T

U

V

W

X

Y

MANAGEMENT ACCOUNTING INTERNET INDEX*

*Note: These Web site addresses may also be accessed at **http://albrecht.swcollege.com**